The Story of Psychology: A Timeline
by Charles L. Brewer, Furman University

B.C.E.

387 — Plato, who believed in innate ideas, suggests that the brain is the seat of mental processes.

335 — Aristotle, who denied the existence of innate ideas, suggests that the heart is the seat of mental processes.

C.E.

1604 — Johannes Kepler describes inverted image on the retina.

1605 — Francis Bacon publishes *The Proficiency and Advancement of Learning*.

1636 — Harvard College is founded.

1637 — René Descartes, the French philosopher and mathematician who proposed mind-body interaction and the doctrine of innate ideas, publishes *A Discourse on Method*.

1690 — John Locke, the British philosopher who rejected Descartes' notion of innate ideas and insisted that the mind at birth is a "blank slate" (*tabula rasa*), publishes *An Essay Concerning Human Understanding*, which stresses empiricism over speculation.

1774 — Franz Mesmer, an Austrian physician, performs his first supposed cure using "animal magnetism" (later called Mesmerism and hypnosis). In **1777** he was expelled from the practice of medicine in Vienna.

1793 — Philippe Pinel releases the first mental patients from their chains at the Bicêtre Asylum in France and advocates more humane treatment of mental patients.

1802 — Thomas Young publishes *A Theory of Color Vision* in England. (His theory was later called the trichromatic theory.)

1808 — Franz Joseph Gall, a German physician, describes phrenology, the belief that the shape of a person's skull reveals mental faculties and character traits.

1834 — Ernst Heinrich Weber publishes *The Sense of Touch*, in which he discusses the just noticeable difference (*jnd*) and what we now call Weber's Law.

1848 — Phineas Gage suffers massive brain damage when a large iron rod accidentally pierces his brain, leaving his intellect and memory intact but altering his personality.

1859 — Charles Darwin publishes *On the Origin of Species by Means of Natural Selection*, synthesizing much previous work on the theory of evolution, including that of Herbert Spencer, who coined the phrase "survival of the fittest."

1861 — Paul Broca, a French physician, discovers an area in the left frontal lobe of the brain (now called Broca's area) that is critical for the production of spoken language.

Turn the page to continue

1901 — Ten founders establish the British Psychological Society.

1905 — Mary Whiton Calkins becomes the first woman president of the APA.

— Ivan Petrovich Pavlov begins publishing studies of conditioning in animals.

— Alfred Binet and Théodore Simon produce the first intelligence test for assessing the abilities and academic progress of Parisian schoolchildren.

1913 — John B. Watson outlines the tenets of behaviorism in a *Psychological Review* article, "Psychology as the Behaviorist Views It."

1914 — During World War I, Robert Yerkes and his staff develop a group intelligence test for evaluating U.S. military personnel, which increases the U.S. public's acceptance of psychological testing.

1920 — Leta Stetter Hollingworth publishes *The Psychology of Subnormal Children*, an early classic. In **1921** she is cited in *American Men of Science* for her research on the psychology of women.

— Francis Cecil Sumner receives a Ph.D. degree in psychology from Clark University, becoming the first African-American to earn a psychology doctorate.

— John B. Watson and Rosalie Rayner report conditioning a fear reaction in a child called "Little Albert."

1921 — Hermann Rorschach, a Swiss psychiatrist, introduces the Rorschach inkblot test.

1923 — Developmental psychologist Jean Piaget publishes *The Language and Thought of the Child*.

1924 — Mary Cover Jones reports reconditioning a fear reaction in a child (Peter), a forerunner of systematic desensitization developed by Joseph Wolpe.

1927 — In *Introduction to the Technique of Child Analysis*, Anna Freud discusses psychoanalysis in the treatment of children.

1929 — Wolfgang Köhler publishes *Gestalt Psychology*, which criticizes behaviorism and outlines essential elements of the Gestalt position and approach.

1931 — Margaret Floy Washburn becomes the first female psychologist (and the second female scientist in any discipline) elected to the U.S. National Academy of Sciences.

1932 — In *The Wisdom of the Body*, Walter B. Cannon coins the term *homeostasis*, discusses the fight-or-flight response, and identifies hormonal changes associated with stress.

Turn the page to continue

1869 — Francis Galton, Charles Darwin's cousin, publishes *Hereditary Genius*, in which he claims that intelligence is inherited. In **1876** he coins the expression "nature and nurture" to correspond with "heredity and environment."

1874 — Carl Wernicke, a German neurologist and psychiatrist, shows that damage to a specific area in the left temporal lobe (now called Wernicke's area) disrupts ability to comprehend or produce spoken or written language.

1878 — G. Stanley Hall receives from Harvard University's Department of Philosophy the first U.S. Ph.D. degree based on psychological research.

1879 — Wilhelm Wundt establishes at the University of Leipzig, Germany, the first psychology laboratory, which becomes a Mecca for psychology students from all over the world.

1883 — G. Stanley Hall, student of Wilhelm Wundt, establishes the first formal U.S. psychology laboratory at Johns Hopkins University.

1885 — Hermann Ebbinghaus publishes *On Memory*, summarizing his extensive research on learning and memory, including the "forgetting curve."

1886 — Joseph Jastrow receives from Johns Hopkins University the first Ph.D. degree in psychology awarded by a Department of Psychology in the United States.

1889 — Alfred Binet and Henri Beaunis establish the first psychology laboratory in France at the Sorbonne, and the first International Congress of Psychology meets in Paris.

1890 — William James, Harvard University philosopher and psychologist, publishes *The Principles of Psychology*, describing psychology as "the science of mental life."

1891 — James Mark Baldwin establishes the first psychology laboratory in the British Commonwealth at the University of Toronto.

1892 — G. Stanley Hall spearheads the founding of the American Psychological Association (APA) and becomes its first president.

1893 — Mary Whiton Calkins and Christine Ladd-Franklin are the first women elected to membership in the APA.

1894 — Margaret Floy Washburn is the first woman to receive a Ph.D. degree in psychology (Cornell University).

— Harvard University denies Mary Whiton Calkins admission to doctoral candidacy because of her gender, despite Hugo Münsterberg's claim that she was the best student he had ever had there.

1896 — John Dewey publishes "The Reflex Arc Concept in Psychology," helping to formalize the school of psychology called functionalism.

1898 — In "Animal Intelligence," Edward L. Thorndike, Columbia University, describes his learning experiments with cats in "puzzle boxes." In **1905**, he proposes the "law of effect."

1900 — Sigmund Freud publishes *The Interpretation of Dreams*, his major theoretical work on psychoanalysis.

1933 — Inez Beverly Prosser becomes the first African-American woman to receive a doctoral degree in psychology from a U.S. institution (Ph.D., University of Cincinnati).

1935 — Christiana Morgan and Henry Murray introduce the Thematic Apperception Test to elicit fantasies from people undergoing psychoanalysis.

1936 — Egas Moniz, Portuguese physician, publishes work on the first frontal lobotomies performed on humans.

1938 — B. F. Skinner publishes *The Behavior of Organisms*, which describes operant conditioning of animals.

— In *Primary Mental Abilities*, Louis L. Thurstone proposes seven such abilities.

— Ugo Cerletti and Lucino Bini use electroshock treatment with a human patient.

1939 — David Wechsler publishes the Wechsler-Bellevue intelligence test, forerunner of the Wechsler Intelligence Scale for Children (WISC) and the Wechsler Adult Intelligence Scale (WAIS).

— Mamie Phipps Clark receives a master's degree from Howard University. In collaboration with Kenneth B. Clark, she later extends her thesis, "The Development of Consciousness of Self in Negro Preschool Children," providing joint research cited in the U.S. Supreme Court's **1954** decision to end racial segregation in public schools.

— Edward Alexander Bott helps found the Canadian Psychological Association. He becomes its first president in **1940**.

— World War II provides many opportunities for psychologists to enhance the popularity and influence of psychology, especially in applied areas.

1943 — Psychologist Starke Hathaway and physician J. Charnley McKinley publish the Minnesota Multiphasic Personality Inventory (MMPI).

1945 — Karen Horney, who criticized Freud's theory of female sexual development, publishes *Our Inner Conflicts*.

1946 — Benjamin Spock's first edition of *The Commonsense Book of Baby and Child Care* appears; the book will influence child rearing in North America for several decades.

1948 — Alfred Kinsey and his colleagues publish *Sexual Behavior in the Human Male*, and they publish *Sexual Behavior in the Human Female* in **1953**.

— B. F. Skinner's novel, *Walden Two*, describes a Utopian community based on positive reinforcement, which becomes a clarion call for applying psychological principles in everyday living, especially communal living.

— Ernest R. Hilgard publishes *Theories of Learning*, which was required reading for several generations of psychology students in North America.

1949 — Raymond B. Cattell publishes the Sixteen Personality Factor Questionnaire (16PF).

Continued on inside back cover

Myers' Psychology for AP®

Second Edition

David G. Myers

**Hope College
Holland, Michigan**

AP® is a trademark registered and/or owned by
the College Board®, which was not involved in the
production of, and does not endorse, this product.

bfw
Worth

WORTH PUBLISHERS

A Macmillan Higher Education Company

Senior Vice President, Editorial, Design, and Media Production: Catherine Woods

Publisher, High School: Ann Heath

Sponsoring Editor, Worth Social Studies: Dora Figueiredo

Development Editors: Trish Morgan, Christine Brune

Senior Marketing Manager: Janie Pierce-Bratcher

Marketing Assistant: Caroline English

Director of Print and Digital Development: Tracey Kuehn

Photo Editor: Bianca Moscatelli

Photo Researcher: Julie Tesser

Art Director: Diana Blume

Cover Designer: Diana Blume

Interior Designer: Marsha Cohen

Layout Designer: Lee McKevitt

Managing Editor: Lisa Kinne

Senior Project Editor: Jane O'Neill

Production Manager: Sarah Segal

Illustration Coordinator: Matthew McAdams

Illustrations: TSI Graphics, Shawn Barber, Keith Kasnot, Matthew McAdams, Evelyn Pence

Composition: TSI Graphics

Printing and Binding: LSC Communications

Library of Congress Control Number: 2014931516

ISBN-10: 1-4641-1307-6

ISBN-13: 978-1-4641-1307-9

©2014, 2011 by Worth Publishers

Printed in the United States of America

Sixth Printing

BFW/Worth Publishers
41 Madison Ave.
New York, NY 10010

All royalties from the sale of this book are assigned to the David and Carol Myers Foundation, which exists to receive and distribute funds to other charitable organizations.

highschool.bfwpub.com/MyersAP2e

Dedication

For our esteemed Content Advisory Board members, with gratitude for their committed and perceptive support of our efforts to assist the teaching of AP® Psychology:

Tina Athanasopoulos	Allison Herzig
Charles Blair-Broeker	Steve Jones
Laura Brandt	Kent Korek
James Costello	Robert McEntarffer
Randal Ernst	Nathaniel Naughton
Nancy Fenton	Debra Park
Amy Fineburg	Kimberly Patterson
Joe Geiger	Hilary Rosenthal
Adam Goodie	Kristin Whitlock

About the Author

DAVID MYERS received his psychology Ph.D. from the University of Iowa. He has spent his career at Hope College in Michigan, where he has taught dozens of introductory psychology sections. Hope College students have invited him to be their commencement speaker and voted him "outstanding professor."

His research and writings have been recognized by the Gordon Allport Intergroup Relations Prize, by a 2010 Honored Scientist award from the Federation of Associations in Behavioral & Brain Sciences, by a 2010 Award for Service on Behalf of Personality and Social Psychology, by a 2013 Presidential Citation from the American Psychological Association (APA) Division 2, and by three honorary doctorates.

Myers' scientific articles have, with support from National Science Foundation grants, appeared in three dozen scientific periodicals, including *Science, American Scientist, Psychological Science,* and *American Psychologist.* In addition to his scholarly writing and his textbooks for introductory and social psychology, he also digests psychological science for the general public. His writings have appeared in four dozen magazines, from *Today's Education* to *Scientific American.* He also has authored five general audience books, including *The Pursuit of Happiness* and *Intuition: Its Powers and Perils.*

David Myers has chaired his city's Human Relations Commission, helped found a thriving assistance center for families in poverty, and spoken to hundreds of college, community, and high school groups (including AP® Psychology conferences, an AP® Psychology Reading, Teachers of Psychology in Secondary Schools, and the National Council for Social Studies Psychology Community). He also served on the APA's working group that created the 2010 revision of the *National Standards for High School Psychology Curricula.*

Drawing on his experience, Myers has written dozens of articles and a book (*A Quiet World*) about hearing loss, and he is advocating a transformation in American assistive listening technology (see www.hearingloop.org). For his leadership, he received an American Academy of Audiology Presidential Award in 2011, the Hearing Loss Association of America Walter T. Ridder Award in 2012, and Oticon's Focus on People Award in 2013.

He bikes to work year-round and plays regular pickup basketball. David and Carol Myers have raised two sons and a daughter, and have one granddaughter.

Content Advisory Board

TINA ATHANASOPOULOS
John Hersey High School, IL
Strive for a 5: Preparing for the AP® Psychology Examination

Tina Athanasopoulos has taught AP® Psychology since 1997 and implemented the AP® Psychology program for District 214 in Illinois. She was on the Test Development Committee for the AP® Psychology exam from 2005 through 2009. She has been involved with the AP® Psychology Reading since 2000 as a Reader, Table Leader, and Exam Leader. She currently serves as the Assistant Chief Reader. Tina has also been a College Board® consultant since 2001 and has presented at College Board® workshops across the country. Currently, Tina is also a professor for North Park University's Education Department.

CHARLES BLAIR-BROEKER
Cedar Falls High School, IA
Charlie Blair-Broeker has taught psychology to over 1500 students since 1978 and is one of only two people who has been at every annual AP® Psychology Reading since the AP® exam was first administered in 1992. He has been a Question Leader, Rubric Writer, Table Leader, and Reader for the AP® Psychology exam, completed a three-year term on the AP® Psychology Test Development Committee, and led many conferences on AP® Psychology. Among Charlie's teaching awards are the Grinnell College Outstanding Iowa Teacher Award, the University of Iowa Distinguished Teacher Award, and the APA Division 2 Teaching Excellence Award.

LAURA BRANDT
Adlai E. Stevenson High School, IL
Strive for a 5: Preparing for the AP® Psychology Examination

Laura Brandt has taught AP® Psychology since 1997 and has been involved with the AP® Psychology Reading since 1999, serving as a Reader, Table Leader, and Question Leader. She also works for the College Board® to facilitate sessions for AP® Psychology instructors. Currently, Laura also teaches AP® Psychology online through the Center for Talent Development at Northwestern University.

JAMES COSTELLO
Alvirne High School, NH
Dr. Jim Costello is a psychology, history, and government teacher in Hudson, NH. Holding a *Juris Doctor* from the University of Notre Dame, he had extensive civil trial experience prior to beginning his teaching career. He has taught psychology and numerous other AP® courses in the ten years since transitioning from the courtroom to the classroom.

RANDAL ERNST
Lincoln Public Schools, NE
Randy Ernst was a member of the initial AP® Psychology Test Development Committee and has served as a Table Leader, Question Leader, and Exam Leader at the annual AP® Psychology Reading. Randy authored the second edition of the College Board's® *Teacher's Guide for Advanced Placement® Psychology*. Randy has taught introductory psychology at both the high school and college level, and has run dozens of psychology-related workshops all over the world. He co-authored the *National Standards for High School Psychology Curricula*. He was part of the APA committee that founded the Teachers of Psychology in Secondary Schools (TOPSS), and was elected TOPSS Chair in 1995. Randy is also an adjunct professor at the University of Nebraska-Lincoln.

NANCY FENTON
Adlai E. Stevenson High School, IL
Nancy Fenton has taught high school psychology since 2004 and has served as an AP® Psychology Reader since 2008. She is currently serving on a panel of teachers reviewing submissions of performance indicators designed to accompany the *National Standards for High School Psychology Curricula*, and as the TOPSS liaison to the APA committee on psychology in schools and education. Nancy is also co-author of the review book *AP® Psychology: All Access*.

JOE GEIGER
Carl Sandburg High School, IL
Joe Geiger has been teaching high school psychology since 1995, and he entered the world of AP® Psychology in 2002. He has been a regular presenter at the National Council for the Social Studies conference for the past eight years. Currently, Joe serves as a vice chair for the National Council for the Social Studies Psychology Community. He also sits as a member of the House of Delegates for the National Council for the Social Studies.

ADAM GOODIE
University of Georgia, GA
Dr. Adam Goodie is a professor of psychology at the University of Georgia, where he teaches the introductory course and

serves as the undergraduate coordinator. As director of the Georgia Decision Lab, he has published over 50 journal articles, books, chapters, and proceedings, and his research has been funded by the National Institute of Mental Health, the National Center for Responsible Gaming, and other agencies. His teaching has been recognized by being awarded the Russell Hall Last Lecture, and he serves as a Reader for the AP® Psychology exam.

KENT KOREK

Germantown High School, WI

Key Contributors Appendix, Lecture PowerPoint® Presentations

Kent Korek has taught psychology since 1978 and AP® Psychology since its inception in 1992. He was first invited to the AP® Psychology Reading in 2005 and was promoted to Table Leader three years later. Kent was endorsed as a College Board® consultant in 2004 and since then has conducted numerous one-day workshops and week-long AP® summer institutes in the United States and Canada. He may be best known as a moderator for the award-winning blog *Teaching High School Psychology* (teachinghighschoolpsychology. blogspot.com).

NATHANIEL NAUGHTON

Arlington Catholic High School, MA

Strive for a 5: Preparing for the AP® Psychology Examination

Nate Naughton is the Social Studies Chairperson at Arlington Catholic High School. He has taught regular psychology since 1995 and AP® Psychology since 2001 when he began his school's AP® Psychology program. Nate has served as an AP® Reader since 2008. He is also an adjunct faculty member at Park University, teaching psychology and liberal education courses.

DEBRA PARK

Rutgers University–Camden, NJ

For 33 years, Debra Park taught psychology at West Deptford High School, and her teaching awards include Gloucester County Teacher of the Year, Rutgers University Public School Educator of the Year, APA Award for Excellence in Teaching Psychology, and the Moffett Memorial Teaching Excellence Award. Debra has served as a Reader for the AP® Psychology Reading. In 2011 she received an APA Presidential Citation for her outstanding contributions to the organization, and currently she serves as the Membership Committee Chair for STP, Division 2 (Teaching of Psychology) of the APA. Debra has taught various psychology and behavior management courses for Rutgers University–Camden for the last 13 years.

KIMBERLY PATTERSON

Cypress Bay High School, FL

Kimberly Patterson teaches in a high school that has been recognized by the College Board® for an exemplary AP® program at a public school. She has been teaching AP® Psychology for over 10 years, has been an AP® Psychology Reader for six years, and has been an AP® Psychology exam question writer for four years. She has spoken at the AP® Annual Conference twice on staying positive about teaching biological bases of the behavior. She has also taught at Palm Beach State University and with North Carolina Virtual Public Schools.

HILARY ROSENTHAL

Glenbrook South High School, IL

Hilary Rosenthal has been teaching AP® Psychology since 1995 in the Glenview, Illinois, area and was named Distinguished Teacher by Glenbrook South High School. She has been part of the annual AP® Psychology Reading as both Reader and Table Leader since 1997. She is currently a part of APA's working group to revise the *National Standards for High School Psychology Curricula*.

KRISTIN WHITLOCK

Viewmont High School, UT

Kristin Whitlock has taught AP® Psychology since 1992 and currently serves as a College Board® Advisor. She serves as part of the administrative team at the annual AP® Psychology Reading, and she authored the College Board's® *AP® Psychology Teacher's Guide*. Kristin has presented at numerous conferences and was awarded a Presidential citation from the APA and the 2005 Moffett Memorial Teaching Excellence Award.

Supplement Authors

AMY FINEBURG
A+ College Ready, AL
Annotated Teacher's Edition, Teacher's Resource Materials

An award-winning teacher, Dr. Amy Fineburg chaired the TOPSS executive board, served as a Reader then Table Leader at the AP® Psychology Reading, and chaired the APA working group that created the 2010 *National Standards for High School Psychology Curricula.* She also wrote the 2003 edition of the *Teacher's Guide for AP® Psychology.* She has contributed numerous articles to AP® Central and is a frequent workshop presenter and consultant for AP® Coordinators for the College Board®. She is an adjunct instructor in psychology at Samford University and is the chief academic officer for A+ College Ready, which works in Alabama to establish and build AP® programs in public schools.

ALLISON HERZIG
Langley High School, VA
Strive for a 5: Preparing for the AP® Psychology Examination

Allison Herzig has been teaching AP® Psychology for 15 years. She has been a Reader and Table Leader at the AP® Psychology Reading since 2002 and has been a workshop consultant for the College Board® for over a decade, running various workshops nationwide for AP® Psychology instructors. Allison has served on the test development committee for the Psychology Praxis, published a sample syllabus in the College Board's® *Teacher Resource Manual,* and authored a curriculum module on intelligence for the College Board®. Allison also currently teaches Methods and Instructional Strategies at American University.

STEVE JONES
Durham Public Schools, NC
Test Bank, Teacher's Resource Materials

Steve Jones is a National Board Certified Teacher who has taught AP® Psychology for 11 years. He has served as chair and as a member at large for the TOPSS committee and established North Carolina Teachers of Psychology. He is a former contributing editor of the *Psychology Teacher Network* quarterly newsletter, published by the APA. He is also a co-founder of the award-winning blog *Teaching High School Psychology* (teachinghighschoolpsychology.blogspot.com).

ROBERT McENTARFFER
Lincoln Public Schools, NE
Test Bank

Dr. Robert McEntarffer is an award-winning psychology teacher who has taught at both the high school and college level. Rob became an AP® Psychology Reader in 1995, was promoted to Table Leader, and served as a Question Leader from 2004 to 2010. He chaired the Assessment Committee at the Psychology Partnerships Project (James Madison University), co-authored *How to Prepare for the Advanced Placement® Psychology Exam,* and won the 2004 Moffett Memorial Teaching Excellence Award. Rob currently works as an assessment specialist for the Lincoln Public School district.

In Appreciation

Reviewers

My gratitude extends to the colleagues who contributed criticism, corrections, and creative ideas related to the content, pedagogy, and format of the tenth edition of *Psychology*. For their expertise and encouragement, and the gifts of their time to the teaching of psychology, I thank the reviewers and consultants listed below.

Lisa Abrams
Hunter College

William Acker
Chino Hills High School (CA)

Geri Acquard
Walter Johnson High School (MD), and Howard Community College

Karen Albertini
Penn State University

Jonathan Appel
Tiffin University

Willow Aureala
Hawaii Community College/University of Hawaii Center, W. H.

Hallie Baker
Muskingum University

Meeta Banerjee
Michigan State University

Joy Berrenberg
University of Colorado, Denver

Joan Bihun
University of Colorado, Denver

Megan Bradley
Frostburg State University

Stephen Brasel
Moody Bible Institute

Sherry Broadwell
Georgia State University

Jane Brown
Athens Technical College

Tamara Brown
University of Kentucky

Mark Carter
Baker University

Jenel Cavazos
University of Oklahoma

Brian Charboneau
Wekiva High School (FL)

Stephen Chew
Samford University

Katherine Clemans
University of Florida

James Collins
Middle Georgia College

Ingrid Cominsky
Onondaga Community College

Corey Cook
University of Florida

Grant Corser
Southern Utah University

Janet Dean
Asbury University

Deanna DeGidio
North Virginia Community College

Beth Dietz-Uhler
Miami University

Stephanie Ding
Del Mar College

William Dragon
Cornell College

Kathryn Dumper
Bainbridge College

David Dunaetz
Azusa Pacific University

Julie Earles
Florida Atlantic University

Kristin Flora
Franklin College

James Foley
The College of Wooster

Nicole Ford
Walter Johnson High School (MD)

Lisa Fozio-Thielk
Waubonsee Community College

Sue Frantz
Highline Community College

Phyllis Freeman
State University of New York, New Paltz

Julia Fullick
Rollins College

Christopher Gade
Dominican University of California

Becky Ganes
Modesto Junior College

Gary Gillund
The College of Wooster

William Goggin
University of Southern Mississippi

Andrea Goldstein
Keiser University

Chris Goode
Georgia State University

Peter Graf
University of British Columbia

Jeffrey Green
Virginia Commonwealth University

Jerry J. Green
Tarrant County College

Stephen Hampe
Utica College

Marissa Harrison
Penn State, Harrisburg

William Hart
University of Alabama

Michael Hendery
Southern New Hampshire University

Patricia Hinton
Hiwassee College

Debra Hollister
Valencia Community College

Richard Houston-Norton
West Texas A & M University

Alishia Huntoon
Oregon Institute of Technology

Matthew Isaak
University of Louisiana, Lafayette

Diana Joy
Community College of Denver

Bethany Jurs
University of Wisconsin, Stout

Richard Keen
Converse College

Barbara Kennedy
Brevard Community College

April Kindrick
South Puget Sound Community College

Kristina Klassen
North Idaho College

Mark Kline
Elon University

Larry Kollman
North Iowa Area Community College

Lee Kooler
Yosemite Community College

Kristine Kovak-Lesh
Ripon University

Elizabeth Lanthier
Northern Virginia Community College

Cathy Lawrenz
Johnson County Community College

Fred Leavitt
California State University, East Bay

Jennifer Levitas
Strayer University

Gary Lewandowski
Monmouth University

Peter Lifton
Northeastern University

Mark Loftis
Tennessee Technological University

Cecile Marczinski
Northern Kentucky University

Monica Marsee
University of New Orleans

Mary-Elizabeth Maynard
Leominster High School (MA)

Judy McCown
University of Detroit Mercy

Todd McKerchar
Jacksonville State University

Michelle Merwin
The University of Tennessee at Martin

Amy Miron
Community College of Baltimore County

Charles Miron
Community College of Baltimore County

Paulina Multhaupt
Macomb Community College

Joel Nadler
Southern Illinois University, Edwardsville

Carmelo Nina
William Paterson University

Wendy North-Ollendorf
Northwestern Connecticut Community College

Margaret Norwood
Community College of Aurora

Lindsay Novak
College of Saint Mary

Michie Odle
State University of New York, Cortland

Caroline Olko
Nassau Community College

Jennifer Peluso
Florida Atlantic University

Marion Perlmutter
University of Michigan

Maura PiLotti
New Mexico Highlands University

Shane Pitts
Birmingham-Southern College

Chantel Prat
University of Washington

William Price
North Country Community College

Chris K. Randall
Kennesaw State University

Jenny Rinehart
University of New Mexico

Vicki Ritts
St. Louis Community College, Meramec

Alan Roberts
Indiana University

Karena Rush
Millersville University

Lisa Sanders
Austin High School (TX)

Catherine Sanderson
Amherst College

Kristina Schaefer
Moorpark College

Cory Scherer
Penn State, Schuylkill

Erin Schoeberl
Mount Saint Mary College

Paul Schulman
State University of New York Institute of Technology

Michael Schumacher
Columbus State Community College

Jane Sheldon
University of Michigan, Dearborn

Mark Sibiky
Marietta College

Lisa Sinclair
University of Winnipeg

Starlette Sinclair
Georgia Institute of Technology

Stephanie Smith
Indiana University Northwest

Michael Spiegler
Providence College

George Spilich
Washington College

Lynn Sprout
Jefferson Community College

Kim Stark-Wroblewski
University of Central Missouri

Krishna Stilianos
Oakland Community College

Jaine Strauss
Macalester College

Robert Strausser
Baptist College for Health Sciences

James Sullivan
Florida State University

Richard Tafalla
University of Wisconsin, Stout

Michael Vallante
Quinsigamond Community College

Amanda Vanderbur
Zionsville Community High School (IN)

Jason Vasquez
Illinois State University

Craig Vickio
Bowling Green State University

Rachel Walker
Charleston Southern University

Lou Ann Wallace
University of Tennessee, Martin Parsons Center

Erica Weisgram
University of Wisconsin, Stevens Point

Elizabeth Weiss
The Ohio State University of Newark

Ryan Wessle
Northwest Missouri State

Robert Westbrook
Washington State Community College

Penny Williams
Jackson Community College

William C. Williams
Spokane Falls Community College

Jennifer Yanowitz
Utica College

Tammy Zacchili
Saint Leo University

Brief Contents

Contents

Unit III

Biological Bases of Behavior / 75

Unit IV

Sensation and Perception / 150

Unit V

States of Consciousness / 217

Unit VI

Learning / 262

Unit VII

Cognition / 316

Unit VIII

Motivation, Emotion, and Stress / 389

Unit IX

Developmental Psychology / 460

Unit X

Personality / 554

Unit XI

Testing and Individual Differences / 606

Unit XII

Abnormal Behavior / 649

Unit XIII

Treatment of Abnormal Behavior / 707

Unit XIV

Social Psychology / 753

How to Get the Most From Your AP® Psychology Resources

The Advanced Placement® (AP®) Psychology course represents a wonderful opportunity for high school students to be challenged by the rigor of a college-level course, while learning life-relevant, mind-expanding concepts from the humanly significant discipline of psychology.

My unwavering vision for *Psychology for AP®* has been to *merge rigorous science with a broad human perspective that engages both mind and heart*. I aim to offer a state-of-the-art introduction to psychological science that speaks to your needs and interests. I aspire to help you understand and appreciate the wonders of your everyday life. And I seek to convey the inquisitive spirit with which psychologists *do* psychology.

HIGH SCHOOL INSIGHT

Creating this book is a team sport. Like so many human achievements, it is the product of a collective intelligence. Woodrow Wilson spoke for me: "I not only use all the brains I have, but all I can borrow."

For this edition, I was fortunate to collaborate closely with an expert Content Advisory Board throughout the development process. The Content Advisory Board understands the needs of the AP® Psychology teacher and student, and provided crucial direction on how to make the content relevant, engaging, and appropriate for a high school classroom. In addition, the Board members provided sage guidance on key content, organizational, and pedagogical issues and ensured that the end-of-module and end-of-unit assessments provide the practice you will need for the questions you will encounter on the AP® exam. More detailed information about our extensive teacher/student support package can be found in the *Annotated Teacher's Edition* and on our catalog page: http://highschool.bfwpub.com/MyersAP2e.

I extend gratitude and admiration to each of our Board members for their enduring contributions to the teaching of psychology. See pages vii through ix for more information about each of these talented educators and assessment writers.

WHAT'S NEW?

The organization of this book is inspired by my goal of providing the ultimate teaching and learning tool for AP® Psychology teachers and students. With this in mind, the second edition has been carefully restructured and extensively updated, while keeping true to the most recently revised College Board® Course Description. It features improvements to the organization and presentation, as well as to our system of supporting student learning and remembering. For a visual walk-through of the features of the book, see pages xxxi through xxxiv.

Key Content Changes

New Research Throughout

My ongoing scrutiny of dozens of scientific periodicals and science news sources, in addition to regular correspondence with researchers, was enhanced by commissioned reviews and countless e-mails from teachers and students. All this supports my integrating the field's most important, thought-provoking, and student-relevant new discoveries. See the table below for details about new coverage.

Key Content Changes in *Myers' Psychology for AP®*, *2nd Edition*

Unit I: Psychology's History and Approaches

- Updated coverage of women in psychology and cross-cultural psychology.
- Introduction of *positive psychology* and *community psychology,* both new key terms.
- Increased coverage of psychology's subfields.

Unit II: Research Methods: Thinking Critically With Psychological Science

- Scientific method is now illustrated with theory about sleep's value for effective learning.
- Includes new survey data examples; *sampling bias* is a new key term.
- Improved clarification of random sampling and random assignment.
- New research demonstrating the dangers of statistical illiteracy, and expanded discussion of descriptive and inferential statistics.

Unit III: Biological Bases of Behavior

- Author's personal MRI experience demonstrates autonomic nervous system in action.
- Includes new coverage of cognitive neural prosthetics.
- New photo shows Phineas Gage as he looked *after* his famous accident.
- Now includes new research on blindsight.
- Several new key terms, including *refractory period, all-or-none response, agonist, antagonist,* and *epigenetics.*

Unit IV: Sensation and Perception

- Both topics covered in clearer and more efficient fashion.
- Expanded discussion and new research examples of selective attention.
- New section covers *embodied cognition,* the blending of tactile and social judgments.
- Includes new coverage of taste-touch sensory interaction, and new cognitive neuroscience research helps explain smell-cognition connection.

Unit V: States of Consciousness

- Expanded coverage and research examples of conscious awareness.
- Adopts the new American Academy of Sleep Medicine classification of sleep stages (REM, NREM-1, NREM-2, and NREM-3).
- Includes new research linking sleep loss and depression in adolescents, and new research support for sleep deprivation lowering immune system functioning.
- New illustration of physiological effects of sleep deprivation.
- Drugs discussion fully updated for DSM-5 (*substance use disorder* and *alcohol use disorder* are new key terms); new table outlines when drug use is a disorder.

Unit VI: Learning

- New biology, cognition, and learning section that more fully explores the biological and cognitive constraints on classical, operant, and observational learning.

- New learning and personal control section.
- New key terms include *cognitive learning, respondent behavior,* and *operant behavior.*
- New research examples of how children will over-imitate adult actions.
- Updated research examples of media violence viewing/violent behavior.

Unit VII: Cognition

- David Myers worked closely with Janie Wilson (professor of psychology at Georgia Southern University and vice president for programming of the Society for the Teaching of Psychology) for this unit's thorough revision.
- Atkinson-Shiffrin's three-stage model de-emphasized in favor of more current theories; coverage of working memory updated and expanded.
- New discussion of the testing effect and other study tips, including best times to study and effects of spacing on memory over time.
- New research on inaccurate autobiographical memories, memory reconsolidation, the misinformation effect, insight, confirmation bias, framing, and why we tend to fear the wrong things.
- New research updates the discussion of babies' productive language development and the nature–nurture debate over language development.
- Neuroscience research updates discussion of language development; coverage of aphasia, Broca's area, and Wernicke's area now appears here.

Unit VIII: Motivation, Emotion, and Stress

- Biochemistry of hunger and the biological and cultural influences on hunger updated.
- New research fully updated for DSM-5 enhances discussion of hormones and sexual behavior.
- New discussion of social networking.
- Theories of emotion coverage reorganized and improved.
- New research tracks positive vs. negative social media posts across days of the week.
- New research supports men's tendency to socially withdraw under stress and women's tendency to *tend and befriend.*
- New research shows health-depleting effects of depression, anxiety, and stress, including the links to genes controlling inflammation.

Unit IX: Developmental Psychology

- Discussion of teratogens expanded to include epigenetics.
- Autism spectrum disorder discussion extensively updated.
- Gender development section expanded and improved with new research.
- New research expands discussion of adolescent identity development to include effects on alcohol abuse and effects of romantic relationships; new social networking research updates peer relationship discussion.
- Sexual development now covered here.

Unit X: Personality

- Modern-day psychodynamic approaches now more clearly distinguished from historical Freudian roots.
- New research expands discussion of modern unconscious mind.
- New research supports value of humanistic psychology's positive regard as well as Big Five personality traits; new social networking research connects texting behavior with Big Five traits.

(continued on the next page)

- New cross-cultural research expands understanding of extraversion and well-being, and new research updates discussion of positive psychology.
- *Self-efficacy* and *narcissism* are new key terms.

Unit XI: Testing and Individual Differences

- New research updates discussion of *g* factor and cognitive abilities predicting later accomplishments.
- New research links emotional intelligence to unconscious processing and updates discussion of neurological measurements of intelligence.
- Research updates clarify discussion of twin studies and heritability and the variability of intelligence in gender, racial, ethnic, and socioeconomic groups.
- New research offers ideas for culturally less-biased intelligence tests and new examples support the effect of expectations on test performance.

Unit XII: Abnormal Behavior

- Fully updated to reflect DSM-5 changes.
- Updated PTSD coverage and related discussion of resilience and posttraumatic growth.
- New research on depression (including high school student population statistics); suicide box expanded to include nonsuicidal self-injury.
- New neuroscience research updates schizophrenia section; includes new risk factors and more research support for risk of maternal virus during midpregnancy.
- New cross-cultural research and art updates eating disorders coverage; antisocial personality disorder coverage updated.

Unit XIII: Treatment of Abnormal Behavior

- Fully updated to reflect DSM-5 changes.
- New case study demonstrates transference in therapy; now covers Ellis' *rational-emotive behavior therapy (REBT),* with new key term and case study.
- Cognitive-behavioral therapy discussion expanded.
- Discussion of aims and benefits of group and family therapy clarified.
- Includes new research on certain psychotherapies working best on specific disorders, with *therapeutic alliance* a new key term.
- Improved antidepressants coverage for anxiety and other disorders.
- New research explores placebo effect in ECT treatment and alternative stimulation procedures.

Unit XIV: Social Psychology

- New research on persuasion uses climate change as central example; Milgram discussion includes cross-cultural, modern-day research replications.
- New coverage of online group polarization.
- New figure tracks prejudice over time in various age groups.
- Updated ingroup and outgroup discussion; new research on categorizing mixed-race people by their minority identity.
- New research on contributors to aggression; new research on prosocial effects of playing positive video games and on violent video games increasing aggression and decreasing compassion and altruism.

Enrichment Modules

- Engaging bonus material that teachers may choose to assign after the AP® exam: influences on drug use, psychology at work, experienced emotions, human flourishing, and animal thinking and language.

New Features

A Flexible Modular Approach

The second edition has been restructured with a modular approach. As in the first edition, the units still correspond to the College Board® AP® Topic Outline. For the second edition, the units have been divided into 3 to 10 modules each. Each module breaks the course material into a pedagogically appropriate "chunk" that is designed to be presented in one or two class periods, with additional class periods for activities, demonstrations, and reinforcement, as needed. The modular approach also makes it easier for you to remember what to study and read for homework.

In addition, the **Numbered Learning Objectives** have been improved and are now used more effectively to promote retention. They appear in statement form at the beginning of each module to help orient you to the material you are about to read. These clear and measurable Learning Objectives provide you with a snapshot preview of the section material, while allowing you to "check off" each objective as you master it. The objectives are repeated in an engaging question form in context within the module, and then used at the end of each module for review.

More AP®-Focused Elements and Study Aids

- **AP® Exam Tips,** found in the margin throughout the text, provide invaluable advice on where to focus and how to avoid pitfalls so that you may be successful in the course and on the exam. These tips also appear compiled in an appendix at the end of the book.
- More **AP® exam practice** is provided in the numerous, high-quality multiple-choice and free-response questions (FRQs) found at the end of each module and unit. These assessments not only test the material learned, but they also mimic AP® questions to train you for what you will see on the exam. The open-ended, conceptual FRQs familiarize you with the kind of synthesis skills you'll need to master the exam.
- A **full-length AP®-style practice exam** is included at the end of the text to ensure you have nailed down the content and are ready to tackle the real test in May.
- A **Key Contributors list** appears at the end of each unit to highlight the most important people you should know in psychology. You can access the **Key Contributors Appendix** at the end of the text, and the *Key Contributors Study Guide* on the Book Companion Site (BCS) to be sure you are familiar with these core contributions to psychology. Access the BCS at www.worthpublishers.com/MyersAP2e.

What Continues?

Alignment With the College Board® Topic Outline

With help from my sharp-eyed editors and Content Advisory Board, I have worked to create an organization that matches up with the College Board's® 2013 topic outline, so that teachers can be sure they are providing their students with the best possible preparation for the AP® exam. This means my text offers the same 14 units, in order, and the same distribution of content coverage among those 14 units. Where the outline has recommended coverage within specific units, you can be sure that you will find that coverage (sometimes with references to more, related coverage elsewhere).

Although the College Board® topic outline is not intended to be an exhaustive list of topics, it represents an excellent starting point—to which I have added coverage based on my own knowledge of what is needed to succeed in other college courses, what's new and important in the world of psychology research, and perhaps most important, what an educated person needs to know. See the opening book pages for a table aligning each College Board® course description topic to the corresponding coverage in this text.

Thoughtful Study Aids

- **Numbered Learning Objective Questions,** as noted earlier, establish reading objectives for each significant section of text and direct your learning.

- **Before You Move On** features, found at the end of major sections of text, include **Ask Yourself questions,** which encourage you to apply new concepts to your own experiences, and **Test Yourself questions** (with answers in Appendix E) that assess mastery and encourage big-picture thinking.
- **Module Review Sections** repeat the numbered objective questions and address them with a bulleted summary. **Unit Review Sections** include page-referenced Terms and Concepts to Remember as well as a list of Key Contributors discussed in the unit.

Cultural and Gender Diversity Coverage

This text presents a thoroughly cross-cultural perspective on psychology (Table 1)—reflected in research findings, and text and photo examples. Coverage of the psychology of women and men is also thoroughly integrated (Table 2). Discussion of the relevance of cultural and gender diversity begins on the first page of the first unit and continues throughout the text.

Strong Critical Thinking Coverage and Research Emphasis

I aim to introduce you to critical thinking throughout the book. The text includes the following opportunities for you to learn or practice critical thinking skills and to work toward a better understanding of research design principles—both of which are essential to success on the AP® exam.

- Unit II, Research Methods: Thinking Critically With Psychological Science, introduces you to psychology's **research methods,** emphasizing the fallacies of our everyday intuition and common sense and, thus, the need for psychological science. Critical thinking is introduced as a key term in this unit (page 35). The Statistical Reasoning discussion encourages you to focus on thinking smarter by applying simple statistical principles to everyday reasoning.
- Throughout the text, additional opportunities may be found for you to test your understanding of **research design,** with narrative and marginal self-test review questions (with answers following in the narrative, or upside down in a nearby margin).
- **Critical examinations of key issues in psychology** appear throughout the narrative to spark interest and provide important lessons in thinking critically about everyday topics and pop psychology. (Consider, for example, the critical analysis of ESP on page 238.) See Table 3 for a summary of this text's coverage of critical thinking and research-related topics, and for a list of the Thinking Critically About boxes.

Table 1 Culture and Multicultural Experience

In Units I–XIV and the Enrichment Modules, coverage of culture and multicultural experience can be found on the following pages:

Aggression, p. 791	Behavioral effects of culture, p. 130	definition, pp. 776–777	use of, p. 824
AIDS, p. 450		and the self, pp. 598–600	Eating disorders: Western culture and, p. 698
Anger, p. 846	Body ideal, pp. 697–698	shock, pp. 44, 777	
Animal research ethics, pp. 66–67	Categorization, pp. 256–257	Deaf culture, pp. 869, 117, 111, 374, 376, 377	Emotion:
Attraction:	Complementary/alternative medicine, p. 863	Development:	emotion-detecting ability, p. 432
love and marriage, p. 803	Conformity, p. 765	attachment, pp. 492, 495	experiencing, p. 846
speed-dating, p. 799	Corporal punishment practices, pp. 281–282	child-rearing, p. 497	expressing, pp. 435–437, 435–437
Attractiveness, pp. 138, 798–799, 801	Cultural norms, pp. 140, 777, 503–504	cognitive development, p. 484	Enemy perceptions, p. 812
Attribution, social and economic effects of, p. 755	Culture:	social development, p. 492	Fear, p. 367
	context effects, p. 165	Drugs:	Flow, pp. 827–828
		psychological effects of, p. 247	Flynn effect, pp. 621–622

Table 2   The Psychology of Men and Women

In Units I-XIV and the Enrichment Modules, coverage of the psychology of men and women can be found on the following pages:

(continued on the next page)

Table 2 (continued)

sexual behavior,
    pp. 407–408
sexual development,
    pp. 513–514,
    526–527
testosterone-replacement
    therapy, pp. 407–408
Intelligence, pp. 638–639
    bias, p. 642
Leadership:
    transformational, p. 839
Losing weight, p. 403
Marriage, pp. 545, 857
Maturation, pp. 513–514
Menarche, p. 513

Menopause, p. 540
Midlife crisis, p. 544
Molecular genetics: "missing
    women," pp. 781–783,
Obesity:
    health risks, p. 401
Observational learning:
    sexually violent media, p. 309
TV's influence, p. 309
Pornography, p. 408
Posttraumatic stress disorder:
    development of, pp. 664–665
Prejudice, pp. 357, 780–783
Psychological disorders, rates
    of, p. 658

Rape, p. 787
Religiosity and: life expectancy,
    p. 864
REM sleep, arousal in, p. 229
Romantic love, pp. 803–804
Savant syndrome, p. 609
Schizophrenia, pp. 685–686
Sense of smell, pp. 206–207
Sexual attraction, p. 138
Sexual fantasies , p. 410
Sexuality, pp. 406–410
    adolescent, pp. 527–531
    evolutionary explanation,
        pp. 138–139
    external stimuli, p. 409

Sleep, p. 235
Stereotyping, p. 164
Stress:
    and depression, p. 453
    and health and sexual
        abuse, p. 859
    and heart disease,
        p. 452
    and HIV, p. 450
    and the immune system,
        p. 448
    response, pp. 445–446
Suicide, pp. 676–677
Women in psychology,
    pp. 4–5

Table 3 Critical Thinking and Research Emphasis

Critical Thinking boxes and emphasis on research can be found on the following pages:

**Thinking Critically
About . . . boxes:**
The Fear Factor—Why We
    Fear the Wrong Things,
    pp. 366–367
Lie Detection, p. 428
How to Be a "Successful"
    Astrologer or Palm
    Reader, pp. 579–580
ADHD—Normal High
    Energy or Genuine
    Disorder?, p. 652
Insanity and Responsibility,
    p. 656
"Regressing" from Unusual
    to Usual, p. 730
Complementary and
    Alternative Medicine,
    p. 863

**Critical Examinations of
Pop Psychology:**
The need for psychological
    science, p. 30
Perceiving order in random
    events, pp. 33–34
Do we use only 10 percent
    of our brains?,
    p. 109
Critiquing the evolutionary
    perspective, p. 139

Is there extrasensory
    perception?, pp. 167–169
Can hypnosis enhance
    recall? Coerce action? Be
    therapeutic? Alleviate pain?,
    pp. 220–221
Has the concept of "addiction"
    been stretched too far?, p. 248
Near-death experiences,
    p. 255
How much credit (or blame) do
    parents deserve?, p. 510
How valid is the Rorschach
    test?, p. 567
Is repression a myth?, pp. 562–563
Is Freud credible?, pp. 562–563
Is psychotherapy effective?,
    pp. 728–732
Evaluating alternative therapies,
    pp. 733–734
Do video games teach or release
    violence?, pp. 794–795

**Thinking Critically With
Psychological Science:**
The limits of intuition and
    common sense, pp. 30–34
The scientific attitude, pp. 34–35
"Critical thinking" introduced as
    a key term, pp. 35–36
The scientific method, pp. 38–39

Correlation and causation,
    pp. 48–49
Illusory correlation, p. 50
Exploring cause and effect,
    pp. 50–51
Random assignment, p. 51
Independent and dependent
    variables, pp. 52–53
Statistical reasoning, pp. 56–60
Descriptive statistics, pp. 57–59
Making inferences, pp. 60–61

Scientific Detective Stories:
Is breast milk better than
    formula?, pp. 51–52
Our divided brains, pp. 114–117
Twin and adoption studies,
    pp. 125–128
Parallel processing, pp. 176–178
How do we see in color?,
    pp. 178–179
What affects our sleep
    patterns?, pp. 229–231
Why do we dream?, pp. 241–243
Is hypnosis an extension of
    normal consciousness or an
    altered state?, pp. 221–222
How do we store memories in our
    brains?, pp. 329–334
How are memories constructed?,
    pp. 347–352

Why do we feel hunger?,
    pp. 396–399
The pursuit of happiness:
    Who is happy, and why?,
    pp. 847–853
Why—and in whom—does
    stress contribute to heart
    disease?, pp. 451–453
How a child's mind
    develops, pp. 476–484
Aging and intelligence,
    pp. 625–627
Self-esteem versus
    self-serving bias,
    pp. 596–598
What causes mood
    disorders?, pp. 674–681
Do prenatal viral infections
    increase risk of
    schizophrenia?, p. 688
Is psychotherapy effective?,
    pp. 728–731
Why do people fail to help in
    emergencies?,
    pp. 807–809
How and why is social
    support linked with
    health?, pp. 857–859
Do animals exhibit
    language?, pp. 868–870

Tools for Learning . . .
Getting the Most From This Book

Each unit and its modules are structured with a common set of features designed to help students learn while remaining engaged.

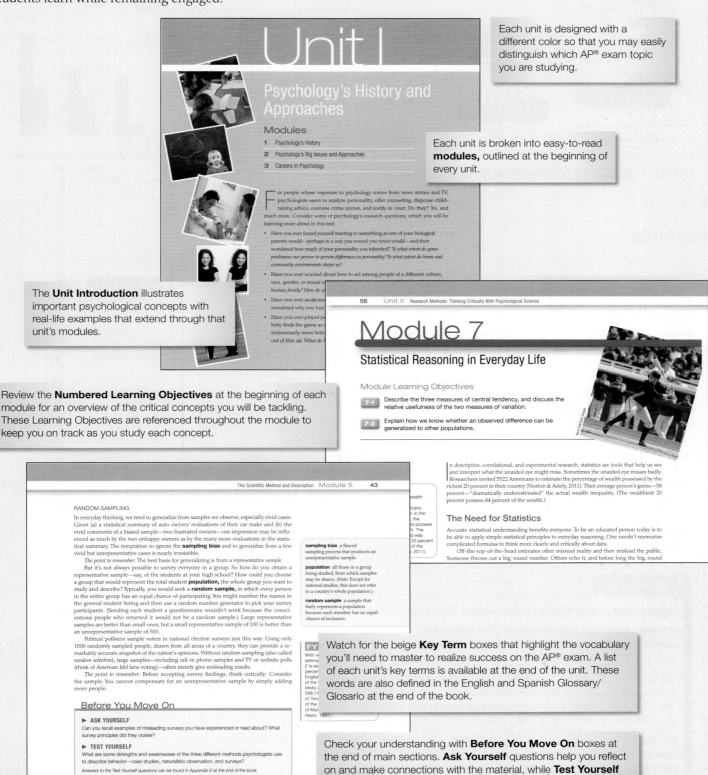

Each unit is designed with a different color so that you may easily distinguish which AP® exam topic you are studying.

Each unit is broken into easy-to-read **modules,** outlined at the beginning of every unit.

The **Unit Introduction** illustrates important psychological concepts with real-life examples that extend through that unit's modules.

Review the **Numbered Learning Objectives** at the beginning of each module for an overview of the critical concepts you will be tackling. These Learning Objectives are referenced throughout the module to keep you on track as you study each concept.

Watch for the beige **Key Term** boxes that highlight the vocabulary you'll need to master to realize success on the AP® exam. A list of each unit's key terms is available at the end of the unit. These words are also defined in the English and Spanish Glossary/ Glosario at the end of the book.

Check your understanding with **Before You Move On** boxes at the end of main sections. **Ask Yourself** questions help you reflect on and make connections with the material, while **Test Yourself** questions assess your mastery of the content you've just read.

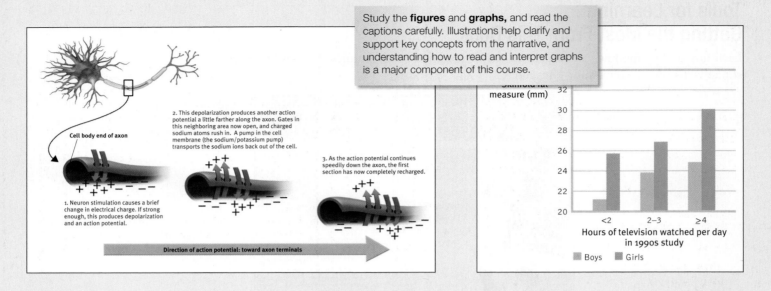

Study the **figures** and **graphs,** and read the captions carefully. Illustrations help clarify and support key concepts from the narrative, and understanding how to read and interpret graphs is a major component of this course.

Features

AP® Exam Tip

Be prepared for at least a multiple-choice question that tests your ability to tell the difference between the James-Lange theory and the Cannon-Bard theory.

Pay attention to the **AP® Exam Tip** boxes, written by longtime AP® teacher Charlie Blair-Broeker. They provide helpful advice on what to pay close attention to and what common pitfalls to avoid so you can succeed on the AP® exam.

FYI

The people who first dissected and labeled the brain used the language of scholars—Latin and Greek. Their words are actually attempts at graphic description: For example, *cortex* means "bark," *cerebellum* is "little brain," and *thalamus* is "inner chamber."

FYI boxes are interesting tidbits of information that help connect the content you're reading with real-life examples and research studies.

Try This

Most of us would be unable to name the order of the songs on our favorite album or playlist. Yet, hearing the end of one piece cues (by association) an anticipation of the next. Likewise, when singing your national anthem, you associate the end of each line with the beginning of the next. (Pick a line out of the middle and notice how much harder it is to recall the *previous* line.)

Connect more deeply with the concepts you're learning by putting them into real-life practice with **Try This** boxes.

Close-up

Improve Your Retention—and Your Grades!

 How can psychological principles help you learn and remember, and do better on the AP® exam?

Do you, like most students, assume that the way to cement your new learning is to reread? What helps even more—and what this book therefore encourages—is repeated self-testing and rehearsal of previously studied material. Memory researchers Henry Roediger and Jeffrey Karpicke (2006) call this phenomenon the **testing effect.** They note that "testing is a powerful means of improving learning, not just assessing it." In one of their studies, students recalled the meaning of 40

in the *Before You Move On* sections. After answerin[g] *Yourself* questions there, you can check your answ[er in Ap]pendix E at the end of this text and reread as needed[.]

Finally, *review:* Read over any notes you have ta[ken,] with an eye on the module's organization, and qui[ckly review] the whole module. Write or say what a concept is [before] reading to check your understanding.

Survey, question, read, retrieve, review. I have organized this book's modules to facilitate your use of the SQ3R study system. Each module begins with a list of objectives that aid your *survey.* Headings and the numbered Learning Objective *Questions* at the beginning of main sections suggest issues

Apply psychological findings to your life with **Close-up** boxes. This feature encourages application of new concepts by providing high-interest, real-life examples.

Thinking Critically About

Does Viewing Media Violence Trigger Violent Behavior?

Was the judge who, in 1993, tried two British 10-year-olds for the murder of a 2-year-old right to suspect that the pair had been influenced by "violent video films"? Were the American media right to wonder if Adam Lanza, the 2012 mass killer of [children] and their teachers at Connecticut's Sandy Hook [S]chool, was influenced by his playing of the vio[lent ga]mes found stockpiled in his home? To understand [how viole]nce viewing leads to violent behavior, research[ers hav]e some 600 correlational and experimental studies [(Anderson &]Gentile, 2008; Comstock, 2008; Murray, 2008). [Correlatio]nal studies do support this link:

[• In the Uni]ted States and Canada, homicide rates doubled between 1957 and 1974, just when TV was introduced and spreading. Moreover, census regions with later dates

people, when irritated, to react more cruelly? To some extent, it does. This is especially so when an attractive person commits seemingly justified, realistic violence that goes unpunished and causes no visible pain or harm (Donnerstein, 1998, 2011).

The violence-viewing effect seems to stem from at least two factors. One is *imitation* (Geen & Thomas, 1986). Children as young as 14 months will imitate acts they observe on TV (Meltzoff & Moore, 1989, 1997). As they watch, their brains simulate the behavior, and after this inner rehearsal they become more likely to act it out. Thus, in one experiment, violent play increased sevenfold immediately after children viewed *Power Rangers* episodes (Boyatzis et al., 1995). As happened in the Bobo doll experiment, children often precisely imitated the models' violent acts—in this case, flying karate kicks.

Prolonged exposure to violence also *desensitizes* viewers.

Exercise your brain with the **Thinking Critically About** boxes. These boxes sharpen your analytical skills by modeling a critical thinking approach to key issues in psychology, and encourage you to apply psychological research to current topics. Before you know it, you'll be thinking like a psychological scientist!

Each module concludes with a unique review.

Test yourself using the **Module Review,** organized by that module's learning objectives, so you can be sure you've mastered all of the key concepts.

Module 9 Review

 9-1 Why are psychologists concerned with human biology?

- Psychologists working from a *biological* perspective study the links between biology and behavior.

- We are biopsychosocial systems, in which biological, psychological, and social-cultural factors interact to influence behav[ior.]

 9-2 What are [the parts of a] neural im[pulse?]

- *Neurons* are the [basic units of the nervous] system, the bod[y's speedy electrochemical information] system.

- A neuron receiv[es signals through its dendrites,] and sends signa[ls through its axon.]

- Some axons are [encased in a myelin sheath, which enables] faster transmiss[ion.]

 9-3 How do nerve cells communicate with other nerve cells?

- When action potentials reach the end of an axon (the axon terminals), they stimulate the release of *neurotransmitters.*

- These chemical messengers carry a message from the sending neuron across a *synapse* to receptor sites on a

Multiple-Choice Questions

1. Multiple sclerosis is a result of degeneration in the
   a. dendrite.
   b. axon.
   c. myelin sheath.
   d. terminal button.
   e. neuron.

2. Junita does not feel like getting out of bed, has lost her appetite, and feels tired for most of the day. Which of the following neurotransmitters likely is in short supply for Junita?
   a. Dopamine   d. Acetylcholine

3. Which neurotransmitter inhibits CNS activity in order to calm a person down during stressful situations?
   a. GABA   d. Dopamine
   b. Norepinephrine   e. Serotonin
   c. Acetylcholine

4. Phrenology has been discredited, but which of the following ideas has its origins in phrenology?
   a. Brain lateralization
   b. Brain cavities contributing to sense of humor
   c. Bumps in the left hemisphere leading to emotional responses

and vitality into

Practice FRQs

1. While hiking, Ken stumbled and fell down a 10-foot drop-off. Upon landing, he sprained his ankle badly. Ken was surprised that he felt very little pain for the first half hour. Explain how the following helped Ken feel little pain in the moments after the injury.
   - Endorphins
   - The synapse

Answer

1 point: Endorphins are natural, opiate-like neurotransmitters linked to controlling pain.

2. Explain the role each of the following plays in sending a message through a neuron.
   - Dendrites
   - Axon
   - Myelin sheath

(3 points)

Improve your retention by testing yourself at the end of each module with **Multiple-Choice Questions** and skill-building **Practice FRQs.**

Each unit ends with a comprehensive AP®-style review.

Unit I Review

Key Terms and Concepts to Remember

empiricism, p. 3

structuralism, p. 4

functionalism, p. 4

experimental psychology, p. 5

behavioral psychology, p. 11

biological psychology, p. 11

applied research, p. 14

industrial-organizational (I/O)

> At the end of each unit, make sure you know all the **Key Terms and Concepts** and can explain the importance of each **Key Contributor** before moving on to the **AP® Exam Practice Questions.**

Key Contributors to Remember

Wilhelm Wundt, p. 3

G. Stanley Hall, p. 3

William James, p. 4

Mary Whiton Calkins, p. 4

John B. Watson, p. 6

B. F. Skinner, p. 6

Sigmund Freud, p. 6

Carl Rogers, p. 6

Jean Piaget, p. 9

Charles Darwin, p. 10

Dorothea Dix, p. 14

AP® Exam Practice Questions

Multiple-Choice Questions

1. Which perspective would be most useful when explaining how people from different countries express anger?

a. Social-cultural
b. Psychodynamic
c. Behavioral

3. Which of the following professionals is required to have a medical degree?

Free-Response Questions

1. Sam Greene noticed an ad for an Internet dating service that claimed more people who used its service are in long-term relationships than people who didn't. Sam, a good critical thinker, knows this isn't enough to claim that the service causes people to find long-term love and wants to create an experiment to investigate. Use the following terms to describe an experiment that would support or dispute the ad's claim.

- Hypothesis
- Random sample

> The **AP®-Style Multiple Choice Questions** and **Free-Response Questions** cover material from the unit to help you check your mastery of everything you've just learned. Once you get everything right, you're ready to move to the next unit!

1 point: Sam would need to operationally define what is meant by use of the Internet service, possibly including a precise number of visits to the website or time spent on the website. The phrase *long-term relationship* would also need an operational definition, possibly by the number of months together or a formal commitment (like engagement or marriage). ↩ Page 39

1 point: In Sam's study, the use of the online dating service is the independent variable. ↩ Page 52

1 point: The number of long-term relationships is the dependent variable. ↩ Page 52

1 point: Sam will need to calculate statistical significance for the experimental findings. In order to claim support for the hypothesis, the results need to show that there is no more than a 5 percent chance the findings are due to chance. ↩ Page 60

Rubric for Free-Response Question 1

1 point: The hypothesis in this context is that the Internet dating service causes (or leads to) long-term relationships. ↩ Page 38

1 point: Since the population of interest for this study should be people who are looking for long-term relationships, selecting a random sample of adults seeking relationships would help assure that the conclusions could be fairly generalized to the dating public. ↩ Page 43

1 point: In this case, participants should be randomly assigned to use of the Internet service (the experimental group) or not (the control group). ↩ Page 51

> The end-of-book **Practice AP®-Style Exam** covers material learned through the entire course, simulating the real exam. This comprehensive test ensures that you get enough practice so you can strive for a 5 on the day of the exam.

Enrichment Modules

Learning about psychology doesn't stop after you take the exam in May. Continue your exploration with Enrichment Modules 81–85, to help round out your course and prepare you for further psychology study in college and beyond.

Innovative Multimedia Supplements Package

For Students

MYERS' PSYCHOLOGY FOR AP®, SECOND EDITION E-BOOK

Our interactive e-Book fully integrates the text with student media. The e-Book also offers a range of customization features including bookmarking, highlighting, note-taking, note-sharing, and flashcards.

FLIP IT VIDEOS

If your teacher has flipped the classroom, you can watch the assigned lecture videos from links on the Book Companion Site at www.worthpublishers.com/MyersAP2e. You may also watch the videos as a refresher while studying, so that you can reflect on what you've learned and formulate meaningful questions to discuss with the teacher or your classmates.

STRIVE FOR A 5: PREPARING FOR THE AP® PSYCHOLOGY EXAMINATION

Prepared by longtime AP® teachers Allison Herzig, Nathaniel Naughton, Laura Brandt, and Tina Athanasopoulos, this supplement serves as a complete study guide and as the optimal preparation resource for the AP® exam. The unit-by-unit study guide reinforces the topics and key concepts covered in the text and on the AP® exam, and the two AP®-style practice tests at the end provide you with the opportunity to tackle the most important piece of the course.

    Strive for a 5 begins with a context-setting, big-picture overview of each unit, along with a practical study tip. Next, there is a detailed, module-by-module review, which is organized as follows:

Before You Read
- Module summary, list of key terms and names in the module

While You Read
- Essential questions to answer for each module, organized by the numbered learning objectives

After You Read
- Application and vocabulary questions for you to practice what you've learned without looking at the book

Check Yourself
- High-level, open-ended questions that require you to synthesize what you've learned throughout the unit

    The test preparation section of *Strive for a 5* is a comprehensive test review resource. To help you focus your efforts, the guide offers detailed test preparation tips, suggestions for setting a test preparation schedule, and advice on how to study effectively and efficiently. The guide includes two sample practice tests simulating the AP® exam, with solutions and sample grading rubrics found on the teacher's website and on the Teacher's Resource CD. Information about purchasing the *Strive for a 5* guide may be found on the catalog page (http://highschool.bfwpub.com/MyersAP2e).

BOOK COMPANION SITE

www.worthpublishers.com/MyersAP2e

The companion website offers valuable tools for both teachers and students. Students can access the following, free of charge:

- Quizzes
- Key Contributors Study Guide
- Flip It videos
- Podcast correlation
- Interactive flashcards that tutor students on all the key terms in the text

For Teachers

Please visit our catalog page (http://highschool.bfwpub.com/MyersAP2e) or see the Teacher's Edition for more information.

Teacher's Edition *(Amy Fineburg, A+ College Ready)*
TE-Book (e-Book version of the Teacher's Edition with integrated supplements)
ExamView® Assessment Suite Test Bank
Teacher's Resource CD
Lecture PowerPoint® Presentation
Book Companion Site

*   *   *

What an amazing success story AP® Psychology has become since 1992, when 3916 students took the first exam. As of 2013, 1.8 million students had sat for AP® Psychology exams, and more than 2 million had taken the course. For me, it has been an honor to support the teaching of our humanly significant discipline to so many of those students, and a great pleasure to have met or corresponded with so many AP® teachers and their students. It is also a keenly felt responsibility. So please do feel free to be in touch with your feedback and suggestions.

With every good wish,

David Myers

www.davidmyers.org

Myers'
Psychology
for AP®

Unit I

Psychology's History and Approaches

Modules

For people whose exposure to psychology comes from news stories and TV, psychologists seem to analyze personality, offer counseling, dispense child-raising advice, examine crime scenes, and testify in court. Do they? *Yes,* and much more. Consider some of psychology's research questions, which you will be learning more about in this text.

- Have you ever found yourself reacting to something as one of your biological parents would—perhaps in a way you vowed you never would—and then wondered how much of your personality you inherited? *To what extent do genes predispose our person-to-person differences in personality? To what extent do home and community environments shape us?*

- Have you ever worried about how to act among people of a different culture, race, gender, or sexual orientation? *In what ways are we alike as members of the human family? How do we differ?*

- Have you ever awakened from a nightmare and, with a wave of relief, wondered why you had such a crazy dream? *How often, and why, do we dream?*

- Have you ever played peekaboo with a 6-month-old and wondered why the baby finds the game so delightful? The infant reacts as though, when you momentarily move behind a door, you actually disappear—only to reappear out of thin air. *What do babies actually perceive and think?*

- Have you ever wondered what fosters school and work success? *Are some people just born smarter? And does sheer intelligence explain why some people get richer, think more creatively, or relate more sensitively?*

- Have you ever become depressed or anxious and wondered whether you'll ever feel "normal"? *What triggers our bad moods—and our good ones? Where is the line between a normal mood swing and a psychological disorder for which someone should seek help?*

- Have you ever wondered how the Internet, video games, and electronic social networks affect people? *How do today's electronic media influence how we think and how we relate?*

Psychology is a science that seeks to answer such questions about us all—how and why we think, feel, and act as we do.

A smile is a smile the world around Throughout this book, you will see examples not only of our cultural and gender diversity but also of the similarities that define our shared human nature. People in different cultures vary in when and how often they smile, but a naturally happy smile *means* the same thing anywhere in the world.

Module 1

Psychology's History

Module Learning Objectives

1-1 Describe how psychology developed from its prescientific roots in early understandings of mind and body to the beginnings of modern science.

1-2 Describe some important milestones in psychology's early development.

1-3 Describe how psychology continued to develop from the 1920s through today.

Psychology's Roots

Once upon a time, on a planet in this neighborhood of the universe, there came to be people. Soon thereafter, these creatures became intensely interested in themselves and in one another: *"Who are we? What produces our thoughts? Our feelings? Our actions? And how are we to understand and manage those around us?"*

Prescientific Psychology

 How did psychology develop from its prescientific roots in early understandings of mind and body to the beginnings of modern science?

We can trace many of psychology's current questions back through human history. These early thinkers wondered: How does our mind work? How does our body relate to our mind? How much of what we know comes built in? How much is acquired through experience? In India, Buddha pondered how sensations and perceptions combine to form ideas. In China, Confucius stressed the power of ideas and of an educated mind. In ancient Israel, Hebrew scholars anticipated today's psychology by linking mind and emotion to the body; people were said to think with their heart and feel with their bowels.

In ancient Greece, the philosopher-teacher Socrates (469–399 B.C.E.) and his student Plato (428–348 B.C.E.) concluded that mind is separable from body and continues after the body dies, and that knowledge is innate—born within us. Unlike Socrates and Plato, who derived principles by logic, Plato's student Aristotle (384–322 B.C.E.) had a love of data. An intellectual ancestor of today's scientists, Aristotle derived principles from careful observations. Moreover, he said knowledge is *not* preexisting (sorry, Socrates and Plato); instead it grows from the experiences stored in our memories.

The next 2000 years brought few enduring new insights into human nature, but that changed in the 1600s, when modern science began to flourish. With it came new theories of human behavior, and new versions of the ancient debates. A frail but brilliant Frenchman named René Descartes (1595–1650) agreed with Socrates and Plato about the existence of innate ideas and mind's being "entirely distinct from body" and able to survive its death. Descartes' concept of mind forced him to conjecture, as people have ever since, how the immaterial mind and physical body communicate. A scientist as well as a philosopher, Descartes dissected animals and concluded that the fluid in the brain's cavities contained "animal spirits." These spirits, he surmised, flowed from the brain through what we call the nerves (which he thought were hollow) to the muscles, provoking movement. Memories formed as experiences opened pores in the brain into which the animal spirits also flowed.

Descartes was right that nerve paths are important and that they enable reflexes. Yet, genius though he was, and standing upon the knowledge accumulated from 99+ percent of our human history, he hardly had a clue of what today's average 12-year-old knows. Indeed, most of the scientific story of our self-exploration—the story told in this book—has been written in but the last historical eye-blink of human time.

Meanwhile, across the English Channel in Britain, science was taking a more down-to-earth form, centered on experiment, experience, and common-sense judgment. Francis Bacon (1561–1626) became one of the founders of modern science, and his influence lingers in the experiments of today's psychological science. Bacon also was fascinated by the human mind and its failings. Anticipating what we have come to appreciate about our mind's hunger to perceive patterns even in random events, he wrote that "the human understanding, from its peculiar nature, easily supposes a greater degree of order and equality in things than it really finds" (*Novum Organuum,* 1620). He also foresaw research findings on our noticing and remembering events that confirm our beliefs: "All superstition is much the same whether it be that of astrology, dreams, omens . . . in all of which the deluded believers observe events which are fulfilled, but neglect and pass over their failure, though it be much more common."

Some 50 years after Bacon's death, John Locke (1632–1704), a British political philosopher, sat down to write a one-page essay on "our own abilities" for an upcoming discussion with friends. After 20 years and hundreds of pages, Locke had completed one of history's greatest late papers (*An Essay Concerning Human Understanding*), in which he famously argued that the mind at birth is a *tabula rasa*—a "blank slate"—on which experience writes. This idea, adding to Bacon's ideas, helped form modern **empiricism,** the idea that what we know comes from experience, and that observation and experimentation enable scientific knowledge.

> **empiricism** the view that knowledge originates in experience and that science should, therefore, rely on observation and experimentation.

Psychological Science Is Born

 What are some important milestones in psychology's early development?

Philosophers' thinking about thinking continued until the birth of psychology as we know it, on a December day in 1879, in a small, third-floor room at Germany's University of Leipzig. There, two young men were helping an austere, middle-aged professor, Wilhelm Wundt, create an experimental apparatus. Their machine measured the time lag between people's hearing a ball hit a platform and their pressing a telegraph key (Hunt, 1993). Curiously, people responded in about one-tenth of a second when asked to press the key as soon as the sound occurred—and in about two-tenths of a second when asked to press the key as soon as they were consciously aware of perceiving the sound. (To be aware of one's awareness takes a little longer.) Wundt was seeking to measure "atoms of the mind"—the fastest and simplest mental processes. So began the first psychological laboratory, staffed by Wundt and by psychology's first graduate students. (In 1883, Wundt's American student G. Stanley Hall went on to establish the first formal U.S. psychology laboratory, at Johns Hopkins University.)

Before long, this new science of psychology became organized into different branches, or schools of thought, each promoted by pioneering thinkers. These early schools included *structuralism, functionalism,* and *behaviorism,* described here (with more on behaviorism in Modules 26–30), and two schools described in later modules: Gestalt psychology (Module 19) and psychoanalysis (Module 55).

Wilhelm Wundt Wundt established the first psychology laboratory at the University of Leipzig, Germany.

Edward Bradford Titchener
Titchener used introspection to search for the mind's structural elements.

Thinking About the Mind's Structure

Soon after receiving his Ph.D. in 1892, Wundt's student Edward Bradford Titchener joined the Cornell University faculty and introduced **structuralism.** As physicists and chemists discerned the structure of matter, so Titchener aimed to discover the structural elements of mind. His method was to engage people in self-reflective *introspection* (looking inward), training them to report elements of their experience as they looked at a rose, listened to a metronome, smelled a scent, or tasted a substance. What were their immediate sensations, their images, their feelings? And how did these relate to one another? Titchener shared with the English essayist C. S. Lewis the view that "there is one thing, and only one in the whole universe which we know more about than we could learn from external observation." That one thing, Lewis said, is ourselves. "We have, so to speak, inside information" (1960, pp. 18–19).

Alas, introspection required smart, verbal people. It also proved somewhat unreliable, its results varying from person to person and experience to experience. Moreover, we often just don't know why we feel what we feel and do what we do. Recent studies indicate that people's recollections frequently err. So do their self-reports about what, for example, has caused them to help or hurt another (Myers, 2002). As introspection waned, so did structuralism.

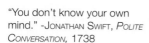

"You don't know your own mind." -JONATHAN SWIFT, *POLITE CONVERSATION*, 1738

Thinking About the Mind's Functions

Hoping to assemble the mind's structure from simple elements was rather like trying to understand a car by examining its disconnected parts. Philosopher-psychologist William James thought it would be more fruitful to consider the evolved functions of our thoughts and feelings. Smelling is what the nose does; thinking is what the brain does. But *why* do the nose and brain do these things? Under the influence of evolutionary theorist Charles Darwin, James assumed that thinking, like smelling, developed because it was *adaptive*—it contributed to our ancestors' survival. Consciousness serves a function. It enables us to consider our past, adjust to our present, and plan our future. As a **functionalist,** James encouraged explorations of down-to-earth emotions, memories, willpower, habits, and moment-to-moment streams of consciousness.

James' greatest legacy, however, came less from his laboratory than from his Harvard teaching and his writing. When not plagued by ill health and depression, James was an impish, outgoing, and joyous man, who once recalled that "the first lecture on psychology I ever heard was the first I ever gave." During one of his wise-cracking lectures, a student interrupted and asked him to get serious (Hunt, 1993). He loved his students, his family, and the world of ideas, but he tired of painstaking chores such as proofreading. "Send me no proofs!" he once told an editor. "I will return them unopened and never speak to you again" (Hunt, 1993, p. 145).

James displayed the same spunk in 1890, when—over the objections of Harvard's president—he admitted Mary Whiton Calkins into his graduate seminar (Scarborough & Furumoto, 1987). (In those years women lacked even the right to vote.) When Calkins joined, the other students (all men) dropped out. So James tutored her alone. Later, she finished all the requirements for a Harvard Ph.D., outscoring all the male students on the qualifying exams. Alas, Harvard denied her the degree she had earned, offering her instead a degree from Radcliffe College, its undergraduate sister school for women. Calkins resisted the unequal treatment and refused the degree. (More than a century

structuralism early school of thought promoted by Wundt and Titchener; used introspection to reveal the structure of the human mind.

functionalism early school of thought promoted by James and influenced by Darwin; explored how mental and behavioral processes function—how they enable the organism to adapt, survive, and flourish.

William James and Mary Whiton Calkins James was a legendary teacher-writer who authored an important 1890 psychology text. He mentored Calkins, who became a pioneering memory researcher and the first woman to be president of the American Psychological Association (APA).

Margaret Floy Washburn The first woman to receive a psychology Ph.D., Washburn synthesized animal behavior research in *The Animal Mind.*

later, psychologists and psychology students were lobbying Harvard to posthumously award Calkins the Ph.D. she earned [*Feminist Psychologist*, 2002].) Calkins nevertheless went on to become a distinguished memory researcher and the APA's first female president in 1905.

When Harvard denied Calkins the claim to being psychology's first female psychology Ph.D., that honor fell to Margaret Floy Washburn, who later wrote an influential book, *The Animal Mind*, and became the second female APA president in 1921. Although Washburn's thesis was the first foreign study Wundt published in his journal, her gender meant she was barred from joining the organization of **experimental psychologists** (who explore behavior and thinking with experiments), despite its being founded by Titchener, her own graduate adviser (Johnson, 1997). What a different world from the recent past—1996 to 2013—when women claimed two-thirds or more of new U.S. psychology Ph.D.s and were 9 of the 18 elected presidents of the science-oriented Association for Psychological Science. In Canada and Europe, too, most recent psychology doctorates have been earned by women.

James' influence reached even further through his dozens of well-received articles, which moved the publisher Henry Holt to offer a contract for a textbook of the new science of psychology. James agreed and began work in 1878, with an apology for requesting two years to finish his writing. The text proved an unexpected chore and actually took him 12 years. (Why am I not surprised?) More than a century later, people still read the resulting *Principles of Psychology* and marvel at the brilliance and elegance with which James introduced psychology to the educated public.

> **experimental psychology** the study of behavior and thinking using the experimental method.

Psychological Science Develops

1-3 How did psychology continue to develop from the 1920s through today?

In psychology's early days, Wundt and Titchener focused on inner sensations, images, and feelings. James, too, engaged in introspective examination of the stream of consciousness and of emotion. Sigmund Freud emphasized the ways emotional responses to childhood experiences and our unconscious thought processes affect our behavior. Thus, until the 1920s, *psychology* was defined as "the science of mental life."

> **AP® Exam Tip**
>
> There are lots of important people in psychology. As you study, focus on the significance of their accomplishments. You are more likely to be tested on what a finding means than who discovered it.

John B. Watson and Rosalie Rayner
Working with Rayner, Watson championed psychology as the science of behavior and demonstrated conditioned responses on a baby who became famous as "Little Albert." (More about Watson's controversial study in Module 26.)

And so it continued until the 1920s, when the first of two larger-than-life American psychologists appeared on the scene. Flamboyant and provocative John B. Watson, and later the equally provocative B. F. Skinner, dismissed introspection and redefined *psychology* as "the scientific study of observable behavior." After all, they said, science is rooted in observation. You cannot observe a sensation, a feeling, or a thought, but you *can* observe and record people's *behavior* as they respond to different situations. They further suggested that our behavior is influenced by learned associations, through a process called *conditioning*. Many agreed, and the **behaviorists** were one of two major forces in psychology well into the 1960s. (More on these psychologists in Modules 26–30.)

The other major force was *Freudian psychology,* which emphasized the ways our unconscious thought processes and our emotional responses to childhood experiences affect our behavior. (In modules to come, we'll look more closely at Sigmund Freud's teachings, including his theory of personality and his views on unconscious sexual conflicts and the mind's defenses against its own wishes and impulses. We will also study the *psychodynamic approach,* which is the updated, modern-day version of Freud's ideas.)

As the behaviorists had done in the early 1900s, two other groups rejected the definition of psychology that was current in the 1960s. The first, the **humanistic psychologists,** led by Carl Rogers and Abraham Maslow, found both Freudian psychology and behaviorism too limiting. Rather than focusing on the meaning of early childhood memories or the learning of conditioned responses, the humanistic psychologists drew attention to ways that current environmental influences can nurture or limit our growth potential, and to the importance of having our needs for love and acceptance satisfied. (More on this in Module 57.)

behaviorism the view that psychology (1) should be an objective science that (2) studies behavior without reference to mental processes. Most research psychologists today agree with (1) but not with (2).

humanistic psychology a historically significant perspective that emphasized the growth potential of healthy people.

B. F. Skinner A leading behaviorist, Skinner rejected introspection and studied how consequences shape behavior.

Sigmund Freud The controversial ideas of this famed personality theorist and therapist have influenced humanity's self-understanding.

The rebellion of a second group of psychologists during the 1960s is now known as the *cognitive revolution,* and it led the field back to its early interest in mental processes, such as the importance of how our mind processes and retains information. Cognitive psychology scientifically explores the ways we perceive, process, and remember information. **Cognitive neuroscience,** an interdisciplinary study, has enriched our understanding of the brain activity underlying mental activity. The cognitive approach has given us new ways to understand ourselves and to treat disorders such as depression, as we shall see in Module 71.

To encompass psychology's concern with observable behavior *and* with inner thoughts and feelings, today we define **psychology** as the *science of behavior and mental processes.* Let's unpack this definition. *Behavior* is anything an organism *does*—any action we can observe and record. Yelling, smiling, blinking, sweating, talking, and questionnaire marking are all observable behaviors. *Mental processes* are the internal, subjective experiences we infer from behavior—sensations, perceptions, dreams, thoughts, beliefs, and feelings.

The key word in psychology's definition is *science.* Psychology, as I will emphasize throughout this book, is less a set of findings than a way of asking and answering questions. My aim, then, is not merely to report results but also to show you how psychologists play their game. You will see how researchers evaluate conflicting opinions and ideas. And you will learn how all of us, whether scientists or simply curious people, can think smarter when describing and explaining the events of our lives.

> **cognitive neuroscience** the interdisciplinary study of the brain activity linked with cognition (including perception, thinking, memory, and language).
>
> **psychology** the science of behavior and mental processes.

Before You Move On

▶ **ASK YOURSELF**

How do you think psychology might change as more and more women contribute their ideas to the field?

▶ **TEST YOURSELF**

What event defined the founding of modern scientific psychology?

Answers to the Test Yourself questions can be found in Appendix E at the end of the book.

Module 1 Review

 1-1 How did psychology develop from its prescientific roots in early understandings of mind and body to the beginnings of modern science?

- Psychology traces its roots back through recorded history to India, China, the Middle East, and Europe. Buddha and Confucius focused on the power and origin of ideas. The ancient Hebrews, Socrates, Plato, and Aristotle pondered whether mind and body are connected or distinct, and whether human ideas are innate or result from experience.

- Descartes and Locke reengaged those ancient debates, with Locke offering his famous description of the mind as a "blank slate" on which experience writes. The ideas of Bacon and Locke contributed to the development of modern *empiricism.*

 1-2 What are some important milestones in psychology's early development?

- Wilhelm Wundt established the first psychological laboratory in 1879 in Germany.

- Two early schools of psychology were *structuralism* and *functionalism.*

- Structuralism, promoted by Wundt and Titchener, used self-reflection to learn about the mind's structure. Functionalism, promoted by James, explored how behavior and thinking function.

 1-3 How did psychology continue to develop from the 1920s through today?

- Early researchers defined *psychology* as a "science of mental life."

- In the 1920s, under the influence of John B. Watson and the *behaviorists,* the field's focus changed to the "scientific study of observable behavior."

- In the 1960s, the *humanistic psychologists* and the *cognitive psychologists* revived interest in the study of mental processes.

- Psychology is now defined as the science of behavior and mental processes.

Multiple-Choice Questions*

1. By seeking to measure "atoms of the mind," who established the first psychology laboratory?
   a. Sigmund Freud
   b. John B. Watson
   c. Wilhelm Wundt
   d. G. Stanley Hall
   e. William James

2. Which philosopher proposed that nerve pathways allowed for reflexes?
   a. Socrates
   b. René Descartes
   c. John Locke
   d. Aristotle
   e. Plato

3. Who coined the term "tabula rasa" (blank slate) to help explain the impact experience has on shaping an individual?
   a. Francis Bacon
   b. René Descartes
   c. John B. Watson
   d. Sigmund Freud
   e. John Locke

4. Which of the following best describes research typical of Wilhelm Wundt's first psychology laboratory?
   a. Examining the unconscious to determine behavior motivation
   b. Using a brain-scanning device to determine the impact events have on brain function
   c. Measuring the reaction time between hearing a sound and pressing a button
   d. Studying helping behavior, based on the premise that people are good
   e. Examining how collective life experiences combine to create individuality

5. With which of the following statements would John B. Watson most likely agree?
   a. Psychology should study the growth potential in all people.
   b. Psychology should study the unconscious.
   c. Psychology should focus on observable behavior.
   d. Psychology should study mental thought processes.
   e. Psychology should study how culture and beliefs impact an individual.

Practice FRQs**

1. The definition of psychology changed as the field evolved during the early years. Why did John B. Watson object to the definition preferred by Wundt, Titchener, and James? What group of psychologists did Watson's ideas influence? How did Watson redefine psychology?

Answer

1 point: Watson objected to the "science of mental life" because he felt it was impossible to be scientific without observation.

1 point: Watson's ideas influenced the behaviorists.

1 point: Watson preferred limiting psychology to behavior, because behavior could be observed and scientifically analyzed.

2. Identify the founder of structuralism, and explain structuralism's four foundational concepts.

(6 points)

Note: If you are a student using these Multiple-Choice Questions for self-testing, please consult with your teacher to check your answers.

** "FRQ" stands for "Free-Response Question." The AP® exam contains two of these essay-style questions, which count for one-third of your final score. The actual FRQs will be complex, requiring you to integrate knowledge from across multiple modules, like the practice questions you will find at the end of each *unit* in this text. These simpler "Practice FRQs" that appear at the end of each *module,* along with a sample grading rubric, will help you get started practicing this skill.

Module 2

Psychology's Big Issues and Approaches

Module Learning Objectives

2-1   Summarize the nature–nurture debate in psychology.

2-2   Describe psychology's three main levels of analysis and related perspectives.

2-3   Identify psychology's main subfields.

2-4   Explain how psychological principles can help you learn and remember, and do better on the AP® exam.

The young science of psychology developed from the more established fields of philosophy and biology. Wundt was both a philosopher and a physiologist. James was an American philosopher. Freud was an Austrian physician. Ivan Pavlov, who pioneered the study of learning (Module 26), was a Russian physiologist. Jean Piaget, the last century's most influential observer of children (Module 47), was a Swiss biologist. These "Magellans of the mind," as Morton Hunt (1993) has called them, illustrate psychology's origins in many disciplines and many countries.

Like those early pioneers, today's psychologists are citizens of many lands. The International Union of Psychological Science has 71 member nations, from Albania to Zimbabwe. In China, the first university psychology department began in 1978; by 2008 there were nearly 200 (Han, 2008; Tversky, 2008). Moreover, thanks to international publications, joint meetings, and the Internet, collaboration and communication now cross borders. Psychology is *growing* and it is *globalizing*. The story of psychology—the subject of this book—continues to develop in many places, at many levels, with interests ranging from the study of nerve cell activity to the study of international conflicts.

Across the world, psychologists are debating enduring issues, viewing behavior from the differing perspectives offered by the subfields in which they teach, work, and do research.

Psychology's Biggest Question

2-1   What is psychology's historic big issue?

Are our human traits present at birth, or do they develop through experience? This has been psychology's biggest and most persistent issue. As we have seen, the debate over the **nature–nurture issue** is ancient. The ancient Greeks debated this, with Plato assuming that we

> **AP® Exam Tip**
>
> Pay close attention to what David Myers, your author, is emphasizing as he tells the story of psychology. When he says the nature–nurture issue is the *biggest* question in psychology, that's a sign. It's a safe bet that this concept will be covered on the AP® exam.

> **nature–nurture issue** the longstanding controversy over the relative contributions that genes and experience make to the development of psychological traits and behaviors. Today's science sees traits and behaviors arising from the interaction of nature and nurture.

Charles Darwin Darwin argued that natural selection shapes behaviors as well as bodies.

natural selection the principle that, among the range of inherited trait variations, those contributing to reproduction and survival will most likely be passed on to succeeding generations.

A nature-made nature–nurture experiment Because identical twins have the same genes, they are ideal participants in studies designed to shed light on hereditary and environmental influences on intelligence, personality, and other traits. Studies of identical and fraternal twins provide a rich array of findings—described in later modules—that underscore the importance of both nature and nurture.

inherit character and intelligence and that certain ideas are also inborn, and Aristotle countering that there is nothing in the mind that does not first come in from the external world through the senses.

In the 1600s, philosophers rekindled the debate. Locke rejected the notion of inborn ideas, suggesting that the mind is a blank slate on which experience writes. Descartes disagreed, believing that some ideas are innate. Descartes' views gained support from a curious naturalist two centuries later. In 1831, an indifferent student but ardent collector of beetles, mollusks, and shells set sail on a historic round-the-world journey. The 22-year-old voyager, Charles Darwin, pondered the incredible species variation he encountered, including tortoises on one island that differed from those on nearby islands. Darwin's 1859 *On the Origin of Species* explained this diversity by proposing the evolutionary process of **natural selection:** From among chance variations, nature selects traits that best enable an organism to survive and reproduce in a particular environment. Darwin's principle of natural selection—what philosopher Daniel Dennett (1996) has called "the single best idea anyone has ever had"—is still with us 150+ years later as biology's organizing principle. Evolution also has become an important principle for twenty-first-century psychology. This would surely have pleased Darwin, for he believed his theory explained not only animal structures (such as a polar bear's white coat) but also animal behaviors (such as the emotional expressions associated with human lust and rage).

The nature–nurture issue recurs throughout this text as today's psychologists explore the relative contributions of biology and experience, asking, for example, how we humans are alike (because of our common biology and evolutionary history) and diverse (because of our differing environments). Are gender differences biologically predisposed or socially constructed? Is children's grammar mostly innate or formed by experience? How are intelligence and personality differences influenced by heredity and by environment? Are sexual behaviors more "pushed" by inner biology or "pulled" by external incentives? Should we treat psychological disorders—depression, for example—as disorders of the brain, disorders of thought, or both?

Such debates continue. Yet over and over again we will see that in contemporary science the nature–nurture tension dissolves: *Nurture works on what nature endows.* Our species is biologically endowed with an enormous capacity to learn and adapt. Moreover, every psychological event (every thought, every emotion) is simultaneously a biological event. Thus, depression can be both a brain disorder and a thought disorder.

Psychology's Three Main Levels of Analysis

2-2   What are psychology's levels of analysis and related perspectives?

Each of us is a complex system that is part of a larger social system. But each of us is also composed of smaller systems, such as our nervous system and body organs, which are composed of still smaller systems—cells, molecules, and atoms.

These tiered systems suggest different **levels of analysis,** which offer complementary outlooks. It's like explaining why horrific school shootings have occurred. Is it because the shooters have brain disorders or genetic tendencies that cause them to be violent? Because they have been rewarded for violent behavior? Because we, in the United States, live in a gun-promoting society that accepts violence? Such perspectives are complementary because "everything is related to everything else" (Brewer, 1996). Together, different levels of analysis form an integrated **biopsychosocial approach,** which considers the influences of biological, psychological, and social-cultural factors (**FIGURE 2.1**).

levels of analysis the differing complementary views, from biological to psychological to social-cultural, for analyzing any given phenomenon.

biopsychosocial approach an integrated approach that incorporates biological, psychological, and social-cultural levels of analysis.

Biological influences:
- natural selection of adaptive traits
- genetic predispositions responding to environment
- brain mechanisms
- hormonal influences

Psychological influences:
- learned fears and other learned expectations
- emotional responses
- cognitive processing and perceptual interpretations

Behavior or mental process

Social-cultural influences:
- presence of others
- cultural, societal, and family expectations
- peer and other group influences
- compelling models (such as in the media)

Figure 2.1
Biopsychosocial approach This integrated viewpoint incorporates various levels of analysis and offers a more complete picture of any given behavior or mental process.

AP® Exam Tip

You will see versions of Figure 2.1 throughout the text. Spend some time right now familiarizing yourself with how the figure's three corners might contribute to behavior or mental processes, the very stuff of psychology.

Each level provides a valuable vantage point for looking at a behavior or mental process, yet each by itself is incomplete. Like different academic disciplines, psychology's varied approaches, or perspectives, ask different questions and have their own limits. One perspective may stress the biological, psychological, or social-cultural level more than another, but the different perspectives described in **TABLE 2.1** on the next page complement one another. Consider, for example, how they shed light on anger.

Views of anger How would each of psychology's levels of analysis explain what's going on here?

Table 2.1 Psychology's Approaches

Perspective	Focus	Sample Questions
Behavioral	How we learn observable responses	How do we learn to fear particular objects or situations? What is the most effective way to alter our behavior, say, to lose weight?
Biological	How the body and brain enable emotions, memories, and sensory experiences; how genes combine with environment to influence individual differences	How do pain messages travel from the hand to the brain? How is blood chemistry linked with moods and motives? To what extent are traits such as intelligence, personality, sexual orientation, and depression attributable to our genes? To our environment?
Cognitive	How we encode, process, store, and retrieve information	How do we use information in remembering? Reasoning? Solving problems?
Evolutionary	How the natural selection of traits has promoted the survival of genes	How does evolution influence behavior tendencies?
Humanistic	How we meet our needs for love and acceptance and achieve self-fulfillment	How can we work toward fulfilling our potential? How can we overcome barriers to our personal growth?
Psychodynamic	How behavior springs from unconscious drives and conflicts	How can someone's personality traits and disorders be explained by unfulfilled wishes and childhood traumas?
Social-cultural	How behavior and thinking vary across situations and cultures	How are we alike as members of one human family? How do we differ as products of our environment?

AP® Exam Tip

These perspectives will come up again and again throughout your AP® Psychology course, and they *will* be on the exam. You need to become very comfortable with the meaning of terms like cognitive, behavioral, and psychodynamic. Ask your teacher for clarification if you are the least bit unclear about what the perspectives mean.

behavioral psychology the scientific study of observable behavior, and its explanation by principles of learning.

biological psychology the scientific study of the links between biological (genetic, neural, hormonal) and psychological processes. (Some biological psychologists call themselves *behavioral neuroscientists, neuropsychologists, behavior geneticists, physiological psychologists,* or *biopsychologists.*)

- Someone working from the **behavioral** perspective might attempt to determine which external stimuli trigger angry responses or aggressive acts.

- Someone working from a **biological** perspective might study brain circuits that cause us to be "red in the face" and "hot under the collar," or how heredity and experience influence our individual differences in temperament.

- Someone working from the **cognitive** perspective might study how our interpretation of a situation affects our anger and how our anger affects our thinking.

- Someone working from the **evolutionary** perspective might analyze how anger facilitated the survival of our ancestors' genes.

- Someone working from the *humanistic* perspective (a historically important approach) might have been interested in understanding how angry feelings affect a person's potential for growth. As we will see, modern-day *positive psychology* incorporates humanistic psychology's emphasis on human flourishing.

- Someone working from the **psychodynamic** perspective (which evolved from Freud's psychoanalysis) might view an outburst as an outlet for unconscious hostility.

- Someone working from the **social-cultural** perspective might explore how expressions of anger vary across cultural contexts.

The point to remember: Like two-dimensional views of a three-dimensional object, each of psychology's perspectives is helpful. But each by itself fails to reveal the whole picture.

Psychology's Subfields

2-3 What are psychology's main subfields?

Picturing a chemist at work, you probably envision a white-coated scientist surrounded by glassware and high-tech equipment. Picture a psychologist at work and you would be right to envision

- a white-coated scientist probing a rat's brain.

- an intelligence researcher measuring how quickly an infant shows boredom by looking away from a familiar picture.

- an executive evaluating a new "healthy lifestyles" training program for employees.

- someone at a computer analyzing data on whether adopted teens' temperaments more closely resemble those of their adoptive parents or their biological parents.

- a therapist listening carefully to a a client's depressed thoughts.

- a researcher visiting another culture and collecting data on variations in human values and behaviors.

- a teacher or writer sharing the joy of psychology with others.

"I'm a social scientist, Michael. That means I can't explain electricity or anything like that, but if you ever want to know about people I'm your man."

The cluster of subfields we call psychology is a meeting ground for different disciplines. "Psychology is a hub scientific discipline," said Association for Psychological Science president John Cacioppo (2007). Thus, it's a perfect home for those with wide-ranging interests. In its diverse activities, from biological experimentation to cultural comparisons, the tribe of psychology is united by a common quest: *describing and explaining behavior and the mind underlying it.* There is even a branch of psychology devoted to studying the measurement of our abilities, attitudes, and traits: **psychometrics.**

cognitive psychology the scientific study of all the mental activities associated with thinking, knowing, remembering, and communicating.

evolutionary psychology the study of the evolution of behavior and mind, using principles of natural selection.

psychodynamic psychology a branch of psychology that studies how unconscious drives and conflicts influence behavior, and uses that information to treat people with psychological disorders.

social-cultural psychology the study of how situations and cultures affect our behavior and thinking.

psychometrics the scientific study of the measurement of human abilities, attitudes, and traits.

Laura Dwight

I see you! A biological psychologist might view this child's delighted response as evidence of brain maturation. A cognitive psychologist might see it as a demonstration of the baby's growing knowledge of his surroundings. For a social-cultural psychologist, the role of grandparents in different societies might be the issue of interest. As you will see throughout this book, these and other perspectives offer complementary views of behavior.

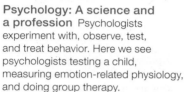

Psychology: A science and a profession Psychologists experiment with, observe, test, and treat behavior. Here we see psychologists testing a child, measuring emotion-related physiology, and doing group therapy.

basic research pure science that aims to increase the scientific knowledge base.

developmental psychology a branch of psychology that studies physical, cognitive, and social change throughout the life span.

educational psychology the study of how psychological processes affect and can enhance teaching and learning.

personality psychology the study of an individual's characteristic pattern of thinking, feeling, and acting.

social psychology the scientific study of how we think about, influence, and relate to one another.

Some psychologists conduct **basic research** that builds psychology's knowledge base. In the pages that follow we will meet a wide variety of such researchers, including

- *biological psychologists* exploring the links between brain and mind.
- **developmental psychologists** studying our changing abilities from womb to tomb.
- *cognitive psychologists* experimenting with how we perceive, think, and solve problems.
- **educational psychologists** studying influences on teaching and learning.
- **personality psychologists** investigating our persistent traits.
- **social psychologists** exploring how we view and affect one another.

(Read on to the next module for a more complete list of what psychologists in various professions do and where they work.)

These and other psychologists also may conduct **applied research,** tackling practical problems. **Industrial-organizational (I/O) psychologists,** for example, use psychology's concepts and methods in the workplace to help organizations and companies select and train employees, boost morale and productivity, design products, and implement systems. Within that domain, **human factors psychologists** focus on the interaction of people, machines, and physical environments. (More on this subject in Enrichment Module 82.)

Although most psychology textbooks focus on psychological science, psychology is also a helping profession devoted to such practical issues as how to have a happy marriage, how to overcome anxiety or depression, and how to raise thriving children. As a science, psychology at its best bases such interventions on *evidence of effectiveness.* **Counseling psychologists** help people to cope with challenges and crises (including academic, vocational, and marital issues) and to improve their personal and social functioning. **Clinical psychologists** assess and treat mental, emotional, and behavior disorders. Both counseling and clinical psychologists administer and interpret tests, provide counseling and therapy, and sometimes conduct basic and applied research. By contrast, **psychiatrists,** who also may provide psychotherapy, are medical doctors licensed to prescribe drugs and otherwise treat physical causes of psychological disorders.

We will study the history of therapy, including the role of pioneering Dorothea Dix, in the Therapy unit. Reformers such as Dix and Philippe Pinel led the way to humane treatment of those with psychological disorders.

To balance historic psychology's focus on human problems, Martin Seligman and others (2002, 2005, 2011) have called for more research on human strengths and human flourishing.

Their **positive psychology** scientifically explores "positive emotions, positive character traits, and enabling institutions." What, they ask, can psychology contribute to a "good life" that engages one's skills, and a "meaningful life" that points beyond oneself?

Rather than seeking to change people to fit their environment, **community psychologists** work to create social and physical environments that are healthy for all (Bradshaw et al., 2009; Trickett, 2009). For example, if school bullying is a problem, some psychologists will seek to change the bullies. Knowing that many students struggle with the transition from elementary to middle school, they might train individual kids how to cope. Community psychologists instead seek ways to adapt the school experience to early adolescent needs. To prevent bullying, they might study how the school and neighborhood foster bullying.

With perspectives ranging from the biological to the social, and with settings from the laboratory to the clinic, psychology relates to many fields. As we will see in Module 3, psychologists teach in medical schools, law schools, and high schools, and they work in hospitals, factories, and corporate offices. They engage in interdisciplinary studies, such as psychohistory (the psychological analysis of historical characters), psycholinguistics (the study of language and thinking), and psychoceramics (the study of crackpots).[1]

Psychology also influences modern culture. Knowledge transforms us. Learning about the solar system and the germ theory of disease alters the way people think and act. Learning about psychology's findings also changes people: They less often judge psychological disorders as moral failings, treatable by punishment and ostracism. They less often regard and treat women as men's mental inferiors. They less often view and rear children as ignorant, willful beasts in need of taming. "In each case," noted Morton Hunt (1990, p. 206), "knowledge has modified attitudes, and, through them, behavior." Once aware of psychology's well-researched ideas—about how body and mind connect, how a child's mind grows, how we construct our perceptions, how we remember (and misremember) our experiences, how people across the world differ (and are alike)—your mind may never again be quite the same.

But bear in mind psychology's limits. Don't expect it to answer the ultimate questions, such as those posed by Russian novelist Leo Tolstoy (1904): "Why should I live? Why should I do anything? Is there in life any purpose which the inevitable death that awaits me does not undo and destroy?"

Although many of life's significant questions are beyond psychology, some very important ones are illuminated by even a first psychology course. Through painstaking research, psychologists have gained insights into brain and mind, dreams and memories, depression and joy. Even the unanswered questions can renew our sense of mystery about "things too wonderful" for us yet to understand. And, as you will see in Modules 4–8, your study of psychology can help teach you how to ask and answer important questions—how to think critically as you evaluate competing ideas and claims.

Psychology deepens our appreciation for how we humans perceive, think, feel, and act. By so doing, it can indeed enrich our lives and enlarge our vision. Throughout this book I hope to help guide you toward that end. As educator Charles Eliot said a century ago: "Books are the quietest and most constant of friends, and the most patient of teachers."

Dorothea Dix (1802–1887)
"I . . . call your attention to the state of the Insane Persons confined within this Commonwealth, in cages."

applied research scientific study that aims to solve practical problems.

industrial-organizational (I/O) psychology the application of psychological concepts and methods to optimizing human behavior in workplaces.

human factors psychology an I/O psychology subfield that explores how people and machines interact and how machines and physical environments can be made safe and easy to use.

counseling psychology a branch of psychology that assists people with problems in living (often related to school, work, or marriage) and in achieving greater well-being.

clinical psychology a branch of psychology that studies, assesses, and treats people with psychological disorders.

psychiatry a branch of medicine dealing with psychological disorders; practiced by physicians who sometimes provide medical (for example, drug) treatments as well as psychological therapy.

positive psychology the scientific study of human functioning, with the goals of discovering and promoting strengths and virtues that help individuals and communities to thrive.

community psychology a branch of psychology that studies how people interact with their social environments and how social institutions affect individuals and groups.

"Once expanded to the dimensions of a larger idea, [the mind] never returns to its original size." -OLIVER WENDELL HOLMES, 1809–1894

---

[1]Confession: I wrote the last part of this sentence on April Fools' Day.

Close-up

Improve Your Retention—and Your Grades!

How can psychological principles help you learn and remember, and do better on the AP® exam?

Do you, like most students, assume that the way to cement your new learning is to reread? What helps even more—and what this book therefore encourages—is repeated self-testing and rehearsal of previously studied material. Memory researchers Henry Roediger and Jeffrey Karpicke (2006) call this phenomenon the **testing effect.** They note that "testing is a powerful means of improving learning, not just assessing it." In one of their studies, students recalled the meaning of 40 previously learned Swahili words much better if tested repeatedly than if they spent the same time restudying the words (Karpicke & Roediger, 2008).

As you will see in Modules 31–33, to master information you must *actively process it.* Your mind is not like your stomach, something to be filled passively; it is more like a muscle that grows stronger with exercise. Countless experiments reveal that people learn and remember best when they put material in their own words, rehearse it, and then retrieve and review it again.

The **SQ3R** study method incorporates these principles (McDaniel et al., 2009; Robinson, 1970). SQ3R is an acronym for its five steps: Survey, Question, Read, Retrieve,[2] Review.

To study a module, first *survey,* taking a bird's-eye view. Scan the headings, and notice how the module is organized.

Before you read each main section, try to answer its numbered Learning Objective Question (for this box: "How can psychological principles help you learn and remember, and do better on the AP® exam?"). Roediger and Bridgid Finn (2010) have found that "trying and failing to retrieve the answer is actually helpful to learning." Those who test their understanding before reading, and discover what they don't yet know, will learn and remember better.

Then *read,* actively searching for the answer to the question. At each sitting, read only as much of the module (usually a single main section) as you can absorb without tiring. Read actively and critically. Ask questions. Take notes. Make the ideas your own: How does what you've read relate to your own life? Does it support or challenge your assumptions? How convincing is the evidence?

Having read a section, *retrieve* its main ideas. *Test yourself.* This will not only help you figure out what you know; the testing itself will help you learn and retain the information more effectively. Even better, test yourself repeatedly. To facilitate this, I offer self-testing opportunities in each module—for example,

in the *Before You Move On* sections. After answering the *Test Yourself* questions there, you can check your answers in Appendix E at the end of this text and reread as needed.

Finally, *review:* Read over any notes you have taken, again with an eye on the module's organization, and quickly review the whole module. Write or say what a concept is before rereading to check your understanding.

Survey, question, read, retrieve, review. I have organized this book's modules to facilitate your use of the SQ3R study system. Each module begins with a list of objectives that aid your *survey.* Headings and the numbered Learning Objective *Questions* at the beginning of main sections suggest issues and concepts you should consider as you *read.* The material is organized into sections of readable length. At the end of main sections is a "Before You Move On" box with Ask Yourself and Test Yourself questions that help you *retrieve* what you know. The Module *Review* provides answers to the learning objective questions along with helpful review questions. The Unit Review offers a list of Key Terms and Key Contributors, along with AP® Exam Practice Questions. Appendix C, Psychological Science's Key Contributors, at the end of the text will also be an important review tool—especially in preparing for the AP® exam. In addition to learning psychology's key concepts and key people, you will also need to learn the style of writing that is required for success on the exam. The sample grading rubrics provided for some of the *Free-Response Questions* (essay-style questions) in the Module and Unit Reviews will help get you started.

Five additional study tips may further boost your learning:

Distribute your study time. One of psychology's oldest findings is that *spaced practice* promotes better retention than *massed practice.* You'll remember material better if you space your time over several study periods—perhaps one hour a day, six days a week—rather than cram it into one long study blitz. For example, rather than trying to read an entire module in a single sitting, read just one main section and then turn to something else. *Interleaving* your study of psychology with your study of other subjects boosts long-term retention and protects against overconfidence (Kornell & Bjork, 2008; Taylor & Rohrer, 2010).

Spacing your study sessions requires a disciplined approach to managing your time. (Richard O. Straub explains time management in a helpful preface at the beginning of this text.)

---

testing effect enhanced memory after retrieving, rather than simply rereading, information. Also sometimes referred to as a *retrieval practice* effect or *test-enhanced learning.*

SQ3R a study method incorporating five steps: Survey, Question, Read, Retrieve, Review.

---

[2] Also sometimes called "*Recite.*"

Close-up *(continued)*

Learn to think critically. Whether you are reading or in class, note people's assumptions and values. What perspective or bias underlies an argument? Evaluate evidence. Is it anecdotal? Or is it based on informative experiments? (More on this in Module 6.) Assess conclusions. Are there alternative explanations?

Process class information actively. Listen for the main ideas and sub-ideas of a lesson. *Write them down.* Ask questions during and after class. In class, as with your homework, process the information actively and you will understand and retain it better. As psychologist William James urged a century ago, *"No reception without reaction, no impression without . . . expression."* Make the information your own. Take notes in your own words. Relate what you read to what you already know. Tell someone else about it. (As any teacher will confirm, to teach is to remember.)

Overlearn. Psychology tells us that overlearning improves retention. We are prone to overestimating how much we know. You may understand a module as you read it, but that feeling of familiarity can be deceptively comforting. By devoting extra study time to testing yourself, you may retain your new knowledge much more effectively.

Be a smart test-taker. If a test contains both multiple-choice questions and an essay question, turn first to the essay. Read the question carefully, noting exactly what the teacher is asking. On the back of a page, pencil in a list of points you'd like to make and then organize them. Before writing, put aside the essay and work through the multiple-choice questions. (As you do so, your mind may continue to mull over the essay question. Sometimes the multiple-choice questions will bring pertinent thoughts to mind.) Then reread the essay question, rethink your answer, and start writing. When you finish, proofread your answer to eliminate spelling and grammatical errors that make you look less competent than you are.

When reading multiple-choice questions, don't confuse yourself by trying to imagine how each choice might be the right one. Instead, try to answer each question as if it were a fill-in-the-blank question. First cover the answers and form a sentence in your mind, recalling what you know to complete the sentence. Then read the answers on the test and find the alternative that best matches your own answer.

Memory experts Elizabeth Bjork and Robert Bjork (2011, p. 63) offer the bottom line for how to improve your retention and your grades:

> Spend less time on the input side and more time on the output side, such as summarizing what you have read from memory or getting together with friends and asking each other questions. Any activities that involve testing yourself—that is, activities that require you to retrieve or generate information, rather than just representing information to yourself—will make your learning both more durable and flexible.

OJO Images Ltd/Alamy

Before You Move On

▶ ASK YOURSELF

When you signed up for this course, what did you think psychology would be all about?

▶ TEST YOURSELF

What are psychology's major levels of analysis?

Answers to the Test Yourself questions can be found in Appendix E at the end of the book.

Module 2 Review

2-1   What is psychology's historic big issue?

- Psychology's biggest and most enduring issue has been the *nature–nurture issue,* which focuses on the relative contributions of genes and experience.

- Charles Darwin's view that *natural selection* shapes behaviors as well as bodies is an important principle in contemporary psychology.

- Today's science emphasizes the interaction of genes and experiences in specific environments.

2-2   What are psychology's levels of analysis and related perspectives?

- The *biopsychosocial approach* integrates information from three differing but complementary levels of analysis: the biological, psychological, and social-cultural.

- This approach offers a more complete understanding than could usually be reached by relying on only one of psychology's current perspectives (*biological, evolutionary, psychodynamic, behavioral, cognitive,* and *social-cultural*) or historically influential perspectives (such as the *humanistic* approach).

2-3   What are psychology's main subfields?

- Within the science of psychology, researchers may conduct *basic research* to increase the field's knowledge base (often in biological, *developmental,* cognitive, *educational, personality,* and *social psychology*) or *applied research* to solve practical problems (in *industrial-organizational* and *human factors psychology*).

- *Psychometric* psychologists study measurement methods.

- Those who engage in psychology as a helping profession may assist people as *counseling psychologists* (helping people with problems in living or achieving greater well-being) or as *clinical psychologists,* studying and assessing people with psychological disorders and treating them with psychotherapy. (*Psychiatrists* also study, assess, and treat people with disorders, but as medical doctors, they may prescribe drugs in addition to psychotherapy.)

- *Positive psychology* attempts to discover and promote traits that help people to thrive.

- *Community psychologists* work to create healthy social and physical environments.

2-4   How can psychological principles help you learn and remember, and do better on the AP® exam?

- The *testing effect* shows that learning and memory are enhanced by actively retrieving, rather than simply rereading, previously studied material.

- The *SQ3R* study method—survey, question, read, retrieve, and review—applies the principles derived from memory research.

- Five additional tips are (1) distribute your study time; (2) learn to think critically; (3) process class information actively; (4) overlearn; (5) be a smart test-taker.

Multiple-Choice Questions

1. Which of the following perspectives is most likely to address how the encoding, storing, and retrieval of information might alter our thoughts?
   a. Behavioral
   b. Psychodynamic
   c. Humanistic
   d. Cognitive
   e. Biological

2. Who among the following would most likely study the interaction of people, machines, and physical environments?
   a. Human factors psychologist
   b. Personality psychologist
   c. Industrial-organizational psychologist
   d. Counseling psychologist
   e. Experimental psychologist

3. Psychiatrists differ from psychologists in that they

    a. help people cope with challenges and crises.

    b. conduct research.

    c. explore how we view and affect one another.

    d. experiment with how people perceive, think, and solve problems.

    e. are medical doctors licensed to prescribe medication.

4. A humanistic psychologist working with some poets might ask which of the following questions?

    a. How can we get them to reach their highest potential?

    b. How did their childhood experiences impact their current behavior?

    c. How have rewards and punishments shaped their behavior?

    d. How do society's attitudes affect their writing topics?

    e. How do their brains differ from those of other successful people?

5. Betsy works in a human resources department. She plans training sessions, recruits people to work for the company, and implements techniques to boost morale around the office. Of the following, Betsy is most likely a(n)

    a. developmental psychologist.

    b. personality psychologist.

    c. counseling psychologist.

    d. educational psychologist.

    e. industrial-organizational psychologist.

Practice FRQs

1. George is said to have an "easy-going" personality. How might the biopsychosocial approach be used to explain an easy-going personality?

Answer

1 point: Biological factors would include George's genetic, physiological, and chemical makeup. For instance, George's easy-going manner may be the result of brain chemistry.

1 point: Psychological factors would include a discussion of how George learned that an easy-going personality makes people want to spend time with him. In response, he keeps anxiety and negative feelings to himself. He has the perception that others do not want to deal with his stress and anxiety.

1 point: Social-cultural factors would include George's family or cultural upbringing and expectations. If those who surround George expect him to be relaxed and laid-back, and this is what is supported in his community, George will be likely to act accordingly.

2. Six months ago, Carlos emigrated from Spain to the United States. Although fluent in English and an honor student in Spain, Carlos has had difficulty completing his assignments since moving to the United States. His parents don't understand why he is not succeeding like he did in his last school. Carlos has quit participating in family traditions.

    Explain how each of the following psychological perspectives might explain Carlos' behavior:

- Psychodynamic
- Cognitive

(2 points)

Module 3

Careers in Psychology

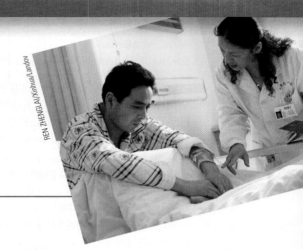

Module Learning Objective

3-1 Describe what psychologists in various professions do and where they work.

This module was written by Jennifer Zwolinski, Associate Professor of Psychology at the University of San Diego.

3-1 What do psychologists in various professions do, and where do they work?

What can you do with a college degree in psychology? Lots!

If you major in psychology, you will graduate with a scientific mind-set and an awareness of basic principles of human behavior (biological mechanisms, development, cognition, psychological disorders, social interaction). This background will prepare you for success in many areas, including business, the helping professions, health services, marketing, law, sales, and teaching. You may even go on to graduate school for specialized training to become a psychology professional. This module describes psychology's specialized subfields. Appendix D, Preparing for Further Psychology Studies, provides tips for preparing to earn a bachelor's, master's, or doctoral degree in psychology, with information about the career options that become available at those varying levels of education.

If you are like most students, you may be unaware of the wide variety of specialties and work settings available in psychology (Terre & Stoddart, 2000). To date, the American Psychological Association (APA) has formed 56 divisions. Let's look at some of the basic research, applied research, and helping profession careers (arranged alphabetically) in the main specialty areas of psychology, most of which require a graduate degree in psychology.

Consulting psychologist Cognitive psychologists may advise businesses on how to operate more effectively by understanding the human factors involved.

Basic Research Subfields

COGNITIVE PSYCHOLOGISTS study thought processes and focus on such topics as perception, language, attention, problem solving, memory, judgment and decision making, forgetting, and intelligence. Research interests include designing computer-based models of thought processes and identifying biological correlates of cognition. As a cognitive psychologist, you might work as a professor, industrial consultant, or human factors specialist in an educational or business setting.

DEVELOPMENTAL PSYCHOLOGISTS conduct research on age-related behavioral changes and apply their scientific knowledge to educational, child-care, policy, and related settings. As a developmental psychologist, you would investigate change across a broad range of topics, including the biological, psychological, cognitive, and social aspects of development. Developmental psychology informs a number of applied fields, including educational psychology, school psychology, child psychopathology, and gerontology. The field also informs public policy in areas such as education and child-care reform, maternal and child health, and attachment and adoption. You would probably specialize in a specific stage of the life span, such as infancy, childhood, adolescence, or middle or late adulthood. Your work setting could be an educational institution, day-care center, youth group program, or senior center.

EDUCATIONAL PSYCHOLOGISTS are interested in the psychological processes involved in learning. They study the relationship between learning and physical and social environments, and they develop strategies for enhancing the learning process. As an educational psychologist, working in a university psychology department or school of education, you might conduct basic research on topics related to learning or develop innovative methods of teaching to enhance the learning process. You might design effective tests, including measures of aptitude and achievement. You might be employed by a school or government agency or charged with designing and implementing effective employee-training programs in a business setting.

AP® Exam Tip

Educational psychologists apply psychology's findings in an effort to improve learning, and *school psychologists* assess and assist individual schoolchildren.

EXPERIMENTAL PSYCHOLOGISTS are a diverse group of scientists who investigate a variety of basic behavioral processes in humans and other animals. Prominent areas of experimental research include comparative methods of science, motivation, learning, thought, attention, memory, perception, and language. Most experimental psychologists identify with a particular subfield, such as cognitive psychology, depending on their interests and training. It is important to note that experimental research methods are not limited to the field of experimental psychology; many other subfields rely on experimental methodology to conduct studies. As an experimental psychologist, you would most likely work in an academic setting, teaching courses and supervising students' research in addition to conducting your own research. Or you might be employed by a research institution, zoo, business, or government agency.

PSYCHOMETRIC AND QUANTITATIVE PSYCHOLOGISTS study the methods and techniques used to acquire psychological knowledge. A psychometrician may update existing neurocognitive or personality tests or devise new tests for use in clinical and school settings or in business and industry. These psychologists also administer, score, and interpret such tests. Quantitative psychologists collaborate with researchers to design, analyze, and interpret the results of research programs. As a psychometric or quantitative psychologist, you will need to be well trained in research methods, statistics, and computer technology. You will most likely be employed by a university or college, testing company, private research firm, or government agency.

SOCIAL PSYCHOLOGISTS are interested in our interactions with others. Social psychologists study how our beliefs, feelings, and behaviors are affected by and influence other people. They study topics such as attitudes, aggression, prejudice, interpersonal attraction, group behavior, and leadership. As a social psychologist, you would probably be a college or university faculty member. You might also work in organizational consultation, market research, or other applied psychology fields, including social neuroscience. Some social psychologists work for hospitals, federal agencies, or businesses performing applied research.

Ted Fitzgerald, Pool/AP Photo

Psychology in court Forensic psychologists apply psychology's principles and methods in the criminal justice system. They may assess witness credibility or testify in court on a defendant's state of mind and future risk.

Applied Research Subfields

FORENSIC PSYCHOLOGISTS apply psychological principles to legal issues. They conduct research on the interface of law and psychology, help to create public policies related to mental health, help law-enforcement agencies in criminal investigations, or consult on jury selection and deliberation processes. They also provide assessment to assist the legal community. Although most forensic psychologists are clinical psychologists, they might have expertise in other areas of psychology, such as social or cognitive psychology. Some also hold law degrees. As a forensic psychologist, you might work in a university psychology department, law school, research organization, community mental health agency, law-enforcement agency, court, or correctional setting.

HEALTH PSYCHOLOGISTS are researchers and practitioners concerned with psychology's contribution to promoting health and preventing disease. As applied psychologists or clinicians, they may help individuals lead healthier lives by designing, conducting, and evaluating programs to stop smoking, lose weight, improve sleep, manage pain, prevent the spread of sexually transmitted infections, or treat psychosocial problems associated with chronic and terminal illnesses. As researchers and clinicians, they identify conditions and practices associated with health and illness to help create effective interventions. In public service, health psychologists study and work to improve government policies and health care systems. As a health psychologist, you could be employed in a hospital, medical school, rehabilitation center, public health agency, college or university, or, if you are also a clinical psychologist, in private practice.

INDUSTRIAL-ORGANIZATIONAL (I/O) PSYCHOLOGISTS study the relationship between people and their working environments. They may develop new ways to increase productivity, improve personnel selection, or promote job satisfaction in an organizational setting. Their interests include organizational structure and change, consumer behavior, and personnel selection and training. As an I/O psychologist, you might conduct workplace training or provide organizational analysis and development. You may find yourself working in business, industry, the government, or a college or university. Or you may be self-employed as a consultant or work for a management consulting firm.

NEUROPSYCHOLOGISTS investigate the relationship between neurological processes (structure and function of the nervous system) and behavior. As a neuropsychologist you might assess, diagnose, or treat central nervous system disorders, such as Alzheimer's disease or stroke. You might also evaluate individuals for evidence of head injuries; learning and developmental disabilities, such as autism spectrum disorder; and other psychiatric disorders, such as attention-deficit/hyperactivity disorder (ADHD). If you are a *clinical neuropsychologist,* you might work in a hospital's neurology, neurosurgery, or psychiatric unit. Neuropsychologists also work in academic settings, where they conduct research and teach.

REHABILITATION PSYCHOLOGISTS are researchers and practitioners who work with people who have lost optimal functioning after an accident, illness, or other event. As a rehabilitation psychologist, you would probably work in a medical rehabilitation institution or hospital. You might also work in a medical school, university, state or federal vocational rehabilitation agency, or in private practice serving people with physical disabilities.

SCHOOL PSYCHOLOGISTS are involved in the assessment of and intervention for children in educational settings. They diagnose and treat cognitive, social, and emotional problems that may negatively influence children's learning or overall functioning at school. As a school psychologist, you would collaborate with teachers, parents, and administrators, making recommendations to improve student learning. You could work in an academic setting, a federal or state government agency, a child guidance center, or a behavioral research laboratory.

Class counselor School psychologists, who have their master's degree in psychology, may find themselves working with students individually or in groups, as well as in a consultative role for their school's administrators.

SPORT PSYCHOLOGISTS study the psychological factors that influence, and are influenced by, participation in sports and other physical activities. Their professional activities include coach education and athlete preparation, as well as research and teaching. Sport psychologists who also have a clinical or counseling degree can apply those skills to working with individuals with psychological problems, such as anxiety or substance abuse, that might interfere with optimal performance. As a sport psychologist, if you were not working in an academic or research setting, you would most likely work as part of a team or organization, or in a private capacity.

The Helping Professions

CLINICAL PSYCHOLOGISTS promote psychological health in individuals, groups, and organizations. Some clinical psychologists specialize in specific psychological disorders. Others treat a range of disorders, from adjustment difficulties to severe psychopathology. Clinical psychologists might engage in research, teaching, assessment, and consultation. Some hold workshops and lectures on psychological issues for other professionals or for the public. Clinical psychologists work in a variety of settings, including private practice, mental health service organizations, schools, universities, industries, legal systems, medical systems, counseling centers, government agencies, and military services.

Athlete assistance Sport psychologists often work directly with athletes to help them improve their performance.

To become a clinical psychologist, you will need to earn a doctorate from a clinical psychology program. The APA sets the standards for clinical psychology graduate programs, offering accreditation (official recognition) to those who meet their standards. In all U.S. states, clinical psychologists working in independent practice must obtain a license to offer services such as therapy and testing.

COMMUNITY PSYCHOLOGISTS move beyond focusing on specific individuals or families and deal with broad problems of mental health in community settings. These psychologists believe that human behavior is powerfully influenced by the interaction between people and their physical, social, political, and economic environments. They seek to promote psychological health by enhancing environmental settings, focusing on preventive measures and crisis intervention, with special attention to the problems of underserved groups and ethnic minorities. Given the shared emphasis on prevention, some community psychologists collaborate with

professionals in other areas, such as public health. As a community psychologist, your work settings could include federal, state, and local departments of mental health, corrections, and welfare. You might conduct research or help evaluate research in health service settings, serve as an independent consultant for a private or government agency, or teach and consult as a college or university faculty member.

COUNSELING PSYCHOLOGISTS help people adjust to life transitions or make lifestyle changes. Although similar to clinical psychologists, counseling psychologists typically help people with adjustment problems rather than severe psychopathology. Like clinical psychologists, counseling psychologists conduct therapy and provide assessments to individuals and groups. As a counseling psychologist, you would emphasize your clients' strengths, helping them to use their own skills, interests, and abilities to cope during transitions. You might find yourself working in an academic setting as a faculty member or administrator or in a university counseling center, community mental health center, business, or private practice. As with clinical psychology, if you plan to work in independent practice you will need to obtain a state license to provide counseling services to the public.

* * *

Coping with disaster After Haiti's disastrous 2010 earthquake, this community psychologist helped survivors cope with the loss of their homes and, for many, the death of family members and friends.

So, the next time someone asks you what you could do with a psychology degree, tell them you will have a lot of options. You might use your acquired skills and understanding to get a job and succeed in any number of fields, or you might pursue graduate school and then career opportunities in associated professions. In any case, what you have learned about behavior and mental processes will surely enrich your life (Hammer, 2003).

Before You Move On

▶ **ASK YOURSELF**

Which of psychology's specialties were you aware of before taking this course? Which seem most interesting to you?

▶ **TEST YOURSELF**

Name the subfields that focus on a) people and their work environments, b) how people change over the life span, c) the human thinking involved in perceiving, remembering, speaking, and decision making, and d) diagnosing and treating psychological disorders.

Answers to the Test Yourself questions can be found in Appendix E at the end of the book.

Module 3 Review

3-1 What do psychologists in various professions do, and where do they work?

- The APA has formed 56 divisions.

- Psychology's specialties include the basic research subfields (cognitive, developmental, educational, experimental, psychometric and quantitative, and social psychology); the applied research subfields (forensic, health, industrial-organizational, neuropsychology, rehabilitation, school, and sport psychology); and the helping professions (clinical, community, and counseling).

- Work settings for psychologists include a wide range of government agencies, industrial and business settings, clinics and counseling centers, health care institutions, schools, universities, and research organizations.

Multiple-Choice Questions

1. Which of the following psychologists most strongly emphasize that human behavior is powerfully influenced by the interaction between people and their physical, social, political, and economic environments?
   a. Community
   b. Clinical
   c. Counseling
   d. Industrial-organizational
   e. Rehabilitation

2. Which of the following psychologists would be most likely to investigate biological, psychological, cognitive, and social changes over time?
   a. Educational
   b. Experimental
   c. Social
   d. Cognitive
   e. Developmental

3. A psychologist investigates the methods teachers use to enhance student learning. With which of the following subfields is the psychologist most likely aligned?
   a. Educational psychology
   b. Experimental psychology
   c. School psychology
   d. Social psychology
   e. Forensic psychology

4. A psychologist works with children whose parents are divorcing. She helps them develop skills they need to cope with the situation. Of the following, what kind of psychologist is most likely helping these children?
   a. Industrial-organizational
   b. Social
   c. Research
   d. Counseling
   e. Community

5. Dwayne is interested in helping people make good decisions regarding their physical well-being. Dwayne should consider a career as a
   a. community psychologist.
   b. social psychologist.
   c. forensic psychologist.
   d. industrial-organizational psychologist.
   e. health psychologist.

Practice FRQs

1. Anisha, a high school junior, has been struggling recently in many areas of her life. She is overweight and spends several hours a day watching television. She is having trouble keeping up in her classes and says she cannot seem to keep her focus. She also is having trouble making friends and "fitting in" at school.
   Explain how the following applied psychologists might attempt to help Anisha's current situation.
   • Health psychologists
   • Social psychologists
   • Counseling psychologists

Answer

1 point: A health psychologist might attempt to find ways to encourage Anisha to lead a more active lifestyle and focus on improving her diet and creating an exercise program. This should help her to lose some weight and become healthier in her daily habits.

1 point: A school psychologist might work with Anisha's parents, teachers, and counselors to determine why she is struggling in her classes and make recommendations for improving her classroom performance.

1 point: A counseling psychologist might work with Anisha to find out why she has recently found numerous aspects of her life more challenging and might work on strategies for helping Anisha cope with challenging situations, such as how to make friends.

2. Hurricane Katrina hit New Orleans in 2005, causing a staggering loss of life and cultural heritage and billions of dollars in damage. How might each of the following have contributed to making life better in New Orleans following the hurricane?
   • Clinical psychologists
   • Social psychologists

(2 points)

Unit I Review

Key Terms and Concepts to Remember

empiricism, p. 3

structuralism, p. 4

functionalism, p. 4

experimental psychology, p. 5

behaviorism, p. 6

humanistic psychology, p. 6

cognitive neuroscience, p. 7

psychology, p. 7

nature–nurture issue, p. 9

natural selection, p. 10

levels of analysis, p. 11

biopsychosocial approach, p. 11

behavioral psychology, p. 12

biological psychology, p. 12

cognitive psychology, p. 12

evolutionary psychology, p. 12

psychodynamic psychology, p. 12

social-cultural psychology, p. 12

psychometrics, p. 13

basic research, p. 14

developmental psychology, p. 14

educational psychology, p. 14

personality psychology, p. 14

social psychology, p. 14

applied research, p. 14

industrial-organizational (I/O)
   psychology, p. 14

human factors psychology, p. 14

counseling psychology, p. 14

clinical psychology, p. 14

psychiatry, p. 14

positive psychology, p. 15

community psychology, p. 15

testing effect, p. 16

SQ3R, p. 16

Key Contributors to Remember

Wilhelm Wundt, p. 3

G. Stanley Hall, p. 3

William James, p. 4

Mary Whiton Calkins, p. 4

Margaret Floy Washburn, p. 5

Sigmund Freud, p. 5

John B. Watson, p. 6

B. F. Skinner, p. 6

Carl Rogers, p. 6

Ivan Pavlov, p. 9

Jean Piaget, p. 9

Charles Darwin, p. 10

Dorothea Dix, p. 14

For more information, see Appendix C, Psychological Science's Key Contributors, at the end of this text.

AP® Exam Practice Questions

Multiple-Choice Questions

1. Which perspective would be most useful when explaining how people from different countries express anger?

  a. Social-cultural   d. Functionalist

  b. Psychodynamic   e. Biological

  c. Behavioral

2. The debate about the relative contributions of biology and experience to human development is most often referred to as what?

  a. Evolutionary analysis

  b. Behaviorism

  c. The cognitive revolution

  d. The nature–nurture issue

  e. Natural selection

3. Which of the following professionals is required to have a medical degree?

  a. Psychiatrist   d. Counselor

  b. Psychologist   e. Psychotherapist

  c. Clinician

4. Which psychological principle best explains why studying an hour a day for a week is more effective than one 7-hour study session?

  a. Testing effect

  b. Distributed practice

  c. SQ3R

  d. Retrieval practice effect

  e. Psychometrics

5. Which of the following kinds of psychologists would most likely explore how we process and remember information?

a. Developmental
b. Biological
c. Social
d. Cognitive
e. Personality

6. According to the behaviorist perspective, psychological science should be rooted in what?

a. Introspection
b. Observation
c. Cultural influences
d. Growth potential
e. Basic needs

7. Which of the following psychologists would most likely conduct psychotherapy?

a. Biological
b. Clinical
c. Industrial-organizational
d. Cognitive
e. Evolutionary

8. Which field of psychology is most interested in studying the link between mental activity and brain activity?

a. Humanistic psychology
b. Gestalt psychology
c. Cognitive neuroscience
d. Psychodynamic perspective
e. Evolutionary perspective

9. What was the main difference between the psychological thinking of Wilhelm Wundt and earlier philosophers who were also interested in thinking and behavior?

a. Wundt was European, earlier philosophers were American.
b. Wundt was the first professor from a major university interested in psychology.
c. Wundt was the first scholar to call himself a psychologist.
d. Wundt used psychotherapy techniques established by Freud to examine the thinking and behavior of healthy individuals.
e. Wundt and his students gathered data about human thinking and behavior in a laboratory setting.

10. Which school of psychology focused on the adaptive nature of thinking and how our consciousness evolves to meet our needs?

a. Functionalist   d. Humanistic
b. Structuralist   e. Psychodynamic
c. Behavioral

11. The study of the importance of satisfying love and acceptance needs best describes which school of psychology?

a. Behavioral
b. Functionalist
c. Humanistic
d. Psychodynamic
e. Structuralist

12. Which of the following statements is the best example of applied research?

a. Investigating personality traits
b. Using psychological concepts to boost worker productivity
c. Experimenting with how people perceive different stimuli
d. Studying the changing abilities of children from ages 2 to 5
e. Exploring the neural changes that occur during adolescence

13. Self-reflective introspection about the elements of experience best describes a technique used by which school of psychology?

a. Darwinists
b. Empiricists
c. Structuralists
d. Behaviorists
e. Psychiatrists

14. Which psychological perspective is most likely to focus on how our interpretation of a situation affects how we react to it?

a. Psychodynamic
b. Biological
c. Social-cultural
d. Evolutionary
e. Cognitive

15. The science of behavior and mental processes is the definition of which field of study?

a. Philosophy
b. Cognitive neuroscience
c. Basic research
d. Psychology
e. Applied research

Free-Response Questions

1. Arianna is nervous around large crowds, and often leaves social situations like school dances and parties because she feels like she might have a panic attack. Her father died when she was a young girl, but she still often has nightmares about his death. Arianna enjoys school, and because she generally receives good grades, she appreciates the positive feedback from her teachers that encourages her to improve her academic skills.

    Using the seven major modern approaches to psychology, explain how each approach might explain Arianna's behavior.

Rubric for Free-Response Question 1

1 point: The *biological approach* would likely attribute Arianna's nervousness to brain chemistry, hormones, or genetic influences. ⟳ Page 12

1 point: The *evolutionary approach* would explore how avoiding social crowds might have been a survival advantage for early humans, such as by reducing exposure to germs and violence. ⟳ Page 12

1 point: The *psychodynamic approach* would examine Arianna's early life and how she dealt with losing her father, focusing on Arianna's childhood experiences and unconscious anxieties. ⟳ Page 12

1 point: The *behavioral approach* would look at how Arianna has learned in the past through rewards and punishments. She may have had a negative experience in a large group in the past and as a result has learned to avoid social gatherings. ⟳ Page 12

1 point: The *cognitive approach* would focus on examining how Arianna perceives situations. Her interpretation of social situations may impact the outcome. ⟳ Page 12

1 point: The *humanistic approach* would look at how Arianna's environment may have hindered her growth and self-fulfillment. ⟳ Page 12

1 point: The *social-cultural approach* would examine how interactions within the cultures Arianna belongs to influence her expectations about social situations. If her family or other cultural influences encourage her to attend social functions, that might influence her to continue to try attending those kinds of events. ⟳ Page 12

2. In thinking of the question of nature versus nurture, explain how each of the following schools of psychology would address this debate.

- Behaviorism
- Biological perspective
- Personality psychologists
- Developmental psychologists

(4 points)

Multiple-choice self-tests and more may be found at www.worthpublishers.com/MyersAP2e

Unit II

Research Methods: Thinking Critically With Psychological Science

Modules

In a difficult moment—after an argument with a loved one, a social embarrassment, or a bad grade—to whom do you turn? For advice and comfort, we often turn to friends and family, or search online. Psychology can also shed insight. Psychologists start with the questions that intrigue all of us: How can we be happier, healthier, and more successful? What can we do to improve our relationships? Why do people act and think as they do? But psychological *science* takes it a step further and uses careful research to separate uninformed opinions from examined conclusions.

Module 4

The Need for Psychological Science

Top Photo Group/Thinkstock/Getty Images

Module Learning Objectives

 Describe how hindsight bias, overconfidence, and the tendency to perceive order in random events illustrate why science-based answers are more valid than those based on intuition and common sense.

 Identify how the three main components of the scientific attitude relate to critical thinking.

 How do hindsight bias, overconfidence, and the tendency to perceive order in random events illustrate why science-based answers are more valid than those based on intuition and common sense?

Some people suppose that psychology merely documents and dresses in jargon what people already know: "So what else is new—you get paid for using fancy methods to prove what everyone knows?" Others place their faith in human intuition: "Buried deep within each and every one of us, there is an instinctive, heart-felt awareness that provides—if we allow it to—the most reliable guide," offered Prince Charles (2000).

Prince Charles has much company, judging from the long list of pop psychology books on "intuitive managing," "intuitive trading," and "intuitive healing." Today's psychological science does document a vast intuitive mind. As we will see, our thinking, memory, and attitudes operate on two levels—conscious and unconscious—with the larger part operating automatically, off-screen. Like jumbo jets, we fly mostly on autopilot.

The limits of intuition Personnel interviewers tend to be overconfident of their gut feelings about job applicants. Their confidence stems partly from their recalling cases where their favorable impression proved right, and partly from their ignorance about rejected applicants who succeeded elsewhere.

Marilyn Angel Wynn/Getty Images

So, are we smart to listen to the whispers of our inner wisdom, to simply trust "the force within"? Or should we more often be subjecting our intuitive hunches to skeptical scrutiny?

This much seems certain: We often underestimate intuition's perils. My geographical intuition tells me that Reno is east of Los Angeles, that Rome is south of New York, that Atlanta is east of Detroit. But I am wrong, wrong, and wrong.

Modules to come will show that experiments have found people greatly overestimating their lie detection accuracy, their eyewitness recollections, their interviewee assessments, their risk predictions, and their stock-picking talents. As a Nobel Prize-winning physicist explained, "The first principle is that you must not fool yourself—and you are the easiest person to fool" (Feynman, 1997).

Indeed, observed novelist Madeleine L'Engle, "The naked intellect is an extraordinarily inaccurate instrument" (1973). Three phenomena—*hindsight bias, judgmental overconfidence, and our tendency to perceive patterns in random events*—illustrate why we cannot rely solely on intuition and common sense.

Did We Know It All Along? Hindsight Bias

Consider how easy it is to draw the bull's eye *after* the arrow strikes. After the stock market drops, people say it was "due for a correction." After the football game, we credit the coach if a "gutsy play" wins the game, and fault the coach for the "stupid play" if it doesn't. After a war or an election, its outcome usually seems obvious. Although history may therefore seem like a series of inevitable events, the actual future is seldom foreseen. No one's diary recorded, "Today the Hundred Years War began."

This **hindsight bias** (also known as the *I-knew-it-all-along phenomenon*) is easy to demonstrate: Give half the members of a group some purported psychological finding, and give the other half an opposite result. Tell the first group, "Psychologists have found that separation weakens romantic attraction. As the saying goes, 'Out of sight, out of mind.'" Ask them to imagine why this might be true. Most people can, and nearly all will then view this true finding as unsurprising.

Tell the second group the opposite, "Psychologists have found that separation strengthens romantic attraction. As the saying goes, 'Absence makes the heart grow fonder.'" People given this untrue result can also easily imagine it, and most will also see it as unsurprising. When two opposite findings both seem like common sense, there is a problem.

Such errors in our recollections and explanations show why we need psychological research. Just asking people how and why they felt or acted as they did can sometimes be misleading—not because common sense is usually wrong, but because common sense more easily describes what *has* happened than what *will* happen. As physicist Niels Bohr reportedly said, "Prediction is very difficult, especially about the future."

Some 100 studies have observed hindsight bias in various countries and among both children and adults (Blank et al., 2007). Nevertheless, our intuition is often right. As Yogi Berra once said, "You can observe a lot by watching." (We have Berra to thank for other gems, such as "Nobody ever comes here—it's too crowded," and "If the people don't want to come out to the ballpark, nobody's gonna stop 'em.") Because we're all behavior watchers, it would be

> "Those who trust in their own wits are fools." -Proverbs 28:26

> "Life is lived forwards, but understood backwards." -Philosopher Søren Kierkegaard, 1813–1855

> **hindsight bias** the tendency to believe, after learning an outcome, that one would have foreseen it. (Also known as the *I-knew-it-all-along phenomenon*.)

> "Anything seems commonplace, once explained." -Dr. Watson to Sherlock Holmes

REUTERS/U.S. Coast Guard/Handout

Hindsight bias When drilling the Deepwater Horizon oil well in 2010, BP employees took some shortcuts and ignored some warning signs, without intending to harm the environment or their company's reputation. *After* the resulting Gulf oil spill, with the benefit of 20/20 hindsight, the foolishness of those judgments became obvious.

AP® Exam Tip

It is quite common for multiple-choice questions on the AP® exam to test your knowledge of "media myths." Pay particular attention when psychological findings run counter to "common sense."

surprising if many of psychology's findings had *not* been foreseen. Many people believe that love breeds happiness, and they are right (we have what Module 40 calls a deep "need to belong"). Indeed, note Daniel Gilbert, Brett Pelham, and Douglas Krull (2003), "good ideas in psychology usually have an oddly familiar quality, and the moment we encounter them we feel certain that we once came close to thinking the same thing ourselves and simply failed to write it down." Good ideas are like good inventions; once created, they seem obvious. (Why did it take so long for someone to invent suitcases on wheels and Post-it Notes?)

But sometimes our intuition, informed by countless casual observations, has it wrong. In later modules we will see how research has overturned popular ideas—that familiarity breeds contempt, that dreams predict the future, and that most of us use only 10 percent of our brain. (See also **TABLE 4.1**.) We will also see how it has surprised us with discoveries about how the brain's chemical messengers control our moods and memories, about other animals' abilities, and about the effects of stress on our capacity to fight disease.

Table 4.1 True or False?
Psychological research discussed in modules to come will either confirm or refute each of these statements (adapted, in part, from Furnham et al., 2003). Can you predict which of these popular ideas have been confirmed and which refuted? (Check your answers at the bottom of this table.)
1. If you want to teach a habit that persists, reward the desired behavior every time, not just intermittently (see Module 27).
2. Patients whose brains are surgically split down the middle survive and function much as they did before the surgery (see Module 13).
3. Traumatic experiences, such as sexual abuse or surviving the Holocaust, are typically "repressed" from memory (see Module 33).
4. Most abused children do *not* become abusive adults (see Module 50).
5. Most infants recognize their own reflection in a mirror by the end of their first year (see Module 47).
6. Adopted siblings usually do not develop similar personalities, even though they are reared by the same parents (see Module 14).
7. Fears of harmless objects, such as flowers, are just as easy to acquire as fears of potentially dangerous objects, such as snakes (see Module 15).
8. Lie detection tests often lie (see Module 41).
9. The brain remains active during sleep (see Modules 22–23).
Answers: 1. F, 2. T, 3. F, 4. T, 5. F, 6. T, 7. F, 8. T, 9. T

Overconfidence

We humans tend to think we know more than we do. Asked how sure we are of our answers to factual questions *(Is Boston north or south of Paris?),* we tend to be more confident than correct.[1] Or consider these three anagrams, which Richard Goranson (1978) asked people to unscramble:

WREAT → WATER

ETRYN → ENTRY

GRABE → BARGE

About how many seconds do you think it would have taken you to unscramble each of these? Did hindsight influence you? Knowing the answers tends to make us overconfident—surely the solution would take only 10 seconds or so, when in reality the average problem solver spends 3 minutes, as you also might, given a similar anagram without the solution: OCHSA.[2]

Are we any better at predicting social behavior? University of Pennsylvania psychologist Philip Tetlock (1998, 2005) collected more than 27,000 expert predictions of world events, such as the future of South Africa or whether Quebec would separate from Canada. His repeated finding: These predictions, which experts made with 80 percent confidence on average, were right less than 40 percent of the time. Nevertheless, even those who erred maintained their confidence by noting they were "almost right." "The Québécois separatists *almost* won the secessionist referendum."

Perceiving Order in Random Events

In our natural eagerness to make sense of our world—what poet Wallace Stevens called our "rage for order"—we are prone to perceive patterns. People see a face on the moon, hear Satanic messages in music, perceive the Virgin Mary's image on a grilled cheese sandwich. Even in random data we often find order, because—here's a curious fact of life—*random sequences often don't look random* (Falk et al., 2009; Nickerson, 2002, 2005). Consider a random coin flip: If someone flipped a coin six times, which of the following sequences of heads (H) and tails (T) would be most likely: HHHTTT or HTTHTH or HHHHHH?

Daniel Kahneman and Amos Tversky (1972) found that most people believe HTTHTH would be the most likely random sequence. Actually, all three are equally likely (or, you might say, equally unlikely). A poker hand of 10 through ace, all of hearts, would seem extraordinary; actually, it would be no more or less likely than any other specific hand of cards (**FIGURE 4.1**).

In actual random sequences, patterns and streaks (such as repeating digits) occur more often than people expect (Oskarsson et al., 2009). To demonstrate this phenomenon for myself, I flipped a coin 51 times, with these results:

1. H	10. T	19. H	28. T	37. T	46. H
2. T	11. T	20. H	29. H	38. T	47. H
3. T	12. H	21. T	30. T	39. H	48. T
4. T	13. H	22. T	31. T	40. T	49. T
5. H	14. T	23. H	32. T	41. H	50. T
6. H	15. T	24. T	33. T	42. H	51. T
7. H	16. H	25. T	34. T	43. H	
8. T	17. T	26. T	35. T	44. H	
9. T	18. T	27. H	36. H	45. T	

Looking over the sequence, patterns jump out: Tosses 10 to 22 provided an almost perfect pattern of pairs of tails followed by pairs of heads. On tosses 30 to 38 I had a "cold hand," with only one head in nine tosses. But my fortunes immediately reversed with a "hot hand"—seven heads out of the next nine tosses. Similar streaks happen, about as often as one would expect in random sequences, in basketball shooting, baseball hitting, and mutual fund stock pickers' selections (Gilovich et al., 1985; Malkiel, 2007; Myers, 2002). These sequences often don't look random and so are overinterpreted. ("When you're hot, you're hot!")

---

[1] Boston is south of Paris.
[2] The anagram solution: CHAOS.

Figure 4.1

Two random sequences Your chances of being dealt either of these hands are precisely the same: 1 in 2,598,960.

What explains these streaky patterns? Was I exercising some sort of paranormal control over my coin? Did I snap out of my tails funk and get in a heads groove? No such explanations are needed, for these are the sorts of streaks found in any random data. Comparing each toss to the next, 23 of the 50 comparisons yielded a changed result—just the sort of near 50-50 result we expect from coin tossing. Despite seeming patterns, the outcome of one toss gives no clue to the outcome of the next.

However, some happenings seem so extraordinary that we struggle to conceive an ordinary, chance-related explanation (as applies to our coin tosses). In such cases, statisticians often are less mystified. When Evelyn Marie Adams won the New Jersey lottery *twice*, newspapers reported the odds of her feat as 1 in 17 trillion. Bizarre? Actually, 1 in 17 trillion are indeed the odds that a given person who buys a single ticket for two New Jersey lotteries will win both times. And given the millions of people who buy U.S. state lottery tickets, statisticians Stephen Samuels and George McCabe (1989) reported, it was "practically a sure thing" that someday, somewhere, someone would hit a state jackpot twice. Indeed, said fellow statisticians Persi Diaconis and Frederick Mosteller (1989), "with a large enough sample, any outrageous thing is likely to happen." An event that happens to but 1 in 1 billion people every day occurs about 7 times a day, 2500 times a year.

The point to remember: Hindsight bias, overconfidence, and our tendency to perceive patterns in random events often lead us to overestimate our intuition. But scientific inquiry can help us sift reality from illusion.

"The really unusual day would be one where nothing unusual happens." -Statistician Persi Diaconis (2002)

The Scientific Attitude: Curious, Skeptical, and Humble

4-2 How do the scientific attitude's three main components relate to critical thinking?

Underlying all science is, first, a hard-headed *curiosity,* a passion to explore and understand without misleading or being misled. Some questions *(Is there life after death?)* are beyond science. Answering them in any way requires a leap of faith. With many other ideas *(Can some people demonstrate ESP?),* the proof is in the pudding. Let the facts speak for themselves.

Magician James Randi has used this *empirical approach* when testing those claiming to see auras around people's bodies:

The Amazing Randi The magician James Randi exemplifies skepticism. He has tested and debunked supposed psychic phenomena.

AP Photo/Alan Diaz

Randi: Do you see an aura around my head?

Aura-seer: Yes, indeed.

Randi: Can you still see the aura if I put this magazine in front of my face?

Aura-seer: Of course.

Randi: Then if I were to step behind a wall barely taller than I am, you could determine my location from the aura visible above my head, right?

Randi told me that no aura-seer has agreed to take this simple test.

No matter how sensible-seeming or wild an idea, the smart thinker asks: *Does it work?* When put to the test, can its predictions be confirmed? Subjected to such scrutiny, crazy-sounding ideas sometimes find support. During the 1700s, scientists scoffed at the notion that meteorites had extraterrestrial origins. When two Yale scientists challenged the conventional opinion, Thomas Jefferson jeered, "Gentlemen, I would rather believe that those two Yankee professors would lie than to believe that stones fell from Heaven." Sometimes scientific inquiry turns jeers into cheers.

More often, science becomes society's garbage disposal, sending crazy-sounding ideas to the waste heap, atop previous claims of perpetual motion machines, miracle cancer cures, and out-of-body travels into centuries past. To sift reality from fantasy, sense from nonsense, therefore requires a scientific attitude: being skeptical but not cynical, open but not gullible.

"To believe with certainty," says a Polish proverb, "we must begin by doubting." As scientists, psychologists approach the world of behavior with a *curious skepticism,* persistently asking two questions: *What do you mean? How do you know?*

When ideas compete, skeptical testing can reveal which ones best match the facts. Do parental behaviors determine children's sexual orientation? Can astrologers predict your future based on the position of the planets at your birth? Is electroconvulsive therapy (delivering an electric shock to the brain) an effective treatment for severe depression? As we will see, putting such claims to the test has led psychological scientists to answer *No* to the first two questions and *Yes* to the third.

Putting a scientific attitude into practice requires not only curiosity and skepticism but also *humility*—an awareness of our own vulnerability to error and an openness to surprises and new perspectives. In the last analysis, what matters is not my opinion or yours, but the truths nature reveals in response to our questioning. If people or other animals don't behave as our ideas predict, then so much the worse for our ideas. This humble attitude was expressed in one of psychology's early mottos: "The rat is always right."

Historians of science tell us that these three attitudes—curiosity, skepticism, and humility—helped make modern science possible. Some deeply religious people today may view science, including psychological science, as a threat. Yet, many of the leaders of the scientific revolution, including Copernicus and Newton, were deeply religious people acting on the idea that "in order to love and honor God, it is necessary to fully appreciate the wonders of his handiwork" (Stark, 2003a,b).

> "I'm a skeptic not because I do not want to believe but because I want to *know*. I believe that the truth is out there. But how can we tell the difference between what we would like to be true and what is actually true? The answer is science." -MICHAEL SHERMER, "I WANT TO BELIEVE," *SCIENTIFIC AMERICAN*, 2009

> "My deeply held belief is that if a god anything like the traditional sort exists, our curiosity and intelligence are provided by such a god. We would be unappreciative of those gifts . . . if we suppressed our passion to explore the universe and ourselves." -CARL SAGAN, *BROCA'S BRAIN*, 1979

Non Sequitur

THE IRRESISTIBLE FORCE MEETS THE IMMOVABLE OBJECT

THE FACTS AS THEY ARE

THE TRUTH AS I SEE IT

WILEY 5-16

Reprinted by permission of Universal Press Syndicate. © 1997 Wiley.

Of course, scientists, like anyone else, can have big egos and may cling to their preconceptions. Nevertheless, the ideal of curious, skeptical, humble scrutiny of competing ideas unifies psychologists as a community as they check and recheck one another's findings and conclusions.

Critical Thinking

The scientific attitude prepares us to think smarter. Smart thinking, called **critical thinking,** examines assumptions, assesses the source, discerns hidden values, confirms evidence, and assesses conclusions. Whether reading a news report or listening to a conversation, critical thinkers ask questions. Like scientists, they wonder: How do they know that? What is this person's agenda? Is the conclusion based on anecdote and gut feelings, or on evidence? Does the evidence justify a cause-effect conclusion? What alternative explanations are possible?

Critical thinking, informed by science, helps clear the colored lenses of our biases. Consider: Does climate change threaten our future, and, if so, is it human-caused? In 2009, climate-action advocates interpreted an Australian heat wave and dust storms as evidence of climate change. In 2010, climate-change skeptics perceived North American bitter cold and East Coast blizzards as discounting global warming. Rather than having their understanding

critical thinking thinking that does not blindly accept arguments and conclusions. Rather, it examines assumptions, assesses the source, discerns hidden values, evaluates evidence, and assesses conclusions.

of climate change swayed by today's weather, or by their own political views, critical thinkers say, "Show me the evidence." Over time, is the Earth actually warming? Are the polar ice caps melting? Are vegetation patterns changing? And is human activity spewing gases that would lead us to expect such changes? When contemplating such issues, critical thinkers will consider the credibility of sources. They will look at the evidence (*"Do the facts support them, or are they just makin' stuff up?"*). They will recognize multiple perspectives. And they will expose themselves to news sources that challenge their preconceived ideas.

Has psychology's critical inquiry been open to surprising findings? The answer, as ensuing modules illustrate, is plainly *Yes*. Believe it or not, massive losses of brain tissue early in life may have minimal long-term effects (see Module 12). Within days, newborns can recognize their mother's odor and voice (see Module 45). After brain damage, a person may be able to learn new skills yet be unaware of such learning (see Modules 31–33). Diverse groups—men and women, old and young, rich and middle class, those with disabilities and without—report roughly comparable levels of personal happiness (see Module 83).

And has critical inquiry convincingly debunked popular presumptions? The answer, as ensuing modules also illustrate, is again *Yes*. The evidence indicates that sleepwalkers are *not* acting out their dreams (see Module 24). Our past experiences are *not* all recorded verbatim in our brains; with brain stimulation or hypnosis, one *cannot* simply "hit the replay button" and relive long-buried or repressed memories (see Module 33). Most people do *not* suffer from unrealistically low self-esteem, and high self-esteem is not all good (see Module 59). Opposites do *not* generally attract (see Module 79). In each of these instances and more, what has been learned is not what is widely believed.

> "The real purpose of the scientific method is to make sure Nature hasn't misled you into thinking you know something you don't actually know." -ROBERT M. PIRSIG, *ZEN AND THE ART OF MOTORCYCLE MAINTENANCE*, 1974

Before You Move On

▶ **ASK YOURSELF**

How might critical thinking help us assess someone's interpretations of people's dreams or their claims to communicate with the dead?

▶ **TEST YOURSELF**

How does the scientific attitude contribute to critical thinking?

Answers to the Test Yourself questions can be found in Appendix E at the end of the book.

Module 4 Review

 4-1 How do hindsight bias, overconfidence, and the tendency to perceive order in random events illustrate why science-based answers are more valid than those based on intuition and common sense?

- *Hindsight bias* (also called the "I-knew-it-all-along phenomenon") is the tendency to believe, after learning an outcome, that we would have foreseen it.

- Overconfidence in our judgments results partly from our bias to seek information that confirms them.

- These tendencies, plus our eagerness to perceive patterns in random events, lead us to overestimate our intuition.

Although limited by the testable questions it can address, scientific inquiry can help us overcome our intuition's biases and shortcomings.

 4-2 How do the scientific attitude's three main components relate to critical thinking?

- The scientific attitude equips us to be curious, skeptical, and humble in scrutinizing competing ideas or our own observations.

- This attitude carries into everyday life as *critical thinking*, which puts ideas to the test by examining assumptions, assessing the source, discerning hidden values, evaluating evidence, and assessing conclusions.

Multiple-Choice Questions

1. After the student council election, a friend tells you he has known for weeks who would be elected president. What does this seem to illustrate?

   a. Skepticism
   b. Critical thinking
   c. Hindsight bias
   d. Overconfidence
   e. Perceiving order in random events

2. While taking a standardized test with randomly scrambled answers, you notice that your last four answers have been "c." Which of the following is true concerning the probability of the next answer being "c"?

   a. It is higher. Once a streak begins, it is likely to last for a while.
   b. It is lower. Since answers are distributed randomly, "c" answers become less common.
   c. It is unaffected by previous answers. It is as likely to be "c" as any other answer.
   d. You should check your previous answers. Four "c's" in a row is impossible.
   e. It is higher. Test constructors trick students by keeping the same answer many times in a row.

3. What do we call the tendency to exaggerate the correctness or accuracy of our beliefs and predictions prior to testing?

   a. Hindsight bias
   b. Overconfidence
   c. Critical thinking
   d. Skepticism
   e. Reliability

4. Which of the following is an example of hindsight bias?

   a. Tom is certain that electric cars will represent 80 percent of vehicles in twenty years and only reads research studies that support his hypothesis.
   b. Liza underestimates how much time it will take her to finish writing her college application essays and as a result fails to meet an important deadline.
   c. Experts predicting world events with 80 percent confidence turned out to be correct less than 40 percent of the time.
   d. Marcy cannot recognize a definition on a flashcard. After turning the card over and viewing the term, she tells herself she knew what the answer was all along.
   e. Dr. Grace overestimates how effectively her new treatment method works because she fails to seek out any evidence refuting her theory.

Practice FRQs

1. Name the three components of the scientific attitude. Provide an example to show how each component contributes to the investigation of competing ideas in psychology.

Answer

1 point: Curiosity, or passion to explore, leads us to questions we want to investigate. Any examples of such questions will serve (For example, Does more money make us happier? Is schizophrenia inherited?).

1 point: Skepticism keeps us from accepting ideas without sound support. The work of The Amazing Randi would be a good example here.

1 point: Humility keeps us open to the possibility of changing our ideas when they are not supported by the data. For example, "the rat is always right."

2. Aziz has read that handwriting reveals important details about personality. Explain how each component of the scientific attitude can help Aziz investigate the accuracy of the information he has read about handwriting analysis.

(3 points)

Module 5

The Scientific Method and Description

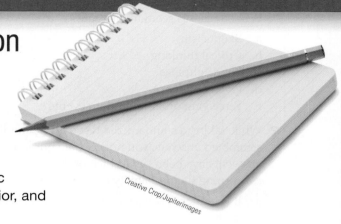

Creative Crop/Jupiterimages

Module Learning Objectives

 Describe how theories advance psychological science.

5-2 Describe how psychologists use case studies, naturalistic observation, and surveys to observe and describe behavior, and explain the importance of random sampling.

sychologists arm their scientific attitude with the *scientific method*—a self-correcting process for evaluating ideas with observation and analysis. In its attempt to describe and explain human nature, psychological science welcomes hunches and plausible-sounding theories. And it puts them to the test. If a theory works—if the data support its predictions—so much the better for that theory. If the predictions fail, the theory will be revised or rejected.

The Scientific Method

5-1 How do theories advance psychological science?

Chatting with friends and family, we often use theory to mean "mere hunch." In science, a **theory** *explains* behaviors or events by offering ideas that *organize* what we have observed. By organizing isolated facts, a theory simplifies. By linking facts with deeper principles, a theory offers a useful summary. As we connect the observed dots, a coherent picture emerges.

A theory about the effects of sleep on memory, for example, helps us organize countless sleep-related observations into a short list of principles. Imagine that we observe over and over that people with good sleep habits tend to answer questions correctly in class, and they do well at test time. We might therefore theorize that sleep improves memory. So far so good: Our principle neatly summarizes a list of facts about the effects of a good night's sleep on memory.

Yet no matter how reasonable a theory may sound—and it does seem reasonable to suggest that sleep could improve memory—we must put it to the test. A good theory produces testable predictions, called **hypotheses.** Such predictions specify what results (what behaviors or events) would support the theory and what results would cast doubt on the theory. To test our theory about the effects of sleep on memory, our hypothesis might be that when sleep deprived, people will remember less from the day before. To test that hypothesis, we might assess how well people remember course materials they studied before a good night's sleep, or before a shortened night's sleep (**FIGURE 5.1**). The results will either confirm our theory or lead us to revise or reject it.

theory an explanation using an integrated set of principles that organizes observations and predicts behaviors or events.

hypothesis a testable prediction, often implied by a theory.

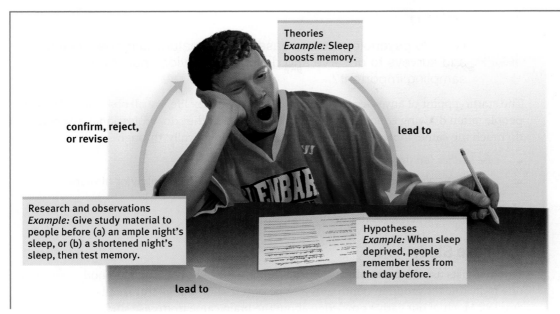

Figure 5.1

The scientific method A self-correcting process for asking questions and observing nature's answers.

Our theories can bias our observations. Having theorized that better memory springs from more sleep, we may see what we expect: We may perceive sleepy people's comments as less insightful. Perhaps you are aware of students who, because they have developed an excellent reputation, can now do no wrong in the eyes of teachers. If they're in the hall during class, nobody worries. Other students can do no good. Because they have behaved badly in the past, even their positive behaviors are viewed suspiciously.

As a check on their biases, psychologists use **operational definitions** when they report their studies. "Sleep deprived," for example, may be defined as "X hours less" than the person's natural sleep. Unlike dictionary definitions, operational definitions describe concepts with precise procedures or measures. These exact descriptions will allow anyone to **replicate** (repeat) the research. Other people can then re-create the study with different participants and in different situations. If they get similar results, we can be confident that the findings are reliable.

Let's summarize. A good theory:

- effectively *organizes* a range of self-reports and observations.
- leads to clear *hypotheses* (predictions) that anyone can use to check the theory.
- often stimulates research that leads to a revised theory which better organizes and predicts what we know. Or, our research may be replicated and supported by similar findings. (This has been the case for sleep and memory studies, as you will see in Module 24.)

We can test our hypotheses and refine our theories in several ways.

- *Descriptive* methods describe behaviors, often by using case studies, surveys, or naturalistic observations.
- *Correlational* methods associate different factors, or *variables.* (You'll see the word *variable* often in descriptions of research. It refers to anything that contributes to a result.)
- *Experimental* methods manipulate variables to discover their effects.

To think critically about popular psychology claims, we need to understand the strengths and weaknesses of these methods.

operational definition a carefully worded statement of the exact procedures (operations) used in a research study. For example, *human intelligence* may be operationally defined as what an intelligence test measures.

replication repeating the essence of a research study, usually with different participants in different situations, to see whether the basic finding extends to other participants and circumstances.

Description

 5-2 How do psychologists use case studies, naturalistic observation, and surveys to observe and describe behavior, and why is random sampling important?

The starting point of any science is description. In everyday life, we all observe and describe people, often drawing conclusions about why they act as they do. Professional psychologists do much the same, though more objectively and systematically, through

- *case studies* (analyses of special individuals).
- *naturalistic observation* (watching and recording the natural behavior of many individuals).
- *surveys* and interviews (by asking people questions).

The Case Study

Psychologists use the **case study,** which is among the oldest research methods, to examine one individual or group in depth in the hope of revealing things true of all of us. Some examples: Much of our early knowledge about the brain came from case studies of individuals who suffered a particular impairment after damage to a certain brain region. Jean Piaget taught us about children's thinking through case studies in which he carefully observed and questioned individual children. Studies of only a few chimpanzees have revealed their capacity for understanding and language. Intensive case studies are sometimes very revealing. They show us what *can* happen, and they often suggest directions for further study.

But individual cases may mislead us if the individual is atypical. Unrepresentative information can lead to mistaken judgments and false conclusions. Indeed, anytime a researcher mentions a finding (*"Smokers die younger: ninety-five percent of men over 85 are nonsmokers"*) someone is sure to offer a contradictory anecdote (*"Well, I have an uncle who smoked two packs a day and lived to 89"*). Dramatic stories and personal experiences (even psychological case examples) command our attention and are easily remembered. Journalists understand that, and so begin an article about bank foreclosures with the sad story of one family put out of their house, not with foreclosure statistics. Stories move us. But stories can mislead. Which of the following do you find more memorable? (1) "In one study of 1300 dream reports concerning a kidnapped child, only 5 percent correctly envisioned the child as dead" (Murray & Wheeler, 1937). (2) "I know a man who dreamed his sister was in a car accident, and two days later she died in a head-on collision!" Numbers can be numbing, but the plural of *anecdote* is not *evidence*. As psychologist Gordon Allport (1954, p. 9) said, "Given a thimbleful of [dramatic] facts we rush to make generalizations as large as a tub."

The point to remember: Individual cases can suggest fruitful ideas. What's true of all of us can be glimpsed in any one of us. But to discern the general truths that cover individual cases, we must answer questions with other research methods.

Naturalistic Observation

A second descriptive method records behavior in natural environments. These **naturalistic observations** range from watching chimpanzee societies in the jungle, to unobtrusively videotaping (and later systematically analyzing) parent-child interactions in different cultures, to recording racial differences in students' self-seating patterns in a school cafeteria.

Like the case study, naturalistic observation does not *explain* behavior. It *describes* it. Nevertheless, descriptions can be revealing. We once thought, for example, that only humans use tools. Then naturalistic observation revealed that chimpanzees sometimes insert a stick in a termite mound and withdraw it, eating the stick's load of termites.

---

case study a descriptive technique in which one individual or group is studied in depth in the hope of revealing universal principles.

naturalistic observation observing and recording behavior in naturally occurring situations without trying to manipulate and control the situation.

"'Well my dear,' said Miss Marple, 'human nature is very much the same everywhere, and of course, one has opportunities of observing it at closer quarters in a village.'" -AGATHA CHRISTIE, *THE TUESDAY CLUB MURDERS*, 1933

Juniors Bildarchiv/F355/Alamy

Freud and Little Hans Sigmund Freud's case study of 5-year-old Hans' extreme fear of horses led Freud to his theory of childhood sexuality. He conjectured that Hans felt unconscious desire for his mother, feared castration by his rival father, and then transferred this fear into his phobia about being bitten by a horse. As Module 56 will explain, today's psychological science discounts Freud's theory of childhood sexuality but acknowledges that much of the human mind operates outside our conscious awareness.

Such unobtrusive naturalistic observations paved the way for later studies of animal thinking, language, and emotion, which further expanded our understanding of our fellow animals. "Observations, made in the natural habitat, helped to show that the societies and behavior of animals are far more complex than previously supposed," chimpanzee observer Jane Goodall noted (1998). Thanks to researchers' observations, we know that chimpanzees and baboons use deception. Psychologists Andrew Whiten and Richard Byrne (1988) repeatedly saw one young baboon pretending to have been attacked by another as a tactic to get its mother to drive the other baboon away from its food. The more developed a primate species' brain, the more likely it is that the animals will display deceptive behaviors (Byrne & Corp, 2004).

Naturalistic observations also illuminate human behavior. Here are four findings you might enjoy.

A natural observer Chimpanzee researcher Frans de Waal (2005) reported, "I am a born observer. . . . When picking a seat in a restaurant I want to face as many tables as possible. I enjoy following the social dynamics—love, tension, boredom, antipathy—around me based on body language, which I consider more informative than the spoken word. Since keeping track of others is something I do automatically, becoming a fly on the wall of an ape colony came naturally to me."

- *A funny finding.* We humans laugh 30 times more often in social situations than in solitary situations. (Have you noticed how seldom you laugh when alone?) As we laugh, 17 muscles contort our mouth and squeeze our eyes, and we emit a series of 75-millisecond vowel-like sounds, spaced about one-fifth of a second apart (Provine, 2001).

- *Sounding out students.* What, really, are college psychology students saying and doing during their everyday lives? To find out, researchers equipped 52 such students from the University of Texas with electronic recorders (Mehl & Pennebaker, 2003). For up to four days, the recorders captured 30 seconds of the students' waking hours every 12.5 minutes, thus enabling the researchers to eavesdrop on more than 10,000 half-minute life slices by the end of the study. On what percentage of the slices do you suppose they found the students talking with someone? What percentage captured the students at a computer? The answers: 28 and 9 percent. (What percentage of *your* waking hours are spent in these activities?)

- *What's on your mind?* To find out what was on the mind of their University of Nevada, Las Vegas, students, researchers gave them beepers (Heavey & Hurlburt, 2008). On a half-dozen occasions, a beep interrupted students' daily activities, signaling them to pull out a notebook and record their inner experience at that moment. When the researchers later coded the reports in categories, they found five common forms of inner experience (**TABLE 5.1** on the next page).

- *Culture, climate, and the pace of life.* Naturalistic observation also enabled researchers to compare the pace of life in 31 countries (Levine & Norenzayan, 1999). (Their operational definition of *pace of life* included walking speed, the speed with which postal clerks completed a simple request, and the accuracy of public clocks.) Their conclusion: Life is fastest paced in Japan and Western Europe, and slower paced in economically less-developed countries. People in colder climates also tend to live at a faster pace (and are more prone to die from heart disease).

Naturalistic observation Researchers at the University of Texas used electronic recorders to sample naturally occurring slices of daily life.

Table 5.1　A Penny for Their Thoughts: The Inner Experience of University Students*

Inner Experience	Example	Frequency
Inner speech	Susan was saying to herself, "I've got to get to class."	26%
Inner seeing	Paul was imagining the face of a best friend, including her neck and head.	34%
Unsymbolized thinking	Alphonse was wondering whether the workers would drop the bricks.	22%
Feeling	Courtney was experiencing anger and its physical symptoms.	26%
Sensory awareness	Fiona was feeling the cold breeze on her cheek and her hair moving.	22%

* More than one experience could occur at once.

Naturalistic observation offers interesting snapshots of everyday life, but it does so without controlling for all the variables that may influence behavior. It's one thing to observe the pace of life in various places, but another to understand what makes some people walk faster than others.

The Survey

> **survey** a technique for ascertaining the self-reported attitudes or behaviors of a particular group, usually by questioning a representative, random sample of the group.

A **survey** looks at many cases in less depth. Researchers do surveys when wanting to estimate, from a representative sample of people, the attitudes or reported behaviors of a whole population. Questions about everything from cell-phone use to political opinions are put to the public. In recent surveys,

- half of all Americans reported experiencing more happiness and enjoyment than worry and stress on the previous day (Gallup, 2010).
- online Canadians reported using new forms of electronic communication and thus receiving 35 percent fewer e-mails in 2010 than 2008 (Ipsos, 2010a).
- 1 in 5 people across 22 countries reported believing that alien beings have come to Earth and now walk among us disguised as humans (Ipsos, 2010b).
- 68 percent of all humans—some 4.6 billion people—say that religion is important in their daily lives (Diener et al., 2011).

But asking questions is tricky, and the answers often depend on the ways questions are worded and respondents are chosen.

WORDING EFFECTS

As we will see in Module 35, even subtle changes in the order or wording of questions—the way we *frame* a question—can have major effects. People are much more approving of "aid to the needy" than of "welfare," of "affirmative action" than of "preferential treatment," of "not allowing" televised cigarette ads and pornography than of "censoring" them, and of "revenue enhancers" than of "taxes." In 2009, three in four Americans in one national survey approved of giving people "a choice" of public, government-run, or private health insurance. Yet in another survey, most Americans were not in favor of "creating a public health care plan administered by the federal government that would compete directly with private health insurance companies" (Stein, 2009). Because wording is such a delicate matter, critical thinkers will reflect on how the phrasing of a question might affect people's expressed opinions.

RANDOM SAMPLING

In everyday thinking, we tend to generalize from samples we observe, especially vivid cases. Given (a) a statistical summary of auto owners' evaluations of their car make and (b) the vivid comments of a biased sample—two frustrated owners—our impression may be influenced as much by the two unhappy owners as by the many more evaluations in the statistical summary. The temptation to ignore the **sampling bias** and to generalize from a few vivid but unrepresentative cases is nearly irresistible.

The point to remember: The best basis for generalizing is from a *representative sample.*

But it's not always possible to survey everyone in a group. So how do you obtain a representative sample—say, of the students at your high school? How could you choose a group that would represent the total student **population,** the whole group you want to study and describe? Typically, you would seek a **random sample,** in which every person in the entire group has an equal chance of participating. You might number the names in the general student listing and then use a random number generator to pick your survey participants. (Sending each student a questionnaire wouldn't work because the conscientious people who returned it would not be a random sample.) Large representative samples are better than small ones, but a small representative sample of 100 is better than an unrepresentative sample of 500.

Political pollsters sample voters in national election surveys just this way. Using only 1500 randomly sampled people, drawn from all areas of a country, they can provide a remarkably accurate snapshot of the nation's opinions. Without random sampling (also called *random selection*), large samples—including call-in phone samples and TV or website polls (think of *American Idol* fans voting)—often merely give misleading results.

The point to remember: Before accepting survey findings, think critically: Consider the sample. You cannot compensate for an unrepresentative sample by simply adding more people.

sampling bias a flawed sampling process that produces an unrepresentative sample.

population all those in a group being studied, from which samples may be drawn. (*Note:* Except for national studies, this does *not* refer to a country's whole population.)

random sample a sample that fairly represents a population because each member has an equal chance of inclusion.

FYI

With very large samples, estimates become quite reliable. *E* is estimated to represent 12.7 percent of the letters in written English. *E*, in fact, is 12.3 percent of the 925,141 letters in Melville's *Moby Dick*, 12.4 percent of the 586,747 letters in Dickens' *A Tale of Two Cities*, and 12.1 percent of the 3,901,021 letters in 12 of Mark Twain's works (*Chance News*, 1997).

Before You Move On

▶ **ASK YOURSELF**

Can you recall examples of misleading surveys you have experienced or read about? What survey principles did they violate?

▶ **TEST YOURSELF**

What are some strengths and weaknesses of the three different methods psychologists use to describe behavior—case studies, naturalistic observation, and surveys?

Answers to the Test Yourself questions can be found in Appendix E at the end of the book.

Module 5 Review

 5-1 How do theories advance psychological science?

- Psychological *theories* are explanations that apply an integrated set of principles to organize observations and generate *hypotheses*—predictions that can be used to check the theory or produce practical applications of it. By testing their hypotheses, researchers can confirm, reject, or revise their theories.

- To enable other researchers to *replicate* the studies, researchers report them using precise *operational definitions* of their procedures and concepts. If others achieve similar results, confidence in the conclusion will be greater.

 5-2 How do psychologists use case studies, naturalistic observation, and surveys to observe and describe behavior, and why is random sampling important?

- Description methods, which include *case studies, naturalistic observations,* and *surveys,* show us what can happen, and they may offer ideas for further study.

- The best basis for generalizing about a *population* is a representative sample; in a *random sample,* every person in the entire population being studied has an equal chance of participating.

- Descriptive methods describe but do not *explain* behavior, because these methods do not control for the many variables that can affect behavior.

Multiple-Choice Questions

1. Why is an operational definition necessary when reporting research findings?

   a. An operational definition allows others to replicate the procedure.
   b. An operational definition provides more context and includes many examples of the concept described.
   c. An operational definition is easier to translate into multiple languages than a dictionary definition.
   d. An operational definition uses more scientific language than a dictionary definition.
   e. An operational definition is not necessary since a dictionary definition will work as well for replication.

2. A researcher looking for gender differences in 3-year-olds observes a preschool class and records how many minutes children of each gender play with dolls. She then compares the two sets of numbers. What type of descriptive research is she conducting?

   a. Case study
   b. National study
   c. Random sample method
   d. Naturalistic observation
   e. Survey

3. Which of the following questions is best investigated by means of a survey?

   a. Is IQ related to grades?
   b. Are violent criminals genetically different from nonviolent criminals?
   c. Does extra sleep improve memory?
   d. What is the best study technique for AP® tests?
   e. Are students more likely to be politically liberal or conservative?

4. A testable prediction that drives research is known as a(n)

   a. theory.
   b. hypothesis.
   c. operational definition.
   d. guess.
   e. random sample.

5. Researchers are interested in finding out if winning Congressional candidates display more positive facial expressions than losing candidates. The researchers attend political debates and record how frequently each candidate displays positive facial expressions. Which research method are the researchers using?

   a. Random sample
   b. Case study
   c. Naturalistic observation
   d. Survey
   e. Interview

6. An individual with an exceptional memory is identified. She is capable of recalling major events, the weather, and what she did on any given date. What research method is being used if a psychologist conducts an in-depth investigation of this individual including questionnaires, brain scans, and memory tests?

 a. Naturalistic observation
 b. Survey
 c. Interview
 d. Case study
 e. Correlational method

7. Which of the following is most important when conducting survey research?

 a. Choosing a representative sample
 b. Choosing a large sample
 c. Choosing a biased sample
 d. Choosing a sample that includes every member of the population
 e. Choosing a sample whose answers will likely support your hypothesis

Practice FRQs

1. A teacher wants to know if nightmares are more common than dreams. He asks volunteers from his second-period class to report how many dreams they had last week. He asks volunteers from his third-period class to report the number of nightmares they had last week. Describe two things wrong with the design of this study.

Answer (2 of the following)

1 point: There is no hypothesis stated.

1 point: In asking for volunteers, the teacher is taking a nonrandom sample that is probably not representative of the population of interest.

1 point: Neither dreams nor nightmares are operationally defined, so they might be interpreted differently by later researchers.

1 point: The research is not blind. The teacher could influence the results by the way he asked questions.

2. Naturalistic observation is a research method used by psychologists to investigate human and animal behavior. Identify three weaknesses of naturalistic observation.

(3 points)

Module 6

Correlation and Experimentation

imagebroker/Alamy

Module Learning Objectives

6-1 Describe positive and negative correlations, and explain how correlational measures can aid the process of prediction but not provide evidence of cause-effect relationships.

6-2 Explain illusory correlations.

6-3 Describe the characteristics of experimentation that make it possible to isolate cause and effect.

"Study finds that increased parental support for college results in lower grades" (Jaschik, 2013). "People with mental illness more likely to be smokers" (Belluck, 2013). What should we make of such news headlines—telling us that students whose parents pay the college bill tend to underachieve, and that smoking is associated with mental illness? Do these correlations indicate that students would achieve more if their parents became less supportive and that stopping smoking could produce better mental health? *No.* Read on.

Correlation

correlation a measure of the extent to which two variables change together, and thus of how well either variable predicts the other.

correlation coefficient a statistical index of the relationship between two variables (from −1.0 to +1.0).

scatterplot a graphed cluster of dots, each of which represents the values of two variables. The slope of the points suggests the direction of the relationship between the two variables. The amount of scatter suggests the strength of the correlation (little scatter indicates high correlation).

6-1 What are positive and negative correlations, and why do they enable prediction but not cause-effect explanation?

Describing behavior is a first step toward predicting it. Naturalistic observations and surveys often show us that one trait or behavior is related to another. In such cases, we say the two **correlate.** A statistical measure (the **correlation coefficient**) helps us figure how closely two things vary together, and thus how well either one predicts the other. Knowing how much aptitude test scores correlate with school success tells us how well the scores predict school success.

Throughout this book we will often ask how strongly two things are related: For example, how closely related are the personality scores of identical twins? How well do intelligence test scores predict career achievement? How closely is stress related to disease? In such cases, **scatterplots** can be very revealing.

Each dot in a scatterplot represents the values of two variables. The three scatterplots in **FIGURE 6.1** illustrate the range of possible correlations from a perfect positive to a perfect negative. (Perfect correlations rarely occur in the "real world.") A correlation is positive if two sets of scores, such as height and weight, tend to rise or fall together.

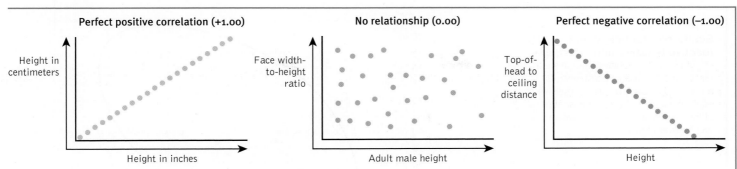

Figure 6.1

Scatterplots, showing patterns of correlation Correlations can range from +1.00 (scores on one measure increase in direct proportion to scores on another) to –1.00 (scores on one measure decrease precisely as scores rise on the other).

Saying that a correlation is "negative" says nothing about its strength or weakness. A correlation is negative if two sets of scores relate inversely, one set going up as the other goes down. The study of Nevada university students' inner speech discussed in Module 5 also included a correlational component. Students' reports of inner speech correlated negatively (–.36) with their scores on another measure: psychological distress. Those who reported more inner speech tended to report slightly *less* psychological distress.

Statistics can help us see what the naked eye sometimes misses. To demonstrate this for yourself, try an imaginary project. Wondering if tall men are more or less easygoing, you collect two sets of scores: men's heights and men's temperaments. You measure the heights of 20 men, and you have someone else independently assess their temperaments (from zero for extremely calm to 100 for highly reactive).

With all the relevant data right in front of you (**TABLE 6.1**), can you tell whether the correlation between height and reactive temperament is positive, negative, or close to zero?

Comparing the columns in Table 6.1, most people detect very little relationship between height and temperament. In fact, the correlation in this imaginary example is positive, +0.63, as we can see if we display the data as a scatterplot. In **FIGURE 6.2** on the next page, moving from left to right, the upward, oval-shaped slope of the cluster of points shows that our two imaginary sets of scores (height and temperament) tend to rise together.

If we fail to see a relationship when data are presented as systematically as in Table 6.1, how much less likely are we to notice them in everyday life? To see what is right in front of us, we sometimes need statistical illumination. We can easily see evidence of gender discrimination when given statistically summarized information about job level, seniority, performance,

Table 6.1 Height and Temperamental Reactivity of 20 Men		
Person	Height in Inches	Temperament
1	80	75
2	63	66
3	61	60
4	79	90
5	74	60
6	69	42
7	62	42
8	75	60
9	77	81
10	60	39
11	64	48
12	76	69
13	71	72
14	66	57
15	73	63
16	70	75
17	63	30
18	71	57
19	68	84
20	70	39

AP® Exam Tip

This is the first of several times in your psychology course that you will see something labeled as being positive or negative. We often think that if something is positive it is good and if it's negative it's bad. That is rarely the case in this course. Here, positive and negative refer only to the direction of the correlation. They say nothing about whether the relationship is desirable or not.

Figure 6.2

Scatterplot for height and reactive temperament This display of data from 20 imagined people (each represented by a data point) reveals an upward slope, indicating a positive correlation. The considerable scatter of the data indicates the correlation is much lower than +1.0.

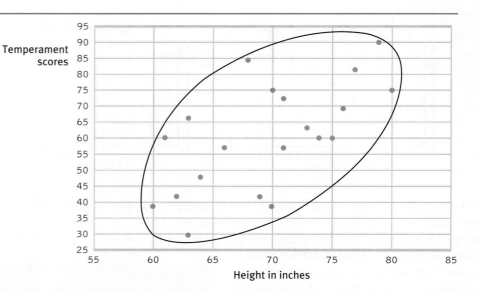

gender, and salary. But we often see no discrimination when the same information dribbles in, case by case (Twiss et al., 1989). See **TABLE 6.2** to test your understanding further.

The point to remember: A correlation coefficient, which can range from −1.0 to +1.0, reveals the extent to which two things relate. The closer the score gets to −1 or +1, the stronger the correlation.

Table 6.2

Test your understanding of correlation. Which of the following news reports are examples of a *positive* correlation, and which are examples of a *negative* correlation? (Check your answers below.)

1. The more children and youth used various media, the less happy they were with their lives (Kaiser, 2010). _____

2. The less sexual content teens saw on TV, the less likely they were to have sex (Collins et al., 2004). _____

3. The longer children were breast-fed, the greater their later academic achievement (Horwood & Ferguson, 1998). _____

4. The more income rose among a sample of poor families, the fewer psychiatric symptoms their children experienced (Costello et al., 2003). _____

ANSWERS: 1. negative, 2. positive, 3. positive, 4. negative

Correlation and Causation

Correlations help us predict. The *New York Times* reports that U.S. counties with high gun ownership rates tend to have high murder rates (Luo, 2011). Gun ownership predicts homicide. What might explain this guns-homicide correlation?

I can almost hear someone thinking, "Well, of course, guns kill people, often in moments of passion." If so, that could be an example of A (guns) causes B (murder). But I can hear other readers saying, "Not so fast. Maybe people in dangerous places buy more guns for self-protection—maybe B causes A." Or maybe some third variable C causes both A and B.

Another example: Self-esteem correlates negatively with (and therefore predicts) depression. (The lower people's self-esteem, the more they are at risk for depression.) So, does low self-esteem *cause* depression? If, based on the correlational evidence, you assume that it does, you have much company. A nearly irresistible thinking error is assuming that an association, sometimes presented as a correlation coefficient, proves causation. But no matter how strong the relationship, it does not.

© Nancy Brown/Getty Images

Correlation need not mean causation Length of marriage correlates with hair loss in men. Does this mean that marriage *causes* men to lose their hair (or that balding men make better husbands)? In this case, as in many others, a third variable probably explains the correlation: Golden anniversaries and baldness both accompany aging.

As options 2 and 3 in **FIGURE 6.3** show, we'd get the same negative correlation between self-esteem and depression if depression caused people to be down on themselves, or if some third variable—such as heredity or brain chemistry—caused both low self-esteem and depression.

This point is so important—so basic to thinking smarter with psychology—that it merits one more example. A survey of over 12,000 adolescents found that the more teens feel loved by their parents, the less likely they are to behave in unhealthy ways—having early sex, smoking, abusing alcohol and drugs, exhibiting violence (Resnick et al., 1997). "Adults have a powerful effect on their children's behavior right through the high school years," gushed an Associated Press (AP) story reporting the finding. But this correlation comes with no built-in cause-effect arrow. The AP could as well have reported, "Well-behaved teens feel their parents' love and approval; out-of-bounds teens more often think their parents are disapproving jerks."

The point to remember (turn the volume up here): *Association does not prove causation.*[1] Correlation indicates the *possibility* of a cause-effect relationship *but does not prove such.* Remember this principle and you will be wiser as you read and hear news of scientific studies.

---

[1]Because many associations are stated as correlations, the famously worded principle is "Correlation does not prove causation." That's true, but it's also true of associations verified by other nonexperimental statistics (Hatfield et al., 2006).

FYI

A *New York Times* writer reported a massive survey showing that "adolescents whose parents smoked were 50 percent more likely than children of nonsmokers to report having had sex." He concluded (would you agree?) that the survey indicated a causal effect—that "to reduce the chances that their children will become sexually active at an early age" parents might "quit smoking" (O'Neil, 2002).

AP® Exam Tip

Take note of how much emphasis is put on this idea. Correlation and association do not prove a cause-effect relationship.

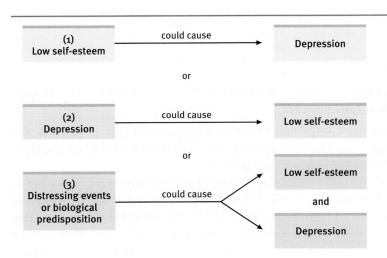

Figure 6.3

Three possible cause-effect relationships People low in self-esteem are more likely to report depression than are those high in self-esteem. One possible explanation of this negative correlation is that a bad self-image causes depressed feelings. But, as the diagram indicates, other cause-effect relationships are possible.

(1) Low self-esteem — could cause → Depression

or

(2) Depression — could cause → Low self-esteem

or

(3) Distressing events or biological predisposition — could cause → Low self-esteem and Depression

Illusory Correlations

6-2   What are illusory correlations?

Correlation coefficients make visible the relationships we might otherwise miss. They also restrain our "seeing" relationships that actually do not exist. A perceived but nonexistent correlation is an **illusory correlation.** When we *believe* there is a relationship between two things, we are likely to *notice* and *recall* instances that confirm our belief (Trolier & Hamilton, 1986).

Because we are sensitive to dramatic or unusual events, we are especially likely to notice and remember the occurrence of two such events in sequence—say, a premonition of an unlikely phone call followed by the call. When the call does not follow the premonition, we are less likely to note and remember the nonevent. Illusory correlations help explain many superstitious beliefs, such as the presumption that infertile couples who adopt become more likely to conceive (Gilovich, 1991). Couples who conceive after adopting capture our attention. We're less likely to notice those who adopt and never conceive, or those who conceive without adopting. In other words, illusory correlations occur when we over-rely on the top left cell of **FIGURE 6.4**, ignoring equally essential information in the other cells.

Such illusory thinking helps explain why for so many years people believed (and many still do) that sugar makes children hyperactive, that getting chilled and wet causes people to catch a cold, and that changes in the weather trigger arthritis pain. We are, it seems, prone to perceiving patterns, whether they're there or not.

The point to remember: When we notice random coincidences, we may forget that they are random and instead see them as correlated. Thus, we can easily deceive ourselves by seeing what is not there.

Figure 6.4

Illusory correlation in everyday life Many people believe infertile couples become more likely to conceive a child after adopting a baby. This belief arises from their attention being drawn to such cases. The many couples who adopt without conceiving or conceive without adopting grab less attention. To determine whether there actually is a correlation between adoption and conception, we need data from all four cells in this figure. (From Gilovich, 1991.)

	Conceive	Do not conceive
Adopt	confirming evidence	disconfirming evidence
Do not adopt	disconfirming evidence	confirming evidence

Michael Newman Jr./PhotoEdit

Experimentation

6-3   What are the characteristics of experimentation that make it possible to isolate cause and effect?

Happy are they, remarked the Roman poet Virgil, "who have been able to perceive the causes of things." How might psychologists perceive causes in correlational studies, such as the correlation between breast feeding and intelligence?

Researchers have found that the intelligence scores of children who were breast-fed as infants are somewhat higher than the scores of children who were bottle-fed (Angelsen et al., 2001; Mortensen et al., 2002; Quinn et al., 2001). In Britain, breast-fed babies have also been more likely than their bottle-fed counterparts to eventually move into a higher social class (Martin et al., 2007). The "breast is best" intelligence effect shrinks when researchers compare breast-fed and bottle-fed children from the same families (Der et al., 2006).

What do such findings mean? Do smarter mothers (who in modern countries more often breast feed) have smarter children? Or, as some researchers believe, do the nutrients of mother's milk contribute to brain development? To find answers to such questions—to isolate cause and effect—researchers can **experiment.** Experiments enable researchers to isolate the effects of one or more variables by (1) manipulating the variables of interest and (2) holding constant ("controlling") other variables. To do so, they often create an **experimental group,** in which people receive the treatment, and a contrasting **control group** that does not receive the treatment.

Lane Oatey/Getty Images

Earlier we mentioned the place of *random sampling* in a well-done survey. Consider now the equally important place of *random assignment* in a well-done experiment. To minimize any preexisting differences between the two groups, researchers **randomly assign** people to the two conditions. Random assignment effectively equalizes the two groups. If one-third of the volunteers for an experiment can wiggle their ears, then about one-third of the people in each group will be ear wigglers. So, too, with ages, attitudes, and other characteristics, which will be similar in the experimental and control groups. Thus, if the groups differ at the experiment's end, we can surmise that the treatment had an effect.

To experiment with breast feeding, one research team randomly assigned some 17,000 Belarus newborns and their mothers either to a breast-feeding promotion group or to a normal pediatric care program (Kramer et al., 2008). At 3 months of age, 43 percent of the infants in the experimental group were being exclusively breast-fed, as were 6 percent in the control group. At age 6, when nearly 14,000 of the children were restudied, those who had been in the breast-feeding promotion group had intelligence test scores averaging six points higher than their control condition counterparts.

No single experiment is conclusive, of course. But randomly assigning participants to one feeding group or the other effectively eliminated all variables except nutrition. This supported the conclusion that breast is indeed best for developing intelligence: If a behavior (such as test performance) changes when we vary an experimental variable (such as infant nutrition), then we infer the variable is having an effect.

The point to remember: Unlike correlational studies, which uncover naturally occurring relationships, an experiment manipulates a variable to determine its effect.

Consider, then, how we might assess therapeutic interventions. Our tendency to seek new remedies when we are ill or emotionally down can produce misleading testimonies. If three days into a cold we start taking vitamin C tablets and find our cold symptoms lessening, we may credit the pills rather than the cold naturally subsiding. In the 1700s, bloodletting seemed effective. People sometimes improved after the treatment; when they didn't, the practitioner inferred the disease was too advanced to be reversed. So, whether or not a remedy is truly effective, enthusiastic users will probably endorse it. To determine its effect, we must control for other variables.

And that is precisely how investigators evaluate new drug treatments and new methods of psychological therapy (Modules 72–73). They randomly assign participants in these studies to research groups. One group receives a treatment (such as a medication). The other group receives a pseudotreatment—an inert placebo (perhaps a pill with no drug in it). The participants are often blind (uninformed) about what treatment, if any, they are receiving. If the study is using a **double-blind procedure,** neither the participants nor the research assistants who administer the drug and collect the data will know which group is receiving the treatment.

---

experiment a research method in which an investigator manipulates one or more factors (independent variables) to observe the effect on some behavior or mental process (the dependent variable). By *random assignment* of participants, the experimenter aims to control other relevant variables.

experimental group in an experiment, the group exposed to the treatment, that is, to one version of the independent variable.

control group in an experiment, the group *not* exposed to the treatment; contrasts with the experimental group and serves as a comparison for evaluating the effect of the treatment.

random assignment assigning participants to experimental and control groups by chance, thus minimizing preexisting differences between the different groups.

double-blind procedure an experimental procedure in which both the research participants and the research staff are ignorant (blind) about whether the research participants have received the treatment or a placebo. Commonly used in drug-evaluation studies.

In such studies, researchers can check a treatment's actual effects apart from the participants' and the staff's belief in its healing powers. Just thinking you are getting a treatment can boost your spirits, relax your body, and relieve your symptoms. This **placebo effect** is well documented in reducing pain, depression, and anxiety (Kirsch, 2010). And the more expensive the placebo, the more "real" it seems to us—a fake pill that costs $2.50 works better than one costing 10 cents (Waber et al., 2008). To know how effective a therapy really is, researchers must control for a possible placebo effect.

Independent and Dependent Variables

Here is a practical experiment: In a not yet published study, Victor Benassi and his colleagues gave college psychology students frequent in-class quizzes. Some items served merely as *review*—students were given questions with answers. Other *self-testing* items required students to actively produce the answers. When tested weeks later on a final exam, students did far better on material on which they had been tested (75 percent correct) rather than merely reviewed (51 percent correct). By a wide margin, testing beat restudy.

This simple experiment manipulated just one factor: the study procedure (reading answers versus self-testing). We call this experimental factor the **independent variable** because we can vary it *independently* of other factors, such as the students' memories, intelligence, and age. These other factors, which can potentially influence the results of the experiment, are called **confounding variables.** Random assignment controls for possible confounding variables.

Experiments examine the effect of one or more independent variables on some measurable behavior, called the **dependent variable** because it can vary *depending* on what takes place during the experiment. Both variables are given precise *operational definitions*, which specify the procedures that manipulate the independent variable (the review versus self-testing study method in this analysis) or measure the dependent variable (final exam performance). These definitions answer the "What do you mean?" question with a level of precision that enables others to repeat the study. (See **FIGURE 6.5** for the previously mentioned breast-milk experiment's design.)

Let's pause to check your understanding using a simple psychology experiment: To test the effect of perceived ethnicity on the availability of a rental house, researchers sent identically worded e-mail inquiries to 1115 Los Angeles-area landlords (Carpusor & Loges, 2006). The researchers varied the ethnic connotation of the sender's name and tracked the percentage of positive replies (invitations to view the apartment in person). "Patrick McDougall," "Said Al-Rahman," and "Tyrell Jackson" received, respectively, 89 percent, 66 percent, and 56 percent invitations. (In this experiment, what was the independent variable? The dependent variable?[2])

placebo [pluh-SEE-bo; Latin for "I shall please"] **effect** experimental results caused by expectations alone; any effect on behavior caused by the administration of an inert substance or condition, which the recipient assumes is an active agent.

independent variable the experimental factor that is manipulated; the variable whose effect is being studied.

confounding variable a factor other than the independent variable that might produce an effect in an experiment.

dependent variable the outcome factor; the variable that may change in response to manipulations of the independent variable.

AP® Exam Tip

The identification of independent and dependent variables is the single most likely concept to be tested on the AP® exam. Experiments are critical to psychology, and independent and dependent variables are critical to experiments.

Figure 6.5

Experimentation To discern causation, psychologists may randomly assign some participants to an experimental group, others to a control group. Measuring the dependent variable (intelligence score in later childhood) will determine the effect of the independent variable (whether breast feeding was promoted).

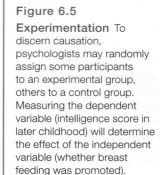

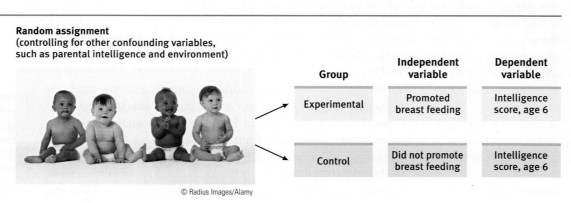

Random assignment (controlling for other confounding variables, such as parental intelligence and environment)

Group	Independent variable	Dependent variable
Experimental	Promoted breast feeding	Intelligence score, age 6
Control	Did not promote breast feeding	Intelligence score, age 6

© Radius Images/Alamy

A key goal of experimental design is **validity,** which means the experiment will test what it is supposed to test. In the rental housing experiment, we might ask, "Did the e-mail inquiries test the effect of perceived ethnicity? Did the landlords' response actually vary with the ethnicity of the name?"

Experiments can also help us evaluate social programs. Do early childhood education programs boost impoverished children's chances for success? What are the effects of different antismoking campaigns? Do school sex-education programs reduce teen pregnancies? To answer such questions, we can experiment: If an intervention is welcomed but resources are scarce, we could use a lottery to randomly assign some people (or regions) to experience the new program and others to a control condition. If later the two groups differ, the intervention's effect will be supported (Passell, 1993).

Let's recap. A *variable* is anything that can vary (infant nutrition, intelligence, TV exposure—anything within the bounds of what is feasible and ethical). Experiments aim to *manipulate* an *independent* variable, *measure* the *dependent* variable, and allow random assignment to *control* all other variables. An experiment has at least two different conditions: an *experimental condition* and a *comparison* or *control condition. Random assignment* works to equate the groups before any treatment effects occur. In this way, an experiment tests the effect of at least one independent variable (what we manipulate) on at least one dependent variable (the outcome we measure). **TABLE 6.3** compares the features of psychology's research methods.

> **validity** the extent to which a test or experiment measures or predicts what it is supposed to.

AP® Exam Tip

Almost 15 pages of text are summarized in this one table. Spend some time with it, as it is information you will likely encounter on the AP® exam.

---

[2]The independent variable, which the researchers manipulated, was the ethnicity-related names. The dependent variable, which they measured, was the positive response rate.

Table 6.3   Comparing Research Methods

Research Method	Basic Purpose	How Conducted	What Is Manipulated	Strengths	Weaknesses
Descriptive	To observe and record behavior	Do case studies, naturalistic observations, or surveys	Nothing	Case studies require only one participant; naturalistic observations may be done when it is not ethical to manipulate variables; surveys may be done quickly and inexpensively (compared with experiments)	Uncontrolled variables mean cause and effect cannot be determined; single cases may be misleading
Correlational	To detect naturally occurring relationships; to assess how well one variable predicts another	Collect data on two or more variables; no manipulation	Nothing	Works with large groups of data, and may be used in situations where an experiment would not be ethical or possible	Does not specify cause and effect
Experimental	To explore cause and effect	Manipulate one or more variables; use random assignment	The independent variable(s)	Specifies cause and effect, and variables are controlled	Sometimes not feasible; results may not generalize to other contexts; not ethical to manipulate certain variables

"If I don't think it's going to work, will it still work?"

Before You Move On

▶ **ASK YOURSELF**

If you were to become a research psychologist, what questions would you like to explore with experiments?

▶ **TEST YOURSELF**

Why, when testing a new drug to control blood pressure, would we learn more about its effectiveness from giving it to half of the participants in a group of 1000 than to all 1000 participants?

Answers to the Test Yourself questions can be found in Appendix E at the end of the book.

Module 6 Review

 What are positive and negative correlations, and why do they enable prediction but not cause-effect explanation?

- In a positive correlation, two variables rise or fall together. In a negative correlation, one item rises as the other falls.

- *Scatterplots* can help us to see *correlations*.

- A *correlation coefficient* can describe the strength and direction of a relationship between two variables, from +1.00 (a perfect positive correlation) through zero (no correlation at all) to −1.00 (a perfect negative correlation).

6-2 What are illusory correlations?

- *Illusory correlations* are random events that we notice and falsely assume are related.

- Patterns or sequences occur naturally in sets of random data, but we tend to interpret these patterns as meaningful connections, perhaps in an attempt to make sense of the world around us.

 What are the characteristics of experimentation that make it possible to isolate cause and effect?

- To discover cause-effect relationships, psychologists conduct *experiments,* manipulating one or more variables of interest and controlling other variables.

- Using *random assignment,* they can minimize *confounding variables,* such as preexisting differences between the *experimental group* (exposed to the treatment) and the *control group* (given a placebo or different version of the treatment).

- The *independent variable* is the factor the experimenter manipulates to study its effect; the *dependent variable* is the factor the experimenter measures to discover any changes occurring in response to the manipulation of the independent variable.

- Studies may use a *double-blind procedure* to avoid the *placebo effect* and researcher's bias.

- An experiment has *validity* if it tests what it is supposed to test.

Multiple-Choice Questions

1. Which of the following is an example of negative correlation?

a. People who spend more time exercising tend to weigh less.

b. Teenage females tend to have fewer speeding tickets than teenage males.

c. Students with low IQ scores tend to have lower grades.

d. As hours studying for a test decrease, so do grades on that test.

e. Students' shoe sizes are not related to their grades.

2. Which of the following is used only in correlation studies?

  a. Double blind
  b. Placebo
  c. Random assignment
  d. Scatterplot
  e. Random sample

3. Researchers have discovered that individuals with lower income levels report having fewer hours of total sleep. Therefore,

  a. income and sleep levels are positively correlated.
  b. income and sleep levels are negatively correlated.
  c. income and sleep levels are inversely correlated.
  d. income and sleep levels are not correlated.
  e. lower income levels cause individuals to have fewer hours of sleep.

4. Which of the following correlation coefficients represents the strongest relationship between two variables?

  a. +.30
  b. +.75
  c. +1.3
  d. −.85
  e. −1.2

5. The purpose of random assignment is to

  a. allow participants in both the experimental and control groups to be exposed to the independent variable.
  b. ensure that every member of the population had an equal chance of being selected to participate in the research.
  c. eliminate the placebo effect.
  d. reduce potential confounding variables.
  e. generate operational definitions for the independent and dependent variables.

Practice FRQs

1. Students with higher scores on anxiety scales were found to have lower scores on standardized tests. What research method would show this relationship? Why can no cause-effect conclusion be drawn from the results?

Answer

1 point: This research method is a correlation study.

1 point: There are three possibilities for causation: Anxiety could cause low test scores, low test scores could cause anxiety, or a third factor could cause both anxiety and low test scores. No conclusions can be drawn about causation because this is not an experiment.

2. Ms. Ledbetter wants to determine if the new review activity she developed will improve student performance on unit exams. She randomly separates 160 students into two groups. Group A reviews for the unit exam in the traditional manner they have always used. Group B participates in the new review activity. After reviewing, both groups are given the same unit exam and their scores are compared. Identify the independent and dependent variables for this experiment.

(2 points)

Module 7

Statistical Reasoning in Everyday Life

Norm Hall/Getty Images

Module Learning Objectives

 7-1 Describe the three measures of central tendency, and discuss the relative usefulness of the two measures of variation.

 7-2 Explain how we know whether an observed difference can be generalized to other populations.

In descriptive, correlational, and experimental research, statistics are tools that help us see and interpret what the unaided eye might miss. Sometimes the unaided eye misses badly. Researchers invited 5522 Americans to estimate the percentage of wealth possessed by the richest 20 percent in their country (Norton & Ariely, 2011). Their average person's guess—58 percent—"dramatically underestimated" the actual wealth inequality. (The wealthiest 20 percent possess 84 percent of the wealth.)

The Need for Statistics

Accurate statistical understanding benefits everyone. To be an educated person today is to be able to apply simple statistical principles to everyday reasoning. One needn't memorize complicated formulas to think more clearly and critically about data.

Off-the-top-of-the-head estimates often misread reality and then mislead the public. Someone throws out a big, round number. Others echo it, and before long the big, round number becomes public misinformation. A few examples:

- *Ten percent of people are lesbians or gay men.* Or is it 2 to 3 percent, as suggested by various national surveys (Module 53)?

- *We ordinarily use but 10 percent of our brain.* Or is it closer to 100 percent (Module 12)?

- *The human brain has 100 billion nerve cells.* Or is it more like 40 billion, as suggested by extrapolation from sample counts (Module 10)?

The point to remember: Doubt big, round, undocumented numbers.

Statistical illiteracy also feeds needless health scares (Gigerenzer et al., 2008, 2009, 2010). In the 1990s, the British press reported a study showing

"Figures can be misleading—so I've written a song which I think expresses the real story of the firm's performance this quarter."

Patrick Hardin/cartoonstock

that women taking a particular contraceptive pill had a 100 percent increased risk of blood clots that could produce strokes. This caused thousands of women to stop taking the pill, leading to a wave of unwanted pregnancies and an estimated 13,000 additional abortions (which also are associated with increased blood clot risk). And what did the study find? A 100 percent increased risk, indeed—but only from 1 in 7000 women to 2 in 7000 women. Such false alarms underscore the need to teach statistical reasoning and to present statistical information more transparently.

Descriptive Statistics

 How do we describe data using three measures of central tendency, and what is the relative usefulness of the two measures of variation?

Once researchers have gathered their data, they may use **descriptive statistics** to organize that data meaningfully. One way to do this is to convert the data into a simple *bar graph,* called a **histogram,** as in **FIGURE 7.1,** which displays a distribution of different brands of trucks still on the road after a decade. When reading statistical graphs such as this, take care. It's easy to design a graph to make a difference look big (Figure 7.1a) or small (Figure 7.1b). The secret lies in how you label the vertical scale (the *y-axis*).

The point to remember: Think smart. When viewing figures in magazines and on television, read the scale labels and note their range.

Measures of Central Tendency

The next step is to summarize the data using some *measure of central tendency,* a single score that represents a whole set of scores. The simplest measure is the **mode,** the most frequently occurring score or scores. The most commonly reported is the **mean,** or arithmetic average—the total sum of all the scores divided by the number of scores. On a divided highway, the median is the middle. So, too, with data: The **median** is the midpoint—the 50th percentile. If you arrange all the scores in order from the highest to the lowest, half will be above the median and half will be below it. In a symmetrical, bell-shaped distribution of scores, the mode, mean, and median scores may be the same or very similar.

descriptive statistics numerical data used to measure and describe characteristics of groups. Includes measures of central tendency and measures of variation.

histogram a bar graph depicting a frequency distribution.

mode the most frequently occurring score(s) in a distribution.

mean the arithmetic average of a distribution, obtained by adding the scores and then dividing by the number of scores.

median the middle score in a distribution; half the scores are above it and half are below it.

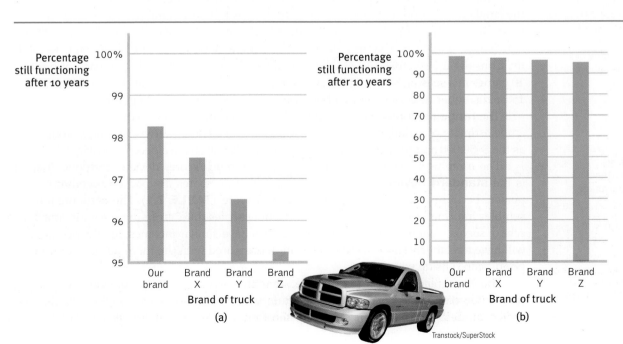

Figure 7.1

Read the scale labels An American truck manufacturer offered graph (a)—with actual brand names included—to suggest the much greater durability of its trucks. Note, however, how the apparent difference shrinks as the vertical scale changes in graph (b).

Transtock/SuperStock

Measures of central tendency neatly summarize data. But consider what happens to the mean when a distribution is lopsided, or **skewed,** by a few way-out scores. With income data, for example, the mode, median, and mean often tell very different stories (**FIGURE 7.2**). This happens because the mean is biased by a few extreme scores. When Microsoft co-founder Bill Gates sits down in an intimate café, its average (mean) customer instantly becomes a billionaire. But the customers' median wealth remains unchanged. Understanding this, you can see how a British newspaper could accurately run the head-line "Income for 62% Is Below Average" (Waterhouse, 1993). Because the bottom *half* of British income earners receive only a *quarter* of the national income cake, most British people, like most people everywhere, make less than the mean. Mean and median tell different true stories.

The point to remember: Always note which measure of central tendency is reported. If it is a mean, consider whether a few atypical scores could be distorting it.

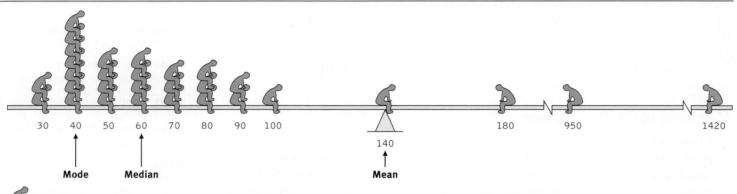

Mode Median Mean

One family   Income per family in thousands of dollars

Figure 7.2

A skewed distribution This graphic representation of the distribution of a village's incomes illustrates the three measures of central tendency—mode, median, and mean. Note how just a few high incomes make the mean—the fulcrum point that balances the incomes above and below—deceptively high.

skewed distribution a representation of scores that lack symmetry around their average value.

range the difference between the highest and lowest scores in a distribution.

standard deviation a computed measure of how much scores vary around the mean score.

Measures of Variation

Knowing the value of an appropriate measure of central tendency can tell us a great deal. But the single number omits other information. It helps to know something about the amount of *variation* in the data—how similar or diverse the scores are. Averages derived from scores with low variability are more reliable than averages based on scores with high variability. Consider a basketball player who scored between 13 and 17 points in each of her first 10 games in a season. Knowing this, we would be more confident that she would score near 15 points in her next game than if her scores had varied from 5 to 25 points.

The **range** of scores—the gap between the lowest and highest scores—provides only a crude estimate of variation. A couple of extreme scores in an otherwise uniform group, such as the $950,000 and $1,420,000 incomes in Figure 7.2, will create a deceptively large range.

The more useful standard for measuring how much scores deviate from one another is the **standard deviation.** It better gauges whether scores are packed together or dispersed, because it uses information from each score (**TABLE 7.1**). The computation assembles information about how much individual scores differ from the mean. If your high school serves a community where most families have similar incomes, family income data will have a relatively small standard deviation compared with the more diverse community population outside your school.

You can grasp the meaning of the standard deviation if you consider how scores tend to be distributed in nature. Large numbers of data—heights, weights, intelligence scores, grades (though not incomes)—often form a symmetrical, *bell-shaped* distribution.

Table 7.1 Standard Deviation Is Much More Informative Than Mean Alone

Note that the test scores in Class A and Class B have the same mean (80), but very different standard deviations, which tell us more about how the students in each class are really faring.

Test Scores in Class A			Test Scores in Class B		
Score	Deviation from the Mean	Squared Deviation	Score	Deviation from the Mean	Squared Deviation
72	−8	64	60	−20	400
74	−6	36	60	−20	400
77	−3	9	70	−10	100
79	−1	1	70	−10	100
82	+2	4	90	+10	100
84	+4	16	90	+10	100
85	+5	25	100	+20	400
87	+7	49	100	+20	400

Total = 640   Sum of (deviations)² = 204   Total = 640   Sum of (deviations)² = 2000

Mean = 640 ÷ 8 = 80   **Mean** = 640 ÷ 8 = 80

Standard deviation =

$$\sqrt{\frac{\text{Sum of (deviations)}^2}{\text{Number of scores}}} = \sqrt{\frac{204}{8}} = 5.0$$

Standard deviation =

$$\sqrt{\frac{\text{Sum of (deviations)}^2}{\text{Number of scores}}} = \sqrt{\frac{2000}{8}} = 15.8$$

Most cases fall near the mean, and fewer cases fall near either extreme. This bell-shaped distribution is so typical that we call the curve it forms the **normal curve.**

As **FIGURE 7.3** shows, a useful property of the normal curve is that roughly 68 percent of the cases fall within one standard deviation on either side of the mean. About 95 percent of cases fall within two standard deviations. Thus, as Module 61 notes, about 68 percent of people taking an intelligence test will score within ±15 points of 100. About 95 percent will score within ±30 points.

normal curve (*normal distribution*) a symmetrical, bell-shaped curve that describes the distribution of many types of data; most scores fall near the mean (about 68 percent fall within one standard deviation of it) and fewer and fewer near the extremes.

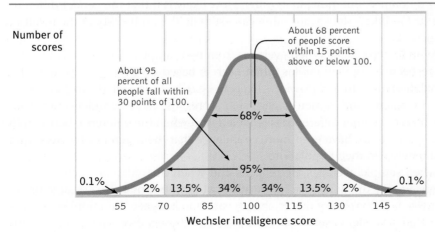

Figure 7.3

The normal curve Scores on aptitude tests tend to form a normal, or bell-shaped, curve. For example, the most commonly used intelligence test, the Wechsler Adult Intelligence Scale, calls the average score 100.

Inferential Statistics

 7-2 How do we know whether an observed difference can be generalized to other populations?

Data are "noisy." The average score in one group (breast-fed babies) could conceivably differ from the average score in another group (bottle-fed babies) not because of any real difference but merely because of chance fluctuations in the people sampled. How confidently, then, can we infer that an observed difference is not just a fluke—a chance result of your sampling? For guidance, we can ask how reliable and significant the differences are. These **inferential statistics** help us determine if results can be generalized to a larger population.

When Is an Observed Difference Reliable?

In deciding when it is safe to generalize from a sample, we should keep three principles in mind.

1. **Representative samples are better than biased samples.** As noted in Module 5, the best basis for generalizing is not from the exceptional and memorable cases one finds at the extremes but from a representative sample of cases. Research never randomly samples the whole human population. Thus, it pays to keep in mind what population a study has sampled.
2. **Less-variable observations are more reliable than those that are more variable.** As we noted in the example of the basketball player whose game-to-game points were consistent, an average is more reliable when it comes from scores with low variability.
3. **More cases are better than fewer.** An eager high school senior visits two university campuses, each for a day. At the first, the student randomly attends two classes and discovers both instructors to be witty and engaging. At the next campus, the two sampled instructors seem dull and uninspiring. Returning home, the student (discounting the small sample size of only two instructors at each institution) tells friends about the "great instructors" at the first school, and the "bores" at the second. Again, we know it but we ignore it: *Averages based on many cases are more reliable* (less variable) than averages based on only a few cases.

The point to remember: Smart thinkers are not overly impressed by a few anecdotes. Generalizations based on a few unrepresentative cases are unreliable.

When Is a Difference Significant?

Perhaps you've compared men's and women's scores on a laboratory test of aggression, and found a gender difference. But individuals differ. How likely is it that the gender difference you found was just a fluke? Statistical testing can estimate the probability of the result occurring by chance.

Here is the underlying logic: When averages from two samples are each reliable measures of their respective populations (as when each is based on many observations that have small variability), then their *difference* is likely to be reliable as well. (Example: The less the variability in women's and in men's aggression scores, the more confidence we would have that any observed gender difference is reliable.) And when the difference between the sample averages is *large,* we have even more confidence that the difference between them reflects a real difference in their populations.

In short, when sample averages are reliable, and when the difference between them is relatively large, we say the difference has **statistical significance.** This means that the observed difference is probably not due to chance variation between the samples.

In judging statistical significance, psychologists are conservative. They are like juries who must presume innocence until guilt is proven. For most psychologists, proof beyond a

inferential statistics numerical data that allow one to generalize—to infer from sample data the probability of something being true of a population.

statistical significance a statistical statement of how likely it is that an obtained result occurred by chance.

PEANUTS

reasonable doubt means not making much of a finding unless the odds of its occurring by chance, if no real effect exists, are less than 5 percent.

When reading about research, you should remember that, given large enough samples, a difference between them may be "statistically significant" yet have little practical significance. For example, comparisons of intelligence test scores among hundreds of thousands of first-born and later-born individuals indicate a highly significant tendency for first-born individuals to have higher average scores than their later-born siblings (Kristensen & Bjerkedal, 2007; Zajonc & Markus, 1975). But because the scores differ by only one to three points, the difference has little practical importance.

The point to remember: Statistical significance indicates the *likelihood* that a result will happen by chance. But this does not say anything about the *importance* of the result.

Before You Move On

▶ **ASK YOURSELF**

Find a graph in a popular magazine ad. How does the advertiser use (or abuse) statistics to make a point?

▶ **TEST YOURSELF**

Can you solve this puzzle?

The registrar's office at the University of Michigan has found that usually about 100 students in Arts and Sciences have perfect grades at the end of their first term at the University. However, only about 10 to 15 students graduate with perfect grades. What do you think is the most likely explanation for the fact that there are more perfect grades after one term than at graduation (Jepson et al., 1983)?

Answers to the Test Yourself questions can be found in Appendix E at the end of the book.

Module 7 Review

7-1 | **How do we describe data using three measures of central tendency, and what is the relative usefulness of the two measures of variation?**

- A measure of central tendency is a single score that represents a whole set of scores. Three such measures are the *mode* (the most frequently occurring score), the *mean* (the arithmetic average), and the *median* (the middle score in a group of data).

- Measures of variation tell us how diverse data are. Two measures of variation are the *range* (which describes the gap between the highest and lowest scores) and the *standard deviation* (which states how much scores vary around the mean, or average, score).

- Scores often form a *normal* (or bell-shaped) *curve.*

7-2 **How do we know whether an observed difference can be generalized to other populations?**

- To feel confident about generalizing an observed difference to other populations, we would want to know that

  - the sample studied was representative of the larger population being studied;

- the observations, on average, had low variability;
- the sample consisted of more than a few cases; and
- the observed difference was *statistically significant.*

Multiple-Choice Questions

1. Which of the following is a measure of variation?

   a. Range
   b. Mean
   c. Mode
   d. Frequency
   e. Median

2. Which statistical measure of central tendency is most affected by extreme scores?

   a. Mean
   b. Median
   c. Mode
   d. Skew
   e. Correlation

3. A researcher calculates statistical significance for her study and finds a 5 percent chance that results are due to chance. Which of the following is an accurate interpretation of this finding?

   a. This is well beyond the range of statistical significance.
   b. This is the minimum result typically considered statistically significant.
   c. This is not statistically significant.
   d. There is no way to determine statistical significance without replication of the study.
   e. Chance or coincidence is unrelated to statistical significance.

4. Descriptive statistics _____, while inferential statistics _____.

   a. indicate the significance of the data; summarize the data
   b. describe data from experiments; describe data from surveys and case studies
   c. are measures of central tendency; are measures of variance
   d. determine if data can be generalized to other populations; summarize data
   e. summarize data; determine if data can be generalized to other populations

5. In a normal distribution, what percentage of the scores in the distribution falls within one standard deviation on either side of the mean?

   a. 34 percent
   b. 40 percent
   c. 50 percent
   d. 68 percent
   e. 95 percent

Practice FRQs

1. Explain the difference between descriptive and inferential statistics in research.

Answer (2 points)

1 point: Descriptive statistics organize and summarize the data collected during research.

1 point: Inferential statistics are used to help determine whether results can be generalized to a larger population through the calculation of statistical significance.

2. The following data set includes information from survey research in a psychology course regarding how many hours each individual in the class spent preparing for the exam.

Student	Amount of hours reported studying
1	2
2	3
3	6
4	8
5	9
6	9
7	21

Examine the data and respond to the following:

- What is the middle score in this distribution? What term is used to describe the middle score?

- What would be the most useful statistic for measuring the variation of the hours spent studying? Why is this statistic a better measure of variation than the range?

(3 points)

Module 8

Frequently Asked Questions About Psychology

wdstock/E+/Getty Images

Module Learning Objectives

8-1 Explain the value of simplified laboratory conditions in illuminating everyday life.

8-2 Discuss whether psychological research can be generalized across cultures and genders.

8-3 Explain why psychologists study animals, and describe the ethical guidelines that safeguard animal research participants.

8-4 Describe the ethical guidelines that safeguard human research participants.

8-5 Examine whether psychology is free of value judgments.

We have reflected on how a scientific approach can restrain biases. We have seen how case studies, naturalistic observations, and surveys help us describe behavior. We have also noted that correlational studies assess the association between two variables, which indicates how well one thing predicts another. We have examined the logic that underlies experiments, which use control conditions and random assignment of participants to isolate the effects of an independent variable on a dependent variable. And we have considered how statistical tools can help us see and interpret the world around us.

Yet, even knowing this much, you may still be approaching psychology with a mixture of curiosity and apprehension. So before we plunge in, let's entertain some frequently asked questions.

Psychology Applied

8-1 Can laboratory experiments illuminate everyday life?

When you see or hear about psychological research, do you ever wonder whether people's behavior in the lab will predict their behavior in real life? For example, does detecting the blink of a faint red light in a dark room have anything useful to say about flying a plane at night? If, after playing violent video games in the lab, teens become more willing to push buttons that they think electrically shock someone, does this indicate that playing shooter games makes someone more likely to commit violence in everyday life?

Before you answer, consider: The experimenter *intends* the laboratory environment to be a simplified reality—one that simulates and controls important features of everyday life. Just as a wind tunnel lets airplane designers re-create airflow forces under controlled conditions, a laboratory experiment lets psychologists re-create psychological forces under controlled conditions.

An experiment's purpose is not to re-create the exact behaviors of everyday life but to test *theoretical principles* (Mook, 1983). In aggression studies, deciding whether to push a button that delivers a shock may not be the same as slapping someone in the face, but the principle is the same. *It is the resulting principles—not the specific findings—that help explain everyday behaviors.*

When psychologists apply laboratory research on aggression to actual violence, they are applying theoretical principles of aggressive behavior, principles they have refined through many experiments. Similarly, it is the principles of the visual system, developed from experiments in artificial settings (such as looking at red lights in the dark), that researchers apply to more complex behaviors such as night flying. And many investigations show that principles derived in the laboratory do typically generalize to the everyday world (Anderson et al., 1999).

The point to remember: Psychological science focuses less on particular behaviors than on seeking general principles that help explain many behaviors. And remember: Although psychological principles may help predict behaviors for groups of people, they minimally predict behavior for any individual. Knowing students' grade level may clue us to their average vocabulary level, but individual students' word power will vary.

8-2   ### Does behavior depend on one's culture and gender?

What can psychological studies done in one time and place—often with people from what researchers call the WEIRD (*W*estern, *E*ducated, *I*ndustrialized, *R*ich, and *D*emocratic) cultures (Henrich et al., 2010) really tell us about people in general? As we will see time and again, **culture**—shared ideas and behaviors that one generation passes on to the next—matters. Our culture shapes our behavior. It influences our standards of promptness and frankness, our attitudes toward premarital sex and varying body shapes, our tendency to be casual or formal, our willingness to make eye contact, our conversational distance, and much, much more. *Collectivist* cultures, for example, emphasize group goals, while *individualist* cultures put a priority on individual goals. Being aware of such differences, we can restrain our assumptions that others will think and act as we do. Given the growing mixing and clashing of cultures, our need for such awareness is urgent.

It is also true, however, that our shared biological heritage unites us as a universal human family. The same underlying processes guide people everywhere.

- People diagnosed with specific learning disorder (formerly called dyslexia) exhibit the same brain malfunction whether they are Italian, French, or British (Paulesu et al., 2001).

- Variation in languages may impede communication across cultures. Yet all languages share deep principles of grammar, and people from opposite hemispheres can communicate with a smile or a frown.

- People in different cultures vary in feelings of loneliness. But across cultures, loneliness is magnified by shyness, low self-esteem, and being unmarried (Jones et al., 1985; Rokach et al., 2002).

> **culture** the enduring behaviors, ideas, attitudes, values, and traditions shared by a group of people and transmitted from one generation to the next.

Soccer shoes? Because culture shapes social behavior, actions that seem ordinary to some may seem odd to others. Yet underlying these differences are powerful similarities. Children everywhere love to play sports such as soccer. But many American children would only play with athletic shoes on a field, not barefoot in the street, as do these Burkina Faso boys.

Alistair Berg/Alamy

We are each in certain respects like all others, like some others, and like no other. Studying people of all races and cultures helps us discern our similarities and our differences, our human kinship and our diversity.

You will see throughout this book that *gender* matters, too. Researchers report gender differences in what we dream, in how we express and detect emotions, and in our risk for alcohol use disorder, depression, and eating disorders. Gender differences fascinate us, and studying them is potentially beneficial. For example, many researchers believe that women carry on conversations more readily to build relationships, while men talk more to give information and advice (Tannen, 2001). Knowing this difference can help us prevent conflicts and misunderstandings in everyday relationships.

But again, psychologically as well as biologically, women and men are overwhelmingly similar. Whether female or male, we learn to walk at about the same age. We experience the same sensations of light and sound. We feel the same pangs of hunger, desire, and fear. We exhibit similar overall intelligence and well-being.

The point to remember: Even when specific attitudes and behaviors vary by gender or across cultures, as they often do, the underlying processes are much the same.

Ethics in Research

8-3 Why do psychologists study animals, and is it ethical to experiment on animals?

Many psychologists study animals because they find them fascinating. They want to understand how different species learn, think, and behave. Psychologists also study animals to learn about people. We humans are not *like* animals, we *are* animals, sharing a common biology. Animal experiments have therefore led to treatments for human diseases—insulin for diabetes, vaccines to prevent polio and rabies, transplants to replace defective organs.

Humans are complex. But the same processes by which we learn are present in rats, monkeys, and even sea slugs. The simplicity of the sea slug's nervous system is precisely what makes it so revealing of the neural mechanisms of learning. Sharing such similarities, should we not respect our animal relatives? "We cannot defend our scientific work with animals on the basis of the similarities between them and ourselves and then defend it morally on the basis of differences," noted Roger Ulrich (1991). The animal protection movement protests the use of animals in psychological, biological, and medical research. Researchers remind us that the animals used worldwide each year in research are but a fraction of 1 percent of the billions of animals killed annually for food. And yearly, for every dog or cat used in an experiment and cared for under humane regulations, 50 others are killed in humane animal shelters (Goodwin & Morrison, 1999).

Some animal protection organizations want to replace experiments on animals with naturalistic observation. Many animal researchers respond that this is not a question of good versus evil but of compassion for animals versus compassion for people. How many of us would have attacked Louis Pasteur's experiments with rabies, which caused some dogs to suffer but led to a vaccine that spared millions of people (and dogs) from agonizing death? And would we really wish to have deprived ourselves of the animal research that led to effective methods of training children with mental disorders, of understanding aging, and of relieving fears and depression? The answers to such questions vary by culture. In Gallup surveys in Canada and the United States, about 60 percent of adults deem medical testing on animals "morally acceptable." In Britain, only 37 percent do (Mason, 2003).

Out of this heated debate, two issues emerge. The basic one is whether it is right to place the well-being of humans above that of animals. In experiments on stress and cancer, is it right that mice get tumors in the hope that people might not? Should some monkeys be

"All people are the same; only their habits differ." -Confucius, 551–479 B.C.E.

"Rats are very similar to humans except that they are not stupid enough to purchase lottery tickets." -Dave Barry, July 2, 2002

"Please do not forget those of us who suffer from incurable diseases or disabilities who hope for a cure through research that requires the use of animals." -Psychologist Dennis Feeney (1987)

exposed to an HIV-like virus in the search for an AIDS vaccine? Is our use and consumption of other animals as natural as the behavior of carnivorous hawks, cats, and whales? Defenders of research on animals argue that anyone who has eaten a hamburger, worn leather shoes, tolerated hunting and fishing, or supported the extermination of crop-destroying or plague-carrying pests has already agreed that, *yes,* it is sometimes permissible to sacrifice animals for the sake of human well-being.

Scott Plous (1993) notes, however, that our compassion for animals varies, as does our compassion for people—based on their perceived similarity to us. As Module 79 explains, we feel more attraction, give more help, and act less aggressively toward similar others. Likewise, we value animals according to their perceived kinship with us. Thus, primates and companion pets get top priority. (Western people raise or trap mink and foxes for their fur, but not dogs or cats.) Other mammals occupy the second rung on the privilege ladder, followed by birds, fish, and reptiles on the third rung, with insects at the bottom. In deciding which animals have rights, we each draw our own cut-off line somewhere across the animal kingdom.

If we give human life first priority, what safeguards should protect the well-being of animals in research? One survey of animal researchers gave an answer. Some 98 percent supported government regulations protecting primates, dogs, and cats, and 74 percent supported regulations providing for the humane care of rats and mice (Plous & Herzog, 2000). Many professional associations and funding agencies already have such guidelines. British Psychological Society guidelines call for housing animals under reasonably natural living conditions, with companions for social animals (Lea, 2000). American Psychological Association (APA) guidelines state that researchers must ensure the "comfort, health, and humane treatment" of animals and minimize "infection, illness, and pain" (APA, 2002). The European Parliament now mandates standards for animal care and housing (Vogel, 2010).

Animals have themselves benefited from animal research. One Ohio team of research psychologists measured stress hormone levels in samples of millions of dogs brought each year to animal shelters. They devised handling and stroking methods to reduce stress and ease the dogs' transition to adoptive homes (Tuber et al., 1999). Other studies have helped improve care and management in animals' natural habitats. By revealing our behavioral kinship with animals and the remarkable intelligence of chimpanzees, gorillas, and other animals, experiments have also led to increased empathy and protection for them. At its best, a psychology concerned for humans and sensitive to animals serves the welfare of both.

> "The greatness of a nation can be judged by the way its animals are treated." -Mahatma Gandhi, 1869–1948

AP Photo/Mary Altaffer

Animal research benefiting animals Thanks partly to research on the benefits of novelty, control, and stimulation, these gorillas are enjoying an improved quality of life in New York's Bronx Zoo.

8-4   What ethical guidelines safeguard human participants?

Does the image of white-coated scientists delivering electric shocks trouble you? If so, you'll be relieved to know that most psychological studies are free of such stress. With people, blinking lights, flashing words, and pleasant social interactions are more common. Moreover, psychology's experiments are mild compared with the stress and humiliation often inflicted by reality TV shows. In one episode of *The Bachelor,* a man dumped his new fiancée—on camera, at the producers' request—for the woman who earlier had finished second (Collins, 2009).

Occasionally, though, researchers do temporarily stress or deceive people, but only when they believe it is essential to a justifiable end, such as understanding and controlling violent behavior or studying mood swings. Some experiments won't work if participants know everything beforehand. (Wanting to be helpful, the participants might try to confirm the researcher's predictions.)

Ethical principles developed by the American Psychological Association (2010), by the British Psychological Society (2009), and by psychologists internationally (Pettifor, 2004), urge researchers to (1) obtain potential participants' **informed consent,** (2) protect them from physical or emotional harm and discomfort, (3) keep information about individual participants confidential, and (4) fully **debrief** people (explain the research afterward). Moreover, most universities (where a great deal of research is conducted) now have an ethics committee—an Institutional Review Board (IRB)—that screens research proposals and safeguards participants' well-being.

The ideal is for a researcher to be sufficiently informative *and* considerate so that participants will leave feeling at least as good about themselves as when they came in. Better yet, they should be repaid by having learned something.

informed consent an ethical principle that research participants be told enough to enable them to choose whether they wish to participate.

debriefing the postexperimental explanation of a study, including its purpose and any deceptions, to its participants.

"It is doubtless impossible to approach any human problem with a mind free from bias."
-Simone de Beauvoir, *The Second Sex,* 1953

Mike Kemp/Getty Images

8-5   Is psychology free of value judgments?

Psychology is definitely not value-free. Values affect what we study, how we study it, and how we interpret results. Researchers' values influence their choice of topics. Should we study worker productivity or worker morale? Sex discrimination or gender differences? Conformity or independence? Values can also color "the facts." As we noted earlier, our preconceptions can bias our observations and interpretations; sometimes we see what we want or expect to see (**FIGURE 8.1**).

Even the words we use to describe something can reflect our values. In psychology and in everyday speech, labels describe and labels evaluate: One person's *rigidity* is another's *consistency*. One person's *faith* is another's *fanaticism*. One country's *enhanced interrogation techniques,* such as cold-water immersion, become *torture* when practiced by its enemies. Our labeling someone as *firm* or *stubborn, careful* or *picky, discreet* or *secretive* reveals our own attitudes.

Figure 8.1

What do you see? Our expectations influence what we perceive. Did you see a duck or a rabbit? Show some friends this image with the rabbit photo above covered up and see if they are more likely to perceive a duck head instead. (From Shepard, 1990.)

Popular applications of psychology also contain hidden values. If you defer to "professional" guidance about how to live—how to raise children, how to achieve self-fulfillment, what to do with sexual feelings, how to get ahead at work—you are accepting value-laden advice. A science of behavior and mental processes can help us reach our goals. But it cannot decide what those goals should be.

If some people see psychology as merely common sense, others have a different concern—that it is becoming dangerously powerful. Is it an accident that astronomy is the oldest science and psychology the youngest? To some, exploring the external universe seems far safer than exploring our own inner universe. Might psychology, they ask, be used to manipulate people?

Knowledge, like all power, can be used for good or evil. Nuclear power has been used to light up cities—and to demolish them. Persuasive power has been used to educate people—and to deceive them. Although psychology does indeed have the power to deceive, its purpose is to enlighten. Every day, psychologists are exploring ways to enhance learning, creativity, and compassion. Psychology speaks to many of our world's great problems—war, overpopulation, prejudice, family crises, crime—all of which involve attitudes and behaviors. Psychology also speaks to our deepest longings—for nourishment, for love, for happiness. Psychology cannot address all of life's great questions, but it speaks to some mighty important ones.

Library of Congress

Psychology speaks In making its historic 1954 school desegregation decision, the U.S. Supreme Court cited the expert testimony and research of psychologists Kenneth Clark and Mamie Phipps Clark (1947). The Clarks reported that, when given a choice between Black and White dolls, most African-American children chose the White doll, which seemingly indicated internalized anti-Black prejudice.

Before You Move On

▶ **ASK YOURSELF**

Were any of this module's Frequently Asked Questions your questions? Do you have other questions or concerns about psychology?

▶ **TEST YOURSELF**

How are human and animal research participants protected?

Answers to the Test Yourself questions can be found in Appendix E at the end of the book.

Module 8 Review

8-1 Can laboratory experiments illuminate everyday life?

- Researchers intentionally create a controlled, artificial environment in the laboratory in order to test general theoretical principles. These general principles help explain everyday behaviors.

8-2 Does behavior depend on one's culture and gender?

- Attitudes and behaviors may vary somewhat by gender or across *cultures,* but because of our shared human kinship, the underlying processes and principles are more similar than different.

8-3 Why do psychologists study animals, and is it ethical to experiment on animals?

- Some psychologists are primarily interested in animal behavior; others want to better understand the physiological and psychological processes shared by humans and other species.

- Government agencies have established standards for animal care and housing. Professional associations and funding agencies also establish guidelines for protecting animals' well-being.

8-4 **What ethical guidelines safeguard human participants?**

- The APA ethics code outlines standards for safeguarding human participants' well-being, including obtaining their *informed consent* and *debriefing* them later.

8-5 **Is psychology free of value judgments?**

- Psychologists' values influence their choice of research topics, their theories and observations, their labels for behavior, and their professional advice.

- Applications of psychology's principles have been used mainly in the service of humanity.

Multiple-Choice Questions

1. Which of the following is more likely to be emphasized in individualist cultures than in collectivist cultures?

  a. Gender differences
  b. Shared goals
  c. Personal achievement
  d. Cooperation with the group
  e. Preservation of tradition

2. What must a researcher do to fulfill the ethical principle of informed consent?

  a. Keep information about participants confidential.
  b. Allow participants to choose whether to take part.
  c. Protect participants from potential harm.
  d. Provide participants with a pre-experimental explanation of the study.
  e. Provide participants with a post-experimental explanation of the study.

3. Which ethical principle requires that at the end of the study participants be told about the true purpose of the research?

  a. Institutional Review Board approval
  b. Informed consent
  c. Confidentiality
  d. Debriefing
  e. Protection from physical harm

4. Which of the following beliefs would most likely be held by an individual in a collectivist culture?

  a. Children should be encouraged to focus on personal goals and aspirations.
  b. Children should be encouraged to develop harmonious relationships.
  c. It is important to be competitive and assertive in order to get ahead in life.
  d. If you want something done well, you should do it yourself.
  e. It is important to satisfy personal needs before those of the larger community.

Practice FRQs

1. Provide three reasons why nonhuman animals are sometimes used in psychological research.

Answer

1 point: Some researchers use nonhuman animals because they are interested in understanding the animals themselves, including their thinking and behaviors.

1 point: Others use nonhuman animals to reduce the complexity that is part of human research. They hope to understand principles that may be similar to those that govern human psychological phenomena.

1 point: Researchers also study nonhuman animals in order to apply the findings in ways that will help both humans and the other animals themselves.

2. Researchers interested in studying stress gave 150 high school seniors a very difficult math exam. After the test, the researchers measured stress by examining physiological changes with extensive medical testing that included drawing blood samples.

- What ethical principle governs what students must be told before the research takes place? What should the potential participants be told?

- What ethical principle governs the appropriate use of the results of the medical testing? What would that principle say about the use of these results?

(8 points)

Unit II Review

Key Terms and Concepts to Remember

hindsight bias, p. 31

critical thinking, p. 35

theory, p. 38

hypothesis, p. 38

operational definition, p. 39

replication, p. 39

case study, p. 40

naturalistic observation, p. 40

survey, p. 42

sampling bias, p. 43

population, p. 43

random sample, p. 43

correlation, p. 46

correlation coefficient, p. 46

scatterplot, p. 46

illusory correlation, p. 50

experiment, p. 51

experimental group, p. 51

control group, p. 51

random assignment, p. 51

double-blind procedure, p. 51

placebo [pluh-SEE-bo] effect, p. 52

independent variable, p. 52

confounding variable, p. 52

dependent variable, p. 52

validity, p. 53

descriptive statistics, p. 57

mode, p. 57

mean, p. 57

median, p. 57

skewed distribution, p. 58

range, p. 58

standard deviation, p. 58

normal curve, p. 59

inferential statistics, p. 60

statistical significance, p. 60

culture, p. 65

informed consent, p. 68

debriefing, p. 68

AP® Exam Practice Questions

Multiple-Choice Questions

1. Which descriptive statistic would a researcher use to describe how close a student's SAT score is to a school's average SAT score?

a. Correlation coefficient

b. Mean

c. Median

d. Standard deviation

e. Range

2. Which method should a psychology researcher use if she is interested in testing whether a specific reward in a classroom situation causes students to behave better?

a. Case study

b. Experiment

c. Survey

d. Naturalistic observation

e. Correlation

3. When a distribution of scores is skewed, which of the following is the most representative measure of central tendency?

a. Inference

b. Standard deviation

c. Mean

d. Median

e. Correlation coefficient

4. A researcher wants to conduct an experiment to determine if eating a cookie before class each day improves student grades. He uses two psychology classes for the experiment, providing daily cookies to one and nothing to the other. At the end of the semester, the researcher compares the final grades of students in the two classes. What is the independent variable for this experiment?

a. The students in the class that received cookies

b. The presence or absence of cookies

c. The students in the class that didn't receive cookies

d. The period of the day that the two classes met

e. Semester grades

5. Which of the following represents naturalistic observation?

   a. Researchers watch and record how elementary school children interact on the playground.
   b. Researchers bring participants into a laboratory to see how they respond to a puzzle with no solution.
   c. A principal looks at the relationship between the number of student absences and their grades.
   d. A social worker visits a family home and gives feedback on family interactions.
   e. Two grandparents sit in the front row to watch their grandson's first piano recital.

6. "Monday morning quarterbacks" rarely act surprised about the outcome of weekend football games. This tendency to believe they knew how the game would turn out is best explained by which psychological principle?

   a. Overconfidence
   b. Hindsight bias
   c. Intuition
   d. Illusory correlation
   e. Random sampling

7. Researchers studying gender have found that

   a. there are more similarities than differences between the genders.
   b. there are no significant cognitive differences between the genders.
   c. there are no significant emotional differences between the genders.
   d. research tools are not capable of determining if there are true differences or not.
   e. differences between the genders are becoming more pronounced over time.

8. A journalism student is writing an article about her school's new cell-phone policy, and she'd like to interview a random sample of students. Which of the following is the best example of a random sample?

   a. The writer arrives at school early and interviews the first five students who come through the main entrance.
   b. The writer pulls the names of five students from a hat that contains all students' names. She interviews the five selected students.
   c. The writer asks her teacher if she can distribute a brief survey to the students in her AP® Psychology class.
   d. The writer passes out brief surveys to 50 students in the hall and uses the 18 surveys returned to her as the basis of her article.
   e. The writer asks the principal for the names of 10 students who have had their cell phones confiscated for a day for violating the policy. She interviews these 10 students.

9. Which of the following is a positive correlation?

   a. As study time decreases, students achieve lower grades.
   b. As levels of self-esteem decline, levels of depression increase.
   c. People who exercise regularly are less likely to be obese.
   d. Gas mileage decreases as vehicle weight increases.
   e. Repeatedly shooting free throws in basketball is associated with a smaller percentage of missed free throws.

10. Why is random assignment of participants to groups an important aspect of a properly designed experiment?

   a. If the participants are randomly assigned, the researcher can assume that the people in each of the groups are pretty similar.
   b. By randomly assigning participants, the researcher knows that whatever is learned from the experiment will also be true for the population from which the participants were selected.
   c. Random assignment keeps expectations from influencing the results of the experiment.
   d. If participants are not randomly assigned, it is impossible to replicate the experiment.
   e. Statistical analysis cannot be performed on an experiment if random assignment is not used.

11. Which of the following demonstrates the need for psychological science?

   a. Psychology's methods are unlike those of any other science.
   b. Psychological experiments are less valuable without psychological science.
   c. Our intuitions about human thinking and behavior are not always accurate.
   d. Intuition does not provide correct answers unless it is applied through the scientific method.
   e. Psychological science research is superior to that of other sciences like biology and physics.

12. Which of the following is a potential problem with case studies?

   a. They provide too much detail and the researcher is likely to lose track of the most important facts.
   b. They are generally too expensive to be economical.
   c. They may be misleading because they don't fairly represent other cases.
   d. They are technically difficult and most researchers don't have the skills to do them properly.
   e. The dependent variable is difficult to operationally define in a case study.

13. Which of the following is *not* an ethical principle regarding research on humans?

   a. Researchers must protect participants from needless harm and discomfort.
   b. Participants must take part in the study on a voluntary basis.
   c. Personal information about individual participants must be kept confidential.
   d. Research studies must be fully explained to participants when the study is completed.
   e. Participants should always be informed of the hypothesis of the study before they agree to participate.

14. There is a negative correlation between TV watching and grades. What can we conclude from this research finding?

   a. We can conclude that a student who watches a lot of TV is likely to have lower grades.
   b. We can conclude that TV watching leads to lower grades.
   c. We can conclude that TV watching leads to higher grades.
   d. We can conclude that the grades students get impact their TV watching habits.
   e. We can conclude that this is an illusory correlation.

15. A scientist's willingness to admit that she is wrong is an example of

   a. curiosity.   d. skepticism.
   b. intelligence.   e. cynicism.
   c. humility.

Free-Response Questions

1. Sam Greene noticed an ad for an Internet dating service that claimed more people who used its service are in long-term relationships than people who didn't. Sam, a good critical thinker, knows this isn't enough to claim that the service causes people to find long-term love and wants to create an experiment to investigate. Use the following terms to describe an experiment that would support or dispute the ad's claim.

   - Hypothesis
   - Random sample
   - Random assignment
   - Operational definitions
   - Independent variable
   - Dependent variable
   - Inferential statistics

Rubric for Free-Response Question 1

1 point: The hypothesis in this context is that the Internet dating service causes (or leads to) long-term relationships. ↻ Page 38

1 point: Since the population of interest for this study should be people who are looking for long-term relationships, selecting a random sample of adults seeking relationships would help assure that the conclusions could be fairly generalized to the dating public. ↻ Page 43

1 point: In this case, participants should be randomly assigned to use of the Internet service (the experimental group) or not (the control group). ↻ Page 51

1 point: Sam would need to operationally define what is meant by use of the Internet service, possibly including a precise number of visits to the website or time spent on the website. The phrase *long-term relationship* would also need an operational definition, possibly by the number of months together or a formal commitment (like engagement or marriage). ↻ Page 39

1 point: In Sam's study, the use of the online dating service is the independent variable. ↻ Page 52

1 point: The number of long-term relationships is the dependent variable. ↻ Page 52

1 point: Sam will need to calculate statistical significance for the experimental findings. In order to claim support for the hypothesis, the results need to show that there is no more than a 5 percent chance the findings are due to chance. ↻ Page 60

2. Dr. Tabor wanted to investigate the relationship between sleep and levels of alertness during a class for American university students. She gave surveys to 150 college freshmen in her introduction to psychology course, asking them to report how many hours they slept each night during a two-week period. Dr. Tabor also had the participants rate their level of alertness on a scale of 1 to 10, with 10 being the most alert each day at the end of class. Dr. Tabor compared the average amount of sleep reported by each participant along with their average score on the alertness scale on a graph to examine the data. The resulting correlation coefficient for Dr. Tabor's data was +0.89. Define each of the following terms and explain how each concept might apply to Dr. Tabor's research.

- Random sample
- Scatterplot
- Wording effects
- Positive correlation
- Operational definition

(10 points)

3. Find at least five problems in the research study described below. Identify the problem and explain how it is a violation of accepted research principles.

Dr. Pauling wanted to study whether vitamin C affects self-esteem. She recruited 200 respondents who arrived at her lab. Participants were told that they were about to participate in a harmless research study, and they needed to sign a release form in case there were harmful side effects from the vitamin C pills. The 100 participants on the right side of the room received a pill with vitamin C and the others on the left received a pill with caffeine. She then gave each group a list of questions to answer in essay form about their self-esteem. When they were finished, she thanked the participants and sent them on their way. After compiling her findings, Dr. Pauling printed the names of the students and their results in the campus newspaper so they would know what the results of the test were. Dr. Pauling concluded that vitamin C had a positive affect on self-esteem.

(5 points)

Multiple-choice self-tests and more may be found at www.worthpublishers.com/MyersAP2e

Unit III

Biological Bases of Behavior

Modules

Imagine that just moments before your death, someone removed your brain from your body and kept it alive by floating it in a tank of fluid while feeding it enriched blood. Would you still be in there? Further imagine that your still-living brain was transplanted into the body of a person whose own brain had been severely damaged. To whose home should the recovered patient return? If you say the patient should return to your home, you illustrate what most of us believe—that we reside in our head. An acquaintance of mine received a new heart from a woman who had received a heart-lung transplant. When the two chanced to meet in their hospital ward, she introduced herself: "I think you have my heart." But only her heart; her self, she assumed, still resided inside her skull. We rightly presume that our brain enables our mind. Indeed, no principle is more central to today's psychology, or to this book, than this: *Everything psychological is simultaneously biological.*

Module 9

Biological Psychology and Neurotransmission

Module Learning Objectives

9-1 Explain why psychologists are concerned with human biology.

9-2 Describe the parts of a neuron, and explain how its impulses are generated.

9-3 Describe how nerve cells communicate with other nerve cells.

9-4 Describe how neurotransmitters influence behavior, and explain how drugs and other chemicals affect neurotransmission.

Biology, Behavior, and Mind

9-1 Why are psychologists concerned with human biology?

Your every idea, every mood, every urge is a biological happening. You love, laugh, and cry with your body. Without your body—your genes, your brain, your appearance—you would, indeed, be nobody. Although we find it convenient to talk separately of biological and psychological influences on behavior, we need to remember: To think, feel, or act without a body would be like running without legs.

"Then it's agreed—you can't have a mind without a brain, but you can have a brain without a mind."

Our understanding of how the brain gives birth to the mind has come a long way. The ancient Greek philosopher Plato correctly located the mind in the spherical head—his idea of the perfect form. His student, Aristotle, believed the mind was in the heart, which pumps warmth and vitality to the body. The heart remains our symbol for love, but science has long since overtaken philosophy on this issue. It's your brain, not your heart, that falls in love.

In the early 1800s, German physician Franz Gall proposed that *phrenology*, studying bumps on the skull, could reveal a person's mental abilities and character traits (**FIGURE 9.1**). At one point, Britain had 29 phrenological societies, and phrenologists traveled North America giving skull readings (Hunt, 1993).

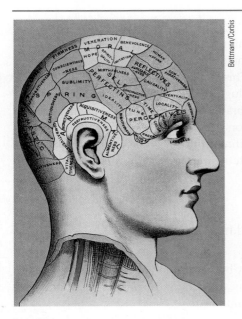

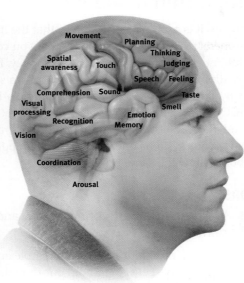

Figure 9.1

A wrongheaded theory Despite initial acceptance of Franz Gall's speculations, bumps on the skull tell us nothing about the brain's underlying functions. Nevertheless, some of his assumptions have held true. Though they are not the functions Gall proposed, different parts of the brain do control different aspects of behavior, as suggested here (from *The Human Brain Book*) and as you will see throughout this unit.

Using a false name, humorist Mark Twain put one famous phrenologist to the test. "He found a cavity [and] startled me by saying that that cavity represented the total absence of the sense of humor!" Three months later, Twain sat for a second reading, this time identifying himself. Now "the cavity was gone, and in its place was . . . the loftiest bump of humor he had ever encountered in his life-long experience!" (Lopez, 2002). Although its initial popularity faded, phrenology succeeded in focusing attention on the *localization of function*—the idea that various brain regions have particular functions.

You and I are living in a time Gall could only dream about. By studying the links between biological activity and psychological events, **biological psychologists** are announcing discoveries about the interplay of our biology and our behavior and mind at an exhilarating pace. Within little more than the past century, researchers seeking to understand the biology of the mind have discovered that

- the body is composed of cells.

- among these are nerve cells that conduct electricity and "talk" to one another by sending chemical messages across a tiny gap that separates them.

- specific brain systems serve specific functions (though not the functions Gall supposed).

- we integrate information processed in these different brain systems to construct our experience of sights and sounds, meanings and memories, pain and passion.

- our adaptive brain is wired by our experience.

We have also realized that we are each a system composed of subsystems that are in turn composed of even smaller subsystems. Tiny cells organize to form body organs. These organs form larger systems for digestion, circulation, and information processing. And those systems are part of an even larger system—the individual, who in turn is a part of a family, culture, and community. Thus, we are *biopsychosocial* systems. To understand our behavior, we need to study how these biological, psychological, and social systems work and interact.

In this unit we start small and build from the bottom up—from nerve cells up to the brain, and then to the environmental influences that interact with our biology. We will also work from the top down, as we consider how our thinking and emotions influence our brain and our health.

"If I were a college student today, I don't think I could resist going into neuroscience."
-Novelist Tom Wolfe, 2004

biological psychology the scientific study of the links between biological (genetic, neural, hormonal) and psychological processes. (Some biological psychologists call themselves *behavioral neuroscientists, neuropsychologists, behavior geneticists, physiological psychologists,* or *biopsychologists.*)

Neural Communication

For scientists, it is a happy fact of nature that the information systems of humans and other animals operate similarly—so similarly that you could not distinguish between small samples of brain tissue from a human and a monkey. This similarity allows researchers to study relatively simple animals, such as squids and sea slugs, to discover how our neural systems operate. It allows them to study other mammals' brains to understand the organization of our own. Cars differ, but all have engines, accelerators, steering wheels, and brakes. An alien could study any one of them and grasp the operating principles. Likewise, animals differ, yet their nervous systems operate similarly. Though the human brain is more complex than a rat's, both follow the same principles.

Neurons

 What are the parts of a neuron, and how are neural impulses generated?

Our body's neural information system is complexity built from simplicity. Its building blocks are **neurons,** or nerve cells. To fathom our thoughts and actions, memories and moods, we must first understand how neurons work and communicate.

Neurons differ, but all are variations on the same theme (**FIGURE 9.2**). Each consists of a *cell body* and its branching fibers. The bushy **dendrite** fibers receive information and conduct it toward the cell body. From there, the cell's lengthy **axon** fiber passes the message through its terminal branches to other neurons or to muscles or glands. Dendrites listen. Axons speak.

Unlike the short dendrites, axons may be very long, projecting several feet through the body. A neuron carrying orders to a leg muscle, for example, has a cell body and axon roughly on the scale of a basketball attached to a rope 4 miles long. Much as home electrical wire is insulated, some axons are encased in a **myelin sheath,** a layer of fatty tissue that insulates them and speeds their impulses. As myelin is laid down up to about age 25, neural efficiency, judgment, and self-control grow (Fields, 2008). If the myelin sheath degenerates, *multiple sclerosis* results: Communication to muscles slows, with eventual loss of muscle control.

Neurons transmit messages when stimulated by signals from our senses or when triggered by chemical signals from neighboring neurons. In response, a neuron fires an impulse, called the **action potential**—a brief electrical charge that travels down its axon.

Depending on the type of fiber, a neural impulse travels at speeds ranging from a sluggish 2 miles per hour to a breakneck 180 miles per hour. But even this top speed is 3 million times slower than that of electricity through a wire. We measure brain activity in

neuron a nerve cell; the basic building block of the nervous system.

dendrites a neuron's bushy, branching extensions that receive messages and conduct impulses toward the cell body.

axon the neuron extension that passes messages through its branches to other neurons or to muscles or glands.

myelin [MY-uh-lin] **sheath** a fatty tissue layer segmentally encasing the axons of some neurons; enables vastly greater transmission speed as neural impulses hop from one sausage-like node to the next.

action potential a neural impulse; a brief electrical charge that travels down an axon.

"I sing the body electric." -Walt Whitman, "Children of Adam" (1855)

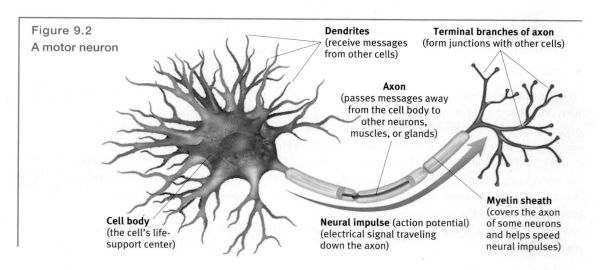

Figure 9.2
A motor neuron

Dendrites (receive messages from other cells)

Terminal branches of axon (form junctions with other cells)

Axon (passes messages away from the cell body to other neurons, muscles, or glands)

Cell body (the cell's life-support center)

Neural impulse (action potential) (electrical signal traveling down the axon)

Myelin sheath (covers the axon of some neurons and helps speed neural impulses)

milliseconds (thousandths of a second) and computer activity in nanoseconds (billionths of a second). Thus, unlike the nearly instantaneous reactions of a high-speed computer, your reaction to a sudden event, such as a book slipping off your desk during class, may take a quarter-second or more. Your brain is vastly more complex than a computer, but slower at executing simple responses. And if you are an elephant—whose round-trip message travel time from a yank on the tail to the brain and back to the tail is 100 times longer than for a tiny shrew—reflexes are slower yet (More et al., 2010).

Like batteries, neurons generate electricity from chemical events. In the neuron's chemistry-to-electricity process, *ions* (electrically charged atoms) are exchanged. The fluid outside an axon's membrane has mostly positively charged ions; a resting axon's fluid interior has mostly negatively charged ions. This positive-outside/negative-inside state is called the *resting potential.* Like a tightly guarded facility, the axon's surface is very selective about what it allows through its gates. We say the axon's surface is *selectively permeable.*

When a neuron fires, however, the security parameters change: The first section of the axon opens its gates, rather like sewer covers flipping open, and positively charged sodium ions flood through the cell membrane (**FIGURE 9.3**). This *depolarizes* that axon section, causing another axon channel to open, and then another, like a line of falling dominos, each tripping the next.

During a resting pause called the **refractory period,** rather like a web page pausing to refresh, the neuron pumps the positively charged sodium ions back outside. Then it can fire again. (In myelinated neurons, as in Figure 9.2, the action potential speeds up by hopping from the end of one myelin "sausage" to the next.) The mind boggles when imagining this electrochemical process repeating up to 100 or even 1000 times a second. But this is just the first of many astonishments.

Each neuron is itself a miniature decision-making device performing complex calculations as it receives signals from hundreds, even thousands, of other neurons. Most signals are *excitatory,* somewhat like pushing a neuron's accelerator. Some are *inhibitory,* more like

refractory period a period of inactivity after a neuron has fired.

"What one neuron tells another neuron is simply how much it is excited." -FRANCIS CRICK, *THE ASTONISHING HYPOTHESIS*, 1994

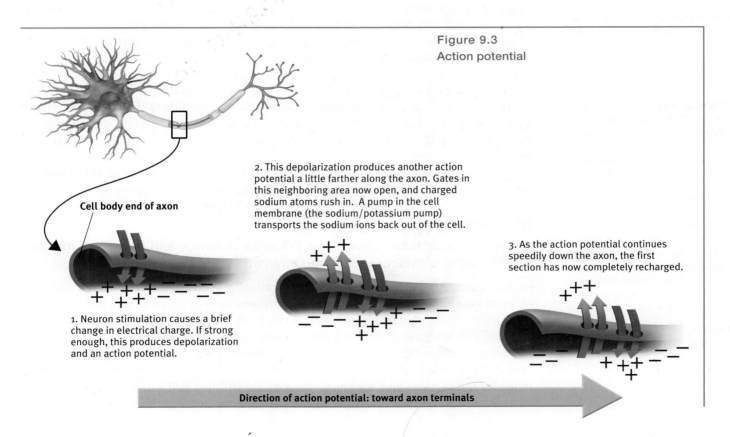

Figure 9.3
Action potential

Cell body end of axon

1. Neuron stimulation causes a brief change in electrical charge. If strong enough, this produces depolarization and an action potential.

2. This depolarization produces another action potential a little farther along the axon. Gates in this neighboring area now open, and charged sodium atoms rush in. A pump in the cell membrane (the sodium/potassium pump) transports the sodium ions back out of the cell.

3. As the action potential continues speedily down the axon, the first section has now completely recharged.

Direction of action potential: toward axon terminals

"All information processing in the brain involves neurons 'talking to' each other at synapses."
-NEUROSCIENTIST SOLOMON H. SNYDER (1984)

pushing its brake. If excitatory signals exceed inhibitory signals by a minimum intensity, or **threshold,** the combined signals trigger an action potential. (Think of it as a class vote: If the excitatory people with their hands up outvote the inhibitory people with their hands down, then the vote passes.) The action potential then travels down the axon, which branches into junctions with hundreds or thousands of other neurons or with the body's muscles and glands.

Increasing the level of stimulation above the threshold will not increase the neural impulse's intensity. The neuron's reaction is an **all-or-none response:** Like guns, neurons either fire or they don't. How, then, do we detect the intensity of a stimulus? How do we distinguish a gentle touch from a big hug? A strong stimulus can trigger *more* neurons to fire, and to fire more often. But it does not affect the action potential's strength or speed. Squeezing a trigger harder won't make a bullet go faster.

How Neurons Communicate

 9-3   How do nerve cells communicate with other nerve cells?

Neurons interweave so intricately that even with a microscope you would have trouble seeing where one neuron ends and another begins. Scientists once believed that the axon of one cell fused with the dendrites of another in an uninterrupted fabric. Then British physiologist Sir Charles Sherrington (1857–1952) noticed that neural impulses were taking an unexpectedly long time to travel a neural pathway. Inferring that there must be a brief interruption in the transmission, Sherrington called the meeting point between neurons a **synapse.**

We now know that the axon terminal of one neuron is in fact separated from the receiving neuron by a *synaptic gap* (or *synaptic cleft*) less than 1 millionth of an inch wide. Spanish anatomist Santiago Ramón y Cajal (1852–1934) marveled at these near-unions of neurons, calling them "protoplasmic kisses." "Like elegant ladies air-kissing so as not to muss their makeup, dendrites and axons don't quite touch," notes poet Diane Ackerman (2004, p. 37). How do the neurons execute this protoplasmic kiss, sending information across the tiny synaptic gap? The answer is one of the important scientific discoveries of our age.

When an action potential reaches the knob-like terminals at an axon's end, it triggers the release of chemical messengers, called **neurotransmitters** (**FIGURE 9.4**). Within 1/10,000th of a second, the neurotransmitter molecules cross the synaptic gap and bind to receptor sites on the receiving neuron—as precisely as a key fits a lock. For an instant, the neurotransmitter unlocks tiny channels at the receiving site, and ions flow in, exciting or inhibiting the receiving neuron's readiness to fire. Then, in a process called **reuptake,** the sending neuron reabsorbs the excess neurotransmitters.

How Neurotransmitters Influence Us

9-4   How do neurotransmitters influence behavior, and how do drugs and other chemicals affect neurotransmission?

In their quest to understand neural communication, researchers have discovered dozens of different neurotransmitters and almost as many new questions: Are certain neurotransmitters found only in specific places? How do they affect our moods, memories, and mental abilities? Can we boost or diminish these effects through drugs or diet?

Later modules explore neurotransmitter influences on hunger and thinking, depression and euphoria, addictions and therapy. For now, let's glimpse how neurotransmitters influence our motions and our emotions. A particular brain pathway may use only one or two neurotransmitters (**FIGURE 9.5**), and particular neurotransmitters may affect specific

Figure 9.4
How neurons communicate

1. Electrical impulses (action potentials) travel down a neuron's axon until reaching a tiny junction known as a *synapse*.

Sending neuron

Action potential

Receiving neuron

Synapse

Sending neuron

Action potential

Synaptic gap

Axon terminal

Receptor sites on receiving neuron

Neurotransmitter

Reuptake

2. When an action potential reaches an axon terminal, it stimulates the release of neurotransmitter molecules. These molecules cross the synaptic gap and bind to receptor sites on the receiving neuron. This allows ions to enter the receiving neuron and excite or inhibit a new action potential.

3. The sending neuron normally reabsorbs excess neurotransmitter molecules, a process called *reuptake*.

behaviors and emotions (**TABLE 9.1** on the next page). But neurotransmitter systems don't operate in isolation; they interact, and their effects vary with the receptors they stimulate. *Acetylcholine (ACh)*, which is one of the best-understood neurotransmitters, plays a role in learning and memory. In addition, it is the messenger at every junction between motor neurons (which carry information from the brain and spinal cord to the body's tissues) and skeletal muscles. When ACh is released to our muscle cell receptors, the muscle contracts. If ACh transmission is blocked, as happens during some kinds of anesthesia, the muscles cannot contract and we are paralyzed.

"When it comes to the brain, if you want to see the action, follow the neurotransmitters."
-Neuroscientist Floyd Bloom (1993)

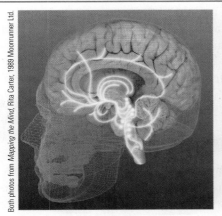

Serotonin pathways

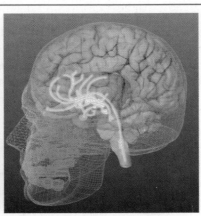

Dopamine pathways

Both photos from *Mapping the Mind*, Rita Carter, 1989 Moonrunner Ltd.

Figure 9.5

Neurotransmitter pathways Each of the brain's differing chemical messengers has designated pathways where it operates, as shown here for serotonin and dopamine (Carter, 1998).

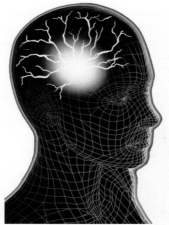

LiquidLibrary/Jupiterimages

Table 9.1 Some Neurotransmitters and Their Functions

Neurotransmitter	Function	Examples of Malfunctions
Acetylcholine (ACh)	Enables muscle action, learning, and memory.	With Alzheimer's disease, ACh-producing neurons deteriorate.
Dopamine	Influences movement, learning, attention, and emotion.	Oversupply linked to schizophrenia. Undersupply linked to tremors and decreased mobility in Parkinson's disease.
Serotonin	Affects mood, hunger, sleep, and arousal.	Undersupply linked to depression. Some antidepressant drugs raise serotonin levels.
Norepinephrine	Helps control alertness and arousal.	Undersupply can depress mood.
GABA (gamma-aminobutyric acid)	A major inhibitory neurotransmitter.	Undersupply linked to seizures, tremors, and insomnia.
Glutamate	A major excitatory neurotransmitter; involved in memory.	Oversupply can overstimulate the brain, producing migraines or seizures (which is why some people avoid MSG, monosodium glutamate, in food).

Researchers made an exciting discovery about neurotransmitters when they attached a radioactive tracer to morphine, showing where it was taken up in an animal's brain (Pert & Snyder, 1973). The morphine, an opiate drug that elevates mood and eases pain, bound to receptors in areas linked with mood and pain sensations. But why would the brain have these "opiate receptors"? Why would it have a chemical lock, unless it also had a natural key to open it?

Researchers soon confirmed that the brain does indeed produce its own naturally occurring opiates. Our body releases several types of neurotransmitter molecules similar to morphine in response to pain and vigorous exercise. These **endorphins** (short for *endogenous* [produced within] m*orphine*) help explain good feelings such as the "runner's high," the painkilling effects of acupuncture, and the indifference to pain in some severely injured people. But once again, new knowledge led to new questions.

HOW DRUGS AND OTHER CHEMICALS ALTER NEUROTRANSMISSION

If indeed the endorphins lessen pain and boost mood, why not flood the brain with artificial opiates, thereby intensifying the brain's own "feel-good" chemistry? One problem is that when flooded with opiate drugs such as heroin and morphine, the brain may stop producing its own natural opiates. When the drug is withdrawn, the brain may then be deprived of any form of opiate, causing intense discomfort. For suppressing the body's own neurotransmitter production, nature charges a price.

Drugs and other chemicals affect brain chemistry at synapses, often by either exciting or inhibiting neurons' firing. **Agonist** molecules may be similar enough to a neurotransmitter to bind to its receptor and mimic its effects. Some opiate drugs are agonists and produce a temporary "high" by amplifying normal sensations of arousal or pleasure.

endorphins [en-DOR-fins] "morphine within"—natural, opiate-like neurotransmitters linked to pain control and to pleasure.

agonist a molecule that, by binding to a receptor site, stimulates a response.

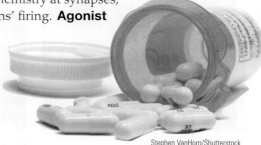

Stephen VanHorn/Shutterstock

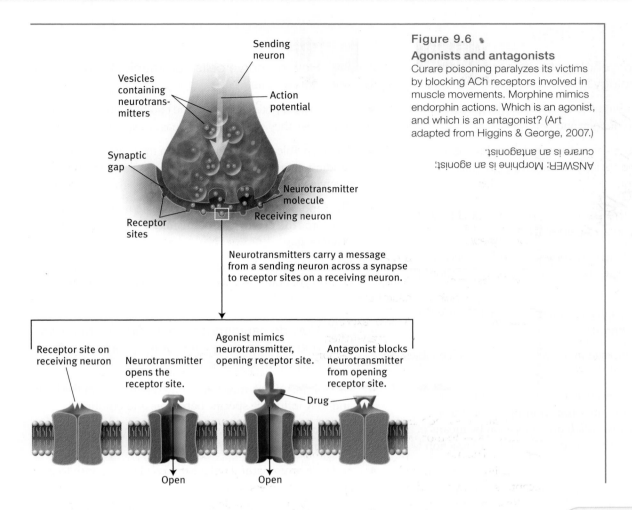

Figure 9.6

Agonists and antagonists
Curare poisoning paralyzes its victims by blocking ACh receptors involved in muscle movements. Morphine mimics endorphin actions. Which is an agonist, and which is an antagonist? (Art adapted from Higgins & George, 2007.)

ANSWER: Morphine is an agonist; curare is an antagonist.

Sending neuron

Vesicles containing neurotrans-mitters

Action potential

Synaptic gap

Neurotransmitter molecule

Receptor sites

Receiving neuron

Neurotransmitters carry a message from a sending neuron across a synapse to receptor sites on a receiving neuron.

Receptor site on receiving neuron

Neurotransmitter opens the receptor site.

Agonist mimics neurotransmitter, opening receptor site.

Antagonist blocks neurotransmitter from opening receptor site.

Drug

Open

Open

Antagonists also bind to receptors but their effect is instead to block a neurotransmitter's functioning. Botulin, a poison that can form in improperly canned food, causes paralysis by blocking ACh release. (Small injections of botulin—Botox—smooth wrinkles by paralyzing the underlying facial muscles.) These antagonists are enough like the natural neurotransmitter to occupy its receptor site and block its effect, as in **FIGURE 9.6**, but are not similar enough to stimulate the receptor (rather like foreign coins that fit into, but won't operate, a candy machine). Curare, a poison some South American Indians have applied to hunting-dart tips, occupies and blocks ACh receptor sites on muscles, producing paralysis in animals struck by the darts.

antagonist a molecule that, by binding to a receptor site, inhibits or blocks a response.

> **AP® Exam Tip**
>
> Be very clear on this. Neurotransmitters are produced inside the body. They can excite and inhibit neural communication. Drugs and other chemicals come from outside the body. They can have an agonistic effect or an antagonistic effect on neurotransmission.

Before You Move On

▶ **ASK YOURSELF**
Can you recall a time when the endorphin response may have protected you from feeling extreme pain?

▶ **TEST YOURSELF**
How do neurons communicate with one another?

Answers to the Test Yourself questions can be found in Appendix E at the end of the book.

Module 9 Review

9-1 Why are psychologists concerned with human biology?

- Psychologists working from a *biological* perspective study the links between biology and behavior.

- We are biopsychosocial systems, in which biological, psychological, and social-cultural factors interact to influence behavior.

9-2 What are the parts of a neuron, and how are neural impulses generated?

- *Neurons* are the elementary components of the nervous system, the body's speedy electrochemical information system.

- A neuron receives signals through its branching *dendrites,* and sends signals through its *axons.*

- Some axons are encased in a *myelin sheath,* which enables faster transmission.

- If the combined received signals exceed a minimum *threshold,* the neuron fires, transmitting an electrical impulse (the *action potential*) down its axon by means of a chemistry-to-electricity process. The neuron's reaction is an *all-or-none process.*

9-3 How do nerve cells communicate with other nerve cells?

- When action potentials reach the end of an axon (the axon terminals), they stimulate the release of *neurotransmitters.*

- These chemical messengers carry a message from the sending neuron across a *synapse* to receptor sites on a receiving neuron.

- The sending neuron, in a process called *reuptake,* then reabsorbs the excess neurotransmitter molecules in the synaptic gap.

- If incoming signals are strong enough, the receiving neuron generates its own action potential and relays the message to other cells.

9-4 How do neurotransmitters influence behavior, and how do drugs and other chemicals affect neurotransmission?

- Neurotransmitters travel designated pathways in the brain and may influence specific behaviors and emotions.

- Acetylcholine (ACh) affects muscle action, learning, and memory.

- *Endorphins* are natural opiates released in response to pain and exercise.

- Drugs and other chemicals affect brain chemistry at synapses.

- *Agonists* excite by mimicking particular neurotransmitters or by blocking their reuptake.

- *Antagonists* inhibit a particular neurotransmitter's release or block its effect.

Multiple-Choice Questions

1. Multiple sclerosis is a result of degeneration in the
   a. dendrite.
   b. axon.
   c. myelin sheath.
   d. terminal button.
   e. neuron.

2. Junita does not feel like getting out of bed, has lost her appetite, and feels tired for most of the day. Which of the following neurotransmitters likely is in short supply for Junita?
   a. Dopamine   d. Acetylcholine
   b. Serotonin   e. Glutamate
   c. Norephinephrine

3. Which neurotransmitter inhibits CNS activity in order to calm a person down during stressful situations?
   a. GABA   d. Dopamine
   b. Norepinephrine   e. Serotonin
   c. Acetylcholine

4. Phrenology has been discredited, but which of the following ideas has its origins in phrenology?
   a. Brain lateralization
   b. Brain cavities contributing to sense of humor
   c. Bumps in the left hemisphere leading to emotional responses
   d. Brain function localization
   e. Belief that the mind pumps warmth and vitality into the body

5. When there is a negative charge inside an axon and a positive charge outside it, the neuron is

   a. in the process of reuptake.

   b. not in the refractory period.

   c. said to have a resting potential.

   d. said to have an action potential.

   e. depolarizing.

6. Morphine elevates mood and eases pain, and is most similar to which of the following?

   a. Dopamine

   b. Serotonin

   c. Endorphins

   d. Acetylcholine

   e. GABA

7. Neurotransmitters cross the _____ to carry information to the next neuron.

   a. synaptic gap

   b. axon

   c. myelin sheath

   d. dendrites

   e. cell body

8. What neurotransmitters are most likely in undersupply in someone who is depressed?

   a. Dopamine and GABA

   b. ACh and norepinephrine

   c. Dopamine and norepinephrine

   d. Serotonin and norepinephrine

   e. Serotonin and glutamate

Practice FRQs

1. While hiking, Ken stumbled and fell down a 10-foot drop-off. Upon landing, he sprained his ankle badly. Ken was surprised that he felt very little pain for the first half hour. Explain how the following helped Ken feel little pain in the moments after the injury.

   • Endorphins

   • The synapse

Answer

1 point: Endorphins are natural, opiate-like neurotransmitters linked to controlling pain.

1 point: The synapse is the space between neurons where neurotransmitters like the endorphins carry information that influences how Ken feels.

2. Explain the role each of the following plays in sending a message through a neuron.

   • Dendrites

   • Axon

   • Myelin sheath

(3 points)

Module 10

The Nervous and Endocrine Systems

Radius Images/Getty Images

Module Learning Objectives

 Describe the functions of the nervous system's main divisions, and identify the three main types of neurons.

 Describe the nature and functions of the endocrine system and its interaction with the nervous system.

nervous system the body's speedy, electrochemical communication network, consisting of all the nerve cells of the peripheral and central nervous systems.

central nervous system (CNS) the brain and spinal cord.

peripheral nervous system (PNS) the sensory and motor neurons that connect the central nervous system (CNS) to the rest of the body.

nerves bundled axons that form neural "cables" connecting the central nervous system with muscles, glands, and sense organs.

sensory (afferent) neurons neurons that carry incoming information from the sensory receptors to the brain and spinal cord.

motor (efferent) neurons neurons that carry outgoing information from the brain and spinal cord to the muscles and glands.

M y nervous system recently gave me an emotional roller-coaster ride. Before sending me into an MRI machine for a routine shoulder scan, a technician asked if I had issues with claustrophobia (fear of enclosed spaces). "No, I'm fine," I assured her, with perhaps a hint of macho swagger. Moments later, as I found myself on my back, stuck deep inside a coffin-sized box and unable to move, my nervous system had a different idea. As claustrophobia overtook me, my heart began pounding and I felt a desperate urge to escape. Just as I was about to cry out for release, I suddenly felt my nervous system having a reverse calming influence. My heart rate slowed and my body relaxed, though my arousal surged again before the 20-minute confinement ended. "You did well!" the technician said, unaware of my roller-coaster ride.

What happens inside our brains and bodies to produce such surging and subsiding emotions? Is the nervous system that stirs us the same nervous system that soothes us?

The Nervous System

 What are the functions of the nervous system's main divisions, and what are the three main types of neurons?

To live is to take in information from the world and the body's tissues, to make decisions, and to send back information and orders to the body's tissues. All this happens thanks to our body's **nervous system** (**FIGURE 10.1**). The brain and spinal cord form the **central nervous system (CNS),** the body's decision maker. The **peripheral nervous system (PNS)** is responsible for gathering information and for transmitting CNS decisions to other body parts. **Nerves,** electrical cables formed of bundles of axons, link the CNS with the body's sensory receptors, muscles, and glands. The optic nerve, for example, bundles a million axons into a single cable carrying the messages each eye sends to the brain (Mason & Kandel, 1991).

Information travels in the nervous system through three types of neurons. **Sensory neurons** carry messages from the body's tissues and sensory receptors inward to the brain and spinal cord for processing. **Motor neurons** carry instructions from the central

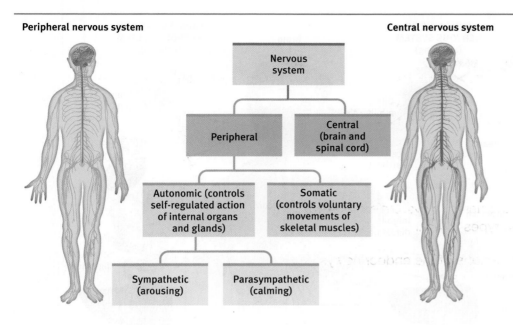

Peripheral nervous system

Central nervous system

Figure 10.1
The functional divisions of the human nervous system

nervous system out to the body's muscles and glands. Between the sensory input and motor output, information is processed in the brain's internal communication system via its **interneurons.** Our complexity resides mostly in our interneuron systems. Our nervous system has a few million sensory neurons, a few million motor neurons, and billions and billions of interneurons.

The Peripheral Nervous System

Our peripheral nervous system has two components—somatic and autonomic. Our **somatic nervous system** enables voluntary control of our skeletal muscles. As the bell signals the end of class, your somatic nervous system reports to your brain the current state of your skeletal muscles and carries instructions back, triggering your body to rise from your seat.

Our **autonomic nervous system (ANS)** controls our glands and the muscles of our internal organs, influencing such functions as glandular activity, heartbeat, and digestion. Like an automatic pilot, this system may be consciously overridden, but usually operates on its own (autonomously).

The autonomic nervous system serves two important, basic functions (**FIGURE 10.2** on the next page). The **sympathetic nervous system** arouses and expends energy. If something alarms or challenges you (such as taking the AP® Psychology exam, or being stuffed in an MRI machine), your sympathetic nervous system will accelerate your heartbeat, raise your blood pressure, slow your digestion, raise your blood sugar, and cool you with perspiration, making you alert and ready for action. When the stress subsides (the AP® exam or MRI is over), your **parasympathetic nervous system** will produce the opposite effects, conserving energy as it calms you by decreasing your heartbeat, lowering your blood sugar, and so forth. In everyday situations, the sympathetic and parasympathetic nervous systems work together to keep us in a steady internal state.

The Central Nervous System

From the simplicity of neurons "talking" to other neurons arises the complexity of the central nervous system's brain and spinal cord.

interneurons neurons within the brain and spinal cord that communicate internally and intervene between the sensory inputs and motor outputs.

somatic nervous system the division of the peripheral nervous system that controls the body's skeletal muscles. Also called the *skeletal nervous system.*

autonomic [aw-tuh-NAHM-ik] **nervous system (ANS)** the part of the peripheral nervous system that controls the glands and the muscles of the internal organs (such as the heart). Its sympathetic division arouses; its parasympathetic division calms.

sympathetic nervous system the division of the autonomic nervous system that arouses the body, mobilizing its energy in stressful situations.

parasympathetic nervous system the division of the autonomic nervous system that calms the body, conserving its energy.

Figure 10.2

The dual functions of the autonomic nervous system The autonomic nervous system controls the more autonomous (or self-regulating) internal functions. Its sympathetic division arouses and expends energy. Its parasympathetic division calms and conserves energy, allowing routine maintenance activity. For example, sympathetic stimulation accelerates heartbeat, whereas parasympathetic stimulation slows it.

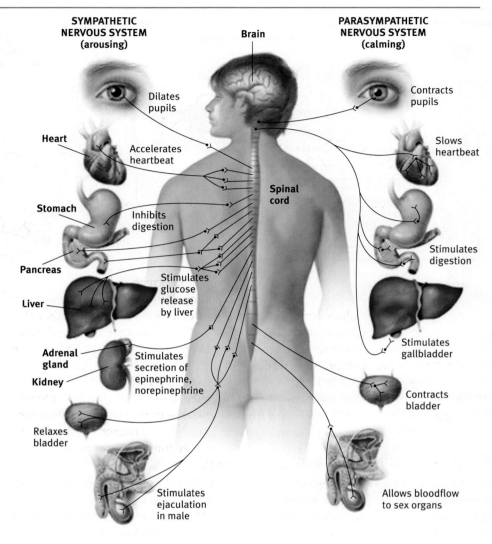

SYMPATHETIC NERVOUS SYSTEM (arousing)

Brain

PARASYMPATHETIC NERVOUS SYSTEM (calming)

Dilates pupils

Contracts pupils

Heart

Accelerates heartbeat

Slows heartbeat

Spinal cord

Stomach

Inhibits digestion

Stimulates digestion

Pancreas

Stimulates glucose release by liver

Liver

Stimulates gallbladder

Adrenal gland

Stimulates secretion of epinephrine, norepinephrine

Kidney

Contracts bladder

Relaxes bladder

Stimulates ejaculation in male

Allows bloodflow to sex organs

BIOLOGY

"The body is made up of millions and millions of crumbs."

© Tom Swick

It is the brain that enables our humanity—our thinking, feeling, and acting. Tens of billions of neurons, each communicating with thousands of other neurons, yield an everchanging wiring diagram. With some 40 billion neurons, each connecting with roughly 10,000 other neurons, we end up with perhaps 400 trillion synapses—places where neurons meet and greet their neighbors (de Courten-Myers, 2005).[1] A grain-of-sand-sized speck of your brain contains some 100,000 neurons and 1 billion "talking" synapses (Ramachandran & Blakeslee, 1998).

The brain's neurons cluster into work groups called *neural networks.* To understand why, Stephen Kosslyn and Olivier Koenig (1992, p. 12) have invited us to "think about why cities exist; why don't people distribute themselves more evenly across the countryside?" Like people networking with people, neurons network with nearby neurons with which they can have short, fast connections. As in **FIGURE 10.3,** each layer's cells connect with various cells in the neural network's next layer. Learning—to play the violin, speak a foreign language, solve a math problem—occurs as experience strengthens connections. Neurons that fire together wire together.

---

[1] Another research team, projecting from representative tissue samples, has estimated that the adult human male brain contains 86 billion neurons—give or take 8 billion (Azevedo et al., 2009). One moral: Distrust big round numbers, such as the familiar, undocumented claim that the human brain contains 100 billion neurons.

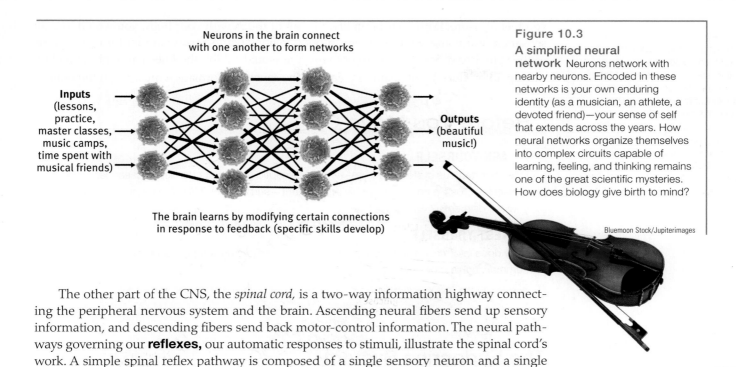

Neurons in the brain connect
with one another to form networks

Inputs
(lessons,
practice,
master classes,
music camps,
time spent with
musical friends)

Outputs
(beautiful
music!)

The brain learns by modifying certain connections
in response to feedback (specific skills develop)

Figure 10.3

**A simplified neural
network** Neurons network with
nearby neurons. Encoded in these
networks is your own enduring
identity (as a musician, an athlete, a
devoted friend)—your sense of self
that extends across the years. How
neural networks organize themselves
into complex circuits capable of
learning, feeling, and thinking remains
one of the great scientific mysteries.
How does biology give birth to mind?

Bluemoon Stock/Jupiterimages

The other part of the CNS, the *spinal cord,* is a two-way information highway connecting the peripheral nervous system and the brain. Ascending neural fibers send up sensory information, and descending fibers send back motor-control information. The neural pathways governing our **reflexes,** our automatic responses to stimuli, illustrate the spinal cord's work. A simple spinal reflex pathway is composed of a single sensory neuron and a single motor neuron. These often communicate through an interneuron. The knee-jerk response, for example, involves one such simple pathway. A headless warm body could do it.

Another such pathway enables the pain reflex (**FIGURE 10.4**). When your finger touches a flame, neural activity (excited by the heat) travels via sensory neurons to interneurons in your spinal cord. These interneurons respond by activating motor neurons leading to the muscles in your arm. Because the simple pain-reflex pathway runs through the spinal cord and right back out, your hand jerks away from the candle's flame *before* your brain receives and responds to the information that causes you to feel pain. That's why it feels as if your hand jerks away not by your choice, but on its own.

Information travels to and from the brain by way of the spinal cord. Were the top of your spinal cord severed, you would not feel pain from your paralyzed body below. Nor would

reflex a simple, automatic
response to a sensory stimulus,
such as the knee-jerk response.

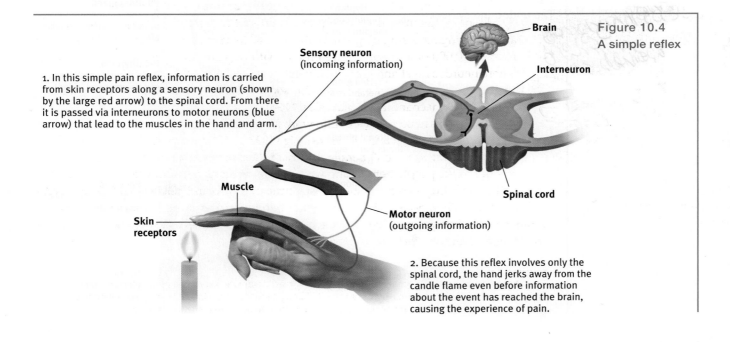

1. In this simple pain reflex, information is carried
from skin receptors along a sensory neuron (shown
by the large red arrow) to the spinal cord. From there
it is passed via interneurons to motor neurons (blue
arrow) that lead to the muscles in the hand and arm.

Sensory neuron
(incoming information)

Brain

Interneuron

Spinal cord

Muscle

**Skin
receptors**

Motor neuron
(outgoing information)

Figure 10.4
A simple reflex

2. Because this reflex involves only the
spinal cord, the hand jerks away from the
candle flame even before information
about the event has reached the brain,
causing the experience of pain.

> "If the nervous system be cut off between the brain and other parts, the experiences of those other parts are nonexistent for the mind. The eye is blind, the ear deaf, the hand insensible and motionless." -WILLIAM JAMES, *PRINCIPLES OF PSYCHOLOGY*, 1890

you feel pleasure. With your brain literally out of touch with your body, you would lose all sensation and voluntary movement in body regions with sensory and motor connections to the spinal cord below its point of injury. You would exhibit the knee jerk without feeling the tap. To produce bodily pain or pleasure, the sensory information must reach the brain.

Before You Move On

▶ **ASK YOURSELF**

Does our nervous system's design—with its synaptic gaps that chemical messenger molecules cross in an imperceptibly brief instant—surprise you? Would you have designed yourself differently?

▶ **TEST YOURSELF**

How does information flow through your nervous system as you pick up a fork? Can you summarize this process?

Answers to the Test Yourself questions can be found in Appendix E at the end of the book.

The Endocrine System

endocrine [EN-duh-krin] **system** the body's "slow" chemical communication system; a set of glands that secrete hormones into the bloodstream.

hormones chemical messengers that are manufactured by the endocrine glands travel through the bloodstream and affect other tissues.

 10-2 What is the nature and what are the functions of the endocrine system, and how does it interact with the nervous system?

So far we have focused on the body's speedy electrochemical information system. Interconnected with your nervous system is a second communication system, the **endocrine system** (**FIGURE 10.5**). The endocrine system's glands secrete another form of chemical messengers, **hormones,** which travel through the bloodstream and affect other tissues, including the brain. When hormones act on the brain, they influence our interest in sex, food, and aggression.

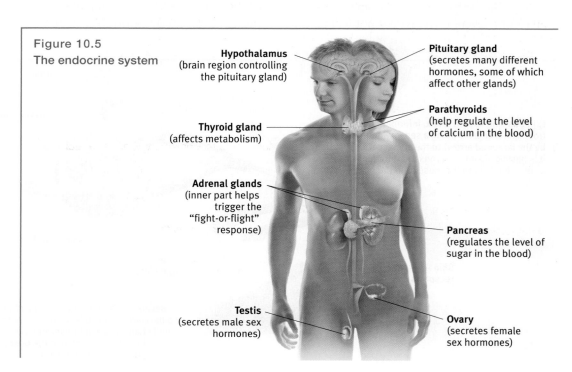

Figure 10.5
The endocrine system

Hypothalamus (brain region controlling the pituitary gland)

Pituitary gland (secretes many different hormones, some of which affect other glands)

Thyroid gland (affects metabolism)

Parathyroids (help regulate the level of calcium in the blood)

Adrenal glands (inner part helps trigger the "fight-or-flight" response)

Pancreas (regulates the level of sugar in the blood)

Testis (secretes male sex hormones)

Ovary (secretes female sex hormones)

Some hormones are chemically identical to neurotransmitters (the chemical messengers that diffuse across a synapse and excite or inhibit an adjacent neuron). The endocrine system and nervous system are therefore close relatives: Both produce molecules that act on receptors elsewhere. Like many relatives, they also differ. The speedy nervous system zips messages from eyes to brain to hand in a fraction of a second. Endocrine messages trudge along in the bloodstream, taking several seconds or more to travel from the gland to the target tissue. If the nervous system's communication delivers messages with the speed of a text message, the endocrine system is more like sending a letter through the mail.

But slow and steady sometimes wins the race. Endocrine messages tend to outlast the effects of neural messages. That helps explain why upset feelings may linger beyond our awareness of what upset us. When this happens, it takes time for us to "simmer down." In a moment of danger, for example, the ANS orders the **adrenal glands** on top of the kidneys to release *epinephrine* and *norepinephrine* (also called *adrenaline* and *noradrenaline*). These hormones increase heart rate, blood pressure, and blood sugar, providing us with a surge of energy, known as the *fight-or-flight* response. When the emergency passes, the hormones— and the feelings of excitement—linger a while.

The most influential endocrine gland is the **pituitary gland,** a pea-sized structure located in the core of the brain, where it is controlled by an adjacent brain area, the *hypothalamus* (more on that shortly). The pituitary releases certain hormones. One is a growth hormone that stimulates physical development. Another, oxytocin, enables contractions associated with birthing, milk flow during nursing, and orgasm. Oxytocin also promotes pair bonding, group cohesion, and social trust (De Dreu et al., 2010). During a laboratory game, those given a nasal squirt of oxytocin rather than a placebo were more likely to trust strangers with their money (Kosfeld et al., 2005).

Pituitary secretions also influence the release of hormones by other endocrine glands. The pituitary, then, is a sort of master gland (whose own master is the hypothalamus). For example, under the brain's influence, the pituitary triggers your sex glands to release sex hormones. These in turn influence your brain and behavior. So, too, with stress. A stressful event triggers your hypothalamus to instruct your pituitary to release a hormone that causes your adrenal glands to flood your body with cortisol, a stress hormone that increases blood sugar.

This feedback system (brain $\rightarrow$ pituitary $\rightarrow$ other glands $\rightarrow$ hormones $\rightarrow$ body and brain) reveals the intimate connection of the nervous and endocrine systems. The nervous system directs endocrine secretions, which then affect the nervous system. Conducting and coordinating this whole electrochemical orchestra is that maestro we call the brain.

adrenal [ah-DREEN-el] **glands** a pair of endocrine glands that sit just above the kidneys and secrete hormones (epinephrine and norepinephrine) that help arouse the body in times of stress.

pituitary gland the endocrine system's most influential gland. Under the influence of the hypothalamus, the pituitary regulates growth and controls other endocrine glands.

Before You Move On

▶ **ASK YOURSELF**

Can you remember feeling an extended period of discomfort after some particularly stressful event? How long did those feelings last?

▶ **TEST YOURSELF**

Why is the pituitary gland called the "master gland"?

Answers to the Test Yourself questions can be found in Appendix E at the end of the book.

Module 10 Review

 10-1 What are the functions of the nervous system's main divisions, and what are the three main types of neurons?

- The *central nervous system (CNS)*—the brain and the spinal cord—is the *nervous system*'s decision maker.

- The *peripheral nervous system (PNS),* which connects the CNS to the rest of the body by means of *nerves,* gathers information and transmits CNS decisions to the rest of the body.

- The two main PNS divisions are the *somatic nervous system* (which enables voluntary control of the skeletal muscles) and the *autonomic nervous system* (which controls involuntary muscles and glands by means of its *sympathetic* and *parasympathetic divisions*).

- Neurons cluster into working networks.

- There are three types of neurons:

  (1) *Sensory neurons* carry incoming information from sense receptors to the brain and spinal cord.

  (2) *Motor neurons* carry information from the brain and spinal cord out to the muscles and glands.

  (3) *Interneurons* communicate within the brain and spinal cord and between sensory and motor neurons.

 10-2 What is the nature and what are the functions of the endocrine system, and how does it interact with the nervous system?

- The *endocrine system* is a set of glands that secrete *hormones* into the bloodstream, where they travel through the body and affect other tissues, including the brain. The *adrenal glands,* for example, release the hormones that trigger the fight-or-flight response.

- The endocrine system's master gland, the *pituitary,* influences hormone release by other glands. In an intricate feedback system, the brain's *hypothalamus* influences the pituitary gland, which influences other glands, which release hormones, which in turn influence the brain.

Multiple-Choice Questions

1. Which of the following carries the information necessary to activate withdrawal of the hand from a hot object?

   a. Sensory neuron
   b. Motor neuron
   c. Interneuron
   d. Receptor neuron
   e. Reflex

2. Hormones are _____ released into the _____.

   a. neurons; neurotransmitters
   b. chemical messengers; bloodstream
   c. electrical messengers; bloodstream
   d. electrical messengers; synapse
   e. chemical messengers; synapse

3. Which division of the nervous system produces the startle response?

   a. Parasympathetic
   b. Central
   c. Somatic
   d. Sympathetic
   e. Autonomic

4. Which of the following endocrine glands may explain unusually tall height in a 12-year-old?

   a. Pituitary
   b. Adrenal
   c. Pancreas
   d. Parathyroid
   e. Testes

5. Which of the following communicates with the pituitary, which in turn controls the endocrine system?

   a. Parathyroids
   b. Autonomic nervous system
   c. Hypothalamus
   d. Spinal cord
   e. Pancreas

6. Which branch of the nervous system calms a person?

   a. Central nervous system
   b. Sympathetic
   c. Parasympathetic
   d. Somatic
   e. Endocrine

7. Epinephrine and norepinephrine increase energy and are released by the

a. thyroid glands.
b. pituitary gland.
c. hypothalamus.
d. thalamus.
e. adrenal glands.

8. Interneurons are said to

a. send messages from specific body parts to the brain.
b. transmit and process information within the brain and spinal cord.
c. act as connectors, supporting other neurons in the brain.
d. send messages from the brain to body parts.
e. influence the pituitary gland.

Practice FRQs

1. While walking barefoot, you step on a piece of glass. Before you have a chance to consciously process what has happened, you draw your foot away from the glass. Identify and explain the three types of neurons that deal with information regarding this painful stimulus.

2. Name and describe the components and subcomponents of the peripheral nervous system.

(4 points)

Answer

1 point: Sensory neurons carry information from the point of the injury to the central nervous system.

1 point: Interneurons are neurons within the brain and spinal cord. Interneurons would help you interpret the pain and enable your brain to send out marching orders.

1 point: Motor neurons carry the instruction from the central nervous system to activate the muscles in your leg and foot.

Module 11

Studying the Brain, and Older Brain Structures

Module Learning Objectives

11-1 Describe several techniques for studying the brain's connections to behavior and mind.

11-2 Describe the components of the brainstem, and summarize the functions of the brainstem, thalamus, and cerebellum.

11-3 Describe the limbic system's structures and functions.

T he brain enables the mind—seeing, hearing, smelling, feeling, remembering, thinking, speaking, dreaming, loving. Moreover, it is the brain that self-reflectively analyzes the brain. When we're thinking *about* our brain, we're thinking *with* our brain—by firing across millions of synapses and releasing billions of neurotransmitter molecules. Neuroscientists tell us that the *mind is what the brain does*. Brain, behavior, and cognition are an integrated whole. But precisely where and how are the mind's functions tied to the brain? Let's first see how scientists explore such questions.

> "I am a brain, Watson. The rest of me is a mere appendix."
> -SHERLOCK HOLMES, IN ARTHUR CONAN DOYLE'S "THE ADVENTURE OF THE MAZARIN STONE"

The Tools of Discovery: Having Our Head Examined

11-1 How do neuroscientists study the brain's connections to behavior and mind?

A century ago, scientists had no tools high-powered yet gentle enough to explore the living human brain. Early case studies of patients by physicians and others helped localize some of the brain's functions. Damage to one side of the brain often caused numbness or paralysis on the body's opposite side, suggesting that the body's right side is wired to the brain's left side, and vice versa. Damage to the back of the brain disrupted vision, and to the left-front part of the brain produced speech difficulties. Gradually, these early explorers were mapping the brain.

Now, within a lifetime, a new generation of neural cartographers is probing and mapping the known universe's most amazing organ. Scientists can selectively **lesion** (destroy) tiny clusters of brain cells, leaving the surrounding tissue unharmed. In the laboratory, such studies have revealed, for example, that damage to one area of the hypothalamus in a rat's brain reduces eating, to the point of starvation, whereas damage in another area produces overeating.

lesion [LEE-zhuhn] tissue destruction. A brain lesion is a naturally or experimentally caused destruction of brain tissue.

Today's neuroscientists can also electrically, chemically, or magnetically *stimulate* various parts of the brain and note the effect. Depending on the stimulated brain part, people may—to name a few examples—giggle, hear voices, turn their head, feel themselves falling, or have an out-of-body experience (Selimbeyoglu & Parvizi, 2010). Scientists can even snoop on the messages of individual neurons. With tips so small they can detect the electrical pulse in a single neuron, modern microelectrodes can, for example, now detect exactly where the information goes in a cat's brain when someone strokes its whisker. Researchers can also eavesdrop on the chatter of billions of neurons and can see color representations of the brain's energy-consuming activity.

Right now, your mental activity is emitting telltale electrical, metabolic, and magnetic signals that would enable neuroscientists to observe your brain at work. Electrical activity in your brain's billions of neurons sweeps in regular waves across its surface. An **electroencephalogram (EEG)** is an amplified readout of such waves. Researchers record the brain waves through a shower-cap-like hat that is filled with electrodes covered with a conductive gel. Studying an EEG of the brain's activity is like studying a car engine by listening to its hum. With no direct access to the brain, researchers present a stimulus repeatedly and have a computer filter out brain activity unrelated to the stimulus. What remains is the electrical wave evoked by the stimulus (**FIGURE 11.1**).

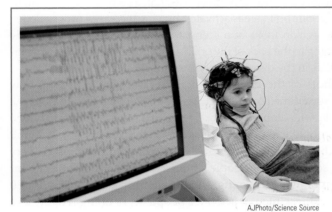

Figure 11.1

An electroencephalogram providing amplified tracings of waves of electrical activity in the brain Here it is displaying the brain activity of this 4-year-old who has epilepsy.

AJPhoto/Science Source

electroencephalogram (EEG) an amplified recording of the waves of electrical activity sweeping across the brain's surface. These waves are measured by electrodes placed on the scalp.

CT (computed tomography) scan a series of X-ray photographs taken from different angles and combined by computer into a composite representation of a slice of the brain's structure. (*Also called CAT scan.*)

PET (positron emission tomography) scan a visual display of brain activity that detects where a radioactive form of glucose goes while the brain performs a given task.

MRI (magnetic resonance imaging) a technique that uses magnetic fields and radio waves to produce computer-generated images of soft tissue. MRI scans show brain anatomy.

"You must look into people, as well as at them," advised Lord Chesterfield in a 1746 letter to his son. Unlike EEGs, newer neuroimaging techniques give us that Superman-like ability to see inside the living brain. For example, the **CT (computed tomography) scan** examines the brain by taking X-ray photographs that can reveal brain damage. Even more dramatic is the **PET (positron emission tomography) scan** (**FIGURE 11.2** on the next page), which depicts brain activity by showing each brain area's consumption of its chemical fuel, the sugar glucose. Active neurons are glucose hogs, and after a person receives temporarily radioactive glucose, the PET scan can track the gamma rays released by this "food for thought" as the person performs a given task. Rather like weather radar showing rain activity, PET-scan "hot spots" show which brain areas are most active as the person does mathematical calculations, looks at images of faces, or daydreams.

In **MRI (magnetic resonance imaging)** brain scans, the person's head is put in a strong magnetic field, which aligns the spinning atoms of brain molecules. Then, a radio-wave pulse momentarily disorients the atoms. When the atoms return to their normal spin, they emit signals that provide a detailed picture of soft tissues, including the brain. MRI scans have revealed a larger-than-average neural area in the left hemisphere of musicians who display perfect pitch (Schlaug et al., 1995). They have also revealed enlarged *ventricles*—fluid-filled brain areas

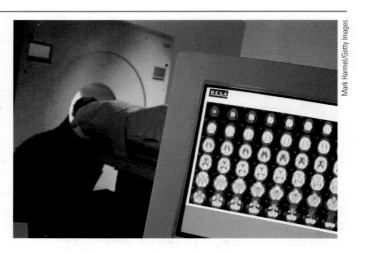

Figure 11.2

The PET scan To obtain a PET scan, researchers inject volunteers with a low and harmless dose of a short-lived radioactive sugar. Detectors around the person's head pick up the release of gamma rays from the sugar, which has concentrated in active brain areas. A computer then processes and translates these signals into a map of the brain at work.

Mark Harmel/Getty Images

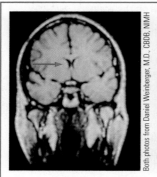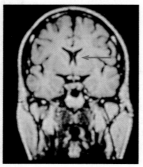

Both photos from Daniel Weinberger, M.D., CBDB, NIMH

Figure 11.3

MRI scan of a healthy individual (left) and a person with schizophrenia (right) Note the enlarged ventricle, the fluid-filled brain region at the tip of the arrow in the image on the right.

fMRI (functional MRI) a technique for revealing bloodflow and, therefore, brain activity by comparing successive MRI scans. fMRI scans show brain function as well as its structure.

(marked by the red arrows in **FIGURE 11.3**)—in some patients who have schizophrenia, a disabling psychological disorder.

A special application of MRI—**fMRI (functional MRI)**—can reveal the brain's functioning as well as its structure. Where the brain is especially active, blood goes. By comparing MRI scans taken less than a second apart, researchers can watch as specific brain areas activate, showing increased oxygen-laden bloodflow. As the person looks at a scene, for example, the fMRI machine detects blood rushing to the back of the brain, which processes visual information (see Figure 12.5, in the discussion of cortex functions in Module 12).

Such snapshots of the brain's changing activity are providing new insights—albeit sometimes overstated (Vul et al., 2009a,b)—into how the brain divides its labor. A mountain of recent fMRI studies suggests which brain areas are most active when people feel pain or rejection, listen to angry voices, think about scary things, feel happy, or become sexually excited. The technology enables a very crude sort of mind reading. After scanning 129 people's brains as they did eight different mental tasks (such as reading, gambling, or rhyming), neuroscientists were able, with 80 percent accuracy, to predict which of these mental activities people were doing (Poldrack et al., 2009). Other studies have explored brain activity associated with religious experience, though without settling the question of whether the brain is producing or perceiving God (Fingelkurts & Fingelkurts, 2009; Inzlicht et al., 2009; Kapogiannis et al., 2009).

* * *

Today's techniques for peering into the thinking, feeling brain are doing for psychology what the microscope did for biology and the telescope did for astronomy. From them we have learned more about the brain in the last 30 years than in the previous 30,000. To be learning about the neurosciences now is like studying world geography while Magellan was exploring the seas. This truly is the golden age of brain science.

Older Brain Structures

11-2 What structures make up the brainstem, and what are the functions of the brainstem, thalamus, and cerebellum?

An animal's capacities come from its brain structures. In primitive animals, such as sharks, a not-so-complex brain primarily regulates basic survival functions: breathing, resting, and feeding. In lower mammals, such as rodents, a more complex brain enables emotion and greater memory. In advanced mammals, such as humans, a brain that processes more information enables increased foresight as well.

AP® Exam Tip

Your author, David Myers, is about to take you on a journey through your brain. Focus on the name of each part, its location within the brain, and what it does. Then it's time to practice, practice, practice.

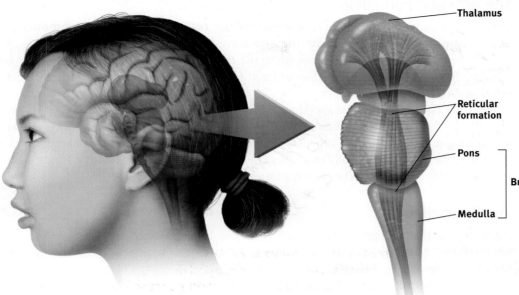

Figure 11.4
The brainstem and thalamus The brainstem, including the pons and medulla, is an extension of the spinal cord. The thalamus is attached to the top of the brainstem. The reticular formation passes through both structures.

This increasing complexity arises from new brain systems built on top of the old, much as the Earth's landscape covers the old with the new. Digging down, one discovers the fossil remnants of the past—brainstem components performing for us much as they did for our distant ancestors. Let's start with the brain's basement and work up to the newer systems.

The Brainstem

The brain's oldest and innermost region is the **brainstem.** It begins where the spinal cord swells slightly after entering the skull. This slight swelling is the **medulla** (**FIGURE 11.4**). Here lie the controls for your heartbeat and breathing. As some brain-damaged patients in a vegetative state illustrate, we need no higher brain or conscious mind to orchestrate our heart's pumping and lungs' breathing. The brainstem handles those tasks.

Just above the medulla sits the *pons,* which helps coordinate movements. If a cat's brainstem is severed from the rest of the brain above it, the animal will still breathe and live—and even run, climb, and groom (Klemm, 1990). But cut off from the brain's higher regions, it won't *purposefully* run or climb to get food.

The brainstem is a crossover point, where most nerves to and from each side of the brain connect with the body's opposite side (**FIGURE 11.5**). This peculiar cross-wiring is but one of the brain's many surprises.

The Thalamus

Sitting atop the brainstem is the **thalamus,** a pair of egg-shaped structures that act as the brain's sensory control center (Figure 11.4). The thalamus receives information from all the senses except smell and routes it to the higher brain regions that deal with seeing, hearing, tasting, and touching. The thalamus also receives some of the higher brain's replies, which it then directs to the medulla and to the cerebellum (see the next page). Think of the thalamus as being to sensory information what London is to England's trains: a hub through which traffic passes en route to various destinations.

brainstem the oldest part and central core of the brain, beginning where the spinal cord swells as it enters the skull; the brainstem is responsible for automatic survival functions.

medulla [muh-DUL-uh] the base of the brainstem; controls heartbeat and breathing.

thalamus [THAL-uh-muss] the brain's sensory control center, located on top of the brainstem; it directs messages to the sensory receiving areas in the cortex and transmits replies to the cerebellum and medulla.

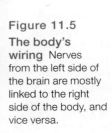

Figure 11.5
The body's wiring Nerves from the left side of the brain are mostly linked to the right side of the body, and vice versa.

Andrew Swift

The Reticular Formation

reticular formation a nerve network that travels through the brainstem and thalamus and plays an important role in controlling arousal.

Inside the brainstem, between your ears, lies the **reticular** ("netlike") **formation,** a neuron network that extends from the spinal cord right up through the thalamus. As the spinal cord's sensory input flows up to the thalamus, some of it travels through the reticular formation, which filters incoming stimuli and relays important information to other brain areas.

In 1949, Giuseppe Moruzzi and Horace Magoun discovered that electrically stimulating the reticular formation of a sleeping cat almost instantly produced an awake, alert animal. When Magoun *severed* a cat's reticular formation without damaging the nearby sensory pathways, the effect was equally dramatic: The cat lapsed into a coma from which it never awakened. The conclusion? The reticular formation enables arousal.

The Cerebellum

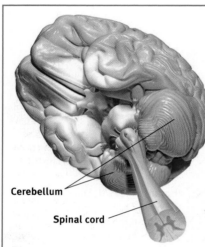

Cerebellum

Spinal cord

Figure 11.6

The brain's organ of agility Hanging at the back of the brain, the cerebellum coordinates our voluntary movements.

Extending from the rear of the brainstem is the baseball-sized **cerebellum,** meaning "little brain," which is what its two wrinkled halves resemble (**FIGURE 11.6**). As you will see in Module 32, the cerebellum enables nonverbal learning and memory. It also helps us judge time, modulate our emotions, and discriminate sounds and textures (Bower & Parsons, 2003). And it coordinates voluntary movement (with assistance from the pons). When a soccer player executes a perfect bicycle kick (above), give his cerebellum some credit. If you injured your cerebellum, you would have difficulty walking, keeping your balance, or shaking hands. Your movements would be jerky and exaggerated. Gone would be any dreams of being a dancer or guitarist. Under alcohol's influence on the cerebellum, coordination suffers, as many a driver has learned after being pulled over and given a roadside test.

Mark Scott/Getty Images

* * *

Note: These older brain functions all occur without any conscious effort. This illustrates another of our recurring themes: *Our brain processes most information outside of our awareness.* We are aware of the *results* of our brain's labor (say, our current visual experience) but not of *how* we construct the visual image. Likewise, whether we are asleep or awake, our brainstem manages its life-sustaining functions, freeing our newer brain regions to think, talk, dream, or savor a memory.

The Limbic System

cerebellum [sehr-uh-BELL-um] the "little brain" at the rear of the brainstem; functions include processing sensory input, coordinating movement output and balance, and enabling nonverbal learning and memory.

limbic system neural system (including the *hippocampus, amygdala,* and *hypothalamus*) located below the cerebral hemispheres; associated with emotions and drives.

11-3 What are the limbic system's structures and functions?

We've considered the brain's oldest parts, but we've not yet reached its newest and highest regions, the *cerebral hemispheres* (the two halves of the brain). Between the oldest and newest brain areas lies the **limbic system** (*limbus* means "border"). This system contains the *amygdala,* the *hypothalamus,* and the *hippocampus* (**FIGURE 11.7**). The hippocampus processes conscious memories. Animals or humans who lose their hippocampus to surgery or injury also lose their ability to form new memories of facts and events. Module 31 explains how our two-track mind processes our memories. For now, let's look at the limbic system's links to emotions such as fear and anger, and to basic motives such as those for food and sex.

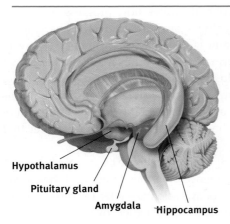

Figure 11.7
The limbic system This neural system sits between the brain's older parts and its cerebral hemispheres. The limbic system's hypothalamus controls the nearby pituitary gland.

Hypothalamus

Pituitary gland

Amygdala   Hippocampus

amygdala [uh-MIG-duh-la] two lima-bean-sized neural clusters in the limbic system; linked to emotion.

hypothalamus [hi-po-THAL-uh-muss] a neural structure lying below (*hypo*) the thalamus; it directs several maintenance activities (eating, drinking, body temperature), helps govern the endocrine system via the pituitary gland, and is linked to emotion and reward.

THE AMYGDALA

Research has linked the **amygdala,** two lima-bean-sized neural clusters, to aggression and fear. In 1939, psychologist Heinrich Klüver and neurosurgeon Paul Bucy surgically removed a rhesus monkey's amygdala, turning the normally ill-tempered animal into the most mellow of creatures. In studies with other wild animals, including the lynx, wolverine, and wild rat, researchers noted the same effect.

What then might happen if we electrically stimulated the amygdala of a normally placid domestic animal, such as a cat? Do so in one spot and the cat prepares to attack, hissing with its back arched, its pupils dilated, its hair on end. Move the electrode only slightly within the amygdala, cage the cat with a small mouse, and now it cowers in terror.

These and other experiments have confirmed the amygdala's role in rage and fear, including the perception of these emotions and the processing of emotional memories (Anderson & Phelps, 2000; Poremba & Gabriel, 2001). But we must be careful. The brain is not neatly organized into structures that correspond to our behavior categories. When we feel or act in aggressive or fearful ways, there is neural activity in many levels of our brain. Even within the limbic system, stimulating structures other than the amygdala can evoke aggression or fear. If you charge your cell phone's dead battery, you can activate the phone and make a call. Yet the battery is merely one link in an integrated system.

Aggression as a brain state Back arched and fur fluffed, this fierce cat is ready to attack. Electrical stimulation of a cat's amygdala provokes angry reactions, suggesting the amygdala's role in aggression. Which ANS division is activated by such stimulation?

ANSWER: The cat would be aroused via its sympathetic nervous system.

Jane Burton/Dorling Kindersley/Getty Images

THE HYPOTHALAMUS

Just below (*hypo*) the thalamus is the **hypothalamus (FIGURE 11.8** on the next page), an important link in the command chain governing bodily maintenance. Some neural clusters in the hypothalamus influence hunger; others regulate thirst, body temperature, and sexual behavior. Together, they help maintain a steady internal state.

As the hypothalamus monitors the state of your body, it tunes into your blood chemistry and any incoming orders from other brain parts. For example, picking up signals from your brain's cerebral cortex that you are thinking about sex, your hypothalamus will secrete hormones. These hormones will in turn trigger the adjacent "master gland," your pituitary (see Figure 11.7), to influence your sex glands to release their hormones. These will intensify the thoughts of sex in your cerebral cortex. (Once again, we see the interplay between the nervous and endocrine systems: The brain influences the endocrine system, which in turn influences the brain.)

AP® Exam Tip

If you ever have to make a guess about brain parts on the AP® exam, the hypothalamus isn't a bad bet. Even though it's small, it has many functions.

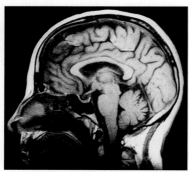

ISM/Phototake

Figure 11.8

The hypothalamus This small but important structure, colored yellow/orange in this MRI scan photograph, helps keep the body's internal environment in a steady state.

"If you were designing a robot vehicle to walk into the future and survive, . . . you'd wire it up so that behavior that ensured the survival of the self or the species—like sex and eating—would be naturally reinforcing."
-CANDACE PERT (1986)

A remarkable discovery about the hypothalamus illustrates how progress in science often occurs—when curious, open-minded investigators make an unexpected observation. Two young McGill University neuropsychologists, James Olds and Peter Milner (1954), were trying to implant an electrode in a rat's reticular formation when they made a magnificent mistake: They placed the electrode incorrectly (Olds, 1975). Curiously, as if seeking more stimulation, the rat kept returning to the location where it had been stimulated by this misplaced electrode. On discovering that they had actually placed the device in a region of the hypothalamus, Olds and Milner realized they had stumbled upon a brain center that provides pleasurable rewards (Olds, 1975).

In a meticulous series of experiments, Olds (1958) went on to locate other "pleasure centers," as he called them. (What the rats actually experience only they know, and they aren't telling. Rather than attribute human feelings to rats, today's scientists refer to *reward centers,* not "pleasure centers.") When allowed to press pedals to trigger their own stimulation in these areas, rats would sometimes do so at a feverish pace—up to 7000 times per hour—until they dropped from exhaustion. Moreover, to get this stimulation, they would even cross an electrified floor that a starving rat would not cross to reach food (**FIGURE 11.9**).

Other limbic system reward centers, such as the *nucleus accumbens* in front of the hypothalamus, were later discovered in many other species, including dolphins and monkeys. In fact, animal research has revealed both a general dopamine-related reward system and specific centers associated with the pleasures of eating, drinking, and sex. Animals, it seems, come equipped with built-in systems that reward activities essential to survival.

Contemporary researchers are experimenting with new ways of using limbic stimulation to control animals' actions in future applications, such as search-and-rescue operations. By rewarding rats for turning left or right, one research team trained previously caged rats to navigate natural environments (Talwar et al., 2002; **FIGURE 11.10**). By pressing buttons on a laptop, the researchers were then able to direct the rat—which carried a receiver, power source, and video camera on a backpack—to turn on cue, climb trees, scurry along branches, and turn around and come back down.

Do humans have limbic centers for pleasure? Indeed we do. To calm violent patients, one neurosurgeon implanted electrodes in such areas. Stimulated patients reported mild pleasure; unlike Olds' rats, however, they were not driven to a frenzy (Deutsch, 1972; Hooper & Teresi, 1986).

Experiments have also revealed the effects of a dopamine-related reward system in people. One research team had people rate the desirability of different vacation destinations. Then, after receiving either a dopamine-increasing drug or a sugar pill, they imagined themselves vacationing at half the locations. A day later, when presented with pairs of vacation spots they

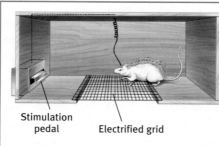

Stimulation pedal   Electrified grid

Figure 11.9

Rat with an implanted electrode With an electrode implanted in a reward center of its hypothalamus, the rat readily crosses an electrified grid, accepting the painful shocks, to press a pedal that sends electrical impulses to that center.

Figure 11.10

Ratbot on a pleasure cruise When stimulated by remote control, a rat could be guided to navigate across a field and even up a tree.

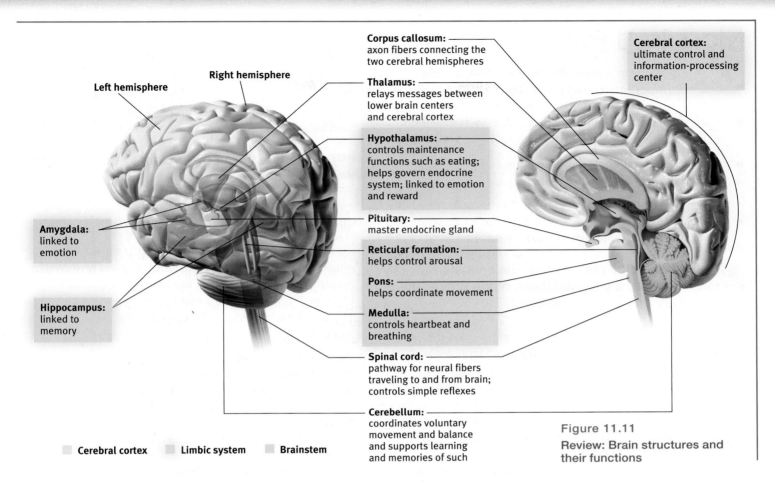

Corpus callosum:
axon fibers connecting the two cerebral hemispheres

Cerebral cortex:
ultimate control and information-processing center

Right hemisphere

Left hemisphere

Thalamus:
relays messages between lower brain centers and cerebral cortex

Hypothalamus:
controls maintenance functions such as eating; helps govern endocrine system; linked to emotion and reward

Pituitary:
master endocrine gland

Amygdala:
linked to emotion

Reticular formation:
helps control arousal

Pons:
helps coordinate movement

Hippocampus:
linked to memory

Medulla:
controls heartbeat and breathing

Spinal cord:
pathway for neural fibers traveling to and from brain; controls simple reflexes

Cerebral cortex   **Limbic system**   **Brainstem**

Cerebellum:
coordinates voluntary movement and balance and supports learning and memories of such

Figure 11.11
Review: Brain structures and their functions

had initially rated equally, only the dopamine takers preferred the places they had imagined under dopamine's influence (Sharot et al., 2009). The participants, it seems, associated the imagined experiences with dopamine-induced pleasant feelings.

Some researchers believe that addictive disorders, such as substance use disorders and binge eating, may stem from malfunctions in natural brain systems for pleasure and well-being. People genetically predisposed to this *reward deficiency syndrome* may crave whatever provides that missing pleasure or relieves negative feelings (Blum et al., 1996).

* * *

FIGURE 11.11 locates the brain areas we've discussed, as well as the *cerebral cortex,* our next topic.

Before You Move On

▶ **ASK YOURSELF**

If one day researchers discover how to stimulate human limbic centers to produce as strong a reaction as found in other animals, do you think this process could be used to reduce the incidence of substance use? Could such use have any negative consequences?

▶ **TEST YOURSELF**

Within what brain region would damage be most likely to disrupt your ability to skip rope? Your ability to sense tastes or sounds? In what brain region would damage perhaps leave you in a coma? Without the very breath and heartbeat of life?

Answers to the Test Yourself questions can be found in Appendix E at the end of the book.

Module 11 Review

 How do neuroscientists study the brain's connections to behavior and mind?

- Case studies and *lesioning* first revealed the general effects of brain damage.

- Modern electrical, chemical, or magnetic stimulation has also revealed aspects of information processing in the brain.

- *CT* and *MRI* scans show anatomy. *EEG, PET,* and *fMRI* (*functional MRI*) recordings reveal brain function.

 What structures make up the brainstem, and what are the functions of the brainstem, thalamus, and cerebellum?

- The *brainstem,* the oldest part of the brain, is responsible for automatic survival functions. Its components are the *medulla* (which controls heartbeat and breathing), the *pons* (which helps coordinate movements), and the *reticular formation* (which affects arousal).

- The *thalamus,* sitting above the brainstem, acts as the brain's sensory control center. The *cerebellum,* attached to the rear of the brainstem, coordinates muscle movement and balance and also helps process sensory information.

11-3 **What are the limbic system's structures and functions?**

- The *limbic system* is linked to emotions, memory, and drives.

- Its neural centers include the hippocampus (which processes conscious memories); the *amygdala* (involved in responses of aggression and fear); and the *hypothalamus* (involved in various bodily maintenance functions, pleasurable rewards, and the control of the endocrine system).

- The pituitary (the "master gland") controls the hypothalamus by stimulating it to trigger the release of hormones.

Multiple-Choice Questions

1. Computer-enhanced X-rays used to create brain images are known as

a. position emission tomography scans.
b. functional magnetic resonance images.
c. computed tomography scans.
d. electroencephalograms.
e. magnetic resonance images.

2. What part of the brain triggers the release of adrenaline to boost heart rate when you're afraid?

a. Amygdala
b. Thalamus
c. Medulla
d. Hippocampus
e. Hypothalamus

3. A gymnast falls and hits her head on the floor. She attempts to continue practicing, but has trouble maintaining balance. What part of her brain has probably been affected?

a. Reticular formation
b. Cerebellum
c. Amygdala
d. Frontal lobe
e. Brainstem

4. Which of the following scanning techniques measures glucose consumption as an indicator of brain activity?

a. CT
b. MRI
c. fMRI
d. PET
e. EEG

5. Which of the following is sometimes referred to as the brain's train hub, because it directs incoming sensory messages (with the exception of smell) to their proper places in the brain?

a. Hypothalamus
b. Pituitary
c. Cerebellum
d. Limbic system
e. Thalamus

6. Which of the following brain areas is responsible for regulating thirst?

a. Reticular activating system
b. Amygdala
c. Hypothalamus
d. Hippocampus
e. Brainstem

7. The hypothalamus is a(n) _____ center for the brain.

a. positioning
b. aggression
c. balance
d. memory
e. reward

8. Which of the following's primary function is processing memories?

a. Cerebral cortex
b. Medulla
c. Corpus callosum
d. Hippocampus
e. Hypothalamus

Practice FRQs

1. Following a brain injury, Mike struggles to control his emotions and has difficulty establishing new memories. What parts of Mike's brain have most likely been affected by his injury?

Answer

1 point: Damage to the amygdala would make it difficult for Mike to control his emotions.

1 point: Damage to the hippocampus would affect Mike's ability to establish new memories.

2. Identify the role of each of the following in listening to and taking notes during a psychology lecture.

• Hippocampus
• Cerebellum
• Cerebral cortex

(3 points)

Module 12

The Cerebral Cortex

Ed Kashi/Corbis

Module Learning Objectives

12-1 Identify the various regions of the cerebral cortex, and describe their functions.

12-2 Discuss the brain's ability to reorganize itself, and define neurogenesis.

12-1 What are the functions of the various cerebral cortex regions?

Older brain networks sustain basic life functions and enable memory, emotions, and basic drives. Newer neural networks within the *cerebrum*—the hemispheres that contribute 85 percent of the brain's weight—form specialized work teams that enable our perceiving, thinking, and speaking. Like other structures above the brainstem (including the thalamus, hippocampus, and amygdala), the cerebral hemispheres come as a pair. Covering those hemispheres, like bark on a tree, is the **cerebral cortex,** a thin surface layer of interconnected neural cells. It is your brain's thinking crown, your body's ultimate control and information-processing center.

As we move up the ladder of animal life, the cerebral cortex expands, tight genetic controls relax, and the organism's adaptability increases. Frogs and other small-cortex amphibians operate extensively on preprogrammed genetic instructions. The larger cortex of mammals offers increased capacities for learning and thinking, enabling them to be more adaptable. What makes us distinctively human mostly arises from the complex functions of our cerebral cortex.

Structure of the Cortex

If you opened a human skull, exposing the brain, you would see a wrinkled organ, shaped somewhat like the meat of an oversized walnut. Without these wrinkles, a flattened cerebral cortex would require triple the area—roughly that of a large pizza. The brain's left and right hemispheres are filled mainly with axons connecting the cortex to the brain's other regions. The cerebral cortex—that thin surface layer—contains some 20 to 23 billion nerve cells and 300 trillion synaptic connections (de Courten-Myers, 2005). Being human takes a lot of nerve.

Supporting these billions of nerve cells are nine times as many spidery **glial cells** ("glue cells"). Neurons are like queen bees; on their own they cannot feed or sheathe themselves. Glial cells are worker bees. They provide nutrients and insulating myelin, guide neural connections, and mop up ions and neurotransmitters. Glia may also play a role in learning and thinking. By "chatting" with neurons they may participate in information transmission and memory (Fields, 2009; Miller, 2005).

---

cerebral [seh-REE-bruhl] **cortex** the intricate fabric of interconnected neural cells covering the cerebral hemispheres; the body's ultimate control and information-processing center.

glial cells (glia) cells in the nervous system that support, nourish, and protect neurons; they may also play a role in learning and thinking.

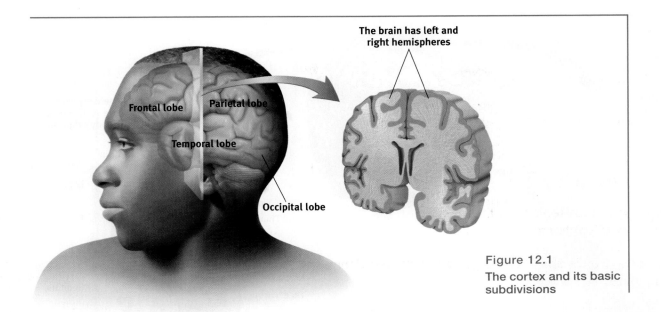

The brain has left and right hemispheres

Frontal lobe   Parietal lobe

Temporal lobe

Occipital lobe

Figure 12.1
The cortex and its basic subdivisions

In more complex animal brains, the proportion of glia to neurons increases. A postmortem analysis of Einstein's brain did not find more or larger-than-usual neurons, but it did reveal a much greater concentration of glial cells than found in an average Albert's head (Fields, 2004).

Each hemisphere's cortex is subdivided into four *lobes,* separated by prominent *fissures,* or folds (**FIGURE 12.1**). Starting at the front of your brain and moving over the top, there are the **frontal lobes** (behind your forehead), the **parietal lobes** (at the top and to the rear), and the **occipital lobes** (at the back of your head). Reversing direction and moving forward, just above your ears, you find the **temporal lobes.** Each of the four lobes carries out many functions, and many functions require the interplay of several lobes.

Functions of the Cortex

More than a century ago, surgeons found damaged cortical areas during autopsies of people who had been partially paralyzed or speechless. This rather crude evidence did not prove that specific parts of the cortex control complex functions like movement or speech. After all, if the entire cortex controlled speech and movement, damage to almost any area might produce the same effect. A TV with its power cord cut would go dead, but we would be fooling ourselves if we thought we had "localized" the picture in the cord.

Motor Functions

Scientists had better luck in localizing simpler brain functions. For example, in 1870, German physicians Gustav Fritsch and Eduard Hitzig made an important discovery: Mild electrical stimulation to parts of an animal's cortex made parts of its body move. The effects were selective: Stimulation caused movement only when applied to an arch-shaped region at the back of the frontal lobe, running roughly ear-to-ear across the top of the brain. Moreover, stimulating parts of this region in the left or right hemisphere caused movements of specific body parts on the *opposite* side of the body. Fritsch and Hitzig had discovered what is now called the **motor cortex.**

MAPPING THE MOTOR CORTEX

Lucky for brain surgeons and their patients, the brain has no sensory receptors. Knowing this, Otfrid Foerster and Wilder Penfield were able to map the motor cortex in hundreds of wide-awake patients by stimulating different cortical areas and observing the body's responses.

frontal lobes portion of the cerebral cortex lying just behind the forehead; involved in speaking and muscle movements and in making plans and judgments.

parietal [puh-RYE-uh-tuhl] **lobes** portion of the cerebral cortex lying at the top of the head and toward the rear; receives sensory input for touch and body position.

occipital [ahk-SIP-uh-tuhl] **lobes** portion of the cerebral cortex lying at the back of the head; includes areas that receive information from the visual fields.

temporal lobes portion of the cerebral cortex lying roughly above the ears; includes the auditory areas, each receiving information primarily from the opposite ear.

motor cortex an area at the rear of the frontal lobes that controls voluntary movements.

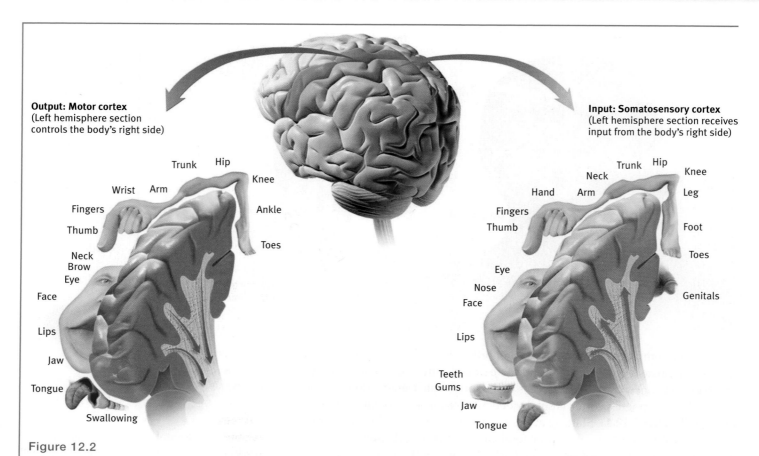

Output: Motor cortex
(Left hemisphere section controls the body's right side)

Trunk Hip
Wrist Arm Knee
Fingers Ankle
Thumb
Neck Toes
Brow
Eye
Face
Lips
Jaw
Tongue
Swallowing

Input: Somatosensory cortex
(Left hemisphere section receives input from the body's right side)

Trunk Hip
Neck Knee
Hand Arm Leg
Fingers Foot
Thumb
Toes
Eye
Nose Genitals
Face
Lips
Teeth
Gums
Jaw
Tongue

Figure 12.2

Left hemisphere tissue devoted to each body part in the motor cortex and the somatosensory cortex As you can see from this classic though inexact representation, the amount of cortex devoted to a body part in the motor cortex (in the frontal lobes) or in the somatosensory cortex (in the parietal lobes) is not proportional to that body part's size. Rather, the brain devotes more tissue to sensitive areas and to areas requiring precise control. Thus, the fingers have a greater representation in the cortex than does the upper arm.

They discovered that body areas requiring precise control, such as the fingers and mouth, occupy the greatest amount of cortical space (**FIGURE 12.2**).

In one of his many demonstrations of motor behavior mechanics, Spanish neuroscientist José Delgado stimulated a spot on a patient's left motor cortex, triggering the right hand to make a fist. Asked to keep the fingers open during the next stimulation, the patient, whose fingers closed despite his best efforts, remarked, "I guess, Doctor, that your electricity is stronger than my will" (Delgado, 1969, p. 114).

More recently, scientists were able to predict a monkey's arm motion a tenth of a second *before* it moved—by repeatedly measuring motor cortex activity preceding specific arm movements (Gibbs, 1996). Such findings have opened the door to research on brain-controlled computers.

BRAIN-COMPUTER INTERFACES

By eavesdropping on the brain, could we enable someone—perhaps a paralyzed person—to move a robotic limb? Could a *brain-computer interface* command a cursor to write an e-mail or search the Internet? To find out, Brown University brain researchers implanted 100 tiny recording electrodes in the motor cortexes of three monkeys (Nicolelis & Chapin, 2002; Serruya et al., 2002). As the monkeys used a joystick to move a cursor to follow a moving red target (to gain rewards), the researchers matched the brain signals with the arm movements. Then they programmed a computer to monitor the signals and operate the joystick. When a monkey merely thought about a move, the mind-reading computer moved the cursor with nearly the same proficiency as had the reward-seeking monkey. In follow-up experiments, two monkeys were trained to control a robot arm that could grasp and deliver food (Velliste et al., 2008), and then a human did the same (**FIGURE 12.3**).

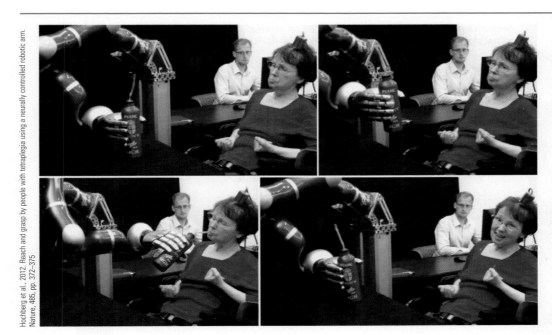

Hochberg et al., 2012. Reach and grasp by people with tetraplegia using a neurally controlled robotic arm. Nature, 485, pp. 372–375

Figure 12.3

Mind over matter A series of strokes left Cathy paralyzed for 15 years, unable to make even simple arm movements. Now, thanks to a tiny, 96-electrode implant in her brain's motor cortex, she is learning to direct a robotic arm with her thoughts (Hochberg et al., 2012).

Clinical trials of such *cognitive neural prosthetics* are now under way with people who have suffered paralysis or amputation (Andersen et al., 2010; Nurmikko et al., 2010). The first patient, a paralyzed 25-year-old man, was able to mentally control a TV, draw shapes on a computer screen, and play video games—all thanks to an aspirin-sized chip with 100 microelectrodes recording activity in his motor cortex (Hochberg et al., 2006). If everything psychological is also biological—if, for example, every thought is also a neural event—then microelectrodes perhaps could detect thoughts well enough to enable people to control events, as suggested by **FIGURE 12.4** on the next page.

Sensory Functions

If the motor cortex sends messages out to the body, where does the cortex receive the incoming messages? Wilder Penfield also identified the cortical area that specializes in receiving information from the skin senses and from the movement of body parts. This area at the front of the parietal lobes, parallel to and just behind the motor cortex, we now call the **somatosensory cortex** (Figure 12.2). Stimulate a point on the top of this band of tissue and a person may report being touched on the shoulder; stimulate some point on the side and the person may feel something on the face.

The more sensitive the body region, the larger the somatosensory cortex area devoted to it (Figure 12.2). Your supersensitive lips project to a larger brain area than do your toes, which is one reason we kiss with our lips rather than touch toes. Rats have a large area of the brain devoted to their whisker sensations, and owls to their hearing sensations.

Scientists have identified additional areas where the cortex receives input from senses other than touch. At this moment, you are receiving visual information in the visual cortex in your occipital lobes, at the very back of your brain (**FIGURES 12.5** and **12.6** on the next page). A bad enough bash there would make you blind. Stimulated there, you might see flashes of light or dashes of color. (In a sense, we *do* have eyes in the back of our head!) From your occipital lobes, visual information goes to other areas that specialize in tasks such as identifying words, detecting emotions, and recognizing faces.

Any sound you now hear is processed by your auditory cortex in your temporal lobes (just above your ears; see Figure 12.6). Most of this auditory information travels

somatosensory cortex area at the front of the parietal lobes that registers and processes body touch and movement sensations.

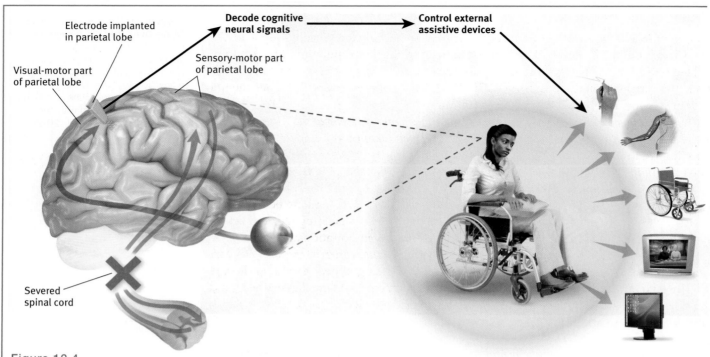

Decode cognitive neural signals

Control external assistive devices

Electrode implanted in parietal lobe

Sensory-motor part of parietal lobe

Visual-motor part of parietal lobe

Severed spinal cord

Figure 12.4

Brain-computer interaction A patient with a severed spinal cord has electrodes planted in a parietal lobe region involved with planning to reach out one's arm. The resulting signal can enable the patient to move a robotic limb, stimulate muscles that activate a paralyzed limb, navigate a wheelchair, control a TV, and use the Internet. (Graphic adapted from Andersen et al., 2010.)

a circuitous route from one ear to the auditory receiving area above your opposite ear. If stimulated there, you might hear a sound. MRI scans of people with schizophrenia reveal active auditory areas in the temporal lobes during auditory hallucinations (Lennox et al., 1999). Even the phantom ringing sound experienced by people with hearing loss is—if heard in one ear—associated with activity in the temporal lobe on the brain's opposite side (Muhlnickel, 1998).

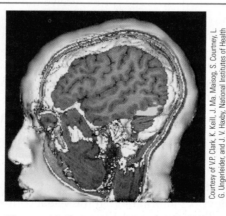

Courtesy of V.P. Clark, K. Keill, J. Ma. Maisog, S. Courtney, L. G. Ungerleider, and J. V. Haxby, National Institutes of Health

Figure 12.5

The brain in action This fMRI (functional MRI) scan shows the visual cortex in the occipital lobes activated (color representation of increased bloodflow) as a research participant looks at a photo. When the person stops looking, the region instantly calms down.

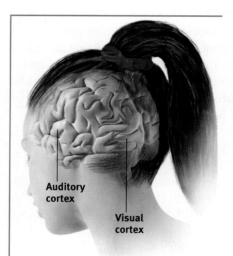

Auditory cortex

Visual cortex

Figure 12.6

The visual cortex and auditory cortex The visual cortex of the occipital lobes at the rear of your brain receives input from your eyes. The auditory cortex, in your temporal lobes—above your ears—receives information from your ears.

Association Areas

So far, we have pointed out small cortical areas that either receive sensory input or direct muscular output. Together, these occupy about one-fourth of the human brain's thin, wrinkled cover. What, then, goes on in the vast regions of the cortex? In these **association areas** (the peach-colored areas in **FIGURE 12.7**), neurons are busy with higher mental functions—many of the tasks that make us human.

Electrically probing an association area won't trigger any observable response. So, unlike the sensory and motor areas, association area functions cannot be neatly mapped. Their silence has led to what Donald McBurney (1996, p. 44) has called "one of the hardiest weeds in the garden of psychology": the claim that we ordinarily use only 10 percent of our brains. (If true, wouldn't this imply a 90 percent chance that a bullet to your brain would land in an unused area?) Surgically lesioned animals and brain-damaged humans bear witness that association areas are not dormant. Rather, these areas interpret, integrate, and act on sensory information and link it with stored memories—a very important part of thinking.

Association areas are found in all four lobes. The *prefrontal cortex* in the forward part of the frontal lobes enables judgment, planning, and processing of new memories. People with damaged frontal lobes may have intact memories, high scores on intelligence tests, and great cake-baking skills. Yet they would not be able to plan ahead to *begin* baking a cake for a birthday party (Huey et al., 2006).

> **association areas** areas of the cerebral cortex that are not involved in primary motor or sensory functions; rather, they are involved in higher mental functions such as learning, remembering, thinking, and speaking.

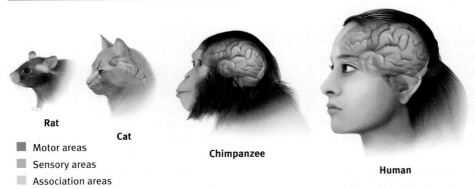

Rat

Cat

Chimpanzee

Human

- ■ Motor areas
- ■ Sensory areas
- ■ Association areas

Figure 12.7

Areas of the cortex in four mammals More intelligent animals have increased "uncommitted" or association areas of the cortex. These vast areas of the brain are responsible for interpreting, integrating, and acting on sensory information and linking it with stored memories.

Frontal lobe damage also can alter personality and remove a person's inhibitions. Consider the classic case of railroad worker Phineas Gage. One afternoon in 1848, Gage, then 25 years old, was packing gunpowder into a rock with a tamping iron. A spark ignited the gunpowder, shooting the rod up through his left cheek and out the top of his skull, leaving his frontal lobes massively damaged (**FIGURE 12.8** on the next page). To everyone's amazement, he was immediately able to sit up and speak, and after the wound healed he returned to work. But the affable, soft-spoken man was now irritable, profane, and dishonest. This person, said his friends, was "no longer Gage." Although his mental abilities and memories were intact, his personality was not. (Although Gage lost his job, he did, over time, adapt to his injury and find work as a stagecoach driver [Macmillan & Lena, 2010].)

More recent studies of people with damaged frontal lobes have revealed similar impairments. Not only may they become less inhibited (without the frontal lobe brakes on their impulses), but their moral judgments may seem unrestrained by normal emotions. Would you advocate pushing someone in front of a runaway boxcar to save five others? Most people do not, but those with damage to a brain area behind the eyes often do (Koenigs et al., 2007). With their frontal lobes ruptured, people's moral compass seems to disconnect from their behavior.

Figure 12.8

A blast from the past
(a) Gage's skull was kept as a medical record. Using measurements and modern neuroimaging techniques, researchers have reconstructed the probable path of the rod through Gage's brain (Damasio et al., 1994). (b) This recently discovered photo shows Gage after his accident. The image has been reversed to show the features correctly. (Early photos, such as this one, were actually mirror images.)

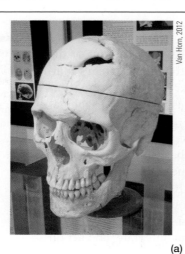
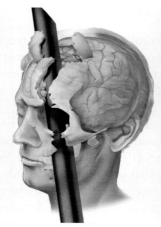

(a)   (b)

Association areas also perform other mental functions. In the parietal lobes, parts of which were large and unusually shaped in Einstein's normal-weight brain, they enable mathematical and spatial reasoning (Witelson et al., 1999). In patients undergoing brain surgery, stimulation of one parietal lobe area produced a feeling of wanting to move an upper limb, the lips, or the tongue (but without any actual movement). With increased stimulation, patients falsely believed they actually had moved. Curiously, when surgeons stimulated a different association area near the motor cortex in the frontal lobes, the patients did move but had no awareness of doing so (Desmurget et al., 2009). These head-scratching findings suggest that our perception of moving flows not from the movement itself, but rather from our intention and the results we expected.

Yet another association area, on the underside of the right temporal lobe, enables us to recognize faces. If a stroke or head injury destroyed this area of your brain, you would still be able to describe facial features and to recognize someone's gender and approximate age, yet be strangely unable to identify the person as, say, Lady Gaga, or even your grandmother.

Nevertheless, we should be wary of using pictures of brain "hot spots" to create a new phrenology that locates complex functions in precise brain areas (Uttal, 2001). Complex mental functions don't reside in any one place. There is no one spot in a rat's small association cortex that, when damaged, will obliterate its ability to learn or remember a maze.

Similarly, the acquisition, development, and use of language depends on both specialized neural networks and their integration. Nineteenth-century research by French physician Paul Broca and German investigator Carl Wernicke led to the discovery of specialized language brain areas. Damage to *Broca's area* disrupts speaking, while damage to *Wernicke's area* disrupts understanding. Today's neuroscience has shown that language functions are distributed across other brain areas as well.

Memory, language, and attention result from the synchronized activity among distinct brain areas (Knight, 2007). Ditto for religious experience. Reports of more than 40 distinct brain regions becoming active in different religious states, such as praying and meditating, indicate that there is no simple "God spot" (Fingelkurts & Fingelkurts, 2009). The big lesson: *Our mental experiences arise from coordinated brain activity.*

The Brain's Plasticity

 To what extent can a damaged brain reorganize itself, and what is neurogenesis?

Our brains are sculpted not only by our genes but also by our experiences. MRI scans show that well-practiced pianists have a larger-than-usual auditory cortex area that encodes piano sounds (Bavelier et al., 2000; Pantev et al., 1998). In Unit IX, we'll focus more on how

FYI

For information on how distinct neural networks in your brain coordinate to enable language, see Module 36.

experience molds the brain. For now, let's turn to another aspect of the brain's **plasticity:** its ability to modify itself after damage.

Some of the effects of brain damage described earlier can be traced to two hard facts: (1) Severed neurons, unlike cut skin, usually do not regenerate. (If your spinal cord were severed, you would probably be permanently paralyzed.) And (2) some brain functions seem preassigned to specific areas. One newborn who suffered damage to temporal lobe facial recognition areas later remained unable to recognize faces (Farah et al., 2000). But there is good news: Some of the brain's neural tissue can *reorganize* in response to damage. Under the surface of our awareness, the brain is constantly changing, building new pathways as it adjusts to little mishaps and new experiences.

Plasticity may also occur after serious damage, especially in young children (Kolb, 1989; see also **FIGURE 12.9**). Constraint-induced therapy aims to rewire brains and improve the dexterity of a brain-damaged child or even an adult stroke victim (Taub, 2004). By restraining a fully functioning limb, therapists force patients to use the "bad" hand or leg, gradually reprogramming the brain. One stroke victim, a surgeon in his fifties, was put to work cleaning tables, with his good arm and hand restrained. Slowly, the bad arm recovered its skills. As damaged-brain functions migrated to other brain regions, he gradually learned to write again and even to play tennis (Doidge, 2007).

The brain's plasticity is good news for those who are blind or deaf. Blindness or deafness makes unused brain areas available for other uses (Amedi et al., 2005). If a blind person uses one finger to read Braille, the brain area dedicated to that finger expands as the sense of touch invades the visual cortex that normally helps people see (Barinaga, 1992a; Sadato et al., 1996). Plasticity also helps explain why some studies find that deaf people have enhanced peripheral vision (Bosworth & Dobkins, 1999). In those people whose native language is sign, the temporal lobe area normally dedicated to hearing waits in vain for stimulation. Finally, it looks for other signals to process, such as those from the visual system.

Similar reassignment may occur when disease or damage frees up other brain areas normally dedicated to specific functions. If a slow-growing left hemisphere tumor disrupts language (which resides mostly in the left hemisphere), the right hemisphere may compensate (Thiel et al., 2006). If a finger is amputated, the somatosensory cortex that received its input will begin to receive input from the adjacent fingers, which then become more sensitive (Fox, 1984).

Although the brain often attempts self-repair by reorganizing existing tissue, it sometimes attempts to mend itself by producing new brain cells. This process, known as

plasticity the brain's ability to change, especially during childhood, by reorganizing after damage or by building new pathways based on experience.

Figure 12.9

Brain plasticity Although the brains of young children show the greatest ability to reorganize and adapt to damage, adult brains also have some capacity for self-repair. Former Arizona Congresswoman Gabrielle Giffords lost her ability to speak after suffering a left-hemisphere gunshot wound. Her medical care included music therapy, where she worked on forming words to familiar songs such as "Happy Birthday." Giffords has since partly recovered her speaking ability. Two years after the shooting, she was able to speak as a surprise witness at a 2013 U.S. Senate hearing on gun legislation.

MIKE THEILER/UPI/ Newscom

neurogenesis the formation of new neurons.

neurogenesis, has been found in adult mice, birds, monkeys, and humans (Jessberger et al., 2008). These baby neurons originate deep in the brain and may then migrate elsewhere and form connections with neighboring neurons (Aimone et al., 2010; Gould, 2007).

Master stem cells that can develop into any type of brain cell have also been discovered in the human embryo. If mass-produced in a lab and injected into a damaged brain, might neural stem cells turn themselves into replacements for lost brain cells? Might we someday be able to rebuild damaged brains, much as we reseed damaged lawns? Might new drugs spur the production of new nerve cells? Stay tuned. Today's biotech companies are hard at work on such possibilities. In the meantime, we can all benefit from other natural promoters of neurogenesis, such as exercise, sleep, and nonstressful but stimulating environments (Iso et al., 2007; Pereira et al., 2007; Stranahan et al., 2006).

Before You Move On

▶ **ASK YOURSELF**

Has what you have learned about how our brains enable our minds affected your view of human nature?

▶ **TEST YOURSELF**

Try moving your right hand in a circular motion, as if polishing a table. Then start your right foot doing the same motion, synchronized with your hand. Now reverse the right foot's motion, but not the hand's. Finally, try moving the *left* foot opposite to the right hand.

1. Why is reversing the right foot's motion so hard?
2. Why is it easier to move the left foot opposite to the right hand?

Answers to the Test Yourself questions can be found in Appendix E at the end of the book.

Module 12 Review

 What are the functions of the various cerebral cortex regions?

- The *cerebral cortex* has two hemispheres, and each hemisphere has four lobes: the *frontal, parietal, occipital,* and *temporal.* Each lobe performs many functions and interacts with other areas of the cortex.

- *Glial cells* support, nourish, and protect neurons and may also play a role in learning and thinking.

- The *motor cortex,* at the rear of the frontal lobes, controls voluntary movements.

- The *somatosensory cortex,* at the front of the parietal lobes, registers and processes body touch and movement sensations.

- Body parts requiring precise control or those that are especially sensitive occupy the greatest amount of space in the motor cortex and somatosensory cortex, respectively.

- Most of the brain's cortex—the major portion of each of the four lobes—is devoted to uncommitted *association areas,* which integrate information involved in learning, remembering, thinking, and other higher-level functions.

- Our mental experiences arise from coordinated brain activity.

12-2 **To what extent can a damaged brain reorganize itself, and what is neurogenesis?**

- If one hemisphere is damaged early in life, the other will pick up many of its functions by reorganizing or building new pathways. This *plasticity* diminishes later in life.

- The brain sometimes mends itself by forming new neurons, a process known as *neurogenesis.*

Multiple-Choice Questions

1. Damage to which of the following could interfere with the ability to plan for the future?
   a. Frontal lobe
   b. Temporal lobe
   c. Parietal lobe
   d. Occipital lobe
   e. Somatosensory cortex

2. In general, damage to _____ disrupts speaking, while damage to _____ disrupts understanding of language.
   a. the frontal lobe; the occipital lobe
   b. the temporal lobe; the frontal lobe
   c. the occipital lobe; the temporal lobe
   d. Wernicke's area; Broca's area
   e. Broca's area; Wernicke's area

3. Stimulation at a point on which of the following may cause a person to report being touched on the knee?
   a. Motor cortex
   b. Cerebellum
   c. Somatosensory cortex
   d. Temporal lobe
   e. Thalamus

4. George can move his hand to sign a document because the _____, located in the _____ lobe of the brain, allows him to activate the proper muscles.
   a. somatosensory cortex; temporal
   b. somatosensory cortex; parietal
   c. motor cortex; parietal
   d. somatosensory cortex; frontal
   e. motor cortex; frontal

5. The most noticeable difference between human brains and other mammalian brains is the size of the
   a. association areas.
   b. frontal lobe.
   c. glial cells.
   d. reticular activating system.
   e. visual cortex.

6. Cognitive neural prosthetics are placed in the brain to help control parts of the
   a. motor cortex.
   b. auditory cortex.
   c. somatosensory cortex.
   d. visual cortex.
   e. parietal lobe.

Practice FRQs

1. Doctors sometimes have to remove a portion of the brain to control life-threatening seizures. Describe what the results of the removal of a portion of the motor cortex would be and explain how this procedure might be affected by brain plasticity.

Answer

1 point: Removing part of the motor cortex will result in paralysis in the parts of the body associated with the removed tissue.

1 point: Because of brain plasticity, the person's brain may be able to change and reorganize new pathways based on experience. This is more likely if the person is a child.

2. Anthony attends a high school band concert. First, identify and explain which two lobes of his brain are most important for watching and listening to the concert. Second, explain which lobe of the brain is most responsible for analyzing the music and finding personal meaning.

(3 points)

Module 13

Brain Hemisphere Organization and the Biology of Consciousness

Monica Murphy/Getty Images

Module Learning Objectives

 13-1 Explain how split-brain research helps us understand the functions of our two brain hemispheres.

 13-2 Explain what is meant by "dual processing," as revealed by today's cognitive neuroscience.

Our Divided Brain

 13-1 What do split brains reveal about the functions of our two brain hemispheres?

Our brain's look-alike left and right hemispheres serve differing functions. This *lateralization* is apparent after brain damage. Research collected over more than a century has shown that accidents, strokes, and tumors in the left hemisphere can impair reading, writing, speaking, arithmetic reasoning, and understanding. Similar lesions in the right hemisphere have effects that are less visibly dramatic.

Does this mean that the right hemisphere is just along for the ride—a silent, "subordinate" or "minor" hemisphere? Many believed this was the case until 1960, when researchers found that the "minor" right hemisphere was not so limited after all. The story of this discovery is a fascinating episode in psychology's history.

Splitting the Brain

In 1961, two Los Angeles neurosurgeons, Philip Vogel and Joseph Bogen, speculated that major epileptic seizures were caused by an amplification of abnormal brain activity bouncing back and forth between the two cerebral hemispheres. If so, they wondered, could they put an end to this biological tennis game by severing the **corpus callosum** (see **FIGURE 13.1**)? This wide band of axon fibers connects the two hemispheres and carries messages between them. Vogel and Bogen knew that psychologists Roger Sperry, Ronald Myers, and Michael Gazzaniga had divided the brains of cats and monkeys in this manner, with no serious ill effects.

So the surgeons operated. The result? The seizures all but disappeared. The patients with these **split brains** were surprisingly normal, their personality and intellect hardly affected. Waking from surgery, one even joked that he had a "splitting headache" (Gazzaniga, 1967). By sharing their experiences, these patients have greatly expanded our understanding of interactions between the intact brain's two hemispheres.

corpus callosum [KOR-pus kah-LOW-sum] the large band of neural fibers connecting the two brain hemispheres and carrying messages between them.

split brain a condition resulting from surgery that isolates the brain's two hemispheres by cutting the fibers (mainly those of the corpus callosum) connecting them.

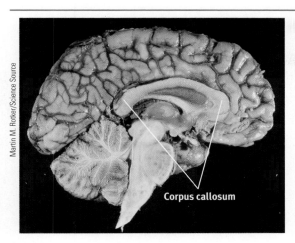

Figure 13.1

The corpus callosum This large band of neural fibers connects the two brain hemispheres. To photograph this half brain, a surgeon separated the hemispheres by cutting through the corpus callosum and lower brain regions.

Martin M. Rotker/Science Source

Corpus callosum

To appreciate these findings, we need to focus for a minute on the peculiar nature of our visual wiring. As **FIGURE 13.2** illustrates, information from the left half of your field of vision goes to your right hemisphere, and information from the right half of your visual field goes to your left hemisphere, which usually controls speech. (Note, however, that each eye receives sensory information from both the right and left visual fields.) Data received by either hemisphere are quickly transmitted to the other across the corpus callosum. In a person with a severed corpus callosum, this information-sharing does not take place.

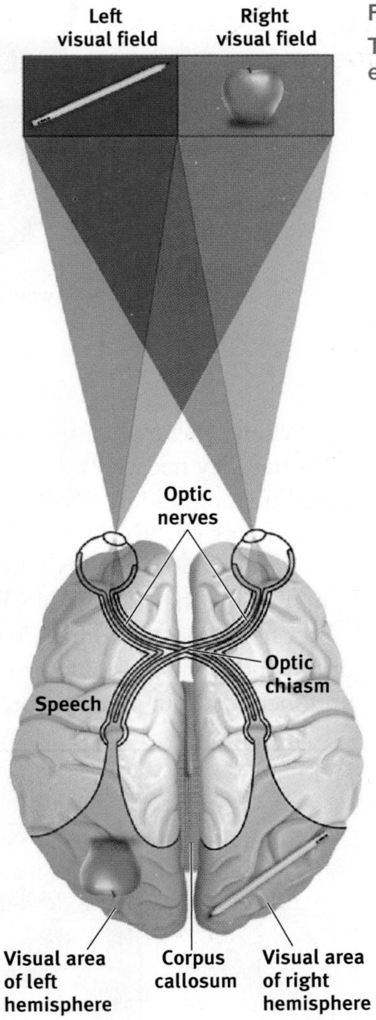

Knowing these facts, Sperry and Gazzaniga could send information to a patient's left or right hemisphere. As the person stared at a spot, they flashed a stimulus to its right or left. They could do this with you, too, but in your intact brain, the hemisphere receiving the information would instantly pass the news to the other side. Because the split-brain surgery had cut the communication lines between the hemispheres, the researchers could, with these patients, quiz each hemisphere separately.

In an early experiment, Gazzaniga (1967) asked these people to stare at a dot as he flashed HE·ART on a screen (**FIGURE 13.3** on the next page). Thus, HE appeared in their left visual field (which transmits to the right hemisphere) and ART in the right field (which transmits to the left hemisphere). When he then asked them to *say* what they had seen, the patients reported that they had seen ART. But when asked to *point* to the word they had seen, they were startled when their left hand (controlled by the right hemisphere) pointed to HE. Given an opportunity to express itself, each hemisphere reported what it had seen. The right hemisphere (controlling the left hand) intuitively knew what it could not verbally report.

Figure 13.2

The information highway from eye to brain

Left visual field

Right visual field

Optic nerves

Optic chiasm

Speech

Visual area of left hemisphere

Corpus callosum

Visual area of right hemisphere

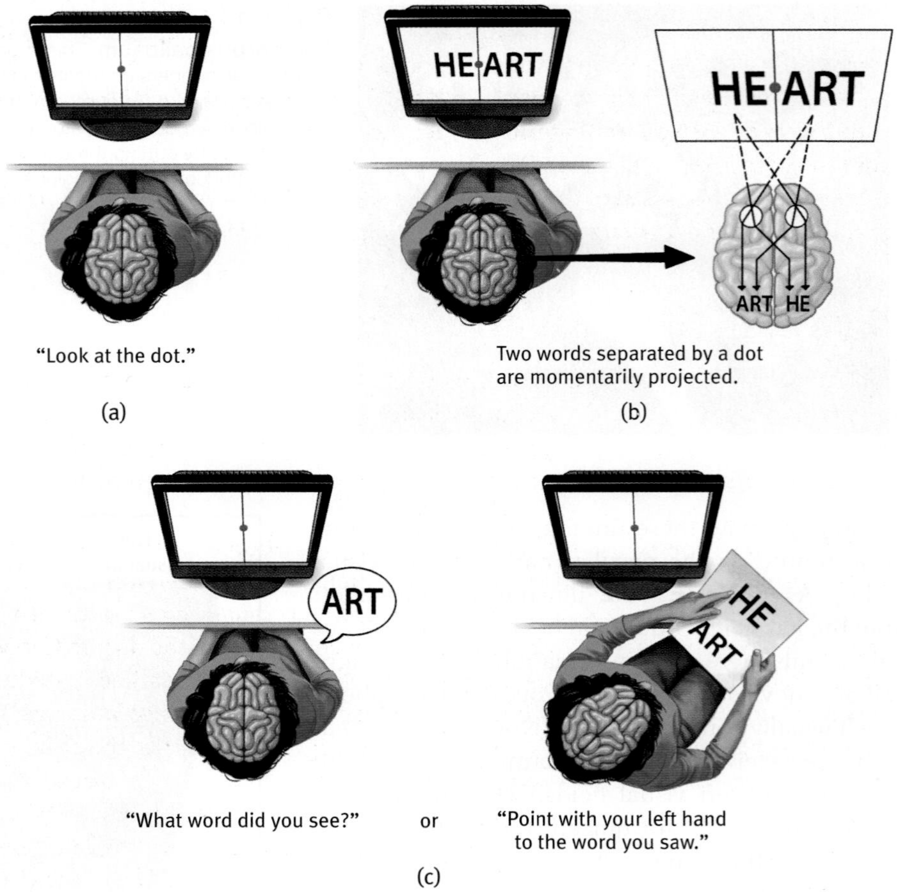

Figure 13.3

Testing the divided brain When an experimenter flashes the word HEART across the visual field, a woman with a split brain reports seeing the portion of the word transmitted to her left hemisphere. However, if asked to indicate with her left hand what she saw, she points to the portion of the word transmitted to her right hemisphere. (From Gazzaniga, 1983.)

"Look at the dot."

(a)

HE·ART

Two words separated by a dot are momentarily projected.

(b)

ART

"What word did you see?" or

HE
ART

"Point with your left hand to the word you saw."

(c)

When a picture of a spoon was flashed to their right hemisphere, the patients could not *say* what they had viewed. But when asked to *identify* what they had viewed by feeling an assortment of hidden objects with their left hand, they readily selected the spoon. If the experimenter said, "Correct!" the patient might reply, "What? Correct? How could I possibly pick out the correct object when I don't know what I saw?" It is, of course, the left hemisphere doing the talking here, bewildered by what the nonverbal right hemisphere knows.

A few people who have had split-brain surgery have been for a time bothered by the unruly independence of their left hand, which might unbutton a shirt while the right hand buttoned it, or put grocery store items back on the shelf after the right hand put them in the cart. It was as if each hemisphere was thinking "I've half a mind to wear my green (blue) shirt today." Indeed, said Sperry (1964), split-brain surgery leaves people "with two separate minds." With a split brain, both hemispheres can comprehend and follow an instruction to copy—*simultaneously*—different figures with the left and right hands (Franz et al., 2000; see also **FIGURE 13.4**). (Reading these reports, I fantasize a patient enjoying a solitary game of "rock, paper, scissors"—left versus right hand.)

"Do not let your left hand know what your right hand is doing."
-MATTHEW 6:3

Figure 13.4

Try this! A person who has undergone split-brain surgery can simultaneously draw two different shapes.

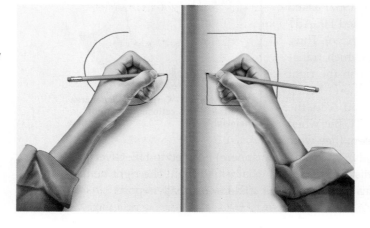

When the "two minds" are at odds, the left hemisphere does mental gymnastics to rationalize reactions it does not understand. If a patient follows an order sent to the right hemisphere ("Walk"), a strange thing happens. Unaware of the order, the left hemisphere doesn't know why the patient begins walking. Yet, when asked why, the patient doesn't say "I don't know." Instead, the interpretive left hemisphere improvises—"I'm going into the house to get a Coke." Gazzaniga (1988), who considers these patients "the most fascinating people on earth," concluded that the conscious left hemisphere is an "interpreter" or press agent that instantly constructs theories to explain our behavior.

Right-Left Differences in the Intact Brain

So, what about the 99.99+ percent of us with undivided brains? Does each of *our* hemispheres also perform distinct functions? Several different types of studies indicate they do. When a person performs a *perceptual* task, for example, brain waves, bloodflow, and glucose consumption reveal increased activity in the *right* hemisphere. When the person speaks or calculates, activity increases in the *left* hemisphere.

A dramatic demonstration of hemispheric specialization happens before some types of brain surgery. To locate the patient's language centers, the surgeon injects a sedative into the neck artery feeding blood to the left hemisphere, which usually controls speech. Before the injection, the patient is lying down, arms in the air, chatting with the doctor. Can you predict what probably happens when the drug puts the left hemisphere to sleep? Within seconds, the person's right arm falls limp. If the left hemisphere is controlling language, the patient will be speechless until the drug wears off. If the drug is injected into the artery to the right hemisphere, the *left* arm will fall limp, but the person will still be able to speak.

To the brain, language is language, whether spoken or signed. Just as hearing people usually use the left hemisphere to process speech, deaf people use the left hemisphere to process sign language (Corina et al., 1992; Hickok et al., 2001). Thus, a left-hemisphere stroke disrupts a deaf person's signing, much as it would disrupt a hearing person's speaking. The same brain area is involved in both (Corina, 1998). (For more on how the brain enables language, see Module 36.)

Although the left hemisphere is adept at making quick, literal interpretations of language, the right hemisphere

- *excels in making inferences* (Beeman & Chiarello, 1998; Bowden & Beeman, 1998; Mason & Just, 2004). Primed with the flashed word *foot,* the left hemisphere will be especially quick to recognize the closely associated word *heel.* But if primed with *foot, cry,* and *glass,* the right hemisphere will more quickly recognize another word distantly related to all three *(cut).* And if given an insight-like problem—"What word goes with *boot, summer,* and *ground?*"—the right hemisphere more quickly than the left recognizes the solution: *camp.* As one patient explained after a right-hemisphere stroke, "I understand words, but I'm missing the subtleties."

- *helps us modulate our speech* to make meaning clear—as when we ask "What's that in the road ahead?" instead of "What's that in the road, a head?" (Heller, 1990).

- *helps orchestrate our sense of self.* People who suffer partial paralysis will sometimes obstinately deny their impairment—strangely claiming they can move a paralyzed limb—if the damage is to the right hemisphere (Berti et al., 2005).

Simply looking at the two hemispheres, so alike to the naked eye, who would suppose they contribute uniquely to the harmony of the whole? Yet a variety of observations—of people with split brains, of people with normal brains, and even of other species' brains—converge beautifully, leaving little doubt that we have unified brains with specialized parts (Hopkins & Cantalupo, 2008; MacNeilage et al., 2009; and see Close-up: Handedness on the next page).

AP® Exam Tip

Notice that David Myers never refers to your left brain or your right brain. You have two brain hemispheres, each with its own responsibilities, *but you only have one brain.* It's very misleading when the media refers to the left brain and the right brain, and this happens frequently.

Close-up

Handedness

Nearly 90 percent of us are primarily right-handed (Leask & Beaton, 2007; Medland et al., 2004; Peters et al., 2006). Some 10 percent of us (somewhat more among males, somewhat less among females) are left-handed. (A few people write with their right hand and throw a ball with their left, or vice versa.) Almost all right-handers (96 percent) process speech primarily in the left hemisphere, which tends to be the slightly larger hemisphere (Hopkins, 2006). Left-handers are more diverse. Seven in ten process speech in the left hemisphere, as right-handers do. The rest either process language in the right hemisphere or use both hemispheres.

IS HANDEDNESS INHERITED?

Judging from prehistoric human cave drawings, tools, and hand and arm bones, this veer to the right occurred long ago (Corballis, 1989; MacNeilage et al., 2009). Right-handedness prevails in all human cultures, and even in monkeys and apes. Moreover, it appears prior to culture's impact: More than 9 in 10 fetuses suck the right hand's thumb (Hepper et al., 1990, 2004). Twin studies indicate only a small genetic influence on individual handedness (Vuoksimaa et al., 2009). But the universal prevalence of right-handers in humans and other primates suggests that either genes or some prenatal factors influence handedness.

> Most people also kick with their right foot, look through a microscope with their right eye, and (had you noticed?) kiss the right way—with their head tilted right (Güntürkün, 2003).

SO, IS IT ALL RIGHT TO BE LEFT-HANDED?

Judging by our everyday conversation, left-handedness is not all right. To be "coming out of left field" is hardly better than to be "gauche" (derived from the French word for "left"). On the other hand, right-handedness is "right on," which any "righteous," "right-hand man" "in his right mind" usually is.

Left-handers are more numerous than usual among those with reading disabilities, allergies, and migraine headaches (Geschwind & Behan, 1984). But in Iran, where students report which hand they write with when taking the university

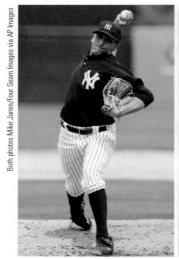

The rarest of baseball players: an ambidextrous pitcher
Using a glove with two thumbs, Minor League New York Yankees pitcher Pat Venditte, shown here in 2012, pitches to right-handed batters with his right hand, then switches to face left-handed batters with his left hand. During his college career at Creighton University, after one switch-hitter switched sides of the plate, Venditte switched pitching arms, which triggered the batter to switch again, and so on. The umpires ultimately ended the comedy routine by applying a little-known rule: A pitcher must declare which arm he will use before throwing his first pitch to a batter (Schwarz, 2007).

entrance exam, lefties have outperformed righties in all subjects (Noroozian et al., 2003). Left-handedness is also more common among musicians, mathematicians, professional baseball and cricket players, architects, and artists, including such luminaries as Michelangelo, Leonardo da Vinci, and Picasso.[1] Although left-handers must tolerate elbow jostling at the dinner table, right-handed desks, and awkward scissors, the pros and cons of being a lefty seem roughly equal.

---

[1] Strategic factors explain the higher-than-normal percentage of lefties in sports. For example, it helps a soccer team to have left-footed players on the left side of the field (Wood & Aggleton, 1989). In golf, however, no left-hander won the Masters tournament until Canadian Mike Weir did so in 2003.

The Biology of Consciousness

13-2 What is the "dual processing" being revealed by today's cognitive neuroscience?

consciousness our awareness of ourselves and our environment.

Today's science explores the biology of **consciousness.** Evolutionary psychologists speculate that consciousness must offer a reproductive advantage (Barash, 2006). Consciousness helps us act in our long-term interests (by considering consequences) rather than merely seeking short-term pleasure and avoiding pain. Consciousness also promotes our survival by anticipating how we seem to others and helping us read their minds: "He looks really angry! I'd better run!"

Such explanations still leave us with the "hard problem": How do brain cells jabbering to one another create our awareness of the taste of a taco, the idea of infinity, the feeling of fright? Today's scientists are pursuing answers.

Cognitive Neuroscience

Scientists assume, in the words of neuroscientist Marvin Minsky (1986, p. 287), that "the mind is what the brain does." We just don't know *how* it does it. Even with all the world's chemicals, computer chips, and energy, we still don't have a clue *how* to make a conscious robot. Yet today's **cognitive neuroscience**—the interdisciplinary study of the brain activity linked with our mental processes—is taking the first small step by relating specific brain states to conscious experiences.

A stunning demonstration of consciousness appeared in brain scans of a noncommunicative patient—a 23-year-old woman who had been in a car accident and showed no outward signs of conscious awareness (Owen et al., 2006). When researchers asked her to *imagine* playing tennis, fMRI scans revealed brain activity in a brain area that normally controls arm and leg movements (**FIGURE 13.5**). Even in a motionless body, the researchers concluded, the brain—and the mind—may still be active. A follow-up study of 22 other "vegetative" patients revealed 3 more who also showed meaningful brain responses to questions (Monti et al., 2010).

Many cognitive neuroscientists are exploring and mapping the conscious functions of the cortex. Based on your cortical activation patterns, they can now, in limited ways, read your mind (Bor, 2010). They can, for example, tell which of 10 similar objects (hammer, drill, and so forth) you are viewing (Shinkareva et al., 2008).

Despite such advances, much disagreement remains. One view sees conscious experiences as produced by the synchronized activity across the brain (Gaillard et al., 2009; Koch & Greenfield, 2007; Schurger et al., 2010). If a stimulus activates enough brainwide coordinated neural activity—with strong signals in one brain area triggering activity elsewhere—it crosses a threshold for consciousness. A weaker stimulus—perhaps a word flashed too briefly to consciously perceive—may trigger localized visual cortex activity that quickly dies out. A stronger stimulus will engage other brain areas, such as those involved with language, attention, and memory. Such reverberating activity (detected by brain scans) is a telltale sign of conscious awareness. How the synchronized activity produces awareness—how matter makes mind—remains a mystery.

> **cognitive neuroscience** the interdisciplinary study of the brain activity linked with cognition (including perception, thinking, memory, and language).

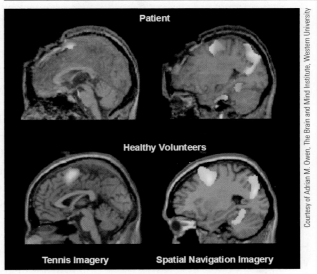

Figure 13.5

Evidence of awareness? When asked to imagine playing tennis or navigating through her home, a vegetative patient's brain (top) exhibited activity similar to a healthy person's brain (bottom). Researchers wonder if such fMRI scans might enable a "conversation" with some unresponsive patients, by instructing them, for example, to answer *yes* to a question by imagining playing tennis and *no* by imagining walking around their home.

Dual Processing: The Two-Track Mind

Many cognitive neuroscience discoveries tell us of a particular brain region (such as the visual cortex mentioned above) that becomes active with a particular conscious experience. Such findings strike many people as interesting but not mind-blowing. (If everything psychological is simultaneously biological, then our ideas, emotions, and spirituality must all, somehow, be embodied.) What *is* mind-blowing to many of us is the growing evidence that we have, so to speak, two minds, each supported by its own neural equipment.

At any moment, you and I are aware of little more than what's on the screen of our consciousness. But beneath the surface, unconscious information processing occurs simultaneously on many parallel tracks. When we look at a bird flying, we are consciously aware of the result of our cognitive processing ("It's a hummingbird!") but not of our subprocessing of the bird's color, form, movement, and distance. One of the grand ideas of recent cognitive neuroscience is that much of our brain work occurs off stage, out of sight. Perception, memory, thinking, language, and attitudes all operate on two levels—a conscious, deliberate

> **AP® Exam Tip**
>
> Dual processing is another one of those big ideas that shows up in several units. Pay attention!

dual processing the principle that information is often simultaneously processed on separate conscious and unconscious tracks.

"high road" and an unconscious, automatic "low road." Today's researchers call this **dual processing.** We know more than we know we know.

Sometimes science confirms widely held beliefs. Other times, as this next story illustrates, science is stranger than science fiction.

During my sojourns at Scotland's University of St. Andrews, I came to know cognitive neuroscientists David Milner and Melvyn Goodale (2008). When overcome by carbon monoxide, a local woman, whom they call D. F., suffered brain damage that left her unable to recognize and discriminate objects visually. Consciously she could see nothing. Yet she exhibited *blindsight*—she would act as if she could see. Asked to slip a postcard into a vertical or horizontal mail slot, she could do so without error. Although unable to report the width of a block in front of her, she could grasp it with just the right finger-thumb distance. If you were to experience temporary blindness (with magnetic pulses to your brain's primary visual cortex area) this, too, would create blindsight—as you correctly guess the color or orientation of an object that you cannot consciously see (Boyer et al., 2005).

How could this be? Don't we have one visual system? Goodale and Milner knew from animal research that the eye sends information simultaneously to different brain areas, which support different tasks (Weiskrantz, 2009, 2010). Sure enough, a scan of D. F.'s brain activity revealed normal activity in the area concerned with reaching for, grasping, and navigating objects, but damage in the area concerned with consciously recognizing objects. (See another example in **FIGURE 13.6.**)

So, would the reverse damage lead to the opposite symptoms? Indeed, there are a few such patients—who can see and recognize objects but have difficulty pointing toward or grasping them.

How strangely intricate is this thing we call vision, conclude Goodale and Milner in their aptly titled book, *Sight Unseen*. We may think of our vision as one system controlling our visually guided actions, but it is actually a dual-processing system. A *visual perception track* enables us "to think about the world"—to recognize things and to plan future actions. A *visual action track* guides our moment-to-moment movements.

On rare occasions, the two conflict. Shown the *hollow face illusion,* people will mistakenly perceive the inside of a mask as a protruding face (**FIGURE 13.7**). Yet they will unhesitatingly and accurately reach into the inverted mask to flick off a buglike target stuck on the face (Króliczak et al., 2006). What their conscious mind doesn't know, their hand does.

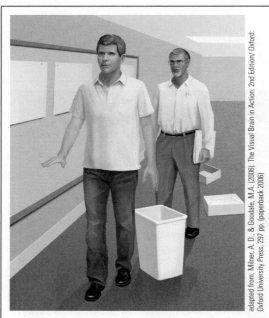

adapted from: Milner, A. D., & Goodale, M.A. (2006). The Visual Brain in Action: 2nd Edition/ Oxford: Oxford University Press, 297 pp. (paperback 2006)

Figure 13.6

When the blind can "see" In a compelling demonstration of blindsight and the two-track mind, a researcher trails a blindsight patient down a cluttered hallway. Although told the hallway was empty, the patient meandered around all the obstacles without any awareness of them.

Figure 13.7

The hollow face illusion We tend to see an illusory protruding face even on an inverted mask (right). Yet research participants will accurately reach for a speck on the face inside the inverted mask, suggesting that our unconscious mind seems to know the truth of the illusion.

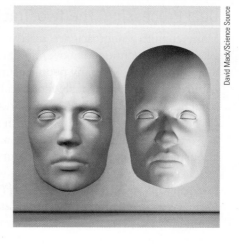

David Mack/Science Source

Another patient, who lost all his left visual cortex—leaving him blind to objects presented on the right side of his field of vision—can nevertheless sense the emotion expressed in faces he does not consciously perceive (De Gelder, 2010). The same is true of normally sighted people whose visual cortex has been disabled with magnetic stimulation. This suggests that brain areas below the cortex are processing emotion-related information.

People often have trouble accepting that much of our everyday thinking, feeling, and acting operates outside our conscious awareness (Bargh & Chartrand, 1999). We are understandably biased to believe that our intentions and deliberate choices rule our lives. But consciousness, though enabling us to exert voluntary control and to communicate our mental states to others, is but the tip of the information-processing iceberg. Being intensely focused on an activity (such as reading this module, I'd love to think) increases your total brain activity no more than 5 percent above its baseline rate. And even when you rest, "hubs of dark energy" are whirling inside your head (Raichle, 2010).

Figure 13.8

Is the brain ahead of the mind? In this study, volunteers watched a computer clock sweep through a full revolution every 2.56 seconds. They noted the time at which they decided to move their wrist. About one-third of a second before that decision, their brain-wave activity jumped, indicating a *readiness potential* to move. Watching a slow-motion replay, the researchers were able to predict when a person was about to decide to move (following which, the wrist did move) (Libet, 1985, 2004). Other researchers, however, question the clock measurement procedure (Miller et al., 2011).

Experiments show that when you move your wrist at will, you consciously experience the decision to move it about 0.2 seconds before the actual movement (Libet, 1985, 2004). No surprise there. But your brain waves jump about 0.35 seconds before you consciously perceive your decision to move (**FIGURE 13.8**)! This readiness potential has enabled researchers (using fMRI brain scans) to predict—with 60 percent accuracy and up to 7 seconds ahead—participants' decisions to press a button with their left or right finger (Soon et al., 2008). The startling conclusion: Consciousness sometimes arrives late to the decision-making party.

Running on automatic pilot allows our consciousness—our mind's CEO—to monitor the whole system and deal with new challenges, while neural assistants automatically take care of routine business. Walking the familiar path to your next class, your feet do the work while your mind rehearses the presentation you're about to give. A skilled tennis player's brain and body respond automatically to an oncoming serve before becoming consciously aware of the ball's trajectory (which takes about three-tenths of a second). Ditto for other skilled athletes, for whom action precedes awareness. *The bottom line:* In everyday life, we mostly function like an automatic point-and-shoot camera, but with a manual (conscious) override.

Our unconscious parallel processing is faster than sequential conscious processing, but both are essential. Sequential processing is skilled at solving new problems, which require our focused attention. Try this: If you are right-handed, you can move your right foot in a smooth counterclockwise circle, and you can write the number 3 repeatedly with your right hand—but probably not at the same time. (Try something equally difficult: Tap a steady beat three times with your left hand while tapping four times with your right hand.) Both tasks require conscious attention, which can be in only one place at a time. If time is nature's way of keeping everything from happening at once, then consciousness is nature's way of keeping us from thinking and doing everything at once.

Before You Move On

▶ **ASK YOURSELF**

What are some examples of things you do on "automatic pilot"? What behaviors require your conscious attention?

▶ **TEST YOURSELF**

What are the mind's two tracks, and what is "dual processing"?

Answers to the Test Yourself questions can be found in Appendix E at the end of the book.

Module 13 Review

 13-1 What do split brains reveal about the functions of our two brain hemispheres?

- *Split-brain* research (experiments on people with a severed *corpus callosum*) has confirmed that in most people, the left hemisphere is the more verbal, and that the right hemisphere excels in visual perception and the recognition of emotion.

- Studies of healthy people with intact brains confirm that each hemisphere makes unique contributions to the integrated functioning of the brain.

13-2 What is the "dual processing" being revealed by today's cognitive neuroscience?

- *Cognitive neuroscientists* and others studying the brain mechanisms underlying consciousness and cognition have discovered that the mind processes information on two separate tracks, one operating at an explicit, conscious level and the other at an implicit, unconscious level. This *dual processing* affects our perception, memory, attitudes, and other cognitions.

Multiple-Choice Questions

1. A split-brain patient has a picture of a dog flashed to his right hemisphere and a cat to his left hemisphere. He will be able to identify the

    a. cat using his right hand.
    b. dog using his right hand.
    c. dog using either hand.
    d. cat using either hand.
    e. cat using his left hand.

2. You are aware that a dog is viciously barking at you, but you are not aware of the type of dog. Later, you are able to describe the type and color of the dog. This ability to process information without conscious awareness best exemplifies which of the following?

    a. Split brain
    b. Blindsight
    c. Consciousness
    d. Cognitive neuroscience
    e. Dual processing

3. Which of the following is most likely to be a function of the left hemisphere?

    a. Speech
    b. Evaluating perceptual tasks
    c. Making inferences
    d. Identifying emotion in other people's faces
    e. Identifying one's sense of self

4. The dual-processing model refers to which of the following ideas?

    a. The right and left hemispheres of the brain both process incoming messages.
    b. Incoming information is processed by both conscious and unconscious tracks.
    c. Each lobe of the brain processes incoming information.
    d. The brain first processes emotional information and then processes analytical information.
    e. The thalamus and hypothalamus work together to analyze incoming sensory information.

Practice FRQs

1. Brain lateralization means that each hemisphere has its own functions. Give an example of both a left hemisphere and a right hemisphere function. Then explain how the two hemispheres communicate with one another.

Answer

1 point: Left hemisphere functions include language, math, and logic.

1 point: Right hemisphere functions include spatial relationships, facial recognition, and patterns.

1 point: The corpus callosum carries information back and forth between the two hemispheres.

2. Because Jerry suffered severe seizures, his neurosurgeon decided to "split his brain." What does this mean? How might a psychologist use people who have had split-brain surgery to determine the location of speech control?

(3 points)

Module 14

Behavior Genetics: Predicting Individual Differences

Module Learning Objectives

14-1 Define *genes,* and describe how behavior geneticists explain our individual differences.

14-2 Identify the potential uses of molecular genetics research.

14-3 Explain what is meant by heritability, and discuss how it relates to individuals and groups.

14-4 Discuss the interaction of heredity and environment.

Behind the story of our human brain—surely the most awesome thing on Earth—is the essence of our universal human attributes and our individual traits. What makes you *you?* In important ways, we are each unique. We look different. We sound different. We have varying personalities, interests, and cultural and family backgrounds.

We are also the leaves of one tree. Our human family shares not only a common biological heritage—cut us and we bleed—but also common behavioral tendencies. Our shared brain architecture predisposes us to sense the world, develop language, and feel hunger through identical mechanisms. Whether we live in the Arctic or the tropics, we prefer sweet tastes to sour. We divide the color spectrum into similar colors. And we feel drawn to behaviors that produce and protect offspring.

Our kinship appears in our social behaviors as well. Whether named Wong, Nkomo, Smith, or Gonzales, we start fearing strangers at about eight months, and as adults we prefer the company of those with attitudes and attributes similar to our own. Coming from different parts of the globe, we know how to read one another's smiles and frowns. As members of one species, we affiliate, conform, return favors, punish offenses, organize hierarchies of status, and grieve a child's death. A visitor from outer space could drop in anywhere and find humans dancing and feasting, singing and worshipping, playing sports and games, laughing and crying, living in families and forming groups. Taken together, such universal behaviors define our human nature.

What causes our striking diversity, and also our shared human nature? How much are human differences shaped by our differing genes? And how much by our *environment*—by every external influence, from maternal nutrition while in the womb to social support while nearing the tomb? To what extent are we formed by our upbringing? By our culture? By our current circumstances? By people's reactions to our genetic dispositions? This module and the next begin to tell the complex story of how our genes (nature) and environments (nurture) define us.

The nurture of nature Parents everywhere wonder: Will my baby grow up to be peaceful or aggressive? Homely or attractive? Successful or struggling at every step? What comes built in, and what is nurtured—and how? Research reveals that nature and nurture together shape our development—every step of the way.

behavior genetics the study of the relative power and limits of genetic and environmental influences on behavior.

environment every external influence, from prenatal nutrition to the people and things around us.

chromosomes threadlike structures made of DNA molecules that contain the genes.

DNA (deoxyribonucleic acid) a complex molecule containing the genetic information that makes up the chromosomes.

genes the biochemical units of heredity that make up the chromosomes; segments of DNA capable of synthesizing proteins.

genome the complete instructions for making an organism, consisting of all the genetic material in that organism's chromosomes.

"Your DNA and mine are 99.9 percent the same. . . . At the DNA level, we are clearly all part of one big worldwide family." -FRANCIS COLLINS, HUMAN GENOME PROJECT DIRECTOR, 2007

Genes: Our Codes for Life

 14-1 What are genes, and how do behavior geneticists explain our individual differences?

If Jaden Agassi, son of tennis stars Andre Agassi and Steffi Graf, grows up to be a tennis star, should we attribute his superior talent to his Grand Slam genes? To his growing up in a tennis-rich environment? To high expectations? Such questions intrigue **behavior geneticists,** who study our differences and weigh the effects and interplay of heredity and **environment.**

Barely more than a century ago, few would have guessed that every cell nucleus in your body contains the genetic master code for your entire body. It's as if every room in Dubai's Burj Khalifa (the world's tallest building) had a book containing the architect's plans for the entire structure. The plans for your own book of life run to 46 chapters—23 donated by your mother's egg and 23 by your father's sperm. Each of these 46 chapters, called a **chromosome,** is composed of a coiled chain of the molecule **DNA** (deoxyribonucleic acid). **Genes,** small segments of the giant DNA molecules, form the words of those chapters (**FIGURE 14.1**). All told, you have 20,000 to 25,000 genes. Genes can be either active (expressed) or inactive. Environmental events "turn on" genes, rather like hot water enabling a tea bag to express its flavor. When turned on, genes provide the code for creating protein molecules, our body's building blocks.

Genetically speaking, every other human is nearly your identical twin. Human **genome** researchers have discovered the common sequence within human DNA. It is this shared genetic profile that makes us humans, rather than chimpanzees or tulips.

Actually, we aren't all that different from our chimpanzee cousins; with them we share about 96 percent of our DNA sequence (Mikkelsen et al., 2005). At "functionally important" DNA sites, reported one molecular genetics team, the human-chimpanzee DNA similarity is 99.4 percent (Wildman et al., 2003). Yet that wee difference matters. Despite

"Thanks for almost everything, Dad."

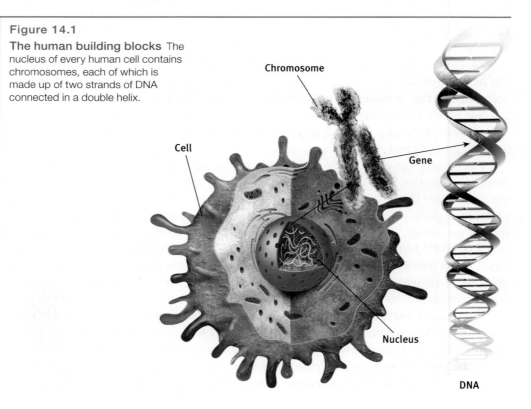

Figure 14.1

The human building blocks The nucleus of every human cell contains chromosomes, each of which is made up of two strands of DNA connected in a double helix.

Chromosome

Cell

Gene

Nucleus

DNA

some remarkable abilities, chimpanzees grunt. Shakespeare intricately wove 17,677 words to form his literary masterpieces.

Small differences matter among chimpanzees, too. Two species, common chimpanzees and bonobos, differ by much less than 1 percent of their genomes, yet they display markedly differing behaviors. Chimpanzees are aggressive and male dominated. Bonobos are peaceable and female led.

Geneticists and psychologists are interested in the occasional variations found at particular gene sites in human DNA. Slight person-to-person variations from the common pattern give clues to our uniqueness—why one person has a disease that another does not, why one person is short and another tall, why one is outgoing and another shy.

Most of our traits are influenced by many genes. How tall you are, for example, reflects the size of your face, vertebrae, leg bones, and so forth—each of which may be influenced by different genes interacting with your environment. Complex traits such as intelligence, happiness, and aggressiveness are similarly influenced by groups of genes. Thus our genetic predispositions—our genetically influenced traits—help explain both our shared human nature and our human diversity.

> "We share half our genes with the banana." -EVOLUTIONARY BIOLOGIST ROBERT MAY, PRESIDENT OF BRITAIN'S ROYAL SOCIETY, 2001

Twin and Adoption Studies

To scientifically tease apart the influences of environment and heredity, behavior geneticists would need to design two types of experiments. The first would control the home environment while varying heredity. The second would control heredity while varying the home environment. Such experiments with human infants would be unethical, but happily for our purposes, nature has done this work for us.

Identical Versus Fraternal Twins

Identical *(monozygotic)* **twins** develop from a single fertilized egg that splits in two. Thus they are *genetically* identical—nature's own human clones (**FIGURE 14.2**). Indeed, they are clones who share not only the same genes but the same conception and uterus, and usually the same birth date and cultural history. Two slight qualifications:

- Although identical twins have the same genes, they don't always have the same *number of copies* of those genes. That helps explain why one twin may be more at risk for certain illnesses (Bruder et al., 2008).
- Most identical twins share a placenta during prenatal development, but one of every three sets has two separate placentas. One twin's placenta may provide slightly better nourishment, which may contribute to identical twin differences (Davis et al., 1995; Phelps et al., 1997; Sokol et al., 1995).

Fraternal *(dizygotic)* **twins** develop from separate fertilized eggs. As womb-mates, they share a fetal environment, but they are genetically no more similar than ordinary brothers and sisters.

Shared genes can translate into shared experiences. A person whose identical twin has Alzheimer's disease, for example, has a 60 percent risk of getting the disease; if the affected twin is fraternal, the risk is 30 percent (Plomin et al., 1997). To study the effects of genes and environments, hundreds of researchers have studied some 800,000 identical and fraternal twin pairs (Johnson et al., 2009).

identical twins *(monozygotic twins)* twins who develop from a single fertilized egg that splits in two, creating two genetically identical organisms.

fraternal twins *(dizygotic twins)* twins who develop from separate fertilized eggs. They are genetically no closer than brothers and sisters, but they share a fetal environment.

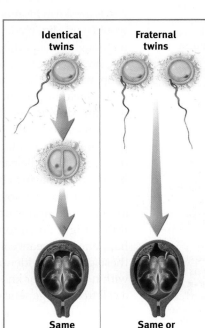

Identical twins **Fraternal twins**

Same sex only Same or opposite sex

Figure 14.2

Same fertilized egg, same genes; different eggs, different genes Identical twins develop from a single fertilized egg, fraternal twins from two.

More twins Curiously, twinning rates vary by race. The rate among Caucasians is roughly twice that of Asians and half that of Africans. In Africa and Asia, most twins are identical. In Western countries, most twins are fraternal, and fraternal twins are increasing with the use of fertility drugs (Hall, 2003; Steinhauer, 1999).

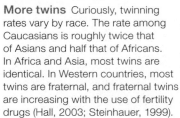

Are identical twins, being genetic clones of each other, also behaviorally more similar than fraternal twins? Studies of thousands of twin pairs in Sweden, Finland, and Australia find that on both extraversion (outgoingness) and neuroticism (emotional instability), identical twins are much more similar than fraternal twins. If genes influence traits such as emotional instability, might they also influence the social effects of such traits? To find out, researchers studied divorce rates among 1500 same-sex, middle-aged twin pairs (McGue & Lykken, 1992). Their result: If you have a fraternal twin who has divorced, the odds of your divorcing are 1.6 times greater than if you have a not-divorced twin. If you have an identical twin who has divorced, the odds of your divorcing are 5.5 times greater. From such data, the researchers estimate that people's differing divorce risks are about 50 percent attributable to genetic factors.

Identical twins, more than fraternal twins, also report being treated alike. So, do their experiences rather than their genes account for their similarity? *No.* Studies have shown that identical twins whose parents treated them alike were not psychologically more alike than identical twins who were treated less similarly (Loehlin & Nichols, 1976). In explaining individual differences, genes matter.

Separated Twins

Imagine the following science fiction experiment: A mad scientist decides to separate identical twins at birth, then rear them in differing environments. Better yet, consider a *true* story:

On a chilly February morning in 1979, some time after divorcing his first wife, Linda, Jim Lewis awoke in his modest home next to his second wife, Betty. Determined that this marriage would work, Jim made a habit of leaving love notes to Betty around the house. As he lay in bed he thought about others he had loved, including his son, James Alan, and his faithful dog, Toy.

Jim was looking forward to spending part of the day in his basement woodworking shop, where he had put in many happy hours building furniture, picture frames, and other items, including a white bench now circling a tree in his front yard. Jim also liked to spend free time driving his Chevy, watching stock-car racing, and drinking Miller Lite beer.

Jim was basically healthy, except for occasional half-day migraine headaches and blood pressure that was a little high, perhaps related to his chain-smoking habit. He had become overweight a while back but had shed some of the pounds. Having undergone a vasectomy, he was done having children.

What was extraordinary about Jim Lewis, however, was that at that same moment (I am not making this up) there existed another man—also named Jim—for whom all these things (right down to the dog's name) were also true.[1] This other Jim—Jim Springer—just happened, 38 years earlier, to have been his fetal partner. Thirty-seven days after their birth, these genetically identical twins were separated, adopted by blue-collar families, and reared with no contact or knowledge of each other's whereabouts until the day Jim Lewis received a call from his genetic clone (who, having been told he had a twin, set out to find him).

FYI

Sweden has the world's largest national twin registry—140,000 living and dead twin pairs—which forms part of a massive registry of 600,000 twins currently being sampled in the world's largest twin study (Wheelwright, 2004; www.genomeutwin.org).

FYI

Twins Lorraine and Levinia Christmas, driving to deliver Christmas presents to each other near Flitcham, England, collided (Shepherd, 1997).

"In some domains it looks as though our identical twins reared apart are . . . just as similar as identical twins reared together. Now that's an amazing finding and I can assure you none of us would have expected that degree of similarity."
-THOMAS BOUCHARD (1981)

---

[1] Actually, this description of the two Jims errs in one respect: Jim Lewis named his son James Alan. Jim Springer named his James Allan.

One month later, the brothers became the first twin pair tested by University of Minnesota psychologist Thomas Bouchard and his colleagues, beginning a study of separated twins that extends to the present (Holden, 1980a,b; Wright, 1998). Their voice intonations and inflections were so similar that, hearing a playback of an earlier interview, Jim Springer guessed "That's me." Wrong—it was his brother. Given tests measuring their personality, intelligence, heart rate, and brain waves, the Jim twins—despite 38 years of separation—were virtually as alike as the same person tested twice. Both married women named Dorothy Jane Scheckelburger. Okay, the last item is a joke. But as Judith Rich Harris (2006) notes, it is hardly weirder than some other reported similarities.

Aided by publicity in magazine and newspaper stories, Bouchard (2009) and his colleagues located and studied 74 pairs of identical twins reared apart. They continued to find similarities not only of tastes and physical attributes but also of personality (characteristic patterns of thinking, feeling, and acting), abilities, attitudes, interests, and even fears.

In Sweden, Nancy Pedersen and her co-workers (1988) identified 99 separated identical twin pairs and more than 200 separated fraternal twin pairs. Compared with equivalent samples of identical twins reared together, the separated identical twins had somewhat less identical personalities. Still, separated twins were more alike if genetically identical than if fraternal. And separation shortly after birth (rather than, say, at age 8) did not amplify their personality differences.

Stories of startling twin similarities do not impress Bouchard's critics, who remind us that "the plural of *anecdote* is not *data*." They contend that if any two strangers were to spend hours comparing their behaviors and life histories, they would probably discover many coincidental similarities. If researchers created a control group of biologically unrelated pairs of the same age, sex, and ethnicity, who had not grown up together but who were as similar to one another in economic and cultural background as are many of the separated twin pairs, wouldn't these pairs also exhibit striking similarities (Joseph, 2001)? Bouchard replies that separated fraternal twins do not exhibit similarities comparable to those of separated identical twins.

Even the more impressive data from personality assessments are clouded by the reunion of many of the separated twins some years before they were tested. Moreover, identical twins share an appearance, and the responses it evokes. Adoption agencies also tend to place separated twins in similar homes. Despite these criticisms, the striking twin-study results helped shift scientific thinking toward a greater appreciation of genetic influences.

FYI

Bouchard's famous twin research was, appropriately enough, conducted in Minneapolis, the "Twin City" (with St. Paul), and home to the Minnesota Twins baseball team.

FYI

Coincidences are not unique to twins. Patricia Kern of Colorado was born March 13, 1941, and named Patricia Ann Campbell. Patricia DiBiasi of Oregon also was born March 13, 1941, and named Patricia Ann Campbell. Both had fathers named Robert, worked as bookkeepers, and at the time of this comparison had children ages 21 and 19. Both studied cosmetology, enjoyed oil painting as a hobby, and married military men, within 11 days of each other. They are not genetically related. (From an AP report, May 2, 1983.)

The twin friars Julian and Adrian Reister—two "quiet, gentle souls"—both died of heart failure, at age 92, on the same day in 2011.

Biological Versus Adoptive Relatives

For behavior geneticists, nature's second real-life experiment—adoption—creates two groups: *genetic relatives* (biological parents and siblings) and *environmental relatives* (adoptive parents and siblings). For any given trait, we can therefore ask whether adopted children are more like their biological parents, who contributed their genes, or their adoptive parents, who contribute a home environment. While sharing that home environment, do adopted siblings also come to share traits?

The stunning finding from studies of hundreds of adoptive families is that people who grow up together, whether biologically related or not, do not much resemble one another in personality (McGue & Bouchard, 1998; Plomin, 2011; Rowe, 1990). In traits such as extraversion and agreeableness, adoptees are more similar to their biological parents than to their caregiving adoptive parents.

The finding is important enough to bear repeating: *The environment shared by a family's children has virtually no discernible impact on their personalities.* Two adopted children reared in the same home are no more likely to share personality traits with each other than with the child down the block. Heredity shapes other primates' personalities, too. Macaque monkeys raised by foster mothers exhibit social behaviors that resemble their biological, rather than foster, mothers (Maestripieri, 2003). Add all this to the similarity of identical twins, whether they grow up together or apart, and the effect of a shared rearing environment seems shockingly modest.

What we have here is perhaps "the most important puzzle in the history of psychology," contended Steven Pinker (2002): *Why are children in the same family so different?* Why does shared family environment have so little effect on children's personalities? Is it because each sibling experiences unique peer influences and life events? Because sibling relationships ricochet off each other, amplifying their differences? Because siblings—despite sharing half their genes—have very different combinations of genes and may evoke very different kinds of parenting? Such questions fuel behavior geneticists' curiosity.

The minimal shared-environment effect does not mean that adoptive parenting is a fruitless venture. The genetic leash may limit the family environment's influence on personality, but parents do influence their children's attitudes, values, manners, faith, and politics (Reifman & Cleveland, 2007). A pair of adopted children or identical twins *will,* especially during adolescence, have more similar religious beliefs if reared together (Koenig et al., 2005). Parenting matters!

Moreover, in adoptive homes, child neglect and abuse and even parental divorce are rare. (Adoptive parents are carefully screened; natural parents are not.) So it is not surprising that, despite a somewhat greater risk of psychological disorder, most adopted children thrive, especially when adopted as infants (Loehlin et al., 2007; van IJzendoorn & Juffer, 2006; Wierzbicki, 1993). Seven in eight report feeling strongly attached to one or both adoptive parents. As children of self-giving parents, they grow up to be more self-giving and altruistic than average (Sharma et al., 1998). Many score higher than their biological parents on intelligence tests, and most grow into happier and more stable adults. In one Swedish study, infant adoptees grew up with fewer problems than were experienced by children whose biological mothers had initially registered them for adoption but then decided to raise the children themselves (Bohman & Sigvardsson, 1990). Regardless of personality differences between parents and their adoptees, most children benefit from adoption.

> "We carry to our graves the essence of the zygote that was first us." -Mary Pipher, *Seeking Peace: Chronicles of the Worst Buddhist in the World*, 2009

> "Mom may be holding a full house while Dad has a straight flush, yet when Junior gets a random half of each of their cards his poker hand may be a loser." -David Lykken (2001)

FYI

The greater uniformity of adoptive homes—mostly healthy, nurturing homes—helps explain the lack of striking differences when comparing child outcomes of different adoptive homes (Stoolmiller, 1999).

LUIS ACOSTA/AFP/Getty Images

Nature or nurture or both? When talent runs in families, as with the Williams sisters for tennis, how do heredity and environment together do their work?

The New Frontier: Molecular Genetics

14-2   What is the promise of molecular genetics research?

Behavior geneticists have progressed beyond asking, "Do genes influence behavior?" The new frontier of behavior-genetics research draws on "bottom-up" **molecular genetics** as it seeks to identify *specific genes* influencing behavior.

As we have already seen, most human traits are influenced by teams of genes. For example, twin and adoption studies tell us that heredity influences body weight, but there is no single "obesity gene." More likely, some genes influence how quickly the stomach tells the brain, "I'm full." Others might dictate how much fuel the muscles need, how many calories are burned off by fidgeting, and how efficiently the body converts extra calories into fat (Vogel, 1999). Given that genes typically are not solo players, a goal of *molecular behavior genetics* is to find some of the many genes that together orchestrate traits such as body weight, sexual orientation, and extraversion (Holden, 2008; Tsankova et al., 2007).

Genetic tests can now reveal at-risk populations for many dozens of diseases. The search continues in labs worldwide, where molecular geneticists are teaming with psychologists to pinpoint genes that put people at risk for such genetically influenced disorders as learning disorder, depression, schizophrenia, and alcohol use disorder. (In Module 67, for example, we will take note of a worldwide research effort to sleuth the genes that make people vulnerable to the emotional swings of bipolar disorder, formerly called manic-depressive disorder.) To tease out the implicated genes, molecular behavior geneticists find families that have had the disorder across several generations. They draw blood or take cheek swabs from both affected and unaffected family members. Then they examine their DNA, looking for differences. "The most powerful potential for DNA," note Robert Plomin and John Crabbe (2000), "is to predict risk so that steps can be taken to prevent problems before they happen."

Aided by inexpensive DNA-scanning techniques, medical personnel are becoming able to give would-be parents a readout on how their fetus' genes differ from the normal pattern and what this might mean. With this benefit come risks. Might labeling a fetus "at risk for a learning disorder" lead to discrimination? Prenatal screening poses ethical dilemmas. In China and India, where boys are highly valued, testing for an offspring's sex has enabled selective abortions resulting in millions—yes, millions—of "missing women."

Assuming it were possible, should prospective parents take their eggs and sperm to a genetics lab for screening before combining them to produce an embryo? Should we enable parents to screen their fertilized eggs for health—and for brains or beauty? Progress is a double-edged sword, raising both hopeful possibilities and difficult problems. By selecting out certain traits, we may deprive ourselves of future Handels and van Goghs, Churchills and Lincolns, Tolstoys and Dickinsons—troubled people all.

molecular genetics the subfield of biology that studies the molecular structure and function of genes.

"I thought that sperm-bank donors remained anonymous."

Heritability

14-3   What is heritability, and how does it relate to individuals and groups?

Using twin and adoption studies, behavior geneticists can mathematically estimate the **heritability** of a trait—the extent to which variation among individuals can be attributed to their differing genes. As Modules 63 and 64 will emphasize, if the heritability of intelligence is, say, 50 percent, this does *not* mean that *your* intelligence is 50 percent genetic. (The heritability of height is 90 percent, but this does not mean that a 60-inch-tall woman can credit

heritability the proportion of variation among individuals that we can attribute to genes. The heritability of a trait may vary, depending on the range of populations and environments studied.

> ### AP® Exam Tip
>
> Heritability is likely to show up on the AP® exam because it's confusing. The key thing to remember is that heritability refers to variation within a group. It does not refer to the impact of nature on an individual. Be clear on both what it is and what it isn't.

her genes for 54 inches and her environment for the other 6 inches.) Rather, it means that genetic influence explains 50 percent of the observed *variation among people*. This point is so often misunderstood that I repeat: We can never say what percentage of an *individual's* personality or intelligence is inherited. It makes no sense to say that your personality is due *x* percent to your heredity and *y* percent to your environment. Heritability refers instead to the extent to which *differences among people* are attributable to genes.

Even this conclusion must be qualified, because heritability can vary from study to study. Consider humorist Mark Twain's (1835–1910) fantasy of raising boys in barrels to age 12, feeding them through a hole. If we were to follow his suggestion, the boys would all emerge with lower-than-normal intelligence scores at age 12. Yet, given their equal environments, their test score differences could be explained only by their heredity. In this case, heritability—differences due to genes—would be near 100 percent.

As environments become more similar, heredity as a source of differences necessarily becomes more important. If all schools were of uniform quality, all families equally loving, and all neighborhoods equally healthy, then heritability would *increase* (because differences due to environment would *decrease*). At the other extreme, if all people had similar heredities but were raised in drastically different environments (some in barrels, some in luxury homes), heritability would be much lower.

"The title of my science project is 'My Little Brother: Nature or Nurture.'"

Can we extend this thinking to differences between groups? If genetic influences help explain individual diversity in traits such as aggressiveness, for example, can the same be said of group differences between men and women, or between people of different races? Not necessarily. Individual differences in height and weight, for example, are highly heritable; yet nutritional rather than genetic influences explain why, as a group, today's adults are taller and heavier than those of a century ago. The two groups differ, but not because human genes have changed in a mere century's eye-blink of time. Although height is 90 percent heritable, South Koreans, with their better diets, average six inches taller than North Koreans, who come from the same genetic stock (Johnson et al., 2009).

As with height and weight, so with personality and intelligence scores: Heritable individual differences need not imply heritable group differences. If some individuals are genetically disposed to be more aggressive than others, that needn't explain why some groups are more aggressive than others. Putting people in a new social context can change their aggressiveness. Today's peaceful Scandinavians carry many genes inherited from their Viking warrior ancestors.

Gene-Environment Interaction

14-4 How do heredity and environment work together?

Among our similarities, the most important—the behavioral hallmark of our species—is our enormous adaptive capacity. Some human traits, such as having two eyes, develop the same in virtually every environment. But other traits are expressed only in particular environments. Go barefoot for a summer and you will develop toughened, callused feet—a biological adaptation to friction. Meanwhile, your shod neighbor will remain a tenderfoot. The difference between the two of you is, of course, an effect of environment. But it is also the product of a biological mechanism—adaptation. Our shared biology enables our developed diversity (Buss, 1991).

An analogy may help: Genes and environment—nature and nurture—work together like two hands clapping. Genes are *self-regulating*. Rather than acting as blueprints that lead to the same result no matter the context, genes react. An African butterfly that is green in summer turns brown in fall, thanks to a temperature-controlled genetic switch. The genes

> "Men's natures are alike; it is their habits that carry them far apart."
> -Confucius, *Analects*, 500 b.c.e.

that produce brown in one situation produce green in another. So, too, people with identical genes but differing experiences will have similar but not identical minds. One twin may fall in love with someone quite different from the co-twin's love.

Asking whether our personality is more a product of our genes or our environment is like asking whether the area of a field is more the result of its length or its width. We could, however, ask whether the differing areas of various fields are more the result of *differences* in their length or their width, and also whether person-to-person personality differences are influenced more by nature or nurture.

To say that genes and experience are *both* important is true. But more precisely, they **interact.** Imagine two babies, one genetically predisposed to be attractive, sociable, and easygoing, the other less so. Assume further that the first baby attracts more affectionate and stimulating care and so develops into a warmer and more outgoing person. As the two children grow older, the more naturally outgoing child more often seeks activities and friends that encourage further social confidence.

What has caused their resulting personality differences? Neither heredity nor experience dances alone. Environments trigger gene activity. And our genetically influenced traits *evoke* significant responses in others. Thus, a child's impulsivity and aggression may evoke an angry response from a teacher who reacts warmly to the child's model classmates. Parents, too, may treat their own children differently; one child elicits punishment, another does not. In such cases, the child's nature and the parents' nurture interact. Neither operates apart from the other. Gene and scene dance together.

Evocative interactions may help explain why identical twins reared in different families recall their parents' warmth as remarkably similar—almost as similar as if they had had the same parents (Plomin et al., 1988, 1991, 1994). Fraternal twins have more differing recollections of their early family life—even if reared in the same family! "Children experience us as different parents, depending on their own qualities," noted Sandra Scarr (1990). Moreover, a selection effect may be at work. As we grow older, we select environments well suited to our natures.

Recall that genes can be either active (expressed, as the hot water activates the tea bag) or inactive. A new field, **epigenetics** (meaning "in addition to" or "above and beyond" genetics), is studying the molecular mechanisms by which environments trigger genetic expression. Although genes have the potential to influence development, environmental triggers can switch them on or off, much as your computer's software directs your printer. One such *epigenetic mark* is an organic methyl molecule attached to part of a DNA strand (**FIGURE 14.3**). It instructs the cell to ignore any gene present in that DNA segment, thereby preventing the DNA from producing the proteins coded by that gene.

Environmental factors such as diet, drugs, and stress can affect the epigenetic molecules that regulate gene expression. In one experiment, infant rats deprived of their mothers' normal licking had more molecules that blocked

Dim154/Shutterstock

> "Heredity deals the cards; environment plays the hand."
> -Psychologist Charles L. Brewer (1990)

interaction the interplay that occurs when the effect of one factor (such as environment) depends on another factor (such as heredity).

epigenetics the study of environmental influences on gene expression that occur without a DNA change.

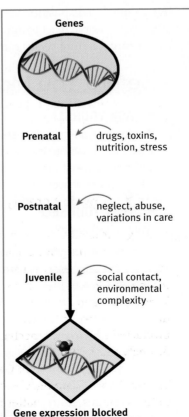

Genes

Prenatal → drugs, toxins, nutrition, stress

Postnatal → neglect, abuse, variations in care

Juvenile → social contact, environmental complexity

Gene expression blocked by epigenetic molecules

Figure 14.3
Epigenetics influences gene expression Life experiences beginning in the womb lay down *epigenetic marks*—often organic methyl molecules—that can block the expression of any gene in the associated DNA segment (from Champagne, 2010).

Gene-environment interaction
Biological appearances have social consequences. People respond differently to recording artist Nicki Minaj and concert violinist Hilary Hahn.

access to the "on" switch for developing the brain's stress hormone receptors. When stressed, the animals had more free-floating stress hormones and were more stressed out (Champagne et al., 2003; Champagne & Mashoodh, 2009). Child abuse may similarly affect its victims. Humans who have committed suicide exhibit the same epigenetic effect if they had suffered a history of child abuse (McGowan et al., 2009). Researchers now wonder if epigenetics might help solve some scientific mysteries, such as why only one member of an identical twin pair may develop a genetically influenced mental disorder, and how experience leaves its fingerprints in our brains.

So, from conception onward, we are the product of a cascade of interactions between our genetic predispositions and our surrounding environments (McGue, 2010). Our genes affect how people react to and influence us. Biological appearances have social consequences. So, forget nature *versus* nurture; think nature *via* nurture.

Before You Move On

▶ **ASK YOURSELF**

Would you want genetic tests on your unborn offspring? What would you do if you knew your child would be destined for hemophilia (a medical condition that interferes with blood clotting)? A specific learning disorder? A high risk of depression? Do you think society would benefit or lose if such embryos were aborted?

▶ **TEST YOURSELF**

What is *heritability*?

Answers to the Test Yourself questions can be found in Appendix E at the end of the book.

Module 14 Review

14-1 What are genes, and how do behavior geneticists explain our individual differences?

- *Genes* are the biochemical units of heredity that make up *chromosomes*, the threadlike coils of *DNA*.

- When genes are "turned on" (expressed), they provide the code for creating the proteins that form our body's building blocks.

- Most human traits are influenced by many genes acting together.

- *Behavior geneticists* seek to quantify genetic and *environmental* influences on our traits, in part through studies of *identical* (monozygotic) *twins, fraternal* (dizygotic) *twins,* and adoptive families.

- Shared family environments have little effect on personality, and the stability of personality suggests a genetic predisposition.

14-2 What is the promise of molecular genetics research?

- *Molecular geneticists* study the molecular structure and function of genes, including those that affect behavior.

- Psychologists and molecular geneticists are cooperating to identify specific genes—or more often, teams of genes—that put people at risk for disorders.

14-3 What is heritability, and how does it relate to individuals and groups?

- *Heritability* describes the extent to which variation among members of a group can be attributed to genes.

- Heritable individual differences (in traits such as height or intelligence) do not necessarily imply heritable group differences. Genes mostly explain why some people are taller than others, but not why people are taller today than they were a century ago.

14-4 How do heredity and environment work together?

- Our genetic predispositions and our surrounding environments *interact.* Environments can trigger gene activity, and genetically influenced traits can evoke responses from others.

- The field of *epigenetics* studies the influences on gene expression that occur without changes in DNA.

Multiple-Choice Questions

1. Human genome (DNA) researchers have discovered that
   a. chimpanzees are completely different than humans, sharing a small DNA sequence percentage.
   b. the occasional variations found at particular gene sites in human DNA are of no interest to science.
   c. many genes do not influence most of our traits.
   d. nearly every other human is your genetically identical twin.
   e. genetic predispositions do not help explain our shared human nature and our human diversity.

2. One reason that identical twins might show slight differences at birth is
   a. they did not develop from a single fertilized egg.
   b. one twin's placenta may have provided slightly better nourishment.
   c. they develop from different sperm.
   d. one twin gestated much longer in the uterus than the other.
   e. their relative positions in the uterus.

3. Generally speaking, heritability is the extent to which
   a. differences among people are accounted for by genes.
   b. an individual's specific traits are due to genes or the environment.
   c. differences among people are due to the environment.
   d. differences among people are due to their cultural heritage.
   e. an individual's height is related to the height of his or her parents.

4. Which of the following is most closely associated with the idea of epigenetics?
   a. Eye color
   b. Gene display based on environmental factors
   c. IQ as a function of educational experiences
   d. Height at birth
   e. Shoe size

5.   Which of the following is an example of gene-environment interaction?

a. Yeh Lin experiences flushing syndrome, which mostly occurs in those of Asian heritage.

b. Alfonso gets food poisoning from eating undercooked meat.

c. Ted gets diabetes, which runs in his family, because he eats too much sugary food.

d. Samantha has a food allergy to shellfish.

e. Jordan has an autoimmune disorder that causes him to lose hair.

Practice FRQs

1. Explain the two positions in the nature–nurture debate.

Answer (2 points)

1 point: Nature refers to the contributions of heredity and inborn, biologically determined aspects of behavior and mental processes.

1 point: Nurture refers to the contributions of environment and the way individuals are raised.

2. What does it mean to say that the heritability of height is 90 percent? What does that tell us about the contribution of genetics to any one person's height?

(2 points)

Module 15

Evolutionary Psychology: Understanding Human Nature

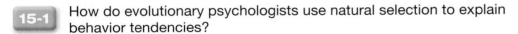

Chris Johnson/Dreamstime.com

Module Learning Objectives

15-1 Describe evolutionary psychologists' use of natural selection to explain behavior tendencies.

15-2 Discuss evolutionary explanations for gender differences in sexuality and mating preferences.

15-3 Summarize the key criticisms of evolutionary psychology, and describe how evolutionary psychologists respond.

15-4 Describe the biopsychosocial approach to individual development.

15-1 How do evolutionary psychologists use natural selection to explain behavior tendencies?

Behavior geneticists explore the genetic and environmental roots of human differences. **Evolutionary psychologists** instead focus mostly on what makes us so much alike. They use Charles Darwin's principle of natural selection to understand the roots of behavior and mental processes. Richard Dawkins (2007) calls **natural selection** "arguably the most momentous idea ever to occur to a human mind." The idea, simplified, is this:

- Organisms' varied offspring compete for survival.

- Certain biological and behavioral variations increase organisms' reproductive and survival chances in their particular environment.

- Offspring that survive are more likely to pass their genes to ensuing generations.

- Thus, over time, population characteristics may change.

To see these principles at work, let's consider a straightforward example in foxes.

> **evolutionary psychology** the study of the evolution of behavior and the mind, using principles of natural selection.
>
> **natural selection** the principle that, among the range of inherited trait variations, those contributing to reproduction and survival will most likely be passed on to succeeding generations.

Natural Selection and Adaptation

A fox is a wild and wary animal. If you capture a fox and try to befriend it, be careful. Stick your hand in the cage and, if the timid fox cannot flee, it may snack on your fingers. Russian scientist Dmitry Belyaev wondered how our human ancestors had domesticated dogs from their equally wild wolf forebears. Might he, within a comparatively short stretch of time, accomplish a similar feat by transforming the fearful fox into a friendly fox?

Eric Isselée/Shutterstock

To find out, Belyaev set to work with 30 male and 100 female foxes. From their offspring he selected and mated the tamest 5 percent of males and 20 percent of females. (He measured tameness by the foxes' responses to attempts to feed, handle, and stroke them.) Over more than 30 generations of foxes, Belyaev and his successor, Lyudmila Trut, repeated that simple procedure. Forty years and 45,000 foxes later, they had a new breed of foxes that, in Trut's (1999) words, are "docile, eager to please, and unmistakably domesticated. . . . Before our eyes, 'the Beast' has turned into 'beauty,' as the aggressive behavior of our herd's wild [ancestors] entirely disappeared." So friendly and eager for human contact are they, so inclined to whimper to attract attention and to lick people like affectionate dogs, that the cash-strapped institute seized on a way to raise funds—marketing its foxes to people as house pets.

Over time, traits that are *selected* confer a reproductive advantage on an individual or a species and will prevail. Animal breeding experiments manipulate genetic selection and show its powers. Dog breeders have given us sheepdogs that herd, retrievers that retrieve, trackers that track, and pointers that point (Plomin et al., 1997). Psychologists, too, have bred animals to be serene or reactive, quick learners or slow.

Does the same process work with naturally occurring selection? Does natural selection explain our human tendencies? Nature has indeed selected advantageous variations from the new gene combinations produced at each human conception and the **mutations** (random errors in gene replication) that sometimes result. But the tight genetic leash that predisposes a dog's retrieving, a cat's pouncing, or an ant's nest building is looser on humans. The genes selected during our ancestral history provide more than a long leash; they endow us with a great capacity to learn and therefore to *adapt* to life in varied environments, from the tundra to the jungle. Genes and experience together wire the brain. Our adaptive flexibility in responding to different environments contributes to our *fitness*—our ability to survive and reproduce.

> **mutation** a random error in gene replication that leads to a change.

Evolutionary Success Helps Explain Similarities

Although our person-to-person differences grab attention, we humans are also strikingly alike. As brothers and sisters in one great human family, we all wake and sleep, think and speak, hunger and thirst. We smile when happy and favor what's familiar more than what is foreign. We return favors, fear snakes, grieve death, and, as social animals, have a need to belong. Beneath our differing skin, we all are kin. Evolutionary psychologist Steven Pinker (2002, p. 73) has noted that it is no wonder our emotions, drives, and reasoning "have a common logic across cultures": Our shared human traits "were shaped by natural selection acting over the course of human evolution."

Our Genetic Legacy

Our behavioral and biological similarities arise from our shared human *genome*, our common genetic profile. No more than 5 percent of the genetic differences among humans arise from population group differences. Some 95 percent of genetic variation exists *within* populations (Rosenberg et al., 2002). The typical genetic difference between two Icelandic villagers or between two Kenyans is much greater than the *average* difference between the two groups. Thus, if after a worldwide catastrophe only Icelanders or Kenyans survived, the human species would suffer only "a trivial reduction" in its genetic diversity (Lewontin, 1982).

And how did we develop this shared human genome? At the dawn of human history, our ancestors faced certain questions: Who is my ally, who my foe? What food should I eat? With whom should I mate? Some individuals answered those questions more successfully than others. For example, women who experienced nausea in the critical first three months of pregnancy were predisposed to avoid certain bitter, strongly flavored, and novel foods. Avoiding such foods has survival value, since they are the very foods most often toxic to embryonic development (Schmitt & Pilcher, 2004). Early humans disposed to eat nourishing rather than poisonous foods survived to contribute their genes to later generations. Those who deemed leopards "nice to pet" often did not.

Similarly successful were those whose mating helped them produce and nurture offspring. Over generations, the genes of individuals not so disposed tended to be lost from the human gene pool. As success-enhancing genes continued to be selected, behavioral tendencies and thinking and learning capacities emerged that prepared our Stone Age ancestors to survive, reproduce, and send their genes into the future, and into you.

Across our cultural differences, we even share "a universal moral grammar," notes evolutionary psychologist Marc Hauser (2006, 2009). Men and women, young and old, liberal and conservative, living in Sydney or Seoul, all respond negatively when asked, "If a lethal gas is leaking into a vent and is headed toward a room with seven people, is it okay to push someone into the vent—saving the seven but killing the one?" And they all respond more approvingly when asked if it's okay to allow someone to fall into the vent, again sacrificing one life but saving seven. Our shared moral instincts survive from a distant past where we lived in small groups in which direct harm-doing was punished, argues Hauser. For all such universal human tendencies, from our intense need to give parental care to our shared fears and lusts, evolutionary theory proposes a one-stop shopping explanation (Schloss, 2009).

As inheritors of this prehistoric genetic legacy, we are predisposed to behave in ways that promoted our ancestors' surviving and reproducing. But in some ways, we are biologically prepared for a world that no longer exists. We love the taste of sweets and fats, which prepared our ancestors to survive famines, and we heed their call from school cafeterias, fast-food outlets, and vending machines. With famine now rare in Western cultures, obesity is truly a growing problem. Our natural dispositions, rooted deep in history, are mismatched with today's junk-food environment and today's threats such as climate change (Colarelli & Dettman, 2003).

Evolutionary Psychology Today

Darwin's theory of evolution has been an organizing principle for biology for a long time. Jared Diamond (2001) noted, "Virtually no contemporary scientists believe that Darwin was basically wrong." Today, Darwin's theory lives on in the *second Darwinian revolution:* the application of evolutionary principles to psychology. In concluding *On the Origin of Species,* Darwin anticipated this, foreseeing "open fields for far more important researches. Psychology will be based on a new foundation" (1859, p. 346).

In modules to come, we'll address questions that intrigue evolutionary psychologists, such as why infants start to fear strangers about the time they become mobile. Why are biological fathers so much less likely than unrelated boyfriends to abuse and murder the children with whom they share a home? Why do so many more people have phobias about spiders, snakes, and heights than about more dangerous threats, such as guns and electricity? And why do we fear air travel so much more than driving?

To see how evolutionary psychologists think and reason, let's pause now to explore their answers to these two questions: How are men and women alike? How and why does men's and women's sexuality differ?

An Evolutionary Explanation of Human Sexuality

 How might an evolutionary psychologist explain gender differences in sexuality and mating preferences?

Having faced many similar challenges throughout history, men and women have adapted in similar ways. Whether male or female, we eat the same foods, avoid the same predators, and perceive, learn, and remember similarly. It is only in those domains where we have faced differing adaptive challenges—most obviously in behaviors related to reproduction—that we differ, say evolutionary psychologists.

FYI

Despite high infant mortality and rampant disease in past millennia, not one of your countless ancestors died childless.

FYI

Those who are troubled by an apparent conflict between scientific and religious accounts of human origins may find it helpful to recall from Module 2 that different perspectives of life can be complementary. For example, the scientific account attempts to tell us *when* and *how;* religious creation stories usually aim to tell about an ultimate *who* and *why.* As Galileo explained to the Grand Duchess Christina, "The Bible teaches how to go to heaven, not how the heavens go."

What evolutionary psychologists study Each word's size in this "word cloud" shows how frequently it has appeared in evolutionary psychology article titles. (Derived by Gregory Webster, Peter Jonason, and Tatiana Schember [2009] from all articles published in *Evolution and Human Behavior* between 1979 and 2008.)
Webster, G. D., Jonason, P. K., & Schember, T. O. (2009). Hot topics and popular papers in evolutionary psychology: Analyses of title words and citation counts in *Evolution and Human Behavior*, 1979–2008. *Evolutionary Psychology, 7*, 348–362.

Gender Differences in Sexuality

And differ we do. Consider men's and women's sex drives. Who thinks more about sex? Masturbates more often? Initiates more sex? Views more pornography? The answers worldwide: *men, men, men,* and *men* (Baumeister et al., 2001; Lippa, 2009; Petersen & Hyde, 2009). No surprise, then, that in one BBC survey of more than 200,000 people in 53 nations, men everywhere more strongly agreed that "I have a strong sex drive" and "It doesn't take much to get me sexually excited" (Lippa, 2008).

Indeed, "with few exceptions anywhere in the world," reported cross-cultural psychologist Marshall Segall and his colleagues (1990, p. 244), "males are more likely than females to initiate sexual activity."

Men also have a lower threshold for perceiving warm responses as a sexual come-on. In study after study, men more often than women attribute a woman's friendliness to sexual interest (Abbey, 1987; Johnson et al., 1991). Misattributing women's cordiality as a come-on helps explain—but does not excuse—men's greater sexual assertiveness (Kolivas & Gross, 2007). The unfortunate results can range from sexual harassment to date rape.

Natural Selection and Mating Preferences

Evolutionary psychologists use natural selection to explain why—worldwide—women's approach to sex is usually more relational, and men's more recreational (Schmitt, 2005, 2007). The explanation goes like this: While a woman usually incubates and nurses one infant at a time, a male can spread his genes through other females. Our natural yearnings are our genes' way of reproducing themselves. In our ancestral history, women most often sent their genes into the future by pairing wisely, men by pairing widely. "Humans are living fossils—collections of mechanisms produced by prior selection pressures," said evolutionary psychologist David Buss (1995).

And what do heterosexual men and women find attractive in a mate? Some desired traits, such as a woman's youthful appearance, cross place and time (Buss, 1994). Evolutionary psychologists say that men who were drawn to healthy, fertile-appearing women—women with smooth skin and a youthful shape suggesting many childbearing years to come—stood a better chance of sending their genes into the future. And sure enough, men feel most attracted to women whose waists (thanks to their genes or their surgeons) are roughly a third narrower than their hips—a sign of future fertility (Perilloux et al., 2010). Moreover, just as evolutionary psychology predicts, men are most attracted to women whose ages in the ancestral past (when ovulation began later than today) would be associated with peak fertility (Kenrick et al., 2009). Thus, teen boys are most excited by a woman several years older than themselves, mid-twenties men prefer women around their own age, and older men prefer younger women. This pattern consistently appears across European singles ads, Indian marital ads, and marriage records from North and South America, Africa, and the Philippines (Singh, 1993; Singh & Randall, 2007).

Women, in turn, prefer stick-around dads over likely cads. They are attracted to men who seem mature, dominant, bold, and affluent, with a potential for long-term mating and investment in their joint offspring (Gangestad & Simpson, 2000; Singh, 1995). In one study of hundreds of Welsh pedestrians, men rated a woman as equally attractive whether pictured at a wheel of a humble Ford Fiesta or a swanky Bentley. Women, however, found the man more attractive if he was in the luxury car (Dunn & Searle, 2010). In another experiment, women skillfully discerned which men most liked looking at baby pictures, and they rated those men higher as potential long-term mates (Roney et al., 2006). From an evolutionary perspective, such attributes connote a man's capacity to support and protect a family (Buss, 1996, 2009; Geary, 1998).

"I had a nice time, Steve. Would you like to come in, settle down, and raise a family?"

There is a principle at work here, say evolutionary psychologists: Nature selects behaviors that increase the likelihood of sending one's genes into the future. As mobile gene machines, we are designed to prefer whatever worked for our ancestors in their environments. They were predisposed to act in ways that would produce grandchildren—had they not been, we wouldn't be here. And as carriers of their genetic legacy, we are similarly predisposed.

Without disputing nature's selection of traits that enhance gene survival, critics see some problems with this explanation of our mating preferences. They believe that the evolutionary perspective overlooks some important influences on human sexuality (see Thinking Critically About: The Evolutionary Perspective on Human Sexuality).

Thinking Critically About

The Evolutionary Perspective on Human Sexuality

15-3 What are the key criticisms of evolutionary psychology, and how do evolutionary psychologists respond?

Evolutionary psychology, say some critics, starts with an effect (such as the gender sexuality difference) and works backward to propose an explanation. They invite us to imagine a different result and reason backward. If men were uniformly loyal to their mates, might we not reason that the children of these committed, supportive fathers would more often survive to perpetuate their genes? Might not men also be better off bonded to one woman—both to increase their odds of impregnation and to keep her from the advances of competing men? Might not a ritualized bond—a marriage—also spare women from chronic male harassment? Such suggestions are, in fact, evolutionary explanations for why humans tend to pair off monogamously (Gray & Anderson, 2010). One can hardly lose at hindsight explanation, which is, said paleontologist Stephen Jay Gould (1997), mere "speculation [and] guesswork in the cocktail party mode."

Some also worry about the social consequences of evolutionary psychology. Does it suggest a genetic determinism that strikes at the heart of progressive efforts to remake society (Rose, 1999)? Does it undercut moral responsibility (Buller, 2005, 2009)? Could it be used to rationalize "high-status men marrying a series of young, fertile women" (Looy, 2001)?

Others argue that evolutionary explanations blur the line between genetic legacy and social-cultural tradition. Show Alice Eagly and Wendy Wood (1999; Eagly, 2009) a culture with gender inequality—where men are providers and women are homemakers—and they will show you a culture where men strongly desire youth and domestic skill in their potential mates, and where women seek status and earning potential in their mates. Show Eagly and Wood a culture with gender equality, and they will show you a culture with smaller gender differences in mate preferences.

Much of who we are is *not* hard-wired, agree evolutionary psychologists. "Evolution forcefully rejects a genetic determinism," insists one research team (Confer et al., 2010). Evolutionary psychologists reassure us that men and women, having faced similar adaptive problems, are far more alike than different, and that humans have a great capacity for learning and social progress. Indeed, natural selection has prepared us to flexibly adjust and respond to varied environments, to adapt and survive, whether we live in igloos or tree houses. Further, they agree that cultures vary, cultures change, and cultural expectations can bend the genders. If socialized to value lifelong commitment, men may sexually bond with one partner; if socialized to accept casual sex, women may willingly have sex with many partners.

Evolutionary psychologists acknowledge struggling to explain some traits and behaviors such as same-sex attraction and suicide (Confer et al., 2010). But they also point to the explanatory and predictive power of evolutionary principles. Evolutionary psychologists predict, and have confirmed, that we tend to favor others to the extent that they share our genes or can later return our favors. They predict, and have confirmed, that human memory should be well-suited to retaining survival-relevant information (such as food locations, for which females exhibit superiority). They predict, and have confirmed, various other male and female mating strategies.

Evolutionary psychologists also remind us that the study of how we came to be need not dictate how we ought to be. Understanding our propensities sometimes helps us overcome them.

"It is dangerous to show a man too clearly how much he resembles the beast, without at the same time showing him his greatness. It is also dangerous to allow him too clear a vision of his greatness without his baseness. It is even more dangerous to leave him in ignorance of both." -BLAISE PASCAL, PENSÉES, 1659

Before You Move On

▶ **ASK YOURSELF**

Whose reasoning do you find most persuasive—that of evolutionary psychologists or their critics? Why?

▶ **TEST YOURSELF**

What are the three main criticisms of evolutionary psychology's explanations?

Answers to the Test Yourself questions can be found in Appendix E at the end of the book.

Reflections on Nature and Nurture

15-4 What is included in the biopsychosocial approach to individual development?

"There are trivial truths and great truths," the physicist Niels Bohr reportedly said in reflecting on the paradoxes of science. "The opposite of a trivial truth is plainly false. The opposite of a great truth is also true." It appears true that our ancestral history helped form us as a species. Where there is variation, natural selection, and heredity, there will be evolution. The unique gene combination created when our mother's egg engulfed our father's sperm predisposed both our shared humanity and our individual differences. This is a great truth about human nature. Genes form us.

But it also is true that our experiences form us. In our families and in our peer relationships, we learn ways of thinking and acting. Differences initiated by our nature may be amplified by our nurture. If genes and hormones predispose males to be more physically aggressive than females, culture may magnify this gender difference through norms that encourage males to be macho and females to be the kinder, gentler sex. If men are encouraged toward roles that demand physical power, and women toward more nurturing roles, each may then exhibit the actions expected of them and find themselves shaped accordingly. Roles remake their players. Presidents in time become more presidential, servants more servile. Gender roles similarly shape us.

But gender roles are converging. Brute strength has become increasingly irrelevant to power and status (think Bill Gates and Hillary Clinton). Thus both women and men are now seen as "fully capable of effectively carrying out organizational roles at all levels," note Wendy Wood and Alice Eagly (2002). And as women's employment in formerly male occupations has increased, gender differences in traditional masculinity or femininity and in what one seeks in a mate have diminished (Twenge, 1997). As the roles we play change over time, we change with them.

* * *

If nature and nurture jointly form us, are we "nothing but" the product of nature and nurture? Are we rigidly determined?

We are the product of nature and nurture (**FIGURE 15.1**), but we are also an open system, as suggested by the biopsychosocial approach (see Module 2). Genes are all pervasive but not all powerful; people may defy their genetic bent to reproduce by electing celibacy. Culture, too, is all pervasive but not all powerful; people may defy peer pressures and do the opposite of the expected. To excuse our failings by blaming our nature and nurture is what philosopher-novelist Jean-Paul Sartre called "bad faith"—attributing responsibility for one's fate to bad genes or bad influences.

San Diego Museum of Man, photograph by Rose Tyson

Culture matters As this exhibit at San Diego's Museum of Man illustrates, children learn their culture. A baby's foot can step into any culture.

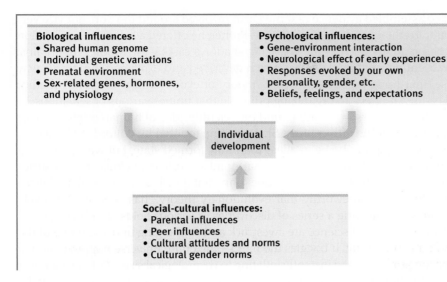

Biological influences:
- Shared human genome
- Individual genetic variations
- Prenatal environment
- Sex-related genes, hormones, and physiology

Psychological influences:
- Gene-environment interaction
- Neurological effect of early experiences
- Responses evoked by our own personality, gender, etc.
- Beliefs, feelings, and expectations

Individual development

Social-cultural influences:
- Parental influences
- Peer influences
- Cultural attitudes and norms
- Cultural gender norms

Figure 15.1
The biopsychosocial approach to individual development

In reality, we are both the creatures and the creators of our worlds. We are—it is a great truth—the products of our genes and environments. Nevertheless (another great truth), the stream of causation that shapes the future runs through our present choices. Our decisions today design our environments tomorrow. Mind matters. The human environment is not like the weather—something that just happens. We are its architects. Our hopes, goals, and expectations influence our future. And that is what enables cultures to vary and to change so quickly.

* * *

I know from my mail and from public opinion surveys that some readers feel troubled by the naturalism and evolutionism of contemporary science. Readers from other nations bear with me, but in the United States there is a wide gulf between scientific and lay thinking about evolution. "The idea that human minds are the product of evolution is . . . unassailable fact," declared a 2007 editorial in *Nature,* a leading science magazine. That sentiment concurs with a 2006 statement of "evidence-based facts" about evolution jointly issued by the national science academies of 66 nations (IAP, 2006). In *The Language of God,* Human Genome Project director Francis Collins (2006, pp. 141, 146), a self-described evangelical Christian, compiles the "utterly compelling" evidence that leads him to conclude that Darwin's big idea is "unquestionably correct." Yet Gallup reports that half of U.S. adults do not believe in evolution's role in "how human beings came to exist on Earth" (Newport, 2007). Many of those who dispute the scientific story worry that a science of behavior (and evolutionary science in particular) will destroy our sense of the beauty, mystery, and spiritual significance of the human creature. For those concerned, I offer some reassuring thoughts.

"Let's hope that it's not true; but if it is true, let's hope that it doesn't become widely known." -LADY ASHLEY, COMMENTING ON DARWIN'S THEORY

When Isaac Newton explained the rainbow in terms of light of differing wavelengths, the poet Keats feared that Newton had destroyed the rainbow's mysterious beauty. Yet, noted Richard Dawkins (1998) in *Unweaving the Rainbow,* Newton's analysis led to an even deeper mystery—Einstein's theory of special relativity. Moreover, nothing about Newton's optics need diminish our appreciation for the dramatic elegance of a rainbow arching across a brightening sky.

Tetyana Kochneva | Dreamstime.com

When Galileo assembled evidence that the Earth revolved around the Sun, not vice versa, he did not offer irrefutable proof for his theory. Rather, he offered a coherent explanation for a variety of observations, such as the changing shadows cast by the Moon's mountains. His explanation eventually won the day because it described and explained things in a way that made sense, that hung together. Darwin's theory of evolution likewise is a coherent view of natural history. It offers an organizing principle that unifies various observations.

Collins is not the only person of faith to find the scientific idea of human origins congenial with his spirituality. In the fifth century, St. Augustine (quoted by Wilford, 1999) wrote, "The universe was brought into being in a less than fully formed state, but was gifted with the capacity to transform itself from unformed matter into a truly marvelous array of structures and life forms." Some 1600 years later, Pope John Paul II in 1996 welcomed a science-religion dialogue, finding it noteworthy that evolutionary theory "has been progressively accepted by researchers, following a series of discoveries in various fields of knowledge."

Meanwhile, many people of science are awestruck at the emerging understanding of the universe and the human creature. It boggles the mind—the entire universe popping out of a point some 14 billion years ago, and instantly inflating to cosmological size. Had the energy of this Big Bang been the tiniest bit less, the universe would have collapsed back on itself. Had it been the tiniest bit more, the result would have been a soup too thin to support life. Astronomer Sir Martin Rees has described *Just Six Numbers* (1999), any one of which, if changed ever so slightly, would produce a cosmos in which life could not exist. Had gravity been a tad bit stronger or weaker, or had the weight of a carbon proton been a wee bit different, our universe just wouldn't have worked.

What caused this almost-too-good-to-be-true, finely tuned universe? Why is there something rather than nothing? How did it come to be, in the words of Harvard-Smithsonian astrophysicist Owen Gingerich (1999), "so extraordinarily right, that it seemed the universe had been expressly designed to produce intelligent, sentient beings"? Is there a benevolent superintelligence behind it all? Have there instead been an infinite number of universes born and we just happen to be the lucky inhabitants of one that, by chance, was exquisitely fine-tuned to give birth to us? Or does that idea violate *Occam's razor,* the principle that we should prefer the simplest of competing explanations? On such matters, a humble, awed, scientific silence is appropriate, suggested philosopher Ludwig Wittgenstein: "Whereof one cannot speak, thereof one must be silent" (1922, p. 189).

Rather than fearing science, we can welcome its enlarging our understanding and awakening our sense of awe. In *The Fragile Species,* Lewis Thomas (1992) described his utter amazement that the Earth in time gave rise to bacteria and eventually to Bach's Mass in B Minor. In a short 4 billion years, life on Earth has come from nothing to structures as complex as a 6-billion-unit strand of DNA and the incomprehensible intricacy of the human brain. Atoms no different from those in a rock somehow formed dynamic entities that became conscious. Nature, says cosmologist Paul Davies (2007), seems cunningly and ingeniously devised to produce extraordinary, self-replicating, information-processing systems—us. Although we appear to have been created from dust, over eons of time, the end result is a priceless creature, one rich with potential beyond our imagining.

Before You Move On

▶ **ASK YOURSELF**

How have your heredity and your environment influenced who you are today? Can you recall an important time when you determined your own fate in a way that was at odds with pressure you felt from either your heredity or your environment?

▶ **TEST YOURSELF**

How does the biopsychosocial approach explain our individual development?

Answers to the Test Yourself questions can be found in Appendix E at the end of the book.

* * *

In this unit we have glimpsed an overriding principle: Everything psychological is simultaneously biological. We have focused on how our thoughts, feelings, and actions arise from our specialized yet integrated brain. In modules to come, we will further explore the significance of the biological revolution in psychology.

From nineteenth-century phrenology to today's neuroscience, we have come a long way. Yet what is unknown still dwarfs what is known. We can describe the brain. We can learn the functions of its parts. We can study how the parts communicate. But how do we get mind out of meat? How does the electrochemical whir in a hunk of tissue the size of a head of lettuce give rise to elation, a creative idea, or that memory of Grandmother?

Much as gas and air can give rise to something different—fire—so also, believed Roger Sperry, does the complex human brain give rise to something different: *consciousness.* The mind, he argued, emerges from the brain's dance of ions, yet is not reducible to it. Cells cannot be fully explained by the actions of atoms, nor minds by the activity of cells. Psychology is rooted in biology, which is rooted in chemistry, which is rooted in physics. Yet psychology is more than applied physics. As Jerome Kagan (1998) reminded us, the meaning of the Gettysburg Address is not reducible to neural activity. Communication is more than air flowing over our vocal cords. Morality and responsibility become possible when we understand the mind as a "holistic system," said Sperry (1992) (**FIGURE 15.2**). We are not mere jabbering robots.

The mind seeking to understand the brain—that is indeed among the ultimate scientific challenges. And so it will always be. To paraphrase cosmologist John Barrow, a brain simple enough to be understood is too simple to produce a mind able to understand it.

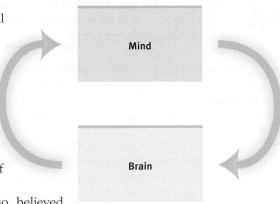

Figure 15.2

Mind and brain as holistic system In Roger Sperry's view, the brain creates and controls the emergent mind, which in turn influences the brain. (Think vividly about biting into a lemon and you may salivate.)

Module 15 Review

 How do evolutionary psychologists use natural selection to explain behavior tendencies?

- *Evolutionary psychologists* seek to understand how our traits and behavior tendencies are shaped by *natural selection,* as genetic variations increasing the odds of reproducing and surviving are most likely to be passed on to future generations.

- Some genetic variations arise from *mutations* (random errors in gene replication), others from new gene combinations at conception.

- Humans share a genetic legacy and are predisposed to behave in ways that promoted our ancestors' surviving and reproducing.

- Charles Darwin's theory of evolution is an organizing principle in biology. He anticipated today's application of evolutionary principles in psychology.

 How might an evolutionary psychologist explain gender differences in sexuality and mating preferences?

- Men tend to have a recreational view of sexual activity; women tend to have a relational view.

- Evolutionary psychologists reason that men's attraction to multiple healthy, fertile-appearing partners increases their chances of spreading their genes widely.

- Because women incubate and nurse babies, they increase their own and their children's chances of survival by searching for mates with the potential for long-term investment in their joint offspring.

15-3 What are the key criticisms of evolutionary psychology, and how do evolutionary psychologists respond?

- Critics argue that evolutionary psychologists (1) start with an effect and work backward to an explanation, (2) do not recognize social and cultural influences, and (3) absolve people from taking responsibility for their sexual behavior.

- Evolutionary psychologists respond that understanding our predispositions can help us overcome them. They also cite the value of testable predictions based on evolutionary principles, as well as the coherence and explanatory power of those principles.

15-4 What is included in the biopsychosocial approach to individual development?

- Individual development results from the interaction of biological, psychological, and social-cultural influences.

- Biological influences include our shared human *genome*; individual variations; prenatal environment; and sex-related genes, hormones, and physiology.

- Psychological influences include gene-environment interactions; the effect of early experiences on neural networks; responses evoked by our own characteristics, such as gender and personality; and personal beliefs, feelings, and expectations.

- Social-cultural influences include parental and peer influences; cultural traditions and values; and cultural gender norms.

Multiple-Choice Questions

1. Which of the following refers to an effect of life experience that leaves a molecular mark that affects gene expression?
- a. Epigenetics
- b. Adaptation
- c. Evolution
- d. Natural selection
- e. Universal moral grammar

2. Which of the following best describes genetic mutation?
- a. Random errors in gene replication
- b. The study of the mind's evolution
- c. The study of behavioral evolution
- d. Passing on successful, inherited traits
- e. Survival of the genetically successful

3. Which of the following is true regarding the initiation of sexual activity?
- a. Men are more likely to initiate sexual activity than women.
- b. Women are more likely to initiate sexual activity than men.
- c. The initiation of sexual activity for both men and women correlates with how many television sitcoms they viewed as children.
- d. Men and women are equally likely to initiate sexual activity.
- e. Who initiates sexual activity is largely determined by culture.

Practice FRQs

1. Explain four of the important ideas behind natural selection.

Answer

1 point: Organisms' varied offspring compete for survival.

1 point: Certain biological and behavioral variations increase an organism's reproductive and survival chances in a particular environment.

1 point: Offspring that survive are more likely to pass their genes to ensuing generations.

1 point: Over time, population characteristics may change.

2. Explain the three major influences on individual development, according to the biopsychosocial approach.

(3 points)

Unit III Review

Key Terms and Concepts to Remember

biological psychology, p. 77

neuron, p. 78

dendrites, p. 78

axon, p. 78

myelin [MY-uh-lin] sheath, p. 78

action potential, p. 78

refractory period, p. 79

threshold, p. 80

all-or-none response, p. 80

synapse [SIN-aps], p. 80

neurotransmitters, p. 80

reuptake, p. 80

endorphins [en-DOR-fins], p. 82

agonist, p. 82

antagonist, p. 83

nervous system, p. 86

central nervous system (CNS), p. 86

peripheral nervous system (PNS), p. 86

nerves, p. 86

sensory (afferent) neurons, p. 86

motor (efferent) neurons, p. 86

interneurons, p. 87

somatic nervous system, p. 87

autonomic [aw-tuh-NAHM-ik] nervous system (ANS), p. 87

sympathetic nervous system, p. 87

parasympathetic nervous system, p. 87

reflex, p. 89

endocrine [EN-duh-krin] system, p. 90

hormones, p. 90

adrenal [ah-DREEN-el] glands, p. 91

pituitary gland, p. 91

lesion [LEE-zhuhn], p. 94

electroencephalogram (EEG), p. 95

CT (computed tomography) scan, p. 95

PET (positron emission tomography) scan, p. 95

MRI (magnetic resonance imaging), p. 95

fMRI (functional MRI), p. 96

brainstem, p. 97

medulla [muh-DUL-uh], p. 97

thalamus [THAL-uh-muss], p. 97

reticular formation, p. 98

cerebellum [sehr-uh-BELL-um], p. 98

limbic system, p. 98

amygdala [uh-MIG-duh-la], p. 99

hypothalamus [hi-po-THAL-uh-muss], p. 99

cerebral [seh-REE-bruhl] cortex, p. 104

glial cells (glia), p. 104

frontal lobes, p. 105

parietal [puh-RYE-uh-tuhl] lobes, p. 105

occipital [ahk-SIP-uh-tuhl] lobes, p. 105

temporal lobes, p. 1050

motor cortex, p. 105

somatosensory cortex, p. 107

association areas, p. 109

plasticity, p. 111

neurogenesis, p. 112

corpus callosum [KOR-pus kah-LOW-sum], p. 114

split brain, p. 114

consciousness, p. 118

cognitive neuroscience, p. 119

dual processing, p. 120

behavior genetics, p. 124

environment, p. 124

chromosomes, p. 124

DNA (deoxyribonucleic acid), p. 124

genes, p. 124

genome, p. 124

identical twins, p. 125

fraternal twins, p. 125

molecular genetics, p. 129

heritability, p. 129

interaction, p. 131

epigenetics, p. 131

evolutionary psychology, p. 135

natural selection, p. 135

mutation, p. 136

Key Contributors to Remember

Paul Broca, p. 110

Carl Wernicke, p. 110

Roger Sperry, p. 114

Michael Gazzaniga, p. 114

Charles Darwin, p. 135

AP® Exam Practice Questions

Multiple-Choice Questions

1. Why do researchers study the brains of nonhuman animals?

a. It is not ethical to study human brains.
b. Human brains are too complex to study meaningfully.
c. The same principles govern neural functioning in all species.
d. It is too expensive to study human brains.
e. The technology is still being developed for the study of human brains.

2. What is the brief electrical charge that travels down an axon called?

a. Action potential
b. Resting potential
c. All-or-none impulse
d. Refractory period
e. Myelination response

3. An individual is having trouble with cognitive tasks related to learning and memory. Which of the following neurotransmitters is most likely to be involved with the problem?

a. Acetylcholine
b. Dopamine
c. Serotonin
d. The endorphins
e. GABA

4. Which is the most influential of the endocrine glands?

a. Pituitary gland
b. Adrenal glands
c. Dendrites
d. Threshold glands
e. Parasympathetic

5. What is the purpose of the myelin sheath?

a. Make the transfer of information across a synapse more efficient
b. Increase the amount of neurotransmitter available in the neuron
c. Reduce the antagonistic effect of certain drugs
d. Establish a resting potential in the axon
e. Speed the transmission of information within a neuron

6. The peripheral nervous system

a. connects the brain to the spinal cord.
b. calms the body after an emergency.
c. is limited to the control of voluntary movement.
d. controls only the arms and the legs.
e. is the part of the nervous system that does not include the brain and the spinal cord.

7. To walk across a street, a person would rely most directly on which division of the nervous system?

a. Central nervous system
b. Sympathetic nervous system
c. Peripheral nervous system
d. Autonomic nervous system
e. Parasympathetic nervous system

8. Opiate drugs such as morphine are classified as what?

a. Antagonists, because they block neurotransmitter receptors for pain
b. Agonists, because they mimic other neurotransmitters' pain-diminishing effects
c. Excitatory neurotransmitters, because they activate pain-control mechanisms
d. Sympathetic nervous system agents, because they prepare the body for a challenge
e. Parasympathetic nervous system agents, because they calm the body

9. Which region of the brain controls our breathing and heartbeat?

a. Pons
b. Corpus callosum
c. Parietal lobe
d. Hippocampus
e. Medulla

10. Which of the following does a PET scan best allow researchers to examine?

a. The presence of tumors in the brain
b. Electrical activity on the surface of the brain
c. The size of the internal structures of the brain
d. The location of strokes
e. The functions of various brain regions

11. A researcher interested in determining the size of a particular area of the brain would be most likely to use what kind of test?

a. Lesion
b. EEG
c. MRI
d. fMRI
e. PET scan

12. Damage to the hippocampus would result in what?

a. Difficulties with balance and coordination
b. Memory problems
c. The false sensation of burning in parts of the body
d. Emotional outbursts
e. Death

13. Surgical stimulation of the somatosensory cortex might result in the false sensation of what?

a. Music
b. Flashes of colored light
c. Someone whispering your name
d. Someone tickling you
e. A bad odor

14. During which task might the right hemisphere of the brain be most active?

a. Solving a mathematical equation
b. Reading
c. Making a brief oral presentation to a class
d. Imagining what a dress would look like on a friend
e. Solving a logic problem

15. Brain plasticity refers to which of the following?

a. Healthy human brain tissue
b. The ability of the brain to transfer information from one hemisphere to the other
c. How a brain gets larger as a child grows
d. A wide variety of functions performed by the human brain
e. The ability of brain tissue to take on new functions

16. When Klüver and Bucy surgically lesioned the amygdala of a rhesus monkey's brain, what was the impact on the monkey's behavior?

a. Lost its ability to coordinate movement
b. Died because its heartbeat became irregular
c. Became less aggressive
d. Lost its memory of where food was stored
e. Sank into an irreversible coma

17. An individual experiences brain damage that produces a coma. Which part of the brain was probably damaged?

a. Corpus callosum
b. Reticular formation
c. Frontal lobe
d. Cerebellum
e. Limbic system

18. Evolutionary psychologists seek to understand how traits and behavioral tendencies have been shaped by what?

a. Natural selection
b. Genes
c. Prenatal nutrition
d. DNA
e. Chromosomes

19. Which is one of the major criticisms of the evolutionary perspective in psychology?

a. It analyzes after the fact using hindsight.
b. It attempts to extend a biological theory into a psychological realm.
c. There is very little evidence to support it.
d. It has not been around long enough to "stand the test of time."
e. It seems to apply in certain cultures but not in others.

20. What was one of the major findings of Thomas Bouchard's study of twins?

a. It demonstrated that peer influence is more important than parental influence in the development of personality traits.
b. It proved that the influence of parental environment becomes more and more important as children grow into adults.
c. He discovered almost unbelievable similarities between adult identical twins who had been separated near birth.
d. Fraternal twins showed almost as much similarity as identical twins when they reached adulthood.
e. It provided evidence that heritability is less important than researchers previously suspected.

21. Which of the following statements has been supported by the research of evolutionary psychologists?

a. Women are attracted to men who appear virile.
b. Men are attracted to women who appear fertile and capable of bearing children.
c. The connection between sex and pleasure is mostly determined by culture.
d. The same factors determine sexual attraction in both males and females.
e. Most adults are attracted to partners that in some way remind them of their parents.

22. Why do researchers find the study of fraternal twins important?

    a. They share similar environments and the same genetic code.

    b. Data collected concerning their similarities is necessary for calculating heritability.

    c. They are the same age and are usually raised in similar environments, but they do not have the same genetic code.

    d. Results allow us to determine exactly how disorders ranging from heart disease to schizophrenia are inherited.

    e. They are typically raised in less similar environments than nontwin siblings.

23. Heritability refers to the percentage of what?

    a. Group variation in a trait that can be explained by environment

    b. Traits shared by identical twins

    c. Traits shared by fraternal twins

    d. Traits shared by adopted children and their birth parents

    e. Group variation in a trait that can be explained by genetics

24. What is the study of specific genes and teams of genes that influence behavior called?

    a. Molecular genetics

    b. Evolutionary psychology

    c. Behavior genetics

    d. Heritability

    e. Natural selection

25. In an effort to reveal genetic influences on personality, researchers use adoption studies mainly for what purpose?

    a. To compare adopted children with nonadopted children

    b. To study the effect of prior neglect on adopted children

    c. To study the effect of a child's age at adoption

    d. To evaluate whether adopted children more closely resemble their adoptive parents or their biological parents

    e. To consider the effects of adoption on a child's manners and values

Free-Response Questions

1. Charlotte is 88 years old and is feeling the effects of her long life. She suffered a stroke five years ago, which left the right side of her body limp. She also sometimes has trouble understanding when she is asked questions. Her doctors believe that she also may be suffering from the beginning stages of Alzheimer's disease. Define each of the following terms and explain how each might contribute to Charlotte's current circumstance.

- Motor cortex
- Acetylcholine
- Association areas
- Plasticity
- Epigenetics

Rubric for Free Response Question 1

1 point: The motor cortex is responsible for directing movements. The left motor cortex controls the right side of the body while the right motor cortex controls the left side of the body. ↪Page 105

1 point: Because Charlotte's right side is limp, the damage from her stroke most likely occurred in the left hemisphere and potentially in her left motor cortex, which would leave her with little muscular control over the right side of her body. ↪Page 105

1 point: Acetylcholine is a neurotransmitter that plays a role in muscle action, learning, and memory. ↪Page 81

1 point: If Charlotte suffers from Alzheimer's disease, it is possible that the neurons responsible for producing acetylcholine have deteriorated. ↪Page 81

1 point: Association areas are the areas of the cerebral cortex not directly involved in motor or sensory functions; rather they are involved in higher-order thought processes such as learning, memory, and thinking. ↪Page 109

1 point: If Charlotte's association areas have been damaged, it may be difficult for her to integrate new ideas. She may also have trouble retrieving memories that were once easily recalled. ↪Page 109

1 point: Plasticity is the brain's ability to create new neural pathways. This often occurs in response to brain injuries and occurs most efficiently in children. ↪Page 111

1 point: Because of Charlotte's age, her brain will not have the ability to build an abundance of new neural networks, and if she has not recovered from her injury in a few months time, she is likely to make little progress in her recovery. ↪Page 111

1 point: Epigenetics is the study of environmental influences on gene expression, which occur without DNA change. ↪Page 131

1 point: Perhaps Charlotte has a predisposition for Alzheimer's disease. If she was in an environment which was not enriching and cognitively engaging, it may have made Alzheimer's disease more likely. On the other hand, despite having a genetic predisposition for Alzheimer's disease, if Charlotte was exposed to an enriching environment, her disposition may not have been expressed. ↪Page 125

2. If a person accidentally touches a pan filled with hot water on the stove, they will immediately move their hand away from the hot pan before yelling out in pain. Use the following terms to explain what is involved in this reaction.

- Neurotransmitters
- The endocrine system
- Thalamus
- Amygdala
- Sensory cortex
- Pain reflex

(6 points)

3. Dr. Nation is a biopsychologist interested in studying genetic influences on brain development. Briefly describe a twin study Dr. Nation might design to investigate the research question: "How do genetics and early environmental influences interact to impact how brains develop?" Use the following terms in context in your description:

- Genes
- Heritability
- Epigenetics
- Fraternal or identical twins
- fMRI

(5 points)

Multiple-choice self-tests and more may be found at www.worthpublishers.com/MyersAP2e

Unit IV

Sensation and Perception

Modules

" I have perfect vision," explains my colleague, Heather Sellers, an acclaimed writer and teacher. Her vision may be fine, but there is a problem with her perception. She cannot recognize faces.

In her memoir, *You Don't Look Like Anyone I Know,* Sellers (2010) tells of awkward moments resulting from her lifelong *prosopagnosia*—face blindness.

> In college, on a date at the Spaghetti Station, I returned from the bathroom and plunked myself down in the wrong booth, facing the wrong man. I remained unaware he was not my date even as my date (a stranger to me) accosted Wrong Booth Guy, and then stormed out of the Station. I can't distinguish actors in movies and on television. I do not recognize myself in photos or videos. I can't recognize my step-sons in the soccer pick-up line; I failed to determine which husband was mine at a party, in the mall, at the market.

Her inability to recognize faces means that people sometimes perceive her as snobby or aloof. "Why did you walk past me?" a neighbor might later ask. Similar to those of us with hearing loss who fake hearing during trite social conversation, Sellers sometimes fakes recognition. She often smiles at people she passes, in case she knows them. Or she pretends to know the person with whom she is talking. (To avoid the stress associated with such perception failures, people with serious hearing loss or with prosopagnosia often shy away from busy social situations.) But there is an upside: When encountering someone who previously irritated her, she typically won't feel ill will, because she doesn't recognize the person.

Unlike Sellers, most of us have (as Module 18 explains) a functioning area on the underside of our brain's right hemisphere that helps us recognize a familiar human face as soon as we detect it—in only one-seventh of a second (Jacques & Rossion, 2006). This ability illustrates a broader principle. *Nature's sensory gifts enable each animal to obtain essential information.* Some examples:

- Frogs, which feed on flying insects, have cells in their eyes that fire only in response to small, dark, moving objects. A frog could starve to death knee-deep in motionless flies. But let one zoom by and the frog's "bug detector" cells snap awake.

- Male silkworm moths' odor receptors can detect one-billionth of an ounce of sex attractant per second released by a female one mile away. That is why silkworms continue to be.

- Human ears are most sensitive to sound frequencies that include human voices, especially a baby's cry.

In this unit, we'll look more closely at what psychologists have learned about how we sense and perceive the world around us.

Module 16

Basic Principles of Sensation and Perception

Beau Lark/Corbis

Module Learning Objectives

16-1 Contrast *sensation* and *perception*, and explain the difference between *bottom-up* and *top-down processing*.

16-2 Discuss how much information we can consciously attend to at once.

16-3 Identify the three steps that are basic to all our sensory systems.

16-4 Distinguish between *absolute* and *difference thresholds*, and discuss whether we can sense and be affected by stimuli below the absolute threshold.

16-5 Explain the function of sensory adaptation.

sensation the process by which our sensory receptors and nervous system receive and represent stimulus energies from our environment.

perception the process of organizing and interpreting sensory information, enabling us to recognize meaningful objects and events.

bottom-up processing analysis that begins with the sensory receptors and works up to the brain's integration of sensory information.

top-down processing information processing guided by higher-level mental processes, as when we construct perceptions drawing on our experience and expectations.

selective attention the focusing of conscious awareness on a particular stimulus.

 What are *sensation* **and** *perception*? **What do we mean by** *bottom-up processing* **and** *top-down processing*?

Sellers' curious mix of "perfect vision" and face blindness illustrates the distinction between sensation and perception. When she looks at a friend, her **sensation** is normal: Her senses detect the same information yours would, and they transmit that information to her brain. And her **perception**—the processes by which her brain organizes and interprets sensory input—is almost normal. Thus, she may recognize people from their hair, gait, voice, or particular physique, just not their face. Her experience is much like the struggle you or I would have trying to recognize a specific penguin in a group of waddling penguins.

In our everyday experiences, sensation and perception blend into one continuous process. In this module, we slow down that process to study its parts, but in real life, our sensory and perceptual processes work together to help us decipher the world around us.

- Our **bottom-up processing** starts at the sensory receptors and works up to higher levels of processing.
- Our **top-down processing** constructs perceptions from the sensory input by drawing on our experience and expectations.

As our brain absorbs the information in **FIGURE 16.1**, bottom-up processing enables our sensory systems to detect the lines, angles, and colors that form the flower and leaves. Using top-down processing we interpret what our senses detect.

But *how* do we do it? How do we create meaning from the blizzard of sensory stimuli bombarding our bodies 24 hours a day? Meanwhile, in a silent, cushioned, inner world, our brain floats in utter darkness. By itself, it sees nothing. It hears nothing. It feels nothing. *So, how does the world out there get in?* To phrase the question scientifically: How do we construct our representations of the external world? How do a campfire's flicker, crackle, and smoky scent activate neural connections? And how, from this living neurochemistry, do we create our conscious experience of the fire's motion and temperature, its aroma and beauty? In search of answers to such questions, let's look at some processes that cut across all our sensory systems. To begin, where is the border between our conscious and unconscious awareness, and what stimuli cross that threshold?

Figure 16.1

What's going on here? Our sensory and perceptual processes work together to help us sort out the complex images, including the hidden couple in Sandro Del-Prete's drawing, *The Flowering of Love.*

Sandro Del-Prete

Selective Attention

 How much information do we consciously attend to at once?

Through **selective attention,** your awareness focuses, like a flashlight beam, on a minute aspect of all that you experience. By one estimate, your five senses take in 11,000,000 bits of information per second, of which you consciously process about 40 (Wilson, 2002). Yet your mind's unconscious track intuitively makes great use of the other 10,999,960 bits. Until reading this sentence, for example, you have been unaware that your shoes are pressing against your feet or that your nose is in your line of vision. Now, suddenly, your attentional spotlight shifts. Your feet feel encased, your nose stubbornly intrudes on the words before you. While focusing on these words, you've also been blocking other parts of your environment from awareness, though your peripheral vision would let you see them easily. You can change that. As you stare at the X below, notice what surrounds these sentences (the edges of the page, the desktop, the floor).

X

A classic example of selective attention is the *cocktail party effect*—your ability to attend to only one voice among many (while also being able to detect your own name in an unattended voice). This effect might have prevented an embarrassing and dangerous situation in

2009, when two commercial airline pilots "lost track of time." Focused on their laptops and conversation, they ignored alarmed air traffic controllers' attempts to reach them as they overflew their Minneapolis destination by 150 miles. If only the controllers had known and spoken the pilots' names.

Selective Attention and Accidents

Text or talk on the phone while driving, or attend to a music player or GPS, and your selective attention will shift back and forth between the road and its electronic competition. But when a demanding situation requires it, you'll probably give the road your full attention. You'll probably also blink less. When focused on a task, such as reading, people blink less than when their mind is wandering (Smilek et al., 2010). If you want to know whether your dinner companion is focused on what you're saying, watch for eyeblinks and hope there won't be too many.

We pay a toll for switching attentional gears, especially when we shift to complex tasks, like noticing and avoiding cars around us. The toll is a slight and sometimes fatal delay in coping (Rubenstein et al., 2001). About 28 percent of traffic accidents occur when people are chatting on cell phones or texting (National Safety Council, 2010). One study tracked long-haul truck drivers for 18 months. The video cameras mounted in their cabs showed they were at 23 times greater risk of a collision while texting (VTTI, 2009). Mindful of such findings, the United States in 2010 banned truckers and bus drivers from texting while driving (Halsey, 2010).

It's not just truck drivers who are at risk. One in four teen drivers with cell phones admit to texting while driving (Pew, 2009). Multitasking comes at a cost: fMRI scans offer a biological account of how multitasking distracts from brain resources allocated to driving. They show that brain activity in areas vital to driving decreases an average 37 percent when a driver is attending to conversation (Just et al., 2008).

Even hands-free cell-phone talking is more distracting than a conversation with passengers, who can see the driving demands and pause the conversation. When University of Sydney researchers analyzed phone records for the moments before a car crash, they found that cell-phone users (even with hands-free sets) were four times more at risk (McEvoy et al., 2005, 2007). Having a passenger increased risk only 1.6 times. This risk difference also appeared in an experiment that asked drivers to pull off at a freeway rest stop 8 miles ahead. Of drivers conversing with a passenger, 88 percent did so. Of those talking on a cell phone, 50 percent drove on by (Strayer & Drews, 2007).

"I wasn't texting. I was building this ship in a bottle."

AP® Exam Tip

You may wish to think about how the information on selective attention relates to something a little less dangerous: studying. The same principles apply. The more time you spend texting, tweeting, and Facebooking, the less focused you'll be on the material you're trying to master. A better strategy is to spend 25 minutes doing schoolwork and schoolwork alone. Then you can reward yourself with a few minutes of social networking.

Driven to distraction In driving-simulation experiments, people whose attention is diverted by cell-phone conversation make more driving errors.

Most European countries and American states now ban hand-held cell phones while driving (Rosenthal, 2009). Engineers are also devising ways to monitor drivers' gaze and to direct their attention back to the road (Lee, 2009).

Selective Inattention

At the level of conscious awareness, we are "blind" to all but a tiny sliver of visual stimuli. Researchers demonstrated this **inattentional blindness** dramatically by showing people a 1-minute video in which images of three black-shirted men tossing a basketball were superimposed over the images of three white-shirted players (Neisser, 1979; Becklen & Cervone, 1983). The viewers' supposed task was to press a key every time a black-shirted player passed the ball. Most focused their attention so completely on the game that they failed to notice a young woman carrying an umbrella saunter across the screen midway through the video (**FIGURE 16.2**). Seeing a replay of the video, viewers were astonished to see her (Mack & Rock, 2000). This inattentional blindness is a by-product of what we are really good at: focusing attention on some part of our environment.

In a repeat of the experiment, smart-aleck researchers Daniel Simons and Christopher Chabris (1999) sent a gorilla-suited assistant through the swirl of players. During its 5- to 9-second cameo appearance, the gorilla paused to thump its chest. Still, half the conscientious pass-counting viewers failed to see it. In another follow-up experiment, only 1 in 4 students engrossed in a cell-phone conversation while crossing a campus square noticed a clown-suited unicyclist in their midst (Hyman et al., 2010). (Most of those not on the phone *did* notice.) Attention is powerfully selective. Your conscious mind is in one place at a time.

Given that most people miss someone in a gorilla or clown suit while their attention is riveted elsewhere, imagine the fun that magicians can have by manipulating our selective attention. Misdirect people's attention and they will miss the hand slipping into the pocket. "Every time you perform a magic trick, you're engaging in experimental psychology," says Teller, a magician and master of mind-messing methods (2009).

Magicians also exploit a form of inattentional blindness called **change blindness.** By selectively riveting our attention on their left hand's dramatic act, we fail to notice changes made with their other hand. In laboratory experiments, viewers didn't notice that, after a brief visual interruption, a big Coke bottle had disappeared, a railing had risen, or clothing color had changed (Chabris & Simons, 2010; Resnick et al., 1997). Focused on giving directions to a construction worker, two out of three people also failed to notice when he was replaced by another worker during a staged interruption (**FIGURE 16.3**). Out of sight, out of mind.

inattentional blindness failing to see visible objects when our attention is directed elsewhere.

change blindness failing to notice changes in the environment.

Figure 16.2

Testing selective attention In this classic experiment, viewers who were attending to basketball tosses among the black-shirted players usually failed to notice the umbrella-toting woman sauntering across the screen. (From Neisser, 1979.)

Figure 16.3
Change blindness While a man (white hair) provides directions to a construction worker, two experimenters rudely pass between them. During this interruption, the original worker switches places with another person wearing different-colored clothing. Most people, focused on their direction giving, do not notice the switch.

An equally astonishing form of inattention is *choice blindness*. At one Swedish supermarket, people tasted two jams, indicated their preference, and then tasted again their preferred jam and explained their preference. Fooled by trick jars (see **FIGURE 16.4**) most people didn't notice that they were actually "retasting" their *non*preferred jam.

Image is from the research paper by Lars Hall, Petter Johansson, and colleagues (2010).

Figure 16.4
Marketplace magic Prankster researchers Lars Hall, Petter Johansson, and colleagues (2010) invited people to sample two jams and pick one to retaste. By flipping the jars after putting the lids back on, the researchers actually induced people to "resample" their nonchosen jam. Yet, even when asked whether they noticed anything odd, most tasters were choice blind. Even when given markedly different jams, they usually failed to notice the switch.

Some stimuli, however, are so powerful, so strikingly distinct, that we experience *pop-out,* as when we notice an angry face in a crowd. We don't choose to attend to these stimuli; they draw our eye and demand our attention.

Our selective attention extends even into our sleep, as we will see.

Transduction

16-3 What three steps are basic to all our sensory systems?

Every second of every day, our sensory systems perform an amazing feat: They convert one form of energy into another. Vision processes light energy. Hearing processes sound waves. All our senses

- *receive* sensory stimulation, often using specialized receptor cells.
- *transform* that stimulation into neural impulses.
- *deliver* the neural information to our brain.

The process of converting one form of energy into another that your brain can use is called **transduction.** Later in this unit, we'll focus on individual sensory systems. How do we see? Hear? Feel pain? Taste? Smell? Keep our balance? In each case, we'll consider these three steps—receiving, transforming, and delivering the information to the brain. We'll also see what **psychophysics** has discovered about the physical energy we can detect and its effects on our psychological experiences.

First, though, let's explore some strengths and weaknesses in our ability to detect and interpret stimuli in the vast sea of energy around us.

transduction conversion of one form of energy into another. In sensation, the transforming of stimulus energies, such as sights, sounds, and smells, into neural impulses our brain can interpret.

psychophysics the study of relationships between the physical characteristics of stimuli, such as their intensity, and our psychological experience of them.

Thresholds

 What are the *absolute* and *difference thresholds*, and do stimuli below the absolute threshold have any influence on us?

At this moment, you and I are being struck by X-rays and radio waves, ultraviolet and infrared light, and sound waves of very high and very low frequencies. To all of these we are blind and deaf. Other animals with differing needs detect a world that lies beyond our experience. Migrating birds stay on course aided by an internal magnetic compass. Bats and dolphins locate prey using sonar, bouncing echoing sound off objects. Bees navigate on cloudy days by detecting invisible (to us) polarized light.

The shades on our own senses are open just a crack, allowing us a restricted awareness of this vast sea of energy. But for our needs, this is enough.

Absolute Thresholds

To some kinds of stimuli we are exquisitely sensitive. Standing atop a mountain on an utterly dark, clear night, most of us could see a candle flame atop another mountain 30 miles away. We could feel the wing of a bee falling on our cheek. We could smell a single drop of perfume in a three-room apartment (Galanter, 1962).

German scientist and philosopher Gustav Fechner (1801–1887) studied our awareness of these faint stimuli and called them our **absolute thresholds**—the minimum stimulation necessary to detect a particular light, sound, pressure, taste, or odor 50 percent of the time. To test your absolute threshold for sounds, a hearing specialist would expose each of your ears to varying sound levels. For each tone, the test would define where half the time you could detect the sound and half the time you could not. That 50-50 point would define your absolute threshold.

Detecting a weak stimulus, or signal, depends not only on the signal's strength (such as a hearing-test tone) but also on our psychological state—our experience, expectations, motivation, and alertness. **Signal detection theory** predicts when we will detect weak signals (measured as our ratio of "hits" to "false alarms") **(FIGURE 16.5)**. Signal detection theorists seek to understand why people respond differently to the same stimuli (have you ever noticed that some teachers are much more likely than others to detect students texting during class?) and why the same person's reactions vary as circumstances change. Exhausted parents will notice the faintest whimper from a newborn's cradle while failing to notice louder, unimportant sounds. Lonely, anxious people at speed-dating events also respond with a low threshold and thus tend to be unselective in reaching out to potential dates (McClure et al., 2010).

> **absolute threshold** the minimum stimulation needed to detect a particular stimulus 50 percent of the time.
>
> **signal detection theory** a theory predicting how and when we detect the presence of a faint stimulus *(signal)* amid background stimulation *(noise)*. Assumes that there is no single absolute threshold and that detection depends partly on a person's experience, expectations, motivation, and alertness.

Try This

Try out this old riddle on a couple of friends. "You're driving a bus with 12 passengers. At your first stop, 6 passengers get off. At the second stop, 3 get off. At the third stop, 2 more get off but 3 new people get on. What color are the bus driver's eyes?" Do your friends detect the signal—who is the bus driver?—amid the accompanying noise?

Figure 16.5

Signal detection What three factors will make it more likely that you correctly detect a text message?

ANSWER: (1) You are expecting a text message. (2) It is important that you see the text message and respond. (3) You are alert.

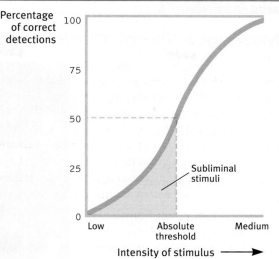

Figure 16.6
Absolute threshold Can I detect this sound? An *absolute threshold* is the intensity at which a person can detect a stimulus half the time. Hearing tests locate these thresholds for various frequency levels. Stimuli below your absolute threshold are subliminal.

Stimuli you cannot detect 50 percent of the time are **subliminal**—below your absolute threshold (**FIGURE 16.6**). Under certain conditions, you can be affected by stimuli so weak that you don't consciously notice them. An unnoticed image or word can reach your visual cortex and briefly **prime** your response to a later question. In a typical experiment, the image or word is quickly flashed, then replaced by a *masking stimulus* that interrupts the brain's processing before conscious perception (Van den Bussche et al., 2009). For example, one experiment subliminally flashed either emotionally positive scenes (kittens, a romantic couple) or negative scenes (a werewolf, a dead body) an instant before participants viewed slides of people (Krosnick et al., 1992). The participants consciously perceived either scene as only a flash of light. Yet the people somehow looked nicer if their image immediately followed unperceived kittens rather than an unperceived werewolf. As other experiments confirm, we can evaluate a stimulus even when we are not aware of it—and even when we are unaware of our evaluation (Ferguson & Zayas, 2009).

How do we feel or respond to what we do not know and cannot describe? An imperceptibly brief stimulus often triggers a weak response that *can* be detected by brain scanning (Blankenburg et al., 2003; Haynes & Rees, 2005, 2006). Only when the stimulus triggers synchronized activity in several brain areas does it reach consciousness (Dehaene, 2009). Once again we see the dual-track mind at work: *Much of our information processing occurs automatically, out of sight, off the radar screen of our conscious mind.*

So can we be controlled by subliminal messages? For more on that question, see Thinking Critically About: Can Subliminal Messages Control Our Behavior? on the next page.

subliminal below one's absolute threshold for conscious awareness.

priming the activation, often unconsciously, of certain associations, thus predisposing one's perception, memory, or response.

"The heart has its reasons which reason does not know." -Pascal, *Pensées*, 1670

Difference Thresholds

To function effectively, we need absolute thresholds low enough to allow us to detect important sights, sounds, textures, tastes, and smells. We also need to detect small differences among stimuli. A musician must detect minute discrepancies when tuning an instrument. Students in the hallway must detect the sound of their friends' voices amid all the other voices. Even after living two years in Scotland, sheep *baa*'s all sound alike to my ears. But not to those of ewes, which I have observed streaking, after shearing, directly to the *baa* of their lamb amid the chorus of other distressed lambs.

Eric Isselée/Shutterstock

Thinking Critically About

Can Subliminal Messages Control Our Behavior?

Hoping to penetrate our unconscious, entrepreneurs offer audio and video programs to help us lose weight, stop smoking, or improve our memories. Soothing ocean sounds may mask messages we cannot consciously hear: "I am thin"; "Smoke tastes bad"; or "I do well on tests—I have total recall of information." Such claims make two assumptions: (1) We can unconsciously sense subliminal (literally, "below threshold") stimuli. (2) Without our awareness, these stimuli have extraordinary suggestive powers. Can we? Do they?

As we have seen, subliminal *sensation* is a fact. Remember that an "absolute" threshold is merely the point at which we can detect a stimulus *half the time*. At or slightly below this threshold, we will still detect the stimulus some of the time.

But does this mean that claims of subliminal *persuasion* are also facts? The near-consensus among researchers is *No*. The laboratory research reveals a *subtle, fleeting* effect. Priming thirsty people with the subliminal word *thirst* might therefore, for a moment, make a thirst-quenching beverage ad more persuasive (Strahan et al., 2002). Likewise, priming thirsty people with Lipton Iced Tea may increase their choosing the primed brand (Karremans et al., 2006; Veltkamp et al., 2011; Verwijmeren et al., 2011a,b). But the subliminal-message hucksters claim something different: a *powerful, enduring* effect on behavior.

To test whether subliminal recordings have this enduring effect, researchers randomly assigned university students to listen daily for 5 weeks to commercial subliminal messages claiming to improve either self-esteem or memory (Greenwald et al., 1991, 1992). But the researchers played a practical joke and switched half the labels. Some students who thought they were receiving affirmations of self-esteem were actually hearing the memory-enhancement message. Others got the self-esteem message but thought their memory was being recharged.

Were the recordings effective? Students' test scores for self-esteem and memory, taken before and after the 5 weeks,

Babs Reingold for Worth Publishers

Subliminal persuasion? Although subliminally presented stimuli *can* subtly influence people, experiments discount attempts at subliminal advertising and self-improvement. (The playful message here is not actually subliminal—because you can easily perceive it.)

revealed no effects. Yet the students *perceived* themselves receiving the benefits they *expected*. Those who *thought* they had heard a memory recording *believed* their memories had improved. Those who thought they had heard a self-esteem recording believed their self-esteem had grown. (Reading this research, one hears echoes of the testimonies that ooze from ads for such products. Some customers, having bought what is not supposed to be heard [and having indeed not heard it!] offer testimonials like, "I really know that your recordings were invaluable in reprogramming my mind.")

Over a decade, Greenwald conducted 16 double-blind experiments evaluating subliminal self-help recordings. His results were uniform: Not one of the recordings helped more than a placebo (Greenwald, 1992). And placebos, you may remember, work only because we *believe* they will work.

The difference threshold In this computer-generated copy of the Twenty-third Psalm, each line of the typeface increases slightly. How many lines are required for you to experience a just noticeable difference?

The LORD is my shepherd;
  I shall not want.
He maketh me to lie down
    in green pastures:
  he leadeth me
    beside the still waters.
He restoreth my soul:
  he leadeth me
    in the paths of righteousness
    for his name's sake.
Yea, though I walk through the valley
    of the shadow of death,
  I will fear no evil:
for thou art with me;
    thy rod and thy staff
    they comfort me.
Thou preparest a table before me
    in the presence of mine enemies:
  thou anointest my head with oil,
    my cup runneth over.
Surely goodness and mercy
    shall follow me
    all the days of my life:
and I will dwell
    in the house of the LORD
    for ever.

The **difference threshold** (or the *just noticeable difference [jnd]*) is the minimum difference a person can detect between any two stimuli half the time. That difference threshold increases with the size of the stimulus. Thus, if you add 1 ounce to a 10-ounce weight, you will detect the difference; add 1 ounce to a 100-ounce weight and you probably will not.

In the nineteenth century, Ernst Weber noted something so simple and so widely applicable that we still refer to it as **Weber's law.** This law states that for an average person to perceive a difference, two stimuli must differ by a constant minimum *percentage* (not a constant *amount*). The exact proportion varies, depending on the stimulus. Two lights, for example, must differ in intensity by 8 percent. Two objects must differ in weight by 2 percent. And two tones must differ in frequency by only 0.3 percent (Teghtsoonian, 1971). For example, to be perceptibly different, a 50-ounce weight must differ from another by about an ounce, a 100-ounce weight by about 2 ounces.

Sensory Adaptation

16-5 What is the function of sensory adaptation?

Entering your neighbors' living room, you smell a musty odor. You wonder how they can stand it, but within minutes you no longer notice it. **Sensory adaptation** has come to your rescue. When we are constantly exposed to a stimulus that does not change, we become less aware of it because our nerve cells fire less frequently. (To experience sensory adaptation, move your watch up your wrist an inch: You will feel it—but only for a few moments.)

Why, then, if we stare at an object without flinching, does it *not* vanish from sight? Because, unnoticed by us, our eyes are always moving. This continual flitting from one spot to another ensures that stimulation on the eyes' receptors continually changes (**FIGURE 16.7**).

What if we actually could stop our eyes from moving? Would sights seem to vanish, as odors do? To find out, psychologists have devised ingenious instruments that maintain a constant image on the eye's inner surface. Imagine that we have fitted a volunteer, Mary, with one of these instruments—a miniature projector mounted on a contact lens (**FIGURE 16.8a** on the next page). When Mary's eye moves, the image from the projector moves as well. So everywhere that Mary looks, the scene is sure to go.

If we project images through this instrument, what will Mary see? At first, she will see the complete image. But within a few seconds, as her sensory system begins to fatigue, things get weird. Bit by bit, the image vanishes, only to reappear and then disappear—often in fragments (Figure 16.8b).

Although sensory adaptation reduces our sensitivity, it offers an important benefit: freedom to focus on *informative* changes in our environment without being distracted by background chatter. Stinky or heavily perfumed classmates don't notice their odor because, like you and me, they adapt to what's constant and detect only change. Our sensory receptors

difference threshold the minimum difference between two stimuli required for detection 50 percent of the time. We experience the difference threshold as a *just noticeable difference* (or *jnd*).

Weber's law the principle that, to be perceived as different, two stimuli must differ by a constant minimum percentage (rather than a constant amount).

sensory adaptation diminished sensitivity as a consequence of constant stimulation.

"We need above all to know about changes; no one wants or needs to be reminded 16 hours a day that his shoes are on." -NEUROSCIENTIST DAVID HUBEL (1979)

Figure 16.7

The jumpy eye Our gaze jumps from one spot to another every third of a second or so, as eye-tracking equipment illustrated in this photograph of Edinburgh's Princes Street Gardens (Henderson, 2007). The circles represent fixations, and the numbers indicate the time of fixation in milliseconds (300 milliseconds = three-tenths of a second).

John M. Henderson

Figure 16.8

Sensory adaptation: Now you see it, now you don't!
(a) A projector mounted on a contact lens makes the projected image move with the eye. (b) Initially, the person sees the stabilized image, but soon she sees fragments fading and reappearing. (From "Stabilized images on the retina," by R. M. Pritchard. Copyright © 1961 Scientific American, Inc. All rights reserved.)

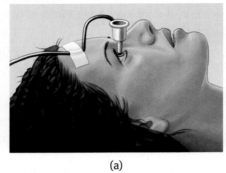

(a)

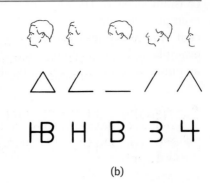

(b)

are alert to novelty; bore them with repetition and they free our attention for more important things. We will see this principle again and again: *We perceive the world not exactly as it is, but as it is useful for us to perceive it.*

Our sensitivity to changing stimulation helps explain television's attention-grabbing power. Cuts, edits, zooms, pans, sudden noises—all demand attention. The phenomenon is irresistible even to TV researchers. One noted that even during interesting conversations, "I cannot for the life of me stop from periodically glancing over to the screen" (Tannenbaum, 2002).

Sensory adaptation even influences our perceptions of emotions. By creating a 50-50 morphed blend of an angry and a scared face, researchers showed that our visual system adapts to a static facial expression by becoming less responsive to it (Butler et al., 2008) (**FIGURE 16.9**).

Sensory adaptation and sensory thresholds are important ingredients in our perceptions of the world around us. Much of what we perceive comes not just from what's "out there" but also from what's behind our eyes and between our ears.

Figure 16.9

Emotion adaptation Gaze at the angry face on the left for 20 to 30 seconds, then look at the center face (looks scared, yes?). Then gaze at the scared face on the right for 20 to 30 seconds, before returning to the center face (now looks angry, yes?).

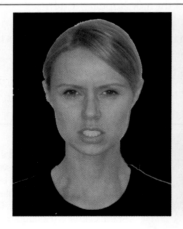
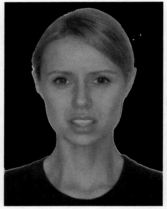

Before You Move On

▶ **ASK YOURSELF**

Can you recall a recent time when, your attention focused on one thing, you were oblivious to something else (perhaps to pain, to someone's approach, or to background music)?

▶ **TEST YOURSELF**

Explain how Heather Sellers' experience of prosopagnosia illustrates the difference between sensation and perception.

Answers to the Test Yourself questions can be found in Appendix E at the end of the book.

Module 16 Review

 What are *sensation* and *perception*? What do we mean by *bottom-up processing* and *top-down processing*?

- *Sensation* is the process by which our sensory receptors and nervous system receive and represent stimulus energies from our environment. *Perception* is the process of organizing and interpreting this information, enabling recognition of meaningful events. Sensation and perception are actually parts of one continuous process.

- *Bottom-up processing* is sensory analysis that begins at the entry level, with information flowing from the sensory receptors to the brain. *Top-down processing* is information processing guided by high-level mental processes, as when we construct perceptions by filtering information through our experience and expectations.

 How much information do we consciously attend to at once?

- We *selectively attend* to, and process, a very limited portion of incoming information, blocking out much and often shifting the spotlight of our attention from one thing to another.

- Focused intently on one task, we often display *inattentional blindness* (including *change blindness*) to other events and changes around us.

 What three steps are basic to all our sensory systems?

- Our senses (1) receive sensory stimulation (often using specialized receptor cells); (2) transform that stimulation into neural impulses; and (3) deliver the neural information to the brain. *Transduction* is the process of converting one form of energy into another.

- Researchers in *psychophysics* study the relationships between stimuli's physical characteristics and our psychological experience of them.

What are the *absolute* and *difference* thresholds, and do stimuli below the absolute threshold have any influence on us?

- Our *absolute threshold* for any stimulus is the minimum stimulation necessary for us to be consciously aware of it 50 percent of the time. *Signal detection theory* predicts how and when we will detect a faint stimulus amid background noise. Individual absolute thresholds vary, depending on the strength of the signal and also on our experience, expectations, motivation, and alertness.

- Our *difference threshold* (also called *just noticeable difference*, or *jnd*) is the difference we can discern between two stimuli 50 percent of the time. *Weber's law* states that two stimuli must differ by a constant percentage (not a constant amount) to be perceived as different.

- *Priming* shows that we can process some information from stimuli below our absolute threshold for conscious awareness. But the effect is too fleeting to enable people to exploit us with *subliminal* messages.

What is the function of sensory adaptation?

- *Sensory adaptation* (our diminished sensitivity to constant or routine odors, sights, sounds, and touches) focuses our attention on informative changes in our environment.

Multiple-Choice Questions

1. What occurs when experiences influence our interpretation of data?

a. Selective attention
b. Transduction
c. Bottom-up processing
d. Top-down processing
e. Signal detection theory

2. What principle states that to be perceived as different, two stimuli must differ by a minimum percentage rather than a constant amount?

a. Absolute threshold
b. Different threshold
c. Signal detection theory
d. Priming
e. Weber's law

3. What do we call the conversion of stimulus energies, like sights and sounds, into neural impulses?

a. Transduction
b. Perception
c. Priming
d. Signal detection theory
e. Threshold

4. Natalia is washing her hands and adjusts the faucet handle until the water feels just slightly hotter than it did before. Natalia's adjustment until she feels a difference is an example of

a. a subliminal stimulus.
b. an absolute threshold.
c. a difference threshold.
d. signal detection.
e. Weber's law.

5. Tyshane went swimming with friends who did not want to get into the pool because the water felt cold. Tyshane jumped in and after a few minutes declared, "It was cold when I first got in, but now my body is used to it. Come on in!" Tyshane's body became accustomed to the water due to

a. perceptual set.
b. absolute threshold.
c. difference threshold.
d. selective attention.
e. sensory adaptation.

Practice FRQs

1. Explain how bottom-up and top-down processes work together to help us decipher the world around us..

Answer

1 point: Bottom-up processing starts at the sensory receptors and works up to higher levels of processing.

1 point: Top-down processing constructs perceptions from the sensory input by drawing on our experience and expectations.

2. Marisol is planning a ski trip for spring break. Define absolute threshold and difference threshold, and explain how each one might play a role in her perception of the winter weather she will experience.

(4 points)

Module 17

Influences on Perception

© Nick Dolding/cultura/Corbis

Module Learning Objectives

17-1 Explain how our expectations, contexts, emotions, and motivation influence our perceptions.

17-2 List the claims of ESP, and discuss the conclusions of most research psychologists after putting these claims to the test.

Perceptual Set

17-1 How do our expectations, contexts, emotions, and motivation influence our perceptions?

As everyone knows, to see is to believe. As we less fully appreciate, to believe is to see. Through experience, we come to expect certain results. Those expectations may give us a **perceptual set,** a set of mental tendencies and assumptions that greatly affects (top-down) what we perceive. Perceptual set can influence what we hear, taste, feel, and see.

Consider: Is the image in the center picture of **FIGURE 17.1** a young woman's profile or an old woman? What we see in such a drawing can be influenced by first looking at either of the two unambiguous versions (Boring, 1930).

Everyday examples of perceptual set abound. In 1972, a British newspaper published unretouched photographs of a "monster" in Scotland's Loch Ness—"the most amazing

> **perceptual set** a mental predisposition to perceive one thing and not another.

Figure 17.1
Perceptual set Show a friend either the left or right image. Then show the center image and ask, "What do you see?" Whether your friend reports seeing a young woman's profile or an old woman may depend on which of the other two drawings was viewed first. In each of those images, the meaning is clear, and it will establish perceptual expectations.

pictures ever taken," stated the paper. If this information creates in you the same expectations it did in most of the paper's readers, you, too, will see the monster in a similar photo in **FIGURE 17.2**. But when a skeptical researcher approached the photos with different expectations, he saw a curved tree limb—as had others the day the photo was shot (Campbell, 1986). With this different perceptual set, you may now notice that the object is floating motionless, with ripples outward in all directions—hardly what we would expect of a lively monster. Once we have formed a wrong idea about reality, we have more difficulty seeing the truth.

Perceptual set can also affect what we hear. Consider the kindly airline pilot who, on a takeoff run, looked over at his depressed co-pilot and said, "Cheer up." Expecting to hear the usual "Gear up," the co-pilot promptly raised the wheels—before they left the ground (Reason & Mycielska, 1982).

Figure 17.2

Believing is seeing What do you perceive? Is this Nessie, the Loch Ness monster, or a log?

Hulton Archive/Getty Images

Perceptual set similarly affects taste. One experiment invited some bar patrons to sample free beer (Lee et al., 2006). When researchers added a few drops of vinegar to a brand-name beer, the tasters preferred it—unless they had been told they were drinking vinegar-laced beer. Then they expected, and usually experienced, a worse taste. In another experiment, preschool children, by a 6-to-1 margin, thought french fries tasted better when served in a McDonald's bag rather than a plain white bag (Robinson et al., 2007).

What determines our perceptual set? As Module 47 will explain, through experience we form concepts, or *schemas,* that organize and allow us to interpret unfamiliar information. Our pre-existing schemas for old women and young women, for monsters and tree limbs, all influence how we interpret ambiguous sensations with top-down processing.

In everyday life, stereotypes about gender (another instance of perceptual set) can color perception. Without the obvious cues of pink or blue, people will struggle over whether to call the new baby "he" or "she." But told an infant is "David," people (especially children) may perceive "him" as bigger and stronger than if the same infant is called "Diana" (Stern & Karraker, 1989). Some differences, it seems, exist merely in the eyes of their beholders.

"We hear and apprehend only what we already half know."
-Henry David Thoreau, *Journal,* 1860

Context Effects

A given stimulus may trigger radically different perceptions, partly because of our differing perceptual set, but also because of the immediate context. Some examples:

Culture and context effects
What is above the woman's head? In a classic study from nearly a half-century ago, most East Africans perceived the woman as balancing a metal box or can on her head and the family as sitting under a tree. Westerners, for whom corners and boxlike architecture were more common, were more likely to perceive the family as being indoors, with the woman sitting under a window. (Adapted from Gregory & Gombrich, 1973.)

- Imagine hearing a noise interrupted by the words "eel is on the wagon." Likely, you would actually perceive the first word as *wheel*. Given "eel is on the orange," you would hear *peel*. This curious phenomenon, discovered by Richard Warren, suggests that the brain can work backward in time to allow a later stimulus to determine how we perceive an earlier one. The context creates an expectation that, top-down, influences our perception (Grossberg, 1995).

- Does the pursuing dog in **FIGURE 17.3** look bigger than the one being pursued? If so, you are experiencing a context effect.

- How tall is the shorter player in **FIGURE 17.4**?

Figure 17.3

The interplay between context and emotional perception The context makes the pursuing dog look bigger than the pursued. It isn't.

Dennis Geppert/Holland Sentinel

Figure 17.4

Big and "little" The "little guy" shown here is actually a 6'9" former Hope College basketball center who would tower over most of us. But he seemed like a short player when matched in a semi-pro game against the world's tallest basketball player at that time, 7'9" Sun Ming Ming from China.

Emotion and Motivation

Perceptions are influenced, top-down, not only by our expectations and by the context, but also by our emotions and motivation.

Hearing sad rather than happy music can predispose people to perceive a sad meaning in spoken homophonic words—*mourning* rather than *morning, die* rather than *dye, pain* rather than *pane* (Halberstadt et al., 1995).

Researchers (Proffitt, 2006a,b; Schnall et al., 2008) have demonstrated the power of emotions with other clever experiments showing that

- walking destinations look farther away to those who have been fatigued by prior exercise.
- a hill looks steeper to those who are wearing a heavy backpack or have just been exposed to sad, heavy classical music rather than light, bouncy music. As with so many of life's challenges, a hill also seems less steep to those with a friend beside them.
- a target seems farther away to those throwing a heavy rather than a light object at it.

Even a softball appears bigger when you are hitting well, observed other researchers, after asking players to choose a circle the size of the ball they had just hit well or poorly (Witt & Proffitt, 2005). When angry, people more often perceive neutral objects as guns (Bauman & DeSteno, 2010).

Motives also matter. Desired objects, such as a water bottle when thirsty, seem closer (Balcetis & Dunning, 2010). This perceptual bias energizes our going for it. Our motives also direct our perception of ambiguous images.

Emotions color our social perceptions, too. Spouses who feel loved and appreciated perceive less threat in stressful marital events—"He's just having a bad day" (Murray et al., 2003). Professional referees, if told a soccer team has a history of aggressive behavior, will assign more penalty cards after watching videotaped fouls (Jones et al., 2002).

* * *

Emotion and motivation clearly influence how we perceive sensations. But what to make of extrasensory perception, which claims that perception can occur apart from sensory input? For more on that question, see Thinking Critically About: ESP—Perception Without Sensation?

> "When you're hitting the ball, it comes at you looking like a grapefruit. When you're not, it looks like a blackeyed pea."
> -Former Major League Baseball player George Scott

Before You Move On

▶ **ASK YOURSELF**
Can you recall a time when your expectations have predisposed how you perceived a person (or group of people)?

▶ **TEST YOURSELF**
What type of evidence shows that, indeed, "there is more to perception than meets the senses"?

Answers to the Test Yourself questions can be found in Appendix E at the end of the book.

Thinking Critically About

ESP—Perception Without Sensation?

 17-2 What are the claims of ESP, and what have most research psychologists concluded after putting these claims to the test?

Without sensory input, are we capable of **extrasensory perception (ESP)**? Are there indeed people—any people—who can read minds, see through walls, or foretell the future? Nearly half of Americans believe there are (AP, 2007; Moore, 2005).

The most testable and, for this unit, most relevant parapsychological concepts are

- *telepathy:* mind-to-mind communication.
- *clairvoyance:* perceiving remote events, such as a house on fire in another state.
- *precognition:* perceiving future events, such as an unexpected death in the next month.

Closely linked is *psychokinesis,* or "mind over matter," such as levitating a table or influencing the roll of a die. (The claim is illustrated by the wry request, "Will all those who believe in psychokinesis please raise my hand?")

If ESP is real, we would need to overturn the scientific understanding that we are creatures whose minds are tied to our physical brains and whose perceptual experiences of the world are built of sensations. Sometimes new evidence does overturn our scientific preconceptions. Science, as we will see throughout this book, offers us various surprises—about the extent of the unconscious mind, about the effects of emotions on health, about what heals and what doesn't, and much more.

Most research psychologists and scientists—including 96 percent of the scientists in the U.S. National Academy of Sciences—are skeptical that paranormal phenomena exist (McConnell, 1991). But reputable universities in many locations, including Great Britain, the Netherlands, and Australia, have added faculty chairs or research units in **parapsychology** (Turpin, 2005). These researchers perform scientific experiments searching for possible ESP and other paranormal phenomena. Before seeing how parapsychologists do research on ESP, let's consider some popular beliefs.

PREMONITIONS OR PRETENSIONS?

Can psychics see into the future? Although one might wish for a psychic stock forecaster, the tallied forecasts of "leading psychics" reveal meager accuracy. During the 1990s, the tabloid psychics were all wrong in predicting surprising events. (Madonna did not become a gospel singer, the Statue of Liberty did not lose both its arms in a terrorist blast, Queen Elizabeth did not abdicate her throne to enter a convent.) And the new-century psychics have missed the big-news events. Where were the psychics on 9/10 when we needed them? Why, despite a $50 million reward offered, could none of them help locate terrorist Osama bin Laden after the horror of 9/11, or step forward to predict the impending stock crashes in 2008? In 30 years, unusual predictions have almost never come true, and psychics have virtually never anticipated any of the year's headline events (Emory, 2004, 2006). In 2010, when a mine collapse trapped 33 miners, the Chilean government reportedly consulted four psychics. Their verdict? "They're all dead" (Kraul, 2010). But 69 days later, all 33 were rescued.

Moreover, the hundreds of psychic visions offered to police departments have been no more accurate than guesses made by others (Nickell, 1994, 2005; Radford, 2010; Reiser, 1982). But their sheer volume does increase the odds of an occasional correct guess, which psychics can then report to the media. Police departments are wise to all this. When researchers asked the police departments of America's 50 largest cities whether they ever had used psychics, 65 percent said *No* (Sweat & Durm, 1993). Of those that had, not one had found them helpful. Vague predictions can also later be interpreted ("retrofitted")

Will you marry me, live happily for 3 years, become bored, pretend to be taking a pottery class but actually be having an affair, then agree to go to marriage counseling to stay together for the sake of our hyperactive son, Derrick?

WHEN PSYCHICS PROPOSE

extrasensory perception (ESP) the controversial claim that perception can occur apart from sensory input; includes telepathy, clairvoyance, and precognition.

parapsychology the study of paranormal phenomena, including ESP and psychokinesis.

(continued on next page)

Thinking Critically About (continued)

to match events that provide a perceptual set for "understanding" them. Nostradamus, a sixteenth-century French psychic, explained in an unguarded moment that his ambiguous prophecies "could not possibly be understood till they were interpreted after the event and by it."

Are the spontaneous "visions" of everyday people any more accurate? Do dreams, for example, foretell the future, as people from both Eastern and Western cultures tend to believe—making some people more reluctant to fly after dreaming of a plane crash (Morewedge & Norton, 2009)? Or do they only seem to do so when we recall or reconstruct them in light of what has already happened? Two Harvard psychologists tested the prophetic power of dreams after superhero aviator Charles Lindbergh's baby son was kidnapped and murdered in 1932, but before the body was discovered (Murray & Wheeler, 1937). When invited to report their dreams about the child, 1300 visionaries submitted dream reports. How many accurately envisioned the child dead? Five percent. And how many also correctly anticipated the body's location—buried among trees? Only 4 of the 1300. Although this number was surely no better than chance, to those 4 dreamers the accuracy of their apparent precognitions must have seemed uncanny.

Given the billions of events in the world each day, and given enough days, some stunning coincidences are sure to occur. By one careful estimate, chance alone would predict that more than a thousand times a day someone on Earth will think of another person and then within the next five minutes will learn of that person's death (Charpak & Broch, 2004). Thus, when explaining an astonishing event, we should "give chance a chance" (Lilienfeld, 2009). With enough time and people, the improbable becomes inevitable.

> "To be sure of hitting the target, shoot first and call whatever you hit the target." -Writer-artist Ashleigh Brilliant, 1933

> "A person who talks a lot is sometimes right." -Spanish proverb

PUTTING ESP TO EXPERIMENTAL TEST

When faced with claims of mind reading or out-of-body travel or communication with the dead, how can we separate bizarre ideas from those that sound strange but are true? At the heart of science is a simple answer: *Test them to see if they work.* If they do, so much the better for the ideas. If they don't, so much the better for our skepticism.

This scientific attitude has led both believers and skeptics to agree that what parapsychology needs is a reproducible phenomenon and a theory to explain it. Parapsychologist Rhea White (1998) spoke for many in saying that "the image of parapsychology that comes to my mind, based on nearly 44 years in the field, is that of a small airplane [that] has been perpetually taxiing down the runway of the Empirical Science Airport since 1882 . . . its movement punctuated occasionally by lifting a few feet off the ground only to bump back down on the tarmac once again. It has never taken off for any sustained flight."

How might we test ESP claims in a controlled, reproducible experiment? An experiment differs from a staged demonstration. In the laboratory, the experimenter controls what the "psychic" sees and hears. On stage, the psychic controls what the audience sees and hears.

The search for a valid and reliable test of ESP has resulted in thousands of experiments. After digesting data from 30 such studies, parapsychologist Lance Storm and his colleagues (2010a,b) concluded that, given participants with experience or belief in ESP, there is "consistent and reliable" parapsychological evidence. Psychologist Ray Hyman (2010), who has been scrutinizing parapsychological research since 1957, replies that if this is the best evidence, it fails to impress: "Parapsychology will achieve scientific acceptability only when it provides a positive theory with . . . independently replicable evidence. This is something it has yet to achieve after more than a century."

Daryl Bem (2011), a respected social psychologist, has been a skeptic of stage psychics; he once quipped that "a psychic is an actor playing the role of a psychic" (1984). Yet he has reignited hopes for replicable evidence with nine experiments that seemed to show people anticipating future events. In one,

> "At the heart of science is an essential tension between two seemingly contradictory attitudes—an openness to new ideas, no matter how bizarre or counterintuitive they may be, and the most ruthless skeptical scrutiny of all ideas, old and new." -Carl Sagan (1987)

> Magician Harry Houdini after fooling Sir Arthur Conan Doyle with a pseudo-psychic trick: "Now I beg of you, Sir Arthur, do not jump to the conclusion that certain things you see are necessarily 'supernatural,' or with the work of 'spirits,' just because you cannot explain them." -Quoted by William Kalush and Larry Sloman, *The Secret Life of Houdini*, 2007

Thinking Critically About *(continued)*

when an erotic scene was about to appear on a screen in one of two randomly selected positions, Cornell University participants guessed right 53.1 percent of the time (beating 50 percent by a small but statistically significant margin). In another, people viewed a set of words, took a recall test of those words, and then rehearsed a randomly selected subset of those words. People better remembered the rehearsed words—even when the rehearsal took place *after* the recall test. The upcoming rehearsal—a future event—apparently affected their ability to recall words.

Bem wonders if his "anomalous" findings reflect an evolutionary advantage to those who can precognitively anticipate future dangers. Critics scoff. "If any of his claims were true," wrote cognitive scientist Douglas Hofstadter (2011), "then all of the bases underlying contemporary science would be toppled, and we would have to rethink everything about the nature of the universe." Moreover, if future events retroactively affect present feelings, then why can't people intuitively predict casino outcomes or stock market futures?

Despite Bem's research having survived critical reviews by a top-tier journal, other critics found the methods "badly flawed" (Alcock, 2011) or the statistical analyses "biased" (Wagenmakers et al., 2011). "A result—especially one of this importance—must recur several times in tests by independent and skeptical researchers to gain scientific credibility," observed astronomer David Helfand (2011). "I have little doubt that Professor Bem's experiments will fail this test."

Anticipating such skepticism, Bem has made his computer materials available to anyone who wishes to replicate his studies, and replications are now under way. One research team has already conducted five replications of Bem's recall experiments at various universities and found no precognition (Galak et al., 2011). Regardless of the outcomes, science will have done its work. It will have been open to a finding that challenges its own worldview, and then, through follow-up research, it will have assessed its validity. And that is how science sifts crazy-sounding ideas, leaving most on the historical waste heap while occasionally surprising us.

One skeptic, magician James Randi, has had a longstanding offer of $1 million to be given "to anyone who proves a genuine psychic power under proper observing conditions" (Randi, 1999; Thompson, 2010). French, Australian, and Indian groups have made similar offers of up to 200,000 euros (CFI, 2003). Large as these sums are, the scientific seal of approval would be worth far more. To refute those who say there is no ESP,

Testing psychic powers in the British population
University of Hertfordshire psychologists created a "mind machine" to see if people can influence or predict a coin toss (Wiseman & Greening, 2002). Using a touch-sensitive screen, visitors to festivals around the country were given four attempts to call heads or tails. Using a random-number generator, a computer then decided the outcome. When the experiment concluded in January 2000, nearly 28,000 people had predicted 110,959 tosses—with 49.8 percent correct.

one need only produce a single person who can demonstrate a single, reproducible ESP event. (To refute those who say pigs can't talk would take but one talking pig.) So far, no such person has emerged.

Before You Move On

▶ **ASK YOURSELF**

Have you ever had what felt like an ESP experience? Can you think of an explanation other than ESP for that experience?

▶ **TEST YOURSELF**

What is the field of study that researches claims of extrasensory perception (ESP)?

Answers to the Test Yourself questions can be found in Appendix E at the end of the book.

Module 17 Review

 17-1 How do our expectations, contexts, emotions, and motivation influence our perceptions?

- *Perceptual set* is a mental predisposition that functions as a lens through which we perceive the world.

- Our learned concepts (schemas) prime us to organize and interpret ambiguous stimuli in certain ways.

- Our physical and emotional context, as well as our motivation, can create expectations and color our interpretation of events and behaviors.

 17-2 What are the claims of ESP, and what have most research psychologists concluded after putting these claims to the test?

- *Parapsychology* is the study of paranormal phenomena, including *extrasensory perception (ESP)* and psychokinesis.

- The three most testable forms of ESP are telepathy (mind-to-mind communication), clairvoyance (perceiving remote events), and precognition (perceiving future events).

- Skeptics argue that (1) to believe in ESP, you must believe the brain is capable of perceiving without sensory input, and (2) researchers have been unable to replicate ESP phenomena under controlled conditions.

Multiple-Choice Questions

1. What do we call a mental predisposition that influences our interpretation of a stimulus?
   a. A context effect
   b. Perceptual set
   c. Extrasensory perception
   d. Emotion
   e. Motivation

2. Kimberly tells her brother to put on a suit on a warm summer day. Kimberly's brother knows to put on a swimsuit instead of a business suit because of
   a. context.
   b. ESP.
   c. precognition.
   d. bottom-up processing.
   e. clairvoyance.

3. Which of the following is produced by perceptual set?
   a. Not noticing that the songs change in a restaurant
   b. Noticing a difference in the weight of a friend from one week to the next
   c. Moving an arm quickly so that a mosquito flies away
   d. Surprise at hearing an Oklahoma cowboy speak with a British accent
   e. Not noticing a watch on your wrist as the day goes on

Practice FRQs

1. Martha is convinced she has extrasensory perception. Explain what Martha's specific abilities would be if she had each of the following forms of ESP:
   - Telepathy
   - Clairvoyance
   - Precognition

   Then, briefly explain why you should doubt her claims.

Answer

1 point: Telepathy: Martha would be able to use mind-to-mind communication; that is, she is able to read someone's mind.

1 point: Clairvoyance: Martha would be able to perceive things happening at a distance; that is, a cousin who lives in another state just burnt her hand on the oven, and Martha feels it.

1 point: Precognition: Martha would be able to see future events happen; that is, she knows a pop quiz will take place next week.

1 point: There has never been a conclusive scientific demonstration of extrasensory ability.

2. How can context effects, emotions, and motivation trigger different perceptions of a single stimulus?
   (3 points)

Module 18

Vision

Module Learning Objectives

18-1 Describe the characteristics of visible light, and explain the process by which the eye transforms light energy into neural messages.

18-2 Describe how the eye and brain process visual information.

18-3 Discuss the theories that help us understand color vision.

18-1 What is the energy that we see as visible light, and how does the eye transform light energy into neural messages?

Our eyes receive light energy and transduce (transform) it into neural messages that our brain then processes into what we consciously see. How does such a taken-for-granted yet remarkable thing happen?

The Stimulus Input: Light Energy

When you look at a bright red tulip, what strikes your eyes is not particles of the color red but pulses of electromagnetic energy that your visual system perceives as red. What we see as visible light is but a thin slice of the whole spectrum of electromagnetic energy, ranging from imperceptibly short gamma waves to the long waves of radio transmission (**FIGURE 18.1**). Other organisms are sensitive to differing portions of the spectrum. Bees, for instance, cannot see what we perceive as red but can see ultraviolet light.

Two physical characteristics of light help determine our sensory experience of them. Light's **wavelength**—the distance from one wave peak to the next

wavelength the distance from the peak of one light or sound wave to the peak of the next. Electromagnetic wavelengths vary from the short blips of cosmic rays to the long pulses of radio transmission.

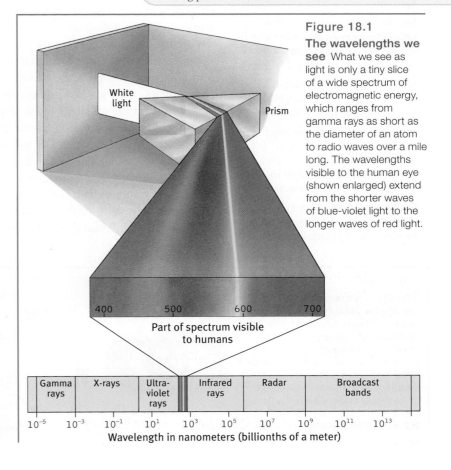

Figure 18.1

The wavelengths we see What we see as light is only a tiny slice of a wide spectrum of electromagnetic energy, which ranges from gamma rays as short as the diameter of an atom to radio waves over a mile long. The wavelengths visible to the human eye (shown enlarged) extend from the shorter waves of blue-violet light to the longer waves of red light.

Figure 18.2

The physical properties of waves (a) Waves vary in *wavelength* (the distance between successive peaks). *Frequency*, the number of complete wavelengths that can pass a point in a given time, depends on the wavelength. The shorter the wavelength, the higher the frequency. Wavelength determines the perceived color of light (and also the *pitch* of sound). (b) Waves also vary in *amplitude* (the height from peak to trough). Wave amplitude determines the *brightness* of colors (and also the loudness of sounds).

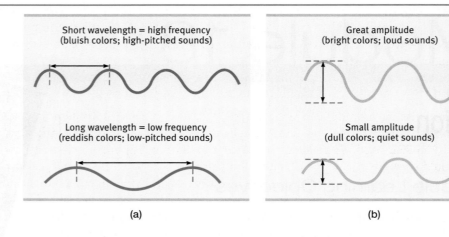

Short wavelength = high frequency
(bluish colors; high-pitched sounds)

Long wavelength = low frequency
(reddish colors; low-pitched sounds)

Great amplitude
(bright colors; loud sounds)

Small amplitude
(dull colors; quiet sounds)

(a)   (b)

hue the dimension of color that is determined by the wavelength of light; what we know as the color names *blue*, *green*, and so forth.

intensity the amount of energy in a light or sound wave, which we perceive as brightness or loudness, as determined by the wave's amplitude.

pupil the adjustable opening in the center of the eye through which light enters.

iris a ring of muscle tissue that forms the colored portion of the eye around the pupil and controls the size of the pupil opening.

lens the transparent structure behind the pupil that changes shape to help focus images on the retina.

retina the light-sensitive inner surface of the eye, containing the receptor rods and cones plus layers of neurons that begin the processing of visual information.

accommodation the process by which the eye's lens changes shape to focus near or far objects on the retina.

(**FIGURE 18.2a**)—determines its **hue** (the color we experience, such as the tulip's red petals or green leaves). **Intensity,** the amount of energy in light waves (determined by a wave's *amplitude*, or height), influences brightness (Figure 18.2b). To understand *how* we transform physical energy into color and meaning, we first need to understand vision's window, the eye.

The Eye

Light enters the eye through the *cornea*, which protects the eye and bends light to provide focus (**FIGURE 18.3**). The light then passes through the **pupil,** a small adjustable opening. Surrounding the pupil and controlling its size is the **iris,** a colored muscle that dilates or constricts in response to light intensity and even to inner emotions. (When we're feeling amorous, our telltale dilated pupils and dark eyes subtly signal our interest.) Each iris is so distinctive that an iris-scanning machine can confirm your identity.

Behind the pupil is a **lens** that focuses incoming light rays into an image on the **retina,** a multilayered tissue on the eyeball's sensitive inner surface. The lens focuses the rays by changing its curvature in a process called **accommodation.**

For centuries, scientists knew that when an image of a candle passes through a small opening, it casts an inverted mirror image on a dark wall behind. If the retina receives this sort of upside-down image, as in Figure 18.3, how can we see the world right side up? The ever-curious Leonardo da Vinci had an idea: Perhaps the eye's watery fluids bend the light rays, reinverting the image to the upright position as it reaches the retina. But then in 1604, the astronomer and optics expert Johannes Kepler showed that the retina does receive upside-down images of the world (Crombie, 1964). And how could we understand such a world? "I leave it," said the befuddled Kepler, "to natural philosophers."

Figure 18.3

The eye Light rays reflected from a candle pass through the cornea, pupil, and lens. The curvature and thickness of the lens change to bring nearby or distant objects into focus on the retina. Rays from the top of the candle strike the bottom of the retina, and those from the left side of the candle strike the right side of the retina. The candle's image on the retina thus appears upside down and reversed.

© Pascal Goetgheluck/
Science Source

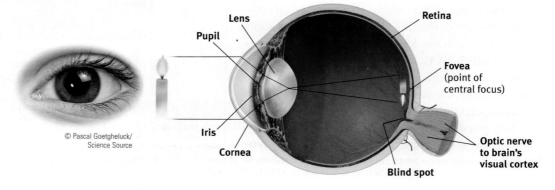

Lens
Pupil
Retina
Fovea
(point of central focus)
Iris
Cornea
Blind spot
Optic nerve to brain's visual cortex

Eventually, the answer became clear: The retina doesn't "see" a whole image. Rather, its millions of receptor cells convert particles of light energy into neural impulses and forward those to the brain. *There,* the impulses are reassembled into a perceived, upright-seeming image.

The Retina

If you could follow a single light-energy particle into your eye, you would first make your way through the retina's outer layer of cells to its buried receptor cells, the **rods** and **cones** (**FIGURE 18.4**). There, you would see the light energy trigger chemical changes that would spark neural signals, activating nearby *bipolar cells.* The bipolar cells in turn would activate the neighboring *ganglion cells,* whose axons twine together like the strands of a rope to form the **optic nerve.** That nerve will carry the information to your brain, where your thalamus stands ready to distribute the information. The optic nerve can send nearly 1 million messages at once through its nearly 1 million ganglion fibers. (The auditory nerve, which enables hearing, carries much less information through its mere 30,000 fibers.) We pay a small price for this eye-to-brain highway. Where the optic nerve leaves the eye, there are no receptor cells—creating a **blind spot** (**FIGURE 18.5** on the next page). Close one eye and you won't see a black hole, however. Without seeking your approval, your brain fills in the hole.

Rods and cones differ in where they're found and in what they do (**TABLE 18.1** on the next page). *Cones* cluster in and around the **fovea,** the retina's area of central focus (see Figure 18.3). Many have their own hotline to the brain: Each one transmits to a single bipolar cell that helps relay the cone's individual message to the visual cortex, which devotes a large area to input from the fovea. These direct connections preserve the cones' precise information, making them better able to detect fine detail.

Rods have no such hotline; they share bipolar cells with other rods, sending combined messages. To experience this rod-cone difference in sensitivity to details, pick a word in this sentence and stare directly at it, focusing its image on the cones in your fovea. Notice that

rods retinal receptors that detect black, white, and gray; necessary for peripheral and twilight vision, when cones don't respond.

cones retinal receptor cells that are concentrated near the center of the retina and that function in daylight or in well-lit conditions. The cones detect fine detail and give rise to color sensations.

optic nerve the nerve that carries neural impulses from the eye to the brain.

blind spot the point at which the optic nerve leaves the eye, creating a "blind" spot because no receptor cells are located there.

fovea the central focal point in the retina, around which the eye's cones cluster.

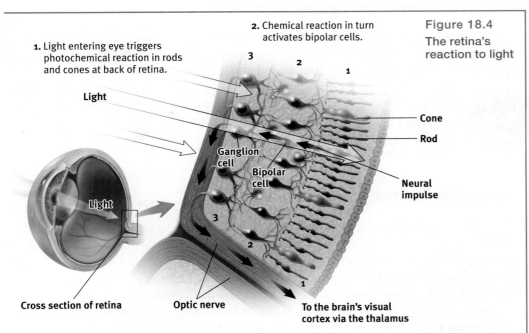

Figure 18.4 The retina's reaction to light

1. Light entering eye triggers photochemical reaction in rods and cones at back of retina.

2. Chemical reaction in turn activates bipolar cells.

Light

Cone

Rod

Ganglion cell

Bipolar cell

Neural impulse

Light

Cross section of retina

Optic nerve

To the brain's visual cortex via the thalamus

3. Bipolar cells then activate the ganglion cells, the axons of which converge to form the optic nerve. This nerve transmits information to the visual cortex (via the thalamus) in the brain.

Figure 18.5

The blind spot There are no receptor cells where the optic nerve leaves the eye. This creates a blind spot in your vision. To demonstrate, first close your left eye, look at the spot, and move the page to a distance from your face at which one of the cars disappears (which one do you predict it will be?). Repeat with the other eye closed—and note that now the other car disappears. Can you explain why?

words a few inches off to the side appear blurred? Their image strikes the outer regions of your retina, where rods predominate. Thus, when driving or biking, you can detect a car in your peripheral vision well before perceiving its details.

Cones also enable you to perceive color. In dim light they become ineffectual, so you see no colors. Rods, which enable black-and-white vision, remain sensitive in dim light. Several rods will funnel their faint energy output onto a single bipolar cell. Thus, cones and rods each provide a special sensitivity—cones to detail and color, and rods to faint light.

Omikron/Science Source

Table 18.1 Receptors in the Human Eye: Rod-Shaped Rods and Cone-Shaped Cones	Cones	Rods
Number	6 million	120 million
Location in retina	Center	Periphery
Sensitivity in dim light	Low	High
Color sensitivity	High	Low
Detail sensitivity	High	Low

When you enter a darkened theater or turn off the light at night, your eyes adapt. Your pupils dilate to allow more light to reach your retina, but it typically takes 20 minutes or more before your eyes fully adapt. You can demonstrate dark adaptation by closing or covering one eye for up to 20 minutes. Then make the light in the room not quite bright enough to read this book with your open eye. Now open the dark-adapted eye and read (easily). This period of dark adaptation matches the average natural twilight transition between the Sun's setting and darkness. How wonderfully made we are.

Andrey Armyagov /Shutterstock

Visual Information Processing

18-2   How do the eye and the brain process visual information?

Visual information percolates through progressively more abstract levels on its path through the thalamus and on to the visual cortex. At the entry level, information processing begins in the retina's neural layers, which are actually brain tissue that has migrated to the eye during early fetal development. These layers don't just pass along electrical impulses; they also help to encode and analyze sensory information. The third neural layer in a frog's eye, for example, contains the "bug detector" cells that fire only in response to moving fly-like stimuli.

After processing by your retina's nearly 130 million receptor rods and cones, information travels to your bipolar cells, then to your million or so ganglion cells, and through their axons making up the optic nerve to your brain. Any given retinal area relays its information to a corresponding location in the visual cortex, in the occipital lobe at the back of your brain (**FIGURE 18.6**).

The same sensitivity that enables retinal cells to fire messages can lead them to misfire, as you can demonstrate for yourself. Turn your eyes to the left, close them, and then gently rub the right side of your right eyelid with your fingertip. Note the patch of light to the left, moving as your finger moves. Why do you see light? Why at the left?

Your retinal cells are so responsive that even pressure triggers them. But your brain interprets their firing as light. Moreover, it interprets the light as coming from the left—the normal direction of light that activates the right side of the retina.

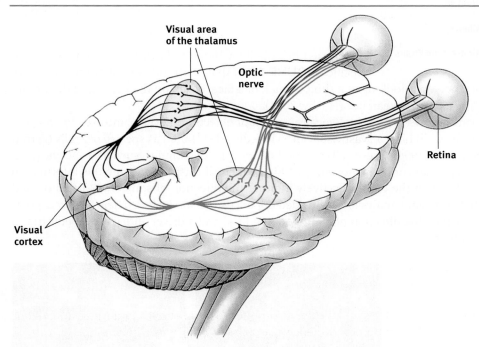

Figure 18.6

Pathway from the eyes to the visual cortex Ganglion axons forming the optic nerve run to the thalamus, where they synapse with neurons that run to the visual cortex.

Feature Detection

David Hubel and Torsten Wiesel (1979) received a Nobel Prize for their work on **feature detectors.** These specialized neurons in the occipital lobe's visual cortex receive information from individual ganglion cells in the retina. Feature detector cells derive their name from their ability to respond to a scene's specific features—to particular edges, lines, angles, and movements. These cells pass this information to other cortical areas, where teams of cells (*supercell clusters*) respond to more complex patterns. As we noted in Module 12, one temporal lobe area by your right ear (**FIGURE 18.7** on the next page) enables you to perceive faces and, thanks to a specialized neural network, to recognize them from varied viewpoints (Connor, 2010). If this region were damaged, you might recognize other forms and objects, but, like Heather Sellers, not familiar faces. When researchers temporarily disrupt the brain's face-processing areas with magnetic pulses, people are unable to recognize faces.

They will, however, be able to recognize houses, because the brain's face-perception occurs separately from its object-perception (McKone et al., 2007; Pitcher et al., 2007). Thus, functional MRI (fMRI) scans show different brain areas activating when people

feature detectors nerve cells in the brain that respond to specific features of the stimulus, such as shape, angle, or movement.

AP® Exam Tip

Warning! Sometimes students spend so much time mastering the parts of the eye that they skim over the part you're about to read. Do not forget that you see with your brain as much as you see with your eyes.

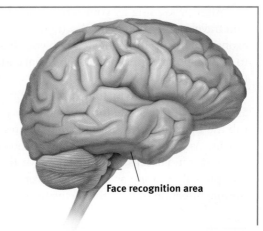

Figure 18.7

Face recognition processing In social animals such as humans, a dedicated brain system (shown here in a right-facing brain) assigns considerable neural bandwidth to the crucial task of face recognition.

Face recognition area

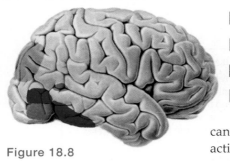

■ Faces

■ Houses

■ Chairs

■ Houses and Chairs

Figure 18.8

The telltale brain Looking at faces, houses, and chairs activates different brain areas in this right-facing brain.

view varied objects (Downing et al., 2001). Brain activity is so specific (**FIGURE 18.8**) that, with the help of brain scans, "we can tell if a person is looking at a shoe, a chair, or a face, based on the pattern of their brain activity," noted one researcher (Haxby, 2001).

Research shows that for biologically important objects and events, monkey brains (and surely ours as well) have a "vast visual encyclopedia" distributed as specialized cells (Perrett et al., 1988, 1992, 1994). These cells respond to one type of stimulus, such as a specific gaze, head angle, posture, or body movement. Other supercell clusters integrate this information and fire only when the cues collectively indicate the direction of someone's attention and approach. This instant analysis, which aided our ancestors' survival, also helps a soccer goal-keeper anticipate the direction of an impending kick, and a driver anticipate a pedestrian's next movement.

Well-developed supercells In this 2011 World Cup match, USA's Abby Wambach instantly processed visual information about the positions and movements of Brazil's defenders and goalkeeper and somehow managed to get the ball around them all and into the net.

parallel processing the processing of many aspects of a problem simultaneously; the brain's natural mode of information processing for many functions, including vision. Contrasts with the step-by-step (serial) processing of most computers and of conscious problem solving.

Parallel Processing

Our brain achieves these and other remarkable feats by means of **parallel processing:** doing many things at once. To analyze a visual scene, the brain divides it into subdimensions—motion, form, depth, color—and works on each aspect simultaneously (Livingstone & Hubel, 1988). We then construct our perceptions by integrating the separate but parallel work of these different visual teams (**FIGURE 18.9**).

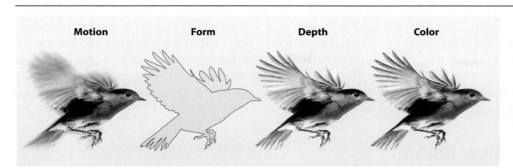

Figure 18.9

Parallel processing Studies of patients with brain damage suggest that the brain delegates the work of processing motion, form, depth, and color to different areas. After taking a scene apart, the brain integrates these subdimensions into the perceived image. How does the brain do this? The answer to this question is the Holy Grail of vision research.

To recognize a face, your brain integrates information projected by your retinas to several visual cortex areas, compares it with stored information, and enables you to recognize the face: *Grandmother!* Scientists are debating whether this stored information is contained in a single cell or distributed over a network. Some supercells—"grandmother cells"—do appear to respond very selectively to 1 or 2 faces in 100 (Bowers, 2009). The whole facial recognition process requires tremendous brain power—30 percent of the cortex (10 times the brain area devoted to hearing).

Destroy or disable a neural workstation for a visual subtask, and something peculiar results, as happened to "Mrs. M." (Hoffman, 1998). Since a stroke damaged areas near the rear of both sides of her brain, she has been unable to perceive movement. People in a room seem "suddenly here or there but I have not seen them moving." Pouring tea into a cup is a challenge because the fluid appears frozen—she cannot perceive it rising in the cup.

After stroke or surgery damage to the brain's visual cortex, others have experienced *blindsight* (a phenomenon we met in Module 13). Shown a series of sticks, they report seeing nothing. Yet when asked to guess whether the sticks are vertical or horizontal, their visual intuition typically offers the correct response. When told, "You got them all right," they are astounded. There is, it seems, a second "mind"—a parallel processing system—operating unseen. These separate visual systems for perception and action illustrate dual processing—the two-track mind.

* * *

Think about the wonders of visual processing. As you look at that tiger in the zoo, information enters your eyes, is transduced, and is sent to your brain as millions of neural impulses. As your brain buzzes with activity, various areas focus on different aspects of the tiger's image. Finally, in some as yet mysterious way, these separate teams pool their work to produce a meaningful image, which you compare with previously stored images and recognize: a crouching tiger (**FIGURE 18.10**).

"I am . . . wonderfully made."
-King David, Psalm 139:14

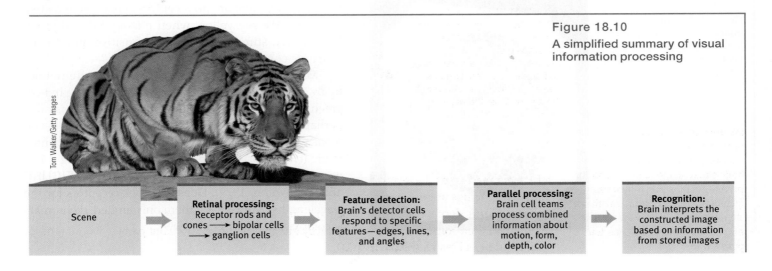

Figure 18.10

A simplified summary of visual information processing

Scene → **Retinal processing:** Receptor rods and cones ⟶ bipolar cells ⟶ ganglion cells → **Feature detection:** Brain's detector cells respond to specific features—edges, lines, and angles → **Parallel processing:** Brain cell teams process combined information about motion, form, depth, color → **Recognition:** Brain interprets the constructed image based on information from stored images

Think, too, about what is happening as you read this page. The printed squiggles are transmitted by reflected light rays onto your retina, which triggers a process that sends formless nerve impulses to several areas of your brain, which integrates the information and decodes meaning, thus completing the transfer of information across time and space from my mind to your mind. That all of this happens instantly, effortlessly, and continuously is indeed awesome. As Roger Sperry (1985) observed, the "insights of science give added, not lessened, reasons for awe, respect, and reverence."

Color Vision

18-3   What theories help us understand color vision?

We talk as though objects possess color: "A tomato is red." Perhaps you have pondered the old question, "If a tree falls in the forest and no one hears it, does it make a sound?" We can ask the same of color: If no one sees the tomato, is it red?

The answer is *No.* First, the tomato is everything *but* red, because it *rejects* (reflects) the long wavelengths of red. Second, the tomato's color is our mental construction. As Isaac Newton (1704) noted, "The [light] rays are not colored." Color, like all aspects of vision, resides not in the object but in the theater of our brain, as evidenced by our dreaming in color.

One of vision's most basic and intriguing mysteries is how we see the world in color. How, from the light energy striking the retina, does the brain manufacture our experience of color—and of such a multitude of colors? Our difference threshold for colors is so low that we can discriminate more than 1 million different color variations (Neitz et al., 2001). At least most of us can. For about 1 person in 50, vision is color deficient—and that person is usually male, because the defect is genetically sex-linked.

Why is some people's vision deficient? To answer that question, we need to understand how normal color vision works. Modern detective work on this mystery began in the nineteenth century, when Hermann von Helmholtz built on the insights of an English physicist, Thomas Young. Knowing that any color can be created by combining the light waves of three primary colors—red, green, and blue—Young and von Helmholtz inferred that the eye must have three corresponding types of color receptors. Years later, researchers measured the response of various cones to different color stimuli and confirmed the **Young-Helmholtz trichromatic (three-color) theory,** which implies that the receptors do their color magic in teams of three. Indeed, the retina has three types of color receptors, each especially sensitive to one of three colors. And those colors are, in fact, red, green, and blue. When we stimulate combinations of these cones, we see other colors. For example, there are no receptors especially sensitive to yellow. We see yellow when mixing red and green light, which stimulates both red-sensitive and green-sensitive cones.

Most people with color-deficient vision are not actually "colorblind." They simply lack functioning red- or green-sensitive cones, or sometimes both. Their vision—perhaps unknown to them, because their lifelong vision *seems* normal—is monochromatic (one-color) or dichromatic (two-color) instead of trichromatic, making it impossible to distinguish the red and green in **FIGURE 18.11** (Boynton, 1979). Dogs, too, lack receptors for the wavelengths of red, giving them only limited, dichromatic color vision (Neitz et al., 1989).

> "Only mind has sight and hearing; all things else are deaf and blind."
> -EPICHARMUS, *FRAGMENTS*, 550 B.C.E.

Young-Helmholtz trichromatic (three-color) theory the theory that the retina contains three different color receptors—one most sensitive to red, one to green, one to blue—which, when stimulated in combination, can produce the perception of any color.

Figure 18.11

Color-deficient vision People who suffer red-green deficiency have trouble perceiving the number within the design.

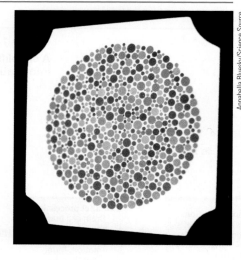

Annabella Bluesky/Science Source

Figure 18.12
Afterimage effect Stare at the center of the flag for a minute and then shift your eyes to the dot in the white space beside it. What do you see? (After tiring your neural response to black, green, and yellow, you should see their opponent colors.) Stare at a white wall and note how the size of the flag grows with the projection distance.

But how is it that people blind to red and green can often still see yellow? And why does yellow appear to be a pure color and not a mixture of red and green, the way purple is of red and blue? As Ewald Hering soon noted, trichromatic theory leaves some parts of the color vision mystery unsolved.

Hering, a physiologist, found a clue in *afterimages.* Stare at a green square for a while and then look at a white sheet of paper, and you will see red, green's *opponent color.* Stare at a yellow square and its opponent color, blue, will appear on the white paper. (To experience this, try the flag demonstration in **FIGURE 18.12**.) Hering surmised that there must be two additional color processes, one responsible for red-versus-green perception, and one for blue-versus-yellow.

Indeed, a century later, researchers also confirmed Hering's **opponent-process theory.** Three sets of opponent retinal processes—*red-green, yellow-blue,* and *white-black*—enable color vision. In the retina and in the thalamus (where impulses from the retina are relayed en route to the visual cortex), some neurons are turned "on" by red but turned "off" by green. Others are turned on by green but off by red (DeValois & DeValois, 1975). Like red and green marbles sent down a narrow tube, "red" and "green" messages cannot both travel at once. So we do not experience a reddish green. (Red and green are thus opponents.) But red and blue travel in separate channels, so we *can* see a reddish-blue magenta.

So how do we explain afterimages, such as in the flag demonstration? By staring at green, we tire our green response. When we then stare at white (which contains all colors, including red), only the red part of the green-red pairing will fire normally.

The present solution to the mystery of color vision is therefore roughly this: Color processing occurs in two stages. The retina's red, green, and blue cones respond in varying degrees to different color stimuli, as the Young-Helmholtz trichromatic theory suggested. Their signals are then processed by the nervous system's opponent-process cells, as Hering's theory proposed.

opponent-process theory the theory that opposing retinal processes (red-green, yellow-blue, white-black) enable color vision. For example, some cells are stimulated by green and inhibited by red; others are stimulated by red and inhibited by green.

Before You Move On

▶ **ASK YOURSELF**
If you were forced to give up one sense, which would it be? Why?

▶ **TEST YOURSELF**
What is the rapid sequence of events that occurs when you see and recognize a friend?

Answers to the Test Yourself questions can be found in Appendix E at the end of the book.

Module 18 Review

 18-1   **What is the energy that we see as visible light, and how does the eye transform light energy into neural messages?**

- The *hue* we perceive in light depends on its *wavelength,* and its brightness depends on its *intensity.*

- After entering the eye and being focused by the *lens,* light energy particles (from a thin slice of the broad spectrum of electromagnetic energy) strike the eye's inner surface, the *retina.* The retina's light-sensitive *rods* and color-sensitive *cones* convert the light energy into neural impulses.

 18-2   **How do the eye and the brain process visual information?**

- After processing by bipolar and ganglion cells in the eyes' retina, neural impulses travel through the *optic nerve,* to the thalamus, and on to the visual cortex. In the visual cortex, *feature detectors* respond to specific features of the visual stimulus. Supercell clusters in other critical brain areas respond to more complex patterns.

- Through *parallel processing,* the brain handles many aspects of vision (color, movement, form, and depth) simultaneously. Other neural teams integrate the results, comparing them with stored information and enabling perceptions.

18-3   **What theories help us understand color vision?**

- *The Young-Helmholtz trichromatic (three-color) theory* proposed that the retina contains three types of color receptors. Contemporary research has found three types of cones, each most sensitive to the wavelengths of one of the three primary colors of light (red, green, or blue).

- Hering's *opponent-process theory* proposed three additional color processes (red-versus-green, blue-versus-yellow, black-versus-white). Contemporary research has confirmed that, en route to the brain, neurons in the retina and the thalamus code the color-related information from the cones into pairs of opponent colors.

- These two theories, and the research supporting them, show that color processing occurs in two stages.

Multiple-Choice Questions

1. Light's _____ is the distance from one wave peak to the next. This dimension determines the _____ we experience.
   a. hue; wavelength
   b. wavelength; hue
   c. hue; intensity
   d. wavelength; intensity
   e. intensity; wavelength

2. What do we call the specialized neurons in the occipital lobe's visual cortex that respond to particular edges, lines, angles, and movements?
   a. Rods
   b. Cones
   c. Foveas
   d. Feature detectors
   e. Ganglion cells

3. Which of the following explains reversed-color afterimages?
   a. Young-Helmholtz trichromatic theory
   b. The blind spot
   c. Hering's opponent-process theory
   d. Feature detectors
   e. Parallel processing

4. Your best friend decides to paint her room an extremely bright electric blue. Which of the following best fits the physical properties of the color's light waves?
   a. No wavelength; large amplitude
   b. Short wavelength; large amplitude
   c. Short wavelength; small amplitude
   d. Long wavelength; large amplitude
   e. No wavelength; small amplitude

5. What do we call the transparent, protective layer that light passes through as it enters the eye?

a. Pupil
b. Iris
c. Cornea
d. Lens
e. Fovea

Practice FRQs

1. As light reflected off an object reaches your eye, it passes through several structures before it reaches the retina. Describe three of these structures, including the function of each.

Answer

1 point: The cornea is at the front of the eye. It bends and focuses the light waves.

1 point: The pupil is the opening through which light enters the eyeball. It is surrounded by the iris, which can expand or contract to allow more or less light to pass through the pupil.

1 point: The lens is the transparent structure behind the pupil that changes shape to help focus images on the retina.

2. Explain two theories of color vision in humans. How does one of them explain color deficiency?

(3 points)

Module 19

Visual Organization and Interpretation

Rob Kavanagh/Alamy

Module Learning Objectives

19-1 Describe Gestalt psychologists' understanding of perceptual organization, and explain how figure-ground and grouping principles contribute to our perceptions.

19-2 Explain how we use binocular and monocular cues to perceive the world in three dimensions and perceive motion.

19-3 Explain how perceptual constancies help us organize our sensations into meaningful perceptions.

19-4 Describe what research on restored vision, sensory restriction, and perceptual adaptation reveals about the effects of experience on perception.

Visual Organization

19-1 How did the Gestalt psychologists understand perceptual organization, and how do figure-ground and grouping principles contribute to our perceptions?

It's one thing to understand how we see shapes and colors. But how do we organize and interpret those sights (or sounds or tastes or smells) so that they become meaningful perceptions—a rose in bloom, a familiar face, a sunset?

Early in the twentieth century, a group of German psychologists noticed that when given a cluster of sensations, people tend to organize them into a **gestalt,** a German word meaning a "form" or a "whole." For example, look at **FIGURE 19.1**. Note that the individual elements of this figure, called a *Necker cube,* are really nothing but eight blue circles, each containing three converging white lines. When we view these elements all together, however, we see a cube that sometimes reverses direction. This phenomenon nicely illustrates a favorite saying of Gestalt psychologists: In perception, the whole may exceed the sum of its parts. If we combine sodium (a corrosive metal) with chlorine (a poisonous gas), something very different emerges—table salt. Likewise, a unique perceived form emerges from a stimulus' components (Rock & Palmer, 1990).

Over the years, the Gestalt psychologists demonstrated many principles we use to organize our sensations into perceptions. Underlying all of them is a fundamental truth: *Our brain does more than register information about the world.* Perception is not just opening a shutter and letting a picture print itself on the brain. We filter incoming information and construct perceptions. Mind matters.

gestalt an organized whole. Gestalt psychologists emphasized our tendency to integrate pieces of information into meaningful wholes.

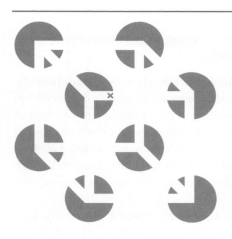

Figure 19.1

A Necker cube What do you see: circles with white lines, or a cube? If you stare at the cube, you may notice that it reverses location, moving the tiny X in the center from the front edge to the back. At times, the cube may seem to float in front of the page, with circles behind it. At other times, the circles may become holes in the page through which the cube appears, as though it were floating behind the page. There is far more to perception than meets the eye. (From Bradley et al., 1976.)

Figure 19.2
Reversible figure and ground

Form Perception

Imagine designing a video-computer system that, like your eye-brain system, can recognize faces at a glance. What abilities would it need?

FIGURE AND GROUND

To start with, the video-computer system would need to separate faces from their backgrounds. Likewise, in our eye-brain system, our first perceptual task is to perceive any object (the *figure*) as distinct from its surroundings (the *ground*). Among the voices you hear at a party, the one you attend to becomes the figure; all others are part of the ground. As you read, the words are the figure; the white paper is the ground. Sometimes the same stimulus can trigger more than one perception. In **FIGURE 19.2,** the **figure-ground** relationship continually reverses—but always we organize the stimulus into a figure seen against a ground.

GROUPING

Having discriminated figure from ground, we (and our video-computer system) must also organize the figure into a *meaningful* form. Some basic features of a scene—such as color, movement, and light-dark contrast—we process instantly and automatically (Treisman, 1987). Our minds bring order and form to stimuli by following certain rules for **grouping**. These rules, identified by the Gestalt psychologists and applied even by infants, illustrate how the perceived whole differs from the sum of its parts (Quinn et al., 2002; Rock & Palmer, 1990). Three examples:

PROXIMITY We group nearby figures together. We see not six separate lines, but three sets of two lines.

CONTINUITY We perceive smooth, continuous patterns rather than discontinuous ones. This pattern could be a series of alternating semicircles, but we perceive it as two continuous lines—one wavy, one straight.

CLOSURE We fill in gaps to create a complete, whole object. Thus we assume that the circles on the right are complete but partially blocked by the (illusory) triangle. Add nothing more than little line segments to close off the circles and your brain stops constructing a triangle. Such principles usually help us construct reality.

figure-ground the organization of the visual field into objects (the *figures*) that stand out from their surroundings (the *ground*).

grouping the perceptual tendency to organize stimuli into coherent groups.

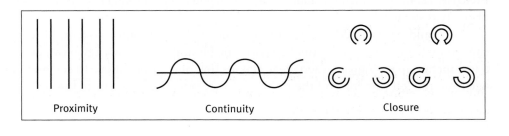

Proximity   Continuity   Closure

Depth Perception

 How do we use binocular and monocular cues to perceive the world in three dimensions and perceive motion?

From the two-dimensional images falling on our retinas, we somehow organize three-dimensional perceptions. **Depth perception** enables us to estimate an object's distance from us. At a glance, we can estimate the distance of an oncoming car or the height of a house. Depth perception is partly innate, as Eleanor Gibson and Richard Walk (1960) discovered using a model of a cliff with a drop-off area (which was covered by sturdy glass). Gibson's inspiration for these **visual cliff** experiments occurred while she was picnicking on the rim of the Grand Canyon. She wondered: Would a toddler peering over the rim perceive the dangerous drop-off and draw back?

Figure 19.3

Visual cliff Eleanor Gibson and Richard Walk devised a miniature cliff with a glass-covered drop-off to determine whether crawling infants can perceive depth. Even when coaxed, infants are reluctant to venture onto the glass over the cliff (Gibson & Walk, 1960).

Back in their Cornell University laboratory, Gibson and Walk placed 6- to 14-month-old infants on the edge of a safe canyon and had the infants' mothers coax them to crawl out onto the glass (**FIGURE 19.3**). Most infants refused to do so, indicating that they could perceive depth.

Had they *learned* to perceive depth? Learning seems to be part of the answer because crawling, no matter when it begins, seems to increase infants' wariness of heights (Campos et al., 1992). Yet, the researchers observed, mobile newborn animals come prepared to perceive depth. Even those with virtually no visual experience—including young kittens, a day-old goat, and newly hatched chicks—will not venture across the visual cliff. Thus, it seems that biology predisposes us to be wary of heights and experience amplifies that fear.

How do we perceive depth? *How* do we transform two differing two-dimensional (2-D) retinal images into a single three-dimensional (3-D) perception? Our brain constructs these perceptions using information supplied by one or both eyes.

BINOCULAR CUES

Try this: With both eyes open, hold two pens or pencils in front of you and touch their tips together. Now do so with one eye closed. With one eye, the task becomes noticeably more difficult, demonstrating the importance of **binocular cues** in judging the distance of nearby objects. Two eyes are better than one.

Because your eyes are about 2½ inches apart, your retinas receive slightly different images of the world. By comparing these two images, your brain can judge how close an object is to you. The greater the **retinal disparity,** or difference between the two images, the closer the object. Try it. Hold your two index fingers, with the tips about half an inch apart, directly in front of your nose, and your retinas will receive quite different views. If you close one eye and then the other, you can see the difference. (You may also create a finger sausage, as in **FIGURE 19.4.**) At a greater distance—say, when you hold your fingers at arm's length—the disparity is smaller.

We could easily build this feature into our video-computer system. Moviemakers can simulate or exaggerate retinal disparity by filming a scene with two cameras placed a few inches apart. Viewers then wear glasses that allow the left eye to see only the image from the left camera, and the right eye to see only the image from the right camera.

depth perception the ability to see objects in three dimensions although the images that strike the retina are two-dimensional; allows us to judge distance.

visual cliff a laboratory device for testing depth perception in infants and young animals.

binocular cues depth cues, such as retinal disparity, that depend on the use of two eyes.

retinal disparity a binocular cue for perceiving depth: By comparing images from the retinas in the two eyes, the brain computes distance—the greater the disparity (difference) between the two images, the closer the object.

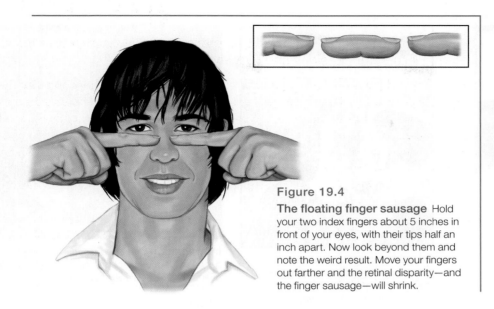

Figure 19.4

The floating finger sausage Hold your two index fingers about 5 inches in front of your eyes, with their tips half an inch apart. Now look beyond them and note the weird result. Move your fingers out farther and the retinal disparity—and the finger sausage—will shrink.

FYI

Carnivorous animals, including humans, have eyes that enable forward focus on a prey and offer binocular vision-enhanced depth perception. Grazing herbivores, such as horses and sheep, typically have eyes on the sides of their skull. Although lacking binocular depth perception, they have sweeping peripheral vision.

The resulting 3-D effect, as 3-D movie fans know, mimics or exaggerates normal retinal disparity. Similarly, twin cameras in airplanes can take photos of terrain for integration into 3-D maps.

MONOCULAR CUES

How do we judge whether a person is 10 or 100 meters away? Retinal disparity won't help us here, because there won't be much difference between the images cast on our right and left retinas. At such distances, we depend on **monocular cues** (depth cues available to each eye separately). See **FIGURE 19.5** on the next page for some examples.

Motion Perception

Imagine that you could perceive the world as having color, form, and depth but that you could not see motion. Not only would you be unable to bike or drive, you would have trouble writing, eating, and walking.

Normally your brain computes motion based partly on its assumption that shrinking objects are retreating (not getting smaller) and enlarging objects are approaching. But you are imperfect at motion perception. Large objects, such as trains, appear to move more slowly than smaller objects, such as cars, moving at the same speed. (Perhaps at an airport you've noticed that jumbo jets seem to land more slowly than little jets.)

To catch a fly ball, softball or cricket players (unlike drivers) want to achieve a collision—with the ball that's flying their way. To accomplish that, they follow an unconscious rule—one they can't explain but know intuitively: Run to keep the ball at a constantly increasing angle of gaze (McBeath et al., 1995). A dog catching a Frisbee does the same (Shaffer et al., 2004).

The brain also perceives continuous movement in a rapid series of slightly varying images (a phenomenon called *stroboscopic movement*). As film animation artists know well, you can create this illusion by flashing 24 still pictures a second. The motion we then see in popular action adventures is not in the film, which merely presents a superfast slide show. We construct that motion in our heads, just as we construct movement in blinking marquees and holiday lights. When two adjacent stationary lights blink on and off in quick succession, we perceive a single light moving back and forth between them. Lighted signs exploit this **phi phenomenon** with a succession of lights that creates the impression of, say, a moving arrow.

monocular cues depth cues, such as interposition and linear perspective, available to either eye alone.

phi phenomenon an illusion of movement created when two or more adjacent lights blink on and off in quick succession.

"Sometimes I wonder: Why is that Frisbee getting bigger? And then it hits me." -ANONYMOUS

"From there to here, from here to there, funny things are everywhere." -DR. SEUSS, *ONE FISH, TWO FISH, RED FISH, BLUE FISH*, 1960

Relative height We perceive objects higher in our field of vision as farther away. Because we assume the lower part of a figure-ground illustration is closer, we perceive it as figure (Vecera et al., 2002). Invert this illustration and the black will become ground, like a night sky.

Image courtesy Shaun P. Vecera, Ph.D., adapted from stimuli that appeared in Vecera et al., 2002

Relative size If we assume two objects are similar in size, *most* people perceive the one that casts the smaller retinal image as farther away.

© Philip Mugridge/Alamy

Interposition *Interpose* means "to come between." If one object partially blocks our view of another, we perceive it as closer.

Relative motion As we move, objects that are actually stable may appear to move. If while riding on a bus you fix your gaze on some point—say, a house—the objects beyond the fixation point will appear to move with you. Objects in front of the point will appear to move backward. The farther an object is from the fixation point, the faster it will seem to move.

Direction of passenger's motion ⟶

Figure 19.5
Monocular depth cues

Linear perspective Parallel lines appear to meet in the distance. The sharper the angle of convergence, the greater the perceived distance.

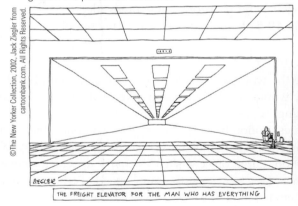

©The New Yorker Collection, 2002, Jack Ziegler from cartoonbank.com. All Rights Reserved.

THE FREIGHT ELEVATOR FOR THE MAN WHO HAS EVERYTHING

Light and shadow Shading produces a sense of depth consistent with our assumption that light comes from above. If you invert this illustration, the hollow will become a hill.

From "Perceiving Shape From Shading" by Vilayanur S. Ramachandran. Copyright © 1988 by Scientific American, Inc. All Rights Reserved.

Perceptual Constancy

19-3 How do perceptual constancies help us organize our sensations into meaningful perceptions?

So far, we have noted that our video-computer system must perceive objects as we do—as having a distinct form, location, and perhaps motion. Its next task is to recognize objects without being deceived by changes in their color, brightness, shape, or size—a top-down process called **perceptual constancy.** Regardless of the viewing angle, distance, and illumination, we can identify people and things in less time than it takes to draw a breath, a feat that would be a monumental challenge for even advanced computers and that has intrigued researchers for decades.

COLOR AND BRIGHTNESS CONSTANCIES

Color does not reside in an object. Our experience of color depends on the object's *context.* If you view an isolated tomato through a paper tube, its color would seem to change as the light—and thus the wavelengths reflected from its surface—changed. But if you viewed that tomato as one item in a bowl of fresh fruit and vegetables, its color would remain roughly constant as the lighting shifts. This perception of consistent color is known as **color constancy.**

Though we take color constancy for granted, this ability is truly remarkable. A blue poker chip under indoor lighting reflects wavelengths that match those reflected by a sunlit gold chip (Jameson, 1985). Yet bring a bluebird indoors and it won't look like a goldfinch. The color is not in the bird's feathers. You and I see color thanks to our brain's computations of the light reflected by an object *relative to the objects surrounding it*. (But only if we grew up with normal light, it seems. Monkeys raised under a restricted range of wavelengths later have great difficulty recognizing the same color when illumination varies [Sugita, 2004].) **FIGURE 19.6** dramatically illustrates the ability of a blue object to appear very different in three different contexts. Yet we have no trouble seeing these disks as blue.

> **perceptual constancy** perceiving objects as unchanging (having consistent shapes, size, brightness, and color) even as illumination and retinal images change.
>
> **color constancy** perceiving familiar objects as having consistent color, even if changing illumination alters the wavelengths reflected by the object.

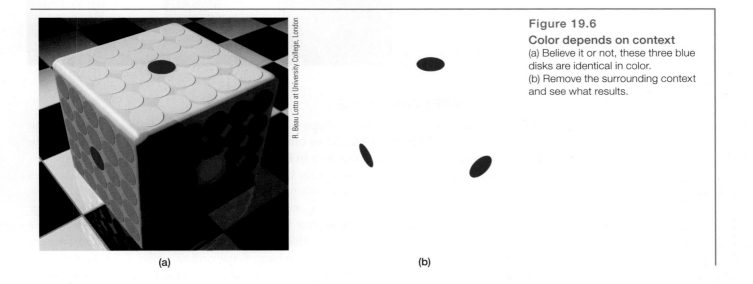

R. Beau Lotto at University College, London

(a)   (b)

Figure 19.6
Color depends on context
(a) Believe it or not, these three blue disks are identical in color.
(b) Remove the surrounding context and see what results.

Similarly, *brightness constancy* (also called *lightness constancy*) depends on context. We perceive an object as having a constant brightness even while its illumination varies. This perception of constancy depends on *relative luminance*—the amount of light an object reflects *relative to its surroundings* (**FIGURE 19.7** on the next page). White paper reflects 90 percent of the light falling on it; black paper, only 10 percent. Although a black paper viewed in sunlight may reflect 100 times more light than does a white paper viewed indoors, it will still look black (McBurney & Collings, 1984). But if you view sunlit black paper through a narrow tube so nothing else is visible, it may look gray, because in bright sunshine it reflects a fair amount of light. View it without the tube and it is again black, because it reflects much less light than the objects around it.

This principle—that we perceive objects not in isolation but in their environmental context—matters to artists, interior decorators, and clothing designers. Our perception of the color and brightness of a wall or of a streak of paint on a canvas is determined not just by the paint in the can but by the surrounding colors. The take-home lesson: *Comparisons govern our perceptions.*

Figure 19.7

Relative luminance Squares A and B are identical in color, believe it or not. (If you don't believe me, photocopy the illustration, cut out the squares, and compare.) But we perceive A as lighter, thanks to its surrounding context.

SHAPE AND SIZE CONSTANCIES

Sometimes an object whose actual shape cannot change *seems* to change shape with the angle of our view (**FIGURE 19.8**). More often, thanks to *shape constancy,* we perceive the form of familiar objects, such as the door in **FIGURE 19.9**, as constant even while our retinas receive changing images of them. Our brain manages this feat thanks to visual cortex neurons that rapidly learn to associate different views of an object (Li & DiCarlo, 2008).

Thanks to *size constancy,* we perceive objects as having a constant size, even while our distance from them varies. We assume a car is large enough to carry people, even when we see its tiny image from two blocks away. This assumption also illustrates the close connection between perceived *distance* and perceived *size*. Perceiving an object's distance gives us cues to its size. Likewise, knowing its general size—that the object is a car—provides us with cues to its distance.

Figure 19.8

Perceiving shape Do the tops of these tables have different dimensions? They appear to. But—believe it or not—they are identical. (Measure and see.) With both tables, we adjust our perceptions relative to our viewing angle.

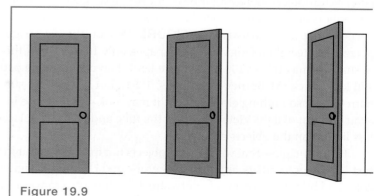

Figure 19.9

Shape constancy A door casts an increasingly trapezoidal image on our retinas as it opens, yet we still perceive it as rectangular.

Even in size-distance judgments, however, we consider an object's context. The dogs in Module 17's Figure 17.3 cast identical images on our retinas. Using linear perspective as a cue (see Figure 19.5), our brain assumes that the pursuing dog is farther away. We therefore perceive it as larger. It isn't.

This interplay between perceived size and perceived distance helps explain several well-known illusions, including the *Moon illusion:* The Moon looks up to 50 percent larger when near the horizon than when high in the sky. Can you imagine why? For at least 22 centuries, scholars have debated this question (Hershenson, 1989). One reason is that cues to objects' distances make the horizon Moon—like the distant dog in Figure 17.3—appear farther away. If it's farther away, our brain assumes, it must be larger than the Moon high in the night sky (Kaufman & Kaufman, 2000). Take away the distance cue, by looking at the horizon Moon (or each dog) through a paper tube, and the object will immediately shrink.

Size-distance relationships also explain why in **FIGURE 19.10** the two same-age girls seem so different in size. As the diagram reveals, the girls are actually about the same size, but the room is distorted. Viewed with one eye through a peephole, the room's trapezoidal walls produce the same images you would see in a normal rectangular room viewed with both eyes. Presented with the camera's one-eyed view, your brain makes the reasonable assumption that the room *is* normal and each girl is therefore the same distance from you. Given the different sizes of the girls' images on your retinas, your brain ends up calculating that the girls must be very different in size.

Perceptual illusions reinforce a fundamental lesson: Perception is not merely a projection of the world onto our brain. Rather, our sensations are disassembled into information bits that our brain, using both bottom-up and top-down processing, then reassembles into its own functional model of the external world. During this reassembly process, our assumptions—such as the usual relationship between distance and size—can lead us astray. *Our brain constructs our perceptions.*

* * *

Form perception, depth perception, motion perception, and perceptual constancies illuminate how we organize our visual experiences. Perceptual organization applies to our other senses, too. It explains why we perceive a clock's steady tick not as a *tick-tick-tick-tick* but as grouped sounds, say, *TICK-tick, TICK-tick.* Listening to an unfamiliar language, we have trouble hearing where one word stops and the next one begins. Listening to our own language, we automatically hear distinct words. This, too, reflects perceptual organization. But it is more, for we even organize a string of letters—THEDOGATEMEAT—into words that make an intelligible phrase, more likely "The dog ate meat" than "The do gate me at" (McBurney & Collings, 1984). This process involves not only the organization we've been discussing, but also interpretation—discerning meaning in what we perceive.

Figure 19.10

The illusion of the shrinking and growing girls This distorted room, designed by Adelbert Ames, appears to have a normal rectangular shape when viewed through a peephole with one eye. The girl in the right corner appears disproportionately large because we judge her size based on the false assumption that she is the same distance away as the girl in the left corner.

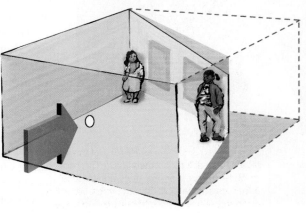

Visual Interpretation

Philosophers have debated whether our perceptual abilities should be credited to our nature or our nurture. To what extent do we *learn* to perceive? German philosopher Immanuel Kant (1724–1804) maintained that knowledge comes from our *inborn* ways of organizing sensory experiences. Indeed, we come equipped to process sensory information. But British philosopher John Locke (1632–1704) argued that through our experiences we also *learn* to perceive the world. Indeed, we learn to link an object's distance with its size. So, just how important is experience? How radically does it shape our perceptual interpretations?

> "Let us then suppose the mind to be, as we say, white paper void of all characters, without any ideas: How comes it to be furnished? . . . To this I answer, in one word, from EXPERIENCE." -JOHN LOCKE, *AN ESSAY CONCERNING HUMAN UNDERSTANDING*, 1690

Experience and Visual Perception

 19-4 What does research on restored vision, sensory restriction, and perceptual adaptation reveal about the effects of experience on perception?

RESTORED VISION AND SENSORY RESTRICTION

Writing to John Locke, William Molyneux wondered whether "a man *born* blind, and now adult, taught by his *touch* to distinguish between a cube and a sphere" could, if made to see, visually distinguish the two. Locke's answer was *No,* because the man would never have *learned* to see the difference.

Molyneux's hypothetical case has since been put to the test with a few dozen adults who, though blind from birth, have gained sight (Gregory, 1978; von Senden, 1932). Most had been born with cataracts—clouded lenses that allowed them to see only diffused light, rather as someone might see a foggy image through a Ping-Pong ball sliced in half. After cataract surgery, the patients could distinguish figure from ground and could sense colors—suggesting that these aspects of perception are innate. But much as Locke supposed, they often could not visually recognize objects that were familiar by touch.

Seeking to gain more control than is provided by clinical cases, researchers have outfitted infant kittens and monkeys with goggles through which they could see only diffuse, un-patterned light (Wiesel, 1982). After infancy, when the goggles were removed, these animals exhibited perceptual limitations much like those of humans born with cataracts. They could distinguish color and brightness, but not the form of a circle from that of a square. Their eyes had not degenerated; their retinas still relayed signals to their visual cortex. But lacking stimulation, the cortical cells had not developed normal connections. Thus, the animals remained functionally blind to shape. Experience guides, sustains, and maintains the brain's neural organization as it forms the pathways that affect our perceptions.

In both humans and animals, similar sensory restrictions later in life do no permanent harm. When researchers cover the eye of an adult animal for several months, its vision will be unaffected after the eye patch is removed. When surgeons remove cataracts that develop during late adulthood, most people are thrilled at the return to normal vision.

The effect of sensory restriction on infant cats, monkeys, and humans suggests there is a *critical period* for normal sensory and perceptual development. Nurture sculpts what nature has endowed. In less dramatic ways, it continues to do so throughout our lives. Despite concerns about their social costs (more on this in Module 78), action video games sharpen spatial skills such as visual attention, eye-hand coordination and speed, and tracking multiple objects (Spence & Feng, 2010).

Experiments on early sensory deprivation provide a partial answer to the enduring question about experience: Does the effect of early experience last a lifetime? For some aspects of perception, the answer is clearly *Yes:* "Use it *soon* or lose it." We retain the imprint of some early sensory experiences far into the future.

Learning to see: At age 3, Mike May lost his vision in an explosion. Decades later, after a new cornea restored vision to his right eye, he got his first look at his wife and children. Alas, although signals were now reaching his visual cortex, it lacked the experience to interpret them. May could not recognize expressions, or faces, apart from features such as hair. Yet he can see an object in motion and has learned to navigate his world and to marvel at such things as dust floating in sunlight (Abrams, 2002).

AP Photo/Marcio Jose Sanchez

PERCEPTUAL ADAPTATION

Given a new pair of glasses, we may feel slightly disoriented, even dizzy. Within a day or two, we adjust. Our **perceptual adaptation** to changed visual input makes the world seem normal again. But imagine a far more dramatic new pair of glasses—one that shifts the apparent location of objects 40 degrees to the left. When you first put them on and toss a ball to a friend, it sails off to the left. Walking forward to shake hands with the person, you veer to the left.

Could you adapt to this distorted world? Baby chicks cannot. When fitted with such lenses, they continue to peck where food grains *seem* to be (Hess, 1956; Rossi, 1968). But we humans adapt to distorting lenses quickly. Within a few minutes your throws would again be accurate, your stride on target. Remove the lenses and you would experience an aftereffect: At first your throws would err in the *opposite* direction, sailing off to the right; but again, within minutes you would readapt.

Indeed, given an even more radical pair of glasses—one that literally turns the world upside down—you could still adapt. Psychologist George Stratton (1896) experienced this when he invented, and for eight days wore, optical headgear that flipped left to right *and* up to down, making him the first person to experience a right-side-up retinal image while standing upright. The ground was up, the sky was down.

At first, when Stratton wanted to walk, he found himself searching for his feet, which were now "up." Eating was nearly impossible. He became nauseated and depressed. But he persisted, and by the eighth day he could comfortably reach for an object in the right direction and walk without bumping into things. When Stratton finally removed the headgear, he readapted quickly.

In later experiments, people wearing the optical gear have even been able to ride a motorcycle, ski the Alps, and fly an airplane (Dolezal, 1982; Kohler, 1962). The world around them still seemed above their heads or on the wrong side. But by actively moving about in these topsy-turvy worlds, they adapted to the context and learned to coordinate their movements.

> **perceptual adaptation** in vision, the ability to adjust to an artificially displaced or even inverted visual field.

Perceptual adaptation "Oops, missed," thought researcher Hubert Dolezal as he viewed the world through inverting goggles. Yet, believe it or not, kittens, monkeys, and humans can adapt to an inverted world.

Before You Move On

▶ **ASK YOURSELF**
Try drawing a realistic depiction of the scene from your window. Which monocular cues will you use in your drawing?

▶ **TEST YOURSELF**
What do we mean when we say that, in perception, "the whole is greater than the sum of its parts"?

Answers to the Test Yourself questions can be found in Appendix E at the end of the book.

Module 19 Review

 How did the Gestalt psychologists understand perceptual organization, and how do figure-ground and grouping principles contribute to our perceptions?

- Gestalt psychologists searched for rules by which the brain organizes fragments of sensory data into *gestalts* (from the German word for "whole"), or meaningful forms. In pointing out that the whole may exceed the sum of its parts, they noted that we filter sensory information and construct our perceptions.

- To recognize an object, we must first perceive it (see it as a *figure*) as distinct from its surroundings (the *ground*). We bring order and form to stimuli by organizing them into meaningful *groups*, following such rules as proximity, continuity, and closure.

 How do we use binocular and monocular cues to perceive the world in three dimensions and perceive motion?

- *Depth perception* is our ability to see objects in three dimensions and judge distance. The *visual cliff* and other research demonstrate that many species perceive the world in three dimensions at, or very soon after, birth.

- *Binocular cues,* such as *retinal disparity,* are depth cues that rely on information from both eyes.

- *Monocular cues* (such as relative size, interposition, relative height, relative motion, linear perspective, and light and shadow) let us judge depth using information transmitted by only one eye.

- As objects move, we assume that shrinking objects are retreating and enlarging objects are approaching.

- A quick succession of images on the retina can create an illusion of movement, as in stroboscopic movement or the *phi phenomenon.*

 How do perceptual constancies help us organize our sensations into meaningful perceptions?

- *Perceptual constancy* enables us to perceive objects as stable despite the changing image they cast on our retinas.
  - *Color constancy* is our ability to perceive consistent color in objects, even though the lighting and wavelengths shift.
  - Brightness (or lightness) constancy is our ability to perceive an object as having a constant lightness even when its illumination—the light cast upon it—changes.
  - Our brain constructs our experience of an object's color or brightness through comparisons with other surrounding objects.
  - Shape constancy is our ability to perceive familiar objects (such as an opening door) as unchanging in shape.
  - Size constancy is perceiving objects as unchanging in size despite their changing retinal images.

- Knowing an object's size gives us clues to its distance; knowing its distance gives clues about its size, but we sometimes misread monocular distance cues and reach the wrong conclusions, as in the Moon illusion.

 What does research on restored vision, sensory restriction, and perceptual adaptation reveal about the effects of experience on perception?

- Experience guides our perceptual interpretations. People blind from birth who gained sight after surgery lack the experience to visually recognize shapes, forms, and complete faces.

- Sensory restriction research indicates that there is a critical period for some aspects of sensory and perceptual development. Without early stimulation, the brain's neural organization does not develop normally.

- People given glasses that shift the world slightly to the left or right, or even upside down, experience *perceptual adaptation.* They are initially disoriented, but they manage to adapt to their new context.

Multiple-Choice Questions

1. A teacher used distortion goggles, which shifted the wearer's gaze 20 degrees, to demonstrate an altered perception. A student wearing the goggles initially bumped into numerous desks and chairs while walking around, but chose to wear the goggles for a half hour. After 30 minutes, the student was able to smoothly avoid obstacles, illustrating the concept of

   a. perceptual adaptation.
   b. visual interpretation.
   c. sensory restriction.
   d. perceptual constancy.
   e. binocular cues.

2. What do we call the illusion of movement that results from two or more stationary, adjacent lights blinking on and off in quick succession?

   a. Phi phenomenon
   b. Perceptual constancy
   c. Binocular cues
   d. Retinal disparity
   e. Depth perception

3. Bryanna and Charles are in a dancing competition. It is easy for spectators to see them against the dance floor because of

   a. the visual cliff.
   b. the phi phenomenon.
   c. color constancy.
   d. sensory restriction.
   e. figure-ground relationships.

4. The view from Narmeen's left eye is slightly different from the view from her right eye. This is due to which depth cue?

   a. Retinal disparity
   b. Relative size
   c. Linear perspective
   d. Relative motion
   e. Convergence

5. Bringing order and form to stimuli, which illustrates how the whole differs from the sum of its parts, is called

   a. grouping.
   b. monocular cue.
   c. binocular cue.
   d. disparity.
   e. motion.

Practice FRQs

1. Look at the **relative size** cartoon in Figure 19.5. Describe how the artist who drew this cartoon incorporated relative size, linear perspective, and interposition to create depth.

Answer

Specific explanations may utilize different aspects of the cartoon.

1 point: Relative size: We know the woman is closer to us than the police officer, because she is drawn larger.

1 point: Linear perspective: We can tell that the sidewalk is receding into the distance, because its sides pinch closer together in the distance.

1 point: Interposition: We know the woman is closer to us than the police officer, because our view of her partially blocks our view of him.

2. Explain the meaning of the word *gestalt* as it applies to perception. Then, apply any two gestalt principles to the perception of food on a plate.

(3 points)

Module 20

Hearing

Leland Bobbé/CORBIS

Module Learning Objectives

20-1 Describe the characteristics of air pressure waves, and explain the process by which the ear transforms sound energy into neural messages.

20-2 Discuss the theories that help us understand pitch perception.

20-3 Describe how we locate sounds.

20-1 What are the characteristics of air pressure waves that we hear as sound, and how does the ear transform sound energy into neural messages?

Like our other senses, our **audition,** or hearing, is highly adaptive. We hear a wide range of sounds, but the ones we hear best are those sounds with frequencies in a range corresponding to that of the human voice. Those with normal hearing are acutely sensitive to faint sounds, an obvious boon for our ancestors' survival when hunting or being hunted, or for detecting a child's whimper. (If our ears were much more sensitive, we would hear a constant hiss from the movement of air molecules.)

We are also remarkably attuned to variations in sounds. We easily detect differences among thousands of possible human voices: Walking between classes, we immediately recognize the voice of a friend behind us. A fraction of a second after a spoken word stimulates the ear's receptors, millions of neurons have simultaneously coordinated in extracting the essential features, comparing them with past experience, and identifying the stimulus (Freeman, 1991).

But not everyone has this ability. Some years ago, on a visit to my childhood home, I communicated with my then 80-year-old mother by writing on her erasable "magic pad." Four years earlier she had transitioned from hearing loss to complete deafness by giving up her now useless hearing aids.

"Do you hear anything?" I wrote.

"No," she answered, her voice still strong although she could not hear it. "Last night your Dad came in and found the TV blasting. Someone had left the volume way up; I didn't hear a thing." (Indeed, my father later explained, he recently tested her by sneaking up while she was reading and giving a loud clap just behind her ear. Her eye never wavered from the page.)

What is it like, I wondered. "A silent world?"

"Yes," she replied. "It's a silent world."

audition the sense or act of hearing.

And for her, with human connections made difficult, it became a socially isolated world. "Not having understood what was said in a group," she reminisced, "I would chime in and say the same thing someone else had just said—and everyone would laugh. I would be so embarrassed, I wanted to fall through the floor." Increasingly, her way of coping was to avoid getting out onto the floor in the first place. She shied away from public events and found excuses to avoid people who didn't understand.

Our exchange left me wondering: Will I—having inherited her progressive hearing loss—also become socially isolated? Or, aided by today's better technology, can I keep my private vow not to repeat her past? Hearing allows mind-to-mind communication and enables connection. Yet many of us can and do connect despite hearing loss—with help from technology, lip-reading, and signing. For me, it's worth the effort. Communicating with others affirms our humanity as social creatures.

So, how does hearing normally work? How do we harvest meaning from the air pressure waves sent from another's mouth?

The Stimulus Input: Sound Waves

Draw a bow across a violin, and you will unleash the energy of sound waves. Jostling molecules of air, each bumping into the next, create waves of compressed and expanded air, like the ripples on a pond circling out from a tossed stone. As we swim in our ocean of moving air molecules, our ears detect these brief air pressure changes. (Exposed to a loud, low bass sound—perhaps from a bass guitar or a cello—we can also *feel* the vibration. We hear by both air and bone conduction.)

The sounds of music A violin's short, fast waves create a high pitch, a cello's longer, slower waves a lower pitch. Differences in the waves' height, or amplitude, also create differing degrees of loudness. (To review the physical properties of light and sound waves, see Figure 18.2 in Module 18.)

Like light waves, sound waves vary in shape. The *amplitude* of sound waves determines their *loudness.* Their length, or **frequency,** determines the **pitch** we experience. Long waves have low frequency—and low pitch. Short waves have high frequency—and high pitch. Sound waves produced by a violin are much shorter and faster than those produced by a cello or a bass guitar.

We measure sounds in *decibels,* with zero decibels representing the absolute threshold for hearing. Every 10 decibels correspond to a tenfold increase in sound intensity. Thus, normal conversation (60 decibels) is 10,000 times more intense than a 20-decibel whisper. And a temporarily tolerable 100-decibel passing subway train is 10 billion times more intense than the faintest detectable sound.

AP® Exam Tip

Note that both light and sound travel in waves. In each case, the amplitude and length of the waves are important.

The Ear

The intricate process that transforms vibrating air into nerve impulses, which our brain decodes as sounds, begins when sound waves enter the outer ear. A mechanical chain reaction begins as the visible *outer ear* channels the waves through the auditory canal to the *eardrum,* a tight membrane, causing it to vibrate (**FIGURE 20.1** on the next page). In the **middle ear** three tiny bones (the *hammer, anvil,* and *stirrup*) pick up the vibrations and transmit them to the **cochlea,** a snail-shaped tube in the **inner ear.** The incoming vibrations cause the cochlea's membrane (the *oval window*) to vibrate, jostling the fluid that fills the tube. This motion causes ripples in the *basilar membrane,* bending the *hair cells* lining its surface, not unlike the wind bending a wheat field. Hair cell movement triggers impulses in the adjacent nerve cells. Axons of those cells converge to form the *auditory nerve,* which sends neural messages (via the thalamus) to the *auditory cortex* in the brain's temporal lobe. From vibrating air to fluid waves to electrical impulses to the brain: Voila! We hear.

frequency the number of complete wavelengths that pass a point in a given time (for example, per second).

pitch a tone's experienced highness or lowness; depends on frequency.

middle ear the chamber between the eardrum and cochlea containing three tiny bones (hammer, anvil, and stirrup) that concentrate the vibrations of the eardrum on the cochlea's oval window.

cochlea [KOHK-lee-uh] a coiled, bony, fluid-filled tube in the inner ear; sound waves traveling through the cochlear fluid trigger nerve impulses.

inner ear the innermost part of the ear, containing the cochlea, semicircular canals, and vestibular sacs.

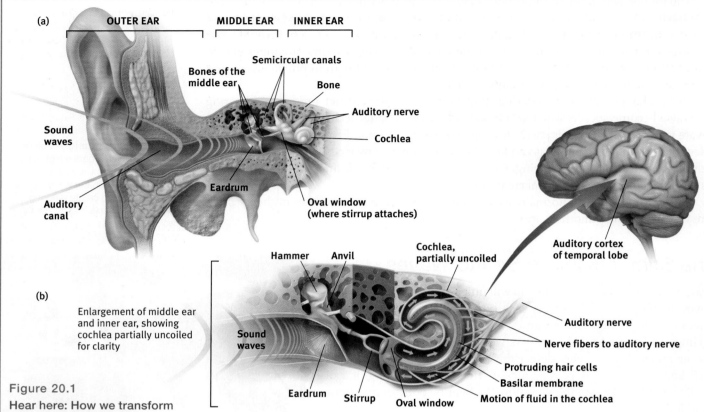

(a)

OUTER EAR | MIDDLE EAR | INNER EAR

Semicircular canals

Bones of the middle ear

Bone

Sound waves

Auditory nerve

Cochlea

Eardrum

Auditory canal

Oval window (where stirrup attaches)

(b)

Enlargement of middle ear and inner ear, showing cochlea partially uncoiled for clarity

Hammer   Anvil   Cochlea, partially uncoiled

Auditory cortex of temporal lobe

Sound waves

Auditory nerve

Nerve fibers to auditory nerve

Eardrum   Stirrup   Oval window

Protruding hair cells

Basilar membrane

Motion of fluid in the cochlea

Figure 20.1

Hear here: How we transform sound waves into nerve impulses that our brain interprets (a) The outer ear funnels sound waves to the eardrum. The bones of the middle ear (hammer, anvil, and stirrup) amplify and relay the eardrum's vibrations through the oval window into the fluid-filled cochlea. (b) As shown in this detail of the middle and inner ear, the resulting pressure changes in the cochlear fluid cause the basilar membrane to ripple, bending the hair cells on its surface. Hair cell movements trigger impulses at the base of the nerve cells, whose fibers converge to form the auditory nerve. That nerve sends neural messages to the thalamus and on to the auditory cortex.

My vote for the most intriguing part of the hearing process is the hair cells—"quivering bundles that let us hear" thanks to their "extreme sensitivity and extreme speed" (Goldberg, 2007). A cochlea has 16,000 of them, which sounds like a lot until we compare that with an eye's 130 million or so photoreceptors. But consider their responsiveness. Deflect the tiny bundles of *cilia* on the tip of a hair cell by the width of an atom—the equivalent of displacing the top of the Eiffel Tower by half an inch—and the alert hair cell, thanks to a special protein at its tip, triggers a neural response (Corey et al., 2004).

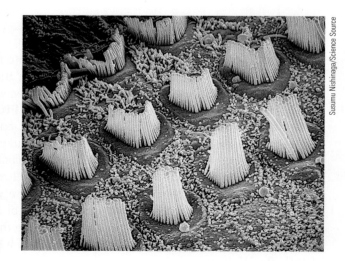

Susumu Nishinaga/Science Source

Be kind to your inner ear's hair cells When vibrating in response to sound, the hair cells shown here lining the cochlea produce an electrical signal.

Damage to the cochlea's hair cell receptors or their associated nerves can cause **sensorineural hearing loss** (or nerve deafness). (A less common form of hearing loss is **conduction hearing loss,** caused by damage to the mechanical system that conducts sound waves to the cochlea.) Occasionally, disease causes sensorineural hearing loss, but more often the culprits are biological changes linked with heredity, aging, and prolonged exposure to ear-splitting noise or music.

Hair cells have been likened to carpet fibers. Walk around on them and they will spring back with a quick vacuuming. But leave a heavy piece of furniture on them for a long time and they may never rebound. As a general rule, if we cannot talk over a noise, it is potentially harmful, especially if prolonged and repeated (Roesser, 1998). Such experiences are common when sound exceeds 100 decibels, as happens in venues from frenzied sports arenas to bagpipe bands to personal music coming through our earphones near maximum volume (**FIGURE 20.2**). Ringing of the ears after exposure to loud machinery or music indicates that we have been bad to our unhappy hair cells. As pain alerts us to possible bodily harm, ringing of the ears alerts us to possible hearing damage. It is hearing's equivalent of bleeding.

The rate of teen hearing loss, now 1 in 5, has risen by one-third since the early 1990s (Shargorodsky et al., 2010). Teen boys more than teen girls or adults blast themselves with loud volumes for long periods (Zogby, 2006). Males' greater noise exposure may help explain why men's hearing tends to be less acute than women's. But male or female, those who spend many hours in a loud nightclub, behind a power mower, or above a jackhammer should wear earplugs. "Condoms or, safer yet, abstinence," say sex educators. "Earplugs or walk away," say hearing educators.

AP Photo/Mark J. Terrill

sensorineural hearing loss hearing loss caused by damage to the cochlea's receptor cells or to the auditory nerves; also called *nerve deafness.*

conduction hearing loss hearing loss caused by damage to the mechanical system that conducts sound waves to the cochlea.

That Baylen may hear When Super Bowl-winning quarterback Drew Brees celebrated New Orleans' 2010 victory amid pandemonium, he used ear muffs to protect the vulnerable hair cells of his son, Baylen.

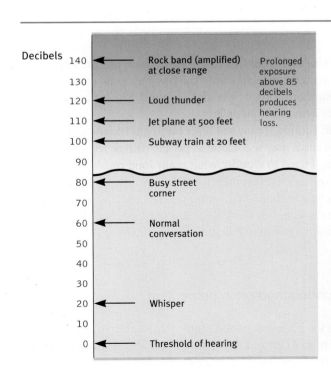

Decibels

140	Rock band (amplified) at close range
130	
120	Loud thunder
110	Jet plane at 500 feet
100	Subway train at 20 feet
90	
80	Busy street corner
70	
60	Normal conversation
50	
40	
30	
20	Whisper
10	
0	Threshold of hearing

Prolonged exposure above 85 decibels produces hearing loss.

Figure 20.2
The intensity of some common sounds

Mark Holloway/Getty Images

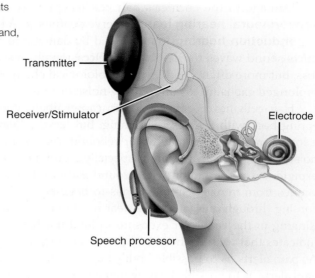

Hardware for hearing Cochlear implants work by translating sounds into electrical signals that are transmitted to the cochlea and, via the auditory nerve, on to the brain.

Transmitter

Receiver/Stimulator

Electrode

Speech processor

cochlear implant a device for converting sounds into electrical signals and stimulating the auditory nerve through electrodes threaded into the cochlea.

For now, the only way to restore hearing for people with nerve deafness is a sort of bionic ear—a **cochlear implant**, which, by 2009, had been given to 188,000 people world-wide (NIDCD, 2011). This electronic device translates sounds into electrical signals that, wired into the cochlea's nerves, convey information about sound to the brain. Cochlear implants given to deaf kittens and human infants seem to trigger an "awakening" of the pertinent brain area (Klinke et al., 1999; Sirenteanu, 1999). They can help children become proficient in oral communication (especially if they receive them as preschoolers or even before age 1) (Dettman et al., 2007; Schorr et al., 2005).

The latest cochlear implants also can help restore hearing for most adults. However, the implants will not enable normal hearing in adults if their brain never learned to process sound during childhood. Similarly, cochlear implants did not enable hearing in deaf-from-birth cats that received them when fully grown rather than as 8-week-old kittens (Ryugo et al., 2010).

Perceiving Loudness

How do we detect loudness? It is not, as I would have guessed, from the intensity of a hair cell's response. Rather, a soft, pure tone activates only the few hair cells attuned to its frequency. Given louder sounds, neighboring hair cells also respond. Thus, the brain can interpret loudness from the *number* of activated hair cells.

If a hair cell loses sensitivity to soft sounds, it may still respond to loud sounds. This helps explain another surprise: Really loud sounds may seem loud to people with or without normal hearing. As a person with hearing loss, I used to wonder what really loud music must sound like to people with normal hearing. Now I realize it sounds much the same; where we differ is in our sensation of soft sounds. This is why we hard-of-hearing people do not want *all* sounds (loud and soft) amplified. We like sound *compressed*—which means harder-to-hear sounds are amplified more than loud sounds (a feature of today's digital hearing aids).

Perceiving Pitch

20-2 What theories help us understand pitch perception?

How do we know whether a sound is the high-frequency, high-pitched chirp of a bird or the low-frequency, low-pitched roar of a truck? Current thinking on how we discriminate pitch, like current thinking on how we discriminate color, combines two theories.

- Hermann von Helmholtz's **place theory** presumes that we hear different pitches because different sound waves trigger activity at different places along the cochlea's basilar membrane. Thus, the brain determines a sound's pitch by recognizing the specific place (on the membrane) that is generating the neural signal. When Nobel laureate-to-be Georg von Békésy (1957) cut holes in the cochleas of guinea pigs and human cadavers and looked inside with a microscope, he discovered that the cochlea vibrated, rather like a shaken bedsheet, in response to sound. High frequencies produced large vibrations near the beginning of the cochlea's membrane. Low frequencies vibrate more of the membrane, including near the end. But a problem remains: Place theory can explain how we hear high-pitched sounds but not low-pitched sounds. The neural signals generated by low-pitched sounds are not so neatly localized on the basilar membrane.

- **Frequency theory** suggests an alternative: The brain reads pitch by monitoring the frequency of neural impulses traveling up the auditory nerve. The whole basilar membrane vibrates with the incoming sound wave, triggering neural impulses to the brain at the same rate as the sound wave. If the sound wave has a frequency of 100 waves per second, then 100 pulses per second travel up the auditory nerve. But again, a problem remains: An individual neuron cannot fire faster than 1000 times per second. How, then, can we sense sounds with frequencies above 1000 waves per second (roughly the upper third of a piano keyboard)?

- Enter the *volley principle:* Like soldiers who alternate firing so that some can shoot while others reload, neural cells can alternate firing. By firing in rapid succession, they can achieve a *combined frequency* above 1000 waves per second. Thus, place theory best explains how we sense *high pitches,* frequency theory best explains how we sense *low pitches,* and some combination of place and frequency seems to handle the *pitches in the intermediate range.*

place theory in hearing, the theory that links the pitch we hear with the place where the cochlea's membrane is stimulated.

frequency theory in hearing, the theory that the rate of nerve impulses traveling up the auditory nerve matches the frequency of a tone, thus enabling us to sense its pitch.

Locating Sounds

20-3 How do we locate sounds?

Why don't we have one big ear—perhaps above our one nose? "All the better to hear you with," as the wolf said to Red Riding Hood. As the placement of our eyes allows us to sense visual depth, so the placement of our two ears allows us to enjoy stereophonic ("three-dimensional") hearing.

Two ears are better than one for at least two reasons. If a car to the right honks, your right ear receives a more *intense* sound, and it receives sound slightly *sooner* than your left ear (**FIGURE 20.3**). Because sound travels 750 miles per hour and our ears are but 6 inches apart, the intensity difference and the time lag are extremely small. A just noticeable difference in the direction of two sound sources corresponds to a time difference of just 0.000027 second! Lucky for us, our supersensitive auditory system can detect such minute differences (Brown & Deffenbacher, 1979; Middlebrooks & Green, 1991).

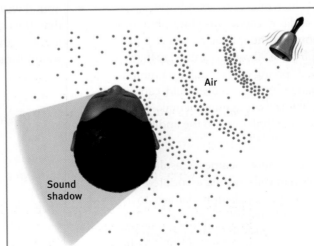

Air

Sound shadow

Figure 20.3

How we locate sounds Sound waves strike one ear sooner and more intensely than the other. From this information, our nimble brain computes the sound's location. As you might therefore expect, people who lose all hearing in one ear often have difficulty locating sounds.

Before You Move On

▶ **ASK YOURSELF**

If you are a hearing person, imagine that you had been born deaf. Do you think your life would be different?

▶ **TEST YOURSELF**

What are the basic steps in transforming sound waves into perceived sound?

Answers to the Test Yourself questions can be found in Appendix E at the end of the book.

Module 20 Review

 20-1 What are the characteristics of air pressure waves that we hear as sound, and how does the ear transform sound energy into neural messages?

- Sound waves are bands of compressed and expanded air. Our ears detect these changes in air pressure and transform them into neural impulses, which the brain decodes as sound.

- Sound waves vary in amplitude, which we perceive as differing loudness, and in *frequency,* which we experience as differing *pitch.*

- The outer ear is the visible portion of the ear. The *middle ear* is the chamber between the eardrum and *cochlea.*

- The *inner ear* consists of the cochlea, semicircular canals, and vestibular sacs.

- Through a mechanical chain of events, sound waves traveling through the auditory canal cause tiny vibrations in the eardrum. The bones of the middle ear (the *hammer, anvil,* and *stirrup*) amplify the vibrations and relay them to the fluid-filled cochlea. Rippling of the basilar membrane, caused by pressure changes in the cochlear fluid, causes movement of the tiny hair cells, triggering neural messages to be sent (via the thalamus) to the auditory cortex in the brain.

- *Sensorineural hearing loss* (or nerve deafness) results from damage to the cochlea's hair cells or their associated nerves. *Conduction hearing loss* results from damage to the mechanical system that transmits sound waves to the cochlea. *Cochlear implants* can restore hearing for some people.

20-2 What theories help us understand pitch perception?

- *Place theory* explains how we hear high-pitched sounds, and *frequency theory* explains how we hear low-pitched sounds. (A combination of the two theories (the volley principle) explains how we hear pitches in the middle range.)
  - *Place theory* proposes that our brain interprets a particular pitch by decoding the place where a sound wave stimulates the cochlea's basilar membrane.
  - *Frequency theory* proposes that the brain deciphers the frequency of the neural impulses traveling up the auditory nerve to the brain.

20-3 How do we locate sounds?

- Sound waves strike one ear sooner and more intensely than the other. The brain analyzes the minute differences in the sounds received by the two ears and computes the sound's source.

Multiple-Choice Questions

1. What type of hearing loss is due to damage to the mechanism that transmits sound waves to the cochlea?

   a. Sensorineural
   b. Window-related
   c. Conduction
   d. Cochlear
   e. Basilar

2. Pitch depends on which of the following?

   a. Amplitude of a sound wave
   b. Number of hair cells stimulated
   c. Strength of nerve impulses traveling up the auditory nerve
   d. Number of sound waves that reach the ear in a given time
   e. Decibels of a sound wave

3. Which of the following reflects the notion that pitch is related to the number of impulses traveling up the auditory nerve in a unit of time?

   a. Place theory
   b. Frequency theory
   c. Volley principle
   d. Sound localization
   e. Stereophonic hearing

4. The three small bones of the ear are located in the

   a. cochlea.
   b. outer ear.
   c. inner ear.
   d. middle ear.
   e. auditory nerve.

Practice FRQs

1. Describe two parts of the ear that transmit sound waves before they reach the hair cells.

Answer

Students may describe any two of the following:

1 point: The eardrum, a tight membrane separating the middle ear from the outer ear.

1 point: The three bones in the middle ear that transmit sound waves between the eardrum and the cochlea.

1 point: The oval window, the point at which vibrations enter the cochlea.

1 point: The cochlea, where the fluid inside vibrates and the hair cells are stimulated.

2. What roles do the outer, middle, and inner ear play in helping a person hear a song on the radio?

(3 points)

Module 21

The Other Senses

© Paul Burns/Corbis

Module Learning Objectives

21-1 Describe the sense of touch.

21-2 Discuss how we best understand and control pain.

21-3 Describe the senses of taste and smell.

21-4 Explain how we sense our body's position and movement.

21-5 Describe how our senses interact.

Although our brain gives seeing and hearing priority in the allocation of cortical tissue, extraordinary happenings occur within our four other senses—our senses of touch, taste, smell, and body position and movement. Sharks and dogs rely on their extraordinary sense of smell, aided by large brain areas devoted to this system. Without our own senses of touch, taste, smell, and body position and movement, we humans would also be seriously handicapped, and our capacities for enjoying the world would be seriously diminished.

Touch

21-1 How do we sense touch?

> "Touch is both the alpha and omega of affection." -WILLIAM JAMES (1890)

Although not the first sense to come to mind, touch is vital. Right from the start, touch is essential to our development. Infant rats deprived of their mother's grooming produce less growth hormone and have a lower metabolic rate—a good way to keep alive until the mother returns, but a reaction that stunts growth if prolonged. Infant monkeys allowed to see, hear, and smell—but not touch—their mother become desperately unhappy; those separated by a screen with holes that allow touching are much less miserable. As we will see in Module 46, premature human babies gain weight faster and go home sooner if they are stimulated by hand massage. As lovers, we yearn to touch—to kiss, to stroke, to snuggle. And even strangers, touching only the other's forearms and separated by a curtain, can communicate anger, fear, disgust, love, gratitude, and sympathy at levels well above chance (Hertenstein et al., 2006).

Humorist Dave Barry may be right to jest that your skin "keeps people from seeing the inside of your body, which is repulsive, and it prevents your organs from falling onto the ground." But skin does much more. Our "sense of touch" is actually a mix of distinct skin senses for pressure, warmth, cold, and pain. Touching various spots on the skin with a soft hair, a warm or cool wire, and the point of a pin reveals that some spots are especially sensitive to pressure, others to warmth, others to cold, still others to pain. Other skin sensations are variations of the basic four (*pressure, warmth, cold,* and *pain*):

- Stroking adjacent pressure spots creates a tickle.
- Repeated gentle stroking of a pain spot creates an itching sensation.
- Touching adjacent cold and pressure spots triggers a sense of wetness, which you can experience by touching dry, cold metal.
- Stimulating nearby cold and warm spots produces the sensation of hot (**FIGURE 21.1**).

Touch sensations involve more than tactile stimulation, however. A self-produced tickle produces less somatosensory cortex activation than does the same tickle from something or someone else (Blakemore et al., 1998). (The brain is wise enough to be most sensitive to unexpected stimulation.)

Pain

21-2 How can we best understand and control pain?

Be thankful for occasional pain. Pain is your body's way of telling you something has gone wrong. Drawing your attention to a burn, a break, or a sprain, pain orders you to change your behavior—"Stay off that turned ankle!" The rare people born without the ability to feel pain may experience severe injury or even die before early adulthood. Without the discomfort that makes us occasionally shift position, their joints fail from excess strain, and without the warnings of pain, the effects of unchecked infections and injuries accumulate (Neese, 1991).

More numerous are those who live with chronic pain, which is rather like an alarm that won't shut off. The suffering of those with persistent or recurring backaches, arthritis, headaches, and cancer-related pain, prompts two questions: What is pain? How might we control it?

Understanding Pain

Our pain experiences vary widely. Women are more pain sensitive than men are (Wickelgren, 2009). Individual pain sensitivity varies, too, depending on genes, physiology, experience, attention, and surrounding culture (Gatchel et al., 2007; Reimann et al., 2010). Thus, feeling pain reflects both bottom-up sensations and top-down processes.

BIOLOGICAL INFLUENCES

There is no one type of stimulus that triggers pain (as light triggers vision). Instead, there are different *nociceptors*—sensory receptors that detect hurtful temperatures, pressure, or chemicals (**FIGURE 21.2** on the next page).

Although no theory of pain explains all available findings, psychologist Ronald Melzack and biologist Patrick Wall's (1965, 1983) classic **gate-control theory** provides a useful model. The spinal cord contains small nerve fibers that conduct most pain signals, and larger fibers that conduct most other sensory signals. Melzack and Wall theorized that the spinal cord contains a neurological "gate." When tissue is injured, the small fibers activate and open the gate, and you feel pain. Large-fiber activity closes the gate, blocking pain signals and preventing them from reaching the brain. Thus, one way to treat chronic pain is to

Figure 21.1

Warm + cold = hot When ice-cold water passes through one coil and comfortably warm water through another, we perceive the combined sensation as burning hot.

"Pain is a gift" So said a doctor studying 13-year-old Ashlyn Blocker. Ashlyn has a rare genetic mutation that prevents her feeling pain. At birth she didn't cry. As a child, she ran around for two days on a broken ankle. She has put her hands on a hot machine and burned the flesh off. And she has reached into boiling water to retrieve a dropped spoon. "Everyone in my class asks me about it, and I say, 'I can feel pressure, but I can't feel pain.' *Pain!* I cannot feel it!" (Heckert, 2010).
Jeff Riedel/Contour by Getty Images

gate-control theory the theory that the spinal cord contains a neurological "gate" that blocks pain signals or allows them to pass on to the brain. The "gate" is opened by the activity of pain signals traveling up small nerve fibers and is closed by activity in larger fibers or by information coming from the brain.

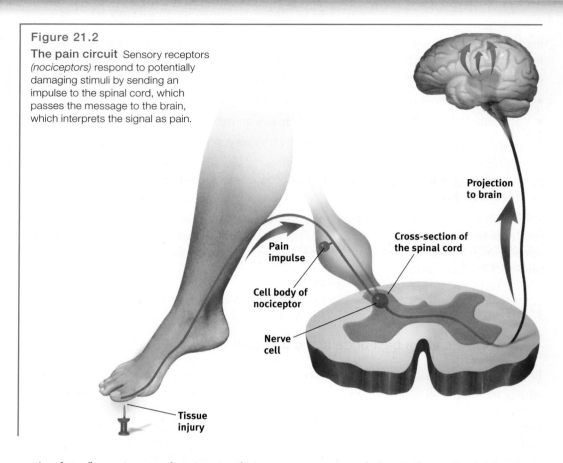

Figure 21.2

The pain circuit Sensory receptors *(nociceptors)* respond to potentially damaging stimuli by sending an impulse to the spinal cord, which passes the message to the brain, which interprets the signal as pain.

Pain impulse

Projection to brain

Cross-section of the spinal cord

Cell body of nociceptor

Nerve cell

Tissue injury

stimulate (by massage, electric stimulation, or acupuncture) "gate-closing" activity in the large neural fibers (Wall, 2000).

But pain is not merely a physical phenomenon of injured nerves sending impulses to a definable brain area—like pulling on a rope to ring a bell. Melzack and Wall noted that brain-to-spinal-cord messages can also close the gate, helping to explain some striking influences on pain. When we are distracted from pain (a psychological influence) and soothed by the release of our naturally painkilling *endorphins* (a biological influence), our experience of pain diminishes. Sports injuries may go unnoticed until the after-game shower. People who carry a gene that boosts the availability of endorphins are less bothered by pain, and their brain is less responsive to pain (Zubieta et al., 2003). Others carry a mutated gene that disrupts pain circuit neurotransmission and experience little pain (Cox et al., 2006). Such discoveries may point the way toward new pain medications that mimic these genetic effects.

The brain can also create pain, as it does in people's experiences of *phantom limb sensations,* when it misinterprets the spontaneous central nervous system activity that occurs in the absence of normal sensory input. As the dreamer may see with eyes closed, so some 7 in 10 amputees may feel pain or movement in nonexistent limbs (Melzack, 1992, 2005). (An amputee may also try to step off a bed onto a phantom limb or to lift a cup with a phantom hand.) Even those born without a limb sometimes perceive sensations from the absent arm or leg. The brain, Melzack (1998) surmises, comes prepared to anticipate "that it will be getting information from a body that has limbs."

A similar phenomenon occurs with other senses. People with hearing loss often experience the sound of silence: phantom sounds—a ringing-in-the-ears sensation known as *tinnitus.* Those who lose vision to glaucoma, cataracts, diabetes, or macular degeneration may experience phantom sights—nonthreatening hallucinations (Ramachandran & Blakeslee, 1998). Some with nerve damage have had taste phantoms, such as ice water seeming sickeningly sweet (Goode, 1999). Others have experienced phantom smells, such as nonexistent rotten food. The point to remember: *We feel, see, hear, taste, and smell with our brain,* which can sense even without functioning senses.

PSYCHOLOGICAL INFLUENCES

The psychological effects of distraction are clear in the stories of athletes who, focused on winning, play through the pain. We also seem to edit our *memories* of pain, which often differ from the pain we actually experienced. In experiments, and after medical procedures, people overlook a pain's duration. Their memory snapshots instead record two factors: their pain's *peak* moment (which can lead them to recall variable pain, with peaks, as worse [Stone et al., 2005]), and how much pain they felt at the *end.*

In one experiment, researchers asked people to immerse one hand in painfully cold water for 60 seconds, and then the other hand in the same painfully cold water for 60 seconds followed by a slightly less painful 30 seconds more (Kahneman et al., 1993). Which experience would you expect to recall as most painful? Curiously, when asked which trial they would prefer to repeat, most preferred the longer trial, with more net pain—but less pain at the end. Physicians have used this principle with patients undergoing colon exams—lengthening the discomfort by a minute, but lessening its intensity (Kahneman, 1999). Although the extended milder discomfort added to their net pain experience, patients experiencing this taper-down treatment later recalled the exam as less painful than did those whose pain ended abruptly. (If, at the end of a painful root canal, the oral surgeon asks if you'd like to go home or to have a few more minutes of milder discomfort, there's a case to be made for prolonging your hurt.)

SOCIAL-CULTURAL INFLUENCES

Our perception of pain also varies with our social situation and our cultural traditions. We tend to perceive more pain when others also seem to be experiencing pain (Symbaluk et al., 1997). This may help explain other apparent social aspects of pain, as when pockets of Australian keyboard operators during the mid-1980s suffered outbreaks of severe pain during typing or other repetitive work—without any discernible physical abnormalities (Gawande, 1998). Sometimes the pain in sprain is mainly in the brain—literally. When feeling empathy for another's pain, a person's own brain activity may partly mirror that of the other's brain in pain (Singer et al, 2004).

Thus, our perception of pain is a biopsychosocial phenomenon (**FIGURE 21.3**). Viewing pain this way can help us better understand how to cope with pain and treat it.

Playing with pain In a 2012 NFL game, Dallas Cowboys quarterback Tony Romo cracked a rib after colliding with an opposing player. He continued playing through the pain, which reclaimed his attention after the game's end.

"When belly with bad pains doth swell, It matters naught what else goes well." -SADI, *THE GULISTAN*, 1258

"Pain is increased by attending to it." -CHARLES DARWIN, *EXPRESSION OF EMOTIONS IN MAN AND ANIMALS*, 1872

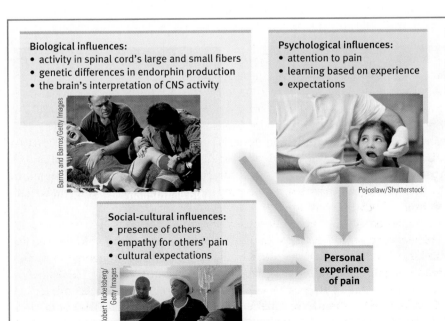

Biological influences:
- activity in spinal cord's large and small fibers
- genetic differences in endorphin production
- the brain's interpretation of CNS activity

Psychological influences:
- attention to pain
- learning based on experience
- expectations

Social-cultural influences:
- presence of others
- empathy for others' pain
- cultural expectations

Personal experience of pain

Figure 21.3

Biopsychosocial approach to pain Our experience of pain is much more than neural messages sent to the brain.

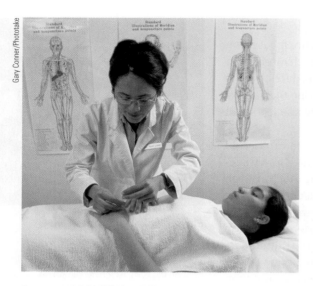

Acupuncture: A jab well done This acupuncturist is attempting to help this woman gain relief from back pain by using needles on points of the patient's hand.

Controlling Pain

If pain is where body meets mind—if it is both a physical and a psychological phenomenon—then it should be treatable both physically and psychologically. Depending on the type of symptoms, pain control clinics select one or more therapies from a list that includes drugs, surgery, acupuncture, electrical stimulation, massage, exercise, hypnosis, relaxation training, and thought distraction.

Even an inert placebo can help, by dampening the central nervous system's attention and responses to painful experiences—mimicking analgesic drugs (Eippert et al., 2009; Wager, 2005). After being injected in the jaw with a stinging saltwater solution, men in one experiment received a placebo said to relieve pain, and they immediately felt better. Being given fake pain-killing chemicals caused the brain to dispense real ones, as indicated by activity in an area that releases natural pain-killing opiates (Scott et al., 2007; Zubieta et al., 2005). "Believing becomes reality," noted one commentator (Thernstrom, 2006), as "the mind unites with the body."

Another experiment pitted two placebos—fake pills and pretend acupuncture—against each other (Kaptchuk et al., 2006). People with persistent arm pain (270 of them) received either sham acupuncture (with trick needles that retracted without puncturing the skin) or blue cornstarch pills that looked like pills often prescribed for strain injury. A fourth of those receiving the nonexistent needle pricks and 31 percent of those receiving the pills complained of side effects, such as painful skin or dry mouth and fatigue. After two months, both groups were reporting less pain, with the fake acupuncture group reporting the greater pain drop.

Distracting people with pleasant images (*"Think of a warm, comfortable environment"*) or drawing their attention away from the painful stimulation (*"Count backward by 3s"*) is an especially effective way to activate pain-inhibiting circuits and to increase pain tolerance (Edwards et al., 2009). A well-trained nurse may distract needle-shy patients by chatting with them and asking them to look away when inserting the needle. For burn victims receiving excruciating wound care, an even more effective distraction comes from immersion in a computer-generated 3-D world, like the snow scene in **FIGURE 21.4**. Functional MRI (fMRI) scans reveal that playing in the virtual reality reduces the brain's pain-related activity (Hoffman, 2004). Because pain is in the brain, diverting the brain's attention may bring relief.

Figure 21.4

Virtual-reality pain control For burn victims undergoing painful skin repair, an escape into virtual reality can powerfully distract attention, thus reducing pain and the brain's response to painful stimulation. The fMRI scans on the right illustrate a lowered pain response when the patient is distracted.

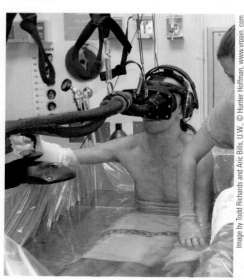

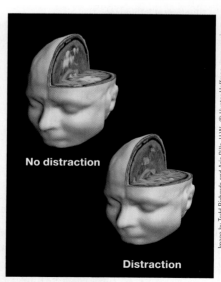

No distraction

Distraction

Taste

21-3 How do we experience taste and smell?

Like touch, our sense of taste involves several basic sensations. Taste's sensations were once thought to be sweet, sour, salty, and bitter, with all others stemming from mixtures of these four (McBurney & Gent, 1979). Then, as investigators searched for specialized nerve fibers for the four taste sensations, they encountered a receptor for what we now know is a fifth—the savory meaty taste of *umami,* best experienced as the flavor enhancer monosodium glutamate (MSG), often used in Chinese and Thai food.

Evolutionary psychologists explain that tastes exist for more than our pleasure (see **TABLE 21.1**). Pleasureful tastes attracted our ancestors to energy- or protein-rich foods that enabled their survival. Aversive tastes deterred them from new foods that might be toxic. We see the inheritance of this biological wisdom in today's 2- to 6-year-olds, who are typically fussy eaters, especially when offered new meats or bitter-tasting vegetables, such as spinach and brussels sprouts (Cooke et al., 2003). Meat and plant toxins were both potentially dangerous sources of food poisoning for our ancestors, especially for children. Given repeated small tastes of disliked new foods, children will, however, typically begin to accept them (Wardle et al., 2003). (Module 38 will explore cultural influences on our taste preferences.)

Taste is a chemical sense. Inside each little bump on the top and sides of your tongue are 200 or more taste buds, each containing a pore that catches food chemicals. Into each taste bud pore, 50 to 100 taste receptor cells project antenna-like hairs that sense food molecules. Some receptors respond mostly to sweet-tasting molecules, others to salty-, sour-, umami-, or bitter-tasting ones. It doesn't take much to trigger a response that alerts your brain's temporal lobe. If a stream of water is pumped across your tongue, the addition of a concentrated salty or sweet taste for but one-tenth of a second will get your attention (Kelling & Halpern, 1983). When a friend asks for "just a taste" of your soft drink, you can squeeze off the straw after a mere instant.

Taste receptors reproduce themselves every week or two, so when you burn your tongue with hot pizza, it hardly matters. However, as you grow older, the number of taste buds decreases, as does taste sensitivity (Cowart, 1981). (No wonder adults enjoy strong-tasting foods that children resist.) Smoking and alcohol use accelerate these declines. Those who lose their sense of taste report that food tastes like "straw" and is hard to swallow (Cowart, 2005).

Essential as taste buds are, there's more to taste than meets the tongue. Expectations can influence taste. When told a sausage roll was "vegetarian," people in one experiment found it decidedly inferior to its identical partner labeled "meat" (Allen et al., 2008). In another experiment, when adults were told that a wine cost $90 rather than its real $10 price, they reported it tasting better and a brain area that responds to pleasant experiences showed more activity (Plassmann et al., 2008).

Table 21.1 The Survival Functions of Basic Tastes	
Taste	Indicates
Sweet	Energy source
Salty	Sodium essential to physiological processes
Sour	Potentially toxic acid
Bitter	Potential poisons
Umami	Proteins to grow and repair tissue

(Adapted from Cowart, 2005.)

Lauren Burke/Jupiterimages

Smell

Life begins with an inhale and ends with an exhale. Between birth and death, you will daily inhale and exhale nearly 20,000 breaths of life-sustaining air, bathing your nostrils in a stream of scent-laden molecules. The resulting experiences of smell *(olfaction)* are strikingly intimate: You inhale something of whatever or whoever it is you smell.

Like taste, smell is a chemical sense. We smell something when molecules of a substance carried in the air reach a tiny cluster of 20 million receptor cells at the top of each

Try This

Impress your friends with your new word for the day: People unable to see are said to experience blindness. People unable to hear experience deafness. People unable to smell experience *anosmia.*

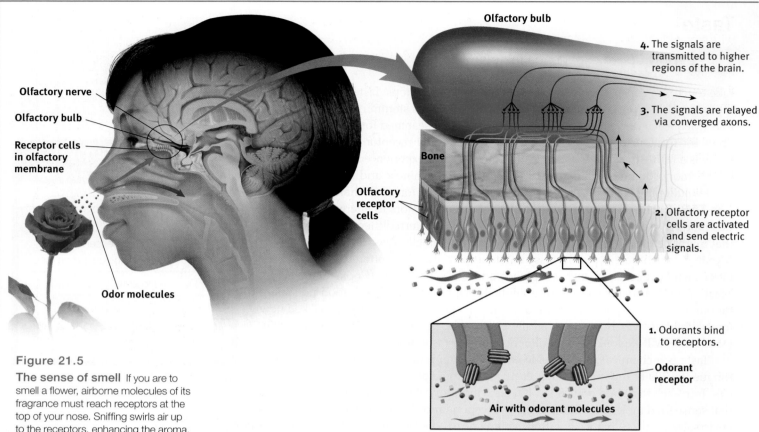

Olfactory bulb

4. The signals are transmitted to higher regions of the brain.

3. The signals are relayed via converged axons.

Bone

2. Olfactory receptor cells are activated and send electric signals.

Olfactory receptor cells

1. Odorants bind to receptors.

Odorant receptor

Air with odorant molecules

Olfactory nerve

Olfactory bulb

Receptor cells in olfactory membrane

Odor molecules

Figure 21.5

The sense of smell If you are to smell a flower, airborne molecules of its fragrance must reach receptors at the top of your nose. Sniffing swirls air up to the receptors, enhancing the aroma. The receptor cells send messages to the brain's olfactory bulb, and then onward to the temporal lobe's primary smell cortex and to the parts of the limbic system involved in memory and emotion.

Tish1/Shutterstock

nasal cavity (**FIGURE 21.5**). These olfactory receptor cells, waving like sea anemones on a reef, respond selectively—to the aroma of a cake baking, to a wisp of smoke, to a friend's fragrance. Instantly, they alert the brain through their axon fibers. Being an old, primitive sense, olfactory neurons bypass the brain's sensory control center, the thalamus.

Research has shown that even nursing infants and their mothers have a literal chemistry to their relationship: They quickly learn to recognize each other's scents (McCarthy, 1986). Aided by smell, a mother fur seal returning to a beach crowded with pups will find her own. Our human sense of smell is less acute than our senses of seeing and hearing. Looking out across a garden, we see its forms and colors in exquisite detail and hear a variety of birds singing, yet we smell little of it without sticking our nose into the blossoms.

Odor molecules come in many shapes and sizes—so many, in fact, that it takes many different receptors to detect them. A large family of genes designs the 350 or so receptor proteins that recognize particular odor molecules (Miller, 2004). Linda Buck and Richard Axel (1991) discovered (in work for which they received a 2004 Nobel Prize) that these receptor proteins are embedded on the surface of nasal cavity neurons. As a key slips into a lock, so odor molecules slip into these receptors. Yet we don't seem to have a distinct receptor for each detectable odor. This suggests that some odors trigger a combination of receptors, in patterns that are interpreted by the olfactory cortex. As the English alphabet's 26 letters can combine to form many words, so odor molecules bind to different receptor arrays, producing the 10,000 odors we can detect (Malnic et al., 1999). It is the combinations of olfactory receptors, which activate different neuron patterns, that allow us to distinguish between the aromas of fresh-brewed and hours-old coffee (Zou et al., 2005).

For humans, the attractiveness of smells depends on learned associations (Herz, 2001). As babies nurse, their preference for the smell of their mother's breast builds. So, too, with other associations. As good experiences are linked with a particular scent, people come to like that scent, which helps explain why people in the United States tend to like the smell of wintergreen (which they associate with candy and gum) more than do those in Great Britain (where it often is associated with medicine). In another example of odors evoking unpleasant emotions, researchers frustrated Brown University students with a rigged computer game in a scented room (Herz et al., 2004). Later, if exposed to the same odor while working on a verbal task, the students' frustration was rekindled and they gave up sooner than others exposed to a different odor or no odor.

The nose knows Humans have some 20 million olfactory receptors. A bloodhound has 220 million (Herz, 2007).

Though it's difficult to recall odors by name, we have a remarkable capacity to recognize long-forgotten odors and their associated memories (Engen, 1987; Schab, 1991). The smell of the sea, the scent of a perfume, or an aroma of a favorite relative's kitchen can bring to mind a happy time. It's a phenomenon the British travel agent chain Lunn Poly understood well. To evoke memories of lounging on sunny, warm beaches, the company once piped the aroma of coconut suntan oil into its shops (Fracassini, 2000).

Our brain's circuitry helps explain an odor's power to evoke feelings and memories (**FIGURE 21.6**). A hotline runs between the brain area receiving information from the nose and the brain's ancient limbic centers associated with memory and emotion. Thus, when put in a foul-smelling room, people expressed harsher judgments of immoral acts (such as lying or keeping a found wallet) and more negative attitudes toward gay men (Inbar et al., 2011; Schnall et al., 2008).

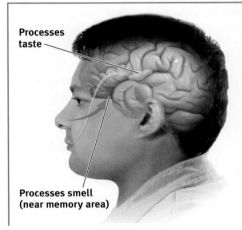

Processes taste

Processes smell (near memory area)

Figure 21.6

Taste, smell, and memory Information from the taste buds (yellow arrow) travels to an area between the frontal and temporal lobes of the brain. It registers in an area not far from where the brain receives information from our sense of smell, which interacts with taste. The brain's circuitry for smell (red area) also connects with areas involved in memory storage, which helps explain why a smell can trigger a memory.

Body Position and Movement

21-4 How do we sense our body's position and movement?

Important sensors in your joints, tendons, and muscles enable your **kinesthesia**—your sense of the position and movement of your body parts. By closing your eyes or plugging your ears you can momentarily imagine being without sight or sound. But what would it be like to live without touch or kinesthetic sense—without, therefore, being able to sense the positions of your limbs when you wake during the night? Ian Waterman of Hampshire, England, knows. In 1972, at age 19, Waterman contracted a rare viral infection that destroyed the nerves enabling his sense of light touch and of body position and movement. People with this condition report feeling disembodied, as though their body is dead, not real, not theirs (Sacks, 1985). With prolonged practice, Waterman has learned to walk and eat—by visually focusing on his limbs and directing them accordingly. But if the lights go out, he crumples to the floor (Azar, 1998). Even for the rest of us, vision interacts with kinesthesia. Stand with your right heel in front of your left toes. Easy. Now close your eyes and you will probably wobble.

A companion **vestibular sense** monitors your head's (and thus your body's) position and movement. The biological gyroscopes for this sense of equilibrium are in your inner ear. The *semicircular canals,* which look like a three-dimensional pretzel (Figure 20.1a), and the *vestibular sacs,* which connect the canals with the cochlea, contain fluid that moves when your head rotates or tilts. This movement stimulates hairlike receptors, which send

kinesthesia [kin-ehs-THEE-see-a] the system for sensing the position and movement of individual body parts.

vestibular sense the sense of body movement and position, including the sense of balance.

Bodies in space These high school competitive cheer team members can thank their inner ears for the information that enables their brains to monitor their bodies' position so expertly.

sensory interaction the principle that one sense may influence another, as when the smell of food influences its taste.

messages to the cerebellum at the back of the brain, thus enabling you to sense your body position and to maintain your balance.

If you twirl around and then come to an abrupt halt, neither the fluid in your semicircular canals nor your kinesthetic receptors will immediately return to their neutral state. The dizzy aftereffect fools your brain with the sensation that you're still spinning. This illustrates a principle that underlies perceptual illusions: Mechanisms that normally give us an accurate experience of the world can, under special conditions, fool us. Understanding how we get fooled provides clues to how our perceptual system works.

Sensory Interaction

21-5 How do our senses interact?

Our senses are not totally separate information channels. In interpreting the world, our brain blends their inputs. Consider what happens to your sense of taste if you hold your nose, close your eyes, and have someone feed you various foods. A slice of apple may be indistinguishable from a chunk of raw potato. A piece of steak may taste like cardboard. Without their smells, a cup of cold coffee may be hard to distinguish from a glass of Gatorade. To savor a taste, we normally breathe the aroma through our nose—which is why eating is not much fun when you have a bad cold. Smell can also change our perception of taste: A drink's strawberry odor enhances our perception of its sweetness. Even touch can influence taste. Depending on its texture, a potato chip "tastes" fresh or stale (Smith, 2011). This is **sensory interaction** at work—the principle that one sense may influence another. Smell + texture + taste = flavor.

Vision and hearing may similarly interact. An almost imperceptible flicker of light is more easily visible when accompanied by a short burst of sound (Kayser, 2007). And a sound may be easier to hear with a visual cue. If I (as a person with hearing loss) watch a video with simultaneous captioning, I have no trouble hearing the words I am seeing (and may therefore think I don't need the captioning). If I then turn off the captioning, I suddenly realize I do need it. The eyes guide the ears (**FIGURE 21.7**).

But what do you suppose happens if the eyes and the ears disagree? What if we *see* a speaker saying one syllable while we *hear* another? Surprise: We may perceive a third syllable that blends both inputs. Seeing the mouth movements for *ga* while hearing *ba* we may perceive *da*. This phenomenon is known as the *McGurk effect*, after its discoverers, psychologist Harry McGurk and his assistant John MacDonald (1976).

Touch also interacts with our other senses. In detecting events, the brain can combine simultaneous touch and visual signals, thanks to neurons projecting from the somatosensory cortex back to the visual cortex (Macaluso et al., 2000). Touch even interacts with hearing. In one experiment, researchers blew a puff of air (such as our mouths produce when saying *pa* and *ta*) on the neck or hands as people heard either these sounds or the more airless sounds *ba* or *da*. To my surprise (and yours?), the people more often misheard

Figure 21.7
Sensory interaction When a hard-of-hearing listener sees an animated face forming the words being spoken at the other end of a phone line, the words become easier to understand (Knight, 2004). The eyes guide the ears.

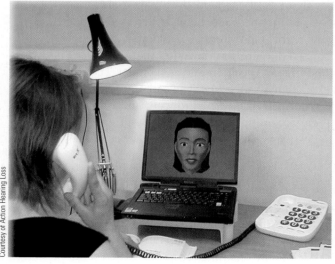

ba or *da* as *pa* or *ta* when played with the faint puff (Gick & Derrick, 2009). Thanks to sensory interaction, they were hearing with their skin.

Our brain even blends our tactile and social judgments:

- After holding a warm drink rather than a cold one, people are more likely to rate someone more warmly, feel closer to them, and behave more generously (IJzerman & Semin, 2009; Williams & Bargh, 2008). Physical warmth promotes social warmth.

- After being given the cold shoulder by others in an experiment, people judge the room as colder than do those treated warmly (Zhong & Leonardelli, 2008). Social exclusion literally feels cold.

- Holding a heavy rather than light clipboard makes job candidates seem more important. Holding rough objects makes social interactions seem more difficult (Ackerman et al., 2010).

- When leaning to the left—by sitting in a left- rather than right-leaning chair, or squeezing a hand-grip with their left hand, or using a mouse with their left hand—people lean more left in their expressed political attitudes (Oppenheimer & Trail, 2010).

These examples of **embodied cognition** illustrate how brain circuits processing our bodily sensations connect with brain circuits responsible for cognition.

So, the senses interact: As we attempt to decipher our world, our brain blends inputs from multiple channels. For many people, an odor, perhaps of mint or chocolate, can evoke a sensation of taste (Stevenson & Tomiczek, 2007). But in a few select individuals, the senses become joined in a phenomenon called *synesthesia,* where one sort of sensation (such as hearing sound) produces another (such as seeing color). Thus, hearing music may activate color-sensitive cortex regions and trigger a sensation of color (Brang et al., 2008; Hubbard et al., 2005). Seeing the number 3 may evoke a taste sensation (Ward, 2003).

* * *

For a summary of our sensory systems, see **TABLE 21.2**. The river of perception is fed by sensation, cognition, and emotion. And that is why we need biological, psychological, and social-cultural levels of analysis.

> **embodied cognition** in psychological science, the influence of bodily sensations, gestures, and other states on cognitive preferences and judgments.

Table 21.2 Summarizing the Senses

Sensory System	Source	Receptors
Vision	Light waves striking the eye	Rods and cones in the retina
Hearing	Sound waves striking the outer ear	Cochlear hair cells in the inner ear
Touch	Pressure, warmth, cold, pain on the skin	Skin receptors detect pressure, warmth, cold, and pain
Taste	Chemical molecules in the mouth	Basic tongue receptors for sweet, sour, salty, bitter, and umami
Smell	Chemical molecules breathed in through the nose	Millions of receptors at top of nasal cavity
Body position—kinesthesia	Any change in position of a body part, interacting with vision	Kinesthetic sensors all over the body
Body movement—vestibular sense	Movement of fluids in the inner ear caused by head/body movement	Hairlike receptors in the semicircular canals and vestibular sacs

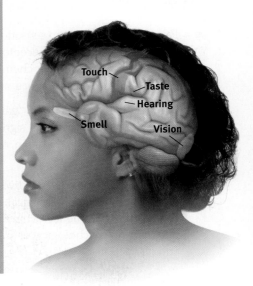

* * *

To feel awe, mystery, and a deep reverence for life, we need look no further than our own perceptual system and its capacity for organizing formless nerve impulses into colorful sights, vivid sounds, and evocative smells. As Shakespeare's Hamlet recognized, "There are more things in Heaven and Earth, Horatio, than are dreamt of in your philosophy." Within our ordinary sensory and perceptual experiences lies much that is truly extraordinary—surely much more than has so far been dreamt of in our psychology.

Before You Move On

▶ **ASK YOURSELF**

Have you ever experienced a feeling that you think could be explained by embodied cognition?

▶ **TEST YOURSELF**

How does our system for sensing smell differ from our sensory systems for vision, touch, and taste?

Answers to the Test Yourself questions can be found in Appendix E at the end of the book.

Module 21 Review

21-1 How do we sense touch?

- Our sense of touch is actually several senses—pressure, warmth, cold, and pain—that combine to produce other sensations, such as "hot."

21-2 How can we best understand and control pain?

- Pain reflects bottom-up sensations (such as input from nociceptors, the sensory receptors that detect hurtful temperatures, pressure, or chemicals) and top-down processes (such as experience, attention, and culture).

- One theory of pain is that a "gate" in the spinal cord either opens to permit pain signals traveling up small nerve fibers to reach the brain, or closes to prevent their passage.

- The biopsychosocial perspective views our perception of pain as the sum of biological, psychological, and social-cultural influences. Pain treatments often combine physical and psychological elements, including placebos and distractions.

21-3 How do we experience taste and smell?

- Taste and smell are chemical senses.

- Taste is a composite of five basic sensations—sweet, sour, salty, bitter, and umami—and of the aromas that interact with information from the taste receptor cells of the taste buds.

- There are no basic sensations for smell. We have some 20 million olfactory receptor cells, with about 350 different receptor proteins.

- Odor molecules trigger combinations of receptors, in patterns that the olfactory cortex interprets. The receptor cells send messages to the brain's olfactory bulb, then to the temporal lobe, and to parts of the limbic system.

21-4 How do we sense our body's position and movement?

- Through *kinesthesia,* we sense the position and movement of our body parts.

- We monitor our body's position and movement, and maintain our balance with our *vestibular sense.*

21-5 How do our senses interact?

- Our senses can influence one another. This *sensory interaction* occurs, for example, when the smell of a favorite food amplifies its taste.

- *Embodied cognition* is the influence of bodily sensations, gestures, and other states on cognitive preferences and judgments.

Multiple-Choice Questions

1. Sensing the position and movement of individual body parts is an example of which sense?

a. Kinesthetic
b. Vestibular
c. Auditory
d. Umami
e. Olfactory

2. Which of the following is the best example of kinesthesia?

a. Awareness of the smell of freshly brewed coffee
b. Ability to feel pressure on your arm
c. Ability to hear a softly ticking clock
d. Ability to calculate where a kicked soccer ball will land from the moment it leaves your foot
e. Awareness of the position of your arms when swimming the backstroke

3. Which of the following is the best example of sensory interaction?

a. Finding that despite its delicious aroma, a weird-looking meal tastes awful
b. Finding that food tastes bland when you have a bad cold
c. Finding it difficult to maintain your balance when you have an ear infection
d. Finding that the cold pool water doesn't feel so cold after a while
e. All of these are examples.

4. Which of the following is most closely associated with hairlike receptors in the semicircular canals?

a. Body position
b. Smell
c. Hearing
d. Pain
e. Touch

Practice FRQs

1. Describe the receptor cells for taste and smell.

Answer

1 point: Taste: Receptor cells in the tongue detect sweet, sour, salty, bitter, and umami.

1 point: Smell: Olfactory cells line the top of the nasal cavity.

2. Briefly explain the biopsychosocial perspective on pain and pain treatment.

(2 points)

Unit IV Review

Key Terms and Concepts to Remember

sensation, p. 152

perception, p. 152

bottom-up processing, p. 152

top-down processing, p. 152

selective attention, p. 152

inattentional blindness, p. 154

change blindness, p. 154

transduction, p. 155

psychophysics, p. 155

absolute threshold, p. 156

signal detection theory, p. 156

subliminal, p. 157

priming, p. 157

difference threshold, p. 158

Weber's law, p. 158

sensory adaptation, p. 159

perceptual set, p. 163

extrasensory perception (ESP), p. 167

parapsychology, p. 167

wavelength, p. 171

hue, p. 172

intensity, p. 172

pupil, p. 172

iris, p. 172

lens, p. 172

retina, p. 172

accommodation, p. 172

rods, p. 173

cones, p. 173

optic nerve, p.173

blind spot, p. 173

fovea, p. 173

feature detectors, p. 175

parallel processing, p. 176

Young-Helmholtz trichromatic (three-color) theory, p. 178

opponent-process theory, p. 179

gestalt, p. 182

figure-ground, p. 183

grouping, p. 183

depth perception, p. 184

visual cliff, p. 184

binocular cues, p. 184

retinal disparity, p. 184

monocular cues, p. 185

phi phenomenon, p. 185

perceptual constancy, p. 186

color constancy, p. 187

perceptual adaptation, p. 191

audition, p. 194

frequency, p. 195

pitch, p. 195

middle ear, p. 195

cochlea [KOHK-lee-uh], p. 195

inner ear, p. 195

sensorineural hearing loss, p. 197

conduction hearing loss, p. 197

cochlear implant, p. 198

place theory, p. 199

frequency theory, p. 199

gate-control theory, p. 203

kinesthesia [kin-ehs-THEE-see-a], p. 209

vestibular sense, p. 209

sensory interaction, p. 210

embodied cognition, p. 211

Key Contributors to Remember

Gustav Fechner, p. 156

Ernst Weber, p. 158

David Hubel, p. 175

Torsten Wiesel, p. 175

AP® Exam Practice Questions

Multiple-Choice Questions

1. What is the purpose of the iris?

  a. To focus light on the retina
  b. To process color
  c. To allow light into the eye
  d. To enable night vision
  e. To detect specific shapes

2. Neurons that fire in response to specific edges, lines, angles, and movements are called what?

  a. Rods
  b. Cones
  c. Ganglion cells
  d. Feature detectors
  e. Bipolar cells

3. Signal detection theory is most closely associated with which perception process?

   a. Vision
   b. Sensory adaptation
   c. Absolute thresholds
   d. Smell
   e. Context effects

4. Which of the following represents perceptual constancy?

   a. We recognize the taste of McDonald's food each time we eat it.
   b. In photos of people, the people almost always are perceived as figure and everything else as ground.
   c. We know that the color of a printed page has not changed as it moves from sunlight into shadow.
   d. From the time they are very young, most people can recognize the smell of a dentist's office.
   e. The cold water in a lake doesn't seem so cold after you have been swimming in it for a few minutes.

5. Our tendency to see faces in clouds and other ambiguous stimuli is partly based on what perception principle?

   a. Selective attention
   b. ESP
   c. Perceptual set
   d. Shape constancy
   e. Bottom-up processing

6. The process by which rods and cones change electromagnetic energy into neural messages is called what?

   a. Adaptation
   b. Accommodation
   c. Parallel processing
   d. Transduction
   e. Perceptual setting

7. Which of the following is most likely to influence our memory of a painful event?

   a. The overall length of the event
   b. The intensity of pain at the end of the event
   c. The reason for the pain
   d. The amount of rest you've had in the 24 hours preceding the event
   e. The specific part of the body that experiences the pain

8. Frequency theory relates to which element of the hearing process?

   a. Rate at which the basilar membrane vibrates
   b. Number of fibers in the auditory nerve
   c. Point at which the basilar membrane exhibits the most vibration
   d. Decibel level of a sound
   e. Number of hair cells in each cochlea

9. Which of the following best represents an absolute threshold?

   a. A guitar player knows that his D string has just gone out of tune.
   b. A photographer can tell that the natural light available for a photograph has just faded slightly.
   c. Your friend amazes you by correctly identifying unlabeled glasses of Coke and Pepsi.
   d. A cook can just barely taste the salt she has added to her soup.
   e. Your mom throws out the milk because she says the taste is "off."

10. Which of the following describes a perception process that the Gestalt psychologists would have been interested in?

   a. Depth perception and how it allows us to survive in the world
   b. Why we see an object near us as closer rather than larger
   c. How an organized whole is formed out of its component pieces
   d. What the smallest units of perception are
   e. The similarities between shape constancy and size constancy

11. Which perception process are the hammer, anvil, and stirrup involved in?

   a. Processing intense colors
   b. Processing information related to our sense of balance
   c. Supporting á structural frame to hold the eardrum
   d. Transmitting sound waves to the cochlea
   e. Holding hair cells that enable hearing

12. Which of the following might result from a disruption of your vestibular sense?

   a. Inability to detect the position of your arm without looking at it
   b. Loss of the ability to detect bitter tastes
   c. Dizziness and a loss of balance
   d. An inability to detect pain
   e. Loss of color vision

13. When we go to the movies, we see smooth continuous motion rather than a series of still images because of which process?

   a. The phi phenomenon
   b. Perceptual set
   c. Stroboscopic movement
   d. Relative motion
   e. Illusory effect

14. Two monocular depth cues are most responsible for our ability to know that a jet flying overhead is at an elevation of several miles. One cue is relative size. What is the other?

a. Relative motion
b. Retinal disparity
c. Interposition
d. Light and shadow
e. Linear perspective

15. Which of the following phrases accurately describes top-down processing?

a. The entry-level data captured by our various sensory systems
b. The effect that our experiences and expectations have on perception
c. Our tendency to scan a visual field from top to bottom
d. Our inclination to follow a predetermined set of steps to process sound
e. The fact that information is processed by the higher regions of the brain before it reaches the lower brain

Free-Response Questions

1. While listening to the orchestra as she dances the lead role in *Swan Lake,* a ballerina concludes her performance with a pirouette, spinning around several times before leaping into the arms of her dance partner.

Discuss how the ballerina relied on the following and how each is important.

- Kinesthetic sense
- Vestibular sense
- Semicircular canals
- Hearing

Rubric for Free Response Question 1

1 point: Kinesthesia will allow the ballerina to sense the position of different parts of her body as she dances the role. Thus, she will know that she is to start by facing the audience and, although she has spun around several times, she will always be aware of where the audience is, and where to put her feet and arms in order to accomplish the choreography. ↻ Page 209

1 point: The vestibular sense enables the dancer to sense her body position and to maintain her balance. ↻ Pages 209–210

1 point: Semicircular canals near her inner ear help the ballerina maintain her sense of balance. She needs this balance as she leaps and spins, and her training allows her to use her vestibular sense to maintain balance rather than become dizzy. ↻ Pages 195 and 209

1 point: The ballerina's sense of hearing allows her to perceive the music and to dance to the correct rhythm of each piece of music. ↻ Pages 194–199

2. Ester is walking to her chemistry class when she notices someone in the distance suddenly duck into a dark doorway. She is suspicious and starts to chase the figure, but misjudges the distance and accidentally runs into the door. She falls down but quickly recovers, and laughs when she discovers that the mystery person is her roommate, who was avoiding Ester, because she had borrowed Ester's favorite sweater without permission and was afraid Ester might be angry.

Use the following terms to explain the perceptual processes involved in this scenario.

- Gate-control theory
- Vestibular sense
- Selective attention
- Signal detection theory
- Binocular cues
- Perceptual set

(6 points)

3. Describe, from the beginning of the process to the end, how your brain is perceiving the words you are reading right now. Use the following terms in your answer.

- Transduction
- Top-down processing
- Retina
- Pupil
- Occipital lobe
- Rods
- Feature detectors

(7 points)

Multiple-choice self-tests and more may be found at www.worthpublishers.com/MyersAP2e

Unit V

States of Consciousness

Modules

Consciousness can be a funny thing. It offers us weird experiences, as when entering sleep or leaving a dream, and sometimes it leaves us wondering who is really in control. After zoning me out with nitrous oxide, my dentist tells me to turn my head to the left. My conscious mind resists: *"No way,"* I silently say. *"You can't boss me around!"* Whereupon my robotic head, ignoring my conscious mind, turns obligingly under the dentist's control.

During my noontime pickup basketball games, I am sometimes mildly irritated as my body passes the ball while my conscious mind is saying, *"No, stop! Sarah is going to intercept!"* Alas, my body completes the pass. Other times, as psychologist Daniel Wegner (2002) noted in *The Illusion of Conscious Will*, people believe their consciousness is controlling their actions when it isn't. In one experiment, two people jointly controlled a computer mouse. Even when their partner (who was actually the experimenter's accomplice) caused the mouse to stop on a predetermined square, the participants perceived that *they* had caused it to stop there.

Then there are those times when consciousness seems to split. Reading *Green Eggs and Ham* to one of my preschoolers for the umpteenth time, my obliging mouth could say the words while my mind wandered elsewhere. And if someone asks what you're doing for lunch while you're texting, it's not a problem. Your thumbs complete the message as you suggest getting tacos.

What do such experiences reveal? Was my drug-induced dental experience akin to people's experiences with other *psychoactive drugs* (mood- and perception-altering substances)? Was my automatic obedience to my dentist like people's responses to a hypnotist? Does a split in consciousness, as when our minds go elsewhere while reading or texting, explain people's behavior while under hypnosis? And during sleep, when do those weird dream experiences occur, and why? Before considering these questions and more, let's ask a fundamental question: What is *consciousness?*

Module 22

Understanding Consciousness and Hypnosis

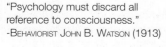

Module Learning Objectives

22-1 Describe the place of consciousness in psychology's history.

22-2 Define *hypnosis*, and describe how a hypnotist can influence a hypnotized subject.

22-3 Discuss whether hypnosis is an extension of normal consciousness or an altered state.

Every science has concepts so fundamental they are nearly impossible to define. Biologists agree on what is alive but not on precisely what life is. In physics, *matter* and *energy* elude simple definition. To psychologists, consciousness is similarly a fundamental yet slippery concept.

Defining Consciousness

22-1 What is the place of consciousness in psychology's history?

At its beginning, *psychology* was "the description and explanation of states of consciousness" (Ladd, 1887). But during the first half of the twentieth century, the difficulty of scientifically studying consciousness led many psychologists—including those in the emerging school of *behaviorism* (Module 26)—to turn to direct observations of behavior. By the 1960s, psychology had nearly lost consciousness and was defining itself as "the science of behavior." Consciousness was likened to a car's speedometer: "It doesn't make the car go, it just reflects what's happening" (Seligman, 1991, p. 24).

After 1960, mental concepts reemerged. Neuroscience advances related brain activity to sleeping, dreaming, and other mental states. Researchers began studying consciousness

"Psychology must discard all reference to consciousness."
-BEHAVIORIST JOHN B. WATSON (1913)

altered by hypnosis and drugs. Psychologists of all persuasions were affirming the importance of *cognition,* or mental processes. Psychology was regaining consciousness.

Most psychologists now define **consciousness** as our awareness of ourselves and our environment. As we saw in Module 13, our conscious awareness is one part of the *dual processing* that goes on in our two-track minds. Although much of our information processing is conscious, much is unconscious and automatic—outside our awareness. Module 16 highlighted our *selective attention,* which directs the spotlight of our awareness, allowing us to assemble information from many sources as we reflect on our past and plan for our future. We are also attentive when we learn a complex concept or behavior. When learning to ride a bike, we focus on obstacles that we have to steer around and on how to use the brakes. With practice, riding a bike becomes semi-automatic, freeing us to focus our attention on other things. As we do so, we experience what the early psychologist William James called a continuous "stream of consciousness," with each moment flowing into the next. Over time, we flit between different *states of consciousness,* including sleeping, waking, and various altered states (**FIGURE 22.1**).

AP® Exam Tip

Note that our modern-day understanding of the unconscious is very different from Sigmund Freud's theory of the unconscious (Module 55). Freud believed the unconscious was a hiding place for our most anxiety-provoking ideas and emotions, and that uncovering those hidden thoughts could lead to healing. Now, most psychologists simply view the unconscious track as one that operates without awareness. Make sure you keep these two ideas of the unconscious straight.

Some states occur spontaneously	Daydreaming	Drowsiness	Dreaming
Some are physiologically induced	Hallucinations	Orgasm	Food or oxygen starvation
Some are psychologically induced	Sensory deprivation	Hypnosis	Meditation

Maria Teijeiro/Getty Images

Stuart Franklin/Magnum Photos

Figure 22.1
States of consciousness
In addition to normal, waking awareness, consciousness comes to us in altered states, including daydreaming and meditating.

Hypnosis

 22-2 What is hypnosis, and what powers does a hypnotist have over a hypnotized subject?

Imagine you are about to be hypnotized. The hypnotist invites you to sit back, fix your gaze on a spot high on the wall, and relax. In a quiet voice the hypnotist suggests, "Your eyes are growing tired. . . . Your eyelids are becoming heavy . . . now heavier and heavier. . . . They are beginning to close. . . . You are becoming more deeply relaxed. . . . Your breathing is now deep and regular. . . . Your muscles are becoming more and more relaxed. Your whole body is beginning to feel like lead."

After a few minutes of this *hypnotic induction,* you may experience **hypnosis.** When the hypnotist suggests, "Your eyelids are shutting so tight that you cannot open them even if you try," it may indeed seem beyond your control to open your eyelids. Told to forget the number 6, you may be puzzled when you count 11 fingers on your hands. Invited to smell a sensuous perfume that is actually ammonia, you may linger delightedly over its pungent odor. Told that you cannot see a certain object, such as a chair, you may indeed report that it is not there, although you manage to avoid the chair when walking around (illustrating once again that two-track mind of yours).

But is hypnosis really an *altered* state of consciousness? Let's start with some frequently asked questions.

Frequently Asked Questions About Hypnosis

Hypnotists have no magical mind-control power. Their power resides in the subjects' openness to suggestion, their ability to focus on certain images or behaviors (Bowers, 1984). But how open to suggestions are we?

consciousness our awareness of ourselves and our environment.

hypnosis a social interaction in which one person (the subject) responds to another person's (the hypnotist's) suggestions that certain perceptions, feelings, thoughts, or behaviors will spontaneously occur.

- **Can anyone experience hypnosis?** To some extent, we are all open to suggestion. When people stand upright with their eyes closed and are told that they are swaying back and forth, most will indeed sway a little. In fact, *postural sway* is one of the items assessed on the Stanford Hypnotic Susceptibility Scale. People who respond to such suggestions without hypnosis are the same people who respond with hypnosis (Kirsch & Braffman, 2001).

  Highly hypnotizable people—say, the 20 percent who can carry out a suggestion not to smell or react to a bottle of ammonia held under their nose—typically become deeply absorbed in imaginative activities (Barnier & McConkey, 2004; Silva & Kirsch, 1992). Many researchers refer to this as hypnotic ability—the ability to focus attention totally on a task, to become imaginatively absorbed in it, to entertain fanciful possibilities.

- **Can hypnosis enhance recall of forgotten events?** Most people believe (wrongly, as Module 32 will explain) that our experiences are all "in there," recorded in our brain and available for recall if only we can break through our own defenses (Loftus, 1980). But 60 years of memory research disputes such beliefs. We do not encode everything that occurs around us. We permanently store only some of our experiences, and we may be unable to retrieve some memories we have stored.

  "Hypnotically refreshed" memories combine fact with fiction. Since 1980, thousands of people have reported being abducted by UFOs, but most such reports have come from people who are predisposed to believe in aliens, are highly hypnotizable, and have undergone hypnosis (Newman & Baumeister, 1996; Nickell, 1996). Without either person being aware of what is going on, a hypnotist's hints—"Did you hear loud noises?"—can plant ideas that become the subject's pseudomemory.

So should testimony obtained under hypnosis be admissible in court? American, Australian, and British courts have agreed it should not. They generally ban testimony from witnesses who have been hypnotized (Druckman & Bjork, 1994; Gibson, 1995; McConkey, 1995).

- **Can hypnosis force people to act against their will?** Researchers have induced hypnotized people to perform an apparently dangerous act: plunging one hand briefly into fuming "acid," then throwing the "acid" in a researcher's face (Orne & Evans, 1965). Interviewed a day later, these people emphatically denied their acts and said they would never follow such orders.

  Had hypnosis given the hypnotist a special power to control others against their will? To find out, researchers Martin Orne and Frederick Evans unleashed that enemy of so many illusory beliefs—the control group. Orne asked other individuals to *pretend* they were hypnotized. Laboratory assistants, unaware that those in the experiment's control group had not been hypnotized, treated both groups the same. The result? All the *un*hypnotized participants (perhaps believing that the laboratory context assured safety) performed the same acts as those who were hypnotized.

- **Can hypnosis be therapeutic?** *Hypnotherapists* try to help patients harness their own healing powers (Baker, 1987). **Posthypnotic suggestions** have helped alleviate headaches, asthma, and stress-related skin disorders.

  In one statistical digest of 18 studies, the average client whose therapy was supplemented with hypnosis showed greater improvement than 70 percent of other therapy patients (Kirsch et al., 1995, 1996). Hypnosis seemed especially helpful for the treatment of obesity. However, drug, alcohol, and smoking addictions have not responded well to hypnosis (Nash, 2001). In controlled studies, hypnosis speeds the disappearance of warts, but so do the same positive suggestions given without hypnosis (Spanos, 1991, 1996).

AP® Exam Tip

Psychological research corrects the mistaken popular belief that hypnosis or other methods can be used to tap into a pure and complete memory bank. You will learn much more about how memory really works when you get to Unit VII.

"Hypnosis is not a psychological truth serum and to regard it as such has been a source of considerable mischief." -Researcher Kenneth Bowers (1987)

FYI

See Module 33 for a more detailed discussion of how people may construct false memories.

"It wasn't what I expected. But facts are facts, and if one is proved to be wrong, one must just be humble about it and start again." -Agatha Christie's Miss Marple

---

posthypnotic suggestion
a suggestion, made during a hypnosis session, to be carried out after the subject is no longer hypnotized; used by some clinicians to help control undesired symptoms and behaviors.

- **Can hypnosis relieve pain?** Hypnosis *can* relieve pain (Druckman & Bjork, 1994; Jensen, 2008). When unhypnotized people put their arm in an ice bath, they feel intense pain within 25 seconds. When hypnotized people do the same after being given suggestions to feel no pain, they indeed report feeling little pain. As some dentists know, light hypnosis can reduce fear, thus reducing hypersensitivity to pain.

  Hypnosis inhibits pain-related brain activity. In surgical experiments, hypnotized patients have required less medication, recovered sooner, and left the hospital earlier than unhypnotized control patients (Askay & Patterson, 2007; Hammond, 2008; Spiegel, 2007). Nearly 10 percent of us can become so deeply hypnotized that even major surgery can be performed without anesthesia. Half of us can gain at least some pain relief from hypnosis. The surgical use of hypnosis has flourished in Europe, where one Belgian medical team has performed more than 5000 surgeries with a combination of hypnosis, local anesthesia, and a mild sedative (Song, 2006).

Hypnotherapy This therapy aims to help people uncover problem-causing thoughts and feelings, or to change an unwanted behavior.

Explaining the Hypnotized State

 Is hypnosis an extension of normal consciousness or an altered state?

We have seen that hypnosis involves heightened suggestibility. We have also seen that hypnotic procedures do not endow a person with special powers but can sometimes help people overcome stress-related ailments and cope with pain. So, just what *is* hypnosis? Psychologists have proposed two explanations.

HYPNOSIS AS A SOCIAL PHENOMENON

Our attentional spotlight and interpretations powerfully influence our ordinary perceptions. Might hypnotic phenomena reflect such workings of normal consciousness, as well as the power of social influence (Lynn et al., 1990; Spanos & Coe, 1992)? Advocates of the *social influence theory of hypnosis* believe they do.

Does this mean that subjects consciously fake hypnosis? *No*—like actors caught up in their roles, they begin to feel and behave in ways appropriate for "good hypnotic subjects." The more they like and trust the hypnotist, the more they allow that person to direct their attention and fantasies (Gfeller et al., 1987). "The hypnotist's ideas become the subject's thoughts," explained Theodore Barber (2000), "and the subject's thoughts produce the hypnotic experiences and behaviors." Told to scratch their ear later when they hear the word *psychology,* subjects will likely do so—but only if they think the experiment is still under way. If an experimenter eliminates their motivation for acting hypnotized—by stating that hypnosis reveals their "gullibility"—subjects become unresponsive. Such findings support the idea that hypnotic phenomena are an extension of normal social and cognitive processes.

These views illustrate a principle that Module 75 emphasizes: *An authoritative person in a legitimate context can induce people—hypnotized or not—to perform some unlikely acts.* Or as hypnosis researcher Nicholas Spanos (1982) put it, "The overt behaviors of hypnotic subjects are well within normal limits."

HYPNOSIS AS DIVIDED CONSCIOUSNESS

Other hypnosis researchers believe hypnosis is more than inducing someone to play the role of "good subject." How, they ask, can we explain why hypnotized subjects sometimes carry out suggested behaviors on cue, even when they believe no one is watching (Perugini et al., 1998)? And why does distinctive brain activity accompany hypnosis (Oakley & Halligan, 2009)? In one experiment, deeply hypnotized people were asked to imagine a color, and areas of their brain activated as if they were really seeing the color. To the hypnotized person's brain, mere imagination had become a compelling hallucination (Kosslyn et al., 2000). In another experiment, researchers invited hypnotizable and nonhypnotizable people to say the color of letters. This is an easy task, but it slows if, say, green letters form the conflicting word RED, a phenomenon known as the *Stroop effect* (Raz et al., 2005). When easily hypnotized people were given a suggestion to focus on the color and to perceive the letters as irrelevant gibberish, they were much less slowed by the word-color conflict. (Brain areas that decode words and detect conflict remained inactive.)

These results would not have surprised famed researcher Ernest Hilgard (1986, 1992), who believed hypnosis involves not only social influence but also a special dual-processing state of **dissociation**—a split between different levels of consciousness. Hilgard viewed hypnotic dissociation as a vivid form of everyday mind splits—similar to doodling while listening to a lecture or typing the end of a sentence while starting a conversation. Hilgard felt that when, for example, hypnotized people lower their arm into an ice bath, as in **FIGURE 22.2**, the hypnosis dissociates the sensation of the pain stimulus (of which the subjects are still aware) from the emotional suffering that defines their experience of pain. The ice water therefore feels cold—very cold—but not painful.

> **dissociation** a split in consciousness, which allows some thoughts and behaviors to occur simultaneously with others.

Figure 22.2

Dissociation or role playing?

A hypnotized woman tested by Ernest Hilgard exhibited no pain when her arm was placed in an ice bath. But asked to press a key if some part of her felt the pain, she did so. To Hilgard, this was evidence of dissociation, or divided consciousness. Proponents of social influence theory, however, maintain that people responding this way are caught up in playing the role of "good subject."

Attention is diverted from a painful ice bath. How?

Divided-consciousness theory:

Hypnosis has caused a split in awareness.

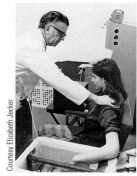

Courtesy Elizabeth Jecker

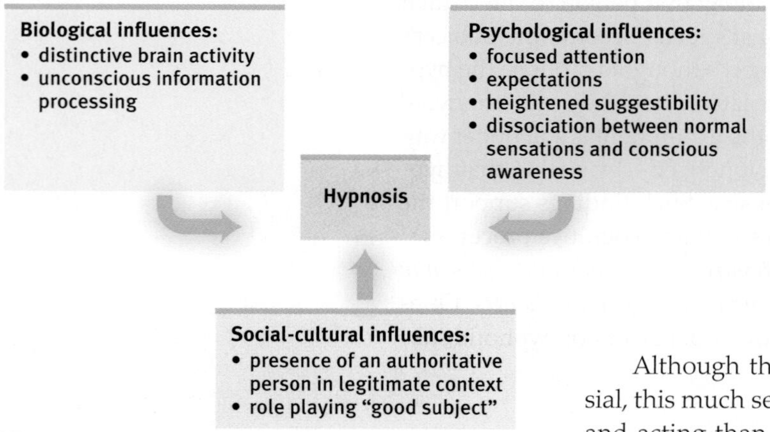

Social influence theory:

The subject is so caught up in the hypnotized role that she ignores the cold.

Biological influences:
• distinctive brain activity
• unconscious information processing

Psychological influences:
• focused attention
• expectations
• heightened suggestibility
• dissociation between normal sensations and conscious awareness

Hypnosis

Social-cultural influences:
• presence of an authoritative person in legitimate context
• role playing "good subject"

Figure 22.3

Levels of analysis for hypnosis Using a biopsychosocial approach, researchers explore hypnosis from complementary perspectives.

Another form of dual processing—*selective attention*—may also play a role in hypnotic pain relief. PET scans show that hypnosis reduces brain activity in a region that processes painful stimuli, but not in the sensory cortex, which receives the raw sensory input (Rainville et al., 1997). Hypnosis does not block sensory input, but it may block our attention to those stimuli. This helps explain why an injured athlete, caught up in the competition, may feel little or no pain until the game ends.

Although the divided-consciousness theory of hypnosis is controversial, this much seems clear: There is, without doubt, much more to thinking and acting than we are conscious of. Our information processing, which starts with selective attention, is divided into simultaneous conscious and nonconscious realms. In hypnosis as in life, *much of our behavior occurs on autopilot.* We have two-track minds (**FIGURE 22.3**).

Before You Move On

▶ **ASK YOURSELF**

You've read about two examples of dissociated consciousness: talking while texting, and thinking about something else while reading a child a bedtime story. Can you think of another example that you have experienced?

▶ **TEST YOURSELF**

When is the use of hypnosis potentially harmful, and when can hypnosis be used to help?

Answers to the Test Yourself questions can be found in Appendix E at the end of the book.

Module 22 Review

 What is the place of consciousness in psychology's history?

- After initially claiming consciousness as its area of study in the nineteenth century, psychologists had abandoned it in the first half of the twentieth century, turning instead to the study of observable behavior because they believed consciousness was too difficult to study scientifically.

- Since 1960, under the influence of cognitive psychology and neuroscience, *consciousness* (our awareness of ourselves and our environment) has resumed its place as an important area of research.

 What is hypnosis, and what powers does a hypnotist have over a hypnotized subject?

- *Hypnosis* is a social interaction in which one person suggests to another that certain perceptions, feelings, thoughts, or behaviors will spontaneously occur.

- Hypnosis does not enhance recall of forgotten events (it may even evoke false memories).

- It cannot force people to act against their will, though hypnotized people, like unhypnotized people, may perform unlikely acts.

- *Posthypnotic suggestions* have helped people harness their own healing powers but have not been very effective in treating addiction. Hypnosis can help relieve pain.

 Is hypnosis an extension of normal consciousness or an altered state?

- Many psychologists believe that hypnosis is a form of normal social influence and that hypnotized people act out the role of "good subject" by following directions given by an authoritative person.

- Other psychologists view hypnosis as a *dissociation*—a split between normal sensations and conscious awareness. Selective attention may also contribute by blocking attention to certain stimuli.

Multiple-Choice Questions

1. What do we call awareness of our environment and ourselves?

a. Selective attention
b. Hypnotism
c. Posthypnotic suggestion
d. Dissociation
e. Consciousness

2. Which of the following is true about daydreaming?

a. It occurs spontaneously.
b. It is physiologically induced.
c. It is psychologically induced.
d. It is considered the same as waking awareness.
e. It is more like meditation than it is like dreaming.

3. Which of the following states of consciousness occurs when one person suggests to another that certain thoughts or behaviors will spontaneously occur?

a. Dreaming
b. Hypnosis
c. Daydreaming
d. Hallucination
e. Waking awareness

4. Which of the following is the term most closely associated with the split in consciousness that allows some thoughts and behaviors to occur simultaneously with others?

a. Consciousness
b. Hypnosis
c. Hallucination
d. Dissociation
e. Meditation

Practice FRQs

1. Identify two states of consciousness that are psychologically induced and two that occur spontaneously.

Answer

1 point: For any two psychologically induced states: sensory deprivation, hypnosis, or meditation.

1 point: For any two spontaneously occurring states: daydreaming, drowsiness, or dreaming.

2. According to the biopsychosocial approach, identify a biological, a psychological, and a social-cultural influence on hypnosis.

(3 points)

Module 23

Sleep Patterns and Sleep Theories

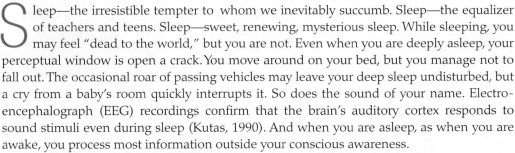

Catchlight Visual Services/Alamy

Module Learning Objectives

23-1   Describe how our biological rhythms influence our daily functioning.

23-2   Describe the biological rhythm of our sleeping and dreaming stages.

23-3   Explain how biology and environment interact in our sleep patterns.

23-4   Describe sleep's functions.

Sleep—the irresistible tempter to whom we inevitably succumb. Sleep—the equalizer of teachers and teens. Sleep—sweet, renewing, mysterious sleep. While sleeping, you may feel "dead to the world," but you are not. Even when you are deeply asleep, your perceptual window is open a crack. You move around on your bed, but you manage not to fall out. The occasional roar of passing vehicles may leave your deep sleep undisturbed, but a cry from a baby's room quickly interrupts it. So does the sound of your name. Electroencephalograph (EEG) recordings confirm that the brain's auditory cortex responds to sound stimuli even during sleep (Kutas, 1990). And when you are asleep, as when you are awake, you process most information outside your conscious awareness.

Many of sleep's mysteries are now being solved as some people sleep, attached to recording devices, while others observe. By recording brain waves and muscle movements, and by observing and occasionally waking sleepers, researchers are glimpsing things that a thousand years of common sense never told us. Perhaps you can anticipate some of their discoveries. Are the following statements true or false?

1.   When people dream of performing some activity, their limbs often move in concert with the dream.
2.   Older adults sleep more than young adults.
3.   Sleepwalkers are acting out their dreams.
4.   Sleep experts recommend treating insomnia with an occasional sleeping pill.
5.   Some people dream every night; others seldom dream.

All these statements (adapted from Palladino & Carducci, 1983) are *false*. To see why, read on.

> "I love to sleep. Do you? Isn't it great? It really is the best of both worlds. You get to be alive and unconscious." -COMEDIAN RITA RUDNER, 1993

Biological Rhythms and Sleep

Like the ocean, life has its rhythmic tides. Over varying periods, our bodies fluctuate, and with them, our minds. Let's look more closely at two of those biological rhythms—our 24-hour biological clock and our 90-minute sleep cycle.

Circadian Rhythm

23-1 How do our biological rhythms influence our daily functioning?

The rhythm of the day parallels the rhythm of life—from our waking at a new day's birth to our nightly return to what Shakespeare called "death's counterfeit." Our bodies roughly synchronize with the 24-hour cycle of day and night by an internal biological clock called the **circadian rhythm** (from the Latin *circa*, "about," and *diem*, "day"). As morning approaches, body temperature rises, then peaks during the day, dips for a time in early afternoon (when many people take siestas), and begins to drop again in the evening. Thinking is sharpest and memory most accurate when we are at our daily peak in circadian arousal. Try pulling an all-nighter or working an occasional night shift. You'll feel groggiest in the middle of the night but may gain new energy when your normal wake-up time arrives.

Eric Isselée/Shutterstock

Age and experience can alter our circadian rhythm. Most teens and young adults are evening-energized "owls," with performance improving across the day (May & Hasher, 1998). Most older adults are morning-loving "larks," with performance declining as the day wears on. By mid-evening, when the night has hardly begun for many young adults, retirement homes are typically quiet. At about age 20 (slightly earlier for women), we begin to shift from being owls to being larks (Roenneberg et al., 2004). Women become more morning oriented as they have children and also as they transition to menopause (Leonhard & Randler, 2009; Randler & Bausback, 2010). Morning types tend to do better in school, to take more initiative, and to be less vulnerable to depression (Randler, 2008, 2009; Randler & Frech, 2009).

Peter Chadwick/Science Source

Sleep Stages

23-2 What is the biological rhythm of our sleeping and dreaming stages?

Sooner or later, sleep overtakes us and consciousness fades as different parts of our brain's cortex stop communicating (Massimini et al., 2005). Yet the sleeping brain remains active and has its own biological rhythm.

About every 90 minutes, we cycle through four distinct sleep stages. This simple fact apparently was unknown until 8-year-old Armond Aserinsky went to bed one night in 1952. His father, Eugene, a University of Chicago graduate student, needed to test an electroencephalograph he had repaired that day (Aserinsky, 1988; Seligman & Yellen, 1987). Placing electrodes near Armond's eyes to record the rolling eye movements then believed to occur during sleep, Aserinsky watched the machine go wild, tracing deep zigzags on the graph paper. Could the machine still be broken? As the night proceeded and the activity recurred, Aserinsky realized that the periods of fast, jerky eye movements were accompanied by energetic brain activity. Awakened during one such episode, Armond reported having a dream. Aserinsky had discovered what we now know as **REM sleep** (rapid *eye* *movement* *sleep*).

Similar procedures used with thousands of volunteers showed the cycles were a normal part of sleep (Kleitman, 1960). To appreciate these studies, imagine yourself as a participant. As the hour grows late, you feel sleepy and yawn in response to reduced brain metabolism. (Yawning, which can be socially contagious, stretches your neck muscles and increases your heart rate, which increases your alertness [Moorcroft, 2003].) When you are ready for bed, a

circadian [ser-KAY-dee-an] **rhythm** the biological clock; regular bodily rhythms (for example, of temperature and wakefulness) that occur on a 24-hour cycle.

REM sleep rapid eye movement sleep; a recurring sleep stage during which vivid dreams commonly occur. Also known as *paradoxical sleep*, because the muscles are relaxed (except for minor twitches) but other body systems are active.

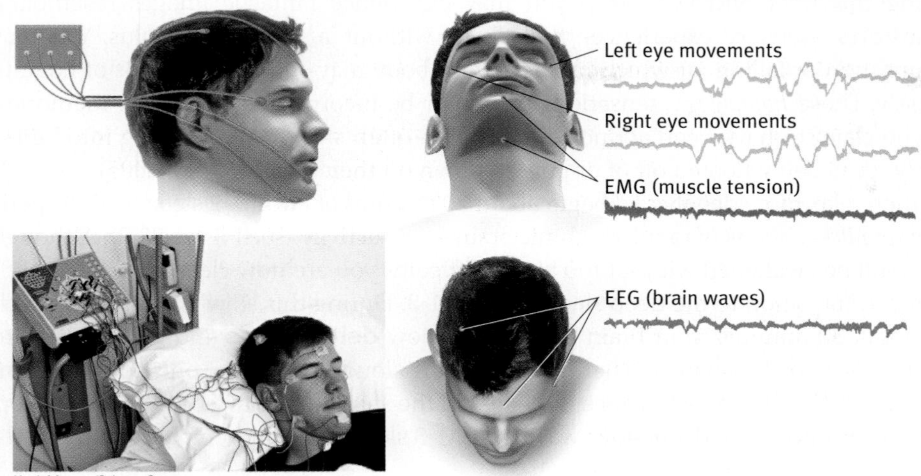

Left eye movements

Right eye movements

EMG (muscle tension)

EEG (brain waves)

Hank Morgan/Science Source

Figure 23.1

Measuring sleep activity Sleep researchers measure brain-wave activity, eye movements, and muscle tension by electrodes that pick up weak electrical signals from the brain, eye, and facial muscles. (From Dement, 1978.)

researcher comes in and tapes electrodes to your scalp (to detect your brain waves), on your chin (to detect muscle tension), and just outside the corners of your eyes (to detect eye movements) (**FIGURE 23.1**). Other devices will record your heart rate, respiration rate, and genital arousal.

When you are in bed with your eyes closed, the researcher in the next room sees on the EEG the relatively slow **alpha waves** of your awake but relaxed state (**FIGURE 23.2**). As you adapt to all this equipment, you grow tired and, in an unremembered moment, slip into **sleep** (**FIGURE 23.3**). The transition is marked by the slowed breathing and the irregular brain waves of non-REM stage 1 sleep. Using the new American Academy of Sleep Medicine classification of sleep stages, this is called NREM-1 (Silber et al., 2008).

In one of his 15,000 research participants, William Dement (1999) observed the moment the brain's perceptual window to the outside world slammed shut. Dement asked this sleep-deprived young man, lying on his back with eyelids taped open, to press a button every time a strobe light flashed in his eyes (about every 6 seconds). After a few minutes the young man missed one. Asked why, he said, "Because there was no flash." But there was a flash. He missed it because (as his brain activity revealed) he had fallen asleep for 2 seconds, missing not only the flash 6 inches from his nose but also the awareness of the abrupt moment of entry into sleep.

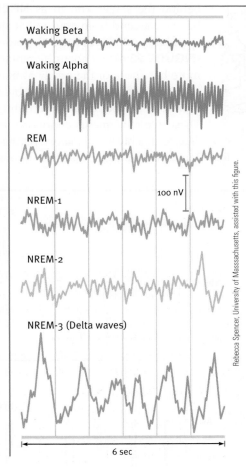

Waking Beta

Waking Alpha

REM

100 nV

NREM-1

NREM-2

NREM-3 (Delta waves)

6 sec

Rebecca Spencer, University of Masssachusetts, assisted with this figure.

Figure 23.2

Brain waves and sleep stages The beta waves of an alert, waking state and the regular alpha waves of an awake, relaxed state differ from the slower, larger delta waves of deep NREM-3 sleep. Although the rapid REM sleep waves resemble the near-waking NREM-1 sleep waves, the body is more aroused during REM sleep than during NREM sleep.

alpha waves the relatively slow brain waves of a relaxed, awake state.

sleep periodic, natural loss of consciousness—as distinct from unconsciousness resulting from a coma, general anesthesia, or hibernation. (Adapted from Dement, 1999.)

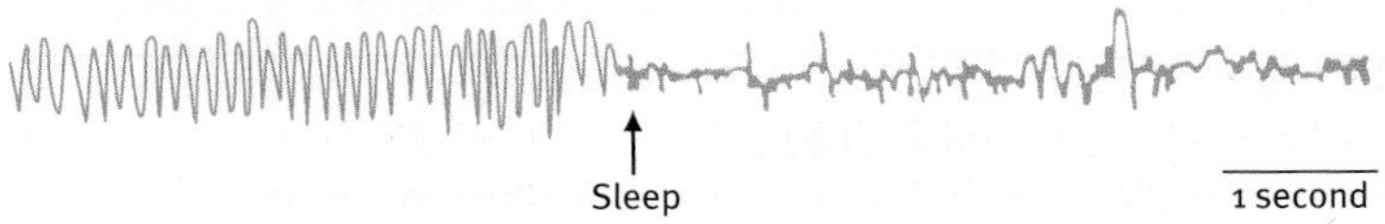

Sleep

1 second

Figure 23.3

The moment of sleep We seem unaware of the moment we fall into sleep, but someone watching our brain waves could tell. (From Dement, 1999.)

hallucinations false sensory experiences, such as seeing something in the absence of an external visual stimulus.

delta waves the large, slow brain waves associated with deep sleep.

NREM sleep non–rapid eye movement sleep; encompasses all sleep stages except for REM sleep.

"Boy are my eyes tired! I had REM sleep all night long."

During this brief NREM-1 sleep you may experience fantastic images resembling **hallucinations**—sensory experiences that occur without a sensory stimulus. You may have a sensation of falling (at which moment your body may suddenly jerk) or of floating weightlessly. These *hypnagogic* sensations may later be incorporated into your memories. People who claim to have been abducted by aliens—often shortly after getting into bed—commonly recall being floated off of or pinned down on their beds (Clancy, 2005).

You then relax more deeply and begin about 20 minutes of NREM-2 sleep, with its periodic *sleep spindles*—bursts of rapid, rhythmic brain-wave activity (see Figure 23.2). Although you could still be awakened without too much difficulty, you are now clearly asleep.

Then you transition to the deep sleep of NREM-3. During this slow-wave sleep, which lasts for about 30 minutes, your brain emits large, slow **delta waves** and you are hard to awaken. Ever say to classmates, "That thunder was so loud last night," only to have them respond, "What thunder?" Those who missed the storm may have been in delta sleep. (It is at the end of the deep, slow-wave NREM-3 sleep that children may wet the bed.)

REM SLEEP

About an hour after you first fall asleep, a strange thing happens. You start to leave behind the stages known as **NREM sleep.** Rather than continuing in deep slumber, you ascend from your initial sleep dive. Returning through NREM-2 (where you spend about half your night), you enter the most intriguing sleep phase—REM sleep (**FIGURE 23.4**). For about 10 minutes, your brain waves become rapid and saw-toothed, more like those of the nearly awake NREM-1 sleep. But unlike NREM-1, during REM sleep your heart rate rises, your breathing becomes rapid and irregular, and every half-minute or so your eyes dart around in momentary bursts of activity behind closed lids.

These eye movements announce the beginning of a dream—often emotional, usually story-like, and richly hallucinatory. Because anyone watching a sleeper's eyes can notice these REM bursts, it is amazing that science was ignorant of REM sleep until 1952.

Figure 23.4

The stages in a typical night's sleep People pass through a multistage sleep cycle several times each night, with the periods of deep sleep diminishing and REM sleep periods increasing in duration. As people age, sleep becomes more fragile, with awakenings common among older adults (Kamel et al., 2006; Neubauer, 1999).

AP® Exam Tip

Study this cycle of sleep carefully. One common mistake that students make is to believe that REM sleep comes directly after deep NREM-3 sleep. As you can see, it does not. Generally, NREM-2 follows NREM-3. Then comes REM.

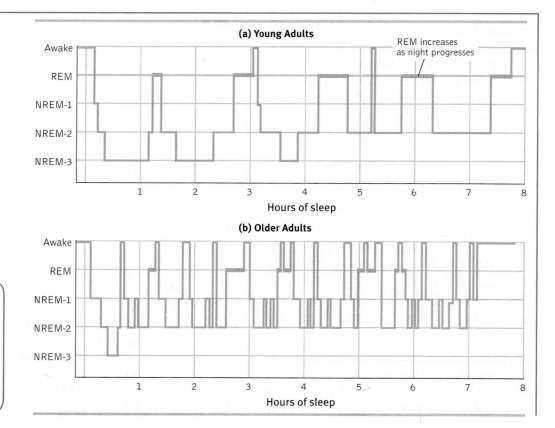

Except during very scary dreams, your genitals become aroused during REM sleep. You have an erection or increased vaginal lubrication, regardless of whether the dream's content is sexual (Karacan et al., 1966). Men's common "morning erection" stems from the night's last REM period, often just before waking.

Your brain's motor cortex is active during REM sleep, but your brainstem blocks its messages. This leaves your muscles relaxed, so much so that, except for an occasional finger, toe, or facial twitch, you are essentially paralyzed. Moreover, you cannot easily be awakened. (This immobility may occasionally linger as you awaken from REM sleep, producing a disturbing experience of *sleep paralysis* [Santomauro & French, 2009].) REM sleep is thus sometimes called *paradoxical* sleep: The body is internally aroused, with waking-like brain activity, yet asleep and externally calm.

The sleep cycle repeats itself about every 90 minutes. As the night wears on, deep NREM-3 sleep grows shorter and disappears. The REM and NREM-2 sleep periods get longer (see Figure 23.4). By morning, we have spent 20 to 25 percent of an average night's sleep—some 100 minutes—in REM sleep. Thirty-seven percent of people report rarely or never having dreams "that you can remember the next morning" (Moore, 2004). Yet even they will, more than 80 percent of the time, recall a dream after being awakened during REM sleep. We spend about 600 hours a year experiencing some 1500 dreams, or more than 100,000 dreams over a typical lifetime—dreams swallowed by the night but not acted out, thanks to REM's protective paralysis.

Uriel Sinai/Getty Images

What Affects Our Sleep Patterns?

23-3 How do biology and environment interact in our sleep patterns?

The idea that "everyone needs 8 hours of sleep" is untrue. Newborns often sleep two-thirds of their day, most adults no more than one-third. Still, there is more to our sleep differences than age. Some of us thrive with fewer than 6 hours per night; others regularly rack up 9 hours or more. Such sleep patterns are genetically influenced (Hor & Tafti, 2009). In studies of fraternal and identical twins, only the identical twins had strikingly similar sleep patterns and durations (Webb & Campbell, 1983). Today's researchers are discovering the genes that regulate sleep in humans and animals (Donlea et al., 2009; He et al., 2009).

Sleep patterns are also culturally influenced. In the United States and Canada, adults average 7 to 8 hours per night (Hurst, 2008; National Sleep Foundation, 2010; Robinson & Martin, 2009). (The weeknight sleep of many students and workers falls short of this average [NSF, 2008].) North Americans are nevertheless sleeping less than their counterparts a century ago. Thanks to modern lighting, shift work, and social media and other diversions, those who would have gone to bed at 9:00 P.M. are now up until 11:00 P.M. or later. With sleep, as with waking behavior, biology and environment interact.

Bright morning light tweaks the circadian clock by activating light-sensitive retinal proteins. These proteins control the circadian clock by triggering signals to the brain's **suprachiasmatic nucleus (SCN)**—a pair of grain-of-rice-sized, 10,000-cell clusters in the hypothalamus (Wirz-Justice, 2009). The SCN does its job in part by causing the brain's pineal gland to decrease its production of the sleep-inducing hormone *melatonin* in the morning and to increase it in the evening (**FIGURE 23.5** on the next page).

suprachiasmatic nucleus (SCN) a pair of cell clusters in the hypothalamus that controls circadian rhythm. In response to light, the SCN causes the pineal gland to adjust melatonin production, thus modifying our feelings of sleepiness.

Figure 23.5

The biological clock Light striking the retina signals the suprachiasmatic nucleus (SCN) to suppress the pineal gland's production of the sleep hormone melatonin. At night, the SCN quiets down, allowing the pineal gland to release melatonin into the bloodstream.

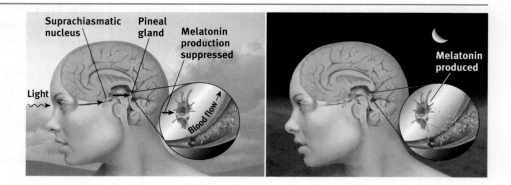

Suprachiasmatic nucleus · Pineal gland · **Melatonin production suppressed** · Light · Blood flow · **Melatonin produced**

Try This

If our natural circadian rhythm were attuned to a 23-hour cycle, would we instead need to discipline ourselves to stay up later at night and sleep in longer in the morning?

FYI

A circadian disadvantage: One study of a decade's 24,121 Major League Baseball games found that teams who had crossed three time zones before playing a multiday series had nearly a 60 percent chance of losing their first game (Winter et al., 2009).

"Sleep faster, we need the pillows." -YIDDISH PROVERB

Being bathed in light disrupts our 24-hour biological clock (Czeisler et al., 1999; Dement, 1999). Curiously—given that our ancestors' body clocks were attuned to the rising and setting Sun of the 24-hour day—many of today's young adults adopt something closer to a 25-hour day, by staying up too late to get 8 hours of sleep. For this, we can thank (or blame) Thomas Edison, inventor of the light bulb. This helps explain why, until our later years, we must discipline ourselves to go to bed and force ourselves to get up. Most animals, too, when placed under unnatural constant illumination will exceed a 24-hour day. Artificial light delays sleep.

Sleep often eludes those who stay up late and sleep in on weekends, and then go to bed earlier on Sunday evening in preparation for the new school week (Oren & Terman, 1998). They are like New Yorkers whose biology is on California time. For North Americans who fly to Europe and need to be up when their circadian rhythm cries *"SLEEP,"* bright light (spending the next day outdoors) helps reset the biological clock (Czeisler et al., 1986, 1989; Eastman et al., 1995).

Sleep Theories

23-4   What are sleep's functions?

So, our sleep patterns differ from person to person and from culture to culture. But why do we have this need for sleep?

Psychologists believe sleep may have evolved for five reasons.

1. **Sleep protects.** When darkness shut down the day's hunting, food gathering, and travel, our distant ancestors were better off asleep in a cave, out of harm's way. Those who didn't try to navigate around rocks and cliffs at night were more likely to leave descendants. This fits a broader principle: A species' sleep pattern tends to suit its ecological niche (Siegel, 2009). Animals with the greatest need to graze and the least ability to hide tend to sleep less. (For a sampling of animal sleep times, see **FIGURE 23.6**.)

2. **Sleep helps us recuperate.** It helps restore and repair brain tissue. Bats and other animals with high waking metabolism burn a lot of calories, producing a lot of *free radicals*, molecules that are toxic to neurons. Sleeping a lot gives resting neurons time to repair themselves, while pruning or weakening unused connections (Gilestro et al., 2009; Siegel, 2003; Vyazovskiy et al., 2008). Think of it this way: When consciousness leaves your house, brain construction workers come in for a makeover.

Figure 23.6

Animal sleep time Would you rather be a brown bat and sleep 20 hours a day or a giraffe and sleep 2 hours daily (data from NIH, 2010)?
Kruglov_Orda/Shutterstock; Courtesy of Andrew D. Myers; Utekhina Anna/Shutterstock; Steffen Foerster Photography/Shutterstock; The Agency Collection/Punchstock; Eric Isselée/Shutterstock; pandapaw/Shutterstock

 20 hours 16 hours  12 hours  10 hours 8 hours 4 hours 2 hours

3. ***Sleep helps restore and rebuild our fading memories of the day's experiences.***
Sleep consolidates our memories—it strengthens and stabilizes neural memory traces
(Racsmány et al., 2010; Rasch & Born, 2008). People trained to perform tasks therefore
recall them better after a night's sleep, or even after a short nap, than after several
hours awake (Stickgold & Ellenbogen, 2008). Among older adults, more sleep leads
to better memory of recently learned material (Drummond, 2010). After sleeping
well, seniors remember more. And in both humans and rats, neural activity during
slow-wave sleep re-enacts and promotes recall of prior novel experiences (Peigneux
et al., 2004; Ribeiro et al., 2004). Sleep, it seems, strengthens memories in a way that
being awake does not.

4. ***Sleep feeds creative thinking.*** On occasion, dreams have inspired noteworthy
literary, artistic, and scientific achievements, such as the dream that clued chemist
August Kekulé to the structure of benzene (Ross, 2006). More commonplace is the
boost that a complete night's sleep gives to our thinking and learning. After working
on a task, then sleeping on it, people solve problems more insightfully than do those
who stay awake (Wagner et al., 2004). They also are better at spotting connections
among novel pieces of information (Ellenbogen et al., 2007). To think smart and see
connections, it often pays to sleep on it.

5. ***Sleep supports growth.*** During deep sleep, the pituitary gland releases a growth
hormone. This hormone is necessary for muscle development. A regular full
night's sleep can also *"dramatically* improve your athletic ability,"* report James
Maas and Rebecca Robbins (see Close-up: Sleep and Athletic Performance).
As we age, we release less of this hormone and spend less time in deep sleep
(Pekkanen, 1982).

Given all the benefits of sleep, it's no wonder that sleep loss hits us so hard.

> "Corduroy pillows make headlines." -ANONYMOUS

Close-up

Sleep and Athletic Performance

Exercise improves sleep. What's not as widely known, report James Maas and Rebecca Robbins (2010), is that sleep improves athletic performance. Well-rested athletes have faster reaction times, more energy, and greater endurance, and teams that build 8 to 10 hours of daily sleep into their training show improved performance. Top violinists also report sleeping 8.5 hours a day on average, and rate practice and sleep as the two most important improvement-fostering activities (Ericsson et al., 1993).

Slow-wave sleep, which occurs mostly in the first half of a night's sleep, produces the human growth hormone necessary for muscle development. REM sleep and NREM-2 sleep, which occur mostly in the final hours of a long night's sleep, help strengthen the neural connections that build enduring memories, including the "muscle memories" learned while practicing tennis or shooting baskets.

The optimal exercise time is late afternoon or early evening, Maas and Robbins advise, when the body's natural cooling is most efficient. Early morning workouts are ill-advised, because they increase the risk of injury and rob athletes of valuable sleep. Heavy workouts within three hours of bedtime should also be avoided because the arousal disrupts falling asleep. Precision muscle training, such as shooting free throws, may, however, benefit when followed by sleep.

Maas has been a sleep consultant for college and professional athletes and teams. On Maas' advice, the Orlando Magic cut early morning practices. He also advised one young woman, Sarah Hughes, who felt stymied in her efforts to excel in figure-skating competition. "Cut the early morning practice," he instructed, as part of the recommended sleep regimen. Soon thereafter, Hughes' performance scores increased, ultimately culminating in her 2002 Olympic gold medal.

AP Photo/Lionel Cironneau

Ample sleep supports skill learning and high performance This was the experience of Olympic gold medalist Sarah Hughes.

Before You Move On

▶ **ASK YOURSELF**

Would you consider yourself a night owl or a morning lark? When do you usually feel most energetic? What time of day works best for you to study?

▶ **TEST YOURSELF**

What five theories explain our need for sleep?

Answers to the Test Yourself questions can be found in Appendix E at the end of the book.

Module 23 Review

 How do our biological rhythms influence our daily functioning?

- Our bodies have an internal biological clock, roughly synchronized with the 24-hour cycle of night and day.

- This *circadian rhythm* appears in our daily patterns of body temperature, arousal, sleeping, and waking. Age and experiences can alter these patterns, resetting our biological clock.

 What is the biological rhythm of our sleeping and dreaming stages?

- We cycle through four distinct *sleep* stages about every 90 minutes.

- Leaving the *alpha waves* of the awake, relaxed stage, we descend into the irregular brain waves of non-REM stage 1 sleep (NREM-1), often with the sensation of falling or floating.

- NREM-2 sleep (in which we spend the most time) follows, lasting about 20 minutes, with its characteristic sleep spindles.

- We then enter NREM-3 sleep, lasting about 30 minutes, with large, slow *delta waves*.

- About an hour after falling asleep, we begin periods of *REM (rapid eye movement) sleep*.

- Most dreaming occurs in this REM stage (also known as paradoxical sleep) of internal arousal but outward paralysis.

- During a normal night's sleep, NREM-3 sleep shortens and REM and NREM-2 sleep lengthens.

23-3 How do biology and environment interact in our sleep patterns?

- Biology—our circadian rhythm as well as our age and our body's production of melatonin (influenced by the brain's suprachiasmatic nucleus)—interacts with cultural expectations and individual behaviors to determine our sleeping and waking patterns.

23-4 What are sleep's functions?

- Sleep may have played a protective role in human evolution by keeping people safe during potentially dangerous periods.

- Sleep also helps restore and repair damaged neurons.

- REM and NREM-2 sleep help strengthen neural connections that build enduring memories.

- Sleep promotes creative problem solving the next day.

- During slow-wave sleep, the pituitary gland secretes human growth hormone, which is necessary for muscle development.

Multiple-Choice Questions

1. Which of the following represents a circadian rhythm?
   a. A burst of growth occurs during puberty.
   b. A full Moon occurs about once a month.
   c. Body temperature rises each day as morning approaches.
   d. When it is summer in the northern hemisphere, it is winter in the southern hemisphere.
   e. Pulse rate increases when we exercise.

2. In which stage of sleep are you likely to experience hypnagogic sensations of falling?
   a. Alpha sleep
   b. NREM-1
   c. NREM-2
   d. NREM-3
   e. REM

3. What is the role of the suprachiasmatic nucleus (SCN) in sleep?
   a. It induces REM sleep approximately every 90 minutes during sleep.
   b. It causes the pineal gland to increase the production of melatonin.
   c. It causes the pituitary gland to increase the release of human growth hormone.
   d. It causes the pituitary gland to decrease the release of human growth hormone.
   e. It causes the pineal gland to decrease the production of melatonin.

4. Which of the following sleep theories emphasizes sleep's role in restoring and repairing brain tissue?
   a. Memory
   b. Protection
   c. Growth
   d. Recuperation
   e. Creativity

Practice FRQs

1. Sleep serves many functions for us. Briefly explain how sleep can
   - provide protection.
   - promote physical growth.

Answer

1 point: Sleep kept our ancestors safe from nighttime dangers.

1 point: Sleep promotes the release of pituitary growth hormone.

2. Name and briefly describe three stages of sleep when rapid eye movements are not occurring.

(3 points)

Module 24

Sleep Deprivation, Sleep Disorders, and Dreams

Module Learning Objectives

24-1 Describe the effects of sleep loss, and identify the major sleep disorders.

24-2 Describe the most common content of dreams.

24-3 Identify proposed explanations for why we dream.

Sleep Deprivation and Sleep Disorders

24-1 How does sleep loss affect us, and what are the major sleep disorders?

When our body yearns for sleep but does not get it, we begin to feel terrible. Trying to stay awake, we will eventually lose. It's easy to spot students who have stayed up late to study for a test or finish a term paper: They are often fighting the "nods" (their heads bobbing downward in seconds-long "microsleeps") as they fight to stay awake.

In the tiredness battle, sleep always wins. In 1989, Michael Doucette was named America's Safest Driving Teen. In 1990, while driving home from college, he fell asleep at the wheel and collided with an oncoming car, killing both himself and the other driver. Michael's driving instructor later acknowledged never having mentioned sleep deprivation and drowsy driving (Dement, 1999).

Effects of Sleep Loss

Today, more than ever, our sleep patterns leave us not only sleepy but drained of energy and feelings of well-being. After a succession of 5-hour nights, we accumulate a sleep debt that need not be entirely repaid but cannot be satisfied by one long sleep. "The brain keeps an accurate count of sleep debt for at least two weeks," reported sleep researcher William Dement (1999, p. 64).

Obviously, then, we need sleep. Sleep commands roughly one-third of our lives—some 25 years, on average. But why?

Allowed to sleep unhindered, most adults will sleep at least 9 hours a night (Coren, 1996). With that much sleep, we awake refreshed, sustain better moods, and perform more efficient and accurate work. The U.S. Navy and the National Institutes of Health have demonstrated the benefits of unrestricted sleep in experiments in which volunteers spent 14 hours daily in bed for at least a week. For the first few days, the volunteers averaged 12 hours of sleep a day or more, apparently paying off a sleep debt that averaged 25 to 30 hours.

That accomplished, they then settled back to 7.5 to 9 hours nightly and felt energized and happier (Dement, 1999). In one Gallup survey (Mason, 2005), 63 percent of adults who reported getting the sleep they needed also reported being "very satisfied" with their personal life (as did only 36 percent of those needing more sleep). And when 909 working women reported on their daily moods, the researchers were struck by what mattered little (such as money, so long as the person was not battling poverty), and what mattered a lot: less time pressure at work and a good night's sleep (Kahneman et al., 2004). Perhaps it's not surprising, then, that when asked if they had felt well rested on the previous day, 3 in 10 Americans said they had not (Pelham, 2010).

College and university students are especially sleep deprived; 69 percent in one national survey reported "feeling tired" or "having little energy" on several or more days in the last two weeks (AP, 2009). In another survey, 28 percent of high school students acknowledged falling asleep in class at least once a week (Sleep Foundation, 2006). The going needn't get boring before students start snoring. (To test whether you are one of the many sleep-deprived students, see **TABLE 24.1.**)

Sleep loss is a predictor of depression. Researchers who studied 15,500 young people, 12 to 18 years old, found that those who slept 5 or fewer hours a night had a 71 percent higher risk of depression than their peers who slept 8 hours or more (Gangwisch et al., 2010). This link does not appear to reflect sleep difficulties caused by depression. When children and youth are followed through time, sleep loss predicts depression rather than

MARK RALSTON/AFP/Getty Images

Sleepless and suffering These fatigued, sleep-deprived earthquake rescue workers in China may experience a depressed immune system, impaired concentration, and greater vulnerability to accidents.

Table 24.1

Cornell University psychologist James Maas has reported that most students suffer the consequences of sleeping less than they should. To see if you are in that group, answer the following true-false questions:

True	False	
....	....	1. I need an alarm clock in order to wake up at the appropriate time.
....	....	2. It's a struggle for me to get out of bed in the morning.
....	....	3. Weekday mornings I hit snooze several times to get more sleep.
....	....	4. I feel tired, irritable, and stressed out during the week.
....	....	5. I have trouble concentrating and remembering.
....	....	6. I feel slow with critical thinking, problem solving, and being creative.
....	....	7. I often fall asleep watching TV.
....	....	8. I often fall asleep in boring meetings or lectures or in warm rooms.
....	....	9. I often fall asleep after heavy meals.
....	....	10. I often fall asleep while relaxing after dinner.
....	....	11. I often fall asleep within five minutes of getting into bed.
....	....	12. I often feel drowsy while driving.
....	....	13. I often sleep extra hours on weekend mornings.
....	....	14. I often need a nap to get through the day.
....	....	15. I have dark circles around my eyes.

If you answered "true" to three or more items, you probably are not getting enough sleep. To determine your sleep needs, Maas recommends that you "go to bed 15 minutes earlier than usual every night for the next week—and continue this practice by adding 15 more minutes each week—until you wake without an alarm clock and feel alert all day." (Sleep Quiz reprinted with permission from James B. Maas, "Sleep to Win!" (Bloomington, IN: AuthorHouse, 2013).)

"So shut your eyes
Kiss me goodbye
And sleep
Just sleep."
-Song by My Chemical Romance

vice versa (Gregory et al., 2009). Moreover, REM sleep's processing of emotional experiences helps protect against depression (Walker & van der Helm, 2009). After a good night's sleep, we often do feel better the next day. And that may help to explain why parentally enforced bedtimes predict less depression, and why pushing back school start time leads to improved adolescent sleep, alertness, and mood (Gregory et al., 2009; Owens et al., 2010).

Even when awake, students often function below their peak. And they know it: Four in five teens and three in five 18- to 29-year-olds wish they could get more sleep on weekdays (Mason, 2003, 2005). Yet that teen who staggers glumly out of bed in response to an unwelcome alarm, yawns through morning classes, and feels half-depressed much of the day may be energized at 11:00 P.M. and mindless of the next day's looming sleepiness (Carskadon, 2002). "Sleep deprivation has consequences—difficulty studying, diminished productivity, tendency to make mistakes, irritability, fatigue," noted Dement (1999, p. 231). A large sleep debt "makes you stupid."

It can also make you fatter. Sleep deprivation increases *ghrelin,* a hunger-arousing hormone, and decreases its hunger-suppressing partner, *leptin* (more on these in Module 38). It also increases cortisol, a stress hormone that stimulates the body to make fat. Sure enough, children and adults who sleep less than normal are fatter than those who sleep more (Chen et al., 2008; Knutson et al., 2007; Schoenborn & Adams, 2008). And experimental sleep deprivation of adults increases appetite and eating (Nixon et al., 2008; Patel et al., 2006; Spiegel et al., 2004; Van Cauter et al., 2007). This may help explain the common weight gain among sleep-deprived students (although a review of 11 studies reveals that the mythical college student's "freshman 15" is, on average, closer to a "first-year 4" [Hull et al., 2007]).

In addition to making us more vulnerable to obesity, sleep deprivation can suppress immune cells that fight off viral infections and cancer (Motivala & Irwin, 2007). One experiment exposed volunteers to a cold virus. Those who had been averaging less than 7 hours sleep a night were 3 times more likely to develop a cold than were those sleeping 8 or more hours a night (Cohen et al., 2009). Sleep's protective effect may help explain why people who sleep 7 to 8 hours a night tend to outlive those who are chronically sleep deprived, and why older adults who have no difficulty falling or staying asleep tend to live longer than their sleep-deprived agemates (Dement, 1999; Dew et al., 2003). When infections do set in, we typically sleep more, boosting our immune cells.

Sleep deprivation slows reactions and increases errors on visual attention tasks similar to those involved in screening airport baggage, performing surgery, and reading X-rays (Lim & Dinges, 2010). Similarly, the result can be devastating for driving, piloting, and equipment operating. Driver fatigue has contributed to an estimated 20 percent of American traffic accidents (Brody, 2002) and to some 30 percent of Australian highway deaths (Maas, 1999). One two-year study examined the driving accident rates of more than 20,000 Virginia 16- to 18-year-olds in two major cities. In one city, the high schools started 75 to 80 minutes later than in the other. The late starters had about 25 percent fewer crashes (Vorona et al., 2011). Consider, too, the timing of four industrial disasters—the 1989 *Exxon Valdez* tanker hitting rocks and spilling millions of gallons of oil on the shores of Alaska; Union Carbide's 1984 release of toxic gas that killed thousands in Bhopal, India; and the 1979 Three Mile Island and 1986 Chernobyl nuclear accidents. All occurred after midnight, when operators in charge were likely to be drowsiest and unresponsive to signals requiring an alert response. Likewise, the 2013 Asiana Airlines crash landing at San Francisco Airport happened at 3:30 A.M. Korea time, after a 10-hour flight from Seoul. When sleepy frontal lobes confront an unexpected situation, misfortune often results.

Stanley Coren capitalized on what is, for many North Americans, a semi-annual sleep-manipulation experiment—the "spring forward" to "daylight savings" time and "fall backward" to "standard" time. Searching millions of records, Coren found that in both Canada and the United States, accidents increased immediately after the time change that shortens sleep (**FIGURE 24.1**).

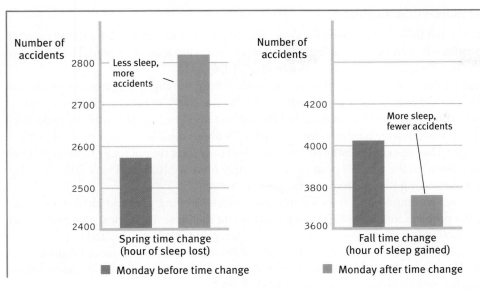

Figure 24.1

Canadian traffic accidents On the Monday after the spring time change, when people lose one hour of sleep, accidents increased, as compared with the Monday before. In the fall, traffic accidents normally increase because of greater snow, ice, and darkness, but they diminished after the time change. (Adapted from Coren, 1996.)

Number of accidents

2800 — Less sleep, more accidents

2700

2600

2500

2400

Spring time change (hour of sleep lost)

Number of accidents

4200

More sleep, fewer accidents

4000

3800

3600

Fall time change (hour of sleep gained)

■ Monday before time change   ■ Monday after time change

FIGURE 24.2 summarizes the effects of sleep deprivation. But there is good news! Psychologists have discovered a treatment that strengthens memory, increases concentration, boosts mood, moderates hunger and obesity, fortifies the disease-fighting immune system, and lessens the risk of fatal accidents. Even better news: The treatment feels good, it can be self-administered, the supplies are limitless, and it's available free! If you are a typical high school student, often going to bed near midnight and dragged out of bed six or seven hours later by the dreaded alarm, the treatment is simple: Each night just add 15 minutes to your sleep. Ignore that last text, resist the urge to check in with friends online, and succumb to sleep, "the gentle tyrant."

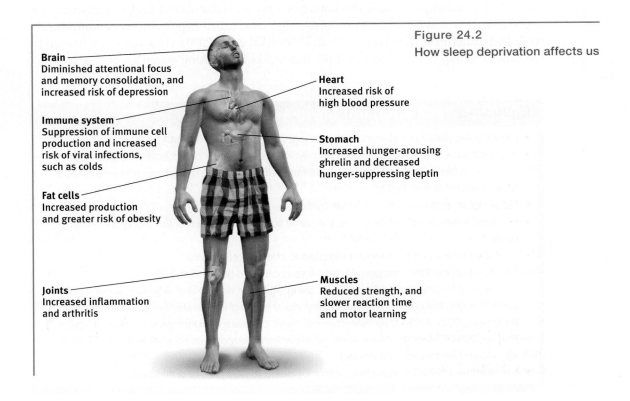

Figure 24.2

How sleep deprivation affects us

Brain
Diminished attentional focus and memory consolidation, and increased risk of depression

Immune system
Suppression of immune cell production and increased risk of viral infections, such as colds

Fat cells
Increased production and greater risk of obesity

Joints
Increased inflammation and arthritis

Heart
Increased risk of high blood pressure

Stomach
Increased hunger-arousing ghrelin and decreased hunger-suppressing leptin

Muscles
Reduced strength, and slower reaction time and motor learning

off the mark.com   by Mark Parisi

LET ME GET THIS STRAIGHT, IT'S BEEN TWO CONSECUTIVE HOURS SINCE YOU'VE SLEPT?

WHEN CATS EXPERIENCE INSOMNIA

> "The lion and the lamb shall lie down together, but the lamb will not be very sleepy." -WOODY ALLEN, IN THE MOVIE *LOVE AND DEATH*, 1975

> "Sleep is like love or happiness. If you pursue it too ardently it will elude you." -WILSE WEBB, *SLEEP: THE GENTLE TYRANT*, 1992

insomnia recurring problems in falling or staying asleep.

narcolepsy a sleep disorder characterized by uncontrollable sleep attacks. The sufferer may lapse directly into REM sleep, often at inopportune times.

MAJOR SLEEP DISORDERS

No matter what their normal need for sleep, 1 in 10 adults, and 1 in 4 older adults, complain of **insomnia**—not an occasional inability to sleep when anxious or excited, but persistent problems in falling or staying asleep (Irwin et al., 2006).

From middle age on, awakening occasionally during the night becomes the norm, not something to fret over or treat with medication (Vitiello, 2009). Ironically, insomnia is worsened by fretting about one's insomnia. In laboratory studies, insomnia complainers do sleep less than others, but they typically overestimate—by about double—how long it takes them to fall asleep. They also underestimate by nearly half how long they actually have slept. Even if we have been awake only an hour or two, we may *think* we have had very little sleep because it's the waking part we remember.

The most common quick fixes for true insomnia—sleeping pills and alcohol—can aggravate the problem, reducing REM sleep and leaving the person with next-day blahs. Such aids can also lead to *tolerance*—a state in which increasing doses are needed to produce an effect. An ideal sleep aid would mimic the natural chemicals that are abundant during sleep, without side effects. Until scientists can supply this magic pill, sleep experts have offered some tips for getting better quality sleep (**TABLE 24.2**).

Falling asleep is not the problem for people with **narcolepsy** (from *narco*, "numbness," and *lepsy*, "seizure"), who have sudden attacks of overwhelming sleepiness, usually lasting less than 5 minutes. Narcolepsy attacks can occur at the most inopportune times, perhaps just after taking a terrific swing at a softball or when laughing loudly, shouting angrily, or having sex (Dement, 1978, 1999). In severe cases, the person collapses directly into a brief period of REM sleep, with loss of muscular tension. People with narcolepsy—1 in 2000 of us, estimated the Stanford University Center for Narcolepsy (2002)—must therefore live with extra caution. As a traffic menace, "snoozing is second only to boozing," says the American Sleep Disorders Association, and those with narcolepsy are especially at risk (Aldrich, 1989).

Researchers have discovered genes that cause narcolepsy in dogs and humans (Miyagawa et al., 2008; Taheri, 2004). Genes help sculpt the brain, and neuroscientists are searching the brain for narcolepsy-linked abnormalities. One team discovered a relative absence of a hypothalamic neural center that produces *orexin* (also called hypocretin), a neurotransmitter linked to alertness (Taheri et al., 2002; Thannickal et al., 2000). (That discovery has led to the clinical testing of a new sleeping pill that works by blocking orexin's arousing activity.)

Table 24.2 Some Natural Sleep Aids

- Exercise regularly but not in the late evening. (Late afternoon is best.)
- Avoid caffeine after early afternoon, and avoid food and drink near bedtime. The exception would be a glass of milk, which provides raw materials for the manufacture of serotonin, a neurotransmitter that facilitates sleep.
- Relax before bedtime, using dimmer light.
- Sleep on a regular schedule (rise at the same time even after a restless night) and avoid naps.
- Hide the clock face so you aren't tempted to check it repeatedly.
- Reassure yourself that temporary sleep loss causes no great harm.
- Realize that for any stressed organism, being vigilant is natural and adaptive. A personal conflict during the day often means a fitful sleep that night (Åkerstedt et al., 2007; Brissette & Cohen, 2002). And a traumatic stressful event can take a lingering toll on sleep (Babson & Feldner, 2010). Managing your stress levels will enable more restful sleeping. (See Modules 43, 44, and 84 for more on stress.)
- If all else fails, settle for less sleep, either by going to bed later or getting up earlier.

Economic recession and stress can rob sleep A National Sleep Foundation (2009) survey found 27 percent of people reporting sleeplessness related to the economy, their personal finances, and employment, as seems evident in this man looking for work.

sleep apnea a sleep disorder characterized by temporary cessations of breathing during sleep and repeated momentary awakenings.

night terrors a sleep disorder characterized by high arousal and an appearance of being terrified; unlike nightmares, night terrors occur during NREM-3 sleep, within two or three hours of falling asleep, and are seldom remembered.

Narcolepsy, it is now clear, is a brain disease; it is not just "in your mind." And this gives hope that narcolepsy might be effectively relieved by a drug that mimics the missing orexin and can sneak through the blood-brain barrier (Fujiki et al., 2003; Siegel, 2000). In the meantime, physicians are prescribing other drugs to relieve narcolepsy's sleepiness in humans.

Although 1 in 20 of us have **sleep apnea,** it was unknown before modern sleep research. *Apnea* means "with no breath," and people with this condition intermittently stop breathing during sleep. After an airless minute or so, decreased blood oxygen arouses them and they wake up enough to snort in air for a few seconds, in a process that repeats hundreds of times each night, depriving them of slow-wave sleep. Apnea sufferers don't recall these episodes the next day. So, despite feeling fatigued and depressed—and hearing their mate's complaints about their loud "snoring"—many are unaware of their disorder (Peppard et al., 2006).

Sleep apnea is associated with obesity, and as the number of obese Americans has increased, so has this disorder, particularly among overweight men, including some football players (Keller, 2007). Other warning signs are loud snoring, daytime sleepiness and irritability, and (possibly) high blood pressure, which increases the risk of a stroke or heart attack (Dement, 1999). If one doesn't mind looking a little goofy in the dark (imagine a snorkeler at a slumber party), the treatment—a mask-like device with an air pump that keeps the sleeper's airway open—can effectively relieve apnea symptoms.

Unlike sleep apnea, **night terrors** target mostly children, who may sit up or walk around, talk incoherently, experience doubled heart and breathing rates, and appear terrified (Hartmann, 1981). They seldom wake up fully during an episode and recall little or nothing the next morning—at most, a fleeting, frightening image. Night terrors are not nightmares (which, like other dreams, typically occur during early morning REM sleep); night terrors usually occur during the first few hours of NREM-3.

Sleepwalking—another NREM-3 sleep disorder—and *sleep talking* are usually childhood disorders, and like narcolepsy, they run in families. (Sleep talking—usually garbled or nonsensical—can occur during any sleep stage [Mahowald & Ettinger, 1990].) Occasional childhood sleepwalking occurs for about one-third of those with a sleepwalking fraternal twin and half of those with a sleepwalking identical twin. The same is true for sleep talking (Hublin et al., 1997, 1998). Sleepwalking is usually harmless. After returning to bed on their own or with the help of a family member, few sleepwalkers recall their trip the next morning. About 20 percent of 3- to 12-year-olds have at least one episode of sleepwalking,

Did Brahms need his own lullabies? Cranky, overweight, and nap-prone, Johannes Brahms exhibited common symptoms of sleep apnea (Margolis, 2000).

Now I lay me down to sleep For many with sleep apnea, a continuous positive airway pressure (CPAP) machine makes for sounder sleeping and better quality of life.

usually lasting 2 to 10 minutes; some 5 percent have repeated episodes (Giles et al., 1994). Young children, who have the deepest and lengthiest NREM-3 sleep, are the most likely to experience both night terrors and sleepwalking. As we grow older and deep NREM-3 sleep diminishes, so do night terrors and sleepwalking. After being sleep deprived, we sleep more deeply, which increases any tendency to sleepwalk (Zadra et al., 2008).

A dreamy take on dreamland The 2010 movie *Inception* creatively played off our interest in finding meaning in our dreams, and in understanding the layers of our consciousness. It further explored the idea of creating false memories through the power of suggestion—an idea we will explore in Module 33.

Photofest/Warner Bros. Pictures

Dreams

Now playing at an inner theater near you: the premiere showing of a sleeping person's vivid dream. This never-before-seen mental movie features captivating characters wrapped in a plot so original and unlikely, yet so intricate and so seemingly real, that the viewer later marvels at its creation.

Waking from a troubling dream, wrenched by its emotions, who among us has not wondered about this weird state of consciousness? How can our brain so creatively, colorfully, and completely construct this alternative world? In the shadowland between our dreaming and waking consciousness, we may even wonder for a moment which is real.

Discovering the link between REM sleep and dreaming opened a new era in dream research. Instead of relying on someone's hazy recall hours or days after having a dream, researchers could catch dreams as they happened. They could awaken people during or within 3 minutes after a REM sleep period and hear a vivid account.

dream a sequence of images, emotions, and thoughts passing through a sleeping person's mind. Dreams are notable for their hallucinatory imagery, discontinuities, and incongruities, and for the dreamer's delusional acceptance of the content and later difficulties remembering it.

"I do not believe that I am now dreaming, but I cannot prove that I am not." -Philosopher Bertrand Russell (1872–1970)

What We Dream

24-2   What do we dream?

Daydreams tend to involve the familiar details of our life—perhaps picturing ourselves explaining to a teacher why a paper will be late, or replaying in our minds personal encounters we relish or regret. REM **dreams**—"hallucinations of the sleeping mind"(Loftus & Ketcham, 1994, p. 67)—are vivid, emotional, and bizarre—so vivid we may confuse them with reality. Awakening from a nightmare, a 4-year-old may be sure there is a bear in the house.

We spend six years of our life in dreams, many of which are anything but sweet. For both women and men, 8 in 10 dreams are marked by at least one negative event or emotion (Domhoff, 2007). Common themes are repeatedly failing in an attempt to do something; of being attacked, pursued, or rejected; or of experiencing misfortune (Hall et al., 1982). Dreams with sexual imagery occur less often than you might think. In one study, only 1 in 10 dreams among young men and 1 in 30 among young women had sexual content (Domhoff, 1996). More commonly, the story line of our dreams incorporates traces of previous days' nonsexual experiences and preoccupations (De Koninck, 2000):

FYI

Would you suppose that people dream if blind from birth? Studies in France, Hungary, Egypt, and the United States all found blind people dreaming of using their nonvisual senses—hearing, touching, smelling, tasting (Buquet, 1988; Taha, 1972; Vekassy, 1977).

- After suffering a trauma, people commonly report nightmares, which help extinguish daytime fears (Levin & Nielsen, 2007, 2009). One sample of Americans recording their dreams during September 2001 reported an increase in threatening dreams following the 9/11 terrorist attacks (Propper et al., 2007).

- After playing the computer game *Tetris* for 7 hours and then being awakened repeatedly during their first hour of sleep, 3 in 4 people reported experiencing images of the game's falling blocks (Stickgold et al., 2000).

"For what one has dwelt on by day, these things are seen in visions of the night." -Menander of Athens (342–292 b.c.e.), *The Principal Fragments*

- Compared with city-dwellers, people in hunter-gatherer societies more often dream of animals (Mestel, 1997). Compared with nonmusicians, musicians report twice as many dreams of music (Uga et al., 2006).

Our two-track mind is also monitoring our environment while we sleep. Sensory stimuli—a particular odor or a phone's ringing—may be instantly and ingeniously woven into the dream story. In a classic experiment, researchers lightly sprayed cold water on dreamers' faces (Dement & Wolpert, 1958). Compared with sleepers who did not get the cold-water treatment, these people were more likely to dream about a waterfall, a leaky roof, or even about being sprayed by someone.

So, could we learn a foreign language by hearing it played while we sleep? If only it were so easy. While sleeping we can learn to associate a sound with a mild electric shock (and to react to the sound accordingly). But we do not remember recorded information played while we are soundly asleep (Eich, 1990; Wyatt & Bootzin, 1994). In fact, anything that happens during the 5 minutes just before we fall asleep is typically lost from memory (Roth et al., 1988). This explains why sleep apnea patients, who repeatedly awaken with a gasp and then immediately fall back to sleep, do not recall the episodes. It also explains why dreams that momentarily awaken us are mostly forgotten by morning. To remember a dream, get up and stay awake for a few minutes.

"Uh-oh. I think I'm having one of those dreams again."

"Follow your dreams, except for that one where you're naked at work." -Attributed to comedian Henny Youngman

Why We Dream

24-3 What are the functions of dreams?

Dream theorists have proposed several explanations of why we dream, including these:

To satisfy our own wishes. In 1900, in his landmark book *The Interpretation of Dreams*, Sigmund Freud offered what he thought was "the most valuable of all the discoveries it has been my good fortune to make." He proposed that dreams provide a psychic safety valve that discharges otherwise unacceptable feelings. He viewed a dream's **manifest content** (the apparent and remembered story line) as a censored, symbolic version of its **latent content,** the unconscious drives and wishes that would be threatening if expressed directly. Although most dreams have no overt sexual imagery, Freud nevertheless believed that most adult dreams could be "traced back by analysis to erotic wishes." Thus, a gun might be a disguised representation of a penis.

Freud considered dreams the key to understanding our inner conflicts. However, his critics say it is time to wake up from Freud's dream theory, which is a scientific nightmare. Based on the accumulated science, "there is no reason to believe any of Freud's specific claims about dreams and their purposes," observed dream researcher William Domhoff (2003). Some contend that even if dreams are symbolic, they could be interpreted any way one wished. Others maintain that dreams hide nothing. A dream about a gun is a dream about a gun. Legend has it that even Freud, who loved to smoke cigars, acknowledged that "sometimes, a cigar is just a cigar." Freud's wish-fulfillment theory of dreams has in large part given way to other theories.

To file away memories. The *information-processing* perspective proposes that dreams may help sift, sort, and fix the day's experiences in our memory. Some studies support this view. When tested the next day after learning a task, those deprived of both slow-wave and REM sleep did not do as well on their new learning as those who slept undisturbed (Stickgold et al., 2000, 2001). People who hear unusual phrases or learn to find hidden visual images before bedtime remember less the next morning if awakened every time they begin REM sleep than they do if awakened during other sleep stages (Empson & Clarke, 1970; Karni & Sagi, 1994).

Brain scans confirm the link between REM sleep and memory. The brain regions that buzz as rats learn to navigate a maze, or as people learn to perform a visual-discrimination

FYI

A popular sleep myth: If you dream you are falling and hit the ground (or if you dream of dying), you die. (Unfortunately, those who could confirm these ideas are not around to do so. Some people, however, have had such dreams and are alive to report them.)

"When people interpret [a dream] as if it were meaningful and then sell those interpretations, it's quackery." -Sleep researcher J. Allan Hobson (1995)

manifest content according to Freud, the remembered story line of a dream (as distinct from its latent, or hidden, content).

latent content according to Freud, the underlying meaning of a dream (as distinct from its manifest content).

task, buzz again during later REM sleep (Louie & Wilson, 2001; Maquet, 2001). So precise are these activity patterns that scientists can tell where in the maze the rat would be if awake. Others, unpersuaded by these studies, note that memory consolidation may also occur during non-REM sleep (Siegel, 2001; Vertes & Siegel, 2005). This much seems true: A night of solid sleep (and dreaming) has an important place in our lives. To sleep, perchance to remember.

This is important news for students, many of whom, observed researcher Robert Stickgold (2000), suffer from a kind of sleep bulimia—binge-sleeping on the weekend. "If you don't get good sleep and enough sleep after you learn new stuff, you won't integrate it effectively into your memories," he warned. That helps explain why high school students with high grades have averaged 25 minutes more sleep a night than their lower-achieving classmates (Wolfson & Carskadon, 1998).

To develop and preserve neural pathways. Perhaps dreams, or the brain activity associated with REM sleep, serve a *physiological* function, providing the sleeping brain with periodic stimulation. This theory makes developmental sense. As you will see in Unit IX, stimulating experiences preserve and expand the brain's neural pathways. Infants, whose neural networks are fast developing, spend much of their abundant sleep time in REM sleep (**FIGURE 24.3**).

To make sense of neural static. Other theories propose that dreams erupt from *neural activation* spreading upward from the brainstem (Antrobus, 1991; Hobson, 2003, 2004, 2009). According to one version, dreams are the brain's attempt to make sense of random neural activity. Much as a neurosurgeon can produce hallucinations by stimulating different parts of a patient's cortex, so can stimulation originating within the brain. These internal stimuli activate brain areas that process visual images, but not the visual cortex area, which receives raw input from the eyes. As Freud might have expected, PET scans of sleeping people also reveal increased activity in the emotion-related limbic system (in the amygdala) during REM sleep. In contrast, frontal lobe regions responsible for inhibition and logical thinking seem to idle, which may explain why we are less inhibited in our dreams than when awake (Maquet et al., 1996). Add the limbic system's emotional tone to the brain's visual bursts and—voila!—we dream. Damage either the limbic system or the visual centers active during dreaming, and dreaming itself may be impaired (Domhoff, 2003).

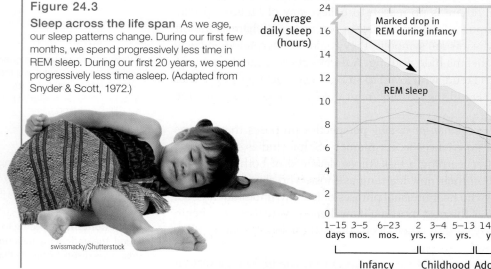
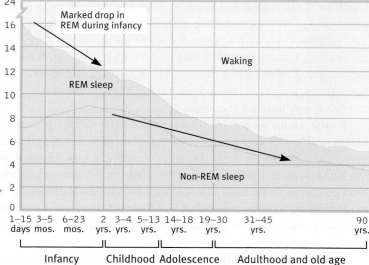

Figure 24.3

Sleep across the life span As we age, our sleep patterns change. During our first few months, we spend progressively less time in REM sleep. During our first 20 years, we spend progressively less time asleep. (Adapted from Snyder & Scott, 1972.)

swissmacky/Shutterstock

Average daily sleep (hours)

Marked drop in REM during infancy

Waking

REM sleep

Non-REM sleep

1–15 days | 3–5 mos. | 6–23 mos. | 2 yrs. | 3–4 yrs. | 5–13 yrs. | 14–18 yrs. | 19–30 yrs. | 31–45 yrs. | 90 yrs.

Infancy | Childhood | Adolescence | Adulthood and old age

To reflect cognitive development. Some dream researchers dispute both the Freudian and neural activation theories, preferring instead to see dreams as part of brain maturation and cognitive development (Domhoff, 2010, 2011; Foulkes, 1999). For example, prior to age 9, children's dreams seem more like a slide show and less like an active story in which the dreamer is an actor. Dreams overlap with waking cognition and feature coherent speech. They simulate reality by drawing on our concepts and knowledge. They engage brain networks that also are active during daydreaming. Unlike the idea that dreams arise from bottom-up brain activation, the cognitive perspective emphasizes our mind's top-down control of our dream content (Nir & Tononi, 2010).

TABLE 24.2 compares major dream theories. Although today's sleep researchers debate dreams' function—and some are skeptical that dreams serve any function—there is one thing they agree on: We need REM sleep. Deprived of it by repeatedly being awakened, people return more and more quickly to the REM stage after falling back to sleep. When finally allowed to sleep undisturbed, they literally sleep like babies—with increased REM sleep, a phenomenon called **REM rebound.** Withdrawing REM-suppressing sleeping medications also increases REM sleep, but with accompanying nightmares.

Most other mammals also experience REM rebound, suggesting that the causes and functions of REM sleep are deeply biological. That REM sleep occurs in mammals—and not in animals such as fish, whose behavior is less influenced by learning—also fits the information-processing theory of dreams.

So does this mean that because dreams serve physiological functions and extend normal cognition, they are psychologically meaningless? Not necessarily. Every psychologically meaningful experience involves an active brain. We are once again reminded of a basic principle: *Biological and psychological explanations of behavior are partners, not competitors.*

REM rebound the tendency for REM sleep to increase following REM sleep deprivation (created by repeated awakenings during REM sleep).

Table 24.2 Dream Theories

Theory	Explanation	Critical Considerations
Freud's wish-fulfillment	Dreams provide a "psychic safety valve"—expressing otherwise unacceptable feelings; contain manifest (remembered) content and a deeper layer of latent content—a hidden meaning.	Lacks any scientific support; dreams may be interpreted in many different ways.
Information-processing	Dreams help us sort out the day's events and consolidate our memories.	But why do we sometimes dream about things we have not experienced?
Physiological function	Regular brain stimulation from REM sleep may help develop and preserve neural pathways.	This does not explain why we experience meaningful dreams.
Neural activation	REM sleep triggers neural activity that evokes random visual memories, which our sleeping brain weaves into stories.	The individual's brain is weaving the stories, which still tells us something about the dreamer.
Cognitive development	Dream content reflects dreamers' cognitive development—their knowledge and understanding.	Does not address the neuroscience of dreams.

Before You Move On

▶ **ASK YOURSELF**

In some places, the school day for teenagers runs from 9:00 A.M. to 4:00 P.M. But in the United States, the teen school day often runs from 8:00 A.M. to 3:00 P.M., or even 7:00 A.M. to 2:00 P.M. Early to rise isn't making kids wise, say critics—it's making them sleepy. For optimal alertness and well-being, teens need 8 to 9 hours of sleep a night. So, should early-start schools move to a later start time, even if it requires buying more buses or switching start times with elementary schools? Or is this impractical, and would it do little to remedy the tired-teen problem?

▶ **TEST YOURSELF**

Are you getting enough sleep? What might you ask yourself to answer this question?

Answers to the Test Yourself questions can be found in Appendix E at the end of the book.

Module 24 Review

24-1 How does sleep loss affect us, and what are the major sleep disorders?

- Sleep deprivation causes fatigue and irritability, and it impairs concentration, productivity, and memory consolidation. It can also lead to depression, obesity, joint pain, a suppressed immune system, and slowed performance (with greater vulnerability to accidents).

- Sleep disorders include *insomnia* (recurring wakefulness); *narcolepsy* (sudden uncontrollable sleepiness or lapsing into REM sleep); *sleep apnea* (the stopping of breathing while asleep; associated with obesity, especially in men); *night terrors* (high arousal and the appearance of being terrified; NREM-3 disorder found mainly in children); sleepwalking (NREM-3 disorder also found mainly in children); and sleep talking.

24-2 What do we dream?

- We usually *dream* of ordinary events and everyday experiences, most involving some anxiety or misfortune.

- Fewer than 10 percent (and less among women) of dreams have any sexual content.

- Most dreams occur during REM sleep; those that happen during NREM sleep tend to be vague fleeting images.

24-3 What are the functions of dreams?

- There are five major views of the function of dreams.

- Freud's wish-fulfillment: Dreams provide a psychic "safety valve," with *manifest content* (story line) acting as a censored version of *latent content* (underlying meaning that gratifies our unconscious wishes).

- Information-processing: Dreams help us sort out the day's events and consolidate them in memory.

- Physiological function: Regular brain stimulation may help develop and preserve neural pathways in the brain.

- Neural activation: The brain attempts to make sense of neural static by weaving it into a story line.

- Cognitive development: Dreams reflect the dreamer's level of development.

- Most sleep theorists agree that REM sleep and its associated dreams serve an important function, as shown by the *REM rebound* that occurs following REM deprivation in humans and other species.

Multiple-Choice Questions

1. Sleep deprivation can lead to weight gain, reduced muscle strength, suppression of the cells that fight common colds, and most likely which of the following?

   a   Increased productivity
   b. Depression
   c. Decreased mistakes on homework
   d. Increased feeling of well-being
   e. Sleep apnea

2. What do we call the sleep disorder that causes you to stop breathing and awaken in order to take a breath?

   a. Narcolepsy
   b. Insomnia
   c. Sleep apnea
   d. Nightmares
   e. Night terrors

3. Which of the following dream theories states that dreams help us sort out the day's events and consolidate our memories?

   a. Information-processing
   b. Wish-fulfillment
   c. Physiological function
   d. Neural activation
   e. Neural disconnection

4. According to research, which of the following are we most likely to experience after sleep deprivation?

   a. Night terrors
   b. Sleep apnea
   c. Manifest content dreams
   d. Narcolepsy
   e. REM rebound

Practice FRQs

1. Identify and briefly describe the three major sleep disorders experienced by adults.

Answer

2 points: Sleep apnea: stops breathing during sleep.

2 points: Narcolepsy: falls asleep suddenly.

2 points: Insomnia: can't fall asleep.

2. Explain the following two theories regarding why we dream. Include a criticism each faces:
   • Freud's theory
   • Neural activation theory

(4 points)

Module 25

Psychoactive Drugs

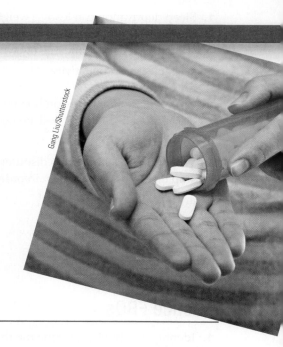

Gang Liu/Shutterstock

Module Learning Objectives

25-1 Define substance use disorders, and explain the roles of tolerance, withdrawal, and addiction.

25-2 Identify the depressants, and describe their effects.

25-3 Identify the stimulants, and describe their effects.

25-4 Identify the hallucinogens, and describe their effects.

et's imagine a day in the life of a legal-drug-using business executive. It begins with a wake-up latte. By midday, several cigarettes have calmed frazzled nerves before an appointment at the plastic surgeon's office for wrinkle-smoothing Botox injections. A diet pill before dinner helps stem the appetite, and its stimulating effects can later be partially offset with a glass of wine and two Tylenol PMs. And if performance needs enhancing, there are beta blockers for onstage performers, Viagra for middle-aged men, hormone-delivering "libido patches" for middle-aged women, and Adderall for those hoping to focus their concentration. Before drifting off into REM-depressed sleep, our hypothetical drug user is dismayed by news reports of pill-sharing, pill-popping students.

Tolerance and Addiction

25-1 What are substance use disorders, and what role do tolerance, withdrawal, and addiction play in these disorders?

Most of us manage to use some nonprescription drugs in moderation and without disrupting our lives. But some of us develop a self-harming **substance use disorder** (**TABLE 25.1**). In such cases, the substances being used are **psychoactive drugs,** chemicals that change perceptions and moods. A drug's overall effect depends not only on its biological effects but also on the psychology of the user's expectations, which vary with social and cultural contexts (Ward, 1994). If one culture assumes that a particular drug produces euphoria (or aggression or sexual arousal) and another does not, each culture may find its expectations fulfilled. In Module 81, we'll take a closer look at these interacting forces in the use and potential abuse of particular psychoactive drugs. But here let's consider how our bodies react to the ongoing use of psychoactive drugs.

Why might a person who rarely drinks alcohol get buzzed on one can of beer while a long-term drinker shows few effects until the second six-pack? The answer is **tolerance.** With continued use of alcohol and some other drugs (marijuana is an exception), the user's brain chemistry adapts to offset the drug effect (a process called *neuroadaptation*). To experience the

substance use disorder continued substance craving and use despite significant life disruption and/or physical risk.

psychoactive drug a chemical substance that alters perceptions and moods.

tolerance the diminishing effect with regular use of the same dose of a drug, requiring the user to take larger and larger doses before experiencing the drug's effect.

Table 25.1 When Is Drug Use a Disorder?

A person may be diagnosed with *substance use disorder* when drug use continues despite significant life disruption. Resulting changes in brain circuits may persist after quitting use of the substance (thus leading to strong cravings when exposed to people and situations that trigger memories of drug use). The severity of substance use disorder varies from *mild* (two to three symptoms) to *moderate* (four to five symptoms) to *severe* (six or more symptoms) (American Psychiatric Association, 2013).

Impaired Control

1. Uses more substance, or for longer, than intended.
2. Tries unsuccessfully to regulate substance use.
3. Spends much time gaining, using, or recovering from substance use.
4. Craves the substance.

Social Impairment

5. Use disrupts obligations at work, school, or home.
6. Continues use despite social problems.
7. Use causes reduced social, recreational, and work activities.

Risky Use

8. Continues use despite hazards.
9. Continues use despite worsening physical or psychological problems.

Drug Action

10. Experiences tolerance (needing more substance for the desired effect).
11. Experiences withdrawal when attempting to end use.

same effect, the user requires larger and larger doses (**FIGURE 25.1**). In chronic alcohol abuse, for example, the person's brain, heart, and liver suffer damage from the excessive amounts of alcohol being "tolerated." Ever-increasing doses of most psychoactive drugs can pose a serious threat to health and may lead to **addiction:** The person craves and uses the substance despite its adverse consequences. (See Thinking Critically About: Addiction on the next page.) The World Health Organization (2008) has reported that, worldwide, 90 million people suffer from such problems related to alcohol and other drugs. Regular users often try to fight their addiction, but abruptly stopping the drug may lead to the undesirable side effects of **withdrawal.**

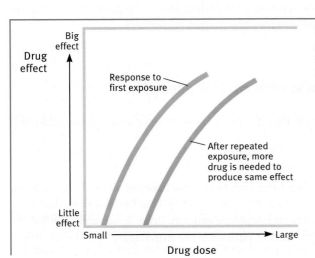

Figure 25.1

Drug tolerance With repeated exposure to a psychoactive drug, the drug's effect lessens. Thus, it takes larger doses to get the desired effect.

Big effect

Drug effect

Response to first exposure

After repeated exposure, more drug is needed to produce same effect

Little effect

Small ———————→ Large

Drug dose

addiction compulsive craving of drugs or certain behaviors (such as gambling) despite known adverse consequences.

withdrawal the discomfort and distress that follow discontinuing an addictive drug or behavior.

Thinking Critically About

Addiction

In recent years, the concept of addiction has been extended to cover many behaviors formerly considered bad habits or even sins. Psychologists debate whether the concept has been stretched too far, and whether addictions are really as irresistible as commonly believed. For example, "even for a very addictive drug like cocaine, only 15 to 16 percent of people become addicted within 10 years of first use," observed Terry Robinson and Kent Berridge (2003).

Addictions can be powerful, and many addicts do benefit from therapy or group support. Alcoholics Anonymous has supported millions of people in overcoming their alcohol addiction. But viewing addiction as an uncontrollable disease can undermine people's self-confidence and their belief that they can change. And that, critics say, would be unfortunate, for many people do voluntarily stop using addictive drugs, without any treatment. Most ex-smokers, for example, have kicked the habit on their own.

The addiction-as-disease-needing-treatment idea has been offered for a host of driven, excessive behaviors—eating, shopping, gambling, work, and sex. However, critics suggest that "addiction" can become an all-purpose excuse when used not as a metaphor ("I'm a science fiction addict") but as reality. Moreover, they note that labeling a behavior doesn't explain it. Attributing serial adultery, as in the case of Tiger Woods, to a "sex addiction" does not explain the sexual impulsiveness (Radford, 2010).

Sometimes, though, behaviors such as gambling, video gaming, or online surfing do become compulsive and dysfunctional,

A social networking addiction?

much like abusive drug taking (Gentile, 2009; Griffiths, 2001; Hoeft et al., 2008). Thus, psychiatry's manual of disorders now includes behavior addictions such as "gambling disorder" and proposes "Internet gaming disorder" for further study (American Psychiatric Association, 2013). Some Internet users, for example, display an apparent inability to resist logging on, and staying on, even when this excessive use impairs their work and relationships (Ko et al., 2005). Stay tuned. Debates over the nature of addiction continue.

Types of Psychoactive Drugs

The three major categories of psychoactive drugs are *depressants, stimulants,* and *hallucinogens.* All do their work at the brain's synapses, inhibiting, stimulating, or mimicking the activity of the brain's own chemical messengers, the neurotransmitters.

Depressants

25-2 What are depressants, and what are their effects?

Depressants are drugs such as alcohol, barbiturates (tranquilizers), and opiates that calm neural activity and slow body functions.

ALCOHOL

True or false? In small amounts, alcohol is a stimulant. *False.* Low doses of alcohol may, indeed, enliven a drinker, but they do so by acting as a *disinhibitor*—they slow brain activity that controls judgment and inhibitions. Alcohol is an equal-opportunity drug: It increases (disinhibits) helpful tendencies, as when tipsy restaurant patrons leave extravagant tips (Lynn, 1988).

AP® Exam Tip

These three categories—depressants, stimulants, and hallucinogens—are important. There are likely to be questions on the AP® exam that will require you to know how a particular psychoactive drug is classified.

depressants drugs (such as alcohol, barbiturates, and opiates) that reduce neural activity and slow body functions.

And it increases harmful tendencies, as when sexually aroused men become more disposed to sexual aggression.

Alcohol + sex = the perfect storm. When drinking, both men and women are more disposed to casual sex (Cooper, 2006; Ebel-Lam et al., 2009). *The urges you would feel if sober are the ones you will more likely act upon when intoxicated.*

SLOWED NEURAL PROCESSING Low doses of alcohol relax the drinker by slowing sympathetic nervous system activity. Larger doses cause reactions to slow, speech to slur, and skilled performance to deteriorate. Paired with sleep deprivation, alcohol is a potent sedative. Add these physical effects to lowered inhibitions, and the result can be deadly. Worldwide, several hundred thousand lives are lost each year in alcohol-related accidents and violent crime. As blood-alcohol levels rise and judgment falters, people's qualms about drinking and driving lessen. In experiments, virtually all drinkers who had insisted when sober that they would not drive under the influence later decided to drive home from a bar, even when given a breathalyzer test and told they were intoxicated (Denton & Krebs, 1990; MacDonald et al., 1995). Alcohol can also be life threatening when heavy drinking follows an earlier period of moderate drinking, which depresses the vomiting response. People may poison themselves with an overdose that their bodies would normally throw up.

Dangerous disinhibition Alcohol consumption leads to feelings of invincibility, which become especially dangerous behind the wheel of a car, such as this one totaled by a teenage drunk driver. This Colorado University Alcohol Awareness Week exhibit prompted many students to post their own anti-drinking pledges (white flags).

MEMORY DISRUPTION Alcohol can disrupt memory formation, and heavy drinking can have long-term effects on the brain and cognition. In rats, at a developmental period corresponding to human adolescence, binge drinking contributes to nerve cell death and reduces the birth of new nerve cells. It also impairs the growth of synaptic connections (Crews et al., 2006, 2007). In humans, heavy drinking may lead to blackouts, in which drinkers are unable to recall people they met the night before or what they said or did while intoxicated. These blackouts result partly from the way alcohol suppresses REM sleep, which helps fix the day's experiences into permanent memories.

The prolonged and excessive drinking that characterizes **alcohol use disorder** can shrink the brain (**FIGURE 25.2**). Girls and young women (who have less of a stomach enzyme that digests alcohol) can become addicted to alcohol more quickly than boys and young men do, and they are at risk for lung, brain, and liver damage at lower consumption levels (CASA, 2003; Wuethrich, 2001).

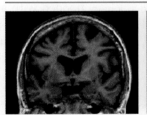 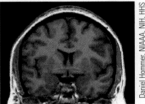

Scan of woman with alcohol use disorder | Scan of woman without alcohol use disorder

Figure 25.2
Disordered drinking shrinks the brain MRI scans show brain shrinkage in women with alcohol use disorder (left) compared with women in a control group (right).

REDUCED SELF-AWARENESS AND SELF-CONTROL In one experiment, those who consumed alcohol (rather than a placebo beverage) were doubly likely to be caught mind-wandering during a reading task, yet were *less* likely to notice that they zoned out (Sayette et al., 2009). Alcohol not only reduces self-awareness, it also produces a sort of "myopia" by focusing attention on an arousing situation (such as a provocation) and distracting attention from normal inhibitions and future consequences (Giancola et al., 2010; Hull et al., 1986; Steele & Josephs, 1990).

Reduced self-awareness may help explain why people who want to suppress their awareness of failures or shortcomings are more likely to drink than are those who feel good about themselves. Losing a business deal, a game, or a romantic partner sometimes elicits a drinking binge.

alcohol use disorder (popularly known as *alcoholism*). Alcohol use marked by tolerance, withdrawal, and a drive to continue problematic use.

EXPECTANCY EFFECTS As with other drugs, expectations influence behavior. When people *believe* that alcohol affects social behavior in certain ways, and believe, rightly or wrongly, that they have been drinking alcohol, they will behave accordingly (Moss & Albery, 2009). In a classic experiment, researchers gave Rutgers University men (who had volunteered for a study on "alcohol and sexual stimulation") either an alcoholic or a nonalcoholic drink (Abrams & Wilson, 1983). (Both had strong tastes that masked any alcohol.) In each group, half the participants thought they were drinking alcohol and half thought they were not. After watching an erotic movie clip, the men who *thought* they had consumed alcohol were more likely to report having strong sexual fantasies and feeling guilt free. Being able to *attribute* their sexual responses to alcohol released their inhibitions—whether or not they had actually consumed any alcohol. Alcohol's effect lies partly in that powerful sex organ, the mind.

BARBITURATES

Like alcohol, the **barbiturate** drugs, or *tranquilizers,* depress nervous system activity. Barbiturates such as Nembutal, Seconal, and Amytal are sometimes prescribed to induce sleep or reduce anxiety. In larger doses, they can impair memory and judgment. If combined with alcohol—as sometimes happens when people take a sleeping pill after an evening of heavy drinking—the total depressive effect on body functions can be lethal.

OPIATES

The **opiates**—opium and its derivatives—also depress neural functioning. When using the opiates, which include *heroin,* a user's pupils constrict, breathing slows, and lethargy sets in as blissful pleasure replaces pain and anxiety. For this short-term pleasure, opiate users may pay a long-term price: a gnawing craving for another fix, a need for progressively larger doses (as tolerance develops), and the extreme discomfort of withdrawal. When repeatedly flooded with an artificial opiate, the brain eventually stops producing *endorphins,* its own opiates. If the artificial opiate is then withdrawn, the brain lacks the normal level of these painkilling neurotransmitters. Those who cannot or choose not to tolerate this state may pay an ultimate price—death by overdose. Opiates include the *narcotics,* such as codeine and morphine, which physicians prescribe for pain relief.

Stimulants

25-3   What are stimulants, and what are their effects?

A **stimulant** excites neural activity and speeds up body functions. Pupils dilate, heart and breathing rates increase, and blood sugar levels rise, causing a drop in appetite. Energy and self-confidence also rise.

Stimulants include caffeine, nicotine, the **amphetamines,** cocaine, methamphetamine ("speed"), and Ecstasy (which is also a mild hallucinogen). People use stimulants to feel alert, lose weight, or boost mood or athletic performance. Unfortunately, stimulants can be addictive, as you may know if you are one of the many who use caffeine daily in your coffee, tea, soda, or energy drinks. Cut off from your usual dose, you may crash into fatigue, headaches, irritability, and depression (Silverman et al., 1992). A mild dose of caffeine typically lasts three or four hours, which—if taken in the evening—may be long enough to impair sleep.

Vasca/Shutterstock

NICOTINE

One of the most addictive stimulants is **nicotine,** found in cigarettes and other tobacco products. Imagine that cigarettes were harmless—except, once in every 25,000 packs, an occasional innocent-looking one is filled with dynamite instead of tobacco. Not such a bad

barbiturates drugs that depress central nervous system activity, reducing anxiety but impairing memory and judgment.

opiates opium and its derivatives, such as morphine and heroin; they depress neural activity, temporarily lessening pain and anxiety.

stimulants drugs (such as caffeine, nicotine, and the more powerful amphetamines, cocaine, Ecstasy, and methamphetamine) that excite neural activity and speed up body functions.

amphetamines drugs that stimulate neural activity, causing speeded-up body functions and associated energy and mood changes.

nicotine a stimulating and highly addictive psychoactive drug in tobacco.

risk of having your head blown off. But with 250 million packs a day consumed worldwide, we could expect more than 10,000 gruesome daily deaths (more than three times the 9/11 fatalities each and every day)—surely enough to have cigarettes banned everywhere.[1]

The lost lives from these dynamite-loaded cigarettes approximate those from today's actual cigarettes. A teen-to-the-grave smoker has a 50 percent chance of dying from the habit, and each year, tobacco kills nearly 5.4 million of its 1.3 billion customers worldwide. (Imagine the outrage if terrorists took down an equivalent of 25 loaded jumbo jets today, let alone tomorrow and every day thereafter.) By 2030, annual deaths are expected to increase to 8 million. That means that *1 billion* twenty-first-century people may be killed by tobacco (WHO, 2008). Eliminating smoking would increase life expectancy more than any other preventive measure.

Those addicted to nicotine find it very hard to quit because tobacco products are as powerfully and quickly addictive as heroin and cocaine. Attempts to quit even within the first weeks of smoking often fail (DiFranza, 2008). As with other addictions, smokers develop *tolerance,* and quitting causes nicotine-withdrawal symptoms, including craving, insomnia, anxiety, irritability, and distractibility. Nicotine-deprived smokers trying to focus on a task experience a tripled rate of mind-wandering (Sayette et al., 2010). When not craving a cigarette, they tend to underestimate the power of such cravings (Sayette et al., 2008).

All it takes to relieve this aversive state is a cigarette—a portable nicotine dispenser. Within 7 seconds, a rush of nicotine signals the central nervous system to release a flood of neurotransmitters (**FIGURE 25.3**). Epinephrine and norepinephrine diminish appetite and boost alertness and mental efficiency. Dopamine and opioids calm anxiety and reduce sensitivity to pain (Nowak, 1994; Scott et al., 2004).

---

[1] This analogy, adapted here with world-based numbers, was suggested by mathematician Sam Saunders, as reported by K. C. Cole (1998).

FYI

Smoke a cigarette and nature will charge you 12 minutes—ironically, just about the length of time you spend smoking it (*Discover*, 1996).

Humorist Dave Barry (1995) recalling why he smoked his first cigarette the summer he turned 15: "Arguments against smoking: 'It's a repulsive addiction that slowly but surely turns you into a gasping, gray-skinned, tumor-ridden invalid, hacking up brownish gobs of toxic waste from your one remaining lung.' Arguments for smoking: 'Other teenagers are doing it.' Case closed! Let's light up!"

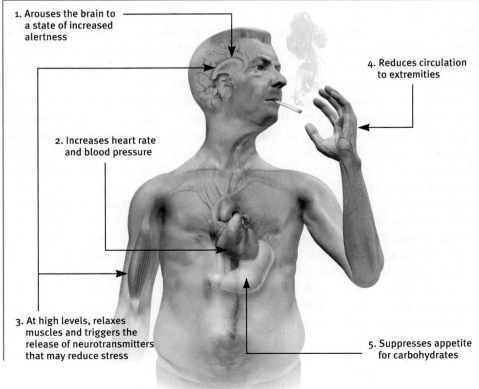

1. Arouses the brain to a state of increased alertness

2. Increases heart rate and blood pressure

3. At high levels, relaxes muscles and triggers the release of neurotransmitters that may reduce stress

4. Reduces circulation to extremities

5. Suppresses appetite for carbohydrates

Figure 25.3

Where there's smoke . . . : The physiological effects of nicotine Nicotine reaches the brain within 7 seconds, twice as fast as intravenous heroin. Within minutes, the amount in the blood soars.

Nic-A-Teen Virtually nobody starts smoking past the vulnerable teen years. Eager to hook customers whose addiction will give them business for years to come, cigarette companies target teens. Portrayals of smoking by popular actors, such as Robert Pattinson in *Remember Me*, entice teens to imitate.

These rewards keep people smoking, even among the 8 in 10 smokers who wish they could stop (Jones, 2007). Each year, fewer than 1 in 7 smokers who want to quit will be able to. Even those who know they are committing slow-motion suicide may be unable to stop (Saad, 2002). Asked "If you had to do it all over again, would you start smoking?" more than 85 percent of adult smokers have answered *No* (Slovic et al., 2002).

Nevertheless, repeated attempts seem to pay off. Half of all Americans who have ever smoked have quit, sometimes aided by a nicotine replacement drug and with encouragement from a counselor or a support group. Success is equally likely whether smokers quit abruptly or gradually (Fiore et al., 2008; Lichtenstein et al., 2010; Lindson et al., 2010). For those who endure, the acute craving and withdrawal symptoms gradually dissipate over the ensuing 6 months (Ward et al., 1997). After a year's abstinence, only 10 percent will relapse in the next year (Hughes et al., 2010). These nonsmokers may live not only healthier but also happier lives. Smoking correlates with higher rates of depression, chronic disabilities, and divorce (Doherty & Doherty, 1998; Vita et al., 1998). Healthy living seems to add both years to life and life to years.

COCAINE

The recipe for Coca-Cola originally included an extract of the coca plant, creating a **cocaine** tonic for tired elderly people. Between 1896 and 1905, Coke was indeed "the real thing." But no longer. Cocaine is now snorted, injected, or smoked. It enters the bloodstream quickly, producing a rush of euphoria that depletes the brain's supply of the neurotransmitters dopamine, serotonin, and norepinephrine (**FIGURE 25.4**). Within the hour, a crash of agitated depression follows as the drug's effect wears off. Many regular cocaine users chasing this high become addicted. In the lab, cocaine-addicted monkeys have pressed levers more than 12,000 times to gain one cocaine injection (Siegel, 1990).

In situations that trigger aggression, ingesting cocaine may heighten reactions. Caged rats fight when given foot shocks, and they fight even more when given cocaine *and* foot shocks. Likewise, humans who voluntarily ingest high doses of cocaine in laboratory experiments impose higher shock levels on a presumed opponent than do those receiving a placebo (Licata et al., 1993). Cocaine use may also lead to emotional disturbances, suspiciousness, convulsions, cardiac arrest, or respiratory failure.

In national surveys, 3 percent of U.S. high school seniors and 6 percent of British 18- to 24-year-olds reported having tried cocaine during the past year (ACMD, 2009; Johnston et al., 2011). Nearly half had smoked *crack,* a faster-working crystallized form of cocaine that produces a briefer but more intense high, followed by a more intense crash. After several hours, the craving for more wanes, only to return several days later (Gawin, 1991).

Cocaine's psychological effects depend in part on the dosage and form consumed, but the situation and the user's expectations and personality also play a role. Given a placebo, cocaine users who *thought* they were taking cocaine often had a cocaine-like experience (Van Dyke & Byck, 1982).

"Cocaine makes you a new man. And the first thing that new man wants is more cocaine." -COMEDIAN GEORGE CARLIN (1937–2008)

---

cocaine a powerful and addictive stimulant, derived from the coca plant, producing temporarily increased alertness and euphoria.

methamphetamine a powerfully addictive drug that stimulates the central nervous system, with speeded-up body functions and associated energy and mood changes; over time, appears to reduce baseline dopamine levels.

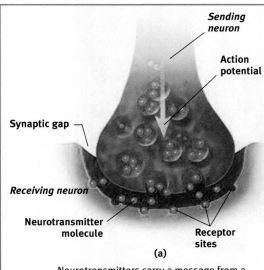
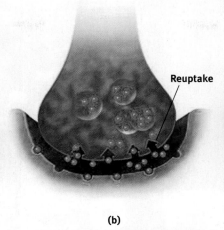
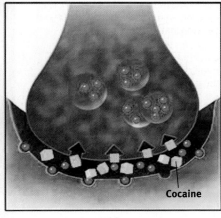

(a)
Neurotransmitters carry a message from a sending neuron across a synapse to receptor sites on a receiving neuron.

(b)
The sending neuron normally reabsorbs excess neurotransmitter molecules, a process called reuptake.

(c)
By binding to the sites that normally reabsorb neurotransmitter molecules, cocaine blocks reuptake of dopamine, norepinephrine, and serotonin (Ray & Ksir, 1990). The extra neurotransmitter molecules therefore remain in the synapse, intensifying their normal mood-altering effects and producing a euphoric rush. When the cocaine level drops, the absence of these neurotransmitters produces a crash.

Figure 25.4
Cocaine euphoria and crash

METHAMPHETAMINE

Methamphetamine is chemically related to its parent drug, *amphetamine* (NIDA, 2002, 2005) but has even greater effects. Methamphetamine triggers the release of the neurotransmitter dopamine, which stimulates brain cells that enhance energy and mood, leading to eight hours or so of heightened energy and euphoria. Its aftereffects may include irritability, insomnia, hypertension, seizures, social isolation, depression, and occasional violent outbursts (Homer et al., 2008). Over time, methamphetamine may reduce baseline dopamine levels, leaving the user with depressed functioning.

ECSTASY

Ecstasy, a street name for **MDMA** (methylenedioxymethamphetamine), is both a stimulant and a mild hallucinogen. As an amphetamine derivative, Ecstasy triggers dopamine release, but its major effect is releasing stored serotonin and blocking its reuptake, thus prolonging serotonin's feel-good flood (Braun, 2001). Users feel the effect about a half-hour after taking an Ecstasy pill. For three or four hours, they experience high energy, emotional elevation, and (given a social context) connectedness with those around them ("I love everyone").

During the 1990s, Ecstasy's popularity soared as a "club drug" taken at nightclubs and all-night raves (Landry, 2002). The drug's popularity crosses national borders, with an estimated 60 million tablets consumed annually in Britain (ACMD, 2009). There are, however, reasons not to be ecstatic about Ecstasy. One is its dehydrating effect, which—when combined with prolonged dancing—can lead to severe overheating, increased

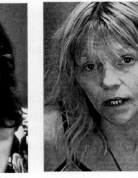

> **AP® Exam Tip**
> Figure 25.4 is an excellent review of how neurotransmitters work. If there is any part of this that you don't understand, head back to Module 9 for a complete explanation.

Dramatic drug-induced decline This woman's methamphetamine addiction led to obvious physical changes. Her decline is evident in these two photos, taken at age 36 (left) and, after four years of addiction, at age 40 (right).

> **Ecstasy (MDMA)** a synthetic stimulant and mild hallucinogen. Produces euphoria and social intimacy, but with short-term health risks and longer-term harm to serotonin-producing neurons and to mood and cognition.

Meth bust As use of the dangerously addictive stimulant methamphetamine has increased, enforcement agencies have increased their efforts to snuff out the labs that produce it.

blood pressure, and death. Another is that long-term, repeated leaching of brain serotonin can damage serotonin-producing neurons, leading to decreased output and increased risk of permanently depressed mood (Croft et al., 2001; McCann et al., 2001; Roiser et al., 2005). Ecstasy also suppresses the disease-fighting immune system, impairs memory, slows thought, and disrupts sleep by interfering with serotonin's control of the circadian clock (Laws & Kokkalis, 2007; Pacifici et al., 2001; Schilt et al., 2007). Ecstasy delights for the night but dispirits the morrow.

Hallucinogens

 What are hallucinogens, and what are their effects?

hallucinogens psychedelic ("mind-manifesting") drugs, such as LSD, that distort perceptions and evoke sensory images in the absence of sensory input.

LSD a powerful hallucinogenic drug; also known as acid *(lysergic acid diethylamide)*.

Hallucinogens distort perceptions and evoke sensory images in the absence of sensory input (which is why these drugs are also called *psychedelics,* meaning "mind-manifesting"). Some, such as LSD and MDMA (Ecstasy), are synthetic. Others, including the mild hallucinogen marijuana, are natural substances.

LSD

Chemist Albert Hofmann created—and on one Friday afternoon in April 1943 accidentally ingested—**LSD** (lysergic acid diethylamide). The result—"an uninterrupted stream of fantastic pictures, extraordinary shapes with intense, kaleidoscopic play of colors"—reminded him of a childhood mystical experience that had left him longing for another glimpse of "a miraculous, powerful, unfathomable reality" (Siegel, 1984; Smith, 2006).

The emotions of an LSD trip vary from euphoria to detachment to panic. The user's current mood and expectations color the emotional experience, but the perceptual distortions and hallucinations have some commonalities. Whether provoked to hallucinate by drugs, loss of oxygen, or extreme sensory deprivation, the brain hallucinates in basically the same way (Siegel, 1982). The experience typically begins with simple geometric forms, such as a lattice, cobweb, or spiral. The next phase consists of more meaningful images; some may be superimposed on a tunnel or funnel, others may be replays of past emotional experiences. As the hallucination peaks, people frequently feel separated from their body and experience dreamlike scenes so real that they may become panic-stricken or harm themselves.

These sensations are strikingly similar to the **near-death experience,** an altered state of consciousness reported by about 15 percent of patients revived from cardiac arrest (Agrillo, 2011; Greyson, 2010). Many describe visions of tunnels (**FIGURE 25.5**), bright lights or beings of light, a replay of old memories, and out-of-body sensations (Siegel, 1980). Given that oxygen deprivation and other insults to the brain are known to produce hallucinations, it is difficult to resist wondering whether a brain under stress manufactures the near-death experience. Following temporal lobe seizures, patients have reported similarly profound mystical experiences. So have solitary sailors and polar explorers while enduring monotony, isolation, and cold (Suedfeld & Mocellin, 1987).

Figure 25.5

Near-death vision or hallucination? Psychologist Ronald Siegel (1977) reported that people under the influence of hallucinogenic drugs often see "a bright light in the center of the field of vision. . . . The location of this point of light create[s] a tunnel-like perspective." This is very similar to others' near-death experiences.

MARIJUANA

For 5000 years, hemp has been cultivated for its fiber. The leaves and flowers of this plant, which are sold as marijuana, contain **THC** (delta-9-tetrahydrocannabinol). Whether smoked (getting to the brain in about 7 seconds) or eaten (causing its peak concentration to be reached at a slower, unpredictable rate), THC produces a mix of effects. *Synthetic marijuana* (also called *K2* or *Spice*) mimics THC. Its harmful side effects, which can include agitation and hallucinations, led to its ingredient becoming illegal under the U.S. Synthetic Drug Abuse Prevention Act of 2012.

Marijuana is a difficult drug to classify. It is a mild hallucinogen, amplifying sensitivity to colors, sounds, tastes, and smells. But like alcohol, marijuana relaxes, disinhibits, and may produce a euphoric high. Both alcohol and marijuana impair the motor coordination, perceptual skills, and reaction time necessary for safely operating an automobile or other machine. "THC causes animals to misjudge events," reported Ronald Siegel (1990, p. 163). "Pigeons wait too long to respond to buzzers or lights that tell them food is available for brief periods; and rats turn the wrong way in mazes."

Marijuana and alcohol also differ. The body eliminates alcohol within hours. THC and its by-products linger in the body for a week or more, which means that regular users experience less abrupt withdrawal and may achieve a high with smaller amounts of the drug than would be needed by occasional users. This is contrary to the usual path of tolerance, in which repeat users need to take larger doses to feel the same effect.

A user's experience can vary with the situation. If the person feels anxious or depressed, using marijuana may intensify these feelings. The more often the person uses marijuana, especially during adolescence and in today's stronger, purified form, the greater the risk of anxiety or depression (Bambico et al., 2010; Hall, 2006; Murray et al., 2007). Daily use bodes a worse outcome than infrequent use.

Marijuana also disrupts memory formation and interferes with immediate recall of information learned only a few minutes before. Such cognitive effects outlast the period of smoking (Messinis et al., 2006). Heavy adult use for over 20 years is associated with a shrinkage of brain areas that process memories and emotions (Yücel et al., 2008). Prenatal exposure through maternal marijuana use impairs brain development (Berghuis et al., 2007; Huizink & Mulder, 2006).

To free up resources to fight crime, some states and countries have passed laws legalizing the possession of small quantities of marijuana. In some cases, legal *medical marijuana* use has been granted to relieve the pain and nausea associated with diseases such

near-death experience an altered state of consciousness reported after a close brush with death (such as by cardiac arrest); often similar to drug-induced hallucinations.

THC the major active ingredient in marijuana; triggers a variety of effects, including mild hallucinations.

as AIDS, glaucoma, and cancer (Munsey, 2010; Watson et al., 2000). In such cases, the Institute of Medicine recommends delivering the THC with medical inhalers. Marijuana smoke, like cigarette smoke, is toxic and can cause cancer, lung damage, and pregnancy complications.

* * *

Despite their differences, the psychoactive drugs summarized in **TABLE 25.2** share a common feature: They trigger negative aftereffects that offset their immediate positive effects and grow stronger with repetition. And this helps explain both tolerance and withdrawal. As the opposing, negative aftereffects grow stronger, it takes larger and larger doses to produce the desired high *(tolerance)*, causing the aftereffects to worsen in the drug's absence *(withdrawal)*. This in turn creates a need to switch off the withdrawal symptoms by taking yet more of the drug (which may lead to *addiction*).

Table 25.2 A Guide to Selected Psychoactive Drugs

Drug	Type	Pleasurable Effects	Adverse Effects
Alcohol	Depressant	Initial high followed by relaxation and disinhibition	Depression, memory loss, organ damage, impaired reactions
Heroin	Depressant	Rush of euphoria, relief from pain	Depressed physiology, agonizing withdrawal
Caffeine	Stimulant	Increased alertness and wakefulness	Anxiety, restlessness, and insomnia in high doses; uncomfortable withdrawal
Methamphetamine	Stimulant	Euphoria, alertness, energy	Irritability, insomnia, hypertension, seizures
Cocaine	Stimulant	Rush of euphoria, confidence, energy	Cardiovascular stress, suspiciousness, depressive crash
Nicotine	Stimulant	Arousal and relaxation, sense of well-being	Heart disease, cancer
Ecstasy (MDMA)	Stimulant; mild hallucinogen	Emotional elevation, disinhibition	Dehydration, overheating, depressed mood, impaired cognitive and immune functioning
Marijuana	Mild hallucinogen	Enhanced sensation, relief of pain, distortion of time, relaxation	Impaired learning and memory, increased risk of psychological disorders, lung damage from smoke

To learn about the influences on drug use, see Module 81.

Before You Move On

► **ASK YOURSELF**

Do you think people can become addicted not only to psychoactive drugs but also to other repetitive, pleasure-seeking behaviors (such as gambling or "Internet game playing")?

► **TEST YOURSELF**

Why do tobacco companies try so hard to get customers hooked as teens?

Answers to the Test Yourself questions can be found in Appendix E at the end of the book.

Module 25 Review

 What are substance use disorders, and what role do tolerance, withdrawal, and addiction play in these disorders?

- Those with a *substance use disorder* may exhibit impaired control, social disruption, risky behavior, and the physical effects of tolerance and withdrawal.

- *Psychoactive drugs* alter perceptions and moods.

- These drugs may produce *tolerance*—requiring larger doses to achieve the desired effect—and *withdrawal*—significant discomfort accompanying efforts to quit.

- *Addiction* is compulsive craving and use of drugs or certain behaviors (such as gambling) despite known adverse consequences.

25-2 What are depressants, and what are their effects?

- *Depressants,* such as alcohol, *barbiturates,* and the *opiates* (which include narcotics), dampen neural activity and slow body functions.

- Alcohol tends to disinhibit, increasing the likelihood that we will act on our impulses, whether harmful or helpful. It also impairs judgment, disrupts memory processes by suppressing REM sleep, and reduces self-awareness and self-control.

- User expectations strongly influence alcohol's behavioral effects.

 What are stimulants, and what are their effects?

- *Stimulants*—including caffeine, *nicotine,* cocaine, the *amphetamines, methamphetamine,* and *Ecstasy*—excite neural activity and speed up body functions, triggering energy and mood changes. All are highly addictive.

- Nicotine's effects make smoking a difficult habit to kick, yet the percentage of Americans who smoke has been dramatically decreasing.

- Cocaine gives users a fast high, followed within an hour by a crash. Its risks include cardiovascular stress and suspiciousness.

- Use of methamphetamines may permanently reduce dopamine production.

- Ecstasy (MDMA) is a combined stimulant and mild hallucinogen that produces euphoria and feelings of intimacy. Its users risk immune system suppression, permanent damage to mood and memory, and (if taken during physical activity) dehydration and escalating body temperatures.

25-4 What are hallucinogens, and what are their effects?

- *Hallucinogens*—such as *LSD* and marijuana—distort perceptions and evoke *hallucinations*—sensory images in the absence of sensory input. The user's mood and expectations influence the effects of LSD, but common experiences are hallucinations and emotions varying from euphoria to panic.

- Marijuana's main ingredient, *THC,* may trigger feelings of disinhibition, euphoria, relaxation, relief from pain, and intense sensitivity to sensory stimuli. It may also increase feelings of depression or anxiety, impair motor coordination and reaction time, disrupt memory formation, and damage lung tissue (because of the inhaled smoke).

Multiple-Choice Questions

1. Which of the following represents drug tolerance?

   a. Hans has grown to accept the fact that his wife likes to have a beer with her dinner, even though he personally does not approve of the use of alcohol.
   b. Jose often wakes up with a headache that lasts until he has his morning cup of coffee.
   c. Pierre enjoys the effect of marijuana and is now using the drug several times a week.
   d. Jacob had to increase the dosage of his pain medication when the old dosage no longer effectively controlled the pain from his chronic back condition.
   e. Chau lost his job and is now homeless as a result of his drug use.

2. Which of the following drugs is classified as an opiate?

   a. Nicotine
   b. Marijuana
   c. Heroin
   d. Methamphetamine
   e. Cocaine

3. Which of the following drugs produces effects similar to a near-death experience?

   a. Ecstasy
   b. Nicotine
   c. Barbiturate
   d. Methamphetamine
   e. LSD

4. Which of the following statements is true of alcohol?

   a. Alcohol is a stimulant because it produces insomnia.
   b. Alcohol is a depressant because it produces bipolar disorder.
   c. Alcohol is a stimulant because people do foolish things while under its influence.
   d. Alcohol is a depressant because it calms neural activity and slows body function.
   e. Alcohol is a stimulant because it increases instances of casual sex.

Practice FRQs

1. Name and compare the effects of the two hallucinogens discussed in the text.

   Answer

   1 point: LSD creates vivid hallucinations and strong emotions.

   1 point: Marijuana creates mild hallucinations, enhanced sensory experiences, and impaired judgment.

2. Three of the most widely used psychoactive drugs—alcohol, caffeine, and nicotine—are legal for large segments of the population. Name the category that each of these drugs belongs to, and describe one effect of each.

   (6 points)

Unit V Review

Key Terms and Concepts to Remember

consciousness, p. 219

hypnosis, p. 219

posthypnotic suggestion, p. 220

dissociation, p. 222

circadian [ser-KAY-dee-an] rhythm, p. 226

REM sleep, p. 226

alpha waves, p. 227

sleep, p. 227

hallucinations, p. 228

delta waves, p. 228

NREM sleep, p. 228

suprachiasmatic nucleus (SCN), p. 229

insomnia, p. 238

narcolepsy, p. 238

sleep apnea, p. 239

night terrors, p. 239

dream, p. 240

manifest content, p. 241

latent content, p. 241

REM rebound, p. 243

substance use disorder, p. 246

psychoactive drug, p. 246

tolerance, p. 246

addiction, p. 247

withdrawal, p. 247

depressants, p. 248

alcohol use disorder, p. 249

barbiturates, p. 250

opiates, p. 250

stimulants, p. 250

amphetamines, p. 250

nicotine, p. 250

cocaine, p. 252

methamphetamine, p. 253

Ecstasy (MDMA), p. 253

hallucinogens, p. 254

LSD, p. 254

near-death experience, p. 255

THC, p. 255

Key Contributors to Remember

William James, p. 219

Ernest Hilgard, p. 222

Sigmund Freud, p. 241

AP® Exam Practice Questions

Multiple-Choice Questions

1. Sudden sleep attacks at inopportune times are symptomatic of which sleep disorder?

a. Sleep apnea

b. Insomnia

c. Night terrors

d. Sleepwalking

e. Narcolepsy

2. Deep sleep occurs in which stage?

a. Hypnagogic

b. REM

c. Alpha

d. NREM-1

e. Delta

3. Recurring problems in falling asleep or staying asleep are characteristic of which sleep disorder?

a. Sleep apnea

b. Narcolepsy

c. Insomnia

d. Sleep talking

e. Sleepwalking

4. What is the pineal gland's role in sleep?

a. Activating the suprachiasmatic nucleus

b. The production of melatonin

c. The location of hypnagogic images

d. Remembering dreams upon waking

e. Emitting alpha waves

5. What are bursts of rapid, rhythmic brain-wave activity that occur during NREM-2 sleep?

   a. Hallucinations
   b. Circadian rhythms
   c. Alpha waves
   d. Sleep spindles
   e. Delta waves

6. Increasing amounts of paradoxical sleep following a period of sleep deprivation is known as what?

   a. Circadian sleep
   b. Sleep shifting
   c. Narcolepsy
   d. Sleep apnea
   e. REM rebound

7. Which of these drugs, which acts as both a stimulant and a hallucinogen, can also cause dangerous dehydration?

   a. LSD
   b. Ecstasy
   c. Alcohol
   d. Cocaine
   e. Caffeine

8. Recent research most consistently supports the effectiveness of hypnosis in which of the following areas?

   a. Pain relief
   b. Recovery of lost memories
   c. Reduction of sleep deprivation
   d. Forcing people to act against their will
   e. Cessation of smoking

9. What are the three major categories of drugs?

   a. Hallucinogens, depressants, and stimulants
   b. Stimulants, barbiturates, and hallucinogens
   c. Amphetamines, barbiturates, and opiates
   d. MDMA, LSD, and THC
   e. Alcohol, caffeine, and nicotine

10. Jarod's muscles are relaxed, his body is basically paralyzed, and he is hard to awaken. Which sleep state is Jarod probably experiencing?

   a. Sleep apnea
   b. Hypnagogic
   c. Paradoxical
   d. Delta
   e. Sleep deprivation

11. The effects of opiates are similar to the effects of which neurotransmitter?

   a. Barbiturates
   b. Endorphins
   c. Tranquilizers
   d. Nembutal
   e. Acetylcholine

12. Slowed reactions, slurred speech, and decreased skill performance are associated with abuse of which drug?

   a. Nicotine
   b. Methamphetamine
   c. Caffeine
   d. Alcohol
   e. Ecstasy

13. What term did Ernest Hilgard use to describe a split between different levels of consciousness?

   a. Hypnagogic imagery
   b. REM sleep
   c. Delta waves
   d. Spindles
   e. Dissociation

14. Psychologists who study the brain's activity during sleep are most likely to use which of these technologies?

   a. MRI
   b. CT scan
   d. PET scan
   d. EEG
   e. EKG

15. What term describes the brain's adaptation to a drug's chemistry, requiring larger and larger doses to experience the same effect?

   a. Withdrawal
   b. Tolerance
   c. Addiction
   d. Substance use disorder
   e. Disinhibiting

Free-Response Questions

1. Different biological changes are associated with different states of consciousness. Explain the biological changes (if any) typically associated with the following consciousness-related concepts:

   - Sleep deprivation
   - REM
   - Tolerance
   - Opiates

Rubric for Free Response Question 1

1 point: Sleep deprivation causes a wide range of biological changes in the body, all associated with decreased performance while awake. These biological changes include lack of energy, falling asleep during the day, changes in appetite, suppression of the immune system, decreased focus and attention, and depressed mood. ⟳ Pages 234–237

1 point: The REM stage of the sleep cycle is associated with dramatic biological changes. Brain waves and breathing become irregular, heart rate increases, and eyes dart back and forth beneath the eyelids. ⟳ Pages 228–229

1 point: After repeated use of some drugs, humans develop tolerance for those substances, meaning that increasing dosages of those drugs are needed to produce the same effect. Tolerance occurs because of biological changes in the brain. The brain's chemistry changes when some psychoactive drugs are repeatedly ingested, interfering with the brain's ability to produce or use some neurotransmitters.
 ⟳ Pages 246–247

1 point: Drugs categorized as opiates cause a range of biological changes in the body. Some of the changes mentioned in the text are: pupil constriction, slower breathing, lethargy, and eventually, painful withdrawal symptoms as the brain loses its ability to produce "natural" endorphins. ⟳ Page 250

2. Ernest, a psychology major, is discussing hypnosis with his roommate, Phil. Phil says: "I can't believe so many people fall for that hypnosis stuff. Hypnosis is just like dreaming. It's just a different state of consciousness, and a dream can affect someone just like a supposed hypnotic state can."

   Explain how Ernest might use the following terms as he discusses the validity of Phil's claims.

   - Posthypnotic suggestion
   - Divided-consciousness theory
   - Social influence theory
   - Dissociation

   (4 points)

3. Consciousness has been defined and studied differently throughout the history of psychology. In your own words, explain how modern psychologists define consciousness, and explain how the following "altered" states of consciousness relate to your definition.

   - Hypnosis
   - Sleep stages
   - Dreams
   - Psychoactive drugs

   (5 points)

Multiple-choice self-tests and more may be found at www.worthpublishers.com/MyersAP2e

Unit VI

Learning

Modules

When a chinook salmon first emerges from its egg in a stream's gravel bed, its genes provide most of the behavioral instructions it needs for life. It knows instinctively how and where to swim, what to eat, and most spectacularly, where to go and when and how to return to its birthplace. Guided by the scent of its home stream, it pursues an upstream odyssey to its ancestral spawning ground and seeks out the best gravel and water flow for breeding. It then mates and, its life mission accomplished, dies.

Unlike salmon, we are not born with a genetic plan for life. Much of what we do we learn from experience. Although we struggle to find the life direction a salmon is born with, our learning gives us more flexibility. We can learn how to build grass huts or snow shelters, submarines or space stations, and thereby adjust to almost any environment. Indeed, nature's most important gift to us may be our *adaptability*—our capacity to learn new behaviors that help us cope with changing circumstances.

Learning breeds hope. What is learnable we can potentially teach—a fact that encourages parents, teachers, coaches, and animal trainers. What has been learned we can potentially change by new learning—an assumption that underlies counseling, psychotherapy, and rehabilitation programs. No matter how unhappy, unsuccessful, or unloving we are, that need not be the end of our story.

262

No topic is closer to the heart of psychology than *learning*. In earlier units we considered how we learn to think critically, and the learning of visual perceptions and of a drug's expected effect. In later units we will see how learning shapes our thoughts and language, our motivations and emotions, our personalities and attitudes. In Unit VII, we will see how the brain stores and retrieves learning.

Module 26

How We Learn and Classical Conditioning

Ken Gillespie Photography/Alamy

Module Learning Objectives

26-1 Define learning, and identify some basic forms of learning.

26-2 Describe the basic components of classical conditioning, and explain behaviorism's view of learning.

26-3 Summarize the processes of acquisition, extinction, spontaneous recovery, generalization, and discrimination.

26-4 Explain why Pavlov's work remains so important, and describe some applications of his work to human health and well-being.

How Do We Learn?

26-1 What is learning, and what are some basic forms of learning?

Psychologists define **learning** as the process of acquiring new and relatively enduring information or behaviors. By learning, we humans are able to adapt to our environments. We learn to expect and prepare for significant events such as food or pain *(classical conditioning)*. We typically learn to repeat acts that bring rewards and to avoid acts that bring unwanted results *(operant conditioning)*. We learn new behaviors by observing events and by watching others, and through language we learn things we have neither experienced nor observed *(cognitive learning)*. But *how* do we learn?

More than 200 years ago, philosophers such as John Locke and David Hume echoed Aristotle's conclusion from 2000 years earlier: We learn by *association*. Our minds naturally

learning the process of acquiring new and relatively enduring information or behaviors.

Most of us would be unable to name the order of the songs on our favorite album or playlist. Yet, hearing the end of one piece cues (by association) an anticipation of the next. Likewise, when singing your national anthem, you associate the end of each line with the beginning of the next. (Pick a line out of the middle and notice how much harder it is to recall the *previous* line.)

It's easy to confuse habituation with sensory adaptation, a concept from Unit IV. Recall that sensory adaptation occurs when one of your sensory systems stops registering the presence of an unchanging stimulus—when you go swimming in a cool pool, for example, the water no longer feels cool after you've been in for a few minutes. Habituation, like sensory adaptation, involves a diminished response, but in this case it's a form of learning rather than a function of the sensory system. If you're exposed to the same stimulus over and over, your response decreases. A friend might sneak up and startle you by yelling "Boo!" But you'll probably startle less when he tries it again two minutes later. That's habituation.

habituation an organism's decreasing response to a stimulus with repeated exposure to it.

associative learning learning that certain events occur together. The events may be two stimuli (as in classical conditioning) or a response and its consequences (as in operant conditioning).

stimulus any event or situation that evokes a response.

connect events that occur in sequence. Suppose you see and smell freshly baked bread, eat some, and find it satisfying. The next time you see and smell fresh bread, you will expect that eating it will again be satisfying. So, too, with sounds. If you associate a sound with a frightening consequence, hearing the sound alone may trigger your fear. As one 4-year-old exclaimed after watching a TV character get mugged, "If I had heard that music, I wouldn't have gone around the corner!" (Wells, 1981).

Learned associations often operate subtly. Give people a red pen (associated with error marking) rather than a black pen and, when correcting essays, they will spot more errors and give lower grades (Rutchick et al., 2010). When voting, people are more likely to support taxes to aid education if their assigned voting place is in a school (Berger et al., 2008).

Learned associations also feed our habitual behaviors (Wood & Neal, 2007). As we repeat behaviors in a given context—sleeping in a certain posture in bed, walking certain routes from class to class, eating popcorn in a movie theater—the behaviors become associated with the contexts. Our next experience of the context then evokes our habitual response. How long does it take to form such habits? To find out, one British research team asked 96 university students to choose some healthy behavior (such as running before dinner or eating fruit with lunch), to do it daily for 84 days, and to record whether the behavior felt automatic (something they did without thinking and would find it hard not to do). On average, behaviors became habitual after about 66 days (Lally et al., 2010). (Is there something you'd like to make a routine part of your life? Just do it every day for two months, or a bit longer for exercise, and you likely will find yourself with a new habit.)

Other animals also learn by association. Disturbed by a squirt of water, the sea slug *Aplysia* protectively withdraws its gill. If the squirts continue, as happens naturally in choppy water, the withdrawal response diminishes. We say the slug **habituates.** But if the sea slug repeatedly receives an electric shock just after being squirted, its response to the squirt instead grows stronger. The animal has associated the squirt with the impending shock.

Complex animals can learn to associate their own behavior with its outcomes. An aquarium seal will repeat behaviors, such as slapping and barking, that prompt people to toss it a herring.

By linking two events that occur close together, both animals are exhibiting **associative learning.** The sea slug associates the squirt with an impending shock; the seal associates slapping and barking with a herring treat. Each animal has learned something important to its survival: predicting the immediate future.

This process of learning associations is *conditioning,* and it takes two main forms:

- In *classical conditioning,* we learn to associate two stimuli and thus to anticipate events. (A **stimulus** is any event or situation that evokes a response.) We learn that a flash of lightning signals an impending crack of thunder; when lightning flashes nearby, we start to brace ourselves (**FIGURE 26.1**).

- In *operant conditioning,* we learn to associate a response (our behavior) and its consequence. Thus we (and other animals) learn to repeat acts followed by good results (**FIGURE 26.2**) and avoid acts followed by bad results.

To simplify, we will explore these two types of associative learning separately. Often, though, they occur together, as on one Japanese cattle ranch, where the clever rancher outfitted his herd with electronic pagers, which he calls from his cell phone. After a week of training, the animals learn to associate two stimuli—the beep on their pager and the arrival of food (classical conditioning). But they also learn to associate their hustling to the food trough with the pleasure of eating (operant conditioning).

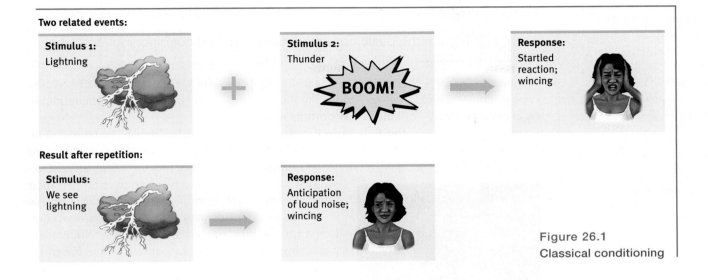

Figure 26.1
Classical conditioning

Conditioning is not the only form of learning. Through **cognitive learning** we acquire mental information that guides our behavior. *Observational learning,* one form of cognitive learning, lets us learn from others' experiences. Chimpanzees, for example, sometimes learn behaviors merely by watching others perform them. If one animal sees another solve a puzzle and gain a food reward, the observer may perform the trick more quickly. So, too, in humans: We look and we learn.

Let's look more closely now at classical conditioning.

Figure 26.2
Operant conditioning

(a) Response: Being polite   (b) Consequence: Getting a treat   (c) Behavior strengthened

cognitive learning the acquisition of mental information, whether by observing events, by watching others, or through language.

Before You Move On

▶ **ASK YOURSELF**

Can you remember some example from your childhood of learning through classical conditioning—perhaps salivating at the sound or smell of some delicious food cooking in your family kitchen? Can you remember an example of operant conditioning, when you repeated (or decided not to repeat) a behavior because you liked (or hated) its consequences? Can you recall watching someone else perform some act and later repeating or avoiding that act?

▶ **TEST YOURSELF**

As we develop, we learn cues that lead us to expect and prepare for good and bad events. We learn to repeat behaviors that bring rewards. And we watch others and learn. What do psychologists call these three types of learning?

Answers to the Test Yourself questions can be found in Appendix E at the end of the book.

classical conditioning a type of learning in which one learns to link two or more stimuli and anticipate events.

behaviorism the view that psychology (1) should be an objective science that (2) studies behavior without reference to mental processes. Most research psychologists today agree with (1) but not with (2).

neutral stimulus (NS) in classical conditioning, a stimulus that elicits no response before conditioning.

Ivan Pavlov "Experimental investigation . . . should lay a solid foundation for a future true science of psychology" (1927).

Classical Conditioning

 What are the basic components of classical conditioning, and what was behaviorism's view of learning?

For many people, the name Ivan Pavlov (1849–1936) rings a bell. His early twentieth-century experiments—now psychology's most famous research—are classics, and the phenomenon he explored we justly call **classical conditioning.**

Pavlov's work laid the foundation for many of psychologist John B. Watson's ideas. In searching for laws underlying learning, Watson (1913) urged his colleagues to discard reference to inner thoughts, feelings, and motives. The science of psychology should instead study how organisms respond to stimuli in their environments, said Watson: "Its theoretical goal is the prediction and control of behavior. Introspection forms no essential part of its methods." Simply said, psychology should be an objective science based on observable behavior.

This view, which influenced North American psychology during the first half of the twentieth century, Watson called **behaviorism.** Pavlov and Watson shared both a disdain for "mentalistic" concepts (such as consciousness) and a belief that the basic laws of learning were the same for all animals—whether dogs or humans. Few researchers today propose that psychology should ignore mental processes, but most now agree that classical conditioning is a basic form of learning by which all organisms adapt to their environment.

Pavlov's Experiments

Pavlov was driven by a lifelong passion for research. After setting aside his initial plan to follow his father into the Russian Orthodox priesthood, Pavlov received a medical degree at age 33 and spent the next two decades studying the digestive system. This work earned him Russia's first Nobel Prize in 1904. But his novel experiments on learning, which consumed the last three decades of his life, earned this feisty scientist his place in history.

Pavlov's new direction came when his creative mind seized on an incidental observation. Without fail, putting food in a dog's mouth caused the animal to salivate. Moreover, the dog began salivating not only at the taste of the food, but also at the mere sight of the food, or at the food dish, or at the person delivering the food, or even at the sound of that person's approaching footsteps. At first, Pavlov considered these "psychic secretions" an annoyance—until he realized they pointed to a simple but important form of learning.

Pavlov and his assistants tried to imagine what the dog was thinking and feeling as it drooled in anticipation of the food. This only led them into fruitless debates. So, to explore the phenomenon more objectively, they experimented. To eliminate other possible influences, they isolated the dog in a small room, secured it in a harness, and attached a device to divert its saliva to a measuring instrument (**FIGURE 26.3**). From the next room, they presented food—first by sliding in a food bowl, later by blowing meat powder into the dog's mouth at a precise moment. They then paired various **neutral stimuli (NS)**—events the dog could see or hear but didn't associate with food—with food in the dog's mouth. If a sight or sound regularly signaled the arrival of food, would the dog learn the link? If so, would it begin salivating in anticipation of the food?

PEANUTS

THE EARS HEAR THE CAN OPENER..

RIGHT AWAY THE STOMACH KNOWS THAT SUPPER IS COMING..

HOW DO THE EARS TELL THE STOMACH?

I'VE NEVER BEEN ABLE TO FIGURE THAT OUT..

Peanuts reprinted with permission of United Features Syndicate

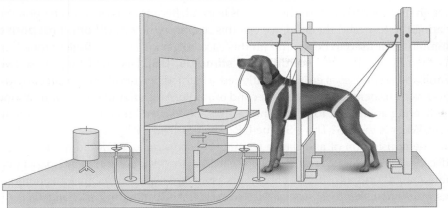

Figure 26.3

Pavlov's device for recording salivation A tube in the dog's cheek collects saliva, which is measured in a cylinder outside the chamber.

The answers proved to be *Yes* and *Yes.* Just before placing food in the dog's mouth to produce salivation, Pavlov sounded a tone. After several pairings of tone and food, the dog, now anticipating the meat powder, began salivating to the tone alone. In later experiments, a buzzer,[1] a light, a touch on the leg, even the sight of a circle set off the drooling. (This procedure works with people, too. When hungry young Londoners viewed abstract figures before smelling peanut butter or vanilla, their brain soon responded in anticipation to the abstract images alone [Gottfried et al., 2003].)

A dog doesn't learn to salivate in response to food in its mouth. Food in the mouth automatically, *unconditionally,* triggers a dog's salivary reflex (**FIGURE 26.4**). Thus, Pavlov called the drooling an **unconditioned response (UR).** And he called the food an **unconditioned stimulus (US).**

---

[1] The "buzzer" (English translation) was perhaps Pavlov's supposed bell—a small electric bell (Tully, 2003).

unconditioned response (UR) in classical conditioning, an unlearned, naturally occurring response (such as salivation) to an unconditioned stimulus (US) (such as food in the mouth).

unconditioned stimulus (US) in classical conditioning, a stimulus that unconditionally—naturally and automatically—triggers a response (UR).

Figure 26.4

Pavlov's classic experiment Pavlov presented a neutral stimulus (a tone) just before an unconditioned stimulus (food in mouth). The neutral stimulus then became a conditioned stimulus, producing a conditioned response.

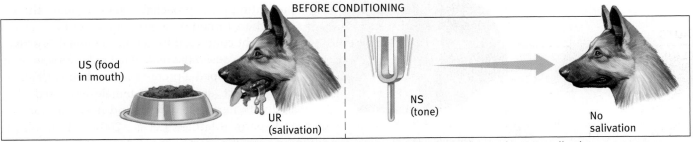

BEFORE CONDITIONING

US (food in mouth) → UR (salivation)

An unconditioned stimulus (US) produces an unconditioned response (UR).

NS (tone) → No salivation

A neutral stimulus produces no salivation response.

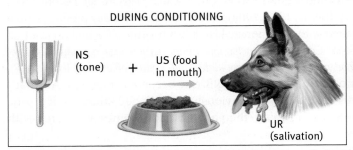

DURING CONDITIONING

NS (tone) + US (food in mouth) → UR (salivation)

The unconditioned stimulus is repeatedly presented just after the neutral stimulus. The unconditioned stimulus continues to produce an unconditioned response.

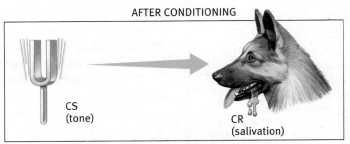

AFTER CONDITIONING

CS (tone) → CR (salivation)

The neutral stimulus alone now produces a conditioned response (CR), thereby becoming a conditioned stimulus (CS).

conditioned response (CR) in classical conditioning, a learned response to a previously neutral (but now conditioned) stimulus (CS).

conditioned stimulus (CS) in classical conditioning, an originally irrelevant stimulus that, after association with an unconditioned stimulus (US), comes to trigger a conditioned response (CR).

acquisition in classical conditioning, the initial stage, when one links a neutral stimulus and an unconditioned stimulus so that the neutral stimulus begins triggering the conditioned response. In operant conditioning, the strengthening of a reinforced response.

higher-order conditioning a procedure in which the conditioned stimulus in one conditioning experience is paired with a new neutral stimulus, creating a second (often weaker) conditioned stimulus. For example, an animal that has learned that a tone predicts food might then learn that a light predicts the tone and begin responding to the light alone. (Also called *second-order conditioning*.)

Salivation in response to the tone, however, is learned. Because it is *conditional* upon the dog's associating the tone and the food, we call this response the **conditioned response (CR).** The stimulus that used to be neutral (in this case, a previously meaningless tone that now triggers the salivation) is the **conditioned stimulus (CS).** Distinguishing these two kinds of stimuli and responses is easy: Conditioned = learned; *un*conditioned = *un*learned.

Let's check your understanding with a second example. An experimenter sounds a tone just before delivering an air puff to your blinking eye. After several repetitions, you blink to the tone alone. What is the NS? The US? The UR? The CS? The CR?[2]

If Pavlov's demonstration of associative learning was so simple, what did he do for the next three decades? What discoveries did his research factory publish in his 532 papers on salivary conditioning (Windholz, 1997)? He and his associates explored five major conditioning processes: *acquisition, extinction, spontaneous recovery, generalization,* and *discrimination.*

ACQUISITION

 In classical conditioning, what are the processes of acquisition, extinction, spontaneous recovery, generalization, and discrimination?

To understand the **acquisition,** or initial learning, of the stimulus-response relationship, Pavlov and his associates had to confront the question of timing: How much time should elapse between presenting the NS (the tone, the light, the touch) and the US (the food)? In most cases, not much—half a second usually works well.

What do you suppose would happen if the food (US) appeared before the tone (NS) rather than after? Would conditioning occur? Not likely. With but a few exceptions, conditioning doesn't happen when the NS follows the US. *Remember, classical conditioning is biologically adaptive because it helps humans and other animals prepare for good or bad events.* To Pavlov's dogs, the originally neutral tone became a (CS) after signaling an important biological event—the arrival of food (US). To deer in the forest, the snapping of a twig (CS) may signal a predator's approach (US). If the good or bad event has already occurred, the tone or the sound won't help the animal prepare.

More recent research on male Japanese quail shows how a CS can signal another important biological event (Domjan, 1992, 1994, 2005). Just before presenting an approachable female quail, the researchers turned on a red light. Over time, as the red light continued to herald the female's arrival, the light caused the male quail to become excited. They developed a preference for their cage's red-light district, and when a female appeared, they mated with her more quickly and released more semen and sperm (Matthews et al., 2007). All in all, the quail's capacity for classical conditioning gives it a reproductive edge.

Eric Isselée/Shutterstock

In humans, too, objects, smells, and sights associated with sexual pleasure can become conditioned stimuli for sexual arousal (Byrne, 1982). Onion breath does not usually produce sexual arousal. But when repeatedly paired with a passionate kiss, it can become a CS and do just that (**FIGURE 26.5**). The larger lesson: *Conditioning helps an animal survive and reproduce—by responding to cues that help it gain food, avoid dangers, locate mates, and produce offspring* (Hollis, 1997).

Through **higher-order conditioning,** a new NS can become a new CS. All that's required is for it to become associated with a previously conditioned stimulus. If a tone regularly signals food and produces salivation, then a light that becomes associated with

[2] NS = tone before procedure; US = air puff; UR = blink to air puff; CS = tone after procedure; CR = blink to tone

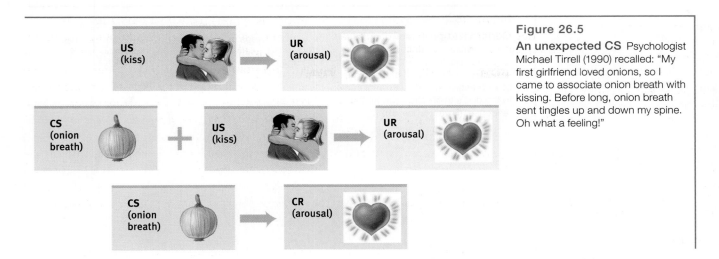

Figure 26.5

An unexpected CS Psychologist Michael Tirrell (1990) recalled: "My first girlfriend loved onions, so I came to associate onion breath with kissing. Before long, onion breath sent tingles up and down my spine. Oh what a feeling!"

the tone may also begin to trigger salivation. Although this higher-order conditioning (also called *second-order conditioning*) tends to be weaker than first-order conditioning, it influences our everyday lives. Imagine that something makes us very afraid (perhaps a guard dog associated with a previous dog bite). If something else, such as the sound of a barking dog, brings to mind that guard dog, the bark alone may make us feel a little afraid.

EXTINCTION AND SPONTANEOUS RECOVERY

What would happen, Pavlov wondered, if after conditioning, the CS occurred repeatedly without the US? If the tone sounded again and again, but no food appeared, would the tone still trigger salivation? The answer was mixed. The dogs salivated less and less, a reaction known as **extinction,** the diminished responding that occurs when the CS (tone) no longer signals an impending US (food). But a different picture emerged when Pavlov allowed several hours to elapse before sounding the tone again. After the delay, the dogs would again begin salivating to the tone (**FIGURE 26.6**). This **spontaneous recovery**— the reappearance of a (weakened) CR after a pause—suggested to Pavlov that extinction was *suppressing* the CR rather than eliminating it.

GENERALIZATION

Pavlov and his students noticed that a dog conditioned to the sound of one tone also responded somewhat to the sound of a new and different tone. Likewise, a dog conditioned to salivate when rubbed would also drool a bit when scratched (Windholz, 1989) or when touched on a different body part (**FIGURE 26.7** on the next page). This tendency to respond likewise to stimuli similar to the CS is called **generalization.**

extinction the diminishing of a conditioned response; occurs in classical conditioning when an unconditioned stimulus (US) does not follow a conditioned stimulus (CS); occurs in operant conditioning when a response is no longer reinforced.

spontaneous recovery the reappearance, after a pause, of an extinguished conditioned response.

generalization the tendency, once a response has been conditioned, for stimuli similar to the conditioned stimulus to elicit similar responses.

AP® Exam Tip

Spontaneous recovery is, in fact, spontaneous. Notice that the extinguished conditioned response returns without any additional pairing with the unconditioned stimulus. It is not a form of acquisition.

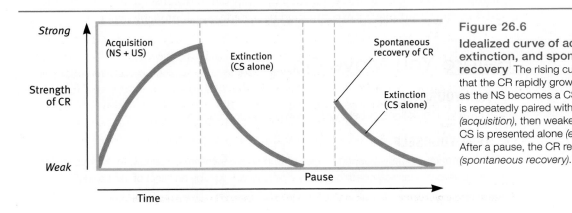

Figure 26.6

Idealized curve of acquisition, extinction, and spontaneous recovery The rising curve shows that the CR rapidly grows stronger as the NS becomes a CS as it is repeatedly paired with the US *(acquisition)*, then weakens as the CS is presented alone *(extinction)*. After a pause, the CR reappears *(spontaneous recovery)*.

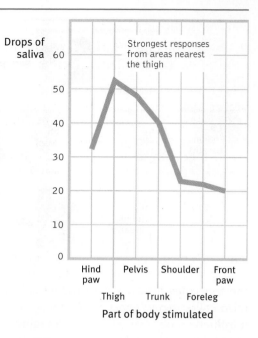

Figure 26.7

Generalization Pavlov demonstrated generalization by attaching miniature vibrators to various parts of a dog's body. After conditioning salivation to stimulation of the thigh, he stimulated other areas. The closer a stimulated spot was to the dog's thigh, the stronger the conditioned response. (From Pavlov, 1927.)

"I don't care if she's a tape dispenser. I love her."

Generalization can be adaptive, as when toddlers taught to fear moving cars also become afraid of moving trucks and motorcycles. And generalized fears can linger. One Argentine writer who underwent torture still recoils with fear when he sees black shoes—his first glimpse of his torturers as they approached his cell. Generalized anxiety reactions have been demonstrated in laboratory studies comparing abused with nonabused children. When an angry face appears on a computer screen, abused children's brain-wave responses are dramatically stronger and longer lasting (Pollak et al., 1998).

Stimuli similar to naturally disgusting objects will, by association, also evoke some disgust, as otherwise desirable fudge does when shaped to resemble dog feces (Rozin et al., 1986). Researchers have also found that we like unfamiliar people more if they look somewhat like someone we've learned to like rather than dislike (Verosky & Todorov, 2010). (They find this by subtly morphing the facial features of someone we've learned to like or dislike onto a novel face.) In each of these human examples, people's emotional reactions to one stimulus have generalized to similar stimuli.

> **AP® Exam Tip**
>
> Generalization and discrimination are introduced in this module, but they don't just apply to classical conditioning. These two concepts will show up in other types of learning as well.

discrimination in classical conditioning, the learned ability to distinguish between a conditioned stimulus and stimuli that do not signal an unconditioned stimulus.

DISCRIMINATION

Pavlov's dogs also learned to respond to the sound of a particular tone and *not* to other tones. This learned ability to *distinguish* between a conditioned stimulus (which predicts the US) and other irrelevant stimuli is called **discrimination.** Being able to recognize differences is adaptive. Slightly different stimuli can be followed by vastly different consequences. Confronted by a guard dog, your heart may race; confronted by a guide dog, it probably will not.

Before You Move On

▶ **ASK YOURSELF**

How have your emotions or behaviors been classically conditioned?

▶ **TEST YOURSELF**

In slasher movies, sexually arousing images of women are sometimes paired with violence against women. Based on classical conditioning principles, what might be an effect of this pairing?

Answers to the Test Yourself questions can be found in Appendix E at the end of the book.

Pavlov's Legacy

 26-4 Why does Pavlov's work remain so important, and what have been some applications of his work to human health and well-being?

What remains today of Pavlov's ideas? A great deal. Most psychologists now agree that classical conditioning is a basic form of learning. Judged by today's knowledge of the interplay of our biology, psychology, and social-cultural environment, Pavlov's ideas were incomplete. But if we see further than Pavlov did, it is because we stand on his shoulders.

Why does Pavlov's work remain so important? If he had merely taught us that old dogs can learn new tricks, his experiments would long ago have been forgotten. Why should we care that dogs can be conditioned to salivate at the sound of a tone? The importance lies first in this finding: *Many other responses to many other stimuli can be classically conditioned in many other organisms*—in fact, in every species tested, from earthworms to fish to dogs to monkeys to people (Schwartz, 1984). Thus, classical conditioning is one way that virtually all organisms learn to adapt to their environment.

Second, *Pavlov showed us how a process such as learning can be studied objectively.* He was proud that his methods involved virtually no subjective judgments or guesses about what went on in a dog's mind. The salivary response is a behavior measurable in cubic centimeters of saliva. Pavlov's success therefore suggested a scientific model for how the young discipline of psychology might proceed—by isolating the basic building blocks of complex behaviors and studying them with objective laboratory procedures.

APPLICATIONS OF CLASSICAL CONDITIONING

Other units in this text—on consciousness, motivation, emotion, health, psychological disorders, and therapy—show how Pavlov's principles can influence human health and well-being. Two examples:

- Former drug users often feel a craving when they are again in the drug-using context—with people or in places they associate with previous highs. Thus, drug counselors advise addicts to steer clear of people and settings that may trigger these cravings (Siegel, 2005).

- Classical conditioning even works on the body's disease-fighting immune system. When a particular taste accompanies a drug that influences immune responses, the taste by itself may come to produce an immune response (Ader & Cohen, 1985).

Pavlov's work also provided a basis for Watson's (1913) idea that human emotions and behaviors, though biologically influenced, are mainly a bundle of conditioned responses. Working with an 11-month-old, Watson and Rosalie Rayner (1920; Harris, 1979) showed how specific fears might be conditioned. Like most infants, "Little Albert" feared loud noises but not white rats. Watson and Rayner presented a white rat and, as Little Albert reached to touch it, struck a hammer against a steel bar just behind his head. After seven repeats of seeing the rat and hearing the frightening noise, Albert burst into tears at the mere sight of the rat. Five days later, he had generalized this startled fear reaction to the sight of a rabbit, a dog, and a sealskin coat, but not to dissimilar objects, such as toys.

For years, people wondered what became of Little Albert. Not until 2009 did some psychologist-sleuths identify him as Douglas Merritte, the son of a campus hospital wet nurse who received $1 for her tot's participation. Sadly, Albert died at age 6, apparently having suffered all his short life from congenital hydrocephalus, complicated later by meningitis. This brain damage probably influenced his behavior during Watson and Rayner's experiment (Beck et al., 2009, 2010; Fridlund et al., 2012a,b). People also wondered what became of Watson. After losing his Johns Hopkins professorship over an affair with Rayner (whom he later married), he joined an advertising agency as the company's resident psychologist. There he used his knowledge of associative learning to conceive many successful advertising campaigns, including one for Maxwell House that helped make the "coffee break" an American custom (Hunt, 1993).

John B. Watson Watson (1924) admitted to "going beyond my facts" when offering his famous boast: "Give me a dozen healthy infants, well-formed, and my own specified world to bring them up in and I'll guarantee to take any one at random and train him to become any type of specialist I might select—doctor, lawyer, artist, merchant-chief, and, yes, even beggar-man and thief, regardless of his talents, penchants, tendencies, abilities, vocations, and race of his ancestors."

Little Albert In Watson and Rayner's experiments, "Little Albert" learned to fear a white rat after repeatedly experiencing a loud noise as the rat was presented. In this experiment, what was the US? The UR? The NS? The CS? The CR?

ANSWERS: The US was the loud noise; the UR was the fear response; the NS was the rat before it was paired with the noise; the CS was the rat after pairing; the CR was fear.

Both images Archives of the History of American Psychology, The University of Akron

The treatment of Little Albert would be unacceptable by today's ethical standards. Also, some psychologists, noting that the infant's fear wasn't learned quickly, had difficulty repeating Watson and Rayner's findings with other children. Nevertheless, Little Albert's learned fears led many psychologists to wonder whether each of us might be a walking repository of conditioned emotions. If so, might extinction procedures or even new conditioning help us change our unwanted responses to emotion-arousing stimuli? One patient, who for 30 years had feared going into an elevator alone, did just that. Following his therapist's advice, he forced himself to enter 20 elevators a day. Within 10 days, his fear had nearly vanished (Ellis & Becker, 1982). With support from AirTran, comedian-writer Mark Malkoff likewise extinguished his fear of flying. He lived on an airplane for 30 days, taking 135 flights that had him in the air 14 hours a day (NPR, 2009). After a week and a half, his fears had faded and he began playing games with fellow passengers. (His favorite antic was the "toilet paper experiment": He'd put one end of a roll in the toilet, unroll the rest down the aisle, and flush. The entire roll would be sucked down in three seconds.) In Units XII and XIII we will see more examples of how psychologists use behavioral techniques to treat emotional disorders and promote personal growth.

Module 26 Review

 What is learning, and what are some basic forms of learning?

- *Learning* is the process of acquiring new and relatively enduring information or behaviors.

- In *associative learning,* we learn that certain events occur together.

- In classical conditioning, we learn to associate two or more stimuli (a *stimulus* is any event or situation that evokes a response).

- In operant conditioning, we learn to associate a response and its consequences.

- Through *cognitive learning,* we acquire mental information that guides our behavior. For example, in observational learning, we learn new behaviors by observing events and watching others.

 What are the basic components of classical conditioning, and what was behaviorism's view of learning?

- *Classical conditioning* is a type of learning in which an organism comes to associate stimuli.

- In classical conditioning, an *NS* is a stimulus that elicits no response before conditioning.

- A *UR* is an event that occurs naturally (such as salivation), in response to some stimulus.

- A *US* is something that naturally and automatically (without learning) triggers the unlearned response (as food in the mouth triggers salivation).

- A *CS* is a previously neutral stimulus (such as a tone) that, after association with a US (such as food) comes to trigger a CR.

- A *CR* is the learned response (salivating) to the originally neutral (but now conditioned) stimulus.

- Ivan Pavlov's work on classical conditioning laid the foundation for *behaviorism,* the view that psychology should be an objective science that studies behavior without reference to mental processes.

- The behaviorists believed that the basic laws of learning are the same for all species, including humans.

 In classical conditioning, what are the processes of acquisition, extinction, spontaneous recovery, generalization, and discrimination?

- In classical conditioning, *acquisition* is associating an NS with the US so that the NS begins triggering the CR.

- Acquisition occurs most readily when the NS is presented just before (ideally, about a half-second before) a US, preparing the organism for the upcoming event. This finding supports the view that classical conditioning is biologically adaptive. Through *higher-order conditioning,* a new NS can become a new CS.

- *Extinction* is diminished responding when the CS no longer signals an impending US.

- *Spontaneous recovery* is the appearance of a formerly extinguished response, following a rest period.

- *Generalization* is the tendency to respond to stimuli that are similar to a CS.

- *Discrimination* is the learned ability to distinguish between a CS and other irrelevant stimuli.

 Why does Pavlov's work remain so important, and what have been some applications of his work to human health and well-being?

- Pavlov taught us that significant psychological phenomena can be studied objectively, and that classical conditioning is a basic form of learning that applies to all species.

- Classical conditioning techniques are used to improve human health and well-being in many areas, including therapy for those recovering from drug addiction and for those overcoming fears. The body's immune system may also respond to classical conditioning.

Multiple-Choice Questions

1. Which of the following is best defined as a relatively permanent change in behavior due to experience?

a. Acquisition
b. Stimulus
c. Learning
d. Habituation
e. Response

2. Lynn is teaching learning. Every time she claps her hands, Charlie turns off the light. When Randy claps in approval of Lynn's presentation, Charlie does not turn the light off. What concept has Charlie demonstrated?

a. Habituation
b. Discrimination
c. Spontaneous recovery
d. Extinction
e. Habituation

3. Classical conditioning is the type of learning in which a person links two or more stimuli and

a. forgets about them.
b. lays them out in sequence.
c. shuts down.
d. anticipates events.
e. receives a reward.

4. In classical conditioning, the unconditioned stimulus

a. naturally triggers a response.
b. is a naturally occurring response.
c. is initially irrelevant, and then comes to trigger a response.
d. objectively studies psychology.
e. is Pavlovian.

5. Students are accustomed to a bell ringing to indicate the end of a class period. The principal decides to substitute popular music for the bell to indicate the end of each class period. Students quickly respond to the music in the same way they did to the bell. What principle does this illustrate?

a. Acquisition
b. Habituation
c. Generalization
d. Functional fixedness
e. Stimulus

6. The work of Ivan Pavlov and John Watson fits best into which of psychology's perspectives?

a. Humanism
b. Gestalt psychology
c. Trait theory
d. Behaviorism
e. Neuropsychology

Practice FRQs

1. Carter's goldfish has been classically conditioned to swim to the top of the fish tank every time the light is turned on. This happened because Carter always turns on the light in the room just before feeding the fish. Identify what each of the following would be in this example, making sure you explain why you know your identification is correct.

- Conditioned response (CR)
- Conditioned stimulus (CS)
- Unconditioned stimulus (US)

2. A researcher paired the sound of a whistle with an air puff to the eye to classically condition Ashley to blink when the whistle alone was sounded. Explain how the researcher could demonstrate the following:

- Generalization
- Extinction
- Spontaneous recovery

(3 points)

Answer

1 point: The goldfish swimming to the top of the tank when the light is turned on is the CR because the fish has learned to behave in this way.

1 point: The light is the CS because the goldfish has learned to respond to this stimulus. The light was initially an NS.

1 point: The food is the US because this stimulus will naturally cause the fish to swim to the top of the tank.

Module 27

Operant Conditioning

Henrik Sorensen

Module Learning Objectives

27-1 Describe operant conditioning, and explain how operant behavior is reinforced and shaped.

27-2 Discuss the differences between positive and negative reinforcement, and identify the basic types of reinforcers.

27-3 Explain how the different reinforcement schedules affect behavior.

27-4 Discuss how punishment and negative reinforcement differ, and explain how punishment affects behavior.

27-5 Describe the controversy over Skinner's views of human behavior.

Operant Conditioning

27-1 What is operant conditioning, and how is operant behavior reinforced and shaped?

It's one thing to classically condition a dog to salivate at the sound of a tone, or a child to fear moving cars. To teach an elephant to walk on its hind legs or a child to say *please,* we turn to operant conditioning.

Classical conditioning and operant conditioning are both forms of associative learning, yet their difference is straightforward:

- *Classical conditioning* forms associations between stimuli (a CS and the US it signals). It also involves *respondent behavior*—actions that are automatic responses to a stimulus (such as salivating in response to meat powder and later in response to a tone).

- In **operant conditioning,** organisms associate their own actions with consequences. Actions followed by reinforcers increase; those followed by punishers often decrease. Behavior that *operates* on the environment to *produce* rewarding or punishing stimuli is called *operant behavior.*

Skinner's Experiments

B. F. Skinner (1904–1990) was a college English major and an aspiring writer who, seeking a new direction, entered psychology graduate school. He went on to become modern behaviorism's most influential and controversial figure. Skinner's work elaborated on what psychologist Edward L. Thorndike (1874–1949) called the **law of effect:** Rewarded

operant conditioning a type of learning in which behavior is strengthened if followed by a reinforcer or diminished if followed by a punisher.

law of effect Thorndike's principle that behaviors followed by favorable consequences become more likely, and that behaviors followed by unfavorable consequences become less likely.

Figure 27.1

Cat in a puzzle box Thorndike used a fish reward to entice cats to find their way out of a puzzle box (right) through a series of maneuvers. The cats' performance tended to improve with successive trials (left), illustrating Thorndike's *law of effect.* (Adapted from Thorndike, 1898.)

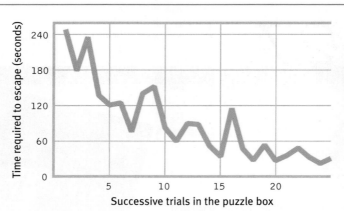

behavior is likely to recur (**FIGURE 27.1**). Using Thorndike's law of effect as a starting point, Skinner developed a behavioral technology that revealed principles of *behavior control.* These principles also enabled him to teach pigeons such unpigeon-like behaviors as walking in a figure 8, playing Ping-Pong, and keeping a missile on course by pecking at a screen target.

Figure 27.2

A Skinner box Inside the box, the rat presses a bar for a food reward. Outside, a measuring device (not shown here) records the animal's accumulated responses.

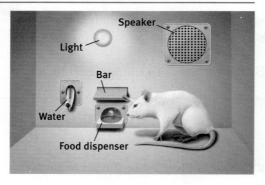

For his pioneering studies, Skinner designed an **operant chamber,** popularly known as a *Skinner box* (**FIGURE 27.2**). The box has a bar (a lever) that an animal presses—or a key (a disc) the animal pecks—to release a reward of food or water. It also has a device that records these responses. This design creates a stage on which rats and others animals act out Skinner's concept of **reinforcement:** any event that strengthens (increases the frequency of) a preceding response. What is reinforcing depends on the animal and the conditions. For people, it may be praise, attention, or a paycheck. For hungry and thirsty rats, food and water work well. Skinner's experiments have done far more than teach us how to pull habits out of a rat. They have explored the precise conditions that foster efficient and enduring learning.

Shaping Behavior

Imagine that you wanted to condition a hungry rat to press a bar. Like Skinner, you could tease out this action with **shaping,** gradually guiding the rat's actions toward the desired behavior. First, you would watch how the animal naturally behaves, so that you could build on its existing behaviors. You might give the rat a bit of food each time it approaches the bar. Once the rat is approaching regularly, you would give the food only when it moves close to the bar, then closer still. Finally, you would require it to touch the bar to get food. With this method of *successive approximations,* you reward responses that are ever-closer to the final desired behavior, and you ignore all other responses. By making rewards contingent on desired behaviors, researchers and animal trainers gradually shape complex behaviors.

Shaping can also help us understand what nonverbal organisms perceive. Can a dog distinguish red and green? Can a baby hear the difference between lower- and higher-pitched tones? If we can shape them to respond to one stimulus and not to another, then we know they can perceive the difference. Such experiments have even shown that some animals can form concepts. When experimenters reinforced pigeons for pecking after

operant chamber in operant conditioning research, a chamber (also known as a *Skinner box*) containing a bar or key that an animal can manipulate to obtain a food or water reinforcer; attached devices record the animal's rate of bar pressing or key pecking.

reinforcement in operant conditioning, any event that *strengthens* the behavior it follows.

shaping an operant conditioning procedure in which reinforcers guide behavior toward closer and closer approximations of the desired behavior.

Reinforcers vary with circumstances What is reinforcing (a heat lamp) to one animal (a cold meerkat) may not be to another (an overheated child). What is reinforcing in one situation (a cold snap at the Taronga Zoo in Sydney) may not be in another (a sweltering summer day).

seeing a human face, but not after seeing other images, the pigeon's behavior showed that it could recognize human faces (Herrnstein & Loveland, 1964). In this experiment, the human face was a **discriminative stimulus.** Like a green traffic light, discriminative stimuli signal that a response will be reinforced. After being trained to discriminate among classes of events or objects—flowers, people, cars, chairs—pigeons can usually identify the category in which a new pictured object belongs (Bhatt et al., 1988; Wasserman, 1993). They have even been trained to discriminate between the music of Bach and Stravinsky (Porter & Neuringer, 1984).

In everyday life, we continually reinforce and shape others' behavior, said Skinner, though we may not mean to do so. Isaac's whining, for example, annoys his dad, but look how he typically responds:

Isaac: Could you take me to the mall?

Father: *(Ignores Isaac and stays focused on his phone)*

Isaac: Dad, I need to go to the mall.

Father: *(distracted)* Uh, yeah, just a minute.

Isaac: DAAAD! The mall!!

Father: Show some manners! Okay, where are my keys. . .

Isaac's whining is reinforced, because he gets something desirable—his dad's attention. Dad's response is reinforced because it gets rid of something aversive—Isaac's whining.

Or consider a teacher who pastes gold stars on a wall chart beside the names of children scoring 100 percent on spelling tests. As everyone can then see, some children consistently do perfect work. The others, who take the same test and may have worked harder than the academic all-stars, get no rewards. The teacher would be better advised to apply the principles of operant conditioning—to reinforce all spellers for gradual improvements (successive approximations toward perfect spelling of words they find challenging).

Types of Reinforcers

27-2 How do positive and negative reinforcement differ, and what are the basic types of reinforcers?

Up to now, we've mainly been discussing **positive reinforcement,** which strengthens a response by *presenting* a typically pleasurable stimulus after a response. But, as we saw in the whining Isaac story, there are *two* basic kinds of reinforcement (**TABLE 27.1** on the next page).

discriminative stimulus
in operant conditioning, a stimulus that elicits a response after association with reinforcement (in contrast to related stimuli not associated with reinforcement).

positive reinforcement
increasing behaviors by presenting positive reinforcers. A positive reinforcer is any stimulus that, when *presented* after a response, strengthens the response.

Shaping a dog to play the piano Using a method of successive approximations, with a food reward for each small step—hopping up on the piano bench, putting her paws on the keys, actually making sounds—this dog was taught to "play" the piano, and now does so frequently!

Table 27.1   Ways to Increase Behavior

Operant Conditioning Term	Description	Examples
Positive reinforcement	Add a desirable stimulus	Pet a dog that comes when you call it; pay the person who paints your house
Negative reinforcement	Remove an aversive stimulus	Take painkillers to end pain; fasten seat belt to end loud beeping

Negative reinforcement *strengthens* a response by *reducing or removing* something negative. Isaac's whining was *positively* reinforced, because Isaac got something desirable—his father's attention. His dad's response to the whining (taking Isaac to the mall) was negatively reinforced, because it ended an aversive event—Isaac's whining. Similarly, taking aspirin may relieve your headache, and pushing the snooze button will silence your annoying alarm. These welcome results provide negative reinforcement and increase the odds that you will repeat these behaviors. For drug addicts, the negative reinforcement of ending withdrawal pangs can be a compelling reason to resume using (Baker et al., 2004). Note that *negative reinforcement is not punishment.* (Some friendly advice: Repeat the last five words in your mind.) Rather, negative reinforcement *removes* a punishing (aversive) event. Think of negative reinforcement as something that provides relief—from that whining teenager, bad headache, or annoying alarm.

Sometimes negative and positive reinforcement coincide. Imagine a worried student who, after goofing off and getting a bad test grade, studies harder for the next test. This increased effort may be *negatively* reinforced by reduced anxiety, and *positively* reinforced by a better grade. Whether it works by reducing something aversive, or by giving something desirable, *reinforcement is any consequence that strengthens behavior.*

HI AND LOIS

PRIMARY AND CONDITIONED REINFORCERS

Getting food when hungry or having a painful headache go away is innately satisfying. These **primary reinforcers** are unlearned. **Conditioned reinforcers,** also called *secondary reinforcers,* get their power through learned association with primary reinforcers. If a rat in a Skinner box learns that a light reliably signals a food delivery, the rat will work to turn on the light. The light has become a conditioned reinforcer. Our lives are filled with conditioned reinforcers—money, good grades, a pleasant tone of voice—each of which has been linked with more basic rewards.

IMMEDIATE AND DELAYED REINFORCERS

Let's return to the imaginary shaping experiment in which you were conditioning a rat to press a bar. Before performing this "wanted" behavior, the hungry rat will engage in a sequence of "unwanted" behaviors—scratching, sniffing, and moving around. If you present food immediately after any one of these behaviors, the rat will likely repeat that rewarded behavior. But what if the rat presses the bar while you are distracted, and you delay giving the reinforcer? If the delay lasts longer than about 30 seconds, the rat will not learn to press the bar. You will have reinforced other incidental behaviors—more sniffing and moving—that intervened after the bar press.

Unlike rats, humans do respond to delayed reinforcers: the paycheck at the end of the week, the good grade at the end of the term, the trophy at the end of the season. Indeed, to function effectively we must learn to delay gratification. In laboratory testing, some 4-year-olds show this ability. In choosing a candy, they prefer having a big one tomorrow to munching on a small one right now. Learning to control our impulses in order to achieve more valued rewards is a big step toward maturity (Logue, 1998a,b). No wonder children who make such choices have tended to become socially competent and high-achieving adults (Mischel et al., 1989).

To our detriment, small but immediate consequences (the enjoyment of late-night videos or texting, for example) are sometimes more alluring than big but delayed consequences (feeling alert tomorrow). For many teens, the immediate gratification of risky, unprotected sex in passionate moments prevails over the delayed gratifications of safe sex or saved sex. And for many people, the immediate rewards of today's gas-guzzling vehicles, air travel, and air conditioning prevail over the bigger future consequences of global climate change, rising seas, and extreme weather.

"Oh, not bad. The light comes on, I press the bar, they write me a check. How about you?"

Reinforcement Schedules

 27-3 How do different reinforcement schedules affect behavior?

In most of our examples, the desired response has been reinforced every time it occurs. But **reinforcement schedules** vary. With **continuous reinforcement,** learning occurs rapidly, which makes this the best choice for mastering a behavior. But extinction also occurs rapidly. When reinforcement stops—when we stop delivering food after the rat presses the bar—the behavior soon stops. If a normally dependable candy machine fails to deliver a chocolate bar twice in a row, we stop putting money into it (although a week later we may exhibit spontaneous recovery by trying again).

Real life rarely provides continuous reinforcement. Salespeople do not make a sale with every pitch. But they persist because their efforts are occasionally rewarded. This persistence is typical with **partial (intermittent) reinforcement** schedules, in which responses are sometimes reinforced, sometimes not. Learning is slower to appear, but *resistance to extinction* is greater than with continuous reinforcement. Imagine a pigeon that has learned to peck a key to obtain food. If you gradually phase out the food delivery until it occurs only rarely, in no predictable pattern, the pigeon may peck 150,000 times without a reward (Skinner, 1953). Gambling machines and lottery tickets reward gamblers in much the same way—occasionally and unpredictably. And like pigeons, slot players keep trying, time and time again. With intermittent reinforcement, hope springs eternal.

Lesson for child caregivers: Partial reinforcement also works with children. *Occasionally* giving in to children's tantrums for the sake of peace and quiet intermittently reinforces the tantrums. This is the very best procedure for making a behavior persist.

Skinner (1961) and his collaborators compared four schedules of partial reinforcement. Some are rigidly fixed, some unpredictably variable.

Fixed-ratio schedules reinforce behavior after a set number of responses. Coffee shops may reward us with a free drink after every 10 purchased. In the laboratory, rats may be reinforced on a fixed ratio of, say, one food pellet for every 30 responses. Once conditioned, animals will pause only briefly after a reinforcer before returning to a high rate of responding (**FIGURE 27.3** on the next page).

---

reinforcement schedule a pattern that defines how often a desired response will be reinforced.

continuous reinforcement reinforcing the desired response every time it occurs.

partial (intermittent) reinforcement reinforcing a response only part of the time; results in slower acquisition of a response but much greater resistance to extinction than does continuous reinforcement.

fixed-ratio schedule in operant conditioning, a reinforcement schedule that reinforces a response only after a specified number of responses.

"The charm of fishing is that it is the pursuit of what is elusive but attainable, a perpetual series of occasions for hope." -SCOTTISH AUTHOR JOHN BUCHAN (1875–1940)

Figure 27.3

Intermittent reinforcement schedules
Skinner's laboratory pigeons produced these response patterns to each of four reinforcement schedules. (Reinforcers are indicated by diagonal marks.) For people, as for pigeons, reinforcement linked to number of responses (a *ratio schedule*) produces a higher response rate than reinforcement linked to amount of time elapsed (an *interval schedule*). But the predictability of the reward also matters. An unpredictable *(variable)* schedule produces more consistent responding than does a predictable *(fixed)* schedule.
Adapted from "Teaching Machines" by B. F. Skinner. Copyright © 1961, Scientific American, Inc. All Rights Reserved.

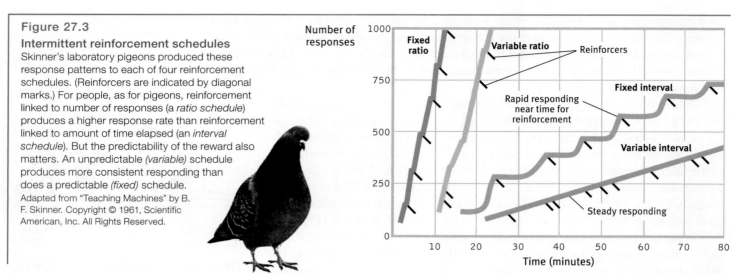

Vitaly Titov & Maria Sidelnikova/Shutterstock

variable-ratio schedule
in operant conditioning, a reinforcement schedule that reinforces a response after an unpredictable number of responses.

fixed-interval schedule
in operant conditioning, a reinforcement schedule that reinforces a response only after a specified time has elapsed.

variable-interval schedule
in operant conditioning, a reinforcement schedule that reinforces a response at unpredictable time intervals.

Variable-ratio schedules provide reinforcers after a seemingly unpredictable number of responses. This is what slot-machine players and fly-casting anglers experience—unpredictable reinforcement—and what makes gambling and fly fishing so hard to extinguish even when both are getting nothing for something. Because reinforcers increase as the number of responses increases, variable-ratio schedules produce high rates of responding.

Fixed-interval schedules reinforce the first response after a fixed time period. Animals on this type of schedule tend to respond more frequently as the anticipated time for reward draws near. People check more frequently for the mail as the delivery time approaches. A hungry child jiggles the Jell-O more often to see if it has set. Pigeons peck keys more rapidly as the time for reinforcement draws nearer. This produces a choppy stop-start pattern rather than a steady rate of response (see Figure 27.3).

Variable-interval schedules reinforce the first response after *varying* time intervals. Like the longed-for responses that finally reward persistence in rechecking e-mail or Facebook, variable-interval schedules tend to produce slow, steady responding. This makes sense, because there is no knowing when the waiting will be over (**TABLE 27.2**).

In general, response rates are higher when reinforcement is linked to the number of responses (a ratio schedule) rather than to time (an interval schedule). But responding is more consistent when reinforcement is unpredictable (a variable schedule) than when it is predictable (a fixed schedule). Animal behaviors differ, yet Skinner (1956) contended

Table 27.2	Schedules of Reinforcement	
	Fixed	Variable
Ratio	*Every so many:* reinforcement after every *nth* behavior, such as buy 10 coffees, get 1 free, or pay per product unit produced	*After an unpredictable number:* reinforcement after a random number of behaviors, as when playing slot machines or fly casting
Interval	*Every so often:* reinforcement for behavior after a fixed time, such as Tuesday discount prices	*Unpredictably often:* reinforcement for behavior after a random amount of time, as in checking for a Facebook response

that the reinforcement principles of operant conditioning are universal. It matters little, he said, what response, what reinforcer, or what species you use. The effect of a given reinforcement schedule is pretty much the same: "Pigeon, rat, monkey, which is which? It doesn't matter. . . . Behavior shows astonishingly similar properties."

Punishment

 27-4 How does punishment differ from negative reinforcement, and how does punishment affect behavior?

Reinforcement increases a behavior; **punishment** does the opposite. A *punisher* is any consequence that *decreases* the frequency of a preceding behavior (**TABLE 27.3**). Swift and sure punishers can powerfully restrain unwanted behavior. The rat that is shocked after touching a forbidden object and the child who is burned by touching a hot stove will learn not to repeat those behaviors. A dog that has learned to come running at the sound of an electric can opener will stop coming if its owner runs the machine to attract the dog and banish it to the basement.

Table 27.3 Ways to Decrease Behavior

Type of Punisher	Description	Examples
Positive punishment	Administer an aversive stimulus	Spray water on a barking dog; give a traffic ticket for speeding
Negative punishment	Withdraw a rewarding stimulus	Take away a teen's driving privileges; revoke a library card for nonpayment of fines

Criminal behavior, much of it impulsive, is also influenced more by swift and sure punishers than by the threat of severe sentences (Darley & Alter, 2011). Thus, when Arizona introduced an exceptionally harsh sentence for first-time drunk drivers, the drunk-driving rate changed very little. But when Kansas City police started patrolling a high crime area to increase the sureness and swiftness of punishment, that city's crime rate dropped dramatically.

How should we interpret the punishment studies in relation to parenting practices? Many psychologists and supporters of nonviolent parenting note four major drawbacks of physical punishment (Gershoff, 2002; Marshall, 2002).

1. *Punished behavior is suppressed, not forgotten. This temporary state may (negatively) reinforce parents' punishing behavior.* The child swears, the parent swats, the parent hears no more swearing and feels the punishment successfully stopped the behavior. No wonder spanking is a hit with so many U.S. parents of 3- and 4-year-olds—more than 9 in 10 of whom acknowledged spanking their children (Kazdin & Benjet, 2003).
2. *Punishment teaches discrimination among situations.* In operant conditioning, *discrimination* occurs when an organism learns that certain responses, but not others, will be reinforced. Did the punishment effectively end the child's swearing? Or did the child simply learn that it's not okay to swear around the house, though okay elsewhere?
3. *Punishment can teach fear.* In operant conditioning, *generalization* occurs when an organism's response to similar stimuli is also reinforced. A punished child may associate fear not only with the undesirable behavior but also with the person who delivered the punishment or the place it occurred. Thus, children may learn to fear a punishing teacher and try to avoid school, or may become more anxious (Gershoff et al., 2010). For such reasons, most European countries and most U.S. states now ban

AP® Exam Tip

Remember that *any kind of reinforcement* (positive, negative, primary, conditioned, immediate, delayed, continuous, or partial) encourages the behavior. *Any kind of punishment* discourages the behavior. Positive and negative do not refer to values—it's not that positive reinforcement (or punishment) is the good kind and negative is the bad. Think of positive and negative mathematically; a stimulus is added with positive reinforcement (or punishment) and a stimulus is subtracted with negative reinforcement (or punishment).

punishment an event that tends to *decrease* the behavior that it follows.

Children see, children do?
Children who often experience physical punishment tend to display more aggression.

B. F. Skinner "I am sometimes asked, 'Do you think of yourself as you think of the organisms you study?' The answer is yes. So far as I know, my behavior at any given moment has been nothing more than the product of my genetic endowment, my personal history, and the current setting" (1983).

hitting children in schools and child-care institutions (www.stophitting.com). Thirty-three countries, including those in Scandinavia, further outlaw hitting by parents, providing children the same legal protection given to spouses.

4. *Physical punishment may increase aggression by modeling aggression as a way to cope with problems.* Studies find that spanked children are at increased risk for aggression (and depression and low self-esteem). We know, for example, that many aggressive delinquents and abusive parents come from abusive families (Straus & Gelles, 1980; Straus et al., 1997).

Some researchers note a problem. Well, *yes,* they say, physically punished children may be more aggressive, for the same reason that people who have undergone psychotherapy are more likely to suffer depression—because they had preexisting problems that triggered the treatments (Larzelere, 2000, 2004). Which is the chicken and which is the egg? Correlations don't hand us an answer.

If one adjusts for preexisting antisocial behavior, then an occasional single swat or two to misbehaving 2- to 6-year-olds looks more effective (Baumrind et al., 2002; Larzelere & Kuhn, 2005). That is especially so if two other conditions are met:

1. The swat is used only as a backup when milder disciplinary tactics, such as a time-out (removing them from reinforcing surroundings), fail.
2. The swat is combined with a generous dose of reasoning and reinforcing.

Other researchers remain unconvinced. After controlling for prior misbehavior, they report that more frequent spankings of young children predict future aggressiveness (Grogan-Kaylor, 2004; Taylor et al., 2010).

Parents of delinquent youths are often unaware of how to achieve desirable behaviors without screaming at or hitting their children (Patterson et al., 1982). Training programs can help transform dire threats ("Apologize right now or I'm taking that cell phone away!") into positive incentives ("You're welcome to have your phone back when you apologize."). Stop and think about it. Aren't many threats of punishment just as forceful, and perhaps more effective, when rephrased positively? Thus, "If you don't get your homework done, I'm not giving you money for a movie!" would better be phrased as . . . .

In classrooms, too, teachers can give feedback on papers by saying, "No, but try this . . ." and "Yes, that's it!" Such responses reduce unwanted behavior while reinforcing more desirable alternatives. Remember: *Punishment tells you what not to do; reinforcement tells you what to do.*

What punishment often teaches, said Skinner, is how to avoid it. Most psychologists now favor an emphasis on reinforcement.

Skinner's Legacy

27-5 Why did Skinner's ideas provoke controversy?

B. F. Skinner stirred a hornet's nest with his outspoken beliefs. He repeatedly insisted that external influences (not internal thoughts and feelings) shape behavior. And he urged people to use operant principles to influence others' behavior at school, work, and home. Knowing that behavior is shaped by its results, he said we should use rewards to evoke more desirable behavior.

Skinner's critics objected, saying that he dehumanized people by neglecting their personal freedom and by seeking to control their actions. Skinner's reply: External consequences already haphazardly control people's behavior. Why not administer those consequences toward human betterment? Wouldn't reinforcers be more humane than the punishments used in homes, schools, and prisons? And if it is humbling to think that our history has shaped us, doesn't this very idea also give us hope that we can shape our future?

Before You Move On

▶ **ASK YOURSELF**

Does your social media behavior (such as checking for new messages) make sense now that you've learned about the different kinds of reinforcement schedules?

▶ **TEST YOURSELF**

Fill in the three blanks below with one of the following terms: negative reinforcement (NR), positive punishment (PP), and negative punishment (NP). The first answer, positive reinforcement (PR) is provided for you.

Type of Stimulus	Give It	Take It Away
Desired (for example, a teen's use of the car):	1. PR	2.
Undesired/aversive (for example, an insult):	3.	4.

Answers to the Test Yourself questions can be found in Appendix E at the end of the book.

Module 27 Review

 What is operant conditioning, and how is operant behavior reinforced and shaped?

- In *operant conditioning,* behaviors followed by reinforcers increase; those followed by punishers often decrease.

- Expanding on Edward Thorndike's *law of effect,* B. F. Skinner and others found that the behavior of rats or pigeons placed in an *operant chamber* (Skinner box) can be *shaped* by using reinforcers to guide closer and closer approximations of the desired behavior.

 How do positive and negative reinforcement differ, and what are the basic types of reinforcers?

- *Reinforcement* is any consequence that strengthens behavior. *Positive reinforcement* adds a desirable stimulus to increase the frequency of a behavior. *Negative reinforcement* removes an aversive stimulus to increase the frequency of a behavior.

- *Primary reinforcers* (such as receiving food when hungry or having nausea end during an illness) are innately satisfying—no learning is required.

- *Conditioned* (or secondary) *reinforcers* (such as cash) are satisfying because we have learned to associate them with more basic rewards (such as the food or medicine we buy with them).

- Immediate reinforcers (such as a purchased treat) offer immediate payback; delayed reinforcers (such as a weekly paycheck) require the ability to delay gratification.

How do different reinforcement schedules affect behavior?

- A *reinforcement schedule* defines how often a response will be reinforced.

- In *continuous reinforcement* (reinforcing desired responses every time they occur), learning is rapid, but so is extinction if rewards cease. In *partial (intermittent) reinforcement* (reinforcing responses only sometimes), initial learning is slower, but the behavior is much more resistant to extinction.

- *Fixed-ratio schedules* reinforce behaviors after a set number of responses; *variable-ratio schedules,* after an unpredictable number.

- *Fixed-interval schedules* reinforce behaviors after set time periods; *variable-interval schedules,* after unpredictable time periods.

 How does punishment differ from negative reinforcement, and how does punishment affect behavior?

- *Punishment* administers an undesirable consequence (such as spanking) or withdraws something desirable (such as taking away a favorite toy) in an attempt to decrease the frequency of a behavior (a child's disobedience).

- Negative reinforcement (taking an aspirin) removes an aversive stimulus (a headache). This desired consequence (freedom from pain) increases the likelihood that the behavior (taking aspirin to end pain) will be repeated.

- Punishment can have undesirable side effects, such as suppressing rather than changing unwanted behaviors; teaching aggression; creating fear; encouraging discrimination (so that the undesirable behavior appears when the punisher is not present); and fostering depression and low self-esteem.

 Why did Skinner's ideas provoke controversy?

- Critics of Skinner's principles believed the approach dehumanized people by neglecting their personal freedom and seeking to control their actions. Skinner replied that people's actions are already controlled by external consequences, and that reinforcement is more humane than punishment as a means for controlling behavior.

Multiple-Choice Questions

1. What do we call the kind of learning in which behavior is strengthened if followed by a reinforcer?
   a. Operant conditioning
   b. Respondent behavior
   c. Classical conditioning
   d. Shaping
   e. Punishment

2. Which of the following best describes a discriminative stimulus?
   a. Something that elicits a response after association with a reinforcer
   b. An innately reinforcing stimulus
   c. Something that when removed increases the likelihood of the behavior
   d. An event that decreases the behavior it follows
   e. An amplified stimulus feeding back information to responses

3. Thorndike's principle that behaviors followed by favorable consequences become more likely is known as what?
   a. Law of effect
   b. Operant conditioning
   c. Shaping
   d. Respondent behavior
   e. Discrimination

4. All of the following are examples of primary reinforcers except a
   a. rat's food reward in a Skinner box.
   b. cold drink on a hot day.
   c. high score on an exam for which a student studied diligently.
   d. hug from a loved one.
   e. large meal following an extended time without food.

Practice FRQs

1. Mom is frustrated because 3-year-old Maya has started to spit frequently. She has decided to temporarily put away one of Maya's toys every time she spits. Mom is going to continue this until Maya has stopped spitting.

   • Explain whether Mom's plan uses reinforcement or punishment.

   • Explain whether Mom's plan is a positive or negative form of reinforcement or punishment.

Answer

1 point: The plan uses punishment, because it is designed to reduce the frequency of spitting.

1 point: This is negative punishment because toys are being taken away from Maya.

2. A business owner is considering different compensation plans for her sales force. Identify what schedule of reinforcement is reflected in each of the following plans, making sure you explain why each answer is correct:

   • The owner will pay a $1,500 bonus each time a hundred units are sold.

   • The owner will have a lottery each month. Each salesperson will get one lottery ticket for every one hundred units sold. The salesperson with the winning ticket will get $5,000.

   • The owner will pay each salesperson a monthly salary that does not depend on units sold.

   (3 points)

Module 28

Operant Conditioning's Applications, and Comparison to Classical Conditioning

Andersen Ross/Blend Images/Corbis

Module Learning Objectives

 Identify some ways to apply operant conditioning principles at school, in sports, at work, at home, and for self-improvement.

 Identify the characteristics that distinguish operant conditioning from classical conditioning.

Applications of Operant Conditioning

28-1 How might Skinner's operant conditioning principles be applied at school, in sports, at work, at home, and for self-improvement?

Would you like to apply operant conditioning principles to your own life—to be a healthier person, a more successful student, or a high-achieving athlete? Reinforcement technologies are at work in schools, sports, workplaces, and homes, and these principles can support our self-improvement as well (Flora, 2004).

AT SCHOOL

Computer-assisted learning
Computers have helped realize Skinner's goal of individually paced instruction with immediate feedback.

Christopher Halloran/Shutterstock

Fifty years ago, Skinner envisioned a day when "teaching machines and textbooks" would shape learning in small steps, immediately reinforcing correct responses. He believed that such machines and texts would revolutionize education and free teachers to focus on each student's special needs. "Good instruction demands two things," Skinner said. "Students must be told immediately whether what they do is right or wrong and, when right, they must be directed to the step to be taken next."

Skinner might be pleased to know that many of his ideals for education are now possible. Teachers used to find it difficult to pace material to each student's rate of learning, and to provide prompt feedback.

Electronic adaptive quizzing does both. Students move through quizzes at their own pace, according to their own level of understanding. And they get immediate feedback on their efforts.

IN SPORTS

The key to shaping behavior in athletic performance, as elsewhere, is first reinforcing small successes and then gradually increasing the challenge. Golf students can learn putting by starting with very short putts, and then, as they build mastery, eventually stepping back farther and farther. Novice batters can begin with half swings at an oversized ball pitched from 10 feet away, giving them the immediate pleasure of smacking the ball. As the hitters' confidence builds with their success and they achieve mastery at each level, the pitcher gradually moves back—to 15, then 22, 30, and 40.5 feet—and eventually introduces a standard baseball. Compared with children taught by conventional methods, those trained by this behavioral method have shown faster skill improvement (Simek & O'Brien, 1981, 1988).

In sports as in the laboratory, the accidental timing of rewards can produce *superstitious behaviors*. If a Skinner box food dispenser gives a pellet of food every 15 minutes, whatever the animal happened to be doing just before the food arrives (perhaps scratching itself) is more likely to be repeated and reinforced, which occasionally can produce a persistent superstitious behavior. Likewise, if a baseball or softball player gets a hit after tapping the plate with the bat, he or she may be more likely to do so again. Over time the player may experience partial reinforcement for what becomes a superstitious behavior.

AT WORK

Knowing that reinforcers influence productivity, many organizations have invited employees to share the risks and rewards of company ownership. Others focus on reinforcing a job well done. Rewards are most likely to increase productivity if the desired performance has been well defined and is achievable. The message for managers? *Reward specific, achievable behaviors, not vaguely defined "merit."*

Operant conditioning also reminds us that reinforcement should be *immediate*. IBM legend Thomas Watson understood. When he observed an achievement, he wrote the employee a check on the spot (Peters & Waterman, 1982). But rewards need not be material or lavish. An effective manager may simply walk the floor and sincerely affirm people for good work, or write notes of appreciation for a completed project. As Skinner said, "How much richer would the whole world be if the reinforcers in daily life were more effectively contingent on productive work?"

AT HOME

As we have seen, parents can learn from operant conditioning practices. Parent-training researchers remind us that by saying, "Get ready for bed" but caving in to protests or defiance, parents reinforce such whining and arguing (Wierson & Forehand, 1994). Exasperated, they may then yell or gesture menacingly. When the child, now frightened, obeys, that reinforces the parents' angry behavior. Over time, a destructive parent-child relationship develops.

AP® Exam Tip

Notice how useful operant conditioning is. People with an understanding of the principles of operant conditioning possess a tremendous tool for changing behavior. If you don't like the way your friends, teachers, coaches, or parents behave, pay attention to the uses of operant conditioning!

"I wrote another five hundred words. Can I have another cookie?"

To disrupt this cycle, parents should remember that basic rule of shaping: *Notice people doing something right and affirm them for it.* Give children attention and other reinforcers when they are behaving *well.* Target a specific behavior, reward it, and watch it increase. When children misbehave or are defiant, don't yell at them or hit them. Simply explain the misbehavior and give them a time-out.

FOR SELF-IMPROVEMENT

Finally, we can use operant conditioning in our own lives (see Close-up: Training Our Partners). To build up your *self-control,* you need to reinforce your own desired behaviors (perhaps to exercise more often) and extinguish the undesired ones (to stop texting while studying, for example). Psychologists suggest taking these steps:

1. *State your goal in measurable terms, and announce it.* You might, for example, aim to boost your study time by an hour a day and share that goal with some close friends.
2. *Monitor how often you engage in your desired behavior.* You might log your current study time, noting under what conditions you do and don't study. (When I began writing textbooks, I logged how I spent my time each day and was amazed to discover how much time I was wasting.)
3. *Reinforce the desired behavior.* To increase your study time, give yourself a reward (a snack or some activity you enjoy) only after you finish your extra hour of study. Agree with your friends that you will join them for weekend activities only if you have met your realistic weekly studying goal.

Close-up

Training Our Partners   By Amy Sutherland

For a book I was writing about a school for exotic animal trainers, I started commuting from Maine to California, where I spent my days watching students do the seemingly impossible: teaching hyenas to pirouette on command, cougars to offer their paws for a nail clipping, and baboons to skateboard.

I listened, rapt, as professional trainers explained how they taught dolphins to flip and elephants to paint. Eventually it hit me that the same techniques might work on that stubborn but lovable species, the American husband.

The central lesson I learned from exotic animal trainers is that I should reward behavior I like and ignore behavior I don't. After all, you don't get a sea lion to balance a ball on the end of its nose by nagging. The same goes for the American husband.

Back in Maine, I began thanking Scott if he threw one dirty shirt into the hamper. If he threw in two, I'd kiss him. Meanwhile, I would step over any soiled clothes on the floor without one sharp word, though I did sometimes kick them

under the bed. But as he basked in my appreciation, the piles became smaller.

I was using what trainers call "approximations," rewarding the small steps toward learning a whole new behavior. . . . Once I started thinking this way, I couldn't stop. At the school in California, I'd be scribbling notes on how to walk an emu or have a wolf accept you as a pack member, but I'd be thinking, "I can't wait to try this on Scott. . . ."

After two years of exotic animal training, my marriage is far smoother, my husband much easier to love. I used to take his faults personally; his dirty clothes on the floor were an affront, a symbol of how he didn't care enough about me. But thinking of my husband as an exotic species gave me the distance I needed to consider our differences more objectively.

Excerpted with permission from Sutherland, A., (2006, June 25). What Shamu taught me about a happy marriage, *New York Times.*

4. *Reduce the rewards gradually.* As your new behaviors become more habitual, give yourself a mental pat on the back instead of a cookie.

In addition, we can literally learn from ourselves. There is some evidence that when we have feedback about our bodily responses, we can sometimes change those responses. (See Close-up: Biofeedback.)

Close-up

Biofeedback

Knowing the damaging effects of stress, could we train people to counteract stress, bringing their heart rate and blood pressure under conscious control? When a few psychologists started experimenting with this idea, many of their colleagues thought them foolish. After all, these functions are controlled by the autonomic ("involuntary") nervous system. Then, in the late 1960s, experiments by respected psychologists made the skeptics wonder. Neal Miller, for one, found that rats could modify their heartbeat if given pleasurable brain stimulation when their heartbeat increased or decreased. Later research revealed that some paralyzed humans could also learn to control their blood pressure (Miller & Brucker, 1979).

Miller was experimenting with **biofeedback,** a system of recording, amplifying, and feeding back information about subtle physiological responses. Biofeedback instruments mirror the results of a person's own efforts, thereby allowing the person to learn techniques for controlling a particular physiological response (**FIGURE 28.1**). After a decade of study, however, researchers decided the initial claims for biofeedback were overblown and oversold (Miller, 1985). A 1995 National Institutes of Health panel declared that biofeedback works best on tension headaches.

> **biofeedback** a system for electronically recording, amplifying, and feeding back information regarding a subtle physiological state, such as blood pressure or muscle tension.

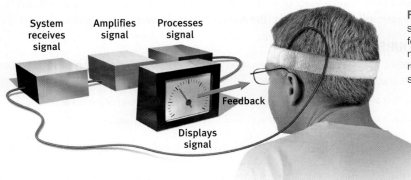

Figure 28.1 **Biofeedback systems** Biofeedback systems—such as this one, which records tension in the forehead muscle of a headache sufferer—allow people to monitor their subtle physiological responses. As this man relaxes his forehead muscle, the pointer on the display screen (or a tone) may go lower.

Contrasting Classical and Operant Conditioning

28-2 How does operant conditioning differ from classical conditioning?

> **respondent behavior** behavior that occurs as an automatic response to some stimulus.
>
> **operant behavior** behavior that operates on the environment, producing consequences.

Both classical and operant conditioning are forms of *associative learning.* Both involve *acquisition, extinction, spontaneous recovery, generalization,* and *discrimination.* But these two forms of learning also differ. Through classical (Pavlovian) conditioning, we associate different stimuli we do not control, and we respond automatically **(respondent behaviors)** (**TABLE 28.1** on the next page). Through operant conditioning, we associate our own behaviors that act on our environment to produce rewarding or punishing stimuli **(operant behaviors)** with their consequences.

As we will next, our biology and cognitive processes influence both classical and operant conditioning.

> "O! This learning, what a thing it is." -WILLIAM SHAKESPEARE, *THE TAMING OF THE SHREW*, 1597

Table 28.1 Comparison of Classical and Operant Conditioning

	Classical Conditioning	Operant Conditioning
Basic idea	Organism associates events.	Organism associates behavior and resulting events.
Response	Involuntary, automatic.	Voluntary, operates on environment.
Acquisition	Associating events; NS is paired with US and becomes CS.	Associating response with a consequence (reinforcer or punisher).
Extinction	CR decreases when CS is repeatedly presented alone.	Responding decreases when reinforcement stops.
Spontaneous recovery	The reappearance, after a rest period, of an extinguished CR.	The reappearance, after a rest period, of an extinguished response.
Generalization	The tendency to respond to stimuli similar to the CS.	Organism's response to similar stimuli is also reinforced.
Discrimination	The learned ability to distinguish between a CS and other stimuli that do not signal a US.	Organism learns that certain responses, but not others, will be reinforced.

Before You Move On

▶ **ASK YOURSELF**

Can you recall a time when a teacher, coach, family member, or employer helped you learn something by shaping your behavior in little steps until you achieved your goal?

▶ **TEST YOURSELF**

Salivating in response to a tone paired with food is a(n) _____ behavior; pressing a bar to obtain food is a(n) _____ behavior.

Answers to the Test Yourself questions can be found in Appendix E at the end of the book.

Module 28 Review

28-1 How might Skinner's operant conditioning principles be applied at school, in sports, at work, at home, and for self-improvement?

- At school, teachers can use shaping techniques to guide students' behaviors, and they can use electronic adaptive quizzing to provide immediate feedback.

- In sports, coaches can build players' skills and self-confidence by rewarding small improvements.

- At work, managers can boost productivity and morale by rewarding well-defined and achievable behaviors.

- At home, parents can reward desired behaviors but not undesirable ones.

- We can shape our own behaviors by stating our goals, monitoring the frequency of desired behaviors, reinforcing desired behaviors, and gradually reducing rewards as behaviors become habitual.

28-2   How does operant conditioning differ from classical conditioning?

- In operant conditioning, an organism learns associations between its own behavior and resulting events; this form of conditioning involves *operant behavior* (behavior that operates on the environment, producing rewarding or punishing consequences).

- In classical conditioning, the organism forms associations between stimuli—events it does not control; this form of conditioning involves *respondent behavior* (automatic responses to some stimulus).

Multiple-Choice Questions

1. What do we call it when the CR decreases as the CS is repeatedly presented alone?

   a. Generalization
   b. Discrimination
   c. Spontaneous recovery
   d. Extinction
   e. Acquisition

2. The basic idea behind classical conditioning is that the organism

   a. associates events.
   b. associates behavior and resulting events.
   c. voluntarily operates on the environment.
   d. associates response with a consequence.
   e. quits responding when reward stops.

3. What do we call the reappearance, after a rest period, of an extinguished response?

   a. Acquisition
   b. Spontaneous recovery
   c. Discrimination
   d. Operant conditioning
   e. Classical conditioning

4. What do we call behavior that occurs as an automatic response to some stimulus?

   a. Respondent behavior
   b. Operant behavior
   c. Extinguished behavior
   d. Biofeedback conditioning
   e. Skinnerian conditioning

5. Superstitious behavior can be produced by

   a. careful manipulation of a classical conditioning experiment.
   b. the accidental timing of rewards.
   c. possession of a large number of traditionally lucky items.
   d. cognitive awareness of superstitious behavior in others.
   e. the change in a reinforcement schedule from ratio to interval.

Practice FRQs

1. Explain two differences between classical and operant conditioning.

Answer

Any two differences described in Table 28.1 can be used to answer. Examples include:

1 point: Classical conditioning involves involuntary responses, but operant conditioning involves voluntary responses.

1 point: In classical conditioning, the learner associates two events (a conditioned stimulus with an unconditioned stimulus). In operant conditioning, the learner associates a behavior with a consequence.

2. Raud is planning to use operant conditioning to help him reach his self-improvement goal of running in his community's 10-kilometer race in July. Explain four things Raud should include in his self-improvement plan.

(4 points)

Module 29

Biology, Cognition, and Learning

Chris Schmidt/Getty Images

Module Learning Objectives

29-1 Explain how biological constraints affect classical and operant conditioning.

29-2 Explain how cognitive processes affect classical and operant conditioning.

29-3 Identify the two ways that people learn to cope with personal problems.

29-4 Describe how a perceived lack of control can affect people's behavior and health.

From drooling dogs, running rats, and pecking pigeons we have learned much about the basic processes of learning. But conditioning principles don't tell us the whole story. Today's learning theorists recognize that learning is the product of the interaction of biological, psychological, and social-cultural influences (**FIGURE 29.1**).

Biological Constraints on Conditioning

29-1 How do biological constraints affect classical and operant conditioning?

Ever since Charles Darwin, scientists have assumed that all animals share a common evolutionary history and thus share commonalities in their makeup and functioning. Pavlov and Watson, for example, believed the basic laws of learning were essentially similar in all animals. So it should make little difference whether one studied pigeons or people. Moreover, it seemed that any natural response could be conditioned to any neutral stimulus.

Limits on Classical Conditioning

In 1956, learning researcher Gregory Kimble proclaimed, "Just about any activity of which the organism is capable can be conditioned and . . . these responses can be conditioned to any stimulus that the organism can perceive" (p. 195). Twenty-five years later, he humbly acknowledged that "half a thousand" scientific reports had proven him wrong (Kimble, 1981). More than the early behaviorists realized, an animal's capacity for conditioning is constrained by its biology. Each species' predispositions prepare it to learn the associations that enhance its survival. Environments are not the whole story.

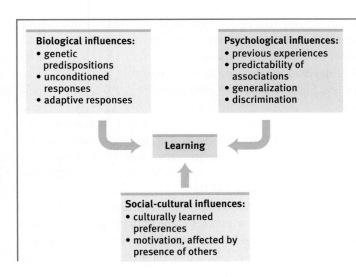

Figure 29.1

Biopsychosocial influences on learning Our learning results not only from environmental experiences, but also from cognitive and biological influences.

Biological influences:
• genetic predispositions
• unconditioned responses
• adaptive responses

Psychological influences:
• previous experiences
• predictability of associations
• generalization
• discrimination

Learning

Social-cultural influences:
• culturally learned preferences
• motivation, affected by presence of others

John Garcia As the laboring son of California farmworkers, Garcia attended school only in the off-season during his early childhood years. After entering junior college in his late twenties, and earning his Ph.D. in his late forties, he received the American Psychological Association's Distinguished Scientific Contribution Award "for his highly original, pioneering research in conditioning and learning." He was also elected to the National Academy of Sciences.

John Garcia was among those who challenged the prevailing idea that all associations can be learned equally well. While researching the effects of radiation on laboratory animals, Garcia and Robert Koelling (1966) noticed that rats began to avoid drinking water from the plastic bottles in radiation chambers. Could classical conditioning be the culprit? Might the rats have linked the plastic-tasting water (a CS) to the sickness (UR) triggered by the radiation (US)?

To test their hunch, Garcia and Koelling exposed the rats to a particular taste, sight, or sound (CS) and later also to radiation or drugs (US) that led to nausea and vomiting (UR). Two startling findings emerged: First, even if sickened as late as several hours after tasting a particular novel flavor, the rats thereafter avoided that flavor. This appeared to violate the notion that for conditioning to occur, the US must immediately follow the CS.

Second, the sickened rats developed aversions to tastes but not to sights or sounds. This contradicted the behaviorists' idea that any perceivable stimulus could serve as a CS. But it made adaptive sense. For rats, the easiest way to identify tainted food is to taste it; if sickened after sampling a new food, they thereafter avoid it. This response, called *taste aversion,* makes it difficult to eradicate a population of "bait-shy" rats by poisoning.

Humans, too, seem biologically prepared to learn some associations rather than others. If you become violently ill four hours after eating contaminated seafood, you will probably develop an aversion to the taste of seafood but usually not to the sight of the associated restaurant, its plates, the people you were with, or the music you heard there. (In contrast, birds, which hunt by sight, appear biologically primed to develop aversions to the *sight* of tainted food [Nicolaus et al., 1983].)

Garcia's early findings on taste aversion were met with an onslaught of criticism. As the German philosopher Arthur Schopenhauer (1788–1860) once said, important ideas are first ridiculed, then attacked, and finally taken for granted. Leading journals refused to publish Garcia's work: The findings are impossible, said some critics. But, as often happens in science, Garcia and Koelling's taste-aversion research is now basic textbook material.

BSIP SA / Alamy

Taste aversion If you became violently ill after eating oysters, you probably would have a hard time eating them again. Their smell and taste would have become a CS for nausea. This learning occurs readily because our biology prepares us to learn taste aversions to toxic foods.

It is also a good example of experiments that begin with the discomfort of some laboratory animals and end by enhancing the welfare of many others. In one conditioned taste-aversion study, coyotes and wolves were tempted into eating sheep carcasses laced with a sickening poison. Thereafter, they developed an aversion to sheep meat; two wolves later penned with a live sheep seemed actually to fear it (Gustavson et al., 1974, 1976). These studies not only saved the sheep from their predators, but also saved the sheep-shunning coyotes and wolves from angry ranchers and farmers who had wanted to destroy them. Similar applications have prevented baboons from raiding African gardens, raccoons from attacking chickens, and ravens and crows from feeding on crane eggs. In all these cases, research helped preserve both the prey and their predators, who occupy an important ecological niche (Dingfelder, 2010; Garcia & Gustavson, 1997).

Such research supports Darwin's principle that natural selection favors traits that aid survival. Our ancestors who readily learned taste aversions were unlikely to eat the same toxic food again and were more likely to survive and leave descendants. Nausea, like anxiety, pain, and other bad feelings, serves a good purpose. Like a low-oil warning on a car dashboard, each alerts the body to a threat (Neese, 1991).

And remember those Japanese quail that were conditioned to get excited by a red light that signaled a receptive female's arrival? Michael Domjan and his colleagues (2004) report that such conditioning is even speedier, stronger, and more durable when the CS is *ecologically relevant*—something similar to stimuli associated with sexual activity in the natural environment, such as the stuffed head of a female quail. In the real world, observes Domjan (2005), conditioned stimuli have a natural association with the unconditioned stimuli they predict.

The tendency to learn behaviors favored by natural selection may help explain why we humans seem to be naturally disposed to learn associations between the color red and sexuality. Female primates display red when nearing ovulation. In human females, enhanced bloodflow produces the red blush of flirtation and sexual excitation. Does the frequent pairing of red and sex—with Valentine's hearts, red-light districts, and red lipstick—naturally enhance men's attraction to women? Experiments (**FIGURE 29.2**) suggest that, without men's awareness, it does (Elliot & Niesta, 2008). In follow-up studies, men who viewed a supposed female conversation partner in a red rather than green shirt chose to sit closer to where they expected her to sit and to ask her more intimate questions (Kayser et al., 2010). And it's not just men: Women tend to perceive men as more attractive when seen on a red background or in red clothing (Elliot et al., 2010).

> "All animals are on a voyage through time, navigating toward futures that promote their survival and away from futures that threaten it. Pleasure and pain are the stars by which they steer." -PSYCHOLOGISTS DANIEL T. GILBERT AND TIMOTHY D. WILSON, "PROSPECTION: EXPERIENCING THE FUTURE," 2007

Animal taste aversion As an alternative to killing wolves and coyotes that preyed on sheep, some ranchers have sickened the animals with lamb laced with a drug.

Figure 29.2

Romantic red In a series of experiments that controlled for other factors (such as the brightness of the image), men found women more attractive and sexually desirable when framed in red (Elliot & Niesta, 2008).

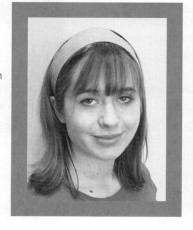

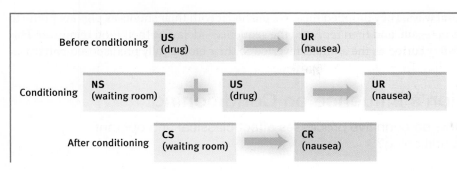

Figure 29.3
Nausea conditioning in cancer patients

A genetic predisposition to associate a CS with a US that follows predictably and immediately is adaptive: Causes often immediately precede effects. Often, but not always, as we saw in the taste-aversion findings. At such times, our predispositions can trick us. When chemotherapy triggers nausea and vomiting more than an hour following treatment, cancer patients may over time develop classically conditioned nausea (and sometimes anxiety) to the sights, sounds, and smells associated with the clinic (**FIGURE 29.3**) (Hall, 1997). Merely returning to the clinic's waiting room or seeing the nurses can provoke these conditioned feelings (Burish & Carey, 1986; Davey, 1992). Under normal circumstances, such revulsion to sickening stimuli would be adaptive.

"Once bitten, twice shy." -G. F. NORTHALL, *FOLK-PHRASES*, 1894

Limits on Operant Conditioning

As with classical conditioning, nature sets limits on each species' capacity for operant conditioning. Mark Twain (1835–1910) said it well: "Never try to teach a pig to sing. It wastes your time and annoys the pig."

We most easily learn and retain behaviors that reflect our biological predispositions. Thus, using food as a reinforcer, you could easily condition a hamster to dig or to rear up, because these are among the animal's natural food-searching behaviors. But you won't be so successful if you use food as a reinforcer to shape face washing and other hamster behaviors that aren't normally associated with food or hunger (Shettleworth, 1973). Similarly, you could easily teach pigeons to flap their wings to avoid being shocked, and to peck to obtain food: Fleeing with their wings and eating with their beaks are natural pigeon behaviors. However, pigeons would have a hard time learning to peck to avoid a shock, or to flap their wings to obtain food (Foree & LoLordo, 1973). The principle: *Biological constraints predispose organisms to learn associations that are naturally adaptive.*

In the early 1940s, University of Minnesota graduate students Marian Breland and Keller Breland witnessed the power of operant conditioning (1961; Bailey & Gillaspy, 2005). Their mentor was B. F. Skinner. Impressed with his results, they began training dogs, cats, chickens, parakeets, turkeys, pigs, ducks, and hamsters. The rest is history. The company they formed spent the next half-century training more than 15,000 animals from 140 species for movies, traveling shows, amusement parks, corporations, and the government. And along the way, the Brelands themselves mentored others, including Sea World's first director of training.

In their early training days, the Brelands presumed that operant principles would work on almost any response an animal could make. But along the way, they too learned about biological constraints. In one act, pigs trained to pick up large wooden "dollars" and deposit them in a piggy bank began to drift back

Natural athletes Animals can most easily learn and retain behaviors that draw on their biological predispositions, such as horses' inborn ability to move around obstacles with speed and agility.

For more information on animal behavior, see books by (I am not making this up) Robin Fox and Lionel Tiger.

to their natural ways. They dropped the coin, pushed it with their snouts as pigs are prone to do, picked it up again, and then repeated the sequence—delaying their food reinforcer. This *instinctive drift* occurred as the animals reverted to their biologically predisposed patterns.

Cognition's Influence on Conditioning

 29-2 How do cognitive processes affect classical and operant conditioning?

Cognitive Processes and Classical Conditioning

In their dismissal of "mentalistic" concepts such as consciousness, Pavlov and Watson underestimated the importance not only of biological constraints on an organism's learning capacity, but also the effects of cognitive processes (thoughts, perceptions, expectations). The early behaviorists believed that rats' and dogs' learned behaviors could be reduced to mindless mechanisms, so there was no need to consider cognition. But Robert Rescorla and Allan Wagner (1972) showed that an animal can learn the *predictability* of an event. If a shock always is preceded by a tone, and then may also be preceded by a light that accompanies the tone, a rat will react with fear to the tone but not to the light. Although the light is always followed by the shock, it adds no new information; the tone is a better predictor. The more predictable the association, the stronger the conditioned response. It's as if the animal learns an *expectancy,* an awareness of how likely it is that the US will occur.

"All brains are, in essence, anticipation machines." -DANIEL C. DENNETT, *CONSCIOUSNESS EXPLAINED,* 1991

Associations can influence attitudes (Hofmann et al., 2010). When British children viewed novel cartoon characters alongside either ice cream *(Yum!)* or brussels sprouts *(Yuck!),* they came to like best the ice-cream-associated characters (Field, 2006). Other researchers have classically conditioned adults' attitudes, using little-known Pokémon characters (Olson & Fazio, 2001). The participants, playing the role of a security guard monitoring a video screen, viewed a stream of words, images, and Pokémon characters. Their task, they were told, was to respond to one target Pokémon character by pressing a button. Unnoticed by the participants, when two other Pokémon characters appeared on the screen, one was consistently associated with various positive words and images (such as *awesome* or a hot fudge sundae); the other appeared with negative words and images (such as *awful* or a cockroach). Without any conscious memory for the pairings, the participants formed more gut-level liking for the characters associated with the positive stimuli.

Follow-up studies indicate that conditioned likes and dislikes are even stronger when people notice and are aware of the associations they have learned (Shanks, 2010). Cognition matters.

Such experiments help explain why classical conditioning treatments that ignore cognition often have limited success. For example, people receiving therapy for alcohol use disorder may be given alcohol spiked with a nauseating drug. Will they then associate alcohol with sickness? If classical conditioning were merely a matter of "stamping in" stimulus associations, we might hope so, and to some extent this does occur (as we will see in Module 71). However, one's awareness that the nausea is induced by the drug, not the alcohol, often weakens the association between drinking alcohol and feeling sick. So, even in classical conditioning, it is (especially with humans) not simply the CS-US association but also the thought that counts.

Cognitive Processes and Operant Conditioning

B. F. Skinner acknowledged the biological underpinnings of behavior and the existence of private thought processes. Nevertheless, many psychologists criticized him for discounting the importance of these influences.

A mere eight days before dying of leukemia in 1990, Skinner stood before the American Psychological Association convention. In this final address, he again resisted the growing belief that cognitive processes (thoughts, perceptions, expectations) have a necessary place in the science of psychology and even in our understanding of conditioning. He viewed "cognitive science" as a throwback to early twentieth-century introspectionism. For Skinner, thoughts and emotions were behaviors that follow the same laws as other behaviors.

Nevertheless, the evidence of cognitive processes cannot be ignored. For example, animals on a fixed-interval reinforcement schedule respond more and more frequently as the time approaches when a response will produce a reinforcer. Although a strict behaviorist would object to talk of "expectations," the animals behave as if they expected that repeating the response would soon produce the reward.

LATENT LEARNING

Evidence of cognitive processes has also come from studying rats in mazes, including classic studies by Edward Chase Tolman (1886–1959) and C. H. Honzik that were done in Skinner's youth. Rats exploring a maze, given no obvious rewards, seem to develop a **cognitive map,** a mental representation of the maze, much like your mental map of your school. This map, and the rats' learning, is not demonstrated until the experimenter places food in the maze's goal box, which motivates the rats to run the maze at least as quickly and efficiently as other rats that were previously reinforced with food for this result (Tolman & Honzik, 1930).

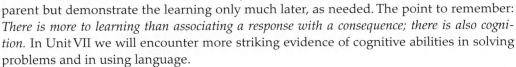

Like people sightseeing in a new town, the exploring rats seemingly experienced **latent learning** during their earlier tours. That learning became apparent only when there was some incentive to demonstrate it. Children, too, may learn from watching a parent but demonstrate the learning only much later, as needed. The point to remember: *There is more to learning than associating a response with a consequence; there is also cognition.* In Unit VII we will encounter more striking evidence of cognitive abilities in solving problems and in using language.

"Bathroom? Sure, it's just down the hall to the left, jog right, left, another left, straight past two more lefts, then right, and it's at the end of the third corridor on your right."

INSIGHT LEARNING

Some learning occurs after little or no systematic interaction with our environment. For example, we may puzzle over a problem, and suddenly, the pieces fall together as we perceive the solution in a sudden flash of **insight**—an abrupt, true-seeming, and often satisfying solution (Topolinski & Reber, 2010). Ten-year-old Johnny Appleton's insight solved a problem that had stumped construction workers: how to rescue a young robin that had fallen into a narrow 30-inch-deep hole in a cement-block wall. Johnny's solution: Slowly pour in sand, giving the bird enough time to keep its feet on top of the constantly rising pile (Ruchlis, 1990).

INTRINSIC MOTIVATION

The cognitive perspective has also shown us the limits of rewards: Promising people a reward for a task they already enjoy can backfire. Excessive rewards can destroy **intrinsic motivation**—the desire to perform a behavior effectively for its own sake. In experiments, children have been promised a payoff for playing with an interesting puzzle or toy. Later, they played with the toy *less* than other unpaid children did (Deci et al., 1999; Tang & Hall, 1995). Likewise, rewarding children with toys or candy for reading diminishes the time they spend reading (Marinak & Gambrell, 2008). It is as if they think, "If I have to be bribed into doing this, it must not be worth doing for its own sake." This overuse of bribes—leading people to see their actions as externally controlled rather than internally appealing—has been called *overjustification.*

cognitive map a mental representation of the layout of one's environment. For example, after exploring a maze, rats act as if they have learned a cognitive map of it.

latent learning learning that occurs but is not apparent until there is an incentive to demonstrate it.

insight a sudden realization of a problem's solution.

intrinsic motivation a desire to perform a behavior effectively for its own sake.

Pure love If this girl were suddenly told that she must look after her baby cousin from now on, she might lose some of the joy that her intrinsic motivation to care for him has provided.

extrinsic motivation a desire to perform a behavior to receive promised rewards or avoid threatened punishment.

To sense the difference between intrinsic motivation and **extrinsic motivation** (behaving in certain ways to gain external rewards or avoid threatened punishment), think about your experience in this course. Are you feeling pressured to finish this reading before a deadline? Worried about your grade? Eager for college credit by doing well on the AP® Exam? If *Yes,* then you are extrinsically motivated (as, to some extent, almost all students must be). Are you also finding the material interesting? Does learning it make you feel more competent? If there were no grade at stake, might you be curious enough to want to learn the material for its own sake? If *Yes,* intrinsic motivation also fuels your efforts.

Youth sports coaches who aim to promote enduring interest in an activity, not just to pressure players into winning, should focus on the intrinsic joy of playing and of reaching one's potential (Deci & Ryan, 1985, 2009). Giving people choices also enhances their intrinsic motivation (Patall et al., 2008). Nevertheless, rewards used to signal a job well done (rather than to bribe or control someone) can be effective (Boggiano et al., 1985). "Most improved player" awards, for example, can boost feelings of competence and increase enjoyment of a sport. Rightly administered, rewards can raise performance and spark creativity (Eisenberger & Aselage, 2009; Henderlong & Lepper, 2002). And extrinsic rewards (such as the college scholarships and jobs that often follow good grades) are here to stay. **TABLE 29.1** compares the biological and cognitive influences on classical and operant conditioning.

Table 29.1	Biological and Cognitive Influences on Conditioning	
	Classical Conditioning	**Operant Conditioning**
Biological predispositions	Natural predispositions constrain what stimuli and responses can easily be associated.	Organisms best learn behaviors similar to their natural behaviors; unnatural behaviors instinctively drift back toward natural ones.
Cognitive processes	Organisms develop expectation that CS signals the arrival of US.	Organisms develop expectation that a response will be reinforced or punished; they also exhibit latent learning, without reinforcement.

Learning and Personal Control

29-3   In what two ways do people learn to cope with personal problems?

coping alleviating stress using emotional, cognitive, or behavioral methods.

problem-focused coping attempting to alleviate stress directly—by changing the stressor or the way we interact with that stressor.

emotion-focused coping attempting to alleviate stress by avoiding or ignoring a stressor and attending to emotional needs related to one's stress reaction.

Problems in life are unavoidable. This fact gives us a clear message: We need to learn to **cope** with the problems in our lives by alleviating the *stress* they cause with emotional, cognitive, or behavioral methods.

Some problems, called stressors, we address directly, with **problem-focused coping.** If our impatience leads to a family fight, we may go directly to that family member to work things out. We tend to use problem-focused strategies when we feel a sense of control over a situation and think we can change the circumstances, or at least change ourselves to deal with the circumstances more capably.

We turn to **emotion-focused coping** when we cannot—or *believe* we cannot—change a situation. If, despite our best efforts, we cannot get along with that family member, we may search for stress relief by reaching out to friends for support and comfort. Emotion-focused strategies can be adaptive, as when we exercise or keep busy with hobbies to avoid thinking about an old addiction. Emotion-focused strategies can be maladaptive, however, as when

Emotion-focused coping
Reaching out to friends can help us attend to our emotional needs in stressful situations.

students worried about not keeping up with the reading in class go out to party to get it off their mind. Sometimes a problem-focused strategy (catching up with the reading) more effectively reduces stress and promotes long-term health and satisfaction.

When challenged, some of us tend to respond with cool problem-focused coping, others with emotion-focused coping (Connor-Smith & Flachsbart, 2007). Our feelings of personal control, our explanatory style, and our supportive connections all influence our ability to cope. So, how might learning influence whether we cope successfully?

Learned Helplessness

29-4   How does a perceived lack of control affect people's behavior and health?

Picture the scene: Two rats receive simultaneous shocks. One can turn a wheel to stop the shocks. The helpless rat, but not the wheel turner, becomes more susceptible to ulcers and lowered immunity to disease (Laudenslager & Reite, 1984). In humans, too, uncontrollable threats trigger the strongest stress responses (Dickerson & Kemeny, 2004).

Feeling helpless and oppressed may lead to a state of passive resignation called **learned helplessness** (**FIGURE 29.4**). Researcher Martin Seligman (1975, 1991) discovered this in some long-ago experiments in which dogs were strapped in a harness and given repeated shocks, with no opportunity to avoid them. Later, when placed in another situation where they *could* escape the punishment by simply leaping a hurdle, the dogs cowered as if without hope. In contrast, animals able to escape the first shocks learned personal control and easily escaped the shocks in the new situation.

Humans can also learn helplessness. When repeatedly faced with traumatic events over which they have no control, people come to feel helpless, hopeless, and depressed.

Perceiving a loss of control, we become more vulnerable to stress and ill health. A famous study of elderly nursing home residents with little perceived control over their activities found that they declined faster and died sooner than those given more control (Rodin, 1986). Workers able to adjust office furnishings and control interruptions and distractions in their work environment have experienced

> **learned helplessness** the hopelessness and passive resignation an animal or human learns when unable to avoid repeated aversive events.

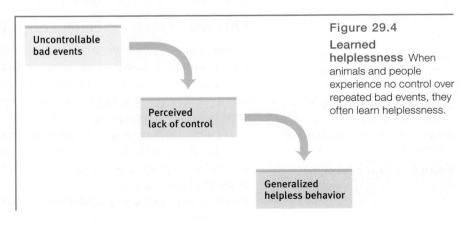

Figure 29.4

Learned helplessness When animals and people experience no control over repeated bad events, they often learn helplessness.

Uncontrollable bad events

Perceived lack of control

Generalized helpless behavior

Happy to have control After working on the building—alongside Habitat for Humanity volunteers—for several months, this family is finally experiencing the joy of having their own new home.

less stress (O'Neill, 1993). Such findings may help explain why British civil service workers at the executive grades have tended to outlive those at clerical or laboring grades, and why Finnish workers with low job stress have been less than half as likely to die of strokes or heart disease as those with a demanding job and little control. The more control workers have, the longer they live (Bosma et al., 1997, 1998; Kivimaki et al., 2002; Marmot et al., 1997).

Increasing self-control—allowing prisoners to move chairs and control room lights and the TV, having workers participate in decision making, offering nursing home patients choices about their environment—noticeably improves health and morale (Humphrey et al., 2007; Wang et al., 2010). In the case of the nursing home patients, 93 percent of those encouraged to exert more control became more alert, active, and happy (Rodin, 1986). As researcher Ellen Langer (1983, p. 291) concluded, "Perceived control is basic to human functioning."

Control may also help explain a well-established link between economic status and longevity (Jokela et al., 2009). In one study of 843 grave markers in an old graveyard in Glasgow, Scotland, those with the costliest, highest pillars (indicating the most affluence) tended to have lived the longest (Carroll et al., 1994). Likewise, those living in Scottish regions with the least overcrowding and unemployment have the greatest longevity. There and elsewhere, high economic status predicts a lower risk of heart and respiratory diseases (Sapolsky, 2005). Wealthy predicts healthy among children, too (Chen, 2004). With higher economic status come reduced risks of low birth weight, infant mortality, smoking, and violence. Even among other primates, individuals at the bottom of the social pecking order have been more likely than their higher-status companions to become sick when exposed to a cold-like virus (Cohen et al., 1997). But high status also entails stress: High-status baboons and monkeys who frequently have to physically defend their dominant position show high stress levels (Sapolsky, 2005).

Why does perceived loss of control predict health problems? Because losing control provokes an outpouring of stress hormones. When rats cannot control shock or when primates or humans feel unable to control their environment, stress hormone levels rise, blood pressure increases, and immune responses drop (Rodin, 1986; Sapolsky, 2005). Captive animals therefore experience more stress and are more vulnerable to disease than are wild animals (Roberts, 1988). Human studies have confirmed that crowding in high-density neighborhoods, prisons, and college and university dorms is another source of diminished feelings of control—and of elevated levels of stress hormones and blood pressure (Fleming et al., 1987; Ostfeld et al., 1987).

INTERNAL VERSUS EXTERNAL LOCUS OF CONTROL

If experiencing a loss of control can be stressful and unhealthy, do people who generally feel in control of their lives enjoy better health? Consider your own feelings of control. Do you believe that your life is beyond your control? That getting a decent summer job depends mainly on being in the right place at the right time? Or do you more strongly believe that what happens to you is your own doing? That being a success is a matter of hard work? Did your parents influence your feelings of control? Did your culture?

Hundreds of studies have compared people who differ in their perceptions of control. On one side are those who have what psychologist Julian Rotter called an **external locus of control**—the perception that chance or outside forces determine their fate. On the other are those who perceive an **internal locus of control,** who believe that they control their own destiny. In study after study, "internals" have achieved more in school and work,

external locus of control the perception that chance or outside forces beyond our personal control determine our fate.

internal locus of control the perception that you control your own fate.

acted more independently, enjoyed better health, and felt less depressed than did "externals" (Lefcourt, 1982; Ng et al., 2006). Moreover, they were better at delaying gratification and coping with various stressors, including marital problems (Miller & Monge, 1986). One study followed 7551 British people for two decades. Those who expressed a more internal locus of control at age 10 exhibited less obesity, hypertension, and distress at age 30 (Gale et al., 2008). Other studies have found that people who believe in free will, or that willpower is controllable, learn better, perform better at work, and are more helpful (Job et al., 2010; Stillman et al., 2010).

Compared with their parents' generation, more Americans now endorse an external locus of control (Twenge et al., 2004). This shift may help explain an associated increase in rates of depression and other psychological disorders in the new generation (Twenge et al., 2010).

DEPLETING AND STRENGTHENING SELF-CONTROL

Self-control is the ability to control impulses and delay short-term gratification for longer-term rewards. In studies, this ability has predicted good adjustment, better grades, and social success (Tangney et al., 2004). Students who planned their day's activities and then lived out their day as planned were also at low risk for depression (Nezlek, 2001).

Self-control often fluctuates. Like a muscle, self-control temporarily weakens after an exertion, replenishes with rest, and becomes stronger with exercise (Baumeister & Exline, 2000; Hagger et al., 2010; Vohs & Baumeister, 2011). Exercising willpower temporarily depletes the mental energy needed for self-control on other tasks (Gailliott & Baumeister, 2007). In one experiment, hungry people who had resisted the temptation to eat chocolate chip cookies abandoned a tedious task sooner than those who had not resisted the cookies. And after expending willpower on laboratory tasks, such as stifling prejudice or saying the color of words (for example, "red" even if the red-colored word was *green*), people were less restrained in their aggressive responses to provocation and in their sexuality (DeWall et al., 2007; Gaillot & Baumeister, 2007).

> **self-control** the ability to control impulses and delay short-term gratification for greater long-term rewards.

Extreme self-control Our ability to exert self-control increases with practice, and some of us have practiced more than others! Magician David Blaine (above) endured standing in a block of ice (in which a small space had been carved out for him) for nearly 62 hours for a stunt in New York's Times Square. A number of performing artists make their living as very convincing human statues, as does this actress (left) performing on The Royal Mile in Edinburgh, Scotland.

Researchers have found that exercising willpower depletes the blood sugar and neural activity associated with mental focus (Inzlicht & Gutsell, 2007). What, then, might be the effect of deliberately boosting people's blood sugar when self-control is depleted? Giving energy-boosting sugar (in a naturally rather than an artificially sweetened lemonade) had a sweet effect: It strengthened people's effortful thinking and reduced their financial impulsiveness (Masicampo & Baumeister, 2008; Wang & Dvorak, 2010). Even dogs can experience both self-control depletion on the one hand and rejuvenation with sugar on the other (Miller et al., 2010).

In the long run, self-control requires attention and energy. With physical exercise and time-managed study programs, people have strengthened their self-control, as seen in both their performance on laboratory tasks and their improved self-management of eating, drinking, smoking, and household chores (Oaten & Cheng, 2006a,b). *The bottom line:* We can grow our willpower muscles—our capacity for self-regulation. But doing so requires some (dare I say it?) willpower.

Before You Move On

▶ **ASK YOURSELF**

How are you intrinsically motivated? What are some extrinsic motivators in your life?

▶ **TEST YOURSELF**

When faced with a situation over which you feel you have no sense of control, is it most effective to use emotion- or problem-focused coping? Why?

Answers to the Test Yourself questions can be found in Appendix E at the end of the book.

Module 29 Review

29-1 How do biological constraints affect classical and operant conditioning?

- Classical conditioning principles, we now know, are constrained by biological predispositions, so that learning some associations is easier than learning others.

- Learning is adaptive: Each species learns behaviors that aid its survival.

- Biological constraints also place limits on operant conditioning. Training that attempts to override biological constraints will probably not endure because animals will revert to predisposed patterns.

29-2 How do cognitive processes affect classical and operant conditioning?

- In classical conditioning, animals may learn when to expect a US and may be aware of the link between stimuli and responses.

- In operant conditioning, *cognitive mapping* and *latent learning* research demonstrate the importance of cognitive processes in learning.

- Other research shows that excessive rewards (driving *extrinsic motivation*) can undermine *intrinsic motivation*.

29-3 In what two ways do people learn to cope with personal problems?

- We use *problem-focused coping* to change the stressor or the way we interact with it.

- We use *emotion-focused coping* to avoid or ignore stressors and attend to emotional needs related to stress reactions.

29-4 How does a perceived lack of control affect people's behavior and health?

- Being unable to avoid repeated aversive events can lead to *learned helplessness*.

- People who perceive an *internal locus of control* achieve more, enjoy better health, and are happier than those who perceive an *external locus of control*.

- *Self-control* requires attention and energy, but it predicts good adjustment, better grades, and social success.

- A perceived lack of control provokes an outpouring of hormones that put people's health at risk.

Multiple-Choice Questions

1. What do we call a desire to perform a behavior in order to receive promised rewards or to avoid threatened punishment?

   a. Latent learning
   b. Extrinsic motivation
   c. Intrinsic motivation
   d. Insight learning
   e. Emotion-focused coping

2. Which ability is a good predictor of good adjustment, better grades, and social success?

   a. Self-control
   b. Locus of control
   c. Problem-focused coping
   d. Learned helplessness
   e. Emotion-focused coping

3. Elephants appear to have the capacity to remember large-scale spaces over long periods. Which of the following best identifies this capacity?

   a. Latent learning   d. Intrinsic motivation
   b. Insight   e. Extrinsic motivation
   c. Cognitive maps

4. The perception that we control our own fate is also called what?

   a. Self-control
   b. Learned helplessness
   c. Internal locus of control
   d. External locus of control
   e. Emotion-focused coping

5. A woman had been pondering a problem for days and was about to give up when, suddenly, the solution came to her. Her experience can be best described as what?

   a. Cognitive mapping
   b. Insight
   c. Operant conditioning
   d. Classical conditioning
   e. Unconscious associative learning

Practice FRQs

1. Provide two specific examples of how biology can influence classical conditioning.

Answer
Any two examples from the module can be used to answer. Possibilities include:

1 point: Garcia's research showed that rats are more likely to develop a classically conditioned aversion to tastes than to sights or sounds.

1 point: Humans are biologically predisposed to form associations between the color red and sexuality.

2. Describe how each of the following can show the impact of cognition on operant conditioning.

   - Latent learning
   - Insight learning
   - Intrinsic motivation

(3 points)

Module 30

Learning by Observation

Module Learning Objectives

30-1 Describe the process of observational learning, and explain how some scientists believe it is enabled by mirror neurons.

30-2 Discuss the impact of prosocial modeling and of antisocial modeling.

30-1 What is observational learning, and how do some scientists believe it is enabled by mirror neurons?

observational learning learning by observing others. Also called *social learning.*

modeling the process of observing and imitating a specific behavior.

Albert Bandura "The Bobo doll follows me wherever I go. The photographs are published in every introductory psychology text and virtually every undergraduate takes introductory psychology. I recently checked into a Washington hotel. The clerk at the desk asked, 'Aren't you the psychologist who did the Bobo doll experiment?' I answered, 'I am afraid that will be my legacy.' He replied, 'That deserves an upgrade. I will put you in a suite in the quiet part of the hotel'" (2005).

Cognition is certainly a factor in **observational learning** (also called *social learning*) in which higher animals, especially humans, learn without direct experience, by watching and imitating others. A child who sees his sister burn her fingers on a hot stove learns not to touch it. We learn our native languages and various other specific behaviors by observing and imitating others, a process called **modeling.**

Picture this scene from an experiment by Albert Bandura, the pioneering researcher of observational learning (Bandura et al., 1961): A preschool child works on a drawing. An adult in another part of the room is building with Tinkertoys. As the child watches, the adult gets up and for nearly 10 minutes pounds, kicks, and throws around the room a large inflated Bobo doll, yelling, "Sock him in the nose. . . . Hit him down. . . . Kick him."

The child is then taken to another room filled with appealing toys. Soon the experimenter returns and tells the child she has decided to save these good toys "for the other children." She takes the now-frustrated child to a third room containing a few toys, including a Bobo doll. Left alone, what does the child do?

Compared with children not exposed to the adult model, those who viewed the model's actions were more likely to lash out at the doll. Observing the aggressive outburst apparently lowered their inhibitions. But *something more* was also at work, for the children imitated the very acts they had observed and used the very words they had heard (**FIGURE 30.1**).

That "something more," Bandura suggests, was this: By watching a model, we experience *vicarious reinforcement* or *vicarious punishment,* and we learn to anticipate a behavior's consequences in situations like those we are observing. We are especially likely to learn from people we perceive

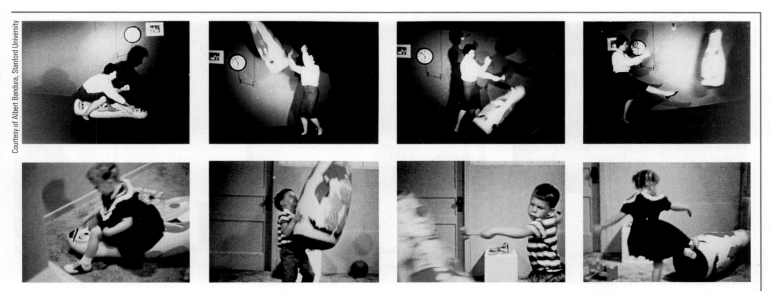

Figure 30.1

The famous Bobo doll experiment Notice how the children's actions directly imitate the adult's.

as similar to ourselves, as successful, or as admirable. Functional MRI scans show that when people observe someone winning a reward (and especially when it's someone likable and similar to themselves) their own brain reward systems activate, much as if they themselves had won the reward (Mobbs et al., 2009). When we identify with someone, we experience their outcomes vicariously. Lord Chesterfield (1694–1773) had the idea: "We are, in truth, more than half what we are by imitation."

Mirrors and Imitation in the Brain

On a 1991 hot summer day in Parma, Italy, a lab monkey awaited its researchers' return from lunch. The researchers had implanted wires next to its motor cortex, in a frontal lobe brain region that enabled the monkey to plan and enact movements. The monitoring device would alert the researchers to activity in that region of the monkey's brain. When the monkey moved a peanut into its mouth, for example, the device would buzz. That day, as one of the researchers reentered the lab, ice cream cone in hand, the monkey stared at him. As the researcher raised the cone to lick it, the monkey's monitor buzzed—as if the motionless monkey had itself moved (Blakeslee, 2006; Iacoboni, 2008, 2009).

The same buzzing had been heard earlier, when the monkey watched humans or other monkeys move peanuts to their mouths. The flabbergasted researchers had, they believed, stumbled onto a previously unknown type of neuron (Rizzolatti et al., 2002, 2006). These presumed **mirror neurons** may provide a neural basis for everyday imitation and observational learning. When a monkey grasps, holds, or tears something, these neurons fire. And they likewise fire when the monkey observes another doing so. When one monkey sees, its neurons mirror what another monkey does.

Imitation is widespread in other species. In one experiment, a monkey watching another selecting certain pictures to gain treats learned to imitate the order of choices (**FIGURE 30.2** on the next page). In other research, rhesus macaque monkeys rarely made up quickly after a fight—unless they grew up with forgiving older macaques. Then, more often than not, their fights, too, were quickly followed by reconciliation (de Waal & Johanowicz, 1993). Rats, pigeons, crows, and gorillas all observe others and learn (Byrne et al., 2011; Dugatkin, 2002).

mirror neurons frontal lobe neurons that some scientists believe fire when performing certain actions or when observing another doing so. The brain's mirroring of another's action may enable imitation and empathy.

Mirror neurons at work?

"Your back is killing me!"

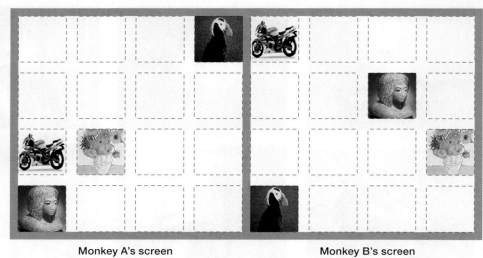

Monkey A's screen   Monkey B's screen

Figure 30.2

Cognitive imitation Monkey A (far left) watched Monkey B touch four pictures on a display screen in a certain order to gain a banana. Monkey A learned to imitate that order, even when shown the same pictures in a different configuration (Subiaul et al., 2004).

As Module 85 describes, chimpanzees observe and imitate all sorts of novel foraging and tool use behaviors, which are then transmitted from generation to generation within their local culture (Hopper et al., 2008; Whiten et al., 2007).

In humans, imitation is pervasive. Our catchphrases, fashions, ceremonies, foods, traditions, morals, and fads all spread by one person copying another. Imitation shapes even very young humans' behavior (Bates & Byrne, 2010). Shortly after birth, a baby may imitate an adult who sticks out his tongue. By 8 to 16 months, infants imitate various novel gestures (Jones, 2007). By age 12 months (**FIGURE 30.3**), they look where an adult is looking (Meltzoff et al., 2009). And by age 14 months, children imitate acts modeled on TV (Meltzoff, 1988; Meltzoff & Moore, 1989, 1997). Even as 2½-year-olds, when many of their mental abilities are near those of adult chimpanzees, young humans surpass chimps at social tasks such as imitating another's solution to a problem (Herrmann et al., 2007). Children see, children do.

So strong is the human predisposition to learn from watching adults that 2- to 5-year-old children *overimitate*. Whether living in urban Australia or rural Africa, they copy even irrelevant adult actions. Before reaching for a toy in a plastic jar, they will first stroke the jar with a feather if that's what they have observed (Lyons et al., 2007). Or, imitating an adult, they will wave a stick over a box and then use the stick to push on a knob that opens the box—when all they needed to do to open the box was to push on the knob (Nielsen & Tomaselli, 2010).

Humans, like monkeys, have brains that support empathy and imitation. Researchers cannot insert experimental electrodes in human brains, but they can use fMRI scans to see brain activity associated with performing and with observing actions. So, is the human

"Children need models more than they need critics." -JOSEPH JOUBERT, *PENSÉES*, 1842

Figure 30.3

Imitation This 12-month-old infant sees an adult look left, and immediately follows her gaze. (From Meltzoff et al., 2009.)

Meltzoff, A. N., Kuhl, P. K., Movellan, J., & Sejnowski, T. J. (2009). Foundations for a new science of learning. Science 325, 284-268

capacity to simulate another's action and to share in another's experience due to specialized mirror neurons? Or is it due to distributed brain networks? That issue is currently being debated (Gallese et al. 2011; Iacoboni, 2008, 2009; Mukamel et al., 2010). Regardless, children's brains enable their empathy and their ability to infer another's mental state, an ability known as *theory of mind.*

The brain's response to observing others makes emotions contagious. Through its neurological echo, our brain simulates and vicariously experiences what we observe. So real are these mental instant replays that we may misremember an action we have observed as an action we have performed (Lindner et al., 2010). But through these reenactments, we grasp others' states of mind. Observing others' postures, faces, voices, and writing styles, we unconsciously synchronize our own to theirs—which helps us feel what they are feeling (Bernieri et al., 1994; Ireland & Pennebaker, 2010). We find ourselves yawning when they yawn, laughing when they laugh.

When observing movie characters smoking, smokers' brains spontaneously simulate smoking, which helps explain their cravings (Wagner et al., 2011). Seeing a loved one's pain, our faces mirror the other's emotion. But as **FIGURE 30.4** shows, so do our brains. In this fMRI scan, the pain imagined by an empathic romantic partner has triggered some of the same brain activity experienced by the loved one actually having the pain (Singer et al., 2004). Even reading fiction may trigger such activity, as we mentally simulate (and vicariously experience) the experiences described (Mar & Oatley, 2008; Speer et al., 2009). The bottom line: *Brain activity underlies our intensely social nature.*

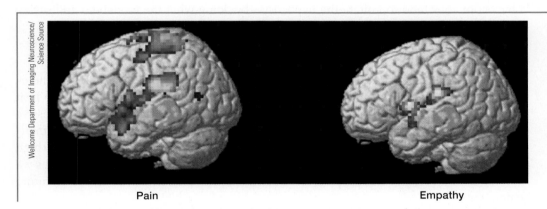

Pain   Empathy

Figure 30.4

Experienced and imagined pain in the brain Brain activity related to actual pain (left) is mirrored in the brain of an observing loved one (right). Empathy in the brain shows up in emotional brain areas, but not in the somatosensory cortex, which receives the physical pain input.

Applications of Observational Learning

30-2 What is the impact of prosocial modeling and of antisocial modeling?

So the big news from Bandura's studies and the mirror-neuron research is that we look, we mentally imitate, and we learn. Models—in our family or neighborhood, or on TV—may have effects, good or bad.

Prosocial Effects

The good news is that **prosocial** (positive, helpful) models can have prosocial effects. Many business organizations effectively use *behavior modeling* to help new employees learn communications, sales, and customer service skills (Taylor et al., 2005). Trainees gain these skills faster when they are able to observe the skills being modeled effectively by experienced workers (or actors simulating them).

prosocial behavior positive, constructive, helpful behavior. The opposite of antisocial behavior.

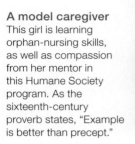

A model caregiver
This girl is learning orphan-nursing skills, as well as compassion from her mentor in this Humane Society program. As the sixteenth-century proverb states, "Example is better than precept."

People who exemplify nonviolent, helpful behavior can also prompt similar behavior in others. India's Mahatma Gandhi and America's Martin Luther King, Jr., both drew on the power of modeling, making nonviolent action a powerful force for social change in both countries. Parents are also powerful models. European Christians who risked their lives to rescue Jews from the Nazis usually had a close relationship with at least one parent who modeled a strong moral or humanitarian concern; this was also true for U.S. civil rights activists in the 1960s (London, 1970; Oliner & Oliner, 1988). The observational learning of morality begins early. Socially responsive toddlers who readily imitate their parents tend to become preschoolers with a strong internalized conscience (Forman et al., 2004).

Models are most effective when their actions and words are consistent. Sometimes, however, models say one thing and do another. To encourage children to read, read to them and surround them with books and people who read. To increase the odds that your children will practice your religion, worship and attend religious activities with them. Many parents seem to operate according to the principle "Do as I *say,* not as I do." Experiments suggest that children learn to do both (Rice & Grusec, 1975; Rushton, 1975). Exposed to a hypocrite, they tend to imitate the hypocrisy—by doing what the model did and saying what the model said.

Antisocial Effects

The bad news is that observational learning may have *antisocial effects.* This helps us understand why abusive parents might have aggressive children, and why many men who beat their wives had wife-battering fathers (Stith et al., 2000). Critics note that being aggressive could be passed along by parents' genes. But with monkeys we know it can be environmental. In study after study, young monkeys separated from their mothers and subjected to high levels of aggression grew up to be aggressive themselves (Chamove, 1980). The lessons we learn as children are not easily replaced as adults, and they are sometimes visited on future generations.

TV shows and Internet videos are a powerful source of observational learning. While watching TV and videos, children may "learn" that bullying is an effective way to control others, that free and easy sex brings pleasure without later misery or disease, or that men should be tough and women gentle. And they have ample time to learn such lessons. During their first 18 years, most children in developed countries spend more time watching TV shows than they spend in school. The average teen watches TV shows more than 4 hours a day; the average adult, 3 hours (Robinson & Martin, 2009; Strasburger et al., 2010).

TV-show viewers are learning about life from a rather peculiar storyteller, one that reflects the culture's mythology but not its reality. Between 1998 and 2006, prime-time violence reportedly increased 75 percent (PTC, 2007). If we include cable programming and video rentals, the violence numbers escalate. An analysis of more than 3000 network and cable programs aired during one closely studied year revealed that nearly 6 in 10 featured violence, that 74 percent of the violence went unpunished, that 58 percent did not show the victims' pain, that nearly half the incidents involved "justified" violence, and that nearly half involved an attractive perpetrator. These conditions define the recipe for the *violence-viewing effect* described in many studies (Donnerstein, 1998, 2011). To read more about this effect, see Thinking Critically About: Does Viewing Media Violence Trigger Violent Behavior?

"The problem with television is that the people must sit and keep their eyes glued to a screen: The average American family hasn't time for it. Therefore the showmen are convinced that . . . television will *never* be a serious competitor of [radio] broadcasting."
-*New York Times*, 1939

Thinking Critically About

Does Viewing Media Violence Trigger Violent Behavior?

Was the judge who, in 1993, tried two British 10-year-olds for the murder of a 2-year-old right to suspect that the pair had been influenced by "violent video films"? Were the American media right to wonder if Adam Lanza, the 2012 mass killer of young children and their teachers at Connecticut's Sandy Hook Elementary School, was influenced by his playing of the violent video games found stockpiled in his home? To understand whether violence viewing leads to violent behavior, researchers have done some 600 correlational and experimental studies (Anderson & Gentile, 2008; Comstock, 2008; Murray, 2008).

Correlational studies do support this link:

- In the United States and Canada, homicide rates doubled between 1957 and 1974, just when TV was introduced and spreading. Moreover, census regions with later dates for TV service also had homicide rates that jumped later.

- White South Africans were first introduced to TV in 1975. A similar near-doubling of the homicide rate began after 1975 (Centerwall, 1989).

- Elementary schoolchildren with heavy exposure to media violence (via TV, videos, and video games) tend to get into more fights (**FIGURE 30.5**). As teens, they are at greater risk for violent behavior (Boxer et al., 2009).

But as we know from Unit II, correlation need not mean causation. So these studies do not prove that viewing violence causes aggression (Freedman, 1988; McGuire, 1986). Maybe aggressive children prefer violent programs. Maybe abused or neglected children are both more aggressive and more often left in front of the TV or computer. Maybe violent programs simply reflect, rather than affect, violent trends.

To pin down causation, psychologists experimented. They randomly assigned some viewers to observe violence and others to watch entertaining nonviolence. Does viewing cruelty prepare people, when irritated, to react more cruelly? To some extent, it does. This is especially so when an attractive person commits seemingly justified, realistic violence that goes unpunished and causes no visible pain or harm (Donnerstein, 1998, 2011).

The violence-viewing effect seems to stem from at least two factors. One is *imitation* (Geen & Thomas, 1986). Children as young as 14 months will imitate acts they observe on TV (Meltzoff & Moore, 1989, 1997). As they watch, their brains simulate the behavior, and after this inner rehearsal they become more likely to act it out. Thus, in one experiment, violent play increased sevenfold immediately after children viewed *Power Rangers* episodes (Boyatzis et al., 1995). As happened in the Bobo doll experiment, children often precisely imitated the models' violent acts—in this case, flying karate kicks.

Prolonged exposure to violence also *desensitizes* viewers. They become more indifferent to it when later viewing a brawl, whether on TV or in real life (Fanti et al., 2009; Rule & Ferguson, 1986). Adult males who spent three evenings watching sexually violent movies became progressively less bothered by the rapes and slashings. Compared with those in a control group, the film watchers later expressed less sympathy for domestic violence victims, and they rated the victims' injuries as less severe (Mullin & Linz, 1995). Likewise, moviegoers were less likely to help an injured woman pick up her crutches if they had just watched a violent rather than a nonviolent movie (Bushman & Anderson, 2009).

Drawing on such findings, the American Academy of Pediatrics (2009) has advised pediatricians that "media violence can contribute to aggressive behavior, desensitization to violence, nightmares, and fear of being harmed." Indeed, an evil psychologist could hardly imagine a better way to make people indifferent to brutality than to expose them to a graded series of scenes, from fights to killings to the mutilations in slasher movies (Donnerstein et al., 1987). Watching cruelty fosters indifference.

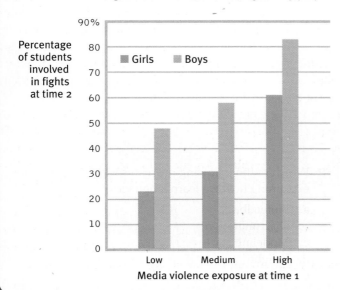

Figure 30.5 **Heavy exposure to media violence predicts future aggressive behavior** Researchers studied more than 400 third- to fifth-graders. After controlling for existing differences in hostility and aggression, the researchers reported increased aggression in those heavily exposed to violent TV, videos, and video games (Gentile et al., 2004).

* * *

Our knowledge of learning principles comes from the work of hundreds of investigators. This unit has focused on the ideas of a few pioneers—Ivan Pavlov, John Watson, B. F. Skinner, and Albert Bandura. They illustrate the impact that can result from single-minded devotion to a few well-defined problems and ideas. These researchers defined the issues and impressed on us the importance of learning. As their legacy demonstrates, intellectual history is often made by people who risk going to extremes in pushing ideas to their limits (Simonton, 2000).

Before You Move On

▶ **ASK YOURSELF**

Who has been a significant role model for you? For whom are you a model?

▶ **TEST YOURSELF**

Jason's parents and older friends all smoke, but they advise him not to. Juan's parents and friends don't smoke, but they say nothing to deter him from doing so. Will Jason or Juan be more likely to start smoking?

Answers to the Test Yourself questions can be found in Appendix E at the end of the book.

Module 30 Review

 30-1 What is observational learning, and how do some scientists believe it is enabled by mirror neurons?

- In *observational learning,* as we observe and imitate others we learn to anticipate a behavior's consequences, because we experience vicarious reinforcement or vicarious punishment.

- Our brain's frontal lobes have a demonstrated ability to mirror the activity of another's brain. The same areas fire when we perform certain actions (such as responding to pain or moving our mouth to form words), as when we observe someone else performing those actions.

30-2 What is the impact of prosocial modeling and of antisocial modeling?

- Children tend to imitate what a model does and says, whether the behavior being *modeled* is *prosocial* (positive, constructive, and helpful) or antisocial.

- If a model's actions and words are inconsistent, children may imitate the hypocrisy they observe.

Multiple-Choice Questions

1. Bandura's famous Bobo doll experiment is most closely associated with which of the following?

   a. Latent learning
   b. Classical conditioning
   c. Operant conditioning
   d. Cognitive maps
   e. Observational learning

2. Which of the following processes is the best term for explaining how we learn languages?

   a. Biofeedback
   b. Discrimination
   c. Modeling
   d. Insight
   e. Creativity

3. Which of the following is the most likely consequence of the brain's tendency to vicariously experience something we observe?

   a. Actual physical injury

   b. The risk of misremembering our own actions

   c. Interference with associative learning

   d. The elimination of classically conditioned responses to stimuli

   e. A confusion between reinforcers and rewards in an operant conditioning setting

4. When is prosocial modeling most effective?

   a. When the model acts in a way consistent with the prosocial lesson

   b. When the model verbally emphasizes the prosocial lesson but acts as she chooses

   c. When the model is predisposed to the prosocial conduct

   d. When the observer has a close personal relationship with the model

   e. When the model is well-known

5. Which of the following is the best synonym for social learning?

   a. Observational learning

   b. Modeling

   c. Mirror neuron imitation

   d. Prosocial model

   e. Imitation

Practice FRQs

1. Explain how Bandura's Bobo doll experiment illustrates each of the following:

   • Modeling

   • Mirror neurons

Answer

1 point: Modeling can be described as the behavior of the child as he or she imitates the adult.

1 point: Mirror neurons on the child's brain presumably would fire the same way when watching the adult or when imitating the adult's behavior.

2. A young boy is left at home with his older brother while their parents drop off the family car for repairs. While the parents are out, the older brother prepares lunch for the young boy. Then the older brother takes the younger brother outside where he entertains him by building several fires with small twigs. Explain how the older brother's conduct is:

   • Prosocial modeling

   • Antisocial modeling

(2 points)

Unit VI Review

Key Terms and Concepts to Remember

learning, p. 263

habituation, p. 264

associative learning, p. 264

stimulus, p. 264

cognitive learning, p. 265

classical conditioning, p. 266

behaviorism, p. 266

neutral stimulus (NS), p. 266

unconditioned response (UR), p. 267

unconditioned stimulus (US), p. 267

conditioned response (CR), p. 268

conditioned stimulus (CS), p. 268

acquisition, p. 268

higher-order conditioning, p. 268

extinction, p. 269

spontaneous recovery, p. 269

generalization, p. 269

discrimination, p. 270

operant conditioning, p. 275

law of effect, p. 275

operant chamber, p. 276

reinforcement, p. 276

shaping, p. 276

discriminative stimulus, p. 277

positive reinforcement, p. 277

negative reinforcement, p. 278

primary reinforcer, p. 278

conditioned reinforcer, p. 278

reinforcement schedule, p. 279

continuous reinforcement, p. 279

partial (intermittent) reinforcement, p. 279

fixed-ratio schedule, p. 279

variable-ratio schedule, p. 280

fixed-interval schedule, p. 280

variable-interval schedule, p. 280

punishment, p. 281

biofeedback, p. 289

respondent behavior, p. 289

operant behavior, p. 289

cognitive map, p. 297

latent learning, p. 297

insight, p. 297

intrinsic motivation, p.297

extrinsic motivation, p. 298

coping, p. 298

problem-focused coping, p. 298

emotion-focused coping, p. 298

learned helplessness, p. 299

external locus of control, p. 300

internal locus of control, p. 300

self-control, p. 301

observational learning, p. 304

modeling, p. 304

mirror neurons, p. 305

prosocial behavior, p. 307

Key Contributors to Remember

Ivan Pavlov, p. 266

John B. Watson, p. 266

B. F. Skinner, p. 275

Edward Thorndike, p. 275

John Garcia, p. 293

Robert Rescorla, p. 296

Edward Tolman, p. 297

Albert Bandura, p. 304

AP® Exam Practice Questions

Multiple-Choice Questions

1. Which of the following most accurately describes an impact of punishment?

a. Punishment is a good way to increase a behavior, as long as it is not used too frequently.

b. Punishment may create problems in the short term but rarely produces long-term side effects.

c. Punishment can be effective at stopping specific behaviors quickly.

d. Punishment typically results in an increase of a behavior that caused the removal of an aversive stimulus.

e. Punishment should never be used (in the opinion of most psychologists), because the damage it causes can never be repaired.

2. Which of the following is an application of shaping?

   a. A mother who wants her daughter to hit a baseball first praises her for holding a bat, then for swinging it, and then for hitting the ball.

   b. A pigeon pecks a disk 25 times for an opportunity to receive a food reinforcement.

   c. A rat presses a bar when a green light is on but not when a red light is on.

   d. A rat gradually stops pressing a bar when it no longer receives a food reinforcement.

   e. A gambler continues to play a slot machine, even though he has won nothing on his last 20 plays, and he has lost a significant amount of money.

3. What is one of the principal functions of mirror neurons?

   a. To allow an organism to replace an unconditioned response with a conditioned response

   b. To help produce intrinsic motivation in some children

   c. To be the mechanism by which the brain accomplishes observational learning

   d. To produce the neural associations that are the basis of both classical and operant conditioning

   e. To explain why modeling prosocial behavior is more effective than modeling negative behavior

4. Which of the following illustrates generalization?

   a. A rabbit that has been conditioned to blink to a tone also blinks when a similar tone is sounded.

   b. A dog salivates to a tone but not to a buzzer.

   c. A light is turned on repeatedly until a rat stops flexing its paw when it's turned on.

   d. A pigeon whose disk-pecking response has been extinguished is placed in a Skinner box three hours later and begins pecking the disk again.

   e. A child is startled when the doorbell rings.

5. What did Albert Bandura's Bobo doll experiments demonstrate?

   a. Children are likely to imitate the behavior of adults.

   b. There may be a negative correlation between televised violence and aggressive behavior.

   c. Children are more likely to copy what adults say than what adults do.

   d. Allowing children to watch too much television is detrimental to their development.

   e. Observational learning can explain the development of fears in children.

6. What did Robert Rescorla and Allan Wagner's experiments establish?

   a. That the acquisition of a CR depends on pairing the CS and the US

   b. That different species respond differently to classical conditioning situations

   c. The current belief that classical conditioning is really a form of operant conditioning

   d. That mirror neurons form the biological basis of classical conditioning

   e. The importance of cognitive factors in classical conditioning

7. What does Edward Thorndike's law of effect state?

   a. The difference between positive and negative reinforcement

   b. That behavior maintained by partial reinforcement is more resistant to extinction than behavior maintained by continuous reinforcement

   c. How shaping can be used to establish operant conditioning

   d. That rewarded behavior is more likely to happen again

   e. The limited effectiveness of punishment

8. Which of the following processes would produce the acquisition of a conditioned response?

   a. Repeatedly present an unconditioned response

   b. Administer the conditioned stimulus without the unconditioned stimulus

   c. Make sure that the conditioned stimulus comes at least one minute before the unconditioned stimulus

   d. Pair a neutral stimulus with an unconditioned stimulus several times

   e. Present the conditioned stimulus until it starts to produce an unconditioned response

9. Which of the following would help determine what stimuli an organism can distinguish between?

   a. Negative reinforcement

   b. A variable-ratio schedule of reinforcement

   c. A fixed-ratio schedule of reinforcement

   d. Extinction

   e. A discriminative stimulus

10. A student studies diligently to avoid the bad feelings associated with a previously low grade on a test. In this case, the studying behavior is being strengthened because of what kind of reinforcement?

   a. Positive reinforcement

   b. Negative reinforcement

   c. Delayed reinforcement

   d. Primary reinforcement

   e. Conditioned reinforcement

11. Taste aversion studies lead researchers to which of the following conclusions?

   a. Taste is the most fundamental of the senses.
   b. There are genetic predispositions involved in taste learning.
   c. Animals must evaluate a situation cognitively before taste aversion develops.
   d. Taste aversion is a universal survival mechanism.
   e. An unconditioned stimulus must occur within seconds of a CS for conditioning to occur.

12. Mary checks her phone every 30 minutes for incoming text messages. Her behavior is being maintained by what kind of reinforcement schedule?

   a. Fixed-interval
   b. Variable-interval
   c. Variable-ratio
   d. Fixed-ratio
   e. Continuous

13. A dog is trained to salivate when it hears a tone associated with food. Then the tone is sounded repeatedly without an unconditioned stimulus until the dog stops salivating. Later, when the tone sounds again, the dog salivates again. This is a description of what part of the conditioning process?

   a. Spontaneous recovery
   b. Extinction
   c. Generalization
   d. Discrimination
   e. Acquisition

14. Latent learning is evidence for which of these conclusions?

   a. Punishment is an ineffective means of controlling behavior.
   b. Negative reinforcement should be avoided when possible.
   c. Cognition plays an important role in operant conditioning.
   d. Conditioned reinforcers are more effective than primary reinforcers.
   e. Shaping is usually not necessary for operant conditioning.

15. Classical and operant conditioning are based on the principles of which psychological perspective?

   a. Cognitive
   b. Biological
   c. Behaviorist
   d. Evolutionary
   e. Humanist

Free-Response Questions

1. Briefly explain how the concepts below could be used to help a child stop throwing temper tantrums.

   - Extinction (operant conditioning)
   - Positive reinforcement
   - Modeling
   - Negative reinforcement
   - Shaping
   - Extinction (classical conditioning)

Rubric for Free Response Question 1

1 point: **Extinction (operant conditioning)** The child might be throwing a temper tantrum because that behavior is being reinforced (for example, it gains the child desired attention from a parent). Extinction could be used to stop the temper tantrum by removing the reinforcement. Without the reinforcement, eventually the behavior (tantrums) should decrease. ↻ Pages 279, 290

1 point: **Positive reinforcement** A positive reinforcement (such as reading a favorite book) could be used to encourage a behavior other than temper tantrums. The child could be given the positive reinforcement after a "prosocial" behavior, such as sharing a toy with a friend instead of throwing a tantrum. ↻ Page 277

1 point: **Modeling** The child might learn to avoid temper tantrums through modeling or observational learning. A parent or other adult could show positive behaviors when disappointed, and the child might imitate this behavior. ↻ Page 304

1 point: **Negative reinforcement** Negative reinforcement occurs when a stimulus is removed, and this removal reinforces a behavior. In this situation, a parent or adult could sit the child on a "time-out" seat as soon as the temper tantrum begins. The child could leave the time out seat as soon as she or he stops crying. The removal of the aversive stimulus of the time out seat could reinforce not crying, and help to stop the temper tantrums. ↻ Page 278

1 point: **Shaping** A parent or other adult could gradually shape the child's negative behavior toward desired behaviors by rewarding successive approximations. For example, a child could first be rewarded for crying more quietly during a tantrum, then for stopping yelling, then for avoiding the tantrum completely. ↻ Page 276

1 point: **Extinction (classical conditioning)** In the context of classical conditioning, a behavior becomes extinct because a neutral stimulus is repeatedly presented without the unconditioned stimulus. For example, a child might have been classically conditioned to throw a tantrum whenever the child's brother is present, because the brother always pinches the child. The tantrums could be made extinct by convincing the brother to stop the pinching. The conditioned stimulus (the brother) is presented to the child without the unconditioned stimulus (the pinching). After repeated pairings, the conditioned response of the tantrum should become extinct. ↻ Pages 269, 290

Multiple-choice self-tests and more may be found at www.worthpublishers.com/MyersAP2e

2. Martin is a sixth-grade teacher who feels he is not able to connect with some of his students. Several of them have had academic problems in the past and although Martin feels that they can do the work, he believes that these students have given up. Explain how Martin could use each of these concepts to learn how best to help his students succeed.

- External locus of control
- Self-control
- Learned helplessness
- Intrinsic motivation

(4 points)

3. Researchers investigating conditioning throughout the history of psychology reached very different conclusions about how humans learn behaviors. Explain how these theorists might explain this example of behavior and response: A child cries when she sees a large pile of peas on her dinner plate.

- Edward Thorndike
- B. F. Skinner
- Ivan Pavlov
- Albert Bandura

(4 points)

Unit VII

Cognition

Modules

I revised this unit's first three modules after collaborating with Janie Wilson, Professor of Psychology at Georgia Southern University and Vice President for Programming of the Society for the Teaching of Psychology.

Throughout history, we humans have both bemoaned our foolishness and celebrated our wisdom. The poet T. S. Eliot was struck by "the hollow men . . . Headpiece filled with straw." But Shakespeare's Hamlet extolled the human species as "noble in reason! . . . infinite in faculties! . . . in apprehension how like a god!" In the preceding units, we have likewise marveled at both our abilities and our errors.

Elsewhere in this text, we study the human brain—three pounds of wet tissue the size of a small cabbage, yet containing circuitry more complex than the planet's telephone networks. We appreciate the amazing abilities of newborns. We marvel at our sensory system, translating visual stimuli into nerve impulses, distributing them for parallel processing, and reassembling them into colorful perceptions. Little wonder that our species has had the collective genius to invent the camera, the car, and the computer; to unlock the atom and crack the genetic code; to travel out to space and into our brain's depths.

Yet we have also seen that our species is kin to the other animals, influenced by the same principles that produce learning in rats and pigeons. We have noted that

316

we not-so-wise humans are easily deceived by perceptual illusions, pseudopsychic claims, and false memories.

In this unit, we encounter further instances of these two images of the human condition—the rational and the irrational. We will ponder our memory's enormous capacity, and the ease with which our two-track mind processes information, with and without our awareness. We will consider how we use and misuse the information we receive, perceive, store, and retrieve. We will look at our gift for language and consider how and why it develops. And we will reflect on how deserving we are of our species name, *Homo sapiens*—wise human.

Module 31

Studying and Building Memories

©Oliver Rossi/Corbis

Module Learning Objectives

31-1 Define *memory*.

31-2 Explain how psychologists describe the human memory system.

31-3 Distinguish between explicit and implicit memories.

31-4 Identify the information we process automatically.

31-5 Explain how sensory memory works.

31-6 Describe the capacity of our short-term and working memory.

31-7 Describe the effortful processing strategies that help us remember new information.

31-8 Describe the levels of processing and their effect on encoding.

B e thankful for memory. We take it for granted, except when it malfunctions. But it is our memory that accounts for time and defines our life. It is our memory that enables us to recognize family, speak our language, find our way home, and locate food and water. It is our memory that enables us to enjoy an experience and then mentally replay and enjoy it again. And it is our memory that occasionally pits us against those whose offenses we cannot forget.

The next three modules deal with memory. Not only is this a significant topic on the AP® exam, it is also one of the most practical topics in psychology, especially if you're a student! Some of your preconceptions about memory may be accurate and some may not. As you read, think about how you can apply what you're learning in order to be a better student.

memory the persistence of learning over time through the encoding, storage, and retrieval of information.

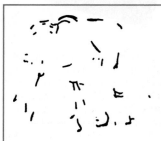

Figure 31.1

What is this? People who had, 17 years earlier, seen the complete image (in Figure 31.4 when you turn the page) were more likely to recognize this fragment, even if they had forgotten the earlier experience (Mitchell, 2006).

In large part, we are what we remember. Without memory—our storehouse of accumulated learning—there would be no savoring of past joys, no guilt or anger over painful recollections. We would instead live in an enduring present, each moment fresh. But each person would be a stranger, every language foreign, every task—dressing, eating, biking—a new challenge. You would even be a stranger to yourself, lacking that continuous sense of self that extends from your distant past to your momentary present.

Studying Memory

31-1   What is memory?

To a psychologist, **memory** is learning that has persisted over time; it is information that has been acquired, stored, and can be retrieved.

Research on memory's extremes has helped us understand how memory works. At age 92, my father suffered a small stroke that had but one peculiar effect. He was as mobile as before. His genial personality was intact. He knew us and enjoyed poring over family photo albums and reminiscing about his past. But he had lost most of his ability to lay down new memories of conversations and everyday episodes. He could not tell me what day of the week it was, or what he'd had for lunch. Told repeatedly of his brother-in-law's death, he was surprised and saddened each time he heard the news.

At the other extreme are people who would be gold medal winners in a memory Olympics. Russian journalist Shereshevskii, or S, had merely to listen while other reporters scribbled notes (Luria, 1968). You and I could parrot back a string of about 7—maybe even 9—digits. S could repeat up to 70, if they were read about 3 seconds apart in an otherwise silent room. Moreover, he could recall digits or words backward as easily as forward. His accuracy was unerring, even when recalling a list as much as 15 years later. "Yes, yes," he might recall. "This was a series you gave me once when we were in your apartment. . . . You were sitting at the table and I in the rocking chair. . . . You were wearing a gray suit. . . ."

Amazing? Yes, but consider your own impressive memory. You remember countless voices, sounds, and songs; tastes, smells, and textures; faces, places, and happenings. Imagine viewing more than 2500 slides of faces and places for 10 seconds each. Later, you see 280 of these slides, paired with others you've never seen. Actual participants in this experiment recognized 90 percent of the slides they had viewed in the first round (Haber, 1970). In a follow-up experiment, people exposed to 2800 images for only 3 seconds each spotted the repeats with 82 percent accuracy (Konkle et al., 2010).

Or imagine yourself looking at a picture fragment, such as the one in **FIGURE 31.1**. Also imagine that you had seen the complete picture for a couple of seconds 17 years earlier. This, too, was a real experiment, and participants who had previously seen the complete drawings were more likely to identify the objects than were members of a control group (Mitchell, 2006). Moreover, the picture memory reappeared even for those who did not consciously recall participating in the long-ago experiment!

How do we accomplish such memory feats? How does our brain pluck information out of the world around us and tuck that information away for later use? How can we remember things we have not thought about for years, yet forget the name of someone we met a minute ago? How are memories stored in our brains? Why will you be likely, later in this module, to misrecall this sentence: *"The angry rioter threw the rock at the window"*? In this and the next two modules, we'll consider these fascinating questions and more, including tips on how we can improve our own memories.

Memory Models

31-2 How do psychologists describe the human memory system?

Architects make miniature house models to help clients imagine their future homes. Similarly, psychologists create memory models to help us think about how our brain forms and retrieves memories. *Information-processing models* are analogies that compare human memory to a computer's operations. Thus, to remember any event, we must

- *get information into our brain,* a process called **encoding.**
- *retain that information,* a process called **storage.**
- later *get the information back out,* a process called **retrieval.**

Like all analogies, computer models have their limits. Our memories are less literal and more fragile than a computer's. Moreover, most computers process information sequentially, even while alternating between tasks. Our dual-track brain processes many things simultaneously (some of them unconsciously) by means of **parallel processing**. As you enter the lunchroom, you simultaneously—in parallel—process information about the people you see, the sounds of voices, and the smell of the food.

To focus on this complex, simultaneous processing, one information-processing model, *connectionism,* views memories as products of interconnected neural networks. Specific memories arise from particular activation patterns within these networks. Every time you learn something new, your brain's neural connections change, forming and strengthening pathways that allow you to interact with and learn from your constantly changing environment.

To explain our memory-forming process, Richard Atkinson and Richard Shiffrin (1968) proposed another model, with three stages:

1. We first record to-be-remembered information as a fleeting **sensory memory.**
2. From there, we process information into **short-term memory,** where we encode it through *rehearsal.*
3. Finally, information moves into **long-term memory** for later retrieval.

Other psychologists have updated this model (**FIGURE 31.2**) to include important newer concepts, including *working memory* and *automatic processing.*

WORKING MEMORY

Alan Baddeley and others (Baddeley, 2001, 2002; Engle, 2002) challenged Atkinson and Shiffrin's view of short-term memory as a small, brief storage space for recent thoughts and experiences. Research shows that this stage is not just a temporary shelf for holding incoming information. It's an active desktop where your brain processes information, making sense of new input and linking it with long-term memories. Whether we hear *eye-screem* as "ice cream" or "I scream" will depend on how the context and our experience guide us in interpreting and encoding the sounds.

encoding the processing of information into the memory system—for example, by extracting meaning.

storage the process of retaining encoded information over time.

retrieval the process of getting information out of memory storage.

parallel processing the processing of many aspects of a problem simultaneously; the brain's natural mode of information processing for many functions. Contrasts with the step-by-step (serial) processing of most computers and of conscious problem solving.

sensory memory the immediate, very brief recording of sensory information in the memory system.

short-term memory activated memory that holds a few items briefly, such as the seven digits of a phone number while dialing, before the information is stored or forgotten.

long-term memory the relatively permanent and limitless storehouse of the memory system. Includes knowledge, skills, and experiences.

AP® Exam Tip

You will see several versions of Figure 31.2 as you work your way through Modules 31, 32, and 33. Pay attention! This model may look confusing now, but will make more and more sense as its components are described in more detail.

Figure 31.2

A modified three-stage processing model of memory Atkinson and Shiffrin's classic three-step model helps us to think about how memories are processed, but today's researchers recognize other ways long-term memories form. For example, some information slips into long-term memory via a "back door," without our consciously attending to it (*automatic processing*). And so much active processing occurs in the short-term memory stage that many now prefer the term *working memory.*

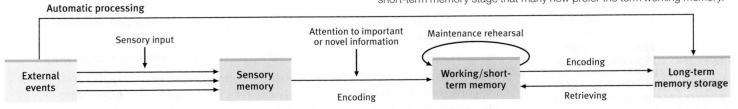

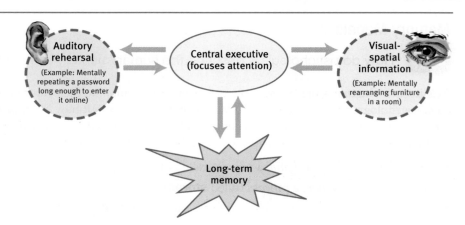

Figure 31.3

Working memory Alan Baddeley's (2002) model of working memory, simplified here, includes *visual* and *auditory rehearsal* of new information. A hypothetical *central executive* (manager) focuses attention and pulls information from long-term memory to help make sense of new information.

To emphasize the active processing that takes place in this middle stage, psychologists use the term **working memory.** Right now, you are using your working memory to link the information you're reading with your previously stored information (Cowan, 2010; Kail & Hall, 2001).

The pages you are reading may enter working memory through vision. You might also repeat the information using auditory rehearsal. As you integrate these memory inputs with your existing long-term memory, your attention is focused. Baddeley (2002) suggested a *central executive* handles this focused processing (**FIGURE 31.3**).

Without focused attention, information often fades. In one experiment, people read and typed new information they would later need, such as "An ostrich's eye is bigger than its brain." If they knew the information would be available online, they invested less energy in remembering, and they remembered the trivia less well (Sparrow et al., 2011). Sometimes Google replaces rehearsal.

Figure 31.4

Now you know People who had seen this complete image were, 17 years later, more likely to recognize the fragment in Figure 31.1.

Before You Move On

▶ **ASK YOURSELF**

How have you used the three parts of your memory system (encoding, storage, and retrieval) in learning something new today?

▶ **TEST YOURSELF**

Memory includes (in alphabetical order) long-term memory, sensory memory, and working/short-term memory. What's the correct order of these three memory stages?

Answers to the Test Yourself questions can be found in Appendix E at the end of the book.

working memory a newer understanding of short-term memory that focuses on conscious, active processing of incoming auditory and visual-spatial information, and of information retrieved from long-term memory.

explicit memory memory of facts and experiences that one can consciously know and "declare." (Also called *declarative memory.*)

effortful processing encoding that requires attention and conscious effort.

automatic processing unconscious encoding of incidental information, such as space, time, and frequency, and of well-learned information, such as word meanings.

implicit memory retention independent of conscious recollection. (Also called *nondeclarative memory.*)

Building Memories: Encoding

Dual-Track Memory: Effortful Versus Automatic Processing

 How do explicit and implicit memories differ?

As we have seen throughout this text, our mind operates on two tracks:

- Atkinson and Shiffrin's model focused on how we process our **explicit memories**—the facts and experiences we can consciously know and declare (thus, also called *declarative memories*). We encode explicit memories through conscious, **effortful processing.**

- Behind the scenes, outside the Atkinson-Shiffrin stages, other information skips the conscious encoding track and barges directly into storage. This **automatic processing,** which happens without our awareness, produces **implicit memories** (also called *nondeclarative memories*).

Automatic Processing and Implicit Memories

31-4 What information do we automatically process?

Our implicit memories include *procedural* memory for automatic skills (such as how to ride a bike) and classically conditioned *associations* among stimuli. Visiting your dentist, you may, thanks to a conditioned association linking the dentist's office with the painful drill, find yourself with sweaty palms. You didn't plan to feel that way when you got to the dentist's office; it happened *automatically*.

Without conscious effort you also automatically process information about

- *space*. While studying, you often encode the place on a page or in your notebook where certain material appears; later, when you want to retrieve information about automatic processing, for example, you may visualize the location of that information on this page.

- *time*. While going about your day, you unintentionally note the sequence of its events. Later, realizing you've left your backpack somewhere, the event sequence your brain automatically encoded will enable you to retrace your steps.

- *frequency*. You effortlessly keep track of how many times things happen, as when you suddenly realize, *This is the third time I've run into her today.*

Our two-track mind engages in impressively efficient information processing. As one track automatically tucks away many routine details, the other track is free to focus on conscious, effortful processing. This reinforces an important principle introduced in Module 18's description of parallel processing: Mental feats such as vision, thinking, and memory may seem to be single abilities, but they are not. Rather, we split information into different components for separate and simultaneous processing.

Effortful Processing and Explicit Memories

Automatic processing happens so effortlessly that it is difficult to shut off. When you see words in your native language, perhaps on the side of a delivery truck, you can't help but read them and register their meaning. *Learning* to read wasn't automatic. You may recall working hard to pick out letters and connect them to certain sounds. But with experience and practice, your reading became automatic. Imagine now learning to read reversed sentences like this:

.citamotua emoceb nac gnissecorp luftroffE

At first, this requires effort, but after enough practice, you would also perform this task much more automatically. We develop many skills in this way. We learn to drive, to text, to speak a new language with effort, but then these tasks become automatic.

SENSORY MEMORY

31-5 How does sensory memory work?

Sensory memory (recall Figure 31.2) feeds our active working memory, recording momentary images of scenes or echoes of sounds. How much of this page could you sense and recall with less exposure than a lightning flash? In one experiment (Sperling, 1960), people viewed three rows of three letters each, for only one-twentieth of a second (**FIGURE 31.5**). After the nine letters disappeared, they could recall only about half of them.

Was it because they had insufficient time to glimpse them? *No.* The researcher, George Sperling, cleverly demonstrated that people actually *could* see and recall all the letters, but only momentarily. Rather than ask them to recall all nine letters at

Figure 31.5

Total recall—briefly When George Sperling flashed a group of letters similar to this for one-twentieth of a second, people could recall only about half the letters. But when signaled to recall a particular row immediately after the letters had disappeared, they could do so with near-perfect accuracy.

K	Z	R
Q	B	T
S	G	N

iconic memory a momentary sensory memory of visual stimuli; a photographic or picture-image memory lasting no more than a few tenths of a second.

echoic memory a momentary sensory memory of auditory stimuli; if attention is elsewhere, sounds and words can still be recalled within 3 or 4 seconds.

once, he sounded a high, medium, or low tone immediately *after* flashing the nine letters. This tone directed participants to report only the letters of the top, middle, or bottom row, respectively. Now they rarely missed a letter, showing that all nine letters were momentarily available for recall.

Sperling's experiment demonstrated **iconic memory,** a fleeting sensory memory of visual stimuli. For a few tenths of a second, our eyes register a photographic or picture-image memory of a scene, and we can recall any part of it in amazing detail. But if Sperling delayed the tone signal by more than half a second, the image faded and participants again recalled only about half the letters. Our visual screen clears quickly, as new images are superimposed over old ones.

We also have an impeccable, though fleeting, memory for auditory stimuli, called **echoic memory** (Cowan, 1988; Lu et al., 1992). Picture yourself in class, as your attention veers to thoughts of the weekend. If your mildly irked teacher tests you by asking, "What did I just say?" you can recover the last few words from your mind's echo chamber. Auditory echoes tend to linger for 3 or 4 seconds.

CAPACITY OF SHORT-TERM AND WORKING MEMORY

31-6 What is the capacity of our short-term and working memory?

George Miller (1956) proposed that short-term memory can retain about seven information bits (give or take two). Other researchers have confirmed that we can, if nothing distracts us, recall about seven digits, or about six letters or five words (Baddeley et al., 1975). How quickly do our short-term memories disappear? To find out, researchers asked people to remember three-consonant groups, such as *CHJ* (Peterson & Peterson, 1959). To prevent rehearsal, the researchers asked them, for example, to start at 100 and count aloud backward by threes. After 3 seconds, people recalled the letters only about half the time; after 12 seconds, they seldom recalled them at all (**FIGURE 31.6**). Without the active processing that we now understand to be a part of our working memory, short-term memories have a limited life.

Working-memory capacity varies, depending on age and other factors. Compared with children and older adults, young adults have more working-memory capacity, so they can use their mental workspace more efficiently. This means their ability to multitask is relatively greater. But whatever our age, we do better and more efficient work when focused, without distractions, on one task at a time. "One of the most stubborn, persistent phenomenon of the mind," notes cognitive psychologist Daniel Willingham (2010), "is that when you do two things at once, you don't do either one as well as when you do them one at a time." *The bottom line:* It's probably a bad idea to try to watch TV, text your friends, and write a psychology paper all at the same time!

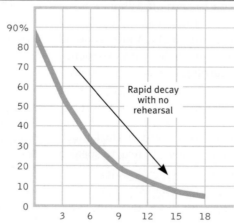

Figure 31.6
Short-term memory decay Unless rehearsed, verbal information may be quickly forgotten. (From Peterson & Peterson, 1959; see also Brown, 1958.)

Percentage who recalled consonants

Rapid decay with no rehearsal

Time in seconds between presentation of consonants and recall request (no rehearsal allowed)

EFFORTFUL PROCESSING STRATEGIES

 31-7 What are some effortful processing strategies that can help us remember new information?

Research shows that several effortful processing strategies can boost our ability to form new memories. Later, when we try to retrieve a memory, these strategies can make the difference between success and failure.

CHUNKING Glance for a few seconds at row 1 of **FIGURE 31.7,** then look away and try to reproduce what you saw. Impossible, yes? But you can easily reproduce the second row, which is no less complex. Similarly, you will probably find row 4 much easier to remember than row 3, although both contain the same letters. And you could remember the sixth cluster more easily than the fifth, although both contain the same words. As these units demonstrate, **chunking** information—organizing items into familiar, manageable units—enables us to recall it more easily. Try remembering 43 individual numbers and letters. It would be impossible, unless chunked into, say, seven meaningful chunks, such as "Try remembering 43 individual numbers and letters." ☺

Figure 31.7

Effects of chunking on memory When we organize information into meaningful units, such as letters, words, and phrases, we recall it more easily. (From Hintzman, 1978.)

1.  ⊲ ⊃ ⊐ ∾ ⊂ Ͷ
2. K L C I S N E

3. KLCISNE NVESE YNA NI CSTTIH TNDO
4. NICKELS SEVEN ANY IN STITCH DONT

5. NICKELS SEVEN ANY IN STITCH DONT SAVES AGO A SCORE TIME AND NINE WOODEN FOUR YEARS TAKE

6. DONT TAKE ANY WOODEN NICKELS FOUR SCORE AND SEVEN YEARS AGO A STITCH IN TIME SAVES NINE

Chunking usually occurs so naturally that we take it for granted. If you are a native English speaker, you can reproduce perfectly the 150 or so line segments that make up the words in the three phrases of item 6 in Figure 31.7. It would astonish someone unfamiliar with the language. I am similarly awed at a Chinese reader's ability to glance at **FIGURE 31.8** and then reproduce all the strokes; or of a varsity basketball player's recall of the positions of the players after a 4-second glance at a basketball play (Allard & Burnett, 1985). We all remember information best when we can organize it into personally meaningful arrangements.

MNEMONICS To help them encode lengthy passages and speeches, ancient Greek scholars and orators also developed **mnemonics** (nih-MON-iks). Many of these memory aids use vivid imagery, because we are particularly good at remembering mental pictures. We more easily remember concrete, visualizable words than we do abstract words. (When I quiz you later, in Module 33, which three of these words—*bicycle, void, cigarette, inherent, fire, process*—will you most likely recall?) If you still recall the rock-throwing rioter sentence, it is probably not only because of the meaning you encoded but also because the sentence painted a mental image.

The *peg-word system* harnesses our superior visual-imagery skill. This mnemonic requires you to memorize a jingle: *"One is a bun; two is a shoe; three is a tree; four is a door; five is a hive; six is sticks; seven is heaven; eight is a gate; nine is swine; ten is a hen."* Without much effort, you will soon be able to count by peg words instead of numbers: *bun, shoe, tree* . . . and then to visually associate the peg words with to-be-remembered items. Now you are ready to challenge anyone to give you a grocery list to remember. Carrots? Stick them into the imaginary bun. Milk? Fill the shoe with it. Paper towels? Drape them over the tree branch. Think *bun, shoe, tree* and you see their associated images: carrots, milk, paper towels. With few errors, you will be able to recall the items in any order and to name any given item (Bugelski et al., 1968). Memory whizzes understand the power of such systems. A study of star performers in the World Memory Championships showed them not to have exceptional intelligence, but rather to be superior at using mnemonic strategies (Maguire et al., 2003).

Chunking and mnemonic techniques combined can be great memory aids for unfamiliar material. Want to remember the colors of the rainbow in order of wavelength? Think of the mnemonic ROY G. BIV (*r*ed, *o*range, *y*ellow, *g*reen, *b*lue, *i*ndigo, *v*iolet). Need to recall the names of North America's five Great Lakes? Just remember HOMES (*H*uron, *O*ntario, *M*ichigan, *E*rie, *S*uperior). In each case, we chunk information into a more familiar form by creating a word (called an *acronym*) from the first letters of the to-be-remembered items.

Figure 31.8

An example of chunking—for those who read Chinese After looking at these characters, can you reproduce them exactly? If so, you are literate in Chinese.

春夏秋冬

chunking organizing items into familiar, manageable units; often occurs automatically.

mnemonics [nih-MON-iks] memory aids, especially those techniques that use vivid imagery and organizational devices.

HIERARCHIES When people develop expertise in an area, they process information not only in chunks but also in *hierarchies* composed of a few broad concepts divided and subdivided into narrower concepts and facts. This section, for example, aims to help you organize some of the memory concepts we have been discussing (**FIGURE 31.9**).

Organizing knowledge in hierarchies helps us retrieve information efficiently, as Gordon Bower and his colleagues (1969) demonstrated by presenting words either randomly or grouped into categories. When the words were organized into categories, recall was two to three times better. Such results show the benefits of organizing what you study—of giving special attention to the module objectives, headings, and Ask Yourself and Test Yourself questions. Taking class and text notes in outline format—a type of hierarchical organization—may also prove helpful.

Figure 31.9

Hierarchies aid retrieval When we organize words or concepts into hierarchical groups, as illustrated here with some of the concepts from this section, we remember them better than when we see them presented randomly.

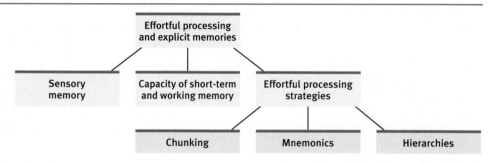

DISTRIBUTED PRACTICE

We retain information (such as classmates' names) better when our encoding is distributed over time. More than 300 experiments over the last century have consistently revealed the benefits of this **spacing effect** (Cepeda et al., 2006). *Massed practice* (cramming) can produce speedy short-term learning and a feeling of confidence. But to paraphrase pioneer memory researcher Hermann Ebbinghaus (1885), those who learn quickly also forget quickly. *Distributed practice* produces better long-term recall. After you've studied long enough to master the material, further study at that time becomes inefficient (Rohrer & Pashler, 2007). Better to spend that extra reviewing time later—a day later if you need to remember something 10 days hence, or a month later if you need to remember something 6 months hence (Cepeda et al., 2008).

Spreading your learning over several months, rather than over a shorter term, can help you retain information for a lifetime. In a 9-year experiment, Harry Bahrick and three of his family members (1993) practiced foreign language word translations for a given number of times, at intervals ranging from 14 to 56 days. Their consistent finding: The longer the space between practice sessions, the better their retention up to 5 years later.

AP® Exam Tip

It's not the studying you do in May that will determine your success on the AP® exam; it's the studying you do now. It's a good idea to take a little time each week to quickly review material from earlier in the course. When was the last time you looked at information from the previous units?

One effective way to distribute practice is *repeated self-testing,* a phenomenon that researchers Henry Roediger and Jeffrey Karpicke (2006) have called the **testing effect.** In this text, for example, the testing questions interspersed throughout and at the end of each module and unit offer such opportunities. Better to practice retrieval (as any exam will demand) than merely to reread material (which may lull you into a false sense of mastery).

The point to remember: Spaced study and self-assessment beat cramming and rereading. Practice may not make perfect, but smart practice—occasional rehearsal with self-testing—makes for lasting memories.

LEVELS OF PROCESSING

31-8 What are the levels of processing, and how do they affect encoding?

spacing effect the tendency for distributed study or practice to yield better long-term retention than is achieved through massed study or practice.

testing effect enhanced memory after retrieving, rather than simply rereading, information. Also sometimes referred to as a *retrieval practice effect* or *test-enhanced learning.*

shallow processing encoding on a basic level based on the structure or appearance of words.

Memory researchers have discovered that we process verbal information at different levels, and that depth of processing affects our long-term retention. **Shallow processing** encodes on a very basic level, such as a word's letters or, at a more intermediate level, a word's sound.

Making things memorable
For suggestions on how to apply the *testing effect* to your own learning, watch this 5-minute YouTube animation: tinyurl.com/HowToRemember.

Deep processing encodes *semantically*, based on the meaning of the words. The deeper (more meaningful) the processing, the better our retention.

In one classic experiment, researchers Fergus Craik and Endel Tulving (1975) flashed words at people. Then they asked the viewers a question that would elicit different levels of processing. To experience the task yourself, rapidly answer the following sample questions:

deep processing encoding semantically, based on the meaning of the words; tends to yield the best retention.

Sample Questions to Elicit Processing	Word Flashed	Yes	No
1. Is the word in capital letters?	CHAIR	_____	_____
2. Does the word rhyme with train?	brain	_____	_____
3. Would the word fit in this sentence? The girl put the _____ on the table.	doll	_____	_____

Which type of processing would best prepare you to recognize the words at a later time? In Craik and Tulving's experiment, the deeper, semantic processing triggered by the third question yielded a much better memory than did the shallower processing elicited by the second question or the very shallow processing elicited by question 1 (which was especially ineffective).

MAKING MATERIAL PERSONALLY MEANINGFUL

If new information is not meaningful or related to our experience, we have trouble processing it. Put yourself in the place of the students whom John Bransford and Marcia Johnson (1972) asked to remember the following recorded passage:

> The procedure is actually quite simple. First you arrange things into different groups. Of course, one pile may be sufficient depending on how much there is to do. . . . After the procedure is completed one arranges the materials into different groups again. Then they can be put into their appropriate places. Eventually they will be used once more and the whole cycle will then have to be repeated. However, that is part of life.

When the students heard the paragraph you have just read, without a meaningful context, they remembered little of it. When told the paragraph described washing clothes (something meaningful to them), they remembered much more of it—as you probably could now after rereading it.

AP® Exam Tip
Are you often pressed for time? The most effective way to cut down on the amount of time you need to spend studying is to increase the meaningfulness of the material. If you can relate the material to your own life—and that's pretty easy when you're studying psychology—it takes less time to master it.

Try This

Here is another sentence I will ask you about later (in Module 33): "The fish attacked the swimmer."

Can you repeat the sentence about the rioter that I gave you at this module's beginning? ("The angry rioter threw . . .") Perhaps, like those in an experiment by William Brewer (1977), you recalled the sentence by the meaning you encoded when you read it (for example, "The angry rioter threw the rock *through* the window") and not as it was written ("The angry rioter threw the rock *at* the window"). Referring to such mental mismatches, researchers have likened our minds to theater directors who, given a raw script, imagine the finished stage production (Bower & Morrow, 1990). Asked later what we heard or read, we recall not the literal text but *what we encoded*. Thus, studying for a test, you may remember your class notes rather than the class itself.

We can avoid some of these mismatches by rephrasing what we see and hear into meaningful terms. From his experiments on himself, German philosopher Hermann Ebbinghaus (1850–1909) estimated that, compared with learning nonsense material, learning meaningful material required one-tenth the effort. As memory researcher Wayne Wickelgren (1977, p. 346) noted, "The time you spend thinking about material you are reading and relating it to previously stored material is about the most useful thing you can do in learning any new subject matter."

Psychologist-actor team Helga Noice and Tony Noice (2006) have described how actors inject meaning into the daunting task of learning "all those lines." They do it by first coming to understand the flow of meaning: "One actor divided a half-page of dialogue into three [intentions]: 'to flatter,' 'to draw him out,' and 'to allay his fears.'" With this meaningful sequence in mind, the actor more easily remembered the lines.

We have especially good recall for information we can meaningfully relate to ourselves. Asked how well certain adjectives describe someone else, we often forget them; asked how well the adjectives describe us, we remember the words well. This tendency, called the *self-reference effect,* is especially strong in members of individualist Western cultures (Symons & Johnson, 1997; Wagar & Cohen, 2003). Information deemed "relevant to me" is processed more deeply and remains more accessible. Knowing this, you can profit from taking time to find personal meaning in what you are studying.

The point to remember: The amount remembered depends both on the time spent learning and on your making it meaningful for deep processing.

Before You Move On

▶ **ASK YOURSELF**

Can you think of three ways to employ the principles in this section to improve your own learning and retention of important ideas?

▶ **TEST YOURSELF**

What would be the most effective strategy to learn and retain a list of names of key historical figures for a week? For a year?

Answers to the Test Yourself questions can be found in Appendix E at the end of the book.

Module 31 Review

31-1 What is memory?

- *Memory* is learning that has persisted over time, through the storage and retrieval of information.

31-2 How do psychologists describe the human memory system?

- Psychologists use memory models to think and communicate about memory.

- Information-processing models involve three processes: *encoding, storage,* and *retrieval.*

- The connectionism information-processing model views memories as products of interconnected neural networks.

- The three processing stages in the Atkinson-Shiffrin model are *sensory memory, short-term memory,* and *long-term memory.* More recent research has updated this model to include two important concepts: (1) *working memory,* to stress the active processing occurring in the second memory stage; and (2) automatic processing, to address the processing of information outside of conscious awareness.

31-3 How do explicit and implicit memories differ?

- Through *parallel processing,* the human brain processes many things simultaneously, on dual tracks.

- *Explicit* (declarative) *memories*—our conscious memories of facts and experiences—form through *effortful processing,* which requires conscious effort and attention.

- *Implicit* (nondeclarative) *memories*—of skills and classically conditioned associations—happen without our awareness, through *automatic processing.*

31-4 What information do we automatically process?

- In addition to skills and classically conditioned associations, we automatically process incidental information about space, time, and frequency.

31-5 How does sensory memory work?

- Sensory memory feeds some information into working memory for active processing there.

- An *iconic memory* is a very brief (a few tenths of a second) sensory memory of visual stimuli; an *echoic memory* is a three- or four-second sensory memory of auditory stimuli.

31-6 What is the capacity of our short-term and working memory?

- Short-term memory capacity is about seven items, plus or minus two, but this information disappears from memory quickly without rehearsal.

- Working memory capacity varies, depending on age, intelligence level, and other factors.

31-7 What are some effortful processing strategies that can help us remember new information?

- Effective effortful processing strategies include *chunking, mnemonics,* hierarchies, and distributed practice sessions.

- The *testing effect* is the finding that consciously retrieving, rather than simply rereading, information enhances memory.

31-8 What are the levels of processing, and how do they affect encoding?

- Depth of processing affects long-term retention.
  - In *shallow processing,* we encode words based on their structure or appearance.
  - Retention is best when we use *deep processing,* encoding words based on their meaning.

- We also more easily remember material that is personally meaningful—the self-reference effect.

Multiple-Choice Questions

1. Caitlin, a fifth grader, is asked to remember her second-grade teacher's name. What measure of retention will Caitlin use to answer this question?

   a. Storage
   b. Recognition
   c. Relearning
   d. Recall
   e. Encoding

2. Working memory is most active during which portion of the information-processing model?

   a. Short-term memory
   b. Sensory memory
   c. Retrieval
   d. Encoding
   e. Long-term memory

3. Your memory of which of the following is an example of implicit memory?

   a. What you had for breakfast yesterday
   b. The need to spend some time reviewing tomorrow for an upcoming psychology quiz
   c. Which way to turn the car key to start the engine
   d. That George Washington was the first President
   e. How exciting it was to get the best birthday present ever

4. Which of the following is the most accurate description of the capacity of short-term and working memory?

   a. Lasts for about 2 days in most circumstances
   b. Lasts for less than half a minute unless you rehearse the information
   c. Is thought to be unlimited—there is always room for more information
   d. Can handle about a half dozen items for each of the tasks you are working on at any time
   e. Can handle about a half dozen items total

5. Which of the following is most likely to lead to semantic encoding of a list of words?

   a. Thinking about how the words relate to your own life
   b. Practicing the words for a single extended period
   c. Breaking up the practice into several relatively short sessions
   d. Noticing where in a sentence the words appear
   e. Focusing on the number of vowels and consonants in the words

Practice FRQs

1. To remember something, we must get information into our brain, retain the information, and later get the information back out. Making sure you use the terms for these three steps of the process, explain how this system would apply if you needed to learn the name of a new student who just enrolled in your school today.

Answer

1 point: Encoding is the process of getting the new student's name into your brain.

1 point: Storage is keeping that name in your memory.

1 point: Retrieval is the process of using that name when greeting the new student later.

2. Last evening, Carlos' mom told him he needed to buy milk today. So, he hopped on his bicycle this morning and headed to the corner store to pick up a gallon. Explain how both implicit and explicit memories were involved in Carlos' errand.

(4 points)

Module 32

Memory Storage and Retrieval

Module Learning Objectives

32-1 Describe the capacity and location of our long-term memories.

32-2 Describe the roles of the frontal lobes and hippocampus in memory processing.

32-3 Describe the roles of the cerebellum and basal ganglia in our memory processing.

32-4 Discuss how emotions affect our memory processing.

32-5 Explain how changes at the synapse level affect our memory processing.

32-6 Explain how memory is measured.

32-7 Describe how external cues, internal emotions, and order of appearance influence memory retrieval.

Memory Storage

32-1 What is the capacity of long-term memory? Are our long-term memories processed and stored in specific locations?

In Arthur Conan Doyle's *A Study in Scarlet,* Sherlock Holmes offers a popular theory of memory capacity:

> I consider that a man's brain originally is like a little empty attic, and you have to stock it with such furniture as you choose. . . . It is a mistake to think that that little room has elastic walls and can distend to any extent. Depend upon it, there comes a time when for every addition of knowledge you forget something that you knew before.

Contrary to Holmes'"memory model," our capacity for storing long-term memories is essentially limitless. Our brains are not like attics, which once filled can store more items only if we discard old ones.

Retaining Information in the Brain

I marveled at my aging mother-in-law, a retired pianist and organist. At age 88, her blind eyes could no longer read music. But let her sit at a keyboard and she would flawlessly play any of hundreds of hymns, including ones she had not thought of for 20 years. Where did her brain store those thousands of sequenced notes?

> "Our memories are flexible and superimposable, a panoramic blackboard with an endless supply of chalk and erasers."
> -ELIZABETH LOFTUS AND KATHERINE KETCHAM, *THE MYTH OF REPRESSED MEMORY,* 1994

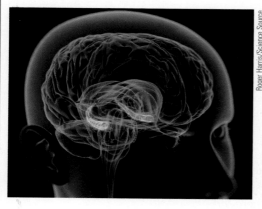

For a time, some surgeons and memory researchers marveled at patients' seeming vivid memories triggered by brain stimulation during surgery. Did this prove that our whole past, not just well-practiced music, is "in there," in complete detail, just waiting to be relived? On closer analysis, the seeming flashbacks appeared to have been invented, not relived (Loftus & Loftus, 1980). In a further demonstration that memories do not reside in single, specific spots, psychologist Karl Lashley (1950) trained rats to find their way out of a maze, then surgically removed pieces of their brain's cortex and retested their memory. No matter which small brain section he removed, the rats retained at least a partial memory of how to navigate the maze.

The point to remember: Despite the brain's vast storage capacity, we do not store information as libraries store their books, in discrete, precise locations. Instead, many parts of the brain interact as we encode, store, and retrieve the information that forms our memories.

EXPLICIT-MEMORY SYSTEM: THE FRONTAL LOBES AND HIPPOCAMPUS

 What roles do the frontal lobes and hippocampus play in memory processing?

As with perception, language, emotion, and much more, memory requires brain networks. The network that processes and stores your explicit memories for facts and episodes includes your frontal lobes and hippocampus. When you summon up a mental encore of a past experience, many brain regions send input to your frontal lobes for working memory processing (Fink et al., 1996; Gabrieli et al., 1996; Markowitsch, 1995). The left and right frontal lobes process different types of memories. Recalling a password and holding it in working memory, for example, would activate the left frontal lobe. Calling up a visual party scene would more likely activate the right frontal lobe.

Cognitive neuroscientists have found that the **hippocampus,** a temporal-lobe neural center located in the limbic system, is the brain's equivalent of a "save" button for explicit memories (**FIGURE 32.1**). Brain scans, such as PET scans of people recalling words, and autopsies of people who had *amnesia* (memory loss) have revealed that new explicit memories of names, images, and events are laid down via the hippocampus (Squire, 1992).

Damage to this structure therefore disrupts recall of explicit memories. Chickadees and other birds can store food in hundreds of places and return to these unmarked caches months later—but not if their hippocampus has been removed (Kamil & Cheng, 2001; Sherry & Vaccarino, 1989). With left-hippocampus damage, people have trouble remembering verbal information, but they have no trouble recalling visual designs and locations. With right-hippocampus damage, the problem is reversed (Schacter, 1996).

Subregions of the hippocampus also serve different functions. One part is active as people learn to associate names with faces (Zeineh et al., 2003). Another part is active as memory champions engage in spatial mnemonics (Maguire et al., 2003b). The rear area, which processes spatial memory, grows bigger the longer a London cabbie has navigated the maze of streets (Maguire et al., 2003a).

Memories are not permanently stored in the hippocampus. Instead, this structure seems to act as a loading dock where the brain registers and temporarily holds the elements of a remembered episode—its smell, feel, sound, and location. Then, like older files shifted to a basement storeroom, memories migrate for storage elsewhere.

Sleep supports memory consolidation. During deep sleep, the hippocampus processes memories for later retrieval. After a training experience, the greater

hippocampus a neural center located in the limbic system; helps process explicit memories for storage.

Figure 32.1

The hippocampus Explicit memories for facts and episodes are processed in the hippocampus and fed to other brain regions for storage.

the hippocampus activity during sleep, the better the next day's memory will be (Peigneux et al., 2004). Researchers have watched the hippocampus and brain cortex displaying simultaneous activity rhythms during sleep, as if they were having a dialogue (Euston et al., 2007; Mehta, 2007). They suspect that the brain is replaying the day's experiences as it transfers them to the cortex for long-term storage. Cortex areas surrounding the hippocampus support the processing and storing of explicit memories (Squire & Zola-Morgan, 1991).

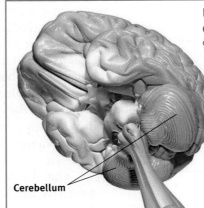

Hippocampus hero Among animals, one contender for champion memorist would be a mere birdbrain—the Clark's Nutcracker—which during winter and spring can locate up to 6000 caches of pine seed it had previously buried (Shettleworth, 1993).

© Tim Zurowski/All Canada Photos/Corbis

IMPLICIT-MEMORY SYSTEM: THE CEREBELLUM AND BASAL GANGLIA

32-3 What roles do the cerebellum and basal ganglia play in our memory processing?

Your hippocampus and frontal lobes are processing sites for your *explicit* memories. But you could lose those areas and still, thanks to automatic processing, lay down *implicit* memories for skills and conditioned associations. Joseph LeDoux (1996) recounted the story of a brain-damaged patient whose amnesia left her unable to recognize her physician as, each day, he shook her hand and introduced himself. One day, she yanked her hand back, for the physician had pricked her with a tack in his palm. The next time he returned to introduce himself she refused to shake his hand but couldn't explain why. Having been *classically conditioned,* she just wouldn't do it.

The *cerebellum* plays a key role in forming and storing the implicit memories created by classical conditioning. With a damaged cerebellum, people cannot develop certain conditioned reflexes, such as associating a tone with an impending puff of air—and thus do not blink in anticipation of the puff (Daum & Schugens, 1996; Green & Woodruff-Pak, 2000). When researchers surgically disrupted the function of different pathways in the cerebellum of rabbits, the rabbits became unable to learn a conditioned eyeblink response (Krupa et al., 1993; Steinmetz, 1999). Implicit memory formation needs the cerebellum (**FIGURE 32.2**).

Figure 32.2 Cerebellum The cerebellum plays an important part in our forming and storing of implicit memories.

Cerebellum

The *basal ganglia,* deep brain structures involved in motor movement, facilitate formation of our procedural memories for skills (Mishkin, 1982; Mishkin et al., 1997). The basal ganglia receive input from the cortex but do not return the favor of sending information back to the cortex for conscious awareness of procedural learning. If you have learned how to ride a bike, thank your basal ganglia.

Our implicit memory system, enabled partly by the cerebellum and basal ganglia, helps explain why the reactions and skills we learned during infancy reach far into our future. Yet as adults, our conscious memory of our first three years is blank, an experience called *infantile amnesia.* In one study, events children experienced and discussed with their mothers at age 3 were 60 percent remembered at age 7 but only 34 percent remembered at age 9 (Bauer et al., 2007). Two influences contribute to infantile amnesia: First, we index much of our explicit memory using words that nonspeaking children have not learned. Second, the hippocampus is one of the last brain structures to mature.

The Amygdala, Emotions, and Memory

32-4 How do emotions affect our memory processing?

Our emotions trigger stress hormones that influence memory formation. When we are excited or stressed, these hormones make more glucose energy available to fuel brain activity, signaling the brain that something important has happened. Moreover, stress hormones provoke the *amygdala* (two limbic system, emotion-processing clusters) to initiate a memory

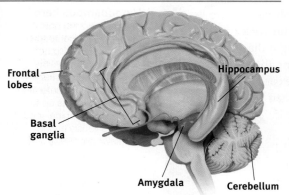

Figure 32.3

Review key memory structures in the brain
Frontal lobes and *hippocampus:* explicit memory formation
Cerebellum and *basal ganglia:* implicit memory formation
Amygdala: emotion-related memory formation

flashbulb memory a clear memory of an emotionally significant moment or event.

Try This

Which is more important—your experiences or your memories of them?

trace in the frontal lobes and basal ganglia and to boost activity in the brain's memory-forming areas (Buchanan, 2007; Kensinger, 2007) (**FIGURE 32.3**). The result? Emotional arousal can sear certain events into the brain, while disrupting memory for neutral events around the same time (Birnbaum et al., 2004; Brewin et al., 2007).

Emotions often persist without our conscious awareness of what caused them. In one ingenious experiment, patients with hippocampal damage (which left them unable to form new explicit memories) watched a sad film and later a happy film. After the viewing, they did not consciously recall the films, but the sad or happy emotion persisted (Feinstein et al., 2010).

Significantly stressful events can form almost indelible (unforgettable) memories. After traumatic experiences—a school shooting, a house fire, a rape—vivid recollections of the horrific event may intrude again and again. It is as if they were burned in: "Stronger emotional experiences make for stronger, more reliable memories," noted James McGaugh (1994, 2003). This makes adaptive sense. Memory serves to predict the future and to alert us to potential dangers. Conversely, weaker emotions mean weaker memories. People given a drug that blocked the effects of stress hormones later had more trouble remembering the details of an upsetting story (Cahill, 1994).

Emotion-triggered hormonal changes help explain why we long remember exciting or shocking events, such as our first kiss or our whereabouts when learning of a loved one's death. In a 2006 Pew survey, 95 percent of American adults said they could recall exactly where they were or what they were doing when they first heard the news of the 9/11 terrorist attacks. This perceived clarity of memories of surprising, significant events leads some psychologists to call them **flashbulb memories.** It's as if the brain commands, "Capture this!"

The people who experienced a 1989 San Francisco earthquake did just that. A year and a half later, they had perfect recall of where they had been and what they were doing (verified by their recorded thoughts within a day or two of the quake). Others' memories for the circumstances under which they merely *heard* about the quake were more prone to errors (Neisser et al., 1991; Palmer et al., 1991).

Our flashbulb memories are noteworthy for their vividness and the confidence with which we recall them. But as we relive, rehearse, and discuss them, these memories may come to err, as misinformation seeps in (Conway et al., 2009; Talarico & Rubin, 2003, 2007).

Synaptic Changes

32-5 How do changes at the synapse level affect our memory processing?

As you read this module and think and learn about memory characteristics and processes, your brain is changing. Given increased activity in particular pathways, neural interconnections are forming and strengthening.

The quest to understand the physical basis of memory—how information becomes embedded in brain matter—has sparked study of the synaptic meeting places where neurons communicate with one another via their neurotransmitter messengers. Eric Kandel and James Schwartz (1982) observed synaptic changes during learning in the sending neurons of the California sea slug, *Aplysia*, a simple animal with a mere 20,000 or so unusually large and accessible nerve cells. Module 26 noted how the sea slug can be classically conditioned (with electric shock) to reflexively withdraw its gills when squirted with water, much as a shell-shocked soldier jumps at the sound of a snapping twig. By observing the slug's neural connections before and after conditioning,

Aplysia The California sea slug, which neuroscientist Eric Kandel studied for 45 years, has increased our understanding of the neural basis of learning.

Art Directors & TRIP/Alamy

Kandel and Schwartz pinpointed changes. When learning occurs, the slug releases more of the neurotransmitter *serotonin* into certain synapses. Those synapses then become more efficient at transmitting signals.

In experiments with people, rapidly stimulating certain memory-circuit connections has increased their sensitivity for hours or even weeks to come. The sending neuron now needs less prompting to release its neurotransmitter, and more connections exist between neurons (**FIGURE 32.4**). This increased efficiency of potential neural firing, called **long-term potentiation (LTP),** provides a neural basis for learning and remembering associations (Lynch, 2002; Whitlock et al., 2006). Several lines of evidence confirm that LTP is a physical basis for memory:

- Drugs that block LTP interfere with learning (Lynch & Staubli, 1991).

- Mutant mice engineered to lack an enzyme needed for LTP couldn't learn their way out of a maze (Silva et al., 1992).

- Rats given a drug that enhanced LTP learned a maze with half the usual number of mistakes (Service, 1994).

- Injecting rats with a chemical that blocked the preservation of LTP erased recent learning (Pastalkova et al., 2006).

After long-term potentiation has occurred, passing an electric current through the brain won't disrupt old memories. But the current will wipe out very recent memories. Such is the experience both of laboratory animals and of severely depressed people given *electroconvulsive therapy* (see Module 73). A blow to the head can do the same. Football players and boxers momentarily knocked unconscious typically have no memory of events just before the knockout (Yarnell & Lynch, 1970). Their working memory had no time to consolidate the information into long-term memory before the lights went out.

Some memory-biology explorers have helped found companies that are competing to develop memory-altering drugs. The target market for memory-boosting drugs includes millions of people with Alzheimer's disease, millions more with *mild neurocognitive disorder* that often becomes Alzheimer's, and countless millions who would love to turn back the clock on age-related memory decline. From expanding memories perhaps will come bulging profits.

In your lifetime, will you have access to safe and legal drugs that boost your fading memory without nasty side effects and without cluttering your mind with trivia best forgotten? That question has yet to be answered. But in the meantime, one safe and free memory enhancer is already available for high schoolers everywhere: effective study techniques followed by adequate *sleep!* (You'll find study tips in Module 2 and at the end of this module, and sleep coverage in Modules 23 and 24.)

> "The biology of the mind will be as scientifically important to this [new] century as the biology of the gene [was] to the twentieth century." -Eric Kandel, acceptance remarks for his 2000 Nobel Prize

long-term potentiation (LTP) an increase in a cell's firing potential after brief, rapid stimulation. Believed to be a neural basis for learning and memory.

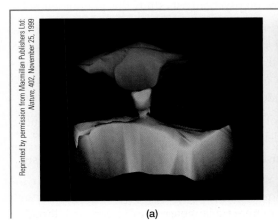
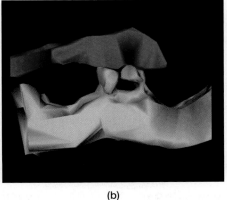

Reprinted by permission from Macmillan Publishers Ltd: *Nature,* 402, November 25, 1999

(a) (b)

Figure 32.4

Doubled receptor sites Electron microscope image (a) shows just one receptor site (gray) reaching toward a sending neuron before long-term potentiation. Image (b) shows that, after LTP, the receptor sites have doubled. This means that the receiving neuron has increased sensitivity for detecting the presence of the neurotransmitter molecules that may be released by the sending neuron. (From Toni et al., 1999.)

FIGURE 32.5 summarizes the brain's two-track memory processing and storage system for implicit (automatic) and explicit (effortful) memories.

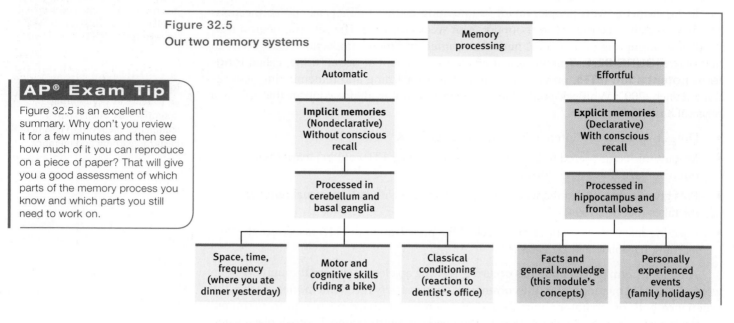

Figure 32.5
Our two memory systems

Before You Move On

▶ **ASK YOURSELF**

Can you name an instance in which stress has helped you remember something, and another instance in which stress has interfered with remembering something?

▶ **TEST YOURSELF**

Your friend tells you that her father experienced brain damage in an accident. She wonders if psychology can explain why he can still play checkers very well but has a hard time holding a sensible conversation. What can you tell her?

Answers to the Test Yourself questions can be found in Appendix E at the end of the book.

Retrieval: Getting Information Out

After the magic of brain encoding and storage, we still have the daunting task of retrieving the information. What triggers retrieval? How do psychologists study this phenomenon?

Measuring Retention

32-6 How is memory measured?

To a psychologist, evidence of memory includes these three *measures of retention:*

- **recall**—retrieving information that is not currently in your conscious awareness but that was learned at an earlier time. A fill-in-the-blank question tests your recall.

- **recognition**—identifying items previously learned. A multiple-choice question tests your recognition.

- **relearning**—learning something more quickly when you learn it a second or later time. When you study for a final exam or engage a language used in early childhood, you will relearn the material more easily than you did initially.

recall a measure of memory in which the person must retrieve information learned earlier, as on a fill-in-the-blank test.

recognition a measure of memory in which the person need only identify items previously learned, as on a multiple-choice test.

relearning a measure of memory that assesses the amount of time saved when learning material again.

Long after you cannot recall most of the people in your high school graduating class, you may still be able to recognize their yearbook pictures from a photographic lineup and pick their names from a list of names. In one experiment, people who had graduated 25 years earlier could not *recall* many of their old classmates, but they could *recognize* 90 percent of their pictures and names (Bahrick et al., 1975). If you are like most students, you, too, could probably recognize more names of Snow White's Seven Dwarfs than you could recall (Miserandino, 1991).

Our recognition memory is impressively quick and vast. "Is your friend wearing a new or old outfit?""Old.""Is this 5-second movie clip from a film you've ever seen?""Yes.""Have you ever seen this person before—this minor variation on the same old human features (two eyes, one nose, and so on)?""No." Before the mouth can form our answer to any of millions of such questions, the mind knows, and knows that it knows.

Remembering things past Even if Taylor Swift and Leonardo DiCaprio had not become famous, their high school classmates would most likely still recognize their high school photos.

Our speed at *relearning* also reveals memory. Hermann Ebbinghaus showed this more than a century ago, in his learning experiments, using nonsense syllables. He randomly selected a sample of syllables, practiced them, and tested himself. To get a feel for his experiments, rapidly read aloud, eight times over, the following list (from Baddeley, 1982), then look away and try to recall the items:

JIH, BAZ, FUB, YOX, SUJ, XIR, DAX, LEQ, VUM, PID, KEL, WAV, TUV, ZOF, GEK, HIW.

The day after learning such a list, Ebbinghaus could recall few of the syllables. But they weren't entirely forgotten. As **FIGURE 32.6** portrays, the more frequently he repeated the list aloud on day 1, the fewer repetitions he required to *relearn* the list on day 2. Additional rehearsal (*overlearning*) of verbal information increases retention, especially when practice is distributed over time. For students, this means that it is important to continue to rehearse course material even after you know it.

The point to remember: Tests of recognition and of time spent relearning demonstrate that *we remember more than we can recall.*

Retrieval Cues

32-7 How do external cues, internal emotions, and order of appearance influence memory retrieval?

Imagine a spider suspended in the middle of her web, held up by the many strands extending outward from her in all directions to different points. If you were to trace a pathway to the spider, you would first need to create a path from one of these anchor points and then follow the strand down into the web.

The process of retrieving a memory follows a similar principle, because memories are held in storage by a web of associations, each piece of information interconnected with others. When you encode into memory a target piece of information, such as the name of the person sitting next to you in class, you associate with it other bits of information about your surroundings, mood, seating position, and so on. These bits can serve as *retrieval cues* that you can later use to access the information. The more retrieval cues you have, the better your chances of finding a route to the suspended memory.

PRIMING

The best retrieval cues come from associations we form at the time we encode a memory—smells, tastes, and sights that can evoke our memory of the associated person or event. To call up visual cues when trying to recall something, we may mentally place ourselves in the

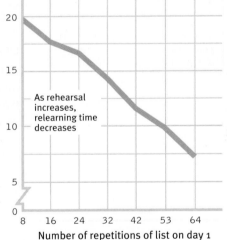

Time in minutes taken to relearn list on day 2

As rehearsal increases, relearning time decreases

Number of repetitions of list on day 1

Figure 32.6

Ebbinghaus' retention curve Ebbinghaus found that the more times he practiced a list of nonsense syllables on day 1, the fewer repetitions he required to relearn it on day 2. Speed of relearning is one measure of memory retention. (From Baddeley, 1982.)

"Memory is not like a container that gradually fills up; it is more like a tree growing hooks onto which memories are hung." -Peter Russell, *The Brain Book*, 1979

priming the activation, often unconsciously, of particular associations in memory.

original context. After losing his sight, British scholar John Hull (1990, p. 174) described his difficulty recalling such details:

> I knew I had been somewhere, and had done particular things with certain people, but where? I could not put the conversations . . . into a context. There was no background, no features against which to identify the place. Normally, the memories of people you have spoken to during the day are stored in frames which include the background.

Often our associations are activated without our awareness. The philosopher-psychologist William James referred to this process, which we call **priming,** as the "wakening of associations." Seeing or hearing the word *rabbit* primes associations with *hare,* even though we may not recall having seen or heard *rabbit* (**FIGURE 32.7**).

Priming is often "memoryless memory"—invisible memory, without your conscious awareness. If, walking down a hallway, you see a poster of a missing child, you may then unconsciously be primed to interpret an ambiguous adult-child interaction as a possible kidnapping (James, 1986). Although you no longer have the poster in mind, it predisposes your interpretation.

Priming can influence behaviors as well. In one study, participants primed with money-related words were less likely to help another person when asked (Vohs et al., 2006). In such cases, money may prime our materialism and self-interest rather than the social norms that encourage us to help (Ariely, 2009).

Seeing or hearing the word *rabbit*

Activates concept

Primes spelling the spoken word *hair/hare* as *h-a-r-e*

Figure 32.7

Priming—awakening associations After seeing or hearing *rabbit*, we are later more likely to spell the spoken word as *h-a-r-e*. The spreading of associations unconsciously activates related associations. This phenomenon is called priming. (Adapted from Bower, 1986.)

CONTEXT-DEPENDENT MEMORY

Putting yourself back in the context where you experienced something can prime your memory retrieval. As **FIGURE 32.8** illustrates, when scuba divers listened to a word list in two different settings (either 10 feet underwater or sitting on the beach), they recalled more words if retested in the same place (Godden & Baddeley, 1975).

You may have experienced similar context effects. Consider this scenario: While taking notes from this book, you realize you need to sharpen your pencil. You get up and walk into another room, but then you cannot remember why. After returning to your desk it hits you: "I wanted to sharpen this pencil!" What happens to create this frustrating experience?

Figure 32.8

The effects of context on memory In this experiment, words heard underwater were best recalled underwater. Words heard on land were best recalled on land. (Adapted from Godden & Baddeley, 1975.)

Olga Khoroshunova/Shutterstock

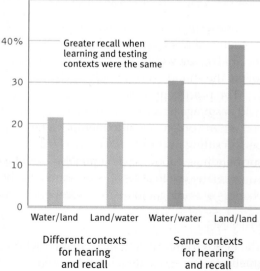

Percentage of words recalled

Greater recall when learning and testing contexts were the same

40%

30

20

10

0

Water/land   Land/water   Water/water   Land/land

Different contexts for hearing and recall

Same contexts for hearing and recall

In one context (desk, reading psychology), you realize your pencil needs sharpening. When you go to the other room and are in a different context, you have few cues to lead you back to that thought. When you are once again at your desk, you are back in the context in which you encoded the thought *("This pencil is dull")*.

In several experiments, one researcher found that a familiar context could activate memories even in 3-month-olds (Rovee-Collier, 1993). After infants learned that kicking a crib mobile would make it move (via a connecting ribbon from the ankle), the infants kicked more when tested again in the same crib with the same bumper than when in a different context.

STATE-DEPENDENT MEMORY

Closely related to context-dependent memory is *state-dependent memory*. What we learn in one state—be it drunk or sober—may be more easily recalled when we are again in that state. What people learn when drunk they don't recall well in *any* state (alcohol disrupts storage). But they recall it slightly better when again drunk. Someone who hides money when drunk may forget the location until drunk again.

Our mood states provide an example of memory's state dependence. Emotions that accompany good or bad events become retrieval cues (Fiedler et al., 2001). Thus, our memories are somewhat **mood congruent.** If you've had a bad evening—your date never showed, your Chicago Cubs hat disappeared, your TV went out 10 minutes before the end of a show—your gloomy mood may facilitate recalling other bad times. Being depressed sours memories by priming negative associations, which we then use to explain our current mood. In many experiments, people put in a buoyant mood—whether under hypnosis or just by the day's events (a World Cup soccer victory for German participants in one study)—have recalled the world through rose-colored glasses (DeSteno et al., 2000; Forgas et al., 1984; Schwarz et al., 1987). They judged themselves competent and effective, other people benevolent, happy events more likely.

"I can't remember what we're arguing about, either. Let's keep yelling, and maybe it will come back to us."

© The New Yorker Collection, 2005, David Sipress from cartoonbank.com. All Rights Reserved.

Knowing this mood-memory connection, we should not be surprised that in some studies *currently* depressed people have recalled their parents as rejecting, punitive, and guilt promoting, whereas *formerly* depressed people's recollections more closely resembled the more positive descriptions given by those who never suffered depression (Lewinsohn & Rosenbaum, 1987; Lewis, 1992). Similarly, adolescents' ratings of parental warmth in one week gave little clue to how they would rate their parents six weeks later (Bornstein et al., 1991). When teens were down, their parents seemed inhuman; as their mood brightened, their parents morphed from devils into angels. In a good or bad mood, we persist in attributing to reality our own changing judgments, memories, and interpretations. In a bad mood, we may read someone's look as a glare and feel even worse. In a good mood, we may encode the same look as interest and feel even better. Passions exaggerate.

This retrieval effect helps explain why our moods persist. When happy, we recall happy events and therefore see the world as a happy place, which helps prolong our good mood. When depressed, we recall sad events, which darkens our interpretations of current events. For those of us with a predisposition to depression, this process can help maintain a vicious, dark cycle.

> "When a feeling was there, they felt as if it would never go; when it was gone, they felt as if it had never been; when it returned, they felt as if it had never gone." -GEORGE MACDONALD, *WHAT'S MINE'S MINE*, 1886

SERIAL POSITION EFFECT

Another memory-retrieval quirk, the **serial position effect,** can leave us wondering why we have large holes in our memory of a list of recent events. Imagine it's your first day in a new job, and your manager is introducing co-workers. As you meet each person, you silently repeat everyone's name, starting from the beginning. As the last person smiles and turns away, you feel confident you'll be able to greet your new co-workers by name the next day.

Don't count on it. Because you have spent more time rehearsing the earlier names than the later ones, those are the names you'll probably recall more easily the next day.

mood-congruent memory the tendency to recall experiences that are consistent with one's current good or bad mood.

serial position effect our tendency to recall best the last (a *recency effect*) and first items (a *primacy effect*) in a list.

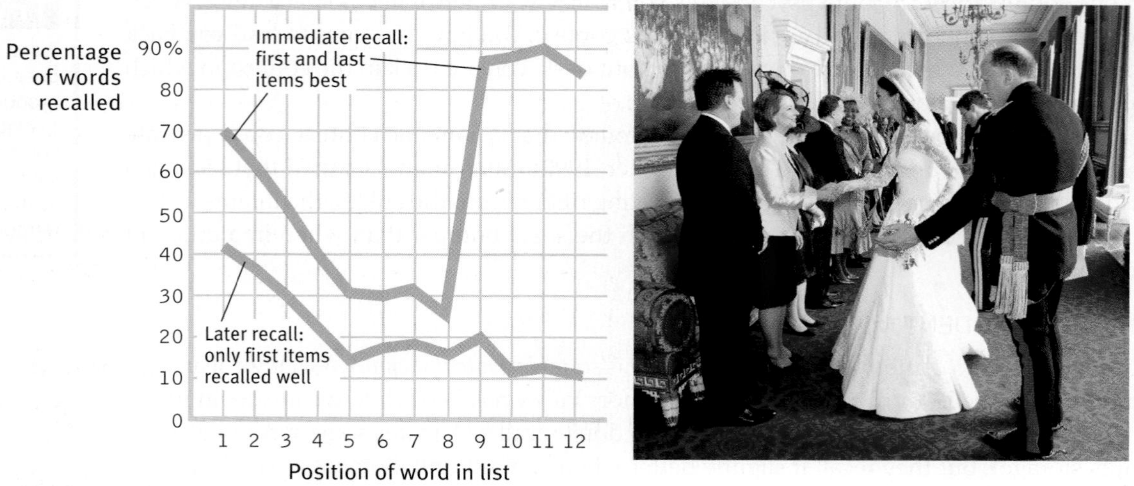

Figure 32.9

The serial position effect Immediately after the royal newlyweds, William and Kate, made their way through the receiving line of special guests, they would probably have recalled the names of the last few people best. But later they may have been able to recall the first few people best.

Percentage of words recalled

Immediate recall: first and last items best

Later recall: only first items recalled well

Position of word in list

In experiments, when people view a list of items (words, names, dates, even odors) and immediately try to recall them in any order, they fall prey to the serial position effect (Reed, 2000). They briefly recall the last items especially quickly and well (*a recency effect*), perhaps because those last items are still in working memory. But after a delay, when they have shifted their attention away from the last items, their recall is best for the first items (*a primacy effect;* see **FIGURE 32.9**).

Before You Move On

▶ **ASK YOURSELF**

What sort of mood have you been in lately? How has your mood colored your memories, perceptions, and expectations?

▶ **TEST YOURSELF**

You have just watched a movie that includes a chocolate factory. After the chocolate factory is out of mind, you nevertheless feel a strange urge for a chocolate bar. How do you explain this in terms of priming?

Answers to the Test Yourself questions can be found in Appendix E at the end of the book.

Module 32 Review

 What is the capacity of long-term memory? Are our long-term memories processed and stored in specific locations?

- Our long-term memory capacity is essentially unlimited.

- Memories are not stored intact in the brain in single spots. Many parts of the brain interact as we form and retrieve memories.

 What are the roles of the frontal lobes and hippocampus in memory processing?

- The frontal lobes and *hippocampus* are parts of the brain network dedicated to explicit memory formation.
  - Many brain regions send information to the frontal lobes for processing.
  - The hippocampus, with the help of surrounding areas of cortex, registers and temporarily holds elements of explicit memories before moving them to other brain regions for long-term storage.

32-3 What roles do the cerebellum and basal ganglia play in our memory processing?

- The cerebellum and basal ganglia are parts of the brain network dedicated to implicit memory formation.
  - The cerebellum is important for storing classically conditioned memories.
  - The basal ganglia are involved in motor movement and help form procedural memories for skills.

- Many reactions and skills learned during our first three years continue into our adult lives, but we cannot consciously remember learning these associations and skills, a phenomenon psychologists call "infantile amnesia."

32-4 How do emotions affect our memory processing?

- Emotional arousal causes an outpouring of stress hormones, which lead to activity in the brain's memory-forming areas. Significantly stressful events can trigger very clear *flashbulb memories.*

32-5 How do changes at the synapse level affect our memory processing?

- *Long-term potentiation (LTP)* appears to be the neural basis for learning and memory. In LTP, neurons become more efficient at releasing and sensing the presence of neurotransmitters, and more connections develop between neurons.

32-6 How is memory measured?

- Evidence of memory may be seen in an ability to *recall* information, *recognize* it, or *relearn* it more easily on a later attempt.

32-7 How do external cues, internal emotions, and order of appearance influence memory retrieval?

- External cues activate associations that help us retrieve memories; this process may occur without our awareness, as it does in *priming.*

- Returning to the same physical context or emotional state *(mood congruency)* in which we formed a memory can help us retrieve it.

- The *serial position effect* accounts for our tendency to recall best the last items (which may still be in working memory) and the first items (which we've spent more time rehearsing) in a list.

Multiple-Choice Questions

1. What two parts of the brain are most involved in explicit memory?
   a. Frontal lobes and basal ganglia
   b. Amygdala and hippocampus
   c. Amygdala and cerebellum
   d. Cerebellum and basal ganglia
   e. Frontal lobes and hippocampus

2. Which of the following statements most accurately reflects the relationship between emotions and memory?
   a. Emotion blocks memory, and it is generally true that we are unable to recall highly emotional events.
   b. Excitement tends to increase the chance that an event will be remembered, but stress decreases the chance that an event will be remembered.
   c. Stress tends to increase the chance that an event will be remembered, but excitement decreases the chance that an event will be remembered.
   d. The effect of emotion on memory depends on the interpretation of the event in the frontal lobes.
   e. Emotion enhances memory because it is important for our survival to remember events that make us emotional.

3. Which of the following is an example of flashbulb memory?

   a. Barry remembers an especially bright sunrise because he was by the ocean and the sunlight reflected off the water.

   b. Robert remembers that correlation does not prove a cause–effect relationship because his teacher emphasized this fact over and over again.

   c. Anna remembers when her father returned from an overseas military deployment because the day was very emotional for her.

   d. Kris has stronger memories of her second grade teacher than she does of her third grade teacher because her second grade teacher has the same name as her neighbor.

   e. Anton remembers a moment from his last homecoming dance because a strobe light seemed to freeze the scene in his imagination.

4. Juan returns to his grandparent's house after a 10-year absence. The flood of memories about his childhood visits is best explained by which of the following?

   a. Recall
   b. Priming
   c. Explicit memory
   d. The serial position effect
   e. Flashbulb memory

5. Which of the following is an example of the primacy effect?

   a. Remembering the most important assignment you have to complete for school tomorrow

   b. Remembering the skills you learned early in life, such as walking

   c. Remembering the last thing your English teacher talked about in class yesterday, but nothing from earlier in the class period

   d. Remembering the names of the first two co-workers you met on the first day of your new job

   e. Remembering that your clocks must be moved ahead one hour when daylight savings time begins in the spring

Practice FRQs

1. Consider an explicit memory, such as a memory of what happened in your science class yesterday.

Explain the process that allows memory to occur at the synaptic level.
Explain the role of two parts of the brain in your memory of the class.

Answer

1 point: Long-term potentiation (LTP) increases the cells' firing potential at the synapse.

1 point: The hippocampus gives the command to "save" a memory.

1 point: The frontal lobes allow you to process the memory information.

2. You have a friend, Rachel, who cannot remember where she left a check she had received from a relative for her birthday. She remembers having drunk several cups of tea the morning she received the check, and she remembers taking it to her bedroom. Explain how Rachel can take advantage of context-dependent memory and state-dependent memory to remember where in her bedroom she left the check.

(2 points)

Module 33

Forgetting, Memory Construction, and Memory Improvement

Module Learning Objectives

33-1 Explain why we forget.

33-2 Explain how misinformation, imagination, and source amnesia influence our memory construction, and describe how we decide whether a memory is real or false.

33-3 Describe the reliability of young children's eyewitness descriptions, and discuss the controversy related to claims of repressed and recovered memories.

33-4 Describe how you can use memory research findings to do better in this and other courses.

Forgetting

33-1 Why do we forget?

Amid all the applause for memory—all the efforts to understand it, all the books on how to improve it—have any voices been heard in praise of forgetting? William James (1890, p. 680) was such a voice: "If we remembered everything, we should on most occasions be as ill off as if we remembered nothing." To discard the clutter of useless or out-of-date information—last year's locker combination, a friend's old phone number, restaurant orders already cooked and served—is surely a blessing. The Russian memory whiz S, whom we met at the beginning of Module 31, was haunted by his junk heap of memories. They dominated his consciousness. He had difficulty thinking abstractly—generalizing, organizing, evaluating. After reading a story, he could recite it but would struggle to summarize its gist.

A more recent case of a life overtaken by memory is "A. J.," whose experience has been studied and verified by a University of California at Irvine research team (Parker et al., 2006). A. J., who has identified herself as Jill Price, compares her memory with "a running movie that never stops. It's like a split screen. I'll be talking to someone and seeing something else. . . . Whenever I see a date flash on the television (or anywhere for that matter) I automatically go back to that day and remember where I was, what I was doing, what day it fell on, and on and on and on and on. It is nonstop, uncontrollable, and totally exhausting." A good memory is helpful, but so is the ability to forget. If a memory-enhancing pill becomes available, it had better not be *too* effective.

> "Amnesia seeps into the crevices of our brains, and amnesia heals." -JOYCE CAROL OATES, "WORDS FAIL, MEMORY BLURS, LIFE WINS," 2001

More often, however, our unpredictable memory dismays and frustrates us. Memories are quirky. My own memory can easily call up such episodes as that wonderful first kiss with the woman I love, or trivial facts like the air mileage from London to Detroit. Then it abandons me when I discover I have failed to encode, store, or retrieve a student's name, or where I left my sunglasses.

Forgetting and the Two-Track Mind

English novelist and critic C. S. Lewis described the forgetting that plagues us all. We are

> bombarded every second by sensations, emotions, thoughts . . . nine-tenths of which [we] must simply ignore. The past [is] a roaring cataract of billions upon billions of such moments: Any one of them too complex to grasp in its entirety, and the aggregate beyond all imagination. . . . At every tick of the clock, in every inhabited part of the world, an unimaginable richness and variety of 'history' falls off the world into total oblivion.

For some, memory loss is severe and permanent. Consider Henry Molaison (known as "H. M.," 1926–2008). For 55 years after having brain surgery to stop severe seizures, Molaison was unable to form new conscious memories. He was, as before his surgery, intelligent and did daily crossword puzzles. Yet, reported neuroscientist Suzanne Corkin (2005), "I've known H. M. since 1962, and he still doesn't know who I am." For about 20 seconds during a conversation he could keep something in mind. When distracted, he would lose what was just said or what had just occurred. Thus, he never could name the current president of the United States (Ogden, 2012).

Molaison suffered from **anterograde amnesia**—he could recall his past, but he could not form new memories. (Those who cannot recall their past—the old information stored in long-term memory—suffer from **retrograde amnesia.**)

Neurologist Oliver Sacks (1985, pp. 26–27) described another patient, Jimmie, who had anterograde amnesia resulting from brain damage. Jimmie had no memories—thus, no sense of elapsed time—beyond his injury in 1945.

When Jimmie gave his age as 19, Sacks set a mirror before him: "Look in the mirror and tell me what you see. Is that a 19-year-old looking out from the mirror?"

Jimmie turned ashen, gripped the chair, cursed, then became frantic: "What's going on? What's happened to me? Is this a nightmare? Am I crazy? Is this a joke?" When his attention was diverted to some children playing baseball, his panic ended, the dreadful mirror forgotten.

Sacks showed Jimmie a photo from *National Geographic*. "What is this?" he asked.

"It's the Moon," Jimmie replied.

"No, it's not," Sacks answered. "It's a picture of the Earth taken from the Moon."

"Doc, you're kidding? Someone would've had to get a camera up there!"

"Naturally."

"Hell! You're joking—how the hell would you do that?" Jimmie's wonder was that of a bright young man from nearly 70 years ago reacting with amazement to his travel back to the future.

Careful testing of these unique people reveals something even stranger: Although incapable of recalling new facts or anything they have done recently, Molaison, Jimmie, and others with similar conditions can learn nonverbal tasks. Shown hard-to-find figures in pictures (in the *Where's Waldo?* series), they can quickly spot them again later. They can find their way to the bathroom, though without being able to tell you where it is. They can learn to read mirror-image writing or do a jigsaw puzzle, and they have even been taught complicated job skills (Schacter, 1992, 1996; Xu & Corkin, 2001). They can be classically conditioned. However, *they do all these things with no awareness of having learned them.*

Molaison and Jimmie lost their ability to form new explicit memories, but their automatic processing ability remained intact. Like Alzheimer's patients,

---

AP® Exam Tip

Retrograde amnesia acts backward in time, just like when you choose a "retro" look for a party and wear clothes from an earlier time.

anterograde amnesia an inability to form new memories.

retrograde amnesia an inability to retrieve information from one's past.

"Waiter, I'd like to order, unless I've eaten, in which case bring me the check."

whose *explicit* memories for new people and events are lost, they can form new *implicit* memories (Lustig & Buckner, 2004). They can learn *how* to do something, but they will have no conscious recall of learning their new skill. Such sad cases confirm that we have two distinct memory systems, controlled by different parts of the brain.

For most of us, forgetting is a less drastic process. Let's consider some of the reasons we forget.

Studying a famous brain Jacopo Annese and other scientists at the University of California, San Diego's Brain Observatory are preserving Henry Molaison's brain for the benefit of future generations. Their careful work will result in a freely available online brain atlas.

Encoding Failure

Much of what we sense we never notice, and what we fail to encode, we will never remember (**FIGURE 33.1**). Age can affect encoding efficiency. The brain areas that jump into action when young adults encode new information are less responsive in older adults. This slower encoding helps explain age-related memory decline (Grady et al., 1995).

But no matter how young we are, we selectively attend to few of the myriad sights and sounds continually bombarding us. When texting during class, students may fail to encode details that their more attentive classmates are encoding for next week's test. Without effort, many potential memories never form.

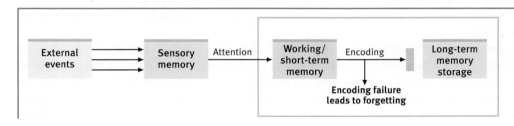

Figure 33.1
Forgetting as encoding failure We cannot remember what we have not encoded.

Storage Decay

Even after encoding something well, we sometimes later forget it. To study the durability of stored memories, Hermann Ebbinghaus (1885) learned more lists of nonsense syllables and measured how much he retained when relearning each list, from 20 minutes to 30 days later. The result, confirmed by later experiments, was his famous forgetting curve: *The course of forgetting is initially rapid, then levels off with time* (**FIGURE 33.2;** Wixted & Ebbesen, 1991).

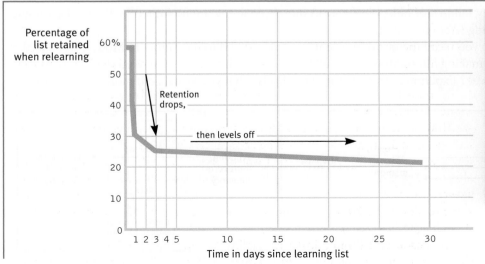

Figure 33.2
Ebbinghaus' forgetting curve After learning lists of nonsense syllables, such as YOX and JIH, Ebbinghaus studied how much he retained up to 30 days later. He found that memory for novel information fades quickly, then levels out. (Adapted from Ebbinghaus, 1885.)

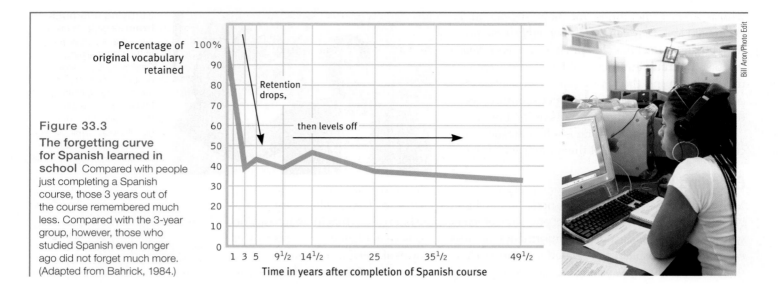

Figure 33.3

The forgetting curve for Spanish learned in school Compared with people just completing a Spanish course, those 3 years out of the course remembered much less. Compared with the 3-year group, however, those who studied Spanish even longer ago did not forget much more. (Adapted from Bahrick, 1984.)

Harry Bahrick (1984) found a similar forgetting curve for Spanish vocabulary learned in school. Compared with those just completing a high school or college Spanish course, people 3 years out of school had forgotten much of what they had learned (**FIGURE 33.3**). However, what people remembered then, they still remembered 25 and more years later. Their forgetting had leveled off.

One explanation for these forgetting curves is a gradual fading of the physical memory trace. Cognitive neuroscientists are getting closer to solving the mystery of the physical storage of memory and are increasing our understanding of how memory storage could decay. Like books you can't find in your high school library, memories may be inaccessible for many reasons. Some were never acquired (not encoded). Others were discarded (stored memories decay). And others are out of reach because we can't retrieve them.

Retrieval Failure

Deaf persons fluent in sign language experience a parallel "tip of the fingers" phenomenon (Thompson et al., 2005).

Often, forgetting is not memories faded but memories unretrieved. We store in long-term memory what's important to us or what we've rehearsed. But sometimes important events defy our attempts to access them (**FIGURE 33.4**). How frustrating when a name lies poised on the tip of our tongue, just beyond reach. Given retrieval cues (*"It begins with an M"*), we may easily retrieve the elusive memory. Retrieval problems contribute to the occasional memory failures of older adults, who more frequently are frustrated by tip-of-the-tongue forgetting (Abrams, 2008).

Do you recall the gist of the sentence I asked you to remember in Module 32's discussion of making information personally meaningful? If not, does the word *shark* serve as a retrieval cue? Experiments show that *shark* (likely what you visualized) more readily retrieves

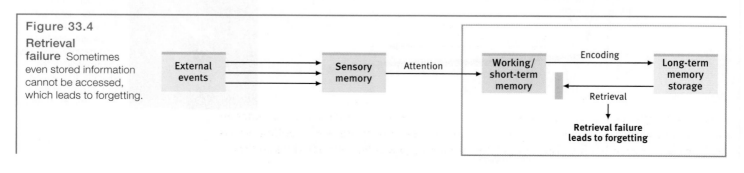

Figure 33.4

Retrieval failure Sometimes even stored information cannot be accessed, which leads to forgetting.

the image you stored than does the sentence's actual word, *fish* (Anderson et al., 1976). (The sentence was *"The fish attacked the swimmer."*)

But retrieval problems occasionally stem from interference and, perhaps, from motivated forgetting.

INTERFERENCE

As you collect more and more information, your mental attic never fills, but it surely gets cluttered. Sometimes the clutter interferes, as new learning and old collide. **Proactive** *(forward-acting)* **interference** occurs when prior learning disrupts your recall of new information. Your well-rehearsed Facebook password may interfere with your retrieval of your newly learned copy machine code.

Retroactive *(backward-acting)* **interference** occurs when new learning disrupts recall of old information. If someone sings new lyrics to the tune of an old song, you may have trouble remembering the original words. It is rather like a second stone tossed in a pond, disrupting the waves rippling out from the first.

Information presented in the hour before sleep is protected from retroactive interference because the opportunity for interfering events is minimized (Diekelmann & Born, 2010; Nesca & Koulack, 1994). Researchers John Jenkins and Karl Dallenbach (1924) first discovered this in a now-classic experiment. Day after day, two people each learned some nonsense syllables, then tried to recall them after up to 8 hours of being awake or asleep at night. As **FIGURE 33.5** shows, forgetting occurred more rapidly after being awake and involved with other activities. The investigators surmised that "forgetting is not so much a matter of the decay of old impressions and associations as it is a matter of interference, inhibition, or obliteration of the old by the new" (1924, p. 612).

The hour before sleep is a good time to commit information to memory (Scullin & McDaniel, 2010), though information presented in the *seconds* just before sleep is seldom remembered (Wyatt & Bootzin, 1994). If you're considering learning *while* sleeping, forget it. We have little memory for information played aloud in the room during sleep, although the ears do register it (Wood et al., 1992).

Old and new learning do not always compete with each other, of course. Previously learned information (Latin) often facilitates our learning of new information (French). This phenomenon is called *positive transfer.*

proactive interference the disruptive effect of prior learning on the recall of new information.

retroactive interference the disruptive effect of new learning on the recall of old information.

AP® Exam Tip

Here's the prefix "retro" again and it means exactly the same thing with interference that it did for amnesia. In both cases, they're exerting an influence back in time.

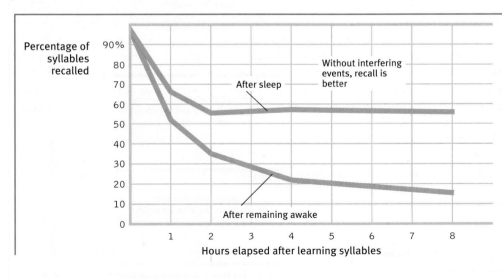

Figure 33.5

Retroactive interference More forgetting occurred when a person stayed awake and experienced other new material. (From Jenkins & Dallenbach, 1924.)

MOTIVATED FORGETTING

To remember our past is often to revise it. Years ago, the huge cookie jar in our kitchen was jammed with freshly baked chocolate chip cookies. Still more were cooling across racks on the counter. Twenty-four hours later, not a crumb was left. Who had taken them?

Fuse/Thinkstock

During that time, my wife, three children, and I were the only people in the house. So while memories were still fresh, I conducted a little memory test. Andy admitted wolfing down as many as 20. Peter thought he had eaten 15. Laura guessed she had stuffed her then-6-year-old body with 15 cookies. My wife, Carol, recalled eating 6, and I remembered consuming 15 and taking 18 more to the office. We sheepishly accepted responsibility for 89 cookies. Still, we had not come close; there had been 160.

Why do our memories fail us? This happens in part because, as Carol Tavris and Elliot Aronson have pointed out, memory is an "unreliable, self-serving historian" (2007, p. 6). Consider one study, in which researchers told some participants about the benefits of frequent toothbrushing. Those individuals then recalled (more than others did) having frequently brushed their teeth in the preceding 2 weeks (Ross et al., 1981).

FIGURE 33.6 reminds us that as we process information, we filter, alter, or lose much of it. So why were my family and I so far off in our estimates of the cookies we had eaten? Was it an *encoding* problem? (Did we just not notice what we had eaten?) Was it a storage problem? (Might our memories of cookies, like Ebbinghaus' memory of nonsense syllables, have melted away almost as fast as the cookies themselves?) Or was the information still intact but not *retrievable* because it would be embarrassing to remember?[1]

Sigmund Freud might have argued that our memory systems self-censored this information. He proposed that we **repress** painful or unacceptable memories to protect

---

[1] One of my cookie-scarfing sons, on reading this in his father's textbook years later, confessed he had fibbed "a little."

repression in psychoanalytic theory, the basic defense mechanism that banishes from consciousness anxiety-arousing thoughts, feelings, and memories.

AP® Exam Tip

There are many references to Sigmund Freud in the text. Most of your knowledge of Freud probably came from popular culture, and it often conflicts with the discoveries of modern researchers. The AP® exam may test your understanding of researchers' views of Freud.

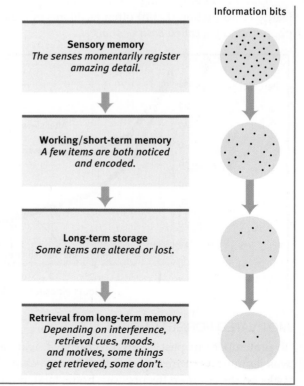

Information bits

Sensory memory
The senses momentarily register amazing detail.

Working/short-term memory
A few items are both noticed and encoded.

Long-term storage
Some items are altered or lost.

Retrieval from long-term memory
Depending on interference, retrieval cues, moods, and motives, some things get retrieved, some don't.

Figure 33.6

When do we forget? Forgetting can occur at any memory stage. As we process information, we filter, alter, or lose much of it.

© The New Yorker Collection, 2008, Michael Maslin from cartoonbank.com. All Rights Reserved.

"Someday we'll look back at this time in our lives and be unable to remember it."

our self-concept and to minimize anxiety. But the repressed memory lingers, he believed, and can be retrieved by some later cue or during therapy. Repression was central to Freud's psychoanalytic theory (more on that in Module 55) and was a popular idea in mid-twentieth-century psychology and beyond. In one study, 9 in 10 university students agreed that "memories for painful experiences are sometimes pushed into unconsciousness" (Brown et al., 1996). Some therapists assume it. Today, however, increasing numbers of memory researchers think repression rarely, if ever, occurs. People succeed in forgetting unwanted neutral information (yesterday's parking place), but it's harder to forget emotional events (Payne & Corrigan, 2007). Thus, we may have intrusive memories of the very traumatic experiences we would most like to forget.

Before You Move On

▶ **ASK YOURSELF**

Most people, especially as they grow older, wish for a better memory. Is that true of you? Or do you more often wish you could better discard old memories?

▶ **TEST YOURSELF**

Can you offer examples of proactive and retroactive interference?

Answers to the Test Yourself questions can be found in Appendix E at the end of the book.

Memory Construction Errors

 How do misinformation, imagination, and source amnesia influence our memory construction? How do we decide whether a memory is real or false?

Memory is not precise. Like scientists who infer a dinosaur's appearance from its remains, we infer our past from stored information plus what we later imagined, expected, saw, and heard. We don't just retrieve memories, we reweave them, noted Daniel Gilbert (2006, p. 79): "Information acquired after an event alters memory of the event." We often construct our memories as we encode them, and every time we "replay" a memory, we replace the original with a slightly modified version (Hardt et al., 2010). (Memory researchers call this *reconsolidation*.) So, in a sense, said Joseph LeDoux (2009), "your memory is only as good as your last memory. The fewer times you use it, the more pristine it is." This means that, to some degree, "all memory is false" (Bernstein & Loftus, 2009b). Let's examine some of the ways we rewrite our past.

Misinformation and Imagination Effects

In more than 200 experiments, involving more than 20,000 people, Elizabeth Loftus has shown how eyewitnesses reconstruct their memories after a crime or an accident. In one experiment, two groups of people watched a film of a traffic accident and then answered questions about what they had seen (Loftus & Palmer, 1974). Those asked, "About how fast were the cars going when they *smashed* into each other?" gave higher speed estimates than those asked, "About how fast were the cars going when they *hit* each other?" A week later, when asked whether they recalled seeing any broken glass, people who had heard *smashed* were more than twice as likely to report seeing glass fragments (**FIGURE 33.7** on the next page). In fact, the film showed no broken glass.

In many follow-up experiments around the world, others have witnessed an event, received or not received misleading information about it, and then taken a memory test. The repeated result is a **misinformation effect:** Exposed to misleading information, we tend to

misinformation effect
incorporating misleading information into one's memory of an event.

"Memory is insubstantial. Things keep replacing it. Your batch of snapshots will both fix and ruin your memory. . . . You can't remember anything from your trip except the wretched collection of snapshots." -Annie Dillard, "To Fashion a Text," 1988

Figure 33.7

Memory construction In this experiment, people viewed a film of a car accident (left). Those who later were asked a leading question recalled a more serious accident than they had witnessed. (From Loftus & Palmer, 1974.)

Leading question: *"About how fast were the cars going when they smashed into each other?"*

Depiction of actual accident   **Memory construction**

misremember. A yield sign becomes a stop sign, hammers become screwdrivers, Coke cans become peanut cans, breakfast cereal becomes eggs, and a clean-shaven man morphs into a man with a mustache (Loftus et al., 1992). So powerful is the misinformation effect that it can influence later attitudes and behaviors (Bernstein & Loftus, 2009).

Just hearing a vivid retelling of an event can implant false memories. One experiment falsely suggested to some Dutch university students that, as children, they became ill after eating spoiled egg salad (Geraerts et al., 2008). After absorbing that suggestion, a significant minority were less likely to eat egg-salad sandwiches, both immediately and 4 months later.

Even repeatedly *imagining* nonexistent actions and events can create false memories. American and British university students were asked to imagine certain childhood events, such as breaking a window with their hand or having a skin sample removed from a finger. One in four of them later recalled the imagined event as something that had really happened (Garry et al., 1996; Mazzoni & Memon, 2003).

Digitally altered photos have also produced this *imagination inflation.* In experiments, researchers have altered photos from a family album to show some family members taking a hot-air balloon ride. After viewing these photos (rather than photos showing just the balloon), children reported more false memories and indicated high confidence in those memories. When interviewed several days later, they reported even richer details of their false memories (Strange et al., 2008; Wade et al., 2002).

In British and Canadian university surveys, nearly one-fourth of students have reported autobiographical memories that they later realized were not accurate (Mazzoni et al., 2010).

DOONESBURY

I empathize. For decades, my cherished earliest memory was of my parents getting off the bus and walking to our house, bringing my baby brother home from the hospital. When, in middle age, I shared that memory with my father, he assured me they did *not* bring their newborn home on the Seattle Transit System. The human mind, it seems, comes with built-in Photoshopping software.

Source Amnesia

Among the frailest parts of a memory is its source. We may recognize someone but have no idea where we have seen the person. We may dream an event and later be unsure whether it really happened. We may misrecall how we learned about something (Henkel et al., 2000). Psychologists are not immune to the process. Famed child psychologist Jean Piaget was startled as an adult to learn that a vivid, detailed memory from his childhood—a nursemaid's thwarting his kidnapping—was utterly false. He apparently constructed the memory from repeatedly hearing the story (which his nursemaid, after undergoing a religious conversion, later confessed had never happened). In attributing his "memory" to his own experiences, rather than to his nursemaid's stories, Piaget exhibited **source amnesia** (also called *source misattribution*). Misattribution is at the heart of many false memories. Authors and songwriters sometimes suffer from it. They think an idea came from their own creative imagination, when in fact they are unintentionally plagiarizing something they earlier read or heard.

Debra Poole and Stephen Lindsay (1995, 2001, 2002) demonstrated source amnesia among preschoolers. They had the children interact with "Mr. Science," who engaged them in activities such as blowing up a balloon with baking soda and vinegar. Three months later, on three successive days, their parents read them a story describing some things the children had experienced with Mr. Science and some they had not. When a new interviewer asked what Mr. Science had done with them—"Did Mr. Science have a machine with ropes to pull?"—4 in 10 children spontaneously recalled him doing things that had happened only in the story.

Source amnesia also helps explain **déjà vu** (French for "already seen"). Two-thirds of us have experienced this fleeting, eerie sense that "I've been in this exact situation before." It happens most commonly to well-educated, imaginative young adults, especially when tired or stressed (Brown, 2003, 2004; McAneny, 1996). Some wonder, "How could I recognize a situation I'm experiencing for the first time?" Others may think of reincarnation ("I must have experienced this in a previous life") or precognition ("I viewed this scene in my mind before experiencing it").

The key to déjà vu seems to be familiarity with a stimulus without a clear idea of where we encountered it before (Cleary, 2008). Normally, we experience a feeling of *familiarity* (thanks to temporal lobe processing) before we consciously remember details (thanks to hippocampus and frontal lobe processing). When these functions (and brain regions) are out of sync, we may experience a feeling of familiarity without conscious recall. Our amazing brains try to make sense of such an improbable situation, and we get an eerie feeling that we're reliving some earlier part of our life. After all, the situation is familiar, even though we have no idea why. Our source amnesia forces us to do our best to make sense of an odd moment.

Discerning True and False Memories

Because the misinformation effect and source amnesia happen outside our awareness, it is nearly impossible to sift suggested ideas out of the larger pool of real memories (Schooler et al., 1986). Perhaps you can recall describing a childhood experience to a friend and filling in memory gaps with reasonable guesses and assumptions. We all do it, and after more retellings, those guessed details—now absorbed into our memories—may feel as real as if we had actually experienced them (Roediger et al., 1993). Much as perceptual illusions may seem like real perceptions, unreal memories feel like real memories.

> "It isn't so astonishing, the number of things I can remember, as the number of things I can remember that aren't so." -MARK TWAIN (1835–1910)

Try This

In the discussion of mnemonics in Module 31, I gave you six words and told you I would quiz you about them later. How many of these words can you now recall? Of these, how many are high-imagery words? How many are low-imagery? (You can check your list against the six inverted words below.)

Bicycle, void, cigarette, inherent, fire, process

> "Do you ever get that strange feeling of vujà dé? Not déjà vu; vujà dé. It's the distinct sense that, somehow, something just happened that has never happened before. Nothing seems familiar. And then suddenly the feeling is gone. Vujà dé." -COMEDIAN GEORGE CARLIN (1937–2008), IN *FUNNY TIMES*, DECEMBER 2001

source amnesia attributing to the wrong source an event we have experienced, heard about, read about, or imagined. (Also called *source misattribution*.) Source amnesia, along with the misinformation effect, is at the heart of many false memories.

déjà vu that eerie sense that "I've experienced this before." Cues from the current situation may unconsciously trigger retrieval of an earlier experience.

False memories can be very persistent. Imagine that I were to read aloud a list of words such as *candy, sugar, honey,* and *taste.* Later, I ask you to recognize the presented words from a larger list. If you are at all like the people tested by Henry Roediger and Kathleen McDermott (1995), you would err three out of four times—by falsely remembering a nonpresented similar word, such as *sweet.* We more easily remember the gist than the words themselves.

Memory construction helps explain why 79 percent of 200 convicts exonerated by later DNA testing had been misjudged based on faulty eyewitness identification (Garrett, 2008). It explains why "hypnotically refreshed" memories of crimes so easily incorporate errors, some of which originate with the hypnotist's leading questions *("Did you hear loud noises?").* It explains why dating partners who fell in love have overestimated their first impressions of one another *("It was love at first sight"),* while those who broke up underestimated their earlier liking *("We never really clicked")* (McFarland & Ross, 1987). How people feel today tends to be how they recall they have always felt (Mazzoni & Vannucci, 2007; and recall from Module 4 our tendency to *hindsight bias*). As George Vaillant (1977, p. 197) noted after following adult lives through time, "It is all too common for caterpillars to become butterflies and then to maintain that in their youth they had been little butterflies. Maturation makes liars of us all."

Children's Eyewitness Recall

33-3 How reliable are young children's eyewitness descriptions, and why are reports of repressed and recovered memories so hotly debated?

If memories can be sincere, yet sincerely wrong, might children's recollections of sexual abuse be prone to error? "It would be truly awful to ever lose sight of the enormity of child abuse," observed Stephen Ceci (1993). Yet Ceci and Maggie Bruck's (1993, 1995) studies of children's memories have made them aware of how easily children's memories can be molded. For example, they asked 3-year-olds to show on anatomically correct dolls where a pediatrician had touched them. Of the children who had not received genital examinations, 55 percent pointed to either genital or anal areas.

In other experiments, the researchers studied the effect of suggestive interviewing techniques (Bruck & Ceci, 1999, 2004). In one study, children chose a card from a deck of possible happenings, and an adult then read the card to them. For example, "Think real hard, and tell me if this ever happened to you. Can you remember going to the hospital with a mousetrap on your finger?" In interviews, the same adult repeatedly asked children to think about several real and fictitious events. After 10 weeks of this, a new adult asked the same question. The stunning result: 58 percent of preschoolers produced false (often vivid) stories regarding one or more events they had never experienced (Ceci et al., 1994). Here's one of those stories:

> My brother Colin was trying to get Blowtorch [an action figure] from me, and I wouldn't let him take it from me, so he pushed me into the wood pile where the mousetrap was. And then my finger got caught in it. And then we went to the hospital, and my mommy, daddy, and Colin drove me there, to the hospital in our van, because it was far away. And the doctor put a bandage on this finger.

Given such detailed stories, professional psychologists who specialize in interviewing children could not reliably separate the real memories from the false ones. Nor could the children themselves. The above child, reminded that his parents had told him several times that the mousetrap incident never happened—that he had imagined it—protested, "But it really did happen. I remember it!" In another experiment, preschoolers merely overheard an erroneous remark that a magician's missing rabbit had gotten loose in their classroom. Later, when the children were suggestively questioned, 78 percent of them recalled actually seeing the rabbit (Principe et al., 2006). "[The] research leads me to worry about the possibility of false allegations. It is not a tribute to one's scientific integrity to walk down the middle of the road if the data are more to one side," said Ceci (1993).

© Darren Matthews/Alamy

Does this mean that children can never be accurate eyewitnesses? *No.* When questioned about their experiences in neutral words they understood, children often accurately recalled what happened and who did it (Goodman, 2006; Howe, 1997; Pipe, 1996). And when interviewers used less suggestive, more effective techniques, even 4- to 5-year-old children produced more accurate recall (Holliday & Albon, 2004; Pipe et al., 2004). Children were especially accurate when they had not talked with involved adults prior to the interview and when their disclosure was made in a first interview with a neutral person who asked nonleading questions.

Repressed or Constructed Memories of Abuse?

The research on source amnesia and the misinformation effect raises concerns about therapist-guided "recovered" memories. There are two tragedies related to adult recollections of child abuse. One happens when people don't believe abuse survivors who tell their secret. The other happens when innocent people are falsely accused.

Some well-intentioned therapists have reasoned with patients that "people who've been abused often have your symptoms, so you probably were abused. Let's see if, aided by hypnosis or drugs, or helped to dig back and visualize your trauma, you can recover it." Patients exposed to such techniques may then form an image of a threatening person. With further visualization, the image grows more vivid. The patient ends up stunned, angry, and ready to confront or sue the remembered abuser. The accused person (often a parent or relative) is equally stunned and devastated, and vigorously denies the accusation.

Critics are not questioning most therapists' professionalism. Nor are they questioning the accusers' sincerity; even if false, their memories are heartfelt. Critics' charges are specifically directed against clinicians who use "memory work" techniques, such as "guided imagery," hypnosis, and dream analysis to recover memories. "Thousands of families were cruelly ripped apart," with "previously loving adult daughters" suddenly accusing fathers (Gardner, 2006). Irate clinicians have countered that those who argue that recovered memories of abuse never happen are adding to abused people's trauma and playing into the hands of child molesters.

In an effort to find a sensible common ground that might resolve psychology's "memory war," professional organizations (the American Medical, American Psychological, and American Psychiatric Associations; the Australian Psychological Society; the British Psychological Society; and the Canadian Psychiatric Association) have convened study panels and issued public statements. Those committed to protecting abused children and those committed to protecting wrongly accused adults have agreed on the following:

- *Sexual abuse happens.* And it happens more often than we once supposed. Although sexual abuse can leave its victims at risk for problems ranging from sexual dysfunction to depression (Freyd et al., 2007), there is no characteristic "survivor syndrome"—no group of symptoms that lets us spot victims of sexual abuse (Kendall-Tackett et al., 1993).

- *Injustice happens.* Some innocent people have been falsely convicted. And some guilty people have evaded responsibility by casting doubt on their truth-telling accusers.

- *Forgetting happens.* Many of those actually abused were either very young when abused or may not have understood the meaning of their experience—circumstances under which forgetting is common. Forgetting isolated past events, both negative and positive, is an ordinary part of everyday life.

- *Recovered memories are commonplace.* Cued by a remark or an experience, we all recover memories of long-forgotten events, both pleasant and unpleasant. What many psychologists debate is twofold: Does the unconscious mind sometimes *forcibly repress* painful experiences? If so, can these experiences be retrieved by certain therapist-aided techniques? (Memories that surface naturally are more likely to be verified [Geraerts et al., 2007].)

- *Memories of things happening before age 3 are unreliable.* We cannot reliably recall happenings from our first three years. As noted earlier, this infantile amnesia happens because our brain pathways have not yet developed enough to form the kinds of memories we will form later in life. Most psychologists—including most clinical and counseling psychologists—therefore doubt "recovered" memories of abuse during infancy (Gore-Felton et al., 2000; Knapp & VandeCreek, 2000). The older a child was when suffering sexual abuse, and the more severe the abuse, the more likely it is to be remembered (Goodman et al., 2003).

- *Memories "recovered" under hypnosis or the influence of drugs are especially unreliable.* Under hypnosis, people will incorporate all kinds of suggestions into their memories, even memories of "past lives."

- *Memories, whether real or false, can be emotionally upsetting.* Both the accuser and the accused may suffer when what was born of mere suggestion becomes, like an actual trauma, a stinging memory that drives bodily stress (McNally, 2003, 2007). Some people knocked unconscious in unremembered accidents know this all too well. They have later developed stress disorders after being haunted by memories they constructed from photos, news reports, and friends' accounts (Bryant, 2001).

So, does *repression* of threatening memories ever occur? Or is this concept—the cornerstone of Freud's theory and of so much popular psychology—misleading? In Modules 55 and 56, we will return to this hotly debated issue. For now, this much appears certain: The most common response to a traumatic experience (witnessing a loved one's murder, being terrorized by a hijacker or a rapist, losing everything in a natural disaster) is not banishment of the experience into the unconscious. Rather, such experiences are typically etched on the mind as vivid, persistent, haunting memories (Porter & Peace, 2007). As Robert Kraft (2002) said of the experience of those trapped in the Nazi death camps, "Horror sears memory, leaving . . . the consuming memories of atrocity."

Before You Move On

▶ **ASK YOURSELF**

Could you be an impartial jury member in a trial of a parent accused of sexual abuse based on a recovered memory, or of a therapist being sued for creating a false memory of abuse? Why or why not?

▶ **TEST YOURSELF**

How would source amnesia affect us if we were to remember all of our waking experiences as well as all of our dreams?

Answers to the Test Yourself questions can be found in Appendix E at the end of the book.

Improving Memory

 How can you use memory research findings to do better in this and other courses?

Biology's findings benefit medicine. Botany's findings benefit agriculture. So, too, can psychology's research on memory benefit education. Here, for easy reference, is a summary of some research-based suggestions that could help you remember information when you need it. The SQ3R (*S*urvey, *Q*uestion, *R*ead, *R*etrieve, *R*eview) study technique introduced in Module 2 incorporates several of these strategies:

Rehearse repeatedly. To master material, use distributed (spaced) practice. To learn a concept, give yourself many separate study sessions. Take advantage of life's little intervals—riding a bus, walking to lunch, waiting for class to start. New memories are weak; exercise them and they will strengthen. To memorize specific facts or figures, Thomas Landauer (2001) has advised, "rehearse the name or number you are trying to memorize, wait a few seconds, rehearse again, wait a little longer, rehearse again, then wait longer still and rehearse yet again. The waits should be as long as possible without losing the information." Reading complex material with minimal rehearsal yields little retention. Rehearsal and critical reflection help more. It pays to study actively.

Make the material meaningful. You can build a network of retrieval cues by taking text and class notes in your own words. Apply the concepts to your own life. Form images. Understand and organize information. Relate the material to what you already know or have experienced. As William James (1890) suggested, "Knit each new thing on to some acquisition already there." Restate concepts in your own words. Mindlessly repeating someone else's words won't supply many retrieval cues. On an exam, you may find yourself stuck when a question uses phrasing different from the words you memorized.

Thinking and memory Actively thinking as we read, by rehearsing and relating ideas, and by making the material personally meaningful, yields the best retention.

Activate retrieval cues. Mentally re-create the situation and the mood in which your original learning occurred. Jog your memory by allowing one thought to cue the next.

Use mnemonic devices. Associate items with peg words. Make up a story that incorporates vivid images of the items. Chunk information into acronyms. Create rhythmic rhymes (*"i before e, except after c"*).

Minimize interference. Study before sleep. Do not schedule back-to-back study times for topics that are likely to interfere with each other, such as Spanish and French.

Sleep more. During sleep, the brain reorganizes and consolidates information for long-term memory. Sleep deprivation disrupts this process.

Test your own knowledge, both to rehearse it and to find out what you don't yet know. Don't be lulled into overconfidence by your ability to recognize information. Test your recall using the Test Yourself items found throughout each unit, and the numbered Learning Objective Questions at the end of each module. Outline sections. Define the terms and concepts listed at each unit's end before turning back to their definitions. Try the Multiple-Choice and Practice FRQ questions at the end of each module, and take the AP® Exam Practice Questions at the end of each unit.

Before You Move On

▶ **ASK YOURSELF**

Which of the study and memory strategies suggested in this section will work best for you?

▶ **TEST YOURSELF**

What are the recommended memory strategies you just read about? (One advised rehearsing to-be-remembered material. What were the others?)

Answers to the Test Yourself questions can be found in Appendix E at the end of the book.

Module 33 Review

33-1   Why do we forget?

- *Anterograde amnesia* is an inability to form new memories.

- *Retrograde amnesia* is an inability to retrieve old memories.

- Normal forgetting happens because we have never encoded information; because the physical trace has decayed; or because we cannot retrieve what we have encoded and stored.

- Retrieval problems may result from *proactive* (forward-acting) *interference,* as prior learning interferes with recall of new information, or from *retroactive* (backward-acting) *interference,* as new learning disrupts recall of old information.

- Some believe that motivated forgetting occurs, but researchers have found little evidence of *repression.*

33-2   How do misinformation, imagination, and source amnesia influence our memory construction? How do we decide whether a memory is real or false?

- In experiments demonstrating the *misinformation effect,* people have formed false memories, by incorporating misleading details, either after receiving wrong information after an event, or after repeatedly *imagining* and rehearsing something that never happened.

- When we reassemble a memory during retrieval, we may attribute it to the wrong source *(source amnesia).* Source amnesia may help explain *déjà vu.*

- False memories feel like real memories and can be persistent but are usually limited to the gist of the event.

33-3   How reliable are young children's eyewitness descriptions, and why are reports of repressed and recovered memories so hotly debated?

- Children are susceptible to the misinformation effect, but if questioned in neutral words they understand, they can accurately recall events and people involved in them.

- The debate (between memory researchers and some well-meaning therapists) focuses on whether most memories of early childhood abuse are repressed and can be recovered during therapy using "memory work" techniques using leading questions or hypnosis.

- Psychologists now agree that (1) sexual abuse happens; (2) injustice happens; (3) forgetting happens; (4) recovered memories are commonplace; (5) memories of things that happened before age 3 are unreliable; (6) memories "recovered" under hypnosis or the influence of drugs are especially unreliable; and (7) memories, whether real or false, can be emotionally upsetting.

33-4   How can you use memory research findings to do better in this and other courses?

- Memory research findings suggest the following strategies for improving memory: Study repeatedly, make material meaningful, activate retrieval cues, use mnemonic devices, minimize interference, sleep more, and test yourself to be sure you can retrieve, as well as recognize, material.

Multiple-Choice Questions

1. Which of the following is an example of anterograde amnesia?
   a. Halle has no memories of the first 10 years of her life.
   b. William has lost his memory of the 2 weeks before he had surgery to remove a benign brain tumor.
   c. Louis can remember his past, but has not been able to form new long-term memories since experiencing a brain infection 4 years ago.
   d. Maddie can't remember the details of when she was mugged downtown 6 months ago.
   e. Kalund struggles in school because he consistently misremembers what his teachers said in class.

2. Muhammad has been in his school cafeteria hundreds of times. It is a large room, and there are nine free-standing pillars that support the roof. One day, to illustrate the nature of forgetting, Muhammad's teacher asks him how many pillars there are in the cafeteria. Muhammad has difficulty answering the question, but finally replies that he thinks there are six pillars. What memory concept does this example illustrate?
   a. Storage decay
   b. Retrograde amnesia
   c. Proactive interference
   d. Retroactive interference
   e. Encoding failure

3. What does Hermann Ebbinghaus' forgetting curve show about the nature of storage decay?

   a. The rate of forgetting increases as time goes on.

   b. The rate of forgetting decreases as time goes on.

   c. The rate of forgetting does not change as time goes on.

   d. The rate of forgetting varies according to the motivation of the learner.

   e. The rate of forgetting varies according to the emotional state of the learner.

4. Which of the following is an example of proactive interference?

   a. You can't recall your locker combination from sixth grade because your current locker combination interferes.

   b. You can't recall your new cell phone number because your old number interferes.

   c. You can't recall what you studied in first period because what you studied in fourth period interferes.

   d. You can't recall what you studied on Monday because what you studied on Tuesday interferes.

   e. You can't recall who won the state swim meet last year because the winner of this year's meet interferes.

5. The text discusses therapist-guided "recovered" memories. Which of the following statements represents an appropriate conclusion about this issue?

   a. Therapists who use hypnosis are likely to help their patients retrieve repressed memories.

   b. Statistics indicate that childhood sexual abuse rarely occurs; therefore, recovered memories of such abuse must be false.

   c. Memories are only rarely recovered; once you are unable to retrieve a memory you will probably never be able to retrieve it.

   d. One indicator of whether a recovered memory is true is the patient's emotional response; only true recovered memories are emotionally upsetting.

   e. Since the brain is not sufficiently mature to store accurate memories of events before the age of 3, memories from the first 3 years of life are not reliable.

Practice FRQs

1. Tasnia feels like she encodes material well, but still forgets the material on test day. Explain how her forgetting might be related to problems with each of the following:

- Storage
- Retrieval

Answer

1 point: Forgetting may be related to the decay of stored material.

1 point: Forgetting may be related to interference during retrieval (or motivated forgetting).

2. Your younger sister has asked you for help because she feels she cannot remember class material well enough to get good grades on her tests. Provide three specific pieces of advice that she should consider, making sure that your advice is based on psychological science.

(3 points)

Module 34

Thinking, Concepts, and Creativity

Module Learning Objectives

34-1 Define *cognition,* and describe the functions of concepts.

34-2 Identify the factors associated with creativity, and describe ways of promoting creativity.

I n some ways, we humans are, as we will see, dim-witted. We fear the wrong things. We allow the day's hot or cold weather to color our judgments of global climate change. We tend to be overconfident in our judgments and to persevere in clinging to discredited beliefs. Yet we also display remarkable mental powers. Our intelligence, creativity, and language mark us as "little less than the angels."

> **cognition** all the mental activities associated with thinking, knowing, remembering, and communicating.
>
> **concept** a mental grouping of similar objects, events, ideas, or people.
>
> **prototype** a mental image or best example of a category. Matching new items to a prototype provides a quick and easy method for sorting items into categories (as when comparing feathered creatures to a prototypical bird, such as a robin).

Thinking and Concepts

34-1 What is cognition, and what are the functions of concepts?

Let's begin our study of **cognition**—the mental activities associated with thinking, knowing, remembering, and communicating information—by appreciating our human smarts.

Consider, for example, our ability to form **concepts**—mental groupings of similar objects, events, ideas, and people. The concept *chair* includes many items—a baby's high chair, a reclining chair, a dentist's chair—all of which are for sitting. Concepts simplify our thinking. Imagine life without them. We would need a different name for every person, event, object, and idea. We could not ask a child to "throw the ball" because there would be no concept of *throw* or *ball.* Instead of saying, "They were angry," we would have to describe expressions, intensities, and words. Concepts such as *ball* and *anger* give us much information with little cognitive effort.

We often form our concepts by developing **prototypes**—a mental image or best example of a category (Rosch, 1978). People more quickly agree that "a robin is a bird" than that "a penguin is a bird." For most of us, the robin is the birdier bird; it more closely resembles our bird prototype. And the more closely something matches our prototype of a concept—bird or car—the more readily we recognize it as an example of the concept.

Once we place an item in a category, our memory of it later shifts toward the category prototype, as it did for Belgian students who viewed ethnically blended faces. For example, when viewing a blended face in which 70 percent of the features were Caucasian and 30 percent were Asian, the students categorized the

"Attention, everyone! I'd like to introduce the newest member of our family."

face as Caucasian. Later, as their memory shifted toward the Caucasian prototype, they were more likely to remember an 80 percent Caucasian face than the 70 percent Caucasian they had actually seen (Corneille et al., 2004). Likewise, if shown a 70 percent Asian face, they later remembered a more prototypically Asian face. So, too, with gender: People who viewed 70 percent male faces categorized them as male (no surprise there) and then later misremembered them as even more prototypically male (Huart et al., 2005).

Move away from our prototypes, and category boundaries may blur. Is a tomato a fruit? Is a 17-year-old female a girl or a woman? Is a whale a fish or a mammal? Because a whale fails to match our "mammal" prototype, we are slower to recognize it as a mammal. Similarly, when symptoms don't fit one of our disease prototypes, we are slow to perceive an illness (Bishop, 1991). People whose heart attack symptoms (shortness of breath, exhaustion, a dull weight in the chest) don't match their heart attack prototype (sharp chest pain) may not seek help. And when behaviors don't fit our discrimination prototypes—of White against Black, male against female, young against old—we often fail to notice prejudice. People more easily detect male prejudice against females than female against males or female against females (Inman & Baron, 1996; Marti et al., 2000). Concepts speed and guide our thinking. But they don't always make us wise.

© Oleksiy Maksymenko/agefotostock

Toying with our prototypes It takes a bit longer to conceptualize a Smart Car as an actual car, because it looks more like a toy than our mental prototype for *car*.

Creativity

34-2 What is creativity, and what fosters it?

Pierre de Fermat, a seventeenth-century mischievous genius, challenged mathematicians of his day to match his solutions to various number theory problems. His most famous challenge—*Fermat's last theorem*—baffled the greatest mathematical minds, even after a $2 million prize (in today's dollars) was offered in 1908 to whoever first created a proof.

Princeton mathematician Andrew Wiles had pondered the problem for more than 30 years and had come to the brink of a solution. One morning, out of the blue, the final "incredible revelation" struck him. "It was so indescribably beautiful; it was so simple and so elegant. I couldn't understand how I'd missed it. . . . It was the most important moment of my working life" (Singh, 1997, p. 25).

Wiles' incredible moment illustrates **creativity**—the ability to produce ideas that are both novel and valuable (Hennessey & Amabile, 2010). Studies suggest that a certain level of aptitude—a score above 120 on a standard intelligence test—supports creativity. Those who score exceptionally high in quantitative aptitude as 13-year-olds are more likely to obtain graduate science and math degrees and create published or patented work (Park et al., 2008; Robertson et al., 2010). Intelligence matters. Yet, there is more to creativity than what intelligence tests reveal. Indeed, the two kinds of thinking engage different brain areas. Intelligence tests, which typically demand a single correct answer, require **convergent thinking.** Injury to the left parietal lobe damages this ability. Creativity tests (*How many uses can you think of for a brick?*) require **divergent thinking.** Injury to certain areas of the frontal lobes can leave reading, writing, and arithmetic skills intact but destroy imagination (Kolb & Whishaw, 2006).

Although there is no agreed-upon creativity measure—there is no Creativity Quotient (CQ) corresponding to an Intelligence Quotient (IQ) score—Robert Sternberg and his colleagues have identified five components of creativity (Sternberg, 1988, 2003; Sternberg & Lubart, 1991, 1992):

1. *Expertise*—a well-developed base of knowledge—furnishes the ideas, images, and phrases we use as mental building blocks. "Chance favors only the prepared mind," observed Louis Pasteur. The more blocks we have, the more chances we have to combine them in novel ways. Wiles' well-developed base of knowledge put the needed theorems and methods at his disposal.

creativity the ability to produce novel and valuable ideas.

convergent thinking narrows the available problem solutions to determine the single best solution.

divergent thinking expands the number of possible problem solutions (creative thinking that diverges in different directions).

2. **Imaginative thinking skills** provide the ability to see things in novel ways, to recognize patterns, and to make connections. Having mastered a problem's basic elements, we redefine or explore it in a new way. Copernicus first developed expertise regarding the solar system and its planets, and then creatively defined the system as revolving around the Sun, not the Earth. Wiles' imaginative solution combined two partial solutions.

3. **A venturesome personality** seeks new experiences, tolerates ambiguity and risk, and perseveres in overcoming obstacles. Wiles risked much of his time in pursuit of his dream and persevered in near-isolation from the mathematics community partly to stay focused and avoid distraction.

4. **Intrinsic motivation** is being driven more by interest, satisfaction, and challenge than by external pressures (Amabile & Hennessey, 1992). Creative people focus less on extrinsic motivators—meeting deadlines, impressing people, or making money—than on the pleasure and stimulation of the work itself. Asked how he solved such difficult scientific problems, Isaac Newton reportedly answered, "By thinking about them all the time." Wiles concurred: "I was so obsessed by this problem that . . . I was thinking about it all the time—[from] when I woke up in the morning to when I went to sleep at night" (Singh & Riber, 1997).

5. **A creative environment** sparks, supports, and refines creative ideas. After studying the careers of 2026 prominent scientists and inventors, Dean Keith Simonton (1992) noted that the most eminent were mentored, challenged, and supported by their colleagues. Many had the emotional intelligence needed to network effectively with peers. Even Wiles stood on the shoulders of others and wrestled his problem with the collaboration of a former student. Creativity-fostering environments support innovation, team-building, and communication (Hülsheger et al., 2009). They also support contemplation. After Jonas Salk solved a problem that led to the polio vaccine while in a monastery, he designed the Salk Institute to provide contemplative spaces where scientists could work without interruption (Sternberg, 2006). Google has estimated that nearly half its product innovations have been sparked during the 20 percent of employee time reserved for unstructured creative thinking (Mayer, 2006).

Imaginative thinking Cartoonists often display creativity as they see things in new ways or make unusual connections.

"For the love of God, is there a doctor in the house?"

For those seeking to boost the creative process, research offers some ideas:

- *Develop your expertise.* Ask yourself what you care about and most enjoy. Follow your passion and become an expert at something.

- *Allow time for incubation.* Given sufficient knowledge available for novel connections, a period of inattention to a problem ("sleeping on it") allows for unconscious processing to form associations (Zhong et al., 2008). So think hard on a problem, then set it aside and come back to it later.

- *Set aside time for the mind to roam freely.* Take time away from attention-absorbing television, social networking, and video gaming. Jog, go for a long walk, or meditate.

- *Experience other cultures and ways of thinking.* Living abroad sets the creative juices flowing. Even after controlling for other variables, students who have spent time abroad are more adept at working out creative solutions to problems (Leung et al., 2008; Maddux et al., 2009, 2010). Multicultural experiences expose us to multiple perspectives and facilitate flexible thinking.

A creative environment

Before You Move On

▶ **ASK YOURSELF**

Imagine patiently waiting your turn at a store, and then having some late-arriving adults served before you. The clerk also checks inside your bag as you leave the store. What is a prototype, and what sort of "teenager" prototype does the clerk seem to have in mind?

▶ **TEST YOURSELF**

According to Robert Sternberg, what are the five components of creativity?

Answers to the Test Yourself questions can be found in Appendix E at the end of the book.

Module 34 Review

 34-1 What is cognition, and what are the functions of concepts?

- *Cognition* refers to all the mental activities associated with thinking, knowing, remembering, and communicating.

- We use *concepts,* mental groupings of similar objects, events, ideas, or people, to simplify and order the world around us.

- We form most concepts around *prototypes,* or best examples of a category.

34-2 What is creativity, and what fosters it?

- *Creativity,* the ability to produce novel and valuable ideas, correlates somewhat with intelligence, but beyond an intelligence test score of 120, that correlation dwindles.

- Sternberg has proposed that creativity has five components: expertise, imaginative thinking skills; a venturesome personality; intrinsic motivation; and a creative environment that sparks, supports, and refines creative ideas.

Multiple-Choice Questions

1. Which of the following is the best term for mental activities associated with remembering, thinking, and knowing?

    a. Cognition
    b. Concepts
    c. Prototypes
    d. Convergent thinking
    e. Divergent thinking

2. Which of the following is the best phrase for the narrowing of available problem solutions with the goal of determining the best solution?

    a. Allowing for incubation
    b. Divergent thinking
    c. Developing expertise
    d. Convergent thinking
    e. Experiencing other cultures

3. Producing valuable and novel ideas best defines which of the following?

    a. Prototyping
    b. Cognition
    c. Intrinsic motivation
    d. Venturesome personality
    e. Creativity

Practice FRQs

1. Compare the notions of concept and prototype.

Answer

1 point: A concept is a mental grouping of similar objects, events, ideas, and people.

1 point: A prototype is a mental image or best example of a category.

2. Identify and explain four of the five components of creativity mentioned in this module.

(4 points)

Module 35

Solving Problems and Making Decisions

Module Learning Objectives

35-1 Describe the cognitive strategies that assist our problem solving, and identify the obstacles that hinder it.

35-2 Explain what is meant by intuition, and describe how the representativeness and availability heuristics, overconfidence, belief perseverance, and framing influence our decisions and judgments.

35-3 Describe how smart thinkers use intuition.

Problem Solving: Strategies and Obstacles

35-1 What cognitive strategies assist our problem solving, and what obstacles hinder it?

One tribute to our rationality is our problem-solving skill. What's the best route around this traffic jam? How should we handle a friend's criticism? How can we get in the house without our keys?

Some problems we solve through *trial and error*. Thomas Edison tried thousands of light bulb filaments before stumbling upon one that worked. For other problems, we use **algorithms,** step-by-step procedures that guarantee a solution. But step-by-step algorithms can be laborious and exasperating. To find a word using the 10 letters in *SPLOYOCHYG*, for example, you could try each letter in each of the 10 positions—907,200 permutations in all. Rather than give you a computing brain the size of a beach ball, nature resorts to **heuristics,** simpler thinking strategies. Thus, you might reduce the number of options in the *SPLOYOCHYG* example by grouping letters that often appear together (*CH* and *GY*) and excluding rare letter combinations (such as two *Y*'s together). By using heuristics and then applying trial and error, you may hit on the answer. Have you guessed it?[1]

Sometimes, no problem-solving strategy seems to be at work at all, and we arrive at a solution to a problem with **insight**. Teams of researchers have identified brain activity associated with sudden flashes of insight (Kounios & Beeman, 2009; Sandkühler & Bhattacharya, 2008). They gave people a problem: Think of a word that will form a compound word or phrase with each of three other words in a set (such as *pine, crab,* and *sauce*), and press a button to sound a bell when you know the answer. (If you need a hint: The word is a fruit.[2]) EEGs or fMRIs (functional MRIs) revealed the problem solver's brain activity.

AP® Exam Tip

There are several sample problems for you to enjoy in this section. It can be very interesting to ask several of your friends to try to solve them, too. Have them talk through the problem out loud and you will gain some understanding of the processes they are using.

algorithm a methodical, logical rule or procedure that guarantees solving a particular problem. Contrasts with the usually speedier—but also more error-prone—use of *heuristics*.

heuristic a simple thinking strategy that often allows us to make judgments and solve problems efficiently; usually speedier but also more error-prone than *algorithms*.

insight a sudden realization of a problem's solution; contrasts with strategy-based solutions.

---

[1] Answer to SPLOYOCHYG anagram: PSYCHOLOGY.
[2] The word is apple: pineapple, crabapple, applesauce.

Heuristic searching To search for hot cocoa mix, you could search every supermarket aisle (an algorithm), or check the breakfast, beverage, and baking supplies sections (heuristics). The heuristics approach is often speedier, but an algorithmic search guarantees you will find it eventually.

In the first experiment, about half the solutions were by a sudden Aha! insight. Before the Aha! moment, the problem solvers' frontal lobes (which are involved in focusing attention) were active, and there was a burst of activity in the right temporal lobe, just above the ear (**FIGURE 35.1**).

We are also not the only creatures to display insight, as psychologist Wolfgang Köhler (1925) demonstrated in an experiment with Sultan, a chimpanzee. Köhler placed a piece of fruit and a long stick outside Sultan's cage. Inside the cage, he placed a short stick, which Sultan grabbed, using it to try to reach the fruit. After several failed attempts, he dropped the stick and seemed to survey the situation. Then suddenly, as if thinking "Aha!" Sultan jumped up and seized the short stick again. This time, he used it to pull in the longer stick—which he then used to reach the fruit. What is more, apes will even exhibit foresight, by storing a tool they can use to retrieve food the next day (Mulcahy & Call, 2006).

Insight strikes suddenly, with no prior sense of "getting warmer" or feeling close to a solution (Knoblich & Oellinger, 2006; Metcalfe, 1986). When the answer pops into mind (*apple!*), we feel a happy sense of satisfaction. The joy of a joke may similarly lie in our sudden comprehension of an unexpected ending or a double meaning: "You don't need a parachute to skydive. You only need a parachute to skydive twice."

Inventive as we are, other cognitive tendencies may lead us astray. For example, we more eagerly seek out and favor evidence verifying our ideas than evidence refuting them (Klayman & Ha, 1987; Skov & Sherman, 1986). Peter Wason (1960) demonstrated this tendency, known as **confirmation bias,** by giving British university students the three-number sequence 2-4-6 and asking them to guess the rule he had used to devise the series. (The rule was simple: any three ascending numbers.) Before submitting answers, students generated their own three-number sets and Wason told them whether their sets conformed to his rule. Once *certain* they had the rule, they could announce it. The result? Seldom right but never in doubt. Most students formed a wrong idea *("Maybe it's counting by twos")* and then searched only for confirming evidence (by testing 6-8-10, 100-102-104, and so forth).

"Ordinary people," said Wason (1981), "evade facts, become inconsistent, or systematically defend themselves against the threat of new information relevant to the issue." Thus, once people form a belief—that vaccines cause autism spectrum disorder, that President Barack Obama is a Kenyan-born Muslim, that gun control does (or does not) save lives—they prefer belief-confirming information. The results can be momentous. The U.S. war against Iraq was launched on the belief that Saddam Hussein possessed weapons of mass destruction (WMD) that posed an immediate threat. When that assumption turned out to be false, the bipartisan U.S. Senate Select Committee on Intelligence (2004) identified confirmation bias as partly to blame: Administration analysts "had a tendency to accept information which supported [their presumptions] . . . more readily than information which contradicted" them. Sources denying such weapons were deemed "either lying or

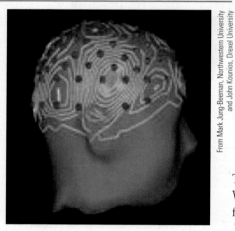

Figure 35.1

The Aha! moment A burst of right temporal lobe activity accompanied insight solutions to word problems (Jung-Beeman et al., 2004). The red dots designate EEG electrodes. The light gray lines show the distribution of high-frequency activity accompanying insight. The insight-related activity is centered in the right temporal lobe (yellow area).

confirmation bias a tendency to search for information that supports our preconceptions and to ignore or distort contradictory evidence.

"The human understanding, when any proposition has been once laid down . . . forces everything else to add fresh support and confirmation." -Francis Bacon, *Novum Organum*, 1620

not knowledgeable about Iraq's problems," while those sources who reported ongoing WMD activities were seen as "having provided valuable information."

Once we incorrectly represent a problem, it's hard to restructure how we approach it. If the solution to the matchstick problem in **FIGURE 35.2** eludes you, you may be experiencing *fixation*—an inability to see a problem from a fresh perspective. (For the solution, turn the page to see **FIGURE 35.3**.)

A prime example of fixation is **mental set,** our tendency to approach a problem with the mind-set of what has worked for us previously. Indeed, solutions that worked in the past often do work on new problems. Consider:

Given the sequence *O-T-T-F-?-?-?,* what are the final three letters?

Most people have difficulty recognizing that the three final letters are *F*(ive), *S*(ix), and *S*(even). But solving this problem may make the next one easier:

Given the sequence *J-F-M-A-?-?-?,* what are the final three letters? (If you don't get this one, ask yourself what month it is.)

As a perceptual set predisposes what we perceive, a mental set predisposes how we think; sometimes this can be an obstacle to problem solving, as when our mental set from our past experiences with matchsticks predisposes us to arrange them in two dimensions.

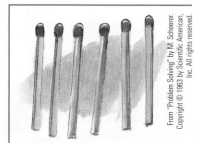

Figure 35.2
The matchstick problem How would you arrange six matches to form four equilateral triangles?

Forming Good and Bad Decisions and Judgments

 What is intuition, and how can the representativeness and availability heuristics, overconfidence, belief perseverance, and framing influence our decisions and judgments?

When making each day's hundreds of judgments and decisions *(Is it worth the bother to take a jacket? Can I trust this person? Should I shoot the basketball or pass to the player who's hot?),* we seldom take the time and effort to reason systematically. We just follow our **intuition,** our fast, automatic, unreasoned feelings and thoughts. After interviewing policy makers in government, business, and education, social psychologist Irving Janis (1986) concluded that they "often do not use a reflective problem-solving approach. How do they usually arrive at their decisions? If you ask, they are likely to tell you . . . they do it mostly by *the seat of their pants.*"

When we need to act quickly, the mental shortcuts we call *heuristics* enable snap judgments. Thanks to our mind's automatic information processing, intuitive judgments are instantaneous and usually effective. However, research by cognitive psychologists Amos Tversky and Daniel Kahneman (1974) on the *representativeness* and *availability heuristics* showed how these generally helpful shortcuts can lead even the smartest people into dumb decisions.[3]

---

[3] Tversky and Kahneman's joint work on decision making received a 2002 Nobel Prize; sadly, only Kahneman was alive to receive the honor.

"The problem is I can't tell the difference between a deeply wise, intuitive nudge from the Universe and one of my own bone-headed ideas!"

"Kahneman and his colleagues and students have changed the way we think about the way people think." -American Psychological Association President, Sharon Brehm, 2007

"In creating these problems, we didn't set out to fool people. All our problems fooled us, too." Amos Tversky (1985)

"Intuitive thinking [is] fine most of the time. . . . But sometimes that habit of mind gets us in trouble." Daniel Kahneman (2005)

mental set a tendency to approach a problem in one particular way, often a way that has been successful in the past.

intuition an effortless, immediate, automatic feeling or thought, as contrasted with explicit, conscious reasoning.

Figure 35.3

Solution to the matchstick problem To solve this problem, you must view it from a new perspective, breaking the fixation of limiting solutions to two dimensions.

The Representativeness Heuristic

To judge the likelihood of things in terms of how well they represent particular prototypes is to use the **representativeness heuristic.** To illustrate, consider:

> A stranger tells you about a person who is short, slim, and likes to read poetry, and then asks you to guess whether this person is more likely to be a professor of classics at an Ivy League university or a truck driver (adapted from Nisbett & Ross, 1980). Which would be the better guess?

Did you answer "professor"? Many people do, because the description seems more *representative* of Ivy League scholars than of truck drivers. The representativeness heuristic enabled you to make a snap judgment. But it also led you to ignore other relevant information. When I help people think through this question, the conversation goes something like this:

Question: First, let's figure out how many professors fit the description. How many Ivy League universities do you suppose there are?

Answer: Oh, about 10, I suppose.

Question: How many classics professors would you guess there are at each?

Answer: Maybe 4.

Question: Okay, that's 40 Ivy League classics professors. What fraction of these are short and slim?

Answer: Let's say half.

Question: And, of these 20, how many like to read poetry?

Answer: I'd say half—10 professors.

Question: Okay, now let's figure how many truck drivers fit the description. How many truck drivers do you suppose there are?

Answer: Maybe 400,000.

Question: What fraction are short and slim?

Answer: Not many—perhaps 1 in 8.

Question: Of these 50,000, what percentage like to read poetry?

Answer: Truck drivers who like poetry? Maybe 1 in 100—oh, oh, I get it— that leaves 500 short, slim, poetry-reading truck drivers.

Comment: Yup. So, even if we accept your stereotype that the description is more representative of classics professors than of truck drivers, the odds are 50 to 1 that this person is a truck driver.

The representativeness heuristic influences many of our daily decisions. To judge the likelihood of something, we intuitively compare it with our mental representation of that category—of, say, what truck drivers are like. If the two match, that fact usually overrides other considerations of statistics or logic.

The Availability Heuristic

The **availability heuristic** operates when we estimate the likelihood of events based on how mentally available they are. Casinos entice us to gamble by signaling even small wins with bells and lights—making them vividly memorable—while keeping big losses soundlessly invisible.

The availability heuristic can lead us astray in our judgments of other people, too. Anything that makes information "pop" into mind—its vividness, recency, or distinctiveness—can make it seem commonplace. If someone from a particular ethnic or religious group commits a terrorist act, as happened on September 11, 2001, when Islamic extremists killed

representativeness heuristic judging the likelihood of things in terms of how well they seem to represent, or match, particular prototypes; may lead us to ignore other relevant information.

availability heuristic estimating the likelihood of events based on their availability in memory; if instances come readily to mind (perhaps because of their vividness), we presume such events are common.

nearly 3000 people in the United States in coordinated terrorist attacks, our readily available memory of the dramatic event may shape our impression of the whole group.

Even during that horrific year, terrorist acts claimed comparatively few lives. Yet when the statistical reality of greater dangers (see **FIGURE 35.4**) was pitted against a single vivid case, the memorable case won, as emotion-laden images of terror exacerbated our fears (Sunstein, 2007).

We often fear the wrong things. We fear flying because we play in our heads some air disaster. We fear letting our children walk to school because we play in our heads tapes of abducted and brutalized children. We fear swimming in ocean waters because we replay *Jaws* in our heads. Even just passing by a person who sneezes and coughs heightens our perceptions of various health risks (Lee et al., 2010). And so, thanks to these readily available images, we come to fear extremely rare events. (Turn the page to see Thinking Critically About: The Fear Factor—Why We Fear the Wrong Things.)

Meanwhile, the lack of comparably available images of global climate change—which some scientists regard as a future "Armageddon in slow motion"—has left most people little concerned (Pew, 2007). The vividness of a recent local cold day reduces their concern about long-term global warming and overwhelms less memorable scientific data (Li et al., 2011). Dramatic outcomes make us gasp; probabilities we hardly grasp. As of 2013, some 60 nations—including Canada, many in Europe, and the United States—have, however, sought to harness the positive power of vivid, memorable images by putting eye-catching warnings and graphic photos on cigarette packages (Riordan, 2013). This campaign may work, where others have failed. As psychologist Paul Slovic (2007) points out, we reason emotionally and neglect probabilities. We overfeel and underthink. In one experiment, donations to a starving 7-year-old child were greater when her image was *not* accompanied by statistical information about the millions of needy African children like her (Small et al., 2007). "If I look at the mass, I will never act," Mother Teresa reportedly said. "If I look at the one, I will." "The more who die, the less we care," noted Slovic (2010).

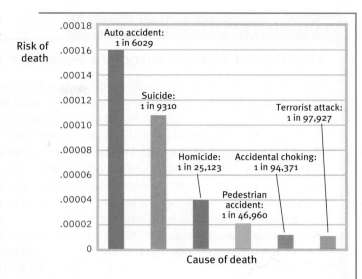

Figure 35.4

Risk of death from various causes in the United States, 2001 (Data assembled from various government sources by Randall Marshall et al., 2007.)

Overconfidence

Sometimes our judgments and decisions go awry simply because we are more confident than correct. Across various tasks, people overestimate their performance (Metcalfe, 1998). If 60 percent of people correctly answer a factual question, such as "Is absinthe a liqueur or a precious stone?," they will typically average 75 percent confidence (Fischhoff et al., 1977). (It's a licorice-flavored liqueur.) This tendency to overestimate the accuracy of our knowledge and judgments is **overconfidence.**

It was an overconfident BP that, before its exploded drilling platform spewed oil into the Gulf of Mexico, downplayed safety concerns, and then downplayed the spill's magnitude (Mohr et al., 2010; Urbina, 2010). It is overconfidence that drives stockbrokers and investment managers to market their ability to outperform stock market averages, despite overwhelming evidence to the contrary (Malkiel, 2004). A purchase of stock X, recommended by a broker who judges this to be the time to buy, is usually balanced by a sale made by someone who judges this to be the time to sell. Despite their confidence, buyer and seller cannot both be right.

History is full of leaders who were more confident than correct. And classrooms are full of overconfident students who expect to finish assignments and write papers ahead of schedule (Buehler et al., 1994). In fact, the projects generally take about twice the number of days predicted.

overconfidence the tendency to be more confident than correct—to overestimate the accuracy of our beliefs and judgments.

"Don't believe everything you think." -Bumper sticker

Thinking Critically About

The Fear Factor—Why We Fear the Wrong Things

After the 9/11 attacks, many people feared flying more than driving. In a 2006 Gallup survey, only 40 percent of Americans reported being "not afraid at all" to fly. Yet from 2005 to 2007 Americans were—mile for mile—170 times more likely to die in an automobile or pickup truck crash than on a scheduled flight (National Safety Council, 2010). In 2009 alone, 33,808 Americans were killed in motor vehicle accidents—that's 650 dead people each week. Meanwhile, in 2009 (as in 2007 and 2008) zero died from airline accidents on scheduled flights.

In a late 2001 essay, I calculated that if—because of 9/11— we flew 20 percent less and instead drove half those unflown miles, about 800 more people would die in the year after 9/11 (Myers, 2001). German psychologist Gerd Gigerenzer (2004, 2006) later checked this estimate against actual accident data. (Why didn't I think of that?) U.S. traffic deaths did indeed increase significantly in the last three months of 2001 (**FIGURE 35.5**). By the end of 2002, Gigerenzer estimated, 1600 Americans had "lost their lives on the road by trying to avoid the risk of flying." Despite our greater fear of flying, flying's greatest danger is, for most people, the drive to the airport.

Why do we fear the wrong things? Why do we judge terrorism to be a greater risk than accidents? Psychologists have identified four influences that feed fear and cause us to ignore higher risks.

1. *We fear what our ancestral history has prepared us to fear.* Human emotions were road tested in the Stone Age. Our old brain prepares us to fear yesterday's risks: snakes, lizards, and spiders (which combined now kill a tiny fraction of the number killed by modern-day threats, such as cars and cigarettes). Yesterday's risks also prepare us to fear confinement and heights, and therefore flying.

2. *We fear what we cannot control.* Driving we control; flying we do not.

3. *We fear what is immediate.* The dangers of flying are mostly telescoped into the moments of takeoff and landing. The dangers of driving are diffused across many moments to come, each trivially dangerous.

4. *Thanks to the availability heuristic, we fear what is most readily available in memory.* Powerful, vivid images, like that of United Flight 175 slicing into the World Trade Center, feed our judgments of risk. Thousands of safe car trips have extinguished our anxieties about driving. Similarly, we remember (and fear) widespread disasters (hurricanes, tornadoes, earthquakes) that kill people dramatically, in bunches. But we fear too little the less dramatic threats that claim lives quietly, one by one, continuing into the distant future. Bill Gates has noted that each year a half-million children worldwide die from rotavirus. This is the equivalent of four 747s full of children *every day,* and we hear nothing of it (Glass, 2004).

ssuaphotos/Shutterstock

©Motoring Picture Library/Alamy

Figure 35.5

Scared onto deadly highways Images of 9/11 etched a sharper image in American minds than did the millions of fatality-free flights on U.S. airlines during 2002 and after. Dramatic events are readily available to memory, and they shape our perceptions of risk. In the three months after 9/11, those faulty perceptions led more Americans to travel, and some to die, by car. (Adapted from Gigerenzer, 2004.)

Monthly U.S. Traffic Deaths

Oct.–Dec. 2001: 353 excess deaths

Number of traffic deaths, 2001

Average number of traffic deaths, 1996–2000

(y-axis: 2200 to 3600; x-axis: Jan. Feb. March April May June July Aug. Sept. Oct. Nov. Dec.)

The Perils and Powers of Intuition

35-3 How do smart thinkers use intuition?

We have seen how our irrational thinking can plague our efforts to see problems clearly, make wise decisions, form valid judgments, and reason logically. Moreover, these perils of intuition feed gut fears and prejudices. And they persist even when people are offered extra pay for thinking smart, even when they are asked to justify their answers, and even when they are expert physicians or clinicians (Shafir & LeBoeuf, 2002). So, are our heads indeed filled with straw?

Good news: Cognitive scientists are also revealing intuition's powers. Here is a summary of some of the high points:

- *Intuition is huge.* Recall from Module 16 that through *selective attention,* we can focus our conscious awareness on a particular aspect of all we experience. Our mind's unconscious track, however, makes good use intuitively of what we are not consciously processing. Today's cognitive science offers many examples of unconscious influences on our judgments (Custers & Aarts, 2010). Consider: Most people guess that the more complex the choice, the smarter it is to make decisions rationally rather than intuitively (Inbar et al., 2010). Actually, Dutch psychologists have shown that in making complex decisions, we benefit by letting our brain work on a problem without thinking about it (Strick et al., 2010). In one series of experiments, they showed three groups of people complex information (about apartments or roommates or art posters or soccer football matches). They invited one group to state their preference immediately after reading information about each of four options. A second group, given several minutes to analyze the information, made slightly smarter decisions. But wisest of all, in study after study, was the third group, whose attention was distracted for a time, enabling their minds to process the complex information unconsciously. Critics of this research remind us that deliberate, conscious thought also is part of smart thinking (Gonzáles-Vallejo et al., 2008; Lassiter et al., 2009; Newell et al., 2008; Payne et al., 2008). Nevertheless, letting a problem "incubate" while we attend to other things can pay dividends (Sio & Ormerod, 2009). Facing a difficult decision involving lots of facts, we're wise to gather all the information we can, and then say, "Give me some time *not* to think about this." By taking time to sleep on it, we let our unconscious mental machinery work on, and await, the intuitive result of our unconscious processing.

- *Intuition is usually adaptive.* Our instant, intuitive reactions enable us to react quickly. Our fast and frugal heuristics, for example, enable us to intuitively assume that fuzzy looking objects are far away—which they usually are, except on foggy mornings. Our learned associations surface as gut feelings, the intuitions of our two-track mind. If a stranger looks like someone who previously harmed or threatened us, we may—without consciously recalling the earlier experience—react warily. People's automatic, unconscious associations with a political position can even predict their future decisions *before* they consciously make up their minds (Galdi et al., 2008).

- *Intuition is recognition born of experience.* It is implicit knowledge—what we've learned but can't fully explain, such as how to ride a bike. We see this tacit expertise in chess masters playing "blitz chess," where every move is made after barely more than a glance. They can look at a board and intuitively know the right move (Burns, 2004). We see it in experienced nurses, firefighters, art critics, car mechanics, and hockey players. And in you, too, for anything in which you have developed a special skill. In each case, what feels like instant intuition is an acquired ability to size up a situation in an eyeblink. As Nobel laureate psychologist Herbert Simon (2001) observed, intuition is analysis "frozen into habit."

Hmm . . . male or female?
When acquired expertise becomes an automatic habit, as it is for experienced chicken sexers, it feels like intuition. At a glance, they just know the sex of the chick, yet cannot easily tell you how they know.

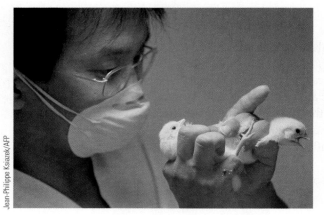

Jean-Philippe Ksiazek/AFP

The bottom line: Intuition can be perilous, especially when we overfeel and underthink, as we do when judging risks. Today's psychological science reminds us to check our intuitions against reality, but also enhances our appreciation for intuition. Our two-track mind makes sweet harmony as smart, critical thinking listens to the creative whispers of our vast unseen mind, and then evaluates evidence, tests conclusions, and plans for the future.

Try This

What time is it now? When I asked you (in the section on overconfidence) to estimate how quickly you would finish this module, did you underestimate or overestimate?

Before You Move On

▶ **ASK YOURSELF**

People's perceptions of risk, often biased by vivid images from movies or the news, are surprisingly unrelated to actual risks. (People may hide in the basement during thunderstorms but fail to buckle their seat belts in the car.) What are the things you fear? Are some of those fears out of proportion to statistical risk? Are you failing, in other areas of your life, to take reasonable precautions?

▶ **TEST YOURSELF**

The availability heuristic is a quick-and-easy but sometimes misleading guide to judging reality. What is the availability heuristic?

Answers to the Test Yourself questions can be found in Appendix E at the end of the book.

Module 35 Review

35-1 What cognitive strategies assist our problem solving, and what obstacles hinder it?

- An *algorithm* is a methodical, logical rule or procedure (such as a step-by-step description for evacuating a building during a fire) that guarantees a solution to a problem.

- A *heuristic* is a simpler strategy (such as running for an exit if you smell smoke) that is usually speedier than an algorithm but is also more error-prone.

- *Insight* is not a strategy-based solution, but rather a sudden flash of inspiration that solves a problem.

- Obstacles to problem solving include *confirmation bias,* which predisposes us to verify rather than challenge our hypotheses, and fixation, such as *mental set,* which may prevent us from taking the fresh perspective that would lead to a solution.

35-2 What is intuition, and how can the representativeness and availability heuristics, overconfidence, belief perseverance, and framing influence our decisions and judgments?

- *Intuition* is the effortless, immediate, automatic feeling or thoughts we often use instead of systematic reasoning.

- Heuristics enable snap judgments. *The representativeness heuristic* leads us to judge the likelihood of things in terms of how they represent our prototype for a group of items. Using the *availability heuristic,* we judge the likelihood of things based on how readily they come to mind, which often leads us to fear the wrong things.

- *Overconfidence* can lead us to overestimate the accuracy of our beliefs.

- When a belief we have formed and explained has been discredited, belief perseverance may cause us to cling to that belief. A remedy for *belief perseverance* is to consider how we might have explained an opposite result.

- *Framing* is the way a question or statement is worded. Subtle wording differences can dramatically alter our responses.

35-3 How do smart thinkers use intuition?

- Smart thinkers welcome their intuitions (which are usually adaptive), but when making complex decisions they gather as much information as possible and then take time to let their two-track mind process all available information.

- As people gain expertise, they grow adept at making quick, shrewd judgments.

Multiple-Choice Questions

1. What is another term for a methodical, logical rule that guarantees solving a particular problem?
   a. Heuristic
   b. Algorithm
   c. Insight
   d. Mental set
   e. Confirmation bias

2. Which of the following is the tendency to search for supportive information of preconceptions while ignoring contradictory evidence?
   a. Confirmation bias
   b. Intuition
   c. Mental set
   d. Availability heuristic
   e. Overconfidence

3. What is another word for the way an issue is presented to you?
   a. Intuition
   b. Insight
   c. Framing
   d. Overconfidence
   e. Perseverance

4. When instances come readily to mind, we often presume such events are common. What of the following is the term for this phenomenon?
   a. Intuition insight
   b. Confirmation bias
   c. Belief perseverance
   d. Mental set
   e. Availability heuristic

Practice FRQs

1. Name and define two problem-solving strategies. Next, explain an advantage each has over the other.

Answer

1 point: An algorithm is a step-by-step procedure that guarantees a solution.

1 point: A heuristic is a simple thinking strategy that often allows us to make quick judgments.

1 point: Algorithm advantage: More likely to produce a correct solution.

1 point: Heuristic advantage: Often faster than using an algorithm.

2. Explain how each of the following can lead to inaccurate judgments: overconfidence, mental set, and confirmation bias.

(3 points)

Module 36

Thinking and Language

Module Learning Objectives

36-1 Describe the structural components of a language.

36-2 Identify the milestones in language development.

36-3 Describe how we acquire language.

36-4 Identify the brain areas involved in language processing and speech.

36-5 Describe the relationship between language and thinking, and discuss the value of thinking in images.

language our spoken, written, or signed words and the ways we combine them to communicate meaning.

magine an alien species that could pass thoughts from one head to another merely by pulsating air molecules in the space between them. Perhaps these weird creatures could inhabit a future science fiction movie?

Actually, we are those creatures. When we speak, our brain and voice apparatus conjure up air pressure waves that we send banging against another's eardrum—enabling us to transfer thoughts from our brain into theirs. As cognitive scientist Steven Pinker (1998) has noted, we sometimes sit for hours "listening to other people make noise as they exhale, because those hisses and squeaks contain *information*." And thanks to all those funny sounds created in our heads from the air pressure waves we send out, we get people's attention, we get them to do things, and we maintain relationships (Guerin, 2003). Depending on how you vibrate the air after opening your mouth, you may get slapped or kissed.

Language transmits knowledge Whether spoken, written, or signed, language—the original wireless communication—enables mind-to-mind information transfer, and with it the transmission of civilization's accumulated knowledge across generations.

But **language** is more than vibrating air. As I create this paragraph, my fingers on a keyboard generate electronic binary numbers that are translated into squiggles of dried carbon pressed onto the page in front of you. When transmitted by reflected light rays into your retina, the printed squiggles trigger formless nerve impulses that project to several areas of your brain, which integrate the information, compare it with stored information, and decode meaning. Thanks to language, information is moving from my mind to yours. Monkeys mostly know what they see. Thanks to language (spoken, written, or signed) we comprehend much that we've never seen and that our distant ancestors never knew.

Today, notes Daniel Gilbert (2006), "The average newspaper boy in Pittsburgh knows more about the universe than did Galileo, Aristotle, Leonardo, or any of those other guys who were so smart they only needed one name."

To Pinker (1990), language is "the jewel in the crown of cognition." If you were able to retain one cognitive ability, make it language, suggests researcher Lera Boroditsky (2009). Without sight or hearing, you could still have friends, family, and a job. But without language, could you have these things? "Language is so fundamental to our experience, so deeply a part of being human, that it's hard to imagine life without it."

Language Structure

36-1 What are the structural components of a language?

Consider how we might go about inventing a language. For a spoken language, we would need three building blocks:

- **Phonemes** are the smallest distinctive sound units in a language. To say *bat*, English speakers utter the phonemes *b, a,* and *t.* (Phonemes aren't the same as letters. *Chat* also has three phonemes—*ch, a,* and *t.*) Linguists surveying nearly 500 languages have identified 869 different phonemes in human speech, but no language uses all of them (Holt, 2002; Maddieson, 1984). English uses about 40; other languages use anywhere from half to more than twice that many. As a general rule, consonant phonemes carry more information than do vowel phonemes. *The treth ef thes stetement shed be evedent frem thes bref demenstretien.*

- **Morphemes** are the smallest units that carry meaning in a given language. In English, a few morphemes are also phonemes—the personal pronoun *I* and the *s* that indicates plural, for instance. But most morphemes combine two or more phonemes. Some, like *bat* or *gentle,* are words. Others—like the prefix *pre-* in *preview* or the suffix *-ed* in *adapted*—are parts of words.

- **Grammar** is the system of rules that enables us to communicate with one another. Grammatical rules guide us in deriving meaning from sounds *(semantics)* and in ordering words into sentences *(syntax).*

Language becomes increasingly complex as we move from one level to the next. In English, for example, 40 or so phonemes can be combined to form more than 100,000 morphemes, which alone or in combination produce the 616,500 word forms in the *Oxford English Dictionary.* Using those words, we can then create an infinite number of sentences, most of which (like this one) are original. Like life constructed from the genetic code's simple alphabet, language is complexity built of simplicity. I know that you can know why I worry that you think this sentence is starting to get too complex, but that complexity—and our capacity to communicate and comprehend it—is what distinguishes human language capacity (Hauser et al., 2002; Premack, 2007).

Language Development

Make a quick guess: How many words will you have learned during the years between your first birthday and your high school graduation? Although you use only 150 words for about half of what you say, you will have learned about 60,000 words in your native language during those years (Bloom, 2000; McMurray, 2007). That averages (after age 2) to nearly 3500 words each year, or nearly 10 each day! How you do it—how those 3500 words so far outnumber the roughly 200 words your schoolteachers are consciously teaching you each year—is one of the great human wonders.

phoneme in a language, the smallest distinctive sound unit.

morpheme in a language, the smallest unit that carries meaning; may be a word or a part of a word (such as a prefix).

grammar in a language, a system of rules that enables us to communicate with and understand others. In a given language, *semantics* is the set of rules for deriving meaning from sounds, and *syntax* is the set of rules for combining words into grammatically sensible sentences.

AP® Exam Tip

It is sometimes challenging to keep these building blocks straight. Phonemes are sounds. It may help to remember that phones carry sounds. Morphemes have meaning, and both words begin with the letter *m.*

"Let me get this straight now. Is what you want to build a jean factory or a gene factory?"

Jaimie Duplass/Shutterstock

Could you even state all your language's rules of syntax (the correct way to string words together to form sentences)? Most of us cannot. Yet, before you were able to add 2 + 2, you were creating your own original and grammatically appropriate sentences. As a preschooler, you comprehended and spoke with a facility that puts to shame college students struggling to learn a foreign language.

We humans have an astonishing facility for language. With remarkable efficiency, we sample tens of thousands of words in our memory, effortlessly assemble them with near-perfect syntax, and spew them out, three words a second (Vigliocco & Hartsuiker, 2002). Seldom do we form sentences in our minds before speaking them. Rather we organize them on the fly as we speak. And while doing all this, we also adapt our utterances to our social and cultural context, following rules for speaking *(How far apart should we stand?)* and listening *(Is it OK to interrupt?)*. Given how many ways there are to mess up, it's amazing that we can master this social dance. So when and how does it happen?

When Do We Learn Language?

 What are the milestones in language development?

RECEPTIVE LANGUAGE

Children's language development moves from simplicity to complexity. Infants start without language (*in fantis* means "not speaking"). Yet by 4 months of age, babies can recognize differences in speech sounds (Stager & Werker, 1997). They can also read lips: They prefer to look at a face that matches a sound, so we know they can recognize that *ah* comes from wide open lips and *ee* from a mouth with corners pulled back (Kuhl & Meltzoff, 1982). This marks the beginning of the development of babies' *receptive language,* their ability to understand what is said to and about them. At 7 months and beyond, babies grow in their power to do what you and I find difficult when listening to an unfamiliar language: to segment spoken sounds into individual words. Moreover, their adeptness at this task, as judged by their listening patterns, predicts their language abilities at ages 2 and 5 (Newman et al., 2006).

PRODUCTIVE LANGUAGE

Babies' *productive language,* their ability to produce words, matures after their receptive language. They recognize noun-verb differences—as shown by their responses to a misplaced noun or verb—earlier than they utter sentences with nouns and verbs (Bernal et al., 2010).

Before nurture molds babies' speech, nature enables a wide range of possible sounds in the **babbling stage,** beginning around 4 months of age. Many of these spontaneously uttered sounds are consonant-vowel pairs formed by simply bunching the tongue in the front of the mouth *(da-da, na-na, ta-ta)* or by opening and closing the lips *(ma-ma),* both of which babies do naturally for feeding (MacNeilage & Davis, 2000). Babbling is not an imitation of adult speech—it includes sounds from various languages, including those not spoken in the household. From this early babbling, a listener could not identify an infant as being, say, French, Korean, or Ethiopian. Deaf infants who observe their deaf parents signing begin to babble more with their hands (Petitto & Marentette, 1991).

By the time infants are about 10 months old, their babbling has changed so that a trained ear can identify the household language (de Boysson-Bardies et al., 1989). Without exposure to other languages, babies lose their ability to hear and produce sounds and tones found outside their native language (Meltzoff et al., 2009; Pallier et al., 2001). Thus, by adulthood, those who speak only English cannot discriminate certain sounds in Japanese speech.

babbling stage beginning at about 4 months, the stage of speech development in which the infant spontaneously utters various sounds at first unrelated to the household language.

Nor can Japanese adults with no training in English hear the difference between the English *r* and *l*. For a Japanese-speaking adult, *la-la-ra-ra* may sound like the same syllable repeated. (Does this astonish you as it does me?) A Japanese-speaking person told that the train station is "just after the next light" may wonder, "The next what? After the street veering right, or farther down, after the light?"

Around their first birthday, most children enter the **one-word stage.** They have already learned that sounds carry meanings, and if repeatedly trained to associate, say, *fish* with a picture of a fish, 1-year-olds will look at a fish when a researcher says, "Fish, fish! Look at the fish!" (Schafer, 2005). They now begin to use sounds—usually only one barely recognizable syllable, such as *ma* or *da*—to communicate meaning. But family members quickly learn to understand, and gradually the infant's language conforms more to the family's language. Across the world, baby's first words are often nouns that label objects or people (Tardif et al., 2008). At this one-word stage, a single inflected word ("Doggy!") may equal a sentence. ("Look at the dog out there!")

At about 18 months, children's word learning explodes from about a word per week to a word per day. By their second birthday, most have entered the **two-word stage** (**TABLE 36.1**). They start uttering two-word sentences in **telegraphic speech.** Like today's text messages or yesterday's telegrams that charged by the word (TERMS ACCEPTED. SEND MONEY), a 2-year-old's speech contains mostly nouns and verbs *(Want juice)*. Also like telegrams, it follows rules of syntax: The words are in a sensible order. English-speaking children typically place adjectives before nouns—*white house* rather than *house white*. Spanish reverses this order, as in *casa blanca*.

"Got idea. Talk better. Combine words. Make sentences."

one-word stage the stage in speech development, from about age 1 to 2, during which a child speaks mostly in single words.

two-word stage beginning about age 2, the stage in speech development during which a child speaks mostly in two-word statements.

telegraphic speech early speech stage in which a child speaks like a telegram—"go car"—using mostly nouns and verbs.

Table 36.1 Summary of Language Development

Month (approximate)	Stage
4	Infant babbles many speech sounds ("Ah-goo").
10	Babbling resembles household language ("Ma-ma").
12	Child enters one-word stage ("Kitty!").
24	Child engages in two-word, telegraphic speech ("Get ball.").
24+	Language develops rapidly into complete sentences.

Moving out of the two-word stage, children quickly begin uttering longer phrases (Fromkin & Rodman, 1983). If they get a late start on learning a particular language, such as after receiving a cochlear implant or being adopted by a family in another country, their language development still proceeds through the same sequence, although usually at a faster pace (Ertmer et al., 2007; Snedeker et al., 2007). By early elementary school, children understand complex sentences and begin to enjoy the humor conveyed by double meanings: "You never starve in the desert because of all the sand-which-is there."

Explaining Language Development

 How do we acquire language?

The world's 7000 or so languages are structurally very diverse (Evans & Levinson, 2009). Linguist Noam Chomsky has nonetheless argued that all languages do share some basic elements, which he calls *universal grammar.* All human languages, for example, have nouns, verbs, and adjectives as grammatical building blocks. Moreover, said Chomsky, we humans are born with a built-in predisposition to learn grammar rules, which helps explain why preschoolers pick up language so readily and use grammar so well. It happens so naturally—as naturally as birds learn to fly—that training hardly helps.

Susan Meiselas/Magnum Photos

Creating a language Brought together as if on a desert island (actually a school), Nicaragua's young deaf children over time drew upon sign gestures from home to create their own Nicaraguan Sign Language, complete with words and intricate grammar. Our biological predisposition for language does not create language in a vacuum. But activated by a social context, nature and nurture work creatively together (Osborne, 1999; Sandler et al., 2005; Senghas & Coppola, 2001).

We are not, however, born with a built-in *specific* language. Europeans and Native Australia–New Zealand populations, though geographically separated for 50,000 years, can readily learn each others' languages (Chater et al., 2009). And whatever language we experience as children, whether spoken or signed, we all readily learn its specific grammar and vocabulary (Bavelier et al., 2003). But no matter what language we learn, we start speaking it mostly in nouns *(kitty, da-da)* rather than in verbs and adjectives (Bornstein et al., 2004). Biology and experience work together.

STATISTICAL LEARNING

When adults listen to an unfamiliar language, the syllables all run together. A young Sudanese couple new to North America and unfamiliar with English might, for example, hear *United Nations* as "Uneye Tednay Shuns." Their 7-month-old daughter would not have this problem. Human infants display a remarkable ability to learn statistical aspects of human speech. Their brains not only discern word breaks, they statistically analyze which syllables, as in "hap-py-ba-by," most often go together. After just two minutes of exposure to a computer voice speaking an unbroken, monotone string of nonsense syllables *(bidakupadotigo-labubidaku . . .)*, 8-month-old infants were able to recognize (as indicated by their attention) three-syllable sequences that appeared repeatedly (Saffran et al., 1996, 2009).

In further testimony to infants' surprising knack for soaking up language, research shows that 7-month-olds can learn simple sentence structures. After repeatedly hearing syllable sequences that follow one rule (an ABA pattern, such as *ga-ti-ga* and *li-na-li*), infants listened longer to syllables in a different sequence (an ABB pattern, such as *wo-fe-fe,* rather than *wo-fe-wo*). Their detecting the difference between the two patterns supports the idea that babies come with a built-in readiness to learn grammatical rules (Marcus et al., 1999).

CRITICAL PERIODS

Could we train adults to perform this same feat of statistical analysis later in the human life span? Many researchers believe not. Childhood seems to represent a *critical* (or "sensitive") *period* for mastering certain aspects of language before the language-learning window closes (Hernandez & Li, 2007). People who learn a second language as adults usually speak it with the accent of their native language, and they also have difficulty mastering the new grammar. In one experiment, Korean and Chinese immigrants considered 276 English sentences (*"Yesterday the hunter shoots a deer"*) and decided whether they were grammatically correct or incorrect (Johnson & Newport, 1991). All had been in the United States for approximately 10 years: Some had arrived in early childhood, others as adults. As **FIGURE 36.1** reveals, those who learned their second language early learned it best. The older one is when moving to a new country, the harder it will be to learn its language and to absorb its culture (Cheung et al., 2011; Hakuta et al., 2003).

The window on language learning closes gradually in early childhood. Later-than-usual exposure to language (at age 2 or 3) unleashes the idle language capacity of a child's brain, producing a rush of language. But

©Roy Morsch/CORBIS

A natural talent We humans come with a remarkable capacity to soak up language. But the particular language we learn reflects our unique interactions with others.

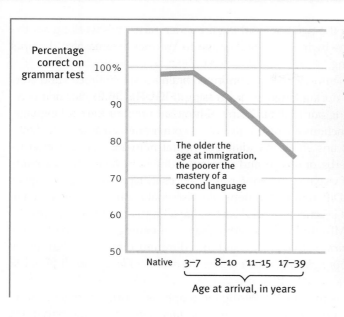

Figure 36.1

Our ability to learn a new language diminishes with age Ten years after coming to the United States, Asian immigrants took an English grammar test. Although there is no sharply defined critical period for second language learning, those who arrived before age 8 understood American English grammar as well as native speakers did. Those who arrived later did not. (From Johnson & Newport, 1991.)

The older the age at immigration, the poorer the mastery of a second language

by about age 7, those who have not been exposed to either a spoken or a signed language gradually lose their ability to master *any* language.

The impact of early experiences is evident in language learning in the 90+ percent of prelingually deaf children born to hearing-nonsigning parents. These children typically do not experience language during their early years. Natively deaf children who learn sign language after age 9 never learn it as well as those who lose their hearing at age 9 after learning English. They also never learn English as well as other natively deaf children who learned sign in infancy (Mayberry et al., 2002). Those who learn to sign as teens or adults are like immigrants who learn English after childhood: They can master basic words and learn to order them, but they never become as fluent as native signers in producing and comprehending subtle grammatical differences (Newport, 1990). As a flower's growth will be stunted without nourishment, so, too, children will typically become linguistically stunted if isolated from language during the critical period for its acquisition.

The Brain and Language

36-4   What brain areas are involved in language processing and speech?

We think of speaking and reading, or writing and reading, or singing and speaking as merely different examples of the same general ability—language. But consider this curious finding: **Aphasia,** an impairment of language, can result from damage to any of several cortical areas. Even more curious, some people with aphasia can speak fluently but cannot read (despite good vision), while others can comprehend what they read but cannot speak. Still others can write but not read, read but not write, read numbers but not letters, or sing but not speak. These cases suggest that language is complex, and that different brain areas must serve different language functions.

Indeed, in 1865, French physician Paul Broca reported that after damage to an area of the left frontal lobe (later called **Broca's area**) a person would struggle to *speak* words while still being able to sing familiar songs and comprehend speech.

In 1874, German investigator Carl Wernicke discovered that after damage to an area of the left temporal lobe (**Wernicke's area**) people could speak only meaningless words. Asked to describe a picture that showed two boys stealing cookies behind a woman's back, one patient responded: "Mother is away her working her work to get her better, but when

***No* means *No*—no matter how you say it!** Deaf children of deaf-signing parents and hearing children of hearing parents have much in common. They develop language skills at about the same rate, and they are equally effective at opposing parental wishes and demanding their way.

aphasia impairment of language, usually caused by left-hemisphere damage either to Broca's area (impairing speaking) or to Wernicke's area (impairing understanding).

Broca's area controls language expression—an area of the frontal lobe, usually in the left hemisphere, that directs the muscle movements involved in speech.

Wernicke's area controls language reception—a brain area involved in language comprehension and expression; usually in the left temporal lobe.

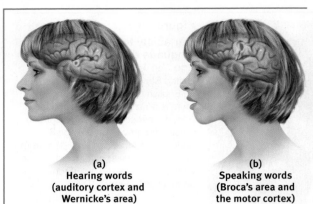

(a)
Hearing words
(auditory cortex and
Wernicke's area)

(b)
Speaking words
(Broca's area and
the motor cortex)

Figure 36.2
Brain activity when hearing and speaking words

"It is the way systems interact and have a dynamic interdependence that is—unless one has lost all sense of wonder—quite awe-inspiring." -Simon Conway Morris, "The Boyle Lecture," 2005

AP® Exam Tip

You'll notice that even though the brain was one of the major topics in Unit III, it keeps coming up. Each time it does provides you with an opportunity to go back and review what you learned previously about the brain. Rehearse frequently, and you will not have much to relearn before the AP® exam.

she's looking the two boys looking the other part. She's working another time" (Geschwind, 1979). Damage to Wernicke's area also disrupts understanding.

Today's neuroscience has confirmed brain activity in Broca's and Wernicke's areas during language processing (**FIGURE 36.2**). But neuroscience is refining our understanding of how our brain processes language. Language functions are distributed across other brain areas as well. Functional MRI scans show that different neural networks are activated by nouns and verbs, or objects and actions; by different vowels; and by reading stories of visual versus motor experiences (Shapiro et al., 2006; Speer et al., 2009). Different neural networks also enable one's native language and a second language learned later in life (Perani & Abutalebi, 2005).

And here's another funny fMRI finding. Jokes that play on meaning (*"Why don't sharks bite lawyers? . . . Professional courtesy"*) are processed in a different brain area than jokes that play on words (*"What kind of lights did Noah use on the ark? . . . Flood lights"*) (Goel & Dolan, 2001).

The big point to remember is this: In processing language, as in other forms of information processing, *the brain operates by dividing its mental functions—speaking, perceiving, thinking, remembering—into subfunctions*. Your conscious experience of reading this page *seems* indivisible, but your brain is computing each word's form, sound, and meaning using different neural networks (Posner & Carr, 1992). We saw this also in Module 18's discussion of vision, for which the brain engages specialized subtasks, such as discerning depth, movement, form, and color. And in vision as in language, a localized trauma that destroys one of these neural work teams may cause people to lose just one aspect of processing. In visual processing, a stroke may destroy the ability to perceive movement but not color. In language processing, a stroke may impair the ability to speak distinctly without harming the ability to read.

Think about it: What you experience as a continuous, indivisible stream of experience is actually but the visible tip of a subdivided information-processing iceberg.

* * *

Returning to our debate about how deserving we humans are of our name *Homo sapiens*, let's pause to issue an interim report card. On decision making and risk assessment, our error-prone species might rate a C+. On problem solving, where humans are inventive yet vulnerable to fixation, we would probably receive a better mark, perhaps a B. On cognitive efficiency, our fallible but quick heuristics earn us an A. And when it comes to our creativity, and our learning and using language, the awestruck experts would surely award the human species an A+.

Before You Move On

▶ **ASK YOURSELF**

There has been controversy at some universities about allowing fluency in sign language to fulfill a second-language requirement for an undergraduate degree. As you start planning for your own college years, what is your opinion?

▶ **TEST YOURSELF**

If children are not yet speaking, is there any reason to think they would benefit from parents and other caregivers reading to them?

Answers to the Test Yourself questions can be found in Appendix E at the end of the book.

Language and Thought

 What is the relationship between language and thinking, and what is the value of thinking in images?

Thinking and language intricately intertwine. Asking which comes first is one of psychology's chicken-and-egg questions. Do our ideas come first and we wait for words to name them? Or are our thoughts conceived in words and therefore unthinkable without them?

Language Influences Thinking

Linguist Benjamin Lee Whorf (1956) contended that language determines the way we think: "Language itself shapes a [person's] basic ideas." The Hopi, who have no past tense for their verbs, could not readily *think* about the past, said Whorf.

Whorf's **linguistic determinism** hypothesis is too extreme. We all think about things for which we have no words. (Can you think of a shade of blue you cannot name?) And we routinely have *unsymbolized* (wordless, imageless) thoughts, as when someone, while watching two men carry a load of bricks, wondered whether the men would drop them (Heavey & Hurlburt, 2008; Hurlburt & Akhter, 2008).

Nevertheless, to those who speak two dissimilar languages, such as English and Japanese, it seems obvious that a person may think differently in different languages (Brown, 1986). Unlike English, which has a rich vocabulary for self-focused emotions such as anger, Japanese has more words for interpersonal emotions such as sympathy (Markus & Kitayama, 1991). Many bilingual individuals report that they have different senses of self, depending on which language they are using (Matsumoto, 1994). In one series of studies with bilingual Israeli Arabs (who speak both Arabic and Hebrew), participants thought differently about their social world, with differing automatic associations with Arabs and Jews, depending on which language the testing session used (Danziger & Ward, 2010).

Bilingual individuals may even reveal different personality profiles when taking the same test in their two languages (Dinges & Hull, 1992). This happened when China-born, bilingual students at the University of Waterloo in Ontario were asked to describe themselves in English or Chinese (Ross et al., 2002). The English-language self-descriptions fit typical Canadian profiles: Students expressed mostly positive self-statements and moods. Responding in Chinese, the same students gave typically Chinese self-descriptions: They reported more agreement with Chinese values and roughly equal positive and negative self-statements and moods. "Learn a new language and get a new soul," says a Czech proverb. Similar personality changes have been shown when bicultural, bilingual Americans and Mexicans shifted between the cultural frames associated with English and Spanish (Ramírez-Esparza et al., 2006).

So our words may not *determine* what we think, but they do *influence* our thinking (Boroditsky, 2011). We use our language in forming categories. In Brazil, the isolated Piraha tribespeople have words for the numbers 1 and 2, but numbers above that are simply "many." Thus, if shown 7 nuts in a row, they find it very difficult to lay out the same number from their own pile (Gordon, 2004).

Words also influence our thinking about colors. Whether we live in New Mexico, New South Wales, or New Guinea, we *see* colors much the same, but we use our native language to *classify* and *remember* colors (Davidoff, 2004; Roberson et al., 2004, 2005). If your language is English, you might view three colors and call two of them "yellow" and one of them "blue." Later you would likely see and recall the yellows as being more similar. But if you are a member of Papua New Guinea's Berinmo tribe, which has words for two different shades of yellow, you would more speedily perceive and better recall the distinctions between the two yellows. And if your language is Russian, which has distinct names for different shades of blue, such as *goluboy* and *sinly,* you might remember the blue better. Words matter.

Try This

To find out what we have learned about thinking and language in other animals, see Module 85.

Try This

Before reading on, use a pen or pencil to sketch this idea: "The girl pushes the boy." Now see the inverted comment below.

How did you illustrate "the girl pushes the boy"? Anne Maass and Aurora Russo (2003) report that people whose language that people whose language reads from left to right mostly position the pushing girl on the left. Those who read and write Arabic, a right-to-left language, mostly place her on the right. This spatial bias appears only in those old enough to have learned their culture's writing system (Dobel et al., 2007).

linguistic determinism
Whorf's hypothesis that language determines the way we think.

Culture and color
In Papua New Guinea, Berinmo children have words for different shades of "yellow," so they might more quickly spot and recall yellow variations. Here and everywhere, "the languages we speak profoundly shape the way we think, the way we see the world, the way we live our lives," notes psychologist Lera Boroditsky (2009).

Prisma Bildagentur AG/Alamy

"All words are pegs to hang ideas on." -HENRY WARD BEECHER, PROVERBS FROM PLYMOUTH PULPIT, 1887

Perceived differences grow when we assign different names to colors. On the color spectrum, blue blends into green—until we draw a dividing line between the portions we call "blue" and "green." Although equally different on the color spectrum, two different items that share the same color name (as the two "blues" do in **FIGURE 36.3**, contrast B) are harder to distinguish than two items with different names ("blue" and "green," as in Figure 36.3, contrast A) (Özgen, 2004).

Given words' subtle influence on thinking, we do well to choose our words carefully. Does it make any difference whether I write, "A child learns language as *he* interacts with *his* caregivers" or "Children learn language as *they* interact with *their* caregivers"? Many studies have found that it does. When hearing the generic *he* (as in "the artist and his work"), people are more likely to picture a male (Henley, 1989; Ng, 1990). If *he* and *his* were truly gender free, we shouldn't skip a beat when hearing that "man, like other mammals, nurses his young."

To expand language is to expand the ability to think. As Unit IX points out, young children's thinking develops hand in hand with their language (Gopnik & Meltzoff, 1986). Indeed, it is very difficult to think about or conceptualize certain abstract ideas (commitment, freedom, or rhyming) without language! And what is true for preschoolers is true for everyone: *It pays to increase your word power.* That's why most textbooks, including this one, introduce new words—to teach new ideas and new ways of thinking. And that's also why psychologist Steven Pinker (2007) titled his book on language *The Stuff of Thought.*

Increased word power helps explain what McGill University researcher Wallace Lambert (1992; Lambert et al., 1993) calls the *bilingual advantage.* Although their vocabulary in each language is somewhat smaller than that of people speaking a single language, bilingual people are skilled at inhibiting one language while using the other. And thanks to their well-practiced "executive control" over language, they also are better at inhibiting their attention to irrelevant information (Bialystock & Craik, 2010). This superior attentional control is evident from 7 months of age into adulthood (Emmorey et al., 2008; Kovacs & Mehler, 2009).

Lambert helped devise a Canadian program that immerses English-speaking children in French. (The number of non-Quebec children enrolled rose from 65,000 in 1981 to 300,000 in 2007 [Statistics Canada, 2010].) For most of their first three years in school, the English-speaking children are taught entirely in French, and thereafter gradually shift to classes mostly in English. Not surprisingly, the children attain a natural French fluency unrivaled by other methods of language teaching. Moreover, compared with similarly capable children in control groups, they do so without detriment to their English fluency, and with increased aptitude scores, creativity, and appreciation for French-Canadian culture (Genesee & Gándara, 1999; Lazaruk, 2007).

Whether we are in the linguistic minority or majority, language links us to one another. Language also connects us to the past and the future. "To destroy a people, destroy their language," observed poet Joy Harjo.

Figure 36.3

Language and perception When people view blocks of equally different colors, they perceive those with different names as more different. Thus the "green" and "blue" in contrast A may appear to differ more than the two similarly different blues in contrast B (Özgen, 2004).

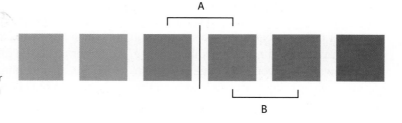

Thinking in Images

When you are alone, do you talk to yourself? Is "thinking" simply conversing with yourself? Without a doubt, words convey ideas. But aren't there times when ideas precede words? To turn on the cold water in your bathroom, in which direction do you turn the handle? To answer, you probably thought not in words but with *implicit* (nondeclarative, procedural) memory—a mental picture of how you do it (see Module 31).

Indeed, we often think in images. Artists think in images. So do composers, poets, mathematicians, athletes, and scientists. Albert Einstein reported that he achieved some of his greatest insights through visual images and later put them into words. Pianist Liu Chi Kung showed the value of thinking in images. One year after placing second in the 1958 Tschaikovsky piano competition, Liu was imprisoned during China's cultural revolution. Soon after his release, after seven years without touching a piano, he was back on tour, the critics judging his musicianship better than ever. How did he continue to develop without practice? "I did practice," said Liu, "every day. I rehearsed every piece I had ever played, note by note, in my mind" (Garfield, 1986).

For someone who has learned a skill, such as ballet dancing, even *watching* the activity will activate the brain's internal simulation of it, reported one British research team after collecting fMRIs as people watched videos (Calvo-Merino et al., 2004). So, too, will imagining a physical experience, which activates some of the same neural networks that are active during the actual experience (Grèzes & Decety, 2001). Small wonder, then, that mental practice has become a standard part of training for Olympic athletes (Suinn, 1997).

One experiment on mental practice and basketball foul shooting tracked the University of Tennessee women's team over 35 games (Savoy & Beitel, 1996). During that time, the team's free-throw shooting increased from approximately 52 percent in games following standard physical practice to some 65 percent after mental practice. Players had repeatedly imagined making foul shots under various conditions, including being "trash-talked" by their opposition. In a dramatic conclusion, Tennessee won the national championship game in overtime, thanks in part to their foul shooting.

Mental rehearsal can also help you achieve an academic goal, as researchers demonstrated with two groups of introductory psychology students facing a midterm exam 1 week later (Taylor et al., 1998). (Scores of other students formed a control group, not engaging in any mental simulation.) The first group spent 5 minutes each day visualizing themselves scanning the posted grade list, seeing their A, beaming with joy, and feeling proud. This *outcome simulation* had little effect, adding only 2 points to their exam-scores average. Another group spent 5 minutes each day visualizing themselves effectively studying—reading the textbook, going over notes, eliminating distractions, declining an offer to go out. This *process simulation* paid off: This second group began studying sooner, spent more time at it, and beat the others' average by 8 points. *The point to remember:* It's better to spend your fantasy time planning how to get somewhere than to dwell on the imagined destination.

* * *

What, then, should we say about the relationship between thinking and language? As we have seen, language influences our thinking. But if thinking did not also affect language, there would never be any new words. And new words and new combinations of old words express new ideas. The basketball term *slam dunk* was coined after the act itself had become fairly common. So, let us say that *thinking affects our language, which then affects our thought* (**FIGURE 36.4**).

Figure 36.4

The interplay of thought and language The traffic runs both ways between thinking and language. Thinking affects our language, which affects our thought.

Psychological research on thinking and language mirrors the mixed views of our species by those in fields such as literature and religion. The human mind is simultaneously capable of striking intellectual failures and of striking intellectual power. Misjudgments are common and can have disastrous consequences. So we do well to appreciate our capacity for error. Yet our efficient heuristics often serve us well. Moreover, our ingenuity at problem solving and our extraordinary power of language mark humankind as almost "infinite in faculties."

Before You Move On

▶ **ASK YOURSELF**

Do you use certain words or gestures that only your family or closest circle of friends would understand? Can you envision using these words or gestures to construct a language, as the Nicaraguan children did in building their version of sign language?

▶ **TEST YOURSELF**

To say that "words are the mother of ideas" assumes the truth of what concept?

Answers to the Test Yourself questions can be found in Appendix E at the end of the book.

Module 36 Review

 What are the structural components of a language?

- *Phonemes* are a *language's* basic units of sound.

- *Morphemes* are the elementary units of meaning.

- *Grammar*—the system of rules that enables us to communicate—includes semantics (rules for deriving meaning) and syntax (rules for ordering words into sentences).

 What are the milestones in language development?

- Language development's timing varies, but all children follow the same sequence.

- Receptive language (the ability to understand what is said to or about you) develops before productive language (the ability to produce words).

- At about 4 months of age, infants *babble,* making sounds found in languages from all over the world.

- By about 10 months, their babbling contains only the sounds found in their household language.

- Around 12 months of age, children begin to speak in single words. This *one-word stage* evolves into *two-word* (*telegraphic*) utterances before their second birthday, after which they begin speaking in full sentences.

 How do we acquire language?

- Linguist Noam Chomsky has proposed that all human languages share a universal grammar—the basic building blocks of language—and that humans are born with a predisposition to learn language.

- We acquire specific language through learning as our biology and experience interact.

- Childhood is a critical period for learning to speak or sign fluently.

 What brain areas are involved in language processing and speech?

- Two important language- and speech-processing areas are *Broca's area,* a region of the frontal lobe that controls language expression, and *Wernicke's area,* a region in the left temporal lobe that controls language reception (and also assists with expression).

- Language processing is spread across other brain areas as well, where different neural networks handle specific linguistic subtasks.

36-5 What is the relationship between language and thinking, and what is the value of thinking in images?

- Although Benjamin Lee Whorf's *linguistic determinism* hypothesis suggested that language determines thought, it is more accurate to say that language influences thought.

- Different languages embody different ways of thinking, and immersion in bilingual education can enhance thinking.

- We often think in images when we use nondeclarative (procedural) memory (our automatic memory system for motor and cognitive skills and classically conditioned associations).

- Thinking in images can increase our skills when we mentally practice upcoming events.

Multiple-Choice Questions

1. What do we call the smallest distinctive sound units in language?

  a. Structure
  b. Morphemes
  c. Grammar
  d. Phonemes
  e. Thoughts

2. Which of the following best identifies the early speech stage in which a child speaks using mostly nouns and verbs?

  a. Two-word stage
  b. Babbling stage
  c. One-word stage
  d. Telegraphic speech
  e. Grammar

3. The prefix "pre" in "preview" or the suffix "ed" in "adapted" are examples of

  a. phonemes.
  b. morphemes.
  c. babbling.
  d. grammar.
  e. intuition.

4. Evidence of words' subtle influence on thinking best supports the notion of

  a. Wernicke's area.
  b. Broca's area.
  c. linguistic determinism.
  d. babbling.
  e. aphasia.

Practice FRQs

1. Name and define the three building blocks of spoken language.

Answer

1 point: Phoneme: the smallest distinctive sound unit.

1 point: Morpheme: the smallest unit carrying meaning in language.

1 point: Grammar: the system of rules that enable communication.

2. What is aphasia, and how does it relate to Broca's and Wernicke's areas?

(3 points)

Unit VII Review

Key Terms and Concepts to Remember

memory, p. 318

encoding, p. 319

storage, p. 319

retrieval, p. 319

parallel processing, p. 319

sensory memory, p. 319

short-term memory, p. 319

long-term memory, p. 319

working memory, 320

explicit memory, p. 320

effortful processing, p. 320

automatic processing, p. 320

implicit memory, p. 320

iconic memory, p. 322

echoic memory, p. 322

chunking, p. 323

mnemonics [nih-MON-iks], p. 323

spacing effect, p. 324

testing effect, p. 324

shallow processing, p. 324

deep processing, p. 325

hippocampus, p. 330

flashbulb memory, p. 332

long-term potentiation (LTP), p. 333

recall, p. 334

recognition, p. 334

relearning, p. 334

priming, p. 336

mood-congruent memory, p. 337

serial position effect, p. 337

anterograde amnesia, p. 342

retrograde amnesia, p. 342

proactive interference, p. 345

retroactive interference, p. 345

repression, p. 346

misinformation effect, p. 347

source amnesia, p. 349

déjà vu, p. 349

cognition, p. 356

concept, p. 356

prototype, p. 356

creativity, p. 357

convergent thinking, p. 357

divergent thinking, p. 357

algorithm, p. 361

heuristic, p. 361

insight, p. 361

confirmation bias, p. 362

mental set, p. 363

intuition, p. 363

representativeness heuristic, p. 364

availability heuristic, p. 364

overconfidence, p. 365

belief perseverance, p. 367

framing, p. 368

language, p. 372

phoneme, p. 373

morpheme, p. 373

grammar, p. 373

babbling stage, p. 374

one-word stage, p. 375

two-word stage, p. 375

telegraphic speech, p. 375

aphasia, p. 377

Broca's area, p. 377

Wernicke's area, p. 377

linguistic determinism, p. 379

Key Contributors to Remember

Richard Atkinson, p. 319

Richard Shiffrin, p. 319

George A. Miller, p. 322

Hermann Ebbinghaus, p. 324

Eric Kandel, p. 332

Elizabeth Loftus, p. 347

Robert Sternberg, p. 357

Wolfgang Köhler, p. 362

Amos Tversky, p. 363

Daniel Kahneman, p. 363

Steven Pinker, p. 372

Noam Chomsky, p. 375

Paul Broca, p. 377

Carl Wernicke, p. 377

Benjamin Lee Whorf, p. 379

AP® Exam Practice Questions

Multiple-Choice Questions

1. What does the "magical number seven, plus or minus two" refer to?
   a. The ideal number of times to rehearse information in the first encoding session
   b. The number of seconds information stays in short-term memory without rehearsal
   c. The capacity of short-term memory
   d. The number of seconds information stays in echoic storage
   e. The number of years most long-term memories last

2. Which of the following describes long-term potentiation (LTP)?
   a. When attempting to retrieve information, it is easier to recognize than to recall.
   b. Constructed memories have the potential to be either accurate or inaccurate.
   c. Changes in synapses allow for more efficient transfer of information.
   d. Implicit memories are processed by the cerebellum instead of by the hippocampus.
   e. Information is transferred from working memory to long-term memory.

3. Which of the following abilities is an example of implicit memory?
   a. Riding a bicycle while talking to your friend about something that happened in class
   b. Retrieving from memory the details of an assignment that is due tomorrow
   c. Vividly recalling significant events like the 9/11 attacks on New York City and Washington, D.C.
   d. Remembering the details of your last birthday party
   e. Recognizing names and pictures of your classmates many years after they have graduated

4. Which of the following statements concerning memory is true?
   a. Hypnosis, when used as a component of therapy, usually improves the accuracy of memory.
   b. One aspect of memory that is usually accurate is the source of the remembered information.
   c. Children's memories of abuse are more accurate than other childhood memories.
   d. Memories we are more certain of are more likely to be accurate.
   e. Memories are often a blend of correct and incorrect information.

5. The basketball players could remember the main points of their coach's halftime talk, but not her exact words. This is because they encoded the information
   a. semantically.
   b. iconically.
   c. implicitly.
   d. shallowly.
   e. automatically.

6. When someone provides his phone number to another person, he usually pauses after the area code and again after the next three numbers. This pattern underscores the importance of which memory principle?
   a. Chunking
   b. The serial position effect
   c. Semantic encoding
   d. Auditory encoding
   e. Recognition

7. Which of the following is true regarding the role of the amygdala in memory?
   a. The amygdala help process implicit memories.
   b. The amygdala support Freud's ideas about memory because they allow us to repress memories of trauma.
   c. The amygdala produce long-term potentiation in the brain.
   d. The amygdala help make sure we remember events that trigger strong emotional responses.
   e. The amygdala are active when the retrieval of a long-term memory is primed.

8. Which of the following illustrates the serial position effect?
   a. The only name Kensie remembers from the people she met at the party is Spencer because she thought he was particularly good looking.
   b. Kimia has trouble remembering information from the book's first unit when she reviews for semester finals.
   c. It's easy for Brittney to remember that carbon's atomic number is 6 because her birthday is on December 6.
   d. Kyle was not able to remember the names of all of his new co-workers after one week on the job, but he could remember them after two weeks.
   e. Alp is unable to remember the middle of a list of vocabulary words as well as he remembers the first or last words on the list.

9. Mnemonic devices are *least* likely to be dependent upon which of the following?
   a. Imagery
   b. Acronyms
   c. Rhymes
   d. Chunking
   e. Massed rehearsal

10. You are more likely to remember psychology information in your psychology classroom than in other environments because of what memory principle?
   a. Mood congruence
   b. Context effects
   c. State-dependency
   d. Proactive interference
   e. Retroactive interference

11. Which of the following kinds of information is *not* likely to be automatically processed?
   a. Space information
   b. Time information
   c. Frequency information
   d. New information
   e. Rehearsed information

12. Which of the following is an example of source amnesia?
   a. Iva can't remember the details of a horrifying event because she has repressed them.
   b. Mary has entirely forgotten about an incident in grade school until her friend reminds her of the event.
   c. Michael can't remember this year's locker combination because he confuses it with last year's combination.
   d. Stephen misremembers a dream as something that really happened.
   e. Anna, who is trying to lose weight, is unable to remember several of the between-meal snacks she had yesterday.

13. Which of the following is an accurate conclusion based on Hermann Ebbinghaus' forgetting curve research?
   a. Most forgetting occurs early on and then levels off
   b. We forget more rapidly as time passes
   c. Forgetting is relatively constant over time
   d. Forgetting is related to many factors, but time is not one of them
   e. We are more likely to forget items in the middle of a list than at the beginning or the end

14. "Chair," "freedom," and "ball" are all examples of what?
   a. Phonemes
   b. Heuristics
   c. Concepts
   d. Telegraphic utterances
   e. Prototypes

15. People are more concerned about a medical procedure when told it has a 10 percent death rate than they are when told it has a 90 percent survival rate. Which psychological concept explains this difference in concern?
   a. Belief perseverance
   b. Insight
   c. Intuition
   d. Framing
   e. Confirmation bias

16. Which of the following illustrates a heuristic?
   a. Calculating the area of a rectangle by multiplying the length times the width
   b. Using news reports of corporate fraud to estimate how much business fraud occurs in American business
   c. Looking in each room of your home to find your sleeping cat
   d. Following a new recipe to bake a cake for your friend
   e. Trying every key on your mom's key ring until you find the one that unlocks the seldom-used storeroom in the basement

17. Which of the following most likely represents a prototype for the concept indicated in parentheses?
   a. A whale (mammal)
   b. An ostrich (bird)
   c. A beanbag chair (chair)
   d. An igloo (house)
   e. A golden retriever (dog)

18. The inability to see a problem from a fresh perspective is called what?
   a. Confirmation bias
   b. Insight
   c. Representativeness
   d. Fixation
   e. Availability

19. Which phrase best describes the concept of phonemes?
   a. Units of meaning in a language
   b. A form of syntax
   c. The basis of grammar
   d. Units of sound in a language
   e. A form of telegraphic speech

20. Which concept best explains why people often underestimate the amount of time it will take to complete a project?
   a. Belief perseverance
   b. Framing
   c. Intuition
   d. The availability heuristic
   e. Overconfidence

21. Which of the following is not one of Robert Sternberg's components of creativity?
   a. A venturesome personality
   b. Imaginative thinking skills
   c. A creative environment
   d. A position of ignorance
   e. Intrinsic motivation

22. Which of the following demonstrates the representativeness heuristic?
   a. Deciding that a new kid in school is a nerd because he looks like a nerd
   b. Fearing air travel because of memories of plane crashes
   c. Checking in every drawer to find some matches because matches are usually in drawers
   d. Having the solution to a word problem pop into your head because you have just successfully solved a similar problem
   e. Applying for jobs in several local grocery stores because your best friend just got a job in a grocery store

23. Benjamin Lee Whorf's linguistic determinism hypothesis relates to what aspect of the power of language?
   a. How thinking influences language
   b. How language influences thinking
   c. The role of the language acquisition device
   d. The importance of critical periods in language development
   e. The development of language in nonhuman animals

24. According to Noam Chomsky, what is the most essential environmental stimulus necessary for language acquisition?
   a. Exposure to language in early childhood
   b. Instruction in grammar
   c. Reinforcement for babbling and other early verbal behaviors
   d. Imitation and drill
   e. Linguistic determinism

Free-Response Questions

1. Jacque learned to speak Italian when she was in the first grade and was able to speak, read, and write Italian fairly well by the fourth grade. She moved to a new school system that did not have Italian as a choice for World Languages, so she decided to take Spanish. Sometimes she found herself saying and writing words in Italian as she completed her Spanish assignments. Often, she remembered the vocabulary in Italian before she said the word in Spanish. Sometimes she felt like knowing Italian helped her learn Spanish, but sometimes she thought it just confused her! When Jacque was in her Spanish classroom, she felt more at ease with the Spanish language. When she went to an Italian restaurant, she enjoyed being able to read the menu to her friends if it was written in Italian.

Briefly define each concept and use an example to show how each concept is related to Jacque's experiences.
- Working memory
- Explicit memory
- Effortful processing
- Context-dependent memory
- Proactive interference

Explain how these brain structures play a role in Jacque's memory processing.
- Hippocampus
- Amygdala

Rubric for Free Response Question 1

1 point: Working memory is a newer understanding of short-term memory that focuses on conscious, active processing of incoming auditory and visual-spatial information, and of information retrieved from long-term memory. Possible example: Jacque has to focus on what the teacher is saying and recall the correct vocabulary word when she is asked a question. ↻ Page 319

1 point: Explicit memory is memory of facts and experiences that one can consciously know and "declare." (Also called *declarative memory*.) Possible example: Defining vocabulary words in any language relies on explicit memory.
↻ Page 321

1 point: Effortful processing is encoding that requires attention and conscious effort. Possible example: When reading, Jacque has to pay attention to the words and sentence construction to understand what is being conveyed. ↻ Page 321

1 point: Context-dependent memory refers to the need to put yourself back in the context where you experienced something to prime your memory retrieval. Possible example: Jacque seems to be able to remember her Spanish best when in her Spanish classroom. ↻ Page 336

1 point: Proactive interference is the disruptive effect of prior learning on the recall of new information. Possible example: Jacque learned Italian before she learned Spanish, and so sometimes her prior knowledge of Italian interferes with her recall of Spanish words. ↻ Page 345

1 point: The hippocampus is a brain area important to the storage of new learning. Possible example: Since the left hippocampus is important to storage and recall of verbal information—new terms, vocabulary, and so on—Jacque's hippocampus must be very active during her language classes. ↻ Page 330

1 point: The amygdala is involved in intense emotional experiences, which affect related memory formation. Possible example: When Jacque is stressed about mixing up her Spanish with Italian words, the stress may cause her to have trouble recalling the information because of hormones that are released. Her positive emotions, experienced in the Italian restaurant, may also be related to the amygdala.
↻ Pages 331–332

2. Our cognitive processes can enhance or inhibit memory, decision making, problem solving, and communication. Explain how each of the following may both help and hurt cognitive functioning.
   - Mental set
   - Availability heuristic
   - Prototypes
   - Critical (or sensitive) period for language development
   - Stress effects on memory

   (10 points)

3. George, a senior in high school, was reminiscing with his friends about their first homecoming dance.

   A. Explain how each of the following psychological terms could *help* George's recollection or memory of his freshman-year homecoming dance.
   - Flashbulb memory
   - Mood-congruent effect

   B. Explain how each of the following psychological terms could *hinder* George's recollection or memory of his freshman-year homecoming dance.
   - Serial position effect
   - Retroactive interference
   - Misinformation effect

   (5 points)

Multiple-choice self-tests and more may be found at www.worthpublishers.com/MyersAP2e

Unit VIII

Motivation, Emotion, and Stress

Modules

After an ill-fated Saturday morning in the spring of 2003, experienced mountaineer Aron Ralston understood how motivation can energize and direct behavior. Having bagged nearly all of Colorado's tallest peaks, Ralston ventured some solo canyon hiking that seemed so risk-free he didn't bother to tell anyone where he was going. In Utah's narrow Bluejohn Canyon, just 150 yards above his final rappel, he was climbing over an 800-pound rock when disaster struck: It shifted and pinned his right wrist and arm. He was, as the title of his book says, caught *Between a Rock and a Hard Place*.

Realizing no one would be rescuing him, Ralston tried with all his might to dislodge the rock. Then, with a dull pocketknife, he tried chipping away at it. When that, too, failed, he rigged up ropes to lift the rock. Alas, nothing worked. Hour after hour, then cold night after cold night, he was stuck.

By Tuesday, he had run out of food and water. On Wednesday, as thirst and hunger gnawed, he began saving and sipping his own urine. Using his video recorder, he said good-bye to family and friends, for whom he now felt intense love: "So

Lucas Oleniuk/Toronto Star via Getty Images

again love to everyone. Bring love and peace and happiness and beautiful lives into the world in my honor. Thank you. Love you."

On Thursday, surprised to find himself still alive, Ralston had a seemingly divine insight into his reproductive future, a vision of a preschool boy being scooped up by a one-armed man. With this inspiration, he summoned his remaining strength and his enormous will to live and, over the next hour, willfully broke his arm bones and then proceeded to use that dull knife to cut off his arm. He put on a tourniquet, chopped the last piece of skin, and, after 127 hours, broke free. He then rappelled with his bleeding half-arm down a 65-foot cliff and hiked 5 miles before finding someone. He was, in his own words, "just reeling with this euphoria . . . having been dead and standing in my grave, leaving my last will and testament, etching 'Rest in peace' on the wall, all of that, gone and then replaced with having my life again. It was undoubtedly the sweetest moment that I will ever experience" (Ralston, 2004). Ralston's thirst and hunger, his sense of belonging to others, and his brute will to live and become a father highlight *motivation's* energizing and directing power.

His intense emotional experiences of love and joy demonstrate the close ties between our feelings, or *emotions,* and our motivated behaviors. In this unit, we explore our motivations and emotions, and the health effects of intense or prolonged emotions such as anger and stress.

Module 37

Motivational Concepts

Module Learning Objective

37-1 Define *motivation* as psychologists use the term, and identify the perspectives useful for studying motivated behavior.

"What do you think . . . should we get started on that motivation research or not?"

37-1 How do psychologists define *motivation?* From what perspectives do they view motivated behavior?

Our **motivations** arise from the interplay between nature (the bodily "push") and nurture (the "pulls" from our thought processes and culture). Consider four perspectives for viewing motivated behaviors. *Instinct theory* (now replaced by the *evolutionary perspective*) focuses on genetically predisposed behaviors. *Drive-reduction theory* focuses on how our inner pushes and external pulls interact. *Arousal theory* focuses on finding the right level of stimulation. And Abraham Maslow's *hierarchy of needs* describes how some of our needs take priority over others.

Instincts and Evolutionary Psychology

Early in the twentieth century, as the influence of Charles Darwin's evolutionary theory grew, it became fashionable to classify all sorts of behaviors as instincts. If people criticized themselves, it was because of their "self-abasement instinct." If they boasted, it reflected their "self-assertion instinct." After scanning 500 books, one sociologist compiled a list of 5759 supposed human instincts! Before long, this fad for naming instincts collapsed under its own weight. Rather than *explaining* human behaviors, the early instinct theorists were simply *naming* them. It was like "explaining" a bright child's low grades by labeling the child an "underachiever." To name a behavior is *not* to explain it.

To qualify as an **instinct,** a complex behavior must have a fixed pattern throughout a species and be unlearned (Tinbergen, 1951). Such behaviors are common in other species (Module 26 described salmon returning to their birthplace, and Module 48 will describe imprinting in birds). Human behavior, too, exhibits certain unlearned fixed patterns, including infants' innate reflexes for rooting and sucking.

Although *instinct theory* failed to explain most human motives, *evolutionary psychology's* underlying assumption that genes predispose species-typical behavior remains as strong as ever. We saw this in Module 29's discussion of animals' biological predispositions to learn certain behaviors. And we will see this in later discussions of how evolution might influence our phobias, our helping behaviors, and our romantic attractions.

motivation a need or desire that energizes and directs behavior

instinct a complex, unlearned behavior that is rigidly patterned throughout a species.

Same motive, different wiring
The more complex the nervous system, the more adaptable the organism. Both humans and weaverbirds satisfy their need for shelter in ways that reflect their inherited capacities. Human behavior is flexible; we can learn whatever skills we need to build a house. The bird's behavior pattern is fixed; it can build only this kind of nest.

Drives and Incentives

When the original instinct theory of motivation collapsed, it was replaced by **drive-reduction theory**—the idea that a physiological need creates an aroused state that drives the organism to reduce the need by, say, eating or drinking. With few exceptions, when a physiological need increases, so does a psychological *drive*—an aroused, motivated state.

The physiological aim of drive reduction is **homeostasis**—the maintenance of a steady internal state. An example of homeostasis (literally "staying the same") is the body's temperature-regulation system, which works like a room thermostat. Both systems operate through feedback loops: Sensors feed room temperature to a control device. If the room temperature cools, the control device switches on the furnace. Likewise, if our body temperature cools, blood vessels constrict to conserve warmth, and we feel driven to put on more clothes or seek a warmer environment (**FIGURE 37.1**).

drive-reduction theory the idea that a physiological need creates an aroused tension state (a drive) that motivates an organism to satisfy the need.

homeostasis a tendency to maintain a balanced or constant internal state; the regulation of any aspect of body chemistry, such as blood glucose, around a particular level.

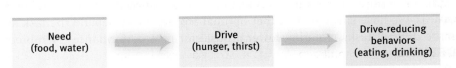

Figure 37.1
Drive-reduction theory Drive-reduction motivation arises from *homeostasis*—an organism's natural tendency to maintain a steady internal state. Thus, if we are water deprived, our thirst drives us to drink and to restore the body's normal state.

Need (food, water) → Drive (hunger, thirst) → Drive-reducing behaviors (eating, drinking)

FYI

Recall from Module 29 that we are also motivated by both *intrinsic* and *extrinsic* rewards.

Not only are we *pushed* by our need to reduce drives, we also are *pulled* by **incentives**—positive or negative stimuli that lure or repel us. This is one way our individual learning histories influence our motives. Depending on our learning, the aroma of good food, whether freshly baked pizza or freshly toasted ants, can motivate our behavior. So can the sight of those we find attractive or threatening.

When there is both a need and an incentive, we feel strongly driven. The food-deprived person who smells baking bread feels a strong hunger drive. In the presence of that drive, the baking bread becomes a compelling incentive. For each motive, we can therefore ask, "How is it pushed by our inborn physiological needs and pulled by incentives in the environment?"

Optimum Arousal

We are much more than homeostatic systems, however. *Optimal arousal theory* holds that some motivated behaviors actually *increase* arousal. Well-fed animals will leave their shelter to explore and gain information, seemingly in the absence of any need-based drive. Curiosity drives monkeys to monkey around trying to figure out how to unlock a latch that opens nothing or how to open a window that allows them to see outside their room (Butler, 1954). It drives the 9-month-old infant to investigate every accessible corner of the house. It drives you to read this text, and it drives the scientists whose work this text discusses. And it drives explorers and adventurers such as Aron Ralston and George Mallory. Asked why he wanted to climb Mount Everest, the *New York Times* reported that Mallory answered, "Because it is there." Those who, like Mallory and Ralston, enjoy high arousal are most likely to seek out intense music, novel foods, and risky behaviors (Zuckerman, 1979). They are "sensation-seekers."

Driven by curiosity Baby monkeys and young children are fascinated by things they've never handled before. Their drive to explore the relatively unfamiliar is one of several motives that do not fill any immediate physiological need.

So, human motivation aims not to eliminate arousal but to seek optimum levels of arousal. Having all our biological needs satisfied, we feel driven to experience stimulation and we hunger for information. We are "infovores," said neuroscientists Irving Biederman and Edward Vessel (2006), after identifying brain mechanisms that reward us for acquiring information. Lacking stimulation, we feel bored and look for a way to increase arousal to some optimum level. However, with too much stimulation comes stress, and we then look for a way to decrease arousal.

Two early-twentieth-century psychologists studied the relationship of arousal to performance and identified what we now call the **Yerkes-Dodson law,** suggesting that moderate arousal would lead to optimal performance (Yerkes & Dodson, 1908). When taking an exam, for example, it pays to be moderately aroused—alert but not trembling with nervousness. We have since learned that optimal arousal levels depend the task as well, with more difficult tasks requiring lower arousal for best performance (Hembree, 1988) (**FIGURE 37.2**).

incentive a positive or negative environmental stimulus that motivates behavior.

Yerkes-Dodson law the principle that performance increases with arousal only up to a point, beyond which performance decreases.

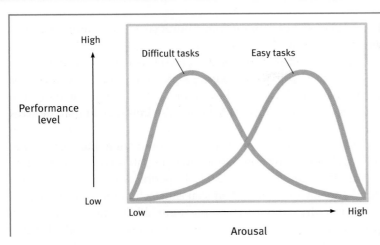

Figure 37.2
Arousal and performance

A Hierarchy of Motives

Some needs take priority over others. At this moment, with your needs for air and water hopefully satisfied, other motives—such as your desire to achieve (discussed in Module 82)—are energizing and directing your behavior. Let your need for water go unsatisfied and your thirst will preoccupy you. Just ask Aron Ralston. Deprived of air, your thirst would disappear.

Abraham Maslow (1970) described these priorities as a **hierarchy of needs** (**FIGURE 37.3**). At the base of this pyramid are our physiological needs, such as those for food and water. Only if these needs are met are we prompted to meet our need for safety, and then to satisfy our needs to give and receive love and to enjoy self-esteem. Beyond this, said Maslow (1971), lies the need to actualize one's full potential. (More on self-esteem and self-actualization in Modules 57 and 59.)

Near the end of his life, Maslow proposed that some people also reach a level of self-transcendence. At the self-actualization level, people seek to realize their own potential.

hierarchy of needs Maslow's pyramid of human needs, beginning at the base with physiological needs that must first be satisfied before higher-level safety needs and then psychological needs become active.

"Hunger is the most urgent form of poverty." -ALLIANCE TO END HUNGER, 2002

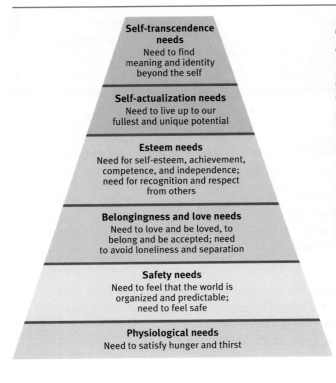

Self-transcendence needs
Need to find meaning and identity beyond the self

Self-actualization needs
Need to live up to our fullest and unique potential

Esteem needs
Need for self-esteem, achievement, competence, and independence; need for recognition and respect from others

Belongingness and love needs
Need to love and be loved, to belong and be accepted; need to avoid loneliness and separation

Safety needs
Need to feel that the world is organized and predictable; need to feel safe

Physiological needs
Need to satisfy hunger and thirst

Figure 37.3

Maslow's hierarchy of needs Once our lower-level needs are met, we are prompted to satisfy our higher-level needs. (From Maslow, 1970.) For survivors of the disastrous tornadoes that swept across the Midwest and Southeastern United States in 2011, satisfying very basic needs for water, food, and safety became top priority. Higher-level needs on Maslow's hierarchy, such as respect, self-actualization, and meaning, become far less important during such times.

At the self-transcendence level, people strive for meaning, purpose, and communion that is beyond the self, that is *transpersonal* (Koltko-Rivera, 2006).

Maslow's hierarchy is somewhat arbitrary; the order of such needs is not universally fixed. People have starved themselves to make a political statement. Today's evolutionary psychologists concur with the first four levels of Maslow's needs pyramid. But they note that gaining and retaining mates, and parenting offspring, are also universal human motives (Kenrick et al., 2010).

Nevertheless, the simple idea that some motives are more compelling than others provides a framework for thinking about motivation. Worldwide life-satisfaction surveys support this basic idea (Oishi et al., 1999; Tay & Diener, 2011). In poorer nations that lack easy access to money and the food and shelter it buys, financial satisfaction more strongly predicts feelings of well-being. In wealthy nations, where most are able to meet basic needs, home-life satisfaction is a better predictor. Self-esteem matters most in individualist nations, whose citizens tend to focus more on personal achievements than on family and community identity. (**TABLE 37.1** summarizes the strengths and weaknesses of the different perspectives on motivation.)

In the ensuing modules, we will consider four representative motives, beginning at the physiological level with hunger and working up through sexual motivation and the need to belong. At each level, we shall see how experience interacts with biology.

Table 37.1

Motivational Theory	Strength	Weakness
Instinct Theory and *Evolutionary Psychology*	Evolutionary psychology helps explain behavioral similarities due to adaptations from our ancestral past.	Instinct theory explains animal behavior better than human behavior; humans have few true instincts.
Drive-Reduction Theory	Explains our motivation to reduce arousal by meeting basic needs, such as hunger or thirst.	Does not explain why some motivated behaviors *increase* arousal.
Optimal Arousal Theory	Explains that motivated behaviors may decrease *or* increase arousal.	Does not explain our motivation to address our more complex social needs.
Maslow's Hierarchy of Needs	Incorporates the idea that we have various *levels* of needs, including lower-level physiological and safety needs, and higher-level social, self-esteem, actualization, and meaning needs.	The order of needs may change in some circumstances. Evolutionary psychologists note the absence in the hierarchy of the universal human motives to find a mate and reproduce.

Before You Move On

▶ **ASK YOURSELF**

Consider your own experiences in relation to Maslow's hierarchy of needs. Have you ever experienced true hunger or thirst that displaced your concern for other, higher-level needs? Do you usually feel safe? Loved? Confident? How often do you feel you are able to address what Maslow called your "self-actualization" needs?

▶ **TEST YOURSELF**

While on a long road trip, you suddenly feel very hungry. You see a diner that looks pretty deserted and creepy, but you are *really* hungry, so you stop anyway. What motivational perspective would most easily explain this behavior, and why?

Answers to the Test Yourself questions can be found in Appendix E at the end of the book.

Module 37 Review

 37-1 How do psychologists define *motivation?* From what perspectives do they view motivated behavior?

- *Motivation* is a need or desire that energizes and directs behavior.

- The *instinct*/evolutionary perspective explores genetic influences on complex behaviors.

- *Drive-reduction theory* explores how physiological needs create aroused tension states (drives) that direct us to satisfy those needs. Environmental *incentives* can intensify drives. Drive-reduction's goal is *homeostasis,* maintaining a steady internal state.

- Optimal arousal theory proposes that some behaviors (such as those driven by curiosity) do not reduce physiological needs but rather are prompted by a search for an optimum level of arousal.

- Abraham Maslow's *hierarchy of needs* proposes a pyramid of human needs, from basic needs such as hunger and thirst up to higher-level needs such as self-actualization and self-transcendence.

Multiple-Choice Questions

1. Which of the following is an unlearned, complex behavior exhibited by all members of a species?

   a. Reflex
   b. Drive
   c. Incentive
   d. Instinct
   e. Motive

2. Which of the following is an aroused motivational state created by a physiological need?

   a. Drive
   b. Instinct
   c. Incentive
   d. Reflex
   e. Motive

3. Which of the following is a conclusion that can be drawn from the Yerkes-Dodson law?

   a. Performance on easy tasks is best when arousal is low.
   b. Performance is best when arousal is extremely high.
   c. Performance is best when arousal is extremely low.
   d. Performance on difficult tasks is best when arousal is high.
   e. Performance is best when arousal is moderate.

4. Which of the following is the lowest priority motive in Abraham Maslow's hierarchy of needs?

   a. Belongingness and love needs
   b. Physiological needs
   c. Esteem needs
   d. Self-actualization needs
   e. Self-transcendence needs

Practice FRQs

1. How can you use Maslow's hierarchy of needs to explain why a
   - hungry young person would steal?
   - lonely new student in a school would join a club?
   - successful artist would continue to invest tremendous effort in her career?

Answer

1 point: A hungry young person would steal because of a physiological need.

1 point: A lonely new student would join a club to meet belongingness and love needs.

1 point: A successful artist would still work hard to satisfy the need for self-actualization.

2. Describe how three different motivational theories could explain a young man's desire to become an excellent soccer player.

(3 points)

Module 38

Hunger Motivation

Module Learning Objectives

38-1   Describe the physiological factors that produce hunger.

38-2   Discuss cultural and situational factors that influence hunger.

38-3   Discuss the factors that predispose some people to become and remain obese.

The power of physiological needs was vividly demonstrated when Ancel Keys and his research team (1950) conducted a now-classic study of semistarvation. They first fed 36 male volunteers (all wartime conscientious objectors) just enough to maintain their initial weight. Then, for six months, they cut this food level in half. The effects soon became visible. Without thinking about it, the men began conserving energy. They appeared sluggish and dull. After dropping rapidly, their body weights stabilized at about 25 percent below their starting point.

As Maslow might have guessed, the men became food obsessed. They talked food. They daydreamed food. They collected recipes, read cookbooks, and feasted their eyes on delectable forbidden food. Preoccupied with their unmet basic need, they lost interest in sex and social activities. As one man reported, "If we see a show, the most interesting part of it is contained in scenes where people are eating. I couldn't laugh at the funniest picture in the world, and love scenes are completely dull."

The semistarved men's preoccupations illustrate how activated motives can hijack our consciousness. As journalist Dorothy Dix (1861–1951) observed, "Nobody wants to kiss when they are hungry." When we're hungry, thirsty, fatigued, or sexually aroused, little else seems to matter. When we're not, food, water, sleep, or sex just don't seem like such big things in life, now or ever.

> "Nature often equips life's essentials—sex, eating, nursing—with built-in gratification."
> -FRANS DE WAAL, "MORALS WITHOUT GOD?," 2010

"Never hunt when you're hungry."

In studies, people in a motivational "hot" state (from fatigue, hunger, or sexual arousal) have easily recalled such feelings in their own past and have perceived them as driving forces in others' behavior (Nordgren et al., 2006, 2007). (You may recall from Module 32 a parallel effect of our current good or bad mood on our memories.) Grocery shop with an empty stomach and you are more likely to see those jelly-filled doughnuts as just what you've always loved and will be wanting tomorrow. *Motives matter mightily.*

> "The full person does not understand the needs of the hungry." -IRISH PROVERB

The Physiology of Hunger

 What physiological factors produce hunger?

Deprived of a normal food supply, Keys' semistarved volunteers were clearly hungry. But what precisely triggers hunger? Are the pangs of an empty stomach the source of hunger? So it seemed to A. L. Washburn. Working with Walter Cannon (Cannon & Washburn, 1912), Washburn agreed to swallow a balloon attached to a recording device (**FIGURE 38.1**). When inflated to fill his stomach, the balloon transmitted his stomach contractions. Washburn supplied information about his *feelings* of hunger by pressing a key each time he felt a hunger pang. The discovery: Washburn was indeed having stomach contractions whenever he felt hungry.

Can hunger exist without stomach pangs? To answer that question, researchers removed some rats' stomachs and created a direct path to their small intestines (Tsang, 1938). Did the rats continue to eat? Indeed they did. Some hunger persists similarly in humans whose stomachs have been removed as a treatment for ulcers or cancer. So the pangs of an empty stomach are not the *only* source of hunger. What else might trigger hunger?

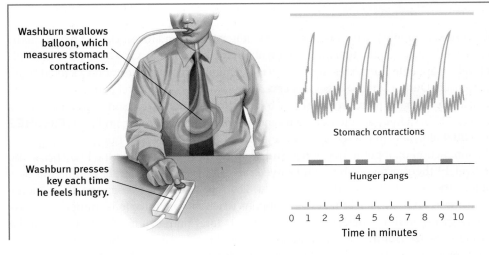

Washburn swallows balloon, which measures stomach contractions.

Washburn presses key each time he feels hungry.

Stomach contractions

Hunger pangs

0 1 2 3 4 5 6 7 8 9 10
Time in minutes

Figure 38.1

Monitoring stomach contractions

Using this procedure, Washburn showed that stomach contractions (transmitted by the stomach balloon) accompany our feelings of hunger (indicated by a key press). (From Cannon, 1929.)

Body Chemistry and the Brain

Somehow, somewhere, your body is keeping tabs on the energy it takes in and the energy it uses. If this weren't true, you would be unable to maintain a stable body weight. A major source of energy in your body is the blood sugar **glucose.** If your blood glucose level drops, you won't consciously feel this change, but your stomach, intestines, and liver will signal your brain to motivate eating. Your brain, which is automatically monitoring your blood chemistry and your body's internal state, will then trigger hunger.

> **glucose** the form of sugar that circulates in the blood and provides the major source of energy for body tissues. When its level is low, we feel hunger.

How does the brain integrate these messages and sound the alarm? The work is done by several neural areas, some housed deep in the brain within the hypothalamus (**FIGURE 38.2**). This neural traffic intersection includes areas that influence eating. For example, one neural arc (called the *arcuate nucleus*) has a center that secretes appetite-stimulating hormones, and another center that secretes appetite-suppressing hormones. Explorations of this neural area and others reveal that when an appetite-enhancing center is stimulated electrically, well-fed animals begin to eat. If the area is destroyed, even starving animals have no interest in food. The opposite occurs when an appetite-suppressing area is stimulated: Animals will stop eating. Destroy this area and animals will eat and eat, and become extremely fat (Duggan & Booth, 1986; Hoebel & Teitelbaum, 1966) (**FIGURE 38.3**).

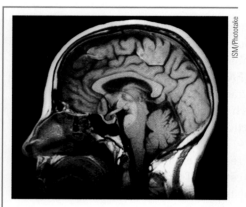

Figure 38.2

The hypothalamus As we saw in Module 11, the hypothalamus (colored orange) performs various body maintenance functions, including control of hunger.

Figure 38.3

Evidence for the brain's control of eating The fat mouse on the left has nonfunctioning leptin receptors.

set point the point at which an individual's "weight thermostat" is supposedly set. When the body falls below this weight, an increase in hunger and a lowered metabolic rate may act to restore the lost weight.

basal metabolic rate the body's resting rate of energy expenditure.

Blood vessels supply the hypothalamus, enabling it to respond to our current blood chemistry as well as to incoming neural information about the body's state. One of its tasks is monitoring levels of appetite hormones, such as *ghrelin,* a hunger-arousing hormone secreted by an empty stomach. During bypass surgery for severe obesity, surgeons seal off part of the stomach. The remaining stomach then produces much less ghrelin, and the person's appetite lessens (Lemonick, 2002). Other appetite hormones include *insulin, leptin, orexin,* and *PYY;* **FIGURES 38.3** and **38.4** illustrate and describe how they influence your feelings of hunger.

The interaction of appetite hormones and brain activity suggests that the body has some sort of "weight thermostat." When semistarved rats fall below their normal weight, this system signals the body to restore the lost weight. The rats' hunger increases and their energy output decreases. If body weight rises—as happens when rats are force fed—hunger decreases and energy expenditure increases. In this way, rats (and humans) tend to hover around a stable weight, or **set point,** influenced in part by heredity (Keesey & Corbett, 1983).

We humans (and other species, too) vary in our **basal metabolic rate,** a measure of how much energy we use to maintain basic body functions when our body is at rest. But we share a common response to decreased food intake: Our basal metabolic rate drops, as it did for participants in Keys' experiment. After 24 weeks of semistarvation, they stabilized at three-quarters of their normal weight, although they were taking in only *half* their previous calories. How did their bodies achieve this dieter's nightmare? They reduced their energy expenditure, partly by being less active, but partly by dropping their basal metabolic rate by 29 percent.

Some researchers have suggested that the idea of a biologically *fixed* set point is too rigid to explain some things. One thing it doesn't address is that slow, sustained changes in body weight can alter a person's set point (Assanand et al., 1998). Another is that when we

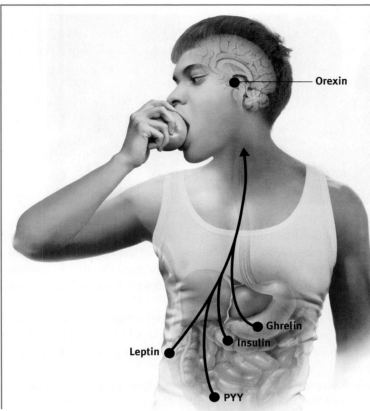

Figure 38.4
The appetite hormones
- *Insulin:* Hormone secreted by pancreas; controls blood glucose.
- *Ghrelin:* Hormone secreted by empty stomach; sends "I'm hungry" signals to the brain.
- *Orexin:* Hunger-triggering hormone secreted by hypothalamus.
- *Leptin:* Protein hormone secreted by fat cells; when abundant, causes brain to increase metabolism and decrease hunger.
- *PYY:* Digestive tract hormone; sends "I'm not hungry" signals to the brain.

have unlimited access to a wide variety of tasty foods, we tend to overeat and gain weight (Raynor & Epstein, 2001). And set points don't explain why psychological factors influence hunger. For all these reasons, some prefer the looser term *settling point* or *set range* to indicate the level at which a person's weight settles in response to caloric intake and energy use. As we will see next, these factors are influenced by environment as well as biology.

"Never get a tattoo when you're drunk and hungry."

The Psychology of Hunger

38-2 What cultural and situational factors influence hunger?

We have seen that our eagerness to eat is pushed by our body chemistry and brain activity. Yet there is more to hunger than meets the stomach. This was strikingly apparent when trickster researchers tested two patients who had no memory for events occurring more than a minute ago (Rozin et al., 1998). If offered a second lunch 20 minutes after eating a normal lunch, both patients readily consumed it . . . and usually a third meal offered 20 minutes after they finished the second. This suggests that one part of our decision to eat is our memory of the time of our last meal. As time passes, we think about eating again, and those thoughts trigger feelings of hunger.

Taste Preferences: Biology and Culture

Body chemistry and environmental factors together influence not only the when of hunger, but also the what—our taste preferences. When feeling tense or depressed, do you crave starchy, carbohydrate-laden foods? Carbohydrates such as pasta, chips, and sweets help boost levels of the neurotransmitter serotonin, which has calming effects. When stressed, even rats find it extra rewarding to scarf Oreos (Artiga et al., 2007; Boggiano et al., 2005).

An acquired taste People everywhere learn to enjoy the fatty, bitter, or spicy foods common in their culture. For these Alaska Natives (left), but not for most other North Americans, whale blubber is a tasty treat. For Peruvians (right), roasted guinea pig is similarly delicious.

Our preferences for sweet and salty tastes are genetic and universal, but conditioning can intensify or alter those preferences. People given highly salted foods may develop a liking for excess salt (Beauchamp, 1987). People sickened by a food may develop an aversion to it. (The frequency of children's illnesses provides many chances for them to learn to avoid certain foods.)

Our culture teaches us that some foods are acceptable but others are not. Bedouins enjoy eating the eye of a camel, which most North Americans would find repulsive. North Americans and Europeans also shun horse, dog, and rat meat, all of which are prized elsewhere.

But there is biological wisdom to many of our taste preferences. Environments can influence the human genetics that affect diet and taste. In places where agriculture has produced milk, for example, survival patterns have favored people with lactose tolerance (Arjamaa & Vuorisalo, 2010). And in hot climates (where foods spoil more quickly) recipes often include spices that inhibit the growth of bacteria (**FIGURE 38.5**). India averages nearly 10 spices per meat recipe; Finland, 2 spices. Pregnant women's food dislikes—and the nausea associated with them—peak about the tenth week, when the developing embryo is most vulnerable to toxins.

Rats tend to avoid unfamiliar foods (Sclafani, 1995). So do we, especially those that are animal based. This *neophobia* (dislike of things unfamiliar) surely was adaptive for our ancestors by protecting them from potentially toxic substances. In time, though, most people who repeatedly sample an initially novel fruit drink or ethnic food come to appreciate the new taste (Pliner, 1982, Pliner et al., 1993).

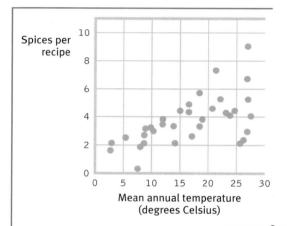

Figure 38.5
Hot cultures like hot spices

Situational Influences on Eating

To a surprising extent, situations also control our eating—a phenomenon psychologists have called the *ecology of eating.* Here are three situations you may have noticed but underestimated:

- Do you eat more when eating with others? Most of us do (Herman et al., 2003; Hetherington et al., 2006). After a party, you may realize you've overeaten. This happens because the presence of others tends to amplify our natural behavior tendencies. (You'll hear more about *social facilitation* in Module 76.)

- *Unit bias* occurs with similar mindlessness. Working with researchers at France's National Center for Scientific Research, Andrew Geier and his colleagues (2006) explored a possible explanation of why French waistlines are smaller than American waistlines. From soda drinks to yogurt sizes, the French offer foods in smaller portion sizes. Does it matter? (One could as well order two small sandwiches as one large one.) To find out, the investigators offered people varieties of free snacks. For example, in the lobby of an apartment house, they laid out either full or half pretzels, big or little Tootsie Rolls, or a big bowl of M&M's with either a small or large serving scoop. Their consistent result: Offered a supersized standard portion, people put away more calories. In other studies (Wansink, 2006, 2007), even nutrition experts helped themselves to 31 percent more ice cream when given a big bowl rather than a small one, and 15 percent more when scooping with a big rather than a small scoop. Portion size matters.

- *Food variety* also stimulates eating. Offered a dessert buffet, we eat more than we do when asked to choose a portion from one favorite dessert. For our early ancestors, these behaviors were adaptive. When foods were abundant and varied, eating more provided a wide range of vitamins and minerals and produced fat that protected them during winter cold or famine. When a bounty of varied foods was unavailable, eating less extended the food supply until winter or famine ended (Polivy et al., 2008; Remick et al., 2009).

Cooking shows increase appetites but not healthful home cooking Julia Child was once the only chef on TV. Today dozens of U.S. cooking shows are broadcast to millions of viewers daily. Yet fewer Americans than ever are home cooking their own, more healthful meals (Pollan, 2009). Nations that devote more time to food preparation at home tend to have lower rates of obesity (Cutler et al., 2003).

Obesity and Weight Control

38-3 What factors predispose some people to become and remain obese?

Obesity can be socially toxic, by affecting both how you are treated and how you feel about yourself. Obesity has been associated with lower psychological well-being, especially among women, and increased risk of depression (de Wit et al., 2010; Luppino et al., 2010; Mendes, 2010a). Obese 6- to 9-year-olds are 60 percent more likely to suffer bullying (Lumeng et al., 2010). And, as we will see, obesity has physical health risks as well. Yet few overweight people win the battle of the bulge. Why? And why do some people gain weight while others eat the same amount and seldom add a pound?

The Physiology of Obesity

Our bodies store fat for good reasons. Fat is an ideal form of stored energy—a high-calorie fuel reserve to carry the body through periods when food is scarce—a common occurrence in our prehistoric ancestors' world. No wonder that in many developing societies today (as in Europe in earlier centuries) people find heavier bodies attractive: Obesity signals affluence and social status (Furnham & Baguma, 1994; Swami et al., 2011).

In parts of the world where food and sweets are now abundantly available, the rule that once served our hungry distant ancestors—*When you find energy-rich fat or sugar, eat it!*—has become dysfunctional. Pretty much everywhere this book is being read, people have a growing problem. The World Health Organization (WHO) (2007) has estimated that more than 1 billion people worldwide are overweight, and 300 million of them are clinically *obese,* defined by the WHO as a *body mass index* (BMI) of 30 or more. (See www.cdc.gov/healthyweight/assessing/bmi to calculate your BMI.) In the United States, the adult obesity rate has more than doubled in the last 40 years, reaching 34 percent, and child-teen obesity has quadrupled (Flegal et al., 2010).

Significant obesity increases the risk of diabetes, high blood pressure, heart disease, gallstones, arthritis, and certain types of cancer, thus increasing health care costs and shortening life expectancy (de Gonzales et al., 2010; Jarrett et al., 2010; Sun et al., 2009). Recent research also has linked women's obesity to their risk of late-life cognitive decline, including Alzheimer's disease and brain tissue loss (Bruce-Keller et al., 2009; Whitmer et al., 2008). One experiment found improved memory performance 12 weeks after severely obese people had weight-loss surgery and lost significant weight. Those not having the surgery showed some further cognitive decline (Gunstad et al., 2011).

Research on the physiology of obesity challenges the stereotype of severely overweight people being weak-willed gluttons.

> "Americans, on average, report that they weigh 177 pounds, but would like to weigh 161."
> -ELIZABETH MENDES, WWW.GALLUP.COM, 2010

SET POINT AND METABOLISM

Once we become fat, we require less food to maintain our weight than we did to attain it. Fat has a lower metabolic rate than does muscle—it takes less food energy to maintain. When an overweight person's body drops below its previous set (or settling) point, the person's hunger increases and metabolism decreases. Thus, the body adapts to starvation by burning off fewer calories.

Lean people also seem naturally disposed to move about. They burn more calories than do energy-conserving overweight people who tend to sit still longer (Levine et al., 2005). These individual differences in resting metabolism help explain why two people of the same height, age, and activity level can maintain the same weight, even if one of them eats much less than the other does.

THE GENETIC FACTOR

Do our genes predispose us to fidget or sit still? Studies do reveal a genetic influence on body weight. Consider two examples:

- Despite shared family meals, adoptive siblings' body weights are uncorrelated with one another or with those of their adoptive parents. Rather, people's weights resemble those of their biological parents (Grilo & Pogue-Geile, 1991).

- Identical twins have closely similar weights, even when reared apart (Hjelmborg et al., 2008; Plomin et al., 1997). Across studies, their weight correlates +.74. The much lower +.32 correlation among fraternal twins suggests that genes explain two-thirds of our varying body mass (Maes et al., 1997).

THE FOOD AND ACTIVITY FACTORS

Genes tell an important part of the obesity story. But environmental factors are mighty important, too.

Studies in Europe, Japan, and the United States show that children and adults who suffer from *sleep loss* are more vulnerable to obesity (Keith et al., 2006; Nedeltcheva et al., 2010; Taheri, 2004a,b). With sleep deprivation, the levels of leptin (which reports body fat to the brain) fall, and ghrelin (the appetite-stimulating stomach hormone) rise.

Social influence is another factor. One 32-year study of 12,067 people found them most likely to become obese when a friend became obese (Christakis & Fowler, 2007). If the obese friend was a close one, the odds of likewise becoming obese almost tripled. Moreover, the correlation among friends' weights was not simply a matter of seeking out similar people as friends. Friends matter.

The strongest evidence that environment influences weight comes from *our fattening world* (**FIGURE 38.6**). What explains this growing problem? Changing *food consumption* and *activity levels* are at work. We are eating more and moving less, with lifestyles approaching those of animal feedlots (where farmers fatten inactive animals). In the United States, jobs requiring moderate physical activity declined from about 50 percent in 1960 to 20 percent in 2011 (Church et al., 2011).

The "bottom" line: New stadiums, theaters, and subway cars—but not airplanes—are widening seats to accommodate the girth growth (Hampson, 2000; Kim & Tong, 2010). Washington State Ferries abandoned a 50-year-old standard: "Eighteen-inch butts are a thing of the past" (Shepherd, 1999). New York City, facing a large problem with Big Apple bottoms, has mostly replaced 17.5-inch bucket-style subway seats with bucketless seats (Hampson, 2000). In the end, today's people need more room.

We will revisit this lesson in Unit XI's study of individual differences. There can be high levels of heritability (genetic influence on individual differences in such things as intelligence) without heredity explaining group differences. Genes mostly determine why one person today is heavier than another. Environment mostly determines why people today

Corey Nolen/Aurora Open/Corbis

"We put fast food on every corner, we put junk food in our schools, we got rid of [physical education classes], we put candy and soda at the checkout stand of every retail outlet you can think of. The results are in. It worked." -HAROLD GOLDSTEIN, EXECUTIVE DIRECTOR OF THE CALIFORNIA CENTER FOR PUBLIC HEALTH ADVOCACY, 2009, WHEN IMAGINING A VAST U.S. NATIONAL EXPERIMENT TO ENCOURAGE WEIGHT GAIN

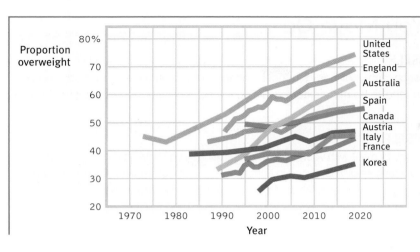

Figure 38.6

Past and projected overweight rates, by the Organization for Economic Cooperation and Development

are heavier than their counterparts 50 years ago. Our eating behavior also demonstrates the now-familiar interaction among biological, psychological, and social-cultural factors. For tips on shedding unwanted pounds, see Close-up: Waist Management.

Close-up

Waist Management

Perhaps you are shaking your head: "Slim chance I have of becoming and staying thin." People struggling with obesity are well advised to seek medical evaluation and guidance. For others who wish to take off a few pounds, researchers have offered these tips.

Begin only if you feel motivated and self-disciplined. For most people, permanent weight loss requires making a career of staying thin—a lifelong change in eating habits combined with increased exercise.

Exercise and get enough sleep. Inactive people are often overweight (**FIGURE 38.7**). Especially when supported by 7 to 8 hours of sleep a night, exercise empties fat cells, builds muscle, speeds up metabolism, and helps lower your settling point (Bennett, 1995; Kolata, 1987; Thompson et al., 1982).

Minimize exposure to tempting food cues. Food shop only on a full stomach. Keep tempting foods out of the house, and store other appealing foods out of sight.

Limit variety and eat healthy foods. Given more variety, people consume more; eat simple meals with whole grains, fruits, and vegetables. Healthy fats, such as those found in olive oil and fish, help regulate appetite and artery-clogging cholesterol (Taubes, 2001, 2002). Better crispy greens than Krispy Kremes.

Reduce portion sizes. Serve food with smaller bowls, plates, and utensils.

Don't starve all day and eat one big meal at night. This eating pattern, common among overweight people, slows metabolism. Moreover, those who eat a balanced breakfast are, by late morning, more alert and less fatigued (Spring et al., 1992).

Beware of the binge. Especially for men, eating slowly can lead to eating less (Martin et al., 2007). Among people who do consciously restrain their eating, drinking alcohol or feeling anxious or depressed can unleash the urge to eat (Herman & Polivy, 1980).

Before eating with others, decide how much you want to eat. Eating with friends can distract us from monitoring our own eating (Ward & Mann, 2000).

Remember, most people occasionally lapse. A lapse need not become a full collapse.

Connect to a support group. Join with others, either face-to-face or online, with whom you can share your goals and progress (Freedman, 2011).

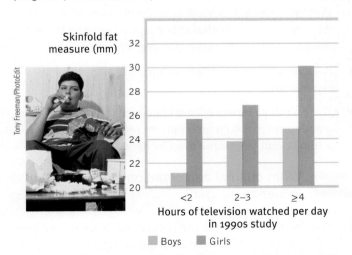

Figure 38.7 **American idle: Couch potatoes beware—TV watching correlates with obesity** As lifestyles have become more sedentary and TV watching has increased, so has the percentage of overweight people in Britain, Canada, and the United States (Pagani et al., 2010). When California children were placed in a TV-reduction educational program, they watched less—and lost weight (Robinson, 1999). Don't watch TV? Then watch out for other screen time that keeps your motor idling.

Before You Move On

▶ **ASK YOURSELF**

Do you feel in touch with your body's hunger signals? Do you eat when your body needs food? Or do you tend to be more externally influenced by enticing foods even when you're full?

▶ **TEST YOURSELF**

You've skipped lunch to meet with your guidance counselor so you haven't eaten anything in eight hours. As your favorite dish is placed in front of you, your mouth waters. Even imagining this may set your mouth to watering. What triggers this anticipatory salivation?

Answers to the Test Yourself questions can be found in Appendix E at the end of the book.

Module 38 Review

 What physiological factors produce hunger?

- Hunger's pangs correspond to the stomach's contractions, but hunger also has other causes.

- Neural areas in the brain, some within the hypothalamus, monitor blood chemistry (including *glucose* level) and incoming information about the body's state.

- Appetite hormones include insulin (controls blood glucose); ghrelin (secreted by an empty stomach); orexin (secreted by the hypothalamus); leptin (secreted by fat cells); and PYY (secreted by the digestive tract).

- *Basal metabolic rate* is the body's resting rate of energy expenditure.

- The body may have a *set point* (a biologically fixed tendency to maintain an optimum weight) or a looser settling point (also influenced by the environment).

 What cultural and situational factors influence hunger?

- Hunger also reflects our memory of when we last ate and our expectation of when we should eat again.

- Humans as a species prefer certain tastes (such as sweet and salty), but our individual preferences are also influenced by conditioning, culture, and situation.

- Some taste preferences, such as the avoidance of new foods, or of foods that have made us ill, have survival value.

38-3 **What factors predispose some people to become and remain obese?**

- Genes and environment interact to produce obesity.
  - Obesity correlates with depression, especially among women.
  - Twin and adoption studies indicate that body weight is also genetically influenced.
  - Environmental influences include lack of exercise, an abundance of high-calorie food, and social influence.

- Those wishing to lose weight are advised to make a lifelong change in habits: Get enough sleep; boost energy expenditure through exercise; limit variety and minimize exposure to tempting food cues; eat healthy foods and reduce portion sizes; space meals throughout the day; beware of the binge; monitor eating during social events; forgive the occasional lapse; and connect to a support group.

Multiple-Choice Questions

1. Which of the following is the major source of energy in your body?

   a. PYY
   b. Arcuate nucleus
   c. Hypothalamus
   d. Ghrelin
   e. Glucose

2. Which of the following is the best term or phrase for the body's resting rate of energy expenditure?

   a. Hunger
   b. Set point
   c. Basal metabolic rate
   d. Body chemistry
   e. Settling point

3. Which of the following statements is true?

   a. We eat less dessert when there are three different desserts available.
   b. Serving sizes in France are generally larger than in the United States.
   c. Offered a supersized portion, most of us consume fewer calories.
   d. We eat more when we're around others.
   e. Food variety generally decreases appetite.

Practice FRQs

1. Explain the activity of the appetite hormones insulin and leptin.

Answer

1 point: Insulin controls blood glucose.

1 point: Leptin causes the brain to increase metabolism and decrease hunger.

2. Explain the difference between set point and basal metabolic rate.

(2 points)

Module 39

Sexual Motivation

Steve Cole/Getty Images

Module Learning Objectives

39-1 Describe the human sexual response cycle, and identify the dysfunctions that disrupt it.

39-2 Discuss the impact of hormones, and external and internal stimuli, on human sexual motivation.

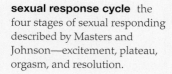

sexual response cycle the four stages of sexual responding described by Masters and Johnson—excitement, plateau, orgasm, and resolution.

"It is a near-universal experience, the invisible clause on one's birth certificate stipulating that one will, upon reaching maturity, feel the urge to engage in activities often associated with the issuance of more birth certificates." -Science writer Natalie Angier, 2007

Sex is part of life. Had this not been so for all your ancestors, you would not be reading this book. Sexual motivation is nature's clever way of making people procreate, thus enabling our species' survival. When two people feel an attraction, they hardly stop to think of themselves as guided by their genes. As the pleasure we take in eating is nature's method of getting our body nourishment, so the desires and pleasures of sex are our genes' way of preserving and spreading themselves. Life is sexually transmitted.

The Physiology of Sex

Like hunger, sexual arousal depends on the interplay of internal and external stimuli. To understand sexual motivation, we must consider both.

The Sexual Response Cycle

  What is the human sexual response cycle, and what dysfunctions disrupt it?

In the 1960s, gynecologist-obstetrician William Masters and his collaborator Virginia Johnson (1966) made headlines by recording the physiological responses of volunteers who masturbated or had intercourse. With the help of 382 female and 312 male volunteers—a somewhat atypical sample, consisting only of people able and willing to display arousal and orgasm while being observed in a laboratory—Masters and Johnson monitored or filmed more than 10,000 sexual "cycles." Their description of the **sexual response cycle** identified four stages. During the initial *excitement phase,* men's and women's genital areas become engorged with blood, a woman's vagina expands and secretes lubricant, and her breasts and nipples may enlarge.

In the *plateau phase,* excitement peaks as breathing, pulse, and blood pressure rates continue to increase. The penis becomes fully engorged and some fluid—frequently containing enough live sperm to enable conception—may appear at its tip. Vaginal secretion continues to increase.

Masters and Johnson observed muscle contractions all over the body during *orgasm;* these were accompanied by further increases in breathing, pulse, and blood pressure rates.

At orgasm, pulse rate surges from about 70 to 115 beats per minute (Jackson, 2009). A woman's arousal and orgasm facilitate conception by positioning the uterus to receive sperm, and drawing the sperm further inward. A woman's orgasm therefore not only reinforces intercourse, which is essential to natural reproduction, it also increases retention of deposited sperm (Furlow & Thornhill, 1996).

The pleasurable feeling of sexual release apparently is much the same for both sexes. In one study, a panel of experts could not reliably distinguish between descriptions of orgasm written by men and those written by women (Vance & Wagner, 1976). University of Groningen neuroscientist Gert Holstege and his colleagues (2003a,b) understand why. They discovered that when men and women undergo PET scans while having orgasms, the same subcortical brain regions glow. And when people who are passionately in love undergo fMRI scans while viewing photos of their beloved or of a stranger, men's and women's brain responses to their partner are pretty similar (Fisher et al., 2002).

The body gradually returns to its unaroused state as the engorged genital blood vessels release their accumulated blood—relatively quickly if orgasm has occurred, relatively slowly otherwise. (It's like the nasal tickle that goes away rapidly if you have sneezed, slowly otherwise.) During this *resolution phase,* the male enters a **refractory period,** lasting from a few minutes to a day or more, during which he is incapable of another orgasm. The female's much shorter refractory period may enable her to have more orgasms if restimulated during or soon after resolution.

Sexual Dysfunctions and Paraphilias

Masters and Johnson sought not only to describe the human sexual response cycle but also to understand and treat the inability to complete it. **Sexual dysfunctions** are problems that consistently impair sexual arousal or functioning. Some involve sexual motivation, especially lack of sexual energy and arousability. For men, others include *erectile disorder* (inability to have or maintain an erection) and *premature ejaculation.* For women, the problem may be pain or *female orgasmic disorder* (distress over infrequently or never experiencing orgasm). In separate surveys of some 3000 Boston women and 32,000 other American women, about 4 in 10 reported a sexual problem, such as orgasmic disorder or low desire, but only about 1 in 8 reported that this caused personal distress (Lutfey et al., 2009; Shifren et al., 2008). Most women who experience sexual distress relate it to their emotional relationship with the partner during sex (Bancroft et al., 2003).

Men and women with sexual dysfunctions can often be helped through therapy. In behaviorally oriented therapy, for example, men learn ways to control their urge to ejaculate, and women are trained to bring themselves to orgasm. Starting with the introduction of Viagra in 1998, erectile disorder has been routinely treated by taking a pill.

Sexual dysfunction involves problems with arousal or sexual functioning. People with *paraphilias* such as exhibitionism, fetishism, and pedophilia, do experience sexual arousal, but they direct it in unusual ways. The American Psychiatric Association (2013) only classifies such behavior as disordered if

- a person experiences distress from their unusual sexual interest or
- the sexual desire or behavior entails harm or risk of harm to others.

Hormones and Sexual Behavior

 How do hormones, and external and internal stimuli, influence human sexual motivation?

Sex hormones have two effects: They direct the physical development of male and female sex characteristics, and (especially in nonhuman animals) they activate sexual behavior. In most mammals, nature neatly synchronizes sex with fertility. The female becomes sexually receptive

refractory period a resting period after orgasm, during which a man cannot achieve another orgasm.

sexual dysfunction a problem that consistently impairs sexual arousal or functioning.

In a National Center for Health Statistics survey of adult Americans, using computer-assisted self-interviews that guaranteed privacy, nearly 98 percent of 30- to 59-year-olds reported having had sex with someone (Fryar et al., 2007).

(in other animals, being "in heat") when secretion of the female hormones, the **estrogens** (such as estradiol), peaks during ovulation. In experiments, researchers can stimulate receptivity by injecting female animals with an estrogen. Male hormone levels are more constant, and hormone injection does not so easily manipulate the sexual behavior of male animals (Feder, 1984). Nevertheless, castrated male rats—having lost their testes, which manufacture the male sex hormone **testosterone**—gradually lose much of their interest in receptive females. They gradually regain it if injected with testosterone.

In humans, hormones more loosely influence sexual behavior, although sexual desire rises slightly at ovulation among women with mates (Pillsworth et al., 2004). When at peak fertility in their menstrual cycle, women express increased preference for masculine faces and ability to detect sexual orientation, but also increased apprehensiveness of men perceived as potentially sexually coercive (Eastwick, 2009; Little et al., 2008; Navarrete et al., 2009; Rule et al., 2011). One study invited partnered women not at risk for pregnancy to keep a diary of their sexual activity. (These women were either using intrauterine devices or had undergone surgery to prevent pregnancy.) On the days around ovulation, intercourse was 24 percent more frequent (Wilcox et al., 2004).

Women's sexuality differs from that of other mammalian females in being more responsive to testosterone level (van Anders & Dunn, 2009). If a woman's natural testosterone level drops, as happens with removal of the ovaries or adrenal glands, her sexual interest may wane. But testosterone-replacement therapy sometimes restores diminished sexual appetite. That is the finding of experiments with hundreds of surgically or naturally menopausal women, for whom a testosterone-replacement patch restored sexual activity, arousal, and desire more than did a placebo (Braunstein et al., 2005; Buster et al., 2005; Petersen & Hyde, 2011). For men with abnormally low testosterone levels, testosterone-replacement therapy often increases sexual desire and also energy and vitality (Yates, 2000).

In men, normal fluctuations in testosterone levels, from man to man and hour to hour, have little effect on sexual drive (Byrne, 1982). Indeed, fluctuations in male hormones are partly a *response* to sexual stimulation. In the presence of an attractive female, Australian skateboarders' testosterone surges, which contributes to riskier moves and more crash landings (Ronay & von Hippel, 2010). Thus, sexual arousal can be a cause as well as a consequence of increased testosterone levels.

Although normal short-term hormonal changes have little effect on men's and women's desire, large hormonal shifts over the life span have a greater effect. A person's interest in dating and sexual stimulation usually increases with the pubertal surge in sex hormones. If the hormonal surge is precluded—as it was during the 1600s and 1700s for prepubertal boys who were castrated to preserve their soprano voices for Italian opera—the normal development of sex characteristics and sexual desire does not occur (Peschel & Peschel, 1987). When adult men are castrated, sex drive typically falls as testosterone levels decline sharply (Hucker & Bain, 1990). Male sex offenders taking Depo-Provera, a drug that reduces testosterone levels to that of a prepubertal boy, similarly lose much of their sexual urge (Bilefsky, 2009; Money et al., 1983). In later life, as sex hormone levels decline, the frequency of sexual fantasies and intercourse declines as well (Leitenberg & Henning, 1995).

To summarize: We might compare human sex hormones, especially testosterone, to the fuel in a car. Without fuel, a car will not run. But if the fuel level is minimally adequate, adding more fuel to the gas tank won't change how the car runs. The analogy is imperfect, because hormones and sexual motivation interact. However, it correctly suggests that biology is a necessary but not sufficient explanation of human sexual behavior. The hormonal fuel is essential, but so are the psychological stimuli that turn on the engine, keep it running, and shift it into high gear.

estrogens sex hormones, such as estradiol, secreted in greater amounts by females than by males and contributing to female sex characteristics. In nonhuman female mammals, estrogen levels peak during ovulation, promoting sexual receptivity.

testosterone the most important of the male sex hormones. Both males and females have it, but the additional testosterone in males stimulates the growth of the male sex organs in the fetus and the development of the male sex characteristics during puberty.

"Fill'er up with testosterone."

The Psychology of Sex

Hunger and sex are different sorts of motivations. Hunger responds to a *need.* If we do not eat, we die. Sex is not in this sense a need. (We may feel like dying, but we do not.) Nevertheless, there are similarities between hunger and sexual motivation. Both depend on internal physiological factors. Both reflect the interplay of excitatory and inhibitory responses—the body's acceleration and braking systems (Bancroft et al., 2009). And both are influenced by external and imagined stimuli, and by cultural expectations (**FIGURE 39.1**).

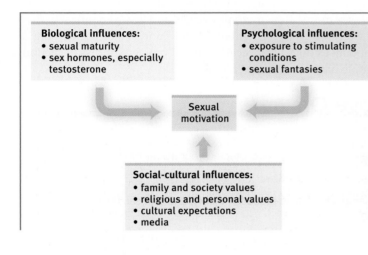

Figure 39.1

Levels of analysis for sexual motivation Compared with our motivation for eating, our sexual motivation is less influenced by biological factors. Psychological and social-cultural factors play a bigger role.

External Stimuli

Many studies confirm that men become aroused when they see, hear, or read erotic material. Surprising to many (because sexually explicit materials are marketed mostly to men) is that most women—at least the less-inhibited women who volunteer to participate in such studies—report or exhibit nearly as much arousal to the same stimuli (Heiman, 1975; Stockton & Murnen, 1992). (Their brains do, however, respond differently, with fMRI scans revealing a more active amygdala in men viewing erotica [Hamann et al., 2004].) In 132 such experiments, men's feelings of sexual arousal have much more closely mirrored their (more obvious) genital response than have women's (Chivers et al., 2010).

People may find sexual arousal either pleasing or disturbing. (Those who wish to control their arousal often limit their exposure to such materials, just as those wishing to control hunger limit their exposure to tempting cues.) With repeated exposure, the emotional response to any erotic stimulus often lessens, or *habituates.* During the 1920s, when Western women's hemlines first reached the knee, an exposed leg was a mildly erotic stimulus.

Can sexually explicit material have adverse effects? Research indicates that it can. Depictions of women being sexually coerced—and liking it—tend to increase viewers' acceptance of the false idea that women enjoy rape, and they tend to increase male viewers' willingness to hurt women (Malamuth & Check, 1981; Zillmann, 1989). Viewing images of sexually attractive women and men may also lead people to devalue their own partners and relationships. After male collegians viewed TV or magazine depictions of sexually attractive women, they often found an average woman, or their own girlfriend or wife, less attractive (Kenrick & Gutierres, 1980; Kenrick et al., 1989; Weaver et al., 1984). Viewing X-rated sex films similarly tends to diminish people's satisfaction with their own sexual partner (Zillmann, 1989). Perhaps reading or watching erotica creates expectations that few men and women can fulfill.

"Ours is a society which stimulates interest in sex by constant titillation. . . . Cinema, television, and all the formidable array of our marketing technology project our very effective forms of titillation and our prejudices about man as a sexy animal into every corner of every hovel in the world." -GERMAINE GREER, 1984

Imagined Stimuli

The brain, it has been said, is our most significant sex organ. The stimuli inside our heads—our imagination—can influence sexual arousal and desire. People who, because of a spinal-cord injury, have no genital sensation can still feel sexual desire (Willmuth, 1987). Consider, too, the erotic potential of dreams. Sleep researchers have discovered that genital arousal accompanies all types of dreams, even though most dreams have no sexual content. But in nearly all men and some 40 percent of women, dreams sometimes contain sexual imagery that leads to orgasm (Wells, 1986). In men, nighttime orgasm and nocturnal emissions ("wet dreams") are more likely when orgasm has not occurred recently.

About 95 percent of both men and women say they have sexual fantasies. Men (whether gay or straight) fantasize about sex more often, more physically, and less romantically. They also prefer less personal and faster-paced sexual content in books and videos (Leitenberg & Henning, 1995). Fantasizing about sex does *not* indicate a sexual problem or dissatisfaction. If anything, sexually active people have more sexual fantasies.

Before You Move On

▶ **ASK YOURSELF**

What psychological and social-cultural factors have affected your sexual motivation?

▶ **TEST YOURSELF**

How might the evolutionary perspective, drive-reduction theory, and arousal theory explain our sexual motivation?

Answers to the Test Yourself questions can be found in Appendix E at the end of the book.

Module 39 Review

 What is the human sexual response cycle, and what dysfunctions disrupt it?

- William Masters and Virginia Johnson described four stages in the human *sexual response cycle:* excitement, plateau, orgasm (which seems to involve similar feelings and brain activity in males and females), and resolution.

- In the resolution phase, males experience a *refractory period,* during which renewed arousal and orgasm are impossible.

- *Sexual dysfunctions* are problems that consistently impair sexual arousal or functioning. They can often be successfully treated by behaviorally oriented therapy or drug therapy.

 How do hormones, and external and internal stimuli, influence human sexual motivation?

- The female *estrogen* and male *testosterone* hormones influence human sexual behavior less directly than they influence sexual behavior in other species. Short-term shifts in testosterone level are normal in men, partly in response to stimulation.

- External stimuli can trigger sexual arousal in both men and women, although the activated brain areas differ somewhat.
  - Men respond more specifically to sexual depictions involving their preferred sex.
  - Sexually explicit material may lead people to perceive their partners as comparatively less appealing and to devalue their relationships. Imagined stimuli (dreams and fantasies) also influence sexual arousal.

Multiple-Choice Questions

1. Which of the following best describes the relationship between gender and orgasm?
   a. You can use fMRIs to identify when orgasm occurs in men, but this method is unreliable in women.
   b. Men describe orgasm in physical terms and women describe orgasm in emotional terms.
   c. Orgasm activates subcortical regions in men and cortical regions in women.
   d. Men and women describe orgasm similarly.
   e. Orgasm serves evolutionary purposes in women but not in men.

2. About _____ percent of the population experience sexual fantasies.
   a. 95
   b. 68
   c. 50
   d. 35
   e. 20

3. Which of the following is true concerning the effect of sex hormones?
   a. Hormone injections can be used to easily manipulate sexual behavior in males but not in females.
   b. Hormone injections can be used to easily manipulate sexual behavior in both males and females.
   c. Sex hormones have a more direct effect on nonhuman animals than on humans.
   d. The levels of sex hormones are more constant in females than in males.
   e. While studies have shown that ovulation is associated with changes in women's fantasies, they have not established an association between ovulation and women's sexual behavior.

Practice FRQs

1. Describe one influence on sexual motivation from each of the following categories:
   - Biological
   - Psychological
   - Social-cultural

   Answer

   1 point: Biological: hormones, sexual orientation.

   1 point: Psychological: exposure to sexually stimulating material, fantasizing.

   1 point: Social-cultural: religious and personal values, media.

2. Name and briefly describe the four stages of the sexual response cycle identified by Masters and Johnson.

   (4 points)

Module 40

Social Motivation: Affiliation Needs

Module Learning Objectives

 Describe the evidence that points to our human affiliation need—our need to belong.

 Describe how social networking influences us.

 What evidence points to our human affiliation need—our need to belong?

The social stigma attached to obesity may bother an overweight person as much as, or more than, the health concerns. Why? We are what Greek philosopher Aristotle called *the social animal.* Cut off from friends or family—alone in prison or at a new school or in a foreign land—most people feel keenly their lost connections with important others. This deep *need to belong*—our *affiliation need*—seems to be a basic human motivation (Baumeister & Leary, 1995). Although healthy people vary in their wish for privacy and solitude, most of us seek to affiliate with others, even to become strongly attached to certain others in enduring, close relationships. Human beings, contended personality theorist Alfred Adler, have an "urge to community" (Ferguson, 1989, 2001, 2010). Our psychological needs drive our adaptive behaviors and, when satisfied, enhance our psychological well-being (Sheldon, 2011).

The Benefits of Belonging

Social bonds boosted our early ancestors' chances of survival. Adults who formed attachments were more likely to reproduce and to co-nurture their offspring to maturity. Attachment bonds helped keep those children close to their caregivers, protecting them from many threats. Indeed, to be "wretched" literally means, in its Middle English origin *(wrecche),* to be without kin nearby.

Cooperation also enhanced survival. In solo combat, our ancestors were not the toughest predators. But as hunters, they learned that six hands were better than two. As food gatherers, they gained protection from two-footed and four-footed enemies by traveling in groups. Those who felt a need to belong survived and reproduced most successfully, and their genes now predominate. We are innately social creatures. People in every society on Earth belong to groups and (as Module 77 explains) prefer and favor "us" over "them."

Do you have close friends—people with whom you freely disclose your ups and downs? Having someone who rejoices with us over good news helps us feel even better about the good news, as well as about the friendship (Reis et al., 2010). The need to belong runs deeper, it seems, than the need to be rich. One study found that *very* happy university students were distinguished not by their money but by their "rich and satisfying close relationships" (Diener & Seligman, 2002).

> "We must love one another or die." -W. H. AUDEN, "SEPTEMBER 1, 1939"

The need to belong colors our thoughts and emotions. We spend a great deal of time thinking about actual and hoped-for relationships. When relationships form, we often feel joy. Falling in mutual love, people have been known to feel their cheeks ache from their irrepressible grins. Asked, "What is necessary for your happiness?" or "What is it that makes your life meaningful?" most people have mentioned—before anything else—close, satisfying relationships with family, friends, or romantic partners (Berscheid, 1985). Happiness hits close to home.

Consider: What was your most satisfying moment in the past week? Researchers asked that question of American and South Korean collegians, then asked them to rate how much that moment had satisfied various needs (Sheldon et al., 2001). In both countries, the peak moment had contributed most to satisfaction of self-esteem and relatedness-belonging needs. When our need for relatedness is satisfied in balance with two other basic psychological needs—*autonomy* (a sense of personal control) and *competence*—we experience a deep sense of well-being, and our self-esteem rides high (Deci & Ryan, 2002, 2009; Milyavskaya et al., 2009; Sheldon & Niemiec, 2006). Indeed, *self-esteem* is a gauge of how valued and accepted we feel (Leary et al., 1998).

Is it surprising, then, that so much of our social behavior aims to increase our feelings of belonging? To gain acceptance, we generally conform to group standards. We monitor our behavior, hoping to make a good impression. We spend billions on clothes, cosmetics, and diet and fitness aids—all motivated by our search for love and acceptance.

By drawing a sharp circle around "us," the need to belong feeds both deep attachments and menacing threats. Out of our need to define a "we" come loving families, faithful friendships, and team spirit, but also teen gangs, ethnic rivalries, and fanatic nationalism.

For good or for bad, we work hard to build and maintain our relationships. Familiarity breeds liking, not contempt. Thrown together in groups at school, at band camp, on a hiking trip, we behave like magnets, moving closer, forming bonds. Parting, we feel distress. We promise to call, to write, to come back for reunions.

This happens in part because feelings of love activate brain reward and safety systems. In one experiment involving exposure to heat, deeply-in-love university students felt markedly less pain when looking at their beloved's picture (rather than viewing someone else's photo or being distracted by a word task) (Younger et al., 2010). Pictures of our loved ones also activate a brain region associated with safety—the prefrontal cortex—that dampens feelings of physical pain (Eisenberger et al., 2011). Love is a natural painkiller.

Even when bad relationships break, people suffer. In one 16-nation survey, and in repeated U.S. surveys, separated and divorced people have been half as likely as married people to say they were "very happy" (Inglehart, 1990; NORC, 2010). After such separations, loneliness and anger—and sometimes even a strange desire to be near the former partner—linger. For those in abusive relationships, the fear of being alone sometimes seems worse than the certainty of emotional or physical pain.

Children who move through a series of foster homes or through repeated family relocations know the fear of being alone. After repeated disruption of budding attachments, they may have difficulty forming deep attachments (Oishi & Schimmack, 2010b). The evidence is clearest at the extremes—the children who grow up in institutions without a sense of belonging to anyone, or who are locked away at home and severely neglected. Too many become withdrawn, frightened, speechless. Feeling insecurely attached to others during childhood can persist into adulthood, in two main forms (Fraley et al., 2011). Some display *insecure anxious attachment,* constantly craving acceptance but remaining vigilant to signs of possible rejection. Others are trapped in *insecure avoidant attachment,* feeling such discomfort over getting close to others that they employ avoidant strategies to maintain their distance.

Photodisc/Jupiterimages

The need to connect Six days a week, women from the Philippines work as "domestic helpers" in 154,000 Hong Kong households. On Sundays, they throng to the central business district to picnic, dance, sing, talk, and laugh. "Humanity could stage no greater display of happiness," reported one observer (*Economist*, 2001).

AP Photo/Vincent Yu

No matter how secure our early years were, we all experience anxiety, loneliness, jealousy, or guilt when something threatens or dissolves our social ties. Much as life's best moments occur when close relationships begin—making a new friend, falling in love, having a baby—life's worst moments happen when close relationships end (Jaremka et al., 2011). Bereaved, we may feel life is empty, pointless. Even the first weeks living on a college campus away from home can be distressing.

For immigrants and refugees moving alone to new places, the stress and loneliness can be depressing. After years of placing individual families in isolated communities, U.S. immigration policies began to encourage *chain migration* (Pipher, 2002). The second refugee Sudanese family settling in a town generally has an easier adjustment than the first.

Social isolation can put us at risk for mental decline and ill health (Cacioppo & Hawkley, 2009). But if feelings of acceptance and connection increase, so will self-esteem, positive feelings, and the desire to help rather than hurt others (Blackhart et al., 2009; Buckley & Leary, 2001).

The Pain of Being Shut Out

Can you recall feeling excluded or ignored or shunned? Perhaps you received the silent treatment. Perhaps people avoided you or averted their eyes in your presence or even mocked you behind your back. If you are like others, even being in a group speaking a different language may have left you feeling excluded, a linguistic outsider (Dotan-Eliaz et al., 2009). In one mock-interview study, women felt more excluded if interviewers used gender-exclusive language (*he, his, him*) rather than inclusive (*his or her*) or neutral (*their*) language (Stout & Dasgupta, 2011).

All these experiences are instances of *ostracism*—of social exclusion (Williams 2007, 2009). Worldwide, humans use many forms of ostracism—exile, imprisonment, solitary confinement—to punish, and therefore control, social behavior. For children, even a brief time-out in isolation can be punishing. Asked to describe personal episodes that made them feel especially *bad* about themselves, people will—about four times in five—describe a relationship difficulty (Pillemer et al., 2007). Feelings of loneliness can also spread from person to person like a disease, through one's acquaintances (Cacioppo et al., 2009).

Being shunned—given the cold shoulder or the silent treatment, with others' eyes avoiding yours—threatens one's need to belong (Williams & Zadro, 2001). "It's the meanest thing you can do to someone, especially if you know they can't fight back. I never should have been born," said Lea, a lifelong victim of the silent treatment by her mother and grandmother. Like Lea, people often respond to ostracism with depressed moods, initial efforts to restore their acceptance, and then withdrawal. After two years of silent treatment by his employer, Richard reported, "I came home every night and cried. I lost 25 pounds, had no self-esteem and felt that I wasn't worthy."

To experience ostracism is to experience real pain, as social psychologist Kipling Williams and his colleagues were surprised to discover in their studies of *cyberostracism* (Gonsalkorale & Williams, 2006). (Perhaps you can recall the feeling of being unfriended or having few followers on a social networking site, being ignored in a chat room, or having a text message or e-mail go unanswered.) Such ostracism, they discovered, takes a toll: It elicits increased activity in brain areas, such as the *anterior cingulate cortex,* that also activate in response to physical pain (Kross et al., 2011; Lieberman & Eisenberger, 2009). That helps explain another surprising finding: The pain-reliever acetaminophen (as in Tylenol and Anacin) lessens *social* as well as physical pain (DeWall et al., 2010). Across cultures, people use the same words (for example, *hurt, crushed*) for social pain and physical pain (MacDonald & Leary, 2005). Psychologically, we seem to experience social pain with the same emotional unpleasantness that marks physical pain.

Enduring the pain of ostracism Caucasian cadets at the United States Military Academy at West Point ostracized Henry Flipper for years, hoping he would drop out. He somehow resisted their cruelty and in 1877 became the first African-American West Point graduate.

The Granger Collection, New York

Social acceptance and rejection Successful participants on the reality TV show *Survivor* form alliances and gain acceptance among their peers. The rest receive the ultimate social punishment as they are "voted off the island."

Pain, whatever its source, focuses our attention and motivates corrective action. Rejected and unable to remedy the situation, people may seek new friends or relieve stress in a strengthened religious faith (Aydin et al., 2010). Or they may turn nasty. In a series of experiments, researchers (Baumeister et al., 2002; Twenge et al., 2001, 2002, 2007) told some students (who had taken a personality test) that they were "the type likely to end up alone later in life," or that people they had met didn't want them in a group that was forming. They told other students that they would have "rewarding relationships throughout life," or that "everyone chose you as someone they'd like to work with." Those excluded became much more likely to engage in self-defeating behaviors and to underperform on aptitude tests. The rejection also interfered with their empathy for others and made them more likely to act in disparaging or aggressive ways against those who had excluded them (blasting them with noise, for example). "If intelligent, well-adjusted, successful . . . students can turn aggressive in response to a small laboratory experience of social exclusion," noted the research team, "it is disturbing to imagine the aggressive tendencies that might arise from . . . chronic exclusion from desired groups in actual social life." Indeed, as Williams (2007) has observed, ostracism "weaves through case after case of school violence."

Connecting and Social Networking

40-2 How does social networking influence us?

As social creatures, we live for connection. Asked what he had learned from studying 238 Harvard University men from the 1930s to the end of their lives, researcher George Vaillant (2009) replied, "The only thing that really matters in life are your relationships to other people." A South African Zulu saying captures the idea: *Umuntu ngumuntu ngabantu*—"a person is a person through other persons."

Mobile Networks and Social Media

Look around and see humans connecting: talking, texting, posting, chatting, social gaming, e-mailing. The changes in how we connect have been fast and vast:

- Cell phones have been history's most rapidly adopted technology. At the end of 2010, the world had 7.1 billion people and 6.8 billion mobile cell-phone subscriptions (ITU, 2013). Asia and Europe have lead the way. In 2012 in India, 925 million people had mobile phone access—more than had a home toilet (Krishna, 2012; Mishra, 2013). American youth have kept up with the world: In 2013, 78 percent of 12- to 17-year-olds were cell-phone users (Pew, 2013).

"There's no question in my mind about what stands at the heart of the communication revolution—the human desire to connect."
-SKYPE PRESIDENT JOSH SILVERMAN, 2009

Image Source/SuperStock

- Texting and e-mailing have been displacing phone talking, which by 2009 accounted for less than half of U.S. mobile network traffic (Wortham, 2010). In Canada and elsewhere, e-mailing has declined, displaced by texting, Facebook, and other messaging technology (IPSOS, 2010a). Speedy texting is not really writing, said one observer (McWhorter, 2012), but rather a new form of conversation—"fingered speech."

- For many, it's as though friends, for better or worse, are always present. How many of us are using social networking sites, such as Facebook or Twitter? Among 2010's entering American collegians, 94 percent were (Pryor et al., 2011). With a "critical mass" of your friends on a social network, its lure becomes hard to resist. Such is our need to belong. Check in or miss out.

The Social Effects of Social Networking

By connecting like-minded people, the Internet serves as a social amplifier. It also functions as an online dating matchmaker (more on those topics in Module 79). As electronic communication has become part of our "new normal," researchers have explored how these changes have affected our relationships.

HAVE SOCIAL NETWORKING SITES MADE US MORE, OR LESS, SOCIALLY ISOLATED?

In the Internet's early years, when online communication in chat rooms and during social games was mostly between strangers, the adolescents and adults who spent more time online spent less time with friends (Kraut et al., 1998; Mesch, 2001; Nie, 2001). As a result, their offline relationships suffered. Even in more recent times, lonely people have tended to spend greater-than-average time online (Bonetti et al., 2010; Stepanikova et al., 2010). Social networkers have been less likely to know their real-world neighbors and "64 percent less likely than non-Internet users to rely on neighbors for help in caring for themselves or a family member" (Pew, 2009).

But the Internet has also diversified our social networks. I am now connected to other hearing-technology advocates across the world and perhaps you, too, have found a group of kindred spirits online. Despite the decrease in neighborliness, social networking seems mostly to have strengthened our connections with people we already know (DiSalvo, 2010; Valkenburg & Peter, 2009). If your social networking helps you connect with friends, stay in touch with extended family, or find support in facing challenges, then you are not alone (Rainie et al., 2011). For many, though, being alone is not the problem. If you are like other students, two days of social networking deprivation would be followed by a glut of online time, much as you would eat voraciously after a two-day food fast (Sheldon et al., 2011). Social networks connect us, but they can also become gigantic time- and attention-sucking diversions. For some research-based strategies, see Close-up: Managing Your Social Networking.

Close-up

Managing Your Social Networking

In today's world, each of us is challenged to find a healthy balance between our real-world time with people and our online sharing. In both Taiwan and the United States, excessive online socializing and gaming have been associated with lower grades (Chen & Fu, 2008; Kaiser Family Foundation, 2010). In one U.S. survey, 47 percent of the heaviest users of the Internet and other media were receiving mostly C grades or lower, as were just 23 percent of the lightest users (Kaiser Family Foundation, 2010). The heaviest users may be almost constantly connected, sometimes even awakening during the night long enough to reply to a text but not long enough to remember it the next day.

If you're trying to maintain a healthy balance between online connecting and real-world responsibilities, experts offer these practical suggestions:

- *Monitor your time.* Keep a log of how you use your time. Then ask yourself, "Does my time use reflect my priorities? Am I spending more time online than I intended? Is my time online interfering with school or work performance? Have family or friends commented on this?"

- *Monitor your feelings.* Again, ask yourself, "Am I emotionally distracted by online preoccupations? When I disconnect and move on to another activity, how do I feel?"

- *"Hide" your more distracting online friends.* And in your own postings, practice the golden rule. Before you post,

ask yourself, "Is this something I'd care about reading if someone else posted it?"

- *Try turning off your mobile devices or leaving them elsewhere.* Selective attention—the flashlight of your mind—can be in only one place at a time. When you want to study or work productively, squelch the temptation to check for messages, posts, or e-mails. And disable sound alerts and pop-ups. These distractions can interrupt your work and hijack your attention just when you've managed to get focused.

- *Try a social networking fast (give it up for an hour, a day, or a week) or a time-controlled social media diet (check in only after homework is done, or only during a predetermined break).* Take notes on what you're losing and gaining on your new "diet."

- *Replenish your focus with a nature walk.* University of Michigan researchers have reported that a walk in the woods, unlike walking on a busy street, replenishes people's capacity for focused attention (Berman et al., 2008). People learn better after a peaceful walk that restores their fatigued attention.

> "The solution is not to bemoan technology but to develop strategies of self-control, as we do with every other temptation in life." -Psychologist Steven Pinker, "Mind Over Mass Media," 2010

DOES ELECTRONIC COMMUNICATION STIMULATE HEALTHY SELF-DISCLOSURE?

As we will see in Module 84, confiding in others can be a healthy way of coping with day-to-day challenges. When communicating electronically rather than face to face, we often are less focused on others' reactions, less self-conscious, and thus less inhibited. We become more willing to share joys, worries, and vulnerabilities. Sometimes this is taken to an extreme, as when teens send photos of themselves they later regret, or cyberbullies hound a victim, or hate groups post messages promoting bigotry or crimes. More often, however, the increased self-disclosure serves to deepen friendships (Valkenburg & Peter, 2009).

Although electronic networking pays dividends, nature has designed us for face-to-face communication, which appears to be the better predictor of life satisfaction (Killingsworth & Gilbert, 2010; Lee et al., 2011). Texting and e-mailing are rewarding, but eye-to-eye conversation with family and friends is even more so.

DO SOCIAL NETWORKING PROFILES AND POSTS REFLECT PEOPLE'S ACTUAL PERSONALITIES?

We've all heard stories of Internet predators hiding behind false personalities, values, and motives. Generally, however, social networks reveal people's real personalities. In one study, participants completed a personality test twice. In one test, they described their "actual personality"; in the other, they described their "ideal self." Volunteers then used the participants' Facebook profiles to create an independent set of personality ratings. The ratings based on Facebook profiles were much closer to the participants' actual personalities than to their ideal personalities (Back et al., 2010). In another study, people who seemed most likable on their Facebook page also seemed most likable in face-to-face meetings (Weisbuch et al., 2009). Your online profiles may indeed reflect the real you!

DOES SOCIAL NETWORKING PROMOTE NARCISSISM? *Narcissism* is self-esteem gone awry. Narcissistic people are self-important, self-focused, and self-promoting. Some personality tests assess narcissism with items such as "I like to be the center of attention." Given our constant social comparison—our measuring ourselves against others—many social networkers can't resist comparing numbers of friends. (Evolutionary psychologist Robin Dunbar [1992, 2010] estimates we can have meaningful, supportive relationships with about 150 people— a typical size of tribal villages.)

Those who score high on narcissism are especially active on social networking sites. They collect more superficial "friends." They offer more staged, glamorous photos. And, not surprisingly, they *seem* more narcissistic to strangers viewing their pages (Buffardi & Campbell, 2008).

For narcissists, social networking sites are more than a gathering place; they are a feeding trough. In one study, college students were randomly assigned either to edit and explain their online profile for 15 minutes, or to use that time to study and explain a Google Maps routing (Freeman & Twenge, 2010). After completing their tasks, all were tested. Who then scored higher on a narcissism measure? Those who had spent the time focused on themselves.

* * *

We have seen that identifiable physiological mechanisms drive some motives, such as hunger (though learned tastes and cultural expectations matter, too). Other motives, such as our need for affiliation, are more obviously driven by psychological factors, such as the social rewards that come from belonging. What unifies all motives is their common effect: the energizing and directing of behavior.

Before You Move On

▶ **ASK YOURSELF**

Have there been times when you felt out of the loop with family and friends, or even ostracized by them? How did you respond?

▶ **TEST YOURSELF**

How might the evolutionary perspective, drive-reduction theory, and arousal theory explain our affiliation needs?

Answers to the Test Yourself questions can be found in Appendix E at the end of the book.

Module 40 Review

 40-1   **What evidence points to our human affiliation need—our need to belong?**

- Our need to affiliate or belong—to feel connected and identified with others—had survival value for our ancestors, which may explain why humans in every society live in groups.

- Because of their need to belong, people suffer when socially excluded, and they may engage in self-defeating behaviors (performing below their ability) or in antisocial behaviors.

- Feeling loved activates brain regions associated with reward and safety systems.

- Social isolation can put us at risk mentally and physically.

40-2   **How does social networking influence us?**

- We connect with others through social networking, strengthening our relationships with those we already know.

- When networking, people tend toward increased self-disclosure.

- Working out strategies for self-control and disciplined use can help people maintain a healthy balance between social networking and school and work performance.

Multiple-Choice Questions

1. If you are trying to maintain a healthy balance between connecting with others online and a real-world perspective, which of the following suggestions should you follow?
   a. Monitor your feelings.
   b. Dismiss the notion of logging online time.
   c. Interact often with your more distracting online friends.
   d. Decrease physical activity.
   e. Try a social networking marathon.

2. Which of the following statements about mobile networks and social media is accurate?
   a. There are more home toilets in India than there are cell phones.
   b. Cell phones have been history's most rapidly adopted technology.
   c. Fewer than 75 percent of American youth are cell-phone users.
   d. Phone calling has displaced texting.
   e. Texting has declined in Canada and elsewhere because of e-mail.

3. Which of the following words or phrases best identifies our gauge of how valued and accepted we feel?
   a. Hope   d. Self-esteem
   b. Autonomy   e. Ostracism
   c. Competence

Practice FRQs

1. Explain three potentially negative effects of social networking.

Answer

1 point each for explaining any of the following:

   Isolates us from others
   Can become a time-sucking diversion
   Can become an attention-sucking diversion
   People may self-disclose too much
   Can make us feel emotionally distracted
   Other effects (use teacher discretion)

2. Explain three things you can do to manage your social networking.

(3 points)

Module 41

Theories and Physiology of Emotion

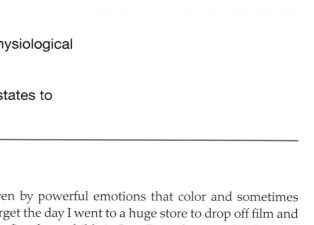

Paul Simcock/Corbis

Module Learning Objectives

41-1 Describe how arousal and expressive behaviors interact in emotion.

41-2 Explain whether we can experience emotions without consciously interpreting and labeling them.

41-3 Describe the link between emotional arousal and the autonomic nervous system, and discuss the relationship between arousal and performance.

41-4 Discuss whether different emotions activate different physiological and brain-pattern responses.

41-5 Discuss the effectiveness of polygraphs in using body states to detect lies.

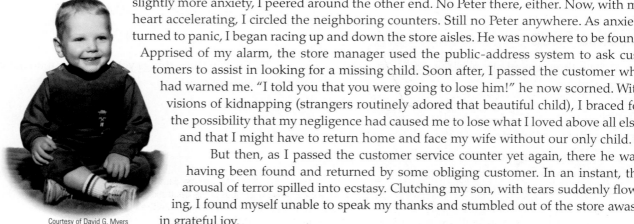

Motivated behavior often is driven by powerful emotions that color and sometimes disrupt our lives. I will never forget the day I went to a huge store to drop off film and brought along Peter, my toddler first-born child. As I set Peter down on his feet and prepared to complete the paperwork, a passerby warned, "You'd better be careful or you'll lose that boy!" Not more than a few breaths later, after dropping the film in the slot, I turned and found no Peter beside me.

With mild anxiety, I peered around one end of the counter. No Peter in sight. With slightly more anxiety, I peered around the other end. No Peter there, either. Now, with my heart accelerating, I circled the neighboring counters. Still no Peter anywhere. As anxiety turned to panic, I began racing up and down the store aisles. He was nowhere to be found. Apprised of my alarm, the store manager used the public-address system to ask customers to assist in looking for a missing child. Soon after, I passed the customer who had warned me. "I told you that you were going to lose him!" he now scorned. With visions of kidnapping (strangers routinely adored that beautiful child), I braced for the possibility that my negligence had caused me to lose what I loved above all else, and that I might have to return home and face my wife without our only child.

But then, as I passed the customer service counter yet again, there he was, having been found and returned by some obliging customer. In an instant, the arousal of terror spilled into ecstasy. Clutching my son, with tears suddenly flowing, I found myself unable to speak my thanks and stumbled out of the store awash in grateful joy.

Courtesy of David G. Myers

Where do such emotions come from? Why do we have them? What are they made of? Emotions don't exist just to give us interesting experiences. They are our body's adaptive response, increasing our chances of survival. When we face challenges, emotions focus our attention and energize our actions (Cyders & Smith, 2008). Our heart races. Our pace quickens. All our senses go on high alert. Receiving unexpected good news, we may find our eyes tearing up. We raise our hands triumphantly. We feel exuberance and a newfound confidence. Yet negative and prolonged emotions can harm our health.

Cognition and Emotion

41-1 How do arousal and expressive behaviors interact in emotion?

As my panicked search for Peter illustrates, **emotions** are a mix of *bodily arousal* (heart pounding); *expressive behaviors* (quickened pace); and *conscious experience,* including thoughts ("Is this a kidnapping?") and feelings (panic, fear, joy).

The puzzle for psychologists is figuring out how these three pieces fit together. To do that, we need answers to two big questions:

- A chicken-and-egg debate: Does your bodily arousal come *before, after,* or *at the same time as* your emotional feelings? (Did I first notice my racing heart and faster step, and then feel terror about losing Peter? Or did my sense of fear come first, stirring my heart and legs to respond?)

- How do *thinking* (cognition) and *feeling* interact? Does cognition always come before emotion? (Did I think about a kidnapping threat before I reacted emotionally?)

Historical emotion theories, as well as current research, have sought to answer these questions.

Historical Emotion Theories

JAMES-LANGE THEORY: AROUSAL COMES BEFORE EMOTION

Common sense tells most of us that we cry because we are sad, lash out because we are angry, tremble because we are afraid. First comes conscious awareness, then the feeling. But to pioneering psychologist William James, this commonsense view of emotion had things backwards. Rather, "We feel sorry because we cry, angry because we strike, afraid because we tremble" (1890, p. 1066). James' idea was also proposed by Danish physiologist Carl Lange, and so is called the **James-Lange theory.** James and Lange would guess that I noticed my racing heart and then, shaking with fright, felt the whoosh of emotion. My feeling of fear followed my body's response.

Joy expressed According to the James-Lange theory, we don't just smile because we share our teammates' joy. We also share the joy because we are smiling with them.

> **FYI**
>
> Not only emotion, but most psychological phenomena (vision, sleep, memory, sex, and so forth) can be approached these three ways—physiologically, behaviorally, and cognitively.

> **emotion** a response of the whole organism, involving
> (1) physiological arousal,
> (2) expressive behaviors, and
> (3) conscious experience.
>
> **James-Lange theory** the theory that our experience of emotion is our awareness of our physiological responses to emotion-arousing stimuli.

CANNON-BARD THEORY: AROUSAL AND EMOTION OCCUR SIMULTANEOUSLY

Physiologist Walter Cannon (1871–1945) disagreed with James and Lange. Does a racing heart signal fear or anger or love? The body's responses—heart rate, perspiration, and body temperature—are too similar, and they change too slowly, to *cause* the different emotions, said Cannon. He, and later another physiologist, Philip Bard, concluded that our bodily responses and experienced emotions occur separately but simultaneously. So, according to the **Cannon-Bard theory,** my heart began pounding *as* I experienced fear. The emotion-triggering stimulus traveled to my sympathetic nervous system, causing my body's arousal. *At the same time,* it traveled to my brain's cortex, causing my awareness of my emotion. My pounding heart did not cause my feeling of fear, nor did my feeling of fear cause my pounding heart.

The Cannon-Bard theory has been challenged by studies of people with severed spinal cords, including a survey of 25 soldiers who suffered such injuries in World War II (Hohmann, 1966). Those with *lower-spine injuries,* who had lost sensation only in their legs, reported little change in their emotions' intensity. Those with *high spinal cord injury,* who could feel nothing below the neck, did report changes. Some reactions were much less intense than before the injuries. Anger, one man confessed, "just doesn't have the heat to it that it used to. It's a mental kind of anger." Other emotions, those expressed mostly in body areas above the neck, were felt *more* intensely. These men reported increases in weeping, lumps in the throat, and getting choked up when saying good-bye, worshipping, or watching a touching movie. Our bodily responses seemingly feed our experienced emotions.

But most researchers now agree that our emotions also involve cognition (Averill, 1993; Barrett, 2006). Whether we fear the man behind us on the dark street depends entirely on whether we interpret his actions as threatening or friendly.

Cognition Can Define Emotion: Schachter and Singer

41-2 To experience emotions, must we consciously interpret and label them?

Stanley Schachter and Jerome Singer (1962) believed that an emotional experience requires a conscious interpretation of arousal: Our physical reactions and our thoughts (perceptions, memories, and interpretations) together create emotion. In their **two-factor theory,** emotions therefore have two ingredients: physical arousal and cognitive appraisal.

Consider how arousal spills over from one event to the next. Imagine arriving home after an invigorating run and finding a message that you got a longed-for job. With arousal lingering from the run, would you feel more elated than if you received this news after awakening from a nap?

To explore this *spillover effect,* Schachter and Singer injected college men with the hormone epinephrine, which triggers feelings of arousal. Picture yourself as a participant: After receiving the injection, you go to a waiting room, where you find yourself with another person (actually an accomplice of the experimenters) who is acting either euphoric or irritated. As you observe this person, you begin to feel your heart race, your body flush, and your breathing become more rapid. If you had been told to expect these effects from the injection, what would you feel? The actual volunteers felt little emotion—because they attributed their arousal to the drug. But if you had been told the injection would produce no effects, what would you feel? Perhaps you would react as another group of participants did. They "caught" the apparent emotion of the other person in the waiting room. They became happy if the accomplice was acting euphoric, and testy if the accomplice was acting irritated.

Cannon-Bard theory the theory that an emotion-arousing stimulus simultaneously triggers (1) physiological responses and (2) the subjective experience of emotion.

two-factor theory the Schachter-Singer theory that to experience emotion one must (1) be physically aroused and (2) cognitively label the arousal.

The spillover effect Arousal from a soccer match can fuel anger, which can descend into rioting or other violent confrontations.

Reuters/CORBIS

This discovery—that a stirred-up state can be experienced as one emotion or another, depending on how we interpret and label it—has been replicated in dozens of experiments (Reisenzein, 1983; Sinclair et al., 1994; Zillmann, 1986). As researcher Daniel Gilbert (2006) has noted, "Feelings that one interprets as fear in the presence of a sheer drop may be interpreted as lust in the presence of a sheer blouse." *The point to remember:* Arousal fuels emotion; cognition channels it.

Cognition May Not Precede Emotion: Zajonc, LeDoux, and Lazarus

But is the heart always subject to the mind? Must we *always* interpret our arousal before we can experience an emotion? Robert Zajonc [ZI-yence] (1980, 1984a) contended that we actually have many emotional reactions apart from, or even before, our interpretation of a situation. Perhaps you can recall liking something or someone immediately, without knowing why.

In earlier modules, we noted that when people repeatedly view stimuli flashed too briefly for them to interpret, they come to prefer those stimuli. Unaware of having previously seen them, they nevertheless rather like them. We have an acutely sensitive automatic radar for emotionally significant information, such that even a subliminally flashed stimulus can prime us to feel better or worse about a follow-up stimulus (Murphy et al., 1995; Zeelenberg et al., 2006). In experiments, thirsty people were given a fruit-flavored drink after viewing a subliminally flashed (thus unperceived) face. Those exposed to a happy face drank about 50 percent more than those exposed to a neutral face (Berridge & Winkielman, 2003). Those flashed an angry face drank substantially less.

Neuroscientists are charting the neural pathways of both "bottom-up" and "top-down" emotions (Ochsner et al., 2009). Our emotional responses can follow two different brain pathways. Some emotions (especially more complex feelings like hatred and love) travel a "high road." A stimulus following this path would travel (by way of the thalamus) to the brain's cortex (**FIGURE 41.1a**). There, it would be analyzed and labeled before the command is sent out, via the amygdala (an emotion-control center), to respond.

But sometimes our emotions (especially simple likes, dislikes, and fears) take what Joseph LeDoux (2002) has called the "low road," a neural shortcut that bypasses the cortex. Following the low-road pathway, a fear-provoking stimulus would travel from the eye or ear (again via the thalamus) directly to the amygdala (Figure 41.1b). This shortcut, bypassing the cortex, enables our greased-lightning emotional response before our intellect intervenes. Like speedy

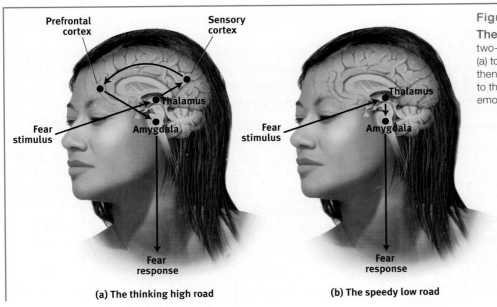

Figure 41.1

The brain's pathways for emotions In the two-track brain, sensory input may be routed (a) to the cortex (via the thalamus) for analysis and then transmission to the amygdala; or (b) directly to the amygdala (via the thalamus) for an instant emotional reaction.

(a) The thinking high road

(b) The speedy low road

Figure 41.2

The brain's sensitivity to threats
Even when fearful eyes (left) were flashed too briefly for people to consciously perceive them, fMRI scans revealed that their hypervigilant amygdala was alerted (Whalen et al., 2004). The eyes on the right did not have this effect.

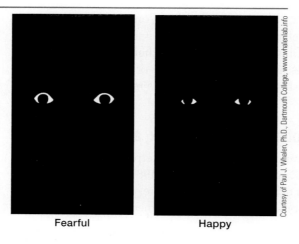

Fearful   Happy

Courtesy of Paul J. Whalen, Ph.D., Dartmouth College, www.whalenlab.info

reflexes that also operate apart from the brain's thinking cortex, the amygdala reactions are so fast that we may be unaware of what's transpired (Dimberg et al., 2000). In one fascinating experiment, researchers used fMRI scans to observe the amygdala's response to subliminally presented fearful eyes (**FIGURE 41.2**) (Whalen et al., 2004). Although they were flashed too quickly for people to consciously perceive them, the fearful eyes triggered increased amygdala activity. A control condition that presented happy eyes did not trigger this activity.

The amygdala sends more neural projections up to the cortex than it receives back, which makes it easier for our feelings to hijack our thinking than for our thinking to rule our feelings (LeDoux & Armony, 1999). Thus, in the forest, we can jump at the sound of rustling bushes nearby and leave it to our cortex to decide later whether the sound was made by a snake or by the wind. Such experiences support Zajonc's belief that *some* of our emotional reactions involve no deliberate thinking.

Emotion researcher Richard Lazarus (1991, 1998) conceded that our brain processes vast amounts of information without our conscious awareness, and that some emotional responses do not require *conscious* thinking. Much of our emotional life operates via the automatic, speedy low road. But, he asked, how would we *know* what we are reacting to if we did not in some way appraise the situation? The appraisal may be effortless and we may not be conscious of it, but it is still a mental function. To know whether a stimulus is good or bad, the brain must have some idea of what it is (Storbeck et al., 2006). Thus, said Lazarus, emotions arise when we *appraise* an event as harmless or dangerous, whether we truly *know* it is or not. We appraise the sound of the rustling bushes as the presence of a threat. Later, we realize that it was "just the wind."

So, as Zajonc and LeDoux have demonstrated, some emotional responses—especially simple likes, dislikes, and fears—involve no conscious thinking (**FIGURE 41.3**). We may fear a big spider, even if we "know" it is harmless. Such responses are difficult to alter by changing our thinking. We may automatically like one person more than another. This instant appeal can even influence our political decisions if we vote (as many people do) for a candidate we *like* over the candidate expressing positions closer to our own (Westen, 2007).

But as Lazarus, Schachter, and Singer predicted, our memories, expectations, and interpretations also influence our feelings about politics. Moreover, highly emotional people are intense partly because of their interpretations. They may *personalize* events as being somehow directed at them, and they may *generalize* their experiences by blowing single incidents out of proportion (Larsen et al., 1987). Thus, learning to *think* more positively can help people *feel* better. Although the emotional low road functions automatically, the thinking high road allows us to retake some control over our emotional life. Together, automatic emotion and conscious thinking weave the fabric of our emotional lives. (**TABLE 41.1** summarizes these emotion theories.)

Figure 41.3

Two pathways for emotions
Zajonc and LeDoux have emphasized that some emotional responses are immediate, before any conscious appraisal. Lazarus, Schachter, and Singer emphasized that our appraisal and labeling of events also determine our emotional responses.

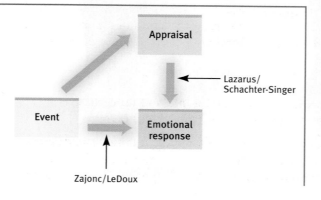

Appraisal

Lazarus/
Schachter-Singer

Event

Emotional
response

Zajonc/LeDoux

Table 41.1 Summary of Emotion Theories

Theory	Explanation of Emotions	Example
James-Lange	Emotions arise from our awareness of our specific bodily responses to emotion-arousing stimuli.	We observe our heart racing after a threat and then feel afraid.
Cannon-Bard	Emotion-arousing stimuli trigger our bodily responses and simultaneous subjective experience.	Our heart races at the same time that we feel afraid.
Schachter-Singer	Our experience of emotion depends on two factors: general arousal and a conscious cognitive label.	We may interpret our arousal as fear or excitement, depending on the context.
Zajonc; LeDoux	Some embodied responses happen instantly, without conscious appraisal.	We automatically feel startled by a sound in the forest before labeling it as a threat.
Lazarus	Cognitive appraisal ("Is it dangerous or not?")—sometimes without our awareness—defines emotion.	The sound is "just the wind."

AP® Exam Tip

Table 41.1 is an excellent summary of the theories of emotion. They are presented in the order of appearance historically. Notice that cognition, a hugely important factor in the modern theories, is not mentioned in the first two theories.

Before You Move On

► **ASK YOURSELF**

Can you remember a time when you began to feel upset or uneasy and only later labeled those feelings?

► **TEST YOURSELF**

Christine is holding her 8-month-old baby when a fierce dog appears out of nowhere and, with teeth bared, leaps for the baby's face. Christine immediately ducks for cover to protect the baby, screams at the dog, then notices that her heart is banging in her chest and she's broken out in a cold sweat. How would the James-Lange, Cannon-Bard, and two-factor theories explain Christine's emotional reaction?

Answers to the Test Yourself questions can be found in Appendix E at the end of the book.

Embodied Emotion

Whether you are falling in love or grieving a death, you need little convincing that emotions involve the body. Feeling without a body is like breathing without lungs. Some physical responses are easy to notice. Other emotional responses we experience without awareness.

Emotions and the Autonomic Nervous System

 What is the link between emotional arousal and the autonomic nervous system? How does arousal affect performance?

As we saw in Module 10, in a crisis, the *sympathetic division* of your *autonomic nervous system (ANS)* mobilizes your body for action, directing your adrenal glands to release the stress hormones epinephrine (adrenaline) and norepinephrine (noradrenaline)

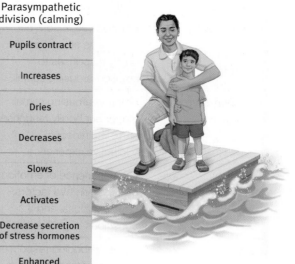

Autonomic Nervous System Controls Physiological Arousal

Sympathetic division (arousing)		Parasympathetic division (calming)
Pupils dilate	EYES	Pupils contract
Decreases	SALIVATION	Increases
Perspires	SKIN	Dries
Increases	RESPIRATION	Decreases
Accelerates	HEART	Slows
Inhibits	DIGESTION	Activates
Secrete stress hormones	ADRENAL GLANDS	Decrease secretion of stress hormones
Reduced	IMMUNE SYSTEM FUNCTIONING	Enhanced

Figure 41.4

Emotional arousal Like a crisis control center, the autonomic nervous system arouses the body in a crisis and calms it when danger passes.

(**FIGURE 41.4**). To provide energy, your liver pours extra sugar into your bloodstream. To help burn the sugar, your respiration increases to supply needed oxygen. Your heart rate and blood pressure increase. Your digestion slows, diverting blood from your internal organs to your muscles. With blood sugar driven into the large muscles, running becomes easier. Your pupils dilate, letting in more light. To cool your stirred-up body, you perspire. If wounded, your blood would clot more quickly.

As we saw in Module 37, the *Yerkes-Dodson law* explains that arousal affects performance in different ways, depending on the task. When taking an exam, it pays to be moderately aroused—alert but not trembling with nervousness (**FIGURE 41.5**). But too little arousal (as when sleepy) can be disruptive, and, as we'll see later in this unit, prolonged high arousal can tax the body.

When the crisis passes, the *parasympathetic division* of your ANS gradually calms your body, as stress hormones slowly leave your bloodstream. After your next crisis, think of this: Without any conscious effort, your body's response to danger is wonderfully coordinated and adaptive—preparing you to *fight or flee*.

Figure 41.5

Arousal and performance
Performance peaks at lower levels of arousal for difficult tasks, and at higher levels for easy or well-learned tasks. (1) How might this phenomenon affect runners? (2) How might this phenomenon affect anxious test-takers facing a difficult exam? (3) How might the performance of anxious students be affected by relaxation training?

ANSWERS: (1) Runners tend to excel when aroused by competition. (2) High anxiety in test-takers may disrupt their performance. (3) Teaching anxious students how to relax before an exam can enable them to perform better (Hembree, 1988).

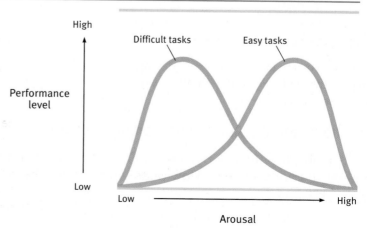

The Physiology of Emotions

41-4 Do different emotions activate different physiological and brain-pattern responses?

Imagine conducting an experiment measuring the physiological responses of emotion. In each of four rooms, you have someone watching a movie: In the first, the person is viewing a horror show; in the second, an anger-provoking film; in the third, a sexually arousing film; in the fourth, a boring film. From the control center you monitor each person's perspiration, breathing, and heart rate. Could you tell who is frightened? Who is angry? Who is sexually aroused? Who is bored?

Emotional arousal Elated excitement and panicky fear involve similar physiological arousal. That allows us to flip rapidly between the two emotions.

With training, you could probably pick out the bored viewer. But discerning physiological differences among fear, anger, and sexual arousal would be much more difficult (Barrett, 2006). Different emotions do not have sharply distinct biological signatures.

Nor do they engage sharply distinct brain regions. Consider the broad emotional portfolio of the *insula,* a neural center deep inside the brain. The insula is activated when we experience various social emotions, such as lust, pride, and disgust. In brain scans, it becomes active when people bite into some disgusting food, smell the same disgusting food, think about biting into a disgusting cockroach, or feel moral disgust over a sleazy business exploiting a saintly widow (Sapolsky, 2010).

Nevertheless, despite their similarities, sexual arousal, fear, anger, and disgust *feel* different to you and me, and they often *look* different to others. We may appear "paralyzed with fear" or "ready to explode." Research has pinpointed some real, though subtle, physiological distinctions and brain-pattern distinctions among the emotions. For example, the finger temperatures and hormone secretions that accompany fear and rage do sometimes differ (Ax, 1953; Levenson, 1992). Fear and joy, although they prompt similar increased heart rate, stimulate different facial muscles. During fear, your brow muscles tense. During joy, muscles in your cheeks and under your eyes pull into a smile (Witvliet & Vrana, 1995).

Some emotions also differ in their brain circuits (Panksepp, 2007). Compared with observers watching angry faces, those watching (and subtly mimicking) fearful faces show more activity in their amygdala (Whalen et al., 2001). Brain scans and EEG recordings show that emotions also activate different areas of the brain's cortex. When you experience negative emotions such as disgust, your right prefrontal cortex tends to be more active than the left. Depression-prone people, and those with generally negative personalities, also show more right frontal lobe activity (Harmon-Jones et al., 2002).

Positive moods tend to trigger more left frontal lobe activity. People with positive personalities—exuberant infants and alert, enthusiastic, energized, and persistently goal-directed adults—also show more activity in the left frontal lobe than in the right (Davidson, 2000, 2003; Urry et al., 2004). Indeed, the more a person's baseline frontal lobe activity tilts left—or is made to tilt left by perceptual activity—the more upbeat the person typically is (Drake & Myers, 2006).

To sum up, we can't easily see differences in emotions from tracking heart rate, breathing, and perspiration. But facial expressions and brain activity can vary with the emotion. So, do we, like Pinocchio, give off telltale signs when we lie? For more on that question, see Thinking Critically About: Lie Detection.

"No one ever told me that grief felt so much like fear. I am not afraid, but the sensation is like being afraid. The same fluttering in the stomach, the same restlessness, the yawning. I keep on swallowing." -C. S. Lewis, *A Grief Observed*, 1961

FYI

In 1966, a young man named Charles Whitman killed his wife and mother and then climbed to the top of a tower at the University of Texas and shot 38 people. An autopsy later revealed a tumor pressing against his amygdala, which may have contributed to his violence.

Thinking Critically About

Lie Detection

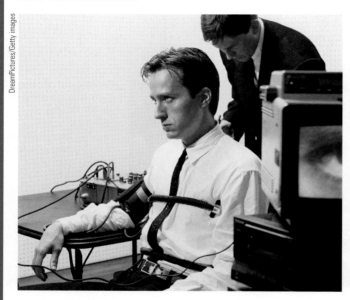

Can polygraph tests like this identify liars? To learn more, read on.

41-5 How effective are polygraphs in using body states to detect lies?

Can a *lie detector*—a **polygraph**—reveal lies? Polygraphs don't literally detect lies. Instead, they measure emotion-linked changes in breathing, cardiovascular activity, and perspiration. If you were taking this test, an examiner would monitor these responses as you answered questions. She might ask, "In the last 20 years, have you ever taken something that didn't belong to you?" This item is a control question, aimed at making everyone a little nervous. If you lie and say *"No!"* (as many people do) the polygraph will detect arousal. This response will establish a baseline, a useful comparison for your responses to *critical questions ("Did you ever steal anything from your previous employer?")*. If your responses to critical questions are weaker than to control questions, the examiner will infer you are telling the truth.

Critics point out two problems: First, our physiological arousal is much the same from one emotion to another. Anxiety, irritation, and guilt all prompt similar physiological reactivity. Second, many innocent people do respond with heightened tension to the accusations implied by the critical questions (**FIGURE 41.6**). Many rape victims, for example, "fail" these tests when reacting emotionally but truthfully (Lykken, 1991).

polygraph a machine, commonly used in attempts to detect lies, that measures several of the physiological responses (such as perspiration and cardiovascular and breathing changes) accompanying emotion.

A 2002 U.S. National Academy of Sciences report noted that "no spy has ever been caught [by] using the polygraph." It is not for lack of trying. The FBI, CIA, and Departments of Defense and Energy in the United States have tested tens of thousands of employees, and polygraph use in Europe has also increased (Meijer & Verschuere, 2010). Meanwhile Aldrich Ames, a Russian spy within the CIA, went undetected. Ames took many "polygraph tests and passed them all," noted Robert Park (1999). "Nobody thought to investigate the source of his sudden wealth—after all, he was passing the lie detector tests."

A more effective approach to lie detection uses a *guilty knowledge test,* which also assesses a suspect's physiological responses to crime-scene details known only to the police and the guilty person (Ben-Shakhar & Elaad, 2003). If a camera and computer had been stolen, for example, only a guilty person should react strongly to the brand names of the stolen items. Given enough such specific probes, an innocent person will seldom be wrongly accused.

Research teams are now exploring new ways to nab liars. Psychologist Paul Ekman (2003) has done research (and has trained law enforcement officers) in detecting fleeting signals of deceit in facial expressions. Eyeblinks, for example, decrease during the cognitive demands of lying and increase afterward (Leal & Vrij, 2008). Other researchers are developing software that analyzes facial microexpressions (Adelson, 2004; Newman et al., 2003) or compares the language of truth-tellers and of liars (who use fewer first-person pronouns and more negative-emotion words).

"Forensic neuroscience" researchers are going straight to the seat of deceit—the brain. EEG recordings have revealed brain waves that indicate familiarity with crime information. fMRI scans have shown liars' brains activating in places that honest people's brains do not (Langleben et al., 2006, 2008; Lui & Rosenfeld, 2009). Pinocchio's giveaway signal of lying may be not the length of his nose, but rather the telltale activity in places such as his left frontal lobe and anterior cingulate cortex, which become active when the brain inhibits truth telling. A new U.S. $10 million Law and Neuroscience Project, led by psychologist Michael Gazzaniga, aims to assess appropriate uses of the new technology in identifying terrorists, convicting criminals, and protecting the

Thinking Critically About *(continued)*

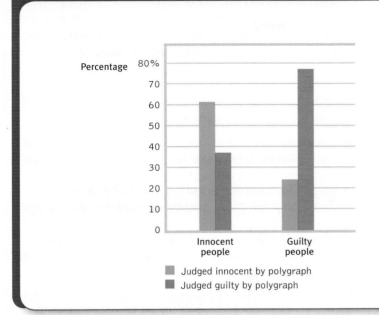

Judged innocent by polygraph
Judged guilty by polygraph

innocent. In 2010, a U.S. federal court declared that fMRI lie detection is not yet ready for courtroom use (Miller, 2010). Many neuroscientists concur (Gazzaniga, 2011; Wagner, 2010). Others argue that jurors' and judges' seat-of-the-pants judgments "are worse than the science that is excluded" (Schauer, 2010).

Figure 41.6 How often do lie detection tests lie? In one study, polygraph experts interpreted the polygraph data of 100 people who had been suspects in theft crimes (Kleinmuntz & Szucko, 1984). Half the suspects were guilty and had confessed; the other half had been proven innocent. Had the polygraph experts been the judges, more than one-third of the innocent would have been declared guilty, and one-fourth of the guilty would have been declared innocent.

Before You Move On

▶ **ASK YOURSELF**

Can you think of a recent time when you noticed your body's reactions to an emotionally charged situation, such as a difficult social setting or perhaps even a test or game you were worrying about in advance? Did you perceive the situation as a challenge or a threat? How well did you do?

▶ **TEST YOURSELF**

How do the two divisions of the autonomic nervous system affect our emotional responses?

Answers to the Test Yourself questions can be found in Appendix E at the end of the book.

Module 41 Review

41-1 How do arousal and expressive behaviors interact in emotion?

- *Emotions* are psychological responses of the whole organism involving an interplay among physiological arousal, expressive behaviors, and conscious experience.

- Theories of emotion generally address two major questions: (1) Does physiological arousal come before, after, or at the same time as emotional feelings, and (2) how do cognition and feeling interact?

- The *James-Lange theory* maintains that emotional feelings follow our body's response to emotion-inducing stimuli.

- The *Cannon-Bard theory* proposes that our body responds to emotion at the same time that we experience the emotion (one does not cause the other).

41-2 To experience emotions, must we consciously interpret and label them?

- The Schachter-Singer *two-factor theory* holds that our emotions have two ingredients, physical arousal and a cognitive label, and the cognitive labels we put on our states of arousal are an essential ingredient of emotion.

- Lazarus agreed that many important emotions arise from our interpretations or inferences.

- Zajonc and LeDoux, however, believe that some simple emotional responses occur instantly, not only outside our conscious awareness, but before any cognitive processing occurs. This interplay between emotion and cognition illustrates our dual-track mind.

41-3 What is the link between emotional arousal and the autonomic nervous system? How does arousal affect performance?

- The arousal component of emotion is regulated by the autonomic nervous system's sympathetic (arousing) and parasympathetic (calming) divisions.

- Performance peaks at lower levels of arousal for difficult tasks, and at higher levels for easy or well-learned tasks.

41-4 Do different emotions activate different physiological and brain-pattern responses?

- Emotions may be similarly arousing, but some subtle physiological responses, such as facial muscle movements, distinguish them.

- More meaningful differences have been found in activity in some brain pathways and cortical areas and in the hormone secretions associated with different emotions.

41-5 How effective are polygraphs in using body states to detect lies?

- *Polygraphs,* which measure several physiological indicators of emotion, are not accurate enough to justify widespread use in business and law enforcement. The use of guilty knowledge questions and new forms of technology may produce better indications of lying.

Multiple-Choice Questions

1. One night Samar became frightened when she was startled by a noise while walking down the street alone. Which theory of emotion would say that her fear resulted from the startle response alone?
   a. James-Lange
   b. Cannon-Bard
   c. Two-factor
   d. Lazarus
   e. Schachter-Singer

2. The Cannon-Bard theory of emotion states that
   a. emotional response occurs before cognition.
   b. physiological response occurs before emotional response.
   c. emotional response occurs before physiological response.
   d. cognition occurs before emotional response.
   e. physiological response and emotion occur independently and simultaneously.

3. Which of the following is an example of cognitive appraisal?

   a. Randal is happy all day because he is savoring the wonderful events of yesterday.

   b. Charles is frightened in a dark alley because he remembers stories of others being attacked in dark alleys.

   c. Sherika labels the arousal she is feeling as attraction because she is in the presence of a good-looking young man.

   d. Dora is angry because she cannot figure out how to convince her husband to take her to Hawaii.

   e. Ann is frustrated because traffic has made her late for an important meeting.

4. Which of the following characterizes the "low road" neural pathway to emotions?

   a. Information travels directly from the thalamus to the amygdala.

   b. The emotion results more slowly than it would via the "high road."

   c. It is an example of top-down processing.

   d. It is more likely to be utilized for complex feelings.

   e. It passes through the brain's cortex.

Practice FRQs

1. Explain the role of conscious thinking in emotion according to the theory that some emotions take the high road while others take the low road.

Answer

1 point: The high-road theory argues that conscious thinking occurs before the emotion.

1 point: The low-road theory argues that conscious awareness does not occur until after the emotional response.

2. Lynn's boyfriend has not replied to her last three text messages. Lynn is experiencing anger, increased blood pressure, and rapid breathing. Analyze this situation using both the James-Lange and the Cannon-Bard theories of emotion.

(2 points)

Module 42

Expressed Emotion

Ocean/Corbis

Module Learning Objectives

42-1 Describe our ability to communicate nonverbally, and discuss gender differences in this capacity.

42-2 Discuss the culture-specific and culturally universal aspects of nonverbal expressions of emotion.

42-3 Describe how facial expressions influence our feelings.

FYI

To learn more about our experienced emotions of anger and happiness, see Module 83.

E xpressive behavior implies emotion. Dolphins, with smiles seemingly plastered on their faces, appear happy. To decipher people's emotions we read their bodies, listen to their voice tones, and study their faces. Does nonverbal language vary with culture—or is it universal? And do our expressions influence our experienced emotions?

Detecting Emotion in Others

42-1 How do we communicate nonverbally? How do the genders differ in this capacity?

To Westerners, a firm handshake conveys an outgoing, expressive personality (Chaplin et al., 2000). A gaze, an averted glance, or a stare communicate intimacy, submission, or dominance (Kleinke, 1986). When two people are passionately in love, they typically spend time—quite a bit of time—gazing into each other's eyes (Rubin, 1970). Would such gazes stir these feelings between strangers? To find out, researchers asked unacquainted male-female pairs to gaze intently for two minutes either at each other's hands or into each other's eyes. After separating, the eye gazers reported feeling a tingle of attraction and affection (Kellerman et al., 1989).

Most of us read nonverbal cues well. Shown 10 seconds of video from the end of a speed-dating interaction, people can often detect whether one person is attracted to another (Place et al., 2009). We are especially good at detecting nonverbal threats. In a series of subliminally flashed words, we more often sense the presence of negative ones, such as *snake* or *bomb* (Dijksterhuis & Aarts, 2003). In a crowd of faces, a single angry face "pops out" faster than a single happy one (Hansen & Hansen, 1988; Pinkham et al., 2010). And even when hearing another language, most of us readily detect anger (Scherer et al., 2001).

Network Photographers/Alamy

A silent language of emotion Hindu classic dance uses the face and body to effectively convey 10 different emotions (Hejmadi et al., 2000).

Pollak, S.D, and Kistler, D.J. (2002). Proceedings of the National Academy of Sciences USA, 99: 13, 9072–9076.

Figure 42.1

Experience influences how we perceive emotions
Viewing the morphed middle face, evenly mixing fear with anger, physically abused children were more likely than nonabused children to perceive the face as angry (Pollak & Kistler, 2002; Pollak & Tolley-Schell, 2003).

Experience can sensitize us to particular emotions, as shown by experiments using a series of faces (like those in **FIGURE 42.1**) that morph from fear (or sadness) to anger. Viewing such faces, physically abused children are much quicker than other children to spot the signals of anger. Shown a face that is 60 percent fear and 40 percent anger, they are as likely to perceive anger as fear. Their perceptions become sensitively attuned to glimmers of danger that nonabused children miss.

Hard-to-control facial muscles reveal signs of emotions you may be trying to conceal. Lifting just the inner part of your eyebrows, which few people do consciously, reveals distress or worry. Eyebrows raised and pulled together signal fear. Activated muscles under the eyes and raised cheeks suggest a natural smile, called a *Duchenne smile* in honor of the French physician who described it. A feigned smile, such as one we make for a photographer, often is frozen in place for several seconds, then suddenly switched off. Authentic smiles tend to be briefer and to fade less abruptly (Bugental, 1986).

Our brains are rather amazing detectors of subtle expressions. Just *how* amazing was clear when researchers filmed teachers talking to unseen schoolchildren (Babad et al., 1991). A mere 10-second clip of either the teacher's voice or face provided enough clues for both young and old viewers to determine whether the teacher liked and admired a child. In other experiments, even glimpsing a face for one-tenth of a second enabled people to judge people's attractiveness or trustworthiness or to rate politicians' competence and predict their voter support (Willis & Todorov, 2006). "First impressions . . . occur with astonishing speed," note Christopher Olivola and Alexander Todorov (2010).

Despite our brain's emotion-detecting skill, we find it difficult to detect deceiving expressions (Porter & ten Brinke, 2008). In one digest of 206 studies of discerning truth from lies, people were just 54 percent accurate—barely better than a coin toss (Bond & DePaulo, 2006). Moreover, contrary to claims that some experts can spot lies, the available research indicates that virtually no one—save perhaps police professionals in high-stakes situations—beats chance by much (Bond & DePaulo, 2008; O'Sullivan et al., 2009). The behavioral differences between liars and truth-tellers are too minute for most people to detect (Hartwig & Bond, 2011).

Which of researcher Paul Ekman's smiles is feigned, which natural? The smile on the right engages the facial muscles of a natural smile.

Some of us are, however, more sensitive than others to physical cues. In one study, hundreds of people were asked to name the emotion in brief film clips they watched. The clips showed portions of a person's emotionally expressive face or body, sometimes accompanied by a garbled voice (Rosenthal et al., 1979). For example, after a 2-second scene revealing only the face of an upset woman, the researchers would ask whether the woman was criticizing someone for being late or was talking about her divorce. Given such "thin slices," some people were much better emotion detectors than others. Introverts tend to excel at reading others' emotions, while extraverts are generally easier to read (Ambady et al., 1995).

Gestures, facial expressions, and voice tones, which are absent in written communication, convey important information. Those who listen to 30 seconds of people describing their marital separation can better predict their current and future adjustment than can those who read a script of the recording (Mason et al., 2010). Electronic communications provide impoverished nonverbal cues. To partly remedy that, we sometimes accompany our text messages, e-mails, and online posts with emotion cues (ROFL!). The absence of expressive e-motion can make for ambiguous emotion. Without the vocal nuances that signal whether a statement is serious, kidding, or sarcastic, we are in danger of communicating our own egocentrism, as people misinterpret our "just kidding" message (Kruger et al., 2005).

Gender, Emotion, and Nonverbal Behavior

Is women's intuition, as so many believe, superior to men's? After analyzing 125 studies of sensitivity to nonverbal cues, Judith Hall (1984, 1987) concluded that women generally do surpass men at reading people's emotional cues when given "thin slices" of behavior. Women have also surpassed men in other assessments of emotional cues, such as deciding whether a male-female couple is a genuine romantic couple or a posed phony couple, and in discerning which of two people in a photo is the other's supervisor (Barnes & Sternberg, 1989).

Women's nonverbal sensitivity helps explain their greater emotional literacy. Invited by Lisa Feldman Barrett and her colleagues (2000) to describe how they would feel in certain situations, men described simpler emotional reactions. You might like to try this yourself: Ask some people how they might feel when saying good-bye to friends after graduation. Barrett's work suggests you are more likely to hear young men say, simply, "I'll feel bad," and to hear young women express more complex emotions: "It will be bittersweet; I'll feel both happy and sad."

Women's skill at decoding others' emotions may also contribute to their greater emotional responsiveness (Vigil, 2009). In studies of 23,000 people from 26 cultures around the world, women more than men reported themselves open to feelings (Costa et al., 2001). That helps explain the extremely strong perception that emotionality is "more true of women"— a perception expressed by nearly 100 percent of 18- to 29-year-old Americans (Newport, 2001). But the perception of women's emotionality also feeds—and is fed by—people's attributing women's emotionality to their disposition and men's to their circumstances: "She's emotional. He's having a bad day" (Barrett & Bliss-Moreau, 2009).

One exception: Anger strikes most people as a more masculine emotion. Quickly: Imagine an angry face. What gender is the person? If you're like 3 in 4 Arizona State University students, you imagined a male (Becker et al., 2007). The researchers also found that when a gender-neutral face was made to look angry, most people perceived it as male. If the face was smiling, they were more likely to perceive it as female (**FIGURE 42.2**).

When surveyed, women are also far more likely than men to describe themselves as empathic. If you have *empathy*, you identify with others and imagine what it must be like to walk in their shoes. You rejoice with those who rejoice and weep with those who weep. Children and adults who skillfully infer others' thoughts and feelings tend to enjoy positive peer relationships (Gleason et al., 2009).

Obvious emotions Graphic novel authors use facial expressions and other design elements to express emotion, reducing the need to explain how the characters are feeling.

Figure 42.2

Male or female? Researchers manipulated a gender-neutral face. People were more likely to see it as a male when it wore an angry expression, and as a female when it wore a smile (Becker et al., 2007).

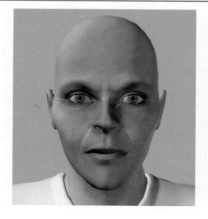
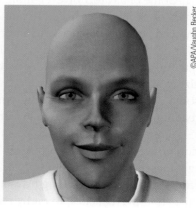

Physiological measures of empathy, such as one's heart rate while seeing another's distress, confirm a gender gap, though a smaller one than is indicated in survey self-reports (Eisenberg & Lennon, 1983; Rueckert et al., 2010). Females are also more likely to *express* empathy—to cry and to report distress when observing someone in distress. As **FIGURE 42.3** shows, this gender difference was clear in videotapes of male and female students watching film clips that were sad (children with a dying parent), happy (slapstick comedy), or frightening (a man nearly falling off the ledge of a tall building) (Kring & Gordon, 1998). Women also tend to experience emotional events, such as viewing pictures of mutilation, more deeply, with more brain activation in areas sensitive to emotion. And they are better at remembering the scenes three weeks later (Canli et al., 2002).

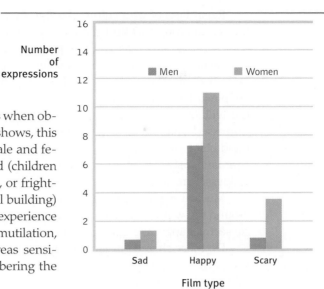

Figure 42.3

Gender and expressiveness
Male and female film viewers did not differ dramatically in self-reported emotions or physiological responses. But the women's faces *showed* much more emotion. (From Kring & Gordon, 1998.)

Culture and Emotional Expression

42-2 How are nonverbal expressions of emotion understood within and across cultures?

The meaning of *gestures* varies with the culture. Former U.S. President Richard Nixon learned this while traveling in Brazil; he made the North American "A-OK" sign, not realizing it was a crude insult to Brazilians. The importance of cultural definitions of gestures and other body language was again demonstrated in 1968, when North Korea publicized photos of supposedly happy officers from a captured U.S. Navy spy ship. In the photo, three men had raised their middle finger, telling their captors it was a "Hawaiian good luck sign" (Fleming & Scott, 1991).

Do facial expressions also have different meanings in different cultures? To find out, two investigative teams showed photographs of various facial expressions to people in different parts of the world and asked them to guess the emotion (Ekman et al., 1975, 1987, 1994; Izard, 1977, 1994). You can try this matching task yourself by pairing the six emotions with the six faces of **FIGURE 42.4**.

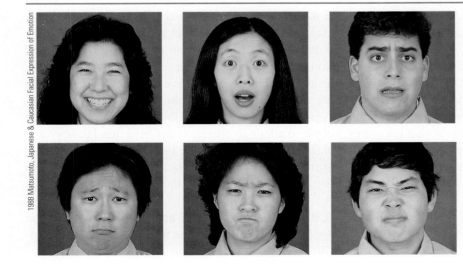

1988 Matsumoto, Japanese & Caucasian Facial Expression of Emotion

Figure 42.4

Culture-specific or culturally universal expressions?
As people of differing cultures and races, do our faces speak differing languages? Which face expresses disgust? Anger? Fear? Happiness? Sadness? Surprise? (From Matsumoto & Ekman, 1989.) See inverted answers below.

From left to right, top to bottom: happiness, surprise, fear, sadness, anger, disgust.

Regardless of your cultural background, you probably did pretty well. A smile's a smile the world around. Ditto for anger, and to a lesser extent the other basic expressions (Elfenbein & Ambady, 1999). (There is no culture where people frown when they are happy.)

Facial expressions do convey some nonverbal accents that provide clues to one's culture (Marsh et al., 2003). Thus data from 182 studies show slightly enhanced accuracy when people judge emotions from their own culture (Elfenbein & Ambady, 2002, 2003a,b). Still, the telltale signs of emotion generally cross cultures. The world over, children cry when distressed, shake their heads when defiant, and smile when they are happy. So, too, with blind children who have never seen a face (Eibl-Eibesfeldt, 1971). People blind from birth spontaneously exhibit the common facial expressions associated with such emotions as joy, sadness, fear, and anger (Galati et al., 1997).

Musical expressions also cross cultures. Happy and sad music feels happy and sad around the world. Whether you live in an African village or a European city, fast-paced music seems happy, and slow-paced music seems sadder (Fritz et al., 2009).

Do these shared emotional categories reflect shared cultural experiences, such as movies and TV broadcasts seen around the world? Apparently not. Paul Ekman and his team asked isolated people in New Guinea to respond to such statements as, "Pretend your child has died." When North American collegians viewed the taped responses, they easily read the New Guineans' facial reactions.

So we can say that facial muscles speak a universal language. This discovery would not have surprised Charles Darwin (1809–1882) who argued that in prehistoric times, before our ancestors communicated in words, they communicated threats, greetings, and submission with facial expressions. Their shared expressions helped them survive (Hess & Thibault, 2009). A sneer, for example, retains elements of an animal baring its teeth in a snarl. Emotional expressions may enhance our survival in other ways, too. Surprise raises the eyebrows and widens the eyes, enabling us to take in more information. Disgust wrinkles the nose, closing it from foul odors.

Smiles are social as well as emotional events. Bowlers seldom smile when they score a strike; they smile when they turn to face their companions (Jones et al., 1991; Kraut & Johnston, 1979). Euphoric Olympic gold-medal winners typically don't smile when they are awaiting their ceremony. But they wear broad grins when interacting with officials and facing the crowd and cameras (Fernández-Dols & Ruiz-Belda, 1995). Thus, a glimpse at competitors' spontaneous expressions following an Olympic judo competition gives a very good clue to who won, no matter their country (Matsumoto et al., 2006). Even natively blind athletes, who have never observed smiles, display the same social smiles in such situations (Matsumoto & Willingham, 2009).

Although we share a universal facial language, it has been adaptive for us to interpret faces in particular contexts (**FIGURE 42.5**). People judge an angry face set in a frightening situation as afraid. They judge a fearful face set in a painful situation as pained (Carroll & Russell, 1996). Movie directors harness this phenomenon by creating contexts and soundtracks that amplify our perceptions of particular emotions.

Although cultures share a universal facial language for basic emotions, they differ in how *much* emotion they express. Those that encourage individuality, as in Western Europe, Australia, New Zealand, and North America, display mostly visible emotions (van Hemert et al., 2007). Those that encourage people to adjust to others, as in China, tend to have less visible displays of personal emotions (Matsumoto et al., 2009; Tsai et al., 2007). In Japan, people infer emotion more from the surrounding context. Moreover, the mouth, which is so expressive in North Americans, conveys less emotion than do the telltale eyes (Masuda et al., 2008; Yuki et al., 2007).

Cultural differences also exist *within* nations. The Irish and their Irish-American descendants tend to be more expressive than Scandinavians and their Scandinavian-

Figure 42.5

We read faces in context
Whether we perceive the man in the top row as disgusted or angry depends on which body his face appears on (Aviezer et al., 2008). In the second row, tears on a face make its expression seem sadder (Provine et al., 2009).

American descendants (Tsai & Chentsova-Dutton, 2003). And that reminds us of a familiar lesson: Like most psychological events, emotion is best understood not only as a biological and cognitive phenomenon, but also as a social-cultural phenomenon.

The Effects of Facial Expressions

42-3 How do our facial expressions influence our feelings?

As William James (1890) struggled with feelings of depression and grief, he came to believe that we can control emotions by going "through the outward movements" of any emotion we want to experience. "To feel cheerful," he advised, "sit up cheerfully, look around cheerfully, and act as if cheerfulness were already there."

Studies of the emotional effects of facial expressions reveal precisely what James might have predicted. Expressions not only communicate emotion, they also amplify and regulate it. In *The Expression of the Emotions in Man and Animals,* Charles Darwin (1872) contended that "the free expression by outward signs of an emotion intensifies it. . . . He who gives way to violent gestures will increase his rage."

Was Darwin right? You can test his hypothesis: Fake a big grin. Now scowl. Can you feel the "smile therapy" difference? Participants in dozens of experiments have felt a difference. For example, James Laird and his colleagues (1974, 1984, 1989) subtly induced students to make a frowning expression by asking them to "contract these muscles" and "pull your brows together" (supposedly to help the researchers attach facial electrodes). The results? The students reported feeling a little angry. So, too, for other basic emotions. For example, people reported feeling more fear than anger, disgust, or sadness when made to construct a fearful expression: "Raise your eyebrows. And open your eyes wide. Move your whole head back, so that your chin is tucked in a little bit, and let your mouth relax and hang open a little" (Duclos et al., 1989).

"Whenever I feel afraid
I hold my head erect
And whistle a happy tune."
-RICHARD RODGERS AND OSCAR HAMMERSTEIN, THE KING AND I, 1958

facial feedback effect
the tendency of facial muscle states to trigger corresponding feelings such as fear, anger, or happiness.

This **facial feedback effect** has been repeated many times, in many places, for many basic emotions (**FIGURE 42.6**). Just activating one of the smiling muscles by holding a pen in the teeth (rather than with the lips, which activates a frowning muscle) is enough to make cartoons seem more amusing (Strack et al., 1988). A heartier smile—made not just with the mouth but with raised cheeks that crinkle the eyes—enhances positive feelings even more when you are reacting to something pleasant or funny (Soussignan, 2001). Smile warmly on the outside and you feel better on the inside. When smiling, you will even more quickly understand sentences that describe pleasant events (Havas et al., 2007). Scowl and the whole world seems to scowl back.

So your face is more than a billboard that displays your feelings; it also feeds your feelings. No wonder depressed patients reportedly feel better after between-the-eyebrows Botox injections that paralyze the frowning muscles (Finzi & Wasserman, 2006). Two months after the treatment, 9 of the 10 nonfrowning patients given this treatment were no longer depressed. Follow-up studies have found that Botox paralysis of the frowning muscles slows people's reading of sadness or anger-related sentences, and it slows activity in emotion-related brain circuits (Havas et al., 2010; Hennenlotter et al., 2008). In such ways, Botox smooths life's emotional wrinkles.

Other researchers have observed a similar *behavior feedback* phenomenon (Snodgrass et al., 1986). You can duplicate the participants' experience: Walk for a few minutes with short, shuffling steps, keeping your eyes downcast. Now walk around taking long strides, with your arms swinging and your eyes looking straight ahead. Can you feel your mood shift? Going through the motions awakens the emotions.

Likewise, people perceive ambiguous behaviors differently depending on which finger they move up and down while reading a story. (This was said to be a study of the effect of using finger muscles "located near the reading muscles on the motor cortex.") If participants read the story while moving an extended middle finger, the story behaviors seemed more hostile. If read with a thumb up, they seemed more positive. Hostile gestures prime hostile perceptions (Chandler & Schwarz, 2009; Goldin-Meadow & Beilock, 2010).

You can use your understanding of feedback effects to become more empathic: Let your own face mimic another person's expression. Acting as another acts helps us feel what another feels (Vaughn & Lanzetta, 1981). Indeed, natural mimicry of others' emotions helps explain why emotions are contagious (Dimberg et al., 2000; Neumann & Strack, 2000). Primates also ape one another, and such synchronized expressions help bond them (and us) together (de Waal, 2009). One social worker with Moebius syndrome, a rare facial paralysis disorder, struggled to make emotional connections with Hurricane Katrina refugees. When people made a sad expression, "I wasn't able to return it. I tried to do so with words and tone of voice, but it was no use. Stripped of the facial expression, the emotion just dies there, unshared" (Carey, 2010).

Figure 42.6

How to make people smile without telling them to smile
Do as Kazuo Mori and Hideko Mori (2009) did with students in Japan: Attach rubber bands to the sides of the face with adhesive bandages, and then run them either over the head or under the chin. (1) Based on the facial feedback effect, how might students report feeling when the rubber bands raise their cheeks as though in a smile? (2) How might students report feeling when the rubber bands pull their cheeks downward?

ANSWERS: (1) Most students report feeling more happy than sad when their cheeks are raised upward. (2) Most students report feeling more sad than happy when their cheeks are pulled downward.

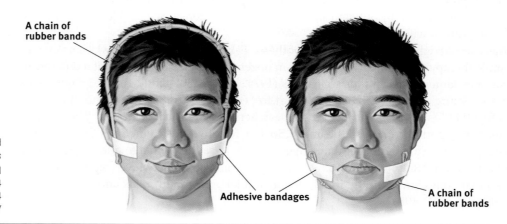

A chain of rubber bands

Adhesive bandages

A chain of rubber bands

* * *

How do our emotions, personality, attitudes, and behaviors influence our risk of disease? What can we do to prevent illness and promote health? To study how stress and healthy and unhealthy behaviors influence health and illness, psychologists and physicians created the interdisciplinary field of *behavioral medicine*, integrating behavioral and medical knowledge. **Health psychology** provides psychology's contribution to behavioral medicine. Let's consider some of psychology's findings on stress and ways of coping with it.

> **health psychology** a subfield of psychology that provides psychology's contribution to behavioral medicine.

Before You Move On

▶ **ASK YOURSELF**

Can you think of one situation in which you would like to change the way you feel, and create a simple plan for doing so? For instance, if you would like to feel more cheerful on your way to class tomorrow morning rather than dragging yourself there, you might try walking briskly—with head held high and a pleasant expression on your face.

▶ **TEST YOURSELF**

Who tends to express more emotion—men or women? How do we know the answer to that question?

Answers to the Test Yourself questions can be found in Appendix E at the end of the book.

Module 42 Review

  How do we communicate nonverbally? How do the genders differ in this capacity?

- Much of our communication is through body movements, facial expressions, and voice tones. Even seconds-long filmed slices of behavior can reveal feelings.

- Women tend to read emotional cues more easily and to be more empathic.

  How are nonverbal expressions of emotion understood within and across cultures?

- The meaning of gestures varies with culture, but facial expressions, such as those of happiness and fear, are common the world over.

- Cultures also differ in the amount of emotion they express.

  How do our facial expressions influence our feelings?

- Research on the *facial feedback effect* shows that our facial expressions can trigger emotional feelings and signal our body to respond accordingly.

- We also mimic others' expressions, which helps us empathize.

Multiple-Choice Questions

1. What do we call the tendency of facial muscle states to trigger corresponding feelings such as fear, anger, or happiness?
   a. Culture-specific expression
   b. Moebius syndrome
   c. Botox
   d. Facial feedback effect
   e. Culturally universal expression

2. Which of the following statements is most accurate regarding emotion?
   a. Smiles are neither social nor emotional events.
   b. Inhabitants of individualist countries are more likely to display nonverbal emotions than inhabitants of collectivist countries.
   c. Mouths convey more emotion than eyes.
   d. Natively blind people who have never seen a smile will never generate a smile.
   e. Cultures share a universal facial language for basic emotions.

3. Which subfield of psychology provides psychology's contribution to behavioral medicine?
   a. Cognitive
   b. Health
   c. Clinical
   d. Educational
   e. Community

Practice FRQs

1. Name the phenomenon describing the impact facial expressions can have on our disposition, and give an example.

Answer

1 point: The facial feedback effect.

1 point: For example, smiling makes you feel happy and frowning makes you feel a little angry.

2. Name four pieces of evidence that suggest women are more empathic than men.

(4 points)

Module 43

Stress and Health

Module Learning Objective

43-1 Identify events that provoke stress responses, and describe how we respond and adapt to stress.

How often do you experience stress in your daily life? Never? Rarely? Sometimes? Or frequently? When pollsters put a similar question to college students, some 85 percent recalled experiencing stress during the last three months—and most said it had disrupted their schoolwork at least once (AP, 2009). On entering college or university, 18 percent of men and 41 percent of women reported having been "frequently overwhelmed" by all they had to do during the past year (Pryor et al., 2012).

For many students, the high school years, with their new relationships and more demanding challenges, prove stressful. Deadlines become relentless and intense at the end of each term. The time demands of volunteering, sports, music and theater, work, college prep courses, and college applications combine with occasional family tensions and success pressures. Sometimes it's enough to give you a headache or disrupt sleep.

Stress often strikes without warning. Imagine being 21-year-old Ben Carpenter on the world's wildest and fastest wheelchair ride. As he crossed an intersection on a sunny summer afternoon in 2007, the light changed. A large truck, whose driver didn't see him, started moving into the intersection. As they bumped, Ben's wheelchair turned to face forward, and its handles got stuck in the truck's grille. Off they went, the driver unable to hear Ben's cries for help. As they sped down the highway about an hour from my home, passing motorists caught the bizarre sight of a truck pushing a wheelchair at 50 miles per hour and started calling 911. (The first caller: "You are not going to believe this. There is a semi truck pushing a guy in a wheelchair on Red Arrow highway!") Lucky for Ben, one passerby was an undercover police officer. Pulling a quick U-turn, he followed the truck to its destination a couple of miles from where the wild ride had started, and informed the disbelieving driver that he had a passenger hooked in his grille. "It was very scary," said Ben, who has muscular dystrophy. In this section, we explore stress—what it is and how it affects us.

FYI

In Module 84, we take a close look at some ways we can reduce the stress in our lives, so that we can flourish in both body and mind.

Extreme stress Ben Carpenter experienced the wildest of rides after his wheelchair got stuck in a truck's grille.

Stress: Some Basic Concepts

43-1   What events provoke stress responses, and how do we respond and adapt to stress?

Stress is a slippery concept. We sometimes use the word informally to describe threats or challenges ("Ben was under a lot of stress"), and at other times our responses ("Ben experienced acute stress"). To a psychologist, the dangerous truck ride was a *stressor.* Ben's physical and emotional responses were a *stress reaction.* And the process by which he related to the threat was *stress.* Thus, **stress** is the process of appraising and responding to a threatening or challenging event (**FIGURE 43.1**). Stress arises less from events themselves than from how we appraise them (Lazarus, 1998). One person, alone in a house, ignores its creaking sounds and experiences no stress; someone else suspects an intruder and becomes alarmed. One person regards a new job as a welcome challenge; someone else appraises it as risking failure.

> **stress** the process by which we perceive and respond to certain events, called *stressors,* that we appraise as threatening or challenging.

When short-lived, or when perceived as challenges, stressors can have positive effects. A momentary stress can mobilize the immune system for fending off infections and healing wounds (Segerstrom, 2007). Stress also arouses and motivates us to conquer problems. In a Gallup World Poll, those who were stressed but not depressed reported being energized and satisfied with their lives—the opposite of the lethargy of those depressed but not stressed (Ng et al., 2009). Championship athletes, successful entertainers, and great teachers and leaders all thrive and excel when aroused by a challenge (Blascovich et al., 2004). Having conquered cancer or rebounded from a lost job, some people emerge with stronger self-esteem and a deepened spirituality and sense of purpose. Indeed, some stress early in life is conducive to later emotional resilience (Landauer & Whiting, 1979). Adversity can beget growth.

Extreme or prolonged stress can harm us. Children who suffer severe or prolonged abuse are later at risk of chronic disease (Repetti et al., 2002). Troops who had posttraumatic stress reactions to heavy combat in the Vietnam war later suffered greatly elevated rates of circulatory, digestive, respiratory, and infectious diseases (Boscarino, 1997). People who lose their jobs, especially later in their working life, are at increased risk of heart problems and death (Gallo et al., 2006; Sullivan & von Wachter, 2009).

So there is an interplay between our heads and our health. Before exploring that interplay, let's look more closely at stressors and stress reactions.

Stressors—Things That Push Our Buttons

Stressors fall into three main types: catastrophes, significant life changes, and daily hassles. All can be toxic.

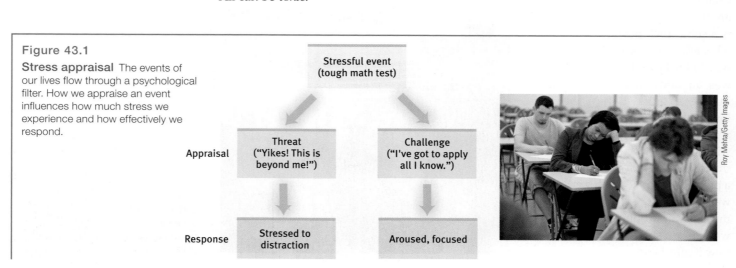

Figure 43.1

Stress appraisal The events of our lives flow through a psychological filter. How we appraise an event influences how much stress we experience and how effectively we respond.

Stressful event
(tough math test)

Appraisal

Threat
("Yikes! This is beyond me!")

Challenge
("I've got to apply all I know.")

Response

Stressed to distraction

Aroused, focused

Roy Mehta/Getty Images

CATASTROPHES

Catastrophes are unpredictable large-scale events, such as wars, earthquakes, floods, wildfires, and famines. Nearly everyone appraises catastrophes as threatening. We often give aid and comfort to one another after such events, but damage to emotional and physical health can be significant. In surveys taken in the three weeks after the 9/11 terrorist attacks, for example, two-thirds of Americans said they were having some trouble concentrating and sleeping (Wahlberg, 2001). In the New York area, people were especially likely to report such symptoms, and sleeping pill prescriptions rose by a reported 28 percent (HMHL, 2002a; NSF, 2001). In the four months after Hurricane Katrina, New Orleans' suicide rate reportedly tripled (Saulny, 2006).

Toxic stress Unpredictable large-scale events, such as the severe earthquake that devastated Haiti in 2010, trigger significant levels of stress-related ills. When an earthquake struck Los Angeles in 1994, sudden-death heart attacks increased fivefold. Most occurred in the first two hours after the quake and near its center and were unrelated to physical exertion (Muller & Verrier, 1996).

For those who respond to catastrophes by relocating to another country, the stress is twofold. The trauma of uprooting and family separation combine with the challenges of adjusting to the new culture's language, ethnicity, climate, and social norms (Pipher, 2002; Williams & Berry, 1991). In the first half-year, before their morale begins to rebound, newcomers often experience culture shock and deteriorating well-being (Markovizky & Samid, 2008). Such relocations may become increasingly common because of climate change in years to come.

SIGNIFICANT LIFE CHANGES

Life transitions are often keenly felt. Even happy events, such as getting married, can be stressful. Other changes—graduating from high school, leaving home for college, losing a job, having a loved one die—often happen during young adulthood. The stress of those years was clear in a survey in which 15,000 Canadian adults were asked whether "You are trying to take on too many things at once." Responses indicated highest stress levels among young adults (Statistics Canada, 1999). Young adult stress appeared again when 650,000 Americans were asked if they had experienced a lot of stress "yesterday" (**FIGURE 43.2**).

Some psychologists study the health effects of life changes by following people over time. Others compare the life changes recalled by those who have or have not suffered a specific health problem, such as a heart attack. These studies indicate that people recently widowed, fired, or divorced are more vulnerable to disease (Dohrenwend et al., 1982; Strully, 2009). In one Finnish study of 96,000 widowed people, their risk of death doubled in the week following their partner's death (Kaprio et al., 1987). Experiencing a cluster of crises—losing a job, home, and partner, for example—puts one even more at risk.

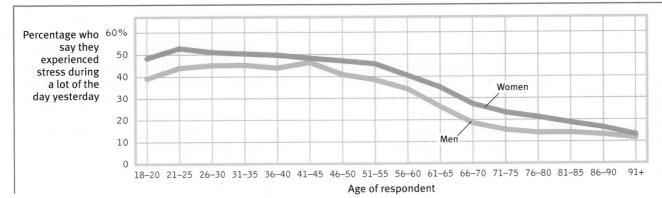

Percentage who say they experienced stress during a lot of the day yesterday

Age of respondent

Figure 43.2

Age and stress
A Gallup-Healthways survey of more than 650,000 Americans during 2008 and 2009 found daily stress highest among younger adults (Newport & Pelham, 2009).

DAILY HASSLES

Events don't have to remake our lives to cause stress. Stress also comes from *daily hassles*—rush-hour traffic, aggravating siblings, long lunch lines, too many things to do, family frustrations, and friends who don't respond to calls or texts (Kohn & Macdonald, 1992; Repetti et al., 2009; Ruffin, 1993). Some people can simply shrug off such hassles. For others, however, the everyday annoyances add up and take a toll on health and well-being.

Many people face more significant daily hassles. As the Great Recession of 2008–2009 bottomed out, Americans' most oft-cited stressors related to money (76 percent), work (70 percent), and the economy (65 percent) (APA, 2010). Such stressors are well-known to residents of impoverished areas, where many people routinely face inadequate income, unemployment, solo parenting, and overcrowding.

Prolonged stress takes a toll on our cardiovascular system. Daily pressures may be compounded by anti-gay prejudice or racism, which—like other stressors—can have both psychological and physical consequences (Pascoe & Richman, 2009; Rostosky et al., 2010; Swim et al., 2009). Thinking that some of the people you encounter each day will dislike you, distrust you, or doubt your abilities makes daily life stressful. Such stress takes a toll on the health of many African-Americans, driving up blood pressure levels (Ong et al., 2009; Mays et al., 2007).

The Stress Response System

Medical interest in stress dates back to Hippocrates (460–377 b.c.e.). In the 1920s, Walter Cannon (1929) confirmed that the stress response is part of a unified mind-body system. He observed that extreme cold, lack of oxygen, and emotion-arousing events all trigger an outpouring of the stress hormones epinephrine and norepinephrine from the core of the adrenal glands. When alerted by any of a number of brain pathways, the sympathetic nervous system (see Figure 41.4) increases heart rate and respiration, diverts blood from digestion to the skeletal muscles, dulls feelings of pain, and releases sugar and fat from the body's stores. All this prepares the body for the wonderfully adaptive response that Cannon called *fight or flight.*

Since Cannon's time, physiologists have identified an additional stress response system. On orders from the cerebral cortex (via the hypothalamus and pituitary gland), the outer part of the adrenal glands secretes *glucocorticoid* stress hormones such as *cortisol.* The two systems work at different speeds, explains biologist Robert Sapolsky (2003): "In a fight-or-flight scenario, epinephrine is the one handing out guns; glucocorticoids are the ones drawing up blueprints for new aircraft carriers needed for the war effort." The epinephrine guns were firing at high speed during an experiment inadvertently conducted on a British Airways San Francisco to London flight. Three hours after takeoff, a mistakenly played message told passengers the plane was about to crash into the sea. Although the flight crew immediately recognized the error and tried to calm the terrified passengers, several required medical assistance (Associated Press, 1999).

Canadian scientist Hans Selye's (1936, 1976) 40 years of research on stress extended Cannon's findings. His studies of animals' reactions to various stressors, such as electric shock and surgery, helped make stress a major concept in both psychology and medicine. Selye proposed that the body's adaptive response to stress is so general that, like a single burglar alarm, it sounds, no matter what intrudes. He named this response the **general adaptation syndrome (GAS),** and he saw it as a three-phase process (**FIGURE 43.3**). Let's say you suffer a physical or an emotional trauma. In Phase 1, you have an *alarm reaction,* as your sympathetic nervous system is suddenly activated. Your heart rate zooms. Blood is diverted to your skeletal muscles. You feel the faintness of shock.

With your resources mobilized, you are now ready to fight back. During Phase 2, *resistance,* your temperature, blood pressure, and respiration remain high. Your adrenal glands

> "You've got to know when to hold 'em; know when to fold 'em. Know when to walk away, and know when to run." -KENNY ROGERS, "THE GAMBLER," 1978

general adaptation syndrome (GAS) Selye's concept of the body's adaptive response to stress in three phases—alarm, resistance, exhaustion.

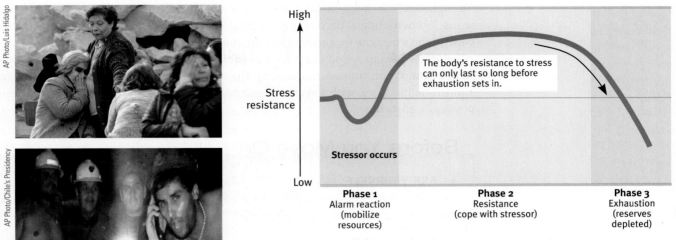

The body's resistance to stress can only last so long before exhaustion sets in.

High

Stress resistance

Low

Stressor occurs

Phase 1
Alarm reaction
(mobilize
resources)

Phase 2
Resistance
(cope with stressor)

Phase 3
Exhaustion
(reserves
depleted)

Figure 43.3

Selye's general adaptation syndrome When a gold and copper mine in Chile collapsed in 2010, family and friends rushed to the scene, fearing the worst. Many of those holding vigil outside the mine were nearly exhausted with the stress of waiting and worrying when, after 18 days, they received news that all 33 of the miners inside were alive and well.

pump hormones into your bloodstream. You are fully engaged, summoning all your resources to meet the challenge.

As time passes, with no relief from stress, your body's reserves begin to run out. You have reached Phase 3, *exhaustion*. With exhaustion, you become more vulnerable to illness or even, in extreme cases, collapse and death.

Selye's basic point: Although the human body copes well with temporary stress, prolonged stress can damage it. The brain's production of new neurons slows and some neural circuits degenerate (Dias-Ferreira et al., 2009; Mirescu & Gould, 2006). One study found shortening of *telomeres,* pieces of DNA at the ends of chromosomes, in women who suffered enduring stress as caregivers for children with serious disorders (Epel et al., 2004). Telomere shortening is a normal part of the aging process; when telomeres get too short, the cell can no longer divide and it ultimately dies. The most stressed women had cells that looked a decade older than their chronological age, which may help explain why severe stress seems to age people. Even fearful, easily stressed rats have been found to die sooner (after about 600 days) than their more confident siblings, which average 700-day life spans (Cavigelli & McClintock, 2003).

Fortunately, there are other options for dealing with stress. One is a common response to a loved one's death: Withdraw. Pull back. Conserve energy. Faced with an extreme disaster, such as a ship sinking, some people become paralyzed by fear. Another stress response, found especially among women, is to seek and give support (Taylor et al., 2000, 2006). This **tend-and-befriend** response is demonstrated in the outpouring of help after natural disasters.

Facing stress, men more often than women tend to socially withdraw, turn to alcohol, or become aggressive. Women more often respond to stress by nurturing and banding together. This may in part be due to *oxytocin,* a stress-moderating hormone associated with pair bonding in animals and released by cuddling, massage, and breast feeding in humans

"You may be suffering from what's known as full-nest syndrome."

tend-and-befriend response
under stress, people (especially women) often provide support to others (tend) and bond with and seek support from others (befriend).

(Campbell, 2010; Taylor, 2006). Gender differences in stress responses are reflected in brain scans: Women's brains become more active in areas important for face processing and empathy; men's become less active (Mather et al., 2010).

It often pays to spend our resources in fighting or fleeing an external threat. But we do so at a cost. When stress is momentary, the cost is small. When stress persists, we may pay a much higher price, with lowered resistance to infections and other threats to mental and physical well-being.

Before You Move On

▶ **ASK YOURSELF**

How often is your stress response system activated? What are some of the things that have triggered a fight-or-flight response for you?

▶ **TEST YOURSELF**

What two processes happen simultaneously when our stress response system is activated? What happens if the stress is continuous?

Answers to the Test Yourself questions can be found in Appendix E at the end of the book.

Module 43 Review

 43-1 What events provoke stress responses, and how do we respond and adapt to stress?

- *Stress* is the process by which we appraise and respond to stressors (catastrophic events, significant life changes, and daily hassles) that challenge or threaten us.

- Walter Cannon viewed the stress response as a "fight-or-flight" system.

- Later researchers identified an additional stress-response system in which the adrenal glands secrete glucocorticoid stress hormones.

- Hans Selye proposed a general three-phrase (alarm-resistance-exhaustion) *general adaptation syndrome (GAS)*.

- Prolonged stress can damage neurons, hastening cell death.

- Facing stress, women may have a *tend-and-befriend* response; men may withdraw socially, turn to alcohol, or become aggressive.

Multiple-Choice Questions

1. Which of the following is an example of stress?

   a. Ray is tense and anxious as he has to decide which college to attend.
   b. Sunga is assigned an extra shift at work.
   c. Joe's parents are allowing him to stay home alone while they go away for a weekend.
   d. Linda remembers to repay a friend the $10 she owes her.
   e. Enrico learns of a traffic accident on the Interstate.

2. The general adaptation syndrome (GAS) begins with

   a. resistance.   d. alarm.
   b. appraisal.   e. challenge.
   c. exhaustion.

3. Which of the following is likely to result from the release of oxytocin?

   a. A fight-or-flight response   d. Elevated hunger
   b. A tend-and-befriend response   e. Exhaustion
   c. Social isolation

Practice FRQs

1. Xavier has a huge math test coming up next Tuesday. Explain two ways appraisal can determine how stress will influence his test performance.

Answer

1 point: If Xavier interprets the test as a challenge he will be aroused and focused in a way that could improve his test performance.

1 point: If Xavier interprets the test as a threat he will be distracted by stress in a way that is likely to harm his test performance.

2. Name and briefly describe the three phases of Hans Selye's general adaptation syndrome (GAS).

(3 points)

Module 44

Stress and Illness

Module Learning Objectives

44-1 Describe how stress makes us more vulnerable to disease.

44-2 Explain why some of us are more prone than others to coronary heart disease.

 44-1 How does stress make us more vulnerable to disease?

Not so long ago, the term *psychosomatic* described psychologically caused physical symptoms. In common usage, the term came to mean that the symptoms were unreal—"merely" psychosomatic. To avoid such connotations and to better describe the genuine physiological effects of psychological states, most experts today refer instead to stress-related **psychophysiological illnesses,** such as hypertension and some headaches. Stress also leaves us less able to fight off disease. The field of **psychoneuroimmunology** studies these mind-body interactions (Kiecolt-Glaser, 2009). This awkward name makes sense when said slowly: Your thoughts and feelings *(psycho)* influence your brain *(neuro),* which influences the endocrine hormones that affect your disease-fighting *immune* system. And this field is the study of *(ology)* those interactions.

Hundreds of experiments reveal the nervous and endocrine systems' influence on the immune system (Sternberg, 2009). You can think of the immune system as a complex surveillance system. When it functions properly, it keeps you healthy by isolating and destroying bacteria, viruses, and other invaders. Four types of cells are active in these search-and-destroy missions (**FIGURE 44.1**). Two are types of white blood cells, called **lymphocytes.** *B lymphocytes* mature in the *b*one marrow and release antibodies that fight bacterial infections. *T lymphocytes* form in the *t*hymus and other lymphatic tissue and attack cancer cells, viruses, and foreign substances—even "good" ones, such as transplanted organs. The third agent is the *macrophage* ("big eater"), which identifies, pursues, and ingests harmful invaders and worn-out cells. And, finally, the *natural killer cells* (NK cells) pursue diseased cells (such as those infected by viruses or cancer). Your age, nutrition, genetics, body temperature, and stress all influence your immune system's activity.

When your immune system doesn't function properly, it can err in two directions. Responding too strongly, it may attack the body's own tissues, causing some forms of arthritis or an allergic reaction. Underreacting, it may allow a dormant herpes virus to erupt or cancer cells to multiply. Women are immunologically stronger than men, making them less susceptible to infections, but this very strength also makes them more susceptible to self-attacking diseases, such as lupus and multiple sclerosis (Morell, 1995; Pido-Lopez et al., 2001).

Your immune system is not a headless horseman. The brain regulates the secretion of stress hormones, which suppresses the disease-fighting lymphocytes. Immune suppression appears when animals are stressed by physical restraints, unavoidable electric shocks, noise, crowding, cold water, social defeat, or separation from their mothers (Maier et al., 1994). One six-month study monitored immune responses in 43 monkeys (Cohen et al., 1992).

psychophysiological illness literally, "mind-body" illness; any stress-related physical illness, such as hypertension and some headaches.

psychoneuroimmunology the study of how psychological, neural, and endocrine processes together affect the immune system and resulting health.

lymphocytes the two types of white blood cells that are part of the body's immune system: *B lymphocytes* form in the *b*one marrow and release antibodies that fight bacterial infections; *T lymphocytes* form in the *t*hymus and other lymphatic tissue and attack cancer cells, viruses, and foreign substances.

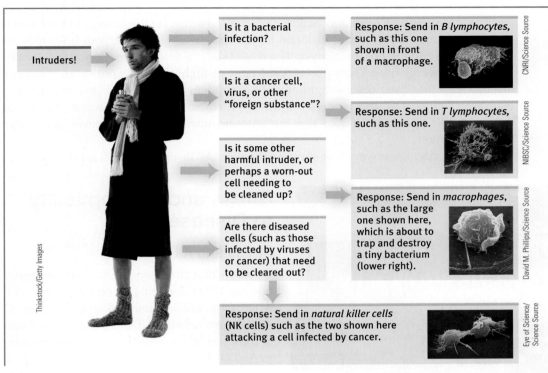

Figure 44.1

A simplified view of immune responses

Intruders!

Is it a bacterial infection? → Response: Send in *B lymphocytes*, such as this one shown in front of a macrophage. *CNRI/Science Source*

Is it a cancer cell, virus, or other "foreign substance"? → Response: Send in *T lymphocytes*, such as this one. *NIBSC/Science Source*

Is it some other harmful intruder, or perhaps a worn-out cell needing to be cleaned up? → Response: Send in *macrophages*, such as the large one shown here, which is about to trap and destroy a tiny bacterium (lower right). *David M. Phillips/Science Source*

Are there diseased cells (such as those infected by viruses or cancer) that need to be cleared out? → Response: Send in *natural killer cells* (NK cells) such as the two shown here attacking a cell infected by cancer. *Eye of Science/Science Source*

Thinkstock/Getty Images

Twenty-one were stressed by being housed with new roommates—three or four new monkeys—each month. By the end of the experiment, the socially disrupted monkeys' immune systems were weaker than those of monkeys left in stable groups. Human immune systems react similarly. Two examples:

- *Surgical wounds heal more slowly in stressed people.* In one experiment, dental students received punch wounds (precise small holes punched in the skin). Compared with wounds placed during summer vacation, those placed three days before a major exam healed 40 percent more slowly (Kiecolt-Glaser et al., 1998). Marriage conflict also slows punch-wound healing (Kiecolt-Glaser et al., 2005).

- *Stressed people are more vulnerable to colds.* Researchers dropped a cold virus into the noses of stressed and relatively unstressed people (**FIGURE 44.2**). Among those living stress-filled lives, 47 percent developed colds. Among those living relatively free of stress, only 27 percent did. In follow-up research, the happiest and most relaxed people were likewise markedly less vulnerable to an experimentally delivered cold virus (Cohen et al., 2003, 2006). Other studies reveal that major life stress increases the risk of a respiratory infection (Pedersen et al., 2010).

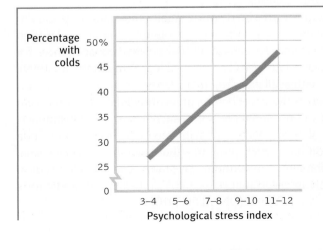

Percentage with colds

50%
45
40
35
30
25
0

3–4 5–6 7–8 9–10 11–12

Psychological stress index

LAURENT BSIP/YAKOU/SCIENCE PHOTO LIBRARY

Figure 44.2

Stress and colds In an experiment by Sheldon Cohen and colleagues (1991), people with the highest life stress scores were also most vulnerable when exposed to an experimentally delivered cold virus.

The stress effect on immunity makes physiological sense. It takes energy to track down invaders, produce swelling, and maintain fevers. Thus, when diseased, your body reduces muscular energy output by inactivity and increased sleep. Stress does the opposite. It creates a competing energy need. During an aroused fight-or-flight reaction, your stress responses divert energy from your disease-fighting immune system and send it to your muscles and brain (see Figure 41.4). This renders you more vulnerable to illness. *The bottom line:* Stress does not make us sick, but it does alter our immune functioning, which leaves us less able to resist infection.

Let's consider some ways that stress might affect AIDS, cancer, and heart disease.

Africa is ground zero for AIDS In Ghana, the Ministry of Health uses these informative billboards as part of prevention efforts.

Stress and Susceptibility to Disease

Stress and AIDS

We know that stress suppresses immune functioning. What does this mean for people with AIDS *(acquired immune deficiency syndrome)*? As its name tells us, AIDS is an immune disorder, caused by the *human immunodeficiency virus (HIV)*. AIDS has become the world's fourth leading cause of death and Africa's number one killer.

Ironically, if a disease is spread by human contact (as AIDS is, through the exchange of bodily fluids, primarily semen and blood), and if it kills slowly (as AIDS does), it can be lethal to more people. Those who acquire HIV often spread it in the highly contagious first few weeks before they know they are infected. Worldwide, some 2.6 million people—slightly more than half of them women—became infected with HIV in 2009, often without their awareness (UNAIDS, 2010). Years after the initial infection, when AIDS appears, people have difficulty fighting off other diseases, such as pneumonia. More than 25 million people worldwide have died of AIDS (UNAIDS, 2010). (In the United States, where "only" a half-million of these fatalities have occurred, AIDS has killed more people than did combat in all the twentieth-century wars.)

Stress cannot give people AIDS. But could stress and negative emotions speed the transition from HIV infection to AIDS in someone already infected? Might stress predict a faster decline in those with AIDS? The answer to both questions seems to be *Yes* (Bower et al., 1998; Kiecolt-Glaser & Glaser, 1995; Leserman et al., 1999). HIV-infected men who experience stressful events, such as the loss of a partner, exhibit somewhat greater immune suppression and travel a faster course in this disease.

Would efforts to reduce stress help control the disease? Again, the answer appears to be *Yes.* Educational initiatives, bereavement support groups, cognitive therapy, relaxation training, and exercise programs that reduce stress have all had positive consequences for HIV-positive people (Baum & Posluszny, 1999; McCain et al., 2008; Schneiderman, 1999). But the benefits are small, compared with available drug treatments.

Although AIDS is now more treatable than ever before, preventing HIV infection is a far better option. This is the focus of many educational programs, such as the ABC (*a*bstinence, *b*eing faithful, *c*ondom use) program that has been used with seeming success in Uganda (Altman, 2004; USAID, 2004). In addition to such programs that seek to influence sexual norms and behaviors, today's "combination prevention" programs also include medical strategies (such as drugs and male circumcision that reduce HIV transmission) and efforts to reduce social inequalities that increase HIV risk (UNAIDS, 2010).

FYI

In North America and Western Europe, 74 percent of people with AIDS are men. In Sub-Saharan Africa, 60 percent of people with AIDS are women (UNAIDS, 2010).

Stress and Cancer

Stress does not create cancer cells. But in a healthy, functioning immune system, lymphocytes, macrophages, and NK cells search out and destroy cancer cells and cancer-damaged cells. If stress weakens the immune system, might this weaken a person's ability to fight off cancer? To explore a possible connection between stress and cancer, experimenters have implanted tumor cells in rodents or given them *carcinogens* (cancer-producing substances). They then exposed some rodents to uncontrollable stress, such as inescapable shocks, which weakened their immune systems. Those rodents were indeed more prone to developing cancer (Sklar & Anisman, 1981). Their tumors developed sooner and grew larger than in nonstressed rodents.

Does this stress-cancer link also hold with humans? The results are mixed. Some studies find that people are at increased risk for cancer within a year after experiencing depression, helplessness, or bereavement (Chida et al., 2008; Steptoe et al., 2010). In one large Swedish study, the risk of colon cancer was 5.5 times greater among people with a history of workplace stress than among those who reported no such problems. This difference was not attributable to group differences in age, smoking, drinking, or physical characteristics (Courtney et al., 1993). Other studies, however, have found no link between stress and human cancer (Coyne et al., 2010; Petticrew et al., 1999, 2002). Concentration camp survivors and former prisoners of war, for example, do not have elevated cancer rates.

One danger in hyping reports on emotions and cancer is that some patients may then blame themselves for their illness: "If only I had been more expressive, relaxed, and hopeful." A corollary danger is a "wellness macho" among the healthy, who take credit for their "healthy character" and lay a guilt trip on the ill: "She has cancer? That's what you get for holding your feelings in and being so nice." Dying thus becomes the ultimate failure.

It's important enough to repeat: *Stress does not create cancer cells.* At worst, it may affect their growth by weakening the body's natural defenses against multiplying malignant cells (Antoni & Lutgendorf, 2007). Although a relaxed, hopeful state may enhance these defenses, we should be aware of the thin line that divides science from wishful thinking. The powerful biological processes at work in advanced cancer or AIDS are not likely to be completely derailed by avoiding stress or maintaining a relaxed but determined spirit (Anderson, 2002; Kessler et al., 1991). And that explains why research consistently indicates that psychotherapy does not extend cancer patients' survival (Coyne et al., 2007, 2009; Coyne & Tennen, 2010).

Stress and Heart Disease

 Why are some of us more prone than others to coronary heart disease?

Stress is much more closely linked to **coronary heart disease,** North America's leading cause of death. In this disease, the blood vessels that nourish the heart muscle gradually close. Hypertension and a family history of the disease increase the risk of coronary heart disease. So do many behavioral factors (smoking, obesity, a high-fat diet, physical inactivity), physiological factors (an elevated cholesterol level), and psychological factors (stress responses and personality traits).

In some classic studies, Meyer Friedman, Ray Rosenman, and their colleagues tested the idea that stress increases vulnerability to heart disease by measuring the blood cholesterol level and clotting speed of 40 U.S. male tax accountants at different times of year (Friedman & Rosenman, 1974; Friedman & Ulmer, 1984). From January through March, the test results were completely normal. Then, as the accountants began scrambling to finish their clients' tax returns before the April 15 filing deadline, their cholesterol and clotting measures rose to dangerous levels. In May and June, with the deadline past, the measures returned to normal. Stress predicted heart attack risk for these men. The researchers' hunch had paid off, launching a classic nine-year study of more than 3000 healthy men, aged 35 to 59.

"I didn't give myself cancer."
-Mayor Barbara Boggs Sigmund (1939–1990), Princeton, New Jersey

FYI

When organic causes of illness are unknown, it is tempting to invent psychological explanations. Before the germ that causes tuberculosis (TB) was discovered, personality explanations of TB were popular (Sontag, 1978).

coronary heart disease
the clogging of the vessels that nourish the heart muscle; the leading cause of death in many developed countries.

Tony Freeman/Photo Edit

"The fire you kindle for your enemy often burns you more than him." -CHINESE PROVERB

Type A Friedman and Rosenman's term for competitive, hard-driving, impatient, verbally aggressive, and anger-prone people.

Type B Friedman and Rosenman's term for easygoing, relaxed people.

At the start of the study, the researchers interviewed each man for 15 minutes, noting his work and eating habits, manner of talking, and other behavioral patterns. Those who seemed the most reactive, competitive, hard-driving, impatient, time-conscious, supermotivated, verbally aggressive, and easily angered they called **Type A.** The roughly equal number who were more easygoing they called **Type B.** Which group do you suppose turned out to be the most coronary-prone?

Nine years later, 257 men had suffered heart attacks, and 69 percent of them were Type A. Moreover, not one of the "pure" Type Bs—the most mellow and laid back of their group—had suffered a heart attack.

As often happens in science, this exciting discovery provoked enormous public interest. But after that initial honeymoon period, researchers wanted to know more. Was the finding reliable? If so, what is the toxic component of the Type A profile: Time-consciousness? Competitiveness? Anger?

More than 700 studies have now explored possible psychological correlates or predictors of cardiovascular health (Chida & Hamer, 2008; Chida & Steptoe, 2009). These reveal that Type A's toxic core is negative emotions—especially the anger associated with an aggressively reactive temperament. As we will see in Module 83's discussion of anger, when we are harassed or challenged, our active sympathetic nervous system redistributes bloodflow to our muscles, pulling it away from our internal organs. One of those organs, the liver, which normally removes cholesterol and fat from the blood, can't do its job. Type A individuals are more often "combat ready." Thus, excess cholesterol and fat may continue to circulate in their blood and later get deposited around the heart. Further stress—sometimes conflicts brought on by their own abrasiveness—may trigger altered heart rhythms. In people with weakened hearts, this altered pattern can cause sudden death (Kamarck & Jennings, 1991). Hostility also correlates with other risk factors, such as smoking, drinking, and obesity (Bunde & Suls, 2006). In important ways, people's minds and hearts interact.

Hundreds of other studies of young and middle-aged men and women have confirmed the finding that people who react with anger over little things are the most coronary-prone. Suppressing negative emotions only heightens the risk (Kupper & Denollet, 2007). One study followed 13,000 middle-aged people for 5 years. Among those with normal blood pressure, people who had scored high on anger were three times more likely to have had heart attacks, even after researchers controlled for smoking and weight (Williams et al., 2000). Another study followed 1055 male medical students over an average of 36 years. Those who had reported being hot tempered were five times more likely to have had a heart attack by age 55 (Chang et al., 2002). As others have noted, rage "seems to lash back and strike us in the heart muscle" (Spielberger & London, 1982).

Pessimism seems to be similarly toxic. One study followed 1306 initially healthy men who a decade earlier had scored as optimists, pessimists, or neither. Even after other risk factors such as smoking had been ruled out, pessimists were more than twice as likely as optimists to develop heart disease (**FIGURE 44.3**) (Kubzansky et al., 2001).

Figure 44.3

Pessimism and heart disease A Harvard School of Public Health team found pessimistic men at doubled risk of developing heart disease over a 10-year period. (From Kubzansky et al., 2001.)

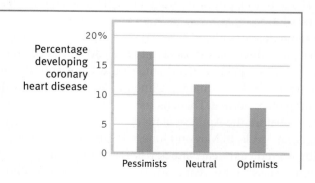

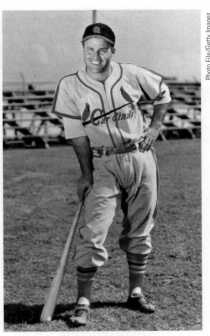

Depression, too, can be lethal. Happy people tend to be healthier and to outlive their unhappy peers (Diener & Chan, 2011; Siahpush et al., 2008). Even a big, happy smile predicts longevity, as Ernest Abel and Michael Kruger (2010) discovered when they examined the photographs of 150 Major League Baseball players who had appeared in the 1952 *Baseball Register* and had died by 2009. On average, the nonsmilers had died at 73, compared with an average 80 years for those with a broad, genuine smile.

The accumulated evidence from 57 studies suggests that "depression substantially increases the risk of death, especially death by unnatural causes and cardiovascular disease" (Wulsin et al., 1999). After following 63,469 women over a dozen years, researchers found more than a doubled rate of heart attack death among those who initially scored as depressed (Whang et al., 2009). In the years following a heart attack, people with high scores for depression are four times more likely than their low-scoring counterparts to develop further heart problems (Frasure-Smith & Lesperance, 2005). Depression is disheartening.

> "A cheerful heart is a good medicine, but a downcast spirit dries up the bones." -PROVERBS 17:22

Depressed people tend to smoke more and exercise less (Whooley et al., 2008), but stress itself is also disheartening:

- When following 17,415 middle-aged American women, researchers found an 88 percent increased risk of heart attacks among those facing significant work stress (Slopen et al., 2010).

- In Denmark, a study of 12,116 female nurses found that those reporting "much too high" work pressures had a 40 percent increased risk of heart disease (Allesøe et al., 2010).

- In the United States, a 10-year study of middle-aged workers found that involuntary job loss more than doubled their risk of a heart attack (Gallo et al., 2006). A 14-year study of 1059 women found that those with five or more trauma-related stress symptoms had three times the normal risk of heart disease (Kubzansky et al., 2009).

Research suggests that heart disease and depression may both result when chronic stress triggers persistent inflammation (Matthews, 2005; Miller & Blackwell, 2006). After a heart attack, stress and anxiety increase the risk of death or of another attack (Roest et al., 2010). As we have seen, stress disrupts the body's disease-fighting immune system, enabling the body to focus its energies on fleeing or fighting the threat. Yet stress hormones enhance one immune response, the production of proteins that contribute to inflammation. Thus, people who experience social threats, including children raised in harsh families, are more prone to inflammation responses (Dickerson et al., 2009; Miller & Chen, 2010). Inflammation fights infections; if you cut yourself, inflammation recruits infection-fighting cells. But persistent inflammation can produce problems such as asthma or clogged arteries, and worsen depression (see **FIGURE 44.4**). Researchers are now uncovering the molecular mechanisms by which stress, in some people, activates genes that control inflammation (Cole et al., 2010).

* * *

We can view the stress effect on our disease resistance as a price we pay for the benefits of stress (**FIGURE 44.5** on the next page). Stress invigorates our lives by arousing and motivating us. An unstressed life would hardly be challenging or productive.

Figure 44.4

Stress→inflammation→heart disease and depression
Gregory Miller and Ekin Blackwell (2006) report that chronic stress leads to persistent inflammation, which heightens the risk of both depression and clogged arteries.

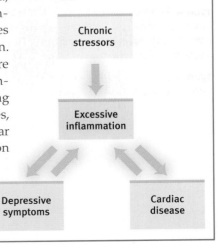

Figure 44.5

Stress can have a variety of health-related consequences This is especially so when stress is experienced by angry, depressed, or anxious people. Job and income loss caused by the recent economic recession has created stress for many people, such as this jobless Japanese man living in a Tokyo "capsule hotel."

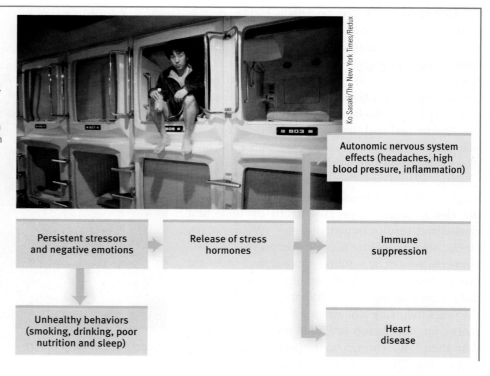

Ko Sasaki/The New York Times/Redux

Autonomic nervous system effects (headaches, high blood pressure, inflammation)

Persistent stressors and negative emotions → Release of stress hormones → Immune suppression

Unhealthy behaviors (smoking, drinking, poor nutrition and sleep)

Heart disease

Behavioral medicine research provides a reminder of one of contemporary psychology's overriding themes: *Mind and body interact; everything psychological is simultaneously physiological.* Psychological states are physiological events that influence other parts of our physiological system. Just pausing to *think* about biting into an orange section—the sweet, tangy juice from the pulpy fruit flooding across your tongue—can trigger salivation. As the Indian sage Santi Parva recognized more than 4000 years ago, "Mental disorders arise from physical causes, and likewise physical disorders arise from mental causes." There is an interplay between our heads and our health. We are biopsychosocial systems.

Before You Move On

▶ **ASK YOURSELF**

Are there changes you could make to avoid the persistent stressors in your life?

▶ **TEST YOURSELF**

Which component of the Type A personality has been linked most closely to coronary heart disease?

Answers to the Test Yourself questions can be found in Appendix E at the end of the book.

Module 44 Review

 44-1 How does stress make us more vulnerable to disease?

- *Psychoneuroimmunologists* study mind-body interactions, including *psychophysiological* illnesses, such as hypertension and some headaches.

- Stress diverts energy from the immune system, inhibiting the activities of its *B* and *T lymphocytes,* macrophages, and NK cells.

- Stress does not cause diseases such as AIDS and cancer, but by altering our immune functioning it may make us more vulnerable to them and influence their progression.

44-2 Why are some of us more prone than others to coronary heart disease?

- *Coronary heart disease,* North America's number one cause of death, has been linked with the reactive, anger-prone *Type A* personality.

- Compared with relaxed, easygoing *Type B* personalities, Type A people secrete more of the hormones that accelerate the buildup of plaque on the heart's artery walls.

- Chronic stress also contributes to persistent inflammation, which heightens the risk of clogged arteries and depression.

Multiple-Choice Questions

1. Which of the following best identifies any stress-related physical illness, such as hypertension and some headaches?

    a. Bacterial infection
    b. Psychoneuroimmunology
    c. Allergic reaction
    d. Psychophysiological illness
    e. Viral infection

2. What is North America's leading cause of death?

    a. Psychosomatic disorders
    b. Coronary heart disease
    c. Cancer
    d. Depression
    e. Stroke

3. What did a famous Harvard University public health study identify as a factor that doubles the risk of heart disease?

    a. Optimism
    b. Apathy
    c. Pessimism
    d. Competitiveness
    e. AIDS

Practice FRQs

1. Explain the two types of people identified by Friedman and Rosenman in their study on stress responses and personality traits.

Answer

1 point: Type A people are competitive, hard-driving, impatient, verbally aggressive, and anger prone.

1 point: Type B people are easygoing and relaxed.

2. Explain the difference between *B* lymphocytes and *T* lymphocytes.

(2 points)

Unit VIII Review

Key Terms and Concepts to Remember

motivation, p. 390

instinct, p. 391

drive-reduction theory, p. 391

homeostasis, p. 391

incentive, p. 392

Yerkes-Dodson law, p. 392

hierarchy of needs, p. 393

glucose, p. 397

set point, p. 398

basal metabolic rate, p. 398

sexual response cycle, p. 406

refractory period, p. 407

sexual dysfunction, p. 407

estrogens, p. 408

testosterone, p. 408

emotion, p. 421

James-Lange theory, p. 421

Cannon-Bard theory, p. 422

two-factor theory, p. 422

polygraph, p. 428

facial feedback effect, p. 438

health psychology, p. 439

stress, p. 442

general adaptation syndrome (GAS),
   p. 444

tend and befriend response, p. 445

psychophysiological illness, p. 448

psychoneuroimmunology, p. 448

lymphocytes, p. 448

coronary heart disease, p. 451

Type A, p. 452

Type B, p. 452

Key Contributors to Remember

Abraham Maslow, p. 393

William Masters, p. 406

Virginia Johnson, p. 406

William James, p. 421

Stanley Schachter, p. 422

Hans Selye, p. 444

AP® Exam Practice Questions

Multiple-Choice Questions

1. Which theory explains that physiological needs create an aroused state that motivates an organism to reduce the need?

a. Instinct theory

b. Drive-reduction theory

c. Achievement motivation

d. Arousal theory

e. Hierarchy of needs

2. Attempts to control social behavior by using the punishing effects of isolation is an example of

a. attachment disorder.

b. ostracism.

c. exploitation.

d. wanting to belong.

e. conforming.

3. Which theory explains why, even when our biological needs are satisfied, we may still feel driven to experience stimulation?

a. Incentive   d. Arousal theory

b. Homeostasis   e. Physiology

c. Instinct

4. Why does further weight loss come slowly following a rapid loss during the initial three weeks of a rigorous diet?

a. The number of fat cells makes further weight loss impossible.

b. When a person's hunger increases, metabolism increases.

c. When an obese person's set point has been reached, weight loss increases dramatically.

d. The body reacts as if it's being starved and metabolic rates drop.

e. An obese person cannot maintain a rigorous weight loss diet.

5. Research on semistarvation found that men who were given just enough food to stabilize their weight at 25 percent below their starting weight

a. became obsessed with physical exercise.
b. were more interpersonally outgoing.
c. showed increases in mental cognition.
d. were in a state of homeostasis.
e. lost interest in social activities.

6. Which of the following is the best biological explanation for why the human body stores fat?

a. Fat signals affluence and social status.
b. Fat is a fuel reserve during periods when food is scarce.
c. Fat is a display of abundant food sources.
d. Fat keeps the body warm in winter climates.
e. Fat combats the global epidemic of diabetes.

7. What do we call a need or desire that energizes and directs behavior?

a. Incentive
b. Refractory period
c. Emotion
d. Motivation
e. Instinct

8. Which of the following actions is a violation of Maslow's hierarchy of needs?

a. A person who moves to a new city gets an apartment before beginning to make friends.
b. A very hungry reality show contestant searches for food before trying to win a competition.
c. A professor spends time socially with her colleagues before she works on her own research.
d. An artist works to win a local award before spending time on his own personal projects.
e. An athlete follows a "no pain, no gain" motto rather than stopping for rest and nourishment.

9. What term refers to the ability of the body's physiological processes to maintain a balanced or constant internal state?

a. Hierarchy of needs
b. Basal metabolic rate
c. Homeostasis
d. Instinct
e. Motivation

10. A person who eats excessively and never seems to feel full may have which of the following conditions?

a. Tumor in the hypothalamus
b. Too much insulin
c. Stomach ulcer
d. Stomach bypass surgery
e. Too much of the hormone PYY

11. Which of the following is one of the stages of the sexual response cycle described by Masters and Johnson?

a. Expulsion
b. Plateau
c. Attraction
d. Compensation
e. Depolarization

12. Emotions are a mix of consciously experienced thoughts, expressive behaviors, and physiological arousal. Which theory emphasized the importance of consciously experienced thoughts?

a. Facial feedback theory
b. James-Lange theory
c. Arousal and performance theory
d. Fight-or-flight theory
e. Schachter-Singer two-factor theory

13. Surveys conducted with people who have high spinal cord injuries suggest to researchers that emotions are

a. entirely cognitive, requiring no physical response to be intense.
b. largely dependent upon our bodily responses and behaviors.
c. mostly a social response to surrounding factors.
d. mostly a cultural reaction to context.
e. mostly psychological.

14. The stress hormones epinephrine and norepinephrine are released from where?

a. Parasympathetic nervous system
b. Hippocampus
c. Brain stem
d. Adrenal glands
e. Hypothalamus

15. When hearing emotions conveyed in another language, what emotion can people most readily detect?

a. Sadness
b. Happiness
c. Anger
d. Fear
e. Surprise

16. Brain scans and EEG recordings indicate that positive emotions are associated with high levels of activity in which brain section?

a. Right temporal lobe
b. Cerebellum
c. Left frontal lobe
d. Left temporal lobe
e. Right parietal lobe

17. Which one of the following statements about stress is *true*?

  a. Surgical wounds heal more slowly in stressed humans.
  b. Stress has no effect on those exposed to cold viruses.
  c. There is no correlation between stress and longevity.
  d. Stress makes us more resistant to infection and heart disease.
  e. Anxiety, irritation, and guilt all prompt very different physiological responses.

18. Which of the following statements about nonverbal expression is *true*?

  a. People blind from birth do not usually exhibit common facial expressions.
  b. The meaning of gestures is the same across cultures.
  c. Facial signs of emotion are generally understood across world cultures.
  d. People from different cultures have difficulty understanding nonverbal expressions.
  e. Nonverbal expression is not reliably interpreted within a culture.

19. Which psychological concept would predict that smiling warmly on the outside would cause you to feel better on the inside?

  a. Relative deprivation
  b. Mimicry
  c. Empathy
  d. Facial feedback
  e. Catharsis

20. After an alarming event, your temperature, blood pressure, and respiration are high, and you have an outpouring of hormones. Hans Selye would most likely guess that you are in which general adaptation syndrome phase?

  a. Exhaustion
  b. Resistance
  c. Immobilization
  d. Collapse
  e. Shock

Free-Response Questions

1. Bill is applying for admission to the University of Michigan and has completed the entire process except for writing his application essay. He is very nervous about writing the essay because it is such an important part of the acceptance process and the topic he was assigned is very challenging.

   Explain how each of the following psychological concepts might relate to how Bill feels five months later when he receives a letter of acceptance from the University of Michigan.

- Maslow's hierarchy

- James-Lange theory

- Cannon-Bard theory

- Schachter-Singer two-factor theory

Rubric for Free Response Question 1

1 point: According to Maslow's hierarchy, Bill's decision to apply to the University of Michigan is the result of a need or drive (motivation) to achieve the higher psychological needs of belonging, esteem, self-actualization, or self-transcendence. Bill is able to focus on these higher-level needs because his physiological and safety needs have already been met. ↻ Page 393

1 point: According to the James-Lange theory, when Bill receives the letter in the mail, his heart races and his breathing increases, which causes his brain to automatically interpret this experience as the emotion of excitement.
Note: Bill may exhibit any emotion as long as the physical arousal occurs prior to the experience of the emotion. ↻ Page 421

1 point: According to the Cannon-Bard theory, when Bill receives the letter in the mail, his heart races and his breathing increases at the same time that he experiences the emotion of excitement. He simultaneously experiences an increase in physiological arousal and the emotion of happiness. ↻ Page 422

1 point: According to the Schachter-Singer two-factor theory, when Bill opens his letter, he experiences an increase in physical arousal and determines that he is experiencing happiness based on his memories and thoughts.
Note: Bill may exhibit any emotion as long as the response includes a physical arousal and a cognitive labeling of that emotion. ↻ Page 422

2. Hope's soccer team is playing in the championship game today. Hope knows the opposing team is the defending champion and that this will be a challenging game. Explain how the following theories apply to Hope's performance and reactions during the game.

- Yerkes-Dodson law
- Affiliation needs
- Schachter-Singer theory of emotion

(3 points)

Multiple-choice self-tests and more may be found at www.worthpublishers.com/MyersAP2e

3. Franz is 17 and wants to lose 15 pounds. Explain how the following factors might contribute to the success or failure of his weight-loss attempt.

- Social influence
- Set point
- Sleep
- Incentive theory

(4 points)

Unit IX

Developmental Psychology

Modules

Life is a journey, from womb to tomb. So it is for me, and so it will be for you. My story, and yours, began when a man and a woman together contributed 20,000+ genes to an egg that became a unique person. Those genes coded the protein building blocks that, with astonishing precision, formed our bodies and predisposed our traits. My grandmother bequeathed to my mother a rare hearing loss pattern, which she, in turn, gave to me (the least of her gifts). My father was an amiable extravert, and sometimes I forget to stop talking. As a child, my talking was impeded by painful stuttering, for which Seattle Public Schools gave me speech therapy.

Along with my parents' nature, I also received their nurture. Like you, I was born into a particular family and culture, with its own way of viewing the world. My values have been shaped by a family culture filled with talking and laughter, by

460

a religious culture that speaks of love and justice, and by an academic culture that encourages critical thinking (asking, What do you mean? How do you know?).

We are formed by our genes, and by our contexts, so our stories will differ. But in many ways we are each like nearly everyone else on Earth. Being human, you and I have a need to belong. My mental video library, which began after age 4, is filled with scenes of social attachment. Over time, my attachments to parents loosened as peer friendships grew. After lacking confidence to date in high school, I fell in love with a college classmate and married at age 20. Natural selection disposes us to survive and perpetuate our genes. Sure enough, two years later a child entered our lives, and I experienced a new form of love that surprised me with its intensity.

But life is marked by change. That child now lives 2000 miles away, and one of his two siblings has found her calling in South Africa. The tight rubber bands linking parent and child have loosened, as yours likely have as well.

Change also marks most vocational lives, which for me transitioned from a teen working in the family insurance agency, to a premed chemistry major and hospital aide, to (after discarding my half-completed medical school applications) a psychology professor and author. I predict that in 10 years you, too, will be doing things you do not currently anticipate.

Stability also marks our development: We experience a continuous self. When I look in the mirror, I do not see the person I once was, but I feel like the person I have always been. I am the same person who, as a late teen, played basketball and discovered love. A half-century later, I still play basketball and still love (with less passion but more security) the life partner with whom I have shared life's griefs and joys.

Continuity morphs through stages—growing up, raising children, enjoying a career, and, eventually, life's final stage, which will demand my presence. As I wend my way through this cycle of life and death, I am mindful that life is a journey, a continuing process of development, seeded by nature and shaped by nurture, animated by love and focused by work, begun with wide-eyed curiosity and completed, for those blessed to live to a good old age, with peace and never-ending hope.

Module 45

Developmental Issues, Prenatal Development, and the Newborn

David Greedy/Lonely Planet Images/Getty Images

Module Learning Objectives

45-1   Identify three issues that have engaged developmental psychologists.

45-2   Discuss the course of prenatal development, and explain how teratogens affect that development.

45-3   Describe some abilities of the newborn, noting how researchers are able to identify their mental abilities.

---

developmental psychology a branch of psychology that studies physical, cognitive, and social change throughout the life span.

> **AP® Exam Tip**
>
> All three of these issues are important for development. Nature and nurture, of course, weaves its way through almost every module. It is one of the topics most likely to be on the AP® exam.

> "Nature is all that a man brings with him into the world; nurture is every influence that affects him after his birth." -FRANCIS GALTON, *ENGLISH MEN OF SCIENCE*, 1874

Developmental Psychology's Major Issues

45-1   What three issues have engaged developmental psychologists?

Developmental psychology examines our physical, cognitive, and social development across the life span, with a focus on three major issues:

1. *Nature and nurture:* How does our genetic inheritance (our *nature*) interact with our experiences (our *nurture*) to influence our development?
2. *Continuity and stages:* What parts of development are gradual and continuous, like riding an escalator? What parts change abruptly in separate stages, like climbing rungs on a ladder?
3. *Stability and change:* Which of our traits persist through life? How do we change as we age?

Let's reflect now on these three development issues.

Nature and Nurture

The gene combination created when our mother's egg engulfed our father's sperm helped form us, as individuals. Genes predispose both our shared humanity and our individual differences.

But it is also true that our experiences form us. In the womb, in our families, and in our peer social relationships, we learn ways of thinking and acting. Even differences initiated by our nature may be amplified by our nurture. We are not formed by either nature or nurture, but by their interrelationships—their *interaction*. Biological, psychological, and social-cultural forces interact.

Mindful of how others differ from us, however, we often fail to notice the similarities stemming from our shared biology. Regardless of our culture, we humans share the same life cycle. We speak to our infants in similar ways and respond similarly to their coos and cries (Bornstein et al., 1992a,b). All over the world, the children of warm and supportive parents feel better about themselves and are less hostile than are the children of punishing and rejecting parents (Rohner, 1986; Scott et al., 1991). Although ethnic groups differ in school achievement and delinquency, the differences are "no more than skin deep." To the extent that family structure, peer influences, and parental education predict behavior in one of these ethnic groups, they do so for the others as well. Compared with the person-to-person differences within groups, the differences between groups are small.

Continuity and Stages

Do adults differ from infants as a giant redwood differs from its seedling—a difference created by gradual, cumulative growth? Or do they differ as a butterfly differs from a caterpillar—a difference of distinct stages?

Stages of the life cycle

Generally speaking, researchers who emphasize experience and learning see development as a slow, continuous shaping process. Those who emphasize biological maturation tend to see development as a sequence of genetically predisposed stages or steps: Although progress through the various stages may be quick or slow, everyone passes through the stages in the same order.

Are there clear-cut stages of psychological development, as there are physical stages such as walking before running? The stage theories of Jean Piaget on cognitive development, Lawrence Kohlberg on moral development, and Erik Erikson on psychosocial development propose that such stages do exist (as summarized in **FIGURE 45.1**). But some research casts doubt on the idea that life proceeds through neatly defined, age-linked stages. Young children have some abilities Piaget attributed to later stages. Kohlberg's work reflected a worldview characteristic of individualist cultures and emphasized thinking over acting. And adult life does not progress through a fixed, predictable series of steps. Chance events can influence us in ways we would never have predicted.

Nevertheless, the concept of *stage* remains useful. The human brain does experience growth spurts during childhood and puberty that correspond roughly to Piaget's stages (Thatcher et al., 1987). And stage theories contribute a developmental perspective on the whole life span, by suggesting how people of one age think and act differently when they arrive at a later age.

> **FYI**
>
> Another stage theory, Sigmund Freud's ideas about how personality develops, is discussed in Unit X.

Figure 45.1
Comparing the stage theories (With thanks to Dr. Sandra Gibbs, Muskegon Community College, for inspiring this.)

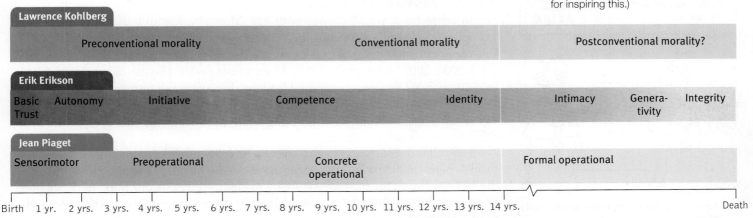

Stability and Change

As we follow lives through time, do we find more evidence for stability or change? If re-united with a long-lost grade-school friend, do we instantly realize that "it's the same old Andy"? Or do people we befriend during one period of life seem like strangers at a later period? (At least one acquaintance of mine would choose the second option. He failed to recognize a former classmate at his 40-year college reunion. The aghast classmate pointed out that she was his long-ago first wife.)

Research reveals that we experience both stability and change. Some of our characteristics, such as *temperament* (our emotional reactivity and intensity), are very stable:

- One study followed 1000 3-year-old New Zealanders through time. It found that preschoolers who were low in conscientiousness and self-control were more vulnerable to ill health, substance abuse, arrest, and single parenthood by age 32 (Moffitt et al., 2011).

Smiles predict marital stability
In one study of 306 college alums, one in four with yearbook expressions like the one on the left later divorced, as did only 1 in 20 with smiles like the one on the right (Hertenstein et al., 2009).

- Another study found that hyperactive, inattentive 5-year-olds required more teacher effort at age 12 (Houts et al., 2010).

- Another research team interviewed adults who, 40 years earlier, had their talkativeness, impulsiveness, and humility rated by their elementary school teachers (Nave et al., 2010). To a striking extent, the personalities persisted.

"At 70, I would say the advantage is that you take life more calmly. You know that 'this, too, shall pass'!" -ELEANOR ROOSEVELT, 1954

"As at 7, so at 70," says a Jewish proverb. The widest smilers in childhood and college photos are, years later, the ones most likely to enjoy enduring marriages (Hertenstein et al., 2009). While one in four of the weakest college smilers eventually divorced, only 1 in 20 of the widest smilers did so. As people grow older, personality gradually stabilizes (Ferguson, 2010; Hopwood et al., 2011; Kandler et al., 2010). The struggles of the present may be laying a foundation for a happier tomorrow.

We cannot, however, predict all of our eventual traits based on our early years of life (Kagan et al., 1978, 1998). Some traits, such as social attitudes, are much less stable than temperament, especially during the impressionable late adolescent years (Krosnick & Alwin, 1989; Moss & Susman, 1980). Older children and adolescents learn new ways of coping. Although delinquent children have elevated rates of later work problems, substance abuse, and crime, many confused and troubled children blossom into mature, successful adults (Moffitt et al., 2002; Roberts et al., 2001; Thomas & Chess, 1986). Happily for them, life is a process of becoming.

BEFORE   AFTER

As adults grow older, there is continuity of self.

In some ways, we *all* change with age. Most shy, fearful toddlers begin opening up by age 4, and most people become more conscientious, stable, agreeable, and self-confident in the years after adolescence (Lucas & Donnellan, 2009; Roberts et al., 2003, 2006, 2008; Shaw et al., 2010). Many irresponsible 16-year-olds have matured into 40-year-old business or cultural leaders. (If you are the former, you aren't done yet.) Such changes can occur without changing a person's position *relative to others* of the same age. The hard-driving young adult may mellow by later life, yet still be a relatively driven senior citizen.

Life requires *both* stability and change. Stability provides our identity. It enables us to depend on others and be concerned about the healthy development of the children in our lives. Our trust in our ability to change gives us our hope for a brighter future. It motivates our concerns about present influences and lets us adapt and grow with experience.

Before You Move On

▶ **ASK YOURSELF**

Are you the same person you were as a preschooler? As an 8-year-old? As a 12-year-old? How are you different? How are you the same?

▶ **TEST YOURSELF**

What findings in psychology support the concept of stages in development and the idea of stability in personality across the life span? What findings challenge these ideas?

Answers to the Test Yourself questions can be found in Appendix E at the end of the book.

AP® Exam Tip

Almost every topic in psychology holds personal relevance, but development stands out. As you work your way through this unit, think of how the material relates to you, your relatives, and your friends. The more often you do this, the easier it will be to remember the material.

Prenatal Development and the Newborn

45-2 What is the course of prenatal development, and how do teratogens affect that development?

Conception

Nothing is more natural than a species reproducing itself. And nothing is more wondrous. With humans, the process starts when a woman's ovary releases a mature egg—a cell roughly the size of the period at the end of this sentence. The woman was born with all the immature eggs she would ever have, although only 1 in 5000 will ever mature and be released. A man, in contrast, begins producing sperm cells at puberty. For the rest of his life, 24 hours a day, he will be a nonstop sperm factory, with the rate of production—in the beginning more than 1000 sperm during the second it takes to read this phrase—slowing with age.

Like space voyagers approaching a huge planet, the 200 million or more deposited sperm begin their race upstream, approaching a cell 85,000 times their own size. The relatively few reaching the egg release digestive enzymes that eat away its protective coating (**FIGURE 45.2a**). As soon as one sperm penetrates that coating and is welcomed in (Figure 45.2b), the egg's surface blocks out the others. Before half a day elapses, the egg nucleus and the sperm nucleus fuse. The two have become one. Consider it your

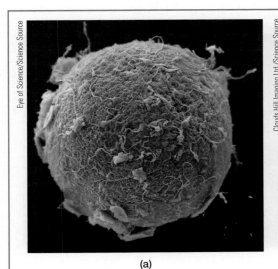
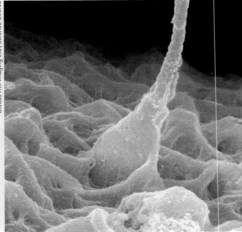

(a)

(b)

Figure 45.2

Life is sexually transmitted
(a) Sperm cells surround an egg. (b) As one sperm penetrates the egg's jellylike outer coating, a series of chemical events begins that will cause sperm and egg to fuse into a single cell. If all goes well, that cell will subdivide again and again to emerge 9 months later as a 100-trillion-cell human being.

most fortunate of moments. Among 200 million sperm, the one needed to make you, in combination with that one particular egg, won the race. And so it was for innumerable generations before us. If any one of our ancestors had been conceived with a different sperm or egg, or died before conceiving, or not chanced to meet the partner or . . . the mind boggles at the improbable, unbroken chain of events that produced you and me.

Prenatal Development

Fewer than half of all fertilized eggs, called **zygotes,** survive beyond the first 2 weeks (Grobstein, 1979; Hall, 2004). But for you and me, good fortune prevailed. One cell became 2, then 4—each just like the first—until this cell division had produced some 100 identical cells within the first week. Then the cells began to differentiate—to specialize in structure and function. How identical cells do this—as if one decides "I'll become a brain, you become intestines!"—is a puzzle that scientists are just beginning to solve.

About 10 days after conception, the zygote attaches to the mother's uterine wall, beginning approximately 37 weeks of the closest human relationship. The zygote's inner cells become the **embryo** (**FIGURE 45.3a**). The outer cells become the *placenta*, the life-link that transfers nutrients and oxygen from mother to embryo. A healthy and well-nourished mother helps form a healthy baby-to-be. Over the next 6 weeks, the embryo's organs begin to form and function. The heart begins to beat.

For 1 in 270 sets of parents, though, there is a bonus. Two heartbeats will reveal that the zygote, during its early days of development, has split into two. If all goes well, two genetically identical babies will start life together some 8 months later (Module 14).

By 9 weeks after conception, an embryo looks unmistakably human (Figure 45.3b). It is now a **fetus** (Latin for "offspring" or "young one"). During the sixth month, organs such as the stomach have developed enough to give the fetus a good chance of survival if born prematurely.

At each prenatal stage, genetic and environmental factors affect our development. By the sixth month, microphone readings taken inside the uterus reveal that the fetus is responsive to sound and is exposed to the sound of its mother's muffled voice (Ecklund-Flores, 1992; Hepper, 2005). Immediately after birth, emerging from living 38 or so weeks underwater, newborns prefer her voice to another woman's or to their father's (Busnel et al., 1992; DeCasper et al., 1984, 1986, 1994). They also prefer hearing their mother's language. If she spoke two languages during pregnancy, they display interest in both (Byers-Heinlein et al., 2010). And just after birth, the melodic ups and downs of newborns' cries bear the tuneful signature of their mother's native tongue (Mampe et al., 2009). Babies born

zygote the fertilized egg; it enters a 2-week period of rapid cell division and develops into an embryo.

embryo the developing human organism from about 2 weeks after fertilization through the second month.

fetus the developing human organism from 9 weeks after conception to birth.

Figure 45.3

Prenatal development (a) The embryo grows and develops rapidly. At 40 days, the spine is visible and the arms and legs are beginning to grow. (b) By the end of the second month, when the fetal period begins, facial features, hands, and feet have formed. (c) As the fetus enters the fourth month, its 3 ounces could fit in the palm of your hand.

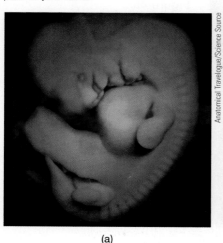

(a)

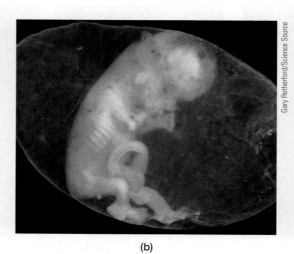

(b)

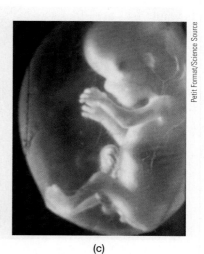

(c)

to French-speaking mothers tend to cry with the rising intonation of French; babies born to German-speaking mothers cry with the falling tones of German. Would you have guessed? The learning of language begins in the womb.

In the 2 months before birth, fetuses demonstrate learning in other ways, as when they adapt to a vibrating, honking device placed on their mother's abdomen (Dirix et al., 2009). Like people who adapt to the sound of trains in their neighborhood, fetuses get used to the honking. Moreover, 4 weeks later, they recall the sound (as evidenced by their blasé response, compared with reactions of those not previously exposed).

Sounds are not the only stimuli fetuses are exposed to in the womb. In addition to transferring nutrients and oxygen from mother to fetus, the placenta screens out many harmful substances, but some slip by. **Teratogens,** agents such as viruses and drugs, can damage an embryo or fetus. This is one reason pregnant women are advised not to drink alcoholic beverages. A pregnant woman never drinks alone. As alcohol enters her bloodstream, and her fetus', it depresses activity in both their central nervous systems. Alcohol use during pregnancy may prime the woman's offspring to like alcohol and may put them at risk for heavy drinking and alcohol use disorder during their teens. In experiments, when pregnant rats drank alcohol, their young offspring later displayed a liking for alcohol's taste and odor (Youngentob et al., 2007, 2009).

Even light drinking or occasional binge drinking can affect the fetal brain (Braun, 1996; Ikonomidou et al., 2000; Sayal et al., 2009). Persistent heavy drinking puts the fetus at risk for birth defects and for future behavior problems, hyperactivity, and lower intelligence. For 1 in about 800 infants, the effects are visible as **fetal alcohol syndrome (FAS),** marked by lifelong physical and mental brain abnormalities (May & Gossage, 2001). The fetal damage may occur because alcohol has an *epigenetic effect:* It leaves chemical marks on DNA that switch genes abnormally on or off (Liu et al., 2009).

The Competent Newborn

 What are some newborn abilities, and how do researchers explore infants' mental abilities?

Babies come with software preloaded on their neural hard drives. Having survived prenatal hazards, we as newborns came equipped with automatic reflex responses ideally suited for our survival. We withdrew our limbs to escape pain. If a cloth over our face interfered with our breathing, we turned our head from side to side and swiped at it.

New parents are often in awe of the coordinated sequence of reflexes by which their baby gets food. Thanks to the *rooting reflex,* when something touches their cheek, babies turn toward that touch, open their mouth, and vigorously root for a nipple. Finding one, they automatically close on it and begin *sucking*—which itself requires a coordinated sequence of reflexive *tonguing, swallowing,* and *breathing.* Failing to find satisfaction, the hungry baby may cry—a behavior parents find highly unpleasant and very rewarding to relieve.

FYI

Prenatal development
zygote: conception to 2 weeks
embryo: 2 to 9 weeks
fetus: 9 weeks to birth

"You shall conceive and bear a son. So then drink no wine or strong drink." -JUDGES 13:7

---

teratogens (literally, "monster maker") agents, such as chemicals and viruses, that can reach the embryo or fetus during prenatal development and cause harm.

fetal alcohol syndrome (FAS) physical and cognitive abnormalities in children caused by a pregnant woman's heavy drinking. In severe cases, signs include a small, out-of-proportion head and abnormal facial features.

"I felt like a man trapped in a woman's body. Then I was born." -COMEDIAN CHRIS BLISS

Prepared to feed and eat Animals are predisposed to respond to their offsprings' cries for nourishment.

The pioneering American psychologist William James presumed that the newborn experiences a "blooming, buzzing confusion," an assumption few people challenged until the 1960s. But then scientists discovered that babies can tell you a lot—if you know how to ask. To ask, you must capitalize on what babies can do—gaze, suck, turn their heads. So, equipped with eye-tracking machines and pacifiers wired to electronic gear, researchers set out to answer parents' age-old questions: What can my baby see, hear, smell, and think?

habituation decreasing responsiveness with repeated stimulation. As infants gain familiarity with repeated exposure to a visual stimulus, their interest wanes and they look away sooner.

Consider how researchers exploit **habituation**—a decrease in responding with repeated stimulation. We saw this earlier when fetuses adapted to a vibrating, honking device placed on their mother's abdomen. The novel stimulus gets attention when first presented. With repetition, the response weakens. This seeming boredom with familiar stimuli gives us a way to ask infants what they see and remember.

An example: Researchers have used *visual preference* to "ask" 4-month-olds how they recognize cats and dogs (Quinn, 2002; Spencer et al., 1997). First, they showed the infants a series of images of either cats or dogs. Then they showed them hybrid cat-dog images (**FIGURE 45.4**). Which of those two animals do you think the infants would find more novel (measured in looking time) after seeing a series of cats? It was the hybrid animal with the dog's head (and vice versa if they previously viewed dogs). This suggests that infants, like adults, focus first on the face, not the body.

Figure 45.4

Quick—which is the cat? Researchers used cat-dog hybrid images such as these to test how infants categorize animals.

Indeed, even as newborns, we prefer sights and sounds that facilitate social responsiveness. We turn our heads in the direction of human voices. We gaze longer at a drawing of a face-like image (**FIGURE 45.5**). We prefer to look at objects 8 to 12 inches away. Wonder of wonders, that just happens to be the approximate distance between a nursing infant's eyes and its mother's (Maurer & Maurer, 1988).

Figure 45.5

Newborns' preference for faces When shown these two stimuli with the same elements, Italian newborns spent nearly twice as many seconds looking at the face-like image (Johnson & Morton, 1991). Canadian newborns display the same apparently inborn preference to look toward faces (Mondloch et al., 1999).

Within days after birth, our brain's neural networks were stamped with the smell of our mother's body. Week-old nursing babies, placed between a gauze pad from their mother's bra and one from another nursing mother, have usually turned toward the smell of their own mother's pad (MacFarlane, 1978). What's more, that smell preference lasts. One experiment capitalized on the fact that some nursing mothers in a French maternity ward applied a balm with a chamomile scent to prevent nipple soreness (Delaunay-El Allam, et al., 2010). Twenty-one months later, their toddlers preferred playing with chamomile-scented toys! Their peers who had not sniffed the scent while breast feeding showed no such preference. (This makes one wonder: Will adults who as babies associated chamomile scent with their mother's breast become devoted chamomile tea drinkers?

Before You Move On

▶ **ASK YOURSELF**

Are you surprised by the news of infants' competencies? Remember hindsight bias from Module 4? Is this one of those cases where it feels like you "knew it all along"?

▶ **TEST YOURSELF**

Your friend's older sister—a regular drinker—hopes to become pregnant soon and has stopped drinking. Why is this a good idea? What negative effects might alcohol consumed during pregnancy have on a developing fetus?

Answers to the Test Yourself questions can be found in Appendix E at the end of the book.

Module 45 Review

 What three issues have engaged developmental psychologists?

- *Developmental psychologists* study physical, mental, and social changes throughout the life span.

- They focus on three issues: nature and nurture (the interaction between our genetic inheritance and our experiences); continuity and stages (whether development is gradual and continuous or a series of relatively abrupt changes); and stability and change (whether our traits endure or change as we age).

 What is the course of prenatal development, and how do teratogens affect that development?

- The life cycle begins at conception, when one sperm cell unites with an egg to form a *zygote.*

- The zygote's inner cells become the *embryo,* and in the next 6 weeks, body organs begin to form and function.

- By 9 weeks, the *fetus* is recognizably human.

- *Teratogens* are potentially harmful agents that can pass through the placental screen and harm the developing embryo or fetus, as happens with *fetal alcohol syndrome.*

 What are some newborn abilities, and how do researchers explore infants' mental abilities?

- Babies are born with sensory equipment and reflexes that facilitate their survival and their social interactions with adults. For example, they quickly learn to discriminate their mother's smell and sound.

- Researchers use techniques that test *habituation,* such as the visual-preference procedure, to explore infants' abilities.

Multiple-Choice Questions

1. Alcohol is a teratogen that can slip through the _____ and damage the fetus or embryo.

  a.   placenta
  b.   nervous system
  c.   womb
  d.   brainstem
  e.   zygote

2. Even as newborns, we prefer sights and sounds that facilitate social responsiveness. This can be seen by a newborn's preference for

  a.   soft music.
  b.   face-like images.
  c.   low pitched sounds.
  d.   soft colors.
  e.   loud music.

3. As infants gain familiarity with repeated exposure to a visual stimulus, their interest wanes and they look away sooner. The decrease in an infant's responsiveness is called

  a.   concentration.
  b.   teratogens.
  c.   habituation.
  d.   stability.
  e.   transference.

4. Which question expresses the developmental issue of stability and change?

  a.   Are individuals more similar or different from each other?
  b.   How much of development occurs in distinct stages?
  c.   How much of development is determined by genetics?
  d.   To what extent do certain traits persist through the life span?
  e.   Which traits are most affected by life changes and experience?

5. What is the prenatal development sequence?

  a.   Zygote, embryo, fetus
  b.   Fetus, zygote, embryo
  c.   Embryo, zygote, fetus
  d.   Zygote, fetus, embryo
  e.   Fetus, embryo, zygote

6. Some people think development occurs much in the way a tree grows, slowly and steadily adding one ring each year. Others think that there are rather abrupt developmental jumps, like the transformation of a tadpole into a frog. Which of the following issues would this difference of opinion relate to?

  a.   Nature and nurture
  b.   Maturation and learning
  c.   Prenatal and neonatal
  d.   Stability and change
  e.   Continuity and stages

7. Which of the following is the longest prenatal stage?

  a.   Teratogen
  b.   Conception
  c.   Zygote
  d.   Embryo
  e.   Fetus

Practice FRQs

1. What is habituation? How is this phenomenon used by researchers in examining newborns' abilities?

Answer

1 point: Habituation is the decrease in responding with repeated stimulation.

1 point: Researchers use habituation to see what infants recognize and remember.

2. Three major issues are addressed by psychologists in the study of human development. Identify and state how all three might be considered to explain how children's traits and abilities develop.

(3 points)

Module 46

Infancy and Childhood: Physical Development

Module Learning Objectives

 Describe some developmental changes in brain and motor abilities during infancy and childhood.

46-2 Describe how an infant's developing brain begins processing memories.

 During infancy and childhood, how do the brain and motor skills develop?

During infancy, a baby grows from newborn to toddler, and during childhood from toddler to teenager. We all traveled this path, with its physical, cognitive, and social milestones.

As a flower unfolds in accord with its genetic instructions, so do we. **Maturation**—the orderly sequence of biological growth—decrees many of our commonalities. We stand before walking. We use nouns before adjectives. Severe deprivation or abuse can retard development. Yet the genetic growth tendencies are inborn. Maturation (nature) sets the basic course of development; experience (nurture) adjusts it. Once again, we see genes and scenes interacting.

Brain Development

In your mother's womb, your developing brain formed nerve cells at the explosive rate of nearly one-quarter million per minute. The developing brain cortex actually overproduces neurons, with the number peaking at 28 weeks and then subsiding to a stable 23 billion or so at birth (Rabinowicz et al., 1996, 1999; de Courten-Myers, 2002).

From infancy on, brain and mind—neural hardware and cognitive software—develop together. On the day you were born, you had most of the brain cells you would ever have. However, your nervous system was immature: After birth, the branching neural networks that eventually enabled you to walk, talk, and remember had a wild growth spurt (**FIGURE 46.1** on the next page). From ages 3 to 6, the most rapid growth was in your frontal lobes, which enable rational planning. This explains why preschoolers display a rapidly developing ability to control their attention and behavior (Garon et al., 2008).

The association areas—those linked with thinking, memory, and language—are the last cortical areas to develop. As they do, mental abilities surge (Chugani & Phelps, 1986; Thatcher et al., 1987). Fiber pathways supporting language and agility proliferate into puberty. A use-it-or-lose-it *pruning process* shuts down unused links and strengthens others (Paus et al., 1999; Thompson et al., 2000).

> "It is a rare privilege to watch the birth, growth, and first feeble struggles of a living human mind."
> -ANNIE SULLIVAN, IN HELEN KELLER'S *THE STORY OF MY LIFE*, 1903

maturation biological growth processes that enable orderly changes in behavior, relatively uninfluenced by experience.

AP® Exam Tip

Note that maturation, to developmental psychologists, is a biological sequence. This is much more precise than the general notion that maturation means to become more adult-like.

Figure 46.1
Drawings of human cerebral cortex sections In humans, the brain is immature at birth. As the child matures, the neural networks grow increasingly more complex.

At birth   3 months   15 months

Motor Development

The developing brain enables physical coordination. As an infant's muscles and nervous system mature, skills emerge. With occasional exceptions, the motor development sequence is universal. Babies roll over before they sit unsupported, and they usually crawl on all fours before they walk (**FIGURE 46.2**). These behaviors reflect not imitation but a maturing nervous system; blind children, too, crawl before they walk.

There are, however, individual differences in timing. In the United States, for example, 25 percent of all babies walk by age 11 months, 50 percent within a week after their first birthday, and 90 percent by age 15 months (Frankenburg et al., 1992). The recommended infant *back-to-sleep position* (putting babies to sleep on their backs to reduce the risk of a smothering crib death) has been associated with somewhat later crawling but not with later walking (Davis et al., 1998; Lipsitt, 2003).

FYI

In the eight years following the 1994 launch of a U.S. Back to Sleep educational campaign, the number of infants sleeping on their stomach dropped from 70 to 11 percent—and SIDS (Sudden Infant Death Syndrome) deaths fell by half (Braiker, 2005).

Figure 46.2
Triumphant toddlers Sit, crawl, walk, run—the sequence of these motor development milestones is the same the world around, though babies reach them at varying ages.

Genes guide motor development. Identical twins typically begin walking on nearly the same day (Wilson, 1979). Maturation—including the rapid development of the cerebellum at the back of the brain—creates our readiness to learn walking at about age 1. Experience before that time has a limited effect. The same is true for other physical skills, including bowel and bladder control. Before necessary muscular and neural maturation, don't expect pleading or punishment to produce successful toilet training.

Brain Maturation and Infant Memory

46-2 How does an infant's developing brain begin processing memories?

Can you recall your first day of preschool or your third birthday party? Our earliest memories seldom predate our third birthday. We see this *infantile amnesia* in the memories of some preschoolers who experienced an emergency fire evacuation caused by a burning popcorn maker. Seven years later, they were able to recall the alarm and what caused it—*if* they were 4 to 5 years old at the time. Those experiencing the event as 3-year-olds could not remember the cause and usually misrecalled being already outside when the alarm sounded (Pillemer, 1995). Other studies confirm that the average age of earliest conscious memory is 3½ years (Bauer, 2002, 2007). As children mature, from 4 to 6 to 8 years, childhood amnesia is giving way, and they become increasingly capable of remembering experiences, even for a year or more (Bruce et al., 2000; Morris et al., 2010). The brain areas underlying memory, such as the hippocampus and frontal lobes, continue to mature into adolescence (Bauer, 2007).

"This is the path to adulthood. You're here."

Apart from constructed memories based on photos and family stories, we *consciously* recall little from before age 4. Yet our brain was processing and storing information during those early years. In 1965, while finishing her doctoral work in psychology, Carolyn Rovee-Collier observed a nonverbal infant memory. She was also a new mom, whose colicky 2-month-old, Benjamin, could be calmed by moving a crib mobile. Weary of hitting the mobile, she strung a cloth ribbon connecting the mobile to Benjamin's foot. Soon, he was kicking his foot to move the mobile. Thinking about her unintended home experiment, Rovee-Collier realized that, contrary to popular opinion in the 1960s, babies are capable of learning. To know for sure that her son wasn't just a whiz kid, she repeated the experiment with other infants (Rovee-Collier, 1989, 1999). Sure enough, they, too, soon kicked more when hitched to a mobile, both on the day of the experiment and the day after. They had learned the link between moving legs and moving mobiles. If, however, she hitched them to a different mobile the next day, the infants showed no learning, indicating that they remembered the original mobile and recognized the difference. Moreover, when tethered to the familiar mobile a month later, they remembered the association and again began kicking (**FIGURE 46.3**).

Traces of forgotten childhood languages may also persist. One study tested English-speaking British adults who had no conscious memory of the Hindi or Zulu they had spoken as children. Yet, up to age 40, they could relearn subtle sound contrasts in these languages that other people could *not* learn (Bowers et al., 2009). What the conscious mind does not know and cannot express in words, the nervous system somehow remembers.

Figure 46.3

Infant at work Babies only 3 months old can learn that kicking moves a mobile, and they can retain that learning for a month. (From Rovee-Collier, 1989, 1997.)

Before You Move On

▶ **ASK YOURSELF**

What do you tend to regard as your earliest memory? Now that you know about infantile amnesia, has your opinion changed about the accuracy of that memory?

▶ **TEST YOURSELF**

What is the biological growth process that explains why most children begin walking by about 12 to 15 months?

Answers to the Test Yourself questions can be found in Appendix E at the end of the book.

Module 46 Review

 46-1 During infancy and childhood, how do the brain and motor skills develop?

- The brain's nerve cells are sculpted by heredity and experience. Their interconnections multiply rapidly after birth, a process that continues until puberty, when a pruning process begins shutting down unused connections.

- Complex motor skills—sitting, standing, walking—develop in a predictable sequence, though the timing of that sequence is a function of individual *maturation* and culture.

46-2 How does an infant's developing brain begin processing memories?

- We have no conscious memories of events occurring before about age 3½, in part because major brain areas have not yet matured.

Multiple-Choice Questions

1. As the infant's brain develops, some neural pathways will decay if not used. This use-it-or-lose-it process is known as

  a. motor development.
  b. pruning.
  c. spacing.
  d. accommodation.
  e. maturation.

2. Which of the following depends least on the maturation process?

  a. Riding a bike
  b. Writing
  c. Talking
  d. Bladder control
  e. Telling time

3. Which of the following is true of the early formation of brain cells?

  a. They form at a constant rate throughout the prenatal period.
  b. They begin forming slowly, and then the rate increases throughout prenatal development.
  c. They form slowly during the prenatal period, and then the rate increases after birth.
  d. They form at a constantly increasing rate prenatally and in early childhood.
  e. They are overproduced early in the prenatal period, and then the rate decreases and stabilizes.

4. Neural networks grow more complex by

  a. branching outward to form multiple connections.
  b. keeping the nervous system immature.
  c. controlling one another with a restricted response system.
  d. limiting connections.
  e. associating behaviors that would not normally be associated together.

Practice FRQs

1. Define and give an example of maturation. Define infantile amnesia and explain how maturation contributes to this phenomenon.

Answer

1 point: Maturation is the orderly changes in behavior that result from biological processes that are relatively unaffected by experience.

1 point: Various examples will serve here, such as the normal development of motor skills (e.g., rolling over, crawling) or bladder and bowel control.

1 point: Infantile amnesia is our inability to remember events that occurred before we are about 3½ years old.

1 point: The brain areas underlying memory need to mature before we can remember accurately. This maturation doesn't happen until after the age of 3.

2. Three types of development are listed below. Give a specific example of each.

- Brain development
- Motor development
- Infant memory

(3 points)

Module 47

Infancy and Childhood: Cognitive Development

Image Source/Getty Images

Module Learning Objectives

 Describe how a child's mind develops from the perspectives of Piaget, Vygotsky, and today's researchers.

 Explain how autism spectrum disorder affects development.

Jean Piaget (1896–1980) "If we examine the intellectual development of the individual or of the whole of humanity, we shall find that the human spirit goes through a certain number of stages, each different from the other" (1930).

© Bill Anderson/Science Source

> **AP® Exam Tip**
>
> Jean Piaget is such an important person in the history of psychology that it's likely there will be at least one question about him on the AP® exam.

cognition all the mental activities associated with thinking, knowing, remembering, and communicating.

 From the perspectives of Piaget, Vygotsky, and today's researchers, how does a child's mind develop?

Somewhere on your precarious journey "from egghood to personhood" (Broks, 2007), you became conscious. When was that, and how did your mind unfold from there? Developmental psychologist Jean Piaget [pee-ah-ZHAY] spent his life searching for the answers to such questions. He studied children's **cognitive** development—all the mental activities associated with thinking, knowing, remembering, and communicating. His interest began in 1920, when he was in Paris developing questions for children's intelligence tests. While administering the tests, Piaget became intrigued by children's wrong answers, which were often strikingly similar among same-age children. Where others saw childish mistakes, Piaget saw intelligence at work.

A half-century spent with children convinced Piaget that a child's mind is not a miniature model of an adult's. Thanks partly to his work, we now understand that children reason *differently* than adults, in "wildly illogical ways about problems whose solutions are self-evident to adults" (Brainerd, 1996).

Piaget's studies led him to believe that a child's mind develops through a series of stages, in an upward march from the newborn's simple reflexes to the adult's abstract reasoning power. Thus, an 8-year-old can comprehend things a toddler cannot, such as the analogy that "getting an idea is like having a light turn on in your head," or that a miniature slide is too small for sliding, and a miniature car is much too small to get into (**FIGURE 47.1**).

Piaget's core idea is that the driving force behind our intellectual progression is an unceasing struggle to make sense of our experiences. To this end, the maturing brain

Both photos: Courtesy of Judy DeLoache

Figure 47.1

Scale errors Psychologists report that 18- to 30-month-old children may fail to take the size of an object into account when trying to perform impossible actions with it (DeLoache, Uttal, & Rosengren, 2004). At left, a 21-month-old attempts to slide down a miniature slide. At right, a 24-month-old opens the door to a miniature car and tries to step inside.

builds **schemas,** concepts or mental molds into which we pour our experiences (**FIGURE 47.2**). By adulthood we have built countless schemas, ranging from *cats* and *dogs* to our concept of *love*.

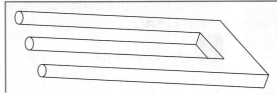

Figure 47.2

An impossible object Look carefully at the "devil's tuning fork." Now look away—no, better first study it some more—and then look away and draw it. . . . Not so easy, is it? Because this tuning fork is an impossible object, you have no schema for such an image.

To explain how we use and adjust our schemas, Piaget proposed two more concepts. First, we **assimilate** new experiences—we interpret them in terms of our current understandings (schemas). Having a simple schema for *dog*, for example, a toddler may call all four-legged animals *dogs*. But as we interact with the world, we also adjust, or **accommodate,** our schemas to incorporate information provided by new experiences. Thus, the child soon learns that the original *dog* schema is too broad and accommodates by refining the category (**FIGURE 47.3**).

Figure 47.3

Pouring experience into mental molds We use our existing schemas to *assimilate* new experiences. But sometimes we need to *accommodate* (adjust) our schemas to include new experiences.

(a) Two-year-old Alexandra has learned the schema for *doggy* from her picture books.

(b) Alexandra sees a cat and calls it a *doggy*. She is trying to assimilate this new animal into an existing schema. Her mother tells her, "No, it's a *cat*."

(c) Alexandra accommodates her schema for furry four-legged animals, distinguishing dogs from cats. Over time her schemas become more sophisticated as she learns to distinguish the pets of family and friends by name.

schema a concept or framework that organizes and interprets information.

assimilation interpreting our new experiences in terms of our existing schemas.

accommodation adapting our current understandings (schemas) to incorporate new information.

Piaget's Theory and Current Thinking

Piaget believed that children construct their understanding of the world while interacting with it. Their minds experience spurts of change, followed by greater stability as they move from one cognitive plateau to the next, each with distinctive characteristics that permit specific kinds of thinking. In Piaget's view, cognitive development consisted of four major stages—*sensorimotor, preoperational, concrete operational,* and *formal operational.*

Sensorimotor Stage

In the **sensorimotor stage,** from birth to nearly age 2, babies take in the world through their senses and actions—through looking, hearing, touching, mouthing, and grasping. As their hands and limbs begin to move, they learn to make things happen.

Very young babies seem to live in the present: Out of sight is out of mind. In one test, Piaget showed an infant an appealing toy and then flopped his beret over it. Before the age of 6 months, the infant acted as if it ceased to exist. Young infants lack **object permanence**—the awareness that objects continue to exist when not perceived. By 8 months, infants begin exhibiting memory for things no longer seen. If you hide a toy, the infant will momentarily look for it (**FIGURE 47.4**). Within another month or two, the infant will look for it even after being restrained for several seconds.

Figure 47.4

Object permanence Infants younger than 6 months seldom understand that things continue to exist when they are out of sight. But for this older infant, out of sight is definitely not out of mind.

So does object permanence in fact blossom at 8 months, much as tulips blossom in spring? Today's researchers think not. They believe object permanence unfolds gradually, and they see development as more continuous than Piaget did. Even young infants will at least momentarily look for a toy where they saw it hidden a second before (Wang et al., 2004).

Researchers also believe Piaget and his followers underestimated young children's competence. Consider these simple experiments:

- *Baby physics:* Like adults staring in disbelief at a magic trick (the *"Whoa!"* look), infants look longer at an unexpected and unfamiliar scene of a car seeming to pass through a solid object, a ball stopping in midair, or an object violating object permanence by magically disappearing (Baillargeon, 1995, 2008; Wellman & Gelman, 1992).

- *Baby math:* Karen Wynn (1992, 2000) showed 5-month-olds one or two objects (**FIGURE 47.5a**). Then she hid the objects behind a screen, and visibly removed or added one (Figure 47.5d). When she lifted the screen, the infants sometimes did a double take, staring longer when shown a wrong number of objects (Figure 47.5f). But were they just responding to a greater or smaller *mass* of objects, rather than a change in *number* (Feigenson et al., 2002)? Later experiments showed that babies' number sense extends to larger numbers, to ratios, and to such things as drumbeats and motions (Libertus & Brannon, 2009; McCrink & Wynn, 2004; Spelke & Kinzler, 2007). If accustomed to a Daffy Duck puppet jumping three times on stage, they showed surprise if it jumped only twice.

Clearly, infants are smarter than Piaget appreciated. Even as babies, we had a lot on our minds.

sensorimotor stage in Piaget's theory, the stage (from birth to about 2 years of age) during which infants know the world mostly in terms of their sensory impressions and motor activities.

object permanence the awareness that things continue to exist even when not perceived.

Figure 47.5

Baby math Shown a numerically impossible outcome, 5-month-old infants stare longer. (From Wynn, 1992.)

Then either: possible outcome
(e) Screen drops revealing 1 object

(a) Objects placed in case

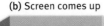

(b) Screen comes up

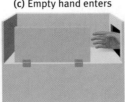

(c) Empty hand enters

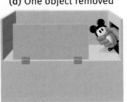

(d) One object removed

or: impossible outcome
(f) Screen drops revealing 2 objects

Preoperational Stage

Piaget believed that until about age 6 or 7, children are in a **preoperational stage**—too young to perform *mental operations* (such as imagining an action and mentally reversing it). For a 5-year-old, the milk that seems "too much" in a tall, narrow glass may become an acceptable amount if poured into a short, wide glass. Focusing only on the height dimension, this child cannot perform the operation of mentally pouring the milk back. Before about age 6, said Piaget, children lack the concept of **conservation**—the principle that quantity remains the same despite changes in shape (**FIGURE 47.6**).

Piaget did not view the stage transitions as abrupt. Even so, *symbolic thinking* (representing things with words and images) appears at an earlier age than he supposed. Judy DeLoache (1987) discovered this when she showed children a model of a room and hid a model toy in it (a miniature stuffed dog behind a miniature couch). The 2½-year-olds easily remembered where to find the miniature toy, but they could not use the model to locate an actual stuffed dog behind a couch in a real room. Three-year-olds—only 6 months older—usually went right to the actual stuffed animal in the real room, showing they *could* think of the model as a symbol for the room. Piaget probably would have been surprised.

EGOCENTRISM

Piaget contended that preschool children are **egocentric:** They have difficulty perceiving things from another's point of view. Asked to "show Mommy your picture," 2-year-old Gabriella holds the picture up facing her own eyes. Three-year-old Gray makes himself "invisible" by putting his hands over his eyes, assuming that if he can't see his grandparents,

> **preoperational stage**
> in Piaget's theory, the stage (from about 2 to about 6 or 7 years of age) during which a child learns to use language but does not yet comprehend the mental operations of concrete logic.
>
> **conservation** the principle (which Piaget believed to be a part of concrete operational reasoning) that properties such as mass, volume, and number remain the same despite changes in the forms of objects.
>
> **egocentrism** in Piaget's theory, the preoperational child's difficulty taking another's point of view.

> **AP® Exam Tip**
>
> Careful! *Egocentric* is not the same as egotistical. Egocentric means you can't take someone else's point of view. Egotistical means you're pretty full of yourself.

Bianca Moscatelli/Worth Publishers

Figure 47.6

Piaget's test of conservation This preoperational child does not yet understand the principle of conservation of substance. When the milk is poured into a tall, narrow glass, it suddenly seems like "more" than when it was in the shorter, wider glass. In another year or so, she will understand that the quantity stays the same.

"It's too late, Roger—they've seen us."

Roger has not outgrown his early childhood egocentrism.

they can't see him. Children's conversations also reveal their egocentrism, as one young boy demonstrated (Phillips, 1969, p. 61):

"Do you have a brother?"
"Yes."
"What's his name?"
"Jim."
"Does Jim have a brother?"
"No."

Like Gabriella, TV-watching preschoolers who block your view of the TV assume that you see what they see. They simply have not yet developed the ability to take another's viewpoint. Even teens and adults often overestimate the extent to which others share our opinions and perspectives, a trait known as the *curse of knowledge.* We assume that something will be clear to others if it is clear to us, or that text message recipients will "hear" our "just kidding" intent (Epley et al., 2004; Kruger et al., 2005). Children are even more susceptible to this tendency.

> **theory of mind** people's ideas about their own and others' mental states—about their feelings, perceptions, and thoughts, and the behaviors these might predict.

THEORY OF MIND

When Little Red Riding Hood realized her "grandmother" was really a wolf, she swiftly revised her ideas about the creature's intentions and raced away. Preschoolers, although still egocentric, develop this ability to infer others' mental states when they begin forming a **theory of mind** (a term first coined by psychologists to describe chimpanzees' seeming ability to read intentions [Premack & Woodruff, 1978]).

Figure 47.7

Testing children's theory of mind This simple problem illustrates how researchers explore children's presumptions about others' mental states. (Inspired by Baron-Cohen et al., 1985.)

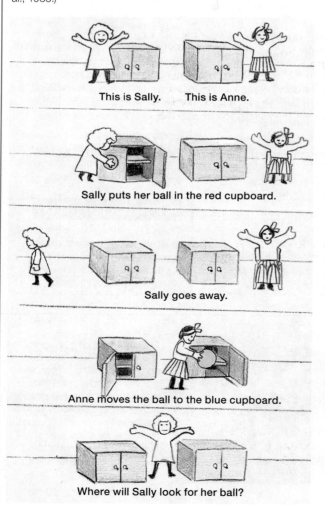

This is Sally.   This is Anne.

Sally puts her ball in the red cupboard.

Sally goes away.

Anne moves the ball to the blue cupboard.

Where will Sally look for her ball?

Infants as young as 7 months show some knowledge of others' beliefs (Kovács et al., 2010). With time, the ability to take another's perspective develops. They come to understand what made a playmate angry, when a sibling will share, and what might make a parent buy a toy. And they begin to tease, empathize, and persuade. Between about 3½ and 4½, children worldwide come to realize that others may hold false beliefs (Callaghan et al., 2005; Sabbagh et al., 2006). Researchers showed Toronto children a Band-Aids box and asked them what was inside (Jenkins & Astington, 1996). Expecting Band-Aids, the children were surprised to discover that the box actually contained pencils. Asked what a child who had never seen the box would think was inside, 3-year-olds typically answered "pencils." By age 4 to 5, the children's theory of mind had leapt forward, and they anticipated their friends' false belief that the box would hold Band-Aids.

In a follow-up experiment, children viewed a doll named Sally leaving her ball in a red cupboard (**FIGURE 47.7**). Another doll, Anne, then moves the ball to a blue cupboard. Researchers then pose a question: When Sally returns, where will she look for the ball? Children with *autism spectrum disorder* (ASD; see Close-up: Autism Spectrum Disorder and "Mind-Blindness") have difficulty understanding that Sally's state of mind differs from their own— that Sally, not knowing the ball has been moved, will return to the red cupboard. They also have difficulty reflecting on their own mental states. They are, for example, less likely to use the personal pronouns *I* and *me.* Deaf children with hearing parents and minimal communication opportunities have had similar difficulty inferring others' states of mind (Peterson & Siegal, 1999).

Autism Spectrum Disorder and "Mind-Blindness"

47-2 How does autism spectrum disorder affect development?

Diagnoses of **autism spectrum disorder (ASD),** a disorder marked by social deficiencies and repetitive behaviors, have been increasing, according to recent estimates. Once believed to affect 1 in 2500 children, ASD now affects 1 in 110 American children and about 1 in 100 in Britain (CDC, 2009; Lilienfeld & Arkowitz, 2007; NAS, 2011). The increase in ASD diagnoses has been offset by a decrease in the number of children considered "cognitively disabled" or "learning disabled," which suggests a relabeling of children's disorders (Gernsbacher et al., 2005; Grinker, 2007; Shattuck, 2006). A massive $6.7 billion National Children's Study now under way aims to enroll 100,000 pregnant women in 105 countries and to follow their babies until they turn 21—partly in hopes of explaining the rising rates of ASD, as well as premature births, childhood obesity, and asthma (Belluck, 2010; Murphy, 2008).

The underlying source of ASD's symptoms seems to be poor communication among brain regions that normally work together to let us take another's viewpoint. This effect appears to result from ASD-related genes interacting with the environment (State & Šestan, 2012). People with ASD are therefore said to have an *impaired theory of mind* (Rajendran & Mitchell, 2007; Senju et al., 2009). They have difficulty inferring others' thoughts and feelings. They do not appreciate that playmates and parents might view things differently. Mind reading that most of us find intuitive *(Is that face conveying a smirk or a sneer?)* is difficult for those with ASD. Most children learn that another child's pouting mouth signals sadness, and that twinkling eyes mean happiness or mischief. A child with ASD fails to understand these signals (Frith & Frith, 2001).

> **autism spectrum disorder (ASD)** a disorder that appears in childhood and is marked by significant deficiencies in communication and social interaction, and by rigidly fixated interests and repetitive behaviors.

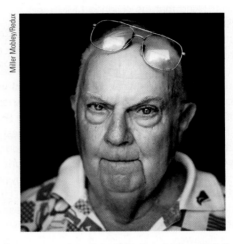

"Autism" case number 1 In 1943, Donald Gray Triplett, an "odd" child with unusual gifts and social deficits, was the first person to receive the diagnosis of a previously unreported condition, which psychiatrist Leo Kanner termed "autism." (After a 2013 change in the diagnosis manual, his condition is now called autism spectrum disorder.) In 2010, at age 77, Triplett was still living in his family home and Mississippi town, where he often played golf (Donvan & Zucker, 2010).

In hopes of a cure, desperate parents have sometimes subjected children to dubious therapies (Shute, 2010).

ASD (formerly referred to as "autism") has differing levels of severity. "High-functioning" individuals generally have normal intelligence, and they often have an exceptional skill or talent in a specific area. But they lack social and communication skills, and they tend to become distracted by minor and unimportant stimuli (Remington et al., 2009). Those at the spectrum's lower end are unable to use language at all.

ASD afflicts four boys for every girl. Psychologist Simon Baron-Cohen believes this hints at one way to understand this disorder. He has argued that ASD represents an "extreme male brain" (2008, 2009). Although there is some overlap between the sexes, he believes that boys are better "systemizers." They tend to understand things according to rules or laws, for example, as in mathematical and mechanical systems. Children exposed to high levels of the male sex hormone *testosterone* in the womb may develop more masculine and autistic traits (Auyeung et al, 2009).

In contrast, girls are naturally predisposed to be "empathizers," Baron-Cohen contends. They are better at reading facial

Autism spectrum disorder This speech-language pathologist is helping a boy with ASD learn to form sounds and words. ASD is marked by deficient social communication and difficulty grasping others' states of mind.

(Continued on next page)

Close-up (continued)

expressions and gestures, though less so if given testosterone (van Honk et al., 2011).

Biological factors, including genetic influences and abnormal brain development, contribute to ASD (State & Šestan, 2012). Childhood MMR vaccinations do not (Demicheli et al., 2012). Based on a fraudulent 1998 study—"the most damaging medical hoax of the last 100 years" (Flaherty, 2011)—some parents were misled into thinking that the childhood MMR vaccine increased risk of ASD. The unfortunate result was a drop in vaccination rates and an increase in cases of measles and mumps. Some unvaccinated children suffered long-term harm or even death.

Twin and sibling studies provide some evidence for biology's influence. If one identical twin is diagnosed with ASD, the chances are 50 to 70 percent that the co-twin will be as well (Lichtenstein et al., 2010; Sebat et al., 2007). A younger sibling of a child with ASD also is at a heightened risk (Sutcliffe, 2008). Random genetic mutations in sperm-producing cells may also play a role. As men age, these mutations become more frequent, which may help explain why an over-40 man has a much higher risk of fathering a child with ASD than does a man under 30 (Reichenberg et al., 2007). Researchers are now sleuthing ASD's telltale signs in the brain's synaptic and gray matter (Crawley, 2007; Ecker et al., 2010; Garber, 2007).

Biology's role in ASD also appears in brain-function studies. People without ASD often yawn after seeing others yawn. And as they view and imitate another's smiling or frowning, they feel something of what the other is feeling. Not so among those with ASD, who are less imitative and show much less activity in brain areas involved in mirroring others' actions (Dapretto et al., 2006; Perra et al., 2008; Senju et al., 2007). When people with ASD watch another person's hand move-ments, for example, their brain displays less than normal mir-roring activity (Oberman & Ramachandran, 2007; Théoret et al., 2005). Scientists are continuing to explore and vigorously debate the idea that the brains of people with ASD have "bro-ken mirrors" (Gallese et al., 2011).

Seeking to "systemize empathy," Baron-Cohen and his Cambridge University colleagues (2007; Golan et al., 2010) collaborated with Britain's National Autistic Society and a film production company. Knowing that television shows with ve-hicles have been popular among kids with ASD, they created animations that grafted emotion-conveying faces onto toy tram, train, and tractor characters in a pretend boy's bedroom (**FIGURE 47.8**). After the boy leaves for school, the charac-ters come to life and have experiences that lead them to dis-play various emotions (which I predict you would enjoy viewing at www.thetransporters.com). The children were surprisingly able to generalize what they had learned to a new, real con-text. By the intervention's end, their previously deficient ability to recognize emotions on real faces now equaled that of chil-dren without ASD.

"The neighbor's dog has bitten people before. He is barking at Louise."

Point to the face that shows how Louise is feeling.

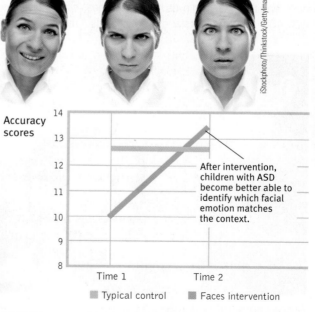

Figure 47.8

Transported into a world of emotion (a) A research team at Cambridge University's Autism Research Centre introduced children with ASD to emotions experienced and displayed by toy vehicles. (b) After 4 weeks of viewing animations, the children displayed a markedly increased ability to recognize emotions not only in the toy faces but also in humans.

After intervention, children with ASD become better able to identify which facial emotion matches the context.

Accuracy scores

■ Typical control   ■ Faces intervention

(a) Emotion-conveying faces were grafted onto toy trains.

(b) Children matched the correct face with the story and photo. (The graph above shows data from two trials.)

Concrete Operational Stage

By age 6 or 7, said Piaget, children enter the **concrete operational stage.** Given concrete (physical) materials, they begin to grasp conservation. Understanding that change in form does not mean change in quantity, they can mentally pour milk back and forth between glasses of different shapes. They also enjoy jokes that use this new understanding:

> Mr. Jones went into a restaurant and ordered a whole pizza for his dinner. When the waiter asked if he wanted it cut into 6 or 8 pieces, Mr. Jones said, "Oh, you'd better make it 6, I could never eat 8 pieces!" (McGhee, 1976)

Piaget believed that during the concrete operational stage, children become able to comprehend mathematical transformations and conservation. When my daughter, Laura, was 6, I was astonished at her inability to reverse simple arithmetic. Asked, "What is 8 plus 4?" she required 5 seconds to compute "12," and another 5 seconds to then compute 12 minus 4. By age 8, she could answer a reversed question instantly.

Formal Operational Stage

By age 12, our reasoning expands from the purely concrete (involving actual experience) to encompass abstract thinking (involving imagined realities and symbols). As children approach adolescence, said Piaget, many become capable of thinking more like scientists. They can ponder hypothetical propositions and deduce consequences: *If* this, *then* that. Systematic reasoning, what Piaget called **formal operational** thinking, is now within their grasp.

Although full-blown logic and reasoning await adolescence, the rudiments of formal operational thinking begin earlier than Piaget realized. Consider this simple problem:

> If John is in school, then Mary is in school. John is in school. What can you say about Mary?

Formal operational thinkers have no trouble answering correctly. But neither do most 7-year-olds (Suppes, 1982). **TABLE 47.1** summarizes the four stages in Piaget's theory.

AP® Exam Tip

One good way to master the developmental milestones in Piaget's theory is to see them in action. If you know children of various ages, you can test them using some of the ideas presented in this section. Hide a toy from an infant to see object permanence in action. Pour water between two differently shaped glasses to see if a preschooler understands conservation.

Table 47.1 Piaget's Stages of Cognitive Development

Typical Age Range	Description of Stage	Developmental Phenomena
Birth to nearly 2 years	*Sensorimotor* Experiencing the world through senses and actions (looking, hearing, touching, mouthing, and grasping)	• Object permanence • Stranger anxiety
About 2 to about 6 or 7 years	*Preoperational* Representing things with words and images (symbolic thinking); using intuitive rather than logical reasoning	• Pretend play • Egocentrism
6 or 7 to 11 years	*Concrete operational* Thinking logically about concrete events; grasping concrete analogies and performing arithmetical operations	• Conservation • Mathematical transformations
About 12 through adulthood	*Formal operational* Abstract reasoning	• Abstract logic • Potential for mature moral reasoning

Jamie Grill/Getty Images

Pretend play

Lev Vygotsky (1896–1934)
Vygotsky, a Russian developmental psychologist pictured here with his daughter, studied how a child's mind feeds on the language of social interaction.

An Alternative Viewpoint: Lev Vygotsky's Scaffolding

As Piaget was forming his theory of cognitive development, Russian psychologist Lev Vygotsky was also studying how children think and learn. He noted that by age 7, they increasingly think in words and use words to solve problems. They do this, he said, by internalizing their culture's language and relying on inner speech (Fernyhough, 2008). Parents who say *"No, no!"* when pulling a child's hand away from a cake are giving the child a self-control tool. When the child later needs to resist temptation, he may likewise say *"No, no!"* Second graders who muttered to themselves while doing math problems grasped third-grade math better the following year (Berk, 1994). Whether out loud or inaudibly, talking to themselves helps children control their behavior and emotions and master new skills.

Where Piaget emphasized how the child's mind grows through interaction with the physical environment, Vygotsky emphasized how the child's mind grows through interaction with the *social* environment. If Piaget's child was a young scientist, Vygotsky's was a young apprentice. By mentoring children and giving them new words, parents and others provide a temporary *scaffold* from which children can step to higher levels of thinking (Renninger & Granott, 2005). Language, an important ingredient of social mentoring, provides the building blocks for thinking, noted Vygotsky (who was born the same year as Piaget, but died prematurely of tuberculosis).

Effective mentoring occurs when children are developmentally ready to learn a new skill. For Vygotsky, a child's *zone of proximal development* was the zone between what a child can and can't do—it's what a child can do with help. When learning to ride a bike, it's the developmental zone in which a child can ride with training wheels or a steadying parental hand.

Reflecting on Piaget's Theory

"Assessing the impact of Piaget on developmental psychology is like assessing the impact of Shakespeare on English literature." -Developmental psychologist Harry Beilin (1992)

What remains of Piaget's ideas about the child's mind? Plenty—enough to merit his being singled out by *Time* magazine as one of the twentieth century's 20 most influential scientists and thinkers and rated in a survey of British psychologists as the last century's greatest psychologist (*Psychologist,* 2003). Piaget identified significant cognitive milestones and stimulated worldwide interest in how the mind develops. His emphasis was less on the ages at which children typically reach specific milestones than on their sequence. Studies around the globe, from aboriginal Australia to Algeria to North America, have confirmed that human cognition unfolds basically in the sequence Piaget described (Lourenco & Machado, 1996; Segall et al., 1990).

However, today's researchers see development as more continuous than did Piaget. By detecting the beginnings of each type of thinking at earlier ages, they have revealed conceptual abilities Piaget missed. Moreover, they see formal logic as a smaller part of cognition than he did. Piaget would not be surprised that today, as part of our own cognitive development, we are adapting his ideas to accommodate new findings.

Implications for Parenting and Teaching

"Childhood has its own way of seeing, thinking, and feeling, and there is nothing more foolish than the attempt to put ours in its place." -Philosopher Jean-Jacques Rousseau, 1798

Future parents and teachers remember: Young children are incapable of adult logic. Preschoolers who block one's view of the TV simply have not learned to take another's viewpoint. What seems simple and obvious to us—pestering a cat will lead to scratches—may be incomprehensible to a 3-year-old. Also remember that children are not passive receptacles waiting to be filled with knowledge. Better to build on what they already know, engaging them in concrete demonstrations and stimulating them to think for themselves. And, finally, accept children's cognitive immaturity as adaptive. It is nature's strategy for keeping children close to protective adults and providing time for learning and socialization (Bjorklund & Green, 1992).

Before You Move On

▶ **ASK YOURSELF**

Can you recall a time when you misheard some song lyrics because you assimilated them into your own schema? (For hundreds of examples of this phenomenon, visit www.kissthisguy.com.)

▶ **TEST YOURSELF**

Use Piaget's first three stages of cognitive development to explain why children are not just miniature adults in the way they think.

Answers to the Test Yourself questions can be found in Appendix E at the end of the book.

Module 47 Review

47-1

From the perspectives of Piaget, Vygotsky, and today's researchers, how does a child's mind develop?

- In his theory of *cognitive* development, Jean Piaget proposed that children actively construct and modify their understanding of the world through the processes of *assimilation* and *accommodation.* They form *schemas* that help them organize their experiences.

- Progressing from the simplicity of the *sensorimotor stage* of the first two years, in which they develop *object permanence,* children move to more complex ways of thinking.

- In the *preoperational stage* (about age 2 to about 6 or 7), they develop a *theory of mind,* but they are *egocentric* and unable to perform simple logical operations.

- At age 6 or 7, they enter the *concrete operational stage* and are able to comprehend the principle of *conservation.*

- By about age 12, children enter the *formal operational stage* and can reason systematically.

- Research supports the sequence Piaget proposed, but it also shows that young children are more capable, and their development is more continuous, than he believed.

- Lev Vygotsky's studies of child development focused on the ways a child's mind grows by interacting with the social environment. In his view, parents and caretakers provide temporary scaffolds enabling children to step to higher levels of learning.

47-2 **How does autism spectrum disorder affect development?**

- ASD is marked by social deficiencies and repetitive behaviors.

- Genetic influences contribute to ASD, as does the male hormone testosterone.

Multiple-Choice Questions

1. Your friend's baby brother, Matt, loves to play with his pet cat. When he sees a puppy, he points and calls it "Mi Mi," which is what he calls his cat. Matt is demonstrating Piaget's process of

   a. conservation.
   b. accommodation.
   c. cognition.
   d. object permanence.
   e. assimilation.

2. If you showed a 2-year-old that you'd hidden a toy behind the bed in a model of her bedroom, she would not be able to find the toy in her real bedroom because she lacks

   a. analytical thinking.
   b. random thinking.
   c. symbolic thinking.
   d. schematic thinking.
   e. egocentric thinking.

3. Vygotsky called the space between what a child could learn with and without help the

   a. theory of mind.
   b. zone of abstract logic.
   c. zone of abstract reasoning.
   d. zone of proximal development.
   e. zone of developmental readiness.

4. Which of the following is a current belief of researchers that differs from Piaget's original theories?

   a. Infants simply have less information about the world than older children and adults.
   b. Object permanence develops earlier than Piaget believed.
   c. Infants learn more by verbal explanations than Piaget believed.
   d. Accommodation is a process that doesn't occur in young children.
   e. Schemas don't form until later than Piaget believed.

5. Which of the following cognitive abilities is possible only at the formal operational stage?

   a. Reversing arithmetic operations
   b. Using a theory of mind to predict the behavior of others
   c. Using hypothetical situations as the basis of moral reasoning
   d. Using symbolic thinking for pretend play
   e. Understanding basic physics to recognize impossible situations

6. Which of the following identifies children's difficulty seeing another's perspective?

   a. Abstract thinker
   b. Role player
   c. Egocentric thinker
   d. A child who understands conservation
   e. A child who demonstrates high mental operations

7. Which of the following would indicate that a child understood conservation?

   a. She would continue to seek a toy hidden under a blanket.
   b. She would "hide" in a game of hide-and-seek by covering her eyes with her hands.
   c. She would believe that a clay snake would have the same amount of clay as the clay ball that was used to make it.
   d. She would recognize that 7 + 3 involves the same mathematical relationship as 10 − 7.
   e. She would be able to comprehend the logic of if-then statements.

Practice FRQs

1. Describe Lev Vygotsky's ideas on the role of language, scaffolding, and the zone of proximal development in cognitive development. How did his theory differ from that of Jean Piaget?

Answer

1 point: Vygotsky believed that as children grow, they increasingly use words to solve problems and think. Adults help with this process by giving them words to internalize behaviors.

1 point: Scaffolding is the way in which parents and others mentor children to promote cognitive growth, often through providing new words to describe a situation.

1 point: The zone of proximal development marks the border between what children can learn on their own or with help.

1 point: The major difference is that Piaget thought cognitive development resulted from children's interactions with their physical environment, while Vygotsky believed they learned through social interactions.

2. Define and give an example of each of the cognitive milestones listed below:

- Object permanence
- Conservation
- Theory of mind

(3 points)

Module 48

Infancy and Childhood: Social Development

© Sean Cayton/The Image Works

Module Learning Objectives

48-1 Describe how parent-infant attachment bonds form.

48-2 Describe how psychologists study attachment differences, and discuss their findings about the effect of temperament and parenting.

48-3 Discuss how childhood neglect, abuse, or family disruption affect children's attachments.

48-4 Discuss the effect of day care on children.

48-5 Trace the onset and development of children's self-concept.

48-6 Describe three parenting styles, and explain how children's traits relate to them.

48-1 How do parent-infant attachment bonds form?

From birth, babies in all cultures are social creatures, developing an intense bond with their caregivers. Infants come to prefer familiar faces and voices, then to coo and gurgle when given a parent's attention. At about 8 months, soon after object permanence emerges and children become mobile, a curious thing happens: They develop **stranger anxiety.** They may greet strangers by crying and self-protectively reaching for familiar caregivers. "No! Don't leave me!" their distress seems to say. Children this age have schemas for familiar faces; when they cannot assimilate the new face into these remembered schemas, they become distressed (Kagan, 1984). Once again, we see an important principle: *The brain, mind, and social-emotional behavior develop together.*

stranger anxiety the fear of strangers that infants commonly display, beginning by about 8 months of age.

attachment an emotional tie with another person; shown in young children by their seeking closeness to the caregiver and showing distress on separation.

Origins of Attachment

One-year-olds typically cling tightly to a parent when they are frightened or expect separation. Reunited after being apart, they shower the parent with smiles and hugs. No social behavior is more striking than the intense and mutual infant-parent bond. This **attachment** bond is a powerful survival impulse that keeps infants close to their caregivers. Infants become attached to those—typically their parents—who are comfortable and familiar. For many years, psychologists reasoned that infants became attached to those who satisfied their need for nourishment. It made sense. But an accidental finding overturned this explanation.

Body Contact

During the 1950s, University of Wisconsin psychologists Harry Harlow and Margaret Harlow bred monkeys for their learning studies. To equalize experiences and to isolate any disease, they separated the infant monkeys from their mothers shortly after birth and raised them in sanitary individual cages, which included a cheesecloth baby blanket (Harlow et al., 1971). Then came a surprise: When their blankets were taken to be laundered, the monkeys became distressed.

The Harlows recognized that this intense attachment to the blanket contradicted the idea that attachment derives from an association with nourishment. But how could they show this more convincingly? To pit the drawing power of a food source against the contact comfort of the blanket, they created two artificial mothers. One was a bare wire cylinder with a wooden head and an attached feeding bottle, the other cylinder wrapped with terry cloth.

When raised with both, the monkeys overwhelmingly preferred the comfy cloth mother (**FIGURE 48.1**). Like other infants clinging to their live mothers, the monkey babies would cling to their cloth mothers when anxious. When exploring their environment, they used her as a *secure base,* as if attached to her by an invisible elastic band that stretched only so far before pulling them back. Researchers soon learned that other qualities—rocking, warmth, and feeding—made the cloth mother even more appealing.

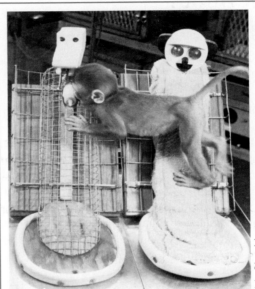

Figure 48.1
The Harlows' monkey mothers
Psychologists Harry Harlow and Margaret Harlow raised monkeys with two artificial mothers—one a bare wire cylinder with a wooden head and an attached feeding bottle, the other a cylinder with no bottle but covered with foam rubber and wrapped with terry cloth. The Harlows' discovery surprised many psychologists: The infants much preferred contact with the comfortable cloth mother, even while feeding from the nourishing mother.

Harlow Primate Laboratory

Human infants, too, become attached to parents who are soft and warm and who rock, feed, and pat. Much parent-infant emotional communication occurs via touch (Hertenstein et al., 2006), which can be either soothing (snuggles) or arousing (tickles). Human attachment also consists of one person providing another with a secure base from which to explore and a safe haven when distressed. As we mature, our secure base and safe haven shift—from parents to peers and partners (Cassidy & Shaver, 1999). But at all ages we are social creatures. We gain strength when someone offers, by words and actions, a safe haven: "I will be here. I am interested in you. Come what may, I will support you" (Crowell & Waters, 1994).

Familiarity

Contact is one key to attachment. Another is familiarity. In many animals, attachments based on familiarity form during a **critical period**—an optimal period when certain events must take place to facilitate proper development (Bornstein, 1989). For goslings, ducklings, or chicks, that period falls in the hours shortly after hatching, when the first moving object they see is normally their mother. From then on, the young fowl follow her, and her alone.

Konrad Lorenz (1937) explored this rigid attachment process, called **imprinting.** He wondered: What would ducklings do if he was the first moving creature they observed? What they did was follow him around: Everywhere that Konrad went, the ducks were sure to go. Although baby birds imprint best to their own species, they also will imprint to a variety of moving objects—an animal of another species, a box on wheels, a bouncing ball (Colombo, 1982; Johnson, 1992). Once formed, this attachment is difficult to reverse.

FYI

For some people, a perceived relationship with God functions as do other attachments, by providing a secure base for exploration and a safe haven when threatened (Granqvist et al., 2010; Kirkpatrick, 1999).

critical period an optimal period early in the life of an organism when exposure to certain stimuli or experiences produces normal development.

imprinting the process by which certain animals form strong attachments during an early-life critical period.

Imprinting Whooping cranes normally learn to migrate by following their parents. These cranes, hand-raised from eggs, have imprinted on a crane-costumed ultralight pilot, who then guided them to winter nesting grounds (Mooallem, 2009).

Children—unlike ducklings—do not imprint. However, they do become attached, during a less precisely defined *sensitive period,* to what they've known. *Mere exposure* to people and things fosters fondness (see Module 79). Children like to reread the same books, rewatch the same movies, reenact family traditions. They prefer to eat familiar foods, live in the same familiar neighborhood, attend school with the same old friends. You may even have noticed your own preference for familiar music, familiar daily routines, and familiar class seating locations. Familiarity is a safety signal. Familiarity breeds content.

Attachment Differences: Temperament and Parenting

48-2 How have psychologists studied attachment differences, and what have they learned about the effects of temperament and parenting?

What accounts for children's attachment differences? To answer this question, Mary Ainsworth (1979) designed the *strange situation* experiment. She observed mother-infant pairs at home during their first 6 months. Later she observed the 1-year-old infants in a strange situation (usually a laboratory playroom). Such research has shown that about 60 percent of infants display *secure attachment.* In their mother's presence they play comfortably, happily exploring their new environment. When she leaves, they become distressed; when she returns, they seek contact with her.

Other infants avoid attachment or show *insecure attachment,* marked either by anxiety or avoidance of trusting relationships. They are less likely to explore their surroundings; they may even cling to their mother. When she leaves, they either cry loudly and remain upset or seem indifferent to her departure and return (Ainsworth, 1973, 1989; Kagan, 1995; van IJzendoorn & Kroonenberg, 1988).

Ainsworth and others found that sensitive, responsive mothers—those who noticed what their babies were doing and responded appropriately—had infants who exhibited secure attachment (De Wolff & van IJzendoorn, 1997). Insensitive, unresponsive mothers—mothers who attended to their babies when they felt like doing so but ignored them at other times—often had infants who were insecurely attached. The Harlows' monkey studies, with unresponsive artificial mothers, produced even more striking effects. When put in strange situations without their artificial mothers, the deprived infants were terrified (**FIGURE 48.2**).

But is attachment style the *result* of parenting? Or is attachment style the result of genetically influenced **temperament**—a person's characteristic emotional reactivity and intensity?

As most parents will tell you after having their second child, babies differ even before gulping their first breath. Heredity predisposes temperament differences (Rothbart, 2007).

temperament a person's characteristic emotional reactivity and intensity.

AP® Exam Tip

Note that temperament is a contribution from the nature side of the nature–nurture debate.

From their first weeks of life, some infants are reactive, intense, and fidgety. Others are easygoing, quiet, and placid. *Difficult* babies are more irritable, intense, and unpredictable. *Easy* babies are cheerful, relaxed, and predictable in feeding and sleeping. *Slow-to-warm-up* infants tend to resist or withdraw from new people and situations (Chess & Thomas, 1987; Thomas & Chess, 1977). And temperament differences typically persist. Consider:

- The most emotionally reactive newborns tend also to be the most reactive 9-month-olds (Wilson & Matheny, 1986; Worobey & Blajda, 1989).

- Exceptionally inhibited and fearful 2-year-olds often are still relatively shy as 8-year-olds; about half will become introverted adolescents (Kagan et al., 1992, 1994).

- The most emotionally intense preschoolers tend to be relatively intense young adults (Larsen & Diener, 1987). In one study of more than 900 New Zealanders, emotionally reactive and impulsive 3-year-olds developed into somewhat more impulsive, aggressive, and conflict-prone 21-year-olds (Caspi, 2000).

The genetic effect appears in physiological differences. Anxious, inhibited infants have high and variable heart rates and a reactive nervous system. When facing new or strange situations, they become more physiologically aroused (Kagan & Snidman, 2004). One form of a gene that regulates the neurotransmitter serotonin predisposes a fearful temperament and, in combination with unsupportive caregiving, an inhibited child (Fox et al., 2007). Such evidence adds to the emerging conclusion that our biologically rooted temperament helps form our enduring personality (McCrae et al., 2000, 2007; Rothbart et al., 2000).

By neglecting such inborn differences, the parenting studies, noted Judith Harris (1998), are like "comparing foxhounds reared in kennels with poodles reared in apartments." So to separate nature and nurture, we would need to vary parenting while controlling temperament. (Pause and think: If you were the researcher, how might you have done this?)

One Dutch researcher's solution was to randomly assign 100 temperamentally difficult 6- to 9-month-olds to either an experimental group, in which mothers received personal training in sensitive responding, or to a control group, in which they did not (van den Boom, 1990, 1995). At 12 months of age, 68 percent of the infants in the experimental group were rated securely attached, as were only 28 percent of the control group infants. Other studies support the idea that intervention programs can increase parental sensitivity and, to a lesser extent, infant attachment security (Bakermans-Kranenburg et al., 2003; Van Zeijl et al., 2006).

As these examples indicate, researchers have more often studied mother care than father care. Infants who lack a caring mother are said to suffer "maternal deprivation";

Figure 48.2
Social deprivation and fear
In the Harlows' experiments, monkeys raised with artificial mothers were terror-stricken when placed in strange situations without those mothers. (Today's climate of greater respect for animal welfare prevents such primate studies.)

"Oh, he's cute, all right, but he's got the temperament of a car alarm."

Full-time dad Financial analyst Walter Cranford, shown here with his baby twins, is one of a growing number of stay-at-home dads. Cranford says the experience has made him appreciate how difficult the work can be: "Sometimes at work you can just unplug, but with this you've got to be going all the time."

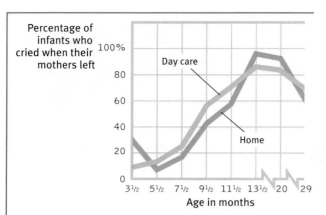

Figure 48.3

Infants' distress over separation from parents In an experiment, groups of infants were left by their mothers in an unfamiliar room. In both groups, the percentage who cried when the mother left peaked at about 13 months. Whether the infant had experienced day care made little difference. (From Kagan, 1976.)

Jouke van Keulen/Shutterstock

those lacking a father's care merely experience "father absence." This reflects a wider attitude in which "fathering a child" has meant impregnating, and "mothering" has meant nurturing. But fathers are more than just mobile sperm banks. Across nearly 100 studies worldwide, a father's love and acceptance have been comparable to a mother's love in predicting their offspring's health and well-being (Rohner & Veneziano, 2001). In one mammoth British study following 7259 children from birth to adulthood, those whose fathers were most involved in parenting (through outings, reading to them, and taking an interest in their education) tended to achieve more in school, even after controlling for other factors such as parental education and family wealth (Flouri & Buchanan, 2004).

Children's anxiety over separation from parents peaks at around 13 months, then gradually declines (**FIGURE 48.3**). This happens whether they live with one parent or two, are cared for at home or in a day-care center, live in North America, Guatemala, or the Kalahari Desert. Does this mean our need for and love of others also fades away? Hardly. Our capacity for love grows, and our pleasure in touching and holding those we love never ceases. The power of early attachment does nonetheless gradually relax, allowing us to move out into a wider range of situations, communicate with strangers more freely, and stay emotionally attached to loved ones despite distance.

Attachment Styles and Later Relationships

Developmental theorist Erik Erikson (1902–1994), working with his wife, Joan Erikson, believed that securely attached children approach life with a sense of **basic trust**—a sense that the world is predictable and reliable. He attributed basic trust not to environment or inborn temperament, but to early parenting. He theorized that infants blessed with sensitive, loving caregivers form a lifelong attitude of trust rather than fear. (Later, we'll consider Erikson's other stages of development.)

Although debate continues, many researchers now believe that our early attachments form the foundation for our adult relationships and our comfort with affection and intimacy (Birnbaum et al., 2006; Fraley et al., 2013). Our adult styles of romantic love tend to exhibit either secure, trusting attachment; insecure, anxious attachment; or the avoidance of attachment (Feeney & Noller, 1990; Rholes & Simpson, 2004; Shaver & Mikulincer, 2007). These adult attachment styles in turn affect relationships with one's own children, as avoidant people find parenting more stressful and unsatisfying (Rholes et al., 2006).

Attachment style is also associated with motivation (Elliot & Reis, 2003). Securely attached people exhibit less fear of failure and a greater drive to achieve. But say this for those (nearly half of all humans) who exhibit insecure attachments: Anxious or avoidant tendencies have helped our groups detect or escape dangers (Ein-Dor et al., 2010).

"Out of the conflict between trust and mistrust, the infant develops hope, which is the earliest form of what gradually becomes faith in adults." -ERIK ERIKSON (1983)

basic trust according to Erik Erikson, a sense that the world is predictable and trustworthy; said to be formed during infancy by appropriate experiences with responsive caregivers.

Deprivation of Attachment

48-3 Does childhood neglect, abuse, or family disruption affect children's attachments?

If secure attachment nurtures social trust, what happens when circumstances prevent a child from forming attachments? In all of psychology, there is no sadder research literature. Babies locked away at home under conditions of abuse or extreme neglect are often withdrawn, frightened, even speechless. The same is true of those raised in institutions without the stimulation and attention of a regular caregiver, as was tragically illustrated during the

"What is learned in the cradle, lasts to the grave." -FRENCH PROVERB

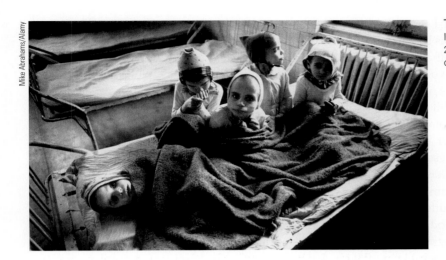

The deprivation of attachment
In this Romanian orphanage, the 250 children between ages 1 and 5 outnumbered caregivers 15 to 1.

1970s and 1980s in Romania. Having decided that economic growth for his impoverished country required more human capital, Nicolae Ceaușescu, Romania's Communist dictator, outlawed contraception, forbade abortion, and taxed families with fewer than five children. The birthrate indeed skyrocketed. But unable to afford the children they had been coerced into having, many families abandoned them to government-run orphanages with untrained and overworked staff. Child-to-caregiver ratios often were 15 to 1 (and you thought babysitting triplets was a strain), so the children were deprived of healthy attachment with at least one adult. When tested after Ceaușescu was assassinated in 1989, these children had lower intelligence scores and double the 20 percent rate of anxiety symptoms found in children assigned to quality foster care settings (Nelson et al., 2009). Dozens of other studies across 19 countries have confirmed that orphaned children tend to fare better on later intelligence tests if raised in family homes. This is especially so for those placed at an early age (van IJzendoorn et al., 2008).

Most children growing up under adversity (as did the surviving children of the Holocaust) are *resilient;* they withstand the trauma and become normal adults (Helmreich, 1992; Masten, 2001). So do most victims of childhood sexual abuse, noted Harvard researcher Susan Clancy (2010), while emphasizing that using children for sex is revolting and never the victim's fault.

But others, especially those who experience no sharp break from their abusive past, don't bounce back so readily. The Harlows' monkeys raised in total isolation, without even an artificial mother, bore lifelong scars. As adults, when placed with other monkeys their age, they either cowered in fright or lashed out in aggression. When they reached sexual maturity, most were incapable of mating. If artificially impregnated, females often were neglectful, abusive, even murderous toward their first-born. Another primate experiment confirmed the abuse-breeds-abuse phenomenon. In one study, 9 of 16 females who had been abused by their mothers became abusive parents, as did *no* female raised by a nonabusive mother (Maestripieri, 2005).

In humans, too, the unloved may become the unloving. Most abusive parents—and many condemned murderers—have reported being neglected or battered as children (Kempe & Kempe, 1978; Lewis et al., 1988). Some 30 percent of people who have been abused later abuse their children—a rate lower than that found in the primate study, but four times the U.S. national rate of child abuse (Dumont et al., 2007; Kaufman & Zigler, 1987).

Although most abused children do *not* later become violent criminals or abusive parents, extreme early trauma may nevertheless leave footprints on the brain. Abused children exhibit hypersensitivity to angry faces (Pollak, 2008). As adults, they exhibit stronger startle responses (Jovanovic et al., 2009). If repeatedly threatened and attacked while young, normally placid golden hamsters grow up to be cowards when caged with same-sized hamsters, or bullies when caged with weaker ones (Ferris, 1996). Such animals show changes in the brain chemical serotonin, which calms aggressive impulses. A similarly sluggish serotonin response has been found in abused children who become aggressive teens and adults. "Stress can set off a ripple of hormonal changes that permanently wire a child's brain to cope with a malevolent world," concluded abuse researcher Martin Teicher (2002).

Such findings help explain why young children who have survived severe or prolonged physical abuse, childhood sexual abuse, or wartime atrocities are at increased risk for health problems, psychological disorders, substance abuse, and criminality (Freyd et al., 2005; Kendall-Tackett et al., 1993, 2004; Wegman & Stetler, 2009). Abuse victims are at considerable risk for depression *if* they carry a gene variation that spurs stress-hormone production (Bradley et al., 2008). As we will see again and again, behavior and emotion arise from a particular environment interacting with particular genes.

Adults also suffer when attachment bonds are severed. Whether through death or separation, a break produces a predictable sequence. Agitated preoccupation with the lost partner is followed by deep sadness and, eventually, the beginnings of emotional detachment and a return to normal living (Hazan & Shaver, 1994). Newly separated couples who have long ago ceased feeling affection are sometimes surprised at their desire to be near the former partner. Deep and longstanding attachments seldom break quickly. Detaching is a process, not an event.

Day Care

48-4   How does day care affect children?

In the mid-twentieth century, when mom-at-home was the social norm, researchers asked, "Is day care bad for children? Does it disrupt children's attachments to their parents?" For the high-quality day-care programs usually studied, the answer was *No*. In *Mother Care/Other Care,* developmental psychologist Sandra Scarr (1986) explained that children are "biologically sturdy individuals . . . who can thrive in a wide variety of life situations." Scarr spoke for many developmental psychologists, whose research has uncovered no major impact of maternal employment on children's development, attachments, and achievements (Friedman & Boyle, 2008; Goldberg et al., 2008; Lucas-Thompson et al., 2010).

Research then shifted to the effects of differing quality of day care on different types and ages of children (Vandell et al., 2010). Scarr (1997) explained: Around the world, "high-quality child care consists of warm, supportive interactions with adults in a safe, healthy, and stimulating environment. . . . Poor care is boring and unresponsive to children's needs." Even well-run orphanages can produce healthy, thriving children. In Africa and Asia, where more and more children are losing parents to AIDS and other diseases, orphanages typically are unlike those in Ceauşescu's Romania, and the children living in quality orphanages fare about as well as those living in communities (Whetten et al., 2009).

Children's ability to thrive under varied types of responsive caregiving should not surprise us, given cultural variations in attachment patterns. Westernized attachment features one or two caregivers and their offspring. In other cultures, such as the Efe of Zaire, multiple caregivers are the norm (Field, 1996; Whaley et al., 2002). Even before the mother holds her newborn, the baby is passed among several women. In the weeks to come, the infant will be constantly held (and fed) by other women. The result is strong multiple attachments.

One ongoing study in 10 American cities has followed 1100 children since the age of 1 month. The researchers found that

An example of high-quality day care Research has shown that young children thrive socially and intellectually in safe, stimulating environments with a ratio of one caregiver for every three or four children.

AP Photo/Imperial Valley Press, Cuauhtemoc Beltran

at ages 4½ to 6, children who had spent the most time in day care had slightly advanced thinking and language skills. They also had an increased rate of aggressiveness and defiance (NICHD, 2002, 2003, 2006). To developmental psychologist Eleanor Maccoby (2003), the positive correlation between the increased rate of problem behaviors and time spent in child care suggested "some risk for some children spending extended time in some day-care settings as they're now organized." But the child's temperament, the parents' sensitivity, and the family's economic and educational level influenced aggression more than time spent in day care.

There is little disagreement that the children who merely exist for 9 hours a day in understaffed centers deserve better. What all children need is a consistent, warm relationship with people whom they can learn to trust. The importance of such relationships extends beyond the preschool years, as Finnish psychologist Lea Pulkkinen (2006) observed in her career-long study of 285 individuals tracked from age 8 to 42. Her finding—that adult monitoring of children predicts favorable outcomes—led her to undertake, with support from Finland's parliament, a nationwide program of adult-supervised activities for all first and second graders (Pulkkinen, 2004; Rose, 2004).

Self-Concept

48-5 How do children's self-concepts develop?

Self-awareness Mirror images fascinate infants from the age of about 6 months. Only at about 18 months, however, does the child recognize that the image in the mirror is "me."

Infancy's major social achievement is attachment. *Childhood's* major social achievement is a positive sense of self. By the end of childhood, at about age 12, most children have developed a **self-concept**—an understanding and assessment of who they are. (Their *self-esteem* is how they feel about who they are.) Parents often wonder when and how this sense of self develops. "Is my baby girl aware of herself—does she know she is a person distinct from everyone else?"

Of course we cannot ask the baby directly, but we can again capitalize on what she can do—letting her *behavior* provide clues to the beginnings of her self-awareness. In 1877, biologist Charles Darwin offered one idea: Self-awareness begins when we recognize ourselves in a mirror. To see whether a child recognizes that the girl in the mirror is indeed herself, researchers sneakily dabbed color on the nose. At about 6 months, children reach out to touch their mirror image as if it were another child (Courage & Howe, 2002; Damon & Hart, 1982, 1988, 1992). By 15 to 18 months, they begin to touch their own noses when they see the colored spot in the mirror (Butterworth, 1992; Gallup & Suarez, 1986). Apparently, 18-month-olds have a schema of how their face should look, and they wonder, "What is that spot doing on *my* face?"

Self-aware animals After prolonged exposure to mirrors, several species—chimpanzees, orangutans, gorillas, dolphins, elephants, and magpies—have similarly demonstrated self-recognition of their mirror image (Gallup, 1970; Reis & Marino, 2001; Prior et al., 2008). In an experiment by Joshua Plotnik and colleagues (2006), Happy, an Asian elephant, when facing a mirror, repeatedly used her trunk to touch an "X" painted above her eye (but not a similar mark above the other eye that was visible only under black light). As one report said, "She's Happy and she knows it!"

> **self-concept** all our thoughts and feelings about ourselves, in answer to the question, "Who am I?"

By school age, children's self-concept has blossomed into more detailed descriptions that include their gender, group memberships, psychological traits, and similarities and differences compared with other children (Newman & Ruble, 1988; Stipek, 1992). They come to see themselves as good and skillful in some ways but not others. They form a concept of which traits, ideally, they would like to have. By age 8 or 10, their self-image is quite stable.

Children's views of themselves affect their actions. Children who form a positive self-concept are more confident, independent, optimistic, assertive, and sociable (Maccoby, 1980). So how can parents encourage a positive yet realistic self-concept?

Parenting Styles

48-6 What are three parenting styles, and how do children's traits relate to them?

Some parents spank, some reason. Some are strict, some are lax. Some show little affection, some liberally hug and kiss. Do such differences in parenting styles affect children?

The most heavily researched aspect of parenting has been how, and to what extent, parents seek to control their children. Investigators have identified three parenting styles:

1. *Authoritarian* parents impose rules and expect obedience: "Don't interrupt." "Keep your room clean." "Don't stay out late or you'll be grounded." "Why? Because I said so."
2. *Permissive* parents submit to their children's desires. They make few demands and use little punishment.
3. *Authoritative* parents are both demanding and responsive. They exert control by setting rules and enforcing them, but they also explain the reasons for rules. And, especially with older children, they encourage open discussion when making the rules and allow exceptions.

Too hard, too soft, and just right, these styles have been called, especially by pioneering researcher Diana Baumrind and her followers. Research indicates that children with the highest self-esteem, self-reliance, and social competence usually have warm, concerned, *authoritative* parents (Baumrind, 1996; Buri et al., 1988; Coopersmith, 1967). Those with authoritarian parents tend to have less social skill and self-esteem, and those with permissive parents tend to be more aggressive and immature. The participants in most studies have been middle-class White families, and some critics suggest that effective parenting may vary by culture. Yet studies with families of other races and in more than 200 cultures worldwide have confirmed the social and academic correlates of loving and authoritative parenting (Rohner & Veneziano, 2001; Sorkhabi, 2005; Steinberg & Morris, 2001). For example, two studies of thousands of Germans found that those whose parents had maintained a curfew exhibited better adjustment and greater achievements in young adulthood than did those with permissive parents (Haase et al., 2008). And the effects are stronger when children are embedded in *authoritative communities* with connected adults who model a good life (Commission on Children at Risk, 2003).

A word of caution: The association between certain parenting styles (being firm but open) and certain childhood outcomes (social competence) is correlational. *Correlation is not causation.* Here are two possible alternative explanations for this parenting-competence link.

- Children's traits may influence parenting. Parental warmth and control vary somewhat from child to child, even in the same family (Holden & Miller, 1999). Perhaps socially mature, agreeable, easygoing children *evoke* greater trust and warmth from their parents. Twin studies have supported this possibility (Kendler, 1996).
- Some underlying third factor may be at work. Perhaps, for example, competent parents and their competent children share genes that predispose social competence. Twin studies have also supported this possibility (South et al., 2008).

> **AP® Exam Tip**
>
> It's understandable if you are struggling to remember the differences between authoritarian and authoritative—these words are exactly the same through the first nine letters! Maybe it will help to realize that authoritative parents will engage in a little more give and take, and that the words *give* and *authoritative* both end in the letters *ive*.

Parents who struggle with conflicting advice should remember that *all advice reflects the advice-giver's values.* For those who prize unquestioning obedience from a child, an authoritarian style may have the desired effect. For those who value children's sociability and self-reliance, authoritative firm-but-open parenting is advisable.

Culture and Child Raising

Child-raising practices reflect cultural values that vary across time and place. Do you prefer children who are independent or children who comply? If you live in a Westernized culture, the odds are you prefer independence. "You are responsible for yourself," Western families and schools tell their children. "Follow your conscience. Be true to yourself. Discover your gifts. Think through your personal needs." A half-century and more ago, Western cultural values placed greater priority on obedience, respect, and sensitivity to others (Alwin, 1990; Remley, 1988). "Be true to your traditions," parents then taught their children. "Be loyal to your heritage and country. Show respect toward your parents and other superiors." Cultures can change.

Cultures vary Parents everywhere care about their children, but raise and protect them differently depending on the surrounding culture. Parents raising children in New York City keep them close. In Scotland's Orkney Islands' town of Stromness, social trust has enabled parents to park their toddlers outside shops.

Many Asians and Africans live in cultures that value emotional closeness. Rather than being given their own bedrooms and entrusted to day care, infants and toddlers may sleep with their mothers and spend their days close to a family member (Morelli et al., 1992; Whiting & Edwards, 1988). These cultures encourage a strong sense of *family self*—a feeling that what shames the child shames the family, and what brings honor to the family brings honor to the self.

Children across place and time have thrived under various child-raising systems. Upper-class British parents traditionally handed off routine caregiving to nannies, then sent their 10-year-olds off to boarding school. These children generally grew up to be pillars of British society, as did their parents and their boarding-school peers. In the African Gusii society, babies nurse freely but spend most of the day on their mother's back—with lots of body contact but little face-to-face and language interaction. When the mother becomes pregnant again, the toddler is weaned and handed over to someone else, often an older sibling. Westerners may wonder about the negative effects of this lack of verbal interaction, but then the African Gusii may in turn wonder about Western mothers pushing their babies around in strollers and leaving them in playpens (Small, 1997). Such diversity in child raising cautions us against presuming that our culture's way is the only way to raise children successfully.

Parental involvement promotes development Parents in every culture facilitate their children's discovery of their world, but cultures differ in what they deem important. Asian cultures place more emphasis on school and hard work than do North American cultures. This may help explain why Japanese and Taiwanese children get higher scores on mathematics achievement tests.

* * *

The investment in raising a child buys many years not only of joy and love but of worry and irritation. Yet for most people who become parents, a child is one's biological and social legacy—one's personal investment in the human future. To paraphrase psychiatrist Carl Jung, we reach backward into our parents and forward into our children, and through their children into a future we will never see, but about which we must therefore care.

Before You Move On

▶ **ASK YOURSELF**

How would you describe your own temperament? Is it similar to that of other family members, or quite different?

▶ **TEST YOURSELF**

What distinguishes imprinting from attachment?

Answers to the Test Yourself questions can be found in Appendix E at the end of the book.

Module 48 Review

48-1 How do parent-infant attachment bonds form?

- At about 8 months, soon after object permanence develops, children separated from their caregivers display *stranger anxiety.*

- Infants form *attachments* not simply because parents gratify biological needs but, more important, because they are comfortable, familiar, and responsive.

- Ducks and other animals have a more rigid attachment process, called *imprinting*, that occurs during a *critical period.*

48-2 How have psychologists studied attachment differences, and what have they learned about the effects of temperament and parenting?

- Attachment has been studied in strange situation experiments, which show that some children are securely attached and others are insecurely attached.

- Sensitive, responsive parents tend to have securely attached children.

- Adult relationships seem to reflect the attachment styles of early childhood, lending support to Erik Erikson's idea that *basic trust* is formed in infancy by our experiences with responsive caregivers.

- Yet it's become clear that *temperament*—our characteristic emotional reactivity and intensity—also plays a huge role in how our attachment patterns form.

48-3 Does childhood neglect, abuse, or family disruption affect children's attachments?

- Children are very resilient, but those who are moved repeatedly, severely neglected by their parents, or otherwise prevented from forming attachments by an early age may be at risk for attachment problems.

48-4 How does day care affect children?

- Quality day care, with responsive adults interacting with children in a safe and stimulating environment, does not appear to harm children's thinking and language skills.

- Some studies have linked extensive time in day care with increased aggressiveness and defiance, but other factors— the child's temperament, the parents' sensitivity, and the family's economic and educational levels and culture— also matter.

48-5 How do children's self-concepts develop?

- *Self-concept,* an understanding and evaluation of who we are, emerges gradually.
  - At 15 to 18 months, children recognize themselves in a mirror.
  - By school age, they can describe many of their own traits, and by ages 8 to 10 their self-image is stable.

48-6 What are three parenting styles, and how do children's traits relate to them?

- Parenting styles—authoritarian, permissive, and authoritative—reflect varying degrees of control.
- Children with high self-esteem tend to have authoritative parents and to be self-reliant and socially competent, but the direction of cause and effect in this relationship is not clear.

Multiple-Choice Questions

1. An 18-month-old typically recognizes herself in a mirror. This self-awareness contributes to
   a. self-assurance.
   b. self-concept.
   c. self-esteem.
   d. self-actualization.
   e. self-determination.

2. In the attachment studies conducted with infant monkeys, what did the Harlows find?
   a. Nutrition was the most important factor in attachment.
   b. Contact comfort was the most important factor in attachment.
   c. The surrogate mother's appearance was the most important attachment factor.
   d. Monkeys were equally likely to become attached to either surrogate mother.
   e. The monkeys didn't form attachments to the surrogate mothers.

3. What do we call an optimal window of opportunity for proper development?
   a. Attachment
   b. The critical period
   c. The social period
   d. Imprinting
   e. Mere exposure

4. Which of the following identifies the parenting style most likely to ground a teen who had missed a curfew—and to explain the rationale for doing so, after considering the teen's reasons?
   a. Authoritative
   b. Authoritarian
   c. Permissive
   d. Secure attachment
   e. Insecure attachment

5. Which of the following would be considered a sign of secure attachment in a 1-year-old?
   a. Showing no sign of stranger anxiety, whether the parent is present or not
   b. Paying no attention to a parent who returns after a brief separation
   c. Showing anger at the parent after a brief separation
   d. Becoming distressed when the parent leaves and seeking contact on return
   e. Not reacting to a parent leaving or returning after a brief separation

6. Who identified secure and insecure attachment?
   a. Sigmund Freud
   b. Konrad Lorenz
   c. Jean Piaget
   d. Mary Ainsworth
   e. Jerome Kagan

Practice FRQs

1. Name and describe the three types of infant temperaments.

Answer

1 point: Easy: These babies are easygoing, cheerful, predictable, and placid.

1 point: Difficult: These babies are emotionally reactive, intense, irritable, and unpredictable.

1 point: Slow to warm up: These babies resist and withdraw from new people or situations.

2. Name and describe Diana Baumrind's three parenting styles.

(3 points)

Module 49

Gender Development

Module Learning Objectives

49-1 Discuss gender similarities and differences in psychological traits.

49-2 Discuss the importance of gender roles and gender typing in development.

gender the socially constructed roles and characteristics by which a culture defines *male* and *female*.

As we saw in Module 34, we humans share an irresistible urge to organize our worlds into simple categories. Among the ways we classify people—as tall or short, fat or slim, smart or dull—one stands out: Before or at your birth, everyone wanted to know, "Boy or girl?" From that time on, your sex (your biological status, defined by your chromosomes and anatomy) helped define your **gender,** the socially constructed roles and characteristics by which your culture defines *male* and *female.* Guided by our culture, our gender influences our social development.

How Are We Alike? How Do We Differ?

49-1 What are some gender similarities and differences in aggression, social power, and social connectedness?

Having faced similar adaptive challenges, we are in most ways alike. Tell me whether you are male or female and you give me virtually no clues to your vocabulary, intelligence, and happiness, or to the mechanisms by which you see, hear, learn, and remember. Your "opposite" sex is, in reality, your very similar sex. At conception, you received 23 chromosomes from your mother and 23 from your father. Of those 46 chromosomes, 45 are unisex—the same for males and females. (In Module 53, we'll return to that forty-sixth chromosome.)

But males and females do differ, and differences command attention—stimulating more than 18,000 studies (Ellis et al., 2008). Some much-talked-about gender differences are actually quite modest, as Janet Shibley Hyde (2005) illustrated by graphically representing male and female self-esteem scores across many studies (**FIGURE 49.1**). Other differences are more striking. Compared with the average man, the average woman enters puberty 2 years sooner, and her life span is 5 years longer. She carries 70 percent more fat, has 40 percent less muscle, and is 5 inches shorter. She expresses emotions more freely, can smell fainter odors, and is offered help more often. She can become sexually re-aroused soon after orgasm. She is also doubly vulnerable to depression and anxiety, and her risk of developing an eating disorder is 10 times greater than the average man's. Yet, he is some 4 times more likely to commit suicide or develop alcohol use disorder. He is also more likely to be diagnosed with autism spectrum disorder, color-blindness, attention-deficit/hyperactivity disorder as a child, and antisocial personality disorder as an adult. Choose your gender and pick your vulnerability.

FYI

Pink and blue baby outfits offer another example of how cultural norms vary and change. "The generally accepted rule is pink for the boy and blue for the girl," declared the publication *Earnshaw's Infants' Department* in June 1918 (Maglaty, 2011). "The reason is that pink being a more decided and stronger color is more suitable for the boy, while blue, which is more delicate and dainty, is prettier for the girls."

AP® Exam Tip

There is a lot of information in this section. One good way to process these differences and similarities between genders is to consider which facts fit prevailing stereotypes and which don't. You may even want to keep a list.

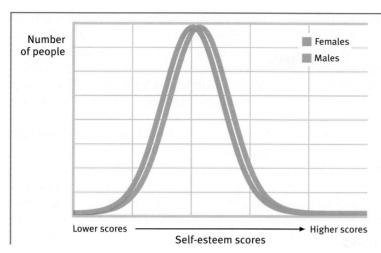

Lower scores ⟶ Higher scores
Self-esteem scores

Figure 49.1

Much ado about a small difference in self-esteem These two normal distributions differ by the approximate magnitude of the gender difference in self-esteem, averaged over all available samples (Hyde, 2005). Moreover, such comparisons illustrate differences between the average woman and man. The variation among individual women greatly exceeds this difference, as it also does among individual men.

Gender differences appear throughout this book. For now, let's consider some gender differences in aggression, social power, and social connectedness. (Note that these differences between the *average* woman and man do not necessarily describe any individual woman or man.)

Gender and Aggression

In surveys, men admit to more **aggression** than women do. This aggression gender gap pertains to harmful physical aggression, rather than indirect or verbal relational aggression such as ostracism or spreading rumors. As John Archer (2004, 2006, 2009) has noted, based on statistical digests of dozens of studies, women may be slightly more likely to commit acts of relational aggression, such as passing along malicious gossip. The gap appears in everyday life at various ages and in various cultures, especially cultures with gender inequality (Archer, 2009).

Men's tendency to behave more aggressively can be seen in experiments where they deliver what they believe are more painful electric shocks (Card et al., 2008). Violent crime rates illustrate the gender difference even more strikingly. The male-to-female arrest ratio for murder, for example, is 9 to 1 in the United States and 8 to 1 in Canada (FBI, 2009; Statistics Canada, 2010). Throughout the world, fighting, warring, and hunting are primarily men's activities (Wood & Eagly, 2002, 2007). Men also express more support for war. The Iraq war, for example, was consistently supported more by American men than by American women (Newport et al., 2007).

Gender difference in aggression Around the world, fighting, violent crime, and blowing things up are mostly men's activities. This is why many were surprised to hear that female suicide bombers were responsible for the 2010 Moscow subway bombing that killed dozens.

Gender and Social Power

Close your eyes and imagine two adults standing side by side. The one on the left is dominant, forceful, and independent. The one on the right is submissive, nurturing, and socially connected.

Did you see the person on the left as a man, and the one on the right as a woman? If so, you are not alone.

Around the world, from Nigeria to New Zealand, people perceive such power differences between men and women (Williams & Best, 1990). Indeed, in most societies men *do* place more importance on power and achievement and *are* socially dominant (Schwartz &

aggression any physical or verbal behavior intended to hurt or destroy.

Rubel-Lifschitz, 2009). When groups form, whether as juries or companies, leadership tends to go to males (Colarelli et al., 2006). When salaries are paid, those in traditionally male occupations receive more. And when political leaders are elected, they usually are men, who held 80 percent of the seats in the world's governing parliaments in 2011 (IPU, 2011). If perceived to be hungry for political power (thus violating gender norms), women more than men suffer voter backlash (Okimoto & Brescoll, 2010). Men's power hunger is more expected and accepted.

As leaders, men tend to be more *directive,* even autocratic. Women tend to be more *democratic,* more welcoming of subordinates' input in decision making (Eagly & Carli, 2007; van Engen & Willemsen, 2004). When people interact, men are more likely to utter opinions, women to express support (Aries, 1987; Wood, 1987). In everyday behavior, men tend to act as powerful people often do: They are more likely to talk assertively, interrupt, initiate touches, and stare. And they smile and apologize less (Leaper & Ayres, 2007; Major et al., 1990; Schumann & Ross, 2010). Such behaviors help sustain social power inequities.

Gender and Social Connectedness

In the 1980s, many developmental psychologists believed that all children struggle to create a separate, independent identity. Research by Carol Gilligan and her colleagues (1982, 1990), however, suggested that this struggle describes Western individualist males more than relationship-oriented females. Gilligan believed females tend to differ from males both in being less concerned with viewing themselves as separate individuals and in being more concerned with "making connections." Indeed, later research has found that females are more *interdependent* than males, and this difference surfaces early. In children's play, boys typically form large groups. Their games tend to be active and competitive, with little intimate discussion (Rose & Rudolph, 2006). Studies have found that girls usually play in smaller groups, often with one friend. Their play is less competitive and more imitative of social relationships (Maccoby, 1990; Roberts, 1991).

As adults, women take more pleasure in talking face to face, and they more often use conversation to explore relationships. Men enjoy doing activities side by side and tend to use conversation to communicate solutions (Tannen, 1990; Wright, 1989). The communication difference is apparent in student e-mails: In one New Zealand study, people could correctly guess the author's gender two-thirds of the time (Thomson & Murachver, 2001).

Gender differences also appear in phone-based communication. In the United States, the average teen girl sends double the number of text messages of the average teen boy (Lenhart, 2010). In France, women have made 63 percent of phone calls and, when talking to a woman, stayed connected longer (7.2 minutes) than have men when talking to other men (4.6 minutes) (Smoreda & Licoppe, 2000).

Every man for himself, or tend and befriend? Gender differences in the way we interact with others begin to appear at a very young age.

Women worldwide have oriented their interests and vocations more to people and less to things (Eagly, 2009; Lippa, 2005, 2006, 2008). One analysis of more than a half-million people's responses to various interest inventories revealed that "men prefer working with things and women prefer working with people" (Su et al., 2009). On entering college, American men are seven times more likely than women to express interest in computer science, and they contribute 87 percent of Wikipedia articles (Cohen, 2011; Pryor et al., 2011). In the workplace, women have been less driven by money and status and more often opted for reduced work hours (Pinker, 2008). In the home, they have been five times more likely than men to claim primary responsibility for taking care of children (*Time,* 2009).

Women's emphasis on caring helps explain another interesting finding: Although 69 percent of people have said they have a close relationship with their father, 90 percent said they feel close to their mother (Hugick, 1989). When wanting understanding and someone with whom to share worries and hurts, both men and women usually turn to women, and both have reported their friendships with women to be more intimate, enjoyable, and nurturing (Rubin, 1985; Sapadin, 1988). And when coping with their own stress, women more than men turn to others for support—they *tend and befriend* (Tamres et al., 2002; Taylor, 2002).

Gender differences in social connectedness, power, and other traits peak in late adolescence and early adulthood—the very years most commonly studied (also the years of dating and mating). As teenagers, girls become progressively less assertive and more flirtatious; boys become more domineering and unexpressive. Following the birth of a first child, parents (women especially) become more traditional in their gender-related attitudes and behavior (Ferriman et al., 2009; Katz-Wise et al., 2010). But studies have shown that by age 50, parenthood-related gender differences subside. Men become more empathic and less domineering, and women—especially those with paid employment—become more assertive and self-confident (Kasen et al., 2006; Maccoby, 1998).

What explains our diversity? How much does biology bend the genders? To what extent are we shaped by our cultures? A biopsychosocial view suggests both are important, thanks to the interplay among our biological dispositions, our developmental experiences, and our current situations (Eagly, 2009).

> "In the long years liker must they grow; The man be more of woman, she of man." -ALFRED LORD TENNYSON, *THE PRINCESS*, 1847

gender role a set of expected behaviors for males or for females.

role a set of expectations (norms) about a social position, defining how those in the position ought to behave.

The Nurture of Gender: Our Culture

 How do gender roles and gender typing influence gender development?

For most people, their biological sex and their gender are tightly interwined. What biology initiates (as we will see in Module 53), culture accentuates.

Gender Roles

Culture is everything shared by a group and transmitted across generations. We can see culture's shaping power in **gender roles**—the social expectations that guide men's and women's behavior. (In psychology, as in the theater, a **role** refers to a cluster of prescribed actions, the behaviors we expect of those who occupy a particular social position.)

Gender roles vary over time and place. In North America, men were traditionally expected to initiate dates, drive the car, and pick up the check. Women were expected to decorate the home, buy and care for the children's clothes, and select the wedding gifts. Up through the 1990s, Mom (about 90 percent of the time in two-parent U.S. families) stayed home with a sick child, arranged for the babysitter, and called the doctor (Maccoby, 1995). Even in recent years, compared with employed women, employed men in the United States have daily spent about an hour and a half more on

"Sex brought us together, but gender drove us apart."

the job and about one hour less on household activities and caregiving (Amato et al., 2007; Bureau of Labor Statistics, 2004; Fisher et al., 2006). Ditto Australia, where, compared with men, women have devoted 54 percent more time to unpaid household work and 71 percent more time to child care (Trewin, 2001).

Other societies have different expectations. In nomadic societies of food-gathering people, there is little division of labor by sex. Boys and girls receive much the same upbringing. In agricultural societies, where women work in the nearby fields and men roam while herding livestock, children have typically been socialized into more distinct gender roles (Segall et al., 1990; Van Leeuwen, 1978).

Among industrialized countries, gender roles and attitudes vary widely. Australia and the Scandinavian countries offer the greatest gender equity, Middle Eastern and North African countries the least (Social Watch, 2006). And consider: Would you agree that "when jobs are scarce, men should have more rights to a job?" In the United States, Britain, and Spain, about one in eight adults agree. In Nigeria, Pakistan, and India, about four in five do (Pew, 2010). We are one species, but my, how we differ.

The gendered tsunami In Sri Lanka, Indonesia, and India, the gendered division of labor helps explain the excess of female deaths from the 2004 tsunami. In some villages, 80 percent of those killed were women, who were mostly at home while the men were more likely to be at sea fishing or doing out-of-the-home chores (Oxfam, 2005).

To see how gender role attitudes vary over time, consider women's voting rights. At the opening of the twentieth century, only one country—New Zealand—granted women the right to vote (Briscoe, 1997). By the late 1960s and early 1970s, women had become a force in the voting booth and the workplace in many countries. Nearly 50 percent of employed Americans are now women, as are 54 percent of college graduates, up from 36 percent in just four decades (Fry & Cohn, 2010). In today's postindustrial economy, the jobs expected to grow the most in the years ahead are the ones women have gravitated toward—those that require not size and strength but social intelligence, open communication, and the ability to sit still and focus (Rosin, 2010). These are big gender changes in but a thin slice of history.

Gender roles can smooth social relations, avoiding irritating discussions about whose job it is to get the car fixed and who should buy the birthday presents. But these quick and easy assumptions come at a cost: If we deviate from conventions, we may feel anxious.

How Do We Learn to Be Male or Female?

Gender identity is a person's sense of being male or female. **Social learning theory** assumes that children acquire this identity by observing and imitating others' gender-linked behaviors and by being rewarded or punished for acting in certain ways themselves ("Nicole, you're such a good mommy to your dolls"; "Big boys don't cry, Alex."). Some critics have objected, saying that parental modeling and rewarding of male-female differences aren't enough to explain **gender typing,** the way some children seem more attuned than others to traditional male or female roles (Lytton & Romney, 1991). In fact, even in families that discourage traditional gender typing, children organize themselves into "boy worlds" and "girl worlds," each guided by rules for what boys and girls do.

Cognition (thinking) also matters. In your own childhood you formed concepts that helped you make sense of your world. One of these was your *gender schema,* your framework for organizing boy-girl characteristics (Bem, 1987, 1993). This gender schema then became a lens through which you viewed your experiences.

Gender schemas form early in life, and social learning helps form them. Before age 1, you began to discriminate male and female voices and faces (Martin et al., 2002). After age 2, language forced you to begin organizing your world on the basis of gender. English, for example, uses the pronouns *he* and *she;* other languages classify objects as masculine ("*le* train") or feminine ("*la* table").

FYI

In Module 30, we explored how children can learn—including the aggressive behavior modeled in Albert Bandura's famous Bobo doll experiment—by observing others.

---

gender identity our sense of being male or female.

social learning theory the theory that we learn social behavior by observing and imitating and by being rewarded or punished.

gender typing the acquisition of a traditional masculine or feminine role.

Young children are "gender detectives" (Martin & Ruble, 2004). Once they grasp that two sorts of people exist—and that they are of one sort—they search for clues about gender, and they find them in language, dress, toys, and songs. Girls, they may decide, are the ones with long hair. Having divided the human world in half, 3-year-olds will then like their own kind better and seek them out for play. And having compared themselves with their concept of gender, they will adjust their behavior accordingly. ("I am male—thus, masculine, strong, aggressive," or "I am female—therefore, feminine, sweet,

The social learning of gender Children observe and imitate parental models.

and helpful.") These rigid boy-girl stereotypes peak at about age 5 or 6. If the new neighbor is a boy, a 6-year-old girl may assume he just cannot share her interests. For young children, gender looms large.

For some people, comparing themselves with their culture's concepts of gender produces feelings of confusion and discord. **Transgender** people's *gender identity* (their sense of being male or female) or *gender expression* (their communication of gender identity through behavior or appearance) differs from that typical of their birth sex (APA, 2010). A person may feel like a man in a woman's body, or a woman in a man's body. These include *transsexual* people, who live, or wish to live, as members of the gender opposite to their birth sex, often aided by medical treatment that supports gender reassignment. Note that gender identity is distinct from *sexual orientation* (the direction of one's sexual attraction). Transgender people may be heterosexual, homosexual, bisexual, or asexual.

Some transgender persons express their gender identity by dressing as a person of the other biological sex typically would. Most cross-dressers are biological males, the majority of whom feel an attraction to females (APA, 2010).

Transgender contestant In 2012, Jenna Talackova became the first transgender beauty pageant contestant in this Miss Universe Canada contest in Toronto. Talackova was born a male but had sex-reassignment surgery.

"The more I was treated as a woman, the more woman I became." -WRITER JAN MORRIS, MALE-TO-FEMALE TRANSSEXUAL

transgender an umbrella term describing people whose gender identity or expression differs from that associated with their birth sex.

Before You Move On

▶ **ASK YOURSELF**

Do you consider yourself strongly gender typed or not strongly gender typed? What factors do you think have contributed to your feelings of masculinity or femininity?

▶ **TEST YOURSELF**

What are gender roles, and what do their variations tell us about our human capacity for learning and adaptation?

Answers to the Test Yourself questions can be found in Appendix E at the end of the book.

Module 49 Review

 49-1 What are some gender similarities and differences in aggression, social power, and social connectedness?

- *Gender* refers to the socially constructed roles and characteristics by which a culture defines "male" and "female."

- We are more alike than different, thanks to our similar genetic makeup—we see, hear, learn, and remember similarly. Males and females do differ in body fat, muscle, height, age of onset of puberty, life expectancy, and vulnerability to certain disorders.

- Men admit to more *aggression* than women do, and they are more likely to be physically aggressive. Women's aggression is more likely to be relational.

- In most societies, men have more social power, and their leadership style tends to be directive, whereas women's is more democratic.

- Women focus more on social connectedness, and they "tend and befriend."

49-2 How do gender roles and gender typing influence gender development?

- *Gender roles,* the behaviors a culture expects from its males and females, vary across place and time.

- *Social learning theory* proposes that we learn *gender identity*—our sense of being male or female—as we learn other things: through reinforcement, punishment, and observation. Critics argue that cognition also plays a role because modeling and rewards cannot explain *gender typing*.

- *Transgender* people's gender identity or expression differs from their birth sex. Their sexual orientation may be heterosexual, homosexual, bisexual, or asexual.

Multiple-Choice Questions

1. According to research, which type of aggression is more common among males than females?
   a. Harmful physical aggression
   b. Indirect nonphysical aggression
   c. Verbal aggression
   d. Ostracism
   e. Spreading rumors

2. Gender _____ are the social expectations that guide men and women's behavior. Gender _____ is a person's sense of being male or female.
   a. concepts; role
   b. preferences; role
   c. roles; preference
   d. roles; identity
   e. roles; preference

3. Which of the following is generally true of males?
   a. They have a longer life span.
   b. They are more likely to have a democratic leadership style.
   c. They are more likely to commit suicide.
   d. They are more likely to be diagnosed with depression.
   e. They are more likely to be diagnosed with anxiety.

4. Diego likes to play sports and video games whereas Sara likes to sing, dance, and play "house." This example best depicts which of the following?
   a. Gender identity
   b. Gender typing
   c. Gender schema
   d. Social learning theory
   e. Gender expression

5. Carol Gilligan's research emphasizes prominent female characteristics, especially
   a. spatial abilities.
   b. making social connections.
   c. playing in large groups.
   d. talking a great deal.
   e. playing in competitive groups.

Practice FRQs

1. What are gender roles? What are gender schemas? How does social learning contribute to the formation of each?

Answer

1 point: Gender roles are the cultural norms for expected behaviors for males and females.

1 point: Gender schemas are the cognitive ways in which we organize boy-girl characteristics.

1 point: Social learning contributes to gender schema formation by the observation of gender roles, the rewarding of gender-appropriate behaviors, and the ways in which gender is discussed.

2. Give an example of a biological, a psychological, and a social factor that might contribute to gender differences.
(3 points)

Module 50

Parents, Peers, and Early Experiences

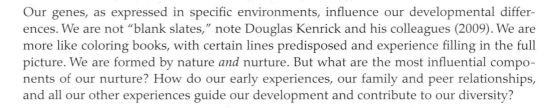

Module Learning Objectives

50-1 Describe how early experiences can modify the brain.

50-2 Describe the ways in which parents and peers shape children's development.

Our genes, as expressed in specific environments, influence our developmental differences. We are not "blank slates," note Douglas Kenrick and his colleagues (2009). We are more like coloring books, with certain lines predisposed and experience filling in the full picture. We are formed by nature *and* nurture. But what are the most influential components of our nurture? How do our early experiences, our family and peer relationships, and all our other experiences guide our development and contribute to our diversity?

Experience and Brain Development

50-1 How do early experiences modify the brain?

The formative nurture that conspires with nature begins at conception, as we have seen, with the prenatal environment in the womb. Embryos receive differing nutrition and varying levels of exposure to toxic agents. Nurture then continues outside the womb, where our early experiences foster brain development.

Our genes dictate our overall brain architecture, but experience fills in the details, developing neural connections and preparing our brain for thought and language and other later experiences. So how do early experiences leave their "marks" in the brain? Mark Rosenzweig, David Krech, and their colleagues (1962) opened a window on that process when they raised some young rats in solitary confinement and others in a communal playground. When they later analyzed the rats' brains, those raised in the enriched environment, which simulated a natural environment, usually developed a heavier and thicker brain cortex (**FIGURE 50.1**).

Stringing the circuits young
String musicians who started playing before age 12 have larger and more complex neural circuits controlling the note-making left-hand fingers than do string musicians whose training started later (Elbert et al., 1995).

Rosenzweig was so surprised by this discovery that he repeated the experiment several times before publishing his findings (Renner & Rosenzweig, 1987; Rosenzweig, 1984). So great are the effects that, shown brief video clips of rats, you could tell from their activity and curiosity whether their environment had been impoverished or enriched (Renner & Renner, 1993). After 60 days in the enriched environment, the rats' brain weights increased 7 to 10 percent and the number of synapses mushroomed by about 20 percent (Kolb & Whishaw, 1998).

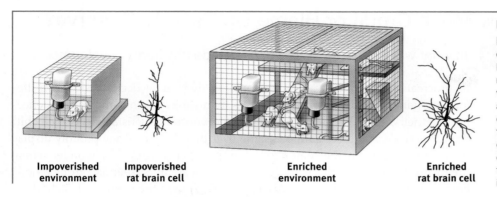

Figure 50.1

Experience affects brain development Mark Rosenzweig, David Krech, and their colleagues raised rats either alone in an environment without playthings, or with other rats in an environment enriched with playthings changed daily. In 14 of 16 repetitions of this basic experiment, rats in the enriched environment developed significantly more cerebral cortex (relative to the rest of the brain's tissue) than did those in the impoverished environment.

Impoverished environment   **Impoverished rat brain cell**   **Enriched environment**   **Enriched rat brain cell**

Such results have motivated improvements in environments for laboratory, farm, and zoo animals—and for children in institutions. Stimulation by touch or massage also benefits infant rats and premature babies (Field et al., 2007). "Handled" infants of both species develop faster neurologically and gain weight more rapidly. By giving preemies massage therapy, neonatal intensive care units now help them to go home sooner (Field et al., 2006).

Both nature and nurture sculpt our synapses. After brain maturation provides us with an abundance of neural connections, our experiences trigger a pruning process. Sights and smells, touches and tugs activate and strengthen connections. Unused neural pathways weaken. Like forest pathways, popular tracks are broadened and less-traveled ones gradually disappear. The result by puberty is a massive loss of unemployed connections.

Here at the juncture of nurture and nature is the biological reality of early childhood learning. During early childhood—while excess connections are still on call—youngsters can most easily master such skills as the grammar and accent of another language. Lacking any exposure to language before adolescence, a person will never master any language (see Module 36). Likewise, lacking visual experience during the early years, those whose vision is restored by cataract removal never achieve normal perceptions (see Module 19). The brain cells normally assigned to vision have died or been diverted to other uses. The maturing brain's rule: Use it or lose it.

Although normal stimulation during the early years is critical, the brain's development does not end with childhood. As we saw in Module 12's discussion of brain plasticity, our neural tissue is ever changing and new neurons are born. If a monkey pushes a lever with the same finger several thousand times a day, brain tissue controlling that finger changes to reflect the experience. Human brains work similarly (**FIGURE 50.2**). Whether learning to keyboard or skateboard, we perform with increasing skill as our brain incorporates the learning (Ambrose, 2010).

> "Genes and experiences are just two ways of doing the same thing—wiring synapses." -JOSEPH LEDOUX, THE SYNAPTIC SELF, 2002

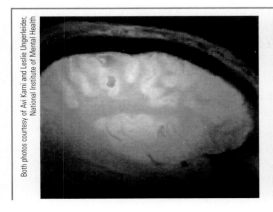
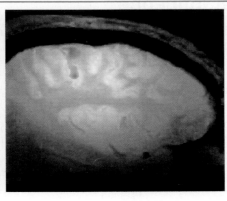

Both photos courtesy of Avi Karni and Leslie Ungerleider, National Institute of Mental Health

Figure 50.2

A trained brain A well-learned fingertapping task activates more motor cortex neurons (orange area, right) than were active in the same brain before training (left). (From Karni et al., 1998.)

How Much Credit or Blame Do Parents Deserve?

50-2   In what ways do parents and peers shape children's development?

"To be frank, officer, my parents never set boundaries."

"So I blame you for everything— whose fault is that?"

"If you want to blame your parents for your own adult problems, you are entitled to blame the genes they gave you, but you are not entitled—by any facts I know— to blame the way they treated you. . . . We are not prisoners of our past." -Martin Seligman, *What You Can Change and What You Can't*, 1994

In procreation, a woman and a man shuffle their gene decks and deal a life-forming hand to their child-to-be, who is then subjected to countless influences beyond their control. Parents, nonetheless, feel enormous satisfaction in their children's successes, and feel guilt or shame over their failures. They proudly display their "my child is on the honor roll" bumper sticker. And they wonder where they went wrong with the teenager who is repeatedly suspended from school. Freudian psychiatry and psychology have been among the sources of such ideas, by blaming problems from asthma to schizophrenia on "bad mothering." Society has reinforced such parent blaming: Believing that parents shape their offspring as a potter molds clay, people readily praise parents for their children's virtues and blame them for their children's vices. Popular culture endlessly proclaims the psychological harm toxic parents inflict on their fragile children. No wonder having and raising children can seem so risky.

But do parents really produce future adults with an inner wounded child by being (take your pick from the toxic-parenting lists) overbearing—or uninvolved? Pushy—or ineffectual? Overprotective—or distant? Are children really so easily wounded? If so, should we then blame our parents for our failings, and ourselves for our children's failings? Or does talk of wounding fragile children through normal parental mistakes trivialize the brutality of real abuse?

Parents do matter. The power of parenting is clearest at the extremes: the abused children who become abusive, the neglected who become neglectful, the loved but firmly handled who become self-confident and socially competent. The power of the family environment also appears in the remarkable academic and vocational successes of children of people who fled from Vietnam and Cambodia—successes attributed to close-knit, supportive, even demanding families (Caplan et al., 1992).

Yet in personality measures, shared environmental influences from the womb onward typically account for less than 10 percent of children's differences. In the words of behavior geneticists Robert Plomin and Denise Daniels (1987; Plomin, 2011), "Two children in the same family are [apart from their shared genes] as different from one another as are pairs of children selected randomly from the population." To developmental psychologist Sandra Scarr (1993), this implied that "parents should be given less credit for kids who turn out great and blamed less for kids who don't." Knowing children are not easily sculpted by parental nurture, perhaps parents can relax a bit more and love their children for who they are.

Peer Influence

As children mature, what other experiences do the work of nurturing? At all ages, but especially during childhood and adolescence, we seek to fit in with our groups and are influenced by them (Harris, 1998, 2000):

- Preschoolers who disdain a certain food often will eat that food if put at a table with a group of children who like it.

- Children who hear English spoken with one accent at home and another in the neighborhood and at school will invariably adopt the accent of their peers, not their parents. Accents (and slang) reflect culture, "and children get their culture from their peers," notes Judith Rich Harris (2007).

- Teens who start smoking typically have friends who model smoking, suggest its pleasures, and offer cigarettes (J. S. Rose et al., 1999; R. J. Rose et al., 2003). Part of this peer similarity may result from a *selection effect,* as kids seek out peers with similar attitudes and interests. Those who smoke (or don't) may select as friends those who also smoke (or don't).

"Men resemble the times more than they resemble their fathers."
-Ancient Arab proverb

Howard Gardner (1998) has concluded that parents and peers are complementary:

Parents are more important when it comes to education, discipline, responsibility, orderliness, charitableness, and ways of interacting with authority figures. Peers are more important for learning cooperation, for finding the road to popularity, for inventing styles of interaction among people of the same age. Youngsters may find their peers more interesting, but they will look to their parents when contemplating their own futures. Moreover, parents [often] choose the neighborhoods and schools that supply the peers.

This power to select a child's neighborhood and schools gives parents an ability to influence the culture that shapes the child's peer group. And because neighborhood influences matter, parents may want to become involved in intervention programs that aim at a whole school or neighborhood. If the vapors of a toxic climate are seeping into a child's life, that climate—not just the child—needs reforming. Even so, peers are but one medium of cultural influence. As a purported African proverb declares, and former U.S. Secretary of State Hillary Clinton has popularized, "It takes a village to raise a child."

Peer power As we develop, we play, date, and partner with peers. No wonder children and youths are so sensitive and responsive to peer influences.

Before You Move On

▶ **ASK YOURSELF**

To what extent, and in what ways, have your peers and your parents helped shape who you are?

▶ **TEST YOURSELF**

To predict whether a teenager smokes, ask how many of the teen's friends smoke. One explanation for this correlation is peer influence. What's another?

Answers to the Test Yourself questions can be found in Appendix E at the end of the book.

Module 50 Review

50-1 How do early experiences modify the brain?

- As a child's brain develops, neural connections grow more numerous and complex. Experiences then trigger a pruning process, in which unused connections weaken and heavily used ones strengthen.

- Early childhood is an important period for shaping the brain, but throughout our lives our brain modifies itself in response to our learning.

50-2 In what ways do parents and peers shape children's development?

- Parents influence their children in areas such has manners and political and religious beliefs, but not in other areas, such as personality.

- As children attempt to fit in with their peers, they tend to adopt their culture—styles, accents, slang, attitudes.

- By choosing their children's neighborhoods and schools, parents exert some influence over peer group culture.

Multiple-Choice Questions

1. According to Plomin and Daniels, "Two children in the same family are [apart from their shared genes] as different from _____ as are pairs of children selected randomly from the population."
   a. their parents
   b. their grandparents
   c. their friends
   d. one another
   e. their cousins

2. Compared with rats raised in an enriched environment, which of the following is true of rats raised in isolation?
   a. Their brain cortex is less developed.
   b. Though neurologically similar, they fear other rats.
   c. Their brains have more connections.
   d. They have a thicker brain cortex.
   e. The differences between the two groups are not statistically significant.

3. What is the *primary* means by which parents influence the behavior of their children?
   a. Parenting style
   b. Genetic contributions
   c. Prenatal environment
   d. Teaching cooperation
   e. Rewarding achievement

4. Neurologically, what is the function of pruning?
   a. Pruning creates new connections between synapses through repeated experiences.
   b. Pruning reduces the negative effects of teratogens by eliminating neural waste.
   c. Pruning increases the weight of the brain through enriching experiences.
   d. Pruning creates areas in the brain used in learning mathematics.
   e. Pruning eliminates unused neural pathways.

Practice FRQs

1. Compare and contrast the influence parents and peers have on a child's development, giving one example for each.

Answer

2 points: Parents influence a child's (1) quality of life, (2) attachments and beliefs, (3) exposure to peer culture via neighborhood and schools.

2 points: Peers influence a child's (1) tastes and styles, (2) accents and slang, and (3) substance use.

2. Provide two examples of how children seek to fit in with their groups and are influenced by them.

(2 points)

Module 51

Adolescence: Physical and Cognitive Development

Module Learning Objectives

 Define *adolescence,* and identify the major physical changes during this period.

 Describe adolescent cognitive and moral development, according to Piaget, Kohlberg, and later researchers.

 How is *adolescence* defined, and what physical changes mark this period?

Many psychologists once believed that childhood sets our traits. Today's developmental psychologists see development as lifelong. As this *life-span perspective* emerged, psychologists began to look at how maturation and experience shape us not only in infancy and childhood, but also in adolescence and beyond. Your story is still being written. **Adolescence**— the years spent morphing from child to adult—starts with the physical beginnings of sexual maturity and ends with the social achievement of independent adult status. In some cultures, where teens are self-supporting, this means that adolescence hardly exists.

G. Stanley Hall (1904), one of the first psychologists to describe adolescence, believed that the tension between biological maturity and social dependence creates a period of "storm and stress." Indeed, after age 30, many who grew up in independence-fostering Western cultures look back on their teenage years as a time they would not want to relive, a time when their peers' social approval was imperative, their sense of direction in life was in flux, and their feeling of alienation from their parents was deepest (Arnett, 1999; Macfarlane, 1964).

But for many, adolescence is a time of vitality without the cares of adulthood, a time of rewarding friendships, heightened idealism, and a growing sense of life's exciting possibilities.

> **adolescence** the transition period from childhood to adulthood, extending from puberty to independence.

> **Try This**
> How will you look back on your life 10 years from now? Are you making choices that someday you will recollect with satisfaction?

Physical Development

Adolescence begins with *puberty,* the time when we mature sexually. Puberty follows a surge of hormones, which may intensify moods and which trigger a series of bodily changes, described in Module 53.

Just as in the earlier life stages, the *sequence* of physical changes in puberty (for example, breast buds and visible pubic hair before *menarche*—the first menstrual period) is far more predictable than their *timing.* Some girls start their growth spurt at 9, some boys as late as age 16. Though such variations have little effect on height at maturity, they may have psychological consequences: It is not only when we mature that counts, but how people react to our physical development.

Erik Isakson/JupiterImages

For boys, early maturation has mixed effects. Boys who are stronger and more athletic during their early teen years tend to be more popular, self-assured, and independent, though also more at risk for alcohol use, delinquency, and premature sexual activity (Conley & Rudolph, 2009; Copeland et al., 2010; Lynne et al., 2007). For girls, early maturation can be a challenge (Mendle et al., 2007). If a young girl's body and hormone-fed feelings are out of sync with her emotional maturity and her friends' physical development and experiences, she may begin associating with older adolescents or may suffer teasing or sexual harassment (Ge & Natsuaki, 2009).

An adolescent's brain is also a work in progress. Until puberty, brain cells increase their connections, like trees growing more roots and branches. Then, during adolescence comes a selective pruning of unused neurons and connections (Blakemore, 2008). What we don't use, we lose.

As teens mature, their frontal lobes also continue to develop. The growth of *myelin,* the fatty tissue that forms around axons and speeds neurotransmission, enables better communication with other brain regions (Kuhn, 2006; Silveri et al., 2006). These developments bring improved judgment, impulse control, and long-term planning.

Maturation of the frontal lobes nevertheless lags behind that of the emotional limbic system. Puberty's hormonal surge and limbic system development help explain teens' occasional impulsiveness, risky behaviors, and emotional storms—slamming doors and turning up the music (Casey et al., 2008). No wonder younger teens (whose unfinished frontal lobes aren't yet fully equipped for making long-term plans and curbing impulses) so often succumb to the tobacco corporations, which most adult smokers could tell them they will later regret. Teens actually don't underestimate the risks of smoking—or fast driving or unprotected sex. They just, when reasoning from their gut, weigh the immediate benefits more heavily (Reyna & Farley, 2006; Steinberg, 2007, 2010). They seek thrills and rewards, but they can't yet locate the brake pedal controlling their impulses.

© The New Yorker Collection, 2006, Barbara Smaller from cartoonbank.com. All Rights Reserved.

"Young man, go to your room and stay there until your cerebral cortex matures."

So, when Junior drives recklessly and academically self-destructs, should his parents reassure themselves that "he can't help it; his frontal cortex isn't yet fully grown"? They can at least take hope: The brain with which Junior begins his teens differs from the brain with which he will end his teens. Unless he slows his brain development with heavy drinking—leaving him prone to impulsivity and addiction—his frontal lobes will continue maturing until about age 25 (Beckman, 2004; Crews et al., 2007).

In 2004, the American Psychological Association joined seven other medical and mental health associations in filing U.S. Supreme Court briefs arguing against the death penalty for 16- and 17-year-olds. The briefs documented the teen brain's immaturity "in areas that bear upon adolescent decision making." Teens are "less guilty by reason of adolescence," suggested psychologist Laurence Steinberg and law professor Elizabeth Scott (2003; Steinberg et al., 2009). In 2005, by a 5-to-4 margin, the Court concurred, declaring juvenile death penalties unconstitutional.

> "If a gun is put in the control of the prefrontal cortex of a hurt and vengeful 15-year-old, and it is pointed at a human target, it will very likely go off." -National Institutes of Health brain scientist Daniel R. Weinberger, "A Brain Too Young for Good Judgment," 2001

Cognitive Development

51-2 How did Piaget, Kohlberg, and later researchers describe adolescent cognitive and moral development?

During the early teen years, reasoning is often self-focused. Adolescents may think their private experiences are unique, something parents just could not understand: "But, Mom, you don't really know how it feels to be in love" (Elkind, 1978). Capable of thinking about their own thinking, and about other people's thinking, they also begin imagining what others are thinking about *them*. (They might worry less if they understood their peers' similar self-absorption.) Gradually, though, most begin to reason more abstractly.

Developing Reasoning Power

When adolescents achieve the intellectual summit Jean Piaget called *formal operations,* they apply their new abstract reasoning tools to the world around them. They may think about what is ideally possible and compare that with the imperfect reality of their society, their parents, and even themselves. They may debate human nature, good and evil, truth and justice. Their sense of what's fair changes from simple equality to equity—to what's proportional to merit (Almås et al., 2010). Having left behind the concrete images of early childhood, they may now seek a deeper conception of God and existence (Elkind, 1970; Worthington, 1989). Reasoning hypothetically and deducing consequences also enables adolescents to detect inconsistencies and spot hypocrisy in others' reasoning. This can lead to heated debates with parents and silent vows never to lose sight of their own ideals (Peterson et al., 1986).

> "When the pilot told us to brace and grab our ankles, the first thing that went through my mind was that we must all look pretty stupid." -JEREMIAH RAWLINGS, AGE 12, AFTER A 1989 DC-10 CRASH IN SIOUX CITY, IOWA

Demonstrating their reasoning ability Although they supported different candidates in the 2012 U.S. presidential election, these teens were all demonstrating their ability to think logically about abstract topics. According to Piaget, they were in the final cognitive stage, formal operations.

Developing Morality

Two crucial tasks of childhood and adolescence are discerning right from wrong and developing character—the psychological muscles for controlling impulses. To be a moral person is to *think* morally and *act* accordingly. Jean Piaget and Lawrence Kohlberg proposed that moral reasoning guides moral actions. A newer view builds on psychology's game-changing new recognition that much of our functioning occurs not on the "high road" of deliberate, conscious thinking but on the "low road" of unconscious, automatic thinking.

MORAL REASONING

Piaget (1932) believed that children's moral judgments build on their cognitive development. Agreeing with Piaget, Lawrence Kohlberg (1981, 1984) sought to describe the development of *moral reasoning,* the thinking that occurs as we consider right and wrong. Kohlberg posed moral dilemmas (for example, whether a person should steal medicine to save a loved one's life) and asked children, adolescents, and adults whether the action was right or wrong. He then analyzed their answers for evidence of stages of moral thinking. His findings led him to propose three basic levels of moral thinking: preconventional, conventional, and postconventional (**TABLE 51.1** on the next page).

Moral reasoning Some Staten Island, New York, residents faced a moral dilemma in 2012 when Superstorm Sandy caused disastrous flooding. Should they risk their lives to try to rescue family, friends, and neighbors in dangerously flooded areas?

Table 51.1 Kohlberg's Levels of Moral Thinking

Level (approximate age)	Focus	Example
Preconventional morality (before age 9)	Self-interest; obey rules to avoid punishment or gain concrete rewards.	"If you save your wife, you'll be a hero."
Conventional morality (early adolescence)	Uphold laws and rules to gain social approval or maintain social order.	"If you steal the drug, everyone will think you're a criminal."
Postconventional morality (adolescence and beyond)	Actions reflect belief in basic rights and self-defined ethical principles.	"People have a right to live."

Kohlberg claimed these levels form a moral ladder. As with all stage theories, the sequence is unvarying. We begin on the bottom rung and ascend to varying heights. Kohlberg's critics have noted that his postconventional stage is culturally limited, appearing mostly among people who prize individualism (Eckensberger, 1994; Miller & Bersoff, 1995).

Moral Intuition

Psychologist Jonathan Haidt (2002, 2006, 2010) believes that much of our morality is rooted in *moral intuitions*—"quick gut feelings, or affectively laden intuitions." According to this intuitionist view, the mind makes moral judgments as it makes aesthetic judgments—quickly and automatically. We *feel* disgust when seeing people engaged in degrading or subhuman acts. Even a disgusting taste in the mouth heightens people's disgust over various moral digressions (Eskine et al., 2011). We *feel* elevation—a tingly, warm, glowing feeling in the chest—when seeing people display exceptional generosity, compassion, or courage. These feelings in turn trigger moral reasoning, says Haidt.

One woman recalled driving through her snowy neighborhood with three young men as they passed "an elderly woman with a shovel in her driveway. I did not think much of it, when one of the guys in the back asked the driver to let him off there. . . . When I saw him jump out of the back seat and approach the lady, my mouth dropped in shock as I realized that he was offering to shovel her walk for her." Witnessing this unexpected goodness triggered elevation: "I felt like jumping out of the car and hugging this guy. I felt like singing and running, or skipping and laughing. I felt like saying nice things about people" (Haidt, 2000).

"Could human morality really be run by the moral emotions," Haidt wonders, "while moral reasoning struts about pretending to be in control?" Consider the desire to punish. Laboratory games reveal that the desire to punish wrongdoings is mostly driven not by reason (such as an objective calculation that punishment deters crime) but rather by emotional reactions, such as moral outrage (Darley, 2009). After the emotional fact, moral reasoning—our mind's press secretary—aims to convince us and others of the logic of what we have intuitively felt.

This intuitionist perspective on morality finds support in a study of moral paradoxes. Imagine seeing a runaway trolley headed for five people. All will certainly be killed unless you throw a switch that diverts the trolley onto another track, where it will kill one person. Should you throw the switch? Most say *Yes.* Kill one, save five.

Now imagine the same dilemma, except that your opportunity to save the five requires you to push a large stranger onto the tracks, where he will die as his body stops the trolley. Kill one, save five? The logic is the same, but most say *No.* Seeking to understand why, a Princeton research team led by Joshua Greene (2001) used brain imaging to spy on people's neural responses as they contemplated such dilemmas. Only when given the body-pushing type of moral dilemma did their brain's emotion areas activate. Despite the identical logic, the personal dilemma engaged emotions that altered moral judgment.

While the new moral psychology illustrates the many ways moral intuitions trump moral reasoning, others reaffirm the importance of moral reasoning. The religious and moral reasoning of the Amish, for example, shapes their practices of forgiveness, communal life, and modesty (Narvaez, 2010). Joshua Greene (2010) likens our moral cognition to a camera. Usually, we rely on the automatic point-and-shoot. But sometimes we use reason to manually override the camera's automatic impulse.

> "It is a delightful harmony when doing and saying go together."
> -Michel Eyquem de Montaigne (1533–1592)

MORAL ACTION

Our moral thinking and feeling surely affect our moral talk. But sometimes talk is cheap and emotions are fleeting. Morality involves *doing* the right thing, and what we do also depends on social influences. As political theorist Hannah Arendt (1963) observed, many Nazi concentration camp guards during World War II were ordinary "moral" people who were corrupted by a powerfully evil situation.

Today's character education programs tend to focus on the whole moral package—thinking, feeling, and *doing* the right thing. As children's *thinking* matures, their *behavior* also becomes less selfish and more caring (Krebs & Van Hesteren, 1994; Miller et al., 1996). Today's programs also teach children *empathy* for others' feelings, and the self-discipline needed to restrain one's own impulses—to delay small gratifications now to enable bigger rewards later. Those who do learn to *delay gratification* become more socially responsible, academically successful, and productive (Funder & Block, 1989; Mischel et al., 1988, 1989). In service-learning programs, teens tutor, clean up their neighborhoods, and assist the elderly. The result? The teens' sense of competence and desire to serve increase, and their school absenteeism and drop-out rates diminish (Andersen, 1998; Piliavin, 2003). Moral action feeds moral attitudes.

"This might not be ethical. Is that a problem for anybody?"

Before You Move On

▶ **ASK YOURSELF**

Can you recall making an impulsive decision when you were younger that you later regretted? Would you approach the situation differently today?

▶ **TEST YOURSELF**

Describe Kohlberg's three levels of moral reasoning.

Answers to the Test Yourself questions can be found in Appendix E at the end of the book.

Module 51 Review

51-1 How is *adolescence* defined, and what physical changes mark this period?

- *Adolescence* is the transition period from childhood to adulthood, extending from puberty to social independence.

- For boys, early maturation has mixed effects; for girls, early maturation can be a challenge.

- The brain's frontal lobes mature and myelin growth increases during adolescence and the early twenties, enabling improved judgment, impulse control, and long-term planning.

51-2 How did Piaget, Kohlberg, and later researchers describe adolescent cognitive and moral development?

- Piaget theorized that adolescents develop a capacity for formal operations and that this development is the foundation for moral judgment.

- Lawrence Kohlberg proposed a stage theory of moral reasoning, from a preconventional morality of self-interest, to a conventional morality concerned with upholding laws and social rules, to (in some people) a postconventional morality of universal ethical principles.

- Other researchers believe that morality lies in moral intuition and moral action as well as thinking.

- Some critics argue that Kohlberg's postconventional level represents morality from the perspective of individualist cultures.

Multiple-Choice Questions

1. The growth of _____ around axons speeds neurotransmission, enabling better communication between the frontal lobe and other brain regions.

   a. neurons
   d. myelin
   b. the cell body
   e. synapses
   c. dendrites

2. The maturation of the brain's _____ lags behind the development of the limbic system, which may explain the impulsivity of teenagers compared with adults.

   a. frontal lobes
   d. parietal lobes
   b. temporal lobes
   e. corpus collosum
   c. occipital lobes

3. _____ believed that a child's moral judgments build on cognitive development. _____ agreed and sought to describe the development of moral reasoning.

   a. Kohlberg; Erikson
   d. Piaget; Erikson
   b. Erikson; Kohlberg
   e. Haidt; Hall
   c. Piaget; Kohlberg

4. Which level of moral reasoning includes a focus on upholding laws in order to gain social approval?

   a. Collectivist
   d. Postconventional
   b. Preconventional
   e. Formal operational
   c. Conventional

5. What development in adolescents allows for greater impulse control?

   a. The hormonal surge of early adolescence
   b. Hindbrain changes associated with the onset of puberty
   c. Frontal lobe maturation in late adolescence
   d. Limbic system development in mid-adolescence
   e. A decrease in myelin production throughout adolescence

6. Which of Jean Piaget's stages describes typical adolescent thinking?

   a. Sensorimotor
   d. Formal operational
   b. Preoperational
   e. Accommodation
   c. Concrete operational

7. Which of the following correctly describes one of Kohlberg's levels of moral reasoning?

   a. Preconventional stage, where one follows moral principles
   b. Conventional stage, where individualism is foremost
   c. Conventional stage, where it is imperative to uphold the law and follow rules
   d. Preconventional stage, where moral judgment depends on rewards and punishments
   e. Postconventional stage, where it is imperative to uphold the law and follow rules

Practice FRQs

1. Describe how the ideas of Lawrence Kohlberg and Jonathan Haidt differ in regard to the development of morality.

Answer

1 point: Lawrence Kohlberg focused on moral reasoning and the way people *think* about moral situations.

1 point: Jonathan Haidt focused on moral intuition and the way people *feel* about moral situations.

2. Name two biological changes related to sexual maturity in adolescence and briefly describe one change in neurological development in adolescence.

(3 points)

Module 52

Adolescence: Social Development and Emerging Adulthood

Module Learning Objectives

52-1 Describe the social tasks and challenges of adolescence.

52-2 Contrast parental and peer influences during adolescence.

52-3 Discuss the characteristics of emerging adulthood.

52-1 What are the social tasks and challenges of adolescence?

Theorist Erik Erikson (1963) contended that each stage of life has its own *psychosocial* task, a crisis that needs resolution. Young children wrestle with issues of *trust*, then *autonomy* (independence), then *initiative*. School-age children strive for *competence*, feeling able and productive. But for people your age, the task is to synthesize past, present, and future possibilities into a clearer sense of self (**TABLE 52.1** on the next page). Adolescents wonder, "Who am I as an individual? What do I want to do with my life? What values should I live by? What do I believe in?" Erikson called this quest the adolescent's *search for identity.*

As sometimes happens in psychology, Erikson's interests were bred by his own life experience. As the son of a Jewish mother and a Danish Gentile father, Erikson was "doubly an outsider," reported Morton Hunt (1993, p. 391). He was "scorned as a Jew in school but mocked as a Gentile in the synagogue because of his blond hair and blue eyes." Such episodes fueled his interest in the adolescent struggle for identity.

Forming an Identity

To refine their sense of identity, adolescents in individualist cultures usually try out different "selves" in different situations. They may act out one self at home, another with friends, and still another at school or on Facebook. If two situations overlap—as when a teenager brings friends home—the discomfort can be considerable. The teen asks, "Which self should I be? Which is the real me?" The resolution is a self-definition that unifies the various selves into a consistent and comfortable sense of who one is—an **identity.**

For both adolescents and adults, group identities are often formed by how we differ from those around us. When living in Britain, I become conscious of my Americanness. When spending time with my daughter in Africa, I become conscious of my minority (White) race. When surrounded by women, I am mindful of my gender identity. For international students, for those of a minority ethnic group, for people with a disability, for those on a team, a **social identity** often forms around their distinctiveness.

> "Somewhere between the ages of 10 and 13 (depending on how hormone-enhanced their beef was), children entered adolescence, a.k.a. 'the de-cutening.'" -JON STEWART ET AL., *EARTH (THE BOOK)*, 2010

AP® Exam Tip

This is not the only place in the book that the author discusses Erik Erikson's stage theory. For example, trust was discussed on page 492. Integrity comes up on page 548. Table 52.1 pulls it all together in one place for you.

identity our sense of self; according to Erikson, the adolescent's task is to solidify a sense of self by testing and integrating various roles.

social identity the "we" aspect of our self-concept; the part of our answer to "Who am I?" that comes from our group memberships.

Competence vs. inferiority

Intimacy vs. isolation

Table 52.1 Erikson's Stages of Psychosocial Development

Stage (approximate age)	Issue	Description of Task
Infancy (to 1 year)	Trust vs. mistrust	If needs are dependably met, infants develop a sense of basic trust.
Toddlerhood (1 to 3 years)	Autonomy vs. shame and doubt	Toddlers learn to exercise their will and do things for themselves, or they doubt their abilities.
Preschool (3 to 6 years)	Initiative vs. guilt	Preschoolers learn to initiate tasks and carry out plans, or they feel guilty about their efforts to be independent.
Elementary school (6 years to puberty)	Competence vs. inferiority	Children learn the pleasure of applying themselves to tasks, or they feel inferior.
Adolescence (teen years into 20s)	Identity vs. role confusion	Teenagers work at refining a sense of self by testing roles and then integrating them to form a single identity, or they become confused about who they are.
Young adulthood (20s to early 40s)	Intimacy vs. isolation	Young adults struggle to form close relationships and to gain the capacity for intimate love, or they feel socially isolated.
Middle adulthood (40s to 60s)	Generativity vs. stagnation	In middle age, people discover a sense of contributing to the world, usually through family and work, or they may feel a lack of purpose.
Late adulthood (late 60s and up)	Integrity vs. despair	Reflecting on his or her life, an older adult may feel a sense of satisfaction or failure.

"Self-consciousness, the recognition of a creature by itself as a 'self,' [cannot] exist except in contrast with an 'other,' a something which is not the self."
-C. S. Lewis, *The Problem of Pain*, 1940

But not always. Erikson noticed that some adolescents forge their identity early, simply by adopting their parents' values and expectations. (Traditional, less individualist cultures teach adolescents who they are, rather than encouraging them to decide on their own.) Other adolescents may adopt an identity defined in opposition to parents but in conformity with a particular peer group—jocks, preps, geeks, band kids, debaters.

Most young people do develop a sense of contentment with their lives. When American teens were asked whether a series of statements described them, 81 percent said *Yes* to "I would choose my life the way it is right now." The other 19 percent agreed that "I wish I were somebody else" (Lyons, 2004). Reflecting on their existence, 75 percent of American collegians say they "discuss religion/spirituality" with friends, "pray," and agree that "we are all spiritual beings" and "search for meaning/purpose in life" (Astin et al., 2004; Bryant & Astin, 2008). This would not surprise Stanford psychologist William Damon and his colleagues (2003), who have contended that a key task of adolescence is to achieve a purpose—a desire to accomplish something personally meaningful that makes a difference to the world beyond oneself.

The late teen years, when many people like you in industrialized countries begin attending college or working full time, provide new opportunities for trying out possible roles. Here is something for you to remember: Many college seniors have achieved a clearer identity and a more positive self-concept than they had as first-year students (Waterman, 1988).

Who shall I be today? By varying the way they look, adolescents try out different "selves." Although we eventually form a consistent and stable sense of identity, the self we present may change with the situation.

This could be one of the reasons why the first year of college is such a challenge. Collegians who have achieved a clear sense of identity are less prone to self-destructive behavior such as alcohol misuse (Bishop et al., 2005).

Several nationwide studies indicate that young Americans' self-esteem falls during the early to midteen years, and, for girls, depression scores often increase. But then self-image rebounds during the late teens and twenties (Robins et al., 2002; Twenge & Campbell, 2001; Twenge & Nolen-Hoeksema, 2002). Late adolescence and early adulthood are also when agreeableness and emotional stability scores increase (Klimstra et al., 2009; Lucas and Donnellan, 2011).

Erikson contended that the adolescent identity stage is followed in young adulthood by a developing capacity for **intimacy**, the ability to form emotionally close relationships. Romantic relationships, which tend to be emotionally intense, are reported by some two in three North American 17-year-olds, but fewer among those in collectivist countries such as China (Collins et al., 2009; Li et al., 2010). Those who enjoy high-quality (intimate, supportive) relationships with family and friends tend also to enjoy similarly high-quality romantic relationships in adolescence, which set the stage for healthy adult relationships. Such relationships are, for most of us, a source of great pleasure. When Mihaly Csikszentmihalyi [chick-SENT-me-hi] and Jeremy Hunter (2003) used a beeper to sample the daily experiences of American teens, they found them unhappiest when alone and happiest when with friends. As Aristotle long ago recognized, we humans are "the social animal." Relationships matter.

intimacy in Erikson's theory, the ability to form close, loving relationships; a primary developmental task in late adolescence and early adulthood.

AP® Exam Tip

Careful! In the media, to describe a relationship as intimate usually implies that it is sexual. Erikson means something different. In his theory, an intimate relationship may or may not be sexual (and a sexual relationship may or may not be intimate).

Parent and Peer Relationships

52-2 How do parents and peers influence adolescents?

This next research finding will not surprise you: As adolescents in Western cultures seek to form their own identities, they begin to pull away from their parents (Shanahan et al., 2007). The preschooler who can't be close enough to her mother, who loves to touch and cling to her, becomes the 14-year-old who wouldn't be caught dead holding hands with Mom. The transition occurs gradually. By adolescence, arguments occur more often, usually over mundane things—household chores, bedtime, homework (Tesser et al., 1989). Parent-child conflict during the transition to adolescence tends to be greater with first-born than with second-born children, and greater with mothers than with fathers (Burk et al., 2009; Shanahan et al., 2007).

"She says she's someone from your past who gave birth to you, and raised you, and sacrificed everything so you could have whatever you wanted."

For a minority of parents and their adolescents, differences lead to real splits and great stress (Steinberg & Morris, 2001). But most disagreements are at the level of harmless bickering. And most adolescents—6000 of them in 10 countries, from Australia to Bangladesh to Turkey—said they like their parents (Offer et al., 1988). "We usually get along but . . . ," adolescents often reported (Galambos, 1992; Steinberg, 1987).

Positive parent-teen relations and positive peer relations often go hand in hand. High school girls who have the most affectionate relationships with their mothers tend also to enjoy the most intimate friendships with girlfriends (Gold & Yanof, 1985). And teens who feel close to their parents tend to be healthy and happy and to do well in school (Resnick et al., 1997). Of course, we can state this correlation the other way: Misbehaving teens are more likely have tense relationships with parents and other adults.

"It's you who don't understand me—I've been fifteen, but you have never been forty-eight."

Adolescence is typically a time of diminishing parental influence and growing peer influence. Asked in a survey if they had "ever had a serious talk" with their child about illegal drugs, 85 percent of American parents answered *Yes.* But if the parents had indeed given this earnest advice, many teens had apparently tuned it out: Only 45 percent could recall such a talk (Morin & Brossard, 1997).

Heredity does much of the heavy lifting in forming individual temperament and personality differences, and peer influences do much of the rest. Most teens are herd animals. They talk, dress, and act more like their peers than their parents. What their friends are, they often become, and what "everybody's doing," they often do. In teen calls to hotline counseling services, peer relationships have been the most discussed topic (Boehm et al., 1999). The average U.S. teen sends 60 text messages per day (Pew, 2012). Many adolescents become absorbed by social networking, sometimes with a compulsive use that produces "Facebook fatigue."

Online communication stimulates intimate self-disclosure—both for better (support groups) and for worse (online predators and extremist groups) (Subrahmanyam & Greenfield, 2008; Valkenburg & Peter, 2009).

Nine times out of ten, it's all about peer pressure.

For those who feel excluded, the pain is acute. "The social atmosphere in most high schools is poisonously clique-driven and exclusionary," observed social psychologist Elliot Aronson (2001). Most excluded "students suffer in silence. . . . A small number act out in violent ways against their classmates." Those who withdraw are vulnerable to loneliness, low self-esteem, and depression (Steinberg & Morris, 2001). Peer approval matters.

Teens see their parents as having more influence in other areas—for example, in shaping their religious faith and in thinking about college and career choices (*Emerging Trends*, 1997). A Gallup Youth Survey reveals that most share their parents' political views (Lyons, 2005).

Emerging Adulthood

52-3   What is emerging adulthood?

In the Western world, adolescence now roughly corresponds to the teen years. At earlier times, and in other parts of the world today, this slice of life has been much smaller (Baumeister & Tice, 1986). Shortly after sexual maturity, young people would assume adult responsibilities and status. The event might be celebrated with an elaborate initiation—a public *rite of passage.* The new adult would then work, marry, and have children.

When schooling became compulsory in many Western countries, independence was put on hold until after graduation. From Europe to Australia, adolescents are now taking more time to establish themselves as adults. In the United States, for example, the average age at first marriage has increased more than 4 years since 1960 (to 28 for men, 26 for women). In 1960, 3 in 4 women and 2 in 3 men had, by age 30, finished school, left home, become financially independent, married, and had a child. Today, fewer than half of 30-year-old women and one-third of men have achieved these five milestones (Henig, 2010). Delayed independence has overlapped with an earlier onset of puberty. Earlier sexual maturity is related both to girls' increased body fat (which can support pregnancy and nursing) and to weakened parent-child bonds, including absent fathers (Ellis, 2004).

"When I was your age, I was an adult."

Together, later independence and earlier sexual maturity have widened the once-brief interlude between biological maturity and social independence (**FIGURE 52.1**). In prosperous communities, the time from 18 to the mid-twenties is an increasingly not-yet-settled phase of life, which some now call **emerging adulthood** (Arnett, 2006, 2007; Reitzle, 2006). No longer adolescents, these emerging adults, having not yet assumed full adult responsibilities and independence, feel "in between." After high school, those who enter the job market or go to college may be managing their own time and priorities more than ever before. Yet they may be doing so from their parents' home—unable to afford their own place and perhaps still emotionally dependent as well. Recognizing today's more gradually emerging adulthood, the U.S. government now allows dependent children up to age 26 to remain on their parents' health insurance (Cohen, 2010).

> **emerging adulthood** for some people in modern cultures, a period from the late teens to mid-twenties, bridging the gap between adolescent dependence and full independence and responsible adulthood.

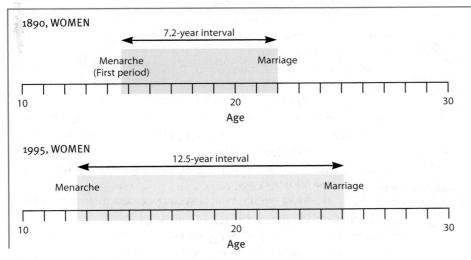

Figure 52.1

The transition to adulthood is being stretched from both ends In the 1890s, the average interval between a woman's first menstrual period and marriage, which typically marked a transition to adulthood, was about 7 years; in industrialized countries today it is about 12 years (Guttmacher, 1994, 2000). Although many adults are unmarried, later marriage combines with prolonged education and earlier menarche to help stretch out the transition to adulthood.

Before You Move On

▶ **ASK YOURSELF**

What have been your best and worst experiences during adolescence? How have your experiences been influenced by environmental factors, such as your cultural context, and how have they been influenced by your inborn traits?

▶ **TEST YOURSELF**

How has the transition from childhood to adulthood changed in Western cultures in the last century or so?

Answers to the Test Yourself questions can be found in Appendix E at the end of the book.

Module 52 Review

 52-1 What are the social tasks and challenges of adolescence?

- Erikson theorized that each life stage has its own psychosocial task, and that a chief task of adolescence is solidifying one's sense of self—one's *identity.* This often means "trying on" a number of different roles.

- *Social identity* is the part of the self-concept that comes from a person's group memberships.

 52-2 How do parents and peers influence adolescents?

- During adolescence, parental influence diminishes and peer influence increases.

- Adolescents adopt their peers' ways of dressing, acting, and communicating.

- Parents have more influence in religion, politics, and college and career choices.

52-3 What is emerging adulthood?

- The transition from adolescence to adulthood is now taking longer.

- *Emerging adulthood* is the period from age 18 to the mid-twenties, when many young people are not yet fully independent. But critics note that this stage is found mostly in today's Western cultures.

Multiple-Choice Questions

1. According to Erikson, you develop your _____, a part of who you are, from your group memberships.
   a. self-interest
   b. social identity
   c. social self
   d. self-esteem
   e. self-consciousness

2. In many Western societies, it is common for adolescents to graduate high school, go to college, and still live at home with their parents. They have not yet assumed full adult responsibilities and independence. Psychologists have identified this period of time as
   a. adulthood.
   b. early adulthood.
   c. emerging adulthood.
   d. late adolescence.
   e. role confusion.

3. Which is true of social relations during the teen years?
   a. As teens distance themselves from parents, peer relationships become more important.
   b. High school girls who have the poorest relationships with their mothers have the most intense friendships with peers.
   c. Parental influence peaks during mid to late adolescence.
   d. Most adolescents have serious disagreements with parents, leading to great social stress.
   e. Teens are generally more concerned with family relationships than peer relationships.

4. According to Erikson, what is the primary developmental task for adolescents?
   a. Trust versus mistrust
   b. Initiative versus guilt
   c. Competence versus inferiority
   d. Identity versus role confusion
   e. Intimacy versus isolation

5. Compared with the late nineteenth century, what is true about the transition from childhood to adulthood in Western cultures?

   a. It starts earlier and is completed earlier.
   b. It starts later and is completed later.
   c. It starts later and is completed earlier.
   d. It starts earlier and is completed later.
   e. It has not changed.

6. Megan, a third grader, is having trouble with math. She is starting to do poorly in other subjects, because she feels she cannot master math. Based on Erikson's stages of psychosocial development, which stage is Megan in?

   a. Autonomy versus shame and doubt
   b. Initiative versus guilt
   c. Competence versus inferiority
   d. Identity versus role confusion
   e. Intimacy versus isolation

7. Boez is a 2-year-old boy who is in the process of potty training. When Boez urinates in the potty, he has a sense of pride. If Boez urinates in his pants, he runs and hides. According to Erikson, in which psychosocial stage is Boez?

   a. Autonomy versus shame and doubt
   b. Initiative versus guilt
   c. Competence versus inferiority
   d. Identity versus role confusion
   e. Intimacy versus isolation

Practice FRQs

1. What is emerging adulthood? Name two trends that have led to adding this to the stages of life.

Answer

1 point: Emerging adulthood is the period in modern Western cultures during the late teens to the mid-twenties that bridges the gap between adolescent dependence and adult independence.

2 points: Longer years of schooling and later age of marriage and moving out of the family home are the trends that have led to this new stage.

2. Name and describe Erik Erikson's stages of psychosocial development for infancy (first year) and middle adulthood (40s to 60s).

(4 points)

Module 53

Sexual Development

Module Learning Objectives

53-1 Explain how biological sex is determined, and describe the role of sex hormones in gender development.

53-2 Describe some of the ways that sexual development varies.

53-3 Discuss the factors that reduce the risk of sexually transmitted infections.

53-4 Discuss the factors that influence teenagers' sexual behaviors and use of contraceptives.

53-5 Summarize what research has taught us about sexual orientation.

Image Source/Getty Images

53-1 How is our biological sex determined, and how do sex hormones influence prenatal and adolescent development?

In domains where we face similar challenges—regulating heat with sweat, preferring foods that nourish, growing calluses where the skin meets friction—men and women are similar. Even when describing the ideal mate, both prize traits such as "kind," "honest," and "intelligent." But in mating-related domains, evolutionary psychologists contend, males differ from females whether they are elephants or elephant seals, rural peasants or corporate presidents (Geary, 2010). Our biology may influence our gender differences in two ways: genetically, by our differing *sex chromosomes,* and physiologically, from our differing concentrations of *sex hormones.*

Prenatal Sexual Development

As noted earlier, males and females are variations on a single form—of the 46 chromosomes, 45 are unisex. So great is this similarity that until seven weeks after conception, you were anatomically indistinguishable from someone of the other sex. Then your genes activated your biological sex. Male or female, your sex was determined by your father's contribution to your twenty-third pair of chromosomes, the two sex chromosomes. You received an **X chromosome** from your mother. From your father, you received the one chromosome that is not unisex—either another X chromosome, making you a girl, or a **Y chromosome,** making you a boy.

The Y chromosome includes a single gene which, about seven weeks after conception, throws a master switch triggering the testes to develop and to produce the principal male hormone, **testosterone.** This hormone starts the development of male sex organs. Females also have testosterone, but less of it.

X chromosome the sex chromosome found in both men and women. Females have two X chromosomes; males have one. An X chromosome from each parent produces a female child.

Y chromosome the sex chromosome found only in males. When paired with an X chromosome from the mother, it produces a male child.

testosterone the most important of the male sex hormones. Both males and females have it, but the additional testosterone in males stimulates the growth of the male sex organs in the fetus and the development of the male sex characteristics during puberty.

Another key period for sexual differentiation falls during the fourth and fifth prenatal months. During this period, sex hormones bathe the fetal brain and influence its wiring. Different patterns for males and females develop under the influence of the male's greater testosterone and the female's ovarian hormones (Hines, 2004; Udry, 2000).

Adolescent Sexual Development

Pronounced physical differences emerge during adolescence, when boys and girls enter **puberty** and mature sexually. A surge of hormones triggers a two-year period of rapid physical development, usually beginning at about age 11 in girls and at about age 13 in boys. A year or two before that, however, boys and girls often feel the first stirrings of physical attraction (McClintock & Herdt, 1996).

About the time of puberty, boys' growth propels them to greater height than their female counterparts (**FIGURE 53.1**). During this growth spurt, the **primary sex characteristics**—the reproductive organs and external genitalia—develop dramatically. So do **secondary sex characteristics,** the nonreproductive traits such as breasts and hips in girls, facial hair and deepened voice in boys, and pubic and underarm hair in both sexes (**FIGURE 53.2** on the next page).

In various countries, girls are developing breasts earlier (sometimes before age 10) and reaching puberty earlier than in the past. This phenomenon is variously attributed to increased body fat, increased hormone-mimicking chemicals, and increased stress related to family disruption (Biro et al., 2010).

Puberty's landmarks are the first ejaculation in boys (*spermarche),* usually by about age 14, and the first menstrual period in girls (**menarche**—meh-NAR-key), usually within a year of age 12½ (Anderson et al., 2003). Menarche appears to occur a few months earlier, on average, for girls who have experienced stresses related to father absence, sexual abuse, or insecure attachments (Belsky et al., 2010; Vigil et al., 2005; Zabin et al., 2005). Girls who have

puberty the period of sexual maturation, during which a person becomes capable of reproducing.

primary sex characteristics the body structures (ovaries, testes, and external genitalia) that make sexual reproduction possible.

secondary sex characteristics nonreproductive sexual traits, such as female breasts and hips, male voice quality, and body hair.

menarche [meh-NAR-key] the first menstrual period.

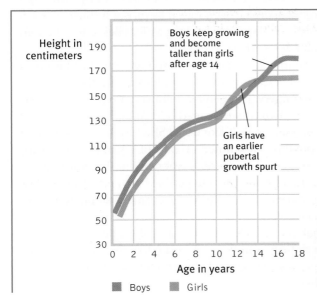

Boys keep growing and become taller than girls after age 14

Girls have an earlier pubertal growth spurt

Height in centimeters

Age in years

Boys   Girls

Figure 53.1

Height differences Throughout childhood, boys and girls are similar in height. At puberty, girls surge ahead briefly, but then boys overtake them at about age 14. (Data from Tanner, 1978.) Studies suggest that sexual development and growth spurts are beginning somewhat earlier than was the case a half-century ago (Herman-Giddens et al., 2001).

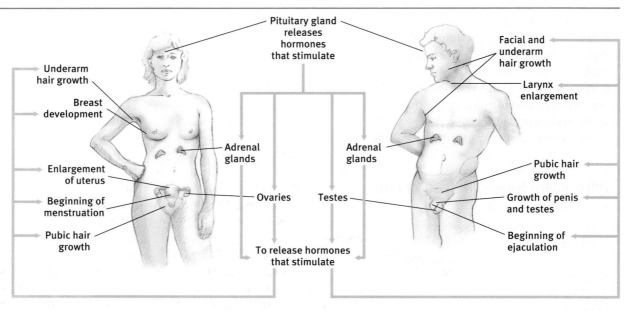

Figure 53.2

Body changes at puberty At about age 11 in girls and age 13 in boys, a surge of hormones triggers a variety of physical changes.

been prepared for menarche usually experience it as a positive life transition. Studies have shown that nearly all adult women recall their first menstrual period and remember experiencing a mixture of feelings—pride, excitement, embarrassment, and apprehension (Greif & Ulman, 1982; Woods et al., 1983). Most men have similarly recalled their first ejaculation, which usually occurs as a nocturnal emission (Fuller & Downs, 1990).

Variations on Sexual Development

53-2 What are some of the ways that sexual development varies?

Sometimes nature blurs the biological line between males and females. Atypical hormone exposure or sensitivity may cause atypical fetal development. *Intersex* individuals are born with intermediate or unusual combinations of male and female physical features. Genetic males, for example, may be born with normal male hormones and testes but without a penis or with a very small one.

Until recently, pediatricians and other medical experts often recommended surgery to create a female identity for these children. One study reviewed 14 cases of boys who had undergone early sex-reassignment surgery and had been raised as girls. Of those cases, 6 had later declared themselves as males, 5 were living as females, and 3 had an unclear gender identity (Reiner & Gearhart, 2004).

Although not born with an intersex condition, a little boy who lost his penis during a botched circumcision became a famous case illustrating the problems involved in sex-reassignment surgery. His parents followed a psychiatrist's advice to raise him as a girl rather than as a damaged boy. Alas, "Brenda" Reimer was not like most other girls. "She" didn't like dolls. She tore her dresses with rough-and-tumble play. At puberty she wanted no part of kissing boys. Finally, Brenda's parents explained what had happened, whereupon "Brenda" immediately rejected the assigned female identity. He cut his hair and chose a male name, David. He eventually married a woman and became a stepfather. And, sadly, he later committed suicide (Colapinto, 2000).

The bottom line: "Sex matters," concluded the National Academy of Sciences (2001). In combination with the environment, sex-related genes and physiology "result in behavioral and cognitive differences between males and females." Nature and nurture work together.

Gender in the spotlight Dramatic improvements in South African track star Caster Semenya's race times prompted the International Association of Athletics Federations to undertake sex testing in 2009. Semenya was reported to be intersex—with physical characteristics of both males and females—though she was officially cleared to continue competing as a woman. Semenya declared, "God made me the way I am and I accept myself. I am who I am" (*YOU*, 10 September 2009).

Cameron Spencer/Getty Images

Sexually Transmitted Infections

53-3 How can sexually transmitted infections be prevented?

Rates of *sexually transmitted infections* (*STIs*; also called *STDs* for *sexually transmitted diseases*) are rising, and two-thirds of the new infections have occurred in people under 25 (CASA, 2004). Teenage girls, because of their not yet fully mature biological development and lower levels of protective antibodies, are especially vulnerable (Dehne & Riedner, 2005; Guttmacher, 1994). A Centers for Disease Control study of sexually experienced 14- to 19-year-old U.S. females found 39.5 percent had STIs (Forhan et al., 2008).

Consider this: If someone uses a birth control method that is 98 percent effective in preventing pregnancy or infection, a 2 percent chance of failure in the first such use accumulates to a risk of nearly 50 percent after 30 such uses. Moreover, when people feel drawn to a partner, they become motivated to underestimate risks (Knäuper et al, 2005).

Condoms offer only limited protection against certain skin-to-skin STIs, such as herpes, but they do reduce other risks (Medical Institute, 1994; NIH, 2001). The effects were clear when Thailand promoted 100 percent condom use by commercial sex workers. Over a 4-year period, as condom use soared from 14 to 94 percent, the annual number of bacterial STIs plummeted from 410,406 to 27,362 (WHO, 2000).

Across the available studies, condoms also have been 80 percent effective in preventing transmission of *HIV* (*human immunodeficiency virus*—the virus that causes **AIDS**) from an infected partner (Weller & Davis-Beaty, 2002; WHO, 2003). Although AIDS can be transmitted by other means, such as needle sharing during drug use, its sexual transmission is most common. Women's AIDS rates are increasing fastest, partly because the virus is passed from man to woman much more often than from woman to man. A man's semen can carry more of the virus than can a woman's vaginal and cervical secretions. The HIV-infected semen can also linger for days in a woman's vagina and cervix, increasing the time of exposure (Allen & Setlow, 1991; WHO, 2004).

Most people recently diagnosed with AIDS in the United States have been ages 25 to 44 (CDC, 2013a). Given AIDS' long incubation period, it's unsurprising that 39 percent of new HIV diagnoses in the United States were among those even younger—13- to 29-year-olds (CDC, 2013b). In 2009, the death of 1.8 million people with AIDS worldwide left behind countless grief-stricken partners and millions of orphaned children (UNAIDS, 2010). Sub-Saharan Africa is home to two-thirds of those infected with HIV, and medical treatment and care for the dying are sapping the region's social resources.

Many people assume that oral sex falls in the category of "safe sex," but recent studies show a significant link between oral sex and transmission of STIs, such as the *human papilloma virus (HPV)*. Risks rise with the number of sexual partners (Gillison et al., 2012). Most HPV infections can now be prevented with a vaccination administered before sexual contact.

AIDS (acquired immune deficiency syndrome) a life-threatening, sexually transmitted infection caused by the *human immunodeficiency virus* (HIV). AIDS depletes the immune system, leaving the person vulnerable to infections.

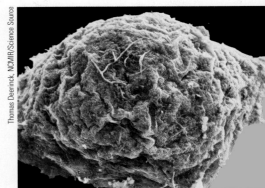

An HIV-infected cell

Teen Pregnancy

53-4 What factors influence teenagers' sexual behaviors and use of contraceptives?

Adolescents' physical maturation fosters a sexual dimension to their emerging identity. Yet sexual expression varies dramatically with time and culture. Among American women born before 1900, a mere 3 percent had experienced premarital sex by age 18 (Smith, 1998). A century later, about half of U.S. ninth- to twelfth-graders reported having had sexual intercourse (CDC, 2010). Teen intercourse rates are roughly similar in Western Europe and in Latin America, but much lower in Arab and Asian countries and among North Americans of Asian descent (McLaughlin et al., 1997; Wellings et al., 2006). Given the wide variation across time and place, it's no surprise that twin research has found that environmental factors accounted for almost three-fourths of the individual variation in age of sexual initiation (Bricker et al., 2006). Family and cultural values matter.

Compared with European teens, American teens have a higher rate of STIs and also of teen pregnancy (Call et al., 2002; Sullivan/Anderson, 2009). What environmental factors contribute to teen pregnancy?

Minimal communication about birth control Many teenagers are uncomfortable discussing contraception with their parents, partners, and peers. Teens who talk freely with parents, and who are in an exclusive relationship with a partner with whom they communicate openly, are more likely to use contraceptives (Aspy et al., 2007; Milan & Kilmann, 1987).

Guilt related to sexual activity In another survey, 72 percent of sexually active 12- to 17-year-old American girls said they regretted having had sex (Reuters, 2000). Sexual inhibitions or ambivalence can restrain sexual activity, but if passion overwhelms intentions they may also reduce attempts at birth control (Gerrard & Luus, 1995; MacDonald & Hynie, 2008).

Alcohol use Sexually active teens are typically alcohol-using teens (Zimmer-Gembeck & Helfand, 2008), and those who use alcohol prior to sex are less likely to use condoms (Kotchick et al., 2001). By depressing the brain centers that control judgment, inhibition, and self-awareness, alcohol disarms normal restraints, a phenomenon well known to sexually coercive males.

Mass media norms of unprotected promiscuity Media help write the "social scripts" that affect our perceptions and actions. So what sexual scripts do today's media write on our minds? An average hour of prime-time television on the three major U.S. networks has contained 15 sexual acts, words, and innuendos. The partners were usually unmarried, with no prior romantic relationship, and few communicated any concern for birth control or STIs (Brown et al., 2002; Kunkel, 2001; Sapolsky & Tabarlet, 1991). The more sexual content adolescents view (even when controlling for other predictors of early sexual activity), the more likely they are to perceive their peers as sexually active, to develop sexually permissive attitudes, and to experience early intercourse (Escobar-Chaves et al., 2005; Martino et al., 2005; Ward & Friedman, 2006). (See Close-up: The Sexualization of Girls.)

Recently, there has been a greater emphasis on teen abstinence within some comprehensive sex-education programs. A government-commissioned study of four urban, school-based abstinence programs found that 49 percent of students not participating had sex over the next four to six years. And how many participating in the abstinence programs did so? An identical 49 percent (Trenholm et al., 2007). A National Longitudinal Study of Adolescent Health followed abstinence pledgers and nonpledgers (matched samples of similarly conservative teens who had never had sex). Five years later, the pledgers—82 percent of whom denied having ever pledged—were just as likely to have had premarital sex (Rosenbaum, 2009). However, a more recent experiment offered African-American middle school students an abstinence education program rooted in social psychological theory and research. In the ensuing two years, only 34 percent of those who participated started having sex, compared with 49 percent of those randomly assigned to a health promotion control group (Jemmott et al., 2010).

The National Longitudinal Study of Adolescent Health among 12,000 teens found several factors that predicted sexual restraint:

- *High intelligence* Teens with high rather than average intelligence test scores more often delayed sex, partly because they appreciated possible negative consequences and were more focused on future achievement than on here-and-now pleasures (Halpern et al., 2000).

- *Religious engagement* Actively religious teens have more often reserved sexual activity for adulthood (Lucero et al., 2008).

"All of us who make motion pictures are teachers, teachers with very loud voices." -FILM PRODUCER GEORGE LUCAS, ACADEMY AWARD CEREMONIES, 1992

Close-up

The Sexualization of Girls

As you have surely noticed, TV, the Internet, music videos and lyrics, movies, magazines, sports media, and advertising often portray women and even girls as sexual objects. The frequent result, according to both an American Psychological Association task force (2007) and the Scottish Parliament (2010), is harm to their self-image, and unhealthy sexual development.

Sexualization occurs when girls

- are led to value themselves in terms of their sexual appeal.

- compare themselves to narrowly defined beauty standards.

- see themselves as sexual beings for others' use.

© T.Arroyo/JPegFoto/
PictureGroup via AP IMAGES

In experiments, the APA task force reported, being made self-conscious about one's body, such as by wearing a swimsuit, disrupts thinking when doing math computations or logical reasoning. Sexualization also contributes to eating disorders and depression, and to unrealistic expectations regarding sexuality.

Mindful of today's sexualizing media, the APA has some suggestions for countering these messages. Parents, teachers, and others can teach girls "to value themselves for who they are rather than how they look." They can teach boys "to value girls as friends, sisters, and girlfriends, rather than as sexual objects." And they can help girls and boys develop "media literacy skills" that enable them to recognize and resist the message that women are sexual objects and that a thin, sexy look is all that matters.

- *Father presence* In studies that followed hundreds of New Zealand and U.S. girls from age 5 to 18, a father's absence was linked to sexual activity before age 16 and to teen pregnancy (Ellis et al., 2003). These associations held even after adjusting for other adverse influences, such as poverty. Close family attachments—families that eat together and where parents know their teens' activities and friends—also predicted later sexual initiation (Coley et al., 2008).

- *Participation in service learning programs* Several experiments have found that teens volunteering as tutors or teachers' aides, or participating in community projects, had lower pregnancy rates than were found among comparable teens randomly assigned to control conditions (Kirby, 2002; O'Donnell et al., 2002). Researchers are unsure why. Does service learning promote a sense of personal competence, control, and responsibility? Does it encourage more future-oriented thinking? Or does it simply reduce opportunities for unprotected sex?

Keeping abreast of hypersexuality An analysis of the 60 top-selling video games found 489 characters, 86 percent of whom were males (like most of the game players). The female characters were much more likely than the male characters to be "hypersexualized"—partially nude or revealingly clothed, with large breasts and tiny waists (Downs & Smith, 2010).

Eidos Scripps Howard Photo Service/Newscom

Sexual Orientation

53-5 What has research taught us about sexual orientation?

We express the *direction* of our sexual interest in our **sexual orientation**—our enduring sexual attraction toward members of our own sex *(homosexual orientation)*, the other sex *(heterosexual orientation)*, or both sexes *(bisexual orientation)*. As far as we know, all cultures in all times have been predominantly heterosexual (Bullough, 1990). Some cultures have condemned same-sex relations. (In Kenya and Nigeria, 98 percent have thought homosexuality is "never justified" [Pew, 2006].) Others have accepted same-sex marriage, which by 2013 had become legal in 14 countries. But in both cases, heterosexuality prevails and homosexuality endures.

sexual orientation an enduring sexual attraction toward members of either one's own sex (homosexual orientation), the other sex (heterosexual orientation), or both sexes (bisexual orientation).

FYI

In one British survey, of the 18,876 people contacted, 1 percent were seemingly asexual, having "never felt sexually attracted to anyone at all" (Bogaert, 2004, 2006b).

Driven to suicide In 2010, Rutgers University student Tyler Clementi jumped off this bridge after his intimate encounter with another man reportedly became known. Reports then surfaced of other gay teens who had reacted in a similarly tragic fashion after being taunted. Since 2010, Americans—especially those under 30—have been increasingly supportive of those with same-sex orientations.

FYI

Note that the scientific question is not "What causes homosexuality?" (or "What causes heterosexuality?") but "What causes differing sexual orientations?" In pursuit of answers, psychological science compares the backgrounds and physiology of people whose sexual orientations *differ*.

How many people are exclusively homosexual? About 10 percent, as the popular press has often assumed? Nearly 25 percent, as average Americans estimated in a 2011 Gallup survey (Morales, 2011)? Not according to more than a dozen national surveys that have explored sexual orientation in Europe and the United States, using methods protecting the respondents' anonymity. The most accurate figure seems to be about 3 percent of men and 1 or 2 percent of women, or perhaps a tad more if allowing for some underreporting (Chandra et al., 2011; Gates & Newport, 2012; Herbenick et al., 2010a,b). Fewer than 1 percent of survey respondents—for example, only 12 people out of 7076 Dutch adults in one survey (Sandfort et al., 2001)—have reported being actively bisexual. A larger number of adults—13 percent of women and 5 percent of men in a U.S. National Center for Health Statistics survey—report some same-sex sexual contact during their lives (Chandra et al., 2011). And still more have had an occasional homosexual fantasy.

What does it feel like to be the "odd man (or woman) out" in a heterosexual culture? If you are heterosexual, one way to understand is to imagine how you would feel if you were socially isolated for openly admitting or displaying your feelings toward someone of the other sex. How would you react if you overheard people making crude jokes about heterosexual people, or if most movies, TV shows, and advertisements portrayed (or implied) homosexuality? And how would you answer if your family members were pleading with you to change your heterosexual lifestyle and to enter into a homosexual marriage?

Facing such reactions, homosexual people often struggle with their sexual orientation. They may at first try to ignore or deny their desires, hoping they will go away. But they don't. The feelings typically persist, as do those of heterosexual people—who are similarly incapable of becoming homosexual (Haldeman, 1994, 2002; Myers & Scanzoni, 2005).

Most of today's psychologists therefore view sexual orientation as neither willfully chosen nor willfully changed. "Efforts to change sexual orientation are unlikely to be successful and involve some risk of harm," declared a 2009 American Psychological Association report. In 1973, the American Psychiatric Association dropped homosexuality from its list of "mental illnesses." In 1993, the World Health Organization did the same, as did Japan's and China's psychiatric associations in 1995 and 2001. Some have noted that rates of depression and attempted suicide are higher among gays and lesbians. Many psychologists believe, however, that these symptoms may result from experiences with bullying, harassment, and discrimination (Sandfort et al., 2001; Warner et al., 2004). "Homosexuality, in and of itself, is not associated with mental disorders or emotional or social problems," declared the American Psychological Association (2007).

Thus, sexual orientation in some ways is like handedness: Most people are one way, some the other. A very few are ambidextrous. Regardless, the way one is endures.

This conclusion is most strongly established for men. Compared with men's sexual orientation, women's tends to be less strongly felt and may be more variable (Chivers, 2005; Diamond, 2008; Peplau & Garnets, 2000). Men's lesser *erotic plasticity* (sexual variability) is apparent in many ways (Baumeister, 2000). Adult women's sexual drive and interests are more flexible and varying than are adult men's. Women, more than men, for example, prefer to alternate periods of high sexual activity with periods of almost none. They are also more likely than men to feel and act on bisexual attractions (Mosher et al., 2005).

Environment and Sexual Orientation

So, our sexual orientation is something we do not choose and (especially for males) seemingly cannot change. Where then, do these preferences come from? Let's look first at possible environmental influences on sexual orientation. To see if you can anticipate the conclusions that have emerged from hundreds of studies, try answering *Yes* or *No* to these questions:

1. Is homosexuality linked with problems in a child's relationships with parents, such as with a domineering mother and an ineffectual father, or a possessive mother and a hostile father?

2. Does homosexuality involve a fear or hatred of people of the other sex, leading individuals to direct their desires toward members of their own sex?
3. Is sexual orientation linked with levels of sex hormones currently in the blood?
4. As children, were most homosexuals molested, seduced, or otherwise sexually victimized by an adult homosexual?

The answer to all these questions has been *No* (Storms, 1983). In a search for possible environmental influences on sexual orientation, Kinsey Institute investigators interviewed nearly 1000 homosexuals and 500 heterosexuals. They assessed nearly every imaginable psychological cause of homosexuality—parental relationships, childhood sexual experiences, peer relationships, and dating experiences (Bell et al., 1981; Hammersmith, 1982). Their findings: Homosexuals were no more likely than heterosexuals to have been smothered by maternal love or neglected by their father. And consider this: If "distant fathers" were more likely to produce homosexual sons, then shouldn't boys growing up in father-absent homes more often be gay? (They are not.) And shouldn't the rising number of such homes have led to a noticeable increase in the gay population? (It has not.) Most children raised by gay or lesbian parents grow up straight and well-adjusted (Gartrell & Bos, 2010).

A bottom line has emerged from a half-century's theory and research: If there are environmental factors that influence sexual orientation, we do not yet know what they are.

Personal values affect sexual orientation less than they affect other forms of sexual behavior Compared with people who rarely attend religious services, for example, those who attend regularly are one-third as likely to have lived together before marriage, and they report having had many fewer sex partners. But (if male) they are just as likely to be homosexual (Smith, 1998).

Biology and Sexual Orientation

The lack of evidence for environmental causes of homosexuality has motivated researchers to explore possible biological influences. They have considered

- evidence of homosexuality in other species,
- gay-straight brain differences,
- genetics, and
- prenatal hormones.

SAME-SEX ATTRACTION IN OTHER SPECIES

In Boston's Public Gardens, caretakers have solved the mystery of why a much-loved swan couple's eggs never hatch. Both swans are female. In New York City's Central Park Zoo, penguins Silo and Roy spent several years as devoted same-sex partners. At least occasional same-sex relations have been observed in several hundred species (Bagemihl, 1999). Grizzlies, gorillas, monkeys, flamingos, and owls are all on the long list. Among rams, for example, some 7 to 10 percent (to sheep-breeding ranchers, the "duds") display same-sex attraction by shunning ewes and seeking to mount other males (Perkins & Fitzgerald, 1997). Some degree of homosexual behavior seems a natural part of the animal world.

Juliet and Juliet Boston's beloved swan couple, "Romeo and Juliet," were discovered actually to be, as are many other animal partners, a same-sex pair.

GAY-STRAIGHT BRAIN DIFFERENCES

Researcher Simon LeVay (1991) studied sections of the hypothalamus (a brain structure linked to emotion) taken from deceased heterosexual and homosexual people. As a gay man, LeVay wanted to do "something connected with my gay identity." To avoid biasing the results, he did a *blind study,* without knowing which donors were gay or straight. After 9 months of peering through his microscope at a hypothalamus cell cluster that seemed to come in different sizes, he consulted the donor records. The cell cluster was reliably larger in heterosexual men than in women and homosexual men. "I was almost in a state of shock," LeVay said (1994). "I took a walk by myself on the cliffs over the ocean. I sat for half an hour just thinking what this might mean."

It should not surprise us that brains differ with sexual orientation. Remember, *everything psychological is simultaneously biological*. But when did the brain difference begin? At conception? During childhood or adolescence? Did experience produce the difference? Or was it genes or prenatal hormones (or genes via prenatal hormones)?

LeVay does not view this cell cluster as an "on-off button" for sexual orientation. Rather, he believes it is an important part of a brain pathway that is active during sexual behavior. He agrees that sexual behavior patterns could influence the brain's anatomy. (Neural pathways in our brain do grow stronger with use.) In fish, birds, rats, and humans, brain structures vary with experience—including sexual experience (Breedlove, 1997). But LeVay believes it more likely that brain anatomy influences sexual orientation. His hunch seems confirmed by the discovery of a similar difference found between the 7 to 10 percent of male sheep that display same-sex attraction and the 90+ percent attracted to females (Larkin et al., 2002; Roselli et al., 2002, 2004). Moreover, such differences seem to develop soon after birth, perhaps even before birth (Rahman & Wilson, 2003).

Since LeVay's discovery, other researchers have reported additional gay-straight brain activity differences. One is an area of the hypothalamus that governs sexual arousal (Savic et al., 2005). When straight women were given a whiff of a scent derived from men's sweat (which contains traces of male hormones), this area became active. Gay men's brains responded similarly to the men's scent. Straight men's brains did not. They showed the arousal response only to a female hormone sample. In a similar study, lesbians' responses differed from those of straight women (Kranz & Ishai, 2006; Martins et al., 2005).

GENETIC INFLUENCES

Three lines of evidence suggest a genetic influence on sexual orientation.

FAMILY STUDIES Researchers have speculated about possible reasons why "gay genes" might persist in the human gene pool, given that same-sex couples cannot naturally reproduce. One possible answer is kin selection. Recall from Module 15 the evolutionary psychology reminder that many of our genes also reside in our biological relatives. Perhaps, then, gay people's genes live on through their supporting the survival and reproductive success of their nieces, nephews, and other relatives (who also carry many of the same genes). Gay men make generous uncles, suggests one study of Samoans (Vasey & VanderLaan, 2010).

An alternative "fertile females" theory suggests that maternal genetics may also be at work (Bocklandt et al., 2006). Homosexual men tend to have more homosexual relatives on their mother's side than on their father's (Camperio-Ciani et al., 2004, 2009; Zietsch et al., 2008). And the relatives on the mother's side also produce more offspring than do the maternal relatives of heterosexual men. Perhaps the genes that dispose women to be strongly attracted to men, and therefore to have more children, also dispose some men to be attracted to men (LeVay, 2011).

TWIN STUDIES Twin studies indicate that genes influence sexual orientation. Identical twins (who have identical genes) are somewhat more likely than fraternal twins (whose genes are not identical) to share a homosexual orientation (Alanko et al., 2010; Långström et al., 2008, 2010). However, because sexual orientation differs in many identical twin pairs (especially female twins), other factors must also play a role.

FRUIT FLY STUDIES Laboratory experiments on fruit flies have altered a single gene and changed the flies' sexual orientation and behavior (Dickson, 2005). During courtship, females acted like males (pursuing other females) and males acted like females (Demir & Dickson, 2005). With humans, it's likely that multiple genes, possibly in interaction with other influences, shape sexual orientation. In search of such genetic markers, one study financed by the U.S. National Institutes of Health is analyzing the genes of more than 1000 gay brothers.

PRENATAL INFLUENCES

Twins share not only genes, but also a prenatal environment. Two sets of findings indicate that prenatal environment matters.

First, in humans, a critical period for brain development seems to fall between the middle of the second and fifth months after conception (Ellis & Ames, 1987; Gladue, 1990; Meyer-Bahlburg, 1995). Exposure to the hormone levels typically experienced by female fetuses during this period may predispose a person (female or male) to be attracted to males in later life. When pregnant sheep were injected with testosterone during a similar critical period, their female offspring later showed homosexual behavior (Money, 1987).

Second, the mother's immune system may play a role in the development of sexual orientation. Men who have older brothers are somewhat more likely to be gay—about one-third more likely for each additional older brother (Blanchard, 1997, 2008; Bogaert, 2003). If the odds of homosexuality are roughly 2 percent among first sons, they would rise to nearly 3 percent among second sons, 4 percent for third sons, and so on for each additional older brother (see **FIGURE 53.3**). The reason for this curious effect—called the *older-brother* or *fraternal birth-order effect*—is unclear. But the explanation does seem biological. The effect does not occur among adopted brothers (Bogaert, 2006). Researchers suspect the mother's immune system may have a defensive response to substances produced by male fetuses. After each pregnancy with a male fetus, the maternal antibodies may become stronger and may prevent the fetal brain from developing in a typical male pattern.

> "Modern scientific research indicates that sexual orientation is . . . partly determined by genetics, but more specifically by hormonal activity in the womb." -GLENN WILSON AND QAZI RAHMAN, *BORN GAY: THE PSYCHOBIOLOGY OF SEX ORIENTATION*, 2005

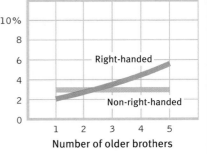

Figure 53.3

The fraternal birth-order effect Researcher Ray Blanchard (2008) offered these approximate curves depicting a man's likelihood of homosexuality as a function of his number of older brothers. This correlation has been found in several studies, but only among right-handed men (as about 9 in 10 men are).

GAY-STRAIGHT TRAIT DIFFERENCES

On several traits, gays and lesbians appear to fall midway between straight females and males (**TABLE 53.1**; see also LeVay, 2011; Rahman & Koerting, 2008). Gay men tend to

---

Table 53.1 Biological Correlates of Sexual Orientation

Gay-straight trait differences

Sexual orientation is part of a package of traits. Studies—some in need of replication—indicate that homosexuals and heterosexuals differ in the following biological and behavioral traits:

- spatial abilities
- fingerprint ridge counts
- auditory system development
- handedness
- occupational preferences
- relative finger lengths
- gender nonconformity
- age of onset of puberty in males
- male body size
- sleep length
- physical aggression
- walking style

On average (the evidence is strongest for males), results for gays and lesbians fall between those of straight men and straight women. Three biological influences—brain, genetic, and prenatal—may contribute to these differences.

Brain differences

- One hypothalamic cell cluster is smaller in women and gay men than in straight men.
- Gay men's hypothalamus reacts as do straight women's to the smell of sex-related hormones.

Genetic influences

- Shared sexual orientation is higher among identical twins than among fraternal twins.
- Sexual attraction in fruit flies can be genetically manipulated.
- Male homosexuality often appears to be transmitted from the mother's side of the family.

Prenatal influences

- Altered prenatal hormone exposure may lead to homosexuality in humans and other animals.
- Men with several older biological brothers are more likely to be gay, possibly due to a maternal immune-system reaction.

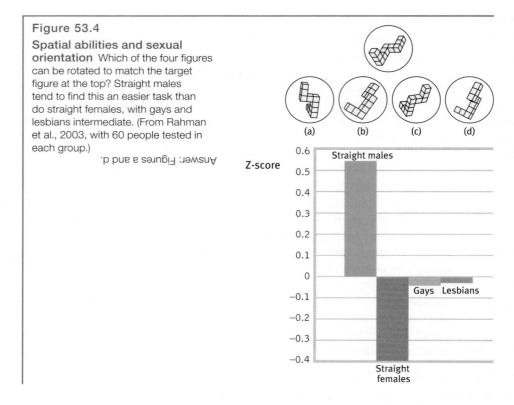

Figure 53.4

Spatial abilities and sexual orientation Which of the four figures can be rotated to match the target figure at the top? Straight males tend to find this an easier task than do straight females, with gays and lesbians intermediate. (From Rahman et al., 2003, with 60 people tested in each group.)

Answer: Figures a and d.

be shorter and lighter than straight men—a difference that appears even at birth. Women in same-sex marriages were mostly heavier than average at birth (Bogaert, 2010; Frisch & Zdravkovic, 2010). Data from 20 studies have also revealed handedness differences: Homosexual participants were 39 percent more likely to not be right-handed (Blanchard, 2008; Lalumière et al., 2000).

Gay-straight spatial abilities also differ. On mental rotation tasks such as the one illustrated in **FIGURE 53.4** (Vandenberg & Kuse, 1978), straight men tend to outscore straight women but the scores of gays and lesbians fall between those of straight men and women (Rahman et al., 2003). But straight women and gays both outperform straight men at remembering objects' spatial locations in tasks like those found in memory games (Hassan & Rahman, 2007).

* * *

"There is no sound scientific evidence that sexual orientation can be changed." -UK ROYAL COLLEGE OF PSYCHIATRISTS, 2009

The consistency of the brain, genetic, and prenatal findings has swung the pendulum toward a biological explanation of sexual orientation (LeVay, 2011; Rahman & Koerting, 2008). Although "much remains to be discovered," concludes Simon LeVay (2011, p. xvii), "the same processes that are involved in the biological development of our bodies and brains as male or female are also involved in the development of sexual orientation."

Before You Move On

▶ **ASK YOURSELF**

What do you think would be an effective strategy for reducing teen pregnancy?

▶ **TEST YOURSELF**

What factors have been found to predict sexual restraint among teens?

Answers to the Test Yourself questions can be found in Appendix E at the end of the book.

Module 53 Review

 How is our biological sex determined, and how do sex hormones influence prenatal and adolescent development?

- Both sex chromosomes and sex hormones influence development.

- Biological sex is determined by the father's contribution to the twenty-third pair of chromosomes.
  - The mother always contributes an *X chromosome.*
  - The father may also contribute an X chromosome, producing a female, or a *Y chromosome,* producing a male by triggering additional *testosterone* release and the development of male sex organs.

- During *puberty,* both *primary* and *secondary sex characteristics* develop.

- Sex-related genes and physiology influence behavioral and cognitive gender differences between males and females.

 What are some of the ways that sexual development varies?

- Intersex individuals are born with intermediate or unusual combinations of male and female characteristics.

- Research suggests sex-reassignment surgery can be problematic.

 How can sexually transmitted infections be prevented?

- Safe-sex practices help prevent sexually transmitted infections (STIs).

- Condoms are especially effective in preventing transmission of HIV, the virus that causes *AIDS.*

- A vaccination administered before sexual contact can prevent most human papilloma virus infections.

53-4 **What factors influence teenagers' sexual behaviors and use of contraceptives?**

- Rates of teen intercourse vary from culture to culture and era to era.

- Factors contributing to teen pregnancy include minimal communication about birth control with parents, partners, and peers; guilt related to sexual activity; alcohol use; and mass media norms of unprotected and impulsive sexuality.

- High intelligence, religious engagement, father presence, and participation in service learning programs have been predictors of teen sexual restraint.

53-5 **What has research taught us about sexual orientation?**

- *Sexual orientation* is an enduring sexual attraction toward members of one's own sex (homosexual orientation), the other sex (heterosexual orientation), or both sexes (bisexual orientation).

- Sexual orientation is not an indicator of mental health.

- There is no evidence that environmental influences determine sexual orientation.

- Evidence for biological influences includes the presence of same-sex attraction in many animal species; straight-gay differences in body and brain characteristics; higher rates in certain families and in identical twins; exposure to certain hormones during critical periods of prenatal development; and the fraternal birth-order effect.

Multiple-Choice Questions

1. Which of the following is an example of a primary sex characteristic?

   a. Nonreproductive traits such as breasts and hips in girls

   b. Facial hair in boys

   c. Deepened voice in boys

   d. Pubic and underarm hair in both sexes

   e. Reproductive organs in both sexes

2. Which of the following is a *primary* sex characteristic that changes at puberty?

   a. A growth spurt in height, especially for boys

   b. Development of breasts for girls

   c. Full development of external genitalia in both sexes

   d. Facial hair and deepened voice for boys

   e. Appearance of pubic and underarm hair in both sexes

3. Which of the following has been shown to be the most effective intervention to reduce teen pregnancies?

   a. Abstinence-only sex education in schools

   b. Participation in service learning programs

   c. Increasing guilt related to sexual activity

   d. Taking a pledge to remain abstinent

   e. Increased exposure to sexual content in the media

Practice FRQs

1. Provide examples of a primary and a secondary sex characteristic for both males and females.

Answer

1 point: Male primary sex characteristics include growth of penis and testes and first ejaculation (spermarche).

1 point: Male secondary sex characteristics include pubic hair, body hair, widening of the shoulders, and lower voice.

1 point: Female primary sex characteristics include menarche and full development of external genitalia.

1 point: Female secondary sex characteristics include pubic hair, body hair, widening of the hips, and growth of breasts.

2. Explain three examples of evidence that suggests a genetic influence on sexual orientation.

(3 points)

Module 54

Adulthood: Physical, Cognitive, and Social Development

Module Learning Objectives

54-1 Identify the physical changes that occur during middle and late adulthood.

54-2 Assess the impact of aging on memory.

54-3 Discuss the themes and influences that mark the social journey from early adulthood to death.

54-4 Describe trends in people's self-confidence and life satisfaction across the life span.

54-5 Describe the range of reactions to the death of a loved one.

The unfolding of people's adult lives continues across the life span. It is, however, more difficult to generalize about adulthood stages than about life's early years. If you know that James is a 1-year-old and Jamal is a 10-year-old, you could say a great deal about each child. Not so with adults who differ by a similar number of years. The boss may be 30 or 60; the marathon runner may be 20 or 50; the 19-year-old may be a parent who supports a child or a child who receives an allowance. Yet our life courses are in some ways similar. Physically, cognitively, and especially socially, we differ at age 50 from our 25-year-old selves. In the discussion that follows, we recognize these differences and use three terms: *early adulthood* (roughly twenties and thirties), *middle adulthood* (to age 65), and *late adulthood* (the years after 65). Within each of these stages, people will vary widely in physical, psychological, and social development.

Physical Development

54-1 What physical changes occur during middle and late adulthood?

Like the declining daylight after the summer solstice, our physical abilities—muscular strength, reaction time, sensory keenness, and cardiac output—all begin an almost imperceptible decline in our mid-twenties. Athletes are often the first to notice. World-class sprinters and swimmers peak by their early twenties. Women—who mature earlier than men—also peak earlier. But most of us—especially those of us whose daily lives do not require top physical performance—hardly perceive the early signs of decline.

menopause the time of natural cessation of menstruation; also refers to the biological changes a woman experiences as her ability to reproduce declines.

Physical Changes in Middle Adulthood

Post-40 athletes know all too well that physical decline gradually accelerates. During early and middle adulthood, physical vigor has less to do with age than with a person's health and exercise habits. Many of today's physically fit 50-year-olds run 4 miles with ease, while sedentary 25-year-olds find themselves huffing and puffing up two flights of stairs.

Aging also brings a gradual decline in fertility, especially for women. For a 35- to 39-year-old woman, the chances of getting pregnant after a single act of intercourse are only half those of a woman 19 to 26 (Dunson et al., 2002). Men experience a gradual decline in sperm count, testosterone level, and speed of erection and ejaculation. Women experience **menopause,** as menstrual cycles end, usually within a few years of age 50. Expectations and attitudes influence the emotional impact of this event. Is it a sign of lost femininity and growing old? Or is it liberation from menstrual periods and fears of pregnancy? For men, too, expectations can influence perceptions. Some experience distress related to a perception of declining virility and physical capacities, but most age without such problems.

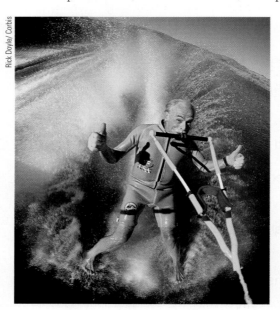

Adult abilities vary widely
97-year-olds: Don't try this. In 2002, George Blair became the world's oldest barefoot water skier, just days after reaching age 87. And he did it again in 2012, at age 97!

With age, sexual activity lessens. Nevertheless, most men and women remain capable of satisfying sexual activity, and most express satisfaction with their sex life. This was true of 70 percent of Canadians surveyed (ages 40 to 64) and 75 percent of Finns (ages 65 to 74) (Kontula & Haavio-Mannila, 2009; Wright, 2006). In another survey, 75 percent of respondents reported being sexually active into their eighties (Schick et al., 2010). And in an American Association of Retired Persons sexuality survey, it was not until age 75 or older that most women and nearly half of men reported little sexual desire (DeLamater & Sill, 2005). Given good health and a willing partner, the flames of desire, though simmered down, live on. As Alex Comfort (1992, p. 240) jested, "The things that stop you having sex with age are exactly the same as those that stop you riding a bicycle (bad health, thinking it looks silly, no bicycle)."

Physical Changes in Later Life

Is old age "more to be feared than death" (Juvenal, *Satires*)? Or is life "most delightful when it is on the downward slope" (Seneca, *Epistulae ad Lucilium*)? What is it like to grow old?

STRENGTH AND STAMINA

Although physical decline begins in early adulthood, we are not usually acutely aware of it until later life, when the stairs get steeper, the print gets smaller, and other people seem to mumble more. Muscle strength, reaction time, and stamina diminish in late adulthood. As a lifelong basketball player, I find myself increasingly not racing for that loose ball. But even diminished vigor is sufficient for normal activities. Moreover, exercise slows aging. Active older adults tend to be mentally quick older adults. Physical exercise not only enhances muscles, bones, and energy and helps to prevent obesity and heart disease, it also stimulates brain cell development and neural connections, thanks perhaps to increased oxygen and nutrient flow (Erickson et al., 2010; Pereira et al., 2007).

"Happy fortieth. I'll take the muscle tone in your upper arms, the girlish timbre of your voice, your amazing tolerance for caffeine, and your ability to digest french fries. The rest of you can stay."

"For some reason, possibly to save ink, the restaurants had started printing their menus in letters the height of bacteria." -DAVE BARRY, *DAVE BARRY TURNS FIFTY*, 1998

SENSORY ABILITIES

With age, visual sharpness diminishes, and distance perception and adaptation to light-level changes are less acute. The eye's pupil shrinks and its lens becomes less transparent, reducing the amount of light reaching the retina: A 65-year-old retina receives only about one-third as much light as its 20-year-old counterpart (Kline & Schieber, 1985). Thus, to see as well as a 20-year-old when reading or driving, a 65-year-old needs three times as much light—a reason for buying cars with untinted windshields. This also explains why older people sometimes ask people your age, "Don't you need better light for reading?"

The senses of smell and hearing also diminish. In Wales, teens' loitering around a convenience store has been discouraged by a device that emits an aversive high-pitched sound almost no one over 30 can hear (Lyall, 2005).

HEALTH

For those growing older, there is both bad and good news about health. The bad news: The body's disease-fighting immune system weakens, making older adults more susceptible to life-threatening ailments, such as cancer and pneumonia. The good news: Thanks partly to a lifetime's accumulation of antibodies, people over 65 suffer fewer short-term ailments, such as common flu and cold viruses. One study found they were half as likely as 20-year-olds and one-fifth as likely as preschoolers to suffer upper respiratory flu each year (National Center for Health Statistics, 1990).

Pascal Parrot/Sygma/Corbis · Pascal Parrot/Sygma/Corbis

World record for longevity? French woman Jeanne Calment, the oldest human in history with authenticated age, died in 1998 at age 122. At age 100, she was still riding a bike. At age 114, she became the oldest film actor ever, by portraying herself in *Vincent and Me.* She is shown at left at age 20 in 1895.

THE AGING BRAIN

Up to the teen years, we process information with greater and greater speed (Fry & Hale, 1996; Kail, 1991). But compared with you, older people take a bit more time to react, to solve perceptual puzzles, even to remember names (Bashore et al., 1997; Verhaeghen & Salthouse, 1997). The neural processing lag is greatest on complex tasks (Cerella, 1985; Poon, 1987). At video games, most 70-year-olds are no match for a 20-year-old.

Slower neural processing combined with diminished sensory abilities can increase accident risks. As **FIGURE 54.1** indicates, fatal accident rates per mile driven increase sharply after age 75. By age 85, they exceed the 16-year-old level. Nevertheless, because older people drive less, they account for fewer than 10 percent of crashes (Coughlin et al., 2004).

Brain regions important to memory begin to atrophy during aging (Schacter, 1996). In early adulthood, a small, gradual net loss of brain cells begins, contributing by age 80 to a brain-weight reduction of 5 percent or so. Earlier, we noted that late-maturing frontal lobes

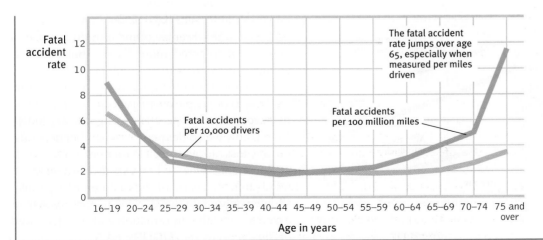

The fatal accident rate jumps over age 65, especially when measured per miles driven

Fatal accidents per 10,000 drivers

Fatal accidents per 100 million miles

Fatal accident rate — 12, 10, 8, 6, 4, 2, 0

Age in years — 16–19, 20–24, 25–29, 30–34, 35–39, 40–44, 45–49, 50–54, 55–59, 60–64, 65–69, 70–74, 75 and over

Figure 54.1

Age and driver fatalities Slowing reactions contribute to increased accident risks among those 75 and older, and their greater fragility increases their risk of death when accidents happen (NHTSA, 2000). Would you favor driver exams based on performance, not age, to screen out those whose slow reactions or sensory impairments indicate accident risk?

"I am still learning." -MICHELANGELO, 1560, AT AGE 85

help account for teen impulsivity. Late in life, atrophy of the inhibition-controlling frontal lobes seemingly explains older people's occasional blunt questions and comments ("Have you put on weight?") (von Hippel, 2007).

As noted earlier, exercise helps counteract some effects of brain aging. It aids memory by stimulating the development of neural connections and by promoting neurogenesis, the birth of new nerve cells, in the hippocampus. Sedentary older adults randomly assigned to aerobic exercise programs exhibit enhanced memory, sharpened judgment, and reduced risk of *neurocognitive disorder* (formerly called "dementia") (Colcombe et al., 2004; Liang et al., 2010; Nazimek, 2009).

Exercise also helps maintain the telomeres, which protect the ends of chromosomes (Cherkas et al., 2008; Erickson, 2009; Pereira et al., 2007). With age, telomeres wear down, much as the tip of a shoelace frays. This wear is accentuated by smoking, obesity, or stress. As telomeres shorten, aging cells may die without being replaced with perfect genetic replicas (Epel, 2009).

The message for seniors is clear: We are more likely to rust from disuse than to wear out from overuse.

Cognitive Development

54-2 How does memory change with age?

Among the most intriguing developmental psychology questions is whether adult cognitive abilities, such as memory, intelligence, and creativity, parallel the gradually accelerating decline of physical abilities.

As we age, we remember some things well. Looking back in later life, people asked to recall the one or two most important events over the last half-century tend to name events from their teens or twenties (Conway et al., 2005; Rubin et al., 1998). Whatever people experience around this time of life—the election of Barack Obama, the events of 9/11, the civil rights movement—becomes pivotal (Pillemer, 1998; Schuman & Scott, 1989). Our teens and twenties are a time of so many memorable "firsts"—first kiss, first job, first day at college or university, first meeting of in-laws.

Early adulthood is indeed a peak time for some types of learning and remembering. In one test of recall, people (1205 of them) watched videotapes as 14 strangers said their names, using a common format: "Hi, I'm Larry" (Crook & West, 1990). Then those strangers reappeared and gave additional details. For example, they said, "I'm from Philadelphia," providing more visual *and* voice cues for remembering the person's name. As **FIGURE 54.2** shows, after a second and third replay of the introductions, everyone remembered more names, but younger adults consistently surpassed older adults.

Perhaps it is not surprising, then, that nearly two-thirds of people over age 40 say their memory is worse than it was 10 years ago (KRC, 2001). In fact, how well older people remember depends on the task. In another experiment (Schonfield & Robertson, 1966), when asked to *recognize* 24 words they had earlier tried to memorize, people showed only a minimal decline in memory. When asked to *recall* that information without clues, the decline was greater (**FIGURE 54.3**).

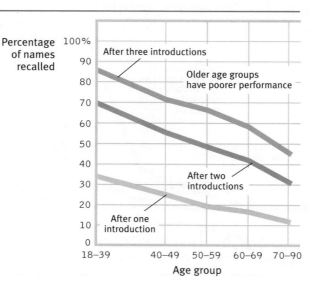

Figure 54.2

Tests of recall Recalling new names introduced once, twice, or three times is easier for younger adults than for older ones. (Data from Crook & West, 1990.)

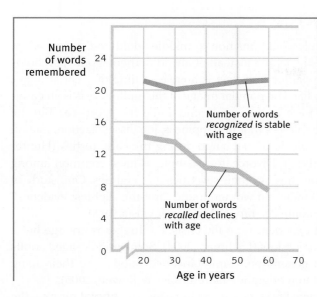

Figure 54.3

Recall and recognition in adulthood In this experiment, the ability to *recall* new information declined during early and middle adulthood, but the ability to *recognize* new information did not. (From Schonfield & Robertson, 1966.)

In our capacity to learn and remember, as in other areas of development, we differ. Younger adults vary in their abilities to learn and remember, but 70-year-olds vary much more. "Differences between the most and least able 70-year-olds become much greater than between the most and least able 50-year-olds," reports Oxford researcher Patrick Rabbitt (2006). Some 70-year-olds perform below nearly all 20-year-olds; other 70-year-olds match or outdo the average 20-year-old.

No matter how quick or slow we are, remembering seems also to depend on the type of information we are trying to retrieve. If the information is meaningless—nonsense syllables or unimportant events—then the older we are, the more errors we are likely to make. If the information is *meaningful,* older people's rich web of existing knowledge will help them to hold it. But they may take longer than younger adults to *produce* the words and things they know: Quick-thinking game show winners are usually young or middle-aged adults (Burke & Shafto, 2004). Older people's capacity to learn and remember *skills* declines less than their verbal recall (Graf, 1990; Labouvie-Vief & Schell, 1982; Perlmutter, 1983).

Module 62 explores another dimension of cognitive development: intelligence. As we will see, **cross-sectional studies** (comparing people of different ages) and **longitudinal studies** (restudying the same people over time) have identified mental abilities that do and do not change as people age. Age is less a predictor of memory and intelligence than is proximity to death. Tell me whether someone is 8 months or 8 years from death and, regardless of age, you've given me a clue to that person's mental ability. Especially in the last three or four years of life, cognitive decline typically accelerates (Wilson et al., 2007). Researchers call this near-death drop *terminal decline* (Backman & MacDonald, 2006).

Try This

What experiences from your high school years do you think you may never forget? (These years, and the next few, will be among the times of your life you may remember most easily when you are 50.)

cross-sectional study a study in which people of different ages are compared with one another.

longitudinal study research in which the same people are restudied and retested over a long period.

Social Development

54-3 What themes and influences mark our social journey from early adulthood to death?

Many differences between younger and older adults are created by significant life events. A new job means new relationships, new expectations, and new demands. Marriage brings the joy of intimacy and the stress of merging two lives. The three years surrounding the birth of a child bring increased life satisfaction for most parents (Dyrdal & Lucas, 2011). The death of a loved one creates an irreplaceable loss. Do these adult life events shape a sequence of life changes?

Adulthood's Ages and Stages

As people enter their forties, they undergo a transition to middle adulthood, a time when they realize that life will soon be mostly behind instead of ahead of them. Some psychologists have argued that for many the *midlife transition* is a crisis, a time of great struggle, regret, or even feeling struck down by life. The popular image of the midlife crisis is an early-forties man who forsakes his family for a younger girlfriend and a hot sports car. But the fact—reported by large samples of people—is that unhappiness, job dissatisfaction, marital dissatisfaction, divorce, anxiety, and suicide do *not* surge during the early forties (Hunter & Sundel, 1989; Mroczek & Kolarz, 1998). Divorce, for example, is most common among those in their twenties, suicide among those in their seventies and eighties. One study of emotional instability in nearly 10,000 men and women found "not the slightest evidence" that distress peaks anywhere in the midlife age range (McCrae & Costa, 1990).

For the 1 in 4 adults who report experiencing a life crisis, the trigger is not age but a major event, such as illness, divorce, or job loss (Lachman, 2004). Some middle-aged adults describe themselves as a "sandwich generation," simultaneously supporting their aging parents and their emerging adult children or grandchildren (Riley & Bowen, 2005).

Life events trigger transitions to new life stages at varying ages. The **social clock**—the definition of "the right time" to leave home, get a job, marry, have children, or retire—varies from era to era and culture to culture. The social clock still ticks, but people feel freer about being out of sync with it.

Even *chance events* can have lasting significance, by deflecting us down one road rather than another (Bandura, 1982). Albert Bandura (2005) recalls the ironic true story of a book editor who came to one of Bandura's lectures on the "Psychology of Chance Encounters and Life Paths"—and ended up marrying the woman who happened to sit next to him. The sequence that led to my authoring this book (which was not my idea) began with my being seated near, and getting to know, a distinguished colleague at an international conference. Chance events can change our lives.

> **social clock** the culturally preferred timing of social events such as marriage, parenthood, and retirement.

> "The important events of a person's life are the products of chains of highly improbable occurrences." -JOSEPH TRAUB, "TRAUB'S LAW," 2003

Adulthood's Commitments

Two basic aspects of our lives dominate adulthood. Erik Erikson called them *intimacy* (forming close relationships) and *generativity* (being productive and supporting future generations). Researchers have chosen various terms—*affiliation* and *achievement, attachment* and *productivity, connectedness* and *competence.* Sigmund Freud (1935) put it most simply: The healthy adult, he said, is one who can *love* and *work.*

LOVE

We typically flirt, fall in love, and commit—one person at a time. "Pair-bonding is a trademark of the human animal," observed anthropologist Helen Fisher (1993). From an evolutionary perspective, relatively monogamous pairing makes sense: Parents who cooperated to nurture their children to maturity were more likely to have their genes passed along to posterity than were parents who didn't.

Adult bonds of love are most satisfying and enduring when marked by a similarity of interests and values, a sharing of emotional and material support, and intimate self-disclosure (see Module 79). Couples who seal their love with commitment—via (in one Vermont study) marriage for heterosexual couples and civil unions for homosexual couples—more often endure (Balsam et al., 2008). Marriage bonds are especially likely to last when couples marry after age 20 and are well educated. Compared with their counterparts of 50 years ago, people in Western countries *are* better educated and marrying later. Yet, ironically, they are nearly twice as likely to divorce. (Both Canada and the United States

now have about one divorce for every two marriages, and in Europe, divorce is only slightly less common.) The divorce rate partly reflects women's lessened economic dependence and men's and women's rising expectations. We now hope not only for an enduring bond, but also for a mate who is a wage earner, caregiver, intimate friend, and warm and responsive lover.

Might test-driving life together in a "trial marriage" minimize divorce risk? In one Gallup survey of American twenty-somethings, 62 percent thought it would (Whitehead & Popenoe, 2001). In reality, in Europe, Canada, and the United States, those who cohabit before marriage have had *higher* rates of divorce and marital dysfunction than those who did not cohabit (Jose et al., 2010). The risk appears greatest for those cohabiting prior to engagement (Goodwin et al., 2010; Rhoades et al., 2009).

American children born to cohabiting parents are about five times more likely to experience their parents' separation than are children born to married parents (Osborne et al., 2007). Two factors contribute. First, cohabiters tend to be initially less committed to the ideal of enduring marriage. Second, they become even less marriage supporting while cohabiting.

Nonetheless, the institution of marriage endures. Worldwide, reports the United Nations, 9 in 10 heterosexual adults marry. And marriage is a predictor of happiness, sexual satisfaction, income, and physical and mental health (Scott et al., 2010). National Opinion Research Center surveys of nearly 50,000 Americans since 1972 reveal that 40 percent of married adults, though only 23 percent of unmarried adults, have reported being "very happy." Lesbian couples, too, report greater well-being than those who are alone (Peplau & Fingerhut, 2007; Wayment & Peplau, 1995). Moreover, neighborhoods with high marriage rates typically have low rates of social pathologies such as crime, delinquency, and emotional disorders among children (Myers & Scanzoni, 2005).

Marriages that last are not always devoid of conflict. Some couples fight but also shower each other with affection. Other couples never raise their voices yet also seldom praise each other or nuzzle. Both styles can last. After observing the interactions of 2000 couples, John Gottman (1994) reported one indicator of marital success: at least a five-to-one ratio of positive to negative interactions. Stable marriages provide five times more instances of smiling, touching, complimenting, and laughing than of sarcasm, criticism, and insults. So, if you want to predict which newlyweds will stay together, don't pay attention to how passionately they are in love. The couples who make it are more often those who refrain from putting down their partners. To prevent a cancerous negativity, successful couples learn to fight fair (to state feelings without insulting) and to steer conflict away from chaos with comments like "I know it's not your fault" or "I'll just be quiet for a moment and listen."

Often, love bears children. For most people, this most enduring of life changes is a happy event. "I feel an overwhelming love for my children unlike anything I feel for anyone else," said 93 percent of American mothers in a national survey (Erickson & Aird, 2005). Many fathers feel the same. A few weeks after the birth of my first child I was suddenly struck by a realization: "So *this* is how my parents felt about me?"

When children begin to absorb time, money, and emotional energy, satisfaction with the marriage itself may decline (Doss et al., 2009). This is especially likely among employed women who, more than they expected, carry the traditional burden of doing the chores at home. Putting effort into creating an equitable relationship can thus pay double dividends: a more satisfying marriage, which breeds better parent-child relations (Erel & Burman, 1995).

Although love bears children, children eventually leave home. This departure is a significant and sometimes difficult event. For most people, however, an empty nest is a happy place (Adelmann et al., 1989; Gorchoff et al., 2008). Many parents experience a "postlaunch honeymoon," especially if they maintain close relationships with their children (White & Edwards, 1990). As Daniel Gilbert (2006) has said, "The only known symptom of 'empty nest syndrome' is increased smiling."

Love Intimacy, attachment, commitment—love by whatever name—is central to healthy and happy adulthood.

Try This

What do you think? Does marriage correlate with happiness because marital support and intimacy breed happiness, because happy people more often marry and stay married, or both?

"Our love for children is so unlike any other human emotion. I fell in love with my babies so quickly and profoundly, almost completely independently of their particular qualities. And yet 20 years later I was (more or less) happy to see them go—I had to be happy to see them go. We are totally devoted to them when they are little and yet the most we can expect in return when they grow up is that they regard us with bemused and tolerant affection." -DEVELOPMENTAL PSYCHOLOGIST ALISON GOPNIK, "THE SUPREME INFANT," 2010

Job satisfaction and life satisfaction Work can provide us with a sense of identity and competence and opportunities for accomplishment. Perhaps this is why challenging and interesting occupations enhance people's happiness.

WORK

For many adults, the answer to "Who are you?" depends a great deal on the answer to "What do you do?" For women and men, choosing a career path is difficult, especially during bad economic times. Even in the best of times, few students in their first two years of college or university can predict their later careers.

In the end, happiness is about having work that fits your interests and provides you with a sense of competence and accomplishment. It is having a close, supportive companion who cheers your accomplishments (Gable et al., 2006). And for some, it includes having children who love you and whom you love and feel proud of.

Well-Being Across the Life Span

54-4   Do self-confidence and life satisfaction vary with life stages?

> "When you were born, you cried and the world rejoiced. Live your life in a manner so that when you die the world cries and you rejoice." -NATIVE AMERICAN PROVERB

To live is to grow older. This moment marks the oldest you have ever been and the youngest you will henceforth be. That means we all can look back with satisfaction or regret, and forward with hope or dread. When asked what they would have done differently if they could relive their lives, people's most common answer has been "Taken my education more seriously and worked harder at it" (Kinnier & Metha, 1989; Roese & Summerville, 2005). Other regrets—"I should have told my father I loved him," "I regret that I never went to Europe"—have also focused less on mistakes made than on the things one *failed* to do (Gilovich & Medvec, 1995).

From the teens to midlife, people typically experience a strengthening sense of identity, confidence, and self-esteem (Huang, 2010; Robins & Trzesniewski, 2005). In later life, challenges arise: Income shrinks. Work is often taken away. The body deteriorates. Recall fades. Energy wanes. Family members and friends die or move away. The great enemy, death, looms ever closer. And for those in the terminal decline phase, life satisfaction does decline as death approaches (Gerstorf et al., 2008).

Small wonder that most presume that happiness declines in later life (Lacey et al., 2006). But worldwide, as Gallup researchers discovered, most find that the over-65 years are not notably unhappy (**FIGURE 54.4**). If anything, positive feelings, supported by enhanced emotional control, grow after midlife, and negative feelings subside (Stone et al., 2010; Urry & Gross, 2010). Older adults increasingly use words that convey positive emotions (Pennebaker & Stone, 2003), and they attend less and less to negative information. Compared with younger adults, for example, they are slower to perceive negative faces and more attentive to positive news (Carstensen & Mikels, 2005; Scheibe & Carstensen, 2010). Older adults also have fewer problems in their social relationships (Fingerman & Charles, 2010), and they experience less intense anger, stress, and worry (Stone et al., 2010).

Figure 54.4

Age and life satisfaction The Gallup Organization asked 142,682 people worldwide to rate their lives on a ladder, from 0 ("the worst possible life") to 10 ("the best possible life"). Age gave no clue to life satisfaction (Crabtree, 2010).

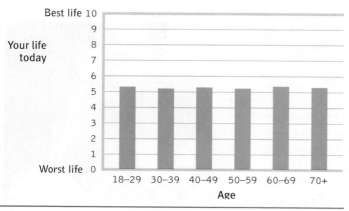

The aging brain may help nurture these positive feelings. Brain scans of older adults show that the amygdala, a neural processing center for emotions, responds less actively to negative events (but not to positive events), and it interacts less with the hippocampus, a brain memory-processing center (Mather et al., 2004; St. Jacques et al., 2009; Williams et al., 2006). Brain-wave reactions to negative images also diminish with age (Kisley et al., 2007).

Moreover, at all ages, the bad feelings we associate with negative events fade faster than do the good feelings we associate with positive events (Walker et al., 2003). This contributes to most older people's sense that life, on balance, has been mostly good. Given that growing older is an outcome of living (an outcome most prefer to early dying), the positivity of later life is comforting. Thanks to biological, psychological, and social-cultural influences, more and more people flourish into later life (**FIGURE 54.5**).

> "At 20 we worry about what others think of us. At 40 we don't care what others think of us. At 60 we discover they haven't been thinking about us at all." -ANONYMOUS

> "The best thing about being 100 is no peer pressure." -LEWIS W. KUESTER, 2005, ON TURNING 100

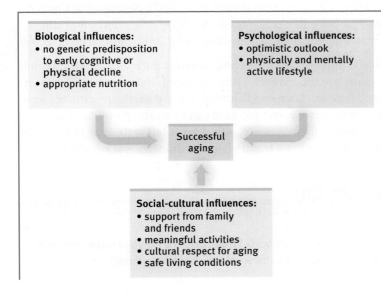

Biological influences:
• no genetic predisposition to early cognitive or physical decline
• appropriate nutrition

Psychological influences:
• optimistic outlook
• physically and mentally active lifestyle

Successful aging

Social-cultural influences:
• support from family and friends
• meaningful activities
• cultural respect for aging
• safe living conditions

Figure 54.5

Biopsychosocial influences on successful aging Numerous biological, psychological, and social-cultural factors affect the way we age. With the right genes, we have a good chance of aging successfully if we maintain a positive outlook and stay mentally and physically active as well as connected to family and friends in the community.

Death and Dying

 A loved one's death triggers what range of reactions?

Warning: If you begin reading the next paragraph, you will die.

But of course, if you hadn't read this, you would still die in due time. Death is our inevitable end. Most of us will also suffer and cope with the deaths of relatives and friends. Usually, the most difficult separation is from a spouse—a loss suffered by five times more women than men. When, as usually happens, death comes at an expected late-life time, grieving may be relatively short-lived.

Grief is especially severe when a loved one's death comes suddenly and before its expected time on the social clock. The sudden illness or accident claiming a 45-year-old life partner or a child may trigger a year or more of memory-laden mourning that eventually subsides to a mild depression (Lehman et al., 1987).

For some, however, the loss is unbearable. One Danish long-term study of more than 1 million people found that about 17,000 of them had suffered the death of a child under 18. In the five years following that death, 3 percent of them had a first psychiatric hospitalization. This rate was 67 percent higher than the rate recorded for parents who had not lost a child (Li et al., 2005).

Even so, reactions to a loved one's death range more widely than most suppose. Some cultures encourage public weeping and wailing; others hide grief. Within any culture,

> "Love—why, I'll tell you what love is: It's you at 75 and her at 71, each of you listening for the other's step in the next room, each afraid that a sudden silence, a sudden cry, could mean a lifetime's talk is over." -BRIAN MOORE, THE LUCK OF GINGER COFFEY, 1960

individuals differ. Given similar losses, some people grieve hard and long, others less so (Ott et al., 2007). Contrary to popular misconceptions, however,

> "Consider, friend, as you pass by, as you are now, so once was I. As I am now, you too shall be. Prepare, therefore, to follow me."
> -SCOTTISH TOMBSTONE EPITAPH

- terminally ill and bereaved people do not go through identical predictable stages, such as denial before anger (Friedman & James, 2008; Nolen-Hoeksema & Larson, 1999). A Yale study following 233 bereaved individuals through time did, however, find that yearning for the loved one reached a high point four months after the loss, with anger peaking, on average, about a month later (Maciejewski et al., 2007).

- those who express the strongest grief immediately do not purge their grief more quickly (Bonanno & Kaltman, 1999; Wortman & Silver, 1989).

- bereavement therapy and self-help groups offer support, but there is similar healing power in the passing of time, the support of friends, and the act of giving support and help to others (Baddeley & Singer, 2009; Brown et al., 2008; Neimeyer & Carrier, 2009). Grieving spouses who talk often with others or receive grief counseling adjust about as well as those who grieve more privately (Bonanno, 2004; Stroebe et al., 2005).

We can be grateful for the waning of death-denying attitudes. Facing death with dignity and openness helps people complete the life cycle with a sense of life's meaningfulness and unity—the sense that their existence has been good and that life and death are parts of an on-going cycle. Although death may be unwelcome, life itself can be affirmed even at death. This is especially so for people who review their lives not with despair but with what Erik Erikson called a sense of *integrity*—a feeling that one's life has been meaningful and worthwhile.

Before You Move On

▶ **ASK YOURSELF**

In what ways are you looking forward to adulthood? What concerns do you have about your own transition into adulthood, and how do you think you might address them?

▶ **TEST YOURSELF**

Research has shown that living together before marriage predicts an increased likelihood of future divorce. Can you imagine two possible explanations for this correlation?

Answers to the Test Yourself questions can be found in Appendix E at the end of the book.

Module 54 Review

 54-1 What physical changes occur during middle and late adulthood?

- Muscular strength, reaction time, sensory abilities, and cardiac output begin to decline in the late twenties and continue to decline throughout middle adulthood (roughly age 40 to 65) and late adulthood (the years after 65).

- Women's period of fertility ends with *menopause* around age 50; men have no similar age-related sharp drop in hormone levels or fertility.

- In late adulthood, the immune system weakens, increasing susceptibility to life-threatening illnesses.

- Chromosome tips (telomeres) wear down, reducing the chances of normal genetic replication.

- But for some, longevity-supporting genes, low stress, and good health habits enable better health in later life.

54-2 How does memory change with age?

- As the years pass, recall begins to decline, especially for meaningless information, but recognition memory remains strong.

- Developmental researchers study age-related changes (such as memory) with *cross-sectional studies* (comparing people of different ages) and *longitudinal studies* (retesting the same people over a period of years).

- "Terminal decline" describes the cognitive decline in the final few years of life.

54-3 What themes and influences mark our social journey from early adulthood to death?

- Adults do not progress through an orderly sequence of age-related social stages. Chance events can determine life choices.

- The *social clock* is a culture's preferred timing for social events, such as marriage, parenthood, and retirement.

- Adulthood's dominant themes are love and work, which Erikson called intimacy and generativity.

54-4 Do self-confidence and life satisfaction vary with life stages?

- Self-confidence tends to strengthen across the life span.

- Surveys show that life satisfaction is unrelated to age. Positive emotions increase after midlife and negative ones decrease.

54-5 A loved one's death triggers what range of reactions?

- People do not grieve in predictable stages, as was once supposed.

- Strong expressions of emotion may not purge grief, and bereavement therapy is not significantly more effective than grieving without such aid.

- Erikson viewed the late-adulthood psychosocial task as developing a sense of integrity (versus despair).

Multiple-Choice Questions

1. Which of the following changes does *not* occur with age?
   a. Visual sharpness diminishes.
   b. Distance perception is less acute.
   c. Adaptation to light-level changes is less rapid.
   d. The lens of the eye becomes more transparent.
   e. Senses of smell and hearing diminish.

2. As telomeres shorten, aging cells may die without being replaced with perfect genetic replicas. This process is slowed by
   a. smoking.
   b. obesity.
   c. stress.
   d. aging.
   e. exercise.

3. According to Erikson, which of the following is a dominant goal of adulthood?
   a. Competence
   b. Generativity
   c. Performance
   d. Identity
   e. Connectedness

4. The aging brain may help nurture positive feelings that are reported by many older adults. Brain scans of older adults show that the _____, a neural processing center for emotions, responds less actively to negative events (but not to positive events), and it interacts less with the hippocampus, a brain memory-processing center.
   a. amygdala
   b. hypothalamus
   c. pineal gland
   d. thyroid gland
   e. thalamus

5. Which of the following is true of menopause?

   a. Both men and women experience menopause around the age of 50.

   b. Men experience menopause around 50 years of age, but women experience menopause around 65 years of age.

   c. Women experience menopause around 50 years of age, but men experience menopause around 65 years of age.

   d. Women experience menopause around the age of 50, but men don't experience menopause.

   e. Men experience menopause around the age of 65, but women don't experience menopause.

6. Which of the following would be considered an example of Erikson's concept of generativity?

   a. A 25-year-old meets and marries the love of his life.

   b. A 35-year-old earns a lot of money, though she doesn't particularly enjoy her job.

   c. An 85-year-old looks back at a life well-lived and feels satisfied.

   d. A 40-year-old takes pride in her work and how she has raised her children.

   e. A 20-year-old decides to become a physician.

7. The _____ is a culturally determined timetable for certain events, such as having children and retirement.

   a. critical period

   b. menopause

   c. intimacy phase

   d. attachment stage

   e. social clock

Practice FRQs

1. Describe two changes in cognitive ability during adulthood. What is one factor that can prevent the steepest decline?

Answer

1 point: There is a decline in recall over the course of adulthood.

1 point: There is a decline in speed of processing over the adult years.

1 point: Exercise can prevent the steepest decline.

2. Numerous biological, psychological, and social-cultural factors affect the way we age. Explain one example for each of the three that contributes to successful aging.

(3 points)

Unit IX Review

Key Terms and Concepts to Remember

developmental psychology, p. 462

zygote, p. 466

embryo, p. 466

fetus, p. 466

teratogens, p. 467

fetal alcohol syndrome (FAS), p. 467

habituation, p. 468

maturation, p. 471

cognition, p.476

schema, p. 477

assimilation, p. 477

accommodation, p. 477

sensorimotor stage, p. 478

object permanence, p. 478

preoperational stage, p. 479

conservation, p. 479

egocentrism, p. 479

theory of mind, p. 480

autism spectrum disorder (ASD), p. 481

concrete operational stage, p. 483

formal operational stage, p. 483

stranger anxiety, p. 488

attachment, p. 488

critical period, p. 489

imprinting, p. 489

temperament, p. 490

basic trust, p. 492

self-concept, p. 495

gender, p. 500

aggression, p. 501

gender role, p. 503

role, p. 503

gender identity, p. 504

social learning theory, p. 504

gender typing, p. 504

transgender, p. 505

adolescence, p. 513

identity, p. 519

social identity, p. 519

intimacy, p. 521

emerging adulthood, p. 523

X chromosome, p. 526

Y chromosome, p. 526

testosterone, p. 526

puberty, p. 527

primary sex characteristics, p. 527

secondary sex characteristics, p. 527

menarche [meh-NAR-key], p. 527

AIDS (acquired immune deficiency syndrome), p. 529

sexual orientation, p. 531

menopause, p. 540

cross-sectional study, p. 543

longitudinal study, p. 543

social clock, p. 544

Key Contributors to Remember

Jean Piaget, p. 476

Lev Vygotsky, p. 484

Konrad Lorenz, p. 489

Harry Harlow, p. 489

Margaret Harlow, p. 489

Mary Ainsworth, p. 490

Diana Baumrind, p. 496

Carol Gilligan, p. 502

Albert Bandura, pp. 504, 544

Lawrence Kohlberg, p. 515

Erik Erikson, p. 519

Sigmund Freud, p. 544

AP® Exam Practice Questions

Multiple-Choice Questions

1. What aspect of development did Jean Piaget's development theory focus on?

a. Social

b. Moral

c. Cognitive

d. Physical

e. Ego

2. According to Erikson's psychosocial theory of development, the crisis that needs resolution for adolescents involves the search for what?

a. Trust

b. Identity

c. Autonomy

d. Initiative

e. Worth

3. What is the correct term for a period of time when certain events must take place in order to facilitate proper development?

a. Conservation stage
b. Preoperational stage
c. Attachment period
d. Critical period
e. Assimilation step

4. Which of the following statements about the impact of aging is *true*?

a. During old age, many of the brain's neurons die.
b. If we live to be 90 or older, most of us will eventually become senile.
c. Older people become less susceptible to short-term illnesses.
d. Recognition memory—the ability to identify things previously experienced—declines with age.
e. Life satisfaction peaks in the 50s and then gradually declines after age 65.

5. According to Lawrence Kohlberg, what stage of moral development is exhibited when actions are judged "right" because they flow from basic ethical principles?

a. Postconventional
b. Preconventional
c. Conventional
d. Preoperational
e. Formal operational

6. According to Mary Ainsworth's research on attachment, what would a child need most to become "securely attached"?

a. Consistent, responsive caregivers
b. The right temperament
c. A terry cloth-wrapped "surrogate" mother
d. An imprinting experience shortly after birth
e. Enriched motor development experiences

7. Temperament refers to what aspect of an infant's development?

a. Susceptibility to infection and disease
b. Emotional reactivity
c. General intelligence
d. Level of optimism
e. Ability to learn from situations

8. How does fluid intelligence change as we age?

a. Decreases slowly with age
b. Has not been measured over time
c. Increases slowly with age
d. Does not change until about age 75
e. Remains unchanged if we exercise

9. Once a sperm penetrates the cell wall of an egg and fertilizes it, this structure is known as what?

a. An embryo
b. A fetus
c. Placenta
d. A teratogen
e. A zygote

10. Social development researchers suggest that infancy's major social achievement is attachment. Childhood's major social achievement is developing which of the following?

a. Basic trust
b. Into a sexually mature person
c. Intimacy
d. A positive sense of self
e. Object permanence

11. Most adolescents can ponder and debate human nature, good and evil, truth and justice. According to Piaget, this thinking ability is due to the emergence of which stage?

a. Concrete operational
b. Sensorimotor
c. Preoperational
d. Formal operational
e. Accommodation

12. Cultural norms related to when to leave home, get a job, or marry are referred to as what?

a. Social clock
b. Midlife crisis
c. Critical period
d. Life span
e. Theory of mind

13. The more often the stimulus is presented, the weaker the response becomes. What do developmental researchers call this decrease in response intensity due to repeated stimulation?

a. Stagnation
b. Attachment
c. Autonomy
d. Imprinting
e. Habituation

14. Eleanor Maccoby's research found which of the following factors to be the *least* positively correlated with problem behavior in preschool children?

a. Parent income
b. Parent education level
c. Time spent in day care
d. Child's temperament
e. Parent sensitivity

15. Which of these is an example of a longitudinal study?

a. The depth perception of infants is measured once a month for 6 months in a row, starting at six months.

b. In the same month, researchers compare the reaction time of 20 sixth graders and 20 first graders.

c. The memory of one group of 50-year-old adults is measured and then 20 years later compared to a different group of 70-year-olds.

d. A psychologist develops a case study of a woman who is 102 by interviewing her twice a week for 12 weeks.

e. Researchers compare curiosity ratings of a group of toddlers with that same group's SAT scores 15 years later.

Free-Response Questions

1. Adolescence has been called a time of "storm and stress." Describe how each of the following brain areas or psychological concepts might contribute to this storm and stress.

- Limbic system activity
- Frontal lobe development
- Formal operational abilities
- Erikson's identity versus role confusion stage
- Early physical maturation for girls

Rubric for Free Response Question 1

1 point: The limbic system is primed by surges of hormones at puberty, which may lead some adolescents to seek excitement and, possibly, behave impulsively. ↻ Page 514

1 point: Frontal lobes, which are necessary for judgment and planning, continue to develop during adolescence and into the early twenties. Unused pathways are pruned and myelin speeds the connection between the frontal lobes and other areas of the brain. Without completed frontal lobe development, adolescents are often unable to exert adult impulse control. They may be more likely to indulge in risky and/or illegal behaviors despite understanding the possible consequences. ↻ Pages 471, 514

1 point: When adolescents reach the formal operational stage, they have all of the cognitive abilities of earlier stages and can also think abstractly and hypothetically. With the ability to compare reality with a hypothetical ideal, adolescents may be disappointed in what exists, may detect hypocrisy, or may argue with those around them about how to achieve a more just world. ↻ Page 483

1 point: During Erikson's identity versus role confusion stage, teenagers seek a sense of identity. Adolescents typically try out different versions of "self" before adopting a comfortable identity. This process can be difficult and can lead to conflicts with friends and family. ↻ Pages 519–521

1 point: Early maturation puts some girls out of sync with their emotional development and friends' experiences. They may begin associating with older teens or endure teasing or sexual harassment. ↻ Page 514

2. Piaget, Erikson, and Kohlberg described several cognitive, social, and moral reasoning stages of adolescence. Illustrate each of the following stages.

- Concrete operational
- Formal operational
- Identity versus role confusion
- Intimacy versus isolation
- Conventional level
- Postconventional level

(6 points)

3. Cruz and Eva have a 7-year-old son. He is in the second grade and is extremely obedient. He has many friends, most of whom are on a baseball team with him.

What advice might each of the researchers below give to Cruz and Eva about their son's development?

- Jean Piaget (cognitive development)
- Harry and Margaret Harlow (attachment)
- Lawrence Kohlberg (moral levels of thinking)
- Albert Bandura (social learning theory)
- Erik Erikson (psychosocial development)
- Diana Baumrind (parenting styles)
- Lev Vygotsky (scaffolding)

(7 points)

Multiple-choice self-tests and more may be found at www.worthpublishers.com/MyersAP2e

Unit X

Personality

Modules

Lord of the Rings hobbit-hero Frodo Baggins knew that throughout his difficult journey there was one who would never fail him—his loyal and ever-cheerful companion, Sam Gamgee. Even before they left their beloved homes in the Shire, Frodo warned Sam that the journey would not be easy.

"It is going to be very dangerous, Sam. It is already dangerous. Most likely neither of us will come back."

"If you don't come back, sir, then I shan't, that's certain," said Sam. "[The Elves told me] 'Don't you leave him!' Leave him! I said. I never mean to. I am going with him, if he climbs to the Moon; and if any of those Black Riders try to stop him, they'll have Sam Gamgee to reckon with." (J.R.R. Tolkien, *The Fellowship of the Ring,* 1954, p. 96)

And so they did! Later in the story, when it becomes clear that Frodo's path will lead him into the dreaded land of Mordor, it is Sam who insists he will be at Frodo's side, come what may. It is Sam who lifts Frodo's spirits with songs and stories from their boyhood. And it is Sam whom Frodo leans upon when he can barely take another step. When Frodo is overcome by the evil of the ring he carries, it is Sam who saves him. In the end, it is Sam who helps Frodo successfully reach the end of his journey. Sam Gamgee—cheerful, optimistic, emotionally stable—never falters in his faithfulness or his belief that they will overcome the threatening darkness.

As he appears and reappears throughout the series, Tolkien's Sam Gamgee exhibits the distinctive and enduring behaviors that define **personality**—a person's characteristic pattern of thinking, feeling, and acting. Earlier units have focused on our similar ways of developing, perceiving, learning, remembering, thinking, and feeling. This unit focuses on what makes us each unique.

Much of this book deals with personality. We have considered biological influences on personality, personality development across the life span, and personality-related aspects of learning, motivation, emotion, and health. In later units we will study social influences on personality and disorders of personality.

Two historically significant theories have become part of our cultural legacy. Sigmund Freud's *psychoanalytic* theory proposed that childhood sexuality and unconscious motivations influence personality. The *humanistic* approach focused on our inner capacities for growth and self-fulfillment. These sweeping perspectives on human nature laid the foundation for later personality theorists and are complemented by what this unit goes on to explore: newer scientific research of specific aspects of personality. Today's personality researchers study the basic dimensions of personality, the biological roots of these dimensions, and the interaction of persons and environments. They also study self-esteem, self-serving bias, and cultural influences on one's sense of self. And they study the unconscious mind—with findings that probably would have surprised Freud himself.

> **personality** an individual's characteristic pattern of thinking, feeling, and acting.

Module 55

Freud's Psychoanalytic Perspective: Exploring the Unconscious

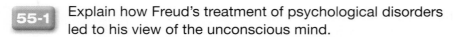

Module Learning Objectives

55-1 Explain how Freud's treatment of psychological disorders led to his view of the unconscious mind.

55-2 Describe Freud's view of personality.

55-3 Identify Freud's developmental stages.

55-4 Describe Freud's views on how people defend themselves against anxiety.

55-5 Discuss how contemporary psychologists view Freud's psychoanalytic perspective.

F reud's work is so well known that you may assume it's the most important theory in psychology. It's not. However, Freud was the first to focus clinical attention on the unconscious mind, and he is part of psychology's historical development.

Sigmund Freud, 1856–1939
"I was the only worker in a new field."

Psychoanalytic Theory's Core Ideas

55-1 How did Sigmund Freud's treatment of psychological disorders lead to his view of the unconscious mind?

Ask 100 people on the street to name a notable deceased psychologist, suggested Keith Stanovich (1996, p. 1), and "Freud would be the winner hands down." In the popular mind, he is to psychology's history what Elvis Presley is to rock music's history. Freud's influence not only lingers in psychiatry and clinical psychology, but also in literary and film interpretation. Almost 9 in 10 American college courses that reference psychoanalysis are outside of psychology departments (Cohen, 2007). His early twentieth-century concepts penetrate our twenty-first-century language. Without realizing their source, we may speak of *ego, repression, projection, sibling rivalry, Freudian slips,* and *fixation.* So, who was Freud, and what did he teach?

Like all of us, Sigmund Freud was a product of his times. His Victorian era was a time of tremendous discovery and scientific advancement, but it is also known today as a time of sexual repression and male dominance. Men's and women's roles were clearly defined, with male superiority assumed and only male sexuality generally acknowledged (discreetly).

Long before entering the University of Vienna in 1873, young Freud showed signs of independence and brilliance. He so loved reading plays, poetry, and philosophy that he once ran up a bookstore debt beyond his means. As a teen he often took his evening meal in his tiny bedroom in order to lose no time from his studies. After medical school he set up a private practice specializing in nervous disorders. Before long, however, he faced patients whose disorders made no neurological sense. For example, a patient might have lost all feeling in a hand—yet there is no sensory nerve that, if damaged, would numb the entire hand and nothing else. Freud's search for a cause for such disorders set his mind running in a direction destined to change human self-understanding.

Might some neurological disorders have psychological causes? Observing patients led Freud to his "discovery" of the unconscious. He speculated that lost feeling in one's hand might be caused by a fear of touching one's genitals; that unexplained blindness or deafness might be caused by not wanting to see or hear something that aroused intense anxiety. After some early unsuccessful trials with hypnosis, Freud turned to **free association,** in which he told the patient to relax and say whatever came to mind, no matter how embarrassing or trivial. He assumed that a line of mental dominoes had fallen from his patients' distant past to their troubled present. Free association, he believed, would allow him to retrace that line, following a chain of thought leading into the patient's unconscious, where painful unconscious memories, often from childhood, could be retrieved and released. Freud called his theory of personality and the associated treatment techniques **psychoanalysis.**

Basic to Freud's theory was his belief that the mind is mostly hidden (**FIGURE 55.1**). Our conscious awareness is like the part of an iceberg that floats above the surface. Beneath our awareness is the larger **unconscious** mind with its thoughts, wishes, feelings, and memories. Some of these thoughts we store temporarily in a *preconscious* area, from which we can retrieve them into conscious awareness. Of greater interest to Freud was the mass of unacceptable passions and thoughts that he believed we *repress,* or forcibly block from our consciousness because they would be too unsettling to acknowledge. Freud believed that without our awareness, these troublesome feelings and ideas powerfully influence us, sometimes gaining expression in disguised forms—the work we choose, the beliefs we hold, our daily habits, our troubling symptoms.

AP® Exam Tip

The boldfaced key terms that you read in this module are all quite famous terms. Even though modern psychology rejects many of the specifics of psychoanalysis, the fame of Freud's concepts makes them likely topics for AP® exam questions.

free association in psychoanalysis, a method of exploring the unconscious in which the person relaxes and says whatever comes to mind, no matter how trivial or embarrassing.

psychoanalysis Freud's theory of personality that attributes thoughts and actions to unconscious motives and conflicts; the techniques used in treating psychological disorders by seeking to expose and interpret unconscious tensions.

unconscious according to Freud, a reservoir of mostly unacceptable thoughts, wishes, feelings, and memories. According to contemporary psychologists, information processing of which we are unaware.

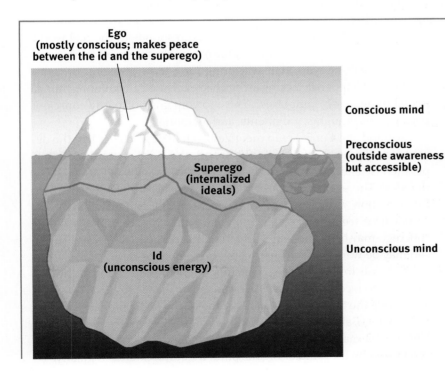

Ego
(mostly conscious; makes peace between the id and the superego)

Conscious mind

Preconscious
(outside awareness but accessible)

Superego
(internalized ideals)

Id
(unconscious energy)

Unconscious mind

Figure 55.1

Freud's idea of the mind's structure Psychologists have used an iceberg image to illustrate Freud's idea that the mind is mostly hidden beneath the conscious surface. Note that the id is totally unconscious, but ego and superego operate both consciously and unconsciously. Unlike the parts of a frozen iceberg, however, the id, ego, and superego interact.

"Good morning, beheaded—uh, I mean beloved."

For Freud the determinist, nothing was ever accidental. He believed he could glimpse the unconscious seeping not only into people's free associations, beliefs, habits, and symptoms but also into slips of the tongue and pen. He illustrated with a financially stressed patient who, not wanting any large pills, said, "Please do not give me any bills, because I cannot swallow them." Similarly, Freud viewed jokes as expressions of repressed sexual and aggressive tendencies, and dreams as the "royal road to the unconscious." The remembered content of dreams (their *manifest content*) he believed to be a censored expression of the dreamer's unconscious wishes (the dream's *latent content*). In his dream analyses, Freud searched for patients' inner conflicts.

Personality Structure

55-2   What was Freud's view of personality?

> "I remember your name perfectly but I just can't think of your face."
> -Oxford professor W. A. Spooner (1844–1930), famous for his linguistic flip-flops (*spoonerisms*). Spooner rebuked one student for "fighting a liar in the quadrangle" and another who "hissed my mystery lecture," adding "You have tasted two worms."

AP® Exam Tip

Be careful: It's easy to confuse Freud's three layers of the mind (conscious, preconscious, and unconscious) with the three parts of personality (id, ego, superego).

In Freud's view, human personality—including its emotions and strivings—arises from a conflict between impulse and restraint—between our aggressive, pleasure-seeking biological urges and our internalized social controls over these urges. Freud believed personality arises from our efforts to resolve this basic conflict—to express these impulses in ways that bring satisfaction without also bringing guilt or punishment. To understand the mind's dynamics during this conflict, Freud proposed three interacting systems: the *id, ego,* and *superego* (Figure 55.1).

The **id**'s unconscious psychic energy constantly strives to satisfy basic drives to survive, reproduce, and aggress. The id operates on the *pleasure principle:* It seeks immediate gratification. To envision an id-dominated person, think of a newborn infant crying out for satisfaction, caring nothing for the outside world's conditions and demands. Or think of people with a present rather than future time perspective—those who abuse tobacco, alcohol, and other drugs, and would sooner party now than sacrifice today's pleasure for future success and happiness (Keough et al., 1999).

"Fifty is plenty." "Hundred and fifty."

The ego struggles to reconcile the demands of superego and id, said Freud.

As the **ego** develops, the young child responds to the real world. The ego, operating on the *reality principle,* seeks to gratify the id's impulses in realistic ways that will bring long-term pleasure. (Imagine what would happen if, lacking an ego, we expressed all our unrestrained sexual or aggressive impulses.) The ego contains our partly conscious perceptions, thoughts, judgments, and memories.

Around age 4 or 5, Freud theorized, a child's ego recognizes the demands of the newly emerging **superego,** the voice of our moral compass (conscience) that forces the ego to consider not only the real but the *ideal.* The superego focuses on how we *ought* to behave. It strives for perfection, judging actions and producing positive feelings of pride or negative feelings of guilt. Someone with an exceptionally strong superego may be virtuous yet guilt-ridden; another with a weak superego may be wantonly self-indulgent and remorseless.

Because the superego's demands often oppose the id's, the ego struggles to reconcile the two. It is the personality "executive," mediating among the impulsive demands of the id, the restraining demands of the superego, and the real-life demands of the external world. If chaste Jane feels sexually attracted to John, she may satisfy both id and superego by joining a volunteer organization that John attends regularly.

Personality Development

55-3   What developmental stages did Freud propose?

Analysis of his patients' histories convinced Freud that personality forms during life's first few years. He concluded that children pass through a series of **psychosexual stages,** during which the id's pleasure-seeking energies focus on distinct pleasure-sensitive areas of the body called *erogenous zones* (**TABLE 55.1**). Each stage offers its own challenges, which Freud saw as conflicting tendencies.

Table 55.1 Freud's Psychosexual Stages

Stage	Focus
Oral (0–18 months)	Pleasure centers on the mouth—sucking, biting, chewing
Anal (18–36 months)	Pleasure focuses on bowel and bladder elimination; coping with demands for control
Phallic (3–6 years)	Pleasure zone is the genitals; coping with incestuous sexual feelings
Latency (6 to puberty)	A phase of dormant sexual feelings
Genital (puberty on)	Maturation of sexual interests

Freud believed that during the *phallic stage,* for example, boys seek genital stimulation, and they develop both unconscious sexual desires for their mother and jealousy and hatred for their father, whom they consider a rival. Given these feelings, he thought boys also experience guilt and a lurking fear of punishment, perhaps by castration, from their father. Freud called this collection of feelings the **Oedipus complex** after the Greek legend of Oedipus, who unknowingly killed his father and married his mother. Some psychoanalysts in Freud's era believed that girls experienced a parallel *Electra complex.*

Children eventually cope with the threatening feelings, said Freud, by repressing them and by identifying with (trying to become like) the rival parent. It's as though something inside the child decides, "If you can't beat 'em [the parent of the same sex], join 'em." Through this **identification** process, children's superegos gain strength as they incorporate many of their parents' values. Freud believed that identification with the same-sex parent provides what psychologists now call our *gender identity*—our sense of being male or female.

id a reservoir of unconscious psychic energy that, according to Freud, strives to satisfy basic sexual and aggressive drives. The id operates on the *pleasure principle,* demanding immediate gratification.

ego the largely conscious, "executive" part of personality that, according to Freud, mediates among the demands of the id, superego, and reality. The ego operates on the *reality principle,* satisfying the id's desires in ways that will realistically bring pleasure rather than pain.

superego the part of personality that, according to Freud, represents internalized ideals and provides standards for judgment (the conscience) and for future aspirations.

psychosexual stages the childhood stages of development (oral, anal, phallic, latency, genital) during which, according to Freud, the id's pleasure-seeking energies focus on distinct erogenous zones.

Oedipus [ED-uh-puss] **complex** according to Freud, a boy's sexual desires toward his mother and feelings of jealousy and hatred for the rival father.

identification the process by which, according to Freud, children incorporate their parents' values into their developing superegos.

Identification I want to be like Dad.

"Oh, for goodness' sake! Smoke!"

Freud presumed that our early childhood relations—especially with our parents and caregivers—influence our developing identity, personality, and frailties.

In Freud's view, conflicts unresolved during earlier psychosexual stages could surface as maladaptive behavior in the adult years. At any point in the oral, anal, or phallic stages, strong conflict could lock, or **fixate,** the person's pleasure-seeking energies in that stage. A person who had been either orally overindulged or deprived (perhaps by abrupt, early weaning) might fixate at the oral stage. This orally fixated adult could exhibit either passive dependence (like that of a nursing infant) or an exaggerated denial of this dependence (by acting tough or uttering biting sarcasm). Or the person might continue to seek oral gratification by smoking or excessive eating. In such ways, Freud suggested, the twig of personality is bent at an early age.

Freud's ideas of sexuality were controversial in his own time. "Freud was called a dirty-minded pansexualist and Viennese libertine," notes historian of psychology Morton Hunt (2007, p. 211). Today his ideas of Oedipal conflict and castration anxiety are disputed even by later *psychodynamic* theorists and therapists (see Module 56) (Shedler, 2010b). Yet we still teach them as part of the history of Western ideas.

Defense Mechanisms

55-4 How did Freud think people defend themselves against anxiety?

Anxiety, said Freud, is the price we pay for civilization. As members of social groups, we must control our sexual and aggressive impulses, not act them out. But sometimes the ego fears losing control of this inner war between the id and superego. The presumed result is a dark cloud of unfocused anxiety that leaves us feeling unsettled but unsure why.

Freud proposed that the ego protects itself with **defense mechanisms**—tactics that reduce or redirect anxiety by distorting reality. Defense mechanisms protect our self-understanding. For Freud, *all defense mechanisms function indirectly and unconsciously.* Just as the body unconsciously defends itself against disease, so also does the ego unconsciously defend itself against anxiety. For example, **repression** banishes anxiety-arousing wishes and feelings from consciousness. According to Freud, *repression underlies all the other defense mechanisms.* However, because repression is often incomplete, repressed urges may appear as symbols in dreams or as slips of the tongue in casual conversation. **TABLE 55.2** describes a sampling of seven other well-known defense mechanisms.

fixation according to Freud, a lingering focus of pleasure-seeking energies at an earlier psychosexual stage, in which conflicts were unresolved.

defense mechanisms in psychoanalytic theory, the ego's protective methods of reducing anxiety by unconsciously distorting reality.

repression in psychoanalytic theory, the basic defense mechanism that banishes from consciousness anxiety-arousing thoughts, feelings, and memories.

Regression: Faced with a mild stressor, children and young orangutans will seek protection and comfort from their caregivers. Freud might have interpreted these behaviors as regression, a retreat to an earlier developmental stage.

Table 55.2 Seven Defense Mechanisms

Freud believed that *repression,* the basic mechanism that banishes anxiety-arousing impulses, enables other defense mechanisms, seven of which are listed here.

Defense Mechanism	Unconscious Process Employed to Avoid Anxiety-Arousing Thoughts or Feelings	Example
Regression	Retreating to a more infantile psychosexual stage, where some psychic energy remains fixated.	A little boy reverts to the oral comfort of thumb sucking in the car on the way to his first day of school.
Reaction formation	Switching unacceptable impulses into their opposites.	Repressing angry feelings, a person displays exaggerated friendliness.
Projection	Disguising one's own threatening impulses by attributing them to others.	"The thief thinks everyone else is a thief" (an El Salvadoran saying).
Rationalization	Offering self-justifying explanations in place of the real, more threatening unconscious reasons for one's actions.	A habitual drinker says she drinks with her friends "just to be sociable."
Displacement	Shifting sexual or aggressive impulses toward a more acceptable or less threatening object or person.	A little girl kicks the family dog after her mother sends her to her room.
Sublimation	Transferring of unacceptable impulses into socially valued motives.	A man with aggressive urges becomes a surgeon.
Denial	Refusing to believe or even perceive painful realities.	A partner denies evidence of his loved one's affair.

Evaluating Freud's Psychoanalytic Perspective

55-5 How do contemporary psychologists view Freud's psychoanalysis?

Modern Research Contradicts Many of Freud's Ideas

We critique Freud from an early twenty-first-century perspective, a perspective that itself will be subject to revision. Freud did not have access to neurotransmitter or DNA studies, or to all that we have since learned about human development, thinking, and emotion. To criticize his theory by comparing it with today's thinking, some say, is like criticizing Henry Ford's Model T by comparing it with today's hybrid cars. (How tempting it always is to judge people in the past from our perspective in the present.)

But both Freud's admirers and his critics agree that recent research contradicts many of his specific ideas. Today's developmental psychologists see our development as lifelong, not fixed in childhood. They doubt that infants' neural networks are mature enough to sustain as much emotional trauma as Freud assumed. Some think Freud overestimated parental influence and underestimated peer influence. They also doubt that conscience and gender identity form as the child resolves the Oedipus complex at age 5 or 6. We gain our gender identity earlier and become strongly masculine or feminine even without a same-sex parent present. And they note that Freud's ideas about childhood sexuality arose from his skepticism of stories of childhood sexual abuse told by his female patients—stories that some scholars believe he attributed to their own childhood sexual wishes and conflicts (Esterson, 2001; Powell & Boer, 1994).

> **AP® Exam Tip**
>
> The differences between these defense mechanisms aren't always clear. For example, *repression* can be found in almost every example. Focus on the key feature of each given example. If the key feature is seeing your own impulse in someone else, it's projection. If the key feature is shifting your aggression from one target to another, it's displacement.

> "Many aspects of Freudian theory are indeed out of date, and they should be: Freud died in 1939, and he has been slow to undertake further revisions."
> -Psychologist Drew Westen (1998)

As we saw in Module 24, new ideas about why we dream dispute Freud's belief that dreams disguise and fulfill wishes. And slips of the tongue can be explained as competition between similar verbal choices in our memory network. Someone who says "I don't want to do that—it's a lot of brothel" may simply be blending *bother* and *trouble* (Foss & Hakes, 1978). Researchers find little support for Freud's idea that defense mechanisms disguise sexual and aggressive impulses (though our cognitive gymnastics do indeed work to protect our self-esteem). History also has failed to support another of Freud's ideas—that suppressed sexuality causes psychological disorders. From Freud's time to ours, sexual inhibition has diminished; psychological disorders have not.

Psychologists also criticize Freud's theory for its scientific shortcomings. Recall from Module 5 that good scientific theories explain observations and offer testable hypotheses. Freud's theory rests on few objective observations, and parts of it offer few testable hypotheses. (For Freud, his own recollections and interpretations of patients' free associations, dreams, and slips were evidence enough.)

What is the most serious problem with Freud's theory? It offers after-the-fact explanations of any characteristic (of one person's smoking, another's fear of horses, another's sexual orientation) yet fails to *predict* such behaviors and traits. If you feel angry at your mother's death, you illustrate his theory because "your unresolved childhood dependency needs are threatened." If you do not feel angry, you again illustrate his theory because "you are repressing your anger." That, said Calvin Hall and Gardner Lindzey (1978, p. 68), "is like betting on a horse after the race has been run." A good theory makes testable predictions.

> "We are arguing like a man who should say, 'If there were an invisible cat in that chair, the chair would look empty; but the chair does look empty; therefore there is an invisible cat in it.'" -C. S. LEWIS, *FOUR LOVES*, 1958

So, should psychology post an "Allow Natural Death" order on this old theory? Freud's supporters object. To criticize Freudian theory for not making testable predictions is, they say, like criticizing baseball for not being an aerobic exercise, something it was never intended to be. Freud never claimed that psychoanalysis was predictive science. He merely claimed that, looking back, psychoanalysts could find meaning in their clients' state of mind (Rieff, 1979).

Supporters also note that some of Freud's ideas *are* enduring. It was Freud who drew our attention to the unconscious and the irrational, to our self-protective defenses, to the importance of human sexuality, and to the tension between our biological impulses and our social well-being. It was Freud who challenged our self-righteousness, punctured our pretensions, and reminded us of our potential for evil.

Modern Research Challenges the Idea of Repression

Psychoanalytic theory rests on the assumption that the human mind often *represses* offending wishes, banishing them into the unconscious until they resurface, like long-lost books in a dusty attic. Recover and resolve childhood's conflicted wishes, and emotional healing should follow. Repression became a widely accepted concept, used to explain hypnotic phenomena and psychological disorders. Some of Freud's followers extended repression to explain apparently lost and recovered memories of childhood traumas (Boag, 2006; Cheit, 1998; Erdelyi,

2006). In one survey, 88 percent of university students believed that painful experiences commonly get pushed out of awareness and into the unconscious (Garry et al., 1994).

Today's researchers agree that we sometimes spare our egos by neglecting threatening information (Green et al., 2008). Yet, many contend that repression, if it ever occurs, is a rare mental response to terrible trauma. Even those who have witnessed a parent's murder or survived Nazi death camps retain their unrepressed memories of the horror (Helmreich, 1992, 1994; Malmquist, 1986; Pennebaker, 1990). "Dozens of formal studies have yielded not a single convincing case of repression in the entire literature on trauma," concluded personality researcher John Kihlstrom (2006).

Some researchers do believe that extreme, prolonged stress, such as the stress some severely abused children experience, might disrupt memory by damaging the hippocampus (Schacter, 1996). But the far more common reality is that high stress and associated stress hormones *enhance* memory (see Module 32). Indeed, rape, torture, and other traumatic events haunt survivors, who experience unwanted flashbacks. They are seared onto the soul. "You see the babies," said Holocaust survivor Sally H. (1979). "You see the screaming mothers. You see hanging people. You sit and you see that face there. It's something you don't forget."

> "The overall findings . . . seriously challenge the classical psychoanalytic notion of repression." -Psychologist Yacov Rofé, "Does Repression Exist?" 2008

> "During the Holocaust, many children . . . were forced to endure the unendurable. For those who continue to suffer [the] pain is still present, many years later, as real as it was on the day it occurred." -Eric Zillmer, Molly Harrower, Barry Ritzler, and Robert Archer, The Quest for the Nazi Personality, 1995

Before You Move On

▶ **ASK YOURSELF**
Which of Freud's presumed defense mechanisms have you found yourself employing?

▶ **TEST YOURSELF**
How does today's psychological science assess Freud's theory?

Answers to the Test Yourself questions can be found in Appendix E at the end of the book.

Module 55 Review

- *Personality* is an individual's characteristic pattern of thinking, feeling, and acting.

- Sigmund Freud's theory of *psychoanalysis* is not the most important theory in psychology, but his famous work is historically and culturally significant.

55-1 How did Sigmund Freud's treatment of psychological disorders lead to his view of the unconscious mind?

- In treating patients whose disorders had no clear physical explanation, Freud concluded that these problems reflected unacceptable thoughts and feelings, hidden away in the *unconscious* mind.

- To explore this hidden part of a patient's mind, Freud used *free association* and dream analysis.

55-2 What was Freud's view of personality?

- Freud believed that personality results from conflict arising from the interaction among the mind's three systems: the *id* (pleasure-seeking impulses), *ego* (reality-oriented executive), and *superego* (internalized set of ideals, or conscience).

55-3 What developmental stages did Freud propose?

- Freud believed children pass through five *psychosexual stages* (oral, anal, phallic, latency, and genital).

- Unresolved conflicts at any stage can leave a person's pleasure-seeking impulses *fixated* (stalled) at that stage.

55-4 How did Freud think people defend themselves against anxiety?

- For Freud, anxiety was the product of tensions between the demands of the id and superego. The ego copes by using unconscious *defense mechanisms,* such as *repression,* which he viewed as the basic mechanism underlying and enabling all the others.

55-5 How do contemporary psychologists view Freud's psychoanalysis?

- Today's psychologists give Freud credit for drawing attention to the vast unconscious, to the importance of our sexuality, and to the conflict between biological impulses and social restraints.

- But Freud's concept of repression, and his view of the unconscious as a collection of repressed and unacceptable thoughts, wishes, feelings, and memories, have not survived scientific scrutiny. Freud offered after-the-fact explanations, which are hard to test scientifically.

- Research does not support many of Freud's specific ideas, such as the view that development is fixed in childhood. (We now know it is lifelong.)

Multiple-Choice Questions

1. Free association is

a. a method of exploring the unconscious.
b. another name for hypnosis.
c. the major function of the superego.
d. an ego defense mechanism.
e. a method of dream analysis.

2. According to Freud, which of the following is true of the ego?

a. It focuses on how we ought to behave.
b. It is the source of guilt.
c. It is the part of the personality present at birth.
d. It strives to satisfy basic drives.
e. It operates under the reality principle.

3. Which of the following represents Freud's Oedipus complex?

a. Yutao has begun to suffer from the same recurrent nightmares he had as a child.
b. Madeline manifests repressed anxiety because of guilt she experienced when she disappointed her parents during toilet training.
c. Five-year-old Anagha is taking on many of her mother's values through a process of identification.
d. Four-year-old Carlos is experiencing unconscious sexual desire for his mother and unconscious hatred for his father.
e. Elle has begun to overeat and smoke cigarettes as a college student, indicating a degree of oral fixation.

4. According to Freud, which of the following defense mechanisms underlies all of the others?

a. Repression   d. Projection
b. Reaction formation e. Regression
c. Displacement

Practice FRQs

1. Name what Freud believed to be the three parts of the mind and describe the role of each.

Answer

1 point: The conscious mind is what a person is aware of.

1 point: The preconscious mind is a temporary holding place from which memories and feelings can be easily retrieved.

1 point: The unconscious mind is the hidden holding place for unacceptable passions and thoughts.

2. Nadina is struggling to decide whether to buy a new sweater that she really cannot afford. What role would each of the three parts of her personality (as theorized by Freud) play in her decision?

(3 points)

Module 56

Psychodynamic Theories and Modern Views of the Unconscious

Module Learning Objectives

56-1 Identify which of Freud's ideas were accepted or rejected by his followers.

56-2 Describe projective tests and how they are used, and discuss some criticisms of them.

56-3 Describe the modern view of the unconscious.

P**sychodynamic theories** of personality view our behavior as emerging from the interaction between the conscious and unconscious mind, including associated motives and conflicts. These theories are descended from Freud's historical *psychoanalytic theory,* but the modern-day approaches differ in important ways.

> **psychodynamic theories**
> modern-day approaches that view personality with a focus on the unconscious and the importance of childhood experiences.

The Neo-Freudian and Psychodynamic Theorists

56-1 Which of Freud's ideas did his followers accept or reject?

Freud's writings were controversial, but they soon attracted followers, mostly young, ambitious physicians who formed an inner circle around their strong-minded leader. These pioneering psychoanalysts, whom we often call *neo-Freudians,* accepted Freud's basic ideas: the personality structures of id, ego, and superego; the importance of the unconscious; the shaping of personality in childhood; and the dynamics of anxiety and the defense mechanisms. But they broke off from Freud in two important ways. First, they placed more emphasis on the conscious mind's role in interpreting experience and in coping with the environment. And second, they doubted that sex and aggression were all-consuming motivations. Instead, they tended to emphasize loftier motives and social interactions.

Alfred Adler and Karen Horney [HORN-eye], for example, agreed with Freud that childhood is important. But they believed that childhood *social,* not sexual, tensions are crucial for personality formation (Ferguson, 2003). Adler (who had proposed the still-popular idea of the *inferiority complex*) himself struggled to overcome childhood illnesses and accidents, and he believed that much of our behavior is driven by efforts to conquer childhood inferiority feelings that trigger our strivings for superiority and power. Horney said childhood anxiety triggers our desire for love and security. She also countered Freud's assumptions, arising as they did in his conservative culture, that women have weak superegos and suffer "penis envy," and she attempted to balance the bias she detected in his masculine view of psychology.

Alfred Adler "The individual feels at home in life and feels his existence to be worthwhile just so far as he is useful to others and is overcoming feelings of inferiority" (*Problems of Neurosis*, 1964).

Karen Horney "The view that women are infantile and emotional creatures, and as such, incapable of responsibility and independence is the work of the masculine tendency to lower women's self-respect" (*Feminine Psychology*, 1932).

Carl Jung "From the living fountain of instinct flows everything that is creative; hence the unconscious is the very source of the creative impulse" (*The Structure and Dynamics of the Psyche*, 1960).

collective unconscious Carl Jung's concept of a shared, inherited reservoir of memory traces from our species' history.

Carl Jung—Freud's disciple-turned-dissenter—placed less emphasis on social factors and agreed with Freud that the unconscious exerts a powerful influence. But to Jung [Yoong], the unconscious contains more than our repressed thoughts and feelings. He believed we also have a **collective unconscious,** a common reservoir of images, or *archetypes,* derived from our species' universal experiences. Jung said that the collective unconscious explains why, for many people, spiritual concerns are deeply rooted and why people in different cultures share certain myths and images, such as mother as a symbol of nurturance. (Most of today's psychodynamic psychologists discount the idea of inherited experiences. But many psychodynamic and other psychological theorists do believe that our shared evolutionary history shaped some universal dispositions.)

Some of Freud's ideas have been incorporated into the diversity of modern perspectives that make up psychodynamic theory. "Most contemporary [psychodynamic] theorists and therapists are not wedded to the idea that sex is the basis of personality," noted Drew Westen (1996). They "do not talk about ids and egos, and do not go around classifying their patients as oral, anal, or phallic characters." What they do assume, with Freud and with much support from today's psychological science, is that much of our mental life is unconscious. With Freud, they also assume that we often struggle with inner conflicts among our wishes, fears, and values, and that childhood shapes our personality and ways of becoming attached to others.

Assessing Unconscious Processes

56-2 What are projective tests, how are they used, and what are some criticisms of them?

Personality assessment tools are useful to those who study personality or provide therapy. Such tools differ because they are tailored to specific theories. How might psychodynamic clinicians attempt to assess personality characteristics?

The first requirement would be some sort of a road into the unconscious, to unearth the residue of early childhood experiences, to move beneath surface pretensions and reveal hidden conflicts and impulses. Objective assessment tools, such as agree-disagree or true-false questionnaires, would be inadequate because they would merely tap the conscious surface.

ScienceCartoonsPlus.com

"The forward thrust of the antlers shows a determined personality, yet the small sun indicates a lack of self-confidence...."

Projective tests aim to provide this "psychological X-ray" by asking test-takers to describe an ambiguous stimulus or tell a story about it. Henry Murray introduced one such test, the **Thematic Apperception Test (TAT),** in which a person views an ambiguous picture and then makes up a story about it (**FIGURE 56.1**). The clinician may presume that any hopes, desires, and fears that people see in the ambiguous image are projections of their own inner feelings or conflicts.

The most widely used projective test left some blots on the name of Swiss psychiatrist Hermann Rorschach [ROAR-shock]. He based his famous **Rorschach inkblot test,** in which people describe what they see in a series of inkblots (**FIGURE 56.2**), on a childhood game. He and his friends would drip ink on a paper, fold it, and then say what they saw in the resulting blot (Sdorow, 2005). Do you see predatory animals or weapons? Perhaps you have aggressive tendencies. But is this a reasonable assumption?

Clinicians' and critics' answers differ. Some clinicians cherish the Rorschach, even offering Rorschach-based assessments of criminals' violence potential to judges. Others view it as a helpful diagnostic tool, a source of suggestive leads, or an icebreaker and a revealing interview technique. The Society for Personality Assessment (2005) commends "its responsible use" (which would *not* include inferring past childhood sexual abuse). And—in response to past criticisms of test scoring and interpretation (Sechrest et al., 1998)—a research-based, computer-aided tool has been designed to improve agreement among raters and enhance the test's validity (Erdberg, 1990; Exner, 2003).

But the evidence is insufficient to its revilers, who insist the Rorschach is no emotional MRI. They argue that only a few of the many Rorschach-derived scores, such as ones for hostility and anxiety, have demonstrated *validity*—predicting what they are supposed to predict (Wood, 2006). Moreover, they say, these tests do not yield consistent results—they are not *reliable*. Inkblot assessments diagnose many normal adults as pathological (Wood et al., 2003, 2006, 2010). Alternative projective assessment techniques fare little better. "Even seasoned professionals can be fooled by their intuitions and their faith in tools that lack strong evidence of effectiveness," warned Scott Lilienfeld, James Wood, and Howard Garb (2001). "When a substantial body of research demonstrates that old intuitions are wrong, it is time to adopt new ways of thinking."

Figure 56.1

The TAT This clinician presumes that the hopes, fears, and interests expressed in this boy's descriptions of a series of ambiguous pictures in the Thematic Apperception Test (TAT) are projections of his inner feelings.

"The Rorschach Inkblot Test has been resoundingly discredited. I call it the Dracula of psychological tests, because no one has been able to drive a stake through the cursed thing's heart." -CAROL TAVRIS, "MIND GAMES: PSYCHOLOGICAL WARFARE BETWEEN THERAPISTS AND SCIENTISTS," 2003

"We don't see things as they are; we see things as we are." -THE TALMUD

projective test a personality test, such as the Rorschach, that provides ambiguous stimuli designed to trigger projection of one's inner dynamics.

Thematic Apperception Test (TAT) a projective test in which people express their inner feelings and interests through the stories they make up about ambiguous scenes.

Rorschach inkblot test the most widely used projective test, a set of 10 inkblots, designed by Hermann Rorschach; seeks to identify people's inner feelings by analyzing their interpretations of the blots.

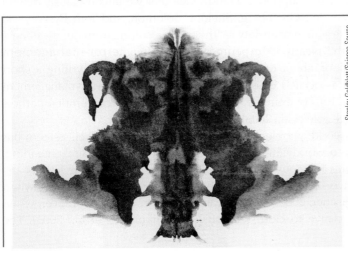

Figure 56.2

The Rorschach test In this projective test, people tell what they see in a series of symmetrical inkblots. Some who use this test are confident that the interpretation of ambiguous stimuli will reveal unconscious aspects of the test-taker's personality.

The Modern Unconscious Mind

56-3 How has modern research developed our understanding of the unconscious?

Freud was right about a big idea that underlies today's psychodynamic thinking: We indeed have limited access to all that goes on in our minds (Erdelyi, 1985, 1988, 2006; Norman, 2010). Our two-track mind has a vast out-of-sight realm.

Nevertheless, many of today's research psychologists now think of the unconscious not as seething passions and repressive censoring but as cooler information processing that occurs without our awareness. To these researchers, the unconscious also involves

- the schemas that automatically control our perceptions and interpretations (Module 17).

- the priming by stimuli to which we have not consciously attended (Modules 16 and 32).

- the right hemisphere brain activity that enables the split-brain patient's left hand to carry out an instruction the patient cannot verbalize (Module 13).

- the implicit memories that operate without conscious recall, even among those with amnesia (Module 33).

- the emotions that activate instantly, before conscious analysis (Module 41).

- the self-concept and stereotypes that automatically and unconsciously influence how we process information about ourselves and others (Module 77).

false consensus effect the tendency to overestimate the extent to which others share our beliefs and our behaviors.

terror-management theory a theory of death-related anxiety; explores people's emotional and behavioral responses to reminders of their impending death.

More than we realize, we fly on autopilot. Our lives are guided by off-screen, out-of-sight, unconscious information processing. The unconscious mind is huge. This understanding of unconscious information processing is more like the pre-Freudian view of an underground, unattended stream of thought from which spontaneous behavior and creative ideas surface (Bargh & Morsella, 2008).

Research has also supported Freud's idea of our unconscious defense mechanisms. For example, Roy Baumeister and his colleagues (1998) found that people tend to see their foibles and attitudes in others, a phenomenon that Freud called projection and that today's researchers call the **false consensus effect,** the tendency to overestimate the extent to which others share our beliefs and behaviors. People who cheat on their taxes or break speed limits tend to think many others do likewise. People who are happy, kind, and trustworthy tend to see others as the same (Wood et al., 2010).

Evidence also confirms the unconscious mechanisms that defend self-esteem, such as reaction formation. Defense mechanisms, Baumeister concluded, are motivated less by the seething impulses that Freud presumed than by our need to protect our self-image.

Finally, recent history has supported Freud's idea that we unconsciously defend ourselves against anxiety. Jeff Greenberg, Sheldon Solomon, and Tom Pyszczynski (1997) proposed that one source of anxiety is "the terror resulting from our awareness of vulnerability and death." Nearly 300 experiments testing their **terror-management theory** show that thinking about one's mortality—for example, by writing a short essay on dying and its associated emotions—provokes various terror-management defenses (Burke et al., 2010). For example, death anxiety increases contempt for others and esteem for oneself (Koole et al., 2006).

Faced with a threatening world, people act not only to enhance their self-esteem but also to adhere more strongly to worldviews that answer questions about life's meaning. The prospect of death promotes religious sentiments, and deep religious convictions enable people to be less defensive—less likely to rise in defense of their worldview—when reminded of death (Jonas & Fischer, 2006; Norenzayan & Hansen, 2006). Moreover, when contemplating death, people cleave to close relationships (Mikulincer et al., 2003). The

"It says, 'Someday you will die.'"

"I don't want to attain immortality through my work; I want to attain immortality by not dying." -FILM DIRECTOR AND ACTOR WOODY ALLEN

events of 9/11—a striking experience of the terror of death—led trapped World Trade Center occupants to spend their last moments calling loved ones, and led most Americans to reach out to family and friends.

> "I sought the Lord, and he answered me and delivered me out of all my terror." -PSALM 34:4

Before You Move On

▶ **ASK YOURSELF**

What understanding and impressions of Freud did you bring to this unit? Are you surprised to find that some of his ideas (especially the big idea of our unconscious mind) had merit?

▶ **TEST YOURSELF**

What methods have been used by psychodynamic clinicians to assess unconscious processes?

Answers to the Test Yourself questions can be found in Appendix E at the end of the book.

Module 56 Review

- *Psychodynamic theories,* which descended from Freud's historically important work, view personality from the perspective that behavior is a dynamic interaction between the conscious and unconscious mind.

 56-1 Which of Freud's ideas did his followers accept or reject?

- Freud's early followers, the neo-Freudians, accepted many of his ideas. They differed in placing more emphasis on the conscious mind and in stressing social motives more than sexual or aggression motives.

- Contemporary psychodynamic theorists and therapists reject Freud's emphasis on sexual motivation. They stress, with support from modern research findings, the view that much of our mental life is unconscious, and they believe that our childhood experiences influence our adult personality and attachment patterns.

56-2 What are projective tests, how are they used, and what are some criticisms of them?

- *Projective tests* attempt to assess personality by showing people vague stimuli with many possible interpretations; answers reveal unconscious motives.

- One such test, the *Rorschach inkblot test,* has low reliability and validity.

56-3 How has modern research developed our understanding of the unconscious?

- Current research confirms that we do not have full access to all that goes on in our mind, but the current view of the unconscious is not that of a hidden storehouse filled with repressed feelings and thoughts.

- Researchers see the unconscious as a separate and parallel track of information processing that occurs outside our awareness, such as schemas that control our perceptions; priming; implicit memories of learned skills; instantly activated emotions; self-concepts and stereotypes that filter information about ourselves and others; and mechanisms that defend our self-esteem and deter anxiety, such as the *false consensus effect*/projection and *terror management.*

Multiple-Choice Questions

1. What did Carl Jung call the shared, inherited reservoir of memory traces from our species' history?

   a. Neurosis
   b. Archetypes
   c. Collective unconscious
   d. Inferiority complex
   e. Terror management

2. Scott Lilienfeld, James Wood, and Howard Garb (2001) wrote, "When a substantial body of research demonstrates that old intuitions are wrong, it is time to adopt new ways of thinking." What were they talking about?

   a. MRI test
   b. Rorschach inkblot test
   c. Freud's work on the id and ego
   d. Psychodynamic theories
   e. Modern views of the unconscious

3. According to the text, many research psychologists think of _____ as an information processor that works without our awareness.

   a. the TAT
   b. the id
   c. repression
   d. defense mechanisms
   e. the unconscious

Practice FRQs

1. Name and accurately describe two projective tests.

Answer

1 point: Thematic Apperception Test (TAT)

1 point: In the TAT, someone is asked to tell a story about a picture.

1 point: Rorschach Inkblot Test

1 point: In the Rorschach, someone is asked to state what he or she sees in an inkblot.

2. Explain and give an example of the false consensus effect.

(2 points)

Module 57

Humanistic Theories

Module Learning Objectives

57-1 Describe how humanistic psychologists viewed personality, and explain their goal in studying personality.

57-2 Explain how humanistic psychologists assessed a person's sense of self.

57-3 Describe how humanistic theories have influenced psychology, and discuss the criticisms they have faced.

57-1 How did humanistic psychologists view personality, and what was their goal in studying personality?

By the 1960s, some personality psychologists had become discontented with the sometimes bleak focus on drives and conflicts in psychodynamic theory and the mechanistic psychology of B. F. Skinner's behaviorism (see Modules 27 and 28). In contrast to Freud's study of the base motives of "sick" people, these **humanistic theorists** focused on the ways people strive for self-determination and self-realization. In contrast to behaviorism's scientific objectivity, they studied people through their own self-reported experiences and feelings.

Two pioneering theorists—Abraham Maslow (1908–1970) and Carl Rogers (1902–1987)—offered a "third-force" perspective that emphasized human potential. Like *psychoanalytic theory,* the humanistic theories have been an important part of psychology's history.

Abraham Maslow's Self-Actualizing Person

Maslow proposed that we are motivated by a *hierarchy of needs* (Module 37). If our physiological needs are met, we become concerned with personal safety; if we achieve a sense of security, we then seek to love, to be loved, and to love ourselves; with our love needs satisfied, we seek self-esteem. Having achieved self-esteem, we ultimately seek **self-actualization** (the process of fulfilling our potential) and *self-transcendence* (meaning, purpose, and communion beyond the self).

Maslow (1970) developed his ideas by studying healthy, creative people rather than troubled clinical cases. He based his description of self-actualization on a study of those, such as Abraham Lincoln, who seemed notable for their rich and productive lives. Maslow reported that such people shared certain characteristics: They were self-aware and self-accepting, open and spontaneous, loving and caring, and not paralyzed by others' opinions. Secure in their sense of who they were, their interests were problem-centered rather than self-centered. They focused their energies on a particular task, one they often regarded as their mission in life.

humanistic theories view personality with a focus on the potential for healthy personal growth.

self-actualization according to Maslow, one of the ultimate psychological needs that arises after basic physical and psychological needs are met and self-esteem is achieved; the motivation to fulfill one's potential.

Abraham Maslow (1908–1970)
"Any theory of motivation that is worthy of attention must deal with the highest capacities of the healthy and strong person as well as with the defensive maneuvers of crippled spirits" (*Motivation and Personality,* 1970, p. 33).

Most enjoyed a few deep relationships rather than many superficial ones. Many had been moved by spiritual or personal *peak experiences* that surpassed ordinary consciousness.

These, said Maslow, are mature adult qualities, ones found in those who have learned enough about life to be compassionate, to have outgrown their mixed feelings toward their parents, to have found their calling, to have "acquired enough courage to be unpopular, to be unashamed about being openly virtuous, etc." Maslow's work with college students led him to speculate that those likely to become self-actualizing adults were likable, caring, "privately affectionate to those of their elders who deserve it," and "secretly uneasy about the cruelty, meanness, and mob spirit so often found in young people."

Carl Rogers' Person-Centered Perspective

Fellow humanistic psychologist Carl Rogers agreed with much of Maslow's thinking. Rogers believed that people are basically good and are endowed with self-actualizing tendencies. Unless thwarted by an environment that inhibits growth, each of us is like an acorn, primed for growth and fulfillment. Rogers' (1980) *person-centered perspective* (also called *client-centered perspective*) held that a growth-promoting climate required three conditions.

- *Genuineness:* When people are *genuine,* they are open with their own feelings, drop their facades, and are transparent and self-disclosing.

- *Acceptance:* When people are *accepting,* they offer **unconditional positive regard,** an attitude of grace that values us even knowing our failings. It is a profound relief to drop our pretenses, confess our worst feelings, and discover that we are still accepted. In a good marriage, a close family, or an intimate friendship, we are free to be spontaneous without fearing the loss of others' esteem.

- *Empathy:* When people are *empathic,* they share and mirror other's feelings and reflect their meanings. "Rarely do we listen with real understanding, true empathy," said Rogers. "Yet listening, of this very special kind, is one of the most potent forces for change that I know."

Genuineness, acceptance, and empathy are, Rogers believed, the water, sun, and nutrients that enable people to grow like vigorous oak trees. For "as persons are accepted and prized, they tend to develop a more caring attitude toward themselves" (Rogers, 1980, p. 116). As persons are empathically heard, "it becomes possible for them to listen more accurately to the flow of inner experiencings."

Writer Calvin Trillin (2006) recalls an example of parental genuineness and acceptance at a camp for children with severe disorders, where his wife, Alice, worked. L., a "magical child," had genetic diseases that meant she had to be tube-fed and could walk only with difficulty. Alice recalled,

> One day, when we were playing duck-duck-goose, I was sitting behind her and she asked me to hold her mail for her while she took her turn to be chased around the circle. It took her a while to make the circuit, and I had time to see that on top of the pile [of mail] was a note from her mom. Then I did something truly awful. . . . I simply had to know what this child's parents could have done to make her so spectacular, to make her the most optimistic, most enthusiastic, most hopeful human being I had ever encountered. I snuck a quick look at the note, and my eyes fell on this sentence: "If God had given us all of the children in the world to choose from, L., we would only have chosen you." Before L. got back to her place in the circle, I showed the note to Bud, who was sitting next to me. "Quick. Read this," I whispered. "It's the secret of life."

Maslow and Rogers would have smiled knowingly. For them a central feature of personality is one's **self-concept**—all the thoughts and feelings we have in response to the question, "Who am I?" If our self-concept is positive, we tend to act and perceive the world

---

unconditional positive regard according to Rogers, an attitude of total acceptance toward another person.

self-concept all our thoughts and feelings about ourselves, in answer to the question, "Who am I?"

A father *not* offering unconditional positive regard:

"Just remember, son, it doesn't matter whether you win or lose—unless you want Daddy's love."

positively. If it is negative—if in our own eyes we fall far short of our *ideal self*—said Rogers, we feel dissatisfied and unhappy. A worthwhile goal for therapists, parents, teachers, and friends is therefore, he said, to help others know, accept, and be true to themselves.

Assessing the Self

 How did humanistic psychologists assess a person's sense of self?

Humanistic psychologists sometimes assessed personality by asking people to fill out questionnaires that would evaluate their self-concept. One questionnaire, inspired by Carl Rogers, asked people to describe themselves both as they would *ideally* like to be and as they *actually* are. When the ideal and the actual self are nearly alike, said Rogers, the self-concept is positive. Assessing his clients' personal growth during therapy, he looked for successively closer ratings of actual and ideal selves.

Some humanistic psychologists believed that any standardized assessment of personality, even a questionnaire, is depersonalizing. Rather than forcing the person to respond to narrow categories, these humanistic psychologists presumed that interviews and intimate conversation would provide a better understanding of each person's unique experiences.

Evaluating Humanistic Theories

 How have humanistic theories influenced psychology? What criticisms have they faced?

One thing said of Freud can also be said of the humanistic psychologists: Their impact has been pervasive. Maslow's and Rogers' ideas have influenced counseling, education, child raising, and management.

They have also influenced—sometimes in ways they did not intend—much of today's popular psychology. Is a positive self-concept the key to happiness and success? Do acceptance and empathy nurture positive feelings about oneself? Are people basically good and capable of self-improvement? Many people answer *Yes, Yes,* and *Yes.* Responding to a 1992 *Newsweek* Gallup poll, 9 in 10 people rated self-esteem as very important for "motivating a person to work hard and succeed." Given a choice, today's North American collegians say they'd rather get a self-esteem boost, such as a compliment or good grade on a paper, than enjoy a favorite food (Bushman et al., 2011). Humanistic psychology's message has been heard.

The prominence of the humanistic perspective set off a backlash of criticism. First, said the critics, its concepts are vague and *subjective.* Consider Maslow's description of self-actualizing people as open, spontaneous, loving, self-accepting, and productive. Is this a scientific description? Isn't it merely a description of the theorist's own values and ideals? Maslow, noted M. Brewster Smith (1978), offered impressions of his own personal heroes. Imagine another theorist who began with a different set of heroes—perhaps Napoleon, John D. Rockefeller, Sr., and Margaret Thatcher. This theorist would likely describe self-actualizing people as "undeterred by others' needs and opinions," "motivated to achieve," and "comfortable with power."

Critics also objected to the idea that, as Rogers put it, "The only question which matters is, 'Am I living in a way which is deeply satisfying to me, and which truly expresses me?'" (quoted by Wallach & Wallach, 1985). The *individualism* encouraged by humanistic psychology—trusting and acting on one's feelings, being true to oneself, fulfilling oneself—can, the critics have said, lead to self-indulgence, selfishness, and an erosion of moral restraints (Campbell & Specht, 1985; Wallach & Wallach, 1983). Indeed, it is those who focus beyond themselves who are most likely to experience social support, to enjoy life, and to cope effectively with stress (Crandall, 1984).

Humanistic psychologists reply that a secure, nondefensive self-acceptance is actually the first step toward loving others. Indeed, people who feel intrinsically liked and accepted—for who they are, not just for their achievements—exhibit less-defensive attitudes (Schimel et al., 2001).

A final accusation leveled against humanistic psychology is that it is *naive*, that it fails to appreciate the reality of our human capacity for evil. Faced with climate change, overpopulation, terrorism, and the spread of nuclear weapons, we may become apathetic from either of two rationalizations. One is a starry-eyed optimism that denies the threat ("People are basically good; everything will work out"). The other is a dark despair ("It's hopeless; why try?"). Action requires enough realism to fuel concern and enough optimism to provide hope. Humanistic psychology, say the critics, encourages the needed hope but not the equally necessary realism about evil.

"We do pretty well when you stop to think that people are basically good."

Before You Move On

▶ **ASK YOURSELF**

Have you had someone in your life who accepted you unconditionally? Do you think this person helped you to know yourself better and to develop a better image of yourself?

▶ **TEST YOURSELF**

What does it mean to be "empathic"? To be "self-actualized"?

Answers to the Test Yourself questions can be found in Appendix E at the end of the book.

Module 57 Review

 How did humanistic psychologists view personality, and what was their goal in studying personality?

- The *humanistic* psychologists' view of personality focused on the potential for healthy personal growth and people's striving for self-determination and self-realization.

- Abraham Maslow proposed that human motivations form a hierarchy of needs; if basic needs are fulfilled, people will strive toward *self-actualization* and self-transcendence.

- Carl Rogers' person-centered perspective suggested that the ingredients of a growth-promoting environment are genuineness, acceptance (including *unconditional positive regard*), and empathy.

- The *self-concept* was a central feature of personality for both Maslow and Rogers.

 How did humanistic psychologists assess a person's sense of self?

- Some rejected any standardized assessments and relied on interviews and conversations.

- Rogers sometimes used questionnaires in which people described their ideal and actual selves, which he later used to judge progress during therapy.

 How have humanistic theories influenced psychology? What criticisms have they faced?

- Humanistic psychology helped renew interest in the concept of self.

- Critics have said that humanistic psychology's concepts were vague and subjective, its values self-centered, and its assumptions naively optimistic.

Multiple-Choice Questions

1. Which of the following theories offers a special focus on the potential for healthy personal growth?
   a. Neo-Freudian
   b. Psychodynamic
   c. Humanistic
   d. Behavioral
   e. Functionalist

2. What do we call the process of fulfilling our potential?
   a. Free association
   b. Self-transcendence
   c. Unconditional positive regard
   d. Self-concept
   e. Self-actualization

3. Humanistic psychologists often prefer to assess personality by
   a. having a person write out answers to questions.
   b. sitting down and talking to a person.
   c. getting a person to describe what he or she sees in ambiguous inkblots.
   d. having a person describe their dreams.
   e. putting a person in a stressful situation to see how he or she behaves under pressure.

4. Which of the following is an example of unconditional positive regard?
   a. Mr. and Mrs. Prohaska, who have been married for 37 years, credit the success of their marriage to the fact that each has been able to accept the faults of the other without criticism.
   b. Seven-year-old Michaela gets her allowance each week whether she does her chores or not.
   c. Ms. Lopez, a second grade teacher, puts a smiley face sticker on her students' papers when they have done a good job.
   d. John got a promotion and a raise at work after filling in for a sick manager one day and doing a better job than the manager had done previously.
   e. Chen's parents usually praise him when he does well and ignore him when he engages in minor misbehavior.

Practice FRQs

1. Describe the three conditions that Carl Rogers believed were necessary for a growth-promoting climate.

Answer

1 point: Genuineness, where people are open with their feelings.

1 point: Acceptance, which includes unconditional positive regard, where people are accepted despite their faults and failures.

1 point: Empathy, where the therapist shares and mirrors the feelings of others.

2. Describe three criticisms that have been made of humanistic psychology.

(3 points)

Module 58

Trait Theories

Module Learning Objectives

58-1 Explain how psychologists use traits to describe personality.

58-2 Describe personality inventories, and discuss their strengths and weaknesses as trait-assessment tools.

58-3 Identify the traits that seem to provide the most useful information about personality variation.

58-4 Discuss whether research supports the consistency of personality traits over time and across situations.

58-1   How do psychologists use traits to describe personality?

Rather than focusing on unconscious forces and thwarted growth opportunities, some researchers attempt to define personality in terms of stable and enduring behavior patterns, such as Sam Gamgee's loyalty and optimism. This perspective can be traced in part to a remarkable meeting in 1919, when Gordon Allport, a curious 22-year-old psychology student, interviewed Sigmund Freud in Vienna. Allport soon discovered just how preoccupied the founder of psychoanalysis was with finding hidden motives, even in Allport's own behavior during the interview. That experience ultimately led Allport to do what Freud did not do—to describe personality in terms of fundamental **traits**—people's characteristic behaviors and conscious motives (such as the curiosity that actually motivated Allport to see Freud). Meeting Freud, said Allport, "taught me that [psychoanalysis], for all its merits, may plunge too deep, and that psychologists would do well to give full recognition to manifest motives before probing the unconscious." Allport came to define personality in terms of identifiable behavior patterns. He was concerned less with *explaining* individual traits than with *describing* them.

Like Allport, Isabel Briggs Myers (1987) and her mother, Katharine Briggs, wanted to describe important personality differences. They attempted to sort people according to Carl Jung's personality types, based on their responses to 126 questions. The *Myers-Briggs Type Indicator (MBTI),* available in 21 languages, has been taken by more than 2 million people a year, mostly for counseling, leadership training, and work-team development (CPP, 2008). It offers choices, such as "Do you usually value sentiment more than logic, or value logic more than sentiment?" Then it counts the test-taker's preferences, labels them as indicating, say, a "feeling type" or "thinking type," and feeds them back to the person in complimentary terms. Feeling types, for example, are told they are sensitive to values and are "sympathetic, appreciative, and tactful"; thinking types are told they "prefer an objective standard of truth" and are "good at analyzing." (Every type has its strengths, so everyone is affirmed.)

Most people agree with their announced type profile, which mirrors their declared preferences. They may also accept their label as a basis for being matched with work partners

> **trait** a characteristic pattern of behavior or a disposition to feel and act, as assessed by self-report inventories and peer reports.

and tasks that supposedly suit their temperaments. A National Research Council report noted, however, that despite the test's popularity in business and career counseling, its initial use outran research on its value as a predictor of job performance, and "the popularity of this instrument in the absence of proven scientific worth is troublesome" (Druckman & Bjork, 1991, p. 101; see also Pittenger, 1993). Although research on the MBTI has been accumulating since those cautionary words were expressed, the test remains mostly a counseling and coaching tool, not a research instrument.

Exploring Traits

Classifying people as one or another distinct personality type fails to capture their full individuality. We are each a unique complex of multiple traits. So how else could we describe our personalities? We might describe an apple by placing it along several trait dimensions—relatively large or small, red or green, sweet or sour. By placing people on several trait dimensions simultaneously, psychologists can describe countless individual personality variations. (Remember from Module 18 that variations on just three color dimensions—hue, saturation, and brightness—create many thousands of colors.)

What trait dimensions describe personality? If you had an upcoming blind date, what personality traits might give you an accurate sense of the person? Allport and his associate H. S. Odbert (1936) counted all the words in an unabridged dictionary with which one could describe people. There were almost 18,000! How, then, could psychologists condense the list to a manageable number of basic traits?

Factor Analysis

One technique is *factor analysis,* a statistical procedure used to identify clusters of test items that tap basic components of intelligence (such as spatial ability or verbal skill). Imagine that people who describe themselves as outgoing also tend to say that they like excitement and practical jokes and dislike quiet reading. Such a statistically correlated cluster of behaviors reflects a basic factor, or trait—in this case, *extraversion.*

British psychologists Hans Eysenck and Sybil Eysenck [EYE-zink] believed that we can reduce many of our normal individual variations to two or three dimensions, including *extraversion–introversion* and *emotional stability–instability* (**FIGURE 58.1**). People in 35 countries around the world, from China to Uganda to Russia, have taken the *Eysenck Personality Questionnaire.* When their answers were analyzed, the extraversion and emotionality factors inevitably emerged as basic personality dimensions (Eysenck, 1990, 1992). The Eysencks believed that these factors are genetically influenced, and research supports this belief.

Stephen Colbert: The extravert
Trait labels such as *extraversion* can describe our temperament and typical behaviors.

Figure 58.1

Two personality dimensions
Map makers can tell us a lot by using two axes (north–south and east–west). Two primary personality factors (extraversion–introversion and stability–instability) are similarly useful as axes for describing personality variation. Varying combinations define other, more specific traits. (From Eysenck & Eysenck, 1963.) Those who are naturally introverted, such as primatologist Jane Goodall, may be particularly gifted in field studies. Successful entertainers, including recording artist Katy Perry, are often natural extraverts.

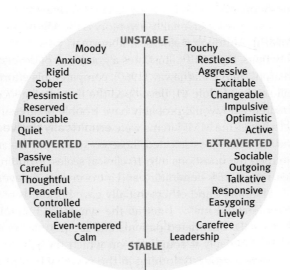

personality inventory
a questionnaire (often with *true-false* or *agree-disagree* items) on which people respond to items designed to gauge a wide range of feelings and behaviors; used to assess selected personality traits.

Minnesota Multiphasic Personality Inventory (MMPI)
the most widely researched and clinically used of all personality tests. Originally developed to identify emotional disorders (still considered its most appropriate use), this test is now used for many other screening purposes.

empirically derived test a test (such as the MMPI) developed by testing a pool of items and then selecting those that discriminate between groups.

Biology and Personality

Brain-activity scans of extraverts add to the growing list of traits and mental states that have been explored with brain-imaging procedures. (That list includes intelligence, impulsivity, addictive cravings, lying, sexual attraction, aggressiveness, empathy, spiritual experience, and even racial and political attitudes [Olson, 2005].) Such studies indicate that extraverts seek stimulation because their normal *brain arousal* is relatively low. For example, PET scans show that a frontal lobe area involved in behavior inhibition is less active in extraverts than in introverts (Johnson et al., 1999). Dopamine and dopamine-related neural activity tend to be higher in extraverts (Wacker et al., 2006).

Erik Lam/Shutterstock

Our biology influences our personality in other ways as well. As you may recall from the twin and adoption studies in Module 14, our *genes* have much to say about the behavioral style that helps define our personality. Jerome Kagan, for example, has attributed differences in children's shyness and inhibition to their *autonomic nervous system reactivity*. Given a reactive autonomic nervous system, we respond to stress with greater anxiety and inhibition. The fearless, curious child may become the rock-climbing or fast-driving adult.

Other researchers report that personality differences among dogs (in energy, affection, reactivity, and curious intelligence) are as evident, and as consistently judged, as personality differences among humans (Gosling et al., 2003; Jones & Gosling, 2005). Monkeys, chimpanzees, orangutans, and even birds also have stable personalities (Weiss et al., 2006). Among the Great Tit (a European relative of the American chickadee), bold birds more quickly inspect new objects and explore trees (Groothuis & Carere, 2005; Verbeek et al., 1994). By selective breeding, researchers can produce bold or shy birds. Both have their place in natural history. In lean years, bold birds are more likely to find food; in abundant years, shy birds feed with less risk.

Assessing Traits

 What are personality inventories, and what are their strengths and weaknesses as trait-assessment tools?

If stable and enduring traits guide our actions, can we devise valid and reliable tests of them? Several trait assessment techniques exist—some more valid than others (see Thinking Critically About: How to Be a "Successful" Astrologer or Palm Reader). Some provide quick assessments of a single trait, such as extraversion, anxiety, or self-esteem. **Personality inventories**—longer questionnaires covering a wide range of feelings and behaviors—assess several traits at once.

The classic personality inventory is the **Minnesota Multiphasic Personality Inventory (MMPI).** Although it assesses "abnormal" personality tendencies rather than normal personality traits, the MMPI illustrates a good way of developing a personality inventory. One of its creators, Starke Hathaway (1960), compared his effort with that of Alfred Binet. Binet, as you will see in Module 61, developed the first intelligence test by selecting items that identified children who would probably have trouble progressing normally in French schools. Like Binet's items, the MMPI items were **empirically derived.** From a large pool of items, Hathaway and his colleagues selected those on which particular diagnostic groups differed. They then grouped the questions into 10 clinical scales, including scales that assess depressive tendencies, masculinity–femininity, and introversion–extraversion.

Hathaway and others initially gave hundreds of true-false statements ("No one seems to understand me"; "I get all the sympathy I should"; "I like poetry") to groups of psychologically disordered patients and to "normal" people. They retained any statement—no matter how silly it sounded—on which the patient group's answer differed from that of the normal group. "Nothing in the newspaper interests me except the comics" may seem senseless, but it just so happened that depressed people were more likely to answer *True*.

Thinking Critically About

How to Be a "Successful" Astrologer or Palm Reader

> "A petite fortune-teller who escapes from prison is a small medium at large." -ANONYMOUS

Can we discern people's traits from the alignment of the stars and planets at the time of their birth? From their handwriting? From lines on their palms?

Astronomers scoff at the naiveté of astrology—the constellations have shifted in the millennia since astrologers formulated their predictions (Kelly, 1997, 1998). Humorists mock it: "No offense," writes Dave Barry, "but if you take the horoscope seriously your frontal lobes are the size of Raisinets." Psychologists instead ask questions: Does it work? Can astrologers surpass chance when given someone's birth date and asked to identify the person from a short lineup of different personality descriptions? Can people pick out their own horoscopes from a lineup of horoscopes? Do people's astrological signs correlate with predicted traits?

The consistent answers have been *No, No, No,* and *No* (British Psychological Society, 1993; Carlson, 1985; Kelly, 1997; Reichardt, 2010). For example, one researcher examined census data from 20 million married people in England and Wales and found that "astrological sign has no impact on the probability of marrying—and staying married to—someone of any other sign" (Voas, 2008).

Graphologists, who make predictions from handwriting samples, have similarly been found to do no better than chance when trying to discern people's occupations from examining several pages of their handwriting (Beyerstein & Beyerstein, 1992; Dean et al., 1992). Nevertheless, graphologists—and introductory psychology students—will often perceive correlations between personality and handwriting even where there are none (King & Koehler, 2000).

If all these perceived correlations evaporate under close scrutiny, how do astrologers, palm readers, and crystal-ball gazers persuade millions of people worldwide to buy their services? Ray Hyman (1981), palm reader turned research psychologist, has revealed some of their suckering methods.

The first technique, the "stock spiel," builds on the observation that each of us is in some ways like no one else and in other ways just like everyone. That some things are true of us all enables the "seer" to offer statements that seem impressively accurate: "I sense that you worry about things more than you let on, even to your best friends." A number of such generally true statements can be combined into a personality description. Imagine that you take a personality test and then receive the following character sketch:

You have a strong need for other people to like and to admire you. You have a tendency to be critical of yourself. . . . You pride yourself on being an independent thinker and do not accept other opinions without satisfactory proof. You have found it unwise to be too frank in revealing yourself to others. At times you are extraverted, affable, sociable; at other times you are introverted, wary, and reserved. Some of your aspirations tend to be pretty unrealistic (Davies, 1997; Forer, 1949).

In experiments, college students have received stock assessments like this one, drawn from statements in a newsstand astrology book. When they thought the bogus, generic feedback was prepared just for them and when it was favorable, they nearly always rated the description as either "good" or "excellent" (Davies, 1997). Even skeptics, given a flattering description attributed to an astrologer, begin to think that "maybe there's something to this astrology stuff after all" (Glick et al., 1989). An astrologer, it has been said, is someone "prepared to tell you what you think of yourself" (Jones, 2000). This acceptance of stock, positive descriptions is called the *Barnum effect,* named in honor of master showman P. T. Barnum's dictum, "We've got something for everyone."

A second technique used by seers is to "read" our clothing, physical features, gestures, and reactions. An expensive wedding ring and black dress might, for example, suggest a wealthy woman who was recently widowed.

(continued)

Thinking Critically About (continued)

You, too, could read such clues, says Hyman. If people seek you out for a reading, start with some safe sympathy: "I sense you're having some problems lately. You seem unsure what to do. I get the feeling another person is involved." Then tell them what they want to hear. Memorize some Barnum statements from astrology and fortune-telling manuals and use them liberally. Tell people it is their responsibility to cooperate by relating your message to their specific experiences. Later they will recall that you predicted those specific details. Phrase statements as questions, and when you detect a positive response assert the statement strongly. Finally, be a good listener, and later, in different words, reveal to people what they earlier revealed to you. If you dupe them, they will come.

Better yet, beware of those who, by exploiting people with these techniques, are fortune takers rather than fortune tellers.

"Perhaps you'd like a second opinion?"

(Nevertheless, people have had fun spoofing the MMPI with their own mock items: "Weeping brings tears to my eyes," "Frantic screams make me nervous," and "I stay in the bathtub until I look like a raisin" [Frankel et al., 1983].) Today's MMPI-2 also has scales assessing, for instance, work attitudes, family problems, and anger.

In contrast to the subjectivity of most projective tests, personality inventories are scored objectively—so objectively that a computer can administer and score them. (The computer can also provide descriptions of people who previously responded similarly.) Objectivity does not, however, guarantee validity. For example, individuals taking the MMPI for employment purposes can give socially desirable answers to create a good impression. But in so doing they may also score high on a *lie scale* that assesses faking (as when people respond *false* to a universally true statement such as "I get angry sometimes"). The objectivity of the MMPI has contributed to its popularity and to its translation into more than 100 languages.

The Big Five Factors

 58-3 Which traits seem to provide the most useful information about personality variation?

Today's trait researchers believe that simple trait factors, such as the Eysencks' introverted–extraverted and unstable–stable dimensions, are important, but they do not tell the whole story. A slightly expanded set of factors—dubbed the *Big Five*—does a better job (Costa & McCrae, 2009). Work by Paul Costa, Robert McCrae, and others shows that where we fall on these five dimensions (conscientiousness, agreeableness, neuroticism, openness, and extraversion; see **TABLE 58.1**), reveals much of what there is to say about our personality. Around the world—across 56 nations and 29 languages in one study (Schmitt et al., 2007)—people describe others in terms roughly consistent with this list. The Big Five may not be the last word. (Some researchers report it takes only two or three factors—such as conscientiousness, agreeableness, and extraversion—to describe the basic personality dimensions [Block, 2010; De Raad et al., 2010].) But for now, at least, five is the winning number in the personality lottery (Heine & Buchtel, 2009; McCrae, 2009). The Big Five—today's "common currency for personality psychology" (Funder, 2001)—has been the most active personality research topic since the early 1990s and is currently our best approximation of the basic trait dimensions.

Table 58.1 The "Big Five" Personality Factors

(*Memory tip:* Picturing a CANOE will help you recall these.)

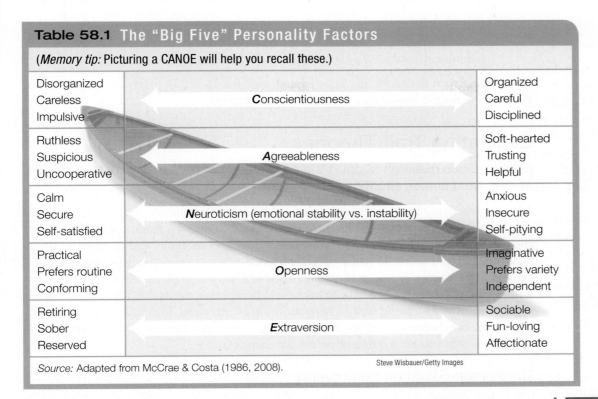

Disorganized Careless Impulsive	**C**onscientiousness	Organized Careful Disciplined
Ruthless Suspicious Uncooperative	**A**greeableness	Soft-hearted Trusting Helpful
Calm Secure Self-satisfied	**N**euroticism (emotional stability vs. instability)	Anxious Insecure Self-pitying
Practical Prefers routine Conforming	**O**penness	Imaginative Prefers variety Independent
Retiring Sober Reserved	**E**xtraversion	Sociable Fun-loving Affectionate

Source: Adapted from McCrae & Costa (1986, 2008).   Steve Wisbauer/Getty Images

Big Five research has explored various questions:

- **How stable are these traits?** In adulthood, the Big Five traits are quite stable, with some tendencies (emotional instability, extraversion, and openness) waning a bit during early and middle adulthood, and others (agreeableness and conscientiousness) rising (McCrae, 2011; Vaidya et al., 2002). Conscientiousness increases the most during people's twenties, as people mature and learn to manage their jobs and relationships. Agreeableness increases the most during people's thirties and continues to increase through their sixties (Srivastava et al., 2003).

- **How heritable are they?** Heritability (the extent to which individual differences are attributable to genes) varies with the diversity of people studied, but it generally runs 50 percent or a tad more for each dimension, and genetic influences are similar in different nations (Loehlin et al., 1998; Yamagata et al., 2006). Many genes, each having small effects, combine to influence our traits (McCrae et al., 2010). Researchers have also identified brain areas associated with the various Big Five traits, such as a frontal lobe area that is sensitive to reward and is larger in extraverts (DeYoung et al., 2010).

- **Do the Big Five traits predict our actual behaviors?** Yes. If people report being outgoing, conscientious, and agreeable, "they probably are telling the truth," reports Big Five researcher Robert McCrae (2011). Here are some examples:
  - Shy introverts are more likely than extraverts to prefer communicating by e-mail rather than face-to-face (Hertel et al., 2008).
  - Highly conscientious people earn better high school and university grades (Poropat, 2009). They also are more likely to be morning types (sometimes called "larks"); evening types ("owls") are marginally more extraverted (Jackson & Gerard, 1996).
  - If one partner scores lower than the other on agreeableness, stability, and openness, marital and sexual satisfaction may suffer (Botwin et al., 1997; Donnellan et al., 2004).

> **AP® Exam Tip**
>
> Table 58.1 is an excellent summary of the Big Five personality factors and what they mean.

- Our traits infuse our language. In text messaging, extraversion predicts use of personal pronouns, agreeableness predicts positive-emotion words, and neuroticism (emotional instability) predicts negative-emotion words (Holtgraves, 2011).

By exploring such questions, Big Five research has sustained trait psychology and renewed appreciation for the importance of personality. Traits matter.

Evaluating Trait Theories

58-4 Does research support the consistency of personality traits over time and across situations?

Are our personality traits stable and enduring? Or does our behavior depend on where and with whom we find ourselves? J.R.R. Tolkien created characters, like the loyal Sam Gamgee, whose personality traits were consistent across various times and places. The Italian playwright Luigi Pirandello had a different view. For him, personality was ever-changing, tailored to the particular role or situation. In one of Pirandello's plays, Lamberto Laudisi describes himself: "I am really what you take me to be; though, my dear madam, that does not prevent me from also being really what your husband, my sister, my niece, and Signora Cini take me to be—because they also are absolutely right!" To which Signora Sirelli responds, "In other words you are a different person for each of us."

The Person-Situation Controversy

Who, then, typifies human personality, Tolkien's consistent Sam Gamgee or Pirandello's inconsistent Laudisi? Both. Our behavior is influenced by the interaction of our inner disposition with our environment. Still, the question lingers: Which is more important? Are we *more* as Tolkien or as Pirandello imagined us to be?

When we explore this *person-situation controversy,* we look for genuine personality traits that persist over time *and* across situations. Are some people dependably conscientious and others unreliable, some cheerful and others dour, some friendly and outgoing and others shy? If we are to consider friendliness a trait, friendly people must act friendly at different times and places. Do they?

In earlier chapters, we considered research that has followed lives through time. We noted that some scholars (especially those who study infants) are impressed with personality change; others are struck by personality stability during adulthood. As **FIGURE 58.2** illustrates, data from 152 long-term studies reveal that personality trait scores are positively correlated with scores obtained seven years later, and that as people grow older their personality stabilizes. Interests may change—the avid collector of tropical fish may become an avid gardener. Careers may change—the determined salesperson may become a determined social worker. Relationships may change—the hostile spouse may start over with a

> "There is as much difference between us and ourselves, as between us and others."- MICHEL DE MONTAIGNE, *ESSAYS*, 1588

FYI

Roughly speaking, the temporary, external influences on behavior are the focus of social psychology, and the enduring, inner influences are the focus of personality psychology. In actuality, behavior always depends on the interaction of persons with situations.

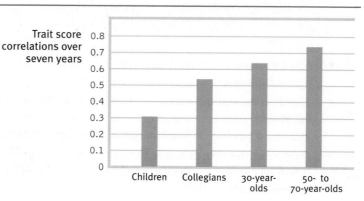

Figure 58.2

Personality stability With age, personality traits become more stable, as reflected in the stronger correlation of trait scores with follow-up scores seven years later. (Data from Roberts & DelVecchio, 2000.)

new partner. But most people recognize their traits as their own, note Robert McCrae and Paul Costa (1994), "and it is well that they do. A person's recognition of the inevitability of his or her one and only personality is . . . the culminating wisdom of a lifetime."

So most people—including most psychologists—would probably side with Tolkien's assumption of stability of personality traits. Moreover, our traits are socially significant. They influence our health, our thinking, and our job performance (Deary & Matthews, 1993; Hogan, 1998). Studies that follow lives through time show that personality traits rival socioeconomic status and cognitive ability as predictors of mortality, divorce, and occupational attainment (Roberts et al., 2007).

Although our personality *traits* may be both stable and potent, the consistency of our specific *behaviors* from one situation to the next is another matter. As Walter Mischel (1968, 2009) has pointed out, people do not act with predictable consistency. Mischel's studies of college students' conscientiousness revealed but a modest relationship between a student's being conscientious on one occasion (say, showing up for class on time) and being similarly conscientious on another occasion (say, turning in assignments on time). Pirandello would not have been surprised. If you've noticed how outgoing you are in some situations and how reserved you are in others, perhaps you're not surprised either (though for certain traits, Mischel reports, you may accurately assess yourself as more consistent).

This inconsistency in behaviors also makes personality test scores weak predictors of behaviors. People's scores on an extraversion test, for example, do not neatly predict how sociable they actually will be on any given occasion. If we remember such results, says Mischel, we will be more cautious about labeling and pigeonholing individuals. Years in advance, science can tell us the phase of the Moon for any given date. A day in advance, meteorologists can often predict the weather. But we are much further from being able to predict how *you* will feel and act tomorrow.

However, people's *average* outgoingness, happiness, or carelessness over many situations is predictable (Epstein, 1983a,b). When rating someone's shyness or agreeableness, this consistency enables people who know someone well to agree on their ratings (Kenrick & Funder, 1988). By collecting snippets of people's daily experience via body-worn recording devices, Matthias Mehl and his colleagues (2006) confirmed that extraverts really do talk more. (I have repeatedly vowed to cut back on my jabbering and joking during my noontime pickup basketball games with friends. Alas, moments later, the irrepressible chatterbox inevitably reoccupies my body.) As our best friends can verify, we do have genetically influenced personality traits. And those traits even lurk in our

- *music preferences.* Classical, jazz, blues, and folk music lovers tend to be open to experience and verbally intelligent; country, pop, and religious music lovers tend to be cheerful, outgoing, and conscientious (Rentfrow & Gosling, 2003, 2006). On first meeting, students often disclose their music preferences to one another; in doing so, they are swapping information about their personalities.

- *bedrooms and offices.* Our personal spaces display our identity and leave a behavioral residue (in our scattered laundry or neat desktop). And that helps explain why just a few minutes' inspection of our living and working spaces can enable someone to assess with reasonable accuracy our conscientiousness, our openness to new experiences, and even our emotional stability (Gosling et al., 2002, 2008).

"Mr. Coughlin over there was the founder of one of the first motorcycle gangs."

"I'm going to France—I'm a different person in France."

ICP-UK/Alamy

Joe Baraban/Alamy

Room with a cue Even at "zero acquaintance," people can discern something of others' personality from glimpsing their website, bedroom, or office.

- *personal websites.* Is a personal website or an online profile also a canvas for self-expression? Or is it an opportunity for people to present themselves in false or misleading ways? It's more the former (Back et al., 2010; Gosling et al., 2007; Marcus et al., 2006). Visitors to personal websites quickly gain important clues to the creator's extraversion, conscientiousness, and openness to experience. Even mere pictures of people, and their associated clothes, expressions, and postures, can give clues to personality (Naumann et al., 2009).

- *electronic communication.* If you have ever felt you could detect others' personality from their writing voice, you are right!! (What a cool, exciting finding!!!) People's ratings of others' personalities based solely on their e-mails or blogs correlate with actual personality scores on measures such as extraversion and neuroticism (Gill et al., 2006; Oberlander & Gill, 2006; Yarkoni, 2010). Extraverts, for example, use more adjectives.

In unfamiliar, formal situations—perhaps as a guest in the home of a person from another culture—our traits remain hidden as we carefully attend to social cues. In familiar, informal situations—just hanging out with friends—we feel less constrained, allowing our traits to emerge (Buss, 1989). In these informal situations, our expressive styles—our animation, manner of speaking, and gestures—are impressively consistent. That's why those very thin slices of someone's behavior—even just three 2-second clips of a teacher—can be revealing (Ambady & Rosenthal, 1992, 1993).

Some people are naturally expressive (and therefore talented at pantomime and charades); others are less expressive (and therefore better poker players). To evaluate people's voluntary control over their expressiveness, researchers asked people to *act* as expressive or inhibited as possible while stating opinions (DePaulo et al., 1992). The remarkable findings: Inexpressive people, even when feigning expressiveness, were less expressive than expressive people acting naturally. Similarly, expressive people, even when trying to seem inhibited, were less inhibited than inexpressive people acting naturally. It's hard to be someone you're not, or not to be who you are.

To sum up, we can say that at any moment the immediate situation powerfully influences a person's behavior. Social psychologists have assumed, albeit without much evidence, that this is especially so when a "strong situation" makes clear demands (Cooper & Withey, 2009). We can better predict drivers' behavior at traffic lights from knowing the color of the lights than from knowing the drivers' personalities. Thus, professors may perceive certain students as subdued (based on their classroom behavior), but friends may perceive them as pretty wild (based on their party behavior). Averaging our behavior across many occasions does, however, reveal distinct personality traits. Traits exist. We differ. And our differences matter.

Before You Move On

▶ **ASK YOURSELF**

Where would you place yourself on the five personality dimensions—conscientiousness, agreeableness, neuroticism (emotional stability versus instability), openness, and extraversion? Where might your family and friends place you?

▶ **TEST YOURSELF**

What is the person-situation controversy?

Answers to the Test Yourself questions can be found in Appendix E at the end of the book.

Module 58 Review

 58-1 How do psychologists use traits to describe personality?

- *Trait* theorists see personality as a stable and enduring pattern of behavior. They describe our differences rather than trying to explain them.

- Using factor analysis, they identify clusters of behavior tendencies that occur together. Genetic predispositions influence many traits.

58-2 What are personality inventories, and what are their strengths and weaknesses as trait-assessment tools?

- *Personality inventories* (such as the *MMPI*) are questionnaires on which people respond to items designed to gauge a wide range of feelings and behaviors.

- Test items are *empirically derived,* and the tests are objectively scored. But people can fake their answers to create a good impression, and the ease of computerized testing may lead to misuse of the tests.

 58-3 Which traits seem to provide the most useful information about personality variation?

- The Big Five personality factors—conscientiousness, agreeableness, neuroticism, openness, and extraversion (CANOE)—currently offer the clearest picture of personality. These factors are stable and appear to be found in all cultures.

58-4 Does research support the consistency of personality traits over time and across situations?

- A person's average traits persist over time and are predictable over many different situations. But traits cannot predict behavior in any one particular situation.

Multiple-Choice Questions

1. Which of the following is the best term or phrase for a characteristic pattern of behavior or a disposition to feel and act?
   a. Myers-Briggs Indicator
   b. Factor analysis
   c. Introversion
   d. Extroversion
   e. Trait

2. Which of the following is a "Big Five" personality factor?
   a. Seriousness
   b. Neuroticism
   c. Dutifulness
   d. Dominance
   e. Abstractedness

3. Which of the following is best described along a continuum ranging from ruthless and suspicious to helpful and trusting?
   a. Conscientiousness
   b. Agreeableness
   c. Openness
   d. Extraversion
   e. Perfectionism

4. Which of the following is true based on "Big Five" personality traits research?
   a. Highly conscientious people are likely to be evening people or "owls."
   b. Highly conscientious people get poor grades.
   c. Married partners scoring the same on agreeableness are more likely to experience marital dissatisfaction.
   d. Shy introverts are more likely to prefer communicating through e-mail instead of in person.
   e. Neuroticism predicts the use of positive-emotion words in text messages.

Practice FRQs

1. Explain one weakness and one strength of the Minnesota Multiphasic Personality Inventory (MMPI).

Answer

1 point: One point for any strength (for example, the MMPI is empirically derived, assesses several traits at once, or is easily scored).

1 point: One point for any weakness (for example, the MMPI test-taker might not answer honestly, or validity is not guaranteed).

2. Explain Hans and Sybil Eysenck's personality dimensions.

(4 points)

Module 59

Social-Cognitive Theories and Exploring the Self

Module Learning Objectives

59-1 Identify the psychologist who first proposed the social-cognitive perspective, and describe how social-cognitive theorists view personality development.

59-2 Describe how social-cognitive researchers explore behavior, and state the criticism they have faced.

59-3 Explain why psychology has generated so much research on the self, and discuss the importance of self-esteem to psychology and to human well-being.

59-4 Discuss some evidence for self-serving bias, and contrast defensive and secure self-esteem.

59-5 Discuss how individualist and collectivist cultures influence people.

Social-Cognitive Theories

59-1 Who first proposed the social-cognitive perspective, and how do social-cognitive theorists view personality development?

Today's psychological science views individuals as biopsychosocial organisms. The **social-cognitive perspective** on personality proposed by Albert Bandura (1986, 2006, 2008) emphasizes the interaction of our traits with our situations. Much as nature and nurture always work together, so do individuals and their situations.

Those who take the **behavioral approach** to personality development emphasize the effects of learning. We are conditioned to repeat certain behaviors, and we learn by observing and imitating others. For example, a child with a very controlling parent may learn to follow orders rather than think independently, and may exhibit a more timid personality.

Social-cognitive theorists do consider the behavioral perspective, including others' influence. (That's the "social" part.) However, they also emphasize the importance of mental processes: What we *think* about our situations affects our behavior. (That's the "cognitive" part.) Instead of focusing solely on how our environment *controls* us, as behaviorists do, social-cognitive theorists focus on how we and our environment *interact:* How do we interpret and respond to external events? How do our schemas, our memories, and our expectations influence our behavior patterns?

social-cognitive perspective
views behavior as influenced by the interaction between people's traits (including their thinking) and their social context.

behavioral approach
in personality theory, this perspective focuses on the effects of learning on our personality development.

reciprocal determinism
the interacting influences of behavior, internal cognition, and environment.

Reciprocal Influences

Bandura (1986, 2006) views the person-environment interaction as **reciprocal determinism.** "Behavior, internal personal factors, and environmental influences," he said, "all operate as interlocking determinants of each other" (**FIGURE 59.1**). For example, children's TV-viewing habits (past behavior) influence their viewing preferences (internal factor), which influence how television (environmental factor) affects their current behavior. The influences are mutual.

Figure 59.1

Reciprocal determinism
The social-cognitive perspective proposes that our personalities are shaped by the interaction of our personal traits (including our thoughts and feelings), our environment, and our behaviors.

Courtesy of Joslyn Brugh

Internal personal factors (thoughts and feelings about risky activities)

Behavior (learning to rock climb)

Environmental factors (rock-climbing friends)

Consider three specific ways in which individuals and environments interact:

1. *Different people choose different environments.* The school you attend, the reading you do, the TV programs you watch, the music you listen to, the friends you associate with—all are part of an environment you participated in choosing, based partly on your dispositions (Funder, 2009; Ickes et al., 1997). You choose your environment and it then shapes you.

2. *Our personalities shape how we interpret and react to events.* Anxious people, for example, are attuned to potentially threatening events (Eysenck et al., 1987). Thus, they perceive the world as threatening, and they react accordingly.

3. *Our personalities help create situations to which we react.* Many experiments reveal that how we view and treat people influences how they in turn treat us. If we expect someone to be angry with us, we may give the person a cold shoulder, touching off the very anger we expect. If we have an easygoing, positive disposition, we will likely enjoy close, supportive friendships (Donnellan et al., 2005; Kendler, 1997).

Figure 59.2

The biopsychosocial approach to the study of personality As with other psychological phenomena, personality is fruitfully studied at multiple levels.

In such ways, we are both the products and the architects of our environments.

If all this has a familiar ring, it may be because it parallels and reinforces a pervasive theme in psychology and in this book: *Behavior emerges from the interplay of external and internal influences.* Boiling water turns an egg hard and a potato soft. A threatening environment turns one person into a hero, another into a scoundrel. Extraverts enjoy greater well-being in an extraverted culture than an introverted one (Fulmer et al., 2010). *At every moment,* our behavior is influenced by our biology, our social and cultural experiences, and our cognition and dispositions (**FIGURE 59.2**).

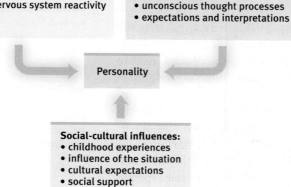

Biological influences:
• genetically determined temperament
• autonomic nervous system reactivity
• brain activity

Psychological influences:
• learned responses
• unconscious thought processes
• expectations and interpretations

Personality

Social-cultural influences:
• childhood experiences
• influence of the situation
• cultural expectations
• social support

Optimism Versus Pessimism

Recall from Module 29 that we learn to cope with life's challenges in various ways. In studying how we interact with our environment, social-cognitive psychologists emphasize our sense of *personal control*—whether we learn to see ourselves as controlling, or as controlled by, our environment. One measure of how helpless or effective you feel is where you stand on optimism-pessimism. How do you characteristically explain negative and positive events? Perhaps you have known students whose *attributional style* is pessimistic—who attribute poor performance to their lack of ability ("I can't do this") or to situations enduringly beyond their control ("There is nothing I can do about it"). Such students are more likely to continue getting low grades than are students who adopt the more hopeful attitude that effort, good study habits, and self-discipline can make a difference (Noel et al., 1987; Peterson & Barrett, 1987). Mere fantasies do not fuel motivation and success. Realistic positive expectations do (Oettingen & Mayer, 2002).

Attributional style also matters when dating couples wrestle with conflicts. Optimists and their partners see each other as engaging constructively, and they then tend to feel more supported and satisfied with the resolution and with their relationship (Srivastava et al., 2006). Expect good things from others, and often you will get what you expect. Such studies helped point Martin Seligman toward proposing a more positive psychology (see Close-up: Toward a More Positive Psychology on the next page).

Positive expectations often motivate eventual success.

"We just haven't been flapping them hard enough."

EXCESSIVE OPTIMISM

Positive thinking in the face of adversity can pay dividends, but so, too, can a dash of realism (Schneider, 2001). Realistic anxiety over possible future failures can fuel energetic efforts to avoid the dreaded fate (Goodhart, 1986; Norem, 2001; Showers, 1992). Concerned about failing an upcoming test, students may study thoroughly and outperform their equally able but more confident peers. Asian-American students express somewhat greater pessimism than their European-American counterparts, which Edward Chang (2001) suspects helps explain their often impressive academic achievements. Success requires enough optimism to provide hope and enough pessimism to prevent complacency. We want our airline pilots to be mindful of worst-possible outcomes.

Excessive optimism can blind us to real risks. Neil Weinstein (1980, 1982, 1996) has shown how our natural positive-thinking bias can promote "an unrealistic optimism about future life events." Most late adolescents see themselves as much less vulnerable than their peers to the HIV virus that causes AIDS (Abrams, 1991). Most college students perceive themselves as less likely than their average classmate to develop drinking problems, drop out of school, have a heart attack by age 40, or go deeply into debt on their high-interest credit cards (Yang et al., 2006). If overconfident of our ability to control an impulse such as the urge to smoke, we are more likely to expose ourselves to temptations—and to fail (Nordgren et al., 2009). Those who optimistically deny the power and effects of smoking or venture into ill-fated relationships remind us that blind optimism can be self-defeating.

People also display illusory optimism about their groups. Throughout a National Football League season, fans of all teams correctly guessed that other teams would win about 50 percent of the games. But they incorrectly guessed, on average (across teams and weeks), that their own team stood about a 2 in 3 chance of winning (Massey et al., 2011). This optimistic and illogical bias persisted despite their team's experience and monetary incentives for accuracy.

Our natural positive-thinking bias does seem to vanish, however, when we are bracing ourselves for feedback, such as test results (Carroll et al., 2006). (Have you ever noticed that, as a big game nears its end, the outcome seems more in doubt when your team is ahead than when it is behind?) Positive illusions also vanish after a traumatic personal experience—as they did for victims of a catastrophic California earthquake, who had to give up their illusions of being less vulnerable than others to earthquakes (Helweg-Larsen, 1999).

Close-up

Toward a More Positive Psychology

During its first century, psychology understandably focused much of its attention on understanding and alleviating negative states. Psychologists have studied abuse and anxiety, depression and disease, prejudice and poverty. Since 1887, articles on selected negative emotions have outnumbered those on positive emotions by 17 to 1.

In ages past, notes American Psychological Association past-president Martin Seligman (2002), times of relative peace and prosperity have enabled cultures to turn their attention from repairing weakness and damage to promoting "the highest qualities of life." Prosperous fifth-century Athens nurtured philosophy and democracy. Flourishing fifteenth-century Florence nurtured great art. Victorian England, flush with the bounty of the British Empire, nurtured honor, discipline, and duty. In this millennium, Seligman believes, thriving Western cultures have a parallel opportunity to create, as a "humane, scientific monument," a more **positive psychology**—a psychology concerned not only with weakness and damage but also with strength and virtue. Thanks to his own leadership, the new positive psychology movement has gained strength, with supporters in 77 countries from Croatia to China (IPPA, 2009, 2010; Seligman, 2004, 2011).

Positive psychology shares with humanistic psychology an interest in advancing human fulfillment, but its methodology is scientific. Positive psychology science is exploring

- *positive well-being*—which assesses exercises and interventions aimed at increasing happiness (Schueller, 2010; Sin & Lyubomirsky, 2009),

- *positive health*—which studies how positive emotions enhance and sustain physical well-being (Seligman, 2008; Seligman et al., 2011),

- *positive neuroscience*—which explores the biological foundations of positive emotions, resilience, and social behavior (www.posneuroscience.org), and

- *positive education*—which evaluates educational efforts to increase students' engagement, resilience, character strengths, optimism, and sense of meaning (Seligman et al., 2009).

"Positive psychology," say Seligman and colleagues (2005), "is an umbrella term for the study of positive emotions, positive character traits, and enabling institutions." Taken together, satisfaction with the past, happiness with the present, and optimism about the future define the movement's first pillar: *positive emotions.* Happiness, Seligman argues, is a by-product of a pleasant, engaged, and meaningful life.

Courtesy of Martin E. P. Seligman

Martin E. P. Seligman "The main purpose of a positive psychology is to measure, understand, and then build the human strengths and the civic virtues."

Positive psychology is about building not just a pleasant life, says Seligman, but also a good life that engages one's skills, and a meaningful life that points beyond oneself. Thus, the second pillar, *positive character,* focuses on exploring and enhancing creativity, courage, compassion, integrity, self-control, leadership, wisdom, and spirituality.

The third pillar, *positive groups, communities, and cultures,* seeks to foster a positive social ecology. This includes healthy families, communal neighborhoods, effective schools, socially responsible media, and civil dialogue.

Will psychology have a more positive mission in this century? Without slighting the need to repair damage and cure disease, positive psychology's proponents hope so. With *American Psychologist* and British *Psychologist* special issues devoted to positive psychology; with many new books; with networked scientists working in worldwide research groups; and with prizes, research awards, summer institutes, and a graduate program promoting positive psychology scholarship, these psychologists have reason to be positive.

positive psychology the scientific study of optimal human functioning; aims to discover and promote strengths and virtues that enable individuals and communities to thrive.

BLINDNESS TO ONE'S OWN INCOMPETENCE

Ironically, people often are most overconfident when most incompetent. That, say some researchers, is because it often takes competence to recognize competence (Kruger & Dunning, 1999). They found that most students scoring at the low end of grammar and logic tests believed they had scored in the top half. If you do not know what good grammar is, you may be unaware that your grammar is poor. This "ignorance of one's own incompetence" phenomenon has a parallel, as I can confirm, in hard-of-hearing people's difficulty recognizing their own hearing loss. We're not so much "in denial" as we are simply unaware of what we don't hear. If I fail to hear my friend calling my name, the friend notices my inattention. But for me it's a nonevent. I hear what I hear—which, to me, seems pretty normal.

The difficulty in recognizing one's own incompetence helps explain why so many low-scoring students are dumbfounded after doing badly on a test. If you don't know all the Scrabble word possibilities you've overlooked, you may feel pretty smart—until someone points them out. As experiments that re-create this phenomenon have demonstrated, our ignorance of what we don't know helps sustain our confidence in our own abilities (Caputo & Dunning, 2005). Once part of our self-concept, our self-assessments also influence how we perceive our performance. Thinking we're good at something drives how we perceive ourselves doing (Critcher & Dunning, 2009).

> "The living-room [Scrabble] player is lucky. . . . He has no idea how miserably he fails with almost every turn, how many possible words or optimal plays slip by unnoticed." -Stefan Fatsis, *Word Freak*, 2001

DOONESBURY

To judge one's competence and predict one's future performance, it pays to invite others' assessments (Dunning, 2006). Based on studies in which both individuals and their acquaintances predict their future, we can hazard some advice: If you're an AP® psychology student preparing for the exam, and you want to predict how well you will do, don't rate yourself—ask your teacher for a candid evaluation. If you're a Naval officer and need to assess your leadership ability—don't rate yourself, ask your fellow officers. And if you're in love and want to predict whether it will last, don't listen to your heart—ask your friends.

Assessing Behavior in Situations

59-2 How do social-cognitive researchers explore behavior, and what criticism have they faced?

Social-cognitive psychologists explore how people interact with situations. To predict behavior, they often observe behavior in realistic situations.

Assessing behavior in situations Reality TV shows, such as Donald Trump's *The Apprentice*, may take "show me" job interviews to the extreme, but they do illustrate a valid point. Seeing how a potential employee behaves in a job-relevant situation helps predict job performance.

One ambitious example was the U.S. Army's World War II strategy for assessing candidates for spy missions. Rather than using paper-and-pencil tests, Army psychologists subjected the candidates to simulated undercover conditions. They tested their ability to handle stress, solve problems, maintain leadership, and withstand intense interrogation without blowing their cover. Although time-consuming and expensive, this assessment of behavior in a realistic situation helped predict later success on actual spy missions (OSS Assessment Staff, 1948). Modern studies indicate that assessment center exercises are more revealing of visible dimensions, such as communication ability, than others, such as inner achievement drive (Bowler & Woehr, 2006).

Military and educational organizations and many Fortune 500 companies are adopting assessment center strategies (Bray et al., 1991, 1997; Eurich et al., 2009). AT&T has observed prospective managers doing simulated managerial work. Student teachers are observed and evaluated several times during the term they spend in your school. Many colleges assess students' potential via internships and student teaching and assess potential faculty members' teaching abilities by observing them teach. Armies assess their soldiers by observing them during military exercises. Most American cities with populations of 50,000 or more have used assessment centers in evaluating police officers and firefighters (Lowry, 1997).

These procedures exploit the principle that the best means of predicting future behavior is neither a personality test nor an interviewer's intuition. Rather, it is *the person's past behavior patterns in similar situations* (Mischel, 1981; Ouellette & Wood, 1998; Schmidt & Hunter, 1998). As long as the situation and the person remain much the same, the best predictor of future job performance is past job performance; the best predictor of future grades is past grades; the best predictor of future aggressiveness is past aggressiveness; the best predictor of drug use in young adulthood is drug use in high school. If you can't check the person's past behavior, the next-best thing is to create an assessment situation that simulates the task so you can see how the person handles it (Lievens et al., 2009; Meriac et al., 2008).

Evaluating Social-Cognitive Theories

Social-cognitive theories of personality sensitize researchers to how situations affect, and are affected by, individuals. More than other personality theories, they build from psychological research on learning and cognition. (See **TABLE 59.1** for a comparison of personality theories.)

Critics charge that social-cognitive theories focus so much on the situation that they fail to appreciate the person's inner traits. Where is the person in this view of personality, ask the dissenters, and where are human emotions? True, the situation does guide our behavior. But, say the critics, in many instances our unconscious motives, our emotions, and our pervasive traits shine through. Personality traits have been shown to predict behavior at work, love, and play. Our biologically influenced traits really do matter. Consider Percy Ray Pridgen and Charles Gill. Each faced the same situation: They had jointly won a $90 million lottery jackpot (Harriston, 1993). When Pridgen learned of the winning numbers, he began trembling uncontrollably, huddled with a friend behind a bathroom door while confirming the win, then sobbed. When Gill heard the news, he told his wife and then went to sleep.

* * *

As we have seen, researchers investigate personality using various methods that serve differing purposes. For a synopsis and comparison of these methods, see **TABLE 59.2**.

Table 59.1 Comparing the Major Personality Theories

Personality Theory	Key Proponents	Assumptions	View of Personality
Psychoanalytic	Freud	Emotional disorders spring from unconscious dynamics, such as unresolved sexual and other childhood conflicts, and fixation at various developmental stages. Defense mechanisms fend off anxiety.	Personality consists of pleasure-seeking impulses (the id), a reality-oriented executive (the ego), and an internalized set of ideals (the superego).
Psychodynamic	Adler, Horney, Jung	The unconscious and conscious minds interact. Childhood experiences and defense mechanisms are important.	The dynamic interplay of conscious and unconscious motives and conflicts shape our personality.
Humanistic	Rogers, Maslow	Rather than examining the struggles of sick people, it's better to focus on the ways people strive for self-realization.	If our basic human needs are met, people will strive toward self-actualization. In a climate of unconditional positive regard, we can develop self-awareness and a more realistic and positive self-concept.
Trait	Allport, Eysenck, McCrae, Costa	We have certain stable and enduring characteristics, influenced by genetic predispositions.	Scientific study of traits has isolated important dimensions of personality, such as the Big Five traits (conscientiousness, agreeableness, neuroticism, openness, and extraversion).
Social-Cognitive	Bandura	Our traits and the social context interact to produce our behaviors.	Conditioning and observational learning interact with cognition to create behavior patterns.

Table 59.2 Comparing Research Methods to Investigate Personality

Research Method	Description	Perspectives Incorporating This Method	Benefits	Weaknesses
Case study	In-depth study of one individual.	Psychoanalytic, humanistic	Less expensive than other methods.	May not generalize to the larger population.
Survey	Systematic questioning of a random sample of the population.	Trait, social-cognitive, positive psychology	Results tend to be reliable and can be generalized to the larger population.	May be expensive; correlational findings.
Projective tests (e.g., TAT and Rorschach)	Ambiguous stimuli designed to trigger projection of inner dynamics.	Psychodynamic	Designed to get beneath the conscious surface of a person's self-understanding; may be a good ice-breaker.	Results have weak validity and reliability.
Personality inventories, such as the MMPI (to determine scores on Big Five personality factors)	Objectively scored groups of questions designed to identify personality dispositions.	Trait	Generally reliable and empirically validated.	Explore limited number of traits.
Observation	Studying how individuals react in different situations.	Social-cognitive	Allows researchers to study the effects of environmental factors on the way an individual's personality is expressed.	Results may not apply to the larger population.
Experimentation	Manipulate variables, with random assignment to conditions.	Social-cognitive	Discerns cause and effect.	Some variables cannot feasibly or ethically be manipulated.

Before You Move On

▶ **ASK YOURSELF**

Are you a pessimist? Do you tend to have low expectations and to attribute bad events to your inability or to circumstances beyond your control? Or are you an optimist, perhaps even being excessively optimistic at times? How has either tendency influenced your choices thus far?

▶ **TEST YOURSELF**

What do social-cognitive psychologists consider the best way to predict a person's future behavior?

Answers to the Test Yourself questions can be found in Appendix E at the end of the book.

self in contemporary psychology, assumed to be the center of personality, the organizer of our thoughts, feelings, and actions.

spotlight effect overestimating others' noticing and evaluating our appearance, performance, and blunders (as if we presume a spotlight shines on us).

Exploring the Self

59-3 Why has psychology generated so much research on the self? How important is self-esteem to psychology and to human well-being?

Psychology's concern with people's sense of self dates back at least to William James, who devoted more than 100 pages of his 1890 *Principles of Psychology* to the topic. By 1943, Gordon Allport lamented that the self had become "lost to view." Although humanistic psychology's later emphasis on the self did not instigate much scientific research, it did help renew the concept of self and keep it alive. Now, more than a century after James, the self is one of Western psychology's most vigorously researched topics. Every year, new studies galore appear on self-esteem, self-disclosure, self-awareness, self-schemas, self-monitoring, and so forth. Even neuroscientists have searched for self, by identifying a central frontal lobe region that activates when people respond to self-reflective questions about their traits and dispositions (Damasio, 2010; Mitchell, 2009). Underlying this research is an assumption that the **self,** as organizer of our thoughts, feelings, and actions, is the center of personality.

One example of thinking about self is the concept of possible selves put forth by Hazel Markus and her colleagues (Cross & Markus, 1991; Markus & Nurius, 1986). Your possible selves include your visions of the self you dream of becoming—the rich self, the successful self, the loved and admired self. They also include the self you fear becoming—the unemployed self, the lonely self, the academically failed self. Such possible selves motivate us by laying out specific goals and calling forth the energy to work toward them. University of Michigan students in a combined undergraduate/medical school program earn higher grades if they undergo the program with a clear vision of themselves as successful doctors. Dreams do often give birth to achievements.

Our self-focused perspective may motivate us, but it can also lead us to presume too readily that others are noticing and evaluating us. Thomas Gilovich (1996) demonstrated this **spotlight effect** by having individual Cornell University students don Barry Manilow T-shirts before entering a room with other students. Feeling self-conscious (even in the 1990s, singer Barry Manilow was not cool), the T-shirt wearers guessed that nearly half their peers would take note of the shirt as they walked in. In reality, only 23 percent did. This absence of attention applies not only to our dorky clothes and bad hair but also to our nervousness, irritation, or attraction: Fewer

Possible selves By giving them a chance to try out many possible selves, pretend games offer children important opportunities to develop emotionally, socially, and cognitively. This young girl may or may not grow up to be a physician, but playing adult roles will certainly bear fruit in terms of an expanded vision of what she might become.

"The first step to better times is to imagine them." -CHINESE FORTUNE COOKIE people notice than we presume (Gilovich & Savitsky, 1999). Others are also less aware than we suppose of the variability—the ups and downs—of our appearance and performance (Gilovich et al., 2002). Even after a blunder (setting off a library alarm, showing up in the wrong clothes), we stick out like a sore thumb less than we imagine (Savitsky et al., 2001). Knowing about the spotlight effect can be empowering. Help public speakers to understand that their natural nervousness is not so apparent to their audience and their speaking performance improves (Savitsky & Gilovich, 2003).

The Benefits of Self-Esteem

How we feel about ourselves is also important. High **self-esteem**—a feeling of self-worth—pays dividends. So does **self-efficacy,** our sense of competence on a task. People who feel good about themselves (who strongly agree with self-affirming questionnaire statements such as, "I am fun to be with") have fewer sleepless nights. They succumb less easily to pressures to conform. They are more persistent at difficult tasks; they are less shy, anxious, and lonely. And they are just plain happier (Greenberg, 2008; Orth et al., 2008, 2009).

If feeling bad, they think they deserve better and thus make more effort to repair their mood (Wood et al., 2009).

But is high self-esteem the horse or the cart? Is it really "the armor that protects kids" from life's problems (McKay, 2000)? Some psychologists have their doubts (Baumeister, 2006; Dawes, 1994; Leary, 1999; Seligman, 1994, 2002). Children's academic self-efficacy—their confidence that they can do well in a subject—predicts school achievement. But general self-image does not (Marsh & Craven, 2006; Swann et al., 2007; Trautwein et al., 2006). Maybe self-esteem simply reflects reality. Maybe feeling good *follows* doing well. Maybe it's a side effect of meeting challenges and surmounting difficulties. Maybe self-esteem is a gauge that reads out the state of our relationships with others. If so, isn't pushing the gauge artificially higher ("You are special") akin to forcing a car's low fuel gauge to display "full"? And if problems and failures cause low self-esteem, won't the best boost therefore come not from our repeatedly telling children how wonderful they are but from their own effective coping and hard-won achievements?

However, experiments do reveal an *effect* of low self-esteem. Temporarily deflate people's self-image (say, by telling them they did poorly on an aptitude test or by disparaging their personality) and they will be more likely to disparage others or to express heightened racial prejudice (Ybarra, 1999). Those who are negative about themselves also tend to be oversensitive and judgmental (Baumgardner et al., 1989; Pelham, 1993). In experiments, people made to feel insecure often become excessively critical, as if to impress others with their own brilliance (Amabile, 1983). Such findings are consistent with Maslow's and Rogers' presumptions that a healthy self-image pays dividends. Accept yourself and you'll find it easier to accept others. Disparage yourself and you will be prone to the floccinaucinihilipilification[1] of others. Said more simply, some "love their neighbors as themselves"; others loathe their neighbors as themselves. People who are down on themselves tend to be down on other things and people.

"When kids increase in self-control, their grades go up later. But when kids increase their self-esteem, there is no effect on their grades." -Angela Duckworth, *In Character* interview, 2009

self-esteem one's feelings of high or low self-worth.

self-efficacy one's sense of competence and effectiveness.

---

[1] I couldn't resist throwing that in. But don't worry, you won't be tested on floccinaucinihilipilification, which is the act of estimating something as worthless (and was the longest nontechnical word in the first edition of the *Oxford English Dictionary*).

Self-Serving Bias

59-4 What evidence reveals self-serving bias, and how do defensive and secure self-esteem differ?

Carl Rogers (1958) once objected to the religious doctrine that humanity's problems arise from excessive self-love, or pride. He noted that most people he had known "despise themselves, regard themselves as worthless and unlovable." Mark Twain had a similar idea: "No man, deep down in the privacy of his heart, has any considerable respect for himself."

Actually, most of us have a good reputation with ourselves. In studies of self-esteem, even those who score relatively low respond in the midrange of possible scores. (A low-self-esteem person responds to statements such as "I have good ideas" with qualifying adjectives such as *somewhat* or *sometimes*.) Moreover, one of psychology's most provocative and firmly established recent conclusions concerns our potent **self-serving bias**—our readiness to perceive ourselves favorably (Mezulis et al., 2004; Myers, 2008). Consider:

People accept more responsibility for good deeds than for bad, and for successes than for failures. Athletes often privately credit their victories to their own prowess, and their losses to bad breaks, lousy officiating, or the other team's exceptional performance. After receiving poor grades on a test, most students in a half-dozen studies criticized the test, not themselves. On insurance forms, drivers have explained accidents in such words as: "An invisible car came out of nowhere, struck my car, and vanished." "As I reached an intersection, a hedge sprang up, obscuring my vision, and I did not see the other car." "A pedestrian hit me and went under my car." The question "What have I done to deserve this?" is one we usually ask of our troubles, not our successes—those, we assume we deserve.

Most people see themselves as better than average. This is true for nearly any commonplace behavior that is subjectively assessed and socially desirable:

- In national surveys, most business executives say they are more ethical than their average counterpart.

- In several studies, 90 percent of business managers and more than 90 percent of college professors rated their performance as superior to that of their average peer.

- In the National Survey of Families and Households, 49 percent of men said they provided half or more of the child care, though only 31 percent of their wives or partners saw things that way (Galinsky et al., 2008).

- In Australia, 86 percent of people rate their job performance as above average, and only 1 percent as below average.

The phenomenon, which reflects the overestimation of self rather than the underestimation of others (Epley & Dunning, 2000), is less striking in Asia, where people value modesty (Falk et al., 2009; Heine & Hamamura, 2007). Yet self-serving biases have been observed worldwide: among Dutch, Australian, and Chinese students; Japanese drivers; Indian Hindus; and French people of most walks of life. In every one of 53 countries surveyed, people expressed self-esteem above the midpoint of the most widely used scale (Schmitt & Allik, 2005).

Ironically, people even see themselves as more immune than others to self-serving bias (Pronin, 2007). The world, it seems, is Garrison Keillor's fictional Lake Wobegon writ

self-serving bias a readiness to perceive oneself favorably.

"If you are like most people, then like most people, you don't know you're like most people. Science has given us a lot of facts about the average person, and one of the most reliable of these facts is the average person doesn't see herself as average."
-DANIEL GILBERT, *STUMBLING ON HAPPINESS*, 2006

PEANUTS

large—a place where "all the women are strong, all the men are good-looking, and all the children are above average." And so are the pets. Three in four owners believe their pet is smarter than average (Nier, 2004).

Threatened egotism, more than low self-esteem, it seems, predisposes aggression. This is true even in childhood, when the recipe for frequent fighting mixes high self-esteem with social rejection. The most aggressive children tend to have high self-regard that gets punctured by other kids' dislike (van Boxtel et al., 2004).

An adolescent or adult whose swelled head is deflated by insults is potentially dangerous. Finding their self-esteem threatened, people with large egos may react violently. "Aryan pride" fueled Nazi atrocities. "These biases have the effect of making wars more likely to begin and more difficult to end," noted Daniel Kahneman and Jonathan Renshon (2007).

Brad Bushman and Roy Baumeister (1998; Bushman et al., 2009) experimented with what they call the "dark side of high self-esteem." They had 540 undergraduate volunteers write a brief essay, in response to which another supposed student gave them either praise ("Great essay!") or stinging criticism ("One of the worst essays I have read!"). Then the essay writers played a reaction-time game against the other student. After wins, they could assault their opponent with noise of any intensity for any duration.

Can you anticipate the result? After criticism, those with inflated high self-esteem were "exceptionally aggressive." They delivered three times the auditory torture of those with normal self-esteem. "Encouraging people to feel good about themselves when they haven't earned it" poses problems, Baumeister (2001) concluded. "Conceited, self-important individuals turn nasty toward those who puncture their bubbles of self-love."

Are self-serving perceptions on the rise in North America? Some researchers believe they are. From 1980 to 2007, popular song lyrics became more self-focused (DeWall et al., 2011). From 1988 to 2008, self-esteem scores increased among American collegians, high schoolers, and especially middle school students (Gentile et al., 2010). On one prominent self-esteem inventory on which 40 is the highest possible self-esteem score, 51 percent of 2008 collegians scored 35 or more.

Narcissism—excessive self-love and self-absorption—is also rising, reports psychologist Jean Twenge (2006; Twenge & Foster, 2010). After tracking self-importance across the last several decades, Twenge found that what she calls *Generation Me* (born in the 1980s and 1990s) is expressing more narcissism by agreeing more often with statements such as, "If I ruled the world, it would be a better place," or "I think I am a special person." Agreement with such narcissistic statements correlates with materialism, the desire to be famous, inflated expectations, more hookups with fewer committed relationships, more gambling, and more cheating, all of which have been increasing as narcissism has increased.

Some critics of the concept of self-serving bias claim that it overlooks those who feel worthless and unlovable: If self-serving bias prevails, why do so many people disparage themselves? For four reasons:

- Self-directed put-downs can be *subtly strategic:* They elicit reassuring strokes. Saying "No one likes me" may at least elicit "But not everyone has met you!"

- Before an important event, such as a game or a test, self-disparaging comments *prepare us for possible failure.* The coach who extols the superior strength of the upcoming opponent makes a loss understandable, a victory noteworthy.

- A self-disparaging "How could I have been so stupid!" can help us *learn from our mistakes.*

TOO MUCH COFFEE MAN BY SHANNON WHEELER

AND GOD CREATED SELF-WORTH

© Shannon Wheeler

"The enthusiastic claims of the self-esteem movement mostly range from fantasy to hogwash. The effects of self-esteem are small, limited, and not all good."
-ROY BAUMEISTER (1996)

narcissism excessive self-love and self-absorption.

- Self-disparagement frequently *pertains to one's old self.* Asked to remember their really bad behaviors, people recall things from long ago; good behaviors more easily come to mind from their recent past (Escobedo & Adolphs, 2010). People are much more critical of their distant past selves than of their current selves—even when they have not changed (Wilson & Ross, 2001). "At 18, I was a jerk; today I'm more sensitive." In their own eyes, chumps yesterday, champs today.

Even so, it's true: All of us some of the time, and some of us much of the time, do feel inferior—especially when we compare ourselves with those who are a step or two higher on the ladder of status, looks, income, or ability. The deeper and more frequently we have such feelings, the more unhappy, even depressed, we are. But for most people, thinking has a naturally positive bias.

> "If you compare yourself with others, you may become vain and bitter; for always there will be greater and lesser persons than yourself." -Max Ehrmann, "Desiderata," 1927

While recognizing the dark side of self-serving bias and self-esteem, some researchers prefer isolating the effects of two types of self-esteem—defensive and secure (Kernis, 2003; Lambird & Mann, 2006; Ryan & Deci, 2004). *Defensive self-esteem* is fragile. It focuses on sustaining itself, which makes failures and criticism feel threatening. Such egotism exposes one to perceived threats, which feed anger and disorder, note Jennifer Crocker and Lora Park (2004).

Secure self-esteem is less fragile, because it is less contingent on external evaluations. To feel accepted for who we are, and not for our looks, wealth, or acclaim, relieves pressures to succeed and enables us to focus beyond ourselves. By losing ourselves in relationships and purposes larger than self, Crocker and Park add, we may achieve a more secure self-esteem and greater quality of life.

Before You Move On

▶ **ASK YOURSELF**

What possible selves do you dream of—or fear—becoming? To what extent do these imagined selves motivate you now?

▶ **TEST YOURSELF**

In a 1997 Gallup poll, White Americans estimated 44 percent of their fellow White Americans to be high in prejudice (scoring them 5 or higher on a 10-point scale). How many rated themselves similarly high in prejudice? Just 14 percent. What phenomenon does this illustrate?

Answers to the Test Yourself questions can be found in Appendix E at the end of the book.

Culture and the Self

59-5 How do individualist and collectivist cultures influence people?

Imagine that someone were to rip away your social connections, making you a solitary refugee in a foreign land. How much of your identity would remain intact?

If as our solitary traveler you pride yourself on your **individualism,** a great deal of your identity would remain intact—the very core of your being, the sense of "me," the awareness of your personal convictions and values. Individualists (often people from North America, Western Europe, Australia, or New Zealand) give relatively greater priority to personal goals and define their identity mostly in terms of personal attributes (Schimmack et al., 2005). They strive for personal control and individual achievement. In American culture, with its relatively big *I* and small *we*, 85 percent of people have agreed that it is possible "to pretty much be who you want to be" (Sampson, 2000).

individualism giving priority to one's own goals over group goals and defining one's identity in terms of personal attributes rather than group identifications.

Individualists share the human need to belong. They join groups. But they are less focused on group harmony and doing their duty to the group (Brewer & Chen, 2007). And being more self-contained, they more easily move in and out of social groups. They feel relatively free to switch places of worship, switch jobs, or even leave their extended families and migrate to a new place. Marriage is often for as long as they both shall love.

If set adrift in a foreign land as a **collectivist,** you might experience a greater loss of identity. Cut off from family, groups, and loyal friends, you would lose the connections that have defined who you are. In a collectivist culture, group identifications provide a sense of belonging, a set of values, a network of caring individuals, an assurance of security. In return, collectivists have deeper, more stable attachments to their groups—their family, clan, or company. In South Korea, for example, people place less value on expressing a consistent, unique self-concept, and more on tradition and shared practices (Choi & Choi, 2002).

Valuing communal solidarity means placing a premium on preserving group spirit and ensuring that others never lose face. What people say reflects not only what they feel (their inner attitudes) but what they presume others feel (Kashima et al., 1992). Avoiding direct confrontation, blunt honesty, and uncomfortable topics, collectivists often defer to others' wishes and display a polite, self-effacing humility (Markus & Kitayama, 1991). Elders and superiors receive respect, and duty to family may trump personal career and mate preferences (Zhang & Kline, 2009). In new groups, people may be shy and more easily embarrassed than their individualist counterparts (Singelis et al., 1995, 1999). Compared with Westerners, people in Japanese and Chinese cultures, for example, exhibit greater shyness toward strangers and greater concern for social harmony and loyalty (Bond, 1988; Cheek & Melchior, 1990; Triandis, 1994). When the priority is "we," not "me," that individualized latte—"decaf, single shot, skinny, extra hot"—that feels so good to a North American in a coffee shop might sound more like a selfish demand in Seoul (Kim & Markus, 1999).

Collectivist culture Although the United States is largely individualist, many cultural subgroups remain collectivist. This is true for many Alaska Natives, who demonstrate respect for tribal elders, and whose identity springs largely from their group affiliations.

To be sure, there is diversity within cultures. Even in the most individualist countries, some people manifest collectivist values. Within many countries, there are also distinct cultures related to one's religion, economic status, and region (Cohen, 2009). And in collectivist Japan, a spirit of individualism marks the "northern frontier" island of Hokkaido (Kitayama et al., 2006). But in general, people (especially men) in competitive, individualist cultures have more personal freedom, are less geographically bound to their families, enjoy more privacy, and take more pride in personal achievements (**TABLE 59.3** on the next page).

"One needs to cultivate the spirit of sacrificing the *little me* to achieve the benefits of the *big me*." -CHINESE SAYING

Considerate collectivists Japan's collectivist values, including duty to others and social harmony, were on display after the devastating 2011 earthquake and tsunami. Virtually no looting was reported, and residents remained calm and orderly, as shown here while waiting for drinking water.

collectivism giving priority to the goals of one's group (often one's extended family or work group) and defining one's identity accordingly.

Table 59.3 Value Contrasts Between Individualism and Collectivism

Concept	Individualism	Collectivism
Self	Independent (identity from individual traits)	Interdependent (identity from belonging)
Life task	Discover and express one's uniqueness	Maintain connections, fit in, perform role
What matters	Me—personal achievement and fulfillment; rights and liberties; self-esteem	Us—group goals and solidarity; social responsibilities and relationships; family duty
Coping method	Change reality	Accommodate to reality
Morality	Defined by individuals (self-based)	Defined by social networks (duty-based)
Relationships	Many, often temporary or casual; confrontation acceptable	Few, close and enduring; harmony valued
Attributing behavior	Behavior reflects one's personality and attitudes	Behavior reflects social norms and roles

Sources: Adapted from Thomas Schoeneman (1994) and Harry Triandis (1994).

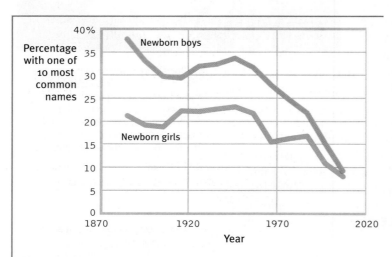

Figure 59.3

A child like no other Americans' individualist tendencies are reflected in their choice of names for their babies. In recent years, the percentage of American babies receiving one of that year's 10 most common names has plunged. (Adapted from Twenge et al., 2010.)

They even prefer unusual names, as psychologist Jean Twenge noticed while seeking a name for her first child. Over time, the most common American names listed by year on the U.S. Social Security baby names website were becoming less desirable. When she and her colleagues (2010) analyzed the first names of 325 million American babies born between 1880 and 2007, they confirmed this trend. As **FIGURE 59.3** illustrates, the percentage of boys and girls given one of the 10 most common names for their birth year has plunged, especially in recent years. (No wonder my parents, who welcomed my arrival in a less individualist age, gave me such a common first name.)

The individualist-collectivist divide appeared in reactions to medals received during the 2000 and 2002 Olympic games. U.S. gold medal winners and the U.S. media covering them attributed the achievements mostly to the athletes themselves (Markus et al., 2006). "I think I just stayed focused," explained swimming gold medalist Misty Hyman. "It was time to show the world what I could do. I am just glad I was able to do it." Japan's gold medalist in the women's marathon, Naoko Takahashi, had a different explanation: "Here is the best coach in the world, the best manager in the world, and all of the people who support me—all of these things were getting together and became a gold medal." Even when describing friends, Westerners tend to use trait-describing adjectives (*"she is helpful"*), whereas East Asians more often use verbs that describe behaviors in context (*"she helps her friends"*) (Heine & Buchtel, 2009; Maass et al., 2006).

Individualism's benefits can come at the cost of more loneliness, higher divorce and homicide rates, and more stress-related disease (Popenoe, 1993; Triandis et al., 1988). Demands for more romance and personal fulfillment in marriage can subject relationships to more pressure (Dion & Dion, 1993). In one survey, "keeping romance alive" was rated as important to a good marriage by 78 percent of U.S. women but only 29 percent of Japanese women (*American Enterprise*, 1992). In China, love songs often express enduring commitment and friendship (Rothbaum & Tsang, 1998): "We will be together from now on. . . . I will never change from now to forever."

Before You Move On

▶ **ASK YOURSELF**

Which concept best describes you—collectivist or individualist? Do you fit completely in either category, or are you sometimes a collectivist and sometimes an individualist?

▶ **TEST YOURSELF**

How do individualist and collectivist cultures differ?

Answers to the Test Yourself questions can be found in Appendix E at the end of the book.

Module 59 Review

 Who first proposed the social-cognitive perspective, and how do social-cognitive theorists view personality development?

- Albert Bandura first proposed the *social-cognitive perspective,* which views personality as the product of the interaction between a person's traits (including thinking) and the situation—the social context.

- The *behavioral approach* contributes an understanding that our personality development is affected by learned responses.

- Social-cognitive researchers apply principles of learning, as well as cognition and social behavior, to personality.

- *Reciprocal determinism* is a term describing the interaction and mutual influence of behavior, internal personal factors, and environmental factors.

- Research on how we interact with our environment evolved into research on the effects of optimism and pessimism, which led to a broader *positive psychology.*

 How do social-cognitive researchers explore behavior, and what criticism have they faced?

- Social-cognitive researchers tend to believe that the best way to predict someone's behavior in a given situation is to observe that person's behavior in similar situations.

- They have been faulted for underemphasizing the importance of unconscious dynamics, emotions, and inner traits. Their response is that the social-cognitive perspective builds on psychology's well-established concepts of learning and cognition and reminds us of the power of situations.

 Why has psychology generated so much research on the self? How important is self-esteem to psychology and to human well-being?

- The *self* is the center of personality, organizing our thoughts, feelings, and actions.

- Considering possible selves helps motivate us toward positive development, but focusing too intensely on ourselves can lead to the *spotlight effect.*

- High *self-esteem* (our feeling of self-worth) is beneficial, but unrealistically high self-esteem is dangerous (linked to aggressive behavior) and fragile.

- *Self-efficacy* is our sense of competence.

 What evidence reveals self-serving bias, and how do defensive and secure self-esteem differ?

- *Self-serving bias* is our tendency to perceive ourselves favorably, as when viewing ourselves as better than average or when accepting credit for our successes but not blame for our failures.

- Defensive self-esteem is fragile, focuses on sustaining itself, and views failure or criticism as a threat.

- Secure self-esteem enables us to feel accepted for who we are.

59-5 How do individualist and collectivist cultures influence people?

● Within any culture, the degree of *individualism* or *collectivism* varies from person to person. Cultures based on self-reliant individualism, like those found in North America and Western Europe, tend to value personal independence and individual achievement. They define identity in terms of self-esteem, personal goals and attributes, and personal rights and liberties. Cultures based on socially connected collectivism, like those in many parts of Asia and Africa, tend to value interdependence, tradition, and harmony, and they define identity in terms of group goals, commitments, and belonging to one's group.

Multiple-Choice Questions

1. Who of the following is considered the leading advocate of personality's social-cognitive approach?
   a. Gordon Allport
   b. Carl Jung
   c. Karen Horney
   d. Carl Rogers
   e. Albert Bandura

2. The way we explain negative and positive events is called
   a. personal control.
   b. reciprocal determinism.
   c. positive psychology.
   d. attributional style.
   e. situational assessment.

3. Which of the following is an example of an assessment likely to be used by a social-cognitive psychologist?
   a. A student teacher is formally observed and evaluated in front of the classroom.
   b. A person applying for a managerial position takes the Myers-Briggs Type Indicator.
   c. A defendant in a criminal case is interviewed by a court-appointed psychologist.
   d. In a premarriage counseling session, a young couple responds to ambiguous inkblots.
   e. A depressed young man is asked by his therapist to relax on a couch and talk about whatever comes to mind.

4. Which of the following is an example of self-efficacy?
   a. Manuela believes others are always watching her.
   b. Abraham believes he is a good person.
   c. Rasheed believes he is a competent skater.
   d. Saundra believes it rained because she's been wishing for rain for days.
   e. Igor maintains his optimism despite doing poorly in his math class.

5. Which of the following is most likely to be true of a person from an individualistic culture?
   a. His behavior would be a reflection of his personality and attitudes.
   b. He would cope by accommodating to reality.
   c. He would view his life task as fitting in and maintaining connections.
   d. He would strive to develop a few close and enduring relationships.
   e. He would focus on his duty to his family.

Practice FRQs

1. Briefly describe the two main components of the self-serving bias.

Answer

1 point: People are more likely to take credit for their successes than their failures.

1 point: Most people see themselves as above average.

2. Heidi is an exceptionally avid reader of books. Explain how the three types of factors in reciprocal determinism might interact to support Heidi's desire to read.

(3 points)

Unit X Review

Key Terms and Concepts to Remember

personality, p. 555

free association, p. 557

psychoanalysis, p. 557

unconscious, p. 557

id, p. 558

ego, p. 558

superego, p. 558

psychosexual stages, p. 559

Oedipus [ED-uh-puss] complex, p. 559

identification, p. 559

fixation, p. 560

defense mechanisms, p. 560

repression, p. 560

psychodynamic theories, p. 565

collective unconscious, p. 566

projective test, p. 567

Thematic Apperception Test (TAT), p. 567

Rorschach inkblot test, p. 567

false consensus effect, p. 568

terror-management theory, p. 568

humanistic theories, p. 571

self-actualization, p. 571

unconditional positive regard, p. 572

self-concept, p. 572

trait, p. 576

personality inventory, p. 578

Minnesota Multiphasic Personality Inventory (MMPI), p. 578

empirically derived test, p. 578

social-cognitive perspective, p. 587

behavioral approach, p. 587

reciprocal determinism, p. 588

positive psychology, p. 590

self, p. 594

spotlight effect, p. 594

self-esteem, p. 595

self-efficacy, p. 595

self-serving bias, p. 596

narcissism, p. 597

individualism, p. 598

collectivism, p. 599

Key Contributors to Remember

Sigmund Freud, p. 556

Alfred Adler p. 565

Karen Horney, p. 565

Carl Jung, p. 566

Abraham Maslow, p. 571

Carl Rogers, p. 572

Robert McCrae, pp. 580, 583

Paul Costa, pp. 580, 583

Albert Bandura, p. 587

Martin Seligman, p. 590

AP® Exam Practice Questions

Multiple-Choice Questions

1. A question on the Minnesota Multiphasic Personality Inventory (MMPI) such as "I get angry sometimes" is included to determine what about the test-taker?

a. Whether the person has a personality disorder.

b. If the person needs immediate help for anger management.

c. If the person is more extraverted than introverted.

d. Whether the person has a stronger id or superego.

e. If the person is answering the questions truthfully.

2. Albert Bandura proposed the social-cognitive perspective, which

a. explains the nature–nurture debate.

b. predicts human behavior.

c. focuses on how our environment controls us.

d. explains human motivation.

e. emphasizes the interaction of our traits with our situations.

3. According to Sigmund Freud, which of the following defense mechanisms buries threatening or upsetting events in the unconscious?

a. Regression
d. Projection
b. Displacement
e. Rationalization
c. Repression

4. Athletes who often privately credit their victories to their own abilities, and their losses to bad breaks, lousy officiating, or the other team's exceptional performance, are exhibiting which psychological concept?

a. A low self-esteem
b. The self-serving bias
c. Pessimism
d. The spotlight effect
e. Incompetence

5. What did Abraham Maslow call the process of fulfilling our potential?

a. Love needs
b. Self-esteem
c. Self-actualization
d. Self-transcendence
e. Hierarchy of needs

6. Which term is defined as all the thoughts and feelings we have in response to the question, "Who am I?"

a. Self-concept
d. Empathy
b. Ideal self
e. Self-acceptance
c. Self-esteem

7. What did Sigmund Freud call his theory of personality and the associated treatment techniques?

a. Psychoanalysis
b. Humanism
c. The self-concept
d. Psychosexual stages
e. Free association

8. Which term describes questionnaires that cover a wide range of feelings and behaviors and are designed to assess several traits?

a. Factor analysis studies
b. Peer reports
c. Achievement tests
d. Cognition tests
e. Personality inventories

9. Someone from a collectivist culture is more likely to do what?

a. Develop a strong sense of self
b. Give priority to group goals
c. Form casual, often temporary relationships
d. Achieve personal goals
e. Focus on how they are different from the group

10. Critics of humanistic psychology have suggested that this theory fails to appreciate the reality of our human capacity for which of the following?

a. Empathy
d. Evil
b. Love
e. Laziness
c. Negativity

11. Amy was sure everyone noticed how nervous she was when she spoke in front of the entire school, but later no one that she talked to mentioned it. What is the term for the belief that others are always noticing and evaluating us more than they really are?

a. Self-monitoring
b. Self-schemas
c. Possible selves
d. The spotlight effect
e. The social-cognitive perspective

12. In Brad Bushman and Roy Baumeister's research, how did people with unrealistically high self-esteem react when they were criticized?

a. They became exceptionally aggressive.
b. Many were more receptive to the criticism.
c. Some became easily depressed.
d. Most worked harder to do better the next time.
e. They quit the task without completing it.

13. According to Carl Rogers, when we are in a good marriage, a close family, or an intimate friendship, we are free to be spontaneous without fearing the loss of others' esteem. What did he call this accepting attitude?

a. A peak experience
b. Unconditional positive regard
c. Self-transcendence
d. Humanistic psychology
e. Our self-concept

14. Children's TV-viewing habits (past behavior) influence their viewing preferences (internal personal factor), which influence how television (environmental factor) affects their current behavior. What is this an example of?

a. Personal control
b. Learned helplessness
c. Reciprocal determinism
d. The Big Five traits
e. Implicit learning

Free-Response Questions

1. One important difference between psychological perspectives on personality involves how each perspective tries to measure personality. Briefly explain how each of the following perspectives views personality measurement, using appropriate psychological terminology.

- Psychodynamic perspective
- Humanistic perspective
- Trait theorists

Rubric for Free-Response Question 1

1 point: The psychodynamic perspective views the goal of personality measurement as revealing the unconscious conflicts and impulses that drive and create our personality. Projective tests (such as the TAT or Rorschach test) are used to allow individuals to "project" their unconscious desires and impulses on to the test so that they are revealed to the therapist and client. ↻ Pages 565–567

1 point: Humanistic theorists are skeptical about attempts to measure personality. They view personality tests and other attempts at measuring and quantifying personality as potentially depersonalizing, reducing the complexity of a person to one of a few generalized categories. ↻ Page 573

1 point: Trait theorists attempt to measure personality through personality inventories, such as the MMPI. They are most interested in knowing where a person fits on each of the Big Five personality factors. ↻ Pages 578–582

Multiple-choice self-tests and more may be found at www.worthpublishers.com/MyersAP2e

2. Alejandro has joined an online dating service in an attempt to meet some new people. He met a woman named Sakura through the website and agreed to go out on a date with her because they have many things in common.

Explain how the following concepts could relate to Alejandro and Sakura's date:

- Self-concept
- Self-efficacy
- Extraversion/introversion
- Spotlight effect

(4 points)

3. Maylin has a negative attitude and is disrespectful to her peers. She is unhappy at work and has not been performing at her job as well as in the past. Unfortunately, Maylin blames her co-workers for mistakes that have been made and feels as if the world is against her.

A. Explain how each of the following psychological concepts might explain Maylin's *negative* or *unpleasant* behavior.

- Self-serving bias
- Displacement

B. Explain how each of the following psychological concepts might *help* Maylin become more positive in her daily life.

- Self-actualization
- Sublimation
- Unconditional positive regard

(6 points)

Unit XI

Testing and Individual Differences

Modules

Three huge controversies have sparked recent debate in and beyond psychology. First is the "memory war," over whether traumatic experiences are repressed and can later be recovered, with therapeutic benefit. The second great controversy is the "gender war," over the extent to which nature and nurture shape our behaviors as men and women. In this unit, we meet the "intelligence war": Does each of us have an inborn general mental capacity (intelligence), and can we quantify this capacity as a meaningful number?

School boards, courts, and scientists debate the use and fairness of tests that assess people's mental abilities and assign them a score. Is intelligence testing a constructive way to guide people toward suitable opportunities? Or is it a potent, discriminatory weapon camouflaged as science? First, some basic questions:

- What is intelligence?

- How can we best assess it?

- To what extent does it result from heredity and from environmental influence?

- What do test score differences among individuals and groups really mean? Should we use such differences to track the abilities of public school students? To admit them to colleges or universities? To hire them?

This unit offers answers. It identifies a variety of mental gifts. And it concludes that the recipe for high achievement blends talent and grit.

Module 60

Introduction to Intelligence

Module Learning Objectives

60-1 Discuss the difficulty of defining *intelligence.*

60-2 Present arguments for and against considering intelligence as one general mental ability.

60-3 Compare Gardner's and Sternberg's theories of intelligence.

60-4 Describe the four components of emotional intelligence.

60-5 Describe the relationship between intelligence and brain anatomy.

60-6 Describe the relationship between intelligence and neural processing speed.

60-1 How is *intelligence* defined?

Psychologists debate: Should we consider intelligence as one aptitude or many? As linked to cognitive speed? As neurologically measurable? On this much, intelligence experts agree: Intelligence is a concept and not a "thing."

In many research studies, *intelligence* has been operationally defined as whatever intelligence tests measure, which has tended to be school smarts. But intelligence is not a quality like height or weight, which has the same meaning to everyone around the globe. People assign the term *intelligence* to the qualities that enable success in their own time and in their own culture (Sternberg & Kaufman, 1998). In the Amazon rain forest, *intelligence* may be understanding the medicinal qualities of local plants. In a North American high school, it may be mastering difficult concepts in tough courses. In both locations, **intelligence** is the ability to learn from experience, solve problems, and use knowledge to adapt to new situations. An **intelligence test** assesses people's mental abilities and compares them with others, using numerical scores.

> **intelligence** mental quality consisting of the ability to learn from experience, solve problems, and use knowledge to adapt to new situations.
>
> **intelligence test** a method for assessing an individual's mental aptitudes and comparing them with those of others, using numerical scores.

Hands-on healing The socially constructed concept of intelligence varies from culture to culture. This natural healer in India displays his intelligence in his knowledge about his medicinal plants and understanding of the needs of the people he is helping.

Hemis/Alamy

Is Intelligence One General Ability or Several Specific Abilities?

60-2 What are the arguments for and against considering intelligence as one general mental ability?

You probably know some people with talents in science, others who excel in social studies, and still others gifted in athletics, art, music, or dance. You may also know a talented artist who is stumped by the simplest math problem, or a brilliant math student with little aptitude for literary discussion. Are all these people intelligent? Could you rate their intelligence on a single scale? Or would you need several different scales?

Charles Spearman (1863–1945) believed we have one **general intelligence** (often shortened to *g*). He granted that people often have special abilities that stand out and he helped develop **factor analysis,** a statistical procedure that identifies clusters of related items. But Spearman also found that those who score high in one area, such as verbal intelligence, typically score higher than average in other areas, such as spatial or reasoning ability. Spearman believed a common skill set, the *g* factor, underlies all intelligent behavior, from navigating the sea to excelling in school.

This idea of a general mental capacity expressed by a single intelligence score was controversial in Spearman's day, and so it remains. One of Spearman's early opponents was L. L. Thurstone (1887–1955). Thurstone gave 56 different tests to people and mathematically identified seven clusters of primary mental abilities (word fluency, verbal comprehension, spatial ability, perceptual speed, numerical ability, inductive reasoning, and memory). Thurstone did not rank people on a single scale of general aptitude. But when other investigators studied these profiles, they detected a persistent tendency: Those who excelled in one of the seven clusters generally scored well on the others. So, the investigators concluded, there was still some evidence of a *g* factor.

We might, then, liken mental abilities to physical abilities. Athleticism is not one thing but many. The ability to run fast is distinct from the eye-hand coordination required to throw a ball on target. A champion weightlifter rarely has the potential to be a skilled ice skater. Yet there remains some tendency

© Ocean/Corbis

general intelligence (g) a general intelligence factor that, according to Spearman and others, underlies specific mental abilities and is therefore measured by every task on an intelligence test.

factor analysis a statistical procedure that identifies clusters of related items (called *factors*) on a test; used to identify different dimensions of performance that underlie a person's total score.

for good things to come packaged together—for running speed and throwing accuracy to correlate, thanks to general athletic ability. So, too, with intelligence. Several distinct abilities tend to cluster together and to correlate enough to define a general intelligence factor.

Satoshi Kanazawa (2004, 2010) argues that general intelligence evolved as a form of intelligence that helps people solve *novel* problems—how to stop a fire from spreading, how to find food during a drought, how to reunite with one's tribe on the other side of a flooded river. More common problems—such as how to mate or how to read a stranger's face or how to find your way back to camp—require a different sort of intelligence. Kanazawa asserts that general intelligence scores *do* correlate with the ability to solve various novel problems (like those found in academic and many vocational situations) but do *not* much correlate with individuals' skills in *evolutionarily familiar* situations—such as marrying and parenting, forming close friendships, and navigating without maps. No wonder academic and social skills may come in different bodies.

Theories of Multiple Intelligences

 60-3 How do Gardner's and Sternberg's theories of multiple intelligences differ?

Since the mid-1980s, some psychologists have sought to extend the definition of *intelligence* beyond Spearman's and Thurstone's academic smarts.

GARDNER'S EIGHT INTELLIGENCES

Howard Gardner (1983, 2006) views intelligence as multiple abilities that come in different packages. Brain damage, for example, may destroy one ability but leave others intact. And consider people with **savant syndrome,** who often score low on intelligence tests but have an island of brilliance (Treffert & Wallace, 2002). Some have virtually no language ability, yet are able to compute numbers as quickly and accurately as an electronic calculator, or identify the day of the week corresponding to any given historical date, or render incredible works of art or musical performance (Miller, 1999). About 4 in 5 people with savant syndrome are males, and many also have autism spectrum disorder (ASD; see Module 47).

The late memory whiz Kim Peek, a savant who did not have ASD, was the inspiration for the movie *Rain Man.* In 8 to 10 seconds, he could read and remember a page. During his lifetime, he memorized 9000 books, including Shakespeare and the Bible. He learned maps from the front of phone books and could provide GPS-like travel directions within any major U.S. city. Yet he could not button his clothes. And he had little capacity for abstract concepts. Asked by his father at a restaurant to "lower your voice," he slid lower in his chair to lower his voice box. Asked for Lincoln's Gettysburg Address, he responded, "227 North West Front Street. But he only stayed there one night—he gave the speech the next day" (Treffert & Christensen, 2005).

Using such evidence, Gardner argues that we do not have *an* intelligence, but rather *multiple intelligences* (**FIGURE 60.1** on the next page), including the verbal and mathematical aptitudes assessed by standard tests. Thus, the computer programmer, the poet, the street-smart adolescent who becomes a crafty executive, and the basketball team's point guard exhibit different kinds of intelligence (Gardner, 1998a).

Wouldn't it be nice if the world were so just that being weak in one area would be compensated by genius in another? Alas, say Gardner's critics, the world is not just (Ferguson, 2009; Scarr, 1989). Recent research, using factor analysis, has confirmed that there *is* a general intelligence factor (Johnson et al., 2008): *g* matters. It predicts performance on various complex tasks and in various jobs (Gottfredson,

> "***g*** is one of the most reliable and valid measures in the behavioral domain . . . and it predicts important social outcomes such as educational and occupational levels far better than any other trait." -Behavior geneticist Robert Plomin (1999)

savant syndrome a condition in which a person otherwise limited in mental ability has an exceptional specific skill, such as in computation or drawing.

Islands of genius: Savant syndrome Matt Savage, an award-winning jazz musician, is a Berklee College of Music graduate who has released many albums. His success has been hard-won given his early childhood diagnosis of what is now called autism spectrum disorder, which came with struggles to communicate and an initial inability to tolerate sounds of any kind.

Joanne Rathe/The Boston Globe via Getty Images

Figure 60.1
Gardner's eight intelligences

NATURALIST
LINGUISTIC
INTERPERSONAL
LOGICAL-MATHEMATICAL
INTRAPERSONAL
MUSICAL
BODILY-KINESTHETIC
SPATIAL

grit in psychology, grit is passion and perseverance in the pursuit of long-term goals.

Try This

For more on how self-disciplined grit feeds achievement, see Module 82.

2002a,b, 2003a,b; see also **FIGURE 60.2**). Much as jumping ability is not a predictor of jumping performance when the bar is set a foot off the ground—but becomes a predictor when the bar is set higher—so extremely high cognitive ability scores predict exceptional attainments, such as doctoral degrees and publications (Kuncel & Hezlett, 2010).

Even so, "success" is not a one-ingredient recipe. High intelligence may help you get into a good college and ultimately a desired profession, but it won't make you successful once there. The recipe for success combines talent with **grit:** Those who become highly successful tend also to be conscientious, well-connected, and doggedly energetic.

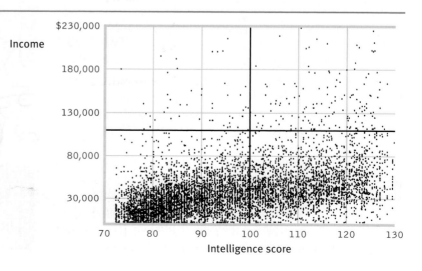

Figure 60.2

Smart and rich? Jay Zagorsky (2007) tracked 7403 participants in the U.S. National Longitudinal Survey of Youth across 25 years. As shown in this scatterplot, their intelligence scores shared a small but significant correlation (+.30) with their later income. Each dot indicates a given youth's intelligence score and later adult income.

K. Anders Ericsson (2002, 2007; Ericsson et al., 2007) reports a *10-year rule:* A common ingredient of expert performance in chess, dancing, sports, computer programming, music, and medicine is "about 10 years of intense, daily practice." Various animal species, including bees, birds, and chimps, likewise require time and experience to acquire peak expertise in skills such as foraging (Helton, 2008). As with humans, animal performance therefore tends to peak near midlife.

Spatial intelligence genius In 1998, World Checkers Champion Ron "Suki" King of Barbados set a new record by simultaneously playing 385 players in 3 hours and 44 minutes. Thus, while his opponents often had hours to plot their game moves, King could only devote about 35 seconds to each game. Yet he still managed to win all 385 games!

"You have to be careful, if you're good at something, to make sure you don't think you're good at other things that you aren't necessarily so good at. . . . Because I've been very successful at [software development] people come in and expect that I have wisdom about topics that I don't."
-BILL GATES (1998)

STERNBERG'S THREE INTELLIGENCES

Robert Sternberg (1985, 1999, 2003) agrees that there is more to success than traditional intelligence and also agrees with Gardner's idea of multiple intelligences. But he proposes a *triarchic theory* of three, not eight, intelligences:

- *Analytical (academic problem-solving) intelligence* is assessed by traditional intelligence tests, which present well-defined problems having a single right answer. Such tests predict school grades reasonably well and vocational success more modestly.

- *Creative intelligence* is demonstrated in reacting adaptively to novel situations and generating novel ideas. Many inventions result from such creative problem solving.

- *Practical intelligence* is required for everyday tasks, which may be ill-defined, with multiple solutions. Managerial success, for example, depends less on academic problem-solving skills than on a shrewd ability to manage oneself, one's tasks, and other people. Sternberg and Richard Wagner (1993, 1995) offer a test of practical managerial intelligence that measures skill at writing effective memos, motivating people, delegating tasks and responsibilities, reading people, and promoting one's own career. Business executives who score relatively high on this test tend to earn high salaries and receive high performance ratings.

"*You're wise, but you lack tree smarts.*"

With support from the U.S. College Board® (which administers the Advanced Placement® Program as well as the widely used SAT Reasoning Test™ to U.S. college and university applicants), Sternberg (2006, 2007, 2010) and a team of collaborators have developed new measures of creativity (such as thinking up a caption for an untitled cartoon) and practical thinking (such as figuring out how to move a large bed up a winding staircase). Their initial data indicate that these more comprehensive assessments improve prediction of American students' first-year college grades, and they do so with reduced ethnic-group differences.

Although Gardner and Sternberg differ on specific points, they agree that multiple abilities can contribute to life success. They also agree that the differing varieties of giftedness add spice to life and challenges for education. Under their influence, many teachers have been trained to appreciate such variety and to apply multiple intelligence theory in their classrooms.

Street smarts This child selling candy on the streets of Manaus, Brazil, is developing practical intelligence at a very young age.

Emotional Intelligence

60-4 What are the four components of emotional intelligence?

Also distinct from academic intelligence is *social intelligence*—the know-how involved in successfully comprehending social situations. People with high social intelligence can read social situations the way a skilled football player reads the defense or a seafarer reads the weather. The concept was first proposed in 1920 by psychologist Edward Thorndike, who noted, "The best mechanic in a factory may fail as a foreman for lack of social intelligence" (Goleman, 2006, p. 83). Later psychologists have marveled that high-aptitude people are "not, by a wide margin, more effective . . . in achieving better marriages, in successfully raising their children, and in achieving better mental and physical well-being" (Epstein & Meier, 1989). Others have explored the difficulty that some smart people have processing and managing social information (Cantor & Kihlstrom, 1987; Weis & Süß, 2007). This idea is especially significant for an aspect of social intelligence that John Mayer, Peter Salovey, and David Caruso (2002, 2008) have called **emotional intelligence.** They have developed a test that assesses four emotional intelligence components:

- *Perceiving* emotions (to recognize them in faces, music, and stories)
- *Understanding* emotions (to predict them and how they change and blend)
- *Managing* emotions (to know how to express them in varied situations)
- *Using* emotions to enable adaptive or creative thinking

Mayer, Salovey, and Caruso caution against stretching "emotional intelligence" to include varied traits such as self-esteem and optimism. Rather, emotionally intelligent people are both socially and self-aware. And in both the United States and Germany, those scoring high on managing emotions enjoy higher-quality interactions with friends (Lopes et al., 2004). They avoid being hijacked by overwhelming depression, anxiety, or anger. Being sensitive to emotional cues, they know what to say to soothe a grieving friend, encourage a colleague, and manage a conflict.

Emotional intelligence is less a matter of conscious effort than of one's unconscious processing of emotional information (Fiori, 2009). Yet the outgrowths of this automatic processing become visible. Across dozens of studies in many countries, those scoring high in emotional intelligence exhibit somewhat better job performance (Joseph & Newman, 2010; Van Rooy & Viswesvaran, 2004; Zeidner et al., 2008). They also can delay gratification in pursuit of long-range rewards, rather than being overtaken by immediate impulses. They are emotionally in tune with others, and thus often succeed in career, marriage, and parenting situations where academically smarter (but emotionally less intelligent) people fail (Cherniss, 2010a,b; Ciarrochi et al., 2006).

Brain damage reports have provided extreme examples of the results of diminished emotional intelligence in people with high general intelligence. Neuroscientist Antonio Damasio (1994) tells of Elliot, who had a brain tumor removed: "I never saw a tinge of emotion in my many hours of conversation with him, no sadness, no impatience, no frustration." Shown disturbing pictures of injured people, destroyed communities, and natural disasters, Elliot showed—and realized he felt—no emotion. He knew but he could not feel. Unable to intuitively adjust his behavior in response to others' feelings, Elliot lost his job. He went bankrupt. His marriage collapsed. He remarried and divorced again. At last report, he was dependent on a disability check and custodial care from a sibling.

Some scholars, however, are concerned that emotional intelligence stretches the concept of intelligence too far. Multiple-intelligence man Howard Gardner (1999b) welcomes our stretching the concept into such realms as music and information about ourselves and others. But let us also, he says, respect emotional sensitivity, creativity, and motivation as important but different. Stretch "intelligence" to include everything we prize and it will lose its meaning.

Is Intelligence Neurologically Measurable?

You know it: You are smarter than some people and not as smart as others. Question: What in that heart of smarts—your brain—creates this difference? Is it your brain's relative *size?* The amount of certain brain *tissue?* Your brain networks' *efficiency?*

Brain Size and Complexity

60-5 To what extent is intelligence related to brain anatomy?

After the brilliant English poet Lord Byron died in 1824, doctors discovered that his brain was a massive 5 pounds, not the normal 3 pounds. Three years later, Beethoven died and his brain was found to have exceptionally numerous and deep convolutions. Such observations set brain scientists off studying the brains of other geniuses (Burrell, 2005). Do people with big brains have big smarts?

Alas, some geniuses had small brains, and some dim-witted criminals had brains like Byron's. More recent studies that directly measure brain volume using MRI scans do reveal correlations of about +.33 between brain size (adjusted for body size) and intelligence score (Carey, 2007; McDaniel, 2005). Bigger is better.

One review of 37 brain-imaging studies revealed associations between intelligence and brain size and activity in specific areas, especially within the frontal and parietal lobes (Jung & Haier, 2007; Tang et al., 2010). Intelligence is having ample gray matter (mostly neural cell bodies) plus ample white matter (axons) that make for efficient communication between brain centers (Deary et al., 2009; Haier et al., 2009).

Sandra Witelson would not have been surprised. With the brains of 91 Canadians as a comparison base, Witelson and her colleagues (1999) seized an opportunity to study Einstein's brain. Although not notably heavier or larger in total size than the typical Canadian's brain, Einstein's brain was 15 percent larger in the parietal lobe's lower region—which just happens to be a center for processing mathematical and spatial information.

> **AP® Exam Tip**
>
> Do not continue on if you can't remember what terms like *MRI*, *parietal lobe*, and *axon* mean. Now is the time to head back to Unit III for a review. If you do this sort of review frequently, you'll have much better command of the material on the day of the AP® exam.

Brain Function

60-6 To what extent is intelligence related to neural processing speed?

The correlations between brain anatomy and intelligence only begin to explain intelligence differences. Searching for other explanations, neuroscientists are studying the brain's functioning.

As people contemplate a variety of questions like those found on intelligence tests, a frontal lobe area just above the outer edge of the eyebrows becomes especially active—in the left brain for verbal questions, and on both sides for spatial questions (Duncan et al., 2000). Information from various brain areas seems to converge here, suggesting to researcher John Duncan (2000) that it may be a "global workspace for organizing and coordinating information" and that some people may be "blessed with a workspace that functions very, very well."

Functioning well means functioning efficiently. Brain scans reveal that smart people use less energy to solve problems (Haier, 2009). They are like skilled athletes, for whom agile moves can seem effortless. Agile minds come with agile brains.

So, are more intelligent people literally more quick-witted, much as today's speedier computer chips enable ever more powerful computing? On some tasks they seem to be. Verbal intelligence scores are predictable from the speed with which people retrieve information from memory (Hunt, 1983). Those who recognize quickly that *sink* and *wink* are different words, or that *A* and *a* share the same name, tend to score high in verbal ability. Extremely precocious 12- to 14-year-old college students are especially quick in responding to such tasks (Jensen, 1989). To try to define *quick-wittedness,* researchers are taking a close look at speed of perception and speed of neural processing.

Figure 60.3

An inspection time task
A stimulus is flashed before being overridden by a masking image. How long would you need to glimpse the stimulus at the left to answer the question? People who can perceive the stimulus very quickly tend to score somewhat higher on intelligence tests. (Adapted from Deary & Stough, 1996.)

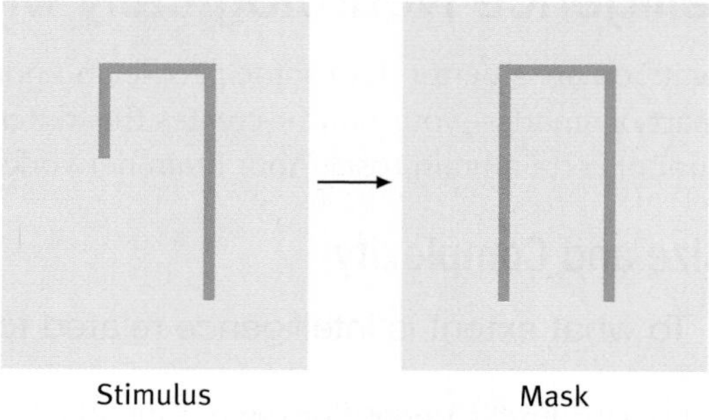

Stimulus   Mask

Question: Long side on left or right?

Across many studies, the correlation between intelligence score and the speed of taking in perceptual information tends to be about +.3 to +.5 (Deary & Der, 2005; Sheppard & Vernon, 2008). A typical experiment flashes an incomplete stimulus, as in **FIGURE 60.3,** then a *masking image*—another image that overrides the lingering afterimage of the incomplete stimulus. The researcher then asks participants whether the long side appeared on the right or left. Those whose brains require the least inspection time to register a simple stimulus tend to score somewhat higher on intelligence tests (Caryl, 1994; Deary & Caryl, 1993; Reed & Jensen, 1992).

Perhaps people who process more quickly accumulate more information. Or perhaps, as one Australian-Dutch research team has found, processing speed and intelligence correlate not because one causes the other but because they share an underlying genetic influence (Luciano et al., 2005).

* * *

For a summary of Spearman's, Thurstone's, Gardner's, and Sternberg's theories, see **TABLE 60.1.**

Table 60.1 Comparing Theories of Intelligence

Theory	Summary	Strengths	Other Considerations
Spearman's general intelligence (g)	A basic intelligence predicts our abilities in varied academic areas.	Different abilities, such as verbal and spatial, do have some tendency to correlate.	Human abilities are too diverse to be encapsulated by a single general intelligence factor.
Thurstone's primary mental abilities	Our intelligence may be broken down into seven factors: word fluency, verbal comprehension, spatial ability, perceptual speed, numerical ability, inductive reasoning, and memory.	A single *g* score is not as informative as scores for seven primary mental abilities.	Even Thurstone's seven mental abilities show a tendency to cluster, suggesting an underlying *g* factor.
Gardner's multiple intelligences	Our abilities are best classified into eight independent intelligences, which include a broad range of skills beyond traditional school smarts.	Intelligence is more than just verbal and mathematical skills. Other abilities are equally important to our human adaptability.	Should all of our abilities be considered *intelligences*? Shouldn't some be called talents?
Sternberg's triarchic theory	Our intelligence is best classified into three areas that predict real-world success: analytical, creative, and practical.	These three facets can be reliably measured.	1. These three facets may be less independent than Sternberg thought and may actually share an underlying *g* factor. 2. Additional testing is needed to determine whether these facets can reliably predict success.

Before You Move On

▶ **ASK YOURSELF**

The modern concept of multiple intelligences (as proposed by Gardner and Sternberg) assumes that the analytical school smarts measured by traditional intelligence tests are important abilities but that other abilities are also important. Different people have different gifts. What are yours?

▶ **TEST YOURSELF**

Joseph, a Harvard Law School student, has a straight-A average, writes for the *Harvard Law Review,* and will clerk for a Supreme Court justice next year. His grandmother, Judith, is very proud of him, saying he is way more intelligent than she ever was. But Joseph is also very proud of Judith: As a young woman, she was imprisoned by the Nazis. When the war ended, she walked out of Germany, contacted an agency helping refugees, and began a new life in the United States as an assistant chef in her cousin's restaurant. According to the definition of intelligence in this unit, is Joseph the only intelligent person in this story? Why or why not?

Answers to the Test Yourself questions can be found in Appendix E at the end of the book.

Module 60 Review

 60-1 How is *intelligence* defined?

- *Intelligence* is a mental quality consisting of the ability to learn from experience, solve problems, and use knowledge to adapt to new situations.

- An *intelligence test* aims to assess these qualities and compare them with those of others, using a numerical score.

60-2 What are the arguments for and against considering intelligence as one general mental ability?

- Charles Spearman proposed that we have one *general intelligence (g).* He helped develop *factor analysis,* a statistical procedure that identifies clusters of related mental abilities.

- L. L. Thurstone disagreed and identified seven different clusters of mental abilities. Yet a tendency remained for high scorers in one cluster to score high in other clusters.

- Studies indicate that *g* scores are most predictive in novel situations and do not much correlate with skills in evolutionarily familiar situations.

60-3 How do Gardner's and Sternberg's theories of multiple intelligences differ?

- *Savant syndrome* seems to support Howard Gardner's view that we have multiple intelligences. He proposed eight independent intelligences: linguistic, logical-mathematical, musical, spatial, bodily-kinesthetic, intrapersonal, interpersonal, and naturalist.

- Robert Sternberg's triarchic theory proposes three intelligence areas that predict real-world skills: analytical (academic problem solving), creative, and practical.

60-4 What are the four components of emotional intelligence?

- *Emotional intelligence,* which is an aspect of social intelligence, is the ability to perceive, understand, manage, and use emotions.

- Emotionally intelligent people achieve greater personal and professional success.

- Some critics question whether calling these abilities "intelligence" stretches that concept too far.

60-5 To what extent is intelligence related to brain anatomy?

- Some studies have found a positive correlation between intelligence score and brain size and activity, especially in the frontal and parietal lobes.

- Ample gray matter and white matter enable efficient communication between brain circuits.

60-6 To what extent is intelligence related to neural processing speed?

- People who score high on intelligence tests tend also to have agile brains and score high in speed of perception and speed of neural processing.

- The direction of correlation has not been determined, and some third factor may influence both intelligence and processing speed.

Multiple-Choice Questions

1. According to Robert Sternberg, what kind of intelligence is assessed by traditional intelligence tests?
   a. Linguistic
   b. Practical
   c. Creative
   d. Spatial
   e. Analytical

2. According to Charles Spearman and others, which of the following underlies specific mental abilities and is measured by every task on an intelligence test?
   a. Savant syndrome
   b. General intelligence (g)
   c. Factor analysis
   d. Intelligence
   e. Emotional intelligence

3. Of the following, which term best describes the condition in which a person with limited mental ability excels at a specific skill such as computation?
   a. Savant syndrome
   b. g factor
   c. Creative intelligence
   d. Emotional intelligence
   e. Street smarts

4. Which of the following is not a component of emotional intelligence?
   a. Understanding emotions
   b. Perceiving emotions
   c. Using emotions
   d. Managing emotions
   e. Inventing emotions

Practice FRQs

1. Give a summary, a strength, and a weakness of Charles Spearman's idea of general intelligence.

Answer

1 point: General intelligence is basic intelligence that predicts our abilities in varied academic areas.

1 point: A strength of this idea is that different abilities, such as verbal and spatial, tend to correlate.

1 point: A weakness of this idea is that human abilities are too diverse to be explained by a single general intelligence factor.

2. Name and describe Robert Sternberg's three intelligences.

(3 points)

Module 61

Assessing Intelligence

Module Learning Objectives

61-1 Discuss the history of intelligence testing.

61-2 Distinguish between aptitude and achievement tests.

61-3 Explain the meaning of standardization, and describe the normal curve.

61-4 Explain the meanings of reliability and validity.

How do we assess intelligence? And what makes a test credible? Answering these questions begins with a look at why psychologists created tests of mental abilities and how they have used those tests.

The Origins of Intelligence Testing

61-1 When and why were intelligence tests created?

Some societies concern themselves with promoting the collective welfare of the family, community, and society. Other societies emphasize individual opportunity. Plato, a pioneer of the individualist tradition, wrote more than 2000 years ago in *The Republic* that "no two persons are born exactly alike; but each differs from the other in natural endowments, one being suited for one occupation and the other for another." As heirs to Plato's individualism, people in Western societies have pondered how and why individuals differ in mental ability.

Western attempts to assess such differences began in earnest over a century ago. The English scientist Francis Galton (1822–1911) had a fascination with measuring human traits. When his cousin Charles Darwin proposed that nature selects successful traits through the survival of the fittest, Galton wondered if it might be possible to measure "natural ability" and to encourage those of high ability to mate with one another. At the 1884 London Exposition, more than 10,000 visitors received his assessment of their "intellectual strengths" based on such things as reaction time, sensory acuity, muscular power, and body proportions. But alas, on these measures, well-regarded adults and students did not outscore others. Nor did the measures correlate with one another.

Although Galton's quest for a simple intelligence measure failed, he gave us some statistical techniques that we still use (as well as the phrase "nature and nurture"). And his persistent belief in the inheritance of genius—reflected in his book, *Hereditary Genius*—illustrates an important lesson from both the history of intelligence research and the history of science: Although science itself strives for objectivity, individual scientists are affected by their own assumptions and attitudes.

Alfred Binet "Some recent philosophers have given their moral approval to the deplorable verdict that an individual's intelligence is a fixed quantity, one which cannot be augmented. We must protest and act against this brutal pessimism" (Binet, 1909, p. 141).

"The IQ test was invented to predict academic performance, nothing else. If we wanted something that would predict life success, we'd have to invent another test completely." -SOCIAL PSYCHOLOGIST ROBERT ZAJONC (1984b)

mental age a measure of intelligence test performance devised by Binet; the chronological age that most typically corresponds to a given level of performance. Thus, a child who does as well as the average 8-year-old is said to have a mental age of 8.

Stanford-Binet the widely used American revision (by Terman at Stanford University) of Binet's original intelligence test.

intelligence quotient (IQ) defined originally as the ratio of mental age (*ma*) to chronological age (*ca*) multiplied by 100 (thus, IQ = *ma/ca* × 100). On contemporary intelligence tests, the average performance for a given age is assigned a score of 100, with scores assigned to relative performance above or below average.

Alfred Binet: Predicting School Achievement

The modern intelligence-testing movement began at the turn of the twentieth century, when France passed a law requiring that all children attend school. Some children, including many newcomers to Paris, seemed incapable of benefiting from the regular school curriculum and in need of special classes. But how could the schools objectively identify children with special needs?

The French government hesitated to trust teachers' subjective judgments of children's learning potential. Academic slowness might merely reflect inadequate prior education. Also, teachers might prejudge children on the basis of their social backgrounds. To minimize bias, France's minister of public education in 1904 commissioned Alfred Binet (1857–1911) and others to study the problem.

Binet and his collaborator, Théodore Simon, began by assuming that all children follow the same course of intellectual development but that some develop more rapidly. On tests, therefore, a "dull" child should perform as does a typical younger child, and a "bright" child as does a typical older child. Thus, their goal became measuring each child's **mental age,** the level of performance typically associated with a certain chronological age. The average 9-year-old, then, has a mental age of 9. Children with below-average mental ages, such as 9-year-olds who perform at the level of typical 7-year-olds, would struggle with age-appropriate schoolwork.

To measure mental age, Binet and Simon theorized that mental aptitude, like athletic aptitude, is a general capacity that shows up in various ways. After testing a variety of reasoning and problem-solving questions on Binet's two daughters, and then on "bright" and "backward" Parisian schoolchildren, Binet and Simon identified items that would predict how well French children would handle their schoolwork.

Note that Binet and Simon made no assumptions concerning *why* a particular child was slow, average, or precocious. Binet personally leaned toward an environmental explanation. To raise the capacities of low-scoring children, he recommended "mental orthopedics" that would help develop their attention span and self-discipline. He believed his intelligence test did not measure inborn intelligence as a meter stick measures height. Rather, it had a single practical purpose: to identify French schoolchildren needing special attention. Binet hoped his test would be used to improve children's education, but he also feared it would be used to label children and limit their opportunities (Gould, 1981).

Lewis Terman: The Innate IQ

Binet's fears were realized soon after his death in 1911, when others adapted his tests for use as a numerical measure of inherited intelligence. This began when Stanford University professor Lewis Terman (1877–1956) found that the Paris-developed questions and age norms worked poorly with California schoolchildren. Adapting some of Binet's original items, adding others, and establishing new age norms, Terman extended the upper end of the test's range from teenagers to "superior adults." He also gave his revision the name it retains today—the **Stanford-Binet.** For Terman, intelligence tests revealed the intelligence with which a person was born.

From such tests, German psychologist William Stern derived the famous **intelligence quotient,** or **IQ.** The IQ is simply a person's mental age divided by chronological age and multiplied by 100 to get rid of the decimal point:

$$IQ = \frac{\text{mental age}}{\text{chronological age}} \times 100$$

Thus, an average child, whose mental and chronological ages are the same, has an IQ of 100. But an 8-year-old who answers questions as would a typical 10-year-old has an IQ of 125.

The original IQ formula worked fairly well for children but not for adults. (Should a 40-year-old who does as well on the test as an average 20-year-old be assigned an IQ of only 50?) Most current intelligence tests, including the Stanford-Binet, no longer compute an IQ in this manner (though the term *IQ* still lingers as a shorthand expression for "intelligence test score"). Instead, they represent the test-taker's performance *relative to the average performance of others the same age.* This average performance is arbitrarily assigned a score of 100, and about two-thirds of all test-takers fall between 85 and 115.

Mrs. Randolph takes mother's pride too far.

Terman promoted the widespread use of intelligence testing. His motive was to "take account of the inequalities of children in original endowment" by assessing their "vocational fitness." In sympathy with Francis Galton's *eugenics*—a much-criticized nineteenth-century movement that proposed measuring human traits and using the results to encourage only smart and fit people to reproduce—Terman (1916, pp. 91–92) envisioned that the use of intelligence tests would "ultimately result in curtailing the reproduction of feeble-mindedness and in the elimination of an enormous amount of crime, pauperism, and industrial inefficiency" (p. 7).

With Terman's help, the U.S. government developed new tests to evaluate both newly arriving immigrants and World War I army recruits—the world's first mass administration of an intelligence test. To some psychologists, the results indicated the inferiority of people not sharing their Anglo-Saxon heritage. Such findings were part of the cultural climate that led to a 1924 immigration law that reduced Southern and Eastern European immigration quotas to less than one-fifth of those for Northern and Western Europe.

Binet probably would have been horrified that his test had been adapted and used to draw such conclusions. Indeed, such sweeping judgments became an embarrassment to most of those who championed testing. Even Terman came to appreciate that test scores reflected not only people's innate mental abilities but also their education, native language, and familiarity with the culture assumed by the test. Abuses of the early intelligence tests serve to remind us that science can be value-laden. Behind a screen of scientific objectivity, ideology sometimes lurks.

> **AP® Exam Tip**
>
> David Myers did not use the terms *nature* or *nurture* as he described the contributions of Binet and Terman, but he dropped many hints that should allow you to figure out who leaned toward the nature position and who leaned toward the nurture position. Can you do it?

Modern Tests of Mental Abilities

61-2 What's the difference between achievement and aptitude tests?

By this point in your life, you've faced dozens of ability tests: school tests of basic reading and math skills, course exams, intelligence tests, and driver's license exams, to name just a few. Psychologists classify such tests as either **achievement tests,** intended to *measure* what you have learned, or **aptitude tests,** intended to *predict* your ability to learn a new skill. Exams covering what you have learned in this course (like the AP® Exam) are achievement tests. A college entrance exam, which seeks to predict your ability to do college work, is an aptitude test—a "thinly disguised intelligence test," says Howard Gardner (1999a). Indeed, total scores on the U.S. SAT® correlated +.82 with general intelligence scores in a national sample of 14- to 21-year-olds (Frey & Detterman, 2004; **FIGURE 61.1** on the next page).

> **achievement test** a test designed to assess what a person has learned.
>
> **aptitude test** a test designed to predict a person's future performance; aptitude is the capacity to learn.

Figure 61.1

Close cousins: Aptitude and intelligence scores A scatterplot shows the close correlation between intelligence scores and verbal and quantitative SAT® scores. (From Frey and Detterman, 2004.)

Intelligence score (IQ)

SAT® scores (verbal + quantitative)

Wechsler Adult Intelligence Scale (WAIS) the WAIS is the most widely used intelligence test; contains verbal and performance (nonverbal) subtests.

Matching patterns Block design puzzles test visual abstract processing ability. Wechsler's individually administered intelligence test comes in forms suited for adults and children.

Psychologist David Wechsler created what is now the most widely used individual intelligence test, the **Wechsler Adult Intelligence Scale (WAIS),** with a version for school-age children (the *Wechsler Intelligence Scale for Children [WISC]*), and another for preschool children. The latest (2008) edition of the WAIS consists of 15 subtests, including these:

- *Similarities*—Reasoning the commonality of two objects or concepts, such as "In what way are wool and cotton alike?"

- *Vocabulary*—Naming pictured objects, or defining words ("What is a guitar?")

- *Block design*—Visual abstract processing, such as "Using the four blocks, make one just like this."

- *Letter-number sequencing*—On hearing a series of numbers and letters, repeat the numbers in ascending order, and then the letters in alphabetical order: "R-2-C-1-M-3."

It yields not only an overall intelligence score, as does the Stanford-Binet, but also separate scores for verbal comprehension, perceptual organization, working memory, and processing speed. Striking differences among these scores can provide clues to cognitive strengths or weaknesses that teachers or therapists can build upon. For example, a low verbal comprehension score combined with high scores on other subtests could indicate a reading or language disability. Other comparisons can help a psychologist or psychiatrist establish a rehabilitation plan for a stroke patient. Such uses are possible, of course, only when we can trust the test results.

Principles of Test Construction

61-3   What are standardization and the normal curve?

To be widely accepted, psychological tests must meet three criteria: They must be *standardized, reliable,* and *valid.* The Stanford-Binet and Wechsler tests meet these requirements.

Standardization

The number of questions you answer correctly on an intelligence test would tell us almost nothing. To evaluate your performance, we need a basis for comparing it with others' performance. To enable meaningful comparisons, test-makers first give the test to a representative sample of people. When you later take the test following the same procedures, your score

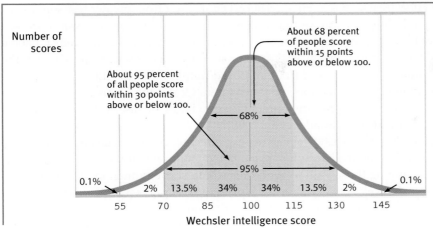

Figure 61.2

The normal curve Scores on aptitude tests tend to form a normal, or bell-shaped, curve around an average score. For the Wechsler scale, for example, the average score is 100.

can be compared with the sample's scores to determine your position relative to others. This process of defining meaningful scores relative to a pretested group is called **standardization.**

Group members' scores typically are distributed in a bell-shaped pattern that forms the **normal curve** shown in **FIGURE 61.2**. No matter what we measure—height, weight, or mental aptitude—people's scores tend to form this roughly symmetrical shape. On an intelligence test, we call the midpoint, the average score, 100. Moving out from the average toward either extreme, we find fewer and fewer people. For both the Stanford-Binet and Wechsler tests, a person's score indicates whether that person's performance fell above or below the average. As Figure 61.2 shows, a performance higher than all but 2 percent of all scores earns an intelligence score of 130. A performance lower than 98 percent of all scores earns an intelligence score of 70.

To keep the average score near 100, the Stanford-Binet and Wechsler scales are periodically restandardized. If you took the WAIS Fourth Edition recently, your performance was compared with a standardization sample who took the test during 2007, not to David Wechsler's initial 1930s sample. If you compared the performance of the most recent standardization sample with that of the 1930s sample, do you suppose you would find rising or declining test performance? Amazingly—given that college entrance aptitude scores were dropping during the 1960s and 1970s—intelligence test performance was improving. This worldwide phenomenon is called the *Flynn effect,* in honor of New Zealand researcher James Flynn (1987, 2009b, 2010), who first calculated its magnitude. As **FIGURE 61.3** indicates, the average person's intelligence test score in 1920 was—by today's standard—only a 76! Such rising performance has been observed in 29 countries, from Canada to rural Australia (Ceci & Kanaya, 2010). Although the gains have recently reversed in Scandinavia, the historic increase is now widely accepted as an important phenomenon (Lynn, 2009; Teasdale & Owen, 2005, 2008).

standardization defining uniform testing procedures and meaningful scores by comparison with the performance of a pretested group.

normal curve the symmetrical, bell-shaped curve that describes the distribution of many physical and psychological attributes. Most scores fall near the average, and fewer and fewer scores lie near the extremes.

AP® Exam Tip

Can you remember why the intelligence test scores in Figure 61.2 are marked off in 15-point intervals? Do the 68 percent and 95 percent areas seem familiar? They should—you've seen this graph before. It's Figure 7.3 from the module on statistical reasoning. Intelligence tests are being used to illustrate that 68 percent of a population will be within one standard deviation of the mean for normally distributed data. Ninety-five percent will be within two standard deviations.

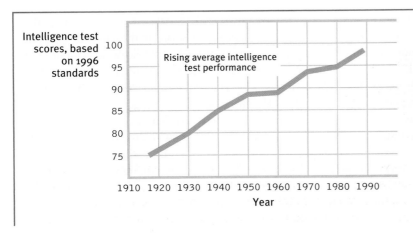

Figure 61.3

Getting smarter? In every country studied, intelligence test performance rose during the twentieth century, as shown here with U.S. Wechsler and Stanford-Binet test performance between 1918 and 1989. In Britain, test scores have risen 27 points since 1942. (From Hogan, 1995.) Very recent data indicate this trend may have leveled off or may even be reversing.

The Flynn effect's cause has been a mystery. Did it result from greater test sophistication? (But the gains began before testing was widespread and have even been observed among preschoolers.) Better nutrition? As the nutrition explanation would predict, people have gotten not only smarter but taller. But in post-war Britain, notes Flynn (2009a), the lower-class children gained the most from improved nutrition but the intelligence performance gains were greater among upper-class children. Or did the Flynn effect stem from more education? More stimulating environments? Less childhood disease? Smaller families and more parental investment (Sundet et al., 2008)?

Regardless of what combination of factors explains the rise in intelligence test scores, the phenomenon counters one concern of some hereditarians—that the higher twentieth-century birthrates among those with lower scores would shove human intelligence scores downward (Lynn & Harvey, 2008). Seeking to explain the rising scores, and mindful of global mixing, one scholar has even speculated about the influence of a genetic phenomenon comparable with "hybrid vigor," which occurs in agriculture when cross-breeding produces corn or livestock superior to the parent plants or animals (Mingroni, 2004, 2007).

Reliability

61-4   What are reliability and validity?

Knowing where you stand in comparison to a standardization group still won't tell us much about your intelligence unless the test has **reliability**—unless it yields dependably consistent scores. To check a test's reliability, researchers retest people. They may use the same test or they may split the test in half to see whether odd-question scores and even-question scores agree. If the two scores generally agree, or *correlate,* the test is reliable. The higher the correlation between the *test-retest* or the *split-half* scores, the higher the test's reliability. The tests we have considered so far—the Stanford-Binet, the WAIS, and the WISC—all have reliabilities of about +.9, which is very high. When retested, people's scores generally match their first score closely.

Validity

High reliability does not ensure a test's **validity**—the extent to which the test actually measures or predicts what it promises. If you use an inaccurate tape measure to measure people's heights, your height report would have high reliability (consistency) but low validity. It is enough for some tests that they have **content validity,** meaning the test taps the pertinent behavior, or *criterion.* The road test for a driver's license has content validity because it samples the tasks a driver routinely faces. Course exams have content validity if they assess one's mastery of a representative sample of course material. But we expect intelligence tests to have **predictive validity:** They should predict the criterion of future performance, and to some extent they do.

Are general aptitude tests as predictive as they are reliable? As critics are fond of noting, the answer is plainly *No.* The predictive power of aptitude tests is fairly strong in the early school years, but later it weakens. Academic aptitude test scores are reasonably good predictors of achievement for children ages 6 to 12, where the correlation between intelligence score and school performance is about +.6 (Jensen, 1980). Intelligence scores correlate even more closely with scores on *achievement tests:* +.81 in one comparison of 70,000 English children's intelligence scores at age 11 with their academic achievement in national exams at age 16 (Deary et al., 2007, 2009). The SAT® exam, used in the United States as a college entrance exam, is less successful in predicting first-year college grades. (The correlation, which is less than +.5, is, however, a bit higher when adjusting for high scorers electing tougher courses [Berry & Sackett, 2009; Willingham et al., 1990].) By the time we get to the Graduate Record Examination® (GRE®; an aptitude test similar to the SAT® exam but for those applying to graduate school), the correlation with graduate school performance is an even more modest but still significant +.4 (Kuncel & Hezlett, 2007).

reliability the extent to which a test yields consistent results, as assessed by the consistency of scores on two halves of the test, on alternate forms of the test, or on retesting.

validity the extent to which a test measures or predicts what it is supposed to. (See also *content validity* and *predictive validity.*)

content validity the extent to which a test samples the behavior that is of interest.

predictive validity the success with which a test predicts the behavior it is designed to predict; it is assessed by computing the correlation between test scores and the criterion behavior. (Also called *criterion-related validity.*)

AP® Exam Tip

Be careful! The terms *reliability* and *validity* have more precise meanings to psychologists than they do to the general public.

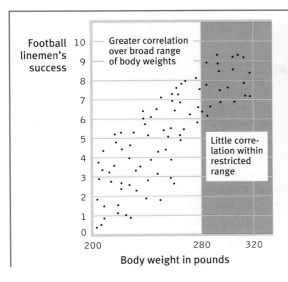

Figure 61.4

Diminishing predictive power Let's imagine a correlation between football linemen's body weight and their success on the field. Note how insignificant the relationship becomes when we narrow the range of weight to 280 to 320 pounds. As the range of data under consideration narrows, its predictive power diminishes.

Why does the predictive power of aptitude scores diminish as students move up the educational ladder? Consider a parallel situation: Among all American and Canadian football linemen, body weight correlates with success. A 300-pound player tends to overwhelm a 200-pound opponent. But within the narrow 280- to 320-pound range typically found at the professional level, the correlation between weight and success becomes negligible (**FIGURE 61.4**). The narrower the *range* of weights, the lower the predictive power of body weight becomes. If an elite university takes only those students who have very high aptitude scores, those scores cannot possibly predict much. This will be true even if the test has excellent predictive validity with a more diverse sample of students. So, when we validate a test using a wide range of people but then use it with a restricted range of people, it loses much of its predictive validity.

Before You Move On

▶ **ASK YOURSELF**

Are you working to the potential reflected in your standardized test scores? What, other than your aptitude, is affecting your school performance?

▶ **TEST YOURSELF**

What was the purpose of Binet's pioneering intelligence test?

Answers to the Test Yourself questions can be found in Appendix E at the end of the book.

Module 61 Review

 When and why were intelligence tests created?

- In the late 1800s, Francis Galton, who believed that genius was inherited, attempted but failed to construct a simple intelligence test.

- In France in 1904, Alfred Binet, who tended toward an environmental explanation of intelligence differences, started the modern intelligence-testing movement by developing questions to measure children's *mental age* and thus predict progress in the school system.

- During the early twentieth century, Lewis Terman of Stanford University revised Binet's work for use in the United States.
  - Terman believed intelligence is inherited, and he thought his *Stanford-Binet* could help guide people toward appropriate opportunities.
  - During this period, intelligence tests were sometimes used to "document" scientists' assumptions about the innate inferiority of certain ethnic and immigrant groups.

61-2   What's the difference between achievement and aptitude tests?

- *Achievement tests* are designed to assess what you have learned.

- *Aptitude tests* are designed to predict what you can learn.

- The *WAIS (Wechsler Adult Intelligence Scale),* an aptitude test, is the most widely used intelligence test for adults.

 61-3   What are standardization and the normal curve?

- *Standardization* establishes a basis for meaningful score comparisons by giving a test to a representative sample of future test-takers.

- The distribution of test scores often forms a *normal* (bell-shaped) *curve* around the central average score, with fewer and fewer scores at the extremes.

61-4   What are reliability and validity?

- *Reliability* is the extent to which a test yields consistent results (on two halves of the test, or when people are retested).

- *Validity* is the extent to which a test measures or predicts what it is supposed to.
  - A test has *content validity* if it samples the pertinent behavior (as a driving test measures driving ability).
  - It has *predictive validity* if it predicts a behavior it was designed to predict. (Aptitude tests have predictive ability if they can predict future achievements.)

Multiple-Choice Questions

1. A test-developer defines uniform testing procedures and meaningful scores by comparison with the performance of a pretested group. Which of the following best describes this process?

a. Reliability testing
b. Validation
c. Content validation
d. Standardization
e. Predictive validity

2. Which of the following best describes the extent to which a test yields consistent results upon retesting?

a. Content validity
b. Validity
c. Reliability
d. Predictive validity
e. Normal curve

3. Which of the following can be used to demonstrate that only about 2 percent of the population scores are at least two standard deviations above the mean on an intelligence test?

a. Reliability test
b. Aptitude test
c. Predictive validity test
d. Test-retest procedure
e. Normal curve

Practice FRQs

1. What are the fundamental differences between achievement and aptitude tests?

Answer

1 point: Achievement tests are designed to assess what a person has learned.

1 point: An aptitude test is designed to predict a person's future performance.

2. Name and briefly describe the three essential principals of test construction.

(3 points)

Module 62

The Dynamics of Intelligence

Module Learning Objectives

62-1 Describe the stability of intelligence scores over the life span.

62-2 Describe the traits of those at the low and high intelligence extremes.

W e now can address some age-old questions about the dynamics of human intelligence—about its stability over the life span, and about the extremes of intelligence.

Stability or Change?

62-1 How stable are intelligence scores over the life span?

If we retested people periodically throughout their lives, would their intelligence scores be stable? Let's first explore the stability of mental abilities in later life.

Aging and Intelligence

What happens to our broader intellectual muscles as we age? Do they gradually decline, as does our body strength (even if relative intellectual and muscular strength in later life is predictable from childhood)? Or do they remain constant? The quest for answers to these questions illustrates psychology's self-correcting process. This research developed in phases.

PHASE I: CROSS-SECTIONAL EVIDENCE FOR INTELLECTUAL DECLINE

In *cross-sectional studies*, researchers at one point in time test and compare people of various ages. In such studies, researchers have consistently found that older adults give fewer correct answers on intelligence tests than do younger adults. WAIS-creator, David Wechsler (1972) therefore concluded that "the decline of mental ability with age is part of the general [aging] process of the organism as a whole." For a long time, this rather dismal view went unchallenged. Many corporations established mandatory retirement policies, assuming the companies would benefit by replacing aging workers with younger, presumably more capable, employees. As "everyone knows," you can't teach an old dog new tricks.

PHASE II: LONGITUDINAL EVIDENCE FOR INTELLECTUAL STABILITY

After colleges in the 1920s began giving intelligence tests to entering students, several psychologists saw their chance to study intelligence *longitudinally*. They retested the same **cohort**—the same group of people—over a period of years (Schaie & Geiwitz, 1982). What they found was a surprise: Until late in life, intelligence remained stable (**FIGURE 62.1** on the next page). On some tests, it even increased.

cohort a group of people from a given time period.

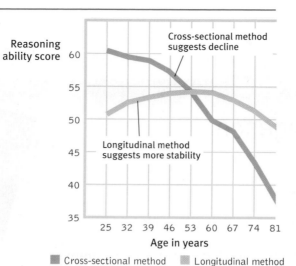

Figure 62.1

Cross-sectional versus longitudinal testing of intelligence at various ages In this test of one type of verbal intelligence (inductive reasoning), the cross-sectional method produced declining scores with age. The longitudinal method (in which the same people were retested over a period of years) produced a slight rise in scores well into adulthood. (Adapted from Schaie, 1994.)

How then are we to account for the cross-sectional findings? In retrospect, researchers saw the problem. When cross-sectional studies compared 70-year-olds and 30-year-olds, they compared people not only of two different ages but of two different eras. They compared generally less-educated people (born, say, in the early 1900s) with better-educated people (born after 1950), people raised in large families with people raised in smaller families, people growing up in less affluent families with people raised in more affluent families.

With this more optimistic view, the myth that intelligence sharply declines with age was laid to rest. At age 70, John Rock developed the birth control pill. At age 81—and 17 years from the end of his college football coaching career—Amos Alonzo Stagg was named coach of the year. At age 89, architect Frank Lloyd Wright designed New York City's Guggenheim Museum. As "everyone knows," given good health you're never too old to learn.

PHASE III: IT ALL DEPENDS

With "everyone knowing" two different and opposing facts about age and intelligence, something was clearly wrong. As it turns out, longitudinal studies have their own potential pitfalls. Those who survive to the end of longitudinal studies may be bright, healthy people whose intelligence is least likely to decline. (Perhaps people who died younger and were removed from the study had declining intelligence.) Adjusting for the loss of participants, as did a study following more than 2000 people over age 75 in Cambridge, England, reveals a steeper intelligence decline, especially after 85 (Brayne et al., 1999).

Research is further complicated by the finding that intelligence is not a single trait, but rather several distinct abilities. Intelligence tests that assess speed of thinking may place older adults at a disadvantage because of their slower neural processing. Meeting old friends on the street, names rise to the mind's surface more slowly—"like air bubbles in molasses," said David Lykken (1999). But slower processing need not mean less intelligence. In four studies in which players were given 15 minutes to complete *New York Times* crossword puzzles, the highest average performance was achieved by adults in their fifties, sixties, and seventies (Salthouse, 2004). "Wisdom" tests assessing "expert knowledge about life in general and good judgment and advice about how to conduct oneself in the face of complex, uncertain circumstances" also suggested that older adults more than hold their own on such tasks (Baltes et al., 1993, 1994, 1999).

So the answers to our age-and-intelligence questions depend on what we assess and how we assess it. **Crystallized intelligence**—our accumulated knowledge as reflected in vocabulary and analogies tests—*increases* up to old age. **Fluid intelligence**—our ability to reason speedily and abstractly, as when solving novel logic problems—*decreases* beginning in the twenties and thirties, slowly up to age 75 or so, then more rapidly, especially after age 85 (Cattell, 1963; Horn, 1982; Salthouse, 2009). With age we lose and we win. We lose recall memory and processing speed, but we gain vocabulary knowledge (**FIGURE 62.2**). Our decisions also become less distorted by negative emotions such as anxiety, depression, and anger (Blanchard-Fields, 2007; Carstensen & Mikels, 2005). And despite their lesser fluid intelligence, older adults also show increased social reasoning, such as by taking multiple perspectives, appreciating knowledge limits, and thus offering helpful wisdom in times of social conflict (Grossman et al., 2010).

FYI

Like older people, older gorillas process information more slowly (Anderson et al., 2005).

"Knowledge is knowing a tomato is a fruit; wisdom is not putting it in a fruit salad." -Anonymous

crystallized intelligence our accumulated knowledge and verbal skills; tends to increase with age.

fluid intelligence our ability to reason speedily and abstractly; tends to decrease during late adulthood.

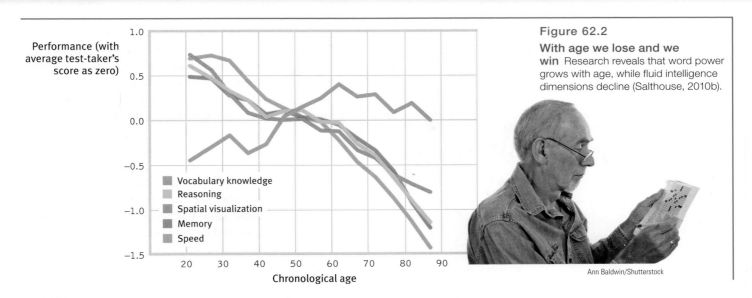

Figure 62.2

With age we lose and we win Research reveals that word power grows with age, while fluid intelligence dimensions decline (Salthouse, 2010b).

Ann Baldwin/Shutterstock

These cognitive differences help explain why older adults are less likely to embrace new technologies (Charness & Boot, 2009). In 2010, only 31 percent of Americans ages 65 and older had broadband Internet at home, compared with 80 percent of adults under 30 (Pew, 2010). The age-related cognitive differences also help explain some curious findings about creativity. Mathematicians and scientists produce much of their most creative work during their late twenties or early thirties. In literature, history, and philosophy, people tend to produce their best work in their forties, fifties, and beyond—after accumulating more knowledge (Simonton, 1988, 1990). Poets, for example, who depend on fluid intelligence, reach their peak output earlier than prose authors, who need a deeper knowledge reservoir. This finding holds in every major literary tradition, for both living and dead languages.

Stability Over the Life Span

Now what about the stability of intelligence scores early in life? Except for extremely impaired or very precocious children, casual observation and intelligence tests before age 3 only modestly predict children's future aptitudes (Humphreys & Davey, 1988; Tasbihsazan et al., 2003). For example, children who are early talkers—speaking in sentences typical of 3-year-olds by age 20 months—are not especially likely to be reading by age 4½ (Crain-Thoreson & Dale, 1992). (A better predictor of early reading is having parents who have read lots of stories to their child.) Even Albert Einstein was slow in learning to talk (Quasha, 1980).

By age 4, however, children's performance on intelligence tests begins to predict their adolescent and adult scores. The consistency of scores over time increases with the age of the child. The remarkable stability of aptitude scores by late adolescence is seen in a U.S. Educational Testing Service® study of 23,000 students who took the SAT® exam and then later took the GRE® (Angoff, 1988). On either test, verbal scores correlated only modestly with math scores—revealing that these two aptitudes are distinct. Yet scores on the SAT® exam verbal test correlated +.86 with the scores on the GRE® verbal tests taken four to five years later. An equally astonishing +.86 correlation occurred between the two math tests. Given the time lapse and differing educational experiences of these 23,000 students, the stability of their aptitude scores is remarkable.

Ian Deary and his colleagues (2004, 2009) set a record for long-term follow-up. Their amazing longitudinal studies have been enabled by their country, Scotland, doing something that no nation has done before or since. On June 1, 1932, essentially every child in the country who had been born in 1921—87,498 children around age 11—was given an intelligence test. The aim was to identify working-class children who would benefit from

"In youth we learn, in age we understand." -Marie Von Ebner-Eschenbach, *Aphorisms*, 1883

"My dear Adele, I am 4 years old and I can read any English book. I can say all the Latin substantives and adjectives and active verbs besides 52 lines of Latin poetry." -Francis Galton, letter to his sister, 1827

FYI

Ironically, SAT® exam and GRE® scores correlate better with each other than either does with its intended criterion, school achievement. Thus, their reliability far exceeds their predictive validity. If either test was much affected by coaching, luck, or how one feels on the test day (as so many people believe), such reliability would be impossible.

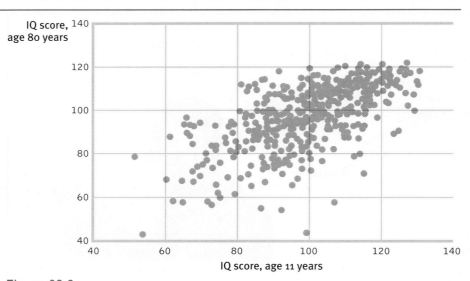

Figure 62.3

Intelligence endures When Ian Deary and his colleagues (2004) retested 80-year-old Scots, using an intelligence test they had taken as 11-year-olds, their scores across seven decades correlated +.66. (When 207 survivors were again retested at age 87, the correlation with their age 11 scores was +.51 [Gow et al., 2011].)

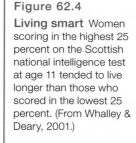

"Whether you live to collect your old-age pension depends in part on your IQ at age 11."
-Ian Deary, "Intelligence, Health, and Death," 2005

further education. Sixty-five years later to the day, Patricia Whalley, the wife of Deary's co-worker, Lawrence Whalley, discovered the test results on dusty storeroom shelves at the Scottish Council for Research in Education, not far from Deary's Edinburgh University office. "This will change our lives," Deary replied when Whalley told him the news.

And so it has, with dozens of studies of the stability and the predictive capacity of these early test results. For example, when the intelligence test administered to 11-year-old Scots in 1932 was readministered to 542 survivors as turn-of-the-millennium 80-year-olds, the correlation between the two sets of scores—after almost 70 years of varied life experiences—was striking (**FIGURE 62.3**). A later study that followed Scots born in 1936 from ages 11 to 70 confirmed the remarkable stability of intelligence, independent of life circumstance (Johnson et al., 2010).

High-scoring 11-year-olds also were more likely to be living independently as 77-year-olds and were less likely to have suffered the cognitive erosion of Alzheimer's disease (Starr et al., 2000; Whalley et al., 2000). Among girls scoring in the highest 25 percent, 70 percent were still alive at age 76—as were only 45 percent of those scoring in the lowest 25 percent (**FIGURE 62.4**). (World War II prematurely ended the lives of many of the male test-takers.) Follow-up studies with other large samples confirm the phenomenon: More intelligent children and adults live healthier and longer (Deary et al., 2008, 2010; Der et al., 2009; Weiss et al., 2009). One study that followed 93 nuns found that those exhibiting less verbal ability in essays written when entering convents in their teens were more at risk for Alzheimer's disease after age 75 (Snowdon et al., 1996).

Pause a moment: Have you any ideas why more intelligent people might live longer? Deary (2008) reports four possible explanations:

1. Intelligence facilitates more education, better jobs, and a healthier environment.
2. Intelligence encourages healthy living: less smoking, better diet, more exercise.
3. Prenatal events or early childhood illnesses might have influenced both intelligence and health.
4. A "well-wired body," as evidenced by fast reaction speeds, perhaps fosters both intelligence and longevity.

Figure 62.4

Living smart Women scoring in the highest 25 percent on the Scottish national intelligence test at age 11 tended to live longer than those who scored in the lowest 25 percent. (From Whalley & Deary, 2001.)

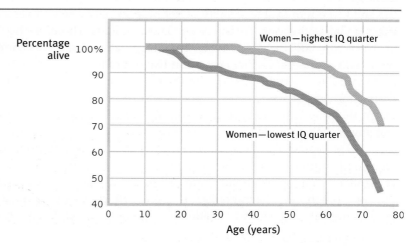

Extremes of Intelligence

 62-2 What are the traits of those at the low and high intelligence extremes?

One way to glimpse the validity and significance of any test is to compare people who score at the two extremes of the normal curve. The two groups should differ noticeably, and they do.

The Low Extreme

At one extreme of the normal curve are those with unusually low intelligence test scores. To be labeled as having an **intellectual disability** (formerly referred to as *mental retardation*), a person must have both a low test score and difficulty adapting to the normal demands of independent living. American Association on Intellectual and Developmental Disabilities guidelines specify performance that is approximately two standard deviations below average (Schalock et al., 2010). For an intelligence test with 100 as average and a standard deviation of 15, that means (allowing for some variation in one's test score) an IQ of approximately 70 or below. The second criterion is a comparable limitation in adaptive behavior as expressed in

- *conceptual skills,* such as language, literacy, and concepts of money, time, and number,
- *social skills,* such as interpersonal skills, social responsibility, and the ability to follow basic rules and laws and avoid being victimized, and
- *practical skills,* such as daily personal care, occupational skill, and travel and health care.

Intellectual disability is a developmental condition that is apparent before age 18, sometimes with a known physical cause. **Down syndrome,** for example, is a disorder of varying severity caused by an extra chromosome 21 in the person's genetic makeup.

Consider one reason why people diagnosed with a mild intellectual disability—those just below the 70 score—might be better able to live independently today than many decades ago, when they were institutionalized. Recall that, thanks to the Flynn effect, the tests have been periodically restandardized. As that happened, individuals who scored near 70 on earlier tests suddenly lost about 6 IQ points. Two people with the same ability level could thus be classified differently, depending on when they were tested (Kanaya et al., 2003; Reynolds et al., 2010). As the boundary shifts, more people become eligible for special education and for Social Security payments for those with an intellectual disability. And in the United States (one of only a few industrialized countries with the death penalty), fewer people are eligible for execution—the U.S. Supreme Court ruled in 2002 that the execution of people with an intellectual disability is "cruel and unusual punishment." For people near that score of 70, intelligence testing can be a high-stakes competition. And so it was for Teresa Lewis, a "dependant personality" with limited intellect, who was executed by the state of Virginia in 2010. Lewis, whose reported IQ score was 72, reportedly agreed to a plot in which two men killed her husband and stepson in exchange for a split of a life insurance payout (Eckholm, 2010). If only she had scored 69.

intellectual disability a condition of limited mental ability, indicated by an intelligence score of 70 or below and difficulty in adapting to the demands of life. (Formerly referred to as *mental retardation.*)

Down syndrome a condition of mild to severe intellectual disability and associated physical disorders caused by an extra copy of chromosome 21.

Mainstreaming in Chile Most Chilean children with Down syndrome attend separate schools for children with special needs. However, this boy is a student at the Altamira School, where children with differing abilities share the classrooms.

The High Extreme

In one famous project begun in 1921, Lewis Terman studied more than 1500 California schoolchildren with IQ scores over 135. Contrary to the popular notion that intellectually gifted children are frequently maladjusted, Terman's high-scoring children, like those in later studies, were healthy, well-adjusted, and unusually successful academically (Koenen et al., 2009; Lubinski, 2009a; Stanley, 1997). When restudied over the next seven decades, most people in Terman's group (the "Termites") had attained high levels of education (Austin et al., 2002; Holahan & Sears, 1995). They included many doctors, lawyers, professors, scientists, and writers, but no Nobel Prize winners.

FYI

Terman did test two future Nobel laureates in physics but they failed to score above his gifted sample cutoff (Hulbert, 2005).

The extremes of intelligence
Moshe Kai Cavalin completed his third college degree by the time he was 14, when the math major graduated from UCLA. According to his mother, he first picked up a college textbook and started reading it at age 2.

> "Joining Mensa means that you are a genius. . . . I worried about the arbitrary 132 cutoff point, until I met someone with an IQ of 131 and, honestly, he was a bit slow on the uptake." -COMEDIAN STEVE MARTIN, 1997

A more recent study of precocious youths who aced the math SAT® exam at age 13—by scoring in the top quarter of 1 percent of their age group—were at age 33 twice as likely to have patents as were those in the bottom quarter of the top 1 percent (Wai et al., 2005). Compared with the math aces, 13-year-olds scoring high on verbal aptitude were more likely to have become humanities professors or written a novel (Park et al., 2007). About 1 percent of Americans earn doctorates. But among those scoring in the top 1 in 10,000—on the mere two-hour SAT® at age 12 or 13—more than half have done so (Lubinski, 2009b).

These whiz kids remind me of Jean Piaget, who by age 15 was publishing scientific articles on mollusks and who went on to become the twentieth century's most famous developmental psychologist (Hunt, 1993). Children with extraordinary academic gifts are sometimes more isolated, introverted, and in their own worlds (Winner, 2000). But most thrive.

Is there a gifted education program at your school? There are critics who question many of the assumptions of currently popular "talented and gifted child" programs, such as the belief that only 3 to 5 percent of children are gifted and that it pays to identify and "track" these special few—segregating them in special classes and giving them academic enrichment not available to their peers. Critics note that tracking by aptitude sometimes creates a self-fulfilling prophecy: Those implicitly labeled "ungifted" may be influenced to become so (Lipsey & Wilson, 1993; Slavin & Braddock, 1993). Denying lower-ability students opportunities for enriched education can widen the achievement gap between ability groups and increase their social isolation from one another (Carnegie, 1989; Stevenson & Lee, 1990). Because minority and low-income youth are more often placed in lower academic groups, tracking can also promote segregation and prejudice—hardly, note critics, a healthy preparation for working and living in a multicultural society.

Critics and proponents of gifted education do, however, agree on this: Children have differing gifts, whether at math, verbal reasoning, art, or social leadership. Educating children as if all were alike is as naive as assuming that giftedness is something, like blue eyes, that you either have or do not have. One need not hang labels on children to affirm their special talents and to challenge them all at the frontiers of their own ability and understanding. By providing *appropriate developmental placement* suited to each child's talents, we can promote both equity and excellence for all (Colangelo et al., 2004; Lubinski & Benbow, 2000; Sternberg & Grigorenko, 2000).

Before You Move On

► **ASK YOURSELF**

How do you feel about mainstreaming children of all ability levels in the same classroom? What evidence are you using to support your view?

► **TEST YOURSELF**

The Smiths have enrolled their 2-year-old son in a special program that promises to assess his IQ and, if he places in the top 5 percent of test-takers, to create a plan that will guarantee his admission to a top university at age 18. Why is this endeavor of questionable value?

Answers to the Test Yourself questions can be found in Appendix E at the end of the book.

Module 62 Review

 62-1 How stable are intelligence scores over the life span?

- Cross-sectional studies (comparing people of different ages) and longitudinal studies (retesting the same *cohort* over a period of years) have shown that *fluid intelligence* declines in older adults, in part because neural processing slows. *Crystallized intelligence* tends to increase.

- The stability of intelligence test scores increases with age.
  - At age 4, scores fluctuate somewhat but begin to predict adolescent and adult scores.
  - By early adolescence, scores are very stable and predictive.

62-2 What are the traits of those at the low and high intelligence extremes?

- An intelligence test score of or below 70 is one diagnostic criterion for the diagnosis of *intellectual disability* (others are limited conceptual, social, and practical skills). People with this diagnosis vary from near-normal to requiring constant aid and supervision.

- *Down syndrome* is a developmental disorder caused by an extra copy of chromosome 21.

- High-scoring people tend to be healthy and well-adjusted, as well as unusually successful academically.
  - Schools sometimes "track" such children, separating them from students with lower scores. Such programs can become self-fulfilling prophecies as both groups live up to—or down to—others' perceptions and expectations.

Multiple-Choice Questions

1. Which of the following is a longitudinal study?
a. Researchers test the intelligence of all the students in a high school.
b. Intelligence tests are given to the residents of a nursing home.
c. Researchers randomly select 50 students from a high school with 2000 students. The 50 students are given intelligence tests.
d. A group of college juniors is given an extensive battery of tests over a period of 2 days.
e. A group of kindergartners is given an intelligence test. They are retested every other year for 30 years.

2. Which of the following best represents crystallized intelligence?
a. Jake can solve math word problems quickly.
b. Grandpa Milt is good at crossword puzzles.
c. Aliyah has a knack for training dogs.
d. Anna writes creative computer programs.
e. Heng bakes excellent chocolate chip cookies.

3. Who conducted a famous study of high IQ children?
a. Lewis Terman
b. David Wechsler
c. Robert Sternberg
d. Howard Gardner
e. Alfred Binet

4. Intellectual disability is defined by both IQ and which of the following?
a. Chronological age
b. Mental age
c. Adaptive ability
d. Physical condition
e. Heritability

Practice FRQs

1. Name and describe the two main types of evidence used to determine whether there is an intellectual decline as people age.

Answer

2 points: Cross-sectional evidence, which comes from studies that examine several age groups at once.

2 points: Longitudinal evidence, which comes from studies that examine the same group of people over a long period of time.

2. Explain three reasons why more intelligent people might live longer.

(3 points)

Module 63

Studying Genetic and Environmental Influences on Intelligence

Module Learning Objectives

63-1 Discuss the evidence for a genetic influence on intelligence, and explain what is meant by heritability.

63-2 Discuss the evidence for environmental influences on intelligence.

"I told my parents that if grades were so important they should have paid for a smarter egg donor."

heritability the proportion of variation among individuals that we can attribute to genes. The heritability of a trait may vary, depending on the range of populations and environments studied.

63-1 What evidence points to a genetic influence on intelligence, and what is heritability?

Intelligence runs in families. But why? Are our intellectual abilities mostly inherited? Or are they molded by our environment?

Few issues arouse such passion or have such serious political implications. Consider: If we mainly inherit our differing mental abilities, and if success reflects those abilities, then people's socioeconomic standing will correspond to their inborn differences. This could lead to those on top believing their intellectual birthright justifies their social positions.

But if mental abilities are primarily nurtured by our environments, then children from disadvantaged environments can expect to lead disadvantaged lives. In this case, people's standing will result from their unequal opportunities.

For now, as best we can, let's set aside such political implications and examine the evidence.

Twin and Adoption Studies

Do people who share the same genes also share mental abilities? As you can see from **FIGURE 63.1**, which summarizes many studies, the answer is clearly *Yes.* Consider:

- The intelligence test scores of identical twins raised together are virtually as similar as those of the same person taking the same test twice (Lykken, 1999; Plomin, 2001). (The scores of fraternal twins, who share only about half their genes, are much less similar.) Estimates of the **heritability** of intelligence—the extent to which intelligence test score variation can be attributed to genetic variation—range from 50 to 80 percent (Johnson et al., 2009; Neisser et al., 1996; Plomin, 2003). Identical twins also exhibit substantial similarity (and heritability) in specific talents, such as music, math, and sports (Vinkhuyzen et al., 2009).

- Brain scans reveal that identical twins' brains are built and function similarly. They have similar gray and white matter volume (Deary et al., 2009). Their brains (unlike those of fraternal twins) are virtually the same in areas associated with verbal and spatial intelligence (Thompson et al., 2001). And their brains show similar activity while doing mental tasks (Koten et al., 2009).

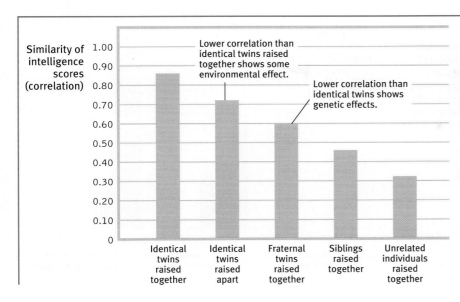

Lower correlation than identical twins raised together shows some environmental effect.

Lower correlation than identical twins shows genetic effects.

Figure 63.1

Intelligence: Nature and nurture The most genetically similar people have the most similar intelligence scores. Remember: 1.0 indicates a perfect correlation; zero indicates no correlation at all. (Data from McGue et al., 1993.)

- Are there known genes for genius? Today's researchers have identified chromosomal regions important to intelligence, and they have pinpointed specific genes that seemingly influence variations in intelligence and learning disorders (Dick, 2007; Plomin & Kovas, 2005; Posthuma & de Geus, 2006). But intelligence appears to be *polygenetic,* involving many genes, with each gene accounting for much less than 1 percent of intelligence variations (Butcher et al., 2008). Intelligence is like height, suggests Wendy Johnson (2010): 54 specific gene variations together have accounted for 5 percent of our individual differences in height, leaving the rest yet to be discovered. Do we really need to discover them all—or is it enough to know that few individual genes have a big effect on height, or intelligence? What matters is the combination of many genes.

> **AP® Exam Tip**
>
> Figure 63.1 is worth spending some time on. Try grabbing a study buddy and explaining whether each of the five conditions provides more support for nature or more for nurture. In most cases, it's some of each and you have to look at comparisons between categories to really be able to draw conclusions.

Other evidence points to the effects of environment. Twin studies show some environmental contribution to IQ score variation among top scorers (Brant et al., 2009; Kirkpatrick et al., 2009). Where environments vary widely, as they do among children of less-educated parents, environmental differences are more predictive of intelligence scores (Rowe et al., 1999; Tucker-Drob et al., 2011; Turkheimer et al., 2003). Studies also show that adoption enhances the intelligence scores of mistreated or neglected children (van IJzendoorn & Juffer, 2005, 2006).

Seeking to disentangle genes and environment, researchers have compared the intelligence test scores of adopted children with those of (a) their adoptive siblings, (b) their biological parents (the providers of their genes), and (c) their adoptive parents, the providers of their home environment. During childhood, the intelligence test scores of adoptive siblings correlate modestly. Over time, adopted children accumulate experience in their differing adoptive families. So would you expect the family-environment effect to grow with age and the genetic-legacy effect to shrink?

If you would, behavior geneticists have a stunning surprise for you. Mental similarities between adopted children and their adoptive families wane with age, until the correlation approaches zero by adulthood (McGue et al., 1993). Genetic influences—not environmental ones—become more apparent as we accumulate life experience. Identical twins' similarities, for example, continue or increase into their eighties. Thus, report Ian Deary and his colleagues (2009), the heritability of general intelligence increases from "about 30 percent" in early childhood to "well over 50 percent in adulthood." In one massive study of 11,000 twin pairs in four

"Selective breeding has given me an aptitude for the law, but I still love fetching a dead duck out of freezing water."

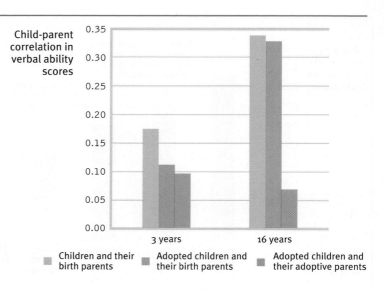

Figure 63.2

Who do adopted children resemble in verbal ability? As the years went by in their adoptive families, children's verbal ability scores became modestly more like their *biological* parents' scores. (Adapted from Plomin & DeFries, 1998.)

Child-parent correlation in verbal ability scores

- Children and their birth parents
- Adopted children and their birth parents
- Adopted children and their adoptive parents

> "There are more studies addressing the genetics of *g* [general intelligence] than any other human characteristic."
> -ROBERT PLOMIN (1999)

countries, the heritability of *g* increased from 41 percent in middle childhood to 55 percent in adolescence to 66 percent in young adulthood (Haworth et al., 2010). Similarly, adopted children's verbal ability scores over time become more like those of their biological parents (**FIGURE 63.2**). Who would have guessed?

Environmental Influences

 What does evidence reveal about environmental influences on intelligence?

Genes make a difference. Even if we were all raised in the same intellectually stimulating environment, we would have differing aptitudes. But life experiences also matter. Human environments are rarely as impoverished as the dark and barren cages inhabited by deprived rats that develop thinner-than-normal brain cortexes (see Module 50). Yet severe deprivation also leaves footprints on the human brain.

Early Environmental Influences

Nowhere is the intertwining of biology and experience more apparent than in impoverished human environments such as J. McVicker Hunt (1982) observed in a destitute Iranian orphanage. The typical child Hunt observed there could not sit up unassisted at age 2 or walk at age 4. The little care the infants received was not in response to their crying, cooing, or other behaviors, so the children developed little sense of personal control over their environment. They were instead becoming passive "glum lumps." Extreme deprivation was bludgeoning native intelligence—a finding confirmed by other studies of children raised in poorly run orphanages in Romania and elsewhere (Nelson, et al., 2009; van IJzendoorn et al., 2008).

Aware of both the dramatic effects of early experiences and the impact of early intervention, Hunt began a program of *tutored human enrichment*. He trained caregivers to play language-fostering games with 11 infants, imitating the babies' babbling, then engaging them in vocal follow-the-leader, and finally teaching them sounds from the Persian language. The results were dramatic. By 22 months of age,

Devastating neglect Some Romanian orphans, such as this child in the Leaganul Pentru Copii orphanage in 1990, had minimal interaction with caregivers, and suffered delayed development.

Josef Polleross/The Image Works

the infants could name more than 50 objects and body parts, and so charmed visitors that most were adopted—an unprecedented success for the orphanage.

Hunt's findings are an extreme case of a more general finding: Among those economically impoverished, environmental conditions can depress cognitive development. Schools with many poverty-level children often have less-qualified teachers, as one study of 1450 Virginia schools found. So these children may receive a less-enriched education. And even after controlling for poverty, having less-qualified teachers predicted lower achievement scores (Tuerk, 2005). Malnutrition also plays a role. Relieve infant malnutrition with nutritional supplements, and poverty's effect on physical and cognitive development lessens (Brown & Pollitt, 1996).

Do studies of such early interventions indicate that providing an "enriched" environment can "give your child a superior intellect," as some popular products claim? Most experts are doubtful (Bruer, 1999). Although malnutrition, sensory deprivation, and social isolation can retard normal brain development, there is no environmental recipe for fast-forwarding a normal infant into a genius. All babies should have normal exposure to sights, sounds, and speech. Beyond that, Sandra Scarr's (1984) verdict still is widely shared: "Parents who are very concerned about providing special educational lessons for their babies are wasting their time."

Still, explorations of intelligence promotion continue. Some parents, after exposing their 12- to 18-month-old babies to educational DVDs such as from the *Baby Einstein* series, have observed their baby's vocabulary growing. To see whether such cognitive growth is a result of the DVD exposure, or simply of infants' natural language explosion, two research teams assigned babies to DVD exposure or a control group (DeLoache et al., 2010; Reichert et al., 2010). Their common finding: The two groups' word-learning did not differ.

Schooling and Intelligence

Later in childhood, schooling is one intervention that pays intelligence score dividends. Schooling and intelligence interact, and both enhance later income (Ceci & Williams, 1997, 2009). Hunt was a strong believer in the ability of education to boost children's chances for success by developing their cognitive and social skills. Indeed, his 1961 book, *Intelligence and Experience,* helped launch Project Head Start in 1965, a U.S. government-funded preschool program that serves more than 900,000 children, most of whom come from families below the poverty level (Head Start, 2010). Does it succeed? Generally, the aptitude benefits dissipate over time (reminding us that life experience *after* Head Start matters, too). Psychologist Edward Zigler, the program's first director, nevertheless believed there are long-term benefits (Ripple & Zigler, 2003; Zigler & Styfco, 2001).

Genes and experience together weave the intelligence fabric. (Recall from Module 14 that *epigenetics* is one field that studies this nature–nurture meeting place.) But what we accomplish with our intelligence depends also on our own beliefs and motivation. One analysis of 72,431 collegians found that study motivation and study skills rivaled previous grades and aptitude as predictors of academic achievement (Credé & Kuncel, 2008). Motivation even affects intelligence test performance. Four dozen studies show that, when promised money for doing well, adolescents score higher (Duckworth et al., 2011).

Psychologist Carol Dweck (2006, 2007, 2008) reports that believing intelligence is biologically set and unchanging can lead to a "fixed mindset." Believing intelligence is changeable, a "growth mindset" results in a focus on learning and growing. As collegians, these believers also tend to happily flourish (Howell, 2009). Dweck has developed interventions that effectively teach young teens that the brain is like a muscle that grows stronger with use as neuron connections grow. Indeed, as we noted earlier, superior achievements in fields from sports to science to music arise from disciplined effort and sustained practice (Ericsson et al., 2007).

Before You Move On

▶ **ASK YOURSELF**

How have genetic and environmental influences shaped your intelligence?

▶ **TEST YOURSELF**

As society succeeds in creating equality of opportunity, it will also increase the heritability of ability. The heritability of intelligence scores will be greater in a society marked by equal opportunity than in a society of peasants and aristocrats. Why?

Answers to the Test Yourself questions can be found in Appendix E at the end of the book.

Module 63 Review

 What evidence points to a genetic influence on intelligence, and what is heritability?

- Studies of twins, family members, and adoptees indicate a significant hereditary contribution to intelligence scores.

- Intelligence seems to be polygenetic, and researchers are searching for genes that exert an influence.

- *Heritability* is the proportion of variation among individuals that can be attributed to genes.

 What does evidence reveal about environmental influences on intelligence?

- Studies of twins, family members, and adoptees also provide evidence of environmental influences.

- Test scores of identical twins raised apart are slightly less similar (though still very highly correlated) than the scores of identical twins raised together.

- Studies of children raised in extremely impoverished environments with minimal social interaction indicate that life experiences can significantly influence intelligence test performance.

- No evidence supports the idea that normal, healthy children can be molded into geniuses by growing up in an exceptionally enriched environment.

Multiple-Choice Questions

1. Heritability relates to the
   a. percentage of a person's intelligence that is due to environmental influences.
   b. percentage of a person's intelligence that is due to genetics.
   c. correlation of intelligence test scores among family members.
   d. extent to which variability among individuals' intelligence scores can be attributed to genetic variation.
   e. genetic stability of intelligence over time.

2. The correlation between the IQ scores of fraternal twins raised together is lower than IQ scores of identical twins raised together. What conclusion can be drawn from this data?
   a. Nothing, because the type of twin has not been held constant.
   b. Nothing, because there is no comparison between twins and adopted children.
   c. Nothing, because cultural differences have not been considered.
   d. There is a genetic effect on intelligence.
   e. There is an environmental effect on intelligence.

3. Which of the following is true of the mental similarities between adoptive children and their adoptive parents as they age?

 a. Adoptive children become much more similar to their adoptive families over time.

 b. Adoptive children become slightly more similar to their adoptive families over time.

 c. There is hardly any similarity, either when the adoptive children are young or when they are older.

 d. Adoptive children become slightly less similar to their adoptive families over time.

 e. Adoptive children become much less similar to their adoptive families over time.

4. According to Carol Dweck, students are often hampered by a "fixed mindset." This means they believe:

 a. intelligence is biologically set and unchangeable.

 b. it is never good to change your mind once it is made up.

 c. intelligence can be "repaired" by doing specific mental exercises.

 d. they have already done everything they can to improve.

 e. problems can only be solved a particular way.

Practice FRQs

1. Explain two environmental interventions that might help poverty-level schoolchildren develop better cognitive skills.

Answer

1 point: The presence of more highly qualified teachers is positively correlated with higher student achievement.

1 point: Nutritional supplements can help alleviate the effects of the poor nutrition that often accompanies economic poverty.

2. Explain whether each of the following comparisons indicates a greater influence of genetics on intelligence or a greater influence of environment on intelligence.

 • The correlation of intelligence test scores for identical twins raised *together* is about +.85. For identical twins raised *apart,* the correlation is about +.72.

 • The correlation of intelligence scores for identical twins raised together is about +.85. For fraternal twins raised together, it is about +.60.

(2 points)

Module 64

Group Differences and the Question of Bias

Hugh Sitton/Corbis

Module Learning Objectives

64-1 Describe how and why the genders differ in mental ability scores.

64-2 Describe how and why racial and ethnic groups differ in mental ability scores.

64-3 Discuss whether intelligence tests are inappropriately biased.

Group Differences in Intelligence Test Scores

If there were no group differences in aptitude scores, psychologists could politely debate hereditary and environmental influences in their ivory towers. But there are group differences. What are they? And what shall we make of them?

Gender Similarities and Differences

64-1 How and why do the genders differ in mental ability scores?

In science, as in everyday life, differences, not similarities, excite interest. Compared with the anatomical and physiological similarities between men and women, our differences are minor. In that 1932 testing of all Scottish 11-year-olds, for example, girls' average intelligence score was 100.6 and boys' was 100.5 (Deary et al., 2003). So far as *g* is concerned, boys and girls, men and women, are the same species.

Yet, most people find differences more newsworthy. Girls are better spellers, more verbally fluent, better at locating objects, better at detecting emotions, and more sensitive to touch, taste, and color (Halpern et al., 2007). Boys outperform girls in tests of spatial ability and complex math problems, though in math computation and overall math performance, boys and girls hardly differ (Else-Quest et al., 2010; Hyde & Mertz, 2009; Lindberg et al., 2010). Males' mental ability scores also vary more than females'. Thus, boys worldwide outnumber girls at both the low extreme and the high extreme (Machin & Pekkarinen, 2008; Strand et al., 2006). Boys, for example, are more often found in special education classes. And among 12- to 14-year-olds scoring extremely high (700 or higher) on the SAT® exam math section, boys outnumber girls 4 to 1 (Wai et al., 2010).

The most reliable male edge appears in spatial ability tests like the one shown in **FIGURE 64.1**. The solution requires speedily rotating three-dimensional objects in one's mind (Collins & Kimura, 1997; Halpern, 2000). Today, such skills help when fitting suitcases into a car trunk, playing chess, or doing certain types of geometry problems. From an evolutionary perspective, those same skills would have helped our ancestral fathers track prey and make their way home (Geary, 1995, 1996; Halpern et al., 2007). The survival of our ancestral mothers may have benefited more from a keen memory for the location of edible plants—a legacy that lives today in women's superior memory for objects and their location.

Which two circles contain a configuration of blocks identical to the one in the circle at the left?

Standard   Alternatives

Figure 64.1

The mental rotation test This is a test of spatial abilities. (From Vandenberg & Kuse, 1978.) See inverted answer below.

ANSWER: The first and fourth alternatives.

But experience also matters. One experiment found that playing action video games boosts spatial abilities (Feng et al., 2007). And you probably won't be surprised to know that among entering American collegians, six times as many men (23 percent) as women (4 percent) report playing video/computer games six or more hours a week (Pryor et al., 2010).

Evolutionary psychologist Steven Pinker (2005) argues that biological as well as social influences appear to affect gender differences in life priorities (women's greater interest in people versus men's in money and things), in risk-taking (with men more reckless), and in math reasoning and spatial abilities. Such differences are, he notes, observed across cultures, stable over time, influenced by prenatal hormones, and observed in genetic boys raised as girls. Culturally influenced preferences also help explain women selecting people- rather than math-intensive vocations (Ceci & Williams, 2010, 2011).

Other critics urge us to remember that social expectations and divergent opportunities shape boys' and girls' interests and abilities (Crawford et al., 1995; Eccles et al., 1990). Gender-equal cultures, such as Sweden and Iceland, exhibit little of the gender math gap found in gender-unequal cultures, such as Turkey and Korea (Guiso et al., 2008).

Nature or nurture? At this 2005 Google Inc.-sponsored computer coding competition, programmers competed for cash prizes and possible jobs. What do you think accounted for the fact that only one of the 100 finalists was female?

Racial and Ethnic Similarities and Differences

 How and why do racial and ethnic groups differ in mental ability scores?

Fueling the group-differences debate are two other disturbing but agreed-upon facts:

- Racial groups differ in their average intelligence test scores.

- High-scoring people (and groups) are more likely to attain high levels of education and income.

There are many group differences in average intelligence test scores. New Zealanders of European descent outscore native Maori New Zealanders. Israeli Jews outscore Israeli Arabs. Most Japanese outscore most Burakumin, a stigmatized Japanese minority. Those who can hear outscore those born deaf (Braden, 1994; Steele, 1990; Zeidner, 1990). And White Americans have outscored Black Americans. This Black-White difference has diminished somewhat in recent years, especially among children (Dickens & Flynn, 2006; Nisbett, 2009). Such *group* differences provide little basis for judging individuals. Worldwide, women outlive men by 4 years, but knowing only that you are male or female won't tell us much about how long you will live.

We have seen that heredity contributes to *individual* differences in intelligence. But group differences in a heritable trait may be entirely environmental. Consider one of nature's experiments: Allow some children to grow up hearing their culture's dominant language, while others, born deaf, do not. Then give both groups an intelligence test rooted in

© Larry Williams/CORBIS

the dominant language, and (no surprise) those with expertise in that language will score highest. Although individual performance differences may be substantially genetic, the group difference is not (**FIGURE 64.2**).

Might the racial gap be similarly environmental? Consider:

Genetics research reveals that under the skin, the races are remarkably alike. The average genetic difference between two Icelandic villagers or between two Kenyans greatly exceeds the group difference between Icelanders and Kenyans (Cavalli-Sforza et al., 1994; Rosenberg et al., 2002). Moreover, looks can deceive. Light-skinned Europeans and dark-skinned Africans are genetically closer than are dark-skinned Africans and dark-skinned Aboriginal Australians.

Race is not a neatly defined biological category. Some scholars argue that there is a reality to race, noting that there are genetic markers for race (the continent of one's ancestry), that medical risks (such as skin cancer or high blood pressure) vary by race, and that most people self-identify with a given race (Hunt & Carlson, 2007). Behavioral traits may also vary by race. "No runner of Asian or European descent—a majority of the world's population—has broken 10 seconds in the 100-meter dash, but dozens of runners of West African descent have done so," observed psychologist David Rowe (2005). Many social scientists, though, see race primarily as a social construction without well-defined physical boundaries, as each race blends seamlessly into the race of its geographical neighbors (Helms et al., 2005; Smedley & Smedley, 2005). People with varying ancestry may categorize themselves in the same race. Moreover, with increasingly mixed ancestries, more and more people defy neat racial categorization and self-identify as multiracial (Pauker et al., 2009).

The intelligence test performance of today's better-fed, better-educated, and more test-prepared population exceeds that of the 1930s population—by a greater margin than the intelligence test score of the average White today exceeds that of the average Black. One research review noted that the average IQ test performance of today's sub-Saharan Africans is the same as Brit-

Figure 64.2

Group differences and environmental impact Even if the variation between members within a group reflects genetic differences, the average difference between groups may be wholly due to the environment. Imagine that seeds from the same mixture are sown in different soils. Although height differences *within* each window box will be genetic, the height difference *between* the two groups will be environmental. (From Lewontin, 1976.)

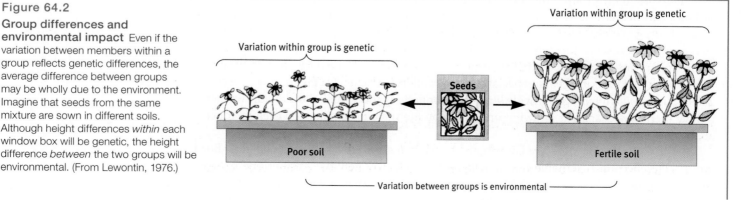

Variation within group is genetic

Variation within group is genetic

Seeds

Poor soil

Fertile soil

Variation between groups is environmental

ish adults in 1948, with the possibility of similar gains to come, given improved nutrition, economic development, and education (Wicherts et al., 2010). No one attributes generational group differences to genetics.

When Blacks and Whites have or receive the same pertinent knowledge, they exhibit similar information-processing skill. "The data support the view that cultural differences in the provision of information may account for racial differences in IQ," report researchers Joseph Fagan and Cynthia Holland (2007).

Schools and culture matter. Countries whose economies create a large wealth gap between rich and poor tend also to have a large rich/poor IQ gap (Nisbett, 2009). Moreover, educational policies such as kindergarten attendance, school discipline, and instructional time per year predict national differences in intelligence and knowledge tests (Rindermann & Ceci, 2009). Asian students outperform North American students on math achievement and aptitude tests. This difference may reflect conscientiousness more than competence. Asian students also attend school 30 percent more days per year and spend much more time in and out of school studying math (Geary et al., 1996; Larson & Verma, 1999; Stevenson, 1992).

In different eras, different ethnic groups have experienced golden ages—periods of remarkable achievement. Twenty-five-hundred years ago, it was the Greeks and the Egyptians, then the Romans; in the eighth and ninth centuries, genius seemed to reside in the Arab world; 500 years ago it was the Aztec Indians and the peoples of Northern Europe. Today, people marvel at Asians' technological genius and Jews' cultural success. In today's United States, Jews are 2 percent of the population, 21 percent of Ivy League student bodies, 37 percent of Academy Award–winning directors, and 51 percent of Pulitzer Prize winners for nonfiction; worldwide, they have been 27 percent of Nobel physics laureates and 54 percent of world chess champions (Brooks, 2010). Cultures rise and fall over centuries; genes do not. That fact makes it difficult to attribute a natural superiority to any race.

Moreover, consider the striking results of a national study that looked back over the mental test performances of White and Black young adults after graduation from college. From eighth grade through the early high school years, the average aptitude score of the White students increased, while that of the Black students decreased—creating a gap that reached its widest point at about the time that high school students like you take college admissions tests. But during college, the Black students' scores increased "more than four times as much" as those of their White counterparts, thus greatly decreasing the aptitude gap. "It is not surprising," concluded researcher Joel Myerson and his colleagues (1998), "that as Black and White students complete more grades in high school environments that differ in quality, the gap in cognitive test scores widens. At the college level, however, where Black and White students are exposed to educational environments of comparable quality . . . many Blacks are able to make remarkable gains, closing the gap in test scores."

Nature's own morphing Nature draws no sharp boundaries between races, which blend gradually one into the next around the Earth. Thanks to the human urge to classify, however, people socially define themselves in racial categories, which become catchall labels for physical features, social identity, and nationality.

© Rob Howard/ Corbis;
© David Turnley/Corbis;
© Barbara Bannister; Gallo Images/ Corbis;
© Dave Bartruff/Corbis;
© Haruyoshi Yamaguchi/Corbis;
© Richard T. Nowitz/Corbis;
© Owen Franken/Corbis;
© John-Francis Bourke/zefa/Corbis

"Do not obtain your slaves from Britain, because they are so stupid and so utterly incapable of being taught." -CICERO, 106–43 B.C.E.

The Question of Bias

64-3   Are intelligence tests inappropriately biased?

If one assumes that race is a meaningful concept, the debate over race differences in intelligence divides into three camps, note Earl Hunt and Jerry Carlson (2007):

- There are genetically disposed race differences in intelligence.
- There are socially influenced race differences in intelligence.
- There are race differences in test scores, but the tests are inappropriate or biased.

Are intelligence tests biased? The answer depends on which of two very different definitions of *bias* we use.

Two Meanings of Bias

We consider a test biased if it detects not only innate differences in intelligence but also performance differences caused by cultural experiences. This in fact happened to Eastern European immigrants in the early 1900s. Lacking the experience to answer questions about their new culture, many were classified as feeble-minded.

In this popular sense, intelligence tests are biased. They measure your developed abilities, which reflect, in part, your education and experiences. You may have read examples of intelligence test items that make middle-class assumptions (for example, that a cup goes with a saucer). Do such items bias the test against those who do not use saucers? Could such questions explain racial differences in test performance? If so, are tests a vehicle for discrimination, consigning potentially capable children, some of whom may have a different native language, to dead-end classes and jobs? And could creating culture-neutral questions—such as by assessing people's ability to learn novel words, sayings, and analogies—enable culture-fair aptitude tests (Fagan & Holland, 2007, 2009)?

Defenders of the existing aptitude tests note that racial group differences persist on nonverbal items, such as counting digits backward (Jensen, 1983, 1998). Moreover, they add, blaming the test for a group's lower scores is like blaming a messenger for bad news. Why blame the tests for exposing unequal experiences and opportunities? If, because of malnutrition, people were to suffer stunted growth, would you blame the measuring stick that reveals it? If unequal past experiences predict unequal future achievements, a valid aptitude test will detect such inequalities.

The second meaning of *bias*—its *scientific* meaning—is different. It hinges on a test's validity—on whether it predicts future behavior only for some groups of test-takers. For example, if the SAT® exam accurately predicted the college achievement of women but not that of men, then the test would be biased. In this statistical meaning of the term, the near-consensus among psychologists (as summarized by the U.S. National Research Council's Committee on Ability Testing and the American Psychological Association's Task Force on Intelligence) is that the major U.S. aptitude tests are *not* biased (Hunt & Carlson, 2007; Neisser et al., 1996; Wigdor & Garner, 1982). The tests' predictive validity is roughly the same for women and men, for Blacks and Whites, and for rich and poor. If an intelligence test score of 95 predicts slightly below-average grades, that rough prediction usually applies equally to all.

> "Political equality is a commitment to universal human rights, and to policies that treat people as individuals rather than representatives of groups; it is not an empirical claim that all groups are indistinguishable." -Steven Pinker (2006)

Test-Takers' Expectations

Throughout this text, we have seen that our expectations and attitudes can influence our perceptions and behaviors, and we find this effect in intelligence testing. When Steven Spencer and his colleagues (1997) gave a difficult math test to equally capable men and women, women did not do as well—except when they had been led to expect that women usually do as well as men on the test. Otherwise, the women apparently felt apprehensive, which affected their performance. With Claude Steele and Joshua Aronson, Spencer (2002) also observed this self-fulfilling **stereotype threat** with Black students. When reminded of their race just before taking verbal aptitude tests, they performed worse. Follow-up experiments confirm that negatively stereotyped minorities and women may have unrealized academic potential (Nguyen & Ryan, 2008; Walton & Spencer, 2009). If, when taking an exam, you are worried that your type often doesn't do well, your self-doubts and self-monitoring may hijack your working memory and impair your performance (Schmader, 2010). For such reasons, stereotype threat may also impair attention and learning (Inzlicht & Kang, 2010; Rydell et al., 2010).

stereotype threat a self-confirming concern that one will be evaluated based on a negative stereotype.

> "Math class is tough!" -"Teen talk" talking Barbie doll (introduced July 1992, recalled October 1992)

Critics note that stereotype threat does not fully account for the Black-White aptitude score difference (Sackett et al., 2004, 2008). But it does help explain why Blacks have scored higher when tested by Blacks than when tested by Whites (Danso & Esses, 2001; Inzlicht & Ben-Zeev, 2000). It gives us insight into why women have scored higher on math tests with no male test-takers present, and why women's chess play drops sharply when they *think* they are playing a male opponent (Maass et al., 2008). And it explains "the Obama effect"—

the finding that African-American adults performed better if taking a verbal aptitude test administered immediately after watching Barack Obama's stereotype-defying nomination acceptance speech or just after his 2008 presidential victory (Marx et al., 2009).

Steele (1995, 2010) concludes that telling students they probably won't succeed (as is sometimes implied by remedial "minority support" programs) functions as a stereotype that can erode performance. Over time, such students may detach their self-esteem from academics and look for recognition elsewhere. Indeed, as African-American boys progress from eighth to twelfth grade, there is a growing disconnect between their grades and their self-esteem and they tend to underachieve (Osborne, 1997). One experiment randomly assigned some African-American seventh-graders to write for 15 minutes about their most important values (Cohen et al., 2006, 2009). That simple exercise in self-affirmation had the apparent effect of boosting their semester grade point average by 0.26 in a first experiment and 0.34 in a replication. Minority students in university programs that challenge them to believe in their potential, or to focus on the idea that intelligence is malleable and not fixed, have likewise produced markedly higher grades and had lower dropout rates (Wilson, 2006).

What, then, can we realistically conclude about aptitude tests and bias? The tests are indeed biased (appropriately so, some would say) in one sense—sensitivity to performance differences caused by cultural experience. But they are not biased in the scientific sense of failing to make valid statistical predictions for different groups.

Bottom line: Are the tests discriminatory? Again, the answer can be *Yes* or *No.* In one sense, *Yes,* their purpose is to discriminate—to distinguish among individuals. In another sense, *No,* their purpose is to reduce discrimination by reducing reliance on subjective criteria for school and job placement—who you know, what school you're from, or whether you are the "right kind of person." Civil service aptitude tests, for example, were devised to discriminate more fairly and objectively by reducing the political, racial, and ethnic discrimination that preceded their use. Banning aptitude tests would lead those who decide on jobs and admissions to rely more on other considerations, such as personal opinion.

Perhaps, then, our goals for tests of mental abilities should be threefold. First, we should realize the benefits Alfred Binet foresaw—to enable schools to recognize who might profit most from early intervention. Second, we must remain alert to Binet's fear that intelligence test scores may be misinterpreted as literal measures of a person's worth and potential. Third, we must remember that the competence that general intelligence tests sample is important; it helps enable success in some life paths. But it reflects only one aspect of personal competence. Our practical intelligence and emotional intelligence matter, too, as do other forms of creativity, talent, and character. Because there are many ways of being successful, our differences are variations of human adaptability.

Finally, life's great achievements result not only from "can do" abilities but also from "will do" motivation. Competence + Diligence → Accomplishment.

Untestable compassion
Intelligence test scores are only one part of the picture of a whole person. They don't measure the abilities, talent, and commitment of, for example, people who devote their lives to helping others.

"Almost all the joyful things of life are outside the measure of IQ tests." -Madeleine L'Engle, *A Circle of Quiet,* 1972

"[Einstein] showed that genius equals brains plus tenacity squared." -Walter Isaacson, "Einstein's Final Quest," 2009

Before You Move On

▶ **ASK YOURSELF**

How have your expectations influenced your own test performance? What steps could you take to control this influence?

▶ **TEST YOURSELF**

What is the difference between a test that is biased culturally, and a test that is biased in terms of its validity?

Answers to the Test Yourself questions can be found in Appendix E at the end of the book.

Module 64 Review

 How and why do the genders differ in mental ability scores?

- Males and females tend to have the same average intelligence test scores. They differ in some specific abilities.

- Girls are better spellers, more verbally fluent, better at locating objects, better at detecting emotions, and more sensitive to touch, taste, and color.

- Boys outperform girls at spatial ability and related mathematics, though girls outperform boys in math computation. Boys also outnumber girls at the low and high extremes of mental abilities.

- Psychologists debate evolutionary, brain-based, and cultural explanations of such gender differences.

 How and why do racial and ethnic groups differ in mental ability scores?

- Racial and ethnic groups differ in their average intelligence test scores.

- The evidence suggests that environmental differences are largely, perhaps entirely, responsible for these group differences.

64-3 **Are intelligence tests inappropriately biased?**

- Aptitude tests aim to predict how well a test-taker will perform in a given situation. So they are necessarily "biased" in the sense that they are sensitive to performance differences caused by cultural experience.

- By "inappropriately biased," psychologists mean that a test predicts less accurately for one group than for another. In this sense, most experts consider the major aptitude tests unbiased.

- *Stereotype threat*, a self-confirming concern that one will be evaluated based on a negative stereotype, affects performance on all kinds of tests.

Multiple-Choice Questions

1. Which of the following is true of boys compared with girls?

a. Boys have a higher average intelligence score.
b. Boys are better spellers than girls.
c. Boys are better at detecting emotions.
d. Boys are more verbally fluent.
e. Boys are more likely to have extremely low intelligence scores.

2. Which of the following provides the best evidence that race is more of a social construct than a biological category?

a. People of varying ancestry may categorize themselves in the same race.
b. The races arose in different continents.
c. Behavior traits (like running speed) are associated with race.
d. Skin cancer rates vary by race.
e. The incidence of high blood pressure varies by race.

3. According to most experts, intelligence tests are not biased because

a. the average scores for various racial and ethnic groups do not differ by much.
b. the tests do a pretty good job of predicting what they are supposed to predict.
c. cultural background has little influence on test scores.
d. scores on the test are not very stable even when you don't consider race.
e. scores are increasing for almost all groups because of the Flynn effect.

Practice FRQs

1. Robert and Maya are having an argument about whether intelligence tests are biased. Robert thinks they are but Maya insists they are not. How can they both be right?

2. Explain three reasons why racial differences in intelligence might be caused by environmental factors.

(3 points)

Answer

1 point: Intelligence tests can be considered biased because they, in part, measure experience. Therefore, people from a middle-class, or higher, background are at an advantage.

1 point: Intelligence tests do a good job of predicting the future no matter what demographic group the test-taker is from. In other words, children who do well on intelligence tests are likely to do well in school no matter what their economic or ethnic background is. Likewise, children from all backgrounds who do poorly on the tests do poorly in school.

Unit XI Review

Key Terms and Concepts to Remember

intelligence, p. 607

intelligence test, p. 607

general intelligence (g), p. 608

factor analysis, p. 608

savant syndrome, p. 609

grit, p. 610

emotional intelligence, p. 612

mental age, p. 618

Stanford-Binet, p. 618

intelligence quotient (IQ), p. 618

achievement test, p. 619

aptitude test, p. 619

Wechsler Adult Intelligence Scale (WAIS), p. 620

standardization, p. 621

normal curve, p. 621

reliability, p. 622

validity, p. 622

content validity, p. 622

predictive validity, p. 622

cohort, p. 625

crystallized intelligence, p. 626

fluid intelligence, p. 626

intellectual disability, p. 629

Down syndrome, p. 629

heritability, p. 632

stereotype threat, p. 642

Key Contributors to Remember

Charles Spearman, p. 608

L. L. Thurstone, p. 608

Howard Gardner, p. 609

Robert Sternberg, p. 611

Francis Galton, p. 617

Alfred Binet, p. 618

Louis Terman, p. 618

David Wechsler, p. 620

Carol Dweck, p. 635

AP® Exam Practice Questions

Multiple-Choice Questions

1. Children are said to have an intellectual disability if they have difficulty adapting to the demands of independent living and have IQ scores below

 a. 60.
 b. 70.
 c. 80.
 d. 90.
 e. 100.

2. Charles Spearman's *g* refers to

 a. general intelligence.
 b. grouped intelligence factors.
 c. genetic intelligence.
 d. generated creativity.
 e. generalized reliability.

3. What would be true of a thermometer that always reads three degrees off?

 a. It is valid but not reliable.
 b. It is both reliable and valid.
 c. It is neither reliable nor valid.
 d. It is not valid, but you cannot determine if it is reliable from the information given.
 e. It is reliable but not valid.

4. In general, males score higher than females on tests of

 a. spelling.
 b. verbal fluency.
 c. emotion detection.
 d. spatial ability.
 e. sensitivity to touch, taste, and odor.

5. Achievement tests are to aptitude tests as

 a. verbal performance is to spatial performance.
 b. elementary school skills are to secondary school skills.
 c. measurement is to prediction.
 d. reliability is to validity.
 e. general intelligence is to multiple intelligences.

6. Howard Gardner found evidence of multiple intelligences in individuals who scored low on intelligence but had an area of exceptional ability—for example, to make complex calculations. These people have

 a. the Flynn effect.
 b. savant syndrome.
 c. advanced mental age.
 d. Wechsler syndrome.
 e. intelligence heritability.

7. Which of the following is one of Robert Sternberg's types of intelligence?

 a. Naturalistic intelligence
 b. General intelligence
 c. Practical intelligence
 d. Savant intelligence
 e. Kinesthetic intelligence

8. The Flynn effect refers to the

 a. superiority of certain racial and ethnic groups on intelligence tests.
 b. extreme scores (very high and very low scores) that are more common for males than females on math tests.
 c. stereotype threat that might cause some Black students to underperform on standardized tests.
 d. predictive ability of intelligence tests.
 e. gradual improvement in intelligence test scores over the last several decades.

9. The ability to perceive, understand, manage, and use emotions is called

 a. interpersonal intelligence.
 b. general intelligence.
 c. practical intelligence.
 d. emotional intelligence.
 e. adaptive intelligence.

10. Heritability of intelligence refers to

 a. the extent to which a person's intelligence is caused by genetics.
 b. the effect of adoption on the intelligence of adopted children.
 c. the amount of group variation in intelligence that can be attributed to genetics.
 d. the extent to which the quality of schools and other environmental factors determine intelligence.
 e. the correlation between intelligence test scores of identical twins.

11. Recent research about brain size and function suggests that

 a. the occipital lobe is more active when people are thinking about questions on intelligence tests.
 b. people who are smarter use less energy when solving problems.
 c. there is no correlation between processing speed and IQ scores.
 d. people with larger brains are always smarter than those with smaller brains.
 e. subjects with larger parietal lobes tended to process information more slowly.

12. The most widely used modern intelligence test was developed by

  a. Alfred Binet.
  b. Louis Terman.
  c. Robert Sternberg.
  d. David Wechsler.
  e. Howard Gardner.

13. Students who do well on college entrance exams generally do well in their first year of college. This helps establish that these exams have

  a. predictive validity.
  b. split-half reliability.
  c. content validity.
  d. test-retest reliability.
  e. standard validity.

14. The purpose of Alfred Binet's early intelligence test was to

  a. predict how children would do in school.
  b. identify differences among ethnic and racial groups.
  c. help French graduates find the occupation in which they were most likely to succeed.
  d. establish the scientific definition of intelligence.
  e. facilitate "genetic breeding" experiments.

15. The original formula for a child's intelligence quotient compared a child's

  a. aptitude to his or her school performance.
  b. mental age to his or her chronological age.
  c. intelligence to his or her siblings' intelligence.
  d. intelligence to his or her parents' intelligence.
  e. math intelligence to his or her verbal intelligence.

Free-Response Questions

1. Shervin is a high school student who excels in academics and usually scores very high on academic standardized tests. His friend, Hany, struggles in his coursework and with standardized tests, but is a brilliant pianist and dancer.

  For each of the following intelligence theorists, briefly explain the psychologist's intelligence theory and identify how the theory might describe Shervin's and Hany's intelligence.

  - Howard Gardner
  - Robert Sternberg
  - Charles Spearman

Rubric for Free Response Question

1 point: Gardner believed that there are eight intelligences: linguistic, musical, logical-mathematical, spatial, bodily-kinesthetic, intrapersonal, interpersonal, and naturalist. Individuals with the condition of savant syndrome exemplify his theory because they may score low on traditional intelligence tests, but have an extraordinary skill such as musical ability. ↻ Pages 609–611

1 point: Gardner might describe Shervin as having high logical-mathematical and linguistic intelligence, and Hany as having high musical and bodily-kinesthetic intelligence. ↻ Page 610

1 point: Sternberg's triarchic intelligence theory describes intelligence as a combination of three independent factors: creative, academic, and practical intelligence. ↻ Page 611

1 point: Sternberg might predict that Shervin would score high in academic intelligence and Hany might score high in creative intelligence. ↻ Page 611

1 point: According to Spearman's general intelligence theory, each individual has a general, underlying mental ability that can be measured. Spearman defined (and measured) intelligence as this general ability, which expresses itself on different mental tasks. For example, if an individual is above average academically in English, then he will most likely be at least average, if not above average academically in other subjects as well (such as math). ↻ Pages 608–609

1 point: Spearman might predict that Shervin would score high on his test of general intelligence, but Hany would not since creativity in music and dance is not included as an aspect or expression of intelligence. ↻ Page 608

2. The principal of a new elementary school wants to give an IQ test to all students when they enter the school. The students will then be placed in groups of students of similar IQ scores. The principal assures the community that this plan is supported by scientific research and will improve education for all students, regardless of their ability.

  - Using evidence, present an argument for or against intelligence testing for children early in life.
  - Using evidence, present an argument for or against schools that "track" children based on intelligence test scores, separating high scorers from students with lower scores.
  - Using evidence, present an argument supporting the claim that environmental influences affect intelligence.
  - Using evidence, present an argument supporting the claim that labeling or tracking students could lead to stereotype threat.

(4 points)

3. Professor Emic wants to first develop an intelligence test that can be used cross-culturally, and then to assess the reliability and validity of that test.

Briefly explain how Professor Emic could examine the following characteristics about this new intelligence test:

- Standardization
- Reliability
- Validity
- Bias

(4 points)

Multiple-choice self-tests and more may be found at www.worthpublishers.com/MyersAP2e

Unit XII

Abnormal Behavior

Modules

I felt the need to clean my room at home in Indianapolis every Sunday and would spend four to five hours at it. I would take every book out of the bookcase, dust and put it back. . . . I couldn't stop.

Marc, diagnosed with obsessive-compulsive disorder (from Summers, 1996)

Whenever I get depressed it's because I've lost a sense of self. I can't find reasons to like myself. I think I'm ugly. I think no one likes me.

Greta, diagnosed with depression (from Thorne, 1993, p. 21)

Voices, like the roar of a crowd, came. I felt like Jesus; I was being crucified.

Stuart, diagnosed with schizophrenia (from Emmons et al., 1997)

People are fascinated by the exceptional, the unusual, the abnormal. "The sun shines and warms and lights us and we have no curiosity to know why this is so," observed Ralph Waldo Emerson, "but we ask the reason of all evil, of pain, and hunger, and [unusual] people."

Why such fascination with disturbed people? Even when we are well, do we see in them something of ourselves? At various moments, all of us feel, think, or act the way disturbed people do much of the time. We, too, get anxious, depressed, withdrawn, suspicious, or deluded, just less intensely and more briefly. No wonder studying psychological disorders sometimes evokes an eerie sense of self-recognition, one that illuminates our own personality. "To study the abnormal is the best way of understanding the normal," proposed William James (1842–1910).

649

Another reason for our curiosity is that so many of us have felt, either personally or through friends or family, the bewilderment and pain of a psychological disorder that may bring unexplained physical symptoms, irrational fears, or a feeling that life is not worth living. Indeed, as members of the human family, most of us will at some point encounter a person with a psychological disorder.

The World Health Organization (WHO, 2010) reports that, worldwide, some 450 million people suffer from mental or behavioral disorders. These disorders account for 15.4 percent of the years of life lost due to death or disability—scoring slightly below cardiovascular conditions and slightly above cancer (Murray & Lopez, 1996). Rates and symptoms of psychological disorders vary by culture, but two terrible maladies appear more consistently worldwide: depression and schizophrenia.

Module 65

Introduction to Psychological Disorders

chinaface/Getty Images

Module Learning Objectives

65-1   Discuss how we draw the line between normality and disorder.

65-2   Discuss the controversy over the diagnosis of attention-deficit/hyperactivity disorder.

65-3   Contrast the medical model with the biopsychosocial approach to psychological disorders.

65-4   Describe how and why clinicians classify psychological disorders.

65-5   Explain why some psychologists criticize the use of diagnostic labels.

65-6   Discuss the prevalence of psychological disorders, and summarize the findings on the link between poverty and serious psychological disorders.

Most people would agree that someone who is too depressed to get out of bed for weeks at a time has a psychological disorder. But what about those who, having experienced a loss, are unable to resume their usual social activities? Where should we draw the line between sadness and depression? Between zany creativity and bizarre irrationality? Between normality and abnormality? Let's start with these questions:

- How should we *define* psychological disorders?
- How should we *understand* disorders? How do underlying biological factors contribute to disorder? How do troubling environments influence our well-being? And how do these effects of nature and nurture interact?
- How should we *classify* psychological disorders? And can we do so in a way that allows us to help people without stigmatizing them with *labels?*

> "Who in the rainbow can draw the line where the violet tint ends and the orange tint begins? Distinctly we see the difference of the colors, but where exactly does the one first blendingly enter into the other? So with sanity and insanity." -HERMAN MELVILLE, *BILLY BUDD, SAILOR*, 1924

Defining Psychological Disorders

65-1 How should we draw the line between normality and disorder?

A **psychological disorder** is a syndrome marked by a "clinically significant disturbance in an individual's cognition, emotion regulation, or behavior" (American Psychiatric Association, 2013). Disturbed, or *dysfunctional*, behaviors are *maladaptive*—they interfere with normal day-to-day life. An intense fear of spiders may be abnormal, but if it doesn't interfere with your life, it is not a disorder. Marc's cleaning rituals (from this unit's opening) did interfere with his work and leisure. If occasional sad moods persist and become disabling, they may signal a psychological disorder. Distress often accompanies dysfunctional behaviors. Marc, Greta, and Stuart were all distressed by their behaviors or emotions.

Over time, definitions of what makes for a "significant disturbance" have varied. From 1952 through December 9, 1973, homosexuality was classified as a mental illness. By day's end on December 10, it was not. The American Psychiatric Association had dropped homosexuality as a disorder because more and more of its members no longer viewed it as a psychological problem. (Later research revealed that the stigma and stresses that often accompany homosexuality, however, increase the risk of mental health problems [Hatzenbuehler et al., 2009; Meyer, 2003].) In this new century, controversy swirls over the frequent diagnosing of children with *attention-deficit/hyperactivity disorder* (see Thinking Critically About: ADHD—Normal High Energy or Disordered Behavior? on the next page).

> **psychological disorder**
> a syndrome marked by a clinically significant disturbance in an individual's cognition, emotion regulation, or behavior. (Adapted from American Psychiatric Association, 2013.)

Carol Beckwith

iStock/Thinkstock

Culture and normality Young men of the West African Wodaabe tribe put on elaborate makeup and costumes to attract women. Young American men may buy flashy cars with loud stereos to do the same. Each culture may view the other's behavior as abnormal.

Understanding Psychological Disorders

65-3 How do the medical model and the biopsychosocial approach understand psychological disorders?

To explain puzzling behavior, people in earlier times often presumed the work of strange forces—the movements of the stars, godlike powers, or evil spirits. Had you lived during the Middle Ages, you might have said, "The devil made him do it," and you might have

Yesterday's "therapy" In other times and places, psychologically disordered people sometimes received brutal treatments, including the trephination evident in this Stone Age skull. Drilling skull holes like these may have been an attempt to release evil spirits and cure those with mental disorders. Did this patient survive the "cure"?

John W. Verano

approved of a cure to rid the evil force by exorcising the demon. Until the last two centuries, "mad" people were sometimes caged in zoo-like conditions or given "therapies" appropriate to a demon: beatings, burning, or castration. In other times, therapy included pulling teeth, removing lengths of intestines, cauterizing the clitoris, or giving transfusions of animal blood (Farina, 1982).

Thinking Critically About

ADHD—Normal High Energy or Disordered Behavior?

65-2 Why is there controversy over attention-deficit/hyperactivity disorder?

Eight-year-old Todd has always been energetic. At home, he chatters away and darts from one activity to the next, rarely settling down to read a book or focus on a game. At play, he is reckless and overreacts when playmates bump into him or take one of his toys. At school, his exasperated teacher complains that fidgety Todd doesn't listen, follow instructions, or stay in his seat and do his lessons. As he matures to adulthood, Todd's hyperactivity likely will subside, but his inattentiveness may persist (Kessler et al., 2010).

If taken for a psychological evaluation, Todd may be diagnosed with **attention-deficit/hyperactivity disorder (ADHD),** as are some 11 percent of American 4- to 17-year-olds who display its key symptoms (extreme inattention, hyperactivity, and impulsivity) (Schwarz & Cohen, 2013). Studies also find 2.5 percent of adults—though a diminishing number with age—exhibiting ADHD symptoms (Simon et al., 2009). Psychiatry's new diagnostic manual loosens the criteria for adult ADHD, leading critics to fear increased diagnosis and overuse of prescription drugs (Frances, 2012).

To skeptics, being distractible, fidgety, and impulsive sounds like a "disorder" caused by a single genetic variation: a Y chromosome. And sure enough, ADHD is diagnosed three times more often in boys than in girls. Does energetic child + boring school = ADHD overdiagnosis? Is the label being applied to healthy schoolchildren who, in more natural outdoor environments, would seem perfectly normal?

Skeptics think so. In the decade after 1987, they note, the proportion of American children being treated for ADHD nearly quadrupled (Olfson et al., 2003). How commonplace the diagnosis is depends in part on teacher referrals. Some teachers refer lots of kids for ADHD assessment, others none. ADHD rates have varied by a factor of 10 in different counties of New York State (Carlson, 2000). Although African-American youth display more ADHD symptoms than do Caucasian youth, they less often receive an ADHD diagnosis (Miller et al., 2009). Depending on where they live, children who are "a persistent pain in the neck in school" are often diagnosed with ADHD and given powerful prescription drugs, notes Peter Gray (2010). But the problem resides less in the child, he argues, than in today's abnormal environment

that forces children to do what evolution has not prepared them to do—to sit for long hours in chairs.

On the other side of the debate are those who argue that the more frequent diagnoses of ADHD today reflect increased awareness of the disorder, especially in those areas where rates are highest. They acknowledge that diagnoses can be subjective and sometimes inconsistent—ADHD is not as objectively defined as is a broken arm. Nevertheless, declared the World Federation for Mental Health (2005), "there is strong agreement among the international scientific community that ADHD is a real neurobiological disorder whose existence should no longer be debated." A consensus statement by 75 researchers noted that in neuroimaging studies, ADHD has associations with abnormal brain activity patterns (Barkley et al., 2002).

What, then, is known about ADHD's causes? It is not caused by too much sugar or poor schools. There is mixed evidence suggesting that extensive TV watching and video gaming are associated with reduced cognitive self-regulation and ADHD (Bailey et al., 2011; Courage & Setliff, 2010; Ferguson, 2011). ADHD often coexists with a learning disorder or with defiant and temper-prone behavior. ADHD is *heritable,* and research teams are sleuthing the culprit genes and abnormal neural pathways (Nikolas & Burt, 2010; Poelmans et al., 2011; Volkow et al., 2009; Williams et al., 2010). It is treatable with medications such as Ritalin and Adderall, which are considered stimulants but help calm hyperactivity and increase the ability to sit and focus on a task—and to progress normally in school (Barbaresi et al., 2007). Psychological therapies, such as those focused on shaping behaviors in the classroom and at home, have also helped address the distress of ADHD (Fabiano et al., 2008).

The bottom line: Extreme inattention, hyperactivity, and impulsivity can derail social, academic, and vocational achievements, and these symptoms can be treated with medication and other therapies. But the debate continues over whether normal rambunctiousness is too often diagnosed as a psychiatric disorder, and whether there is a cost to the long-term use of stimulant drugs in treating ADHD.

---

attention-deficit/hyperactivity disorder (ADHD)
a psychological disorder marked by the appearance by age 7 of one or more of three key symptoms: extreme inattention, hyperactivity, and impulsivity.

The Medical Model

In opposition to brutal treatments, reformers, including Philippe Pinel (1745–1826) in France, insisted that madness is not demon possession but a sickness of the mind caused by severe stresses and inhumane conditions. For Pinel and others, "moral treatment" included boosting patients' morale by unchaining them and talking with them, and by replacing brutality with gentleness, isolation with activity, and filth with clean air and sunshine. While such measures did not often cure patients, they were certainly more humane.

By the 1800s, the discovery that syphilis infects the brain and distorts the mind drove further gradual reform. Hospitals replaced asylums, and the medical world began searching for physical causes and treatments of mental disorders. Today, this **medical model** is recognizable in the terminology of the mental *health* movement: A mental *illness* (also called a psycho*pathology*) needs to be *diagnosed* on the basis of its *symptoms* and *treated* through *therapy*, which may include time in a psychiatric *hospital*.

The medical perspective has gained credibility from recent discoveries that genetically influenced abnormalities in brain structure and biochemistry contribute to many disorders. But as we will see, psychological factors, such as chronic or traumatic stress, also play an important role.

> **medical model** the concept that diseases, in this case psychological disorders, have physical causes that can be *diagnosed, treated,* and, in most cases, *cured,* often through treatment in a *hospital.*

Dance in a Madhouse, 1917 (litho), Bellows, George Wesley (1882–1925)/ San Diego Museum of Art, USA/Museum Purchase/The Bridgeman Art Library

"Moral treatment" Under Philippe Pinel's influence, hospitals sometimes sponsored patient dances, often called "lunatic balls," depicted in this painting by George Bellows (*Dance in a Madhouse*).

The Biopsychosocial Approach

Today's psychologists contend that all behavior, whether called normal or disordered, arises from the interaction of nature (genetic and physiological factors) and nurture (past and present experiences). To presume that a person is "mentally ill," they say, attributes the condition to a "sickness" that must be identified and cured. But difficulty in the person's environment, the person's current interpretations of events, or the person's bad habits and poor social skills may also be factors.

Evidence of such effects comes from links between specific disorders and cultures (Beardsley, 1994; Castillo, 1997). Cultures differ in their sources of stress, and they produce different ways of coping. The eating disorders anorexia nervosa and bulimia nervosa, for example, have occurred mostly in Western cultures. In Malaysia, *amok* describes a sudden outburst of violent behavior (thus the phrase "run amok"). Latin America lays claim to *susto,* a condition marked by severe anxiety, restlessness, and a fear of black magic. *Taijin-kyofusho,* social anxiety about one's appearance combined with a readiness to blush and a fear of eye contact, appears in Japan, as does the extreme withdrawal of *hikikomori.* Such disorders may share an underlying dynamic (such as anxiety) while differing in the symptoms (an eating problem or a type of fear) manifested in a particular culture.

But not all disorders are culture-bound. Depression and schizophrenia occur worldwide. From Asia to Africa and across the Americas, schizophrenia's symptoms often include irrationality and incoherent speech.

> **FYI**
>
> Increasingly, North American disorders, such as eating disorders, are, along with McDonald's and MTV, spreading across the globe (Watters, 2010).

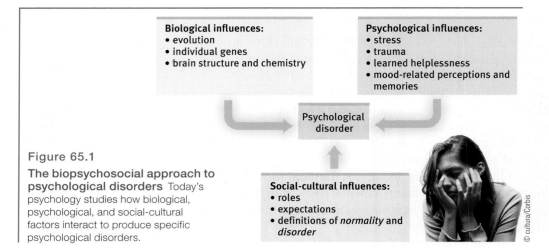

Biological influences:
• evolution
• individual genes
• brain structure and chemistry

Psychological influences:
• stress
• trauma
• learned helplessness
• mood-related perceptions and memories

Psychological disorder

Social-cultural influences:
• roles
• expectations
• definitions of *normality* and *disorder*

© cultura/Corbis

Figure 65.1

The biopsychosocial approach to psychological disorders Today's psychology studies how biological, psychological, and social-cultural factors interact to produce specific psychological disorders.

To assess the whole set of influences—genetic predispositions and physiological states, inner psychological dynamics, and social and cultural circumstances—the biopsychosocial model helps (**FIGURE 65.1**). This approach recognizes that mind and body are inseparable. Negative emotions contribute to physical illness, and physical abnormalities contribute to negative emotions. We are mind embodied and socially embedded.

Classifying Psychological Disorders

65-4   How and why do clinicians classify psychological disorders?

In biology and the other sciences, classification creates order. To classify an animal as a "mammal" says a great deal—that it is warm-blooded, has hair or fur, and nourishes its young with milk. In psychiatry and psychology, too, classification orders and describes symptoms. To classify a person's disorder as "schizophrenia" suggests that the person talks incoherently; hallucinates or has delusions (bizarre beliefs); shows either little emotion or inappropriate emotion; or is socially withdrawn. "Schizophrenia" provides a handy shorthand for describing a complex disorder.

In psychiatry and psychology, diagnostic classification aims not only to describe a disorder but also to predict its future course, imply appropriate treatment, and stimulate research into its causes. Indeed, to study a disorder we must first name and describe it. The most common system for describing disorders and estimating how often they occur is the American Psychiatric Association's 2013 *Diagnostic and Statistical Manual of Mental Disorders,* now in its fifth edition (**DSM-5**). Physicians and mental health workers use the detailed "diagnostic criteria and codes" in the DSM-5 to guide medical diagnoses and define who is eligible for treatments, including medication. For example, a person may be diagnosed with and treated for "insomnia disorder" if he or she meets *all* of the following criteria:

- Is dissatisfied with sleep quantity or quality (difficulty initiating, maintaining, or returning to sleep).

- Sleep disturbance causes distress or impairment in everyday functioning.

- Occurs at least three nights per week.

- Present for at least three months.

- Occurs despite adequate opportunity for sleep.

- Is not explained by another sleep disorder (such as narcolepsy).

- Is not caused by substance use or abuse.

- Is not caused by other mental disorders or medical conditions.

In this new DSM edition, some diagnostic labels have changed. For example, "autism" and "Asperger's syndrome" are no longer included; they have been combined into "autism spectrum disorder." "Mental retardation" has become "intellectual disability." New categories include "hoarding disorder" and "binge-eating disorder."

> **FYI**
>
> A book of case illustrations accompanying the previous DSM edition provides several examples for this unit.

DSM-5 the American Psychiatric Association's *Diagnostic and Statistical Manual of Mental Disorders,* Fifth Edition; a widely used system for classifying psychological disorders.

Some new or altered diagnoses are controversial. "Disruptive mood dysregulation disorder" is a new DSM-5 diagnosis for children "who exhibit persistent irritability and frequent episodes of behavior outbursts three or more times a week for more than a year." Will this diagnosis assist parents who struggle with unstable children, or will it "turn temper tantrums into a mental disorder" and lead to overmedication, as the chair of the previous DSM edition has warned (Frances, 2012)?

Critics have long faulted the DSM for casting too wide a net and bringing "almost any kind of behavior within the compass of psychiatry" (Eysenck et al., 1983). They worry that the DSM-5 will extend the pathologizing of everyday life—for example, by turning bereavement grief into depression and boyish rambunctiousness into ADHD (Frances, 2013). Others respond that depression and hyperactivity, though needing careful definition, are genuine disorders even, for example, those triggered by a major life stress such as a death when the grief does not go away (Kendler, 2011; Kupfer, 2012).

"I'm always like this, and my family was wondering if you could prescribe a mild depressant."

Labeling Psychological Disorders

65-5 Why do some psychologists criticize the use of diagnostic labels?

The DSM has other critics who register a more fundamental complaint—that these labels are at best arbitrary and at worst value judgments masquerading as science. Once we label a person, we view that person differently (Farina, 1982). Labels create preconceptions that guide our perceptions and our interpretations.

In a now-classic study of the biasing power of labels, David Rosenhan (1973) and seven others went to hospital admissions offices, complaining of "hearing voices" saying *empty, hollow,* and *thud.* Apart from this complaint and giving false names and occupations, they answered questions truthfully. All eight normal people were misdiagnosed with disorders.

Should we be surprised? As one psychiatrist noted, if someone swallows blood, goes to an emergency room, and spits it up, should we fault the doctor for diagnosing a bleeding ulcer? Surely not. But what followed the diagnosis in the Rosenhan study was startling. Until being released an average of 19 days later, the "patients" exhibited no further symptoms such as hearing voices. Yet after analyzing their (quite normal) life histories, clinicians were able to "discover" the causes of their disorders, such as reacting with mixed emotions about a parent. Even the routine behavior of taking notes was misinterpreted as a symptom.

Labels matter. When people in another experiment watched videotaped interviews, those told the interviewees were job applicants perceived them as normal (Langer et al., 1974, 1980). Those who thought they were watching psychiatric or cancer patients perceived them as "different from most people." Therapists who thought an interviewee was a psychiatric patient perceived him as "frightened of his own aggressive impulses," a "passive, dependent type," and so forth. A label can, as Rosenhan discovered, have "a life and an influence of its own."

Surveys in Europe and North America have demonstrated the stigmatizing power of labels (Page, 1977). Getting a job or finding a place to rent can be a challenge for those known to be just released from prison—or a mental hospital. But as we are coming to understand that many psychological disorders are diseases of the brain, not failures of character, the stigma seems to be lifting (Solomon, 1996). Public figures are feeling freer to "come out" and speak with candor about their struggles with disorders such as depression. And the more contact people have with individuals with disorders, the more accepting their attitudes are (Kolodziej & Johnson, 1996). People express greatest sympathy for people whose disorders are gender atypical—for men suffering depression (which is more common among women), or for women plagued by alcohol use disorder (Wirth & Bodenhausen, 2009).

"One of the unpardonable sins, in the eyes of most people, is for a man to go about unlabeled. The world regards such a person as the police do an unmuzzled dog, not under proper control." -T. H. HUXLEY, *EVOLUTION AND ETHICS,* 1893

"My sister suffers from a bipolar disorder and my nephew from schizoaffective disorder. There has, in fact, been a lot of depression and alcoholism in my family and, traditionally, no one ever spoke about it. It just wasn't done. The stigma is toxic." -ACTRESS GLENN CLOSE, "MENTAL ILLNESS: THE STIGMA OF SILENCE," 2009

Accurate portrayal
Recent films have offered some realistic depictions of psychological disorders. *Black Swan* (2010), shown here, portrayed a main character suffering a delusional disorder. *Temple Grandin* (2010) dramatized a lead character who successfully copes with autism spectrum disorder. *A Single Man* (2009) depicted depression.

Protozoa Pictures/Phoenix Pictures/The Kobal Collection

Nevertheless, stereotypes linger in media portrayals of psychological disorders. Some are reasonably accurate and sympathetic. But too often people with disorders are portrayed as objects of humor or ridicule (*As Good as It Gets),* as homicidal maniacs (Hannibal Lecter in *Silence of the Lambs*), or as freaks (Nairn, 2007). Apart from the few who experience threatening delusions and hallucinated voices that command a violent act, and from those whose dysfunctionality includes substance abuse, mental disorders seldom lead to violence (Douglas et al., 2009; Elbogen & Johnson, 2009; Fazel et al., 2009, 2010). In real life, people with disorders are more likely to be the *victims* of violence than the perpetrators (Marley & Bulia, 2001). Indeed, reported the U.S. Surgeon General's Office (1999, p. 7), "There is very little risk of violence or harm to a stranger from casual contact with an individual who has a mental disorder." (Although most people with psychological disorders are not violent, those who are create a moral dilemma for society. For more on this topic, see Thinking Critically About: Insanity and Responsibility.)

Thinking Critically About

Insanity and Responsibility

"My brain . . . my genes . . . my bad upbringing made me do it." Such defenses were anticipated by Shakespeare's Hamlet. If I wrong someone when not myself, he explained, "then Hamlet does it not, Hamlet denies it. Who does it then? His madness." Such is the essence of a legal insanity defense. "Insanity" is a legal rather than a psychological concept, and was created in 1843 after a deluded Scotsman tried to shoot the prime minister (who he thought was persecuting him) but killed an assistant by mistake. Like U.S. President Ronald Reagan's near-assassin, John Hinckley, Scotsman Daniel M'Naghten was sent to a mental hospital rather than to prison.

In both cases, the public was outraged. "Hinckley Insane, Public Mad," declared one headline. They were mad again when a deranged Jeffrey Dahmer in 1991 admitted murdering 15 young men and eating parts of their bodies. They were mad in 1998 when 15-year-old Kip Kinkel, driven by "those voices in my head," killed his parents and two fellow Springfield, Oregon, students and wounded 25 others. They were mad in 2002 when Andrea Yates, after being taken off her antipsychotic medication, was tried in Texas for drowning her five children. And they were mad in 2011, when an irrational Jared Loughner gunned down a crowd of people, including survivor Congresswoman Gabrielle Giffords, in an Arizona supermarket parking lot. Following their arrest, most of these people were sent to jails, not hospitals. (Hinckley was sent to a psychiatric hospital and later, after another trial, Yates was instead hospitalized.) As Yates' fate illustrates, 99 percent of those whose insanity defense is accepted are nonetheless institutionalized, often for as long as those convicted of crimes (Lilienfeld & Arkowitz, 2011).

HANDOUT/Reuters/Corbis

Jail or hospital? Jared Lee Loughner was charged with the 2011 Tucson, Arizona, shooting that killed six people and left over a dozen others injured, including U.S. Representative Gabrielle Giffords. Loughner had a history of mental health issues, including paranoid beliefs, and was diagnosed with schizophrenia. Usually, however, schizophrenia is only associated with violence when accompanied by substance abuse (Fazel et al., 2009).

Most people with psychological disorders are not violent. But what should society do with those who are? What do we do with disturbed individuals who mow down innocents at movie theaters and schools? Sometimes there is nothing to be done, as in the case of the 2012 Sandy Hook Elementary School tragedy in Connecticut, where the shooter's final fatal shot was self-inflicted. Many people who have been executed or are now on death row have been limited by intellectual disability or motivated by delusional voices. The State of Arkansas forced one murderer with schizophrenia, Charles Singleton, to take two anti-psychotic drugs—in order to make him mentally competent, so that he could then be put to death.

Which of Yates' two juries made the right decision? The first, which decided that people who commit such rare but terrible crimes should be held responsible? Or the second, which decided to blame the "madness" that clouds their vision? As we come to better understand the biological and environmental basis for all human behavior, from generosity to vandalism, when should we—and should we not—hold people accountable for their actions?

Not only can labels bias perceptions, they can also change reality. When teachers are told certain students are "gifted," when students expect someone to be "hostile," or when interviewers check to see whether someone is "extraverted," they may act in ways that elicit the very behavior expected (Snyder, 1984). Someone who was led to think you are nasty may treat you coldly, leading you to respond as a mean-spirited person would. Labels can serve as self-fulfilling prophecies.

But let us remember the *benefits* of diagnostic labels. Mental health professionals use labels to communicate about their cases, to comprehend the underlying causes, and to discern effective treatment programs. Diagnostic definitions also inform patient self-understandings. And they are useful in research that explores the causes and treatments of disordered behavior.

Rates of Psychological Disorders

 How many people suffer, or have suffered, from a psychological disorder? Is poverty a risk factor?

Who is most vulnerable to psychological disorders? At what times of life? To answer such questions, various countries have conducted lengthy, structured interviews with representative samples of thousands of their citizens. After asking hundreds of questions that probed for symptoms—"Has there ever been a period of two weeks or more when you felt like you wanted to die?"—the researchers have estimated the current, prior-year, and lifetime prevalence of various disorders.

How many people have, or have had, a psychological disorder? More than most of us suppose:

- The U.S. National Institute of Mental Health (2008, based on Kessler et al., 2005) estimates that 26 percent of adult Americans "suffer from a diagnosable mental disorder in a given year" (**TABLE 65.1**).

- A large-scale World Health Organization (2004a) study—based on 90-minute interviews of 60,463 people—estimated the number of prior-year mental disorders in 20 countries. As **FIGURE 65.2** displays, the lowest rate of reported mental disorders was in Shanghai, the highest rate in the United States. Moreover, immigrants to the United States from Mexico, Africa, and Asia average better mental health than their native U.S. counterparts (Breslau et al., 2007; Maldonado-Molina et al., 2011). For example, compared with people who have recently immigrated from Mexico, Mexican-Americans born in the United States are at greater risk of mental disorder—a phenomenon known as the *immigrant paradox* (Schwartz et al., 2010).

Table 65.1 Percentage of Americans Reporting Selected Psychological Disorders in the Past Year

Psychological Disorder	Percentage
Generalized anxiety	3.1
Social anxiety disorder	6.8
Phobia of specific object or situation	8.7
Mood disorder	9.5
Obsessive-compulsive disorder (OCD)	1.0
Schizophrenia	1.1
Posttraumatic stress disorder (PTSD)	3.5
Attention-deficit/ hyperactivity disorder (ADHD)	4.1
Any mental disorder	26.2

Source: National Institute of Mental Health, 2008.

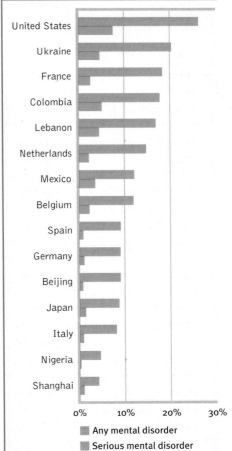

Figure 65.2

Prior-year prevalence of disorders in selected areas From World Health Organization (WHO, 2004a) interviews in 20 countries.

Who is most vulnerable to mental disorders? As we have seen, the answer varies with the disorder. One predictor of mental disorder, poverty, crosses ethnic and gender lines. The incidence of serious psychological disorders has been doubly high among those below the poverty line (CDC, 1992). Like so many other correlations, the poverty-disorder association raises a chicken-and-egg question: Does poverty cause disorders? Or do disorders cause poverty? It is both, though the answer varies with the disorder. Schizophrenia understandably leads to poverty. Yet the stresses and demoralization of poverty can also precipitate disorders, especially depression in women and substance use disorder in men (Dohrenwend et al., 1992). In one natural experiment on the poverty-pathology link, researchers tracked rates of behavior problems in North Carolina Native American children as economic development enabled a dramatic reduction in their community's poverty rate. As the study began, children of poverty exhibited more deviant and aggressive behaviors. After four years, children whose families had moved above the poverty line exhibited a 40 percent decrease in the behavior problems, while those who continued in their previous positions below or above the poverty line exhibited no change (Costello et al., 2003).

As **TABLE 65.2** indicates, there is a wide range of risk and protective factors for mental disorders. At what times of life do disorders strike? Usually by early adulthood. "Over 75 percent of our sample with any disorder had experienced its first symptoms by age 24," reported Lee Robins and Darrel Regier (1991, p. 331). The symptoms of antisocial personality disorder and of phobias are among the earliest to appear, at a median age of 8 and 10, respectively. Symptoms of alcohol use disorder, obsessive-compulsive disorder, bipolar disorder, and schizophrenia appear at a median age near 20. Major depression often hits somewhat later, at a median age of 25. Such findings make clear the need for research and treatment to help the growing number of people, especially teenagers and young adults, who suffer the bewilderment and pain of a psychological disorder.

Table 65.2 Risk and Protective Factors for Mental Disorders

Risk Factors	Protective Factors
Academic failure	Aerobic exercise
Birth complications	Community offering empowerment, opportunity, and security
Caring for chronically ill or patients with neurocognitive disorder	Economic independence
Child abuse and neglect	Effective parenting
Chronic insomnia	Feelings of mastery and control
Chronic pain	Feelings of security
Family disorganization or conflict	Literacy
Low birth weight	Positive attachment and early bonding
Low socioeconomic status	Positive parent-child relationships
Medical illness	Problem-solving skills
Neurochemical imbalance	Resilient coping with stress and adversity
Parental mental illness	Self-esteem
Parental substance abuse	Social and work skills
Personal loss and bereavement	Social support from family and friends
Poor work skills and habits	
Reading disabilities	
Sensory disabilities	
Social incompetence	
Stressful life events	
Substance abuse	
Trauma experiences	

Source: World Health Organization (WHO, 2004b,c).

Although mindful of the pain, we can also be encouraged by the many successful people—including Leonardo da Vinci, Isaac Newton, and Leo Tolstoy—who pursued brilliant careers while enduring psychological difficulties. So have 18 U.S. presidents, including the periodically depressed Abraham Lincoln, according to one psychiatric analysis of their biographies (Davidson et al., 2006). The bewilderment, fear, and sorrow caused by psychological disorders are real. But, as Unit XIII shows, hope, too, is real.

Before You Move On

▶ **ASK YOURSELF**

How would you draw the line between sending disturbed criminals to prisons or to mental hospitals? Would the person's history (for example, having suffered child abuse) influence your decisions?

▶ **TEST YOURSELF**

What is the biopsychosocial approach, and why is it important in our understanding of psychological disorders?

Answers to the Test Yourself questions can be found in Appendix E at the end of the book.

Module 65 Review

 How should we draw the line between normality and disorder?

- According to psychologists and psychiatrists, a *psychological disorder* is a syndrome marked by a clinically significant disturbance in an individual's cognition, emotion regulation, or behavior.

 Why is there some controversy over attention-deficit/hyperactivity disorder?

- A child who by age 7 displays extreme inattention, hyperactivity, and impulsivity may be diagnosed with *attention-deficit/hyperactivity disorder (ADHD)* and treated with medication and other therapy.

- The controversy centers on whether the growing number of ADHD cases reflects overdiagnosis or increased awareness of the disorder. Long-term effects of stimulant-drug treatment for ADHD are not yet known.

 How do the medical model and the biopsychosocial approach understand psychological disorders?

- The *medical model* assumes that psychological disorders are mental illnesses with physical causes that can be diagnosed, treated, and, in most cases, cured through therapy, sometimes in a hospital.

- The biopsychosocial approach assumes that three sets of influences—biological (evolution, genetics, brain structure and chemistry), psychological (stress, trauma, learned helplessness, mood-related perceptions and memories), and social-cultural (roles, expectations, definitions of "normality" and "disorder")—interact to produce specific psychological disorders.

 How and why do clinicians classify psychological disorders?

- The American Psychiatric Association's *DSM-5* (*Diagnostic and Statistical Manual of Mental Disorders,* **Fifth Edition**) contains diagnostic labels and descriptions that provide a common language and shared concepts for communication and research.

- Some critics believe the DSM editions have become too detailed and extensive.

65-5 Why do some psychologists criticize the use of diagnostic labels?

- Other critics view DSM diagnoses as arbitrary labels that create preconceptions which bias perceptions of the labeled person's past and present behavior. The legal label, "insanity," raises moral and ethical questions about whether society should hold people with disorders responsible for their violent actions.

- Most people with disorders are nonviolent and are more likely to be victims than attackers.

65-6 How many people suffer, or have suffered, from a psychological disorder? Is poverty a risk factor?

- Psychological disorder rates vary, depending on the time and place of the survey. In one multinational survey, rates for any disorder ranged from less than 5 percent (Shanghai) to more than 25 percent (the United States).

- Poverty is a risk factor: Conditions and experiences associated with poverty contribute to the development of psychological disorders. But some disorders, such as schizophrenia, can drive people into poverty.

Multiple-Choice Questions

1. Which of the following describes the idea that psychological disorders can be diagnosed and treated?

 a. Taijin-kyofusho
 b. The DSM
 c. The biopsychosocial approach
 d. Amok
 e. The medical model

2. Which of the following is the primary purpose of the DSM?

 a. Diagnosis of mental disorders
 b. Selection of appropriate psychological therapies for mental disorders
 c. Placement of mental disorders in appropriate cultural context
 d. Selection of appropriate medicines to treat mental disorders
 e. Understanding the causes of mental disorders

3. Which of the following disorders do Americans report most frequently?

 a. Schizophrenia
 b. Mood disorders
 c. Posttraumatic stress disorder (PTSD)
 d. Obsessive-compulsive disorder (OCD)
 e. Attention-deficit/hyperactivity disorder (ADHD)

Practice FRQs

1. Name and describe the two major approaches to understanding psychological disorders.

Answer

2 points: The medical model, which is an attempt to first diagnose and then treat psychological disorders.

2 points: The biopsychosocial approach, which is an attempt to understand psychological disorders as an interaction of biological, psychological, and social-cultural factors.

2. Explain two criticisms of the DSM.

(2 points)

Module 66

Anxiety Disorders, Obsessive-Compulsive Disorder, and Posttraumatic Stress Disorder

Module Learning Objectives

66-1 Identify the different anxiety disorders.

66-2 Describe obsessive-compulsive disorder.

66-3 Describe posttraumatic stress disorder.

66-4 Describe how the learning and biological perspectives explain anxiety disorders, OCD, and PTSD.

66-1 What are the different anxiety disorders?

Anxiety is part of life. Speaking in front of a class, peering down from a ladder, or waiting to play in a big game, any one of us might feel anxious (even seasoned performers like Green Day's Billie Joe Armstrong, whose anxiety and substance abuse resulted in cancelled concerts in 2012 and 2013). At times we may feel enough anxiety to avoid making eye contact or talking with someone—"shyness," we call it. Fortunately for most of us, our uneasiness is not intense and persistent.

Some of us, however, are more prone to notice and remember threats (Mitte, 2008). This tendency may place us at risk for one of the **anxiety disorders,** marked by distressing, persistent anxiety or dysfunctional anxiety-reducing behaviors. We will consider these three:

- *Generalized anxiety disorder,* in which a person is unexplainably and continually tense and uneasy

- *Panic disorder,* in which a person experiences sudden episodes of intense dread

- *Phobias,* in which a person is intensely and irrationally afraid of a specific object or situation

Two other disorders involve anxiety, though the DSM-5 now classifies them separately:

- *Obsessive-compulsive disorder,* in which a person is troubled by repetitive thoughts or actions

- *Posttraumatic stress disorder,* in which a person has lingering memories, nightmares, and other symptoms for weeks after a severely threatening, uncontrollable event

anxiety disorders psychological disorders characterized by distressing, persistent anxiety or maladaptive behaviors that reduce anxiety.

Snapshots

Obsessing about obsessive-compulsive disorder

Generalized Anxiety Disorder

For the past two years, Tom, a 27-year-old electrician, has been bothered by dizziness, sweating palms, heart palpitations, and ringing in his ears. He feels edgy and sometimes finds himself shaking. With reasonable success, he hides his symptoms from his family and co-workers. But he allows himself few other social contacts, and occasionally he has to leave work. His family doctor and a neurologist can find no physical problem.

Tom's unfocused, out-of-control, agitated feelings suggest a **generalized anxiety disorder**, which is marked by pathological worry. The symptoms of this disorder are commonplace; their persistence, for six months or more, is not. People with this condition—two-thirds are women (McLean & Anderson, 2009)—worry continually, and they are often jittery, agitated, and sleep-deprived. Concentration is difficult as attention switches from worry to worry, and their tension and apprehension may leak out through furrowed brows, twitching eyelids, trembling, perspiration, or fidgeting.

One of generalized anxiety disorder's worst characteristics is that the person may not be able to identify, and therefore deal with or avoid, its cause. To use Sigmund Freud's term, the anxiety is *free-floating*. Generalized anxiety disorder is often accompanied by depressed mood, but even without depression it tends to be disabling (Hunt et al., 2004; Moffitt et al., 2007b). Moreover, it may lead to physical problems, such as high blood pressure.

Many people with generalized anxiety disorder were maltreated and inhibited as children (Moffitt et al., 2007a). As time passes, however, emotions tend to mellow, and by age 50, generalized anxiety disorder becomes fairly rare (Rubio & López-Ibor, 2007).

Panic Disorder

Panic disorder entails an anxiety tornado. Panic strikes suddenly, wreaks havoc, and disappears. For the 1 person in 75 with this disorder, anxiety suddenly escalates into a terrifying *panic attack*—a minutes-long episode of intense fear that something horrible is about to happen. Heart palpitations, shortness of breath, choking sensations, trembling, or dizziness typically accompany the panic, which may be misperceived as a heart attack or other serious physical ailment. Smokers have at least a doubled risk of panic disorder (Zvolensky & Bernstein, 2005). Because nicotine is a stimulant, lighting up doesn't lighten up.

One woman recalled suddenly feeling "hot and as though I couldn't breathe. My heart was racing and I started to sweat and tremble and I was sure I was going to faint. Then my fingers started to feel numb and tingly and things seemed unreal. It was so bad I wondered if I was dying and asked my husband to take me to the emergency room. By the time we got there (about 10 minutes) the worst of the attack was over and I just felt washed out" (Greist et al., 1986).

Phobias

Phobias are anxiety disorders in which an irrational fear causes the person to avoid some object, activity, or situation. Many people accept their phobias and live with them, but others are incapacitated by their efforts to avoid the feared situation. Marilyn, an otherwise healthy and happy 28-year-old, fears thunderstorms so intensely that she feels anxious as soon as a weather forecaster mentions possible storms later in the week. If her husband is away and a storm is forecast, she may stay with a close relative. During a storm, she hides from windows and buries her head to avoid seeing the lightning.

Other *specific phobias* may focus on animals, insects, heights, blood, or enclosed spaces (**FIGURE 66.1**). People avoid the stimulus that arouses the fear, hiding during thunderstorms or avoiding high places.

Not all phobias have such specific triggers. **Social anxiety disorder** (formerly called *social phobia*) is shyness taken to an extreme. Those with social anxiety disorder,

generalized anxiety disorder an anxiety disorder in which a person is continually tense, apprehensive, and in a state of autonomic nervous system arousal.

panic disorder an anxiety disorder marked by unpredictable, minutes-long episodes of intense dread in which a person experiences terror and accompanying chest pain, choking, or other frightening sensations. Often followed by worry over a possible next attack.

phobia an anxiety disorder marked by a persistent, irrational fear and avoidance of a specific object, activity, or situation.

social anxiety disorder intense fear of social situations, leading to avoidance of such. (Formerly called *social phobia.*)

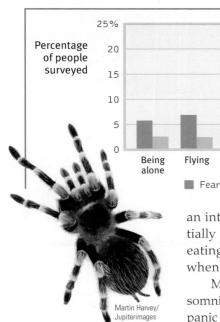

Martin Harvey/
Jupiterimages

Figure 66.1

Some common and uncommon specific fears This Dutch national interview study identified the commonality of various specific fears. A strong fear becomes a phobia if it provokes a compelling but irrational desire to avoid the dreaded object or situation. (From Delpa et al., 2008.)

an intense fear of being scrutinized by others, avoid potentially embarrassing social situations, such as speaking up, eating out, or going to parties—or will sweat or tremble when doing so.

Much as fretting over insomnia may, ironically, cause insomnia, so worries about anxiety—perhaps fearing another panic attack, or fearing anxiety-caused sweating in public—can amplify anxiety symptoms (Olatunji & Wolitzky-Taylor, 2009). People who have experienced several panic attacks may come to avoid situations where the panic has struck before. If the fear is intense enough, it may become **agoraphobia,** fear or avoidance of situations in which escape might be difficult or help unavailable when panic strikes. Given such fear, people may avoid being outside the home, in a crowd, on a bus, or on an elevator.

After spending five years sailing the world, Charles Darwin began suffering panic disorder at age 28. Because of the attacks, he moved to the country, avoided social gatherings, and traveled only in his wife's company. But the relative seclusion did free him to focus on developing his evolutionary theory. "Even ill health," he reflected, "has saved me from the distraction of society and its amusements" (quoted in Ma, 1997).

agoraphobia fear or avoidance of situations, such as crowds or wide open places, where one has felt loss of control and panic.

obsessive-compulsive disorder (OCD) a disorder characterized by unwanted repetitive thoughts (obsessions) and/or actions (compulsions).

Obsessive-Compulsive Disorder

66-2   What is obsessive-compulsive disorder?

As with generalized anxiety and phobias, we can see aspects of **obsessive-compulsive disorder (OCD)** in our everyday behavior. We all may at times be obsessed with senseless or offensive thoughts that will not go away. Or we may engage in compulsive behaviors, perhaps lining up books and pencils "just so" before studying.

Obsessive thoughts and compulsive behaviors cross the fine line between normality and disorder when they persistently interfere with everyday living and cause distress. Checking to see you locked the door is normal; checking 10 times is not. Washing your hands is normal; washing so often that your skin becomes raw is not. (**TABLE 66.1** on the next page offers more examples.) At some time during their lives, often during their late teens or twenties, 2 to 3 percent of people cross that line from normal preoccupations and fussiness to debilitating disorder (Karno et al., 1988). Although the person knows them to be irrational, the anxiety-fueled obsessive thoughts become so haunting, the compulsive rituals so senselessly time-consuming, that effective functioning becomes impossible.

Making everything perfect Soccer star David Beckham has openly discussed his obsessive-compulsive tendencies, which have driven him to line up objects in pairs or to spend hours straightening furniture (Adams, 2011).

Stephen Dunn/Getty Images

Table 66.1 Common Obsessions and Compulsions Among Children and Adolescents With Obsessive-Compulsive Disorder

Thought or Behavior	Percentage Reporting Symptom
Obsessions (repetitive *thoughts*)	
Concern with dirt, germs, or toxins	40
Something terrible happening (fire, death, illness)	24
Symmetry, order, or exactness	17
Compulsions (repetitive *behaviors*)	
Excessive hand washing, bathing, toothbrushing, or grooming	85
Repeating rituals (in/out of a door, up/down from a chair)	51
Checking doors, locks, appliances, car brakes, homework	46

Source: Adapted from Rapoport, 1989.

posttraumatic stress disorder (PTSD) a disorder characterized by haunting memories, nightmares, social withdrawal, jumpy anxiety, numbness of feeling, and/or insomnia that lingers for four weeks or more after a traumatic experience.

OCD is more common among teens and young adults than among older people (Samuels & Nestadt, 1997). A 40-year follow-up study of 144 Swedish people diagnosed with the disorder found that, for most, the obsessions and compulsions had gradually lessened, though only 1 in 5 had completely recovered (Skoog & Skoog, 1999).

Posttraumatic Stress Disorder

66-3 What is posttraumatic stress disorder?

As an Iraq war soldier, Jesse "saw the murder of children, women. It was just horrible for anyone to experience." After calling in a helicopter strike on one house where he had seen ammunition crates carried in, he heard the screams of children from within. "I didn't know there were kids there," he recalls. Back home in Texas, he suffered "real bad flashbacks" (Welch, 2005).

Our memories exist in part to protect us in the future. So there is biological wisdom in not being able to forget our most emotional or traumatic experiences—our greatest embarrassments, our worst accidents, our most horrid experiences. But sometimes, for some of us, the unforgettable takes over our lives. The complaints of battle-scarred veterans such as Jesse—recurring haunting memories and nightmares, a numbed social withdrawal, jumpy anxiety, insomnia—are typical of what once was called "shellshock" or "battle fatigue" and now is called **posttraumatic stress disorder (PTSD)** (Babson & Feldner, 2010; Yufik & Simms, 2010). What defines and explains PTSD is less the event itself than the severity and persistence of the trauma memory (Rubin et al., 2008).

PTSD symptoms have also been reported by survivors of accidents, disasters, and violent and sexual assaults (including an estimated two-thirds of prostitutes) (Brewin et al., 1999; Farley et al., 1998; Taylor et al., 1998). A month after the 9/11 terrorist attacks, a survey of Manhattan residents indicated that 8.5 percent were suffering PTSD, most as a result of the attack (Galea et al., 2002). Among those living near the World Trade Center, 20 percent reported such telltale signs as nightmares, severe anxiety, and fear of public places (Susser et al., 2002).

Bringing the war home Nearly a quarter of a million Iraq and Afghanistan war veterans have been diagnosed with PTSD or traumatic brain injury (TBI). Many vets participate in an intensive recovery program using deep breathing, massage, and group and individual discussion techniques to treat their PTSD or TBI.

Lynn Johnson/National Geographic Society/Corbis

To pin down the frequency of this disorder, the U.S. Centers for Disease Control (1988) compared 7000 Vietnam combat veterans with 7000 noncombat veterans who served during the same years. On average, according to a reanalysis, 19 percent of all Vietnam veterans reported PTSD symptoms. The rate varied from 10 percent among those who had never seen combat to 32 percent among those who had experienced heavy combat (Dohrenwend et al., 2006). Similar variations in rates have been found among more recent combat veterans and among people who have experienced a natural disaster or have been kidnapped, held captive, tortured, or raped (Brewin et al., 2000; Brody, 2000; Kessler, 2000; Stone, 2005; Yaffe et al., 2010).

The toll seems at least as high for veterans of the Iraq war, where 1 in 6 U.S. combat infantry personnel has reported symptoms of PTSD, depression, or severe anxiety in the months after returning home (Hoge et al., 2006, 2007). In one study of 103,788 veterans returning from Iraq and Afghanistan, 1 in 4 was diagnosed with a psychological disorder, most frequently PTSD (Seal et al., 2007).

So what determines whether a person suffers PTSD after a traumatic event? Research indicates that the greater one's emotional distress during a trauma, the higher the risk for posttraumatic symptoms (Ozer et al., 2003). Among New Yorkers who witnessed the 9/11 attacks, PTSD was doubled for survivors who were inside rather than outside the World Trade Center (Bonanno et al., 2006). And the more frequent an assault experience, the more adverse the long-term outcomes tend to be (Golding, 1999). In the 30 years after the Vietnam war, veterans who came home with a PTSD diagnosis had twice the normal likelihood of dying (Crawford et al., 2009).

A sensitive limbic system seems to increase vulnerability, by flooding the body with stress hormones again and again as images of the traumatic experience erupt into consciousness (Kosslyn, 2005; Ozer & Weiss, 2004). Brain scans of PTSD patients suffering memory flashbacks reveal an aberrant and persistent right temporal lobe activation (Engdahl et al., 2010). Genes may also play a role. In one study, combat-exposed men had identical twins who did not experience combat. But these nonexposed co-twins still tended to share their brother's risk for cognitive difficulties, such as unfocused attention. Such findings suggest that some PTSD symptoms may actually be genetically predisposed (Gilbertson et al., 2006).

Some psychologists believe that PTSD has been overdiagnosed, due partly to a broadening definition of *trauma* (Dobbs, 2009; McNally, 2003). PTSD is actually infrequent, say those critics, and well-intentioned attempts to have people relive the trauma may exacerbate their emotions and pathologize normal stress reactions (Wakefield & Spitzer, 2002). "Debriefing" survivors right after a trauma by getting them to revisit the experience and vent emotions has actually proven generally ineffective and sometimes harmful (Bonanno et al., 2010).

Researchers have noted the impressive *survivor resiliency* of those who do *not* develop PTSD (Bonanno et al., 2010). About half of adults experience at least one traumatic event in their lifetime, but only about 1 in 10 women and 1 in 20 men develop PTSD (Olff et al., 2007; Ozer & Weiss, 2004; Tolin & Foa, 2006). More than 9 in 10 New Yorkers, although stunned and grief-stricken by 9/11, did *not* respond pathologically. By the following January, the stress symptoms of the rest had mostly subsided (Galea et al., 2002). Similarly, most combat-stressed veterans and most political dissidents who survive dozens of episodes of torture do not later exhibit PTSD (Mineka & Zinbarg, 1996). Likewise, the Holocaust survivors in 71 studies "showed remarkable resilience." Despite some lingering stress symptoms, most experienced essentially normal physical health and cognitive functioning (Barel et al., 2010).

Psychologist Peter Suedfeld (1998, 2000; Cassel & Suedfeld, 2006), who as a boy survived the Holocaust under deprived conditions while his mother died in Auschwitz, has documented the *resilience* of Holocaust survivors, most of whom have lived productive lives. "It is not always true that 'What doesn't kill you makes you stronger,' but it is often true," he reports. And "what doesn't kill you may reveal to you just how strong you really are."

Indeed, suffering can lead to "benefit finding" (Aspinwall & Tedeschi, 2010a,b; Helgeson et al., 2006), and to what Richard Tedeschi and Lawrence Calhoun (2004) call **posttraumatic growth.** Tedeschi and Calhoun have found that the struggle with challenging crises, such as

FYI

A $125 million, five-year U.S. Army program is currently assessing the well-being of 800,000 soldiers and training them in emotional resilience (Stix, 2011).

posttraumatic growth positive psychological changes as a result of struggling with extremely challenging circumstances and life crises.

facing cancer, often leads people later to report an increased appreciation for life, more meaningful relationships, increased personal strength, changed priorities, and a richer spiritual life. This idea—that suffering has transformative power—is also found in Judaism, Christianity, Hinduism, Buddhism, and Islam. The idea is confirmed by research with ordinary people. Compared with those with traumatic life histories and with those unchallenged by any significant adversity, people whose life history includes *some* adversity tend to enjoy better mental health and well-being (Seery et al., 2010). Out of even our worst experiences some good can come. Like the body, the mind has great recuperative powers and may grow stronger with exertion.

Understanding Anxiety Disorders, OCD, and PTSD

66-4 How do the learning and biological perspectives explain anxiety disorders, OCD, and PTSD?

Anxiety is both a feeling and a cognition, a doubt-laden appraisal of one's safety or social skill. How do these anxious feelings and cognitions arise? Freud's psychoanalytic theory proposed that, beginning in childhood, people *repress* intolerable impulses, ideas, and feelings and that this submerged mental energy sometimes produces mystifying symptoms, such as anxiety. Today's psychologists have instead turned to two contemporary perspectives—learning and biological.

The Learning Perspective

CLASSICAL AND OPERANT CONDITIONING

When bad events happen unpredictably and uncontrollably, anxiety or other disorders often develop (Field, 2006b; Mineka & Oehlberg, 2008). Recall from Unit VI that dogs learn to fear neutral stimuli associated with shock and that infants come to fear furry objects associated with frightening noises. Using classical conditioning, researchers have also created chronically anxious, ulcer-prone rats by giving them unpredictable electric shocks (Schwartz, 1984). Like assault victims who report feeling anxious when returning to the scene of the crime, the rats become apprehensive in their lab environment. This link between conditioned fear and general anxiety helps explain why anxious or traumatized people are hyperattentive to possible threats, and how panic-prone people come to associate anxiety with certain cues (Bar-Haim et al., 2007; Bouton et al., 2001). In one survey, 58 percent of those with social anxiety disorder experienced their disorder after a traumatic event (Ost & Hugdahl, 1981).

AP® Exam Tip

This is a good time to return to Unit VI and review the principles of classical and operant conditioning.

Through conditioning, the short list of naturally painful and frightening events can multiply into a long list of human fears. My car was once struck by another whose driver missed a stop sign. For months afterward, I felt a twinge of unease when any car approached from a side street. Marilyn's phobia of thunderstorms may have been similarly conditioned during a terrifying or painful experience associated with a thunderstorm.

Two specific learning processes can contribute to these disorders. The first, *stimulus generalization,* occurs, for example, when a person attacked by a fierce dog later develops a fear of *all* dogs. The second learning process, *reinforcement,* helps maintain our phobias and compulsions after they arise. Avoiding or escaping the feared situation reduces anxiety, thus reinforcing the phobic behavior. Feeling anxious or fearing a panic attack, a person may go inside and be reinforced by feeling calmer (Antony et al., 1992). Compulsive behaviors operate similarly. If washing your hands relieves your feelings of anxiety, you may wash your hands again when those feelings return.

OBSERVATIONAL LEARNING

We may also learn fear through observational learning—by observing others' fears. Susan Mineka (1985, 2002) sought to explain why nearly all monkeys reared in the wild fear snakes, yet lab-reared monkeys do not. Surely, most wild monkeys do not actually suffer snake bites.

Do they learn their fear through observation? To find out, Mineka experimented with six monkeys reared in the wild (all strongly fearful of snakes) and their lab-reared offspring (virtually none of which feared snakes). After repeatedly observing their parents or peers refusing to reach for food in the presence of a snake, the younger monkeys developed a similar strong fear of snakes. When retested three months later, their learned fear persisted. Humans likewise learn fears by observing others (Olsson et al., 2007).

COGNITION

Observational learning is not the only cognitive influence on feelings of anxiety. As the next unit's discussion of cognitive-behavioral therapy illustrates, our interpretations and irrational beliefs can also cause feelings of anxiety. Whether we interpret the creaky sound in the old house simply as the wind or as a possible knife-wielding intruder determines whether we panic. People with anxiety disorder also tend to be *hypervigilant.* A pounding heart becomes a sign of a heart attack. A lone spider near the bed becomes a likely infestation. An everyday disagreement with a friend or boss spells possible doom for the relationship. Anxiety is especially common when people cannot switch off such intrusive thoughts and perceive a loss of control and sense of helplessness (Franklin & Foa, 2011).

The Biological Perspective

There is, however, more to anxiety, OCD, and PTSD than conditioning, observational learning, and cognition. The biological perspective can help us understand why few people develop lasting phobias after suffering traumas, why we learn some fears more readily, and why some individuals are more vulnerable.

NATURAL SELECTION

We humans seem biologically prepared to fear threats faced by our ancestors. Our phobias focus on such specific fears: spiders, snakes, and other animals; enclosed spaces and heights; storms and darkness. (Those fearless about these occasional threats were less likely to survive and leave descendants.) Thus, even in Britain, with only one poisonous snake species, people often fear snakes. And preschool children more speedily detect snakes in a scene than flowers, caterpillars, or frogs (LoBue & DeLoache, 2008). It is easy to condition and hard to extinguish fears of such "evolutionarily relevant" stimuli (Coelho & Purkis, 2009; Davey, 1995; Öhman, 2009).

Our modern fears can also have an evolutionary explanation. For example, a fear of flying may come from our biological predisposition to fear confinement and heights. Moreover, consider what people tend *not* to learn to fear. World War II air raids produced remarkably few lasting phobias. As the air blitzes continued, the British, Japanese, and German populations became not more panicked, but rather more indifferent to planes outside their immediate neighborhoods (Mineka & Zinbarg, 1996). Evolution has not prepared us to fear bombs dropping from the sky.

Just as our phobias focus on dangers faced by our ancestors, our compulsive acts typically exaggerate behaviors that contributed to our species' survival. Grooming gone wild becomes hair pulling. Washing up becomes ritual hand washing. Checking territorial boundaries becomes rechecking an already locked door (Rapoport, 1989).

GENES

Some people are more anxious than others. Genes matter. Pair a traumatic event with a sensitive, high-strung temperament and the result may be a new phobia (Belsky & Pluess, 2009). Some of us have genes that make us like orchids—fragile, yet capable of beauty under favorable circumstances. Others of us are like dandelions—hardy, and able to thrive in varied circumstances (Ellis & Boyce, 2008).

Among monkeys, fearfulness runs in families. Individual monkeys react more strongly to stress if their close biological relatives are anxiously reactive (Suomi, 1986).

Fearless The biological perspective helps us understand why most people would be too afraid to try U.S. Olympic snowboarder Shaun White's tricks. White is less vulnerable to a fear of heights than most of us!

In humans, vulnerability to anxiety disorders rises when an afflicted relative is an identical twin (Hettema et al., 2001; Kendler et al., 1992, 1999, 2002a,b). Identical twins also may develop similar phobias, even when raised separately (Carey, 1990; Eckert et al., 1981). One pair of 35-year-old female identical twins independently became so afraid of water that each would wade in the ocean backward and only up to the knees.

Given the genetic contribution to anxiety disorders, researchers are now sleuthing the culprit genes. One research team has identified 17 genes that appear to be expressed with typical anxiety disorder symptoms (Hovatta et al., 2005). Other teams have found genes associated specifically with OCD (Dodman et al., 2010; Hu et al., 2006).

Genes influence disorders by regulating neurotransmitters. Some studies point to an anxiety gene that affects brain levels of *serotonin,* a neurotransmitter that influences sleep and mood (Canli, 2008). Other studies implicate genes that regulate the neurotransmitter *glutamate* (Lafleur et al., 2006; Welch et al., 2007). With too much glutamate, the brain's alarm centers become overactive.

THE BRAIN

Generalized anxiety, panic attacks, PTSD, and even obsessions and compulsions are manifested biologically as an overarousal of brain areas involved in impulse control and habitual behaviors. When the disordered brain detects that something is amiss, it seems to generate a mental hiccup of repeating thoughts or actions (Gehring et al., 2000). Brain scans of people with OCD reveal elevated activity in specific brain areas during behaviors such as compulsive hand washing, checking, ordering, or hoarding (Insel, 2010; Mataix-Cols et al., 2004, 2005). As **FIGURE 66.2** shows, the *anterior cingulate cortex,* a brain region that monitors our actions and checks for errors, seems especially likely to be hyperactive in those with OCD (Maltby et al., 2005). Fear-learning experiences that traumatize the brain can also create fear circuits within the amygdala (Etkin & Wager, 2007; Kolassa & Elbert, 2007; Maren, 2007). Some antidepressant drugs dampen this fear-circuit activity and its associated obsessive-compulsive behavior.

Fears can also be blunted by giving people drugs, such as propranolol or D-Cycloserine, as they recall and then rerecord ("reconsolidate") a traumatic experience (Kindt et al., 2009; Norberg, et al., 2008). Although they don't forget the experience, the associated emotion is largely erased.

Figure 66.2

An obsessive-compulsive brain Neuroscientists Nicholas Maltby, David Tolin, and their colleagues (2005) used functional MRI scans to compare the brains of those with and without OCD as they engaged in a challenging cognitive task. The scans of those with OCD showed elevated activity in the anterior cingulate cortex in the brain's frontal area (indicated by the yellow area on the far right).

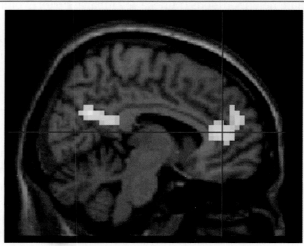

Before You Move On

▶ **ASK YOURSELF**

Can you recall a fear that you have learned? What role, if any, was played by fear conditioning and by observational learning?

▶ **TEST YOURSELF**

How do generalized anxiety disorder, panic disorder, phobias, obsessive-compulsive disorder, and posttraumatic stress disorder differ?

Answers to the Test Yourself questions can be found in Appendix E at the end of the book.

Module 66 Review

66-1 What are the different anxiety disorders?

- Anxious feelings and behaviors are classified as an *anxiety disorder* only when they form a pattern of distressing, persistent anxiety or maladaptive behaviors that reduce anxiety.

- People with *generalized anxiety disorder* feel persistently and uncontrollably tense and apprehensive, for no apparent reason.

- In the more extreme *panic disorder,* anxiety escalates into periodic episodes of intense dread.

- Those with a *phobia* may be irrationally afraid of a specific object, activity, or situation.

- Two other disorders (obsessive-compulsive disorder and posttraumatic stress disorder) involve anxiety (though they are classified separately from the anxiety disorders).

66-2 What is obsessive-compulsive disorder?

- Persistent and repetitive thoughts (obsessions) and actions (compulsions) characterize *obsessive-compulsive disorder (OCD).*

66-3 What is posttraumatic stress disorder?

- Symptoms of *posttraumatic stress disorder (PTSD)* include four or more weeks of haunting memories, nightmares, social withdrawal, jumpy anxiety, and sleep problems following some traumatic experience.

66-4 How do the learning and biological perspectives explain anxiety disorders, OCD, and PTSD?

- The learning perspective views anxiety disorders, OCD, and PTSD as products of fear conditioning, stimulus generalization, fearful-behavior reinforcement, and observational learning of others' fears and cognitions (interpretations, irrational beliefs, and hypervigilance).

- The biological perspective considers the role that fears of life-threatening animals, objects, or situations played in natural selection and evolution; genetic predispositions for high levels of emotional reactivity and neurotransmitter production; and abnormal responses in the brain's fear circuits.

Multiple-Choice Questions

1. What do we call an anxiety disorder marked by a persistent, irrational fear and avoidance of a specific object, activity, or situation?
   a. Obsessive-compulsive disorder
   b. Phobia
   c. Panic disorder
   d. Generalized anxiety disorder
   e. Posttraumatic stress disorder

2. A person troubled by repetitive thoughts or actions is most likely experiencing which of the following?
   a. Generalized anxiety disorder
   b. Posttraumatic stress disorder
   c. Panic disorder
   d. Obsessive-compulsive disorder
   e. Fear conditioning

3. The key difference between obsessions and compulsions is that compulsions involve repetitive
   a. thoughts.
   b. experiences.
   c. behaviors.
   d. memories.
   e. concerns.

Practice FRQs

1. Name the two contemporary perspectives used by psychologists to understand anxiety disorders. Then explain how or what psychologists study within each perspective.

Answer

1 point: The learning perspective

1 point: Psychologists using the learning perspective study fear conditioning, observational learning, or cognitive processes.

1 point: The biological perspective

1 point: Psychologists using the biological perspective study natural selection, genes, or the brain.

2. Name and describe two anxiety disorders. *(4 points)*

Module 67

Mood Disorders

Module Learning Objectives

 67-1 Define *mood disorders*, and contrast major depressive disorder and bipolar disorder.

67-2 Describe how the biological and social-cognitive perspectives explain mood disorders.

67-3 Discuss the factors that affect suicide and self-injury, and identify important warning signs to watch for in suicide-prevention efforts.

67-1 What are mood disorders? How does major depressive disorder differ from bipolar disorder?

The emotional extremes of **mood disorders** come in two principal forms: (1) *major depressive disorder,* with its prolonged hopelessness and lethargy, and (2) *bipolar disorder* (formerly called *manic-depressive disorder*), in which a person alternates between depression and *mania,* an overexcited, hyperactive state.

> **mood disorders** psychological disorders characterized by emotional extremes. See *major depressive disorder, mania,* and *bipolar disorder.*

Major Depressive Disorder

If you are like most high school students, at some time during this year—more likely the dark months of winter than the bright days of summer—you will probably experience some of depression's symptoms. You may feel deeply discouraged about the future, dissatisfied with your life, or socially isolated. You may lack the energy to get things done or even to force yourself out of bed; be unable to concentrate, eat, or sleep normally; or even wonder if you would be better off dead. Perhaps academic success came easily to you in middle school, and now you find that disappointing grades jeopardize your goals. Maybe social stresses, such as feeling you don't belong or experiencing the end of a romance, have plunged you into despair. And maybe brooding has at times only worsened your self-torment. Likely you think you are more alone in having such negative feelings than you really are (Jordan et al., 2011). In one survey of American high school students, 29 percent "felt so sad or hopeless almost every day for 2 or more weeks in a row that they stopped doing some usual activities" (CDC, 2008). In another national survey, of American collegians, 31 percent agreed when asked if in the past year they had at some time "felt so depressed that it was difficult to function" (ACHA, 2009). Misery has more company than most suppose.

Although phobias are more common, depression is the number-one reason people seek mental health services. At some point during their lifetime, depression plagues 12 percent of Canadian adults and 17 percent of U.S. adults (Holden, 2010; Patten et al., 2006). Moreover, it is the leading cause of disability worldwide (WHO, 2002). In any given year, a depressive episode plagues 5.8 percent of men and 9.5 percent of women, reports the World Health Organization.

> "My life had come to a sudden stop. I was able to breathe, to eat, to drink, to sleep. I could not, indeed, help doing so; but there was no real life in me." -LEO TOLSTOY, *MY CONFESSION,* 1887

major depressive disorder
a mood disorder in which a person experiences, in the absence of drugs or another medical condition, two or more weeks with five or more symptoms, at least one of which must be either (1) depressed mood or (2) loss of interest or pleasure.

As anxiety is a response to the threat of future loss, depressed mood is often a response to past and current loss. About one in four people diagnosed with depression is debilitated by a significant loss, such as a loved one's death, a ruptured marriage, or a lost job (Wakefield et al., 2007). To feel bad in reaction to profoundly sad events is to be in touch with reality. In such times, there is an up side to being down. Sadness is like a car's low-fuel light—a signal that warns us to stop and take appropriate measures. Recall that, biologically speaking, life's purpose is not happiness but survival and reproduction. Coughing, vomiting, swelling, and pain protect the body from dangerous toxins. Similarly, depression is a sort of psychic hibernation: It slows us down, defuses aggression, helps us let go of unattainable goals, and restrains risk taking (Andrews & Thomson, 2009a,b; Wrosch & Miller, 2009). To grind temporarily to a halt and ruminate, as depressed people do, is to reassess one's life when feeling threatened, and to redirect energy in more promising ways (Watkins, 2008). Even mild sadness can improve people's recall, make them more discerning, and help them make complex decisions (Forgas, 2009). There is sense to suffering.

But when does this response become seriously maladaptive? Joy, contentment, sadness, and despair are different points on a continuum, points at which any of us may be found at any given moment. The difference between a blue mood after bad news and a mood disorder is like the difference between gasping for breath after a hard run and being chronically short of breath.

Major depressive disorder occurs when at least five signs of depression last two or more weeks (**TABLE 67.1**). To sense what major depression feels like, suggest some clinicians, imagine combining the anguish of grief with the sluggishness of bad jet lag.

Adults diagnosed with *persistent depressive disorder* (also called *dysthymia*) experience a mildly depressed mood more often than not for at least two years (American Psychiatric Association, 2013). They also display at least two of the following symptoms:

1. Problems regulating appetite
2. Problems regulating sleep
3. Low energy
4. Low self-esteem
5. Difficulty concentrating and making decisions
6. Feelings of hopelessness

Table 67.1   Diagnosing Major Depressive Disorder
The DSM-5 classifies major depressive disorder as the presence of at least five of the following symptoms over a two-week period of time (including depressed mood or loss of interest or pleasure). The symptoms must cause near-daily distress or impairment and not be attributable to substance use or another medical or mental illness.
• Depressed mood most of the day
• Markedly diminished interest or pleasure in activities most of the day
• Significant weight loss or gain when not dieting, or significant decrease or increase in appetite
• Insomnia or sleeping too much
• Physical agitation or lethargy
• Fatigue or loss of energy
• Feeling worthless, or excessive or inappropriate guilt
• Problems in thinking, concentrating, or making decisions
• Recurrent thoughts of death and suicide

Bipolar Disorder

With or without therapy, episodes of major depression usually end, and people temporarily or permanently return to their previous behavior patterns. However, some people rebound to, or sometimes start with, the opposite emotional extreme—the euphoric, hyperactive, wildly optimistic state of **mania.** If depression is living in slow motion, mania is fast forward. Alternating between depression and mania (week to week, and not day to day or moment to moment) signals **bipolar disorder.**

Adolescent mood swings, from rage to bubbly, can, when prolonged, produce a bipolar diagnosis. Between 1994 and 2003, U.S. National Center for Health Statistics annual physician surveys revealed an astonishing 40-fold increase in diagnoses of bipolar disorder in those 19 and under—from an estimated 20,000 to 800,000 (Carey, 2007; Flora & Bobby, 2008; Moreno et al., 2007). The new popularity of the diagnosis, given in two-thirds of the cases to boys, has been a boon to companies whose drugs are prescribed to lessen mood swings. The DSM-5 will likely reduce the number of child and adolescent bipolar diagnoses, by classifying as *disruptive mood dysregulation disorder* some of those with emotional volatility (Miller, 2010).

During the manic phase, people with bipolar disorder are typically overtalkative, overactive, and elated (though easily irritated); have little need for sleep; and show fewer sexual inhibitions. Speech is loud, flighty, and hard to interrupt. They find advice irritating. Yet they need protection from their own poor judgment, which may lead to reckless spending or unsafe sex.

In milder forms, mania's energy and free-flowing thinking does fuel creativity. George Frideric Handel, who may have suffered from a mild form of bipolar disorder, composed his nearly four-hour-long *Messiah* (1742) during three weeks of intense, creative energy (Keynes, 1980). Robert Schumann composed 51 musical works during two years of mania (1840 and 1849) and none during 1844, when he was severely depressed (Slater & Meyer, 1959). Those who rely on precision and logic, such as architects, designers, and journalists, suffer bipolar disorder less often than do those who rely on emotional expression and vivid imagery (Ludwig, 1995). Composers, artists, poets, novelists, and entertainers seem especially prone (Jamison, 1993, 1995; Kaufman & Baer, 2002; Ludwig, 1995).

FYI

For some people suffering depressive disorders or bipolar disorder, symptoms may have a *seasonal pattern.* Depression may regularly return each fall or winter, and mania (or a reprieve from depression) may dependably arrive with spring. For many others, winter darkness simply means more blue moods. When asked "Have you cried today?" Americans have agreed more often in the winter.

Percentage who cried

	Men	Women
August	4%	7%
December	8%	21%

Source: Time/CNN survey, 1994.

mania   a mood disorder marked by a hyperactive, wildly optimistic state.

bipolar disorder   a mood disorder in which a person alternates between the hopelessness and lethargy of depression and the overexcited state of mania. (Formerly called *manic-depressive disorder.*)

**Actress
Catherine Zeta-Jones**
Wirelmage/Getty Images

**Humorist
Samuel Clemens (Mark Twain)**
The Granger Collection

**Writer
Virginia Woolf**
George C. Beresford/Hulton Getty Pictures Library

**Movie Producer
Tim Burton**
Jemal Countess/Getty Images

Creativity and bipolar disorder   There are many creative artists, composers, writers, and musical performers with bipolar disorder. Madeleine L'Engle wrote in *A Circle of Quiet* (1972): "All the people in history, literature, art, whom I most admire: Mozart, Shakespeare, Homer, El Greco, St. John, Chekhov, Gregory of Nyssa, Dostoevsky, Emily Brontë: not one of them would qualify for a mental-health certificate."

Jennifer Graylock

Life after depression Writer J. K. Rowling reports suffering acute depression—a "dark time," with suicidal thoughts—between ages 25 and 28. It was, she said, a "terrible place" that did, however, form a foundation that allowed her "to come back stronger" (McLaughlin, 2010).

It is as true of emotions as of everything else: What goes up comes down. Before long, the elated mood either returns to normal or plunges into a depression. Though bipolar disorder is much less common than major depressive disorder, it is often more dysfunctional, claiming twice as many lost workdays yearly (Kessler et al., 2006). Among adults, it afflicts men and women about equally.

Understanding Mood Disorders

67-2 How do the biological and social-cognitive perspectives explain mood disorders?

In thousands of studies, psychologists have been accumulating evidence to help explain mood disorders and suggest more effective ways to treat and prevent them. Researcher Peter Lewinsohn and his colleagues (1985, 1998, 2003) summarized the facts that any theory of depression must explain, including the following:

- *Many behavioral and cognitive changes accompany depression.* People trapped in a depressed mood are inactive and feel unmotivated. They are sensitive to negative happenings (Peckham et al., 2010). They more often recall negative information. They expect negative outcomes (my team will lose, my grades will fall, my love will fail). When the mood lifts, these behavioral and cognitive accompaniments disappear. Nearly half the time, people also exhibit symptoms of another disorder, such as anxiety or substance use disorder.

- *Depression is widespread.* Its commonality suggests that its causes, too, must be common.

- *Women's risk of major depression is nearly double men's.* When Gallup in 2009 asked more than a quarter-million Americans if they had ever been diagnosed with depression, 13 percent of men and 22 percent of women said they had (Pelham, 2009). This gender gap has been found worldwide **(FIGURE 67.1)**. The trend begins in adolescence; preadolescent girls are not more depression-prone than are boys (Hyde et al., 2008).

Figure 67.1

Gender and major depression Interviews with 89,037 adults in 18 countries (10 shown here) confirm what many smaller studies have found: Women's risk of major depression is nearly double that of men's.

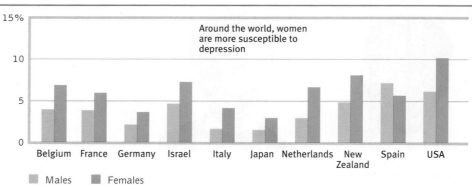

Percentage of adults experiencing major depression in previous 12 months

Around the world, women are more susceptible to depression

Belgium   France   Germany   Israel   Italy   Japan   Netherlands   New Zealand   Spain   USA

■ Males   ■ Females

The factors that put women at risk for depression (genetic predispositions, child abuse, low self-esteem, marital problems, and so forth) similarly put men at risk (Kendler et al., 2006). Yet women are more vulnerable to disorders involving internalized states, such as depression, anxiety, and inhibited sexual desire. Men's disorders tend to be more external—alcohol use disorder, antisocial conduct, lack of impulse control. When women get sad, they often get sadder than men do. When men get mad, they often get madder than women do.

- *Most major depressive episodes self-terminate.* Although therapy often helps and tends to speed recovery, most people suffering major depression eventually return to normal even without professional help. The plague of depression comes and, a few weeks or months later, it goes, though for about half of people it eventually recurs (Burcusa & Iacono, 2007; Curry et al., 2011; Hardeveld et al., 2010). For only about 20 percent is the condition chronic (Klein, 2010). On average, patients with major depression today will spend about three-fourths of the next decade in a normal, nondepressed state (Furukawa et al., 2009). Recovery is more likely to be permanent the later the first episode strikes, the longer the person stays well, the fewer the previous episodes, the less stress experienced, and the more social support received (Belsher & Costello, 1988; Fergusson & Woodward, 2002; Kendler et al., 2001).

The emotional lives of men and women?

- *Stressful events related to work, marriage, and close relationships often precede depression.* A family member's death, a job loss, a marital crisis, or a physical assault increase one's risk of depression (Kendler et al., 2008; Monroe & Reid, 2009; Orth et al., 2009). If stress-related anxiety is a "crackling, menacing brushfire," notes biologist Robert Sapolsky (2003), "depression is a suffocating heavy blanket thrown on top of it." One long-term study (Kendler, 1998) tracked rates of depression in 2000 people. The risk of depression ranged from less than 1 percent among those who had experienced no stressful life event in the preceding month to 24 percent among those who had experienced three such events in that month.

- *With each new generation, depression is striking earlier (now often in the late teens) and affecting more people, with the highest rates in developed countries among young adults.* This is true in Canada, the United States, England, France, Germany, Italy, Lebanon, New Zealand, Puerto Rico, and Taiwan (Collishaw et al., 2007; Cross-National Collaborative Group, 1992; Kessler et al., 2010; Twenge et al., 2008). In one study, 12 percent of Australian adolescents reported symptoms of depression (Sawyer et al., 2000). Most hid it from their parents; almost 90 percent of those parents perceived their depressed teen as *not* suffering depression. In North America, today's young adults are three times more likely than their grandparents to report having recently—or ever—suffered depression (despite the grandparents' many more years of being at risk). The increase appears partly authentic, but it may also reflect today's young adults' greater willingness to disclose depression.

> "I see depression as the plague of the modern era." -Lewis Judd, former chief, National Institute of Mental Health, 2000

Today's researchers propose biological and cognitive explanations of depression, often combined in a biopsychosocial approach.

The Biological Perspective

GENETIC INFLUENCES

Mood disorders run in families. As one researcher noted, emotions are "postcards from our genes" (Plotkin, 1994). The risk of major depression and bipolar disorder increases if you have a parent or sibling with the disorder (Sullivan et al., 2000). If one identical twin is diagnosed with major depressive disorder, the chances are about 1 in 2 that at some time the other twin will be, too. If one identical twin has bipolar disorder, the chances are 7 in 10 that the other twin will at some point be diagnosed similarly. Among fraternal twins, the corresponding odds are just under 2 in 10 (Tsuang & Faraone, 1990). The greater similarity among identical twins holds even among twins raised apart (DiLalla et al., 1996). Summarizing the major twin studies, one research team estimated the heritability (extent to which individual differences are attributable to genes) of major depression at 37 percent (**FIGURE 67.2** on the next page).

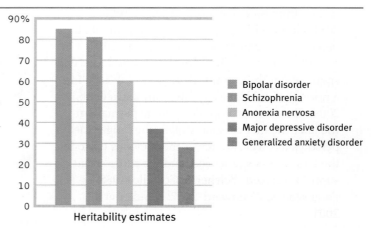

Figure 67.2

The heritability of various psychological disorders
Researchers Joseph Bienvenu, Dimitry Davydow, and Kenneth Kendler (2011) aggregated data from studies of identical and fraternal twins to estimate the heritability of bipolar disorder, schizophrenia, anorexia nervosa, major depressive disorder, and generalized anxiety disorder.

Legend:
- Bipolar disorder
- Schizophrenia
- Anorexia nervosa
- Major depressive disorder
- Generalized anxiety disorder

Heritability estimates

Moreover, adopted people who suffer a mood disorder often have close biological relatives who suffer mood disorders, develop alcohol use disorder, or commit suicide (Wender et al., 1986). (Close-up: Suicide and Self-Injury reports other research findings.)

Close-up

Suicide and Self-Injury

 67-3 What factors affect suicide and self-injury, and what are some of the important warning signs to watch for in suicide prevention efforts?

> ""But life, being weary of these worldly bars, / Never lacks power to dismiss itself." -WILLIAM SHAKESPEARE, JULIUS CAESAR, 1599

Each year nearly 1 million despairing people worldwide will elect a permanent solution to what might have been a temporary problem. Comparing the suicide rates of different groups, researchers have found

- **national differences:** Britain's, Italy's, and Spain's suicide rates are little more than half those of Canada, Australia, and the United States. Austria's and Finland's are about double (WHO, 2011). Within Europe, people in the most suicide-prone country (Belarus) have been 16 times more likely to kill themselves than those in the least (Georgia).

- **racial differences:** Within the United States, Whites kill themselves twice as often as Blacks (AAS, 2010).

- **gender differences:** Women are much more likely than men to attempt suicide (WHO, 2011). But men are two to four times more likely (depending on the country) to actually end their lives. Men use more lethal methods, such as firing a bullet into the head, the method of choice in 6 of 10 U.S. suicides.

- **age differences and trends:** In late adulthood, rates increase, peaking in middle age and beyond. In the last half of the twentieth century, the global rate of annual suicide deaths nearly doubled (WHO, 2008).

- **other group differences:** Suicide rates are much higher among the rich, the nonreligious, and those who are single, widowed, or divorced (Hoyer & Lund, 1993; Stack, 1992; Stengel, 1981). When facing an unsupportive environment, including family or peer rejection, gay and lesbian youth are at increased risk of attempting suicide (Goldfried, 2001; Haas et al., 2011; Hatzenbuehler, 2011).

- **day of the week differences:** 25 percent of suicides occur on Wednesdays (Kposowa & D'Auria, 2009).

The risk of suicide is at least five times greater for those who have been depressed than for the general population (Bostwick & Pankratz, 2000). People seldom commit suicide while in the depths of depression, when energy and initiative are lacking. The risk increases when they begin to rebound and become capable of following through. Among people with alcohol use disorder, 3 percent die by suicide. This rate is roughly 100 times greater than the rate for people without alcohol use disorder (Murphy & Wetzel, 1990; Sher, 2006).

Because suicide is so often an impulsive act, environmental barriers (such as jump barriers on high bridges and the unavailability of loaded guns) can reduce suicides (Anderson, 2008). Although common sense might suggest that a determined person would simply find another way to complete the act, such restrictions give time for self-destructive impulses to subside.

Social suggestion may trigger suicide. Following highly publicized suicides and TV programs featuring suicide, known suicides increase. So do fatal auto and private airplane "accidents." One six-year study tracked suicide cases among all 1.2 million people who lived in metropolitan Stockholm at any time during the 1990s

(continued)

Close-up (continued)

(Hedström et al., 2008). Men exposed to a family suicide were 8 times more likely to commit suicide than were nonexposed men. Although that phenomenon may be partly attributable to family genes, shared genetic predispositions do not explain why men exposed to a co-worker's suicide were 3.5 times more likely to commit suicide, compared with nonexposed men.

Suicide is not necessarily an act of hostility or revenge. The elderly sometimes choose death as an alternative to current or future suffering. In people of all ages, suicide may be a way of switching off unendurable pain and relieving a perceived burden on family members. "People desire death when two fundamental needs are frustrated to the point of extinction," notes Thomas Joiner (2006, p. 47): "The need to belong with or connect to others, and the need to feel effective with or to influence others." Suicidal urges typically arise when people feel disconnected from others, and a burden to them (Joiner, 2010), or when they feel defeated and trapped by an inescapable situation (Taylor et al., 2011). Thus, suicide rates increase a bit during economic recessions (Luo et al., 2011). Suicidal thoughts also may increase when people are driven to reach a goal or standard—to become thin or straight or rich—and find it unattainable (Chatard & Selimbegović, 2011).

In hindsight, families and friends may recall signs they believe should have forewarned them—verbal hints, giving possessions away, or withdrawal and preoccupation with death. To judge from surveys of 84,850 people across 17 nations, about 9 percent of people at some point in their lives have thought seriously of suicide. About 30 percent of these (3 percent of people) actually attempt it (Nock et al., 2008). For only about 1 in 25 does the attempt become their final act (AAS, 2009). Of those who die, one-third had tried to kill themselves previously. Most discussed it beforehand. So, if a friend talks suicide to you, it's important to listen and to direct the person to professional help. Anyone who threatens suicide is at least sending a signal of feeling desperate or despondent.

NONSUICIDAL SELF-INJURY

Suicide is not the only way to send a message or deal with distress. Some people, especially adolescents and young adults, may engage in *nonsuicidal self-injury (NSSI)* (**FIGURE 67.3**). Such behavior includes cutting or burning the skin, hitting oneself, pulling hair out, inserting objects under the nails or skin, and self-administered tattooing (Fikke et al., 2011).

Why do people hurt themselves? Those who do so tend to be less able to tolerate emotional distress, are extremely self-critical, and often have poor communication and problem-solving skills (Nock, 2010). They engage in NSSI to

- gain relief from intense negative thoughts through the distraction of pain,
- ask for help and gain attention,
- relieve guilt by self-punishment
- get others to change their negative behavior (bullying, criticism), or
- to fit in with a peer group.

Does NSSI lead to suicide? Usually not. Those who engage in NSSI are typically *suicide gesturers,* not *suicide attempters* (Nock & Kessler, 2006). Suicide gesturers engage in NSSI as a desperate but non-life-threatening form of communication or when they are feeling overwhelmed. But NSSI has been shown to be a risk factor for future suicide attempts (Wilkinson & Goodyer, 2011). If people do not get help, their nonsuicidal behavior may escalate to suicidal ideation and finally, to attempted suicide.

Figure 67.3

Rates of nonfatal self-injury in the U.S. Self-injury rates peak higher for females than for males (CDC, 2009).

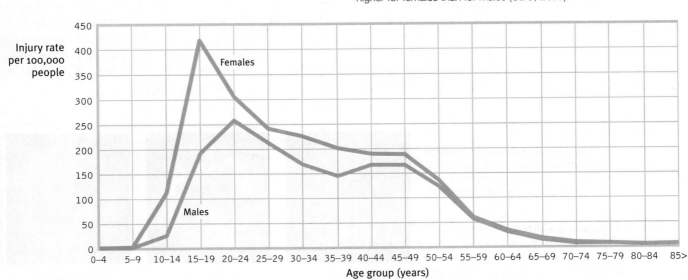

To tease out the genes that put people at risk for depression, some researchers have turned to *linkage analysis.* After finding families in which the disorder appears across several generations, geneticists examine DNA from affected and unaffected family members, looking for differences. Linkage analysis points us to a chromosome neighborhood, note behavior genetics researchers Robert Plomin and Peter McGuffin (2003); "a house-to-house search is then needed to find the culprit gene." Such studies are reinforcing the view that depression is a complex condition. Many genes work together, producing a mosaic of small effects that interact with other factors to put some people at greater risk. If the culprit gene variations can be identified—with chromosome 3 genes implicated in separate British and American studies (Breen et al., 2011; Pergadia et al., 2011)—they may open the door to more effective drug therapy.

THE DEPRESSED BRAIN

Using modern technology, researchers are also gaining insight into brain activity during depressed and manic states, and into the effects of certain neurotransmitters during these states. One study gave 13 elite Canadian swimmers the wrenching experience of watching a video of the swim in which they failed to make the Olympic team or failed at the Olympic games (Davis et al., 2008). Functional MRI scans showed the disappointed swimmers experiencing brain activity patterns akin to those of patients with depressed moods.

Many studies have found diminished brain activity during slowed-down depressive states, and more activity during periods of mania (**FIGURE 67.4**). The left frontal lobe and an adjacent brain reward center are active during positive emotions, but less active during depressed states (Davidson et al., 2002; Heller et al., 2009). In one study of people with severe depression, MRI scans also found their frontal lobes 7 percent smaller than normal (Coffey et al., 1993). Other studies show that the hippocampus, the memory-processing center linked with the brain's emotional circuitry, is vulnerable to stress-related damage.

Bipolar disorder likewise correlates with brain structure. Neuroscientists have found structural differences, such as decreased axonal white matter or enlarged fluid-filled ventricles, in the brains of people with bipolar disorder (Kempton et al., 2008; van der Schot et al., 2009).

Neurotransmitter systems influence mood disorders. Norepinephrine, which increases arousal and boosts mood, is scarce during depression and overabundant during mania. (Drugs that alleviate mania reduce norepinephrine.) Many people with a history of depression also have a history of habitual smoking, and smoking increases one's risk for future depression (Pasco et al. 2008). This may indicate an attempt to self-medicate with inhaled nicotine, which can temporarily increase norepinephrine and boost mood (HMHL, 2002b).

Researchers are also exploring a second neurotransmitter, serotonin (Carver et al., 2008). One well-publicized study of New Zealand young adults found that the recipe for depression combined two necessary ingredients—significant life stress plus a variation on a serotonin-controlling gene (Caspi et al., 2003; Moffitt et al., 2006). Depression arose from the interaction of an adverse environment plus a genetic susceptibility, but not from either alone. But stay tuned: The story of gene-environment interactions is still being written, as other researchers debate the reliability of this result (Caspi et al., 2010; Karg et al., 2011; Munafò et al., 2009; Risch et al., 2009; Uher & McGuffin, 2010).

> **AP® Exam Tip**
>
> You can review brain scanning techniques, neurotransmitters, and brain structures in Unit III.

Figure 67.4

The ups and downs of bipolar disorder These top-facing PET scans show that brain energy consumption rises and falls with the patient's emotional switches. Areas where the brain rapidly consumes glucose are shown in red in these images.

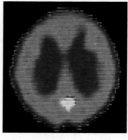
Depressed state
(May 17)

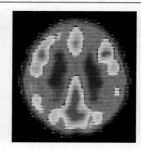
Manic state
(May 18)

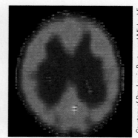
Depressed state
(May 27)

Courtesy of Drs. Lewis Baxter and Michael E. Phelps, UCLA School of Medicine

Drugs that relieve depression tend to increase norepinephrine or serotonin supplies by blocking either their reuptake (as Prozac, Zoloft, and Paxil do with serotonin) or their chemical breakdown. Repetitive physical exercise, such as jogging, reduces depression as it increases serotonin (Ilardi, 2009; Jacobs, 1994). Boosting serotonin may promote recovery from depression by stimulating hippocampus neuron growth (Airan et al., 2007; Jacobs et al., 2000).

What's good for the heart is also good for the brain and mind. People who eat a heart-healthy "Mediterranean diet" (heavy on vegetables, fish, and olive oil) have a comparatively low risk of developing heart disease, late-life cognitive decline, and depression—all of which are associated with inflammation (Dowlati et al., 2010; Sánchez-Villegas et al., 2009; Tangney et al., 2011). Excessive alcohol use also correlates with depression—mostly because alcohol misuse leads to depression (Fergusson et al., 2009).

The Social-Cognitive Perspective

Depression is a whole-body disorder. Biological influences contribute to depression but don't fully explain it. The social-cognitive perspective explores the roles of thinking and acting.

Depressed people view life through the dark glasses of low self-esteem (Orth et al., 2009). Their intensely negative assumptions about themselves, their situation, and their future lead them to magnify bad experiences and minimize good ones. Listen to Norman, a Canadian college professor, recalling his depression:

> I [despaired] of ever being human again. I honestly felt subhuman, lower than the lowest vermin. Furthermore, I was self-deprecatory and could not understand why anyone would want to associate with me, let alone love me. . . . I was positive that I was a fraud and a phony and that I didn't deserve my Ph.D. I didn't deserve to have tenure; I didn't deserve to be a Full Professor. . . . I didn't deserve the research grants I had been awarded; I couldn't understand how I had written books and journal articles. . . . I must have conned a lot of people. (Endler, 1982, pp. 45–49)

Research reveals how *self-defeating beliefs* and a *negative explanatory style* feed depression's vicious cycle.

NEGATIVE THOUGHTS AND NEGATIVE MOODS INTERACT

Self-defeating beliefs may arise from *learned helplessness.* As we saw in Module 29, both dogs and humans act depressed, passive, and withdrawn after experiencing uncontrollable painful events. Learned helplessness is more common in women than in men, and women may respond more strongly to stress (Hankin & Abramson, 2001; Mazure et al., 2002; Nolen-Hoeksema, 2001, 2003). For example, 38 percent of women and 17 percent of men entering U. S. colleges and universities report feeling at least occasionally "overwhelmed by all I have to do" (Pryor et al., 2006). (Men report spending more of their time in "light anxiety" activities such as sports, TV watching, and partying, possibly avoiding activities that might make them feel overwhelmed.) This may help explain why, beginning in their early teens, women are nearly twice as vulnerable to depression. Susan Nolen-Hoeksema (2003) believed women's higher risk of depression relates to what she described as their tendency to *overthink,* to ruminate. **Rumination**—staying focused on a problem (thanks to the continuous firing of a frontal lobe area that sustains attention)—can be adaptive (Altamirano et al., 2010; Andrews & Thomson, 2009a,b). But when it is relentless, self-focused rumination diverts us from thinking about other life tasks and produces a negative emotional inertia (Kuppens et al., 2010).

But why do life's unavoidable failures lead only some people to become depressed? The answer lies partly in their *explanatory style*—who or what they blame for their failures (or credit for their successes). Think of how you might feel if you failed a test. If you can externalize the blame ("What an unfair test!"), you are more likely to feel angry. If you blame yourself, you probably will feel stupid and depressed.

Michael Marsland

Susan Nolen-Hoeksema (1959–2013) "This epidemic of morbid meditation is a disease that women suffer much more than men. Women can ruminate about anything and everything—our appearance, our families, our career, our health." (*Women Who Think Too Much: How to Break Free of Overthinking and Reclaim Your Life*, 2003)

rumination compulsive fretting; *overthinking* about our problems and their causes.

"I have learned to accept my mistakes by referring them to a personal history which was not of my making." -B. F. SKINNER (1983)

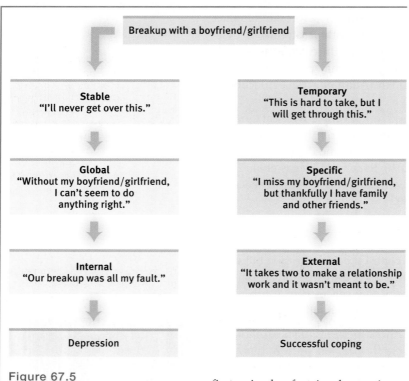

Breakup with a boyfriend/girlfriend

Stable
"I'll never get over this."

Temporary
"This is hard to take, but I will get through this."

Global
"Without my boyfriend/girlfriend, I can't seem to do anything right."

Specific
"I miss my boyfriend/girlfriend, but thankfully I have family and other friends."

Internal
"Our breakup was all my fault."

External
"It takes two to make a relationship work and it wasn't meant to be."

Depression

Successful coping

Figure 67.5
Explanatory style and depression After a negative experience, a depression-prone person may respond with a negative explanatory style.

So it is with depressed people, who tend to explain bad events in terms that are *stable* ("It's going to last forever"), *global* ("It's going to affect everything I do"), and *internal* ("It's all my fault") (**FIGURE 67.5**). Depression-prone people respond to bad events in an especially self-focused, self-blaming way (Mor & Winquist, 2002; Pyszczynski et al., 1991; Wood et al., 1990a,b). Their self-esteem fluctuates more rapidly up with boosts and down with threats (Butler et al., 1994).

The result of these pessimistic, overgeneralized, self-blaming attributions may be a depressing sense of hopelessness (Abramson et al., 1989; Panzarella et al., 2006). As Martin Seligman has noted, "A recipe for severe depression is preexisting pessimism encountering failure" (1991, p. 78). What then might we expect of new college students who are not depressed but do exhibit a pessimistic explanatory style? Lauren Alloy and her collaborators (1999) monitored Temple University and University of Wisconsin students every 6 weeks for 2.5 years. Among those identified as having a pessimistic thinking style, 17 percent had a first episode of major depression, as did only 1 percent of those who began college with an optimistic thinking style.

Seligman (1991, 1995) has contended that depression is common among young Westerners because the rise of individualism and the decline of commitment to religion and family have forced young people to take personal responsibility for failure or rejection. In non-Western cultures, where close-knit relationships and cooperation are the norm, major depression is less common and less tied to self-blame over personal failure (WHO, 2004a). In Japan, for example, depressed people instead tend to report feeling shame over letting others down (Draguns, 1990a).

PEANUTS

Might Charlie Brown be helped by an optimism-training program?

Permission of United Features Syndicate, Inc.

There is, however, a chicken-and-egg problem with the social-cognitive explanation of depression. Self-defeating beliefs, negative attributions, and self-blame *coincide* with a depressed mood and are *indicators* of depression. But do they *cause* depression, any more than a speedometer's reading causes a car's speed? Before or after being depressed, people's thoughts are less negative. Perhaps this is because, as we noted in our discussion of state-dependent memory (Module 32), a depressed mood triggers negative thoughts. If you temporarily put people in a bad or sad mood, their memories, judgments, and expectations suddenly become more pessimistic.

DEPRESSION'S VICIOUS CYCLE

Depression, as we have seen, is often brought on by stressful experiences—losing a job, getting divorced or rejected, suffering physical trauma—by anything that disrupts our sense of who we are and why we are worthy human beings. This disruption in turn leads

"Man never reasons so much and becomes so introspective as when he suffers, since he is anxious to get at the cause of his sufferings." -LUIGI PIRANDELLO, *SIX CHARACTERS IN SEARCH OF AN AUTHOR*, 1922

to brooding, which amplifies negative feelings. But being withdrawn, self-focused, and complaining can by itself elicit rejection (Furr & Funder, 1998; Gotlib & Hammen, 1992). In one study, researchers Stephen Strack and James Coyne (1983) noted that "depressed persons induced hostility, depression, and anxiety in others and got rejected. Their guesses that they were not accepted were not a matter of cognitive distortion." Indeed, people in the throes of depression are at high risk for divorce, job loss, and other stressful life events. Weary of the person's fatigue, hopeless attitude, and lethargy, a spouse may threaten to leave or a boss may begin to question the person's competence. (This provides another example of genetic-environmental interaction: People genetically predisposed to depression more often experience depressing events.) The losses and stress only serve to compound the original depression. Rejection and depression feed each other. Misery may love another's company, but company does not love another's misery.

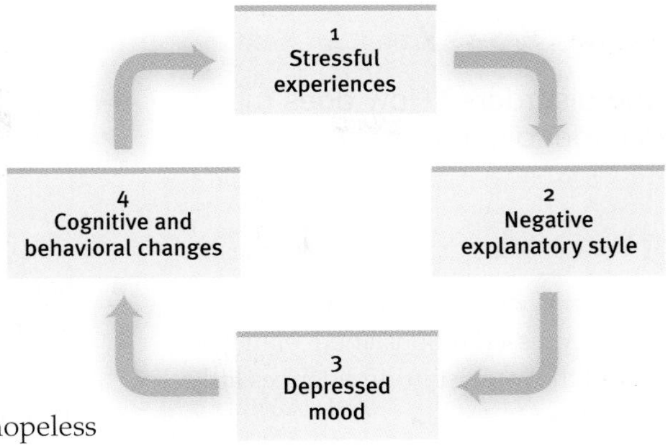

We can now assemble some of the pieces of the depression puzzle (**FIGURE 67.6**): (1) Negative, stressful events interpreted through (2) a ruminating, pessimistic explanatory style create (3) a hopeless, depressed state that (4) hampers the way the person thinks and acts. This, in turn, fuels (1) negative, stressful experiences such as rejection.

None of us is immune to the dejection, diminished self-esteem, and negative thinking brought on by rejection or defeat. As Edward Hirt and his colleagues (1992) demonstrated, even small losses can temporarily sour our thinking. They studied some avid Indiana University basketball fans who seemed to regard the team as an extension of themselves. After the fans watched their team lose or win, the researchers asked them to predict the team's future performance and their own. After a loss, the morose fans offered bleaker assessments not only of the team's future but also of their own likely performance at throwing darts, solving anagrams, and getting a date. When things aren't going our way, it may seem as though they never will.

It is a cycle we can all recognize. Bad moods feed on themselves: When we *feel* down, we *think* negatively and remember bad experiences. On the brighter side, we can break the cycle of depression at any of these points—by moving to a different environment, by reversing our self-blame and negative attributions, by turning our attention outward, or by engaging in more pleasant activities and more competent behavior.

Winston Churchill called depression a "black dog" that periodically hounded him. Poet Emily Dickinson was so afraid of bursting into tears in public that she spent much of her adult life in seclusion (Patterson, 1951). As each of these lives reminds us, people can and do struggle through depression. Most regain their capacity to love, to work, and even to succeed at the highest levels.

Figure 67.6

The vicious cycle of depressed thinking Cognitive therapists attempt to break this cycle, as we will see in Module 71, by changing the way depressed people process events. Psychiatrists attempt to alter with medication the biological roots of persistently depressed moods.

"Some cause happiness wherever they go; others, whenever they go." -Irish writer Oscar Wilde (1854–1900)

Before You Move On

▶ **ASK YOURSELF**

Has your high school experience been a challenging time for you? What advice would you have for other students about to enter high school?

▶ **TEST YOURSELF**

What is the most common psychological disorder? What is the disorder for which people most often seek treatment?

Answers to the Test Yourself questions can be found in Appendix E at the end of the book.

Module 67 Review

 67-1 What are mood disorders? How does major depressive disorder differ from bipolar disorder?

- *Mood disorders* are characterized by emotional extremes.

- A person with *major depressive disorder* experiences two or more weeks of seriously depressed moods and feelings of worthlessness, and takes little interest in, and derives little pleasure from, most activities.

- A person with the less common condition of *bipolar disorder* experiences not only depression but also *mania*—episodes of hyperactive and wildly optimistic, impulsive behavior.

 67-2 How do the biological and social-cognitive perspectives explain mood disorders?

- The biological perspective on depression focuses on genetic predispositions and on abnormalities in brain structures and function (including those found in neurotransmitter systems).

- The social-cognitive perspective views depression as an ongoing cycle of stressful experiences (interpreted through negative beliefs, attributions, and memories) leading to negative moods and actions and fueling new stressful experiences.

67-3 What factors affect suicide and self-injury, and what are some of the important warning signs to watch for in suicide-prevention efforts?

- Suicide rates differ by nation, race, gender, age group, income, religious involvement, marital status, and (for gay and lesbian youth) social support structure.

- Those with depression are more at risk for suicide than others are, but social suggestion, health status, and economic and social frustration are also contributing factors.

- Environmental barriers (such as jump barriers) are effective in preventing suicides.

- Forewarnings of suicide may include verbal hints, giving away possessions, withdrawal, preoccupation with death, and discussing one's own suicide.

- Nonsuicidal self-injury (NSSI) does not usually lead to suicide but may escalate to suicidal thoughts and acts if untreated.

- People who engage in NSSI do not tolerate stress well and tend to be self-critical, with poor communication and problem-solving skills.

Multiple-Choice Questions

1. Which of the following is NOT a symptom of major depressive disorder?
   a. Weight gain or loss
   b. Auditory hallucinations
   c. Sleep disturbance
   d. Inappropriate guilt
   e. Problems concentrating

2. Which of the following is true of depression?
   a. Depression usually develops during middle age.
   b. Depression usually happens without major cognitive or behavioral changes.
   c. A major depressive episode usually gets worse and worse unless it's treated.
   d. True depression is usually not related to stress in one's work or relationships.
   e. Compared with men, nearly twice as many women have been diagnosed with depression.

3. Which of the following is true of suicide?
   a. Marijuana use is related to suicide, but alcohol use is not.
   b. Women are more likely to end their lives than men.
   c. Suicide is a bigger problem among the poor than the rich.
   d. In the United States, suicide is more common among Whites than Blacks.
   e. Married individuals are more likely to commit suicide than single people.

4. Based on brain scans, which of the following is true of brain function and mood?

   a. The brain is more active during manic episodes and less active during depressive episodes.

   b. The brain is less active during manic episodes and more active during depressive episodes.

   c. There is no consistent relationship between brain activity and mood.

   d. The brain is more active than normal during both manic and depressive episodes.

   e. The brain is less active than normal during both manic and depressive episodes.

5. Xavier, who has a negative explanatory style, is most likely to get depressed after failing a math test if he believes that he failed because

   a. he is not good at math and never will be.

   b. his teacher made it impossible to learn the material.

   c. he was sick on the day he took the test.

   d. his parents have been putting too much pressure on him and he panicked on the test.

   e. the testing room was very hot and stuffy.

Practice FRQs

1. Christina became depressed after being laid off from her job. Her therapist thinks it's because she has a stable, global, and internal explanatory style. Illustrate each of these three attributes by writing a possible thought Christina might have for each one.

Answer

1 point: Stable thought (For example, "I have always had trouble holding down a job").

1 point: Global thought (For example, "Everything in my life is messed up").

1 point: Internal thought (For example, "It's all my fault I lost this job").

2. Identify and describe the two major symptoms of bipolar disorder.

(4 points)

Module 68

Schizophrenia

Module Learning Objectives

68-1 Describe the patterns of thinking, perceiving, and feeling that characterize schizophrenia.

68-2 Contrast chronic and acute schizophrenia.

68-3 Discuss how brain abnormalities and viral infections help explain schizophrenia.

68-4 Discuss the evidence for genetic influences on schizophrenia, and describe some factors that may be early warning signs of schizophrenia in children.

---

schizophrenia a psychological disorder characterized by delusions, hallucinations, disorganized speech, and/or diminished or inappropriate emotional expression.

psychosis a psychological disorder in which a person loses contact with reality, experiencing irrational ideas and distorted perceptions.

delusions false beliefs, often of persecution or grandeur, that may accompany psychotic disorders.

AP® Exam Tip

It is common for the AP® exam to measure your awareness of various "media myths" about psychology. One of the most common of these myths is that schizophrenia means "split personality" or "multiple personality." Read this section carefully to achieve an accurate understanding of what schizophrenia is—and isn't.

Imagine trying to communicate with Maxine, a young woman with schizophrenia whose thoughts spill out in no logical order. Her biographer, Susan Sheehan (1982, p. 25), observed her saying aloud to no one in particular, "This morning, when I was at Hillside [Hospital], I was making a movie. I was surrounded by movie stars. . . . I'm Mary Poppins. Is this room painted blue to get me upset? My grandmother died four weeks after my eighteenth birthday."

Nearly 1 in 100 people (about 60 percent men) develop schizophrenia, with an estimated 24 million across the world suffering from this dreaded disorder (Abel et al., 2010; WHO, 2011).

Symptoms of Schizophrenia

68-1 What patterns of thinking, perceiving, and feeling characterize schizophrenia?

Literally translated, **schizophrenia** means "split mind." It refers *not* to a multiple-personality split but rather to a split from reality that shows itself in disturbed perceptions, disorganized thinking and speech, and diminished, inappropriate emotions. As such, it is the chief example of a **psychosis,** a *psychotic disorder* marked by irrationality and lost contact with reality.

Disorganized Thinking and Disturbed Perceptions

As Maxine's strange monologue illustrates, the thinking of a person with schizophrenia is fragmented, bizarre, and often distorted by false beliefs called **delusions** ("I'm Mary Poppins"). Those with *paranoid* tendencies are particularly prone to delusions of persecution. Even within sentences, jumbled ideas may create what is called *word salad.* One young man begged for "a little more allegro in the treatment," and suggested that "liberationary movement with a view to the widening of the horizon" will "ergo extort some wit in lectures."

A person with schizophrenia may have **hallucinations** (sensory experiences without sensory stimulation). They may see, feel, taste, or smell things that are not there. Most often, however, the hallucinations are auditory, frequently voices making insulting remarks or giving orders. The voices may tell the patient that she is bad or that she must burn herself with a cigarette lighter. Imagine your own reaction if a dream broke into your waking consciousness. When the unreal seems real, the resulting perceptions are at best bizarre, at worst terrifying.

Disorganized thoughts may result from a breakdown in *selective attention.* Recall from Module 16 that we normally have a remarkable capacity for giving our undivided attention to one set of sensory stimuli while filtering out others. Those with schizophrenia cannot do this. Thus, irrelevant, minute stimuli, such as the grooves on a brick or the inflections of a voice, may distract their attention from a bigger event or a speaker's meaning. As one former patient recalled, "What had happened to me . . . was a breakdown in the filter, and a hodge-podge of unrelated stimuli were distracting me from things which should have had my undivided attention" (MacDonald, 1960, p. 218). This selective-attention difficulty is but one of dozens of cognitive differences associated with schizophrenia (Reichenberg & Harvey, 2007).

© Craig Geiser

Art by someone diagnosed with schizophrenia
Commenting on the kind of artwork shown here (from Craig Geiser's 2010 art exhibit in Michigan), poet and art critic John Ashbery wrote: "The lure of the work is strong, but so is the terror of the unanswerable riddles it proposes."

Diminished and Inappropriate Emotions

The expressed emotions of schizophrenia are often utterly inappropriate, split off from reality (Kring & Caponigro, 2010). Maxine laughed after recalling her grandmother's death. On other occasions, she cried when others laughed, or became angry for no apparent reason. Others with schizophrenia lapse into an emotionless state of *flat affect.* Most also have difficulty perceiving facial emotions and reading others' states of mind (Green & Horan, 2010; Kohler et al., 2010).

Motor behavior may also be inappropriate. Some perform senseless, compulsive acts, such as continually rocking or rubbing an arm. Others, who exhibit *catatonia,* may remain motionless for hours and then become agitated.

As you can imagine, such disorganized thinking, disturbed perceptions, and inappropriate emotions profoundly disrupt social relationships and make it difficult to hold a job. Even those with *dissociative identity disorder,* which we'll discuss later in this unit, may continue to function in everyday life, but less so those with schizophrenia. During their most severe periods, those with schizophrenia live in a private inner world, preoccupied with illogical ideas and unreal images. Given a supportive environment and medication, over 40 percent of schizophrenia patients will have periods of a year or more of normal life experience (Jobe & Harrow, 2010). Many others remain socially withdrawn and isolated or rejected throughout much of their lives (Hooley, 2010).

Onset and Development of Schizophrenia

68-2   How do chronic and acute schizophrenia differ?

Schizophrenia typically strikes as young people are maturing into adulthood. Although it only afflicts 1 in 100 people, it knows no national boundaries, and it affects both males and females—though men tend to be struck earlier, more severely, and slightly more often (Aleman et al., 2003; Picchioni & Murray, 2007).

"When someone asks me to explain schizophrenia I tell them, you know how sometimes in your dreams you are in them yourself and some of them feel like real nightmares? My schizophrenia was like I was walking through a dream. But everything around me was real. At times, today's world seems so boring and I wonder if I would like to step back into the schizophrenic dream, but then I remember all the scary and horrifying experiences." -STUART EMMONS, WITH CRAIG GEISER, KALMAN J. KAPLAN, AND MARTIN HARROW, *LIVING WITH SCHIZOPHRENIA*, 1997

hallucination false sensory experience, such as seeing something in the absence of an external visual stimulus.

For some, schizophrenia will appear suddenly, seemingly as a reaction to stress. For others, as was the case with Maxine, schizophrenia develops gradually, emerging from a long history of social inadequacy and poor school performance (MacCabe et al., 2008). No wonder those predisposed to schizophrenia often end up in the lower socioeconomic levels, or even homeless.

We have thus far described schizophrenia as if it were a single disorder. Actually, it varies. Schizophrenia patients with *positive symptoms* may experience hallucinations, talk in disorganized and deluded ways, and exhibit inappropriate laughter, tears, or rage. Those with *negative symptoms* have toneless voices, expressionless faces, or mute and rigid bodies. Thus, positive symptoms are the *presence* of inappropriate behaviors, and negative symptoms are the *absence* of appropriate behaviors.

When schizophrenia is a slow-developing process (called *chronic,* or *process, schizophrenia*), recovery is doubtful (WHO, 1979). Those with chronic schizophrenia often exhibit the persistent and incapacitating negative symptom of social withdrawal (Kirkpatrick et al., 2006). Men, whose schizophrenia develops on average four years earlier than women's, more often exhibit negative symptoms and chronic schizophrenia (Räsänen et al., 2000). When previously well-adjusted people develop schizophrenia rapidly (called *acute,* or *reactive, schizophrenia*) following particular life stresses, recovery is much more likely. They more often have the positive symptoms that are responsive to drug therapy (Fenton & McGlashan, 1991, 1994; Fowles, 1992).

Understanding Schizophrenia

Schizophrenia is not only the most dreaded psychological disorder but also one of the most heavily researched. Most of the new research studies link it with brain abnormalities and genetic predispositions. Schizophrenia is a disease of the brain manifest in symptoms of the mind.

Brain Abnormalities

68-3 How do brain abnormalities and viral infections help explain schizophrenia?

Might imbalances in brain chemistry underlie schizophrenia? Scientists have long known that strange behavior can have strange chemical causes. The saying "mad as a hatter" refers to the psychological deterioration of British hatmakers whose brains, it was later discovered, were slowly poisoned as they moistened the brims of mercury-laden felt hats with their tongue and lips (Smith, 1983). As we saw in Module 25, scientists are clarifying the mechanism by which chemicals such as LSD produce hallucinations. These discoveries hint that schizophrenia symptoms might have a biochemical key.

© mikeledray/Shutterstock

DOPAMINE OVERACTIVITY

Researchers discovered one such key when they examined schizophrenia patients' brains after death and found an excess of receptors for *dopamine*—a sixfold excess for the so-called D4 dopamine receptor (Seeman et al., 1993; Wong et al., 1986). They now speculate that such a hyper-responsive dopamine system may intensify brain signals in schizophrenia, creating positive symptoms such as hallucinations and paranoia (Grace, 2010). As we might therefore expect, drugs that block dopamine receptors often lessen these symptoms; drugs that increase dopamine levels, such as amphetamines and cocaine, sometimes intensify them (Seeman, 2007; Swerdlow & Koob, 1987).

FYI

Most schizophrenia patients smoke, often heavily. Nicotine apparently stimulates certain brain receptors, which helps focus attention (Diaz et al., 2008; Javitt & Coyle, 2004).

ABNORMAL BRAIN ACTIVITY AND ANATOMY

Modern brain-scanning techniques reveal that many people with chronic schizophrenia have abnormal activity in multiple brain areas. Some have abnormally low brain activity in the frontal lobes, which are critical for reasoning, planning, and problem solving (Morey et al., 2005; Pettegrew et al., 1993; Resnick, 1992). People diagnosed with schizophrenia also display a noticeable decline in the brain waves that reflect synchronized neural firing in the frontal lobes (Spencer et al., 2004; Symond et al., 2005). Out-of-sync neurons may disrupt the integrated functioning of neural networks, possibly contributing to schizophrenia symptoms.

One study took PET scans of brain activity while people were hallucinating (Silbersweig et al., 1995). When participants heard a voice or saw something, their brain became vigorously active in several core regions, including the thalamus, a structure deep in the brain that filters incoming sensory signals and transmits them to the cortex. Another PET scan study of people with paranoia found increased activity in the amygdala, a fear-processing center (Epstein et al., 1998).

Many studies have found enlarged, fluid-filled areas and a corresponding shrinkage and thinning of cerebral tissue in people with schizophrenia (Goldman et al., 2009; Wright et al., 2000). Some studies have even found such abnormalities in the brains of people who would *later* develop this disorder and in their close relatives (Karlsgodt et al., 2010). The greater the brain shrinkage, the more severe the thought disorder (Collinson et al., 2003; Nelson et al., 1998; Shenton, 1992). One smaller-than-normal area is the cortex. Another is the corpus callosum connection between the two hemispheres (Arnone et al., 2008). Another is the thalamus, which may explain why people with schizophrenia have difficulty filtering sensory input and focusing attention (Andreasen et al., 1994; Ellison-Wright et al., 2008). The bottom line of various studies is that schizophrenia involves not one isolated brain abnormality but problems with several brain regions and their interconnections (Andreasen, 1997, 2001).

Naturally, scientists wonder what causes these abnormalities. Some point to mishaps during prenatal development or delivery (Fatemi & Folsom, 2009; Walker et al., 2010). Risk factors for schizophrenia include low birth weight, maternal diabetes, older paternal age, and oxygen deprivation during delivery (King et al., 2010). Famine may also increase risks. People conceived during the peak of the Dutch wartime famine later displayed a doubled rate of schizophrenia, as did those conceived during the famine that occurred from 1959 to 1961 in eastern China (St. Clair et al., 2005; Susser et al., 1996).

MATERNAL VIRUS DURING MIDPREGNANCY

Consider another possible culprit: a midpregnancy viral infection that impairs fetal brain development (Patterson, 2007). Can you imagine some ways to test this fetal-virus idea? Scientists have asked the following:

- *Are people at increased risk of schizophrenia if, during the middle of their fetal development, their country experienced a flu epidemic?* The repeated answer is *Yes* (Mednick et al., 1994; Murray et al., 1992; Wright et al., 1995).

- *Are people born in densely populated areas, where viral diseases spread more readily, at greater risk for schizophrenia?* The answer, confirmed in a study of 1.75 million Danes, is *Yes* (Jablensky, 1999; Mortensen, 1999).

- *Are those born during the winter and spring months—after the fall-winter flu season—also at increased risk?* Although the increase is small, just 5 to 8 percent, the answer is again *Yes* (Fox, 2010; Torrey et al., 1997, 2002).

Studying the neurophysiology of schizophrenia Psychiatrist E. Fuller Torrey has collected the brains of hundreds of those who died as young adults and suffered disorders such as schizophrenia and bipolar disorder.

- *In the Southern Hemisphere, where the seasons are the reverse of the Northern Hemisphere, are the months of above-average schizophrenia births similarly reversed?* Again, the answer is *Yes,* though somewhat less so. In Australia, for example, people born between August and October are at greater risk—*unless* they migrated from the Northern Hemisphere, in which case their risk is greater if they were born between January and March (McGrath et al., 1995, 1999).

- *Are mothers who report being sick with influenza during pregnancy more likely to bear children who develop schizophrenia?* In one study of nearly 8000 women, the answer was *Yes.* The schizophrenia risk increased from the customary 1 percent to about 2 percent—but only when infections occurred during the second trimester (Brown et al., 2000). Maternal influenza infection during pregnancy also affects brain development in monkeys (Short et al., 2010).

- *Does blood drawn from pregnant women whose offspring develop schizophrenia show higher-than-normal levels of antibodies that suggest a viral infection?* In one study of 27 women whose children later developed schizophrenia, the answer was *Yes* (Buka et al., 2001). And the answer was again *Yes* in a huge California study, which collected blood samples from some 20,000 pregnant women during the 1950s and 1960s (Brown et al., 2004). Another study found traces of a specific retrovirus (HERV) in nearly half of people with schizophrenia and virtually none in healthy people (Perron et al., 2008).

These converging lines of evidence suggest that fetal-virus infections play a contributing role in the development of schizophrenia. They also strengthen the recommendation that "women who will be more than three months pregnant during the flu season" have a flu shot (CDC, 2003).

Why might a second-trimester maternal flu bout put fetuses at risk? Is it the virus itself? The mother's immune response to it? Medications taken (Wyatt et al., 2001)? Does the infection weaken the brain's supportive glial cells, leading to reduced synaptic connections (Moises et al., 2002)? In time, answers may become available.

Genetic Factors

68-4 Are there genetic influences on schizophrenia? What factors may be early warning signs of schizophrenia in children?

Fetal-virus infections do appear to increase the odds that a child will develop schizophrenia. But this theory cannot tell us why only 2 percent of women who catch the flu during their second trimester of pregnancy bear children who develop schizophrenia. Might people also inherit a predisposition to this disorder? The evidence strongly suggests that, *Yes,* some do. The nearly 1-in-100 odds of any person's being diagnosed with schizophrenia become about 1 in 10 among those whose sibling or parent has the disorder, and close to 1 in 2 if the affected sibling is an identical twin (**FIGURE 68.1**). Although only a dozen or so such cases are on record, the co-twin of an identical twin with schizophrenia retains that 1-in-2 chance even when the twins are reared apart (Plomin et al., 1997).

Remember, though, that identical twins also share a prenatal environment. About two-thirds also share a placenta and the blood it supplies; the other one-third have two single placentas. If an identical twin has schizophrenia, the co-twin's chances of being similarly afflicted are 6 in 10 if they shared a placenta. If they had separate placentas, as do fraternal twins, the chances are only 1 in 10 (Davis et al., 1995a,b; Phelps et al., 1997). Twins who share a placenta are more likely to

Figure 68.1

Risk of developing schizophrenia The lifetime risk of developing schizophrenia varies with one's genetic relatedness to someone having this disorder. Across countries, barely more than 1 in 10 fraternal twins, but some 5 in 10 identical twins, share a schizophrenia diagnosis. (Adapted from Gottesman, 2001.)

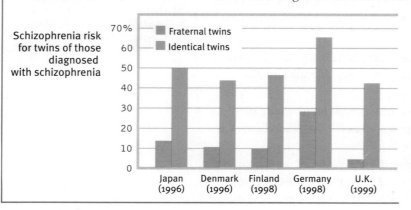

Schizophrenia risk for twins of those diagnosed with schizophrenia

experience the same prenatal viruses. So it is possible that shared germs as well as shared genes produce identical twin similarities.

Adoption studies, however, confirm that the genetic link is real (Gottesman, 1991). Children adopted by someone who develops schizophrenia seldom "catch" the disorder. Rather, adopted children have an elevated risk if a *biological* parent is diagnosed with schizophrenia.

With the genetic factor established, researchers are now sleuthing specific genes that, in some combination, might predispose schizophrenia-inducing brain abnormalities (Levinson et al., 2011; Mitchell & Porteous, 2011; Vacic et al., 2011; Wang et al., 2010). (It is not our genes but our brains that directly control our behavior.) Some of these genes influence the effects of dopamine and other neurotransmitters in the brain. Others affect the production of *myelin,* a fatty substance that coats the axons of nerve cells and lets impulses travel at high speed through neural networks.

Schizophrenia in identical twins
When twins differ, only the one afflicted with schizophrenia typically has enlarged, fluid-filled cranial cavities (right) (Suddath et al., 1990). The difference between the twins implies some nongenetic factor, such as a virus, is also at work.

Although the genetic contribution to schizophrenia is beyond question, the genetic formula is not as straightforward as the inheritance of eye color. Genome studies of thousands of individuals with and without schizophrenia indicate that schizophrenia is influenced by many genes, each with very small effects (International Schizophrenia Consortium, 2009; Pogue-Geile & Yokley, 2010). Recall from Module 14 that *epigenetic* (literally "in addition to genetic") factors influence gene expression. Like hot water activating the tea bag, environmental factors such as prenatal viral infections, nutritional deprivation, and maternal stress can "turn on" the genes that predispose schizophrenia. Identical twins' differing histories in the womb and beyond explain why only one of them may show differing gene expressions (Walker et al., 2010). As we have so often seen, nature and nurture interact. Neither hand claps alone.

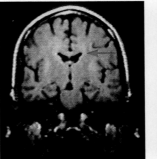 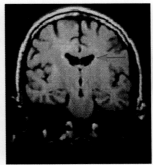

No schizophrenia   **Schizophrenia**

Both photos: From Daniel Weinberger, M.D., CBDB, NIMH

Thanks to our expanding understanding of genetic and brain influences on maladies such as schizophrenia, the general public more and more attributes psychiatric disorders to biological factors (Pescosolido et al., 2010). In 2007, one privately funded new research center announced its ambitious aim: "To unambiguously diagnose patients with psychiatric disorders based on their DNA sequence in 10 years' time" (Holden, 2007). In 2010, $120 million in start-up funding launched a bold new effort to study the neuroscience and genetics of schizophrenia and other psychiatric disorders (Kaiser, 2010). So, can scientists develop genetic tests that reveal who is at risk? If so, will people in the future subject their embryos to genetic testing (and gene repair or abortion) if they are at risk for this or some other psychological or physical malady? Might they take their egg and sperm to a genetics lab for screening before combining them to produce an embryo? Or will children be tested for genetic risks and given appropriate preventive treatments? In this brave new twenty-first-century world, such questions await answers.

Psychological Factors

If prenatal viruses and genetic predispositions do not, by themselves, cause schizophrenia, neither do family or social factors alone. It remains true, as Susan Nicol and Irving Gottesman (1983) noted almost three decades ago, that "no environmental causes have been discovered that will invariably, or even with moderate probability, produce schizophrenia in persons who are not related to" a person with schizophrenia.

Hoping to identify environmental triggers of schizophrenia, several investigators are following the development of "high-risk" children, such as those born to a parent with schizophrenia or exposed to prenatal risks (Freedman et al., 1998; Olin & Mednick, 1996; Susser, 1999). One study followed 163 teens and early-twenties adults who had two relatives with schizophrenia. During the 2.5-year study, the 20 percent who developed schizophrenia displayed some tendency to withdraw socially and behave oddly before the onset of

FYI

The odds of any four people picked at random all being diagnosed with schizophrenia are 1 in 100 million. But genetically identical sisters Nora, Iris, Myra, and Hester Genain all have the disease. Two of the sisters have more severe forms of the disorder than the others, suggesting the influence of environmental as well as biological factors.

the disorder (Johnstone et al., 2005). By comparing the experiences of high-risk and low-risk children who do versus do not develop schizophrenia, researchers have so far pinpointed the following possible early warning signs:

- A mother whose schizophrenia was severe and long-lasting
- Birth complications, often involving oxygen deprivation and low birth weight
- Separation from parents
- Short attention span and poor muscle coordination
- Disruptive or withdrawn behavior
- Emotional unpredictability
- Poor peer relations and solo play

* * *

Most of us can relate more easily to the ups and downs of mood disorders than to the strange thoughts, perceptions, and behaviors of schizophrenia. Sometimes our thoughts do jump around, but in the absence of disorder we do not talk nonsensically. Occasionally we feel unjustly suspicious of someone, but we do not fear that the world is plotting against us. Often our perceptions err, but rarely do we see or hear things that are not there. We have felt regret after laughing at someone's misfortune, but we rarely giggle in response to bad news. At times we just want to be alone, but we do not live in social isolation. However, millions of people around the world do talk strangely, suffer delusions, hear nonexistent voices, see things that are not there, laugh or cry at inappropriate times, or withdraw into private imaginary worlds. The quest to solve the cruel puzzle of schizophrenia therefore continues, and more vigorously than ever.

Before You Move On

▶ **ASK YOURSELF**

Do you think the media accurately portray the behavior of people suffering from schizophrenia? Why or why not?

▶ **TEST YOURSELF**

How do researchers believe that biological and environmental factors interact in the onset of schizophrenia?

Answers to the Test Yourself questions can be found in Appendix E at the end of the book.

Module 68 Review

 What patterns of thinking, perceiving, and feeling characterize schizophrenia?

- *Schizophrenia* is a disorder that typically strikes during late adolescence, affects men slightly more than women, and seems to occur in all cultures.

- Symptoms are disorganized and delusional thinking, disturbed perceptions, and diminished or inappropriate emotions.

- *Delusions* are false beliefs; *hallucinations* are sensory experiences without sensory stimulation.

 How do chronic and acute schizophrenia differ?

- Schizophrenia symptoms may be positive (the presence of inappropriate behaviors) or negative (the absence of appropriate behaviors).

- In chronic (or process) schizophrenia, the disorder develops gradually and recovery is doubtful.

- In acute (or reactive) schizophrenia, the onset is sudden, in reaction to stress, and the prospects for recovery are brighter.

 How do brain abnormalities and viral infections help explain schizophrenia?

- People with schizophrenia have increased dopamine receptors, which may intensify brain signals, creating positive symptoms such as hallucinations and paranoia.

- Brain abnormalities associated with schizophrenia include enlarged, fluid-filled cerebral cavities and corresponding decreases in the cortex.

- Brain scans reveal abnormal activity in the frontal lobes, thalamus, and amygdala.

- Interacting malfunctions in multiple brain regions and their connections may produce schizophrenia's symptoms.

- Possible contributing factors include viral infections or famine conditions during the mother's pregnancy and low weight or oxygen deprivation at birth.

 Are there genetic influences on schizophrenia? What factors may be early warning signs of schizophrenia in children?

- Twin and adoption studies indicate that the predisposition to schizophrenia is inherited, and environmental factors influence gene expression to enable this disorder, which is found worldwide.

- No environmental causes invariably produce schizophrenia.

- Possible early warning signs of later development of schizophrenia include both biological factors (a mother with severe and long-lasting schizophrenia; oxygen deprivation and low weight at birth; short attention span and poor muscle coordination) as well as psychological factors (disruptive or withdrawn behavior; emotional unpredictability; poor peer relations and solo play).

Multiple-Choice Questions

1. Which of the following is the best term or phrase for a false belief, often of persecution, that may accompany psychotic disorders?

a. Psychosis
b. Schizophrenia
c. Delusion
d. Split mind
e. Dissociative identity disorder

2. Which of the following is true?

a. Those born during winter and spring are less likely to develop schizophrenia later in life.
b. People born in densely populated areas are less likely to develop schizophrenia later in life.
c. Fetuses exposed to flu virus are more likely to develop schizophrenia later in life.
d. Maternal influenza during pregnancy does not affect brain development in monkeys.
e. The retrovirus HERV is found more often in people who do not develop schizophrenia.

3. According to research, which of the following has been identified as an early warning sign of schizophrenia?

a. Emotional predictability
b. Poor peer relations and solo play
c. Long attention span
d. Good muscle coordination
e. High birth weight

Practice FRQs

1. Name three possible warning signs of schizophrenia.

Answer

Score 1 point for any of the following (up to 3) possibilities.

- A mother whose schizophrenia was severe and long-lasting
- Birth complications, often involving oxygen deprivation and low weight
- Separation from parents
- Short attention span and poor muscle coordination
- Disruptive or withdrawn behavior
- Emotional unpredictability
- Poor peer relations and solo play

2. Name and explain two brain abnormalities that help us understand schizophrenia.

(4 points)

Module 69

Other Disorders

Mary Evans/C20TH FOX/TWENTIETH CENTURY FOX/
Ronald Grant/Everett Collection

Module Learning Objectives

69-1 Describe somatic symptom and related disorders.

69-2 Describe dissociative disorders, and discuss why they are controversial.

69-3 Explain how anorexia nervosa, bulimia nervosa, and binge-eating disorder demonstrate the influence of psychological and genetic forces.

68-4 Contrast the three clusters of personality disorders, and describe the behaviors and brain activity that characterize the antisocial personality.

Somatic Symptom and Related Disorders

69-1 What are somatic symptom and related disorders?

Among the most common problems bringing people into doctors' offices are "medically unexplained illnesses" (Johnson, 2008). Ellen becomes dizzy and nauseated in the late afternoon—shortly before she expects her husband home. Neither her primary care physician nor the neurologist he sent her to could identify a physical cause. They suspect her symptoms have an unconscious psychological origin, possibly triggered by her mixed feelings about her husband. In a **somatic symptom disorder** such as Ellen's, the distressing symptoms take a somatic (bodily) form without apparent physical causes. One person may have a variety of complaints—vomiting, dizziness, blurred vision, difficulty in swallowing. Another may experience severe and prolonged pain.

Culture has a big effect on people's physical complaints and how they explain them (Kirmayer & Sartorius, 2007). In China, psychological explanations of anxiety and depression are socially less acceptable than in many Western countries, and people less often express the emotional aspects of distress. The Chinese appear more sensitive to—and more willing to report—the physical symptoms of their distress (Ryder et al., 2008). Mr. Wu, a 36-year-old technician in Hunan, illustrates one of China's most common psychological disorders (Spitzer & Skodol, 2000). He finds work difficult because of his insomnia, fatigue, weakness, and headaches. Chinese herbs and Western medicines provide no relief. To his Chinese clinician, who treats the bodily symptoms, he seems not so much depressed as exhausted. Similar, generalized bodily complaints have often been observed in African cultures (Binitie, 1975).

somatic symptom disorder a psychological disorder in which the symptoms take a somatic (bodily) form without apparent physical cause. (See *conversion disorder* and *illness anxiety disorder*.)

conversion disorder a disorder in which a person experiences very specific genuine physical symptoms for which no physiological basis can be found. (Also called *functional neurological symptom disorder.*)

illness anxiety disorder a disorder in which a person interprets normal physical sensations as symptoms of a disease. (Formerly called *hypochondriasis.*)

dissociative disorders disorders in which conscious awareness becomes separated (dissociated) from previous memories, thoughts, and feelings.

Even to people in the West, somatic symptoms are familiar. To a lesser extent, we have all experienced inexplicable physical symptoms under stress. It is little comfort to be told that the problem is "all in your head." Although the symptoms may be psychological in origin, they are nevertheless genuinely felt.

One rare type of disorder, more common in Freud's day than in ours, is **conversion disorder** (also known as *functional neurological symptom disorder),* so called because anxiety presumably is converted into a physical symptom. (As we noted in Module 55, Freud's effort to treat and understand psychological disorders stemmed from his puzzlement over ailments that had no physiological basis.) A patient with a conversion disorder might, for example, lose sensation in a way that makes no neurological sense. Yet the physical symptoms would be real; sticking pins in the affected area would produce no response. Other conversion disorder symptoms might be unexplained paralysis, blindness, or an inability to swallow. In each case, the person would be strangely indifferent to the problem.

As you can imagine, somatic symptom and related disorders send people not to a psychologist or psychiatrist but to a physician. This is especially true of those who experience **illness anxiety disorder** (formerly called *hypochondriasis*). In this relatively common disorder, people interpret normal sensations (a stomach cramp today, a headache tomorrow) as symptoms of a dreaded disease. Sympathy or temporary relief from everyday demands may reinforce such complaints. No amount of reassurance by any physician convinces the patient that the trivial symptoms do not reflect a serious illness. So the patient moves on to another physician, seeking and receiving more medical attention—but failing to confront the disorder's psychological root.

Before You Move On

▶ **ASK YOURSELF**
Can you recall (as most people can) times when you have fretted needlessly over a normal bodily sensation?

▶ **TEST YOURSELF**
What does *somatic* mean?

Answers to the Test Yourself questions can be found in Appendix E at the end of the book.

Dissociative Disorders

69-2 What are dissociative disorders, and why are they controversial?

Among the most bewildering disorders are the rare **dissociative disorders.** These are disorders of consciousness, in which a person appears to experience a sudden loss of memory or change in identity, often in response to an overwhelmingly stressful situation. Chris Sizemore's story, told in the book and movie *The Three Faces of Eve,* gave early visibility to what is now called *dissociative identity disorder.* One Vietnam veteran who was haunted by his comrades' deaths, and who had left his World Trade Center office shortly before the 9/11 attack, disappeared en route to work one day and was discovered six months later in a Chicago homeless shelter, reportedly with no memory of his identity or family (Stone, 2006). In such *fugue state* cases, the person's conscious awareness is said to *dissociate* (become separated) from painful memories, thoughts, and feelings. (Note that this explanation presumes the existence of repressed memories, which, as we noted in Modules 33 and 56, have been questioned by memory researchers.)

Dissociation itself is not so rare. Now and then, many people may have a sense of being unreal, of being separated from their body, of watching themselves as if in a movie.

Sometimes we may say, "I was not myself at the time." Perhaps you can recall getting up to go somewhere and ending up at some unintended location while your mind was preoccupied elsewhere. Or perhaps you can play a well-practiced tune on a guitar or piano while talking to someone. Facing trauma, dissociative detachment may actually protect a person from being overwhelmed by emotion.

Dissociative Identity Disorder

A massive dissociation of self from ordinary consciousness characterizes those with **dissociative identity disorder (DID),** in which two or more distinct identities are said to alternately control the person's behavior. Each personality has its own voice and mannerisms. Thus the person may be prim and proper one moment, loud and flirtatious the next. Typically, the original personality denies any awareness of the other(s).

People diagnosed with DID (formerly called *multiple personality disorder*) are usually not violent, but cases have been reported of dissociations into a "good" and a "bad" (or aggressive) personality—a modest version of the Dr. Jekyll/Mr. Hyde split immortalized in Robert Louis Stevenson's story. One unusual case involved Kenneth Bianchi, accused in the "Hillside Strangler" rapes and murders of 10 California women. During a hypnosis session with Bianchi, psychologist John Watkins (1984) "called forth" a hidden personality: "I've talked a bit to Ken, but I think that perhaps there might be another part of Ken that . . . maybe feels somewhat differently from the part that I've talked to. . . . Would you talk with me, Part, by saying, 'I'm here'?" Bianchi answered "Yes" and then claimed to be "Steve."

Speaking as Steve, Bianchi stated that he hated Ken because Ken was nice and that he (Steve), aided by a cousin, had murdered women. He also claimed Ken knew nothing about Steve's existence and was innocent of the murders. Was Bianchi's second personality a ruse, simply a way of disavowing responsibility for his actions? Indeed, Bianchi—a practiced liar who had read about multiple personality in psychology books—was later convicted.

Understanding Dissociative Identity Disorder

Skeptics question whether DID is a genuine disorder or an extension of our normal capacity for personality shifts. Nicholas Spanos (1986, 1994, 1996) asked college students to pretend they were accused murderers being examined by a psychiatrist. Given the same hypnotic treatment Bianchi received, most spontaneously expressed a second personality. This discovery made Spanos wonder: Are dissociative identities simply a more extreme version of our capacity to vary the "selves" we present—as when we display a goofy, loud self while hanging out with friends, and a subdued, respectful self around grandparents? Are clinicians who discover multiple personalities merely triggering role-playing by fantasy-prone people? Do these patients, like actors who commonly report "losing themselves" in their roles, then convince themselves of the authenticity of their own role enactments? Spanos was no stranger to this line of thinking. In a related research area, he had also raised these questions about the hypnotic state. Given that most DID patients are highly hypnotizable, whatever explains one condition—dissociation or role playing—may help explain the other.

Skeptics also find it suspicious that the disorder is so localized in time and space. Between 1930 and 1960, the number of DID diagnoses in North America was 2 per decade. In the 1980s, when the DSM contained the first formal code for this disorder, the number of reported cases had exploded to more than 20,000 (McHugh, 1995a). The average number of displayed personalities also mushroomed—from 3 to 12 per patient (Goff & Simms, 1993). Outside North America, the disorder is much less prevalent, although in other cultures some people are said to be "possessed" by an alien spirit (Aldridge-Morris, 1989; Kluft, 1991). In Britain, DID—which some have considered "a wacky American fad" (Cohen, 1995)—is rare. In India and Japan, it is essentially nonexistent (or at least unreported).

The "Hillside Strangler" Kenneth Bianchi is shown here at his trial.

dissociative identity disorder (DID) a rare dissociative disorder in which a person exhibits two or more distinct and alternating personalities. Formerly called *multiple personality disorder.*

"Pretense may become reality."
-Chinese proverb

"Would it be possible to speak with the personality that pays the bills?"

"Though this be madness, yet there is method in 't." -WILLIAM SHAKESPEARE, *HAMLET*, 1600

Such findings, skeptics say, point to a cultural phenomenon—a disorder created by therapists in a particular social context (Merskey, 1992). Rather than being provoked by trauma, dissociative symptoms tend to be exhibited by suggestible, fantasy-prone people (Giesbrecht et al., 2008, 2010). Patients do not enter therapy saying "Allow me to introduce myselves." Rather, note these skeptics, some therapists go fishing for multiple personalities: "Have you ever felt like another part of you does things you can't control? Does this part of you have a name? Can I talk to the angry part of you?" Once patients permit a therapist to talk, by name, "to the part of you that says those angry things," they begin acting out the fantasy. Like actors who lose themselves in their roles, vulnerable patients may "become" the parts they are acting out. The result may be the experience of another self.

Other researchers and clinicians believe DID is a real disorder. They find support for this view in the distinct brain and body states associated with differing personalities (Putnam, 1991). Handedness, for example, sometimes switches with personality (Henninger, 1992). Ophthalmologists have detected shifting visual acuity and eye-muscle balance as patients switched personalities, changes that did not occur among control group members trying to simulate DID (Miller et al., 1991). Dissociative disorder patients also have exhibited heightened activity in brain areas associated with the control and inhibition of traumatic memories (Elzinga et al., 2007).

Researchers and clinicians have interpreted DID symptoms from psychodynamic and learning perspectives. Both views agree that the symptoms are ways of dealing with anxiety. Psychodynamic theorists see them as defenses against the anxiety caused by the eruption of unacceptable impulses; a wanton second personality enables the discharge of forbidden impulses. Learning theorists see dissociative disorders as behaviors reinforced by anxiety reduction.

Other clinicians include dissociative disorders under the umbrella of posttraumatic stress disorder—a natural, protective response to "histories of childhood trauma" (Putnam, 1995; Spiegel, 2008). Many DID patients recall suffering physical, sexual, or emotional abuse as children (Gleaves, 1996; Lilienfeld et al., 1999). In one study of 12 murderers diagnosed with DID, 11 had suffered severe, torturous child abuse (Lewis et al., 1997). One was set afire by his parents. Another was used in child pornography and was scarred from being made to sit on a stove burner. Some critics wonder, however, whether vivid imagination or therapist suggestion contributes to such recollections (Kihlstrom, 2005).

So the debate continues. On one side are those who believe multiple personalities are the desperate efforts of the traumatized to detach from a horrific existence. On the other are the skeptics who think DID is a condition contrived by fantasy-prone, emotionally vulnerable people, and constructed out of the therapist-patient interaction. If the skeptics' view wins, predicted psychiatrist Paul McHugh (1995b), "this epidemic will end in the way that the witch craze ended in Salem. The [multiple personality phenomenon] will be seen as manufactured."

Before You Move On

▶ **ASK YOURSELF**

In a more normal way, do you ever flip between displays of different aspects of your personality?

▶ **TEST YOURSELF**

The psychodynamic and learning perspectives agree that dissociative identity disorder symptoms are ways of dealing with anxiety. How do their explanations differ?

Answers to the Test Yourself questions can be found in Appendix E at the end of the book.

Eating Disorders

69-3 How do anorexia nervosa, bulimia nervosa, and binge-eating disorder demonstrate the influence of psychological and genetic forces?

Our bodies are naturally disposed to maintain a steady weight, including stored energy reserves for times when food becomes unavailable. Yet sometimes psychological influences overwhelm biological wisdom. This becomes painfully clear in three eating disorders.

- **Anorexia nervosa** typically begins as a weight-loss diet. People with anorexia—usually adolescents and 9 times out of 10 females—drop significantly below normal weight. Yet they feel fat, fear being fat, and remain obsessed with losing weight, and sometimes exercise excessively. About half of those with anorexia display a binge-purge-depression cycle.

- **Bulimia nervosa** may also be triggered by a weight-loss diet, broken by gorging on forbidden foods. Binge-purge eaters—mostly women in their late teens or early twenties—eat in spurts, sometimes influenced by friends who are bingeing (Crandall, 1988). In a cycle of repeating episodes, overeating is followed by compensatory purging (through vomiting or laxative use), fasting, or excessive exercise (Wonderlich et al., 2007). Preoccupied with food (craving sweet and high-fat foods), and fearful of becoming overweight, binge-purge eaters experience bouts of depression and anxiety during and following binges (Hinz & Williamson, 1987; Johnson et al., 2002). Unlike anorexia, bulimia is marked by weight fluctuations within or above normal ranges, making the condition easy to hide.

- Those who do significant binge eating, followed by remorse—but do not purge, fast, or exercise excessively—are said to have **binge-eating disorder.**

A national study funded by the U.S. National Institute of Mental Health reported that, at some point during their lifetime, 0.6 percent of people meet the criteria for anorexia, 1 percent for bulimia, and 2.8 percent for binge-eating disorder (Hudson et al., 2007). So, how can we explain these disorders?

Eating disorders do *not* provide (as some have speculated) a telltale sign of childhood sexual abuse (Smolak & Murnen, 2002; Stice, 2002). The family environment may provide a fertile ground for the growth of eating disorders in other ways, however.

- Mothers of girls with eating disorders tend to focus on their own weight and on their daughters' weight and appearance (Pike & Rodin, 1991).

- Families of bulimia patients have a higher-than-usual incidence of childhood obesity and negative self-evaluation (Jacobi et al., 2004).

- Families of anorexia patients tend to be competitive, high-achieving, and protective (Pate et al., 1992; Yates, 1989, 1990).

Those with eating disorders often have low self-evaluations, set perfectionist standards, fret about falling short of expectations, and are intensely concerned with how others perceive them (Pieters et al., 2007; Polivy & Herman, 2002; Sherry & Hall, 2009). Some of these factors also predict teen boys' pursuit of unrealistic muscularity (Ricciardelli & McCabe, 2004).

Genetics also influence susceptibility to eating disorders. Twins are more likely to share the disorder if they are identical rather than fraternal (Culbert et al., 2009; Klump et al., 2009; Root et al., 2010). Scientists are now searching for culprit genes, which may influence the body's available serotonin and estrogen (Klump & Culbert, 2007).

But these disorders also have cultural and gender components. Ideal shapes vary across culture and time. In impoverished areas of the world, including much of Africa—where plumpness means prosperity and thinness can signal poverty or illness—bigger

Dying to be thin Anorexia was identified and named in the 1870s, when it appeared among affluent adolescent girls (Brumberg, 2000). Many modern-day celebrities, including Lady Gaga, have struggled publicly with eating disorders.

Jeff Kravitz/FilmMagic for MTV/Getty Images

anorexia nervosa an eating disorder in which a person (usually an adolescent female) maintains a starvation diet despite being significantly (15 percent or more) underweight.

bulimia nervosa an eating disorder in which a person alternates binge eating (usually of high-calorie foods) with purging (by vomiting or laxative use), excessive exercise, or fasting.

binge-eating disorder significant binge-eating episodes, followed by distress, disgust, or guilt, but without the compensatory purging or fasting that marks bulimia nervosa.

"Gee, I had no idea you were married to a supermodel."

"Skeletons on Parade" A newspaper article used this headline in criticizing the display of superthin models. Do such models make self-starvation fashionable?

"Why do women have such low self-esteem? There are many complex psychological and societal reasons, by which I mean Barbie." -DAVE BARRY, 1999

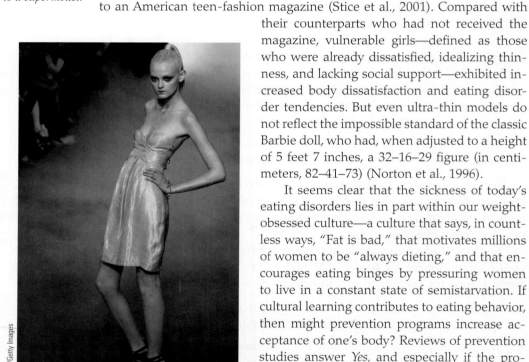

seems better (Knickmeyer, 2001; Swami et al., 2010). Bigger does not seem better in Western cultures, where, according to 222 studies of 141,000 people, the rise in eating disorders over the last 50 years has coincided with a dramatic increase in women having a poor body image (Feingold & Mazzella, 1998).

Those most vulnerable to eating disorders are also those (usually women or gay men) who most idealize thinness and have the greatest body dissatisfaction (Feldman & Meyer, 2010; Kane, 2010; Stice et al., 2010). Should it surprise us, then, that when women view real and doctored images of unnaturally thin models and celebrities, they often feel ashamed, depressed, and dissatisfied with their own bodies—the very attitudes that predispose eating disorders (Grabe et al., 2008; Myers & Crowther, 2009; Tiggemann & Miller, 2010)? Researchers tested this modeling idea by giving some adolescent girls (but not others) a 15-month subscription to an American teen-fashion magazine (Stice et al., 2001). Compared with their counterparts who had not received the magazine, vulnerable girls—defined as those who were already dissatisfied, idealizing thinness, and lacking social support—exhibited increased body dissatisfaction and eating disorder tendencies. But even ultra-thin models do not reflect the impossible standard of the classic Barbie doll, who had, when adjusted to a height of 5 feet 7 inches, a 32–16–29 figure (in centimeters, 82–41–73) (Norton et al., 1996).

It seems clear that the sickness of today's eating disorders lies in part within our weight-obsessed culture—a culture that says, in countless ways, "Fat is bad," that motivates millions of women to be "always dieting," and that encourages eating binges by pressuring women to live in a constant state of semistarvation. If cultural learning contributes to eating behavior, then might prevention programs increase acceptance of one's body? Reviews of prevention studies answer *Yes,* and especially if the programs are interactive and focused on girls over age 15 (Stice et al., 2007; Vocks et al., 2010).

Personality Disorders

 What are the three clusters of personality disorders? What behaviors and brain activity characterize the antisocial personality?

Some dysfunctional behavior patterns impair people's social functioning without depression or delusions. Among them are **personality disorders**—disruptive, inflexible, and enduring behavior patterns that impair one's social functioning. Anxiety is a feature of one cluster of these disorders, such as a fearful sensitivity to rejection that predisposes the withdrawn *avoidant personality disorder.* A second cluster expresses eccentric or odd behaviors, such as the emotionless disengagement of the *schizoid personality disorder.* A third cluster exhibits dramatic or impulsive behaviors, such as the attention-getting *histrionic personality disorder* and the self-focused and self-inflating *narcissistic personality disorder.*

personality disorders
psychological disorders characterized by inflexible and enduring behavior patterns that impair social functioning.

No remorse Dennis Rader, known as the "BTK killer" in Kansas, was convicted in 2005 of killing 10 people over a 30-year span. Rader exhibited the extreme lack of conscience that marks antisocial personality disorder.

> **AP® Exam Tip**
>
> Notice how different antisocial personality disorder is from the other disorders you have studied in this unit. Because individuals with antisocial personality disorder so often behave badly, they tend to be viewed differently from people with disorders such as depression or phobia.

Antisocial Personality Disorder

The most troubling and heavily researched personality disorder is the **antisocial personality disorder.** The person (sometimes called a *sociopath* or a *psychopath*) is typically a male whose lack of conscience becomes plain before age 15, as he begins to lie, steal, fight, or display unrestrained sexual behavior (Cale & Lilienfeld, 2002). About half of such children become antisocial adults—unable to keep a job, irresponsible as a spouse and parent, and assaultive or otherwise criminal (Farrington, 1991). When the antisocial personality combines a keen intelligence with amorality, the result may be a charming and clever con artist, a ruthless corporate executive (*Snakes in Suits* is a book on antisocial behavior in business)—or worse.

"Thursday is out. I have jury duty."

Many criminals, like this one, exhibit a sense of conscience and responsibility in other areas of their life, and thus do not exhibit antisocial personality disorder.

Despite their remorseless and sometimes criminal behavior, criminality is not an essential component of antisocial behavior (Skeem & Cooke, 2010). Moreover, many criminals do not fit the description of antisocial personality disorder. Why? Because they actually show responsible concern for their friends and family members.

Antisocial personalities behave impulsively, and then feel and fear little (Fowles & Dindo, 2009). The results sometimes are horrifying, as they were in the case of Henry Lee Lucas. He killed his first victim when he was 13. He felt little regret then or later. He confessed that, during his 32 years of crime, he had brutally beaten, suffocated, stabbed, shot, or mutilated some 360 women, men, and children. For the last 6 years of his reign of terror, Lucas teamed with Elwood Toole, who reportedly slaughtered about 50 people he "didn't think was worth living anyhow" (Darrach & Norris, 1984).

Understanding Antisocial Personality Disorder

Antisocial personality disorder is woven of both biological and psychological strands. No single gene codes for a complex behavior such as crime, but twin and adoption studies reveal that biological relatives of those with antisocial and unemotional tendencies are at increased risk for antisocial behavior (Larsson et al., 2007; Livesley & Jang, 2008). Molecular geneticists have identified some specific genes that are more common in those with antisocial personality disorder (Gunter et al., 2010). The genetic vulnerability of people

> **antisocial personality disorder** a personality disorder in which a person (usually a man) exhibits a lack of conscience for wrongdoing, even toward friends and family members. May be aggressive and ruthless or a clever con artist.

Adrenaline excretion (ng/min.)

Males with criminal convictions as adults had lower levels of arousal as 13-year-olds

- ■ No criminal conviction
- ■ Criminal conviction

Figure 69.1

Cold-blooded arousability and risk of crime Levels of the stress hormone adrenaline were measured in two groups of 13-year-old Swedish boys. In both stressful and nonstressful situations, those who would later be convicted of a crime as 18- to 26-year-olds showed relatively low arousal. (From Magnusson, 1990.)

with antisocial and unemotional tendencies appears as a fearless approach to life. Awaiting aversive events, such as electric shocks or loud noises, they show little autonomic nervous system arousal (Hare, 1975; van Goozen et al., 2007). Long-term studies have shown that their levels of stress hormones were lower than average when they were youngsters, before committing any crime (**FIGURE 69.1**). Three-year-olds who are slow to develop conditioned fears are later more likely to commit a crime (Gao et al., 2010).

Other studies have found that preschool boys who later became aggressive or antisocial adolescents tended to be impulsive, uninhibited, unconcerned with social rewards, and low in anxiety (Caspi et al., 1996; Tremblay et al., 1994). If channeled in more productive directions, such fearlessness may lead to courageous heroism, adventurism, or star-level athleticism (Poulton & Milne, 2002). Lacking a sense of social responsibility, the same disposition may produce a cool con artist or killer (Lykken, 1995). The genes that put people at risk for antisocial behavior also put people at risk for substance use disorders, which helps explain why these disorders often appear in combination (Dick, 2007).

Genetic influences, often in combination with child abuse, help wire the brain (Dodge, 2009). Adrian Raine (1999, 2005) compared PET scans of 41 murderers' brains with those from people of similar age and sex. Raine found reduced activity in the murderers' frontal lobes, an area of the cortex that helps control impulses (**FIGURE 69.2**). This reduction was especially apparent in those who murdered impulsively. In a follow-up study, Raine and his team (2000) found that violent repeat offenders had 11 percent less frontal lobe tissue than normal. This helps explain why people with antisocial personality disorder exhibit marked deficits in frontal lobe cognitive functions, such as planning, organization, and inhibition (Morgan & Lilienfeld, 2000). Compared with people who feel and display empathy, their brains also respond less to facial displays of others' distress (Deeley et al., 2006).

A biologically based fearlessness, as well as early environment, helps explain the reunion of long-separated sisters Joyce Lott, 27, and Mary Jones, 29—in a South Carolina prison where both were sent on drug charges. After a newspaper story about their reunion, their long-lost half-brother Frank Strickland called. He explained it would be a while before he could come see them—because he, too, was in jail, on drug, burglary, and larceny charges (Shepherd et al., 1990).

Genetics alone is hardly the whole story of antisocial crime, however. A study of criminal tendencies among young Danish men illustrates the usefulness of a complete biopsychosocial approach. Another Adrian Raine-led study (1996) checked criminal records on nearly 400 men at ages 20 to 22, knowing that these men either had experienced biological risk factors at birth (such as premature birth) or came from family backgrounds marked by

Figure 69.2

Murderous minds Researchers have found reduced activation in a murderer's frontal lobes. This brain area (shown in a left-facing brain) helps brake impulsive, aggressive behavior (Raine, 1999).

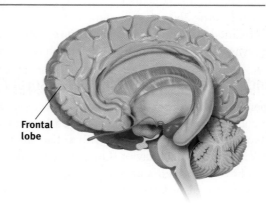

Frontal lobe

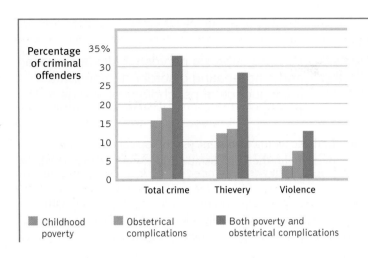

Figure 69.3

Biopsychosocial roots of crime Danish male babies whose backgrounds were marked both by obstetrical complications and social stresses associated with poverty were twice as likely to be criminal offenders by ages 20 to 22 as those in either the biological or social risk groups. (From Raine et al., 1996.)

poverty and family instability. The researchers then compared each of these two groups with a third *biosocial* group whose lives were marked by *both* the biological and social risk factors. The biosocial group had double the risk of committing a crime (**FIGURE 69.3**). Similar findings emerged from a famous study that followed 1037 children for a quarter-century: Two combined factors—childhood maltreatment and a gene that altered neurotransmitter balance—predicted antisocial problems (Caspi et al., 2002). Neither "bad" genes alone nor a "bad" environment alone predisposed later antisocial behavior. Rather, genes predisposed some children to be more sensitive to maltreatment. Within "genetically vulnerable segments of the population," environmental influences matter—for better or for worse (Belsky et al., 2007; Moffitt, 2005).

With antisocial behavior, as with so much else, nature and nurture interact and together leave their marks on the brain. To explore the neural basis of antisocial behavior, neuroscientists are identifying brain activity differences in criminals who display antisocial personality disorder. Shown emotionally evocative photographs, such as a man holding a knife to a woman's throat, they display lower heart rate and perspiration responses, and less activity in brain areas that typically respond to emotional stimuli (Harenski et al., 2010; Kiehl & Buckholtz, 2010). They also display a hyper-reactive dopamine reward system that predisposes their impulsive drive to do something rewarding, despite the consequences (Buckholtz et al., 2010). Such data provide another reminder: Everything psychological is also biological.

Before You Move On

▶ **ASK YOURSELF**

Given what we have learned in earlier units about the powers and limits of parental influence, how much do you think parental training might affect the risk of a child's developing antisocial personality disorder?

▶ **TEST YOURSELF**

What contribution do genes make to the development of antisocial personality disorder?

Answers to the Test Yourself questions can be found in Appendix E at the end of the book.

Module 69 Review

 69-1 **What are somatic symptom and related disorders?**

- *Somatic symptom disorder* presents a somatic (bodily) symptom—some physiologically unexplained but genuinely felt ailment.

- With *conversion disorder* (also called functional neurological symptom disorder), anxiety appears converted to a physical symptom that has no reasonable neurological basis.

- The more common *illness anxiety disorder* is the interpretation of normal sensations as a dreaded disorder.

 69-2 **What are dissociative disorders, and why are they controversial?**

- *Dissociative disorders* are conditions in which conscious awareness seems to become separated from previous memories, thoughts, and feelings.

- Skeptics note that *dissociative identity disorder,* formerly known as multiple personality disorder, increased dramatically in the late twentieth century, that it is rarely found outside North America, and that it may reflect role-playing by people who are vulnerable to therapists' suggestions. Others view this disorder as a manifestation of feelings of anxiety, or as a response learned when behaviors are reinforced by anxiety-reduction.

69-3 **How do anorexia nervosa, bulimia nervosa, and binge-eating disorder demonstrate the influence of psychological and genetic forces?**

- In these eating disorders, psychological factors may overwhelm the homeostatic drive to maintain a balanced internal state.

- Despite being significantly underweight, people with *anorexia nervosa* (usually adolescent females) continue to diet because they view themselves as fat.

- Those with *bulimia nervosa* (usually females in their teens and twenties) secretly binge and then compensate by purging, fasting, or excessively exercising.

- Those with *binge-eating disorder* binge but do not follow bingeing with purging, fasting, or exercise.

- Cultural pressures, low self-esteem, and negative emotions interact with stressful life experiences and genetics to produce eating disorders.

69-4 **What are the three clusters of personality disorders? What behaviors and brain activity characterize the antisocial personality?**

- *Personality disorders* are disruptive, inflexible, and enduring behavior patterns that impair social functioning.

- These disorders form clusters, based on three main characteristics: (1) anxiety; (2) eccentric or odd behaviors; and (3) dramatic or impulsive behaviors.

- *Antisocial personality disorder* is characterized by a lack of conscience and, sometimes, by aggressive and fearless behavior. Genetic predispositions may interact with the environment to produce the altered brain activity associated with antisocial personality disorder.

Multiple-Choice Questions

1. Adela regularly interprets ordinary physical symptoms like stomach cramps and headaches as serious medical problems. Her doctor is unable to convince her that her problems are not serious. Adela suffers from
   a. illness anxiety disorder.
   b. conversion disorder.
   c. fugue state.
   d. dissociative identity disorder.
   e. anorexia nervosa.

2. Which of the following is the diagnosis given to people with multiple personalities?
   a. Schizophrenia
   b. Antisocial personality disorder
   c. Fugue state
   d. Conversion disorder
   e. Dissociative identity disorder

3. Which of the following is the defining characteristic of antisocial personality disorder?

   a. Violence

   b. Lack of conscience

   c. Mood swings

   d. Unexplained physical symptoms

   e. Committing serial murders

Practice FRQs

1. Name and briefly describe three eating disorders.

Answer

1 point: Anorexia nervosa is a disorder in which the individuals starve themselves despite being significantly underweight.

1 point: Bulimia nervosa is a disorder in which the individual alternates between bingeing and purging.

1 point: Binge-eating disorder is a disorder in which the individual binges without purging.

2. Dissociative identity disorder (DID) is among the most controversial of all psychological disorders. Briefly describe the disorder. Then, provide one piece of evidence that supports the existence of the disorder and one piece of evidence that would indicate the disorder might not be genuine.

(3 points)

Unit XII Review

Key Terms and Concepts to Remember

psychological disorder, p. 651

attention-deficit/hyperactivity disorder (ADHD), p. 652

medical model, p. 653

DSM-5, p. 654

anxiety disorders, p. 661

generalized anxiety disorder, p. 662

panic disorder, p. 662

phobia, p. 662

social anxiety disorder, p. 662

agoraphobia, p. 663

obsessive-compulsive disorder (OCD), p. 663

posttraumatic stress disorder (PTSD), p. 664

posttraumatic growth, p. 665

mood disorders, p. 671

major depressive disorder, p. 672

mania, p. 673

bipolar disorder, p. 673

rumination, p. 679

schizophrenia, p. 684

psychosis, p. 684

delusions, p. 684

hallucination, p. 685

somatic symptom disorder, p. 693

conversion disorder, p. 694

illness anxiety disorder, p. 694

dissociative disorders, p. 694

dissociative identity disorder (DID), p. 695

anorexia nervosa, p. 697

bulimia nervosa, p. 697

binge-eating disorder, p. 697

personality disorders, p. 698

antisocial personality disorder, p. 699

AP® Exam Practice Questions

Multiple-Choice Questions

1. Which of the following statements is *false?*

a. Many behavioral and cognitive changes accompany depression.

b. Someone suffering from depression will get better only with therapy or medication.

c. Compared with men, women are nearly twice as vulnerable to major depression.

d. Stressful events related to work, marriage, and close relationships often precede depression.

e. With each new generation, depression is striking earlier and affecting more people.

2. The risk of major depression and bipolar disorder dramatically increases if you

a. have suffered a debilitating injury.

b. have an adoptive parent that has the disorder.

c. have a parent or sibling with the disorder.

d. have a life-threatening illness.

e. have above-average intelligence.

3. What do mental health professionals call a clinically significant disturbance in an individual's cognition, emotion regulation, or behavior?

a. An interaction of nature and nurture

b. A physiological state

c. A genetic predisposition

d. A psychological factor

e. A psychological disorder

4. Adolescent mood swings might be misdiagnosed as which psychological disorder?

a. Schizophrenia

b. Temper tantrums

c. Oppositional defiant disorder

d. Bipolar disorder

e. ADHD

5. A split from reality that shows itself in disorganized thinking, disturbed perceptions, and/or diminished or inappropriate emotions is associated with which psychological disorder?

a. Schizophrenia

b. Phobias

c. Depression

d. Bipolar disorder

e. Anxiety

6. The nearly 1-in-100 odds of any person being diagnosed with schizophrenia become about 1 in 10 among those

a. who also suffer anxiety disorder.

b. whose sibling or parent has the disorder.

c. who have been diagnosed with depression.

d. who live with someone diagnosed with schizophrenia.

e. whose identical twin has schizophrenia.

7. Which of the following can be characterized as a compulsion?

a. Worry about exposure to germs or toxins

b. Fear that something terrible is about to happen

c. Concern with making sure things are in symmetrical order

d. Anxiety when objects are not lined up in an exact pattern

e. Checking repeatedly to see if doors are locked

8. Sensory experiences without sensory stimulation are called

a. word salads.

b. delusions.

c. paranoid thoughts.

d. ruminations.

e. hallucinations.

9. What is the most common reason people seek mental health services?

a. Depression

b. Bipolar disorder

c. Posttraumatic stress disorder

d. Dissociative identity disorder

e. Illness anxiety disorder

10. Brain-scanning techniques reveal what kinds of brain activity differences in people with chronic schizophrenia?

a. Abnormally high brain activity in the frontal lobes

b. An increase in the brain waves that reflect synchronized neural firing

c. Abnormal activity in multiple brain areas

d. Decreased activity in the amygdala

e. A lack of dopamine receptors

11. Which personality disorder is associated with a lack of regret over violating others' rights?

a. Antisocial personality disorder

b. Avoidant personality disorder

c. Schizoid personality disorder

d. Histrionic personality disorder

e. Narcissistic personality disorder

12. What term refers to thoughts about who or what we blame for our successes and failures?

a. Stability

b. Emotional memory

c. The social-cognitive perspective

d. Explanatory style

e. Dissociative reasoning

13. Although some psychological disorders are culture-bound, others are universal. Which of the following disorders is found in every known culture?

a. Bulimia nervosa

b. Anorexia nervosa

c. Susto

d. Schizophrenia

e. Taijin-kyofusho

14. Modern psychologists contend that all behavior, whether it is called normal or disordered, arises from the interaction of

a. genetics and physiology.

b. children and parents.

c. experience and wisdom.

d. inborn tendencies and drives.

e. nature and nurture.

15. Which of the following are symptoms of generalized anxiety disorder?

a. Unexplainable and continual tension

b. Sudden episodes of intense dread

c. Irrational and intense fear of a specific object or situation

d. Repetitive thoughts or actions

e. Nightmares for weeks after a severe, uncontrollable event

Free-Response Questions

1. After reading her AP® Psychology text, Jane starts to wonder if all young people have some kind of psychological disorder. First, briefly explain what you might say to Jane about the criteria psychologists use when diagnosing mental illnesses. Then, briefly explain the symptoms associated with the following diagnoses and how age might be related to each diagnosis:

- ADHD
- Anorexia nervosa
- OCD
- Bipolar disorder

Rubric for Free-Response Question 1

1 point: Psychologists define a disorder as a significant disturbance in thinking, emotion, and/or behavior that is maladaptive. Jane's general statement that all young people have a psychological disorder doesn't make sense in this context: It's not likely that all young people have significant disturbances that interfere with their day-to-day lives. ↻ page 651

1 point: ADHD: The symptoms of ADHD involve inattention, hyperactivity, and impulsivity. ADHD is diagnosed more often in young people, but some adults are also diagnosed with ADHD. ↻ page 652

1 point: Anorexia nervosa: The symptoms of anorexia nervosa involve a starvation diet that results in a person weighing at least 15 percent less than he or she should. Often the symptoms of anorexia nervosa appear in adolescence since body image is likely to be a focus during this time of life, but people of any age might suffer from this disorder. ↻ page 697

1 point: OCD: The symptoms of OCD involve unwanted repetitive thoughts (obsessions) and actions (compulsions). This disorder is more commonly diagnosed in teens and young adults. ↻ pages 663–664

1 point: Bipolar disorder: The symptoms of bipolar disorder involve alternating between mania and depression. Some psychologists think that adolescent mood swings might have caused the increase in this diagnosis among young people in recent years. ↻ pages 673–674

2. Describe what the terms *obsession* and *compulsion* refer to in the context of obsessive-compulsive disorder. Then, briefly explain

- an example of a common obsession experienced by individuals with obsessive-compulsive disorder.
- an example of a common compulsion experienced by individuals with obsessive-compulsive disorder.
- how the learning perspective explains compulsions.
- how the biological perspective explains compulsions.

(6 points)

3. Psychologists organize psychological disorders into categories (in publications such as the DSM-5) in order to communicate commonalities and differences among psychological disorders, and to imply appropriate treatment and encourage future research. For each of the psychological disorders below, explain what psychological disorder category it should be organized into, and why it "belongs" in that category.

- Major depressive disorder
- Dissociative identity disorder
- Panic disorder
- Phobias

(4 points)

Multiple-choice self-tests and more may be found at
www.worthpublishers.com/MyersAP2e

Unit XIII

Treatment of Abnormal Behavior

Modules

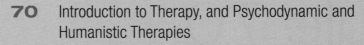

Kay Redfield Jamison, an award-winning clinical psychologist and world expert on the emotional extremes of bipolar disorder, knows her subject firsthand. "For as long as I can remember," she recalled in *An Unquiet Mind*, "I was frighteningly, although often wonderfully, beholden to moods. Intensely emotional as a child, mercurial as a young girl, first severely depressed as an adolescent, and then unrelentingly caught up in the cycles of manic-depressive illness [now known as bipolar disorder] by the time I began my professional life, I became, both by necessity and intellectual inclination, a student of moods" (1995, pp. 4–5). Her life was blessed with times of intense sensitivity and passionate energy. But like her father's, it was also at times plagued by reckless spending, racing conversation, and sleeplessness, alternating with swings into "the blackest caves of the mind."

Then, "in the midst of utter confusion," she made a sane and profoundly helpful decision. Risking professional embarrassment she made an appointment with a therapist, a psychiatrist she would visit weekly for years to come.

He kept me alive a thousand times over. He saw me through madness, despair, wonderful and terrible love affairs, disillusionments and triumphs, recurrences of illness, an almost fatal suicide attempt, the death of a man I greatly loved, and the enormous pleasures and aggravations of my professional life. . . . He was very tough, as well as very kind, and even though he understood more than anyone how much I felt I was losing—in energy, vivacity, and originality—by taking medication, he never was seduced into losing sight of the overall perspective of how costly, damaging, and life threatening my illness was. . . . Although I went to him to be treated for an illness, he taught me . . . the total beholdenness of brain to mind and mind to brain (pp. 87–88).

"Psychotherapy heals," Jamison reports. "It makes some sense of the confusion, reins in the terrifying thoughts and feelings, returns some control and hope and possibility from it all."

Module 70

Introduction to Therapy, and Psychodynamic and Humanistic Therapies

Image Source RF/Sydney Bourne/Getty Images

Module Learning Objectives

70-1 Discuss how *psychotherapy, biomedical therapy,* and an *eclectic approach* to therapy differ.

70-2 Discuss the goals and techniques of psychoanalysis, and describe how they have been adapted in psychodynamic therapy.

70-3 Identify the basic themes of humanistic therapy, and describe the specific goals and techniques of Rogers' client-centered approach.

The long history of efforts to treat psychological disorders has included a bewildering mix of harsh and gentle methods. Well-meaning individuals have cut holes in people's heads and restrained, bled, or "beat the devil" out of them. But they also have given warm baths and massages and placed people in sunny, serene environments. They have administered drugs and electric shocks. And they have talked with their patients about childhood experiences, current feelings, and maladaptive thoughts and behaviors.

Reformers Philippe Pinel and Dorothea Dix pushed for gentler, more humane treatments and for constructing mental hospitals. Since the 1950s, the introduction of effective drug therapies and community-based treatment programs have emptied most of those hospitals.

Introduction to Therapy

70-1 How do *psychotherapy, biomedical therapy,* and an *eclectic approach* to therapy differ?

Today's therapies can be classified into two main categories. In **psychotherapy,** a trained therapist uses psychological techniques to assist someone seeking to overcome difficulties or achieve personal growth. **Biomedical therapy** offers medication or other biological treatments.

Many therapists combine techniques. Jamison received psychotherapy in her meetings with her psychiatrist, and she took medications to control her wild mood swings. Many psychotherapists describe themselves as taking an **eclectic approach,** using a blend of psychotherapies. Like Jamison, many patients also can receive psychotherapy combined with medication.

Let's look first at the psychotherapeutic "talk therapies." Among the dozens of types of psychotherapy, we will look at the most influential. Each is built on one or more of psychology's major theories: psychodynamic, humanistic, behavioral, and cognitive. Most of these techniques can be used one-on-one or in groups. We'll explore psychodynamic and humanistic therapies in this module, and behavior, cognitive, and group therapies in Module 71.

The history of treatment Visitors to eighteenth-century mental hospitals paid to gawk at patients, as though they were viewing zoo animals. William Hogarth's (1697–1764) painting captured one of these visits to London's St. Mary of Bethlehem hospital (commonly called Bedlam).

Psychoanalysis and Psychodynamic Therapy

70-2 What are the goals and techniques of psychoanalysis, and how have they been adapted in psychodynamic therapy?

Sigmund Freud's **psychoanalysis** was the first of the psychological therapies. Few clinicians today practice therapy as Freud did, but his work deserves discussion as part of the foundation for treating psychological disorders.

Goals

Psychoanalytic theory presumes that healthier, less anxious living becomes possible when people release the energy they had previously devoted to id-ego-superego conflicts (see Module 55). Freud assumed that we do not fully know ourselves. There are threatening things that we seem to want not to know—that we disavow or deny. "We can have loving feelings and hateful feelings toward the same person," notes Jonathan Shedler (2009), and "we can desire something and also fear it."

psychotherapy treatment involving psychological techniques; consists of interactions between a trained therapist and someone seeking to overcome psychological difficulties or achieve personal growth.

biomedical therapy prescribed medications or procedures that act directly on the person's physiology.

eclectic approach an approach to psychotherapy that, depending on the client's problems, uses techniques from various forms of therapy.

psychoanalysis Sigmund Freud's therapeutic technique. Freud believed the patient's free associations, resistances, dreams, and transferences—and the therapist's interpretations of them—released previously repressed feelings, allowing the patient to gain self-insight.

Freud's therapy aimed to bring patients' repressed or disowned feelings into conscious awareness. By helping them reclaim their unconscious thoughts and feelings and giving them *insight* into the origins of their disorders, he aimed to help them reduce growth-impeding inner conflicts.

Techniques

Psychoanalysis is historical reconstruction. Psychoanalytic theory emphasizes the formative power of childhood experiences and their ability to mold the adult. Thus, it aims to unearth one's past in hope of unmasking the present. After discarding hypnosis as an unreliable excavator, Freud turned to *free association*.

"I'm more interested in hearing about the eggs you're hiding from yourself."

Imagine yourself as a patient using free association. First, you relax, perhaps by lying on a couch. As the psychoanalyst sits out of your line of vision, you say aloud whatever comes to mind. At one moment, you're relating a childhood memory. At another, you're describing a dream or recent experience. It sounds easy, but soon you notice how often you edit your thoughts as you speak. You pause for a second before uttering an embarrassing thought. You omit what seems trivial, irrelevant, or shameful. Sometimes your mind goes blank or you find yourself unable to remember important details. You may joke or change the subject to something less threatening.

To the analyst, these mental blocks indicate **resistance.** They hint that anxiety lurks and you are defending against sensitive material. The analyst will note your resistances and then provide insight into their meaning. If offered at the right moment, this **interpretation**—of, say, your not wanting to talk about your mother—may illuminate the underlying wishes, feelings, and conflicts you are avoiding. The analyst may also offer an explanation of how this resistance fits with other pieces of your psychological puzzle, including those based on analysis of your dream content.

Over many such sessions, your relationship patterns surface in your interaction with your therapist. You may find yourself experiencing strong positive or negative feelings for your analyst. The analyst may suggest you are **transferring** feelings, such as dependency or mingled love and anger, that you experienced in earlier relationships with family members or other important people. By exposing such feelings, you may gain insight into your current relationships.

Relatively few U.S. therapists now offer traditional psychoanalysis. Much of its underlying theory is not supported by scientific research (Module 56). Analysts' interpretations cannot be proven or disproven. And psychoanalysis takes considerable time and money, often years of several sessions per week. Some of these problems have been addressed in the modern psychodynamic perspective that has evolved from psychoanalysis.

Psychodynamic Therapy

Therapists who use **psychodynamic therapy** techniques don't talk much about id, ego, and superego. Instead they try to help people understand their current symptoms. They focus on themes across important relationships, including childhood experiences and the therapist relationship. Rather than lying on a couch, out of the therapist's line of vision, patients meet with their therapist face to face. These meetings take place once or twice a week (rather than several times per week), and often for only a few weeks or months (rather than several years).

In these meetings, patients explore and gain perspective into defended-against thoughts and feelings. Therapist David Shapiro (1999, p. 8) illustrates with the case of a young man who had told women that he loved them, when knowing well that he didn't. They expected it, so he said it. But later with his wife, who wishes he would say that he loves her, he finds he "cannot" do that—"I don't know why, but I can't."

"I haven't seen my analyst in 200 years. He was a strict Freudian. If I'd been going all this time, I'd probably almost be cured by now." -Woody Allen, after awakening from suspended animation in the movie *Sleeper*

resistance in psychoanalysis, the blocking from consciousness of anxiety-laden material.

interpretation in psychoanalysis, the analyst's noting supposed dream meanings, resistances, and other significant behaviors and events in order to promote insight.

transference in psychoanalysis, the patient's transfer to the analyst of emotions linked with other relationships (such as love or hatred for a parent).

psychodynamic therapy therapy deriving from the psychoanalytic tradition that views individuals as responding to unconscious forces and childhood experiences, and that seeks to enhance self-insight.

Therapist: Do you mean, then, that if you could, you would like to?

Patient: Well, I don't know. . . . Maybe I can't say it because I'm not sure it's true. Maybe I don't love her.

Further interactions reveal that he can't express real love because it would feel "mushy" and "soft" and therefore unmanly. He is "in conflict with himself, and he is cut off from the nature of that conflict." Shapiro noted that with such patients, who are estranged from themselves, therapists using psychodynamic techniques "are in a position to introduce them to themselves. We can restore their awareness of their own wishes and feelings, and their awareness, as well, of their reactions against those wishes and feelings."

Psychodynamic therapies may also help reveal past relationship troubles as the origin of current difficulties. Jonathan Shedler (2010a) recalls his patient Jeffrey's complaints of difficulty getting along with his colleagues and wife, who saw him as hypercritical. Jeffrey then "began responding to me as if I were an unpredictable, angry adversary." Shedler seized this opportunity to help Jeffrey recognize the relationship pattern, and its roots in the attacks and humiliation he experienced from his alcohol-abusing father—and to work through and let go of this defensive responding to people.

Interpersonal psychotherapy, a brief (12- to 16-session) variation of psychodynamic therapy, has effectively treated depression (Cuijpers, 2011). Although interpersonal psychotherapy aims to help people gain insight into the roots of their difficulties, its goal is symptom relief in the here and now. Rather than focusing mostly on undoing past hurts and offering interpretations, the therapist concentrates primarily on current relationships and on helping people improve their relationship skills.

The case of Anna, a 34-year-old married professional, illustrates these goals. Five months after receiving a promotion, with accompanying increased responsibilities and longer hours, Anna experienced tensions with her husband over his wish for a second child. She began feeling depressed, had trouble sleeping, became irritable, and was gaining weight. A therapist using psychodynamic techniques might have helped Anna gain insight into her angry impulses and her defenses against anger. A therapist applying interpersonal techniques would concur but would also engage her thinking on more immediate issues—how she could balance work and home, resolve the dispute with her husband, and express her emotions more effectively (Markowitz et al., 1998).

Face-to-face therapy
In contemporary psychodynamic therapy, the couch has disappeared. But the influence of psychoanalytic theory continues in some areas, as the therapist seeks information from the patient's childhood and helps the person bring unconscious feelings into conscious awareness.

Humanistic Therapies

 70-3 What are the basic themes of humanistic therapy? What are the specific goals and techniques of Rogers' client-centered approach?

The humanistic perspective (Module 57) has emphasized people's inherent potential for self-fulfillment. Like psychodynamic therapies, humanistic therapies have attempted to reduce growth-impeding inner conflicts by providing clients with new insights. Indeed, the psychodynamic and humanistic therapies are often referred to as **insight therapies.** But humanistic therapy differs from psychoanalytic therapy in many other ways:

> **insight therapies** a variety of therapies that aim to improve psychological functioning by increasing a person's awareness of underlying motives and defenses.

- *Humanistic therapy aims to boost people's self-fulfillment by helping them grow in self-awareness and self-acceptance.*

- *Promoting this growth, not curing illness, is the focus of therapy.* Thus, those in therapy became "clients" or just "persons" rather than "patients" (a change many other therapists have adopted).

- *The path to growth is taking immediate responsibility for one's feelings and actions, rather than uncovering hidden determinants.*

- *Conscious thoughts are more important than the unconscious.*

- *The present and future are more important than the past.* The goal is to explore feelings as they occur, rather than achieve insights into the childhood origins of the feelings.

Carl Rogers (1902–1987) developed the widely used humanistic technique he called **client-centered therapy,** which focuses on the person's conscious self-perceptions. In this *nondirective therapy,* the therapist listens, without judging or interpreting, and seeks to refrain from directing the client toward certain insights.

Believing that most people possess the resources for growth, Rogers (1961, 1980) encouraged therapists to exhibit *acceptance, genuineness,* and *empathy.* When therapists enable their clients to feel unconditionally accepted, when they drop their façades and genuinely express their true feelings, and when they empathically sense and reflect their clients' feelings, the clients may deepen their self-understanding and self-acceptance (Hill & Nakayama, 2000). As Rogers (1980, p. 10) explained,

> Hearing has consequences. When I truly hear a person and the meanings that are important to him at that moment, hearing not simply his words, but him, and when I let him know that I have heard his own private personal meanings, many things happen. There is first of all a grateful look. He feels released. He wants to tell me more about his world. He surges forth in a new sense of freedom. He becomes more open to the process of change.
>
> I have often noticed that the more deeply I hear the meanings of the person, the more there is that happens. Almost always, when a person realizes he has been deeply heard, his eyes moisten. I think in some real sense he is weeping for joy. It is as though he were saying, "Thank God, somebody heard me. Someone knows what it's like to be me."

"Hearing" refers to Rogers' technique of **active listening**—echoing, restating, and seeking clarification of what the person expresses (verbally or nonverbally) and acknowledging the expressed feelings. Active listening is now an accepted part of therapeutic counseling practices in many high schools, colleges, and clinics. The counselor listens attentively and interrupts only to restate and confirm feelings, to accept what is being expressed, or to seek clarification. The following brief excerpt between Rogers and a male client illustrates how he sought to provide a psychological mirror that would help clients see themselves more clearly.

Rogers: Feeling that now, hm? That you're just no good to yourself, no good to anybody. Never will be any good to anybody. Just that you're completely worthless, huh?—Those really are lousy feelings. Just feel that you're no good at all, hm?

Client: Yeah. *(Muttering in low, discouraged voice)* That's what this guy I went to town with just the other day told me.

Rogers: This guy that you went to town with really told you that you were no good? Is that what you're saying? Did I get that right?

Client: M-hm.

Rogers: I guess the meaning of that if I get it right is that here's somebody that—meant something to you and what does he think of you? Why, he's told you that he thinks you're no good at all. And that just really knocks the props out from under you. *(Client weeps quietly.)* It just brings the tears. *(Silence of 20 seconds)*

Client: *(Rather defiantly)* I don't care though.

Rogers: You tell yourself you don't care at all, but somehow I guess some part of you cares because some part of you weeps over it.

(Meador & Rogers, 1984, p. 167)

Can a therapist be a perfect mirror, without selecting and interpreting what is reflected? Rogers conceded that one cannot be *totally* nondirective. Nevertheless, he believed that the therapist's most important contribution is to accept and understand the client. Given a nonjudgmental, grace-filled environment that provides **unconditional positive regard,** people may accept even their worst traits and feel valued and whole.

"We have two ears and one mouth that we may listen the more and talk the less." -Zeno, 335–263 b.c.e., *Diogenes Laertius*

client-centered therapy
a humanistic therapy, developed by Carl Rogers, in which the therapist uses techniques such as active listening within a genuine, accepting, empathic environment to facilitate clients' growth. (Also called *person-centered therapy.*)

active listening empathic listening in which the listener echoes, restates, and clarifies. A feature of Rogers' client-centered therapy.

unconditional positive regard
a caring, accepting, nonjudgmental attitude, which Carl Rogers believed would help clients to develop self-awareness and self-acceptance.

Active listening Carl Rogers (right) empathized with a client during this group therapy session.

If you want to listen more actively in your own relationships, three Rogerian hints may help:

1. *Paraphrase.* Rather than saying "I know how you feel," check your understanding by summarizing the person's words in your own words.
2. *Invite clarification.* "What might be an example of that?" may encourage the person to say more.
3. *Reflect feelings.* "It sounds frustrating" might mirror what you're sensing from the person's body language and intensity.

Before You Move On

▶ **ASK YOURSELF**

Think of your closest friends. Do they tend to express more empathy than those you don't feel as close to? How have your own active listening skills changed as you've gotten older?

▶ **TEST YOURSELF**

In psychoanalysis, what does it mean when we refer to transference, resistance, and interpretation?

Answers to the Test Yourself questions can be found in Appendix E at the end of the book.

Module 70 Review

 70-1 How do *psychotherapy, biomedical therapy,* and an *eclectic approach* to therapy differ?

- *Psychotherapy* is treatment involving psychological techniques; it consists of interactions between a trained therapist and someone seeking to overcome psychological difficulties or achieve personal growth.

- The major psychotherapies derive from psychology's psychodynamic, humanistic, behavioral, and cognitive perspectives.

- *Biomedical therapy* treats psychological disorders with medications or procedures that act directly on a patient's physiology.

- An *eclectic approach* combines techniques from various forms of psychotherapy.

70-2 What are the goals and techniques of psychoanalysis, and how have they been adapted in psychodynamic therapy?

- Through *psychoanalysis,* Sigmund Freud tried to give people self-insight and relief from their disorders by bringing anxiety-laden feelings and thoughts into conscious awareness.
  - Techniques included using free association and *interpretation* of instances of *resistance* and *transference.*

- Contemporary *psychodynamic therapy* has been influenced by traditional psychoanalysis but is briefer, less expensive, and more focused on helping the client find relief from current symptoms.
  - Therapists help clients understand themes that run through past and current relationships.
  - Interpersonal therapy is a brief 12- to 16-session form of psychodynamic therapy that has been effective in treating depression.

70-3 What are the basic themes of humanistic therapy, and what are the specific goals and techniques of Rogers' client-centered approach?

- Both psychoanalytic and humanistic therapies are *insight therapies*—they attempt to improve functioning by increasing clients' awareness of motives and defenses.

- Humanistic therapy's goals have included helping clients grow in self-awareness and self-acceptance; promoting personal growth rather than curing illness; helping clients take responsibility for their own growth; focusing on conscious thoughts rather than unconscious motivations; and seeing the present and future as more important than the past.

- Carl Rogers' *client-centered therapy* proposed that therapists' most important contributions are to function as a psychological mirror through *active listening* and to provide a growth-fostering environment of *unconditional positive regard,* characterized by genuineness, acceptance, and empathy.

Multiple-Choice Questions

1. Many clinical psychologists incorporate a variety of approaches into their therapy. They are said to take a(n) _____ approach.

a. transference
b. biomedical
c. psychoanalytic
d. eclectic
e. psychodynamic

2. What do psychodynamic therapists call the blocking of anxiety-laden material from the conscious?

a. Resistance
b. Interpretation
c. Transference
d. Face-to-face therapy
e. Interpersonal psychotherapy

3. Which of the following is one of the ways humanistic therapies differ from psychoanalytic therapies?

   a. Humanist therapies believe the past is more important than the present and future.
   b. Humanist therapies boost self-fulfillment by decreasing self-acceptance.
   c. Humanist therapies believe the path to growth is found by uncovering hidden determinants.
   d. Humanist therapies believe that unconscious thoughts are more important than conscious thoughts.
   e. Humanist therapies focus on promoting growth, not curing illness.

4. Which of the following is a feature of client-centered therapy?

   a. Free association
   b. Active listening
   c. Resistance
   d. Freudian interpretation
   e. Medical/biological treatment

Practice FRQs

1. Explain what psychoanalysis is, and then discuss the relationship of transference and resistance to the therapy.

Answer

1 point: Psychoanalysis is a Freudian therapy that seeks to get patients to release repressed feelings to gain self-insight.

1 point: Transference is the patient's transfer of emotion to the analyst.

1 point: Resistance is the blocking of consciousness (by the patient) of anxiety-laden material.

2. Explain what client-centered therapy is, then describe the two major techniques of the therapy.

(3 points)

Module 71

Behavior, Cognitive, and Group Therapies

Richard T. Nowitz/CORBIS

Module Learning Objectives

71-1   Explain how the basic assumption of behavior therapy differs from those of psychodynamic and humanistic therapies, and describe the techniques used in exposure therapies and aversive conditioning.

71-2   State the main premise of therapy based on operant conditioning principles, and describe the views of its proponents and critics.

71-3   Discuss the goals and techniques of cognitive therapy and of cognitive-behavioral therapy.

71-4   Discuss the aims and benefits of group and family therapy.

> **behavior therapy** therapy that applies learning principles to the elimination of unwanted behaviors.

Behavior Therapies

71-1   How does the basic assumption of behavior therapy differ from those of psychodynamic and humanistic therapies? What techniques are used in exposure therapies and aversive conditioning?

The insight therapies assume that many psychological problems diminish as self-awareness grows. Psychodynamic therapies expect problems to subside as people gain insight into their unresolved and unconscious tensions. Humanistic therapies expect problems to diminish as people get in touch with their feelings. Proponents of **behavior therapy,** however, doubt the healing power of self-awareness. (You can become aware of why you are highly anxious during tests and still be anxious.) They assume that problem behaviors *are* the problems, and the application of learning principles can eliminate them. Rather than delving deeply below the surface looking for inner causes, therapies using behavioral techniques view maladaptive symptoms—such as phobias or sexual dysfunctions—as learned behaviors that can be replaced by constructive behaviors.

Classical Conditioning Techniques

AP® Exam Tip

Before you read the next several pages of this module, you may want to quickly review the material on classical and operant conditioning in Unit VI.

One cluster of behavior therapies derives from principles developed in Ivan Pavlov's early twentieth-century conditioning experiments (Module 26). As Pavlov and others showed, we learn various behaviors and emotions through classical conditioning. Could maladaptive symptoms be examples of conditioned responses? If so, might reconditioning be a solution? Learning theorist O. H. Mowrer thought so and developed a successful conditioning therapy for chronic bed-wetters. The child sleeps on a liquid-sensitive pad connected to an alarm. Moisture on the pad triggers the alarm, waking the child. With sufficient repetition, this association of bladder relaxation with waking up stops the bed-wetting. In three out of four cases the treatment is effective, and the success provides a boost to the child's self-image (Christophersen & Edwards, 1992; Houts et al., 1994).

Another example: If a claustrophobic fear of elevators is a learned aversion to the stimulus of being in a confined space, then might one unlearn that association by undergoing another round of conditioning to replace the fear response? **Counterconditioning** pairs the trigger stimulus (in this case, the enclosed space of the elevator) with a new response (relaxation) that is incompatible with fear. Indeed, behavior therapists have successfully counterconditioned people with such fears. Two specific counterconditioning techniques—*exposure therapy* and *aversive conditioning*—replace unwanted responses.

EXPOSURE THERAPIES

Picture this scene reported in 1924 by psychologist Mary Cover Jones: Three-year-old Peter is petrified of rabbits and other furry objects. Jones plans to replace Peter's fear of rabbits with a conditioned response incompatible with fear. Her strategy is to associate the fear-evoking rabbit with the pleasurable, relaxed response associated with eating.

As Peter begins his midafternoon snack, Jones introduces a caged rabbit on the other side of the huge room. Peter, eagerly munching away on his crackers and drinking his milk, hardly notices. On succeeding days, she gradually moves the rabbit closer and closer. Within two months, Peter is tolerating the rabbit in his lap, even stroking it while he eats. Moreover, his fear of other furry objects subsides as well, having been *countered,* or replaced, by a relaxed state that cannot coexist with fear (Fisher, 1984; Jones, 1924).

Unfortunately for those who might have been helped by her counterconditioning procedures, Jones' story of Peter and the rabbit did not immediately become part of psychology's lore. It was more than 30 years later that psychiatrist Joseph Wolpe (1958; Wolpe & Plaud, 1997) refined Jones' technique into what are now the most widely used types of behavior therapies: **exposure therapies,** which expose people to what they normally avoid or escape (behaviors that get reinforced by reduced anxiety). Exposure therapies have them face their fear, and thus overcome their fear of the fear response itself. As people can habituate to the sound of a train passing their new apartment, so, with repeated exposure, can they become less anxiously responsive to things that once petrified them (Rosa-Alcázar et al., 2008; Wolitzky-Taylor et al., 2008).

One widely used exposure therapy is **systematic desensitization.** Wolpe assumed, as did Jones, that you cannot be simultaneously anxious and relaxed. Therefore, if you can repeatedly relax when facing anxiety-provoking stimuli, you can gradually eliminate your anxiety. The trick is to proceed gradually. Let's see how this might work with social anxiety disorder. Imagine yourself afraid of public speaking. A therapist might first ask for your help in constructing a hierarchy of anxiety-triggering speaking situations. Yours might range from mildly anxiety-provoking situations, perhaps speaking up in a small group of friends, to panic-provoking situations, such as having to address a large audience.

Next, using *progressive relaxation,* the therapist would train you to relax one muscle group after another, until you achieve a blissful state of complete relaxation and comfort. Then the therapist would ask you to imagine, with your eyes closed, a mildly anxiety-arousing situation: You are having coffee with a group of friends and are trying to decide whether to speak up. If imagining the scene causes you to feel any anxiety, you would signal your tension by raising your finger, and the therapist would instruct you to switch off the mental image and go back to deep relaxation. This imagined scene is repeatedly paired with relaxation until you feel no trace of anxiety.

The therapist would progress up the constructed anxiety hierarchy, using the relaxed state to desensitize you to each imagined situation. After several sessions, you move to actual situations and practice what you had only imagined before, beginning with relatively easy tasks and gradually moving to more anxiety-filled ones. Conquering your anxiety in an actual situation, not just in your imagination, raises your self-confidence (Foa & Kozak, 1986; Williams, 1987). Eventually, you may even become a confident public speaker.

---

counterconditioning behavior therapy procedures that use classical conditioning to evoke new responses to stimuli that are triggering unwanted behaviors; include *exposure therapies* and *aversive conditioning.*

exposure therapies behavioral techniques, such as *systematic desensitization* and *virtual reality exposure therapy,* that treat anxieties by exposing people (in imagination or actual situations) to the things they fear and avoid.

systematic desensitization a type of exposure therapy that associates a pleasant, relaxed state with gradually increasing anxiety-triggering stimuli. Commonly used to treat phobias.

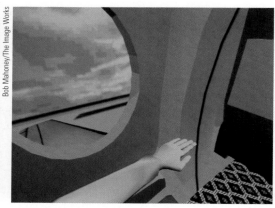

Virtual reality exposure therapy Virtual reality technology exposes people to vivid simulations of feared stimuli, such as a plane's takeoff.

When an anxiety-arousing situation is too expensive, difficult, or embarrassing to re-create, **virtual reality exposure therapy** offers an efficient middle ground. Wearing a head-mounted display unit that projects a three-dimensional virtual world, you would view a lifelike series of scenes that would be tailored to your particular fear and shift as your head turned. Experiments led by several research teams have treated many different people with many different fears—flying, heights, particular animals, and public speaking (Parsons & Rizzo, 2008). People who fear flying, for example, can peer out a virtual window of a simulated plane, feel vibrations, and hear the engine roar as the plane taxis down the runway and takes off. In studies comparing control groups with people experiencing virtual reality exposure therapy, the therapy has provided greater relief from real-life fear (Hoffman, 2004; Krijn et al., 2004).

Developments in virtual reality therapy suggest the likelihood of increasingly sophisticated simulated worlds in which people, using avatars (computer representations of themselves), try out new behaviors in virtual environments (Gorini, 2007). For example, someone with social anxiety disorder might visit virtual parties or group discussions, which others join over time.

AVERSIVE CONDITIONING

In systematic desensitization, the goal is substituting a positive (relaxed) response for a negative (fearful) response to a *harmless* stimulus. In **aversive conditioning,** the goal is substituting a negative (aversive) response for a positive response to a *harmful* stimulus (such as alcohol). Thus, aversive conditioning is the reverse of systematic desensitization—it seeks to condition an aversion to something the person *should* avoid.

The procedure is simple: It associates the unwanted behavior with unpleasant feelings. To treat nail biting, one can paint the fingernails with a nasty-tasting nail polish (Baskind, 1997). To treat alcohol use disorder, an aversion therapist offers the client appealing drinks laced with a drug that produces severe nausea. By linking alcohol with violent nausea (recall the taste-aversion experiments with rats and coyotes in Module 29), the therapist seeks to transform the person's reaction to alcohol from positive to negative (**FIGURE 71.1**).

virtual reality exposure therapy an anxiety treatment that progressively exposes people to electronic simulations of their greatest fears, such as airplane flying, spiders, or public speaking.

aversive conditioning a type of counterconditioning that associates an unpleasant state (such as nausea) with an unwanted behavior (such as drinking alcohol).

Figure 71.1

Aversion therapy for alcohol use disorder After repeatedly imbibing an alcoholic drink mixed with a drug that produces severe nausea, some people with a history of alcohol use disorder develop at least a temporary conditioned aversion to alcohol. (Remember: US is unconditioned stimulus, UR is unconditioned response, NS is neutral stimulus, CS is conditioned stimulus, and CR is conditioned response.)

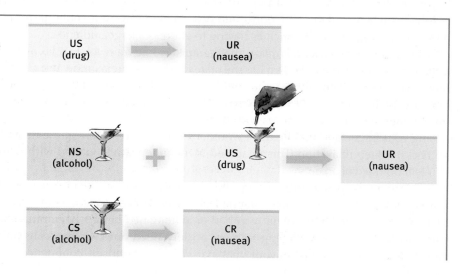

Does aversive conditioning work? In the short run it may. Arthur Wiens and Carol Menustik (1983) studied 685 patients with alcohol use disorder who completed an aversion therapy program at a Portland, Oregon, hospital. One year later, after returning for several booster treatments of alcohol-sickness pairings, 63 percent were still successfully abstaining. But after three years, only 33 percent had remained abstinent.

The problem is that cognition influences conditioning. People know that outside the therapist's office they can drink without fear of nausea. Their ability to discriminate between the aversive conditioning situation and all other situations can limit the treatment's effectiveness. Thus, therapists often use aversive conditioning in combination with other treatments.

Operant Conditioning

 What is the main premise of therapy based on operant conditioning principles, and what are the views of its proponents and critics?

Pioneering researcher B. F. Skinner helped us understand the basic concept in operant conditioning (Modules 27 and 28) that voluntary behaviors are strongly influenced by their consequences. Knowing this, today's therapists can practice *behavior modification*—reinforcing desired behaviors, and withholding reinforcement for undesired behaviors. Using operant conditioning to solve specific behavior problems has raised hopes for some otherwise hopeless cases. Children with intellectual disabilities have been taught to care for themselves. Socially withdrawn children with autism spectrum disorder (ASD) have learned to interact. People with schizophrenia have been helped to behave more rationally in their hospital ward. In such cases, therapists use positive reinforcers to shape behavior in a step-by-step manner, rewarding closer and closer approximations of the desired behavior.

In extreme cases, treatment must be intensive. One study worked with 19 withdrawn, uncommunicative 3-year-olds with ASD. Each participated in a 2-year program in which their parents spent 40 hours a week attempting to shape their behavior (Lovaas, 1987). The combination of positively reinforcing desired behaviors, and ignoring or punishing aggressive and self-abusive behaviors, worked wonders for some. By first grade, 9 of the 19 children were functioning successfully in school and exhibiting normal intelligence. In a group of 40 comparable children not undergoing this effortful treatment, only one showed similar improvement. (Ensuing studies suggested that positive reinforcement without punishment was most effective.)

Rewards used to modify behavior vary. For some people, the reinforcing power of attention or praise is sufficient. Others require concrete rewards, such as food. In institutional settings, therapists may create a **token economy.** When people display appropriate behavior, such as getting out of bed, washing, dressing, eating, talking coherently, cleaning up their rooms, or playing cooperatively, they receive a token or plastic coin as a positive reinforcer. Later, they can exchange their accumulated tokens for various rewards, such as candy, TV time, trips to town, or better living quarters. Token economies have been successfully applied in various settings (homes, classrooms, hospitals, institutions for juvenile offenders) and among members of various populations (including disturbed children and people with schizophrenia and other mental disabilities).

Critics of behavior modification express two concerns. The first is practical: *How durable are the behaviors?* Will people become so dependent on extrinsic rewards that the appropriate behaviors will stop when the reinforcers stop? Proponents of behavior modification believe the behaviors will endure if therapists wean patients from the tokens by shifting them toward other, real-life rewards, such as social approval. They also point out that the appropriate behaviors themselves can be intrinsically rewarding. For example, as a withdrawn person becomes more socially competent, the intrinsic satisfactions of social interaction may help the person maintain the behavior.

token economy an operant conditioning procedure in which people earn a token of some sort for exhibiting a desired behavior and can later exchange the tokens for various privileges or treats.

The second concern is ethical: *Is it right for one human to control another's behavior?* Those who set up token economies deprive people of something they desire and decide which behaviors to reinforce. To critics, this whole process has an authoritarian taint. Advocates reply that some patients request the therapy. Moreover, control already exists; rewards and punishers are already maintaining destructive behavior patterns. So why not reinforce adaptive behavior instead? Treatment with positive rewards is more humane than being institutionalized or punished, advocates argue, and the right to effective treatment and an improved life justifies temporary deprivation.

Cognitive Therapies

71-3 What are the goals and techniques of cognitive therapy and of cognitive-behavioral therapy?

We have seen how behavior therapies treat specific fears and problem behaviors. But how do they deal with major depression? Or with generalized anxiety disorder, in which anxiety has no focus and developing a hierarchy of anxiety-triggering situations is difficult? Therapists treating these less clearly defined psychological problems have had help from the same *cognitive revolution* that has profoundly changed other areas of psychology during the last half-century.

Cognitive therapy for eating disorders aided by journaling Cognitive therapists guide people toward new ways of explaining their good and bad experiences. By recording positive events and how she has enabled them, this woman may become more mindful of her self-control and more optimistic.

cognitive therapy therapy that teaches people new, more adaptive ways of thinking; based on the assumption that thoughts intervene between events and our emotional reactions.

"Life does not consist mainly, or even largely, of facts and happenings. It consists mainly of the storm of thoughts that are forever blowing through one's mind." -MARK TWAIN, 1835–1910

The **cognitive therapies** assume that our thinking colors our feelings (**FIGURE 71.2**). Between the event and our response lies the mind. Self-blaming and overgeneralized explanations of bad events are often an integral part of the vicious cycle of depression (see Module 67). The depressed person interprets a suggestion as criticism, disagreement as dislike, praise as flattery, friendliness as pity. Ruminating on such thoughts sustains the negative thinking. If such thinking patterns can be learned, then surely they can be replaced. Cognitive therapists therefore try in various ways to teach people new, more constructive ways of thinking. If people are miserable, they can be helped to change their minds.

Figure 71.2

A cognitive perspective on psychological disorders The person's emotional reactions are produced not directly by the event but by the person's thoughts in response to the event.

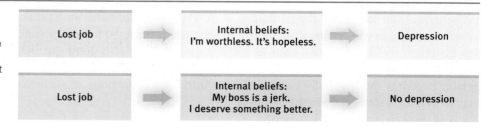

| Lost job | → | Internal beliefs: I'm worthless. It's hopeless. | → | Depression |
| Lost job | → | Internal beliefs: My boss is a jerk. I deserve something better. | → | No depression |

Rational-Emotive Behavior Therapy

According to Albert Ellis (1962, 1987, 1993), the creator of **rational-emotive behavior therapy (REBT),** many problems arise from irrational thinking. For example, he described a disturbed woman and suggested how therapy might challenge her illogical, self-defeating assumptions (Ellis, 2011, pp. 198–199):

> [She] does not merely believe it is undesirable if her lover rejects her. She tends to believe, also, that (a) it is awful; (b) she cannot stand it; (c) she should not, *must* not be rejected; (d) she will never be accepted by any desirable partner; (e) she is a worthless person because one lover has rejected her; and (f) she deserves to be rejected for being so worthless. Such common covert hypotheses are illogical, unrealistic, and destructive. . . . They can be easily elicited and demolished by any scientist worth his or her salt; and the rational-emotive therapist is exactly that: an exposing and nonsense-annihilating scientist.

Change people's thinking by revealing the "absurdity" of their self-defeating ideas, the sharp-tongued Ellis believed, and you will change their self-defeating feelings and enable healthier behaviors.

> **rational-emotive behavior therapy (REBT)** a confrontational cognitive therapy, developed by Albert Ellis, that vigorously challenges people's illogical, self-defeating attitudes and assumptions.

Aaron Beck's Therapy for Depression

Cognitive therapist Aaron Beck also believes that changing people's thinking can change their functioning, though he has a gentler approach. Originally trained in Freudian techniques, Beck analyzed the dreams of depressed people. He found recurring negative themes of loss, rejection, and abandonment that extended into their waking thoughts. Such negativity even extends into therapy, as clients recall and rehearse their failings and worst impulses (Kelly, 2000). With cognitive therapy, Beck and his colleagues (1979) have sought to reverse clients' *catastrophizing* beliefs about themselves, their situations, and their futures. Gentle questioning seeks to reveal irrational thinking, and then to persuade people to remove the dark glasses through which they view life (Beck et al., 1979, pp. 145–146):

Client: I agree with the descriptions of me but I guess I don't agree that the way I think makes me depressed.

Beck: How do you understand it?

Client: I get depressed when things go wrong. Like when I fail a test.

Beck: How can failing a test make you depressed?

Client: Well, if I fail I'll never get into law school.

Beck: So failing the test means a lot to you. But if failing a test could drive people into clinical depression, wouldn't you expect everyone who failed the test to have a depression? . . . Did everyone who failed get depressed enough to require treatment?

Client: No, but it depends on how important the test was to the person.

Beck: Right, and who decides the importance?

Client: I do.

Beck: And so, what we have to examine is your way of viewing the test (or the way that you think about the test) and how it affects your chances of getting into law school. Do you agree?

Client: Right.

Beck: Do you agree that the way you interpret the results of the test will affect you? You might feel depressed, you might have trouble sleeping, not feel like eating, and you might even wonder if you should drop out of the course.

Client: I have been thinking that I wasn't going to make it. Yes, I agree.

Beck: Now what did failing mean?

Client: *(tearful)* That I couldn't get into law school.

Beck: And what does that mean to you?

Client: That I'm just not smart enough.

Beck: Anything else?

Client: That I can never be happy.

Beck: And how do these thoughts make you feel?

Client: Very unhappy.

Beck: So it is the meaning of failing a test that makes you very unhappy. In fact, believing that you can never be happy is a powerful factor in producing unhappiness. So, you get yourself into a trap—by definition, failure to get into law school equals "I can never be happy."

PEANUTS

Drawing by Charles Schulz; ©1956. Reprinted by permission of United Features Syndicate.

We often think in words. Therefore, getting people to change what they say to themselves is an effective way to change their thinking. Perhaps you can identify with the anxious students who, before a test, make matters worse with self-defeating thoughts: "This test's probably going to be impossible. All these other students seem so relaxed and confident. wish I were better prepared. Anyhow, I'm so nervous I'll forget everything." To change such negative self-talk, Donald Meichenbaum (1977, 1985) offered *stress inoculation training:* teaching people to restructure their thinking in stressful situations. Sometimes it may be enough simply to say more positive things to oneself: "Relax. The test may be hard, but it will be hard for everyone else, too. I studied harder than most people. Besides, I don't need a perfect score to get a good grade in this class." After being trained to dispute their negative thoughts, depression-prone children, teens, and college students exhibit a greatly reduced rate of future depression (Seligman, 2002; Seligman et al., 2009). To a large extent, it *is* the thought that counts. **TABLE 71.1** provides a sampling of techniques commonly used in cognitive therapy.

Table 71.1 Selected Cognitive Therapy Techniques

Aim of Technique	Technique	Therapists' Directives
Reveal beliefs	Question your interpretations	Explore your beliefs, revealing faulty assumptions such as "I must be liked by everyone."
	Rank thoughts and emotions	Gain perspective by ranking your thoughts and emotions from mildly to extremely upsetting.
Test beliefs	Examine consequences	Explore difficult situations, assessing possible consequences and challenging faulty reasoning.
	Decatastrophize thinking	Work through the actual worst-case consequences of the situation you face (it is often not as bad as imagined). Then determine how to cope with the real situation you face.
Change beliefs	Take appropriate responsibility	Challenge total self-blame and negative thinking, noting aspects for which you may be truly responsible, as well as aspects that aren't your responsibility.
	Resist extremes	Develop new ways of thinking and feeling to replace maladaptive habits. For example, change from thinking "I am a total failure" to "I got a failing grade on that paper, and I can make these changes to succeed next time."

Cognitive-Behavioral Therapy

Cognitive-behavioral therapy (CBT), a widely practiced integrative therapy, aims not only to alter the way people think (cognitive therapy), but also to alter the way they act (behavior therapy). It seeks to make people aware of their irrational negative thinking, to replace it with new ways of thinking, *and to practice* the more positive approach in everyday settings. Behavioral change is typically addressed first, followed by sessions on cognitive change; the therapy concludes with a focus on maintaining both and preventing relapses.

Anxiety and mood disorders share a common problem: emotion regulation (Aldao & Nolen-Hoeksema, 2010). An effective CBT program for these emotional disorders trains people both to replace their catastrophizing thinking with more realistic appraisals, and, as homework, to practice behaviors that are incompatible with their problem (Kazantzis et al., 2010a,b; Moses & Barlow, 2006). A person might, for example, keep a log of daily situations associated with negative and positive emotions, and engage more in activities that lead them to feeling good. Or those who fear social situations might be assigned to practice approaching people.

CBT may also be useful with obsessive-compulsive disorder. In one study, people learned to prevent their compulsive behaviors by relabeling their obsessive thoughts (Schwartz et al., 1996). Feeling the urge to wash their hands again, they would tell themselves, "I'm having a compulsive urge," and attribute it to their brain's abnormal activity, as previously viewed in their PET scans. Instead of giving in to the urge, they would then spend 15 minutes in an enjoyable, alternative behavior, such as practicing an instrument, taking a walk, or gardening. This helped "unstick" the brain by shifting attention and engaging other brain areas. For two or three months, the weekly therapy sessions continued, with relabeling and refocusing practice at home. By the study's end, most participants' symptoms had diminished and their PET scans revealed normalized brain activity. Many other studies confirm CBT's effectiveness for those with anxiety, depression, or anorexia nervosa (Covin et al., 2008; Mitte, 2005; Norton & Price, 2007). Studies have also found that cognitive-behavioral skills can be effectively taught and therapy conducted over the Internet (Barak et al., 2008; Kessler et al., 2009; Marks & Cavanaugh, 2009; Stross, 2011).

> "The trouble with most therapy is that it helps you to feel better. But you don't get better. You have to back it up with action, action, action." -Therapist Albert Ellis (1913–2007)

cognitive-behavioral therapy (CBT) a popular integrative therapy that combines cognitive therapy (changing self-defeating thinking) with behavior therapy (changing behavior).

group therapy therapy conducted with groups rather than individuals, permitting therapeutic benefits from group interaction.

Group and Family Therapies

71-4 | What are the aims and benefits of group and family therapy?

Group Therapy

Except for traditional psychoanalysis, most therapies may also occur in small groups. **Group therapy** does not provide the same degree of therapist involvement with each client. However, it offers benefits:

- *It saves therapists' time and clients' money,* often with no less effectiveness than individual therapy (Fuhriman & Burlingame, 1994).

- *It offers a social laboratory for exploring social behaviors and developing social skills.* Therapists frequently suggest group therapy for people experiencing frequent conflicts or whose behavior distresses others. For up to 90 minutes weekly, the therapist guides people's interactions as they discuss issues and try out new behaviors.

Group Therapy ABC Family's and *Seventeen Magazine's* 2011 film *Cyberbully* realistically portrayed main characters attending group therapy, where they found they were not alone in their troublesome feelings.

Photograph Courtesy of Muse Entertainment Enterprises Inc.

- *It enables people to see that others share their problems.* It can be a relief to discover that you are not alone—to learn that others, despite their composure, experience some of the same troublesome feelings and behaviors.

- *It provides feedback as clients try out new ways of behaving.* Hearing that you look poised, even though you feel anxious and self-conscious, can be very reassuring.

Family Therapy

One special type of group interaction, **family therapy,** assumes that no person is an island: We live and grow in relation to others, especially our families. We struggle to differentiate ourselves from our families, but we also need to connect with them emotionally. Some of our problem behaviors arise from the tension between these two tendencies, which can create family stress.

Unlike most psychotherapy, which focuses on what happens inside the person's own skin, family therapists work with multiple family members to heal relationships and to mobilize family resources. They tend to view the family as a system in which each person's actions trigger reactions from others, and they help family members discover their role within their family's social system. A child's rebellion, for example, affects and is affected by other family tensions. Therapists also attempt—usually with some success, research suggests—to open up communication within the family or to help family members discover new ways of preventing or resolving conflicts (Hazelrigg et al., 1987; Shadish et al., 1993).

Self-Help Groups

Many people also participate in self-help and support groups (Yalom, 1985). One analysis of online support groups and more than 14,000 self-help groups reported that most support groups focus on stigmatized or hard-to-discuss illnesses (Davison et al., 2000). AIDS patients, for example, are 250 times more likely than hypertension patients to be in support groups. Those struggling with anorexia and alcohol use disorder often join groups; those with migraines and ulcers usually do not. People with hearing loss have national organizations with local chapters; people with vision loss more often cope on their own.

The grandparent of support groups, Alcoholics Anonymous (AA), reports having more than 2 million members in 114,000 groups worldwide. Its famous 12-step program, emulated by many other self-help groups, asks members to admit their powerlessness, to seek help from a higher power and from one another, and (the twelfth step) to take the message to others in need of it. In one eight-year, $27 million investigation, AA participants reduced their drinking sharply, although so did those assigned to cognitive-behavioral therapy or to "motivational therapy" (Project Match, 1997). Other studies have similarly found that 12-step programs such as AA have helped reduce alcohol use disorder comparably with other treatment interventions (Ferri et al., 2006; Moos & Moos, 2005). The more meetings members attend, the greater their alcohol abstinence (Moos & Moos, 2006). In one study of 2300 veterans who sought treatment for alcohol use disorder, a high level of AA involvement was followed by diminished alcohol problems (McKellar et al., 2003).

In an individualistic age, with more and more people living alone or feeling isolated, the popularity of support groups—for the addicted, the bereaved, the divorced, or simply those seeking fellowship and growth—seems to reflect a longing for community and connectedness. More than 100 million Americans belong to small religious, interest, or self-help groups that meet regularly—and 9 in 10 report that group members "support each other emotionally" (Gallup, 1994).

* * *

For a synopsis of the modern forms of psychotherapy we've been discussing, see **TABLE 71.2.**

FYI

With more than 2 million members worldwide, AA is said to be "the largest organization on Earth that nobody wanted to join" (Finlay, 2000).

family therapy therapy that treats the family as a system. Views an individual's unwanted behaviors as influenced by, or directed at, other family members.

Table 71.2 Comparing Modern Psychotherapies

Therapy	Presumed Problem	Therapy Aim	Therapy Technique
Psychodynamic	Unconscious conflicts from childhood experiences	Reduce anxiety through self-insight.	Interpret patients' memories and feelings.
Client-centered	Barriers to self-understanding and self-acceptance	Enable growth via unconditional positive regard, genuineness, and empathy.	Listen actively and reflect clients' feelings.
Behavior	Dysfunctional behaviors	Relearn adaptive behaviors; extinguish problem ones.	Use classical conditioning (via exposure or aversion therapy) or operant conditioning (as in token economies).
Cognitive	Negative, self-defeating thinking	Promote healthier thinking and self-talk.	Train people to dispute negative thoughts and attributions.
Cognitive-behavioral	Self-harmful thoughts and behaviors	Promote healthier thinking and adaptive behaviors.	Train people to counter self-harmful thoughts and to act out their new ways of thinking.
Group and family	Stressful relationships	Heal relationships.	Develop an understanding of family and other social systems, explore roles, and improve communication.

Before You Move On

▶ **ASK YOURSELF**

Critics say that behavior modification techniques, such as those used in token economies, are inhumane. Do you agree or disagree? Why?

▶ **TEST YOURSELF**

What is the major distinction between the underlying assumptions in insight therapies and in behavior therapies?

Answers to the Test Yourself questions can be found in Appendix E at the end of the book.

Module 71 Review

 71-1 How does the basic assumption of behavior therapy differ from those of psychodynamic and humanistic therapies? What techniques are used in exposure therapies and aversive conditioning?

- *Behavior therapies* are not insight therapies. Their goal is to apply learning principles to modify problem behaviors.

- Classical conditioning techniques, including *exposure therapies* (such as *systematic desensitization* or *virtual reality exposure therapy*) and *aversive conditioning,* attempt to change behaviors through *counterconditioning*—evoking new responses to old stimuli that trigger unwanted behaviors.

 71-2 What is the main premise of therapy based on operant conditioning principles, and what are the views of its proponents and critics?

- Therapy based on operant conditioning principles uses behavior modification techniques to change unwanted behaviors through positively reinforcing desired behaviors and ignoring or punishing undesirable behaviors.

- Critics maintain that (1) techniques such as those used in *token economies* may produce behavior changes that disappear when rewards end, and (2) deciding which behaviors should change is authoritarian and unethical.

- Proponents argue that treatment with positive rewards is more humane than punishing people or institutionalizing them for undesired behaviors.

71-3 What are the goals and techniques of cognitive therapy and of cognitive-behavioral therapy?

- The *cognitive therapies,* such as Aaron Beck's cognitive therapy for depression, assume that our thinking influences our feelings, and that the therapist's role is to change clients' self-defeating thinking by training them to view themselves in more positive ways.

- *Rational-emotive behavior therapy (REBT)* is a confrontational cognitive therapy that actively challenges irrational beliefs.

- The widely researched and practiced *cognitive-behavioral therapy (CBT)* combines cognitive therapy and behavior therapy by helping clients regularly act out their new ways of thinking and talking in their everyday life.

71-4 What are the aims and benefits of group and family therapy?

- *Group therapy* sessions can help more people and costs less per person than individual therapy would. Clients may benefit from exploring feelings and developing social skills in a group situation, from learning that others have similar problems, and from getting feedback on new ways of behaving.

- *Family therapy* views a family as an interactive system and attempts to help members discover the roles they play and to learn to communicate more openly and directly.

Multiple-Choice Questions

1. Dr. Welle tries to help her clients by teaching them to modify the things they do when under stress or experiencing symptoms. This means that Dr. Welle engages in _____ therapy.

   a. behavior
   b. cognitive
   c. group
   d. rational-emotive behavior
   e. client-centered

2. Mary Cover Jones helped a little boy named Peter overcome his fear of rabbits by gradually moving a rabbit closer to him each day while he was eating his snack. This was one of the first applications of

   a. group therapy.
   b. virtual reality exposure therapy.
   c. aversive therapy.
   d. exposure therapy.
   e. cognitive therapy.

3. On which of the following are token economies based?

a. Classical conditioning
b. Operant conditioning
c. Group therapy
d. Cognitive therapy
e. Cognitive-behavioral therapy

4. Which of the following is considered a benefit of group therapy?

a. It is the most effective therapy for children.
b. It is particularly effective in the treatment of antisocial personality disorder.
c. It is particularly effective in the treatment of schizophrenia.
d. It is the only setting proven effective for virtual reality exposure therapy.
e. It saves time and money when compared with other forms of therapy.

Practice FRQs

1. Name and describe two specific types of group therapy.

Answer

1 point: Family therapy is a means of treating an entire family as an interdependent system.

1 point: Self-help groups, such as Alcoholics Anonymous (AA), are groups of individuals who share a similar problem working together to overcome that problem.

2. Explain what systematic desensitization is, then describe the two major components of the therapy.

(3 points)

Module 72

Evaluating Psychotherapies and Prevention Strategies

RubberBall/SuperStock

Module Learning Objectives

72-1 Discuss whether psychotherapy works as interpreted by clients, clinicians, and outcome research.

72-2 Describe which psychotherapies are most effective for specific disorders.

72-3 Discuss how alternative therapies fare under scientific scrutiny.

72-4 Describe the three elements shared by all forms of psychotherapy.

72-5 Discuss how culture, gender, and values influence the therapist-client relationship.

72-6 Identify some guidelines for selecting a therapist.

72-7 Explain the rationale of preventive mental health programs.

Evaluating Psychotherapies

Advice columnists frequently urge their troubled letter writers to get professional help: "Don't give up. Find a therapist who can help you. Make an appointment."

Many Americans share this confidence in psychotherapy's effectiveness. Before 1950, psychiatrists were the primary providers of mental health care. Today's providers include clinical and counseling psychologists; clinical social workers; clergy; marital and school counselors; and psychiatric nurses. With such an enormous outlay of time as well as money, effort, and hope, it is important to ask: Are the millions of people worldwide justified in placing their hopes in psychotherapy?

Is Psychotherapy Effective?

72-1   Does psychotherapy work? Who decides?

The question, though simply put, is not simple to answer. Measuring therapy's effectiveness is not like taking your body's temperature to see if your fever has gone away. If you and I were to undergo psychotherapy, how would we assess its effectiveness? By how we feel about our progress? By how our therapist feels about it? By how our friends and family feel about it? By how our behavior has changed?

CLIENTS' PERCEPTIONS

If clients' testimonials were the only measuring stick, we could strongly affirm the effectiveness of psychotherapy. When 2900 *Consumer Reports* readers (1995; Kotkin et al., 1996; Seligman, 1995) related their experiences with mental health professionals, 89 percent said they were at least "fairly well satisfied." Among those who recalled feeling *fair* or *very poor* when beginning therapy, 9 in 10 now were feeling *very good, good,* or at least *so-so.* We have their word for it—and who should know better?

We should not dismiss these testimonials lightly. But for several reasons, client testimonials do not persuade psychotherapy's skeptics:

- **People often enter therapy in crisis.** When, with the normal ebb and flow of events, the crisis passes, people may attribute their improvement to the therapy.

- **Clients may need to believe the therapy was worth the effort.** To admit investing time and money in something ineffective is like admitting to having one's car serviced repeatedly by a mechanic who never fixes it. Self-justification is a powerful human motive.

- **Clients generally speak kindly of their therapists.** Even if the problems remain, say the critics, clients "work hard to find something positive to say. The therapist had been very understanding, the client had gained a new perspective, he learned to communicate better, his mind was eased, anything at all so as not to have to say treatment was a failure" (Zilbergeld, 1983, p. 117).

As earlier units document, we are prone to selective and biased recall and to making judgments that confirm our beliefs. Consider the testimonials gathered in a massive experiment with over 500 Massachusetts boys, aged 5 to 13 years, many of whom seemed bound for delinquency. By the toss of a coin, half the boys were assigned to a 5-year treatment program. The treated boys were visited by counselors twice a month. They participated in community programs, and they received academic tutoring, medical attention, and family assistance as needed. Some 30 years later, Joan McCord (1978, 1979) located 485 participants, sent them questionnaires, and checked public records from courts, mental hospitals, and other sources. Was the treatment successful?

Client testimonials yielded encouraging results, even glowing reports. Some men noted that, had it not been for their counselors, "I would probably be in jail," "My life would have gone the other way," or "I think I would have ended up in a life of crime." Court records offered apparent support: Even among the "difficult" boys in the treatment group, 66 percent had no official juvenile crime record.

But recall psychology's most powerful tool for sorting reality from wishful thinking: the *control group.* For every boy in the treatment group, there was a similar boy in a control group, receiving no counseling. Of these untreated men, *70 percent* had no juvenile record. On several other measures, such as a record of having committed a second crime, alcohol use disorder, death rate, and job satisfaction, the untreated men exhibited slightly *fewer* problems. The glowing testimonials of those treated had been unintentionally deceiving.

CLINICIANS' PERCEPTIONS

Do clinicians' perceptions give us any more reason to celebrate? Case studies of successful treatment abound. The problem is that clients justify entering psychotherapy by emphasizing their unhappiness and justify leaving by emphasizing their well-being. Therapists treasure compliments from clients as they say good-bye or later express their gratitude, but they hear little from clients who experience only temporary relief and seek out new therapists for their recurring problems. Thus, the same person—with the same recurring anxieties, depression, or marital difficulty—may be a "success" story in several therapists' files.

Because people enter therapy when they are extremely unhappy, and usually leave when they are less extremely unhappy, most therapists, like most clients, testify to therapy's success—regardless of the treatment (see Thinking Critically About: "Regressing" From Unusual to Usual on the next page).

Trauma These women were mourning the tragic loss of lives and homes in the 2010 earthquake in China. Those who suffer through such trauma may benefit from counseling, though many people recover on their own, or with the help of supportive relationships with family and friends. "Life itself still remains a very effective therapist," noted psychodynamic therapist Karen Horney (*Our Inner Conflicts*, 1945).

Feng Li/Getty Images

Thinking Critically About

"Regressing" From Unusual to Usual

Clients' and therapists' perceptions of therapy's effectiveness are vulnerable to inflation from two phenomena. One is the *placebo effect*—the power of belief in a treatment. If you think a treatment is going to be effective, it just may be (thanks to the healing power of your positive expectations).

The second phenomenon is **regression toward the mean**—the tendency for unusual events (or emotions) to "regress" (return) to their average state. Thus, extraordinary happenings (feeling low) tend to be followed by more ordinary ones (a return to our more usual state). Indeed, when things hit bottom, whatever we try—going to a psychotherapist, starting yoga, doing aerobic exercise—is more likely to be followed by improvement than by further descent.

> "Once you become sensitized to it, you see regression everywhere."
>
> Psychologist Daniel Kahneman (1985)

The point may seem obvious, yet we regularly miss it: We sometimes attribute what may be a normal regression (the expected return to normal) to something we have done. Consider:

- Students who score much lower or higher on a test than they usually do are likely, when retested, to return toward their average.

- Unusual ESP subjects who defy chance when first tested nearly always lose their "psychic powers" when retested (a phenomenon parapsychologists have called the decline effect).

- Coaches often yell at their players after an unusually bad first half. They may then feel rewarded for having done so when the team's performance improves (returns to normal) during the second half.

In each case, the cause-effect link may be genuine. Each may, however, be an instance of the natural tendency for behavior to regress from the unusual to the more usual. And this defines the task for therapy-efficacy research: Does the client's improvement following a particular therapy exceed what could be expected from the placebo and regression effects alone, shown by comparison with control groups?

regression toward the mean the tendency for extreme or unusual scores to fall back (regress) toward their average.

OUTCOME RESEARCH

How, then, can we objectively measure the effectiveness of psychotherapy if neither clients nor clinicians can tell us? How can we determine which people and problems are best helped, and by what type of psychotherapy?

In search of answers, psychologists have turned to controlled research studies. Similar research in the 1800s transformed the field of medicine. Physicians, skeptical of many of the fashionable treatments (bleeding, purging, infusions of plant and metal substances), began to realize that many patients got better on their own, without these treatments, and that others died despite them. Sorting fact from superstition required observing patients with and without a particular treatment. Typhoid fever patients, for example, often improved after being bled, convincing most physicians that the treatment worked. Not until a control group was given mere bed rest—and 70 percent were observed to improve after five weeks of fever—did physicians learn, to their shock, that the bleeding was worthless (Thomas, 1992).

In psychology, the opening challenge to the effectiveness of psychotherapy was issued by British psychologist Hans Eysenck (1952). Launching a spirited debate, he summarized studies showing that two-thirds of those receiving psychotherapy for nonpsychotic disorders improved markedly. To this day, no one disputes that optimistic estimate.

Why, then, are we still debating psychotherapy's effectiveness? Because Eysenck also reported similar improvement among *untreated* persons, such as those who were on waiting lists. With or without psychotherapy, he said, roughly two-thirds improved noticeably. Time was a great healer.

Later research revealed shortcomings in Eysenck's analyses; his sample was small (only 24 studies of psychotherapy outcomes in 1952). Today, hundreds of studies are available. The best are *randomized clinical trials,* in which researchers randomly assign people on a waiting list to therapy or to no therapy, and later evaluate everyone, using tests and assessments by others who don't know whether therapy was given. The results of many such studies are then digested by means of **meta-analysis,** a statistical procedure that combines the conclusions of a large number of different studies. Simply said, meta-analyses give us the bottom-line results of lots of studies.

Psychotherapists welcomed the first meta-analysis of some 475 psychotherapy outcome studies (Smith et al., 1980). It showed that the average therapy client ends up better off than 80 percent of the untreated individuals on waiting lists (**FIGURE 72.1**). The claim is modest—by definition, about 50 percent of untreated people also are better off than the average untreated person. Nevertheless, Mary Lee Smith and her colleagues exulted that "psychotherapy benefits people of all ages as reliably as schooling educates them, medicine cures them, or business turns a profit" (p. 183).

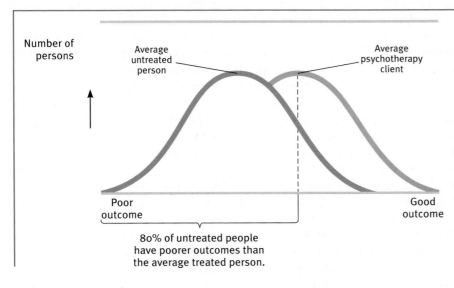

Figure 72.1

Treatment versus no treatment These two normal distribution curves based on a meta-analysis (combining data from 475 studies) show the improvement of untreated people and psychotherapy clients. The outcome for the average therapy client surpassed that for 80 percent of the untreated people. (Adapted from Smith et al., 1980.)

Dozens of subsequent summaries have now examined this question. Their verdict echoes the results of the earlier outcome studies: *Those not undergoing therapy often improve, but those undergoing therapy are more likely to improve more quickly, and with less risk of relapse.*

Is psychotherapy also cost-effective? Again, the answer is *Yes.* Studies show that when people seek psychological treatment, their search for other medical treatment drops—by 16 percent in one digest of 91 studies (Chiles et al., 1999). Given the staggering annual cost of psychological disorders and substance abuse—including crime, accidents, lost work, and treatment—psychotherapy is a good investment, much like money spent on prenatal and well-baby care. Both *reduce* long-term costs. Boosting employees' psychological well-being, for example, can lower medical costs, improve work efficiency, and diminish absenteeism.

But note that the claim—that psychotherapy, *on average,* is somewhat effective—refers to no one therapy in particular. It is like reassuring lung-cancer patients that "on average," medical treatment of health problems is effective. What people want to know is the effectiveness of a *particular* treatment for their specific problems.

meta-analysis a procedure for statistically combining the results of many different research studies.

The Relative Effectiveness of Different Psychotherapies

 Are some psychotherapies more effective than others for specific disorders?

So what can we tell people considering psychotherapy, and those paying for it, about *which* psychotherapy will be most effective for their problem? The statistical summaries and surveys fail to pinpoint any one type of therapy as generally superior (Smith et al., 1977, 1980). Clients seemed equally satisfied, *Consumer Reports* concluded, whether treated by a psychiatrist, psychologist, or social worker; whether seen in a group or individual context; whether the therapist had extensive or relatively limited training and experience (Seligman, 1995). Other studies concur. There is little if any connection between clinicians' experience, training, supervision, and licensing and their clients' outcomes (Luborsky et al., 2002; Wampold, 2007).

So, was the dodo bird in Alice in Wonderland right: "Everyone has won and all must have prizes"? Not quite. Some forms of therapy get prizes for particular problems, though there is often an overlapping—or comorbidity—of disorders. Behavioral conditioning therapies, for example, have achieved especially favorable results with specific behavior problems, such as bed-wetting, phobias, compulsions, marital problems, and sexual dysfunctions (Baker et al., 2008; Hunsley & DiGiulio, 2002; Shadish & Baldwin, 2005). Psychodynamic therapy has helped treat depression and anxiety (Driessen et al., 2010; Leichsenring & Rabung, 2008; Shedler, 2010b). And new studies confirm cognitive and cognitive-behavioral therapy's effectiveness in coping with anxiety, posttraumatic stress disorder, and depression (Baker et al., 2008; De Los Reyes & Kazdin, 2009; Stewart & Chambliss, 2009; Tolin, 2010).

Moreover, we can say that therapy is most effective when the problem is clear-cut (Singer, 1981; Westen & Morrison, 2001). Those who experience phobias or panic and those who are unassertive can hope for improvement. Those with less-focused problems, such as depression and anxiety, usually benefit in the short term but often relapse later. And those with the negative symptoms of chronic schizophrenia or a desire to change their entire personality are unlikely to benefit from therapy alone (Pfammatter et al., 2006; Zilbergeld, 1983). The more specific the problem, the greater the hope.

But no prizes—and little or no scientific support—go to certain other therapies (Arkowitz & Lilienfeld, 2006). We would all therefore be wise to avoid energy therapies that propose to manipulate people's invisible energy fields, recovered-memory therapies that aim to unearth "repressed memories" of early child abuse (Module 33), and rebirthing therapies that engage people in reenacting the supposed trauma of their birth.

As with some medical treatments, it's possible for psychological treatments not only to be ineffective but harmful—by making people worse or preventing their getting better (Barlow, 2010; Castonguay et al., 2010; Dimidjian & Hollon, 2010). The National Science and Technology Council cites the Scared Straight program (seeking to deter children and youth from crime) as an example of well-intentioned programs that have proved ineffective or even harmful. The evaluation question—which therapies get prizes and which do not?—lies at the heart of what some call psychology's civil war. To what extent should science guide both clinical practice and the willingness of health care providers and insurers to pay for therapy?

On the one side are research psychologists using scientific methods to extend the list of well-defined and validated therapies for various disorders. They decry clinicians who "give more weight to their personal experiences" (Baker et al., 2008). On the other side are nonscientist therapists who view their practice as more art than science, saying that people are too complex and therapy too intuitive to describe in a manual or test in an experiment. Between these two factions stand the science-oriented clinicians, who aim to base practice on evidence and make mental health professionals accountable for effectiveness.

To encourage **evidence-based practice** in psychology, the American Psychological Association and others (2006; Baker et al., 2008; Levant & Hasan, 2008) have followed the Institute of Medicine's lead, advocating that clinicians integrate the best available research with clinical expertise and with patient preferences and characteristics. Available therapies "should be rigorously evaluated" and then applied by clinicians who are mindful of their skills and of each patient's unique situation (**FIGURE 72.2**). Increasingly, insurer and government support for mental health services requires evidence-based practice. In 2007, for example, Britain's National Health Service announced that it would pour the equivalent of $600 million into training new mental health workers in evidence-based practices (such as cognitive-behavioral therapy) and to disseminating information about such treatments (DeAngelis, 2008).

"Whatever differences in treatment efficacy exist, they appear to be extremely small, at best." -BRUCE WAMPOLD ET AL., 1997

"Different sores have different salves." -ENGLISH PROVERB

evidence-based practice clinical decision making that integrates the best available research with clinical expertise and patient characteristics and preferences.

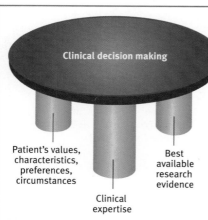

Figure 72.2

Evidence-based clinical decision making The ideal clinical decision making is a three-legged stool, upheld by research evidence, clinical expertise, and knowledge of the patient.

Evaluating Alternative Therapies

72-3 How do alternative therapies fare under scientific scrutiny?

The tendency of many abnormal states of mind to regress to normal, combined with the placebo effect, creates fertile soil for pseudotherapies. Bolstered by anecdotes, heralded by the media, and broadcast on the Internet, alternative therapies can spread like wildfire. In one national survey, 57 percent of those with a history of anxiety attacks and 54 percent of those with a history of depression had used alternative treatments, such as herbal medicine, massage, and spiritual healing (Kessler et al., 2001).

Testimonials aside, what does the evidence say? This is a tough question, because there is no evidence for or against most of them, though their proponents often feel personal experience is evidence enough. Some, however, have been the subject of controlled research. Let's consider two of them. As we do, remember that sifting sense from nonsense requires the scientific attitude: being skeptical but not cynical, open to surprises but not gullible.

EYE MOVEMENT DESENSITIZATION AND REPROCESSING (EMDR)

EMDR (eye movement desensitization and reprocessing) is a therapy adored by thousands and dismissed by thousands more as a sham—"an excellent vehicle for illustrating the differences between scientific and pseudoscientific therapy techniques," suggested James Herbert and seven others (2000). Francine Shapiro (1989, 2007) developed EMDR while walking in a park and observing that anxious thoughts vanished as her eyes spontaneously darted about. Offering her novel anxiety treatment to others, she had people imagine traumatic scenes while she triggered eye movements by waving her finger in front of their eyes, supposedly enabling them to unlock and reprocess previously frozen memories. Tens of thousands of mental health professionals from more than 75 countries have since undergone training (EMDR, 2011). Not since the similarly charismatic Franz Anton Mesmer introduced *animal magnetism* (hypnosis) more than two centuries ago (also after feeling inspired by an outdoor experience) has a new therapy attracted so many devotees so quickly.

Does it work? For 84 to 100 percent of single-trauma victims participating in four studies, the answer is *Yes,* reports Shapiro (1999, 2002). Moreover, the treatment need take no more than three 90-minute sessions. The Society of Clinical Psychology task force on empirically validated treatments acknowledges that EMDR is "probably efficacious" for the treatment of nonmilitary posttraumatic stress disorder (Chambless et al., 1997; see also Bisson & Andrew, 2007; Rodenburg et al., 2009; Seidler & Wagner, 2006).

Why, wonder the skeptics, would rapidly moving one's eyes while recalling traumas be therapeutic? Some argue that eye movements serve to relax or distract patients, thus allowing the memory-associated emotions to extinguish (Gunter & Bodner, 2008). Others believe that eye movements in themselves are *not* the therapeutic ingredient. Trials in which people imagined traumatic scenes and tapped a finger, or just stared straight ahead while the therapist's finger wagged, have produced therapeutic results (Devilly, 2003). EMDR does work better than doing nothing, acknowledge the skeptics (Lilienfeld & Arkowitz, 2007b), but many suspect that what is therapeutic is the combination of exposure therapy—repeatedly associating with traumatic memories a safe and reassuring context that provides some emotional distance from the experience—and a robust placebo effect. Had Mesmer's pseudotherapy been compared with no treatment at all, it, too (thanks to the healing power of positive belief), might have been found "probably efficacious," observed Richard McNally (1999).

> "Studies indicate that EMDR is just as effective with fixed eyes. If that conclusion is right, what's useful in the therapy (chiefly behavioral desensitization) is not new, and what's new is superfluous." -*Harvard Mental Health Letter*, 2002

LIGHT EXPOSURE THERAPY

Have you ever found yourself oversleeping, gaining weight, and feeling lethargic during the dark mornings and overcast days of winter? There likely was a survival advantage to your distant ancestors' slowing down and conserving energy during the dark days of winter. For some people, however, especially women and those living far from the equator, the wintertime

SEASONAL FUND-RAISING FOR THE YOUNG ENTREPRENEUR

GOT WINTER BLUES?! LIGHT Therapy 5¢

©2009 Kathryn LeMieux, distributed by King Features Syndicate

blahs constitute a seasonal pattern for major depressive disorder. To counteract these dark spirits, National Institute of Mental Health researchers the early 1980s had an idea: Give people a timed daily dose of intense light. Sure enough, people reported they felt better.

Was this a bright idea, or another dim-witted example of the placebo effect? Research sheds some light. One study exposed some people with a seasonal pattern in their depression symptoms to 90 minutes of bright light and others to a sham placebo treatment—a hissing "negative ion generator" about which the staff expressed similar enthusiasm (but which was not even turned on). After four weeks, 61 percent of those exposed to morning light had greatly improved, as had 50 percent of those exposed to evening light and 32 percent of those exposed to the placebo (Eastman et al., 1998). Other studies have found that 30 minutes of exposure to 10,000-lux white fluorescent light produced relief for more than half the people receiving morning light therapy (Flory et al., 2010; Terman et al., 1998, 2001). From 20 carefully controlled trials we have a verdict (Golden et al., 2005; Wirz-Justice, 2009): Morning bright light does indeed dim depression symptoms for many of those suffering in a seasonal pattern. Moreover, it does so as effectively as taking antidepressant drugs or undergoing cognitive-behavioral therapy (Lam et al., 2006; Rohan et al., 2007). The effects are clear in brain scans; light therapy sparks activity in a brain region that influences the body's arousal and hormones (Ishida et al., 2005).

Light therapy To counteract winter depression, some people spend time each morning exposed to intense light that mimics natural outdoor light. Light boxes with the appropriate intensity are available from health supply and lighting stores.

Commonalities Among Psychotherapies

72-4 What three elements are shared by all forms of psychotherapy?

Why have studies found little correlation between therapists' training and experience and clients' outcomes? In search of some answers, Jerome Frank (1982), Marvin Goldfried (Goldfried & Padawer, 1982), Hans Strupp (1986), and Bruce Wampold (2001, 2007) have studied the common ingredients of various therapies. They suggest that all therapies offer at least three benefits:

- **Hope for demoralized people** People seeking therapy typically feel anxious, depressed, devoid of self-esteem, and incapable of turning things around. What any therapy offers is the expectation that, with commitment from the therapy seeker, things can and will get better. This belief, apart from any therapeutic technique, may function as a placebo, improving morale, creating feelings of self-efficacy, and diminishing symptoms (Prioleau et al., 1983).

- **A new perspective** Every therapy also offers people a plausible explanation of their symptoms and an alternative way of looking at themselves or responding to their world. Armed with a believable fresh perspective, they may approach life with a new attitude, open to making changes in their behaviors and their views of themselves.

- **An empathic, trusting, caring relationship** To say that therapy outcome is unrelated to training and experience is not to say all *therapists* are equally effective. No matter what therapeutic technique they use, effective therapists are empathic people who seek to understand another's experience; who communicate their care and concern to the client; and who earn the client's trust through respectful listening, reassurance, and advice. Marvin Goldfried and his associates (1998) found these qualities in recorded therapy sessions from 36 recognized master therapists. Some took a cognitive-behavioral approach, others emphasized psychodynamic teachings. Regardless, the striking finding was how *similar* they were. At key moments, the empathic therapists of both persuasions would help clients evaluate themselves, link one aspect of their life with another, and gain insight into their interactions with others.

The emotional bond between therapist and client—the **therapeutic alliance**—is a key aspect of effective therapy (Klein et al., 2003; Wampold, 2001). One U.S. National Institute of Mental Health depression-treatment study confirmed that the most effective therapists were those who were perceived as most empathic and caring and who established the closest therapeutic bonds with their clients (Blatt et al., 1996). That all therapies offer hope through a fresh perspective offered by a caring person is what also enables paraprofessionals (briefly trained caregivers) to assist so many troubled people so effectively (Christensen & Jacobson, 1994).

These three common elements are also part of what the growing numbers of self-help and support groups offer their members. And they are part of what traditional healers have offered (Jackson, 1992). Healers everywhere—special people to whom others disclose their suffering, whether psychiatrists, witch doctors, or shamans—have listened in order to understand and to empathize, reassure, advise, console, interpret, or explain (Torrey, 1986). Such qualities may explain why people who feel supported by close relationships—who enjoy the fellowship and friendship of caring people—are less likely to need or seek therapy (Frank, 1982; O'Connor & Brown, 1984).

A caring relationship Effective therapists form a bond of trust with their clients.

* * *

To recap, people who seek help usually improve. So do many of those who do not undergo psychotherapy, and that is a tribute to our human resourcefulness and our capacity to care for one another. Nevertheless, though the therapist's orientation and experience appear not to matter much, people who receive some psychotherapy usually improve more than those who do not. People with clear-cut, specific problems tend to improve the most.

Culture, Gender, and Values in Psychotherapy

 How do culture, gender, and values influence the therapist-client relationship?

therapeutic alliance a bond of trust and mutual understanding between a therapist and client, who work together constructively to overcome the client's problem.

All therapies offer hope, and nearly all therapists attempt to enhance their clients' sensitivity, openness, personal responsibility, and sense of purpose (Jensen & Bergin, 1988). But in matters of diversity, therapists differ from one another and may differ from their clients (Delaney et al., 2007; Kelly, 1990).

These differences can become significant when a therapist from one culture or gender meets a client from another. In North America, Europe, and Australia, for example, most therapists reflect their culture's individualism, which often gives priority to personal desires and identity, particularly for men. Clients who are immigrants from Asian countries, where people are mindful of others' expectations, may have trouble relating to therapies that require them to think only of their own well-being. And women seeking therapy who are from a collectivist culture might be doubly discomfited. Such differences help explain minority populations' reluctance to use mental health services and their tendency to prematurely terminate therapy (Chen et al., 2009; Sue, 2006). In one experiment, Asian-American clients matched with counselors who shared their cultural values (rather than mismatched with those who did not) perceived more counselor empathy and felt a stronger alliance with the counselor (Kim et al., 2005). Recognizing that therapists and clients may differ in their values, communication styles, and language, American Psychological Association–accredited therapy training programs now provide training in cultural sensitivity and recruit members of underrepresented cultural groups.

Another area of potential conflict related to values is religion. Highly religious people may prefer and benefit from religiously similar therapists (Masters, 2010; Smith et al., 2007; Wade et al., 2006). They may have trouble establishing an emotional bond with a therapist who does not share their values.

Albert Ellis, who advocated the aggressive rational-emotive behavior therapy (REBT), and Allen Bergin, co-editor of the *Handbook of Psychotherapy and Behavior Change,* illustrated how sharply therapists can differ, and how those differences can affect their view of a healthy person. Ellis (1980) assumed that "no one and nothing is supreme," that "self-gratification" should be encouraged, and that "unequivocal love, commitment, service, and . . . fidelity to any interpersonal commitment, especially marriage, leads to harmful consequences." Bergin (1980) assumed the opposite—that "because God is supreme, humility and the acceptance of divine authority are virtues," that "self-control and committed love and self-sacrifice are to be encouraged," and that "infidelity to any interpersonal commitment, especially marriage, leads to harmful consequences."

Bergin and Ellis disagreed more radically than most therapists on what values are healthiest. In so doing, however, they agreed on a more general point: Psychotherapists' personal beliefs influence their practice. Because clients tend to adopt their therapists' values (Worthington et al., 1996), some psychologists believe therapists should divulge those values more openly. (For those thinking about seeking therapy, Close-up: A Consumer's Guide to Psychotherapists offers some tips on when to seek help and how to start searching for a therapist who shares your perspective and goals.)

Close-up

A Consumer's Guide to Psychotherapists

 What should a person look for when selecting a therapist?

Life for everyone is marked by a mix of serenity and stress, blessing and bereavement, good moods and bad. So, when should we seek a mental health professional's help? The American Psychological Association offers these common trouble signals:

- Feelings of hopelessness
- Deep and lasting depression
- Self-destructive behavior, such as substance use disorder
- Disruptive fears

- Sudden mood shifts
- Thoughts of suicide
- Compulsive rituals, such as hand washing
- Hearing voices or seeing things that others don't experience

In looking for a therapist, you may want to have a preliminary consultation with two or three. High school counseling offices are generally good starting points, and may offer some free services. You can describe your problem and learn each therapist's treatment approach. You can ask questions about the therapist's values, credentials (**TABLE 72.1**), and fees. And you can assess your own feelings about each of them. The emotional bond between therapist and client is perhaps the most important factor in effective therapy.

TABLE 72.1
Therapists and Their Training

Type	Description
Clinical psychologists	Most are psychologists with a Ph.D. (includes research training) or Psy.D. (focuses on therapy) supplemented by a supervised internship and, often, postdoctoral training. About half work in agencies and institutions, half in private practice.
Psychiatrists	Psychiatrists are physicians who specialize in the treatment of psychological disorders. Not all psychiatrists have had extensive training in psychotherapy, but as M.D.s or D.O.s they can prescribe medications. Thus, they tend to see those with the most serious problems. Many have their own private practice.
Clinical or psychiatric social workers	A two-year master of social work graduate program plus postgraduate supervision prepares some social workers to offer psychotherapy, mostly to people with everyday personal and family problems. About half have earned the National Association of Social Workers' designation of clinical social worker.
Counselors	Marriage and family counselors specialize in problems arising from family relations. Clergy provide counseling to countless people. Abuse counselors work with substance abusers and with spouse and child abusers and their victims. Mental health and other counselors may be required to have a two-year master's degree.

Preventing Psychological Disorders

72-7 What is the rationale for preventive mental health programs?

We have seen that lifestyle change can help *reverse* some of the symptoms of psychological disorders. Might such change also *prevent* some disorders by building individuals' **resilience**—an ability to cope with stress and recover from adversity? Faced with unforeseen trauma, most adults exhibit resilience. This was true of New Yorkers in the aftermath of the September 11 terrorist attacks, especially those who enjoyed supportive close relationships and who had not recently experienced other stressful events (Bonanno et al., 2007). More than 9 in 10 New Yorkers, although stunned and grief-stricken by 9/11, did *not* have a dysfunctional stress reaction. By the following January, the stress symptoms of those who did were mostly gone (Person et al., 2006). Even in groups of combat-stressed veterans and political rebels who have survived dozens of episodes of torture, most do not later exhibit posttraumatic stress disorder (Mineka & Zinbarg, 1996).

Psychotherapies and biomedical therapies tend to locate the cause of psychological disorders within the person with the disorder. We infer that people who act cruelly must be cruel and that people who act "crazy" must be "sick." We attach labels to such people, thereby distinguishing them from "normal" folks. It follows, then, that we try to treat "abnormal" people by giving them insight into their problems, by changing their thinking, by helping them gain control with drugs.

There is an alternative viewpoint: We could interpret many psychological disorders as understandable responses to a disturbing and stressful society. According to this view, it is not just the person who needs treatment, but also the person's social context. Better to prevent a problem by reforming a sick situation and by developing people's coping competencies than to wait for a problem to arise and then treat it.

A story about the rescue of a drowning person from a rushing river illustrates this viewpoint: Having successfully administered first aid to the first victim, the rescuer spots another struggling person and pulls her out, too. After a half-dozen repetitions, the rescuer suddenly turns and starts running away while the river sweeps yet another floundering person into view. "Aren't you going to rescue that fellow?" asks a bystander. "Heck no," the rescuer replies. "I'm going upstream to find out what's pushing all these people in."

Preventive mental health is upstream work. It seeks to prevent psychological casualties by identifying and alleviating the conditions that cause them. As George Albee (1986) pointed out, there is abundant evidence that poverty, meaningless work, constant criticism, unemployment, racism, sexism, and heterosexism undermine people's sense of competence, personal control, and self-esteem. Such stresses increase their risk of depression, alcohol use disorder, and suicide.

We who care about preventing psychological casualties should, Albee contended, support programs that alleviate these demoralizing situations. We eliminated smallpox not by treating the afflicted but by inoculating the unafflicted. We conquered yellow fever by controlling mosquitoes. Preventing psychological problems means empowering those who feel helpless, changing environments that breed loneliness, renewing the disintegrating family, promoting communication training for couples, and bolstering parents' and teachers' skills. "Everything aimed at improving the human condition, at making life more fulfilling and meaningful, may be considered part of primary prevention of mental or emotional disturbance" (Kessler & Albee, 1975, p. 557). That includes the cognitive training that promotes positive thinking in children at risk for depression (Brunwasser et al., 2009; Gillham et al., 2006; Stice et al., 2009). A 2009 National Research Council and Institute of Medicine report—*Preventing Mental, Emotional, and Behavioral Disorders Among Young People*—offers encouragement. It documents that intervention efforts often based on cognitive-behavioral therapy principles significantly boost child and adolescent flourishing. Through such preventive efforts and healthy lifestyles, fewer of us will fall into the rushing river of psychological disorders.

resilience the personal strength that helps most people cope with stress and recover from adversity and even trauma.

"It is better to prevent than to cure." -PERUVIAN FOLK WISDOM

"Mental disorders arise from physical ones, and likewise physical disorders arise from mental ones." -THE MAHABHARATA, 200 B.C.E.

Before You Move On

▶ **ASK YOURSELF**

Can you think of a specific way that improving the environment in your own community might prevent some psychological disorders among its residents?

▶ **TEST YOURSELF**

What is the difference between preventive mental health and psychological or biomedical therapy?

Answers to the Test Yourself questions can be found in Appendix E at the end of the book.

Module 72 Review

 Does psychotherapy work? Who decides?

- Clients' and therapists' positive testimonials cannot prove that therapy is actually effective, and the placebo effect and *regression toward the mean* (the tendency for extreme or unusual scores to fall back toward their average) make it difficult to judge whether improvement occurred because of the treatment.

- Using *meta-analyses* to statistically combine the results of hundreds of randomized psychotherapy outcome studies, researchers have found that those not undergoing treatment often improve, but those undergoing psychotherapy are more likely to improve more quickly, and with less chance of relapse.

 Are some psychotherapies more effective than others for specific disorders?

- No one type of psychotherapy is generally superior to all others. Therapy is most effective for those with clear-cut, specific problems.

- Some therapies—such as behavior conditioning for treating phobias and compulsions—are more effective for specific disorders.

- Psychodynamic therapy helped treat depression and anxiety, and cognitive and cognitive-behavioral therapies have been effective in coping with anxiety, obsessive-compulsive disorder, posttraumatic stress disorder, and depression.

- *Evidence-based practice* integrates the best available research with clinicians' expertise and patients' characteristics, preferences, and circumstances.

 How do alternative therapies fare under scientific scrutiny?

- Controlled research has found some benefits of eye movement desensitization and reprocessing (EMDR) therapy for PTSD, though possibly for reasons unrelated to eye movements.

- Light exposure therapy does seem to relieve depression symptoms for those with a seasonal pattern of major depressive disorder by activating a brain region that influences arousal and hormones.

 What three elements are shared by all forms of psychotherapy?

- All psychotherapies offer new hope for demoralized people; a fresh perspective; and (if the therapist is effective) an empathic, trusting, and caring relationship.

- The emotional bond of trust and understanding between therapist and client—the *therapeutic alliance*—is an important element in effective therapy.

 How do culture, gender, and values influence the therapist-client relationship?

- Therapists differ in the values that influence their goals in therapy and their views of progress. These differences may create problems if therapists and clients differ in their cultural, gender, or religious perspectives.

What should a person look for when selecting a therapist?

- A person seeking therapy may want to ask about the therapist's treatment approach, values, credentials, and fees.

- An important consideration is whether the therapy seeker feels comfortable and able to establish a bond with the therapist.

72-7 **What is the rationale for preventive mental health programs?**

- Preventive mental health programs are based on the idea that many psychological disorders could be prevented by changing oppressive, esteem-destroying environments into more benevolent, nurturing environments that foster growth, self-confidence, and *resilience*.

Multiple-Choice Questions

1. Which of the following does the text's author call psychology's most powerful tool for sorting reality from wishful thinking?
   a. ESP or "psychic powers"
   b. Regression toward the mean
   c. Client perception
   d. Control group
   e. Placebo effect

2. Which of the following best describes meta-analysis?
   a. Evidenced-based practice
   b. A treatment versus no treatment group
   c. A tendency for smaller scores to move toward the average
   d. Regressing from unusual to usual
   e. A way to combine the results of lots of studies

3. Which of the following is the best phrase for a bond of trust and mutual understanding between a therapist and client who are working to overcome the client's problem?
   a. Therapeutic alliance
   b. EMDR
   c. Evidence-based practice
   d. Meta-analysis
   e. Outcome research

Practice FRQs

1. Explain the three sides of evidence-based clinical decision making.

Answer

1 point: Using the best available research evidence.

1 point: Clinical expertise.

1 point: Using a patient's values, preferences, and circumstances.

2. Psychotherapies have many common ingredients. Identify three commonly agreed-upon benefits of psychotherapies.

(3 points)

Module 73

The Biomedical Therapies

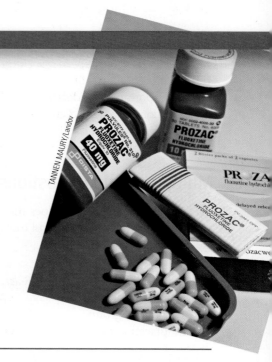

Module Learning Objectives

73-1 Identify and describe the drug therapies, and explain how double-blind studies help researchers evaluate a drug's effectiveness.

73-2 Describe the use of brain stimulation techniques and psychosurgery in treating specific disorders.

73-3 Describe how, by taking care of themselves with a healthy lifestyle, people might find some relief from depression, and explain how this reflects our being biopsychosocial systems.

P sychotherapy is one way to treat psychological disorders. The other, often used with serious disorders, is biomedical therapy—physically changing the brain's functioning by altering its chemistry with drugs, or affecting its circuitry with electroconvulsive shock, magnetic impulses, or psychosurgery. Primary care providers prescribe most drugs for anxiety and depression, followed by psychiatrists and, in some states, psychologists.

psychopharmacology the study of the effects of drugs on mind and behavior.

Drug Therapies

73-1 What are the drug therapies? How do double-blind studies help researchers evaluate a drug's effectiveness?

By far the most widely used biomedical treatments today are the drug therapies. Since the 1950s, discoveries in **psychopharmacology** (the study of drug effects on mind and behavior) have revolutionized the treatment of people with severe disorders, liberating hundreds of thousands from hospital confinement. Thanks to drug therapy—and to efforts to minimize involuntary hospitalization and to support people through community mental health programs—the resident population of mental hospitals is a small fraction of what it was a half-century ago. For some unable to care for themselves, however, release from hospitals has meant homelessness, not liberation.

Almost any new treatment, including drug therapy, is greeted by an initial wave of enthusiasm as many people apparently improve. But that enthusiasm often diminishes after researchers subtract the rates of (1) normal recovery among untreated persons and (2) recovery due to the placebo effect, which arises from the positive expectations of patients and mental health workers alike. So, to evaluate the effectiveness of any new drug, researchers give half the patients the drug, and the other half a similar-appearing placebo. Because neither the staff nor the patients know who gets which, this is called a *double-blind procedure*. The good news: In double-blind studies, some drugs have proven useful.

Drug or placebo effect? For many people, depression lifts while taking an antidepressant drug. But people given a placebo may experience the same effect. Double-blind clinical trials suggest that, especially for those with severe depression, antidepressant drugs do have at least a modest clinical effect.

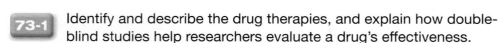

"Our psychopharmacologist is a genius."

Antipsychotic Drugs

The revolution in drug therapy for psychological disorders began with the accidental discovery that certain drugs, used for other medical purposes, calmed patients with *psychoses* (disorders in which hallucinations or delusions indicate some loss of contact with reality). These **antipsychotic drugs,** such as chlorpromazine (sold as Thorazine), dampened responsiveness to irrelevant stimuli. Thus, they provided the most help to patients experiencing positive symptoms of schizophrenia, such as auditory hallucinations and paranoia (Lehman et al., 1998; Lenzenweger et al., 1989).

The molecules of most conventional antipsychotic drugs are antagonists; they are similar enough to molecules of the neurotransmitter dopamine to occupy its receptor sites and block its activity. This finding reinforces the idea that an overactive dopamine system contributes to schizophrenia.

Antipsychotics also have powerful side effects. Some produce sluggishness, tremors, and twitches similar to those of Parkinson's disease (Kaplan & Saddock, 1989). Long-term use of antipsychotics can produce *tardive dyskinesia,* with involuntary movements of the facial muscles (such as grimacing), tongue, and limbs. Although not more effective in controlling schizophrenia symptoms, many of the newer-generation antipsychotics, such as risperidone (Risperdal) and olanzapine (Zyprexa), have fewer of these effects. These drugs may, however, increase the risk of obesity and diabetes (Buchanan et al., 2010; Tiihonen et al., 2009).

Antipsychotics, combined with life-skills programs and family support, have given new hope to many people with schizophrenia (Guo, 2010). Hundreds of thousands of patients have left the wards of mental hospitals and returned to work and to near-normal lives (Leucht et al., 2003).

Antianxiety Drugs

Like alcohol, **antianxiety drugs,** such as Xanax or Ativan, depress central nervous system activity (and so should not be used in combination with alcohol). Antianxiety drugs are often used in combination with psychological therapy. One antianxiety drug, the antibiotic D-cycloserine, acts upon a receptor that, in combination with behavioral treatments, facilitates the extinction of learned fears. Experiments indicate that the drug enhances the benefits of exposure therapy and helps relieve the symptoms of posttraumatic stress disorder and obsessive-compulsive disorder (Davis, 2005; Kushner et al., 2007).

A criticism sometimes made of the behavior therapies—that they reduce symptoms without resolving underlying problems—is also made of drug therapies. Unlike the behavior therapies, however, these substances may be used as an ongoing treatment. "Popping a Xanax" at the first sign of tension can create a learned response; the immediate relief reinforces a person's tendency to take drugs when anxious. Antianxiety drugs can also be addicting. After heavy use, people who stop taking them may experience increased anxiety, insomnia, and other withdrawal symptoms.

Over the dozen years at the end of the twentieth century, the rate of outpatient treatment for anxiety disorders, obsessive-compulsive disorder, and posttraumatic stress disorder nearly doubled. The proportion of psychiatric patients receiving medication during that time increased from 52 to 70 percent (Olfson et al., 2004). And the new standard drug treatment for anxiety disorders? Antidepressants.

Antidepressant Drugs

The **antidepressants** were named for their ability to lift people up from a state of depression, and this was their main use until recently. The label is a bit of a misnomer now that these drugs are increasingly being used to successfully treat anxiety disorders, obsessive-compulsive disorder, and posttraumatic stress disorder. These drugs are agonists; they work by increasing the availability of certain neurotransmitters, such as norepinephrine or serotonin, which

FYI

Perhaps you can guess an occasional side effect of L-dopa, a drug that raises dopamine levels for Parkinson's patients: hallucinations.

antipsychotic drugs drugs used to treat schizophrenia and other forms of severe thought disorder.

antianxiety drugs drugs used to control anxiety and agitation.

antidepressant drugs drugs used to treat depression, anxiety disorders, obsessive-compulsive disorder, and posttraumatic stress disorder. (Several widely used antidepressant drugs are *selective serotonin reuptake inhibitors—SSRIs.*)

© John Greim/Age fotostock

elevate arousal and mood and appear scarce when a person experiences feelings of depression or anxiety. Fluoxetine, which tens of millions of users worldwide have known as Prozac, falls into this category of drugs. The most commonly prescribed drugs in this group, including Prozac and its cousins Zoloft and Paxil, work by blocking the reabsorption and removal of serotonin from synapses (**FIGURE 73.1**). Given their use in treating disorders other than depression—from anxiety to strokes—this group of drugs is most often called *SSRIs (selective serotonin reuptake inhibitors)* rather than antidepressants (Kramer, 2011). Some of the older antidepressant drugs work by blocking the reabsorption or breakdown of both norepinephrine and serotonin. Though effective, these dual-action drugs have more potential side effects, such as dry mouth, weight gain, hypertension, or dizzy spells (Anderson, 2000; Mulrow, 1999). Administering them by means of a patch, bypassing the intestines and liver, helps reduce such side effects (Bodkin & Amsterdam, 2002).

After the introduction of SSRI drugs, the percentage of patients receiving medication for depression jumped dramatically, from 70 percent in 1987, the year before SSRIs were introduced, to 89 percent in 2001 (Olfson et al., 2003; Stafford et al., 2001). From 1996 to 2005, the number of Americans prescribed antidepressant drugs doubled, from 13 to 27 million (Olfson & Marcus, 2009). Between 2002 and 2007 in Australia, antidepressant drug use increased 41 percent (Hollingworth et al., 2010).

Be advised: Patients with depression who begin taking antidepressants do not wake up the next day singing "It's a beautiful day"! Although the drugs begin to influence neurotransmission within hours, their full psychological effect often requires four weeks. One possible reason for the delay is that increased serotonin promotes *neurogenesis*—the birth of new brain cells, perhaps reversing stress-induced loss of neurons (Becker & Wojtowicz, 2007; Jacobs, 2004).

Antidepressant drugs are not the only way to give the body a lift. Aerobic exercise, which calms people who feel anxious and energizes those who feel depressed, does about as much good for some people with mild to moderate depression, and has additional positive side effects (more on this topic later in this module). Cognitive therapy, by helping people reverse their habitual negative thinking style, can boost the drug-aided relief from depression and reduce the post-treatment risk of relapse (Hollon et al., 2002; Keller et al., 2000; Vittengl et al., 2007). Better yet, some studies suggest, is to attack depression (and anxiety) from both below and above (Cuijpers et al., 2010; Walkup et al., 2008). Use antidepressant drugs (which work, bottom-up, on the emotion-forming limbic system) in conjunction with cognitive-behavioral therapy (which works top-down, starting with changed frontal lobe activity).

Figure 73.1

Biology of antidepressants
Shown here is the action of Prozac, which partially blocks the reuptake of serotonin.

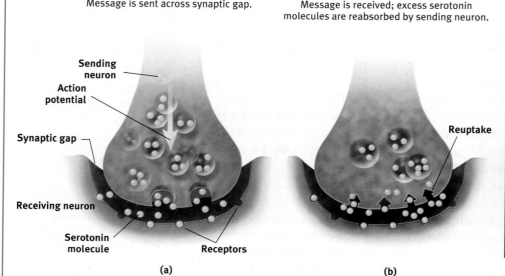

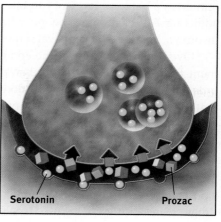

Message is sent across synaptic gap.

Message is received; excess serotonin molecules are reabsorbed by sending neuron.

Prozac partially blocks normal reuptake of the neurotransmitter serotonin; excess serotonin in synapse enhances its mood-lifting effect.

Sending neuron

Action potential

Synaptic gap

Receiving neuron

Serotonin molecule

Receptors

Reuptake

Serotonin

Prozac

(a)　　　(b)　　　(c)

Researchers generally agree that people with depression often improve after a month on antidepressants. But after allowing for natural recovery and the placebo effect, how big is the drug effect? Not big, report Irving Kirsch and his colleagues (1998, 2002, 2010). Their analyses of double-blind clinical trials indicate that the placebo effect accounted for about 75 percent of the active drug's effect. In a follow-up review that included unpublished clinical trials, the antidepressant drug effect was again modest (Kirsch et al., 2008). The placebo effect was less for those with severe depression, which made the added benefit of the drug somewhat greater for them. "Given these results, there seems little reason to prescribe antidepressant medication to any but the most severely depressed patients, unless alternative treatments have failed," Kirsch concluded (BBC, 2008). A newer analysis confirms that the antidepressant benefit compared with placebos is "minimal or nonexistent, on average, in patients with mild or moderate symptoms." For those folks, aerobic exercise or psychotherapy is often effective. But among patients with "very severe" depression, the medication advantage becomes "substantial" (Fournier et al., 2010).

"If this doesn't help you don't worry, it's a placebo."

> "No twisted thought without a twisted molecule." -ATTRIBUTED TO PSYCHOLOGIST RALPH GERARD

Mood-Stabilizing Medications

In addition to antipsychotic, antianxiety, and antidepressant drugs, psychiatrists have *mood-stabilizing drugs* in their arsenal. For those suffering the emotional highs and lows of bipolar disorder, the simple salt *lithium* can be an effective mood stabilizer. Australian physician John Cade discovered this in the 1940s when he administered lithium to a patient with severe mania and the patient became perfectly well in less than a week (Snyder, 1986). After suffering mood swings for years, about 7 in 10 people with bipolar disorder benefit from a long-term daily dose of this cheap salt, which helps prevent or ease manic episodes and, to a lesser extent, lifts depression (Solomon et al., 1995). It also protects neural health, thus reducing bipolar patients' vulnerability to significant cognitive decline (Kessing et al., 2010).

Lithium also reduces bipolar patients' risk of suicide—to about one-sixth of bipolar patients not taking lithium (Tondo et al., 1997). Lithium amounts in drinking water have also correlated with lower suicide rates (across 18 Japanese cities and towns) and lower crime rates (across 27 Texas counties) (Ohgami et al., 2009; Schrauzer & Shrestha, 1990, 2010; Terao et al., 2010). Although we do not fully understand why, lithium works. And so does Depakote, a drug originally used to treat epilepsy and more recently found effective in the control of manic episodes associated with bipolar disorder.

> "Lithium prevents my seductive but disastrous highs, diminishes my depressions, clears out the wool and webbing from my disordered thinking, slows me down, gentles me out, keeps me from ruining my career and relationships, keeps me out of a hospital, alive, and makes psychotherapy possible." -KAY REDFIELD JAMISON, *AN UNQUIET MIND*, 1995

Brain Stimulation

 73-2 How are brain stimulation and psychosurgery used in treating specific disorders?

Electroconvulsive Therapy

A more controversial brain manipulation occurs through shock treatment, or **electroconvulsive therapy (ECT)**. When ECT was first introduced in 1938, the wide-awake patient was strapped to a table and jolted with roughly 100 volts of electricity to the brain, producing racking convulsions and brief unconsciousness. ECT therefore gained a barbaric image, one that lingers. Today, however, the patient receives a general anesthetic and a muscle relaxant (to prevent injury from seizures) before a psychiatrist delivers 30 to 60 seconds of electrical current (**FIGURE 73.2** on the next page). Within 30 minutes, the patient awakens and remembers nothing of the treatment or of the preceding hours. After three such sessions each week for two to four weeks, 80 percent or more of people receiving ECT improve markedly, showing some memory loss for the treatment period but no discernible brain damage.

> **electroconvulsive therapy (ECT)** a biomedical therapy for severely depressed patients in which a brief electric current is sent through the brain of an anesthetized patient.

> **FYI**
>
> The medical use of electricity is an ancient practice. Physicians treated the Roman Emperor Claudius (10 B.C.E.–54 C.E.) for headaches by pressing electric eels to his temples.

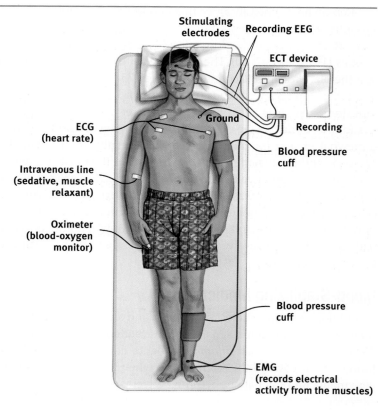

Figure 73.2

Electroconvulsive therapy
Although controversial, ECT is often
an effective treatment for depression
that does not respond to drug
therapy. "Electroconvulsive" is no
longer accurate because patients
are now given a drug that prevents
injurious seizures.

ECT proponent In her book, *Shock:
The Healing Power of Electroconvulsive
Therapy* (2006), Kitty Dukakis writes,
"I used to . . . be unable to shake the
dread even when I was feeling good,
because I knew the bad feelings would
return. ECT has wiped away that
foreboding. It has given me a sense of
control, of hope."

Study after study confirms that ECT is an effective treatment for severe depression in
"treatment-resistant" patients who have not responded to drug therapy (Bailine et al.,
2010; Fink, 2009; UK ECT Review Group, 2003). An editorial in the *Journal of the American Medical Association* concluded that "the results of ECT in treating severe depression
are among the most positive treatment effects in all of medicine" (Glass, 2001).

How does ECT alleviate severe depression? After more than 70 years, no one
knows for sure. One recipient likened ECT to the smallpox vaccine, which was saving lives before we knew how it worked. Others think of it as rebooting their cerebral
computer. But what makes it therapeutic? Perhaps the shock-induced seizures calm
neural centers where overactivity produces depression. ECT, like antidepressant
drugs and exercise, also appears to boost the production of new brain cells (Bolwig
& Madsen, 2007).

Skeptics have raised one other possible explanation for how ECT works: as a placebo
effect. Most ECT studies have failed to contain a control condition in which people are
randomly assigned to receive the same general anesthesia and simulated ECT without the
shock. When given this placebo treatment, note John Read and Richard Bentall (2010),
the positive expectation is therapeutic, though a Food and Drug Administration (2011)
research review concludes that ECT is more effective than a placebo, especially in the
short run.

ECT is now administered with briefer pulses, sometimes only to the brain's right side
and with less memory disruption (HMHL, 2007). Yet no matter how impressive the results,
the idea of electrically shocking people still strikes many as barbaric, especially given our
ignorance about why ECT works. Moreover, about 4 in 10 ECT-treated patients relapse into
depression within six months (Kellner et al., 2006). Nevertheless, in the minds of many psychiatrists and patients, ECT is a lesser evil than severe depression's misery, anguish, and risk
of suicide. As research psychologist Norman Endler (1982) reported after ECT alleviated his
deep depression, "A miracle had happened in two weeks."

Alternative Neurostimulation Therapies

Two other neural stimulation techniques—magnetic stimulation and deep-brain stimulation—are raising hopes for gentler alternatives that jump-start neural circuits in the depressed brain.

MAGNETIC STIMULATION

Depressed moods seem to improve when repeated pulses surge through a magnetic coil held close to a person's skull (**FIGURE 73.3**). The painless procedure—called **repetitive transcranial magnetic stimulation (rTMS)**—is performed on wide-awake patients over several weeks. Unlike ECT, the rTMS procedure produces no seizures, memory loss, or other serious side effects. (Headaches can result.)

   Initial studies have found "modest" positive benefits of rTMS (Daskalakis et al., 2008; George et al., 2010; López-Ibor et al., 2008). How it works is unclear. One possible explanation is that the stimulation energizes the brain's left frontal lobe, which is relatively inactive during depression (Helmuth, 2001). Repeated stimulation may cause nerve cells to form new functioning circuits through the process of long-term potentiation. (See Module 32 for more details on long-term potentiation.)

repetitive transcranial magnetic stimulation (rTMS) the application of repeated pulses of magnetic energy to the brain; used to stimulate or suppress brain activity.

FYI

A meta-analysis of 17 clinical experiments found that one other stimulation procedure alleviates depression: massage therapy (Hou et al., 2010).

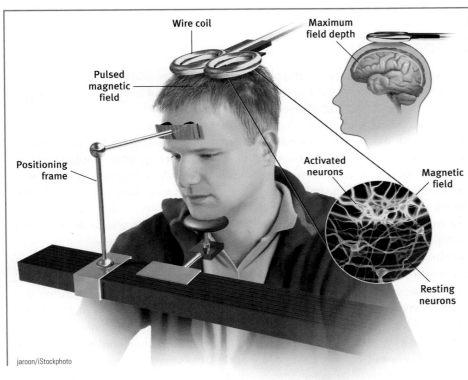

Wire coil
Maximum field depth
Pulsed magnetic field
Positioning frame
Activated neurons
Magnetic field
Resting neurons

jaroon/iStockphoto

Figure 73.3

Magnets for the mind Repetitive transcranial magnetic stimulation (rTMS) sends a painless magnetic field through the skull to the surface of the cortex. Pulses can be used to stimulate or dampen activity in various cortical areas. (From George, 2003.)

DEEP-BRAIN STIMULATION

Other patients whose depression has resisted both drugs that flood the body and ECT that jolts at least half the brain have benefited from an experimental treatment pinpointed at a depression center in the brain. Neuroscientist Helen Mayberg and her colleagues (2005, 2006, 2007, 2009) have been focusing on a neural hub that bridges the thinking frontal lobes to the limbic system. This area, which is overactive in the brain of a depressed or temporarily sad person, calms when treated by ECT or antidepressants. To experimentally excite neurons that inhibit this negative emotion-feeding activity, Mayberg drew upon the deep-brain stimulation technology sometimes used to treat Parkinson's tremors. Among an initial 20 patients receiving implanted electrodes and a pacemaker stimulator, 12 experienced relief, which was sustained over three to six years of follow-up (Kennedy et al., 2011).

A depression switch?
By comparing the brains of patients with and without depression, researcher Helen Mayberg identified a brain area that appears active in people who are depressed or sad, and whose activity may be calmed by deep-brain stimulation.

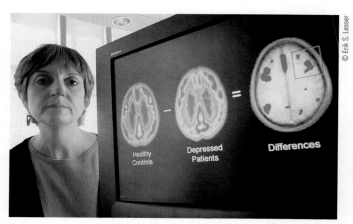

psychosurgery surgery that removes or destroys brain tissue in an effort to change behavior.

lobotomy a psychosurgical procedure once used to calm uncontrollably emotional or violent patients. The procedure cut the nerves connecting the frontal lobes to the emotion-controlling centers of the inner brain.

Some felt suddenly more aware and became more talkative and engaged; others improved only slightly if at all. Future research will explore whether Mayberg has discovered a switch that can lift depression. Other researchers are following up on reports that deep-brain stimulation can offer relief to people with obsessive-compulsive disorder (Rabins et al., 2009).

Psychosurgery

Because its effects are irreversible, **psychosurgery**—surgery that removes or destroys brain tissue—is the most drastic and the least-used biomedical intervention for changing behavior. In the 1930s, Portuguese physician Egas Moniz developed what became the best-known psychosurgical operation: the **lobotomy.** Moniz found that cutting the nerves connecting the frontal lobes with the emotion-controlling centers of the inner brain calmed uncontrollably emotional and violent patients. In what would later become a crude but easy and inexpensive procedure that took only about 10 minutes, a neurosurgeon would shock the patient into a coma, hammer an icepick-like instrument through each eye socket into the brain, and then wiggle it to sever connections running up to the frontal lobes. Between 1936 and 1954, tens of thousands of severely disturbed people were "lobotomized" (Valenstein, 1986).

Although the intention was simply to disconnect emotion from thought, a lobotomy's effect was often more drastic: It usually decreased the person's misery or tension, but also produced a permanently lethargic, immature, uncreative person. During the 1950s, after some 35,000 people had been lobotomized in the United States alone, calming drugs became available and psychosurgery was largely abandoned. Today, lobotomies are history. But more precise, microscale psychosurgery is sometimes used in extreme cases. For example, if a patient suffers uncontrollable seizures, surgeons can deactivate the specific nerve clusters that cause or transmit the convulsions. MRI-guided precision surgery is also occasionally done to cut the circuits involved in severe obsessive-compulsive disorder (Carey, 2009, 2011; Sachdev & Sachdev, 1997). Because these procedures are irreversible, they are controversial and neurosurgeons perform them only as a last resort.

Failed lobotomy This 1940 photo shows Rosemary Kennedy (center) at age 22 with brother (and future U.S. president) John and sister Jean. A year later her father, on medical advice, approved a lobotomy that was promised to control her reportedly violent mood swings. The procedure left her confined to a hospital with an infantile mentality until her death in 2005 at age 86.

Therapeutic Lifestyle Change

 73-3 How, by taking care of themselves with a healthy lifestyle, might people find some relief from depression, and how does this reflect our being biopsychosocial systems?

The effectiveness of the biomedical therapies reminds us of a fundamental lesson: We find it convenient to talk of separate psychological and biological influences, but everything psychological is also biological (**FIGURE 73.4**). Every thought and feeling depends on the functioning brain. Every creative idea, every moment of joy or anger, every period of depression emerges from the electrochemical activity of the living brain. The influence is two-way: When psychotherapy relieves obsessive-compulsive behavior, PET scans reveal a calmer brain (Schwartz et al., 1996).

Anxiety disorders, obsessive-compulsive disorder, posttraumatic stress disorder, major depression, bipolar disorder, and schizophrenia are all biological events. As we have seen over and again, *a human being is an integrated biopsychosocial system.* For years, we have considered the health of our bodies and minds separately. That neat separation no longer seems valid. Stress affects body chemistry and health. And chemical imbalances, whatever their cause, can produce schizophrenia, depression, and other mental disorders.

That lesson is being applied by Stephen Ilardi (2009) in training seminars promoting *therapeutic lifestyle change.* Human brains and bodies were designed for physical activity and social engagement, they note. Our ancestors hunted, gathered, and built in groups, with little evidence of disabling depression. Indeed, those whose way of life entails strenuous physical activity, strong community ties, sunlight exposure, and plenty of sleep (think of foraging bands in Papua New Guinea, or Amish farming communities in North America) rarely experience depression. For both children and adults, outdoor activity in natural environments—perhaps a walk in the woods—reduces stress and promotes health (NEEF, 2011; Phillips, 2011). "Simply put: humans were never designed for the sedentary, disengaged, socially isolated, poorly nourished, sleep-deprived pace of twenty-first-century American life."

The Ilardi team was also impressed by research showing that regular aerobic exercise and a complete night's sleep boost mood and energy. So they invited small groups of people with depression to undergo a 12-week training program with the following goals:

- *Aerobic exercise,* 30 minutes a day, at least 3 times weekly (increasing fitness and vitality, stimulating endorphins)

- *Adequate sleep,* with a goal of 7 to 8 hours a night (increasing energy and alertness, boosting immunity)

- *Light exposure,* at least 30 minutes each morning with a light box (amplifying arousal, influencing hormones)

- *Social connection,* with less alone time and at least two meaningful social engagements weekly (satisfying the human need to belong)

- *Antirumination,* by identifying and redirecting negative thoughts (enhancing positive thinking)

- *Nutritional supplements,* including a daily fish oil supplement with omega-3 fatty acids (supporting healthy brain functioning)

In one study of 74 people, 77 percent of those who completed the program experienced relief from depressive symptoms, compared with 19 percent in those assigned to a treatment-as-usual control condition. Future research will seek to replicate this striking result of lifestyle change, and also to identify which of the treatment components (additively or in some combination) produce the therapeutic effect. In the meantime, there seems little reason to doubt the truth of the Latin adage, *Mens sana in corpore sano:* "A healthy mind in a healthy body."

TABLE 73.1 on the next page summarizes some aspects of the biomedical therapies we've discussed.

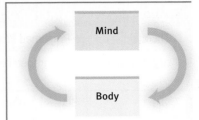

Figure 73.4
Mind-body interaction The biomedical therapies assume that mind and body are a unit: Affect one and you will affect the other.

Healthier lifestyles Researchers suggest that therapeutic lifestyle change can be an effective antidote for people with depression. The changes include managing sleep time, spending more time outdoors (or with a light box), getting more exercise, and developing more social connections.

Table 73.1 Comparing Biomedical Therapies

Therapy	Presumed Problem	Therapy Aim	Therapy Technique
Drug therapies	Neurotransmitter malfunction	Control symptoms of psychological disorders.	Alter brain chemistry through drugs.
Brain stimulation	Severe, "treatment-resistant" depression	Alleviate depression that is unresponsive to drug therapy.	Stimulate brain through electroconvulsive shock, magnetic impulses, or deep-brain stimulation.
Psychosurgery	Brain malfunction	Relieve severe disorders.	Remove or destroy brain tissue.
Therapeutic lifestyle change	Stress and unhealthy lifestyle	Restore healthy biological state.	Alter lifestyle through adequate exercise, sleep, and other changes.

Before You Move On

▶ **ASK YOURSELF**

If a troubled friend asked, how would you summarize the available biomedical therapies?

▶ **TEST YOURSELF**

How do researchers evaluate the effectiveness of particular drug therapies?

Answers to the Test Yourself questions can be found in Appendix E at the end of the book.

Module 73 Review

 73-1 What are the drug therapies? How do double-blind studies help researchers evaluate a drug's effectiveness?

- *Psychopharmacology,* the study of drug effects on mind and behavior, has helped make drug therapy the most widely used biomedical therapy.

- *Antipsychotic drugs,* used in treating schizophrenia, block dopamine activity. Side effects may include tardive dyskinesia (with involuntary movements of facial muscles, tongue, and limbs) or increased risk of obesity and diabetes.

- *Antianxiety drugs,* which depress central nervous system activity, are used to treat anxiety disorders, obsessive-compulsive disorder, and posttraumatic stress disorder. These drugs can be physically and psychologically addictive.

- *Antidepressant drugs,* which increase the availability of serotonin and norepinephrine, are used for depression, with modest effectiveness beyond that of placebo drugs. The antidepressants known as selective serotonin reuptake inhibitors (SSRIs) are now used to treat other disorders, including strokes, anxiety disorders, obsessive-compulsive disorder, and posttraumatic stress disorder.

- Lithium and Depakote are mood stabilizers prescribed for those with bipolar disorder.

- Studies may use a double-blind procedure to avoid the placebo effect and researchers' bias.

73-2 How are brain stimulation and psychosurgery used in treating specific disorders?

- *Electroconvulsive therapy (ECT),* in which a brief electric current is sent through the brain of an anesthetized patient, is an effective treatment for severely depressed people who have not responded to other therapy.

- Newer alternative treatments for depression include *repetitive transcranial magnetic stimulation (rTMS)* and, in preliminary clinical experiments, deep-brain stimulation that calms an overactive brain region linked with negative emotions.

- *Psychosurgery* removes or destroys brain tissue in hopes of modifying behavior.
  - Radical psychosurgical procedures such as the *lobotomy* were once popular, but neurosurgeons now rarely perform brain surgery to change behavior or moods.
  - Brain surgery is a last-resort treatment because its effects are irreversible.

73-3 How, by taking care of themselves with a healthy lifestyle, might people find some relief from depression, and how does this reflect our being biopsychosocial systems?

- Depressed people who undergo a program of aerobic exercise, adequate sleep, light exposure, social engagement, negative-thought reduction, and better nutrition often gain some relief.

- In our integrated biopsychosocial system, stress affects our body chemistry and health; chemical imbalances can produce depression; and social support and other lifestyle changes can lead to relief of symptoms.

Multiple-Choice Questions

1. Which neurotransmitter is affected by antipsychotic medications?

a. Epinephrine
b. Dopamine
c. Norepinephrine
d. Acetylcholine
e. Serotonin

2. Which of the following is most effectively treated with electroconvulsive therapy (ECT)?

a. Psychosis
b. Schizophrenia
c. Obsessive-compulsive disorder
d. Depression
e. Generalized anxiety disorder

3. Which of the following was the purpose of lobotomies?

a. To alleviate depression
b. To minimize delusions and hallucinations
c. To "erase" troubling memories
d. To recover repressed memories
e. To separate the reasoning centers of the brain from the emotional centers

Practice FRQs

1. Identify the category of drugs used to treat schizophrenia and the category of drugs used to treat obsessive-compulsive disorder. Then explain what each of these two categories of drugs does inside the brain.

Answer

2 points: Antipsychotic medications are the preferred drug treatment for schizophrenia. They work by blocking dopamine receptors.

2 points: Antidepressant medications are the preferred drug treatment for obsessive-compulsive disorder. They work by blocking the reuptake of serotonin.

2. Briefly describe four therapeutic lifestyle changes advocated by Stephen Ilardi, and describe their benefits.

(4 points)

Unit XIII Review

Key Terms and Concepts to Remember

psychotherapy, p. 709

biomedical therapy, p. 709

eclectic approach, p. 709

psychoanalysis, p. 709

resistance, p. 710

interpretation, p. 710

transference, p. 710

psychodynamic therapy, p. 710

insight therapies, p. 711

client-centered therapy, p. 712

active listening, p. 712

unconditional positive regard, p. 712

behavior therapy, p. 716

counterconditioning, p. 717

exposure therapies, p. 717

systematic desensitization, p. 717

virtual reality exposure therapy, p. 718

aversive conditioning, p. 718

token economy, p. 719

cognitive therapy, p. 720

rational-emotive behavior therapy (REBT), p. 721

cognitive-behavioral therapy (CBT), p. 723

group therapy, p. 723

family therapy, p. 724

regression toward the mean, p. 730

meta-analysis, p. 731

evidence-based practice, p. 732

therapeutic alliance, p. 735

resilience, p. 737

psychopharmacology, p. 740

antipsychotic drugs, p. 741

antianxiety drugs, p. 741

antidepressant drugs, p. 741

electroconvulsive therapy (ECT), p. 743

repetitive transcranial magnetic stimulation (rTMS), p. 745

psychosurgery, p. 746

lobotomy, p. 746

Key Contributors to Remember

Sigmund Freud, p. 709

Carl Rogers, p. 712

Mary Cover Jones, p. 717

Joseph Wolpe, p. 717

B. F. Skinner, p. 719

Albert Ellis, p. 721

Aaron Beck, p. 721

AP® Exam Practice Questions

Multiple-Choice Questions

1. In an effort to help a child overcome a fear of dogs, a therapist pairs a trigger stimulus (something associated with dogs) with a new stimulus that causes a response that is incompatible with fear (for example, an appealing snack or toy). Which clinical orientation is this therapist using?

a. Psychodynamic

b. Behavioral

c. Biomedical

d. Client-centered

e. Humanistic

2. Which of the following is a similarity between humanistic and psychoanalytic therapies?

a. Both approaches focus on the present more than the past.

b. Both approaches are more concerned with conscious than unconscious feelings.

c. Both approaches focus on taking immediate responsibility for one's feelings.

d. Both approaches focus on growth instead of curing illness.

e. Both approaches are generally considered insight therapies.

3. A psychotherapist who uses a blend of therapies is practicing what kind of approach?

a. Eclectic
b. Psychodynamic
c. Cognitive
d. Cognitive-behavioral
e. Humanistic

4. Some patients whose depression resists drugs have benefited from which experimental treatment?

a. Transference
b. Meta-analysis
c. Antipsychotic drugs
d. Deep-brain stimulation
e. Resistance

5. Which kind of drug is most closely associated with increasing the availability of norepinephrine or serotonin?

a. Antidepressant
b. Antipsychotic
c. Antianxiety
d. Mood-stabilizing
e. Muscle relaxant

6. Which of the following is seen as an effective treatment for severe depression that does not respond to drug therapy?

a. Lobotomy
b. Token economy
c. ECT
d. Crisis debriefing
e. EMDR therapy

7. Echoing, restating, and seeking clarification of what a person expresses (verbally or nonverbally) in a therapy session is called

a. active listening.
b. virtual reality exposure therapy.
c. systematic desensitization.
d. family therapy.
e. classical conditioning.

8. In the context of psychoanalytic theory, experiencing strong positive or negative feelings for your analyst is a sign of what?

a. Counterconditioning
b. Meta-analysis
c. Transference
d. Tardive dyskinesia
e. Aversive conditioning

9. In which kind of therapy would the therapist be most likely to note the following during a session: "Blocks in the flow of free associations indicate resistance"?

a. Cognitive therapy
b. Psychoanalysis
c. Client-centered therapy
d. Behavioral therapy
e. Person-centered therapy

10. Which kind of therapy below is most closely associated with the goal of altering thoughts and actions?

a. Aversive conditioning
b. Psychodynamic
c. Client-centered
d. Family
e. Cognitive-behavioral

11. Allowing people to discover, in a social context, that others have problems similar to their own is a unique benefit of what kind of therapy?

a. Psychodynamic
b. Psychopharmacological
c. Group
d. Cognitive
e. Humanistic

12. Which of the following therapeutic approaches is scientifically supported?

a. Recovered-memory therapies
b. Rebirthing therapies
c. Cognitive therapy
d. Energy therapies
e. Crisis debriefing

13. Most antipsychotic drugs mimic a certain neurotransmitter by blocking its activity at the receptor sites. These drugs affect which one of the following neurotransmitters?

a. Adrenaline
b. Epinephrine
c. Serotonin
d. Dopamine
e. Acetylcholine

14. Which of the following is *not* recommended by therapists as a way to help prevent or get over depression?

a. Recovered-memory therapies
b. Aerobic exercise
c. Light exposure
d. Increased social connections
e. Antirumination strategies

15. A psychotherapist states, "Getting people to change what they say to themselves is an effective way to change their thinking." This statement best exemplifies which kind of therapeutic approach?

a. Behavioral
b. Psychodynamic
c. Biomedical
d. Cognitive
e. Active listening

Free-Response Questions

1. Your friend Lawrence recently confided in you that he has been diagnosed with major depression. He heard about several different kinds of treatments: psychodynamic therapy, exposure therapy, REBT, SSRIs, and rTMS. Explain what you would tell Lawrence about how each type of therapy works and whether research indicates that it might be an effective treatment for major depression.

Rubric for Free-Response Question 1

1 point: Psychodynamic therapy involves a therapist and client attempting to gain perspective and insight into a client's unconscious conflicts and anxieties. Outcome research indicates that psychodynamic therapy has had success with depression symptoms. ↻ Pages 710–711

1 point: Exposure therapy exposes people to the things that they fear and avoid in order to reduce the fear or anxiety. This type of therapy is specifically focused on reducing specific anxiety symptoms and is not designed to treat depression. ↻ Pages 717–718

1 point: Albert Ellis' rational-emotive behavior therapy (REBT), a type of cognitive therapy, attempts to stop irrational thinking by challenging a person's illogical, self-defeating assumptions. Since many of the symptoms of major depression involve negative, pessimistic thinking, this treatment is worth exploring as a treatment for depression. ↻ Page 721

1 point: SSRIs, such as Zoloft, Paxil, and Prozac, work by partially blocking the reabsorption and removal of serotonin from synapses. The fact that more serotonin remains in the synapses serves to reduce the symptoms of depression. ↻ Pages 741–743

1 point: Repetitive transcranial magnetic stimulation (rTMS) sends repeated pulses of magnetic energy into the brain, usually into the left frontal lobe. This approach has proven effective in the treatment of depression. ↻ Page 745

2. For each of the following pairs, first define the particular type of treatment referenced, then explain the rationale for using this therapy to treat an individual with the particular disorder with which it is paired.

- Bipolar disorder and the biomedical approach
- Phobias and systematic desensitization
- Dissociative identity disorder and psychoanalysis
- Addiction and group therapy
- Depression and rational-emotive behavior therapy (REBT)

(5 points)

3. Different therapies rely on different underlying psychological perspectives about causes and explanations of thinking and behavior. List at least one specific therapeutic technique for each of the psychological approaches below and explain how that technique uses that psychological approach.

- Biological
- Cognitive
- Behavioral

(3 points)

Multiple-choice self-tests and more may be found at www.worthpublishers.com/MyersAP2e

Unit XIV

Social Psychology

Modules

D irk Willems faced a moment of decision in 1569. Threatened with torture and death as a member of a persecuted religious minority, he escaped from his Asperen, Holland, prison and fled across an ice-covered pond. His stronger and heavier jailer pursued him but fell through the ice and, unable to climb out, pled for help.

With his freedom in front of him, Willems acted with ultimate selflessness. He turned back and rescued his pursuer, who, under orders, took him back to captivity. A few weeks later Willems was condemned to be "executed with fire, until death ensues." For his martyrdom, present-day Asperen has named a street in honor of its folk hero (Toews, 2004).

What drives people to feel contempt for religious minorities such as Dirk Willems, and to act so spitefully? And what motivated the selflessness of Willems' response, and of so many who have died trying to save others? Indeed, what motivates any of us when we volunteer kindness and generosity toward others?

As such examples demonstrate, we are social animals. We may assume the best or the worst in others. We may approach them with closed fists or open arms. But as the novelist Herman Melville remarked, "We cannot live for ourselves alone. Our lives are connected by a thousand invisible threads." *Social psychologists* explore these connections by scientifically studying how we *think about, influence,* and *relate* to one another.

Module 74

Attribution, Attitudes, and Actions

Frances Roberts/Alamy

Module Learning Objectives

 74-1 Identify what social psychologists study, and discuss how we tend to explain others' behavior and our own.

 74-2 Explain whether what we think affects what we do, and whether what we do affects what we think.

74-1 What do social psychologists study? How do we tend to explain others' behavior and our own?

Personality psychologists (Unit X) focus on the person. They study the personal traits and dynamics that explain why *different people* may act differently *in a given situation*, such as the one Willems faced. (Would you have helped the jailer out of the icy water?) **Social psychologists** focus on the situation. They study the social influences that explain why *the same person* will act differently in *different situations*. Might the jailer have acted differently— opting not to march Willems back to jail—under differing circumstances?

The Fundamental Attribution Error

social psychology the scientific study of how we think about, influence, and relate to one another.

attribution theory the theory that we explain someone's behavior by crediting either the situation or the person's disposition.

fundamental attribution error the tendency for observers, when analyzing others' behavior, to underestimate the impact of the situation and to overestimate the impact of personal disposition.

Our social behavior arises from our social cognition. Especially when the unexpected occurs, we want to understand and explain why people act as they do. After studying how people explain others' behavior, Fritz Heider (1958) proposed an **attribution theory:** We can attribute the behavior to the person's stable, enduring traits (a *dispositional attribution*). Or we can attribute it to the situation (a *situational attribution*).

For example, in class, we notice that Juliette seldom talks. At the game, Jack talks nonstop. That must be the sort of people they are, we decide. Juliette must be shy and Jack outgoing. Such attributions—to their dispositions—can be valid, because people do have enduring personality traits. But sometimes we fall prey to the **fundamental attribution error** (Ross, 1977): We overestimate the influence of personality and underestimate the influence of situations. In class, Jack may be as quiet as Juliette. Catch Juliette as the lead in the high school musical and you may hardly recognize your quiet classmate.

David Napolitan and George Goethals (1979) demonstrated the fundamental attribution error in an experiment with Williams College students. They had students talk, one at a time, with a young woman who acted either cold and critical or warm and friendly. Before the talks, the researchers told half the students that the woman's behavior would be spontaneous. They told the other half the truth—that they had instructed her to *act* friendly (or unfriendly).

Did hearing the truth affect students' impressions of the woman? Not at all! If the woman acted friendly, both groups decided she really was a warm person. If

SelectStock/Getty Images

she acted unfriendly, both decided she really was a cold person. They attributed her behavior to her personal disposition *even when told that her behavior was situational*—that she was merely acting that way for the purposes of the experiment.

The fundamental attribution error appears more often in some cultures than in others. Individualist Westerners more often attribute behavior to people's personal traits. People in East Asian cultures are somewhat more sensitive to the power of the situation (Heine & Ruby, 2010; Kitayama et al., 2009). This difference has appeared in experiments that asked people to view scenes, such as a big fish swimming. Americans focused more on the individual fish, and Japanese people more on the whole scene (Chua et al., 2005; Nisbett, 2003).

We all commit the fundamental attribution error. Consider: Is your AP® psychology teacher shy or outgoing? If you answer "outgoing," remember that you know your teacher from one situation—the classroom, which demands outgoing behavior. Your teacher (who observes his or her own behavior not only in the classroom, but also with family, in meetings, when traveling) might say, "Me, outgoing? It all depends on the situation. In class or with good friends, yes, I'm outgoing. But at professional meetings, I'm really rather shy." Outside their assigned roles, teachers seem less teacherly, presidents less presidential, lawyers less legalistic.

When we explain *our own* behavior, we are sensitive to how our behavior changes with the situation (Idson & Mischel, 2001). After behaving badly, for example, we recognize how the situation affected our actions (recall the *self-serving bias* discussed in Module 59). What about our own intentional and admirable actions? Those we attribute not to situations but to our own good reasons (Malle, 2006; Malle et al., 2007). We also are sensitive to the power of the situation when we explain the behavior of people we know well and have seen in different contexts. We are most likely to commit the fundamental attribution error when a stranger acts badly. Having only seen that red-faced fan screaming at the referee in the heat of competition, we may assume he is a bad person. But outside the stadium, he may be a good neighbor and a great parent.

Researchers have reversed the perspectives of actor and observer. They filmed two people interacting, with a camera behind each person. Then they showed each person a replay—filmed from the other person's perspective. This reversed their attributions of the behaviors (Lassiter & Irvine, 1986; Storms, 1973). Seeing things from the actor's perspective, the observers better appreciated the situation. (As we act, our eyes look outward; we see others' faces, not our own.) Taking the observer's point of view, the actors became more aware of their own personal style.

Reflecting on our past selves of 5 or 10 years ago also switches our perspective. Our present self adopts the observer's perspective and attributes our past behavior mostly to our traits (Pronin & Ross, 2006). In another 5 or 10 years, your today's self may seem like another person.

The way we explain others' actions, attributing them to the person or the situation, can have important real-life effects (Fincham & Bradbury, 1993; Fletcher et al., 1990). A person must decide whether to interpret another's friendliness as genuine, or motivated by self-interest (she just needs a ride). A jury must decide whether a shooting was malicious or in self-defense. A voter must decide whether a candidate's promises will be kept or forgotten. A partner must decide whether a loved one's tart-tongued remark reflects a bad day or a mean disposition.

Finally, consider the social and economic effects of attribution. How do we explain poverty or unemployment? In Britain, India, Australia, and the United States political conservatives tend to place the blame on the personal dispositions of the poor and unemployed: "People generally get what they deserve. Those who don't work are freeloaders. Those who take initiative can still get ahead" (Furnham, 1982; Pandey et al., 1982; Wagstaff, 1982; Zucker & Weiner, 1993). Political liberals (and social scientists) are more likely to blame past and present situations: "If you or I

FYI

Some 7 in 10 college women report having experienced a man misattributing her friendliness as a sexual come-on (Jacques-Tiura et al., 2007).

"Otis, shout at that man to pull himself together."

An attribution question Whether we attribute poverty and homelessness to social circumstances or to personal dispositions affects and reflects our political views.

had to live with the same poor education, lack of opportunity, and discrimination, would we be any better off?" To understand and prevent terrorism, they say, consider the situations that breed terrorists. Better to drain the swamps than swat the mosquitoes.

The point to remember: Our attributions—to a person's disposition or to the situation—have real consequences.

Attitudes and Actions

 Does what we think affect what we do, or does what we do affect what we think?

Attitudes are feelings, often influenced by our beliefs, that predispose our reactions to objects, people, and events. If we *believe* someone is threatening us, we may *feel* fear and anger toward the person and *act* defensively. The traffic between our attitudes and our actions is two-way. Our attitudes affect our actions. And our actions affect our attitudes.

Attitudes Affect Actions

Consider the climate-change debate. On one side are climate-change activists: "Almost all climate scientists are of one mind about the threat of global warming," reports *Science* magazine (Kerr, 2009). "It's real, it's dangerous, and the world needs to take action immediately." On the other side are climate-change deniers: The number of Americans who told Gallup pollsters that global warming is "generally exaggerated" increased from 30 percent in 2006 to 48 percent in 2010, and then dropped to 42 percent in 2012 (Saad, 2013).

Knowing that public attitudes affect public policies, activists on both sides are aiming to persuade. Persuasion efforts generally take two forms:

- **Peripheral route persuasion** doesn't engage systematic thinking, but does produce fast results as people respond to incidental cues (such as endorsements by respected people) and make snap judgments. A perfume ad may lure us with images of beautiful or famous people in love.

- **Central route persuasion** offers evidence and arguments that aim to trigger favorable thoughts. It occurs mostly when people are naturally analytical or involved in the issue. Environmental advocates may show us evidence of rising temperatures, melting glaciers, rising seas, and northward shifts in vegetation and animal life. Because it is more thoughtful and less superficial, it is more durable and more likely to influence behavior.

Those who attempt to persuade us are trying to influence our behavior by changing our attitudes. But other factors, including the situation, also influence behavior. Strong social pressures, for example, can weaken the attitude-behavior connection (Wallace et al., 2005).

attitude feelings, often influenced by our beliefs, that predispose us to respond in a particular way to objects, people, and events.

peripheral route persuasion occurs when people are influenced by incidental cues, such as a speaker's attractiveness.

central route persuasion occurs when interested people focus on the arguments and respond with favorable thoughts.

In roll-call votes, politicians will sometimes vote what their supporters demand, despite privately disagreeing with those demands (Nagourney, 2002). In such cases, external pressure overrides the attitude-behavior link.

Attitudes are especially likely to affect behavior when external influences are minimal, and when the attitude is stable, specific to the behavior, and easily recalled (Glasman & Albarracín, 2006). One experiment used vivid, easily recalled information to persuade people that sustained tanning put them at risk for future skin cancer. One month later, 72 percent of the participants, and only 16 percent of those in a waitlist control group, had lighter skin (McClendon & Prentice-Dunn, 2001). Persuasion changed attitudes, which changed behavior.

Actions Affect Attitudes

Now consider a more surprising principle: Not only will people stand up for what they believe, they also will believe more strongly in what they have stood up for. Many streams of evidence confirm that *attitudes follow behavior* (**FIGURE 74.1**).

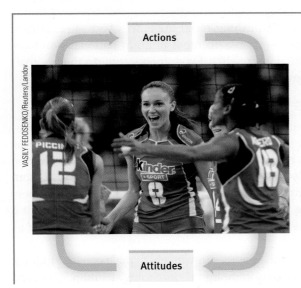

Figure 74.1
Attitudes follow behavior
Cooperative actions, such as those performed by people on sports teams, feed mutual liking. Such attitudes, in turn, promote positive behavior.

THE FOOT-IN-THE-DOOR PHENOMENON

How would you react if someone induced you to act against your beliefs? In many cases, people adjust their attitudes. During the Korean war, many U.S. prisoners of war were held in war camps run by Chinese communists. Without using brutality, the captors secured the prisoners' collaboration in various activities. Some merely ran errands or accepted favors. Others made radio appeals and false confessions. Still others informed on other prisoners and divulged military information. When the war ended, 21 prisoners chose to stay with the communists. More returned home "brainwashed"—convinced that communism was a good thing for Asia.

How did the Chinese captors achieve these amazing results? A key ingredient was their effective use of the **foot-in-the-door phenomenon:** They knew that people who agreed to a small request would find it easier to comply later with a larger one. The Chinese began with harmless requests, such as copying a trivial statement, but gradually escalated their demands (Schein, 1956). The next statement to be copied might list flaws of capitalism. Then, to gain privileges, the prisoners participated in group discussions, wrote self-criticisms, or uttered public confessions. After doing so, they often adjusted their beliefs to be more consistent with their public acts. The point is simple: To get people to agree to something big, start small and build (Cialdini, 1993). A trivial act makes the next act easier. Succumb to a temptation, and you will find the next temptation harder to resist.

foot-in-the-door phenomenon
the tendency for people who have first agreed to a small request to comply later with a larger request.

In dozens of experiments, researchers have coaxed people into acting against their attitudes or violating their moral standards, with the same result: Doing becomes believing. After giving in to a request to harm an innocent victim—by making nasty comments or delivering electric shocks—people begin to disparage their victim. After speaking or writing on behalf of a position they have qualms about, they begin to believe their own words.

Fortunately, the attitudes-follow-behavior principle works with good deeds as well. The foot-in-the-door tactic has helped boost charitable contributions, blood donations, and product sales. In one classic experiment, researchers posing as safe-driving volunteers asked Californians to permit the installation of a large, poorly lettered "Drive Carefully" sign in their front yards. Only 17 percent consented. They approached other home owners with a small request first: Would they display a 3-inch-high "Be a Safe Driver" sign? Nearly all readily agreed. When reapproached two weeks later to allow the large, ugly sign in their front yards, 76 percent consented (Freedman & Fraser, 1966). To secure a big commitment, it often pays to put your foot in the door: Start small and build.

Racial attitudes likewise follow behavior. In the years immediately following the introduction of school desegregation in the United States and the passage of the Civil Rights Act of 1964, White Americans expressed diminishing racial prejudice. And as Americans in different regions came to act more alike—thanks to more uniform national standards against discrimination—they began to think more alike. Experiments confirm the observation: Moral action strengthens moral convictions.

ROLE PLAYING AFFECTS ATTITUDES

When you adopt a new **role**—when you leave middle school and start high school, become a college student, or begin a new job—you strive to follow the social prescriptions. At first, your behaviors may feel phony, because you are *acting* a role. Soldiers may at first feel they are playing war games. Newlyweds may feel they are "playing house." Before long, however, what began as playacting in the theater of life becomes you. Researchers have confirmed this effect by assessing people's attitudes before and after they adopt a new role, sometimes in laboratory situations, sometimes in everyday situations, such as before and after taking a job.

Role playing morphed into real life in one famous study in which male college students volunteered to spend time in a simulated prison. Stanford psychologist Philip Zimbardo (1972) randomly assigned some volunteers to be guards. He gave them uniforms, clubs, and whistles and instructed them to enforce certain rules. Others became prisoners, locked in barren cells and forced to wear humiliating outfits. For a day or two, the volunteers self-consciously "played" their roles. Then the simulation became real—too real. Most guards developed disparaging attitudes, and some devised cruel and degrading routines. One by one, the prisoners broke down, rebelled, or became passively resigned. After only six days, Zimbardo called off the study.

> "Fake it until you make it."
> -ALCOHOLICS ANONYMOUS SAYING

role a set of expectations (norms) about a social position, defining how those in the position ought to behave.

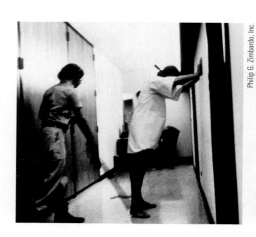

The power of the situation In his 1972 Stanford Prison simulation, Philip Zimbardo created a toxic situation (left). Those assigned to the guard role soon degraded the prisoners. In real life in 2004, some U.S. military guards tormented Iraqi prisoners at the U.S.-run Abu Ghraib prison (right). To Zimbardo (2004, 2007), it was a bad barrel rather than a few bad apples that led to the Abu Ghraib atrocities: "When ordinary people are put in a novel, evil place, such as most prisons, Situations Win, People Lose."

Role playing can train torturers (Staub, 1989). In the early 1970s, the Greek military government eased men into their roles. First, a trainee stood guard outside an interrogation cell. After this "foot in the door" step, he stood guard inside. Only then was he ready to become actively involved in the questioning and torture. What we do, we gradually become.

Yet people differ. In Zimbardo's Stanford Prison simulation and in other atrocity-producing situations, some people have succumbed to the situation and others have not (Carnahan & McFarland, 2007; Haslam & Reicher, 2007; Mastroianni & Reed, 2006; Zimbardo, 2007). Person and situation interact. Much as water dissolves salt but not sand, so toxic situations corrupt some people but not others (Johnson, 2007).

COGNITIVE DISSONANCE: RELIEF FROM TENSION

So far we have seen that actions can affect attitudes, sometimes turning prisoners into collaborators, doubters into believers, and compliant guards into abusers. But why? One explanation is that when we become aware that our attitudes and actions don't coincide, we experience tension, or *cognitive dissonance*. To relieve such tension, according to Leon Festinger's (1957) **cognitive dissonance theory,** we often bring our attitudes into line with our actions.

Dozens of experiments have explored this cognitive dissonance phenomenon. Many have made people feel responsible for behavior that clashed with their attitudes and had foreseeable consequences. In one of these experiments, you might agree for a measly $2 to help a researcher by writing an essay that supports something you don't believe in (perhaps a school vending machine tax). Feeling responsible for the statements (which are inconsistent with your attitudes), you would probably feel dissonance, especially if you thought an administrator would be reading your essay. To reduce the uncomfortable tension you might start believing your phony words. At such times, it's as if we rationalize, "If I chose to do it (or say it), I must believe in it." The less coerced and more responsible we feel for a troubling act, the more dissonance we feel. The more dissonance we feel, the more motivated we are to find consistency, such as changing our attitudes to help justify the act.

The pressure to reduce dissonance helps explain the evolution of American attitudes toward the U.S. invasion of Iraq. When the war began, the stated reason for the invasion was the presumed threat of Saddam Hussein's weapons of mass destruction (WMD). Would the war be justified if Iraq did not have WMD? Only 38 percent of Americans surveyed said it would be (Gallup, 2003). Nearly 80 percent believed such weapons would be found (Duffy, 2003; Newport et al., 2003). When no WMD were found, many Americans felt dissonance, which was heightened by their awareness of the war's financial and human costs, by scenes of chaos in Iraq, and by inflamed anti-American and pro-terrorist sentiments in some parts of the world.

To reduce dissonance, some people revised their memories of the war's rationale. The invasion then became a movement to liberate an oppressed people and promote democracy in the Middle East. Before long, 58 percent of Americans—a majority—said they supported the war even if no WMD were found (Gallup, 2003).

The attitudes-follow-behavior principle has a heartening implication: We cannot directly control all our feelings, but we can influence them by altering our behavior. (Recall from Module 42 the emotional effects of facial expressions and of body postures.) If we are down in the dumps, we can do as cognitive-behavioral therapists advise and talk in more positive, self-accepting ways with fewer self-put-downs. If we are unloving, we can become more loving by behaving as if we were so—by doing thoughtful things, expressing affection, giving affirmation. That helps explain why teens' doing volunteer work promotes a compassionate identity. "Assume a virtue, if you have it not," says Hamlet to his mother. "For use can almost change the stamp of nature." Pretense can become reality. Conduct sculpts character. What we do we become.

The point to remember: Cruel acts shape the self. But so do acts of good will. Act as though you like someone, and you soon may. Changing our behavior can change how we think about others and how we feel about ourselves.

Regarding U.S. President Lyndon Johnson's commitment to the Vietnam war: "A president who justifies his actions only to the public might be induced to change them. A president who has justified his actions to himself, believing that he has the truth, becomes impervious to self-correction." -CAROL TAVRIS AND ELLIOT ARONSON, *MISTAKES WERE MADE (BUT NOT BY ME)*, 2007

cognitive dissonance theory the theory that we act to reduce the discomfort (dissonance) we feel when two of our thoughts (cognitions) are inconsistent. For example, when we become aware that our attitudes and our actions clash, we can reduce the resulting dissonance by changing our attitudes.

"Sit all day in a moping posture, sigh, and reply to everything with a dismal voice, and your melancholy lingers. . . . If we wish to conquer undesirable emotional tendencies in ourselves, we must . . . go through the outward movements of those contrary dispositions which we prefer to cultivate." -WILLIAM JAMES, *PRINCIPLES OF PSYCHOLOGY*, 1890

Before You Move On

▶ **ASK YOURSELF**

Do you have an attitude or tendency you would like to change? Using the attitudes-follow-behavior principle, how might you go about changing that attitude?

▶ **TEST YOURSELF**

Driving to school one snowy day, Marco narrowly misses a car that slides through a red light. "Slow down! What a terrible driver," he thinks to himself. Moments later, Marco himself slips through an intersection and yelps, "Wow! These roads are awful. The city plows need to get out here." What social psychology principle has Marco just demonstrated? Explain.

Answers to the Test Yourself questions can be found in Appendix E at the end of the book.

Module 74 Review

 What do social psychologists study? How do we tend to explain others' behavior and our own?

- *Social psychologists* focus on how we think about, influence, and relate to one another. They study the social influences that explain why the same person will act differently in different situations.

- When explaining others' behavior, we may commit the *fundamental attribution error* (underestimating the influence of the situation and overestimating the effects of personality). When explaining our own behavior, we more readily attribute it to the influence of the situation.

 Does what we think affect what we do, or does what we do affect what we think?

- *Attitudes* are feelings, often influenced by our beliefs, that predispose us to respond in certain ways.

- *Peripheral route persuasion* uses incidental cues (such as celebrity endorsement) to try to produce fast but relatively thoughtless changes in attitudes.

- *Central route persuasion* offers evidence and arguments to trigger thoughtful responses.

- When other influences are minimal, attitudes that are stable, specific, and easily recalled can affect our actions.

- Actions can modify attitudes, as in the *foot-in-the-door phenomenon* (complying with a large request after having agreed to a small request) and role playing (acting a social part by following guidelines for expected behavior).

- When our attitudes don't fit with our actions, *cognitive dissonance theory* suggests that we will reduce tension by changing our attitudes to match our actions.

Multiple-Choice Questions

1. What do we call the tendency for observers to underestimate the impact of the situation and overestimate the impact of personal disposition?

   a. Peripheral route persuasion
   b. Social psychology
   c. Attribution theory
   d. Fundamental attribution error
   e. Central route persuasion

2. Which of the following best describes a feeling, often influenced by a belief, that predisposes one to respond in a particular way to people and events?

   a. Central route persuasion
   b. Anger
   c. Emotion
   d. Foot-in-the-door phenomenon
   e. Attitude

3. Which of the following best explains why we act to reduce the discomfort we feel when two of our thoughts are inconsistent?

   a. Cognitive dissonance theory
   b. Power of the situation
   c. Foot-in-the-door phenomenon
   d. Role theory
   e. Fundamental attribution error

Practice FRQs

1. Explain the fundamental attribution error.

Answer

1 point: The fundamental attribution error occurs when we are analyzing someone's behavior.

2 points: In order for the fundamental attribution error to occur, the person analyzing must underestimate the role of the situation and overestimate the disposition of the person whose behavior is being analyzed.

2. Explain the difference between peripheral route persuasion and central route persuasion.

(4 points)

Module 75

Conformity and Obedience

Module Learning Objectives

75-1 Describe automatic mimicry, and explain how conformity experiments reveal the power of social influence.

75-2 Describe what we learned about the power of social influence from Milgram's obedience experiments.

> "Have you ever noticed how one example—good or bad—can prompt others to follow? How one illegally parked car can give permission for others to do likewise? How one racial joke can fuel another?" -MARIAN WRIGHT EDELMAN, *THE MEASURE OF OUR SUCCESS*, 1992

Social psychology's great lesson is the enormous power of social influence. This influence can be seen in our conformity, our obedience to authority, and our group behavior. Suicides, bomb threats, airplane hijackings, and UFO sightings all have a curious tendency to come in clusters. On most high school campuses, jeans are the dress code; on New York's Wall Street or London's Bond Street, dress suits are the norm. When we know how to act, how to groom, how to talk, life functions smoothly. Armed with social influence principles, advertisers, fundraisers, and campaign workers aim to sway our decisions to buy, to donate, to vote. Isolated with others who share their grievances, dissenters may gradually become rebels, and rebels may become terrorists. Let's examine the pull of these social strings. How strong are they? How do they operate? When do we break them?

Conformity: Complying With Social Pressures

75-1 What is automatic mimicry, and how do conformity experiments reveal the power of social influence?

Conforming to nonconformity
Are these students asserting their individuality or identifying themselves with others of the same microculture?

Automatic Mimicry

Fish swim in schools. Birds fly in flocks. And humans, too, tend to go with their group, to think what it thinks and do what it does. Behavior is contagious. Chimpanzees are more likely to yawn after observing another chimpanzee yawn (Anderson et al., 2004). Ditto for humans. If one of us yawns, laughs, coughs, stares at the sky, or checks a cell phone, others in our group will soon do the same. Like the chameleon lizards that take on the color of their surroundings, we humans take on the emotional tones of those around us. Just hearing someone reading a neutral text in either a happy- or sad-sounding voice creates "mood contagion" in listeners (Neumann & Strack, 2000). We are natural mimics, unconsciously imitating others' expressions, postures, and voice tones.

Tanya Chartrand and John Bargh captured this mimicry, which they call the *chameleon effect* (Chartrand & Bargh, 1999). They had students work in a room alongside another person, who was actually a confederate working for the experimenters. Sometimes the confederates rubbed their own face. Sometimes they shook their foot. Sure enough, the students tended to rub their face when with the face-rubbing person and shake their foot when with the foot-shaking person. Other studies have found people synchronizing their grammar to match material they are reading or people they are hearing (Ireland & Pennebaker, 2010). Perhaps we should not be surprised then that intricate studies show that obesity, sleep loss, drug use, loneliness, and happiness spread through social networks (Christakis & Fowler, 2009). We and our friends form a social system.

Automatic mimicry helps us to *empathize*—to feel what others are feeling. This helps explain why we feel happier around happy people than around depressed people. It also helps explain why studies of groups of British nurses and accountants have revealed *mood linkage*—sharing up and down moods (Totterdell et al., 1998). Empathic people yawn more after seeing others yawn (Morrison, 2007). And empathic mimicking fosters fondness (van Baaren et al., 2003, 2004). Perhaps you've noticed that when someone nods their head as you do and echoes your words, you feel a certain rapport and liking?

Suggestibility and mimicry sometimes lead to tragedy. In the eight days following the 1999 shooting rampage at Colorado's Columbine High School, every U.S. state except Vermont experienced threats of copycat violence. Pennsylvania alone recorded 60 such threats (Cooper, 1999). Sociologist David Phillips and his colleagues (1985, 1989) found that suicides, too, sometimes increase following a highly publicized suicide. In the wake of screen idol Marilyn Monroe's suicide on August 5, 1962, for example, the number of suicides in the United States exceeded the usual August count by 200.

What causes behavior clusters? Do people act similarly because of their influence on one another? Or because they are simultaneously exposed to the same events and conditions? Seeking answers to such questions, social psychologists have conducted experiments on group pressure and conformity.

> "When I see synchrony and mimicry—whether it concerns yawning, laughing, dancing, or aping—I see social connection and bonding." -PRIMATOLOGIST FRANS DE WAAL "THE EMPATHY INSTINCT," 2009

NON SEQUITUR by WILEY

BANKING on the YOUTH MARKET...

TATTOO & PIERCING

BE LIKE ALL YOUR FRIENDS AND EXPRESS YOUR INDIVIDUALITY

OPEN

Conformity and Social Norms

Suggestibility and mimicry are subtle types of **conformity**—adjusting our behavior or thinking toward some group standard. To study conformity, Solomon Asch (1955) devised a simple test. As a participant in what you believe is a study of visual perception, you arrive in time to take a seat at a table with five other people. The experimenter asks the group to state, one by one, which of three comparison lines is identical to a standard line. You see clearly that the answer is Line 2, and you await your turn to say so. Your boredom begins to show when the next set of lines proves equally easy.

Now comes the third trial, and the correct answer seems just as clear-cut (**FIGURE 75.1** on the next page). But the first person gives what strikes you as a wrong answer: "Line 3." When the second person and then the third and fourth give the same wrong

> **conformity** adjusting our behavior or thinking to coincide with a group standard.

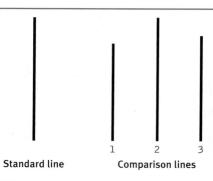

Standard line   Comparison lines

Figure 75.1

Asch's conformity experiments
Which of the three comparison lines
is equal to the standard line? What
do you suppose most people would
say after hearing five others say, "Line
3"? In this photo from one of Asch's
experiments, the student in the center
shows the severe discomfort that
comes from disagreeing with the
responses of other group members
(in this case, accomplices of the
experimenter).

answer, you sit up straight and squint. When the fifth person agrees with the first four, you feel your heart begin to pound. The experimenter then looks to you for your answer. Torn between the unanimity voiced by the five others and the evidence of your own eyes, you feel tense and suddenly unsure. You hesitate before answering, wondering whether you should suffer the discomfort of being the oddball. What answer do you give?

In Asch's experiments, college students, answering questions alone, erred less than 1 percent of the time. But what about when several others—confederates working for the experimenter—answered incorrectly? Although most people told the truth even when others did not, Asch was disturbed by his result: More than one-third of the time, these "intelligent and well-meaning" college students were then "willing to call white black" by going along with the group.

Later investigations have not always found as much conformity as Asch found, but they have revealed that we are more likely to conform when we

- are made to feel incompetent or insecure.

- are in a group with at least three people.

- are in a group in which everyone else agrees. (If just one other person disagrees, the odds of our disagreeing greatly increase.)

- admire the group's status and attractiveness.

- have not made a prior commitment to any response.

- know that others in the group will observe our behavior.

- are from a culture that strongly encourages respect for social standards.

Why do we so often think what others think and do what they do? Why in college residence halls do students' attitudes become more similar to those living near them (Cullum & Harton, 2007)? Why in college classrooms are hand-raised answers to controversial questions less diverse than anonymous electronic clicker responses (Stowell et al., 2010)? Why do we clap when others clap, eat as others eat, believe what others believe, say what others say, even see what others see?

Frequently, we conform to avoid rejection or to gain social approval. In such cases, we are responding to **normative social influence.** We are sensitive to *social norms*—understood rules for accepted and expected behavior—because the price we pay for being different can be severe. We need to belong. To get along, we go along.

At other times, we conform because we want to be accurate. Groups provide information, and only an uncommonly stubborn person will never listen to others. "Those who never retract their opinions love themselves more than they love truth," observed Joseph Joubert, an eighteenth-century French essayist. When we accept others' opinions about reality, we are responding to **informational social influence.** As Rebecca Denton demonstrated in 2004, sometimes it pays to assume others are right and to follow their lead. Denton set a record for the furthest distance driven on the wrong side of a British divided highway—30 miles, with only one minor sideswipe, before the motorway ran out and police were able

normative social influence
influence resulting from a person's
desire to gain approval or avoid
disapproval.

informational social influence
influence resulting from one's
willingness to accept others'
opinions about reality.

to puncture her tires. Denton, who was intoxicated, later explained that she thought the hundreds of other drivers coming at her were all on the wrong side of the road (Woolcock, 2004).

Is conformity good or bad? The answer depends partly on our culturally influenced values. Western Europeans and people in most English-speaking countries tend to prize individualism. People in many Asian, African, and Latin American countries place a higher value on honoring group standards. In social influence experiments across 17 countries, conformity rates have been lower in individualist cultures (Bond & Smith, 1996). American university students, for example, tend to see themselves, in domains ranging from consumer purchases to political views, as less conforming than others (Pronin et al., 2007). We are, in our own eyes, individuals amid a crowd of sheep.

"I love the little ways you're identical to everyone else."

Obedience: Following Orders

75-2 What did Milgram's obedience experiments teach us about the power of social influence?

Social psychologist Stanley Milgram (1963, 1974), a student of Solomon Asch, knew that people often give in to social pressures. But how would they respond to outright commands? To find out, he undertook what became social psychology's most famous, controversial, and influential experiments (Benjamin & Simpson, 2009).

Imagine yourself as one of the nearly 1000 people who took part in Milgram's 20 experiments. You respond to an advertisement for participants in a Yale University psychology study of the effect of punishment on learning. Professor Milgram's assistant asks you and another person to draw slips from a hat to see who will be the "teacher" and who will be the "learner." You draw the "teacher" slip and are asked to sit down in front of a machine, which has a series of labeled switches. The learner, a mild and submissive-seeming man, is led to an adjoining room and strapped into a chair. From the chair, wires run through the wall to "your" machine. You are given your task: Teach and then test the learner on a list of word pairs. If the learner gives a wrong answer, you are to flip a switch to deliver a brief electric shock. For the first wrong answer, you will flip the switch labeled "15 Volts—Slight Shock." With each succeeding error, you will move to the next higher voltage. The researcher demonstrates by flipping the first switch. Lights flash, relay switches click on, and an electric buzzing fills the air.

The experiment begins, and you deliver the shocks after the first and second wrong answers. If you continue, you hear the learner grunt when you flick the third, fourth, and fifth switches. After you activate the eighth switch ("120 Volts—Moderate Shock"), the learner cries out that the shocks are painful. After the tenth switch ("150 Volts—Strong Shock"), he begins shouting. "Get me out of here! I won't be in the experiment anymore! I refuse to go on!" You draw back, but the stern experimenter prods you: "Please continue—the experiment requires that you continue." You resist, but the experimenter insists, "It is absolutely essential that you continue," or "You have no other choice, you *must* go on."

If you obey, you hear the learner shriek in apparent agony as you continue to raise the shock level after each new error. After the 330-volt level, the learner refuses to answer and falls silent. Still, the experimenter pushes you toward the final, 450-volt switch. Ask the question, he says, and if no correct answer is given, administer the next shock level.

Would you follow the experimenter's commands to shock someone? At what level would you refuse to obey? Milgram asked that question in a survey before he started his experiments. Most people were sure they would stop playing such a sadistic-seeming role soon after the learner first indicated pain, certainly before he shrieked in agony. Forty psychiatrists agreed with that prediction when Milgram asked them. Were the predictions accurate? Not even close. When Milgram conducted the experiment with men aged 20 to 50, he was astonished. More than 60 percent complied fully—right up to the last switch.

Stanley Milgram (1933–1984)
This social psychologist's obedience experiments "belong to the self-understanding of literate people in our age" (Sabini, 1986).

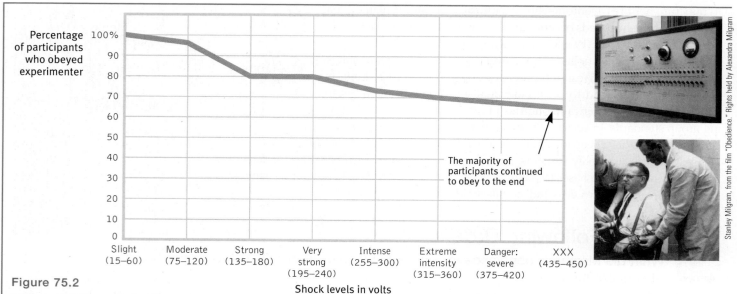

Percentage of participants who obeyed experimenter

100%
90
80
70
60
50
40
30
20
10
0

The majority of participants continued to obey to the end

Slight (15–60)   Moderate (75–120)   Strong (135–180)   Very strong (195–240)   Intense (255–300)   Extreme intensity (315–360)   Danger: severe (375–420)   XXX (435–450)

Shock levels in volts

Stanley Milgram, from the film "Obedience." Rights held by Alexandra Milgram

Figure 75.2

Milgram's follow-up obedience experiment In a repeat of the earlier experiment, 65 percent of the adult male "teachers" fully obeyed the experimenter's commands to continue. They did so despite the "learner's" earlier mention of a heart condition and despite hearing cries of protest after they administered what they thought were 150 volts and agonized protests after 330 volts. (Data from Milgram, 1974.)

Even when Milgram ran a new study, with 40 new teachers, and the learner complained of a "slight heart condition," the results were similar. A full 65 percent of the new teachers obeyed every one of the experimenter's commands, right up to 450 volts (**FIGURE 75.2**).

Cultures change over time. Are people today less likely to obey an order to hurt someone? To find out, Jerry Burger (2009) replicated Milgram's basic experiment. Seventy percent of the participants obeyed up to the 150-volt point, a slight reduction from Milgram's result. And in a French reality TV show replication, 80 percent of people, egged on by a cheering audience, obeyed and tortured a screaming victim (de Moraes, 2010).

Could Milgram's findings reflect some aspect of gender behavior found only in males? *No.* In 10 later studies, women obeyed at rates similar to men's (Blass, 1999).

Did the teachers figure out the hoax—that no real shock was being delivered and the learner was in fact a confederate who was pretending to feel pain? Did they realize the experiment was really testing their willingness to comply with commands to inflict punishment? *No.* The teachers typically displayed genuine distress: They perspired, trembled, laughed nervously, and bit their lips.

Milgram's use of deception and stress triggered a debate over his research ethics. In his own defense, Milgram pointed out that, after the participants learned of the deception and actual research purposes, virtually none regretted taking part (though perhaps by then the participants had reduced their dissonance). When 40 of the teachers who had agonized most were later interviewed by a psychiatrist, none appeared to be suffering emotional aftereffects. All in all, said Milgram, the experiments provoked less enduring stress than university students experience when facing and failing big exams (Blass, 1996).

In later experiments, Milgram discovered some things that do influence people's behavior. When he varied the situation, the percentage of participants who fully obeyed ranged from 0 to 93 percent. Obedience was highest when

- *the person giving the orders was close at hand and was perceived to be a legitimate authority figure.* (Such was the case in 2005 when Temple University's basketball coach sent a 250-pound bench player, Nehemiah Ingram, into a game with instructions to commit "hard fouls." Following orders, Ingram fouled out in four minutes after breaking an opposing player's right arm.)

- *the authority figure was supported by a prestigious institution.* (Compliance was somewhat lower when Milgram dissociated his experiments from Yale University.)

- *the victim was depersonalized or at a distance, even in another room.* (Similarly, many soldiers in combat either have not fired their rifles at an enemy they can see, or have not aimed them properly. Such refusals to kill were rare among soldiers who were operating long-distance artillery or aircraft weapons [Padgett, 1989].)

- *there were no role models for defiance.* (Teachers did not see any other participant disobey the experimenter.)

The power of legitimate, close-at-hand authorities was apparent among those who followed orders to carry out the Holocaust atrocities. Obedience alone does not explain the Holocaust. Anti-Semitic ideology produced eager killers as well (Mastroianni, 2002). But obedience was a factor. In the summer of 1942, nearly 500 middle-aged German reserve police officers were dispatched to German-occupied Jozefow, Poland. On July 13, the group's visibly upset commander informed his recruits, mostly family men, of their orders. They were to round up the village's Jews, who were said to be aiding the enemy. Able-bodied men would be sent to work camps, and all the rest would be shot on the spot.

The commander gave the recruits a chance to refuse to participate in the executions. Only about a dozen immediately refused. Within 17 hours, the remaining 485 officers killed 1500 helpless women, children, and elderly, shooting them in the back of the head as they lay face down. Hearing the victims' pleas, and seeing the gruesome results, some 20 percent of the officers did eventually dissent, managing either to miss their victims or to wander away and hide until the slaughter was over (Browning, 1992). In real life, as in Milgram's experiments, those who resisted did so early, and they were the minority.

Another story was being played out in the French village of Le Chambon. There, French Jews destined for deportation to Germany were sheltered by villagers who openly defied orders to cooperate with the "New Order." The villagers' Protestant ancestors had themselves been persecuted, and their pastors taught them to "resist whenever our adversaries will demand of us obedience contrary to the orders of the Gospel" (Rochat, 1993). Ordered by police to give a list of sheltered Jews, the head pastor modeled defiance: "I don't know of Jews, I only know of human beings." Without realizing how long and terrible the war would be, or how much punishment and poverty they would suffer, the resisters made an initial commitment to resist. Supported by their beliefs, their role models, their interactions with one another, and their own initial acts, they remained defiant to the war's end.

Lest we presume that obedience is always evil and resistance is always good, consider the obedience of British soldiers who, in 1852, were traveling with civilians aboard the steamship *Birkenhead*. As they neared their South African port, the *Birkenhead* became impaled on a rock. To calm the passengers and permit an orderly exit of civilians via the three available lifeboats, soldiers who were not assisting the passengers or working the pumps lined up at parade rest. "Steady, men!" said their officer as the lifeboats pulled away. Heroically, no one frantically rushed to claim a lifeboat seat. As the boat sank, all were plunged into the sea, most to be drowned or devoured by sharks. For almost a century, noted James Michener (1978), "the Birkenhead drill remained the measure by which heroic behavior at sea was measured."

The power of disobedience. The American civil rights movement was ignited when one African American woman, Rosa Parks, was arrested after spontaneously refusing to relinquish her Montomery, Alabama, bus seat to a White man.

The "Birkenhead drill" To calm and give priority to passengers, soldiers obeyed orders to line up on deck as their ship sank.

Lessons From the Obedience Studies

What do the Milgram experiments teach us about ourselves? How does flicking a shock switch relate to everyday social behavior? Recall from Module 6 that psychological experiments aim not to re-create the literal behaviors of everyday life but to capture and explore the underlying processes that shape those behaviors. Participants in the Milgram experiments confronted a dilemma we all face frequently: Do I adhere to my own standards, or do I respond to others?

In these experiments and their modern replications, participants were torn. Should they respond to the pleas of the victim or the orders of the experimenter? Their moral sense warned them not to harm another, yet it also prompted them to obey the experimenter and to be a good research participant. With kindness and obedience on a collision course, obedience usually won.

These experiments demonstrated that strong social influences can make people conform to falsehoods or capitulate to cruelty. Milgram saw this as the fundamental lesson of this work: "Ordinary people, simply doing their jobs, and without any particular hostility on their part, can become agents in a terrible destructive process" (1974, p. 6).

Focusing on the end point—450 volts, or someone's real-life reprehensible deceit or violence—we can hardly comprehend the inhumanity. But we ignore how they get there, in tiny increments. Milgram did not entrap his teachers by asking them first to zap learners with enough electricity to make their hair stand on end. Rather, he exploited the foot-in-the-door effect, beginning with a little tickle of electricity and escalating step by step. In the minds of those throwing the switches, the small action became justified, making the next act tolerable. In Jozefow and Le Chambon, as in Milgram's experiments, those who resisted usually did so early. After the first acts of compliance or resistance, attitudes began to follow and justify behavior.

So it happens when people succumb, gradually, to evil. In any society, great evils sometimes grow out of people's compliance with lesser evils. The Nazi leaders suspected that most German civil servants would resist shooting or gassing Jews directly, but they found them surprisingly willing to handle the paperwork of the Holocaust (Silver & Geller, 1978). Milgram found a similar reaction in his experiments. When he asked 40 men to administer the learning test while someone else did the shocking, 93 percent complied. Cruelty does not require devilish villains. All it takes is ordinary people corrupted by an evil situation. Ordinary students may follow orders to haze initiates into their group. Ordinary employees may follow orders to produce and market harmful products. Ordinary soldiers may follow orders to punish and then torture prisoners (Lankford, 2009).

> "I was only following orders." -ADOLF EICHMANN, DIRECTOR OF NAZI DEPORTATION OF JEWS TO CONCENTRATION CAMPS

> "The normal reaction to an abnormal situation is abnormal behavior." -JAMES WALLER, BECOMING EVIL: HOW ORDINARY PEOPLE COMMIT GENOCIDE AND MASS KILLING, 2007

Before You Move On

► **ASK YOURSELF**

How have you found yourself conforming, or perhaps "conforming to nonconformity"? In what ways have you seen others identifying themselves with those of the same culture or microculture?

► **TEST YOURSELF**

What types of situations have researchers found to be most likely to encourage obedience in participants?

Answers to the Test Yourself questions can be found in Appendix E at the end of the book.

Module 75 Review

 75-1 What is automatic mimicry, and how do conformity experiments reveal the power of social influence?

- Automatic mimicry (the chameleon effect), our tendency to unconsciously imitate others' expressions, postures, and voice tones, is a form of *conformity*.

- Solomon Asch and others have found that we are most likely to adjust our behavior or thinking to coincide with a group standard when (a) we feel incompetent or insecure, (b) our group has at least three people, (c) everyone else agrees, (d) we admire the group's status and attractiveness, (e) we have not already committed to another response, (f) we know we are being observed, and (g) our culture encourages respect for social standards.

- We may conform to gain approval *(normative social influence)* or because we are willing to accept others' opinions as new information *(informational social influence)*.

75-2 What did Milgram's obedience experiments teach us about the power of social influence?

- Stanley Milgram's experiments—in which people obeyed orders even when they thought they were harming another person—demonstrated that strong social influences can make ordinary people conform to falsehoods or give in to cruelty.

- Obedience was highest when (a) the person giving orders was nearby and was perceived as a legitimate authority figure; (b) the research was supported by a prestigious institution; (c) the victim was depersonalized or at a distance; and (d) there were no role models for defiance.

Multiple-Choice Questions

1. Which of the following is an example of conformity?
   a. Malik has had a series of dogs over the years. Each has learned to curl up at his feet when he was watching television.
   b. Renee begins to buy the same brand of sweatshirt that most of the kids in her school are wearing.
   c. Jonah makes sure to arrive home before his curfew because he knows he will be grounded if he doesn't.
   d. Yuri makes sure to arrive home before her curfew because she does not want her parents to be disappointed in her.
   e. Terry cranks it up a notch during volleyball practice because the team captain has been on her case for not showing enough effort.

2. Groundbreaking research on obedience was conducted by
   a. Albert Bandura.
   b. Solomon Asch.
   c. Philip Zimbardo.
   d. Stanley Milgram.
   e. John Bargh.

3. Classic studies of obedience indicate that about _____ of the participants were willing to administer what they believed to be 450-volt shocks to other humans.
   a. one-tenth
   b. one-half
   c. one-third
   d. one-fourth
   e. two-thirds

4. Obedience to authority when the authority figure is asking someone to shock another person is highest when
   a. the person receiving orders has witnessed others defy the authority figure.
   b. the person receiving orders wonders whether the person giving orders has legitimate authority.
   c. the victim receiving the shocks is physically near the person receiving orders.
   d. the authority figure is from a prestigious institution.
   e. the person receiving the orders is female.

Practice FRQs

1. Define conformity and obedience. Then, provide an example of each.

Answer

1 point: Conformity is adjusting our behavior or thinking to coincide with a group standard.

1 point: Obedience is following the orders of an authority figure.

1 point: Any correct example of conformity. Answers will vary.

1 point: Any correct example of obedience. Answers will vary.

2. Stanley Milgram's research on obedience triggered a debate over ethics. Explain the concern and Milgram's defense.

(2 points)

Module 76

Group Behavior

Module Learning Objectives

76-1 Describe how our behavior is affected by the presence of others.

76-2 Explain group polarization and groupthink, and discuss the power of the individual.

76-3 Describe how behavior is influenced by cultural norms.

76-1 How is our behavior affected by the presence of others?

Imagine yourself standing in a room, holding a fishing pole. Your task is to wind the reel as fast as you can. On some occasions you wind in the presence of another participant who is also winding as fast as possible. Will the other's presence affect your own performance?

In one of social psychology's first experiments, Norman Triplett (1898) found that adolescents would wind a fishing reel faster in the presence of someone doing the same thing. He and later social psychologists studied how others' presence affects our behavior. Group influences operate in such simple groups—one person in the presence of another—and in more complex groups.

Social Facilitation

Triplett's finding—of strengthened performance in others' presence—is called **social facilitation.** But on tougher tasks (learning nonsense syllables or solving complex multiplication problems), people perform worse when observers or others working on the same task are present. Further studies revealed that the presence of others sometimes helps and sometimes hinders performance (Guerin, 1986; Zajonc, 1965). Why? Because when others observe us, we become aroused, and this arousal amplifies our other reactions. It strengthens our most *likely* response—the correct one on an easy task, an incorrect one on a difficult task. Thus, expert pool players who made 71 percent of their shots when alone made 80 percent when four people came to watch them (Michaels et al., 1982). Poor shooters, who made 36 percent of their shots when alone, made only 25 percent when watched.

The energizing effect of an enthusiastic audience probably contributes to the home advantage that has shown up in studies of more than a quarter-million college and professional athletic events in various countries (Jamieson, 2010). Home teams win about 6 in 10 games (somewhat fewer for baseball, cricket, and football, somewhat more for basketball, rugby, and soccer—see **TABLE 76.1** on the next page).

social facilitation improved performance on simple or well-learned tasks in the presence of others.

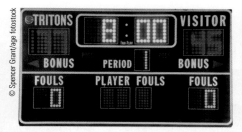

Table 76.1 Home Advantage in Team Sports		
Sport	Games Studied	Home Team Winning Percentage
Baseball	120,576	55.6%
Cricket	513	57.0
American football	11,708	57.3
Ice hockey	50,739	59.5
Basketball	30,174	62.9
Rugby	2,653	63.7
Soccer	40,380	67.4

Source: From Jeremy Jamieson (2010).

The point to remember: What you do well, you are likely to do even better in front of an audience, especially a friendly audience. What you normally find difficult may seem all but impossible when you are being watched.

Social facilitation also helps explain a funny effect of crowding. Comedians and actors know that a "good house" is a full one. Crowding triggers arousal, which, as we have seen, strengthens other reactions, too. Comedy routines that are mildly amusing to people in an uncrowded room seem funnier in a densely packed room (Aiello et al., 1983; Freedman & Perlick, 1979). And in experiments, when participants have been seated close to one another, they liked a friendly person even more, an unfriendly person even less (Schiffenbauer & Schiavo, 1976; Storms & Thomas, 1977). So, for an energetic class or event, choose a room or set up seating that will just barely accommodate everyone.

Social Loafing

Social facilitation experiments test the effect of others' presence on performance on an individual task, such as shooting pool. But what happens to performance when people perform the task as a group? In a team tug-of-war, for example, do you suppose your effort would be more than, less than, or the same as the effort you would exert in a one-on-one tug-of-war? To find out, a University of Massachusetts research team asked blindfolded students "to pull as hard as you can" on a rope. When they fooled the students into believing three others were also pulling behind them, they exerted only 82 percent as much effort as when they thought they were pulling alone (Ingham et al., 1974). And consider what happened when blindfolded people seated in a group clapped or shouted as loud as they could while hearing (through headphones) other people clapping or shouting loudly (Latané, 1981). When they thought they were part of a group effort, the participants produced about one-third less noise than when clapping or shouting "alone."

Working hard, or hardly working? In group projects, social loafing often occurs, as individuals free ride on the efforts of others.

Bibb Latané and his colleagues (1981; Jackson & Williams, 1988) described this diminished effort as **social loafing.** Experiments in the United States, India, Thailand, Japan, China, and Taiwan have recorded social loafing on various tasks, though it was especially common among men in individualist cultures (Karau & Williams, 1993). What causes social loafing? Three things:

- People acting as part of a group feel less accountable, and therefore worry less about what others think.

- Group members may view their individual contributions as dispensable (Harkins & Szymanski, 1989; Kerr & Bruun, 1983).

- When group members share equally in the benefits, regardless of how much they contribute, some may slack off (as you perhaps have observed on group assignments). Unless highly motivated and strongly identified with the group, people may *free ride* on others' efforts.

> **social loafing** the tendency for people in a group to exert less effort when pooling their efforts toward attaining a common goal than when individually accountable.
>
> **deindividuation** the loss of self-awareness and self-restraint occurring in group situations that foster arousal and anonymity.

Deindividuation

We've seen that the presence of others can arouse people (social facilitation), or it can diminish their feelings of responsibility (social loafing). But sometimes the presence of others does both. The uninhibited behavior that results can range from a food fight to vandalism or rioting. This process of losing self-awareness and self-restraint, called **deindividuation,** often occurs when group participation makes people both *aroused* and *anonymous*. In one experiment, New York University women dressed in depersonalizing Ku Klux Klan–style hoods. Compared with identifiable women in a control group, the hooded women delivered twice as much electric shock to a victim (Zimbardo, 1970). (As in all such experiments, the "victim" did not actually receive the shocks.)

Deindividuation During England's 2011 riots and looting, rioters were disinhibited by social arousal and by the anonymity provided by darkness and their hoods and masks. Later, some of those arrested expressed bewilderment over their own behavior.

Deindividuation thrives, for better or for worse, in many different settings. Tribal warriors who depersonalize themselves with face paints or masks are more likely than those with exposed faces to kill, torture, or mutilate captured enemies (Watson, 1973). Online, Internet trolls and bullies, who would never say "You're so fake" to someone's face, will hide behind anonymity. Whether in a mob, at a rock concert, at a ballgame, or at worship, when we shed self-awareness and self-restraint, we become more responsive to the group experience—bad or good.

* * *

We have examined the conditions under which being in the *presence* of others can motivate people to exert themselves or tempt them to free ride on the efforts of others, make easy tasks easier and difficult tasks harder, and enhance humor or fuel mob violence. Research also shows that *interacting* with others can similarly have both bad and good effects.

Group Polarization

76-2 What are group polarization and groupthink, and how much power do we have as individuals?

Over time, initial differences between groups of college students tend to grow. If the first-year students at College X tend to be artistic and those at College Y tend to be business-savvy, those differences will probably be even greater by the time they graduate. Similarly, gender differences tend to widen over time, as Eleanor Maccoby (2002) noted from her decades of observing gender development. Girls talk more intimately than boys do and play

Figure 76.1

Group polarization If a group is like-minded, discussion strengthens its prevailing opinions. Talking over racial issues increased prejudice in a high-prejudice group of high school students and decreased it in a low-prejudice group (Myers & Bishop, 1970).

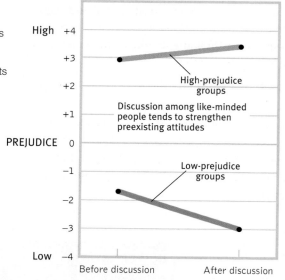

Discussion among like-minded people tends to strengthen preexisting attitudes

High-prejudice groups

Low-prejudice groups

PREJUDICE

High +4
+3
+2
+1
0
−1
−2
−3
Low −4

Before discussion   After discussion

group polarization

the enhancement of a group's prevailing inclinations through discussion within the group.

"What explains the rise of facism in the 1930s? The emergence of student radicalism in the 1960s? The growth of Islamic terrorism in the 1990s?. . . The unifying theme is simple: *When people find themselves in groups of like-minded types, they are especially likely to move to extremes.* [This] is the phenomenon of group polarization." -CASS SUNSTEIN, *GOING TO EXTREMES*, 2009

and fantasize less aggressively; these differences will be amplified as boys and girls interact mostly with their own gender.

In each case, the beliefs and attitudes we bring to a group grow stronger as we discuss them with like-minded others. This process, called **group polarization,** can have beneficial results, as when it amplifies a sought-after spiritual awareness or reinforces the resolve of those in a self-help group. But it can also have dire consequences. George Bishop and I discovered that when high-prejudice students discussed racial issues, they became *more* prejudiced (**FIGURE 76.1**). (Low-prejudice students became even more accepting.) Thus ideological separation + deliberation = polarization between groups.

Group polarization can feed extremism and even suicide terrorism. Analysis of terrorist organizations around the world reveals that the terrorist mentality does not erupt suddenly, on a whim (McCauley, 2002; McCauley & Segal, 1987; Merari, 2002). It usually begins slowly, among people who share a grievance. As they interact in isolation (sometimes with other "brothers" and "sisters" in camps) their views grow more and more extreme. Increasingly, they categorize the world as "us" against "them" (Moghaddam, 2005; Qirko, 2004). The like-minded echo chamber will continue to polarize people, speculated a 2006 U.S. National Intelligence estimate: "We assess that the operational threat from self-radicalized cells will grow."

When I got my start in social psychology with experiments on group polarization, I never imagined the potential dangers, or the creative possibilities, of polarization in *virtual* groups. Electronic communication and social networking have created virtual town halls where people can isolate themselves from those whose perspective differs. People read blogs that reinforce their views, and those blogs link to kindred blogs (**FIGURE 76.2**). As the Internet connects the like-minded and pools their ideas, climate-change skeptics, those who believe they've been abducted by aliens, and conspiracy theorists find support for their shared ideas and suspicions. White supremacists may become more racist. And militia members may become more terrorism prone. In the echo chambers of virtual worlds, as in the real world, separation + conversation = polarization.

But the Internet-as-social-amplifier can also work for good. Social networking sites connect friends and family members sharing common interests or coping with challenges. Peacemakers, cancer survivors, and bereaved parents can find strength and solace from kindred

Figure 76.2

Like minds network in the blogosphere Blue liberal blogs link mostly to one another, as do red conservative blogs. (The intervening colors display links across the liberal-conservative boundary.) Each blog's size reflects the number of other blogs linking to it. (From Lazer et al., 2009.)

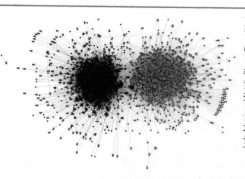

Lada Adamic and Natalie Glance. The political blogosphere and the 2004 U.S. election: Divided they blog. In Proceedings of the 3rd International Workshop on Link Discovery, pages 36–43, 2005.

spirits. By amplifying shared concerns and ideas, Internet-enhanced communication can also foster social ventures. (I know this personally from social networking with others with hearing loss to transform U. S. assistive-listening technology.)

The point to remember: By linking and magnifying the inclinations of like-minded people, the Internet can be very, very bad, but also very, very good.

Groupthink

So group interaction can influence our personal decisions. Does it ever distort important national decisions? Consider the "Bay of Pigs fiasco." In 1961, President John F. Kennedy and his advisers decided to invade Cuba with 1400 CIA-trained Cuban exiles. When the invaders were easily captured and soon linked to the U.S. government, Kennedy wondered in hindsight, "How could we have been so stupid?"

Social psychologist Irving Janis (1982) studied the decision-making procedures leading to the ill-fated invasion. He discovered that the soaring morale of the recently elected president and his advisers fostered undue confidence. To preserve the good feeling, group members suppressed or self-censored their dissenting views, especially after President Kennedy voiced his enthusiasm for the scheme. Since no one spoke strongly against the idea, everyone assumed the support was unanimous. To describe this harmonious but unrealistic group thinking, Janis coined the term **groupthink.**

Later studies showed that groupthink—fed by overconfidence, conformity, self-justification, and group polarization—contributed to other fiascos as well. Among them were the failure to anticipate the 1941 Japanese attack on Pearl Harbor; the escalation of the Vietnam war; the U.S. Watergate cover-up; the Chernobyl nuclear reactor accident (Reason, 1987); the U.S. space shuttle *Challenger* explosion (Esser & Lindoerfer, 1989); and the Iraq war, launched on the false idea that Iraq had weapons of mass destruction (U.S. Senate Intelligence Committee, 2004).

Despite the dangers of groupthink, two heads are better than one in solving many problems. Knowing this, Janis also studied instances in which U.S. presidents and their advisers collectively made good decisions, such as when the Truman administration formulated the Marshall Plan, which offered assistance to Europe after World War II, and when the Kennedy administration successfully prevented the Soviets from installing missiles in Cuba. In such instances—and in the business world, too, Janis believed—groupthink is prevented when a leader welcomes various opinions, invites experts' critiques of developing plans, and assigns people to identify possible problems. Just as the suppression of dissent bends a group toward bad decisions, so open debate often shapes good ones. This is especially so with diverse groups, whose varied perspectives often enable creative or superior outcomes (Nemeth & Ormiston, 2007; Page, 2007). None of us is as smart as all of us.

The Power of Individuals

In affirming the power of social influence, we must not overlook the power of individuals. *Social control* (the power of the situation) and *personal control* (the power of the individual) interact. People aren't billiard balls. When feeling coerced, we may react by doing the opposite of what is expected, thereby reasserting our sense of freedom (Brehm & Brehm, 1981).

Committed individuals can sway the majority and make social history. Were this not so, communism would have remained an obscure theory, Christianity would be a small Middle Eastern sect, and Rosa Parks' refusal to sit at the back of the bus would not have ignited the U.S. civil rights movement. Technological history, too, is often made by innovative minorities who overcome the majority's resistance to change. To many, the railroad was a nonsensical idea; some farmers even feared that train noise would prevent hens from laying eggs. People

> "One of the dangers in the White House, based on my reading of history, is that you get wrapped up in groupthink and everybody agrees with everything, and there's no discussion and there are no dissenting views." -BARACK OBAMA, DECEMBER 1, 2008, PRESS CONFERENCE

> "Truth springs from argument among friends." -PHILOSOPHER DAVID HUME, 1711–1776

> "If you have an apple and I have an apple and we exchange apples then you and I will still each have one apple. But if you have an idea and I have an idea and we exchange these ideas, then each of us will have two ideas." -ATTRIBUTED TO DRAMATIST GEORGE BERNARD SHAW, 1856–1950

groupthink the mode of thinking that occurs when the desire for harmony in a decision-making group overrides a realistic appraisal of alternatives.

Gandhi As the life of Hindu nationalist and spiritual leader Mahatma Gandhi powerfully testifies, a consistent and persistent minority voice can sometimes sway the majority. Gandhi's nonviolent appeals and fasts were instrumental in winning India's independence from Britain in 1947.

derided Robert Fulton's steamboat as "Fulton's Folly." As Fulton later said, "Never did a single encouraging remark, a bright hope, a warm wish, cross my path." Much the same reaction greeted the printing press, the telegraph, the incandescent lamp, and the typewriter (Cantril & Bumstead, 1960).

The power of one or two individuals to sway majorities is *minority influence* (Moscovici, 1985). In studies of groups in which one or two individuals consistently express a controversial attitude or an unusual perceptual judgment, one finding repeatedly stands out: When you are the minority, you are far more likely to sway the majority if you hold firmly to your position and don't waffle. This tactic won't make you popular, but it may make you influential, especially if your self-confidence stimulates others to consider *why* you react as you do. Even when a minority's influence is not yet visible, people may privately develop sympathy for the minority position and rethink their views (Wood et al., 1994). The powers of social influence are enormous, but so are the powers of the committed individual.

Cultural Influences

76-3 How do cultural norms affect our behavior?

Compared with the narrow path taken by flies, fish, and foxes, the road along which environment drives us is wider. The mark of our species—nature's great gift to us—is our ability to learn and adapt. We come equipped with a huge cerebral hard drive ready to receive cultural software.

Culture is the behaviors, ideas, attitudes, values, and traditions shared by a group of people and transmitted from one generation to the next (Brislin, 1988; Cohen, 2009). Human nature, notes Roy Baumeister (2005), seems designed for culture. We are social animals, but more. Wolves are social animals; they live and hunt in packs. Ants are incessantly social, never alone. But "culture is a better way of being social," notes Baumeister. Wolves function pretty much as they did 10,000 years ago. You and I enjoy things unknown to most of our century-ago ancestors, including electricity, indoor plumbing, antibiotics, and the Internet. Culture works.

Other animals exhibit the rudiments of culture. Primates have local customs of tool use, grooming, and courtship. Younger chimpanzees and macaque monkeys sometimes invent customs—potato washing, in one famous example—and pass them on to their peers and offspring. But human culture does more. It supports our species' survival and reproduction by enabling social and economic systems that give us an edge.

Thanks to our mastery of language, we humans enjoy the *preservation of innovation*. Within the span of this day, I have, thanks to my culture, made good use of Post-it Notes, Google, and digital hearing technology. Moreover, culture enables an efficient *division of labor*. Although one lucky person gets his name on this book's cover, the product actually results from the coordination and commitment of a team of people, no one of whom could produce it alone.

Across cultures, we differ in our language, our monetary systems, our sports, which fork—if any—we eat with, even which side of the road we drive on. But beneath these differences is our great similarity—our capacity for culture. Culture transmits the customs and beliefs that enable us to communicate, to exchange money for things, to play, to eat, and to drive with agreed-upon rules and without crashing into one another.

culture the enduring behaviors, ideas, attitudes, values, and traditions shared by a group of people and transmitted from one generation to the next.

Variation Across Cultures

We see our adaptability in cultural variations among our beliefs and our values, in how we raise our children and bury our dead, and in what we wear (or whether we wear anything at all). I am ever mindful that the readers of this book are culturally diverse. You and your ancestors reach from Australia to Africa and from Singapore to Sweden.

Riding along with a unified culture is like biking with the wind: As it carries us along, we hardly notice it is there. When we try riding *against* the wind, we feel its force. Face to face with a different culture, we become aware of the cultural winds. Stationed in Iraq, Afghanistan, and Kuwait, American and European soldiers were reminded how liberal their home cultures were.

Humans in varied cultures nevertheless share some basic moral ideas, as we noted earlier. Even before they can walk, babies display a moral sense by showing disapproval of what's wrong or naughty (Bloom, 2010). Yet each cultural group also evolves its own **norms**—rules for accepted and expected behavior. The British have a norm for orderly waiting in line. Many South Asians use only the right hand's fingers for eating. Sometimes social expectations seem oppressive: "Why should it matter how I dress?" Yet, norms grease the social machinery and free us from self-preoccupation.

When cultures collide, their differing norms often befuddle. Should we greet people by shaking hands or kissing each cheek? The answer depends on the surrounding culture. Learning when to clap or bow, how to order at a new restaurant, and what sorts of gestures and compliments are appropriate help us avoid accidental insults and embarrassment.

When we don't understand what's expected or accepted, we may experience *culture shock.* People from Mediterranean cultures have perceived northern Europeans as efficient but cold and preoccupied with punctuality (Triandis, 1981). People from time-conscious Japan—where bank clocks keep exact time, pedestrians walk briskly, and postal clerks fill requests speedily—have found themselves growing impatient when visiting Indonesia, where clocks keep less accurate time and the pace of life is more leisurely (Levine & Norenzayan, 1999). In adjusting to their host countries, the first wave of U.S. Peace Corps volunteers reported that two of their greatest culture shocks, after the language differences, were the differing pace of life and the people's differing sense of punctuality (Spradley & Phillips, 1972).

> **norm** an understood rule for accepted and expected behavior. Norms prescribe "proper" behavior.

Variation Over Time

Like biological creatures, cultures vary and compete for resources, and thus evolve over time (Mesoudi, 2009). Consider how rapidly cultures may change. English poet Geoffrey Chaucer (1342–1400) is separated from a modern Briton by only 25 generations, but the two would converse with great difficulty. In the thin slice of history since 1960, most Western cultures have changed with remarkable speed. Middle-class people today fly to places they once only read about. They enjoy the convenience of air-conditioned housing, online shopping, anywhere-anytime electronic communication, and—enriched by doubled per-person real income—eating out more than twice as often as did their grandparents back in the culture of 1960. Many minority groups enjoy expanded human rights. And, with greater economic independence, today's women more often marry for love and less often endure abusive relationships (Circle of Prevention, 2002).

But some changes seem not so wonderfully positive. Had you fallen asleep in the United States in 1960 and awakened today, you would open your eyes to a culture with more divorce and depression. You would also find North Americans—like their counterparts in Britain, Australia, and New Zealand—spending more hours at work, fewer hours with friends and family, and fewer hours asleep (BLS, 2011; Putnam, 2000).

Whether we love or loathe these changes, we cannot fail to be impressed by their breathtaking speed. And we cannot explain them by changes in the human gene pool, which evolves far too slowly to account for high-speed cultural transformations. Cultures vary. Cultures change. And cultures shape our lives.

Before You Move On

▶ **ASK YOURSELF**

What two examples of social influence have you experienced this week? (Remember, influence may be informational.)

▶ **TEST YOURSELF**

You are organizing a Town Hall–style meeting of fiercely competitive political candidates. To add to the fun, friends have suggested handing out masks of the candidates' faces for supporters to wear. What phenomenon might these masks engage?

Answers to the Test Yourself questions can be found in Appendix E at the end of the book.

Module 76 Review

 How is our behavior affected by the presence of others?

- In *social facilitation,* the mere presence of others arouses us, improving our performance on easy or well-learned tasks but decreasing it on difficult ones.

- In *social loafing,* participating in a group project makes us feel less responsible, and we may free ride on others' efforts.

- When the presence of others both arouses us and makes us feel anonymous, we may experience *deindividuation*—loss of self-awareness and self-restraint.

 What are group polarization and groupthink, and how much power do we have as individuals?

- In *group polarization,* group discussions with like-minded others strengthen members' prevailing beliefs and attitudes. Internet communication magnifies this effect, for better and for worse.

- *Groupthink* is driven by a desire for harmony within a decision-making group, overriding realistic appraisal of alternatives.

- The power of the individual and the power of the situation interact. A small minority that consistently expresses its views may sway the majority.

76-3 **How do cultural norms affect our behavior?**

- A *culture* is a set of behaviors, ideas, attitudes, values, and traditions shared by a group and transmitted from one generation to the next.

- Cultural *norms* are understood rules that inform members of a culture about accepted and expected behaviors.

- Cultures differ across time and space.

Multiple-Choice Questions

1. What do we call the improved performance on simple or well-learned tasks in the presence of others?

   a. Social facilitation
   b. Group behavior
   c. Social loafing
   d. Deindividuation
   e. Group polarization

2. Which of the following terms or phrases best describes the behavior of rowdy fans yelling obscenities at a football or soccer referee after a controversial penalty has been called?

   a. Culture
   b. Social facilitation
   c. Groupthink
   d. Deindividuation
   e. Group polarization

3. Which of the following is most likely to occur when the desire for harmony in a decision-making group overrides a realistic appraisal of alternatives?

   a. Group polarization
   b. Groupthink
   c. Social loafing
   d. Norming
   e. Prejudice

4. What do we call the enduring behaviors, ideas, attitudes, values, and traditions shared by a group of people and transmitted from one generation to the next?

   a. Deindividuation
   b. Norms
   c. Social facilitation
   d. Culture
   e. Social control

Practice FRQs

1. Describe the three causes of social loafing.

Answer

1 point: People acting as part of a group feel less accountable.

1 point: Group members may view their individual contributions as dispensable.

1 point: Unless highly motivated and strongly identified with the group, people may free ride on others' efforts.

2. Define groupthink and group polarization. Then, provide an example of each.

(4 points)

Module 77

Prejudice and Discrimination

Module Learning Objectives

 77-1   Define *prejudice*, and identify its social and emotional roots.

 77-2   Identify the cognitive roots of prejudice.

W e have sampled how we *think* about and *influence* one another. Now we come to social psychology's third focus—how we *relate* to one another. What causes us to harm or to help or to fall in love? How can we move a destructive conflict toward a just peace? We will ponder the bad and the good: from prejudice and aggression to attraction, altruism, and peacemaking.

Prejudice

 77-1   What is *prejudice?* What are its social and emotional roots?

Prejudice means "prejudgment." It is an unjustifiable and usually negative attitude toward a group—often a different cultural, ethnic, or gender group. Like all attitudes, prejudice is a three-part mixture of

- *beliefs* (in this case, called **stereotypes**).
- *emotions* (for example, hostility or fear).
- predispositions to *action* (to discriminate).

Ethnocentrism—assuming the superiority of one's ethnic group—is one example of prejudice. To *believe* that a person of another ethnicity is somehow inferior or threatening, to *feel* dislike for that person, and to be hesitant to hire or date that person is to be prejudiced. Prejudice is a negative *attitude*. **Discrimination** is a negative *behavior*.

How Prejudiced Are People?

To assess prejudice, we can observe what people say and what they do. Americans' expressed gender and racial attitudes have changed dramatically in the last half-century. The one-third of Americans who in 1937 told Gallup pollsters that they would vote for a qualified woman whom their party nominated for president soared to 89 percent in 2007 (Gallup Brain, 2008; Jones & Moore, 2003). Nearly everyone now agrees that women and men should receive the same pay for the same job, and that children of all races should attend the same schools.

---

prejudice   an unjustifiable and usually negative *attitude* toward a group and its members. Prejudice generally involves stereotyped beliefs, negative feelings, and a predisposition to discriminatory action.

stereotype   a generalized (sometimes accurate but often overgeneralized) *belief* about a group of people.

discrimination   unjustifiable negative *behavior* toward a group and its members.

FYI

Percentage of 2010 American marriages to someone whose race or ethnicity differed from one's own:

Whites	9%
Blacks	17%
Hispanics	26%
Asians	28%

Source: Wang, 2012

Paolo Bruno/Getty Images

Support for all forms of racial contact, including interracial dating (**FIGURE 77.1**), has also dramatically increased. Among 18- to 29-year old Americans, 9 in 10 now say they would be fine with a family member marrying someone of a different race (Pew, 2010).

Yet as *overt* prejudice wanes, *subtle* prejudice lingers. Despite increased verbal support for interracial marriage, many people admit that in socially intimate settings (dating, dancing, marrying) they would feel uncomfortable with someone of another race. And many people who *say* they would feel upset with someone making racist slurs actually, when hearing such racism, respond indifferently (Kawakami et al., 2009). In Western Europe, where many "guest workers" and refugees settled at the end of the twentieth century, "modern prejudice"—rejecting immigrant minorities as job applicants for supposedly nonracial reasons—has been replacing blatant prejudice (Jackson et al., 2001; Lester, 2004; Pettigrew, 1998, 2006). A slew of recent experiments illustrates that prejudice can be not only subtle but also automatic and unconscious (see Close-up: Automatic Prejudice on the next page).

Nevertheless, overt prejudice persists in many places. Just ask Italy's AC Milan soccer star Kevin-Prince Boateng (pictured at the beginning of this module), of Ghanaian descent, who strode off the field in protest after being subjected to racial taunts from spectators. And in the aftermath of the 9/11 terrorist attacks and the Iraq and Afghanistan wars, 4 in 10 Americans acknowledged "some feelings of prejudice against Muslims," and about half of non-Muslims in Western Europe and the United States perceived Muslims as "violent" (Saad, 2006; Wike & Grim, 2007). With Americans feeling threatened by Arabs, and as opposition to Islamic mosques and immigration flared in 2010, one national observer noted that "Muslims are one of the last minorities in the United States that it is still possible to demean openly" (Kristof, 2010; Lyons et al., 2010). Muslims reciprocated the negativity, with most in Jordan, Egypt, Turkey, and Britain seeing Westerners as "greedy" and "immoral."

In most places in the world, gays and lesbians cannot comfortably acknowledge who they are and whom they love. Gender prejudice and discrimination persist, too. Despite gender equality in intelligence scores, people have tended to perceive their fathers as more intelligent than their mothers (Furnham & Rawles, 1995). In Saudi Arabia, women are not allowed to drive. In Western countries, we pay more to those (usually men) who care for our streets than to those (usually women) who care for our children. Worldwide, women are more likely to live in poverty (Lipps, 1999), and two-thirds of illiterate adults are women (CIA, 2010).

Unwanted female infants are no longer left out on a hillside to die of exposure, as was the practice in ancient Greece. Yet natural female mortality and the normal male-to-female newborn ratio (105-to-100) hardly explain the world's estimated 163 million

"Unhappily, the world has yet to learn how to live with diversity."
-Pope John Paul II, Address to the United Nations, 1995

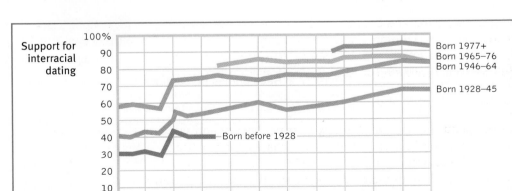

Figure 77.1

Prejudice over time Americans' approval of interracial dating has soared over the past quarter-century (Pew, 2010).

Close-up

Automatic Prejudice

As we have seen throughout this book, the human mind processes thoughts, memories, and attitudes on two different tracks. Sometimes that processing is explicit—on the radar screen of our awareness. To an even greater extent, it is implicit—below the radar, leaving us unaware of how our attitudes are influencing our behavior. Modern studies indicate that prejudice is often implicit, an automatic attitude that is an unthinking knee-jerk response. Consider these findings:

Implicit Racial Associations Using Implicit Association Tests, researchers have demonstrated that even people who deny harboring racial prejudice may carry negative associations (Greenwald et al., 1998, 2009). (By 2011, nearly 5 million people had taken the Implicit Association Test, as you can at www.implicit.harvard.edu.) For example, 9 in 10 White respondents took longer to identify pleasant words (such as *peace* and *paradise*) as "good" when presented with Black-sounding names (such as *Latisha* and *Darnell*) rather than White-sounding names (such as *Katie* and *Ian*). Moreover, people who more quickly associate good things with White names or faces also are the quickest to perceive anger and apparent threat in Black faces (Hugenberg & Bodenhausen, 2003).

Although the test is useful for studying automatic prejudice, critics caution against using it to assess or label individuals (Blanton et al., 2006, 2007, 2009). Defenders counter that implicit biases predict behaviors that range from simple acts of friendliness to the evaluation of work quality (Greenwald et al., 2009). In the 2008 U.S. presidential election, implicit as well as explicit prejudice predicted voters' support for candidate Barack Obama, whose election in turn served to reduce implicit prejudice (Bernstein et al., 2010; Payne et al., 2010).

Unconscious Patronization When White university women evaluated a flawed essay said to be written by a Black fellow student, they gave markedly higher ratings and never expressed the harsh criticisms they assigned to flawed essays supposedly written by White students (Harber, 1998). Did the evaluators calibrate their evaluations to their racial stereotypes, leading to less exacting standards and a patronizing attitude? In real-world evaluations, such low expectations and the resulting "inflated praise and insufficient criticism" could hinder minority student achievement, the researcher noted. (To preclude such bias, many teachers read essays while "blind" to their authors.)

Race-Influenced Perceptions Our expectations influence our perceptions. In 1999, Amadou Diallo was accosted as he approached his apartment house doorway by police officers looking for a rapist. When he pulled out his wallet, the officers, perceiving a gun, riddled his body with 19 bullets from 41 shots. Curious about this killing of an unarmed man, two research teams reenacted the situation (Correll et al., 2002, 2007; Greenwald et al., 2003). They asked viewers to press buttons quickly to "shoot" or not shoot men who suddenly appeared on screen. Some of the on-screen men held a gun. Others held a harmless object, such as a flashlight or bottle. People (both Blacks and Whites, in one study) more often shot Black men holding the harmless objects. Priming people with a flashed Black rather than White face also makes them more likely to misperceive a flashed tool as a gun (**FIGURE 77.2**).

Reflexive Bodily Responses Even people who consciously express little prejudice may give off telltale signals as their body responds selectively to another's race. Neuroscientists can detect these signals when people look at White and Black faces. The viewers' implicit prejudice may show up in facial-muscle responses and in the activation of their emotion-processing amygdala (Cunningham et al., 2004; Eberhardt, 2005; Stanley et al., 2008).

If your own gut check reveals you sometimes have feelings you would rather not have about other people, remember this: It is what we *do* with our feelings that matters. By monitoring our feelings and actions, and by replacing old habits with new ones based on new friendships, we can work to free ourselves from prejudice.

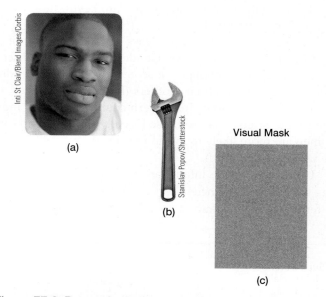

Visual Mask

(a)

(b)

(c)

Figure 77.2 Race primes perceptions In experiments by Keith Payne (2006), people viewed (a) a White or Black face, immediately followed by (b) a gun or hand tool, which was then followed by (c) a visual mask. Participants were more likely to misperceive a tool as a gun when it was preceded by a Black rather than White face.

(say that number slowly) "missing women" (Hvistendahl, 2011). In many places, sons are valued more than daughters. With testing that enables sex-selective abortions, several Asian countries have experienced a shortfall in female births (**FIGURE 77.3**). Although China has declared that sex-selective abortions—gender genocide—are now a criminal offense, the country's newborn sex ratio is still 118 boys for every 100 girls (Hvistendahl,

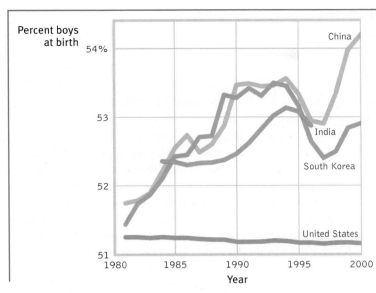

Figure 77.3

Missing girls In several Asian countries, especially in China, which has mandated one-child families, boy babies are overrepresented (Abrevaya, 2009). In China, this overrepresentation still occurred in 2009: 54.5 percent of babies were boys and only 45.5 percent were girls (Hvistendahl, 2010).

2009, 2010, 2011), and 95 percent of the children in Chinese orphanages are girls (Webley, 2009). With males under age 20 exceeding females by 32 million, many Chinese bachelors will be unable to find mates (Zhu et al., 2009).

In the United States, a striking sex-ratio bias appears among Chinese, Korean, and Asian Indian parents with a third child. Sons outnumber daughters by 50 percent after two previous girl births. Given a previous boy birth, or given Caucasian parents, there is no sex-ratio bias (Almond & Edlund, 2008).

Studies have shown, however, that most people *feel* more positively about women in general than they do about men (Eagly, 1994; Haddock & Zanna, 1994). Worldwide, people see women as having some traits (such as nurturance, sensitivity, and less aggressiveness) that most people prefer (Glick et al., 2004; Swim, 1994). That may explain why women tend to like women more than men like men (Rudman & Goodwin, 2004). And perhaps that is also why people prefer slightly feminized computer-generated faces—men's and women's—to slightly masculinized faces. Researcher David Perrett and his colleagues (1998) have speculated that a slightly feminized male face connotes kindness, cooperativeness, and other traits of a good father. When the British Broadcasting Corporation invited 18,000 women to guess which of the men in **FIGURE 77.4** was most likely to place a personal ad seeking a "special lady to love and cherish forever," which one do you think they picked?

(a)   (b)

Figure 77.4

Who do you like best? Which one placed an ad seeking "a special lady to love and cherish forever"? (See answer below.)

Research suggests that subtly feminized features convey a likable image, which people tend to associate more with committed dads than with promiscuous cads. Thus, 66 percent of the women picked computer-generated face (b) in response to both of these questions.

Social Roots of Prejudice

Why does prejudice arise? Social inequalities and divisions are partly responsible.

SOCIAL INEQUALITIES

just-world phenomenon the tendency for people to believe the world is just and that people therefore get what they deserve and deserve what they get.

When some people have money, power, and prestige and others do not, the "haves" usually develop attitudes that justify things as they are. The **just-world phenomenon** reflects an idea we commonly teach our children—that good is rewarded and evil is punished. From this it is but a short leap to assume that those who succeed must be good and those who suffer must be bad. Such reasoning enables the rich to see both their own wealth and the poor's misfortune as justly deserved.

Are women naturally unassertive and sensitive? This common perception suggests that women are well-suited for the caretaking tasks they have traditionally performed (Hoffman & Hurst, 1990). In an extreme case, slave "owners" perceived slaves as innately lazy, ignorant, and irresponsible—as having the very traits that justified enslaving them. Stereotypes rationalize inequalities.

Victims of discrimination may react with either self-blame or anger (Allport, 1954). Either reaction can feed prejudice through the classic *blame-the-victim* dynamic. Do the circumstances of poverty breed a higher crime rate? If so, that higher crime rate can be used to justify discrimination against those who live in poverty.

"If the King destroys a man, that's proof to the King it must have been a bad man." -THOMAS CROMWELL, IN ROBERT BOLT'S *A MAN FOR ALL SEASONS*, 1960

US AND THEM: INGROUP AND OUTGROUP

ingroup "Us"—people with whom we share a common identity.

outgroup "Them"—those perceived as different or apart from our ingroup.

ingroup bias the tendency to favor our own group.

We have inherited our Stone Age ancestors' need to belong, to live and love in groups. There was safety in solidarity (those who didn't band together left fewer descendants). Whether hunting, defending, or attacking, 10 hands were better than 2. Dividing the world into "us" and "them" entails racism and war, but it also provides the benefits of communal solidarity. Thus we cheer for our groups, kill for them, die for them. Indeed, we define who we are partly in terms of our groups. Through our *social identities* we associate ourselves with certain groups and contrast ourselves with others (Hogg, 1996, 2006; Turner, 1987, 2007). When Ian identifies himself as a man, an Aussie, a University of Sydney student, a Catholic, and a MacGregor, he knows who he is, and so do we.

Evolution prepared us, when encountering strangers, to make instant judgments: friend or foe? Those from our group, those who look like us, and also those who *sound* like us—with accents like our own—we instantly tend to like, from childhood onward (Gluszek & Dovidio, 2010; Kinzler et al., 2009). Mentally drawing a circle defines "us," the **ingroup.** But the social definition of who you are also states who you are not. People outside that circle are "them," the **outgroup.** An **ingroup bias**—a favoring of our own group—soon follows. Even arbitrarily creating us-them groups by tossing a coin creates this bias. In experiments, people have favored their own group when dividing any rewards (Tajfel, 1982; Wilder, 1981).

The urge to distinguish enemies from friends predisposes prejudice against strangers (Whitley, 1999). To Greeks of the classical era, all non-Greeks were "barbarians." In our own era, most students believe their school is better than all other schools in town. Perhaps you can recall being most conscious of your school identity when competing with an archrival school. Many high school students form cliques—jocks, gamers, stoners, theater types, LGBT supporters—and disparage those outside their own group. Even chimpanzees

The ingroup Basketball fans, shown here from my own college during a game against their archrival, share a social identity that defines "us" (the ingroup) and "them" (the outgroup).

have been seen to wipe clean the spot where they were touched by a chimpanzee from another group (Goodall, 1986). They also display ingroup empathy, by yawning more after seeing ingroup (rather than outgroup) members yawn (Campbell & de Waal, 2011).

Ingroup bias explains the cognitive power of partisanship (Cooper, 2010; Douthat, 2010). In the United States in the late 1980s, most Democrats believed inflation had risen under Republican president Ronald Reagan (it had dropped). In 2010, most Republicans believed that taxes had increased under Democrat president Barack Obama (for most, they had decreased).

Emotional Roots of Prejudice

Prejudice springs not only from the divisions of society but also from the passions of the heart. **Scapegoat theory** notes that when things go wrong, finding someone to blame can provide a target for anger. Following 9/11, some outraged people lashed out at innocent Arab-Americans. Others called for eliminating Saddam Hussein, the Iraqi leader whom Americans had been grudgingly tolerating. "Fear and anger create aggression, and aggression against citizens of different ethnicity or race creates racism and, in turn, new forms of terrorism," noted Philip Zimbardo (2001). A decade after 9/11, anti-Muslim animosities still flared, with mosque burnings and efforts to block an Islamic community center near New York City's Ground Zero.

Evidence for the scapegoat theory of prejudice comes from high prejudice levels among economically frustrated people, and from experiments in which a temporary frustration intensifies prejudice. Students who experience failure or are made to feel insecure often restore their self-esteem by disparaging a rival school or another person (Cialdini & Richardson, 1980; Crocker et al., 1987). To boost our own sense of status, it helps to have others to denigrate. That is why a rival's misfortune sometimes provides a twinge of pleasure. By contrast, those made to feel loved and supported become more open to and accepting of others who differ (Mikulincer & Shaver, 2001).

Negative emotions nourish prejudice. When facing death, fearing threats, or experiencing frustration, people cling more tightly to their ingroup and their friends. As the terror of death heightens patriotism, it also produces loathing and aggression toward "them"—those who threaten our world (Pyszczynski et al., 2002, 2008). The few individuals who lack fear and its associated amygdala activity—such as children with the genetic disorder Williams syndrome—also display a notable lack of racial stereotypes and prejudice (Santos et al., 2010).

Cognitive Roots of Prejudice

77-2 What are the cognitive roots of prejudice?

Prejudice springs from a culture's divisions, the heart's passions, and also from the mind's natural workings. Stereotyped beliefs are a by-product of how we cognitively simplify the world.

FORMING CATEGORIES

One way we simplify our world is to categorize. A chemist categorizes molecules as organic and inorganic. A football coach categorizes offensive players as quarterbacks, running backs, and wide receivers. Therapists categorize psychological disorders. Human beings categorize people by race, with mixed-race people often assigned to their minority identity. Despite his mixed-race background and being raised by a White mother and White grandparents, Barack Obama has been perceived by White Americans as Black. Researchers believe this happens because, after learning the features of a familiar racial group, the observer's selective attention is drawn to the distinctive features of the less-familiar minority. Jamin Halberstadt and his colleagues (2011) illustrated this learned-association effect by showing New Zealanders blended Chinese-Caucasian faces. Compared with

"For if [people were] to choose out of all the customs in the world [they would] end by preferring their own." -GREEK HISTORIAN HERODOTUS, 440 B.C.E.

scapegoat theory the theory that prejudice offers an outlet for anger by providing someone to blame.

"If the Tiber reaches the walls, if the Nile does not rise to the fields, if the sky doesn't move or the Earth does, if there is famine, if there is plague, the cry is at once: 'The Christians to the lion!'" -TERTULLIAN, *APOLOGETICUS*, 197 C.E.

"The misfortunes of others are the taste of honey." -JAPANESE SAYING

AP® Exam Tip

Pause for a minute and try to identify examples of the just-world phenomenon, ingroup bias, and scapegoating in your own school. Are there a few or a lot?

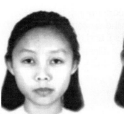     

| 100% Chinese | 80% Chinese 20% Caucasian | 60% Chinese 40% Caucasian | 40% Chinese 60% Caucasian | 20% Chinese 80% Caucasian | 100% Caucasian |

Dr. Jamin Halberstadt, Steven J. Sherman, Jeff Sherman, and Gillian Rhodes

Figure 77.5

Categorizing mixed-race people When New Zealanders quickly classified 104 photos by race, those of European descent more often than those of Chinese descent classified the ambiguous middle two as Chinese (Halberstadt et al., 2011).

participants of Chinese descent, European-descent New Zealanders more readily classified ambiguous faces as Chinese (see **FIGURE 77.5**).

In categorizing people into groups, however, we often stereotype them. We recognize how greatly *we* differ from other individuals in *our* groups. But we overestimate the homogeneity of other groups (we perceive *outgroup homogeneity*). "They"—the members of some other group—seem to look and act alike, while "we" are more diverse (Bothwell et al., 1989). To those in one ethnic group, members of another often seem more alike than they really are in attitudes, personality, and appearance. Our greater recognition for faces of our own race—called the **other-race effect** (also called the *cross-race effect* or *own-race bias*)—emerges during infancy, between 3 and 9 months of age (Gross, 2009; Kelly et al., 2007).

With effort and with experience, people get better at recognizing individual faces from another group (Hugenberg et al., 2010). People of European descent, for example, more accurately identify individual African faces if they have watched a great deal of basketball on television, exposing them to many African-heritage faces (Li et al., 1996). And the longer Chinese people have resided in a Western country, the less they exhibit the other-race effect (Hancock & Rhodes, 2008).

REMEMBERING VIVID CASES

As we saw in Module 35's discussion of the availability heuristic, we often judge the frequency of events by instances that readily come to mind. In a classic experiment, researchers showed two groups of University of Oregon students lists containing information about 50 men (Rothbart et al., 1978). The first group's list included 10 men arrested for *nonviolent* crimes, such as forgery. The second group's list included 10 men arrested for *violent* crimes, such as assault. Later, both groups were asked how many men on their list had committed *any* sort of crime. The second group overestimated the number. Vivid (violent) cases are more readily available to our memory and feed our stereotypes (**FIGURE 77.6**).

BELIEVING THE WORLD IS JUST

As we noted earlier, people often justify their prejudices by blaming victims. If the world is just, "people must get what they deserve." As one German civilian is said to have remarked when visiting the Bergen-Belsen concentration camp shortly after World War II, "What terrible criminals these prisoners must have been to receive such treatment."

other-race effect the tendency to recall faces of one's own race more accurately than faces of other races. Also called the *cross-race effect* or the *own-race bias*.

Figure 77.6

Vivid cases feed stereotypes The 9/11 Muslim terrorists created, in many minds, an exaggerated stereotype of Muslims as terrorism prone. Actually, reported a U.S. National Research Council panel on terrorism, when offering this inexact illustration, most terrorists are not Muslim and "the vast majority of Islamic people have no connection with and do not sympathize with terrorism" (Smelser & Mitchell, 2002).

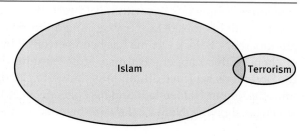

Hindsight bias is also at work here (Carli & Leonard, 1989). Have you ever heard people say that rape victims, abused spouses, or people with AIDS got what they deserved? In some countries, such as Pakistan, women who have been raped have sometimes been sentenced to severe punishment for having violated a law against adultery (Mydans, 2002). In one experiment illustrating the blame-the-victim phenomenon, people were given a detailed account of a date that ended with the woman being raped (Janoff-Bulman et al., 1985). They perceived the woman's behavior as at least partly to blame, and in hindsight, they thought, "She should have known better." (Blaming the victim also serves to reassure people that it couldn't happen to them.) Others, given the same account with the rape ending deleted, did not perceive the woman's behavior as inviting rape.

People also have a basic tendency to justify their culture's social systems (Jost et al., 2009; Kay et al, 2009). We're inclined to see the way things are as the way they ought to be. This natural conservatism makes it difficult to legislate major social changes, such as health care or climate-change policies. Once such policies are in place, our "system justification" tends to preserve them.

Before You Move On

▶ **ASK YOURSELF**
What are some examples of ingroup bias in your community?

▶ **TEST YOURSELF**
What is the difference between prejudice and discrimination?

Answers to the Test Yourself questions can be found in Appendix E at the end of the book.

Module 77 Review

 77-1 What is *prejudice*? What are its social and emotional roots?

- *Prejudice* is an unjustifiable, usually negative attitude toward a group and its members.

- Prejudice's three components are beliefs (often *stereotypes*), emotions, and predispositions to action (*discrimination*).

- Overt prejudice in North America has decreased over time, but implicit prejudice—an automatic, unthinking attitude—continues.

- The social roots of prejudice include social inequalities and divisions.
  - Higher-status groups often justify their privileged position with the *just-world phenomenon*.
  - We tend to favor our own group (*ingroup bias*) as we divide ourselves into "us" (the *ingroup*) and "them" (the *outgroup*).

- Prejudice can also be a tool for protecting our emotional well-being, as when we focus our anger by blaming events on a *scapegoat*.

77-2 What are the cognitive roots of prejudice?

- The cognitive roots of prejudice grow from our natural ways of processing information: forming categories, remembering vivid cases, and believing that the world is just and our own and our culture's ways of doing things are the right ways.

Multiple-Choice Questions

1. Which of the following is the primary distinction between prejudice and discrimination?

  a. Prejudice is cognitive and discrimination is behavioral.

  b. Prejudice is based on anger and discrimination is based on fear.

  c. Prejudice is a legal term and discrimination is a psychological term.

  d. Discrimination typically develops in infancy and prejudice typically develops in adolescence.

  e. Discrimination is primarily caused by nature and prejudice is primarily caused by nurture.

2. Which of the following is true of prejudice in recent years?

  a. Both overt and subtle prejudice have shown steady and equal increases.

  b. Subtle prejudice has been decreasing more than overt prejudice.

  c. Both overt and subtle prejudice have been increasing, but overt prejudice is increasing at a faster rate.

  d. Both overt and subtle prejudice have been increasing, but subtle prejudice is increasing at a faster rate.

  e. Overt prejudice has been decreasing more than subtle prejudice.

3. Which of the following accurately describes the just-world phenomenon?

  a. It's the reduction in prejudice that has resulted from improvements in our laws and judicial system.

  b. It's the reduction in discrimination that has resulted from improvements in our laws and judicial system.

  c. It's the belief that most people get what they deserve and deserve what they get.

  d. It's the tendency of people to deny that prejudice is still a problem.

  e. It's our mind's desire to categorize daily events as either "fair" or "unfair."

4. Which of the following is an example of ingroup bias?

  a. Hinata talked only to her five best friends when she was in ninth grade.

  b. Sabrina has been a New York Yankee fan since she was in fourth grade.

  c. Kimia believes she is the best student in her AP® Psychology class, but her grades are not as good as several students.

  d. Francisco believes he is the best student in his AP® Psychology class, and in fact he has the highest test average.

  e. Derek believes his t-ball team is the best in the league.

5. A member of one racial group viciously beats someone from a different racial group. The incident is widely publicized in the local media. Which of the following terms best describes this incident?

  a. Scapegoat theory

  b. Vivid case

  c. Just-world phenomenon

  d. Other-race effect

  e. Ingroup bias

Practice FRQs

1. Describe the three major components of prejudice.

Answer

1 point: Stereotyped judgments, which are generalized, negative beliefs about a group of people.

1 point: Negative emotions, such as hostility or fear, toward the members of a group.

1 point: A predisposition to discriminate against members of a group.

2. Describe an example of a social root of prejudice, an emotional root of prejudice, and a cognitive root of prejudice.

(3 points)

Module 78

Aggression

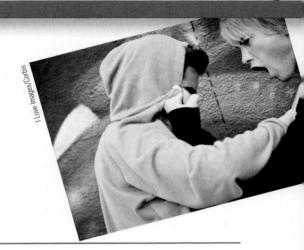

Module Learning Objectives

 Explain how psychology's definition of *aggression* differs from everyday usage, and identify the biological factors that make us more prone to hurt one another.

 Outline psychological and social-cultural triggers of aggression.

78-1 How does psychology's definition of *aggression* differ from everyday usage? What biological factors make us more prone to hurt one another?

aggression any physical or verbal behavior intended to hurt or destroy.

Prejudice hurts, but aggression often hurts more. In psychology, **aggression** is any physical or verbal behavior intended to hurt or destroy, whether done out of hostility or as a calculated means to an end. The assertive, persistent salesperson is not aggressive. Nor is the dentist who makes you wince with pain. But the person who passes along a vicious rumor about you, the person who verbally assaults you, and the attacker who mugs you for your money are aggressive.

Aggressive behavior emerges from the interaction of biology and experience. For a gun to fire, the trigger must be pulled; with some people, as with hair-trigger guns, it doesn't take much to trip an explosion. Let's look first at some biological factors that influence our thresholds for aggressive behavior, then at the psychological factors that pull the trigger.

The Biology of Aggression

Aggression varies too widely from culture to culture, era to era, and person to person to be considered an unlearned instinct. But biology does *influence* aggression. We can look for biological influences at three levels—genetic, neural, and biochemical.

Genetic Influences

Genes influence aggression. We know this because animals have been bred for aggressiveness—sometimes for sport, sometimes for research. The effect of genes also appears in human twin studies (Miles & Carey, 1997; Rowe et al., 1999). If one identical twin admits to "having a violent temper," the other twin will often independently admit the same. Fraternal twins are much less likely to respond similarly. Researchers continue to search for genetic markers in those who commit the most violence. (One is already well known and is carried by half the human race: the Y chromosome.)

"It's a guy thing."

Neural Influences

There is no one spot in the brain that controls aggression. Aggression is a complex behavior, and it occurs in particular contexts. But animal and human brains have neural systems that, given provocation, will either inhibit or facilitate aggressive behavior (Denson, 2011; Moyer, 1983). Consider:

- Researchers implanted a radio-controlled electrode in the brain of the domineering leader of a caged monkey colony. The electrode was in an area that, when stimulated, inhibits aggression. When researchers placed the control button for the electrode in the colony's cage, one small monkey learned to push it every time the boss became threatening.

- A neurosurgeon, seeking to diagnose a disorder, implanted an electrode in the amygdala of a mild-mannered woman. Because the brain has no sensory receptors, she was unable to feel the stimulation. But at the flick of a switch she snarled, "Take my blood pressure. Take it now," then stood up and began to strike the doctor.

- Studies of violent criminals have revealed diminished activity in the frontal lobes, which play an important role in controlling impulses. If the frontal lobes are damaged, inactive, disconnected, or not yet fully mature, aggression may be more likely (Amen et al., 1996; Davidson et al., 2000; Raine, 1999, 2005).

Biochemical Influences

Our genes engineer our individual nervous systems, which operate electrochemically. The hormone testosterone, for example, circulates in the bloodstream and influences the neural systems that control aggression. A raging bull will become a gentle Ferdinand when castration reduces its testosterone level. The same is true of mice. When injected with testosterone, gentle, castrated mice once again become aggressive.

Humans are less sensitive to hormonal changes. But as men age, their testosterone levels—and their aggressiveness—diminish. Hormonally charged, aggressive 17-year-olds mature into hormonally quieter and gentler 70-year-olds. Also, violent criminals tend to be muscular young males with higher-than-average testosterone levels, lower-than-average intelligence scores, and low levels of the neurotransmitter serotonin (Dabbs et al., 2001a; Pendick, 1994). Men more than women tend to have wide faces, a testosterone-linked trait, rather than roundish or long faces. And men's facial width is a predictor of their aggressiveness (Carré et al., 2009; Stirrat & Perrett, 2010).

High testosterone correlates with irritability, assertiveness, impulsiveness, and low tolerance for frustration—qualities that predispose somewhat more aggressive responses to provocation or competition for status (Dabbs et al., 2001b; Harris, 1999; McAndrew, 2009). Among both teenage boys and adult men, high testosterone levels correlate with delinquency, hard drug use, and aggressive-bullying responses to frustration (Berman et al., 1993; Dabbs & Morris, 1990; Olweus et al., 1988). Drugs that sharply reduce testosterone levels subdue men's aggressive tendencies.

> "We could avoid two-thirds of all crime simply by putting all able-bodied young men in cryogenic sleep from the age of 12 through 28." -DAVID T. LYKKEN, *THE ANTISOCIAL PERSONALITIES*, 1995

A lean, mean fighting machine—the testosterone-laden female hyena The hyena's unusual embryology pumps testosterone into female fetuses. The result is revved-up young female hyenas who seem born to fight.

Another drug that sometimes circulates in the bloodstream—alcohol—*unleashes* aggressive responses to frustration. In police data and prison surveys, as in experiments, aggression-prone people are more likely to drink, and they are more likely to become violent when intoxicated (White et al., 1993). People who have been drinking commit 4 in 10 violent crimes and 3 in 4 acts of spousal abuse (Karberg & James, 2005). Alcohol's effects are both biological and psychological (Bushman, 1993; Ito et al., 1996; Taylor & Chermack, 1993). Those who only *think* they've imbibed alcohol will be somewhat affected, but so, too, will those who have had alcohol unknowingly slipped into a drink. Unless people are distracted, alcohol tends to focus their attention on a provocation rather than on inhibitory cues (Giancola & Corman, 2007). Alcohol also inclines people to interpret ambiguous acts (such as a bump in a crowd) as provocations (Bègue et al., 2010).

Psychological and Social-Cultural Factors in Aggression

 78-2 What psychological and social-cultural factors may trigger aggressive behavior?

Biological factors influence the ease with which aggression is triggered. But what psychological and social-cultural factors pull the trigger?

Aversive Events

Suffering sometimes builds character. In laboratory experiments, however, those made miserable have often made others miserable (Berkowitz, 1983, 1989). This phenomenon is called the **frustration-aggression principle:** Frustration creates anger, which can spark aggression. One analysis of 27,667 hit-by-pitch Major League Baseball incidents between 1960 and 2004 revealed this link (Timmerman, 2007). Pitchers were most likely to hit batters when

- they had been frustrated by the previous batter hitting a home run.
- the current batter had hit a home run the last time at bat.
- a teammate had been hit by a pitch in the previous half-inning.

Other aversive stimuli—hot temperatures, physical pain, personal insults, foul odors, cigarette smoke, crowding, and a host of others—can also evoke hostility. In laboratory experiments, when people get overheated, they think, feel, and act more aggressively. In baseball games, the number of hit batters rises with the temperature (Reifman et al., 1991; see **FIGURE 78.1**). And in the wider world, violent crime and spousal abuse rates have been higher during hotter years, seasons, months, and days (Anderson & Anderson, 1984).

> **frustration-aggression principle**
> the principle that frustration—the blocking of an attempt to achieve some goal—creates anger, which can generate aggression.

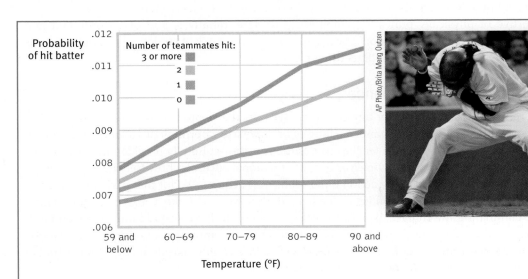

Figure 78.1

Temperature and retaliation Richard Larrick and his colleagues (2011) looked for occurrences of batters hit by pitchers during 4,566,468 pitcher-batter matchups across 57,293 Major League Baseball games since 1952. The probability of a hit batter increased if one or more of the pitcher's teammates had been hit, and also with temperature.

From the available data, Craig Anderson and his colleagues (2000; 2011) have projected that, other things being equal, global warming of 4 degrees Fahrenheit (about 2 degrees centigrade) would induce tens of thousands of additional assaults and murders—and that's before the added violence inducement from climate-change-related drought, poverty, food insecurity, and migration.

Reinforcement and Modeling

AP® Exam Tip

David Myers points out that this section is an application of material that was introduced in Unit VI. You should go back there for a quick review if you don't recognize the basic components of operant conditioning and observational learning in this material.

Aggression may be a natural response to aversive events, but learning can alter natural reactions. As Unit VI explained, we learn when our behavior is reinforced, and we learn by watching others.

In situations where experience has taught us that aggression pays, we are likely to act aggressively again. Children whose aggression has successfully intimidated other children may become bullies. Animals that have successfully fought to get food or mates become increasingly ferocious. To foster a kinder, gentler world we had best model and reward sensitivity and cooperation from an early age, perhaps by training parents to discipline without modeling violence.

Parents of delinquent youth frequently cave in to (reward) their children's tears and temper tantrums. Then, exasperated, they discipline with beatings (Patterson et al., 1982, 1992).

Parent-training programs often advise parents to avoid modeling violence by screaming and hitting. Instead, parents should reinforce desirable behaviors and frame statements positively. ("When you finish loading the dishwasher you can go play," rather than "If you don't load the dishwasher, there'll be no playing.")

One *aggression-replacement program* worked with juvenile offenders and gang members and their parents. It taught both generations new ways to control anger, and more thoughtful approaches to moral reasoning (Goldstein et al., 1998). The result? The youths' re-arrest rates dropped.

Different cultures model, reinforce, and evoke different tendencies toward violence. For example, crime rates are higher (and average happiness is lower) in countries marked by a great disparity between rich and poor (Triandis, 1994). In the United States, cultures and families that experience minimal father care also have high violence rates (Triandis, 1994). Even after controlling for parental education, race, income, and teen motherhood, American male youths from father-absent homes have double their peers' incarceration rate (Harper & McLanahan, 2004).

Violence can also vary by culture within a country. Richard Nisbett and Dov Cohen (1996) analyzed violence among White Americans in southern towns settled by Scots-Irish herders whose tradition emphasized "manly honor," the use of arms to protect one's flock, and a history of coercive slavery. Compared with their White counterparts in New England towns settled by the more traditionally peaceful Puritan, Quaker, and Dutch farmer-artisans, the cultural descendants of those herders have triple the homicide rates and are more supportive of physically punishing children, of warfare initiatives, and of uncontrolled gun ownership. "Culture-of-honor" states also have higher rates of students bringing weapons to school and of school shootings (Brown et al., 2009).

Media Models for Violence

social script culturally modeled guide for how to act in various situations.

Parents are hardly the only aggression models. In the United States and elsewhere, TV shows, films, video games, and YouTube offer supersized portions of violence. Repeatedly viewing on-screen violence teaches us **social scripts**—culturally provided mental files for how to act. When we find ourselves in new situations, uncertain how to behave, we rely on social scripts. After so many action films, teens may acquire a script that plays in their head when they face real-life conflicts. Challenged, they may "act like a man" by intimidating or eliminating the threat. Likewise, after viewing the multiple sexual innuendoes and acts found in most prime-time TV shows—often involving impulsive or short-term relationships—youths may acquire sexual scripts they later enact in real-life relationships (Kunkel et al., 2001; Sapolsky & Tabarlet, 1991).

Music lyrics also write social scripts. In one set of experiments, German university men administered hotter chili sauce to a woman and recalled more negative feelings and beliefs about women after listening to woman-hating song lyrics. Man-hating song lyrics had a similar effect on the aggressive behavior of women listeners (Fischer & Greitemeyer, 2006).

Sexual aggression is sometimes modeled in X-rated films and pornography. Content analyses have revealed that most X-rated films depict quick, casual sex between strangers, but sometimes also provide scenes of rape and sexual exploitation of women by men (Cowan et al., 1988; NCTV, 1987; Yang & Linz, 1990). These scenes often include enactments of the *rape myth*—the idea that some women invite or enjoy rape and get "swept away" while being "taken." (In actuality, rape is traumatic, and it frequently harms women's reproductive and psychological health [Golding, 1996].) Most rapists accept this myth (Brinson, 1992). So do many men and women who watch a great deal of TV: Compared with those who watch little television, heavy viewers are more accepting of the rape myth (Kahlor & Morrison, 2007). Might sexually explicit media models in the $97 billion global pornography business contribute to sexually aggressive tendencies (D'Orlando, 2011)?

Most consumers of child and adult pornography commit no known sexual crimes (Seto, 2009). But they are more likely to accept the rape myth as reality (Kingston et al., 2009). Canadian and U.S. sex offenders acknowledge a greater-than-usual appetite for sexually explicit and sexually violent materials—materials typically labeled as pornography (Kingston et al., 2009; Marshall, 1989, 2000; Oddone-Paolucci et al., 2000). The Los Angeles Police Department, for example, reported that pornography was "conspicuously present" in 62 percent of its extrafamilial child sexual abuse cases during the 1980s (Bennett, 1991). High pornography consumption also has predicted greater sexual aggressiveness among university men, even after controlling for other predictors of antisocial behavior (Vega & Malamuth, 2007). But critics object. Since 1990, the reported U.S. rape rate has declined while pornography consumption has increased (Ferguson & Hartley, 2009). And aren't many sexual aggressors merely, as sex researcher John Money (1988) suspected, using pornography "as an alibi to explain to themselves what otherwise is inexplicable"?

People heavily exposed to televised crime see the world as more dangerous. People heavily exposed to pornography see the world as more sexual. Repeatedly watching X-rated films, even nonviolent films, has many effects (Kingston et al., 2009). One's own partner seems less attractive (Module 39). Extramarital sex seems less troubling (Zillmann, 1989). A woman's friendliness seems more sexual. Sexual aggression seems less serious (Harris, 1994; Zillmann, 1989). These effects feed the ingredients of coercion against women.

In one experiment, undergraduates viewed six brief, sexually explicit films each week for six weeks (Zillmann & Bryant, 1984). A control group viewed nonerotic films during the same six-week period. Three weeks later, both groups read a newspaper report about a man convicted but not yet sentenced for raping a hitchhiker. When asked to suggest an appropriate prison term, viewers of the sexually explicit films recommended sentences half as long as those recommended by the control group.

Experiments cannot elicit actual sexual violence, but they can assess a man's willingness to hurt a woman. Often the research gauges the effect of violent versus nonviolent erotic films on men's willingness to deliver supposed electric shocks to women who had earlier provoked them. These experiments suggest that it's less the eroticism than the depictions of sexual *violence* (whether in R-rated slasher films or X-rated films) that most directly affect men's acceptance and performance of aggression against women.

To a lesser extent, nonviolent pornography can also influence aggression. In a series of studies, Nathaniel Lambert and his colleagues (2011) used various methods to explore pornography's effects on aggression against relationship partners. They found that pornography consumption predicted both self-reported aggression and laboratory noise blasts to their partner, and that abstaining from customary pornography consumption decreased aggression (while abstaining from their favorite food did not).

AP® Exam Tip

In the experiment described here, can you identify the independent and dependent variables? It's great practice to do this every time you read about an experiment.

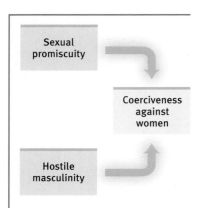

Figure 78.2

Men who sexually coerce women The recipe for coercion against women combines an impersonal approach to sex with a hostile masculinity. (Adapted from Malamuth, 1996.)

Neil Malamuth (1996) has shown that sexually coercive men typically are sexually promiscuous and hostile in their relationships with women (**FIGURE 78.2**). Several factors can create a predisposition to sexual violence (Malamuth et al., 1991, 1995). They include media influences but also dominance motives, disinhibition by alcohol, and a history of child abuse. Still, media depictions of violence can disinhibit and desensitize; viewing sexual violence fosters hostile, domineering attitudes and behaviors; and viewing pornography leads viewers to trivialize rape, devalue their partners, and engage in uncommitted sex. Media influence is not a minor issue.

Might public consciousness be raised by making people aware of the information you have just been reading? In the 1940s, movies often depicted African-Americans as childlike, superstitious buffoons, images we would not tolerate today. Many hope that entertainers, producers, and audiences might someday look back with embarrassment on the days when movies "entertained" us with scenes of sexual coercion, torture, and mutilation.

Do Violent Video Games Teach Social Scripts for Violence?

Violent video games became an issue for public debate after teenagers in more than a dozen places seemed to mimic the carnage in the shooter games they had so often played (Anderson, 2004a). In 2002, two Grand Rapids, Michigan, teens and a man in his early twenties spent part of a night drinking beer and playing *Grand Theft Auto III*. Using simulated cars, they ran down pedestrians, then beat them with fists, leaving a bloody body behind (Kolker, 2002). The same teens and man then went out for a real drive. Spotting a 38-year-old man on a bicycle, they ran him down with their car, got out, stomped and punched him, and returned home to play the game some more. (The victim, a father of three, died six days later.)

As we noted in Module 30, observing media violence tends to desensitize people to cruelty and prime them to respond aggressively when provoked. Does this violence-viewing effect extend to playing violent video games? Should parents worry about the ways actively role-playing aggression will affect their children? Experiments indicate that playing positive games has positive effects. For example, playing *Lemmings,* where a goal is to help others, increases real-life helping (Greitemeyer & Osswald, 2010). So, might a parallel effect occur after playing games that enact violence?

When combining data from 400 studies with 130,296 participants, Craig Anderson and his colleagues (2010) found such an effect: Playing violent video games increased aggression. The finding held for youth and for young adults; in North America, Japan, and Western Europe; and with each of three major research designs (correlational, experimental, and longitudinal). In a 2010 statement submitted for a U.S. Supreme Court case, Anderson was joined by more than 100 social scientists in explaining that "the psychological processes underlying such effects are well understood and include: imitation; observational learning; priming of cognitive, emotional, and behavioral scripts; physiological arousal; and emotional desensitization."

Consider some evidence:

- University men who spent the most hours playing violent video games tended to be the most physically aggressive (for example, more likely to acknowledge having hit or attacked someone else) (Anderson & Dill, 2000).

- People randomly assigned to play a game involving bloody murders with groaning victims (rather than to play nonviolent *Myst*) became more hostile. On a follow-up task, they also were more likely to blast intense noise at a fellow student.

- People with extensive experience in violent video gaming display desensitization to violence, as shown by blunted brain responses; they also are less likely to help an injured victim (Bartholow et al., 2006; Bushman & Anderson, 2009).

- After playing a violent rather than a neutral or prosocial video game, people become more likely to express dehumanized perceptions of immigrant outgroups (Greitemeyer & McLatchie, 2011).

REUTERS/Andrew Berwick via www.freak.no/Handout

Coincidence or cause? In 2011, Norwegian Anders Behring Breivik bombed government buildings in Oslo, and then went to a youth camp where he shot and killed 69 people, mostly teens. As a player of first-person shooter games, Breivik stirred debate when he commented that "I see MW2 *[Modern Warfare 2]* more as a part of my training-simulation than anything else." Did his violent game playing contribute to his violence, or was it a mere coincidental association? To explore such questions, psychologists experiment.

Young adolescents who play a lot of violent video games see the world as more hostile. Compared with nongaming kids, they get into more arguments and fights and get worse grades (Gentile, 2009). Ah, but is this merely because naturally hostile kids are drawn to such games? Apparently not. Comparisons of gamers and nongamers who scored low in hostility revealed a difference in the number of reported fights: 38 percent of the violent-game players had been in fights, versus only 4 percent of the nongamers. Over time, the nongamers became more likely to have fights only if they started playing the violent games (Anderson, 2004a). Another study, with German adolescents, found that today's violent game playing predicts future aggression, but today's aggression does not predict future game playing (Möller & Krahé, 2008). Some researchers believe that, due partly to the more active participation and rewarded violence of game play, violent video games have even greater effects on aggressive behavior and cognition than do violent TV shows and movies (Anderson et al., 2007). The effects of violent gaming, some say, are comparable to the toxic effects of asbestos or second-hand smoke exposure (Bushman et al., 2010). "Playing violent video games probably will not turn your child into a psychopathic killer," acknowledges researcher Brad Bushman (2011), "but I would want to know how the child treats his or her parents, how they treat their siblings, how much compassion they have."

Others are unimpressed by violent-game-effect findings (Ferguson & Kilburn, 2010). They note that from 1996 to 2006, youth violence was declining while video game sales were increasing. Moreover, some point out that avid game players are quick and sharp: they develop speedy reaction times and enhanced visual skills (Dye et al., 2009; Green et al., 2010). The focused fun of game playing can satisfy basic needs for a sense of competence, control, and social connection (Przbylski et al., 2010). That helps explain why, in one experiment, elementary school boys randomly selected to receive a game system spent enormous amounts of time on it over the next four months, with diminished time spent on schoolwork and with more academic problems (Weis & Cerankosky, 2010).

This much seems clear. Aggressive thoughts can lead to violent behavior and role playing can increase aggressive thoughts and emotions. As the Greek philosopher Aristotle observed, "We are what we repeatedly do."

Nevertheless, a 2011 Supreme Court decision overturned a California state law that banned violent video game sales to children (much like the ban on sales of sexually explicit materials to children). The First Amendment's free speech guarantee protects even offensive games, said the court's majority, which was unpersuaded by the evidence of harm. But the debate goes on. "What sense does it make to forbid selling to a 13-year-old a magazine with an image of a nude woman," wrote Justice Stephen Breyer, in a dissenting opinion, "while protecting the sale to that 13-year-old of an interactive video game in which he actively, but virtually, binds and gags the woman, then tortures and kills her?"

* * *

To sum up, significant behaviors, such as violence, usually have many determinants, making any single explanation an oversimplification. Asking what causes violence is therefore like asking what causes cancer. Asbestos exposure, for example, is indeed a cancer cause, albeit only one among many. Research reveals many different biological, psychological, and social-cultural influences on aggressive behavior. Like so much else, aggression is a biopsychosocial phenomenon (**FIGURE 78.3**).

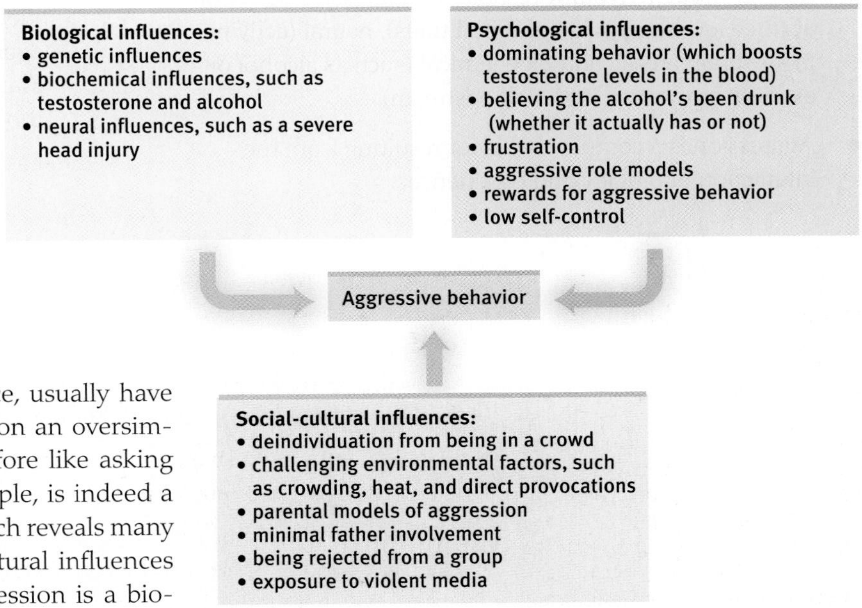

Figure 78.3

Biopsychosocial understanding of aggression Because many factors contribute to aggressive behavior, there are many ways to change such behavior, including learning anger management and communication skills, and avoiding violent media and video games.

Biological influences:
- genetic influences
- biochemical influences, such as testosterone and alcohol
- neural influences, such as a severe head injury

Psychological influences:
- dominating behavior (which boosts testosterone levels in the blood)
- believing the alcohol's been drunk (whether it actually has or not)
- frustration
- aggressive role models
- rewards for aggressive behavior
- low self-control

Aggressive behavior

Social-cultural influences:
- deindividuation from being in a crowd
- challenging environmental factors, such as crowding, heat, and direct provocations
- parental models of aggression
- minimal father involvement
- being rejected from a group
- exposure to violent media

It is also important to note that many people are leading gentle, even heroic lives amid personal and social stresses, reminding us again that individuals differ. The person matters. That people vary over time and place reminds us that environments also differ. Yesterday's plundering Vikings have become today's peace-promoting Scandinavians. Situations matter. Like all behavior, aggression arises from the interaction of persons and situations.

Before You Move On

▶ **ASK YOURSELF**

Do you think there should be laws to prevent children's exposure to violent media? Why or why not?

▶ **TEST YOURSELF**

What psychological, biological, and social-cultural influences interact to produce aggressive behaviors?

Answers to the Test Yourself questions can be found in Appendix E at the end of the book.

Module 78 Review

 78-1 How does psychology's definition of *aggression* differ from everyday usage? What biological factors make us more prone to hurt one another?

- In psychology, *aggression* is any physical or verbal behavior intended to hurt or destroy.

- Biology influences our threshold for aggressive behaviors at three levels: genetic (inherited traits), neural (activity in key brain areas), and biochemical (such as alcohol or excess testosterone in the bloodstream).

- Aggression is a complex behavior resulting from the interaction of biology and experience.

 78-2 What psychological and social-cultural factors may trigger aggressive behavior?

- Frustration (*frustration-aggression principle*), previous reinforcement for aggressive behavior, and observing an aggressive role model can all contribute to aggression.
  - Media portrayals of violence provide *social scripts* that children learn to follow.
  - Viewing sexual violence contributes to greater aggression toward women.
  - Playing violent video games increases aggressive thoughts, emotions, and behaviors.

Multiple-Choice Questions

1. A friend fails to meet an achievement goal. As a result, he gets angry and behaves aggressively. Which of the following terms best identifies this chain of events?

   a. Aggression
   b. Fundamental attribution error
   c. Frustration-aggression principle
   d. Social scripts
   e. Biopsychosocial hypothesis

2. What do we call culturally modeled guides for how to act in various situations?

   a. Aggressive behavior
   b. Cultures of honor
   c. Reinforcement modeling
   d. Social scripts
   e. Social-cultural influences

3. Which of the following is an example of a social-cultural influence on aggressive behavior?

   a. Exposure to violent media
   b. Frustration
   c. Testosterone
   d. Believing you've drunk alcohol
   e. Genetics

Practice FRQs

1. Using the biopsychosocial model, give a biological influence, social-cultural influence, and a psychological influence on aggressive behavior.

Answer

1 point: Biological: genetics, biochemicals (for example, testosterone), or neural (for example, severe frontal lobe injury).

1 point: Social-cultural: exposure to violent media, rejection from a group, or parental models of aggression.

1 point: Psychological: frustration, aggressive role models, or rewards for aggressive behavior.

2. Define social scripts and the frustration-aggression principle. Then, provide an example of each.

(4 points)

Module 79

Attraction

Klaus Tiedge/Corbis

Module Learning Objectives

79-1 Explain why we befriend or fall in love with some people but not others.

79-2 Describe how romantic love typically changes as time passes.

---

mere exposure effect
the phenomenon that repeated exposure to novel stimuli increases liking of them.

Rex USA

Familiarity breeds acceptance
When this rare white penguin was born in the Sydney, Australia, zoo, his tuxedoed peers ostracized him. Zookeepers thought they would need to dye him black to gain acceptance. But after three weeks of contact, the other penguins came to accept him.

Pause a moment and think about your relationships with two people—a close friend, and someone who has stirred your feelings of romantic love. What psychological chemistry binds us together in these special sorts of attachments that help us cope with all other relationships? Social psychology suggests some answers.

The Psychology of Attraction

79-1 Why do we befriend or fall in love with some people but not others?

We endlessly wonder how we can win others' affection and what makes our own affections flourish or fade. Does familiarity breed contempt, or does it intensify affection? Do birds of a feather flock together, or do opposites attract? Is beauty only skin deep, or does attractiveness matter greatly? To explore these questions, let's consider three ingredients of our liking for one another: proximity, attractiveness, and similarity.

Proximity

Before friendships become close, they must begin. *Proximity*—geographic nearness—is friendship's most powerful predictor. Proximity provides opportunities for aggression, but much more often it breeds liking. Study after study reveals that people are most inclined to like, and even to marry, those who live in the same neighborhood, who sit nearby in class, who work in the same office, who share the same parking lot, who eat in the same cafeteria. Look around. Mating starts with meeting. (For more on modern ways to connect people, see Close-up: Online Matchmaking and Speed Dating.)

Proximity breeds liking partly because of the **mere exposure effect.** Repeated exposure to novel stimuli increases our liking for them. This applies to nonsense syllables, musical selections, geometric figures, Chinese characters, human faces, and the letters of our own name (Moreland & Zajonc, 1982; Nuttin, 1987; Zajonc, 2001). We are even somewhat more likely to marry someone whose first or last name resembles our own (Jones et al., 2004).

So, within certain limits, familiarity breeds fondness (Bornstein, 1989, 1999). Researchers demonstrated this by having four equally attractive women silently attend a

Close-up

Online Matchmaking and Speed Dating

Those who have not found a romantic partner in their immediate proximity may cast a wider net by joining the estimated 30 million people who each year try one of the some 1500 online dating services (Ellin, 2009). Online matchmaking works mostly by expanding the pool of potential mates (Finkel et al., 2012a,b).

Although published research on the effectiveness of Internet matchmaking services is sparse, this much seems well established: Some people, including occasional predators, dishonestly represent their age, attractiveness, occupation, or other details, and thus are not who they seem to be. Nevertheless, Katelyn McKenna and John Bargh and their colleagues have offered a surprising finding: Compared with relationships formed in person, Internet-formed friendships and romantic relationships have been, on average, more likely to last beyond two years (Bargh et al. 2002, 2004; McKenna & Bargh, 1998, 2000; McKenna et al., 2002). In one of their studies, people disclosed more, with less posturing, to those whom they met online. When conversing online with someone for 20 minutes, they felt more liking for that person than they did for someone they had met and talked with face to face. This was true even when (unknown to them) it was the same person! Internet friendships often feel as real and important to people as in-person relationships. That helps explain why one-third of American marriages occur among partners who met online, and why those marriages are slightly more stable and satisfying than marriages that began offline (Cacioppo et al., 2013).

Speed dating pushes the search for romance into high gear. In a process pioneered by a matchmaking Jewish rabbi,

AND DO YOU, FUNNYGRL@BIZONE.NET, TAKE HARLEY99@COMCO.COM...

THEY MET ONLINE.

© Dave Coverly

people meet a succession of prospective partners, either in person or via webcam (Bower, 2009). After a 3- to 8-minute conversation, people move on to the next person. (In an in-person meeting, one partner—usually the woman—remains seated and the other circulates.) Those who want to meet again can arrange for future contacts. For many participants, 4 minutes is enough time to form a feeling about a conversational partner and to register whether the partner likes them (Eastwick & Finkel, 2008a,b).

Researchers have quickly realized that speed dating offers a unique opportunity for studying influences on our first impressions of potential romantic partners. Among recent findings are these:

- Men are more transparent. Observers (male or female) watching videos of speed-dating encounters can read a man's level of romantic interest more accurately than a woman's (Place et al., 2009).

- Given more options, people's choices become more superficial. Meeting lots of potential partners leads people to focus on more easily assessed characteristics, such as height and weight (Lenton & Francesconi, 2010). This was true even when researchers controlled for time spent with each partner.

- Men wish for future contact with more of their speed dates; women tend to be more choosy. But this gender difference disappears if the conventional roles are reversed, so that men stay seated while women circulate (Finkel & Eastwick, 2009).

200-student class for zero, 5, 10, or 15 class sessions (Moreland & Beach, 1992). At the end of the course, students were shown slides of each woman and asked to rate her attractiveness. The most attractive? The ones they'd seen most often. The phenomenon would come as no surprise to the young Taiwanese man who wrote more than 700 letters to his girlfriend, urging her to marry him. She did marry—the mail carrier (Steinberg, 1993).

No face is more familiar than your own. And that helps explain an interesting finding by Lisa DeBruine (2004): We like other people when their faces incorporate some morphed features of our own. When DeBruine (2002) had

Ben Pruchnie/Getty Images

The mere exposure effect
The mere exposure effect applies even to ourselves. Because the human face is not perfectly symmetrical, the face we see in the mirror is not the same face our friends see. Most of us prefer the familiar mirror image, while our friends like the reverse (Mita et al., 1977). The Maggie Smith (actor) known to her fans is at left. The person she sees in the mirror each morning is shown at right, and that's the photo she would probably prefer.

Beauty grows with mere exposure Herman Miller, Inc.'s famed Aeron chair initially received high comfort ratings but abysmal beauty ratings. To some it looked like "lawn furniture" or "a giant prehistoric insect" (Gladwell, 2005). But then, with design awards, media visibility, and imitators, the ugly duckling came to be the company's best-selling chair ever and to be seen as beautiful. With people, too, beauty lies partly in the beholder's eye and can grow with exposure.

> "Personal beauty is a greater recommendation than any letter of introduction." -ARISTOTLE, *APOTHEGEMS*, 330 B.C.E.

FYI

Percentage of Men and Women Who "Constantly Think About Their Looks"

	Men	Women
Canada	18%	20%
United States	17	27
Mexico	40	45
Venezuela	47	65

From Roper Starch survey, reported by McCool (1999).

McMaster University students (both men and women) play a game with a supposed other player, they were more trusting and cooperative when the other person's image had some of their own facial features morphed into it. In me I trust.

For our ancestors, the mere exposure effect had survival value. What was familiar was generally safe and approachable. What was unfamiliar was more often dangerous and threatening. Evolution may therefore have hard-wired into us the tendency to bond with those who are familiar and to be wary of those who are unfamiliar (Zajonc, 1998). If so, gut-level prejudice against those who are culturally different could be a primitive, automatic emotional response (Devine, 1995). It's what we do with our knee-jerk prejudice that matters, say researchers. Do we let those feelings control our behavior? Or do we monitor our feelings and act in ways that reflect our conscious valuing of human equality?

Physical Attractiveness

Once proximity affords us contact, what most affects our first impressions? The person's sincerity? Intelligence? Personality? Hundreds of experiments reveal that it is something far more superficial: physical appearance. This finding is unnerving for most of us who were taught that "beauty is only skin deep" and that "appearances can be deceiving."

In one early study, researchers randomly matched new University of Minnesota students for a Welcome Week dance (Walster et al., 1966). Before the dance, the researchers gave each student a battery of personality and aptitude tests, and they rated each student's level of physical attractiveness. On the night of the blind date, the couples danced and talked for more than two hours and then took a brief intermission to rate their dates. What determined whether they liked each other? Only one thing seemed to matter: appearance. Both the men and the women liked good-looking dates best. Women are more likely than men to say that another's looks don't affect them (Lippa, 2007). But studies show that a man's looks do affect women's behavior (Feingold, 1990; Sprecher, 1989; Woll, 1986). Speed-dating experiments confirm that attractiveness influences first impressions for both sexes (Belot & Francesconi, 2006; Finkel & Eastwick, 2008).

Physical attractiveness also predicts how often people date and how popular they feel. It affects initial impressions of people's personalities. We don't assume that attractive people are more compassionate, but we do perceive them as healthier, happier, more sensitive, more successful, and more socially skilled (Eagly et al., 1991; Feingold, 1992; Hatfield & Sprecher, 1986). Attractive, well-dressed people are more likely to make a favorable impression on potential employers, and they tend to be more successful in their jobs (Cash & Janda, 1984; Langlois et al., 2000; Solomon, 1987). Income analyses show a penalty for plainness or obesity and a premium for beauty (Engemann & Owyang, 2005).

An analysis of 100 top-grossing films since 1940 found that attractive characters were portrayed as morally superior to unattractive characters (Smith et al., 1999). But Hollywood modeling doesn't explain why, to judge from their gazing times, even babies prefer attractive over unattractive faces (Langlois et al., 1987). So do some blind people, as University of Birmingham professor John Hull (1990, p. 23) discovered after going blind. A colleague's remarks on a woman's beauty would strangely affect his feelings. He found this "deplorable. . . . What can it matter to me what sighted men think of women . . . yet I do care what sighted men think, and I do not seem able to throw off this prejudice."

For those who find importance of looks unfair and unenlightened, two attractiveness findings may be reassuring. First, people's attractiveness is surprisingly unrelated to their self-esteem and happiness (Diener et al., 1995; Major et al., 1984). Unless we have just compared ourselves with superattractive people, few of us (thanks, perhaps, to the mere exposure effect) view ourselves as unattractive (Thornton & Moore, 1993). Second, strikingly attractive people are sometimes suspicious that praise for their work may simply be a reaction to their looks. Less attractive people are more likely to accept praise as sincere (Berscheid, 1981).

In the eye of the beholder Conceptions of attractiveness vary by culture. Yet some adult physical features, such as a youthful form and face, seem attractive everywhere.

Beauty is in the eye of the culture. Hoping to look attractive, people across the globe have pierced their noses, lengthened their necks, bound their feet, and dyed or painted their skin and hair. They have gorged themselves to achieve a full figure or liposuctioned fat to achieve a slim one, applied chemicals hoping to rid themselves of unwanted hair or to regrow wanted hair, strapped on leather garments to make their breasts seem smaller or surgically filled their breasts with silicone and put on Wonderbras to make them look bigger. Cultural ideals also change over time. For women in North America, the ultra-thin ideal of the Roaring Twenties gave way to the soft, voluptuous Marilyn Monroe ideal of the 1950s, only to be replaced by today's lean yet busty ideal.

If we're not born attractive, we may try to buy beauty. Americans now spend more on beauty supplies than on education and social services combined. Still not satisfied, millions undergo plastic surgery, teeth capping and whitening, Botox skin smoothing, and laser hair removal (ASPS, 2010).

Some aspects of attractiveness, however, do cross place and time (Cunningham et al., 2005; Langlois et al., 2000). By providing reproductive clues, bodies influence sexual attraction. As evolutionary psychologists explain (Module 15), men in many cultures, from Australia to Zambia, judge women as more attractive if they have a youthful, fertile appearance, suggested by a low waist-to-hip ratio (Karremans et al., 2010; Perilloux et al., 2010; Platek & Singh, 2010). Women feel attracted to healthy-looking men, but especially—and the more so when ovulating—to those who seem mature, dominant, masculine, and affluent (Gallup & Frederick, 2010; Gangestad et al., 2010). But faces matter, too. When people separately rate opposite-sex faces and bodies, the face tends to be the better predictor of overall physical attractiveness (Currie & Little, 2009; Peters et al., 2007).

People everywhere also seem to prefer physical features—noses, legs, physiques—that are neither unusually large nor small. An averaged face is attractive (**FIGURE 79.1**). In one clever demonstration, researchers digitized the faces of up to 32 college students and used a computer to average them (Langlois & Roggman, 1990). Students

Figure 79.1

Average is attractive Which of these faces offered by University of St. Andrews psychologist David Perrett (2002, 2010) is most attractive? Most people say it's the face on the right—of a nonexistent person that is the average composite of these 3 plus 57 other actual faces.

Extreme makeover Greater wealth and concerns about appearance in China have led to increasing numbers of women seeking to alter their appearance. This woman underwent six months of grueling plastic surgery to transform her eyes, nose, chin, breasts, abdomen, bottom, legs, and skin in hopes of obtaining a career in film.

judged the averaged, composite faces as more attractive than 96 percent of the individual faces. One reason is that averaged faces are symmetrical, and people with symmetrical faces and bodies are more sexually attractive (Rhodes et al., 1999; Singh, 1995; Thornhill & Gangestad, 1994). Merge either half of your face with its mirror image and your symmetrical new face would boost your attractiveness a notch.

Our feelings also influence our attractiveness judgments. Imagine two people. The first is honest, humorous, and polite. The second is rude, unfair, and abusive. Which one is more attractive? Most people perceive the person with the appealing traits as also more physically attractive (Lewandowski et al., 2007). Those we like we find attractive. In a Rodgers and Hammerstein musical, Prince Charming asks Cinderella, "Do I love you because you're beautiful, or are you beautiful because I love you?" Chances are it's both. As we see our loved ones again and again, their physical imperfections grow less noticeable and their attractiveness grows more apparent (Beaman & Klentz, 1983; Gross & Crofton, 1977). Shakespeare said it in *A Midsummer Night's Dream:* "Love looks not with the eyes, but with the mind." Come to love someone and watch beauty grow.

Similarity

So proximity has brought you into contact with someone, and your appearance has made an acceptable first impression. What now influences whether you will become friends? As you get to know each other better, will the chemistry be better if you are opposites or if you are alike?

It makes a good story—extremely different types living in harmonious union: Rat, Mole, and Badger in *The Wind in the Willows,* Frog and Toad in Arnold Lobel's books. The stories delight us by expressing what we seldom experience, for in real life, opposites *retract* (Rosenbaum, 1986). Compared with randomly paired people, friends and couples are far more likely to share common attitudes, beliefs, and interests (and, for that matter, age, religion, race, education, intelligence, smoking behavior, and economic status).

Moreover, the more alike people are, the more their liking endures (Byrne, 1971). Journalist Walter Lippmann was right to suppose that love lasts "when the lovers love many things together, and not merely each other." Similarity breeds content. Dissimilarity often fosters disfavor, which helps explain many straight men's disapproval of gay men who are doubly dissimilar from themselves in sexual orientation and gender roles (Lehavot & Lambert, 2007).

Proximity, attractiveness, and similarity are not the only determinants of attraction. We also like those who like us. This is especially so when our self-image is low. When we believe someone likes us, we feel good and respond to them warmly, which leads them to like us even more (Curtis & Miller, 1986). To be liked is powerfully rewarding.

Indeed, all the findings we have considered so far can be explained by a simple *reward theory of attraction:* We will like those whose behavior is rewarding to us, and we will continue relationships that offer more rewards than costs. When people live or work in close proximity with us, it costs less time and effort to develop the friendship and enjoy its benefits. When people are attractive, they are aesthetically pleasing, and associating with them can be socially rewarding. When people share our views, they reward us by validating our own.

Romantic Love

79-2 How does romantic love typically change as time passes?

Sometimes people move quickly from initial impressions, to friendship, to the more intense, complex, and mysterious state of romantic love. If love endures, temporary passionate love will mellow into a lingering companionate love (Hatfield, 1988).

Passionate Love

A key ingredient of **passionate love** is arousal. The two-factor theory of emotion (Module 41) can help us understand this intense positive absorption in another (Hatfield, 1988). That theory assumes that:

- Emotions have two ingredients—*physical arousal* plus *cognitive appraisal.*
- Arousal from any source can enhance one emotion or another, depending on how we interpret and label the arousal.

In tests of the two-factor theory, college men have been aroused by fright, by running in place, by viewing erotic materials, or by listening to humorous or repulsive monologues. They were then introduced to an attractive woman and asked to rate her (or their girlfriend). Unlike unaroused men, the stirred-up men attributed some of their arousal to the woman or girlfriend, and felt more attracted to her (Carducci et al., 1978; Dermer & Pyszczynski, 1978; White & Kight, 1984).

A sample experiment: Researchers studied people crossing two bridges above British Columbia's rocky Capilano River (Dutton & Aron, 1974, 1989). One, a swaying footbridge, was 230 feet above the rocks; the other was low and solid. The researchers had an attractive young woman intercept men coming off each bridge, and ask their help in filling out a short questionnaire. She then offered her phone number in case they wanted to hear more about her project. Far more of those who had just crossed the high bridge—which left their hearts pounding—accepted the number and later called the woman. To be revved up and to associate some of that arousal with a desirable person is to feel the pull of passion. Adrenaline makes the heart grow fonder. And when sexual desire is supplemented by a growing attachment, the result is the passion of romantic love (Berscheid, 2010).

Companionate Love

Although the desire and attachment of romantic love often endure, the intense absorption in the other, the thrill of the romance, the giddy "floating on a cloud" feelings typically fade. Does this mean the French are correct in saying that "love makes the time pass and time makes love pass"? Or can friendship and commitment keep a relationship going after the passion cools?

The evidence indicates that, as love matures, it becomes a steadier **companionate love**—a deep, affectionate attachment (Hatfield, 1988). The flood of passion-facilitating hormones (testosterone, dopamine, adrenaline) subsides and another hormone, oxytocin, supports feelings of trust, calmness, and bonding with the mate. In the most satisfying of marriages, attraction and sexual desire endure, minus the obsession of early stage romance (Acevedo & Aron, 2009).

There may be adaptive wisdom to the shift from passion to attachment (Reis & Aron, 2008). Passionate love often produces children, whose survival is aided by the parents' waning obsession with each other. Failure to appreciate passionate love's limited half-life can doom a relationship (Berscheid et al., 1984). Indeed, recognizing the short duration of obsessive passionate love, some societies deem such feelings to be an irrational reason for marrying. Better, they say, to choose (or have someone choose for you) a partner with a compatible background and interests. Non-Western cultures, where people rate love less important for marriage, do have lower divorce rates (Levine et al., 1995).

Snapshots at jasonlove.com

Bill looked at Susan, Susan at Bill. Suddenly death didn't seem like an option. This was love at first sight.

FYI

Note the difference between lust (immediate desire) and romantic love (desire + attachment).

---

passionate love an aroused state of intense positive absorption in another, usually present at the beginning of a love relationship.

companionate love the deep affectionate attachment we feel for those with whom our lives are intertwined.

"When two people are under the influence of the most violent, most insane, most delusive, and most transient of passions, they are required to swear that they will remain in that excited, abnormal, and exhausting condition continuously until death do them part." -George Bernard Shaw, "Getting Married," 1908

HI & LOIS

One key to a gratifying and enduring relationship is **equity.** When equity exists—when both partners receive in proportion to what they give—their chances for sustained and satisfying companionate love are good (Gray-Little & Burks, 1983; Van Yperen & Buunk, 1990). In one national survey, "sharing household chores" ranked third, after "faithfulness" and a "happy sexual relationship," on a list of nine things people associated with successful marriages. "I like hugs. I like kisses. But what I really love is help with the dishes," summarized the Pew Research Center (2007).

Equity's importance extends beyond marriage. Mutually sharing self and possessions, making decisions together, giving and getting emotional support, promoting and caring about each other's welfare—all of these acts are at the core of every type of loving relationship (Sternberg & Grajek, 1984). It's true for lovers, for parent and child, and for intimate friends.

Another vital ingredient of loving relationships is **self-disclosure,** the revealing of intimate details about ourselves—our likes and dislikes, our dreams and worries, our proud and shameful moments. "When I am with my friend," noted the Roman statesman Seneca, "me thinks I am alone, and as much at liberty to speak anything as to think it." Self-disclosure breeds liking, and liking breeds self-disclosure (Collins & Miller, 1994). As one person reveals a little, the other reciprocates, the first then reveals more, and on and on, as friends or lovers move to deeper and deeper intimacy (Baumeister & Bratslavsky, 1999).

One experiment marched student pairs through 45 minutes of increasingly self-disclosing conversation—from "When did you last sing to yourself?" to "When did you last cry in front of another person? By yourself?" Others spent the time with small-talk questions, such as "What was your high school like?" (Aron et al., 1997). By the experiment's end, those experiencing the escalating intimacy felt remarkably close to their conversation partner, much closer than did the small-talkers.

Intimacy can also grow from pausing to ponder and write our feelings. In another study, researchers invited one person from each of 86 dating couples to spend 20 minutes a day over three days either writing their deepest thoughts and feelings about the relationship or writing merely about their daily activities (Slatcher & Pennebaker, 2006). Those who had written about their feelings expressed more emotion in their instant messages with their partners in the days following, and 77 percent were still dating three months later (compared with 52 percent of those who had written about their activities).

In addition to equity and self-disclosure, a third key to enduring love is *positive support*. While relationship conflicts are inevitable, we can ask ourselves whether our communications more often express sarcasm or support, scorn or sympathy, sneers or smiles. For unhappy couples,

equity a condition in which people receive from a relationship in proportion to what they give to it.

self-disclosure revealing intimate aspects of oneself to others.

Love is an ancient thing In 2007, a 5000- to 6000-year-old "Romeo and Juliet" young couple was unearthed locked in embrace, near Rome.

disagreements, criticisms, and put downs are routine. For happy couples in enduring relationships, positive interactions (compliments, touches, laughing) outnumber negative interactions (sarcasm, disapproval, insults) by at least 5 to 1 (Gottman, 2007; see also Sullivan et al., 2010).

In the mathematics of love, self-disclosing intimacy + mutually supportive equity = enduring companionate love.

Before You Move On

▶ **ASK YOURSELF**

When you think of some of the older couples you know, which ones seem to experience companionate love? How do you think they've achieved it?

▶ **TEST YOURSELF**

How does being physically attractive influence others' perceptions?

Answers to the Test Yourself questions can be found in Appendix E at the end of the book.

Module 79 Review

 79-1 Why do we befriend or fall in love with some people but not others?

- Proximity (geographical nearness) increases liking, in part because of the *mere exposure effect*—exposure to novel stimuli increases liking of those stimuli.

- Physical attractiveness increases social opportunities and improves the way we are perceived.

- Similarity of attitudes and interests greatly increases liking, especially as relationships develop. We also like those who like us.

 79-2 How does romantic love typically change as time passes?

- Intimate love relationships start with *passionate love*—an intensely aroused state.

- Over time, the strong affection of *companionate love* may develop, especially if enhanced by an *equitable* relationship and by intimate *self-disclosure*.

Multiple-Choice Questions

1. Which of the following terms describes our geographic nearness to another person?

   a. Mere exposure effect
   b. Proximity
   c. Similarity
   d. Ingroup bias
   e. Symmetry

2. Which of the following is an example of the mere exposure effect?

   a. Adrianna has started arriving tardy to her second period class to avoid a group of kids in the hall who constantly tease her.
   b. Abe has biked the same route to school so many times that he no longer has to think about where to turn.
   c. Daiyu has seen the same toothpaste ad on television a hundred times. Each time she sees it she hates it more.
   d. Abdul has always loved dogs, so he adopted one from the local shelter.
   e. Guiren didn't like sushi the first couple times he tried it, but his friend encouraged him to keep eating it and now it's one of his favorite foods.

3. Which of the following is an aspect of physical attractiveness that appears to be true across cultures?

   a. Indications of reproductive health
   b. Height
   c. Weight
   d. Size of the ears
   e. Shape of the chin

4. Over time, which of the following is typically true of the relationship between passionate love and companionate love?

   a. Passionate and companionate love both decrease.
   b. Passionate love increases and companionate love decreases.
   c. Passionate and companionate love both increase.
   d. Passionate love decreases and companionate love increases.
   e. There is no consistent relationship between the levels of passionate love and companionate love.

Practice FRQs

1. List the three major factors that influence attraction.

Answer

1 point: Proximity, which is geographic nearness.

1 point: Physical attractiveness.

1 point: Similarity.

2. Describe one key factor present in passionate love and two key factors present in companionate love.

(3 points)

Module 80

Altruism, Conflict, and Peacemaking

Paul Conklin/Photo Edit

Module Learning Objectives

80-1 Identify the times when people are most—and least—likely to help.

80-2 Discuss how social exchange theory and social norms explain helping behavior.

80-3 Explain how social traps and mirror-image perceptions fuel social conflict.

80-4 Discuss how we can transform feelings of prejudice, aggression, and conflict into attitudes that promote peace.

Altruism

80-1 When are people most—and least—likely to help?

Altruism is an unselfish concern for the welfare of others. In rescuing his jailer, Dirk Willems exemplified altruism (Unit XIV opener). So also did Carl Wilkens and Paul Rusesabagina in Kigali, Rwanda. Wilkens, a Seventh Day Adventist missionary, was living there in 1994 with his family when Hutu militia began to slaughter the Tutsi. The U.S. government, church leaders, and friends all implored Wilkens to leave. He refused. After evacuating his family, and even after every other American had left Kigali, he alone stayed and contested the 800,000-person genocide. When the militia came to kill him and his Tutsi servants, Wilkens' Hutu neighbors deterred them. Despite repeated death threats, he spent his days running roadblocks to take food and water to orphanages and to negotiate, plead, and bully his way through the bloodshed, saving lives time and again. "It just seemed the right thing to do," he later explained (Kristof, 2004).

Elsewhere in Kigali, Rusesabagina, a Hutu married to a Tutsi and the acting manager of a luxury hotel, was sheltering more than 1200 terrified Tutsis and moderate Hutus. When international peacekeepers abandoned the city and hostile militia threatened his guests in the "Hotel Rwanda" (as it came to be called in a 2004 movie), the courageous Rusesabagina began cashing in past favors. He bribed the militia and telephoned influential people abroad to exert pressure on local authorities, thereby sparing the lives of the hotel's occupants from the surrounding chaos.

Both Wilkens and Rusesabagina were displaying altruism. Altruism became a major concern of social psychologists after an especially vile act of sexual violence. On March 13, 1964, a stalker repeatedly stabbed Kitty Genovese, then raped her as she lay dying outside her Queens, New York, apartment at 3:30 A.M. "Oh, my God, he stabbed me!"

altruism unselfish regard for the welfare of others.

"Probably no single incident has caused social psychologists to pay as much attention to an aspect of social behavior as Kitty Genovese's murder." -R. LANCE SHOTLAND (1984)

Genovese screamed into the early morning stillness. "Please help me!" Windows opened and lights went on as neighbors (38 of them, said an initial *New York Times* report, though that number was later contested) heard her screams. Her attacker fled and then returned to stab and rape her again. Not until he had fled for good did anyone so much as call the police, at 3:50 A.M.

Bystander Intervention

Reflecting on initial reports of the Genovese murder and other such tragedies, most commentators were outraged by the bystanders' "apathy" and "indifference." Rather than blaming the onlookers, social psychologists John Darley and Bibb Latané (1968b) attributed their inaction to an important situational factor—the presence of others. Given certain circumstances, they suspected, most of us might behave similarly.

After staging emergencies under various conditions, Darley and Latané assembled their findings into a decision scheme: We will help only if the situation enables us first to *notice* the incident, then to *interpret* it as an emergency, and finally to *assume responsibility* for helping (**FIGURE 80.1**). At each step, the presence of others can turn us away from the path that leads to helping.

Figure 80.1

The decision-making process for bystander intervention Before helping, one must first notice an emergency, then correctly interpret it, and then feel responsible. (From Darley & Latané, 1968b.)

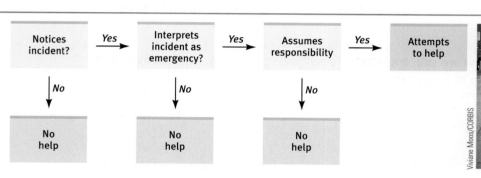

Darley and Latané reached their conclusions after interpreting the results of a series of experiments. For example, they simulated a physical emergency in their laboratory as students participated in a discussion over an intercom. Each student was in a separate cubicle, and only the person whose microphone was switched on could be heard. When his turn came, one student (an accomplice of the experimenters) made sounds as though he were having an epileptic seizure, and he called for help (Darley & Latané, 1968a).

How did the other students react? As **FIGURE 80.2** shows, those who believed only they could hear the victim—and therefore thought they alone were responsible for helping him—usually went to his aid. Students who thought others also could hear the victim's cries were more likely to ignore the victim. When more people shared responsibility for helping—when there was a *diffusion of responsibility*—any single listener was less likely to help.

Hundreds of additional experiments have confirmed this **bystander effect.** For example, researchers and their assistants took 1497 elevator rides in three cities and "accidentally" dropped coins or pencils in front of 4813 fellow passengers (Latané & Dabbs, 1975). When alone with the person in need, 40 percent helped; in the presence of 5 other bystanders, only 20 percent helped.

Observations of behavior in thousands of such situations—relaying an emergency phone call, aiding a stranded motorist, donating blood, picking up dropped books, contributing money, giving time—show that the *best* odds of our helping someone occur when

- the person appears to need and deserve help.
- the person is in some way similar to us.
- the person is a woman.

bystander effect the tendency for any given bystander to be less likely to give aid if other bystanders are present.

AP® Exam Tip

Common sense suggests that you would be more likely to get help if there are more people around, but research on the bystander effect has in fact shown just the opposite is true. This concept often shows up on the AP® exam, so be sure you understand it.

- we have just observed someone else being helpful.
- we are not in a hurry.
- we are in a small town or rural area.
- we are feeling guilty.
- we are focused on others and not preoccupied.
- we are in a good mood.

This last result, that happy people are helpful people, is one of the most consistent findings in all of psychology. As poet Robert Browning (1868) observed, "Oh, make us happy and you make us good!" It doesn't matter how we are cheered. Whether by being made to feel successful and intelligent, by thinking happy thoughts, by finding money, or even by receiving a posthypnotic suggestion, we become more generous and more eager to help (Carlson et al., 1988). And given a feeling of elevation after witnessing or learning of someone else's self-giving deed, our helping will become even more pronounced (Schnall et al., 2010).

So happiness breeds helpfulness. But it's also true that helpfulness breeds happiness. Making charitable donations activates brain areas associated with reward (Harbaugh et al., 2007). That helps explain a curious finding: People who give money away are happier than those who spend it almost entirely on themselves. In one experiment, researchers gave people an envelope with cash and instructions either to spend it on themselves or to spend it on others (Dunn et al., 2008). Which group was happiest at the day's end? It was, indeed, those assigned to the spend-it-on-others condition.

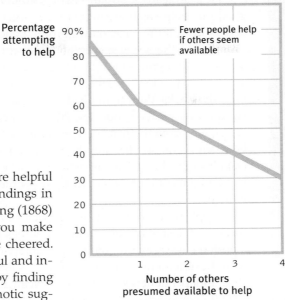

Figure 80.2

Responses to a simulated physical emergency When people thought they alone heard the calls for help from a person they believed to be having an epileptic seizure, they usually helped. But when they thought four others were also hearing the calls, fewer than one-third responded. (From Darley & Latané, 1968a.)

The Norms for Helping

 How do social exchange theory and social norms explain helping behavior?

Why do we help? One widely held view is that self-interest underlies all human interactions, that our constant goal is to maximize rewards and minimize costs. Accountants call it *cost-benefit analysis.* Philosophers call it *utilitarianism.* Social psychologists call it **social exchange theory.** If you are pondering whether to donate blood, you may weigh the costs of doing so (time, discomfort, and anxiety) against the benefits (reduced guilt, social approval, and good feelings). If the rewards exceed the costs, you will help.

Others believe that we help because we have been socialized to do so, through norms that prescribe how we *ought* to behave. Through socialization, we learn the **reciprocity norm,** the expectation that we should return help, not harm, to those who have helped us. In our relations with others of similar status, the reciprocity norm compels us to give (in favors, gifts, or social invitations) about as much as we receive.

The reciprocity norm kicked in after Dave Tally, a Tempe, Arizona, homeless man, found $3300 in a backpack that had been lost by an Arizona State University student headed to buy a used car (Lacey, 2010). Instead of using the cash for much-needed bike repairs, food, and shelter, Tally turned the backpack in to the social service agency where he volunteered. To reciprocate Tally's help, the student thanked him with a reward. Hearing about Tally's self-giving deeds, dozens of others also sent him money and job offers.

social exchange theory the theory that our social behavior is an exchange process, the aim of which is to maximize benefits and minimize costs.

reciprocity norm an expectation that people will help, not hurt, those who have helped them.

Subway hero Wesley Autrey "I don't feel like I did something spectacular; I just saw someone who needed help."

We also learn a **social-responsibility norm:** that we should help those who need our help—young children and others who cannot give as much as they receive—even if the costs outweigh the benefits. Construction worker Wesley Autrey exemplified the social-responsibility norm on January 2, 2007. He and his 6- and 4-year-old daughters were awaiting a New York City subway train when, before them, a man collapsed in a seizure, got up, then stumbled to the platform's edge and fell onto the tracks. With train headlights approaching, "I had to make a split decision," Autrey later recalled (Buckley, 2007). His decision, as his girls looked on in horror, was to leap from the platform, push the man off the tracks and into a foot-deep space between them, and lay atop him. As the train screeched to a halt, five cars traveled just above his head, leaving grease on his knit cap. When Autrey cried out, "I've got two daughters up there. Let them know their father is okay," the onlookers erupted into applause.

People who attend weekly religious services often are admonished to practice the social-responsibility norm, and sometimes they do. In American surveys, they have reported twice as many volunteer hours spent helping the poor and infirm, compared with those who rarely or never attend religious services (Hodgkinson & Weitzman, 1992; Independent Sector, 2002). Between 2006 and 2008, Gallup polls sampled more than 300,000 people across 140 countries, comparing those "highly religious" (who said religion was important to them and who had attended a religious service in the prior week) with those less religious. The highly religious, despite being poorer, were about 50 percent more likely to report having "donated money to a charity in the last month" and to have volunteered time to an organization (Pelham & Crabtree, 2008). Although positive social norms encourage generosity and enable group living, conflicts often divide us.

Conflict and Peacemaking

We live in surprising times. With astonishing speed, recent democratic movements swept away totalitarian rule in Eastern European and Arab countries, and hopes for a new world order displaced the Cold War chill. And yet, the twenty-first century began with terrorist acts and war. *Every day,* the world has continued to spend more than $3 billion for arms and armies—money that could have been used for housing, nutrition, education, and health care. Knowing that wars begin in human minds, psychologists have wondered: What in the human mind causes destructive conflict? How might the perceived threats of social diversity be replaced by a spirit of cooperation?

Elements of Conflict

 How do social traps and mirror-image perceptions fuel social conflict?

To a social psychologist, a **conflict** is a perceived incompatibility of actions, goals, or ideas. The elements of conflict are much the same, whether we are speaking of nations at war, cultural groups feuding within a society, or partners sparring in a relationship. In each situation, people become enmeshed in potentially destructive processes that can produce results no one wants. Among these processes are social traps and distorted perceptions.

SOCIAL TRAPS

In some situations, we support our collective well-being by pursuing our personal interests. As capitalist Adam Smith wrote in *The Wealth of Nations* (1776), "It is not from the benevolence of the butcher, the brewer, or the baker that we expect our dinner, but from their regard to their own interest." In other situations, we harm our collective well-being by pursuing our personal interests. Such situations are **social traps.**

social-responsibility norm an expectation that people will help those needing their help.

conflict a perceived incompatibility of actions, goals, or ideas.

social trap a situation in which the conflicting parties, by each rationally pursuing their self-interest rather than the good of the group, become caught in mutually destructive behavior.

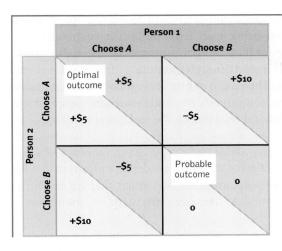

Figure 80.3

Social-trap game matrix By pursuing our self-interest and not trusting others, we can end up losers. To illustrate this, imagine playing the game on the left. The light-orange triangles show the outcomes for Person 1, which depend on the choices made by both players. If you were Person 1, would you choose A or B? (This game is called a *non-zero-sum* game because the outcomes need not add up to zero; both sides can win or both can lose.)

Consider the simple game matrix in **FIGURE 80.3**, which is similar to those used in experiments with countless thousands of people. Both sides can win or both can lose, depending on the players' individual choices. Pretend you are Person 1, and that you and Person 2 will each receive the amount shown after you separately choose either *A* or *B*. (You might invite someone to look at the matrix with you and take the role of Person 2.) Which do you choose—*A* or *B*?

You and Person 2 are caught in a dilemma. If you both choose *A*, you both benefit, making $5 each. Neither of you benefits if you both choose *B*, for neither of you makes anything. Nevertheless, on any single trial you serve your own interests if you choose *B*: You can't lose, and you might make $10. But the same is true for the other person. Hence, the social trap: As long as you both pursue your own immediate best interest and choose *B*, you will both end up with nothing—the typical result—when you could have made $5.

Many real-life situations similarly pit our individual interests against our communal well-being. Individual whalers reasoned that the few whales they took would not threaten the species and that if they didn't take them others would anyway. The result: Some species of whales became endangered. Ditto for the buffalo hunters of yesterday and the elephant-tusk poachers of today. Individual car owners and home owners reason, "It would cost me comfort or money to buy a more fuel-efficient car and furnace. Besides, the fossil fuels I burn don't noticeably add to the greenhouse gases." When enough others reason similarly, the collective result threatens disaster—climate change, rising seas, and more extreme weather.

Not in my ocean! Many people support alternative energy sources, including wind turbines. But proposals to construct wind farms in real-world neighborhoods elicit less support. One such proposal, for locating wind turbines off the coast of Massachusetts' Nantucket Island, produced heated debate over the future benefits of clean energy versus the costs of altering treasured ocean views and, possibly, migratory bird routes.

Social traps challenge us to find ways of reconciling our right to pursue our personal well-being with our responsibility for the well-being of all. Psychologists have therefore explored ways to convince people to cooperate for their mutual betterment—through agreed-upon *regulations,* through better *communication,* and through promoting *awareness* of our responsibilities toward community, nation, and the whole of humanity (Dawes, 1980; Linder, 1982; Sato, 1987). Given effective regulations, communication, and awareness, people more often cooperate, whether it be in playing a laboratory game or the real game of life.

ENEMY PERCEPTIONS

Psychologists have noted that those in conflict have a curious tendency to form diabolical images of one another. These distorted images are, ironically, so similar that we call them **mirror-image perceptions:** As we see "them"—as untrustworthy, with evil intentions— so "they" see us. Each demonizes the other.

Mirror-image perceptions can often feed a vicious cycle of hostility. If Juan believes Maria is annoyed with him, he may snub her, causing her to act in ways that justify his perception. As with individuals, so with countries. Perceptions can become **self-fulfilling prophecies**. They may confirm themselves by influencing the other country to react in ways that seem to justify them.

> **mirror-image perceptions**
> mutual views often held by conflicting people, as when each side sees itself as ethical and peaceful and views the other side as evil and aggressive.
>
> **self-fulfilling prophecy** a belief that leads to its own fulfillment.

Participants tend to see their own actions as responses to provocation, not as the causes of what happens next. Perceiving themselves as returning tit for tat, they often hit back harder, as University College London volunteers did in one experiment (Shergill et al., 2003). Their task: After feeling pressure on their own finger, they were to use a mechanical device to press on another volunteer's finger. Although told to reciprocate with the same amount of pressure, they typically responded with about 40 percent more force than they had just experienced. Despite seeking only to respond in kind, their touches soon escalated to hard presses, much as when each child after a fight claims that "I just poked him, but he hit me harder."

Perceived provocations feed similar cycles of hostility on the world stage. In 2001, newly elected U.S. President George W. Bush spoke of Saddam Hussein: "Some of today's tyrants are gripped by an implacable hatred of the United States of America. They hate our friends, they hate our values, they hate democracy and freedom and individual liberty. Many care little for the lives of their own people." Hussein reciprocated the perception in 2002. The United States, he said, is "an evil tyrant," with Satan as its protector. It lusts for oil and aggressively attacks those who "defend what is right."

The point is not that truth must lie midway between two such views (one may be more accurate). The point is that enemy perceptions often form mirror images. Moreover, as enemies change, so do perceptions. In American minds and media, the "bloodthirsty, cruel, treacherous" Japanese of World War II later became our "intelligent, hardworking, self-disciplined, resourceful allies" (Gallup, 1972).

Promoting Peace

80-4 How can we transform feelings of prejudice, aggression, and conflict into attitudes that promote peace?

How can we make peace? Can contact, cooperation, communication, and conciliation transform the antagonisms fed by prejudice and conflicts into attitudes that promote peace? Research indicates that, in some cases, they can.

CONTACT

Does it help to put two conflicting parties into close contact? It depends. When contact is noncompetitive and between parties of equal status, such as fellow store clerks, it typically helps. Initially prejudiced co-workers of different races have, in such circumstances, usually come to accept one another. This finding is confirmed by a statistical digest of more than 500 studies of face-to-face contact with outgroups (such as ethnic minorities, the elderly, and those with disabilities). Among the quarter-million people studied across 38 nations, contact has been correlated with, or in experimental studies has led to, more positive attitudes (Pettigrew & Tropp, 2011). Some examples:

- With interracial contact, South African Whites' and Blacks' "attitudes [have moved] into closer alignment" (Dixon et al, 2007; Finchilescu & Tredoux, 2010). In South Africa, as elsewhere, the contact effect is somewhat less for lower-status ethnic groups' views of higher-status groups (Durrheim & Dixon, 2010; Gibson & Claassen, 2010).

- Heterosexuals' attitudes toward gay people are influenced not only by what they know but also by whom they know (Smith et al., 2009). In surveys, the reason people most often give for becoming more supportive of same-sex marriage is "having friends, family or acquaintances who are gay or lesbian" (Pew, 2013).

- Friendly contact, say between Blacks and Whites, improves attitudes not only toward one another, but also toward other outgroups, such as Hispanics (Tausch et al., 2010).

- Even indirect contact with an outgroup member (via story reading or through a friend who has an outgroup friend) has reduced prejudice (Cameron & Rutland, 2006; Pettigrew et al., 2007).

However, contact is not always enough. In most desegregated schools, ethnic groups resegregate themselves in the lunchrooms and classrooms, and on the school grounds (Alexander & Tredoux, 2010; Clack et al., 2005; Schofield, 1986). People in each group often think that they would welcome more contact with the other group, but they assume the other group does not reciprocate the wish (Richeson & Shelton, 2007). "I don't reach out to them, because I don't want to be rebuffed; they don't reach out to me, because they're just not interested." When such mirror-image misperceptions are corrected, friendships may then form and prejudices melt.

> "You cannot shake hands with a clenched fist." -Indira Gandhi, 1971

COOPERATION

To see if enemies could overcome their differences, researcher Muzafer Sherif (1966) set a conflict in motion. He separated 22 Oklahoma City boys into two separate camp areas. Then he had the two groups compete for prizes in a series of activities. Before long, each group became intensely proud of itself and hostile to the other group's "sneaky," "smart-alecky stinkers." Food wars broke out. Cabins were ransacked. Fistfights had to be broken up by camp counselors. Brought together, the two groups avoided each other, except to taunt and threaten. Little did they know that within a few days, they would be friends.

Sherif accomplished this by giving them **superordinate goals**—shared goals that could be achieved only through cooperation. When he arranged for the camp water supply to "fail," all 22 boys had to work together to restore water. To rent a movie in those pre-DVD days, they all had to pool their resources. To move a stalled truck, the boys needed to combine their strength, pulling and pushing together. Having used isolation and competition to make strangers into enemies, Sherif used shared predicaments and goals to turn enemies into friends. What reduced conflict was not mere contact, but *cooperative* contact.

> **superordinate goals** shared goals that override differences among people and require their cooperation.

A shared predicament likewise had a powerfully unifying effect in the weeks after 9/11. Patriotism soared as Americans felt "we" were under attack. Gallup-surveyed approval of "our President" shot up from 51 percent the week before the attack to a highest-ever 90 percent level 10 days after (Newport, 2002). In chat groups and everyday speech, even the word *we* (relative to *I*) surged in the immediate aftermath (Pennebaker, 2002).

AFP/Getty Images

Striving for peace The road to reconciliation in the Middle East may be arduous, but as former U.N. Secretary-General Kofi Annan noted in his Nobel lecture, "Most of us have overlapping identities which unite us with very different groups. We *can* love what we are, without hating what—and who—we are *not*. We can thrive in our own tradition, even as we learn from others" (2001). Pictured here are Palestinian statesman Mahmoud Abbas, Israeli Prime Minister Benjamin Netanyahu, and U. S. President Barack Obama.

At such times, cooperation can lead people to define a new, inclusive group that dissolves their former sub-groups (Dovidio & Gaertner, 1999). To accomplish this, you might seat members of two groups not on opposite sides, but alternately around a table. Give them a new, shared name. Have them work together. Then watch "us" and "them" become "we." After 9/11, one 18-year-old New Jersey man described this shift in his own social identity: "I just thought of myself as Black. But now I feel like I'm an American, more than ever" (Sengupta, 2001). In a real experiment, White Americans who read a news-paper article about a terrorist threat against all Americans subsequently expressed reduced prejudice against Black Americans (Dovidio et al., 2004).

If cooperative contact between rival group members encourages positive attitudes, might this principle bring people together in multicultural schools? Could interracial friendships replace competitive classroom situations with cooperative ones? Could cooperative learning maintain or even enhance student achievement? Experiments with adolescents from 11 countries confirm that, in each case, the answer is *Yes* (Roseth et al., 2008). In the classroom as in the sports arena, members of interracial groups who work together on projects typically come to feel friendly toward one another. Knowing this, thousands of teachers have made interracial cooperative learning part of their classroom experience.

The power of cooperative activity to make friends of former enemies has led psycholo-gists to urge increased international exchange and cooperation. As we engage in mutually beneficial trade, as we work to protect our common destiny on this fragile planet, and as we become more aware that our hopes and fears are shared, we can transform misperceptions that feed conflict into feelings of solidarity based on common interests.

COMMUNICATION

When real-life conflicts become intense, a third-party mediator—a marriage counselor, labor mediator, diplomat, community volunteer—may facilitate much-needed communi-cation (Rubin et al., 1994). Mediators help each party to voice its viewpoint and to un-derstand the other's needs and goals. If successful, mediators can replace a competitive *win-lose* orientation with a cooperative *win-win* orientation that leads to a mutually ben-eficial resolution. A classic example: Two friends, after quarreling over an orange, agreed to

AP Photo/Grant Hindsley

Superordinate goals override differences Cooperative efforts to achieve shared goals are an effective way to break down social barriers.

split it. One squeezed his half for juice. The other used the peel from her half to flavor a cake. If only the two had understood each other's motives, they could have hit on the win-win solution of one having all the juice, the other all the peel.

CONCILIATION

Understanding and cooperative resolution are most needed, yet least likely, in times of anger or crisis (Bodenhausen et al., 1994; Tetlock, 1988). When conflicts intensify, images become more stereotyped, judgments more rigid, and communication more difficult, or even impossible. Each party is likely to threaten, coerce, or retaliate. In the weeks before the Persian Gulf war, the first President George Bush threatened, in the full glare of publicity, to "kick Saddam's ass." Saddam Hussein communicated in kind, threatening to make Americans "swim in their own blood."

"To begin with, I would like to express my sincere thanks and deep appreciation for the opportunity to meet with you. While there are still profound differences between us, I think the very fact of my presence here today is a major breakthrough."

Under such conditions, is there an alternative to war or surrender? Social psychologist Charles Osgood (1962, 1980) advocated a strategy of *Graduated and Reciprocated Initiatives in Tension-Reduction,* nicknamed **GRIT.** In applying GRIT, one side first announces its recognition of mutual interests and its intent to reduce tensions. It then initiates one or more small, conciliatory acts. Without weakening one's retaliatory capability, this modest beginning opens the door for reciprocity by the other party. Should the enemy respond with hostility, one reciprocates in kind. But so, too, with any conciliatory response.

> **GRIT** *Graduated and Reciprocated Initiatives in Tension-Reduction*—a strategy designed to decrease international tensions.

In laboratory experiments, small conciliatory gestures—a smile, a touch, a word of apology—have allowed both parties to begin edging down the tension ladder to a safer rung where communication and mutual understanding can begin (Lindskold et al., 1978, 1988). In a real-world international conflict, U.S. President John F. Kennedy's gesture of stopping atmospheric nuclear tests began a series of reciprocated conciliatory acts that culminated in the 1963 atmospheric test-ban treaty.

As working toward shared goals reminds us, we are more alike than different. Civilization advances not by conflict and cultural isolation, but by tapping the knowledge, the skills, and the arts that are each culture's legacy to the whole human race. Thanks to cultural sharing, every modern society is enriched by a cultural mix (Sowell, 1991). We have China to thank for paper and printing and for the magnetic compass that opened the great explorations. We have Egypt to thank for trigonometry. We have the Islamic world and India's Hindus to thank for our Arabic numerals. While celebrating and claiming these diverse cultural legacies, we can also welcome the enrichment of today's social diversity. We can view ourselves as instruments in a human orchestra. And we—this book's worldwide readers—can therefore each affirm our own culture's heritage while building bridges of communication, understanding, and cooperation across our cultural traditions.

Before You Move On

▶ **ASK YOURSELF**

Do you regret not getting along with some friend or family member? How might you go about reconciling that relationship?

▶ **TEST YOURSELF**

Why didn't anybody help Kitty Genovese? What social relations principle did this incident illustrate?

Answers to the Test Yourself questions can be found in Appendix E at the end of the book.

* * *

If you just finished reading this book, your introduction to psychological science is completed. Our tour of psychological science has taught me much—and you, too?—about our moods and memories, about the reach of our unconscious, about how we flourish and struggle, about how we perceive our physical and social worlds, and about how our biology and culture in turn shape us. My hope, as your guide on this tour, is that you have shared some of my fascination, grown in your understanding and compassion, and sharpened your critical thinking. I also hope you enjoyed the ride.

With every good wish in your future endeavors (including the AP® exam!),
David G. Myers
www.davidmyers.org

Module 80 Review

80-1 When are people most—and least—likely to help?

- *Altruism* is unselfish regard for the well-being of others.

- We are most likely to help when we (a) notice an incident, (b) interpret it as an emergency, and (c) assume responsibility for helping. Other factors, including our mood and our similarity to the victim, also affect our willingness to help.

- We are least likely to help if other bystanders are present (the *bystander effect*).

80-2 How do social exchange theory and social norms explain helping behavior?

- *Social exchange theory* is the view that we help others because it is in our own self-interest; in this view, the goal of social behavior is maximizing personal benefits and minimizing costs.

- Others believe that helping results from socialization, in which we are taught guidelines for expected behaviors in social situations, such as the *reciprocity norm* and the *social-responsibility norm*.

80-3 How do social traps and mirror-image perceptions fuel social conflict?

- A *conflict* is a perceived incompatibility of actions, goals, or ideas.

- *Social traps* are situations in which people in conflict pursue their own individual self-interest, harming the collective well-being.

- Individuals and cultures in conflict also tend to form *mirror-image perceptions* that may become *self-fulfilling prophecies:* Each party views the opponent as untrustworthy and evil-intentioned, and itself as an ethical, peaceful victim.

80-4 How can we transform feelings of prejudice, aggression, and conflict into attitudes that promote peace?

- Peace can result when individuals or groups work together to achieve *superordinate* (shared) *goals.*

- Research indicates that four processes—contact, cooperation, communication, and conciliation—help promote peace.

Multiple-Choice Questions

1. Which of the following is the best term or phrase for the unselfish concern for the welfare of others?

  a. Assuming responsibility
  b. Bystander intervention
  c. Altruism
  d. Bystander effect
  e. Diffusion of responsibility

2. Which of the following maintains that our social behavior is an exchange process that minimizes costs?

  a. Social-responsibility norm
  b. Bystander apathy
  c. Reciprocity norm
  d. Social exchange theory
  e. Biopsychosocial hypothesis

3. What do we call a situation in which the conflicting parties, by rationally pursuing their self-interest, become caught in mutually destructive behavior?

   a. Social trap

   b. Conflict

   c. Bystander intervention

   d. Diffusion of responsibility

   e. Social-responsibility norm

4. What do we call a belief that leads to its own fulfillment?

   a. Superordinate goal

   b. Mirror-image perception

   c. Enemy perception

   d. Social trap

   e. Self-fulfilling prophecy

Practice FRQs

1. According to Darley and Latané, what three things must happen for a bystander to intervene?

Answer

1 point: The bystander must notice the event.

1 point: The bystander must interpret the incident as an emergency.

1 point: The bystander must assume responsibility.

2. The author identifies two "enemy perceptions." Name and describe both.

(4 points)

Unit XIV Review

Key Terms and Concepts to Remember

social psychology, p. 754

attribution theory, p. 754

fundamental attribution error, p. 754

attitude, p. 756

peripheral route persuasion, p. 756

central route persuasion, p. 756

foot-in-the-door phenomenon, p. 757

role, p. 758

cognitive dissonance theory, p. 759

conformity, p. 763

normative social influence, p. 764

informational social influence, p. 764

social facilitation, p. 771

social loafing, p. 773

deindividuation, p. 773

group polarization, p. 774

groupthink, p. 775

culture, p. 776

norm, p. 777

prejudice, p. 780

stereotype, p. 780

discrimination, p. 780

just-world phenomenon, p. 784

ingroup, p. 784

outgroup, p. 784

ingroup bias, p. 784

scapegoat theory, p. 785

other-race effect, p. 786

aggression, p. 789

frustration-aggression principle, p. 791

social script, p. 792

mere exposure effect, p. 798

passionate love, p. 803

companionate love, p. 803

equity, p. 804

self-disclosure, p. 804

altruism, p. 807

bystander effect, p. 808

social exchange theory, p. 809

reciprocity norm, p. 809

social-responsibility norm, p. 810

conflict, p. 810

social trap, p. 810

mirror-image perceptions, p. 812

self-fulfilling prophecy, p. 812

superordinate goals, p. 813

GRIT, p. 815

Key Contributors to Remember

Philip Zimbardo, p. 758

Leon Festinger, p. 759

Solomon Asch, p. 763

Stanley Milgram, p. 765

AP® Exam Practice Questions

Multiple-Choice Questions

1. The enhancement of a group's prevailing tendencies occurs when people within a group discuss an idea that most of them either favor or oppose. What is this tendency called?

a. Group polarization
b. Deindividuation
c. The just-world phenomenon
d. Discrimination
e. Categorization

2. Which of the following statements about the foot-in-the-door phenomenon is *false?*

a. People who agree to a small action are less likely to agree to a larger one later.
b. The Chinese army took advantage of this phenomenon in the thought control program they used on prisoners during the Korean War.
c. To get people to agree to something big, start small and build.
d. Succumb to a temptation and you will find the next temptation harder to resist.
e. This phenomenon has been used to boost charitable contributions, blood donations, and product sales.

3. According to research on the bystander effect, which of the following people is most likely to stop and help a stranger?

a. Jacob is on his way to a doctor's appointment with his young son.
b. Xavier lives in a crowded city.
c. Malika is in a terrible mood, having just learned that she failed her midterm exam.
d. Ciera just saw a young girl offering her arm to help an older woman cross the street.
e. Mahmood is lost in thought as he walks to work, thinking about his upcoming presentation.

4. Believing that your school is better than all the other schools in town is an example of what psychological concept?

a. Ingroup bias
b. Conformity
c. Scapegoat theory
d. Discrimination
e. Groupthink

5. People frequently credit or blame either internal dispositions or external situations for others' behavior. What is this tendency called?

a. The foot-in-the-door phenomenon
b. The fundamental attribution error
c. Attribution
d. Social psychology
e. Social thinking

6. Researchers have found that people tend to become more hostile in situations when they are exposed to aversive stimuli, such as heat or personal insults. What is the term for this tendency?

a. The proximity effect
b. GRIT
c. The frustration-aggression principle
d. Social scripting
e. Deindividuation

7. Galileo's notion that the earth revolved around the sun was in opposition to the widespread beliefs of his day. What social psychological principle is this an example of?

a. Social thinking
b. Group polarization
c. Conformity
d. A stereotype
e. Minority influence

8. Physical or verbal behavior intended to hurt or destroy is called

a. the mere exposure effect.
b. hindsight bias.
c. aggression.
d. the just-world phenomenon.
e. the other-race effect.

9. What tension occurs when we become aware that our attitudes and actions don't coincide?

a. Role playing
b. The fundamental attribution error
c. Social pressure
d. Social influence
e. Cognitive dissonance

10. Which of the following *least* describes prejudice?

   a. An unjustifiable attitude toward a group

   b. Schemas that influence how we notice and interpret events

   c. Preconceived ideas that bias our impressions of others' behavior

   d. A physical behavior intended to hurt or destroy

   e. Automatic and unconscious thoughts and behaviors

11. Which social psychology principle influences people to perform a task better in the presence of others?

   a. Compliance

   b. Group polarization

   c. Social facilitation

   d. Conformity

   e. Social loafing

12. Becoming less self-conscious and less restrained when in a group situation is referred to as

   a. social loafing.

   b. deindividuation.

   c. social facilitation.

   d. obedience.

   e. cognitive dissonance.

13. If Juan believes Ngoc is annoyed with him, he may snub her, causing her to act in ways that justify his perception. What concept is this an example of?

   a. Superordinate goals

   b. Tension-reduction

   c. A social trap

   d. A mirror-image perception

   e. Self-fulfilling prophecy

14. Which of the following is the most complete definition of conformity?

   a. Sharing a mood with others

   b. Unconsciously mimicking the behaviors and reactions of others

   c. Changing thoughts about a situation in order to please an authority figure

   d. Adjusting our behavior or thinking toward some group standard

   e. Bringing our attitudes in line with our actions

15. Sophia was not sure she would like the new driver of her school bus, but during the year she realized she was looking forward to greeting him in the morning and hearing one of his corny jokes. Which concept best explains her change in perception?

   a. Similarity

   b. Ingroup bias

   c. Companionate attraction

   d. Social trap

   e. Mere exposure effect

Free-Response Questions

1. Abi moved from her small rural hometown to a large city to pursue her singing career. She was hired for an important and popular choral performance. She is nervous but excited about this new opportunity. Explain how the following social psychology factors might affect her experiences in the "big city."
   - Self-fulfilling prophecy
   - Frustration-aggression model
   - Social facilitation
   - Reciprocity norm

Rubric for Free Response Question 1

1 point: Self-fulfilling prophecy: Abi may think that she is not talented enough to compete with all of the other singers in the performance. Because of her low expectations of herself, she may not perform to the best of her ability. ↺ Page 812

1 point: Frustration-aggression model: If Abi does not progress to her satisfaction, and experiences frustration as her career stagnates, she may lash out at her colleagues either physically or verbally or even try to railroad others' careers to further her own. ↺ Page 791

1 point: Social facilitation: Abi has been singing for a number of years. Because this is a well-practiced activity, Abi's performance should be enhanced by the presence of others. Because she will have larger crowds in the "big city," Abi's performance should improve in front of larger crowds. ↺ Page 771

1 point: Reciprocity norm: If Abi receives gifts (such as flowers) from the audience, she may be motivated to give an extra effort in her performances. If the audience perceives that Abi is throwing herself completely into her performance and exhausting herself trying to entertain them, they each will be more likely to applaud and cheer because the reciprocity norm indicates we will often return the efforts or feelings of others. ↺ Page 809

2. Peter and Manuela met in their high school senior year psychology class. They sat near each other and were often partnered during class discussions and group work. They were both on the swim team and often volunteered at the same homelessness prevention shelter. By the end of the year, they became good friends. Later, Manuela and Peter attended the same college, and after graduation they became engaged. When they attended their five-year high school reunion it was obvious to their friends from high school that they were a very happy couple.

   Explain the *reward theory of attraction* and give an example to show how each of the following factors may have influenced Manuela and Peter's developing relationship from high school through college.
   - Proximity
   - Equity
   - Self-disclosure
   - Companionate love

   (5 points)

3. Dutch is in his first year as a student at a large university. At the urging of some friends, he attended a "pep rally" on the night prior to the football game. At the rally, the marching band played the university's fight song and Dutch began singing along as they did. The head football coach then gave a rousing speech and Dutch joined with the hundreds of other students to cheer him. Although Dutch had not paid attention to the football team prior to the rally, he enthusiastically participated in the rally, even going so far as to have an image of the team's mascot painted on his face. The following day, he attended the game and since has become an avid fan of the football team.

   Analyze Dutch's behavior at the rally and afterwards, using each of the following principles of social psychology:
   - Peripheral route persuasion
   - Central route persuasion
   - Automatic mimicry
   - Social facilitation
   - Deindividuation

   (5 points)

Multiple-choice self-tests and more may be found at www.worthpublishers.com/MyersAP2e

Enrichment Modules

Modules

Module 81

Influences on Drug Use

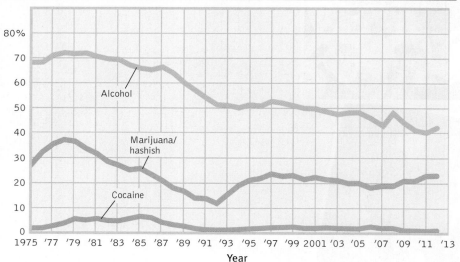

R. Wright/Corbis

Module Learning Objective

 Explain why some people become regular users of consciousness-altering drugs.

 Why do some people become regular users of consciousness-altering drugs?

Drug use by North American youth increased during the 1970s. Then, with increased drug education and a more realistic and deglamorized media depiction of taking drugs, drug use declined sharply. After the early 1990s, the cultural antidrug voice softened, and drugs for a time were again glamorized in some music and films. Consider these marijuana-related trends:

- In the University of Michigan's annual survey of 15,000 U.S. high school seniors, the proportion who believe there is "great risk" in regular marijuana use rose from 35 percent in 1978 to 79 percent in 1991, then retreated to 44 percent in 2012 (Johnston et al., 2013).

- After peaking in 1978, marijuana use by U.S. high school seniors declined through 1992, then rose, but has recently been tapering off (**FIGURE 81.1**). Among Canadian 15- to 24-year-olds, 23 percent report using marijuana monthly, weekly, or daily (Health Canada, 2012).

Figure 81.1

Trends in drug use The percentage of U.S. high school seniors who report having used alcohol, marijuana, or cocaine during the past 30 days declined from the late 1970s to 1992, when it partially rebounded for a few years. (From Johnston et al., 2013.)

For some adolescents, occasional drug use represents thrill seeking. Why, though, do others become regular drug users? In search of answers, researchers have engaged biological, psychological, and social-cultural levels of analysis.

Biological Influences

Some people may be biologically vulnerable to particular drugs. For example, evidence accumulates that heredity influences some aspects of alcohol use problems, especially those appearing by early adulthood (Crabbe, 2002):

- Adopted individuals are more susceptible to alcohol use disorder if one or both biological parents have a history of it.

- Having an identical rather than fraternal twin with alcohol use disorder puts one at increased risk for alcohol problems (Kendler et al., 2002). In marijuana use also, identical twins more closely resemble each other than do fraternal twins.

- Boys who at age 6 are excitable, impulsive, and fearless (genetically influenced traits) are more likely as teens to smoke, drink, and use other drugs (Masse & Tremblay, 1997).

- Researchers have bred rats and mice that prefer alcoholic drinks to water. One such strain has reduced levels of the brain chemical NPY. Mice engineered to *overproduce* NPY are very sensitive to alcohol's sedating effect and drink little (Thiele et al., 1998).

- Researchers have identified genes that are more common among people and animals predisposed to alcohol use disorder, and they are seeking genes that contribute to tobacco addiction (NIH, 2006; Nurnberger & Bierut, 2007). These culprit genes seemingly produce deficiencies in the brain's natural dopamine reward system: While triggering temporary dopamine-produced pleasure, the addictive drugs disrupt normal dopamine balance. Studies of how drugs reprogram the brain's reward systems raise hopes for anti-addiction drugs that might block or blunt the effects of alcohol and other drugs (Miller, 2008; Wilson & Kuhn, 2005).

> **FYI**
>
> **Warning signs of alcohol use disorder**
>
> - Drinking binges
> - Craving alcohol
> - Use results in unfulfilled work, school, or home tasks
> - Failing to honor a resolve to drink less
> - Continued use when risky
> - Avoiding family or friends when drinking

Psychological and Social-Cultural Influences

Throughout this text, you have seen that biological, psychological, and social-cultural influences interact to produce behavior. So, too, with disordered drug use (**FIGURE 81.2**). One psychological factor that has appeared in studies of youth and young adults is the feeling that life is meaningless and directionless (Newcomb & Harlow, 1986). This feeling is common among school dropouts who subsist without job skills, without privilege, and with little hope.

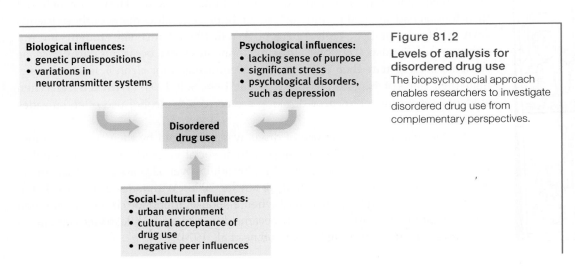

Biological influences:
- genetic predispositions
- variations in neurotransmitter systems

Psychological influences:
- lacking sense of purpose
- significant stress
- psychological disorders, such as depression

Disordered drug use

Social-cultural influences:
- urban environment
- cultural acceptance of drug use
- negative peer influences

Figure 81.2

Levels of analysis for disordered drug use
The biopsychosocial approach enables researchers to investigate disordered drug use from complementary perspectives.

Sometimes the psychological influence is obvious. Many heavy users of alcohol, marijuana, and cocaine have experienced significant stress or failure and are depressed. Girls with a history of depression, eating disorders, or sexual or physical abuse are at risk for substance addiction. So are youth undergoing school or neighborhood transitions (CASA, 2003; Logan et al., 2002). Collegians who have not yet achieved a clear identity are also at greater risk (Bishop et al., 2005). By temporarily dulling the pain of self-awareness, alcohol and other drugs may offer a way to avoid coping with depression, anger, anxiety, or insomnia. As Unit VI explained, behavior is often controlled more by its immediate consequences than by its later ones.

Especially for teenagers, drug use can have social roots. For example, teens are exposed to smoking in movies. Those with a lot of exposure are three times as likely as other teens to try smoking and become smokers. And that correlation is not a result of personality, parenting style, or family economics, which researchers controlled for (Heatherton & Sargent, 2009). Most teen drinking is done for social reasons, not as a way to cope with problems (Kuntsche et al., 2005). When young unmarried adults leave home, alcohol and other drug use increases; when they marry and have children, it decreases (Bachman et al., 1997).

Rates of drug use also vary across cultural and ethnic groups. One survey of 100,000 teens in 35 European countries found that marijuana use in the prior 30 days ranged from zero to 1 percent in Romania and Sweden to 20 to 22 percent in Britain, Switzerland, and France (ESPAD, 2003). Independent U.S. government studies of drug use in households nationwide and among high schoolers in all regions reveal that African-American teens have sharply lower rates of drinking, smoking, and cocaine use (Johnston et al., 2007). Alcohol and other drug addiction rates have also been low among those actively religious, and extremely low among Orthodox Jews, Mormons, the Amish, and Mennonites (Trimble, 1994; Yeung et al., 2009). Relatively drug-free small towns and rural areas tend to constrain any genetic predisposition to drug use (Legrand et al., 2005). So does active parental monitoring (Lac & Crano, 2009). For those whose genetic predispositions nudge them toward substance use, cities offer more opportunities and less supervision.

Whether in cities or rural areas, peers influence attitudes about drugs. They also throw the parties and provide (or don't provide) the drugs. If an adolescent's friends use drugs, the odds are that he or she will, too. If the friends do not, the opportunity may not even arise. Teens who come from happy families, who do not begin drinking before age 15, and who do well in school tend not to use drugs, largely because they rarely associate with those who do (Bachman et al., 2007; Hingson et al., 2006; Odgers et al., 2008).

Peer influence is more than what friends do or say. Adolescents' expectations—what they *believe* friends are doing and favoring—influence their behavior (Vitória et al., 2009). One study surveyed sixth graders in 22 U.S. states. How many believed their friends had smoked marijuana? About 14 percent. How many of those friends acknowledged doing so? Only 4 percent (Wren, 1999). University students are not immune to such misperceptions: Drinking dominates social occasions partly because students overestimate their fellow students' enthusiasm for alcohol and underestimate their views of its risks (Prentice & Miller, 1993; Self, 1994) (**TABLE 81.1**). When students' overestimates of peer drinking are corrected, alcohol use often subsides (Moreira et al., 2009).

People whose beginning use of drugs was influenced by their peers are more likely to stop using when friends stop or their social network changes (Kandel & Raveis, 1989). One study that followed 12,000 adults over 32 years found that smokers tend to quit in clusters (Christakis & Fowler, 2008). Within a social network, the odds of a person's quitting increased when a spouse, friend, or co-worker stopped smoking. Similarly, most soldiers who became drug addicted while in Vietnam ceased their drug use after returning home (Robins et al., 1974).

SNAPSHOTS

Once upon a time, peer pressure caused Bob to start smoking.

RESTAURANT

Twenty years later, it forces him to quit.

© Jason Love

Table 81.1	Facts About "Higher" Education
• College and university students drink more alcohol than their nonstudent peers and exhibit 2.5 times the general population's rate of substance abuse.
• Fraternity and sorority members report nearly twice the binge drinking rate of nonmembers.
• Since 1993, campus smoking rates have declined, alcohol use has been steady, and abuse of prescription opioids, stimulants, tranquilizers, and sedatives has increased, as has marijuana use.

Source: NCASA, 2007.

As always with correlations, the traffic between friends' drug use and our own may be two-way: Our friends influence us. Social networks matter. But we also select as friends those who share our likes and dislikes.

What do the findings on drug use suggest for drug prevention and treatment programs? Three channels of influence seem possible:

- Educate young people about the long-term costs of a drug's temporary pleasures.
- Help young people find other ways to boost their self-esteem and purpose in life.
- Attempt to modify peer associations or to "inoculate" youths against peer pressures by training them in refusal skills.

People rarely abuse drugs if they understand the physical and psychological costs, feel good about themselves and the direction their lives are taking, and are in a peer group that disapproves of using drugs. These educational, psychological, and social-cultural factors may help explain why 26 percent of U.S. high school dropouts, but only 6 percent of those with a postgraduate education, report smoking (CDC, 2011).

Before You Move On

▶ **ASK YOURSELF**

Drinking dominates parties when students overestimate other students' enthusiasm for alcohol. Do you think such misperceptions exist at your high school? How might you find out?

▶ **TEST YOURSELF**

Studies have found that people who begin drinking in their early teens are much more likely to exhibit alcohol use disorder than those who begin at age 21 or after. What possible explanations might there be for this correlation between early use and later abuse?

Answers to the Test Yourself questions can be found in Appendix E at the end of the book.

Module 81 Review

 81-1 Why do some people become regular users of consciousness-altering drugs?

- Some people may be biologically vulnerable to particular drugs, such as alcohol.

- Psychological factors (such as stress, depression, and hopelessness) and social factors (such as peer pressure) combine to lead many people to experiment with—and sometimes become addicted to—drugs. Cultural and ethnic groups have differing rates of drug use.

- Each type of influence—biological, psychological, and social-cultural—offers a possible path for drug prevention and treatment programs.

Multiple-Choice Questions

1. Which of the following is true of 6-year-old boys who are more likely to use drugs when they become teenagers?

   a. They are introverted.
   b. They have difficulty learning to read.
   c. They are prone to temper tantrums.
   d. They are isolated from their peers.
   e. They are excitable, impulsive, and fearless.

2. Which of the following is most clearly a biological influence on disordered drug use?

   a. Significant stress
   b. Variations in neurotransmitter systems
   c. An urban environment
   d. Peer influence
   e. A lack of purpose

3. Which of the following statements most accurately reflects the relationship between drinking and expectations among U.S. college students? The students

   a. typically overestimate the percentage of fellow students who drink.
   b. accurately estimate the percentage of fellow students who drink.
   c. tend to slightly underestimate the percentage of fellow students who drink.
   d. tend to greatly underestimate the percentage of fellow students who drink.
   e. tend to be inaccurate in their estimates of the percentage of fellow students who drink, but there is no clear pattern to their inaccuracies.

Practice FRQ

1. Briefly explain one biological, one psychological, and one social-cultural influence on drug use.

(3 points)

Module 82

Psychology at Work

Module Learning Objectives

82-1 Explain the concept of *flow,* and identify three subfields of industrial-organizational psychology.

82-2 Describe how personnel psychologists help organizations with employee selection, work placement, and performance appraisal.

82-3 Define *achievement motivation,* and describe the role of organizational psychologists.

82-4 Describe some effective leadership techniques.

82-5 Describe human factors psychologists' work to create user-friendly machines and work settings.

Psychology at Work

82-1 What is *flow,* and what are the three subfields of industrial-organizational psychology?

For most of us, work is life's biggest single waking activity. To live is to work. Work helps satisfy several levels of need identified in Maslow's hierarchy of needs. Work supports us. Work connects us. Work defines us. Meeting someone for the first time, and wondering "Who are you?" we may ask, "So, what do you do?"

Amy Wrzesniewski and her colleagues (1997, 2001) have identified person-to-person variations in people's attitudes toward their work. Across various occupations, some people view their work as a *job,* an unfulfilling but necessary way to make money. Others view their work as a *career,* an opportunity to advance from one position to a better position. The rest—those who view their work as a *calling,* a fulfilling and socially useful activity—report the highest satisfaction with their work and with their lives.

This finding would not surprise Mihaly Csikszentmihalyi (1990, 1999). He has observed that people's quality of life increases when they are purposefully engaged. Between the anxiety of being overwhelmed and stressed, and the apathy of being underwhelmed and bored, lies a zone in which people experience **flow.** Can you recall being in a zoned-out flow state while playing a video game or text messaging? If so, then perhaps you can sympathize with the two Northwest Airlines pilots who in 2009 were so focused on their laptops that they missed Earth-to-pilot messages from their control tower. The pilots flew 150 miles past their Minneapolis destination—and lost their jobs.

FYI

Sometimes, notes Gene Weingarten (2002), a humor writer knows "when to just get out of the way." Here are some sample job titles from the U.S. Department of Labor *Dictionary of Occupational Titles:* Animal impersonator, human projectile, banana ripening-room supervisor, impregnator, impregnator helper, dope sprayer, finger waver, rug scratcher, egg smeller, bottom buffer, cookie breaker, brain picker, hand pouncer, bosom presser, and mother repairer.

flow a completely involved, focused state of consciousness, with diminished awareness of self and time, resulting from optimal engagement of one's skills.

industrial-organizational (I/O) psychology the application of psychological concepts and methods to optimizing human behavior in workplaces.

personnel psychology an I/O psychology subfield that focuses on employee recruitment, selection, placement, training, appraisal, and development.

organizational psychology an I/O psychology subfield that examines organizational influences on worker satisfaction and productivity and facilitates organizational change.

human factors psychology an I/O psychology subfield that explores how people and machines interact and how machines and physical environments can be made safe and easy to use.

Disrupted flow Internet-related distractions can disrupt flow. It takes time to refocus mental concentration after the distraction of an e-mail or a text.

Csikszentmihalyi [chick-SENT-me-hi] formulated the flow concept after studying artists who spent hour after hour painting or sculpting with enormous concentration. Immersed in a project, they worked as if nothing else mattered, and then, when finished, they promptly forgot about it. The artists seemed driven less by the external rewards of producing art—money, praise, promotion—than by the intrinsic rewards of creating the work.

Csikszentmihalyi's later observations—of dancers, chess players, surgeons, writers, parents, mountain climbers, sailors, and farmers; of Australians, North Americans, Koreans, Japanese, and Italians; of people from their teens to their golden years—confirmed an overriding principle: It's exhilarating to flow with an activity that fully engages our skills. Flow experiences boost our sense of self-esteem, competence, and well-being. Idleness may sound like bliss, but purposeful work enriches our lives. Busy people are happier (Hsee et al., 2010; Robinson & Martin, 2008). One research team interrupted people on about a quarter-million occasions (using a smart-phone app), and found people's minds wandering 47 percent of the time. They were, on average, happier when *not* mind-wandering (Killingsworth & Gilbert, 2010).

In many nations, work has been changing, from farming to manufacturing to *knowledge work*. More and more work is outsourced to temporary employees and consultants or done by telecommuters who communicate electronically from virtual workplaces in remote locations. As work changes, will our attitudes toward our work also change? Will our satisfaction with work increase or decrease? Will the *psychological contract*—the sense of mutual obligations between workers and employers—become more or less trusting and secure? These are among the questions that fascinate psychologists who study work-related behavior.

Industrial-organizational (I/O) psychology applies psychology's principles to the workplace (see Close-up: I/O Psychology at Work). Here we consider three of I/O psychology's subfields:

- **Personnel psychology** applies psychology's methods and principles to selecting and evaluating workers. Personnel psychologists match people with jobs, by identifying and placing well-suited candidates.

- **Organizational psychology** considers how work environments and management styles influence worker motivation, satisfaction, and productivity. Organizational psychologists modify jobs and supervision in ways that boost morale and productivity.

- **Human factors psychology** explores how machines and environments can be optimally designed to fit human abilities. Human factors psychologists study people's natural perceptions and inclinations to create user-friendly machines and work settings.

Close-up

I/O Psychology at Work

As scientists, consultants, and management professionals, industrial-organizational psychologists are found working in varied areas:

PERSONNEL PSYCHOLOGY

Selecting and placing employees

- Developing and validating assessment tools for selecting, placing, and promoting workers
- Analyzing job content
- Optimizing worker placement

Training and developing employees

- Identifying needs
- Designing training programs
- Evaluating training programs

Appraising performance

- Developing criteria
- Measuring individual performance
- Measuring organizational performance

ORGANIZATIONAL PSYCHOLOGY

Developing organizations

- Analyzing organizational structures
- Maximizing worker satisfaction and productivity
- Facilitating organizational change

Enhancing quality of work life

- Expanding individual productivity
- Identifying elements of satisfaction
- Redesigning jobs

HUMAN FACTORS (ENGINEERING) PSYCHOLOGY

- Designing optimum work environments
- Optimizing person-machine interactions
- Developing systems technologies

Source: Adapted from the Society of Industrial and Organizational Psychology (www.siop.org).

Personnel Psychology

 82-2 How do personnel psychologists help organizations with employee selection, work placement, and performance appraisal?

Psychologists can assist organizations at various stages of selecting and assessing employees. They may help identify needed job skills, decide upon selection methods, recruit and evaluate applicants, introduce and train new employees, and appraise their performance.

Harnessing Strengths

As a new AT&T human resource executive, psychologist Mary Tenopyr (1997) was assigned to solve a problem: Customer-service representatives were failing at a high rate. After concluding that many of the hires were ill-matched to the demands of their new job, Tenopyr developed a new selection instrument:

1. She asked new applicants to respond to various questions (without as yet making any use of their responses).
2. She followed up later to assess which of the applicants excelled on the job.
3. She identified the individual items on the earlier test that best predicted who would succeed.

The happy result of her data-driven work was a new test that enabled AT&T to identify likely-to-succeed customer-service representatives. Personnel selection techniques such as this one aim to match people's strengths with work that enables them and their organization to flourish. Marry the strengths of people with the tasks of organizations, and the result is often prosperity and profit.

Artistic strengths At age 21, Henri Matisse was a sickly and often depressed lawyer's clerk. When his mother gave him a box of paints to cheer him up one day, he felt the darkness lift and his energy surge. He began to fill his days with painting and drawing and went on to art school and a life as one of the world's great painters. For Matisse, doing art felt like "a comfortable armchair." That is how exercising our strengths often feels.

Your strengths are any enduring qualities that can be productively applied. Are you naturally curious? Persuasive? Charming? Persistent? Competitive? Analytical? Empathic? Organized? Articulate? Neat? Mechanical? Any such trait, if matched with suitable work, can function as a strength (Buckingham, 2007). (See Close-up: Discovering Your Strengths.)

Gallup researchers Marcus Buckingham and Donald Clifton (2001) have argued that the first step to a stronger organization is instituting a strengths-based selection system. Thus, as a manager, you would first identify a group of the most effective people in any role—the ones you would want to hire more of—and compare their strengths with those of a group of the least effective people in that role. In defining these groups, you would try to measure performance as objectively as possible. In one Gallup study of more than 5000 telecommunications customer-service representatives, those evaluated most favorably by their managers were strong in "harmony" and "responsibility," while those actually rated most effective by customers were strong in energy, assertiveness, and eagerness to learn.

An example: If you needed to hire new people in software development, and you had discovered that your best software developers are analytical, disciplined, and eager to learn, you would focus employment ads less on experience than on the identified strengths. Thus "Do you take a logical and systematic approach to problem solving *[analytical]*? Are you a perfectionist who strives for timely completion of your projects *[disciplined]*? Do you want to master Java, C++, and PHP *[eager to learn]*? If you can say *yes* to these questions, then please call . . ."

Identifying people's strengths and matching strengths to work is a first step toward workplace effectiveness. Personnel managers use various tools to assess applicants' strengths and decide who is best suited to the job (Sackett & Lievens, 2008). In Module 59, we explored personality tests and "assessment centers" that enable observations of behaviors on simulated job tasks. And in Module 61, we saw how psychologists assess candidates using ability tests. Here we'll consider the job interview.

Close-up

Discovering Your Strengths

You can use some of the techniques personnel psychologists have developed to identify your own strengths and pinpoint types of work that will likely prove satisfying and successful. Buckingham and Clifton (2001) have suggested asking yourself these questions:

- What activities give me pleasure? (Bringing order out of chaos? Playing host? Helping others? Challenging sloppy thinking?)

- What activities leave me wondering, "When can I do this again?" (Rather than, "When will this be over?")

- What sorts of challenges do I relish? (And which do I dread?)

- What sorts of tasks do I learn easily? (And which do I struggle with?)

Some people find themselves in flow—their skills engaged and time flying—when teaching or selling or writing or cleaning or consoling or creating or repairing. If an activity feels good, if it comes easily, if you look forward to it, then look deeper and see your strengths at work.

Satisfied and successful people devote far less time to correcting their deficiencies than to accentuating their strengths. Top performers are "rarely well rounded," Buckingham and Clifton found (p. 26). Instead, they have sharpened their existing skills. Given the persistence of our traits and temperaments, we should focus not on our deficiencies, but rather on identifying and employing our talents. There may be limits to the benefits of assertiveness training if you are extremely shy, of public speaking courses if you tend to be nervous and soft-spoken, or of drawing classes if you express your artistic side in stick figures. To discover and develop your strengths, might you try out for a play or a sport, join a club, or volunteer in your community?

Identifying your talents can help you recognize the activities you learn quickly and find absorbing. Knowing your strengths, you can develop them further. FYI: For a free (it only requires registration) assessment of your strengths, visit www.authentichappiness.sas.upenn.edu and select "Brief Strengths Test."

DO INTERVIEWS PREDICT PERFORMANCE?

Interviewers tend to feel confident in their ability to predict long-term job performance from an unstructured, get-acquainted interview. What's therefore shocking is how error-prone those predictions are. Whether predicting job or graduate school success, interviewers' judgments are weak predictors. From their review of 85 years of personnel-selection research, I/O psychologists Frank Schmidt and John Hunter (1998; Schmidt, 2002) determined that for all but less-skilled jobs, general mental ability best predicts on-the-job performance. Subjective overall evaluations from informal interviews are more useful than handwriting analysis (which is worthless). But informal interviews are less informative than aptitude tests, work samples, job knowledge tests, and past job performance. If there's a contest between what our gut tells us about someone and what test scores, work samples, and past performance tell us, we should distrust our gut.

THE INTERVIEWER ILLUSION

Richard Nisbett (1987) has labeled interviewers' overrating their discernment as the *interviewer illusion*. "I have excellent interviewing skills, so I don't need reference checking as much as someone who doesn't have my ability to read people," is a comment sometimes heard by I/O consultants. Four factors explain this gap between interviewers' overconfidence and the resulting reality:

- *Interviews disclose the interviewee's good intentions, which are less revealing than habitual behaviors* (Ouellette & Wood, 1998). Intentions matter. People can change. But the best predictor of the person we will be is the person we have been. Compared with work-avoiding university students, those who engage in their tasks are more likely, a decade and more later, to be engaged workers (Salmela-Aro et al., 2009). Educational attainments predict job performance partly because people who have shown up for school each day and done their tasks also tend to show up for work and do their tasks (Ng & Feldman, 2009). Wherever we go, we take ourselves along.

- *Interviewers more often follow the successful careers of those they have hired than the successful careers of those they have rejected and lost track of.* This missing feedback prevents interviewers from getting a reality check on their hiring ability.

- *Interviewers presume that people are what they seem to be in the interview situation.* As Module 74 explained, when meeting others, we discount the enormous influence of varying situations and mistakenly presume that what we see is what we will get. But mountains of research on everything from chattiness to conscientiousness reveal that how we behave reflects not only our enduring traits, but also the details of the particular situation (such as wanting to impress in a job interview).

- *Interviewers' preconceptions and moods color how they perceive interviewees' responses* (Cable & Gilovich, 1998; Macan & Dipboye, 1994). If interviewers instantly like a person who perhaps is similar to themselves, they may interpret the person's assertiveness as indicating "confidence" rather than "arrogance." If told certain applicants have been prescreened, interviewers are disposed to judge them more favorably.

Traditional *unstructured interviews* do provide a sense of someone's personality—their expressiveness, warmth, and verbal ability, for example. But unstructured interviews also give interviewees considerable power to control the impression they are making in the interview situation (Barrick et al., 2009). The interview may thus create a false impression of the person's behavior toward others in different situations. Hoping to improve prediction and selection, personnel psychologists have put people in simulated work situations, scoured sources for information on past performance, aggregated evaluations from multiple interviews, administered tests, and developed job-specific interviews.

"Interviews are a terrible predictor of performance." -LASZLO BOCK, GOOGLE'S VICE PRESIDENT, PEOPLE OPERATIONS, 2007

"Between the idea and reality . . . falls the shadow." -T. S. ELIOT, THE HOLLOW MEN, 1925

structured interviews
an interview process that asks the same job-relevant questions of all applicants, each of whom is rated on established scales.

STRUCTURED INTERVIEWS

Unlike casual conversation aimed at getting a feel for someone, **structured interviews** offer a disciplined method of collecting information. A personnel psychologist may analyze a job, script questions, and train interviewers. The interviewers then put the same questions, in the same order, to all applicants, and rate each applicant on established scales.

In an unstructured interview, someone might ask, "How organized are you?" "How well do you get along with people?" or "How do you handle stress?" Street-smart applicants know how to score high: "Although I sometimes drive myself too hard, I handle stress by prioritizing and delegating, and by making sure I leave time for sleep and exercise."

By contrast, structured interviews pinpoint strengths (attitudes, behaviors, knowledge, and skills) that distinguish high performers in a particular line of work. The process includes outlining job-specific situations and asking candidates to explain how they would handle them, and how they handled similar situations in their prior employment. "Tell me about a time when you were caught between conflicting demands, without time to accomplish both. How did you handle that?"

To reduce memory distortions and bias, the interviewer takes notes and makes ratings as the interview proceeds and avoids irrelevant and follow-up questions. The structured interview therefore feels less warm, but that can be explained to the applicant: "This conversation won't typify how we relate to each other in this organization."

A review of 150 findings revealed that structured interviews had double the predictive accuracy of unstructured seat-of-the-pants interviews (Schmidt & Hunter, 1998; Wiesner & Cronshaw, 1988). Structured interviews also reduce bias, such as against overweight applicants (Kutcher & Bragger, 2004). Thanks partly to its greater reliability and partly to its job-analysis focus, the predictive power of one structured interview is roughly equal to that of the average judgment from three or four unstructured interviews (Huffcutt et al., 2001; Schmidt & Zimmerman, 2004).

If, instead, we let our intuitions bias the hiring process, notes Malcolm Gladwell (2000, p. 86), then "all we will have done is replace the old-boy network, where you hired your nephew, with the new-boy network, where you hire whoever impressed you most when you shook his hand. Social progress, unless we're careful, can merely be the means by which we replace the obviously arbitrary with the not so obviously arbitrary."

To recap, personnel psychologists assist organizations in analyzing jobs, recruiting well-suited applicants, selecting and placing employees, and appraising their performance (**FIGURE 82.1**)—the topic we turn to next.

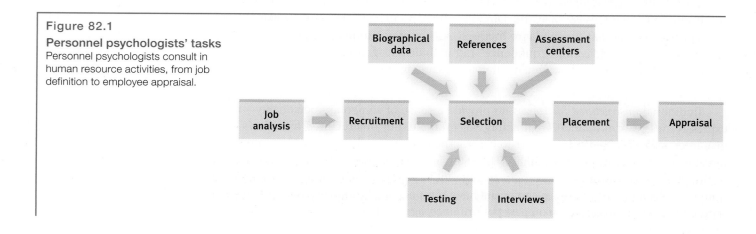

Figure 82.1

Personnel psychologists' tasks
Personnel psychologists consult in human resource activities, from job definition to employee appraisal.

Appraising Performance

Performance appraisal serves organizational purposes: It helps decide who to retain, how to appropriately reward and pay people, and how to better harness employee strengths, sometimes with job shifts or promotions. Performance appraisal also serves individual purposes: Feedback affirms workers' strengths and helps motivate needed improvements.

Performance appraisal methods include

- *checklists* on which supervisors simply check specific behaviors that describe the worker ("always attends to customers' needs," "takes long breaks").

- *graphic rating scales* on which a supervisor checks, perhaps on a five-point scale, how often a worker is dependable, productive, and so forth.

- *behavior rating scales* on which a supervisor checks scaled behaviors that describe a worker's performance. If rating the extent to which a worker "follows procedures," the supervisor might mark the employee somewhere between "often takes shortcuts" and "always follows established procedures" (Levy, 2003).

Figure 82.2
360-degree feedback
With multisource 360-degree feedback, our knowledge, skills, and behaviors are rated by ourselves and surrounding others. Teachers, for example, may be rated by students, their principal, and their colleagues. After receiving all these ratings, teachers discuss the 360-degree feedback with their principal.

In some organizations, performance feedback comes not only from supervisors but also from all organizational levels. If you join an organization that practices *360-degree feedback* (**FIGURE 82.2**), you will rate yourself, your manager, and your other colleagues, and you will be rated by your manager, other colleagues, and customers (Green, 2002). The net result is often more open communication and more complete appraisal.

Performance appraisal, like other social judgments, is vulnerable to bias (Murphy & Cleveland, 1995). *Halo errors* occur when one's overall evaluation of an employee, or of a personal trait such as friendliness, biases ratings of specific work-related behaviors, such as reliability. *Leniency* and *severity errors* reflect evaluators' tendencies to be either too easy or too harsh on everyone. *Recency errors* occur when raters focus only on easily remembered recent behavior. By using multiple raters and developing objective, job-relevant performance measures, personnel psychologists seek to support their organizations while also helping employees perceive the appraisal process as fair.

Before You Move On

▶ **ASK YOURSELF**

What have you learned about your own strengths and about the kind of career you might see yourself pursuing?

▶ **TEST YOURSELF**

A human resources director explains to you that "I don't bother with tests or references. It's all about the interview." Based on I/O psychology research, what concerns does this raise?

Answers to the Test Yourself questions can be found in Appendix E at the end of the book.

Organizational Psychology: Motivating Achievement

 What is *achievement motivation?* What is the role of organizational psychologists?

The appraisal of work and the matching of talents to work matter, but so does overall motivation. Before considering how organizational psychologists assist with efforts to motivate employees and keep them engaged, let's take a closer look at why any employee might want to pursue high standards or difficult goals.

Grit

Think of someone you know who strives to succeed by excelling at any task where evaluation is possible. Now think of someone who is less driven. Psychologist Henry Murray (1938) defined the first person's **achievement motivation** as a desire for significant accomplishment, for mastering skills or ideas, for control, and for attaining a high standard.

As you might expect from their persistence and eagerness for realistic challenges, people with high achievement motivation do achieve more. One study followed the lives of 1528 California children whose intelligence test scores were in the top 1 percent. Forty years later, when researchers compared those who were most and least successful professionally, they found a motivational difference. Those most successful were more ambitious, energetic, and persistent. As children, they had more active hobbies. As adults, they participated in more groups and favored being sports participants to being spectators (Goleman, 1980). Gifted children are able learners. Accomplished adults are tenacious doers. Most of us are energetic doers when starting and finishing a project. It's easiest—have you noticed?—to "get stuck in the middle," which is when high achievers keep going (Bonezzi et al., 2011).

In other studies of both secondary school and university students, self-discipline has been a better predictor of school performance, attendance, and graduation honors than intelligence scores have been. When combined with a positive enthusiasm, sustained, gritty effort predicts success for teachers, too—with their students making good academic progress (Duckworth et al., 2009). "Discipline outdoes talent," concluded researchers Angela Duckworth and Martin Seligman (2005, 2006).

Discipline also refines talent. By their early twenties, top violinists have accumulated some 10,000 lifetime practice hours—double the practice time of other violin students aiming to be teachers (Ericsson, 2001, 2006, 2007). Researchers report a *10-year rule:* World-class experts in a field typically have invested 10 years and at least 10,000 hours to "intense, daily practice" (Ericsson, 2002, 2007; Simon & Chase, 1973). A study of outstanding scholars, athletes, and artists found that all were highly motivated and self-disciplined, willing to dedicate hours every day to the pursuit of their goals (Bloom, 1985). These superstar achievers were distinguished not so much by their extraordinary natural talent as by their extraordinary daily discipline.

What distinguishes extremely successful individuals from their equally talented peers, notes Duckworth, is **grit**—passionate dedication to an ambitious, long-term goal. Although intelligence is distributed like a bell curve, achievements are not. That tells us that achievement

---

> "Genius is 1% inspiration and 99% perspiration." -THOMAS EDISON (1847–1931)

achievement motivation
a desire for significant accomplishment, for mastery of skills or ideas, for control, and for attaining a high standard.

grit in psychology, grit is passion and perseverance in the pursuit of long-term goals.

Calum's road: What grit can accomplish Having spent his life on the Scottish island of Raasay, farming a small patch of land, tending its lighthouse, and fishing, Malcolm ("Calum") MacLeod (1911–1988) felt anguished. His local government repeatedly refused to build a road that would enable vehicles to reach his north end of the island. With the once-flourishing population there having dwindled to two—MacLeod and his wife—he responded with heroic determination. One spring morning in 1964, MacLeod, then in his fifties, gathered an ax, a chopper, a shovel, and a wheelbarrow. By hand, he began to transform the existing footpath into a 1.75-mile road (Miers, 2009).

"With a road," a former neighbor explained, "he hoped new generations of people would return to the north end of Raasay," restoring its culture (Hutchinson, 2006). Day after day he worked through rough hillsides, along hazardous cliff faces, and over peat bogs. Finally, 10 years later, he completed his supreme achievement. The road, which the government has since surfaced, remains a visible example of what vision plus determined grit can accomplish. It bids us each to ponder: What "roads"—what achievements—might we, with sustained effort, build in the years before us?

From Calum's Road by Roger Hutchinson, reproduced courtesy of Birlinn Ltd.

involves much more than raw ability. That is why organizational psychologists seek ways to engage and motivate ordinary people doing ordinary jobs. And that is why training students in "hardiness"—resilience under stress—leads to better grades (Maddi et al., 2009).

Satisfaction and Engagement

Partly because work is such a big part of life, I/O psychologists study employee satisfaction. Satisfaction with work feeds satisfaction with life (Bowling et al., 2010; and see Close-up: Doing Well While Doing Good—"The Great Experiment"). Moreover, as we saw in Module 29, decreased job stress feeds improved health.

> "The only place success comes before work is in the dictionary."
> -FORMER GREEN BAY PACKERS FOOTBALL COACH VINCE LOMBARDI

Satisfied employees also contribute to successful organizations. Positive moods at work enhance creativity, persistence, and helpfulness (Brief & Weiss, 2002; Kaplan et al., 2009). Are engaged, happy workers also less often absent? Less likely to quit? Less prone to theft? More punctual? More productive? Conclusive evidence of satisfaction's benefits is, some have said, the Holy Grail of I/O psychology. Statistical digests of prior research have found a modest positive correlation between individual job satisfaction and performance (Judge et al., 2001; Ng et al., 2009; Parker et al., 2003). In one analysis of 4500 employees at 42 British manufacturing companies, the most productive workers tended to be those in satisfying work environments (Patterson et al., 2004). But does satisfaction *produce* better job performance?

Close-up

Doing Well While Doing Good—"The Great Experiment"

At the end of the 1700s, the New Lanark, Scotland, cotton mill had more than 1000 workers. Many were children drawn from Glasgow's poorhouses. They worked 13-hour days and lived in grim conditions. Their education and sanitation were neglected. Theft and drunkenness were commonplace. Most families occupied just one room.

On a visit to Glasgow, Welsh-born Robert Owen—an idealistic young cotton-mill manager—chanced to meet and fall in love with the mill owner's daughter. After their wedding, Owen, with several partners, purchased the mill and on the first day of the 1800s took control as its manager. Before long, he began what he said was "the most important experiment for the happiness of the human race that had yet been instituted at any time in any part of the world" (Owen, 1814). The exploitation of child and adult labor was, he observed, producing unhappy and inefficient workers. Believing that better working and living conditions could pay economic dividends, he undertook numerous innovations: a nursery for preschool children, education for older children (with encouragement rather than corporal punishment), Sundays off, health care, paid sick days, unemployment pay for days when the mill could not operate, and a company store selling goods at reduced prices.

Owen also innovated a goals- and worker-assessment program that included detailed records of daily productivity and costs. By each employee's workstation, one of four colored boards indicated that person's performance for the previous day. Owen could walk through the mill and at a glance see how individuals were performing. There was, he said, "no beating, no abusive language. . . . I merely looked at the person and then at the [color]. . . . I could at once see by the expression [which color] was shown."

The commercial success that followed was essential to sustaining what became a movement toward humanitarian reforms. By 1816, with decades of profitability still ahead, Owen believed he had demonstrated "that society may be formed so as to exist without crime, without poverty, with health greatly improved, with little if any misery, and with intelligence and happiness increased a hundredfold." Although his Utopian vision has not been fulfilled, Owen's great experiment did lay the groundwork for employment practices that have today become accepted in much of the world.

Courtesy of New Lanark Mills World Heritage Site

The great experiment New Lanark Mills, which today is preserved as a World Heritage Site (www.newlanark.org), provided an influential demonstration of how industries could do well while doing good. In its heyday, New Lanark was visited by many European royals and reformers who came to observe its vibrant workforce and prosperous business.

An engaged employee Mohamed Mamow, left, is joined by his employer in saying the Pledge of Allegiance as he becomes a U.S. citizen. Mamow and his wife met in a Somali refugee camp and now are parents of five children, whom he supports by working as a machine operator. Mindful of his responsibility—"I don't like to lose my job. I have a responsibility for my children and my family"—he arrives for work a half hour early and tends to every detail on his shift. "He is an extremely hard-working employee," noted his employer, and "a reminder to all of us that we are really blessed" (Roelofs, 2010).

The debate continues, with one analysis of past research indicating that satisfaction and performance correlate because both reflect job self-esteem ("I matter around here") and a sense that efforts control rewards (Bowling, 2007).

Nevertheless, some organizations do have a knack for cultivating more engaged and productive employees. In the United States, the *Fortune* "100 Best Companies to Work For" have also produced markedly higher-than-average returns for their investors (Fulmer et al., 2003). Other positive data come from the biggest-ever I/O study, an analysis of Gallup data from more than 198,000 employees in nearly 8000 business units of 36 large companies (including some 1100 bank branches, 1200 stores, and 4200 teams or departments). James Harter, Frank Schmidt, and Theodore Hayes (2002) explored correlations between various measures of organizational success and *employee engagement*—the extent of workers' involvement, enthusiasm, and identification with their organizations (**TABLE 82.1**). They found that engaged workers (compared with disengaged workers who are just putting in time) know what's expected of them, have what they need to do their work, feel fulfilled in their work, have regular opportunities to do what they do best, perceive that they are part of something significant, and have opportunities to learn and develop. They also found that business units with engaged employees have more loyal customers, less turnover, higher productivity, and greater profits.

Table 82.1 Three Types of Employees
Engaged: working with passion and feeling a profound connection to their company or organization.
Not engaged: putting in the time but investing little passion or energy into their work.
Actively disengaged: unhappy workers undermining what their colleagues accomplish.

Source: Adapted from Gallup via Crabtree, 2005.

But what causal arrows explain this correlation between business success and employee morale and engagement? Does success boost morale, or does high morale boost success? In a follow-up longitudinal study of 142,000 workers, Harter and his colleagues (2010) found that over time, employee attitudes predicted future business success (more than the other way around). Another analysis compared companies with top-quartile versus below-average employee engagement levels. Over a three-year period, earnings grew 2.6 times faster for the companies with highly engaged workers (Ott, 2007).

Managing Well

82-4   What are some effective leadership techniques?

Every leader dreams of managing in ways that enhance people's satisfaction, engagement, and productivity and their organization's success. Effective leaders harness job-relevant strengths, set goals, and choose an appropriate leadership style.

HARNESSING JOB-RELEVANT STRENGTHS

"The major challenge for CEOs over the next 20 years will be the effective deployment of human assets," observed Marcus Buckingham (2001). That challenge is "about psychology. It's about getting [individuals] to be more productive, more focused, more fulfilled than [they were] yesterday." To do so, he and others have maintained, effective leaders want first to select the right people. Then, they aim to discern their employees' natural talents, adjust their work roles to suit their talents, and develop those talents into great strengths (**FIGURE 82.3**). For example, should every teacher at a high school be expected to teach the same level and number of students and engage in the same number of extracurricular activities? Or should each job description be tailored to harness a specific person's unique strengths?

As noted earlier in the discussion of personnel psychologists, our temperament and our traits tend to follow us throughout our lives. Managers who excel spend less time trying to instill talents that are not there and more time developing and drawing out what is there. Kenneth Tucker (2002) has noted that effective managers

- start by helping people identify and measure their talents.

- match tasks to talents and then give people freedom to do what they do best.

- care how their people feel about their work.

- reinforce positive behaviors through recognition and reward.

Thus, rather than focusing on weaknesses and packing people off to training seminars to fix those problems, good managers focus training time on educating people about their strengths and building upon them (which means not promoting people into roles ill-suited to their strengths). In Gallup surveys, 77 percent of engaged workers, and only 23 percent of not-engaged workers, strongly agreed that "my supervisor focuses on my strengths or positive characteristics" (Krueger & Killham, 2005).

Celebrating engaged and productive employees in every organizational role builds upon a basic principle of operant conditioning (Modules 27 and 28): To teach a behavior, catch a person doing something right and reinforce it. It sounds simple, but many managers are like parents who, when a child brings home near-perfect scores, focus on the one low score in a troublesome biology class and ignore the rest. "Sixty-five percent of Americans received NO praise or recognition in the workplace last year," reported the Gallup Organization (2004).

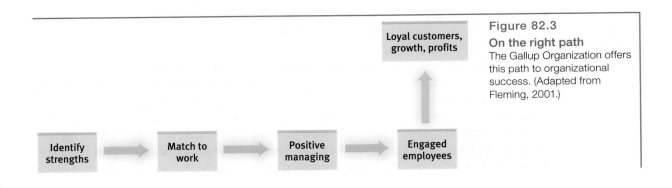

Figure 82.3

On the right path
The Gallup Organization offers this path to organizational success. (Adapted from Fleming, 2001.)

Positive coaching Larry Brown has been an adviser to the youth sports organization Positive Coaching Alliance. He was observed during practices offering his players 4 to 5 positive comments for every negative comment (Insana, 2005). In 2004, he coached his underdog Detroit Pistons to the National Basketball Association championship.

SETTING SPECIFIC, CHALLENGING GOALS

In everyday life, our achievement goals sometimes involve approaching high levels of mastery or performance (such as mastering the material for this class and getting a high grade) and sometimes involve avoiding failure (Elliot & McGregor, 2001). In many situations, specific, challenging goals motivate achievement, especially when combined with progress reports (Johnson et al., 2006; Latham & Locke, 2007). Specific, measurable objectives, such as "finish gathering the history paper information by Friday," serve to direct attention, promote effort, motivate persistence, and stimulate creative strategies.

When people state goals together with *subgoals* and *implementation intentions*—action plans that specify when, where, and how they will march toward achieving those goals—they become more focused in their work, and on-time completion becomes more likely (Burgess et al., 2004; Fishbach et al., 2006; Koestner et al., 2002). Through a task's ups and downs, people best sustain their mood and motivation when they focus on immediate goals (such as daily study) rather than distant goals (such as a course grade). Better to have one's nose to the grindstone than one's eye on the ultimate prize (Houser-Marko & Sheldon, 2008). Thus, before beginning each new edition of this book, my editor, my associates, and I *manage by objectives*—we agree on target dates for the completion and editing of each unit draft. If we focus on achieving each of these short-term goals, the prize—an on-time book—takes care of itself. So, to motivate high productivity, effective leaders work with people to define explicit goals, subgoals, and implementation plans, and then provide feedback on progress.

CHOOSING AN APPROPRIATE LEADERSHIP STYLE

Leadership varies from a boss-focused directive style to a democratic style that empowers workers in setting goals and strategies. Which works best may depend on the situation and the leader. The best leadership style for leading a discussion may not be the best style for leading troops on a charge (Fiedler, 1981). Moreover, different leaders are suited to different styles. Some excel at **task leadership**—setting standards, organizing work, and focusing attention on goals. Being goal-oriented, task leaders are good at keeping a group centered on its mission. Typically, they have a directive style, which can work well if the leader is bright enough to give good orders (Fiedler, 1987).

Other managers excel at **social leadership**—explaining decisions, mediating conflicts, and building high-achieving teams (Evans & Dion, 1991). Social leaders often have a democratic style: They delegate authority and welcome the participation of team members. Many experiments show that social leadership is good for morale. Subordinates usually feel more satisfied

> **task leadership** goal-oriented leadership that sets standards, organizes work, and focuses attention on goals.

> **social leadership** group-oriented leadership that builds teamwork, mediates conflict, and offers support.

> "I'm the decider, and I decide what's best." -FORMER U.S. PRESIDENT GEORGE W. BUSH, 2006

HE'D BE BETTER IF HE WERE MORE DECISIVE.

AUTOCRATIC.

HE'S GOOD ON IDEAS, BUT NOT SO GOOD ON FOLLOW-THROUGH.

HIS PROBLEM IS HE DOESN'T KNOW HOW TO SET CLEAR GOALS.

I'D LIKE HIM BETTER IF HE WERE MORE COMPASSIONATE.

HE DOESN'T TAKE CRITICISM WELL AT ALL.

NOT CONSISTENT.

OPEN TO SUGGESTIONS.

and motivated, and perform better, when they participate in decision making (Cawley et al., 1998; Pereira & Osburn, 2007). Moreover, groups solve problems with greater "collective intelligence" when group members are sensitive to one another and participate equally (Woolley et al., 2010).

Because effective leadership styles vary with the situation and the person, the once-popular *great person theory of leadership*—that all great leaders share certain traits—now seems overstated (Vroom & Jago, 2007; Wielkiewicz & Stelzner, 2005). The same coach may seem great or inferior depending on the strength of the team and its competition. But a leader's personality does matter (Zaccaro, 2007). Effective leaders tend to be neither extremely assertive (impairing social relationships) or unassertive (limiting task leadership) (Ames, 2008). Effective leaders of laboratory groups, work teams, and large corporations also tend to exude *charisma* (House & Singh, 1987; Shamir et al., 1993). Their charisma blends a goal-based *vision*, clear *communication*, and optimism that *inspires* others to follow.

In one study of 50 Dutch companies, the firms with highest morale had chief executives who most inspired their colleagues "to transcend their own self-interests for the sake of the collective" (de Hoogh et al., 2004). *Transformational leadership* of this kind motivates others to identify with and commit themselves to the group's mission. Transformational leaders, many of whom are natural extraverts, articulate high standards, inspire people to share their vision, and offer personal attention (Bono & Judge, 2004). The frequent result is more engaged, trusting, and effective workers (Turner et al., 2002). As leaders, women more than men tend to exhibit transformational leadership qualities. Alice Eagly (2007) believes this helps explain why companies with women in top management have tended to enjoy superior financial results, even after controlling for such variables as company size.

Peter Smith and Monir Tayeb (1989) compiled data from studies in India, Taiwan, and Iran indicating that effective managers—whether in coal mines, banks, or government offices—often exhibit a high degree of *both* task and social leadership. As achievement-minded people, effective managers certainly care about how well work is done, yet at the same time they are sensitive to their subordinates' needs. In one national survey of U. S. workers, those in family-friendly organizations offering flexible-time hours reported feeling greater loyalty to their employers (Roehling et al., 2001). A work environment that satisfies one's need to belong also energizes employees. Employees who enjoy high-quality colleague relationships also engage their work with more vigor (Carmeli et al., 2009). Gallup researchers have asked more than 15 million employees worldwide if they have a "best friend at work." The 30 percent who do "are *seven times* as likely to be engaged in their jobs" as those who don't, report Tom Rath and James Harter (2010).

Many successful businesses have also increased employee participation in making decisions, a management style common in Sweden and Japan and, increasingly, elsewhere (Naylor, 1990; Sundstrom et al., 1990). Although managers often think better of work they have directly supervised, studies reveal a *voice effect:* If given a chance to voice their opinion during a decision-making process, people will respond more positively to the decision (van den Bos & Spruijt, 2002). They will also feel more empowered, and likely, therefore, more creative (Hennessey & Amabile, 2010; Huang et al., 2010). And, as we noted earlier, positive, engaged employees are a mark of thriving organizations.

The ultimate in employee participation is the employee-owned company. One such company in my town, the Fleetwood Group, is a 165-employee manufacturer of educational furniture and wireless electronic clickers. When its founder gave 45 percent of the company to his employees, who later bought out other family stockholders, Fleetwood became one of the United States' first companies with an employee stock ownership plan (ESOP). Today, every employee owns part of the company, and as a group they own 100 percent. The more years employees work, the more they own, yet no one owns more than 5 percent. Like every corporate president, Doug Ruch works for his stockholders—who also just happen to be his employees.

As a company that endorses faith-inspired "servant leadership" and "respect and care for each team member-owner," Fleetwood is free to place people above profits. Thus, when orders

"Good leaders don't ask more than their constituents can give, but they often ask—and get—more than their constituents intended to give or thought it was possible to give." -JOHN W. GARDNER, *EXCELLENCE*, 1984

lagged during the recent recession, the employee-owners decided that job security meant more to them than profits. So the company paid otherwise idle workers to do community service—answering phones at nonprofit agencies, building Habitat for Humanity houses, and the like.

Fleetwood employees "act like they own the place," notes Ruch. Employee ownership attracts and retains talented people, "drives dedication," and gives Fleetwood "a sustainable competitive advantage," he contends. With stock growth averaging 17 percent a year, Fleetwood was named the 2006 National ESOP of the year.

We have considered *personnel psychology* (the I/O subfield that focuses on employee selection, placement, appraisal, and development). And we have considered *organizational psychology* (the I/O subfield that focuses on worker satisfaction and productivity, and on organizational change). Finally, we turn to *human factors psychology,* which explores the human-machine interface.

Before You Move On

▶ **ASK YOURSELF**

Are you highly motivated, or not highly motivated, to achieve in school? How has this affected your academic success? How might you improve upon your own achievement levels?

▶ **TEST YOURSELF**

What are the two basic types of leadership, and how do the most effective managers employ these leadership strategies?

Answers to the Test Yourself questions can be found in Appendix E at the end of the book.

The Human Factor

 How do human factors psychologists work to create user-friendly machines and work settings?

Designs sometimes neglect the human factor. Psychologist Donald Norman, an MIT alumnus with a Ph.D., bemoaned the complexity of assembling his new HDTV, related components, and seven remotes into a usable home theater system: "I was VP of Advanced Technology at Apple. I can program dozens of computers in dozens of languages. I understand television, really, I do. . . . It doesn't matter: I am overwhelmed."

How much easier life might be if engineers would routinely work with human factors psychologists to test their designs and instructions on real people. Human factors psychologists help to design appliances, machines, and work settings that fit our natural perceptions and inclinations. Bank automatic teller machines (ATMs) are internally more complex than remote controls ever were, yet, thanks to human factors psychologists working with engineers, ATMs are easier to operate. Digital recorders have solved the TV recording problem with a simple select-and-click menu system ("record that one"). Apple has similarly engineered easy usability with the iPhone and iPad.

Norman (2001) hosts a website (www.jnd.org) that illustrates good designs that fit people (**FIGURE 82.4**). Human factors psychologists also work at designing efficient environments. An ideal kitchen layout, researchers have found, stores needed items close to their usage point and near eye level. It locates work areas to enable doing tasks in order, such as with a refrigerator, stove, and sink in a triangle. It creates counters that enable hands to work at or slightly below elbow height (Boehm-Davis, 2005).

Understanding human factors can help prevent accidents. By studying the human factor in driving accidents, psychologists seek to devise ways to reduce the distractions, fatigue,

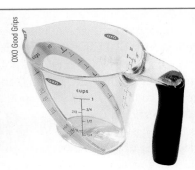

Figure 82.4

Designing products that fit people Human factors psychologist Donald Norman offers these and other examples of effectively designed products.

The Ride On Carry On foldable chair attachment, "designed by a flight attendant mom," enables a small suitcase to double as a stroller.

The Oxo measuring cup allows the user to see the quantity from above.

The Chatsford Teapot comes with a built-in strainer.

and inattention that contribute to 1.3 million annual worldwide traffic fatalities (Lee, 2008). Two-thirds of commercial air accidents have been caused by human error (Nickerson, 1998). After beginning commercial flights in the 1960s, the Boeing 727 was involved in several landing accidents caused by pilot error. Psychologist Conrad Kraft (1978) noted a common setting for these accidents: All took place at night, and all involved landing short of the runway after crossing a dark stretch of water or unilluminated ground. Kraft reasoned that, beyond the runway, city lights would project a larger retinal image if on rising terrain. This would make the ground seem farther away than it was. By re-creating these conditions in flight simulations, Kraft discovered that pilots were deceived into thinking they were flying higher than their actual altitudes (**FIGURE 82.5**). Aided by Kraft's finding, the airlines began requiring the co-pilot to monitor the altimeter—calling out altitudes during the descent—and the accidents diminished.

Later Boeing psychologists worked on other human factors problems (Murray, 1998): How should airlines best train and manage mechanics to reduce the maintenance errors that underlie about 50 percent of flight delays and 15 percent of accidents? What illumination and typeface would make on-screen flight data easiest to read? How could warning messages be most effectively worded—as an action statement ("Pull Up") rather than a problem statement ("Ground Proximity")?

Consider, finally, the available *assistive listening* technologies in various theaters, auditoriums, and places of worship. One technology, commonly available in the United States, requires a headset attached to a pocket-sized receiver that detects infrared or FM signals from the room's sound system. The well-meaning people who design, purchase, and install these systems correctly understand that the technology puts sound directly into the user's ears. Alas, few people with hearing loss undergo the hassle and embarrassment of locating, requesting, wearing, and returning a conspicuous headset. Most such units therefore sit in closets. Britain, the Scandinavian countries, and Australia have instead installed *loop systems* (see www.hearingloop.org) that broadcast customized sound directly through a person's own hearing aid. When suitably equipped, a hearing aid can be transformed by a discrete touch of a switch into an in-the-ear loudspeaker. Offered convenient, inconspicuous, personalized sound, many more people elect to use assistive listening.

Designs that enable safe, easy, and effective interactions between people and technology often seem obvious after the fact. Why, then, aren't they more common? Technology developers sometimes mistakenly assume that others share their expertise—that what's clear to them will similarly be clear to others (Camerer et al., 1989; Nickerson, 1999). When people rap their knuckles on a table to convey a familiar tune (try this with a friend), they

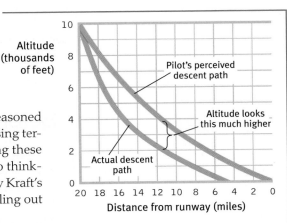

Figure 82.5

The human factor in accidents Lacking distance cues when approaching a runway from over a dark surface, pilots simulating a night landing tended to fly too low. (From Kraft, 1978.)

The human factor in safe landings Advanced cockpit design and rehearsed emergency procedures aided pilot Chesley "Sully" Sullenberger, a U.S. Air Force Academy graduate who studied psychology and human factors. In January 2009, Sullenberger's instantaneous decisions safely guided his disabled airplane onto New York City's Hudson River, where all 155 of the passengers and crew were safely evacuated.

AP Photo/Steven Day

often expect their listener to recognize it. But for the listener, this is a near-impossible task (Newton, 1991). When you know a thing, it's hard to mentally simulate what it's like not to know, and that is called the *curse of knowledge*.

The point to remember: Designers and engineers should consider human abilities and behaviors by designing things to fit people, user-testing their inventions before production and distribution, and being mindful of the curse of knowledge.

Before You Move On

▶ **ASK YOURSELF**

What situations have you experienced (using new technology, visiting new or remodeled building spaces, taking various modes of transportation), where the design did not work well? What situations have you experienced in which planners did a particularly good job matching machines and physical environments to our abilities and expectations?

▶ **TEST YOURSELF**

One of the ways human factors psychologists seek to reduce users' frustration and to improve safety is by watching out for the curse of knowledge. What exactly is this tendency?

Answers to the Test Yourself questions can be found in Appendix E at the end of the book.

Module 82 Review

 82-1 What is *flow,* and what are the three subfields of industrial-organizational psychology?

- *Flow* is a completely involved, focused state of consciousness with diminished awareness of self and time. It results from fully engaging one's skills.

- I/O psychology's three subfields are *personnel, organizational,* and *human factor*s psychology.

 82-2 How do personnel psychologists help organizations with employee selection, work placement, and performance appraisal?

- Personnel psychologists work with organizations to devise selection methods for new employees; recruit and evaluate applicants; design and evaluate training programs; identify people's strengths; analyze job content; and appraise individual and organizational performance.

- Subjective interviews foster the interviewer illusion; *structured interviews* pinpoint job-relevant strengths and are better predictors of performance.

- Checklists, graphic rating scales, and behavior rating scales are useful performance appraisal methods.

82-3 What is *achievement motivation?* What is the role of organizational psychologists?

- *Achievement motivation* is the desire for significant accomplishment, for mastery of skills and ideas, for control, and for rapidly attaining a high standard.

- Organizational psychologists examine influences on worker satisfaction and productivity and facilitate organizational change. Employee satisfaction and engagement tend to correlate with organizational success.

82-4 What are some effective leadership techniques?

- Effective leaders harness job-relevant strengths; set specific challenging goals; and choose an appropriate leadership style. Leadership style may be goal-oriented *(task leadership),* or group-oriented *(social leadership),* or some combination of the two.

82-5 How do human factors psychologists work to create user-friendly machines and work settings?

- Human factors psychologists contribute to human safety and improved design by encouraging developers and designers to consider human perceptual abilities, to avoid the curse of knowledge, and to test users to reveal perception-based problems.

Multiple-Choice Questions

1. Which of the following is the best term or phrase for a completely involved state of consciousness with diminished awareness of self and time?

 a. Flow
 b. I/O psychology
 c. Personnel psychology
 d. Strengths
 e. Achievement motivation

2. According to Angela Duckworth, passion and perseverance in the pursuit of long-term goals describes

 a. wellness.
 b. job analysis.
 c. engagement.
 d. grit.
 e. task leadership.

3. The overall goal of 360-degree feedback is

 a. self-rating.
 b. achievement motivation.
 c. performance appraisal.
 d. selection.
 e. performance.

Practice FRQ

1. Describe engaged, not engaged, and actively disengaged employees.

(3 points)

Module 83

Experienced Emotion: Anger and Happiness

Ron Levine/Getty Images

Module Learning Objectives

83-1 Name some basic emotions, and describe two dimensions psychologists use to differentiate them.

83-2 Identify the causes and consequences of anger.

83-3 Identify the causes and consequences of happiness.

83-1 What are some basic emotions, and what two dimensions help differentiate them?

How many distinct emotions are there? Carroll Izard (1977) isolated 10 basic emotions (joy, interest-excitement, surprise, sadness, anger, disgust, contempt, fear, shame, and guilt), most of which are present in infancy (**FIGURE 83.1**). Jessica Tracy and Richard Robins (2004) believe that pride is also a distinct emotion, signaled by a small smile, head slightly tilted back, and an open posture. And Phillip Shaver and his colleagues (1996) believe that love, too, may be a basic emotion. But Izard has argued that other emotions are combinations of these 10, with love, for example, being a mixture of joy and interest-excitement.

Figure 83.1

Infants' naturally occurring emotions
To identify the emotions present from birth, Carroll Izard analyzed the facial expressions of infants.

Petr Jilek/Shutterstock

Patrick Donehue/Science Source

JGI/Jamie Grill/Blend Images/Corbis

(a) Joy (mouth forming smile, cheeks lifted, twinkle in eye)

(b) Anger (brows drawn together and downward, eyes fixed, mouth squarish)

(c) Interest (brows raised or knitted, mouth softly rounded, lips may be pursed)

Lynn Koenig/Flickr/Getty Images

Viewstock/Corbis

Ariel Alvarez/Getty Images

Vladimir Godnik/Getty Images

(d) Disgust (nose wrinkled, upper lip raised)

(e) Surprise (brows raised, eyes widened, mouth rounded in oval shape)

(f) Sadness (brow's inner corners raised, mouth corners drawn down)

(g) Fear (brows level, drawn in and up, eyelids lifted, mouth corners retracted)

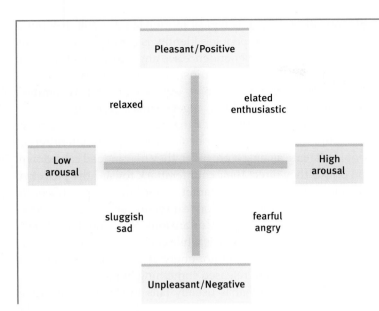

Figure 83.2

Two dimensions of emotion
James Russell, David Watson, Auke Tellegen, and others have described emotions as variations on two dimensions—*arousal* (low versus high) and *valence* (pleasant versus unpleasant feeling).

The ingredients of emotion include not only physiology and expressive behavior but also our conscious experience. Across the world, people place emotional experience along the two dimensions illustrated in **FIGURE 83.2**—positive-versus-negative *valence,* and low-versus-high *arousal* (Russell et al., 1989, 1999a,b, 2009; Watson et al., 1999). Any emotion is some combination of feeling good versus bad, and of being aroused and energized or not. On the valence and arousal dimensions, *terrified* is more frightened (more unpleasant and aroused) than *afraid, enraged* is angrier than *angry, delighted* is happier than *happy.*

Let's take a closer look at anger and happiness. What functions do they serve? What influences our experience of each?

Anger

83-2   What are the causes and consequences of anger?

Anger, the sages have said, is "a short madness" (Horace, 65–8 B.C.E.) that "carries the mind away" (Virgil, 70–19 B.C.E.) and can be "many times more hurtful than the injury that caused it" (Thomas Fuller, 1654–1734). But they have also said that "noble anger" (William Shakespeare, 1564–1616) "makes any coward brave" (Cato, 234–149 B.C.E.) and "brings back . . . strength" (Virgil).

Facing a threat or challenge, fear triggers flight but anger triggers fight—each at times an adaptive behavior. What makes us angry? Sometimes anger is a response to someone's perceived misdeeds, especially when the person's act seems willful, unjustified, and avoidable (Averill, 1983). But small hassles and blameless annoyances—foul odors, high temperatures, dead cell phones, aches and pains—also have the power to make us angry (Berkowitz, 1990).

Anger can harm us: Chronic hostility is linked to heart disease. How, then, can we rid ourselves of our anger? In a Gallup teen survey, boys more than girls reported walking away from the situation or working it off with exercise; girls more often reported talking with a friend, listening to music, or writing (Ray, 2005). Popular books and articles sometimes advise that releasing angry feelings can be better than internalizing them. When irritated, should we lash out at the offender? Are advice columnists right in urging us to teach children to vent their anger? Are "recovery" therapists right in encouraging us to rage at our dead parents, imaginatively curse the boss, or confront our childhood abuser?

Blowing off steam with vuvuzelas

catharsis in psychology, the idea that "releasing" aggressive energy (through action or fantasy) relieves aggressive urges.

"Anger will never disappear so long as thoughts of resentment are cherished in the mind."
- THE BUDDHA, 500 B.C.E.

SIX CHIX

The catharsis idea: Is it true?

Encouraging people to vent their rage is typical in individualist cultures, but it would seldom be heard in cultures where people's identity is centered more on the group. People who keenly sense their *inter*dependence see anger as a threat to group harmony (Markus & Kitayama, 1991). In Tahiti, for instance, people learn to be considerate and gentle. In Japan, from infancy on, angry expressions are less common than in American culture, where in recent politics, anger seems all the rage.

The Western vent-your-anger advice presumes that we can achieve emotional release, or **catharsis,** through aggressive action or fantasy. Experimenters report that *sometimes* when people retaliate against a provoker, they may indeed calm down. But this tends to be true only *if* they direct their counterattack toward the provoker, *if* their retaliation seems justifiable, and *if* their target is not intimidating (Geen & Quanty, 1977; Hokanson & Edelman, 1966). In short, expressing anger can be *temporarily* calming if it does not leave us feeling guilty or anxious. My daughter, a South African resident, experienced a temporary catharsis while cheering on her new country in a World Cup soccer match. "Every time I got angry at Uruguay, blowing that vuvuzela and joining the chorus of dissent released something in me."

Despite the temporary afterglow, catharsis usually fails to cleanse one's rage. More often, expressing anger breeds more anger. For one thing, it may provoke further retaliation, thus escalating a minor conflict into a major confrontation. For another, expressing anger can magnify anger. (Recall the behavior feedback research: *Acting* angry can make us *feel* angrier.) Anger's backfire potential appeared in a study of 100 frustrated engineers and technicians just laid off by an aerospace company (Ebbesen et al., 1975). Researchers asked some workers questions that released hostility, such as, "What instances can you think of where the company has not been fair with you?" After expressing their anger, the workers later filled out a questionnaire that assessed their attitudes toward the company. Had the opportunity to "drain off" their hostility reduced it? Quite the contrary. These people expressed *more* hostility than those who had discussed neutral topics.

Other studies support this finding. In one, people who had been provoked were asked to wallop a punching bag while ruminating about the person who had angered them. Later, when given a chance for revenge, they became even more aggressive. "Venting to reduce anger is like using gasoline to put out a fire," concluded the researcher, Brad Bushman (2002).

When anger fuels physically or verbally aggressive acts we later regret, it becomes maladaptive. Anger primes prejudice. After 9/11, Americans who responded with anger more than fear displayed intolerance for immigrants and Muslims (DeSteno et al., 2004; Skitka et al., 2004). Angry outbursts that temporarily calm us are dangerous in another way: They may be reinforcing and therefore habit forming. If stressed managers find they can drain off some of their tension by berating an employee, then the next time they feel irritated and tense they may be more likely to explode again. Think about it: The next time you are angry you are likely to repeat whatever relieved (and reinforced) your anger in the past.

What, then, is the best way to handle our anger? Experts offer two suggestions. First, wait. You can bring down the level of physiological arousal of anger by waiting. "It is true of the body as of arrows," noted Carol Tavris (1982), "what goes up must come down. Any emotional arousal will simmer down if you just wait long enough." Second, deal with anger in a way that involves neither being chronically angry over every little annoyance, nor sulking and rehearsing your grievances. Ruminating inwardly about the causes of your anger serves only to increase it (Rusting & Nolen-Hoeksema, 1998). Calm yourself by exercising, playing an instrument, or talking it through with a friend.

Anger is not always wrong. Used wisely, it can communicate strength and competence (Tiedens, 2001). It can benefit a relationship when it expresses a grievance in ways that promote reconciliation rather than retaliation. Controlled expressions of anger are more adaptive than either hostile outbursts or pent-up angry feelings. When James Averill (1983) asked people to recall or keep careful records of their experiences with anger, they often recalled reacting assertively rather than hurtfully. Their anger frequently led them to talk things over with the offender, thereby lessening the aggravation. Civility means not only keeping silent about trivial irritations but also communicating important ones clearly and assertively. A nonaccusing statement of feeling—perhaps letting a sibling know that "I get irritated when you mess up my room while I'm away"—can help resolve the conflicts that cause anger.

What if someone's behavior really hurts you, and you cannot resolve the conflict? Research commends the age-old response of forgiveness. Without letting the offender off the hook or inviting further harm, forgiveness releases anger and calms the body. To explore the bodily effects of forgiveness, Charlotte Witvliet and her co-researchers (2001) invited college students to recall an incident where someone had hurt them. As the students mentally rehearsed forgiveness, their negative feelings—and their perspiration, blood pressure, heart rate, and facial tension—all were lower than when they rehearsed their grudges.

Happiness

83-3   What are the causes and consequences of happiness?

Our state of happiness or unhappiness colors everything. Happy people perceive the world as safer and feel more confident. They make decisions and cooperate more easily, and are more tolerant. They rate job applicants more favorably, savor their positive past experiences without dwelling on the negative, and are more socially connected. They live healthier and more energized and satisfied lives (Briñol et al., 2007; Liberman et al., 2009; Mauss et al., 2011). When your mood is gloomy, life as a whole seems depressing and meaningless—and you think more skeptically and attend more critically to your surroundings. Let your mood brighten, and your thinking broadens and becomes more playful and creative (Baas et al., 2008; Forgas, 2008b; Fredrickson, 2006).

This helps explain why college students' happiness helps predict their life course. In one study, women with natural, happy smiles in 1950s college yearbook photos were more likely to be happily married in middle age (Harker & Keltner, 2001). In another study, which surveyed thousands of U.S. college students in 1976 and restudied them at age 37, happy students had gone on to earn significantly more money than their less-happy-than-average peers (Diener et al., 2002). When we are happy, our relationships, self-image, and hopes for the future also seem more promising.

Moreover—and this is one of psychology's most consistent findings—happiness doesn't just feel good, it does good. In study after study, a mood-boosting experience (finding money, succeeding on a challenging task, recalling a happy event) has made people more likely to give money, pick up someone's dropped papers, volunteer time, and do other good deeds. Psychologists call it the **feel-good, do-good phenomenon** (Salovey, 1990). (The reverse is also true: Doing good also promotes good feeling, a phenomenon harnessed by some happiness coaches as they assign people to perform a daily "random act of kindness" and to record the results.)

William James was writing about the importance of happiness ("the secret motive for all [we] do") as early as 1902. With the twenty-first century rise of *positive psychology* (see Module 59) have come many studies of **subjective well-being**—our feelings of happiness (sometimes defined as a high ratio of positive to negative feelings) or sense of satisfaction with life.

The Short Life of Emotional Ups and Downs

Are some days of the week happier than others? In what is surely psychology's biggest-ever data sample, social psychologist Adam Kramer (at my request and in cooperation with Facebook) did a naturalistic observation of emotion words in "billions" of status updates. After eliminating exceptional days, such as holidays, he tracked the frequency of positive and negative emotion words by day of the week. The most positive moods days? Friday and Saturday (**FIGURE 83.3** on the next page). For you, too?

feel-good, do-good phenomenon people's tendency to be helpful when already in a good mood.

subjective well-being self-perceived happiness or satisfaction with life. Used along with measures of objective well-being (for example, physical and economic indicators) to evaluate people's quality of life.

Figure 83.3

Using web science to track happy days

Adam Kramer (personal correspondence, 2010) tracked positive and negative emotion words in many "billions" (the exact number is proprietary information) of status updates of U.S. Facebook users between September 7, 2007 and November 17, 2010.

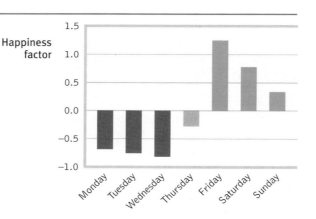

Over the long run, our emotional ups and downs tend to balance out. This is true even over the course of the day (**FIGURE 83.4**). Positive emotion rises over the early to middle part of most days and then drops off (Kahneman et al., 2004; Watson, 2000). A stressful event—an argument, a sick child, a car problem—can trigger a bad mood. No surprise there. But by the next day, the gloom nearly always lifts (Affleck et al., 1994; Bolger et al., 1989; Stone & Neale, 1984). If anything, people tend to rebound from a bad day to a *better-than-usual* good mood the following day.

Even when negative events drag us down for longer periods, our bad mood usually ends. Those involved in romantic relationships expect their lives would be deflated by a breakup. Actually, after a recovery period, their happiness level is about the same as for those who don't break up (Gilbert et al., 1998).

Grief over the loss of a loved one or anxiety after a severe trauma (such as child abuse, rape, or the terrors of war) can linger. But usually, even tragedy is not permanently depressing. People who become blind or paralyzed usually recover near-normal levels of day-to-day happiness. So do those who must go on kidney dialysis or have permanent colostomies (Gerhart et al., 1994; Riis et al., 2005; Smith et al., 2009). And in European studies, 8- to 12-year-olds with cerebral palsy experienced normal psychological well-being (Dickinson et al., 2007).

People mostly cope well with a permanent disability, although they may not rebound all the way back to their former emotions (Diener et al., 2006; Smith et al., 2009). A major disability leaves people less happy than average, yet much happier than able-bodied people with depression (Kübler et al., 2005; Lucas, 2007a,b; Oswald & Powdthavee, 2006; Schwartz & Estrin, 2004). "If you are a paraplegic," explained Daniel Kahneman (2005), "you will gradually start thinking of other things, and the more time you spend thinking of other things the less miserable you are going to be." Contrary to what many people believe, most patients "locked in" a motionless body do not indicate they want to die (Bruno et al., 2008, 2011; Smith & Delargy, 2005).

The surprising reality: *We overestimate the duration of our emotions and underestimate our resiliency and capacity to adapt.* (As one who inherited hearing loss with a trajectory toward that of my mother, who spent the last 13 years of her life completely deaf, I take heart from these findings.)

Courtesy of Anna Putt

Human resilience Seven weeks after her 1994 wedding, Anna Putt of South Midlands, England, shown here with her husband, Des, suffered a brainstem stroke that left her "locked-in." For months after, she recalled, "I was paralyzed from the neck down and was unable to communicate. These were VERY frightening times. But with encouragement from family, friends, faith, and medical staff, I tried to keep positive." In the ensuing three years, she became able to "talk" (by nodding at letters), to steer an electric wheelchair with her head, and to use a computer (with head movements that guide a cursor). Despite her paralysis, she has reported that "I enjoy going out in the fresh air. My motto is 'Don't look back, move forward.' God would not want me to stop trying and I have no intention of doing so. Life is what you make of it!"

"Weeping may tarry for the night, but joy comes with the morning."
- Psalm 30:5

Figure 83.4

Moods across the day

When psychologist David Watson (2000) sampled nearly 4500 mood reports from 150 people, he found this pattern of variation from the average levels of positive and negative emotions.

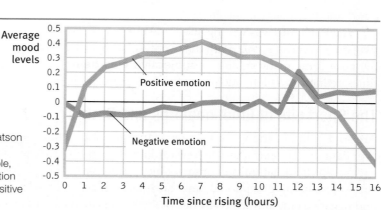

Wealth and Well-Being

"Do you think you would be happier if you made more money?" *Yes,* replied 73 percent of Americans in a 2006 Gallup poll. How important is "Being very well off financially?" *Very important,* say many entering U.S. collegians (**FIGURE 83.5**). Some 3 in 4 students rate their top two objectives (among 21) as being "very well off" and "raising a family," and they grade them "extremely important" or "essential."

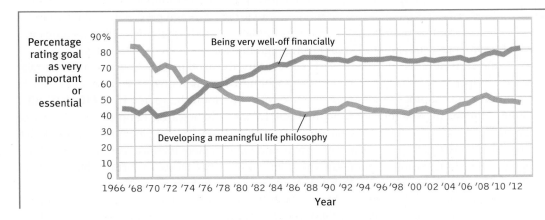

Figure 83.5

The changing materialism of entering collegians Surveys of more than 200,000 entering U.S. collegians per year have revealed an increasing desire for wealth after 1970. (From *The American Freshman* surveys, UCLA, 1966 to 2012.)

And to a point, wealth does correlate with well-being. Consider:

- In most countries, and especially in poor countries, individuals with lots of money are typically happier than those who struggle to afford life's basic needs (Diener & Biswas-Diener, 2009; Howell & Howell, 2008; Lucas & Schimmack, 2009). And, as we saw in Module 29, they often enjoy better health than those stressed by poverty and lack of control over their lives.

- People in rich countries also experience greater well-being than those in poor countries (Diener et al., 2009; Inglehart, 2008; **FIGURE 83.6**). The same is true for those in higher-income American states (Oswald & Wu, 2010).

So, it seems that money enough to buy your way out of hunger and hopelessness also buys some happiness. But once one has enough money for comfort and security, piling up more and more matters less and less. Ever more money does allow us to enjoy more things

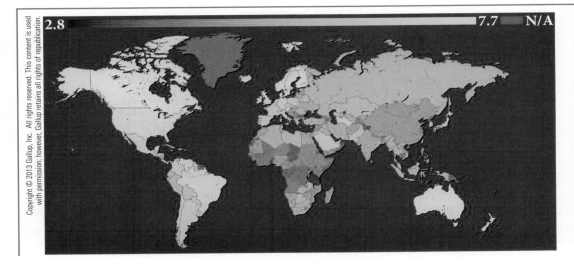

Figure 83.6

Well-being across the planet The Gallup World Poll has surveyed nearly a half-million people across countries representing 99 percent of the human population. One question invited people to imagine a 10-step ladder, where 10 is "the best possible life for you" and 0 is "the worst possible life for you." "On which step of the ladder would you say you personally feel you stand?" As you can see, people in the wealthier countries of North America, Western Europe, and Australia and New Zealand have tended to rate their lives higher. (Courtesy The Gallup Organization, 2011.)

"Money won't make you happy, Waldron. So instead of a raise, I'm giving a Prozac."

and feel more control over our lives, but it does less to increase our *feelings* of happiness (Diener et al., 2009; Kahneman & Deaton, 2010). That's partly because of the *diminishing returns* phenomenon (familiar to economists as *diminishing marginal utility*). Experiencing luxury diminishes our savoring of life's simpler pleasures (Quoidbach et al., 2010). If you experience a friend's hot new smart-phone technology, your old phone—once so cool—may pale by comparison.

As Robert Cummins (2006) confirms with Australian data, the power of more money to increase happiness is significant at low incomes and diminishes as income rises. A $1000 annual wage increase does a lot more for the average person in Malawi than for the average person in Switzerland. This implies, he adds, that raising low incomes will do more to increase happiness than raising high incomes.

And consider this: During the last half-century, the average U.S. citizen's buying power almost tripled. Did this greater wealth—enabling twice as many cars per person, not to mention iPods, laptops, and smart phones—also buy more happiness? As **FIGURE 83.7** shows, the average American, though certainly richer, is not a bit happier. In 1957, some 35 percent said they were "very happy," as did slightly fewer—32 percent—in 2008. Much the same has been true of Europe, Australia, and Japan, where increasing real incomes have *not* produced increasing happiness (Australian Unity, 2008; Diener & Biswas-Diener, 2002, 2009; Di Tella & MacCulloch, 2010). Ditto China, where living standards have risen but satisfaction has not (Brockmann et al., 2009). These findings lob a bombshell at modern materialism: *Economic growth in affluent countries has provided no apparent boost to morale or social well-being.*

Ironically, in every culture, those who strive hardest for wealth have tended to live with lower well-being (Ryan, 1999), especially when those hard-driving people were seeking money to prove themselves, gain power, or show off rather than support their families (Niemiec et al., 2009; Srivastava et al., 2001). Those who instead strive for intimacy, personal growth, and contribution to the community experience a higher quality of life (Kasser, 2002, 2011).

"Australians are three times richer than their parents and grandparents were in the 1950s, but they are not happier." - *A Manifesto for Well-Being*, 2005

Figure 83.7

Does money buy happiness? It surely helps us to avoid certain types of pain. Yet, though buying power has almost tripled since the 1950s, the average American's reported happiness has remained almost unchanged. (Happiness data from National Opinion Research Center surveys; income data from *Historical Statistics of the United States* and *Economic Indicators*.)

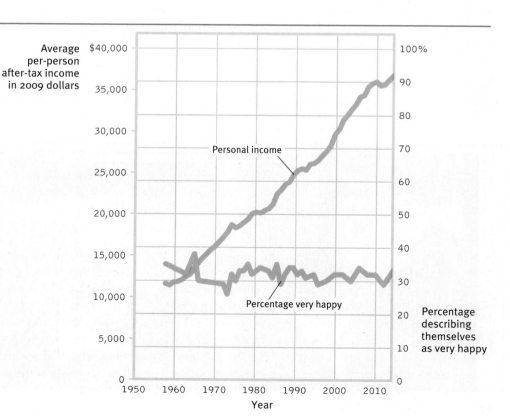

Two Psychological Phenomena: Adaptation and Comparison

Two psychological principles explain why, for those who are not poor, more money buys little more than a temporary surge of happiness and why our emotions seem attached to elastic bands that pull us back from highs or lows. In its own way, each principle suggests that happiness is relative.

HAPPINESS IS RELATIVE TO OUR OWN EXPERIENCE

The **adaptation-level phenomenon** describes our tendency to judge various stimuli in comparison with our past experiences. As psychologist Harry Helson (1898–1977) explained, we adjust our *neutral* levels—the points at which sounds seem neither loud nor soft, temperatures neither hot nor cold, events neither pleasant nor unpleasant—based on our experience. We then notice and react to variations up or down from these levels.

Thus, if our current condition—our income, academic average, or social prestige—improves, we feel an initial surge of pleasure, come to consider this new level normal, and require something even better to give us another surge of happiness. I can recall the childhood thrill of watching my family's first 12-inch, black-and-white TV. Years later, after watching movies on a family member's 60-inch high-definition flat screen, I adapted upward, and became unimpressed by my once wonderful 27-inch TV. Yesterday's marvelous becomes today's mundane.

HI & LOIS

So, could we ever create a permanent social paradise? Probably not (Campbell, 1975; Di Tella & MacCulloch, 2010). People who have experienced a recent windfall—from a lottery, an inheritance, or a surging economy—typically feel some elation (Diener & Oishi, 2000; Gardner & Oswald, 2007). So would you, if you woke up tomorrow to your Utopia—perhaps a world with no bills, no ills, perfect scores, someone who loves you unreservedly. But after a time, you would gradually recalibrate your adaptation level, and you would adjust your new neutral level to include these new experiences. Before long, you would again sometimes feel gratified (when events exceed your expectations) and sometimes feel deprived (when they fall below), and sometimes feel neutral. *The point to remember:* Feelings of satisfaction and dissatisfaction, success and failure are judgments we make based on our prior experience. Satisfaction, as Richard Ryan (1999) said, "has a short half life." Ditto disappointment, which means that you may bounce back from a setback sooner than you expect.

HAPPINESS IS RELATIVE TO OTHERS' SUCCESS

We are always comparing ourselves with others. And whether we feel good or bad depends on who those others are (Lyubomirsky, 2001). We are slow-witted or clumsy only when others are smarter or more agile. This sense that we are worse off than others with whom we compare ourselves is the concept of **relative deprivation.**

During World War II, U.S. Air Corps soldiers experienced a relatively rapid promotion rate. Nevertheless, many individual soldiers were frustrated about their own comparatively slow promotion rates (Merton & Kitt, 1950). Seeing so many others being promoted apparently inflated the soldiers' expectations. Likewise, the economic surge that has made some urban Chinese newly affluent appears to have fueled among other Chinese a sense of relative deprivation (Burkholder, 2005a,b).

"No happiness lasts for long." - SENECA, *AGAMEMNON*, 60 C.E.

"Continued pleasures wear off . . . . Pleasure is always contingent upon change and disappears with continuous satisfaction." - DUTCH PSYCHOLOGIST NICO FRIJDA (1988)

adaptation-level phenomenon our tendency to form judgments (of sounds, of lights, of income) relative to a neutral level defined by our prior experience.

relative deprivation the perception that we are worse off relative to those with whom we compare ourselves.

"I have a 'fortune cookie maxim' that I'm very proud of: Nothing in life is quite as important as you think it is while you are thinking about it. So, nothing will ever make you as happy as you think it will." - NOBEL LAUREATE PSYCHOLOGIST DANIEL KAHNEMAN, GALLUP INTERVIEW, "WHAT WERE THEY THINKING?" 2005

When expectations soar above attainments, the result is disappointment. Relative deprivation showed up again when Alex Rodriguez achieved a 10-year, $275 million baseball contract. His deal surely made him temporarily happy, but it likely also diminished other star players' satisfaction with their lesser, multimillion-dollar contracts. Satisfaction stems less from our income than our income rank (Boyce et al., 2010). Better to make $50,000 when others make $25,000 than to make $100,000 when one's friends, neighbors, and co-workers make $200,000 (Solnick & Hemenway, 1998, 2009).

Such comparisons help us understand why the middle- and upper-income people in a given country, who can compare themselves with the relatively poor, tend to be more satisfied with life than are their less-fortunate compatriots. Nevertheless, once people reach a moderate income level, further increases buy little more happiness. Why? Because as people climb the ladder of success they mostly compare themselves with local peers who are at or above their current level (Gruder, 1977; Suls & Tesch, 1978; Zell & Alicke, 2010). "Beggars do not envy millionaires, though of course they will envy other beggars who are more successful," noted Bertrand Russell (1930, p. 90). Thus, "Napoleon envied Caesar, Caesar envied Alexander, and Alexander, I daresay, envied Hercules, who never existed. You cannot, therefore, get away from envy by means of success alone, for there will always be in history or legend some person even more successful than you are" (pp. 68–69).

Just as comparing ourselves with those who are better off creates envy, so counting our blessings as we compare ourselves with those worse off boosts our contentment. In one study, University of Wisconsin-Milwaukee women considered others' deprivation and suffering (Dermer et al., 1979). They viewed vivid depictions of how grim life was in Milwaukee in 1900. They imagined and then wrote about various personal tragedies, such as being burned and disfigured. Later, the women expressed greater satisfaction with their own lives. Similarly, when mildly depressed people have read about someone who was even more depressed, they felt somewhat better (Gibbons, 1986). "I cried because I had no shoes," states a Persian saying, "until I met a man who had no feet."

Predictors of Happiness

Happy people share many characteristics (**TABLE 83.1**). But why are some people normally so joyful and others so somber? Here, as in so many other areas, the answer is found in the interplay between nature and nurture.

Genes matter. In one study of 254 identical and fraternal twins, about 50 percent of the difference among people's happiness ratings was heritable (Lykken & Tellegen, 1996). Other twin studies report similar or slightly less heritability (Bartels & Boomsma, 2009; Lucas, 2008; Nes et al., 2010). Identical twins raised apart are often similarly happy.

"Researchers say I'm not happier for being richer, but do you know how much researchers make?"

Table 83.1 Happiness Is . . .	
Researchers Have Found That Happy People Tend to	**However, Happiness Seems Not Much Related to Other Factors, Such as**
Have high self-esteem (in individualist countries).	Age.
Be optimistic, outgoing, and agreeable.	Gender (women are more often depressed, but also more often joyful).
Have close friendships or a satisfying marriage.	Parenthood (having children or not).
Have work and leisure that engage their skills.	Physical attractiveness.
Have an active religious faith.	
Sleep well and exercise.	

Sources: Summarized from DeNeve & Cooper (1998), Diener et al. (2003), Headey et al. (2010), Lucas et al. (2004), Myers (1993, 2000), Myers & Diener (1995, 1996), and Steel et al. (2008). Veenhoven (2009) offers a database of 11,000+ correlates of happiness at www.worlddatabaseofhappiness.eur.nl.

But our personal history and our culture matter, too. On the personal level, as we have seen, our emotions tend to balance around a level defined by our experience. On the cultural level, groups vary in the traits they value. Self-esteem and achievement matter more to Westerners, who value individualism. Social acceptance and harmony matter more to those in communal cultures such as Japan that stress family and community (Diener et al., 2003; Uchida & Kitayama, 2009).

Depending on our genes, our outlook, and our recent experiences, our happiness seems to fluctuate around our "happiness set point," which disposes some people to be ever upbeat and others more negative. Even so, after following thousands of lives over two decades, researchers have determined that our satisfaction with life is not fixed (Lucas & Donnellan, 2007). Happiness rises and falls, and can be influenced by factors that are under our control. A striking example: In a long-term German study, married partners were as similarly satisfied with their lives as were identical twins (Schimmack & Lucas, 2007). Genes matter. But as this study hints, relationship quality matters, too. (For research-based hints on enhancing your own happiness, see Close-up: Want to Be Happier?)

FYI

Studies of chimpanzees in zoos reveal that happiness in chimpanzees, as rated by 200 employees, is also genetically influenced (Weiss et al., 2000, 2002).

Close-up

Want to Be Happier?

Your happiness, like your cholesterol level, is genetically influenced. Yet as cholesterol is also influenced by diet and exercise, so happiness is partly under your control (Nes, 2010; Sin & Lyubomirsky, 2009). Here are some research-based suggestions for improving your mood and increasing your satisfaction with life.

Realize that enduring happiness may not come from financial success. We adapt to change by adjusting our expectations. Neither wealth, nor any other circumstance we long for, will guarantee happiness.

Take control of your time. Happy people feel in control of their lives. To master your use of time, set goals and divide them into daily aims. This may be frustrating at first because we all tend to overestimate how much we will accomplish in any given day. The good news is that we generally *underestimate* how much we can accomplish in a year, given just a little progress every day.

Act happy. As you saw in Module 42, people who were manipulated into a smiling expression felt better. So put on a happy face. Talk as *if* you feel positive self-esteem, are optimistic, and are outgoing. We can often act our way into a happier state of mind.

Seek work and leisure that engage your skills. Happy people often are in a zone called *flow*—absorbed in tasks that challenge but don't overwhelm them. Passive forms of leisure (watching TV) often provide less flow experience than socializing, hiking, or creative work. Money also buys more happiness when spent on experiences that you can look forward to, enjoy, and remember than when spent on material stuff (Carter & Gilovich, 2010). As pundit Art Buchwald said, "The best things in life aren't things."

Join the "movement" movement. Aerobic exercise can relieve mild depression and anxiety as it promotes health and energy. Sound minds reside in sound bodies. Off your duffs, couch potatoes!

Give your body the sleep it wants. Happy people live active lives yet reserve time for renewing sleep and solitude. Many people suffer from sleep debt, with resulting fatigue, diminished alertness, and gloomy moods.

Give priority to close relationships. Intimate friendships can help you weather difficult times. Confiding is good for soul and body. Compared with unhappy people, happy people engage in less superficial small talk and more meaningful conversations (Mehl et al., 2010). So resolve to nurture your closest relationships by *not* taking your loved ones for granted. This means displaying to them the sort of kindness you display to others, affirming them, playing together, and sharing together.

Focus beyond self. Reach out to those in need. Happiness increases helpfulness (those who feel good do good). But doing good also makes one feel good.

Count your blessings and record your gratitude. Keeping a gratitude journal heightens well-being (Emmons, 2007; Seligman et al., 2005). Try pausing each day to savor good moments, and to record positive events and why they occurred. Express your gratitude to others.

Nurture your spiritual self. For many people, faith provides a support community, a reason to focus beyond self, and a sense of purpose and hope. That helps explain why people active in faith communities report greater-than-average happiness and often cope well with crisis.

Digested from David G. Myers, *The Pursuit of Happiness* (Harper).

RubberBall Selects/Alamy

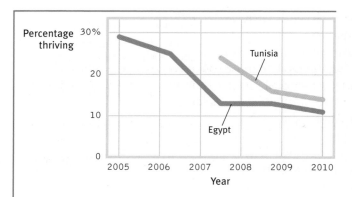

Figure 83.8

Declining well-being in Egypt and Tunisia prior to popular revolts In Gallup surveys, the percentage of people who were "thriving" (rating their life satisfaction 7 or higher and projecting their next five years at 8 or higher on a 10-step scale) declined in advance of 2011 demonstrations that led to a change of government (Clifton & Morales, 2011).

If we can enhance our happiness on an individual level, could we use happiness research to refocus our national priorities more on advancing psychological well-being? Many psychologists believe we could. Diener (2006, 2009), (2006), supported by 52 colleagues, has proposed ways in which nations might measure national well-being. "Policymakers should be interested in subjective well-being not only because of its inherent value to citizens, but also because individuals' subjective well-being can have positive spillover benefits for the society as a whole." Happiness research offers new ways to assess the impacts of various public policies, argue Diener and his colleagues. Happy societies are not only prosperous, but also places where people trust one another, feel free, and enjoy close relationships (Oishi & Schimmack, 2010). Thus, when debating the minimum wage, economic inequality, tax rates, divorce laws, health care, and neighborhood planning, people's psychological well-being should be a prime consideration—a point now affirmed by the Canadian, French, German, and British governments, which have added well-being measures to their national agendas (Cohen, 2011; Gertner, 2010; Stiglitz, 2009). The predictive power of national well-being assessments was apparent in 2011, as the governments of Egypt and Tunisia first succumbed to popular uprisings in the aftermath of declining life satisfaction (**FIGURE 83.8**).

Before You Move On

▶ **ASK YOURSELF**

If we learn our emotional responses, we may be able to learn new responses to replace old ones. Would you like to change any of your emotional responses? Do you feel you are too easily provoked to anger, for instance? How might you go about changing your behavior or your thinking in order to change your emotional reactions?

▶ **TEST YOURSELF**

What things do (and do not) predict self-reported happiness?

Answers to the Test Yourself questions can be found in Appendix E at the end of the book.

Module 83 Review

 What are some basic emotions, and what two dimensions help differentiate them?

- Caroll Izard's 10 basic emotions are joy, interest-excitement, surprise, sadness, anger, disgust, contempt, fear, shame, and guilt.

- The two dimensions of emotion are positive-versus-negative valence, and low-versus-high arousal.

83-2 **What are the causes and consequences of anger?**

- Anger is most often evoked by misdeeds that we interpret as willful, unjustified, and avoidable. But smaller frustrations and blameless annoyances can also trigger anger.

- Emotional *catharsis* may be temporarily calming, but in the long run it does not reduce anger. Rehearsing anger can make us more angry.

- Controlled assertions of feelings may resolve conflicts, and forgiveness may rid us of angry feelings.

83-3   What are the causes and consequences of happiness?

- A good mood brightens people's perceptions of the world and makes them more willing to help others (the *feel-good, do-good phenomenon*).

- The moods triggered by good or bad events seldom last beyond that day. Even significant good events, such as sudden wealth, seldom increase happiness for long.

- Happiness is relative to our own experiences (the *adaptation-level phenomenon*) and to others' success (the *relative deprivation* principle).

- Some individuals seem genetically predisposed to be happier than others. Cultures, which vary in the traits they value and the behaviors they expect and reward, also influence personal levels of happiness.

Multiple-Choice Questions

1. The idea that releasing aggressive energy will relieve aggressive urges is called
   a. subjective well-being.
   b. the adaptation-level phenomenon.
   c. resilience.
   d. catharsis.
   e. valence.

2. Which of the following do psychologists say is the best way to handle anger?
   a. Venting with a friend about the source of your anger
   b. Dealing with the situation right away so the anger does not build
   c. Playing violent video games so the anger can subside
   d. Waiting for the arousal to subside
   e. Keeping the source of anger to yourself so it cannot cause additional problems

3. Which of the following is an example of the feel-good, do-good phenomenon?
   a. Anagha tries to keep her 2-year-old son from becoming upset for any reason.
   b. Niko is praised by his teacher and later volunteers to help his mother clean the garage.
   c. Carrsan felt satisfied after helping the ecology club pick up trash around the school.
   d. Maggie's parents doubled her allowance when she was nice to her sister all day.
   e. Rowen was glad to finally be over the flu so he could return to his volunteer work.

4. Which of the following accurately represents the relationship between happiness and wealth?
   a. Rapidly increasing wealth is associated with a slight decrease in happiness because of relative deprivation.
   b. Increased wealth increases happiness equally for almost everybody.
   c. There is no relationship between wealth and happiness.
   d. Gradually increasing wealth is associated with a slight decrease in happiness because of the adaptation-level phenomenon.
   e. Increased wealth increases happiness for people who don't have enough money to meet their basic needs.

Practice FRQ

1. Describe two factors that are associated with happiness and two that are not.

(4 points)

Module 84

Human Flourishing

Module Learning Objectives

84-1 Discuss the links among basic outlook on life, social support, stress, and health.

84-2 Discuss the advantages of aerobic exercise as a way to manage stress and improve well-being.

84-3 Describe how relaxation and meditation might influence stress and health.

84-4 Define *complementary and alternative medicine,* and explain how it is best assessed through scientific research.

84-5 Describe what is meant by the faith factor, and offer some possible explanations for the link between religious involvement and longevity.

Promoting Health

Promoting health begins with implementing strategies that prevent illness and enhance wellness. Traditionally, people have thought about their health only when something goes wrong—visiting a physician for diagnosis and treatment. That, say **health psychologists,** is like ignoring a car's maintenance and going to a mechanic only when the car breaks down. Health maintenance includes alleviating stress, preventing illness, and promoting well-being.

> **health psychology** a subfield of psychology that provides psychology's contribution to behavioral medicine.

Optimism and Health

84-1 What are the links among basic outlook on life, social support, stress, and health?

One aspect of our health and our coping with stress is our outlook—what we expect from the world. *Pessimists* expect things to go badly. *Optimists* agree with statements such as, "In uncertain times, I usually expect the best." People with an optimistic outlook expect to have more control, to cope better with stressful events, and to enjoy better health (Aspinwall & Tedeschi, 2010; Carver et al., 2010; Rasmussen et al., 2009). During the last month of a semester, students previously identified as optimistic reported less fatigue and fewer coughs, aches, and pains. And during the stressful first few weeks of law school, those who were optimistic ("It's unlikely that I will fail") enjoyed better moods and stronger immune systems (Segerstrom et al., 1998). Optimists also respond to stress with smaller increases in blood pressure, and they recover more quickly from heart bypass surgery.

Consider the consistency and startling magnitude of the optimism and positive emotions factor in several other studies:

- One research team followed 941 Dutch people, ages 65 to 85, for nearly a decade (Giltay et al., 2004, 2007). Among those in the lowest optimism quartile, 57 percent died, as did only 30 percent of the top optimism quartile.

- When Finnish researchers followed 2428 men for up to a decade, the number of deaths among those with a bleak, hopeless outlook was more than double that found among their optimistic counterparts (Everson et al., 1996). American researchers found the same when following 4256 Vietnam-era veterans (Phillips et al., 2009).

- A now-famous study followed up on 180 Catholic nuns who had written brief autobiographies at about 22 years of age and had thereafter lived similar lifestyles. Those who had expressed happiness, love, and other positive feelings in their autobiographies lived an average 7 years longer than their more dour counterparts (Danner et al., 2001). By age 80, some 54 percent of those expressing few positive emotions had died, as had only 24 percent of the most positive spirited.

> The oldest Holocaust survivor explaining her 107 years: "In a word: optimism. I look at the good. When you are relaxed, your body is always relaxed." - Alice Herz-Sommer, 2010

Social Support

Social support—feeling liked and encouraged by intimate friends and family—promotes both happiness and health. In massive investigations, some following thousands of people for several years, close relationships have predicted health. People are less likely to die early if supported by close relationships (Uchino, 2009). When Brigham Young University researchers combined data from 148 studies totaling more than 300,000 people worldwide, they confirmed a striking effect of social support (Holt-Lunstad et al., 2010). During the studies, those with ample social connections had survival rates about 50 percent greater than those with meager connections. The impact of meager connections appeared roughly equal to the effect of smoking 15 cigarettes a day or having alcohol use disorder, and double the effect of not exercising or being obese. People aren't the only creatures to benefit from friends. Among baboons, strong social bonds with relatives and friends similarly predicts longevity (Silk et al., 2010).

People need people. Some fill this need by connecting with friends, family, co-workers, members of a faith community, or other support groups. Others connect in positive, happy, supportive marriages. People in low-conflict marriages live longer, healthier lives than the unmarried (De Vogli et al., 2007; Kaplan & Kronick, 2006; Sbarra, 2009). This correlation holds regardless of age, sex, race, and income (National Center for Health Statistics, 2004). One seven-decade-long study found that at age 50, healthy aging is better predicted by a good marriage than by a low cholesterol level (Vaillant, 2002). But the married versus never-married health gap has shrunk (Liu, 2009).

How can we explain the link between social support and health? Is it because middle-aged and older adults who live alone are more likely to smoke, be obese, and have high cholesterol—and therefore to have a doubled risk of heart attacks (Nielsen et al., 2006)? Or because healthy people are more supportive and marriage-prone? Possibly. But research indicates some other possibilities.

Social support calms us and reduces blood pressure and stress hormones. More than 50 studies support this finding (Graham et al., 2006; Uchino et al., 1996, 1999). To see if social support might calm people's response to threats, one research team subjected happily married women, while lying in an fMRI machine, to the threat of electric shock to an ankle (Coan et al., 2006). During the experiment, some women held their husband's hand. Others held the hand of an unknown person or no hand at all. While awaiting the occasional

Laughter among friends is good medicine Laughter arouses us, massages muscles, and then leaves us feeling relaxed (Robinson, 1983). Humor (though not hostile sarcasm) may defuse stress, ease pain, and strengthen immune activity (Ayan, 2009; Berk et al., 2001; Kimata, 2001). People who laugh a lot also tend to have lower rates of heart disease (Clark et al., 2001).

Mark Andersen/Getty Images

"Woe to one who is alone and falls and does not have another to help." - Ecclesiastes 4:10

shocks, women holding their husband's hand showed less activity in threat-responsive areas. This soothing benefit was greatest for those reporting the highest-quality marriages. Supportive family and friends—human and nonhuman—help buffer threats. After stressful events, Medicare patients who have a dog or other companionable pet are less likely to visit their doctor (Siegel, 1990). (See Close-up: Pets Are Friends, Too.)

Social support fosters stronger immune functioning. Volunteers in studies of resistance to cold viruses showed this effect (Cohen et al., 1997, 2004). In those studies, healthy volunteers inhaled nasal drops laden with a cold virus and were quarantined and observed for five days. (In these experiments, more than 600 volunteers received $800 each to endure this experience.) Age, race, sex, smoking, and other health habits being equal, those with the most social ties were least likely to catch a cold. If they did catch one, they produced less mucus. More sociability meant less susceptibility. The cold fact is that the effect of social ties is nothing to sneeze at!

Close relationships give us an opportunity for "open heart therapy," a chance to confide painful feelings (Frattaroli, 2006). Talking about a stressful event can temporarily arouse us, but in the long run it calms us by calming limbic system activity (Lieberman et al., 2007; Mendolia & Kleck, 1993). In one study, 33 Holocaust survivors spent two hours recalling their experiences, many in intimate detail never before disclosed (Pennebaker et al., 1989). In the weeks following, most watched a tape of their recollections and showed it to family and friends. Those who were most self-disclosing had the most improved health 14 months later. Confiding is good for the body and the soul. In another study of surviving spouses of people who had committed suicide or died in car accidents, those who bore their grief alone had more health problems than those who could express it openly (Pennebaker & O'Heeron, 1984).

Close-up

Pets Are Friends, Too

Have you ever wished for a friend who would love you just as you are? One who would never judge you? Who would be there for you, no matter your mood? For many tens of millions of people that friend exists, and it is a loyal dog or a friendly cat.

Many people describe their pet as a cherished family member who helps them feel calm, happy, and valued. Can pets also help people handle stress? If so, might pets have healing power? The evidence is, as yet, mixed and meager (Herzog, 2010). But Deborah Wells (2009) and Karen Allen (2003) have reported that pets have sometimes been found to increase the odds of survival after a heart attack, to relieve depression among AIDS patients, and to lower the level of blood pressure and blood lipids that contribute to cardiovascular risk. As nursing pioneer Florence Nightingale (1860) foresaw, "A small pet animal is often an excellent companion for the sick." In one study, women's blood pressure rose as they struggled with challenging math problems in the presence of a best friend or even a spouse, but much less so when accompanied by their dog (Allen, 2003).

So, would pets be good medicine for people who do not have pets? To find out, Allen experimented. The participants

were a group of stockbrokers who lived alone, described their work as stressful, and had high blood pressure. She randomly selected half to adopt an animal shelter cat or dog. When later facing stress, all participants experienced higher blood pressure. But among the new pet owners, the increase was less than half as high as the increase in the no-pet group. The effect was greatest for pet owners with few social contacts or friends. Allen's conclusion: For lowering blood pressure, pets are no substitute for effective drugs and exercise. But for those who enjoy animals, and especially for those who live alone, they are a healthy pleasure.

"Well, I think you're wonderful"

Suppressing emotions can be detrimental to physical health. When health psychologist James Pennebaker (1985) surveyed more than 700 undergraduate women, about 1 in 12 of them reported a traumatic sexual experience in childhood. The sexually abused women—especially those who had kept their secret to themselves—reported more headaches and stomach ailments than did other women who had experienced nonsexual traumas, such as parental death or divorce. Another study, of 437 Australian ambulance drivers, confirmed the ill effects of suppressing one's emotions after witnessing traumas (Wastell, 2002).

Even writing about personal traumas in a diary can help (Burton & King, 2008; Hemenover, 2003; Lyubomirsky et al., 2006). In one experiment, volunteers who did so had fewer health problems during the ensuing four to six months (Pennebaker, 1990). As one participant explained, "Although I have not talked with anyone about what I wrote, I was finally able to deal with it, work through the pain instead of trying to block it out. Now it doesn't hurt to think about it."

If we are aiming to exercise more, drink less, quit smoking, or be a healthy weight, our social ties can tug us away from or toward our goal. Studies of networks of thousands of people followed over years suggest that clusters of friends may "infect" one another with either bad health practices or good behaviors (Christakis & Fowler, 2009). Obesity, for example, spreads within networks in ways that seem not merely to reflect people's seeking out similar others.

Reducing Stress

Having a sense of control (Module 29), developing more optimistic thinking, and building social support can help us *experience* less stress and thus improve our health. Moreover, these factors interrelate: People who are upbeat about themselves and their future tend also to enjoy health-promoting social ties (Stinson et al., 2008). But sometimes we cannot alleviate stress and simply need to *manage* our stress. Aerobic exercise, relaxation, meditation, and spiritual communities may help us gather inner strength and lessen stress effects.

Aerobic Exercise

 How effective is aerobic exercise as a way to manage stress and improve well-being?

Aerobic exercise is sustained, oxygen-consuming exercise—such as jogging, swimming, or biking—that increases heart and lung fitness. It's hard to find bad things to say about exercise. By one estimate, moderate exercise adds not only to your quantity of life—two additional years, on average—but also to your quality of life, with more energy and better mood (Seligman, 1994).

Exercise helps fight heart disease by strengthening the heart, increasing bloodflow, keeping blood vessels open, and lowering both blood pressure and the blood pressure reaction to stress (Ford, 2002; Manson, 2002). Compared with inactive adults, people who exercise suffer half as many heart attacks (Powell et al., 1987; Visich & Fletcher, 2009). Exercise makes the muscles hungry for the fats that, if not used by the muscles, contribute to clogged arteries (Barinaga, 1997). In one 20-year study of adult Finnish twins, other things being equal, daily conditioning exercise reduced death risk by 43 percent (Kujala et al., 1998). Regular exercise in later life also predicts better cognitive functioning and reduced risk of neurocognitive disorder and Alzheimer's disease (Kramer & Erickson, 2007).

The genes passed down to us from our distant ancestors were those that enabled the physical activity essential to hunting, foraging, and farming. In muscle cells, those genes, when activated by exercise, respond by producing proteins. In the modern inactive person, these genes

aerobic exercise sustained exercise that increases heart and lung fitness; may also alleviate depression and anxiety.

"Is there anyone here who specializes in stress management?"

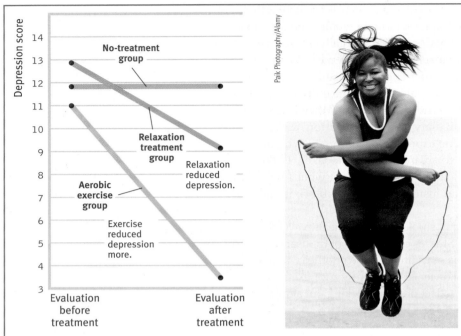

Figure 84.1

Aerobic exercise and depression Mildly depressed college women who participated in an aerobic exercise program showed markedly reduced depression, compared with those who did relaxation exercises or received no treatment. (From McCann & Holmes, 1984.)

produce lower quantities of proteins and leave us susceptible to more than 20 chronic diseases, such as type-2 diabetes, cardiovascular disease, Alzheimer's disease, and cancer (Booth & Neufer, 2005). Inactivity is thus potentially toxic.

Does exercise also boost the spirit? Many studies reveal that aerobic exercise can reduce stress, depression, and anxiety. Americans, Canadians, and Britons who do aerobic exercise at least three times a week manage stress better, exhibit more self-confidence, feel more vigor, and feel less depressed and fatigued than their inactive peers (McMurray, 2004; Mead et al., 2010; Puetz et al., 2006). And in a 21-country survey of university students, physical exercise was a "strong" and consistent predictor of life satisfaction (Grant et al., 2009).

But we could state this observation another way: Stressed and depressed people exercise less. These findings are correlations, and cause and effect are unclear. To sort out cause and effect, researchers experiment. They randomly assign stressed, depressed, or anxious people either to an aerobic exercise group or to a control group. One classic experiment randomly assigned mildly depressed female college students to three groups. One-third participated in a program of aerobic exercise. Another third took part in a program of relaxation exercises. The remaining third (the control group) formed a no-treatment group (McCann & Holmes, 1984). As **FIGURE 84.1** shows, 10 weeks later, the women in the aerobic exercise program reported the greatest decrease in depression. Many had, quite literally, run away from their troubles. Dozens of other experiments confirm that exercise prevents or reduces depression and anxiety (Conn, 2010; Rethorst et al., 2009; Windle et al., 2010). Vigorous exercise provides a substantial and immediate mood boost (Watson, 2000). Even a 10-minute walk stimulates two hours of increased well-being by raising energy levels and lowering tension (Thayer, 1987, 1993).

Some studies indicate that not only is exercise as effective as drugs, it better prevents symptom recurrence (Babyak et al., 2000; Salmon, 2001). In exploring *why* aerobic exercise alleviates negative emotions, researchers have found that exercise in some ways works like an antidepressant drug. Exercise increases arousal, thus counteracting depression's low-arousal state. It often leads to muscle relaxation and sounder sleep. It also orders up mood-boosting chemicals from our body's internal pharmacy—neurotransmitters such as norepinephrine, serotonin, and the endorphins (Jacobs, 1994; Salmon, 2001). And it may foster *neurogenesis.* In mice, exercise causes the brain to produce a molecule that acts as a natural antidepressant, by stimulating the production of new, stress-resistant neurons (Hunsberger et al., 2007; Reynolds, 2009; van Praag, 2009). On a simpler level, the sense of accomplishment and improved physique and body image that often accompany a successful exercise

The mood boost When one's energy or spirits are sagging, few things reboot the day better than exercising (as I can confirm from my daily noontime basketball). Aerobic exercise appears to counteract depression partly by increasing arousal (replacing depression's low-arousal state) and by doing naturally what antidepressants do—increasing the brain's serotonin activity.

routine may enhance one's self-image, leading to a better emotional state. Exercise (at least a half-hour on five or more days of the week) is like a drug that prevents and treats disease, increases energy, calms anxiety, and boosts mood—a drug we would all take, if available. Yet few people (only 1 in 4 in the United States) take advantage of it (Mendes, 2010).

RELAXATION AND MEDITATION

 In what ways might relaxation and meditation influence stress and health?

In the late 1960s, some respected psychologists wondered if we could learn to counteract our stress responses by altering our thinking and lifestyle. As we learned in Module 28, they began experimenting with *biofeedback,* a system of recording, amplifying, and feeding back information about subtle physiological responses, many controlled by the autonomic nervous system. However, a decade of study revealed only limited effectiveness, with biofeedback working best on tension headaches (Miller, 1985; NIH, 1995).

Simple methods of relaxation, which require no expensive equipment, produce many of the results biofeedback once promised. Figure 84.1 pointed out that aerobic exercise reduces depression. But did you notice in that figure that depression also decreased among women in the relaxation treatment group? More than 60 studies have found that relaxation procedures can also help alleviate headaches, hypertension, anxiety, and insomnia (Nestoriuc et al., 2008; Stetter & Kupper, 2002). Such findings would not surprise Meyer Friedman and his colleagues (whose classic studies of stress and heart disease were discussed in Module 44). They tested relaxation in a program designed to help hard-driving Type A heart attack survivors reduce their risk of future attacks, by randomly assigning hundreds of middle-aged men to one of two groups. The first group received standard advice from cardiologists about medications, diet, and exercise habits. The second group received similar advice, but they also were taught ways of modifying their lifestyles. They learned to slow down and relax by walking, talking, and eating more slowly. They learned to smile at others and laugh at themselves. They learned to admit their mistakes; to take time to enjoy life; and to renew their religious faith. The training paid off (**FIGURE 84.2**). During the next three years, the group that learned to modify their lifestyle had half as many repeat heart attacks as did the first group. This, wrote the exuberant Friedman, was an unprecedented, spectacular reduction in heart attack recurrence. A smaller-scale British study similarly divided heart-attack-prone people into control and lifestyle modification groups (Eysenck & Grossarth-Maticek, 1991). During the next 13 years, that study also showed a 50 percent reduction in death rate among people trained to alter their thinking and lifestyle. After suffering a heart attack at age 55, Friedman started taking his own behavioral medicine—and lived to age 90 (Wargo, 2007).

Figure 84.2

Recurrent heart attacks and lifestyle modification The San Francisco Recurrent Coronary Prevention Project offered counseling from a cardiologist to survivors of heart attacks. Those who were also guided in modifying their Type A lifestyle suffered fewer repeat heart attacks. (From Friedman & Ulmer, 1984.)

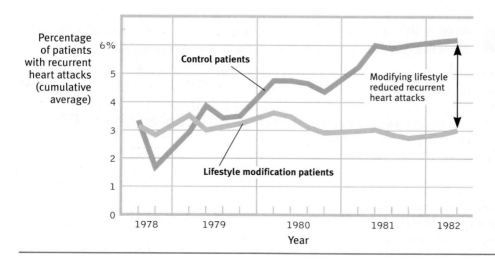

FYI

Meditation is a modern phenomenon with a long history: "Sit down alone and in silence. Lower your head, shut your eyes, breathe out gently, and imagine yourself looking into your own heart. . . . As you breathe out, say 'Lord Jesus Christ, have mercy on me.' . . . Try to put all other thoughts aside. Be calm, be patient, and repeat the process very frequently" (Gregory of Sinai, died 1346).

FYI

And then there are the mystics who seek to use the mind's power to enable novocaine-free cavity repair. Their aim: transcend dental medication.

Cardiologist Herbert Benson (1996) became intrigued with reports that experienced meditators could lower their blood pressure, heart rate, and oxygen consumption and raise their fingertip temperature. His research led him to what he now calls the *relaxation response*, a state of calm marked by relaxed muscles, slowed breathing and heart rate, and decreased blood pressure. According to Benson, relaxation practiced once or twice daily has lasting stress-reducing benefits.

To experience the relaxation response, the Benson-Henry Institute for Mind Body Medicine recommends these steps: Sit quietly in a comfortable position. Close your eyes. Relax your muscles, starting with your feet, then your calves, and upward through your thighs, shoulders, neck, and head. Breathe slowly. As you exhale each breath, repeat a focus word, phrase, or prayer—something drawn from your own belief system. When other thoughts intrude, don't worry. Just return to your repetition and continue for 10 to 20 minutes. When finished, sit quietly for another minute or two, then open your eyes and sit for a few more moments.

Tibetan Buddhists deep in meditation and Franciscan nuns deep in centering prayer report a diminished sense of self, space, and time. Brain scans reveal the neural footprints of such spiritual feelings during these mystical experiences: A part of the parietal lobe that tracks our location in space is less active than usual, and a frontal lobe area involved in focused attention is more active (Cahn & Polich, 2006; Newberg & D'Aquili, 2001). Another difference appears in the brain's left frontal lobe. In Buddhist monks who are experienced in meditation, this area displays elevated levels of activity usually associated with positive emotions.

Was this high rate of activity a *result* of meditation, or simply a correlation unrelated to cause and effect? To find out, the researchers experimented, comparing "before" and "after" brain scans of volunteers who were not experienced meditators (Davidson et al., 2003). First, they took baseline scans of volunteers' normal levels of brain activity. They then randomly assigned them either to a control group or to an eight-week course in *mindfulness meditation*, which has been shown to lessen anxiety and depression (Hofmann et al., 2010). Compared with both the control group and their own baseline, the meditation participants showed noticeably more left-hemisphere activity after the training, and they also had improved immune functioning. Such effects may help explain the results of another study, which found that hypertension patients assigned to meditation training had (compared with other treatment groups) a 30 percent lower cardiovascular death rate over the ensuing 19 years (Schneider et al., 2005). This benefit may result from the lessened anxiety and improved mood that accompanies meditation (Hofmann et al., 2010). The U.S. National Institutes of Health include relaxation and meditation techniques as part of complementary and alternative medicine. For more on that topic, see Thinking Critically About: Complementary and Alternative Medicine.

FAITH COMMUNITIES AND HEALTH

84-5 What is the faith factor, and what are some possible explanations for the link between religious involvement and longevity?

A wealth of studies has revealed another curious correlation, called the *faith factor*. Religiously active people tend to live longer than those who are not religiously active. In the twenty-first century's first decade alone, some 1800 studies explored connections between spirituality and health and healing (Koenig et al., 2011). In one study, researchers compared the death rates for 3900 Israelis living in either one of two groups of communities. The first group contained 11 religiously orthodox collective settlements; the second group contained 11 matched, nonreligious collective settlements (Kark et al., 1996). The researchers found that, over a 16-year period, "belonging to a religious collective was associated with a strong protective effect" not explained by age or economic differences. In every age group, religious community members were about half as likely to have died as were their nonreligious counterparts. This difference is roughly comparable to the gender difference in mortality.

Thinking Critically About

Complementary and Alternative Medicine

 84-4 What is *complementary and alternative medicine,* and how is it best assessed through scientific research?

In China, herbal therapies have long flourished, as have acupuncture and acupressure therapies that claim to correct "imbalances of energy flow" (called Qi or Chi) at identifiable points close to the skin. In Germany, herbal remedies and homeopathy are popular. Such remedies are part of **complementary and alternative medicine (CAM)**, which also includes relaxation, massage therapy, spiritual healing, chiropractic, and aromatherapy. Facing political pressure to explore CAM techniques, the U.S. National Institutes of Health (NIH) established the National Center for Complementary and Alternative Medicine, which the center defines as health care treatments not taught widely in medical schools, not usually reimbursed by insurance companies, and not used in hospitals (**TABLE 84.1**).

> **complementary and alternative medicine (CAM)**
> as yet unproven health care treatments intended to supplement (complement) or serve as alternatives to conventional medicine, and which typically are not widely taught in medical schools, used in hospitals, or reimbursed by insurance companies. When research shows a therapy to be safe and effective, it usually then becomes part of accepted medical practice.

So what shall we make of CAM? Some aspects, such as lifestyle changes and stress management, have acknowledged validity. And certain techniques have proved useful for specific ailments, as acupuncture, massage therapy, and aromatherapy have for pain relief in cancer patients (Fellowes et al., 2004). Do the other aspects offer, as some believe, a new medical paradigm?

Critics point out that people consult physicians for diagnosable, curable diseases and turn to CAM techniques for either

TABLE 84.1
Five Domains of Complementary and Alternative Medicine

Alternative medical systems	Therapies used in place of conventional medicine, including homeopathy in Western cultures and traditional Chinese medicine and Ayurveda practices in non-Western cultures.
Mind-body interventions	Techniques designed to enhance the mind's capacity to affect bodily functions and symptoms, including meditation, prayer, mental healing, and therapies using creative outlets such as art, music, or dance.
Biologically based therapies	Therapies using natural substances such as herbs, foods, and vitamins.
Manipulative and body-based methods	Techniques such as chiropractic or osteopathic manipulation and massage therapy, which manipulate or move one or more body parts.
Energy therapies	Techniques using presumed energy fields. Biofield therapies, such as qi gong, Reiki, and therapeutic touch, are intended to affect energy fields that purportedly surround and penetrate the human body. Bioelectromagnetic-based therapies involve the unconventional use of electromagnetic fields, such as pulsed or magnetic fields.

Source: Adapted from the National Center for Complementary and Alternative Medicine, NIH http://nccam.nih.gov/health/whatiscam.

incurable illnesses or when well but feeling subpar. And given two influences—*spontaneous remission* and the *placebo effect*—CAM practices are bound to seem effective, whether they are or not. Thus, an otherwise healthy person with a cold may try an herbal remedy and then credit the natural disappearance of symptoms to CAM. During cyclical diseases, such as arthritis and allergies, CAM may seem especially effective as people seek therapy during the downturn and presume its effectiveness during the ensuing upturn.

The healing power of belief was clear in one German study of 302 migraine headache patients, which found that 51 percent of those receiving acupuncture treatment found relief, as did only 15 percent of those in a waiting list control group. But among a third group that received "sham acupuncture" (needles inserted at nonacupuncture points), 53 percent enjoyed relief. Such results indicate "a powerful placebo effect" (Linde et al., 2005).

(continued)

Thinking Critically About (continued)

As always, the way to discern what works and what does not is to experiment: Randomly assign patients to receive the therapy or a placebo control. Then ask the critical question: When neither the therapist nor the patient knows who is getting the real therapy, is the real therapy effective?

Much of today's mainstream medicine began as yesterday's alternative medicine. Natural botanical life has given us digitalis (from purple foxglove), morphine (from the opium poppy), and penicillin (from penicillium mold). In each case, the active ingredient was verified in controlled trials. We have medical and public health science to thank for the antibiotics, vaccines, surgical procedures, sanitation, and emergency medicine that helped lengthen our life expectancy by three decades during the last century.

"CAM changes continually," notes the National Center for Complementary and Alternative Medicine (2006), "as those therapies that are proven to be safe and effective become adopted into conventional health care." Indeed, said *New England Journal of Medicine* editors Marcia Angell and Jerome Kassirer (1998), "There cannot be two kinds of medicine—conventional and alternative. There is only medicine that has been adequately tested and medicine that has not, medicine that works and medicine that may or may not work. Once a treatment has been tested rigorously, it no longer matters whether it was considered alternative at the outset."

How should we interpret such findings? Skeptical researchers remind us that correlations can leave many factors uncontrolled (Sloan et al., 1999, 2000, 2002, 2005). Here is one obvious possibility: Women are more religiously active than men, and women outlive men. Does religious involvement merely reflect this gender-longevity link? One 8-year study by the U.S. National Institutes of Health, for example, followed 92,395 women, ages 50 to 79. Even after controlling for many factors, women attending religious services weekly (or more) experienced an approximately 20 percent reduced risk of death during the study period (Schnall et al., 2010). But the association between religious involvement and life expectancy is also found among men (Benjamins et al., 2010; McCullough et al., 2000, 2005, 2009). A 28-year study that followed 5286 Californians found that, after controlling for age, gender, ethnicity, and education, frequent religious attenders were 36 percent less likely to have died in any year (**FIGURE 84.3**). In another 8-year controlled study of more than 20,000 people (Hummer et al., 1999), this effect translated into a life expectancy at age 20 of 83 years for frequent attenders at religious services and 75 years for infrequent attenders.

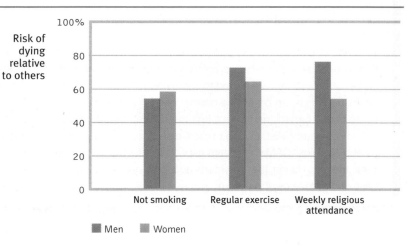

Figure 84.3

Predictors of longer life: Not smoking, frequent exercise, and regular religious attendance Epidemiologist William Strawbridge and his co-workers (1997, 1999; Oman et al., 2002) followed 5286 Alameda, California, adults over 28 years. After adjusting for age and education, the researchers found that not smoking, regular exercise, and religious attendance all predicted a lowered risk of death in any given year. Women attending weekly religious services, for example, were only 54 percent as likely to die in a typical study year as were nonattenders.

Risk of dying relative to others

■ Men ■ Women

These correlational findings do not indicate that nonattenders can add 8 years to their lives if they start attending services and change nothing. But the findings do indicate that religious involvement is a *predictor* of health and longevity, just as nonsmoking and exercise are. Can you imagine what intervening variables might account for the correlation?

First, religion promotes *self-control* (McCullough & Willoughby, 2009). Religiously active people therefore tend to have healthier lifestyles; they smoke and drink much less (Koenig & Vaillant, 2009; Park, 2007; Strawbridge et al., 2001). One Gallup survey of 550,000 Americans found that 15 percent of the very religious were smokers, as were 28 percent of those non-religious (Newport et al., 2010). But such lifestyle differences are not great enough to explain the dramatically reduced mortality in the religious settlements, say the Israeli researchers. In American studies, too, about 75 percent of the longevity difference remained when research-ers controlled for unhealthy behaviors, such as inactivity and smoking (Musick et al., 1999).

Could *social support* explain the faith factor (Ai et al., 2007; George et al., 2002)? In Judaic, Christian, and Islamic religions, faith is a communal experience. To belong to one of these faith communities is to have access to a support network. Religiously active people are there for one another when misfortune strikes. Moreover, religion encourages marriage, another predictor of health and longevity. In the Israeli religious settlements, for example, divorce has been almost nonexistent. But even after controlling for social support, gender, unhealthy behaviors, and preexisting health problems, the mortality studies still find that religiously engaged people tend to live longer (Chida et al., 2009).

Researchers therefore speculate that a third set of intervening variables help protect religious-ly active people from stress and enhance their well-being. Those benefits may flow from a stable, coherent worldview, a sense of hope for the long-term future, feelings of ultimate acceptance, and the relaxed meditation of prayer or Sabbath observance (**FIGURE 84.4**). These variables might also help to explain other recent findings among the religiously active, such as healthier immune functioning, fewer hospital admissions, and, for AIDS patients, fewer stress hormones and longer survival (Ironson et al., 2002; Koenig & Larson, 1998; Lutgendorf et al., 2004).

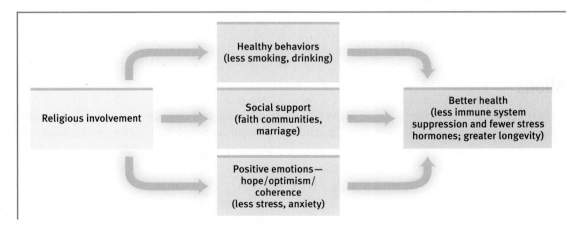

Figure 84.4

Possible explanations for the correlation between religious involvement and health/longevity

Before You Move On

▶ **ASK YOURSELF**

What techniques do you currently use to manage stress and promote health? In what ways might you improve your stress management and increase well-being?

▶ **TEST YOURSELF**

Those who frequently attend religious services live longer, on average, than those who attend infrequently or not at all. What type of research finding is this, and what explanations might it have?

Answers to the Test Yourself questions can be found in Appendix E at the end of the book.

Module 84 Review

 84-1 What are the links among basic outlook on life, social support, stress, and health?

- Studies of people with an optimistic outlook show that their blood pressure does not increase as sharply in response to stress, their recovery from heart bypass surgery is faster, and their life expectancy is longer, compared with their pessimistic counterparts.

- Social support promotes health by calming us, reducing blood pressure and stress hormones, and by fostering stronger immune functioning.

 84-2 How effective is aerobic exercise as a way to manage stress and improve well-being?

- *Aerobic exercise* is sustained, oxygen-consuming activity that increases heart and lung fitness.

- It increases arousal, leads to muscle relaxation and sounder sleep, triggers the production of neurotransmitters, and enhances self-image. It can relieve depression and, in later life, is associated with better cognitive functioning and longer life.

 84-3 In what ways might relaxation and meditation influence stress and health?

- Relaxation and meditation have been shown to reduce stress by relaxing muscles, lowering blood pressure, improving immune functioning, and lessening anxiety and depression.

 84-4 What is *complementary and alternative medicine*, and how is it best assessed through scientific research?

- *Complementary and alternative medicine (CAM)* comprises unproven health care treatments intended to serve as supplements or alternatives to conventional medicine; they are not widely taught in medical schools, used in hospitals, or reimbursed by insurance companies.

- To isolate real CAM treatment effects from placebo effects and spontaneous recovery influences, researchers experiment, randomly assigning people to experimental and control conditions.

 84-5 What is the faith factor, and what are some possible explanations for the link between religious involvement and longevity?

- The faith factor is the finding that religiously active people tend to live longer than those who are not religiously active. Possible explanations may include the effect of intervening variables, such as the healthy behaviors, social support, or positive emotions often found among people who regularly attend religious services.

Multiple-Choice Questions

1. What kind of sustained, oxygen-consuming exercise increases heart and lung fitness?

  a. Meditative
  b. Aerobic
  c. Alternative
  d. Communal
  e. Social

2. Which of the following best describes the group of remedies that include aromatherapy, spiritual healing, and relaxation?

  a. Complementary and alternative medicine
  b. Wellness
  c. Social support
  d. Optimism and health
  e. Immune function support

3. In which complementary and alternative medicine domain would we find therapies such as herbs and vitamins?

  a. Manipulative and body-based methods
  b. Mind-body interventions
  c. Alternative medical system
  d. Biologically based therapies
  e. Energy therapies

Practice FRQ

1. Describe three factors that may account for the relationship between religion and better health.

(3 points)

Module 85

Animal Thinking and Language

Module Learning Objectives

85-1 Describe what is known about thinking in other species.

85-2 Discuss what we know about other species' capacity for language.

Do Other Species Share Our Cognitive Skills?

85-1 What do we know about thinking in other species?

Other animals are smarter than we often realize. As the pioneering psychologist Margaret Floy Washburn explained in her 1908 book, *The Animal Mind,* animal consciousness and intelligence can be inferred from their behavior. Module 34 described animals displaying insight, but here are some other animal tricks.

USING CONCEPTS AND NUMBERS

Even pigeons—mere birdbrains—can sort objects (pictures of cars, cats, chairs, flowers) into categories, or concepts. Shown a picture of a never-before-seen chair, the pigeon will reliably peck a key that represents "chairs" (Wasserman, 1995). The great apes also form concepts, such as "cat" and "dog." After monkeys learn these concepts, certain frontal lobe neurons in their brains fire in response to new "catlike" images, others to new "doglike" images (Freedman et al., 2001).

Until his death in 2007, Alex, an African Grey parrot, categorized and named objects (Pepperberg, 2006, 2009). Among his jaw-dropping numerical skills was the ability to comprehend numbers up to 6. He could speak the number of objects. He could add two small clusters of objects and announce the sum. He could indicate which of two numbers was greater. And he gave correct answers when shown various groups of objects. Asked, for example, "What color four?" (meaning "What's the color of the objects of which there are four?"), he could speak the answer.

USING TOOLS AND TRANSMITTING CULTURE

Like humans, many other species invent behaviors and transmit cultural patterns to their peers and offspring (Boesch-Achermann & Boesch, 1993). Forest-dwelling chimpanzees select different tools for different purposes—a heavy stick for making holes, a light, flexible stick for fishing for termites (Sanz et al., 2004). They break off the reed or stick, strip off any leaves, carry it to a termite mound, twist it just so, and carefully remove it. Termites for lunch! (This is very reinforcing for a chimpanzee.) One anthropologist, trying to mimic the animal's deft fishing moves, failed miserably.

Researchers have found at least 39 local customs related to chimpanzee tool use, grooming, and courtship (Whiten & Boesch, 2001). One group may slurp termites directly from a stick, another group may pluck them off individually. One group may break nuts with a stone hammer, another with a wooden hammer. These group differences, along with differing styles of communication and hunting, are not genetic; they are the chimpanzee version of cultural diversity. Several experiments have brought chimpanzee cultural transmission into the laboratory (Horner et al., 2006). If Chimpanzee A obtains food either by sliding or by lifting a door, Chimpanzee B will then typically do the same to get food. And so will Chimpanzee C after observing Chimpanzee B. Across a chain of six animals, chimpanzees see, and chimpanzees do. Other animals have also shown surprising cognitive talents (**FIGURE 85.1**).

Figure 85.1

Tool-using animals (a) New Caledonian crows studied by Christopher Bird and Nathan Emery (2009) quickly learned to raise the water level in a tube and nab a floating worm by dropping stones into the water. Other crows have used twigs to probe for insects, and bent strips of metal to reach food. (b) Capuchin monkeys have learned not only to use heavy rocks to crack open palm nuts, but also to test stone hammers and select a sturdier, less crumbly one (Visalberghi et al., 2009). (c) One male chimpanzee in Sweden's Furuvik Zoo was observed every morning collecting stones into a neat little pile, which later in the day he used as ammunition to pelt visitors (Osvath, 2009). (d) Dolphins form coalitions, cooperatively hunt, and learn tool use from one another (Bearzi & Stanford, 2010). This bottlenose dolphin in Shark Bay, Western Australia, belongs to a small group that uses marine sponges as protective nose guards when probing the sea floor for fish (Krützen et al., 2005).

(a) (b) (c) (d)

OTHER COGNITIVE SKILLS

A baboon knows everyone's voice within its 80-member troop (Jolly, 2007). Sheep can recognize and remember individual faces (Morell, 2008). Chimpanzees and two species of monkeys can even read your intent. They would show more interest in a food container you have intentionally grasped rather than in one you flopped your hand on, as if by accident (Wood et al., 2007). Great apes and dolphins have demonstrated self-awareness by recognizing themselves in a mirror. So have elephants, which in tests also display their abilities to learn, remember, discriminate smells, empathize, cooperate, teach, and spontaneously use tools (Byrne et al., 2009). As social creatures, chimpanzees have shown altruism, cooperation, and group aggression. Like humans, they will kill their neighbor to gain land, and they grieve over dead relatives (Anderson et al., 2010; Biro et al., 2010; Mitani et al., 2010).

There is no question that other species display many remarkable cognitive skills. But one big question remains: Do they, like humans, exhibit language?

Do Other Species Have Language?

85-2   What do we know about other species' capacity for language?

Humans have long and proudly proclaimed that language sets us above all other animals. "When we study human language," asserted linguist Noam Chomsky (1972), "we are approaching what some might call the 'human essence,' the qualities of mind that are, so far as we know, unique [to humans]."

If in our use of language we humans are, as the psalmist long ago rhapsodized, "little lower than God," where, then, do other animals fit in the scheme of things? Are they "little lower than humans"? Let's see what research on animal language can tell us.

Without doubt, animals show impressive comprehension and communication. Consider vervet monkeys. They sound different alarm cries for different predators: a barking call for a leopard, a cough for an eagle, and a chuttering for a snake. Hearing the leopard alarm, other vervets climb the nearest tree. Hearing the eagle alarm, they rush into the bushes. Hearing the snake chutter, they stand up and scan the ground (Byrne, 1991). To indicate such things as a type of threat—an eagle, leopard, falling tree, or neighboring group— monkeys will combine six different calls into a 25-call sequence (Balter, 2010). But is this language, in the sense that humans use language? This question has launched thousands of studies, most of them with chimpanzees.

In the late 1960s, psychologists Allen Gardner and Beatrix Gardner (1969) aroused enormous scientific and public interest when they built on chimpanzees' natural tendencies for gestured communication and taught sign language to a chimpanzee named Washoe (c. 1965–2007). After 4 years, Washoe could use 132 signs; by her life's end, she was using 245 signs (Metzler et al., 2010; Sanz et al., 1998). After moving to a Central Washington University primate center, Washoe and other chimpanzees showed continued vocabulary growth (Metzler et al., 2010).

During the 1970s, as more and more reports came in, it seemed apes might indeed be "little lower than human." One *New York Times* reporter, having learned sign language from his deaf parents, visited Washoe and exclaimed, "Suddenly I realized I was conversing with a member of another species in my native tongue." Other chimpanzees were stringing signs together to form sentences, as Washoe did, signing, "You me go out, please." Some word combinations seemed very creative—saying *water bird* for "swan" or *elephant baby* for a long-nosed Pinocchio doll, or *apple-which-is-orange* for "orange" (Patterson, 1978; Rumbaugh, 1977).

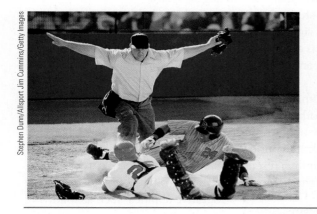

Talking hands Chimpanzees' use of sign language builds upon their natural gestured words (such as a hand extended for "I want some"). Human language appears to have evolved from such gestured communications (Corballis, 2002, 2003; Pollick & de Waal, 2007). Even today, gestures are naturally associated with spontaneous speech, especially speech that has spatial content. Both gesture and speech communicate, and when they convey the same rather than different information (as they do in baseball's sign language), we humans understand faster and more accurately (Hostetter, 2011; Kelly et al., 2010). Outfielder William Hoy, the first deaf player to join the major leagues (1892), invented hand signals for "Strike!" "Safe!" (shown here) and "Yerr out!" (Pollard, 1992). Referees in all sports now use invented signs, and fans are fluent in sports sign language.

By the late 1970s, some psychologists were growing skeptical. Were the chimps language champs or were the researchers chumps? Consider, said the skeptics:

- Ape vocabularies and sentences are simple, rather like those of a 2-year-old child. And unlike speaking or signing children, who easily soak up dozens of new words a week (and 60,000 by adulthood), apes gain their limited vocabularies only with great difficulty (Wynne, 2004, 2008). Saying that apes can learn language because they can sign words is like saying humans can fly because they can jump.

- Chimpanzees can make signs or push buttons in sequence to get a reward. But pigeons, too, can peck a sequence of keys to get grain (Straub et al., 1979). The apes' signing might be nothing more than aping their trainers' signs and learning that certain arm movements produce rewards (Terrace, 1979).

Comprehending canine Border collie Rico has a 200 (human) word vocabulary. If asked to retrieve a toy with a name he has never heard, Rico will pick out a new toy from a group of familiar items (Kaminski et al., 2004). Hearing that name for the second time four weeks later, Rico more often than not retrieves the same toy. Another border collie, Chaser, has set an animal record by learning 1022 object names (Pilley & Reid, 2011). Like a 3-year-old child, she can also categorize them by function and shape. She can "fetch a ball" or "fetch a doll."

- Studies of *perceptual* set (Module 17) show that when information is unclear, we tend to see what we want or expect to see. Interpreting chimpanzee signs as language may be little more than the trainers' wishful thinking (Terrace, 1979). When Washoe signed *water bird,* she may have been separately naming *water* and *bird*.

- "Give orange me give eat orange me eat orange . . ." is a far cry from the exquisite syntax of a 3-year-old (Anderson, 2004; Pinker, 1995). To the child, "You tickle" and "Tickle you" communicate different ideas. A chimpanzee, lacking human syntax, might use the same sequence of signs for both phrases.

Controversy can stimulate progress, and in this case, it triggered more evidence of chimpanzees' abilities to think and communicate. One surprising finding was that Washoe trained her adopted son Loulis to use the signs she had learned. It started like this. After her second infant died, Washoe became withdrawn when told, "Baby dead, baby gone, baby finished." Two weeks later, researcher caretaker Roger Fouts (1992, 1997) signed better news: "I have baby for you." Washoe reacted with instant excitement. Hair on end, she swaggered and panted while signing over and again, "Baby, my baby." It took several hours for the foster mom and infant to warm to each other, but then Washoe broke the ice by signing, "Come baby" and cuddling Loulis. In the months that followed, Loulis, without human assistance, picked up 68 signs, simply by observing Washoe and three other language-trained chimps signing together.

Even more stunning was a report that Kanzi, a bonobo with a reported 384-word vocabulary, could understand syntax (rules of word order) in spoken English (Savage-Rumbaugh et al., 1993, 2009). Kanzi happened onto language while observing his adoptive mother during her language training. To someone who doesn't understand syntax, "Can you show me the light?" and "Can you bring me the [flash]light?" and "Can you turn the light on?" might all seem the same. Kanzi, who appears to have the grammatical abilities of a human 2-year-old, knows the difference. Given stuffed animals and asked—for the first time—to "make the dog bite the snake," he put the snake to the dog's mouth.

So, how should we interpret these studies? Are humans the only language-using species? If by *language* we mean verbal or signed expression of complex grammar, most psychologists would now agree that humans alone possess language. If we mean, more simply, an ability to communicate through a meaningful sequence of symbols, then apes are indeed capable of language.

One thing is certain: Studies of animal language and thinking have moved psychologists toward a greater appreciation of other species, not only for the traits we share with them but also for their own remarkable abilities. In the past, many psychologists doubted that other species could plan, form concepts, count, use tools, show compassion, or use language (Thorpe, 1974). Today, thanks to animal researchers, we know better. It's true that humans alone are capable of complex sentences. Moreover, 2½-year-old children display some

But is this language? Chimpanzees' ability to express themselves in American Sign Language (ASL) raises questions about the very nature of language. Here, the trainer is asking, "What is this?" The sign in response is "Baby." Does the response constitute language?

cognitive abilities, such as following an actor's gaze to a target, that are unmatched even by chimpanzees (Herrmann et al., 2010). Nevertheless, other species do exhibit insight, show family loyalty, communicate with one another, care for one another, and transmit cultural patterns across generations. Accepting and working out what this means in terms of the moral rights of other animals is an unfinished task for our own thinking species.

Before You Move On

▶ **ASK YOURSELF**

Can you think of a time when you felt an animal was communicating with you? How might you put such intuition to a test?

▶ **TEST YOURSELF**

If your dog barks at a stranger at the front door, does this qualify as language? What if the dog yips in a telltale way to let you know she needs to go out?

Answers to the Test Yourself questions can be found in Appendix E at the end of the book.

Module 85 Review

 85-1   What do we know about thinking in other species?

- Researchers make inferences about other species' consciousness and intelligence based on behavior. The main focus of such research has been the great apes, but other species have also been studied.

- Evidence to date shows that other species can use concepts, numbers, and tools, and they can transmit learning from one generation to the next (cultural transmission). They also show insight, self-awareness, altruism, cooperation, grief, and an ability to read intentions.

85-2   What do we know about other species' capacity for language?

- A number of great apes (mostly chimpanzees) have learned to communicate with humans by signing or by pushing buttons wired to a computer, have developed vocabularies of nearly 400 words, have communicated by stringing these words together, have taught their skills to younger animals, and have some understanding of syntax.

- But only humans communicate in complex sentences. Nevertheless, primates' and other animals' impressive abilities to think and communicate challenge humans to consider what this means about the moral rights of other species.

Multiple-Choice Questions

1. Which of the following is an example of an animal using concepts?

   a. A parrot correctly answers the question, "What color four?"
   b. A dog identifies the scent of her owner.
   c. A parrot learns to say phrases.
   d. A dog fetches a thrown stick.
   e. A parrot quiets when the cover is put over his cage at night.

2. All of the following species have shown evidence of tool use except:

   a. humans.   c. monkeys.   e. dogs.
   b. crows.   d. dolphins.

3. Do species other than humans possess language?

   a. Yes. Recent studies with chimpanzees have proven beyond doubt that they use language.
   b. No. Animals have never shown language beyond the ability to recognize words.
   c. The answer depends on how you define language.
   d. No. Animals that seem to use language can only do so for a matter of days before loss of memory leads to rapid fading of language ability.
   e. Yes. Animals can develop vocabularies similar to young children.

Practice FRQ

1. Provide a specific example from the text of animal thinking, animal tool use, and animal language.

(3 points)

Enrichment Modules Review

Key Terms and Concepts to Remember

flow, p. 827

industrial-organizational (I/O) psychology, p. 828

personnel psychology, p. 828

organizational psychology, p. 828

human factors psychology, p. 828

structured interviews, p. 832

achievement motivation, p. 834

grit, p. 834

task leadership, p. 838

social leadership, p. 838

catharsis, p. 846

feel-good, do-good phenomenon, p. 847

subjective well-being, p. 847

adaptation-level phenomenon, p. 851

relative deprivation, p. 851

health psychology, p. 856

aerobic exercise, p. 859

complementary and alternative medicine (CAM), p. 863

Multiple-choice self-tests and more may be found at www.worthpublishers.com/MyersAP2e

Appendix A: Practice AP®-Style Exam

1. The Big Five model suggests that people can be rated along the dimensions of conscientiousness, agreeableness, neuroticism, openness, and extraversion. This theory is best associated with which of the following?
   a. Trait theory
   b. Psychodynamic theory
   c. The cognitive approach
   d. The humanistic approach
   e. The biological approach

2. Warren has a bacterial infection that has affected the ability of the rods in his eyes to function correctly. This should have the greatest impact on which of the following?
   a. Visual clarity
   b. Peripheral vision
   c. Color vision
   d. Hearing high-frequency sounds
   e. Hearing low-frequency sounds

3. Seeking out information that supports our previously held beliefs, while discounting information that questions those beliefs, is an obstacle to problem solving known as
   a. functional fixedness.
   b. a logical fallacy.
   c. overconfidence.
   d. mental set.
   e. confirmation bias.

4. Joe is taking a new job on the night shift next week. His supervisors have informed him that initially he may have some problems with his level of alertness and his memory as he adjusts to his new schedule. Joe's supervisors are sharing with Joe their knowledge of
   a. circadian rhythms.
   b. REM sleep.
   c. sleep spindles.
   d. the social clock.
   e. NREM sleep.

5. A researcher who is trying to determine how social-cultural changes might be correlated with the incidence of bipolar disorder would be most interested in which of the following?
   a. The brain changes in a person with bipolar disorder as measured by a PET scan
   b. Scientific measures of the heritability of the disorder
   c. The correlation between rates of poverty and cases of the disorder
   d. Neurotransmitter levels in patients diagnosed with the disorder
   e. The number of close biological relatives who also suffer from mood disorders

6. Zeina cocked her head to the side immediately when she heard the fire truck's siren. Turning her head enabled each ear to detect a slightly different intensity of sound, thus enabling her to determine the siren's
   a. timbre.
   b. pitch.
   c. frequency.
   d. location.
   e. tone.

7. A police officer who asks a witness to recall details about someone suspected of a crime would be asking the witness to
   a. listen to recordings of several voices to determine if the suspect's voice is detected.
   b. select the suspect from a visual lineup of several similar people.
   c. describe the suspect's physical qualities to a police sketch artist.
   d. determine if the suspect's motive for the shooting seems believable.
   e. imagine a scenario in which the suspect could have acted in self-defense.

8. People diagnosed with OCD suffer from compulsions. Which of the following is a compulsion?
   a. Renee persistently thinks about the possible death of her loved ones.
   b. Eric frequently worries that there may be germs on his hands.
   c. Brianna has an ongoing worry that she might have left the oven on at home.
   d. Stefan often feels great anxiety if things are not in exact order in his room.
   e. Tyrik flips the light switch on and off seven times each time he walks in the front door.

9. When a person performs a heroic act solely for public praise, she is on which developmental level according to Lawrence Kohlberg?

   a. Preconventional
   b. Postconventional
   c. Conventional
   d. Concrete operational
   e. Formal operational

10. The bus driver was surprised when her first passenger asked her to turn the music down, because she thought the volume was fine. When the passenger said something, though, the driver realized the sound was too loud. The bus driver's initial indifference to the volume can best be understood because

    a. the volume was below her absolute threshold.
    b. the driver had a decreased ability to determine the music's pitch.
    c. the just noticeable difference of the music was too great.
    d. the driver had adapted to the volume of the music.
    e. the driver was using bottom-up processing instead of top-down processing.

11. A rat jumps each time it sees a green light flash, because the green light has always appeared just before an electric shock. In classical conditioning, the initial learning of the connection between the light and the shock is referred to as

    a. spontaneous recovery.
    b. extinction.
    c. generalization.
    d. accommodation.
    e. acquisition.

12. Which of the following examples is the best illustration of cognitive dissonance?

    a. The cult member who admires the leader of his group and follows the leader without doubt
    b. The teacher who reprimands a student who she feels could do much better academically
    c. The soldier who receives orders from a superior that violate his personal moral beliefs
    d. The librarian who dreams of returning to graduate school to become a professor
    e. The student who gives up trying to master calculus because it seems too hard

13. At their high school reunion, many attendees recalled exactly where they were 20 years before when they realized the school was on fire. Strong memories of an emotionally significant moment are referred to as

    a. flashbulb memories.
    b. state-dependent memories.
    c. short-term memories.
    d. sensory memories.
    e. critical period memories.

14. Of the following, which pair are both used to reveal activity in a person's brain?

    a. CT scan and PET scan
    b. X-ray and fMRI
    c. fMRI and MRI
    d. PET scan and fMRI
    e. CT scan and MRI

15. A therapist who believes in giving patients positive reinforcements when they behave appropriately is most likely to use which of the following techniques?

    a. Systematic desensitization
    b. Token economy
    c. Aversive conditioning
    d. Transference
    e. Exposure therapy

16. Phil complained to his doctor that the sleeping pill the doctor previously prescribed no longer was effective at the original dosage. To his doctor's dismay, Phil confided that he had been taking more than the recommended amount of the drug to get the same effect. Phil's increasing intake of the drug reflects the condition known as

    a. withdrawal.
    b. sensory overload.
    c. tolerance.
    d. addiction.
    e. REM rebound.

17. Students who have recently learned "correlation does not equal causation" should be most cautious of the findings in which news headline below?

    a. "Coffee drinkers live longer, surveys say."
    b. "101-year-old man still healthy and happy."
    c. "Flu shots lower the risk of infection by 87% in lab studies."
    d. "Skim milk consumption tied to decreased neuron growth in studies of mice."
    e. "Observers note men less likely than women to wash their hands in public restrooms."

18. The symptoms of schizophrenia can be categorized as positive or negative. Which of the following symptoms can be considered positive?

    a. Hallucinations
    b. Flat affect
    c. Social withdrawal
    d. Catatonia
    e. Toneless vocal patterns

19. Mary Ainsworth designed the "strange situation" experiment in order to determine

    a. how creative young children could be in novel environments.

    b. whether children had developed a secure attachment to their mothers.

    c. if children were more motivated by social anxiety than by peer pressure.

    d. if the parenting style of mothers affected their children's temperament.

    e. if early signs of imprinting in young children could be reversed.

20. A principal wants to make this year's Halloween night dance safer because of vandalism and inappropriate behavior in the gym last year. She decides to increase the lighting in the parking lots, ban students from wearing masks over their faces, and increase the number of video cameras near the gym. These ideas are most closely linked to the principle of

    a. group polarization.

    b. social facilitation.

    c. superordinate goals.

    d. deindividuation.

    e. minority influence.

21. Longitudinal studies suggest that certain characteristics of children, such as conscientiousness and self-control, were very stable when those children became adults. Psychologists use what term to refer to these aspects of personality that appear early in life and which appear to be stable?

    a. Schema

    b. Reflex

    c. Temperament

    d. Fixation

    e. Sensory adaptation

22. One way to determine if infants can perceive a certain stimulus is to measure how long they gaze at the item before looking away. Psychologists use what term to refer to the concept that infants tend to decrease their rate of responding when a stimulus is repeated and no longer novel?

    a. Sensory adaptation

    b. Infantile amnesia

    c. Perceptual set

    d. Perceptual constancy

    e. Habituation

23. An injury that leads to the loss of binocular vision would have the greatest impact on

    a. visual acuity.

    b. color perception.

    c. peripheral vision.

    d. depth perception.

    e. selective attention.

24. The stage of sleep in which an EEG would detect the bursts of rhythmic activity known as sleep spindles is called

    a. REM sleep.

    b. NREM-1.

    c. NREM-2.

    d. NREM-3.

    e. hypnagogic sleep.

25. Ulric's doctor suggested that he consider moving to an area where there is greater sunlight or purchasing a light box that emits a bright light. Given these treatment options, Ulric's doctor must have diagnosed Ulric with

    a. attention-deficit/hyperactivity disorder.

    b. a seasonal pattern for depressive disorders or bipolar disorder.

    c. posttraumatic stress disorder.

    d. antisocial personality disorder.

    e. agoraphobia.

26. Damage to which of the following brain areas would create the most difficulty in interpreting feelings of heat and cold?

    a. Motor cortex

    b. Sensory cortex

    c. Frontal lobe

    d. Temporal lobe

    e. Occipital lobe

27. A substance that interrupts neural transmission by fitting into a receptor site but not activating it, or by preventing another neurotransmitter from accessing the receptor site, is known as

    a. an agonist.

    b. an antagonist.

    c. an endorphin.

    d. a hormone.

    e. the synaptic cleft.

28. Which of the following coefficients reflects the strongest correlation between two variables?

    a. 0.42

    b. −0.31

    c. 0.74

    d. −0.88

    e. 0.86

29. After Donnie realized the "intruder" in his home was just his mother returning unexpectedly, his breathing began to slow down, his heart rate decreased, and his digestion began again. These changes were coordinated by the

    a. limbic system.

    b. parasympathetic nervous system.

    c. sympathetic nervous system.

    d. afferent neurons.

    e. efferent neurons.

30. The oldest theory about human motivation, which focuses on unlearned, complex patterns of behavior present throughout a species, is known as
    a. arousal theory.
    b. drive-reduction theory.
    c. instinct theory.
    d. extrinsic motivation.
    e. the hierarchy of needs.

31. Prefixes and suffixes are small groups of letters that when added to the beginning or ending of words alter the definition of those words. Prefixes and suffixes, then, are examples of
    a. phonemes.
    b. morphemes.
    c. algorithms.
    d. accommodation.
    e. assimilation.

32. Which of the following most accurately describes a projective test?
    a. A test designed to reveal a person's inner ability to do a task he or she has not tried before.
    b. A test that shows a person's true preferences, based on responses to multiple-choice questions.
    c. A test that indicates the level of indifference to pain that a person experiences.
    d. A test created to see if one has an anxiety-inducing problem, but is instead claiming that others have that problem.
    e. A test that prompts a person to reveal hidden conflicts by responding to ambiguous stimuli.

33. Mr. Winters is a trainer who encourages his clients to lose weight. Instead of simply rewarding them when their weight declines, he is rewarding them each time they behave in ways that would reduce weight: each time they exercise, decline high-calorie foods, or even take the stairs at work. Reinforcing each time one gets closer to a desired behavior is known as
    a. conforming.
    b. extinguishing.
    c. social loafing.
    d. shaping.
    e. classical conditioning.

34. Often restaurants will require groups of eight or more to pay a tip of 18 percent. This is based on the belief that in larger parties, individuals will often leave a smaller tip because "someone else will pay more." These restaurant owners, then, are aware of the impact of
    a. the fundamental attribution error.
    b. the power of the situation.
    c. hindsight bias.
    d. confirmation bias.
    e. diffusion of responsibility.

35. In a research study, Dr. Regalis has participants listen to different kinds of music while she uses a brain scan to examine their brain functioning. Dr. Regalis is most likely studying which part of the brain?
    a. Temporal lobe
    b. Occipital lobe
    c. Broca's area
    d. Motor cortex
    e. Corpus callosum

36. As a patient experiences an anxiety attack, he may experience a series of changes that are coordinated by the sympathetic nervous system. Which one of the following would the patient experience?
    a. Decreased heart rate
    b. Slower breathing
    c. Decreased salivation
    d. Constricted pupils
    e. Increased rate of digestion

37. Joanna's grandmother told her, "When we were little, we couldn't afford new clothes, so our mother made us dresses out of potato sacks." Joanna's great-grandmother's ability to envision how a potato sack could be used as material for a dress suggests that she was able to overcome
    a. confirmation bias.
    b. functional fixedness.
    c. algorithms.
    d. divergent thinking.
    e. belief bias.

38. Research has found that individuals suffering from schizophrenia have an excess number of receptors for the neurotransmitter
    a. acetylcholine.
    b. norepinephrine.
    c. GABA.
    d. dopamine.
    e. serotonin.

39. Modern psychodynamic counselors are likely to emphasize
    a. the role of the id, ego, and superego.
    b. the importance of early childhood experiences.
    c. long, intensive therapy sessions over a period of many years.
    d. fixations that may have stemmed from repressed sexual urges.
    e. a patient's responses to Rorschach inkblots.

40. Which of the following is an example of variable-ratio reinforcement?

a. College acceptance letters arrive around the date of April 1.
b. Percy gives his dog a cookie whenever his dog walks by strangers without barking.
c. Esmeralda disliked the substitute teacher, so she scowled every time she looked at him.
d. Judy discovered a shark's tooth after several hours of searching for one on the beach.
e. When Stu had been working on his homework for one hour, his mother allowed him to go outside and play.

41. What perspective is sometimes referred to as the "third force," since it offered a more optimistic alternative to Freud's psychoanalysis and Skinner's behaviorism?

a. Biological psychology
b. Humanistic psychology
c. Cognitive psychology
d. Evolutionary psychology
e. Social-cultural psychology

42. The type of therapy that is most likely to emphasize a social-cultural approach by focusing on the patient's environment is

a. family therapy.
b. rational-emotive behavioral therapy.
c. cognitive therapy for depression.
d. psychopharmacological treatments.
e. aversive therapy.

43. Which part of the brain would be most involved in maintaining homeostasis in body temperature?

a. Prefrontal cortex
b. Temporal lobe
c. Thalamus
d. Hypothalamus
e. Amygdala

44. Unexplained physical symptoms, including headaches, pain, and digestive problems, which cannot be explained by physical or mental causes, may be diagnosed as

a. mood disorders.
b. personality disorders.
c. somatoform disorders.
d. dissociative disorders.
e. eating disorders.

45. A psychologist who uses aversive therapy to treat a child's bed-wetting problem is using which of the following approaches?

a. Cognitive
b. Biological
c. Behavioral
d. Evolutionary
e. Social-cultural

46. Psychologist David Wechsler has created tests for adults and children that are designed to reveal their

a. intelligence.
b. aptitude.
c. achievement.
d. personality characteristics.
e. symptoms of psychological disorders.

47. In order to follow the ethical principles for research as established by the APA, psychologists should

a. recruit participants for experiments by placing ads in college newspapers.
b. publish the full results, including participant information, of their research online.
c. keep their operational definitions secret so that they cannot be copied by other researchers.
d. debrief the participants after the conclusion of the research.
e. allow minors to choose to be participants if they wish to.

48. Which of the following statements is most typical of the approach of a cognitive therapist?

a. "Let's go back to your statement about your happiness as a child."
b. "When you say 'No one likes me' that's illogical, because you do have close friends."
c. "What I hear you saying is you are angry, and I can hear the frustration in your voice."
d. "I'm going to start teaching you to relax, and then we'll slowly deal with your phobia."
e. "I think that prescribing you an SSRI will increase your positive mood over the next few weeks."

49. Dr. Alscott has examined two sets of data from his research. In the first set, the standard deviation was very small, while in the second set there was a much larger standard deviation. Based on this information, what conclusion can be drawn from these two sets?

a. The median was greater than the mean in the second set.
b. The mean was greater than the median in the second set.
c. The standard deviation in both sets revealed a positive correlation between the data.
d. Most data points were closer to the mean in the first set than in the second.
e. Most data points were closer to the mean in the second set than in the first.

50. "The curious paradox is that when I accept myself just as I am, then I can change." This core idea in humanistic psychology is a quotation from

a. Sigmund Freud.
b. Carl Rogers.
c. Aaron Beck.
d. Carl Jung.
e. B. F. Skinner.

51. Hans Selye argued that our bodies produce a similar reaction to all kinds of stress, and the longer this response continues, the more exhausted we become. He named this process
a. the opponent-process theory.
b. systematic desensitization.
c. general adaptation syndrome.
d. global assessment of functioning.
e. triarchic intelligence.

52. "Both the left and the right hemisphere may be conscious simultaneously in different, even in mutually conflicting, mental experiences that run along in parallel." This quotation by neuropsychologist Roger Sperry refers to his Nobel Prize–winning research on the effects of severing which part of the brain?
a. Amygdala
b. Brainstem
c. Corpus callosum
d. Thalamus
e. Pituitary gland

53. Martin Seligman developed the concept of learned helplessness, the tendency of organisms to give up in situations in which they feel their efforts make no difference. This concept is closely linked to which of the following psychological disorders?
a. Agoraphobia
b. Schizophrenia
c. Depression
d. Generalized anxiety disorder
e. Histrionic personality disorder

54. John Watson's development of the concept of behaviorism was influenced most strongly by the work of
a. Wilhelm Wundt.
b. the Gestalt psychologists.
c. John Locke.
d. B. F. Skinner.
e. Ivan Pavlov.

55. Psychologists Walk and Gibson attempted to determine whether infants had developed the ability to perceive depth by
a. having them crawl over what appeared to be a sharp ledge.
b. measuring how long they looked at novel stimuli.
c. throwing soft foam balls to them and seeing how they would react.
d. showing them a simulation of birds flying at their faces.
e. seeing if they reached for a toy when it was held slightly beyond the reach of their arms.

56. Systematic desensitization would most likely be used as a treatment for which of the following disorders?
a. Arachnophobia
b. Schizophrenia
c. Bipolar disorder
d. Hypochondriasis
e. Tardive dyskinesia

57. A manager at an ice cream store wants to increase sales, so he creates a program to rank his employees' sales. His goal is to give a cash prize each week to the employee who has sold the highest number of ice cream cones. His strategy is based on the idea of
a. a personal fable.
b. intrinsic motivation.
c. extrinsic motivation.
d. the collective unconscious.
e. self-efficacy.

58. The fire alarm has gone off so many times in their new school that Susannah and Tia don't even flinch when they hear it. In fact, they even remained in the school library during a fire drill because they assumed it was another malfunction. Their failure to respond like they once did to the fire alarm shows the process of
a. acquisition.
b. discrimination.
c. accommodation.
d. extinction.
e. assimilation.

59. Dr. Anders wants to investigate how people of different ages communicate via the Internet, so she does an experiment with three groups of three different ages: 18–21, 47–50, and 75–78. Concurrently comparing how people of different ages behave is an example of which of the following kinds of research?
a. Case study
b. Longitudinal
c. Cross-sectional
d. Factor analysis
e. Qualitative research

60. In studies, reminding female test-takers that women historically have done poorly on a similar test can lead to lower test performance—particularly when compared with the scores of women who weren't given such information. This decline in performance is an example of
a. stereotype threat.
b. hindsight bias.
c. the mere exposure effect.
d. social facilitation.
e. negative transference.

61. Research suggests that there is a connection between parenting style and social skills. Children with lower scores on measures of social skills and self-esteem tend to have parents who are

a. authoritative.
b. permissive.
c. authoritarian.
d. neglecting.
e. demonstrative.

62. Dr. Kirk worked with the government to create new standards for people seeking jobs as airport security screeners, including assessments in the interview process, designs for the flow of the security process itself, and measures for evaluating the job performance of these screeners. Which career category best fits Dr. Kirk's work?

a. Developmental
b. Clinical
c. Forensic
d. Industrial-organizational
e. Community

63. Which emotion theory places the greatest emphasis on physiological changes happening first, which are then followed by an experience of an emotion?

a. Schachter-Singer theory
b. James-Lange theory
c. Cannon-Bard theory
d. Arousal theory
e. Incentive theory

64. Although the group of senior citizens beat the teenagers in a trivia contest based on history, they were not nearly as successful in a competition that required them to quickly learn the rules of a new video game. This is most likely due to the decline of which of the following as humans age?

a. Learned helplessness
b. Cognitive dissonance
c. Fluid intelligence
d. Crystallized intelligence
e. Elaborative rehearsal

65. Which of these statements is most accurate about REM sleep?

a. These periods are the longest at the beginning of the sleep period, then get shorter through the night.
b. These periods are the shortest at the beginning of the sleep period, then get longer through the night.
c. During these periods, brain activity is as reduced as muscle activity.
d. The brainstem continues to pass on motor activity signals to the rest of the body during REM sleep.
e. The dreams during this stage are frequently interrupted by sleep spindles.

66. Random-dot stereograms are pictures that have an image hidden among the dots. Humans can often see these hidden images because each eye has a slightly different image projected on its retina, allowing us to see depth. Which term best describes this process?

a. Motion parallax
b. Convergence
c. Retinal disparity
d. Relative height
e. Linear perspective

67. A therapist tells a CEO that the reason he yells and screams at his staff is due to behavior he learned as a child. When he was a child, he threw temper tantrums in order to get his way. What is the term for this defense mechanism?

a. Regression
b. Reaction formation
c. Projection
d. Rationalization
e. Sublimation

68. During a dental procedure, Xavier is injected with a drug that is designed to greatly reduce his pain by interfering with the sending of pain signals. At the neural level, the drug is preventing

a. action potentials from being transmitted.
b. neurotransmitters from being reabsorbed by neurons.
c. potassium ions from being released at the terminal buttons.
d. pain signals from being clearly interpreted in the sensory cortex.
e. the myelin sheath from protecting the axon.

69. A babysitter cuts a sandwich into three equal pieces, then keeps two and gives one to the child she is caring for. The child is upset that this is unfair, so the babysitter divides the child's piece into two. Since each of them now has two pieces, the child is content. According to Jean Piaget, this is because the child lacks

a. accommodation.
b. assimilation.
c. formal operational knowledge.
d. sensorimotor ability.
e. conservation.

70. A young gymnast works out many hours each day to prepare for a national competition. This schedule means that she has to forgo opportunities to socialize with her peers, and makes it hard to have a romantic relationship. The gymnast's willingness to give up some kinds of affection in order to pursue athletic achievements is at odds with whose theory of human motivation?

a. Abraham Maslow
b. Henry Murray
c. Philip Zimbardo
d. David McClelland
e. Solomon Asch

71. Seven-year-old Daniel was able to see that the dot-to-dot puzzle was going to form a picture of a tiger even before he started drawing on the puzzle. Which Gestalt principle helped Daniel perceive the tiger from all the unconnected dots?
    a. Proximity
    b. Continuity
    c. Bipolar cues
    d. Retinal disparity
    e. Closure

72. In an experiment by Stanley Schachter and Jerome Singer, participants labeled their arousal as joyous or irritable, depending on the people they were with. This experiment established that emotions are not only physiological but are also
    a. psychodynamic.
    b. humanistic.
    c. biological.
    d. cognitive.
    e. behavioral.

73. A tumor cut off bloodflow to a small section of Gia's brain, and as a result she struggled to understand the words that were being spoken to her. The damage to Gia's brain was probably localized in her
    a. Wernicke's area.
    b. Broca's area.
    c. hippocampus.
    d. hypothalamus.
    e. brainstem.

74. According to the behavioral perspective, the purpose of punishment is to
    a. make a person sorry for the behavior he has committed.
    b. associate a positive consequence with a negative consequence.
    c. make a behavior less likely to happen again.
    d. allow the behavior to only occur again during a spontaneous recovery.
    e. extinguish the response permanently.

75. When Eli initially joined an online group against increased government spending, he only had mild views on the topic. If he continues in the group and rarely gets information from alternate sources with opposing views, what might be the outcome?
    a. He might become deindividuated and express views against the group's beliefs.
    b. He might use social facilitation to spread the group's views more widely online.
    c. He might use confirmation bias to seek out sources that challenge his beliefs.
    d. His and the group members' views might become intensified over time.
    e. His and the group members' views might begin to become more varied over time.

76. When hiring for a new creative director for an advertising agency, Amina decided that the number one criteria she desired was a person who could devise numerous ways to solve problems. A person talented in this area would most likely be good at
    a. divergent thinking.
    b. convergent thinking.
    c. belief perseverance.
    d. solving crossword puzzles.
    e. doing arithmetic.

77. The personality test that is based on the writings of Carl Jung is the
    a. Minnesota Multiphasic Personality Inventory.
    b. Draw-A-Person test.
    c. Rorschach inkblot test.
    d. Thematic Apperception Test.
    e. Myers-Briggs Type Indicator.

78. Jason was watching the TV news and spotted a young man on a video running away from the police who were attempting to stop him. "He's running, so he must be a bad man," said Jason to his father. Jason's statement is an example of
    a. the availability heuristic.
    b. the representativeness heuristic.
    c. stereotype threat.
    d. the fundamental attribution error.
    e. cognitive dissonance.

79. The sound of a sizzling steak or the smell of a warm apple pie might strongly tempt people to relish eating them. In the study of motivation, the sound and smell are considered to be
    a. incentives.
    b. arousal-inducing.
    c. drives.
    d. self-actualization needs.
    e. fixed action patterns.

80. In the early twentieth century, French psychologists led by Alfred Binet developed the first test for intelligence to be given to French school children for the purpose of
    a. selecting the most capable to be trained as future leaders.
    b. identifying those who might be wasting their talents and not taking school seriously.
    c. testing whether French teachers merited higher pay.
    d. evaluating the quality of French schools.
    e. finding children who were struggling academically.

81. "We were not surprised to discover that contact comfort was an important basic affectional or love variable, but we did not expect it to overshadow so completely the variable of nursing . . ." This quotation was written by which of the following psychologists?
    a. Harry Harlow
    b. Konrad Lorenz
    c. B. F. Skinner
    d. John B. Watson
    e. Mary Ainsworth

82. An experimenter finds a difference between an experimental group and a control group that is less likely due to chance and more likely due to the manipulation of the independent variable. This finding then is most likely to be
    a. a replication.
    b. statistically significant.
    c. below the margin of error.
    d. reliable, but not valid.
    e. valid, but not reliable.

83. The mere exposure effect reinforces the belief that the most important predictor in whether two people might be friends is
    a. similarity of religious and political views.
    b. similar interests in the arts and culture.
    c. their physical attractiveness.
    d. their social status and level of income.
    e. their proximity to each other.

84. Albert Bandura believed that children could learn not only by doing behaviors themselves, but also by watching models perform those behaviors. His ideas expanded the idea of learning to include
    a. observational learning.
    b. classical conditioning.
    c. operant conditioning.
    d. latent learning.
    e. rote learning.

85. Which of the following is an example of a self-fulfilling prophecy?
    a. David has had trouble in math in the past, so in his new math class he gives up on the first day.
    b. Ivy does not think her teacher has treated her fairly, so she complains to her principal.
    c. Samuel's teacher puts him in a group with struggling students, and Samuel, normally a good student, responds by doing very poor work. The next week he is placed in the same group.
    d. Rachel writes a letter to the editor about her concerns with the city council, and as a result her social studies teacher praises her in class.
    e. Nyah's father takes her out of an advanced class because she is struggling at first, but she responds by working even harder and making better grades in all of her classes.

86. Noam Chomsky departed from B. F. Skinner's beliefs about language, arguing that
    a. language is only possible during a critical period, and not afterward.
    b. simple mastery of phonemes and morphemes does not equal a language.
    c. the rules of syntax were more crucial to understanding language than semantics.
    d. language is innate and not merely developed through reinforcement.
    e. language is just as possible in animals as in humans, given enough time and training.

87. Paul was unable to correctly identify the right shade of blue his wife wanted at the paint store, so he purchased various hues and brought them home. Apparently the ability to detect the varieties of the different blues fell below Paul's
    a. signal detection.
    b. absolute threshold.
    c. difference threshold.
    d. excitatory level.
    e. inhibitory level.

88. Teachers at York High School were dismayed at a new test they would be required to take to demonstrate their ability as educators. Rather than a test of content knowledge or of teaching techniques, the new test would measure their reaction time to a series of rapidly flashed abstract images and words. Despite the assurances of the test's creator, the teachers argued that a test like this would have low
    a. content validity.
    b. diagnostic validity.
    c. split-half reliability.
    d. test-retest reliability.
    e. psychometric ratings.

89. In Stanley Milgram's experiments on obedience, he discovered that participants were less obedient when
    a. the person giving the orders was close at hand and was perceived to be a legitimate authority figure.
    b. the authority figure was supported by a prestigious institution.
    c. the victim was depersonalized or at a distance.
    d. Milgram dissociated his experiments from Yale University.
    e. there were no role models for defiance.

90. The work of Elizabeth Loftus and other researchers has led to significant changes in the way courts and police officers think about
    a. the traumatic effects of solitary confinement.
    b. whether patients with schizophrenia can be forced to take medication against their will.
    c. whether the insanity defense is a legitimate method for handling legally insane individuals.
    d. whether spouses should be forced to testify against their spouses on the witness stand.
    e. the accuracy of eyewitness testimony and identification.

91. The developmental theories of Lev Vygotsky differed from those of Jean Piaget in that Vygotsky
    a. emphasized the role of the social environment.
    b. thought that Piaget ignored the psychosexual development of children.
    c. questioned Piaget's focus on adult development.
    d. focused more on moral development.
    e. thought that the spiritual component of children's growth was essential.

92. Dorothea Dix was a passionate advocate for
    a. reform in the treatment of the mentally ill.
    b. the elimination of culturally-biased IQ tests.
    c. identifying and reducing the self-fulfilling prophecy in schools.
    d. changing the way disorders are classified in the DSM-5.
    e. creating an alternative to the use of psychopharmacological medication.

93. For those who focus on the biological approach, important evidence for whether someone who has been diagnosed with depression is improving is
    a. the quality of their statements about their own abilities and attitudes.
    b. whether the number of contacts with their friends and families has increased.
    c. whether they have begun to establish and work toward long-term goals.
    d. whether the serotonin levels in their blood have increased.
    e. if they have no suicidal thoughts or intentions.

94. Instead of methodically poring through the atlas to find the correct map, Ivan just flipped to the section of the book where he thought it might be. Using a strategy based on a hunch rather than examining each page carefully involves the use of
    a. an algorithm.
    b. a heuristic.
    c. a syllogism.
    d. insight.
    e. framing.

95. On the very first day of class, Mr. Boyarsky gave his students a test. When some complained, he responded that he wanted to know what their talents were, so he was giving them a test to predict what kind of skills they might learn best, and what kinds of jobs they might like to do one day. Mr. Boyarsky's test was
    a. an aptitude test.
    b. an intelligence test.
    c. an achievement test.
    d. a personality test.
    e. a projective test.

96. When basketball star Michael Jordan graduated as one of a small number of geography majors from college, the average starting salary for a geography major soared by several hundred thousand dollars. In a situation like this, where a small amount of data greatly inflates the average, it is better to use which measure of central tendency?
    a. Mean
    b. Median
    c. Range
    d. Standard deviation
    e. Variation

97. Damage to what part of a neuron might result in slowed or incomplete neural transmission along the axon?
    a. Cell body
    b. Mitochondria
    c. Dendrite
    d. Myelin sheath
    e. Synapse

98. Dr. Warren is testing the link between the consumption of caffeine and a person's memory. She randomly divides 300 participants into three groups and gives each participant an energy drink to consume. Some of the drinks have high levels of caffeine, some have medium amounts, and some have none at all—but they all taste the same. About 30 minutes later, she has the participants play a memory game on the computer where they have to match faces and names together. At the end of the game, the computer thanks them for playing, and their scores are sent to Dr. Warren's lab. The dependent variable in the experiment is
    a. how quickly the participants matched the names and faces.
    b. the participants' scores from the memory game.
    c. the amount of caffeine they consumed.
    d. their explanations about how they played the game.
    e. the amount of caffeine they consume in a typical week.

99. The independent variable in the experiment described in question 98 is
    a. how quickly the participants matched the names and faces.
    b. the participants' scores from the memory game.
    c. the amount of caffeine they consumed.
    d. their explanations about how they played the game.
    e. the amount of caffeine they consume in a typical week.

100. A person who has an external locus of control is most likely to explain success or failure on a math test as due to
    a. how difficult the questions were.
    b. whether he had effectively studied enough.
    c. whether he had been able to understand the course material.
    d. how well prepared he had been prior to taking the course.
    e. the amount of time he had set aside to study.

Free-Response Questions

1. Psychology professors Elliott and Elizabeth are co-writing a book about what kinds of behaviors lead to feelings of happiness.

   A. Explain what kinds of research studies Elliott and Elizabeth should look for as they investigate what kinds of behaviors cause feelings of happiness. Use the following terms in your explanation. Note: definitions alone will not score.
      - Experimental method
      - Correlational method
      - Operational definition

   B. Discuss what Elliott and Elizabeth are likely to discover as they research psychological studies regarding the relationship between the following psychological factors and happiness.
      - REM sleep
      - Serotonin
      - Facial feedback effect

2. Charlie has been teaching for 25 years and was just assigned a student teacher, Randy. Charlie wants to advise Randy about effective teaching methods.

   A. What advice should Charlie give Randy about the effectiveness of the following kinds of techniques and whether they might help motivate students in their classroom?
      - Classical conditioning
      - Positive reinforcement
      - Positive punishment

   B. Randy is interested in teaching students study skills that will help them learn and retain information. Discuss how the following concepts might help or get in the way of effective studying.
      - Semantic encoding
      - State-dependent memory
      - Serial position effect

   C. Finally, Charlie wants to advise Randy about how to develop a healthy classroom atmosphere. How could Charlie use the following concepts in his advice about building a useful classroom culture?
      - Ingroup bias
      - Superordinate goals

Appendix B: AP® Exam Tips

Unit I

Module 1

Page 2: To assist your active learning of psychology, Learning Objectives are grouped together at the start of each module, and then framed as questions that appear at the beginning of major sections.

Page 3: Every question on the AP® Psychology exam will reflect the fact that psychology is a science built on the tradition of Wundt and his laboratory. Correct answers on the test are based on what research has revealed; not on "common sense"!

Page 5: There are lots of important people in psychology. As you study, focus on the significance of their accomplishments. You are more likely to be tested on what a finding means than who discovered it.

Page 7: Memory research reveals a *testing effect:* We retain information much better if we actively retrieve it by self-testing and rehearsing. To bolster your learning and memory, take advantage of all the self-testing opportunities you'll find throughout this text. These "Before You Move On" sections will appear at the end of each main section of text. The *Ask Yourself* questions will help you make the material more meaningful to your own life (and therefore more memorable). You can check your answers to the *Test Yourself* review questions in Appendix E at the end of the book.

Module 2

Page 9: Pay close attention to what David Myers, your author, is emphasizing as he tells the story of psychology. When he says the nature–nurture issue is the *biggest* question in psychology, that's a sign. It's a safe bet that this concept will be covered on the AP® exam.

Page 11: You will see versions of Figure 2.1 throughout the text. Spend some time right now familiarizing yourself with how the figure's three corners might contribute to behavior or mental processes, the very stuff of psychology.

Page 12: These perspectives will come up again and again throughout your AP® Psychology course, and they *will* be on the exam. You need to become very comfortable with the meaning of terms like cognitive, behavioral, and psychodynamic. Ask your teacher for clarification if you are the least bit unclear about what the perspectives mean.

Page 14: Take careful note of the fact that psychiatry is a medical specialty and not a part of psychology. Can you summarize the similarities and differences among counseling psychologists, clinical psychologists, and psychiatrists?

Module 3

Page 20: You are about to read about a lot of career possibilities in psychology. Note the division between basic subfields and applied subfields. The work of some of these specialties is pretty obvious (it's not that hard to figure out in general what an educational psychologist or a health psychologist might do). Devote extra attention to those specialties that may be unfamiliar to you.

Page 21: *Educational psychologists* apply psychology's findings in an effort to improve learning, and *school psychologists* assess and assist individual schoolchildren.

Unit II

Module 4

Page 32: It is quite common for multiple-choice questions on the AP® exam to test your knowledge of "media myths." Pay particular attention when psychological findings run counter to "common sense."

Module 5

Page 38: As you read this module, keep in mind that the scientific method is a set of principles and procedures, not a list of facts. You will be expected to understand how the science of psychology is done, not just what it has discovered.

Module 6

Page 47: This is the first of several times in your psychology course that you will see something labeled as being positive or negative. We often think that if something is positive it is good and if it's negative it's bad. That is rarely the case in this course. Here, positive and negative refer only to the direction of the correlation. They say nothing about whether the relationship is desirable or not.

Page 49: Take note of how much emphasis is put on this idea. Correlation and association do not prove a cause-effect relationship.

Page 52: The identification of independent variables (IV) and dependent variables (DV) is the single most likely concept to be tested on the AP® exam. Experiments are critical to psychology, and independent and dependent variables are critical to experiments.

Page 53: Almost 15 pages of text are summarized in Table 6.3. Spend some time with it, as it is information you will likely encounter on the AP® exam.

Module 7

Page 56: Do math and statistics scare you? Take a couple of deep breaths and relax before continuing. You will not be asked to do difficult computations on the AP® exam. Nothing will be beyond the scope of simple mental math. You need to focus on the concepts. Why do these statistics exist? How can they help us understand the real world?

Page 61: Sometimes a phrase that is frequently used in the media has a more specific meaning when used in psychology. That's the case with the phrase "statistically significant." Make sure you know the precise meaning.

Unit III

Module 9

Page 77: There is a ton of vocabulary in this unit. However, learning vocabulary is really not so hard: The secret is to work on it every day. Try flash cards. Work with a study buddy. Impress your non-psych friends with your new vocabulary. Just don't leave it until the night before the test. If you rehearse the vocabulary throughout the unit, you will do better on the unit test. The big bonus is that you will also retain far more information for the AP® exam.

Page 80: So far, you have been learning about how just one neuron operates. The action potential is the mechanism for communication *within* a single neuron. Now you are moving on to a discussion of two neurons and how communication occurs *between* them. Very different, but equally important.

Page 82: As the text indicates, there are dozens of different neurotransmitters. Though there's no way to predict exactly which ones you'll see on the AP® exam, it's quite possible that the ones in Table 9.1 are ones you'll be asked about.

Page 83: Be very clear on this. Neurotransmitters are produced inside the body. They can excite and inhibit neural communication. Drugs and other chemicals come from outside the body. They can have an agonistic effect or an antagonistic effect on neurotransmission.

Module 10

Page 87: You've heard the word peripheral before, right? How does your knowledge of peripheral vision help you understand what the peripheral nervous system is? It's always good to create mental linkages between what you're learning and what you already know.

Module 11

Page 96: Your author, David Myers, is about to take you on a journey through your brain. Focus on the name of each part, its location within the brain, and what it does. Then it's time to practice, practice, practice.

Page 99: If you ever have to make a guess about brain parts on the AP® exam, the hypothalamus isn't a bad bet. Even though it's small, it has many functions.

Module 13

Page 115: The classic split-brain studies are famous in psychology, which means they are likely to show up on the AP® exam.

Page 117: Notice that David Myers never refers to your left brain or your right brain. You have two brain hemispheres, each with its own responsibilities, *but you only have one brain.* It's very misleading when the media refers to the left brain and the right brain, and this happens frequently.

Page 119: Dual processing is another one of those big ideas that shows up in several units. Pay attention!

Module 14

Page 130: Heritability is likely to show up on the AP® exam because it's confusing. The key thing to remember is that heritability refers to variation within a group. It does not refer to the impact of nature on an individual. Be clear both on what it is and what it isn't.

Unit IV

Module 15

Page 153: You may wish to think about how the information on selective attention relates to something a little less dangerous: studying. The same principles apply. The more time you spend texting, tweeting, and Facebooking, the less focused you'll be on the material you're trying to master. A better strategy is to spend 25 minutes doing schoolwork and schoolwork alone. Then you can reward yourself with a few minutes of social networking.

Module 18

Page 173: There's a lot of vocabulary here. Make sure you understand the name and the function of each of the parts of the eye. To learn how all the parts fit together, it may help to make rough sketches (you don't need to be an artist to try this!) and then compare your sketches to Figures 18.3 and 18.4. You'll be better off making several quick, rough sketches than one time-consuming, nicely drawn one.

Page 175: Warning! Sometimes students spend so much time mastering the parts of the eye that they skim over the part you're about to read. Do not forget that you see with your brain as much as you see with your eyes.

Module 19

Page 182: The Necker cube is an excellent vehicle for understanding the distinction between sensation and perception. The only visual stimuli are the blue wedges. The circles, lines, and cube are all the products of perception—they are in your mind and not on the page.

Page 186: The illustrations in Figure 19.5 provide you with excellent opportunities to practice identifying monocular depth cues. To really demonstrate your understanding, look for these cues in other drawings and photographs. There are almost always cues to identify.

Module 20

Page 194: Pay attention to how many pages are devoted to each of the senses. Not only does this represent the complexity of the sensory system, it also represents how likely you are to find questions about that system on the AP® exam. More pages are devoted to vision than hearing, and vision questions are somewhat more likely to appear on the exam.

Page 195: Note that both light and sound travel in waves. In each case, the amplitude and length of the waves are important.

Unit V

Module 22

Page 219: Note that our modern-day understanding of the unconscious is very different from Sigmund Freud's theory of the unconscious (Module 55). Freud believed the unconscious was a hiding place for our most anxiety-provoking ideas and emotions, and that uncovering those hidden thoughts could lead to healing. Now, most psychologists simply view the unconscious track as one that operates without awareness. Make sure you keep these two ideas of the unconscious straight.

Page 220: Psychological research corrects the mistaken popular belief that hypnosis or other methods can be used to tap into a pure and complete memory bank. You will learn much more about how memory really works when you get to Unit VII.

Module 23

Page 228: Study this cycle of sleep carefully. One common mistake that students make is to believe that REM sleep comes directly after deep NREM-3 sleep. As you can see, it does not. Generally, NREM-2 follows NREM-3. Then comes REM.

Module 24

Page 236: Many students try to get by on less and less sleep to try to fit everything in. The irony is that if you stay up too late studying, it can be counterproductive. Sleep deprivation makes it difficult to concentrate and increases the likelihood you will make silly mistakes on tests. The impact on your immune system means you are more likely to get sick. To be the best student you can be, make sleep a priority.

Module 25

Page 248: These three categories—depressants, stimulants, and hallucinogens—are important. There are likely to be questions on the AP® exam that will require you to know how a particular psychoactive drug is classified.

Page 253: Figure 25.4 is an excellent review of how neurotransmitters work. If there is any part of this that you don't understand, head back to Module 9 for a complete explanation.

Unit VI

Module 26

Page 264: It's easy to confuse habituation with sensory adaptation, a concept from Unit IV. Recall that sensory adaptation occurs when one of your sensory systems stops registering the presence of an unchanging stimulus—when you go swimming in a cool pool, for example, the water no longer feels cool after you've been in for a few minutes. Habituation, like sensory adaptation, involves a diminished response, but in this case it's a form of learning rather than a function of the sensory system. If you're exposed to the same stimulus over and over, your response decreases. A friend might sneak up and startle you by yelling "Boo!" But you'll probably startle less when he tries it again two minutes later. That's habituation.

Page 269: Spontaneous recovery is, in fact, spontaneous. Notice that the extinguished conditioned response returns without any additional pairing with the unconditioned stimulus. It is not a form of acquisition.

Page 270: Generalization and discrimination are introduced in this module, but they don't just apply to classical conditioning. These two concepts will show up in other types of learning as well.

Module 27

Page 275: Don't be fooled by the fact that classical conditioning is presented before operant conditioning. Classical conditioning was understood before operant conditioning, but operant conditioning has a larger impact on our day-to-day lives.

Page 280: The word "interval" in schedules of reinforcement means that an interval of time must pass before reinforcement. There is nothing the learner can do to shorten the interval. The word "ratio" refers to the ratio of responses to reinforcements. If the learner responds with greater frequency, there will be more reinforcements.

Page 281: Remember that *any kind of reinforcement* (positive, negative, primary, conditioned, immediate, delayed, continuous, or partial) encourages the behavior. *Any kind of punishment* discourages the behavior. Positive and negative do not refer to values—it's not that positive reinforcement (or punishment) is the good kind and negative is the bad. Think of positive and negative mathematically; a stimulus is added with positive reinforcement (or punishment) and a stimulus is subtracted with negative.

Module 28

Page 287: Notice how useful operant conditioning is. People with an understanding of the principles of operant conditioning possess a tremendous tool for changing behavior. If you don't like the way your friends, teachers, coaches, or parents behave, pay attention to the uses of operant conditioning!

Module 29

Page 292: In the middle of the twentieth century, behaviorism was the dominant perspective in psychology, with little attention paid to the influence of biology and cognition in learning. Now we know better. As you read through this module, notice how important biological and cognitive factors are for understanding learning.

Module 30

Page 304: Bandura's Bobo doll experiment is one of the most famous in psychology. It shows up frequently on the AP® exam.

Unit VII

Module 31

Page 318: The next three modules (31–33) deal with memory. Not only is this a significant topic on the AP® exam, it is also one of the most practical topics in psychology, especially if you're a student! Some of your preconceptions about memory may be accurate and some may not. As you read, think about how you can apply what you're learning in order to be a better student.

Page 319: You will see several versions of Figure 31.2 as you work your way through Modules 31, 32, and 33. Pay attention! This model may look confusing now, but will make more and more sense as its components are described in more detail.

Page 324: It's not the studying you do in May that will determine your success on the AP® exam; it's the studying you do now. It's a good idea to take a little time each week to quickly review material from earlier in the course. When was the last time you looked at information from the previous units?

Page 325: Are you often pressed for time? The most effective way to cut down on the amount of time you need to spend studying is to increase the meaningfulness of the material. If you can relate the material to your own life—and that's pretty easy when you're studying psychology—it takes less time to master it.

Module 32

Page 334: Figure 32.5 is an excellent summary. Why don't you review it for a few minutes and then see how much of it you can reproduce on a piece of paper? That will give you a good assessment of which parts of the memory process you know and which parts you still need to work on.

Module 33

Page 342: Retrograde amnesia acts backward in time, just like when you choose a "retro" look for a party and wear clothes from an earlier time.

Page 345: Here's the prefix "retro" again and it means exactly the same thing with interference that it did for amnesia. In both cases, they're exerting an influence back in time.

Page 346: There are many references to Sigmund Freud in the text. Most of your knowledge of Freud probably came from popular culture, and it often conflicts with the discoveries of modern researchers. The AP® exam may test your understanding of researchers' views of Freud.

Page 347: Read this entire section particularly carefully. Many people harbor misconceptions about how memory works, and a lot of the misconceptions are dealt with in the next few pages. Memory does *not* function like a video recorder!

Module 35

Page 361: There are several sample problems for you to enjoy in this section. It can be very interesting to ask several of your friends to try to solve them, too. Have them talk through the problem out loud and you will gain some understanding of the processes they are using.

Module 36

Page 373: It is sometimes challenging to keep these building blocks straight. Phonemes are sounds. It may help to remember that phones carry sounds. Morphemes have meaning, and both words begin with the letter *m.*

Page 376: You'll notice that even though the brain was one of the major topics in Unit III, it keeps coming up. Each time it does provides you with an opportunity to go back and review what you learned previously about the brain. Rehearse frequently, and you will not have much to relearn before the AP® exam.

Unit VIII

Module 37

Page 390: The introduction to Module 37 is important, because it informs you how the whole module is organized. Read it carefully now and perhaps return to it as a review when you are through with the module.

Page 391: Note that this section illustrates psychology's biological perspective.

Page 392: Read carefully! Homeostasis is *not* a motivation theory, but rather a biological principle that applies to some motivational theories (like drive-reduction).

Module 39

Page 408: The central principle here is that there are many biological processes that govern human behavior less rigidly than they govern the behavior of other species. Because of our highly developed brain, sex hormones have less control over our behavior than they do over other animals' behavior.

Module 40

Page 415: Free-response questions on the AP® exam often ask students to apply psychological principles to real-life situations. It's easy to imagine a question that deals with social media.

Module 41

Page 421: Be prepared for at least a multiple-choice question that tests your ability to tell the difference between the James-Lange theory and the Cannon-Bard theory.

Page 423: Note the connections here to previous units. This paragraph relates to the nature of consciousness. The next paragraph relates to sensation and perception.

Page 425: Table 41.1 is an excellent summary of the theories of emotion. They are presented in the order they appeared historically. Notice that cognition, a hugely important factor in the modern theories, is not mentioned in the first two theories.

Unit IX

Module 45

Page 462: All three of these issues are important for development. Nature and nurture, of course, weaves its way through almost every module. It is one of the topics most likely to be on the AP® exam.

Page 465: Almost every topic in psychology holds personal relevance, but development stands out. As you work your way through this unit, think of how the material relates to you, your relatives, and your friends. The more often you do this, the easier it will be to remember the material.

Module 46

Page 471: Note that maturation, to developmental psychologists, is a biological sequence. This is much more precise than the general notion that maturation means to become more adult-like.

Module 47

Page 476: Jean Piaget is such an important person in the history of psychology that it's likely there will be at least one question about him on the AP® exam.

Page 479: Careful! *Egocentric* is not the same as egotistical. Egocentric means you can't take someone else's point of view. Egotistical means you're pretty full of yourself.

Page 483: One good way to master the developmental milestones in Piaget's theory is to see them in action. If you know children of various ages, you can test them using some of the ideas presented in this section. Hide a toy from an infant to see object permanence in action. Pour water between two differently shaped glasses to see if a preschooler understands conservation.

Module 48

Page 490: Note that temperament is a contribution from the nature side of the nature and nurture debate.

Page 496: It's understandable if you are struggling to remember the differences between authoritarian and authoritative—these words are exactly the same through the first nine letters! Maybe it will help to realize that authoritative parents will engage in a little more give and take, and that the words *give* and *authoritative* both end in the letters *ive*.

Module 49

Page 500: There is a lot of information in this section. One good way to process these differences and similarities between genders is to consider which facts fit prevailing stereotypes and which don't. You may even want to keep a list.

Module 51

Page 516: Kohlberg's is an important stage theory. There are often AP® exam questions on this topic. It's very important to understand that the stage you're in doesn't depend on *what* you decide to do (for example, steal the medicine), it depends on *why* you decide to do it.

Module 52

Page 519: This is not the only place in the book that the author discusses Erik Erikson's stage theory. For example, trust was discussed on page 492. Integrity comes up on page 548. Table 52.1 pulls it all together in one place for you.

Page 521: Careful! In the media, to describe a relationship as intimate usually implies that it is sexual. Erikson means something different. In his theory, an intimate relationship may or may not be sexual (and a sexual relationship may or may not be intimate).

Module 54

Page 542: This section is a good example of the complexity of seemingly simple questions. It seems like one should be able to answer a question like "Does memory decline with age?" with a straightforward *yes* or *no*. People are complex. Development is complex. We should not be surprised to learn that many factors influence memory in adulthood.

Unit X

Module 55

Page 557: The boldfaced key terms that you read in this module are all quite famous terms. Even though modern psychology rejects many of the specifics of psychoanalysis, the fame of Freud's concepts makes them likely topics for AP® exam questions.

Page 558: Be careful: It's easy to confuse Freud's three layers of the mind (conscious, preconscious, and unconscious) with the three parts of personality (id, ego, superego).

Page 561: The lines between these defense mechanisms aren't always clear. For example, *repression* can be found in almost every example. Focus on the key feature of each given example. If the key feature is seeing your own impulse in someone else, it's projection. If the key feature is shifting your aggression from one target to another, it's displacement.

Module 56

Page 568: It's very important to understand the differences between Freud's view of the unconscious and modern psychology's view of the unconscious. Read this section carefully.

Module 57

Page 573: Frequently, terms that begin with "self-" (like *self-actualization* or *self-concept*) are terms that are grounded in the humanistic perspective.

Module 58

Page 578: You are not likely to be asked questions about the specific traits in Figure 58.1. Focus instead on the two main dimensions (extraversion–introversion and stability–instability), and use the traits to get a sense of what the main dimensions mean. For example, stable people demonstrate leadership, and they are calm, even-tempered, and carefree.

Page 578: This is the third time you've encountered the idea of assessing personality. As with the psychodynamic and humanistic theories, psychologists working from the trait perspective have also tried to establish their own unique ways of measuring personality—in this instance by measuring our traits. There are scientifically sound *personality inventories* in use in psychological research, but beware of the hundreds of self-assessments available online that are neither reliable nor valid.

Page 581: Table 58.1 is an excellent summary of the Big Five personality factors and what they mean.

Module 59

Page 592: Tables 59.1 and 59.2 summarize a whole unit's worth of information. Study them well to be clear on the distinctions separating the major approaches to personality.

Page 595: It's important to note the difference between *self-esteem* and *self-efficacy*. Although your feeling of self-worth might be related to your beliefs about how competent you are, they are not the same thing.

Unit XI

Module 60

Page 608: David Myers identified three "huge controversies" in the unit opener. All three are covered extensively in this book, and all three will probably show up on the AP® exam.

Page 613: Do not continue on if you can't remember what terms like *MRI, parietal lobe,* and *axon* mean. Now is the time to head back to Unit III for a review. If you do this sort of review frequently, you'll have much better command of the material on the day of the AP® exam.

Module 61

Page 619: David Myers did not use the terms *nature* or *nurture* as he described the contributions of Binet and Terman, but he dropped many hints that should allow you to figure out who leaned toward the nature position and who leaned toward the nurture position. Can you do it?

Page 621: Can you remember why the intelligence test scores in Figure 61.2 are marked off in 15-point intervals? Do the 68 percent and 95 percent areas seem familiar? They should—you've seen this graph before. It's Figure 7.3 from the module on statistical reasoning. Intelligence tests are being used to illustrate that 68 percent of a population will be within one standard deviation of the mean for normally distributed data. Ninety-five percent will be within two standard deviations.

Page 622: Be careful! The terms *reliability* and *validity* have more precise meanings to psychologists than they do to the general public.

Module 63

Page 633: Figure 63.1 is worth spending some time on. Try grabbing a study buddy and explaining whether each of the five conditions provides more support for nature or more for nurture. In most cases, it's some of each and you have to look at comparisons between categories to really be able to draw conclusions.

Unit XII

Module 65

Page 656: Notice that the term "insanity" comes out of the legal system. It is not a psychological or medical diagnosis and does not appear in DSM-5.

Module 66

Page 662: The way disorders are classified can be confusing, so it's worth taking some time to keep the organization straight. Sometimes, there is a broad classification that includes more specific disorders—the broad category of anxiety disorders, for example, includes generalized anxiety disorder, panic disorder, and phobia. Other times, there is just one level of classification. Obsessive-compulsive disorder and posttraumatic stress disorder do not fit into broader categories.

Page 666: This is a good time to return to Unit VI and review the principles of classical and operant conditioning.

Module 67

Page 678: You can review brain scanning techniques, neurotransmitters, and brain parts in Unit III.

Module 68

Page 684: It is common for the AP® Psychology exam to include items to see if you are aware of various "media myths" about psychology. One of the most common of these myths is that schizophrenia means split or multiple personality. Read this section carefully to achieve an accurate understanding of what schizophrenia is—and isn't.

Page 685: Are you clear about the difference between delusions and hallucinations? Delusions are false *thoughts.* Hallucinations are false *sensory experiences.*

Module 69

Page 699: Notice how different antisocial personality disorder is from the other disorders you have studied in this unit. Because individuals with antisocial personality disorder so often behave badly (according to society's standards of right and wrong), they tend to be viewed differently than people with disorders like depression or phobia.

Unit XIII

Module 70

Page 709: Most of the treatments discussed in this unit come from the perspectives you've been dealing with since Unit I. As you reach each major section—like the upcoming one on psychoanalytic and psychodynamic therapy—try to anticipate how someone from that perspective would approach therapy (in other words, "What would Freud do?"). This should help you organize and retain the information as you read.

Page 710: Psychoanalytic treatment is the public image of psychology. If you were to ask people to sketch a psychologist at work, you would see lots of sketches of therapists taking notes while they were seated behind patients on couches. Keep in mind that most therapy nowadays is very different from this image, and psychology careers stretch well beyond therapy.

Page 712: You can remember *Acceptance, Genuineness,* and *Empathy* as "AGE."

Module 71

Page 716: Before you read the next several pages, you may want to quickly review the material on classical and operant conditioning in Unit VI.

Page 720: Behavior therapies focus on what you do. Cognitive therapies focus on what you think. That's a very basic distinction, but critically important for your understanding.

Module 72

Page 731: You will need to understand what basic statistical concepts are, but you will not need to do any actual calculations on the AP® exam.

Module 73

Page 741: The discussion of drug therapies is a great opportunity for you to review information about neurotransmitters and brain function. See Unit III if you need to brush up on these topics.

Unit XIV

Module 74

Page 754: Many students have not heard of the *fundamental attribution error* before taking a course in psychology. This concept often shows up on the AP® exam, so be sure you understand this well.

Module 75

Page 765: Three of the most famous research projects in psychology were done by social psychologists, and you've now read about them all. Milgram, Asch, and Zimbardo (from the last module) are all likely to appear on the AP® exam.

Module 76

Page 771: As you work through this material, identify examples in your own life. Then, compare your examples with a classmate's. This is a great way to make psychology come alive and to study effectively.

Module 77

Page 781: It's worth spending a little time focusing on the distinction between discrimination and prejudice. They are related, but different. The most important thing to note is that prejudice is cognitive in nature. Discrimination, on the other hand, is behavior motivated by prejudice.

Page 785: Pause for a minute and try to identify examples of the just-world phenomenon, in-group bias, and scapegoating in your own school. Are there a few or a lot?

Module 78

Page 789: Notice that you're back to a nature and nurture analysis again. The biology section is, of course, the nature component. When you get to the psychological and social-cultural factors in a few pages, that's nurture.

Page 792: Dave Myers points out that this section is an application of material that was introduced in Unit VI. You should go back there for a quick review if you don't recognize the basic components of operant conditioning and observational learning in this material.

Page 793: In the experiment described here, can you identify the independent and dependent variables? It's great practice to do this every time you read about an experiment.

Module 79

Page 798: Can you remember the other use of the term *proximity* earlier in the course? It was one of the Gestalt principles from Unit IV, Sensation and Perception.

Module 80

Page 808: Common sense suggests that you would be more likely to get help if there are more people around, but research on the bystander effect has in fact shown just the opposite is true. This concept often shows up on the AP® exam, so be sure you understand it.

Appendix C: Psychological Science's Key Contributors

APPENDIX D: Preparing for Further Psychology Studies

This appendix was written by Jennifer Zwolinski, University of San Diego.

As noted in Module 3, there is much that you can do with a psychology degree. In that module you learned about the work different types of psychologists do and where they do it. You are in the right place here for answers to important questions about pursuing the study of psychology: Will psychology be the right major for you? What are the various levels of psychology education, and what kinds of jobs are available at those levels? What are some ways you can improve your chances of admission to graduate school?

The Psychology Major

How Do You Know If Psychology Is the Right Major for You?

You can start by answering these questions to see if you would be well matched with a major in psychology. Do you

- enjoy learning about how and why we think and behave in the ways we do?
- appreciate the value of applying the scientific method to answer questions?
- have an interest in a career that requires interpersonal skills?
- want to learn critical thinking and analytical skills?
- want to learn communication and presentation skills?
- want to gain computer skills in data processing and skills in research methodology, such as assessment and statistics?
- want to work in human or animal services?
- have a desire to apply psychological principles to understand or solve personal, social, organizational, or environmental problems?

If you answered *Yes* to most or all of these questions, then psychology may be the right major for you.

How Popular Is the Psychology Major?

Psychology is a very popular major. After business and accounting majors (13 percent and 8 percent, respectively), psychology, nursing, and elementary education are tied for the third most popular majors (each 4 percent of all majors) (Carnevale et al., 2011). In 2008, more than 92,000 psychology majors graduated with a bachelor's degree in psychology from U.S. colleges and universities (Mulvey & Grus, 2010) (**FIGURE D.1**).

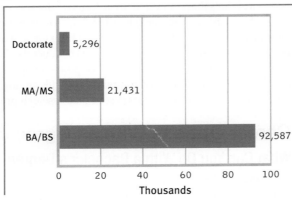

Figure D.1

Number of psychology degrees conferred by level of degree, 2008 Adapted from APA Center for Workforce Studies, January 2010. *Source:* U.S. Dept. of Education, National Center for Education Statistics, Integrated Postsecondary Data System Completion Survey. *Note:* Doctorate degree includes Psy.D.

Who Is Studying Psychology at the Undergraduate and Graduate Levels?

From 2008 to 2009, 77 percent of those graduating with bachelor's degrees in psychology were women. This tendency for most degree recipients in psychology to be women was also observed for master's degrees (80 percent) and doctoral degrees (73 percent). Women were most likely to earn specialized doctorate degrees in developmental and child psychology, whereas men were somewhat more likely to focus on cognitive and psycholinguistic psychology (U.S. Department of Education, National Center for Education Statistics, 2010) (**FIGURE D.2**).

Figure D.2

Psychology doctorate degrees awarded by subfield and sex, 2009 Adapted from APA Center for Workforce Studies, January 2011. *Sources:* NSF/NIH/USED/USDA/ NEH/NASA, 2009 Survey of Earned Doctorates.

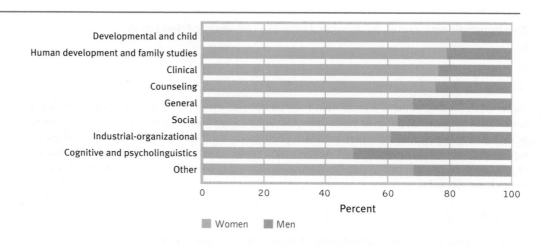

What Are the Main Reasons That Undergraduate Students Choose to Study Psychology?

One study found that the number one reason psychology majors chose their major was a positive experience in their introduction to psychology course (Marrs et al., 2007). Other research has found that the top five reasons students choose a psychology major are because it provides the ability to help others, incorporates interesting subject matter, produces a better understanding of self and others, includes good career or salary potential, and offers the ability to conduct research (Mulvey & Grus, 2010).

What Types of Skills Will You Learn as a Psychology Major?

Studies suggest that psychology majors learn a set of skills not offered by other social science majors. These include communication, information gathering, interpersonal management, and research methodology (Kruger & Zechmeister, 2001, as cited in Wegenek & Buskist, 2010).

The psychology major's skill set prepares graduates for numerous opportunities in the professional world and a range of graduate training options. The skills include an ability to work and get along with others, a desire and willingness to learn new things, adaptability to changing situations, and a capacity for problem solving (Landrum, 2001). Psychology majors also have a number of methodological skills that result from their focus on the scientific study of human and animal behavior. The study of statistics and research methodology contributes to a scientific mind-set that emphasizes exploring and managing uncertainty, critical thinking and analytical skills, and logical thinking abilities. Being able to analyze data using statistics, conduct database searches, and integrate multiple sources of information is helpful in a number of professional settings. Prospective employers appreciate the excellent written and verbal communication skills among students who master American Psychological Association (APA) style and present their research projects at conferences.

Career Options With a Degree in Psychology

What Can You Do With a Bachelor's Degree in Psychology?

If you major in psychology, you will have several possible career paths to follow. First, you might consider employment after graduation in a variety of professional settings. Here are the top five occupations for graduates with a bachelor's degree in psychology (Carnevale et al., 2011):

1.   Management
2.   Office work
3.   Community Service
4.   Sales
5.   Education

Here are the top five industries in which graduates with a bachelor's degree in psychology may be found working (Carnevale et al., 2011):

1.   Health service
2.   Education
3.   Financial services
4.   Public administration
5.   Professional services

If you choose to work more directly in the field of psychology, a bachelor's degree will qualify you to work as an assistant to psychologists, researchers, or other professionals in community mental health centers, vocational rehabilitation offices, and correctional programs (U.S. Bureau of Labor Statistics, 2012).

A second option for psychology majors is to pursue a master's degree or doctorate in psychology. Snyder and Dillow (2010) estimate that 20 to 24 percent of psychology baccalaureate recipients continue on to study psychology in graduate school (approximately 8 to 10 percent pursue doctorates).

A third option is to pursue advanced training in other disciplines, such as law, business, education, or medicine.

Drew Appleby and his colleagues (2010) prepared a list of 171 careers that would be of interest to psychology majors—including those pursuing advanced degrees. The list (see www.tinyurl.com/PsychologyCareers) includes links for more information about professional responsibilities, salaries, and job outlook for each of these positions.

How Can You Maximize Your College Success and Later Job Prospects With a Major in Psychology?

There are some things that all psychology majors can do to maximize success in college and, later, in the job market. Employers who hire people with only a bachelor's degree tend to favor individuals with strong interpersonal skills and practical experience as well as a good education (Cannon, 2005). It's not too early for you to begin planning how you can use your upcoming college education to improve your chances for success after college. Betsy Morgan and Ann Korschgen (2009) offer the following helpful tips for succeeding in college and increasing your chances of getting a job after graduation. Many of these tools will benefit students who plan to apply to graduate school as well.

On the job with a B.A. There are psychology-related jobs available even for those with only a B.A. degree. For example, this case manager working for a mental health organization in Florida is conducting a survey of the homeless people in her county in order to consider the best ways to address their needs.

1.   *Get to know your instructors.* Talk with them about the field of psychology and get their advice on your career plan. Ask them to support you on an independent study internship or research project. By learning more about your skills and future aims, faculty members can help you accomplish your goals. This may even result in an enthusiastic reference for future employment.

2.   *Familiarize yourself with available resources, such as campus career services and alumni.* If you are searching for a part-time job during your studies (or a full-time job after graduation), career services can help you to identify and market your job skills and to emphasize the knowledge and abilities you have in your resume. They can also help you to network with other alumni who are working in your area of interest and who can help you prepare for the career that you want.

3.   *Volunteer some of your time and talent to campus or community organizations, such as Psi Chi (the International Honor Society in Psychology) or your college's psychology club.* In addition to showing that you are an active citizen in your department, you will gain important skills, such as meeting and event planning, how to work with a group, and improved communication skills, all of which enhance your marketability.

© Lyttle, Melissa/St. Petersburg Times/ZUMA Press

4. *Participate in an internship experience.* Many employers want students to gain relevant experience outside the classroom. Internships are offered during the school year and during the summer break. Some are paid and others are not, but you may be able to earn course credit while completing an internship. In addition to trying out a possible career and gaining relevant work experience before you graduate, you will increase your support network of mentors who can provide supervision and support for your career goals. And you may be able to request letters of support when you apply for jobs or to graduate school.

5. *Take courses that support your interests.* Although the psychology major offers a range of skills that will benefit you, don't assume the psychology curriculum will offer all the skills necessary in your area of interest. Add courses to increase your knowledge base and skills. This will show prospective employers that your specific interests are in line with the demands of the job.

What Type of Salary Can You Expect With a Degree in Psychology? Will a Graduate Degree Increase Your Salary?

A 2009 study found that earnings increase with education and that higher levels of educational attainment will almost always yield greater financial rewards (Carnevale et al., 2011). Although these figures will be dated by the time you read this, they still provide a basis of comparison. In 2009, the median salary for psychology majors with a bachelor's degree was $45,000. When considering baccalaureates from 171 majors, the median earnings varied greatly—from $29,000 for counseling psychology majors to $120,000 for petroleum engineering majors.

When considering new doctoral recipients in 2009, the overall median starting salary was $64,000. Women reported a median salary that was $8,000 lower than that reported by men ($62,000 versus $70,000, respectively). Median salaries reported by ethnic minorities were similar to those indicated by nonminorities: $65,000 (Michalski et al., 2011).

Among psychologists with new doctoral level degrees in 2009, clinical psychologists working in criminal justice earned the highest median starting salary, $80,500. Psychology graduates with doctoral degrees working in consulting firms ($75,000) and those working in applied psychology positions ($73,332) tended to have the next two highest median salaries (Michalski et al., 2011).

Of course, earning potential should not be the only reason that individuals choose a major. Job satisfaction is another important consideration.

What Kind of Job Satisfaction Can You Expect If You Are Working in a Psychology Field?

In a study of 27,000 Americans, the most satisfying jobs were found to be those that involve "caring for, teaching and protecting others and creative pursuits" (Smith, 2007, pp. 1–2). Most of the occupations with the highest-ranking happiness levels among workers involved helping others, using technical and scientific expertise, or using creativity (pp. 1–2). A bachelor's degree in psychology can increase the likelihood that you will be working in a job that fosters these skills (Landrum, 2009).

Positive job satisfaction has also been observed among individuals who attend graduate school in psychology. In 2009, 72 percent of new doctorate recipients indicated that their primary occupational position was their first choice. Most new graduates with a Ph.D. are fairly satisfied with their current position in terms of salary, benefits, opportunities for personal development, supervisors, colleagues, and working conditions (Michalski et al., 2011).

Postgraduate Degrees

In addition to a higher salary and strong job satisfaction, a graduate degree in psychology will give you proficiency in an area of psychological specialization. According to the U.S. Bureau of Labor Statistics (2012), psychologists with advanced degrees held approximately 174,000 jobs in 2010. Employment for psychologists is expected to grow 22 percent from 2010 to 2020, which is faster than the average for all occupations.

What's the Difference Between a Master's Degree and a Doctorate Degree in Psychology?

Both degrees will prepare you for more specialized training in psychology and open your job opportunities in the field of psychology beyond the bachelor's degree. However, the work settings for individuals with a psychology degree vary somewhat by type of graduate degree. Psychologists with a doctorate work primarily in universities and colleges; most people with a master's degree work in other educational institutions (such as elementary and secondary schools) and in for-profit companies (Mulvey & Grus, 2010) (**FIGURE D.3**).

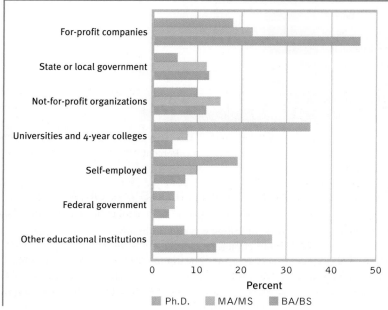

Figure D.3
Work settings for psychology degree recipients, 2006
Adapted from APA Center for Workforce Studies, January 2010. *Sources:* National Science Foundation/Division of Science Resources Statistics, Various Surveys, 2006. *Note:* Psy.D.s are not included in this information.

You might acquire a master's degree to do specialized work in psychology. A master's requires at least two years of full-time graduate study in a specific subfield of psychology. In addition to specialized course work, requirements usually include practical experience in an applied setting and/or a master's thesis on an original research project. As a graduate with a master's degree, you might handle research and data collection and analysis in a university, government, or private industry setting. You might work under the supervision of a psychologist with a doctorate, providing some clinical service such as therapy or testing. Or you might find a job in the health, government, industry, or education fields. You might also acquire a master's degree as a stepping stone for more advanced study in a doctoral program in psychology, which will considerably expand the number of employment opportunities available to you (Super & Super, 2001).

You will probably need five to seven years of graduate study in a specific subfield of psychology to get your doctoral degree. The degree you choose to pursue will depend on your career goals. You will probably choose to earn a doctor of philosophy (Ph.D.) in psychology if your career goals are geared toward conducting research, or possibly a doctor of psychology (Psy.D.) if you are more interested in pursuing professional practice (clinical or therapeutic work). Training for the Ph.D. culminates in a dissertation (an extensive research paper you will be required to defend orally) based on original research. Courses in quantitative research methods, which include the use of computer-based analysis, are an important part of graduate study and are necessary to complete the dissertation. Psy.D. training may be based on clinical work and examinations rather than a dissertation. It is important to note, however, that psychologists with Psy.D. degrees are not the only ones who work in professional practice. Many psychologists who earn a Ph.D. in clinical or counseling psychology

Clinician in training Those interested in professional practice can obtain either a Ph.D. in clinical or counseling psychology, or a Psy.D., which focuses on clinical or therapeutic work.

conduct research and also work in professional settings. If you pursue clinical and counseling psychology programs, you should expect at least a one-year internship in addition to the regular course work, clinical practice, and research.

FIGURE D.4 shows, by subfield, the Ph.D.s earned in the field of psychology in the United States in 2009, the most recent year for which these data are available (Mulvey, 2011). As you can see, clinical psychology is the most popular specialty area among people with doctorates in psychology.

Figure D.4

Psychology doctorates awarded by subfield, 2009 Adapted from APA Center for Workforce Studies, January 2011. *Source:* NSF/NIH/USED/USDA/NEH/NASA, 2009 Survey of Earned Doctorates.

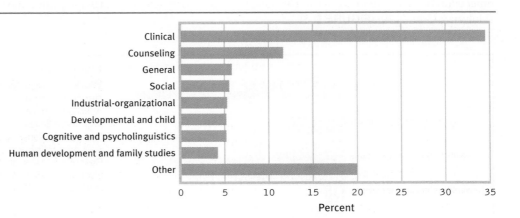

Preparing Early for Graduate Study in Psychology

Competition for openings for advanced degree programs in psychology is keen. If you plan to go to graduate school after college, there are a number of things you can do in advance to maximize your chances of gaining admission to the school of your choice.

The first step is to take full advantage of your opportunities in high school. By enrolling in challenging elective courses and working hard to develop an academic skill set, you will have paved the way for success in college. Successful students also take the time to learn effective study skills and to establish disciplined study habits. Involve yourself in extracurricular activities, gain some experience in the world of work by taking on a part-time job, and look for opportunities to volunteer in your school and community. In addition to helping you grow as a person, becoming a well-rounded student with high standards helps you to earn scholarships and increases your chances of being accepted by the colleges and universities of particular interest to you.

During your first year on campus, continue to maximize opportunities and obtain the experience needed to gain admission to a competitive program. Kristy Arnold and Kelly Horrigan (2002) offer a number of suggestions to facilitate this process.

Membership benefits Members of the Psi Chi Honor Society, such as those meeting here, enjoy educational and professional benefits. They may attend special Psi Chi sessions at psychological conventions, apply for research grants in psychology or other academic awards, and read about research advances in the society's journal *Eye on Psi Chi.* (See www.psichi.org for more information.)

1. *Network.* Get to know the psychology department and its faculty members by attending activities and meetings. This strategy will be especially helpful when you apply to graduate school or for a professional position, because many applications require two to three letters of reference. Become involved in psychology clubs and in Psi Chi. These meetings connect students who have similar interests and expose them to a broader study of the field.

2. *Become actively involved in research as early as possible.* Start by doing simple tasks such as data entry and data collection, and over time you will be prepared to conduct your own research project under the supervision of a research mentor. To test your interest in academic careers and to build your skills for future study in psychology, consider applying for summer research positions through your university or through other organizations such as the American Psychological Association Summer Science Fellowship (SSF) program or the National Science Foundation Research Experiences for Undergraduates (REU) program.

3. *Volunteer or get a job in a psychology-related field.* Getting involved will show your willingness to apply psychological concepts to real-world settings. Further, it will showcase your ability to juggle a number of tasks successfully, such as work and school—an important skill for graduate school success.

4. *Maintain good grades and prepare early for the GRE®.* Demonstrate the ability to do well in graduate school with successful completion of challenging courses, especially those related to your interests. (See the Close-up box in Module 2 and the final section in Module 33 for tips on how to do well in this and other courses, and how to improve your retention of the information you are learning.) In your junior year, you should begin studying for the Graduate Record Exam® (GRE®), the standardized test that applicants to graduate school must complete. Many graduate programs in psychology require both the General GRE® and the Psychology subject tests. If you start preparing early and maintain high grades, you will be ready for success in your graduate school application and study.

For More Information

How Can You Learn More About the Psychology Major and the Field of Psychology?

1. Talk with as many people as possible who have experience in the discipline of psychology. Your psychology teacher or school counselor may have some tips. Try to learn about opportunities to contact psychology majors, graduate students, instructors, and advisors, as well as other professionals who trained in psychology or work in the field.

2. Read books, such as those listed at the end of this appendix.

3. Take advantage of online resources. These resources can help you determine whether you would be well matched for a major and a career in psychology.

    *   Watch online videos showcasing different careers in psychology, such as those at www.drkit.org/psychology/.

    *   Play the Career Interest Game (www.career.missouri.edu/career-interest-game).

    *   Get more information about specific jobs in psychology from the Bureau of Labor Statistics (www.tinyurl.com/PsychologyJobs), the Occupational Information Network (O*NET for short; www.onetcenter.org/), and the Occupational Outlook Handbook (OOH; www.bls.gov/ooh/).

    *   Visit the websites of the American Psychological Association (www.apa.org) and Association for Psychological Science (www.psychologicalscience.org/). The APA has a lot to offer high school students who are interested in learning more about psychology. To learn more about membership at the high school level (which includes subscriptions to APA journals and mobile apps), visit www.apa.org/membership/hs-student/index.aspx. You can also become a member of the Psychology Student Network (www.apa.org/ed/precollege/psn/index.aspx).

    *   Learn more about the honor societies in psychology, Psi Chi (www.psichi.org) and Psi Beta (www.psibeta.org).

What Are Some Books That Can Help You to Learn More About the Major, Careers, and Graduate School in Psychology?

American Psychological Association (2007). *Getting in: A step-by-step plan for gaining admission to graduate school in psychology* (2nd ed.). Washington, DC: Author.

American Psychological Association (2013). *Graduate study in psychology, 2014 edition.* Washington, DC: Author.

Kracen, A. C., & Wallace, I. J. (Eds.) (2008). *Applying to graduate school in psychology: Advice from successful students and prominent psychologists.* Washington, DC: American Psychological Association.

Kuther, T., & Morgan, R. D. (2010). *Careers in psychology: Opportunities in a changing world* (3rd ed.). Boston, MA: Wadsworth Cengage.

Landrum, E. (2009). *Finding jobs with a psychology bachelor's degree: Expert advice for launching your career.* Washington, DC: American Psychological Association.

Morgan, B., & Korschgen, A. (2009). *Majoring in psychology? Career options for psychology undergraduates* (4th ed.). Boston, MA: Pearson.

Schultheiss, D. E. P. (2008). *Psychology as a major: Is it right for me and what can I do with my degree?* Washington, DC: American Psychological Association.

Sternberg, R. (Ed.) (2006). *Career paths in psychology: Where your degree can take you* (2nd ed.). Washington, DC: American Psychological Association.

Wegenek, A. R., & Buskist, W. (2010). *The insider's guide to the psychology major. Everything you need to know about the degree and the profession.* Washington, DC: American Psychological Association

Appendix E: Answers to Test Yourself Questions

Unit I

Psychology's History and Approaches

Module 1 Psychology's History

What event defined the founding of modern scientific psychology?

Answer: The founding of scientific psychology is often attributed to Wilhelm Wundt's opening of the University of Leipzig psychology laboratory in 1879. The new science of psychology was soon organized into different schools of thought, including *structuralism* (founded by Edward Bradford Titchener, using introspection to explore the elemental structure of the human mind) and *functionalism* (founded by William James, focusing on how mental and behavioral processes enable organisms to adapt, survive, and flourish). James also wrote an important psychology textbook, completed in 1890.

Module 2 Psychology's Big Issues and Approaches

What are psychology's major levels of analysis?

Answer: Psychology's three major levels of analysis are the biological, psychological, and social-cultural. The complementary insights of psychologists studying behavior and mental processes from the behavioral, biological, cognitive, evolutionary, humanistic, psychodynamic, and social-cultural perspectives offer a richer understanding than could usually be gained from any one viewpoint alone.

Module 3 Careers in Psychology

Name the subfields that focus on (a) people and their work environments, (b) how people change over the life span, (c) the human thinking involved in perceiving, remembering, speaking, and decision making, and (d) diagnosing and treating psychological disorders.

Answer: These subfields are (a) industrial-organizational psychology, (b) developmental psychology, (c) cognitive psychology, (d) clinical psychology.

Unit II

Research Methods: Thinking Critically With Psychological Science

Module 4 The Need for Psychological Science

How does the scientific attitude contribute to critical thinking?

Answer: The scientific attitude combines (1) *curiosity* about the world around us, (2) *skepticism* toward various claims and ideas, and (3) *humility* about one's own understanding. Evaluating evidence, assessing conclusions, and examining our own assumptions are essential parts of critical thinking.

Module 5 The Scientific Method and Description

What are some strengths and weaknesses of the three different methods psychologists use to describe behavior— case studies, naturalistic observation, and surveys?

Answer: *Case studies* offer in-depth insights that may offer clues to what's true of others—or may, if the case is atypical, mislead. *Naturalistic observation* enables the study of behavior undisturbed by researchers. But the lack of control may leave cause and effect ambiguous. *Surveys* can accurately reveal the tendencies of large populations. But if the questions are leading, or if nonrandom samples are queried, the results can again mislead us.

Module 6 Correlation and Experimentation

Why, when testing a new drug to control blood pressure, would we learn more about its effectiveness from giving it to half of the participants in a group of 1000 than to all 1000 participants?

Answer: To determine the drug's effectiveness, we must compare its effect on those *randomly assigned* to receive it (the *experimental group*) with the other half of the participants (*control group*), who receive a *placebo*. If we gave the drug to all 1000 participants, we would have no way of knowing if the drug is serving as a placebo or if it is actually medically effective.

Module 7 Statistical Reasoning in Everyday Life

Can you solve this puzzle?

The registrar's office at the University of Michigan has found that usually about 100 students in Arts and Sciences have perfect grades at the end of their first term at the University. However, only about 10 to 15 students graduate with perfect grades. What do you think is the most likely explanation for the fact that there are more perfect grades after one term than at graduation (Jepson et al., 1983)?

Answer: Most students in the study came up with plausible causes for the drop in grades, such as, "Students tend to work harder at the beginning of their college careers than toward the end." Fewer than a third recognized the statistical phenomenon clearly at work: Averages based on fewer courses are more variable, which guarantees a greater number of extremely low and high grades at the end of the first term.

Module 8 Frequently Asked Questions About Psychology

How are human and animal research participants protected?

Answer: Animal protection legislation, laboratory regulation and inspection, and local ethics committees serve to protect human and animal welfare. At universities, Institutional Review Boards screen research proposals. Ethical principles developed by international psychological organizations urge researchers using human participants to obtain *informed consent,* to protect them from harm and discomfort, to treat their personal information confidentially, and to fully *debrief* all participants.

Unit III

Biological Bases of Behavior

Module 9 Biological Psychology and Neurotransmission

How do neurons communicate with one another?

Answer: A neuron fires when excitatory inputs exceed inhibitory inputs by a sufficient threshold. When the resulting impulse reaches the axon's end, it triggers the release of chemical messengers called *neurotransmitters.* After crossing a tiny space between one neuron's terminal branch and the next neuron's dendrite (the *synaptic gap*), these molecules chemically activate receptor sites on neighboring neurons.

Module 10 The Nervous and Endocrine Systems

How does information flow through your nervous system as you pick up a fork? Can you summarize this process?

Answer: Your central nervous system's hungry brain activates and guides the muscles of your arm and hand via your peripheral nervous system's motor neurons. As you pick up the fork, your brain processes the information from your sensory nervous system, enabling it to continue to guide the fork to your mouth. The functional circle starts with sensory input, continues with interneuron processing by the central nervous system, and finishes with motor output.

Why is the pituitary gland called the "master gland"?

Answer: Responding to signals from the hypothalamus, the pituitary releases hormones that trigger other endocrine glands to secrete hormones that in turn influence brain and behavior.

Module 11 Studying the Brain, and Older Brain Structures

Within what brain region would damage be most likely to disrupt your ability to skip rope? Your ability to sense tastes or sounds? In what brain region would damage perhaps leave you in a coma? Without the very breath and heartbeat of life?

Answer: These regions are, respectively, the *cerebellum,* the *thalamus,* the *reticular formation,* and the *medulla.* These questions assess your understanding of the essential functions of the lower-level brain areas.

Module 12 The Cerebral Cortex

Try moving your right hand in a circular motion, as if polishing a table. Then start your right foot doing the same motion, synchronized with your hand. Now reverse the right foot's motion, but not the hand's. Finally, try moving the *left* foot opposite to the right hand.

1. Why is reversing the right foot's motion so hard?
2. Why is it easier to move the left foot opposite to the right hand?

Answer: 1. The right limbs' opposed activities interfere with each other because both are controlled by the same (left) side of your brain. 2. Opposite sides of your brain control your left and right limbs, so the reversed motion causes less interference.

Module 13 Brain Hemisphere Organization and the Biology of Consciousness

What are the mind's two tracks, and what is "dual processing"?

Answer: The human brain has separate conscious and unconscious tracks that process information simultaneously. In vision, for example, the visual action track normally guides our conscious visual processing, while the visual perception track normally operates unconsciously, enabling our quick recognition of objects.

Module 14 Behavior Genetics: Predicting Individual Differences

What is *heritability*?

Answer: *Heritability* is the proportion of variation among individuals that we can attribute to genes. *Note:* Heritability is *not* the extent to which an *individual's* traits are genetically determined. Rather, it is the extent to which variation *among* individuals is due to their differing genes. For any trait, heritability can vary, depending on the population and range of environments studied.

Module 15 Evolutionary Psychology: Understanding Human Nature

What are the three main criticisms of evolutionary psychology's explanations?

Answer: Critics of evolutionary psychology's explanations point out that (1) they start with an effect and work backward to propose an explanation; (2) unethical and immoral men could use such explanations to rationalize their behavior toward women; and (3) this explanation overlooks the effects of cultural expectations and socialization.

How does the biopsychosocial approach explain our individual development?

Answer: The biopsychosocial approach considers all the factors that influence our individual development: biological factors (including evolution, genes, hormones, and brains), psychological factors (including our experiences, beliefs, feelings, and expectations), and social-cultural factors (including parental and peer influences and cultural attitudes and norms).

Unit IV

Sensation and Perception

Module 16 Basic Principles of Sensation and Perception

Explain how Heather Sellers' experience of prosopagnosia illustrates the difference between sensation and perception.

Answer: Heather Sellers' *sensation* is normal, and her *perception* is nearly so, but her brain is lacking the functional area that helps us recognize a familiar human face. While her bottom-up physical sensory system receives and represents stimuli, a problem with her top-down mental process of organizing and interpreting sensory input results in her inability to recognize faces.

Module 17 Influences on Perception

What type of evidence shows that, indeed, "there is more to perception than meets the senses"?

Answer: We construct our perceptions based on both sensory input and—experiments show—on our assumptions, expectations, schemas, and perceptual sets, often influenced by the surrounding context.

What is the field of study that researches claims of extrasensory perception (ESP)?

Answer: It is called parapsychology, because it studies paranormal phenomena that are claimed to occur apart from any sensory input.

Module 18 Vision

What is the rapid sequence of events that occurs when you see and recognize a friend?

Answer: Light waves reflect off the person and travel into your eye, where the receptor cells in your retina convert the light waves' energy into neural impulses sent to your brain. Your brain then processes the subdimensions of this visual input—including color, depth, movement, and form—separately but simultaneously. It interprets this information based on previously stored information and your expectations into a conscious perception of your friend.

Module 19 Visual Organization and Interpretation

What do we mean when we say that, in perception, "the whole is greater than the sum of its parts"?

Answer: Gestalt psychologists used this saying to describe our perceptual tendency to organize clusters of sensations into meaningful forms or coherent groups.

Module 20 Hearing

What are the basic steps in transforming sound waves into perceived sound?

Answer: The *outer ear* collects sound waves, which are translated into mechanical waves by the *middle ear* and turned into fluid waves in the *inner ear.* The *auditory nerve* then translates the energy into electrical waves and sends them to the brain, which perceives and interprets the sound.

Module 21 The Other Senses

How does our system for sensing smell differ from our sensory systems for vision, touch, and taste?

Answer: We have two types of retinal receptors, four basic touch senses, and five taste sensations. But we have no basic smell receptors. Instead, different combinations of odor receptors send messages to the brain, enabling us to recognize some 10,000 discernible odors.

Unit V
States of Consciousness

Module 22 Understanding Consciousness and Hypnosis

When is the use of hypnosis potentially harmful, and when can hypnosis be used to help?

Answer: Hypnosis can be harmful if used to "hypnotically refresh" memories, which may plant false memories. But posthypnotic suggestions have helped alleviate some ailments, and hypnosis can also help control pain.

Module 23 Sleep Patterns and Sleep Theories

What five theories explain our need for sleep?

Answer: (1) Sleep has survival value. (2) Sleep helps restore and repair brain tissue. (3) During sleep we strengthen memory traces. (4) Sleep fuels creativity. (5) Sleep plays a role in the growth process.

Module 24 Sleep Deprivation, Sleep Disorders, and Dreams

Are you getting enough sleep? What might you ask yourself to answer this question?

Answer: You could start with the true/false questions in James Maas' sleep deprivation quiz in Table 24.1. Also, William Dement (1999, p. 73) has suggested considering these questions: "How often do you think about taking a quick snooze? How often do you rub your eyes and yawn during the day? How often do you feel like you really need some coffee?" Dement concluded that "each of these is a warning of a sleep debt that you ignore at your peril."

Module 25 Psychoactive Drugs

Why do tobacco companies try so hard to get customers hooked as teens?

Answer: Nicotine is powerfully addictive, expensive, and deadly. Those who start paving the neural pathways when young may find it very hard to stop using nicotine. As a result, tobacco companies may have lifelong customers.

Unit VI
Learning

Module 26 How We Learn and Classical Conditioning

As we develop, we learn cues that lead us to expect and prepare for good and bad events. We learn to repeat behaviors that bring rewards. And we watch others and learn. What do psychologists call these three types of learning?

Answer: Through *classical conditioning,* we learn cues that lead us to expect and prepare for good and bad events. Through *operant conditioning,* we learn to repeat behaviors that bring rewards. Through *cognitive learning,* we watch others and learn.

In slasher movies, sexually arousing images of women are sometimes paired with violence against women. Based on classical conditioning principles, what might be an effect of this pairing?

Answer: If viewing an attractive nude or semi-nude woman (a US) elicits sexual arousal (a UR), then pairing the US with a new stimulus (violence against women) could turn the violence into a conditioned stimulus (CS) that also becomes sexually arousing, a conditioned response (CR).

Module 27 Operant Conditioning

Fill in the three blanks below with one of the following terms: negative reinforcement (NR), positive punishment (PP), and negative punishment (NP). The first answer, positive reinforcement (PR), is provided for you.

Type of Stimulus	Give It	Take It Away
Desired (for example, a teen's use of the car):	1. PR	2. NP
Undesired/aversive (for example, an insult):	3. PP	4. NR

Module 28 Operant Conditioning's Applications, and Comparison to Classical Conditioning

Salivating in response to a tone paired with food is a(n) _____ behavior; pressing a bar to obtain food is a(n) _____ behavior.

Answer: Salivating in response to a tone paired with food is an example of respondent behavior, while pressing a bar to obtain food is an example of operant behavior.

Module 29 Biology, Cognition, and Learning

When faced with a situation over which you feel you have no sense of control, is it most effective to use emotion- or problem-focused coping? Why?

Answer: It is better to use emotion-focused coping because it helps to alleviate stress and attends to our emotional needs in situations that we feel we cannot change. Emotion-focused coping (such as hanging out with friends before a big test), can become maladaptive, however, when a problem-focused strategy (such as studying) would have been more effective.

Module 30 Learning by Observation

Jason's parents and older friends all smoke, but they advise him not to. Juan's parents and friends don't smoke, but they say nothing to deter him from doing so. Will Jason or Juan be more likely to start smoking?

Answer: Jason may be more likely to smoke, because observational learning studies suggest that children tend to do as others do and say what they say.

Unit VII
Cognition

Module 31 Studying and Building Memories

Memory includes (in alphabetical order) long-term memory, sensory memory, and working/short-term memory. What's the correct order of these three memory stages?

Answer: Sensory memory, working/short-term memory, long-term memory.

What would be the most effective strategy to learn and retain a list of names of key historical figures for a week? For a year?

Answer: For a week: Make the names personally meaningful. For a year: Take advantage of the spacing effect by spreading your learning over several months.

Module 32 Memory Storage and Retrieval

Your friend tells you that her father experienced brain damage in an accident. She wonders if psychology can explain why he can still play checkers very well but has a hard time holding a sensible conversation. What can you tell her?

Answer: Our *explicit* (declarative) memories differ from our *implicit* (nondeclarative) memories of skills and procedures, such as playing checkers. Our implicit memories are processed by more ancient brain areas, which apparently escaped damage during the accident.

You have just watched a movie that includes a chocolate factory. After the chocolate factory is out of mind, you nevertheless feel a strange urge for a chocolate bar. How do you explain this in terms of priming?

Answer: *Priming* is the activation (often without our awareness) of associations. Seeing a chocolate factory in a movie, for example, might temporarily predispose you to crave a chocolate treat. Although you might not consciously remember the chocolate factory, it may prime how you interpret or recall events.

Module 33 Forgetting, Memory Construction, and Memory Improvement

Can you offer examples of proactive and retroactive interference?

Answer: *Proactive* (forward-acting) *interference* occurs when earlier learning disrupts your recall of a later experience. Proactive interference has occurred if learning names of new classmates in your first class makes it more difficult to learn the new names in your second class or if the combination of last year's lock makes it difficult to learn the new combination for this year's lock. *Retroactive interference* has occurred if those new classmate's names in the second class, or that new combination, interferes with your memory of the first class student names or last year's lock.

How would source amnesia affect us if we were to remember all of our waking experiences as well as all of our dreams?

Answer: Real experiences would be confused with those we dreamed. When meeting someone, we might therefore be unsure whether we were reacting to something they previously did or to something we dreamed they did. William Dement (1999, p. 298) thinks this "would put a great burden on your sanity. . . . I truly believe that the wall of memory is a blessed protection."

What are the recommended memory strategies you just read about? (One advised rehearsing to-be-remembered material. What were the others?)

Answer: Study repeatedly to boost long-term recall, and schedule spaced (not crammed) study times. Spend more time rehearsing or actively thinking about the material. Make the material personally meaningful, with well-organized and vivid associations. Refresh your memory by returning to contexts and moods to activate retrieval cues. Use mnemonic devices. Minimize interference. Plan for a complete night's sleep. Test yourself repeatedly—retrieval practice is a proven retention strategy.

Module 34 Thinking, Concepts, and Creativity

According to Robert Sternberg, what are the five components of creativity?

Answer: Sternberg identified expertise, imaginative thinking skills, a venturesome personality, intrinsic motivation, and a creative environment as the five components of creativity.

Module 35 Solving Problems and Making Decisions

The availability heuristic is a quick-and-easy but sometimes misleading guide to judging reality. What is the availability heuristic?

Answer: The *availability heuristic* is our tendency to judge the likeliness of an event by how easily we can recall instances of it. Like all heuristics, this guide is efficient. But it can mislead, as it does when we attempt to judge various risks (for example, of plane travel).

Module 36 Thinking and Language

If children are not yet speaking, is there any reason to think they would benefit from parents and other caregivers reading to them?

Answer: Indeed there is, because well before age 1 children are learning to detect words among the stream of spoken sounds and to discern grammatical rules. Before age 1, they also are babbling with the phonemes of their own language. More than many parents realize, their infants are soaking up language. As researcher Peter Jusczyk reminds us, "Little ears are listening."

To say that "words are the mother of ideas" assumes the truth of what concept?

Answer: This phrase supports the *linguistic determinism hypothesis,* which asserts that language determines thought. Research indicates that this position is too extreme, but language does *influence* what we perceive and think.

Unit VIII
Motivation, Emotion, and Stress

Module 37 Motivational Concepts

While on a long road trip, you suddenly feel very hungry. You see a diner that looks pretty deserted and creepy, but you are *really* hungry, so you stop anyway. What motivational perspective would most easily explain this behavior, and why?

Answer: *Drive-reduction theory*—the idea that physical needs create an aroused state that drives us to reduce the need—helps explain your behavior.

Module 38 Hunger Motivation

You've skipped lunch to meet with your guidance counselor, so you haven't eaten anything in eight hours. As your favorite dish is placed in front of you, your mouth waters. Even imagining this may set your mouth to watering. What triggers this anticipatory salivation?

Answer: You, like Pavlov's dogs, have learned through *classical conditioning* to respond to the cues—the sight and aroma—that signal the food about to enter your mouth. Both *physiological cues* (eight hours of deprivation have left you with low blood sugar) and *psychological cues* (the anticipation of the tasty meal) have heightened your experienced hunger.

Module 39 Sexual Motivation

How might the evolutionary perspective, drive-reduction theory, and arousal theory explain our sexual motivation?

Answer: *Evolutionary perspective:* Those motivated to have sex were more likely to leave descendants—us—than were others who lacked sexual motivation. *Drive-reduction theory:* Hormonal influences create a driven (physiologically aroused) state that compels us to reduce the drive. *Arousal theory:* People sometimes *seek* the pleasure and stimulation of arousal.

Module 40 Social Motivation: Affiliation Needs

How might the evolutionary perspective, drive-reduction theory, and arousal theory explain our affiliation needs?

Answer: *Evolutionary perspective:* Our ancestors hunted and survived threats as group-dwelling creatures, finding food and safety in numbers. As their descendants, we therefore are disposed to live in groups, connected to supportive others. *Drive-reduction theory:* Being threatened and afraid drives us to find safety in the company of others (thus reducing our aroused state). *Arousal theory:* We welcome optimal levels of arousal, and the presence of others is arousing.

Module 41 Theories and Physiology of Emotion

Christine is holding her 8-month-old baby when a fierce dog appears out of nowhere and, with teeth bared, leaps for the baby's face. Christine immediately ducks for cover to protect the baby, screams at the dog, then notices that her heart is banging in her chest and she's broken out in a cold sweat. How would the James-Lange, Cannon-Bard, and two-factor theories explain Christine's emotional reaction?

Answer: *James-Lange theory:* Christine's emotional reaction consists of her awareness of her physiological responses to the dog attack. *Cannon-Bard theory:* Christine's fear experience happened simultaneously with her physiological arousal. Schachter and Singer's *two-factor theory:* Christine's emotional reaction stemmed from her interpreting and labeling the arousal.

How do the two divisions of the autonomic nervous system affect our emotional responses?

Answer: The *sympathetic division* of the ANS arouses us for more intense experiences of emotion, pumping out the stress hormones epinephrine and norepinephrine to prepare our body for fight or flight. The *parasympathetic division* of the ANS takes over when a crisis passes, restoring our body to a calm physiological and emotional state.

Module 42 Expressed Emotion

Who tends to express more emotion—men or women? How do we know the answer to that question?

Answer: Women tend to surpass men not only as emotion detectors but also at expressing certain emotions (though men have slightly surpassed women in conveying anger). Researchers discovered this by showing people brief, silent clips of men's and women's faces expressing various emotions and by observing who is most skilled at reading and sending emotions.

Module 43 Stress and Health

What two processes happen simultaneously when our stress response system is activated? What happens if the stress is continuous?

Answer: When alerted to a negative, uncontrollable event, our sympathetic nervous system arouses us. Heart rate and respiration increase. Blood is diverted from digestion to the skeletal muscles. The body releases sugar and fat. All this prepares the body for the fight-or-flight-response.

Module 44 Stress and Illness

Which component of the Type A personality has been linked most closely to coronary heart disease?

Answer: Feeling angry and negative much of the time has been most closely tied to heart disease.

Unit IX
Developmental Psychology

Module 45 Developmental Issues, Prenatal Development, and the Newborn

What findings in psychology support the concept of stages in development and the idea of stability in personality across the life span? What findings challenge these ideas?

Answer: The idea of stages in development is supported by the work of Piaget (cognitive development), Kohlberg (moral development), and Erikson (psychosocial development), but it is challenged by findings that suggest change is more gradual and less culturally universal than these theorists supposed. Some personality traits, such as temperament, do exhibit remarkable stability across many years. But we do change in other ways, such as in our social attitudes, especially during life's early years.

Your friend's older sister—a regular drinker—hopes to become pregnant soon and has stopped drinking. Why is this a good idea? What negative effects might alcohol consumed during pregnancy have on a developing fetus?

Answer: There is no known safe amount of alcohol during pregnancy, so your friend's older sister is wise to quit drinking before becoming pregnant. Harmful effects may occur even before a woman knows she is pregnant. If a woman drinks persistently and heavily during her pregnancy, the fetus will be at risk for severe physical and cognitive impairments (such as occurs with *fetal alcohol syndrome*).

Module 46 Infancy and Childhood: Physical Development

What is the biological growth process that explains why most children begin walking by about 12 to 15 months?

Answer: This process is called *maturation,* which enables orderly changes in behavior, relatively unchanged by experience.

Module 47 Infancy and Childhood: Cognitive Development

Use Piaget's first three stages of cognitive development to explain why children are not just miniature adults in the way they think.

Answer: Infants in the *sensorimotor stage* tend to be focused only on their own perceptions of the world and may, for example, be unaware that objects continue to exist when unseen. A *preoperational* child is still egocentric and incapable of appreciating simple logic, such as the reversibility of operations. A preteen in the *concrete operational stage* is beginning to think logically about concrete events but not about abstract concepts.

Module 48 Infancy and Childhood: Social Development

What distinguishes imprinting from attachment?

Answer: Attachment is the normal process by which we form emotional ties with important others. Imprinting occurs in certain animals that have a critical period very early in their development during which they must form their attachments, and they do so in an inflexible manner.

Module 49 Gender Development

What are gender roles, and what do their variations tell us about our human capacity for learning and adaptation?

Answer: *Gender roles* are sets of expected behaviors for females and for males. Gender roles vary widely in different cultures, which is proof that we are very capable of learning and adapting to the social demands of different environments.

Module 50 Parents, Peers, and Early Experiences

To predict whether a teenager smokes, ask how many of the teen's friends smoke. One explanation for this correlation is peer influence. What's another?

Answer: There may also be a *selection effect.* Adolescents tend to select similar others and sort themselves into like-minded groups—the jocks, the geeks, the druggies, and so forth. Those who smoke may similarly seek out other teenagers who also smoke.

Module 51 Adolescence: Physical and Cognitive Development

Describe Kohlberg's three levels of moral reasoning.

Answer: Preconventional morality focuses on upholding laws and social rules, conventional morality focuses on self-interest, and postconventional morality focuses on self-defined ethical principles.

Module 52 Adolescence: Social Development and Emerging Adulthood

How has the transition from childhood to adulthood changed in Western cultures in the last century or so?

Answer: In little more than a century, the gap between puberty and adult independence has widened from about 7 years to about 12 years. This longer adolescence gives us a chance to grow up a bit more before facing the "real world," but it also comes with its share of stressors, as sexually mature teens must wait many years before achieving true independence. In Western nations, this has led to a postadolescent, not-yet-settled phase of life known as *emerging adulthood.*

Module 53 Sexual Development

What factors have been found to predict sexual restraint among teens?

Answer: Teen sexual restraint is found more often among teens with high intelligence, religious engagement, family environments with a father presence, and among those who participate in service learning programs.

Module 54 Adulthood: Physical, Cognitive, and Social Development

Research has shown that living together before marriage predicts an increased likelihood of future divorce. Can you imagine two possible explanations for this correlation?

Answer: William Axinn and Arland Thornton (1992) have reported data supporting two explanations. (1) The first explanation is an example of a *selection effect*—our tendency to seek out others who are similar to us. Cohabitation attracts people who are more open to terminating unsatisfying relationships. People who cohabit bring a more individualistic ethic to marriage, are more likely to see close relationships as temporary and fragile, are more accepting of divorce, and are about three times more likely after marriage to have an affair (Forste & Tanfer, 1996). (2) Axinn and Thornton's second explanation illustrates the *causal effect* of the experience of cohabitation. Over time, those who cohabit tend to become more approving of dissolving an unfulfilling union. This divorce-accepting attitude increases the odds of later divorce.

Unit X
Personality

Module 55 Freud's Psychoanalytic Perspective: Exploring the Unconscious

How does today's psychological science assess Freud's theory?

Answer: It was Freud who drew our attention to the unconscious and the irrational, to our self-protective defenses, to the importance of human sexuality, and to the tension between our biological impulses and our social well-being. But both Freud's admirers and his critics agree that recent research contradicts many of his specific ideas. It does not support *repression* or Freud's view of the unconscious (but instead views the unconscious as part of our two-track mind). Other modern research has led today's psychologists to see our development as lifelong, not fixed in childhood, and dreams and slips of the tongue not to illustrate urges and conflicts as Freud believed. It's also important to recognize, from a psychological science perspective, that Freudian theory does not enable predictions, and it tends to explain things after the fact.

Module 56 Psychodynamic Theories and Modern Views of the Unconscious

What methods have been used by psychodynamic clinicians to assess unconscious processes?

Answer: Projective tests, such as the *Thematic Apperception Test (TAT)* and the *Rorschach inkblot test,* are personality assessment tools psychodynamic clinicians have used with the aim of assessing unconscious processes. Critics say that projective tests such as the Rorschach have little validity and are not reliable.

Module 57 Humanistic Theories

What does it mean to be "empathic"? To be "self-actualized"?

Answer: To be *empathic* is to share and mirror another person's feelings. Carl Rogers believed that people nurture growth in others by being empathic. Abraham Maslow viewed *self-actualization*—the motivation to fulfill one's potential—as one of the ultimate psychological needs that arises after our physical needs are met. (The other ultimate psychological need is *self-transcendence*—meaning, purpose, and communion beyond the self.)

Module 58 Trait Theories

What is the person-situation controversy?

Answer: The *person-situation controversy* is the question of whether personality traits are consistent over time and across situations. Traits do tend to be consistent, though specific behaviors may vary with time and place.

Module 59 Social-Cognitive Theories and Exploring the Self

What do social-cognitive psychologists consider the best way to predict a person's future behavior?

Answer: Examining a person's past behavior patterns in similar situations is the best way to predict that person's future behavior.

In a 1997 Gallup poll, White Americans estimated 44 percent of their fellow White Americans to be high in prejudice (scoring them 5 or higher on a 10-point scale). How many rated themselves similarly high in prejudice? Just 14 percent. What phenomenon does this illustrate?

Answer: This illustrates the general tendency to see ourselves as superior to the average other, which is an example of *self-serving bias.*

How do individualist and collectivist cultures differ?

Answer: A culture that favors *individualism* gives priority to personal goals over group goals; people in that culture will tend to define their identity in terms of their own personal attributes. A culture that favors *collectivism* gives priority to group goals over individual goals; people in collectivist cultures tend to define their identity in terms of group identifications. Cultures vary in the extent to which they favor individualism or collectivism.

Unit XI

Testing and Individual Differences

Module 60 Introduction to Intelligence

Joseph, a Harvard Law School student, has a straight-A average, writes for the *Harvard Law Review*, and will clerk for a Supreme Court justice next year. His grandmother, Judith, is very proud of him, saying that he is way more intelligent than she ever was. But Joseph is also very proud of Judith: As a young woman, she was imprisoned by the Nazis. When the war ended, she walked out of Germany, contacted an agency helping refugees, and began a new life in the United States as an assistant chef in her cousin's restaurant. According to the definition of *intelligence* in this module, is Joseph the only intelligent person in this story? Why or why not?

Answer: Joseph is not the only intelligent person in this story. *Intelligence* is the ability to learn from experience, solve problems, and use knowledge to adapt to new situations. Judith certainly demonstrates this quality as well, given all that she has accomplished.

Module 61 Assessing Intelligence

What was the purpose of Binet's pioneering intelligence test?

Answer: Binet's original test and those built upon it were designed to predict school achievement. Binet hoped that by determining a child's *mental age*, or the age that typically corresponds to level of performance, he could help children be placed appropriately in school classrooms with others of similar abilities.

Module 62 The Dynamics of Intelligence

The Smiths have enrolled their 2-year-old son in a special program that promises to assess his IQ and, if he places in the top 5 percent of test-takers, to create a plan that will guarantee his admission to a top university at age 18. Why is this endeavor of questionable value?

Answer: This is a waste of money at best. First, IQ tests given before age 3 are only modestly reliable predictors of adult intelligence. Second, admission to a top university depends on more than simple IQ. Third, there are no known training programs that could guarantee this result. The Smiths would do better to read to their child, which predicts early reading and love of reading.

Module 63 Studying Genetic and Environmental Influences on Intelligence

As society succeeds in creating equality of opportunity, it will also increase the heritability of ability. The heritability of intelligence scores will be greater in a society marked by equal opportunity than in a society of peasants and aristocrats. Why?

Answer: Perfect environmental equality would create 100 percent heritability—because genes alone would account for any remaining human differences.

Module 64 Group Differences and the Question of Bias

What is the difference between a test that is biased culturally, and a test that is biased in terms of its validity?

Answer: A test may be *culturally* biased if higher scores are achieved by those with certain cultural experiences. That same test may not be biased in terms of *validity* if it predicts what it is supposed to predict. For example, the SAT® may be culturally biased in favor of those with experience in the U.S. school system, but it does still accurately predict U.S. college success.

Unit XII

Abnormal Behavior

Module 65 Introduction to Psychological Disorders

What is the biopsychosocial approach, and why is it important in our understanding of psychological disorders?

Answer: Biological, psychological, and social-cultural influences combine to produce psychological disorders. This broad perspective helps us understand that our well-being is affected by our genes, brain functioning, inner thoughts and feelings, and the influence of our social and cultural environment.

Module 66 Anxiety Disorders, Obsessive-Compulsive Disorder, and Posttraumatic Stress Disorder

How do generalized anxiety disorder, panic disorder, phobias, obsessive-compulsive disorder, and posttraumatic stress disorder differ?

Answer: *Generalized anxiety disorder* is unfocused tension, apprehension, and arousal. *Panic disorder* is marked by unpredictable periods of terror and intense dread accompanied by frightening physical sensations. Those with *phobias* focus anxiety on specific feared objects or situations. People suffering *obsessive-compulsive disorder* express anxiety through unwanted repetitive thoughts (obsessions) or actions (compulsions). In *posttraumatic stress disorder (PTSD)*, anxiety may be accompanied by recurring memories and nightmares, social withdrawal, and insomnia for periods of four or more weeks after a traumatic event.

Module 67 Mood Disorders

What is the most common psychological disorder? What is the disorder for which people most often seek treatment?

Answer: Phobias are the most common psychological disorders, but the disorder for which people most often seek treatment is depression.

Module 68 Schizophrenia

How do researchers believe that biological and environmental factors interact in the onset of schizophrenia?

Answer: *Schizophrenia* has powerful biological roots, as evidenced by findings that those suffering from schizophrenia have increased receptors for the neurotransmitter dopamine (which may intensify the positive symptoms of schizophrenia); abnormal activity in the frontal lobes, thalamus, and amygdala; and such brain abnormalities as fluid-filled cerebral cavities. Malfunctions in multiple brain regions and their connections apparently interact to produce the symptoms of schizophrenia. Yet environment must play some role, because identical twins don't always share the expression of this disorder, and there is increasing evidence that a virus suffered by the mother during midpregnancy can contribute to that baby's later developing schizophrenia.

Module 69 Other Disorders

What does *somatic* mean?

Answer: Somatic symptoms are bodily symptoms. A *somatic disorder* is one in which symptoms take a somatic (bodily) form without apparent physical cause.

The psychodynamic and learning perspectives agree that dissociative identity disorder symptoms are ways of dealing with anxiety. How do their explanations differ?

Answer: The psychodynamic explanation of DID symptoms is that they are defenses against anxiety generated by unacceptable urges. The learning perspective attempts to explain these symptoms as behaviors that have been reinforced by relieving anxiety in the past. Others attempt to explain DID symptoms as detachment resulting from horrific experiences, such as childhood abuse.

What contribution do genes make to the development of antisocial personality disorder?

Answer: *Antisocial personality disorder*—in which a person exhibits a lack of conscience for wrongdoing—seems to have a strong genetic component. Twin and adoption studies show that biological relatives of people with this disorder are at increased risk for antisocial behavior. But the tendency to be fearless, when combined with a sense of social responsibility, can lead to heroism, adventurism, or athletic success. Genetic predispositions may interact with the environment to produce the altered brain activity associated with antisocial personality disorder.

Unit XIII
Treatment of Abnormal Behavior

Module 70 Introduction to Therapy, and Psychodynamic and Humanistic Therapies

In psychoanalysis, what does it mean when we refer to transference, resistance, and interpretation?

Answer: In psychoanalysis, patients may experience strong feelings for their analyst, which is called *transference*. Patients are said to demonstrate anxiety when they put up mental blocks around sensitive memories—showing *resistance*. The analyst will attempt to offer insight into the underlying anxiety by offering an *interpretation* of the mental blocks.

Module 71 Behavior, Cognitive, and Group Therapies

What is the major distinction between the underlying assumptions in insight therapies and in behavior therapies?

Answer: The *insight therapies*—psychodynamic and humanistic therapies—seek to relieve problems by providing an understanding of their origins. *Behavior therapies* assume the problem behavior *is* the problem and treat it directly, paying less attention to its origins.

Module 72 Evaluating Psychotherapies and Prevention Strategies

What is the difference between preventive mental health and psychological or biomedical therapy?

Answer: Psychological and biomedical therapies attempt to relieve people's suffering from psychological disorders. Preventive mental health attempts to prevent suffering by identifying and eliminating the conditions that cause disorders, and by building individuals' *resilience*.

Module 73 The Biomedical Therapies

How do researchers evaluate the effectiveness of particular drug therapies?

Answer: Ideally, researchers assign people to treatment and no-treatment conditions to see if those who receive the drug therapy improve more than those who don't. Double-blind controlled studies are most effective. If neither the therapist nor the client knows which participants have received the drug treatment, then any difference between the treated and untreated groups will reflect the treatment's actual effect.

Unit XIV
Social Psychology

Module 74 Attribution, Attitudes, and Actions

Driving to school one snowy day, Marco narrowly misses a car that slides through a red light. "Slow down! What a terrible driver," he thinks to himself. Moments later, Marco himself slides through an intersection and yelps, "Wow! These roads are awful. The city plows need to get out here." What social psychology principle has Marco just demonstrated? Explain.

Answer: By attributing the other person's behavior to the person ("What a terrible driver.") and his own, similar behavior to the situation ("These roads are awful."), Marco has exhibited the *fundamental attribution error.*

Module 75 Conformity and Obedience

What types of situations have researchers found to be most likely to encourage obedience in participants?

Answer: The Milgram studies showed that people were most likely to follow orders when the experimenter was nearby and was a legitimate authority figure, the victim was not nearby, and there were no models for defiance.

Module 76 Group Behavior

You are organizing a Town Hall–style meeting of fiercely competitive political candidates. To add to the fun, friends have suggested handing out masks of the candidates' faces for supporters to wear. What phenomenon might these masks engage?

Answer: The anonymity provided by the masks, combined with the arousal of the contentious setting, might create *deindividuation* (lessened self-awareness and self-restraint).

Module 77 Prejudice and Discrimination

What is the difference between prejudice and discrimination?

Answer: Prejudice is an unjustifiable and usually negative *attitude* toward a group and its members, while unjustifiable negative *behavior* is discrimination.

Module 78 Aggression

What psychological, biological, and social-cultural influences interact to produce aggressive behaviors?

Answer: Our biology (our genes, neural systems, and biochemistry—including testosterone and alcohol levels) influences our tendencies to be aggressive. Psychological factors (such as frustration, previous rewards for aggressive acts, and observation of others' aggression) can trigger any aggressive tendencies we may have. Social influences, such as exposure to violent media, and cultural influences, such as whether we've grown up in a "culture of honor" or had a father-absent home, can also affect our aggressive responses.

Module 79 Attraction

How does being physically attractive influence others' perceptions?

Answer: Being physically attractive tends to elicit positive first impressions. People tend to assume that attractive people are healthier, happier, and more socially skilled than others are.

Module 80 Altruism, Conflict, and Peacemaking

Why didn't anybody help Kitty Genovese? What social relations principle did this incident illustrate?

Answer: In the presence of others, an individual is less likely to notice a situation, correctly interpret it as an emergency, and then take responsibility for offering help. The Kitty Genovese case demonstrated this *bystander effect,* as each witness assumed many others were also aware of the event.

Enrichment Modules

Module 81 Influences on Drug Use

Studies have found that people who begin drinking in their early teens are much more likely to exhibit alcohol use disorder than those who begin at age 21 or after. What possible explanations might there be for this correlation between early use and later abuse?

Answer: Possible explanations include (a) a biological predisposition to both early use and later abuse, (b) brain changes and taste preferences induced by early use, and (c) enduring habits, attitudes, activities, or peer relationships that foster alcohol misuse.

Module 82 Psychology at Work

A human resources director explains to you that "I don't bother with tests or references. It's all about the interview." Based on I/O psychology research, what concerns does this raise?

Answer: (1) Interviewers may presume people are what they seem to be in interviews. (2) Interviewers' preconceptions and moods color how they perceive interviewees' responses. (3) Interviewers tend to track the successful careers of those they hire, not the successful careers of those they reject. (4) Interviews tend to disclose prospective workers' good intentions, not their habitual behaviors.

What are the two basic types of leadership, and how do the most effective managers employ these leadership strategies?

Answer: *Task leadership* is goal-oriented. Managers using this style set standards, organize work, and focus attention on goals. *Social leadership* is group-oriented. Managers using this style build teamwork, mediate conflict, and offer support. Research indicates that effective managers exhibit both task and social leadership, depending on the situation and the person.

One of the ways human factors psychologists seek to reduce users' frustration and to improve safety is by watching out for the *curse of knowledge.* What exactly is this tendency?

Answer: The *curse of knowledge* is the tendency for engineers and other designers to assume falsely that others share their knowledge—that what's clear to them will be similarly clear to others.

Module 83 Experienced Emotion: Anger and Happiness

What things do (and do not) predict self-reported happiness?

Answer: People's age, sex, and income give only modest clues to their happiness. Their personality traits, close relationships, "flow" in work and leisure, and religious faith do provide clues.

Module 84 Human Flourishing

Those who frequently attend religious services live longer, on average, than those who attend infrequently or not at all. What type of research finding is this, and what explanations might it have?

Answer: This is a correlational finding—frequent attendance at religious services is associated with (and predicts) health and longevity. But this is not a cause-effect statement. Longevity may be associated with religiosity because women (who tend to live longer than men) attend services more regularly, or because people in poor health are not able to attend services. But even controlling for these factors, the relationship remains, which indicates that the connection could reflect the healthy behaviors, stress-reducing social support, relaxed meditative state, optimistic outlook, and enhanced well-being often experienced by religiously active people.

Module 85 Animal Thinking and Language

If your dog barks at a stranger at the front door, does this qualify as language? What if the dog yips in a telltale way to let you know she needs to go out?

Answer: These are definitely communications. But if language consists of words and the grammatical rules we use to combine them to communicate meaning, few scientists would label a dog's barking and yipping as language.

Glossary

absolute threshold the minimum stimulation needed to detect a particular stimulus 50 percent of the time. (p. 156)

accommodation (1) in sensation and perception, the process by which the eye's lens changes shape to focus near or far objects on the retina. (p. 172) (2) in developmental psychology, adapting our current understandings (schemas) to incorporate new information. (p. 477)

achievement motivation a desire for significant accomplishment; for mastery of skills or ideas; for control; and for attaining a high standard. (p. 834)

achievement test a test designed to assess what a person has learned. (p. 619)

acquisition in classical conditioning, the initial stage, when one links a neutral stimulus and an unconditioned stimulus so that the neutral stimulus begins triggering the conditioned response. In operant conditioning, the strengthening of a reinforced response. (p. 268)

action potential a neural impulse; a brief electrical charge that travels down an axon. (p. 78)

active listening empathic listening in which the listener echoes, restates, and clarifies. A feature of Rogers' client-centered therapy. (p. 712)

adaptation-level phenomenon our tendency to form judgments (of sounds, of lights, of income) relative to a neutral level defined by our prior experience. (p. 851)

addiction compulsive craving of drugs or certain behaviors (such as gambling) despite known adverse consequences. (p. 247)

adolescence the transition period from childhood to adulthood, extending from puberty to independence. (p. 513)

adrenal [ah-DREEN-el] **glands** a pair of endocrine glands that sit just above the kidneys and secrete hormones (epinephrine and norepinephrine) that help arouse the body in times of stress. (p. 91)

aerobic exercise sustained exercise that increases heart and lung fitness; may also alleviate depression and anxiety. (p. 859)

aggression any physical or verbal behavior intended to hurt or destroy. (pp. 501, 789)

agonist a molecule that, by binding to a receptor site, stimulates a response. (p. 82)

agoraphobia fear or avoidance of situations, such as crowds or wide-open places, where one has felt loss of control and panic. (p. 663)

AIDS (acquired immune deficiency syndrome) a life-threatening, sexually transmitted infection caused by the *human immunodeficiency virus* (HIV). AIDS depletes the immune system, leaving the person vulnerable to infections. (p. 529)

alcohol use disorder (popularly known as *alcoholism*). Alcohol use marked by tolerance, withdrawal, and a drive to continue problematic use. (p. 249)

algorithm a methodical, logical rule or procedure that guarantees solving a particular problem. Contrasts with the usually speedier—but also more error-prone—use of *heuristics*. (p. 361)

all-or-none response a neuron's reaction of either firing (with a full-strength response) or not firing. (p. 80)

alpha waves the relatively slow brain waves of a relaxed, awake state. (p. 227)

altruism unselfish regard for the welfare of others. (p. 807)

amphetamines drugs that stimulate neural activity, causing speeded-up body functions and associated energy and mood changes. (p. 250)

amygdala [uh-MIG-duh-la] two lima-bean-sized neural clusters in the limbic system; linked to emotion. (p. 99)

anorexia nervosa an eating disorder in which a person (usually an adolescent female) maintains a starvation diet despite being significantly (15 percent or more) underweight. (p. 697)

antagonist a molecule that, by binding to a receptor site, inhibits or blocks a response. (pp. 83, 342)

anterograde amnesia an inability to form new memories. (p. 342)

antianxiety drugs drugs used to control anxiety and agitation. (p. 741)

antidepressant drugs drugs used to treat depression, anxiety disorders, obsessive-compulsive disorder, and posttraumatic stress disorder. (Several widely used antidepressant drugs are *selective serotonin reuptake inhibitors—SSRIs*.) (p. 741)

antipsychotic drugs drugs used to treat schizophrenia and other forms of severe thought disorder. (p. 741)

antisocial personality disorder a personality disorder in which a person (usually a man) exhibits a lack of conscience for wrongdoing, even toward friends and family members. May be aggressive and ruthless or a clever con artist. (p. 699)

anxiety disorders psychological disorders characterized by distressing, persistent anxiety or maladaptive behaviors that reduce anxiety. (p. 661)

aphasia impairment of language, usually caused by left-hemisphere damage either to Broca's area (impairing speaking) or to Wernicke's area (impairing understanding). (p. 377)

applied research scientific study that aims to solve practical problems. (p. 14)

aptitude test a test designed to predict a person's future performance; aptitude is the capacity to learn. (p. 619)

assimilation interpreting our new experiences in terms of our existing schemas. (p. 477)

association areas areas of the cerebral cortex that are not involved in primary motor or sensory functions; rather, they are involved in higher mental functions such as learning, remembering, thinking, and speaking. (p. 109)

associative learning learning that certain events occur together. The events may be two stimuli (as in classical conditioning) or a response and its consequences (as in operant conditioning). (p. 264)

attachment an emotional tie with another person; shown in young children by their seeking closeness to the caregiver and showing distress on separation. (p. 488)

attention-deficit/hyperactivity disorder (ADHD) a psychological disorder marked by the appearance by age 7 of one or more of three key symptoms: extreme inattention, hyperactivity, and impulsivity. (p. 652)

attitude feelings, often influenced by our beliefs, that predispose us to respond in a particular way to objects, people, and events. (p. 756)

attribution theory the theory that we explain someone's behavior by crediting either the situation or the person's disposition. (p. 754)

audition the sense or act of hearing. (p. 194)

autism spectrum disorder (ASD) a disorder that appears in childhood and is marked by significant deficiencies in communication and social interaction, and by rigidly fixated interests and repetitive behaviors. (p. 481)

automatic processing unconscious encoding of incidental information, such as space, time, and frequency, and of well-learned information, such as word meanings. (p. 320)

autonomic [aw-tuh-NAHM-ik] **nervous system (ANS)** the part of the peripheral nervous system that controls the glands and the muscles of the internal organs (such as the heart). Its sympathetic division arouses; its parasympathetic division calms. (p. 87)

availability heuristic estimating the likelihood of events based on their availability in memory; if instances come readily to mind (perhaps because of their vividness), we presume such events are common. (p. 364)

aversive conditioning a type of counterconditioning that associates an unpleasant state (such as nausea) with an unwanted behavior (such as drinking alcohol). (p. 718)

axon the neuron extension that passes messages through its branches to other neurons or to muscles or glands. (p. 78)

babbling stage beginning at about 4 months, the stage of speech development in which the infant spontaneously utters various sounds at first unrelated to the household language. (p. 374)

barbiturates drugs that depress central nervous system activity, reducing anxiety but impairing memory and judgment. (p. 250)

basal metabolic rate the body's resting rate of energy expenditure. (p. 398)

basic research pure science that aims to increase the scientific knowledge base. (p. 14)

basic trust according to Erik Erikson, a sense that the world is predictable and trustworthy; said to be formed during infancy by appropriate experiences with responsive caregivers. (p. 492)

behavior genetics the study of the relative power and limits of genetic and environmental influences on behavior. (p. 124)

behavior therapy therapy that applies learning principles to the elimination of unwanted behaviors. (p. 716)

behavioral approach in personality theory, this perspective focuses on the effects of learning on our personality development. (p. 587)

behavioral psychology the scientific study of observable behavior, and its explanation by principles of learning. (p. 12)

behaviorism the view that psychology (1) should be an objective science that (2) studies behavior without reference to mental processes. Most research psychologists today agree with (1) but not with (2). (pp. 6, 266)

belief perseverance clinging to one's initial conceptions after the basis on which they were formed has been discredited. (p. 367)

binge-eating disorder significant binge-eating episodes, followed by distress, disgust, or guilt, but without the compensatory purging or fasting that marks bulimia nervosa. (p. 697)

binocular cues depth cues, such as retinal disparity, that depend on the use of two eyes. (p. 184)

biofeedback a system for electronically recording, amplifying, and feeding back information regarding a subtle physiological state, such as blood pressure or muscle tension. (p. 289)

biological psychology the scientific study of the links between biological (genetic, neural, hormonal) and psychological processes. (Some biological psychologists call themselves *behavioral neuroscientists, neuropsychologists, behavior geneticists, physiological psychologists, or biopsychologists.*) (pp. 12, 77)

biomedical therapy prescribed medications or procedures that act directly on the person's physiology. (p. 709)

biopsychosocial approach an integrated approach that incorporates biological, psychological, and social-cultural levels of analysis. (p. 11)

bipolar disorder a mood disorder in which a person alternates between the hopelessness and lethargy of depression and the overexcited state of mania. (Formerly called *manic-depressive disorder.*) (p. 673)

blind spot the point at which the optic nerve leaves the eye, creating a "blind" spot because no receptor cells are located there. (p. 173)

bottom-up processing analysis that begins with the sensory receptors and works up to the brain's integration of sensory information. (p. 152)

brainstem the oldest part and central core of the brain, beginning where the spinal cord swells as it enters the skull; the brainstem is responsible for automatic survival functions. (p. 97)

Broca's area controls language expression—an area of the frontal lobe, usually in the left hemisphere, that directs the muscle movements involved in speech. (p. 377)

bulimia nervosa an eating disorder in which a person alternates binge eating (usually of high-calorie foods) with purging (by vomiting or laxative use) or fasting. (p. 697)

bystander effect the tendency for any given bystander to be less likely to give aid if other bystanders are present. (p. 808)

Cannon-Bard theory the theory that an emotion-arousing stimulus simultaneously triggers (1) physiological responses and (2) the subjective experience of emotion. (p. 422)

case study a descriptive technique in which one individual or group is studied in depth in the hope of revealing universal principles. (p. 40)

catharsis in psychology, the idea that "releasing" aggressive energy (through action or fantasy) relieves aggressive urges. (p. 846)

central nervous system (CNS) the brain and spinal cord. (p. 86)

central route persuasion occurs when interested people focus on the arguments and respond with favorable thoughts. (p. 756)

cerebellum [sehr-uh-BELL-um] the "little brain" at the rear of the brainstem; functions include processing sensory input, coordinating movement output and balance, and enabling nonverbal learning and memory. (p. 98)

cerebral [seh-REE-bruhl] **cortex** the intricate fabric of interconnected neural cells covering the cerebral hemispheres; the body's ultimate control and information-processing center. (p. 104)

change blindness failing to notice changes in the environment. (p. 154)

chromosomes threadlike structures made of DNA molecules that contain the genes. (p. 124)

chunking organizing items into familiar, manageable units; often occurs automatically. (p. 323)

circadian [ser-KAY-dee-an] **rhythm** the biological clock; regular bodily rhythms (for example, of temperature and wakefulness) that occur on a 24-hour cycle. (p. 226)

classical conditioning a type of learning in which one learns to link two or more stimuli and anticipate events. (p. 266)

client-centered therapy a humanistic therapy, developed by Carl Rogers, in which the therapist uses techniques such as active listening within a genuine, accepting, empathic environment to facilitate clients' growth. (Also called *person-centered therapy*.) (p. 712)

clinical psychology a branch of psychology that studies, assesses, and treats people with psychological disorders. (p. 14)

cocaine a powerful and addictive stimulant, derived from the coca plant, producing temporarily increased alertness and euphoria. (p. 252)

cochlea [KOHK-lee-uh] a coiled, bony, fluid-filled tube in the inner ear; sound waves traveling through the cochlear fluid trigger nerve impulses. (p. 195)

cochlear implant a device for converting sounds into electrical signals and stimulating the auditory nerve through electrodes threaded into the cochlea. (p. 198)

cognition all the mental activities associated with thinking, knowing, remembering, and communicating. (pp. 356, 476)

cognitive dissonance theory the theory that we act to reduce the discomfort (dissonance) we feel when two of our thoughts (cognitions) are inconsistent. For example, when we become aware that our attitudes and our actions clash, we can reduce the resulting dissonance by changing our attitudes. (p. 759)

cognitive learning the acquisition of mental information, whether by observing events, by watching others, or through language. (p. 265)

cognitive map a mental representation of the layout of one's environment. For example, after exploring a maze, rats act as if they have learned a cognitive map of it. (p. 297)

cognitive neuroscience the interdisciplinary study of the brain activity linked with cognition (including perception, thinking, memory, and language). (pp. 7, 119)

cognitive psychology the scientific study of all the mental activities associated with thinking, knowing, remembering, and communicating. (p. 12)

cognitive therapy therapy that teaches people new, more adaptive ways of thinking; based on the assumption that thoughts intervene between events and our emotional reactions. (p. 720)

cognitive-behavioral therapy (CBT) a popular integrative therapy that combines cognitive therapy (changing self-defeating thinking) with behavior therapy (changing behavior). (p. 723)

cohort a group of people from a given time period. (p. 625)

collective unconscious Carl Jung's concept of a shared, inherited reservoir of memory traces from our species' history. (p. 566)

collectivism giving priority to the goals of one's group (often one's extended family or work group) and defining one's identity accordingly. (p. 599)

color constancy perceiving familiar objects as having consistent color, even if changing illumination alters the wavelengths reflected by the object. (p. 187)

community psychology a branch of psychology that studies how people interact with their social environments and how social institutions affect individuals and groups. (p. 15)

companionate love the deep affectionate attachment we feel for those with whom our lives are intertwined. (p. 803)

complementary and alternative medicine (CAM) as yet unproven health care treatments intended to supplement (complement) or serve as alternatives to conventional medicine, and which typically are not widely taught in medical schools, used in hospitals, or reimbursed by insurance companies. When research shows a therapy to be safe and effective, it usually then becomes part of accepted medical practice. (p. 863)

concept a mental grouping of similar objects, events, ideas, or people. (p. 356)

concrete operational stage in Piaget's theory, the stage of cognitive development (from about 6 or 7 to 11 years of age) during which children gain the mental operations that enable them to think logically about concrete events. (p. 483)

conditioned reinforcer a stimulus that gains its reinforcing power through its association with a primary reinforcer; also known as a *secondary reinforcer*. (p. 278)

conditioned response (CR) in classical conditioning, a learned response to a previously neutral (but now conditioned) stimulus (CS). (p. 268)

conditioned stimulus (CS) in classical conditioning, an originally irrelevant stimulus that, after association with an unconditioned stimulus (US), comes to trigger a conditioned response (CR). (p. 268)

conduction hearing loss hearing loss caused by damage to the mechanical system that conducts sound waves to the cochlea. (p. 197)

cones retinal receptor cells that are concentrated near the center of the retina and that function in daylight or in well-lit conditions. The cones detect fine detail and give rise to color sensations. (p. 173)

confirmation bias a tendency to search for information that supports our preconceptions and to ignore or distort contradictory evidence. (p. 362)

conflict a perceived incompatibility of actions, goals, or ideas. (p. 810)

conformity adjusting our behavior or thinking to coincide with a group standard. (p. 763)

confounding variable a factor other than the independent variable that might produce an effect in an experiment. (p. 52)

consciousness our awareness of ourselves and our environment. (pp. 118, 219)

conservation the principle (which Piaget believed to be a part of concrete operational reasoning) that properties such as mass, volume, and number remain the same despite changes in the forms of objects. (p. 479)

content validity the extent to which a test samples the behavior that is of interest. (p. 622)

continuous reinforcement reinforcing the desired response every time it occurs. (p. 279)

control group in an experiment, the group *not* exposed to the treatment; contrasts with the experimental group and serves as a comparison for evaluating the effect of the treatment. (p. 51)

convergent thinking narrows the available problem solutions to determine the single best solution. (p. 357)

conversion disorder a disorder in which a person experiences very specific genuine physical symptoms for which no physiological basis can be found. (Also called *functional neurological symptom disorder*.) (p. 694)

coping alleviating stress using emotional, cognitive, or behavioral methods. (p. 298)

coronary heart disease the clogging of the vessels that nourish the heart muscle; the leading cause of death in many developed countries. (p. 451)

corpus callosum [KOR-pus kah-LOW-sum] the large band of neural fibers connecting the two brain hemispheres and carrying messages between them. (p. 114)

correlation a measure of the extent to which two variables change together, and thus of how well either variable predicts the other. (p. 46)

correlation coefficient a statistical index of the relationship between two variables (from −1 to +1). (p. 46)

counseling psychology a branch of psychology that assists people with problems in living (often related to school, work, or marriage) and in achieving greater well-being. (p. 14)

counterconditioning behavior therapy procedures that use classical conditioning to evoke new responses to stimuli that are triggering unwanted behaviors; include *exposure therapies* and *aversive conditioning*. (p. 717)

creativity the ability to produce novel and valuable ideas. (p. 357)

critical period an optimal period early in the life of an organism when exposure to certain stimuli or experiences produces normal development. (p. 489)

critical thinking thinking that does not blindly accept arguments and conclusions. Rather, it examines assumptions, assesses the source, discerns hidden values, evaluates evidence, and assesses conclusions. (p. 35)

cross-sectional study a study in which people of different ages are compared with one another. (p. 543)

crystallized intelligence our accumulated knowledge and verbal skills; tends to increase with age. (p. 626)

CT (computed tomography) scan a series of X-ray photographs taken from different angles and combined by computer into a composite representation of a slice of the brain's structure. (Also called *CAT scan*.) (p. 95)

culture the enduring behaviors, ideas, attitudes, values, and traditions shared by a group of people and transmitted from one generation to the next. (pp. 65, 776)

debriefing the postexperimental explanation of a study, including its purpose and any deceptions, to its participants. (p. 68)

deep processing encoding semantically, based on the meaning of the words; tends to yield the best retention. (p. 325)

defense mechanisms in psychoanalytic theory, the ego's protective methods of reducing anxiety by unconsciously distorting reality. (p. 560)

deindividuation the loss of self-awareness and self-restraint occurring in group situations that foster arousal and anonymity. (p. 773)

déjà vu that eerie sense that "I've experienced this before." Cues from the current situation may unconsciously trigger retrieval of an earlier experience. (p. 349)

delta waves the large, slow brain waves associated with deep sleep. (p. 228)

delusions false beliefs, often of persecution or grandeur, that may accompany psychotic disorders. (p. 684)

dendrites a neuron's bushy, branching extensions that receive messages and conduct impulses toward the cell body. (p. 78)

dependent variable the outcome factor; the variable that may change in response to manipulations of the independent variable. (p. 52)

depressants drugs (such as alcohol, barbiturates, and opiates) that reduce neural activity and slow body functions. (p. 248)

depth perception the ability to see objects in three dimensions although the images that strike the retina are two-dimensional; allows us to judge distance. (p. 184)

descriptive statistics numerical data used to measure and describe characteristics of groups. Includes measures of central tendency and measures of variation. (p. 57)

developmental psychology a branch of psychology that studies physical, cognitive, and social change throughout the life span. (pp. 14, 462)

difference threshold the minimum difference between two stimuli required for detection 50 percent of the time. We experience the difference threshold as a *just noticeable difference* (or *jnd*). (p. 158)

discrimination (1) in classical conditioning, the learned ability to distinguish between a conditioned stimulus and stimuli that do not signal an unconditioned stimulus. (p. 270) (2) in social psychology, unjustifiable negative *behavior* toward a group and its members. (p. 780)

discriminative stimulus in operant conditioning, a stimulus that elicits a response after association with reinforcement (in contrast to related stimuli not associated with reinforcement). (p. 277)

dissociation a split in consciousness, which allows some thoughts and behaviors to occur simultaneously with others. (p. 222)

dissociative disorders disorders in which conscious awareness becomes separated (dissociated) from previous memories, thoughts, and feelings. (p. 694)

dissociative identity disorder (DID) a rare dissociative disorder in which a person exhibits two or more distinct and alternating personalities. Formerly called *multiple personality disorder*. (p. 695)

divergent thinking expands the number of possible problem solutions (creative thinking that diverges in different directions). (p. 357)

DNA *(deoxyribonucleic acid)* a complex molecule containing the genetic information that makes up the chromosomes. (p. 124)

double-blind procedure an experimental procedure in which both the research participants and the research staff are ignorant (blind) about whether the research participants have received the treatment or a placebo. Commonly used in drug-evaluation studies. (p. 51)

Down syndrome a condition of mild to severe intellectual disability and associated physical disorders caused by an extra copy of chromosome 21. (p. 629)

dream a sequence of images, emotions, and thoughts passing through a sleeping person's mind. Dreams are notable for their hallucinatory imagery, discontinuities, and incongruities, and for the dreamer's delusional acceptance of the content and later difficulties remembering it. (p. 240)

drive-reduction theory the idea that a physiological need creates an aroused tension state (a drive) that motivates an organism to satisfy the need. (p. 391)

DSM-5 the American Psychiatric Association's *Diagnostic and Statistical Manual of Mental Disorders,* Fifth Edition; a widely used system for classifying psychological disorders. (p. 654)

dual processing the principle that information is often simultaneously processed on separate conscious and unconscious tracks. (p. 120)

echoic memory a momentary sensory memory of auditory stimuli; if attention is elsewhere, sounds and words can still be recalled within 3 or 4 seconds. (p. 322)

eclectic approach an approach to psychotherapy that, depending on the client's problems, uses techniques from various forms of therapy. (p. 709)

Ecstasy (MDMA) a synthetic stimulant and mild hallucinogen. Produces euphoria and social intimacy, but with short-term health risks and longer-term harm to serotonin-producing neurons and to mood and cognition. (p. 253)

educational psychology the study of how psychological processes affect and can enhance teaching and learning. (p. 14)

effortful processing encoding that requires attention and conscious effort. (p. 320)

ego the largely conscious, "executive" part of personality that, according to Freud, mediates among the demands of the id, superego, and reality. The ego operates on the *reality principle,* satisfying the id's desires in ways that will realistically bring pleasure rather than pain. (p. 558)

egocentrism in Piaget's theory, the preoperational child's difficulty taking another's point of view. (p. 479)

electroconvulsive therapy (ECT) a biomedical therapy for severely depressed patients in which a brief electric current is sent through the brain of an anesthetized patient. (p. 743)

electroencephalogram (EEG) an amplified recording of the waves of electrical activity sweeping across the brain's surface. These waves are measured by electrodes placed on the scalp. (p. 95)

embodied cognition in psychological science, the influence of bodily sensations, gestures, and other states on cognitive preferences and judgments. (p. 211)

embryo the developing human organism from about 2 weeks after fertilization through the second month. (p. 466)

emerging adulthood for some people in modern cultures, a period from the late teens to mid-twenties, bridging the gap between adolescent dependence and full independence and responsible adulthood. (p. 523)

emotion a response of the whole organism, involving (1) physiological arousal, (2) expressive behaviors, and (3) conscious experience. (p. 421)

emotional intelligence the ability to perceive, understand, manage, and use emotions. (p. 612)

emotion-focused coping attempting to alleviate stress by avoiding or ignoring a stressor and attending to emotional needs related to one's stress reaction. (p. 298)

empirically derived test a test (such as the MMPI) developed by testing a pool of items and then selecting those that discriminate between groups. (p. 578)

empiricism the view that knowledge originates in experience and that science should, therefore, rely on observation and experimentation. (p. 3)

encoding the processing of information into the memory system—for example, by extracting meaning. (p. 319)

endocrine [EN-duh-krin] **system** the body's "slow" chemical communication system; a set of glands that secrete hormones into the bloodstream. (p. 90)

endorphins [en-DOR-fins] "morphine within"—natural, opiate-like neurotransmitters linked to pain control and to pleasure. (p. 82)

environment every external influence, from prenatal nutrition to the people and things around us. (p. 124)

epigenetics the study of environmental influences on gene expression that occur without a DNA change. (p. 131)

equity a condition in which people receive from a relationship in proportion to what they give to it. (p. 804)

estrogens sex hormones, such as estradiol, secreted in greater amounts by females than by males and contributing to female sex characteristics. In nonhuman female mammals, estrogen levels peak during ovulation, promoting sexual receptivity. (p. 408)

evidence-based practice clinical decision making that integrates the best available research with clinical expertise and patient characteristics and preferences. (p. 732)

evolutionary psychology the study of the evolution of behavior and mind, using principles of natural selection. (pp. 12, 135)

experiment a research method in which an investigator manipulates one or more factors (independent variables) to observe the effect on some behavior or mental process (the dependent variable). By *random assignment* of participants, the experimenter aims to control other relevant variables. (p. 51)

experimental group in an experiment, the group exposed to the treatment, that is, to one version of the independent variable. (p. 51)

experimental psychology the study of behavior and thinking using the experimental method. (p. 5)

explicit memory memory of facts and experiences that one can consciously know and "declare." (Also called *declarative memory.*) (p. 320)

exposure therapies behavioral techniques, such as *systematic desensitization* and *virtual reality exposure therapy,* that treat anxieties by exposing people (in imagination or actual situations) to the things they fear and avoid. (p. 717)

external locus of control the perception that chance or outside forces beyond our personal control determine our fate. (p. 300)

extinction the diminishing of a conditioned response; occurs in classical conditioning when an unconditioned stimulus (US) does not follow a conditioned stimulus (CS); occurs in operant conditioning when a response is no longer reinforced. (p. 269)

extrasensory perception (ESP) the controversial claim that perception can occur apart from sensory input; includes telepathy, clairvoyance, and precognition. (p. 167)

extrinsic motivation a desire to perform a behavior to receive promised rewards or avoid threatened punishment. (p. 298)

facial feedback effect the tendency of facial muscle states to trigger corresponding feelings such as fear, anger, or happiness. (p. 438)

factor analysis a statistical procedure that identifies clusters of related items (called *factors*) on a test; used to identify different dimensions of performance that underlie a person's total score. (p. 608)

false consensus effect the tendency to overestimate the extent to which others share our beliefs and our behaviors. (p. 568)

family therapy therapy that treats the family as a system. Views an individual's unwanted behaviors as influenced by, or directed at, other family members. (p. 724)

feature detectors nerve cells in the brain that respond to specific features of the stimulus, such as shape, angle, or movement. (p. 175)

feel-good, do-good phenomenon people's tendency to be helpful when already in a good mood. (p. 847)

fetal alcohol syndrome (FAS) physical and cognitive abnormalities in children caused by a pregnant woman's heavy drinking. In severe cases, signs include a small, out-of-proportion head and abnormal facial features. (p. 467)

fetus the developing human organism from 9 weeks after conception to birth. (p. 466)

figure-ground the organization of the visual field into objects (the *figures*) that stand out from their surroundings (the *ground*). (p. 183)

fixation according to Freud, a lingering focus of pleasure-seeking energies at an earlier psychosexual stage, in which conflicts were unresolved. (p. 560)

fixed-interval schedule in operant conditioning, a reinforcement schedule that reinforces a response only after a specified time has elapsed. (p. 280)

fixed-ratio schedule in operant conditioning, a reinforcement schedule that reinforces a response only after a specified number of responses. (p. 279)

flashbulb memory a clear memory of an emotionally significant moment or event. (p. 332)

flow a completely involved, focused state of consciousness, with diminished awareness of self and time, resulting from optimal engagement of one's skills. (p. 827)

fluid intelligence our ability to reason speedily and abstractly; tends to decrease during late adulthood. (p. 626)

fMRI (functional MRI) a technique for revealing bloodflow and, therefore, brain activity by comparing successive MRI scans. fMRI scans show brain function as well as its structure. (p. 96)

foot-in-the-door phenomenon the tendency for people who have first agreed to a small request to comply later with a larger request. (p. 757)

formal operational stage in Piaget's theory, the stage of cognitive development (normally beginning about age 12) during which people begin to think logically about abstract concepts. (p. 483)

fovea the central focal point in the retina, around which the eye's cones cluster. (p. 173)

framing the way an issue is posed; how an issue is framed can significantly affect decisions and judgments. (p. 368)

fraternal twins (*dizygotic twins*) twins who develop from separate fertilized eggs. They are genetically no closer than brothers and sisters, but they share a fetal environment. (p. 125)

free association in psychoanalysis, a method of exploring the unconscious in which the person relaxes and says whatever comes to mind, no matter how trivial or embarrassing. (p. 557)

frequency the number of complete wavelengths that pass a point in a given time (for example, per second). (p. 195)

frequency theory in hearing, the theory that the rate of nerve impulses traveling up the auditory nerve matches the frequency of a tone, thus enabling us to sense its pitch. (p. 199)

frontal lobes portion of the cerebral cortex lying just behind the forehead; involved in speaking and muscle movements and in making plans and judgments. (p. 105)

frustration-aggression principle the principle that frustration—the blocking of an attempt to achieve some goal—creates anger, which can generate aggression. (p. 791)

functionalism early school of thought promoted by James and influenced by Darwin; explored how mental and behavioral processes function—how they enable the organism to adapt, survive, and flourish. (p. 4)

fundamental attribution error the tendency for observers, when analyzing others' behavior, to underestimate the impact of the situation and to overestimate the impact of personal disposition. (p. 754)

gate-control theory the theory that the spinal cord contains a neurological "gate" that blocks pain signals or allows them to pass on to the brain. The "gate" is opened by the activity of pain signals traveling up small nerve fibers and is closed by activity in larger fibers or by information coming from the brain. (p. 203)

gender the socially constructed roles and characteristics by which a culture defines *male* and *female*. (p. 500)

gender identity our sense of being male or female. (p. 504)

gender role a set of expected behaviors for males or for females. (p. 503)

gender typing the acquisition of a traditional masculine or feminine role. (p. 504)

general adaptation syndrome (GAS) Selye's concept of the body's adaptive response to stress in three phases—alarm, resistance, exhaustion. (p. 444)

general intelligence (*g*) a general intelligence factor that, according to Spearman and others, underlies specific mental abilities and is therefore measured by every task on an intelligence test. (p. 608)

generalization the tendency, once a response has been conditioned, for stimuli similar to the conditioned stimulus to elicit similar responses. (p. 269)

generalized anxiety disorder an anxiety disorder in which a person is continually tense, apprehensive, and in a state of autonomic nervous system arousal. (p. 662)

genes the biochemical units of heredity that make up the chromosomes; segments of DNA capable of synthesizing proteins. (p. 124)

genome the complete instructions for making an organism, consisting of all the genetic material in that organism's chromosomes. (p. 124)

gestalt an organized whole. Gestalt psychologists emphasized our tendency to integrate pieces of information into meaningful wholes. (p. 182)

glial cells (glia) cells in the nervous system that support, nourish, and protect neurons; they may also play a role in learning and thinking. (p. 104)

glucose the form of sugar that circulates in the blood and provides the major source of energy for body tissues. When its level is low, we feel hunger. (p. 397)

grammar in a language, a system of rules that enables us to communicate with and understand others. In a given language, *semantics* is the set of rules for deriving meaning from sounds, and *syntax* is the set of rules for combining words into grammatically sensible sentences. (p. 373)

GRIT *Graduated and Reciprocated Initiatives in Tension-Reduction*—a strategy designed to decrease international tensions. (p. 815)

grit in psychology, grit is passion and perseverance in the pursuit of long-term goals. (pp. 610, 834)

group polarization the enhancement of a group's prevailing inclinations through discussion within the group. (p. 774)

group therapy therapy conducted with groups rather than individuals, permitting therapeutic benefits from group interaction. (p. 723)

grouping the perceptual tendency to organize stimuli into coherent groups. (p. 183)

groupthink the mode of thinking that occurs when the desire for harmony in a decision-making group overrides a realistic appraisal of alternatives. (p. 775)

habituation decreasing responsiveness with repeated stimulation. As infants gain familiarity with repeated exposure to a visual stimulus, their interest wanes and they look away sooner. (pp. 264, 468)

hallucinations false sensory experiences, such as seeing something in the absence of an external visual stimulus. (pp. 228, 685)

hallucinogens psychedelic ("mind-manifesting") drugs, such as LSD, that distort perceptions and evoke sensory images in the absence of sensory input. (pp. 439, 856)

health psychology a subfield of psychology that provides psychology's contribution to behavioral medicine. (pp. 439, 856)

heritability the proportion of variation among individuals that we can attribute to genes. The heritability of a trait may vary, depending on the range of populations and environments studied. (pp. 129, 632)

heuristic a simple thinking strategy that often allows us to make judgments and solve problems efficiently; usually speedier but also more error-prone than *algorithms*. (p. 361)

hierarchy of needs Maslow's pyramid of human needs, beginning at the base with physiological needs that must first be satisfied before higher-level safety needs and then psychological needs become active. (p. 393)

higher-order conditioning a procedure in which the conditioned stimulus in one conditioning experience is paired with a new neutral stimulus, creating a second (often weaker) conditioned stimulus. For example, an animal that has learned that a tone predicts food might then learn that a light predicts the tone and begin responding to the light alone. (Also called *second-order conditioning.*) (p. 268)

hindsight bias the tendency to believe, after learning an outcome, that one would have foreseen it. (Also known as the *I-knew-it-all-along phenomenon.*) (p. 31)

histogram a bar graph depicting a frequency distribution. (p. 57)

hippocampus a neural center located in the limbic system; helps process explicit memories for storage. (p. 330)

homeostasis a tendency to maintain a balanced or constant internal state; the regulation of any aspect of body chemistry, such as blood glucose, around a particular level. (p. 391)

hormones chemical messengers that are manufactured by the endocrine glands, travel through the bloodstream, and affect other tissues. (p. 90)

hue the dimension of color that is determined by the wavelength of light; what we know as the color names *blue, green,* and so forth. (p. 172)

human factors psychology an I/O psychology subfield that explores how people and machines interact and how machines and physical environments can be made safe and easy to use. (pp. 14, 828)

humanistic psychology a historically significant perspective that emphasized the growth potential of healthy people. (p. 6)

humanistic theories view personality with a focus on the potential for healthy personal growth. (p. 571)

hypnosis a social interaction in which one person (the subject) responds to another person's (the hypnotist's) suggestion that certain perceptions, feelings, thoughts, or behaviors will spontaneously occur. (p. 219)

hypothalamus [hi-po-THAL-uh-muss] a neural structure lying below (*hypo*) the thalamus; it directs several maintenance activities (eating, drinking, body temperature), helps govern the endocrine system via the pituitary gland, and is linked to emotion and reward. (p. 99)

hypothesis a testable prediction, often implied by a theory. (p. 38)

iconic memory a momentary sensory memory of visual stimuli; a photographic or picture-image memory lasting no more than a few tenths of a second. (p. 322)

id a reservoir of unconscious psychic energy that, according to Freud, strives to satisfy basic sexual and aggressive drives. The id operates on the *pleasure principle,* demanding immediate gratification. (p. 558)

identical twins (*monozygotic twins*) twins who develop from a single fertilized egg that splits in two, creating two genetically identical organisms. (p. 125)

identification the process by which, according to Freud, children incorporate their parents' values into their developing superegos. (p. 559)

identity our sense of self; according to Erikson, the adolescent's task is to solidify a sense of self by testing and integrating various roles. (p. 519)

illness anxiety disorder a disorder in which a person interprets normal physical sensations as symptoms of a disease. (Formerly called *hypochondriasis.*) (p. 694)

illusory correlation the perception of a relationship where none exists. (p. 50)

implicit memory retention independent of conscious recollection. (Also called *nondeclarative memory.*) (p. 320)

imprinting the process by which certain animals form strong attachments during an early life critical period. (p. 489)

inattentional blindness failing to see visible objects when our attention is directed elsewhere. (p. 154)

incentive a positive or negative environmental stimulus that motivates behavior. (p. 392)

independent variable the experimental factor that is manipulated; the variable whose effect is being studied. (p. 52)

individualism giving priority to one's own goals over group goals and defining one's identity in terms of personal attributes rather than group identifications. (p. 598)

industrial-organizational (I/O) psychology the application of psychological concepts and methods to optimizing human behavior in workplaces. (pp. 14, 828)

inferential statistics numerical data that allow one to generalize—to infer from sample data the probability of something being true of a population. (p. 60)

informational social influence influence resulting from one's willingness to accept others' opinions about reality. (p. 764)

informed consent an ethical principle that research participants be told enough to enable them to choose whether they wish to participate. (p. 68)

ingroup "Us"—people with whom we share a common identity. (p. 784)

ingroup bias the tendency to favor our own group. (p. 784)

inner ear the innermost part of the ear, containing the cochlea, semicircular canals, and vestibular sacs. (p. 195)

insight a sudden realization of a problem's solution; contrasts with strategy-based solutions. (pp. 297, 361)

insight therapies a variety of therapies that aim to improve psychological functioning by increasing a person's awareness of underlying motives and defenses. (p. 711)

insomnia recurring problems in falling or staying asleep. (p. 238)

instinct a complex behavior that is rigidly patterned throughout a species and is unlearned. (p. 391)

intellectual disability a condition of limited mental ability, indicated by an intelligence score of 70 or below and difficulty in adapting to the demands of life. (Formerly referred to as *mental retardation.*) (p. 629)

intelligence mental quality consisting of the ability to learn from experience, solve problems, and use knowledge to adapt to new situations. (p. 607)

intelligence quotient (IQ) defined originally as the ratio of mental age *(ma)* to chronological age *(ca)* multiplied by 100 (thus, *IQ = ma/ca* × 100). On contemporary intelligence tests, the average performance for a given age is assigned a score of 100, with scores assigned to relative performance above or below average. (p. 618)

intelligence test a method for assessing an individual's mental aptitudes and comparing them with those of others, using numerical scores. (p. 607)

intensity the amount of energy in a light or sound wave, which we perceive as brightness or loudness, as determined by the wave's amplitude. (p. 172)

interaction the interplay that occurs when the effect of one factor (such as environment) depends on another factor (such as heredity). (p. 131)

internal locus of control the perception that you control your own fate. (p. 300)

interneurons neurons within the brain and spinal cord that communicate internally and intervene between the sensory inputs and motor outputs. (p. 87)

interpretation in psychoanalysis, the analyst's noting supposed dream meanings, resistances, and other significant behaviors and events in order to promote insight. (p. 710)

intimacy in Erikson's theory, the ability to form close, loving relationships; a primary developmental task in late adolescence and early adulthood. (p. 521)

intrinsic motivation a desire to perform a behavior effectively for its own sake. (p. 297)

intuition an effortless, immediate, automatic feeling or thought, as contrasted with explicit, conscious reasoning. (p. 363)

iris a ring of muscle tissue that forms the colored portion of the eye around the pupil and controls the size of the pupil opening. (p. 172)

James-Lange theory the theory that our experience of emotion is our awareness of our physiological responses to emotion-arousing stimuli. (p. 421)

just-world phenomenon the tendency for people to believe the world is just and that people therefore get what they deserve and deserve what they get. (p. 784)

kinesthesia [kin-ehs-THEE-see-a] the system for sensing the position and movement of individual body parts. (p. 209)

language our spoken, written, or signed words and the ways we combine them to communicate meaning. (p. 372)

latent content according to Freud, the underlying meaning of a dream (as distinct from its manifest content). (p. 241)

latent learning learning that occurs but is not apparent until there is an incentive to demonstrate it. (p. 297)

law of effect Thorndike's principle that behaviors followed by favorable consequences become more likely, and that behaviors followed by unfavorable consequences become less likely. (p. 275)

learned helplessness the hopelessness and passive resignation an animal or human learns when unable to avoid repeated aversive events. (p. 299)

learning the process of acquiring new and relatively enduring information or behaviors. (p. 263)

lens the transparent structure behind the pupil that changes shape to help focus images on the retina. (p. 172)

lesion [LEE-zhuhn] tissue destruction. A brain lesion is a naturally or experimentally caused destruction of brain tissue. (p. 94)

levels of analysis the differing complementary views, from biological to psychological to social-cultural, for analyzing any given phenomenon. (p. 11)

limbic system neural system (including the *hippocampus, amygdala,* and *hypothalamus*) located below the cerebral hemispheres; associated with emotions and drives. (p. 98)

linguistic determinism Whorf's hypothesis that language determines the way we think. (p. 379)

lobotomy a psychosurgical procedure once used to calm uncontrollably emotional or violent patients. The procedure cut the nerves connecting the frontal lobes to the emotion-controlling centers of the inner brain. (p. 746)

longitudinal study research in which the same people are restudied and retested over a long period. (p. 543)

long-term memory the relatively permanent and limitless storehouse of the memory system. Includes knowledge, skills, and experiences. (p. 319)

long-term potentiation (LTP) an increase in a cell's firing potential after brief, rapid stimulation. Believed to be a neural basis for learning and memory. (p. 333)

LSD a powerful hallucinogenic drug; also known as acid (*lysergic acid diethylamide*). (p. 254)

lymphocytes the two types of white blood cells that are part of the body's immune system: *B lymphocytes* form in the bone marrow and release antibodies that fight bacterial infections; *T lymphocytes* form in the thymus and other lymphatic tissue and attack cancer cells, viruses, and foreign substances. (p. 448)

major depressive disorder a mood disorder in which a person experiences, in the absence of drugs or another medical condition, two or more weeks with five or more symptoms, at least one of which must be either (1) depressed mood or (2) loss of interest or pleasure. (p. 672)

mania a mood disorder marked by a hyperactive, wildly optimistic state. (p. 673)

manifest content according to Freud, the remembered story line of a dream (as distinct from its latent, or hidden, content). (p. 241)

maturation biological growth processes that enable orderly changes in behavior, relatively uninfluenced by experience. (p. 471)

mean the arithmetic average of a distribution, obtained by adding the scores and then dividing by the number of scores. (p. 57)

median the middle score in a distribution; half the scores are above it and half are below it. (p. 57)

medical model the concept that diseases, in this case psychological disorders, have physical causes that can be *diagnosed, treated*, and, in most cases, *cured*, often through treatment in a *hospital*. (p. 653)

medulla [muh-DUL-uh] the base of the brainstem; controls heartbeat and breathing. (p. 97)

memory the persistence of learning over time through the encoding, storage, and retrieval of information. (p. 318)

menarche [meh-NAR-key] the first menstrual period. (p. 527)

menopause the time of natural cessation of menstruation; also refers to the biological changes a woman experiences as her ability to reproduce declines. (p. 540)

mental age a measure of intelligence test performance devised by Binet; the chronological age that most typically corresponds to a given level of performance. Thus, a child who does as well as the average 8-year-old is said to have a mental age of 8. (p. 618)

mental set a tendency to approach a problem in one particular way, often a way that has been successful in the past. (p. 362)

mere exposure effect the phenomenon that repeated exposure to novel stimuli increases liking of them. (p. 798)

meta-analysis a procedure for statistically combining the results of many different research studies. (p. 731)

methamphetamine a powerfully addictive drug that stimulates the central nervous system, with speeded-up body functions and associated energy and mood changes; over time, appears to reduce baseline dopamine levels. (p. 253)

middle ear the chamber between the eardrum and cochlea containing three tiny bones (hammer, anvil, and stirrup) that concentrate the vibrations of the eardrum on the cochlea's oval window. (p. 195)

Minnesota Multiphasic Personality Inventory (MMPI) the most widely researched and clinically used of all personality tests. Originally developed to identify emotional disorders (still considered its most appropriate use), this test is now used for many other screening purposes. (p. 578)

mirror neurons frontal lobe neurons that some scientists believe fire when performing certain actions or when observing another doing so. The brain's mirroring of another's action may enable imitation and empathy. (p. 304)

mirror-image perceptions mutual views often held by conflicting people, as when each side sees itself as ethical and peaceful and views the other side as evil and aggressive. (p. 812)

misinformation effect incorporating misleading information into one's memory of an event. (p. 347)

mnemonics [nih-MON-iks] memory aids, especially those techniques that use vivid imagery and organizational devices. (p. 323)

mode the most frequently occurring score(s) in a distribution. (p. 57)

modeling the process of observing and imitating a specific behavior. (p. 304)

molecular genetics the subfield of biology that studies the molecular structure and function of genes. (p. 129)

monocular cues depth cues, such as interposition and linear perspective, available to either eye alone. (p. 185)

mood disorders psychological disorders characterized by emotional extremes. See *major depressive disorder, mania,* and *bipolar disorder.* (p. 671)

mood-congruent memory the tendency to recall experiences that are consistent with one's current good or bad mood. (p. 337)

morpheme in a language, the smallest unit that carries meaning; may be a word or a part of a word (such as a prefix). (p. 373)

motivation a need or desire that energizes and directs behavior. (p. 390)

motor (efferent) neurons neurons that carry outgoing information from the brain and spinal cord to the muscles and glands. (p. 86)

motor cortex an area at the rear of the frontal lobes that controls voluntary movements. (p. 105)

MRI (magnetic resonance imaging) a technique that uses magnetic fields and radio waves to produce computer-generated images of soft tissue. MRI scans show brain anatomy. (p. 95)

mutation a random error in gene replication that leads to a change. (p. 136)

myelin [MY-uh-lin] **sheath** a fatty tissue layer segmentally encasing the axons of some neurons; enables vastly greater transmission speed as neural impulses hop from one node to the next. (p. 78)

narcissism excessive self-love and self-absorption. (p. 597)

narcolepsy a sleep disorder characterized by uncontrollable sleep attacks. The sufferer may lapse directly into REM sleep, often at inopportune times. (p. 238)

natural selection the principle that, among the range of inherited trait variations, those contributing to reproduction and survival will most likely be passed on to succeeding generations. (pp. 10, 135)

naturalistic observation observing and recording behavior in naturally occurring situations without trying to manipulate and control the situation. (p. 40)

nature–nurture issue the longstanding controversy over the relative contributions that genes and experience make to the development of psychological traits and behaviors. Today's science sees traits and behaviors arising from the interaction of nature and nurture. (p. 9)

near-death experience an altered state of consciousness reported after a close brush with death (such as through cardiac arrest); often similar to drug-induced hallucinations. (p. 255)

negative reinforcement increasing behaviors by stopping or reducing negative stimuli. A negative reinforcer is any stimulus that, when *removed* after a response, strengthens the response. (*Note:* Negative reinforcement is not punishment.) (p. 278)

nerves bundled axons that form neural "cables" connecting the central nervous system with muscles, glands, and sense organs. (p. 86)

nervous system the body's speedy, electrochemical communication network, consisting of all the nerve cells of the peripheral and central nervous systems. (p. 86)

neurogenesis the formation of new neurons. (p. 112)

neuron a nerve cell; the basic building block of the nervous system. (p. 78)

neurotransmitters chemical messengers that cross the synaptic gaps between neurons. When released by the sending neuron, neurotransmitters travel across the synapse and bind to receptor sites on the receiving neuron, thereby influencing whether that neuron will generate a neural impulse. (p. 80)

neutral stimulus (NS) in classical conditioning, a stimulus that elicits no response before conditioning. (p. 266)

nicotine a stimulating and highly addictive psychoactive drug in tobacco. (p. 250)

night terrors a sleep disorder characterized by high arousal and an appearance of being terrified; unlike nightmares, night terrors occur during NREM-3 sleep, within two or three hours of falling asleep, and are seldom remembered. (p. 239)

norm an understood rule for accepted and expected behavior. Norms prescribe "proper" behavior. (p. 777)

normal curve (*normal distribution*) a symmetrical, bell-shaped curve that describes the distribution of many types of data; most scores fall near the mean (about 68 percent fall within one standard deviation of it) and fewer and fewer near the extremes. (pp. 59, 621)

normative social influence influence resulting from a person's desire to gain approval or avoid disapproval. (p. 764)

NREM sleep nonrapid eye movement sleep; encompasses all sleep stages except for REM sleep. (p. 228)

object permanence the awareness that things continue to exist even when not perceived. (p. 478)

observational learning learning by observing others. (Also called *social learning.*) (p. 304)

obsessive-compulsive disorder (OCD) a disorder characterized by unwanted repetitive thoughts (obsessions) and/or actions (compulsions). (p. 663)

occipital [ahk-SIP-uh-tuhl] **lobes** portion of the cerebral cortex lying at the back of the head; includes areas that receive information from the visual fields. (p. 105)

Oedipus [ED-uh-puss] **complex** according to Freud, a boy's sexual desires toward his mother and feelings of jealousy and hatred for the rival father. (p. 559)

one-word stage the stage in speech development, from about age 1 to 2, during which a child speaks mostly in single words. (p. 375)

operant behavior behavior that operates on the environment, producing consequences. (p. 289)

operant chamber in operant conditioning research, a chamber (also known as a *Skinner box*) containing a bar or key that an animal can manipulate to obtain a food or water reinforcer; attached devices record the animal's rate of bar pressing or key pecking. (p. 276)

operant conditioning a type of learning in which behavior is strengthened if followed by a reinforcer or diminished if followed by a punisher. (p. 275)

operational definition a carefully worded statement of the exact procedures (operations) used in a research study. For example, *human intelligence* may be operationally defined as what an intelligence test measures. (p. 39)

opiates opium and its derivatives, such as morphine and heroin; they depress neural activity, temporarily lessening pain and anxiety. (p. 250)

opponent-process theory the theory that opposing retinal processes (red-green, yellow-blue, white-black) enable color vision. For example, some cells are stimulated by green and inhibited by red; others are stimulated by red and inhibited by green. (p. 179)

optic nerve the nerve that carries neural impulses from the eye to the brain. (p. 173)

organizational psychology an I/O psychology subfield that examines organizational influences on worker satisfaction and productivity and facilitates organizational change. (p. 828)

other-race effect the tendency to recall faces of one's own race more accurately than faces of other races. (Also called the *cross-race effect* and the *own-race bias.*) (p. 786)

outgroup "Them"—those perceived as different or apart from our ingroup. (p. 784)

overconfidence the tendency to be more confident than correct—to overestimate the accuracy of our beliefs and judgments. (p. 365)

panic disorder an anxiety disorder marked by unpredictable, minutes-long episodes of intense dread in which a person experiences terror and accompanying chest pain, choking, or other frightening sensations. Often followed by worry over a possible next attack. (p. 662)

parallel processing the processing of many aspects of a problem simultaneously; the brain's natural mode of information processing for many functions, including vision. Contrasts with the step-by-step (serial) processing of most computers and of conscious problem solving. (pp. 176, 319)

parapsychology the study of paranormal phenomena, including ESP and psychokinesis. (p. 167)

parasympathetic nervous system the division of the autonomic nervous system that calms the body, conserving its energy. (p. 87)

parietal [puh-RYE-uh-tuhl] **lobes** portion of the cerebral cortex lying at the top of the head and toward the rear; receives sensory input for touch and body position. (p. 105)

partial (intermittent) reinforcement reinforcing a response only part of the time; results in slower acquisition of a response but much greater resistance to extinction than does continuous reinforcement. (p. 279)

passionate love an aroused state of intense positive absorption in another, usually present at the beginning of a love relationship. (p. 803)

perception the process of organizing and interpreting sensory information, enabling us to recognize meaningful objects and events. (p. 152)

perceptual adaptation in vision, the ability to adjust to an artificially displaced or even inverted visual field. (p. 191)

perceptual constancy perceiving objects as unchanging (having consistent shapes, size, brightness, and color) even as illumination and retinal images change. (p. 186)

perceptual set a mental predisposition to perceive one thing and not another. (p. 163)

peripheral nervous system (PNS) the sensory and motor neurons that connect the central nervous system (CNS) to the rest of the body. (p. 86)

peripheral route persuasion occurs when people are influenced by incidental cues, such as a speaker's attractiveness. (p. 756)

personality an individual's characteristic pattern of thinking, feeling, and acting. (p. 555)

personality disorders psychological disorders characterized by inflexible and enduring behavior patterns that impair social functioning. (p. 698)

personality inventory a questionnaire (often with *true-false* or *agree-disagree* items) on which people respond to items designed to gauge a wide range of feelings and behaviors; used to assess selected personality traits. (p. 578)

personality psychology the study of an individual's characteristic pattern of thinking, feeling, and acting. (p. 14)

personnel psychology an I/O psychology subfield that focuses on employee recruitment, selection, placement, training, appraisal, and development. (p. 828)

PET (positron emission tomography) scan a visual display of brain activity that detects where a radioactive form of glucose goes while the brain performs a given task. (p. 95)

phi phenomenon an illusion of movement created when two or more adjacent lights blink on and off in quick succession. (p. 185)

phobia an anxiety disorder marked by a persistent, irrational fear and avoidance of a specific object, activity, or situation. (p. 662)

phoneme in a language, the smallest distinctive sound unit. (p. 373)

pitch a tone's experienced highness or lowness; depends on frequency. (p. 195)

pituitary gland the endocrine system's most influential gland. Under the influence of the hypothalamus, the pituitary regulates growth and controls other endocrine glands. (p. 91)

place theory in hearing, the theory that links the pitch we hear with the place where the cochlea's membrane is stimulated. (p. 199)

placebo [pluh-SEE-bo; Latin for "I shall please"] **effect** experimental results caused by expectations alone; any effect on behavior caused by the administration of an inert substance or condition, which the recipient assumes is an active agent. (p. 52)

plasticity the brain's ability to change, especially during childhood, by reorganizing after damage or by building new pathways based on experience. (p. 111)

polygraph a machine, commonly used in attempts to detect lies, that measures several of the physiological responses (such as perspiration and cardiovascular and breathing changes) accompanying emotion. (p. 428)

population all those in a group being studied, from which samples may be drawn. (*Note:* Except for national studies, this does *not* refer to a country's whole population.) (p. 43)

positive psychology the scientific study of human functioning, with the goals of discovering and promoting strengths and virtues that help individuals and communities to thrive. (pp. 15, 590)

positive reinforcement increasing behaviors by presenting positive reinforcers. A positive reinforcer is any stimulus that, when *presented* after a response, strengthens the response. (p. 277)

posthypnotic suggestion a suggestion, made during a hypnosis session, to be carried out after the subject is no longer hypnotized; used by some clinicians to help control undesired symptoms and behaviors. (p. 220)

posttraumatic growth positive psychological changes as a result of struggling with extremely challenging circumstances and life crises. (p. 665)

posttraumatic stress disorder (PTSD) a disorder characterized by haunting memories, nightmares, social withdrawal, jumpy anxiety, numbness of feeling, and/or insomnia that lingers for four weeks or more after a traumatic experience. (p. 664)

predictive validity the success with which a test predicts the behavior it is designed to predict; it is assessed by computing the correlation between test scores and the criterion behavior. (Also called *criterion-related validity*.) (pp. 345, 622)

prejudice an unjustifiable and usually negative *attitude* toward a group and its members. Prejudice generally involves stereotyped beliefs, negative feelings, and a predisposition to discriminatory action. (p. 780)

preoperational stage in Piaget's theory, the stage (from about 2 to about 6 or 7 years of age) during which a child learns to use language but does not yet comprehend the mental operations of concrete logic. (p. 479)

primary reinforcer an innately reinforcing stimulus, such as one that satisfies a biological need. (p. 278)

primary sex characteristics the body structures (ovaries, testes, and external genitalia) that make sexual reproduction possible. (p. 527)

priming the activation, often unconsciously, of certain associations, thus predisposing one's perception, memory, or response. (pp. 157, 336)

proactive interference the disruptive effect of prior learning on the recall of new information. (p. 345)

problem-focused coping attempting to alleviate stress directly—by changing the stressor or the way we interact with that stressor. (p. 298)

projective test a personality test, such as the Rorschach, that provides ambiguous stimuli designed to trigger projection of one's inner dynamics. (p. 567)

prosocial behavior positive, constructive, helpful behavior. The opposite of antisocial behavior. (p. 307)

prototype a mental image or best example of a category. Matching new items to a prototype provides a quick and easy method for sorting items into categories (as when comparing feathered creatures to a prototypical bird, such as a robin). (p. 356)

psychiatry a branch of medicine dealing with psychological disorders; practiced by physicians who sometimes provide medical (for example, drug) treatments as well as psychological therapy. (p. 15)

psychoactive drug a chemical substance that alters perceptions and moods. (p. 246)

psychoanalysis (1) Sigmund Freud's theory of personality that attributes thoughts and actions to unconscious motives and conflicts; the techniques used in treating psychological disorders by seeking to expose and interpret unconscious tensions. (p. 557) (2) Freud's therapeutic technique. Freud believed the patient's free associations, resistances, dreams, and transferences—and the therapist's interpretations of them—released previously repressed feelings, allowing the patient to gain self-insight. (p. 709)

psychodynamic psychology a branch of psychology that studies how unconscious drives and conflicts influence behavior, and uses that information to treat people with psychological disorders. (p. 12)

psychodynamic theories modern-day approaches that view personality with a focus on the unconscious and the importance of childhood experiences. (p. 565)

psychodynamic therapy therapy deriving from the psychoanalytic tradition that views individuals as responding to unconscious forces and childhood experiences, and that seeks to enhance self-insight. (p. 710)

psychological disorder a syndrome marked by a clinically significant disturbance in an individual's cognition, emotion regulation, or behavior. (Adapted from American Psychiatric Association, 2013.) (p. 651)

psychology the science of behavior and mental processes. (p. 7)

psychometrics the scientific study of the measurement of human abilities, attitudes, and traits. (p. 13)

psychoneuroimmunology the study of how psychological, neural, and endocrine processes together affect the immune system and resulting health. (p. 448)

psychopharmacology the study of the effects of drugs on mind and behavior. (p. 740)

psychophysics the study of relationships between the physical characteristics of stimuli, such as their intensity, and our psychological experience of them. (p. 155)

psychophysiological illness literally, "mind-body" illness; any stress-related physical illness, such as hypertension and some headaches. (p. 448)

psychosexual stages the childhood stages of development (oral, anal, phallic, latency, genital) during which, according to Freud, the id's pleasure-seeking energies focus on distinct erogenous zones. (p. 559)

psychosis a psychological disorder in which a person loses contact with reality, experiencing irrational ideas and distorted perceptions. (p. 684)

psychosurgery surgery that removes or destroys brain tissue in an effort to change behavior. (p. 746)

psychotherapy treatment involving psychological techniques; consists of interactions between a trained therapist and someone seeking to overcome psychological difficulties or achieve personal growth. (p. 709)

puberty the period of sexual maturation, during which a person becomes capable of reproducing. (p. 527)

punishment an event that tends to *decrease* the behavior that it follows. (p. 281)

pupil the adjustable opening in the center of the eye through which light enters. (p. 172)

random assignment assigning participants to experimental and control groups by chance, thus minimizing preexisting differences between the different groups. (p. 51)

random sample a sample that fairly represents a population because each member has an equal chance of inclusion. (p. 43)

range the difference between the highest and lowest scores in a distribution. (p. 58)

rational-emotive behavior therapy (REBT) a confrontational cognitive therapy, developed by Albert Ellis, that vigorously challenges people's illogical, self-defeating attitudes and assumptions. (p. 721)

recall a measure of memory in which the person must retrieve information learned earlier, as on a fill-in-the-blank test. (p. 334)

reciprocal determinism the interacting influences of behavior, internal cognition, and environment. (p. 588)

reciprocity norm an expectation that people will help, not hurt, those who have helped them. (p. 809)

recognition a measure of memory in which the person need only identify items previously learned, as on a multiple-choice test. (p. 334)

reflex a simple, automatic response to a sensory stimulus, such as the knee-jerk response. (p. 89)

refractory period (1) a period of inactivity after a neuron has fired. (p. 79) (2) a resting period after orgasm, during which a man cannot achieve another. (p. 407)

regression toward the mean the tendency for extreme or unusual scores to fall back (regress) toward their average. (p. 730)

reinforcement in operant conditioning, any event that *strengthens* the behavior it follows. (p. 276)

reinforcement schedule a pattern that defines how often a desired response will be reinforced. (p. 279)

relative deprivation the perception that we are worse off relative to those with whom we compare ourselves. (p. 851)

relearning a measure of memory that assesses the amount of time saved when learning material again. (p. 334)

reliability the extent to which a test yields consistent results, as assessed by the consistency of scores on two halves of the test, on alternate forms of the test, or on retesting. (p. 622)

REM rebound the tendency for REM sleep to increase following REM sleep deprivation (created by repeated awakenings during REM sleep). (p. 243)

REM sleep rapid eye movement sleep; a recurring sleep stage during which vivid dreams commonly occur. Also known as *paradoxical sleep*, because the muscles are relaxed (except for minor twitches) but other body systems are active. (p. 226)

repetitive transcranial magnetic stimulation (rTMS) the application of repeated pulses of magnetic energy to the brain; used to stimulate or suppress brain activity. (p. 745)

replication repeating the essence of a research study, usually with different participants in different situations, to see whether the basic finding extends to other participants and circumstances. (p. 39)

representativeness heuristic judging the likelihood of things in terms of how well they seem to represent, or match, particular prototypes; may lead us to ignore other relevant information. (p. 364)

repression in psychoanalytic theory, the basic defense mechanism that banishes from consciousness anxiety-arousing thoughts, feelings, and memories. (pp. 346, 560)

resilience the personal strength that helps most people cope with stress and recover from adversity and even trauma. (p. 737)

resistance in psychoanalysis, the blocking from consciousness of anxiety-laden material. (p. 710)

respondent behavior behavior that occurs as an automatic response to some stimulus. (p. 289)

reticular formation a nerve network that travels through the brainstem and thalamus and plays an important role in controlling arousal. (p. 98)

retina the light-sensitive inner surface of the eye, containing the receptor rods and cones plus layers of neurons that begin the processing of visual information. (p. 172)

retinal disparity a binocular cue for perceiving depth: By comparing images from the retinas in the two eyes, the brain computes distance—the greater the disparity (difference) between the two images, the closer the object. (p. 184)

retrieval the process of getting information out of memory storage. (p. 319)

retroactive interference the disruptive effect of new learning on the recall of old information. (p. 345)

retrograde amnesia an inability to retrieve information from one's past. (p. 342)

reuptake a neurotransmitter's reabsorption by the sending neuron. (p. 80)

rods retinal receptors that detect black, white, and gray; necessary for peripheral and twilight vision, when cones don't respond. (p. 173)

role a set of expectations (norms) about a social position, defining how those in the position ought to behave. (pp. 503, 758)

Rorschach inkblot test the most widely used projective test, a set of 10 inkblots, designed by Hermann Rorschach; seeks to identify people's inner feelings by analyzing their interpretations of the blots. (p. 567)

rumination compulsive fretting; *overthinking* about our problems and their causes. (p. 679)

sampling bias a flawed sampling process that produces an unrepresentative sample. (p. 43)

savant syndrome a condition in which a person otherwise limited in mental ability has an exceptional specific skill, such as in computation or drawing. (p. 609)

scapegoat theory the theory that prejudice offers an outlet for anger by providing someone to blame. (p. 785)

scatterplot a graphed cluster of dots, each of which represents the values of two variables. The slope of the points suggests the direction of the relationship between the two variables. The amount of scatter suggests the strength of the correlation (little scatter indicates high correlation). (p. 46)

schema a concept or framework that organizes and interprets information. (p. 477)

schizophrenia a psychological disorder characterized by delusions, hallucinations, disorganized speech, and/or diminished or inappropriate emotional expression. (p. 684)

secondary sex characteristics nonreproductive sexual traits, such as female breasts and hips, male voice quality, and body hair. (p. 527)

selective attention the focusing of conscious awareness on a particular stimulus. (p. 152)

self in contemporary psychology, assumed to be the center of personality, the organizer of our thoughts, feelings, and actions. (p. 594)

self-actualization according to Maslow, one of the ultimate psychological needs that arises after basic physical and psychological needs are met and self-esteem is achieved; the motivation to fulfill one's potential. (p. 571)

self-concept all our thoughts and feelings about ourselves, in answer to the question, "Who am I?" (pp. 492, 572)

self-control the ability to control impulses and delay short-term gratification for greater long-term rewards. (p. 301)

self-disclosure revealing intimate aspects of oneself to others. (p. 804)

self-efficacy one's sense of competence and effectiveness. (p. 595)

self-esteem one's feelings of high or low self-worth. (p. 595)

self-fulfilling prophecy a belief that leads to its own fulfillment. (p. 812)

self-serving bias a readiness to perceive oneself favorably. (p. 596)

sensation the process by which our sensory receptors and nervous system receive and represent stimulus energies from our environment. (p. 152)

sensorimotor stage in Piaget's theory, the stage (from birth to about 2 years of age) during which infants know the world mostly in terms of their sensory impressions and motor activities. (p. 478)

sensorineural hearing loss hearing loss caused by damage to the cochlea's receptor cells or to the auditory nerves. (Also called *nerve deafness*.) (p. 197)

sensory (afferent) neurons neurons that carry incoming information from the sensory receptors to the brain and spinal cord. (p. 86)

sensory adaptation diminished sensitivity as a consequence of constant stimulation. (p. 159)

sensory interaction the principle that one sense may influence another, as when the smell of food influences its taste. (p. 210)

sensory memory the immediate, very brief recording of sensory information in the memory system. (p. 319)

serial position effect our tendency to recall best the last (a recency effect) and first items (a primacy effect) in a list. (p. 337)

set point the point at which an individual's "weight thermostat" is supposedly set. When the body falls below this weight, an increase in hunger and a lowered metabolic rate may act to restore the lost weight. (p. 398)

sexual dysfunction a problem that consistently impairs sexual arousal or functioning. (p. 407)

sexual orientation an enduring sexual attraction toward members of either one's own sex (homosexual orientation), the other sex (heterosexual orientation), or both sexes (bisexual orientation). (p. 531)

sexual response cycle the four stages of sexual responding described by Masters and Johnson—excitement, plateau, orgasm, and resolution. (p. 406)

shallow processing encoding on a basic level based on the structure or appearance of words. (p. 324)

shaping an operant conditioning procedure in which reinforcers guide behavior toward closer and closer approximations of the desired behavior. (p. 276)

short-term memory activated memory that holds a few items briefly, such as the seven digits of a phone number while dialing, before the information is stored or forgotten. (p. 319)

signal detection theory a theory predicting how and when we detect the presence of a faint stimulus (*signal*) amid background stimulation (*noise*). Assumes there is no single absolute threshold and that detection depends partly on a person's experience, expectations, motivation, and alertness. (p. 156)

skewed distribution a representation of scores that lack symmetry around their average value. (p. 58)

sleep periodic, natural loss of consciousness—as distinct from unconsciousness resulting from a coma, general anesthesia, or hibernation. (Adapted from Dement, 1999.) (p. 227)

sleep apnea a sleep disorder characterized by temporary cessations of breathing during sleep and repeated momentary awakenings. (p. 239)

social anxiety disorder intense fear of social situations, leading to avoidance of such. (Formerly called *social phobia*.) (p. 662)

social clock the culturally preferred timing of social events such as marriage, parenthood, and retirement. (p. 544)

social exchange theory the theory that our social behavior is an exchange process, the aim of which is to maximize benefits and minimize costs. (p. 809)

social facilitation improved performance on simple or well-learned tasks in the presence of others. (p. 771)

social identity the "we" aspect of our self-concept; the part of our answer to "Who am I?" that comes from our group memberships. (p. 519)

social leadership group-oriented leadership that builds teamwork, mediates conflict, and offers support. (p. 838)

social learning theory the theory that we learn social behavior by observing and imitating and by being rewarded or punished. (p. 504)

social loafing the tendency for people in a group to exert less effort when pooling their efforts toward attaining a common goal than when individually accountable. (p. 773)

social psychology the scientific study of how we think about, influence, and relate to one another. (pp. 14, 754)

social script culturally modeled guide for how to act in various situations. (p. 792)

social trap a situation in which the conflicting parties, by each rationally pursuing their self-interest rather than the good of the group, become caught in mutually destructive behavior. (p. 810)

social-cognitive perspective views behavior as influenced by the interaction between people's traits (including their thinking) and their social context. (p. 587)

social-cultural psychology the study of how situations and cultures affect our behavior and thinking. (p. 12)

social-responsibility norm an expectation that people will help those needing their help. (p. 810)

somatic nervous system the division of the peripheral nervous system that controls the body's skeletal muscles. (Also called the *skeletal nervous system*.) (p. 87)

somatic symptom disorder a psychological disorder in which the symptoms take a somatic (bodily) form without apparent physical cause. (See *conversion disorder* and *illness anxiety disorder*.) (p. 693)

somatosensory cortex area at the front of the parietal lobes that registers and processes body touch and movement sensations. (p. 107)

source amnesia attributing to the wrong source an event we have experienced, heard about, read about, or imagined. (Also called *source misattribution*.) Source amnesia, along with the misinformation effect, is at the heart of many false memories. (p. 349)

spacing effect the tendency for distributed study or practice to yield better long-term retention than is achieved through massed study or practice. (p. 324)

split brain a condition resulting from surgery that isolates the brain's two hemispheres by cutting the fibers (mainly those of the corpus callosum) connecting them. (p. 114)

spontaneous recovery the reappearance, after a pause, of an extinguished conditioned response. (p. 269)

spotlight effect overestimating others' noticing and evaluating our appearance, performance, and blunders (as if we presume a spotlight shines on us). (p. 594)

SQ3R a study method incorporating five steps: *Survey, Question, Read, Retrieve, Review*. (p. 16)

standard deviation a computed measure of how much scores vary around the mean score. (p. 58)

standardization defining uniform testing procedures and meaningful scores by comparison with the performance of a pretested group. (p. 621)

Stanford-Binet the widely used American revision (by Terman at Stanford University) of Binet's original intelligence test. (p. 618)

statistical significance a statistical statement of how likely it is that an obtained result occurred by chance. (p. 60)

stereotype a generalized (sometimes accurate but often overgeneralized) *belief* about a group of people. (p. 780)

stereotype threat a self-confirming concern that one will be evaluated based on a negative stereotype. (p. 642)

stimulants drugs (such as caffeine, nicotine, and the more powerful amphetamines, cocaine, Ecstasy, and methamphetamine) that excite neural activity and speed up body functions. (p. 250)

stimulus any event or situation that evokes a response. (p. 264)

storage the process of retaining encoded information over time. (p. 319)

stranger anxiety the fear of strangers that infants commonly display, beginning by about 8 months of age. (p. 488)

stress the process by which we perceive and respond to certain events, called *stressors*, that we appraise as threatening or challenging. (p. 442)

structuralism early school of thought promoted by Wundt and Titchener; used introspection to reveal the structure of the human mind. (p. 4)

structured interviews an interview process that asks the same job-relevant questions of all applicants, each of whom is rated on established scales. (p. 832)

subjective well-being self-perceived happiness or satisfaction with life. Used along with measures of objective well-being (for example, physical and economic indicators) to evaluate people's quality of life. (p. 847)

subliminal below one's absolute threshold for conscious awareness. (p. 157)

substance use disorder continued substance craving and use despite significant life disruption and/or physical risk. (p. 246)

superego the part of personality that, according to Freud, represents internalized ideals and provides standards for judgment (the conscience) and for future aspirations. (p. 558)

superordinate goals shared goals that override differences among people and require their cooperation. (p. 813)

suprachiasmatic nucleus (SCN) a pair of cell clusters in the hypothalamus that controls circadian rhythm. In response to light, the SCN causes the pineal gland to adjust melatonin production, thus modifying our feelings of sleepiness. (p. 229)

survey a technique for ascertaining the self-reported attitudes or behaviors of a particular group, usually by questioning a representative, random sample of the group. (p. 42)

sympathetic nervous system the division of the autonomic nervous system that arouses the body, mobilizing its energy in stressful situations. (p. 87)

synapse [SIN-aps] the junction between the axon tip of the sending neuron and the dendrite or cell body of the receiving neuron. The tiny gap at this junction is called the *synaptic gap* or *synaptic cleft.* (p. 80)

systematic desensitization a type of exposure therapy that associates a pleasant, relaxed state with gradually increasing anxiety-triggering stimuli. Commonly used to treat phobias. (p. 717)

task leadership goal-oriented leadership that sets standards, organizes work, and focuses attention on goals. (p. 838)

telegraphic speech early speech stage in which a child speaks like a telegram—"go car"—using mostly nouns and verbs. (p. 375)

temperament a person's characteristic emotional reactivity and intensity. (p. 490)

temporal lobes portion of the cerebral cortex lying roughly above the ears; includes the auditory areas, each receiving information primarily from the opposite ear. (p. 105)

tend and befriend under stress, people (especially women) often provide support to others (tend) and bond with and seek support from others (befriend). (p. 445)

teratogens (literally, "monster makers") agents, such as chemicals and viruses, that can reach the embryo or fetus during prenatal development and cause harm. (p. 467)

terror-management theory a theory of death-related anxiety; explores people's emotional and behavioral responses to reminders of their impending death. (p. 568)

testing effect enhanced memory after retrieving, rather than simply rereading, information. Also sometimes referred to as a *retrieval practice* effect or *test-enhanced learning.* (pp. 16, 324)

testosterone the most important of the male sex hormones. Both males and females have it, but the additional testosterone in males stimulates the growth of the male sex organs in the fetus and the development of the male sex characteristics during puberty. (pp. 408, 526)

thalamus [THAL-uh-muss] the brain's sensory control center, located on top of the brainstem; it directs messages to the sensory receiving areas in the cortex and transmits replies to the cerebellum and medulla. (p. 97)

THC the major active ingredient in marijuana; triggers a variety of effects, including mild hallucinations. (p. 255)

Thematic Apperception Test (TAT) a projective test in which people express their inner feelings and interests through the stories they make up about ambiguous scenes. (p. 567)

theory an explanation using an integrated set of principles that organizes observations and predicts behaviors or events. (p. 38)

theory of mind people's ideas about their own and others' mental states—about their feelings, perceptions, and thoughts, and the behaviors these might predict. (p. 480)

therapeutic alliance a bond of trust and mutual understanding between a therapist and client, who work together constructively to overcome the client's problem. (p. 735)

threshold the level of stimulation required to trigger a neural impulse. (p. 80)

token economy an operant conditioning procedure in which people earn a token of some sort for exhibiting a desired behavior and can later exchange the tokens for various privileges or treats. (p. 719)

tolerance the diminishing effect with regular use of the same dose of a drug, requiring the user to take larger and larger doses before experiencing the drug's effect. (p. 246)

top-down processing information processing guided by higher-level mental processes, as when we construct perceptions drawing on our experience and expectations. (p. 152)

trait a characteristic pattern of behavior or a disposition to feel and act, as assessed by self-report inventories and peer reports. (p. 576)

transduction conversion of one form of energy into another. In sensation, the transforming of stimulus energies, such as sights, sounds, and smells, into neural impulses our brain can interpret. (p. 155)

transference in psychoanalysis, the patient's transfer to the analyst of emotions linked with other relationships (such as love or hatred for a parent). (p. 710)

transgender an umbrella term describing people whose gender identity or expression differs from that associated with their birth sex. (p. 505)

two-factor theory the Schachter-Singer theory that to experience emotion one must (1) be physically aroused and (2) cognitively label the arousal. (p. 422)

two-word stage beginning about age 2, the stage in speech development during which a child speaks mostly in two-word statements. (p. 375)

Type A Friedman and Rosenman's term for competitive, hard-driving, impatient, verbally aggressive, and anger-prone people. (p. 452)

Type B Friedman and Rosenman's term for easygoing, relaxed people. (p. 452)

unconditional positive regard a caring, accepting, nonjudgmental attitude, which Carl Rogers believed would help clients to develop self-awareness and self-acceptance. (pp. 572, 712)

unconditioned response (UR) in classical conditioning, an unlearned, naturally occurring response (such as salivation) to an unconditioned stimulus (US) (such as food in the mouth). (p. 267)

unconditioned stimulus (US) in classical conditioning, a stimulus that unconditionally—naturally and automatically—triggers a response (UR). (p. 267)

unconscious according to Freud, a reservoir of mostly unacceptable thoughts, wishes, feelings, and memories. According to contemporary psychologists, information processing of which we are unaware. (p. 557)

validity the extent to which a test measures or predicts what it is supposed to. (See also *content validity* and *predictive validity*.) (pp. 53, 622)

variable-interval schedule in operant conditioning, a reinforcement schedule that reinforces a response at unpredictable time intervals. (p. 280)

variable-ratio schedule in operant conditioning, a reinforcement schedule that reinforces a response after an unpredictable number of responses. (p. 280)

vestibular sense the sense of body movement and position, including the sense of balance. (p. 209)

virtual reality exposure therapy an anxiety treatment that progressively exposes people to electronic simulations of their greatest fears, such as airplane flying, spiders, or public speaking. (p. 718)

visual cliff a laboratory device for testing depth perception in infants and young animals. (p. 184)

wavelength the distance from the peak of one light or sound wave to the peak of the next. Electromagnetic wavelengths vary from the short blips of cosmic rays to the long pulses of radio transmission. (p. 171)

Weber's law the principle that, to be perceived as different, two stimuli must differ by a constant minimum percentage (rather than a constant amount). (p. 158)

Wechsler Adult Intelligence Scale (WAIS) the WAIS is the most widely used intelligence test; contains verbal and performance (nonverbal) subtests. (p. 620)

Wernicke's area controls language reception—a brain area involved in language comprehension and expression; usually in the left temporal lobe. (p. 377)

withdrawal the discomfort and distress that follow discontinuing an addictive drug or behavior. (p. 247)

working memory a newer understanding of short-term memory that focuses on conscious, active processing of incoming auditory and visual-spatial information, and of information retrieved from long-term memory. (p. 320)

X chromosome the sex chromosome found in both men and women. Females have two X chromosomes; males have one. An X chromosome from each parent produces a female child. (p. 526)

Y chromosome the sex chromosome found only in males. When paired with an X chromosome from the mother, it produces a male child. (p. 526)

Yerkes-Dodson law the principle that performance increases with arousal only up to a point, beyond which performance decreases. (p. 392)

Young-Helmholtz trichromatic (three-color) theory the theory that the retina contains three different color receptors—one most sensitive to red, one to green, one to blue—which, when stimulated in combination, can produce the perception of any color. (p. 178)

zygote the fertilized egg; it enters a 2-week period of rapid cell division and develops into an embryo. (p. 466)

Glosario en Español

absolute threshold/umbral absoluto estímulo mínimo necesario para detectar un estímulo particular el 50 por ciento del tiempo. (p. 156)

accommodation/adaptación (1) ajuste de nuestros conceptos actuales (esquemas) con el propósito de incorporar nueva información. (p. 172) (2) proceso por el que el lente del ojo cambia de forma para enfocar objetos cercanos o lejanos en la retina. (p. 477)

achievement motivation/motivación de logro deseo de alcanzar un logro significativo; de dominar destrezas o ideas; de control; y de lograr un nivel muy alto. (p. 834)

achievement test/prueba de rendimiento prueba diseñada para evaluar lo que una persona ha aprendido. (p. 619)

acquisition/adquisición fase inicial del condicionamiento clásico en la que se asocia un estímulo neutro con un estímulo no condicionado de manera que el estímulo neutro comience a provocar la respuesta condicionada. En el condicionamiento operante, se refiere a la consolidación de una respuesta reforzada. (p. 268)

action potential/potencial de acción impulso neural; carga eléctrica breve que se transmite por un axón. (p. 78)

active listening/escucha activa escucha empática en la que el oyente hace eco, reitera y clarifica. Una característica de la terapia de Rogers centrada en el cliente. (p. 712)

adaptation-level phenomenon/fenómeno del nivel de adaptación nuestra tendencia de formar juicios (de sonidos, de luces, de ingreso) relacionado a un nivel neutro definido por nuestra experiencia de antes. (p. 851)

addiction/adicción deseo compulsivo de usar drogas o llevar a cabo determinadas conductas (como apostar), a pesar de consecuencias desfavorables ya conocidas. (p. 247)

adolescence/adolescencia período de transición de la niñez a la madurez, extendiéndose de la pubertad a la independencia. (p. 513)

adrenal glands/glándulas suprarrenales par de glándulas endocrinas localizadas en la parte superior de los riñones. Estas glándulas secretan hormonas (epinefrina y norepinefrina) que estimulan el cuerpo en momentos de estrés. (p. 91)

aerobic exercise/ejercicio aeróbico ejercicio continuo que fortalece el corazón y los pulmones; también puede aliviar la depresión y la ansiedad. (p. 859)

aggression/agresión comportamiento expresado de manera física o verbal con el propósito de herir o destruir. (pp. 501, 789)

agonist/agonista molécula que, al unirse a un receptor, estimula una respuesta. (p. 82)

agoraphobia/agorafobia temor o tendencia a evitar situaciones, como las multitudes o los espacios abiertos, en las que se ha sentido una pérdida de control o pánico. (p. 663)

AIDS (acquired immune deficiency syndrome)/SIDA (síndrome de inmunodeficiencia adquirida) infección de transmisión sexual, potencialmente mortal, causada por el *virus de la inmunodeficiencia humana* (VIH). El SIDA deteriora el sistema inmunológico, de manera que la persona se vuelve vulnerable a las infecciones. (p. 529)

alcohol use disorder/trastorno por consumo de alcohol (popularmente conocido como *alcoholismo*) Consumo de alcohol caracterizado por la tolerancia, la abstinencia y un impulso por continuar con su uso problemático. (p. 249)

algorithm/algoritmo regla o procedimiento metódico y lógico que garantiza la solución de un problema particular. Se contrapone al uso de la *heurística,* que es normalmente más rápido, pero también con más posibilidades de cometer errores. (p. 361)

all-or-none response/respuesta del todo o nada reacción en la que una neurona emite una descarga (con una respuesta completa) o no lo hace. (p. 80)

alpha waves/ritmo alfa ritmo con ondas cerebrales relativamente lentas que corresponden a un estado relajado y de vigilia. (p. 227)

altruism/altruismo consideración desinteresada por el bienestar de otros. (p. 807)

amphetamines/anfetaminas drogas que estimulan la actividad neural, causando aceleración de las funciones corporales y de los niveles de energía asociadas con estas así como cambios de humor. (p. 250)

amygdala/amígdala dos grupos neurales del tamaño de un frijol que forman parte del sistema límbico; están ligados a las emociones. (p. 99)

anorexia nervosa/anorexia nervosa o nerviosa trastorno alimenticio en el que una persona (generalmente una muchacha adolescente) se somete a una dieta de hambre a pesar de estar muy por debajo de su peso normal (15 por ciento o más). (p. 697)

antagonist/antagonista molécula que, al unirse a un receptor, inhibe o bloquea una respuesta. (pp. 83, 342)

anterograde amnesia/amnesia anterógrada incapacidad de generar nuevos recuerdos. (p. 342)

antianxiety drugs/medicamentos contra la ansiedad medicamentos que se emplean para controlar la ansiedad y la agitación. (p. 741)

antidepressant drugs/medicamentos antidepresivos medicamentos que se emplean para tratar la depresión y los trastornos de ansiedad, obsesivo compulsivo y de estrés postraumático. (Entre los medicamentos antidepresivos más utilizados están los *inhibidores selectivos de la recaptación de la serotonina; SSRI por sus siglas en inglés*). (p. 741)

antipsychotic drugs/medicamentos antipsicóticos medicamentos que se emplean para tratar la esquizofrenia y otros tipos de trastornos graves del pensamiento. (p. 741)

antisocial personality disorder/trastorno antisocial de la personalidad trastorno de la personalidad que se manifiesta cuando la persona (generalmente un hombre) no exhibe sentimiento de culpa por actuar con maldad, incluso hacia los amigos y miembros de la familia. Puede ser agresivo y cruel o un estafador listo. (p. 699)

anxiety disorders/trastornos de ansiedad trastornos psicológicos que se caracterizan por la preocupación y ansiedad crónicas o comportamientos desadaptados que reducen la ansiedad. (p. 661)

aphasia/afasia disfunción del lenguaje generalmente causado por una lesión al hemisferio izquierdo, ya sea en el área de Broca (problemas de articulación) o en el área de Wernicke (problemas de comprensión). (p. 377)

applied research/investigación aplicada estudio científico cuyo objetivo es resolver los problemas prácticos. (p. 14)

aptitude tests/prueba de aptitud prueba diseñada para predecir la actuación de una persona en el futuro; la *aptitud* es la capacidad de aprender. (p. 619)

assimilation/asimilación interpretación de nuevas experiencias según los esquemas previamente existentes. (p. 477)

association areas/áreas de asociación áreas de la corteza cerebral que no están involucradas en las funciones motoras o sensoriales primarias; más bien, están involucradas en las funciones mentales superiores como el aprender, recordar, pensar y hablar. (p. 109)

associative learning/aprendizaje asociativo el aprender que ciertos eventos ocurren juntos. Los eventos pueden ser dos estímulos (como en el condicionamiento clásico) o una respuesta y sus consecuencias (como en el condicionamiento operante). (p. 264)

attachment/apego vínculo emocional con otra persona; mostrado en niños pequeños quienes buscan cercanía física con la persona que los cuida y muestran angustia cuando se les separa de quien los cuida. (p. 488)

attention-deficit hyperactivity disorder (ADHD)/trastorno de déficit de atención con hiperactividad trastorno psicológico marcado por la aparición antes de los 7 años de uno o más de estos tres síntomas clave: falta de atención extrema, hiperactividad e impulsividad. (p. 652)

attitude/actitud sentimientos, a menudo basados en nuestras creencias, que nos predisponen para responder de una manera particular a objetos, personas y eventos. (p. 756)

attribution theory/teoría de atribución teoría que propone que explicamos la conducta de una persona atribuyéndosela a la situación o a la disposición de esa persona. (p. 754)

audition/audición sentido o acto de oír. (p. 194)

autism spectrum disorder (ASD)/trastorno del espectro autista (TEA) trastorno que se manifiesta en la niñez y que está marcado por deficiencias en la comunicación y la interacción social, y por intereses obsesivos y comportamientos repetitivos. (p. 481)

automatic processing/procesamiento automático codificación inconsciente de información incidental, tal como el espacio, el tiempo y la frecuencia, y de información bien sabida, como el significado de las palabras. (p. 320)

autonomic nervous system (ANS)/sistema nervioso autonómico (SNA) parte del sistema nervioso periférico que controla las glándulas y los músculos de los órganos internos (como el corazón). El sistema nervioso simpático alerta al cuerpo; el sistema nervioso parasimpático lo calma. (p. 87)

availability heuristic/heurística de disponibilidad acto de estimar la probabilidad de un evento, basándose en la facilidad con la que es rememorado. Si los casos vienen prontamente a la mente (quizás debido a su intensidad), presumimos que tales eventos son comunes. (p. 364)

aversive conditioning/condicionamiento aversivo tipo de contracondicionamiento en el cual los efectos desagradables (como la náusea) son asociados con comportamientos no deseados (como beber alcohol). (p. 718)

axon/axón prolongación de una neurona a través de la cual transmite mensajes a otras neuronas, o bien a músculos o glándulas, mediante ramificaciones. (p. 78)

babbling stage/fase balbuciente fase del desarrollo del lenguaje que comienza aproximadamente a los 4 meses de edad, y en la cual el infante espontáneamente emite diversos sonidos que al principio no están relacionados con el idioma de la casa. (p. 374)

barbiturates/barbitúricos drogas que deprimen la actividad del sistema nervioso central, reduciendo la ansiedad, pero que afectan la memoria y el discernimiento. (p. 250)

basal metabolic rate/tasa de metabolismo basal cantidad de energía requerida por el organismo en reposo. (p. 398)

basic research/investigación básica ciencia pura que tiene como propósito aumentar la base del conocimiento científico. (p. 14)

basic trust/confianza básica según Erik Erikson, la percepción de que el mundo es predecible y fidedigno; esta percepción se forma durante la infancia a través de experiencias apropiadas con cuidadores sensibles. (p. 492)

behavior genetics/genética del comportamiento estudio del poder relativo y de los límites de las influencias genéticas y ambientales en el comportamiento. (p. 124)

behavior therapy/terapia del comportamiento terapia que aplica los principios de aprendizaje para lograr la eliminación de comportamientos no deseados. (p. 716)

behavioral approach/enfoque conductista en la teoría de la personalidad, perspectiva centrada en los efectos que tiene el aprendizaje en el desarrollo de nuestra personalidad. (p. 587)

behavioral psychology/psicología conductista el estudio científico del comportamiento observable, y su explicación por los principios de aprendizaje. (p. 12)

behaviorism/conductismo posición de que la psicología (1) debe ser una ciencia objetiva que (2) estudia el comportamiento sin referencia a los procesos mentales. La mayoría de los psicólogos en investigación hoy están de acuerdo con (1) pero no con (2). (pp. 6, 266)

belief perseverance/perseverancia de las creencias adhesión a las concepciones iniciales aun después de que la base para estas creencias ha sido desacreditada. (p. 367)

binge-eating disorder/trastorno de alimentación compulsiva episodios significativos de ingestión compulsiva de alimentos, seguidos de angustia, indignación o sentimientos de culpabilidad, que no están seguidos de las purgas o los ayunos con propósitos compensatorios que caracterizan a la bulimia nerviosa. (p. 697)

binocular cues/indicadores binoculares indicadores de profundidad, tales como la disparidad de la retina, que dependen del uso de los dos ojos. (p. 184)

biofeedback/bioretroalimentación sistema para registrar, amplificar y retroalimentar información por vía electrónica en relación con un estado psicológico sutil, como la presión arterial o la tensión muscular (p. 289)

biological psychology/psicología biológica estudio científico de las conexiones entre los procesos biológicos (genéticos, neurales, hormonales) y psicológicos. (Algunos biopsicólogos se denominan *neurocientíficos conductuales, neuropsicólogos, geneticistas de la conducta, psicólogos fisiológicos o biopsicólogos*). (pp. 12, 77)

biomedical therapy/terapia biomédica medicamentos recetados o procedimientos médicos que actúan directamente en la fisiología de la persona. (p. 709)

biopsychosocial approach/enfoque biopsicosocial enfoque integrado que incorpora niveles de análisis biológicos, psicológicos y socioculturales. (p. 11)

bipolar disorder/trastorno bipolar trastorno que afecta el estado de ánimo; la persona alterna entre la desesperanza y el letargo de la depresión y el estado eufórico de la manía. (Anteriormente se denominaba *trastorno maníaco-depresivo*). (p. 673)

blind spot/punto ciego punto en el que el nervio óptico abandona el ojo, creando un punto "ciego" porque allí no se encuentra ninguna célula receptora. (p. 173)

bottom-up processing/procesamiento de abajo para arriba análisis que empieza con los receptores sensoriales y continúa para arriba hasta que llega al centro de integración sensorial del cerebro. (p. 152)

brainstem/tronco encefálico parte más antigua y meollo del cerebro, empezando donde la médula espinal se inflama al entrar en el cráneo; el tronco encefálico es responsable por las funciones automáticas de supervivencia. (p. 97)

Broca's area/área de Broca controla la producción del lenguaje; área del lóbulo frontal, generalmente del hemisferio izquierdo, que dirige los movimientos musculares involucrados en el lenguaje. (p. 377)

bulimia nervosa/bulimia nerviosa trastorno de la alimentación por el que una persona alterna episodios de ingestión compulsiva (generalmente de alimentos de alto contenido calórico) con purgas (por vómitos o uso de laxantes) o períodos de ayuno. (p. 697)

bystander effect/efecto espectador tendencia que tienen las personas a no brindar ayuda si hay otras personas presentes. (p. 808)

Cannon-Bard theory/teoría de Cannon-Bard teoría según la cual un estímulo que despierta emociones simultáneamente puede provocar (1) respuestas fisiológicas y (2) la experiencia subjetiva de la emoción. (p. 422)

case study/caso técnica descriptiva en la cual se estudia a un individuo o grupo a profundidad con la esperanza de revelar principios universales. (p. 40)

catharsis/catarsis en psicología, la idea de que "librar" la energía agresiva (a través de acción o fantasía) alivia los impulsos agresivos. (p. 846)

central nervous system (CNS)/sistema nervioso central (SNC) el cerebro y la médula espinal. (p. 86)

central route persuasion/persuasión por ruta central se observa cuando las personas interesadas se concentran en los argumentos y responden con pensamientos favorables. (p. 756)

cerebellum/cerebelo "cerebro pequeño" situado en la parte posterior del tronco encefálico; sus funciones incluyen procesar los estímulos sensoriales, coordinar el movimiento y el equilibrio, y permitir el aprendizaje no verbal y el funcionamiento de la memoria. (p. 98)

cerebral cortex/corteza cerebral tejido intrincado de células neurales interconectadas que cubren los hemisferios cerebrales; el centro de control y procesamiento de información del cuerpo. (p. 104)

change blindness/ceguera al cambio incapacidad de percibir cambios en el entorno. (p. 154)

chromosomes/cromosomas estructuras semejantes a hilos conformados de moléculas de ADN que contienen los genes. (p. 124)

chunking/división en pedazos el organizar los datos en unidades familiares y manejables; a menudo se da de manera automática. (p. 323)

circadian rhythm/ritmo circadiano reloj biológico; ritmos regulares del cuerpo (por ejemplo, temperatura y estado de vigilia) que ocurren en ciclos de 24 horas. (p. 226)

classical conditioning/condicionamiento clásico tipo de aprendizaje en el cual un individuo aprende a asociar dos o más estímulos y a anticipar hechos. (p. 266)

client-centered therapy/terapia centrada en el cliente terapia humanística, desarrollada por Carl Rogers, en la cual el terapeuta utiliza técnicas como el escuchar activamente dentro de un ambiente real de aceptación y empatía a fin de facilitar el crecimiento de los clientes. (También se la conoce como *terapia centrada en la persona*). (p. 712)

clinical psychology/psicología clínica rama de la psicología que estudia, evalúa y trata a las personas con trastornos psicológicos. (p. 14)

cocaine/cocaína estimulante potente y adictivo que se deriva de la planta de coca. Genera una actitude temporal de alerta y euforia. (p. 252)

cochlea/cóclea estructura ósea en forma de tubo enrollado en espiral, llena de fluidos, que se encuentra en el oído interno. A través de la cóclea las ondas sonoras activan los impulsos nerviosos. (p. 195)

cochlear implant/implante coclear dispositivo que convierte sonidos en signos eléctricos y estimula el nervio auditorio a través de electrodos implantados en la cóclea. (p. 198)

cognition/cognición todas las actividades mentales asociadas con el pensar, saber, recordar y comunicar. (pp. 356, 476)

cognitive dissonance theory/teoría de la disonancia cognitiva teoría que dice que cuando tenemos dos opiniones (cogniciones) que se contradicen, hacemos algo para reducir ese malestar (disonancia). Por ejemplo, cuando percibimos que nuestras actitudes y nuestras acciones chocan, podemos reducir la disonancia resultante cambiando nuestras actitudes. (p. 759)

cognitive learning/aprendizaje cognitivo adquisición de información mental, ya sea mediante la observación de eventos o de personas, o bien mediante el lenguaje. (p. 265)

cognitive map/mapa cognitivo representación mental del propio entorno. Por ejemplo, después de explorar un laberinto, las ratas se comportan como si hubiesen aprendido un mapa cognitivo de este. (p. 297)

cognitive neuroscience/neurociencia cognitiva estudio interdisciplinario de la actividad cerebral relacionada con la cognición (incluye la percepción, el pensamiento, la memoria y el lenguaje). (pp. 7, 119)

cognitive psychology/psicología cognoscitiva estudio científico de todas las actividades mentales relacionadas con el pensamiento, el saber, la memoria y la comunicación. (p. 12)

cognitive therapy/terapia cognitiva terapia que enseña a los pacientes a pensar y actuar de modos más realistas y adaptativos. Está basada en el supuesto de que los pensamientos intervienen entre los eventos y nuestras reacciones emocionales. (p. 720)

cognitive-behavioral therapy (CBT)/terapia cognitiva-conductual (TCC) terapia popular que integra la terapia cognitiva (cambiar el pensamiento de autoderrota) y la terapia conductual (modificar la conducta). (p. 723)

cohort/cohorte grupo de personas en un período determinado. (p. 625)

collective unconscious/inconsciente colectivo concepto de Carl Jung de un depósito de memorias de la historia de nuestra especie compartido por la humanidad. (p. 566)

collectivism/colectivismo el dar prioridad a las metas del grupo al que se pertenece (generalmente la familia extendida o el grupo de trabajo), definiendo de esta manera la propia identidad. (p. 599)

color constancy/constancia de color el percibir que los objetos familiares parecen mantener la apariencia cromática incluso cuando las ondas reflejadas por el objeto se ven alteradas por un cambio de iluminación. (p. 187)

community psychology/psicología comunitaria rama de la psicología que estudia la interacción entre las personas y sus ambientes sociales, así como también la manera en la que las instituciones sociales afectan a los individuos y los grupos. (p. 15)

companionate love/amor compañero apego afectuoso profundo que sentimos por aquellos con quienes nuestras vidas se entrelazan. (p. 803)

complementary and alternative medicine (CAM)/medicina complementaria y alternativa tratamientos de salud que aún no se han puesto a prueba y tienen el propósito de complementar o de servir como alternativas a la medicina convencional; generalmente no se enseñan en las escuelas de medicina, no son utilizados en los hospitales, ni son reembolsados por las compañías de seguros. Cuando los estudios demuestran que una terapia es segura y eficaz, por lo general esta pasa a formar parte de la práctica médica aceptada. (p. 863)

concept/concepto agrupación mental de objetos, eventos, ideas, o personas con características similares. (p. 356)

concrete operational stage/etapa del pensamiento lógico-concreto en la teoría de Piaget, la fase del desarrollo cognitivo (desde aproximadamente los 6 o 7 años hasta los 11 años de edad) durante la cual los niños desarrollan las operaciones mentales que les permiten pensar lógicamente sobre eventos concretos. (p. 483)

conditioned reinforcer/refuerzo condicionado estímulo que debe asociarse con un refuerzo primario para adquirir sus propiedades de reforzamiento. También se lo conoce como *refuerzo secundario*. (p. 278)

conditioned response (CR)/respuesta condicionada (RC) en el condicionamiento clásico, una respuesta aprendida a un estímulo previamente neutral (pero ahora condicionado) (p. 268)

conditioned stimulus (CS)/estímulo condicionado (EC) en el condicionamiento clásico, un estímulo originalmente irrelevante que, después de ser asociado con un estímulo incondicionado (EI) produce una respuesta condicionada (RC). (p. 268)

conduction hearing loss/pérdida auditiva conductiva pérdida de audición causada por daño al sistema mecánico que conduce las ondas sonoras a la cóclea. (p. 197)

cones/conos células receptoras de la retina que se concentran cerca del centro de la retina y que funcionan a la luz del día o en condiciones con buena iluminación. Los conos ayudan a percibir el color y los pequeños detalles. (p. 173)

confirmation bias/predisposición a buscar confirmación tendencia a buscar información que confirme nuestras ideas preconcebidas y a ignorar o distorsionar la evidencia contradictoria. (p. 362)

conflict/conflicto incompatibilidad percibida de acciones, metas o ideas. (p. 810)

conformity/conformidad el adaptar nuestro comportamiento o pensamiento para que coincida con una norma del grupo. (p. 763)

confounding variable/variable de confusión factor distinto de la variable independiente, que podría provocar un efecto en un experimento. (p. 52)

consciousness/conciencia percepción de nosotros mismos y de nuestro ambiente. (pp. 118, 219)

conservation/conservación principio de que las propiedades como la masa, el volumen y el número no varían a pesar de los cambios en las formas de los objetos. (Piaget era de la opinión de que este formaba parte de la etapa operacional concreta). (p. 479)

content validity/validez de contenido grado en el cual una prueba promueve el comportamiento que es de interés. (p. 622)

continuous reinforcement/refuerzo continuo el reforzar la respuesta deseada cada vez que ocurre. (p. 279)

control group/grupo control en un experimento, el grupo que *no* está expuesto al tratamiento; contrasta con el grupo experimental y sirve como comparación para evaluar el efecto del tratamiento. (p. 51)

convergent thinking/pensamiento convergente pensamiento que consiste en ir descartando las posibles soluciones a un problema hasta encontrar la mejor. (p. 357)

conversion disorder/trastorno de conversión trastorno en el que una persona experimenta síntomas físicos genuinos y muy específicos que no se pueden relacionar con una base fisiológica. (También se lo conoce como *trastorno por síntomas neurológicos funcionales*). (p. 694)

coping/afrontamiento el aliviar el estrés utilizando métodos emocionales, cognitivos o conductuales. (p. 298)

coronary heart disease/cardiopatía coronaria obstrucción de los vasos que nutren el músculo cardiaco; la causa principal de muerte en muchos países desarrollados. (p. 451)

corpus callosum/cuerpo calloso banda grande de fibras neurales que conecta los dos hemisferios del cerebro y lleva mensajes entre ellos. (p. 114)

correlation/correlación medida del grado en que dos variables cambian simultáneamente y, por ende, si es que una de ellas es capaz de predecir la otra. (p. 46)

correlation coefficient/coeficiente de correlación índice estadístico de la relación entre dos variables (de −1 a +1). (p. 46)

counseling psychology/psicología de orientación rama de la psicología que ayuda a las personas con sus problemas de la vida diaria (a menudo relacionados con la escuela, el trabajo o el matrimonio) y a aumentar su bienestar. (p. 14)

counterconditioning/contracondicionamiento procedimiento de terapia conductual en el que se emplea el condicionamiento clásico para producir nuevas respuestas a estímulos que provocan conductas no deseadas; incluye las *terapias de exposición* y el *condicionamiento aversivo*. (p. 717)

creativity/creatividad habilidad de producir ideas originales y valiosas. (p. 357)

critical period/período crítico período óptimo poco después el nacimiento cuando la exposición de un organismo a ciertos estímulos o experiencias produce un desarrollo normal. (p. 489)

critical thinking/pensamiento crítico pensamiento que no acepta argumentos y conclusiones a ciegas. Más bien examina las suposiciones, evalúa la fuente, percibe los valores ocultos, analiza la evidencia y evalúa las conclusiones. (p. 35)

cross-sectional study/estudio transversal estudio en el que se comparan personas de diferentes edades. (p. 543)

crystallized intelligence/inteligencia cristalizada el conocimiento y las destrezas verbales que acumulamos; tiende a aumentar con la edad. (p. 626)

CT (computed tomography) scan/tomografía computarizada (TC) una serie de fotografías de rayos X tomadas desde ángulos diferentes y combinadas mediante un ordenador en una representación compuesta de una sección de la estructura del cerebro. (También llamada *CAT scan* en inglés). (p. 95)

culture/cultura comportamientos duraderos, ideas, actitudes y tradiciones compartidos por un grupo de personas y transmitidos de una generación a la siguiente. (pp. 65, 776)

debriefing/aclaración postexperimental explicación de un estudio, incluyendo su finalidad y los posibles engaños, a sus participantes. (p. 68)

deep processing/procesamiento profundo codificación sistemática basada en el significado de las palabras; suele incrementar la retención. (p. 325)

defense mechanisms/mecanismos de defensa en la teoría psicoanalítica, los métodos de protección del ego para reducir la ansiedad distorsionando la realidad inconscientemente. (p. 560)

deindividuation/desindividualización pérdida de identidad personal y del autocontrol en situaciones de grupo que fomentan la excitación y el anonimato. (p. 773)

déjà vu/déjà vu sensación de haber vivido antes una experiencia específica. Señales de la presente situación pueden de manera subconsciente activar la recuperación de una experiencia previa. (p. 349)

delta waves/sondas delta ondas cerebrales amplias y lentas asociadas con el sueño profundo. (p. 228)

delusions/delirios creencias falsas, a menudo de persecución o grandeza, que pueden acompañar los trastornos psicóticos. (p. 684)

dendrites/dendritas extensiones ramificadas de una neurona que reciben los mensajes y emiten impulsos hacia el cuerpo celular. (p. 78)

dependent variable/variable dependiente factor resultante; la variable que puede cambiar en respuesta a cambios en la variable independiente. (p. 52)

depressants/depresivos drogas (como el alcohol, barbitúricos y opiatos) que reducen la actividad neuronal y lentifican las funciones corporales. (p. 248)

depth perception/percepción de profundidad habilidad de ver objetos en tres dimensiones aunque las imágenes percibidas por la retina son bidimensionales. Esto nos permite juzgar la distancia. (p. 184)

descriptive statistics/estadística descriptiva datos numéricos utilizados para medir y describir las características de los grupos. Incluye las medidas de la tendencia central y de la variación. (p. 57)

developmental psychology/psicología del desarrollo rama de la psicología que estudia el cambio físico, cognitivo y social a lo largo de la vida. (pp. 14, 462)

difference threshold/umbral diferencial diferencia mínima requerida para distinguir un estímulo de otro el 50 por ciento de las veces. Experimentamos el umbral diferencial como una *diferencia apenas perceptible* (o *dap*). (p. 158)

discrimination/discriminación (1) en el condicionamiento clásico, la habilidad adquirida de distinguir entre un estímulo condicionado y aquellos estímulos que no señalan un estímulo sin condición. (p. 270) (2) en la psicología social, el *comportamiento* negativo injustificable hacia un grupo y sus miembros. (p. 780)

discriminative stimulus/estímulo discriminativo en el condicionamiento operante, un estímulo que provoca una respuesta después de la asociación con el refuerzo (en contraste a los estímulos relacionados no relacionados con el refuerzo). (p. 277)

dissociation/disociación separación de la conciencia que permite que algunos pensamientos y comportamientos ocurran simultáneamente con otros. (p. 222)

dissociative disorders/trastornos disociativos trastornos en los que el conocimiento consciente se separa (se disocia) de los recuerdos, pensamientos y sentimientos anteriores. (p. 694)

dissociative identity disorder (DID)/trastorno de identidad disociativo (TID) trastorno disociativo poco común en el que una persona exhibe dos o más personalidades distintas que se alternan. Anteriormente se denominaba *trastorno de personalidad múltiple.* (p. 695)

divergent thinking/pensamiento divergente pensamiento que consiste en expandir el número de posibles soluciones a un problema (pensamiento creativo que diverge en diferentes direcciones). (p. 357)

DNA (*deoxyribonucleic acid*)/ADN (*ácido desoxirribonucleico*) molécula compleja que contiene la información genética de la que se constituyen los cromosomas. (p. 124)

double-blind procedure/procedimiento doble ciego procedimiento experimental en el cual los participantes y el personal de la investigación ignoran (están ciegos) si los participantes de la investigación han recibido el tratamiento o un placebo. Normalmente se utiliza en los estudios de evaluación de drogas. (p. 51)

Down syndrome/síndrome de Down retraso mental de leve a severo y trastornos físicos asociados provocados por una copia adicional del cromosoma 21. (p. 629)

dream/sueño sucesión de imágenes, emociones y pensamientos que pasan a través de la mente de una persona durmiente. Los sueños se caracterizan por su fantasía alucinante, falta de ilación e incongruencias, y por la aceptación delirante del contenido de estos de parte del soñador y las dificultades posteriores para recordarlo. (p. 240)

drive-reduction theory/teoría de la reducción del impulso idea que una necesidad fisiológica crea un estado de mayor tensión (un impulso) que motiva al organismo a satisfacer esta necesidad. (p. 391)

DSM-5/DSM-5 *Manual diagnóstico y estadístico de trastornos mentales* de la Asociación psiquiátrica estadounidense, quinta edición; sistema de amplia difusión para la clasificación de trastornos psicológicos. (p. 654)

dual processing/procesamiento dual principio que afirma que la información a menudo se procesa por vías conscientes e inconscientes separadas. (p. 120)

echoic memory/memoria ecoica memoria sensorial-auditiva de corto plazo; aunque la atención esté en otra parte, se pueden recordar sonidos y palabras en los siguientes 3 o 4 segundos. (p. 322)

eclectic approach/aproximación ecléctica enfoque de la psicoterapia que, dependiendo de los problemas del cliente, utiliza técnicas de distintas formas de terapia. (p. 709)

Ecstasy (MDMA)/éxtasis (MDMA) estimulante sintético y alucinógeno leve. Produce euforia e intimidad social, pero tiene riesgos de salud a corto plazo. Además, a largo plazo daña las neuronas que producen la serotonina, y afecta el ánimo y el proceso de cognición. (p. 253)

educational psychology/psicología educativa el estudio de cómo los procesos psicológicos afectan y pueden mejorar la enseñanza y el aprendizaje. (p. 14)

effortful processing/procesamiento con esfuerzo codificación que requiere atención y esfuerzo conscientes. (p. 320)

ego/ego parte en gran medida consciente y "ejecutiva" de la personalidad que, de acuerdo a Freud, media entre las demandas del id, el superego y la realidad. El ego opera bajo el *principio de realidad,* satisfaciendo los deseos del id en formas que de manera realista le brindarán placer y no dolor. (p. 558)

egocentrism/egocentrismo en la teoría de Piaget, la dificultad de los niños en la etapa preoperacional de aceptar el punto de vista ajeno. (p. 479)

electroconvulsive therapy (ECT)/terapia electroconvulsiva (TEC) terapia biomédica para pacientes severamente deprimidos en la que una corriente eléctrica de corta duración se envía a través del cerebro de un paciente anestesiado. (p. 743)

electroencephalogram (EEG)/electroencefalograma (EEG) registro en el que se amplifican las ondas de actividad eléctrica que recorren el cerebro. Estas ondas son medidas a través de electrodos colocados en el cuero cabelludo. (p. 95)

embodied cognition/cognición corpórea en psicología, la influencia que tienen las sensaciones corporales, los gestos y otros estados en las preferencias cognitivas y en la formación de juicios. (p. 211)

embryo/embrión etapa de desarrollo en el organismo humano a partir de las 2 semanas de fertilización hasta el segundo mes. (p. 466)

emerging adulthood/adultez emergente entre algunos individuos de culturas modernas, etapa aproximadamente entre el final de la adolescencia y los veinticinco años de edad, en que se trata de salvar la brecha que se da entre la dependencia adolescente y la independencia completa del adulto responsable. (p. 523)

emotion/emoción reacción que involucra a todo el organismo, e incluye (1) excitación fisiológica, (2) comportamientos expresivos y (3) experiencia consciente. (p. 421)

emotional intelligence/inteligencia emocional habilidad de percibir, entender, administrar y utilizar las emociones. (p. 612)

emotion-focused coping/afrontamiento centrado en la emoción el intentar aliviar el estrés evitando o ignorando los estresores, y atendiendo a las necesidades emocionales relacionadas con la reacción al estrés. (p. 298)

empirically derived test/prueba empíricamente derivada prueba (tal como el MMPI) desarrollada a partir de un grupo de ítems y escogiendo aquellos que discriminan entre grupos. (p. 578)

empiricism/empirismo la visión de que el conocimiento se origina en la experiencia y de que ciencia debe, por lo tanto, basarse en la observación y la experimentación. (p. 3)

encoding/codificación el procesar información al sistema de memoria, por ejemplo, extrayendo el significado. (p. 319)

endocrine system/sistema endocrino sistema "lento" de comunicación química del cuerpo; un conjunto de glándulas que secretan hormonas al torrente sanguíneo. (p. 90)

endorphins/endorfinas "morfina interna"; neurotransmisores naturales similares a los opiatos que están asociados con el control del dolor y con el placer. (p. 82)

environment/entorno toda influencia que no es de carácter genético, desde la nutrición prenatal hasta las personas y cosas que nos rodean. (p. 124)

epigenetics/epigenética estudio de las influencias del ambiente en la expresión génica sin que lleguen a producirse cambios en el ADN. (p. 131)

equity/equidad condición en la cual las personas reciben de manera proporcional lo que aportan a una relación. (p. 804)

estrogens/estrógenos hormonas sexuales, por ejemplo, el estradiol, secretadas en mayor cantidad en la mujer que en el hombre, que contribuye a formar las características sexuales de la mujer. En las mamíferas no humanas, los niveles de estrógeno alcanzan el nivel máximo durante la ovulación, promoviendo la receptividad sexual. (p. 408)

evidence-based practice/práctica basada en la evidencia toma de decisiones que combina los mejores estudios disponibles con la experiencia clínica y las características y preferencias del paciente. (p. 732)

evolutionary psychology/psicología evolutiva el estudio de la evolución de la conducta y la mente que utiliza los principios de selección natural. (pp. 12, 135)

experiment/experimento método de investigación en el que un científico manipula uno o más factores (variables independientes) para observar el efecto en algún comportamiento o proceso mental (la variable dependiente). La *asignación aleatoria* de participantes tiene como finalidad controlar otras variables relevantes. (p. 51)

experimental group/grupo experimental durante un experimento, grupo que está expuesto al tratamiento, o sea, a una versión de la variable independiente. (p. 51)

experimental psychology/psicología experimental el estudio de la conducta y el pensamiento por medio del método experimental. (p. 5)

explicit memory/memoria explícita recolección consciente de hechos y experiencias que uno puede "declarar." (También denominada *memoria declaratoria*). (p. 320)

exposure therapies/terapias de exposición técnicas conductistas, como la *insensibilización sistemática* y la *terapia de exposición a una realidad virtual,* que tratan los estados de ansiedad exponiendo a las personas (en situaciones imaginarias o reales) a las cosas que temen y evitan. (p. 717)

external locus of control/locus de control externo percepción de que nuestra suerte o las fuerzas externas que existen más allá de nuestro control determinan nuestro destino. (p. 300)

extinction/extinción debilitación de la respuesta condicionada (RC); en el condicionamiento clásico ocurre cuando el estímulo incondicionado (EI) no viene detrás del estímulo condicionado (EC). En el condicionamiento operante la extinción ocurre cuando ya no se refuerza una respuesta específica. (p. 269)

extrasensory perception (ESP)/percepción extrasensorial (PES) afirmación controvertida de que es posible percibir por medios distintos de los sentidos; incluye la telepatía, la clarividencia y la precognición. (p. 167)

extrinsic motivation/motivación extrínseca deseo de desempeñar un comportamiento con el propósito de recibir recompensas prometidas o evitar amenazas de castigo. (p. 298)

facial feedback effect/efecto de la reacción facial la tendencia de que los estados de los músculos faciales provoquen sentimientos acordes como el temor, la ira o la felicidad. (p. 438)

factor analysis/análisis factorial procedimiento estadístico que identifica grupos de artículos relacionados (llamados *factores*) en una prueba. Se utiliza para identificar distintas dimensiones de desempeño que determinan el puntaje total que recibe una persona. (p. 608)

false consensus effect/efecto del falso consenso tendencia a sobrestimar el grado en el que otros comparten nuestras creencias y conductas. (p. 568)

family therapy/terapia de familia terapia en la que se considera que la familia es un sistema. Según esta terapia, los comportamientos no deseados de un individuo son influenciados por otros miembros de la familia o dirigidos a estos. (p. 724)

feature detectors/detectores de características neuronas en el cerebro que responden a características específicas de un estímulo tales como forma, ángulo o movimiento. (p. 175)

feel-good, do-good phenomenon/fenómeno de sentirse bien, hacer el bien tendencia a ser serviciales cuando estamos de buen humor. (p. 847)

fetal alcohol syndrome (FAS)/síndrome de alcoholismo fetal (SAF) anomalías físicas y cognitivas en los niños causadas por la ingestión excesiva de alcohol por parte de las madres durante el embarazo. En casos agudos, los síntomas incluyen cráneo desproporcionadamente pequeño y características faciales anormales. (p. 467)

fetus/feto organismo humano en vías de desarrollo a partir de las 9 semanas de concepción hasta el nacimiento. (p. 466)

figure-ground/figura-fondo organización del campo visual en objetos (*figuras*) que se distinguen de sus ambientes (*fondos*). (p. 183)

fixation/fijación según Freud, un permanente foco de energía en busca de placer en una etapa psicosexual temprana cuando los conflictos todavía no estaban resueltos. (p. 560)

fixed-interval schedule/programa de intervalo fijo en el condicionamiento operante, un programa de refuerzo que solo refuerza una respuesta después de un lapso de tiempo específico. (p. 280)

fixed-ratio schedule/programa de frecuencia fija en el condicionamiento operante, un programa de refuerzo que solo refuerza una respuesta después de un número específico de respuestas. (p. 279)

flashbulb memory/memoria de flash memoria clara de un momento o evento emocionalmente significativo. (p. 332)

flow/flujo el sentirse completamente involucrado y concentrado en una actividad, de manera que se pierde la conciencia del yo y del tiempo. En consecuencia, se emplean las habilidades en todo su potencial. (p. 827)

fluid intelligence/inteligencia fluida capacidad que tenemos de razonar rápidamente y de manera abstracta; tiende a disminuir en los adultos muy mayores. (p. 626)

fMRI (functional magnetic resonance imaging)/imágenes de resonancia magnética funcional (IRMf) técnica para observar la circulación sanguínea y, por lo tanto, la actividad cerebral comparando resultados sucesivos de exámenes de resonancia magnética. Los resultados del examen de resonancia magnética funcional muestran la función y la estructura del cerebro. (p. 96)

foot-in-the-door phenomenon/fenómeno de pie en la puerta tendencia de la gente que ha accedido a algo pequeño en primer lugar, a después satisfacer una demanda más grande. (p. 757)

formal operational stage/período operacional formal en la teoría de Piaget, el período en el desarrollo cognitivo (normalmente empieza alrededor de los 12 años) durante el que la persona empieza a pensar lógicamente sobre conceptos abstractos. (p. 483)

fovea/fóvea punto central de enfoque de la retina alrededor del cual se agrupan los conos del ojo. (p. 173)

framing/enmarcamiento manera como se presenta una situación; el cómo se enmarca una situación puede afectar de manera significativa las decisiones y juicios. (p. 368)

fraternal twins (dizygotic twins)/mellizos (gemelos dicigóticos) se desarrollan de dos óvulos fecundados distintos. Genéticamente no están más cercanos que los hermanos y hermanas; pero comparten un medio ambiente fetal. (p. 125)

free association/asociación libre en psicoanálisis, un método de explorar el inconsciente en el que la persona se relaja y dice lo primero que le viene a la mente, no importa cuán trivial o incómodo sea. (p. 557)

frequency/frecuencia número de ondas completas que pasan un punto en un tiempo dado (por ejemplo, por segundo). (p. 195)

frequency theory/teoría de frecuencia en la audición, la teoría que postula que la proporción de impulsos nerviosos que viaja por el nervio auditivo es igual a la frecuencia de un tono, permitiéndonos percibir el tono. (p. 199)

frontal lobes/lóbulos frontales parte de la corteza cerebral que se halla inmediatamente detrás de la frente; tiene que ver con el habla y los movimientos musculares, así como la planificación y la formación de opiniones. (p. 105)

frustration-aggression principle/principio de frustración-agresión principio de que la frustración —el bloqueo de un intento para lograr alguna meta— crea ira, la cual puede generar agresión. (p. 791)

functionalism/funcionalismo escuela de psicología promovida por James e influida por Darwin; exploraba el funcionamiento de nuestros procesos mentales y conductuales, y cómo estos permiten que el organismo se adapte, sobreviva y prospere. (p. 4)

fundamental attribution error/error fundamental de la atribución tendencia de los observadores, al analizar la conducta de otra persona, a subestimar el impacto de la situación y a sobrestimar el impacto de la disposición personal. (p. 754)

gate-control theory/teoría de control de la puerta del dolor teoría que postula que la médula espinal contiene una "puerta" neurológica que bloquea las señales de dolor o les permite proseguir al cerebro. La "puerta" se abre por la actividad de las señales de dolor que viajan a través de pequeñas fibras nerviosas y se cierra por la actividad en las fibras más grandes o por información procedente del cerebro. (p. 203)

gender/género roles y características establecidos por la sociedad por los cuales una cultura define *hombre* y *mujer*. (p. 500)

gender identity/identidad de género sensación que tenemos de ser hombre o mujer. (p. 504)

gender role/rol de género expectativas de cómo las mujeres y los hombres deben comportarse. (p. 503)

gender typing/tipificación de género adquisición de un rol masculino o femenino tradicional. (p. 504)

general adaptation syndrome (GAS)/síndrome de adaptación general (SAG) concepto de Selye que afirma que la respuesta de adaptación del cuerpo al estrés se presenta en tres etapas: alarma, resistencia y agotamiento. (p. 444)

general intelligence (*g*)/factor g de inteligencia general factor de inteligencia general que de acuerdo a Spearman y otros subyace habilidades mentales específicas y es por lo tanto cuantificado por cada tarea de las pruebas de inteligencia. (p. 608)

generalization/generalización tendencia, una vez que una respuesta ha sido condicionada, a que los estímulos similares al estímulo condicionado provoquen respuestas similares. (p. 269)

generalized anxiety disorder/trastorno de ansiedad generalizado trastorno de ansiedad en el que la persona está constantemente tensa, aprensiva, y en estado de excitación del sistema nervioso autonómico. (p. 662)

genes/genes unidades bioquímicas de la herencia que constituyen los cromosomas; segmentos de ADN capaces de sintetizar proteínas. (p. 124)

genome/genoma instrucciones completas para crear un organismo; consiste de todo el material genético en los cromosomas de ese organismo. (p. 124)

gestalt/Gestalt un todo organizado. Los psicólogos de la Gestalt pusieron énfasis en nuestra tendencia a integrar segmentos de información en todos significativos. (p. 182)

glial cells (glia)/células gliales células en el sistema nervioso que sostienen, nutren y protegen a las neuronas; posiblemente cumplan una función en el aprendizaje y el pensamiento. (p. 104)

glucose/glucosa forma de azúcar que circula en la sangre y provee de la mayor fuente de energía a los tejidos del cuerpo. Cuando su nivel es bajo, sentimos hambre. (p. 397)

grammar/gramática en un idioma, un sistema de reglas que nos permite comunicarnos y entendernos con otros. La *semántica* es el conjunto de reglas que permiten deducir el significado de los sonidos y la *sintaxis* es el conjunto de reglas que establecen cómo se deben combinar palabras para formar oraciones gramáticamente correctas. (p. 373)

GRIT/estrategia de de-escalamiento paso a paso GRIT (por sus siglas en inglés) estrategia diseñada para disminuir las tensiones internacionales. (p. 815)

grit/tenacidad en psicología, la tenacidad es la pasión y la perseverancia en la búsqueda de metas a largo plazo. (pp. 610, 834)

group polarization/efecto de polarización de grupo fortalecimiento de las posiciones imperantes en un grupo a través de discusiones del grupo. (p. 774)

group therapy/terapia grupal terapia realizada con grupos, en lugar de individuos, que aprovecha los beneficios terapéuticos de la interacción grupal. (p. 723)

grouping/agrupamiento tendencia perceptiva de organizar los estímulos en grupos coherentes. (p. 183)

groupthink/pensamiento del grupo modo de pensar que ocurre cuando el deseo de armonía en un grupo de toma de decisiones anula la evaluación objetiva de las alternativas. (p. 775)

habituation/habituación atgenuación de la respuesta por una estimulación repetitiva. Conforme los infantes se familiarizan con un estímulo visual debido su exposición repetida a este, su interés desaparece y miran para otro lado más pronto. (pp. 264, 468)

hallucinations/alucinaciones experiencias sensoriales falsas, como ver algo sin recibir ningún estímulo visual externo. (pp. 228, 685)

hallucinogens/alucinógenos drogas psicodélicas ("que se manifiestan en la mente"), como el LSD, que distorsionan las percepciones y evocan imágenes sensoriales sin ninguna inducción sensorial. (pp. 439, 856)

health psychology/psicología de salud subdivisión de la psicología que contribuye a la medicina conductual. (pp. 439, 856)

heritability/heredabilidad proporción de variación entre individuos que podemos atribuir a los genes. La heredabilidad de una característica puede variar dependiendo del rango de las poblaciones y de los ambientes estudiados. (pp. 129, 632)

heuristic/heurística simple estrategia de pensamiento que nos permite formar juicios y resolver problemas de manera eficiente. Normalmente es más rápida que el utilizar *algoritmos;* pero también puede conducir a más errores. (p. 361)

hierarchy of needs/jerarquía de necesidades pirámide de necesidades humanas de Maslow, empezando en la base con las necesidades fisiológicas que se deben satisfacer antes de que se activen las necesidades de seguridad de nivel superior y luego las necesidades psicológicas. (p. 393)

higher-order conditioning/condicionamiento de orden superior procedimiento en el que el estímulo condicionado de una experiencia condicionada se presenta a la vez que un nuevo estímulo neutral, creando un segundo (por lo general más débil) estímulo condicionado. Por ejemplo, un animal que ha aprendido que un tono precede un alimento, podría aprender que una luz precede el tono y comenzar a responder solo a la luz. (También se denomina *condicionamiento de segundo orden*). (p. 268)

hindsight bias/distorsión retrospectiva tendencia a creer, después de saber un resultado, que uno lo habría previsto. (También se lo conoce como *el fenómeno de "yo ya lo sabía"*). (p. 31)

histogram/histograma gráfica de barras que muestra una distribución de frecuencia. (p. 57)

hippocampus/hipocampo centro neuronal que es parte del sistema límbico y contribuye al procesamiento de memorias explícitas para almacenarlas. (p. 330)

homeostasis/homeóstasis tendencia a mantener un estado interior equilibrado o constante; la regulación de cualquier aspecto químico del cuerpo, como la glucosa en sangre, a un nivel específico. (p. 391)

hormones/hormonas mensajeros químicos producidos por las glándulas endocrinas que circulan en el torrente sanguíneo y afectan a otros tejidos. (p. 90)

hue/tono dimensión del color determinada por la longitud de la onda luminosa; lo que conocemos como los nombres de los colores: *azul, verde,* etc. (p. 172)

human factors psychology/psicología de factores humanos división de la psicología industrial y organizacional que explora cómo las personas y máquinas actúan recíprocamente, y cómo las máquinas y los ambientes físicos pueden hacerse seguros y fáciles de usar. (pp. 14, 828)

humanistic psychology/psicología humanista perspectiva históricamente significativa que enfatizaba el potencial de crecimiento de las personas sanas. (p. 6)

humanistic theories/teorías humanistas teorías que analizan la personalidad enfocándose en el potencial del individuo para lograr una evolución personal sana. (p. 571)

hypnosis/hipnosis interacción social en la que una persona (el sujeto) responde a la sugerencia de otra (el hipnotizador) de que ciertas percepciones, sentimientos, pensamientos o comportamientos ocurrirán espontáneamente. (p. 219)

hypothalamus/hipotálamo estructura neural localizada debajo (*hipo*) del tálamo; regula varias actividades de mantenimiento (comer, beber y la temperatura corporal), contribuye a dirigir el sistema endocrino a través de la glándula pituitaria, y está conectado con las emociones y las recompensas. (p. 99)

hypothesis/hipótesis predicción comprobable, a menudo implicada por una teoría. (p. 38)

iconic memory/memoria icónica tipo de memoria sensorial momentánea que reacciona a los estímulos visuales; memoria fotográfica o de imágenes que dura solo unas décimas de segundo. (p. 322)

id/id depósito de energía psíquica inconsciente que, según Freud, se esfuerza por satisfacer los impulsos sexuales y agresivos esenciales. El id opera bajo el *principio de placer,* exigiendo satisfacción inmediata. (p. 558)

identical twins (*monozygotic twins*)**/gemelos** (*gemelos monocigóticos*) se desarrollan a partir de un solo óvulo fecundado que se divide en dos, creando dos organismos con características genéticas idénticas. (p. 125)

identification/identificación proceso en el que, según Freud, los niños incorporan los valores de sus padres en sus súper-egos en vías de desarrollo. (p. 559)

identity/identidad idea que tenemos de nosotros mismos; según Erikson, el adolescente tiene la tarea de solidificar su sentido de identidad probando e integrando diversos roles. (p. 519)

illness anxiety disorder/trastorno de ansiedad por enfermedad trastorno por el que una persona interpreta las sensaciones físicas normales como síntomas de una enfermedad. (Anteriormente se denominaba *hipocondría*). (p. 694)

illusory correlation/correlación ilusoria percepción de una relación dónde no hay ninguna. (p. 50)

implicit memory/memoria implícita retención que es independiente de la memoria consciente. (También se denomina *memoria no declarativa*). (p. 320)

imprinting/impronta proceso en el que ciertos animales forman apegos durante un período crítico muy temprano en la vida. (p. 489)

inattentional blindness/ceguera por falta de atención el no ver los objetos visibles cuando nuestra atención se dirige a otra parte. (p. 154)

incentive/incentivo estímulo medioambiental positivo o negativo que motiva el comportamiento. (p. 392)

independent variable/variable independiente factor experimental que se manipula; la variable cuyo efecto es el objeto de estudio. (p. 52)

individualism/individualismo el dar prioridad a las propias metas sobre las metas del grupo y definir la propia identidad en términos de los atributos personales en lugar de las identificaciones del grupo. (p. 598)

industrial-organizational (I/O) psychology/psicología industrial y organizacional aplicación de conceptos y métodos psicológicos para optimizar el comportamiento humano en los lugares de trabajo. (pp. 14, 828)

inferential statistics/estadística inferencial datos numéricos que permiten generalizar, es decir, inferir a partir de una muestra de datos la probabilidad de que algo sea verdadero para una población. (p. 60)

informational social influence/influencia social informativa influencia resultante de la disposición de una persona para aceptar la opinión de los otros acerca de la realidad. (p. 764)

informed consent/consentimiento informado un principio ético que obliga a proporcionar a los participantes de una investigación los datos necesarios para que puedan decidir si efectivamente desean participar. (p. 68)

ingroup/endogrupo "nosotros": personas con las que tenemos una identidad en común. (p. 784)

ingroup bias/favoritismo del endogrupo tendencia a favorecer al grupo al que pertenecemos. (p. 784)

inner ear/oído interno parte más profunda de la oreja; contiene la cóclea, los canales semicirculares y el vestíbulo. (p. 195)

insight/sagacidad comprensión súbita de la solución a un problema; contrasta con las soluciones basadas en estrategias. (pp. 297, 361)

insight therapies/terapias psicodinámicas variedad de terapias que tienen el propósito de mejorar el funcionamiento psicológico aumentando el nivel de conciencia que tiene una persona de sus motivos y defensas subyacentes. (p. 711)

insomnia/insomnio problemas recurrentes para dormir o quedarse dormido. (p. 238)

instinct/instinto comportamiento complejo que está arraigado y es innato en cada especie. (p. 391)

intellectual disability/discapacidad intelectual cuadro de capacidad mental limitada marcada por un cociente intelectual de 70 o menos, y por la dificultad de adaptarse a las exigencias de la vida. (Anteriormente se conocía como *retraso mental*). (p. 629)

intelligence/inteligencia calidad mental que consiste en la habilidad de aprender de la experiencia, resolver problemas y utilizar el conocimiento para adaptarse a nuevas situaciones. (p. 607)

intelligence quotient (IQ)/cociente intelectual (CI) definido originalmente como la proporción entre la edad mental (*em*) y edad cronológica (*ec*) multiplicada por 100 (por ende, $CI = ed/ec \times 100$). En las pruebas de inteligencia contemporáneas, al desempeño promedio de cada grupo etario se le asigna una puntuación de 100 y las puntuaciones correspondientes al desempeño relativo son mayores o menores que ese promedio. (p. 618)

intelligence test/prueba de inteligencia método para evaluar las aptitudes mentales de un individuo y compararlas con las de otros utilizando puntajes numéricos. (p. 607)

intensity/intensidad cantidad de energía en una onda luminosa o sonora que percibimos como brillo o intensidad sonora, determinada por la amplitud de la onda. (p. 172)

interaction/interacción acción que se ejerce recíprocamente cuando el efecto de un factor (como el ambiente) depende de otro factor (como la herencia). (p. 131)

internal locus of control/locus de control interno impresión de que controlamos nuestro propio destino. (p. 300)

interneurons/interneuronas neuronas del cerebro y la médula espinal que se comunican internamente e intervienen entre la estimulación sensorial y las respuestas motoras. (p. 87)

interpretation/interpretación en psicoanálisis, las observaciones del analista con relación al supuesto significado de los sueños, las resistencias, y otros comportamientos y eventos significativos, a fin de promover la sagacidad. (p. 710)

intimacy/intimidad en la teoría de Erikson, la habilidad de formar relaciones íntimas, amorosas. Una de las tareas principales del desarrollo de la adolescencia tardía y la adultez temprana. (p. 521)

intrinsic motivation/motivación intrínseca deseo de expresar un comportamiento eficazmente por el comportamiento en sí. (p. 297)

intuition/intuición sensación o pensamiento no esforzado, inmediato y automático, que contrasta con el razonamiento explícito y consciente. (p. 363)

iris/iris anillo de tejido muscular que forma la porción coloreada del ojo alrededor de la pupila y controla el tamaño de la apertura de la pupila. (p. 172)

James-Lange theory/teoría de James-Lange teoría que postula que nuestra experiencia emocional es nuestra conciencia de nuestras respuestas fisiológicas a los estímulos que despiertan nuestras emociones. (p. 421)

just-world phenomenon/hipótesis del "mundo justo" tendencia a creer que el mundo es justo y que las personas consiguen lo que se merecen y se merecen lo que consiguen. (p. 784)

kinesthesia/cinética sistema que siente la posición y el movimiento de las partes individuales de cuerpo. (p. 209)

language/lenguaje palabras habladas, escritas o en señas y las maneras en que las combinamos para comunicar significado. (p. 372)

latent content/contenido latente según Freud, el significado subyacente de un sueño (distinto de su contenido manifiesto). (p. 241)

latent learning/aprendizaje latente aprendizaje que ocurre pero que no es aparente hasta que surge un incentivo para demostrarlo. (p. 297)

law of effect/ley de efecto principio de Thorndike según el cual los comportamientos seguidos de consecuencias favorables se vuelven más probables y los comportamientos seguidos de consecuencias desfavorables se vuelven menos probables. (p. 275)

learned helplessness/indefensión aprendida indefensión y resignación pasiva que un animal o un ser humano desarrollan cuando son incapaces de evitar repetidos eventos de aversión. (p. 299)

learning/aprendizaje proceso de adquirir información o comportamientos nuevos y relativamente permanentes. (p. 263)

lens/lente estructura transparente detrás de la pupila que cambia de forma para ayudar a enfocar las imágenes en la retina. (p. 172)

lesion/lesión destrucción del tejido. Una lesión cerebral es una destrucción del tejido cerebral ya sea por efectos naturales o experimentales. (p. 94)

levels of analysis/niveles de análisis las distintas opiniones complementarias desde las biológicas, pasando por las psicológicas, hasta las socio-culturales, para analizar cualquier fenómeno. (p. 11)

limbic system/sistema límbico sistema neuronal (que incluye el *hipocampo*, la *amígdala* y el *hipotálamo*) ubicado debajo de los hemisferios cerebrales; está asociado con las emociones y los instintos. (p. 98)

linguistic determinism/determinismo lingüístico hipótesis de Whorf según la cual el lenguaje determina la manera que pensamos. (p. 379)

lobotomy/lobotomía procedimiento psicoquirúrgico que se utilizó en una época para calmar a pacientes violentos o que padecían de emociones incontrolables. Mediante este procedimiento se separaba la conexión entre los lóbulos frontales y los centros de control de las emociones en las partes interiores del cerebro. (p. 746)

longitudinal study/estudio longitudinal investigación en la que las mismas personas son estudiadas y reexaminadas por un tiempo largo. (p. 543)

long-term memory/memoria a largo plazo tipo de memoria relativamente permanente e ilimitada. Incluye el conocimiento, las habilidades y las experiencias. (p. 319)

long-term potentiation (LTP)/potenciación a largo plazo (PLP) aumento en la eficiencia de una célula con estimulaciones breves y rápidas . Se cree que esta es la base neuronal para el aprendizaje y la memoria. (p. 333)

LSD/LSD droga alucinógena poderosa; también conocido como ácido *(dietilamida del ácido lisérgico).* (p. 254)

lymphocytes/linfocitos los dos tipos de glóbulos blancos que forman parte del sistema inmunológico: *los linfocitos del tipo B* se forman en la médula ósea y liberan anticuerpos que combaten las infecciones bacterianas; *los linfocitos del tipo T* se forman en el timo y en otro tejido linfático y atacan las células cancerosas, los virus y las sustancias extrañas. (p. 448)

major depressive disorder/trastorno depresivo mayor trastorno del estado de ánimo en el cual una persona (sin una condición médica y sin el uso de drogas) presenta cinco o más síntomas por un período mínimo de dos semanas; al menos uno de esos síntomas debe ser (1) depresión o (2) falta de interés o placer. (p. 672)

mania/manía trastorno del estado de ánimo marcado por una condición hiperactiva y desenfrenadamente optimista. (p. 673)

manifest content/contenido manifiesto según Freud, recuerdo de los eventos del sueño (distinto de su contenido latente u oculto). (p. 241)

maturation/maduración procesos biológicos de crecimiento que permiten los cambios estructurados en el comportamiento y que no están relativamente influenciados por la experiencia. (p. 471)

mean/media promedio aritmético de una distribución obtenidos sumando todos los puntajes y dividiendo el total por el número de puntajes. (p. 57)

median/mediana punto medio en una distribución; la mitad de los puntajes están por encima y la mitad están por debajo de la mediana. (p. 57)

medical model/modelo médico concepto que sostiene que las enfermedades (en este caso, los trastornos psíquicos) tienen causas físicas que pueden *diagnosticarse, tratarse* y, en la mayoría de los casos, *curarse,* por lo general mediante un tratamiento en un *hospital.* (p. 653)

medulla/médula base del tronco encefálico; controla el latido del corazón y la respiración. (p. 97)

memory/memoria el aprender de manera persistente a través del tiempo mediante la codificación, el almacenaje y la recuperación de la información. (p. 318)

menarche/menarquía primer período menstrual. (p. 527)

menopause/menopausia período en que la menstruación desaparece de manera natural; también se refiere a los cambios biológicos que una mujer experimenta al declinar su capacidad reproductora. (p. 540)

mental age/edad mental medida de desempeño en pruebas de inteligencia diseñada por Bidet. La edad cronológica normalmente corresponde a un nivel dado de desempeño. Por ende, una criatura que se desempeña como una persona normal de 8 años, tiene una edad mental de 8 años. (p. 618)

mental set/predisposición mental tendencia a tratar de resolver un problema de una manera en particular que, usualmente, ya ha funcionado en el pasado. (p. 362)

mere exposure effect/efecto de la mera exposición fenómeno que sostiene que la exposición repetida a estímulos novedosos aumenta su atracción. (p. 798)

meta-analysis/metaanálisis procedimiento para combinar estadísticamente los resultados de distintos estudios de investigación. (p. 731)

methamphetamine/metanfetamina droga poderosamente adictiva que estimula el sistema nervioso central con funciones corporales aceleradas y cambios de energía y estado de ánimo. Aparentemente, con el tiempo reduce los niveles mínimos de dopamina. (p. 253)

middle ear/oído medio cámara entre el tímpano y cóclea que contiene tres huesos diminutos (martillo, yunque y estribo) que concentran las vibraciones del tímpano en la ventana ovalado de la cóclea. (p. 195)

Minnesota Multiphasic Personality Inventory (MMPI)/Inventario multifásico de personalidad de Minesota (MMPI, por sus siglas en inglés) la prueba de personalidad más investigada y clínicamente utilizada. Esta prueba, originalmente desarrollada para identificar trastornos emocionales (todavía se considera que este es su uso más apropiado), hoy en día se utiliza con muchos otros propósitos. (p. 578)

mirror neurons/neuronas espejo neuronas del lóbulo frontal que, según algunos científicos, descargan impulsos cuando se realizan determinadas acciones o cuando se observa a otro hacerlas. Este proceso cerebral de reflejar las acciones de otro puede posibilitar la imitación y la empatía. (p. 304)

mirror-image perceptions/percepciones especulares opiniones mutuas que generalmente mantienen los individuos con sentimientos encontrados, por ejemplo, cuando uno de ellos se considera ético y pacífico y percibe al otro como malvado y agresivo. (p. 812)

misinformation effect/efecto de desinformación el incorporar información engañosa en nuestros recuerdos de un evento. (p. 347)

mnemonics/mnemónica ayudas de memoria, sobre todo esas técnicas que utilizan imágenes vívidas y dispositivos organizacionales. (p. 323)

mode/moda el puntaje o puntajes que ocurren con mayor frecuencia en una distribución. (p. 57)

modeling/modelado proceso de observar e imitar un comportamiento específico. (p. 304)

molecular genetics/genética molecular división de la biología que estudia la estructura molecular y la función de los genes. (p. 129)

monocular cues/indicaciones monoculares señales de profundidad como la interposición y la perspectiva lineal, que pueden ser extraídas de las imágenes de cada uno de los ojos. (p. 185)

mood disorders/trastornos del estado de ánimo trastornos psicológicos caracterizados por estados extremos de ánimo. Véase *trastorno depresivo mayor, manía y trastorno bipolar.* (p. 671)

mood-congruent memory/memoria congruente con el humor tendencia a rememorar las experiencias que son consistentes con nuestro humor actual, bueno o malo. (p. 337)

morpheme/morfema en el lenguaje, la unidad más pequeña de significado; puede ser una palabra o parte de una palabra (como un prefijo). (p. 373)

motivation/motivación necesidad o deseo que da energía y dirige el comportamiento. (p. 390)

motor (efferent) neurons/neuronas motrices (eferentes) neuronas que transmiten la información del cerebro y la médula espinal hacia los músculos y las glándulas. (p. 86)

motor cortex/corteza motriz área en la parte posterior de los lóbulos frontales que controla los movimientos voluntarios. (p. 105)

MRI (magnetic resonance imaging)/IRM (imágenes por resonancia magnética) técnica que utiliza campos magnéticos y ondas de radio para producir imágenes de tejidos blandos generadas por computadora. Las IRM permiten observar la anatomía cerebral. (p. 95)

mutation/mutación error aleatorio en la réplica de los genes que tiene como resultado un cambio. (p. 136)

myelin sheath/vaina de mielina capa de tejido graso que encasilla los axones de algunas neuronas, facilitando una mayor velocidad de transmisión, ya que los impulsos neuronales saltan de un nódulo al siguiente. (p. 78)

narcissism/narcisismo autoestima exagerada y egotismo. (p. 597)

narcolepsy/narcolepsia trastorno del sueño caracterizado por ataques de somnolencia irresistibles con el sueño REM ocurriendo al inicio del sueño, a menudo en momentos inoportunos. (p. 238)

natural selection/selección natural principio según el cual, entre la variedad de rasgos heredados, aquellos que contribuyen a la reproducción y la supervivencia tienen gran probabilidad de pasar a las generaciones futuras. (pp. 10, 135)

naturalistic observation/observación naturalista el observar y registrar la conducta en situaciones reales sin tratar de manipular y controlar la situación. (p. 40)

nature-nurture issue/relación entre herencia y crianza larga controversia sobre las contribuciones relativas de los genes y la experiencia en el desarrollo de los rasgos psicológicos y las conductas. La ciencia actual considera que los rasgos y las conductas surgen de la interacción entre la naturaleza y la crianza. (p. 9)

near-death experience/experiencia al borde de la muerte estado de alteración experimentado por personas que llegan al borde de la muerte (por ejemplo, a causa de un paro cardíaco). Son similares a las alucinaciones inducidas por las drogas. (p. 255)

negative reinforcement/refuerzo negativo aumento de conductas como consecuencia de la omisión o reducción de un estímulo negativo. Aquí se *omite* un estímulo después de una respuesta, y como consecuencia se refuerza dicha respuesta. (*Nota:* El refuerzo negativo no es castigo). (p. 278)

nerves/nervios conjunto de axones que forman "cables" neurales que conectan el sistema nervioso central con los músculos, las glándulas y los órganos de los sentidos. (p. 86)

nervous system/sistema nervioso veloz red electroquímica de comunicación del cuerpo que consiste de todas las células nerviosas del sistema periférico y del sistema nervioso central. (p. 86)

neurogenesis/neurogénesis formación de nuevas neuronas. (p. 112)

neuron/neurona célula nerviosa; el componente básico del sistema nervioso. (p. 78)

neurotransmitters/neurotransmisores mensajeros químicos que atraviesan los espacios intersinápticos entre las neuronas. Cuando son liberados por una neurona emisora, los neurotransmisores pasan a través de la sinapsis y se acomodan en los receptores de la neurona receptora, influyendo en la generación de un impulso neural por parte de dicha neurona. (p. 80)

neutral stimulus (NS)/estímulo neutro (EN) en el condicionamiento clásico, estímulo que no provoca respuesta antes del condicionamiento. (p. 266)

nicotine/nicotina droga psicoactiva estimulante y altamente adictiva que se encuentra en el tabaco. (p. 250)

night terrors/terrores nocturnos trastorno del sueño caracterizado por una gran excitación y la apariencia de estar aterrorizado; a diferencia de las pesadillas, los terrores nocturnos ocurren durante el sueño NREM-3, dos o tres horas después de dormirse, y raramente se recuerdan. (p. 239)

norm/norma regla entendida de comportamiento aceptado y esperado. Las normas prescriben el comportamiento "apropiado". (p. 777)

normal curve/curva normal (*distribución normal*) curva simétrica en forma de campana que describe la distribución de muchos tipos de datos. La mayoría de los puntajes están cerca de la media (aproximadamente el 68 por ciento están dentro de una desviación estándar de esta) y disminuyen en número conforme se acercan a los extremos. (pp. 59, 621)

normative social influence/influencia social normativa influencia que resulta del deseo de una persona de ganar la aprobación o evitar la desaprobación. (p. 764)

NREM sleep/sueño de NREM (por sus siglas en inglés) sueño en el que no hay un movimiento ocular rápido; abarca todas las etapas del sueño, salvo la REM. (p. 228)

object permanence/permanencia de objeto conocimiento de que las cosas existen aunque no las percibamos. (p. 478)

observational learning/aprendizaje observacional el aprender observando a otros. (También se lo conoce como *aprendizaje social*). (p. 304)

obsessive-compulsive disorder (OCD)/trastorno obsesivo-compulsivo (TOC) trastorno caracterizado por pensamientos (obsesiones) o acciones (compulsiones) que son repetitivos y no deseados. (p. 663)

occipital lobes/lóbulos occipitales porción de la corteza cerebral ubicada en la parte posterior de la cabeza; incluye las áreas que reciben información de los campos visuales. (p. 105)

Oedipus complex/complejo de Edipo según Freud, los deseos sexuales de un muchacho hacia su madre y sentimientos de celos y odio para el padre rival. (p. 559)

one-word stage/etapa holofrástica etapa en el desarrollo del habla en la que el niño, de entre 1 y 2 años, se expresa principalmente con palabras aisladas. (p. 375)

operant behavior/comportamiento operante comportamiento que opera en el ambiente, produciendo consecuencias. (p. 289)

operant chamber/cámara operante en los estudios del condicionamiento operante, cámara (también conocida como *caja de Skinner*) equipada con una barra o llave que un animal manipula para obtener un reforzador de comida o agua; unos dispositivos llevan un registro de las veces en que el animal aprieta la barra o picotea la llave. (p. 276)

operant conditioning/condicionamiento operante aprendizaje donde el comportamiento se consolida si está seguido por un refuerzo o se atenúa si está seguido por un castigo. (p. 275)

operational definition/definición operacional manifestación cuidadosamente redactada de los procedimientos exactos (operaciones) utilizados en una investigación. Por ejemplo, la *inteligencia humana* puede ser operacionalmente definida como lo que mide una prueba de inteligencia. (p. 39)

opiates/opiatas el opio y sus derivados, tales como la morfina y la heroína; deprimen la actividad neuronal, disminuyendo el dolor y la ansiedad temporalmente. (p. 250)

opponent-process theory/teoría de los procesos opuestos teoría según la cual los procesos opuestos en la retina (rojo-verde, amarillo-azul, blanco-negro) permiten la visión de colores. Por ejemplo, algunas células son estimuladas por el verde e inhibidas por el rojo; otras son estimuladas por el rojo e inhibidas por el verde. (p. 179)

optic nerve/nervio óptico nervio que transporta los impulsos neuronales del ojo al cerebro. (p. 173)

organizational psychology/psicología organizacional subdivisión de la psicología industrial y organizacional que examina las influencias organizacionales en la satisfacción y productividad de los trabajadores, y facilita los cambios organizacionales. (p. 828)

other-race effect/efecto de otras razas tendencia a recordar con mayor precisión los rostros de individuos de la raza a la cual uno pertenece que los rostros de individuos de otras razas. (También se denomina *efecto interracial*). (p. 786)

outgroup/exogrupo "ellos": personas que consideramos distintas o ajenas a nuestro endogrupo. (p. 784)

overconfidence/confianza excesiva tendencia a estar más seguros de nosotros mismos que a estar en lo cierto, o sea, de sobreestimar la exactitud de nuestras creencias y opiniones. (p. 365)

panic disorder/trastorno de pánico trastorno de ansiedad marcado por episodios impredecibles de aprehensión intensa que pueden durar varios minutos. Incluyen dolor de pecho, sofocamiento y otras sensaciones atemorizantes. Estos episodios suelen ir seguidos del temor por un posible ataque futuro. (p. 662)

parallel processing/procesamiento paralelo procesamiento simultáneo de varias partes de un problema; el modo natural del cerebro de procesar la información de muchas funciones, incluida la visión. Contrasta con el procesamiento paso a paso (en serie) de la mayoría de las computadoras y de la resolución consciente de problemas. (pp. 176, 319)

parapsychology/parapsicología estudio de fenómenos paranormales incluyendo la percepción extrasensorial y la psicoquinesis. (p. 167)

parasympathetic nervous system/sistema nervioso autonómico parasimpático división del sistema nervioso autonómico que calma el cuerpo conservando su energía. (p. 87)

parietal lobes/lóbulos parietales área de la corteza cerebral en la parte superior y hacia la parte posterior de la cabeza que recibe suministro sensorial para el tacto y la posición del cuerpo. (p. 105)

partial (intermittent) reinforcement/refuerzo parcial (intermitente) refuerzo a una respuesta solo parte del tiempo; tiene como resultado la adquisición más lenta de una respuesta pero mucho más resistente a la extinción que el refuerzo continuo. (p. 279)

passionate love/amor apasionado estado excitado de intensa y positiva absorción en otro ser, normalmente presente al comienzo de una relación amorosa. (p. 803)

perception/percepción proceso de organizar e interpretar la información sensorial, permitiéndonos reconocer los objetos y eventos significativos. (p. 152)

perceptual adaptation/adaptación visual habilidad de acomodarnos a un campo visual artificialmente desplazado o hasta invertido. (p. 191)

perceptual constancy/constancia perceptiva percepción de los objetos como inalterables (de forma, tamaño, luminosidad y color constantes) aunque cambien la iluminación y las imágenes en la retina. (p. 186)

perceptual set/predisposición perceptiva predisposición mental para percibir una cosa y no otra. (p. 163)

peripheral nervous system (PNS)/sistema nervioso periférico (SNP) neuronas sensoriales y motrices que conectan el sistema nervioso central (SNC) al resto del cuerpo. (p. 86)

peripheral route persuasion/persuasión por ruta periférica se observa cuando los individuos son influenciados por claves secundarias, por ejemplo, el atractivo físico de un orador. (p. 756)

personality/personalidad forma característica de pensar, sentir y actuar de un individuo. (p. 555)

personality disorders/trastornos de la personalidad trastornos psicológicos caracterizados por modelos de comportamiento inflexibles y duraderos que impiden el funcionamiento social. (p. 698)

personality inventory/inventario de personalidad cuestionario (a menudo con preguntas de *verdadero/falso, estoy de acuerdo/estoy en desacuerdo*) diseñado para medir un amplio rango de sentimientos y comportamientos, utilizados para evaluar ciertos rasgos de personalidad. (p. 578)

personality psychology/psicología de personalidad estudio de la forma característica de pensar, sentir y actuar de un individuo. (p. 14)

personnel psychology/psicología de personal subdivisión de la psicología industrial y organizacional que está enfocada en el reclutamiento, selección, colocación, entrenamiento, evaluación y desarrollo de los empleados. (p. 828)

PET (positron emission tomography)/TEP (tomografía por emisión de positrones) presentación gráfica de la actividad cerebral que detecta por dónde pasa una fórmula radiactiva de glucosa mientras el cerebro realiza una tarea determinada. (p. 95)

phi phenomenon/fenómeno fi ilusión de movimiento creado cuando dos o más luces adyacentes destellan en sucesión rápida. (p. 185)

phobia/fobia trastorno de ansiedad marcado por un temor persistente e irracional y la evasión de un objeto, actividad o situación específicos. (p. 662)

phoneme/fonema en el lenguaje, la unidad de sonido más pequeña. (p. 373)

pitch/tono lo agudo o grave de un sonido. Esta característica depende de la frecuencia. (p. 195)

pituitary gland/glándula pituitaria glándula más influyente del sistema endocrino. Bajo la influencia del hipotálamo, la pituitaria regula el crecimiento y controla otras glándulas endocrinas. (p. 91)

place theory/teoría de ubicación en la audición, la teoría que relaciona al tono que oímos con el lugar donde la membrana de la cóclea se estimula. (p. 199)

placebo effect/efecto de placebo [del latín, "complaceré"] resultados experimentales causados exclusivamente por expectativas; cualquier efecto en el comportamiento causado por el suministro de una sustancia o condición inerte que el sujeto del experimento considera agente activo. (p. 52)

plasticity/plasticidad capacidad del cerebro de cambiar, especialmente durante la niñez, reorganizándose después de sufrir una lesión o formando nuevas conexiones a partir de las experiencias del individuo. (p. 111)

polygraph/polígrafo máquina, usualmente utilizada para intentar detectar mentiras, que mide varias de las respuestas fisiológicas que acompañan la emoción (tales como la transpiración y los cambios cardiovasculares y de respiración). (p. 428)

population/población todos los individuos del grupo estudiado de los que se pueden tomar muestras. (*Nota:* a excepción de los estudios nacionales, esto no se refiere a la población entera de un país). (p. 43)

positive psychology/psicología positiva estudio científico del funcionamiento humano cuyas metas consisten en descubrir y promover las fuerzas y las virtudes que permiten prosperar a individuos y comunidades. (pp. 15, 590)

positive reinforcement/refuerzo positivo el aumentar la probabilidad de una conducta con el uso de refuerzos positivos. Un refuerzo positivo es cualquier estímulo que, *presentado* después de una respuesta, la fortalece. (p. 277)

posthypnotic suggestion/sugestión poshipnótica sugestión hecha durante una sesión de hipnosis, para que el sujeto la cumpla cuando ya no esté hipnotizado; técnica empleada por algunos médicos clínicos para tratar de controlar conductas y síntomas indeseados. (p. 220)

post-traumatic growth/evolución post-traumática cambios psicológicos positivos que resultan de la lucha por superar circunstancias extremadamente difíciles y crisis de vida. (p. 665)

post-traumatic stress disorder (PTSD)/trastorno de estrés post-traumático (TEPT) trastorno caracterizado por recuerdos obsesionantes, pesadillas, aislamiento social, ansiedad asustadiza, insensibilidad o insomnio que dura por cuatro semanas o más después de una experiencia traumática. (p. 664)

predictive validity/validez predictiva éxito con cuál una prueba predice el comportamiento que está diseñada para predecir; se evalúa computando la correlación entre los puntajes de la prueba y el criterio de comportamiento. (También se la denomina *validez de criterio*). (pp. 345, 622)

prejudice/prejuicio *actitud* injustificable y normalmente negativa hacia un grupo y sus miembros. El prejuicio generalmente implica creencias estereotipadas, sentimientos negativos y una predisposición a acción discriminatoria. (p. 780)

preoperational stage/etapa preoperacional en la teoría de Piaget, la etapa (desde los 2 hasta los 6 o 7 años de edad, aproximadamente) durante la que el niño aprende a utilizar el lenguaje; pero todavía no comprende las operaciones mentales de lógica concreta. (p. 479)

primary reinforcer/refuerzo primario estímulo natural de refuerzo, como cuando uno satisface una necesidad biológica. (p. 278)

primary sex characteristics/características sexuales primarias estructuras del cuerpo (ovarios, testículos y genitales externos) que hacen posible la reproducción sexual. (p. 527)

priming/exposición previa activación normalmente inconsciente de ciertas asociaciones mentales que predispone la percepción, la memoria o la respuesta de un individuo. (pp. 157, 336)

proactive interference/interferencia proactiva efecto de interferencia cuando el material que ha sido aprendido anteriormente dificulta recordar la información nueva. (p. 345)

problem-focused coping/resolución enfocada en el problema intento por aliviar la tensión directamente, ya sea cambiando estresor o la manera como interactuamos con este. (p. 298)

projective test/prueba de proyección prueba de personalidad, como la de Rorschach, que proporciona estímulos ambiguos diseñados para activar la proyección de nuestra dinámica interna. (p. 567)

prosocial behavior/comportamiento prosocial comportamiento positivo, constructivo, útil. Lo contrario del comportamiento antisocial. (p. 307)

prototype/prototipo imagen mental o mejor ejemplo de una categoría. La comparación de elementos nuevos con un prototipo proporciona un método rápido y fácil de clasificar por categorías (como al comparar animales de plumas con un prototipo de ave, como el ruiseñor). (p. 356)

psychiatry/psiquiatría división de la medicina que trata con trastornos psicológicos; practicado por médicos que a veces proporcionan tratamientos médicos (por ejemplo, con drogas) así como terapia psicológica. (p. 15)

psychoactive drug/droga psicoactiva sustancia química que altera las percepciones y el humor. (p. 246)

psychoanalysis/psicoanálisis (1) teoría de la personalidad de Sigmund Freud que atribuye los pensamientos y acciones a motivos y conflictos inconscientes; técnicas utilizadas para tratar trastornos psicológicos exponiendo e interpretando las tensiones inconscientes. (p. 557) (2) la técnica terapéutica de Freud. Freud creía que las asociaciones libres, las resistencias, los sueños y la transferencia del paciente—y las interpretaciones del terapeuta sobre ellos—liberaban los sentimientos previamente reprimidos, permitiendo al paciente ganar introspección. (p. 709)

psychodynamic psychology/psicología psicodinámica rama de la psicología que estudia cómo los impulsos y conflictos inconscientes influyen en el comportamiento, y utiliza esa información para tratar a quienes tienen trastornos psicológicos (p. 12)

psychodynamic theories/teorías psicodinámicas enfoques actuales que analizan la personalidad concentrándose en el inconsciente y en la importancia de las experiencias de la niñez. (p. 565)

psychodynamic therapy/terapia psicodinámica (1) terapia derivada de la tradición psicoanalítica, en la que se considera que las personas responden a fuerzas inconscientes y a experiencias de la niñez, y que tiene el propósito de aumentar el conocimiento de uno mismo. (p. 710)

psychological disorder/trastorno psicológico síndrome marcado por una alteración clínicamente significativa de la cognición, la regulación de las emociones o la conducta de un individuo. (Adaptado de la Asociación psiquiátrica estadounidense, 2013). (p. 651)

psychology/psicología estudio científico del comportamiento y de los procesos mentales. (p. 7)

psychometrics/psicometría el estudio científico de la medida de las capacidades, las actitudes y los rasgos humanos. (p. 13)

psychoneuroimmunology/psiconeuroinmunología estudio del efecto de los procesos psicológicos, neurales y endocrinos en el sistema de inmunidad y la salud resultante. (p. 448)

psychopharmacology/psicofarmacología estudio de los efectos de las drogas en la mente y el comportamiento. (p. 740)

psychophysics/psicofísica estudio de las relaciones entre las características físicas de los estímulos, como su intensidad, y nuestra experiencia psicológica de ellos. (p. 155)

psychophysiological illness/enfermedad psicofisiológica término que significa literalmente enfermedad "de la mente y el cuerpo"; cualquier enfermedad física que tenga relación con el estrés, por ejemplo, la hipertensión y ciertos dolores de cabeza. (p. 448)

psychosexual stages/etapas psicosexuales etapas del desarrollo infantil (oral, anal, fálica, latente, genital) durante las cuales, según Freud, la energía del id en busca de placer se enfoca en zonas erógenas específicas. (p. 559)

psychosis/psicosis trastorno psicológico debido al cual la persona pierde contacto con la realidad, dando lugar a ideas irracionales y percepciones distorsionadas. (p. 684)

psychosurgery/psicocirugía cirugía que remueve o destruye tejido cerebral para cambiar el comportamiento. (p. 746)

psychotherapy/psicoterapia tratamiento en el que se emplean técnicas psicológicas; consiste en interacciones entre un terapeuta especializado y una persona que desea superar dificultades psicológicas o lograr una evolución personal. (p. 709)

puberty/pubertad período de maduración sexual durante el cual una persona adquiere la capacidad de reproducirse. (p. 527)

punishment/castigo evento que tiende a *disminuir* el comportamiento que le precede. (p. 281)

pupil/pupila apertura adaptable en el centro del ojo a través del cual la luz ingresa. (p. 172)

random assignment/asignación aleatoria distribución al azar de participantes a grupos experimentales y de control para minimizar las diferencias preexistentes entre los diferentes grupos. (p. 51)

random sample/muestra aleatoria muestra que representa fielmente a una población porque cada elemento tiene igual oportunidad de ser seleccionado. (p. 43)

range/rango diferencia entre el puntaje más alto y el más bajo en una distribución. (p. 58)

rational-emotive behavior therapy (REBT)/terapia racional emotiva conductual (TREC) terapia cognitiva de confrontación formulada por Albert Ellis que desafía con énfasis las actitudes y suposiciones ilógicas y de autoderrota de las personas. (p. 721)

recall/recuerdo medida de la memoria en la que la persona debe recuperar información aprendida con anterioridad, como en las pruebas donde se debe llenar el espacio en blanco. (p. 334)

reciprocal determinism/determinismo recíproco interacción de las influencias de conducta, cognición interna y entorno. (p. 588)

reciprocity norm/norma de reciprocidad expectativa de que las personas ayudarán y no herirán a aquellos que las han ayudado. (p. 809)

recognition/reconocimiento medida de la memoria en la que la persona solo debe identificar los artículos previamente aprendidos, como en una prueba de selección múltiple. (p. 334)

reflex/reflejo reacción simple y automática a un estímulo sensorial, como el reflejo de la rodilla. (p. 89)

refractory period/período refractario (1) período de inactividad neuronal posterior a la descarga de un impulso. (p. 79) (2) período de descanso después de un orgasmo durante el cual el hombre no puede tener otro orgasmo. (p. 407)

regression toward the mean/regresión hacia la media la tendencia que tienen los puntajes extremos o inusuales de revertirse (regresar) hacia el promedio. (p. 730)

reinforcement/refuerzo en el condicionamiento operante, cualquier evento que *fortalece* la conducta que le precede. (p. 276)

reinforcement schedule/programa de refuerzo patrón que define la frecuencia con la que se reforzará una respuesta deseada. (p. 279)

relative deprivation/privación relativa percepción de que uno está peor relativamente que aquellos a los que uno se compara. (p. 851)

relearning/reaprendizaje medida de memoria que evalúa la cantidad de tiempo ahorrado cuando se aprende el material la segunda vez. (p. 334)

reliability/fiabilidad medida en la que una prueba produce resultados parejos que son evaluados por la uniformidad de puntajes en dos partes de la prueba, en diferentes versiones de esta, o bien al administrarla nuevamente. (p. 622)

REM rebound/rebote de REM la tendencia a un aumento marcado del sueño REM como consecuencia de la privación del sueño REM (producida por despertares repetidos durante el sueño REM). (p. 243)

REM sleep/sueño REM (por sus siglas en inglés) sueño con movimiento ocular rápido; etapa recurrente en el sueño durante la cual ocurren sueños vívidos. También se conoce como *sueño paradójico* porque los músculos están relajados (excepto por pequeños espasmos); pero el resto de los sistemas corporales se mantienen activos. (p. 226)

repetitive transcranial magnetic stimulation (rTMS)/estimulación magnética transcraneal repetitiva (EMTr) aplicación repetitiva de pulsos de energía magnética al cerebro; utilizada para estimular o suprimir la actividad cerebral. (p. 745)

replication/replicación el repetir la esencia de un estudio de investigación, usualmente con diferentes participantes y en diferentes situaciones, para ver si las conclusiones básicas se extienden a otros participantes y circunstancias. (p. 39)

representativeness heuristic/heurística de la representatividad estrategia para estimar la probabilidad de un suceso mediante la evaluación de su parecido o concordancia con ciertos prototipos; a veces conduce a ignorar otros datos relevantes. (p. 364)

repression/represión en la teoría psicoanalítica, el mecanismo básico de defensa por medio del cual el sujeto elimina de su consciente aquellos pensamientos, emociones o recuerdos que le producen ansiedad. (pp. 346, 560)

resilience/capacidad de recuperación la fuerza personal que ayuda a la mayoría de las personas a superar el estrés y recuperarse de la adversidad e incluso de los traumas. (p. 737)

resistance/resistencia en psicoanálisis, el bloquear del consciente aquello que está cargado de ansiedad. (p. 710)

respondent behavior/conducta respondiente conducta que ocurre como respuesta automática a un estímulo. (p. 289)

reticular formation/formación reticular red de nervios que atraviesa el tronco encefálico y el tálamo, y que juega un papel importante en el control de la excitación. (p. 98)

retina/retina superficie sensitiva a la luz en la parte interior del ojo que contiene los receptores de luz llamados bastoncillos y conos además de capas de neuronas que inician el procesamiento de la información visual. (p. 172)

retinal disparity/disparidad retiniana clave binocular en la percepción de profundidad. El cerebro calcula distancias comparando las imágenes reflejadas en la retina de cada ojo. Cuanto más grande es la disparidad (diferencia) entre las dos imágenes, más cerca está el objeto. (p. 184)

retrieval/recuperación proceso de sacar la información que está almacenada en la memoria. (p. 319)

retroactive interference/interferencia retroactiva efecto de interferencia cuando el material que ha sido aprendido recientemente dificulta recordar lo aprendido con anterioridad. (p. 345)

retrograde amnesia/amnesia retrógrada incapacidad de recuperar información sobre el propio pasado. (p. 342)

reuptake/reabsorción reabsorción de un neurotransmisor por la neurona emisora. (p. 80)

rods/bastoncillos receptores de la retina que detectan el negro, el blanco y el gris; necesarios para la visión periférica y en la penumbra, cuando los conos no responden. (p. 173)

role/rol conjunto de expectativas (normas) relacionadas a una posición social, definiendo como aquellos en esa posición deben de comportarse. (pp. 503, 758)

Rorschach inkblot test/test de Rorschach la prueba proyectiva más utilizada, que consiste en un conjunto de 10 manchas de tinta, diseñado por Hermann Rorschach; busca identificar los sentimientos internos de las personas analizando sus interpretaciones de las manchas. (p. 567)

rumination/rumiación preocupación compulsiva; *pensar demasiado* en nuestros problemas y sus causas. (p. 679)

sampling bias/sesgo de muestreo proceso de toma de muestras defectuoso que da como resultado una muestra no representativa. (p. 43)

savant syndrome/síndrome de savant condición según la cual una persona de habilidad mental limitada tiene una destreza excepcional en un campo específico como la computación o el dibujo. (p. 609)

scapegoat theory/teoría del chivo expiatorio teoría que propone que el prejuicio ofrece un escape para la cólera porque nos brinda a alguien a quien culpar. (p. 785)

scatterplot/diagramas de dispersión agrupaciones de puntos en una gráfica, cada una de las cuales representa el valor de dos variables. La pendiente de los puntos representa la dirección de la relación entre las dos variables. La magnitud de la dispersión representa la fuerza de la correlación (a menor dispersión, mayor correlación). (p. 46)

schema/esquema concepto o principio que organiza e interpreta la información. (p. 477)

schizophrenia/esquizofrenia trastorno psicológico caracterizado por delirios, alucinaciones, discurso desorganizado o expresiones emocionales insuficientes o inapropiadas. (p. 684)

secondary sex characteristics/características sexuales secundarias características sexuales no reproductivas, como senos y caderas en las mujeres, timbre de voz y vello corporal en los hombres. (p. 527)

selective attention/atención selectiva enfoque de la percepción consciente en un estímulo en particular. (p. 152)

self/el yo en la psicología contemporánea, supuesto centro de la personalidad, organizador de nuestros pensamientos, sentimientos y acciones. (p. 594)

self-actualization/autorrealización según Maslow, una de las necesidades psicológicas fundamentales que surge después de satisfacer las necesidades básicas, físicas y psicológicas, y de lograr la autoestima; motivación de satisfacer nuestro potencial. (p. 571)

self-concept/autoconcepto todos nuestros pensamientos y sentimientos hacia nosotros mismos cuando respondemos a la pregunta: "¿quién soy yo?" (pp. 492, 572)

self-control/autocontrol capacidad de controlar los impulsos y posponer la gratificación a corto plazo a cambio de mayores recompensas a largo plazo. (p. 301)

self-disclosure/autorrevelación el revelar aspectos íntimos de uno mismo a otros. (p. 804)

self-efficacy/autoeficacia percepción que tenemos de nuestra competencia y eficacia. (p. 595)

self-esteem/autoestima sentimiento valorativo positivo o negativo de nuestro ser. (p. 595)

self-fulfilling prophecy/profecía autocumplida creencia que lleva a su propio cumplimiento. (p. 812)

self-serving bias/sesgo de autoservicio tendencia a auto-percatarse de manera favorable. (p. 596)

sensation/sensación proceso por el cual los receptores sensoriales y el sistema nervioso reciben y representan el estímulo del medio ambiente. (p. 152)

sensorimotor stage/etapa sensorio-motriz en la teoría de Piaget, la etapa (desde el nacimiento hasta aproximadamente los 2 años de edad) durante la que los infantes conocen el mundo principalmente en términos de sus impresiones sensoriales y actividades motoras. (p. 478)

sensorineural hearing loss/pérdida sensorio-neuronal del oído pérdida auditiva causada por daño a las células receptoras de la cóclea o a los nervios auditivos. (También se la denomina *sordera del nervio*). (p. 197)

sensory (afferent) neurons/neuronas sensoriales (aferentes) neuronas que transportan al cerebro y a la médula espinal la información proveniente de los receptores sensoriales. (p. 86)

sensory adaptation/adaptación sensorial sensibilidad disminuida como consecuencia del estímulo constante. (p. 159)

sensory interaction/interacción sensorial principio que un sentido puede influir a otro, como cuando el aroma de la comida influye en su sabor. (p. 210)

sensory memory/memoria sensorial registro muy breve e inmediato de la información sensorial en el sistema de la memoria. (p. 319)

serial position effect/efecto de posición serial nuestra tendencia a recordar mejor los últimos y los primeros artículos en una lista (*efectos de recencia* y *de primacía*, respectivamente). (p. 337)

set point/punto fijo punto de equilibrio en el "termostato del peso" de un individuo. Cuando el cuerpo llega a un peso debajo de este punto, se produce un aumento en el hambre y una disminución en el índice metabólico, los cuales pueden actuar para restablecer el peso perdido. (p. 398)

sexual dysfunction/disfunción sexual problema que impide la excitación o el funcionamiento sexual. (p. 407)

sexual orientation/orientación sexual atracción sexual perdurable hacia los miembros del mismo sexo (orientación homosexual), del sexo opuesto (orientación heterosexual) o de ambos (orientación bisexual). (p. 531)

sexual response cycle/ciclo de respuesta sexual las cuatro etapas de respuesta sexual descritas por Masters y Johnson: excitación, meseta, orgasmo y resolución. (p. 406)

shallow processing/procesamiento superficial codificación básica originada en la estructura o el aspecto de las palabras. (p. 324)

shaping/modelado por aproximaciones sucesivas procedimiento del condicionamiento operante donde los refuerzos guían la conducta para que esta se aproxime más y más a la conducta deseada. (p. 276)

short-term memory/memoria a corto plazo memoria activada que retiene algunos elementos por un corto tiempo, tales como los siete dígitos de un número telefónico mientras se marca, antes que la información se almacene o se olvide. (p. 319)

signal detection theory/teoría de la detección de señales teoría que predice cómo y cuándo detectamos la presencia de un estímulo débil (*señal*) a pesar de la estimulación del ambiente (*ruido*). Asume que no hay ningún umbral absoluto y que la detección depende en parte de la experiencia de la persona, de sus expectativas, motivación, y vigilancia. (p. 156)

skewed distribution/distribución asimétrica representación de puntajes que no guardan simetría respecto del valor promedio. (p. 58)

sleep/sueño pérdida del conocimiento que es periódica y natural. Esto es distinto de la inconsciencia que puede resultar del estado de coma, anestesia general, o hibernación. (Adaptado de Dement, 1999). (p. 227)

sleep apnea/apnea del sueño trastorno de sueño caracterizado por cesaciones temporales de respiración durante el sueño y repetidos despertares momentáneos. (p. 239)

social anxiety disorder/trastorno de ansiedad social temor intenso a situaciones sociales que lleva a evitarlas. (Anteriormente se denominaba *fobia social*). (p. 662)

social clock/reloj social manera que la sociedad tiene de marcar el tiempo adecuado de los eventos sociales, tales como matrimonio, paternidad y jubilación. (p. 544)

social exchange theory/teoría del intercambio social teoría que establece que nuestra conducta social es un proceso de intercambio, cuyo objetivo es maximizar los beneficios y minimizar los costos. (p. 809)

social facilitation/facilitación social mejor desempeño en las tareas simples o bien aprendidas en la presencia de otros. (p. 771)

social identity/identidad social dentro de nuestro autoconcepto, parte a la que nos referimos como "nosotros"; la parte de nuestra respuesta a la pregunta "¿quién soy yo?" que tiene que ver con nuestras afiliaciones de grupo. (p. 519)

social leadership/liderazgo social liderazgo orientado hacia el grupo que construye trabajo en grupo, media en el conflicto y ofrece apoyo. (p. 838)

social learning theory/teoría de aprendizaje social teoría que establece que aprendemos la conducta social observando e imitando, y al ser recompensados o castigados. (p. 504)

social loafing/haraganería social tendencia de las personas en un grupo de realizar menos esfuerzo cuando juntan sus esfuerzos para lograr una meta común que cuando son responsables individualmente. (p. 773)

social psychology/psicología social estudio científico de los pensamientos, las influencias y las relaciones que hay entre las personas. (pp. 14, 754)

social script/guión social guía que establece cómo debe actuarse en diversas situaciones en una cultura determinada. (p. 792)

social trap/trampa social situación en la cual las partes en conflicto, cada una persiguiendo racionalmente su propio interés en lugar del bien del grupo, se ven atrapadas en una conducta mutuamente destructiva. (p. 810)

social-cognitive perspective/perspectiva cognitivo-social enfoque según el cual la conducta es influenciada por la interacción entre los rasgos del individuo (incluida la forma de pensar) y su contexto social. (p. 587)

social-cultural psychology/psicología social-cultural el estudio de cómo situaciones y culturas afectan nuestra conducta y pensamiento. (p. 12)

social-responsibility norm/norma de responsabilidad social posibilidad de que las personas ayudarán a quienes las necesiten. (p. 810)

somatic nervous system/sistema nervioso somático división del sistema nervioso periférico que controla los músculos del esqueleto. (También se lo conoce como *sistema nervioso del esqueleto*). (p. 87)

somatic symptom disorder/trastorno de síntoma somático trastorno psicológico en el que los síntomas cobran carácter somático (del cuerpo) sin tener una causa física aparente. (Véase *trastorno de conversión* y *trastorno de ansiedad por enfermedad*). (p. 693)

somatosensory cortex/corteza somatosensorial area en la parte frontal de los lóbulos parietales que registra y procesa las sensaciones corporales de tacto y movimiento. (p. 107)

source amnesia/amnesia de la fuente el atribuir un origen erróneo a un evento que hemos experimentado, oído, leído o imaginado. (También se le conoce como *falsa atribución*). La amnesia de la fuente, así como el efecto de desinformación, es la causa de muchos recuerdos falsos. (p. 349)

spacing effect/efecto del aprendizaje espaciado tendencia a que el estudio o práctica distribuidos logren mejor retención a largo plazo que la que se logra a través de estudio o prácticas masivas. (p. 324)

split brain/cerebro dividido estado a partir de una intervención quirúrgica en el que los dos hemisferios cerebrales quedan incomunicados mediante el corte de las fibras que los conectan (principalmente las del cuerpo calloso). (p. 114)

spontaneous recovery/recuperación espontánea reaparición, después de una pausa, de una respuesta condicionada extinguida. (p. 269)

spotlight effect/efecto reflector sobreestimación de lo que los demás advierten y evalúan de nuestra apariencia, desempeño y desatinos (como si estuviéramos apuntados por un reflector). (p. 594)

SQ3R/método EPL2R técnica de estudio que combina cinco pasos: *e*xplorar, *p*reguntar, *l*eer, *r*ecitar y *r*epasar. (p. 16)

standard deviation/desviación estándar medida calculada de cuánto varían los puntajes alrededor del promedio de la muestra. (p. 58)

standardization/estandarización el definir procedimientos uniformes de evaluación y puntajes significativos mediante la comparación del desempeño de un grupo examinado con anterioridad. (p. 621)

Stanford-Binet/Stanford-Binet revisión estadounidense (por Terman en la Universidad de Stanford) de la prueba original de inteligencia de Binet. Esta prueba revisada es usada extensamente. (p. 618)

statistical significance/significado estadístico declaración estadística de cuán probable es que un resultado se haya obtenido por casualidad. (p. 60)

stereotype/estereotipo *creencia* (a veces acertada, pero frecuentemente demasiado generalizada) sobre las características de un grupo de personas. (p. 780)

stereotype threat/amenaza del estereotipo preocupación personal que reconfirma el temor de ser evaluado sobre un base de un estereotipo negativo. (p. 642)

stimulants/estimulantes drogas —como la cafeína, la nicotina y las anfetaminas más poderosas (cocaína, éxtasis y metanfetamina)— que excitan la actividad neuronal y aceleran las funciones corporales. (p. 250)

stimulus/estímulo cualquier evento o situación que provoque una respuesta. (p. 264)

storage/almacenamiento proceso de retener información codificada a través del tiempo. (p. 319)

stranger anxiety/miedo a los extraños temor a los extraños que los infantes normalmente expresan a partir de los 8 meses, aproximadamente. (p. 488)

stress/estrés proceso a través del cual percibimos y respondemos a ciertos eventos llamados *estresores*, los cuales evaluamos como amenazantes o desafiantes. (p. 442)

structuralism/estructuralismo escuela de los primeros años de la psicología, promovida por Wundt y Titchener, que empleaba la introspección para explorar la estructura de la mente humana. (p. 4)

structured interviews/entrevistas estructuradas proceso mediante el cual en las entrevistas se hace las mismas preguntas a todos los postulantes, cada uno de los cuales será calificado de acuerdo a escalas establecidas. (p. 832)

subjective well-being/bienestar subjetivo percepción de felicidad o satisfacción con la vida. Se utiliza con las medidas de bienestar objetivo (por ejemplo, los indicadores físicos y económicos) para evaluar la calidad de vida de las personas. (p. 847)

subliminal/subliminal debajo del umbral absoluto del nivel de conciencia. (p. 157)

substance use disorder/trastorno por uso de sustancias deseo y uso continuo de una sustancia a pesar del deterioro de la calidad de vida o el riesgo físico. (p. 246)

superego/superego parte de personalidad que, según Freud, representa los ideales interiorizados y provee de las normas para el juicio (la conciencia) y para las aspiraciones futuras. (p. 558)

superordinate goals/metas comunes metas compartidas que hacen caso omiso de las diferencias entre las personas y que requieren su cooperación. (p. 813)

suprachiasmatic nucleus (SCN)/núcleo supraquiasmático (NSQ) dos grupos de células ubicados en el hipotálamo que controlan el ritmo circadiano. El NSQ es el responsable de que la epífisis ajuste la producción de melatonina en respuesta a la luz, alterando así nuestras sensaciones de somnolencia. (p. 229)

survey/encuesta técnica para verificar las actitudes o conductas reportadas por las personas; usualmente se pregunta a una muestra aleatoria y representativa. (p. 42)

sympathetic nervous system/sistema nervioso simpático división del sistema nervioso autonómico que en situaciones estresantes excita al cuerpo y moviliza su energía. (p. 87)

synapse/sinapsis intersección entre el extremo del axón de una neurona emisora y la dendrita o cuerpo celular de una neurona receptora. El pequeño espacio en esta intersección se denomina *espacio intersináptico*. (p. 80)

systematic desensitization/desensibilización sistemática tipo de terapia de exposición en la que se asocia un estado tranquilo y placentero con estímulos graduales que producen ansiedad. Se emplea comúnmente para tratar fobias. (p. 717)

task leadership/liderazgo específico liderazgo orientado a metas específicas que establece las normas, organiza el trabajo y centra la atención en las metas. (p. 838)

telegraphic speech/lenguaje telegráfico etapa en que un niño comienza a hablar expresándose en forma de telegrama ("dame" o "agua") y utilizando principalmente sustantivos y verbos. (p. 375)

temperament/temperamento característica de reactividad emocional e intensidad de una persona. (p. 490)

temporal lobes/lóbulos temporales porción de la corteza cerebral ubicada aproximadamente arriba de las orejas; incluye las áreas auditivas, cada una de las cuales recibe la información auditiva principalmente de la oreja opuesta. (p. 105)

tend and befriend/cuidar y hacer amistades en situaciones estresantes, la gente (especialmente las mujeres) suele acercarse a otras personas para ofrecer su apoyo (cuidar), generar vínculos y buscar respaldo (hacer amistades). (p. 445)

teratogens/teratógenos (literalmente, "fabricantes de monstruos") agentes, como las sustancias químicas o los virus, que pueden afectar al embrión o al feto durante el desarrollo prenatal y causarle daño. (p. 467)

terror-management theory/teoría de la gestión del terror teoría sobre la ansiedad relacionada con la muerte; explora las respuestas emocionales y conductuales de las personas a todo aquello que les haga recordar la muerte propia. (p. 568)

testing effect/efecto del test incremento de la memoria tras recuperar la información, en vez de limitarse a releerla. En ocasiones se lo denomina efecto de *práctica de recuperación de la información* o *aprendizaje por evaluación*. (pp. 16, 324)

testosterone/testosterona la más importante de las hormonas sexuales masculinas. Tanto los hombres como las mujeres la tienen, pero la testosterona adicional en los hombres estimula el crecimiento de los órganos sexuales masculinos en el feto y el desarrollo de las características sexuales masculinas durante la pubertad. (pp. 408, 526)

thalamus/tálamo estructura cerebral ubicada sobre el tronco encefálico que funciona como centro de control para dirigir información a las áreas sensoriales receptivas de la corteza cerebral y transmite respuestas al cerebelo y la médula. (p. 97)

THC/THC principal sustancia activa encontrada en la marihuana; produce distintos efectos incluyendo alucinaciones leves. (p. 255)

Thematic Apperception Test (TAT)/prueba de apercepción temática (PAT) prueba psicológica proyectiva en la que las personas expresan sus sentimientos internos e intereses a través de historias que inventan a partir de escenas ambiguas. (p. 567)

theory/teoría explicación que utiliza un conjunto integrado de principios que organiza las observaciones y predice los comportamientos o eventos. (p. 38)

theory of mind/teoría de la mente ideas de la gente con relación a su estado de ánimo y al estado de ánimo de los demás: sus sentimientos, percepciones y pensamientos, y la conducta que estos puedan predecir. (p. 480)

therapeutic alliance/alianza terapéutica vínculo de confianza y comprensión mutua que se forma entre el terapeuta y el cliente para trabajar juntos de manera constructiva y lograr superar el problema de este último. (p. 735)

threshold/umbral nivel de estímulo requerido para activar un impulso neuronal. (p. 80)

token economy/economía de fichas procedimiento del condicionamiento operante en el cual las personas ganan fichas de algún tipo si exhiben una conducta deseada y luego pueden cambiar las fichas por privilegios o regalos. (p. 719)

tolerance/tolerancia efecto decreciente de la misma dosis de una droga después de un tiempo de uso, requiriendo que el usuario aumente la dosis para poder experimentar el efecto de la droga. (p. 246)

top-down processing/procesamiento de arriba a abajo procesamiento de información dirigida por procesos mentales superiores, como cuando determinamos nuestras percepciones a partir de nuestra experiencia y nuestras expectativas. (p. 152)

trait/rasgo patrón característico de conducta o una disposición para sentir y actuar, tal como los reportaría una autoevaluación o evaluación por nuestros pares. (p. 576)

transduction/transducción cualquier operación que transforma energía de determinado tipo en otro distinto. En el caso de los sistemas sensoriales, el transformar energía de estímulo, como visiones, sonidos y olores, en impulsos neuronales que nuestros cerebros son capaces de interpretar. (p. 155)

transference/transferencia en el psicoanálisis, la transferencia de emociones ligadas a otras relaciones, del paciente al analista (como el amor u odio hacia uno de los padres). (p. 710)

transgender/transexual término abarcador que describe a aquellas personas cuya identidad o expresión sexual difiere de la asociada con el sexo con el que nacieron. (p. 505)

two-factor theory/teoría bifactorial teoría de Schachter y Singer que sostiene que para sentir una emoción, la persona debe (1) experimentar estimulación física y (2) clasificar la estimulación a nivel cognitivo. (p. 422)

two-word stage/etapa de dos palabras a partir de los 2 años, etapa del desarrollo del lenguaje durante la cual el niño emite mayormente frases de dos palabras. (p. 375)

Type A/Tipo A término de Friedman y Rosenman para las personas competitivas, compulsivas, impacientes, verbalmente agresivas y con tendencia a enojarse. (p. 452)

Type B/Tipo B término de Friedman y Rosenman para las personas tolerantes y relajadas. (p. 452)

unconditional positive regard/consideración positiva incondicional según Carl Rogers, actitud que no juzga, bondadosa y sin restricciones que ayuda a los clientes a desarrollar la conciencia y a aceptarse a sí mismos. (pp. 572, 712)

unconditioned response (UR)/respuesta incondicionada (RI) en el condicionamiento clásico, la respuesta no aprendida e innata (como la salivación) que es producida por un estímulo incondicionado (EI) (como la comida en la boca). (p. 267)

unconditioned stimulus (US)/estímulo incondicionado (EI) en el condicionamiento clásico, un estímulo no condicionado -natural y automático- que produce una respuesta (RI). (p. 267)

unconscious/inconciente según Freud, un depósito de pensamientos, deseos, sentimientos y recuerdos en su mayoría inaceptables. Según los psicólogos contemporáneos, el procesamiento de información del cual no estamos alertas. (p. 557)

validity/validez grado en que una prueba mide o predice lo que se supone que debe medir o predecir (véase también *validez de contenido y validez predictiva*). (pp. 53, 622)

variable-interval schedule/programa de intervalo variable en el condicionamiento operante, un programa de refuerzo que refuerza una respuesta después de intervalos de tiempo impredecibles. (p. 280)

variable-ratio schedule/programa de razón variable en el condicionamiento operante, un programa de refuerzo que refuerza una respuesta después de un número impredecible de respuestas. (p. 280)

vestibular sense/sentido vestibular sentido de movimiento del cuerpo y posición, incluyendo el sentido de equilibrio. (p. 209)

virtual reality exposure therapy/terapia de exposición a una realidad virtual tratamiento de ansiedad que progresivamente expone a las personas a simulaciones de sus más grandes miedos, como los vuelos en avión, las arañas o hablar en público. (p. 718)

visual cliff/precipicio visual dispositivo del laboratorio para examinar la percepción de profundidad en los infantes y animales jóvenes. (p. 184)

wavelength/longitud de onda distancia de la cresta de una onda luminosa o sonora a la cresta de la próxima. Las longitudes de onda electromagnéticas varían desde los puntos de luz cortos de los rayos cósmicos hasta los pulsos largos de transmisión de radio. (p. 171)

Weber's law/ley de Weber principio que, para que dos estímulos sean percibidos como diferentes, estos deben variar en un porcentaje mínimo constante (en vez de en una cantidad constante). (p. 158)

Wechsler Adult Intelligence Scale (WAIS)/escala de la Inteligencia de Wechsler para adultos (EIWA) la prueba de inteligencia más ampliamente utilizada; contiene evaluaciones verbales y de desempeño (no verbales). (p. 620)

Wernicke's area/área de Wernicke controla la recepción del lenguaje. Un área del cerebro involucrada en la comprensión y la expresión del lenguaje; generalmente en el lóbulo temporal izquierdo. (p. 377)

withdrawal/síndrome de abstinencia incomodidad y angustia que ocurren luego de descontinuar una droga o comportamiento adictivos. (p. 247)

working memory/memoria activa aproximación nueva a la memoria a corto plazo que involucra el procesamiento consciente y activo de la información auditiva y visual-espacial, además de la recuperación de información de la memoria a largo plazo. (p. 320)

X chromosome/cromosoma X cromosoma del sexo encontrado en hombres y mujeres. Las mujeres tienen dos cromosomas X; los hombres tienen uno. Un cromosoma de X de cada progenitor produce una niña. (p. 526)

Y chromosome/cromosoma Y cromosoma del sexo encontrado solo en los hombres. Cuando se aparea con un cromosoma X de la madre, produce un niño. (p. 526)

Yerkes-Dodson law/ley de Yerkes-Dodson principio según el cual el desempeño mejora con la excitación solo hasta cierto punto; luego, comienza a decaer. (p. 392)

Young-Helmholtz trichromatic (three-color) theory/teoría tricromática (tricolor) de Young-Helmholtz teoría que establece que la retina contiene tres tipos de receptores cromáticos —uno más sensible al rojo, otro al verde, otro al azul— que, cuando se estimulan simultáneamente, pueden producir la percepción de cualquier color. (p. 178)

zygote/cigoto huevo fertilizado, que atraviesa por un período de 2 semanas de división celular rápida y se convierte en un embrión. (p. 466)

References

AAS. (2009, April 25). *USA suicide: 2006 final data.* Prepared for the American Association of Suicidology by J. L. McIntosh (www.suicidology.org). (p. 677)

AAS. (2010, May 23). *U.S.A. suicide: 2007 official final data.* Prepared for the American Association of Suicidology by J. L. McIntosh (www.suicidology.org). (p. 676)

Abbey, A. (1987). Misperceptions of friendly behavior as sexual interest: A survey of naturally occurring incidents. *Psychology of Women Quarterly, 11,* 173–194. (p. 138)

Abel, E. L., & Kruger, M. L. (2010). Smile intensity in photographs predicts longevity. *Psychological Science, 21,* 542–544. (p. 453)

Abel, K. M., Drake, R., & Goldstein, J. M. (2010). Sex differences in schizophrenia. *International Review of Psychiatry, 22,* 417–428. (p. 684)

Abrams, D. B. (1991). AIDS: What young people believe and what they do. Paper presented at the British Association for the Advancement of Science conference. (p. 589)

Abrams, D. B., & Wilson, G. T. (1983). Alcohol, sexual arousal, and self-control. *Journal of Personality and Social Psychology, 45,* 188–198. (p. 250)

Abrams, L. (2008). Tip-of-the-tongue states yield language insights. *American Scientist, 96,* 234–239. (p. 344)

Abrams, M. (2002, June). Sight unseen—Restoring a blind man's vision is now a real possibility through stem-cell surgery. But even perfect eyes cannot see unless the brain has been taught to use them. *Discover, 23,* 54–60. (p. 190)

Abramson, L. Y., Metalsky, G. I., & Alloy, L. B. (1989). Hopelessness depression: A theory-based subtype. *Psychological Review, 96,* 358–372. (p. 680)

Abrevaya, J. (2009). Are there missing girls in the United States? Evidence from birth data. *American Economic Journal: Applied Economics, 1*(2), 1–34. (p. 783)

Acevedo, B. P., & Aron, A. (2009). Does a long-term relationship kill romantic love? *Review of General Psychology, 13,* 59–65. (p. 803)

ACHA. (2009). *American College Health Association-National College Health Assessment II: Reference group executive summary Fall 2008.* Baltimore: American College Health Association. (p. 671)

Ackerman, D. (2004). *An alchemy of mind: The marvel and mystery of the brain.* New York: Scribner. (p. 80)

Ackerman, J. M., Nocera, C. C., & Bargh, J. A. (2010). Incidental haptic sensations influence social judgments and decisions. *Science, 328,* 1712–1715. (p. 211)

ACMD. (2009). *MDMA ('ecstasy'): A review of its harms and classification under the Misuse of Drugs Act 1971.* London: Home Office. (pp. 252, 253)

Adams, S. (2011, February 6). OCD: David Beckham has it—as do over a million other Britons. *The Telegraph* (www.telegraph.co.uk). (p. 663)

Adelmann, P. K., Antonucci, T. C., Crohan, S. F., & Coleman, L. M. (1989). Empty nest, cohort, and employment in the well-being of midlife women. *Sex Roles, 20,* 173–189. (p. 545)

Adelson, R. (2004, August). Detecting deception. *APA Monitor,* pp. 70–73. (p. 428)

Ader, R., & Cohen, N. (1985). CNS-immune system interactions: Conditioning phenomena. *Behavioral and Brain Sciences, 8,* 379–394. (p. 271)

Affleck, G., Tennen, H., Urrows, S., & Higgins, P. (1994). Person and contextual features of daily stress reactivity: Individual differences in relations of undesirable daily events with mood disturbance and chronic pain intensity. *Journal of Personality and Social Psychology, 66,* 329–340. (p. 848)

Agrillo, C. (2011). Near-death experience: Out-of-body and out-of-brain? *Review of General Psychology, 15,* 1–10. (p. 255)

Ai, A. L., Park, C. L., Huang, B., Rodgers, W., & Tice, T. N. (2007). Psychosocial mediation of religious coping styles: A study of short-term psychological distress following cardiac surgery. *Personality and Social Psychology Bulletin, 33,* 867–882. (p. 865)

Aiello, J. R., Thompson, D. D., & Brodzinsky, D. M. (1983). How funny is crowding anyway? Effects of room size, group size, and the introduction of humor. *Basic and Applied Social Psychology, 4,* 193–207. (p. 772)

Aimone, J. B., Jessberger, S., & Gage, F. H. (2010, last modified February 5). Adult neurogenesis. *Scholarpedia* (www.scholarpedia.org). (p. 112)

Ainsworth, M. D. S. (1973). The development of infant-mother attachment. In B. Caldwell & H. Ricciuti (Eds.), *Review of child development research* (Vol. 3). Chicago: University of Chicago Press. (p. 490)

Ainsworth, M. D. S. (1979). Infant-mother attachment. *American Psychologist, 34,* 932–937. (p. 490)

Ainsworth, M. D. S. (1989). Attachments beyond infancy. *American Psychologist, 44,* 709–716. (p. 490)

Airan, R. D., Meltzer, L. A., Roy, M., Gong, Y., Chen, H., & Deisseroth, K. (2007). High-speed imaging reveals neurophysiological links to behavior in an animal model of depression. *Science, 317,* 819–823. (p. 679)

Åkerstedt, T., Kecklund, G., & Axelsson, J. (2007). Impaired sleep after bedtime stress and worries. *Biological Psychology, 76,* 170–173. (p. 238)

Alanko, K., Santtila, P., Harlaar, N., Witting, K., Varjonen, M., Jern, P., Johansson, A., von der Pahlen, B., & Sandnabba, N. K. (2010). Common genetic effects of gender atypical behavior in childhood and sexual orientation in adulthood: A study of Finnish twins. *Archives of Sexual Behavior, 39,* 81–92. (p. 534)

Albee, G. W. (1986). Toward a just society: Lessons from observations on the primary prevention of psychopathology. *American Psychologist, 41,* 891–898. (p. 737)

Alcock, J. (2011, March/April). Back from the future: Parapsychology and the Bem affair. *Skeptical Inquirer,* pp. 31–39. (p. 169)

Aldao, A., & Nolen-Hoeksema, S. (2010). Emotion-regulation strategies across psychopathology: A meta-analytic review. *Clinical Psychology Review, 30,* 217–237. (p. 723)

Aldrich, M. S. (1989). Automobile accidents in patients with sleep disorders. *Sleep, 12,* 487–494. (p. 238)

Aldridge-Morris, R. (1989). *Multiple personality: An exercise in deception.* Hillsdale, NJ: Erlbaum. (p. 695)

Aleman, A., Kahn, R. S., & Selten, J-P. (2003). Sex differences in the risk of schizophrenia: Evidence from meta-analysis. *Archives of General Psychiatry, 60,* 565–571. (p. 686)

Alexander, L., & Tredoux, C. (2010). The spaces between us: A spatial analysis of informal segregation. *Journal of Social Issues, 66,* 367–386. (p. 813)

Allard, F., & Burnett, N. (1985). Skill in sport. *Canadian Journal of Psychology, 39,* 294–312. (p. 323)

Allen, J. R., & Setlow, V. P. (1991). Heterosexual transmission of HIV: A view of the future. *Journal of the American Medical Association, 266,* 1695–1696. (p. 529)

Allen, K. (2003). Are pets a healthy pleasure? The influence of pets on blood pressure. *Current Directions in Psychological Science, 12,* 236–239. (p. 858)

Allen, M. W., Gupta, R., & Monnier, A. (2008). The interactive effect of cultural symbols and human values on taste evaluation. *Journal of Consumer Research, 35,* 294–308. (p. 207)

Allesøe, K., Hundrup, V. A., Thomsen, J. F., & Osler, M. (2010). Psychosocial work environment and risk of ischaemic heart disease in women: The Danish Nurse Cohort Study. *Occupational and Environmental Medicine, 67,* 318–322. (p. 453)

Alloy, L. B., Abramson, L. Y., Whitehouse, W. G., Hogan, M. E., Tashman, N. A., Steinberg, D. L., Rose, D. T., & Donovan, P. (1999). Depressogenic cognitive styles: Predictive validity, information processing and personality characteristics, and developmental origins. *Behaviour Research and Therapy, 37,* 503–531. (p. 680)

Allport, G. W. (1954). *The nature of prejudice.* New York: Addison-Wesley. (pp. 40, 784)

Allport, G. W., & Odbert, H. S. (1936). Trait-names: A psycho-lexical study. *Psychological Monographs, 47*(1). (p. 577)

Almås, I., Cappelen, A. W., Sørensen, E. Ø., & Tungodden, B. (2010). Fairness and the development of inequality acceptance. *Science, 328,* 1176–1178. (p. 515)

Almond, D., & Edlund, L. (2008). Son-biased sex ratios in the 2000 United States Census. *PNAS, 105,* 5681–5682. (p. 783)

Altamirano, L. J., Miyake, A., & Whitmer, A. J. (2010). When mental inflexibility facilitates executive control: Beneficial side effects of ruminative tendencies on goal maintenance. *Psychological Science, 21*, 1377–1382. (p. 679)

Altman, L. K. (2004, November 24). Female cases of HIV found rising worldwide. *New York Times* (www.nytimes.com). (p. 450)

Alwin, D. F. (1990). Historical changes in parental orientations to children. In N. Mandell (Ed.), *Sociological studies of child development* (Vol. 3). Greenwich, CT: JAI Press. (p. 497)

Amabile, T. M. (1983). *The social psychology of creativity.* New York: Springer-Verlag. (p. 595)

Amabile, T. M., & Hennessey, B. A. (1992). The motivation for creativity in children. In A. K. Boggiano & T. S. Pittman (Eds.), *Achievement and motivation: A social-developmental perspective.* New York: Cambridge University Press. (p. 358)

Amato, P. R., Booth, A., Johnson, D. R., & Rogers, S. J. (2007). *Alone together: How marriage in America is changing.* Cambridge, MA: Harvard University Press. (p. 504)

Ambady, N., Hallahan, M., & Rosenthal, R. (1995). On judging and being judged accurately in zero-acquaintance situations. *Journal of Personality and Social Psychology, 69*, 518–529. (p. 433)

Ambady, N., & Rosenthal, R. (1992). Thin slices of expressive behavior as predictors of interpersonal consequences: A meta-analysis. *Psychological Bulletin, 111*, 256–274. (p. 584)

Ambady, N., & Rosenthal, R. (1993). Half a minute: Predicting teacher evaluations from thin slices of nonverbal behavior and physical attractiveness. *Journal of Personality and Social Psychology, 64*, 431–441. (p. 584)

Ambrose, C. T. (2010). The widening gyrus. *American Scientist, 98*, 270–274. (p. 509)

Amedi, A., Merabet, L. B., Bermpohl, F., & Pascual-Leone, A. (2005). The occipital cortex in the blind: Lessons about plasticity and vision. *Current Directions in Psychological Science, 14*, 306–311. (p. 111)

Amen, D. G., Stubblefield, M., Carmichael, B., & Thisted, R. (1996). Brain SPECT findings and aggressiveness. *Annals of Clinical Psychiatry, 8*, 129–137. (p. 790)

American Academy of Pediatrics. (2009). Policy statement—media violence. *Pediatrics, 124*, 1495–1503. (p. 309)

American Enterprise. (1992, January/February). Women, men, marriages & ministers. p. 106. (p. 600)

American Psychiatric Association (2013). *Diagnostic and statistical manual of mental disorders* (Fifth ed.). Arlington, VA: American Psychiatric Publishing. (pp. 247, 248, 407, 651, 672)

American Psychological Association. (2006). Evidence-based practice in psychology (from APA Presidential Task Force on Evidence-Based Practice). *American Psychologist, 61*, 271–285. (p. 732)

American Psychological Association. (2007). Answers to your questions about sexual orientation and homosexuality. (www.apa.org. Accessed December 6, 2007). (p. 532)

American Psychological Association. (2010). *Ethical principles of psychologists and code of conduct.* Washington, DC. (Effective June 1, 2003, as amended 2010). (p. 68)

American Psychological Association, Task Force on the Sexualization of Girls (2010). Report of the APA task force on the sexualization of girls. Retrieved from http://www.apa.org/pi/women/programs/girls/report-full.pdf.

Ames, D. R. (2008). In search of the right touch: Interpersonal assertiveness in organizational life. *Current Directions in Psychological Science, 17*, 381–385. (p. 839)

Andersen, R. A., Hwang, E. J., & Mulliken, G. H. (2010). Cognitive neural prosthetics. *Annual Review of Psychology, 61*, 169–190. (p. 107)

Andersen, S. M. (1998). *Service Learning: A National Strategy for Youth Development.* A position paper issued by the Task Force on Education Policy. Washington, DC: Institute for Communitarian Policy Studies, George Washington University. (p. 517)

Anderson, A. K., & Phelps, E. A. (2000). Expression without recognition: Contributions of the human amygdala to emotional communication. *Psychological Science, 11*, 106–111. (p. 99)

Anderson, B. L. (2002). Biobehavioral outcomes following psychological interventions for cancer patients. *Journal of Consulting and Clinical Psychology, 70*, 590–610. (p. 451)

Anderson, C. A. (2004). An update on the effects of playing violent video games. *Journal of Adolescence, 27*, 113–122. (pp. 794, 795)

Anderson, C. A., & Anderson, D. C. (1984). Ambient temperature and violent crime: Tests of the linear and curvilinear hypotheses. *Journal of Personality and Social Psychology, 46*, 91–97. (p. 791)

Anderson, C. A., Anderson, K. B., Dorr, N., DeNeve, K. M., & Flanagan, M. (2000). Temperature and aggression. In M. P. Zanna (Ed.), *Advances in Experimental Social Psychology.* San Diego: Academic Press. (p. 792)

Anderson, C. A., & Delisi, M. (2011). Implications of global climate change for violence in developed and developing countries. In J. Forgas, A. Kruglanski., & K. Williams (eds.), *The psychology of social conflict and aggression.* New York: Psychology Press. (p. 792)

Anderson, C. A., & Dill, K. E. (2000). Video games and aggressive thoughts, feelings, and behavior in the laboratory and in life. *Journal of Personality and Social Psychology, 78*, 772–790. (p. 794)

Anderson, C. A., & Gentile, D. A. (2008). Media violence, aggression, and public policy. In E. Borgida & S. Fiske (Eds.), *Beyond common sense: Psychological science in the courtroom.* Malden, MA: Blackwell. (p. 309)

Anderson, C. A., Gentile, D. A., & Buckley, K. E. (2007). *Violent video game effects on children and adolescents: Theory, research, and public policy.* New York: Oxford University Press. (p. 795)

Anderson, C. A., Lindsay, J. J., & Bushman, B. J. (1999). Research in the psychological laboratory: Truth or triviality? *Current Directions in Psychological Science, 8*, 3–9. (p. 65)

Anderson, C. A., Shibuya, A., Ihori, N., Swing, E. L., Bushman, B. J., Sakamoto, A., Rothstein, H. R., & Saleem, M. (2010). Violent video game effects on aggression, empathy, and prosocial behavior in Eastern and Western countries: A meta-analytic review. *Psychological Bulletin, 136*, 151–173. (p. 794)

Anderson, I. M. (2000). Selective serotonin reuptake inhibitors versus tricyclic antidepressants: A meta-analysis of efficacy and tolerability. *Journal of Affective Disorders, 58*, 19–36. (p. 742)

Anderson, J. R., Gillies, A., & Lock, L. (2010). Pan thanatology. *Current Biology, 20*, R349–R351. (p. 868)

Anderson, J. R., Myowa-Yamakoshi, M., & Matsuzawa, T. (2004). Contagious yawning in chimpanzees. *Biology Letters, 271*, S468–S470. (p. 762)

Anderson, R. C., Pichert, J. W., Goetz, E. T., Schallert, D. L., Stevens, K. V., & Trollip, S. R. (1976). Instantiation of general terms. *Journal of Verbal Learning and Verbal Behavior, 15*, 667–679. (p. 345)

Anderson, S. (2008, July 6). The urge to end it. *New York Times* (www.nytimes.com). (p. 676)

Anderson, S. E., Dallal, G. E., & Must, A. (2003). Relative weight and race influence average age at menarche: Results from two nationally representative surveys of U.S. girls studied 25 years apart. *Pediatrics, 111*, 844–850. (p. 527)

Anderson, S. R. (2004). *Doctor Dolittle's delusion: Animals and the uniqueness of human language.* New Haven, CT: Yale University Press. (p. 870)

Anderson, U. S., Stoinski, T. S., Bloomsmith, M. A., Marr, M. J., Anderson, D., & Maple, T. L. (2005). Relative numerous judgment and summation in young and old western lowland gorillas. *Journal of Comparative Psychology, 119*, 285–295. (p. 626)

Andreasen, N. C. (1997). Linking mind and brain in the study of mental illnesses: A project for a scientific psychopathology. *Science, 275*, 1586–1593. (p. 687)

Andreasen, N. C. (2001). *Brave new brain: Conquering mental illness in the era of the genome.* New York: Oxford University Press. (p. 687)

Andreasen, N. C., Arndt, S., Swayze, V., II, Cizadlo, T., & Flaum, M. (1994). Thalamic abnormalities in schizophrenia visualized through magnetic resonance image averaging. *Science, 266*, 294–298. (p. 687)

Andrews, P. W., & Thomson, J. A., Jr. (2009a). The bright side of being blue: Depression as an adaptation for analyzing complex problems. *Psychological Review, 116*, 620–654. (pp. 672, 679)

Andrews, P. W., & Thomson, J. A., Jr. (2009b, January/February). Depression's evolutionary roots. *Scientific American Mind*, pp. 57–61. (pp. 672, 679)

Angell, M., & Kassirer, J. P. (1998). Alternative medicine: The risks of untested and unregulated remedies. *New England Journal of Medicine, 17*, 839–841. (p. 864)

Angelsen, N. K., Vik, T., Jacobsen, G., & Bakketeig, L. S. (2001). Breast feeding and cognitive development at age 1 and 5 years. *Archives of Disease in Childhood, 85*, 183–188. (p. 50)

Angoff, W. H. (1988, Winter). A philosophical discussion: The issues of test and item bias. *ETS Developments*, pp. 10–11. (p. 627)

Antoni, M. H., & Lutgendorf, S. (2007). Psychosocial factors and disease progression in cancer. *Current Directions in Psychological Science, 16*, 42–46. (p. 451)

Antony, M. M., Brown, T. A., & Barlow, D. H. (1992). Current perspectives on panic and panic disorder. *Current Directions in Psychological Science, 1*, 79–82. (p. 666)

Antrobus, J. (1991). Dreaming: Cognitive processes during cortical activation and high afferent thresholds. *Psychological Review, 98*, 96–121. (p. 242)

AP. (1999, April 26). Airline passengers mistakenly told plane would crash. *Grand Rapids Press*, p. A3. (p. 444)

AP. (2007). AP-Ipsos poll of 1,013 U.S. adults taken October 16–18, 2007 and distributed via Associated Press. (p. 167)

AP. (2009, May 9). AP-mtvU poll: Financial worries, stress and depression on college campus. www.hosted.ap.org. (pp. 235, 441)

APA. (2002). *Ethical principles of psychologists and code of conduct.* Washington, DC: American Psychological Association. (p. 67)

APA. (2007). Answers to your questions about sexual orientation and homosexuality (www.apa.org. Accessed December 6, 2007). (p. 531)

APA. (2010, accessed July 31). *Answers to your questions about transgender individuals and gender identity.* Washington, DC: American Psychological Association. (p. 505)

APA. (2010, November 9). *Stress in America findings.* Washington, DC: American Psychological Association. (p. 444)

Archer, J. (2004). Sex differences in aggression in real-world settings: A meta-analytic review. *Review of General Psychology, 8*, 291–322. (p. 501)

Archer, J. (2006). Cross-cultural differences in physical aggression between partners: A social-role analysis. *Personality and Social Psychology Review, 10*, 133–153. (p. 501)

Archer, J. (2009). Does sexual selection explain human sex differences in aggression? *Behavioral and Brain Sciences, 32*, 249–311. (p. 501)

Arendt, H. (1963). *Eichmann in Jerusalem: A report on the banality of evil.* New York: Viking Press. (p. 517)

Ariely, D. (2009). *Predictably irrational: The hidden forces that shape our decisions.* New York: HarperCollins. (p. 336)

Aries, E. (1987). Gender and communication. In P. Shaver & C. Henrick (Eds.), *Review of Personality and Social Psychology, 7*, 149–176. (p. 502)

Arjamaa, O., & Vuorisalo, T. (2010). Gene-culture coevolution and human diet. *American Scientist, 98*, 140–147. (p. 400)

Arkowitz, H., & Lilienfeld, S. O. (2006, April/May). Psychotherapy on trial. *Scientific American Mind*, pp. 42–49. (p. 732)

Arnett, J. J. (1999). Adolescent storm and stress, reconsidered. *American Psychologist, 54*, 317–326. (p. 513)

Arnett, J. J. (2006). Emerging adulthood: Understanding the new way of coming of age. In J. J. Arnett & J. L. Tanner (Eds.), *Emerging adults in America: Coming of age in the 21st century*. Washington, DC: American Psychological Association (p. 523)

Arnett, J. J. (2007). Socialization in emerging adulthood: From the family to the wider world, from socialization to self-socialization. In J. E. Grusec & P. D. Hastings (Eds.), *Handbook of socialization: Theory and research*. New York: Guilford Press. (p. 523)

Arnone, D., McIntosh, A. M., Tan, G. M. Y., & Ebmeier, K. P. (2008). Meta-analysis of magnetic resonance imaging studies of the corpus callosum in schizophrenia. *Schizophrenia Research, 101*, 124–132. (p. 687)

Aron, A. P., Melinat, E., Aron, E. N., Vallone, R. D., & Bator, R. J. (1997). The experimental generation of interpersonal closeness: A procedure and some preliminary findings. *Personality and Social Psychology Bulletin, 23*, 363–377. (p. 804)

Aronson, E. (2001, April 13). Newsworthy violence. E-mail to SPSP discussion list, drawing from *Nobody Left to Hate*. New York: Freeman. (p. 522)

Artiga, A. I., Viana, J. B., Maldonado, C. R., Chandler-Laney, P. C., Oswald, K. D., & Boggiano, M. M. (2007). Body composition and endocrine status of long-term stress-induced binge-eating rats. *Physiology and Behavior, 91*, 424–431. (p. 399)

Asch, S. E. (1955). Opinions and social pressure. *Scientific American, 193*, 31–35. (p. 763)

Aserinsky, E. (1988, January 17). Personal communication. (p. 226)

Askay, S. W., & Patterson, D. R. (2007). Hypnotic analgesia. *Expert Review of Neurotherapeutics, 7*, 1675–1683. (p. 221)

Aspinwall, L. G., & Tedeschi, R. G. (2010a). Of babies and bathwater: A reply to Coyne and Tennen's views of positive psychology and health. *Annals of Behavioral Medicine, 39*, 27–34 (p. 665)

Aspinwall, L. G., & Tedeschi, R. G. (2010b). The value of positive psychology for health psychology: Progress and pitfalls in examining the relation of positive phenomena to health. *Annals of Behavioral Medicine, 39*, 4–15. (pp. 665, 856)

ASPS. (2010). *2010 report of the 2009 statistics: National Clearinghouse of Plastic Surgery Statistics.* American Society of Plastic Surgeons (www.plasticsurgery.org). (p. 801)

Aspy, C. B., Vesely, S. K., Oman, R. F., Rodine, S., Marshall, L., & McLeroy, K. (2007). Parental communication and youth sexual behaviour. *Journal of Adolescence, 30*, 449–466. (p. 530)

Assanand, S., Pinel, J. P. J., & Lehman, D. R. (1998). Personal theories of hunger and eating. *Journal of Applied Social Psychology, 28*, 998–1015. (p. 398)

Astin, A. W., Astin, H. S., & Lindholm, J. A. (2004). *Spirituality in higher education: A national study of college students' search for meaning and purpose.* Los Angeles: Higher Education Research Institute, UCLA. (p. 520)

Atkinson, R. C., & Shiffrin, R. M. (1968). Human memory: A control system and its control processes. In K. Spence (Ed.), *The psychology of learning and motivation* (Vol. 2). New York: Academic Press. (p. 319)

Austin, E. J., Deary, I. J., Whiteman, M. C., Fowkes, F. G. R., Pedersen, N. L., Rabbitt, P., Bent, N., & McInnes, L. (2002). Relationships between ability and personality: Does intelligence contribute positively to personal and social adjustment? *Personality and Individual Differences, 32*, 1391–1411. (p. 629)

Australian Unity. (2008). *What makes us happy? The Australian Unity Wellbeing Index.* South Melbourne: Australian Unity. (p. 850)

Auyeung, B., Baron-Cohen, S., Ashwin, E., Knickmeyer, R., Taylor, K., Hackett, G., & Hines, M. (2009). Fetal testosterone predicts sexually differentiated childhood behavior in girls and in boys. *Psychological Science, 20*, 144–148. (p. 481)

Averill, J. R. (1983). Studies on anger and aggression: Implications for theories of emotion. *American Psychologist, 38*, 1145–1160. (pp. 845, 846)

Averill, J. R. (1993). William James's other theory of emotion. In M. E. Donnelly (Ed.), *Reinterpreting the legacy of William James*. Washington, DC: American Psychological Association. (p. 422)

Aviezer, H., Hassin, R. R., Ryan, J., Grady, C., Susskind, J., Anderson, A., Moscovitch, M., & Bentin, S. (2008). Angry, disgusted, or afraid? Studies on the malleability of emotion perception. *Psychological Science, 19*, 724–732. (p. 437)

Ax, A. F. (1953). The physiological differentiation of fear and anger in humans. *Psychosomatic Medicine, 15*, 433–442. (p. 427)

Ayan, S. (2009, April/May). Laughing matters. *Scientific American Mind*, pp. 24–31. (p. 857)

Aydin, N., Fischer, P., & Frey, D. (2010). Turning to God in the face of ostracism: Effects of social exclusion on religiousness. *Personality and Social Psychology Bulletin, 36*, 742–753. (p. 415)

Azar, B. (1998, June). Why can't this man feel whether or not he's standing up? *APA Monitor* (www.apa.org/monitor/jun98/touch.html). (p. 209)

Azevedo, F. A., Carvalho, L. R., Grinberg, L. T., Farfel, J. M., Ferretti, R. E., Leite, R. E., Jacob Filho, W., Lent, R., & Herculano-Houzel, S. (2009). Equal numbers of neuronal and nonneuronal cells make the human brain an isometrically scaled-up primate brain. *Journal of Comparative Neurology, 513*, 532–541. (p. 88)

Baas, M., De Dreu, C. K. W., & Nijstad, B. A. (2008). A meta-analysis of 25 years of mood-creativity research: Hedonic tone, activation, or regulatory focus? *Psychological Bulletin, 134*, 779–806. (p. 847)

Babad, E., Bernieri, F., & Rosenthal, R. (1991). Students as judges of teachers' verbal and nonverbal behavior. *American Educational Research Journal, 28*, 211–234. (p. 433)

Babson, K. A., & Feldner, M. T. (2010). Temporal relations between sleep problems and both traumatic event exposure and PTSD: A critical review of the empirical literature. *Journal of Anxiety Disorders, 24*, 1–15. (pp. 238, 664)

Babyak, M., Blumenthal, J. A., Herman, S., Khatri, P., Doraiswamy, M., Moore, K., Craighead, W. W., Baldewics, T. T., & Krishnan, K. R. (2000). Exercise treatment for major depression: Maintenance of therapeutic benefit at ten months. *Psychosomatic Medicine, 62*, 633–638. (p. 860)

Bachman, J., O'Malley, P. M., Schulenberg, J. E., Johnston, L. D., Freedman-Doan, P., & Messersmith, E. E. (2007). *The education-drug use connection: How successes and failures in school relate to adolescent smoking, drinking, drug use, and delinquency.* Mahwah, NJ: Erlbaum. (p. 824)

Bachman, J., Wadsworth, K., O'Malley, P., Johnston, L., & Schulenberg, J. (1997). *Smoking, drinking, and drug use in young adulthood: The impact of new freedoms and new responsibilities.* Mahwah, NJ: Erlbaum. (p. 824)

Back, M. D., Stopfer, J. M., Vazire, S., Gaddis, S., Schmukle, S. C., Egloff, B., & Gosling, S. D. (2010). Facebook profiles reflect actual personality not self-idealization. *Psychological Science, 21*, 372–374. (pp. 418, 584)

Backman, L., & MacDonald, S. W. S. (2006). Death and cognition: Synthesis and outlook. *European Psychologist, 11*, 224–235. (p. 543)

Baddeley, A. D. (1982). *Your memory: A user's guide.* New York: Macmillan. (p. 335)

Baddeley, A. D. (2001). Is working memory still working? *American Psychologist, 56*, 849–864. (p. 319)

Baddeley, A. D. (2002, June). Is working memory still working? *European Psychologist, 7*, 85–97. (pp. 319, 320)

Baddeley, A. D., Thomson, N., & Buchanan, M. (1975). Word length and the structure of short-term memory. *Journal of Verbal Learning and Verbal Behavior, 14*, 575–589. (p. 322)

Baddeley, J. L., & Singer J. A. (2009). A social interactional model of bereavement narrative disclosure. *Review of General Psychology, 13*, 202–218. (p. 548)

Bagemihl, B. (1999). *Biological exuberance: Animal homosexuality and natural diversity.* New York: St. Martins. (p. 533)

Bahrick, H. P. (1984). Semantic memory content in permastore: 50 years of memory for Spanish learned in school. *Journal of Experimental Psychology: General, 111*, 1–29. (p. 344)

Bahrick, H. P., Bahrick, L. E., Bahrick, A. S., & Bahrick, P. E. (1993). Maintenance of foreign language vocabulary and the spacing effect. *Psychological Science, 4*, 316–321. (p. 324)

Bahrick, H. P., Bahrick, P. O., & Wittlinger, R. P. (1975). Fifty years of memory for names and faces: A cross-sectional approach. *Journal of Experimental Psychology: General, 104*, 54–75. (p. 335)

Bailey, K., West, R., & Anderson, C. A. (2011). The influence of video games on social, cognitive, and affective information processing. In J. Decety & J. Cacioppo (eds.), *Handbook of social neuroscience.* New York: Oxford. (p. 652)

Bailey, R. E., & Gillaspy, J. A., Jr. (2005). Operant psychology goes to the fair: Marian and Keller Breland in the popular press, 1947–1966. *The Behavior Analyst, 28*, 143–159. (p. 295)

Bailine, S., & 10 others. (2010). Elctroconvulsive therapy is equally effective in unipolar and bipolar depression. *Acta Psychiatrica Scandinavica, 121*, 431–436. (p. 744)

Baillargeon, R. (1995). A model of physical reasoning in infancy. In C. Rovee-Collier & L. P. Lipsitt (Eds.), *Advances in infancy research* (Vol. 9). Stamford, CT: Ablex. (p. 478)

Baillargeon, R. (2008). Innate ideas revisited: For a principle of persistence in infants' physical reasoning. *Perspectives in Psychological Science, 3*, 2–13. (p. 478)

Baker, E. L. (1987). The state of the art of clinical hypnosis. *International Journal of Clinical and Experimental Hypnosis, 35*, 203–214. (p. 220)

Baker, T. B., McFall, R. M., & Shoham, V. (2008). Current status and future prospects of clinical psychology: Toward a scientifically principled approach to mental and behavioral health care. *Psychological Science in the Public Interest, 9*, 67–103. (p. 732)

Baker, T. B., Piper, M. E., McCarthy, D. E., Majeskie, M. R., & Fiore, M. C. (2004). Addiction motivation reformulated: An affective processing model of negative reinforcement. *Psychological Review, 111*, 33–51. (p. 278)

Bakermans-Kranenburg, M. J., van IJzendoorn, M. H., & Juffer, F. (2003). Less is more: Meta-analyses of sensitivity and attachment interventions in early childhood. *Psychological Bulletin, 129*, 195–215. (p. 491)

Balcetis, E., & Dunning, D. (2010). Wishful seeing: More desired objects are seen as closer. *Psychological Science, 21*, 147–152. (p. 166)

Balsam, K. F., Beauchaine, T. P., Rothblum, E. S., & Solomon, S. E. (2008). Three-year follow-up of same-sex couples who had civil unions in Vermont, same-sex couples not in civil unions, and heterosexual married couples. *Developmental Psychology, 44*, 102–116. (p. 544)

Balter, M. (2010). Animal communication helps reveal roots of language. *Science, 328*, 969–970. (p. 869)

Baltes, P. B. (1993). The aging mind: Potential and limits. *The Gerontologist, 33*, 580–594. (p. 626)

Baltes, P. B. (1994). Life-span developmental psychology: On the overall landscape of human development. Invited address, American Psychological Association convention. (p. 626)

Baltes, P. B., & Baltes, M. M. (1999, September-October). Harvesting the fruits of age: Growing older, growing wise. *Science and the Spirit*, pp. 11–14. (p. 626)

Bambico, F. R., Nguyen N-T., Katz, N., & Gobbi, G. (2010). Chronic exposure to cannabinoids during adolescence but not during adulthood impairs emotional behaviour and monoaminergic neurotransmission. *Neurobiology of Disease, 37*, 641–655. (p. 255)

Bancroft, J., Graham, C. A., Janssen, E., & Sanders, S. A. (2009). The dual control model: Current status and future directions. *Journal of Sex Research, 46*, 121–142. (p. 409)

Bancroft, J., Loftus, J., & Long, J. S. (2003). Distress about sex: A national survey of women in heterosexual relationships. *Archives of Sexual Behavior, 32*, 193–208. (p. 407)

Bandura, A. (1982). The psychology of chance encounters and life paths. *American Psychologist, 37*, 747–755. (p. 544)

Bandura, A. (1986). *Social foundations of thought and action: A social-cognitive theory.* Englewood Cliffs, NJ: Prentice-Hall. (pp. 587, 588)

Bandura, A. (2005) The evolution of social cognitive theory. In K. G. Smith & M. A. Hitt (Eds.), *Great minds in management: The process of theory development.* Oxford: Oxford University Press. (pp. 304, 544)

Bandura, A. (2006). Toward a psychology of human agency. *Perspectives on Psychological Science, 1*, 164–180. (pp. 587, 588)

Bandura, A. (2008). An agentic perspective on positive psychology. In S. J. Lopez (Ed.), *The science of human flourishing.* Westport, CT: Praeger. (p. 587)

Bandura, A., Ross, D., & Ross, S. A. (1961). Transmission of aggression through imitation of aggressive models. *Journal of Abnormal and Social Psychology, 63*, 575–582. (p. 304)

Barak, A., Hen, L., Boniel-Nissim, M., & Shapira, N. (2008). A comprehensive review and a meta-analysis of the effectiveness of Internet-based psychotherapeutic interventions. *Journal of Technology in Human Services, 26*, 108–160. (p. 723)

Barash, D. P. (2006, July 14). I am, therefore I think. *Chronicle of Higher Education*, pp. B9–B10. (p. 118)

Barbaresi, W. J., Katusic, S. K. I., Colligan, R. C., Weaver, A. L., & Jacobsen, S. J. (2007). Modifiers of long-term school outcomes for children with attention-deficit/hyperactivity disorder: Does treatment with stimulant medication make a difference? Results from a population-based study. *Journal of Developmental and Behavioral Pediatrics, 28*, 274–287. (p. 652)

Barber, T. X. (2000). A deeper understanding of hypnosis: Its secrets, its nature, its essence. *American Journal of Clinical Hypnosis, 42*, 208–272. (p. 221)

Barel, E., Van IJzendoorn, M. H., Sagi-Schwartz, A., & Bakermans-Kranenburg, M. J. (2010). Surving the Holocaust: A meta-analysis of the long-term sequelae of a genocide. *Psychological Bulletin, 136*, 677–698. (p. 665)

Bargh, J. A., & Chartrand, T. L. (1999). The unbearable automaticity of being. *American Psychologist, 54*, 462–479. (p. 121)

Bargh, J. A., & McKenna, K. Y. A. (2004). The Internet and social life. *Annual Review of Psychology, 55*, 573–590. (p. 799)

Bargh, J. A., McKenna, K. Y. A., & Fitzsimons, G. M. (2002). Can you see the real me? Activation and expression of the "true self" on the Internet. *Journal of Social Issues, 58*, 33–48. (p. 799)

Bargh, J. A., & Morsella, E. (2008). The unconscious mind. *Perspectives on Psychological Science, 3*, 73–79. (p. 568)

Bar-Haim, Y., Lamy, D., Pergamin, L., Bakermans-Kranenburg, M. J., & van IJzendoorn, M. H. (2007). Threat-related attentional bias in anxious and nonanxious individuals: A meta-analytic study. *Psychological Bulletin, 133*, 1–24. (p. 666)

Barinaga, M. B. (1992). The brain remaps its own contours. *Science, 258*, 216–218. (p. 111)

Barinaga, M. B. (1997). How exercise works its magic. *Science, 276*, 1325. (p. 859)

Barkley, R. A., & 74 others. (2002). International consensus statement (January 2002). *Clinical Child and Family Psychology Review, 5*, 2. (p. 652)

Barlow, D. H. (2010). Negative effects from psychological treatments: A perspective. *American Psychologist, 65*, 13–20. (p. 732)

Barnes, M. L., & Sternberg, R. J. (1989). Social intelligence and decoding of nonverbal cues. *Intelligence, 13*, 263–287. (p. 434)

Barnier, A. J., & McConkey, K. M. (2004). Defining and identifying the highly hypnotizable person. In M. Heap, R. J. Brown, & D. A. Oakley (Eds.), *High hypnotisability: Theoretical, experimental and clinical issues.* London: Brunner-Routledge. (p. 220)

Baron-Cohen, S. (2008). Autism, hypersystemizing, and truth. *Quarterly Journal of Experimental Psychology, 61*, 64–75. (p. 481)

Baron-Cohen, S. (2009). Autism: The empathizing-systemizing (E-S) theory. *The Year in Cognitive Neuroscience, 1156,* 68–80. (p. 481)

Baron-Cohen, S., Golan, O., Chapman, E., & Granader, Y. (2007). Transported to a world of emotion. *The Psychologist, 20,* 76–77. (p. 482)

Baron-Cohen, S., Leslie, A. M., & Frith, U. (1985). Does the autistic child have a "theory of mind"? *Cognition, 21,* 37–46. (p. 480)

Barrett, L. F. (2006). Are emotions natural kinds? *Perspectives on Psychological Science, 1,* 28–58. (pp. 422, 427)

Barrett, L. F., & Bliss-Moreau, E. (2009). She's emotional. He's having a bad day: Attributional explanations for emotion stereotypes. *Emotion, 9,* 649–658. (p. 434)

Barrett, L. F., Lane, R. D., Sechrest, L., & Schwartz, G. E. (2000). Sex differences in emotional awareness. *Personality and Social Psychology Bulletin, 26,* 1027–1035. (p. 434)

Barrick, M. R., Shaffer, J. A., & DeGrassi, S. W. (2009). What you see may not be what you get: Relationships among self-presentation tactics and ratings of interview and job performance. *Journal of Applied Psychology, 94,* 1304–1411. (p. 831)

Barry, D. (1995, September 17). Teen smokers, too, get cool, toxic, waste-blackened lungs. *Asbury Park Press,* p. D3. (p. 251)

Bartels, M., & Boomsma, D. I. (2009). Born to be happy? The etiology of subjective well-being. *Behavior Genetics, 39,* 605–615. (p. 852)

Bartholow, B. C., Bushman, B. J., & Sestir, M. A. (2006). Chronic violent video game exposure and desensitization to violence: Behavioral and event-related brain potential data. *Journal of Experimental Social Psychology, 42,* 532–539. (p. 794)

Bashore, T. R., Ridderinkhof, K. R., & van der Molen, M. W. (1997). The decline of cognitive processing speed in old age. *Current Directions in Psychological Science, 6,* 163–169. (p. 541)

Baskind, D. E. (1997, December 14). Personal communication, from Delta College. (p. 718)

Bates, L. A., & Byrne, R. W. (2010, September/October). Imitation: What animal imitation tells us about animal cognition. *Wiley Interdisciplinary Reviews: Cognitive Science, 1,* 685–695. (p. 306)

Bauer, P. J. (2002). Long-term recall memory: Behavioral and neurodevelopmental changes in the first 2 years of life. *Current Directions in Psychology, 11,* 137–141. (p. 473)

Bauer, P. J. (2007). Recall in infancy: A neurodevelopmental account. *Current Directions in Psychological Science, 16,* 142–146. (p. 473)

Bauer, P. J., Burch, M. M., Scholin, S. E., & Güler, O. E. (2007). Using cue words to investigate the distribution of autobiographical memories in childhood. *Psychological Science, 18,* 910–916. (p. 331)

Baum, A., & Posluszny, D. M. (1999). Health psychology: Mapping biobehavioral contributions to health and illness. *Annual Review of Psychology, 50,* 137–163. (p. 450)

Bauman, J., & DeSteno, D. (2010). Emotion guided threat detection: Expecting guns where there are none. *Journal of Personality and Social Psychology, 99,* 595–610. (p. 166)

Baumeister, R. F. (1989). The optimal margin of illusion. *Journal of Social and Clinical Psychology, 8,* 176–189. (p. 367)

Baumeister, R. F. (1996). Should schools try to boost self-esteem? Beware the dark side. *American Educator, 20,* 43. (p. 597)

Baumeister, R. F. (2000). Gender differences in erotic plasticity: The female sex drive as socially flexible and responsive. *Psychological Bulletin, 126,* 347–374. (p. 532)

Baumeister, R. F. (2001, April). Violent pride: Do people turn violent because of self-hate, or self-love? *Scientific American,* 96–101. (p. 597)

Baumeister, R. F. (2005). *The cultural animal: Human nature, meaning, and social life.* New York: Oxford University Press. (p. 776)

Baumeister, R. F. (2006, August/September). Violent pride. *Scientific American Mind,* 54–59. (p. 595)

Baumeister, R. F., & Bratslavsky, E. (1999). Passion, intimacy, and time: Passionate love as a function of change in intimacy. *Personality and Social Psychology Review, 3,* 49–67. (p. 804)

Baumeister, R. F., Catanese, K. R., & Vohs, K. D. (2001). Is there a gender difference in strength of sex drive? Theoretical views, conceptual distinctions, and a review of relevant evidence. *Personality and Social Psychology Review, 5,* 242–273. (p. 138)

Baumeister, R. F., Dale, K., & Sommer, K. L. (1998). Freudian defense mechanisms and empirical findings in modern personality and social psychology: Reaction formation, projection, displacement, undoing, isolation, sublimation, and denial. *Journal of Personality, 66,* 1081–1125. (p. 568)

Baumeister, R. F., & Exline, J. J. (2000). Self-control, morality, and human strength. *Journal of Social and Clinical Psychology, 19,* 29–42. (p. 301)

Baumeister, R. F., & Leary, M. R. (1995). The need to belong: Desire for interpersonal attachments as a fundamental human motivation. *Psychological Bulletin, 117,* 497–529. (p. 412)

Baumeister, R. F., & Tice, D. M. (1986). How adolescence became the struggle for self: A historical transformation of psychological development. In J. Suls & A. G. Greenwald (Eds.), *Psychological perspectives on the self* (Vol. 3). Hillsdale, NJ: Erlbaum. (p. 522)

Baumeister, R. F., Twenge, J. M., & Nuss, C. K. (2002). Effects of social exclusion on cognitive processes: Anticipated aloneness reduces intelligent thought. *Journal of Personality and Social Psychology, 83,* 817–827. (p. 415)

Baumgardner, A. H., Kaufman, C. M., & Levy, P. E. (1989). Regulating affect interpersonally: When low esteem leads to greater enhancement. *Journal of Personality and Social Psychology, 56,* 907–921. (p. 595)

Baumrind, D. (1996). The discipline controversy revisited. *Family Relations, 45,* 405–414. (p. 496)

Baumrind, D., Larzelere, R. E., & Cowan, P. A. (2002). Ordinary physical punishment: Is it harmful? Comment on Gershoff (2002). *Psychological Bulletin, 128,* 602–611. (p. 282)

Bavelier, D., Newport, E. L., & Supalla, T. (2003). Children need natural languages, signed or spoken. *Cerebrum, 5*(1), 19–32. (p. 376)

Bavelier, D., Tomann, A., Hutton, C., Mitchell, T., Corina, D., Liu, G., & Neville, H. (2000). Visual attention to the periphery is enhanced in congenitally deaf individuals. *Journal of Neuroscience, 20,* 1–6. (p. 110)

BBC. (2008, February 26). Anti-depressants 'of little use.' *BBC News* (www.news.bbc.co.uk). (p. 743)

Beaman, A. L., & Klentz, B. (1983). The supposed physical attractiveness bias against supporters of the women's movement: A meta-analysis. *Personality and Social Psychology Bulletin, 9,* 544–550. (p. 802)

Beardsley, L. M. (1994). Medical diagnosis and treatment across cultures. In W. J. Lonner & R. Malpass (Eds.), *Psychology and culture.* Boston: Allyn & Bacon. (p. 653)

Bearzi, M., & Stanford, C. (2010). A bigger, better brain. *American Scientist, 98,* 402–409. (p. 868)

Beauchamp, G. K. (1987). The human preference for excess salt. *American Scientist, 75,* 27–33. (p. 400)

Beck, A. T., Rush, A. J., Shaw, B. F., & Emery, G. (1979). *Cognitive therapy of depression.* New York: Guilford Press. (p. 721)

Beck, H. P., Levinson, S., & Irons, G. (2009). Finding Little Albert: A journey to John B. Watson's infant laboratory. *American Psychologist, 64,* 605–614. (p. 271)

Beck, H. P., Levinson, S., & Irons, G. (2010). The evidence supports Douglas Merritte as Little Albert. *American Psychologist, 65,* 301–303. (p. 271)

Becker, D. V., Kenrick, D. T., Neuberg, S. L., Blackwell, K. C., & Smith, D. M. (2007). The confounded nature of angry men and happy women. *Journal of Personality and Social Psychology, 92,* 179–190. (p. 434)

Becker, S., & Wojtowicz, J. M. (2007). A model of hippocampal neurogenesis in memory and mood disorders. *Trends in Cognitive Sciences, 11,* 70–76. (p. 742)

Becklen, R., & Cervone, D. (1983). Selective looking and the noticing of unexpected events. *Memory and Cognition, 11,* 601–608. (p. 154)

Beckman, M. (2004). Crime, culpability, and the adolescent brain. *Science, 305,* 596–599. (p. 514)

Beeman, M. J., & Chiarello, C. (1998). Complementary right- and left-hemisphere language comprehension. *Current Directions in Psychological Science, 7,* 2–8. (p. 117)

Bègue, L., Bushman, B. J., Giancola, P. R., Subra, B., & Rosset, E. (2010). "There is no such thing as an accident," especially when people are drunk. *Personality and Social Psychology Bulletin, 36,* 1301–1304. (p. 791)

Beilin, H. (1992). Piaget's enduring contribution to developmental psychology. *Developmental Psychology, 28,* 191–204. (p. 484)

Bell, A. P., Weinberg, M. S., & Hammersmith, S. K. (1981). *Sexual preference: Its development in men and women.* Bloomington: Indiana University Press. (p. 533)

Belluck, P. (2010, February 16). Wanted: Volunteers, all pregnant. *New York Times* (www.nytimes.com). (p. 481)

Belluck, P. (2013, February 5). People with mental illness more likely to be smokers, study finds. *New York Times* (www.nytimes.com). (p. 46)

Belot, M., & Francesconi, M. (2006, November). *Can anyone be 'the one'? Evidence on mate selection from speed dating.* London: Centre for Economic Policy Research (www.cepr.org). (p. 800)

Belsher, G., & Costello, C. G. (1988). Relapse after recovery from unipolar depression: A critical review. *Psychological Bulletin, 104,* 84–96. (p. 675)

Belsky, J., Bakermans-Kranenburg, M. J., & van IJzendoorn, M. H. (2007). For better *and* for worse: Differential susceptibility to environmental influences. *Current Directions in Psychological Science, 16,* 300–304. (p. 701)

Belsky, J., Houts, R. M., & Fearon, R. M. P. (2010). Infant attachment security and the timing of puberty: Testing an evolutionary hypothesis. *Psychological Science, 21,* 1195–1201. (p. 527)

Belsky, J., & Pluess, M. (2009). Beyond diathesis stress: Differential susceptibility to environmental influences. *Psychological Bulletin, 135,* 885–908. (p. 667)

Bem, D. J. (1984). Quoted in *The Skeptical Inquirer, 8,* 194. (p. 168)

Bem, D. J. (2011). Feeling the future: Experimental evidence for anomalous retroactive influences on cognition and affect. *Journal of Personality and Social Psychology, 100,* 407–425. (p. 168)

Bem, S. L. (1987). Masculinity and femininity exist only in the mind of the perceiver. In J. M. Reinisch, L. A. Rosenblum, & S. A. Sanders (Eds.), *Masculinity/femininity: Basic perspectives.* New York: Oxford University Press. (p. 504)

Bem, S. L. (1993). *The lenses of gender.* New Haven, CT: Yale University Press. (p. 504)

Benjamin, L. T., Jr., & Simpson, J. A. (2009). The power of the situation: The impact of Milgram's obedience studies on personality and social psychology. *American Psychologist, 64,* 12–19. (p. 765)

Benjamins, M. R., Ellison, C. G., & Rogers, R. G. (2010). Religious involvement and mortality risk among pre-retirement aged U.S. adults. In C. E. Ellison & R. A. Hummer (Eds.), *Religion, families, and health: Population-based research in the United States.* New Brunswick, NJ: Rutgers University Press. (p. 864)

Bennett, R. (1991, February). Pornography and extrafamilial child sexual abuse: Examining the relationship. Unpublished manuscript, Los Angeles Police Department Sexually Exploited Child Unit. (p. 793)

Bennett, W. I. (1995). Beyond overeating. *New England Journal of Medicine, 332,* 673–674. (p. 403)

Ben-Shakhar, G., & Elaad, E. (2003). The validity of psychophysiological detection of information with the guilt knowledge test: A meta-analytic review. *Journal of Applied Psychology, 88,* 131–151. (p. 428)

Benson, H. (1996). *Timeless healing: The power and biology of belief.* New York: Scribner. (p. 862)

Berger, J., Meredith, M., & Wheeler, S. C. (2008). Does where you vote affect how you vote? The impact of environmental cues on voting behavior. *Proceedings of the National Academy of Science, 105*(26), 8846–8849. (p. 264)

Berghuis, P., & 16 others. (2007). Hardwiring the brain: Endocannabinoids shape neuronal connectivity. *Science, 316,* 1212–1216. (p. 255)

Bergin, A. E. (1980). Psychotherapy and religious values. *Journal of Consulting and Clinical Psychology, 48,* 95–105. (p. 736)

Berk, L. E. (1994, November). Why children talk to themselves. *Scientific American,* pp. 78–83. (p. 484)

Berk, L. S., Felten, D. L., Tan, S. A., Bittman, B. B., & Westengard, J. (2001). Modulation of neuroimmune parameters during the eustress of humor-associated mirthful laughter. *Alternative Therapies, 7,* 62–76. (p. 857)

Berkowitz, L. (1983). Aversively stimulated aggression: Some parallels and differences in research with animals and humans. *American Psychologist, 38,* 1135–1144. (p. 791)

Berkowitz, L. (1989). Frustration-aggression hypothesis: Examination and reformulation. *Psychological Bulletin, 106,* 59–73. (p. 791)

Berkowitz, L. (1990). On the formation and regulation of anger and aggression: A cognitive-neoassociationistic analysis. *American Psychologist, 45,* 494–503. (p. 845)

Berman, M., Gladue, B., & Taylor, S. (1993). The effects of hormones, Type A behavior pattern, and provocation on aggression in men. *Motivation and Emotion, 17,* 125–138. (p. 790)

Berman, M. G., Jonides, J., & Kaplan, S. (2008). The cognitive benefits of interacting with nature. *Psychological Science, 19,* 1207–1212. (p. 417)

Bernal, S., Dehaene-Lambertz, G., Millotte, S. & Christophe, A. (2010). Two-year-olds compute syntactic structure on-line. *Developmental Science, 13,* 69–76. (p. 374)

Bernieri, F., Davis, J., Rosenthal, R., & Knee, C. (1994). Interactional synchrony and rapport: Measuring synchrony in displays devoid of sound and facial affect. *Personality and Social Psychology Bulletin, 20,* 303–311. (p. 307)

Bernstein, D. M., & Loftus, E. F. (2009a). The consequences of false memories for food preferences and choices. *Perspectives on Psychological Science, 4,* 135–139. (p. 348)

Bernstein, D. M., & Loftus, E. F. (2009b). How to tell if a particular memory is true or false. *Perspectives on Psychological Science, 4,* 370–374. (p. 347)

Bernstein, M. J., Young, S. G., & Claypool, H. M. (2010). Is Obama's win a gain for Blacks? Changes in implicit racial prejudice following the 2008 election. *Social Psychology, 41,* 147–151. (p. 782)

Berridge, K. C., & Winkielman, P. (2003). What is an unconscious emotion? (The case of unconscious "liking"). *Cognition and Emotion, 17,* 181–211. (p. 423)

Berry, C. M., & Sackett, P. R. (2009). Individual differences in course choice result in underestimation of the validity of college admissions systems. *Psychological Science, 20,* 822–830. (p. 622)

Berscheid, E. (1981). An overview of the psychological effects of physical attractiveness and some comments upon the psychological effects of knowledge of the effects of physical attractiveness. In G. W. Lucker, K. Ribbens, & J. A. McNamara (Eds.), *Psychological aspects of facial form* (Craniofacial growth series). Ann Arbor: Center for Human Growth and Development, University of Michigan. (p. 800)

Berscheid, E. (1985). Interpersonal attraction. In G. Lindzey & E. Aronson (Eds.), *The handbook of social psychology.* New York: Random House. (p. 413)

Berscheid, E. (2010). Love in the fourth dimension. *Annual Review of Psychology, 61,* 1–25. (p. 803)

Berscheid, E., Gangestad, S. W., & Kulakowski, D. (1984). Emotion in close relationships: Implications for relationship counseling. In S. D. Brown & R. W. Lent (Eds.), *Handbook of counseling psychology.* New York: Wiley. (p. 803)

Berti, A., Cottini, G., Gandola, M., Pia, L., Smania, N., Stracciari, A., Castiglioni, I., Vallar, G., & Paulesu, E. (2005). Shared cortical anatomy for motor awareness and motor control. *Science, 309,* 488–491. (p. 117)

Beyerstein, B., & Beyerstein, D. (Eds.). (1992). *The write stuff: Evaluations of graphology.* Buffalo, NY: Prometheus Books. (p. 579)

Bhatt, R. S., Wasserman, E. A., Reynolds, W. F., Jr., & Knauss, K. S. (1988). Conceptual behavior in pigeons: Categorization of both familiar and novel examples from four classes of natural and artificial stimuli. *Journal of Experimental Psychology: Animal Behavior Processes, 14,* 219–234. (p. 277)

Bialystok, E., & Craik, F. I. M. (2010). Cognitive and linguistic processing in the bilingual mind. *Current Directions in Psychological Science, 19,* 19–23. (p. 380)

Biederman, I., & Vessel, E. A. (2006). Perceptual pleasure and the brain. *American Scientist, 94,* 247–253. (p. 392)

Bienvenu, O. J., Davydow, D. S., & Kendler, K. S. (2011). Psychiatric 'diseases' *versus* behavioral disorders and degree of genetic influence. *Psychological Medicine, 41,* 33–40. (p. 676)

Bilefsky, D. (2009, March 11). Europeans debate castration of sex offenders. *New York Times* (www.nytimes.com). (p. 408)

Binet, A. (1909). *Les idées modernes sur les enfants.* Paris: Flammarion (quoted by A. Clarke & A. Clarke, Born to be bright. *The Psychologist, 19,* 409. (p. 618)

Binitie, A. (1975) A factor-analytical study of depression across cultures (African and European). *British Journal of Psychiatry, 127,* 559–563. (p. 693)

Bird, C. D., & Emery, N. J. (2009). Rooks use stones to raise the water level to reach a floating worm. *Current Biology, 19,* 1410–1414. (p. 868)

Birnbaum, G. E., Reis, H. T., Mikulincer, M., Gillath, O., & Orpaz, A. (2006). When sex is more than just sex: Attachment orientations, sexual experience, and relationship quality. *Journal of Personality and Social Psychology, 91,* 929–943. (p. 492)

Birnbaum, S. G., Yuan, P. X., Wang, M., Vijayraghavan, S., Bloom, A. K., Davis, D. J., Gobeski, K. T., Sweatt, J. D., Manhi, H. K., & Arnsten, A. F. T. (2004). Protein kinase C overactivity impairs prefrontal cortical regulation of working memory. *Science, 306,* 882–884. (p. 332)

Biro, D., Humle, T., Koops, K., Sousa, C., Hayashi, M., & Matsuzawa, T. (2010). Chimpanzee mothers at Bossou, Guinea carry the mummified remains of their dead infants. *Current Biology, 20,* R351–R352. (p. 868)

Biro, F. M., & 9 others. (2010). Pubertal assessment method and baseline characteristics in a mixed longitudinal study of girls. *Pediatrics, 126,* e583–e590. (p. 527)

Bishop, D. I., Weisgram, E. S., Holleque, K. M., Lund, K. E., & Wheeler, J. R. (2005). Identity development and alcohol consumption: Current and retrospective self-reports by college students. *Journal of Adolescence, 28,* 523–533. (pp. 521, 824)

Bishop, G. D. (1991). Understanding the understanding of illness: Lay disease representations. In J. A. Skelton & R. T. Croyle (Eds.), *Mental representation in health and illness.* New York: Springer-Verlag. (p. 357)

Bisson, J., & Andrew, M. (2007). Psychological treatment of post-traumatic stress disorder (PTSD). *Cochrane Database of Systematic Reviews 2007,* Issue 3. Art. No. CD003388. (p. 733)

Bjork, E. L., & Bjork, R. (2011). Making things hard on yourself, but in a good way: Creating desirable difficulties to enhance learning. In M. A. Gernsbacher, M. A. Pew, L. M. Hough, & J. R. Pomerantz (eds.), *Psychology and the real world.* New York: Worth Publishers. (p. 17)

Bjorklund, D. F., & Green, B. L. (1992). The adaptive nature of cognitive immaturity. *American Psychologist, 47,* 46–54. (p. 485)

Blackhart, G. C., Nelson, B. C., Knowles, M. L., & Baumeister, R. F. (2009). Rejection elicits emotional reactions but neither causes immediate distress nor lowers self-esteem: A meta-analytic review of 192 studies on social exclusion. *Personality and Social Psychology Bulletin, 13,* 269–309. (p. 414)

Blakemore, S-J. (2008). Development of the social brain during adolescence. *Quarterly Journal of Experimental Psychology, 61,* 40–49. (p. 514)

Blakemore, S-J., Wolpert, D. M., & Frith, C. D. (1998). Central cancellation of self-produced tickle sensation. *Nature Neuroscience, 1,* 635–640. (p. 203)

Blakeslee, S. (2006, January 10). Cells that read minds. *New York Times* (www.nytimes.com). (p. 305)

Blanchard, R. (1997). Birth order and sibling sex ratio in homosexual versus heterosexual males and females. *Annual Review of Sex Research, 8,* 27–67. (p. 535)

Blanchard, R. (2008a). Review and theory of handedness, birth order, and homosexuality in men. *Laterality, 13,* 51–70. (pp. 535, 536)

Blanchard, R. (2008b). Sex ratio of older siblings in heterosexual and homosexual, right-handed and non-right-handed men. *Archives of Sexual Behavior, 37,* 977–981. (p. 535)

Blanchard-Fields, F. (2007). Everyday problem solving and emotion: An adult developmental perspective. *Current Directions in Psychological Science, 16,* 26–31. (p. 626)

Blank, H., Musch, J., & Pohl, R. F. (2007). Hindsight bias: On being wise after the event. *Social Cognition, 25,* 1–9. (p. 31)

Blankenburg, F., Taskin, B., Ruben, J., Moosmann, M., Ritter, P., Curio, G., & Villringer, A. (2003). Imperceptive stimuli and sensory processing impediment. *Science, 299,* 1864. (p. 157)

Blanton, H., Jaccard, J., Christie, C., & Gonzales, P. M. (2007). Plausible assumptions, questionable assumptions and post hoc rationalizations: Will the real IAT please stand up? *Journal of Experimental Social Psychology, 43,* 399–409. (p. 782)

Blanton, H., Jaccard, J., Gonzales, P. M., & Christie, C. (2006). Decoding the implicit association test: Implications for criterion prediction. *Journal of Experimental Social Psychology, 42,* 192–212. (p. 782)

Blanton, H., Jaccard, J., Klick, J., Mellers, B., Mitchell, G., & Tetlock, P. E. (2009). Strong claims and weak evidence: Reassessing the predictive validity of the IAT. *Journal of Applied Psychology, 94,* 567–582. (p. 782)

Blascovich, J., Seery, M. D., Mugridge, C. A., Norris, R. K., & Weisbuch, M. (2004). Predicting athletic performance from cardiovascular indexes of challenge and threat. *Journal of Experimental Social Psychology, 40,* 683–688. (p. 442)

Blass, T. (1996). Stanley Milgram: A life of inventiveness and controversy. In G. A. Kimble, C. A. Boneau, & M. Wertheimer (Eds.), *Portraits of pioneers in psychology* (Vol. II). Washington, DC and Mahwah, NJ: American Psychological Association and Lawrence Erlbaum Publishers. (p. 766)

Blass, T. (1999). The Milgram paradigm after 35 years: Some things we now know about obedience to authority. *Journal of Applied Social Psychology, 29,* 955–978. (p. 766)

Blatt, S. J., Sanislow, C. A., III, Zuroff, D. C., & Pilkonis, P. (1996). Characteristics of effective therapists: Further analyses of data from the National Institute of Mental Health Treatment of Depression Collaborative Research Program. *Journal of Consulting and Clinical Psychology, 64,* 1276–1284. (p. 735)

Block, J. (2010). The five-factor framing of personality and beyond: Some ruminations. *Psychological Inquiry, 21,* 2–25. (p. 580)

Bloom, B. C. (Ed.). (1985). *Developing talent in young people.* New York: Ballantine. (p. 834)

Bloom, F. E. (1993, January/February). What's new in neurotransmitters. *Brain-Work,* pp. 7–9. (p. 81)

Bloom, P. (2000). *How children learn the meanings of words.* Cambridge, MA: MIT Press. (p. 373)

Bloom, P. (2010, May 6). The moral life of babies. *New York Times Magazine* (www.nytimes.com). (p. 777)

Blum, K., Cull, J. G., Braverman, E. R., & Comings, D. E. (1996). Reward deficiency syndrome. *American Scientist, 84,* 132–145. (p. 101)

Boag, S. (2006). Freudian repression, the common view, and pathological science. *Review of General Psychology, 10,* 74–86. (p. 562)

Boahen, K. (2005, May). Neuromorphic microchips. *Scientific American,* 56–63. (p. 196)

Bocklandt, S., Horvath, S., Vilain, E., & Hamer, D. H. (2006). Extreme skewing of X chromosome inactivation in mothers of homosexual men. *Human Genetics, 118,* 691–694. (p. 534)

Bodenhausen, G. V., Sheppard, L. A., & Kramer, G. P. (1994). Negative affect and social judgment: The differential impact of anger and sadness. *European Journal of Social Psychology, 24,* 45–62. (p. 815)

Bodkin, J. A., & Amsterdam, J. D. (2002). Transdermal selegiline in major depression: A double-blind, placebo-controlled, parallel-group study in outpatients. *American Journal of Psychiatry, 159,* 1869–1875. (p. 742)

Boehm, K. E., Schondel, C. K., Marlowe, A. L., & Manke-Mitchell, L. (1999). Teens' concerns: A national evaluation. *Adolescence, 34,* 523–528. (p. 522)

Boehm-Davis, D. A. (2005). Improving product safety and effectiveness in the home. In R. S. Nickerson (Ed.), *Reviews of human factors and ergonomics.* (Vol. 1). Santa Monica, CA: Human Factors and Ergonomics Society, 219–253. (p. 840)

Boesch-Achermann, H., & Boesch, C. (1993). Tool use in wild chimpanzees: New light from dark forests. *Current Directions in Psychological Science, 2,* 18–21. (p. 867)

Bogaert, A. F. (2003). Number of older brothers and sexual orientation: New texts and the attraction/behavior distinction in two national probability samples. *Journal of Personality and Social Psychology, 84,* 644–652. (p. 535)

Bogaert, A. F. (2004). Asexuality: Prevalence and associated factors in a national probability sample. *Journal of Sex Research, 41,* 279–287. (p. 532)

Bogaert, A. F. (2006). Biological versus nonbiological older brothers and men's sexual orientation. *Proceedings of the National Academy of Sciences, 103,* 10771–10774. (pp. 532, 535)

Bogaert, A. F. (2010). Physical development and sexual orientation in men and women: An analysis of NATSAL-2000. *Archives of Sexual Behavior, 39,* 110–116. (p. 536)

Boggiano, A. K., Harackiewicz, J. M., Bessette, M. M., & Main, D. S. (1985). Increasing children's interest through performance-contingent reward. *Social Cognition, 3,* 400–411. (p. 298)

Boggiano, M. M., Chandler, P. C., Viana, J. B., Oswald, K. D., Maldonado, C. R., & Wauford, P. K. (2005). Combined dieting and stress evoke exaggerated responses to opioids in binge-eating rats. *Behavioral Neuroscience, 119,* 1207–1214. (p. 399)

Bohman, M., & Sigvardsson, S. (1990). Outcome in adoption: Lessons from longitudinal studies. In D. Brodzinsky & M. Schechter (Eds.), *The psychology of adoption.* New York: Oxford University Press. (p. 128)

Bolger, N., DeLongis, A., Kessler, R. C., & Schilling, E. A. (1989). Effects of daily stress on negative mood. *Journal of Personality and Social Psychology, 57,* 808–818. (p. 848)

Bolwig, T. G., & Madsen, T. M. (2007). Electroconvulsive therapy in melancholia: The role of hippocampal neurogenesis. *Acta Psychiatrica Scandinavica, 115,* 130–135. (p. 744)

Bonanno, G. A. (2004). Loss, trauma, and human resilience: Have we underestimated the human capacity to thrive after extremely aversive events? *American Psychologist, 59,* 20–28. (p. 548)

Bonanno, G. A., Brewin, C. R., Kaniasty, K., & La Greca, A. M. (2010). Weighing the costs of disaster: Consequences, risks, and resilience in individuals, families, and communities. *Psychological Science in the Public Interest, 11,* 1–49. (p. 665)

Bonanno, G. A., Galea, S., Bucciarelli, A., & Vlahov, D. (2006). Psychological resilience after disaster. *Psychological Science, 17,* 181–186. (p. 665)

Bonanno, G. A., Galea, S., Bucciarelli, A., & Vlahov, D. (2007). What predicts psychological resilience after disaster? The role of demographics, resources, and life stress. *Journal of Consulting and Clinical Psychology, 75(5),* 671–682. (p. 737)

Bonanno, G. A., & Kaltman, S. (1999). Toward an integrative perspective on bereavement. *Psychological Bulletin, 125,* 760–777. (p. 548)

Bond, C. F., Jr., & DePaulo, B. M. (2006). Accuracy of deception judgments. *Personality and Social Psychology Review, 10,* 214–234. (p. 433)

Bond, C. F., Jr., & DePaulo, B. M. (2008). Individual differences in detecting deception: Accuracy and bias. *Psychological Bulletin, 134,* 477–492. (p. 433)

Bond, M. H. (1988). Finding universal dimensions of individual variation in multi-cultural studies of values: The Rokeach and Chinese values surveys. *Journal of Personality and Social Psychology, 55,* 1009–1015. (p. 599)

Bond, R., & Smith, P. B. (1996). Culture and conformity: A meta-analysis of studies using Asch's (1952b, 1956) line judgment task. *Psychological Bulletin, 119,* 111–137. (p. 765)

Bonetti, L., Campbell, M. A., & Gilmore, L. (2010). The relationship of loneliness and social anxiety with children's and adolescents' online communication. *Cyberpsychology, Behavior, and Social Networking, 13,* 279–285. (p. 416)

Bonezzi, A., Brendl, C. M., & DeAngelis, M. (2011). Stuck in the middle: The psychophysics of goal pursuit. *Psychological Science, 22,* 607–612. (p. 834)

Bono, J. E., & Judge, T. A. (2004). Personality and transformational and transactional leadership: A meta-analysis. *Journal of Applied Psychology, 89,* 901–910. (p. 839)

Booth, F. W., & Neufer, P. D. (2005). Exercise controls gene expression. *American Scientist, 93,* 28–35. (p. 860)

Bor, D. (2010, July/August). The mechanics of mind reading. *Scientific American,* pp. 52–57. (p. 119)

Boring, E. G. (1930). A new ambiguous figure. *American Journal of Psychology, 42,* 444–445. (p. 163)

Bornstein, M. H., Cote, L. R., Maital, S., Painter, K., Park, S-Y., Pascual, L., Pecheux, M-G., Ruel, J., Venute, P., & Vyt, A. (2004). Cross-linguistic analysis of vocabulary in young children: Spanish, Dutch, French, Hebrew, Italian, Korean, and American English. *Child Development, 75,* 1115–1139. (p. 376)

Bornstein, M. H., Tal, J., Rahn, C., Galperin, C. Z., Pecheux, M-G., Lamour, M., Toda, S., Azuma, H., Ogino, M., & Tamis-LeMonda, C. S. (1992a). Functional analysis of the contents of maternal speech to infants of 5 and 13 months in four cultures: Argentina, France, Japan, and the United States. *Developmental Psychology, 28,* 593–603. (p. 463)

Bornstein, M. H., Tamis-LeMonda, C. S., Tal, J., Ludemann, P., Toda, S., Rahn, C. W., Pecheux, M-G., Azuma, H., & Vardi, D. (1992b). Maternal responsiveness to infants in three societies: The United States, France, and Japan. *Child Development, 63,* 808–821. (p. 463)

Bornstein, R. F. (1989). Exposure and affect: Overview and meta-analysis of research, 1968–1987. *Psychological Bulletin, 106,* 265–289. (pp. 489, 798)

Bornstein, R. F. (1999). Source amnesia, misattribution, and the power of unconscious perceptions and memories. *Psychoanalytic Psychology, 16,* 155–178. (p. 798)

Bornstein, R. F., Galley, D. J., Leone, D. R., & Kale, A. R. (1991). The temporal stability of ratings of parents: Test-retest reliability and influence of parental contact. *Journal of Social Behavior and Personality, 6,* 641–649. (p. 337)

Boroditsky, L. (2009, June 12). How does our language shape the way we think? www.edge.org. (pp. 373, 380)

Boroditsky, L. (2011, February). How language shapes thought. *Scientific American,* 63–65. (p. 379)

Boscarino, J. A. (1997). Diseases among men 20 years after exposure to severe stress: Implications for clinical research and medical care. *Psychosomatic Medicine, 59,* 605–614. (p. 442)

Bosma, H., Marmot, M. G., Hemingway, H., Nicolson, A. C., Brunner, E., & Stansfeld, S. A. (1997). Low job control and risk of coronary heart disease in Whitehall II (prospective cohort) study. *British Medical Journal, 314,* 558–565. (p. 300)

Bosma, H., Peter, R., Siegrist, J., & Marmot, M. (1998). Two alternative job stress models and the risk of coronary heart disease. *American Journal of Public Health, 88,* 68–74. (p. 300)

Bostwick, J. M., & Pankratz, V. S. (2000). Affective disorders and suicide risk: A re-examination. *American Journal of Psychiatry, 157,* 1925–1932. (p. 676)

Bosworth, R. G., & Dobkins, K. R. (1999). Left-hemisphere dominance for motion processing in deaf signers. *Psychological Science, 10,* 256–262. (p. 111)

Bothwell, R. K., Brigham, J. C., & Malpass, R. S. (1989). Cross-racial identification. *Personality and Social Psychology Bulletin, 15,* 19–25. (p. 786)

Botwin, M. D., Buss, D. M., & Shackelford, T. K. (1997). Personality and mate preferences: Five factors in mate selection and marital satisfaction. *Journal of Personality, 65,* 107–136. (p. 581)

Bouchard, T. J., Jr. (1981, December 6). Interview on *Nova:* Twins [program broadcast by the Public Broadcasting Service]. (p. 126)

Bouchard, T. J., Jr. (2009). Genetic influences on human intelligence (Spearman's *g*): How much? *Annals of Human Biology, 36,* 527–544. (p. 127)

Bouton, M. E., Mineka, S., & Barlow, D. H. (2001). A modern learning theory perspective on the etiology of panic disorder. *Psychological Review, 108,* 4–32. (p. 666)

Bowden, E. M., & Beeman, M. J. (1998). Getting the right idea: Semantic activation in the right hemisphere may help solve insight problems. *Psychological Science, 9,* 435–440. (p. 117)

Bower, B. (2009, February 14). The dating go round. *Science News,* 22–25. (p. 799)

Bower, G. H. (1986). Prime time in cognitive psychology. In P. Eelen (Ed.), *Cognitive research and behavior therapy: Beyond the conditioning paradigm.* Amsterdam: North Holland Publishers. (p. 336)

Bower, G. H., Clark, M. C., Lesgold, A. M., & Winzenz, D. (1969). Hierarchical retrieval schemes in recall of categorized word lists. *Journal of Verbal Learning and Verbal Behavior, 8,* 323–343. (p. 324)

Bower, G. H., & Morrow, D. G. (1990). Mental models in narrative comprehension. *Science, 247,* 44–48. (p. 326)

Bower, J. E., Kemeny, M. E., Taylor, S. E., & Fahey, J. L. (1998). Cognitive processing, discovery of meaning, CD4 decline, and AIDS-related mortality among bereaved HIV-seropositive men. *Journal of Consulting and Clinical Psychology, 66,* 979–986. (p. 450)

Bower, J. M., & Parsons, L. M. (2003, August). Rethinking the "lesser brain." *Scientific American,* 50–57. (p. 98)

Bowers, J. S. (2009). On the biological plausibility of grandmother cells: Implications for neural network theories in psychology and neuroscience. *Psychological Review, 116,* 220–251. (p. 177)

Bowers, J. S., Mattys, S. L., & Gage, S. H. (2009). Preserved implicit knowledge of a forgotten childhood language. *Psychological Science, 20,* 1064–1069. (p. 473)

Bowers, K. S. (1984). Hypnosis. In N. Endler & J. M. Hunt (Eds.), *Personality and behavioral disorders* (2nd ed.). New York: Wiley. (p. 219)

Bowers, K. S. (1987, July). Personal communication. (p. 220)

Bowler, M. C., & Woehr, D. J. (2006). A meta-analytic evaluation of the impact of dimension and exercise factors on assessment center ratings. *Journal of Applied Psychology, 91,* 1114–1124. (p. 592)

Bowling, N. A. (2007). Is the job satisfaction-job performance relationship spurious? A meta-analytic examination. *Journal of Vocational Behavior, 71,* 167–185. (p. 835)

Bowling, N. A., Eschleman, K. J., & Wang, Q. (2010). A meta-analytic examination of the relationship between job satisfaction and subjective well-being. *Journal of Occupational and Organizational Psychology, 83,* 915–934. (p. 835)

Boxer, P., Huesmann, L. R., Bushman, B. J., O'Brien, M., & Moceri, D. (2009). The role of violent media preference in cumulative developmental risk for violence and general aggression. *Journal of Youth and Adolescence, 38,* 417–428. (p. 309)

Boyatzis, C. J., Matillo, G. M., & Nesbitt, K. M. (1995). Effects of the "Mighty Morphin Power Rangers" on children's aggression with peers. *Child Study Journal, 25,* 45–55. (p. 309)

Boyce, C. J., Brown, G. D. A., & Moore, S. C. (2010). Money and happiness: Rank of income, not income, affects life satisfaction. *Psychological Science, 21,* 471–475. (p. 852)

Boyer, J. L., Harrison, S., & Ro, T. (2005). Unconscious processing of orientation and color without primary visual cortex. *Proceedings of the National Academy of Sciences, 102,* 16875–16879 (www.pnas.org). (p. 120)

Boynton, R. M. (1979). *Human color vision.* New York: Holt, Rinehart & Winston. (p. 178)

Braden, J. P. (1994). *Deafness, deprivation, and IQ.* New York: Plenum. (p. 639)

Bradley, D. R., Dumais, S. T., & Petry, H. M. (1976). Reply to Cavonius. *Nature, 261,* 78. (p. 183)

Bradley, R. B., & 15 others. (2008). Influence of child abuse on adult depression: Moderation by the corticotropin-releasing hormone receptor gene. *Archives of General Psychiatry, 65,* 190–200. (p. 494)

Bradshaw, C., Sawyer, A., O'Brennan, L. (2009). A social disorganization perspective on bullying-related attitudes and behaviors: The influence of school context. *American Journal of Community Psychology, 43,* 204–220. (p. 15)

Braiker, B. (2005, October 18). A quiet revolt against the rules on SIDS. *New York Times* (www.nytimes.com). (p. 472)

Brainerd, C. J. (1996). Piaget: A centennial celebration. *Psychological Science, 7,* 191–195. (p. 476)

Branas, C. C., Richmond, T. S., Culhane, D. P., Ten Have, T. R., & Wiebe, D. J. (2009). Investigating the link between gun possession and gun assault. *American Journal of Public Health, 99,* 2034–2040. (p. 789)

Brandon, S., Boakes, J., Glaser, D., & Green, R. (1998). Recovered memories of childhood sexual abuse: Implications for clinical practice. *British Journal of Psychiatry, 172,* 294–307. (p. 352)

Brang, D., Edwards, L., Ramachandran, V. S., & Coulson, S. (2008). Is the sky 2? Contextual priming in grapheme-color synaesthesia. *Psychological Science, 19,* 421–428. (p. 211)

Bransford, J. D., & Johnson, M. K. (1972). Contextual prerequisites for understanding: Some investigations of comprehension and recall. *Journal of Verbal Learning and Verbal Behavior, 11,* 717–726. (p. 325)

Brant, A. M., Haberstick, B. C., Corley, R. P., Wadsworth, S. J., DeFries, J. C., & Hewitt, J. K. (2009). The developmental etiology of high IQ. *Behavior Genetics, 39,* 393–405. (p. 633)

Braun, S. (1996). New experiments underscore warnings on maternal drinking. *Science, 273,* 738–739. (p. 467)

Braun, S. (2001, Spring). Seeking insight by prescription. *Cerebrum,* pp. 10–21. (p. 253)

Braunstein, G. D., Sundwall, D. A., Katz, M., Shifren, J. L., Buster, J. E., Simon, J. A., Bachman, G., Aguirre, O. A., Lucas, J. D., Rodenberg, C., Buch, A., & Watts, N. B. (2005). Safety and efficacy of a testosterone patch for the treatment of hypoactive sexual desire disorder in surgically menopausal women: A randomized, placebo-controlled trial. *Archives of Internal Medicine, 165,* 1582–1589. (p. 408)

Bray, D. W., & Byham, W. C. (1991, Winter). Assessment centers and their derivatives. *Journal of Continuing Higher Education,* pp. 8–11. (p. 592)

Bray, D. W., & Byham, W. C., interviewed by Mayes, B. T. (1997). Insights into the history and future of assessment centers: An interview with Dr. Douglas W. Bray and Dr. William Byham. *Journal of Social Behavior and Personality, 12,* 3–12. (p. 592)

Brayne, C., Spiegelhalter, D. J., Dufouil, C., Chi, L-Y., Dening, T. R., Paykel, E. S., O'Connor, D. W., Ahmed, A., McGee, M. A., & Huppert, F. A. (1999). Estimating the true extent of cognitive decline in the old old. *Journal of the American Geriatrics Society, 47,* 1283–1288. (p. 626)

Breedlove, S. M. (1997). Sex on the brain. *Nature, 389,* 801. (p. 534)

Breen, G., & 27 others. (2011, May). A genome-wide significant linkage for severe depression on chromosome 3: The depression network study. *American Journal of Psychiatry, 167,* 949–957. (p. 678)

Brehm, S., & Brehm, J. W. (1981). *Psychological reactance: A theory of freedom and control.* New York: Academic Press. (p. 775)

Breland, K., & Breland, M. (1961). The misbehavior of organisms. *American Psychologist, 16,* 661–664. (p. 295)

Breslau, J., Aguilar-Gaxiola, S., Borges, G., Kendler, K. S., Su, M., & Kessler, R. C. (2007). Risk for psychiatric disorder among immigrants and their US-born descendants. *Journal of Nervous and Mental Disease, 195,* 189–195. (p. 657)

Brewer, C. L. (1990). Personal correspondence. (p. 131)

Brewer, C. L. (1996). Personal communication. (p. 11)

Brewer, M. B., & Chen, Y-R. (2007). Where (who) are collectives in collectivism? Toward conceptual clarification of individualism and collectivism. *Psychological Review, 114,* 133–151. (p. 599)

Brewer, W. F. (1977). Memory for the pragmatic implications of sentences. *Memory & Cognition, 5,* 673–678. (p. 326)

Brewin, C. R., Andrews, B., Rose, S., & Kirk, M. (1999). Acute stress disorder and posttraumatic stress disorder in victims of violent crime. *American Journal of Psychiatry, 156,* 360–366 (p. 664)

Brewin, C. R., Andrews, B., & Valentine, J. D. (2000). Meta-analysis of risk factors for posttraumatic stress disorder in trauma-exposed adults. *Journal of Consulting and Clinical Psychology, 68,* 748–766. (p. 665)

Brewin, C. R., Kleiner, J. S., Vasterling J. J., & Field, A. P. (2007). Memory for emotionally neutral information in posttraumatic stress disorder: A meta-analytic investigation. *Journal of Abnormal Psychology, 116,* 448–463. (p. 332)

Bricker, J. B., Stallings, M. C., Corley, R. P., Wadsworth, S. J., Bryan, A., Timberlake, D. S., Hewitt, J. K., Caspi, A., Hofer, S. M., Rhea, S. A., & DeFries, J. C. (2006). Genetic and environmental influences on age at sexual initiation in the Colorado Adoption Project. *Behavior Genetics, 36,* 820–832. (p. 530)

Brief, A. P., & Weiss, H. M. (2002). Organizational behavior: Affect in the workplace. *Annual Review of Psychology, 53,* 279–307. (p. 835)

Briñol, P., Petty, R. E., & Barden, J. (2007). Happiness versus sadness as a determinant of thought confidence in persuasion: A self-validation analysis. *Journal of Personality and Social Psychology, 93,* 711–727. (p. 847)

Briscoe, D. (1997, February 16). Women lawmakers still not in charge. *Grand Rapids Press,* p. A23. (p. 504)

Brislin, R. W. (1988). Increasing awareness of class, ethnicity, culture, and race by expanding on students' own experiences. In I. Cohen (Ed.), *The G. Stanley Hall Lecture Series.* Washington, DC: American Psychological Association. (p. 776)

Brissette, I., & Cohen, S. (2002). The contribution of individual differences in hostility to the associations between daily interpersonal conflict, affect, and sleep. *Personality and Social Psychology Bulletin, 28,* 1265–1274. (p. 238)

British Psychological Society. (1993). Ethical principles for conducting research with human participants. *The Psychologist: Bulletin of the British Psychological Society, 6,* 33–36. (p. 579)

British Psychological Society. (2009). *Code of ethics and conduct.* Leicester, UK. (p. 68)

Brockmann, H., Delhey, J., Welzel, C., & Yuan, H. (2009). The China puzzle: Falling happiness in a rising economy. *Journal of Happiness Studies, 10,* 387–405. (p. 850)

Brody, J. E. (2000, March 21). When post-traumatic stress grips youth. *New York Times* (www.nytimes.com). (p. 665)

Brody, J. E. (2002, November 26). When the eyelids snap shut at 65 miles an hour. *New York Times* (www.nytimes.com). (p. 236)

Brody, J. E. (2003, September). Addiction: A brain ailment, not a moral lapse. *New York Times* (www.nytimes.com). (p. 247)

Broks, P. (2007, April). The mystery of consciousness. *Prospect* (www.prospect-magazine.co.uk). (p. 476)

Brooks, D. (2010, January 12). The Tel Aviv cluster. *New York Times* (www.nytimes.com). (p. 641)

Brown, A. S. (2003). A review of the déjà vu experience. *Psychological Bulletin, 129,* 394–413. (p. 349)

Brown, A. S. (2004). *The déjà vu experience.* East Sussex, England: Psychology Press. (p. 349)

Brown, A. S., Begg, M. D., Gravenstein, S., Schaefer, C. A., Wyatt, R. J., Bresnahan, M., Babulas, V. P., & Susser, E. S. (2004). Serologic evidence of prenatal influenza in the etiology of schizophrenia. *Archives of General Psychiatry, 61,* 774–780. (p. 688)

Brown, A. S., Schaefer, C. A., Wyatt, R. J., Goetz, R., Begg, M. D., Gorman, J. M., & Susser, E. S. (2000). Maternal exposure to respiratory infections and adult schizophrenia spectrum disorders: A prospective birth cohort study. *Schizophrenia Bulletin, 26,* 287–295. (p. 688)

Brown, E. L., & Deffenbacher, K. (1979). *Perception and the senses.* New York: Oxford University Press. (p. 199)

Brown, J. A. (1958). Some tests of the decay theory of immediate memory. *Quarterly Journal of Experimental Psychology, 10,* 12–21. (p. 322)

Brown, J. D., Steele, J. R., & Walsh-Childers, K. (2002). *Sexual teens, sexual media: Investigating media's influence on adolescent sexuality.* Mahwah, NJ: Erlbaum. (p. 530)

Brown, J. L., & Pollitt, E. (1996, February). Malnutrition, poverty and intellectual development. *Scientific American,* 38–43. (p. 635)

Brown, R. (1986). Linguistic relativity. In S. H. Hulse & B. F. Green, Jr. (Eds.), *One hundred years of psychological research in America.* Baltimore: Johns Hopkins University Press. (p. 379)

Brown, R. P., Osterman, L. L., & Barnes, C. D. (2009). School violence and the culture of honor. *Psychological Science, 20,* 1400–1405. (p. 792)

Brown, S. L., Brown, R. M., House, J. S., & Smith, D. M. (2008). Coping with spousal loss: Potential buffering effects of self-reported helping behavior. *Personality and Social Psychology Bulletin, 34,* 849–861. (p. 548)

Brown, S. W., Garry, M., Loftus, E., Silver, B., DuBois, K., & DuBreuil, S. (1996). People's beliefs about memory: Why don't we have better memories? Paper presented at the American Psychological Society convention. (p. 347)

Browning, C. (1992). *Ordinary men: Reserve police battalion 101 and the final solution in Poland.* New York: HarperCollins. (p. 767)

Bruce, D., Dolan, A., & Phillips-Grant, K. (2000). On the transition from childhood amnesia to the recall of personal memories. *Psychological Science, 11,* 360–364. (p. 473)

Bruce-Keller, A. J., Keller, J. N., & Morrison, C. D. (2009). Obesity and vulnerability of the CNS. *Biochemica et Biophysica Acta, 1792,* 395–400. (p. 401)

Bruck, M., & Ceci, S. J. (1999). The suggestibility of children's memory. *Annual Review of Psychology, 50,* 419–439. (p. 350)

Bruck, M., & Ceci, S. J. (2004). Forensic developmental psychology: Unveiling four common misconceptions. *Current Directions in Psychological Science, 15,* 229–232. (p. 350)

Bruder, C. E. G., & 22 others. (2008). Phenotypically concordant and discordant monozygotic twins display different DNA copy-number-variation profiles. *American Journal of Human Genetics, 82,* 763–771. (p. 125)

Bruer, J. T. (1999). *The myth of the first three years: A new understanding of early brain development and lifelong learning.* New York: Free Press. (p. 635)

Brumberg, J. J. (2000). *Fasting girls: The history of anorexia nervosa.* New York: Vintage. (p. 697)

Bruno, M-A., Bernheim, J. L., Ledoux, D., Pellas, F., Demertzi, A., & Laureys, S. (2011). A survey on self-assessed well-being in a cohort of chronic locked-in syndrome patients: Happy majority, miserable minority. *BMJ Open.* bmjopen. bmj.com/content/early/2011/02/16/bmjopen-2010-000039.short?rss=1.1. (p. 848)

Bruno, M-A., Pellas, F., & Laureys, S. (2008). Quality of life in locked-in syndrome survivors. In J. L. Vincent (ed.), *2008 yearbook of intensive care and emergency medicine.* New York: Springer. (p. 848)

Brunwasser, S. M., Gillham, J. E., & Kim, E. S. (2009). A meta-analytic review of the Penn Resiliency Program's effect on depressive symptoms. *Journal of Consulting and Clinical Psychology, 77,* 1042–1054. (p. 737)

Bryant, A. N., & Astin, H. A. (2008). The correlates of spiritual struggle during the college years. *Journal of Higher Education, 79,* 1–27. (p. 520)

Bryant, R. A. (2001). Posttraumatic stress disorder and traumatic brain injury: Can they co-exist? *Clinical Psychology Review, 21,* 931–948. (p. 352)

Buchanan, R. W., & 10 others. (2010). The 2009 schizophrenia PORT psychopharmacological treatment recommendations and summary statements. *Schizophrenia Bulletin, 36,* 71–93. (p. 741)

Buchanan, T. W. (2007). Retrieval of emotional memories. *Psychological Bulletin, 133,* 761–779. (p. 332)

Buck, L. B., & Axel, R. (1991). A novel multigene family may encode odorant receptors: A molecular basis for odor recognition. *Cell, 65,* 175–187. (p. 208)

Buckholtz, J. W., & 13 others. (2010). Mesolimbic dopamine reward system hypersensitivity in individuals with psychopathic traits. *Nature Neuroscience, 13,* 419–421. (p. 701)

Buckingham, M. (2001, August). Quoted by P. LaBarre, "Marcus Buckingham thinks your boss has an attitude problem." *The Magazine* (fastcompany.com/online/49/buckingham.html). (p. 837)

Buckingham, M. (2007). *Go put your strengths to work: 6 powerful steps to achieve outstanding performance.* New York: Free Press. (p. 830)

Buckingham, M., & Clifton, D. O. (2001). *Now, discover your strengths.* New York: Free Press. (p. 830)

Buckley, C. (2007, January 3). Man is rescued by stranger on subway tracks. *New York Times* (www.nytimes.com). (p. 810)

Buckley, K. E., & Leary, M. R. (2001). Perceived acceptance as a predictor of social, emotional, and academic outcomes. Paper presented at the Society of Personality and Social Psychology annual convention. (p. 414)

Buehler, R., Griffin, D., & Ross, M. (1994). Exploring the "planning fallacy": Why people underestimate their task completion times. *Journal of Personality and Social Psychology, 67,* 366–381. (p. 365)

Buffardi, L. E., & Campbell, W. K. (2008). Narcissism and social networking web sites. *Personality and Social Psychology Bulletin, 34,* 1303–1314. (p. 418)

Bugelski, B. R., Kidd, E., & Segmen, J. (1968). Image as a mediator in one-trial paired-associate learning. *Journal of Experimental Psychology, 76,* 69–73. (p. 323)

Bugental, D. B. (1986). Unmasking the "polite smile": Situational and personal determinants of managed affect in adult-child interaction. *Personality and Social Psychology Bulletin, 12,* 7–16. (p. 433)

Buka, S. L., Tsuang, M. T., Torrey, E. F., Klebanoff, M. A., Wagner, R. L., & Yolken, R. H. (2001). Maternal infections and subsequent psychosis among offspring. *Archives of General Psychiatry, 58,* 1032–1037. (p. 688)

Buller, D. J. (2005). *Adapting minds: Evolutionary psychology and the persistent quest for human nature.* Cambridge, MA: MIT Press/Bradford Books. (p. 139)

Buller, D. J. (2009, January). Four fallacies of pop evolutionary psychology. *Scientific American,* 74–81. (p. 139)

Bullough, V. (1990). The Kinsey scale in historical perspective. In D. P. McWhirter, S. A. Sanders, & J. M. Reinisch (Eds.), *Homosexuality/heterosexuality: Concepts of sexual orientation.* New York: Oxford University Press. (p. 531)

Bunde, J., & Suls, J. (2006). A quantitative analysis of the relationship between the Cook-Medley Hostility Scale and traditional coronary artery disease risk factors. *Health Psychology, 25,* 493–500. (p. 452)

Buquet, R. (1988). Le rêve et les déficients visuels (Dreams and the visually impaired). *Psychanalyse-a-l'Universite, 13,* 319–327. (p. 240)

Burcusa, S. L., & Iacono, W. G. (2007). Risk for recurrence in depression. *Clinical Psychology Review, 27,* 959–985. (p. 675)

Bureau of Labor Statistics. (2004, September 14). *American time-user survey summary.* Washington, DC: United States Department of Labor (www.bls.gov). (p. 504)

Burger, J. M. (2009). Replicating Milgram: Would people still obey today? *American Psychologist, 64,* 1–11. (p. 766)

Burgess, M., Enzle, M. E., & Schmaltz, R. (2004). Defeating the potentially deleterious effects of externally imposed deadlines: Practitioners' rules-of-thumb. *Personality and Social Psychology Bulletin, 30,* 868–877. (p. 838)

Buri, J. R., Louiselle, P. A., Misukanis, T. M., & Mueller, R. A. (1988). Effects of parental authoritarianism and authoritativeness on self-esteem. *Personality and Social Psychology Bulletin, 14,* 271–282. (p. 496)

Burish, T. G., & Carey, M. P. (1986). Conditioned aversive responses in cancer chemotherapy patients: Theoretical and developmental analysis. *Journal of Counseling and Clinical Psychology, 54,* 593–600. (p. 295)

Burk, W. J., Denissen, J., Van Doorn, M. D., Branje, S. J. T., & Laursen, B. (2009). The vicissitudes of conflict measurement: Stability and reliability in the frequency of disagreements. *European Psychologist, 14,* 153–159. (p. 521)

Burke, B. L., Martens, A., & Faucher, E. H. (2010). Two decades of terror management theory: A meta-analysis of mortality salience research. *Personality and Social Psychology Review, 14,* 155–195. (p. 568)

Burke, D. M., & Shafto, M. A. (2004). Aging and language production. *Current Directions in Psychological Science, 13,* 21–24. (p. 543)

Burkholder, R. (2005a, January 11). Chinese far wealthier than a decade ago—but are they happier? *Gallup Poll News Service* (www.gallup.com). (p. 851)

Burkholder, R. (2005b, January 18). China's citizens optimistic, yet not entirely satisfied. *Gallup Poll News Service* (www.gallup.com). (p. 851)

Burns, B. C. (2004). The effects of speed on skilled chess performance. *Psychological Science, 15,* 442–447. (p. 369)

Burrell, B. (2005). *Postcards from the brain museum: The improbable search for meaning in the matter of famous minds.* New York: Broadway Books. (p. 613)

Burris, C. T., & Branscombe, N. R. (2005). Distorted distance estimation induced by a self-relevant national boundary. *Journal of Experimental Social Psychology, 41,* 305–312. (p. 380)

Burton, C. M., & King, L. A. (2008). Effects of (very) brief writing on health: The two-minute miracle. *British Journal of Health Psychology, 13,* 9–14. (p. 859)

Bushman, B. J. (1993). Human aggression while under the influence of alcohol and other drugs: An integrative research review. *Current Directions in Psychological Science, 2,* 148–152. (p. 791)

Bushman, B. J. (2002). Does venting anger feed or extinguish the flame? Catharsis, rumination, distraction, anger, and aggressive responding. *Personality and Social Psychology Bulletin, 28,* 724–731. (p. 846)

Bushman, B. J. (2011, July 7). Quoted in S. Vendantam, "It's a duel: How do violent video games affect kids?" www.npr.org. (p. 795)

Bushman, B. J., & Anderson, C. A. (2009). Comfortably numb: Desensitizing effects of violent media on helping others. *Psychological Science, 20,* 273–277. (pp. 309, 794)

Bushman, B. J., & Baumeister, R. F. (1998). Threatened egotism, narcissism, self-esteem, and direct and displaced aggression: Does self-love or self-hate lead to violence? *Journal of Personality and Social Psychology, 75,* 219–229. (p. 597)

Bushman, B. J., Baumeister, R. F., Thomaes, S., Ryu, E., Begeer, S., & West, S. G. (2009). Looking again, and harder, for a link between low self-esteem and aggression. *Journal of Personality, 77,* 427–446. (p. 597)

Bushman, B. J., Moeller, S. J., & Crocker, J. (2011). Sweets, sex, or self-esteem? Comparing the value of self-esteem boosts with other pleasant rewards. *Journal of Personality, 79*(5), 993–1012. (p. 573)

Bushman, B. J., Rothstein, H. R., & Anderson, C. A. (2010). Much ado about something: Violent video game effects and a school of red herring: Reply to Ferguson and Kilburn (2010). *Psychological Bulletin, 136*, 182–187. (p. 795)

Busnel, M. C., Granier-Deferre, C., & Lecanuet, J. P. (1992, October). Fetal audition. *New York Academy of Sciences, 662*, 118–134. (p. 466)

Buss, A. H. (1989). Personality as traits. *American Psychologist, 44*, 1378–1388. (p. 584)

Buss, D. M. (1991). Evolutionary personality psychology. *Annual Review of Psychology, 42*, 459–491. (p. 130)

Buss, D. M. (1994). The strategies of human mating: People worldwide are attracted to the same qualities in the opposite sex. *American Scientist, 82*, 238–249. (p. 138)

Buss, D. M. (1995). Evolutionary psychology: A new paradigm for psychological science. *Psychological Inquiry, 6*, 1–30. (p. 138)

Buss, D. M. (1996). Sexual conflict: Evolutionary insights into feminism and the "battle of the sexes." In D. M. Buss & N. M. Malamuth (Eds.), *Sex, power, conflict: Evolutionary and feminist perspectives.* New York: Oxford University Press. (p. 138)

Buss, D. M. (2009). The great struggles of life: Darwin and the emergence of evolutionary psychology. *American Psychologist, 64*, 140–148. (p. 138)

Buster, J. E., Kingsberg, S. A., Aguirre, O., Brown, C., Breaux, J. G., Buch, A., Rodenberg, C. A., Wekselman, K., & Casson, P. (2005). Testosterone patch for low sexual desire in surgically menopausal women: A randomized trial. *Obstetrics and Gynecology, 105*(5), 944–952. (p. 408)

Butcher, L. M., Davis, O. S. P., Craig, I. W., & Plomin, R. (2008). Genome-wide quantitative trait locus association scan of general cognitive ability using pooled DNA and 500K single nucleotide polymorphism microarrays. *Genes, Brain and Behavior, 7*, 435–446. (p. 633)

Butler, A., Oruc, I., Fox, C. J., & Barton, J. J. S. (2008). Factors contributing to the adaptation aftereffects of facial expression. *Brain Research, 1191*, 116–126. (p. 160)

Butler, A. C., Hokanson, J. E., & Flynn, H. A. (1994). A comparison of self-esteem lability and low trait self-esteem as vulnerability factors for depression. *Journal of Personality and Social Psychology, 66*, 166–177. (p. 680)

Butler, R. A. (1954, February). Curiosity in monkeys. *Scientific American*, pp. 70–75. (p. 392)

Butterworth, G. (1992). Origins of self-perception in infancy. *Psychological Inquiry, 3*, 103–111. (p. 495)

Byers-Heinlein, K., Burns, T. C., & Werker, J. F. (2010). The roots of bilingualism in newborns. *Psychological Science, 21*, 343–348. (p. 466)

Byrne, D. (1971). *The attraction paradigm.* New York: Academic Press. (p. 802)

Byrne, D. (1982). Predicting human sexual behavior. In A. G. Kraut (Ed.), *The G. Stanley Hall Lecture Series* (Vol. 2). Washington, DC: American Psychological Association. (pp. 268, 408)

Byrne, R. W. (1991, May/June). Brute intellect. *The Sciences*, 42–47. (p. 869)

Byrne, R. W., Bates, L. A., & Moss, C. J. (2009). Elephant cognition in primate perspective. *Comparative Cognition & Behavior Reviews, 4*, 1–15. (p. 868)

Byrne, R. W., & Corp, N. (2004). Neocortex size predicts deception in primates. *Proceedings of the Royal Society B, 271*, 1693–1699. (p. 41)

Byrne, R. W., Hobaiter, C., & Klailova, M. (2011). Local traditions in gorilla manual skill: Evidence for observational learning of behavioral organization. *Animal Cognition*, 1–11. (p. 305)

Cable, D. M., & Gilovich, T. (1998). Looked over or overlooked? Prescreening decisions and post-interview evaluations. *Journal of Personality and Social Psychology, 83*, 501–508. (p. 831)

Cacioppo, J. T. (2007). Better interdisciplinary research through psychological science. *APS Observer, 20*, 3, 48–49. (p. 13)

Cacioppo, J. T., Fowler, J. H., & Christakis, N. A. (2009). Alone in the crowd: The structure and spread of loneliness in a large social network. *Journal of Personality and Social Psychology, 97*, 977–991. (p. 414)

Cacioppo, J. T., & Hawkley, L. C. (2009). Perceived social isolation and cognition. *Trends in Cognitive Sciences, 13*, 447–454. (p. 414)

Cacioppo, J. T., Cacioppo, S., Gonzaga, G. C., Ogburn, E. L., & Vander-Weele, T. J. (2013). Marital satisfaction and break-ups differ across on-line and off-line meeting venues. *PNAS Proceedings of the National Academy of Sciences of the United States of America, 110*(25), 10135–10140. (p. 799)

Cahill, L. (1994). (Beta)-adrenergic activation and memory for emotional events. *Nature, 371*, 702–704. (p. 332)

Cahn, B. R., & Polich, J. (2006). Meditation states and traits: EEG, ERP, and neuroimaging studies. *Psychological Bulletin, 132*, 180–211. (p. 862)

Cale, E. M., & Lilienfeld, S. O. (2002). Sex differences in psychopathy and anti-social personality disorder: A review and integration. *Clinical Psychology Review, 22*, 1179–1207. (p. 699)

Call, K. T., Riedel, A. A., Hein, K., McLoyd, V., Petersen, A., & Kipke, M. (2002). Adolescent health and well-being in the twenty-first century: A global perspective. *Journal of Research on Adolescence, 12*, 69–98. (p. 530)

Callaghan, T., Rochat, P., Lillard, A., Claux, M. L., Odden, H., Itakura, S., Tapanya, S., & Singh, S. (2005). Synchrony in the onset of mental-state reasoning. *Psychological Science, 16*, 378–384. (p. 480)

Calvo-Merino, B., Glaser, D. E., Grèzes, J., Passingham, R. E., & Haggard, P. (2004). Action observation and acquired motor skills: An fMRI study with expert dancers. *Cerebral Cortex, 15*, 1243–1249. (p. 381)

Camerer, C. F., Loewenstein, G., & Weber, M. (1989). The curse of knowledge in economic settings: An experimental analysis. *Journal of Political Economy, 97*, 1232–1254. (p. 841)

Cameron, L., & Rutland, A. (2006). Extended contact through story reading in school: Reducing children's prejudice toward the disabled. *Journal of Social Issues, 62*, 469–488. (p. 813)

Campbell, A. (2010). Oxytocin and human social behavior. *Personality and Social Psychology Review, 14*, 281–205. (p. 446)

Campbell, D. T. (1975). On the conflicts between biological and social evolution and between psychology and moral tradition. *American Psychologist, 30*, 1103–1126. (p. 851)

Campbell, D. T., & Specht, J. C. (1985). Altruism: Biology, culture, and religion. *Journal of Social and Clinical Psychology, 3*(1), 33–42. (p. 573)

Campbell, M. W., & de Waal, F. B. M. (2011). Ingroup-outgroup bias in contagious yawning by chimpanzees supports link to empathy. *PLoS One, 6*, e18283. (p. 785)

Campbell, S. (1986). *The Loch Ness Monster: The evidence.* Willingborough, Northamptonshire, U.K.: Acquarian Press. (p. 164)

Camperio-Ciani, A., Corna, F., & Capiluppi, C. (2004). Evidence for maternally inherited factors favouring male homosexuality and promoting female fecundity. *Proceedings of the Royal Society of London B, 271*, 2217–2221. (p. 534)

Camperio-Ciani, A., Lemmola, F., & Blecher, S. R. (2009). Genetic factors increase fecundity in female maternal relatives of bisexual men as in homosexuals. *Journal of Sexual Medicine, 6*, 449–455. (p. 534)

Campos, J. J., Bertenthal, B. I., & Kermoian, R. (1992). Early experience and emotional development: The emergence of wariness of heights. *Psychological Science, 3*, 61–64. (p. 184)

Canli, T. (2008, February/March). The character code. *Scientific American Mind*, pp. 53–57. (p. 668)

Canli, T., Desmond, J. E., Zhao, Z., & Gabrieli, J. D. E. (2002). Sex differences in the neural basis of emotional memories. *Proceedings of the National Academy of Sciences, 99*, 10789–10794. (p. 435)

Cannon, W. B. (1929). *Bodily changes in pain, hunger, fear, and rage.* New York: Branford. (pp. 397, 444)

Cannon, W. B., & Washburn, A. L. (1912). An explanation of hunger. *American Journal of Physiology, 29*, 441–454. (p. 397)

Cantor, N., & Kihlstrom, J. F. (1987). *Personality and social intelligence.* Englewood Cliffs, NJ: Prentice-Hall. (p. 612)

Cantril, H., & Bumstead, C. H. (1960). *Reflections on the human venture.* New York: New York University Press. (p. 776)

Caplan, N., Choy, M. H., & Whitmore, J. K. (1992, February). Indochinese refugee families and academic achievement. *Scientific American*, 36–42. (p. 510)

Caputo, D., & Dunning, D. (2005). What you don't know: The role played by errors of omission in imperfect self-assessments. *Journal of Experimental Social Psychology*, 488–505. (p. 591)

Card, N. A., Stucky, B. C., Sawalani, G. M., & Little, T. D. (2008). Direct and indirect aggression during childhood and adolescence: A meta-analytic review of gender differences, intercorrelations, and relations to maladjustment. *Child Development, 79*, 1185–1229. (p. 501)

Carducci, B. J., Cosby, P. C., & Ward, D. D. (1978). Sexual arousal and interpersonal evaluations. *Journal of Experimental Social Psychology, 14*, 449–457. (p. 803)

Carey, B. (2007, September 4). Bipolar illness soars as a diagnosis for the young. *New York Times* (www.nytimes.com). (p. 673)

Carey, B. (2009, November 27). Surgery for mental ills offers both hope and risk. *New York Times* (www.nytimes.com). (p. 746)

Carey, B. (2010). Seeking emotional clues without facial cues. *New York Times* (www.nytimes.com). (p. 438)

Carey, B. (2011, February 14). Wariness on surgery of the mind. *New York Times* (www.nytimes.com). (p. 746)

Carey, D. P. (2007). Is bigger really better? The search for brain size and intelligence in the twenty-first century. In S. Della Sala (Ed.), *Tall tales about the mind and brain: Separating fact from fiction.* Oxford: Oxford University Press. (p. 613)

Carey, G. (1990). Genes, fears, phobias, and phobic disorders. *Journal of Counseling and Development, 68*, 628–632. (p. 668)

Carli, L. L., & Leonard, J. B. (1989). The effect of hindsight on victim derogation. *Journal of Social and Clinical Psychology, 8*, 331–343. (p. 787)

Carlson, C. L. (2000). ADHD is overdiagnosed. In R. L. Atkinson, R. C. Atkinson, E. E. Smith, D. J. Bem, & S. Nolen-Hoeksema (Eds.), *Hilgard's introduction to psychology* (13th ed.). Fort Worth: Harcourt. (p. 652)

Carlson, M., Charlin, V., & Miller, N. (1988). Positive mood and helping behavior: A test of six hypotheses. *Journal of Personality and Social Psychology, 55*, 211–229. (p. 809)

Carlson, S. (1985). A double-blind test of astrology. *Nature, 318*, 419–425. (p. 579)

Carmeli, A., Ben-Hador, B., Waldman, D. A., & Rupp, D. E. (2009). How leaders cultivate social capital and nurture employee vigor: Implications for job performance. *Journal of Applied Psychology, 94*, 1553–1561. (p. 839)

Carnahan, T., & McFarland, S. (2007). Revisiting the Stanford Prison Experiment: Could participant self-selection have led to the cruelty? *Personality and Social Psychology Bulletin, 33*, 603–614. (p. 758)

Carnegie Council on Adolescent Development. (1989, June). *Turning points: Preparing American youth for the 21st century.* (The report of the Task Force on Education of Young Adolescents.) New York: Carnegie Corporation. (p. 630)

Carpusor, A., & Loges, W. E. (2006). Rental discrimination and ethnicity in names. *Journal of Applied Social Psychology, 36*, 934–952. (p. 52)

Carré, J. M., McCormick, C. M., & Mondloch, C. J. (2009). Facial structure is a reliable cue of aggressive behavior. *Psychological Science, 20*, 1194–1198. (p. 790)

Carroll, D., Davey Smith, G., & Bennett, P. (1994, March). Health and socioeconomic status. *The Psychologist*, pp. 122–125. (p. 300)

Carroll, J. M., & Russell, J. A. (1996). Do facial expressions signal specific emotions? Judging emotion from the face in context. *Journal of Personality and Social Psychology, 70*, 205–218. (p. 436)

Carroll, P., Sweeny, K., & Shepperd, J. A. (2006). Forsaking optimism. *Review of General Psychology, 10*, 56–73. (p. 589)

Carskadon, M. A. (2002). *Adolescent sleep patterns: Biological, social, and psychological influences.* New York: Cambridge University Press. (p. 236)

Carstensen, L. L., & Mikels, J. A. (2005). At the intersection of emotion and cognition: Aging and the positivity effect. *Current Directions in Psychological Science, 14*, 117–121. (pp. 546, 626)

Carter, R. (1998). *Mapping the mind.* Berkeley: University of California Press. (p. 81)

Carter, T. J., & Gilovich, T. (2010). The relative relativity of material and experiential purchases. *Journal of Personality and Social Psychology, 98*, 146–159. (p. 853)

Carver, C. S., Johnson, S. L., & Joormann, J. (2008). Serotonergic function, two-mode models of self-regulation, and vulnerability to depression: What depression has in common with impulsive aggression. *Psychological Bulletin, 134*, 912–943. (p. 678)

Carver, C. S., Scheier, M. F., & Segerstrom, S. C. (2010). Optimism. *Clinical Psychology Review, 30*, 879–889. (p. 856)

Caryl, P. G. (1994). Early event-related potentials correlate with inspection time and intelligence. *Intelligence, 18*, 15–46. (p. 614)

CASA. (2003). *The formative years: Pathways to substance abuse among girls and young women ages 8–22.* New York: National Center on Addiction and Substance Use, Columbia University. (pp. 249, 824)

CASA. (2004). *CASA 2004 teen survey.* National Center on Addiction and Substance Abuse, Columbia University (www.casacolumbia.org). (p. 529)

Casey, B. J., Getz, S., & Galvan, A. (2008). The adolescent brain. *Developmental Review, 28*, 62–77. (p. 514)

Cash, T., & Janda, L. H. (1984, December). The eye of the beholder. *Psychology Today*, 46–52. (p. 800)

Caspi, A. (2000). The child is father of the man: Personality continuities from childhood to adulthood. *Journal of Personality and Social Psychology, 78*, 158–172. (p. 491)

Caspi, A., Hariri, A. R., Holmes, A., Uher, R., & Moffitt, T. E. (2010), Genetic sensitivity to the environment: The case of the serotonin transporter gene and its implications for studying complex diseases and traits. *American Journal of Psychiatry, 167*, 509–527. (p. 678)

Caspi, A., Harrington, H., Milne, B., Amell, J. W., Theodore, R. F., & Moffitt, T. E. (2003). Children's behavioral styles at age 3 are linked to their adult personality traits at age 26. *Journal of Personality, 71*, 496–513. (p. 678)

Caspi, A., McClay, J., Moffitt, T., Mill, J., Martin, J., Craig, I. W., Taylor, A., & Poulton, R. (2002). Role of genotype in the cycle of violence in maltreated children. *Science, 297*, 851–854. (p. 701)

Caspi, A., Moffitt, T. E., Newman, D. L., & Silva, P. A. (1996). Behavioral observations at age 3 years predict adult psychiatric disorders: Longitudinal evidence from a birth cohort. *Archives of General Psychiatry, 53*, 1033–1039. (p. 700)

Cassel, L., & Suedfeld, P. (2006). Salutogenesis and autobiographical disclosure among Holocaust survivors. *The Journal of Positive Psychology, 1*, 212–225. (p. 665)

Cassidy, J., & Shaver, P. R. (1999). *Handbook of attachment.* New York: Guilford. (p. 489)

Castillo, R. J. (1997). *Culture and mental illness: A client-centered approach.* Pacific Grove, CA: Brooks/Cole. (p. 653)

Castonguay, L. G., Boswell, J. F., Constantino, M. J., Goldfried, M. R., & Hill, C. E. (2010). Training implications of harmful effects of psychological treatments. *American Psychologist, 65*, 34–49. (p. 732)

Cattell, R. B. (1963). Theory of fluid and crystallized intelligence: A critical experiment. *Journal of Educational Psychology, 54*, 1–22. (p. 626)

Cavalli-Sforza, L., Menozzi, P., & Piazza, A. (1994). *The history and geography of human genes.* Princeton, NJ: Princeton University Press. (p. 640)

Cavigelli, S. A., & McClintock, M. K. (2003). Fear of novelty in infant rats predicts adult corticosterone dynamics and an early death. *Proceedings of the National Academy of Sciences, 100*, 16131–16136. (p. 445)

Cawley, B. D., Keeping, L. M., & Levy, P. E. (1998). Participation in the performance appraisal process and employee reactions: A meta-analytic review of field investigations. *Journal of Applied Psychology, 83*, 615–633. (p. 838)

CDC. (1992, September 16). *Serious mental illness and disability in the adult household population: United States, 1989.* Advance Data No. 218 from Vital and Health Statistics, National Center for Health Statistics. (p. 658)

CDC. (2003). *Who should get a flu shot (influenza vaccine).* National Center for Infectious Diseases (http://www.cdc.gov/ncidod/diseases/flu/who.htm). (p. 688)

CDC. (2008). National youth risk behavior survey overview. Centers for Disease Control and Prevention (www.cdc.gov). (p. 671)

CDC. (2009). *Self-harm, all injury causes, nonfatal injuries and rates per 100,000.* National Center for Injury Prevention and Control. http://webappa.cdc.gov/cgi-bin/broker.exe. (p. 677)

CDC. (2009, December 18). Prevalence of autism spectrum disorders—Autism and developments disabilities monitoring network, United States, 2006 (corresponding author: Catherine Rice). *MMWR, 58*(SS10), 1–20. (www.cdc.gov). (p. 481)

CDC. (2010, June 4). Youth risk behavior surveillance—United States, 2009. *Morbidity and Mortality Weekly, 59*SS05, 1–142 (by D. K. Eaton & 13 others). (p. 529)

CDC. (2011, accessed April 20). *Who's at risk? Tobacco use—smoking.* Centers for Disease Control and Prevention (cdc.gov/vitalsigns/TobaccoUse/Smoking/Risk.html). (p. 825)

CDC. (2013a, April 23). HIV/AIDS: Statistical overview. Centers for Disease Control and Prevention (www.cdc.gov/hiv/statistics/basics/index.html). (p. 529)

CDC. (2013b, April 24). HIV among youth. Centers for Disease Control and Prevention (http://www.cdc.gov/hiv/risk/age/youth/index.html). (p. 529)

Ceci, S. J. (1993). Cognitive and social factors in children's testimony. Master lecture, American Psychological Association convention. (p. 350)

Ceci, S. J., & Bruck, M. (1993). Child witnesses: Translating research into policy. *Social Policy Report* (Society for Research in Child Development), *7*(3), 1–30. (p. 350)

Ceci, S. J., & Bruck, M. (1995). *Jeopardy in the courtroom: A scientific analysis of children's testimony.* Washington, DC: American Psychological Association. (p. 350)

Ceci, S. J., Huffman, M. L. C., Smith, E., & Loftus, E. F. (1994). Repeatedly thinking about a non-event: Source misattributions among preschoolers. *Consciousness and Cognition, 3,* 388–407. (p. 350)

Ceci, S. J., & Kanaya, T. (2010). "Apples and oranges are both round": Furthering the discussion on the Flynn effect. *Journal of Psychoeducational Assessment, 28,* 441–447. (p. 621)

Ceci, S. J., & Williams, W. M. (1997). Schooling, intelligence, and income. *American Psychologist, 52,* 1051–1058. (p. 635)

Ceci, S. J., & Williams, W. M. (2009). *The mathematics of sex: How biology and society conspire to limit talented women and girls.* New York: Oxford University Press. (p. 635)

Ceci, S. J., & Williams, W. M. (2010). Sex differences in math-intensive fields. *Current Directions in Psychological Science, 19,* 275–279. (p. 639)

Ceci, S. J., & Williams, W. M. (2011). Understanding current causes of women's underrepresentation in science. *Proceedings of the National Academy of Sciences, 108.* 3157–3162. (p. 639)

Centers for Disease Control Vietnam Experience Study. (1988). Health status of Vietnam veterans. *Journal of the American Medical Association, 259,* 2701–2709. (p. 665)

Centerwall, B. S. (1989). Exposure to television as a risk factor for violence. *American Journal of Epidemiology, 129,* 643–652. (p. 309)

Cepeda, N. J., Pashler, H., Vul, E., Wixted, J. T., & Rohrer, D. (2006). Distributed practice in verbal recall tasks: A review and quantitative synthesis. *Psychological Bulletin, 132,* 354–380. (p. 324)

Cepeda, N. J., Vul, E., Rohrer, D., Wixed, J. T., & Pashler, H. (2008). Spacing effects in learning: A temporal ridgeline of optimal retention. *Psychological Science, 19,* 1095–1102. (p. 324)

Cerella, J. (1985). Information processing rates in the elderly. *Psychological Bulletin, 98,* 67–83. (p. 541)

CFI. (2003, July). *International developments. Report.* Amherst, NY: Center for Inquiry International. (p. 169)

Chabris, C. F., & Simons, D. (2010). *The invisible gorilla: And other ways our intuitions deceive us.* New York: Crown. (p. 154)

Chambless, D. L., Baker, M. J., Baucom, D. H., Beutler, L. E., Calhoun, K. S., Crits-Christoph, P., Daiuto, A., DeRubeis, R., Detweiler, J., Haaga, D. A. F., Johnson, S. B., McCurry, S., Mueser, K. T., Pope, K. S., Sanderson, W. C., Shoham, V., Stickle, T., Williams, D. A., & Woody, S. R. (1997). Update on empirically validated therapies, II. *The Clinical Psychologist, 51*(1), 3–16. (p. 733)

Chamove, A. S. (1980). Nongenetic induction of acquired levels of aggression. *Journal of Abnormal Psychology, 89,* 469–488. (p. 308)

Champagne, F. A. (2010). Early adversity and developmental outcomes: Interaction between genetics, epigenetics, and social experiences across the life span. *Perspectives on Psychological Science, 5,* 564–574. (p. 131)

Champagne, F. A., Francis, D. D., Mar, A., & Meaney, M. J. (2003). Naturally-occurring variations in maternal care in the rat as a mediating influence for the effects of environment on the development of individual differences in stress reactivity. *Physiology & Behavior, 79,* 359–371. (p. 132)

Champagne, F. A., & Mashoodh, R. (2009). Genes in context: Gene-environment interplay and the origins of individual differences in behavior. *Current Directions in Psychological Science, 18,* 127–131. (p. 132)

Chance News. (1997, 25 November). More on the frequency of letters in texts. Dart.Chance@Dartmouth.edu. (p. 43)

Chandler, J., & Schwarz, N. (2009). How extending your middle finger affects your perception of others: Learned movements influence concept accessibility. *Journal of Experimental Social Psychology, 45,* 123–128. (p. 438)

Chandra, A., Mosher, W. D., & Copen, C. (2011, March). Sexual behavior, sexual attraction, and sexual identity in the United States: Data from the 2006–2008 National Survey of Family Growth. *National Health Statistics Reports,* No. 36 (Centers for Disease Control and Prevention). (p. 532)

Chang, E. C. (2001). Cultural influences on optimism and pessimism: Differences in Western and Eastern construals of the self. In E. C. Chang (Ed.), *Optimism and pessimism.* Washington, DC: APA Books. (p. 589)

Chang, P. P., Ford, D. E., Meoni, L. A., Wang, N-Y., & Klag, M. J. (2002). Anger in young men and subsequent premature cardiovascular disease: The precursors study. *Archives of Internal Medicine, 162,* 901–906. (p. 452)

Chaplin, W. F., Phillips, J. B., Brown, J. D., Clanton, N. R., & Stein, J. L. (2000). Handshaking, gender, personality, and first impressions. *Journal of Personality and Social Psychology, 79,* 110–117. (p. 432)

Charness, N., & Boot, W. R. (2009). Aging and information technology use. *Current Directions in Psychological Science, 18,* 253–258. (p. 627)

Charpak, G., & Broch, H. (2004). *Debunked! ESP, telekinesis, and other pseudoscience.* Baltimore, MD: Johns Hopkins University Press. (p. 168)

Chartrand, T. L., & Bargh, J. A. (1999). The chameleon effect: The perception-behavior link and social interaction. *Journal of Personality and Social Psychology, 76,* 893–910. (p. 763)

Chatard, A., & Selimbegović, L. (2011). When self-destructive thoughts flash through the mind: Failure to meet standards affects the accessibility of suicide-related thoughts. *Journal of Personality and Social Psychology, 100,* 587–605. (p. 677)

Chater, N., Reali, F., & Christiansen, M. H. (2009). Restrictions on biological adaptation in language evolution. *PNAS, 106,* 1015–1020. (p. 376)

Cheek, J. M., & Melchior, L. A. (1990). Shyness, self-esteem, and self-consciousness. In H. Leitenberg (Ed.), *Handbook of social and evaluation anxiety.* New York: Plenum. (p. 599)

Cheit, R. E. (1998). Consider this, skeptics of recovered memory. *Ethics & Behavior, 8,* 141–160. (p. 562)

Chen, A. W., Kazanjian, A., & Wong, H. (2009). Why do Chinese Canadians not consult mental health services: Health status, language or culture? *Transcultural Psychiatry, 46,* 623–640. (p. 735)

Chen, E. (2004). Why socioeconomic status affects the health of children: A psychosocial perspective. *Current Directions in Psychological Science, 13,* 112–115. (p. 300)

Chen, S-Y., & Fu, Y-C. (2008). Internet use and academic achievement: Gender differences in early adolescence. *Adolescence, 44,* 797–812. (p. 417)

Chen, X., Beydoun, M. A., & Wang, Y. (2008). Is sleep duration associated with childhood obesity? A systematic review and meta-analysis. *Obesity, 16,* 265–274. (p. 236)

Cherkas, L. F., Hunkin, J. L., Kato, B. S., Richards, J. B., Gardner, J. P., Surdulescu, G. L., Kimura, M., Lu, X., Spector, T. D., & Aviv, A. (2008). The association between physical activity in leisure time and leukocyte telomere length. *Archives of Internal Medicine, 168,* 154–158. (p. 542)

Cherniss, C. (2010a). Emotional intelligence: Toward clarification of a concept. *Industrial and Organizational Psychology, 3,* 110–126. (p. 612)

Cherniss, C. (2010b). Emotional intelligence: New insights and further clarifications. *Industrial and Organizational Psychology, 3,* 183–191. (p. 612)

Chess, S., & Thomas, A. (1987). *Know your child: An authoritative guide for today's parents.* New York: Basic Books. (p. 491)

Cheung, B. Y., Chudek, M., & Heine, S. J. (2011). Evidence for a sensitive period for acculturation: Younger immigrants report acculturating at a faster rate. *Psychological Science, 22,* 147–152. (p. 376)

Chida, Y., & Hamer, M. (2008). Chronic psychosocial factors and acute physiological responses to laboratory-induced stress in healthy populations: A quantitative review of 30 years of investigations. *Psychological Bulletin, 134,* 829–885. (p. 452)

Chida, Y., Hamer, M., Wardle, J., & Steptoe, A. (2008). Do stress-related psychosocial factors contribute to cancer incidence and survival? *Nature Reviews: Clinical Oncology, 5,* 466–475. (p. 451)

Chida, Y., & Steptoe, A. (2009). The association of anger and hostility with future coronary heart disease: A meta-analytic review of prospective evidence. *Journal of the American College of Cardiology, 17,* 936–946. (p. 452)

Chida, Y., Steptoe, A., & Powell, L. H. (2009). Religiosity/spirituality and mortality. *Psychotherapy and Psychosomatics, 78,* 81–90. (p. 865)

Chiles, J. A., Lambert, M. J., & Hatch, A. L. (1999). The impact of psychological interventions on medical cost offset: A meta-analytic review. *Clinical Psychology: Science and Practice, 6,* 204–220. (p. 731)

Chivers, M. L. (2005). A brief review and discussion of sex differences in the specificity of sexual arousal. *Sexual and Relationship Therapy, 20,* 377–390. (p. 532)

Chivers, M. L., Seto, M. C., Lalumière, M. L., Laan, E., & Grimbos, T. (2010). Agreement of self-reported and genital measures of sexual arousal in men and women: A meta-analysis. *Archives of Sexual Behavior, 39,* 5–56. (p. 409)

Choi, I., & Choi, Y. (2002). Culture and self-concept flexibility. *Personality and Social Psychology Bulletin, 28*, 1508–1517. (p. 599)

Chomsky, N. (1972). *Language and mind.* New York: Harcourt Brace. (p. 868)

Christakis, N. A., & Fowler, J. H. (2007). The spread of obesity in a large social network over 32 years. *New England Journal of Medicine, 357*, 370–379. (p. 402)

Christakis, N. A., & Fowler, J. H. (2008, May). The collective dynamics of smoking in a large social network. *New England Journal of Medicine, 358*(21), 2249–2258. (p. 824)

Christakis, N. A., & Fowler, J. H. (2009). *Connected: The surprising power of social networks and how they shape our lives.* New York: Little, Brown. (pp. 763, 859)

Christensen, A., & Jacobson, N. S. (1994). Who (or what) can do psychotherapy: The status and challenge of nonprofessional therapies. *Psychological Science, 5*, 8–14. (p. 735)

Christophersen, E. R., & Edwards, K. J. (1992). Treatment of elimination disorders: State of the art 1991. *Applied & Preventive Psychology, 1*, 15–22. (p. 717)

Chua, H. F., Boland, J. E., & Nisbett, R. E. (2005). Cultural variation in eye movements during scene perception. *Proceedings of the National Academy of Sciences, 102*, 12629–12633. (p. 755)

Chugani, H. T., & Phelps, M. E. (1986). Maturational changes in cerebral function in infants determined by 18FDG positron emission tomography. *Science, 231*, 840–843. (p. 471)

Church, T. S., Thomas, D. M., Tudor-Locke, C., Katzmarzyk, P. T., Earnest, C. P., Rodarte, R. Q., Martin, C. K., Blair, S. N., & Bouchard, C. (2011). Trends over 5 decades in U.S. occupation-related physical activity and their associations with obesity. *PLoS ONE, 6*(5), e19657. (p. 402)

CIA. (2010). *The World Fact Book:* Literacy. Washington, D.C.: CIA (https://www.cia.gov/library/publications/the-world-factbook/fields/2103.html). (p. 781)

Cialdini, R. B. (1993). *Influence: Science and practice* (3rd ed.). New York: HarperCollins. (p. 757)

Cialdini, R. B., & Richardson, K. D. (1980). Two indirect tactics of image management: Basking and blasting. *Journal of Personality and Social Psychology, 39*, 406–415. (p. 785)

Ciarrochi, J., Forgas, J. P., & Mayer, J. D. (2006). *Emotional intelligence in everyday life* (2nd ed.). New York: Psychology Press. (p. 612)

Clack, B., Dixon, J., & Tredoux, C. (2005). Eating together apart: Patterns of segregation in a multi-ethnic cafeteria. *Journal of Community and Applied Social Psychology, 15*, 1–16. (p. 813)

Clancy, S. A. (2005). *Abducted: How people come to believe they were kidnapped by aliens.* Cambridge, MA: Harvard University Press. (p. 228)

Clancy, S. A. (2010). *The trauma myth: The truth about the sexual abuse of children—and its aftermath.* New York: Basic Books. (p. 493)

Clark, A., Seidler, A., & Miller, M. (2001). Inverse association between sense of humor and coronary heart disease. *International Journal of Cardiology, 80*, 87–88. (p. 857)

Clark, K. B., & Clark, M. P. (1947). Racial identification and preference in Negro children. In T. M. Newcomb & E. L. Hartley (Eds.), *Readings in social psychology.* New York: Holt. (p. 69)

Cleary, A. M. (2008). Recognition memory, familiarity, and déjà vu experiences. *Current Directions in Psychological Science, 17*, 353–357. (p. 349)

Clifton, J., & Morales, L. (2011, February 2). Egyptians', Tunisians' wellbeing plummets despite GDP gains. *Gallup* (www.gallup.com). (p. 854)

Coan, J. A., Schaefer, H. S., & Davidson, R. J. (2006). Lending a hand: Social regulation of the neural response to threat. *Psychological Science, 17*, 1032–1039. (p. 857)

Coelho, C. M., & Purkis, H. (2009). The origins of specific phobias: Influential theories and current perspectives. *Review of General Psychology, 13*, 335–348. (p. 667)

Coffey, C. E., Wilkinson, W. E., Weiner, R. D., Parashos, I. A., Djang, W. T., Webb, M. C., Figiel, G. S., & Spritzer, C. E. (1993). Quantitative cerebral anatomy in depression: A controlled magnetic resonance imaging study. *Archives of General Psychiatry, 50*, 7–16. (p. 678)

Cohen, A. B. (2009). Many forms of culture. *American Psychologist, 64*, 194–204. (pp. 599, 776)

Cohen, D. (1995, June 17). Now we are one, or two, or three. *New Scientist*, pp. 14–15. (p. 695)

Cohen, G. L., Garcia, J., Apfel, N., & Master, A. (2006). Reducing the racial achievement gap: A social-psychological intervention. *Science, 313*, 1307–1310. (p. 643)

Cohen, G. L., Garcia, J., Purdie-Vaughns, V., Apfel, N., Brzustoski, P. (2009). Recursive processes in self-affirmation: Intervening to close the minority achievement gap. *Science, 324*, 400–403. (p. 643)

Cohen, N. (2011, January 30). Define gender gap? Look up Wikipedia's contributor list. *New York Times* (www.nytimes.com). (p. 503)

Cohen, P. (2007, November 15). Freud is widely taught at universities, except in the psychology department. *New York Times* (www.nytimes.com). (p. 556)

Cohen, P. (2010, June 11). Long road to adulthood is growing even longer. *New York Times* (www.nytimes.com). (p. 523)

Cohen, R. (2011, March 12). The happynomics of life. *New York Times* (www.nytimes.com). (p. 854)

Cohen, S. (2004). Social relationships and health. *American Psychologist, 59*, 676–684. (p. 858)

Cohen, S., Doyle, W. J., Alper, C. M., Janicki-Deverts, D., & Turner, R. B. (2009). Sleep habits and susceptibility to the common cold. *Archives of Internal Medicine, 169*, 62–67. (p. 236)

Cohen, S., Doyle, W. J., Skoner, D. P., Rabin, B. S., & Gwaltney, J. M., Jr. (1997). Social ties and susceptibility to the common cold. *Journal of the American Medical Association, 277*, 1940–1944. (pp. 300, 858)

Cohen, S., Doyle, W. J., Turner, R., Alper, C. M., & Skoner, D. P. (2003). Sociability and susceptibility to the common cold. *Psychological Science, 14*, 389–395. (p. 449)

Cohen, S., Kaplan, J. R., Cunnick, J. E., Manuck, S. B., & Rabin, B. S. (1992). Chronic social stress, affiliation, and cellular immune response in nonhuman primates. *Psychological Science, 3*, 301–304. (pp. 448, 449)

Cohen, S., & Pressman, S. D. (2006). Positive affect and health. *Current Directions in Psychological Science, 15*, 122–125. (p. 449)

Cohen, S., Tyrrell, D. A. J., & Smith, A. P. (1991). Psychological stress and susceptibility to the common cold. *New England Journal of Medicine, 325*, 606–612. (p. 449)

Colangelo, N., Assouline, S. G., & Gross, M. U. M. (2004). *A nation deceived: How schools hold back America's brightest students* (Vols. I and II). (The Templeton National Report on Acceleration.) Iowa City, IA: College of Education, University of Iowa. (p. 630)

Colapinto, J. (2000). *As nature made him: The boy who was raised as a girl.* New York: HarperCollins. (p. 528)

Colarelli, S. M., & Dettman, J. R. (2003). Intuitive evolutionary perspectives in marketing. *Psychology and Marketing, 20*, 837–865. (p. 137)

Colarelli, S. M., Spranger, J. L., & Hechanova, M. R. (2006). Women, power, and sex composition in small groups: An evolutionary perspective. *Journal of Organizational Behavior, 27*, 163–184. (p. 502)

Colcombe, S. J., Kramer, A. F., Erickson, K. I., Scalf, P., McAuley, E., Cohen, N. J., Webb, A., Jerome, G. J., Marquex, D. X., & Elavsky, S. (2004). Cardiovascular fitness, cortical plasticity, and aging. *Proceedings of the National Academy of Sciences, 101*, 3316–3321. (p. 542)

Cole, K. C. (1998). *The universe and the teacup: The mathematics of truth and beauty.* New York: Harcourt Brace. (p. 251)

Cole, S. W., Arevalo, J. M. G., Takahashi, R., Sloan, E. K., Lutgendorf, S. K., Sood, A. K., Sheridan, J. F., & Seeman, T. E. (2010). Computational identification of gene-social envnironment interaction at the human *IL6* locus. *PNAS, 107*, 5681–5686. (p. 453)

Coley, R. L., Medeiros, B. L., & Schindler, H. (2008). Using sibling differences to estimate effects of parenting on adolescent sexual risk behaviors. *Journal of Adolescent Health, 43*, 133–140. (p. 531)

Collins, D. W., & Kimura, D. (1997). A large sex difference on a two-dimensional mental rotation task. *Behavioral Neuroscience, 111*, 845–849. (p. 638)

Collins, F. (2006). *The language of God.* New York: Free Press. (p. 141)

Collins, G. (2009, March 9). The rant list. *New York Times* (nytimes.com). (p. 68)

Collins, N. L., & Miller, L. C. (1994). Self-disclosure and liking: A meta-analytic review. *Psychological Bulletin, 116*, 457–475. (p. 804)

Collins, R. L., Elliott, M. N., Berry, S. H., Danouse, D. E., Kunkel, D., Hunter, S. B., & Miu, A. (2004). Watching sex on television predicts adolescent initiation of sexual behavior. *Pediatrics, 114*, 280–289. (p. 48)

Collins, W. A., Welsh, D. P., & Furman, W. (2009). Adolescent romantic relationships. *Annual Review of Psychology, 60*, 631–652. (p. 521)

Collinson, S. L., MacKay, C. E., James, A. C., Quested, D. J., Phillips, T., Roberts, N., & Crow, T. J. (2003). Brain volume, asymmetry and intellectual impairment in relation to sex in early-onset schizophrenia. *British Journal of Psychiatry, 183,* 114–120. (p. 687)

Collishaw, S., Pickles, A., Natarajan, L., & Maughan, B. (2007, June). 20-year trends in depression and anxiety in England. Paper presented at the Thirteenth Scientific Meeting on The Brain and the Developing Child, London. (p. 675)

Colombo, J. (1982). The critical period concept: Research, methodology, and theoretical issues. *Psychological Bulletin, 91,* 260–275. (p. 489)

Comfort, A. (1992). *The new joy of sex.* New York: Pocket. (p. 540)

Commission on Children at Risk. (2003). *Hardwired to connect: The new scientific case for authoritative communities.* New York: Institute for American Values. (p. 496)

Comstock, G. (2008). A sociological perspective on television violence and aggression. *American Behavioral Scientist, 51,* 1184–1211. (p. 309)

Confer, J. C., Easton, J. A., Fleischman, D. S., Goetz, C. D., Lewis, D. M. G., Perilloux, C., & Buss, D. M. (2010). Evolutionary psychology: Controversies, questions, prospects, and limitations. *American Psychologist, 65,* 110–126. (p. 139)

Conley, C. S., & Rudolph, K. D. (2009). The emerging sex difference in adolescent depression: Interacting contributions of puberty and peer stress. *Development and Psychopathology, 21,* 593–620. (p. 514)

Conn, V. S. (2010). Depressive symptom outcomes of physical activity interventions: Meta-analysis findings. *Annals of Behavioral Medicine, 39,* 128–138. (p. 860)

Connor, C. E. (2010). A new viewpoint on faces. *Science, 330,* 764–765. (p. 175)

Connor-Smith, J. K., & Flachsbart, C. (2007). Relations between personality and coping: A meta-analysis. *Journal of Personality and Social Psychology, 93,* 1080–1107. (p. 299)

Consumer Reports. (1995, November). Does therapy help? 734–739. (p. 729)

Conway, A. R. A., Skitka, L. J., Hemmerich, J. A., & Kershaw, T. C. (2009). Flashbulb memory for 11 September 2001. *Applied Cognitive Psychology, 23,* 605–623. (p. 332)

Conway, M. A., Wang, Q., Hanyu, K., & Haque, S. (2005). A cross-cultural investigation of autobiographical memory. On the universality and cultural variation of the reminiscence bump. *Journal of Cross-Cultural Psychology, 36,* 739–749. (p. 542)

Cooke, L. J., Wardle, J., & Gibson, E. L. (2003). Relationship between parental report of food neophobia and everyday food consumption in 2–6-year-old children. *Appetite, 41,* 205–206. (p. 207)

Cooper, K. J. (1999, May 1). This time, copycat wave is broader. *Washington Post* (www.washingtonpost.com). (p. 763)

Cooper, M. (2010, October 18). From Obama, the tax cut nobody heard of. *New York Times* (www.nytimes.com). (p. 785)

Cooper, M. L. (2006). Does drinking promote risky sexual behavior? A complex answer to a simple question. *Current Directions in Psychological Science, 15,* 19–23. (p. 249)

Cooper, W. H., & Withey, M. J. (2009). The strong situation hypothesis. *Personality and Social Psychology Review, 13,* 62–72. (p. 584)

Coopersmith, S. (1967). *The antecedents of self-esteem.* San Francisco: Freeman. (p. 496)

Copeland, W., Shanahan, L., Miller, S., Costello, E. J., Angold, A., & Maughan, B. (2010). Outcomes of early pubertal timing in young women: A prospective population-based study. *American Journal of Psychiatry, 167,* 1218–1225. (p. 514)

Corballis, M. C. (1989). Laterality and human evolution. *Psychological Review, 96,* 492–505. (p. 118)

Corballis, M. C. (2002). *From hand to mouth: The origins of language.* Princeton, NJ: Princeton University Press. (p. 869)

Corballis, M. C. (2003). From mouth to hand: Gesture, speech, and the evolution of right-handedness. *Behavioral and Brain Sciences, 26,* 199–260. (p. 869)

Coren, S. (1996). *Sleep thieves: An eye-opening exploration into the science and mysteries of sleep.* New York: Free Press. (pp. 234, 237)

Corey, D. P., & 15 others. (2004). TRPA1 is a candidate for the mechanosensitive transduction channel of vertebrate hair cells. *Nature, 432,* 723–730. (p. 196)

Corina, D. P. (1998). The processing of sign language: Evidence from aphasia. In B. Stemmer & H. A. Whittaker (Eds.), *Handbook of neurolinguistics.* San Diego: Academic Press. (p. 117)

Corina, D. P., Vaid, J., & Bellugi, U. (1992). The linguistic basis of left hemisphere specialization. *Science, 255,* 1258–1260. (p. 117)

Corkin, S., quoted by R. Adelson (2005, September). Lessons from H. M. *Monitor on Psychology, 59.* (p. 342)

Corneille, O., Huart, J., Becquart, E., & Brédart, S. (2004). When memory shifts toward more typical category exemplars: Accentuation effects in the recollection of ethnically ambiguous faces. *Journal of Personality and Social Psychology, 86,* 236–250. (p. 357)

Correll, J., Park, B., Judd, C. M., & Wittenbrink, B. (2002). The police officer's dilemma: Using ethnicity to disambiguate potentially threatening individuals. *Journal of Personality and Social Psychology, 83,* 1314–1329. (p. 782)

Correll, J., Park, B., Judd, C. M., Wittenbrink, B., Sadler, M. S., & Keesee, T. (2007). Across the thin blue line: Police officers and racial bias in the decision to shoot. *Journal of Personality and Social Psychology, 92,* 1006–1023. (p. 782)

Costa, P. T., Jr., & McCrae, R. R. (2009). The five-factor model and the NEO inventories. In J. N. Butcher (ed.), *Oxford handbook of personality assessment.* New York: Oxford University Press. (p. 580)

Costa, P. T., Jr., Terracciano, A., & McCrae, R. R. (2001). Gender differences in personality traits across cultures: Robust and surprising findings. *Journal of Personality and Social Psychology, 81,* 322–331. (p. 434)

Costello, E. J., Compton, S. N., Keeler, G., & Angold, A. (2003). Relationships between poverty and psychopathology: A natural experiment. *Journal of the American Medical Association, 290,* 2023–2029. (pp. 48, 658)

Coughlin, J. F., Mohyde, M., D'Ambrosio, L. A., & Gilbert, J. (2004). *Who drives older driver decisions?* Cambridge, MA: MIT Age Lab. (p. 541)

Couli, J. T., Vidal, F., Nazarian, B., & Macar, F. (2004). Functional anatomy of the attentional modulation of time estimation. *Science, 303,* 1506–1508. (p. 828)

Courage, M. L., & Howe, M. L. (2002). From infant to child: The dynamics of cognitive change in the second year of life. *Psychological Bulletin, 128,* 250–277. (p. 495)

Courage, M. L., & Setliff, A. E. (2010). When babies watch television: Attention-getting, attention-holding, and the implications for learning from video material. *Developmental Review, 30,* 220–238. (p. 652)

Courtney, J. G., Longnecker, M. P., Theorell, T., & de Verdier, M. G. (1993). Stressful life events and the risk of colorectal cancer. *Epidemiology, 4,* 407–414. (p. 451)

Covin, R., Ouimet, A. J., Seeds, P. M., & Dozois, D. J. A. (2008). A meta-analysis of CBT for pathological worry among clients with GAD. *Journal of Anxiety Disorders, 22,* 108–116. (p. 723)

Cowan, G., Lee, C., Levy, D., & Snyder, D. (1988). Dominance and inequality in X-rated videocassettes. *Psychology of Women Quarterly, 12,* 299–311. (p. 793)

Cowan, N. (1988). Evolving conceptions of memory storage, selective attention, and their mutual constraints within the human information-processing system. *Psychological Bulletin, 104,* 163–191. (p. 322)

Cowan, N. (2010). The magical mystery four: How is working memory capacity limited, and why? *Current Directions in Psychological Science, 19,* 51–57. (p. 320)

Cowart, B. J. (1981). Development of taste perception in humans: Sensitivity and preference throughout the life span. *Psychological Bulletin, 90,* 43–73. (p. 207)

Cowart, B. J. (2005). Taste, our body's gustatory gatekeeper. *Cerebrum, 7*(2), 7–22. (p. 207)

Cox, J. J., & 18 others. (2006). An *SCN9A* channelopathy causes congenital inability to experience pain. *Nature, 444,* 894–898. (p. 204)

Coyne, J. C., Ranchor, A. V., & Palmer, S. C. (2010). Meta-analysis of stress-related factors in cancer. *Nature Reviews: Clinical Oncology, 7,* doi: 10.1038/ncponc1134-c1. (p. 451)

Coyne, J. C., Stefanek, M., & Palmer, S. C. (2007). Psychotherapy and survival in cancer: The conflict between hope and evidence. *Psychological Bulletin, 133,* 367–394. (p. 451)

Coyne, J. C., & Tennen, H. (2010). Positive psychology in cancer care: Bad science, exaggerated claims, and unproven medicine. *Annals of Behavioral Medicine, 39,* 16–26. (p. 451)

Coyne, J. C., Thombs, B. C., Stefanek, M., & Palmer, S. C. (2009). Time to let go of the illusion that psychotherapy extends the survival of cancer patients: Reply to Kraemer, Kuchler, and Spiegel (2009). *Psychological Bulletin, 135,* 179–182. (p. 451)

CPP. (2008). *Myers-Briggs Type Indicator(r) assessment (MBTI(r)).* CPP, Inc. (www.cpp.com). (p. 576)

Crabbe, J. C. (2002). Genetic contributions to addiction. *Annual Review of Psychology, 53,* 435–462. (p. 823)

Crabtree, S. (2005, January 13). Engagement keeps the doctor away. *Gallup Management Journal* (gmj.gallup.com). (p. 836)

Crabtree, S. (2010, July 14). Personal correspondence (Gallup Organization). (p. 546)

Craik, F. I. M., & Tulving, E. (1975). Depth of processing and the retention of words in episodic memory. *Journal of Experimental Psychology: General, 104,* 268–294. (p. 325)

Crain-Thoreson, C., & Dale, P. S. (1992). Do early talkers become early readers? Linguistic precocity, preschool language, and emergent literacy. *Developmental Psychology, 28,* 421–429. (p. 627)

Crandall, C. S. (1988). Social contagion of binge eating. *Journal of Personality and Social Psychology, 55,* 588–598. (p. 697)

Crandall, J. E. (1984). Social interest as a moderator of life stress. *Journal of Personality and Social Psychology, 47,* 164–174. (p. 573)

Crawford, E. F., Drescher, K. D., & Rosen, C. S. (2009). Predicting mortality in veterans with posttraumatic stress disorder thirty years after Vietnam. *Journal of Nervous and Mental Disease, 197,* 260–265. (p. 665)

Crawford, M., Chaffin, R., & Fitton, L. (1995). Cognition in social context. Learning and Individual Differences, Special Issue: Psychological and psychobiological perspectives on sex differences in cognition: 1. *Theory and Research, 7,* 341–362. (p. 639)

Crawley, J. N. (2007). Testing hypotheses about autism. *Science, 318,* 56–57. (p. 482)

Credé, M., & Kuncel, N. R. (2008). Study habits, skills, and attitudes: The third pillar supporting collegiate academic performance. *Perspectives on Psychological Science, 3,* 425–453. (p. 635)

Crews, F. T., He, J., & Hodge, C. (2007). Adolescent cortical development: A critical period of vulnerability for addiction. *Pharmacology, Biochemistry and Behavior, 86,* 189–199. (pp. 249, 514)

Crews, F. T., Mdzinarishvili, A., Kim, D., He, J., & Nixon, K. (2006). Neurogenesis in adolescent brain is potently inhibited by ethanol. *Neuroscience, 137,* 437–445. (p. 249)

Critcher, C. R., & Dunning, D. (2009). How chronic self-views influence (and mislead) self-assessments of task performance: Self-views shape bottom-up experiences with the task. *Journal of Personality and Social Psychology, 97,* 931–945. (p. 591)

Crocker, J., & Park, L. E. (2004). The costly pursuit of self-esteem. *Psychological Bulletin, 130,* 392–414. (p. 598)

Crocker, J., Thompson, L. L., McGraw, K. M., & Ingerman, C. (1987). Downward comparison, prejudice, and evaluation of others: Effects of self-esteem and threat. *Journal of Personality and Social Psychology, 52,* 907–916. (p. 785)

Croft, R. J., Klugman, A., Baldeweg, T., & Gruzelier, J. H. (2001). Electrophysiological evidence of serotonergic impairment in long-term MDMA ("Ecstasy") users. *American Journal of Psychiatry, 158,* 1687–1692. (p. 254)

Crombie, A. C. (1964, May). Early concepts of the senses and the mind. *Scientific American,* pp. 108–116. (p. 172)

Crook, T. H., & West, R. L. (1990). Name recall performance across the adult life-span. *British Journal of Psychology, 81,* 335–340. (p. 542)

Cross, S., & Markus, H. (1991). Possible selves across the life span. *Human Development, 34,* 230–255. (p. 594)

Cross-National Collaborative Group. (1992). The changing rate of major depression. *Journal of the American Medical Association, 268,* 3098–3105. (p. 675)

Crowell, J. A., & Waters, E. (1994). Bowlby's theory grown up: The role of attachment in adult love relationships. *Psychological Inquiry, 5,* 1–22. (p. 489)

Csikszentmihalyi, M. (1990). *Flow: The psychology of optimal experience.* New York: Harper & Row. (p. 827)

Csikszentmihalyi, M. (1999). If we are so rich, why aren't we happy? *American Psychologist, 54,* 821–827. (p. 827)

Csikszentmihalyi, M., & Hunter, J. (2003). Happiness in everyday life: The uses of experience sampling. *Journal of Happiness Studies, 4,* 185–199. (p. 521)

Cuijpers, P., Geraedts, A. S., van Oppen, P., Andersson, G., Markowitz, J. C., & van Straten, A. (2011). Interpersonal psychotherapy for depression: A meta-analysis. *American Journal of Psychiatry, 168,* 581–592. (p. 711)

Cuijpers, P., van Straten, A., Schuurmans, J., van Oppen, P., Hollon, S. D., & Andersson, G. (2010). Psychotherapy for chronic major depression and dysthymia: A meta-analysis. *Clinical Psychology Review, 30,* 51–62.(p. 742)

Culbert, K. M., Burt, S. A., McGue, M., Iacono, W. G., & Klump, K. L. (2009). Puberty and the genetic diathesis of disordered eating attitudes and behaviors. *Journal of Abnormal Psychology, 118,* 788–796. (p. 697)

Cullum, J., & Harton, H. C. (2007). Cultural evolution: Interpersonal influence, issue importance, and the development of shared attitudes in college residence halls. *Personality and Social Psychology Bulletin, 33,* 1327–1339. (p. 764)

Cummins, R. A. (2006, April 4). *Australian Unity Wellbeing Index: Survey 14.1.* Australian Centre on Quality of Life, Deakin University, Melbourne; Report 14.1. (p. 850)

Cunningham, M. R., & others. (2005). "Their ideas of beauty are, on the whole, the same as ours": Consistency and variability in the cross-cultural perception of female physical attractiveness. *Journal of Personality and Social Psychology, 68,* 261–279. (p. 801)

Cunningham, W. A., Johnson, M. K., Raye, C. L., Gatenby, J. C., Gore, J. C., & Banaji, M. R. (2004). Separable neural components in the processing of Black and White faces. *Psychological Science, 15,* 806–813. (p. 782)

Currie, T. E., & Little, A. C. (2009). The relative importance of the face and body in judgments of human physical attractiveness. *Evolution and Human Behavior, 30,* 409–416. (p. 801)

Curry, J., & 22 others. (2011). Recovery and recurrence following treatment for adolescent major depression. *Archives of General Psychiatry, 68,* 263–269. (p. 675)

Curtis, R. C., & Miller, K. (1986). Believing another likes or dislikes you: Behaviors making the beliefs come true. *Journal of Personality and Social Psychology, 51,* 284–290. (p. 802)

Custers, R., & Aarts, H. (2010). The unconscious will: How the pursuir of goals operates outside of conscious awareness. *Science, 329,* 47–50. (p. 369)

Cutler, D. M., Glaeser, E. L., & Shapiro, J. M. (2003, Summer). Why have Americans become more obese? *Journal of Economic Perspectives, 17,* 93–118. (p. 401)

Cyders, M. A., & Smith, G. T. (2008). Emotion-based dispositions to rash action: Positive and negative urgency. *Psychological Bulletin, 134,* 807–828. (p. 421)

Czeisler, C. A., Allan, J. S., Strogatz, S. H., Ronda, J. M., Sanchez, R., Rios, C. D., Freitag, W. O., Richardson, G. S., & Kronauer, R. E. (1986). Bright light resets the human circadian pacemaker independent of the timing of the sleep-wake cycle. *Science, 233,* 667–671. (p. 230)

Czeisler, C. A., Duffy, J. F., Shanahan, T. L., Brown, E. N., Mitchell, J. F., Rimmer, D. W., Ronda, J. M., Silva, E. J., Allan, J. S., Emens, J. S., Dijk, D-J., & Kronauer, R. E. (1999). Stability, precision, and near-24-hour period of the human circadian pacemaker. *Science, 284,* 2177–2181. (p. 230)

Czeisler, C. A., Kronauer, R. E., Allan, J. S., & Duffy, J. F. (1989). Bright light induction of strong (type O) resetting of the human circadian pacemaker. *Science, 244,* 1328–1333. (p. 230)

Dabbs, J. M., Jr., Bernieri, F. J., Strong, R. K., Campo, R., & Milun, R. (2001b). Going on stage: Testosterone in greetings and meetings. *Journal of Research in Personality, 35,* 27–40. (p. 790)

Dabbs, J. M., Jr., & Morris, R. (1990). Testosterone, social class, and antisocial behavior in a sample of 4,462 men. *Psychological Science, 1,* 209–211. (p. 790)

Dabbs, J. M., Jr., Riad, J. K., & Chance, S. E. (2001a). Testosterone and ruthless homicide. *Personality and Individual Differences, 31,* 599–603. (p. 790)

Damasio, A. R. (1994). *Descartes error: Emotion, reason, and the human brain.* New York: Grossett/Putnam & Sons. (p. 612)

Damasio, A. R. (2010). *Self comes to mind: Constructing the conscious brain.* New York: Pantheon. (p. 594)

Damasio, H., Grabowski, T., Frank, R., Galaburda, A. M., & Damasio, A. R. (1994). The return of Phineas Gage: Clues about the brain from the skull of a famous patient. *Science, 264,* 1102–1105. (p. 110)

Damon, W., & Hart, D. (1982). The development of self-understanding from infancy through adolescence. *Child Development, 53,* 841–864. (p. 495)

Damon, W., & Hart, D. (1988). *Self-understanding in childhood and adolescence.* Cambridge: Cambridge University Press. (p. 495)

Damon, W., & Hart, D. (1992). Self-understanding and its role in social and moral development. In M. H. Bornstein & M. E. Lamb (Eds.), *Developmental psychology: An advanced textbook* (3rd ed.). Hillsdale, NJ: Lawrence Erlbaum. (p. 495)

Damon, W., Menon, J., & Bronk, K. (2003). The development of purpose during adolescence. *Applied Developmental Science, 7,* 119–128. (p. 520)

Danner, D. D., Snowdon, D. A., & Friesen, W. V. (2001). Positive emotions in early life and longevity: Findings from the Nun Study. *Journal of Personality and Social Psychology, 80,* 804–813. (p. 857)

Danso, H., & Esses, V. (2001). Black experimenters and the intellectual test performance of white participants: The tables are turned. *Journal of Experimental Social Psychology, 37*, 158–165. (p. 642)

Danziger, S., & Ward, R. (2010). Language changes implicit associations between ethnic groups and evaluation in bilinguals. *Psychological Science, 21*, 799–800. (p. 379)

Dapretto, M., Davies, M. S., Pfeifer, J. H., Scott, A. A., Sigman, M., Bookheimer, S. Y., & Iacoboni, M. (2006). Understanding emotions in others: Mirror neuron dysfunction in children with autism spectrum disorders. *Nature Neuroscience, 9*, 28–30. (p. 482)

Darley, J. M. (2009). Morality in the law: The psychological foundations of citizens' desires to punish transgressions. *Annual Review of Law and Social Science, 5*, 1–23. (p. 516)

Darley, J. M., & Alter, A. L. (2011). Behavioral issues of punishment and deterrence. In E. Shafir (Ed.), *The behavioral foundations of policy.* Princeton, NJ: Princeton University Press and the Russell Sage Foundation. (p. 281)

Darley, J. M., & Latané, B. (1968a). Bystander intervention in emergencies: Diffusion of responsibility. *Journal of Personality and Social Psychology, 8*, 377–383. (pp. 808, 809)

Darley, J. M., & Latané, B. (1968b, December). When will people help in a crisis? *Psychology Today*, 54–57, 70–71. (p. 808)

Darrach, B., & Norris, J. (1984, August). An American tragedy. *Life*, 58–74. (p. 699)

Darwin, C. (1859). *On the origin of species by means of natural selection.* London: John Murray. (p. 137)

Darwin, C. (1872). *The expression of the emotions in man and animals.* London: John Murray, Albemarle Street. (p. 437)

Daskalakis, Z. J., Levinson, A. J., & Fitzgerald, P. B. (2008). Repetitive transcranial magnetic stimulation for major depressive disorder: A review. *Canadian Journal of Psychiatry, 53*, 555–564. (p. 745)

Daum, I., & Schugens, M. M. (1996). On the cerebellum and classical conditioning. *Psychological Science, 5*, 58–61. (p. 331)

Davey, G. C. L. (1992). Classical conditioning and the acquisition of human fears and phobias: A review and synthesis of the literature. *Advances in Behavior Research and Therapy, 14*, 29–66. (p. 295)

Davey, G. C. L. (1995). Preparedness and phobias: Specific evolved associations or a generalized expectancy bias? *Behavioral and Brain Sciences, 18*, 289–297. (p. 667)

Davidoff, J. (2004). Coloured thinking. *The Psychologist, 17*, 570–572. (p. 379)

Davidson, J. R. T., Connor, K. M., & Swartz, M. (2006). Mental illness in U.S. presidents between 1776 and 1974: A review of biographical sources. *Journal of Nervous and Mental Disease, 194*, 47–51. (p. 659)

Davidson, R. J. (2000). Affective style, psychopathology, and resilience: Brain mechanisms and plasticity. *American Psychologist, 55*, 1196–1209. (pp. 427, 790)

Davidson, R. J. (2003). Affective neuroscience and psychophysiology: Toward a synthesis. *Psychophysiology, 40*, 655–665. (p. 427)

Davidson, R. J., Kabat-Zinn, J., Schumacher, J., Rosenkranz, M., Muller, D., Santorelli, S. F., Urbanowski, F., Harrington, A., Bonus, K., & Sheridan, J. F. (2003). Alterations in brain and immune function produced by mindfulness meditation. *Psychosomatic Medicine, 65*, 564–570. (p. 862)

Davidson, R. J., Pizzagalli, D., Nitschke, J. B., & Putnam, K. (2002). Depression: Perspectives from affective neuroscience. *Annual Review of Psychology, 53*, 545–574. (p. 678)

Davies, M. F. (1997). Positive test strategies and confirmatory retrieval processes in the evaluation of personality feedback. *Journal of Personality and Social Psychology, 73*, 574–583. (p. 579)

Davies, P. (2007). *Cosmic jackpot: Why our universe is just right for life.* Boston: Houghton-Mifflin. (p. 142)

Davis, B. E., Moon, R. Y., Sachs, H. C., & Ottolini, M. C. (1998). Effects of sleep position on infant motor development. *Pediatrics, 102*, 1135–1140. (p. 472)

Davis, H., IV, Liotti, M., Ngan, E. T., Woodward, T. S., Van Sellenberg, J. X., van Anders, S. M., Smith, A., & Mayberg, H. S. (2008). FMRI BOLD signal changes in elite swimmers while viewing videos of personal failures. *Brain Imaging and Behavior, 2*, 94–104. (p. 678)

Davis, J. O., & Phelps, J. A. (1995a). Twins with schizophrenia: Genes or germs? *Schizophrenia Bulletin, 21*, 13–18. (p. 688)

Davis, J. O., Phelps, J. A., & Bracha, H. S. (1995). Prenatal development of monozygotic twins and concordance for schizophrenia. *Schizophrenia Bulletin, 21*, 357–366. (pp. 125, 688)

Davis, M. (2005). Searching for a drug to extinguish fear. *Cerebrum, 7*(3), 47–58. (p. 741)

Davison, K. P., Pennebaker, J. W., & Dickerson, S. S. (2000). Who talks? The social psychology of illness support groups. *American Psychologist, 55*, 205–217. (p. 724)

Dawes, R. M. (1980). Social dilemmas. *Annual Review of Psychology, 31*, 169–193. (p. 812)

Dawes, R. M. (1994). *House of cards: Psychology and psychotherapy built on myth.* New York: Free Press. (p. 595)

Dawkins, R. (1998). *Unweaving the rainbow.* Boston: Houghton Mifflin. (p. 141)

Dawkins, R. (2007, July 1). Inferior design. *New York Times* (www.nytimes.com). (p. 135)

Dean, G. A., Kelly, I. W., Saklofske, D. H., & Furnham, A. (1992). Graphology and human judgment. In B. Beyerstein & D. Beyerstein (Eds.), *The write stuff: Evaluations of graphology.* Buffalo, NY: Prometheus Books. (p. 579)

DeAngelis, T. (2008, February). U.K. gives huge boost to psychologists. *Monitor on Psychology*, p. 51. (p. 732)

Deary, I. J. (2008). Why do intelligent people live longer? *Nature, 456*, 175–176. (p. 628)

Deary, I. J., Batty, G. D., & Gale, C. R. (2008). Bright children become enlightened adults. *Psychological Science, 19*, 1–6. (p. 628)

Deary, I. J., & Caryl, P. G. (1993). Intelligence, EEG and evoked potentials. In P. A. Vernon (Ed.), *Biological approaches to the study of human intelligence.* Norwood, NJ: Ablex. (p. 614)

Deary, I. J., & Der, G. (2005). Reaction time explains IQ's association with death. *Psychological Science, 16*, 64–69. (p. 614)

Deary, I. J., Johnson, W., & Houlihan, L. M. (2009). Genetic foundations of human intelligence. *Human Genetics, 126*, 215–232. (pp. 613, 632, 633)

Deary, I. J., & Matthews, G. (1993). Personality traits are alive and well. *The Psychologist: Bulletin of the British Psychological Society, 6*, 299–311. (p. 583)

Deary, I. J., Penke, L., & Johnson, W. (2009). The neuroscience of human intelligence differences. *Nature Reviews: Neuroscience, 11*, 201–211. (p. 627)

Deary, I. J., & Stough, C. (1996). Intelligence and inspection time: Achievements, prospects, and problems. *American Psychologist, 51*, 599–608. (p. 614)

Deary, I. J., Strand, S., Smith, P., & Fernandes, C. (2007). Intelligence and educational achievement. *Intelligence, 35*, 13–21. (p. 622)

Deary, I. J., Thorpe, G., Wilson, V., Starr, J. M., & Whalley, L. J. (2003). Population sex differences in IQ at age 11: The Scottish mental survey 1932. *Intelligence, 31*, 533–541. (p. 638)

Deary, I. J., Weiss, A., & Batty, G. D. (2010) Intelligence and personality as predictors of illness and death: How researchers in differential psychology and chronic disease epidemiology are collaborating to understand and address health inequalities. *Psychological Science in the Public Interest, 11*, 53–79. (p. 628)

Deary, I. J., Whalley, L. J., & Starr, J. M. (2009). *A lifetime of intelligence: Follow-up studies of the Scottish Mental Surveys of 1932 and 1947.* Washington, DC: American Psychological Association. (pp. 622, 628)

Deary, I. J., Whiteman, M. C., Starr, J. M., Whalley, L. J., & Fox, H. C. (2004). The impact of childhood intelligence on later life: Following up the Scottish mental surveys of 1932 and 1947. *Journal of Personality and Social Psychology, 86*, 130–147. (p. 627)

de Boysson-Bardies, B., Halle, P., Sagart, L., & Durand, C. (1989). A cross linguistic investigation of vowel formats in babbling. *Journal of Child Language, 16*, 1–17. (p. 374)

DeBruine, L. M. (2002). Facial resemblance enhances trust. *Proceedings of the Royal Society of London, 269*, 1307–1312. (p. 799)

DeBruine, L. M. (2004). Facial resemblance increases the attractiveness of same-sex faces more than other-sex faces. *Proceedings of the Royal Society of London B, 271*, 2085–2090. (p. 799)

DeCasper, A. J., Lecanuet, J-P, Busnel, M-C, Granier-Deferre, C., et al. (1994). Fetal reactions to recurrent maternal speech. *Infant Behavior and Development, 17*, 159–164. (p. 466)

DeCasper, A. J., & Prescott, P. A. (1984). Human newborns' perception of male voices: Preference, discrimination and reinforcing value. *Developmental Psychobiology, 17*, 481–491. (p. 466)

DeCasper, A. J., & Spence, M. J. (1986). Prenatal maternal speech influences newborns' perception of speech sounds. *Infant Behavior and Development, 9,* 133–150. (p. 466)

Deci, E. L., Koestner, R., & Ryan, R. M. (1999, November). A meta-analytic review of experiments examining the effects of extrinsic rewards on intrinsic motivation. *Psychological Bulletin, 125(6),* 627–668. (p. 297)

Deci, E. L., & Ryan, R. M. (1985). *Intrinsic motivation and self-determination in human behavior.* New York: Plenum Press. (p. 298)

Deci, E. L., & Ryan, R. M. (Eds.). (2002). *Handbook of self-determination research.* Rochester, NY: University of Rochester Press. (p. 413)

Deci, E. L., & Ryan, R. M. (2009). Self-determination theory: A consideration of human motivational universals. In P. J. Corr & G. Matthews (eds.), *The Cambridge Handbook of Personality Psychology.* New York: Cambridge University Press. (pp. 298, 413)

de Courten-Myers, G. M. (2002, May 9). Personal correspondence. (p. 471)

de Courten-Myers, G. M. (2005, February 4). Personal correspondence (estimating total brain neurons, extrapolating from her carefully estimated 20 to 23 billion cortical neurons). (pp. 88, 104)

De Dreu, C. K. W., Greer, L. L., Handgraaf, M. J. J., Shalvi, S., Van Kleef, G. A., Baas, M., Ten Velden, F. S., Van Dijk, E., & Feith, S. W. W. (2010). The neuropeptide oxytocin regulated parochial altruism in intergroup conflict among humans. *Science, 328,* 1409–1411. (p. 91)

Deeley, Q., Daly, E., Surguladze, S., Tunstall, N., Mezey, G., Beer, D., Ambikapathy, A., Robertson, D., Giampietro, V., Brammer, M. J., Clarke, A., Dowsett, J., Fahy, T., Phillips, M. L., & Murphy, D. G. (2006). Facial emotion processing in criminal psychopathy. *British Journal of Psychiatry, 189,* 533–539. (p. 700)

De Gelder, B. (2010, May). Uncanny sight in the blind. *Scientific American,* pp. 61–65. (p. 121)

de Gonzales, A. B., & 33 others. (2010). Body-mass index and mortality among 1.46 million white adults. *New England Journal of Medicine, 363,* 2211–2219. (p. 401)

Dehaene, S. (2009, November 24). Signatures of consciousness. *Edge is Paris.* www.Edge.org. (p. 157)

Dehne, K. L., & Riedner, G. (2005). *Sexually transmitted infections among adolescents: The need for adequate health services.* Geneva: World Health Organization. (p. 529)

de Hoogh, A. H. B., den Hartog, D. N., Koopman, P. L., Thierry, H., van den Berg, P. T., van der Weide, J. G., & Wilderom, C. P. M. (2004). Charismatic leadership, environmental dynamism, and performance. *European Journal of Work and Organisational Psychology, 13,* 447–471. (p. 839)

De Koninck, J. (2000). Waking experiences and dreaming. In M. Kryger, T. Roth, & W. Dement (Eds.), *Principles and practice of sleep medicine, 3rd ed.* Philadelphia: Saunders. (p. 240)

DeLamater, J. D., & Sill, M. (2005). Sexual desire in later life. *Journal of Sex Research, 42,* 138–149. (p. 540)

Delaney, H. D., Miller, W. R., & Bisonó, A. M. (2007). Religiosity and spirituality among psychologists: A survey of clinician members of the American Psychological Association. *Professional Psychology: Research and Practice, 38,* 538–546. (p. 735)

Delaunay-El Allam, M., Soussignan, R., Patris, B., Marlier, L., & Schaal, B. (2010). Long-lasting memory for an odor acquired at the mother's breast. *Developmental Science, 13,* 849–863. (p. 469)

Delgado, J. M. R. (1969). *Physical control of the mind: Toward a psychocivilized society.* New York: Harper & Row. (p. 106)

DeLoache, J. S. (1987). Rapid change in the symbolic functioning of very young children. *Science, 238,* 1556–1557. (p. 479)

DeLoache, J. S., Chiong, C., Sherman, K., Islam, N., Vanderborght, M., Troseth, G. L., Strouse, G. A., & O'Doherty, K. (2010). Do babies learn from baby media? *Psychological Science, 21,* 1570–1574. (p. 635)

DeLoache, J. S., Uttal, D. H., & Rosengren, K. S. (2004). Scale errors offer evidence for a perception-action dissociation early in life. *Science, 304,* 1027–1029. (p. 477)

De Los Reyes, A., & Kazdin, A. E. (2009). Identifying evidence-based interventions for children and adolescents using the range of possible changes model: A meta-analytic illustration. *Behavior Modification, 33,* 583–617. (p. 732)

Dement, W. C. (1978). *Some must watch while some must sleep.* New York: Norton. (pp. 227, 238)

Dement, W. C. (1999). *The promise of sleep.* New York: Delacorte Press. (pp. 227, 230, 234, 235, 236, 238, 239)

Dement, W. C., & Wolpert, E. A. (1958). The relation of eye movements, body mobility, and external stimuli to dream content. *Journal of Experimental Psychology, 55,* 543–553. (p. 241)

Demicheli, V., Rivetti, A., Debalini, M. G., & Di Pietrantonj, C. (2012, February 15). Vaccines for measles, mumps and rubella in children. *Cochrane Database of Systematic Reviews,* Issue 2, CD004407. (p. 482)

Demir, E., & Dickson, B. J. (2005). Fruitless splicing specifies male courtship behavior in *Drosophila. Cell, 121,* 785–794. (p. 534)

de Moraes, L. (2010, March 18). Reality show contestants willing to kill in French experiment. *Washington Post* (www.washingtonpost.com). (p. 766)

DeNeve, K. M., & Cooper, H. (1998). The happy personality: A meta-analysis of 137 personality traits and subjective well-being. *Psychological Bulletin, 124,* 197–229. (p. 852)

Dennett, D. C. (1991). *Consciousness explained.* Boston: Little, Brown. (p. 296)

Dennett, D. C. (1996, September 9). Quoted by Ian Parker, Richard Dawkins' evolution. *The New Yorker,* pp. 41–45. (p. 10)

Denson, T. F. (2011). A social neuroscience perspective on the neurobiological bases of aggression. In P. R. Shaver, & M. Mikulincer (Eds.), *Human aggression and violence: Causes, manifestations, and consequences.* Washington, DC: U. S. American Psychological Association. (p. 790)

Denton, K., & Krebs, D. (1990). From the scene to the crime: The effect of alcohol and social context on moral judgment. *Journal of Personality and Social Psychology, 59,* 242–248. (p. 249)

DePaulo, B. M., Blank, A. L., Swaim, G. W., & Hairfield, J. G. (1992). Expressiveness and expressive control. *Personality and Social Psychology Bulletin, 18,* 276–285. (p. 584)

Depla, M. F. I. A., ten Have, M. L., van Balkom, A. J. L. M., & de Graaf, R. (2008). Specific fears and phobias in the general population: Results from the Netherlands Mental Health Survey and Incidence Study (NEMESIS). *Social Psychiatry and Psychiatric Epidemiology, 43,* 200–208. (p. 663)

Der, G., Batty, G. D., & Deary, I. J. (2006). Effect of breast feeding on intelligence in children: Prospective study, sibling pairs analysis, and meta-analysis. *British Medical Journal, 333,* 945. (p. 50)

Der, G., Batty, G. D., & Deary, I. J. (2009). The association between IQ in adolescence and a range of health outcomes at 40 in the 1979 US National Longitudinal Study of Youth. *Intelligence, 37,* 573–580. (p. 628)

De Raad, B., Barelds, D. P. H., Levert, E., Ostendorf, F., Mlačić, B., Di Blas, L., Hřebíčková, M., Szirmák, Z., Szarota, P., Perugini, M., Church, A. T., & Katigbak, M. S. (2010). Only three factors of personality description are fully replicable across languages: A comparison of 14 trait taxonomies. *Journal of Personality and Social Psychology, 98,* 160–173. (p. 580)

Dermer, M., Cohen, S. J., Jacobsen, E., & Anderson, E. A. (1979). Evaluative judgments of aspects of life as a function of vicarious exposure to hedonic extremes. *Journal of Personality and Social Psychology, 37,* 247–260. (p. 852)

Dermer, M., & Pyszczynski, T. A. (1978). Effects of erotica upon men's loving and liking responses for women they love. *Journal of Personality and Social Psychology, 36,* 1302–1309. (p. 803)

Desmurget, M., Reilly, K. T., Richard, N., Szathmari, A., Mottolese, C., & Sirigu, A. (2009). Movement intention after parietal cortex stimulation in humans. *Science, 324,* 811–813. (p. 110)

DeSteno, D., Dasgupta, N., Bartlett, M. Y., & Cajdric, A. (2004). Prejudice from thin air: The effect of emotion on automatic intergroup attitudes. *Psychological Science, 15,* 319–324. (p. 846)

DeSteno, D., Petty, R. E., Wegener, D. T., & Rucker, D. D. (2000). Beyond valence in the perception of likelihood: The role of emotion specificity. *Journal of Personality and Social Psychology, 78,* 397–416. (p. 337)

Dettman, S. J., Pinder, D., Briggs, R. J. S., Dowell, R. C., & Leigh, J. R. (2007). Communication development in children who receive the cochlear implant younger than 12 months: Risk versus benefits. *Ear and Hearing, 28*(2), Supplement 11S–18S. (p. 198)

Deutsch, J. A. (1972, July). Brain reward: ESP and ecstasy. *Psychology Today,* 46–48. (p. 100)

DeValois, R. L., & DeValois, K. K. (1975). Neural coding of color. In E. C. Carterette & M. P. Friedman (Eds.), *Handbook of perception: Vol. V. Seeing.* New York: Academic Press. (p. 179)

Devilly, G. J. (2003). Eye movement desensitization and reprocessing: A chronology of its development and scientific standing. *Scientific Review of Mental Health Practice, 1,* 113–118. (p. 733)

Devine, P. G. (1995). Prejudice and outgroup perception. In A. Tesser (Ed.), *Advanced social psychology.* New York: McGraw-Hill. (p. 800)

De Vogli, R., Chandola, T., & Marmot, M. G. (2007). Negative aspects of close relationships and heart disease. *Archives of Internal Medicine, 167,* 1951–1957. (p. 857)

Dew, M. A., Hoch, C. C., Buysse, D. J., Monk, T. H., Begley, A. E., Houck, P. R., Hall, M., Kupfer, D. J., Reynolds, C. F., III (2003). Healthy older adults' sleep predicts all-cause mortality at 4 to 19 years of follow-up. *Psychosomatic Medicine, 65,* 63–73. (p. 236)

de Waal, F. B. M. (2005, September 23). We're all Machiavellians. *Chronicle of Higher Education.* (p. 41)

de Waal, F. B. M. (2009, October). The empathy instinct. *Discover,* pp. 54–57. (pp. 438, 763)

de Waal, F. B. M., & Johanowicz, D. L. (1993). Modification of reconciliation behavior through social experience: An experiment with two macaque species. *Child Development, 64,* 897–908. (p. 305)

DeWall, C. N., Baumeister, R. F., Stillman, T. F., & Gaillot, M. T. (2007). Violence restrained: Effects of self-regulation and its depletion on aggression. *Journal of Experimental Social Psychology, 43,* 62–76. (p. 301)

DeWall, C. N., MacDonald, G., Webster, G. D., Masten, C. L., Baumeister, R. F., Powell, C., Combs, D., Schurtz, D. R., Stillman, T. F., Tice, D. M., & Eisenberger, N. I. (2010). Acetaminophen reduces social pain: Behavioral and neural evidence. *Psychological Science, 21,* 931–937. (p. 414)

DeWall, C. N., Pond, R. S., Jr., Campbell, W. K., & Twenge, J. M. (2011). Tuning in to psychological change: Linguistic markers of psychological traits and emotions over time in popular U.S. song lyrics. *Psychology of Aesthetics, Creativity, and the Arts,* in press. (p. 597)

De Wit, L., Luppino, F., van Straten, A., Penninx, B., Zitman, F., & Cuijpers, P. (2010). Depression and obesity: A meta-analysis of community-based studies. *Psychiatry Research, 178,* 230–235. (p. 401)

De Wolff, M. S., & van IJzendoorn, M. H. (1997). Sensitivity and attachment: A meta-analysis on parental antecedents of infant attachment. *Child Development, 68,* 571–591. (p. 490)

DeYoung, C. G., Hirsch, J. B., Shane, M. S., Papademetris, X., Rajeevan, N., & Gray, J. R. (2010). Testing predictions from personality neuroscience: Brain structure and the Big Five. *Psychological Science, 21,* 820–828. (p. 581)

Diaconis, P. (2002, August 11). Quoted by L. Belkin, The odds of that. *New York Times* (www.nytimes.com). (p. 34)

Diaconis, P., & Mosteller, F. (1989). Methods for studying coincidences. *Journal of the American Statistical Association, 84,* 853–861. (p. 34)

Diamond, J. (2001, February). A tale of two reputations: Why we revere Darwin and give Freud a hard time. *Natural History,* pp. 20–24. (p. 137)

Diamond, L. (2008). *Sexual fluidity: Understanding women's love and desire.* Cambridge, MA: Harvard University Press. (p. 532)

Dias-Ferreira, E., Sousa, J. C., Melo, I., Morgado, P., Mesquita, A. R., Cerqueira, J. J., Costa, R. M., & Sousa, N. (2009). Chronic stress causes frontostriatal reorganization and affects decision-making. *Science, 325,* 621–625. (p. 445)

Diaz, F. J., Velásquez, D. M., Susce, M. T., & de Leon, J. (2008). The association between schizophrenia and smoking: Unexplained by either the illness or the prodromal period. *Schizophrenia Research, 104,* 214–219. (p. 686)

Dick, D. M. (2007). Identification of genes influencing a spectrum of externalizing psychopathology. *Current Directions in Psychological Science, 16,* 331–335. (pp. 633, 700)

Dickens, W. T., & Flynn, J. R. (2006). Black Americans reduce the racial IQ gap: Evidence from standardization samples. *Psychological Science, 17,* 913–920. (p. 639)

Dickerson, S. S., Gable, S. L., Irwin, M. R., Aziz, N., & Kemeny, M. E. (2009). Social-evaluative threat and proinflammatory cytokine regulation: An experimental laboratory investigation. *Psychological Science, 20,* 1237–1243. (p. 453)

Dickerson, S. S., & Kemeny, M. E. (2004). Acute stressors and cortisol responses: A theoretical integration and synthesis of laboratory research. *Psychological Bulletin, 130,* 355–391. (p. 299)

Dickinson, H. O., Parkinson, K. M., Ravens-Sieberer, U., Schirripa, G., Thyen, U., Arnaud, C., Beckung, E., Fauconnier, J., McManus, V., Michelsen, S. I., Parkes, J., & Colver, A. F. (2007). Self-reported quality of life of 8–12-year-old children with cerebral palsy: A cross-sectional European study. *Lancet, 369,* 2171–2178. (p. 848)

Dickson, B. J. (2005, June 3). Quoted in E. Rosenthal, For fruit flies, gene shift tilts sex orientation. *New York Times* (www.nytimes.com). (p. 534)

Diekelmann, S., & Born, J. (2010). The memory function of sleep. *Nature Neuroscience, 11,* 114–126. (p. 345)

Diener, E. (2006). Guidelines of national indicators of subjective well-being and ill-being. *Journal of Happiness Studies, 7,* 397–404. (p. 854)

Diener, E., & Biswas-Diener, R. (2002). Will money increase subjective well-being? A literature review and guide to needed research. *Social Indicators Research, 57,* 119–169. (p. 850)

Diener, E., & Biswas-Diener, R. (2009). *Rethinking happiness: The science of psychological wealth.* Malden, MA: Wiley Blackwell. (pp. 849, 850)

Diener, E., & Chan, M. (2011). Happy people live longer: Subjective well-being contributes to health and longevity. *Applied Psychology: Health and Well-Being, 3,* 1–43. (p. 453)

Diener, E., Lucas, R. E., & Scollon, C. N. (2006). Beyond the hedonic treadmill: Revising the adaptation theory of well-being. *American Psychologist, 61,* 305–314. (p. 848)

Diener, E., Ng, W., Harter, J., & Arora, R. (2009). Wealth and happiness across the world: Material prosperity predicts life evaluation, while psychosocial prosperity predicts positive feeling. Unpublished manuscript, University of Illinois and the Gallup Organization. (pp. 849, 850)

Diener, E., Nickerson, C., Lucas, R. E., & Sandvik, E. (2002). Dispositional affect and job outcomes. *Social Indicators Research, 59,* 229–259. (p. 847)

Diener, E., & Oishi, S. (2000). Money and happiness: Income and subjective well-being across nations. In E. Diener & E. M. Suh (Eds.), *Subjective well-being across cultures.* Cambridge, MA: MIT Press. (p. 851)

Diener, E., Oishi, S., & Lucas, R. E. (2003). Personality, culture, and subjective well-being: Emotional and cognitive evaluations of life. *Annual Review of Psychology, 54,* 403–425. (pp. 852, 853)

Diener, E., & Seligman, M. E. P. (2002). Very happy people. *Psychological Science, 13,* 81–84. (p. 412)

Diener, E., Tay, L., & Myers, D. G. (2011). The religion paradox: If religion makes people happy, why are so many dropping out? *Journal of Personality and Social Psychology, 101,* 1278–1290. (p. 42)

Diener, E., Wolsic, B., & Fujita, F. (1995). Physical attractiveness and subjective well-being. *Journal of Personality and Social Psychology, 69,* 120–129. (p. 800)

DiFranza, J. R. (2008, May). Hooked from the first cigarette. *Scientific American,* pp. 82–87. (p. 251)

Dijksterhuis, A., & Aarts, H. (2003). On wildebeests and humans: The preferential detection of negative stimuli. *Psychological Science, 14,* 14–18. (p. 432)

DiLalla, D. L., Carey, G., Gottesman, I. I., & Bouchard, T. J., Jr. (1996). Heritability of MMPI personality indicators of psychopathology in twins reared apart. *Journal of Abnormal Psychology, 105,* 491–499. (p. 675)

Dimberg, U., Thunberg, M., & Elmehed, K. (2000). Unconscious facial reactions to emotional facial expressions. *Psychological Science, 11,* 86–89. (pp. 424, 438)

Dimidjian, S., & Hollon, S. D. (2010). How would we know if psychotherapy were harmful? *American Psychologist, 65,* 21–33. (p. 732)

Dinges, N. G., & Hull, P. (1992). Personality, culture, and international studies. In D. Lieberman (Ed.), *Revealing the world: An interdisciplinary reader for international studies.* Dubuque, IA: Kendall-Hunt. (p. 379)

Dingfelder, S. F. (2010, November). A second chance for the Mexican wolf. *Monitor on Psychology,* pp. 20–21. (p. 294)

Dion, K. K., & Dion, K. L. (1993). Individualistic and collectivistic perspectives on gender and the cultural context of love and intimacy. *Journal of Social Issues, 49,* 53–69. (p. 600)

Dirix, C. E. H., Nijhuis, J. G., Jongsma, H. W., & Hornstra, G. (2009). Aspects of fetal learning and memory. *Child Development, 80,* 1251–1258. (p. 467)

DiSalvo, D. (2010, January/February). Are social networks messing with your head? *Scientific American Mind,* pp. 48–55. (p. 416)

Discover. (1996, May). A fistful of risks. Pp. 82–83. (p. 251)

Di Tella, R., & MacCulloch, R. (2010). Happiness adaptation to income beyond "basic needs." In E. Diener, J. Helliwell, & D. Kahneman (eds.), *International Differences in Well-Being,* pp. 217–247. New York: Oxford University Press. (pp. 850, 851)

Dixon, J., Durrheim, K., & Tredoux, C. (2007). Intergroup contact and attitudes toward the principle and practice of racial equality. *Psychological Science, 18,* 867–872. (p. 813)

Dobbs, D. (2009, April). The post-traumatic stress trap. *Scientific American,* pp. 64–69. (p. 665)

Dobel, C., Diesendruck, G., & Bölte, J. (2007). How writing system and age influence spatial representations of actions: A developmental, cross-linguistic study. *Psychological Science, 18,* 487–491. (p. 379)

Dodge, K. A. (2009). Mechanisms of gene-environment interaction effects in the development of conduct disorder. *Perspectives on Psychological Science, 4,* 408–414. (p. 700)

Dodman, N. H., Karlsson, E. K., Moon-Fanelli, A., Galdzicka, M., Perloski, M., Shuster, L., Lindblad-Toh, K., & Ginns, E. I. (2010). A canine chromosome 7 locus confers compulsive disorder susceptibility. *Molecular Psychiatry 15,* 8–10. (p. 668)

Doherty, E. W., & Doherty, W. J. (1998). Smoke gets in your eyes: Cigarette smoking and divorce in a national sample of American adults. *Families, Systems, and Health, 16,* 393–400. (p. 252)

Dohrenwend, B. P., Levav, I., Shrout, P. E., Schwartz, S., Naveh, G., Link, B. G., Skodol, A. E., & Stueve, A. (1992). Socioeconomic status and psychiatric disorders: The causation-selection issue. *Science, 255,* 946–952. (p. 658)

Dohrenwend, B. P., Pearlin, L., Clayton, P., Hamburg, B., Dohrenwend, B. P., Riley, M., & Rose, R. (1982). Report on stress and life events. In G. R. Elliott & C. Eisdorfer (Eds.), *Stress and human health: Analysis and implications of research* (A study by the Institute of Medicine/National Academy of Sciences). New York: Springer. (p. 443)

Dohrenwend, B. P., Turner, J. B., Turse, N. A., Adams, B. G., Koenen, K. C., & Marshall, R. (2006). The psychological risks of Vietnam for U.S. veterans: A revisit with new data and methods. *Science, 313,* 979–982. (p. 665)

Doidge, N. (2007). *The brain that changes itself.* New York: Viking. (p. 111)

Dolezal, H. (1982). *Living in a world transformed.* New York: Academic Press. (p. 191)

Domhoff, G. W. (1996). *Finding meaning in dreams: A quantitative approach.* New York: Plenum. (p. 240)

Domhoff, G. W. (2003). *The scientific study of dreams: Neural networks, cognitive development, and content analysis.* Washington, DC: APA Books. (pp. 241, 242)

Domhoff, G. W. (2007). Realistic simulations and bizarreness in dream content: Past findings and suggestions for future research. In D. Barrett & P. McNamara (Eds.), *The new science of dreaming: Content, recall, and personality characteristics.* Westport, CT: Praeger. (p. 240)

Domhoff, G. W. (2010). *The case for a cognitive theory of dreams.* Unpublished manuscript: University of California at Santa Cruz (dreamresearch.net/Library/domhoff_2010.html). (p. 243)

Domhoff, G. W. (2011). The neural substrate for dreaming: Is it a subsystem of the default network? *Consciousness and Cognition, 20*(4), 1163–74. (p. 243)

Domjan, M. (1992). Adult learning and mate choice: Possibilities and experimental evidence. *American Zoologist, 32,* 48–61. (p. 268)

Domjan, M. (1994). Formulation of a behavior system for sexual conditioning. *Psychonomic Bulletin & Review, 1,* 421–428. (p. 268)

Domjan, M. (2005). Pavlovian conditioning: A functional perspective. *Annual Review of Psychology, 56.* (pp. 268, 294)

Domjan, M., Cusato, B., & Krause, M. (2004). Learning with arbitrary versus ecological conditioned stimuli: Evidence from sexual conditioning. *Psychonomic Bulletin & Review, 11,* 232–246. (p. 294)

Donlea, J. M., Ramanan, N., & Shaw, P. J. (2009). Use-dependent plasticity in clock neurons regulates sleep need in *Drosophila. Science, 324,* 105–108. (p. 229)

Donnellan, M. B., Conger, R. D., & Bryant, C. M. (2004). The Big Five and enduring marriages. *Journal of Research in Personality, 38,* 481–504. (p. 581)

Donnellan, M. B., Trzesniewski, K. H., Robins, R. W., Moffitt, T. E., & Caspi, A. (2005). Low self-esteem is related to aggression, antisocial behavior, and delinquency. *Psychological Science, 16,* 328–335. (p. 588)

Donnerstein, E. (1998). Why do we have those new ratings on television. Invited address to the National Institute on the Teaching of Psychology. (pp. 308, 309)

Donnerstein, E. (2011). The media and aggression: From TV to the Internet. In J. Forgas, A. Kruglanski, & K. Williams (eds.), *The psychology of social conflict and aggression.* New York: Psychology Press. (pp. 308, 309)

Donnerstein, E., Linz, D., & Penrod, S. (1987). *The question of pornography.* New York: Free Press. (p. 309)

Donvan, J., & Zucker, C. (2010, October). Autism's first child. *The Atlantic* (www.theatlantic.com). (p. 481)

D'Orlando, F. (2011). The demand for pornography. *Journal of Happiness Studies, 12,* 51–75. (p. 793)

Doss, B. D., Rhoades, G. K., Stanley, S. M., & Markman, H. J. (2009). The effect of the transition to parenthood on relationship quality: An 8-year prospective study. *Journal of Personality and Social Psychology, 96,* 601–619. (p. 545)

Dotan-Eliaz, O., Sommer, K. L., & Rubin, S. (2009). Multilingual groups: Effects of linguistic ostracism on felt rejection and anger, coworker attraction, perceived team potency, and creative performance. *Basic and Applied Social Psychology, 31,* 363–375. (p. 414)

Douglas, K. S., Guy, L. S., & Hart, S. D. (2009). Psychosis as a risk factor for violence to others: A meta-analysis. *Psychological Bulletin, 135,* 679–706. (p. 656)

Douthat, R. (2010, November 28). The partisan mind. *New York Times* (www.nytimes.com). (p. 785)

Dovidio, J. F., & Gaertner, S. L. (1999). Reducing prejudice: Combating intergroup biases. *Current Directions in Psychological Science, 8,* 101–105. (p. 813)

Dovidio, J. F., ten Vergert, M., Stewart, T. L., Gaertner, S. L., Johnson, J. D., Esses, V. M., Riek, B. M., & Pearson, A. R. (2004). Perspective and prejudice: Antecedents and mediating mechanisms. *Personality and Social Psychology Bulletin, 30,* 1537–1549. (p. 814)

Dowlati, Y., Herrmann, N., Swardfager, W., Liu, H., Sham, L., Reim, E. K., & Lanctôt, K. (2010). A meta-analysis of cytokines in major depression. *Biological Psychiatry, 67,* 466–457. (p. 679)

Downing, P. E., Jiang, Y., & Shuman, M. (2001). A cortical area selective for visual processing of the human body. *Science, 293,* 2470–2473. (p. 176)

Downs, E., & Smith, S. L. (2010). Keeping abreast of hypersexuality: A video game character content analysis. *Sex Roles, 62,* 721–733. (p. 531)

Draguns, J. G. (1990). Normal and abnormal behavior in cross-cultural perspective: Specifying the nature of their relationship. *Nebraska Symposium on Motivation 1989, 37,* 235–277. (p. 680)

Drake, R. A., & Myers, L. R. (2006). Visual attention, emotion, and action tendency: Feeling active or passive. *Cognition and Emotion, 20,* 608–622. (p. 427)

Driessen, E., Cuijpers, P., de Maat, S. C. M., Abbas, A. A., de Jonghe, F., & Dekker, J. J. M. (2010). The efficacy of short-term psychodynamic psychotherapy for depression: A meta-analysis. *Clinical Psychology Review, 30,* 25–36. (p. 732)

Druckman, D., & Bjork, R. A. (1991). *In the mind's eye: Enhancing human performance.* National Academy Press: Washington, DC. (p. 577)

Druckman, D., & Bjork, R. A. (Eds.) (1994). *Learning, remembering, believing: Enhancing human performance.* Washington, DC: National Academy Press. (pp. 220, 221)

Drummond, S. (2010). Relationship between changes in sleep and memory in older adults. Presentation at AAAS 2010 Annual Meeting, University of California, San Diego, CA. (p. 231)

Duckworth, A. L., Quinn, P. D., Lynam, D. R., Loeber, R., & Stouthamer-Loeber, M. (2011). Role of test motivation in intelligence testing. *PNAS, 108,* 7716–7720. (p. 635)

Duckworth, A. L., Quinn, P. D., & Seligman, M. E. P. (2009). Positive predictors of teacher effectiveness. *Journal of Positive Psychology, 4,* 540–547. (p. 834)

Duckworth, A. L., & Seligman, M. E. P. (2005). Discipline outdoes talent: Self-discipline predicts academic performance in adolescents. *Psychological Science, 12,* 939–944. (p. 834)

Duckworth, A. L., & Seligman, M. E. P. (2006). Self-discipline gives girls the edge: Gender in self-discipline, grades, and achievement tests. *Journal of Educational Psychology, 98,* 198–208. (p. 834)

Duclos, S. E., Laird, J. D., Sexter, M., Stern, L., & Van Lighten, O. (1989). Emotion-specific effects of facial expressions and postures on emotional experience. *Journal of Personality and Social Psychology, 57,* 100–108. (p. 437)

Duffy, M. (2003, June 9). Weapons of mass disappearance. *Time,* pp. 28–33. (p. 759)

Dugatkin, L. A. (2002, Winter). Watching culture shape even guppy love. *Cerebrum,* pp. 51–66. (p. 305)

Duggan, J. P., & Booth, D. A. (1986). Obesity, overeating, and rapid gastric emptying in rats with ventromedial hypothalamic lesions. *Science, 231,* 609–611. (p. 398)

Dukakis, K. (2006). *Shock: The healing power of electroconvulsive therapy.* Avery Press. (p. 744)

Dumont, K. A., Widom, C. S., Czaja, S. J. (2007). Predictors of resilience in abused and neglected children grown-up: The role of individual and neighborhood characteristics. *Child Abuse & Neglect, 31,* 255–274. (p. 493)

Dunbar, R. I. M. (1992, June). Neocortex size as a constraint on group size in primates. *Journal of Human Evolution, 22,* 469–493. (p. 418)

Dunbar, R. I. M. (2010, December 25). You've got to have (150) friends. *New York Times* (www.nytimes.com). (p. 418)

Duncan, J. (2000, July 21). Quoted by N. Angier, Study finds region of brain may be key problem solver. *New York Times* (www.ny times.com). (p. 613)

Duncan, J., Seitz, R. J., Kolodny, J., Bor, D., Herzog, H., Ahmed, A., Newell, F. N., & Emslie, H. (2000). A neural basis of general intelligence. *Science, 289,* 457–460. (p. 613)

Dunn, E. W., Aknin, L. B., & Norton, M. I. (2008). Spending money on others promotes happiness. *Science, 319,* 1687–1688. (p. 809)

Dunn, M., & Searle, R. (2010). Effect of manipulated prestige-car ownership on both sex attractiveness ratings. *British Journal of Psychology, 101,* 69–80. (p. 138)

Dunning, D. (2006). Strangers to ourselves? *The Psychologist, 19,* 600–603. (p. 591)

Dunson, D. B., Colombo, B., & Baird, D. D. (2002). Changes with age in the level and duration of fertility in the menstrual cycle. *Human Reproduction, 17,* 1399–1403. (p. 540)

Durrheim, K., & Dixon, J. (2010). Racial contact and change in South Africa. *Journal of Social Issues, 66,* 273–288. (p. 813)

Dutton, D. G., & Aron, A. P. (1974). Some evidence for heightened sexual attraction under conditions of high anxiety. *Journal of Personality and Social Psychology, 30,* 510–517. (p. 803)

Dutton, D. G., & Aron, A. P. (1989). Romantic attraction and generalized liking for others who are sources of conflict-based arousal. *Canadian Journal of Behavioural Sciences, 21,* 246–257. (p. 803)

Dweck, C. S. (2006). *Mindset: The new psychology of success.* New York: Random House. (p. 635)

Dweck, C. S. (2007, November 28). The secret to raising smart kids. *Scientific American Mind,* pp. 36–43 (http://www.sciam.com). (p. 635)

Dweck, C. S. (2008). Can personality be changed? The role of beliefs in personality and change. *Current Directions in Psychological Science, 17,* 391–394. (p. 635)

Dye, M. W. G., Green, C. S., & Bavelier, D. (2009). Increasing speed of processing with action video games. *Current Directions in Psychological Science, 18,* 321–326. (p. 795)

Dyrdal, G. M., & Lucas, R. E. (2011). Reaction and adaptation to the birth of a child: A couple level analysis. Unpublished manuscript, Michigan State University. (p. 543)

Eagly, A. H. (1994). Are people prejudiced against women? Donald Campbell Award invited address, American Psychological Association convention. (p. 783)

Eagly, A. H. (2007). Female leadership advantage and disadvantage: Resolving the contradictions. *Psychology of Women Quarterly, 31,* 1–12. (p. 839)

Eagly, A. H. (2009). The his and hers of prosocial behavior: An examination of the social psychology of gender. *American Psychologist, 64,* 644–658. (pp. 139, 503)

Eagly, A. H., Ashmore, R. D., Makhijani, M. G., & Kennedy, L. C. (1991). What is beautiful is good, but . . .: A meta-analytic review of research on the physical attractiveness stereotype. *Psychological Bulletin, 110,* 109–128. (p. 800)

Eagly, A. H., & Carli, L. (2007). *Through the labyrinth: The truth about how women become leaders.* Cambridge, MA: Harvard University Press. (p. 502)

Eagly, A. H., & Wood, W. (1999). The origins of sex differences in human behavior: Evolved dispositions versus social roles. *American Psychologist, 54,* 408–423. (p. 139)

Eastman, C. L., Boulos, Z., Terman, M., Campbell, S. S., Dijk, D-J., & Lewy, A. J. (1995). Light treatment for sleep disorders: Consensus report. VI. Shift work. *Journal of Biological Rhythms, 10,* 157–164. (p. 230)

Eastman, C. L., Young, M. A., Fogg, L. F., Liu, L., & Meaden, P. M. (1998). Bright light treatment of winter depression: A placebo-controlled trial. *Archives of General Psychiatry, 55,* 883–889. (p. 734)

Eastwick, P. W. (2009). Beyond the Pleistocene: Using phylogeny and constraint to inform the evolutionary psychology of human mating. *Psychological Bulletin, 135,* 794–821. (p. 408)

Eastwick, P. W., & Finkel, E. J. (2008a). Speed-dating as a methodological innovation. *The Psychologist, 21,* 402–403. (p. 799)

Eastwick, P. W., & Finkel, E. J. (2008b). Sex differences in mate preferences revisited: Do people know what they initially desire in a romantic partner? *Journal of Personality and Social Psychology, 94,* 245–264. (p. 799)

Ebbesen, E. B., Duncan, B., & Konecni, V. J. (1975). Effects of content of verbal aggression on future verbal aggression: A field experiment. *Journal of Experimental Social Psychology, 11,* 192–204. (p. 846)

Ebbinghaus, H. (1885). Über das Gedächtnis. Leipzig: Duncker & Humblot. Cited in R. Klatzky, (1980), *Human memory: Structures and processes.* San Francisco: Freeman. (p. 343)

Ebbinghaus, H. (1885/1964). *Memory: A contribution to experimental psychology* (H. A. Ruger & C. E. Bussenius, Trans.). New York: Dover. (p. 324)

Ebel-Lam, A. P., MacDonald, T. K., Zanna, M. P., & Fong, G. T. (2009). An experimental investigation of the interactive effects of alcohol and sexual arousal on intentions to have unprotected sex. *Basic and Applied Social Psychology, 31,* 226–233. (p. 249)

Eberhardt, J. L. (2005). Imaging race. *American Psychologist, 60,* 181–190. (p. 782)

Eccles, J. S., Jacobs, J. E., & Harold, R. D. (1990). Gender role stereotypes, expectancy effects, and parents' socialization of gender differences. *Journal of Social Issues, 46,* 183–201. (p. 639)

Eckensberger, L. H. (1994). Moral development and its measurement across cultures. In W. J. Lonner & R. Malpass (Eds.), *Psychology and culture.* Boston: Allyn and Bacon. (p. 516)

Ecker, C., & 10 others. (2010). Describing the brain in autism in five dimensions—Magnetic resonance imaging-assisted diagnosis of autism spectrum disorder using a multiparameter classification approach. *Journal of Neuroscience, 30,* 10612–10623. (p. 482)

Eckert, E. D., Heston, L. L., & Bouchard, T. J., Jr. (1981). MZ twins reared apart: Preliminary findings of psychiatric disturbances and traits. In L. Gedda, P. Paris, & W. D. Nance (Eds.), *Twin research: Vol. 3. Pt. B. Intelligence, personality, and development.* New York: Alan Liss. (p. 668)

Eckholm, E. (2010, September 21). Woman on death row runs out of appeals. *New York Times* (www.nytimes.com). (p. 629)

Ecklund-Flores, L. (1992). The infant as a model for the teaching of introductory psychology. Paper presented to the American Psychological Association annual convention. (p. 466)

Economist. (2001, December 20). An anthropology of happiness. *The Economist* (www.economist.com/world/asia). (p. 413)

Edwards, R. R., Campbell, C., Jamison, R. N., & Wiech, K. (2009). The neurobiological underpinnings of coping with pain. *Current Directions in Psychological Science, 18,* 237–241. (p. 206)

Eibl-Eibesfeldt, I. (1971). *Love and hate: The natural history of behavior patterns.* New York: Holt, Rinehart & Winston. (p. 436)

Eich, E. (1990). Learning during sleep. In R. B. Bootzin, J. F. Kihlstrom, & D. L. Schacter (Eds.), *Sleep and cognition.* Washington, DC: American Psychological Association. (p. 241)

Ein-Dor, T., Mikulincer, M., Doron, G., & Shaver, P. R. (2010). The attachment paradox: How can so many of us (the insecure ones) have no adaptive advantages? *Perspectives on Psychological Science, 5,* 123–141. (p. 492)

Eippert, F., Finsterbush, J., Bingel, U., & Büchel, C. (2009). Direct evidence for spinal cord involvement in placebo analgesia. *Science, 326,* 404. (p. 206)

Eisenberg, N., & Lennon, R. (1983). Sex differences in empathy and related capacities. *Psychological Bulletin, 94,* 100–131. (p. 435)

Eisenberger, N. I., Master, S. L., Inagaki, T. K., Taylor, S. E., Shirinyan, D., Lieberman, M. D., & Nalifoff, B. D. (2011). Attachment figures activate a safety signal-related neural region and reduce pain experience. *Proceedings of the National Academy of Sciences, 108,* 11721–11726. (p. 413)

Eisenberger, R., & Aselage, J. (2009). Incremental effects of reward on experienced performance pressure: Positive outcomes for intrinsic interest and creativity. *Journal of Organizational Behavior, 30,* 95–117. (p. 298)

Ekman, P. (1994). Strong evidence for universals in facial expressions: A reply to Russell's mistaken critique. *Psychological Bulletin, 115,* 268–287. (p. 435)

Ekman, P. (2003). *Emotions revealed: Recognizing faces and feelings to improve communication and emotional life.* New York: Times Books. (p. 428)

Ekman, P., & Friesen, W. V. (1975). *Unmasking the face.* Englewood Cliffs, NJ: Prentice-Hall. (p. 435)

Ekman, P., Friesen, W. V., O'Sullivan, M., Chan, A., Diacoyanni-Tarlatzis, I., Heider, K., Krause, R., LeCompte, W. A., Pitcairn, T., Ricci-Bitti, P. E.,

Scherer, K., Tomita, M., & Tzavaras, A. (1987). Universals and cultural differences in the judgments of facial expressions of emotion. *Journal of Personality and Social Psychology, 53,* 712–717. (p. 435)

Elbert, T., Pantev, C., Wienbruch, C., Rockstroh, B., & Taub, E. (1995). Increased cortical representation of the fingers of the left hand in string players. *Science, 270,* 305–307. (p. 508)

Elbogen, E. B., & Johnson, S. C. (2009). The intricate link between violence and mental disorder: Results from the National Epidemiologic Survey on Alcohol and Related Conditions. *Archives of General Psychiatry, 66,* 152–161. (p. 656)

Elfenbein, H. A., & Ambady, N. (1999). *Does it take one to know one? A meta-analysis of the universality and cultural specificity of emotion recognition.* Unpublished manuscript, Harvard University. (p. 436)

Elfenbein, H. A., & Ambady, N. (2002). On the universality and cultural specificity of emotion recognition: A meta-analysis. *Psychological Bulletin, 128,* 203–235. (p. 436)

Elfenbein, H. A., & Ambady, N. (2003a). Universals and cultural differences in recognizing emotions. *Current Directions in Psychological Science, 12,* 159–164. (p. 436)

Elfenbein, H. A., & Ambady, N. (2003b). When familiarity breeds accuracy: Cultural exposure and facial emotion recognition. *Journal of Personality and Social Psychology, 85,* 276–290. (p. 436)

Elkind, D. (1970). The origins of religion in the child. *Review of Religious Research, 12,* 35–42. (p. 515)

Elkind, D. (1978). *The child's reality: Three developmental themes.* Hillsdale, NJ: Erlbaum. (p. 514)

Ellenbogen, J. M., Hu, P. T., Payne, J. D., Titone, D., & Walker, M. P. (2007). Human relational memory requires time and sleep. *Proceedings of the National Academy of Sciences, 104,* 7723–7728. (p. 231)

Ellin, A. (2009, February 12). The recession. Isn't it romantic? *New York Times* (www.nytimes.com). (p. 799)

Elliot, A. J., Kayser, D. N., Greitemeyer, T., Lichtenfeld, S., Gramzow, R. H., Maier, M. A., & Liu, H. (2010). Red, rank, and romance in women viewing men. *Journal of Experimental Psychology: General, 139,* 399–417. (p. 294)

Elliot, A. J., & McGregor, H. A. (2001). A 2x2 achievement goal framework. *Journal of Personality and Social Psychology, 80,* 501–519. (p. 838)

Elliot, A. J., & Niesta, D. (2008). Romantic red: Red enhances men's attraction to women. *Journal of Personality and Social Psychology, 95,* 1150–1164. (p. 294)

Elliot, A. J., & Reis, H. T. (2003). Attachment and exploration in adulthood. *Journal of Personality and Social Psychology, 85,* 317–331. (p. 492)

Ellis, A. (1962). *Reason and emotion in psychotherapy.* Secaucus, NJ: Citadel Press. (p. 721)

Ellis, A. (1980). Psychotherapy and atheistic values: A response to A. E. Bergin's "Psychotherapy and religious values." *Journal of Consulting and Clinical Psychology, 48,* 635–639. (p. 736)

Ellis, A. (1987). The impossibility of achieving consistently good mental health. *American Psychologist, 42,* 364–375. (p. 721)

Ellis, A. (1993). Changing rational-emotive therapy (RET) to rational emotive behavior therapy (REBT). *The Behavior Therapist, 16,* 257–258. (p. 721)

Ellis, A. (2011). Rational emotive behavior therapy. In R. J. Corsini & D. Wedding (Eds.). *Current psychotherapies.* Belmont, CA: Brooks Cole. (p. 721)

Ellis, A., & Becker, I. M. (1982). *A guide to personal happiness.* North Hollywood, CA: Wilshire Book Co. (p. 272)

Ellis, B. J. (2004). Timing of pubertal maturation in girls: An integrated life history approach. *Psychological Bulletin, 130,* 920–958. (p. 523)

Ellis, B. J., Bates, J. E., Dodge, K. A., Fergusson, D. M., John, H. L., Pettit, G. S., & Woodward, L. (2003). Does father absence place daughters at special risk for early sexual activity and teenage pregnancy? *Child Development, 74,* 801–821. (p. 531)

Ellis, B. J., & Boyce, W. T. (2008). Biological sensitivity to context. *Current Directions in Psychological Science, 17,* 183–187. (p. 667)

Ellis, L., & Ames, M. A. (1987). Neurohormonal functioning and sexual orientation: A theory of homosexuality-heterosexuality. *Psychological Bulletin, 101,* 233–258. (p. 535)

Ellis, L., Hershberger, S., Field, E., Wersinger, S., Pellis, S., Geary, D., Palmer, C., Hovenga, K., Hetsroni, A., & Karadi, K. (2008). *Sex differences: Summarizing more than a century of scientific research.* New York: Psychology Press. (p. 500)

Ellison-Wright, I., Glahn, D. C., Laird, A. R., Thelen, S. M., & Bullmore, E. (2008). The anatomy of first-episode and chronic schizophrenia: An anatomical likelihood estimation meta-analysis. *American Journal of Psychiatry, 165,* 1015–1023. (p. 687)

Else-Quest, N. M., Hyde, J. S., & Linn, M. C. (2010). Cross-national patterns of gender differences in mathematics: A meta-analysis. *Psychological Bulletin, 136,* 103–127. (p. 638)

Elzinga, B. M., Ardon, A. M., Heijnis, M. K., De Ruiter, M. B., Van Dyck, R., & Veltman, D. J. (2007). Neural correlates of enhanced working-memory performance in dissociative disorder: A functional MRI study. *Psychological Medicine, 37,* 235–245. (p. 696)

EMDR. (2011, February 18). E-mail correspondence from Robbie Dunton, EMDR Institute (www.emdr.org). (p. 733)

Emerging Trends. (1997, September). *Teens turn more to parents than friends on whether to attend church.* Princeton, NJ: Princeton Religion Research Center. (p. 522)

Emery, G., Jr. (2004). *Psychic predictions 2004.* Committee for the Scientific Investigation of Claims of the Paranormal (www.csicop.org). (p. 167)

Emery, G., Jr. (2006, January 17). Psychic predictions 2005. *Skeptical Inquirer* (www.csicop.org). (p. 167)

Emmons, R. A. (2007). *Thanks! How the new science of gratitude can make you happier.* Boston: Houghton Mifflin. (p. 853)

Emmons, S., Geisler, C., Kaplan, K. J., & Harrow, M. (1997). *Living with schizophrenia.* Muncie, IN: Taylor and Francis (Accelerated Development). (pp. 649, 685)

Emmorey, K., Luk, G., Pyers, J. E., & Bialystok, E. (2008). The source of enhanced cognitive control in bilinguals. *Psychological Science, 19,* 1201–1206. (p. 380)

Empson, J. A. C., & Clarke, P. R. F. (1970). Rapid eye movements and remembering. *Nature, 227,* 287–288. (p. 241)

Endler, N. S. (1982). *Holiday of darkness: A psychologist's personal journey out of his depression.* New York: Wiley. (pp. 679, 744)

Engdahl, B., Leuthold, A. C., Tan, H-R. M., Lewis, S. M., Winskowski, A. M., & Georgopoulos, A. P. (2010). Post-traumatic stress disorder: A right temporal lobe syndrome? *Journal of Neural Engineering, 7,* 066005. (p. 665)

Engemann, K. M., & Owyang, M. T. (2005, April). So much for that merit raise: The link between wages and appearance. *Regional Economist* (www.stlouisfed.org). (p. 800)

Engen, T. (1987). Remembering odors and their names. *American Scientist, 75,* 497–503. (p. 209)

Engle, R. W. (2002). Working memory capacity as executive attention. *Current Directions in Psychological Science, 11,* 19–23. (p. 319)

Epel, E. S. (2009). Telomeres in a life-span perspective: A new"psychobiomarker"? *Current Directions in Psychological Science, 18,* 6–9. (p. 542)

Epel, E. S., Blackburn, E. H., Lin, J., Dhabhar, F. S., Adler, N. E., Morrow, J. D., & Cawthon, R. M. (2004). Accelerated telomere shortening in response to life stress. *Proceedings of the National Academy of Sciences, 101,* 17312–17315. (p. 445)

Epley, N., & Dunning, D. (2000). Feeling "holier than thou": Are self-serving assessments produced by errors in self- or social prediction? *Journal of Personality and Social Psychology, 79,* 861–875. (p. 596)

Epley, N., Keysar, B., Van Boven, L., & Gilovich, T. (2004). Perspective taking as egocentric anchoring and adjustment. *Journal of Personality and Social Psychology, 87,* 327–339. (p. 480)

Epstein, J., Stern, E., & Silbersweig, D. (1998). Mesolimbic activity associated with psychosis in schizophrenia: Symptom-specific PET studies. In J. F. McGinty (Ed.), *Advancing from the ventral striatum to the extended amygdala: Implications for neuropsychiatry and drug use.* In honor of Lennart Heimer. *Annals of the New York Academy of Sciences, 877,* 562–574. (p. 687)

Epstein, S. (1983a). Aggregation and beyond: Some basic issues on the prediction of behavior. *Journal of Personality, 51,* 360–392. (p. 583)

Epstein, S. (1983b). The stability of behavior across time and situations. In R. Zucker, J. Aronoff, & A. I. Rabin (Eds.), *Personality and the prediction of behavior.* San Diego, CA: Academic Press. (p. 583)

Epstein, S., & Meier, P. (1989). Constructive thinking: A broad coping variable with specific components. *Journal of Personality and Social Psychology, 57,* 332–350. (p. 612)

Erdberg, P. (1990). Rorschach assessment. In G. Goldstein & M. Hersen (Eds.), *Handbook of psychological assessment,* 2nd ed. New York: Pergamon. (p. 567)

Erdelyi, M. H. (1985). *Psychoanalysis: Freud's cognitive psychology*. New York: Freeman. (p. 568)

Erdelyi, M. H. (1988). Repression, reconstruction, and defense: History and integration of the psychoanalytic and experimental frameworks. In J. Singer (Ed.), *Repression: Defense mechanism and cognitive style*. Chicago: University of Chicago Press. (p. 568)

Erdelyi, M. H. (2006). The unified theory of repression. *Behavioral and Brain Sciences, 29*, 499–551. (pp. 562, 563, 568)

Erel, O., & Burman, B. (1995). Interrelatedness of marital relations and parent-child relations: A meta-analytic review. *Psychological Bulletin, 118*, 108–132. (p. 545)

Erickson, K. I. (2009). Aerobic fitness is associated with hippocampal volume in elderly humans. *Hippocampus, 19*, 1030–1039. (p. 542)

Erickson, K. I., & 9 others. (2010). Physical activity predicts gray matter volume in late adulthood: The Cardiovascular Health Study. *Neurology, 75*, 1415–1422. (p. 540)

Erickson, M. F., & Aird, E. G. (2005). *The motherhood study: Fresh insights on mothers' attitudes and concerns*. New York: The Motherhood Project, Institute for American Values. (p. 545)

Ericsson, K. A. (2001). Attaining excellence through deliberate practice: Insights from the study of expert performance. In M. Ferrari (Ed.), *The pursuit of excellence in education*. Hillsdale, NJ: Erlbaum. (p. 834)

Ericsson, K. A. (2002). Attaining excellence through deliberate practice: Insights from the study of expert performance. In C. Desforges & R. Fox (Eds.), *Teaching and learning: The essential readings*. Malden, MA: Blackwell Publishers. (p. 611)

Ericsson, K. A. (2006). The influence of experience and deliberate practice on the development of superior expert performance. In K. A. Ericsson, N. Charness, P. J. Feltovich, & R. R. Hoffman (Eds.), *The Cambridge handbook of expertise and expert performance*. Cambridge: Cambridge University Press. (p. 834)

Ericsson, K. A. (2007). Deliberate practice and the modifiability of body and mind: Toward a science of the structure and acquisition of expert and elite performance. *International Journal of Sport Psychology, 38*, 4–34. (pp. 611, 635, 834)

Ericsson, K. A., Krampe, R. T., & Tesch-Römer, C. (1993). The role of deliberate practice in the acquisition of expert performance. *Psychological Review, 100*, 363–406. (p. 231)

Ericsson, K. A., Roring, R. W., & Nandagopal, K. (2007). Giftedness and evidence for reproducibly superior performance: An account based on the expert performance framework. *High Ability Studies, 18*, 3–56. (p. 611)

Erikson, E. H. (1963). *Childhood and society*. New York: Norton. (p. 519)

Erikson, E. H. (1983, June). A conversation with Erikson (by E. Hall). *Psychology Today*, 22–30. (p. 492)

Ertmer, D. J., Young, N. M., & Nathani, S. (2007). Profiles of focal development in young cochlear implant recipients. *Journal of Speech, Language, and Hearing Research, 50*, 393–407. (p. 375)

Escobar-Chaves, S. L., Tortolero, S., Markham, C., Low, B., Eitel, P., Thickstun, P. (2005). Impact of the media on adolescent attitudes and behaviors. *Pediatrics, 116*, 303–326. (p. 530)

Escobedo, J. R., & Adolphs, R. (2010). Becoming a better person: Temporal remoteness biases autobiographical memories for moral events. *Emotion, 10*, 511–518. (p. 598)

Eskine, K. J., Kacinik, N. A., & Prinz, J. J. (2011). A bad taste in the mouth: Gustatory disgust influences moral judgment. *Psychological Science, 22*, 295–299. (p. 516)

ESPAD. (2003). *Summary of the 2003 findings*. European School Survey Project on Alcohol and Other Drugs. (www.espad.org). (p. 824)

Esser, J. K., & Lindoerfer, J. S. (1989). Groupthink and the space shuttle *Challenger* accident: Toward a quantitative case analysis. *Journal of Behavioral Decision Making, 2*, 167–177. (p. 775)

Esterson, A. (2001). The mythologizing of psychoanalytic history: Deception and self-deception in Freud's accounts of the seduction theory episode. *History of Psychiatry, 12*, 329–352. (p. 561)

Etkin, A., & Wager, T. D. (2007). Functional neuroimaging of anxiety: A meta-analysis of emotional processing in PTSD, social anxiety disorder, and specific phobia. *American Journal of Psychiatry, 164*, 1476–1488. (p. 668)

Eurich, T. L., Krause, D. E., Cigularov, K., & Thornton, G. C., III (2009). Assessment centers: Current practices in the United States. *Journal of Business Psychology, 24*, 387–407. (p. 592)

Euston, D. R., Tatsuno, M., & McNaughton, B. L. (2007). Fast-forward playback of recent memory sequences in prefrontal cortex during sleep. *Science, 318*, 1147–1150. (p. 331)

Evans, C. R., & Dion, K. L. (1991). Group cohesion and performance: A meta-analysis. *Small Group Research, 22*, 175–186. (p. 838)

Evans, G. W., Palsane, M. N., & Carrere, S. (1987). Type A behavior and occupational stress: A cross-cultural study of blue-collar workers. *Journal of Personality and Social Psychology, 52*, 1002–1007. (p. 452)

Evans, N., & Levinson, S. C. (2009). The myth of language universals: Language diversity and its importance for cognitive science. *Behavioral and Brain Sciences, 32*, 429–492. (p. 375)

Everson, S. A., Goldberg, D. E., Kaplan, G. A., Cohen, R. D., Pukkala, E., Tuomilehto, J., & Salonen, J. T. (1996). Hopelessness and risk of mortality and incidence of myocardial infarction and cancer. *Psychosomatic Medicine, 58*, 113–121. (p. 857)

Exner, J. E. (2003). *The Rorschach: A comprehensive system*, 4th edition. Hoboken, NJ: Wiley. (p. 567)

Eysenck, H. J. (1952). The effects of psychotherapy: An evaluation. *Journal of Consulting Psychology, 16*, 319–324. (p. 730)

Eysenck, H. J. (1990, April 30). An improvement on personality inventory. *Current Contents: Social and Behavioral Sciences, 22*(18), 20. (p. 577)

Eysenck, H. J. (1992). Four ways five factors are *not* basic. *Personality and Individual Differences, 13*, 667–673. (p. 577)

Eysenck, H. J., & Grossarth-Maticek, R. (1991). Creative novation behaviour therapy as a prophylactic treatment for cancer and coronary heart disease: Part II—Effects of treatment. *Behaviour Research and Therapy, 29*, 17–31. (p. 861)

Eysenck, H. J., Wakefield, J. A., Jr., & Friedman, A. F. (1983). Diagnosis and clinical assessment: The DSM-III. *Annual Review of Psychology, 34*, 167–193. (p. 655)

Eysenck, M. W., MacLeod, C., & Mathews, A. (1987). Cognitive functioning and anxiety. *Psychological Research, 49*, 189–195. (p. 588)

Eysenck, S. B. G., & Eysenck, H. J. (1963). The validity of questionnaire and rating assessments of extraversion and neuroticism, and their factorial stability. *British Journal of Psychology, 54*, 51–62. (p. 577)

Faber, N. (1987, July). Personal glimpse. *Reader's Digest*, p. 34. (p. 357)

Fabiano, G. A., Pelham, W. E., Jr., Coles, E. K., Gnagy, E. M., Chronis-Tuscano, A., & O'Connor, B. C. (2008). A meta-analysis of behavioral treatments for attention-deficit/hyperactivity disorder. *Clinical Psychology Review, 29*, 129–140. (p. 652)

Fagan, J. F., & Holland, C. R. (2007). Equal opportunity and racial differences in IQ. *Intelligence, 30*, 361–387. (pp. 641, 642)

Fagan, J. F., & Holland, C. R. (2009). Culture-fair prediction of academic achievement. *Intelligence, 37*, 62–67. (p. 642)

Falk, C. F., Heine, S. J., Yuki, M., & Takemura, K. (2009). Why do Westerners self-enhance more than East Asians? *European Journal of Personality, 23*, 183–203. (p. 596)

Falk, R., Falk, R., & Ayton, P. (2009). Subjective patterns of randomness and choice: Some consequences of collective responses. *Journal of Experimental Psychology: Human Perception and Performance, 35*, 203–224. (p. 33)

Fanti, K. A., Vanman, E., Henrich, C. C., & Avraamides, M. N. (2009). Desensitization to media violence over a short period of time. *Aggressive Behavior, 35*, 179–187. (p. 309)

Farah, M. J., Rabinowitz, C., Quinn, G. E., & Liu, G. T. (2000). Early commitment of neural substrates for face recognition. *Cognitive Neuropsychology, 17*, 117–124. (p. 111)

Farina, A. (1982). The stigma of mental disorders. In A. G. Miller (Ed.), *In the eye of the beholder*. New York: Praeger. (pp. 652, 655)

Farley, M., Baral, I., Kiremire, M., & Sezgin, U. (1998). Prostitution in five countries: Violence and post-traumatic stress disorder. *Feminism and Psychology, 8*, 405–426. (p. 664)

Farrington, D. P. (1991). Antisocial personality from childhood to adulthood. *The Psychologist: Bulletin of the British Psychological Society, 4*, 389–394. (p. 699)

Fatemi, S. H., & Folsom, T. D. (2009). The neurodevelopmental hypothesis of schizophrenia, revisited. *Schizophrenia Bulletin, 35*, 528–548. (p. 687)

Fazel, S., Langstrom, N., Hjern, A., Grann, M., & Lichtenstein, P. (2009). Schizophrenia, substance abuse, and violent crime. *Journal of the American Medical Association,, 301*, 2016–2023. (p. 656)

Fazel, S., Lichtenstein, P., Grann, M., Goodwin, G. M., & Långström, N. (2010). bipolar disorder and violent crime: new evidence from population-based longitudinal studies and systematic review. *Archives of General Psychiatry, 67,* 931–938. (p. 656)

FBI. (2009). *Uniform Crime Reports.* Table 3. Washington, DC: Federal Bureau of Investigation. (p. 501)

Feder, H. H. (1984). Hormones and sexual behavior. *Annual Review of Psychology, 35,* 165–200. (p. 408)

Feeney, D. M. (1987). Human rights and animal welfare. *American Psychologist, 42,* 593–599. (p. 66)

Feeney, J. A., & Noller, P. (1990). Attachment style as a predictor of adult romantic relationships. *Journal of Personality and Social Psychology, 58, 281–291.* (p. 492)

Feigenson, L., Carey, S., & Spelke, E. (2002). Infants' discrimination of number vs. continuous extent. *Cognitive Psychology, 44,* 33–66. (p. 478)

Feingold, A. (1990). Gender differences in effects of physical attractiveness on romantic attraction: A comparison across five research paradigms. *Journal of Personality and Social Psychology, 59,* 981–993. (p. 800)

Feingold, A. (1992). Good-looking people are not what we think. *Psychological Bulletin, 111,* 304–341. (p. 800)

Feingold, A., & Mazzella, R. (1998). Gender differences in body image are increasing. *Psychological Science, 9,* 190–195. (p. 698)

Feinstein, J. S., Duff, M. C., & Tranel, D. (2010, April 27). Sustained experiences of emotion after loss of memory in patients with amnesia. *Proceedings of the National Academy of Sciences, 107,* 7674–7679. (p. 332)

Feldman, M. B., & Meyer, I. H. (2010). Comorbidity and age of onset of eating disorders in gay men, lesbians, and bisexuals. *Psychiatry research, 180,* 126–131. (p. 698)

Fellowes, D., Barnes, K., & Wilkinson, S. (2004). Aromatherapy and massage for symptom relief in patients with cancer. *The Cochrane Library, 3,* Oxford, England: Update Software. (p. 863)

Feng, J., Spence, I., & Pratt, J. (2007). Playing an action video game reduces gender differences in spatial cognition. *Psychological Science, 18,* 850–855. (p. 639)

Fenton, W. S., & McGlashan, T. H. (1991). Natural history of schizophrenia subtypes: II. Positive and negative symptoms and long-term course. *Archives of General Psychiatry, 48,* 978–986. (p. 686)

Fenton, W. S., & McGlashan, T. H. (1994). Antecedents, symptom progression, and long-term outcome of the deficit syndrome in schizophrenia. *American Journal of Psychiatry, 151,* 351–356. (p. 686)

Ferguson, C. J. (2009, June 14). Not every child is secretly a genius. *The Chronicle Review* (http://chronicle.com/article/Not-Every-Child-Is-Secretly/48001). (p. 609)

Ferguson, C. J. (2010). A meta-analysis of normal and disordered personality across the life span. *Journal of Personality and Social Psychology, 98,* 659–667. (p. 464)

Ferguson, C. J., Coulson, M., & Barnett, J. (2011). A meta-analysis of pathological gaming prevalence and comorbidity with mental health, academic and social problems. *Journal of Psychiatric Research, 45,* 1573–1578. (p. 641)

Ferguson, C. J., & Hartley, R. D. (2009). The pleasure is momentary . . . the expense damnable? The influence of pornography on rape and sexual assault. *Aggression and Violent Behavior, 14,* 323–329. (p. 793)

Ferguson, C. J., & Kilburn, J. (2010). Much ado about nothing: The misestimation and overinterpretation of violent video game effects in Eastern and Western nations: Comment on Anderson et al. (2010). *Psychological Bulletin, 136,* 174–178. (pp. 412, 795)

Ferguson, E. D. (1989). Adler's motivational theory: An historical perspective on belonging and the fundamental human striving. *Individual Psychology, 45,* 354–361. (p. 412)

Ferguson, E. D. (2001). Adler and Dreikurs: Cognitive-social dynamic innovators. *Journal of Individual Psychology, 57,* 324–341. (p. 412)

Ferguson, E. D. (2003). Social processes, personal goals, and their intertwining: Their importance in Adlerian theory and practice. *Journal of Individual Psychology, 59,* 136–144. (p. 565)

Ferguson, M. J., & Zayas, V. (2009). Automatic evaluation. *Current Directions in Psychological Science, 18,* 362–366. (p. 157)

Fergusson, D. M., Boden, J. M., & Horwood, L. J. (2009). Tests of causal links between alcohol abuse or dependence and major depression. *Archives of General Psychiatry, 66,* 260–266. (p. 679)

Fergusson, D. M., & Woodward, L. G. (2002). Mental health, educational, and social role outcomes of adolescents with depression. *Archives of General Psychiatry, 59,* 225–231. (p. 675)

Fernandez-Dols, J-M., & Ruiz-Belda, M-A. (1995). Are smiles a sign of happiness? Gold medal winners at the Olympic Games. *Journal of Personality and Social Psychology, 69,* 1113–1119. (p. 436)

Fernyhough, C. (2008). Getting Vygotskian about theory of mind: Mediation, dialogue, and the development of social understanding. *Developmental Review, 28,* 225–262. (p. 484)

Ferri, M., Amato, L., & Davoli, M. (2006). Alcoholics Anonymous and other 12-step programmes for alcohol dependence. *Cochrane Database of Systematic Reviews,* Issue 3. Art. No.: CD005032. (p. 724)

Ferriman, K., Lubinski, D., & Benbow, C. P. (2009). Work preferences, life values, and personal views of top math/science graduate students and the profoundly gifted: Developmental changes and gender differences during emerging adulthood and parenthood. *Journal of Personality and Social Psychology, 97,* 517–522. (p. 503)

Ferris, C. F. (1996, March). The rage of innocents. *The Sciences,* pp. 22–26. (p. 493)

Festinger, L. (1957). *A theory of cognitive dissonance.* Stanford: Stanford University Press. (p. 759)

Feynman, R. (1997). Quoted by E. Hutchings (Ed.), *"Surely you're joking, Mr. Feynman."* New York: Norton. (p. 30), 357

Fiedler, F. E. (1981). Leadership effectiveness. *American Behavioral Scientist, 24,* 619–632. (p. 838)

Fiedler, F. E. (1987, September). When to lead, when to stand back. *Psychology Today,* 26–27. (p. 838)

Fiedler, K., Nickel, S., Muehlfriedel, T., & Unkelbach, C. (2001). Is mood congruency an effect of genuine memory or response bias? *Journal of Experimental Social Psychology, 37,* 201–214. (p. 337)

Field, A. P. (2006a). I don't like it because it eats sprouts: Conditioning preferences in children. *Behaviour Research and Therapy, 44,* 439–455. (p. 296)

Field, A. P. (2006b). Is conditioning a useful framework for understanding the development and treatment of phobias? *Clinical Psychology Review, 26,* 857–875. (p. 666)

Field, T. (1996). Attachment and separation in young children. *Annual Review of Psychology, 47,* 541–561. (p. 494)

Field, T., Diego, M., & Hernandez-Reif, M. (2007). Massage therapy research. *Developmental Review, 27,* 75–89. (p. 509)

Field, T., Hernandez-Reif, M., Feijo, L., & Freedman, J. (2006). Prenatal, perinatal and neonatal stimulation: A survey of neonatal nurseries. *Infant Behavior & Development, 29,* 24–31. (p. 509)

Fields, R. D. (2004, April). The other half of the brain. *Scientific American,* 54–61. (p. 105)

Fields, R. D. (2008, March). White matter. *Scientific American,* 54–61. (p. 78)

Fields, R. D. (2009). *The other brain: From dementia to schizophrenia, how new discoveries about the brain are revolutionizing medicine and science.* New York: Simon & Schuster. (p. 104)

Fikke, L. T., Melinder, A., & Landrø, N. I. (2011). Executive functions are impaired in adolescents engaging in non-suicidal self-injury. *Psychological Medicine, 41,* 601–610. (p. 677)

Fincham, F. D., & Bradbury, T. N. (1993). Marital satisfaction, depression, and attributions: A longitudinal analysis. *Journal of Personality and Social Psychology, 64,* 442–452. (p. 755)

Finchilescu, G., & Tredoux, C. (eds.) (2010). Intergroup relations in post apartheid South Africa: Change, and obstacles to change. *Journal of Social Issues, 66,* 223–236. (p. 813)

Fingelkurts, A. A., & Fingelkurts, A. A. (2009). Is our brain hardwired to produce God, or is our brain hardwired to perceive God? A systematic review on the role of the brain in mediating religious experience. *Cognitive Processes, 10,* 293–326. (pp. 96, 110)

Fingerman, K. L., & Charles, S. T. (2010). It takes two to tango: Why older people have the best relationships. *Current Directions in Psychological Science, 19,* 172–176. (p. 546)

Fink, G. R., Markowitsch, H. J., Reinkemeier, M., Bruckbauer, T., Kessler, J., & Heiss, W-D. (1996). Cerebral representation of one's own past: Neural networks involved in autobiographical memory. *Journal of Neuroscience, 16,* 4275–4282. (p. 330)

Fink, M. (2009). *Electroconvulsive therapy: A guide for professionals and their patients.* New York: Oxford University Press. (p. 744)

Finkel, E. J., & Eastwick, P. W. (2008). Speed-dating. *Current Directions in Psychological Science, 17*, 193–197. (p. 800)

Finkel, E. J., & Eastwick, P. W. (2009). Arbitrary social norms influence sex differences in romantic selectivity. *Psychological Science 20*, 1290–1295. (p. 799)

Finkel, E. J., Eastwick, P. W., Karney, B. R., Reis, H. T., & Sprecher, S. (2012a, September/October). Dating in a digital world. *Scientific American Mind*, 26–33. (p. 799)

Finkel, E. J., Eastwick, P. W., Karney, B. R., Reis, H. T., & Sprecher, S. (2012b). Online dating: A critical analysis from the perspective of psychological science. *Psychological Science in the Public Interest, 13*, 3–66. (p. 799)

Finlay, S. W. (2000). Influence of Carl Jung and William James on the origin of Alcoholics Anonymous. *Review of General Psychology, 4*, 3–12. (p. 724)

Finzi, E., & Wasserman, E. (2006). Treatment of depression with botulinum toxin A: A case series. *Dermatological Surgery, 32*, 645–650. (p. 438)

Fiore, M. C., & 23 others. (2008). *Treating tobacco use and dependence: 2008 update. Clinical practice guideline*. Rockville, MD: U.S. Department of Health and Human Services, Public Health Service. (p. 252)

Fiori, M. (2009). A new look at emotional intelligence: A dual-process framework. *Personality and Social Psychology Review, 13*, 21–44. (p. 612)

Fischer, P., & Greitemeyer, T. (2006). Music and aggression: The impact of sexual-aggressive song lyrics on aggression-related thoughts, emotions, and behavior toward the same and the opposite sex. *Personality and Social Psychology Bulletin, 32*, 1165–1176. (p. 793)

Fischhoff, B. (1982). Debiasing. In D. Kahneman, P. Slovic, & A. Tversky (Eds.), *Judgment under uncertainty: Heuristics and biases*. New York: Cambridge University Press. (p. 367)

Fischhoff, B., Slovic, P., & Lichtenstein, S. (1977). Knowing with certainty: The appropriateness of extreme confidence. *Journal of Experimental Psychology: Human Perception and Performance, 3*, 552–564. (p. 365)

Fishbach, A., Dhar, R., & Zhang, Y. (2006). Subgoals as substitutes or complements: The role of goal accessibility. *Journal of Personality and Social Psychology, 91*, 232–242. (p. 838)

Fisher, H. E. (1993, March/April). After all, maybe it's biology. *Psychology Today*, 40–45. (p. 544)

Fisher, H. E., Aron, A., Mashek, D., Li, H., & Brown, L. L. (2002). Defining the brain systems of lust, romantic attraction, and attachment. *Archives of Sexual Behavior, 31*, 413–419. (p. 407)

Fisher, H. T. (1984). Little Albert and Little Peter. *Bulletin of the British Psychological Society, 37*, 269. (p. 717)

Fisher, K., Egerton, M., Gershuny, J. I., & Robinson, J. P. (2006). Gender convergence in the American Heritage Time Use Study (AHTUS). *Social Indicators Research, 82*, 1–33. (p. 504)

Flaherty, D. K. (2011). The vaccine-autism connection: a public health crisis caused by unethical medical practices and fraudulent science. *Annals of Pharmacotherapy, 45*, 1302–1304. (p. 482)

Flegal, K. M., Carroll, M. D., Ogden, C. L., & Curtin, L. R. (2010). Prevalence and trends in obesity among US adults, 1999–2008. *Journal of the American Medical Association, 303*, 235–241. (p. 401)

Fleming, I., Baum, A., & Weiss, L. (1987). Social density and perceived control as mediator of crowding stress in high-density residential neighborhoods. *Journal of Personality and Social Psychology, 52*, 899–906. (p. 300)

Fleming, J. H. (2001, Winter/Spring). Introduction to the special issue on linkage analysis. *The Gallup Research Journal*, i–vi. (p. 837)

Fleming, J. H., & Scott, B. A. (1991). The costs of confession: The Persian Gulf War POW tapes in historical and theoretical perspective. *Contemporary Social Psychology, 15*, 127–138. (p. 435)

Fletcher, G. J. O., Fitness, J., & Blampied, N. M. (1990). The link between attributions and happiness in close relationships: The roles of depression and explanatory style. *Journal of Social and Clinical Psychology, 9*, 243–255. (p. 755)

Flora, S. R. (2004). *The power of reinforcement*. Albany, NY: SUNY Press. (p. 286)

Flora, S. R., & Bobby, S. E. (2008, September/October). The bipolar bamboozle. *Skeptical Inquirer*, 41–45. (p. 673)

Flory, R., Ametepe, J., & Bowers, B. (2010). A randomized, placebo-controlled trial of bright light and high-density negative air ions for treatment of Season Affective Disorder. *Psychiatry Research, 177*, 101–108. (p. 734)

Flouri, E., & Buchanan, A. (2004). Early father's and mother's involvement and child's later educational outcomes. *British Journal of Educational Psychology, 74*, 141–153. (p. 492)

Flynn, J. R. (1987). Massive IQ gains in 14 nations: What IQ tests really measure. *Psychological Bulletin, 101*, 171–191. (p. 621)

Flynn, J. R. (2009a). Requiem for nutrition as the cause of IQ gains: Raven's gains in Britain 1938–2008. *Economics and Human Biology, 7*, 18–27. (p. 622)

Flynn, J. R. (2009b). *What is intelligence? Beyond the Flynn effect* (expanded edition). Cambridge: Cambridge University Press. (p. 621)

Flynn, J. R. (2010). Problems with IQ gains: The huge vocabulary gap. *Journal of Psychoeducational Assessment, 28*, 412–433. (p. 621)

Foa, E. B., & Kozak, M. J. (1986). Emotional processing of fear: Exposure to corrective information. *Psychological Bulletin, 99*, 20–35. (p. 717)

Food and Drug Administration. (2011). FDA Executive Summary. Prepared for the January 27–28, 2011 meeting of the Neurological Devices Panel (www.fda.gov) (p. 744)

Ford, E. S. (2002). Does exercise reduce inflammation? Physical activity and B-reactive protein among U.S. adults. *Epidemiology, 13*, 561–569. (p. 859)

Foree, D. D., & LoLordo, V. M. (1973). Attention in the pigeon: Differential effects of food-getting versus shock-avoidance procedures. *Journal of Comparative and Physiological Psychology, 85*, 551–558. (p. 295)

Forer, B. R. (1949). The fallacy of personal validation: A classroom demonstration of gullibility. *Journal of Abnormal and Social Psychology, 44*, 118–123. (p. 579)

Forgas, J. P. (2008). Affect and cognition. *Perspectives on Psychological Science, 3*, 94–101. (p. 847)

Forgas, J. P. (2009, November/December). Think negative! *Australian Science*, 14–17. (p. 672)

Forgas, J. P., Bower, G. H., & Krantz, S. E. (1984). The influence of mood on perceptions of social interactions. *Journal of Experimental Social Psychology, 20*, 497–513. (p. 337)

Forhan, S. E., Gottlieb, S. L., Sternberg, M. R., Xu, F., Datta, D., Berman, S., & Markowitz, L. (2008). Prevalence of sexually transmitted infections and bacterial vaginosis among female adolescents in the United States: Data from the National Health and Nutrition Examination Survey (NHANES) 2003–2004. Paper presented to the 2008 National STD Prevention Conference, Chicago, Illinois. (p. 529)

Forman, D. R., Aksan, N., & Kochanska, G. (2004). Toddlers' responsive imitation predicts preschool-age conscience. *Psychological Science, 15*, 699–704. (p. 308)

Foss, D. J., & Hakes, D. T. (1978). *Psycholinguistics: An introduction to the psychology of language*. Englewood Cliffs, NJ: Prentice-Hall. (p. 562)

Foulkes, D. (1999). *Children's dreaming and the development of consciousness*. Cambridge, MA: Harvard University Press. (p. 243)

Fournier, J. C., DeRubeis, R. J., Hollon, S. D., Dimidjian, S., Amsterdam, J. D., Shelton, R. C., & Fawcett, J. (2010). Antidepressant drug effects and depression severity: A patient-level meta-analysis. *Journal of the American Medical Association, 303*, 47–53. (p. 743)

Fouts, R. S. (1992). Transmission of a human gestural language in a chimpanzee mother-infant relationship. *Friends of Washoe, 12/13*, 2–8. (p. 870)

Fouts, R. S. (1997). *Next of kin: What chimpanzees have taught me about who we are*. New York: Morrow. (p. 870)

Fowles, D. C. (1992). Schizophrenia: Diathesis-stress revisited. *Annual Review of Psychology, 43*, 303–336. (p. 686)

Fowles, D. C., & Dindo, L. (2009). Temperament and psychopathy: A dual-pathway model. *Current Directions in Psychological Science, 18*, 179–183. (p. 699)

Fox, D. (2010, June). The insanity virus. *Discover*, 58–64. (p. 687)

Fox, J. L. (1984). The brain's dynamic way of keeping in touch. *Science, 225*, 820–821. (p. 111)

Fox, N. A., Hane, A. E., & Pine, D. S. (2007). Plasticity for affective neurocircuitry. *Current Directions in Psychological Science, 16*, 1–5. (p. 491)

Fozard, J. L., & Popkin, S. J. (1978). Optimizing adult development: Ends and means of an applied psychology of aging. *American Psychologist, 33*, 975–989. (p. 541)

Fracassini, C. (2000, August 27). Holidaymakers led by the nose in sales quest. *Scotland on Sunday*. (p. 209)

Fraley, R. C., Roisman, G. I., Booth-LaForce, C., Owen, M. T., & Holland, A. S. (2013). Interpersonal and genetic origins of adult attachment styles: A longitudinal study from infancy to early adulthood. *Journal of Personality and Social Psychology, 104*, 817–838. (p. 492)

Fraley, R. C., Vicary, A. M., Brumbaugh, C. C., & Roisman, G. I. (2011). Patterns of stability in adult attachment: An empirical test of two models of continuity and change. *Journal of Personality and Social Psychology, 101,* 974–992. (p. 413)

Frances, A. J. (2012, December 2). DSM-5 is guide not Bible—Ignore its ten worst changes. www.psychologytoday.com/blog/dsm5-in-distress/201212/dsm-5-is-guide-not-bible-ignore-its-ten-worst-changes. (pp. 652, 655)

Frances, A. J. (2013). *Saving normal: An insider's revolt against out-of-control psychiatric diagnosis, DSM-5, big pharma, and the medicalization of ordinary life.* New York: HarperCollins. (p. 655)

Frank, J. D. (1982). Therapeutic components shared by all psychotherapies. In J. H. Harvey & M. M. Parks (Eds.), *The Master Lecture Series: Vol. 1. Psychotherapy research and behavior change.* Washington, DC: American Psychological Association. (pp. 734, 735)

Frank, R. (1999). *Luxury fever: Why money fails to satisfy in an era of excess.* New York: Free Press. (p. 778)

Frankel, A., Strange, D. R., & Schoonover, R. (1983). CRAP: Consumer rated assessment procedure. In G. H. Scherr & R. Liebmann-Smith (Eds.), *The best of The Journal of Irreproducible Results.* New York: Workman Publishing. (p. 580)

Frankenburg, W., Dodds, J., Archer, P., Shapiro, H., & Bresnick, B. (1992). The Denver II: A major revision and restandardization of the Denver Developmental Screening Test. *Pediatrics, 89,* 91–97. (p. 472)

Franklin, M., & Foa, E. B. (2011). Treatment of obsessive-compulsive disorder. *Annual Review of Clinical Psychology, 7,* 229–243. (p. 667)

Franz, E. A., Waldie, K. E., & Smith, M. J. (2000). The effect of callosotomy on novel versus familiar bimanual actions: A neural dissociation between controlled and automatic processes? *Psychological Science, 11,* 82–85. (p. 116)

Frasure-Smith, N., & Lesperance, F. (2005). Depression and coronary heart disease: Complex synergism of mind, body, and environment. *Current Directions in Psychological Science, 14,* 39–43. (p. 453)

Frattaroli, J. (2006). Experimental disclosure and its moderators: A meta-analysis. *Psychological Bulletin, 132,* 823–865. (p. 858)

Fredrickson, B. L. (2006). The broaden-and-build theory of positive emotions. In M. Csikszentmihalyi & I. S. Csikszentmihalyi (Eds.), *A life worth living: Contributions to positive psychology.* New York: Oxford University Press. (p. 847)

Freedman, D. H. (2011, February). How to fix the obesity crisis. *Scientific American,* 40–47. (p. 403)

Freedman, D. J., Riesenhuber, M., Poggio, T., & Miller, E. K. (2001). Categorical representation of visual stimuli in the primate prefrontal cortex. *Science, 291,* 312–316. (p. 867)

Freedman, J. L. (1988). Television violence and aggression: What the evidence shows. In S. Oskamp (Ed.), *Television as a social issue.* Newbury Park, CA: Sage. (p. 309)

Freedman, J. L., & Fraser, S. C. (1966). Compliance without pressure: The foot-in-the-door technique. *Journal of Personality and Social Psychology, 4,* 195–202. (p. 757)

Freedman, J. L., & Perlick, D. (1979). Crowding, contagion, and laughter. *Journal of Experimental Social Psychology, 15,* 295–303. (p. 772)

Freedman, L. R., Rock, D., Roberts, S. A., Cornblatt, B. A., & Erlenmeyer-Kimling, L. (1998). The New York high-risk project: Attention, anhedonia and social outcome. *Schizophrenia Research, 30,* 1–9. (p. 689)

Freeman, E. C., & Twenge, J. M. (2010, January). Using MySpace increases the endorsement of narcissistic personality traits. Poster presented at the annual conference of the Society for Personality and Social Psychology, Las Vegas, NV. (p. 418)

Freeman, W. J. (1991, February). The physiology of perception. *Scientific American,* 78–85. (p. 194)

Freud, S. (1935; reprinted 1960). *A general introduction to psychoanalysis.* New York: Washington Square Press. (p. 544)

Frey, M. C., & Detterman, D. K. (2004). Scholastic assessment or g? The relationship between the Scholastic Assessment Test and general cognitive ability. *Psychological Science, 15,* 373–378. (pp. 619, 620)

Freyd, J. J., DePrince, A. P., & Gleaves, D. H. (2007). The state of betrayal trauma theory: Reply to McNally—Conceptual issues and future directions. *Memory, 15,* 295–311. (p. 351)

Freyd, J. J., Putnam, F. W., Lyon, T. D., Becker-Blease, K. A., Cheit, R. E., Siegel, N. B., & Pezdek, K. (2005). The science of child sexual abuse. *Science, 308,* 501. (p. 494)

Fridlund, A. J., Beck, H. P., Goldie, W. D., & Irons, G. (2012a). Little Albert: A neurologically impaired child. *History of Psychology, 15*(4), 302–327. (p. 271)

Fridlund, A. J., Beck, H. P., Goldie, W. D., & Irons, G. (2012b). Little Albert: Answering the criticism. *The Psychologist, 25,* 258. (p. 271)

Friedman, H. S., & Rosenman, R. (1974). *Type A behavior and your heart.* New York: Knopf. (p. 451)

Friedman, M., & Ulmer, D. (1984). *Treating Type A behavior—and your heart.* New York: Knopf. (pp. 451, 861)

Friedman, R., & James, J. W. (2008). The myth of the sages of dying, death and grief. *Skeptic, 14*(2), 37–41. (p. 548)

Friedman, S. L., & Boyle, D. E. (2008). Attachment in US children experiencing nonmaternal care in the early 1990s. *Attachment & Human Development, 10,* 225–261. (p. 494)

Frijda, N. H. (1988). The laws of emotion. *American Psychologist, 43,* 349–358. (p. 851)

Frisch, M., & Zdravkovic, S. (2010). Body size at birth and same-sex marriage in young adulthood. *Archives of Sexual Behavior, 39,* 117–123. (p. 536)

Frith, U., & Frith, C. (2001). The biological basis of social interaction. *Current Directions in Psychological Science, 10,* 151–155. (p. 481)

Fritz, T., Jentschke, S., Gosselin, N., Sammler, D., Peretz, I., Turner, R., Friederici, A., & Koelsch, S. (2009). Universal recognition of three basic emotions in music. *Current Biology, 19,* 573–576. (p. 436)

Fromkin, V., & Rodman, R. (1983). *An introduction to language* (3rd ed.). New York: Holt, Rinehart & Winston. (p. 375)

Fry, A. F., & Hale, S. (1996). Processing speed, working memory, and fluid intelligence: Evidence for a developmental cascade. *Psychological Science, 7,* 237–241. (p. 541)

Fry, R., & Cohn, D. (2010, January 19). Women, men and the new economics of marriage. Pew Research Center (pewresearch.org). (p. 504)

Fryar, C., Hirsch, R., Porter, K. S., Kottiri, B., Brody, D. J., & Louis, T. (2007, June 28). Drug use and sexual behavior reported by adults: United States, 1999–2002. *Advance Data: From Vital and Health Statistics,* Number 384 (Centers for Disease Control and Prevention). (p. 407)

Fuhriman, A., & Burlingame, G. M. (1994). Group psychotherapy: Research and practice. In A. Fuhriman & G. M. Burlingame (Eds.), *Handbook of group psychotherapy.* New York: Wiley. (p. 723)

Fujiki, N., Yoshida, Y., Ripley, B., Mignot, E., & Nishino, S. (2003). Effects of IV and ICV hypocretin-1 (Orexin A) in hypocretin receptor-2 gene mutated narcoleptic dogs and IV hypocretin-1 replacement therapy in a hypocretin-ligand-deficient narcoleptic dog. *Sleep, 26,* 953–959. (p. 239)

Fuller, M. J., & Downs, A. C. (1990). Spermarche is a salient biological marker in men's development. Poster presented at the American Psychological Society convention. (p. 528)

Fulmer, C. A., Gelfand, M. J., Kruglanski, A. W., Kim-Prieto, C., Diener, E., Pierro, A., & Higgins, E. T. (2010). On "feeling right" in cultural contexts: How person-culture match affects self-esteem and subjective well-being. *Psychological Science, 21,* 1563–1569. (p. 588)

Fulmer, I. S., Gerhart, B., & Scott, K. S. (2003). Are the 100 best better? An empirical investigation of the relationship between being a "great place to work" and firm performance. *Personnel Psychology, 56,* 965–993. (p. 836)

Funder, D. C. (2001). Personality. *Annual Review of Psychology, 52,* 197–221. (p. 580)

Funder, D. C. (2009). Persons, behaviors and situations: An agenda for personality psychology in the postwar era. *Journal of Research in Personality, 43,* 155–162. (p. 588)

Funder, D. C., & Block, J. (1989). The role of ego-control, ego-resiliency, and IQ in delay of gratification in adolescence. *Journal of Personality and Social Psychology, 57,* 1041–1050. (p. 517)

Furlow, F. B., & Thornhill, R. (1996, January/February). The orgasm wars. *Psychology Today,* 42–46. (p. 407)

Furnham, A. (1982). Explanations for unemployment in Britain. *European Journal of Social Psychology, 12,* 335–352. (p. 755)

Furnham, A., & Baguma, P. (1994). Cross-cultural differences in the evaluation of male and female body shapes. *International Journal of Eating Disorders, 15,* 81–89. (p. 401)

Furnham, A., Callahan, I., & Rawles, R. (2003). Adults' knowledge of general psychology. *European Psychologist, 8,* 101–116. (p. 32)

Furnham, A., & Rawles, R. (1995). Sex differences in the estimation of intelligence. *Journal of Social Behavior and Personality, 10,* 741–748. (p. 781)

Furr, R. M., & Funder, D. C. (1998). A multimodal analysis of personal negativity. *Journal of Personality and Social Psychology, 74,* 1580–1591. (p. 681)

Furukawa, T. A., Yoshimura, R., Harai, H., Imaizumi, T., Takeuchi, H., Kitamua, T., & Takahashi, K. (2009). How many well vs. unwell days can you expect over 10 years, once you become depressed? *Acta Psychiatrica Scandinavica, 119,* 290–297. (p. 675)

Gable, S. L., Gonzaga, G. C., & Strachman, A. (2006). Will you be there for me when things go right? Supportive responses to positive event disclosures. *Journal of Personality and Social Psychology, 91,* 904–917. (p. 546)

Gabrieli, J. D. E., Desmond, J. E., Demb, J. E., Wagner, A. D., Stone, M. V., Vaidya, C. J., & Glover, G. H. (1996). Functional magnetic resonance imaging of semantic memory processes in the frontal lobes. *Psychological Science, 7,* 278–283. (p. 330)

Gaillard, R., Dehaene, S., Adam, C., Clémenceau, S., Hasboun, D., Baulac, M., Cohen, L., & Naccache, L. (2009). Converging intracranial markers of conscious access. *PLoS Biology, 7*(e), e1000061. (p. 119)

Gaillot, M. T., & Baumeister, R. F. (2007). Self-regulation and sexual restraint: Dispositionally and temporarily poor self-regulatory abilities contribute to failures at restraining sexual behavior. *Personality and Social Psychology Bulletin, 33,* 173–186. (p. 301)

Galak, J., LeBoeuf, R. A., Nelson, L., & Simmons, J. P. (2012), Correcting the past: Failures to replicate psi. *Journal of Personality and Social Psychology, 103,* 993–948. (p. 169)

Galambos, N. L. (1992). Parent-adolescent relations. *Current Directions in Psychological Science, 1,* 146–149. (p. 522)

Galanter, E. (1962). Contemporary psychophysics. In R. Brown, E. Galanter, E. H. Hess, & G. Mandler (Eds.), *New directions in psychology.* New York: Holt Rinehart & Winston. (p. 156)

Galati, D., Scherer, K. R., & Ricci-Bitti, P. E. (1997). Voluntary facial expression of emotion: Comparing congenitally blind with normally sighted encoders. *Journal of Personality and Social Psychology, 73,* 1363–1379. (p. 436)

Galdi, S., Arcuri, L., & Gawronski, B. (2008). Automatic mental associations predict future choices of undecided decision-makers. *Science, 321,* 1100–1102. (p. 369)

Gale, C. R., Batty, G. D., & Deary, I. J. (2008). Locus of control at age 10 years and health outcomes and behaviors at age 30 years: The 1970 British Cohort Study. *Psychosomatic Medicine, 70,* 397–403. (p. 301)

Galea, S., Boscarino, J., Resnick, H., & Vlahov, D. (2002). Mental health in New York City after the September 11 terrorist attacks: Results from two population surveys. In R. W. Manderscheid & M. J. Henderson (Eds.), *Mental-Health, United States, 2001.* Washington, DC: U.S. Government Printing Office. (pp. 664, 665)

Galinsky, E., Aumann, K., & Bond, J. T. (2008). *Times are changing: Gender and generation at work and at home.* Work and Families Institute (www.familiesandwork.org). (p. 596)

Gallese, V., Gernsbacher, M. A., Heyes, C., Hickok, G., & Iacoboni, M. (2011). Mirror neuron forum. *Perspectives on Psychological Science, 6,* 369–407. (pp. 307, 482)

Gallo, W. T., Teng, H. M., Falba, T. A., Kasl, S. V., Krumholz, H. M., & Bradley, E. H. (2006). The impact of late career job loss on myocardial infarction and stroke: A 10 year follow up using the health and retirement survey. *Occupational and Environmental Medicine, 63,* 683–687. (p. 442, 453)

Gallup. (2010, accessed June 28). Gallup daily: U.S. mood. Based on the Gallup-Healthways well-being index. www.gallup.com. (p. 42)

Gallup Brain. (2008, accessed February 20). Woman for president: Question qn2f, March, 2007 wave. Brain.Gallup.com. (p. 780)

Gallup Organization. (2003, July 8). American public opinion about Iraq. *Gallup Poll News Service* (www.gallup.com). (p. 759)

Gallup Organization. (2004, August 16). 65% of Americans receive NO praise or recognition in the workplace. E-mail from Tom Rath: bucketbook@gallup.com. (p. 838)

Gallup, G. G., Jr. (1970). Chimpanzees: Self-recognition. *Science, 167,* 86–87. (p. 495)

Gallup, G. G., Jr., & Frederick, D. A. (2010). The science of sex appeal: An evolutionary perspective. *Review of General Psychology, 14,* 240–250. (p. 801)

Gallup, G. G., Jr., & Suarez, S. D. (1986). Self-awareness and the emergence of mind in humans and other primates. In J. Suls & A. G. Greenwald (Eds.), *Psychological perspectives on the self* (Vol. 3.). Hillsdale, NJ: Erlbaum. (p. 495)

Gallup, G. H. (1972). *The Gallup poll: Public opinion 1935–1971* (Vol. 3). New York: Random House. (p. 812)

Gallup, G. H., Jr. (1994, October). Millions finding care and support in small groups. *Emerging Trends,* 2–5. (p. 724)

Gangestad, S. W., & Simpson, J. A. (2000). The evolution of human mating: Trade-offs and strategic pluralism. *Behavioral and Brain Sciences, 23,* 573–587. (p. 138)

Gangestad, S. W., Thornhill, R., & Garver-Apgar, C. E. (2010). Men's facial masculinity predicts changes in their female partners' sexual interests across the ovulatory cycle, whereas men's intelligence does not. *Evolution and Human Behavior, 31,* 412–424. (p. 801)

Gangwisch, J. E., Babiss, L. A., Malaspina, D., Turner, J. B., Zammit, G. K., & Posner, K. (2010). Earlier parental set bedtimes as a protective factor against depression and suicidal ideation. *Sleep, 33,* 97–106. (p. 235)

Gao, Y., Raine, A., Venables, P. H., Dawson, M. E., & Mednick, S. A. (2010). Association of poor child fear conditioning and adult crime. *American Journal of Psychiatry, 167,* 56–60. (p. 700)

Garber, K. (2007). Autism's cause may reside in abnormalities at the synapse. *Science, 317,* 190–191. (p. 482)

Garcia, J., & Gustavson, A. R. (1997, January). Carl R. Gustavson (1946–1996): Pioneering wildlife psychologist. *APS Observer,* 34–35. (p. 294)

Garcia, J., & Koelling, R. A. (1966). Relation of cue to consequence in avoidance learning. *Psychonomic Science, 4,* 123–124. (p. 293)

Gardner, H. (1983). *Frames of mind: The theory of multiple intelligences.* New York: Basic Books. (p. 609)

Gardner, H. (1998a, March 19). An intelligent way to progress. *The Independent* (London), p. E4. (p. 609)

Gardner, H. (1998b, November 5). Do parents count? *New York Review of Books* (www.nybooks.com). (p. 511)

Gardner, H. (1999a, February). Who owns intelligence? *Atlantic Monthly,* 67–76. (p. 619)

Gardner, H. (1999b). *Multiple views of multiple intelligence.* New York: Basic Books. (p. 612)

Gardner, H. (2006). *The development and education of the mind: The selected works of Howard Gardner.* New York: Routledge/Taylor & Francis. (pp. 351, 609)

Gardner, J., & Oswald, A. J. (2007). Money and mental well-being: A longitudinal study of medium-sized lottery wins. *Journal of Health Economics, 6,* 49–60. (p. 851)

Gardner, R. A., & Gardner, B. I. (1969). Teaching sign language to a chimpanzee. *Science, 165,* 664–672. (p. 869)

Garfield, C. (1986). *Peak performers: The new heroes of American business.* New York: Morrow. (p. 381)

Garon, N., Bryson, S. E., & Smith, I. M. (2008). Executive function in preschoolers: A review using an integrative framework. *Psychological Bulletin, 134,* 31–60. (p. 471)

Garrett, B. L. (2008). Judging innocence. *Columbia Law Review, 108,* 55–142. (p. 350)

Garry, M., Loftus, E. F., & Brown, S. W. (1994). Memory: A river runs through it. *Consciousness and Cognition, 3,* 438–451. (p. 563)

Garry, M., Manning, C. G., Loftus, E. F., & Sherman, S. J. (1996). Imagination inflation: Imagining a childhood event inflates confidence that it occurred. *Psychonomic Bulletin & Review, 3,* 208–214. (p. 348)

Gartrell, N., & Bos, H. (2010). U.S. national longitudinal lesbian family study: Psychological adjustment of 17-year-old adolescents. *Pediatrics, 126,* 28–36. (p. 533)

Gatchel, R. J., Peng, Y. B., Peters, M. L., Fuchs, P. N., & Turk, D. C. (2007). The biopsychosocial approach to chronic pain: Scientific advances and future directions. *Psychological Bulletin, 133,* 581–624. (p. 203)

Gates, G. J., & Newport, F. (2012, October 18). Special report: 3.4% of U.S. adults identify as LGBT. www.gallup.com. (p. 532)

Gates, W. (1998, July 20). Charity begins when I'm ready (interview). *Fortune* (www.pathfinder.com/fortune/1998/980720/bil7.html). (p. 611)

Gawande, A. (1998, September 21). The pain perplex. *The New Yorker,* 86–94. (p. 205)

Gawin, F. H. (1991). Cocaine addiction: Psychology and neurophysiology. *Science, 251,* 1580–1586. (p. 252)

Gazzaniga, M. S. (1967, August). The split brain in man. *Scientific American,* 24–29. (pp. 114, 115)

Gazzaniga, M. S. (1983). Right hemisphere language following brain bisection: A 20–year perspective. *American Psychologist, 38,* 525–537. (p. 116)

Gazzaniga, M. S. (1988). Organization of the human brain. *Science, 245,* 947–952. (p. 117)

Gazzaniga, M. S. (2011, April). Neuroscience in the courtroom. *Scientific American,* 54–59. (p. 429)

Ge, X., & Natsuaki, M. N. (2009). In search of explanations for early pubertal timing effects on developmental psychopathology. *Current Directions in Psychological Science, 18,* 327–441. (p. 514)

Geary, D. C. (1995). Sexual selection and sex differences in spatial cognition. *Learning and Individual Differences, 7,* 289–301. (p. 638)

Geary, D. C. (1996). Sexual selection and sex differences in mathematical abilities. *Behavioral and Brain Sciences, 19,* 229–247. (p. 638)

Geary, D. C. (1998). *Male, female: The evolution of human sex differences.* Washington, DC: American Psychological Association. (p. 138)

Geary, D. C. (2010). *Male, female: The evolution of human sex differences* (2nd ed.). Washington, DC: American Psychological Association. (p. 526)

Geary, D. C., Salthouse, T. A., Chen, G-P., & Fan, L. (1996). Are East Asian versus American differences in arithmetical ability a recent phenomenon? *Developmental Psychology, 32,* 254–262. (p. 641)

Geen, R. G., & Quanty, M. B. (1977). The catharsis of aggression: An evaluation of a hypothesis. In L. Berkowitz (Ed.), *Advances in experimental social psychology* (Vol. 10). New York: Academic Press. (p. 846)

Geen, R. G., & Thomas, S. L. (1986). The immediate effects of media violence on behavior. *Journal of Social Issues, 42*(3), 7–28. (p. 309)

Gehring, W. J., Wimke, J., & Nisenson, L. G. (2000). Action monitoring dysfunction in obsessive-compulsive disorder. *Psychological Science, 11*(1), 1–6. (p. 668)

Geier, A. B., Rozin, P., & Doros, G. (2006). Unit bias: A new heuristic that helps explain the effects of portion size on food intake. *Psychological Science, 17,* 521–525. (p. 400)

Gelman, D. (1989, May 15). Voyages to the unknown. *Newsweek,* 66–69. (p. 436)

Genesee, F., & Gándara, P. (1999). Bilingual education programs: A cross-national perspective. *Journal of Social Issues, 55,* 665–685. (p. 380)

Gentile, B., Twenge, J. M., & Campbell, W. K. (2010). Birth cohort differences in self-esteem, 1988–2008: A cross-temporal meta-analysis. *Review of General Psychology, 14,* 261–268. (p. 597)

Gentile, D. A. (2009). Pathological video-game use among youth ages 8 to 18: A national study. *Psychological Science, 20,* 594–602. (pp. 248, 795)

Gentile, D. A., Lynch, P. J., Linder, J. R., & Walsh, D. A. (2004). The effects of violent video game habits on adolescent hostility, aggressive behaviors, and school performance. *Journal of Adolescence, 27,* 5–22. (p. 309)

George, L. K., Ellison, C. G., & Larson, D. B. (2002). Explaining the relationships between religious involvement and health. *Psychological Inquiry, 13,* 190–200. (p. 865)

George, M. S. (2003, September). Stimulating the brain. *Scientific American,* 67–73. (p. 745)

George, M. S., & 12 others. (2010). Daily left prefrontal transcranial magnetic stimulation therapy for major depressive disorder: A sham-controlled randomized trial. *Archives of General Psychiatry, 67,* 507–516. (p. 745)

Geraerts, E., Bernstein, D. M., Merckelbach, H., Linders, C., Raymaekers, L., & Loftus, E. F. (2008). Lasting false beliefs and their behavioral consequences. *Psychological Science, 19,* 749–753. (p. 348)

Geraerts, E., Schooler, J. W., Merckelbach, H., Jelicic, M., Hauer, B. J. A., & Ambadar, Z. (2007). The reality of recovered memories: Corroborating continuous and discontinuous memories of childhood sexual abuse. *Psychological Science, 18,* 564–568. (p. 351)

Gerhart, K. A., Koziol-McLain, J., Lowenstein, S. R., & Whiteneck, G. G. (1994). Quality of life following spinal cord injury: Knowledge and attitudes of emergency care providers. *Annals of Emergency Medicine, 23,* 807–812. (p. 848)

Gernsbacher, M. A., Dawson, M., & Goldsmith, H. H. (2005). Three reasons not to believe in an autism epidemic. *Current Directions in Psychological Science, 14,* 55–58. (p. 481)

Gerrard, M., & Luus, C. A. E. (1995). Judgments of vulnerability to pregnancy: The role of risk factors and individual differences. *Personality and Social Psychology Bulletin, 21,* 160–171. (p. 530)

Gershoff, E. T. (2002). Parental corporal punishment and associated child behaviors and experiences: A meta-analytic and theoretical review. *Psychological Bulletin, 128,* 539–579. (p. 281)

Gershoff, E. T., Grogan-Kaylor, A., Lansford, J. E., Chang, L., Zelli, A., Deater-Deckard, K., & Dodge, K. A. (2010). Parent discipline practices in an international sample: Associations with child behaviors and moderation by perceived normativeness. *Child Development, 81,* 487–502. (p. 282)

Gerstorf, D., Ram, N., Röcke, C., Lindenberger, U., & Smith, J. (2008). Decline in life satisfaction in old age: Longitudinal evidence for links to distance-to-death. *Psychology and Aging, 23,* 154–168. (p. 546)

Gertner, J. (2010, May 10). The rise and fall of the G.D.P. *New York Times* (www.nytimes.com). (p. 854)

Geschwind, N. (1979, September). Specializations of the human brain. *Scientific American, 241,* 180–199. (p. 378)

Geschwind, N., & Behan, P. O. (1984). Laterality, hormones, and immunity. In N. Geschwind & A. M. Galaburda (Eds.), *Cerebral dominance: The biological foundations.* Cambridge, MA: Harvard University Press. (p. 118)

Gfeller, J. D., Lynn, S. J., & Pribble, W. E. (1987). Enhancing hypnotic susceptibility: Interpersonal and rapport factors. *Journal of Personality and Social Psychology, 52,* 586–595. (p. 221)

Giancola, P. R., & Corman, M. D. (2007). Alcohol and aggression: A test of the attention-allocation model. *Psychological Science, 18,* 649–655. (p. 791)

Giancola, P. R., Josephs, R. A., Parrott, D. J., & Duke, A. A. (2010). Alcohol myopia revisited: Clarifying aggression and other acts of disinhibition through a distorted lens. *Perspectives on Psychological Science, 5,* 265–278. (p. 249)

Gibbons, F. X. (1986). Social comparison and depression: Company's effect on misery. *Journal of Personality and Social Psychology, 51,* 140–148. (p. 852)

Gibbs, W. W. (1996, June). Mind readings. *Scientific American,* 34–36. (p. 106)

Gibson, E. J., & Walk, R. D. (1960, April). The "visual cliff." *Scientific American,* 64–71. (p. 184)

Gibson, H. B. (1995, April). Recovered memories. *The Psychologist,* 153–154. (p. 220)

Gibson, J. L., & Claassen, C. (2010). Racial reconciliation in South Africa: Interracial contact. *Journal of Social Issues, 66,* 255–272. (p. 813)

Gick, B., & Derrick, D. (2009). Aero-tactile integration in speech perception. *Nature, 462,* 502–504. (p. 211)

Giesbrecht, T., Lynn, S. J., Lilienfeld, S. O., & Merckelbach, H. (2008). Cognitive processes in dissociation: An analysis of core theoretical assumptions. *Psychological Bulletin, 134,* 617–647. (p. 696)

Giesbrecht, T., Lynn, S. J., Lilienfeld, S. O., & Merckelbach, H. (2010). Cognitive processes, trauma, and dissociation—Misconceptions and misrepresentations: Reply to Bremner (2010). *Psychological Bulletin, 136,* 7–11. (p. 696)

Gigerenzer, G. (2004). Dread risk, September 11, and fatal traffic accidents. *Psychological Science, 15,* 286–287. (p. 366)

Gigerenzer, G. (2006). Out of the frying pan into the fire: Behavioral reactions to terrorist attacks. *Risk Analysis, 26,* 347–351. (p. 366)

Gigerenzer, G. (2010). *Rationality for mortals: How people cope with uncertainty.* New York: Oxford University Press. (p. 56)

Gigerenzer, G., Gaissmaier, W., Kurz-Milcke, E., Schwartz, L. M., & Woloshin, S. (2008). Helping doctors and patients make sense of health statistics. *Psychological Science in the Public Interest, 8,* 53–96. (p. 56)

Gigerenzer, G., Gaissmaier, W., Kurz-Milcke, E., Schwartz, L. M., & Woloshin, S. (2009, April/May). Knowing your chances. *Scientific American Mind,* 44–51. (p. 56)

Gilbert, D. T. (2006). *Stumbling on happiness.* New York: Knopf. (pp. 373, 347, 423, 545, 596)

Gilbert, D. T., Pelham, B. W., & Krull, D. S. (2003). The psychology of good ideas. *Psychological Inquiry, 14,* 258–260. (p. 32)

Gilbert, D. T., Pinel, E. C., Wilson, T. D., Blumberg, S. J., & Wheatley, T. P. (1998). Immune neglect: A source of durability bias in affective forecasting. *Journal of Personality and Social Psychology, 75,* 617–638. (p. 848)

Gilbertson, M. W., Paulus, L. A., Williston, S. K., Gurvits, T. V., Lasko, N. B., Pitman, R. K., & Orr, S. P. (2006). Neurocognitive function in monozygotic twins discordant for combat exposure: Relationship to posttraumatic stress disorder. *Journal of Abnormal Psychology, 115,* 484–495. (p. 665)

Giles, D. E., Dahl, R. E., & Coble, P. A. (1994). Childbearing, developmental, and familial aspects of sleep. In J. M. Oldham & M. B. Riba (Eds.), *Review of psychiatry* (Vol. 13). Washington, DC: American Psychiatric Press. (p. 240)

Gilestro, G. F., Tononi, G., & Cirelli, C. (2009). Widespread changes in synaptic markers as a function of sleep and wakefulness in *Drosophila*. *Science, 324*, 109–112. (p. 230)

Gill, A. J., Oberlander, J., & Austin, E. (2006). Rating e-mail personality at zero acquaintance. *Personality and Individual Differences, 40*, 497–507. (p. 584)

Gillham, J. E., Hamilton, J., Freres, D. R., Patton, K. & Gallop, R. (2006). Preventing depression among early adolescents in the primary care setting: A randomized controlled study of the Penn Resiliency Program. *Journal of Abnormal Child Psychology, 34*, 195–211. (p. 737)

Gilligan, C. (1982). *In a different voice: Psychological theory and women's development.* Cambridge, MA: Harvard University Press. (p. 502)

Gilligan, C., Lyons, N. P., & Hanmer, T. J. (Eds.). (1990). *Making connections: The relational worlds of adolescent girls at Emma Willard School.* Cambridge, MA: Harvard University Press. (p. 502)

Gillison, M. L., Broutian, T., Pickard, R. K. L., Tong, Z-Y., Xiao, W., Kahle, L., Graubard, B. I., & Chaturvedi, A. K. (2012). Prevalence of oral HPV infection in the United States, 2009–2010. *Journal of the American Medical Association, 307*(7), 693–703. (p. 529)

Gilovich, T. (1991). *How we know what isn't so: The fallibility of human reason in everyday life.* New York: Free Press. (p. 50)

Gilovich, T. (1996). The spotlight effect: Exaggerated impressions of the self as a social stimulus. Unpublished manuscript, Cornell University. (p. 594)

Gilovich, T., Kruger, J., & Medvec, V. H. (2002). The spotlight effect revisited: Overestimating the manifest variability of our actions and appearance. *Journal of Experimental Social Psychology, 38*, 93–99. (p. 595)

Gilovich, T., & Medvec, V. H. (1995). The experience of regret: What, when, and why. *Psychological Review, 102*, 379–395. (p. 546)

Gilovich, T. & Savitsky, K. (1999). The spotlight effect and the illusion of transparency: Egocentric assessments of how we are seen by others. *Current Directions in Psychological Science, 8*, 165–168. (p. 595)

Gilovich, T., Vallone, R., & Tversky, A. (1985). The hot hand in basketball: On the misperception of random sequences. *Cognitive Psychology, 17*, 295–314. (p. 33)

Giltay, E. J., Geleijnse, J. M., Zitman, F. G., Buijsse, B., & Kromhout, D. (2007). Lifestyle and dietary correlates of dispositional optimism in men: The Zutphen Elderly Study. *Journal of Psychosomatic Research, 63*, 483–490. (p. 857)

Giltay, E. J., Geleijnse, J. M., Zitman, F. G., Hoekstra, T., & Schouten, E. G. (2004). Dispositional optimism and all-cause and cardiovascular mortality in a prospective cohort of elderly Dutch men and women. *Archives of General Psychiatry, 61*, 1126–1135. (p. 857)

Gingerich, O. (1999, February 6). Is there a role for natural theology today? *The Real Issue* (www.origins.org/real/n9501/natural.html). (p 142)

Gladue, B. A. (1990). Hormones and neuroendocrine factors in atypical human sexual behavior. In J. R. Feierman (Ed.), *Pedophilia: Biosocial dimensions.* New York: Springer-Verlag. (p. 535)

Gladwell, M. (2000, May 9). The new-boy network: What do job interviews really tell us? *New Yorker*, 68–86. (p. 832)

Gladwell, M. (2005). *Blink: The power of thinking without thinking.* New York: Little, Brown. (p. 802)

Glasman, L. R., & Albarracin, D. (2006). Forming attitudes that predict future behavior: A meta-analysis of the attitude-behavior relation. *Psychological Bulletin, 132*, 778–822. (p. 757)

Glass, R. I. (2004). Perceived threats and real killers. *Science, 304*, 927. (p. 366)

Glass, R. M. (2001). Electroconvulsive therapy: Time to bring it out of the shadows. *Journal of the American Medical Association, 285*, 1346–1348. (p. 744)

Gleason, K. A., Jensen-Campbell, L. A., & Ickes, W. (2009). The role of empathic accuracy in adolescents' peer relations and adjustment. *Personality and Social Psychology Bulletin, 35*, 997–1011. (p. 434)

Gleaves, D. H. (1996). The sociocognitive model of dissociative identity disorder: A reexamination of the evidence. *Psychological Bulletin, 120*, 42–59. (p. 696)

Glick, P., & 15 others. (2004). Bad but bold: Ambivalent attitudes toward men predict gender inequality in 16 nations. *Journal of Personality and Social Psychology, 86*, 713–728. (p. 783)

Glick, P., Gottesman, D., & Jolton, J. (1989). The fault is not in the stars: Susceptibility of skeptics and believers in astrology to the Barnum effect. *Personality and Social Psychology Bulletin, 15*, 572–583. (p. 579)

Gluszek, A., & Dovidio, J. F. (2010). The way *they* speak: A social psychological perspective on the stigma of nonnative accents in communication. *Personality and Social Psychology Review, 14*, 214–237. (p. 784)

Godden, D. R., & Baddeley, A. D. (1975). Context-dependent memory in two natural environments: On land and underwater. *British Journal of Psychology, 66*, 325–331. (p. 336)

Goel, V., & Dolan, R. J. (2001). The functional anatomy of humor: Segregating cognitive and affective components. *Nature Neuroscience, 4*, 237–238. (p. 378)

Goff, D. C., & Simms, C. A. (1993). Has multiple personality disorder remained consistent over time? *Journal of Nervous and Mental Disease, 181*, 595–600. (p. 695)

Golan, O., Ashwin, E., Granader, Y., McClintock, S., Day, K., Leggett, V., & Baron-Cohen, S. (2010). Enhancing emotion recognition in children with autism spectrum conditions: An intervention using animated vehicles with real emotional faces. *Journal of Autism Development and Disorders, 40*, 269–279. (p. 482)

Gold, M., & Yanof, D. S. (1985). Mothers, daughters, and girlfriends. *Journal of Personality and Social Psychology, 49*, 654–659. (p. 522)

Goldberg, J. (2007, accessed May 31). *Quivering bundles that let us hear.* Howard Hughes Medical Institute (www.hhmi.org/senses/c120.html). (p. 196)

Goldberg, W. A., Prause, J., Lucas-Thompson, R., & Himsel, A. (2008). Maternal employment and children's achievement in context: A meta-analysis of four decades of research. *Psychological Bulletin, 134*, 77–108. (p. 494)

Golden, R. N., Gaynes, B. N., Ekstrom, R. D., Hamer, R. M., Jacobsen, F. M., Suppes, T., Wisner, K. L., & Nemeroff, C. B. (2005). The efficacy of light therapy in the treatment of mood disorders: A review and meta-analysis of the evidence. *American Journal of Psychiatry, 162*, 656–662. (p. 734)

Goldfried, M. R. (2001). Integrating gay, lesbian, and bisexual issues into mainstream psychology. *American Psychologist, 56*, 977–988. (p. 676)

Goldfried, M. R., & Padawer, W. (1982). Current status and future directions in psychotherapy. In M. R. Goldfried (Ed.), *Converging themes in psychotherapy: Trends in psychodynamic, humanistic, and behavioral practice.* New York: Springer. (p. 734)

Goldfried, M. R., Raue, P. J., & Castonguay, L. G. (1998). The therapeutic focus in significant sessions of master therapists: A comparison of cognitive-behavioral and psychodynamic-interpersonal interventions. *Journal of Consulting and Clinical Psychology, 66*, 803–810. (p. 734)

Golding, J. M. (1996). Sexual assault history and women's reproductive and sexual health. *Psychology of Women Quarterly, 20*, 101–121. (p. 793)

Golding, J. M. (1999). Sexual-assault history and the long-term physical health problems: Evidence from clinical and population epidemiology. *Current Directions in Psychological Science, 8*, 191–194. (p. 665)

Goldin-Meadow, S., & Beilock, S. L. (2010). Action's influence on thought: The case of gesture. *Perspectives on Psychological Science, 5*, 664–674. (p. 438)

Goldman, A. L., Pezawas, L., Mattay, V. S., Fischl, B., Verchinski, B. A., Chen, Q., Weinberger, D. R., & Meyer-Lindenberg, A. (2009). Widespread reductions of cortical thickness in schizophrenia and spectrum disorders and evidence of heritability. *Archives of General Psychiatry, 66*, 467–477. (p. 687)

Goldstein, A. P., Glick, B., & Gibbs, J. C. (1998). *Aggression replacement training: A comprehensive intervention for aggressive youth* (rev. ed.). Champaign, IL: Research Press. (p. 792)

Goleman, D. (1980, February). 1,528 little geniuses and how they grew. *Psychology Today*, 28–53. (p. 834)

Goleman, D. (2006). *Social intelligence.* New York: Bantam Books. (p. 612)

Gonsalkorale, K., & Williams, K. D. (2006). The KKK would not let me play: Ostracism even by a despised outgroup hurts. *European Journal of Social Psychology, 36*, 1–11. (p. 414)

González-Vallejo, C., Lassiter, G. D., Bellezza, F. S., & Lindberg, M. J. (2008). "Save angels perhaps": A critical examination of unconscious thought theory and the deliberation-without-attention effect. *Review of General Psychology, 12*, 282–296. (p. 369)

Goodall, J. (1968). The behaviour of free-living chimpanzees in the Gombe Stream Reserve. *Animal Behaviour Monographs, 1*, 161–311. (p. 510)

Goodall, J. (1986). *The chimpanzees of Gombe: Patterns of behavior.* Cambridge, MA: Harvard University Press. (p. 785)

Goodall, J. (1998). Learning from the chimpanzees: A message humans can understand. *Science, 282*, 2184–2185. (p. 41)

Goode, E. (1999, April 13). If things taste bad, 'phantoms' may be at work. *New York Times* (www.nytimes.com). (p. 204)

Goodhart, D. E. (1986). The effects of positive and negative thinking on performance in an achievement situation. *Journal of Personality and Social Psychology, 51,* 117–124. (p. 589)

Goodman, G. S. (2006). Children's eyewitness memory: A modern history and contemporary commentary. *Journal of Social Issues, 62,* 811–832. (p 351)

Goodman, G. S., Ghetti, S., Quas, J. A., Edelstein, R. S., Alexander, K. W., Redlich, A. D., Cordon, I. M., & Jones, D. P. H. (2003). A prospective study of memory for child sexual abuse: New findings relevant to the repressed-memory controversy. *Psychological Science, 14,* 113–118. (p. 352)

Goodstein, L., & Glaberson, W. (2000, April 9). The well-marked roads to homicidal rage. *New York Times* (www.nytimes.com). (p. 592)

Goodwin, F. K., & Morrison, A. R. (1999). Scientists in bunkers: How appeasement of animal rights activism has failed. *Cerebrum, 1(2),* 50–62. (p. 66)

Goodwin, P. Y., Mosher, W. D., & Chandra, A. (2010). Marriage and cohabitation in the United States: A statistical portrait based on Cycle 6 (2002) of the National Survey of Family Growth. National Center for Health Statistics. *Vital Health Statistics, 23*(28). (p. 545)

Gopnik, A., & Meltzoff, A. N. (1986). Relations between semantic and cognitive development in the one-word stage: The specificity hypothesis. *Child Development, 57,* 1040–1053. (p. 380)

Goranson, R. E. (1978). *The hindsight effect in problem solving.* Unpublished manuscript, cited by G. Wood (1984), Research methodology: A decision-making perspective. In A. M. Rogers & C. J. Scheirer (Eds.), *The G. Stanley Hall Lecture Series* (Vol. 4). Washington, DC. (p. 32)

Gorchoff, S. M., John, O. P., & Helson, R. (2008). Contextualizing change in marital satisfaction during middle age. *Psychological Science, 19,* 1194–1200. (p. 545)

Gordon, P. (2004). Numerical cognition without words: Evidence from Amazonia. *Science, 306,* 496–499. (p. 379)

Gore-Felton, C., Koopman, C., Thoresen, C., Arnow, B., Bridges, E., & Spiegel, D. (2000). Psychologists' beliefs and clinical characteristics: Judging the veracity of childhood sexual abuse memories. *Professional Psychology: Research and Practice, 31,* 372–377. (p. 352)

Gorini, A. (2007). Virtual worlds, real healing. *Science, 318,* 1549. (p. 718)

Gosling, S. D. (2008). *Snoop: What your stuff says about you.* New York: Basic Books. (p. 583)

Gosling, S. D., Gladdis, S., & Vazire, S. (2007). Personality impressions based on Facebook profiles. Paper presented to the Society for Personality and Social Psychology meeting. (p. 584)

Gosling, S. D., Ko, S. J., Mannarelli, T., & Morris, M. E. (2002). A room with a cue: Personality judgments based on offices and bedrooms. *Journal of Personality and Social Psychology, 82,* 379–398. (p. 583)

Gosling, S. D., Kwan, V. S. Y., & John, O. P. (2003). A dog's got personality: A cross-species comparative approach to personality judgments in dogs and humans. *Journal of Personality and Social Psychology, 85,* 1161–1169. (p. 578)

Gotlib, I. H., & Hammen, C. L. (1992). *Psychological aspects of depression: Toward a cognitive-interpersonal integration.* New York: Wiley. (p. 681)

Gottesman, I. I. (1991). *Schizophrenia genesis: The origins of madness.* New York: Freeman. (p. 689)

Gottesman, I. I. (2001). Psychopathology through a life span—genetic prism. *American Psychologist, 56,* 867–881. (p. 688)

Gottfredson, L. S. (2002a). g: Highly general and highly practical. In R. J. Sternberg & E. L. Grigorenko (Eds.), *The general factor of intelligence: How general is it?* Mahwah, NJ: Erlbaum. (p. 610)

Gottfredson, L. S. (2002b). Where and why g matters: Not a mystery. *Human Performance, 15,* 25–46. (p. 610)

Gottfredson, L. S. (2003a). Dissecting practical intelligence theory: Its claims and evidence. *Intelligence, 31,* 343–397. (p. 610)

Gottfredson, L. S. (2003b). On Sternberg's "Reply to Gottfredson." *Intelligence, 31,* 415–424. (p. 610)

Gottfried, J. A., O'Doherty, J., & Dolan, R. J. (2003). Encoding predictive reward value in human amygdala and orbitofrontal cortex. *Science, 301,* 1104–1108. (p. 267)

Gottman, J. (2007). *Why marriages succeed or fail—2007 publication.* London: Bloomsbury. (p. 805)

Gottman, J., with Silver, N. (1994). *Why marriages succeed or fail.* New York: Simon & Schuster. (p. 545)

Gould, E. (2007). How widespread is adult neurogenesis in mammals? *Nature Neuroscience, 8,* 481–488. (p. 112)

Gould, S. J. (1981). *The mismeasure of man.* New York: Norton. (p. 618)

Gould, S. J. (1997, June 12). Darwinian fundamentalism. *The New York Review of Books, XLIV*(10), 34–37. (p. 139)

Gow, A. J., Johnson, W., Pattie, A., Brett, C. E., Roberts, B., Starr, J. M., & Deary, I. J. (2011). Stability and change in intelligence from age 11 to ages 70, 79, and 87: The Lothian birth cohorts of 1921 and 1936. *Psychology and Aging, 26,* 232–240. (p. 628)

Grabe, S., Ward, L. M., & Hyde, J. S. (2008). The role of the media in body image concerns among women: A meta-analysis of experimental and correlational studies. *Psychological Bulletin, 134,* 460–476. (p. 698)

Grace, A. A. (2010). Ventral hippocampus, interneurons, and schizophrenia: A new understanding of the pathophysiology of schizophrenia and its implications for treatment and prevention. *Current Directions in Psychological Science, 19,* 232–237. (p. 686)

Grady, C. L., & McIntosh, A. R., Horwitz, B., Maisog, J. M., Ungeleider, L. G., Mentis, M. J., Pietrini, P., Schapiro, M. B., & Haxby, J. V. (1995). Age-related reductions in human recognition memory due to impaired encoding. *Science, 269,* 218–221. (p. 343)

Graf, P. (1990). Life-span changes in implicit and explicit memory. *Bulletin of the Psychonomic Society, 28,* 353–358. (p. 543)

Graham, J. E., Christian, L. M., & Kiecolt-Glaser, J. K. (2006). Marriage, health, and immune function. In S. R. H. Beach & others (Eds.), *Relational processes and DSM-V: Neuroscience, assessment, prevention, and treatment.* Washington, DC: American Psychiatric Association. (p. 857)

Granqvist, P., Mikulincer, M., & Shaver, P. R. (2010). Religion as attachment: Normative processes and individual differences. *Personality and Social Psychology Review, 14,* 49–59. (p. 489)

Grant, N., Wardle, J., & Steptoe, A. (2009). The relationship between life satisfaction and health behavior: A cross-cultural analysis of young adults. *International Journal of Behavioral Medicine, 16,* 259–268. (p. 860)

Gray, P. B. (2010, July 7). ADHD and school: The problem of assessing normalcy in an abnormal environment. *Psychology Today Blog* (www.psychologytoday.com). (p. 652)

Gray, P. B., & Anderson, K. G. (2010). *Fatherhood: Evolution and human paternal behavior.* Cambridge, MA: Harvard University Press. (p. 139)

Gray-Little, B., & Burks, N. (1983). Power and satisfaction in marriage: A review and critique. *Psychological Bulletin, 93,* 513–538. (p. 804)

Green, B. (2002). Listening to leaders: Feedback on 360-degree feedback one year later. *Organizational Development Journal, 20,* 8–16. (p. 833)

Green, C. S., Pouget, A., & Bavelier, D. (2010). Improved probabilistic inference, as a general learning mechanism with action video games. *Current Biology, 20,* 1573–1579. (p. 795)

Green, J. D., Sedikides, C., & Gregg, A. P. (2008). Forgotten but not gone: The recall and recognition of self-threatening memories. *Journal of Experimental Social Psychology, 44,* 547–561. (p. 563)

Green, J. T., & Woodruff-Pak, D. S. (2000). Eyeblink classical conditioning: Hippocampal formation is for neutral stimulus associations as cerebellum is for association-response. *Psychological Bulletin, 126,* 138–158. (p. 331)

Green, M. F., & Horan, W. P. (2010). Social cognition in schizophrenia. *Current Directions in Psychological Science, 19,* 243–248. (p. 685)

Greenberg, J. (2008). Understanding the vital human quest for self-esteem. *Perspectives on Psychological Science, 3,* 48–55. (p. 595)

Greenberg, J., Solomon, S., & Pyszczynski, T. (1997). Terror management theory of self-esteem and cultural worldviews: Empirical assessments and conceptual refinements. *Advances in Social Psychology, 29,* 61–142. (p. 568)

Greene, J. (2010). *Remarks to An Edge conference: The new science of morality.* www.edge.org. (p. 517)

Greene, J., Sommerville, R. B., Nystrom, L. E., Darley, J. M., & Cohen, J. D. (2001). An fMRI investigation of emotional engagement in moral judgment. *Science, 293,* 2105. (p. 516)

Greenwald, A. G. (1992). Subliminal semantic activation and subliminal snake oil. Paper presented to the American Psychological Association Convention, Washington, DC. (p. 158)

Greenwald, A. G., McGhee, D. E., & Schwartz, J. L. K. (1998). Measuring individual differences in implicit cognition: The implicit association test. *Journal of Personality and Social Psychology, 74*, 1464–1480. (p. 782)

Greenwald, A. G., Oakes, M. A., & Hoffman, H. (2003). Targets of discrimination: Effects of race on responses to weapons holders. *Journal of Experimental Social Psychology, 39*, 399. (p. 782)

Greenwald, A. G., Poehlman, T. A., Uhlmann, E. L., & Banaji, M. R. (2009). Understanding and using the implicit association test: III. Meta-analysis of the predictive validity. *Journal of Personality and Social Psychology, 97*, 17–41. (p. 782)

Greenwald, A. G., Spangenberg, E. R., Pratkanis, A. R., & Eskenazi, J. (1991). Double-blind tests of subliminal self-help audiotapes. *Psychological Science, 2*, 119–122. (p. 158)

Greer, G. (1984, April). The uses of chastity and other paths to sexual pleasures. *MS, 53*–60, 96. (p. 409)

Gregory, A. M., Rijksdijk, F. V., Lau, J. Y., Dahl, R. E., & Eley, T. C. (2009). The direction of longitudinal associations between sleep problems and depression symptoms: A study of twins aged 8 and 10 years. *Sleep, 32*, 189–199. (p. 236)

Gregory, R. L. (1978). *Eye and brain: The psychology of seeing* (3rd ed.). New York: McGraw-Hill. (p. 190)

Gregory, R. L., & Gombrich, E. H. (Eds.). (1973). *Illusion in nature and art.* New York: Charles Scribner's Sons. (p. 165)

Greif, E. B., & Ulman, K. J. (1982). The psychological impact of menarche on early adolescent females: A review of the literature. *Child Development, 53*, 1413–1430. (p. 528)

Greist, J. H., Jefferson, J. W., & Marks, I. M. (1986). *Anxiety and its treatment: Help is available.* Washington, DC: American Psychiatric Press. (p. 662)

Greitemeyer, T., & McLatchie, N. (2011). Denying humanness to others: A newly discovered mechanism by which violent video games increase aggressive behavior. *Psychological Science, 22*, 655–659. (p. 794)

Greitemeyer, T., & Osswald, S. (2010). Effects of prosocial video games on prosocial behavior. *Journal of Personality and Social Psychology, 98*, 211–221. (p. 794)

Greyson, B. (2010). Implications of near-death experiences for a postmaterialist psychology. *Review of Religion and Spirituality, 2*, 37–45. (p. 255)

Grèzes, J., & Decety, J. (2001). Functional anatomy of execution, mental simulation, observation, and verb generation of actions: A meta-analysis. *Human Brain Mapping, 12*, 1–19. (p. 381)

Griffiths, M. (2001). Sex on the Internet: Observations and implications for Internet sex addiction. *Journal of Sex Research, 38*, 333–342. (p. 248)

Grilo, C. M., & Pogue-Geile, M. F. (1991). The nature of environmental influences on weight and obesity: A behavior genetic analysis. *Psychological Bulletin, 110*, 520–537. (p. 402)

Grinker, R. R. (2007). *Unstrange minds: Remapping the world of autism.* New York: Basic Books. (p. 481)

Grobstein, C. (1979, June). External human fertilization. *Scientific American*, 57–67. (p. 466)

Grogan-Kaylor, A. (2004). The effect of corporal punishment on antisocial behavior in children. *Social Work Research, 28*, 153–162. (p. 282)

Groothuis, T. G. G., & Carere, C. (2005). Avian personalities: Characterization and epigenesis. *Neuroscience and Biobehavioral Reviews, 29*, 137–150. (p. 578)

Gross, A. E., & Crofton, C. (1977). What is good is beautiful. *Sociometry, 40*, 85–90. (p. 802)

Gross, T. F. (2009). Own-ethnicity bias in the recognition of Black, East Asian, Hispanic, and White faces. *Basic and Applied Social Psychology, 31*, 128–135. (p. 786)

Grossberg, S. (1995). The attentive brain. *American Scientist, 83*, 438–449. (p. 165)

Grossmann, I., Na, J., Varnum, M. E. W., Park, D. C., Kitayama, S., & Nisbett, R. E. (2010). Reasoning about social conflicts improves into old age. *PNAS, 107*, 7246–7250. (p. 626)

Gruder, C. L. (1977). Choice of comparison persons in evaluating oneself. In J. M. Suls & R. L. Miller (Eds.), *Social comparison processes.* New York: Hemisphere. (p. 852)

Guerin, B. (1986). Mere presence effects in humans: A review. *Journal of Personality and Social Psychology, 22*, 38–77. (p. 771)

Guerin, B. (2003). Language use as social strategy: A review and an analytic framework for the social sciences. *Review of General Psychology, 7*, 251–298. (p. 372)

Guiso, L., Monte, F., Sapienza, P., & Zingales, L. (2008). Culture, gender, and math. *Science, 320*, 1164–1165. (p. 639)

Gunstad, J., Strain, G., Devlin, M. J., Wing, R., Cohen, R. A., Paul, R. H., Crosby, R. D., & Mitchell, J. E. (2011). Improved memory function 12 weeks after bariatric surgery. *Surgery for Obesity and Related Diseases, 7*, 465–472. (p. 401)

Gunter, R. W., & Bodner, G. E. (2008). How eye movements affect unpleasant memories: Support for a working-memory account. *Behaviour Research and Therapy, 46*, 913–931. (p. 733)

Gunter, T. D., Vaughn, M. G., & Philibert, R. A. (2010). Behavioral genetics in antisocial spectrum disorders and psychopathy: A review of the recent literature. *Behavioral Sciences and the Law, 28*, 148–173. (p. 699)

Güntürkün, O. (2003). Adult persistence of head-turning asymmetry. *Nature, 421*, 711. (p. 118)

Guo, X., & 19 others. (2010). Effect of antipsychotic medication alone vs combined with psychosocial intervention on outcomes of early-stage schizophrenia. *Archives of General Psychiatry, 67*, 895–904. (p. 741)

Gustavson, C. R., Garcia, J., Hankins, W. G., & Rusiniak, K. W. (1974). Coyote predation control by aversive conditioning. *Science, 184*, 581–583. (p. 294)

Gustavson, C. R., Kelly, D. J., & Sweeney, M. (1976). Prey-lithium aversions I: Coyotes and wolves. *Behavioral Biology, 17*, 61–72. (p. 294)

Guttmacher Institute. (1994). *Sex and America's teenagers.* New York: Alan Guttmacher Institute. (pp. 523, 529)

Guttmacher Institute. (2000). *Fulfilling the promise: Public policy and U.S. family planning clinics.* New York: Alan Guttmacher Institute. (p. 523)

H., Sally. (1979, August). Videotape recording number T–3, Fortunoff Video Archive of Holocaust Testimonies. New Haven, CT: Yale University Library. (p. 563)

Haas, A. P., & 25 others. (2011). Suicide and suicide risk in lesbian, gay, bisexual, and transgender populations: Review and recommendations. *Journal of Homosexuality, 58*, 10–51. (p. 676)

Haase, C. M., Tomasik, M. J., & Silbereisen, R. K. (2008). Premature behavioral autonomy: Correlates in late adolescence and young adulthood. *European Psychologist, 13*, 255–266. (p. 496)

Haber, R. N. (1970, May). How we remember what we see. *Scientific American*, 104–112. (p. 318)

Haddock, G., & Zanna, M. P. (1994). Preferring "housewives" to "feminists." *Psychology of Women Quarterly, 18*, 25–52. (p. 783)

Hagger, M. S., Wood, C., Stiff, C., & Chatzisarantis, N. L. D. (2010). Ego depletion and the strength model of self-control: A meta-analysis. *Psychological Bulletin, 136*, 495–525. (p. 301)

Haidt, J. (2000). The positive emotion of elevation. *Prevention and Treatment, 3*, article 3 (journals.apa.org/prevention/volume3). (p. 516)

Haidt, J. (2002). The moral emotions. In R. J. Davidson, K. Scherer, & H. H. Goldsmith (Eds.), *Handbook of affective sciences.* New York: Oxford University Press. (p. 516)

Haidt, J. (2006). *The happiness hypothesis: Finding modern truth in ancient wisdom.* New York: Basic Books. (p. 516)

Haidt, J. (2010). Moral psychology must not be based on faith and hope: Commentary on Narvaez. *Perspectives on Psychological Science, 5*, 182–184. (p. 516)

Haier, R. J. (2009, November/December). What does a smart brain look like? *Scientific American Mind*, 26–33. (p. 613)

Haier, R. J., Colom, R., Schroeder, D. H., Condon, C. A., Tang, C., Eaves, E., & Head, K. (2009). Gray matter and intelligence factors: Is there a neuro-*g*? *Intelligence, 37*, 136–144. (p. 613)

Hakuta, K., Bialystok, E., & Wiley, E. (2003). Critical evidence: A test of the critical-period hypothesis for second-language acquisition. *Psychological Science, 14*, 31–38. (p. 376)

Halberstadt, J. B., Niedenthal, P. M., & Kushner, J. (1995). Resolution of lexical ambiguity by emotional state. *Psychological Science, 6*, 278–281. (p. 166)

Halberstadt, J. B., Sherman, S. J., & Sherman, J. W. (2011). Why Barack Obama is black. *Psychological Science, 22*, 29–33. (pp. 785, 786)

Haldeman, D. C. (1994). The practice and ethics of sexual orientation conversion therapy. *Journal of Consulting and Clinical Psychology, 62*, 221–227. (p. 532)

Haldeman, D. C. (2002). Gay rights, patient rights: The implications of sexual orientation conversion therapy. *Professional Psychology: Research and Practice, 33*, 260–264. (p. 532)

Hall, C. S., Dornhoff, W., Blick, K. A., & Weesner, K. E. (1982). The dreams of college men and women in 1950 and 1980: A comparison of dream contents and sex differences. *Sleep, 5*, 188–194. (p. 240)

Hall, C. S., & Lindzey, G. (1978). *Theories of personality* (2nd ed.). New York: Wiley. (p. 562)

Hall, G. (1997). Context aversion, Pavlovian conditioning, and the psychological side effects of chemotherapy. *European Psychologist, 2*, 118–124. (p. 295)

Hall, G. S. (1904). *Adolescence: Its psychology and its relations to physiology, anthropology, sex, crime, religion and education* (Vol. I). New York: Appleton-Century-Crofts. (p. 513)

Hall, J. A. (1984). *Nonverbal sex differences: Communication accuracy and expressive style.* Baltimore: Johns Hopkins University Press. (p. 434)

Hall, J. A. (1987). On explaining gender differences: The case of nonverbal communication. In P. Shaver & C. Hendrick (Eds.), *Review of Personality and Social Psychology, 7*, 177–200. (p. 434)

Hall, J. G. (2003). Twinning. *Lancet, 362*, 735–743. (p. 126)

Hall, L., Johansson, P., Tärning, B., Sikström, S., & Deutgen, T. (2010). Magic at the marketplace: Choice blindness for the taste of jam and the smell of tea. *Cognition, 117*, 54–61. (p. 155)

Hall, S. S. (2004, May). The good egg. *Discover*, 30–39. (p. 466)

Hall, W. (2006). The mental health risks of adolescent cannabis use. *PloS Medicine, 3*(2), e39. (p. 255)

Halpern, C. T., Joyner, K., Udry, J. R., & Suchindran, C. (2000). Smart teens don't have sex (or kiss much either). *Journal of Adolescent Health, 26*(3), 213–215. (p. 530)

Halpern, D. F. (2000). *Sex-related ability differences: Changing perspectives, changing minds.* Mahwah, NJ: Erlbaum. (p. 638)

Halpern, D. F., Benbow, C. P., Geary, D. C., Gur, R. C., Hyde, J. S., & Gernsbacher, M. A. (2007). The science of sex differences in science and mathematics. *Psychological Science in the Public Interest, 8*, 1–51. (p. 638)

Halsey, A., III (2010, January 26). U.S. bans truckers, bus drivers from texting while driving. *Washington Post* (www.washingtonpost.com). (p. 153)

Hamann, S., Herman, R. A., Nolan, C. L., & Wallen, K. (2004). Men and women differ in amygdala response to visual sexual stimuli. *Nature Neuroscience, 7*, 411–416. (p. 409)

Hammer, E. (2003). How lucky you are to be a psychology major. *Eye on Psi Chi*, 4–5. (p. 24)

Hammersmith, S. K. (1982, August). Sexual preference: An empirical study from the Alfred C. Kinsey Institute for Sex Research. Paper presented at the meeting of the American Psychological Association, Washington, DC. (p. 533)

Hammond, D. C. (2008). Hypnosis as sole anesthesia for major surgeries: Historical and contemporary perspectives. *American Journal of Clinical Hypnosis, 51*, 101–121. (p. 221)

Hampson, R. (2000, April 10). In the end, people just need more room. *USA Today*, 19A. (p. 402)

Han, S. (2008, January). Bloom and grow: My view of psychological research in China. *Observer*, 21–22. (p. 9)

Hancock, K. J., & Rhodes, G. (2008). Contact, configural coding and the other-race effect in face recognition. *British Journal of Psychology, 99*, 45–56. (p. 786)

Hankin, B. L., & Abramson, L. Y. (2001). Development of gender differences in depression: An elaborated cognitive vulnerability-transactional stress theory. *Psychological Bulletin, 127*, 773–796. (p. 679)

Hansen, C. H., & Hansen, R. D. (1988). Finding the face-in-the-crowd: An anger superiority effect. *Journal of Personality and Social Psychology, 54*, 917–924. (p. 432)

Harbaugh, W. T., Mayr, U., & Burghart, D. R. (2007). Neural responses to taxation and voluntary giving reveal motives for charitable donations. *Science, 316*, 1622–1625. (p. 809)

Harber, K. D. (1998), Feedback to minorities: Evidence of a positive bias. *Journal of Personality and Social Psychology, 74*, 622–628. (p. 782)

Hardeveld, H. S., De Graaf, R., Nolen, W. A., & Beckman, A. T. F. (2010). Prevalence and predictors of recurrence of major depressive disorder in the adult population. *Acta Psychiatrica Scandinavia, 122*, 184–191. (p. 675)

Hardisty, D. J., Johnson, E. J., & Weber, E. U. (2010). A dirty word or a dirty world? Attribute framing, political affiliation, and query theory. *Psychological Science, 21*, 86–92. (p. 368)

Hardt, O., Einarsson, E. O., & Nader, K. (2010). A bridge over troubled water: Reconsolidation as a link between cognitive and neuroscientific memory research traditions. *Annual Review of Psychology, 61*, 141–167. (p. 347)

Hare, R. D. (1975). Psychophysiological studies of psychopathy. In D. C. Fowles (Ed.), *Clinical applications of psychophysiology.* New York: Columbia University Press. (p. 700)

Harenski, C. L., Harenski, K. A., Shane, M. W., & Kiehl, K. A. (2010). Aberrant neural processing of moral violations in criminal psychopaths. *Journal of Abnormal Psychology, 119*, 863–874. (p. 701)

Harker, L. A., & Keltner, D. (2001). Expressions of positive emotion in women's college yearbook pictures and their relationship to personality and life outcomes across adulthood. *Journal of Personality and Social Psychology, 80*, 112–124. (p. 847)

Harkins, S. G., & Szymanski, K. (1989). Social loafing and group evaluation. *Journal of Personality and Social Psychology, 56*, 934–941. (p. 773)

Harlow, H. F., Harlow, M. K., & Suomi, S. J. (1971). From thought to therapy: Lessons from a primate laboratory. *American Scientist, 59*, 538–549. (p. 489)

Harmon-Jones, E., Abramson, L. Y., Sigelman, J., Bohlig, A., Hogan, M. E., & Harmon-Jones, C. (2002). Proneness to hypomania/mania symptoms or depression symptoms and asymmetrical frontal cortical responses to an anger-evoking event. *Journal of Personality and Social Psychology, 82*, 610–618. (p. 427)

Harper, C., & McLanahan, S. (2004). Father absence and youth incarceration. *Journal of Research on Adolescence, 14*, 369–397. (p. 792)

Harper's (2009, November). Harper's index. *Harper's*, 13. (p. 801)

Harris, B. (1979). Whatever happened to Little Albert? *American Psychologist, 34*, 151–160. (p. 271)

Harris, J. A. (1999). Review and methodological considerations in research on testosterone and aggression. *Aggression and Violent Behavior, 4*, 273–291. (p. 790)

Harris, J. R. (1998). *The nurture assumption.* New York: Free Press. (pp. 491, 510)

Harris, J. R. (2000). Beyond the nurture assumption: Testing hypotheses about the child's environment. In J. G. Borkowski & S. L. Ramey (Eds.), *Parenting and the child's world: Influences on academic, intellectual, and social-emotional development.* Washington, DC: APA Books. (p. 510)

Harris, J. R. (2006). *No two are alike: Human nature and human individuality.* New York: Norton. (p. 127)

Harris, J. R. (2007, August 8). Do pals matter more than parents? *The Times* (www.timesonline.co.uk). (p. 510)

Harris, R. J. (1994). The impact of sexually explicit media. In J. Brant & D. Zillmann (Eds.), *Media effects: Advances in theory and research.* Hillsdale, NJ: Erlbaum. (p. 793)

Harriston, K. A. (1993, December 24). 1 shakes, 1 snoozes: Both win $45 million. *Washington Post* release (in *Tacoma News Tribune*, A1, A2). (p. 592)

Harter, J. K., Schmidt, F. L., Asplund, J. W., Killham, E. A., & Agrawal, S. (2010). Causal impact of employee work perceptions on the bottom line of organizations. *Perspectives on Psychological Science, 5*, 378–389. (p. 836)

Harter, J. K., Schmidt, F. L., & Hayes, T. L. (2002). Business-unit-level relationship between employee satisfaction, employee engagement, and business outcomes: A meta-analysis. *Journal of Applied Psychology, 87*, 268–279. (p. 836)

Hartmann, E. (1981, April). The strangest sleep disorder. *Psychology Today, 14*, 16, 18. (p. 239)

Hartwig, M., & Bond, C. F., Jr. (2011). Why do lie-catchers fail? A lens model meta-analysis of human lie judgments. *Psychological Bulletin, 137*, 643–659. (p. 433)

Harvard Mental Health Letter. (2002, February). EMDR (Eye movement and reprocessing). *Harvard Mental Health Letter, 18*, 4–5. (p. 733)

Haslam, S. A., & Reicher, S. (2007). Beyond the banality of evil: Three dynamics of an interactionist social psychology of tyranny. *Personality and Social Psychology Bulletin, 33*, 615–622. (p. 758)

Hassan, B., & Rahman, Q. (2007). Selective sexual orientation-related differences in object location memory. *Behavioral Neuroscience, 121*, 625–633. (p. 536)

Hatfield, E. (1988). Passionate and companionate love. In R. J. Sternberg & M. L. Barnes (Eds.), *The psychology of love.* New Haven, CT: Yale University Press. (p. 803)

Hatfield, E., & Sprecher, S. (1986). *Mirror, mirror . . . The importance of looks in everyday life.* Albany: State University of New York Press. (p. 800)

Hatfield, J., Faunce, G. J., & Job, R. F. S. (2006). Avoiding confusion surrounding the phrase "correlation does not imply causation." *Teaching of Psychology, 33*, 49–51. (p. 49)

Hathaway, S. R. (1960). *An MMPI handbook* (Vol. 1, Foreword). Minneapolis: University of Minnesota Press. (Revised edition, 1972). (p. 578)

Hatzenbuehler, M. L. (2011). The social environment and suicide attempts in lesbian, gay, and bisexual youth. *Pediatrics, 127,* 896–903. (p. 676)

Hatzenbuehler, M. L., Nolen-Hoeksema, S., & Dovidio, J. (2009). How does stigma "get under the skin?" The mediating role of emotion regulation. *Psychological Science, 20,* 1282–1289. (p. 651)

Hauser, M. D. (2006). *Moral minds: How nature designed our universal sense of right and wrong.* New York: Ecco. (p. 137)

Hauser, M. D. (2009). It seems biology (not religion) equals morality. The Edge (www.edge.org). (p. 137)

Hauser, M. D., Chomsky, N., & Fitch, W. T. (2002). The faculty of language: What is it, who has it, and how did it evolve? *Science, 298,* 1569–1579. (p. 373)

Havas, D. A., Glenberg, A. M., Gutowski, K. A., Lucarelli, M. J., & Davidson, R. J. (2010). Cosmetic use of Botulinum Toxin-A affects processing of emotional language. *Psychological Science, 21,* 895–900. (p. 438)

Havas, D. A., Glenberg, A. M., & Rink, M. (2007). Emotion simulation during language comprehension. *Psychonomic Bulletin & Review, 14,* 436–441. (p. 438)

Haworth, C. M. A., & 23 others. (2010). The heritability of general cognitive ability increases linearly from childhood to young adulthood. *Molecular Psychiatry, 15,* 1112–1120. (p. 634)

Haxby, J. V. (2001, July 7). Quoted by B. Bower, Faces of perception. *Science News,* pp. 10–12. See also J. V. Haxby, M. I. Gobbini, M. L. Furey, A. Ishai, J. L. Schouten & P. Pietrini, Distributed and overlapping representations of faces and objects in ventral temporal cortex. *Science, 293,* 2425–2430. (p. 176)

Haynes, J-D., & Rees, G. (2005). Predicting the orientation of invisible stimuli from activity in human primary visual cortex. *Nature Neuroscience, 8,* 686–691. (p. 157)

Haynes, J-D., & Rees, G. (2006). Decoding mental states from brain activity in humans. *Nature Reviews Neuroscience, 7,* 523–534. (p. 157)

Hazan, C., & Shaver, P. R. (1994). Attachment as an organizational framework for research on close relationships. *Psychological Inquiry, 5,* 1–22. (p. 494)

Hazelrigg, M. D., Cooper, H. M., & Borduin, C. M. (1987). Evaluating the effectiveness of family therapies: An integrative review and analysis. *Psychological Bulletin, 101,* 428–442. (p. 724)

He, Y., Jones, C. R., Fujiki, N., Xu, Y., Guo, B., Holder, J. L., Jr., Rossner, M. J., Nishino, S., & Fu, Y-H. (2009). The transcriptional repressor DEC2 regulates sleep length in mammals. *Science, 325,* 866–870. (p. 229)

Head Start. (2010). Head Start program fact sheet. Office of Head Start, U. S. Department of Health and Human Services (www.acf.hhs.gov/programs/ohs/about/fy2010.html). (p. 635)

Headey, B., Muffels, R., & Wagner, G. G. (2010). Long-running German panel survey shows that personal and economic choices, not just genes, matter for happiness. *PNAS,107,* 17922–17926. (p. 852)

Health Canada (2012). Major findings from the Canadian Alcohol and Drug Use Monitoring Survey (CADUMS) 2011. Health Canada (www.hc-sc.gc.ca/hc-ps/drugs-drogues/stat/index-eng.php). (p. 822)

Heatherton, T. F., & Sargent, J. D. (2009). Does watching smoking in movies promote teenage smoking? *Current Directions in Psychological Science, 18,* 63–67. (p. 824)

Heavey, C. L., & Hurlburt, R. T. (2008). The phenomena of inner experience. *Consciousness and Cognition, 17,* 798–810. (pp. 41, 379)

Heckert, J. (2010, November 15). The hazards of growing up painlessly. *New York Times* (www.nytimes.com). (p. 201)

Hedström, P., Liu, K-Y., & Nordvik, M. K. (2008). Interaction domains and suicides: A population-based panel study of suicides in the Stockholm metropolitan area, 1991–1999. *Social Forces, 2,* 713–740. (p. 677)

Heider, F. (1958). *The psychology of interpersonal relations.* New York: Wiley. (p. 754)

Heiman, J. R. (1975, April). The physiology of erotica: Women's sexual arousal. *Psychology Today,* pp. 90–94. (p. 409)

Heine, S. J., & Buchtel, E. E. (2009). Personality: The universal and the culturally specific. *Annual Review of Psychology, 60,* 369–394. (pp. 580, 600)

Heine, S. J., & Hamamura, T. (2007). In search of East Asian self-enhancement. *Personality and Social Psychology Review, 11,* 4–27. (p. 596)

Heine, S. J., & Ruby, M. B. (2010). Cultural psychology. *Wiley Interdisciplinary Reviews: Cognitive Science, 1,* 254–266. (p. 755)

Hejmadi, A., Davidson, R. J., & Rozin, P. (2000). Exploring Hindu Indian emotion expressions: Evidence for accurate recognition by Americans and Indians. *Psychological Science, 11,* 183–187. (p. 432)

Helfand, D. (2011, January 7). An assault on rationality. *New York Times* (www.nytimes.com). (p. 169)

Helgeson, V. S., Reynolds, K. A., & Tomich, P. L. (2006). A meta-analytic review of benefit finding and growth. *Journal of Consulting and Clinical Psychology, 74,* 797–816. (p. 665)

Heller, A. S., Johnstone, T., Schackman, A. J., Light, S. N., Peterson, M. J., Kolden, G. G., Kalin, N. H., & Davidson, R. J. (2009). Reduced capacity to sustain positive emotion in major depression reflects diminished maintenance of fronto-striatal brain activation. *PNAS, 106,* 22445–22450. (p. 678)

Heller, W. (1990, May/June). Of one mind: Second thoughts about the brain's dual nature. *The Sciences,* 38–44. (p. 117)

Helmreich, W. B. (1992). *Against all odds: Holocaust survivors and the successful lives they made in America.* New York: Simon & Schuster. (pp. 493, 563)

Helmreich, W. B. (1994). Personal correspondence. Department of Sociology, City University of New York. (p. 563)

Helms, J. E., Jernigan, M., & Mascher, J. (2005). The meaning of race in psychology and how to change it: A methodological perspective. *American Psychologist, 60,* 27–36. (p. 640)

Helmuth, L. (2001). Boosting brain activity from the outside in. *Science, 292,* 1284–1286. (p. 745)

Helton, W. S. (2008). Expertise acquisition as sustained learning in humans and other animals: Commonalities across species. *Animal Cognition, 11,* 99–107. (p. 611)

Helweg-Larsen, M. (1999). (The lack of) optimistic biases in response to the 1994 Northridge earthquake: The role of personal experience. *Basic and Applied Social Psychology, 21,* 119–129. (p. 589)

Hembree, R. (1988). Correlates, causes, effects, and treatment of test anxiety. *Review of Educational Research, 58,* 47–77. (pp. 392, 426)

Hemenover, S. H. (2003). The good, the bad, and the healthy: Impacts of emotional disclosure of trauma on resilient self-concept and psychological distress. *Personality and Social Psychology Bulletin, 29,* 1236–1244. (p. 859)

Henderlong, J., & Lepper, M. R. (2002). The effects of praise on children's intrinsic motivation: A review and synthesis. *Psychological Bulletin, 128,* 774–795. (p. 298)

Henderson, J. M. (2007). Regarding scenes. *Current Directions in Psychological Science, 16,* 219–222. (p. 159)

Henig, R. M. (2010, August 18). What is it about 20-somethings? *New York Times* (www.nytimes.com). (p. 523)

Henkel, L. A., Franklin, N., & Johnson, M. K. (2000, March). Cross-modal source monitoring confusions between perceived and imagined events. *Journal of Experimental Psychology: Learning, Memory, & Cognition, 26,* 321–335. (p. 349)

Henley, N. M. (1989). Molehill or mountain? What we know and don't know about sex bias in language. In M. Crawford & M. Gentry (Eds.), *Gender and thought: Psychological perspectives.* New York: Springer-Verlag. (p. 380)

Hennenlotter, A., Dresel, C., Castrop, F., Ceballos Baumann, A., Wohschlager, A., & Haslinger, B. (2008). The link between facial feedback and neural activity within central circuitries of emotion: New insights from botulinum toxin-induced denervation of frown muscles. *Cerebral Cortex, 19,* 537–542. (p. 438)

Hennessey, B. A., & Amabile, T. M. (2010). Creativity. *Annual Review of Psychology, 61,* 569–598. (pp. 357, 839)

Henninger, P. (1992). Conditional handedness: Handedness changes in multiple personality disordered subject reflect shift in hemispheric dominance. *Consciousness and Cognition, 1,* 265–287. (p. 696)

Henrich, J., Heine, S. J., & Norenzayan, A. (2010). The weirdest people in the world? *Behavioral and Brain Sciences, 33,* 61–135. (p. 65)

Hepper, P. (2005). Unravelling our beginnings. *The Psychologist, 18,* 474–477. (p. 466)

Hepper, P. G., Shahidullah, S., & White, R. (1990). Origins of fetal handedness. *Nature, 347,* 431. (p. 118)

Hepper, P. G., Wells, D. L., & Lynch, C. (2004). Prenatal thumb sucking is related to postnatal handedness. *Neuropsychologia, 43,* 313–315. (p. 118)

Herbenick, D., Reece, M., Schick, V., Sanders, S. A., Dodge, B., & Fortenberry, J. D. (2010a). Sexual behavior in the United States: Results from a national probability sample of men and women ages 14–94. *Journal of Sexual Medicine, 7*(suppl. 5): 255–265. (p. 532)

Herbenick, D., Reece, M., Schick, V., Sanders, S. A., Dodge, B., & Fortenberry, J. D. (2010b). Sexual behaviors, relationships, and perceived health among adult women in the United States: Results from a national probability sample. *Journal of Sexual Medicine, 7* (suppl 5), 277–290. (p. 532)

Herbert, J. D., Lilienfeld, S. O., Lohr, J. M., Montgomery, R. W., O'Donohue, W. T., Rosen, G. M., & Tolin, D. F. (2000). Science and pseudoscience in the development of eye movement desensitization and reprocessing: Implications for clinical psychology. *Clinical Psychology Review, 20*, 945–971. (p. 733)

Herman, C. P., & Polivy, J. (1980). Restrained eating. In A. J. Stunkard (Ed.), *Obesity*. Philadelphia: Saunders. (p. 403)

Herman, C. P., Roth, D. A., & Polivy, J. (2003). Effects of the presence of others on food intake: A normative interpretation. *Psychological Bulletin, 129*, 873–886. (p. 400)

Herman-Giddens, M. E., Wang, L., & Koch, G. (2001). Secondary sexual characteristics in boys: Estimates from the National Health and Nutrition Examination Survey III, 1988–1994. *Archives of Pediatrics and Adolescent Medicine, 155*, 1022–1028. (p. 527)

Hernandez, A. E., & Li, P. (2007). Age of acquisition: Its neural and computational mechanisms. *Psychological Bulletin, 133*, 638–650. (p. 376)

Herrmann, E., Call, J., Hernández-Lloreda, M. V., Hare, B., & Tomasello, M. (2007). Humans have evolved specialized skills of social cognition: The cultural intelligence hypothesis. *Science, 317*, 1360–1365. (p. 306)

Herrmann, E., Hernández-Lloreda, V., Call, J., Hare, B., & Tomasello, M. (2010). The structure of individual differences in the cognitive abilities of children and chimpanzees. *Psychological Science, 21*, 102–110. (p. 870)

Herrnstein, R. J., & Loveland, D. H. (1964). Complex visual concept in the pigeon. *Science, 146*, 549–551. (p. 277)

Hershenson, M. (1989). *The moon illusion*. Hillsdale, NJ: Erlbaum. (p. 189)

Hertel, G., Schroer, J., Batinic, B., & Naumann, S. (2008). Do shy people prefer to send e-mail: Personality effects on communication media preferences in threatening and nonthreatening situations. *Social Psychology, 39*, 231–243. (p. 581)

Hertenstein, M. J., Hansel, C., Butts, S., Hile, S. (2009). Smile intensity in photographs predicts divorce later in life. *Motivation & Emotion, 33*, 99–105. (p. 464)

Hertenstein, M. J., Keltner, D., App, B. Bulleit, B., & Jaskolka, A. (2006). Touch communicates distinct emotions. *Emotion, 6*, 528–533. (p. 489)

Hertenstein, M. J., Verkamp, J. M., Kerestes, A. M., & Holmes, R. M. (2006). The communicative functions of touch in humans, nonhumans, primates, and rats: A review and synthesis of the empirical research. *Genetic, Social, and General Psychology Monographs, 132*, 5–94. (pp. 202, 489)

Herz, R. S. (2001). Ah sweet skunk! Why we like or dislike what we smell. *Cerebrum, 3*(4), 31–47. (p. 208)

Herz, R. S. (2007). *The scent of desire: Discovering our enigmatic sense of smell*. New York: Morrow/HarperCollins. (p. 209)

Herz, R. S., Beland, S. L., & Hellerstein, M. (2004). Changing odor hedonic perception through emotional associations in humans. *International Journal of Comparative Psychology, 17*, 315–339. (p. 209)

Herzog, H. (2010). *Some we love, some we hate, some we eat: Why it's so hard to think straight about animals*. New York: Harper. (p. 858)

Hess, E. H. (1956, July). Space perception in the chick. *Scientific American*, 71–80. (p. 191)

Hess, U., & Thibault, P. (2009). Darwin and emotion expression. *American Psychologist, 64*, 120–128. (p. 436)

Hetherington, M. M., Anderson, A. S., Norton, G. N. M., & Newson, L. (2006). Situational effects on meal intake: A comparison of eating alone and eating with others. *Physiology and Behavior, 88*, 498–505. (p. 400)

Hettema, J. M., Neale, M. C., & Kendler, K. S. (2001). A review and meta-analysis of the genetic epidemiology of anxiety disorders. *American Journal of Psychiatry, 158*, 1568–1578. (p. 668)

Hickok, G., Bellugi, U., & Klima, E. S. (2001, June). Sign language in the brain. *Scientific American*, 58–65. (p. 117)

Higgins, E. S., & George, M. S. (2007). *The neuroscience of clinical psychiatry: The pathophysiology of behavior and mental illness*. Hagerstown, MD: Lippincott Williams & Wilkins. (p. 83)

Hilgard, E. R. (1986). *Divided consciousness: Multiple controls in human thought and action*. New York: Wiley. (p. 222)

Hilgard, E. R. (1992). Dissociation and theories of hypnosis. In E. Fromm & M. R. Nash (Eds.), *Contemporary hypnosis research*. New York: Guilford. (p. 222)

Hill, C. E., & Nakayama, E. Y. (2000). Client-centered therapy: Where has it been and where is it going? A comment on Hathaway. *Journal of Clinical Psychology, 56*, 961–875. (p. 712)

Hines, M. (2004). *Brain gender*. New York: Oxford University Press. (p. 527)

Hingson, R. W., Heeren, T., & Winter, M. R. (2006). Age at drinking onset and alcohol dependence. *Archives of Pediatrics & Adolescent Medicine, 160*, 739–746. (p. 824)

Hintzman, D. L. (1978). *The psychology of learning and memory*. San Francisco: Freeman. (p. 323)

Hinz, L. D., & Williamson, D. A. (1987). Bulimia and depression: A review of the affective variant hypothesis. *Psychological Bulletin, 102*, 150–158. (p. 697)

Hirt, E. R., Zillmann, D., Erickson, G. A., & Kennedy, C. (1992). Costs and benefits of allegiance: Changes in fans' self-ascribed competencies after team victory versus defeat. *Journal of Personality and Social Psychology, 63*, 724–738. (p. 681)

Hjelmborg, J. v. B., Fagnani, C., Silventoinen, K., McGue, M., Korkeila, M., Christensen, K., Rissanen, A., & Kaprio, J. (2008). Genetic influences on growth traits of BMI: A longitudinal study of adult twins. *Obesity, 16*, 847–852. (p. 402)

HMHL. (2002a, January). Disaster and trauma. *Harvard Mental Health Letter*, pp. 1–5. (p. 443)

HMHL. (2002b, August). Smoking and depression. *Harvard Mental Health Letter*, 6–7. (p. 678)

HMHL. (2007, February). Electroconvulsive therapy. *Harvard Mental Health Letter*, Harvard Medical School, pp. 1–4. (p. 744)

Hobaiter, C., & Byrne, R. W. (2011). The gestural repertoire of the wild chimpanzee. *Animal Cognition*, DOI: 10.1007/s10071-011-0409-2. (p. 869)

Hobson, J. A. (1995, September). Quoted by C. H. Colt, The power of dreams. *Life*, 36–49. (p. 241)

Hobson, J. A. (2003). *Dreaming: An introduction to the science of sleep*. New York: Oxford. (p. 242)

Hobson, J. A. (2004). *13 dreams Freud never had: The new mind science*. New York: Pi Press. (p. 242)

Hobson, J. A. (2009). REM sleep and dreaming: Towards a theory of protoconsciousness. *Nature Reviews, 10*, 803–814. (p. 242)

Hochberg, L. R., Bacher, D., Jarosiewicz, B., Masse, N. Y., Simeral, J. D., Vogel, J., Haddadin, S., Liu, J., Cash, S. S., van der Smagt, P., & Donoghue, J. P. (2012). Reach and grasp by people with tetraplegia using a neurally controlled robotic arm. *Nature, 485*, 375–375. (p. 107)

Hochberg, L. R., Serruya, M. D., Friehs, G. M., Mukand, J. A., Saleh, M., Caplan, A. H., Branner, A., Chen, D., Penn, R. D., & Donoghue, J. P. (2006). Neuronal ensemble control of prosthetic devices by a human with tetraplegia. *Nature, 442*, 164–171. (p. 107)

Hodgkinson, V. A., & Weitzman, M. S. (1992). *Giving and volunteering in the United States*. Washington, DC: Independent Sector. (p. 810)

Hoebel, B. G., & Teitelbaum, P. (1966). Effects of forcefeeding and starvation on food intake and body weight in a rat with ventromedial hypothalamic lesions. *Journal of Comparative and Physiological Psychology, 61*, 189–193. (p. 398)

Hoeft, F., Watson, C. L., Kesler, S. R., Bettinger, K. E., & Reiss, A. L. (2008). Gender differences in the mesocorticolimbic system during computer game-play. *Journal of Psychiatric Research, 42*, 253–258. (p. 248)

Hoffman, C., & Hurst, N. (1990). Gender stereotypes: Perception or rationalization? *Journal of Personality and Social Psychology, 58*, 197–208. (p. 784)

Hoffman, D. D. (1998). *Visual intelligence: How we create what we see*. New York: Norton. (p. 177)

Hoffman, H. G. (2004, August). Virtual-reality therapy. *Scientific American*, 58–65. (pp. 206, 718)

Hofmann, S. G., Sawyer, A. T., Witt, A. A., & Oh, D. (2010). The effect of mindfulness-based therapy on anxiety and depression: A meta-analytic review. *Journal of Consulting and Clinical Psychology, 78*, 169–183. (pp. 296, 862)

Hofstadter, D. (2011, January 7). A cutoff for craziness. *New York Times* (www.nytimes.com). (p. 169)

Hogan, J. (1995, November). Get smart, take a test. *Scientific American*, 12, 14. (p. 621)

Hogan, R. (1998). Reinventing personality. *Journal of Social and Clinical Psychology, 17*, 1–10. (p. 583)

Hoge, C. W., & Castro, C. A. (2006). Post-traumatic stress disorder in UK and U.S. forces deployed to Iraq. *Lancet, 368*, 837. (p. 665)

Hoge, C. W., Terhakopian, A., Castro, C. A., Messer, S. C., & Engel, C. C. (2007). Association of posttraumatic stress disorder with somatic symptoms, health care visits, and absenteeism among Iraq War veterans. *American Journal of Psychiatry, 164,* 150–153. (p. 665)

Hogg, M. A. (1996). Intragroup processes, group structure and social identity. In W. P. Robinson (Ed.), *Social groups and identities: Developing the legacy of Henri Tajfel.* Oxford: Butterworth Heinemann. (p. 784)

Hogg, M. A. (2006). Social identity theory. In P. J. Burke (Ed.), *Contemporary social psychological theories.* Stanford, CA: Stanford University Press. (p. 784)

Hohmann, G. W. (1966). Some effects of spinal cord lesions on experienced emotional feelings. *Psychophysiology, 3,* 143–156. (p. 422)

Hokanson, J. E., & Edelman, R. (1966). Effects of three social responses on vascular processes. *Journal of Personality and Social Psychology, 3,* 442–447. (p. 846)

Holahan, C. K., & Sears, R. R. (1995). *The gifted group in later maturity.* Stanford, CA: Stanford University Press. (p. 629)

Holden, C. (1980a). Identical twins reared apart. *Science, 207,* 1323–1325. (p. 127)

Holden, C. (1980b, November). Twins reunited. *Science, 80,* 55–59. (p. 127)

Holden, C. (2007). Mental illness: The next frontier. *Science, 317,* 23. (p. 689)

Holden, C. (2008). Parsing the genetics of behavior. *Science, 322,* 892–895. (p. 129)

Holden, C. (2010). Experts map the terrain of mood disorders. *Science, 327,* p. 1068. (p. 671)

Holden, G. W., & Miller, P. C. (1999). Enduring and different: A meta-analysis of the similarity in parents' child rearing. *Psychological Bulletin, 125,* 223–254. (p. 496)

Holliday, R. E., & Albon, A. J. (2004). Minimizing misinformation effects in young children with cognitive interview mnemonics. *Applied Cognitive Psychology, 18,* 263–281. (p. 351)

Hollingworth, S. A., Burgess, P. M., & Whiteford, H. A. (2010). Affective and anxiety disorders: Prevalence, treatment and antidepressant medication use. *Australian and New Zealand Journal of Psychiatry, 44,* 513–519. (p. 742)

Hollis, K. L. (1997). Contemporary research on Pavlovian conditioning: A "new" functional analysis. *American Psychologist, 52,* 956–965. (p. 268)

Hollon, S. D., Thase, M. E., & Markowitz, J. C. (2002). Treatment and prevention of depression. *Psychological Science in the Public Interest, 3,* 39–77. (p. 742)

Holstege, G., Georgiadis, J. R., Paans, A. M. J., Meiners, L. C., van der Graaf, F. H. C. E., & Reinders, A. A. T. S. (2003a). Brain activation during male ejaculation. *Journal of Neuroscience, 23,* 9185–9193. (p. 407)

Holstege, G., Reinders, A. A. T., Paans, A. M. J., Meiners, L. C., Pruim, J., & Georgiadis, J. R. (2003b). *Brain activation during female sexual orgasm. Program No. 727.7.* Washington, DC: Society for Neuroscience. (p. 407)

Holt, L. (2002, August). Reported in "Sounds of speech," p. 26, and in personal correspondence, July 18, 2002. (p. 373)

Holtgraves, T. (2011). Text messaging, personality, and the social context. *Journal of Research in Personality, 45,* 92–99. (p. 582)

Holt-Lunstad, J., Smith, T. B., & Layton, J. B. (2010). Social relationships and mortality risk: A meta-analytic review. *PLoS Medicine, 7* (www.plosmedicine.org. e1000316). (p. 857)

Homer, B. D., Solomon, T. M., Moeller, R. W., Mascia, A., DeRaleau, L., & Halkitis, P. N. (2008). Methamphetamine abuse and impairment of social functioning: A review of the underlying neurophysiological causes and behavioral implications. *Psychological Bulletin, 134,* 301–310. (p. 253)

Hooley, J. M. (2010). Social factors in schizophrenia. *Current Directions in Psychological Science, 19,* 238–242. (p. 685)

Hooper, J., & Teresi, D. (1986). *The three-pound universe.* New York: Macmillan. (p. 100)

Hopkins, E. D., & Cantalupo, C. (2008). Theoretical speculations on the evolutionary origins of hemispheric specialization. *Current Directions in Psychological Science, 17,* 233–237. (p. 117)

Hopkins, W. D. (2006). Comparative and familial analysis of handedness in great apes. *Psychological Bulletin, 132,* 538–559. (p. 118)

Hopper, L. M., Lambeth, S. P., Schapiro, S. J., & Whiten, A. (2008). Observational learning in chimpanzees and children studied through 'ghost' conditions. *Proceedings of the Royal Society B, 275,* 835–840. (p. 306)

Hopwood, C. J., Donnellan, M. B., Blonigen, D. M., Krueger, R. F., McGue, M., Iacono, W. G., & Burt, S. A. (2011). Genetic and environmental influences on personality trait stability and growth during the transition to adulthood: A three-wave longitudinal study. *Journal of Personality and Social Psychology, 100,* 545–556. (p. 464)

Hor, H., & Tafti, M. (2009). How much sleep do we need? *Science, 325,* 825–826. (p. 229)

Horn, J. L. (1982). The aging of human abilities. In J. Wolman (Ed.), *Handbook of developmental psychology.* Englewood Cliffs, NJ: Prentice-Hall. (p. 626)

Horner, V., Whiten, A., Flynn, E., & de Waal, F. B. M. (2006). Faithful replication of foraging techniques along cultural transmission chains by chimpanzees and children. *Proceedings of the National Academy of Sciences, 103,* 13878–13883. (p. 868)

Horwood, L. J., & Fergusson, D. M. (1998). Breastfeeding and later cognitive and academic outcomes. *Pediatrics, 101*(1). (p. 48)

Hostetter, A. B. (2011). When do gestures communicate? A meta-analysis. *Psychological Bulletin, 137,* 297–315. (p. 869)

Hou, W-H., Chiang, P-T., Hsu, T-Y., Chiu, S-Y., & Yen, Y-C. (2010). Treatment effects of massage therapy in depressed people: A meta-analysis. *Journal of Clinical Psychiatry, 71,* 894–901. (p. 745)

House, R. J., & Singh, J. V. (1987). Organizational behavior: Some new directions for I/O psychology. *Annual Review of Psychology, 38,* 669–718. (p. 839)

Houser-Marko, L., & Sheldon, K. M. (2008). Eyes on the prize or nose to the grindstone? The effects of level of goal evaluation on mood and motivation. *Personality and Social Psychology Bulletin, 34,* 1556–1569. (p. 838)

Houts, A. C., Berman, J. S., & Abramson, H. (1994). Effectiveness of psychological and pharmacological treatments for nocturnal enuresis. *Journal of Consulting and Clinical Psychology, 62,* 737–745. (p. 717)

Houts, R. M., Caspi, A., Pianta, R. C., Arseneault, L., & Moffitt, T. E. (2010). The challenging pupil in the classroom: The effect of the child on the teacher. *Psychological Science, 21,* 1802–1810. (p. 464)

Hovatta, I., Tennant, R. S., Helton, R., Marr, R. A., Singer, O., Redwine, J. M., Ellison, J. A., Schadt, E. E., Verma, I. M., Lockhart, D. J., & Barlow, C. (2005). Glyoxalase 1 and glutathione reductase 1 regulate anxiety in mice. *Nature, 438,* 662–666. (p. 668)

Howe, M. L. (1997). Children's memory for traumatic experiences. *Learning and Individual Differences, 9,* 153–174. (p. 351)

Howell, A. J. (2009). Flourishing: Achievement-related correlates of students' well-being. *Journal of Positive Psychology, 4,* 1–13. (p. 635)

Howell, R. T., & Howell, C. J. (2008). The relation of economic status to subjective well-being in developing countries: A meta-analysis. *Psychological Bulletin, 134,* 536–560. (p. 849)

Hoyer, G., & Lund, E. (1993). Suicide among women related to number of children in marriage. *Archives of General Psychiatry, 50,* 134–137. (p. 676)

Hsee, C. K., Yang, A. X., & Wang, L. (2010). Idleness aversion and the need for justifiable busyness. *Psychological Science, 21,* 926–930. (p. 828)

Hu, X-Z., Lipsky, R. H., Zhu, G., Akhtar, L. A., Taubman, J., Greenberg, B. D., Xu, K., Arnold, P. D., Richter, M. A., Kennedy, J. L., Murphy, D. L., & Goldman, D. (2006). Serotonin transporter promoter gain-of-function genotypes are linked to obsessive-compulsive disorder. *American Journal of Human Genetics, 78,* 815–826. (p. 668)

Huang, C. (2010). Mean-level change in self-esteem from childhood through adulthood: Meta-analysis of longitudinal studies. *Review of General Psychology, 14,* 251–260. (p. 546)

Huang, X., Iun, J., Liu, A., & Gong, Y. (2010). Does participative leadership enhance work performance by inducing empowerment or trust? The differential effects on managerial and non-managerial subordinates. *Journal of Organizational Behavior, 31,* 122–143. (p. 839)

Huart, J., Corneille, O., & Becquart, E. (2005). Face-based categorization, context-based categorization, and distortions in the recollection of gender ambiguous faces. *Journal of Experimental Social Psychology, 41,* 598–608. (p. 357)

Hubbard, E. M., Arman, A. C., Ramachandran, V. S., & Boynton, G. M. (2005). Individual differences among grapheme-color synesthetes: Brain-behavior correlations. *Neuron, 45,* 975–985. (p. 211)

Hubel, D. H. (1979, September). The brain. *Scientific American,* 45–53. (p. 159)

Hubel, D. H., & Wiesel, T. N. (1979, September). Brain mechanisms of vision. *Scientific American,* 50–162. (p. 175)

Hublin, C., Kaprio, J., Partinen, M., Heikkila, K., & Koskenvuo, M. (1997). Prevalence and genetics of sleepwalking—A population-based twin study. *Neurology, 48,* 177–181. (p. 239)

Hublin, C., Kaprio, J., Partinen, M., & Koskenvuo, M. (1998). Sleeptalking in twins: Epidemiology and psychiatric comorbidity. *Behavior Genetics, 28,* 289–298. (p. 239)

Hucker, S. J., & Bain, J. (1990). Androgenic hormones and sexual assault. In W. Marshall, R. Law, & H. Barbaree (Eds.), *The handbook on sexual assault.* New York: Plenum. (p. 408)

Hudson, J. I., Hiripi, E., Pope, H. G., & Kessler, R. C. (2007). The prevalence and correlates of eating disorders in the National Comorbidity Survey Replication. *Biological Psychiatry, 61,* 348–358. (p. 697)

Huey, E. D., Krueger, F., & Grafman, J. (2006). Representations in the human prefrontal cortex. *Current Directions in Psychological Science, 15,* 167–171. (p. 109)

Huffcutt, A. I., Conway, J. M., Roth, P. L., & Stone, N. J. (2001). Identification and meta-analytic assessment of psychological constructs measured in employment interviews. *Journal of Applied Psychology, 86,* 897–913. (p. 832)

Hugenberg, K., & Bodenhausen, G. V. (2003). Facing prejudice: Implicit prejudice and the perception of facial threat. *Psychological Science, 14,* 640–643. (p. 782)

Hugenberg, K., Young, S. G., Bernstein, M. J., & Sacco, D. F. (2010). The categorization-individuation model: An integrative account of the other-race recognition deficit. *Psychological Review, 117,* 1168–1187. (p. 786)

Hughes, J. R. (2010). Craving among long-abstinent smokers: An Internet survey. *Nicotine & Tobacco Research, 12,* 459–462. (p. 252)

Hugick, L. (1989, July). Women play the leading role in keeping modern families close. *Gallup Report, No. 286,* p. 27–34. (p. 503)

Huizink, A. C., & Mulder, E. J. (2006). Maternal smoking, drinking or cannabis use during pregnancy and neurobehavioral and cognitive functioning in human offspring. *Neuroscience and Biobehavioral Reviews, 30,* 24–41. (p. 255)

Hulbert, A. (2005, November 20). The prodigy puzzle. *New York Times Magazine* (www.nytimes.com). (p. 629)

Hull, H. R., Morrow, M. L., Dinger, M. K., Han, J. L., & Fields, D. A. (2007, November 20). Characterization of body weight and composition changes during the sophomore year of college. *BMC Women's Health, 7,* 21 (biomedcentral.com). (p. 236)

Hull, J. G., & Bond, C. F., Jr. (1986). Social and behavioral consequences of alcohol consumption and expectancy: A meta-analysis. *Psychological Bulletin, 99,* 347–360. (p. 249)

Hull, J. M. (1990). *Touching the rock: An experience of blindness.* New York: Vintage Books. (pp. 336, 800)

Hülsheger, U. R., Anderson, N., & Salgado, J. F. (2009). Team-level predictors of innovation at work: A comprehensive meta-analysis spanning three decades of research. *Journal of Applied Psychology, 94,* 1128–1145. (p. 358)

Hummer, R. A., Rogers, R. G., Nam, C. B., & Ellison, C. G. (1999). Religious involvement and U.S. adult mortality. *Demography, 36,* 273–285. (p. 864)

Humphrey, S. E., Nahrgang, J. D., & Morgeson, F. P. (2007). Integrating motivational, social, and contextual work design features: A meta-analytic summary and theoretical extension of the work design literature. *Journal of Applied Psychology, 92,* 1332–1356. (p. 300)

Humphreys, L. G., & Davey, T. C. (1988). Continuity in intellectual growth from 12 months to 9 years. *Intelligence, 12,* 183–197. (p. 627)

Hunsberger, J. G., Newton, S. S., Bennett, A. H., Duman, C. H., Russell, D. S., Salton, S. R., & Duman, R. S. (2007). Antidepressant actions of the exercise-regulated gene VGF. *Nature Medicine, 13,* 1476–1482. (p. 860)

Hunsley, J., & Di Giulio, G. (2002). Dodo bird, phoenix, or urban legend? The question of psychotherapy equivalence. *Scientific Review of Mental Health Practice, 1,* 11–22. (p. 732)

Hunt, C., Slade, T., & Andrews, G. (2004). Generalized anxiety disorder and major depressive disorder comorbidity in the National Survey of Mental Health and Well-Being. *Depression and Anxiety, 20,* 23–31. (p. 662)

Hunt, E. (1983). On the nature of intelligence. *Science, 219,* 141–146. (p. 613)

Hunt, E., & Carlson, J. (2007). Considerations relating to the study of group differences in intelligence. *Perspectives on Psychological Science, 2,* 194–213. (pp. 640, 641, 642)

Hunt, J. M. (1982). Toward equalizing the developmental opportunities of infants and preschool children. *Journal of Social Issues, 38*(4), 163–191. (p. 634)

Hunt, M. (1990). *The compassionate beast: What science is discovering about the humane side of humankind.* New York: William Morrow. (p. 15)

Hunt, M. (1993). *The story of psychology.* New York: Doubleday. (pp. 3, 4, 9, 76, 271, 519, 630)

Hunt, M. (2007). *The story of psychology.* New York: Anchor. (p. 560)

Hunter, S., & Sundel, M. (Eds.). (1989). *Midlife myths: Issues, findings, and practice implications.* Newbury Park, CA: Sage. (p. 544)

Hurlburt, R. T., & Akhter, S. A. (2008). Unsymbolized thinking. *Consciousness and Cognition, 17,* 1364–1374. (p. 379)

Hurst, M. (2008, April 22). Who gets any sleep these days? Sleep patterns of Canadians. *Canadian Social Trends.* Statistics Canada Catalogue No. 11–008. (p. 229)

Hutchinson, R. (2006). *Calum's road.* Edinburgh: Burlinn Limited. (p. 834)

Hvistendahl, M. (2009). Making every baby girl count. *Science, 323,* 1164–1166. (p. 782)

Hvistendahl, M. (2010). Has China outgrown the one-child policy? *Science, 329,* 1458–1461. (p. 783)

Hvistendahl, M. (2011). China's population growing slowly, changing fast. *Science, 332,* 650–651. (pp. 782, 783)

Hyde, J. S. (2005). The gender similarities hypothesis. *American Psychologist, 60,* 581–592. (pp. 500, 501)

Hyde, J. S., & Mertz, J. E. (2009). Gender, culture, and mathematics performance. *Proceedings of the National Academy of Sciences, 106,* 8801–8807. (p. 638)

Hyde, J. S., Mezulis, A. H., & Abramson, L. Y. (2008). The ABCs of depression: Integrating affective, biological, and cognitive models to explain the emergence of the gender difference in depression. *Psychological Review, 115,* 291–313. (p. 674)

Hyman, I. E., Jr., Boss, S. M., Wise, B. M., McKenzie, K. E., & Caggiano, J. M. (2010). Did you see the unicycling clown? Inattentional blindness while walking and talking on a cell phone. *Applied Cognitive Psychology, 24*(5), 597–607. (p. 154)

Hyman, R. (1981). Cold reading: How to convince strangers that you know all about them. In K. Frazier (Ed.), *Paranormal borderlands of science.* Buffalo, NY: Prometheus. (p. 579)

Hyman, R. (2010). Meta-analysis that conceals more than it reveals: Comment on Storm et al. (2010). *Psychological Bulletin, 136,* 486–490. (p. 168)

Iacoboni, M. (2008). *Mirroring people: The new science of how we connect with others.* New York: Farrar, Straus & Giroux. (pp. 305, 307)

Iacoboni, M. (2009). Imitation, empathy, and mirror neurons. *Annual Review of Psychology, 60,* 653–670. (pp. 305, 307)

IAP. (2006, June 21). IAP statement on the teaching of evolution. *The Interacademy Panel on International Issues* (www.interacademies.net/iap). (p. 141)

Ickes, W., Snyder, M., & Garcia, S. (1997). Personality influences on the choice of situations. In R. Hogan, J. Johnson, & S. Briggs (Eds.). *Handbook of personality psychology.* San Diego, CA: Academic Press. (p. 588)

Idson, L. C., & Mischel, W. (2001). The personality of familiar and significant people: The lay perceiver as a social-cognitive theorist. *Journal of Personality and Social Psychology, 80,* 585–596. (p. 755)

IJzerman, H., & Semin, G. R. (2009). The thermometer of social relations: Mapping social proximity on temperature. *Psychological Science, 20,* 1214–1220. (p. 211)

Ikonomidou, C., Bittigau, P., Ishimaru, M. J., Wozniak, D. F., Koch, C., Genz, K., Price, M. T., Stefovska, V., Hoerster, F., Tenkova, T., Dikranian, K., & Olney, J. W. (2000). Ethanol-induced apoptotic neurodegeneration and fetal alcohol syndrome. *Science, 287,* 1056–1060. (p. 467)

Ilardi, S. S. (2009). *The depression cure: The six-step program to beat depression without drugs.* Cambridge, MA: De Capo Lifelong Books. (pp. 679, 747)

Inbar, Y., Cone, J., & Gilovich, T. (2010). People's intuitions about intuitive insight and intuitive choice. *Journal of Personality and Social Psychology, 99,* 232–247. (p. 369)

Inbar, Y., Pizarro, D., & Bloom, P. (2011). Disgusting smells cause decreased liking of gay men. Unpublished manuscript, Tillburg University. (p. 209)

Independent Sector. (2002). *Faith and philanthropy: The connection between charitable giving behavior and giving to religion.* Washington, DC: Author. (p. 810)

Ingham, A. G., Levinger, G., Graves, J., & Peckham, V. (1974). The Ringelmann effect: Studies of group size and group performance. *Journal of Experimental Social Psychology, 10,* 371–384. (p. 772)

Inglehart, R. (1990). *Culture shift in advanced industrial society.* Princeton, NJ: Princeton University Press. (p. 413)

Inglehart, R. (2008). Cultural change and democracy in Latin America. In F. Hagopian (Ed.), *Contemporary Catholicism, religious pluralism and democracy in Latin America*. South Bend, IN: Notre Dame University Press, 67–95. (p. 849)

Inman, M. L., & Baron, R. S. (1996). Influence of prototypes on perceptions of prejudice. *Journal of Personality and Social Psychology, 70*, 727–739. (p. 357)

Insana, R. (2005, February 21). Coach says honey gets better results than vinegar (interview with Larry Brown). *USA Today*, 4B. (p. 838)

Insel, T. R. (2010, April). Faulty circuits. *Scientific American*, 44–51. (p. 668)

International Schizophrenia Consortium. (2009). Common polygenic variation contributes to risk of schizophrenia and bipolar disorder. *Nature, 460*, 748–752. (p. 689)

Inzlicht, M., & Ben-Zeev, T. (2000). A threatening intellectual environment: Why females are susceptible to experiencing problem-solving deficits in the presence of males. *Psychological Science, 11*, 365–371. (p. 642)

Inzlicht, M., & Gutsell, J. N. (2007). Running on empty: Neural signals for self-control failure. *Psychological Science, 18*, 933–937. (p. 302)

Inzlicht, M., & Kang, S. K. (2010). Stereotype threat spillover: How coping with threats to social identity affects aggression, eating, decision making, and attention. *Journal of Personality and Social Psychology, 99*, 467–481. (p. 642)

Inzlicht, M., McGregor, I., Hirsh, J. C., & Nash, K. (2009). Neural markers of religious conviction. *Psychological Science, 20*, 385–392. (p. 96)

IPPA. (2009, January 22). Membership letter. International Positive Psychology Association. (p. 590)

IPPA. (2010, August). International conference on positive psychology and education in China, by S. Choong. *The IPPA Newsletter*, International Positive Psychology Association. (p. 590)

IPSOS. (2010a, June 29). Online Canadians report a large 35% decline in the amount of email received. www.ipsos-na.com. (pp. 42, 416)

IPSOS. (2010b, April 8). One in five (20%) global citizens believe that alien beings have come down to earth and walk amongst us in our communities disguised as humans. www.ipsos-na.com. (p. 42)

IPU. (2011). Women in national parliaments: Situation as of 31 November 2011. International Parliamentary Union (www.ipu.org). (p. 502)

Ireland, M. E., & Pennebaker, J. W. (2010). Language style matching in writing: Synchrony in essays, correspondence, and poetry. *Journal of Personality and Social Psychology, 99*, 549–571. (pp. 63, 307)

Ironson, G., Solomon, G. F., Balbin, E. G., O'Cleirigh, C., George, A., Kumar, M., Larson, D., & Woods, T. E. (2002). The Ironson-Woods spiritual/religiousness index is associated with long survival, health behaviors, less distress, and low cortisol in people with HIV/AIDS. *Annals of Behavioral Medicine, 24*, 34–48. (p. 865)

Irwin, M. R., Cole, J. C., & Nicassio, P. M. (2006). Comparative meta-analysis of behavioral interventions for insomnia and their efficacy in middle-aged adults and in older adults 55+ years of age. *Health Psychology, 25*, 3-14. (p. 238)

Isaacson, W. (2009, Spring). Einstein's final quest. In Character. http: //incharacter.org/features/einsteins-final-quest. (p. 643)

Ishida, A., Mutoh, T., Ueyama, T., Brando, H., Masubuchi, S., Nakahara, D., Tsujimoto, G., & Okamura, H. (2005). Light activates the adrenal gland: Timing of gene expression and glucocorticoid release. *Cell Metabolism, 2*, 297–307. (p. 734)

Iso, H., Simoda, S., & Matsuyama, T. (2007). Environmental change during postnatal development alters behaviour. *Behavioural Brain Research, 179*, 90–98. (p. 112)

Ito, T. A., Miller, N., & Pollock, V. E. (1996). Alcohol and aggression: A meta-analysis on the moderating effects of inhibitory cues, triggering events, and self-focused attention. *Psychological Bulletin, 120*, 60–82. (p. 791)

ITU. (2010). The world in 2009: ICT facts and figures. International Telecommunication Union (www.itu.int/ict). (p. 415)

Izard, C. E. (1977). *Human emotions*. New York: Plenum Press. (pp. 435, 844)

Izard, C. E. (1994). Innate and universal facial expressions: Evidence from developmental and cross-cultural research. *Psychological Bulletin, 114*, 288–299. (p. 435)

Jablensky, A. (1999). Schizophrenia: Epidemiology. *Current Opinion in Psychiatry, 12*, 19–28. (p. 687)

Jackson, G. (2009). Sexual response in cardiovascular disease. *Journal of Sex Research, 46*, 233–236. (p. 407)

Jackson, J. M., & Williams, K. D. (1988). Social loafing: A review and theoretical analysis. Unpublished manuscript, Fordham University. (p. 773)

Jackson, J. S., Brown, K. T., Brown, T. N., & Marks, B. (2001). Contemporary immigration policy orientations among dominant-group members in western Europe. *Journal of Social Issues, 57*, 431–456. (p. 781)

Jackson, L. A., & Gerard, D. A. (1996). Diurnal types, the "Big Five" personality factors and other personal characteristics. *Journal of Social Behavior and Personality, 11*, 273–283. (p. 581)

Jackson, S. W. (1992). The listening healer in the history of psychological healing. *American Journal Psychiatry, 149*, 1623–1632. (p. 735)

Jacobi, C., Hayward, C., deZwaan, M., Kraemer, H. C., & Agras, W. S. (2004). Coming to terms with risk factors for eating disorders: Application of risk terminology and suggestions for a general taxonomy. *Psychological Bulletin, 130*, 19–65. (p. 697)

Jacobs, B. L. (1994). Serotonin, motor activity, and depression-related disorders. *American Scientist, 82*, 456–463. (pp. 679, 860)

Jacobs, B. L. (2004). Depression: The brain finally gets into the act. *Current Directions in Psychological Science, 13*, 103–106. (p. 742)

Jacobs, B. L., van Praag, H., & Gage, F. H. (2000). Adult brain neurogenesis and psychiatry: A novel theory of depression. *Molecular Psychiatry, 5*, 262–269. (p. 679)

Jacques, C., & Rossion, B. (2006). The speed of individual face categorization. *Psychological Science, 17*, 485–492. (p. 151)

Jacques-Tiura, A. J., Abbey, A., Parkhill, M. R., & Zawacki, T. (2007). Why do some men misperceive women's sexual intentions more frequently than others do? An application of the confluence model. *Personality and Social Psychology Bulletin, 33*, 1467–1480. (p. 755)

James, K. (1986). Priming and social categorizational factors: Impact on awareness of emergency situations. *Personality and Social Psychology Bulletin, 12*, 462–467. (p. 336)

James, W. (1890). *The principles of psychology* (Vol. 2). New York: Holt. (pp. 90, 200, 341, 353, 421, 437, 759)

Jameson, D. (1985). Opponent-colors theory in light of physiological findings. In D. Ottoson & S. Zeki (Eds.), *Central and peripheral mechanisms of color vision*. New York: Macmillan. (p. 187)

Jamieson, J. P. (2010). The home field advantage in athletics: A meta-analysis. *Journal of Applied Social Psychology, 40*, 1819–1848. (pp. 771, 772)

Jamison, K. R. (1993). *Touched with fire: Manic-depressive illness and the artistic temperament*. New York: Free Press. (p. 673)

Jamison, K. R. (1995). *An unquiet mind*. New York: Knopf. (pp. 673, 707, 743)

Janis, I. L. (1982). *Groupthink: Psychological studies of policy decisions and fiascoes*. Boston: Houghton Mifflin. (p. 775)

Janis, I. L. (1986). Problems of international crisis management in the nuclear age. *Journal of Social Issues, 42*(2), 201–220. (p. 363)

Janoff-Bulman, R., Timko, C., & Carli, L. L. (1985). Cognitive biases in blaming the victim. *Journal of Experimental Social Psychology, 21*, 161–177. (p. 787)

Jaremka, L. M., Gabriel, S., & Carvallo, M. (2011). What makes us feel the best also makes us feel the worst: The emotional impact of independent and interdependent experiences. *Self and Identity, 10*, 44–63. (p. 414)

Jarrett, B., Bloch, G. J., Bennett, D., Bleazard, B., & Hedges, D. (2010). The influence of body mass index, age and gender on current illness: A cross-sectional study. *International Journal of Obesity, 34*, 429–436. (p. 401)

Jaschik, S. (2013, January 14). Study finds that increased parental support for college results in lower grades. *Inside Higher Education* (www.insidehighered. com). (p. 46)

Javitt, D. C., & Coyle, J. T. (2004, January). Decoding schizophrenia. *Scientific American*, 48–55. (p. 686)

Jemmott, J. B., III, Jemmott, L. S., & Fong, G. (2010). Efficacy of a theory-based abstinence-only intervention over 24 months. *Archives of Pediatric and Adolescent Medicine, 164*, 152–159. (p. 530)

Jenkins, J. G., & Dallenbach, K. M. (1924). Oblivescence during sleep and waking. *American Journal of Psychology, 35*, 605–612. (p. 345)

Jenkins, J. M., & Astington, J. W. (1996). Cognitive factors and family structure associated with theory of mind development in young children. *Developmental Psychology, 32*, 70–78. (p. 480)

Jensen, A. R. (1980). *Bias in mental testing*. New York: Free Press. (p. 622)

Jensen, A. R. (1983, August). The nature of the Black-White difference on various psychometric tests: Spearman's hypothesis. Paper presented at the meeting of the American Psychological Association, Anaheim, CA. (p. 642)

Jensen, A. R. (1989). New findings on the intellectually gifted. *New Horizons, 30,* 73–80. (p. 613)

Jensen, A. R. (1998). *The g factor: The science of mental ability.* Westport, CT: Praeger/Greenwood. (p. 642)

Jensen, J. P., & Bergin, A. E. (1988). Mental health values of professional therapists: A national interdisciplinary survey. *Professional Psychology: Research and Practice, 19,* 290–297. (p. 735)

Jensen, M. P. (2008). The neurophysiology of pain perception and hypnotic analgesia: Implications for clinical practice. *American Journal of Clinical Hypnosis, 51,* 123–147. (p. 221)

Jepson, C., Krantz, D. H., & Nisbett, R. E. (1983). Inductive reasoning: Competence or skill. *The Behavioral and Brain Sciences, 3,* 494–501. (p. 61)

Jessberger, S., Aimone, J. B., & Gage, F. H. (2008). Neurogenesis. In *Learning and memory: A comprehensive reference.* Oxford: Elsevier. (p. 112)

Job, V., Dweck, C. S., & Walton, G. M. (2010). Ego depletion–Is it all in your head? Implicit theories about willpower affect self-regulation. *Psychological Science, 21,* 1686–1693. (p. 301)

Jobe, T. H., & Harrow, M. (2010). Schizophrenia course, long-term outcome, recovery, and prognosis. *Current Directions in Psychological Science, 19,* 220–225. (p. 685)

Johnson, C. B., Stockdale, M. S., & Saal, F. E. (1991). Persistence of men's misperceptions of friendly cues across a variety of interpersonal encounters. *Psychology of Women Quarterly, 15,* 463–475. (p. 138)

Johnson, D. L., Wiebe, J. S., Gold, S. M., Andreasen, N. C., Hichwa, R. D., Watkins, G. L., & Ponto, L. L. B. (1999). Cerebral blood flow and personality: A positron emission tomography study. *American Journal of Psychiatry, 156,* 252–257. (p. 578)

Johnson, E. J. & Goldstein, D. (2003). Do defaults save lives? *Science, 302,* 1338–1339. (p. 368)

Johnson, J. A. (2007, June 26). Not so situational. Commentary on the SPSP listserv (spsp-discuss). The status of subjacency in the acquisition of a second language. *Cognition, 39,* 215–258. (p. 758)

Johnson, J. G., Cohen, P., Kotler, L., Kasen, S., & Brook, J. S. (2002). Psychiatric disorders associated with risk for the development of eating disorders during adolescence and early adulthood. *Journal of Consulting and Clinical Psychology, 70,* 1119–1128. (p. 697)

Johnson, J. S., & Newport, E. L. (1991). Critical period effects on universal properties of language: The status of subjacency in the acquisition of a second language. *Cognition, 39,* 215–258. (pp. 376, 377)

Johnson, M. H. (1992). Imprinting and the development of face recognition: From chick to man. *Current Directions in Psychological Science, 1,* 52–55. (p. 489)

Johnson, M. H., & Morton, J. (1991). *Biology and cognitive development: The case of face recognition.* Oxford: Blackwell Publishing. (p. 468)

Johnson, R. E., Chang, C-H., & Lord, R. G. (2006). Moving from cognition to behavior: What the research says. *Psychological Bulletin, 132,* 381–415. (p. 838)

Johnson, S. K. (2008). *Medically unexplained illness: Gender and biopsychosocial implications.* Washington, DC: American Psychological Association. (p. 693)

Johnson, W. (2010). Understanding the genetics of intelligence: Can height help? Can corn oil? *Current Directions in Psychological Science, 19,* 177–182. (p. 633)

Johnson, W., Carothers, A., & Deary, I. J. (2008). Sex differences in variability in general intelligence: A new look at the old question. *Perspectives on Psychological Science, 3,* 518–531. (p. 609)

Johnson, W., Gow, A. J., Corley, J., Starr, J. M., & Deary, I. J. (2010). Location in cognitive and residential space at age 70 reflects a lifelong trait over parental and environmental circumstances: The Lothian Birth Cohort 1936. *Intelligence, 38,* 403–411. (p. 628)

Johnson, W., Turkheimer, E., Gottesman, I. I., & Bouchard, T. J., Jr. (2009). Beyond heritability: Twin studies in behavioral research. *Current Directions in Psychological Science, 18,* 217–220. (pp. 125, 130, 632)

Johnston, L. D., O'Malley, P. M., Bachman, J. G., & Schulenberg, J. E. (2007). *Monitoring the Future national results on adolescent drug use: Overview of key findings, 2006.* Bethesda, MD: National Institute on Drug Abuse. (p. 824)

Johnston, L. D., O'Malley, P. M., Bachman, J. G., & Schulenberg, J. E. (2011). *Monitoring the future national results on adolescent drug use: Overview of key findings, 2010.* Ann Arbor, MI: Institute for Social Research, University of Michigan. (p. 252)

Johnston, L. D., O'Malley, P. M., Bachman, J. G., & Schulenberg, J. E. (2013). *Monitoring the future: National results on drug use: 2012 overview, key findings on adolescent drug use.* Ann Arbor: Institute for Social Research, The University of Michigan. (p. 822)

Johnstone, E. C., Ebmeier, K. P., Miller, P., Owens, D. G. C., & Lawrie, S. M. (2005). Predicting schizophrenia: Findings from the Edinburgh High-Risk Study. *British Journal of Psychiatry, 186,* 18–25. (p. 690)

Joiner, T. E., Jr. (2006). *Why people die by suicide.* Cambridge, MA: Harvard University Press. (p. 677)

Joiner, T. E., Jr. (2010). *Myths about suicide.* Cambridge, MA: Harvard University Press. (p. 677)

Jokela, M., Elovainio, M., Archana, S-M., & Kivimäki, M. (2009). IQ, socioeconomic status, and early death: The US National Longitudinal Survey of Youth. *Psychosomatic Medicine, 71,* 322–328. (p. 300)

Jolly, A. (2007). The social origin of mind. *Science, 317,* 1326. (p. 868)

Jonas, E., & Fischer, P. (2006). Terror management and religion: Evidence that intrinsic religiousness mitigates worldview defense following mortality salience. *Journal of Personality and Social Psychology, 91,* 553–567. (p. 568)

Jones, A. C., & Gosling, S. D. (2005). Temperament and personality in dogs (*Canis familiaris*): A review and evaluation of past research. *Applied Animal Behaviour Science, 95,* 1–53. (p. 578)

Jones, J. M. (2007, July 25). Latest Gallup update shows cigarette smoking near historical lows. *Gallup Poll News Service* (poll.gallup.com). (p. 252)

Jones, J. M., & Moore, D. W. (2003, June 17). Generational differences in support for a woman president. The Gallup Organization (www.gallup.com). (p. 780)

Jones, J. T., Pelham, B. W., Carvallo, M., & Mirenberg, M. C. (2004). How do I love thee? Let me count the Js: Implicit egotism and interpersonal attraction. *Journal of Personality and Social Psychology, 87,* 665–683. (p. 798)

Jones, L. (2000, December). Skeptics New Year quiz. *Skeptical Briefs,* 11. (p. 579)

Jones, M. C. (1924). A laboratory study of fear: The case of Peter. *Journal of Genetic Psychology, 31,* 308–315. (p. 717)

Jones, M. V., Paull, G. C., & Erskine, J. (2002). The impact of a team's aggressive reputation on the decisions of association football referees. *Journal of Sports Sciences, 20,* 991–1000. (p. 166)

Jones, S. S. (2007). Imitation in infancy: The development of mimicry. *Psychological Science, 18,* 593–599. (p. 306)

Jones, S. S., Collins, K., & Hong, H-W. (1991). An audience effect on smile production in 10–month-old infants. *Psychological Science, 2,* 45–49. (p. 436)

Jones, W. H., Carpenter, B. N., & Quintana, D. (1985). Personality and interpersonal predictors of loneliness in two cultures. *Journal of Personality and Social Psychology, 48,* 1503–1511. (p. 65)

Jordan, A. H., Monin, B., Dweck, C. S., Lovett, B. J., John, O. P., & Gross, J. J. (2011). Misery has more company than people think: Underestimating the prevalence of others' negative emotions. *Personality and Social Psychology Bulletin, 37,* 120–135. (p. 671)

Jose, A., O'Leary, D., & Moyer, A. (2010). Does premarital cohabitation predict subsequent marital stability and marital quality? A meta-analysis. *Journal of Marriage and Family, 72,* 105–116. (p. 545)

Joseph, D. L., & Newman, D. A. (2010). Emotional intelligence: An integrative meta-analysis and cascading model. *Journal of Applied Psychology, 95,* 54–78. (p. 612)

Joseph, J. (2001). Separated twins and the genetics of personality differences: A critique. *American Journal of Psychology, 114,* 1–30. (p. 127)

Jost, J. T., Kay, A. C., & Thorisdottir, H. (eds.) (2009). *Social and psychological bases of ideology and system justification.* New York: Oxford University Press. (p. 787)

Jovanovic, T., Blanding, N. Q., Norrholm, S. D., Duncan, E., Bradley, B., & Ressler, K. J. (2009). Childhood abuse is associated with increased startle reactivity in adulthood. *Depression and Anxiety, 26,* 1018–1026. (p. 493)

Judge, T. A., Thoresen, C. J., Bono, J. E., & Patton, G. K. (2001). The job satisfaction/job performance relationship: A qualitative and quantitative review. *Psychological Bulletin, 127,* 376–407. (p. 835)

Jung, R. E., & Haier, R. J. (2007). The Parieto-Frontal Integration Theory (P-FIT) of intelligence: Converging neuroimaging evidence. *Behavioral and Brain Sciences, 30,* 135–187. (p. 613)

Jung-Beeman, M., Bowden, E. M., Haberman, J., Frymiare, J. L., Arambel-Liu, S., Greenblatt, R., Reber, P. J., & Kounios, J. (2004). Neural activity when people solve verbal problems with insight. *PloS Biology* 2(4), e111. (p. 362)

Just, M. A., Keller, T. A., & Cynkar, J. (2008). A decrease in brain activation associated with driving when listening to someone speak. *Brain Research, 1205,* 70–80. (p. 153)

Kagan, J. (1976). Emergent themes in human development. *American Scientist, 64,* 186–196. (p. 492)

Kagan, J. (1984). *The nature of the child.* New York: Basic Books. (p. 488)

Kagan, J. (1995). On attachment. *Harvard Review of Psychiatry, 3,* 104–106. (p. 490)

Kagan, J. (1998). *Three seductive ideas.* Cambridge, MA: Harvard University Press. (pp. 143, 464)

Kagan, J., Arcus, D., Snidman, N., Feng, W. Y., Hendler, J., & Greene, S. (1994). Reactivity in infants: A cross-national comparison. *Developmental Psychology, 30,* 342–345. (p. 491)

Kagan, J., Lapidus, D. R., & Moore, M. (December, 1978). Infant antecedents of cognitive functioning: A longitudinal study. *Child Development, 49*(4), 1005–1023. (p. 464)

Kagan, J., & Snidman, N. (2004). *The long shadow of temperament.* Cambridge, MA: Belknap Press. (p. 491)

Kagan, J., Snidman, N., & Arcus, D. M. (1992). Initial reactions to unfamiliarity. *Current Directions in Psychological Science, 1,* 171–174. (p. 491)

Kahlor, L., & Morrison, D. (2007). Television viewing and rape myth acceptance among college women. *Sex Roles, 56,* 729–739. (p. 793)

Kahneman, D. (1985, June). Quoted by K. McKean, Decisions, decisions. *Discover,* pp. 22–31. (p. 730)

Kahneman, D. (1999). Assessments of objective happiness: A bottom-up approach. In D. Kahneman, E. Diener, & N. Schwartz (Eds.), *Understanding well-being: Scientific perspectives on enjoyment and suffering.* New York: Russell Sage Foundation. (p. 205)

Kahneman, D. (2005a, February 10). Are you happy now? *Gallup Management Journal* interview (www.gmj.gallup.com). (p. 848)

Kahneman, D. (2005b, January 13). What were they thinking? Q&A with Daniel Kahneman. *Gallup Management Journal* (gmj.gallup.com). (p. 851)

Kahneman, D., & Deaton, A. (2010). High income improves evaluation of life but not emotional well-being. *Proceedings of the National Academy of Sciences, 107,* 16489–16493. (p. 850)

Kahneman, D., Fredrickson, B. L., Schreiber, C. A., & Redelmeier, D. A. (1993). When more pain is preferred to less: Adding a better end. *Psychological Science, 4,* 401–405. (p. 205)

Kahneman, D., Krueger, A. B., Schkade, D. A., Schwarz, N., & Stone, A. A. (2004). A survey method for characterizing daily life experience: The day reconstruction method. *Science, 306,* 1776–1780. (pp. 235, 848)

Kahneman, D., & Renshon, J. (2007, January/February). Why hawks win. *Foreign Policy* (www.foreignpolicy.com). (p. 597)

Kahneman, D., & Tversky, A. (1972). Subjective probability: A judgment of representativeness. *Cognitive Psychology, 3,* 430–454. (p. 33)

Kail, R. (1991). Developmental change in speed of processing during childhood and adolescence. *Psychological Bulletin, 109,* 490–501. (p. 541)

Kail, R., & Hall, L. K. (2001). Distinguishing short-term memory from working memory. *Memory & Cognition, 29,* 1–9. (p. 320)

Kaiser Family Foundation. (2010, January). *Generation M²: Media in the lives of 8- to 18-year-olds* (by V. J. Rideout, U. G. Foeher, & D. F. Roberts). Menlo Park, CA: Henry J. Kaiser Family Foundation. (pp. 48, 415, 417, 689)

Kamarck, T., & Jennings, J. R. (1991). Biobehavioral factors in sudden cardiac death. *Psychological Bulletin, 109,* 42–75. (p. 452)

Kamel, N. S., & Gammack, J. K. (2006). Insomnia in the elderly: Cause, approach, and treatment. *American Journal of Medicine, 119,* 463–469. (p. 228)

Kamil, A. C., & Cheng, K. (2001). Way-finding and landmarks: The multiple-bearings hypothesis. *Journal of Experimental Biology, 204,* 103–113. (p. 330)

Kaminski, J., Cali, J., & Fischer, J. (2004). Word learning in a domestic dog: Evidence for "fast mapping." *Science, 304,* 1682–1683. (p. 870)

Kanaya, T., Scullin, M. H., & Ceci, S. J. (2003). The Flynn effect and U.S. policies: The impact of rising IQ scores on American society via mental retardation diagnoses. *American Psychologist, 58,* 778–790. (p. 629)

Kanazawa, S. (2004). General intelligence as a domain-specific adaptation. *Psychological Review, 111,* 512–523. (p. 609)

Kanazawa, S. (2010). Evolutionary psychology and intelligence research. *American Psychologist, 65,* 279–289. (p. 609)

Kandel, D. B., & Raveis, V. H. (1989). Cessation of illicit drug use in young adulthood. *Archives of General Psychiatry, 46,* 109–116. (p. 824)

Kandel, E. R., & Schwartz, J. H. (1982). Molecular biology of learning: Modulation of transmitter release. *Science, 218,* 433–443. (p. 332)

Kandler, C., Bleidorn, W., Riemann, R., Spinath, F. M., Thiel, W., & Angleitner, A. (2010). Sources of cumulative continuity in personality: A longitudinal multiple-rater twin study. *Journal of Personality and Social Psychology, 98,* 995–1008. (p. 464)

Kane, G. D. (2010). Revisiting gay men's body image issues: Exposing the fault lines. *Review of General Psychology, 14,* 311–317. (p. 698)

Kaplan, H. I., & Saddock, B. J. (Eds.). (1989). *Comprehensive textbook of psychiatry, V.* Baltimore, MD: Williams and Wilkins. (p. 741)

Kaplan, R. M., & Kronick, R. G. (2006). Marital status and longevity in the United States population. *Journal of Epidemiology and Community Health, 60,* 760–765. (p. 857)

Kaplan, S., Bradley, J. C., Luchman, J. N., & Haynes, D. (2009). On the role of positive and negative affectivity in job performance: A meta-analytic investigation. *Journal of Applied Psychology, 94,* 162–176. (p. 835)

Kapogiannis, D., Barbey, A. K., Sue, M., Zamboni, G., Krueger, F., & Grafman, J. (2009). Cognitive and neural foundations of religious belief. *PNAS, 106,* 4876–4881. (p. 96)

Kaprio, J., Koskenvuo, M., & Rita, H. (1987). Mortality after bereavement: A prospective study of 95,647 widowed persons. *American Journal of Public Health, 77,* 283–287. (p. 443)

Kaptchuk, T. J., Stason, W. B., Davis, R. B., Legedza, A. R. T., Schnyer, R. N., Kerr, C. E., Stone, D. A., Nam, B. H., Kirsch, I., & Goldman, R. H. (2006). Sham device v inert pill: Randomised controlled trial of two placebo treatments. *British Medical Journal, 332,* 391–397. (p. 206)

Karacan, I., Goodenough, D. R., Shapiro, A., & Starker, S. (1966). Erection cycle during sleep in relation to dream anxiety. *Archives of General Psychiatry, 15,* 183–189. (p. 229)

Karau, S. J., & Williams, K. D. (1993). Social loafing: A meta-analytic review and theoretical integration. *Journal of Personality and Social Psychology, 65,* 681–706. (p. 773)

Karberg, J. C., & James, D. J. (2005, July). Substance dependence, abuse, and treatment of jail inmates, 2002. *Bureau of Justice Statistics Special Report* (NCJ 209588). (p. 791)

Karg, K., Burmeister, M., Shedden, K., & Sen, S. (2011). The serotonin transporter promoters variant (*5-HTTLPR*), stress, and depression meta-analysis revised: Evidence of genetic moderation. *Archives of General Psychiatry, 68,* 444–454. (p. 678)

Kark, J. D., Shemi, G., Friedlander, Y., Martin, O., Manor, O., & Blondheim, S. H. (1996). Does religious observance promote health? Mortality in secular vs. religious kibbutzim in Israel. *American Journal of Public Health, 86,* 341–346. (p. 862)

Karlsgodt, K. H., Sun, D., & Cannon, T. D. (2010). Structural and functional brain abnormalities in schizophrenia. *Current Directions in Psychological Science, 19,* 226–231. (p. 687)

Karni, A., Meyer, G., Rey-Hipolito, C., Jezzard, P., Adams, M. M., Turner, R., & Ungerleider, L. G. (1998). The acquisition of skilled motor performance: Fast and slow experience-driven changes in primary motor cortex. *Proceedings of the National Academy of Sciences, 95,* 861–868. (p. 509)

Karni, A., & Sagi, D. (1994). Dependence on REM sleep for overnight improvement of perceptual skills. *Science, 265,* 679–682. (p. 241)

Karno, M., Golding, J. M., Sorenson, S. B., & Burnam, A. (1988). The epidemiology of obsessive-compulsive disorder in five US communities. *Archives of General Psychiatry, 45,* 1094–1099. (p. 663)

Karpicke, J. D., & Roediger, H. L., III (2008). The critical importance of retrieval for learning. *Science, 319,* 966–968. (p. 16)

Karremans, J. C., Frankenhis, W. E., & Arons, S. (2010). Blind men prefer a low waist-to-hip ratio. *Evolution and Human Behavior, 31,* 182–186. (p. 801)

Karremans, J. C., Stroebe, W., & Claus, J. (2006). Beyond Vicary's fantasies: The impact of subliminal priming and brand choice. *Journal of Experimental Social Psychology, 42,* 792–798. (p. 158)

Kasen, S., Chen, H., Sneed, J., Crawford, T., & Cohen, P. (2006). Social role and birth cohort influences on gender-linked personality traits in women: A 20-year longitudinal analysis. *Journal of Personality and Social Psychology, 91*, 944–958. (p. 503)

Kashima, Y., Siegal, M., Tanaka, K., & Kashima, E. S. (1992). Do people believe behaviours are consistent with attitudes? Towards a cultural psychology of attribution processes. *British Journal of Social Psychology, 31*, 111–124. (p. 599)

Kasser, T. (2002). *The high price of materialism.* Cambridge, MA: MIT Press. (p. 850)

Kasser, T. (2011). Cultural values and the well-being of future generations: A cross-national study. *Journal of Cross-Cultural Psychology, 42, 42*, 206–215. (p. 850)

Katz-Wise, S. L., Priess, H. A., & Hyde, J. S. (2010). Gender-role attitudes and behavior across the transition to parenthood. *Developmental Psychology, 46*, 18–28. (p. 503)

Kaufman, J., & Zigler, E. (1987). Do abused children become abusive parents? *American Journal of Orthopsychiatry, 57*, 186–192. (p. 493)

Kaufman, J. C., & Baer, J. (2002). I bask in dreams of suicide: Mental illness, poetry, and women. *Review of General Psychology, 6*, 271–286. (p. 673)

Kaufman, L., & Kaufman, J. H. (2000). Explaining the moon illusion. *Proceedings of the National Academy of Sciences, 97*, 500–505. (p. 189)

Kawakami, K., Dunn, E., Karmali, F., & Dovidio, J. F. (2009). Mispredicting affective and behavioral responses to racism. *Science, 323*, 276–278. (p. 781)

Kay, A. C., Baucher, D., Peach, J. M., Laurin, K., Friesen, J., Zanna, M. P., & Spencer, S. J. (2009). Inequality, discrimination, and the power of the status quo: Direct evidence for a motivation to see the way things are as the way they should be. *Journal of Personality and social Psychology, 97*, 421–434. (p. 787)

Kayser, C. (2007, April/May). Listening with your eyes. *Scientific American Mind*, 24–29. (p. 210)

Kayser, D. N., Elliot, A. J., & Felman, R. (2010). Red and romantic behavior in men viewing women. *European Journal of Social Psychology, 40*, 901–908. (p. 294)

Kazantzis, N., & Dattilio, F. M. (2010b). Definitions of homework, types of homework and ratings of the importance of homework among psychologists with cognitive behavior therapy and psychoanalytic theoretical orientations. *Journal of Clinical Psychology, 66*, 758–773. (p. 723)

Kazantzis, N., Whittington, C., & Dattilio, F. M. (2010a). Meta-analysis of homework effects in cognitive and behavioral therapy: A replication and extension. *Clinical Psychology: Science and Practice, 17*, 144–156. (p. 723)

Kazdin, A. E., & Benjet, C. (2003). Spanking children: Evidence and issues. *Current Directions in Psychological Science, 12*, 99–103. (p. 281)

Keesey, R. E., & Corbett, S. W. (1983). Metabolic defense of the body weight set-point. In A. J. Stunkard & E. Stellar (Eds.), *Eating and its disorders.* New York: Raven Press. (p. 398)

Keith, S. W., & 19 others. (2006). Putative contributors to the secular increase in obesity: Exploring the roads less traveled. *International Journal of Obesity, 30*, 1585–1594. (p. 402)

Keller, J. (2007, March 9). As football players get bigger, more of them risk a dangerous sleep disorder. *Chronicle of Higher Education*, pp. A43–44. (p. 239)

Keller, M. B., McCullough, J. P., Klein, D. N., Arnow, B., Dunner, D. L., Gelenberg, A. J., Markowitz, J. C., Nemeroff, C. B., Russell, J. M., Thase, M. E., Trivedi, M. H., & Zajecka J. (2000), A comparison of nefazodone, the cognitive behavioral-analysis system of psychotherapy, and their combination for the treatment of chronic depression. *New England Journal of Medicine, 342*, 1462–1470. (p. 742)

Kellerman, J., Lewis, J., & Laird, J. D. (1989). Looking and loving: The effects of mutual gaze on feelings of romantic love. *Journal of Research in Personality, 23*, 145–161. (p. 432)

Kellermann, A. L. (1997). Comment: Gunsmoke—changing public attitudes toward smoking and firearms. *American Journal of Public Health, 87*, 910–913. (p. 789)

Kellermann, A. L., Rivara, F. P., Rushforth, N. B., Banton, H. G., Feay, D. T., Francisco, J. T., Locci, A. B., Prodzinski, J., Hackman, B. B., & Somes, G. (1993). Gun ownership as a risk factor for homicide in the home. *New England Journal of Medicine, 329*, 1084–1091. (p. 789)

Kellermann, A. L., Somes, G., Rivara, F. P., Lee, R. K., & Banton, J. G. (1998). Injuries and deaths due to firearms in the home. *Journal of Trauma, 45*, 263–267. (p. 789)

Kelling, S. T., & Halpern, B. P. (1983). Taste flashes: Reaction times, intensity, and quality. *Science, 219*, 412–414. (p. 207)

Kellner, C. H., & 16 others. (2006). Continuation electroconvulsive therapy vs. pharmacotherapy for relapse prevention in major depression: A multisite study from the Consortium for Research in Electroconvulsive Therapy (CORE). *Archives of General Psychiatry, 63*, 1337–1344 (p. 744)

Kelly, A. E. (2000). Helping construct desirable identities: A self-presentational view of psychotherapy. *Psychological Bulletin, 126*, 475–494. (p. 721)

Kelly, D. J., Quinn, P. C., Slater, A. M., Lee, K., Ge, L., & Pascalis, O. (2007). The other-race effect develops during infancy: Evidence of perceptual narrowing. *Psychological Science, 18*, 1084–1089. (p. 786)

Kelly, I. W. (1997). Modern astrology: A critique. *Psychological Reports, 81*, 1035–1066. (p. 579)

Kelly, I. W. (1998). Why astrology doesn't work. *Psychological Reports, 82*, 527–546. (p. 579)

Kelly, S. D., Özyürek, A., & Maris, E. (2010). Two sides of the same coin: Speech and gesture mutually interact to enhance comprehension. *Psychological Science, 21*, 260–267. (p. 869)

Kelly, T. A. (1990). The role of values in psychotherapy: A critical review of process and outcome effects. *Clinical Psychology Review, 10*, 171–186., 735

Kempe, R. S., & Kempe, C. C. (1978). *Child abuse.* Cambridge, MA: Harvard University Press. (p. 493)

Kempton, M. J., Geddes, J. R., Ettinger, U., Williams, S. C. R., & Grasby, P. M. (2008). Meta-analysis, database, and meta-regression of 98 structural imaging studies in bipolar disorder. *Archives of General Psychiatry, 65*, 1017–1032. (p. 678)

Kendall-Tackett, K. A. (Ed.). (2004). *Health consequences of abuse in the family: A clinical guide for evidence-based practice.* Washington, DC: American Psychological Association. (p. 494)

Kendall-Tackett, K. A., Williams, L. M., & Finkelhor, D. (1993). Impact of sexual abuse on children: A review and synthesis of recent empirical studies. *Psychological Bulletin, 113*, 164–180. (pp. 351, 494)

Kendler, K. S. (1996). Parenting: A genetic-epidemiologic perspective. *The American Journal of Psychiatry, 153*, 11–20. (p. 496)

Kendler, K. S. (1997). Social support: A genetic-epidemiologic analysis. *American Journal of Psychiatry, 154*, 1398–1404. (p. 588)

Kendler, K. S. (1998, January). Major depression and the environment: A psychiatric genetic perspective. *Pharmacopsychiatry, 31*(1), 5–9. (p. 675)

Kendler, K. S. (2011). A statement from Kenneth S. Kendler, M.D., on the proposal to eliminate the grief exclusion criterion from major depression. www.dsm5.org. (p. 655)

Kendler, K. S., Gardner, C. O., & Prescott, C. A. (2006). Toward a comprehensive developmental model for major depression in men. *American Journal of Psychiatry, 163*, 115–124. (p. 674)

Kendler, K. S., Jacobson, K. C., Myers, J., & Prescott, C. A. (2002a). Sex differences in genetic and environmental risk factors for irrational fears and phobias. *Psychological Medicine, 32*, 209–217. (p. 668)

Kendler, K. S., Karkowski, L. M., & Prescott, C. A. (1999). Fears and phobias: Reliability and heritability. *Psychological Medicine, 29*, 539–553. (p. 668)

Kendler, K. S., Myers, J., & Prescott, C. A. (2002b). The etiology of phobias: An evaluation of the stress-diathesis model. *Archives of General Psychiatry, 59*, 242–248. (p. 668)

Kendler, K. S., Myers, J., & Zisook, S. (2008). Does bereavement-related major depression differ from major depression associated with other stressful life events? *American Journal of Psychiatry, 165*, 1449–1455. (p. 675)

Kendler, K. S., Neale, M. C., Kessler, R. C., Heath, A. C., & Eaves, L. J. (1992). Generalized anxiety disorder in women: A population-based twin study. *Archives of General Psychiatry, 49*, 267–272. (p. 668)

Kendler, K. S., Neale, M. C., Thornton, L. M., Aggen, S. H., Gilman, S. E., & Kessler, R. C. (2002). Cannabis use in the last year in a U.S. national sample of twin and sibling pairs. *Psychological Medicine, 32*, 551–554. (p. 823)

Kendler, K. S., Thornton, L. M., & Gardner, C. O. (2001). Genetic risk, number of previous depressive episodes, and stressful life events in predicting onset of major depression. *American Journal of Psychiatry, 158*, 582–586. (p. 675)

Kennedy, S. H., Giacobbe, P., Rizvi, S. J., Placenza, F. M., Nishikawa, Y., Mayberg, H. S., & Lozano, A. M. (2011). Deep brain stimulation for treatment-resistant depression: Follow-up after 3 to 6 years. *American Journal of Psychiatry, 168*, 502–510. (p. 745)

Kenrick, D. T., & Funder, D. C. (1988). Profiting from controversy: Lessons from the person-situation debate. *American Psychologist, 43*, 23–34. (p. 583)

Kenrick, D. T., Griskevicious, V., Neuberg, S. L., & Schaller, M. (2010). Renovating the pyramid of needs: Contemporary extensions build upon ancient foundations. *Perspectives on Psychological Science, 5,* 292–314. (p. 394)

Kenrick, D. T., & Gutierres, S. E. (1980). Contrast effects and judgments of physical attractiveness: When beauty becomes a social problem. *Journal of Personality and Social Psychology, 38,* 131–140. (p. 409)

Kenrick, D. T., Gutierres, S. E., & Goldberg, L. L. (1989). Influence of popular erotica on judgments of strangers and mates. *Journal of Experimental Social Psychology, 25,* 159–167. (p. 409)

Kenrick, D. T., Nieuweboer, S., & Buunk, A. P. (2009). Universal mechanisms and cultural diversity: Replacing the blank slate with a coloring book. In M. Schaller, A. Norenzayan, S. Heine, A. Norenzayan, T. Yamagishi, & T. Kameda (eds.), *Evolution, culture, and the human mind.* Mahwah, NJ: Lawrence Erlbaum. (pp. 138, 508)

Kensinger, E. A. (2007). Negative emotion enhances memory accuracy: Behavioral and neuroimaging evidence. *Current Directions in Psychological Science, 16,* 213–218. (p. 332)

Keough, K. A., Zimbardo, P. G., & Boyd, J. N. (1999). Who's smoking, drinking, and using drugs? Time perspective as a predictor of substance use. *Basic and Applied Social Psychology, 2,* 149–164. (p. 558)

Kernis, M. H. (2003). Toward a conceptualization of optimal self-esteem. *Psychological Inquiry, 14,* 1–26. (p. 598)

Kerr, N. L., & Bruun, S. E. (1983). Dispensability of member effort and group motivation losses: Free-rider effects. *Journal of Personality and Social Psychology, 44,* 78–94. (p. 773)

Kerr, R. A. (2009). Amid worrisome signs of warming, 'climate fatigue' sets in. *Science, 326,* 926–928. (p. 756)

Kessing, L. V., Forman, J. L., & Andersen, P. K. (2010). Does lithium protect against dementia? *Bipolar Disorders, 12,* 87–94. (p. 743)

Kessler, D., Lewis, G., Kaur, S., Wiles, N., King, M., Welch, S., Sharp, D. J., Araya, R., Hollinghurst, S., & Peters, T. J. (2009). Therapist-delivered Internet psychotherapy for depression primary care: A randomized controlled trial. *The Lancet, 374,* 628–634. (p. 723)

Kessler, M., & Albee, G. (1975). Primary prevention. *Annual Review of Psychology, 26,* 557–591. (p. 737)

Kessler, R. C. (2000). Posttraumatic stress disorder: The burden to the individual and to society. *Journal of Clinical Psychiatry, 61*(suppl. 5), 4–12. (p. 665)

Kessler, R. C., & 22 others. (2010). Age differences in the prevalence and comorbidity of DSM-IV major depressive episodes: Results from the WHO World Mental Health Survey Initiative. *Depression and Anxiety, 27,* 351–364. (p. 675)

Kessler, R. C., & 12 others. (2010). Structure and diagnosis of adult attention-deficit/hyperactivity disorder: Analysis of expanded symptom criteria from the adult ADHD Clinical Diagnostic Scale. *Archives of General Psychiatry, 67,* 1168–1178. (p. 652)

Kessler, R. C., Akiskal, H. S., Ames, M., Birnbaum, H., Greenberg, P., Hirschfeld, R. M. A., Jin, R., Merikangas, K. R., Simon, G. E., & Wang, P. S. (2006). Prevalence and effects of mood disorders on work performance in a nationally representative sample of U.S. workers. *American Journal of Psychiatry, 163,* 1561–1568. (p. 674)

Kessler, R. C., Berglund, P., Demler, O., Jin, R., Merikangos, K. R., & Walters, E. E. (2005). Lifetime prevalence and age-of-onset distributions of DSM-IV disorders in the National Comorbidity Survey Replication. *Archives of General Psychiatry, 62,* 593–602. (p. 657)

Kessler, R. C., Foster, C., Joseph, J., Ostrow, D., Wortman, C., Phair, J., & Chmiel, J. (1991). Stressful life events and symptom onset in HIV infection. *American Journal of Psychiatry, 148,* 733–738. (p. 451)

Kessler, R. C., Soukup, J., Davis, R. B., Foster, D. F., Wilkey, S. A., Van Rompay, M. I., & Eisenberg, D. M. (2001). The use of complementary and alternative therapies to treat anxiety and depression in the United States. *American Journal of Psychiatry, 158,* 289–294. (p. 733)

Keynes, M. (1980, December 20/27). Handel's illnesses. *Lancet, 316,* 1354–1355. (p. 673)

Keys, A., Brozek, J., Henschel, A., Mickelsen, O., & Taylor, H. L. (1950). *The biology of human starvation.* Minneapolis: University of Minnesota Press. (p. 396)

Kiecolt-Glaser, J. K. (2009). Psychoneuroimmunology: Psychology's gateway to the biomedical future. *Perspectives on Psychological Science, 4,* 367–369. (p. 448)

Kiecolt-Glaser, J. K., & Glaser, R. (1995). Psychoneuroimmunology and health consequences: Data and shared mechanisms. *Psychosomatic Medicine, 57,* 269–274. (p. 450)

Kiecolt-Glaser, J. K., Loving, T. J., Stowell, J. R., Malarkey, W. B., Lemeshow, S., Dickinson, S. L., & Glaser, R. (2005). Hostile marital interactions, proinflammatory cytokine production, and wound healing. *Archives of General Psychiatry, 62,* 1377–1384. (p. 449)

Kiecolt-Glaser, J. K., Page, G. G., Marucha, P. T., MacCallum, R. C., & Glaser, R. (1998). Psychological influences on surgical recovery: Perspectives from psychoneuroimmunology. *American Psychologist, 53,* 1209–1218. (p. 449)

Kiehl, K. A., & Buckholtz, J. W. (2010, September/October). Inside the mind of a psychopath. *Scientific American Mind,* 22–29. (p. 701)

Kihlstrom, J. F. (2005). Dissociative disorders. *Annual Review of Clinical Psychology, 1,* 227–253. (p. 696)

Kihlstrom, J. F. (2006). Repression: A unified theory of a will-o'-the-wisp. *Behavioral and Brain Sciences, 29,* 523. (p. 563)

Killingsworth, M. A., & Gilbert, D. T. (2010). A wandering mind is an unhappy mind. *Science, 330,* 932. (pp. 417, 828)

Kim, B. S. K., Ng, G. F., & Ahn, A. J. (2005). Effects of client expectation for counseling success, client-counselor worldview match, and client adherence to Asian and European American cultural values on counseling process with Asian Americans. *Journal of Counseling Psychology, 52,* 67–76. (p. 735)

Kim, G., & Tong, A. (2010, February 23). Airline passengers have grown, seats haven't. *Sacramento Bee* (reprinted by *Grand Rapids Press,* B1, B3). (p. 402)

Kim, H., & Markus, H. R. (1999). Deviance or uniqueness, harmony or conformity? A cultural analysis. *Journal of Personality and Social Psychology, 77,* 785–800. (p. 599)

Kimata, H. (2001). Effect of humor on allergen-induced wheal reactions. *Journal of the American Medical Association, 285,* 737. (p. 857)

Kimble, G. A. (1981). *Biological and cognitive constraints on learning.* Washington, DC: American Psychological Association. (p. 292)

Kindt, M., Soeter, M., & Vervliet, B. (2009). Beyond extinction: Erasing human fear responses and preventing the return of fear. *Nature Neuroscience, 12,* 256–258. (p. 668)

King, R. N., & Koehler, D. J. (2000). Illusory correlations in graphological interference. *Journal of Experimental Psychology: Applied, 6,* 336–348. (p. 579)

King, S., St-Hilaire, A., & Heidkamp, D. (2010). Prenatal factors in schizophrenia. *Current Directions in Psychological Science, 19,* 209–221. (p. 687)

Kingston, D. W., Malamuth, N. M., Fedoroff, N. M., & Marshall, W. L. (2009). The importance of individual differences in pornography use: Theoretical perspectives and implications for treating sexual offenders. *Journal of Sex Research, 46,* 216–232. (p. 793)

Kinnier, R. T., & Metha, A. T. (1989). Regrets and priorities at three stages of life. *Counseling and Values, 33,* 182–193. (p. 546)

Kinzler, K. D., Shutts, K., Dejesus, J., & Spelke, E. S. (2009). Accent trumps race in guiding children's social preferences. *Social Cognition, 27,* 623–634. (p. 784)

Kirby, D. (2002). Effective approaches to reducing adolescent unprotected sex, pregnancy, and childbearing. *Journal of Sex Research, 39,* 51–57. (p. 531)

Kirkpatrick, B., Fenton, W. S., Carpenter, W. T., Jr., & Marder, S. R. (2006). The NIMH-MATRICS consensus statement on negative symptoms. *Schizophrenia Bulletin, 32,* 214–219. (p. 686)

Kirkpatrick, L. (1999). Attachment and religious representations and behavior. In J. Cassidy & P. R. Shaver (Eds.), *Handbook of attachment.* New York: Guilford. (p. 489)

Kirkpatrick, R. M., McGue, M., & Iacono, W. G. (2009). Shared-environmental contributions to high cognitive ability. *Behavior Genetics, 39,* 406–416. (p. 633)

Kirmayer, L. J., & Sartorius, N. (2007). Cultural models and somatic syndromes. *Psychosomatic Medicine, 69,* 832–840. (p. 693)

Kirsch, I. (1996). Hypnotic enhancement of cognitive-behavioral weight loss treatments: Another meta-reanalysis. *Journal of Consulting and Clinical Psychology, 64,* 517–519. (p. 220)

Kirsch, I. (2010). *The emperor's new drugs: Exploding the antidepressant myth.* New York: Basic Books. (pp. 52, 743)

Kirsch, I., & Braffman, W. (2001). Imaginative suggestibility and hypnotizability. *Current Directions in Psychological Science, 10,* 57–61. (p. 220)

Kirsch, I., Deacon, B. J., Huedo-Medina, T. B., Scoboria, A., Moore, T. J., & Johnson, B. T. (2008) Initial severity and antidepressant benefits: A meta-analysis of data submitted to the Food and Drug Administration. *Public Library of Science Medicine*, 5, e45. (p. 743)

Kirsch, I., & Lynn, S. J. (1995). The altered state of hypnosis. *American Psychologist*, 50, 846–858. (p. 220)

Kirsch, I., Moore, T. J., Scoboria, A., & Nicholls, S. S. (2002, July 15). New study finds little difference between effects of antidepressants and placebo. *Prevention and Treatment* (journals.apa.org/prevention). (p. 743)

Kirsch, I., & Sapirstein, G. (1998). Listening to Prozac but hearing placebo: A meta-analysis of antidepressant medication. *Prevention and Treatment, 1*, posted June 26 at (journals.apa.org/prevention/volume1). (p. 743)

Kisley, M. A., Wood, S., & Burrows, C. L. (2007). Looking at the sunny side of life: Age-related change in an event-related potential measure of the negativity bias. *Psychological Science, 18*, 838–843. (p. 547)

Kitayama, S., Ishii, K., Imada, T., Takemura, K., & Ramaswamy, J. (2006). Voluntary settlement and the spirit of independence: Evidence from Japan's "northern frontier." *Journal of Personality and Social Psychology, 91*, 369–384. (p. 599)

Kitayama, S., Park, H., Sevincer, A. T., Karasawa, M., & Uskul, A. K. (2009). A cultural task analysis of implicit independence: Comparing North America, Western Europe, and East Asia. *Journal of Personality and Social Psychology, 97*, 236–255 (p. 755)

Kivimaki, M., Leino-Arjas, P., Luukkonen, R., Rihimaki, H., & Kirjonen, J. (2002). Work stress and risk of cardiovascular mortality: Prospective cohort study of industrial employees. *British Medical Journal, 325*, 857. (p. 300)

Klayman, J., & Ha, Y-W. (1987). Confirmation, disconfirmation, and information in hypothesis testing. *Psychological Review, 94*, 211–228. (p. 362)

Klein, D. N. (2010). Chronic depression: Diagnosis and classification. *Current Directions in Psychological Science, 19*, 96–100. (p. 675)

Klein, D. N., & 16 others. (2003). Therapeutic alliance in depression treatment: Controlling for prior change and patient characteristics. *Journal of Consulting and Clinical Psychology, 71*, 997–1006. (p. 735)

Kleinke, C. L. (1986). Gaze and eye contact: A research review. *Psychological Bulletin, 1000*, 78–100. (p. 432)

Kleinmuntz, B., & Szucko, J. J. (1984). A field study of the fallibility of polygraph lie detection. *Nature, 308*, 449–450. (p. 429)

Kleitman, N. (1960, November). Patterns of dreaming. *Scientific American*, 82–88. (p. 226)

Klemm, W. R. (1990). Historical and introductory perspectives on brainstem-mediated behaviors. In W. R. Klemm & R. P. Vertes (Eds.), *Brainstem mechanisms of behavior*. New York: Wiley. (p. 97)

Klimstra, T. A., Hale, W. W., III, Raaijmakers, Q. A. W., Branje, S. J. T., & Meeus, W. H. J. (2009). Maturation of personality in adolescence. *Journal of Personality and Social Psychology, 96*, 898–912. (p. 521)

Kline, D., & Schieber, F. (1985). Vision and aging. In J. E. Birren & K. W. Schaie (Eds.), *Handbook of the psychology of aging*. New York: Van Nostrand Reinhold. (p. 541)

Klinke, R., Kral, A., Heid, S., Tillein, J., & Hartmann, R. (1999). Recruitment of the auditory cortex in congenitally deaf cats by long-term cochlear electro-stimulation. *Science, 285*, 1729–1733. (p. 198)

Kluft, R. P. (1991). Multiple personality disorder. In A. Tasman & S. M. Goldfinger (Eds.), *Review of Psychiatry* (Vol. 10). Washington, DC: American Psychiatric Press. (p. 695)

Klump, K. L., & Culbert, K. M. (2007). Molecular genetic studies of eating disorders: Current status and future directions. *Current Directions in Psychological Science, 16*, 37–41. (p. 697)

Klump, K. L., Suisman, J. L., Burt, S. A., McGue, M., & Iacono, W. G. (2009). Genetic and environmental influences on disordered eating: An adoption study. *Journal of Abnormal Psychology, 118*, 797–805. (p. 697)

Knapp, S., & VandeCreek, L. (2000, August). Recovered memories of childhood abuse: Is there an underlying professional consensus? *Professional Psychology: Research and Practice, 31*, 365–371. (p. 352)

Knäuper, B., Kornik, R., Atkinson, K., Guberman, C., & Aydin, C. (2005). Motivation influences the underestimation of cumulative risk. *Personality and Social Psychology Bulletin, 31*, 1511–1523. (p. 529)

Knickmeyer, E. (2001, August 7). In Africa, big is definitely better. *Seattle Times*, A7. (p. 698)

Knight, R. T. (2007). Neural networks debunk phrenology. *Science, 316*, 1578–1579. (p. 110)

Knight, W. (2004, August 2). *Animated face helps deaf with phone chat*. NewScientist.com. (p. 210)

Knoblich, G., & Oellinger, M. (2006, October/November). The Eureka moment. *Scientific American Mind*, 38–43. (p. 362)

Knutson, K. L., Spiegel, K., Penev, P., & Van Cauter, E. (2007). The metabolic consequences of sleep deprivation. *Sleep Medicine Reviews, 11*, 163–178. (p. 236)

Ko, C-K., Yen, J-Y., Chen, C-C., Chen, S-H., & Yen, C-F. (2005). Proposed diagnostic criteria of Internet addiction for adolescents. *Journal of Nervous and Mental Disease, 193*, 728–733. (p. 248)

Koch, C., & Greenfield, S. (2007, October). How does consciousness happen? *Scientific American*, 76–83. (p. 119)

Koenen, K. C., Moffitt, T. E., Roberts, A. L., Martin, L. T., Kubzansky, L., Harrington, H., Poulton, R., & Caspi, A. (2009). Childhood IQ and adult mental disorders: A test of the cognitive reserve hypothesis. *American Journal of Psychiatry, 166*, 50–57. (p. 629)

Koenig, H. G., King, D. E., & Carson, V. B. (2011). *Handbook of religion and health*. New York: Oxford University Press. (p. 862)

Koenig, H. G., & Larson, D. B. (1998). Use of hospital services, religious attendance, and religious affiliation. *Southern Medical Journal, 91*, 925–932. (p. 865)

Koenig, L. B., McGue, M., Krueger, R. F., & Bouchard, T. J., Jr. (2005). Genetic and environmental influences on religiousness: Findings for retrospective and current religiousness ratings. *Journal of Personality, 73*, 471–488. (p. 128)

Koenig, L. B., & Vaillant, G. E. (2009). A prospective study of church attendance and health over the lifespan. *Health Psychology, 28*, 117–124. (p. 865)

Koenigs, M., Young, L., Adolphs, R., Tranel, D., Cushman, F., Hauser, M., & Damasio, A. (2007). Damage to the prefrontal cortex increases utilitarian moral judgements. *Nature, 446*, 908–911. (p. 109)

Koestner, R., Lekes, N., Powers, T. A., & Chicoine, E. (2002). Attaining personal goals: Self-concordance plus implementation intentions equals success. *Journal of Personality and Social Psychology, 83*, 231–244. (p. 838)

Kohlberg, L. (1981). *The philosophy of moral development: Essays on moral development* (Vol. I). San Francisco: Harper & Row. (p. 515)

Kohlberg, L. (1984). *The psychology of moral development: Essays on moral development* (Vol. II). San Francisco: Harper & Row. (p. 515)

Kohler, C. G., Walker, J. B., Martin, E. A., Healey, K. M., & Moberg, P. J. (2010). Facial emotion perception in schizophrenia: A meta-analytic review. *Schizophrenia Bulletin, 36*, 1009–1019. (p. 685)

Kohler, I. (1962, May). Experiments with goggles. *Scientific American*, 62–72. (p. 191)

Köhler, W. (1925; reprinted 1957). *The mentality of apes*. London: Pelican. (p. 362)

Kohn, P. M., & Macdonald, J. E. (1992). The survey of recent life experiences: A decontaminated hassles scale for adults. *Journal of Behavioral Medicine, 15*, 221–236. (p. 444)

Kolassa, I-T., & Elbert, T. (2007). Structural and functional neuroplasticity in relation to traumatic stress. *Current Directions in Psychological Science, 16*, 321–325. (p. 668)

Kolata, G. (1987). Metabolic catch-22 of exercise regimens. *Science, 236*, 146–147. (p. 403)

Kolb, B. (1989). Brain development, plasticity, and behavior. *American Psychologist, 44*, 1203–1212. (p. 111)

Kolb, B., & Whishaw, I. Q. (1998). Brain plasticity and behavior. *Annual Review of Psychology, 49*, 43–64. (p. 508)

Kolb, B., & Whishaw, I. Q. (2006). *An introduction to brain and behavior* (2nd ed.). New York: Worth Publishers. (p. 357)

Kolivas, E. D., & Gross, A. M. (2007). Assessing sexual aggression: Addressing the gap between rape victimization and perpetration prevalence rates. *Aggression and Violent Behavior, 12*, 315–328. (p. 138)

Kolker, K. (2002, December 8). Video violence disturbs some: Others scoff at influence. *Grand Rapids Press*, A1, A12. (p. 794)

Kolodziej, M. E., & Johnson, B. T. (1996). Interpersonal contact and acceptance of persons with psychiatric disorders: A research synthesis. *Journal of Consulting and Clinical Psychology, 64*, 1387–1396. (p. 655)

Koltko-Rivera, M. E. (2006). Rediscovering the later version of Maslow's hierarchy of needs: Self-transcendence and opportunities for theory, research, and unification. *Review of General Psychology, 10*, 302–317. (p. 394)

Konkle, T., Brady, T. F., Alvarez, G. A., & Oliva, A. (2010). Conceptual distinctiveness supports detailed visual long-term memory for real-world objects. *Journal of Experimental Psychology: General, 139*, 558–578. (p. 318)

Kontula, O., & Haavio-Mannila, E. (2009). The impact of aging on human sexual activity and sexual desire. *Journal of Sex Research, 46,* 46–56. (p. 540)

Koole, S. L., Greenberg, J., & Pyszczynski, T. (2006). Introducing science to the psychology of the soul. *Current Directions in Psychological Science, 15,* 212–216. (p. 568)

Kornell, N., & Bjork, R. A. (2008). Learning concepts and categories: Is spacing the "enemy of induction"? *Psychological Science, 19,* 585–592. (p. 16)

Kosfeld, M., Heinrichs, M., Zak, P. J., Fischbacher, U., & Fehr, E. (2005). Oxytocin increases trust in humans. *Nature, 435,* 673–676. (p. 91)

Kosslyn, S. M. (2005). Reflective thinking and mental imagery: A perspective on the development of posttraumatic stress disorder. *Development and Psychopathology, 17,* 851–863. (p. 665)

Kosslyn, S. M., & Koenig, O. (1992). *Wet mind: The new cognitive neuroscience.* New York: Free Press. (p. 88)

Kosslyn, S. M., Thompson, W. L., Costantini-Ferrando, M. F., Alpert, N. M., & Spiegel, D. (2000). Hypnotic visual illusion alters color processing in the brain. *American Journal of Psychiatry, 157,* 1279–1284. (p. 222)

Kotchick, B. A., Shaffer, A., & Forehand, R. (2001). Adolescent sexual risk behavior: A multi-system perspective. *Clinical Psychology Review, 21,* 493–519. (p. 530)

Koten, J. W., Jr., Wood, G., Hagoort, P., Goebel, R., Propping, P., Willmes, K., & Boomsma, D. I. (2009). Genetic contribution to variation in cognitive function: An fMRI study in twins. *Science, 323,* 1737–1740. (p. 632)

Kotkin, M., Daviet, C., & Gurin, J. (1996). The *Consumer Reports* mental health survey. *American Psychologist, 51,* 1080–1082. (p. 729)

Kounios, J., & Beeman, M. (2009). The *Aha!* moment: The cognitive neuroscience of insight. *Current Directions in Psychological Science, 18,* 210–215. (p. 361)

Kovács, Á. M., & Mehler, J. (2009). Cognitive gains in 7-month-old bilingual infants. *Proceedings of the National Academy of Sciences, 106,* 6556–6560. (p. 380)

Kovács, Á. M., Téglás, E., & Endress, A. D. (2010). The social sense: Susceptibility to others' beliefs in human infants and adults. *Science, 330,* 1830–1834. (p. 480)

Kposowa, A. J., & D'Auria, S. (2009). Association of temporal factors and suicides in the United States, 2000–2004. *Social Psychiatry and Psychiatric Epidemiology, 45,* 433–445. (p. 676)

Kraft, C. (1978). A psychophysical approach to air safety: Simulator studies of visual illusions in night approaches. In H. L. Pick, H. W. Leibowitz, J. E. Singer, A. Steinschneider, & H. W. Stevenson (Eds.), *Psychology: From research to practice.* New York: Plenum Press. (p. 841)

Kraft, R. N. (2002). *Memory perceived: Recalling the Holocaust.* Westport, CT: Praeger. (p. 352)

Kramer, A. (2010). Personal correspondence. (p. 848)

Kramer, A. F., & Erickson, K. I. (2007). Capitalizing on cortical plasticity: Influence of physical activity on cognition and brain function. *Trends in Cognitive Sciences, 11,* 342–348. (p. 859)

Kramer, M. S., & 17 others. (2008). Breastfeeding and child cognitive development: New evidence from a large randomized trial. *Archives of General Psychiatry, 65,* 578–584. (p. 51)

Kramer, P. D. (2011, July 9). In defense of antidepressants. *New York Times* (www.nytimes.com). (p. 742)

Kranz, F., & Ishai, A. (2006). Face perception is modulated by sexual preference. *Current Biology, 16,* 63–68. (p. 534)

Kraul, C. (2010, October 12). Chief engineer knew it would take a miracle. *Los Angeles Times* (www.latimes.com). (p. 167)

Kraus, N., Malmfors, T., & Slovic, P. (1992). Intuitive toxicology: Expert and lay judgments of chemical risks. *Risk Analysis, 12,* 215–232. (p. 368)

Kraut, R. E., & Johnston, R. E. (1979). Social and emotional messages of smiling: An ethological approach. *Journal of Personality and Social Psychology, 37,* 1539–1553. (p. 436)

Kraut, R. E., Patterson, M., Lundmark, V., Kiesler, S., Mukopadhyay, T., & Scherlis, W. (1998). Internet paradox: A social technology that reduces social involvement and psychological well being? *American Psychologist, 53,* 1017–1031. (p. 416)

KRC Research & Consulting. (2001, August 7). Memory isn't quite what it used to be (survey for General Nutrition Centers). *USA Today,* D1. (p. 542)

Krebs, D. L., & Van Hesteren, F. (1994). The development of altruism: Toward an integrative model. *Developmental Review, 14,* 103–158. (p. 517)

Krijn, M., Emmelkamp, P. M. G., Olafsson, R. P., & Biemond, R. (2004). Virtual reality exposure therapy of anxiety disorders: A review. *Clinical Psychology Review, 24,* 259–281. (p. 718)

Kring, A. M., & Caponigro, J. M. (2010). Emotion in schizophrenia: Where feeling meets thinking. *Current Directions in Psychological Science, 19,* 255–259. (p. 685)

Kring, A. M., & Gordon, A. H. (1998). Sex differences in emotion: Expression, experience, and physiology. *Journal of Personality and Social Psychology, 74,* 686–703. (p. 435)

Krishna, B. M. (2012, undated). Can India really build toilets for 800 million people in a decade? *IndiaWest* (www.indiawest.com). (p. 415)

Kristensen, P., & Bjerkedal, T. (2007). Explaining the relation between birth order and intelligence. *Science, 316,* 1717. (p. 61)

Kristof, N. D. (2004, July 21). Saying no to killers. *New York Times* (www.nytimes.com). (p. 807)

Kristof, N. D. (2010, September 18). Message to Muslims: I'm sorry. *New York Times* (www.nytimes.com). (p. 781)

Króliczak, G., Heard, P., Goodale, M. A., & Gregory, R. L. (2006). Dissociation of perception and action unmasked by the hollow-face illusion. *Brain Research, 1080,* 9–16. (p. 120)

Krosnick, J. A. (2010, June 8). The climate majority. *New York Times* (www.nytimes.com). (p. 368)

Krosnick, J. A., & Alwin, D. F. (1989). Aging and susceptibility to attitude change. *Journal of Personality and Social Psychology, 57,* 416–425. (p. 464)

Krosnick, J. A., Betz, A. L., Jussim, L. J., & Lynn, A. R. (1992). Subliminal conditioning of attitudes. *Personality and Social Psychology Bulletin, 18,* 152–162. (p. 157)

Kross, E., Berman, M. G., Mischel, W., Smith, E. E., & Wager, T. D. (2011). Social rejection shares somatosensory representations with physical pain. *PNAS, 108,* 6270–6275. (p. 414)

Krueger, J., & Killham, E. (2005, December 8). At work, feeling good matters. *Gallup Management Journal* (www.gmj.gallup.com). (p. 837)

Kruger, J., & Dunning, D. (1999). Unskilled and unaware of it: How difficulties in recognizing one's own incompetence lead to inflated self-assessments. *Journal of Personality and Social Psychology, 77,* 1121–1134. (p. 591)

Kruger, J., Epley, N., Parker, J., & Ng, Z-W. (2005). Egocentrism over e-mail: Can we communicate as well as we think? *Journal of Personality and Social Psychology, 89,* 925–936. (pp. 434, 480)

Krupa, D. J., Thompson, J. K., & Thompson, R. F. (1993). Localization of a memory trace in the mammalian brain. *Science, 260,* 989–991. (p. 331)

Krützen, M., Mann, J., Heithaus, M. R., Connor, R. C., Bejder, L., & Sherwin, W. B. (2005). Cultural transmission of tool use in bottlenose dolphins. *Proceedings of the National Academy of Sciences, 102,* 8939–8943. (p. 868)

Kübler, A., Winter, S., Ludolph, A. C., Hautzinger, M., & Birbaumer, N. (2005). Severity of depressive symptoms and quality of life in patients with amyotrophic lateral sclerosis. *Neurorehabilitation and Neural Repair, 19*(3), 182–193. (p. 848)

Kubzansky, L. D., Koenen, K. C., Jones, C., & Eaton, W. W. (2009). A prospective study of posttraumatic stress disorder symptoms and coronary heart disease in women. *Health Psychology, 28,* 125–130. (p. 453)

Kubzansky, L. D., Sparrow, D., Vokanas, P., & Kawachi, I. (2001). Is the glass half empty or half full? A prospective study of optimism and coronary heart disease in the normative aging study. *Psychosomatic Medicine, 63,* 910–916. (p. 452)

Kuhl, P. K., & Meltzoff, A. N. (1982). The bimodal perception of speech in infancy. *Science, 218,* 1138–1141. (p. 374)

Kuhn, D. (2006). Do cognitive changes accompany developments in the adolescent brain? *Perspectives on Psychological Science, 1,* 59–67. (p. 514)

Kujala, U. M., Kaprio, J., Sarna, S., & Koskenvuo, M. (1998). Relationship of leisure-time physical activity and mortality: The Finnish twin cohort. *Journal of the American Medical Association, 279,* 440–444. (p. 859)

Kuncel, N. R., & Hezlett, S. A. (2007). Standardized tests predict graduate students' success. *Science, 315,* 1080–1081. (p. 622)

Kuncel, N. R., & Hezlett, S. A. (2010). Fact and fiction in cognitive ability testing for admissions and hiring decisions. *Current Directions in Psychological Science, 19,* 339–345. (p. 610)

Kunkel, D. (2001, February 4). *Sex on TV.* Menlo Park, CA: Henry J. Kaiser Family Foundation (www.kff.org). (p. 530)

Kunkel, D., Cope-Farrar, K., Biely, E., Farinola, W. J. M., & Donnerstein, E. (2001). *Sex on TV (2): A biennial report to the Kaiser Family Foundation.* Menlo Park, CA: Kaiser Family Foundation. (p. 792)

Kuntsche, E., Knibbe, R., Gmel, G., & Engels, R. (2005). Why do young people drink? A review of drinking motives. *Clinical Psychology Review, 25,* 841–861. (p. 824)

Kupfer, D. J. (2012, June 1). Dr Kupfer defends DSM-5. www.medscape.com/viewarticle/764735. (p. 655)

Kuppens, P., Allen, N. B., & Sheeber, L. B. (2010). Emotional inertia and psychological maladjustment. *Psychological Science, 21,* 984–991. (p. 679)

Kupper, N., & Denollet, J. (2007). Type D personality as a prognostic factor in heart disease: Assessment and mediating mechanisms. *Journal of Personality Assessment, 89,* 265–276. (p. 452)

Kushner, M. G., Kim, S. W., Conahue, C., Thuras, P., Adson, D., Kotlyar, M., McCabe, J., Peterson, J., & Foa, E. B. (2007). D-cycloserine augmented exposure therapy for obsessive-compulsive disorder. *Biological Psychiatry, 62,* 835–838. (p. 741)

Kutas, M. (1990). Event-related brain potential (ERP) studies of cognition during sleep: Is it more than a dream? In R. R. Bootzin, J. F. Kihlstrom, & D. Schacter (Eds.), *Sleep and cognition.* Washington, DC: American Psychological Association. (p. 225)

Kutcher, E. J., & Bragger, J. D. (2004). Selection interviews of overweight job applicants: Can structure reduce the bias? *Journal of Applied Social Psychology, 34,* 1993–2022. (p. 832)

Labouvie-Vief, G., & Schell, D. A. (1982). Learning and memory in later life. In B. B. Wolman (Ed.), *Handbook of developmental psychology.* Englewood Cliffs, NJ: Prentice-Hall. (p. 543)

Lac, A., & Crano, W. D. (2009). Monitoring matters: Meta-analytic review reveals the reliable linkage of parental monitoring with adolescent marijuana use. *Perspectives on Psychological Science, 4,* 578–586. (p. 824)

Lacey, H. P., Smith, D. M., & Ubel, P. A. (2006). Hope I die before I get old: Mispredicting happiness across the lifespan. *Journal of Happiness Studies, 7,* 167–182. (p. 546)

Lacey, M. (2010, December 11). He found bag of cash, but did the unexpected. *New York Times* (www.nytimes.com). (p. 809)

Lachman, M. E. (2004). Development in midlife. *Annual Review of Psychology, 55,* 305–331. (p. 544)

Ladd, G. T. (1887). *Elements of physiological psychology.* New York: Scribner's. (p. 218)

Lafleur, D. L., Pittenger, C., Kelmendi, B., Gardner, T., Wasylink, S., Malison, R. T., Sanacora, G., Krystal, J. H., & Coric, V. (2006). N-acetylcysteine augmentation in serotonin reuptake inhibitor refractory obsessive-compulsive disorder. *Psychopharmacology, 184,* 254–256. (p. 668)

Laird, J. D. (1974). Self-attribution of emotion: The effects of expressive behavior on the quality of emotional experience. *Journal of Personality and Social Psychology, 29,* 475–486. (p. 437)

Laird, J. D. (1984). The real role of facial response in the experience of emotion: A reply to Tourangeau and Ellsworth, and others. *Journal of Personality and Social Psychology, 47,* 909–917. (p. 437)

Laird, J. D., Cuniff, M., Sheehan, K., Shulman, D., & Strum, G. (1989). Emotion specific effects of facial expressions on memory for life events. *Journal of Social Behavior and Personality, 4,* 87–98. (p. 437)

Lally, P., Van Jaarsveld, C. H. M., Potts, H. W. W., & Wardle, J. (2010). How are habits formed: Modelling habit formation in the real world. *European Journal of Social Psychology, 40,* 998–1009. (p. 264)

Lalumière, M. L., Blanchard, R., & Zucker, K. J. (2000). Sexual orientation and handedness in men and women: A meta-analysis. *Psychological Bulletin, 126,* 575–592. (p. 536)

Lam, R. W., Levitt, A. J., Levitan, R. D., Enns, M. W., Morehouse, R., Michalak, E. E., & Tam, E. M. (2006). The Can-SAD study: A randomized controlled trial of the effectiveness of light therapy and fluoxetine in patients with winter seasonal affective disorder. *American Journal of Psychiatry, 163,* 805–812. (p. 734)

Lambert, N. M., DeWall, C. N., Bushman, B. J., Tillman, T. F., Fincham, F. D., Pond, R. S., Jr., & Gwinn, A. M. (2011). Lashing out in lust: Effect of pornography on nonsexual, physical aggression against relationship partners. Paper presentation at the Society for Personality and Social Psychology convention. (p. 793)

Lambert, W. E. (1992). Challenging established views on social issues: The power and limitations of research. *American Psychologist, 47,* 533–542. (p. 380)

Lambert, W. E., Genesee, F., Holobow, N., & Chartrand, L. (1993). Bilingual education for majority English-speaking children. *European Journal of Psychology of Education, 8,* 3–22. (p. 380)

Lambird, K. H., & Mann, T. (2006). When do ego threats lead to self-regulation failure? Negative consequences of defensive high self-esteem. *Personality and Social Psychology Bulletin, 32,* 1177–1187. (p. 598)

Landauer, T. (2001, September). Quoted by R. Herbert, You must remember this. *APS Observer, 11.* (p. 353)

Landauer, T. K., & Whiting, J. W. M. (1979). Correlates and consequences of stress in infancy. In R. Munroe, B. Munroe, & B. Whiting (Eds.), *Handbook of cross-cultural human development.* New York: Garland. (p. 442)

Landry, M. J. (2002). MDMA: A review of epidemiologic data. *Journal of Psychoactive Drugs, 34,* 163–169. (p. 253)

Langer, E. J. (1983). *The psychology of control.* Beverly Hills, CA: Sage. (p. 300)

Langer, E. J., & Abelson, R. P. (1974). A patient by any other name . . .: Clinician group differences in labeling bias. *Journal of Consulting and Clinical Psychology, 42,* 4–9. (p. 655)

Langer, E. J., & Imber, L. (1980). The role of mindlessness in the perception of deviance. *Journal of Personality and Social Psychology, 39,* 360–367. (p. 655)

Langleben, D. D., & Dattilio, F. M. (2008). Commentary: The future of forensic functional brain imaging. *Journal of the American Academy of Psychiatry and the Law, 36,* 502–504. (p. 428)

Langleben, D. D., Dattilio, F. M., & Gutheil, T. G. (2006). True lies: Delusions and lie-detection technology. *Journal of Psychiatry and Law, 34,* 351–370. (p. 428)

Langlois, J. H., Kalakanis, L., Rubenstein, A. J., Larson, A., Hallam, M., & Smoot, M. (2000). Maxims or myths of beauty? A meta-analytic and theoretical review. *Psychological Bulletin, 126,* 390–423. (pp. 800, 801)

Langlois, J. H., & Roggman, L. A. (1990). Attractive faces are only average. *Psychological Science, 1,* 115–121. (p. 801)

Langlois, J. H., Roggman, L. A., Casey, R. J., Ritter, J. M., Rieser-Danner, L. A., & Jenkins, V. Y. (1987). Infant preferences for attractive faces: Rudiments of a stereotype? *Developmental Psychology, 23,* 363–369. (p. 800)

Langström, N. H., Rahman, Q., Carlström, E., & Lichtenstein, P. (2008). Genetic and environmental effects on same-sex sexual behavior: A population study of twins in Sweden. *Archives of Sexual Behavior.* (p. 534)

Langström, N. H., Rahman, Q., Carlström, E., & Lichtenstein, P. (2010). Genetic and environmental effects on same-sex sexual behavior: A population study of twins in Sweden. *Archives of Sexual Behavior, 39,* 75–80. (p. 534)

Lankford, A. (2009). Promoting aggression and violence at Abu Ghraib: The U.S. military's transformation of ordinary people into torturers. *Aggression and Violent Behavior, 14,* 388–395. (p. 768)

Larkin, K., Resko, J. A., Stormshak, F., Stellflug, J. N., & Roselli, C. E. (2002). Neuroanatomical correlates of sex and sexual partner preference in sheep. Society for Neuroscience convention. (p. 534)

Larrick, R. P., Timmerman, T. A., & Carton, A. M., & Abrevaya, J. (2011). Temper, temperature, and temptation: Heat-related retaliation in baseball. *Psychological Science, 22,* 423–428. (p. 791)

Larsen, R. J., & Diener, E. (1987). Affect intensity as an individual difference characteristic: A review. *Journal of Research in Personality, 21,* 1–39. (pp. 424, 491)

Larson, R. W., & Verma, S. (1999). How children and adolescents spend time across the world: Work, play, and developmental opportunities. *Psychological Bulletin, 125,* 701–736. (p. 641)

Larsson, H., Tuvblad, C., Rijsdijk, F. V., Andershed, H., Grann, M., & Lichtenstein, P. (2007). A common genetic factor explains the association between psychopathic personality and antisocial behavior. *Psychological Medicine, 37,* 15–26. (p. 699)

Larzelere, R. E. (2000). Child outcomes of non-abusive and customary physical punishment by parents: An updated literature review. *Clinical Child and Family Psychology Review, 3,* 199–221. (p. 282)

Larzelere, R. E., & Kuhn, B. R. (2005). Comparing child outcomes of physical punishment and alternative disciplinary tactics: A meta-analysis. *Clinical Child and Family Psychology Review, 8,* 1–37. (p. 282)

Larzelere, R. E., Kuhn, B. R., & Johnson, B. (2004). The intervention selection bias: An underrecognized confound in intervention research. *Psychological Bulletin, 130,* 289–303. (p. 282)

Lashley, K. S. (1950). In search of the engram. In *Symposium of the Society for Experimental Biology* (Vol. 4). New York: Cambridge University Press. (p. 330)

Lassiter, G. D., & Irvine, A. A. (1986). Video-taped confessions: The impact of camera point of view on judgments of coercion. *Journal of Personality and Social Psychology, 16,* 268–276. (p. 755)

Lassiter, G. D., Lindberg, M. J., Gonzáles-Vallego, C., Bellezza, F. S., & Phillips, N. D. (2009). The deliberation-without-attention effect: Evidence for an artifactual interpretation. *Psychological Science, 20,* 671–675. (p. 369)

Latané, B. (1981). The psychology of social impact. *American Psychologist, 36,* 343–356. (pp. 772, 773)

Latané, B., & Dabbs, J. M., Jr. (1975). Sex, group size and helping in three cities. *Sociometry, 38,* 180–194. (p. 808)

Latham, G. P., & Locke, E. A. (2007). New developments in and directions for goal-setting research. *European Psychologist, 12,* 290–300. (p. 838)

Laudenslager, M. L., & Reite, M. L. (1984). Losses and separations: Immunological consequences and health implications. *Review of Personality and Social Psychology, 5,* 285–312. (p. 299)

Laws, K. R., & Kokkalis, J. (2007). Ecstasy (MDMA) and memory function: A meta-analytic update. *Human Psychopharmacology: Clinical and Experimental, 22,* 381–388. (p. 254)

Lazaruk, W. (2007). Linguistic, academic, and cognitive benefits of French immersion. *Canadian Modern Language Review, 63,* 605–628. (p. 380)

Lazarus, R. S. (1991). Progress on a cognitive-motivational-relational theory of emotion. *American Psychologist, 46,* 352–367. (p. 424)

Lazarus, R. S. (1998). *Fifty years of the research and theory of R. S. Lazarus: An analysis of historical and perennial issues.* Mahwah, NJ: Erlbaum. (pp. 424, 442)

Lazer, D., & 14 others. (2009). Computational social science. *Science, 323,* 721–723. (p. 774)

Lea, S. E. G. (2000). Towards an ethical use of animals. *The Psychologist, 13,* 556–557. (p. 67)

Leal, S., & Vrij, A. (2008). Blinking during and after lying. *Journal of Nonverbal Behavior, 32,* 187–194. (p. 428)

Leaper, C., & Ayres, M. M. (2007). A meta-analytic review of gender variations in adults' language use: Talkativeness, affiliative speech, and assertive speech. *Personality and Social Psychology Review, 11,* 328–363. (p. 502)

Leary, M. R. (1999). The social and psychological importance of self-esteem. In R. M. Kowalski & M. R. Leary (Eds.), *The social psychology of emotional and behavioral problems.* Washington, DC: APA Books. (p. 595)

Leary, M. R., Haupt, A. L., Strausser, K. S., & Chokel, J. T. (1998). Calibrating the sociometer: The relationship between interpersonal appraisals and state self-esteem. *Journal of Personality and Social Psychology, 74,* 1290–1299. (p. 413)

Leask, S. J., & Beaton, A. A. (2007). Handedness in Great Britain. *Laterality, 12,* 559–572. (p. 118)

LeDoux, J. E. (1996). *The emotional brain: The mysterious underpinnings of emotional life.* New York: Simon & Schuster. (p. 331)

LeDoux, J. E. (2002). *The synaptic self.* London: Macmillan. (pp. 423, 509)

LeDoux, J. E. (2009, July/August). Quoted by K. McGowan, Out of the past. *Discover,* pp. 28–37. (p. 347)

LeDoux, J. E., & Armony, J. (1999). Can neurobiology tell us anything about human feelings? In D. Kahneman, E. Diener, & N. Schwartz (Eds.), *Well-being: The foundations of hedonic psychology.* New York: Sage. (p. 424)

Lee, J. D. (2008). Fifty years of driving safety research. *Human Factors, 50,* 521–528. (p. 841)

Lee, J. D. (2009). Can technology get your eyes back on the road? *Science, 324,* 344–346. (p. 154)

Lee, L., Frederick, S., & Ariely, D. (2006). Try it, you'll like it: The influence of expectation, consumption, and revelation on preferences for beer. *Psychological Science, 17,* 1054–1058. (p. 164)

Lee, P. S. N., Leung, L., Lo, V., Xiong, C., & Wu, T. (2011). Internet communication versus face-to-face interaction in quality of life. *Social Indicators Research, 100,* 375–389. (p. 417)

Lee, S. W. S., Schwarz, N., Taubman, D., & Hou, M. (2010). Sneezing in times of a flue pandemic: Public sneezing increases perception of unrelated risks and shifts preferences for federal spending. *Psychological Science, 21,* 375–377. (p. 365)

Lefcourt, H. M. (1982). *Locus of control: Current trends in theory and research.* Hillsdale, NJ: Erlbaum. (p. 301)

Legrand, L. N., Iacono, W. G., & McGue, M. (2005). Predicting addiction. *American Scientist, 93,* 140–147. (p. 824)

Lehavot, K., & Lambert, A. J. (2007). Toward a greater understanding of antigay prejudice: On the role of sexual orientation and gender role violation. *Basic and Applied Social Psychology, 29,* 279–292. (p. 802)

Lehman, A. F., Steinwachs, D. M., Dixon, L. B., Goldman, H. H., Osher, F., Postrado, L., Scott, J. E., Thompson, J. W., Fahey, M., Fischer, P., Kasper, J. A., Lyles, A., Skinner, E. A., Buchanan, R., Carpenter, W. T., Jr., Levine, J., McGlynn, E. A., Rosenheck, R., & Zito, J. (1998). Translating research into practice: The schizophrenic patient outcomes research team (PORT) treatment recommendations. *Schizophrenia Bulletin, 24,* 1–10. (p. 741)

Lehman, D. R., Wortman, C. B., & Williams, A. F. (1987). Long-term effects of losing a spouse or child in a motor vehicle crash. *Journal of Personality and Social Psychology, 52,* 218–231. (p. 547)

Leichsenring, F., & Rabung, S. (2008). Effectiveness of long-term psychodynamic psychotherapy: A meta-analysis. *Journal of the American Medical Association, 300,* 1551–1565. (p. 732)

Leitenberg, H., & Henning, K. (1995). Sexual fantasy. *Psychological Bulletin, 117,* 469–496. (pp. 408, 410)

Lemonick, M. D. (2002, June 3). Lean and hungrier. *Time,* 54. (p. 398)

L'Engle, M. (1972). *A Circle of Quiet.* New York: HarperCollins. (pp. 643, 673)

L'Engle, M. (1973). *A Wind in the Door.* New York: Farrar, Straus and Giroux. (p. 31)

Lenhart, A. (2010, April 20). Teens, cell phones and texting. Pew Internet and American Life Project. Pew Research Center (www.pewresearch.org). (p. 502)

Lennox, B. R., Bert, S., Park, G., Jones, P. B., & Morris, P. G. (1999). Spatial and temporal mapping of neural activity associated with auditory hallucinations. *Lancet, 353,* 644. (p. 108)

Lenton, A. P., & Francesconi, M. (2010). How humans cognitively manage an abundance of mate options. *Psychological Science, 21,* 528–533. (p. 799)

Lenzenweger, M. F., Dworkin, R. H., & Wethington, E. (1989). Models of positive and negative symptoms in schizophrenia: An empirical evaluation of latent structures. *Journal of Abnormal Psychology, 98,* 62–70. (p. 741)

Leonhard, C., & Randler, C. (2009). In sync with the family: Children and partners influence the sleep-wake circadian rhythm and social habits of women. *Chronobiology International, 26,* 510–525. (p. 226)

Leserman, J., Jackson, E. D., Petitto, J. M., Golden, R. N., Silva, S. G., Perkins, D. O., Cai, J., Folds, J. D., & Evans, D. L. (1999). Progression to AIDS: The effects of stress, depressive symptoms, and social support. *Psychosomatic Medicine, 61,* 397–406. (p. 450)

Lester, W. (2004, May 26). AP polls: Nations value immigrant workers. Associated Press release. (p. 781)

Leucht, S., Barnes, T. R. E., Kissling, W., Engel, R. R., Correll, C., & Kane, J. M. (2003). Relapse prevention in schizophrenia with new-generation antipsychotics: A systematic review and exploratory meta-analysis of randomized, controlled trials. *American Journal of Psychiatry, 160,* 1209–1222. (p. 741)

Leung, A. K-Y., Maddux, W. W., Galinsky, A. D., & Chiu, C-Y. (2008). Multicultural experience enhances creativity: The when and how. *American Psychologist, 63,* 169–181. (p. 359)

Levant, R. F., & Hasan, N. T. (2008). Evidence-based practice in psychology. *Professional Psychology: Research and Practice, 39,* 658–662. (p. 732)

LeVay, S. (1991). A difference in hypothalamic structure between heterosexual and homosexual men. *Science, 253,* 1034–1037. (p. 533)

LeVay, S. (1994, March). Quoted in D. Nimmons, Sex and the brain. *Discover,* p. 64–71. (p. 533)

LeVay, S. (2011). *Gay, straight, and the reason why: The science of sexual orientation.* New York: Oxford University Press. (pp. 534, 535, 536)

Levenson, R. W. (1992). Autonomic nervous system differences among emotions. *Psychological Science, 3,* 23–27. (p. 427)

Levin, R., & Nielsen, T. A. (2007). Disturbed dreaming, posttraumatic stress disorder, and affect distress: A review and neurocognitive model. *Psychological Bulletin, 133,* 482–528. (p. 240)

Levin, R., & Nielsen, T. A. (2009). Nightmares, bad dreams, and emotion dysregulation. *Current Directions in Psychological Science, 18*, 84–87. (p. 240)

Levine, J. A., Lanningham-Foster, L. M., McCrady, S. K., Krizan, A. C., Olson, L. R., Kane, P. H., Jensen, M. D., & Clark, M. M. (2005). Interindividual variation in posture allocation: Possible role in human obesity. *Science, 307*, 584–586. (p. 402)

Levine, R. V., & Norenzayan, A. (1999). The pace of life in 31 countries. *Journal of Cross-Cultural Psychology, 30*, 178–205. (pp. 41, 777)

Levine, R. V., Sato, S., Hashimoto, T., & Verma, J. (1995). Love and marriage in eleven cultures. *Journal of Cross-Cultural Psychology, 26*, 554–571. (p. 803)

Levinson, D. F., & 23 others. (2011). Copy number variants in schizophrenia: Confirmation of five previous findings and new evidence for 3q29 microdeletions and VIPR2 duplications. *American Journal of Psychiatry, 168*, 302–316. (p. 689)

Levy, P. E. (2003). Industrial/organizational psychology: Understanding the workplace. Boston: Houghton Mifflin. (p. 833)

Lewandowski, G. W., Jr., Aron, A., & Gee, J. (2007). Personality goes a long way: The malleability of opposite-sex physical attractiveness. *Personality Relationships, 14*, 571–585. (p. 802)

Lewinsohn, P. M., Hoberman, H., Teri, L., & Hautziner, M. (1985). An integrative theory of depression. In S. Reiss & R. Bootzin (Eds.), *Theoretical issues in behavior therapy*. Orlando, FL: Academic Press. (p. 674)

Lewinsohn, P. M., Petit, J., Joiner, T. E., Jr., & Seeley, J. R. (2003). The symptomatic expression of major depressive disorder in adolescents and young adults. *Journal of Abnormal Psychology, 112*, 244–252. (p. 674)

Lewinsohn, P. M., Rohde, P., & Seeley, J. R. (1998). Major depressive disorder in older adolescents: Prevalence, risk factors, and clinical implications. *Clinical Psychology Review, 18*, 765–794. (p. 674)

Lewinsohn, P. M., & Rosenbaum, M. (1987). Recall of parental behavior by acute depressives, remitted depressives, and nondepressives. *Journal of Personality and Social Psychology, 52*, 611–619. (p. 337)

Lewis, C. S. (1960). *Mere Christianity*. New York: Macmillan. (p. 4)

Lewis, D. O., Pincus, J. H., Bard, B., Richardson, E., Prichep, L. S., Feldman, M., & Yeager, C. (1988). Neuropsychiatric, psychoeducational, and family characteristics of 14 juveniles condemned to death in the United States. *American Journal of Psychiatry, 145*, 584–589. (p. 493)

Lewis, D. O., Yeager, C. A., Swica, Y., Pincus, J. H., & Lewis, M. (1997). Objective documentation of child abuse and dissociation in 12 murderers with dissociative identity disorder. *American Journal of Psychiatry, 154*, 1703–1710. (p. 696)

Lewis, M. (1992). Commentary. *Human Development, 35*, 44–51. (p. 337)

Lewontin, R. (1976). Race and intelligence. In N. J. Block & G. Dworkin (Eds.), *The IQ controversy: Critical readings*. New York: Pantheon. (p. 640)

Lewontin, R. (1982). *Human diversity*. New York: Scientific American Library. (p. 136)

Li, J., Laursen, T. M., Precht, D. H., Olsen, J., & Mortensen, P. B. (2005). Hospitalization for mental illness among parents after the death of a child. *New England Journal of Medicine, 352*, 1190–1196. (p. 547)

Li, J. C., Dunning, D., & Malpass, R. L. (1996). Cross-racial identification among European-Americans: Basketball fandom and the contact hypothesis. Unpublished manuscript, Cornell University. (p. 786)

Li, N., & DiCarlo, J. J. (2008). Unsupervised natural experience rapidly alters invariant object representation in visual cortex. *Science, 321*, 1502–1506. (p. 188)

Li, Y., Johnson, E. J., & Zaval, L. (2011). Local warming: Daily temperature change influences belief in global warming. *Psychological Science, 22*, 454–459. (p. 365)

Li, Z. H., Jiang, D., Pepler, D., & Craig, W. (2010). Adolescent romantic relationships in China and Canada: A cross-national comparison. *Internal Journal of Behavioral Development, 34*, 113–120. (p. 521)

Liang, K. Y., Mintun, M. A., Fagan, A. M., Goate, A. M., Bugg, J. M., Holtzman, D. M., Morris, J. C., & Head, D. (2010). Exercise and Alzheimer's disease biomarkers in cognitively normal older adults. *Annals of Neurology, 68*, 311–318. (p. 542)

Liberman, V., Boehm, J. K., Lyubomirsky, S., & Ross, L. D. (2009). Happiness and memory: Affective significance of endowment and contrast. *Emotion, 9*, 666–680. (p. 847)

Libertus, M. E., & Brannon, E. M. (2009). Behavioral and neural basis of number sense in infancy. *Current Directions in Psychological Science, 18*, 346–351. (p. 478)

Libet, B. (1985). Unconscious cerebral initiative and the role of conscious will in voluntary action. *Behavioral and Brain Sciences, 12*, 181–187. (p. 121)

Libet, B. (2004). *Mind time: The temporal factor in consciousness*. Cambridge, MA: Harvard University Press. (p. 121)

Licata, A., Taylor, S., Berman, M., & Cranston, J. (1993). Effects of cocaine on human aggression. *Pharmacology Biochemistry and Behavior, 45*, 549–552. (p. 252)

Lichtenstein, E., Zhu, S-H., & Tedeschi, G. J. (2010). Smoking cessation quitlines: An underrecognized intervention success story. *American Psychologist, 65*, 252–261. (p. 252)

Lichtenstein, P., Calström, E., Råstam, M., Gillberg, C., & Anckarsäter, H. (2010). The genetics of autism spectrum disorders and related neuropsychiatric disorders in childhood. *American Journal of Psychiatry, 167*, 1357–1363. (p. 482)

Lieberman, M. D., & Eisenberger, M. I. (2009). Pains and pleasures of social life. *Science, 323*, 890–893. (p. 414)

Lieberman, M. D., Eisenberger, N. L., Crockett, M. J., Tom, S. M., Pfeifer, J. H., & Way, B. M. (2007). Putting feelings into words: Affect labeling disrupts amygdala activity in response to affective stimuli. *Psychological Science, 18*, 421–428. (p. 858)

Lievens, F., Dilchert, S., & Ones, D. S. (2009). The importance of exercise and dimension factors in assessment centers: Simultaneous examinations of construct-related and criterion-related validity. *Human Performance, 22*, 375–390. (p. 592)

Lilienfeld, S. O. (2009, Winter). Tips for spotting psychological pseudoscience: A student-friendly guide. *Eye of Psi Chi*, pp. 23–26. (p.168)

Lilienfeld, S. O., & Arkowitz, H. (2007a, April/May). Autism: An epidemic. *Scientific American Mind*, 82–83. (p. 481)

Lilienfeld, S. O., & Arkowitz, H. (2007b, December, 2006/January, 2007). Taking a closer look: Can moving your eyes back and forth help to ease anxiety? *Scientific American Mind*, 80–81. (p. 733)

Lilienfeld, S. O., & Arkowitz, H. (2011, January/February). The insanity verdict on trial. *Scientific American*, 64–65. (p. 656)

Lilienfeld, S. O., Lynn, S. J., Kirsch, I., Chaves, J. F., Sarbin, T. R., Ganaway, G. K., & Powell, R. A. (1999). Dissociative identity disorder and the sociocognitive model: Recalling the lessons of the past. *Psychological Bulletin, 125*, 507–523. (p. 696)

Lilienfeld, S. O., Wood, J. M., & Garb, H. N. (2001, May). What's wrong with this picture? *Scientific American*, 81–87. (pp. 567, 570)

Lim, J., & Dinges, D. F. (2010). A meta-analysis of the impact of short-term sleep deprivation on cognitive variables. *Psychological Bulletin, 136*, 375–389. (p. 236)

Lindberg, S. M., Hyde, J. S., Linn, M. C., & Petersen, J. L. (2010). New trends in gender and mathematics performance: A meta-analysis. *Psychological Bulletin, 136*, 1125–1135. (p. 638)

Linde, K., & 10 others. (2005). Acupuncture for patients with migraine: A randomized controlled trial. *Journal of the American Medical Association, 293*, 2118–2125. (p. 863)

Linder, D. (1982). Social trap analogs: The tragedy of the commons in the laboratory. In V. J. Derlega & J. Grzelak (Eds.), *Cooperative and helping behavior: Theories and research*. New York: Academic Press. (p. 812)

Lindner, I., Echterhoff, G., Davidson, P. S. R., & Brand, M. (2010). Observation inflation: Your actions become mine. *Psychological Science, 21*, 1291–1299. (p. 307)

Lindskold, S. (1978). Trust development, the GRIT proposal, and the effects of conciliatory acts on conflict and cooperation. *Psychological Bulletin, 85*, 772–793. (p. 815)

Lindskold, S., & Han, G. (1988). GRIT as a foundation for integrative bargaining. *Personality and Social Psychology Bulletin, 14*, 335–345. (p. 815)

Lindson, N., Aveyard, P., & Hughes, J. R. (2010). Reduction versus abrupt cessation in smokers who want to quit (review). *Cochrane Collaboration* (Cochrane Library, Issue 3, www.thecochranelibrary.com). (p. 252)

Linville, P. W., Fischer, G. W., & Fischhoff, B. (1992). AIDS risk perceptions and decision biases. In J. B. Pryor & G. D. Reeder (Eds.), *The social psychology of HIV infection*. Hillsdale, NJ: Erlbaum. (p. 368)

Lippa, R. A. (2005). *Gender, nature, and nurture* (2nd ed.). Mahwah, NJ: Erlbaum. (p. 503)

Lippa, R. A. (2006). The gender reality hypothesis. *American Psychologist, 61,* 639–640. (p. 503)

Lippa, R. A. (2007). The relation between sex drive and sexual attraction to men and women: A cross-national study of heterosexual, bisexual, and homosexual men and women. *Archives of Sexual Behavior, 36,* 209–222. (p. 800)

Lippa, R. A. (2008) Sex differences and sexual orientation differences in personality: Findings from the BBC Internet survey. *Archives of Sexual Behavior, Special Issue: Biological research on sex-dimorphic behavior and sexual orientation, 37*(1), 173–187. (pp. 138, 503)

Lippa, R. A. (2009). Sex differences in sex drive, sociosexuality, and height across 53 nations: Testing evolutionary and social structural theories. *Archives of Sexual Behavior, 38,* 631–651. (p. 138)

Lipps, H. M. (1999). *A new psychology of women: Gender, culture, and ethnicity.* Mountain View, CA: Mayfield Publishing. (p. 781)

Lipsey, M. W., & Wilson, D. B. (1993). The efficacy of psychological, educational, and behavioral treatment: Confirmation from meta-analyses. *American Psychologist, 48,* 1181–1209. (p. 630)

Lipsitt, L. P. (2003). Crib death: A biobehavioral phenomenon? *Current Directions in Psychological Science, 12,* 164–170. (p. 472)

Little, A. C., Jones, B. C., & DeBruine, L. M. (2008). Preferences for variation in masculinity in real male faces change across the menstrual cycle: Women prefer more masculine faces when they are more fertile. *Personality and Individual Differences, 45,* 478–482. (p. 408)

Liu, H. (2009). Till death do us part: Marital status and mortality trends, 1986–2000. *Journal of Marriage and Family, 71,* 1158–1173. (p. 857)

Liu, Y., Balaraman, Y., Wang, G., Nephew, K. P., & Zhou, F. C. (2009). Alcohol exposure alters DNA methylation profiles in mouse embryos at early neurulation. *Epigenetics, 4,* 500–511. (p. 467)

Livesley, W. J., & Jang, K. L. (2008). The behavioral genetics of personality disorder. *Annual Review of Clinical Psychology, 4,* 247–274. (p. 699)

Livingstone, M., & Hubel, D. (1988). Segregation of form, color, movement, and depth: Anatomy, physiology, and perception. *Science, 240,* 740–749. (p. 176)

LoBue, V., & DeLoache, J. S. (2008). Detecting the snake in the grass: Attention to fear-relevant stimuli by adults and young children. *Psychological Science, 19,* 284–289. (p. 667)

Loehlin, J. C., Horn, J. M., & Ernst, J. L. (2007). Genetic and environmental influences on adult life outcomes: Evidence from the Texas adoption project. *Behavior Genetics, 37,* 463–476. (p. 128)

Loehlin, J. C., McCrae, R. R., & Costa, P. T., Jr. (1998). Heritabilities of common and measure-specific components of the Big Five personality factors. *Journal of Research in Personality, 32,* 431–453. (p. 581)

Loehlin, J. C., & Nichols, R. C. (1976). *Heredity, environment, and personality.* Austin: University of Texas Press. (p. 126)

Loftus, E. F. (1980). *Memory: Surprising new insights into how we remember and why we forget.* Reading, MA: Addison-Wesley. (p. 220)

Loftus, E. F., & Ketcham, K. (1994). *The myth of repressed memory.* New York: St. Martin's Press. (pp. 240, 329)

Loftus, E. F., Levidow, B., & Duensing, S. (1992). Who remembers best? Individual differences in memory for events that occurred in a science museum. *Applied Cognitive Psychology, 6,* 93–107. (p. 348)

Loftus, E. F., & Loftus, G. R. (1980). On the permanence of stored information in the human brain. *American Psychologist, 35,* 409–420. (p. 330)

Loftus, E. F., & Palmer, J. C. (October, 1974). Reconstruction of automobile destruction: An example of the interaction between language and memory. *Journal of Verbal Learning & Verbal Behavior, 13*(5), 585–589. (pp. 347, 348)

Logan, T. K., Walker, R., Cole, J., & Leukefeld, C. (2002). Victimization and substance abuse among women: Contributing factors, interventions, and implications. *Review of General Psychology, 6,* 325–397. (p. 824)

Logue, A. W. (1998a). Laboratory research on self-control: Applications to administration. *Review of General Psychology, 2,* 221–238. (p. 279)

Logue, A. W. (1998b). Self-control. In W. T. O'Donohue, (Ed.), *Learning and behavior therapy.* Boston, MA: Allyn & Bacon. (p. 279)

London, P. (1970). The rescuers: Motivational hypotheses about Christians who saved Jews from the Nazis. In J. Macaulay & L. Berkowitz (Eds.), *Altruism and helping behavior.* New York: Academic Press. (p. 308)

Looy, H. (2001). Sex differences: Evolved, constructed, and designed. *Journal of Psychology and Theology, 29,* 301–313. (p. 139)

Lopes, P. N., Brackett, M. A., Nezlek, J. B., Schutz, A., Sellin, I., & Salovey, P. (2004). Emotional intelligence and social interaction. *Personality and Social Psychology Bulletin, 30,* 1018–1034. (p. 612)

Lopez, D. J. (2002, January/February). Snaring the fowler: Mark Twain debunks phrenology. *Skeptical Inquirer* (www.csicop.org). (p. 77)

López-Ibor, J. J., López-Ibor, M-I., & Pastrana, J. I. (2008). Transcranial magnetic stimulation. *Current Opinion in Psychiatry, 21,* 640–644. (p. 745)

Lord, C. G., Lepper, M. R., & Preston, E. (1984). Considering the opposite: A corrective strategy for social judgment. *Journal of Personality and Social Psychology, 47,* 1231–1247. (p. 368)

Lord, C. G., Ross, L., & Lepper, M. (1979). Biased assimilation and attitude polarization: The effects of prior theories on subsequently considered evidence. *Journal of Personality and Social Psychology, 37,* 2098–2109. (p. 367)

Lorenz, K. (1937). The companion in the bird's world. *Auk, 54,* 245–273. (p. 489)

Louie, K., & Wilson, M. A. (2001). Temporally structured replay of awake hippocampal ensemble activity during rapid eye movement sleep. *Neuron, 29,* 145–156. (p. 242)

Lourenco, O., & Machado, A. (1996). In defense of Piaget's theory: A reply to 10 common criticisms. *Psychological Review, 103,* 143–164. (p. 484)

Lovaas, O. I. (1987). Behavioral treatment and normal educational and intellectual functioning in young autistic children. *Journal of Consulting and Clinical Psychology, 55,* 3–9. (p. 719)

Lowry, P. E. (1997). The assessment center process: New directions. *Journal of Social Behavior and Personality, 12,* 53–62. (p. 592)

Lu, Z-L., Williamson, S. J., & Kaufman, L. (1992). Behavioral lifetime of human auditory sensory memory predicted by physiological measures. *Science, 258,* 1668–1670. (p. 322)

Lubinski, D. (2009a). Cognitive epidemiology: With emphasis on untangling cognitive ability and socioeconomic status. *Intelligence, 37,* 625–633. (p. 629)

Lubinski, D. (2009b). Exceptional cognitive ability: The phenotype. *Behavioral Genetics, 39,* 350–358. (p. 630)

Lubinski, D., & Benbow, C. P. (2000). States of excellence. *American Psychologist,* 137–150. (p. 630)

Luborsky, L., Rosenthal, R., Diguer, L., Andrusyna, T. P., Berman, J. S., Levitt, J. T., Seligman, D. A., & Krause, E. D. (2002). The dodo bird verdict is alive and well—mostly. *Clinical Psychology: Science and Practice, 9,* 2–34. (p. 732)

Lucas, R. E. (2007a). Adaptation and the set-point model of subjective well-being. *Current Directions in Psychological Science, 16,* 75–79. (p. 848)

Lucas, R. E. (2007b). Long-term disability is associated with lasting changes in subjective well-being: Evidence from two nationally representative longitudinal studies. *Journal of Personality and Social Psychology, 92,* 717–730. (p. 848)

Lucas, R. E. (2008). Personality and subjective well-being. In M. Eid & R. Larsen (Eds.), *The science of subjective well-being.* New York: Guilford. (p. 852)

Lucas, R. E., Clark, A. E., Georgellis, Y., & Diener, E. (2004). Unemployment alters the set point for life satisfaction. *Psychological Science, 15,* 8–13. (p. 852)

Lucas, R. E., & Donnellan, M. B. (2007). How stable is happiness? Using the STARTS model to estimate the stability of life satisfaction. *Journal of Research in Personality, 41,* 1091–1098. (p. 853)

Lucas, R. E., & Donnellan, M. B. (2009). Age differences in personality: Evidence from a nationally representative Australian sample. *Developmental Psychology, 45,* 1353–1363. (p. 464)

Lucas, R. E., & Donnellan, M. B. (2011). Personality development across the life span: Longitudinal analyses with a national sample from Germany. *Journal of Personality and Social Psychology, 101,* 847–861. (p. 521)

Lucas, R. E., & Schimmack, U. (2009). Income and well-being: How big is the gap between the rich and the poor? *Journal of Research in Personality, 43,* 75–78. (p. 849)

Lucas-Thompson, R. G., Goldberg, W. A., & Prause, J. (2010). Maternal work early in the lives of children and its distal associations with achievement and behavior problems: A meta-analysis. *Psychological Bulletin, 136,* 915–942. (p. 494)

Lucero, S. M., Kusner, K. G., & Speace, E. A. (2008, May 24). Religiousness and adolescent sexual behavior: A meta-analytic review. Paper presented at Association for Psychological Science Convention. (p. 530)

Luciano, M., Posthuma, D., Wright, M. J., de Geus, E. J. C., Smith, G. A., Geffen, G. M., Boomsma, D. I., & Martin, N. G. (2005). Perceptual speed does not cause intelligence, and intelligence does not cause perceptual speed. *Biological Psychology, 70,* 1–8. (p. 614)

Ludwig, A. M. (1995). *The price of greatness: Resolving the creativity and madness controversy.* New York: Guilford Press. (p. 673)

Lui, M., & Rosenfeld, J. P. (2009). The application of subliminal priming in lie detection: Scenario for identification of members of a terrorist ring. *Psycholphysiology, 46,* 889–903. (p. 428)

Lumeng, J. C., Forrest, P., Appugliese, D. P., Kaciroti, N., Corwyn, R. F., Bradley, R. H. (2010). Weight status as a predictor of being bullied in third through sixth grades. *Pediatrics, 125,* e1301–1307. (p. 401)

Luo, F., Florence, C. S., Quispe-Agnoli, M., Ouyang, L., & Crosby, A. E. (2011). Impact of business cycles on US suicide rates, 1928–2007. *American Journal of Public Health, 101,* 1139–1146. (p. 677)

Luo, M. (2011, January 25). In firearms research, cause is often the missing element. *New York Times* (www.nytimes.com). (p. 48)

Luppino, F. S., de Wit, L. M., Bouvy, P. F., Stijnen, T., Cuijpers, P., Penninx, W. J. H., & Zitman, F. G. (2010). Overweight, obesity, and depression. *Archives of General Psychiatry, 67,* 220–229. (p. 401)

Luria, A. M. (1968). In L. Solotaroff (Trans.), *The mind of a mnemonist.* New York: Basic Books. (p. 318)

Lustig, C., & Buckner, R. L. (2004). Preserved neural correlates of priming in old age and dementia. *Neuron, 42,* 865–875. (p. 343)

Lutfey, K. E., Link, C. L., Rosen, R. C., Wiegel, M., & McKinlay, J. B. (2009). Prevalence and correlates of sexual activity and function in women: Results from the Boston Area Community Health (BACH) survey. *Archives of Sexual Behavior, 38,* 514–527. (p. 407)

Lutgendorf, S. K., Russell, D., Ullrich, P., Harris, T. B., & Wallace, R. (2004). Religious participation, interleukin-6, and mortality in older adults. *Health Psychology, 23,* 465–475. (p. 865)

Lyall, S. (2005, November 29). What's the buzz? Rowdy teenagers don't want to hear it. *New York Times* (www.nytimes.com). (p. 541)

Lykken, D. T. (1991). Science, lies, and controversy: An epitaph for the polygraph. Invited address upon receipt of the Senior Career Award for Distinguished Contribution to Psychology in the Public Interest, American Psychological Association convention. (p. 428)

Lykken, D. T. (1995). *The antisocial personalities.* Hillsdale, NJ: Erlbaum. (pp. 700, 790)

Lykken, D. T. (1999). *Happiness: The Nature and Nurture of Joy and Contentment.* New York: Golden Books. (pp. 626, 632)

Lykken, D. T. (2001). Happiness—stuck with what you've got? *The Psychologist, 14,* 470–473. (p. 128)

Lykken, D. T., & Tellegen, A. (1996). Happiness is a stochastic phenomenon. *Psychological Science, 7,* 186–189. (p. 852)

Lynch, G. (2002). Memory enhancement: The search for mechanism-based drugs. *Nature Neuroscience, 5* (suppl.), 1035–1038. (p. 333)

Lynch, G., & Staubli, U. (1991). Possible contributions of long-term potentiation to the encoding and organization of memory. *Brain Research Reviews, 16,* 204–206. (p. 333)

Lynn, M. (1988). The effects of alcohol consumption on restaurant tipping. *Personality and Social Psychology Bulletin, 14,* 87–91. (p. 248)

Lynn, R. (2009). What has caused the Flynn effect? Secular increases in the development quotients of infants. *Intelligence, 37,* 16–24. (p. 621)

Lynn, R., & Harvey, J. (2008). The decline of the world's intelligence. *Intelligence, 36,* 112–120. (p. 622)

Lynn, S. J., Rhue, J. W., & Weekes, J. R. (1990). Hypnotic involuntariness: A social cognitive analysis. *Psychological Review, 97,* 169–184. (p. 221)

Lynne, S. D., Graber, J. A., Nichols, T. R., Brooks-Gunn, J., & Botvin, G. J. (2007). Links between pubertal timing, peer influences, and externalizing behaviors among urban students followed through middle school. *Journal of Adolescent Health, 40,* 181.e7–181.e13. (p. 514)

Lyons, D. E., Young, A. G., Keil, F. C. (2007). The hidden structure of overimitation. *PNAS, 104,* 19751–10756. (p. 306)

Lyons, L. (2004, February 3). Growing up lonely: Examining teen alienation. *Gallup Poll Tuesday Briefing* (www.gallup.com). (p. 520)

Lyons, L. (2005, January 4). Teens stay true to parents' political perspectives. *Gallup Poll News Service* (www.gallup.com). (p. 522)

Lyons, P. A., Kenworthy, J. B., & Popan, J. R. (2010). Ingroup identification and group-level narcissism as predictors of U.S. citizens' attitudes and behavior toward Arab immigrants. *Personality and Social Psychology Bulletin, 36,* 1267–1280. (p. 781)

Lytton, H., & Romney, D. M. (1991). Parents' differential socialization of boys and girls: A meta-analysis. *Psychological Bulletin, 109,* 267–296. (p. 504)

Lyubomirsky, S. (2001). Why are some people happier than others? The role of cognitive and motivational processes in well-being. *American Psychologist, 56,* 239–249. (p. 851)

Lyubomirsky, S., Sousa, L., & Dickerhoof, R. (2006). The costs and benefits of writing, talking, and thinking about life's triumphs and defeats. *Journal of Personality and Social Psychology, 90*(4), 690–708. (p. 859)

Ma, L. (1997, September). On the origin of Darwin's ills. *Discover, 27.* (p. 663)

Maas, J. B. (1999). *Power sleep. The revolutionary program that prepares your mind and body for peak performance.* New York: HarperCollins. (pp. 235, 236)

Maas, J. B., & Robbins, R. S. (2010). *Sleep for success: Everything you must know about sleep but are too tired to ask.* Bloomington, IN: Author House. (p. 231)

Maass, A., D'Ettole, C., & Cadinu, M. (2008). Checkmate? The role of gender stereotypes in the ultimate intellectual sport. *European Journal of Social Psychology, 38,* 231–245. (p. 642)

Maass, A., Karasawa, M., Politi, F., & Suga, S. (2006). Do verbs and adjectives play different roles in different cultures? A cross-linguistic analysis of person representation. *Journal of Personality and Social Psychology, 90,* 734–750. (p. 600)

Maass, A., & Russo, A. (2003). Directional bias in the mental representation of spatial events: Nature or culture? *Psychological Science, 14,* 296–301. (p. 379)

Macaluso, E., Frith, C. D., & Driver, J. (2000). Modulation of human visual cortex by crossmodal spatial attention. *Science, 289,* 1206–1208. (p. 210)

Macan, T. H., & Dipboye, R. L. (1994). The effects of the application on processing of information from the employment interview. *Journal of Applied Social Psychology, 24,* 1291. (p. 831)

MacCabe, J. H., Lambe, M. P., Cnattingius, S., Torrång, A., Björk, C., Sham, P. C., David, A. S., Murray, R. M., & Hultman, C. M. (2008). Scholastic achievement at age 16 and risk of schizophrenia and other psychoses: A national cohort study. *Psychological Medicine, 38,* 1133–1140. (p. 686)

Maccoby, E. E. (1980). *Social development: Psychological growth and the parent-child relationship.* New York: Harcourt Brace Jovanovich. (p. 496)

Maccoby, E. E. (1990). Gender and relationships: A developmental account. *American Psychologist, 45,* 513–520. (p. 502)

Maccoby, E. E. (1995). Divorce and custody: The rights, needs, and obligations of mothers, fathers, and children. *Nebraska Symposium on Motivation, 42,* 135–172. (p. 503)

Maccoby, E. E. (1998). *The paradox of gender.* Cambridge, MA: Harvard University Press. (p. 503)

Maccoby, E. E. (2002). Gender and group process: A developmental perspective. *Current Directions in Psychological Science, 11,* 54–58. (p. 773)

Maccoby, E. E. (2003, July 22). In Susan Gilbert, Turning a mass of data on child care into advice for parents. *New York Times* (www.nytimes.com). (p. 495)

MacDonald, G., & Leary, M. R. (2005). Why does social exclusion hurt? The relationship between social and physical pain. *Psychological Bulletin, 131,* 202–223. (p. 414)

MacDonald, N. (1960). Living with schizophrenia. *Canadian Medical Association Journal, 82,* 218–221. (p. 685)

MacDonald, T. K., & Hynie, M. (2008). Ambivalence and unprotected sex: Failure to predict sexual activity and decreased condom use. *Journal of Applied Social Psychology, 38,* 1092–1107. (p. 530)

MacDonald, T. K., Zanna, M. P., & Fong, G. T. (1995). Decision making in altered states: Effects of alcohol on attitudes toward drinking and driving. *Journal of Personality and Social Psychology, 68,* 973–985. (p. 249)

MacFarlane, A. (1978, February). What a baby knows. *Human Nature,* 74–81. (p. 468)

Macfarlane, J. W. (1964). Perspectives on personality consistency and change from the guidance study. *Vita Humana, 7,* 115–126. (p. 513)

Machin, S., & Pekkarinen, T. (2008). Global sex differences in test score variability. *Science, 322*, 1331–1332. (p. 638)

Maciejewski, P. K., Zhang, B., Block, S. D., & Prigerson, H. G. (2007). An empirical examination of the stage theory of grief. *Journal of the American Medical Association, 297*, 722–723. (p. 548)

Mack, A., & Rock, I. (2000). *Inattentional blindness.* Cambridge, MA: MIT Press. (p. 154)

Macmillan, M., & Lena, M. L. (2010). Rehabilitating Phineas Gage. *Neuropsychological Rehabilitation, 17*, 1–18. (p. 109)

MacNeilage, P. F., & Davis, B. L. (2000). On the origin of internal structure of word forms. *Science, 288*, 527–531. (p. 374)

MacNeilage, P. F., Rogers, L. J., & Vallortigara, G. (2009, July). Origins of the left and right brain. *Scientific American*, 60–67. (pp. 117, 118)

Maddi, S. R., Harvey, R. H., Khoshaba, D. M., Fazel, M., & Resurreccion, N. (2009). Hardiness training facilitates performance in college. *Journal of Positive Psychology, 4*, 566–577. (p. 834)

Maddieson, I. (1984). *Patterns of sounds.* Cambridge: Cambridge University Press. (p. 373)

Maddux, W. W., Adam, H., & Galinsky, A. D. (2010). When in Rome . . . learn why the Romans do what they do: How multicultural learning experiences facilitate creativity. *Personality and Social Psychology Bulletin, 36*, 731–741. (p. 359)

Maddux, W. W., & Galinsky, A. D. (2009). Cultural borders and mental barriers: The relationship between living abroad and creativity. *Journal of Personality and Social Psychology, 96*, 1047–1061. (p. 359)

Maes, H. H. M., Neale, M. C., & Eaves, L. J. (1997). Genetic and environmental factors in relative body weight and human adiposity. *Behavior Genetics, 27*, 325–351. (p. 402)

Maestripieri, D. (2003). Similarities in affiliation and aggression between cross-fostered rhesus macaque females and their biological mothers. *Developmental Psychobiology, 43*, 321–327. (p. 128)

Maestripieri, D. (2005). Early experience affects the intergenerational transmission of infant abuse in rhesus monkeys. *Proceedings of the National Academy of Sciences, 102*, 9726–9729. (p. 493)

Maglaty, J. (2011, April 8). When did girls start wearing pink? *Smithsonian.com.* (p. 500)

Magnusson, D. (1990). Personality research—challenges for the future. *European Journal of Personality, 4*, 1–17. (p. 700)

Maguire, E. A., Spiers, H. J., Good, C. D., Hartley, T., Frackowiak, R. S. J., & Burgess, N. (2003a). Navigation expertise and the human hippocampus: A structural brain imaging analysis. *Hippocampus, 13*, 250–259. (p. 330)

Maguire, E. A., Valentine, E. R., Wilding, J. M., & Kapur, N. (2003b). Routes to remembering: The brains behind superior memory. *Nature Neuroscience, 6*, 90–95. (pp. 323, 330)

Mahowald, M. W., & Ettinger, M. G. (1990). Things that go bump in the night: The parasomnias revisited. *Journal of Clinical Neurophysiology, 7*, 119–143. (p. 239)

Maier, S. F., Watkins, L. R., & Fleshner, M. (1994). Psychoneuroimmunology: The interface between behavior, brain, and immunity. *American Psychologist, 49*, 1004–1017. (p. 448)

Major, B., Carrington, P. I., & Carnevale, P. J. D. (1984). Physical attractiveness and self-esteem: Attribution for praise from an other-sex evaluator. *Personality and Social Psychology Bulletin, 10*, 43–50. (p. 800)

Major, B., Schmidlin, A. M., & Williams, L. (1990). Gender patterns in social touch: The impact of setting and age. *Journal of Personality and Social Psychology, 58*, 634–643. (p. 502)

Malamuth, N. M. (1996). Sexually explicit media, gender differences, and evolutionary theory. *Journal of Communication, 46*, 8–31. (p. 794)

Malamuth, N. M., & Check, J. V. P. (1981). The effects of media exposure on acceptance of violence against women: A field experiment. *Journal of Research in Personality, 15*, 436–446. (p. 409)

Malamuth, N. M., Linz, D., Heavey, C. L., Barnes, G., & Acker, M. (1995). Using the confluence model of sexual aggression to predict men's conflict with women: A 10-year follow-up study. *Journal of Personality and Social Psychology, 69*, 353–369. (p. 794)

Malamuth, N. M., Sockloskie, R. J., Koss, M. P., & Tanaka, J. S. (1991). Characteristics of aggressors against women: Testing a model using a national sample of college students. *Journal of Consulting and Clinical Psychology, 59*, 670–681. (p. 794)

Maldonado-Molina, M. M., Reingle, J. M., Jennings, W. G., & Prado, G. (2011). Drinking and driving among immigrant and US-born Hispanic young adults: Results from a longitudinal and nationally representative study. *Addictive Behavior, 36*, 381–388. (p. 657)

Malkiel, B. (2004). *A random walk down Wall Street* (8th ed.). New York: Norton. (p. 365)

Malkiel, B. (2007). *A random walk down Wall Street: The time-tested strategy for successful investing* (revised and updated). New York: Norton. (p. 33)

Malle, B. F. (2006). The actor-observer asymmetry in attribution: A (surprising) meta-analysis. *Psychological Bulletin, 132*, 895–919. (p. 755)

Malle, B. F., Knobe, J. M., & Nelson, S. E. (2007). Actor-observer asymmetries in explanations of behavior: New answers to an old question. *Journal of Personality and Social Psychology, 93*, 491–514. (p. 755)

Malmquist, C. P. (1986). Children who witness parental murder: Post-traumatic aspects. *Journal of the American Academy of Child Psychiatry, 25*, 320–325. (p. 563)

Malnic, B., Hirono, J., Sato, T., & Buck, L. B. (1999). Combinatorial receptor codes for odors. *Cell, 96*, 713–723. (p. 208)

Maltby, N., Tolin, D. F., Worhunsky, P., O'Keefe, T. M., & Kiehl, K. A. (2005). Dysfunctional action monitoring hyperactivates frontal-striatal circuits in obsessive-compulsive disorder: An event-related fMRI study. *NeuroImage, 24*, 495–503. (p. 668)

Mampe, B., Friederici, A. D., Christophe, A., & Wermke, K. (2009). Newborns' cry melody is shaped by their native language. *Current Biology, 19*, 1–4. (p. 466)

Manson, J. E. (2002). Walking compared with vigorous exercise for the prevention of cardiovascular events in women. *New England Journal of Medicine, 347*, 716–725. (p. 859)

Maquet, P. (2001). The role of sleep in learning and memory. *Science, 294*, 1048–1052. (p. 242)

Maquet, P., Peters, J-M., Aerts, J., Delfiore, G., Degueldre, C., Luxen, A., & Franck, G. (1996). Functional neuroanatomy of human rapid-eye-movement sleep and dreaming. *Nature, 383*, 163–166. (p. 242)

Mar, R. A., & Oatley, K. (2008). The function of fiction is the abstraction and simulation of social experience. *Perspectives on Psychological Science, 3*, 173–192. (p. 307)

Marcus, B., Machilek, F., & Schütz, A. (2006). Personality in cyberspace: Personal web sites as media for personality expressions and impressions. *Journal of Personality and Social Psychology, 90*, 1014–1031. (p. 584)

Marcus, G. F., Vijayan, S., Rao, S. B., & Vishton, P. M. (1999). Rule learning by seven-month-old infants. *Science, 283*, 77–80. (p. 376)

Maren, S. (2007). The threatened brain. *Science, 317*, 1043–1044. (p. 668)

Margolis, M. L. (2000). Brahms' lullaby revisited: Did the composer have obstructive sleep apnea? *Chest, 118*, 210–213. (p. 239)

Marinak, B. A., & Gambrell, L. B. (2008). Intrinsic motivation and rewards: What sustains young children's engagement with text? *Literacy Research and Instruction, 47*, 9–26. (p. 297)

Markovizky, G., & Samid, Y. (2008). The process of immigrant adjustment: The role of time in determining psychological adjustment. *Journal of Cross-Cultural Psychology, 39*, 782–798. (p. 443)

Markowitsch, H. J. (1995). Which brain regions are critically involved in the retrieval of old episodic memory? *Brain Research Reviews, 21*, 117–127. (p. 330)

Markowitz, J. C., Svartberg, M., & Swartz, H. A. (1998). Is IPT time-limited psychodynamic psychotherapy? *Journal of Psychotherapy Practice and Research, 7*, 185–195. (p. 711)

Marks, I., & Cavanagh, K. (2009). Computer-aided psychological treatments: Evolving issues. *Annual Review of Clinical Psychology, 5*, 121–141. (p. 723)

Markus, H. R., & Kitayama, S. (1991). Culture and the self: Implications for cognition, emotion, and motivation. *Psychological Review, 98*, 224–253. (pp. 379, 599, 846)

Markus, H. R., & Nurius, P. (1986). Possible selves. *American Psychologist, 41*, 954–969. (p. 594)

Markus, H. R., Uchida, Y., Omoregie, H., Townsend, S. S. M., & Kitayama, S. (2006). Going for the gold: Models of agency in Japanese and American contexts. *Psychological Science, 17*, 103–112. (p. 600)

Marley, J., & Bulia, S. (2001). Crimes against people with mental illness: Types, perpetrators and influencing factors. *Social Work, 46*, 115–124. (p. 656)

Marmot, M. G., Bosma, H., Hemingway, H., Brunner, E., & Stansfeld, S. (1997). Contribution to job control and other risk factors to social variations in coronary heart disease incidents. *Lancet, 350,* 235–239. (p. 300)

Marsh, A. A., Elfenbein, H. A., & Ambady, N. (2003). Nonverbal "accents": Cultural differences in facial expressions of emotion. *Psychological Science, 14,* 373–376. (p. 436)

Marsh, H. W., & Craven, R. G. (2006). Reciprocal effects of self-concept and performance from a multidimensional perspective: Beyond seductive pleasure and unidimensional perspectives. *Perspectives on Psychological Science, 1,* 133–163. (p. 595)

Marsh, H. W., & Parker, J. W. (1984). Determinants of student self-concept: Is it better to be a relatively large fish in a small pond even if you don't learn to swim as well? *Journal of Personality and Social Psychology, 47,* 213–231. (p. 852)

Marshall, M. J. (2002). *Why spanking doesn't work.* Springville, UT: Bonneville Books. (p. 281)

Marshall, R. D., Bryant, R. A., Amsel, L., Suh, E. J., Cook, J. M., & Neria, Y. (2007). The psychology of ongoing threat: Relative risk appraisal, the September 11 attacks, and terrorism-related fears. *American Psychologist, 62,* 304–316. (p. 365)

Marshall, W. L. (1989). Pornography and sex offenders. In D. Zillmann & J. Bryant (Eds.), *Pornography: Research advances and policy considerations.* Hillsdale, NJ: Erlbaum. (p. 793)

Marshall, W. L. (2000). Revisiting the use of pornography by sexual offenders: Implications for theory and practice. *Journal of Sexual Aggression, 6,* 67–77. (p. 793)

Marteau, T. M. (1989). Framing of information: Its influences upon decisions of doctors and patients. *British Journal of Social Psychology, 28,* 89–94. (p. 368)

Marti, M. W., Robier, D. M., & Baron, R. S. (2000). Right before our eyes: The failure to recognize non-prototypical forms of prejudice. *Group Processes and Intergroup Relations, 3,* 403–418. 409–416. (p. 357)

Martin, C. K., Anton, S. D., Walden, H., Arnett, C., Greenway, F. L., & Williamson, D. A. (2007). Slower eating rate reduces the food intake of men, but not women: Implications for behavioural weight control. *Behaviour Research and Therapy, 45,* 2349–2359. (p. 403)

Martin, C. L., & Ruble, D. (2004). Children's search for gender cues. *Current Directions in Psychological Science, 13,* 67–70. (p. 505)

Martin, C. L., Ruble, D. N., & Szkrybalo, J. (2002). Cognitive theories of early gender development. *Psychological Bulletin, 128,* 903–933. (p. 504)

Martin, R. J., White, B. D., & Hulsey, M. G. (1991). The regulation of body weight. *American Scientist, 79,* 528–541. (p. 398)

Martin, R. M., Goodall, S. H., Gunnell, D., & Smith, G. D. (2007). Breast feeding in infancy and social mobility: 60-year follow-up of the Boyd Orr cohort. *Archives of Disease in Childhood, 92,* 317–321. (p. 50)

Martin, S. J., Kelly, I. W., & Saklofske, D. H. (1992). Suicide and lunar cycles: A critical review over 28 years. *Psychological Reports, 71,* 787–795. (p. 700)

Martino, S. C., Collins, R. L., Kanouse, D. E., Elliott, M., & Berry, S. H. (2005). Social cognitive processes mediating the relationship between exposure to television's sexual content and adolescents' sexual behavior. *Journal of Personality and Social Psychology, 89,* 914–924. (p. 530)

Martins, Y., Preti, G., Crabtree, C. R., & Wysocki, C. J. (2005). Preference for human body odors is influenced by gender and sexual orientation. *Psychological Science, 16,* 694–701. (p. 534)

Marx, D. M., Ko, S. J., & Friedman, R. A. (2009). The "Obama effect": How a salient role model reduces race-based performance differences. *Journal of Experimental Social Psychology, 45,* 953–956. (p. 643)

Masicampo, E. J., & Baumeister, R. F. (2008). Toward a physiology of dual-process reasoning and judgment: Lemonade, willpower, and the expensive rule-based analysis. *Psychological Science, 19,* 255–260. (p. 302)

Maslow, A. H. (1970). *Motivation and personality* (2nd ed.). New York: Harper & Row. (pp. 393, 571)

Maslow, A. H. (1971). *The farther reaches of human nature.* New York: Viking Press. (p. 393)

Mason, A. E., Sbarra, D. A., & Mehl, M. R. (2010). Thin-slicing divorce: Thirty seconds of information predict changes in psychological adjustment over 90 days. *Psychological Science, 21,* 1420–1422. (p. 433)

Mason, C., & Kandel, E. R. (1991). Central visual pathways. In E. R. Kandel, J. H. Schwartz, & T. M. Jessell (Eds.), *Principles of neural science* (3rd ed.). New York: Elsevier. (p. 86)

Mason, H. (2003a, September 2). Americans, Britons at odds on animal testing. *Gallup Poll News Service* (http://www.gallup.com). (p. 66)

Mason, H. (2003b, March 25). Wake up, sleepy teen. *Gallup Poll Tuesday Briefing* (www.gallup.com). (p. 236)

Mason, H. (2005, January 25). Who dreams, perchance to sleep? *Gallup Poll News Service* (www.gallup.com). (pp. 235, 236)

Mason, R. A., & Just, M. A. (2004). How the brain processes causal inferences in text. *Psychological Science, 15,* 1–7. (p. 117)

Masse, L. C., & Tremblay, R. E. (1997). Behavior of boys in kindergarten and the onset of substance use during adolescence. *Archives of General Psychiatry, 54,* 62–68. (p. 823)

Massey, C., Simmons, J. P., & Armor, D. A. (2011). Hope over experience: Desirability and the persistence of optimism. *Psychological Science, 22,* 274–281. (p. 589)

Massimini, M., Ferrarelli, F., Huber, R., Esser, S. K., Singh, H., & Tononi, G. (2005). Breakdown of cortical effective connectivity during sleep. *Science, 309,* 2228–2232. (p. 226)

Mast, M. S., & Hall, J. A. (2006). Women's advantage at remembering others' appearance: A systematic look at the why and when of a gender difference. *Personality and Social Psychology Bulletin, 32,* 353–364. (p. 801)

Masten, A. S. (2001). Ordinary magic: Resilience processes in development. *American Psychologist, 56,* 227–238. (p. 493)

Masters, K. S. (2010). The role of religion in therapy: Time for psychologists to have a little faith? *Cognitive and Behavioral Practice, 17,* 393–400. (p. 735)

Masters, W. H., & Johnson, V. E. (1966). *Human sexual response.* Boston: Little, Brown. (p. 406)

Mastroianni, G. R. (2002). Milgram and the Holocaust: A reexamination. *Journal of Theoretical and Philosophical Psychology, 22,* 158–173. (p. 767)

Mastroianni, G. R., & Reed, G. (2006). Apples, barrels, and Abu Ghraib. *Sociological Focus, 39,* 239–250. (p. 758)

Masuda, T., Ellsworth, P. C., Mesquita, B., Leu, J., Tanida, S., & Van de Veerdonk, E. (2008). Placing the face in context: Cultural differences in the perception of facial emotion. *Journal of Personality and Social Psychology, 94,* 365–381. (p. 436)

Mataix-Cols, D., Rosario-Campos, M. C., & Leckman, J. F. (2005). A multidimensional model of obsessive-compulsive disorder. *American Journal of Psychiatry, 162,* 228–238. (p. 668)

Mataix-Cols, D., Wooderson, S., Lawrence, N., Brammer, M. J., Speckens, A., & Phillips, M. L. (2004). Distinct neural correlates of washing, checking, and hoarding symptom dimensions in obsessive-compulsive disorder. *Archives of General Psychiatry, 61,* 564–576. (p. 668)

Mather, M., Canli, T., English, T., Whitfield, S., Wais, P., Ochsner, K., Gabrieli, J. D. E., & Carstensen, L. L. (2004). Amygdala responses to emotionally valenced stimuli in older and younger adults. *Psychological Science, 15,* 259–263. (p. 547)

Mather, M., Lighthall, N. R., Nga, L., & Gorlick, M. A. (2010). Sex differences in how stress affects brain activity during face viewing. *NeuroReport, 21,* 933–937. (p. 446)

Matsumoto, D. (1994). *People: Psychology from a cultural perspective.* Pacific Grove, CA: Brooks/Cole. (p. 379)

Matsumoto, D., & Ekman, P. (1989). American-Japanese cultural differences in intensity ratings of facial expressions of emotion. *Motivation and Emotion, 13,* 143–157. (p. 435)

Matsumoto, D., & Willingham, B. (2006). The thrill of victory and the agony of defeat: Spontaneous expressions of medal winners of the 2004 Athens Olympic Games. *Journal of Personality and Social Psychology, 91,* 568–581. (p. 436)

Matsumoto, D., & Willingham, B. (2009). Spontaneous facial expressions of emotion of congenitally and noncongenitally blind individuals. *Journal of Personality and Social Psychology, 96,* 1–10. (p. 436)

Matsumoto, D., Willingham, B., & Olide, A. (2009). Sequential dynamics of culturally moderated facial expressions of emotion. *Psychological Science, 20,* 1269–1275. (p. 436)

Matthews, K. A. (2005). Psychological perspectives on the development of coronary heart disease. *American Psychologist, 60,* 783–796. (p. 453)

Matthews, R. N., Domjan, M., Ramsey, M., & Crews, D. (2007). Learning effects on sperm competition and reproductive fitness. *Psychological Science, 18,* 758–762. (p. 268)

Maurer, D., & Maurer, C. (1988). *The world of the newborn.* New York: Basic Books. (p. 468)

Mauss, I. B., Shallcross, A. J., Troy, A. S., John, O. P., Ferrer, E., Wilhelm, F. H., & Gross, J. J. (2011). Don't hide your happiness! Positive emotion dissociation, social connectedness, and psychological functioning. *Journal of Personality and Social Psychology, 100,* 738–748. (p. 847)

May, C., & Hasher, L. (1998). Synchrony effects in inhibitory control over thought and action. *Journal of Experimental Psychology: Human Perception and Performance, 24,* 363–380. (p. 226)

May, P. A., & Gossage, J. P. (2001). Estimating the prevalence of fetal alcohol syndrome: A summary. *Alcohol Research and Health, 25,* 159–167. (p. 467)

Mayberg, H. S. (2006). Defining neurocircuits in depression: Strategies toward treatment selection based on neuroimaging phenotypes. *Psychiatric Annals, 36,* 259–268. (p. 745)

Mayberg, H. S. (2007). Defining the neural circuitry of depression: Toward a new nosology with therapeutic implications. *Biological Psychiatry, 61,* 729–730. (p. 745)

Mayberg, H. S. (2009). Targeted modulation of neural circuits: A new treatment strategy for depression. *Journal of Clinical Investigation, 119,* 717–25. (p. 745)

Mayberg, H. S., Lozano, A. M., Voon, V., McNeely, H. E., Seminowicz, D., Hamani, C., Schwalb, J. M., & Kennedy, S. H. (2005). Deep brain stimulation for treatment-resistant depression. *Neuron, 45,* 651–660. (p. 745)

Mayberry, R. I., Lock, E., & Kazmi, H. (2002). Linguistic ability and early language exposure. *Nature, 417,* 38. (p. 377)

Mayer, J. D., Salovey, P., & Caruso, D. R. (2002). *The Mayer-Salovey-Caruso emotional intelligence test (MSCEIT).* Toronto: Multi-Health Systems, Inc. (p. 612)

Mayer, J. D., Salovey, P., & Caruso, D. R. (2008). Emotional intelligence: New ability or eclectic traits? *American Psychologist, 63,* 503–517. (p. 612)

Mayer, M. (2006, May 17). License to pursue dreams. Entrepreneurial thought leader speaker series, Stanford Technology Ventures Program (http://ecorner.stanford.edu/authorMaterialInfo.html?mid=1527). (p. 358)

Mays, V. M., Cochran, S. D., & Barnes, N. W. (2007). Race, race-based discrimination, and health outcomes among African Americans. *Annual Review of Psychology, 58,* 201–225. (p. 444)

Mazure, C., Keita, G., & Blehar, M. (2002). *Summit on women and depression: Proceedings and recommendations.* Washington, DC: American Psychological Association (www.apa.org/pi/wpo/women&depression.pdf). (p. 679)

Mazzoni, G., & Memon, A. (2003). Imagination can create false autobiographical memories. *Psychological Science, 14,* 186–188. (p. 348)

Mazzoni, G., Scoboria, A., & Harvey, L. (2010). Nonbelieved memories. *Psychological Science, 21,* 1334–1340. (p. 348)

Mazzoni, G., & Vannucci, M. (2007). Hindsight bias, the misinformation effect, and false autobiographical memories. *Social Cognition, 25,* 203–220. (p. 350)

McAndrew, F. T. (2009). The interacting roles of testosterone and challenges to status in human male aggression. *Aggression and Violent Behavior, 14,* 330–335. (p. 790)

McAneny, L. (1996, September). Large majority think government conceals information about UFO's. *Gallup Poll Monthly,* pp. 23–26. (p. 349)

McBeath, M. K., Shaffer, D. M., & Kaiser, M. K. (1995). How baseball outfielders determine where to run to catch fly balls. *Science, 268,* 569–572. (p. 185)

McBurney, D. H. (1996). *How to think like a psychologist: Critical thinking in psychology.* Upper Saddle River, NJ: Prentice-Hall. (p. 109)

McBurney, D. H., & Collings, V. B. (1984). *Introduction to sensation and perception* (2nd ed.). Englewood Cliffs, NJ: Prentice-Hall. (pp. 187, 189)

McBurney, D. H., & Gent, J. F. (1979). On the nature of taste qualities. *Psychological Bulletin, 86,* 151–167. (p. 207)

McCain, N. L., Gray, D. P., Elswick, R. K., Jr., Robins, J. W., Tuck, I., Walter, J. M., Rausch, S. M., & Ketchum, J. M. (2008). A randomized clinical trial of alternative stress management interventions in persons with HIV infection. *Journal of Consulting and Clinical Psychology, 76,* 431–441. (p. 450)

McCann, I. L., & Holmes, D. S. (1984). Influence of aerobic exercise on depression. *Journal of Personality and Social Psychology, 46,* 1142–1147. (p. 860)

McCann, U. D., Eligulashvili, V., & Ricaurte, G. A. (2001). (+-)3,4-Methylenedioxymethamphetamine ('Ecstasy')-induced serotonin neurotoxicity: Clinical studies. *Neuropsychobiology, 42,* 11–16. (p. 254)

McCarthy, P. (1986, July). Scent: The tie that binds? *Psychology Today, 6,* 10. (p. 208)

McCauley, C. R. (2002). Psychological issues in understanding terrorism and the response to terrorism. In C. E. Stout (Ed.), *The psychology of terrorism* (Vol. 3). Westport, CT: Praeger/Greenwood. (p. 774)

McCauley, C. R., & Segal, M. E. (1987). Social psychology of terrorist groups. In C. Hendrick (Ed.), *Group processes and intergroup relations.* Beverly Hills, CA: Sage. (p. 774)

McClendon, B. T., & Prentice-Dunn, S. (2001). Reducing skin cancer risk: An intervention based on protection motivation theory. *Journal of Health Psychology, 6,* 321–328. (p. 757)

McClintock, M. K., & Herdt, G. (1996, December). Rethinking puberty: The development of sexual attraction. *Current Directions in Psychological Science, 5*(6), 178–183. (p. 527)

McClure, M. J., Lydon, J. E., Baccus, J. R., & Baldwin, M. W. (2010). A signal detection analysis of chronic attachment anxiety at speed dating: Being unpopular is only the first part of the problem. *Personality and Social Psychology Bulletin, 36,* 1024–1036. (p. 156)

McConkey, K. M. (1995). Hypnosis, memory, and the ethics of uncertainty. *Australian Psychologist, 30,* 1–10. (p. 220)

McConnell, R. A. (1991). National Academy of Sciences opinion on parapsychology. *Journal of the American Society for Psychical Research, 85,* 333–365. (p. 167)

McCool, G. (1999, October 26). Mirror-gazing Venezuelans top of vanity stakes. *Toronto Star* (via web.lexis-nexis.com). (p. 800)

McCord, J. (1978). A thirty-year follow-up on treatment effects. *American Psychologist, 33,* 284–289. (p. 729)

McCord, J. (1979). Following up on Cambridge-Somerville. *American Psychologist, 34,* 727. (p. 729)

McCrae, R. R. (2009). The five-factor model of personality traits: Consensus and controversy. In P. J. Corr & G. Matthews, Gerald (eds.). *The Cambridge handbook of personality psychology.* New York: Cambridge University Press. (p. 580)

McCrae, R. R. (2011). Personality theories for the 21st century. *Teaching of Psychology, 38,* 209–214. (p. 581)

McCrae, R. R., & Costa, P. T., Jr. (1986). Clinical assessment can benefit from recent advances in personality psychology. *American Psychologist, 41,* 1001–1003. (p. 581)

McCrae, R. R., & Costa, P. T., Jr. (1990). *Personality in adulthood.* New York: Guilford. (p. 544)

McCrae, R. R., & Costa, P. T., Jr. (1994). The stability of personality: Observations and evaluations. *Current Directions in Psychological Science, 3,* 173–175. (p. 583)

McCrae, R. R., & Costa, P. T., Jr. (2008). The Five-Factor Theory of personality. In O. P. John, R. W., Robins, & L. A. Pervin (eds.), *Handbook of personality: Theory and research* (3rd. ed.). New York: Guilford. (p. 581)

McCrae, R. R., Costa, P. T., Jr., Ostendorf, F., Angleitner, A., Hrebickova, M., Avia, M. D., Sanz, J., Sanchez-Bernardos, M. L., Kusdil, M. E., Woodfield, R., Saunders, P. R., & Smith, P. B. (2000). Nature over nurture: Temperament, personality, and life span development. *Journal of Personality and Social Psychology, 78,* 173–186. (p. 491)

McCrae, R. R., Scally, M., Terraccioani, A., Abecasis, G. R., & Costa, P. T., Jr. (2010). An alternative to the search for single polymorphisms: Toward molecular personality scales for the Five-Factor Model. *Journal of Personality and Social Psychology, 99,* 1014–1024. (p. 581)

McCrae, R. R., Terracciano, A., & Khoury, B. (2007). *Dolce far niente:* The positive psychology of personality stability and invariance. In A. D. Ong & M. H. Van Dulmen (Eds.), *Oxford handbook of methods in positive psychology.* New York: Oxford University Press. (p. 491)

McCrink, K., & Wynn, K. (2004). Large-number addition and subtraction by 9-month-old infants. *Psychological Science, 15,* 776–781. (p. 478)

McCullough, M. E., Hoyt, W. T., Larson, D. B., Koenig, H. G., & Thoresen, C. (2000). Religious involvement and mortality: A meta-analytic review. *Health Psychology, 19,* 211–222. (p. 864)

McCullough, M. E., & Laurenceau, J-P. (2005). Religiousness and the trajectory of self-rated health across adulthood. *Personality and Social Psychology Bulletin, 31,* 560–573. (p. 864)

McCullough, M. E., & Willoughby, B. L. B. (2009). Religion, self-regulation, and self-control: Associations, explanations, and implications. *Psychological Bulletin, 135,* 69–93. (pp. 864, 865)

McDaniel, M. A. (2005). Big-brained people are smarter: A meta-analysis of the relationship between in vivo brain volume and intelligence. *Intelligence, 33*, 337–346. (p. 613)

McDaniel, M. A., Howard, D. C., & Einstein, G. O. (2009). The read-recite-review study strategy: Effective and portable. *Psychological Science, 20*, 516–522. (p. 16)

McEvoy, S. P., Stevenson, M. R., McCartt, A. T., Woodward, M., Haworth, C., Palamara, P., & Ceracelli, R. (2005). Role of mobile phones in motor vehicle crashes resulting in hospital attendance: A case-crossover study. *British Medical Journal, 33*, 428. (p. 153)

McEvoy, S. P., Stevenson, M. R., & Woodward, M. (2007). The contribution of passengers versus mobile phone use to motor vehicle crashes resulting in hospital attendance by the driver. *Accident Analysis and Prevention, 39*, 1170–1176. (p. 153)

McFarland, C., & Ross, M. (1987). The relation between current impressions and memories of self and dating partners. *Psychological Bulletin, 13*, 228–238. (p. 350)

McGaugh, J. L. (1994). Quoted by B. Bower, Stress hormones hike emotional memories. *Science News, 146*, 262. (p. 332)

McGaugh, J. L. (2003). *Memory and emotion: The making of lasting memories.* New York: Columbia University Press. (p. 332)

McGhee, P. E. (June, 1976). Children's appreciation of humor: A test of the cognitive congruency principle. *Child Development, 47*(2), 420–426. (p. 483)

McGowan, P. O., Sasaki, A., D'Alessio, A. C., Dymov, S., Labonté, B., Szyl, M., Turecki, G., & Meaney, M. J. (2009). Epigenetic regulation of the glucocorticoid receptor in human brain associates with childhood abuse. *Nature Neuroscience, 12*, 342–348. (p. 132)

McGrath, J. J., & Welham, J. L. (1999). Season of birth and schizophrenia: A systematic review and meta-analysis of data from the Southern hemisphere. *Schizophrenia Research, 35*, 237–242. (p. 688)

McGrath, J. J., Welham, J., & Pemberton, M. (1995). Month of birth, hemisphere of birth and schizophrenia. *British Journal of Psychiatry, 167*, 783–785. (p. 688)

McGue, M. (2010). The end of behavioral genetics? *Behavioral Genetics, 40*, 284–296. (p. 132)

McGue, M., & Bouchard, T. J., Jr. (1998). Genetic and environmental influences on human behavioral differences. *Annual Review of Neuroscience, 21*, 1–24. (p. 128)

McGue, M., Bouchard, T. J., Jr., Iacono, W. G., & Lykken, D. T. (1993). Behavioral genetics of cognitive ability: A life-span perspective. In R. Plomin & G. E. McClearn (Eds.), *Nature, nurture, and psychology.* Washington, DC: American Psychological Association. (p. 633)

McGue, M., & Lykken, D. T. (1992). Genetic influence on risk of divorce. *Psychological Science, 3*, 368–373. (p. 126)

McGuire, W. J. (1986). The myth of massive media impact: Savings and salvagings. In G. Comstock (Ed.), *Public communication and behavior.* Orlando, FL: Academic Press. (p. 309)

McGurk, H., & MacDonald, J. (1976). Hearing lips and seeing voices. *Nature, 264*, 746–748. (p. 210)

McHugh, P. R. (1995a). Resolved: Multiple personality disorder is an individually and socially created artifact. *Journal of the American Academy of Child and Adolescent Psychiatry, 34*, 957–959. (p. 696)

McHugh, P. R. (1995b). Witches, multiple personalities, and other psychiatric artifacts. *Nature Medicine, 1*(2), 110–114. (p. 695)

McKay, J. (2000). Building self-esteem in children. In M. McKay & P. Fanning (Eds.), *Self-esteem.* New York: New Harbinger/St. Martins. (p. 595)

McKellar, J., Stewart, E., & Humphreys, K. (2003). Alcoholics Anonymous involvement and positive alcohol-related outcomes: Cause, consequence, or just a correlate? A prospective 2-year study of 2,319 alcohol-dependent men. *Journal of Consulting and Clinical Psychology, 71*, 302–308. (p. 724)

McKenna, K. Y. A., & Bargh, J. A. (1998). Coming out in the age of the Internet: Identity "demarginalization" through virtual group participation. *Journal of Personality and Social Psychology, 75*, 681–694. (p. 799)

McKenna, K. Y. A., & Bargh, J. A. (2000). Plan 9 from cyberspace: The implications of the Internet for personality and social psychology. *Personality and Social Psychology Review, 4*, 57–75. (p. 799)

McKenna, K. Y. A., Green, A. S., & Gleason, M. E. J. (2002). What's the big attraction? Relationship formation on the Internet. *Journal of Social Issues, 58*, 9–31. (p. 799)

McKone, E., Kanwisher, N., & Duchaine, B. C. (2007). Can generic expertise explain special processing for faces? *Trends in Cognitive Sciences, 11*, 8–15. (p. 175)

McLaughlin, C. S., Chen, C., Greenberger, E., & Biermeier, C. (1997). Family, peer, and individual correlates of sexual experience among Caucasian and Asian American late adolescents. *Journal of Personality and Social Psychology: Journal of Research on Adolescence, 7*, 33–53. (p. 529)

McLaughlin, M. (2010, October 2). JK Rowling: Depression, the 'terrible place that allowed me to come back stronger.' *The Scotsman* (www.scotsman.com). (p. 674)

McLean, C. P., & Anderson, E. R. (2009). Brave men and timid women? A review of the gender differences in fear and anxiety. *Clinical Psychology Review, 29*, 496–505. (p. 662)

McMurray, B. (2007). Defusing the childhood vocabulary explosion. *Science, 317*, 631. (p. 373)

McMurray, C. (2004, January 13). U.S., Canada, Britain: Who's getting in shape? *Gallup Poll Tuesday Briefing* (www.gallup.com). (p. 860)

McNally, R. J. (1999). EMDR and Mesmerism: A comparative historical analysis. *Journal of Anxiety Disorders, 13*, 225–236. (p. 733)

McNally, R. J. (2003). *Remembering trauma.* Cambridge, MA: Harvard University Press. (pp. 352, 665)

McNally, R. J. (2007). Betrayal trauma theory: A critical appraisal. *Memory, 15*, 280–294. (p. 352)

McNeil, B. J., Pauker, S. G., & Tversky, A. (1988). On the framing of medical decisions. In D. E. Bell, H. Raiffa, & A. Tversky (Eds.), *Decision making: Descriptive, normative, and prescriptive interactions.* New York: Cambridge University Press. (p. 368)

McWhorter, J. (2012, April 23). Talking with your fingers. *New York Times* (www.nytimes.com). (p. 416)

Mead, G. E., Morley, W., Campbell, P., Greig, C. A., McMurdo, M., & Lawlor, D. A. (2010). Exercise for depression. *Cochrane Database Systematic Reviews,* Issue 3. Art. No. CD004366. (p. 860)

Meador, B. D., & Rogers, C. R. (1984). Person-centered therapy. In R. J. Corsini (Ed.), *Current psychotherapies* (3rd ed.). Itasca, IL: Peacock. (p. 712)

Medical Institute for Sexual Health. (1994, April). Condoms ineffective against human papilloma virus. *Sexual Health Update,* p. 2. (p. 529)

Medland, S. E., Perelle, I., De Monte, V., & Ehrman, L. (2004). Effects of culture, sex, and age on the distribution of handedness: An evaluation of the sensitivity of three measures of handedness. *Laterality: Asymmetries of Body, Brain, and Cognition, 9*, 287–297. (p. 118)

Mednick, S. A., Huttunen, M. O., & Machon, R. A. (1994). Prenatal influenza infections and adult schizophrenia. *Schizophrenia Bulletin, 20*, 263–267. (p. 687)

Mehl, M. R., Gosling, S. D., & Pennebaker, J. W. (2006). Personality in its natural habitat: Manifestations and implicit folk theories of personality in daily life. *Journal of Personality and Social Psychology, 90*, 862–877. (p. 583)

Mehl, M. R., & Pennebaker, J. W. (2003). The sounds of social life: A psychometric analysis of students' daily social environments and natural conversations. *Journal of Personality and Social Psychology, 84*, 857–870. (p. 41)

Mehl, M. R., Vazire, S., Holleran, S. E., & Clark, C. S. (2010). Eavesdropping on happiness: Well-being is related to having less small talk and more substantive conversations. *Psychological Science, 21*, 539–541. (p. 853)

Mehta, M. R. (2007). Cortico-hippocampal interaction during up-down states and memory consolidation. *Nature Neuroscience, 10*, 13–15. (p. 331)

Meichenbaum, D. (1977). *Cognitive-behavior modification: An integrative approach.* New York: Plenum Press. (p. 722)

Meichenbaum, D. (1985). *Stress inoculation training.* New York: Pergamon. (p. 722)

Meijer, E. H., & Verschuere, B. (2010). The polygraph and the detection of deception. *Journal of Forensic Psychology Practice, 10*, 525–538. (p. 428)

Meltzoff, A. N. (1988). Infant imitation after a 1-week delay: Long-term memory for novel acts and multiple stimuli. *Developmental Psychology, 24*, 470–476. (p. 306)

Meltzoff, A. N., Kuhl, P. K., Movellan, J., & Sejnowski, T. J. (2009). Foundations for a new science of learning. *Science, 325*, 284–288. (pp. 306, 374)

Meltzoff, A. N., & Moore, M. K. (1989). Imitation in newborn infants: Exploring the range of gestures imitated and the underlying mechanisms. *Developmental Psychology, 25*, 954–962. (pp. 306, 309)

Meltzoff, A. N., & Moore, M. K. (1997). Explaining facial imitation: A theoretical model. *Early Development and Parenting, 6,* 179–192. (pp. 306, 309)

Melzack, R. (1992, April). Phantom limbs. *Scientific American,* 120–126. (p. 204)

Melzack, R. (1998, February). Quoted in Phantom limbs. *Discover,* p. 20. (p. 204)

Melzack, R. (2005). Evolution of the neuromatrix theory of pain. *Pain Practice, 5,* 85–94. (p. 204)

Melzack, R., & Wall, P. D. (1965). Pain mechanisms: A new theory. *Science, 150,* 971–979. (p. 201)

Melzack, R., & Wall, P. D. (1983). *The challenge of pain.* New York: Basic Books. (p. 201)

Mendes, E. (2010a, February 9). Six in 10 overweight or obese in U.S., more in '09 than in '08. www.gallup.com. (p. 401)

Mendes, E. (2010b, June 2). U.S. exercise levels up, but demographic differences remain. www.gallup.com. (p. 861)

Mendle, J., Turkheimer, E., & Emery, R. E. (2007). Detrimental psychological outcomes associated with early pubertal timing in adolescent girls. *Developmental Review, 27,* 151–171. (p. 514)

Mendolia, M., & Kleck, R. E. (1993). Effects of talking about a stressful event on arousal: Does what we talk about make a difference? *Journal of Personality and Social Psychology, 64,* 283–292. (p. 858)

Merari, A. (2002). Explaining suicidal terrorism: Theories versus empirical evidence. Invited address to the American Psychological Association. (p. 774)

Meriac, J. P., Hoffman, B. J., Woehr, D. J., & Fleisher, M. S. (2008). Further evidence for the validity of assessment center dimensions: A meta-analysis of the incremental criterion-related validity of dimension ratings. *Journal of Applied Psychology, 93,* 1042–1052. (p. 592)

Merskey, H. (1992). The manufacture of personalities: The production of multiple personality disorder. *British Journal of Psychiatry, 160,* 327–340. (p. 696)

Merton, R. K., & Kitt, A. S. (1950). Contributions to the theory of reference group behavior. In R. K. Merton & P. F. Lazarsfeld (Eds.), *Continuities in social research: Studies in the scope and method of the American soldier.* Glencoe, IL: Free Press. (p. 851)

Mesch, G. (2001). Social relationships and Internet use among adolescents in Israel. *Social Science Quarterly, 82,* 329–340. (p. 416)

Mesoudi, A. (2009). How cultural evolutionary theory can inform social psychology and vice versa. *Psychological Review, 116,* 929–952. (p. 777)

Messinis, L., Kyprianidou, A., Malefaki, S., & Papathanasopoulos, P. (2006). Neuropsychological deficits in long-term frequent cannabis users. *Neurology, 66,* 737–739. (p. 255)

Mestel, R. (1997, April 26). Get real, Siggi. *New Scientist* (www.newscientist.com/ns/970426/siggi.html). (p. 240)

Metcalfe, J. (1986). Premonitions of insight predict impending error. *Journal of Experimental Psychology: Learning, Memory, and Cognition, 12,* 623–634. (p. 362)

Metcalfe, J. (1998). Cognitive optimism: Self-deception or memory-based processing heuristics. *Personality and Social Psychology Review, 2,* 100–110. (p. 365)

Metzler, D. K., Jensvold, M. L., Fouts, D. H., & Fouts, R. S. (2010, Spring). Vocabulary growth in adult cross-fostered chimpanzees. *Friends of Washoe, 13–16.* (p. 869)

Meyer, I. H. (2003). Prejudice, social stress, and mental health in lesbian, gay, and bisexual populations: Conceptual issues and research evidence. *Psychological Bulletin, 129,* 674–697. (p. 651)

Meyer-Bahlburg, H. F. L. (1995). Psychoneuroendocrinology and sexual pleasure: The aspect of sexual orientation. In P. R. Abramson & S. D. Pinkerton (Eds.), *Sexual nature/sexual culture.* Chicago: University of Chicago Press. (p. 535)

Mezulis, A. M., Abramson, L. Y., Hyde, J. S., & Hankin, B. L. (2004). Is there a universal positivity bias in attributions? A meta-analytic review of individual, developmental, and cultural differences in the self-serving attributional bias. *Psychological Bulletin, 130,* 711–747. (p. 596)

Michaels, J. W., Bloomel, J. M., Brocato, R. M., Linkous, R. A., & Rowe, J. S. (1982). Social facilitation and inhibition in a natural setting. *Replications in Social Psychology, 2,* 21–24. (p. 771)

Michener, J. A. (1978, February 3). External forces and inner voices. Speech at the Chapel of the Four Chaplains, Philadelphia, PA. (p. 767)

Middlebrooks, J. C., & Green, D. M. (1991). Sound localization by human listeners. *Annual Review of Psychology, 42,* 135–159. (p. 199)

Miers, R. (2009, Spring). Calum's road. *Scottish Life,* pp. 36–39, 75. (p. 834)

Mikkelsen, T. S., & 66 others (2005). Initial sequence of the chimpanzee genome and comparison with the human genome. *Nature, 437,* 69–87. (p. 125)

Mikulincer, M., Florian, V., & Hirschberger, G. (2003). The existential function of close relationships: Introducing death into the science of love. *Personality and Social Psychology Review, 7,* 20–40. (p. 568)

Mikulincer, M., & Shaver, P. R. (2001). Attachment theory and intergroup bias: Evidence that priming the secure base schema attenuates negative reactions to out-groups. *Journal of Personality and Social Psychology, 81,* 97–115. (p. 785)

Milan, R. J., Jr., & Kilmann, P. R. (1987). Interpersonal factors in premarital contraception. *Journal of Sex Research, 23,* 289–321. (p. 530)

Miles, D. R., & Carey, G. (1997). Genetic and environmental architecture of human aggression. *Journal of Personality and Social Psychology, 72,* 207–217. (p. 789)

Milgram, S. (1963). Behavioral study of obedience. *Journal of Abnormal & Social Psychology, 67*(4), 371–378. (p. 765)

Milgram, S. (1974). *Obedience to authority.* New York: Harper & Row. (pp. 765, 766, 768)

Miller, G. (2004). Axel, Buck share award for deciphering how the nose knows. *Science, 306,* 207. (p. 208)

Miller, G. (2005). The dark side of glia. *Science, 308,* 778–781. (p. 104)

Miller, G. (2008). Tackling alcoholism with drugs. *Science, 320,* 168–170. (p. 823)

Miller, G. (2010). Anything but child's play. *Science, 327,* 1192–1193. (p. 673)

Miller, G. A. (1956). The magical number seven, plus or minus two: Some limits on our capacity for processing information. *Psychological Review, 63,* 81–97. (p. 322)

Miller, G. E., & Blackwell, E. (2006). Turning up the heat: Inflammation as a mechanism linking chronic stress, depression, and heart disease. *Current Directions in Psychological Science, 15,* 269–272. (p. 453)

Miller, G. E., & Chen, E. (2010). Harsh family climate in early life presages the emergence of a proinflammatory phenotype in adolescence. *Psychological Science, 21,* 848–856. (p. 453)

Miller, H. C., Pattison, K. F., DeWall, C. N., Rayburn-Reeves, R., & Zentall, T. R. (2010). Self-control without a "self"? Common self-control processes in humans and dogs. *Psychological Science, 21,* 534–538. (p. 302)

Miller, J., Shepherdson, P., & Trevena, J. (2011). Effects of clock monitoring on electroencephalographic activity: Is unconscious movement initiation an artifact of the clock? *Psychological Science, 22,* 103–109. (p. 121)

Miller, J. G., & Bersoff, D. M. (1995). Development in the context of everyday family relationships: Culture, interpersonal morality and adaptation. In M. Killen and D. Hart (Eds.), *Morality in everyday life: A developmental perspective.* New York: Cambridge University Press. (p. 516)

Miller, K. I., & Monge, P. R. (1986). Participation, satisfaction, and productivity: A meta-analytic review. *Academy of Management Journal, 29,* 727–753. (p. 301)

Miller, L. K. (1999). The savant syndrome: Intellectual impairment and exceptional skill. *Psychological Bulletin, 125,* 31–46. (p. 609)

Miller, N. E. (1985, February). Rx: biofeedback. *Psychology Today,* 54–59. (pp. 289, 861)

Miller, N. E., & Brucker, B. S. (1979). A learned visceral response apparently independent of skeletal ones in patients paralyzed by spinal lesions. In N. Birbaumer & H. D. Kimmel (Eds.), *Biofeedback and self-regulation.* Hillsdale, NJ: Erlbaum. (p. 289)

Miller, P. A., Eisenberg, N., Fabes, R. A., & Shell, R. (1996). Relations of moral reasoning and vicarious emotion to young children's prosocial behavior toward peers and adults. *Developmental Psychology, 32,* 210–219. (p. 517)

Miller, P. J. O., Aoki, K., Rendell, L. E., & Amano, M. (2008). Stereotypical resting behavior of the sperm whale. *Current Biology, 18,* R21–R23. (p. 226)

Miller, S. D., Blackburn, T., Scholes, G., White, G. L., & Mamalis, N. (1991). Optical differences in multiple personality disorder: A second look. *Journal of Nervous and Mental Disease, 179,* 132–135. (p. 696)

Miller, T. W., Nigg, J. T., & Miller, R. L. (2009). Attention deficit hyperactivity disorder in African American children: What can be concluded from the past ten years. *Clinical Psychology Review, 29,* 77–86. (p. 652)

Milner, A. D., & Goodale, M. A. (2008). Two visual systems re-viewed. *Neuropsychologia, 46,* 774–785. (p. 120)

Milyavskaya, M., Gingras, I., Mageau, G. A., Koestner, R., Gagnon, H., Fang, J., & Bolché, J. (2009). Balance across contexts: Importance of balanced need satisfaction across various life domains. *Personality and Social Psychology Bulletin, 35,* 1031–1045. (p. 413)

Mineka, S. (1985). The frightful complexity of the origins of fears. In F. R. Brush & J. B. Overmier (Eds.), *Affect, conditioning and cognition: Essays on the determinants of behavior.* Hillsdale, NJ: Erlbaum. (p. 666)

Mineka, S. (2002). Animal models of clinical psychology. In N. Smelser & P. Baltes (Eds.), *International encyclopedia of the social and behavioral sciences.* Oxford, England: Elsevier Science. (p. 666)

Mineka, S., & Oehlberg, K. (2008). The relevance of recent developments in classical conditioning to understanding the etiology and maintenance of anxiety disorders. *Acta Psychologica, 127,* 567–580. (p. 666)

Mineka, S., & Zinbarg, R. (1996). Conditioning and ethological models of anxiety disorders: Stress-in-dynamic-context anxiety models. In D. Hope (Ed.), *Perspectives on anxiety, panic, and fear* (Nebraska Symposium on Motivation). Lincoln: University of Nebraska Press. (pp. 665, 667, 737)

Mingroni, M. A. (2004). The secular rise in IQ: Giving heterosis a closer look. *Intelligence, 32,* 65–83. (p. 622)

Mingroni, M. A. (2007). Resolving the IQ paradox: Heterosis as a cause of the Flynn effect and other trends. *Psychological Review, 114,* 806–829. (p. 622)

Minsky, M. (1986). *The society of mind.* New York: Simon & Schuster. (p. 119)

Mirescu, C., & Gould, E. (2006). Stress and adult neurogenesis. *Hippocampus, 16,* 233–238. (p. 445)

Mischel, W. (1968). *Personality and assessment.* New York: Wiley. (p. 583)

Mischel, W. (1981). Current issues and challenges in personality. In L. T. Benjamin, Jr. (Ed.), *The G. Stanley Hall Lecture Series* (Vol. 1). Washington, DC: American Psychological Association. (p. 592)

Mischel, W. (2009). From *Personality and Assessment* (1968) to personality science. *Journal of Research in Personality, 43,* 282–290. (p. 583)

Mischel, W., Shoda, Y., & Peake, P. K. (1988). The nature of adolescent competencies predicted by preschool delay of gratification. *Journal of Personality and Social Psychology, 54,* 687–696. (p. 517)

Mischel, W., Shoda, Y., & Rodriguez, M. L. (1989). Delay of gratification in children. *Science, 244,* 933–938. (pp. 279, 517)

Miserandino, M. (1991). Memory and the seven dwarfs. *Teaching of Psychology, 18,* 169–171. (p. 335)

Mishkin, M. (1982). A memory system in the monkey. *Philosophical Transactions of the Royal Society of London: Biological Sciences, 298,* 83–95. (p. 331)

Mishkin, M., Suzuki, W. A., Gadian, D. G., & Vargha-Khadem, F. (1997). Hierarchical organization of cognitive memory. *Philosophical Transactions of the Royal Society of London: Biological Sciences, 352,* 1461–1467. (p. 331)

Mishra, A., & Mishra, H. (2010). Border bias: The belief that state borders can protect against disasters. *Psychological Science, 21,* 1582–1586. (p. 380)

Mishra, P. (2013, January 27). Mobile phones disrupt India, for better and worse. www.bloomberg.com. (p. 415)

Mita, T. H., Dermer, M., & Knight, J. (1977). Reversed facial images and the mere-exposure hypothesis. *Journal of Personality and Social Psychology, 35,* 597–601. (p. 799)

Mitani, J. C., Watts, D. P., & Amsler, S. J. (2010). Lethal intergroup aggression leads to territorial expansion in wild chimpanzees. *Current Biology, 20,* R507–R509. (p. 868)

Mitchell, D. B. (2006). Nonconscious priming after 17 years: Invulnerable implicit memory? *Psychological Science, 17,* 925–929. (p. 318)

Mitchell, J. P. (2009). Social psychology as a natural kind. *Cell, 13,* 246–251. (p. 594)

Mitchell, K. J., & Porteous, D. J. (2011). Rethinking the genetic architecture of schizophrenia. *Psychological Medicine, 41,* 19–32. (p. 689)

Mitte, K. (2005). Meta-analysis of cognitive-behavioral treatments for generalized anxiety disorder: A comparison with pharmacotherapy. *Psychological Bulletin, 131,* 785–795. (p. 723)

Mitte, K. (2008). Memory bias for threatening information in anxiety and anxiety disorders: A meta-analytic review. *Psychological Bulletin, 134,* 886–911. (p. 661)

Miyagawa, T., & 19 others. (2008). Variant between *CPT1B* and *CHKB* associated with susceptibility to narcolepsy. *Nature Genetics, 40,* 1324–1328. (p. 238)

Mobbs, D., Yu, R., Meyer, M., Passamonti, L., Seymour, B., Calder, A. J., Schweizer, S., Frith, C. D., & Dalgeish, T. (2009). A key role for similarity in vicarious reward. *Science, 324,* 900. (p. 305)

Moffitt, T. E. (2005). The new look of behavioral genetics in developmental psychopathology: Gene-environment interplay in antisocial behaviors. *Psychological Bulletin, 131,* 533–554.(p. 701)

Moffitt, T. E., & 12 others. (2011). A gradient of childhood self-control predicts health, wealth, and public safety. *Proceedings of the National Academy of Sciences, 108,* 2693–2698. (p. 464)

Moffitt, T. E., Caspi, A., Harrington, H., & Milne, B. J. (2002). Males on the life-course-persistent and adolescence-limited antisocial pathways: Follow-up at age 26 years. *Development and Psychopathology, 14,* 179–207. (p. 464)

Moffitt, T. E., Caspi, A., Harrington, H., Milne, B. J., Melchior, M., Goldberg, D., & Poulton, R. (2007a). Generalized anxiety disorder and depression: Childhood risk factors in a birth cohort followed to age 32. *Psychological Medicine, 37,* 441–452. (p. 662)

Moffitt, T. E., Caspi, A., & Rutter, M. (2006). Measured gene-environment interactions in psychopathology: Concepts, research strategies, and implications for research, intervention, and public understanding of genetics. *Perspectives on Psychological Science, 1,* 5–27. (p. 678)

Moffitt, T. E., Harrington, H., Caspi, A., Kim-Cohen, J., Goldberg, D., Gregory, A. M., & Poulton, R. (2007b). Depression and generalized anxiety disorder: Cumulative and sequential comorbidity in a birth cohort followed prospectively to age 32 years. *Archives of General Psychiatry, 64,* 651–660. (p. 662)

Moghaddam, F. M. (2005). The staircase to terrorism: A psychological exploration. *American Psychologist, 60,* 161–169. (p. 774)

Mohr, H., Pritchard, J., & Lush, T. (2010, May 29). BP has been good at downplaying disaster. *Associated Press.* (p. 365)

Moises, H. W., Zoega, T., & Gottesman, I. I. (2002, July 3). The glial growth factors deficiency and synaptic destabilization hypothesis of schizophrenia. *BMC Psychiatry, 2*(8). (www.biomedcentral.com/1471–244X/2/8). (p. 688)

Möller, I., & Krahé, B. A. (2008). Exposure to violent video games and aggression in German adolescents: A longitudinal analysis. *Aggressive Behavior, 34,* 1–14. (p. 795)

Mondloch, C. J., Lewis, T. L., Budreau, D. R., Maurer, D., Dannemiller, J. L., Stephens, B. R., & Kleiner-Gathercoal, K. A. (1999). Face perception during early infancy. *Psychological Science, 10,* 419–422. (p. 468)

Money, J. (1987). Sin, sickness, or status? Homosexual gender identity and psychoneuroendocrinology. *American Psychologist, 42,* 384–399. (p. 535)

Money, J. (1988). *Gay, straight, and in-between.* New York: Oxford University Press. (p. 793)

Money, J., Berlin, F. S., Falck, A., & Stein, M. (1983). *Antiandrogenic and counseling treatment of sex offenders.* Baltimore: Department of Psychiatry and Behavioral Sciences, The Johns Hopkins University School of Medicine. (p. 408)

Monroe, S. M., & Reid, M. W. (2009). Life stress and major depression. *Currents Directions in Psychological Science, 18,* 68–72. (p. 675)

Monti, M. M., Vanhaudenhuyse, A., Coleman, M. R., Boly, M., Pickard, J. D., Tshibanda, L., Owen, A. M., & Laureys, S. (2010). Willful modulation of brain activity in disorders of consciousness. *New England Journal of Medicine, 362,* 579–589. (p. 119)

Mooallem, J. (2009, February 19). Rescue flight. *New York Times Magazine* (www.nytimes.com). (p. 490)

Mook, D. G. (1983). In defense of external invalidity. *American Psychologist, 38,* 379–387. (p. 65)

Moorcroft, W. H. (2003). *Understanding sleep and dreaming.* New York: Kluwer/Plenum. (pp. 226, 242)

Moore, D. W. (2004, December 17). Sweet dreams go with a good night's sleep. *Gallup News Service* (www.gallup.com). (p. 229)

Moore, D. W. (2005, June 16). Three in four Americans believe in paranormal. *Gallup New Service* (www.gallup.com). (p. 167)

Moore, D. W. (2006, February 6). Britons outdrink Canadians, Americans. *Gallup News Service* (poll.gallup.com). (p. 824)

Moos, R. H., & Moos, B. S. (2005). Sixteen-year changes and stable remission among treated and untreated individuals with alcohol use disorders. *Drug and Alcohol Dependence, 80,* 337–347. (p. 724)

Moos, R. H., & Moos, B. S. (2006). Participation in treatment and Alcoholics Anonymous: A 16-year follow-up of initially untreated individuals. *Journal of Clinical Psychology, 62,* 735–750. (p. 724)

Mor, N., & Winquist, J. (2002). Self-focused attention and negative affect: A meta-analysis. *Psychological Bulletin, 128,* 638–662. (p. 680)

Morales, L. (2011, May 27). U.S. adults estimate that 25% of Americans are gay or lesbian. www.gallup.com. (p. 532)

More, H. L., Hutchinson, J. R., Collins, D. F., Weber, D. J., Aung, S. K. H., & Donelan, J. M. (2010). Scaling of sensorimotor control in terrestrial mammals. *Proceedings of the Royal Society B, 277,* 3563–3568. (p. 79)

Moreira, M. T., Smith, L. A., & Foxcroft, D. (2009). Social norms interventions to reduce alcohol misuse in university or college students. *Cochrane Database of Systematic Reviews.* 2009, Issue 3., Art. No.: CD006748. (p. 824)

Moreland, R. L., & Beach, S. R. (1992). Exposure effects in the classroom: The development of affinity among students. *Journal of Experimental Social Psychology, 28,* 255–276. (p. 799)

Moreland, R. L., & Zajonc, R. B. (1982). Exposure effects in person perception: Familiarity, similarity, and attraction. *Journal of Experimental Social Psychology, 18,* 395–415. (p. 798)

Morell, V. (1995). Zeroing in on how hormones affect the immune system. *Science, 269,* 773–775. (p. 448)

Morell, V. (2008, March). Minds of their own: Animals are smarter than you think. *National Geographic,* 37–61. (p. 868)

Morelli, G. A., Rogoff, B., Oppenheim, D., & Goldsmith, D. (1992). Cultural variation in infants' sleeping arrangements: Questions of independence. *Developmental Psychology, 26,* 604–613. (p. 497)

Moreno, C., Laje, G., Blanco, C., Jiang, H., Schmidt, A. B., & Olfson, M. (2007). National trends in the outpatient diagnosis and treatment of bipolar disorder in youth. *Archives of General Psychiatry, 64,* 1032–1039. (p. 673)

Morewedge, C. K., & Norton, M. I. (2009). When dreaming is believing. The (motivated) interpretation of dreams. *Journal of Personality and Social Psychology, 96,* 249–264. (p. 168)

Morey, R. A., Inan, S., Mitchell, T. V., Perkins, D. O., Lieberman, J. A., & Belger, A. (2005). Imaging frontostriatal function in ultra-high-risk, early, and chronic schizophrenia during executive processing. *Archives of General Psychiatry, 62,* 254–262. (p. 687)

Morgan, A. B., & Lilienfeld, S. O. (2000). A meta-analytic review of the relation between antisocial behavior and neuropsychological measures of executive function. *Clinical Psychology Review, 20,* 113–136. (p. 700)

Mori, K., & Mori, H. (2009). Another test of the passive facial feedback hypothesis: When your face smiles, you feel happy. *Perceptual and Motor Skills, 109,* 1–3. (p. 438)

Morin, R., & Brossard, M. A. (1997, March 4). Communication breakdown on drugs. *Washington Post,* A1, A6. (p. 522)

Morris, G., Baker-Ward, L., & Bauer, P. J. (2010). What remains of that day: The survival of children's autobiographical memories across time. *Applied Cognitive Psychology, 24,* 527–544. (p. 473)

Morrison, A. R. (2003). The brain on night shift. *Cerebrum, 5*(3), 23–36. (p. 229)

Morrison, C. (2007). *What does contagious yawning tell us about the mind?* Unpublished manuscript, University of Leeds. (p. 763)

Mortensen, E. L., Michaelsen, K. F., Sanders, S. A., & Reinisch, J. M. (2002). The association between duration of breastfeeding and adult intelligence. *Journal of the American Medical Association, 287,* 2365–2371. (p. 50)

Mortensen, P. B. (1999). Effects of family history and place and season of birth on the risk of schizophrenia. *New England Journal of Medicine, 340,* 603–608. (p. 687)

Moscovici, S. (1985). Social influence and conformity. In G. Lindzey & E. Aronson (Eds.), *The handbook of social psychology* (3rd ed). Hillsdale, N.J.: Erlbaum. (p. 776)

Moses, E. B., & Barlow, D. H. (2006). A new unified treatment approach for emotional disorders based on emotion science. *Current Directions in Psychological Science, 15,* 146–150. (p. 723)

Mosher, W. D., Chandra, A., & Jones, J. (2005, September 15). Sexual behavior and selected health measures: Men and women 15–44 years of age, United States, 2002. *Advance Data from Vital and Health Statistics,* No. 362, National Center for Health Statistics, Centers for Disease Control and Prevention, U.S. Department of Health and Human Services. (p. 532)

Moss, A. C., & Albery, I. P. (2009). A dual-process model of the alcohol-behavior link for social drinking. *Psychological Bulletin, 135,* 516–530. (p. 250)

Moss, H. A., & Susman, E. J. (1980). Longitudinal study of personality development. In O. G. Brim, Jr., & J. Kagan (Eds.), *Constancy and change in human development.* Cambridge, MA: Harvard University Press. (p. 464)

Motivala, S. J., & Irwin, M. R. (2007). Sleep and immunity: Cytokine pathways linking sleep and health outcomes. *Current Directions in Psychological Science, 16,* 21–25. (p. 236)

Moyer, K. E. (1983). The physiology of motivation: Aggression as a model. In C. J. Scheier & A. M. Rogers (Eds.), *G. Stanley Hall Lecture Series* (Vol. 3). Washington, DC: American Psychological Association. (p. 790)

Mroczek, D. K., & Kolarz, D. M. (1998). The effect of age on positive and negative affect: A developmental perspective on happiness. *Journal of Personality and Social Psychology, 75,* 1333–1349. (p. 544)

Muhlnickel, W. (1998). Reorganization of auditory cortex in tinnitus. *Proceedings of the National Academy of Sciences, 95,* 10340–10343. (p. 108)

Mukamel, R., Ekstrom, A. D., Kaplan, J., Iacoboni, M., & Fried, I. (2010). Single-neuron responses in humans during execution and observation of actions. *Current Biology, 20,* 750–756. (p. 307)

Mulcahy, N. J., & Call, J. (2006). Apes save tools for future use. *Science, 312,* 1038–1040. (p. 362)

Muller, J. E., & Verier, R. L. (1996). Triggering of sudden death—Lessons from an earthquake. *New England Journal of Medicine, 334,* 461. (p. 443)

Mullin, C. R., & Linz, D. (1995). Desensitization and resensitization to violence against women: Effects of exposure to sexually violent films on judgments of domestic violence victims. *Journal of Personality and Social Psychology, 69,* 449–459. (p. 309)

Mulrow, C. D. (1999, March). Treatment of depression—newer pharmacotherapies, summary. *Evidence Report/Technology Assessment, 7.* Agency for Health Care Policy and Research, Rockville, MD. (http://www.ahrq.gov/clinic/deprsumm.htm). (p. 742)

Munafò, M. R., Durrant, C., Lewis, G., & Flint, J. (2009). Gene X environment interactions at the serotonin transporter locus. *Biological Psychiatry, 65,* 211–219. (p. 678)

Munsey, C. (2010, June). Medicine or menace? Psychologists' research can inform the growing debate over legalizing marijuana. *Monitor on Psychology,* pp. 50–55. (p. 256)

Murphy, G. E., & Wetzel, R. D. (1990). The lifetime risk of suicide in alcoholism. *Archives of General Psychiatry, 47,* 383–392. (p. 676)

Murphy, K. (2008, October 28). 21-year study of children set to begin. *New York Times* (www.nytimes.com). (p. 481)

Murphy, K. R., & Cleveland, J. N. (1995). *Understanding performance appraisal: Social, organizational, and goal-based perspectives.* Thousand Oaks, CA: Sage. (p. 833)

Murphy, S. T., Monahan, J. L., & Zajonc, R. B. (1995). Additivity of nonconscious affect: Combined effects of priming and exposure. *Journal of Personality and Social Psychology, 69,* 589–602. (p. 423)

Murray, B. (1998, May). Psychology is key to airline safety at Boeing. *The APA Monitor,* 36. (p. 841)

Murray, C. J., & Lopez, A. D. (Eds.). (1996). *The global burden of disease: A comprehensive assessment of mortality and disability from diseases, injuries, and risk factors in 1990 and projected to 2020.* Cambridge, MA: Harvard University Press. (p. 650)

Murray, H. (1938). *Explorations in personality.* New York: Oxford University Press. (p. 834)

Murray, H. A., & Wheeler, D. R. (1937). A note on the possible clairvoyance of dreams. *Journal of Psychology, 3,* 309–313. (pp. 40, 168)

Murray, J. P. (2008). Media violence: The effects are both real and strong. *American Behavioral Scientist, 51,* 1212–1230. (p. 309)

Murray, R., Jones, P., O'Callaghan, E., Takei, N., & Sham, P. (1992). Genes, viruses, and neurodevelopmental schizophrenia. *Journal of Psychiatric Research, 26,* 225–235. (p. 687)

Murray, R. M., Morrison, P. D., Henquet, C., & Di Forti, M. (2007). Cannabis, the mind and society: The hash realities. *Nature Reviews: Neuroscience, 8,* 885–895. (p. 255)

Murray, S. L., Bellavia, G. M., Rose, P., & Griffin, D. W. (2003). Once hurt, twice hurtful: How perceived regard regulates daily marital interactions. *Journal of Personality and Social Psychology, 84,* 126–147. (p. 166)

Musick, M. A., Herzog, A. R., & House, J. S. (1999). Volunteering and mortality among older adults: Findings from a national sample. *Journals of Gerontology, 54B,* 173–180. (p. 865)

Mydans, S. (2002, May 17). In Pakistan, rape victims are the 'criminals.' *New York Times* (www.nytimes.com). (p. 787)

Myers, D. G. (1993). *The pursuit of happiness.* New York: Harper. (pp. 852, 853)

Myers, D. G. (2000). *The American paradox: Spiritual hunger in an age of plenty.* New Haven, CT: Yale University Press. (p. 852)

Myers, D. G. (2001, December). Do we fear the right things? *American Psychological Society Observer,* p. 3. (p. 366)

Myers, D. G. (2002). *Intuition: Its powers and perils.* New Haven, CT: Yale University Press. (pp. 4, 33)

Myers, D. G. (2008). *Social psychology* (9th ed.). New York: McGraw-Hill. (p. 596)

Myers, D. G., & Bishop, G. D. (1970). Discussion effects on racial attitudes. *Science, 169,* 78–79, (p. 774)

Myers, D. G., & Diener, E. (1995). Who is happy? *Psychological Science, 6,* 10–19. (p. 852)

Myers, D. G., & Diener, E. (1996, May). The pursuit of happiness. *Scientific American.* (p. 852)

Myers, D. G., & Scanzoni, L. D. (2005). *What God has joined together?* San Francisco: HarperSanFrancisco. (pp. 532, 545)

Myers, I. B. (1987). *Introduction to type: A description of the theory and applications of the Myers-Briggs Type Indicator.* Palo Alto, CA: Consulting Psychologists Press. (p. 576)

Myers, T. A., & Crowther, J. H. (2009). Social comparison as a predictor of body dissatisfaction: A meta-analytic review. *Journal of Abnormal Psychology, 118,* 683–698. (p. 698)

Myerson, J., Rank, M. R., Raines, F. Q., & Schnitzler, M. A. (1998). Race and general cognitive ability: The myth of diminishing returns to education. *Psychological Science, 9,* 139–142. (p. 641)

Nagourney, A. (2002, September 25). For remarks on Iraq, Gore gets praise and scorn. *New York Times* (www.nytimes.com). (p. 757)

Nairn, R. G. (2007). Media portrayals of mental illness, or is it madness? A review. *Australian Psychologist, 42,* 138–146. (p. 656)

Napolitan, D. A., & Goethals, G. R. (1979). The attribution of friendliness. *Journal of Experimental Social Psychology, 15,* 105–113. (p. 754)

Narvaez, D. (2010). Moral complexity: The fatal attraction of truthiness and the importance of mature moral functioning. *Perspectives on Psychological Science, 5,* 163–181. (p. 517)

NAS (National Autistic Society). (2011, accessed May 11). *Statistics: How many people have autistic spectrum disorders.* www.autism.org.uk. (p. 481)

Nash, M. R. (2001, July). The truth and the hype of hypnosis. *Scientific American,* 47–55. (p. 220)

National Academy of Sciences. (2001). *Exploring the biological contributions to human health: Does sex matter?* Washington, DC: Institute of Medicine, National Academy Press. (p. 528)

National Center for Complementary and Alternative Medicine. (2006). *What is complementary and alternative medicine.* www.nccam.nih.gov/health/whatiscam. (p. 864)

National Center for Health Statistics. (1990). *Health, United States, 1989.* Washington, DC: U.S. Department of Health and Human Services. (p. 541)

National Center for Health Statistics. (2004, December 15). Marital status and health: United States, 1999–2002 (by Charlotte A. Schoenborn). *Advance Data from Vital and Human Statistics, number 351.* Centers for Disease Control and Prevention. (p. 857)

National Institute of Mental Health. (2008). *The numbers count: Mental disorders in America.* (nimh.nih.gov). (p. 657)

National Research Council. (1990). *Human factors research needs for an aging population.* Washington, DC: National Academy Press. (p. 541)

National Safety Council. (2010a, January 12). NSC estimates 1.6 million crashes caused by cell phone use and texting. www.nsc.org. (p. 153)

National Safety Council. (2010b). Transportation mode comparison in *Injury facts 2010 edition.* www.nsc.org. (p. 366)

National Sleep Foundation. (2006). The ABC's of back-to-school sleep schedules: The consequences of insufficient sleep. National Sleep Foundation (press release) (www.sleepfoundation.org). (p. 235)

National Sleep Foundation. (2009) 2009 sleep in America poll: Summary of findings. Washington, DC: National Sleep Foundation (www.sleepfoundation.org). (p. 239)

National Sleep Foundation. (2010, March 8). 2010 sleep in America poll. www.sleepfoundation.org. (p. 229)

Naumann, L. P., Vazire, S., Rentfrow, P. J., & Gosling, S. D. (2009). Personality judgments based on physical appearance. *Personality and Social Psychology Bulletin, 35,* 1661–1671. (p. 584)

Navarrete, C. D., Fessler, D. M. T., Fleischman, D. S., & Geyer, J. (2009). Race bias tracks conception risk across the menstrual cycle. *Psychological Science, 20,* 661–665. (p. 408)

Nave, C. S., Sherman, R. A., Funder, D.C., Hampson, S. E., & Goldberg, L. R. (2010). On the contextual independence of personality: Teachers' assessments predict directly observed behavior after four decades. *Social Psychological and Personality Science, 3,* 1–9. (p. 464)

Naylor, T. H. (1990). Redefining corporate motivation, Swedish style. *Christian Century, 107,* 566–570. (p. 839)

Nazimek, J. (2009). Active body, healthy mind. *The Psychologist, 22,* 206–208. (p. 542)

NCASA. (2007). *Wasting the best and the brightest: Substance abuse at America's colleges and universities.* New York: National Center on Addiction and Drug Abuse, Columbia University. (p. 825)

NCTV News. (1987, July-August). More research links harmful effects to nonviolent porn, 12. (p. 793)

Nedeltcheva, A. V., Kilkus, J. M., Imperial, J., Schoeller, D. A., & Penev, P. D. (2010). Insufficient sleep undermines dietary efforts to reduce adiposity. *Annals of Internal Medicine, 153,* 435–441. (p. 402)

NEEF. (2011; undated, accessed 17 June 2011). *Fact sheet: Children's health and nature.* National Environmental Education Foundation (www.neefusa.org). (p. 747)

Neese, R. M. (1991, November/December). What good is feeling bad? The evolutionary benefits of psychic pain. *The Sciences,* 30–37. (pp. 203, 294)

Neimeyer, R. A., & Currier, J. M. (2009). Grief therapy: Evidence of efficacy and emerging directions. *Current Directions in Psychological Science, 18,* 352–356. (p. 548)

Neisser, U. (1979). The control of information pickup in selective looking. In A. D. Pick (Ed.), *Perception and its development: A tribute to Eleanor J. Gibson.* Hillsdale, NJ: Erlbaum. (p. 154)

Neisser, U., Boodoo, G., Bouchard, T. J., Jr., Boykin, A. W., Brody, N., Ceci, S. J., Halpern, D. F., Loehlin, J. C., Perloff, R., Sternberg, R. J., & Urbina, S. (1996). Intelligence: Knowns and unknowns. *American Psychologist, 51,* 77–101. (pp. 632, 642)

Neisser, U., Winograd, E., & Weldon, M. S. (1991). Remembering the earthquake: "What I experienced" vs. "How I heard the news." Paper presented to the Psychonomic Society convention. (p. 332)

Neitz, J., Carroll, J., & Neitz, M. (2001). Color vision: Almost reason enough for having eyes. *Optics & Photonics News 12,* 26–33. (p. 178)

Neitz, J., Geist, T., & Jacobs, G. H. (1989). Color vision in the dog. *Visual Neuroscience, 3,* 119–125. (p. 178)

Nelson, C. A., III, Furtado, E. Z., Fox, N. A., & Zeanah, C. H., Jr. (2009). The deprived human brain. *American Scientist, 97,* 222–229. (pp. 493, 634)

Nelson, M. D., Saykin, A. J., Flashman, L. A., & Riordan, H. J. (1998). Hippocampal volume reduction in schizophrenia as assessed by magnetic resonance imaging. *Archives of General Psychiatry, 55,* 433–440. (p. 687)

Nemeth, C. J., & Ormiston, M. (2007). Creative idea generation: Harmony versus stimulation. *European Journal of Social Psychology, 37,* 524–535. (p. 775)

Nes, R. B. (2010). Happiness in behaviour genetics: Findings and implications. *Journal of Happiness Studies, 11,* 369–381. (p. 853)

Nes, R. B., Czajkowski, N., & Tambs, K. (2010). Family matters: Happiness in nuclear families and twins. *Behavior Genetics, 40,* 577–590. (p. 852)

Nesca, M., & Koulack, D. (1994). Recognition memory, sleep and circadian rhythms. *Canadian Journal of Experimental Psychology, 48,* 359–379. (p. 345)

Nestoriuc, Y., Rief, W., & Martin, A. (2008). Meta-analysis of biofeedback for tension-type headache: Efficacy, specificity, and treatment moderators. *Journal of Consulting and Clinical Psychology, 76,* 379–396. (p. 861)

Neubauer, D. N. (1999). Sleep problems in the elderly. *American Family Physician, 59,* 2551–2558. (p. 228)

Neumann, R., & Strack, F. (2000). "Mood contagion": The automatic transfer of mood between persons. *Journal of Personality and Social Psychology, 79,* 211–223. (pp. 438, 762)

Newberg, A., & D'Aquili, E. (2001). *Why God won't go away: Brain science and the biology of belief.* New York: Simon & Schuster. (p. 862)

Newcomb, M. D., & Harlow, L. L. (1986). Life events and substance use among adolescents: Mediating effects of perceived loss of control and meaninglessness in life. *Journal of Personality and Social Psychology, 51*, 564–577. (p. 823)

Newell, B. R., Wong, K. Y., Cheung, J. C. H., & Rakow, T. (2008, August 23). Think, blink, or sleep on it? The impact of modes of thought on complex decision making. *Quarterly Journal of Experimental Psychology, 62*, 707–732. (p. 369)

Newman, L. S., & Baumeister, R. F. (1996). Toward an explanation of the UFO abduction phenomenon: Hypnotic, elaboration, extraterrestrial sadomasochism, and spurious memories. *Psychological Inquiry, 7*, 99–126. (p. 220)

Newman, L. S., & Ruble, D. N. (1988). Stability and change in self-understanding: The early elementary school years. *Early Child Development and Care, 40*, 77–99. (p. 496)

Newman, M. L., Pennebaker, J. W., Berry, D. S., & Richards, J. M. (2003). Lying words: Predicting deception from linguistic style. *Personality and Social Psychology Bulletin, 29*, 665–675. (p. 428)

Newman, R., Ratner, N. B., Jusczyk, A. M., Jusczyk, P. W., & Dow, K. A. (2006). Infants' early ability to segment the conversational speech signal predicts later language development: A retrospective analysis. *Developmental Psychology, 42*, 643–655. (p. 374)

Newport, E. L. (1990). Maturational constraints on language learning. *Cognitive Science, 14*, 11–28. (p. 377)

Newport, F. (2001, February). Americans see women as emotional and affectionate, men as more aggressive. *The Gallup Poll Monthly*, 34–38. (p. 434)

Newport, F. (2002, July 29). Bush job approval update. *Gallup News Service* (www.gallup.com/poll/releases/pr020729.asp). (p. 813)

Newport, F. (2007, June 11). Majority of Republicans doubt theory of evolution. *Gallup Poll* (www.galluppoll.com). (p. 141)

Newport, F., Argrawal, S., & Witters, D. (2010, December 23). Very religious Americans lead healthier lives. *Gallup* (www.gallup.com). (p. 865)

Newport, F., Jones, J. M., Saad, L., & Carroll, J. (2007, April 27). Gallup poll review: 10 key points about public opinion on Iraq. *The Gallup Poll* (www.gallup-poll.com). (p. 501)

Newport, F., Moore, D. W., Jones, J. M., & Saad, L. (2003, March 21). Special release: American opinion on the war. *Gallup Poll Tuesday Briefing* (www.gallup.com). (p. 759)

Newport, F., & Pelham, B. (2009, December 14). Don't worry, be 80: Worry and stress decline with age. *Gallup* (www.gallup.com). (p. 443)

Newton, E. L. (1991). The rocky road from actions to intentions. *Dissertation Abstracts International, 51*(8–B), 4105. (p. 842)

Nezlek, J. B. (2001). Daily psychological adjustment and the planfulness of day-to-day behavior. *Journal of Social and Clinical Psychology, 20*, 452–475. (p. 301)

Ng, S. H. (1990). Androcentric coding of *man* and *his* in memory by language users. *Journal of Experimental Social Psychology, 26*, 455–464. (p. 380)

Ng, T. W. H., & Feldman, D. C. (2009). How broadly does education contribute to job performance? *Personnel Psychology, 62*, 89–134. (p. 831)

Ng, T. W. H., Sorensen, K. L., & Eby, L. T. (2006). Locus of control at work: A meta-analysis. *Journal of Organizational Behavior, 27*, 1057–1087. (p. 301)

Ng, T. W. H., Sorensen, K. L., & Yim, F. H. K. (2009a). Does the job satisfaction—job performance relationship vary across cultures? *Journal of Cross-Cultural Psychology, 40*, 761–796. (p. 835)

Ng, W., Diener, E., Aurora, R., & Harter, J. (2009b). Affluence, feelings of stress, and well-being. *Social Indicators Research, 94*, 257–271. (p. 442)

Nguyen, H-H. D., & Ryan, A. M. (2008). Does stereotype threat affect test performance of minorities and women? A meta-analysis of experimental evidence. *Journal of Applied Psychology, 93*, 1314–1334. (p. 642)

NHTSA. (2000). *Traffic safety facts 1999: Older population.* Washington, DC: National Highway Traffic Safety Administration (National Transportation Library, www.ntl.bts.gov). (p. 541)

NICHD. (2006). Child-care effect sizes for the NICHD study of early child care and youth development. *American Psychologist, 61*, 99–116. (p. 495)

NICHD Early Child Care Research Network. (2002). Structure/process/outcome: Direct and indirect effects of caregiving quality on young children's development. *Psychological Science, 13*, 199–206. (p. 495)

NICHD Early Child Care Research Network. (2003). Does amount of time spent in child care predict socioemotional adjustment during the transition to kindergarten? *Child Development, 74*, 976–1005. (p. 495)

Nickell, J. (Ed.). (1994). *Psychic sleuths: ESP and sensational cases.* Buffalo, NY: Prometheus Books. (p. 167)

Nickell, J. (1996, May/June). A study of fantasy proneness in the thirteen cases of alleged encounters in John Mack's abduction. *Skeptical Inquirer*, 18–20, 54. (p. 220)

Nickell, J. (2005, July/August). The case of the psychic detectives. *Skeptical Inquirer* (skeptically.org/skepticism/id10.html). (p. 167)

Nickerson, R. S. (1998). Applied experimental psychology. *Applied Psychology: An International Review, 47*, 155–173. (p. 841)

Nickerson, R. S. (1999). How we know—and sometimes misjudge—what others know: Imputing one's own knowledge to others. *Psychological Bulletin, 125*, 737–759. (p. 841)

Nickerson, R. S. (2002). The production and perception of randomness. *Psychological Review, 109*, 330–357. (p. 33)

Nickerson, R. S. (2005). Bertrand's chord, Buffon's needles, and the concept of randomness. *Thinking & Reasoning, 11*, 67–96. (p. 33)

Nicol, S. E., & Gottesman, I. I. (1983). Clues to the genetics and neurobiology of schizophrenia. *American Scientist, 71*, 398–404. (p. 689)

Nicolaus, L. K., Cassel, J. F., Carlson, R. B., & Gustavson, C. R. (1983). Taste-aversion conditioning of crows to control predation on eggs. *Science, 220*, 212–214. (p. 293)

Nicolelis, M. A. L., & Chapin, J. K. (2002, October). Controlling robots with the mind. *Scientific American*, 46–53. (p. 106)

NIDA. (2002). *Methamphetamine abuse and addiction. Research Report Series.* National Institute on Drug Abuse, NIH Publication No. 02–4210. (p. 253)

NIDA. (2005, May). *Methamphetamine. NIDA Info Facts.* National Institute on Drug Abuse. (p. 253)

NIDCD. (2011). Quick statistics. National Institute on Deafness and Other Communication Disorders (www.nidcd.nih.gov). (p. 198)

Nie, N. H. (2001). Sociability, interpersonal relations and the Internet: Reconciling conflicting findings. *American Behavioral Scientist, 45*, 420–435. (p. 416)

Nielsen, K. M., Faergeman, O., Larsen, M. L., & Foldspang, A. (2006). Danish singles have a twofold risk of acute coronary syndrome: Data from a cohort of 138,290 persons. *Journal of Epidemiology and Community Health, 60*, 721–728. (p. 857)

Nielsen, M., & Tomaseli, K. (2010). Overimitation in Kalahari Bushman children and the origins of human cultural cognition. *Psychological Science, 21*, 729–736. (p. 306)

Niemiec, C. P., Ryan, R. M., & Deci, E. L. (2009). The path taken: Consequences of attaining intrinsic and extrinsic aspirations in post-college life. *Journal of Research in Personality, 43*, 291–306. (p. 850)

Nier, J. A. (2004). Why does the "above average effect" exist? Demonstrating idiosyncratic trait definition. *Teaching of Psychology, 31*, 53–54. (p. 597)

Nightingale, F. (1860/1969). *Notes on nursing.* Mineola, NY: Dover. (p. 858)

NIH. (1995). Integration of behavioral and relaxation approaches into the treatment of chronic pain and insomnia. Bethesda, MD: National Institutes of Health. (p. 863)

NIH. (2001, July 20). *Workshop summary: Scientific evidence on condom effectiveness for sexually transmitted disease (STD) prevention.* Bethesda: National Institute of Allergy and Infectious Diseases, National Institutes of Health. (p. 529)

NIH. (2006, December 4). NIDA researchers complete unprecedented scan of human genome that may help unlock the genetic contribution to tobacco addiction. *NIH News*, National Institutes of Health (www.nih.gov). (p. 823)

NIH. (2010). *Teacher's guide: Information about sleep.* National Institutes of Health (www.science.education.nih.gov). (p. 230)

Nikolas, M. A., & Burt, A. (2010). Genetic and environmental influences on ADHD symptom dimensions of inattention and hyperactivity: A meta-analysis. *Journal of Abnormal Psychology, 119*, 1–17. (p. 652)

Nir, Y., & Tononi, G. (2010). Dreaming and the brain: From phenomenology to neurophysiology. *Trends in Cognitive Sciences, 14*, 88–100. (p. 243)

Nisbett, R. E. (1987). Lay personality theory: Its nature, origin, and utility. In N. E. Grunberg, R. E. Nisbett, & others (Eds.). *A distinctive approach to psychological research: The influence of Stanley Schachter.* Hillsdale, NJ: Erlbaum. (pp. 755, 831)

Nisbett, R. E. (2009). *Intelligence and how to get it: Why schools and culture count.* New York: Norton. (pp. 639, 641)

Nisbett, R. E., & Cohen, D. (1996). *Culture of honor: The psychology of violence in the South.* Boulder, CO: Westview Press. (p. 792)

Nisbett, R. E., & Ross, L. (1980). *Human inference: Strategies and shortcomings of social judgment.* Englewood Cliffs, NJ: Prentice-Hall. (p. 364)

Nixon, G. M., Thompson, J. M. D., Han, D. Y., Becroft, D. M., Clark, P. M., Robinson, E., Waldie, K E., Wild, C. J., Black, P. N., & Mitchell, E. A. (2008). Short sleep duration in middle childhood: Risk factors and consequences. *Sleep, 31,* 71–78. (p. 236)

Nock, M. K. (2010). Self-injury. *Annual Review of Clinical Psychology, 6,* 339–363. (p. 677)

Nock, M. K., Borges, G., Bromet, E. J., Alonso, J., Angermeyer, M., Beautrais, A., Bruffaerts, R., Chiu, W. T., de Girolamo, G., Gluzman, S., de Graaf, R., Gureje, O., Haro, J. M., Huang, Y., Karam, E., Kessler, R. C., Lepine, J. P., Levinson, D., Medina-Mora, M. E., Ono, Y., Posada-Villa, J., Williams, D. (2008). Cross-national prevalence and risk factors for suicidal ideation, plans, and attempts. *British Journal of Psychiatry, 192,* 98–105. (p. 677)

Nock, M. K., & Kessler, R. C. (2006). Prevalence of and risk factors for suicide attempts versus suicide gestures: Analysis of the National Comorbidity Survey. *Journal of Abnormal Psychology, 115,* 616–623. (p. 677)

Noel, J. G., Forsyth, D. R., & Kelley, K. N. (1987). Improving the performance of failing students by overcoming their self-serving attributional biases. *Basic and Applied Social Psychology, 8,* 151–162. (p. 589)

Noice, H., & Noice, T. (2006). What studies of actors and acting can tell us about memory and cognitive functioning. *Current Directions in Psychological Science, 15,* 14–18. (p. 326)

Nolen-Hoeksema, S. (2001). Gender differences in depression. *Current Directions in Psychological Science, 10,* 173–176. (p. 679)

Nolen-Hoeksema, S. (2003). *Women who think too much: How to break free of overthinking and reclaim your life.* New York: Holt. (p. 679)

Nolen-Hoeksema, S., & Larson, J. (1999). *Coping with loss.* Mahwah, NJ: Erlbaum. (p. 548)

Norberg, M. M., Krystal, J. H., & Tolin, D. F. (2008). A meta-analysis of d-cycloserine and the facilitation of fear extinction and exposure therapy. *Biological Psychiatry, 63,* 1118–1126. (p. 668)

NORC. (2010). National Opinion Research Center (University of Chicago) General Social Survey data, 1972 through 2008, accessed via sda.berkeley.edu. (p. 413)

Nordgren, L. F., van der Pligt, J., & van Harreveld, F. (2006). Visceral drives in retrospect: Explanations about the inaccessible past. *Psychological Science, 17,* 635–640. (p. 397)

Nordgren, L. F., van der Pligt, J., & van Harreveld, F. (2007). Evaluating Eve: Visceral states influence the evaluation of impulsive behavior. *Journal of Personality and Social Psychology, 93,* 75–84. (p. 397)

Nordgren, L. F., van Harreveld, F., & van der Pligt, J. (2009). The restraint bias: How the illusion of self-restraint promotes impulsive behavior. *Psychological Science, 20,* 1523–1528. (p. 589)

Norem, J. K. (2001). *The positive power of negative thinking: Using defensive pessimism to harness anxiety and perform at your peak.* New York: Basic Books. (p. 589)

Norenzayan, A., & Hansen, I. G. (2006). Belief in supernatural agents in the face of death. *Personality and Social Psychology Bulletin, 32,* 174–187. (p. 568)

Norman, D. A. (2001). The perils of home theater (www.jnd.org/dn.mss/ ProblemsOfHomeTheater.html). (p. 840)

Norman, E. (2010). "The unconscious" in current psychology. *European Psychologist, 15,* 193–201. (p. 568)

Noroozian, M., Lotfi, J., Gassemzadeh, H., Emami, H., & Mehrabi, Y. (2003). Academic achievement and learning abilities in left-handers: Guilt or gift? *Cortex, 38,* 779–785. (p. 118)

Norton, K. L., Olds, T. S., Olive, S., & Dank, S. (1996). Ken and Barbie at life size. *Sex Roles, 34,* 287–294. (p. 698)

Norton, M. I., & Ariely, D. (2011). Building a better America—One wealth quintile at a time. *Perspectives on Psychological Science, 6,* 9–12. (p. 56)

Norton, P. J., & Price, E. C. (2007). A meta-analytic review of adult cognitive-behavioral treatment outcome across the anxiety disorders. *Journal of Nervous and Mental Disease, 195,* 521–531. (p. 723)

Nowak, R. (1994). Nicotine scrutinized as FDA seeks to regulate cigarettes. *Science, 263,* 1555–1556. (p. 251)

NPR. (2009, July 11). Afraid to fly? Try living on a plane. www.npr.org. (p. 272)

NSF. (2001, October 24). Public bounces back after Sept. 11 attacks, national study shows. *NSF News,* National Science Foundation (www.nsf.gov/od/lpa/ news/press/ol/pr0185.htm). (p. 443)

NSF. (2008). *2008 sleep in America poll.* National Sleep Foundation (sleepfoundation. org). (p. 229)

Nurmikko, A. V., Donoghue, J. P., Hochberg, L. R., Patterson, W. R., Song, Y-K., Bull, C. W., Borton, D. A., Laiwalla, F., Park, S., Ming, Y., & Aceros, J. (2010). *Listening to brain microcircuits for interfacing with external world—Progress in wireless implantable microelectronic neuroengineering devices.* Proceedings of the *IEEE, 98,* 375–388. (p. 107)

Nurnberger, J. I., Jr., & Bierut, L. J. (2007, April). Seeking the connections: Alcoholism and our genes. *Scientific American,* 46–53. (p. 823)

Nuttin, J. M., Jr. (1987). Affective consequences of mere ownership: The name letter effect in twelve European languages. *European Journal of Social Psychology, 17,* 381–402. (p. 798)

Oakley, D. A., & Halligan, P. W. (2009). Hypnotic suggestion and cognitive neuroscience. *Trends in Cognitive Science, 13,* 264–270. (p. 221)

Oaten, M., & Cheng, K. (2006a). Longitudinal gains in self-regulation from regular physical exercise. *British Journal of Health Psychology, 11,* 717–733. (p. 302)

Oaten, M., & Cheng, K. (2006b). Improved self-control: The benefits of a regular program of academic study. *Basic and Applied Social Psychology, 28,* 1–16. (p. 302)

Oberlander, J., & Gill, A. J. (2006). Language with character: A stratified corpus comparison of individual differences in e-mail communication. *Discourse Processes, 42,* 239–270. (p. 584)

Oberman, L. M., & Ramachandran, V. S. (2007). The simulating social mind: The role of the mirror neuron system and simulation in the social and communicative deficits of autism spectrum disorders. *Psychological Bulletin, 133,* 310–327. (p. 482)

Ochsner, K. N., Ray, R. R., Hughes, B., McRae, K., Cooper, J. C., Weber, J., Gabrieli, J. D. E., & Gross, J. J. (2009). Bottom-up and top-down processes in emotion generation: Common and distinct neural mechanisms. *Psychological Science, 20,* 1322–1331. (p. 423)

O'Connor, P., & Brown, G. W. (1984). Supportive relationships: Fact or fancy? *Journal of Social and Personal Relationships, 1,* 159–175. (p. 735)

Oddone-Paolucci, E., Genuis, M., & Violato, C. (2000). A meta-analysis of the published research on the effects of pornography. In C. Violato, E. Oddone-Paolucci, & M. Genuis (Eds.), *The changing family and child development.* Aldershot, England: Ashgate. (p. 793)

Odgers, C. L., Caspi, A., Nagin, D. S., Piquero, A. R., Slutske, W. S., Milne, B. J., Dickson, N., Poulton, R., & Moffitt, T. E. (2008). Is it important to prevent early exposure to drugs and alcohol among adolescents? *Psychological Science, 19,* 1037–1044. (p. 824)

O'Donnell, L., Stueve, A., O'Donnell, C., Duran, R., San Doval, A., Wilson, R. F., Haber, D., Perry, E., & Pleck, J. H. (2002). Long-term reduction in sexual initiation and sexual activity among urban middle schoolers in the reach for health service learning program. *Journal of Adolescent Health, 31,* 93–100. (p. 531)

Oettingen, G., & Mayer, D. (2002). The motivating function of thinking about the future: Expectations versus fantasies. *Journal of Personality and Social Psychology, 83,* 1198–1212. (p. 589)

Offer, D., Ostrov, E., Howard, K. I., & Atkinson, R. (1988). *The teenage world: Adolescents' self-image in ten countries.* New York: Plenum. (p. 522)

Ogden, J. (2012, January 16). HM, the man with no memory. www.psychologytoday. com. (p. 342)

Ohgami, H., Terao, T., Shiotsuki, I., Ishii, N., & Iwata, N. (2009). Lithium levels in drinking water and risk of suicide. *British Journal of Psychiatry, 194,* 464–465. (p. 743)

Öhman, A. (2009). Of snakes and fears: An evolutionary perspective on the psychology of fear. *Scandinavian Journal of Psychology, 50,* 543–552. (p. 667)

Oishi, S., Diener, E. F., Lucas, R. E., & Suh, E. M. (1999). Cross-cultural variations in predictors of life satisfaction: Perspectives from needs and values. *Personality and Social Psychology Bulletin, 25,* 980–990. (p. 394)

Oishi, S., & Schimmack, U. (2010a). Culture and well-being: A new inquiry into the psychological wealth of nations. *Perspectives in Psychological Science, 5,* 463–471. (p. 854)

Oishi, S., & Schimmack, U. (2010b). Residential mobility, well-being, and mortality. *Journal of Personality and Social Psychology, 98*, 980–994. (p. 413)

Okimoto, T. G., & Brescoll, V. L. (2010). The price of power: Power seeking and backlash against female politicians. *Personality and Social Psychology Bulletin, 36*, 923–936. (p. 502)

Olatunji, B. O., & Wolitzky-Taylor, K. B. (2009). Anxiety sensitivity and the anxiety disorders: A meta-analytic review and synthesis. *Psychological Bulletin, 135*, 974–999. (p. 663)

Olds, J. (1958). Self-stimulation of the brain. *Science, 127*, 315–324. (p. 100)

Olds, J. (1975). Mapping the mind onto the brain. In F. G. Worden, J. P. Swazey, & G. Adelman (Eds.), *The neurosciences: Paths of discovery*. Cambridge, MA: MIT Press. (p. 100)

Olds, J., & Milner, P. (1954). Positive reinforcement produced by electrical stimulation of the septal area and other regions of rat brain. *Journal of Comparative and Physiological Psychology, 47*, 419–427. (p. 100)

Olff, M., Langeland, W., Draijer, N., & Gersons, B. P. R. (2007). Gender differences in posttraumatic stress disorder. *Psychological Bulletin, 135*, 183–204. (p. 665)

Olfson, M., Gameroff, M. J., Marcus, S. C., & Jensen, P. S. (2003). National trends in the treatment of attention deficit hyperactivity disorder. *American Journal of Psychiatry, 160*, 1071–1077. (p. 652)

Olfson, M., & Marcus, S. C. (2009). National patterns in antidepressant medication treatment. *Archives of General Psychiatry, 66*, 848–856. (p. 742)

Olfson, M., Marcus, S. C., Wan, G. J., & Geissler, E. C. (2004). National trends in the outpatient treatment of anxiety disorders. *Journal of Clinical Psychiatry, 65*, 1166–1173. (p. 741)

Olfson, M., Shaffer, D., Marcus, S. C., & Greenberg, T. (2003). Relationship between antidepressant medication treatment and suicide in adolescents. *Archives of General Psychiatry, 60*, 978–982. (p. 742)

Olin, S. S., & Mednick, S. A. (1996). Risk factors of psychosis: Identifying vulnerable populations premorbidly. *Schizophrenia Bulletin, 22*, 223–240. (p. 689)

Oliner, S. P., & Oliner, P. M. (1988). *The altruistic personality: Rescuers of Jews in Nazi Europe*. New York: Free Press. (p. 308)

Olivola, C. Y., & Todorov, A. (2010). Elected in 100 milliseconds: Appearance-based trait inferences and voting. *Journal of Nonverbal Behavior, 54*, 83–110. (p. 433)

Olson, M. A., & Fazio, R. H. (2001). Implicit attitude formation through classical conditioning. *Psychological Science, 12*, 413–417. (p. 296)

Olson, S. (2005). Brain scans raise privacy concerns. *Science, 307*, 1548–1550. (p. 578)

Olsson, A., Nearing, K. I., & Phelps, E. A. (2007). Learning fears by observing others: The neural systems of social fear transmission. *Social Cognitive and Affective Neuroscience, 2*, 3–11. (p. 667)

Olweus, D., Mattsson, A., Schalling, D., & Low, H. (1988). Circulating testosterone levels and aggression in adolescent males: A causal analysis. *Psychosomatic Medicine, 50*, 261–272. (p. 790)

Oman, D., Kurata, J. H., Strawbridge, W. J., & Cohen, R. D. (2002). Religious attendance and cause of death over 31 years. *International Journal of Psychiatry in Medicine, 32*, 69–89. (p. 864)

O'Neil, J. (2002, September 3). Vital signs: Behavior: Parent smoking and teenage sex. *New York Times*. (p. 49)

O'Neill, M. J. (1993). The relationship between privacy, control, and stress responses in office workers. Paper presented to the Human Factors and Ergonomics Society convention. (p. 300)

Ong, A. D., Fuller-Rowell, T., & Burrow, A. L. (2009). Racial discrimination and the stress process. *Journal of Personality and Social Psychology, 96*, 1259–1271. (p. 444)

Oppenheimer, D. M., & Trail, T. E. (2010). Why leaning to the left makes you lean to the left: Effects of spatial orientation on political attitudes. *Social Cognition, 28*, 651–661. (p. 211)

Oren, D. A., & Terman, M. (1998). Tweaking the human circadian clock with light. *Science, 279*, 333–334. (p. 230)

Orne, M. T., & Evans, F. J. (1965). Social control in the psychological experiment: Antisocial behavior and hypnosis. *Journal of Personality and Social Psychology, 1*, 189–200. (p. 220)

Orth, U., Robins, R. W., & Meier, L. L. (2009). Disentangling the effects of low self-esteem and stressful events on depression: Findings from three longitudinal studies. *Personality Processes and Individual Differences, 97*, 307–321. (pp. 595, 679)

Orth, U., Robins, R. W., & Roberts, B. W. (2008). Low self-esteem prospectively predicts depression in adolescence and young adulthood. *Journal of Personality and Social Psychology, 95*, 695–708. (p. 595)

Orth, U, Robins, R. W., Trzesniewski, K. H., Maes, J., & Schmitt, M. (2009). Low self-esteem is a risk factor for depressive symptoms from young adulthood to old age. *Journal of Abnormal Psychology, 118*, 472–478. (pp. 675, 679)

Osborne, C., Manning, W. D., & Smock, P. J. (2007). Married and cohabiting parents' relationship stability: A focus on race and ethnicity. *Journal of Marriage and Family, 69*, 1345–1366. (p. 545)

Osborne, J. W. (1997). Race and academic disidentification. *Journal of Educational Psychology, 89*, 728–735. (p. 643)

Osborne, L. (1999, October 27). A linguistic big bang. *New York Times Magazine* (www.nytimes.com). (p. 376)

Osgood, C. E. (1962). *An alternative to war or surrender*. Urbana: University of Illinois Press. (p. 815)

Osgood, C. E. (1980). GRIT: A strategy for survival in mankind's nuclear age? Paper presented at the Pugwash Conference on New Directions in Disarmament. (p. 815)

Oskarsson, A. T., Van Voven, L., McClelland, G. H., & Hastie, R. (2009). What's next? Judging sequences of binary events. *Psychological Bulletin, 135*, 262–285. (p. 33)

OSS Assessment Staff. (1948). *The assessment of men*. New York: Rinehart. (p. 592)

Ost, L. G., & Hugdahl, K. (1981). Acquisition of phobias and anxiety response patterns in clinical patients. *Behaviour Research and Therapy, 16*, 439–447. (p. 666)

Ostfeld, A. M., Kasl, S. V., D'Atri, D. A., & Fitzgerald, E. F. (1987). *Stress, crowding, and blood pressure in prison*. Hillsdale, NJ: Erlbaum. (p. 300)

O'Sullivan, M., Frank, M. G., Hurley, C. M., & Tiwana, J. (2009). Police lie detection accuracy: The effect of lie scenario. *Law and Human Behavior, 33*, 530–538. (p. 433)

Osvath, M. (2009). Spontaneous planning for future stone throwing by a male chimpanzee. *Current Biology, 19*, R190–R191. (p. 868)

Oswald, A. J., & Powdthavee, N. (2006). *Does happiness adapt? A longitudinal study of disability with implications for economists and judges* (Discussion Paper No. 2208). Bonn: Institute for the Study of Labor. (p. 848)

Oswald, A. J., & Wu, S. (2010). Objective confirmation of subjective measures of human well-being: Evidence from the U.S.A. *Science, 327*, 576–579. (p. 849)

Ott, B. (2007, June 14). Investors, take note: Engagement boosts earnings. *Gallup Management Journal* (gmj.gallup.com). (p. 836)

Ott, C. H., Lueger, R. J., Kelber, S. T., & Prigerson, H. G. (2007). Spousal bereavement in older adults: Common, resilient, and chronic grief with defining characteristics. *Journal of Nervous and Mental Disease, 195*, 332–341. (p. 548)

Ouellette, J. A., & Wood, W. (1998). Habit and intention in everyday life: The multiple processes by which past behavior predicts future behavior. *Psychological Bulletin, 124*, 54–74. (pp. 592, 831)

Owen, A. M., Coleman, M. R., Boly, M., Davis, M. H., Laureys, S., & Pickard, J. D. (2006). Detecting awareness in the vegetative state. *Science, 313*, 1402. (p. 119)

Owen, R. (1814). First essay in *New view of society or the formation of character*. Quoted in *The story of New Lamark*. New Lamark Mills, Lamark, Scotland: New Lamark Conservation Trust, 1993. (p. 835)

Owens, J. A., Belon, K., & Moss, P. (2010). Impact of delaying school start time on adolescent sleep, mood, and behavior. *Archives of Pediatric Adolescent Medicine, 164*, 608–614. (p. 236)

Oxfam. (2005, March 26). *Three months on: New figures show tsunami may have killed up to four times as many women as men*. Oxfam Press Release (www.oxfam.org.uk). (p. 504)

Ozer, E. J., Best, S. R., Lipsey, T. L., & Weiss, D. S. (2003). Predictors of posttraumatic stress disorder and symptoms in adults: A meta-analysis. *Psychological Bulletin, 129*, 52–73. (p. 665)

Ozer, E. J., & Weiss, D. S. (2004). Who develops posttraumatic stress disorder? *Current Directions in Psychological Science, 13,* 169–172. (p. 665)

Özgen, E. (2004). Language, learning, and color perception. *Current Directions in Psychological Science, 13,* 95–98. (p. 380)

Pacifici, R., Zuccaro, P., Farre, M., Pichini, S., Di Carlo, S., Roset, P. N., Ortuno, J., Pujadas, M., Bacosi, A., Menoyo, E., Segura, J., & de la Torre, R. (2001). Effects of repeated doses of MDMA ("Ecstasy") on cell-mediated immune response in humans. *Life Sciences, 69,* 2931–2941. (p. 254)

Padgett, V. R. (1989). Predicting organizational violence: An application of 11 powerful principles of obedience. Paper presented to the American Psychological Association convention. (p. 767)

Pagani, L. S., Fitzpatrick, C., Barnett, T. A., & Dubow, E. (2010). Prospective associations between early childhood television exposure and academic, psychosocial, and physical well-being by middle childhood. *Archivers of Pediatric and Adolescent Medicine, 164,* 425–431. (p. 403)

Page, S. (1977). Effects of the mental illness label in attempts to obtain accommodation. *Canadian Journal of Behavioral Science, 9,* 84–90. (p. 655)

Page, S. E. (2007). *The difference: How the power of diversity creates better groups, firms, schools, and societies.* Princeton, NJ: Princeton University Press. (p. 775)

Palladino, J. J., & Carducci, B. J. (1983). "Things that go bump in the night": Students' knowledge of sleep and dreams. Paper presented at the meeting of the Southeastern Psychological Association. (p. 225)

Pallier, C., Colomé, A., & Sebastián-Gallés, N. (2001). The influence of native-language phonology on lexical access: Exemplar-based versus abstract lexical entries. *Psychological Science, 12,* 445–448. (p. 374)

Palmer, S., Schreiber, C., & Box, C. (1991). Remembering the earthquake: "Flashbulb" memory for experienced vs. reported events. Paper presented to the Psychonomic Society convention. (p. 332)

Pandey, J., Sinha, Y., Prakash, A., & Tripathi, R. C. (1982). Right-left political ideologies and attribution of the causes of poverty. *European Journal of Social Psychology, 12,* 327–331. (p. 755)

Panksepp, J. (2007). Neurologizing the psychology of affects: How appraisal-based constructivism and basic emotion theory can coexist. *Perspectives on Psychological Science, 2,* 281–295. (p. 427)

Pantev, C., Oostenveld, R., Engelien, A., Ross, B., Roberts, L. R., & Hoke, M. (1998). Increased auditory cortical representation in musicians. *Nature, 392,* 811–814. (p. 110)

Panzarella, C., Alloy, L. B., & Whitehouse, W. G. (2006). Expanded hopelessness theory of depression: On the mechanisms by which social support protects against depression. *Cognitive Theory and Research, 30,* 307–333. (p. 680)

Park, C. L. (2007). Religiousness/spirituality and health: A meaning systems perspective. *Journal of Behavioral Medicine, 30,* 319–328. (p. 865)

Park, G., Lubinski, D., & Benbow, C. P. (2007). Contrasting intellectual patterns predict creativity in the arts and sciences. *Psychological Science, 18,* 948–952. (p. 630)

Park, G., Lubinski, D., & Benbow, C. P. (2008). Ability differences among people who have commensurate degrees matter for scientific creativity. *Psychological Science, 19,* 957–961. (p. 357)

Park, R. L. (1999, July 12). Liars never break a sweat. *New York Times* (www.nytimes.com). (p. 428)

Parker, C. P., Baltes, B. B., Young, S. A., Huff, J. W., Altmann, R. A., LaCost, H. A., & Roberts, J. E. (2003). Relationships between psychological climate perceptions and work outcomes: A meta-analytic review. *Journal of Organizational Behavior, 24,* 389–416. (p. 835)

Parker, E. S., Cahill, L., & McGaugh, J. L. (2006). A case of unusual autobiographical remembering. *Neurocase, 12,* 35–49. (p. 341)

Parsons, T. D., & Rizzo, A. A. (2008). Affective outcomes of virtual reality exposure therapy for anxiety and specific phobias: A meta-analysis. *Journal of Behavior Therapy and Experimental Psychiatry, 39,* 250–261. (p. 718)

Pasco, J. A., Williams, L. A., Jacks, F. N., Ng, F., Henry, M. J., Nicholson, G. C., Kotowicz, M. A., & Berk, M. (2008). Tobacco smoking as a risk factor for major depressive disorder: Population-based study. *British Journal of Psychiatry, 193,* 322–326. (p. 678)

Pascoe, E. A., & Richman, L. S. (2009). Perceived discrimination and health: A meta-analytic review. *Psychological Bulletin, 135,* 531–554. (p. 444)

Passell, P. (1993, March 9). Like a new drug, social programs are put to the test. *New York Times,* C1, C10. (p. 53)

Pastalkova, E., Serrano, P., Pinkhasova, D., Wallace, E., Fenton, A. A., & Sacktor, T. C. (2006). Storage of spatial information by the maintenance mechanism of LTP. *Science, 313,* 1141–1144. (p. 333)

Patall, E. A., Cooper, H., & Robinson, J. C. (2008). The effects of choice on intrinsic motivation and related outcomes: A meta-analysis of research findings. *Psychological Bulletin, 134,* 270–300. (p. 298)

Pate, J. E., Pumariega, A. J., Hester, C., & Garner, D. M. (1992). Cross-cultural patterns in eating disorders: A review. *Journal of the American Academy of Child and Adolescent Psychiatry, 31,* 802–809. (p. 697)

Patel, S. R., Malhotra, A., White, D. P., Gottlieb, D. J., & Hu, F. B. (2006). Association between reduced sleep and weight gain in women. *American Journal of Epidemiology, 164,* 947–954. (p. 236)

Patten, S. B., Wang, J. L., Williams, J. V. A., Currie, S., Beck, C. A., Maxwell, C. J., & El-Guebaly, N. (2006). Descriptive epidemiology of major depression in Canada. *Canadian Journal of Psychiatry, 51,* 84–90. (p. 671)

Patterson, F. (1978, October). Conversations with a gorilla. *National Geographic,* 438–465. (p. 869)

Patterson, G. R., Chamberlain, P., & Reid, J. B. (1982). A comparative evaluation of parent training procedures. *Behavior Therapy, 13,* 638–650. (pp. 282, 792)

Patterson, G. R., Reid, J. B., & Dishion, T. J. (1992). *Antisocial boys.* Eugene, OR: Castalia. (p. 792)

Patterson, M., Warr, P., & West, M. (2004). Organizational climate and company productivity: The role of employee affect and employee level. *Journal of Occupational and Organizational Psychology, 77,* 193–216. (p. 835)

Patterson, P. H. (2007). Maternal effects on schizophrenia risk. *Science, 318,* 576–577. (p. 687)

Patterson, R. (1951). *The riddle of Emily Dickinson.* Boston: Houghton Mifflin. (p. 681)

Pauker, K., Weisbuch, M., Ambady, N., Sommers, S. R., Adams, R. B., Jr., & Ivcevic, Z. (2009). Not so Black and White: Memory for ambiguous group members. *Journal of Personality and Social Psychology, 96,* 795–810. (p. 640)

Paulesu, E., Demonet, J-F., Fazio, F., McCrory, E., Chanoine, V., Brunswick, N., Cappa, S. F., Cossu, G., Habib, M., Frith, C. D., & Frith, U. (2001). Dyslexia: Cultural diversity and biological unity. *Science, 291,* 2165–2167. (p. 65)

Paus, T., Zijdenbos, A., Worsley, K., Collins, D. L., Blumenthal, J., Giedd, J. N., Rapoport, J. L., & Evans, A. C. (1999). Structural maturation of neural pathways in children and adolescents: In vivo study. *Science, 283,* 1908–1911. (p. 471)

Pavlov, I. (1927). *Conditioned reflexes: An investigation of the physiological activity of the cerebral cortex.* Oxford: Oxford University Press. (pp. 266, 270)

Payne, B. K. (2006). Weapon bias: Split-second decisions and unintended stereotyping. *Current Directions in Psychological Science, 15,* 287–291. (p. 782)

Payne, B. K., & Corrigan, E. (2007). Emotional constraints on intentional forgetting. *Journal of Experimental Social Psychology, 43,* 780–786. (p. 347)

Payne, B. K., Krosnick, J. A., Pasek, J., Lelkes, Y., Akhtar, O., & Tompson, T. (2010). Implicit and explicit prejudice in the 2008 American presidential election. *Journal of Experimental Social Psychology, 46,* 367–374. (p. 782)

Payne, J. W., Samper, A., Bettman, J. R., & Luce, M. F. (2008). Boundary conditions on unconscious thought in complex decision making. *Psychological Science, 19,* 1118–1123. (p. 369)

Peckham, A. D., McHugh, R. K., & Otto, M. W. (2010). A meta-analysis of the magnitude of biased attention in depression. *Depression and Anxiety, 27,* 1135–1142. (p. 674)

Pedersen, A., Zachariae, R., & Bovbjerg, D. H. (2010). Influence of psychological stress on upper respiratory infection—A meta-analysis of prospective studies. *Psychosomatic Medicine, 72,* 823–832. (p. 449)

Pedersen, N. L., Plomin, R., McClearn, G. E., & Friberg, L. (1988). Neuroticism, extraversion, and related traits in adult twins reared apart and reared together. *Journal of Personality and Social Psychology, 55,* 950–957. (p. 127)

Peigneux, P., Laureys, S., Fuchs, S., Collette, F., Perrin, F., Reggers, J., Phillips, C., Degueldre, C., Del Fiore, G., Aerts, J., Luxen, A., & Maquet, P. (2004). Are spatial memories strengthened in the human hippocampus during slow wave sleep? *Neuron, 44,* 535–545. (pp. 231, 331)

Pekkanen, J. (1982, June). Why do we sleep? *Science, 82,* 86. (p. 231)

Pelham, B. W. (1993). On the highly positive thoughts of the highly depressed. In R. F. Baumeister (Ed.), *Self-esteem: The puzzle of low self-regard.* New York: Plenum. (p. 595)

Pelham, B. W. (2009, October 22). About one in six Americans report history of depression. *Gallup* (www.gallup.com). (p. 674)

Pelham, B. W. (2010, February 2). Rest eludes nearly 30% of Americans. *Gallup* (www.gallup.com). (p. 235)

Pelham, B. W., & Crabtree, S. (2008, October 8). Worldwide, highly religious more likely to help others. Gallup Poll (www.gallup.com). (p. 810)

Pendick, D. (1994, January/February). The mind of violence. *Brain Work: The Neuroscience Newsletter*, pp. 1–3, 5. (p. 790)

Pennebaker, J. W. (1985). Traumatic experience and psychosomatic disease: Exploring the roles of behavioral inhibition, obsession, and confiding. *Canadian Psychology, 26,* 82–95. (p. 859)

Pennebaker, J. W. (1990). *Opening up: The healing power of confiding in others.* New York: William Morrow. (pp. 563, 859)

Pennebaker, J. W. (2002, January 28). Personal communication. (p. 813)

Pennebaker, J. W., Barger, S. D., & Tiebout, J. (1989). Disclosure of traumas and health among Holocaust survivors. *Psychosomatic Medicine, 51,* 577–589. (p. 858)

Pennebaker, J. W., & O'Heeron, R. C. (1984). Confiding in others and illness rate among spouses of suicide and accidental death victims. *Journal of Abnormal Psychology, 93,* 473–476. (p. 858)

Pennebaker, J. W., & Stone, L. D. (2003). Words of wisdom: Language use over the life span. *Journal of Personality and Social Psychology, 85,* 291–301. (p. 546)

Peplau, L. A., & Fingerhut, A. W. (2007). The close relationships of lesbians and gay men. *Annual Review of Psychology, 58,* 405–424. (p. 545)

Peplau, L. A., & Garnets, L. D. (2000). A new paradigm for understanding women's sexuality and sexual orientation. *Journal of Social Issues, 56,* 329–350. (p. 532)

Peppard, P. E., Szklo-Coxe, M., Hia, K. M., & Young, T. (2006). Longitudinal association of sleep-related breathing disorder and depression. *Archives of Internal Medicine, 166,* 1709–1715. (p. 239)

Pepperberg, I. M. (2006). Grey parrot numerical competence: A review. *Animal Cognition, 9,* 377–391. (p. 867)

Pepperberg, I. M. (2009). *Alex & me: How a scientist and a parrot discovered a hidden world of animal intelligence—and formed a deep bond in the process.* New York: Harper. (p. 867)

Perani, D., & Abutalebi, J. (2005). The neural basis of first and second language processing. *Current Opinion in Neurobiology, 15,* 202–206. (p. 378)

Pereira, A. C., Huddleston, D. E., Brickman, A. M., Sosunov, A. A., Hen, R., McKhann, G. M., Sloan, R., Gage, F. H., Brown, T. R., & Small, S. A. (2007). An *in vivo* correlate of exercise-induced neurogenesis in the adult dentate gyrus. *Proceedings of the National Academic of Sciences, 104,* 5638–5643. (pp. 112, 540, 542)

Pereira, G. M., & Osburn, H. G. (2007). Effects of participation in decision making on performance and employee attitudes: A quality circles meta-analysis. *Journal of Business Psychology, 22,* 145–153. (pp. 838, 839)

Pergadia, M. L., & 30 others. (2011). A 3p26-3p25 genetic linkage finding for DSM-IV major depression in heavy smoking families. *American Journal of Psychiatry. 168,* 848–852. (p. 678)

Perilloux, H. K., Webster, G. D., & Gaulin, S. J. (2010). Signals of genetic quality and maternal investment capacity: The dynamic effects of fluctuating asymmetry and waist-to-hip ratio on men's ratings of women's attractiveness *Social Psychology and Personalty Science, 1,* 34–42. (pp. 138, 801)

Perkins, A., & Fitzgerald, J. A. (1997). Sexual orientation in domestic rams: Some biological and social correlates. In L. Ellis and L. Ebertz (Eds.), *Sexual orientation: Toward biological understanding.* Westport, CT: Praeger Publishers. (p. 533)

Perlmutter, M. (1983). Learning and memory through adulthood. In M. W. Riley, B. B. Hess, & K. Bond (Eds.), *Aging in society: Selected reviews of recent research.* Hillsdale, NJ: Erlbaum. (p. 543)

Perra, O., Williams, J. H. G., Whiten, A., Fraser, L., Benzie, H., & Perrett, D. I. (2008). Imitation and 'theory of mind' competencies in discrimination of autism from other neurodevelopmental disorders. *Research in Autism Disorders, 2,* 456–468. (p. 482)

Perrett, D. I. (2002, October 1). Perception laboratory, Department of Psychology, University of St. Andrews, Scotland (www.perception.st-and.ac.uk). (p. 801)

Perrett, D. I. (2010). *In your face: The new science of human attraction.* New York: Palgrave Macmillan. (p. 801)

Perrett, D. I., Harries, M., Misflin, A. J., & Chitty, A. J. (1988). Three stages in the classification of body movements by visual neurons. In H. B. Barlow, C. Blakemore, & M. Weston Smith (Eds.), *Images and understanding.* Cambridge: Cambridge University Press. (p. 176)

Perrett, D. I., Hietanen, J. K., Oram, M. W., & Benson, P. J. (1992). Organization and functions of cells responsive to faces in the temporal cortex. *Philosophical Transactions of the Royal Society of London: Series B, 335,* 23–30. (p. 176)

Perrett, D. I., Lee, K. J., Penton-Voak, I., Rowland, D., Yoshikawa, S., Burt, D. M., Henzi, S. P., Castles, D. L., & Akamatsu, S. (1998, August). Effects of sexual dimorphism on facial attractiveness. *Nature, 394,* 884–887. (p. 783)

Perrett, D. I., May, K. A., & Yoshikawa, S. (1994). Facial shape and judgments of female attractiveness. *Nature, 368,* 239–242. (p. 176)

Perron, H, Mekaoui, L, Bernard, C, Veas, F, Stefas, I, & Leboyer, M. (2008). Endogenous retrovirus type W GAG and envelope protein antigenemia in serum of schizophrenic patients. *Biological Psychiatry, 64,* 1019–1023. (p. 688)

Person, C., Tracy, M., & Galea, S. (2006). Risk factors for depression after a disaster. *Journal of Nervous and Mental Disease, 194,* 659–666. (p. 737)

Pert, C. B. (1986). Quoted in J. Hooper & D. Teresi, *The three-pound universe.* New York: Macmillan. (p. 100)

Pert, C. B., & Snyder, S. H. (1973). Opiate receptor: Demonstration in nervous tissue. *Science, 179,* 1011–1014. (p. 82)

Perugini, E. M., Kirsch, I., Allen, S. T., Coldwell, E., Meredith, J., Montgomery, G. H., & Sheehan, J. (1998). Surreptitious observation of responses to hypnotically suggested hallucinations: A test of the compliance hypothesis. *International Journal of Clinical and Experimental Hypnosis, 46,* 191–203. (p. 221)

Peschel, E. R., & Peschel, R. E. (1987). Medical insights into the castrati in opera. *American Scientist, 75,* 578–583. (p. 408)

Pescosolido, B. A., Martin, J. K., Long, J. S., Medina, T. R., Phelan, J. C., & Link, B. G. (2010). "A disease like any other"? A decade of change in public reactions to schizophrenia, depression, and alcohol dependence. *American Journal of Psychiatry, 167,* 1321–1330. (p. 689)

Peters, M., Reimers, S., & Manning, J. T. (2006). Hand preference for writing and associations with selected demographic and behavioral variables in 255,100 subjects: The BBC Internet study. *Brain and Cognition, 62,* 177–189. (p. 118)

Peters, M., Rhodes, G., & Simmons, L. W. (2007). Contributions of the face and body to overall attractiveness. *Animal Behaviour, 73,* 937–942. (p. 801)

Peters, T. J., & Waterman, R. H., Jr. (1982). *In search of excellence: Lessons from America's best-run companies.* New York: Harper & Row. (p. 287)

Petersen, J. L., & Hyde, J. S. (2009) A meta-analytic review of research on gender differences in sexuality, 1993–2007. *Psychological Bulletin, 136,* 21–38. (p. 138)

Petersen, J. L., & Hyde, J. S. (2011). Gender differences in sexual attitudes and behaviors: A review of meta-analytic results and large datasets. *Journal of Sex Research, 48,* 149–165. (p. 408)

Peterson, C., & Barrett, L. C. (1987). Explanatory style and academic performance among university freshmen. *Journal of Personality and Social Psychology, 53,* 603–607. (p. 589)

Peterson, C., Peterson, J., & Skevington, S. (1986). Heated argument and adolescent development. *Journal of Social and Personal Relationships, 3,* 229–240. (p. 515)

Peterson, C., & Siegal, M. (1999). Representing inner worlds: Theory of mind in autistic, deaf, and normal hearing children. *Psychological Science, 10,* 126–129. (p. 480)

Peterson, L. R., & Peterson, M. J. (1959). Short-term retention of individual verbal items. *Journal of Experimental Psychology, 58,* 193–198. (p. 322)

Petitto, L. A., & Marentette, P. F. (1991). Babbling in the manual mode: Evidence for the ontogeny of language. *Science, 251,* 1493–1496. (p. 374)

Pettegrew, J. W., Keshavan, M. S., & Minshew, N. J. (1993). 31P nuclear magnetic resonance spectroscopy: Neurodevelopment and schizophrenia. *Schizophrenia Bulletin, 19,* 35–53. (p. 687)

Petticrew, M., Bell, R., & Hunter, D. (2002). Influence of psychological coping on survival and recurrence in people with cancer: Systematic review. *British Medical Journal, 325,* 1066. (p. 451)

Petticrew, M., Fraser, J. M., & Regan, M. F. (1999). Adverse life events and risk of breast cancer: A meta-analysis. *British Journal of Health Psychology, 4,* 1–17. (p. 451)

Pettifor, J. P. (2004). Professional ethics across national boundaries. *European Psychologist, 9,* 264–272. (p. 68)

Pettigrew, T. F. (1998). Reactions toward the new minorities of western Europe. *Annual Review of Sociology, 24,* 77–103. (p. 781)

Pettigrew, T. F. (2006). A two-level approach to anti-immigrant prejudice and discrimination. In R. Mahalingam (Ed.), *Cultural psychology of immigrants*. Mahwah, NJ: Erlbaum. (p. 781)

Pettigrew, T. F., Christ, O., Wagner, U., & Stellmacher, J. (2007). Direct and indirect intergroup contact effects on prejudice: A normative interpretation. *International Journal of Intercultural Relations, 31*, 411–425. (p. 813)

Pettigrew, T. F., & Tropp, L. R. (2011). *When groups meet: The dynamics of intergroup contact*. New York: Psychology Press. (p. 813)

Pew Research Center. (2006, November 14). Attitudes toward homosexuality in African countries. (pewresearch.org). (p. 531)

Pew Research Center. (2007, January 24). *Global warming: A divide on causes and solutions*. Pew Research Center for the People and the Press. (p. 365)

Pew Research Center. (2007, July 18). Modern marriage: "I like hugs. I like kisses. But what I really love is help with the dishes." Pew Research Center (www.pewresearch.org). (p. 804)

Pew Research Center. (2009, November 4). Social isolation and new technology: How the Internet and mobile phones impact Americans' social networks. Pew Research Center (www.pewresearch.org). (p. 416)

Pew Research Center. (2009, November 16). Teens and distracted driving. Internet & American Life Project, Pew Research Center (www.pewinternet.org). (p. 153)

Pew Research Center. (2010). Home broadband 2010. Pew Internet & American Life Project, Pew Research Center (www.pewinternet.org). (p. 627)

Pew Research Center. (2010, February 1). Almost all millennials accept interracial dating and marriage. Pew Research Center. (www.pewresearch.org). (p. 781)

Pew Research Center. (2010, July 1). Gender equality universally embraced, but inequalities acknowledged. Pew Research Center Publications (pewresearch.org). (p. 504)

Pew Research Center. (2012, March 19). Teens, Smartphones & texting. Pew Research Center (pewresearch.org). (p. 522)

Pew Research Center. (2013). *The global divide on homosexuality: Greater acceptance in more secular and affluent countries*. [Data file]. Retrieved from http://www.pewglobal.org/files/2013/06/Pew-Global-Attitudes-Homosexuality-Report-FINAL-JUNE-4-2013.pdf. (p. 813)

Pew Research Center. (2013). Teens and technology, 2013. Retrieved from: http://www.pewinternet.org/~/media/Files/Reports/2013/PIP_TeensandTechnology2013.pdf. (p. 415)

Pfammatter, M., Junghan, U. M., Brenner, H. D. (2006). Efficacy of psychological therapy in schizophrenia: Conclusions from meta-analyses. *Schizophrenia Bulletin, 32*, S64–S80. (p. 732)

Phelps, J. A., Davis J. O., & Schartz, K. M. (1997). Nature, nurture, and twin research strategies. *Current Directions in Psychological Science, 6*, 117–120. (pp. 125, 688)

Phillips, A. C., Batty, G. D., Gale, C. R., Deary, I. J., Osborn, D., MacIntyre, K., & Carroll, D. (2009). Generalized anxiety disorder, major depressive disorder, and their comorbidity as predictors of all-cause and cardiovascular mortality: The Vietnam Experience Study. *Psychosomatic Medicine, 71*, 395–403. (p. 857)

Phillips, A. L. (2011). A walk in the woods. *American Scientist, 69*, 301–302. (p. 747)

Phillips, D. P. (1985). Natural experiments on the effects of mass media violence on fatal aggression: Strengths and weaknesses of a new approach. In L. Berkowitz (Ed.), *Advances in experimental social psychology* (Vol. 19). Orlando, FL: Academic Press. (p. 763)

Phillips, D. P., Carstensen, L. L., & Paight, D. J. (1989). Effects of mass media news stories on suicide, with new evidence on the role of story content. In D. R. Pfeffer (Ed.), *Suicide among youth: Perspectives on risk and prevention*. Washington, DC: American Psychiatric Press. (p. 763)

Phillips, J. L. (1969). *Origins of intellect: Piaget's theory*. San Francisco: Freeman. (p. 480)

Piaget, J. (1930). *The child's conception of physical causality*. London: Routledge & Kegan Paul. (p. 476)

Piaget, J. (1932). *The moral judgment of the child*. New York: Harcourt, Brace & World. (p. 515)

Picchioni, M. M., & Murray, R. M. (2007). Schizophrenia. *British Medical Journal, 335*, 91–95., 686

Pido-Lopez, J., Imami, N., & Aspinall, R. (2001). Both age and gender affect thymic output: More recent thymic migrants in females than males as they age. *Clinical and Experimental Immunology, 125*, 409–413. (p. 448)

Pieters, G. L. M., de Bruijn, E. R. A., Maas, Y., Hultijn, W., Vandereycken, W., Peuskens, J., & Sabbe, B. G. (2007). Action monitoring and perfectionism in anorexia nervosa. *Brain and Cognition, 63*, 42–50. (p. 697)

Pike, K. M., & Rodin, J. (1991). Mothers, daughters, and disordered eating. *Journal of Abnormal Psychology, 100*, 198–204. (p. 697)

Piliavin, J. A. (2003). Doing well by doing good: Benefits for the benefactor. In C. L. M. Keyes & J. Haidt (Eds.), *Flourishing: Positive psychology and the life well-lived*. Washington, DC: American Psychological Association. (p. 517)

Pillemer, D. B. (1995). What is remembered about early childhood events? Invited paper presentation to the American Psychological Society convention. (p. 473)

Pillemer, D. B. (1998). *Momentous events, vivid memories*. Cambridge, MA: Harvard University Press. (p. 542)

Pillemer, D. B., Ivcevic, Z., Gooze, R. A., & Collins, K. A. (2007). Self-esteem memories: Feeling good about achievement success, feeling bad about relationship distress. *Personality and Social Psychology Bulletin, 33*, 1292–1305. (p. 414)

Pilley, J. W., & Reid, A. K. (2011). Border collie comprehends object names as verbal referents. *Behavioural Processes, 86*, 184–195. (p. 870)

Pillsworth, M. G., Haselton, M. G., & Buss, D. M. (2004). Ovulatory shifts in female desire. *Journal of Sex Research, 41*, 55–65. (p. 408)

Pinker, S. (1990, September-October). Quoted by J. de Cuevas, "No, she held them loosely." *Harvard Magazine*, pp. 60–67. (p. 373)

Pinker, S. (1995). The language instinct. *The General Psychologist, 31*, 63–65. (p. 870)

Pinker, S. (1998). Words and rules. *Lingua, 106*, 219–242. (p. 372)

Pinker, S. (2002, September 9). A biological understanding of human nature: A talk with Steven Pinker. (www.edge.org). (pp. 128, 136)

Pinker, S. (2005, April 22). The science of gender and science. Pinker vs. Spelke: A debate. (www.edge.org). (p. 639)

Pinker, S. (2006, January 1). Groups of people may differ genetically in their average talents and temperaments. (www.edge.org). (p. 642)

Pinker, S. (2007). *The stuff of thought*. New York: Viking. (p. 380)

Pinker, S. (2008). *The sexual paradox: Men, women, and the real gender gap*. New York: Scribner. (p. 503)

Pinkham, A. E., Griffin, M., Baron, R., Sasson, N. J., & Gur, R. C. (2010). The face in the crowd effect: Anger superiority when using real faces and multiple identities. *Emotion, 10*, 141–146. (p. 432)

Pipe, M-E. (1996). Children's eyewitness memory. *New Zealand Journal of Psychology, 25*, 36–43. (p. 351)

Pipe, M-E., Lamb, M. E., Orbach, Y., & Esplin, P. W. (2004). Recent research on children's testimony about experienced and witnessed events. *Developmental Review, 24*, 440–468. (p. 351)

Pipher, M. (2002). *The middle of everywhere: The world's refugees come to our town*. New York: Harcourt Brace. (pp. 414, 443)

Pitcher, D., Walsh, V., Yovel, G., & Duchaine, B. (2007). TMS evidence for the involvement of the right occipital face area in early face processing. *Current Biology, 17*, 1568–1573. (p. 175)

Pittenger, D. J. (1993). The utility of the Myers-Briggs Type Indicator. *Review of Eduational Research, 63*, 467–488. (p. 577)

Place, S. S., Todd, P. M., Penke, L., & Asendorph, J. B. (2009). The ability to judge the romantic interest of others. *Psychological Science, 20*, 22–26. (p. 432, 799)

Plassmann, H., O'Doherty, J., Shiv, B., & Rangel, A. (2008). Marketing actions can modulate neural representations of experienced pleasantness. *Proceedings of the National Academy of Sciences, 105*, 1050–1054. (p. 207)

Platek, S. M., & Singh, D. (2010) Optimal waist-to-hip ratios in women activate neural reward centers in men. PLoS ONE 5(2): e9042. doi: 10.1371/journal.pone.0009042. (p. 801)

Pliner, P. (1982). The effects of mere exposure on liking for edible substances. *Appetite: Journal for Intake Research, 3*, 283–290. (p. 400)

Pliner, P., Pelchat, M., & Grabski, M. (1993). Reduction of neophobia in humans by exposure to novel foods. *Appetite, 20*, 111–123. (p. 400)

Plomin, R. (1999). Genetics and general cognitive ability. *Nature, 402* (Suppl), C25–C29. (pp. 609, 634)

Plomin, R. (2001). Genetics and behaviour. *The Psychologist, 14*, 134–139. (p. 632)

Plomin, R. (2003). General cognitive ability. In R. Plomin, J. C. DeFries, I. W. Craig, & P. McGuffin (Eds.), *Behavioral genetics in a postgenomic world.* Washington, DC: APA Books. (p. 632)

Plomin, R. (2011). Why are children in the same family so different? Nonshared environment three decades later. *International Journal of Epidemiology, 40,* 582–592. (pp. 128, 510)

Plomin, R., & Bergeman, C. S. (1991). The nature of nurture: Genetic influence on "environmental" measures. *Behavioral and Brain Sciences, 14,* 373–427. (p. 131)

Plomin, R., & Crabbe, J. (2000). DNA. *Psychological Bulletin, 126,* 806–828. (p. 129)

Plomin, R., & Daniels, D. (1987). Why are children in the same family so different from one another? *Behavioral and Brain Sciences, 10,* 1–60. (p. 510)

Plomin, R., & DeFries, J. C. (1998, May). The genetics of cognitive abilities and disabilities. *Scientific American,* pp. 62–69. (p. 634)

Plomin, R., DeFries, J. C., McClearn, G. E., & Rutter, M. (1997). *Behavioral genetics.* New York: Freeman. (pp. 125, 136, 402, 688)

Plomin, R., & Kovas, Y. (2005). Generalist genes and learning disabilities. *Psychological Bulletin, 131,* 592–617. (p. 633)

Plomin, R., McClearn, G. E., Pedersen, N. L., Nesselroade, J. R., & Bergeman, C. S. (1988). Genetic influence on childhood family environment perceived retrospectively from the last half of the life span. *Developmental Psychology, 24,* 37–45. (p. 131)

Plomin, R., & McGuffin, P. (2003). Psychopathology in the postgenomic era. *Annual Review of Psychology, 54,* 205–228. (p. 678)

Plomin, R., Reiss, D., Hetherington, E. M., & Howe, G. W. (January, 1994). Nature and nurture: Genetic contributions to measures of the family environment. *Developmental Psychology, 30*(1), 32–43. (p. 131)

Plotkin, H. (1994). *Darwin machines and the nature of knowledge.* Cambridge, MA: Harvard University Press. (p. 675)

Plotnik, J. M., de Waal, F. B. M., & Reiss, D. (2006). Self-recognition in an Asian elephant. *Proceedings of the National Academy of Sciences, 103,* 17053–17057. (p. 495)

Plous, S. (1993). Psychological mechanisms in the human use of animals. *Journal of Social Issues, 49*(1), 11–52. (p. 67)

Plous, S., & Herzog, H. A. (2000). Poll shows researchers favor lab animal protection. *Science, 290,* 711. (p. 67)

Poelmans, G., Pauls, D. L., Buitelaar, J. K., & Franke, B. (2011). Integrated genome-wide association study findings: Identification of a neurodevelopmental network for attention deficit hyperactivity disorder. *American Journal of Psychiatry, 168,* 365–377. (p. 652)

Pogue-Geile, M. F., & Yokley, J. L. (2010). Current research on the genetic contributors to schizophrenia. *Current Directions in Psychological Science, 19,* 214–219. (p. 689)

Poldrack, R. A., Halchenko, Y. O., & Hanson, S. J. (2009). Decoding the large-scale structure of brain function by classifying mental states across individuals. *Psychological Science, 20,* 1364–1372. (p. 96)

Polivy, J., & Herman, C. P. (2002). Causes of eating disorders. *Annual Review of Psychology, 53,* 187–213. (p. 697)

Polivy, J., Herman, C. P., & Coelho, J. S. (2008). Caloric restriction in the presence of attractive food cues: External cues, eating, and weight. *Physiology and Behavior, 94,* 729–733. (p. 401)

Pollak, S. D. (2008). Mechanisms linking early experience and the emergence of emotions. *Current Directions in Psychological Science, 17,* 370–375. (p. 493)

Pollak, S. D., Cicchetti, D., & Klorman, R. (1998). Stress, memory, and emotion: Developmental considerations from the study of child maltreatment. *Developmental Psychopathology, 10,* 811–828. (p. 270)

Pollak, S. D., & Kistler, D. J. (2002). Early experience is associated with the development of categorical representations for facial expressions of emotion. *Proceedings of the National Academy of Sciences, 99,* 9072–9076. (p. 433)

Pollan, M. (2009, August 2). Out of the kitchen, onto the couch. *New York Times* (www.nytimes.com). (p. 401)

Pollard, R. (1992). 100 years in psychology and deafness: A centennial retrospective. Invited address to the American Psychological Association convention, Washington, DC. (p. 869)

Pollick, A. S., & de Waal, F. B. M. (2007). Ape gestures and language evolution. *Proceedings of the National Academic of Sciences, 104,* 8184–8189. (p. 869)

Poole, D. A., & Lindsay, D. S. (1995). Interviewing preschoolers: Effects of nonsuggestive techniques, parental coaching and leading questions on reports of nonexperienced events. *Journal of Experimental Child Psychology, 60,* 129–154. (p. 349)

Poole, D. A., & Lindsay, D. S. (2001). Children's eyewitness reports after exposure to misinformation from parents. *Journal of Experimental Psychology: Applied, 7,* 27–50. (p. 349)

Poole, D. A., & Lindsay, D. S. (2002). Reducing child witnesses' false reports of misinformation from parents. *Journal of Experimental Child Psychology, 81,* 117–140. (p. 349)

Poon, L. W. (1987). Myths and truisms: Beyond extant analyses of speed of behavior and age. Address to the Eastern Psychological Association convention. (p. 541)

Popenoe, D. (1993). The evolution of marriage and the problem of stepfamilies: A biosocial perspective. Paper presented at the National Symposium on Stepfamilies, Pennsylvania State University. (p. 600)

Poremba, A., & Gabriel, M. (2001). Amygdalar efferents initiate auditory thalamic discriminative training-induced neuronal activity. *Journal of Neuroscience, 21,* 270–278. (p. 99)

Poropat, A. E. (2009). A meta-analysis of the five-factor model of personality and academic performance. *Psychological Bulletin, 135,* 322–338. (p. 581)

Porter, D., & Neuringer, A. (1984). Music discriminations by pigeons. *Journal of Experimental Psychology: Animal Behavior Processes, 10,* 138–148. (p. 277)

Porter, S., & Peace, K. A. (2007). The scars of memory: A prospective, longitudinal investigation of the consistency of traumatic and positive emotional memories in adulthood. *Psychological Science, 18,* 435–441. (p. 352)

Porter, S., & ten Brinke, L. (2008). Reading between the lies: Identifying concealed and falsified emotions in universal facial expressions. *Psychological Science, 19,* 508–514. (p. 433)

Posner, M. I., & Carr, T. H. (1992). Lexical access and the brain: Anatomical constraints on cognitive models of word recognition. *American Journal of Psychology, 105,* 1–26. (p. 378)

Posthuma, D., & de Geus, E. J. C. (2006). Progress in the molecular-genetic study of intelligence. *Current Directions in Psychological Science, 15,* 151–155. (p. 633)

Poulton, R., & Milne, B. J. (2002). Low fear in childhood is associated with sporting prowess in adolescence and young adulthood. *Behaviour Research and Therapy, 40,* 1191–1197. (p. 700)

Powell, K. E., Thompson, P. D., Caspersen, C. J., & Kendrick, J. S. (1987). Physical activity and the incidence of coronary heart disease. *Annual Review of Public Health, 8,* 253–287. (p. 859)

Powell, R. A., & Boer, D. P. (1994). Did Freud mislead patients to confabulate memories of abuse? *Psychological Reports, 74,* 1283–1298. (p. 561)

Premack, D. (2007). Human and animal cognition: Continuity and discontinuity. *PNAS, 104,* 13861–13867. (p. 373)

Premack, D., & Woodruff, G. (1978). Does the chimpanzee have a theory of mind? *Behavioral and Brain Sciences, 1,* 515–526. (p. 480)

Prentice, D. A., & Miller, D. T. (1993). Pluralistic ignorance and alcohol use on campus: Some consequences of misperceiving the social norm. *Journal of Personality and Social Psychology, 64,* 243–256. (p. 824)

Prince Charles. (2000). BBC Reith Lecture. (p. 30)

Principe, G. F., Kanaya, T., Ceci, S. J., & Singh, M. (2006). Believing is seeing: How rumors can engender false memories in preschoolers. *Psychological Science, 17,* 243–248. (p. 350)

Prioleau, L., Murdock, M., & Brody, N. (1983). An analysis of psychotherapy versus placebo studies. *The Behavioral and Brain Sciences, 6,* 275–310. (p. 734)

Prior, H., Schwarz, A., & Güntürkün, O. (2008). Mirror-induced behavior in the magpie (*Pica pica*): Evidence of self-recognition. *PloS Biology, 6,* 1642–1650. (p. 495)

Proffitt, D. R. (2006a). Embodied perception and the economy of action. *Perspectives on Psychological Science, 1,* 110–122. (p. 166)

Proffitt, D.R. (2006b). Distance perception. *Current Directions in Psychological Research, 15,* 131–135. (p. 166)

Project Match Research Group. (1997). Matching alcoholism treatments to client heterogeneity: Project MATCH posttreatment drinking outcomes. *Journal of Studies on Alcohol, 58,* 7–29. (p. 724)

Pronin, E. (2007). Perception and misperception of bias in human judgment. *Trends in Cognitive Sciences, 11,* 37–43. (p. 596)

Pronin, E., Berger, J., & Molouki, S. (2007). Alone in a crowd of sheep: Asymmetric perceptions of conformity and their roots in an introspection illusion. *Journal of Personality and Social Psychology, 92,* 585–595. (p. 765)

Pronin, E., & Ross, L. (2006). Temporal differences in trait self-ascription: When the self is seen as an other. *Journal of Personality and Social Psychology, 90,* 197–209. (p. 755)

Propper, R. E., Stickgold, R., Keeley, R., & Christman, S. D. (2007). Is television traumatic? Dreams, stress, and media exposure in the aftermath of September 11, 2001. *Psychological Science, 18,* 334–340. (p. 240)

Provine, R. R. (2001). *Laughter: A scientific investigation.* New York: Penguin. (p. 41)

Provine, R. R., Krosnowski, K. A., & Brocato, N. W. (2009). Tearing: Breakthrough in human emotional signaling. *Evolutionary Psychology, 7,* 52–56. (p. 437)

Pryor, J. H., Eagan, K., Blake, L. P., Hurtado, S., Bertran, J., & Case, M. H. (2012). *The American Freshman: National Norms Fall 2012: Expanded edition.* Higher Education Research Institute, UCLA. (p. 441)

Pryor, J. H., Hurtado, S., DeAngelo, L., Blake, L. P., & Tran, S. (2010). *The American Freshman: National Norms Fall 2009: Expanded edition.* Higher Education Research Institute, UCLA. (p. 639)

Pryor, J. H., Hurtado, S., Saenz, V. B., Korn, J. S., Santos, J. L., & Korn, W. S. (2006). *The American freshman: National norms for fall 2006.* Los Angeles: UCLA Higher Education Research Institute. (p. 679)

Przybylski, A. K., Rigby, C. S., & Ryan, R. M. (2010). A motivational model of video game engagement. *Review of General Psychology, 14,* 154–166. (p. 795)

Psychologist. (2003, April). Who's the greatest? *The Psychologist, 16,* p. 17. (p. 484)

PTC. (2007, January 10). *Dying to entertain: Violence on prime time broadcast TV, 1998 to 2006.* Parents Television Council (www.parentstv.org). (p. 308)

Puetz, T. W., O'Connor, P. J., & Dishman, R. K. (2006). Effects of chronic exercise on feelings of energy and fatigue: A quantitative synthesis. *Psychological Bulletin, 132,* 866–876. (p. 860)

Pulkkinen, L. (2004). A longitudinal study on social development as an impetus for school reform toward an integrated school day. *European Psychologist, 9,* 125–141. (p. 495)

Pulkkinen, L. (2006). The Jyväskylä longitudinal study of personality and social development (JYLS). In L. Pulkkinen, J. Kaprio, & R. J. Rose (Eds.), *Socioemotional development and health from adolescence to adulthood.* Cambridge studies on child and adolescent health. New York: Cambridge University Press. (p. 495)

Putnam, F. W. (1991). Recent research on multiple personality disorder. *Psychiatric Clinics of North America, 14,* 489–502. (p. 696)

Putnam, F. W. (1995). Rebuttal of Paul McHugh. *Journal of the American Academy of Child and Adolescent Psychiatry, 34,* 963. (p. 696)

Putnam, R. (2000). *Bowling alone.* New York: Simon and Schuster. (p. 778)

Pyszczynski, T. A., Hamilton, J. C., Greenberg, J., & Becker, S. E. (1991). Self-awareness and psychological dysfunction. In C. R. Snyder & D. O. Forsyth (Eds.), *Handbook of social and clinical psychology: The health perspective.* New York: Pergamon. (p. 680)

Pyszczynski, T. A., Rothschild, Z., & Abdollahi, A. (2008). Terrorism, violence, and hope for peace: A terror management perspective. *Current Directions in Psychological Science 17,* 318–322. (p. 785)

Pyszczynski, T. A., Solomon, S., & Greenberg, J. (2002). *In the wake of 9/11: The psychology of terror.* Washington, DC: American Psychological Association. (p. 785)

Qirko, H. N. (2004). "Fictive kin" and suicide terrorism. *Science, 304,* 49–50. (p. 774)

Quasha, S. (1980). *Albert Einstein: An intimate portrait.* New York: Forest. (p. 627)

Quinn, P. C. (2002). Category representation in young infants. *Current Directions in Psychological Science, 11,* 66–70. (p. 468)

Quinn, P. C., Bhatt, R. S., Brush, D., Grimes, A., & Sharpnack, H. (2002). Development of form similarity as a Gestalt grouping principle in infancy. *Psychological Science, 13,* 320–328. (p. 183)

Quinn, P. J., Williams, G. M., Najman, J. M., Andersen, M. J., & Bor, W. (2001). The effect of breastfeeding on child development at 5 years: A cohort study. *Journal of Pediatrics & Child Health, 3,* 465–469. (p. 50)

Quoidbach, J., Dunn, E. W., Petrides, K. V., & Mikolajczak, M. (2010). Money giveth, money taketh away: The dual effect of wealth on happiness. *Psychological Science, 21,* 759–763. (p. 850)

Rabbitt, P. (2006). Tales of the unexpected: 25 years of cognitive gerontology. *The Psychologist, 19,* 674–676. (p. 543)

Rabinowicz, T., Dean, D. E., Petetot, J. M., & de Courten-Myers, G. M. (1999). Gender differences in the human cerebral cortex: More neurons in males; more processes in females. *Journal of Child Neurology, 14,* 98–107. (p. 471)

Rabinowicz, T., deCourten-Myers, G. M., Petetot, J. M., Xi, G., & de los Reyes, E. (1996). Human cortex development: Estimates of neuronal numbers indicate major loss late during gestation. *Journal of Neuropathology and Experimental Neurology, 55,* 320–328. (p. 471)

Rabins, P., & 18 others. (2009). Scientific and ethical issues related to deep brain stimulation for disorders of mood, behavior, and thought. *Archives of General Psychiatry, 66,* 931–937. (p. 746)

Racsmány, M., Conway, M. A., & Demeter, G. (2010). Consolidation of episodic memories during sleep: Long-term effects of retrieval practice. *Psychological Science, 21,* 80–85. (p. 231)

Radford, B. (2010, February 18). Tiger Woods and sex addiction: Real disease or easy excuse? LiveScience.com (accessed via news.yahoo.com). (p. 248)

Radford, B. (March/April 2010). The psychic and the serial killer: Examining the 'best case' for psychic detectives. *Skeptical Inquirer, 34*(2): 32–37. (p. 167)

Rahman, Q., & Koerting, J. (2008). Sexual orientation-related differences in allocentric spatial memory tasks. *Hippocampus, 18,* 55–63. (pp. 535, 536)

Rahman, Q., & Wilson, G. D. (2003). Born gay? The psychobiology of human sexual orientation. *Personality and Individual Differences, 34,* 1337–1382. (p. 534)

Rahman, Q., Wilson, G. D., & Abrahams, S. (2003). Biosocial factors, sexual orientation and neurocognitive functioning. *Psychoneuroendocrinology, 29,* 867–881. (p. 536)

Raichle, M. (2010, March). The brain's dark energy. *Scientific American,* pp. 44–49. (p. 121)

Raine, A. (1999). Murderous minds: Can we see the mark of Cain? *Cerebrum: The Dana Forum on Brain Science 1*(1), 15–29. (pp. 700, 790)

Raine, A. (2005). The interaction of biological and social measures in the explanation of antisocial and violent behavior. In D. M. Stoff & E. J. Susman (Eds.) *Developmental psychobiology of aggression.* New York: Cambridge University Press. (pp. 700, 790)

Raine, A., Brennan, P., Mednick, B., & Mednick, S. A. (1996). High rates of violence, crime, academic problems, and behavioral problems in males with both early neuromotor deficits and unstable family environments. *Archives of General Psychiatry, 53,* 544–549. (pp. 700, 701)

Raine, A., Lencz, T., Bihrle, S., LaCasse, L., & Colletti, P. (2000). Reduced prefrontal gray matter volume and reduced autonomic activity in antisocial personality disorder. *Archives of General Psychiatry, 57,* 119–127. (p. 700)

Rainie, L., Purcell, K., Goulet, L. S., & Hampton, K. H. (2011, June 16). Social networking sites and our lives. *Pew Research Center* (pewresearch.org). (p. 416)

Rainville, P., Duncan, G. H., Price, D. D., Carrier, B., & Bushnell, M. C. (1997). Pain affect encoded in human anterior cingulate but not somatosensory cortex. *Science, 277,* 968–971. (p. 222)

Raison, C. L., Klein, H. M., & Steckler, M. (1999). The mood and madness reconsidered. *Journal of Affective Disorders, 53,* 99–106. (p. 700)

Rajendran, G., & Mitchell, P. (2007). Cognitive theories of autism. *Developmental Review, 27,* 224–260. (p. 481)

Ralston, A. (2004). Enough rope. Interview for ABC TV, Australia, by Andrew Denton. (www.abc.net.au/enoughrope/stories/s1227885.htm). (p. 390)

Ramachandran, V. S., & Blakeslee, S. (1998). *Phantoms in the brain: Probing the mysteries of the human mind.* New York: Morrow. (pp. 88, 204)

Ramírez-Esparza, N., Gosling, S. D., Benet-Martínez, V., Potter, J. P., & Pennebaker, J. W. (2006). Do bilinguals have two personalities? A special case of cultural frame switching. *Journal of Research in Personality, 40,* 99–120. (p. 379)

Randi, J. (1999, February 4). 2000 club mailing list e-mail letter. (p. 169)

Randler, C. (2008). Morningness–eveningness and satisfaction with life. *Social Indicators Research, 86,* 297–302. (p. 226)

Randler, C. (2009). Proactive people are morning people. *Journal of Applied Social Psychology, 39,* 2787–2797. (p. 226)

Randler, C., & Bausback, V. (2010). Morningness-eveningness in women around the transition through menopause and its relationship with climacteric complaints. *Biological Rhythm Research, 41*, 415–431. (p. 226)

Randler, C., & Frech, D. (2009). Young people's time-of-day preferences affect their school performance. *Journal of Youth Studies, 12*, 653–667. (p. 226)

Rapoport, J. L. (1989, March). The biology of obsessions and compulsions. *Scientific American*, pp. 83–89. (pp. 664, 667)

Räsänen, S., Pakaslahti, A., Syvalahti, E., Jones, P. B., & Isohanni, M. (2000). Sex differences in schizophrenia: A review. *Nordic Journal of Psychiatry, 54*, 37–45. (p. 686)

Rasch, B., & Born, J. (2008). Reactivation and consolidation of memory during sleep. *Current Directions in Psychological Science, 17*, 188–192. (p. 231)

Rasmussen, H. N., Scheier, M. F., & Greenhouse, J. B. (2009). Optimism and physical health: A meta-analytic review. *Annals of Behavioral Medicine, 37*, 239–256. (p. 856)

Rath, T., & Harter, J. K. (2010, August 19). Your friends and your social wellbeing: Close friendships are vital to health, happiness, and even workplace productivity. *Gallup Business Journal* (http://businessjournal.gallup.com/content/127043/friends-social-wellbeing.aspx). (p. 839)

Ray, J. (2005, April 12). U.S. teens walk away from anger: Boys and girls manage anger differently. *The Gallup Organization* (www.gallup.com). (p. 845)

Ray, O., & Ksir, C. (1990). *Drugs, society, and human behavior* (5th ed.). St. Louis: Times Mirror/Mosby. (p. 253)

Raynor, H. A., & Epstein, L. H. (2001). Dietary variety, energy regulation, and obesity. *Psychological Bulletin, 127*, 325–341. (p. 399)

Raz, A., Fan, J., & Posner, M. I. (2005). Hypnotic suggestion reduces conflict in the human brain. *PNAS, 102*, 9978–9983. (p. 222)

Read, J., & Bentall, R. (2010). The effectiveness of electroconvulsive therapy: A literature review. *Epidemiologica e Psichiatria Sociale, 19*, 333–347. (p. 744)

Reason, J. (1987). The Chernobyl errors. *Bulletin of the British Psychological Society, 40*, 201–206. (p. 775)

Reason, J., & Mycielska, K. (1982). *Absent-minded? The psychology of mental lapses and everyday errors.* Englewood Cliffs, NJ: Prentice-Hall. (p. 164)

Reed, P. (2000). Serial position effects in recognition memory for odors. *Journal of Experimental Psychology: Learning, Memory, and Cognition, 26*, 411–422. (p. 338)

Reed, T. E., & Jensen, A. R. (1992). Conduction velocity in a brain nerve pathway of normal adults correlates with intelligence level. *Intelligence, 16*, 259–272. (p. 614)

Rees, M. (1999). *Just six numbers: The deep forces that shape the universe.* New York: Basic Books. (p. 142)

Reichardt, C. S. (2010). Testing astrological predictions about sex, marriage, and selfishness. *Skeptic Magazine, 15*(4), 40–45. (p. 579)

Reichenberg, A., Gross, R., Weiser, M., Bresnahan, M., Silverman, J., Harlap, S., Rabinoqitz, J., Shulman, C., Malaspina, D., Lubin, G., Knobler, H Y., Davidson, M., & Susser, E. (2007). Advancing paternal age and autism. *Archives of General Psychiatry, 63*, 1026–1032. (p. 482)

Reichenberg, A., & Harvey, P. D. (2007). Neuropsychological impairments in schizophrenia: Integration of performance-based and brain imaging findings. *Psychological Bulletin, 133*, 833–858. (p. 685)

Reichert, R. A., Robb, M. B., Fender, J. G., & Wartella, E. (2010). Word learning from baby videos. *Archives of Pediatrics & Adolescent Medicine, 164*, 432–437. (p. 635)

Reichle, E. D., Reineberg, A. E., & Schooler, J. W. (2010). Eye movements during mindless reading. *Psychological Science, 21*, 1300–1310. (p. 121)

Reifman, A. S., & Cleveland, H. H. (2007). Shared environment: A quantitative review. Paper presented to the Society for Research in Child Development, Boston, MA. (p. 128)

Reifman, A. S., Larrick, R. P., & Fein, S. (1991). Temper and temperature on the diamond: The heat-aggression relationship in major league baseball. *Personality and Social Psychology Bulletin, 17*, 580–585. (p. 791)

Reimann, F., & 24 others. (2010). Pain perception is altered by a nucleotide polymorphism in SCN9A. *PNAS, 107*, 5148–5153. (p. 203)

Reiner, W. G., & Gearhart, J. P. (2004). Discordant sexual identity in some genetic males with cloacal exstrophy assigned to female sex at birth. *New England Journal of Medicine, 350*, 333–341. (p. 528)

Reis, D., & Marino, L. (2001). Mirror self-recognition in the bottlenose dolphin: A case of cognitive convergence. *PNAS, 98*, 5937–5942. (p. 495)

Reis, H. T., & Aron, A. (2008). Love: What is it, why does it matter, and how does it operate? *Perspectives on Psychological Science, 3*, 80–86. (p. 803)

Reis, H. T., Smith, S. M., Carmichael, C. L., Caprariello, P. A., Tsa, F-F., Rodrigues, A., & Maniaci, M. R. (2010). Are you happy for me? How sharing positive events with others provides personal and interpersonal benefits. *Journal of Personality and Social Psychology, 99*, 311–329. (p. 412)

Reisenzein, R. (1983). The Schachter theory of emotion: Two decades later. *Psychological Bulletin, 94*, 239–264. (p. 423)

Reiser, M. (1982). *Police psychology.* Los Angeles: LEHI. (p. 167)

Reitzle, M. (2006). The connections between adulthood transitions and the self-perception of being adult in the changing contexts of East and West Germany. *European Psychologist, 11*, 25–38. (p. 523)

Remick, A. K., Polivy, J., & Pliner, P. (2009). Internal and external moderators of the effect of variety on food intake. *Psychological Bulletin, 135*, 434–451. (p. 401)

Remington, A., Swettenham, J., Campbell, R., & Coleman, M. (2009). Selective attention and perceptual load in autism spectrum disorder. *Psychological Science, 20*, 1388–1393. (p. 481)

Remley, A. (1988, October). From obedience to independence. *Psychology Today*, pp. 56–59. (p. 497)

Renner, M. J., & Renner, C. H. (1993). Expert and novice intuitive judgments about animal behavior. *Bulletin of the Psychonomic Society, 31*, 551–552. (p. 508)

Renner, M. J., & Rosenzweig, M. R. (1987). *Enriched and impoverished environments: Effects on brain and behavior.* New York: Springer-Verlag. (p. 508)

Renninger, K. A., & Granott, N. (2005). The process of scaffolding in learning and development. *New Ideas in Psychology, 23*(3), 111–114. (p. 484)

Rentfrow, P. J., & Gosling, S. D. (2003). The Do Re Mi's of everyday life: The structure and personality correlates of music preferences. *Journal of Personality and Social Psychology, 84*, 1236–1256. (p. 583)

Rentfrow, P. J., & Gosling, S. D. (2006). Message in a ballad: The role of music preferences in interpersonal perception. *Psychological Science, 17*, 236–242. (p. 583)

Repetti, R. L., Taylor, S. E., & Seeman, T. E. (2002). Risky families: Family social environments and the mental and physical health of offspring. *Psychological Bulletin, 128*, 330–366. (p. 442)

Repetti, R. L., Wang, S-W., & Saxbe, D. (2009). Bringing it all back home: How outside stressors shape families' everyday lives. *Current Directions in Psychological Science, 18*, 106–111. (p. 444)

Rescorla, R. A., & Wagner, A. R. (1972). A theory of Pavlovian conditioning: Variations in the effectiveness of reinforcement and nonreinforcement. In A. H. Black & W. F. Perokasy (Eds.), *Classical conditioning II: Current theory.* New York: Appleton-Century-Crofts. (p. 296)

Resnick, M. D., Bearman, P. S., Blum, R. W., Bauman, K. E., Harris, K. M., Jones, J., Tabor, J., Beuhring, T., Sieving, R., Shew, M., Bearinger, L. H., & Udry, J. R. (1997). Protecting adolescents from harm: Findings from the National Longitudinal Study on Adolescent Health. *Journal of the American Medical Association, 278*, 823–832. (pp. 49, 154, 522)

Resnick, S. M. (1992). Positron emission tomography in psychiatric illness. *Current Directions in Psychological Science, 1*, 92–98. (p. 687)

Rethorst, C. D., Wipfli, B. M., & Landers, D. M. (2009). The antidepressive effects of exercise: A meta-analysis of randomized trials. *Sports Medicine, 39*, 491–511. (p. 860)

Reuters. (2000, July 5). Many teens regret decision to have sex (National Campaign to Prevent Teen Pregnancy survey). www.washingtonpost.com. (p. 530)

Reyna, V. F., & Farley, F. (2006). Risk and rationality in adolescent decision making: Implications for theory, practice, and public policy. *Psychological Science in the Public Interest, 7*(1), 1–44. (p. 514)

Reynolds, C. R., Niland, J., Wright, J. E., & Rosenn, M. (2010). Failure to apply the Flynn correction in death penalty litigation: Standard practice of today maybe, but certainly malpractice of tomorrow. *Journal of Psychoeducational Assessment, 28*, 477–481. (p. 629)

Reynolds, G. (2009, November 18). Phys ed: Why exercise makes you less anxious. *New York Times blog* (well.blogs.nytimes.com). (p. 860)

Rhoades, G. K., Stanley, S. M., & Markman, H. J. (2009). The pre-engagement cohabitation effect: A replication and extension of previous findings. *Journal of Family Psychology, 23*, 107–111. (p. 545)

Rhodes, G., Sumich, A., & Byatt, G. (1999). Are average facial configurations attractive only because of their symmetry? *Psychological Science, 10*, 52–58. (p. 802)

Rholes, W. S., & Simpson, J. A. (Eds.) (2004). *Adult attachment: Theory, research, and clinical implications.* New York: Guilford. (p. 492)

Rholes, W. S., Simpson, J. A., & Friedman, M. (2006). Avoidant attachment and the experience of parenting. *Personality and Social Psychology Bulletin, 32,* 275–285. (p. 492)

Ribeiro, R., Gervasoni, D., Soares, E. S., Zhou, Y., Lin, S-C., Pantoja, J., Lavine, M., & Nicolelis, M. A. L. (2004). Long-lasting novelty-induced neuronal reverberation during slow-wave sleep in multiple forebrain areas. *PloS Biology, 2*(1), e37 (www.plosbiology.org). (p. 231)

Ricciardelli, L. A., & McCabe, M. P. (2004). A biopsychosocial model of disordered eating and the pursuit of muscularity in adolescent boys. *Psychological Bulletin, 130,* 179–205. (p. 697)

Rice, M. E., & Grusec, J. E. (1975). Saying and doing: Effects on observer performance. *Journal of Personality and Social Psychology, 32,* 584–593. (p. 308)

Richeson, J. A., & Shelton, J. N. (2007). Negotiating interracial interactions. *Current Directions in Psychological Science, 16,* 316–320. (p. 813)

Rieff, P. (1979). *Freud: The mind of a moralist* (3rd ed.). Chicago: University of Chicago Press. (p. 562)

Riis, J., Loewenstein, G., Baron, J., Jepson, C., Fagerlin, A., & Ubel, P. A. (2005). Ignorance of hedonic adaptation to hemodialysis: A study using ecological momentary assessment. *Journal of Experimental Psychology: General, 134,* 3–9. (p. 848)

Riley, L. D., & Bowen, C. (2005). The sandwich generation: Challenges and coping strategies of multigenerational families. *The Family Journal, 13,* 52–58. (p. 544)

Rindermann, H., & Ceci, S. J. (2009). Educational policy and country outcomes in international cognitive competence studies. *Perspectives on Psychological Science, 4,* 551–577. (p. 641)

Riordan, M. (2013, March 19). Tobacco warning labels: Evidence of effectiveness. Washington, DC: The Campaign for Tobacco-Free Kids (www.tobaccofreekids.org<http://www.tobaccofreekids.org>). (p. 365)

Ripple, C. H., & Zigler, E. F. (2003). Research, policy, and the federal role in prevention initiatives for children. *American Psychologist, 58,* 482–490. (p. 635)

Risch, N., Herrell, R., Lehner, T., Liang, K. Y., Eaves, L., Hoh, J., Griem, A., Ott, J., & Merikangas, K. R. (2009) Interaction between the serotonin transporter gene (5-HTTLPR), stressful life events, and risk of depression: a meta-analysis. *Journal of the American Medical Association, 301,* 2462–2471. (p. 678)

Rizzolatti, G., Fadiga, L., Fogassi, L., & Gallese, V. (2002). From mirror neurons to imitation: Facts and speculations. In A. N. Meltzoff & W. Prinz (Eds.), *The imitative mind: Development, evolution, and brain bases.* Cambridge: Cambridge University Press. (p. 305)

Rizzolatti, G., Fogassi, L., & Gallese, V. (2006, November). Mirrors in the mind. *Scientific American,* pp. 54–61. (p. 305)

Roberson, D., Davidoff, J., Davies, I. R. L., & Shapiro, L. R. (2004). The development of color categories in two languages: A longitudinal study. *Journal of Experimental Psychology: General, 133,* 554–571. (p. 379)

Roberson, D., Davies, I. R. L., Corbett, G. G., & Vandervyver, M. (2005). Free-sorting of colors across cultures: Are there universal grounds for grouping? *Journal of Cognition and Culture, 5,* 349–386. (p. 379)

Roberts, B. W., Caspi, A., & Moffitt, T. E. (2001). The kids are alright: Growth and stability in personality development from adolescence to adulthood. *Journal of Personality and Social Psychology, 81,* 670–683. (p. 464)

Roberts, B. W., Caspi, A., & Moffitt, T. E. (2003). Work experiences and personality development in young adulthood. *Journal of Personality and Social Psychology, 84,* 582–593. (p. 464)

Roberts, B. W., & DelVecchio, W. F. (2000). The rank-order consistency of personality traits from childhood to old age: A quantitative review of longitudinal studies. *Psychological Bulletin, 126,* 3–25. (p. 582)

Roberts, B. W., Kuncel, N. R., Shiner, R., Caspi, A., & Goldberg, L. R. (2007). The power of personality: The comparative validity of personality traits, socioeconomic status, and cognitive ability for predicting important life outcomes. *Perspectives on Psychological Science, 2,* 313–345. (p. 583)

Roberts, B. W., & Mroczek, D. (2008). Personality trait change in adulthood. *Current Directions in Psychological Science, 17,* 31–35. (p. 464)

Roberts, B. W., Walton, K. E., & Viechtbauer, W. (2006). Patterns of mean-level change in personality traits across the life course: A meta-analysis of longitudinal studies. *Psychological Bulletin, 132,* 1-25. (p. 464)

Roberts, L. (1988). Beyond Noah's ark: What do we need to know? *Science, 242,* 1247. (p. 300)

Roberts, T-A. (1991). Determinants of gender differences in responsiveness to others' evaluations. *Dissertation Abstracts International, 51*(8–B). (p. 502)

Robertson, K. F., Smeets, S., Lubinski, D., & Benbow, C. P. (2010). Beyond the threshold hypothesis: Even among the gifted and top math/science graduate students, cognitive abilitieis, vocational interests, and lifestyle preferences matter for career choice, performance, and persistence. *Current Directions in Psychological Science, 19,* 346–351. (p. 357)

Robins, L. N., & Regier, D. A. (Eds.). (1991). *Psychiatric disorders in America.* New York: Free Press. (p. 658)

Robins, L. N., Davis, D. H., & Goodwin, D. W. (1974). Drug use by U.S. Army enlisted men in Vietnam: A follow-up on their return home. *American Journal of Epidemiology, 99,* 235–249. (p. 824)

Robins, R. W., & Trzesniewski, K. H. (2005). Self-esteem development across the lifespan. *Current Directions in Psychological Science, 14*(3), 158–162. (p. 546)

Robins, R. W., Trzesniewski, K. H., Tracy, J. L., Gosling, S. D., & Potter, J. (2002). Global self-esteem across the lifespan. *Psychology and Aging, 17,* 423–434. (p. 521)

Robinson, F. P. (1970). *Effective study.* New York: Harper & Row. (p. 16)

Robinson, J. P., & Martin, S. (2008). What do happy people do? *Social Indicators Research, 89,* 565–571. (p. 828)

Robinson, J. P., & Martin, S. (2009). Changes in American daily life: 1965–2005. *Social Indicators Research, 93,* 47–56. (pp. 229, 308)

Robinson, T. E., & Berridge, K. C. (2003). Addiction. *Annual Review of Psychology, 54,* 25–53. (p. 248)

Robinson, T. N. (1999). Reducing children's television viewing to prevent obesity. *Journal of the American Medical Association, 282,* 1561–1567. (p. 403)

Robinson, T. N., Borzekowski, D. L. G., Matheson, D. M., & Kraemer, H. C. (2007). Effects of fast food branding on young children's taste preferences. *Archives of Pediatric and Adolescent Medicine, 161,* 792–797. (p. 164)

Robinson, V. M. (1983). Humor and health. In P. E. McGhee & J. H. Goldstein (Eds.), *Handbook of humor research: Vol. II. Applied studies.* New York: Springer-Verlag. (p. 857)

Rochat, F. (1993). How did they resist authority? Protecting refugees in Le Chambon during World War II. Paper presented at the American Psychological Association convention. (p. 767)

Rock, I., & Palmer, S. (1990, December). The legacy of Gestalt psychology. *Scientific American,* pp. 84–90. (pp. 182, 183)

Rodenburg, R., Benjamin, A., de Roos, C., Meijer, A. M., & Stams, G. J. (2009). Efficacy of EMDR in children: A meta-analysis. *Clinical Psychology Review, 29,* 599–606. (p. 733)

Rodin, J. (1986). Aging and health: Effects of the sense of control. *Science, 233,* 1271–1276. (pp. 299, 300)

Roediger, H. L., III, & Finn, B. (2010, March/April). The pluses of getting it wrong. *Scientific American Mind,* pp. 39–41. (p. 16)

Roediger, H. L., III, & Karpicke, J. D. (2006). Test-enhanced learning: Taking memory tests improves long-term retention. *Psychological Science, 17,* 249–255. (pp. 16, 324)

Roediger, H. L., III, & McDermott, K. B. (1995). Creating false memories: Remembering words not presented in lists. *Journal of Experimental Psychology: Learning, Memory, and Cognition, 21,* 803–814. (p. 350)

Roediger, H. L., III, Wheeler, M. A., & Rajaram, S. (1993). Remembering, knowing, and reconstructing the past. In D. L. Medin (Ed.), *The psychology of learning and motivation: Advances in research and theory* (Vol. 30). Orlando, FL: Academic Press. (p. 349)

Roehling, P. V., Roehling, M. V., & Moen, P. (2001). The relationship between work-life policies and practices and employee loyalty: A life course perspective. *Journal of Family and Economic Issues, 22,* 141–170. (p. 839)

Roelofs, T. (2010, September 22). Somali refugee takes oath of U.S. citizenship year after his brother. *Grand Rapids Press* (www.mlive.com). (p. 836)

Roenneberg, T., Kuehnle, T., Pramstaller, P. P., Ricken, J., Havel, M., Guth, A., Merrow, M. (2004). A marker for the end of adolescence. *Current Biology, 14,* R1038–9. (p. 226)

Roese, N. J., & Summerville, A. (2005). What we regret most . . . and why. *Personality and Social Psychology Bulletin, 31,* 1273–1285. (p. 546)

Roesser, R. (1998). What you should know about hearing conservation. *Better Hearing Institute* (www.betterhearing.org). (p. 197)

Roest, A. M., Martens, E. J., Denollet, J., & De Jonge, P. (2010). Prognostic association of anxiety post myocardial infarction with mortality and new cardiac events: A meta-analysis. *Psychosomatic Medicine, 72,* 563–569. (p. 453)

Rofé, Y. (2008). Does repression exist? Memory, pathogenic, unconscious and clinical evidence. *Review of General Psychology, 12,* 63–85. (p. 563)

Rogers, C. R. (1958). Reinhold Niebuhr's *The self and the dramas of history:* A criticism. *Pastoral Psychology, 9,* 15–17. (p. 596)

Rogers, C. R. (1961). *On becoming a person: A therapist's view of psychotherapy.* Boston: Houghton Mifflin. (p. 712)

Rogers, C. R. (1980). *A way of being.* Boston: Houghton Mifflin. (pp. 572, 712)

Rohan, K. J., Roecklein, K. A., Lindsey, K. T., Johnson, L. G., Lippy, R. D., Lacy, T. J., & Barton, F. B. (2007). A randomized controlled trial of cognitive-behavioral therapy, light therapy, and their combination for seasonal affective disorder. *Journal of Consulting and Clinical Psychology, 75,* 489–500. (p. 734)

Rohner, R. P. (1986). *The warmth dimension: Foundations of parental acceptance-rejection theory.* Newbury Park, CA: Sage. (p. 463)

Rohner, R. P., & Veneziano, R. A. (2001). The importance of father love: History and contemporary evidence. *Review of General Psychology, 5,* 382–405. (pp. 492, 496)

Rohrer, D., & Pashler, H. (2007). Increasing retention without increasing study time. *Current Directions in Psychological Science, 16,* 183–186. (p. 324)

Roiser, J. P., Cook, L. J., Cooper, J. D., Rubinsztein, D. C., & Sahakian, B. J. (2005). Association of a functional polymorphism in the serotonin transporter gene with abnormal emotional processing in ecstasy users. *American Journal of Psychiatry, 162,* 609–612. (p. 254)

Rokach, A., Orzeck, T., Moya, M., & Exposito, F. (2002). Causes of loneliness in North America and Spain. *European Psychologist, 7,* 70–79. (p. 65)

Ronay, R., & von Hippel, W. (2010). The presence of an attractive woman elevates testosterone and physical risk taking in young men. *Social Psychology and Personality Science, 1,* 57–64. (p. 408)

Roney, J. R., Hanson, K. N., Durante, K. M., & Maestripieri, D. (2006). Reading men's faces: Women's mate attractiveness judgments track men's testosterone and interest in infants. *Proceedings of the Royal Society B, 273,* 2169–2175. (p. 138)

Root, T. L., Thornton, L. M., Lindroos, A. K., Stunkard, A. J., Lichtenstein, P., Pedersen, N. L., Rasmussen, F., & Bulik, C. M. (2010). Shared and unique genetic and environmental influences on binge eating and night eating: A Swedish twin study. *Eating Behaviors, 11,* 92–98. (p. 697)

Rosa-Alcázar, A. I., Sáncez-Meca, J., Gómez-Conesa, A., & Marín-Martínez, F. (2008). Psychological treatment of obsessive-compulsive disorder: A meta-analysis. *Clinical Psychology Review, 28,* 1310–1325. (p. 717)

Rosch, E. (1978). Principles of categorization. In E. Rosch & B. L. Lloyd (Eds.), *Cognition and categorization.* Hillsdale, NJ: Erlbaum. (p. 356)

Rose, A. J., & Rudolph, K. D. (2006). A review of sex differences in peer relationship processes: Potential trade-offs for the emotional and behavioral development of girls and boys. *Psychological Bulletin, 132,* 98–131. (p. 502)

Rose, J. S., Chassin, L., Presson, C. C., & Sherman, S. J. (1999). Peer influences on adolescent cigarette smoking: A prospective sibling analysis. *Merrill-Palmer Quarterly, 45,* 62–84. (p. 511)

Rose, R. J. (2004). Developmental research as impetus for school reform. *European Psychologist, 9,* 142–144. (p. 495)

Rose, R. J., Viken, R. J., Dick, D. M., Bates, J. E., Pulkkinen, L., & Kaprio, J. (2003). It *does* take a village: Nonfamiliar environments and children's behavior. *Psychological Science, 14,* 273–277. (p. 511)

Rose, S. (1999). Precis of lifelines: Biology, freedom, determinism. *Behavioral and Brain Sciences, 22,* 871–921. (p. 139)

Roselli, C. E., Larkin, K., Schrunk, J. M., & Stormshak, F. (2004). Sexual partner preference, hypothalamic morphology and aromatase in rams. *Physiology and Behavior, 83,* 233–245. (p. 534)

Roselli, C. E., Resko, J. A., & Stormshak, F. (2002). Hormonal influences on sexual partner preference in rams. *Archives of Sexual Behavior, 31,* 43–49. (p. 534)

Rosenbaum, J. E. (2009). Patient teenagers? A comparison of the sexual behavior of virginity pledgers and matched nonpledgers. *Pediatrics, 123,* e110–e120. (p. 530)

Rosenbaum, M. (1986). The repulsion hypothesis: On the nondevelopment of relationships. *Journal of Personality and Social Psychology, 51,* 1156–1166. (p. 802)

Rosenberg, N. A., Pritchard, J. K., Weber, J. L., Cann, H. M., Kidd, K. K., Zhivotosky, L. A., & Feldman, M. W. (2002). Genetic structure of human populations. *Science, 298,* 2381–2385. (pp. 136, 640)

Rosenberg, T. (2010, November 1). The opt-out solution. *New York Times* (www.nytimes.com). (p. 368)

Rosenhan, D. L. (1973). On being sane in insane places. *Science, 179,* 250–258. (p. 655)

Rosenthal, E. (2009, November 2). When texting kills, Britain offers path of prison. *New York Times* (www.nytimes.com). (p. 154)

Rosenthal, E. (2010, May 24). Climate fears turn to doubts among Britons. *New York Times* (www.nytimes.com). (p. 368)

Rosenthal, R., Hall, J. A., Archer, D., DiMatteo, M. R., & Rogers, P. L. (1979). The PONS test: Measuring sensitivity to nonverbal cues. In S. Weitz (Ed.), *Nonverbal communication* (2nd ed.). New York: Oxford University Press. (p. 433)

Rosenzweig, M. R. (1984). Experience, memory, and the brain. *American Psychologist, 39,* 365–376. (p. 508)

Rosenzweig, M. R., Krech, D., Bennett, E. L., & Diamond, M. C. (1962). Effects of environmental complexity and training on brain chemistry and anatomy: A replication and extension. *Journal of Comparative and Physiological Psychology, 55,* 429–437. (p. 508)

Roseth, C. J., Johnson, D. W., & Johnson, R. T. (2008). Promoting early adolescents' achievement and peer relationships: The effects of cooperative, competitive, and individualistic goal structures. *Psychological Bulletin, 134,* 223–246. (p. 814)

Rosin, H. (2010, July, August). The end of men. *The Atlantic* (www.theatlantic.com). (p. 504)

Ross, J. (2006, December). Sleep on a problem . . . it works like a dream. *The Psychologist, 19,* 738–740. (p. 231)

Ross, L. (1977). The intuitive psychologist and his shortcomings: Distortions in the attribution process. In L. Berkowitz (Ed.) *Advances in experimental social psychology* (Vol. 10). New York: Academic Press. (p. 754)

Ross, M., McFarland, C., & Fletcher, G. J. O. (1981). The effect of attitude on the recall of personal histories. *Journal of Personality and Social Psychology, 40,* 627–634. (p. 346)

Ross, M., Xun, W. Q. E., & Wilson, A. E. (2002). Language and the bicultural self. *Personality and Social Psychology Bulletin, 28,* 1040–1050. (p. 379)

Rossi, P. J. (1968). Adaptation and negative aftereffect to lateral optical displacement in newly hatched chicks. *Science, 160,* 430–432. (p. 191)

Rostosky, S. S., Riggle, E. D. G., Horne, S. G., Denton, F. N., & Huellemeier, J. D. (2010). Lesbian, gay, and bisexual individuals' psychological reactions to amendments denying access to civil marriage. *American Journal of Orthopsychiatry, 80,* 302–310. (p. 444)

Roth, T., Roehrs, T., Zwyghuizen-Doorenbos, A., Stpeanski, E., & Witting, R. (1988). Sleep and memory. In I. Hindmarch & H. Ott (Eds.), *Benzodiazepine receptor ligans, memory and information processing.* New York: Springer-Verlag. (p. 241)

Rothbart, M., Fulero, S., Jensen, C., Howard, J., & Birrell, P. (1978). From individual to group impressions: Availability heuristics in stereotype formation. *Journal of Experimental Social Psychology, 14,* 237–255. (p. 786)

Rothbart, M. K. (2007). Temperament, development, and personality. *Current Directions in Psychological Science, 16,* 207–212. (p. 490)

Rothbart, M. K., Ahadi, S. A., & Evans, D. E. (2000). Temperament and personality: Origins and outcomes. *Journal of Personality and Social Psychology, 78,* 122–135. (p. 491)

Rothbaum, F., & Tsang, B. Y-P. (1998). Lovesongs in the United States and China: On the nature of romantic love. *Journal of Cross-Cultural Psychology, 29,* 306–319. (p. 600)

Rothman, A. J., & Salovey, P. (1997). Shaping perceptions to motivate healthy behavior: The role of message framing. *Psychological Bulletin, 121,* 3–19. (p. 368)

Rotton, J., & Kelly, I. W. (1985). Much ado about the full moon: A metaanalysis of lunar-lunacy research. *Psychological Bulletin, 97,* 286–306. (p. 700)

Rovee-Collier, C. (1989). The joy of kicking: Memories, motives, and mobiles. In P. R. Solomon, G. R. Goethals, C. M. Kelley, & B. R. Stephens (Eds.), *Memory: Interdisciplinary approaches.* New York: Springer-Verlag. (p. 473)

Rovee-Collier, C. (1993). The capacity for long-term memory in infancy. *Current Directions in Psychological Science, 2,* 130–135. (p. 337)

Rovee-Collier, C. (1997). Dissociations in infant memory: Rethinking the development of implicit and explicit memory. *Psychological Review, 104,* 467–498. (p. 473)

Rovee-Collier, C. (1999). The development of infant memory. *Current Directions in Psychological Science, 8,* 80–85. (p. 473)

Rowe, D. C. (1990). As the twig is bent? The myth of child-rearing influences on personality development. *Journal of Counseling and Development, 68,* 606–611. (p. 128)

Rowe, D. C. (2005). Under the skin: On the impartial treatment of genetic and environmental hypotheses of racial differences. *American Psychologist, 60,* 60–70. (p. 640)

Rowe, D. C., Almeida, D. M., & Jacobson, K. C. (1999). School context and genetic influences on aggression in adolescence. *Psychological Science, 10,* 277–280. (p. 789)

Rowe, D. C., Jacobson, K. C., & Van den Oord, E. J. C. G. (1999). Genetic and environmental influences on vocabulary IQ: Parental education level as moderator. *Child Development, 70*(5), 1151–1162. (p. 633)

Rozin, P., Dow, S., Mosovitch, M., & Rajaram, S. (1998). What causes humans to begin and end a meal? A role for memory for what has been eaten, as evidenced by a study of multiple meal eating in amnesic patients. *Psychological Science, 9,* 392–396. (p 399)

Rozin, P., Millman, L., & Nemeroff, C. (1986). Operation of the laws of sympathetic magic in disgust and other domains. *Journal of Personality and Social Psychology, 50,* 703–712. (p. 270)

Rubenstein, J. S., Meyer, D. E., & Evans, J. E. (2001). Executive control of cognitive processes in task switching. *Journal of Experimental Psychology: Human Perception and Performance, 27,* 763–797. (p. 153)

Rubin, D. C., Berntsen, D., & Bohni, M. K. (2008). A memory-based model of posttraumatic stress disorder: Evaluating basic assumptions underlying the PTSD diagnosis. *Psychological Review, 115,* 985–1011. (p. 664)

Rubin, D. C., Rahhal, T. A., & Poon, L. W. (1998). Things learned in early adulthood are remembered best. *Memory and Cognition, 26,* 3–19. (p. 542)

Rubin, J. Z., Pruitt, D. G., & Kim, S. H. (1994). *Social conflict: Escalation, stalemate, and settlement.* New York: McGraw-Hill. (p. 814)

Rubin, L. B. (1985). *Just friends: The role of friendship in our lives.* New York: Harper & Row. (p. 503)

Rubin, Z. (1970). Measurement of romantic love. *Journal of Personality and Social Psychology, 16,* 265–273. (p. 432)

Rubio, G., & López-Ibor, J. J. (2007). Generalized anxiety disorder: A 40-year follow-up study. *Acta Psychiatrica Scandinavica, 115,* 372–379. (p. 662)

Ruchlis, H. (1990). *Clear thinking: A practical introduction.* Buffalo, NY: Prometheus Books. (p. 297)

Rudman, L. A., & Goodwin, S. A. (2004). Gender differences in automatic in-group bias: Why do women like women more than men like men? *Journal of Personality and Social Psychology, 87,* 494–509. (p. 783)

Rueckert, L., Doan, T., & Branch, B. (2010). Emotion and relationship effects on gender differences in empathy. Presented at the annual meeting of the Association for Psychological Science, Boston, MA, May, 2010. (p. 435)

Ruffin, C. L. (1993). Stress and health—little hassles vs. major life events. *Australian Psychologist, 28,* 201–208. (p. 444)

Rule, B. G., & Ferguson, T. J. (1986). The effects of media violence on attitudes, emotions, and cognitions. *Journal of Social Issues, 42*(3), 29–50. (p. 309)

Rule, N. O., Rosen, K. S., Slepian, M. L., & Ambady, N. (2011). Mating interest improves women's accuracy in judging male sexual orientation. *Psychological Science, 22,* 881–886. (p. 408)

Rumbaugh, D. M. (1977). *Language learning by a chimpanzee: The Lana project.* New York: Academic Press. (p. 869)

Rushton, J. P. (1975). Generosity in children: Immediate and long-term effects of modeling, preaching, and moral judgment. *Journal of Personality and Social Psychology, 31,* 459–466. (p. 308)

Russell, B. (1930/1985). *The conquest of happiness.* London: Unwin Paperbacks. (p. 852)

Russell, J. A. (2009). Emotion, core affect, and psychological construction. *Cognition and Emotion, 23,* 1259–1283. (p. 845)

Russell, J. A., & Carroll, J. M. (1999a, January). On the bipolarity of positive and negative affect. *Psychological Bulletin, 125,* 3–30. (p. 845)

Russell, J. A., & Carroll, J. M. (1999b). The phoenix of bipolarity: Reply to Watson and Tellegan (1999). *Psychological Bulletin, 125,* 611–614. (p. 845)

Russell, J. A., Lewicka, M., & Niit, T. (1989). A cross-cultural study of a circumplex model of affect. *Journal of Personality and Social Psychology, 57,* 848–856. (p. 845)

Rusting, C. L., & Nolen-Hoeksema, S. (1998). Regulating responses to anger: Effects of rumination and distraction on angry mood. *Journal of Personality and Social Psychology, 74,* 790–803. (p. 846)

Rutchick, A. M., Slepian, M. L., & Ferris, B. D. (2010). The pen is mightier than the word: Object priming of evaluative standards. *European Journal of Social Psychology, 40,* 704–708. (p. 264)

Ryan, R. (1999, February 2). Quoted by Alfie Kohn, In pursuit of affluence, at a high price. *New York Times* (www.nytimes.com). (pp. 850, 851)

Ryan, R. M., & Deci, E. L. (2004). Avoiding death or engaging life as accounts of meaning and culture: Comment on Pyszczynski et al. (2004). *Psychological Bulletin, 130,* 473–477. (p. 598)

Rydell, R. J., Rydell, M. T., & Boucher, K. L. (2010). The effect of negative performance stereotypes on learning. *Journal of Personality and Social Psychology, 99,* 883–896. (p. 642)

Ryder, A. G., Yang, J., Zhu, X., Yao, S., Yi, J., Heine, S. J., & Bagby, R. M. (2008). The cultural shaping of depression: Somatic symptoms in China, psychological symptoms in North America? *Journal of Abnormal Psychology, 117,* 300–313. (p. 693)

Ryugo, D. K., Baker, C. A., Montey K. L., Chang, L.Y., Coco, A., Fallon, J. B., Shepherd, R. K. (2010). Synaptic plasticity after chemical deafening and electrical stimulation of the auditory nerve in cats. *Journal of Comparative Neurology, 518,* 1046–1063. (p. 198)

Saad, L. (2002, November 21). Most smokers wish they could quit. *Gallup News Service* (www.gallup.com). (p. 252)

Saad, L. (2006, August 10). Anti-Muslim sentiments fairly commonplace. *Gallup News Service* (poll.gallup.com). (p. 781)

Saad, L. (2013, April 8). Americans' concerns about global warming on the rise. www.gallup.com. (p. 756)

Sabbagh, M. A., Xu, F., Carlson, S. M., Moses, L. J., & Lee, K. (2006). The development of executive functioning and theory of mind: A comparison of Chinese and U.S. preschoolers. *Psychological Science, 17,* 74–81. (p. 480)

Sabini, J. (1986). Stanley Milgram (1933–1984). *American Psychologist, 41,* 1378–1379. (p. 765)

Sachdev, P., & Sachdev, J. (1997). Sixty years of psychosurgery: Its present status and its future. *Australian and New Zealand Journal of Psychiatry, 31,* 457–464. (p. 746)

Sackett, P. R., Borneman, M. J., & Connelly, B. S. (2008). High-stakes testing in higher education and employment: Appraising the evidence for validity and fairness. *American Psychologist, 63,* 215–227. (p. 642)

Sackett, P. R., Hardison, C. M., & Cullen, M. J. (2004). On interpreting stereotype threat as accounting for African American–White differences on cognitive tests. *American Psychologist, 59,* 7–13. (p. 642)

Sackett, P. R., & Lievens, F. (2008). Personnel selection. *Annual Review of Psychology, 59,* 419–450. (p. 830)

Sacks, O. (1985). *The man who mistook his wife for a hat.* New York: Summit Books. (pp. 209, 342)

Sadato, N., Pascual-Leone, A., Grafman, J., Ibanez, V., Deiber, M-P., Dold, G., & Hallett, M. (1996). Activation of the primary visual cortex by Braille reading in blind subjects. *Nature, 380,* 526–528. (p. 111)

Saffran, J. A. (2009). What can statistical learning tell us about infant learning? In A. Woodward & A. Needham (eds.), *Learning and the infant mind.* New York: Oxford University Press. (p. 376)

Saffran, J. R., Aslin, R. N., & Newport, E. L. (1996). Statistical learning by 8-month-old infants. *Science, 274,* 1926–1928. (p. 376)

Sagan, C. (1979). *Broca's brain.* New York: Random House. (p. 35)

Sagan, C. (1987, February 1). The fine art of baloney detection. *Parade.* (p. 168)

Salmela-Aro, K., Tolvanen, A., & Nurmi, J. (2009). Achievement strategies during university studies predict early career burnout and engagement. *Journal of Vocational Behavior, 75,* 162–172. (p. 831)

Salmon, P. (2001). Effects of physical exercise on anxiety, depression, and sensitivity to stress: A unifying theory. *Clinical Psychology Review, 21,* 33–61. (p. 860)

Salovey, P. (1990, January/February). Interview. *American Scientist,* 25–29. (p. 847)

Salthouse, T. A. (2004). What and when of cognitive aging. *Current Directions in Psychological Science, 13,* 140–144. (p. 626)

Salthouse, T. A. (2009). When does age-related cognitive decline begin? *Neurobiology of Aging, 30,* 507–514. (p. 626)

Salthouse, T. A. (2010b). Selective review of cognitive aging. *Journal of the International Neuropsychological Society, 16,* 754–760. (p. 627)

Sampson, E. E. (2000). Reinterpreting individualism and collectivism: Their religious roots and monologic versus dialogic person–other relationship. *American Psychologist, 55,* 1425–1432. (p. 598)

Samuels, J., & Nestadt, G. (1997). Epidemiology and genetics of obsessive-compulsive disorder. *International Review of Psychiatry, 9,* 61–71. (p. 664)

Samuels, S., & McCabe, G. (1989). Quoted by P. Diaconis & F. Mosteller, Methods for studying coincidences. *Journal of the American Statistical Association, 84,* 853–861. (p. 34)

Sánchez-Villegas, A., Delgado-Rodríguez, M., Alonson, A., Schlatter, J., Lahortiga, F., Majem, L. S., & Martínez-González, M. A. (2009). Association of the Mediterranean dietary pattern with the incidence of depression. *Archives of General Psychiatry, 66,* 1090–1098. (p. 679)

Sandfort, T. G. M., de Graaf, R., Bijl, R., & Schnabel, P. (2001). Same-sex sexual behavior and psychiatric disorders. *Archives of General Psychiatry, 58,* 85–91. (p. 532)

Sandkühler, S., & Bhattacharya, J. (2008). Deconstructing insight: EEG correlates of insightful problem solving. *PloS ONE, 3,* e1459 (www.plosone.org). (p. 361)

Sandler, W., Meir, I., Padden, C., & Aronoff, M. (2005). The emergence of grammar: Systematic structure in a new language. *Proceedings of the National Academy of Sciences, 102,* 2261–2265. (p. 376)

Santomauro, J., & French, C. C. (2009). Terror in the night. *The Psychologist, 22,* 672–675. (p. 229)

Santos, A., Meyer-Lindenberg, A., & Deruelle, C. (2010). Absence of racial, but not gender, stereotyping in Williams syndrome children. *Current Biology, 20,* R307–R308. (p. 785)

Sanz, C., Blicher, A., Dalke, K., Gratton-Fabri, L., McClure-Richards, T., & Fouts, R. (1998, Winter-Spring). Enrichment object use: Five chimpanzees' use of temporary and semi-permanent enrichment objects. *Friends of Washoe, 19*(1,2), 9–14. (p. 869)

Sanz, C., Morgan, D., & Gulick, S. (2004). New insights into chimpanzees, tools, and termites from the Congo Basin. *American Naturalist, 164,* 567–581. (p. 867)

Sapadin, L. A. (1988). Friendship and gender: Perspectives of professional men and women. *Journal of Social and Personal Relationships, 5,* 387–403. (p. 503)

Sapolsky, B. S., & Tabarlet, J. O. (1991). Sex in primetime television: 1979 versus 1989. *Journal of Broadcasting and Electronic Media, 35,* 505–516. (pp. 530, 792)

Sapolsky, R. (2003, September). Taming stress. *Scientific American,* pp. 87–95. (pp. 444, 675)

Sapolsky, R. (2005). The influence of social hierarchy on primate health. *Science, 308,* 648–652. (p. 300)

Sapolsky, R. (2010, November 14). This is your brain on metaphors. *New York Times* (www.nytimes.com). (p. 427)

Sato, K. (1987). Distribution of the cost of maintaining common resources. *Journal of Experimental Social Psychology, 23,* 19–31. (p. 812)

Saulny, S. (2006, June 21). A legacy of the storm: Depression and suicide. *New York Times* (www.nytimes.com). (p. 443)

Savage-Rumbaugh, E. S., Murphy, J., Sevcik, R. A., Brakke, K. E., Williams, S. L., & Rumbaugh, D. M., with commentary by Bates, E. (1993). Language comprehension in ape and child. *Monographs of the Society for Research in Child Development, 58* (233), 1–254. (p. 870)

Savage-Rumbaugh, E. S., Rumbaugh, D., & Fields, W. M. (2009). Empirical Kanzi: The ape language controversy revisited. *Skeptic, 15,* 25–33. (p. 870)

Savic, I., Berglund, H., & Lindstrom, P. (2005). Brain response to putative pheromones in homosexual men. *Proceedings of the National Academy of Sciences, 102,* 7356–7361. (p. 534)

Savitsky, K., Epley, N., & Gilovich, T. D. (2001). Do others judge us as harshly as we think? Overestimating the impact of our failures, shortcomings, and mishaps. *Journal of Personality and Social Psychology, 81,* 44–56. (p. 595)

Savitsky, K., & Gilovich, T. D. (2003). The illusion of transparency and the alleviation of speech anxiety. Journal *of Experimental Social Psychology, 39,* 618–625. (p. 595)

Savoy, C., & Beitel, P. (1996). Mental imagery for basketball. *International Journal of Sport Psychology, 27,* 454–462. (p. 381)

Sawyer, M. G., Arney, F. M., Baghurst, P. A., Clark, J. J., Graetz, B. W., Kosky, R. J., Nurcombe, B., Patton, G. C., Prior, M. R., Raphael, B., Rey, J., Whaites, L. C., & Zubrick, S. R. (2000). *The mental health of young people in Australia.* Canberra: Mental Health and Special Programs Branch, Commonwealth Department of Health and Aged Care. (p. 675)

Sayal, K., Heron, J., Golding, J., Alati, R., Smith, G. D., Gray, R., & Emond, A. (2009). Binge pattern of alcohol consumption during pregnancy and childhood mental health outcomes: Longitudinal population-based study. *Pediatrics, 123,* e289. (p. 467)

Sayette, M. A., Loewenstein, G., Griffin, K. M., & Black, J. J. (2008). Exploring the cold-to-hot empathy gap in smokers. *Psychological Science, 19,* 926–932. (p. 251)

Sayette, M. A., Reichle, E. D., & Schooler, J. W. (2009). Lost in the sauce: The effects of alcohol on mind wandering. *Psychological Science, 20,* 747–752. (p. 249)

Sayette, M. A., Schooler, J. W., & Reichle, E. D. (2010). Out for a smoke: The impact of cigarette craving on zoning out during reading. *Psychological Science, 21,* 26–30. (p. 251)

Sbarra, D. A. (2009). Marriage protects men from clinically meaningful elevations in C-reactive protein: Results from the National Social Life, Health, and Aging Project (NSHAP). *Psychosomatic Medicine, 71,* 828–835. (p. 857)

Scarborough, E., & Furumoto, L. (1987). *Untold lives: The first generation of American women psychologists.* New York: Columbia University Press. (p. 4)

Scarr, S. (1984, May). What's a parent to do? A conversation with E. Hall. *Psychology Today,* pp. 58–63. (p. 635)

Scarr, S. (1986). *Mother care/other care.* New York: Basic Books. (p. 494)

Scarr, S. (1989). Protecting general intelligence: Constructs and consequences for interventions. In R. J. Linn (Ed.), *Intelligence: Measurement, theory, and public policy.* Champaign: University of Illinois Press. (p. 609)

Scarr, S. (1990). Back cover comments on J. Dunn & R. Plomin (1990), *Separate lives: Why siblings are so different.* New York: Basic Books. (p. 131)

Scarr, S. (1993, May/June). Quoted by *Psychology Today,* Nature's thumbprint: So long, superparents, p. 16. (p. 510)

Scarr, S. (1997). Why child care has little impact on most children's development. *Current Directions in Psychological Science, 6,* 143–148. (p. 494)

Schab, F. R. (1991). Odor memory: Taking stock. *Psychological Bulletin, 109,* 242–251. (p. 209)

Schachter, S., & Singer, J. E. (1962). Cognitive, social and physiological determinants of emotional state. *Psychological Review, 69,* 379–399. (p. 422)

Schacter, D. L. (1992). Understanding implicit memory: A cognitive neuroscience approach. *American Psychologist, 47,* 559–569.(p. 342)

Schacter, D. L. (1996). *Searching for memory: The brain, the mind, and the past.* New York: Basic Books. (pp. 330, 342, 541, 563)

Schafer, G. (2005). Infants can learn decontextualized words before their first birthday. *Child Development, 76,* 87–96. (p. 375)

Schaie, K. W. (1994). The life course of adult intellectual abilities. *American Psychologist, 49,* 304–313. (p. 626)

Schaie, K. W., & Geiwitz, J. (1982). *Adult development and aging.* Boston: Little, Brown. (p. 625)

Schalock, R. L., Borthwick-Duffy, S., Bradley, V. J., Buntinx, W. H. E., Coulter, D. L., Craig, E. M. (2010). *Intellectual disability: Definition, classification, and systems of supports* (11th edition). Washington, DC: American Association on Intellectual and Developmental Disabilities. (p. 629)

Schauer, F. (2010). Neuroscience, lie-detection, and the law. *Trends in Cognitive Sciences, 14,* 101–103. (p. 429)

Scheibe, S., & Carstensen, L. L. (2010). Emotional aging: Recent findings and future trends. *Journal of Gerontology: Psychological Sciences, 65B,* 135–144. (p. 546)

Schein, E. H. (1956). The Chinese indoctrination program for prisoners of war: A study of attempted brainwashing. *Psychiatry, 19,* 149–172. (p. 757)

Scherer, K. R., Banse, R., & Wallbott, H. G. (2001). Emotion inferences from vocal expression correlate across languages and cultures. *Journal of Cross-Cultural Psychology, 32,* 76–92. (p. 432)

Schick, V., Herbenick, D., Reece, M., Sanders, S. A., Dodge, B., Middlestadt, S. E., & Fortenberry, J. D. (2010). Sexual behaviors, condom use, and sexual health of Americans over 50: Implications for sexual health promotion for older adults. *Journal of Sexual Medicine, 7*(suppl 5), 315–329. (p. 540)

Schiffenbauer, A., & Schiavo, R. S. (1976). Physical distance and attraction: An intensification effect. *Journal of Experimental Social Psychology, 12,* 274–282. (p. 772)

Schilt, T., de Win, M. M. L, Koeter, M., Jager, G., Korf, D. J., van den Brink, W., & Schmand, B. (2007). Cognition in novice Ecstasy users with minimal exposure to other drugs. *Archives of General Psychiatry, 64,* 728–736. (p. 254)

Schimel, J., Arndt, J., Pyszczynski, T., & Greenberg, J. (2001). Being accepted for who we are: Evidence that social validation of the intrinsic self reduces general defensiveness. *Journal of Personality and Social Psychology, 80,* 35–52. (p. 574)

Schimmack, U., & Lucas, R. (2007). Marriage matters: Spousal similarity in life satisfaction. *Schmollers Jahrbuch, 127,* 1–7. (p. 853)

Schimmack, U., Oishi, S., & Diener, E. (2005). Individualism: A valid and important dimension of cultural differences between nations. *Personality and Social Psychology Review, 9,* 17–31. (p. 598)

Schlaug, G., Jancke, L., Huang, Y., & Steinmetz, H. (1995). In vivo evidence of structural brain asymmetry in musicians. *Science, 267,* 699–701. (p. 95)

Schloss, J. (2009). Does evolution explain human nature? Totally, for a Martian. In *Celebrating the bicentenary of the birth of Charles Darwin.* Philadelphia: John Templeton Foundation (www.templeton.org). (p. 137)

Schmader, T. (2010). Stereotype threat deconstructed. *Current Directions in Psychological Science, 19,* 14–18. (p. 642)

Schmidt, F. L. (2002). The role of general cognitive ability and job performance: Why there cannot be a debate. *Human Performance, 15,* 187–210. (p. 831)

Schmidt, F. L., & Hunter, J. E. (1998). The validity and utility of selection methods in personnel psychology: Practical and theoretical implications of 85 years of research findings. *Psychological Bulletin, 124,* 262–274. (pp. 592, 831, 832)

Schmidt, F. L., & Zimmerman, R. D. (2004). A counterintuitive hypothesis about employment interview validity and some supporting evidence. *Journal of Applied Psychology, 89,* 553–561. (p. 832)

Schmitt, D. P. (2005). Sociosexuality from Argentina to Zimbabwe: A 48-nation study of sex, culture, and strategies of human mating. *Behavioral and Brain Sciences, 28,* 247–311. (p. 138)

Schmitt, D. P. (2007). Sexual strategies across sexual orientations: How personality traits and culture relate to sociosexuality among gays, lesbians, bisexuals, and heterosexuals. *Journal of Psychology and Human Sexuality, 18,* 183–214. (p. 138)

Schmitt, D. P., & Allik, J. (2005). Simultaneous administration of the Rosenberg Self-esteem Scale in 53 nations: Exploring the universal and culture-specific features of global self-esteem. *Journal of Personality and Social Psychology, 89,* 623–642. (p. 596)

Schmitt, D. P., Allik, J., McCrae, R. R., & Benet-Martínez, V., with many others. (2007). The geographic distribution of Big Five personality traits: Patterns and profiles of human self-description across 56 nations. *Journal of Cross-Cultural Psychology, 38,* 173–212. (p. 580)

Schmitt, D. P., & Pilcher, J. J. (2004). Evaluating evidence of psychological adaptation: How do we know one when we see one? *Psychological Science, 15,* 643–649. (p. 137)

Schnall, E., Wassertheil-Smoller, S., Swencionis, C., Zemon, V., Tinker, L., O'Sullivan. M. J., Van Horn, K., & Goodwin, M. (2010). The relationship between religion and cardiovascular outcomes and all-cause mortality in the women's health initiative observational study. *Psychology and Health, 25,* 249–263. (p. 809)

Schnall, S., Haidt, J., Clore, G. L., & Jordan, A. (2008). Disgust as embodied moral judgment. *Personality and Social Psychology Bulletin, 34,* 1096–1109. (pp. 166, 209)

Schnall, S., Roper, J., & Fessler, D. M. T. (2010). Elevation leads to altruistic behavior. *Psychological Science, 21,* 315–320. (p. 864)

Schneider, R. H., Alexander, C. N., Staggers, F., Rainforth, M., Salerno, J. W., Hartz, A., Arndt, S., Barnes, V. A., & Nidich, S. (2005). Long-term effects of stress reduction on mortality in persons > or = 55 years of age with systemic hypertension. *American Journal of Cardiology, 95,* 1060–1064. (p. 862)

Schneider, S. L. (2001). In search of realistic optimism: Meaning, knowledge, and warm fuzziness. *American Psychologist, 56,* 250–263. (p. 589)

Schneiderman, N. (1999). Behavioral medicine and the management of HIV/AIDS. *International Journal of Behavioral Medicine, 6,* 3–12. (p. 450)

Schneier, B. (2007, May 17). Virginia Tech lesson: Rare risks breed irrational responses. *Wired* (www.wired.com). (p. 367)

Schoenborn, C. A., & Adams, P. F. (2008). *Sleep duration as a correlate of smoking, alcohol use, leisure-time physical inactivity, and obesity among adults: United States, 2004–2006.* Centers for Disease Control and Prevention (www.cdc.gov/nchs). (p. 236)

Schoeneman, T. J. (1994). Individualism. In V. S. Ramachandran (Ed.), *Encyclopedia of human behavior.* San Diego: Academic Press. (p. 600)

Schofield, J. W. (1986). Black-White contact in desegregated schools. In M. Hewstone & R. Brown (Eds.), *Contact and conflict in intergroup encounters.* Oxford: Basil Blackwell. (p. 813)

Schonfield, D., & Robertson, B. A. (1966). Memory storage and aging. *Canadian Journal of Psychology, 20,* 228–236. (pp. 542, 543)

Schooler, J. W., Gerhard, D., & Loftus, E. F. (1986). Qualities of the unreal. *Journal of Experimental Psychology: Learning, Memory, and Cognition, 12,* 171–181. (p. 349)

Schorr, E. A., Fox, N.A., van Wassenhove, V., & Knudsen, E.I. (2005). Auditory-visual fusion in speech perception in children with cochlear implants. *Proceedings of the National Academy of Sciences, 102,* 18748–18750. (p. 198)

Schrauzer, G. N., & Shrestha, K. P. (1990). Lithium in drinking water and the incidences of crimes, suicides, and arrests related to drug addictions. *Biological Trace Element Research, 25*(2), 105–113. (p. 743)

Schrauzer, G. N., & Shrestha, K. P. (2010). Lithium in drinking water. *British Journal of Psychiatry, 196,* 159. (p. 743)

Schueller, S. M. (2010). Preferences for positive psychology exercises. *Journal of Positive Psychology, 5,* 192–203. (p. 590)

Schuman, H., & Scott, J. (June, 1989). Generations and collective memories. *American Sociological Review, 54*(3), 359–381. (p. 542)

Schumann, K., & Ross, M. (2010). Why women apologize more than men: gender differences in thresholds for perceiving offensive behavior. *Psychological Science, 21,* 1649–1655. (p. 502)

Schurger, A., Pereira, F., Treisman, A., Cohen, J. D. (2010, Jan.). Reproducibility distinguishes conscious from nonconscious neural representations. *Science, 327,* 97–99. (p. 119)

Schwartz, B. (1984). *Psychology of learning and behavior* (2nd ed.). New York: Norton. (pp. 271, 666)

Schwartz, J., & Estrin, J. (2004, November 7). Living for today, locked in a paralyzed body. *New York Times* (www.nytimes.com). (p. 848)

Schwartz, J. M., Stoessel, P. W., Baxter, L. R., Jr., Martin, K. M., & Phelps, M. E. (1996). Systematic changes in cerebral glucose metabolic rate after successful behavior modification treatment of obsessive-compulsive disorder. *Archives of General Psychiatry, 53,* 109–113. (pp. 723, 747)

Schwartz, S. H., & Rubel-Lifschitz, T. (2009). Cross-national variation in the size of sex differences in values: Effects of gender equality. *Journal of Personality and Social Psychology, 97,* 171–185. (pp. 501, 502)

Schwartz, S. J., Unger, J. B., Zamboanga, B. L., & Szapocznik, J. (2010). Rethinking the concept of acculturation: Implications for theory and research. *American Psychologist, 65,* 237–251. (p. 657)

Schwarz, A. (2007, April 6). Throwing batters curves before throwing a pitch. *New York Times* (www.nytimes.com). (p. 118)

Schwarz, A., & Cohen, S. (2013, March 31). A.D.H.D. seen in 11% of U.S. children as diagnoses rise. *New York Times* (www.nytimes.com). (p. 652)

Schwarz, N., Strack, F., Kommer, D., & Wagner, D. (1987). Soccer, rooms, and the quality of your life: Mood effects on judgments of satisfaction with life in general and with specific domains. *European Journal of Social Psychology, 17,* 69–79. (p. 337)

Sclafani, A. (1995). How food preferences are learned: Laboratory animal models. *Proceedings of the Nutrition Society, 54,* 419–427. (p. 400)

Scott, D. J., & others. (2004, November 9). U-M team reports evidence that smoking affects human brain's natural "feel good" chemical system (press release by Kara Gavin). University of Michigan Medical School (www.med.umich.edu). (p. 251)

Scott, D. J., Stohler, C. S., Egnatuk, C. M., Wang, H., Koeppe, R. A., & Zubieta, J-K. (2007). Individual differences in reward responding explain placebo-induced expectations and effects. *Neuron, 55,* 325–336. (p. 206)

Scott, K. M., & 18 others. (2010). Gender and the relationship between marital status and first onset of mood, anxiety and substance use disorders. *Psychological Medicine, 40,* 1495–1505. (p. 545)

Scott, W. A., Scott, R., & McCabe, M. (1991). Family relationships and children's personality: A cross-cultural, cross-source comparison. *British Journal of Social Psychology, 30,* 1–20. (p. 463)

Scottish Parliament. (2010, April). External research on sexualised goods aimed at children. SP Paper 374. scottish.parliament.uk/s3/committees/equal/reports-10/eor10-02.htm. (p. 531)

Scullin, M. K., & McDaniel, M. A. (2010). Remembering to execute a goal: Sleep on it! *Psychological Science, 21,* 1028–1035. (p. 345)

Sdorow, L. M. (2005). The people behind psychology. In B. Perlman, L. McCann, & W. Buskist (Eds.), *Voices of experience: Memorable talks from the National Institute on the Teaching of Psychology.* Washington, DC: American Psychological Society. (p. 567)

Seal, K. H., Bertenthal, D., Miner, C. R., Sen, S., & Marmar, C. (2007). Bringing the war back home: Mental health disorders among 103,788 U.S. veterans returning from Iraq and Afghanistan seen at Department of Veterans Affairs facilities. *Archives of Internal Medicine, 167,* 467–482. (p. 665)

Sebat, J., & 31 others. (2007). Strong association of de novo copy number mutations with autism. *Science, 316,* 445–449. (p. 482)

Sechrest, L., Stickle, T. R., & Stewart, M. (1998). The role of assessment in clinical psychology. In A. Bellack, M. Hersen (Series eds.) & C. R. Reynolds (Vol. ed.), *Comprehensive clinical psychology: Vol 4: Assessment.* New York: Pergamon. (p. 567)

Seeman, P. (2007). Dopamine and schizophrenia. *Scholarpedia, 2*(10), 3634. (www.scholarpedia.org). (p. 686)

Seeman, P., Guan, H-C., & Van Tol, H. H. M. (1993). Dopamine D4 receptors elevated in schizophrenia. *Nature, 365,* 441–445. (p. 686)

Seery, M. D., Holman, E. A., & Silver, R. C. (2010). Whatever does not kill us: Cumulative lifetime adversity, vulnerability, and resilience. *Journal of Personality and Social Psychology, 99,* 1025–1041. (p. 666)

Segall, M. H., Dasen, P. R., Berry, J. W., & Poortinga, Y. H. (1990). *Human behavior in global perspective: An introduction to cross-cultural psychology.* New York: Pergamon. (pp. 138, 484, 504)

Segerstrom, S. C. (2007). Stress, energy, and immunity. *Current Directions in Psychological Science, 16,* 326–330. (p. 442)

Segerstrom, S. C., Taylor, S. E., Kemeny, M. E., & Fahey, J. L. (1998). Optimism is associated with mood, coping, and immune change in response to stress. *Journal of Personality and Social Psychology, 74,* 1646–1655. (p. 856)

Seidler, G. H., & Wagner, F. E. (2006). Comparing the efficacy of EMDR and trauma-focused cognitive-behavioral therapy in the treatment of PTSD: A meta-analytic study. *Psychological Medicine, 36,* 1515–1522. (p. 733)

Self, C. E. (1994). *Moral culture and victimization in residence halls.* Unpublished master's thesis. Bowling Green University. (p. 824)

Seligman, M. E. P. (1975). *Helplessness: On depression, development and death.* San Francisco: Freeman. (p. 299)

Seligman, M. E. P. (1991). *Learned optimism.* New York: Knopf. (pp. 218, 299, 680)

Seligman, M. E. P. (1994). *What you can change and what you can't.* New York: Knopf. (pp. 510, 595, 859)

Seligman, M. E. P. (1995). The effectiveness of psychotherapy: The Consumer Reports study. *American Psychologist, 50,* 965–974. (pp. 680, 729, 732)

Seligman, M. E. P. (2002). *Authentic happiness: Using the new positive psychology to realize your potential for lasting fulfillment.* New York: Free Press. (pp. 14, 590, 595, 722)

Seligman, M. E. P. (2004). Eudaemonia, the good life. A talk with Martin Seligman (www.edge.org), (p. 590)

Seligman, M. E. P. (2008). Positive health. *Applied Psychology, 17,* 3–18. (p. 590)

Seligman, M. E. P. (2011). *Flourish: A visionary new understanding of happiness and well-being.* New York: Free Press. (p. 590)

Seligman, M. E. P., Ernst, R. M., Gillham, J., Reivich, K., & Linkins, M. (2009). Positive education: Positive psychology and classroom interventions. *Oxford Review of Education, 35,* 293–311. (pp. 590, 722)

Seligman, M. E. P., Peterson, C., Barsky, A. J., Boehm, J. K., Kubzansky, L. D., & Park, N. (2011). Positive health and health assets: Reanalysis of longitudinal datasets. Unpublished manuscript, University of Pennsylvania. (pp. 14, 590)

Seligman, M. E. P., Steen, T. A., Park, N., & Peterson, C. (2005). Positive psychology progress: Empirical validation of interventions. *American Psychologist, 60,* 410–421. (pp. 14, 590, 853)

Seligman, M. E. P., & Yellen, A. (1987). What is a dream? *Behavior Research and Therapy, 25,* 1–24. (p. 226)

Selimbeyoglu, A., & Parvizi, J. (2010). Electrical stimulation of the human brain: perceptual and behavioral phenomena reported in the old and new literature. *Frontiers in Human Neuroscience, 4,* 1–11. (p. 95)

Sellers, H. (2010). *You don't look like anyone I know.* New York: Riverhead Books. (p. 150)

Selye, H. (1936). A syndrome produced by diverse nocuous agents. *Nature, 138,* 32. (p. 444)

Selye, H. (1976). *The stress of life.* New York: McGraw-Hill. (p. 444)

Senate Intelligence Committee. (2004, July 9). *Report of the select committee on intelligence on the U.S. intelligence community's prewar intelligence assessments on Iraq.* Washington, DC: Author. (pp. 362, 775)

Senghas, A., & Coppola, M. (2001). Children creating language: How Nicaraguan Sign Language acquired a spatial grammar. *Psychological Science, 12,* 323–328. (p. 376)

Sengupta, S. (2001, October 10). Sept. 11 attack narrows the racial divide. *New York Times* (www.nytimes.com). (p. 814)

Senju, A., Maeda, M., Kikuchi, Y., Hasegawa, T., Tojo, Y., & Osanai, H. (2007). Absence of contagious yawning in children with autism spectrum disorder. *Biology Letters, 3,* 706–708. (p. 482)

Senju, A., Southgate, V., White, S., & Frith, U. (2009). Mindblind eyes: An absence of spontaneous theory of mind in Asperger syndrome. *Science, 325,* 883–885. (p. 481)

Serruya, M. D., Hatsopoulos, N. G., Paninski, L., Fellow, M. R., & Donoghue, J. P. (2002). Instant neural control of a movement signal. *Nature, 416,* 141–142. (p. 106)

Service, R. F. (1994). Will a new type of drug make memory-making easier? *Science, 266,* 218–219. (p. 333)

Seto, M. C. (2009, April 6–7). Assessing the risk posed by child pornography offenders. Paper prepared for the G8 Global Symposium, University of North Carolina. (p. 793)

Shadish, W. R., & Baldwin, S. A. (2005). Effects of behavioral marital therapy: A meta-analysis of randomized controlled trials. *Journal of Consulting and Clinical Psychology, 73,* 6–14. (p. 732)

Shadish, W. R., Montgomery, L. M., Wilson, P., Wilson, M. R., Bright, I., & Okwumabua, T. (1993). Effects of family and marital psychotherapies: A meta-analysis. *Journal of Consulting and Clinical Psychology, 61,* 992–1002. (p. 724)

Shaffer, D. M., Krauchunas, S. M., Eddy, M., & McBeath, M. K. (2004). How dogs navigate to catch Frisbees, *Psychological Science, 15,* 437–441. (p. 185)

Shafir, E., & LeBoeuf, R. A. (2002). Rationality. *Annual Review of Psychology, 53,* 491–517. (p. 369)

Shamir, B., House, R. J., & Arthur, M. B. (1993). The motivational effects of charismatic leadership: A self-concept based theory. *Organizational Science, 4*(4), 577–594. (p. 839)

Shanahan, L., McHale, S. M., Osgood, D. W., & Crouter, A. C. (2007). Conflict frequency with mothers and fathers from middle childhood to late adolescence: Within- and between-families comparisons. *Developmental Psychology, 43,* 539–550. (p. 521)

Shanks, D. R. (2010). Learning: From association to cognition. *Annual Review of Psychology, 61,* 273–301. (p. 296)

Shapiro, D. (1999). *Psychotherapy of neurotic character.* New York: Basic Books. (p. 710)

Shapiro, F. (1989). Efficacy of the eye movement desensitization procedure in the treatment of traumatic memories. *Journal of Traumatic Stress, 2,* 199–223. (p. 733)

Shapiro, F. (1999). Eye movement desensitization and reprocessing (EMDR) and the anxiety disorders: Clinical and research implications of an integrated psychotherapy treatment. *Journal of Anxiety Disorders, 13,* 35–67. (p. 733)

Shapiro, F. (Ed.). (2002). *EMDR as an integrative psychotherapy approach: Experts of diverse orientations explore the paradigm prism.* Washington, DC: APA Books. (p. 733)

Shapiro, F. (2007). EMDR and case conceptualization from an adaptive information processing perspective. In F. Shapiro, F. W. Kaslow, & L. Maxfield (Eds.), *Handbook of EMDR and family therapy processes.* Hoboken, NJ: Wiley. (p. 733)

Shapiro, K. A., Moo, L. R., & Caramazza, A. (2006). Cortical signatures of noun and verb production. *Proceedings of the National Academic of Sciences, 103,* 1644–1649. (p. 378)

Shargorodsky, J., Curhan, S. G., Curhan, G. C., & Eavey, R. (2010). Changes of prevalence of hearing loss in US adolescents. *Journal of the American Medical Association, 304,* 772–778. (p. 197)

Sharma, A. R., McGue, M. K., & Benson, P. L. (1998). The psychological adjustment of United States adopted adolescents and their nonadopted siblings. *Child Development, 69,* 791–802. (p. 128)

Sharot, T., Shiner, T., Brown, A. C., Fan, J., & Dolan, R. J. (2009). Dopamine enhances expectation of pleasure in humans. *Current Biology, 19,* 2077–2080. (p. 101)

Shattuck, P. T. (2006). The contribution of diagnostic substitution to the growing administrative prevalence of autism in US special education. *Pediatrics, 117,* 1028–1037. (p. 481)

Shaver, P. R., & Mikulincer, M. (2007). Adult attachment strategies and the regulation of emotion. In J. J. Gross (Ed.), *Handbook of emotion regulation.* New York: Guilford Press. (p. 492)

Shaver, P. R., Morgan, H. J., & Wu, S. (1996). Is love a basic emotion? *Personal Relationships, 3,* 81–96. (p. 844)

Shaw, B. A., Liang, J., & Krause, N. (2010). Age and race differences in the trajectories of self-esteem. *Psychology and Aging, 25,* 84–94. (p. 464)

Shedler, J. (2009, March 23). That was then, this is now: Psychoanalytic psychotherapy for the rest of us. Unpublished manuscript, Department of Psychiatry, University of Colorado Health Sciences Center. (p. 709)

Shedler, J. (2010a, November/December). Getting to know me. *Scientific American Mind,* pp. 53–5 (p. 711)

Shedler, J. (2010b). The efficacy of psychodynamic psychotherapy. *American Psychologist, 65,* 98–109. (pp. 560, 732)

Sheehan, S. (1982). *Is there no place on earth for me?* Boston: Houghton Mifflin. (p. 684)

Sheldon, K. M., Abad, N., & Hinsch, C. (2011). A two-process view of Facebook use and relatedness need-satisfaction: Disconnection drives use, and connection rewards it. *Journal of Personality and Social Psychology, 100,* 766–775. (pp. 412, 416)

Sheldon, K. M., Elliot, A. J., Kim, Y., & Kasser, T. (2001). What is satisfying about satisfying events? Testing 10 candidate psychological needs. *Journal of Personality and Social Psychology, 80,* 325–339. (p. 413)

Sheldon, K. M., & Niemiec, C. P. (2006). It's not just the amount that counts: Balanced need satisfaction also affects well-being. *Journal of Personality and Social Psychology, 91,* 331–341. (p. 413)

Shenton, M. E. (1992). Abnormalities of the left temporal lobe and thought disorder in schizophrenia: A quantitative magnetic resonance imaging study. *New England Journal of Medicine, 327,* 604–612. (p. 687)

Shepard, R. N. (1990). *Mind sights.* New York: Freeman. (p. 68)

Shepherd, C. (1997, April). News of the weird. *Funny Times,* p. 15. (p. 126)

Shepherd, C. (1999, June). News of the weird. *Funny Times,* p. 21. (p. 402)

Shepherd, C., Kohut, J. J., & Sweet, R. (1990). *More news of the weird.* New York: Penguin/Plume Books. (p. 700)

Sheppard, L. D., & Vernon, P. A. (2008). Intelligence and speed of information-processing: A review of 50 years of research. *Personality and Individual Differences, 44,* 535–551. (p. 614)

Sher, L. (2006). Alcohol consumption and suicide. *QJM: An International Journal of Medicine, 99,* 57–61. (p. 676)

Shergill, S. S., Bays, P. M., Frith, C. D., & Wolpert, D. M. (2003). Two eyes for an eye: The neuroscience of force escalation. *Science, 301,* 187. (p. 812)

Sherif, M. (1966). *In common predicament: Social psychology of intergroup conflict and cooperation.* Boston: Houghton Mifflin. (p. 813)

Sherry, D., & Vaccarino, A. L. (1989). Hippocampus and memory for food caches in black-capped chickadees. *Behavioral Neuroscience, 103,* 308–318. (p. 330)

Sherry, S. B., & Hall, P. A. (2009). The perfectionism model of binge eating: Tests of an integrative model. *Journal of Personality and Social Psychology, 96,* 690–709. (p 697)

Shettleworth, S. J. (1973). Food reinforcement and the organization of behavior in golden hamsters. In R. A. Hinde & J. Stevenson-Hinde (Eds.), *Constraints on learning.* London: Academic Press. (p. 295)

Shettleworth, S. J. (1993). Where is the comparison in comparative cognition? Alternative research programs. *Psychological Science, 4,* 179–184. (p. 331)

Shifren, J. L., Monz, B. U., Russo, P. A., Segreti, A., Johannes, C. B. (2008). Sexual problems and distress in United States women: Prevalence and correlates. *Obstetrics & Gynecology, 112,* 970–978. (p. 407)

Shinkareva, S. V., Mason, R. A., Malave, V. L., Wang, W., Mitchell, T. M., & Just, M. A. (2008, January 2). Using fMRI brain activation to identify cognitive states associated with perceptions of tools and dwellings. *PloS One 3*(1), 31394. (p. 119)

Short, S. J., Lubach, G. R., Karasin, A. I., Olsen, C. W., Styner, M., Knickmeyer, R. C., Gilmore, J. H., & Coe, C. L. (2010). Maternal influenza infection during pregnancy impacts postnatal brain development in the rhesus monkey. *Biological Psychiatry, 67,* 965–973. (p. 688)

Shotland, R. L. (1984, March 12). Quoted in Maureen Dowd, 20 years after the murder of Kitty Genovese, the question remains: Why? *The New York Times,* p. B1. (p. 807)

Showers, C. (1992). The motivational and emotional consequences of considering positive or negative possibilities for an upcoming event. *Journal of Personality and Social Psychology, 63,* 474–484. (p. 589)

Shute, N. (2010, October). Desperate for an autism cure. *Scientific American,* pp. 80–85. (p. 481)

Siahpush, M., Spittal, M., & Singh, G. K. (2008). Happiness and life satisfaction prospectively predict self-rated health, physical health and the presence of limiting long-term health conditions. *American Journal of Health Promotion, 23,* 18–26. (p. 453)

Siegel, J. M. (1990). Stressful life events and use of physician services among the elderly: The moderating role of pet ownership. *Journal of Personality and Social Psychology, 58,* 1081–1086. (p. 857)

Siegel, J. M. (2000, Winter). Recent developments in narcolepsy research: An explanation for patients and the general public. *Narcolepsy Network Newsletter,* pp. 1–2. (p. 239)

Siegel, J. M. (2001). The REM sleep-memory consolidation hypothesis. *Science, 294,* 1058–1063. (p. 242)

Siegel, J. M. (2003, November). Why we sleep. *Scientific American,* pp. 92–97. (p. 230)

Siegel, J. M. (2009). Sleep viewed as a state of adaptive inactivity. *Nature Reviews Neuroscience, 10,* 747–753. (p. 230)

Siegel, R. K. (1977, October). Hallucinations. *Scientific American,* pp. 132–140. (p. 255)

Siegel, R. K. (1980). The psychology of life after death. *American Psychologist, 35,* 911–931. (p. 255)

Siegel, R. K. (1982, October). Quoted by J. Hooper, Mind tripping. *Omni,* pp. 72–82, 159–160. (p. 254)

Siegel, R. K. (1984, March 15). Personal communication. (p. 254)

Siegel, R. K. (1990). *Intoxication.* New York: Pocket Books. (pp. 252, 255)

Siegel, S. (2005). Drug tolerance, drug addiction, and drug anticipation. *Current Directions in Psychological Science, 14,* 296–300. (p. 271)

Silber, M. H., & 11 others. (2008). The visual scoring of sleep in adults. *Journal of Clinical Sleep Medicine, 3,* 121–131. (p. 227)

Silbersweig, D. A., Stern, E., Frith, C., Cahill, C., Holmes, A., Grootoonk, S., Seaward, J., McKenna, P., Chua, S. E., Schnorr, L., Jones, T., & Frackowiak, R. S. J. (1995). A functional neuroanatomy of hallucinations in schizophrenia. *Nature, 378,* 176–179. (p. 687)

Silk, J. B., Beehner, J. C., Bergman, T. J., Crockford, C., Engh, A. L., Moscovice, L. R., Wittig, R. M., Seyfarth, R. M., & Cheney, D. L. (2010). Strong and consistent social bonds enhance the longevity of female baboons. *Current Biology, 20,* 1359–1361. (p. 857)

Silva, A. J., Stevens, C. F., Tonegawa, S., & Wang, Y. (1992). Deficient hippocampal long-term potentiation in alpha-calcium-calmodulin kinase II mutant mice. *Science, 257,* 201–206. (p. 333)

Silva, C. E., & Kirsch, I. (1992). Interpretive sets, expectancy, fantasy proneness, and dissociation as predictors of hypnotic response. *Journal of Personality and Social Psychology, 63,* 847–856. (p. 220)

Silver, M., & Geller, D. (1978). On the irrelevance of evil: The organization and individual action. *Journal of Social Issues, 34,* 125–136. (p. 768)

Silver, N. (2009, December 27). The odds of airborne terror. www.fivethirtyeight.com. (p. 367)

Silveri, M. M., Rohan, M. L., Pimental, P. J., Gruber, S. A., Rosso, I. M., & Yurgelun-Todd, D. A. (2006). Sex differences in the relationship between white matter microstructure and impulsivity in adolescents. *Magnetic Resonance Imaging, 24,* 833–841. (p. 514)

Silverman, K., Evans, S. M., Strain, E. C., & Griffiths, R. R. (1992). Withdrawal syndrome after the double-blind cessation of caffeine consumption. *New England Journal of Medicine, 327,* 1109–1114. (p. 250)

Simek, T. C., & O'Brien, R. M. (1981). *Total golf: A behavioral approach to lowering your score and getting more out of your game.* Huntington, NY: B-MOD Associates. (p. 287)

Simek, T. C., & O'Brien, R. M. (1988). A chaining-mastery, discrimination training program to teach Little Leaguers to hit a baseball. *Human Performance, 1,* 73–84. (p. 287)

Simon, H. A. (2001, February). Quoted by A. M. Hayashi, When to trust your gut. *Harvard Business Review,* pp. 59–65. (p. 369)

Simon, H. A., & Chase, W. G. (1973) Skill in chess. *American Scientist, 61,* 394–403. (p. 834)

Simon, V., Czobor, P., Bálint, S., Mésáros, A., & Bitter, I. (2009). Prevalence and correlates of adult attention-deficit hyperactivity disorder: Meta-analysis. *British Journal of Psychiatry, 194,* 204–211. (p. 652)

Simons, D. J., & Chabris, C. F. (1999). Gorillas in our midst: Sustained inattentional blindness for dynamic events. *Perception, 28,* 1059–1074. (p. 154)

Simonton, D. K. (1988). Age and outstanding achievement: What do we know after a century of research? *Psychological Bulletin, 104,* 251–267. (p. 627)

Simonton, D. K. (1990). Creativity in the later years: Optimistic prospects for achievement. *The Gerontologist, 30,* 626–631. (p. 627)

Simonton, D. K. (1992). The social context of career success and course for 2,026 scientists and inventors. *Personality and Social Psychology Bulletin, 18,* 452–463. (p. 358)

Simonton, D. K. (2000). Methodological and theoretical orientation and the long-term disciplinary impact of 54 eminent psychologists. *Review of General Psychology, 4,* 13–24. (p. 310)

Sin, N. L., & Lyubomirsky, S. (2009). Enhancing well-being and alleviating depressive symptoms with positive psychology interventions: A practice-friendly meta-analysis. *Journal of Clinical Psychology: In Session, 65,* 467–487. (pp. 590, 853)

Sinclair, R. C., Hoffman, C., Mark, M. M., Martin, L. L., & Pickering, T. L. (1994). Construct accessibility and the misattribution of arousal: Schachter and Singer revisited. *Psychological Science, 5,* 15–18. (p. 423)

Singelis, T. M., Bond, M. H., Sharkey, W. F., & Lai, C. S. Y. (1999). Unpackaging culture's influence on self-esteem and embarrassability: The role of self-construals. *Journal of Cross-Cultural Psychology, 30,* 315–341. (p. 599)

Singelis, T. M., & Sharkey, W. F. (1995). Culture, self-construal, and embarrassability. *Cross-Cultural Psychology, 26,* 622–644. (p. 599)

Singer, J. L. (1981). Clinical intervention: New developments in methods and evaluation. In L. T. Benjamin, Jr. (Ed.), *The G. Stanley Hall Lecture Series* (Vol. 1). Washington, DC: American Psychological Association. (p. 732)

Singer, T., Seymour, B., O'Doherty, J., Kaube, H., Dolan, R. J., & Frith, C. (2004). Empathy for pain involves the affective but not sensory components of pain. *Science, 303,* 1157–1162. (pp. 205, 307)

Singh, D. (1993). Adaptive significance of female physical attractiveness: Role of waist-to-hip ratio. *Journal of Personality and Social Psychology, 65,* 293–307. (p. 138)

Singh, D. (1995). Female health, attractiveness, and desirability for relationships: Role of breast asymmetry and waist-to-hip ratio. *Ethology and Sociobiology, 16,* 465–481. (pp. 138, 802)

Singh, D., & Randall, P. K. (2007). Beauty is in the eye of the plastic surgeon: Waist-hip ration (WHR) and women's attractiveness. *Personality and Individual Differences, 43,* 329–340. (p. 138)

Singh, S. (1997). *Fermat's enigma: The epic quest to solve the world's greatest mathematical problem.* New York: Bantam Books. (p. 357)

Singh, S., & Riber, K. A. (1997, November). Fermat's last stand. *Scientific American,* pp. 68–73. (p. 358)

Sio, U. N., & Ormerod, T. C. (2009). Does incubation enhance problem solving? A meta-analtic review. *Psychological Bulletin, 135,* 94–120. (p. 369)

Sireteanu, R. (1999). Switching on the infant brain. *Science, 286,* 59, 61. (p. 198)

Skeem, J. L., & Cooke, D. J. (2010). Is criminal behavior a central component of psychopathy? Conceptual directions for resolving the debate. *Psychological Assessment, 22,* 433–445 (p. 699)

Skinner, B. F. (1953). *Science and human behavior.* New York: Macmillan. (p. 279)

Skinner, B. F. (1956). A case history in scientific method. *American Psychologist, 11,* 221–233. (p. 280)

Skinner, B. F. (1961, November). Teaching machines. *Scientific American,* pp. 91–102. (p. 279)

Skinner, B. F. (1983, September). Origins of a behaviorist. *Psychology Today,* pp. 22–33. (pp. 283, 679)

Skitka, L. J., Bauman, C. W., & Mullen, E. (2004). Political tolerance and coming to psychological closure following the September 11, 2001, terrorist attacks: An integrative approach. *Personality and Social Psychology Bulletin, 30,* 743–756. (p. 846)

Sklar, L. S., & Anisman, H. (1981). Stress and cancer. *Psychological Bulletin, 89,* 369–406. (p. 451)

Skoog, G., & Skoog, I. (1999). A 40-year follow-up of patients with obsessive-compulsive disorder. *Archives of General Psychiatry, 56,* 121–127. (p. 664)

Skov, R. B., & Sherman, S. J. (1986). Information-gathering processes: Diagnosticity, hypothesis-confirmatory strategies, and perceived hypothesis confirmation. *Journal of Experimental Social Psychology, 22,* 93–121. (p. 362)

Slatcher, R. B., & Pennebaker, J. W. (2006) How do I love thee? Let me count the words: The social effects of expressive writing, *Psychological Science, 17,* 660–664. (p. 804)

Slater, E., & Meyer, A. (1959). *Confinia psychiatra.* Basel: S. Karger AG. (p. 673)

Slavin, R. E., & Braddock, J. H., III (1993, Summer). Ability grouping: On the wrong track. *The College Board Review,* pp. 11–18. (p. 630)

Sloan, R. P. (2005). Field analysis of the literature on religion, spirituality, and health. Columbia University (available at www.metanexus.net/tarp). (p. 864)

Sloan, R. P., & Bagiella, E. (2002). Claims about religious involvement and health outcomes. *Annals of Behavioral Medicine, 24,* 14–21. (p. 864)

Sloan, R. P., Bagiella, E., & Powell, T. (1999). Religion, spirituality, and medicine. *Lancet, 353,* 664–667. (p. 864)

Sloan, R. P., Bagiella, E., VandeCreek, L., & Poulos, P. (2000). Should physicians prescribe religious activities? *New England Journal of Medicine, 342,* 1913–1917. (p. 864)

Slopen, N., Glynn, R. J., Buring, J., & Albert, M. A. (2010, November 23). Job strain, job insecurity, and incident cardiovascular disease in the Women's Health Study (Abstract 18520). *Circulation,* A18520 (circ.ahajournals.org). (p. 453)

Slovic, P. (2007). "If I look at the mass I will never act": Psychic numbing and genocide. *Judgment and Decision Making, 2,* 79–95. (p. 365)

Slovic, P. (2010, Winter). The more who die, the less we care: Confronting psychic numbing. *Trauma Psychology* (APA Division 56 Newsletter), pp. 4–8. (p. 365)

Slovic, P., Finucane, M., Peters, E., & MacGregor, D. G. (2002). The affect heuristic. In T. Gilovich, D. Griffin, & D. Kahneman (Eds.), *Intuitive judgment: Heuristics and biases.* New York: Cambridge University Press. (p. 252)

Small, D. A., Loewenstein, G., & Slovic, P. (2007). Sympathy and callousness: The impact of deliberative thought on donations to identifiable and statistical victims. *Organizational Behavior and Human Decision Processes, 102,* 143–153. (p. 365)

Small, M. F. (1997). Making connections. *American Scientist, 85,* 502–504. (p. 497)

Smedley, A., & Smedley, B. D. (2005). Race as biology is fiction, racism as a social problem is real: Anthropological and historical perspectives on the social construction of race. *American Psychologist, 60,* 16–26. (p. 640)

Smelser, N. J., & Mitchell, F. (Eds.). (2002). *Terrorism: Perspectives from the behavioral and social sciences.* Washington, DC: National Research Council, National Academies Press. (p. 786)

Smilek, D., Carriere, J. S. A., & Cheyne, J. A. (2010). Out of mind, out of sight: Eye blinking as indicator and embodiment of mind wandering. *Psychological Science, 21,* 786–789. (p. 153)

Smith, A. (1983). Personal correspondence. (p. 686)

Smith, B. C. (2011, January 16). The senses and the multi-sensory. *World Question Center* (www.edge.org). (p. 210)

Smith, C. (2006, January 7). Nearly 100, LSD's father ponders his "problem child." *New York Times* (www.nytimes.com). (p. 254)

Smith, D. M., Loewenstein, G., Jankovic, A., & Ubel, P. A. (2009). Happily hopeless: Adaptation to a permanent, but not to a temporary, disability. *Health Psychology, 28,* 787–791. (p. 848)

Smith, E., & Delargy, M. (2005). Locked-in syndrome. *British Medical Journal, 330,* 406–409. (p. 848)

Smith, M. B. (1978). Psychology and values. *Journal of Social Issues, 34,* 181–199. (p. 573)

Smith, M. L., & Glass, G. V. (1977). Meta-analysis of psychotherapy outcome studies. *American Psychologist, 32*, 752–760. (p. 731)

Smith, M. L., Glass, G. V., & Miller, R. L. (1980). *The benefits of psychotherapy*. Baltimore: Johns Hopkins Press. (p. 731)

Smith, P. B., & Tayeb, M. (1989). Organizational structure and processes. In M. Bond (Ed.), *The cross-cultural challenge to social psychology*. Newbury Park, CA: Sage. (p. 839)

Smith, S. J., Axelton, A. M., & Saucier, D. A. (2009). The effects of contact on sexual prejudice: A meta-analysis. *Sex Roles, 61*, 178–191. (p. 813)

Smith, S. M., McIntosh, W. D., & Bazzini, D. G. (1999). Are the beautiful good in Hollywood? An investigation of the beauty-and-goodness stereotype on film. *Basic and Applied Social Psychology, 21*, 69–80. (p. 800)

Smith, T. B., Bartz, J., & Richards, P. S. (2007). Outcomes of religious and spiritual adaptations to psychotherapy: A meta-analytic review. *Psychotherapy Research, 17*, 643–655. (p. 735)

Smith, T. W. (1998, December). *American sexual behavior: Trends, sociodemographic differences, and risk behavior*. (National Opinion Research Center GSS Topical Report No. 25). (pp. 529, 533)

Smolak, L., & Murnen, S. K. (2002). A meta-analytic examination of the relationship between child sexual abuse and eating disorders. *International Journal of Eating Disorders, 31*, 136–150. (p. 697)

Smoreda, Z., & Licoppe, C. (2000). Gender-specific use of the domestic telephone. *Social Psychology Quarterly, 63*, 238–252. (p. 502)

Snedeker, J., Geren, J., & Shafto, C. L. (2007). Starting over: International adoption as a natural experiment in language development. *Psychological Science, 18*, 79–86. (p. 375)

Snodgrass, S. E., Higgins, J. G., & Todisco, L. (1986). The effects of walking behavior on mood. Paper presented at the American Psychological Association convention. (p. 438)

Snowdon, D. A., Kemper, S. J., Mortimer, J. A., Greiner, L. H., Wekstein, D. R., & Markesbery, W. R. (1996). Linguistic ability in early life and cognitive function and Alzheimer's disease in late life: Finds from the Nun Study. *Journal of the American Medical Association, 275*, 528–532. (p. 628)

Snyder, F., & Scott, J. (1972). The psychophysiology of sleep. In N. S. Greenfield & R. A. Sterbach (Eds.), *Handbook of psychophysiology*. New York: Holt, Rinehart & Winston. (p. 242)

Snyder, S. H. (1984). Neurosciences: An integrative discipline. *Science, 225*, 1255–1257. (pp. 80, 657)

Snyder, S. H. (1986). *Drugs and the brain*. New York: Scientific American Library. (p. 743)

Social Watch. (2006, March 8). No country in the world treats its women as well as its men (www.socialwatch.org). (p. 504)

Society for Personality Assessment. (2005). The status of the Rorschach in clinical and forensic practice: An official statement by the Board of Trustees of the Society for Personality Assessment. *Journal of Personality Assessment, 85*, 219–237. (p. 567)

Sokol, D. K., Moore, C. A., Rose, R. J., Williams, C. J., Reed, T., & Christian, J. C. (1995). Intrapair differences in personality and cognitive ability among young monozygotic twins distinguished by chorion type. *Behavior Genetics, 25*, 457–466. (p. 125)

Solnick, S. J., & Hemenway, D. (1998). Is more always better?: A survey on positional concerns. *Journal of Economic Behavior & Organization, 37*, 373–383. (p. 852)

Solnick, S. J., & Hemenway, D. (2009). Do spending comparisons affect spending and satisfaction? *Journal of Socio-Economics, 38*, 568–573. (p. 852)

Solomon, D. A., Keitner, G. I., Miller, I. W., Shea, M. T., & Keller, M. B. (1995). Course of illness and maintenance treatments for patients with bipolar disorder. *Journal of Clinical Psychiatry, 56*, 5–13. (p. 743)

Solomon, J. (1996, May 20). Breaking the silence. *Newsweek*, pp. 20–22. (p. 655)

Solomon, M. (1987, December). Standard issue. *Psychology Today*, pp. 30–31. (p. 800)

Song, S. (2006, March 27). Mind over medicine. *Time*, p. 47. (p. 221)

Sontag, S. (1978). *Illness as metaphor*. New York: Farrar, Straus, & Giroux. (p. 451)

Soon, C. S., Brass, M., Heinze, H., & Haynes, J. (2008). Unconscious determinants of free decisions in the human brain. *Nature Neuroscience, 11*, 543–545. (p. 121)

Sørensen, H. J., Mortensen, E. L., Reinisch, J. M., & Mednick, S. A. (2005). Breastfeeding and risk of schizophrenia in the Copenhagen Perinatal Cohort. *Acta Psychiatrica Scandinavica, 112*, 26–29. (p. 686)

Sørensen, H. J., Mortensen, E. L., Reinisch, J. M., & Mednick, S. A. (2006). Height, weight, and body mass index in early adulthood and risk of schizophrenia. *Acta Psychiatrica Scandinavica, 114*, 49–54. (p. 686)

Sorkhabi, N. (2005). Applicability of Baumrind's parent typology to collective cultures: Analysis of cultural explanations of parent socialization effects. *International Journal of Behavioral Development, 29*, 552–563. (p. 496)

Soussignan, R. (2001). Duchenne smile, emotional experience, and autonomic reactivity: A test of the facial feedback hypothesis. *Emotion, 2*, 52–74. (p. 438)

South, S. C., Krueger, R. F., Johnson, W., & Iacono, W. G. (2008). Adolescent personality moderates genetic and environmental influences on relationships with parents. *Journal of Personality and Social Psychology, 94*, 899–912. (p. 496)

Sowell, T. (1991, May/June). Cultural diversity: A world view. *American Enterprise*, pp. 44–55. (p. 815)

Spanos, N. P. (1982). A social psychological approach to hypnotic behavior. In G. Weary & H. L. Mirels (Eds.), *Integrations of clinical and social psychology*. New York: Oxford. (p. 221)

Spanos, N. P. (1986). Hypnosis, nonvolitional responding, and multiple personality: A social psychological perspective. *Progress in Experimental Personality Research, 14*, 1–62. (p. 695)

Spanos, N. P. (1991). Hypnosis, hypnotizability, and hypnotherapy. In C. R. Snyder & D. R. Forsyth (Eds.), *Handbook of social and clinical psychology: The health perspective*. New York: Pergamon Press. (p. 220)

Spanos, N. P. (1994). Multiple identity enactments and multiple personality disorder: A sociocognitive perspective. *Psychological Bulletin, 116*, 143–165. (p. 695)

Spanos, N. P. (1996). *Multiple identities and false memories: A sociocognitive perspective*. Washington, DC: American Psychological Association Books. (pp. 220, 695)

Spanos, N. P., & Coe, W. C. (1992). A social-psychological approach to hypnosis. In E. Fromm & M. R. Nash (Eds.), *Contemporary hypnosis research*. New York: Guilford. (p. 221)

Sparrow, B., Liu, J., & Wegner, D. M. (2011). Google effects on memory: Cognitive consequences of having information at our fingertips. *Science, 333*, 776–778. (p. 320)

Speer, N. K., Reynolds, J. R., Swallow, K. M., & Zacks, J. M. (2009). Reading stories activates neural representations of visual and motor experiences. *Psychological Science, 20*, 989–999. (pp. 307, 378)

Spelke, E. S., & Kinzler, K. D. (2007). Core knowledge. *Developmental Science, 10*, 89–96. (p. 478)

Spence, I., & Feng, J. (2010). Video games and spatial cognition. *Review of General Psychology, 14*, 92–104. (p. 190)

Spencer, J., Quinn, P. C., Johnson, M. H., & Karmiloff-Smith, A. (1997). Heads you win, tails you lose: Evidence for young infants categorizing mammals by head and facial attributes. *Early Development & Parenting, 6*, 113–126. (p. 468)

Spencer, K. M., Nestor, P. G., Perlmutter, R., Niznikiewicz, M. A., Klump, M. C., Frumin, M., Shenton, M. E., & McCarley, R. W. (2004). Neural synchrony indexes disordered perception and cognition in schizophrenia. *Proceedings of the National Academy of Sciences, 101*, 17288–17293. (p. 687)

Spencer, S. J., Steele, C. M., & Quinn, D. M. (1997). Stereotype threat and women's math performance. Unpublished manuscript, Hope College. (p. 642)

Sperling, G. (1960). The information available in brief visual presentations. *Psychological Monographs, 74* (Whole No. 498). (p. 321)

Sperry, R. W. (1964). Problems outstanding in the evolution of brain function. James Arthur Lecture, American Museum of Natural History, New York. Cited by R. Ornstein (1977), *The psychology of consciousness* (2nd ed.). New York: Harcourt Brace Jovanovich. (p. 116)

Sperry, R. W. (1985). Changed concepts of brain and consciousness: Some value implications. *Zygon, 20*, 41–57. (p. 178)

Sperry, R. W. (1992, Summer). Turnabout on consciousness: A mentalist view. *Journal of Mind & Behavior, 13*(3), 259–280. (p. 143)

Spiegel, D. (2007). The mind prepared: Hypnosis in surgery. *Journal of the National Cancer Institute, 99*, 1280–1281. (p. 221)

Spiegel, D. (2008, January 31). *Coming apart: Trauma and the fragmentation of the self*. Dana Foundation (www.dana.org). (p. 696)

Spiegel, K., Leproult, R., L'Hermite-Balériaux, M., Copinschi, G., Penev, P. D., & Van Cauter, E. (2004). Leptin levels are dependent on sleep duration: Relationships with sympathovagal balance, carbohydrate regulation, cortisol, and thyrotropin. *Journal of Clinical Endocrinology and Metabolism, 89*, 5762–5771. (p. 236)

Spielberger, C., & London, P. (1982). Rage boomerangs. *American Health, 1*, 52–56. (p. 452)

Spitzer, R. L., & Skodol, A. E. (2000). *DSM-IV-TR casebook: A learning companion to the Diagnostic and Statistical Manual of Mental Disorders, Fourth Edition, Text Revision.* Washington, DC: American Psychiatric Publications. (p. 693)

Spradley, J. P., & Phillips, M. (1972). Culture and stress: A quantitative analysis. *American Anthropologist, 74*, 518–529. (p. 777)

Sprecher, S. (1989). The importance to males and females of physical attractiveness, earning potential, and expressiveness in initial attraction. *Sex Roles, 21*, 591–607. (p. 800)

Spring, B., Pingitore, R., Bourgeois, M., Kessler, K. H., & Bruckner, E. (1992). The effects and non-effects of skipping breakfast: Results of three studies. Paper presented at the American Psychological Association convention. (p. 403)

Squire, L. R. (1992). Memory and the hippocampus: A synthesis from findings with rats, monkeys, and humans. *Psychological Review, 99*, 195–231. (p. 330)

Squire, L. R., & Zola-Morgan, S. (1991, September 20). The medial temporal lobe memory system. *Science, 253*, 1380–1386. (p. 331)

Srivastava, A., Locke, E. A., & Bartol, K. M. (2001). Money and subject well-being: It's not the money, it's the motives. *Journal of Personality and Social Psychology, 80*, 959–971. (p. 850)

Srivastava, S., John, O. P., Gosling, S. D., & Potter, J. (2003). Development of personality in early and middle adulthood: Set like plaster or persistent change? *Journal of Personality & Social Psychology, 84*, 1041–1053. (p. 581)

Srivastava, S., McGonigal, K. M., Richards, J. M., Butler, E. A., & Gross, J. J. (2006). Optimism in close relationships: How seeing things in a positive light makes them so. *Journal of Personality and Social Psychology, 91*, 143–153. (p. 589)

Stack, S. (1992). Marriage, family, religion, and suicide. In R. Maris, A. Berman, J. Maltsberger, & R. Yufit (Eds.), *Assessment and prediction of suicide.* New York: Guilford Press. (p. 676)

Stafford, R. S., MacDonald, E. A., & Finkelstein, S. N. (2001). National patterns of medication treatment for depression, 1987 to 2001. *Primary Care Companion Journal of Clinical Psychiatry, 3*, 232–235. (p. 742)

Stager, C. L., & Werker, J. F. (1997). Infants listen for more phonetic detail in speech perception than in word-learning tasks. *Nature, 388*, 381–382. (p. 374)

Stanford University Center for Narcolepsy. (2002). Narcolepsy is a serious medical disorder and a key to understanding other sleep disorders. (www.med.stanford.edu/school/Psychiatry/narcolepsy). (p. 238)

Stanley, D., Phelps, E., & Banaji, M. (2008). The neural basis of implicit attitudes. *Current Directions in Psychological Science, 17*, 164–170. (p. 782)

Stanley, J. C. (1997). Varieties of intellectual talent. *Journal of Creative Behavior, 31*, 93–119., 629

Stanovich, K. (1996). *How to think straight about psychology.* New York: Harper-Collins. (p. 556)

Stark, R. (2003a). *For the glory of God: How monotheism led to reformations, science, witch-hunts, and the end of slavery.* Princeton, NJ: Princeton University Press. (p. 35)

Stark, R. (2003b, October-November). False conflict: Christianity is not only compatible with science—it created it. *American Enterprise*, pp. 27–33. (p. 35)

Starr, J. M., Deary, I. J., Lemmon, H., & Whalley, L. J. (2000). Mental ability age 11 years and health status age 77 years. *Age and Ageing, 29*, 523–528. (p. 628)

State, M. W., & Šestan, N. (2012). The emerging biology of autism spectrum disorders. *Science, 337*, 1301–1304. (p. 482)

Statistics Canada. (1999). *Statistical report on the health of Canadians.* Prepared by the Federal, Provincial and Territorial Advisory Committee on Population Health for the Meeting of Ministers of Health, Charlottetown, PEI, September 16–17, 1999. (p. 443)

Statistics Canada. (2010). Languages. Canada year book. 11-402-X. (p. 380)

Statistics Canada. (2010). *Victims and persons accused of homicide, by age and sex.* Table 253-0003. (p. 501)

Staub, E. (1989). *The roots of evil: The psychological and cultural sources of genocide.* New York: Cambridge University Press. (p. 758)

St. Clair, D., Xu, M., Wang, P., Yu, Y., Fang, Y., Zhang, F., Zheng, X., Gu, N., Feng, G., Sham, P., & He, L. (2005). Rates of adult schizophrenia following prenatal exposure to the Chinese famine of 1959–1961. *Journal of the American Medical Association, 294*, 557–562. (p. 687)

Steel, P., Schmidt, J., & Schultz, J. (2008). Refining the relationship between personality and subject well-being. *Psychological Bulletin, 134*, 138–161. (p. 852)

Steele, C. M. (1990, May). A conversation with Claude Steele. *APS Observer*, pp. 11–17. (p. 639)

Steele, C. M. (1995, August 31). Black students live down to expectations. *New York Times* (www.nytimes.com). (p. 643)

Steele, C. M. (2010). *Whistling Vivaldi: And other clues to how stereotypes affect us.* New York: Norton. (p. 643)

Steele, C. M., & Josephs, R. A. (1990). Alcohol myopia: Its prized and dangerous effects. *American Psychologist, 45*, 921–933. (p. 249)

Steele, C. M., Spencer, S. J., & Aronson, J. (2002). Contending with group image: The psychology of stereotype and social identity threat. *Advances in Experimental Social Psychology, 34*, 379–440. (p. 642)

Steenhuysen, J. (2002, May 8). Bionic retina gives six patients partial sight. *Reuters News Service.* (See also www.optobionics.com/artificialretina.htm.). (p. 196)

Stein, S. (2009, August 20). New poll: 77 percent support "choice" of public option. *Huffington Post* (www.huffingtonpost.com). (p. 42)

Steinberg, L. (1987, September). Bound to bicker. *Psychology Today*, pp. 36–39. (p. 522)

Steinberg, L. (2007). Risk taking in adolescence: New perspectives from brain and behavioral science. *Current Directions in Psychological Science, 16*, 55–59. (p. 514)

Steinberg, L. (2010, March). Analyzing adolescence. Interview with Sara Martin. *Monitor on Psychology*, pp. 26–29. (p. 514)

Steinberg, L., Cauffman, E., Woolard, J., Graham, S., & Banich, M. (2009). Are adolescents less mature than adults? Minors' access to abortion, the juvenile death penalty, and the alleged APA "flip-flop." *American Psychologist, 64*, 583–594. (p. 514)

Steinberg, L., & Morris, A. S. (2001). Adolescent development. *Annual Review of Psychology, 52*, 83–110. (pp. 496, 522)

Steinberg, L., & Scott, E. S. (2003). Less guilty by reason of adolescence: Developmental immaturity, diminished responsibility, and the juvenile death penalty. *American Psychologist, 58*, 1009–1018. (p. 514)

Steinberg, N. (1993, February). Astonishing love stories (from an earlier United Press International report). *Games*, p. 47. (p. 799)

Steinhauer, J. (1999, November 29). Number of twins rises: so does parental stress. *New York Times* (www.nytimes.com). (p. 126)

Steinmetz, J. E. (1999). The localization of a simple type of learning and memory: The cerebellum and classical eyeblink conditioning. *Contemporary Psychology, 7*, 72–77. (p. 331)

Stengel, E. (1981). Suicide. In *The new Encyclopaedia Britannica, macropaedia* (Vol. 17, pp. 777–782). Chicago: Encyclopaedia Britannica. (p. 676)

Stepanikova, I., Nie, N. H., & He, X. (2010). Time on the Internet at home, loneliness, and life satisfaction: Evidence from panel time-diary data. *Computers in Human Behavior, 26*, 329–338. (p. 416)

Steptoe, A., Chida, Y., Hamer, M., & Wardle, J. (2010). Author reply: Meta-analysis of stress-related factors in cancer. *Nature Reviews: Clinical Oncology, 7*, 1. doi: 10.1038/ncponc1134-c2. (p. 451)

Stern, M., & Karraker, K. H. (1989). Sex stereotyping of infants: A review of gender labeling studies. *Sex Roles, 20*, 501–522. (p. 164)

Sternberg, E. (2006). A compassionate universe? *Science, 311*, 611–612. (p. 611)

Sternberg, E. M. (2009). *Healing spaces: The science of place and well-being.* Cambridge, MA: Harvard University Press. (p. 448)

Sternberg, R. J. (1985). *Beyond IQ: A triarchic theory of human intelligence.* New York: Cambridge University Press. (p. 611)

Sternberg, R. J. (1988). Applying cognitive theory to the testing and teaching of intelligence. *Applied Cognitive Psychology, 2*, 231–255. (p. 357)

Sternberg, R. J. (1999). The theory of successful intelligence. *Review of General Psychology, 3*, 292–316. (p. 611)

Sternberg, R. J. (2003). Our research program validating the triarchic theory of successful intelligence: Reply to Gottfredson. *Intelligence, 31*, 399–413. (pp. 357, 611)

Sternberg, R. J. (2006). The Rainbow Project: Enhance the SAT through assessments of analytical, practical, and creative skills. *Intelligence, 34*, 321–350. (p. 358)

Sternberg, R. J. (2007, July 6). Finding students who are wise, practical, and creative. *The Chronicle Review* (www.chronicle.com). (p. 611)

Sternberg, R. J. (2010). Assessment of gifted students for identification purposes: New techniques for a new millennium. *Learning and Individual Differences, 20*, 327–336. (p. 611)

Sternberg, R. J., & Grajek, S. (1984). The nature of love. *Journal of Personality and Social Psychology, 47*, 312–329. (p. 804)

Sternberg, R. J., & Grigorenko, E. L. (2000). Theme-park psychology: A case study regarding human intelligence and its implications for education. *Educational Psychology Review, 12*, 247–268. (p. 630)

Sternberg, R. J., & Kaufman, J. C. (1998). Human abilities. *Annual Review of Psychology, 49*, 479–502. (p. 607)

Sternberg, R. J., & Lubart, T. I. (1991). An investment theory of creativity and its development. *Human Development*, 1–31. (p. 357)

Sternberg, R. J., & Lubart, T. I. (1992). Buy low and sell high: An investment approach to creativity. *Psychological Science, 1*, 1–5. (p. 357)

Sternberg, R. J., & Wagner, R. K. (1993). The *g*-ocentric view of intelligence and job performance is wrong. *Current Directions in Psychological Science, 2*, 1–5. (p. 611)

Sternberg, R. J., Wagner, R. K., Williams, W. M., & Horvath, J. A. (1995). Testing common sense. *American Psychologist, 50*, 912–927. (p. 611)

Stetter, F., & Kupper, S. (2002). Autogenic training: A meta-analysis of clinical outcome studies. *Applied Psychophysiology and Biofeedback, 27*, 45–98. (p. 861)

Stevenson, H. W. (1992, December). Learning from Asian schools. *Scientific American*, pp. 70–76. (p. 641)

Stevenson, H. W., & Lee, S-Y. (1990). Contexts of achievement: A study of American, Chinese, and Japanese children. *Monographs of the Society for Research in Child Development, 55* (Serial No. 221, Nos. 1–2). (p. 630)

Stevenson, R. J., & Tomiczek, C. (2007). Olfactory-induced synesthesias: A review and model. *Psychological Bulletin, 133*, 294–309. (p. 211)

Stewart, R. E., & Chambless, D. L. (2009). Cognitive-behavioral therapy for adult anxiety disorders in clinical practice: A meta-analysis of effectiveness studies. *Journal of Consulting and Clinical Psychology, 77*, 595–606. (p. 732)

Stice, E. (2002). Risk and maintenance factors for eating pathology: A meta-analytic review. *Psychological Bulletin, 128*, 825–848. (p. 697)

Stice, E., Ng, J., & Shaw, H. (2010). Risk factors and prodromal eating pathology. *Journal of Child Psychology and Psychiatry, 51*, 518–525. (p. 698)

Stice, E., Shaw, H., Bohon, C., Marti, C. N., & Rohde, P. (2009). A meta-analytic review of depression prevention programs for children and adolescents: Factors that predict magnitude of intervention effects. *Journal of Consulting and Clinical Psychology, 77*, 486–503. (p. 737)

Stice, E., Shaw, H., & Marti, C. N. (2007). A meta-analytic review of eating disorder prevention programs: Encouraging findings. *Annual Review of Clinical Psychology, 3*, 233–257. (p. 698)

Stice, E., Spangler, D., & Agras, W. S. (2001). Exposure to media-portrayed thin-ideal images adversely affects vulnerable girls: A longitudinal experiment. *Journal of Social and Clinical Psychology, 20*, 270–288. (p. 698)

Stickgold, R. (2000, March 7). Quoted by S. Blakeslee, For better learning, researchers endorse "sleep on it" adage. *New York Times*, p. F2. (p. 241)

Stickgold, R., & Ellenbogen, J. M. (2008, August/September). Quiet! Sleeping brain at work. *Scientific American Mind*, pp. 23–29. (p. 231)

Stickgold, R., Hobson, J. A., Fosse, R., & Fosse, M. (2001). Sleep, learning, and dreams: Off-line memory processing. *Science, 294*, 1052–1057. (p. 241)

Stickgold, R., Malia, A., Maquire, D., Roddenberry, D., & O'Connor, M. (2000, October 13). Replaying the game: Hypnagogic images in normals and amnesics. *Science, 290*, 350–353. (pp. 240, 242)

Stiglitz, J. (2009, September 13). Towards a better measure of well-being. *Financial Times* (www.ft.com). (p. 854)

Stillman, T. F., Baumeister, R. F., Vohs, K. D., Lambert, N. M., Fincham, F. D., & Brewer, L. E. (2010). Personal philosophy and personnel achievement: Belief in free will predicts better job performance. *Social Psychological and Personality Science, 1*, 43–50. (p. 301)

Stinson, D. A., Logel, C., Zanna, M. P., Holmes, J. G., Camerson, J. J., Wood, J. V., & Spencer, S. J. (2008). The cost of lower self-esteem: Testing a self- and social-bonds model of health. *Journal of Personality and Social Psychology, 94*, 412–428. (p. 859)

Stipek, D. (1992). The child at school. In M. H. Bornstein & M. E. Lamb (Eds.), *Developmental psychology: An advanced textbook*. Hillsdale, NJ: Erlbaum. (p. 496)

Stirrat, M., & Perrett, D. I. (2010). Valid facial cues to cooperation and trust: Male facial width and trustworthiness. *Psychological Science 21*, 349–354. (p. 790)

Stith, S. M., Rosen, K. H., Middleton, K. A., Busch, A. L., Lunderberg, K., & Carlton, R. P. (2000). The intergenerational transmission of spouse abuse: A meta-analysis. *Journal of Marriage and the Family, 62*, 640–654. (p. 308)

Stix, G. (2011, March). The neuroscience of true grit. *Scientific American, 304*, 28–33. (p. 665)

St. Jacques, P. L., Dolcos, F., & Cabeza, R. (2009). Effects of aging on functional connectivity of the amygdala for subsequent memory of negative pictures: A network analysis of fMRI data. *Psychological Science, 20*, 74–84. (p. 547)

Stockton, M. C., & Murnen, S. K. (1992). Gender and sexual arousal in response to sexual stimuli: A meta-analytic review. Paper presented at the American Psychological Society convention. (p. 409)

Stone, A. A., & Neale, J. M. (1984). Effects of severe daily events on mood. *Journal of Personality and Social Psychology, 46*, 137–144. (p. 848)

Stone, A. A., Schwartz, J. E., Broderick, J. E., & Deaton, A. (2010). A snapshot of the age distribution of psychological well-being in the United States. *PNAS, 107*, 9985–9990. (p. 546)

Stone, A. A., Schwartz, J. E., Broderick, J. E., & Shiffman, S. S. (2005). Variability of momentary pain predicts recall of weekly pain: A consequences of the peak (or salience) memory heuristic. *Personality and Social Psychology Bulletin, 31*, 1340–1346. (p. 205)

Stone, G. (2006, February 17). Homeless man discovered to be lawyer with amnesia. *ABC News* (abcnews.go.com). (p. 694)

Stone, R. (2005). In the wake: Looking for keys to posttraumatic stress. *Science, 310*, 1605. (p. 665)

Stoolmiller, M. (1999). Implications of the restricted range of family environments for estimates of heritability and nonshared environment in behavior-genetic adoption studies. *Psychological Bulletin, 125*, 392–409. (p. 128)

Storbeck, J., Robinson, M. D., & McCourt, M. E. (2006). Semantic processing precedes affect retrieval: The neurological case for cognitive primary in visual processing. *Review of General Psychology, 10*, 41–55. (p. 424)

Storm, L., Tressoldi, P. E., & Di Risio, L. (2010a). A meta-analysis with nothing to hide: Reply to Hyman (2010). *Psychological Bulletin, 136*, 491–494. (p. 168)

Storm, L., Tressoldi, P. E., & Di Risio, L. (2010b). Meta-analysis of free-response studies, 1992–2008: Assessing the noise reduction model in parapsychology *Psychological Bulletin, 136*, 471–485. (p. 168)

Storms, M. D. (1973). Videotape and the attribution process: Reversing actors' and observers' points of view. *Journal of Personality and Social Psychology, 27*, 165–175. (p. 755)

Storms, M. D. (1983). *Development of sexual orientation*. Washington, DC: Office of Social and Ethical Responsibility, American Psychological Association. (p. 533)

Storms, M. D., & Thomas, G. C. (1977). Reactions to physical closeness. *Journal of Personality and Social Psychology, 35*, 412–418. (p. 772)

Stout, J. A., & Dasgupta, N. (2011). When *he* doesn't mean *you*: Gender-exclusive language as ostracism. *Personality and Social Psychology Bulletin, 37*, 75–769. (p. 414)

Stowell, J. R., Oldham, T., & Bennett, D. (2010). Using student response systems ("clickers") to combat conformity and shyness. *Teaching of Psychology, 37*, 135–140. (p. 764)

Strack, F., Martin, L., & Stepper, S. (1988). Inhibiting and facilitating conditions of the human smile: A nonobtrusive test of the facial feedback hypothesis. *Journal of Personality and Social Psychology, 54*, 768–777. (p. 438)

Strack, S., & Coyne, J. C. (1983). Social confirmation of dysphoria: Shared and private reactions to depression. *Journal of Personality and Social Behavior, 44*, 798–806. (p. 681)

Strahan, E. J., Spencer, S. J., & Zanna, M. P. (2002). Subliminal priming and persuasion: Striking while the iron is hot. *Journal of Experimental Social Psychology, 38*, 556–568. (p. 158)

Stranahan, A. M., Khalil, D., & Gould, E. (2006). Social isolation delays the positive effects of running on adult neurogenesis. *Nature Neuroscience, 9*, 526–533. (p. 112)

Strand, S., Deary, I. J., & Smith, P. (2006). Sex differences in cognitive abilities test scores: A UK national picture. *British Journal of Educational Psychology, 76*, 463–480. (p. 638)

Strange, D., Hayne, H., & Garry, M. (2008). A photo, a suggestion, a false memory. *Applied Cognitive Psychology, 22*, 587–603. (p. 348)

Strasburger, V. C., Jordan, A. B., & Donnerstein, E. (2010). Health effects of media on children and adolescents. *Pediatrics, 125*, 756–767. (p. 308)

Stratton, G. M. (1896). Some preliminary experiments on vision without inversion of the retinal image. *Psychological Review, 3*, 611–617. (p. 191)

Straub, R. O., Seidenberg, M. S., Bever, T. G., & Terrace, H. S. (1979). Serial learning in the pigeon. *Journal of the Experimental Analysis of Behavior, 32,* 137–148. (p. 869)

Straus, M. A., & Gelles, R. J. (1980). *Behind closed doors: Violence in the American family.* New York: Anchor/Doubleday. (p. 282)

Straus, M. A., Sugarman, D. B., & Giles-Sims, J. (1997). Spanking by parents and subsequent antisocial behavior of children. *Archives of Pediatric Adolescent Medicine, 151,* 761–767. (p. 282)

Strawbridge, W. J. (1999). Mortality and religious involvement: A review and critique of the results, the methods, and the measures. Paper presented at a Harvard University conference on religion and health, sponsored by the National Institute for Health Research and the John Templeton Foundation. (p. 864)

Strawbridge, W. J., Cohen, R. D., & Shema, S. J. (1997). Frequent attendance at religious services and mortality over 28 years. *American Journal of Public Health, 87,* 957–961. (p. 864)

Strawbridge, W. J., Shema, S. J., Cohen, R. D., & Kaplan, G. A. (2001). Religious attendance increases survival by improving and maintaining good health behaviors, mental health, and social relationships. *Annals of Behavioral Medicine, 23,* 68–74. (p. 865)

Strayer, D. L., & Drews, F A. (2007). Cell-phone-induced driver distraction. *Current Directions in Psychological Science, 16,* 128–131. (p. 153)

Strick, M., Dijksterhuis, A., & van Baaren, R. B. (2010). Unconscious-thought effects take place off-line, not on-line. *Psychological Science, 21,* 484–488. (p. 369)

Stroebe, W., Schut, H., & Stroebe, M. S. (2005). Grief work, disclosure and counseling: Do they help the bereaved? *Clinical Psychology Review, 25,* 395–414. (p. 548)

Stross, R. (2011, July 9). The therapist will see you now, via the web. *New York Times* (www.nytimes.com). (p. 723)

Strully, K. W. (2009). Job loss and health in the U.S. labor market. *Demography, 46,* 221–246. (p. 443)

Strupp, H. H. (1986). Psychotherapy: Research, practice, and public policy (How to avoid dead ends). *American Psychologist, 41,* 120–130. (p. 734)

Su, R., Rounds, J., & Armstrong, P. I. (2009). Men and things, women and people: A meta-analysis of sex differences in interests. *Psychological Bulletin, 135,* 859–884. (p. 503)

Subiaul, F., Cantlon, J. F., Holloway, R. L., & Terrace, H. S. (2004). Cognitive imitation in rhesus macaques. *Science, 305,* 407–410. (p. 306)

Subrahmanyam, K., & Greenfield, P. (2008). Online communication and adolescent relationships. *The Future of Children, 18,* 119–146. (p. 522)

Suddath, R. L., Christison, G. W., Torrey, E. F., Casanova, M. F., & Weinberger, D. R. (1990). Anatomical abnormalities in the brains of monozygotic twins discordant for schizophrenia. *New England Journal of Medicine, 322,* 789–794. (p. 689)

Sue, S. (2006). Research to address racial and ethnic disparities in mental health: Some lessons learned. In S. I. Donaldson, D. E. Berger, & K. Pezdek (Eds.), *Applied psychology: New frontiers and rewarding careers.* Mahwah, NJ: Erlbaum. (p. 735)

Suedfeld, P. (1998). Homo invictus: The indomitable species. *Canadian Psychology, 38,* 164–173. (p. 665)

Suedfeld, P. (2000). Reverberations of the Holocaust fifty years later: Psychology's contributions to understanding persecution and genocide. *Canadian Psychology, 41,* 1–9. (p. 665)

Suedfeld, P., & Mocellin, J. S. P. (1987). The "sensed presence" in unusual environments. *Environment and Behavior, 19,* 33–52. (p. 255)

Sugita, Y. (2004). Experience in early infancy is indispensable for color perception. *Current Biology. 14,* 1267–1271. (p. 187)

Suinn, R. M. (1997). Mental practice in sports psychology: Where have we been, Where do we go? *Clinical Psychology: Science and Practice, 4,* 189–207. (p. 381)

Sullivan, D., & von Wachter, T. (2009). Job displacement and mortality: An analysis using administrative data. *Quarterly Journal of Economics, 124,* 1265–1306. (p. 442)

Sullivan, K. T., Pasch, L. A., Johnson, M. D., & Bradbury, T. N. (2010). Social support, problem solving, and the longitudinal course of newlywed marriage. *Journal of Personality and Social Psychology, 98,* 631–644. (p. 805)

Sullivan, P. F., Neale, M. C., & Kendler, K. S. (2000). Genetic epidemiology of major depression: Review and meta-analysis. *American Journal of Psychiatry, 157,* 1552–1562. (p. 675)

Sullivan/Anderson, A. (2009, March 30). How to end the war over sex ed. *Time,* pp. 40–43. (p. 530)

Suls, J. M., & Tesch, F. (1978). Students' preferences for information about their test performance: A social comparison study. *Journal of Experimental Social Psychology, 8,* 189–197. (p. 852)

Summers, M. (1996, December 9). Mister clean. *People Weekly,* pp. 139–142. (p. 649)

Sun, Q. I., Townsend, M. K., Okereke, O., Franco, O. H., Hu, F. B., & Grodstein, F. (2009). Adiposity and weight change in mid-life in relation to healthy survival after age 70 in women: Prospective cohort study. *British Medical Journal, 339,* b3796. (p. 401)

Sundet, J. M., Borren, I., & Tambs, K. (2008). The Flynn effect is partly caused by changing fertility patterns. *Intelligence, 36,* 183–191. (p. 622)

Sundstrom, E., De Meuse, K. P., & Futrell, D. (1990). Work teams: Applications and effectiveness. *American Psychologist, 45,* 120–133. (p. 839)

Sunstein, C. R. (2007). On the divergent American reactions to terrorism and climate change. *Columbia Law Review, 107,* 503–557. (p. 365)

Suomi, S. J. (1986). Anxiety-like disorders in young nonhuman primates. In R. Gettleman (Ed.), *Anxiety disorders of childhood.* New York: Guilford Press. (p. 667)

Suppes, P. (1982). Quoted by R. H. Ennis, Children's ability to handle Piaget's propositional logic: A conceptual critique. In S. Modgil & C. Modgil (Eds.), *Jean Piaget: Consensus and controversy.* New York: Praeger. (p. 483)

Surgeon General. (1999). *Mental health: A report of the surgeon general.* Rockville, MD: U.S. Department of Health and Human Services. (p. 656)

Susser, E. S. (1999). Life course cohort studies of schizophrenia. *Psychiatric Annals, 29,* 161–165. (p. 689)

Susser, E. S., Herman, D. B., & Aaron, B. (2002, August). Combating the terror of terrorism. *Scientific American,* pp. 70–77. (p. 664)

Susser, E. S., Neugenbauer, R., Hoek, H. W., Brown, A. S., Lin, S., Labovitz, D., & Gorman, J. M. (1996). Schizophrenia after prenatal famine. *Archives of General Psychiatry, 53*(1), 25–31. (p. 687)

Sutcliffe, J. S. (2008). Insights into the pathogenesis of autism. *Science, 321,* 208–209. (p. 482)

Sutherland, A. (2006, June 25). What Shamu taught me about a happy marriage, *New York Times* (www.nytimes.com). (p. 288)

Swami, V., & 60 others. (2010). The attractive female body weight and female body dissatisfaction in 26 countries across 10 world regions: Results of the international body project I. *Personality and Social Psychology Bulletin, 36,* 309–325. (p. 698)

Swami, V., Henderson, G., Custance, D., & Tovée, M. J. (2011). A cross-cultural investigation of men's judgments of female body weight in Britain and Indonesia. *Journal of Cross-Cultural Psychology, 42,* 140–145. (p. 401)

Swann, W. B., Jr., Chang-Schneider, C., & McClarty, K. L. (2007). Do people's self-views matter: Self-concept and self-esteem in everyday life. *American Psychologist, 62,* 84–94. (p. 595)

Sweat, J. A., & Durm, M. W. (1993). Psychics: Do police departments really use them? *Skeptical Inquirer, 17,* 148–158. (p. 167)

Swerdlow, N. R., & Koob, G. F. (1987). Dopamine, schizophrenia, mania, and depression: Toward a unified hypothesis of cortico-stiato-pallido-thalamic function (with commentary). *Behavioral and Brain Sciences, 10,* 197–246. (p. 686)

Swim, J. K. (1994). Perceived versus meta-analytic effect sizes: An assessment of the accuracy of gender stereotypes. *Journal of Personality and Social Psychology, 66,* 21–36. (p. 783)

Swim, J. K., Johnston, K., & Pearson, N. B. (2009). Daily experiences with heterosexism: Relations between heterosexist hassles and psychological well-being. *Journal of Social and Clinical Psychology, 28,* 597–629. (p. 444)

Symbaluk, D. G., Heth, C. D., Cameron, J., & Pierce, W. D. (1997). Social modeling, monetary incentives, and pain endurance: The role of self-efficacy and pain perception. *Personality and Social Psychology Bulletin, 23,* 258–269. (p. 205)

Symond, M. B., Harris, A. W. F., Gordon, E., & Williams, L. M. (2005). "Gamma synchrony" in first-episode schizophrenia: A disorder of temporal connectivity? *American Journal of Psychiatry, 162,* 459–465. (p. 687)

Symons, C. S., & Johnson, B. T. (1997). The self-reference effect in memory: A meta-analysis. *Psychological Bulletin, 121*(3), 371–394. (p. 326)

Taha, F. A. (1972). A comparative study of how sighted and blind perceive the manifest content of dreams. *National Review of Social Sciences, 9*(3), 28. (p. 240)

Taheri, S. (2004). The genetics of sleep disorders. *Minerva Medica, 95,* 203–212. (p. 238)

Taheri, S. (2004a, 20 December). Does the lack of sleep make you fat? *University of Bristol Research News* (www.bristol.ac.uk). (p. 402)

Taheri, S., Lin, L., Austin, D., Young, T., & Mignot, E. (2004b). Short sleep duration is associated with reduced leptin, elevated ghrelin, and increased body mass index. *PloS Medicine, 1*(3), e62. (p. 402)

Taheri, S., Zeitzer, J. M., & Mignot, E. (2002). The role of hypocretins (orexins) in sleep regulation and narcolepsy. *Annual Review of Neuroscience, 25,* 283–313. (p. 238)

Tajfel, H. (Ed.). (1982). *Social identity and intergroup relations.* New York: Cambridge University Press. (p. 784)

Talarico, J. M., & Rubin, D. C. (2003). Confidence, not consistency, characterizes flashbulb memories. *Psychological Science, 14,* 455–461. (p. 332)

Talarico, J. M., & Rubin, D. C. (2007). Flashbulb memories are special after all: in phenomenology, not accuracy. *Applied Cognitive Psychology, 21,* 557–578. (p. 332)

Talwar, S. K., Xu, S., Hawley, E. S., Weiss, S. A., Moxon, K. A., & Chapin, J. K. (2002). Rat navigation guided by remote control. *Nature, 417,* 37–38. (p. 100)

Tamres, L. K., Janicki, D., & Helgeson, V. S. (2002). Sex differences in coping behavior: A meta-analytic review and an examination of relative coping. *Personality and Social Psychology Review, 6,* 2–30. (p. 503)

Tang, C. Y., Eaves, E. L., Ng, J. C., Carpenter, D. M., Mai, X., Schroeder, D. H., Condon, C. A., Coliom, R., & Haier, R. J. (2010). Brain networks for working memory and factors of intelligence assessed in males and females with fMRI and DTI. *Intelligence, 38,* 293–303. (p. 613)

Tang, S-H., & Hall, V. C. (1995). The overjustification effect: A meta-analysis. *Applied Cognitive Psychology, 9,* 365–404. (p. 297)

Tangney, C. C., Kwasny, M. J., Li, H., Wilson, R. S., Evans, D. A., & Morris, M. C. (2011). Adherence to a Mediterranean-type dietary pattern and cognitive decline in a community population. *American Journal of Clinical Nutrition, 93,* 601–607. (p. 679)

Tangney, J. P., Baumeister, R. F., & Boone, A. L. (2004). High self-control predicts good adjustment, less pathology, better grades, and interpersonal success. *Journal of Personality, 72,* 271–324. (p. 301)

Tannen, D. (1990). *You just don't understand: Women and men in conversation.* New York: Morrow. (p. 502)

Tannen, D. (2001). *You just don't understand: Women and men in conversation.* New York: Harper. (p. 66)

Tannenbaum, P. (2002, February). Quoted in R. Kubey & M. Csikszentmihalyi, Television addiction is no mere metaphor. *Scientific American,* pp. 74–80. (p. 160)

Tanner, J. M. (1978). *Fetus into man: Physical growth from conception to maturity.* Cambridge, MA: Harvard University Press. (p. 527)

Tardif, T., Fletcher, P., Liang, W., Zhang, Z., Kaciroti, N., & Marchman, V. A. (2008). Baby's first 10 words. *Developmental Psychology, 44,* 929–938. (p. 375)

Tasbihsazan, R., Nettelbeck, T., & Kirby, N. (2003). Predictive validity of the Fagan test of infant intelligence. *British Journal of Developmental Psychology, 21,* 585–597. (p. 627)

Taub, E. (2004). Harnessing brain plasticity through behavioral techniques to produce new treatments in neurorehabilitation. *American Psychologist, 59,* 692–698. (p. 111)

Taubes, G. (2001). The soft science of dietary fat. *Science, 291,* 2536–2545. (p. 403)

Taubes, G. (2002, July 7). What if it's all been a big fat lie? *New York Times* (www.nytimes.com). (p. 403)

Tausch, N., Hewstone, M., Kenworthy, J. B., Psaltis, C., Schmid, K., Popan, J. R., Cairns, E., & Hughes, J. (2010). Secondary transfer effects of intergroup contact: Alternative accounts and underlying processes. *Journal of Personality and Social Psychology, 99,* 282–302. (p. 813)

Tavris, C. (1982, November). Anger defused. *Psychology Today,* pp. 25–35. (p. 846)

Tavris, C., & Aronson, E. (2007). *Mistakes were made (but not by me).* Orlando, FL: Harcourt. (pp. 346, 758)

Tay, L., & Diener, E. (2011). Needs and subjective well-being around the world. *Journal of Personality and Social Psychology, 101,* 354–365. (p. 394)

Taylor, C. A., Manganello, J. A., Lee, S. J., & Rice, J. C. (2010). Mothers' spanking of 3-year-old children and subsequent risk of children's aggressive behavior. *Pediatrics, 125,* 1057–1065. (p. 282)

Taylor, K., & Rohrer, D. (2010). The effects of interleaved practice. *Applied Cognitive Psychology, 24,* 837–848. (p. 16)

Taylor, P. J., Gooding, P., Wood, A. M., & Tarrier, N. (2011). The role of defeat and entrapment in depression, anxiety, and suicide. *Psychological Bulletin, 137,* 391–420. (p. 677)

Taylor, P. J., Russ-Eft, D. F., & Chan, D. W. L. (2005). A meta-analytic review of behavior modeling training. *Journal of Applied Psychology, 90,* 692–709. (p. 307)

Taylor, S., Kuch, K., Koch, W. J., Crockett, D. J., & Passey, G. (1998). The structure of posttraumatic stress symptoms. *Journal of Abnormal Psychology, 107,* 154–160. (p. 664)

Taylor, S. E. (1989). *Positive illusions.* New York: Basic Books. (p. 367)

Taylor, S. E. (2002). *The tending instinct: How nurturing is essential to who we are and how we live.* New York: Times Books. (p. 503)

Taylor, S. E. (2006). Tend and befriend: Biobehavioral bases of affiliation under stress. *Current Directions in Psychological Science, 15,* 273–277. (pp. 445, 446)

Taylor, S. E., Cousino, L. K., Lewis, B. P., Gruenewald, T. L., Gurung, R. A. R., & Updegraff, J. A. (2000). Biobehavioral responses to stress in females: Tend-and-befriend, not fight-or-flight. *Psychological Review, 107,* 411–430. (p. 445)

Taylor, S. E., Pham, L. B., Rivkin, I. D., & Armor, D. A. (1998). Harnessing the imagination: Mental simulation, self-regulation, and coping. *American Psychologist, 53,* 429–439. (p. 381)

Taylor, S. P., & Chermack, S. T. (1993). Alcohol, drugs and human physical aggression. *Journal of Studies on Alcohol,* Supplement No. 11, 78–88. (p. 791)

Teasdale, T. W., & Owen, D. R. (2005). A long-term rise and recent decline in intelligence test performance: The Flynn effect in reverse. *Personality and Individual Differences, 39,* 837–843. (p. 621)

Teasdale, T. W., & Owen, D. R. (2008). Secular declines in cognitive test scores: A reversal of the Flynn effect. *Intelligence, 36,* 121–126. (p. 621)

Tedeschi, R. G., & Calhoun, L. G. (2004). Posttraumatic growth: Conceptual foundations and empirical evidence. *Psychological Inquiry, 15,* 1–18. (p. 665)

Teghtsoonian, R. (1971). On the exponents in Stevens' law and the constant in Ekinan's law. *Psychological Review, 78,* 71–80. (p. 159)

Teicher, M. H. (2002, March). The neurobiology of child abuse. *Scientific American,* pp. 68–75. (p. 494)

Teller. (2009, April 20). Quoted by J. Lehrer, Magic and the brain: Teller reveals the neuroscience of illusion. *Wired Magazine* (www.wired.com). (p. 154)

Tenopyr, M. L. (1997). Improving the workplace: Industrial/organizational psychology as a career. In R. J. Sternberg (Ed.), *Career paths in psychology: Where your degree can take you.* Washington, DC: American Psychological Association. (p. 829)

Terao, T., Ohgami, H., Shlotsuki, I., Ishil, N., & Iwata, N. (2010). Author's reply. *British Journal of Psychiatry, 196,* 160. (p. 743)

Terman, J. S., Terman, M., Lo, E-S., & Cooper, T. B. (2001). Circadian time of morning light administration and therapeutic response in winter depression. *Archives of General Psychiatry, 58,* 69–73. (p 734)

Terman, L. M. (1916). *The measurement of intelligence.* Boston: Houghton Mifflin. (p. 619)

Terman, M., Terman, J. S., & Ross, D. C. (1998). A controlled trial of timed bright light and negative air ionization for treatment of winter depression. *Archives of General Psychiatry, 55,* 875–882. (p. 734)

Terrace, H. S. (1979, November). How Nim Chimpsky changed my mind. *Psychology Today,* pp. 65–76. (pp. 869, 870)

Terre, L., & Stoddart, R. (2000). Cutting edge specialties for graduate study in psychology. *Eye on Psi Chi, 23–26.* (p. 20)

Tesser, A., Forehand, R., Brody, G., & Long, N. (1989). Conflict: The role of calm and angry parent-child discussion in adolescent development. *Journal of Social and Clinical Psychology, 8,* 317–330. (p. 521)

Tetlock, P. E. (1988). Monitoring the integrative complexity of American and Soviet policy rhetoric: What can be learned? *Journal of Social Issues, 44,* 101–131. (p. 815)

Tetlock, P. E. (1998). Close-call counterfactuals and belief-system defenses: I was not almost wrong but I was almost right. *Journal of Personality and Social Psychology, 75,* 639–652. (p. 33)

Tetlock, P. E. (2005). *Expert political judgement: How good is it? How can we know?* Princeton, NJ: Princeton University Press. (p. 33)

Thaler, R. H., & Sunstein, C. R. (2008). *Nudge: Improving decisions about health, wealth, and happiness.* New Haven, CT: Yale University Press. (p. 368)

Thannickal, T. C., Moore, R. Y., Nienhuis, R., Ramanathan, L., Gulyani, S., Aldrich, M., Cornford, M., & Siegel, J. M. (2000). Reduced number of hypocretin neurons in human narcolepsy. *Neuron, 27,* 469–474. (p. 238)

Thatcher, R. W., Walker, R. A., & Giudice, S. (1987). Human cerebral hemispheres develop at different rates and ages. *Science, 236,* 1110–1113. (pp. 463, 471)

Thayer, R. E. (1987). Energy, tiredness, and tension effects of a sugar snack versus moderate exercise. *Journal of Personality and Social Psychology, 52,* 119–125. (p. 860)

Thayer, R. E. (1993). Mood and behavior (smoking and sugar snacking) following moderate exercise: A partial test of self-regulation theory. *Personality and Individual Differences, 14,* 97–104. (p. 860)

Théoret, H., Halligan, H., Kobayashi, M., Fregni, F., Tager-Flusberg, H., & Pascual-Leone, A. (2005). Impaired motor facilitation during action observation in individuals with autism spectrum disorder. *Current Biology, 15,* R84–R85. (p. 482)

Thernstrom, M. (2006, May 14). My pain, my brain. *New York Times* (www.nytimes.com). (p. 206)

Thiel, A., Hadedank, B., Herholz, K., Kessler, J., Winhuisen, L., Haupt, W. F., & Heiss, W-D. (2006). From the left to the right: How the brain compensates progressive loss of language function. *Brain and Language, 98,* 57–65. (p. 111)

Thiele, T. E., Marsh, D. J., Ste. Marie, L., Bernstein, I. L., & Palmiter, R. D. (1998). Ethanol consumption and resistance are inversely related to neuropeptide Y levels. *Nature, 396,* 366–369. (p. 823)

Thomas, A., & Chess, S. (1977). *Temperament and development.* New York: Brunner/Mazel. (p. 491)

Thomas, A., & Chess, S. (1986). The New York Longitudinal Study: From infancy to early adult life. In R. Plomin & J. Dunn (Eds.), *The study of temperament: Changes, continuities, and challenges.* Hillsdale, NJ: Erlbaum. (p. 464)

Thomas, L. (1983). *The youngest science: Notes of a medicine watcher.* New York: Viking Press. (p. 82)

Thomas, L. (1992). *The fragile species.* New York: Scribner's. (pp. 142, 730)

Thompson, G. (2010). The $1 million dollar challenge. *Skeptic Magazine, 15,* 8–9. (p. 169)

Thompson, J. K., Jarvie, G. J., Lahey, B. B., & Cureton, K. J. (1982). Exercise and obesity: Etiology, physiology, and intervention. *Psychological Bulletin, 91,* 55–79. (p. 403)

Thompson, P. M., Cannon, T. D., Narr, K. L., van Erp, T., Poutanen, V-P., Huttunen, M., Lönnqvist, J., Standerskjöld-Nordenstam, C-G., Kaprio, J., Khaledy, M., Dail, R., Zoumalan, C. I., & Toga, A. W. (2001). Genetic influences on brain structure. *Nature Neuroscience, 4,* 1253–1258. (p. 632)

Thompson, P. M., Giedd, J. N., Woods, R. P., MacDonald, D., Evans, A. C., & Toga, A. W. (2000). Growth patterns in the developing brain detected by using continuum mechanical tensor maps. *Nature, 404,* 190–193. (p. 471)

Thompson, R., Emmorey, K., & Gollan, T. H. (2005). "Tip of the fingers" experiences by Deaf signers. *Psychological Science, 16,* 856–860. (p. 344)

Thomson, R., & Murachver, T. (2001). Predicting gender from electronic discourse. *British Journal of Social Psychology, 40,* 193–208 (and personal correspondence from T. Murachver, May 23, 2002). (p. 502)

Thorndike, E. L. (1898). Animal intelligence: An experimental study of associative processes in animals. *Psychological Review Monograph Supplements, 2,* 4–160. (p. 276)

Thorne, J., with Larry Rothstein. (1993). *You are not alone: Words of experience and hope for the journey through depression.* New York: HarperPerennial. (p. 649)

Thornhill, R., & Gangestad, S. W. (1994). Human fluctuating asymmetry and sexual behavior. *Psychological Science, 5,* 297–302. (p. 802)

Thornton, B., & Moore, S. (1993). Physical attractiveness contrast effect: Implications for self-esteem and evaluations of the social self. *Personality and Social Psychology Bulletin, 19,* 474–480. (p. 800)

Thorpe, W. H. (1974). *Animal nature and human nature.* London: Metheun. (p. 870)

Tiedens, L. Z. (2001). Anger and advancement versus sadness and subjugation: The effect of negative emotion expressions on social status conferral. *Journal of Personality and Social Psychology, 80,* 86–94. (p. 846)

Tiggemann, M., & Miller, J. (2010). The Internet and adolescent girls' weight satisfaction and drive for thinness. *Sex Roles, 63,* 79–90. (p. 698)

Tiihonen, J., Lönnqvist, J., Wahlbeck, K., Klaukka, T., Niskanen, L., Tanskanen, A., Haukka, J. (2009). 11-year follow-up of mortality in patients with schizophrenia: a population-based cohort study (FIN11 study). *Lancet, 374,* 260–267 (p. 741)

Time. (2009, Oct. 14). The state of the American woman. pp. 32–33. (p. 503)

Time/CNN Survey. (1994, December 19). Vox pop: Happy holidays, *Time.* (p. 673)

Timmerman, T. A. (2007). "It was a thought pitch": Personal, situational, and target influences on hit-by-pitch events across time. *Journal of Applied Psychology, 92,* 876–884. (p. 791)

Tinbergen, N. (1951). *The study of instinct.* Oxford: Clarendon. (p. 391)

Tirrell, M. E. (1990). Personal communication. (p. 269)

Toews, P. (2004, December 30). *Dirk Willems: A heart undivided.* Mennonite Brethren Historical Commission (www.mbhistory.org/profiles/dirk.en.html). (p. 753)

Tolin, D. F. (2010). Is cognitive-behavioral therapy more effective than other therapies? A meta-analytic review. *Clinical Psychology Review, 30,* 710–720. (p. 732)

Tolin, D. F., & Foa, E. B. (2006). Sex differences in trauma and posttraumatic stress disorder: A quantitative review of 25 years of research. *Psychological Bulletin, 132,* 959–992. (p. 665)

Tolman, E. C., & Honzik, C. H. (1930). Introduction and removal of reward, and maze performance in rats. *University of California Publications in Psychology, 4,* 257–275. (p. 297)

Tolstoy, L. (1904). *My confessions.* Boston: Dana Estes. (p. 15)

Tondo, L., Jamison, K. R., & Baldessarini, R. J. (1997). Effect of lithium maintenance on suicidal behavior in major mood disorders. In D. M. Stoff & J. J. Mann (Eds.), *The neurobiology of suicide: From the bench to the clinic.* New York: New York Academy of Sciences. (p. 743)

Toni, N., Buchs, P.-A., Nikonenko, I., Bron, C. R., & Muller, D. (1999). LTP promotes formation of multiple spine synapses between a single axon terminal and a dendrite. *Nature, 402,* 421–42. (p. 333)

Topolinski, S., & Reber, R. (2010). Gaining insight into the "aha" experience. *Current Directions in Psychological Science, 19,* 401–405. (p. 297)

Torrey, E. F. (1986). *Witchdoctors and psychiatrists.* New York: Harper & Row. (p. 735)

Torrey, E. F., & Miller, J. (2002). *The invisible plague: The rise of mental illness from 1750 to the present.* New Brunswick, NJ: Rutgers University Press. (p. 687)

Torrey, E. F., Miller, J., Rawlings, R., & Yolken, R. H. (1997). Seasonality of births in schizophrenia and bipolar disorder: A review of the literature. *Schizophrenia Research, 28,* 1–38. (p. 687)

Totterdell, P., Kellett, S., Briner, R. B., & Teuchmann, K. (1998). Evidence of mood linkage in work groups. *Journal of Personality and Social Psychology, 74,* 1504–1515. (p. 763)

Tracy, J. L., & Robins, R. W. (2004). Show your pride: Evidence for a discrete emotion expression. *Psychological Science, 15,* 194–197. (p. 844)

Trautwein, U., Lüdtke, O., Köller, O., & Baumert, J. (2006). Self-esteem, academic self-concept, and achievement: How the learning environment moderates the dynamics of self-concept. *Journal of Personality and Social Psychology, 90,* 334–349. (p. 595)

Treffert, D. A., & Christensen, D. D. (2005, December). Inside the mind of a savant. *Scientific American,* pp. 108–113. (p. 609)

Treffert, D. A., & Wallace, G. L. (2002). Island of genius—The artistic brilliance and dazzling memory that sometimes accompany autism and other disorders hint at how all brains work. *Scientific American, 286,* 76–86. (p. 609)

Treisman, A. (1987). Properties, parts, and objects. In K. R. Boff, L. Kaufman, & J. P. Thomas (Eds.), *Handbook of perception and human performance.* New York: Wiley. (p. 183)

Tremblay, R. E., Pihl, R. O., Vitaro, F., & Dobkin, P. L. (1994). Predicting early onset of male antisocial behavior from preschool behavior. *Archives of General Psychiatry, 51,* 732–739. (p. 700)

Trenholm, C., Devaney, B., Fortson, K., Quay, L., Sheeler, J., & Clark, M. (2007, April). Impacts of four Title V, Section 510 abstinence education programs. Report to U.S. Department of Health and Human Services by Mathematica Policy Research, Inc., Princeton, NJ. (p. 530)

Trewin, D. (2001). *Australian social trends 2001.* Canberra: Australian Bureau of Statistics. (p. 504)

Triandis, H. C. (1981). Some dimensions of intercultural variation and their implications for interpersonal behavior. Paper presented at the American Psychological Association convention. (p. 777)

Triandis, H. C. (1994). *Culture and social behavior.* New York: McGraw-Hill. (pp. 599, 600, 792)

Triandis, H. C., Bontempo, R., Villareal, M. J., Asai, M., & Lucca, N. (1988). Individualism and collectivism: Cross-cultural perspectives on self-ingroup relationships. *Journal of Personality and Social Psychology, 54,* 323–338. (p. 600)

Trickett, E. (2009). Community psychology: Individuals and interventions in community context. *Annual Review of Psychology, 60,* 395–419. (p. 15)

Trillin, C. (2006, March 27). Alice off the page. *The New Yorker,* 44. (p. 572)

Trimble, J. E. (1994). Cultural variations in the use of alcohol and drugs. In W. J. Lonner & R. Malpass (Eds.), *Psychology and culture.* Boston: Allyn & Bacon. (p. 824)

Triplett, N. (1898). The dynamogenic factors in pacemaking and competition. *American Journal of Psychology, 9,* 507–533. (p. 771)

Trolier, T. K., & Hamilton, D. L. (1986). Variables influencing judgments of correlational relations. *Journal of Personality and Social Psychology, 50,* 879–888. (p. 50)

Trut, L. N. (1999). Early canid domestication: The farm-fox experiment. *American Scientist, 87,* 160–169. (p. 136)

Tsai, J. L., & Chentsova-Dutton, Y. (2003). Variation among European Americans in emotional facial expression. *Journal of Cross-Cultural Psychology, 34,* 650–657. (p. 437)

Tsai, J. L., Miao, F. F., Seppala, E., Fung, H. H., & Yeung, D. Y. (2007). Influence and adjustment goals: Sources of cultural differences in ideal affect. *Journal of Personality and Social Psychology, 92,* 1102–1117. (p. 436)

Tsang, Y. C. (1938). Hunger motivation in gastrectomized rats. *Journal of Comparative Psychology, 26,* 1–17. (p. 397)

Tsankova, N., Renthal, W., Kumar, A., & Nestler, E. J. (2007). Epigenetic regulation in psychiatric disorders. *Nature Reviews Neuroscience, 8,* 355–367. (p. 129)

Tsuang, M. T., & Faraone, S. V. (1990). *The genetics of mood disorders.* Baltimore, MD: Johns Hopkins University Press. (p. 675)

Tuber, D. S., Miller, D. D., Caris, K. A., Halter, R., Linden, F., & Hennessy, M. B. (1999). Dogs in animal shelters: Problems, suggestions, and needed expertise. *Psychological Science, 10,* 379–386. (p. 67)

Tucker, K. A. (2002). I believe you can fly. *Gallup Management Journal* (www.gallupjournal.com/CA/st/20020520.asp). (p. 837)

Tucker-Drob, E. M., Rhemtulla, M., Harden, K. P., Turkheimer, E., & Fask, D. (2011). Emergence of a gene x socioeconomic status interaction on infant mental ability between 10 months and 2 years. *Psychological Science, 22,* 125–133. (p. 633)

Tuerk, P. W. (2005). Research in the high-stakes era: Achievement, resources, and No Child Left Behind. *Psychological Science, 16,* 419–425. (p. 635)

Tully, T. (2003). Reply: The myth of a myth. *Current Biology, 13,* R426. (p. 267)

Turkheimer, E., Haley, A., Waldron, M., D'Onofrio, B., & Gottesman, I. I. (2003). Socioeconomic status modifies heritability of IQ in young children. *Psychological Science, 14,* 623–628. (p. 633)

Turner, J. C. (1987). *Rediscovering the social group: A self-categorization theory.* New York: Basil Blackwell. (p. 784)

Turner, J. C. (2007) Self-categorization theory. In R. Baumeister & K. Vohs (Eds.), *Encyclopedia of social psychology.* Thousand Oaks, CA: Sage. (p. 784)

Turner, N., Barling, J., & Zacharatos, A. (2002). Positive psychology at work. In C. R. Snyder & S. J. Lopez (Eds.), *The handbook of positive psychology.* New York: Oxford University Press. (p. 839)

Turpin, A. (2005, April 3). The science of psi. *FT Weekend,* pp. W1, W2. (p. 167)

Tversky, A. (1985, June). Quoted in K. McKean, Decisions, decisions. *Discover,* pp. 22–31. (p. 363)

Tversky, A., & Kahneman, D. (1974). Judgment under uncertainty: Heuristics and biases. *Science, 185,* 1124–1131. (p. 363)

Tversky, B. (2008, June/July). Glimpses of Chinese psychology: Reflections on the APS trip to China. *Observer,* pp. 13–14 (also at psychologicalscience.org/observer). (p. 9)

Twenge, J. M. (1997). Changes in masculine and feminine traits over time: A meta-analysis. *Sex Roles 36*(5–6), 305–325. (p. 140)

Twenge, J. M. (2006). *Generation me.* New York: Free Press. (p. 597)

Twenge, J. M., Abebe, E. M., & Campbell, W. K. (2010). Fitting in or standing out: Trends in American parents' choices for children's names, 1880–2007. *Social Psychology and Personality Science, 1,* 19–25. (pp. 301, 600)

Twenge, J. M., Baumeister, R. F., DeWall, C. N., Ciarocco, N. J., & Bartels, J. M. (2007). Social exclusion decreases prosocial behavior. *Journal of Personality and Social Psychology, 92,* 56–66. (p. 415)

Twenge, J. M., Baumeister, R. F., Tice, D. M., & Stucke, T. S. (2001). If you can't join them, beat them: Effects of social exclusion on aggressive behavior. *Journal of Personality and Social Psychology, 81,* 1058–1069. (p. 415)

Twenge, J. M., & Campbell, W. K. (2001). Age and birth cohort differences in self-esteem: A cross-temporal meta-analysis. *Personality and Social Psychology Review, 5,* 321–344. (p. 521)

Twenge, J. M., Catanese, K. R., & Baumeister, R. F. (2002). Social exclusion causes self-defeating behavior. *Journal of Personality and Social Psychology, 83,* 606–615. (p. 415)

Twenge, J. M., & Foster, J. D. (2010). Birth cohort increases in narcissistic personality traits among American college students, 1982–2009. *Social Psychological and Personality Science, 1,* 99–106. (p. 597)

Twenge, J. M., Gentile, B., DeWall, C. D., Ma, D., & Lacefield, K. (2008). *A growing disturbance: Increasing psychopathology in young people 1938–2007 in a meta-analysis of the MMPI.* Unpublished manuscript, San Diego State University. (p. 675)

Twenge, J. M., & Nolen-Hoeksema, S. (2002). Age, gender, race, socioeconomic status, and birth cohort differences on the children's depression inventory: A meta-analysis. *Journal of Abnormal Psychology, 111,* 578–588. (p. 521)

Twenge, J. M., Zhang, L., & Im, C. (2004). It's beyond my control: A cross-temporal meta-analysis of increasing externality in locus of control, 1960-2002. *Personality and Social Psychology Review, 8,* 308–319. (p. 301)

Twiss, C., Tabb, S., & Crosby, F. (1989). Affirmative action and aggregate data: The importance of patterns in the perception of discrimination. In F. Blanchard & F. Crosby (Eds.), *Affirmative action: Social psychological perspectives.* New York: Springer-Verlag. (p. 48)

Uchida, Y., & Kitayama, S. (2009). Happiness and unhappiness in East and West: Themes and variations. *Emotion, 9,* 441–456. (p. 853)

Uchino, B. N. (2009). Understanding the links between social support and physical health. *Perspectives on Psychological Science, 4,* 236–255. (p. 857)

Uchino, B. N., Cacioppo, J. T., & Kiecolt-Glaser, J. K. (1996). The relationship between social support and physiological processes: A review with emphasis on underlying mechanisms and implications for health. *Psychological Bulletin, 119,* 488–531. (p. 857)

Uchino, B. N., Uno, D., & Holt-Lunstad, J. (1999). Social support, physiological processes, and health. *Current Directions in Psychological Science, 8,* 145–148. (p. 857)

Udry, J. R. (2000). Biological limits of gender construction. *American Sociological Review, 65,* 443–457. (p. 527)

Uga, V., Lemut, M. C., Zampi, C., Zilli, I., & Salzarulo, P. (2006). Music in dreams. *Consciousness and Cognition, 15,* 351–357. (p. 240)

Uher, R., & McGuffin, P. (2010). The moderation by the serotonin transporter gene of environmental adversity in the etiology of depression: 2009 update. *Molecular Psychiatry, 15,* 18–22. (p. 678)

UK ECT Review Group. (2003). Efficacy and safety of electroconvulsive therapy in depressive disorders: A systematic review and meta-analysis. *Lancet, 361,* 799–808. (p. 744)

Ulrich, R. E. (1991). Animal rights, animal wrongs and the question of balance. *Psychological Science, 2,* 197–201. (p. 66)

UNAIDS. (2010). *UNAIDS report on the global AIDS epidemic 2010.* www.unaids.org. (pp. 450, 529)

Urbina, I. (2010, May 29). Documents show early worries about safety of rig. *New York Times* (www.nytimes.com). (p. 365)

Urry, H. L., & Gross, J. J. (2010). Emotion regulation in older age. *Current Directions in Psychological Science, 19,* 352–357. (p. 546)

Urry, H. L., Nitschke, J. B., Dolski, I., Jackson, D. C., Dalton, K. M., Mueller, C. J., Rosenkranz, M. A., Ryff, C. D., Singer, B. H., & Davidson, R. J. (2004). Making a life worth living: Neural correlates of well-being. *Psychological Science, 15,* 367–372. (p. 427)

USAID. (2004, January). *The ABCs of HIV prevention.* www.usaid.gov. (p. 450)

Uttal, W. R. (2001). *The new phrenology: The limits of localizing cognitive processes in the brain.* Cambridge, MA: MIT Press. (p. 110)

Vacic, V., & 29 others. (2011). Duplications of the neuropeptide receptor gene *VIPR2* confer significant risk for schizophrenia. *Nature, 471,* 499–503. (p. 689)

Vaidya, J. G., Gray, E. K., Haig, J., & Watson, D. (2002). On the temporal stability of personality: Evidence for differential stability and the role of life experiences. *Journal of Personality and Social Psychology, 83,* 1469–1484. (p. 581)

Vaillant, G. E. (1977). *Adaptation to life.* New York: Little, Brown. (p. 350)

Vaillant, G. E. (2002). *Aging well: Surprising guideposts to a happier life from the landmark Harvard study of adult development.* Boston: Little, Brown. (p. 857)

Vaillant, G. E. (2009). Quoted by J. W. Shenk, What makes us happy? *The Atlantic* (www.theatlantic.com). (p. 415)

Valenstein, E. S. (1986). *Great and desperate cures: The rise and decline of psychosurgery.* New York: Basic Books. (p. 746)

Valkenburg, P. M., & Peter, J. (2009). Social consequences of the Internet for adolescents: A decade of research. *Current Directions in Psychological Science, 18,* 1–5. (pp. 416, 417, 522)

Van Anders, S. M., & Dunn, E. J. (2009). Are gonadal steroids linked with orgasm perceptions and sexual assertiveness in women and men? *Journal of Sexual Medicine, 6,* 739–751. (p. 408)

van Baaren, R. B., Holland, R. W., Kawakami, K., & van Knippenberg, A. (2004). Mimicry and pro-social behavior. *Psychological Science, 15,* 71–74. (p. 763)

van Baaren, R. B., Holland, R. W., Steenaert, B., & van Knippenberg, A. (2003). Mimicry for money: Behavioral consequences of imitation. *Journal of Experimental Social Psychology, 39,* 393–398. (p. 763)

van Boxtel, H. W., Orobio de Castro, B., & Goossens, F. A. (2004). High self-perceived social competence in rejected children is related to frequent fighting. *European Journal of Developmental Psychology, 1,* 205–214. (p. 597)

Vance, E. B., & Wagner, N. N. (1976). Written descriptions of orgasm: A study of sex differences. *Archives of Sexual Behavior, 5,* 87–98. (p. 407)

Van Cauter, E., Holmback, U., Knutson, K., Leproult, R., Miller, A., Nedeltcheva, A., Pannain, S., Penev, P., Tasali, E., & Spiegel, K. (2007). Impact of sleep and sleep loss on neuroendocrine and metabolic function. *Hormone Research, 67,* Supp. 1: 2–9. (p. 236)

Vandell, D. L., Belsky, J., Burchinal, M., Steinberg, L., Vandergrift, N., & NICHD Early Child Care Research Network (2010). Do effects of early child care extend to age 15 years? Results from the NICHD study of early child care and youth development. *Child Development, 81,* 737–756. (p. 494)

Vandenberg, S. G., & Kuse, A. R. (1978). Mental rotations: A group test of three-dimensional spatial visualization. *Perceptual and Motor Skills, 47,* 599–604. (p. 639)

van den Boom, D. (1990). Preventive intervention and the quality of mother-infant interaction and infant exploration in irritable infants. In W. Koops, H. J. G. Soppe, J. L. van der Linden, P. C. M. Molenaar, & J. J. F. Schroots (Eds.), *Developmental psychology research in The Netherlands.* The Netherlands: Uitgeverij Eburon. Cited by C. Hazan & P. R. Shaver (1994). Deeper into attachment theory. *Psychological Inquiry, 5,* 68–79. (p. 491)

van den Boom, D. C. (1995). Do first-year intervention effects endure? Follow-up during toddlerhood of a sample of Dutch irritable infants. *Child Development, 66,* 1798–1816. (p. 491)

van den Bos, K., & Spruijt, N. (2002). Appropriateness of decisions as a moderator of the psychology of voice. *European Journal of Social Psychology, 32,* 57–72. (p. 839)

Van den Bussche, E., Van Den Noortgate, W., & Reynvoet, B. (2009). Mechanisms of masked priming: A meta-analysis. *Psychological Bulletin, 135,* 452–477. (p. 157)

Van der Schot, A. C., & 11 others. (2009). Influence of genes and environment on brain volumes in twin pairs concordant and discordant for bipolar disorder. *Archives of General Psychiatry, 66,* 142–151. (p. 678)

Van Dyke, C., & Byck, R. (1982, March). Cocaine. *Scientific American,* pp. 128–141. (p. 252)

van Engen, M. L., & Willemsen, T. M. (2004). Sex and leadership styles: A meta-analysis of research published in the 1990s. *Psychological Reports, 94,* 3–18. (p. 502)

van Goozen, S. H. M., Fairchild, G., Snoek, H., & Harold, G. T. (2007). The evidence for a neurobiological model of childhood antisocial behavior. *Psychological Bulletin, 133,* 149–182. (p. 700)

van Hemert, D. A., Poortinga, Y. H., & van de Vijver, F. J. R. (2007). Emotion and culture: A meta-analysis. *Cognition and Emotion, 21,* 913–943. (p. 436)

van Honk, J., Schutter, D. J., Bos, P. A., Kruijt, A-W., Lentje, E. G. & Baron-Cohen, S. (2011). Testosterone administration impairs cognitive empathy in women depending on second-to-fourth digit ratio. *Proceedings of the National Academy of Sciences, 108,* 3448–3452. (p. 482)

van IJzendoorn, M. H., & Juffer, F. (2005). Adoption is a successful natural intervention enhancing adopted children's IQ and school performance. *Current Directions in Psychological Science, 14,* 326–330. (p. 633)

van IJzendoorn, M. H., & Juffer, F. (2006). The Emanual Miller Memorial Lecture 2006: Adoption as intervention. Meta-analytic evidence for massive catch-up and plasticity in physical, socio-emotional, and cognitive development. *Journal of Child Psychology and Psychiatry, 47,* 1228–1245. (pp. 128, 633)

van IJzendoorn, M. H., & Kroonenberg, P. M. (1988). Cross-cultural patterns of attachment: A meta-analysis of the strange situation. *Child Development, 59,* 147–156. (p. 490)

van IJzendoorn, M. H., Luijk, M. P. C. M., & Juffer, F. (2008). IQ of children growing up in children's homes: A meta-analysis on IQ delays in ophanages. *Merrill-Palmer Quarterly, 54,* 341–366. (pp. 493, 634)

Van Leeuwen, M. S. (1978). A cross-cultural examination of psychological differentiation in males and females. *International Journal of Psychology, 13,* 87–122. (p. 504)

van Praag, H. (2009). Exercise and the brain: Something to chew on. *Trends in Neuroscience, 32,* 283–290. (p. 860)

Van Rooy, D. L., & Viswesvaran, C. (2004). Emotional intelligence: A meta-analytic investigation of predictive validity and nomological net. *Journal of Vocational Behavior, 65,* 71–95. (p. 612)

Van Yperen, N. W., & Buunk, B. P. (1990). A longitudinal study of equity and satisfaction in intimate relationships. *European Journal of Social Psychology, 20,* 287–309. (p. 804)

Van Zeijl, J., Mesman, J., Van Ijzendoorn, M. H., Bakermans-Kranenburg, M. J., Juffer, F., Stolk, M. N., Koot, H. M., & Alink, L. R. A. (2006). Attachment-based intervention for enhancing sensitive discipline in mothers of 1- to 3-year-old children at risk for externalizing behavior problems: A randomized controlled trial. *Journal of Consulting and Clinical Psychology, 74,* 994–1005. (p. 491)

Vasey, P. L., & VanderLaan, D. P. (2010). An adaptive cognitive dissociation between willingness to help kin and nonkin in Samoan *Fa'afafine. Psychological Science, 21,* 292–297. (p. 534)

Vaughn, K. B., & Lanzetta, J. T. (1981). The effect of modification of expressive displays on vicarious emotional arousal. *Journal of Experimental Social Psychology, 17,* 16–30. (p. 438)

Vecera, S. P., Vogel, E. K., & Woodman, G. F. (2002). Lower region: A new cue for figure-ground assignment. *Journal of Experimental Psychology: General, 13,* 194–205. (p. 186)

Veenhoven, R. (2009). World data base of happiness: Tool for dealing with the 'data-deluge.' *Psychological Topics, 18,* 221–246. (p. 852)

Vega, V., & Malamuth, N. M. (2007). Predicting sexaul aggression: The role of pornography in the context of general and specific risk factors. *Aggressive Behavior, 33,* 104–117. (p. 793)

Vekassy, L. (1977). Dreams of the blind. *Magyar Pszichologiai Szemle, 34,* 478–491. (p. 240)

Velliste, M., Perel, S., Spalding, M. C., Whitford, A. S., & Schwartz, A. B. (2008). Cortical control of a prosthetic arm for self-feeding. *Nature, 453,* 1098–1101. (p. 106)

Veltkamp, M., Custers, R., & Aarts, H. (2011). Motivating consumer behavior by subliminal conditioning in the absence of basic needs: Striking even while the iron is cold. *Journal of Consumer Psychology, 21,* 49–56. (p. 158)

Verbeek, M. E. M., Drent, P. J., & Wiepkema, P. R. (1994). Consistent individual differences in early exploratory behaviour of male great tits. *Animal Behaviour, 48,* 1113–1121. (p. 578)

Verhaeghen, P., & Salthouse, T. A. (1997). Meta-analyses of age-cognition relations in adulthood: Estimates of linear and nonlinear age effects and structural models. *Psychological Bulletin, 122,* 231–249. (p. 541)

Verosky, S. C., & Todorov, A. (2010). Generalization of affective learning about faces to perceptually similar faces. *Psychological Science, 21,* 779–785. (p. 270)

Vertes, R., & Siegel, J. (2005). Time for the sleep community to take a critical look at the purported role of sleep in memory processing. *Sleep, 28,* 1228–1229. (p. 242)

Verwijmeren, T., Karremans, J. C., Stroebe, W., & Wigboldus, D. H. J. (2011a). The workings and limits of subliminal advertising: The role of habits. *Journal of Consumer Psychology, 21,* 206–213. (p. 158)

Verwijmeren, T., Karremans, J. C., Stroebe, W., Wigboldus, D. H. J., & Ooigen, I. (2011b). Vicary's victory: Subliminal ads in movies work! Poster presented at the Society for Personality and Social Psychology meeting, San Antonio, TX. (p. 158)

Vigil, J. M. (2009). A socio-relational framework of sex differences in the expression of emotion. *Behavioral and Brain Sciences, 32,* 375–428. (p. 434)

Vigil, J. M., Geary, D. C., & Byrd-Craven, J. (2005). A life history assessment of early childhood sexual abuse in women. *Developmental Psychology, 41,* 553–561. (p. 527)

Vigliocco, G., & Hartsuiker, R. J. (2002). The interplay of meaning, sound, and syntax in sentence production. *Psychological Bulletin, 128,* 442–472. (p. 374)

Vinkhuyzen, A. A. E., van der Sluis, S., Posthuma, D., & Boomsma, D. I. (2009). The heritability of aptitude and exceptional talent across different domains in adolescents and young adults. *Behavior Genetics, 39,* 380–392. (p. 632)

Visalberghi, E. Addessi, E., Truppa, V., Spagnoletti, N., Ottoni, E., Izar, P., & Fragaszy, D. (2009). Selection of effective stone tools by wild bearded capuchin monkeys. *Current Biology, 19,* 213–217. (p. 868)

Visich, P. S., & Fletcher, E. (2009). Myocardial infarction. In J. K. Ehrman, P. M., Gordon, P. S. Visich, & S. J. Keleyian (Eds.). *Clinical exercise physiology, 2nd Edition.* Champaign, IL: Human Kinetics. (p. 859)

Vita, A. J., Terry, R. B., Hubert, H. B., & Fries, J. F. (1998). Aging, health risks, and cumulative disability. *New England Journal of Medicine, 338,* 1035–1041. (p. 252)

Vitiello, M. V. (2009). Recent advances in understanding sleep and sleep disturbances in older adults: Growing older does not mean sleeping poorly. *Current Directions in Psychological Science, 18,* 316–320. (p. 238)

Vitória, P. D., Salgueiro, M. F., Silva, S. A., & De Vries, H. (2009). The impact of social influence on adolescent intention to smoke: Combining types and referents of influence. *British Journal of Health Psychology, 14,* 681–699. (p. 824)

Vittengl, J. R., Clark, L. A., Dunn, T. W., & Jarrett, R. B. (2007). Reducing relapse and recurrence in unipolar depression: A comparative meta-analysis of cognitive-behavioral therapy's effects. *Journal of Consulting and Clinical Psychology, 75,* 475–488. (p. 742)

Voas, D. (2008, March/April). Ten million marriages: An astrological detective story. *Skeptical Inquirer,* pp. 52–55. (p. 579)

Vocks, S., Tuschen-Caffier, B., Pietrowsky, R., Rustenbach, S. J., Kersting, A., & Herpertz, S. (2010). Meta-analysis of the effectiveness of psychological and pharmacological treatments for binge eating disorder. *International Journal of Eating Disorders, 43,* 205–217. (p. 698)

Vogel, G. (2010). Long-fought compromise reached on European animal rules. *Science, 329,* 1588–1589. (p. 67)

Vogel, S. (1999). *The skinny on fat: Our obsession with weight control.* New York: W. H. Freeman. (p. 129)

Vohs, K. D., & Baumeister, R. F. (eds.) (2011). *Handbook of self-regulation, 2nd edition.* New York: Guilford. (p. 301)

Vohs, K. D., Mead, N. L., & Goode, M. R. (2006). The psychological consequences of money. *Science, 314,* 1154–1156. (p. 336)

Volkow, N. D., & 12 others. (2009). Evaluating dopamine reward pathway in ADHD: Clinical implications. *Journal of the American Medical Association, 302,* 1084–1091. (p. 652)

von Békésy, G. (1957, August). The ear. *Scientific American,* pp. 66–78. (p. 199)

von Hippel, W. (2007). Aging, executive functioning, and social control. *Current Directions in Psychological Science, 16,* 240–244. (p. 542)

von Senden, M. (1932). *The perception of space and shape in the congenitally blind before and after operation.* Glencoe, IL: Free Press. (p. 190)

Vorona, R. D., Szklo-Coxe, M., Wu, A., Dubik, M., Zhao, Y., & Ware, J. C. (2011). Dissimilar teen crash rates in two neighboring Southeastern Virginia cities with different high school start times. *Journal of Clinical Sleep Medicine, 7,* 145–151. (p. 236)

Vroom, V. H., & Jago, A. G. (2007). The role of the situation in leadership. *American Psychologist, 62,* 17–24. (p. 839)

VTTI. (2009, September). Driver distraction in commercial vehicle operations. Virginia Tech Transportation Institute and U.S. Department of Transportation. (p. 153)

Vul, E., Harris, C., Winkielman, P., & Pashler, H. (2009a). Puzzlingly high correlations in fMRI studies of emotion, personality, and social cognition. *Perspectives on Psychological Science, 4,* 274–290. (p. 96)

Vul, E., Harris, C., Winkielman, P., & Pashler, H. (2009b). Reply to comments on "Puzzlingly high correlations in fMRI studies of emotion, personality, and social cognition." *Perspectives on Psychological Science, 4,* 319–324. (p. 96)

Vuoksimaa, E., Koskenvuo, M., Rose, R. J., & Kaprio, J. (2009). Origins of handedness: A nationwide study of 30,161 adults. *Neuropsychologia, 47,* 1294–1301. (p. 118)

Vyazovskiy, V. V., Cirelli, C., Pfister-Genskow, M., Faraguna, U., & Tononi, G. (2008). Molecular and electrophysiological evidence for net synaptic potentiation in wake and depression in sleep. *Nature Neuroscience, 11,* 200–208. (p. 230)

Waber, R. L., Shiv, B., Carmon, & Ariely, D. (2008). Commercial features of placebo and therapeutic efficacy. *Journal of the American Medical Association, 299,* 1016–1017. (p. 52)

Wacker, J., Chavanon, M-L., & Stemmler, G. (2006). Investigating the dopaminergic basis of extraversion in humans: A multilevel approach. *Journal of Personality and Social Psychology, 91,* 177–187. (p. 578)

Wade, K. A., Garry, M., Read, J. D., & Lindsay, D. S. (2002). A picture is worth a thousand lies: Using false photographs to create false childhood memories. *Psychonomic Bulletin & Review, 9,* 597–603. (p. 348)

Wade, N. G., Worthington, E. L., Jr., & Vogel, D. L. (2006). Effectiveness of religiously tailored interventions in Christian therapy. *Psychotherapy Research, 17,* 91–105. (p. 735)

Wagar, B. M., & Cohen, D. (2003). Culture, memory, and the self: An analysis of the personal and collective self in long-term memory. *Journal of Experimental Social Psychology, 39,* 458–475. (p. 326)

Wagenmakers, E-J., Wetzels, R., Borsboom, D., & van der Maas, H. (2011). Why psychologists must change the way they analyze their data: The case of psi. *Journal of Personality and Social Psychology, 100,* 1–12. (p. 169)

Wager, T. D. (2005). The neural bases of placebo effects in pain. *Current Directions in Psychological Science, 14,* 175–179. (p. 206)

Wagner, A. (2010). Can neuroscience identify lies? In F. E. Bloom et al., *A judge's guide to neuroscience: A concise introduction.* Santa Barbara, CA: University of California, Santa Barbara. (p. 429)

Wagner, D. D., Cin, S. D., Sargent, J. C., Kelley, W. M., & Heatherton, T. F. (2011). Spontaneous action representation in smokers when watching movie characters smoke. *Journal of Neuroscience, 31,* 894–898. (p. 307)

Wagner, U., Gais, S., Haider, H., Verleger, R., & Born, J. (2004). Sleep inspires insight. *Nature, 427,* 352–355. (p. 231)

Wagstaff, G. (1982). Attitudes to rape: The "just world" strikes again? *Bulletin of the British Psychological Society, 13,* 275–283. (p. 755)

Wahlberg, D. (2001, October 11). We're more depressed, patriotic, poll finds. *Grand Rapids Press,* p. A15. (p. 443)

Wai, J., Cacchio, M., Putallaz, M., & Makel, M. C. (2010). Sex differences in the right tail of cognitive abilities: A 30 year examination. *Intelligence, 38,* 412–423. (p. 638)

Wai, J., Lubinski, D., & Benbow, C. P. (2005). Creativity and occupational accomplishments among intellectually precocious youths: An age 13 to age 33 longitudinal study. *Journal of Educational Psychology, 97,* 484–492. (p. 630)

Wakefield, J. C., Schmitz, M.F., First, M. B., & Horwitz, A. V. (2007). Extending the bereavement exclusion for major depression to other losses: Evidence from the National Comorbidity Survey. *Archives of General Psychiatry, 64,* 433–440. (p. 672)

Wakefield, J. C., & Spitzer, R. L. (2002). Lowered estimates—but of what? *Archives of General Psychiatry, 59,* 129–130. (p. 665)

Walker, E., Shapiro, D., Esterberg, M., & Trotman, H. (2010). Neurodevelopment and schizophrenia: Broadening the focus. *Current Directions in Psychological Science, 19,* 204–208. (pp. 687, 689)

Walker, M. P., & van der Helm, E. (2009). Overnight therapy? The role of sleep in emotional brain processing. *Psychological Bulletin, 135,* 731–748. (p. 236)

Walker, W. R., Skowronski, J. J., & Thompson, C. P. (2003). Life is pleasant—and memory helps to keep it that way! *Review of General Psychology, 7,* 203–210. (p 547)

Walkup, J. T., & 12 others. (2008). Cognitive behavioral therapy, sertraline, or a combination in childhood anxiety. *New England Journal of Medicine, 359,* 2753–2766. (p. 742)

Wall, P. D. (2000). *Pain: The science of suffering.* New York: Columbia University Press. (p. 204)

Wallace, D. S., Paulson, R. M., Lord, C. G., & Bond, C. F., Jr. (2005). Which behaviors do attitudes predict? Meta-analyzing the effects of social pressure and perceived difficulty. *Review of General Psychology, 9(3),* 214–227. (p. 756)

Wallach, M. A., & Wallach, L. (1983). *Psychology's sanction for selfishness: The error of egoism in theory and therapy.* New York: Freeman. (p. 573)

Wallach, M. A., & Wallach, L. (1985, February). How psychology sanctions the cult of the self. *Washington Monthly,* pp. 46–56. (p. 573)

Walster (Hatfield), E., Aronson, V., Abrahams, D., & Rottman, L. (1966). Importance of physical attractiveness in dating behavior. *Journal of Personality and Social Psychology, 4,* 508–516. (p. 800)

Walton, G. M., & Spencer, S. J. (2009). Latent ability: Grades and test scores systematically underestimate the intellectual ability of negatively stereotyped students. *Psychological Science, 20,* 1132–1139. (p. 642)

Wampold, B. E. (2001). *The great psychotherapy debate: Models, methods, and findings.* Mahwah, NJ: Erlbaum. (pp. 734, 735)

Wampold, B. E. (2007). Psychotherapy: The humanistic (and effective) treatment. *American Psychologist, 62,* 857–873. (pp. 732, 734)

Wampold, B. E., Mondin, G. W., Moody, M., & Ahn, H. (1997). The flat earth as a metaphor for the evidence for uniform efficacy of bona fide psychotherapies: Reply to Crits-Christoph (1997) and Howard et al. (1997). *Psychological Bulletin, 122,* 226–230. (p. 732)

Wang, K-S., Liu, X-F., & Aragam, N. (2010). A genome-wide meta-analysis identified novel loci associated with schizophrenia and bipolar disorder. *Schizophrenia Research, 124,* 192–199. (p. 689)

Wang, Q., Bowling, N. A., & Eschleman, K. J. (2010). A meta-analytic examination of work and general locus of control. *Journal of Applied Psychology, 95,* 761–768. (p. 300)

Wang, S-H., Baillargeon, R., & Brueckner, L. (2004). Young infants' reasoning about hidden objects: Evidence from violation-of-expectation tasks with test trials only. *Cognition, 93,* 167–198. (p. 478)

Wang, W. (2012, February 16). The rise of intermarriage. *Pew Research Social and Demographic Trends* (www.pewsocialtrends.org). (p. 780)

Wang, X. T., & Dvorak, R. D. (2010). Sweet future: Fluctuating blood glucose levels affect future discounting. *Psychological Science, 21,* 183–188. (p. 302)

Wansink, B. (2007). *Mindless eating: Why we eat more than we think.* New York: Bantam Dell. (p. 401)

Wansink, B., van Ittersum, K., & Painter, J. E. (2006). Ice cream illusions: Bowls, spoons, and self-served portion sizes. *American Journal of Preventive Medicine, 31,* 240–243. (p. 401)

Ward, A., & Mann, T. (2000). Don't mind if I do: Disinhibited eating under cognitive load. *Journal of Personality and Social Psychology, 78,* 753–763. (p. 403)

Ward, C. (1994). Culture and altered states of consciousness. In W. J. Lonner & R. Malpass (Eds.), *Psychology and culture.* Boston: Allyn & Bacon. (p. 246)

Ward, J. (2003). State of the art synaesthesia. *The Psychologist, 16,* 196–199. (p. 211)

Ward, K. D., Klesges, R. C., & Halpern, M. T. (1997). Predictors of smoking cessation and state-of-the-art smoking interventions. *Journal of Social Issues, 53,* 129–145. (p. 252)

Ward, L. M., & Friedman, K. (2006). Using TV as a guide: Associations between television viewing and adolescents' sexual attitudes and behavior. *Journal of Research on Adolescence, 16,* 133–156. (p. 530)

Wardle, J., Cooke, L. J., Gibson, L., Sapochnik, M., Sheiham, A., & Lawson, M. (2003). Increasing children's acceptance of vegetables: A randomized trial of parent-led exposure. *Appetite, 40,* 155–162. (p. 207)

Wargo, E. (2007, December). Understanding the have-knots. *APS Observer,* pp. 18–21. (p. 861)

Warner, J., McKeown, E., Johnson, K., Ramsay, A., Cort, C., & King, M. (2004). Rates and predictors of mental illness in gay men, lesbians and bisexual men and women. *British Journal of Psychiatry, 185,* 479–485. (p. 532)

Wason, P. C. (1960). On the failure to eliminate hypotheses in a conceptual task. *Quarterly Journal of Experimental Psychology, 12,* 129–140. (p. 362)

Wason, P. C. (1981). The importance of cognitive illusions. *The Behavioral and Brain Sciences, 4,* 356. (p. 362)

Wasserman, E. A. (1993). Comparative cognition: Toward a general understanding of cognition in behavior. *Psychological Science, 4,* 156–161. (p. 277)

Wasserman, E. A. (1995). The conceptual abilities of pigeons. *American Scientist, 83,* 246–255. (p. 867)

Wastell, C. A. (2002). Exposure to trauma: The long-term effects of suppressing emotional reactions. *Journal of Nervous and Mental Disorders, 190,* 839–845. (p. 859)

Waterhouse, R. (1993, July 19). Income for 62 percent is below average pay. *The Independent,* p. 4. (p. 58)

Waterman, A. S. (1988). Identity status theory and Erikson's theory: Commonalities and differences. *Developmental Review, 8,* 185–208. (p. 520)

Watkins, E. R. (2008). Constructive and unconstructive repetitive thought. *Psychological Bulletin, 134,* 163–206. (p. 672)

Watkins, J. G. (1984). The Bianchi (L. A. Hillside Strangler) case: Sociopath or multiple personality? *International Journal of Clinical and Experimental Hypnosis, 32,* 67–101. (p. 695)

Watson, D. (2000). *Mood and temperament.* New York: Guilford Press. (p. 848)

Watson, D., Wiese, D., Vaidya, J., & Tellegen, A. (1999). The two general activation systems of affect: Structured findings, evolutionary considerations, and psychobiological evidence. *Journal of Personality and Social Psychology, 76,* 820–838. (p. 845)

Watson, J. B. (1913). Psychology as the behaviorist views it. *Psychological Review, 20,* 158–177. (pp. 218, 266, 271)

Watson, J. B. (1924). The unverbalized in human behavior. *Psychological Review, 31,* 339–347. (p. 271)

Watson, J. B., & Rayner, R. (1920). Conditioned emotional reactions. *Journal of Experimental Psychology, 3,* 1–14. (p. 271)

Watson, R. I., Jr. (1973). Investigation into deindividuation using a cross-cultural survey technique. *Journal of Personality and Social Psychology, 25,* 342–345. (p. 773)

Watson, S. J., Benson, J. A., Jr., & Joy, J. E. (2000). Marijuana and medicine: Assessing the science base: A summary of the 1999 Institute of Medicine report. *Archives of General Psychiatry, 57,* 547–553. (pp. 256, 860)

Watters, E. (2010). *Crazy like us: The globalization of the American psyche.* New York: Free Press. (p. 653)

Wayment, H. A., & Peplau, L. A. (1995). Social support and well-being among lesbian and heterosexual women: A structural modeling approach. *Personality and Social Psychology Bulletin, 21,* 1189–1199. (p. 545)

Weaver, J. B., Masland, J. L., & Zillmann, D. (1984). Effect of erotica on young men's aesthetic perception of their female sexual partners. *Perceptual and Motor Skills, 58,* 929–930. (p. 409)

Webb, W. B. (1992). *Sleep: The gentle tyrant.* Bolton, MA: Anker. (p. 238)

Webb, W. B., & Campbell, S. S. (1983). Relationships in sleep characteristics of identical and fraternal twins. *Archives of General Psychiatry, 40,* 1093–1095. (p. 229)

Webley, K. (2009, June 15). Behind the drop in Chinese adoptions. *Time,* p. 55. (p. 783)

Webster, G. D., Jonason, P. K., & Schember, T. O. (2009). Hot topics and popular papers in evolutionary psychology: Analyses of title words and citation counts in *Evolution and Human Behavior*, 1979–2008. *Evolutionary Psychology, 7,* 348–362. (p. 138)

Wechsler, D. (1972). "Hold" and "Don't Hold" tests. In S. M. Chown (Ed.), *Human aging.* New York: Penguin. (p. 625)

Wegman, H. L., & Stetler, C. (2009). A meta-analytic review of the effects of childhood abuse on medical outcomes in adulthood. *Psychosomatic Medicine, 71,* 805–812. (p. 494)

Wegner, D. M. (2002). *The illusion of conscious will.* Cambridge, MA: MIT Press. (p. 217)

Weinberger, D. R. (2001, March 10). A brain too young for good judgment. *New York Times* (www.nytimes.com). (p. 514)

Weingarten, G. (2002, March 10). Below the beltway. *Washington Post,* p. WO3. (p. 827)

Weinstein, N. D. (1980). Unrealistic optimism about future life events. *Journal of Personality and Social Psychology, 39,* 806–820. (p. 589)

Weinstein, N. D. (1982). Unrealistic optimism about susceptibility to health problems. *Journal of Behavioral Medicine, 5,* 441–460. (p. 589)

Weinstein, N. D. (1996, October 4). 1996 optimistic bias bibliography. (weinstein_c@aesop.rutgers.edu). (p. 589)

Weis, R., & Cerankosky, B. C. (2010). Effects of video-game ownership on young boys' academic and behavioral functioning: A randomized, controlled study. *Psychological Science, 21,* 463–470. (p. 795)

Weis, S., & Suß, H-M. (2007). Reviving the search for social intelligence: A multitrait-multimethod study of its structure and construct validity. *Personality and Individual Differences, 42*, 3–14. (p. 612)

Weisbuch, M., Ivcevic, Z., & Ambady, N. (2009). On being liked on the web and in the "real world": Consistency in first impressions across personal webpages and spontaneous behavior. *Journal of Experimental Social Psychology, 45*, 573–576. (p. 418)

Weiskrantz, L. (2009). *Blindsight*. Oxford: Oxford University Press. (p. 120)

Weiskrantz, L. (2010). Blindsight in hindsight. *The Psychologist, 23*, 356–358. (p. 120)

Weiss, A., Gale, C. R., Batty, G. D., & Deary, I. J. (2009). Emotionally stable, intelligent men live longer: The Vietnam experience study cohort. *Psychosomatic Medicine, 71*, 385–394. (p. 628)

Weiss, A., King, J. E., & Enns, R. M. (2002). Subjective well-being is heritable and genetically correlated with dominance in chimpanzees (Pan troglodytes). *Journal of Personality and Social Psychology, 83*, 1141–1149. (p. 853)

Weiss, A., King, J. E., & Figueredo, A. J. (2000). The heritability of personality factors in chimpanzees (Pan troglodytes). *Behavior Genetics, 30*, 213–221. (p. 853)

Weiss, A., King, J. E., & Perkins, L. (2006). Personality and subjective well-being in orangutans (*Pongo pygmaeus* and *Pongo abelii). Journal of Personality and Social Psychology, 90*, 501–511. (p. 578)

Welch, J. M., Lu, J., Rodriquiz, R. M., Trotta, N. C., Peca, J., Ding, J.-D., Feliciano, C., Chen, M., Adams, J. P., Luo, J., Dudek, S. M., Weinberg, R. J., Calakos, N., Wetsel, W. C., & Feng, G. (2007). Cortico-striatal synaptic defects and OCD-like behaviours in Sapap3-mutant mice. *Nature, 448*, 894–900. (p. 668)

Welch, W. W. (2005, February 28). Trauma of Iraq war haunting thousands returning home. *USA Today* (www.usatoday.com). (p. 664)

Weller, S., & Davis-Beaty, K. (2002). The effectiveness of male condoms in prevention of sexually transmitted diseases (protocol). *Cochrane Database of Systematic Reviews*, Issue 4, Art. No. CD004090. (p. 529)

Wellings, K., Collumbien, M., Slaymaker, E., Singh, S., Hodges, Z., Patel, D., & Bajos, N. (2006). Sexual behaviour in context: A global perspective. *Lancet, 368*, 1706–1728. (p. 529)

Wellman, H. M., & Gelman, S. A. (1992). Cognitive development: Foundational theories of core domains. *Annual Review of Psychology, 43*, 337–375. (p. 478)

Wells, B. L. (1986). Predictors of female nocturnal orgasms: A multivariate analysis. *Journal of Sex Research, 22*, 421–437. (p. 410)

Wells, D. L. (2009). The effects of animals on human health and well-being. *Journal of Social Issues, 65*, 523–543. (p. 858)

Wells, G. L. (1981). Lay analyses of causal forces on behavior. In J. Harvey (Ed.), *Cognition, social behavior and the environment*. Hillsdale, NJ: Erlbaum. (p. 264)

Wender, P. H., Kety, S. S., Rosenthal, D., Schulsinger, F., Ortmann, J., & Lunde, I. (1986). Psychiatric disorders in the biological and adoptive families of adopted individuals with affective disorders. *Archives of General Psychiatry, 43*, 923–929. (p. 676)

Westen, D. (1996). Is Freud really dead? Teaching psychodynamic theory to introductory psychology. Presentation to the Annual Institute on the Teaching of Psychology, St. Petersburg Beach, Florida. (p. 566)

Westen, D. (1998). The scientific legacy of Sigmund Freud: Toward a psychodynamically informed psychological science. *Psychological Bulletin, 124*, 333–371. (p. 561)

Westen, D. (2007). *The political brain: The role of emotion in deciding the fate of the nation*. New York: PublicAffairs. (p. 424)

Westen, D., & Morrison, K. (2001). A multidimensional meta-analysis of treatments for depression, panic, and generalized anxiety disorder: An empirical examination of the status of empirically supported therapies. *Journal of Consulting and Clinical Psychology, 69*, 875–899. (p. 732)

Whalen, P. J., Kagan, J., Cook, R. G., Davis, F. C., Kim, H., Polis, S., McLaren, D. G., Somerville, L. H., McLean, A. A., Maxwell, J. S., & Johnstone, T. (2004). Human amygdala responsibility to masked fearful eye whites. *Science, 302*, 2061. (p. 424)

Whalen, P. J., Shin, L. M., McInerney, S. C., Fisher, H., Wright, C. I., & Rauch, S. L. (2001). A functional MRI study of human amygdala responses to facial expressions of fear versus anger. *Emotion, 1*, 70–83. (p. 427)

Whaley, S. E., Sigman, M., Beckwith, L., Cohen, S. E., & Espinosa, M. P. (2002). Infant-caregiver interaction in Kenya and the United States: The importance of multiple caregivers and adequate comparison samples. *Journal of Cross-Cultural Psychology, 33*, 236–247. (p. 494)

Whalley, L. J., & Deary, I. J. (2001). Longitudinal cohort study of childhood IQ and survival up to age 76. *British Medical Journal, 322*, 1–5. (p. 628)

Whalley, L. J., Starr, J. M., Athawes, R., Hunter, D., Pattie, A., & Deary, I. J. (2000). Childhood mental ability and dementia. *Neurology, 55*, 1455–1459. (p. 628)

Whang, W., Kubzansky, L, D., Kawachi, I., Rexrode, K. M., Kroenke, C. H., Glynn, R. J., Garan, H., & Albert, C. M. (2009). Depression and risk of sudden cardiac death and coronary heart disease in women. *Journal of the American College of Cardiology, 53*, 950–958. (p. 453)

Wheelwright, J. (2004, August). Study the clones first. *Discover*, pp. 44–50. (p. 126)

Whetten, K., Ostermann J., Whetten R.A., Pence B.W., O'Donnell K., Messer L.C., Thielman N.M., & The Positive Outcomes for Orphans (POFO) Research Team. (2009). A comparison of the wellbeing of orphans and abandoned children ages 6–12 in institutional and community-based care settings in 5 less wealthy nations. *PLoS One, 4*, E8169. (p. 494)

White, G. L., & Kight, T. D. (1984). Misattribution of arousal and attraction: Effects of salience of explanations for arousal. *Journal of Experimental Social Psychology, 20*, 55–64. (p. 803)

White, H. R., Brick, J., & Hansell, S. (1993). A longitudinal investigation of alcohol use and aggression in adolescence. *Journal of Studies on Alcohol*, Supplement No. 11, 62–77. (p. 791)

White, L., & Edwards, J. (1990). Emptying the nest and parental well-being: An analysis of national panel data. *American Sociological Review, 55*, 235–242. (p. 545)

White, R. A. (1998). Intuition, heart knowledge, and parapsychology. *Journal of the American Society for Psychical Research, 92*, 158–171. (p. 168)

Whitehead, B. D., & Popenoe, D. (2001). *The state of our unions 2001: The social health of marriage in America*. Rutgers University: The National Marriage Project. (p. 545)

Whiten, A., & Boesch, C. (2001, January). Cultures of chimpanzees. *Scientific American*, pp. 60–67. (p. 867)

Whiten, A., & Byrne, R. W. (1988). Tactical deception in primates. *Behavioral and Brain Sciences, 11*, 233–244, 267–273. (p. 41)

Whiten, A., Spiteri, A., Horner, V., Bonnie, K. E., Lambeth, S. P., Schapiro, S. J., & de Waal, F. B. M. (2007). Transmission of multiple traditions within and between chimpanzee groups. *Current Biology, 17*, 1038–1043. (p. 306)

Whiting, B. B., & Edwards, C. P. (1988). *Children of different worlds: The formation of social behavior*. Cambridge, MA: Harvard University Press. (p. 497)

Whitley, B. E., Jr. (1999). Right-wing authoritarianism, social dominance orientation, and prejudice. *Journal of Personality and Social Psychology, 77*, 126–134. (p. 784)

Whitlock, J. R., Heynen, A. L., Shuler, M. G., & Bear, M. F. (2006). Learning induces long-term potentiation in the hippocampus. *Science, 313*, 1093–1097. (p. 333)

Whitmer, R. A., Gustafson, D. R., Barrett-Connor, E. B., Haan, M. N., Gunderson, E. P., & Yaffe, K. (2008). Central obesity and increased risk of dementia more than three decades later. *Neurology, 71*, 1057–1064. (p. 401)

WHO. (1979). *Schizophrenia: An international followup study*. Chicester, England: Wiley. (p. 686)

WHO. (2000). *Effectiveness of male latex condoms in protecting against pregnancy and sexually transmitted infections*. World Health Organization (www.who.int). (p. 529)

WHO. (2002). *The global burden of disease*. Geneva: World Health Organization (www.who.int/msa/mnh/ems/dalys/intro.htm). (p. 671)

WHO. (2003). *The male latex condom: Specification and guidelines for condom procurement*. Department of Reproductive Health and Research, Family and Community Health, World Health Organization. (p. 529)

WHO. (2004). *Women, girls, HIV, and AIDS*. World Health Organization, Western Pacific Regional Office. (p. 529)

WHO. (2004a). Prevalence, severity, and unmet need for treatment of mental disorders in the World Health Organization World Mental Health Surveys. *Journal of the American Medical Association, 291*, 2581–2590. (pp. 657, 680)

WHO. (2004b). *Prevention of mental disorders: Effective interventions and policy options. Summary report*. Geneva: World Health Organization, Department of Mental Health and Substance Abuse. (p. 658)

WHO. (2004c). *Promoting mental health: Concepts, emerging evidence, practice. Summary report*. Geneva: World Health Organization, Department of Mental Health and Substance Abuse. (p. 658)

WHO. (2007). Obesity and overweight. (www.who.int/dietphysicalactivity/publications/facts/obesity/en/). (p. 401)

WHO. (2008). *Mental health (nearly 1 million annual suicide deaths).* Geneva: World Health Organization (www.who.int/mental_health/en). (p. 676)

WHO. (2008). *WHO report on the global tobacco epidemic, 2008.* Geneva: World Health Organization (www.who.int). (p. 251)

WHO. (2010, September). Mental health: strengthening our response. Geneva: World Health Organization (www.who.int/mediacentre/factsheets/fs220/en/). (p. 650)

WHO. (2011). Country reports and charts available. Geneva: World Health Organization (int/mental_health/prevention/suicide/country_reports/en/index.html). (p. 676)

WHO. (2011). Schizophrenia. Geneva: World Health Organization (www.who.int). (p. 684)

Whooley, M. A., & 11 others. (2008). Depressive symptoms, health behaviors, and risk of cardiovascular events in patients with coronary heart disease. *Journal of the American Medical Association, 300,* 2379–2388. (p. 453)

Whorf, B. L. (1956). Science and linguistics. In J. B. Carroll (Ed.), *Language, thought, and reality: Selected writings of Benjamin Lee Whorf.* Cambridge, MA: MIT Press. (p. 379)

Wicherts, J. M., Dolan, C. V., Carlson, J. S., & van der Maas, H. L. J. (2010). Raven's test performance of sub-Saharan Africans: Mean level, psychometric properties, and the Flynn Effect. *Learning and Individual Differences, 20,* 135–151. (p. 641)

Wickelgren, I. (2009, September/October). I do not feel your pain. *Scientific American Mind,* pp. 51–57. (p. 203)

Wickelgren, W. A. (1977). *Learning and memory.* Englewood Cliffs, NJ: Prentice-Hall. (p. 326)

Wielkiewicz, R. M., & Stelzner, S. P. (2005). An ecological perspective on leadership theory, research, and practice. *Review of General Psychology, 9,* 326–341. (p. 839)

Wiens, A. N., & Menustik, C. E. (1983). Treatment outcome and patient characteristics in an aversion therapy program for alcoholism. *American Psychologist, 38,* 1089–1096. (p. 719)

Wierson, M., & Forehand, R. (1994). Parent behavioral training for child noncompliance: Rationale, concepts, and effectiveness. *Current Directions in Psychological Science, 3,* 146–149. (p. 287)

Wierzbicki, M. (1993). Psychological adjustment of adoptees: A meta-analysis. *Journal of Clinical Child Psychology, 22,* 447–454. (p. 128)

Wiesel, T. N. (1982). Postnatal development of the visual cortex and the influence of environment. *Nature, 299,* 583–591. (p. 190)

Wiesner, W. H., & Cronshow, S. P. (1988). A meta-analytic investigation of the impact of interview format and degree of structure on the validity of the employment interview. *Journal of Occupational Psychology, 61,* 275–290. (p. 832)

Wigdor, A. K., & Garner, W. R. (1982). *Ability testing: Uses, consequences, and controversies.* Washington, DC: National Academy Press. (p. 642)

Wike, R., & Grim, B. J. (2007, October 30). Widespread negativity: Muslims distrust Westerners more than vice versa. *Pew Research Center* (www.pewresearch.org). (p. 781)

Wilcox, A. J., Baird, D. D., Dunson, D. B., McConnaughey, D. R., Kesner, J. S., & Weinberg, C. R. (2004). On the frequency of intercourse around ovulation: Evidence for biological influences. *Human Reproduction, 19,* 1539–1543. (p. 408)

Wilder, D. A. (1981). Perceiving persons as a group: Categorization and intergroup relations. In D. L. Hamilton (Ed.), *Cognitive processes in stereotyping and intergroup behavior.* Hillsdale, NJ: Erlbaum. (p. 784)

Wildman, D. E., Uddin, M., Liu, G., Grossman, L. I., & Goodman, M. (2003). Implications of natural selection in shaping 99.4% nonsynonymous DNA identity between humans and chimpanzees: Enlarging genus Homo. *Proceedings of the National Academy of Sciences, 100,* 7181–7188. (p. 125)

Wilford, J. N. (1999, February 9). New findings help balance the cosmological books. *New York Times* (www.nytimes.com). (p. 142)

Wilkinson, P., & Goodyer, I. (2011). Non-suicidal self-injury. *European Child & Adolescent Psychiatry, 20,* 103–108. (p. 677)

Williams, C. L., & Berry, J. W. (1991). Primary prevention of acculturative stress among refugees. *American Psychologist, 46,* 632–641. (p, 443)

Williams, J. E., & Best, D. L. (1990). *Measuring sex stereotypes: A multination study.* Newbury Park, CA: Sage. (p. 501)

Williams, J. E., Paton, C. C., Siegler, I. C., Eigenbrodt, M. L., Nieto, F. J., & Tyroler, H. A. (2000). Anger proneness predicts coronary heart disease risk: Prospective analysis from the artherosclerosis risk in communities (ARIC) study. *Circulation, 101*(17), 2034–2040. (p. 452)

Williams, K. D. (2007). Ostracism. *Annual Review of Psychology, 58,* 425–452. (pp. 414, 415)

Williams, K. D. (2009). Ostracism: A temporal need-threat model. *Advances in Experimental Social Psychology, 41,* 275–313. (p. 414)

Williams, K. D., & Zadro, L. (2001). Ostracism: On being ignored, excluded and rejected. In M. Leary (Ed.), *Rejection.* New York: Oxford University Press. (p. 414)

Williams, L. E., & Bargh, J. A. (2008). Experiencing physical warmth promotes interpersonal warmth. *Science, 322,* 606–607. (p. 211)

Williams, L. M., Brown, K. J., Palmer, D., Liddell, B. J., Kemp, A. H., Olivieri, G., Peduto, A., & Gordon, E. (2006). The mellow years? Neural basis of improving emotional stability over age. *Journal of Neuroscience, 26,* 6422–6430. (p. 547)

Williams, N. M., & 13 others. (2010). Rare chromosomal deletions and duplications in attention-deficit hyperactivity disorder: A genome-wide analysis. *Lancet, 376,* 1401–1408. (p. 652)

Williams, S. L. (1987). Self-efficacy and mastery-oriented treatment for severe phobias. Paper presented to the American Psychological Association convention. (p. 717)

Willingham, D. T. (2010, Summer). Have technology and multitasking rewired how students learn? *American Educator,* pp. 23–28, 42. (p. 322)

Willingham, W. W., Lewis, C., Morgan, R., & Ramist, L. (1990). *Predicting college grades: An analysis of institutional trends over two decades.* Princeton, NJ: Educational Testing Service. (p. 622)

Willis, J., & Todorov, A. (2006). First impressions: Making up your mind after a 100-ms. exposure to a face. *Psychological Science, 17,* 592–598. (p. 433)

Willmuth, M. E. (1987). Sexuality after spinal cord injury: A critical review. *Clinical Psychology Review, 7,* 389–412. (p. 410)

Wilson, A. E., & Ross, M. (2001). From chump to champ: People's appraisals of their earlier and present selves. *Journal of Personality and Social Psychology, 80,* 572–584. (p. 598)

Wilson, G. D., & Rahman, Q. (2005). *Born Gay: The biology of sex orientation.* London: Peter Owen Publishers. (p. 535)

Wilson, R. S. (1979). Analysis of longitudinal twin data: Basic model and applications to physical growth measures. *Acta Geneticae Medicae et Gemellologiae, 28,* 93–105. (p. 472)

Wilson, R. S., Beck, T. L., Bienias, J. L., & Bennett, D. A. (2007). Terminal cognitive decline: Accelerated loss of cognition in the last years of life. *Psychosomatic Medicine, 69,* 131–137. (p. 543)

Wilson, R. S., & Matheny, A. P., Jr. (1986). Behavior-genetics research in infant temperament: The Louisville twin study. In R. Plomin & J. Dunn (Eds.), *The study of temperament: Changes, continuities, and challenges.* Hillsdale, NJ: Erlbaum. (p. 491)

Wilson, T. D. (2002). *Strangers to ourselves: Discovering the adaptive unconscious.* Cambridge, MA: Harvard University Press. (p. 152)

Wilson, T. D. (2006). The power of social psychological interventions. *Science, 313,* 1251–1252. (p. 643)

Wilson, W. A., & Kuhn, C. M. (2005). How addiction hijacks our reward system. *Cerebrum, 7*(2), 53–66. (p. 823)

Windholz, G. (1989, April-June). The discovery of the principles of reinforcement, extinction, generalization, and differentiation of conditional reflexes in Pavlov's laboratories. *Pavlovian Journal of Biological Science, 26,* 64–74. (p. 269)

Windholz, G. (1997). Ivan P. Pavlov: An overview of his life and psychological work. *American Psychologist, 52,* 941–946. (p. 268)

Windle, G., Hughes, D., Linck, P., Russell, I., & Woods, B. (2010). Is exercise effective in promoting mental well-being in older age? A systematic review. *Aging and Mental Health, 14,* 652–669. (p. 860)

Winner, E. (2000). The origins and ends of giftedness. *American Psychologist, 55,* 159–169. (p. 630)

Winter, W. C., Hammond, W. R., Green, N. H., Zhang, Z., & Bilwise, D. L. (2009). Measuring circadian advantage in major league baseball: A 10-year retrospective study. *International Journal of Sports Physiology and Performance, 4,* 394–401. (p. 230)

Wirth, J. H., & Bodenhausen, G. V. (2009). The role of gender in mental-illness stigma. *Psychological Science, 20*, 169–173. (p. 655)

Wirz-Justice, A. (2009). From the basic neuroscience of circadian clock function to light therapy for depression: On the emergence of chronotherapeutics. *Journal of Affective Disorders, 116*, 159–160. (pp. 229, 734)

Wiseman, R., & Greening, E. (2002). The mind machine: A mass participation experiment into the possible existence of extra-sensory perception. *British Journal of Psychology, 93*, 487–499. (p. 169)

Witelson, S. F., Kigar, D. L., & Harvey, T. (1999). The exceptional brain of Albert Einstein. *The Lancet, 353*, 2149–2153. (pp. 110, 613)

Witt, J. K., & Proffitt, D. R. (2005). See the ball, hit the ball: Apparent ball size is correlated with batting average. *Psychological Science, 16*, 937–938. (p. 166)

Wittgenstein, L. (1922). *Tractatus logico-philosophicus.* New York: Harcourt, Brace. (p. 142)

Witvliet, C. V. O., Ludwig, T., & Vander Laan, K. (2001). Granting forgiveness or harboring grudges: Implications for emotions, physiology, and health. *Psychological Science, 12*, 117–123. (p. 847)

Witvliet, C. V. O., & Vrana, S. R. (1995). Psychophysiological responses as indices of affective dimensions. *Psychophysiology, 32*, 436–443. (p. 427)

Wixted, J. T., & Ebbesen, E. B. (1991). On the form of forgetting. *Psychological Science, 2*, 409–415. (p. 343)

Wolfson, A. R., & Carskadon, M. A. (1998). Sleep schedules and daytime functioning in adolescents. *Child Development, 69*, 875–887. (p. 242)

Wolitzky-Taylor, K. B., Horowitz, J. D., Powers, M. B., & Telch, M. J. (2008). Psychological approaches in the treatment of specific phobias: A meta-analysis. *Clinical Psychology Review, 28*, 1021–1037. (p. 717)

Woll, S. (1986). So many to choose from: Decision strategies in videodating. *Journal of Social and Personal Relationships, 3*, 43–52. (p. 800)

Wolpe, J. (1958). *Psychotherapy by reciprocal inhibition.* Stanford, CA: Stanford University Press. (p. 717)

Wolpe, J., & Plaud, J. J. (1997). Pavlov's contributions to behavior therapy: The obvious and the not so obvious. *American Psychologist, 52*, 966–972. (p. 717)

Wonderlich, S. A., Joiner, T. E., Jr., Keel, P. K., Williamson, D. A., & Crosby, R. D. (2007). Eating disorder diagnoses: Empirical approaches to classification. *American Psychologist, 62*, 167–180. (p. 697)

Wong, D. F., Wagner, H. N., Tune, L. E., Dannals, R. F., et al. (1986). Positron emission tomography reveals elevated D$_2$ dopamine receptors in drug-naive schizophrenics. *Science, 234*, 1588–1593. (p. 686)

Wood, C. J, & Aggleton, J. P. (1989). Handedness in 'fast ball' sports: Do left-handers have an innate advantage? *British Journal of Psychology, 80*, 227–240. (p. 118)

Wood, D., Harms, P., & Vazire, S. (2010). Perceiver effects as projective tests: What your perceptions of others say about you. *Journal of Personality and Social Psychology, 99*, 174–190. (p. 568)

Wood, J. M. (2003, May 19). Quoted by R. Mestel, Rorschach tested: Blot out the famous method? Some experts say it has no place in psychiatry. *Los Angeles Times* (www.latimes.com). (p. 567)

Wood, J. M. (2006, Spring). The controversy over Exner's Comprehensive System for the Rorschach: The critics speak. *Independent Practitioner* (works.bepress.com/james_wood/7). (p. 567)

Wood, J. M., Bootzin, R. R., Kihlstrom, J. F., & Schacter, D. L. (1992). Implicit and explicit memory for verbal information presented during sleep. *Psychological Science, 3*, 236–239. (p. 345)

Wood, J. M., Lilienfeld, S. O., Nezworski, M. T., Garb, H. N., Allen, K. H., & Wildermuth, J. L. (2010). Validity of Rorschach inkblot scores for discriminating psychopaths from nonpsychopaths in forensic populations: A meta-analysis. *Psychological Assessment, 22*, 336–349. (p. 567)

Wood, J. M., Nezworski, M. T., Garb, H. N., & Lilienfeld, S. O. (2006). The controversy over the Exner Comprehensive System and the Society for Personality Assessment's white paper on the Rorschach. *Independent Practitioner, 26.* (p. 567)

Wood, J. N., Glynn, D. D., Phillips, B. C., & Hauser, M. C. (2007). The perception of rational, goal-directed action in nonhuman primates. *Science, 317*, 1402–1405. (p. 868)

Wood, J. V., Heimpel, S. A., Manwell, L. A., & Whittington, E. J. (2009). This mood is familiar and I don't deserve to feel better anyway: Mechanisms underlying self-esteem differences in motivation to repair sad moods. *Journal of Personality and Social Psychology, 96*, 363–380. (p. 595)

Wood, J. V., Saltzberg, J. A., & Goldsamt, L. A. (1990a). Does affect induce self-focused attention? *Journal of Personality and Social Psychology, 58*, 899–908. (p. 680)

Wood, J. V., Saltzberg, J. A., Neale, J. M., Stone, A. A., & Rachmiel, T. B. (1990b). Self-focused attention, coping responses, and distressed mood in everyday life. *Journal of Personality and Social Psychology, 58*, 1027–1036. (p. 680)

Wood, W. (1987). Meta-analytic review of sex differences in group performance. *Psychological Bulletin, 102*, 53–71. (p. 502)

Wood, W., & Eagly, A. H. (2002). A cross-cultural analysis of the behavior of women and men: Implications for the origins of sex differences. *Psychological Bulletin, 128*, 699–727. (pp. 140, 501)

Wood, W., & Eagly, A. H. (2007). Social structural origins of sex differences in human mating. In S. W. Gagestad & J. A. Simpson (Eds.), *The evolution of mind: Fundamental questions and controversies.* New York: Guilford Press. (p. 501)

Wood, W., Lundgren, S., Ouellette, J. A., Busceme, S., & Blackstone, T. (1994). Minority influence: A meta-analytic review of social influence processes. *Psychological Bulletin, 115*, 323–345. (p. 776)

Wood, W., & Neal, D. T. (2007, October). A new look at habits and the habit-goal interface. *Psychological Review, 114*, 843–863. (p. 264)

Woods, N. F., Dery, G. K., & Most, A. (1983). Recollections of menarche, current menstrual attitudes, and premenstrual symptoms. In S. Golub (Ed.), *Menarche: The transition from girl to woman.* Lexington, MA: Lexington Books. (p. 528)

Woolcock, N. (2004, September 3). Driver thought everyone else was on wrong side. *The Times*, p. 22. (p. 765)

Woolley, A. W., Chabris, C. F., Pentland, A., Hasmi, N., & Malone, T. W. (2010). Evidence for a collective intelligence factor in the performance of human groups. *Science, 330*, 686–688. (p. 839)

World Federation for Mental Health. (2005). ADHD: The hope behind the hype (www.wfmh.org). (p. 652)

World Health Organization. (2008). *Mental health and substance abuse: Facts and figures.* Geneva: World Health Organization (www.who.int). (p. 247)

Worobey, J., & Blajda, V. M. (1989). Temperament ratings at 2 weeks, 2 months, and 1 year: Differential stability of activity and emotionality. *Developmental Psychology, 25*, 257–263. (p. 491)

Wortham, J. (2010, May 13). Cellphones now used more for data than for calls. *New York Times* (www.nytimes.com). (p. 416)

Worthington, E. L., Jr. (1989). Religious faith across the life span: Implications for counseling and research. *The Counseling Psychologist, 17*, 555–612. (p. 515)

Worthington, E. L., Jr., Kurusu, T. A., McCulloh, M. E., & Sandage, S. J. (1996). Empirical research on religion and psychotherapeutic processes and outcomes: A 10-year review and research prospectus. *Psychological Bulletin, 119*, 448–487. (p. 736)

Wortman, C. B., & Silver, R. C. (1989). The myths of coping with loss. *Journal of Consulting and Clinical Psychology, 57*, 349–357. (p. 548)

Wren, C. S. (1999, April 8). Drug survey of children finds middle school a pivotal time. *New York Times* (www.nytimes.com). (p. 824)

Wright, I. C., Rabe-Hesketh, S., Woodruff, P. W. R., David, A. S., Murray, R. M., & Bullmore, E. T. (2000). Meta-analysis of regional brain volumes in schizophrenia. *American Journal of Psychiatry, 157*, 16–25. (p. 687)

Wright, J. (2006, March 16). Boomers in the bedroom: Sexual attitudes and behaviours in the boomer generation. Ipsos Reid survey (www.ipsos-na.com). (p. 540)

Wright, P., Takei, N., Rifkin, L., & Murray, R. M. (1995). Maternal influenza, obstetric complications, and schizophrenia. *American Journal of Psychiatry, 152*, 1714–1720. (p. 687)

Wright, P. H. (1989). Gender differences in adults' same- and cross-gender friendships. In R. G. Adams & R. Blieszner (Eds.), *Older adult friendships: Structure and process.* Newbury Park, CA: Sage. (p. 502)

Wright, W. (1998). *Born that way: Genes, behavior, personality.* New York: Knopf. (p. 127)

Wrosch, C., & Miller, G. E. (2009). Depressive symptoms can be useful: Self-regulatory and emotional benefits of dysphoric mood in adolescence. *Journal of Personality and Social Psychology, 96*, 1181–1190. (p. 672)

Wrzesniewski, A., & Dutton, J. E. (2001). Crafting a job: Revisioning employees as active crafters of their work. *Academy of Management Review, 26*, 179–201. (p. 827)

Wrzesniewski, A., McCauley, C. R., Rozin, P., & Schwartz, B. (1997). Jobs, careers, and callings: People's relations to their work. *Journal of Research in Personality, 31,* 21–33. (p. 827)

Wuethrich, B. (2001, March). GETTING STUPID—Surprising new neurological behavioral research reveals that teenagers who drink too much may permanently damage their brains and seriously compromise their ability to learn. *Discover, 56,* 56–64. (p. 249)

Wulsin, L. R., Vaillant, G. E., & Wells, V. E. (1999). A systematic review of the mortality of depression. *Psychosomatic Medicine, 61,* 6–17. (p. 453)

Wyatt, J. K., & Bootzin, R. R. (1994). Cognitive processing and sleep: Implications for enhancing job performance. *Human Performance, 7,* 119–139. (pp. 241, 345)

Wyatt, R. J., Henter, I., & Sherman-Elvy, E. (2001). Tantalizing clues to preventing schizophrenia. *Cerebrum: The Dana Forum on Brain Science, 3,* pp. 15–30. (p. 688)

Wynn, K. (1992). Addition and subtraction by human infants. *Nature, 358,* 749–759. (pp. 478, 479)

Wynn, K. (2000). Findings of addition and subtraction in infants are robust and consistent: reply to Wakeley, Rivera, and Langer. *Child Development, 71,* 1535–1536. (p. 478)

Wynne, C. D. L. (2004). *Do animals think?* Princeton, NJ: Princeton University Press. (p. 869)

Wynne, C. D. L. (2008). Aping language: A skeptical analysis of the evidence for nonhuman primate language. *Skeptic, 13*(4), 10–13. (p. 869)

Xu, Y., & Corkin, S. (2001). H. M. revisits the Tower of Hanoi puzzle. *Neuropsychology, 15,* 69–79. (p. 342)

Yaffe, K., Lindquist, K., Barnes, D., Covinsky, K. E., Neylan, T., Kluse, M., & Marmar, C. (2010). Posttraumatic stress disorder and risk of dementia among U.S. veterans. *Archives of General Psychiatry, 67,* 608–613. (p. 665)

Yalom, I. D. (1985). *The theory and practice of group psychotherapy* (3rd ed.). New York: Basic Books. (p. 724)

Yamagata, S., & 11 others. (2006). Is the genetic structure of human personality universal? A cross-cultural twin study from North America, Europe, and Asia. *Journal of Personality and Social Psychology, 90,* 987–998. (p. 581)

Yang, N., & Linz, D. (1990). Movie ratings and the content of adult videos: The sex-violence ratio. *Journal of Communication, 40*(2), 28–42. (p. 793)

Yang, S., Markoczy, L., & Qi, M. (2006). Unrealistic optimism in consumer credit card adoption. *Journal of Economic Psychology, 28,* 170–185. (p. 589)

Yankelovich Partners. (1995, May/June). Growing old. *American Enterprise,* p. 108. (p. 541)

Yarkoni, T. (2010). Personality in 100,000 words: A large-scale analysis of personality and word use among bloggers. *Journal of Research in Personality, 44,* 363–373. (p. 584)

Yarnell, P. R., & Lynch, S. (1970, April 25). Retrograde memory immediately after concussion. *Lancet,* pp. 863–865. (p. 333)

Yates, A. (1989). Current perspectives on the eating disorders: I. History, psychological and biological aspects. *Journal of the American Academy of Child and Adolescent Psychiatry, 28,* 813–828. (p. 697)

Yates, A. (1990). Current perspectives on the eating disorders: II. Treatment, outcome, and research directions. *Journal of the American Academy of Child and Adolescent Psychiatry, 29,* 1–9. (p. 697)

Yates, W. R. (2000). Testosterone in psychiatry. *Archives of General Psychiatry, 57,* 155–156. (p. 408)

Ybarra, O. (1999). Misanthropic person memory when the need to self-enhance is absent. *Personality and Social Psychology Bulletin, 25,* 261–269. (p. 595)

Yerkes, R. M., & Dodson, J. D. (1908). The relation of strength of stimulus to rapidity of habit-formation. *Journal of Comparative Neurology and Psychology, 18,* 459–482. (p. 392)

Yeung, J. W. K., Chan, Y, & Lee, B. L. K. (2009). Youth religiosity and substance use: A meta-analysis from 1995 to 2007. *Psychological Reports, 105,* 255–266. (p. 824)

Young, R., Sweeting, H., & West, P. (2006). Prevalence of deliberate self harm and attempted suicide within contemporary Goth youth subculture: Longitudinal cohort study. *British Medical Journal, 332,* 1058–1061. (p. 50)

Youngentob, S. L., & Glendinning, J. I. (2009). Fetal ethanol exposure increases ethanol intake by making it smell and taste better. *PNAS, 106,* 5359. (p. 467)

Youngentob, S. L., Kent, P. F., Scheehe, P. R., Molina, J. C., Spear, N. E., & Youngentob, L. M. (2007). Experience-induced fetal plasticity: The effect of gestational ethanol exposure on the behavioral and neurophysiologic olfactory response to ethanol odor in early postnatal and adult rats. *Behavioral Neuroscience, 121,* 1293–1305. (p. 467)

Younger, J., Aron, A., Parke, S., Chatterjee, N., & Mackey, S. (2010) Viewing pictures of a romantic partner reduces experimental pain: involvement of neural reward systems. *PLoS 5*(10): e13309. doi: 10.1371/journal.pone.0013309. (p. 413)

Yücel, M., Solowij, N., Respondek, C., Whittle, S., Fornito, A., Pantelis, C., & Lubman, D. I. (2008). Regional brain abnormalities associated with long-term cannabis use. *Archives of General Psychiatry, 65,* 694–701. (p. 255)

Yufik, T., & Simms, L. J. (2010). A meta-analytic investigation of the structure of posttraumatic stress disorder symptoms. *Journal of Abnormal Psychology, 119,* 764–776. (p. 664)

Yuki, M., Maddux, W. W., & Masuda. T. (2007). Are the windows to the soul the same in the East and West? Cultural differences in using the eyes and mouth as cues to recognize emotions in Japan and the United States. *Journal of Experimental Social Psychology, 43,* 303–311. (p. 436)

Zabin, L. S., Emerson, M. R., & Rowland, D. L. (2005). Child sexual abuse and early menarche: The direction of their relationship and its implications. *Journal of Adolescent Health, 36,* 393–400. (p. 527)

Zaccaro, S. J. (2007). Trait-based perspectives of leadership. *American Psychologist, 62,* 6–16. (p. 839)

Zadra, A., Pilon, M., & Montplaisir, J. (2008). Polysomnographic diagnosis of sleepwalking: Effects of sleep deprivation. *Annals of Neurology, 63,* 513–519. (p. 240)

Zagorsky, J. L. (2007). Do you have to be smart to be rich? The impact of IQ on wealth, income and financial distress. *Intelligence, 35,* 489–501. (p. 610)

Zajonc, R. B. (1965). Social facilitation. *Science, 149,* 269–274. (p. 771)

Zajonc, R. B. (1980). Feeling and thinking: Preferences need no inferences. *American Psychologist, 35,* 151–175. (p. 423)

Zajonc, R. B. (1984a). On the primacy of affect. *American Psychologist, 39,* 117–123. (p. 423)

Zajonc, R. B. (1998). Emotions. In D. Gilbert, S. T. Fiske, & G. Lindzey (Eds.), *Handbook of social psychology* (4th ed.). New York: McGraw-Hill. (p. 800)

Zajonc, R. B. (2001). Mere exposure: A gateway to the subliminal. *Current Directions in Psychological Science, 10,* 224–228. (p. 798)

Zajonc, R. B., & Markus, G. B. (1975). Birth order and intellectual development. *Psychological Review, 82,* 74–88. (p. 61)

Zammit, S., Rasmussen, F., Farahmand, B., Gunnell, D., Lewis, G., Tynelius, P., & Brobert, G. P. (2007). Height and body mass index in young adulthood and risk of schizophrenia: A longitudinal study of 1,347,520 Swedish men. *Acta Psychiatrica Scandinavica, 116,* 378–385. (p. 686)

Zauberman, G., & Lynch, J. G., Jr. (2005). Resource slack and propensity to discount delayed investments of time versus money. *Journal of Experimental Psychology: General, 134,* 23–37. (p. 367)

Zeelenberg, R., Wagenmakers, E-J., & Rotteveel, M. (2006). The impact of emotion on perception. *Psychological Science, 17,* 287–291. (p. 423)

Zeidner, M. (1990). Perceptions of ethnic group modal intelligence: Reflections of cultural stereotypes or intelligence test scores? *Journal of Cross-Cultural Psychology, 21,* 214–231. (p. 639)

Zeidner, M., Roberts, R. D., & Matthews, G. (2008). The science of emotional intelligence: Current consensus and controversies. *European Psychologist, 13,* 64–78. (p. 612)

Zeineh, M. M., Engel, S. A., Thompson, P. M., & Bookheimer, S. Y. (2003). Dynamics of the hippocampus during encoding and retrieval of face-name pairs. *Science, 299,* 577–580. (p. 330)

Zell, E., & Alicke, M. D. (2010). The local dominance effect in self-evaluation: Evidence and explanations. *Personality and Social Psychology Review, 14,* 368–384. (p. 852)

Zhang, S., & Kline, S. L. (2009). Can I make my own decision? A cross-cultural study of perceived social network influence in mate selection. *Journal of Cross-Cultural Psychology, 40,* 3–23. (p. 599)

Zhong, C-B., Dijksterhuis, A., & Galinsky, A. D. (2008). The merits of unconscious thought in creativity. *Psychological Science, 19,* 912–918. (p. 359)

Zhong, C-B., & Leonardelli, G. J. (2008). Cold and lonely: Does social exclusion literally feel cold? *Psychological Science, 19,* 838–842. (p. 211)

Zhu, W. X., Lu, L., & Hesketh, T. (2009). China's excess males, sex selective abortion, and one child policy: Analysis of data from 2005 national intercensus survey. *British Medical Journal, 338,* b1211. (p. 783)

Zietsch, B. P., Morley, K. I., Shekar, S. N., Verweij, K. J. H., Keller, M. C., Macgregor, S., Wright, M. J., Bailey, J. M., & Martin, N. G. (2008). Genetic factors predisposing to homosexuality may increase mating success in heterosexuals. *Evolution and Human Behavior, 29,* 424–433. (p. 534)

Zigler, E. F., & Styfco, S. J. (2001). Extended childhood intervention prepared children for school and beyond. *Journal of the American Medical Association, 285,* 2378–2380. (p.635)

Zilbergeld, B. (1983). *The shrinking of America: Myths of psychological change.* Boston: Little, Brown. (pp. 729, 732)

Zillmann, D. (1986). Effects of prolonged consumption of pornography. Background paper for *The surgeon general's workshop on pornography and public health,* June 22–24. Report prepared by E. P. Mulvey & J. L. Haugaard and released by Office of the Surgeon General on August 4, 1986. (p. 423)

Zillmann, D. (1989). Effects of prolonged consumption of pornography. In D. Zillmann & J. Bryant (Eds.), *Pornography: Research advances and policy considerations.* Hillsdale, NJ: Erlbaum. (pp. 409, 793)

Zillmann, D., & Bryant, J. (1984). Effects of massive exposure to pornography. In N. Malamuth & E. Donnerstein (Eds.), *Pornography and sexual aggression.* Orlando, FL: Academic Press. (p. 793)

Zimbardo, P. G. (1970). The human choice: Individuation, reason, and order versus deindividuation, impulse, and chaos. In W. J. Arnold & D. Levine (Eds.), *Nebraska Symposium on Motivation, 1969.* Lincoln, NE: University of Nebraska Press. (p. 773)

Zimbardo, P. G. (1972, April). Pathology of imprisonment. *Transaction/Society,* pp. 4–8. (p. 758)

Zimbardo, P. G. (2001, September 16). Fighting terrorism by understanding man's capacity for evil. Op-ed essay distributed by spsp-discuss@stolaf.edu. (p. 785)

Zimbardo, P. G. (2004, May 25). *Journalist interview re: Abu Ghraib prison abuses: Eleven answers to eleven questions.* Unpublished manuscript, Stanford University. (p. 758)

Zimbardo, P. G. (2007, September). Person x situation x system dynamics. *The Observer* (Association for Psychological Science), p. 43. (p. 758)

Zimmer-Gembeck, M. J., & Helfand, M. (2008). Ten years of longitudinal research on U.S. adolescent sexual behavior: Developmental correlates of sexual intercourse, and the importance of age, gender and ethnic background. *Developmental Review, 28,* 153–224. (p. 530)

Zogby, J. (2006, March). Survey of teens and adults about the use of personal electronic devices and head phones. *Zogby International.* (p. 197)

Zou, Z., Li, F., & Buck, L. B. (2005). Odor maps in the olfactory cortex. *Proceedings of the National Academy of Sciences, 102,* 7724–7729. (p. 208)

Zubieta, J-K., Bueller, J. A., Jackson, L. R., Scott, D. J., Xu, Y., Koeppe, R. A., Nichols, T. E., & Stohler, C. S. (2005). Placebo effects mediated by endogenous opioid activity on μ-opioid receptors. *Journal of Neuroscience, 25,* 7754–7762. (p. 206)

Zubieta, J-K., Heitzeg, M. M., Smith, Y. R., Bueller, J. A., Xu, K., Xu, Y., Koeppe, R. A., Stohler, C. S., & Goldman, D. (2003). COMT val158met genotype affects μ-opioid neurotransmitter responses to a pain stressor. *Science, 299,* 1240–1243. (p. 204)

Zucker, G. S., & Weiner, B. (1993). Conservatism and perceptions of poverty: An attributional analysis. *Journal of Applied Social Psychology, 23,* 925–943. (p. 755)

Zuckerman, M. (1979). *Sensation seeking: Beyond the optimal level of arousal.* Hillsdale, NJ: Erlbaum. (p. 392)

Zvolensky, M. J., & Bernstein, A. (2005). Cigarette smoking and panic psychopathology. *Current Directions in Psychological Science, 14,* 301–305. (p. 662)

Name Index

Subject Index

Absolute threshold, 156–157
Abstinence education, 530
Abuse
  dissociative disorders and, 696
  false/repressed memories of, 346–347,
    351–352, 732
  long-term effects of, 493–494
  modeling of aggression and, 792
Acceptance, 572
Accidents
  human factors psychology and,
    840–841
  selective attention and, 153–154
  sleep deprivation and, 234, 236
Accommodation
  cognitive, 477
  visual, 172
Acetylcholine (ACh), 81, 82
Achievement
  distributed vs. massed practice and,
    16, 324
  ten-year rule for, 611, 834
Achievement motivation, 833–837
Achievement tests, 619. See also Test(s)
  predictive validity of, 622
Acquired immunodeficiency syndrome
    (AIDS)
  stress and, 450
  transmission of, 529
Acquisition, in classical conditioning,
    268–269, 290
Acronyms, 323
Action potential, 78, 79, 80
Active listening, 712–713
Adaptation. See also Evolution
  classical conditioning and, 266, 268,
    294–295
  happiness and, 851
  intuition and, 368, 369
  natural selection and, 10, 135–136
  nature–nurture issue and, 10
  perceptual, 191
  sensory, 159–160
Adaptation-level threshold, 851
Addiction, 101, 247–248, 256. See also
    Alcohol use disorder;
    Psychoactive drugs
Adolescents
  bipolar disorder in, 673
  brain development in, 514
  cognitive development in, 514–517
  emerging adulthood and, 522–523
  hearing loss in, 197
  identity formation in, 519–521
  impulsivity in, 514
  moral development in, 515–517
  parental influence on, 521–522
  peer relationships of, 521–522, 824
  physical development in, 513–514
  pregnant, 529–531
  preventive mental health programs
    for, 737
  reasoning power in, 515
  sexual development in, 513–514, 523,
    527–528
  social development in, 519–522

Adoption studies, 128
  of depression, 676
  of intelligence, 633–634
  of schizophrenia, 689
Adrenal glands, 91
Adrenaline, 91
Adulthood. See also Aging
  cognitive development in, 542–543
  emerging, 522–523
  life satisfaction in, 436–547
  love and work in, 544–546
  midlife transition in, 544
  milestones in, 523
  physical development in, 539–542
  psychosocial development in, 520
  social development in, 543–548
  stages of, 539, 544
Aerobic exercise, 859. See also Exercise
Affect, in schizophrenia, 685
Affiliation needs, 412–415
Afterimages, opponent-process theory
    and, 179
Aggression, 789–797. See also Violence
  alcohol and, 791
  amygdala and, 99
  anger and, 846
  aversive events and, 791–792
  biochemical influences in, 790
  biology of, 789–791
  biopsychosocial approach to, 795
  cultural factors in, 792
  definition of, 789
  frustration and, 791–792
  gender differences in, 501
  genetic factors in, 789
  modeling of, 304–305, 308–309,
    792–795
  neural influences in, 790
  psychological factors in, 791–796
  punishment and, 282
  reinforcement of, 792
  relational, 501. See also Ostracism
  social isolation and, 415
  social scripts and, 792–795
  social-cultural factors in, 791–796
  testosterone and, 791
  threatened egotism and, 597
Aggression-replacement program, 792
Aging. See also Adulthood
  biopsychosocial approach to, 547
  cognitive changes and, 542–543,
    625–627
  intelligence and, 625–628
  life satisfaction and, 546
  physical changes and, 540–542
  stress and, 445
  successful, 547
Agonists, neurotransmitters and, 82
Agoraphobia, 663
Agreeableness, 581
AIDS
  stress and, 450
  transmission of, 529
Alcohol use, 248–250, 256
  aggression and, 791
  disinhibition and, 248, 249, 250

expectancy effects and, 250
fetal effects of, 467
neural processing and, 249
reward centers and, 101
self-awareness and self-control and,
    249
sexual behavior and, 248–249, 530
trends in, 822
Alcohol use disorder, 249
  aversive therapy for, 718–719
  biological influences in, 823
  genetic factors in, 823
  psychological influences in, 823–825
  social-cultural influence in, 823–825
  suicide and, 676
  warning signs of, 823
Alcoholics Anonymous, 724
Algorithms, 361
All-or-none response, 80
Alpha waves, during sleep, 227
Alternative therapies, 733–734, 863–864
  eye movement desensitization and
    reprocessing therapy, 733
  light exposure therapy, 733–734
Altruism, 807–810
  bystander effect and, 808–809
  definition of, 807
  happiness and, 809
  reciprocity norm and, 809
  social exchange theory and, 809
  social responsibility norm and, 810
Alzheimer's disease, 333, 542
  intelligence and, 628
  obesity and, 401
American Psychological Association
    (APA), 5, 20, 23, 351
  ethical guidelines of, 68
Amnesia. See also Forgetting; Memory
    loss
  anterograde, 342
  brain lesions and, 330
  infantile, 331, 352, 473
  retrograde, 342
  source, 349
Amok, 653
Amphetamines, 250, 253, 256
Amygdala, 98, 99
  age-related changes in, 547
  emotions and, 423–424
  in memory, 331–333
Anal stage, 559–560
Analytical intelligence, 611
Ancient Greece, 2, 9–10
Anger, 845–847
  gender differences in, 434
  health effects of, 452
Animal(s)
  breeding of, 135–136
  cognition in, 867–871
  communication in, 868–870
  same-sex attraction in, 533
  tool use by, 867–868
  use in research, 66–67, 294
Anorexia nervosa, 697–698
  genetic factors in, 676
Anosmia, 207

Antagonists, neurotransmitters and, 83
Anterior cingulate cortex
  in anxiety disorders, 668
  ostracism and, 414
Anterograde amnesia, 342
Antianxiety drugs, 741
Antidepressants, 679, 741–743
Antipsychotics, 741
Antisocial personality disorder, 699–701
Anvil (ear), 195
Anxiety
  adaptive function of, 667
  defense mechanisms and, 560–561,
    568
  free-floating, 662
  psychoanalytic view of, 560–561,
    568–569
  psychodynamic view of, 565
  stranger, 488
Anxiety disorders, 661–670
  aversive conditioning for, 718–719
  biological perspective on, 667–668
  brain activity in, 668
  classification of, 661–670
  cognitive-behavioral therapy for, 723
  drug therapy for, 741
  exercise and, 860
  exposure therapy for, 717–718
  generalized anxiety disorder, 662
  genetic factors in, 667–668
  learning perspective on, 666–667
  natural selection and, 667
  panic disorder, 662
  phobias, 662–663
Aphasia, 377
  Broca's, 377
  Wernicke's, 377
Apnea, sleep, 239, 241
Appetite. See also Eating; Hunger
  regulation of, 236, 397–399
Applied research, 14, 64–66
  careers in, 14, 22–23
Aptitude tests, 619. See also Intelligence
    tests; Test(s)
  bias and, 641–643
  predictive validity of, 622–623, 642
  stability of scores in, 627
  stereotype threat and, 642–643
Archetypes, 566
Arcuate nucleus, hunger and, 398
Arousal, 421–425, 845
  autonomic nervous system in,
    425–426, 573
  motivation and, 392
  passionate love and, 803
  personality and, 578
  physiology of, 425–426
  polygraphs and, 428–429
  sexual. See Sexual arousal
  spillover effect and, 422–423
Asch's conformity study, 763–764
Assimilation, in cognitive development,
    477
Association, vs. correlation, 49
Association areas, 109–110
Association for Psychological Science, 13